The History Today

WHO'S WHO
IN
BRITISH
HISTORY

First published in Great Britain in 2000

By Collins & Brown Limited
London House
Great Eastern Wharf
Parkgate Road
London SW11 4NQ

and

Cima Books
32 Great Sutton Street
London ECIV 0NB

3 5 7 9 8 6 4 2

British Library Cataloguing-in-Publication Data:
A catalogue record for this book is available from the British Library.

ISBN 1-85585-771-5 (hardback)
ISBN 1-85585-876-2 (softback)

Typeset by Saxon Graphics Ltd, Derby
Printed and bound in Great Britain by Bath Press Ltd, Bath

Jacket images (clockwise from left to right)
Richard III, artist unknown, date unknown, by Courtesy of the National
Portrait Gallery, London; *Oliver Cromwell*, by Robert Walker, c. 1649, by
Courtesy of the National Portrait Gallery, London; *Elizabeth I*, by Marcus
Gheeraerts the Younger, *c.* 1592, by Courtesy of the National Portrait Gallery,
London; *Arthur Wellesley, 1st Duke of Wellington*, by Sir Thomas Lawrence,
1814/15, by Courtesy of The Royal Collection © Her Majesty Queen
Elizabeth II; *Mary Godwin* (Wollstonecraft), by John Opie, *c.* 1797, by
Courtesy of the National Portrait Gallery, London; *Winston Spencer Churchill*,
by Walter Stoneman, 1941, by Courtesy of the National Portrait Gallery,
London

The History Today

WHO'S WHO
IN
BRITISH
HISTORY

Edited by Juliet Gardiner

COLLINS & BROWN

LIST OF PERIOD CONTRIBUTORS

55 BC–AD 1068
Professor David Bates, University of Glasgow

1068–1485
Professor John Gillingham, London School of Economics (emeritus)

1485–1660
Professor Diarmaid MacCulloch, St Cross College, Oxford

1660–1801
Joanna Innes, Somerville College, Oxford

1801–2000
Professor John Charmley, University of East Anglia
Juliet Gardiner, Oxford Brookes University

PREFACE

The History Today Who's Who in British History organizes the narrative of British history through the lives of those who participated in that history. The 4,000 alphabetical entries span 2,000 years from an entry on Agricola, AD 40–93, Roman soldier and governor, to one on Ken Livingstone, elected Mayor of London on 4 May 2000.

There are a number of Who's Whos, biographical dictionaries and so-called biographical encyclopaedias published, encompassing the world of art, architecture, economics, politics, science, sport etc., or of a designated age (Tudor England, the Second World War), compendia of women, European statesmen and literary figures and many others. In compiling *The History Today Who's Who in British History* our criteria were rigorously historical. At a particular time who has held – or sought – political power? Who has contributed to the country's economic development? Who particularly represents a social or cultural movement? Whose life might best illuminate a specific moment of change? The categories are political, social, economic, cultural, and entries include ones on scientists, soldiers, sailors, airmen and women, preachers, philosophers, trade unionists, writers, poets, explorers, inventors, invaders, linguists, cartographers, painters, musicians, folklorists, designers, rebels, educationalists, criminals and the victims of judicial injustice and more.

It is not possible even to attempt to be comprehensive given the ambition of the historical range, and there are many candidates for entry whose role or activities suggest inclusion, but restraints of space exclude. Every reader will find some omissions from their concept of the human landscape of British history. Equally they will come across unexpected entries which give a new perspective to the understanding of the beliefs or the material conditions of an age.

The History Today Who's Who in British History starts with the Roman invasion of Britain and ends in 2000 (colonial entries end at independence). This demands engagement with the challenge of including entries on people whose activities are ongoing, whose reputations are unsecured, where considered historical judgement is not possible and such entries, whilst factual and up to date to the beginning of the new millennium will perhaps change as further distance is added. But this is not a process that is unique to the assessment of current figures: historical reputations undergo continual revision, reassessment, recontextualisation and examination. It exemplifies the approach of the *The History Today Who's Who in British History* in its aim to be scholarly, informative and authoritative, but also decisive and provocative, both in the selection and the content of entries.

For that reason in addition to the 4,000 entries there are 50 double and 135 single page essays on major figures in English, Irish, Scottish and Welsh history which discuss in greater length the relevance of such varied figures as King Arthur and the Rothschild family to the project of British history.

There is also the question of balance, both of entries and within entries. Some categories have been omitted: sportsmen and women, most stage actors; and a number of literary figures – particularly in the twentieth century – have been included only if this would illuminate a wider historical context since there is no shortage of works of reference for literary figures. The reader might find some entries surprisingly brief and others of characters of less recognized importance, longer and more discursive. That is because this is a historical Who's Who: two specific examples might best indicate our reasoning. With a biographical approach there can, of course, be no entry under 'Industrial Revolution', yet the uneven development of industrialization in Britain is germane to the nation's history. Thus entries on inventors, entrepreneurs, trade unionists and politicians indicate the part that they played and the context in which they acted, to build up an understanding of the sequential processes of industrialization. Similarly the complexities of the history of Ireland in the nineteenth and twentieth centuries demand that entries on Irish political and cultural figures carry the weight of explanation of this process.

As with *The History Today Companion to British History*, a particular characteristic of the *The History Today Who's Who in British History* is its interpretive approach. The contributors nominated the figures who in their view define the historical period or subject of their expertise: their entries focus attention on this conceptualization. *The History Today Who's Who in British History* intends to represent historical debate and controversy. It is for this reason too that historians may seem to be privileged among the entries. The history that Geoffrey of Monmouth, Froissart, Trevelyan, Namier or E. P. Thompson wrote is as indicative of the time in which they were writing as of their object of study: it insists that history is an unending dialogue between the present and the past long after the lives under review are ended.

There are editorial conventions that may help the reader navigate the *The History Today Who's Who of British History*. Entries are alphabetical and where an essay falls out of sequence, this is indicated; names are usually confined to a single forename unless the person is invariably known by more than one (**BRUNEL, ISAMBARD KINGDOM** is an example) or where it is necessary to distinguish between two or more people with the same surname, who also share a forename (e.g. **CECIL, ROBERT** and **CECIL, ROBERT GASCOYNE**); and where a person used the initials of his or her forenames, this is indicated with brackets as for **SMITH, F(REDERICK) E(DWIN)**. Entries for women use the name by which they are best known, and if that is their married name, their birth name is given in parenthesis in the heading; pseudonyms, name changes, abbreviated names and universally used nick-names are similarly indicated in the heading; the life-dates follow the name of the person concerned, with regnant dates or other dates of office following the position or office to which they relate.

All kings, queens and royal princes and princesses are listed under their forenames even where this creates apparent inconsistencies (e.g. **BOLEYN, THOMAS** but **ANNE BOLEYN**). Peers are listed under their family names (e.g. **WELLESLEY, ARTHUR** not **WELLINGTON, 1ST DUKE OF**) but are cross-referenced from title to family name. Where a name within an entry is set in small capitals, this indicates that the person has a separate entry. In the case of Gaelic names there are several points to note. Two spelling systems have been followed: for historical, linguistic and historiographical reasons, the break comes in 1200. Later medieval scholars tended to use the anglicized versions of Gaelic names since this is how they appeared in contemporary English documents, and this has persisted in subsequent textbook conventions. Thus Séan Ó Néill is more usually Shane O'Neill. Before *c.* 1100 Gaelic names usually had a patronymic which did not function as a surname: by *c.* 1100 surnames were becoming more common, Thus the elements 'mac' ('son of') and 'ua' or 'o' ('grandson/descendant of') are capitalised where that is a surname rather than a patronymic, and listed under the surname. So Domnall ua Néill (?–980) was simply the grandson of a man called Niall, while Aedh Méith Ó Néill employed a surname. Aedth Méith is therefore listed as **Ó NÉILL, AEDH MÉITH**, while Domnall appears as **DOMNALL UA NÉILL**.

The History Today Who's Who in British History was written by historians distinguished in their fields, and for their arduous and inspired work I am immensely grateful to Professor David Bates (University of Glasgow), Professor John Gillingham(emeritus professor London School of Economics), Professor Diarmaid MacCulloch (St. Cross College, Oxford), Joanna Innes (Somerville College, Oxford) and Professor John Charmley (University of East Anglia). In addition a number of other specialists have contributed entries which have broadened and deepened the scope of the *The History Today Who's Who in British History* immeasurably. I would like to thank Dr Duncan Anderson (Royal Military Academy Sandhurst), military history; Dr Thomas Clancy (University of Glasgow), Gaelic orthography; Dr Richard Cockett (Royal Holloway,

University of London), twentieth-century business, politics and popular culture; Dr Michael Drolet (Royal Holloway, University of London), nineteenth and twentieth-century philosophy, literature, art and music; Dr Bernard Foley (University of Liverpool), economic and business history; Dr Austin Gee (Royal Historical Society British National Bibliography project), eighteenth-century history; Dr Matthew Kilburn (New Dictionary of National Biography, Oxford University Press), eighteenth-century history; Dr Keith McClelland (Middlesex University), nineteenth-century radical, labour and trade union history; Dr. Patrick Maume (Queen's University, Belfast), nineteenth and twentieth-century Irish political and cultural history; Dr Richard Noakes (University of Leeds), history of science and medicine; Dr. Chris Rowley, medieval history; Dr David Souden, business and colonial history.

For editorial guidance, help and support I would like to thank Kate Kirby, Colin Ziegler and particularly Ulla Weinberg of Collins & Brown, and Mark Collins and Robin Gurdon of Cima Books. I also owe a debt to the copy editors and proof-readers and in that connection and others, I should like to thank Professor Christopher Elrington. I should also like to acknowledge the help which I have received from Professor Henry Horwitz and from Alexander Gardiner.

Juliet Gardiner
London June 2000

A

A LASCO, JOHN *see* ŁASKI, JAN

A SANCTA CLARA, FRANCISCUS *see* DAVEN-
PORT, CHRISTOPHER

ABBO OF FLEURY, ST (?–1004), monk. From
the distinguished French abbey of Fleury-sur-
Loire, Abbo was invited to teach at the abbey of
Ramsey which had been recently re-established by
St OSWALD, one of the leaders of the English
Tenth-Century Reform. An outstanding scholar,
Abbo taught for two years at Ramsey between 985
and 987, before returning to Fleury to become
Abbot. His protégés include BYRHTFERTH of
Ramsey. Subsequently outstanding in the affairs
of the Church in the French kingdom, he was
killed during a riot at the Gascon abbey of La
Réole, which he was responsible for reforming.

ABBOT, GEORGE (1562–1633), Archbishop of
Canterbury (1611–33). After a distinguished
Oxford career he became Dean of Westminster in
1600. Favour from JAMES I resulted in bishoprics
culminating in Canterbury in 1611. A strong
Calvinist, he was detested by the party of anti-
Calvinist or Arminian clergy led by William LAUD.
In 1621 his reputation as a churchman was
damaged when he accidentally killed a game-
keeper when hunting with a crossbow but, more
important to the political eclipse which followed,
was his continuing advocacy of an ideologically
inspired alliance with the Calvinist Dutch United
Provinces when James was seeking friendship
with Spain. CHARLES I never favoured him and, in
Abbot's last years, Laud was Archbishop in all but
name.

ABBOTT, DIANE (1953–), politician. Born in
London of Jamaican parents, Abbott studied at
Newnham College, Cambridge, and worked as a
race relations officer for the National Council of
Civil Liberties, for a trade union, and for the
Greater London Council and was a Westminster
City Councillor (1982–6) before her election as
Labour MP for Hackney North and Stoke New-
ington in 1987 as Britain's first black woman MP.
Always associated with the hard Left of the
Labour Party, and regarded as a dissident, after

1997 Abbott became increasingly critical of the
New Labour project of Tony BLAIR, particularly
over welfare cuts and the government's policy on
legal issues.

ABERCROMBIE, SIR PATRICK (1879–1957),
town planner. Brought up in Ches., Abercrombie's
early architectural experience was in Liverpool,
where he began to formulate principles of town
planning. In the 1920s he began a series of regional
planning studies, and agitated for a 'green belt' of
undeveloped land around London. As a member of
the 1937 Barlow Royal Commission on the
Distribution of Industrial Population, he had
helped highlight the need to counter the hazards of
industrial and urban concentration; the bombing
and need for reconstruction in the Second World
War gave him the planning opportunity. Between
1941 and 1946 Abercrombie prepared detailed
plans for London and its hinterland, Plymouth,
Hull, the west Midlands and for the first new towns.
Plymouth, with its orbital roads and separation of
traffic from shopping pedestrians, is the best
surviving example of an Abercrombie planning
scheme. Often now condemned by the conservation movement for the scale of demolition his plans
involved, Abercrombie's impact on some of
Britain's townscapes was considerable.

ABERDEEN, 4TH EARL OF *see* GORDON, GEORGE

ACCA, ST (?–740), Bishop of Hexham. One of
the major figures of the so-called Northumbrian
Renaissance of the eighth century, Acca had been
St WILFRID's chaplain and was his successor at
Hexham. He seems to have inspired some of the
work of the main contributors to the renaissance,
supplying material to BEDE and, along with a
kinsman of Wilfrid, commissioning EDDIUS
STEPHANUS to write Wilfrid's *Life*. His memorial
cross can still be seen at Hexham.

ACLAND, SIR RICHARD (1906–90), politician.
A baronet and landowner from Devon, educated at
Oxford, he enjoyed an intermittent political career
with the Liberal Party, being MP for Barnstaple
(Devon) 1935–45, and later with the Labour Party.
The high-point of his political career came during

the Second World War when he became the focus for the growing discontent felt by many radicals at the lack of interest shown by Winston CHURCHILL's Coalition government in social and land reform. He founded the Commonwealth Party, which successfully contested several by-elections. His hopes that the new party would become an integral feature of the new political landscape were dashed by the landslide election victory of the Labour Party in 1945. Acland himself was a Labour MP from 1947 to 1955. He practised what he preached on land reform, being one of the first landowners to give his estate, Killerton, to the nation, in 1947.

ACTON, ELIZABETH (1799–1859), cookery writer. Daughter of a Hastings brewer, she turned from poetry to cookery and in 1845 published *Modern Cookery*, an instant success that played an important role in the development of a middle-class sociability. It remained in print until 1914.

ACTON, SIR JOHN (1st Baron Acton) (1834–1902), historian. Born in Italy, the son of a diplomat, and rejected by Cambridge University, Acton studied for six years with the philosopher and historian Döllinger in Munich. Through his stepfather he met William GLADSTONE, who became his mentor, and Acton was elected to Parliament as a Liberal in 1859; but he was not a success, either in the Commons or the Lords, to which he was elevated in 1869. For most of his life he was best known for his fervent attempts to uphold the doctrines of liberal Catholicism at a time when there was little basis for such a position. An obsessive reader and notetaker, Acton's memorial is in the libraries of books he read rather than wrote (the historian Creighton described him as 'the most learned Englishman alive, but he never writes anything') and the rows of his annotated slips and card indexes now in Cambridge University Library. Nevertheless he was appointed Regius Professor of History at Cambridge in 1895 and in 1896 embarked on the monumental task of editing the *Cambridge Modern History*. While his proposed life's work *A History of Liberty* remained unwritten, *The Times* noted in his obituary that Acton had 'made history respectable'.

ADAM OF USK (*c.* 1352–1430), historian. After taking his doctorate at Oxford, he became a lawyer on the staff of Archbishop Thomas ARUNDEL and was thus an eyewitness to the turbulent events at the end of RICHARD II's reign. After some adventurous years in Rome and on the fringes of the opposition to HENRY IV, in 1411 he was allowed to return to England and to a quieter life. In his *Chronicon*, a continuation of HIGDEN's *Polychronicon*, he covered the period 1377–1421. His work closes with comments on the costs of HENRY V's wars, which that monarch's admirers have always found disquieting.

ADAM, ROBERT (1728–92), architect. He was one of five architect sons of William Adam (1689–1748), also a prominent Scottish architect. Educated at Edinburgh University, Adam formed friendships with some of the future leading lights of the Scottish Enlightenment, including David HUME and Adam SMITH. He travelled in Italy, and on his return in 1762 was made Architect Royal, a post he surrendered in 1768 when elected an MP. Robert and his most celebrated brothers John (1721–92) and James (?–1794) were noted for the refined neoclassicism of their architecture and for their delicate and colourful style of interior design (termed by one critic Adamite frippery). They were chiefly employed in completing or redesigning country houses, e.g. Syon Park, Kedleston and Harewood. Robert Adam's other designs include the university and Charlotte Square in Edinburgh and Fitzroy Square, London. The brothers' most ambitious venture, the Adelphi (Greek for 'brothers'), a speculative Thames-side development south of the Strand in London, combining houses, warehouses and wharves, almost bankrupted them, but they succeeded in disposing of it by lottery in 1774.

ADAMS, GERARD (GERRY) (1948–), Irish politician. From a Republican family background, he became politically active in the 1960s. He sided with the Provisional Irish Republican Army (IRA) in the split from Sinn Féin of 1969–70, and the extent of his involvement with the IRA is a matter of controversy (he was briefly interned but has never been convicted). From the late 1970s he emerged as the leading figure of a younger Northern Ireland-based group which challenged the traditionalist Southern Ireland-based leadership under Ruairi O Bradaigh and argued for the development of community politics as an auxiliary to the military campaign. The H-Block (*see* SANDS, BOBBY) campaign for political prisoner status for Republican prisoners paved the way for the creation of a Sinn Féin political machine, which emerged as a serious political threat to the Social Democratic and Labour Party (SDLP) in the early 1980s, one of its highpoints being Adams's displacement of former SDLP leader Gerry FITT as MP for West Belfast in 1983. The SDLP vote, consolidated in 1984–5, helped by the Anglo-Irish Agreement, and Sinn Féin hopes of major political gains in the Irish Republic, failed to materialize despite its decision to take up seats in the Dáil if elected (leading to the secession of 'Republican Sinn Féin' under O Bradaigh, who saw recognition of the existing state as a step towards abandoning the struggle). Sinn Féin was further isolated by public revulsion at the intensification of violence in the late 1980s (especially the killing of 11 Protestant civilians by a bomb at Enniskillen in 1988), and in 1992 Adams lost West Belfast to the SDLP. Soon after, John HUME and Adams entered negotiations which led to the IRA ceasefire and the involvement of Sinn Féin in the peace process. This brought increased electoral support (in 1997 Adams retook West Belfast, and Sinn Féin elected its first member of the Dáil since 1957) but also led to splits in the Republican movement and the emergence of the Continuity IRA (linked to Republican Sinn Féin) and 'Real IRA', which killed 29 people with a car-bomb in Omagh (Co. Tyrone), in Aug. 1998. Sinn Féin endorsed the Good Friday Agreement in 1998 as a step towards a united Ireland and took seats in the new cross-party Northern Ireland Assembly, but its entitlement to seats on the executive was weakened until the IRA agreed to give up its weapons. Adams has played a significant role in the political evolution of the Republican movement; it remains to be seen how far he can reconcile Sinn Féin's role as an anti-system party with the exercise of political power.

ADAMS, JOHN COUCH (1819–92), astronomer. Adams studied mathematics at Cambridge, where he built his career. In 1843, after studying perturbations in the orbit of the planet Uranus, he predicted the existence of a new planet (later named Neptune) but his prediction was neglected. The French astronomer Urbain Leverrier made a similar prediction at the same time, which led to the observation of the planet by the German astronomer Johann Galle. This was followed by a priority dispute over the discovery of Neptune, but by 1847 credit had to be given to both Adams and Leverrier. He spent the rest of his career at Cambridge as Lowndean Professor of Astronomy and Geometry (1858–92) and Director of the University Observatory (1860–92).

ADAMS, WILLIAM (1832–1906), radical and journalist. Born in Cheltenham and apprenticed as a printer, he was a political activist from his teens: he joined the National Chartist Association in 1848. In the 1850s and 1860s he was a republican, working with W. J. LINTON on the *English Republic*, an internationalist and disciple of the Italian nationalist, Mazzini, and a secularist, contributing to Charles BRADLAUGH's *National Reformer*. Through his writing for the paper he became a leading advocate of the cause of the North in the US Civil War. Most importantly he became the editor of Joseph COWEN's *Newcastle Weekly Chronicle*. Under his editorship (1864–1900) he turned the paper into the most important provincial English radical paper, with a national readership and reputation.

ADAMSON, PATRICK (?1537–92), Archbishop of St Andrews (1575–92). Having studied at St Andrews, he became one of the first Protestant ministers of the Scottish Church after the Reformation, and travelled to France and Geneva. Appointed Archbishop in 1576, he was Ambassador to England in 1583–4, and proved a persistent champion of Episcopacy (Church government by bishops) against those urging a purely Presbyterian system. This won him favour from JAMES VI as well as inevitable hostility from Andrew MELVILLE. A series of political blunders and mounting complaints against him steadily undermined James's support after 1588; in 1591, a broken man, Adamson made a humiliating recantation to his opponents.

ADDINGTON, HENRY (1st Viscount Sidmouth) (1757–1844), politician and Prime Minister (1801–4). A Tory Speaker of the House of Commons from 1789 to 1801, and Prime Minister thereafter, Addington was committed to a policy of peace abroad and retrenchment at home. These seem to have been achieved with the Treaty of Amiens in 1802 and the abolition of the wartime necessity of income tax. However, the treaty turned out to be little more than a truce and Addington was finally forced to resign. Whereas he had been an uninspiringly mediocre Prime Minister and regarded as a placeman, Addington (who was created Viscount Sidmouth in 1805) was a harsh Secretary of State for Home Affairs (1812–22) with but a single response to manifestations of 'distress' in his treatment of Luddite activities and popular radicalism, particularly with the introduction of the repressive Six Acts in 1819 after the Peterloo Massacre.

ADDISON, CHRISTOPHER (1st Viscount Addison) (1869–1951), politician. Addison studied medicine and became a distinguished Professor of Anatomy, but, appalled by the poverty and poor housing that he encountered, he became a Liberal MP in 1910 and used his practical expertise to become one of the great public-health reformers of the twentieth century. A protégé of LLOYD GEORGE, who used Addison's knowledge of public health to frame the National Insurance Bill of 1911, he followed his mentor to the Ministry of Munitions during the First World War and briefly succeeded him as minister in 1917. Addison's opportunity to implement many of his ideas came when he was appointed Minister of Reconstruction in the same year, laying the groundwork for the Ministry of Health which was set up in 1919, with him as its first minister. He was particularly associated with the 1919 Housing and Town Planning Act, which accepted that housing was a social service with cost implications for the government. Addison became increasingly frustrated by Lloyd George's acceptance of cutbacks on housing and social reform in the Conservative dominated post-war Coalition government, and in 1921 he resigned from the government, the only coalition Liberal to do so. In 1929 he was appointed a minister in Ramsay MACDONALD's second Labour government. He later played an important mediating role in ATTLEE's Cabinets of 1945–51 from the House of Lords.

ADDISON, JOSEPH (1672–1719), essayist. Son of a cleric who became Dean of Lichfield, he was educated at Charterhouse, where he met Richard STEELE. As a young Fellow of Magdalen College, Oxford, he gained a reputation as an elegant classical scholar, and attracted the notice of Junto Whig Charles MONTAGU (later Earl of Halifax). Whig patronage was to shape the rest of his career. When sources of funding for him to travel in France and Italy stopped on the death of WILLIAM III and the fall of the Junto, he settled in London, becoming a member of the Whig Kit Kat Club. He held a series of official posts from 1704; in 1709 he became an MP. He lost office with other Whigs in 1711, but regained it on the accession of GEORGE I; in 1717 he became Secretary of State, but ill health prompted his retirement in 1718. Addison's renowned modesty and charm helped establish his position in coffee-house literary circles. In 1709–10 he contributed to Steele's essay paper *The Tatler*, and from 1710 to 1711 co-edited with him the similar *Spectator*. Combining instructions in genteel conduct with mild social satire and aesthetic commentary, these periodicals were spectacularly successful, and were frequently reprinted into the nineteenth century. Also enduringly successful was Addison's declamatory classical drama *Cato* (1713).

ADDISON, THOMAS (1793–1860), physician. Addison studied medicine in Edinburgh and London and became a distinguished physician and teacher at Guy's Hospital, London. Early in his career he made pioneering studies of the then fatal disease of appendicitis, the pathology of lobar pneumonia and the effects of poisons on the human body. He is principally celebrated for linking diseases of supra-renal capsules (now known as adrenal glands) to pernicious anaemia and what became known as 'Addison's disease'.

ADELA (OR ADELIZA) OF LOUVAIN (?–1151), Queen of England (1121–35). The daughter of Godfrey, Duke of Lotharingia and Count of Louvain, she was married to HENRY I in Jan. 1121, a few weeks after the death of Henry's only legitimate son in the wreck of the *White Ship*. Consequently, she was under enormous pressure to produce a male heir. To make this more likely, she was required to stay at Henry's side and, as a result, had no opportunity to act (as did most queens of the Anglo-Norman realm) as Regent in her husband's absence. No child was born, and the succession dispute between STEPHEN and the Empress MATILDA followed Henry's death in 1135. Adela then married William de Albini, Earl of Arundel, and provided an heir before retiring to a nunnery. She was an important patron of Anglo-Norman literature.

ADLER, NATHAN (1803–90), Chief Rabbi of the British Empire (1844–79). German-born, he created the centralized ecclesiastical hierarchy that was a distinctive feature of Anglo-Jewry. He monopolized ecclesiastical and rabbinical authority and was legally recognized as the arbiter on all religious issues within the United Synagogue. The father of the Anglo-Jewish pulpit, he created Jews' College, London (1855), to develop a Jewish variant of the Anglican ministry.

ADOMNÁN (c. 627–704), Abbot of Iona. Born into the Cenél Conaill, the then ruling family of the northern Uí Néill, Adomnán became Abbot of Iona in 679. A respected churchman, scholar and diplomat, he was an influential figure in royal courts throughout northern Britain. BEDE suggests that Adomnán accepted the Roman dating of Easter early in his abbacy, and pushed for its adoption in Ireland and Iona; this is unlikely, however, for nowhere in his writings does he attempt any persuasion to adopt the Roman calculation for Easter and it was not until 716 that Iona itself conformed. In 697 Adomnán promulgated his *Lex Innocentium*, a law protecting non-combatants, which attracted supporting signatories from kings and clerics throughout northern Britain and Ireland, attesting to his charisma and diplomatic skills. Included among his numerous works were *De Locis Sanctis*, a commentary on Virgil and a calendar of saints, although his best-known work is his *Vita Columbae*, an important source both for COLUM CILLE himself and for our understanding of the early medieval Irish Church whose influence was felt throughout much of Europe.

ADRIAN IV (c. 1100–59), Pope (1154–9). Born near St Albans (Herts.), after studying at Paris, he became a canon and then Abbot of St Rufus in Avignon. As Nicholas Breakspear he was made a Cardinal in 1149, and as Papal Legate to Scandinavia in 1152–3 he carried through an important reorganization of the churches there. In Dec. 1154 he was elected Pope, the only English-born one so far, taking the name Adrian (or Hadrian) IV. From 1156 to the end of his pontificate, he was at odds with the Emperor Frederick Barbarossa. Less troubling to him then, but the cause of much harm to his memory since, was his favourable response to HENRY II's request (taken to Rome by JOHN OF SALISBURY) that the Pope give him the right to take possession of Ireland. According to a papal bull, known from its opening word as *Laudabiliter*, in 1155 or 1156 Adrian authorized Henry to invade and take over the island so that he could reform its 'rough and ignorant people'. The authenticity of this document has long been disputed. There is no doubt, however, that the Pope did make such a grant, although Henry II did not act upon it until 1171, and that the text of *Laudabiliter*, whether it is a twelfth-century forgery or not, reflects views of the Irish which were then widespread on the continent (*see* MALACHY) as well as in England; in this sense the fact that Adrian was 'the English pope' is not of great significance.

ADRIAN, DOUGLAS EDGAR (1st Baron Edgar) (1889–1977), physiologist. Adrian studied physiology at Cambridge and qualified in medicine in 1915. He studied shell-shock during the First World War and in 1919 returned to research at Cambridge. Regarded as a founder of neurophysiology, in the 1920s he recorded electrical impulses in individual nerve fibres and showed that the magnitude of impulse is independent of the magnitude and nature of stimulus. He also showed that messages sent to the brain by nerves are coded by the frequency of discharges in the nerves. Subsequently he worked on electrical brain rhythms, research which informed the development of the electro-encephalogram, an apparatus for studying epilepsy and brain injury. For his nerve impulse work, he shared the 1932 Nobel Prize for Medicine with Charles SHERRINGTON.

ÆBBE, ST (?–683), Abbess of Coldingham. Daughter of King ETHELFRITH and sister of King OSWALD of Northumbria, Æbbe, like her brother, fled to Scotland when their family was defeated by King EDWIN. Having converted to Christianity among the Irish associated with COLUM CILLE's abbey of Iona, she returned to Northumbria and founded an Irish-type monastery for men and women at Coldingham. Although the monastery's discipline was criticized by the austere Ionian monk ADOMNÁN, it and Æbbe's career appear to have been basically typical of the sort of aristocratic initiative which took place during the early stages of the conversion of England to Christianity.

AED ALLAN MAC FERGAILE (?–743), King of Ailech and Tara. Belonging to the Cenél nEógain kindred of the northern Uí Néill, Aed defeated the Cenél Conaill in a sea battle in 734 to supplant them as the dominant kindred among the northern Uí Néill, a position which the Cenél Conaill never recovered. The following year he defeated the Ulaid at Fochairt, a victory which would determine the political shape of Louth until the eleventh century. In 736 he secured the kingship of Tara, and thus became head of the Uí Néill confederation. His reign began the period of the alternation of the kingship of Tara between the Cenél nEógain of the northern Uí Néill and the Clann Cholmáin of the southern Uí Néill which would continue unbroken until 944. In 737 Aed and CATHAL MAC FINGUINE, King of Munster, formally recognized the ecclesiastical supremacy of Armagh and in 738 Aed subjugated Leinster, from which arose the contention among the Uí Néill that the kingship of Tara entailed overlordship over Leinster. One of the most powerful and warlike kings of the Uí Néill, he maintained his supremacy until his defeat and death by DOMNALL MIDI MAC MURCHADA in 743.

AED FIND THE FAIR (?–778), King of Dál Riata. Aed succeeded to the kingship in *c.* 748. After the ascendancy of OENGUS, SON OF FERGUS, King of the Picts, over Dál Riata had been reversed, following the defeat of the Picts by TEWDWR, SON OF BELI, King of Strathclyde, in 750, and following Oengus' death in 761, Aed took advantage of Pictish weakness by invading Fortriu in 768. In addition to his military exploits, the statement in the *Scottish Chronicle* that DOMNALL I MAC ALPÍN, King of the Scots (?–862), enforced 'the rights and laws of the kingdom of Aed, son of Eochaid', indicates he also had the reputation as a lawgiver.

AED FINDLAITH MAC NÉILL (?–879), King of Ailech and Tara. Under MAEL SECHNAILL I, King of Tara, the alternation in the kingship of Tara between the Clann Cholmáin of the southern Uí Néill and the Cenél nEógain of the northern Uí Néill, by this time well over a century old, was in danger of becoming hereditary within the Clann Cholmáin alone. In 860, Aed, as head of the Cenél nEógain and thus successor-elect, raised his forces as a reminder of his claim, but dispersed in the face of Mael Sechnaill's advance with the forces of Meath, Leinster, Connacht and Munster. In 861 and 862 he raided Meath in alliance with the Dublin Norse and such reminders that the kingship of Tara, apparently already regarded as the equivalent of 'King of Ireland', should continue to alternate appears to have been acknowledged and resulted in his accession in 862. He proved himself a vigorous king, being particularly active against Norse strongholds in the north of Ireland, but his power in the south did not match that of his predecessor. He was succeeded by FLANN SINNA MAC MAÍL SHECHNAILL in 879.

AED Ó CONCHOBHAIR (?–1274), King of Connacht. Impatient with the temporizing policy of his father, Feidhlimidh (?–1265), who had promised loyalty to HENRY III, he represented a new and more combative generation. In 1258 he met Brian Ó NÉILL at Cael Uisce and, abandoning his own dynasty's claims, recognized Brian's right to the 'kingship of the Irish of Ireland'. This attempt to revive the high-kingship of Ireland is often regarded as the beginning of Irish recovery; after Brian's death Aed continued the fight. According to his obituary he was 'a King who inflicted great defeats on the foreigners, and pulled down their palaces and castles'. But his name, Aedh na nGall (of the foreigners), was derived from his marriage to a daughter of Dubhghall Mac Ruairí, King of the Hebrides, and his subsequent employment of a troop of Scottish galloglasses.

AED OIRDNIDE MAC NÉILL (?–819), King of Ailech and Tara. Head of the Cenél nEógain, the most powerful kindred of the northern Uí Néill, Aed succeeded Donnchad Midi of the Clann Cholmáin as King of Tara, and thus head of the Uí Néill confederation, in 797. He strongly promoted the interests of Armagh and in 804, together with the Abbot of Armagh, held a synod which freed monasteries from military service and where he probably received the ordination which his by-name reflects. His relations with the Church were fractious. In 811, following Aed's violation of their sanctuary, the monastic community of Tallaght boycotted his assembly at Tara so effectively 'that neither horse nor chariot reached it'; while in 817 he seems to have been involved in the death of the Abbot of Raphoe, a daughter foundation of Iona. Aed sought to extend his power southwards: following his accession, he divided Meath, the territory of his southern Uí Néill rivals; and in 804 he managed to subdue Leinster and divide it between lesser local dynasties willing to acknowledge his suzerainty. Subsequent campaigns in Leinster in 809 and 819, however, indicate that this settlement was short-lived and that Aed, despite his strength, was never quite powerful enough to turn his claims to high-kingship of all Ireland into fact.

AED THE FURIOUS (?–878), King of the Scots. A son of CINAED MAC ALPÍN, Aed succeeded his brother CONSTANTÍN I, but reigned for little over a year. As the *Chronicle of the Kings of Scotland* puts it, 'the shortness of his reign has bequeathed nothing memorable to history'. *Berchán's Prophecy* states his epithet to be 'The Furious' and suggests his reign to have been one of lawlessness. He was killed in Strathallan in 878 by his cousin GIRIC I who succeeded him.

AEDÁN MAC GABRÁIN (*c.* 574–*c.* 608), King of Dál Riata. The earliest recorded instance of a royal ordination ceremony in the British Isles is ADOMNÁN's mention of Aedán's ordination as King by COLUM CILLE. Soon after his accession, Aedán attended Colum Cille's convention at Drum Cett (575) to resolve the differences with Aed mac Ainmirech over Scots and Irish Dál Riata, thereby preserving the lands in Ulster which were the original base of the kings of Dál Riata. A powerful king, Aedán plundered Orkney in 580, but was forced to yield to BAETÁN MAC CAIRILL of the Airgialla the following year. This overlordship was thrown off following Baetán's death and Aedán ravaged Man in 583. In *c.* 598 he was defeated in an invasion of southern Pictland. Following the defeat of the Gododdin (*c.* 600), Aedán attempted to reverse Northumbrian expansion under ETHELFRITH, but was defeated at Degsastan in 603; nevertheless, Aedán considerably expanded the territory of Scottish Dál Riata and dominated the seas of north-western Britain.

AEDH MÉITH Ó NÉILL (?–1230), King of Tír Eoghain. He ruled for over 30 years and although paying tribute to King JOHN in 1210 he refused to give the hostages demanded and from then on was generally at odds with the English Crown. In 1223–4 his alliance with Hugh de LACY forced HENRY III's government to restore Hugh to the earldom of Ulster. According to Aedh's obituary he was 'the man among the Irish who most killed and pillaged the foreigners and destroyed their castles'.

ÆLBERHT, Archbishop of York (767–80). A relative of his predecessor EGBERT, Ælberht is most renowned as the teacher of ALCUIN OF YORK, who wrote of his master in glowing terms. A great collector of ornaments and books, and typical of the leading figures of the eighth-century Northumbrian Renaissance, he contributed to making contemporary York into one of the most important religious centres, not just of Britain, but of Europe.

ÆLFFLÆD (?–after 920), Queen of Wessex. The second wife of King EDWARD THE ELDER and the granddaughter of King ETHELRED I, her marriage to Edward (*c.* 900) was undoubtedly motivated by the need to close off the dynastic claims of the descendants of elder brothers of ALFRED THE GREAT. These were forcibly expressed when Ælfflæd's uncle ETHELWOLD contested the succession with Edward. Ælfflæd's political importance is illustrated by her being accorded the unusual distinction of a coronation. Her son Ælfweard was King of Wessex after Edward for 14 days; after his death he was succeeded by ATHEL-STAN. Edward took a third wife, EADGIFU, after Ælfflæd became a nun at Wilton.

ÆLFFLÆD, ST (654–713), Abbess of Whitby. A daughter of King OSWY of Northumbria, she was vowed to God after her father's victory at the Battle of Winwæd in 655. Entrusted to her kinswoman St HILDA, whom she succeeded as Abbess in 680, as joint Abbess with her mother St EANFLÆD, she presided over a period of great literary productivity at Whitby as well as over a time when the abbey moved away from the customs of Iona, initially brought in by St AIDAN, to the Roman customs associated with St WILFRID. Also a friend of St CUTHBERT, she, like Hilda, St ÆBBE and St ÆTHELFRYTH, exemplifies the major role played by women in the conversion of the English to Christianity.

ÆLFGAR (?–c. 1062), Earl of Mercia. The son of Earl LEOFRIC of Mercia and an important participant in English politics on the eve of the Norman Conquest, he was twice exiled from England, probably because of his opposition to the apparently inexorable rise to power of HAROLD II, TOSTIG and other sons of Earl GODWINE of Wessex. He was able to maintain his status and pass his earldom on to his son EDWIN because he could rely on Welsh military support to secure his reinstatement in Mercia.

ÆLFGIFU (?–after 966), Queen of the English. Wife of King EADWIG and sister of the Ealdorman ETHELWEARD, Ælfgifu appears to have suffered because of the complex faction-ridden politics of her husband's short reign. Rivalry with Eadwig's brother EDGAR and a political grouping led by St DUNSTAN and the dowager Queen, EADGIFU, led to her being divorced.

ÆLFGIFU OF NORTHAMPTON (?–after 1040), first wife of King CNUT. Daughter of ÆLFHELM, Ealdorman of Northumbria, she was maintained by Cnut, whom she married in 1013, even though he subsequently married EMMA. The mother of HAROLD HAREFOOT, Ælfgifu remained influential throughout the reign, representing Cnut in Norway in 1030, and she may well have been the power behind the throne during her son's rule.

ÆLFHEAH, ST, Archbishop of Canterbury (1005–12). He drafted, with Archbishop WULF-STAN II of York, some of the important legislation

of ETHELRED II THE UNREADY's reign. He was taken prisoner by the Danish army of THORKELL THE TALL in 1011, and was murdered by the latter's followers in 1012 when he protested against a ransom that the Danes were demanding for his release.

ÆLFHEAH THE BALD (?–951), Bishop of Winchester. Like his near-contemporary, Archbishop ODA of Canterbury, Ælfheah was one of the early patrons of the monastic movement which came to be known as the Tenth-Century Reform. A member of the household of King ATHELSTAN until his appointment to the bishopric of Winchester (c. 935), Ælfheah supported and advanced the early careers of both St DUNSTAN and St ETHELWOLD.

ÆLFHELM (?–1006), Ealdorman of Northumbria. A beneficiary and ultimately a victim of the treacherous politics of the reign of ETHELRED II THE UNREADY, he was appointed Ealdorman of Northumbria in 993 but murdered on Ethelred's instructions by EADRIC STREONA. His daughter, ÆLFGIFU OF NORTHAMPTON, was the first wife/mistress of King CNUT.

ÆLFHERE, Ealdorman of Mercia (956–83). The son of Ealdorman EALHHELM, Ælfhere was one of the most powerful magnates of the reigns of EADWIG and EDGAR. He was particularly notable for his part in the anti-monastic reaction that followed Edgar's death, and in the Tenth-Century Reform. The so-called anti-monastic reaction in the reign of EDWARD THE MARTYR and at the start of the reign of ETHELRED II THE UNREADY is generally seen as being more concerned with property and power than as springing from any anti-religious feeling. Ælfhere was one of a group who exploited the disorders of the period to attack the power of politically influential churchmen such as St ETHELWOLD, Bishop of Winchester. One of his chief rivals was ETHELWINE, Ealdorman of East Anglia.

ÆLFRIC (?–1016), Ealdorman of Hampshire. One of the less successful of king ETHELRED II THE UNREADY's generals, the *Anglo-Saxon Chronicle* accuses him of cowardice and treachery. As with all participants in that disastrous reign, it is possible that the sources have blackened his reputation with hindsight. He died fighting for EDMUND IRONSIDE at the Battle of Ashingdon.

ÆLFRIC OF EYNSHAM (c. 955–c. 1022), scholar. A protégé of St ETHELWOLD, Bishop of Winchester, and the chronicler ETHELWEARD, and one of the major second-generation figures of the Tenth-Century Reform, his writings, with their moral and educational purpose, were typical of his age. They include homilies, sermons, translations of parts of the Bible into Old English, books of Latin grammar, and saints' lives. His comments on the Christian duties of kingship are important, and he is renowned for the quality of his Old English prose.

ÆLFRIC PUTTOC (?–1051), Archbishop of York. A former Prior of Winchester who succeeded WULFSTAN II as Archbishop in 1023, he was less obviously distinguished than his predecessor. In 1026 he was the first Archbishop of York to collect his *pallium* from Rome, thus apparently claiming the same status for York as Canterbury. His known involvements in national politics include advising HARTHACNUT to have his half-brother HAROLD I HAREFOOT's body disinterred and thrown into the Thames. He was a great patron of Beverley Minster.

ÆLFTHRYTH (?–1002), Queen of England. Third wife of King EDGAR and mother of King ETHELRED II THE UNREADY, her notoriety rests on sources from the late eleventh century onwards, which suggest her complicity in the murder of her stepson, EDWARD THE MARTYR, in 978. Some scholars accept her innocence because of the absence of contemporary testimony, while others point to the fact that the murderers were never punished. Although influential until her death, she disappeared from court between 984 and 993, a period when the weak-willed Ethelred allowed Church lands to be plundered.

ÆLFWALD, ST (?–788), King of Northumbria (779–88). The son of King Oswulf (?–759), he was one of the feuding participants in the violent politics of the kingdom of Northumbria in the second half of the eighth century. In 779 he drove out King ETHELRED, the son of his father's supplanter but was himself killed by a nobleman in 788. He was succeeded by his kinsman Osred, who was in turn overthrown by a group of nobles and replaced by the returning Ethelred. A bright light is said to have shone on the spot where Ælfwald was killed and he was venerated as a saint in the renowned early-medieval abbey at Hexham.

ÆLFWINE (?661–79), King of Deira (?670–9). Son of King OSWY of Northumbria and brother of King ECGFRITH, Ælfwine was Sub-King of Deira under Ecgfrith. He was killed at the age of 18 in the great battle on the River Trent with King ETHELRED of Mercia, which effectively transferred predominance among the early kingdoms of Anglo-Saxon England from Northumbria to Mercia. After Ælfwine's time, the former kingdoms of Bernicia and Deira largely disappeared and were incorpo-

rated into the single kingdom of Northumbria, which survived until the second half of the ninth century.

ÆLFWYNN (also known as Lady of the Mercians) (c. 900–?). Daughter of ETHELFLÆD and granddaughter of ALFRED THE GREAT, Ælfwynn succeeded her mother as Lady of the Mercians in 918, but within a year was deprived of this position and taken into Wessex by her uncle King EDWARD THE ELDER. This event represents the final subjugation of Mercia by the kings of Wessex and a landmark in the process by which the latter made themselves kings of all England.

ÆLLE (?–c. 491), King of Sussex. He was the first of the seven kings named by BEDE as exercising overlordship over the various peoples of the early Anglo-Saxon kingdoms, a status described in later sources as that of a Bretwalda. The evidence of later sources credits Ælle with the establishment of the kingdom of the South Saxons (i.e. Sussex) in the late-fifth century, but all specific details of his activities are open to doubt. The kingdom of Sussex established by Ælle seemingly remained pagan until the late seventh century and was eventually suppressed in the time of King OFFA of Mercia.

ÆLLE (?–867), King of Northumbria (867). The last King of Northumbria, Ælle overthrew his brother Osberht but both were killed at York fighting against the Viking 'Great Army' of HALFDAN and IVAR THE BONELESS. Northumbrian power at York was eventually replaced by a Scandinavian kingdom. Ælle has a legendary reputation in saga literature as the man who killed the great Viking warrior RAGNAR LOTHBROK, by throwing him into a snake-pit; the same sources describe Ælle as having been killed by ritual torture by the Vikings.

ÆLRED OF RIEVAULX (1109–67), writer. Author of religious and historical works and the son of an English priest, he spent some years at the court of DAVID I of Scotland before entering in c. 1133 the recently founded Cistercian monastery of Rievaulx, where he became Abbot in 1147. The piety and austerity of the early Cistercians is vividly portrayed in the *Life of Ælred*, written by his friend Walter Daniel. Ælred's treatises *The Mirror of Charity* and *On Spiritual Friendship* provide important material for discussion of interpersonal relationships in medieval England.

ÆTHELTHRYTH, ST (?–679), Queen of Northumbria and Abbess of Ely. The daughter of Anna, King of East Anglia, and founder of the double monastery for men and women at Ely in

673, she is an example of the women of high social standing, such as St ÆLFFLÆD and St HILDA, who played a major part in the development of English monasticism. According to BEDE, her religiosity was shown by her having remained a virgin through two marriages before becoming an abbess. One of the marriages was to King ECGFRITH of Northumbria.

AGILBERT, ST (?–690), churchman. A Frank, educated partly in Ireland, he was appointed to the bishopric of Dorchester-on-Thames (c. 650–663) by King CENWEALH of Wessex in succession to St BIRINUS. Agilbert represents the strong Frankish aristocratic presence in the early Christian Church in England and was a significant influence on St WILFRID. He left England soon after Cenwealh had objected to his foreign speech and divided his diocese. He was appointed Bishop of Paris (668–90). His sculptured tomb can still be seen at Jouarre near Paris.

AGRICOLA see essay on page 10

AHERN, BERTIE (1951–), Taoiseach (Irish Prime Minister). An archetypal political 'fixer' from a working-class background, Ahern was prominent in Fianna Fáil under Charles HAUGHEY. As Minister for Labour 1987–91 he played a vital role in negotiating a national agreement between unions, employers and government which helped to control inflation. Minister for Finance (1991–4), he was seen as Haughey's preferred heir but failed to prevent Albert REYNOLDS's succession. Ahern succeeded Reynolds as party leader after the fall of the 1992–4 Fianna Fáil coalition with Labour and became Taoiseach in 1997, heading a minority Fianna Fáil coalition with the Progressive Democrats. His term as Taoiseach has been marked by a continuing economic boom and the conclusion of the Good Friday Agreement (1998), but also problems of adjustment to European integration, and corruption scandals relating to the Haughey years, which have not severely damaged Ahern himself. His separation from his wife and cohabitation with his secretary is widely seen as symbolizing a change in social attitudes.

AIDAN, ST (?–651), churchman. A monk of Iona during the energetic rule of Abbot SÉGÉNE, Aidan was invited to undertake the conversion of the kingdom of Northumbria by King OSWALD. He must to a degree have built upon the earlier missionary work of PAULINUS but, as a monk in the Irish tradition, his methods were very different. BEDE, in his *Ecclesiastical History*, paints a touching portrait of the ascetic Aidan giving away a magnificent horse that he had received as a

present and eating simple food in the midst of the lavish royal court. Aidan founded the famous monastery of Lindisfarne and was Bishop from 634 to 651. He ensured that Northumbria followed the religious traditions of Iona and Ireland, at least up until King OSWY's Synod of Whitby (664).

AINBCHELLACH (?–719), King of Dál Riata. A son of Ferchar Fota of the Cenél Loairn, Ainbchellach became King in 697. Presumably as a result of a kin feud typical of the period, he was expelled from the kingship in the following year and taken, bound, to Ireland. The circumstances of his captivity are unknown, but the recorded obit of one Finnamail, King of Dál Riata, in 700 suggests that it was he who deposed Ainbchellach, and that he, in turn, was killed by SELBACH, Ainbchellach's brother, who himself seized the kingship. Ainbchellach had escaped by 719, when he attempted to win back his kingdom, only to be killed in a battle with his brother.

AIRY, SIR GEORGE (1801–92), astronomer. As Cambridge University's Lucasian Professor of Mathematics (1826–8) and Plumian Professor of Astronomy (1828–30), Airy promoted the study of mathematics and natural science at the university. As Astronomer Royal (1835–81) he transformed the business of astronomy at the Royal Greenwich Observatory, installing sophisticated instruments and imposing new work regimes for producing accurate observations of astronomical, meteorological and geomagnetic phenomena. Celebrated for his researches on optics and geophysics and his numerous scientific treatises, he organized British expeditions to observe the 1874 and 1882 transits of Venus, projects leading to estimates of the distance between the sun and the earth.

AITKEN, MAXWELL (1st Baron Beaverbrook) (1879–1964), newspaper proprietor and politician. Born in Canada, Aitken set up his own finance company in Ontario, and was a sterling millionaire by the age of 30. In 1910 he emigrated to England where, at the urging of his friend Bonar LAW, he stood for Parliament and was elected Conservative MP for Ashton-under-Lyne (Lancs.). In 1916 he assisted in ousting H. H. ASQUITH as Prime Minister, became Chancellor of the Duchy of Lancaster and served as wartime Minister of Information, with a peerage. Meanwhile he was building up a successful newspaper chain, based on the *Daily Express* into which he had first bought for party propaganda. He used the newspaper's influence to oppose the LLOYD GEORGE coalition in 1922, to pillory Stanley BALDWIN and, from 1929, to promote Empire Free Trade. He also supported EDWARD VIII in the abdication crisis,

continued on page 11

AGRICOLA (Gnaeus Julius Agricola) (AD 40–93)
Roman soldier and Governor of Britain (AD 78–84)

A wealth of information about Agricola is contained in the laudatory biography of him written by his son-in-law TACITUS in 97–8. Although his renown resides primarily on his great military campaigns as Governor, he actually spent three periods in Britain, serving as a legionary tribune at the time of BOUDICCA's revolt in 60–1 and as a legionary commander between 69–73. A member of a noble Roman family residing in southern Gaul, he also filled posts in Asia Minor, Italy and Aquitaine as well as serving as a consul in Rome in 77–8. He was extensively experienced throughout the Roman world, and it is notable that his first two periods of service in Britain coincided with one of the greatest crises in Roman rule and with the time when the advance northwards was resumed, when PETILLIUS CERIALIS defeated the Brigantes and established Roman power as far north as Carlisle.

In a series of annual campaigns, Agricola expanded Roman power in Britain to the furthest limits that it ever reached. In 78 he completed the subjugation of north Wales and Anglesey, which had been pushed forward earlier in the decade by JULIUS FRONTINUS. In 79 he campaigned in the north-west of England, in 80 in lowland and central Scotland as far north as the River Tay, and in 82, after a year spent on consolidation, he advanced into south-west Scotland. In 83 he is known to have campaigned against the Caledonii in modern Perths. and in 84 he advanced much further north, defeating the Caledonian chieftain CALGACUS at the famous Battle of *Mons Graupius*, a site which has never been convincingly identified (the mountain known as Bennachie near Durno, which is near Inverurie in Aberdeens., is the best candidate). According to Tacitus, Agricola's spectacular victory was gained against an army of approximately 30,000 Highlanders. It was not, however, a decisive one because around 20,000 of them escaped and because Agricola was shortly afterwards recalled to Rome, according to Tacitus, by an emperor jealous of his success. Remarkable testimony to Agricola's achievements and plans is the legionary fortress established in *c.* 83 at Inchtuthil, near Dunblane (Perths.), as the centre of a ring of fortifications around the Highlands, which have been traced by archaeological excavation. The new fortress was abandoned and systematically dismantled soon after 86 when the Romans decided to base their troops in the Lowlands.

Tacitus presents Agricola as an exemplary Roman Governor. Britain under his rule is seen as living under a Romanized idyll, as the Governor reversed the unjust taxation policies of his predecessors, encouraged the construction of temples, civic squares, baths and houses according to the Roman manner and made arrangements for British children to be educated in Latin. His famous remark that 'the toga was frequently seen' is indicative of a considerable degree of assimilation, although Tacitus was shrewd enough to observe that what the Britons believed to be part of civilization was in reality all part of their servitude. While Tacitus' purpose of praising Agricola inevitably led to the denigration of his predecessors, it is more than likely that his eulogies indicate the development of peaceful Roman rule, at least in Lowland Britain. Agricola's recall and the subsequent abandonment of any idea of conquering the tribes of Scotland left unsolved the problem of the Roman empire's northern frontier in Britain. In spite of the construction of extensive fortifications by Agricola and his successors, it subsequently proved difficult to hold down even the Lowlands and the decision was taken in the time of the Emperor HADRIAN to locate the frontier on the Solway–Tweed line where remains of parts of Hadrian's famous wall can still be seen. One subsequent brief attempt to move the frontier back northwards, which was made in the time of the Emperor ANTONINUS PIUS, was speedily abandoned. It is easy to see that Agricola's governorship and the following abandonment of his plans represent a decisive turning-point, not only in the history of Roman Britain, but of the British Isles. The completion of the Roman conquest of Scotland would surely have made the course of British history very different.

Agricola's personal reputation is to an extent controversial among historians. With Tacitus as effectively the only written source for his life, it is inevitable that his qualities and achievements should be doubted. It is, for example, difficult to find significant archaeological evidence for urban development during his governorship and much easier to locate it under his predecessors. His wars, although spectacular, were arguably over-ambitious and his failure to defeat his enemies conclusively after *Mons Graupius* could be a mistake. This said, the scale of his achievements remains very great by any standards. And without the literary evidence provided by Tacitus' history, our knowledge of Roman Britain would be much the less.

Tacitus, Agricola (trans., 1978)
Peter Salway, Roman Britain (1981)

organizing the voluntary self-censorship that kept mention of Wallis SIMPSON out of British papers until the crisis broke. The profits and circulation of the *Express* and other newspapers had meanwhile grown steadily; Beaverbrook made many friends and just as many enemies. He was memorably lampooned as Lord Copper in Evelyn WAUGH's novel *Scoop* (1938). His friendship with Winston CHURCHILL earned him the post of Minister of Aircraft Production in 1940; within a short time, as the Battle of Britain was being waged, aircraft production was considerably increased. He subsequently served as Minister of Supply (1941–2), Minister of Production (1942) and Lord Privy Seal (1943–5). He negotiated with the USA over Lend-Lease in 1941, and led calls for a second front to assist the Soviet Union. A passionate advocate of empire, Beaverbrook was opposed to Indian independence. In 1954 he transferred the bulk of his wealth to a charitable foundation. His son Sir Maxwell Aitken (1910–85), who disclaimed the barony, eventually sold the newspaper group to Trafalgar House in 1977.

ALANBROOKE, 1ST VISCOUNT *see* BROOKE, ALAN

ALANE, ALEXANDER *see* ALESIUS, ALEXANDER

ALBAN, ST (?third to fourth century), Christian martyr. A Roman soldier residing in the town of Verulamium (later St Albans), he reputedly sheltered a Christian during a persecution, was himself converted to Christianity and preferred to die rather than hand over the man to whom he had given refuge. The story is first told in an early fifth-century source and, because of its early date, can probably be accepted, despite the relatively slight evidence for persecution in Roman Britain. The martyrdom supposedly took place on what is now the site of the high altar of the abbey church of St Albans, founded by OFFA.

ALBANY, DUKE OF, 1ST *see* STEWART, ROBERT; **2ND** *see* STEWART, MURDAC; **3RD** *see* STEWART, ALEXANDER; **4TH** *see* STEWART, JOHN

ALBEMARLE, 1ST EARL OF *see* KEPPEL, ARNOLD JOOST VAN; **1ST DUKE OF** *see* MONCK, GEORGE

ALBERT OF SAXE-COBURG-GOTHA (1819–61), Prince Consort to Queen VICTORIA. The younger son of the Duke and Duchess of Saxe-Coburg-Gotha, Albert was a studious, serious and frail child who was thoroughly educated at the universities of Brussels and Bonn. At the instigation of his uncle Leopold, Albert first met his cousin Victoria in 1836. He returned to England in 1839 and Victoria, now a reigning monarch, proposed to him, a penniless German princeling, and the 20-year-olds were married in Feb. 1840.

Albert's position at court was never an easy one: his German connections revived the resentment against the dissolute and incompetent Hanoverian monarchs who had occupied the British throne until Victoria's accession, and he was castigated in the press and popular ballads as an opportunistic adventurer. There was no clear role for the husband of a queen regnant in British constitutional practice. The early days of the marriage were frustrating for the capable and hard-working young man who appeared doomed to be a royal cipher. As pregnancies followed in quick succession, however, Victoria increasingly relied on the conscientious and sound judgement of her husband in dealing with affairs of State, and Albert replaced Melbourne (*see* LAMB, WILLIAM) as her political adviser, and thus tempered her strong, partisan pro-Whiggishness by his insistence that the monarch should be above party.

Despite the frustrations of his role, Albert's sober and puritanical nature and his wife's often tempestuous one, the marriage, which bore nine children, was happy and companionable. Albert was a strict but fond father, particularly with his first-born, Vicky, with whom he shared the intellectual rapport that he could not achieve with his wife. Gradually Albert was able to channel his formidable administrative abilities into philanthropic activities and the promotion of the arts and sciences. He also made the royal household more efficient and economical, modernizing Buckingham Palace and rebuilding Osborne House on the Isle of Wight and Balmoral in the Scottish Highlands, where the royal family enjoyed a simple, unceremonial existence.

His most notable achievement was the Great Exhibition, held in a great glass palace erected to Joseph Paxton's design in London's Hyde Park in 1851 to showcase British arts and manufacture. He worked tirelessly to realize the exhibition, which was to prove an unexpected success, attracting six million visitors. It made a profit of around £200,000, which was used to purchase land in South Kensington. 'Albertopolis', as it was dubbed, now houses the four museums of science, natural history, geology, and arts and design.

Albert's premature death, from typhoid, came only four years after he had at last been accorded the title of Prince Consort. The Queen was inconsolable at the loss of her 'beloved angel', and the solid base of a responsible, constitutional monarchy which the couple had worked so assiduously to consolidate was put into jeopardy by the Queen's lengthy withdrawal from public life.

ALCOCK, SIR JOHN (1892–1919), aviator. As test pilot for Vickers he had flown on raids into Turkey with the RAF during the First World War. Alcock and a navigator, Arthur Whitten BROWN, made the first non-stop transatlantic flight, from Newfoundland to Ireland, in 16 hours 27 minutes on 14 June 1919, winning £10,000 given by the *Daily Mail* for the feat. Later that year he was killed in a flying accident.

ALCUIN OF YORK (*c.* 737–804), scholar. A Northumbrian, educated at York in the time of Archbishops EGBERT and ÆLBERHT, who became Charlemagne's leading adviser on intellectual and educational matters, Alcuin was one of a number of Englishmen who found employment in the Frankish kingdoms, and was the most influential Englishman abroad since the time of St BONIFACE. He was a poet and voluminous letter writer as well as a great organizer, and was richly rewarded by Charlemagne for his considerable services.

ALDFRITH (?–705), King of Northumbria (685–705). Son of King OSWY and brother of King ECGFRITH, Aldfrith restored stability to the Northumbrian kingdom after his brother's turbulent reign. He is most important, however, for his extensive patronage of learning which helped to foster the most splendid and productive phase of the Northumbrian Renaissance; it is probable, for example, that two of the greatest surviving manuscripts of the renaissance, the Lindisfarne Gospels and the *Codex Amiatinus*, date from his time. Educated in Ireland, and a pupil of ADOMNÁN of Iona and St ALDHELM of Malmesbury, he was remarkably well educated for a king. His personal connections with Ireland and Iona were undoubtedly significant in restoring peace to northern Britain after his brother's wars of expansion. He was succeeded by his son OSRED.

ALDHELM, ST (*c.* 640–709), churchman and scholar. Abbot of Malmesbury from *c.* 674 and Bishop of Sherborne from 705, he was, like his great contemporary BEDE, a master of all branches of learning then in existence, and is notable for having studied under both Irish and Roman scholars. Written in very difficult Latin (the so-called 'hermeneutic style'), his best-known works are treatises advising his contemporaries on various aspects of the religious life, such as his famous letter on virginity to the nuns of Barking. Extremely influential in the second half of the century, during which England was conclusively converted to Christianity, Aldhelm's career illuminates many aspects of the early Church in Britain. Malmesbury was the most important abbey in southern England during his lifetime.

ALEN, SIR JOHN (?–*c.* 1561), royal servant. Not to be confused with his Irish contemporary John ALLEN. Knighted in 1529, made Irish Master of the Rolls in 1533 and Lord Chancellor in 1538, he headed the group of administrators in the Pale (the heartland of English rule around Dublin) through whom Thomas CROMWELL confronted the power of the GERALDINES; he led the enforcement of HENRY VIII's Reformation in Ireland and gained much ex-monastic property. An early advocate of wholesale colonization of Ireland, he opposed the conciliatory policies of Lord Deputy ST LEGER; Alen's involvement in plots against him led to incarceration in the Fleet Prison and deprival of office in 1546. Nevertheless in 1551 he testified in favour of St Leger against fresh accusations of treason. In MARY I's reign he retired to England.

ALESIUS, ALEXANDER (1500–65), writer. Born Alexander Alane, he adopted his cod-Greek surname meaning 'wanderer' to describe the exile in which he spent most of his career. As a canon of St Andrew's Cathedral, he was traumatized by the martyrdom of Patrick HAMILTON (1528), converted to Lutheranism and fled Scotland for Germany. From 1535 he was in England and a client of Thomas CRANMER and Thomas CROMWELL; although when HENRY VIII forced the passage of the conservative Act of Six Articles (1539) he left to teach in Frankfurt-am-der-Oder, he continued to observe events in Britain, and prepared a summary Latin translation of Cranmer's 1549 Book of Common Prayer. He is important for lively eye-witness comments and reminiscences about the early English Reformation in his numerous writings.

ALEXANDER I (*c.* 1077–1124), King of Scots (1107–24). He was the son of MAEL COLUIM III CENN MÓR and St MARGARET, and married Sybilla, illegitimate daughter of HENRY I. Upon succeeding his brother EDGAR on the throne, he continued his parents' policy of 'reforming' the Scottish Church, bringing in monks and canons from England, e.g. to his new priory at Scone (Perths.). He died childless and was buried at Dunfermline (Fife).

ALEXANDER II (1198–1249), King of Scots (1214–49). The son of WILLIAM I THE LION, he successfully overcame challenges for the throne from the MacWilliam dynasty. Although promised the northern counties of England for his support of the Magna Carta rebellion (1215–17), in the end the Anglo-Scottish agreement of 1217 (which effectively allowed the English King to retain the northern shires) ushered in a peace between the two kingdoms that lasted 80 years. This was formalized by Alexander's marriage to HENRY III's sister Joan in 1221, and then by the Treaty of York (1237), by which Alexander renounced the ancestral claim to Northumbria. Thus the Tweed–Solway line was finally established as the Anglo-Scottish border. He pursued an active western policy, campaigning in Argyll in 1221–2 and putting an end to Galloway's status as a kingdom in 1234. He was on the verge of annexing the Western Isles when he died in 1249 on the island of Kerrera in Oban Bay.

ALEXANDER III (1241–86), King of Scots (1249–86). The son of ALEXANDER II, he was married to HENRY III's daughter MARGARET in 1251. When he was able to take personal control of government 10 years later, he resumed his father's policy of annexing the Western Isles. King Haakon of Norway reacted vigorously, but the drawn Battle of Largs (Ayrs.) in Oct. 1263 and Haakon's death two months later ensured that the western Highlands and Islands would be won for the Scottish Crown. In 1264 the kingdom of Man surrendered to Alexander, and in 1266 the Norwegians agreed to the Treaty of Perth. In 1284, following the deaths of his sons, Alexander secured the recognition of his granddaughter MARGARET, MAID OF NORWAY, as his heir presumptive but, still hoping for a son, he married a second wife, YOLANDE OF DREUX. Five months later, on 18 March 1286, when riding along the cliffs of Kinghorn (Fife), his horse fell and he was killed.

ALEXANDER, HAROLD (1st Earl Alexander of Tunis) (1891–1969), soldier. Son of an Irish aristocrat, educated at Harrow and Sandhurst, commissioned into the Irish Guards, he fought on the Western Front where he was twice wounded, awarded the Military Cross and appointed to the Distinguished Service Order (DSO). After the war Alexander led a Prussian Junker *Freikorps* in Latvia, in the mid 1930s he commanded a brigade on India's North West Frontier, and in 1937 became Britain's youngest Major General. A favourite of Winston CHURCHILL after Dunkirk (May 1940), Alexander badly mishandled the retreat from Burma in March 1942, but managed to place the blame on his subordinate William SLIM. Commanding in the Mediterranean in Aug. 1942, Alexander wisely left strategic thinking to able subordinates like MONTGOMERY, while he used his personal charm to facilitate co-operation between the Allies in the campaigns in Tunisia, Sicily and Italy. After the war, Alexander served as Governor General of Canada (1946–52), then as Minister of Defence (1952–4). The embodiment of the ideal officer, Alexander excelled at the command of small formations and at inter-Allied diplomacy, but

demonstrated little aptitude for the wide areas which lay in between.

ALEXANDRA (1844–1925), Queen Consort. Daughter of the King and Queen of Denmark, and considered to be 'outrageously beautiful', 'Alix' was settled upon by Queen VICTORIA and Prince ALBERT as a suitable wife for their errant oldest son, the future EDWARD VII, always known as Bertie. The second of their two sons and three daughters acceded to the throne as GEORGE V in 1910. Alexandra's dignity and charm endeared her to the British people in the long and frustrating years during which Bertie waited to ascend the throne. He was not a faithful husband: she was a loyal wife, becoming Queen Consort on the death of Victoria in 1901, though the King's illness delayed the coronation until 1903.

ALFRED (?–888), Ealdorman. As an ealdorman, Alfred belonged to an elite group of noblemen responsible for local government in ninth-century and tenth-century Wessex and England. Alfred, who must have played an important role in the defence of Wessex in the reign of ALFRED THE GREAT, would be known only from his surviving will and a reference to his death in the *Anglo-Saxon Chronicle*, except for the fact that he redeemed a magnificent illuminated manuscript, the *Codex Aureus*, from pagan Vikings and presented it to Christ Church, Canterbury. The *Codex Aureus* is now in the collections of the Royal Library in Stockholm.

ALFRED (?–1036), brother of EDWARD THE CONFESSOR. The two fled from England to Normandy in 1013 to escape the Danish armies of SVEIN FORKBEARD and CNUT. Alfred invaded England unsuccessfully in 1036 for motives that are now obscure, although it is at least obvious that he was trying to exploit the confusion that followed Cnut's death. On the orders of Cnut's son, King HAROLD I HAREFOOT, he was captured by Earl GODWINE and killed (perhaps accidentally when his eyes were gouged out) at Ely.

ALFRED THE GREAT see essay on pages 14–15

ALHFRITH (?–664), King of Deira (655–64). Installed by his father OSWY as King of Deira after ETHELWOLD's death at the Battle of the River Winwæd, Alhfrith formed a close alliance with St WILFRID, installing him at Ripon in place of St CUTHBERT and Irish monks from Lindisfarne. Alhfrith may well have been the driving force behind the decision to convene the Synod of Whitby, which decided in favour of the Roman date of Easter as against the Irish (*see* BEDE). It is reasonable to think that this represented not

continued on page 16

ALFRED THE GREAT (849–99)
King of Wessex (871–99)

The fifth son of King ETHELWULF of Wessex and his first wife OSBURH, Alfred ruled during what was undoubtedly one of the decisive periods in English and British history. He became King at a time when the Viking 'Great Army', led by HALFDAN and GUTHRUM, had already overrun the English kingdoms of Northumbria (*see* ÆLLE) and East Anglia (*see* EDMUND, ST). Three of his brothers, ETHELBALD, ETHELBERT and ETHELRED II, were king before him. When the 'Great Army' made its first concerted attack on Wessex in 870–1, the resistance organized jointly by Alfred and Ethelred was eventually sufficient to persuade them to leave. Ethelred, however, died in the midst of the campaign and his young son ETHELWOLD was passed over in favour of Alfred in recognition of the dangers of the times. After this rebuff, the 'Great Army' proceeded to the subjugation of Mercia, driving out Alfred's brother-in-law King BURGRED. A series of campaigns in 875–6 saw the Viking army march right across Wessex to Exeter and drive Alfred to seek refuge in the marshes of Athelney (Som.), from where he emerged to win the crucial Battle of Edington (Wilts.) and to make the advantageous Treaty of Wedmore with Guthrum in 878. After this Alfred was able to consolidate during the 880s to such effect that a second Viking assault in 892–6 did not harass Wessex anywhere nearly as much as the first; Alfred and his allies were able to contain the invaders and either defeat them or convince them that the likelihood of success was small. A marriage alliance involving one of Alfred's daughters and Count Baldwin II of Flanders strengthened ties with a strategically crucial continental power. In the long run, his victories can be seen as a decisive turning-point, since they provided the foundations for the eventual creation of a single English kingdom in the tenth century in the reigns of his successors, most notably those of EDWARD THE ELDER and ATHELSTAN.

Great as Alfred's achievements undoubtedly are, explaining his success poses many problems for historians. Not only are the sources as sparse as they always are for the early Middle Ages, they were in this case all written by individuals who were close to Alfred personally or who were members of his court. We have to approach them in the knowledge that we have only one side of the story. The authenticity and credibility of ASSER's *Vita Alfredi*, the chief source for his personality and attitudes, has been doubted, probably incorrectly. The other main source, the *Anglo-Saxon Chronicle*, focuses almost exclusively on Alfred's conflict with the Vikings; its narrowness not only leaves unanswered many questions about the strategy and the logistics of the campaigns, it also conveys the impression that Alfred's reign was almost entirely preoccupied with conflict with the invaders. While Alfred was undeniably a good and successful warrior, it is probable that he benefited from the weakening of the Viking armies which occurred as a result of the way in which groups left the main army to settle in the kingdoms which they had conquered. Although these texts do indicate that Alfred's policies also included an extensive programme of fortification, law-making, education and religious reform, we have to turn to other sources for more detailed information. Furthermore, there were the elements of ruthlessness in Alfred's behaviour, of a kind which we would probably expect as a matter of course in a successful war-leader, which are not made explicit in sources designed to show him as a moral and justified ruler.

The Treaty of Wedmore (878) between Alfred and Guthrum established a clear frontier between Alfred's territories and the lands under Viking control. It was guaranteed by hostages and included the provision that Guthrum convert to Christianity. It also ensured that a considerable part of the kingdom of Mercia was freed from Viking domination. After the death of King CEOLWULF II in 879, however, the Mercians did not choose another king, but instead placed themselves under the rule of the Ealdorman Ethelred. Although Alfred's specific role in these events is not clear, what is starkly obvious is that he used the situation to advance his own power and prestige. In 883 Ethelred accepted Alfred as his overlord, in 886 the former Mercian town of London was taken over by Wessex and in *c.* 888 Ethelred married Alfred's daughter ETHELFLÆD. Alfred also began to call himself 'King of the Angles and Saxons' rather than 'King of Wessex'. The visit to Alfred's court of ANARAWD AP RHODRI, King of Gwynedd, also enabled Asser to claim that Alfred exercised domination over the Welsh. This enhanced power was underpinned by a major strengthening of royal power within the kingdom of Wessex. It is generally believed that the construction of an extensive network of burhs throughout Wessex prevented the Vikings occupying towns and provisioning their armies in the way that they had done before. During Alfred's reign around 30 sites were fortified, sometimes using surviving Roman or Iron Age fortifications, but also on occasion establishing entirely new sites. Some of the best known of the burhs, such as Winchester and Wallingford, are now considerable towns where the street-plan of the burh is readily observable; others were places of much less importance, such as Cricklade (Wilts.), Langport (Som.) and Great Bedwyn (Wilts.). Placed strategically throughout Wessex, they supplied a co-ordinated system of defence, with each burh within one day's march of another and their garrisons able to provide mutual reinforcement. As with much of Alfred's achievement, the idea was not a new one – the Frankish King Charles the Bald (d. 877) had constructed fortified bridges on the Seine and the Loire to contain Viking armies – but the sheer scale of what was accomplished is truly astonishing. At Wallingford, for example, it has been calculated, on the basis of archaeological research and the document known as the *Burghal Hideage,* which dates from Edward the Elder's reign, that 120,000 man-hours would have been required to construct the 2,800 metres of the ramparts and that there would probably have been a garrison of 2,400. In total, Alfred's burhs would have required a standing army of approximately 27,000 men. Other major developments include a reform of the King's army recruited from thegns holding land throughout the kingdom, which involved dividing it into two halves so that a force was permanently available. He also made efforts to establish a fleet to try to anticipate Viking attacks, but his achievements here seem to have been small.

Alfred is also renowned for his sponsorship of learning and religious reform, activities which need to be placed in their historical context. Like all devout ninth-century contemporaries, Alfred unquestioningly believed that the miseries inflicted on the English people were a consequence of God's anger. The intellectual and religious renaissance was therefore designed to make the kingdom more pleasing in the eyes of God and to raise the morale of the English people. Like the construction of fortifications, it has a great deal in common with the policies of the Carolingian kings. What is remarkable about Alfred's achievements is the speed and scale of what was accomplished. Scholars such as Asser, JOHN THE OLD SAXON, GRIMBALD OF SAINT-BERTIN, PLEGMUND and WÆRFERTH were recruited from elsewhere to spearhead the movement. From 887 Alfred himself set about translating some of the great Christian texts, such as Gregory the Great's *Pastoral Care* and Boëthius' *Consolation of Philosophy*, into English for distribution among his subjects. He also established a court school. Modern scholars are generally agreed that, while Alfred's famous reflections on the decline of learning in England in the preface to the translation of the *Pastoral Care* are undoubtedly an exaggeration, his achievements were very large. They also reveal a king who had made himself literate in order to drive through changes which he believed essential, as well as a highly intelligent man who had reflected deeply on the meaning of some very difficult texts.

The Alfred the Great who emerges from Asser's account of his life is a very humane man who battled against serious, recurrent illness, and who immersed himself totally in the responsibilities which he believed God had placed upon him. While his achievements were enormous, it is important to retain perspective. His military achievement in one sense amounted simply to saving Wessex from the Vikings. It has also already been stressed that his methods of rule owed a great deal to Carolingian example. The traditional elements of his rule can indeed be underlined in other ways; his populous court, for example, illuminates his generosity, a characteristic typical of an early medieval king. His law-code also represents a traditional kingly activity. Its imperiousness and its savage penalties for crime do, however, exude in a special way both the power and the responsibilities of kingship. On the other hand, his seizure of monastic lands, his occupation of London and his manipulation of the succession in favour of his son Edward the Elder all demonstrate a readiness to disregard contemporary norms when it suited his interests. His sense of responsibility led directly to his successors' development of ever stronger control over Mercia. His wife, EALHSWITH, played an unusually small role in politics. What is ultimately striking – and is almost tangible across the centuries – is charisma and authority. Alfred possessed that quality which persuaded others to follow him in the most demanding of enterprises. His sense of the authority of kingship laid a base from which those who came after created a single kingdom of England.

Simon Keynes and Michael Lapidge, Alfred the Great (1983)
Richard Abels, Alfred the Great (1998)

simply religious idealism, but also a conscious drive to weaken his father's power. The fact that Alhfrith is not heard of again after 664 suggests that his father had him removed, and perhaps killed. With the exception of the period when ÆLFWINE was Sub-King, the former kingdoms of Bernicia and Deira largely disappeared after 664 and were incorporated into the single kingdom of Northumbria, which survived until the second half of the ninth century.

ALHMUND, ST (?–802), Prince. The son of ALHRED, King of Northumbria, Alhmund was murdered by St EARDWULF, King of Northumbria, as part of an attempt to secure his kingship by eliminating members of the main rival kindred. Although very little is known about Alhmund's actual life, he was regarded as a saint in the west Midlands, with many churches dedicated to him.

ALHRED (?–after 774), King of Northumbria (765–74). A kinsman of the short-reigned King Oswulf, Alhred overthrew Oswulf's supplanter ETHELWOLD MOLL, but was himself deposed and replaced by Ethelwold's son ETHELRED. He fled to CINIOD, SON OF FERADACH, King of the Picts, but his ultimate fate is unknown. Despite the violence of the times, Alhred has a reputation as a religious reformer and supporter of missionary activity; he is known to have had contacts with St LUL and other missionaries active in what is now Germany. The archbishopric of York was an extremely important educational centre at this time (see ALCUIN OF YORK; EGBERT). Two of his sons, the briefly reigned King Osred (d. 788) and St ALHMUND (d. 802), subsequently met violent deaths.

ALI, TARIQ (1943–), political activist. Born in Lahore, Pakistan, of socialist parents, Ali came to Britain to study at Oxford and was elected President of the Union in 1965, the first Pakistani to hold the position (Benazir Bhutto was the second, in 1976). He worked as a journalist and was the key figure in the anti-Vietnam war student protests in London in 1968: he has subsequently written on politics and made documentary films.

ALLAN, WILLIAM (1813–74), trade-union leader. Born in Ulster to Scottish parents, Allan started work in Scotland aged 12 as a cotton piecer before becoming an engineering apprentice in Glasgow. A keen trade unionist, he joined the Journeymen Steam Engine and Machine Makers' Friendly Society, the largest of the engineering unions, becoming its General Secretary in 1848. He was a major force behind the creation of the Amalgamated Society of Engineers (ASE) in 1851, which united the leading engineering unions.

With Allan as General Secretary (1851–74), the ASE pioneered New Model Unionism, distinguished by centralized executive control, firm financial discipline, high membership contributions, to cover sickness and other benefits, and conciliatory policies towards employers. The ASE became one of the best organized and most influential of unions. Allan was a member of the 'Junta' (see APPLEGARTH, ROBERT), active in the Reform League (1865–8) and treasurer of the Parliamentary Committee of the Trades Union Congress (1871–4). As such he was important in helping to create the image of trade unions as bodies of 'respectable' working men.

ALLEN, JOHN (1476–1534), Archbishop of Dublin. After studying in Oxford and Cambridge, he made a career in ecclesiastical administration, travelling to Italy on business for Archbishop WARHAM. He entered WOLSEY's service and, in 1528, in an effort to build up Wolsey's power in Ireland, was sent there as Archbishop of Dublin and Chancellor. In 1532, by now discredited by Wolsey's fall, he was replaced as Chancellor by his rival George Cromer, Archbishop of Armagh. During the Kildare rising, he was murdered by followers of Lord Thomas FITZGERALD while attempting to flee to England.

ALLEN, MARY (1878–1964), co-founder of the Women's Police Service. A suffragette who was imprisoned three times (once for hurling a brick through a Home Office window), Allen assisted Margery Dawson in forming the Women Police Volunteers shortly after the outbreak of the First World War, originally to protect young women refugees against London predators. Although it had no formal affiliation to the Metropolitan Police and no powers of arrest, the Women's Police Service (WPS), as it became in 1915, was sanctioned by the Home Office. In 1920 the Metropolitan Police issued a summons against Allen, who was Commandant (1919–38), and four other WPS members for impersonating police officers. As a result the women's uniform was modified, the word 'police' dropped and 'auxiliary' used instead.

ALLEN, RALPH (1694–1764), postal innovator. His grandmother was a postmistress in Cornwall, and he was recruited to work in the Bath post office. In 1715 he discovered Jacobite correspondence in the mail and was commended by General WADE. Promoted to Deputy Postmaster, he devised the system of cross-posts, avoiding the delays caused by routing letters through London, and from it made an average of £12,000 a year between 1720 and 1764. Allen bought Combe Down quarries near Bath and played an important part in the redevelopment of the city, creating a market for his stone. He built his home, Prior Park, near the quarries. A friend of POPE (who wrote of him as the 'man of Bath'), WARBURTON and PITT THE ELDER he entertained nobility and royalty. He provided finance and material support for Bath Hospital, opened in 1742. Combining new wealth with social grace and charitable impulses, Allen was the ideal self-made man of the first half of the eighteenth century.

ALLEN, WILLIAM (1532–94), Cardinal. His promising Oxford career was cut short by the restoration of Protestantism by ELIZABETH I. He was at Leuven University in 1561–2, and then returned to England, but in 1565 he fled once more to avoid punishment for his Catholic activism. He inspired the foundation of an English College at Douai (Flanders), pioneering the training of priests to win England back to Roman Catholicism (politics forced a move to Rheims 1578). Resident at Rome from 1582, he was drawn into intrigue against the English government, and supported Spanish plans for invasion which culminated in the 1588 sailing of the Armada. He was made a Cardinal in 1587. His death was a blow to the English Catholic community, left without effective leadership to heal its serious divisions. *See* BLACKWELL, GEORGE.

ALLEN, WILLIAM (?–1867), Fenian activist. On 18 Sept. 1867 Allen led a party of Fenians to rescue the Fenian leader Thomas Kelly from a prison van in Manchester. A police guard was killed; while Kelly escaped several Fenians were captured, and Allen was tried and convicted with four other suspects. Nationalist public opinion in Ireland felt that the men should not be executed because the killing was unintentional and the identification evidence was unsatisfactory (one of those convicted was released when an alibi was produced after the trial), while they were widely seen in Britain as dangerous murderers and incendiaries. Two prisoners were reprieved, but Allen, Michael Larkin and William O'Brien were hanged at Salford (Lancs.) gaol on 23 Nov. 1867. The three became known as the 'Manchester Martyrs'; commemorations were held on the anniversary of their deaths for many years. 'God Save Ireland', written in their memory by the moderate nationalist T. D. Sullivan, became an unofficial nationalist anthem.

ALLENBY, EDMUND (1st Viscount Allenby of Megiddo) (1861–1936), soldier. Born into Notts. gentry, Allenby was commissioned from Sandhurst into the Enniskillen Dragoons (1882), and in the Boer War participated in the relief of Kimberley (Feb. 1900) and in hunting down Boer commandos (1900–2). Large and ill-tempered, Allenby was nicknamed 'the Bull'. Commanding the cavalry division in 1914, he kept the Germans at bay during the retreat from Mons, but as Commander of 3rd Army from Oct. 1915 failed to break the deadlock on the Western Front. Transferred to command in Palestine in June 1917, four months later Allenby employed a deception operation devised by Colonel MEINERTZHAGEN, hooking around the left flank of the Turkish line at Beersheeba to take Jerusalem. Allenby attacked again in the autumn of 1918, driving the Turks back to Anatolia in four weeks, an advance which has been seen as a prototype 'blitzkrieg'.

ALLESTREE, RICHARD (1619–81), writer. Salop.-born and educated at Christ Church, Oxford, he joined the army of CHARLES I during the 1642–6 Civil War and during the 1650s helped maintain semi-clandestine Anglican services in Oxford; at CHARLES II's restoration he was predictably rewarded with Oxford's Regius Chair of Divinity and became Provost of Eton in 1665. Most of his devotional writing was anonymous, and included *The Whole Duty of Man* (1658), a manual of Christian morality which was hugely influential over the next 150 years in establishing the ideal for an ordered, moderately austere Protestant lifestyle.

ALLEYN, EDWARD (1566–1626), actor and educational patron. Born in London, he took over the family innkeeping business while acting with various companies, occasionally joining with James Burbage's company at the Globe. He was considered the main rival to Richard BURBAGE as an actor, starring especially in first performances of Christopher MARLOWE's major works. Finally retiring in 1604 to live on his investments and enjoy himself as artistic patron, he set up as a country gentleman at Dulwich and, having no heirs, he left his large fortune to found a college and almshouses there. Dulwich College inherited his collections, the nucleus of the distinguished art gallery which forms part of the foundation.

ALMA-TADEMA, SIR LAWRENCE (1836–1912), artist. Born in Holland, Alma-Tadema studied art in Antwerp before coming to London in 1869. His detailed, sunlit, authentically textured, almost cinematic genre paintings of delicately luscious yet circumspect figures in classical, often Pompeian, settings and dress ('five o'clock tea antiquity', WHISTLER called it) came to define 'High Victorian' art. With the Victorian rediscovery of the classical world, Alma-Tadema, who also designed furniture and stage sets for Henry IRVING, enjoyed a huge popular success, though one that would not survive the harsh realities of the First World War.

ALMON, JOHN (1737–1805), journalist and bookseller. He came from Liverpool to London in 1759 to work as a printer and hack writer, and in 1761 was hired by the owner of *The Gazetteer* as a political commentator. He opposed the anti-war policies of Bute (*see* STUART, JOHN), campaigned for the recall of PITT THE ELDER, attracting the patronage of Earl Temple (*see* GRENVILLE-TEMPLE, RICHARD) who helped him set up his own bookselling and printing business in Piccadilly. Through Temple, Almon met John WILKES and the two became close. When Wilkes fled abroad, Almon propagandized on his behalf. In 1765 he was tried for libel for publishing *A Letter Concerning Libels* questioning the legality of general warrants, but charges were dropped when the Rockingham (*see* WATSON-WENTWORTH, CHARLES) ministry was formed. Almon was again tried in 1769 when he reprinted a letter of 'Junius' from the *Public Advertiser* urging that GEORGE III be deposed; alone among publishers he was convicted and fined. In 1771 he and Wilkes urged the printer of the *London Evening Post* not to answer charges of contempt before the Commons for printing reports of debates, leading to a clash between the City of London, under Brass CROSBY, and the Commons, and the abandonment of attempts to obstruct such reporting. *The Remembrancer* (1775–84) put the American case to a British audience, and in 1788 he was tried for libel for printing remarks about the King's insanity, and fled abroad. Returning to England, he spent a year in prison, then retired to write his memoirs.

ALPÍN, SON OF EOCHAID, King of the Picts and (?) of Dál Riata (?728–41). One of the four kings contending for supremacy in Pictland during the later 720s, Alpín had secured the overlordship of the Picts by 726 and held it until he was defeated, first, by OENGUS, SON OF FERGUS, and then by NECHTAN in 728. This latter defeat also cost Alpín his 'territories', indicating that he had a recognized power-base in Pictland, although he appears to have descended from the Cenél nGabráin kin-group of Dál Riata. It appears that Alpín subsequently ruled in Dál Riata at some point prior to 741, perhaps for a period of four years, although the history of Dál Riata is confused for this period.

ALPÍN, SON OF EOCHAID (?–?841), King of the Picts and (?) of Dál Riata. Alpín's life and career, as reported in the sources, is contradictory and uncertain. The existence of an earlier ALPÍN, SON OF EOCHAID, King of Picts and, perhaps, of Dál Riata, leads to suspicions that the known rearrangement of the *Chronicle of the Kings of Dál Riata* has been undertaken to provide the famous CINAED MAC ALPÍN with a father who was king. The accounts of Alpín contained within the *Chronicle* are tentative and not all versions give him a place in the king-list; those which do give him a reign of three years. Some versions relate that he was killed in Galloway, having devastated the province in 841; while others state he died a natural death. There is no mention of him in the *Annals of Ulster*, which is otherwise comprehensive in its mention of kings of Dál Riata.

AMBERLEY, LADY KATHERINE (KATE) (1842–74), suffragist. Her parents were the Liberal politician, Lord Stanley of Alderley, and Lady Stanley, who insisted that her daughters received as good an education as her sons. In her teens she came to know the work of John Stuart MILL and Harriet TAYLOR on the enfranchisement of women. In 1864 she married a fellow admirer of Mill and Taylor, John Russell, Viscount Amberley. Through friendship with Harriet's daughter, Helen TAYLOR, she was drawn into feminist circles, supporting the work of Emily DAVIES and Elizabeth Garrett ANDERSON in education and medicine, and becoming an active advocate of women's suffrage from 1870 until her untimely death.

AMBROSIUS AURELIANUS (*fl.* fifth century), Romano-British chieftain. Mentioned by GILDAS as a British leader who gained victories, including his greatest at the Battle of Mount Badon (*c.* 500, at a site which cannot now be located), against the Anglo-Saxons after they had overthrown the British ruler later named by BEDE and NENNIUS as VORTIGERN. All that can realistically be said of Ambrosius, whose name suggests Roman descent, is that he was a chieftain who stemmed the tide of the advance of the Angles and Saxons into southern Britain for some considerable time. Some later sources (rightly or wrongly) identify the victor of Mount Badon as King ARTHUR.

AMERY, LEO(POLD) (1873–1955), politician. It was said of Amery that had he been half a head taller in stature and his speeches half an hour shorter in length he might have become Prime Minister; as it was he had to settle for being the foremost imperialist of his generation. A contemporary of Winston CHURCHILL at Harrow, unlike him he went on to a successful university career at Oxford culminating in a prize fellowship at All Souls. As a young man he was a member of MILNER's kindergarten of young imperialists in South Africa, and from the start of Joseph CHAMBERLAIN's Tariff Reform campaign an enthusiastic supporter of greater imperial federation, a cause to which he devoted his political life. He served on the editorial staff of *The Times* (1899–1909), during which time he wrote a controversial history of the Boer War in which he excoriated the shortcomings of the British military. Elected a Conservative MP in 1911 he remained one until 1945.

He first obtained office in Stanley BALDWIN's government of 1923 and was delighted by the decision to adopt Tariff Reform. But after the defeat in the 1923 election the Conservatives took a more cautious approach to the controversial issue of tariffs, and, although Amery was made Colonial Secretary in 1924, he was unable to influence economic policy, which remained firmly under the Free Trade direction of that renegade Conservative turned renegade Liberal, Churchill. Amery's support for Tariff Reform ensured that he stayed out of power when the National government was formed in 1931, and like Churchill spent most of the next decade in the political wilderness. Although he shared Churchill's opposition to appeasement, he deplored his antediluvian attitude on India, where Amery shared the government's aim of granting it dominion status. His finest hour came in May 1940 during the Commons debate on the Narvik debacle when, at the end of a long but effective speech, he rounded on Neville CHAMBER-LAIN, the son of his political hero Joseph, with the words of Oliver CROMWELL to the Long Parliament, 'You have sat too long here for any good you have been doing. Depart, I say, and let us have done with you. In the name of God, go!'

Churchill made him Secretary of State for India in 1940 but the two men continued to disagree on India, and Amery came to feel that Churchill conceded too much to the USA by way of control over the British economy. The end of the war saw a personal tragedy when his eldest son John was hanged for collaboration with the Nazis, but his final years were comforted by the political success of his son Julian, who later became a Conservative minister under Harold MACMILLAN. Amery died in 1955 having seen his dreams of imperial federation come to nothing.

AMES, WILLIAM (1576–1633), theologian. A student of William PERKINS at Cambridge and a strict Puritan, he moved to the Netherlands and was quickly recognized as a champion of hardline Calvinism in the Dutch Reformed Church's religious conflicts, achieving a Europe-wide reputation as Professor of Theology at Franeker (from 1622). Only a few months before his death, he resigned his chair to lead the English church at Rotterdam. His extensive controversial writings included attacks on the leading Roman controversialist, Cardinal Robert Bellarmine, and works of casuistry (discussing the moral dilemmas of the Christian life) which had a lasting influence on Protestant ethics.

AMHURST, NICHOLAS (1697–1742), poet and journalist. Educated at Merchant Taylor's school, he was expelled from Oxford in 1719 for Whig politics and high living, and became a hack writer in London, issuing periodicals, essays and poems, some with political content. Despite his Whig politics he opposed the WALPOLE government and in 1726 was engaged by Bolingbroke (*see* ST JOHN, HENRY), PULTENEY and their allies to manage *The Craftsman*. Its sustained and well-informed attacks on the ministry, and list of contributors headed by Bolingbroke himself, made it the most successful opposition periodical of its day with a circulation of between 500 and 1,250. Amhurst was imprisoned in 1737 for publishing a libellous article under Colley CIBBER's name. *The Craftsman* ceased soon afterwards, and he died in poverty.

AMIS, SIR KINGSLEY (1922–95), novelist. In his lifetime seen as an 'Angry Young Man' (though one whose ammunition was satire), as the progenitor of the 'campus novel' and latterly as a right-wing curmudgeon, Amis shot to fame when, while a lecturer in English at Swansea, he published *Lucky Jim* (1954), the story of a lower middle-class radical lecturer also at a provincial university, whose fortunes are followed in *That Uncertain Feeling* (1956) and *I Like it Here* (1958), while his creator went on to a fellowship at Peterhouse, Cambridge (1961–3). Amis, who is sometimes credited with being the saviour of the English novel from its post-war lassitude, won the Booker Prize for *The Old Devils* (1986).

AMIS, MARTIN (1949–), novelist. Like his father Kingsley AMIS, he won the Somerset Maugham Prize for his first novel, *The Rachel Papers* (1973), published when he was 24. His slangy vernacular, scabrous observations of post-modern manners and urban decay, in *Dead Babies* (1975), *Success* (1978), *Money* (1984), *London Fields* (1989), *The Information* (1995), and his autobiography, *Experience* (2000) have made him something of a literary cult figure whose life is of considerable interest to the media.

ANARAWD AP RHODRI (?–916), King of Gwynedd. On his succession to the kingship following the death of his father, RHODRI MAWR, the greatest threat to Anarawd came from the Vikings and Mercians. Anarawd, in turn, however, was himself a threat to the security of the southern Welsh kings, who claimed the protection of ALFRED THE GREAT, King of Wessex. This led to an invasion of Gwynedd by ETHELRED, Ealdorman of Mercia, in 881, which was checked by Anarawd at the Battle of Cymryd and resulted in a brief alliance with the Danes of York. This must have proved unsatisfactory for, a little later, Anarawd himself sought an alliance with Alfred, visiting the West-Saxon court, the first known instance of such an occasion in Anglo-Welsh history. In 893–4 Anarawd drove a Danish army from Gwynedd, but he was to be troubled by frequent Viking raids for the remainder of his reign.

ANDERSON, ADELAIDE (MARY) (1863–1936), civil servant. The daughter of a Scottish shipowner, Anderson was educated at Girton College, Cambridge. In 1894 she was appointed by the Home Office as one of the first four women factory inspectors, and from 1897 to 1921 was in charge of the Women's Branch of the Factory Department, an arduous fire-fighting role that took her on investigations into women's working conditions all over Britain. Her aim was both to make the inspectorate more efficient and to maintain its separate status. In 1921 the importance of her work was recognized in the reorganization of the Factory Department, but paradoxically that meant the amalgamation of the men's and women's inspectorates.

ANDERSON, ELIZABETH (née Garrett) (1836–1917), physician. Sister of Millicent FAWCETT, Anderson joined the Society for Promoting the Employment of Women and, impressed by the work of Elizabeth BLACKWELL, Barbara Leigh BODICHON and Emily DAVIES, she decided on a medical career. Her gender prevented her from studying at the established medical schools, which bolstered her ambition to open the British medical profession to women. In 1865 she gained a licence to practise from the Society of Apothecaries, thus becoming the first British woman to qualify in medicine. Subsequently she ran a consultancy from home and in 1866 opened a London dispensary for women and children (now the Elizabeth Garrett Anderson Hospital). In 1870 she was elected to the London School Board, appointed physician to the East London Hospital and granted an MD from Paris University. One of the foremost campaigners for women's education and suffrage, she helped Sophia JEX-BLAKE found the London School of Medicine for Women in 1874 and as Mayor of Aldeburgh (1908) was England's first woman mayor.

ANDERSON, LINDSAY (1923–94), theatre and film director. Anderson was one of a group of directors at the Royal Court Theatre who changed the face of British theatre in the 1950s with their productions of the new wave of playwrights such as John OSBORNE and John Arden. He was particularly associated with Arden, staging his *Sergeant's Musgrave's Dance* (1959) and *The Changing Room* (1971). He went on to direct several films, but none equalled the success of *If* (1968), the quintessential anti-Establishment satire to come out of the English counter-culture of the 1960s.

ANDREW OF WYNTOUN (*c.* 1350–*c.* 1425), poet. Prior of St Serf's Isle (Kinross), he was the author of the *Orygynal Cronykil of Scotland*, a narrative poem in Scots verse retelling the story of Scotland from its legendary beginnings until 1408. When it reaches the year 1286, the poem becomes a heroic saga of the Wars of Scottish Independence against the English.

ANDREWES, LANCELOT (1555–1626), Bishop of Winchester. Master of Pembroke Hall, Cambridge, in 1589, he was one of the few anti-Calvinist academics to have a successful career under ELIZABETH I. His scholarship and brilliant sermons (particularly in the Chapel Royal) won admiration from Elizabeth and JAMES I, leading to appointment first as Dean of Westminster in 1601 and then to various bishoprics from 1605; he was made Dean of the Chapel Royal in 1619. A feline operator in Church politics, he was well-placed through his court influence to be an important early patron of the High Church group of Arminian clergy, who echoed his detestation of Calvinists, his appreciation of the pre-Reformation spiritual heritage of the Church and his interest in Greek Orthodox spirituality and liturgy. One of his sermons inspired T. S. ELIOT's poem *The Journey of the Magi*.

ANDREWS, JOHN (1871–1956), Prime Minister of Northern Ireland. A member of a leading Ulster business dynasty: one brother, Thomas, designed the *Titanic* (and sank with it in 1912); another, James, became Chief Justice of Northern Ireland. Andrews was Northern Ireland Minister for Labour (1921–37) and Minister for Finance (1937–40), and succeeded James CRAIG in 1940. His failure to remove geriatric and incompetent colleagues and public discontent with the government's handling of German air raids led to a party *coup* in 1943 which brought younger Unionist leaders to power under Basil BROOKE. Andrews's son, J. L. O. Andrews, held Cabinet positions under Brooke and Terence O'NEILL in the 1950s and 1960s.

ANDREWS, SIR J.L.O. (1903–86), Irish politician *see* ANDREWS, JOHN

ANEIRIN (*fl. c.* 600), British poet. Of the five poets named by NENNIUS who flourished at this time, only work by Aneirin and TALIESIN survives, but from much later manuscripts. The only surviving work by Aneirin is the epic saga *The Gododdin* which relates, through a series of elegies and eulogies, the fate of a failed military expedition, organized by Mynyddawg Mwynfawr, King of the Gododdin, to halt the northwards expansion of the kings of Deira and Bernicia at the expense of the British kingdoms. Although the expedition failed, the kingdom, centred on Edinburgh, managed to resist expansion by the Angles for a further generation.

ANGERSTEIN, JOHN JULIUS (1735–1823), merchant and connoisseur. He came to England from Russia in 1750 and in 1756 became an insurance underwriter at Edward LLOYD's. He persuaded his colleagues to move to a larger building in which all the marine underwriters in London could be based. Advised by Sir Thomas Lawrence and Benjamin WEST, he built up a substantial art collection, 38 paintings from which were bought by the nation in 1824 for £60,000; these became the nucleus of the National Gallery.

ANGLESEY, 7TH EARL OF see ANNESLEY, ARTHUR

ANGUS, EARL OF, 22ND and **23RD** see DOUGLAS, ARCHIBALD

ANNA (?–c. 654), King of East Anglia (?–c. 654). A nephew of King REDWALD and the successor of Kings SIGEBERHT and Egric, Anna, whose personal qualities were praised by BEDE, was a notable figure in the development of Christianity in southern England. A patron of St FURSA and the father of several saintly daughters who included St ÆTHELTHRYTH, SEAXBURH and ETHELBURH (Abbess of Faremoutiers), he was also responsible for the conversion of King CENWEALH of Wessex. Like his predecessors, he was killed in battle against the aggressive King PENDA of Mercia and was succeeded by ETHELHERE.

ANNANDALE, LORD OF see BRUCE, ROBERT

ANNE, QUEEN see essay on page 22

ANNE BOLEYN see essay on page 23

ANNE NEVILLE (1454–85), Queen of England (1483–5). Younger daughter and co-heiress of Warwick the Kingmaker (see NEVILLE, RICHARD), in 1470 she was betrothed to HENRY VI's son, EDWARD, Prince of Wales. By 1474, however, she was married to Richard of Gloucester, and was crowned Queen in 1483 when he took the throne as RICHARD III. She died in March 1485, a year after the death of their only son. Widespread rumours that Richard had plotted her death forced the King to issue a public denial.

ANNE OF BOHEMIA (1367–94), Queen of England. Sister of King Wenceslas of Bohemia, she married RICHARD II in 1382. She was granted a generous dower and, since she was small and plain, this led to the allegation that the King had paid too high a price 'for a tiny bit of flesh'. But on her death in 1394, Richard, apparently inconsolable, ordered the demolition of Sheen (Surrey), the manor house in which she had died.

ANNE OF CLEVES (1515–57), Queen of England. Second daughter of John, Duke of Cleves, she was selected to be HENRY VIII's fourth wife by Thomas CROMWELL for diplomatic reasons: he was hoping to keep the King wedded to an alliance with Protestant princes in Germany. The Duchy of Cleves had strategic importance, lying between the Low Countries and the German imperial territories, and its Duke was cautiously sympathetic towards the Protestant cause. Henry was delighted with HOLBEIN's portrait of Anne but their first meeting on New Year's Day 1540 was a disaster. Cromwell held him to the marriage, which duly took place on 6 Jan. 1540; Henry still detested Anne and the diplomatic value of Cleves declined. Henry insisted on an annulment of the marriage, so Anne took a handsome settlement of English lands and retired to discreet and comfortable grass widowhood. The affair was the main reason for Cromwell's fall. Anne is often seen through Henry's eyes as a dull and lumpish 'Flanders mare' but her skilful reaction to the crisis and her acquisition of tolerable English from scratch within a few weeks suggest that she was no fool.

ANNE OF DENMARK (1574–1619), Queen of England, Ireland and Scotland. Daughter of Frederick II of Denmark and Norway. Marriage negotiations with JAMES VI began in 1585, but were obstructed by ELIZABETH I. Determined pressure from the Scots nobility led to a proxy wedding in Copenhagen in Aug. 1589 and, with uncharacteristic drama, James collected his bride from Norway in person, in Nov. 1589. James did not share Anne's sympathy for Catholicism, although he consistently sought her tacit approval for his homosexual favourites. After he became King of England as JAMES I, she encouraged English court extravagance in building, art and court entertainment, especially masques (see JONES, INIGO; JONSON, BEN).

ANNESLEY, ARTHUR (7th [5th Annesley] Earl of Anglesey) (c. 1679–1735), politician. His family had both English and Irish estates and titles. Educated at Cambridge, he served three times as MP for the university, before taking his seat in the Lords in 1710. During the ministry of Robert HARLEY he emerged as the leader of those Tory peers who fervently defended the Protestant succession; their support was crucial in the struggle between Harley and Bolingbroke (see ST JOHN, HENRY) for leadership of the ministry in the

continued on page 24

ANNE (1665–1714)
Queen of England, Ireland and Scotland (1702–14)

Second of two children surviving to adulthood of James, Duke of York (later JAMES II), Anne was educated for domestic rather than public life. Though her father converted to Catholicism in her childhood, her uncle CHARLES II, to minimize controversy, had his nieces raised Anglicans. Henry COMPTON, Bishop of London, instilled in Anne a lifelong devotion to the Church of England.

Like her sister MARY, Anne married a staunch Protestant, in her case Prince GEORGE of Denmark (1683); it was agreed that they would reside in England. As she had developed a passionate attachment to Sarah CHURCHILL, once her maid of honour, now married to John CHURCHILL, promising young soldier and diplomat, Anne ensured that Sarah had a place in her household. In 1684 she had a stillborn daughter, only the first such tragedy. Many of her 17 pregnancies were abortive: none of her children lived to adulthood.

Her father became King in 1685, and tried in vain to woo her for Catholicism. Her household became a centre for Protestant courtiers, and she began what she herself termed a treasonable correspondence with her sister Mary and her husband William of Orange (later WILLIAM III). Enraged to hear that her father's second wife, MARY OF MODENA was pregnant, she spread rumours that the pregnancy was fraudulent. She and the Churchills were aware of William's plan to invade, and Prince George and Churchill deserted to join William in late Nov. 1688. Anne evaded house arrest and fled to Nottingham, where Protestant nobles rallied to her. Initially resisting the plan to make William and Mary joint monarchs (giving William's claim precedence over hers), she was persuaded by the Churchills to acquiesce.

Relations between Anne and the new royal couple were not easy, in part because Anne was feared as a possible focus for opposition. She did in fact dabble in political intrigue. Perhaps to pre-empt any accommodation between her father and William and Mary, or to forestall invasion, Churchill (now Earl of Marlborough) tried to persuade James that Anne would in due time support his son's claim. When William, hearing of this, deprived Marlborough of his offices, Anne stood by Marlborough.

In 1700 her last surviving child, the 10-year-old Duke of Gloucester, died. The 1701 Act of Settlement provided that after Anne (and failing heirs of her body) the succession should pass to the next Protestant heir, SOPHIA, Electress of Hanover. Though approving this arrangement, Anne resisted all proposals to bring members of the Hanoverian family to England, perhaps remembering problems associated with her own reversionary court.

William's unexpected death in March 1702 brought Anne to the throne. (Prince George remained merely a consort and died in 1708.) She proved a hard-working monarch, telling ministers pressing her to renege on commitments that she was not to be 'frighted into compliance though I am a woman ... I thank God I have a soul above that'. Like William, she aimed to become prisoner of neither Whigs nor Tories, but to construct mixed ministries. Her succession took place at a time of European crisis: Anne pledged herself to continue William's policy of constructing a new anti-French Grand Alliance which soon led to the war which lasted for most of her reign. Marlborough had been William's chief agent in this policy. Anne made him Captain General, and him and GODOLPHIN the linch-pins of her ministry.

Her first ministry had a significant High Tory element. Anne approved many of their policies, but wearied of their partisanship. In 1704 High Tories were replaced by Robert HARLEY and his moderate Tory associates; in 1705 the Queen swung further towards the Whigs. Anne had long wished to pull the Scots into line over the succession; pressed by her Whig ministers, she backed a more ambitious scheme for parliamentary union, enacted in 1707. She was however beginning to resent Whig assertiveness and so became estranged from Sarah Churchill, a fierce partisan. The Whigs nonetheless continued to accumulate power until, in 1710, they overreached themselves by impeaching the Tory cleric Henry SACHEVERELL. Anne then dismissed Godolphin for Harley and a largely Tory ministry, who ended the war and agreed the Peace of Utrecht (1713), against Whig opposition (Anne had to create 12 new peers to get the peace through the Lords). The Queen's debility made the succession issue pressing; Harley (now Lord Oxford) struggled to control Tories inclined to flirt with the possibility of a Jacobite successor. In 1714, losing confidence in him, Anne decided to back his more vigorous rival Bolingbroke (see ST JOHN, HENRY). It was, however, too late for Bolingbroke to establish his position. As the Queen slipped into her final illness, her ministers persuaded her to appoint the Whig Shrewsbury (see TALBOT, CHARLES) Lord Treasurer. It would fall to him to smooth the way for the Hanoverian succession.

Edward Gregg, Queen Anne (1980)

ANNE BOLEYN (?1501–36)
Queen of England

Daughter of Sir Thomas Boleyn, a courtier and Norfolk and Kentish magnate. She spent 18 months at the court of Margaret of Austria in the Netherlands and seven years in France as a maid of honour and companion to her contemporary Claude of France, first wife of Francis I. As a result of a down-turn in Anglo-French relations, she was recalled to the English court in 1521. Her charm, intelligence and strong personality won her many ardent admirers, who from 1526 included HENRY VIII, tiring of CATHERINE OF ARAGON and beginning to think of the annulment of his marriage. Probably by 1527 they were informally betrothed; by Aug. Henry was approaching the Pope about overturning the dispensation which had made possible his marriage to his elder brother's widow. Events moved tortuously slowly, but Anne began living openly with Henry during 1531; when in 1532 the King determined to secure an annulment unilaterally in England, she was created Marquess of Pembroke in her own right, and she became pregnant towards the end of 1532, possibly after a secret service of marriage. A secret marriage certainly took place on 24 or 25 Jan. 1533, and when a hearing by Thomas CRANMER at Dunstable Priory in May had pronounced the annulment of the King's marriage to Catherine, a pregnant Anne was publicly wedded to the King four days later and crowned Queen, to widespread public disgust. Her first child was not the looked-for son but the future ELIZABETH I (Sept. 1533); nevertheless, Anne's position with Henry did not become dangerous until after a stillbirth of a male child on 29 Jan. 1536. Paradoxically, the death of Catherine earlier that month also undermined Anne's position, since Henry now no longer felt obliged to defend Anne against the continued presence of his former wife. He interpreted the stillbirth as God's judgement on his second marriage, and since he was certain that no fault could be found in him, the problem must lie with Anne. He had already become attracted to JANE SEYMOUR, and in the spring he began to listen to accusations against Anne from those who had always hated her for usurping Catherine's position. Fatally, Anne quarrelled with Thomas CROMWELL over foreign policy and the use of resources from the dissolved monasteries, so he took over the conservative conspiracy against her. On 2 May Anne was arrested on absurd charges of treasonous adultery and of incest with her brother George BOLEYN, Lord Rochford; sent to the Tower, she was convicted by a tribunal presided over by her uncle Thomas HOWARD, 8th Duke of Norfolk, despite vigorously protesting her innocence. Archbishop Cranmer obligingly declared her marriage to Henry null (the grounds for his judgement have mysteriously disappeared), and her daughter was thereby declared illegitimate; no one seems to have pointed out to the King that annulment of the marriage rather undermined a charge of adultery. She was executed on 19 May 1536, by the French method of beheading with a sword (against all English precedent); her supposed lovers had already been killed.

Historians are revising previous jaundiced opinions about Anne promulgated by Roman Catholic commentators, beginning with the Ambassador Eustace CHAPUYS. Quite apart from her importance in precipitating the King's 'Great Matter', she played a major role during her brief 'reign' in promoting religious reform and advancing reformists (evangelicals) to positions of power in the Church. From her years spent in France, she had many contacts with evangelicals in French court circles, who were patronized by Francis I's sister Marguerite, Duchess of Angoulême, and among surviving items from her personal library are a number of beautifully illuminated manuscripts with French evangelical associations. Regardless of charges of incest, she was extremely close to her brother George, a fervent evangelical who was regularly used on diplomatic missions to France, and who personally translated for her a French reformist book by the distinguished French humanist, Jacques Lefèvre d'Étaples (c. 1460–1536). She was enthusiastic for translation of the Bible into English and she alerted Henry to various books on reform, especially William TYNDALE's assertion of royal divine right and analysis of the Church's usurpation of royal power in his *Obedience of a Christian Man* (1528). With her family, she became a powerful patron of Cambridge-educated reformist clergy and advanced their careers: besides Thomas Cranmer and Matthew PARKER, Hugh LATIMER and Nicholas SHAXTON were among the reformers who became bishops during her years of power. Several important Evangelical courtiers, such as Antony DENNY or her doctor William BUTTS, also survived her fall to play important roles in protecting religious reformism later in the reign. It is no exaggeration to say that, uniquely among European reformations, the English Reformation owes its peculiar character to the intervention of two women: Anne and her daughter Elizabeth.

E. W. Ives, Anne Boleyn (1986)

months before ANNE's death. (Sir Thomas HANMER led their counterparts in the Commons.) Anglesey's indecisiveness prevented him from providing the Tories with strong leadership after the accession of GEORGE I.

ANNING, MARY (1799–1847), palaeontologist. Born in Lyme Regis (Dorset), she was the daughter of a cabinetmaker who also peddled fossils to summer visitors. In 1811, aged 12, she unearthed the remains of an entire 10-metre-long ichthyosaurus, sold to the British Museum in 1828. Anning was a self-taught fossil-hunter whose local acuity and delicate touch were rewarded in the 1820s with the excavation of an almost perfect plesiosaurus (1824) and evidence of a flying reptile, *Pterodactylus macronyx* (1829), discoveries that brought her national renown (the tongue-twister 'she sells sea shells on the sea-shore' is supposed to refer to Anning) and a profitable fossil-selling business supplying museums and collectors.

ANSELM, ST *see* essay on pages 26–7

ANSON, GEORGE (1st Baron Anson) (1697–1762), circumnavigator and naval administrator. He entered the navy at 15, and in 1740 he was given command of a squadron of six ships, to harry Spanish trade and possessions in the Pacific (Britain and Spain then being at war). Manned largely with Greenwich Hospital pensioners, the squadron met with serious difficulties in rounding Cape Horn and only Anson's *Centurion* and two other ships reached the Pacific rendezvous at Juan Fernandez Island, and then with only a handful of men fit for duty. By June 1743 only the *Centurion* was left, but the *Manila* galleon was captured. Casualties of the expedition were appalling, over 1,200 men died of disease, but 32 wagons of treasure were paraded through London, and Anson became wealthy for life. As Admiral he defeated a French fleet off Finisterre in 1745, and later, as First Lord of the Admiralty, his reforms of the dockyards, and of naval training and administration, set the foundations for generations of British naval success.

ANTONINUS PIUS (Titus Aurelius Fulvius Boionius Arrius Antoninius), Roman Emperor (AD 138–61). After Roman armies had taken over the Scottish Lowlands for the first time since the campaigns of AGRICOLA, Antoninus, in the early 140s, ordered that the earlier HADRIAN's Wall be replaced by a wall connecting the rivers Clyde and Forth. A turf construction almost 60 kilometres in length, the so-called Antonine Wall, was occupied only until the early 160s when it seems to have been decided that the task of holding down the Scottish Lowlands was too difficult and Hadrian's Wall again became the northern frontier of the Roman empire.

ANTRIM, 2ND EARL AND 1ST MARQUESS OF see MACDONNEL, RANDALL

APPLEGARTH, ROBERT (1834–1924), trade-union leader. Born in Hull, Applegarth worked at various trades from the age of 10 before becoming a joiner. After three years in the USA (1855–8) he settled in Sheffield. There he became an active member of the local carpenters' union, which he led into the newly formed Amalgamated Society of Carpenters and Joiners (ASCJ) in 1861, a New Model Union (*see* ALLAN, WILLIAM). He was its General Secretary (1862–71). Applegarth was a member of the 'Junta', the term later applied to the five trade-union leaders William Allan (Engineers), Applegarth, Edwin Coulson (Bricklayers), Daniel Guile (Iron Moulders) and George Odger (Ladies' Shoemakers) who played a major role through the London Trades Council in shaping the image and policies of trade unionism in the 1860s. They helped to move the unions into politics, for votes for working men (mainly through the Reform League), support for the North and anti-slavery during the US Civil War (1861–5) and Italian nationalism. Applegarth was also a prominent figure (from 1865) in the International Working Men's Association. The ASCJ affiliated to it in 1867, and Applegarth was elected Chairman of the General Council in 1868. He was central to the presentation of the trade-union case to the Royal Commission on Trade Unions (1867–9) and in securing an enhanced and unrivalled degree of legal protection for trade unions by 1875. He was the first working man to be appointed to a royal commission, as a member of the inquiry into the Contagious Diseases Acts in 1871. Subsequently he remained a political and social reformer through work in local government, the advocacy of free and universal elementary education, and improved safety in coal mining and other causes.

ARAM, EUGENE (1704–59), murderer. A schoolteacher in Knaresborough (Yorks.) until he left in 1745 under suspicion of being involved in a fraud committed by Daniel Clark, who had disappeared, Aram taught in schools across England and wrote on linguistics, where he was one of the first to connect Celtic with other European languages. In 1758 he was arrested at Lyme Regis (Dorset) after a man called Houseman had shown the authorities the location of Clark's body and implicated Aram in the murder. Aram was tried, and executed on 6 Aug. 1759.

ARBUTHNOT, JOHN (1667–1735), writer. The son of a Scots Episcopal clergyman, who lost his

ANSELM, ST (1033–1109)

nt and Archbishop of Canterbury (1093–1109)

there until 1056
e quarrelled with
ears of wandering
ering the recently
, where the Prior,
course of religious
which was to make
figures in Latin

Prior in 1063 and
By that time he had
rs and *Meditations*,
al and philosophical
on the relationship
nd the *Proslogion*, in
argument, the 'onto-
istence of God.

us was taken ill and,
Anselm as Archbishop
cration, Anselm, like all
n the rights and privi-
, after Lanfranc's death,
bishopric vacant in order
was inevitable that when
new Archbishop would
more money and military
than Anselm was willing
monks who thought that
acy, the fashions, manners
court were anathema. The
cret of the fact that they
dancing more than listening
of wisdom. The King and
words, yoked together like a
old sheep.

ween the two was exacerbated
ived in a period of momentous
western Europe. A group of
as attacking traditional ideas
nd property. Since one of the
reformers was Gregory VII
they are conventionally called
argued that families distracted
real work and that therefore
be celibate, despite the fact that
st priests had had wives and chil-
ere themselves sons of priests. In
chmen who did not want families
came monks. Now the reformers,
like Anselm, were monks, were

saying that all priests should be more like monks themselves.

In 1072 an Archbishop of Rouen who told a meeting of his clergy that they should give up their wives (although he called them their mistresses) was driven out of the meeting by a hail of stones. This did not deter Anselm from ordering priests, deacons and canons to put away their wives; and he prohibited sons from inheriting their fathers' churches.

Gregorians also argued that the humblest priest was more important than the most powerful king, on the grounds that the soul was more important than the body and priests looked after people's souls, whereas kings only ruled people's bodies. Priests therefore should be 'pure'. Since priests promoted by laymen spent too much time pleasing their patrons and too little looking after the spiritual needs of the people, the reformers began to argue that it was wrong for churchmen to be appointed by laymen. Instead they should be 'freely' chosen by other churchmen.

For centuries kings and other secular rulers down to the level of lords of manors had given land to the Church and often paid for the building of churches; in return they took a share of the revenues of 'their' churches and generally appointed the priests, abbots or bishops who headed those churches. In a ceremony known as 'lay investiture' the newly appointed abbot or bishop received the ring or staff symbolizing his office from the hands of the king who had chosen him. Kings needed the support of their churchmen, not only to pray for them, to hold services and dispense the sacraments, but even in the crudest material terms. The Domesday Book (1086) shows that bishops and abbots held about one quarter of the entire wealth of England. In 1095, the year in which Pope Urban II launched the First Crusade, the Gregorian war-cry 'Free the Church!' was first heard in England.

In that year William II summoned a council to Rockingham to settle a dispute between him and 'his' Archbishop. Anselm told the King that the matter could not be settled in his court, but only by the Pope, since it was to the Pope, as the successor of St Peter, and not to any king or emperor, that Christ had given the keys of heaven. In 1093 Anselm had recognized the King as his lord, had been invested by him and had done homage to him, but

living when the Presbyteria[n]
established Church of Sco[t]
Revolution, Arbuthnot traine[d]
at St Andrews. Settling in
guished himself by his mathem[a]
was elected a Fellow of the Ro[yal]
and physician-extraordinary to
1705. He was friendly with lead[ing]
Robert HARLEY's administration, a[nd]
sympathy with their views wh[en]
published a series of pamphlets at[tacking?]
with France, known as *The History*
was these which established the figu[re]
as the archetypal, bluff but somew[hat]
Englishman. Arbuthnot was a me[mber]
Scriblerus Club in 1713–14 along with
and GAY and collaborated with Pope an[d]
comedy *Three Hours after Marriage*
also wrote medical treatises and built up
able medical practice, with patients
PULTENEY and Chesterfield (*see* STANHOPE

ARCH, JOSEPH (1826–1919), agri[cultural]
labour leader. Son of a Warws. farm labou[rer]
became a Primitive Methodist lay preache[r]
radical critic of the political and social ord[er]
1872–3, he founded the National Agricu[ltural]
Labourers' Union, leading the great
labourers' strike in 1874, the 'Revolt of the Fi[eld]'
and in 1885 he represented north-west Norfol[k]
Parliament. There he became an uncriti[cal]
admirer of the Liberal Party, but is rightly remem[em]
bered for his struggles against poverty and inju[s]
tice in the countryside.

ARDEN, ALICE (?–1551), murderess. In order to
marry Thomas Mosby, a tailor, she conspired with
a group of friends to have her husband, Thomas
Arden of Faversham (Kent), murdered,
witnessing the crime herself. Soon arrested, she
was burnt at the stake in Canterbury; her lover
and eventually six other associates were hanged.
The case caused a great and lasting sensation; it
was the basis of the play *Arden of Feversham*
(anonymous, *c.* 1590) and a popular ballad of 1633.

ARGYLL, EARL OF, 1ST *see* CAMPBELL, COLIN;
4TH, 5TH, 8TH and **9TH** *see* CAMPBELL,
ARCHIBALD; **1ST MARQUESS OF** *see* CAMPBELL,
ARCHIBALD; **DUKE OF, 2ND** *see* CAMPBELL, JOHN;
3RD *see* CAMPBELL, ARCHIBALD

ARKWRIGHT, SIR RICHARD *see* essay on page
28

ARLINGTON, 1ST EARL OF *see* BENNET, HENRY

ARMSTRONG, ROBERT (Baron Armstrong)
(1927–), civil servant. Educated at Eton and

Philosopher, sa[int?]

Born at Aosta in Italy, he lived
when, after his mother's death,
his father and left home. After y[ears?]
he became a monk in 1059, en[tering?]
founded Norman Abbey of Be[c?]
LANFRANC, started him on the
and intellectual development
him one of the outstanding
Christendom.

He succeeded Lanfranc a[s]
was elected Abbot in 1078.
written collections of *Praye[rs]*
and two important theologi[cal]
works, the *Monologion*,
between faith and reason,
which he put forward a ne[w]
logical argument', for the e[xistence]

In 1093 WILLIAM II RUF[US]
expecting to die, he name[d]
of Canterbury. At his cons[ecration]
prelates, swore to maint[ain]
leges of his Church. Since
William had kept the arch[bishopric?]
to exploit its revenues, i[t]
he recovered he and hi[s]
quarrel. Rufus wanted
service from Canterbur[y]
to provide. Moreover, t[he]
long hair meant effemi[nate?]
and morals of William'[s]
courtiers made no s[ecret?]
enjoyed hunting and
to ecclesiastical word
he were, in Anselm'[s]
wild bull and a feeble
The mismatch be[tween?]
by the fact that they
change throughout
radical reformers
about sex, power
most determined
(Pope 1073–85),
Gregorians. They
priests from the[ir]
priests ought to
for centuries mo[re]
dren and many
those days chur[ch]
of their own be
many of who[m]

now he was saying that he owed a higher allegiance to the Pope, a faraway lord with few battalions.

For the first time in the history of these islands, relations between Church and State had been turned into a matter of theory and controversy. Not surprisingly, the other bishops of England told Anselm that he was on his own: 'We will not withdraw the fealty that we owe the King.' Further disputes and lack of support from his colleagues led Anselm to choose exile in 1097, leaving the estates of Canterbury to be taken into the King's hand.

In exile he went to the papal curia. There he was asked to expound the doctrine of the Latin Church at a meeting with representatives of the Greek Church. At Easter 1099 he heard Pope Urban II issue decrees excommunicating all clergy who did homage to laymen for ecclesiastical possessions and all who participated in lay investiture. (Norman and English clergy had not been present when Gregory VII condemned lay investiture in 1078, and so, in 1093, not even the reform-minded Anselm had heard of this decree.) He finished his revolutionary study of the theology of redemption, *Cur Deus Homo*, and he might have carried on quite contentedly as a philosopher in exile had not the sudden death of William II led to his recall in 1100.

The questionable circumstances in which the new King, HENRY I, succeeded to the throne made him invite Anselm back in order to give an appearance of legitimacy to his rule. Although Anselm now refused to do homage, this worked for a while since Henry, a master of procrastination and more devious than his brother, initially found it more convenient to postpone problems rather than provoke a quarrel by confronting them. But Anselm's insistence that papal orders must be obeyed and his consequent refusal to consecrate bishops and abbots whom the King invested eventually made life impossible for everyone and led to his second exile in 1103.

There followed prolonged negotiations between the King and a new Pope, Paschal II, in which it gradually became clear that the Papacy was willing to draw back from Urban II's more extreme policy. Anselm returned to England in 1106 and, in Aug. 1107, he accepted a compromise settlement worked out in discussions at Westminster between King and bishops from which he had been absent. Henry renounced lay investiture, but prelates were to continue to do homage for lands held from the King. In practice the King's wishes continued to be the decisive factor in the making of bishops. Up to a point it can be said that the King had preserved the reality of royal control of the Church in return for giving up the form, but neither side was entirely happy with the compromise. Church State relations remained problematic.

The debate which Anselm had brought to England would rumble on, and for centuries the Papacy would have a bigger say than ever before in the internal affairs of churches throughout the British Isles.

Anselm held a second council of the English Church in 1108 (repeating his earlier legislation on marriage and inheritance), and completed his last theological work, a study of the problem of predestination and freewill. He died on 21 April 1109. In the next few years his devoted follower, EADMER, was able to complete the *Life of Anselm* on which he had been working in the 1090s and which Anselm had ordered him to destroy in 1100. In the 1120s Eadmer, convinced that Anselm had been a saint, added a collection of miracles to the *Life*.

In 1163 Archbishop Thomas BECKET presented a new *Life of Anselm* written by JOHN OF SALISBURY to Pope Alexander III and petitioned for his canonization. The Pope remitted the question to a council of English bishops and from then on Anselm was included among the saints, although not until the eighteenth century was his status as a saint of the Roman Catholic Church put on a more formal basis.

Although Eadmer's *Life* and Anselm's own writings (passionate letters to friends as well as learned treatises) mean that we know a great deal about him, he remains a controversial figure. Was he homosexual? Probably not. Was he ambitious for high office and astute enough to get it? Or was he an other-worldly monk out of his depth in the rough and compromising world of power politics? Eadmer portrayed him as a man who went to sleep at business meetings until he woke up and demolished his opponents' arguments in a few words. Writing to a friend, Anselm said, 'Dearest, you have enlisted in the army of Christ, in which it is necessary not only to drive the Enemy away, but also to use some cunning in doing so'.

Richard W. Southern, Saint Anselm: A Portrait in a Landscape (1990)

ARKWRIGHT, SIR RICHARD (1732–92)
Inventor and industrialist, factory pioneer

Youngest son of a Preston tailor of modest means, he received little formal schooling: his spelling was always execrable. Apprenticed to a barber, in his early twenties he set up in business as a peruke maker and haircutter, in Kirkham (Lancs.). There, in 1755, he married the daughter of a prosperous Presbyterian schoolmaster. After her death he remarried in 1761, and branched out in business by setting up an inn, which did not flourish.

Having a taste for mechanical experiment, he began to develop an effective method of spinning cotton by rollers. For some decades, it had been apparent that shortage of cotton yarn might constrain the expansion of various textile trades, including the Lancs. cloth industry and Midlands stocking-knitting industry. Arkwright sought help from clockmaker John KAY, who had been involved in other such experiments. By 1768, he had designed a machine which improved significantly upon earlier models, and moved to Nottingham, a centre of framework knitting, to develop it – perhaps encouraged by recent innovations in that industry (James HARGREAVES, inventor of the spinning jenny, set up a factory there at the same time). With financial aid from relatives, he applied for a 14-year patent, granted 1769.

With backing from local hosier Samuel Need and his inventor-partner Jedediah STRUTT, Arkwright set up a horse-driven mill to power his machine but, by 1771, the partners had decided to shift the main focus of their activities to Cromford, Derbys., where ample water offered an alternative power-source. The coarse cotton twist produced by their machines was strong enough to serve for warp thread – the thread that bore the greater strain in weaving – making possible the production of pure cotton cloths, not previously much made in Britain. In 1774 Arkwright successfully lobbied for an Act to free British cotton cloth from the high level of duty imposed on imports, arguing that the new industry would give work to many 'British poor', especially those children between the ages of 10 and 12. In 1775, acting without his partners, he sought a further patent for a carding machine, to prepare fibres for spinning.

In the next decade his industrial empire expanded rapidly: he built new mills at several Derbys. locations, in Staffs. and in Lancs. at Birkacre near Chorley – though he abandoned the latter after it was destroyed by local workers worried that machinery would displace men. In 1782 he opened a mill in Manchester, where he experimented, unsuccessfully, with steampower

(in 1789 he was to try again, ordering from BOULTON and James WATT a steam engine for his Nottingham mill). In 1784 he also began exploring opportunities in Scotland, and entered into partnerships to establish mills in Lanarks. and Perths. He also sold machines to other manufacturers: by 1782 he claimed that his machines were in use in eight counties, and giving work to at least 5,000 people.

Arkwright's attempt to retain control over, and charge heavily for, such valuable technology unsurprisingly met resistance. From 1781 to 1785 he battled in court with rival manufacturers wishing to use such machines without hindrance. The first verdict went against Arkwright on the grounds that his patent was obscure and incomplete; he succeeded in having that reversed in 1785, but within a few months his critics broadened their attack, alleging that he had stolen others' ideas, in part through his assistant Kay. Under a torrent of hostile evidence, judgement finally went against him.

His ingenuity, hard work and pre-eminence in the trade were, nonetheless, generally acknowledged. He played a part in the General Chamber of Manufacturers of 1785–6 and, in 1791, a leading role in the agitation against renewing the East India Company's charter when, for a change, he urged the case against monopoly.

So successful was Arkwright's invention, and his exploitation of it, that, after 10 years in the trade, he was in a position to begin enjoying the fruits of enterprise. In 1780 he married off his daughter with a dowry of £15,000; in 1782 he purchased the manor of Willersey, where he built Willersey Castle; he also purchased a London house, in the ADAM brothers Adelphi development. In 1786 he was knighted while presenting GEORGE III with a loyal address; in 1787 he was appointed Sheriff of Derbyshire. He commissioned portraits of himself by fashionable London painter Mather Brown and by Joseph WRIGHT of Derby.

In his 60th year his heart or kidneys suddenly failed and he died within a few days. His son Richard succeeded him in business.

In the nineteenth century he was celebrated both as a pioneer of industrialism and as archetypal self-made man, and likened to such other heroes of the age as NELSON, Wellington (see WELLESLEY, ARTHUR) and Napoleon. The Cromford mill is being restored as an industrial museum.

R. S. Fitton, The Arkwrights: Spinners of Fortune (1989)

though this was staunchly denied by Heath and by later historians of the period.

ARMSTRONG-JONES, ANTHONY (TONY) (1st Earl of Snowdon) (1930–), photographer and ex-royal consort. As Tony Armstrong-Jones, son of the Countess of Rosse, with a studio in Rotherhithe (when East End photographers were an essential part of the 'swinging London' circuit portraying its style in such periodicals as *Vogue* and *Queen*), in 1960 he married Princess MARGARET, the younger sister of Queen ELIZABETH II. The couple's divorce in 1978 was seen as damaging the image of Britain's premier family. It was not, however, to be the last such royal marital rupture of the reign. Snowdon has continued to work as a photographer and maker of television documentaries.

ARNE, THOMAS (1710–78), composer. Born in London and educated at Eton, he defied family hopes that he would be a lawyer and became a composer, writing many operas and oratorios. A composer of the second rank, he is remembered for the tune 'Rule, Britannia' in his setting of the play *Alfred* (1740) commissioned by FREDERICK, Prince of Wales.

ARNOLD, SIR MALCOLM (1921–), composer. Arnold studied composition and the trumpet at the Royal College of Music in 1938, joining the London Philharmonic Orchestra in 1941. He abandoned professional playing and took up full time composition in 1948 and demonstrated an inexhaustible capacity for inventing memorable tunes. He has produced a vast amount of orchestral music, including nine symphonies, more than 20 concerti, four ballets, two operas and numerous film scores, including that for *The Bridge on the River Kwai* (1957), for which he won an Oscar.

ARNOLD, MATTHEW (1822–88), poet and cultural critic. The eldest son of Thomas ARNOLD, he was educated at Winchester, Rugby and Balliol College, Oxford, where he drank a good deal, did not do much work and emerged with a mediocre degree. Following a period as private secretary to the Marquess of Lansdowne (1847–51), he was appointed Inspector of Schools (1851–86). During his tenure of office he did much to expose the deficiencies of English education, largely as a result of the extensive knowledge which he developed of provincial schools, and he became a leading advocate of improved secondary education. His was one of the voices influencing the climate of opinion about middle-class education which shaped the reforms following the Taunton Commission of 1864.

While acting as an Inspector, he was also writing, as a poet and critic. Appointed Professor of Poetry at Oxford (1857–67), in 1867 he wrote 'Dover Beach', a reflection of religious doubt and the contemporary crisis of faith in Protestantism. Much of Arnold's poetry and literary criticism was preoccupied with the supposed mediocrity and philistinism of the English middle classes, a central theme of his most celebrated and influential work, *Culture and Anarchy* (1867). In this essay he saw culture, a term whose importance in later discourses about society owes much to Arnold, as the realization of the human spirit through reason. Like his contemporary CARLYLE, he was deeply troubled by what he saw as the breakdown of good government and the turn to anarchy. Unlike Carlyle, his focus was on the moral void of industry and wealth: he envisaged the possibility of the educated being in the vanguard of a resurgence of cultural values rather than social and moral leadership residing in a strong and authoritarian elite. Arnold shared with Carlyle, however, a belief that race was part of the explanation for the climate of anarchy and philistinism. Liberal individualism, with its stress upon individual rights, narrow-minded nonconformity and worship of machinery and wealth, produced a one-sided humanity of incomplete and 'mutilated' men. To counter this, what was needed was 'sweetness and light'. The claim rested, in good part, on an analysis of the English race, which combined elements of both Hebraism, the 'Semitic tradition', and Hellenism, the 'Aryan tradition'. Puritanism had descended from its search for moral development into mere selfish individualism by the nineteenth century: it was necessary to restore the best in English culture by mobilizing the desire for sweetness and light or the Hellenic elements. While Arnold's contribution to cultural analysis has been influential in the twentieth century through the writings of critics such as T. S. ELIOT, F. R. LEAVIS and Raymond WILLIAMS, the notions of Englishness embodied in his writings have been no less pervasive if less clearly visible.

ARNOLD, THOMAS (1795–1842), educationalist. Headmaster of Rugby school in 1828, he initiated a reformed, more broadly based curriculum and a disciplinary code which involved less of the bullying and violence with which Rugby and other schools had been associated. Rugby under Arnold became the prototype for the regeneration of the English public school system. His brand of muscular Christianity is well captured in Thomas Hughes's novel *Tom Brown's Schooldays* (1857), which is modelled on Arnold's Rugby.

ARNÓR THÓRDARSON (c. 1046–75), poet. He spent much of his life at the court of Earl THORFINN THE MIGHTY of Orkney. A considerable amount of his poetry survives, including verse devoted to the Norwegian King HARALD HARDRAADA. His writings illuminate a career spent travelling around the seas of northern Europe and show that he and the northern parts of Britain in which he lived were profoundly immersed in an Icelandic and Scandinavian cultural world.

ARRAN, EARL OF, 1ST see BOYD, THOMAS; **2ND, 3RD** and **4TH** see HAMILTON, JAMES; **5TH** see STEWART, JAMES

ART MAC MURROUGH see ART MÓR MAC MURCHADHA

ART MÓR MAC MURCHADHA (ART MAC MURROUGH) (?–c. 1416), King of Leinster (1375–1416). In 1391 the English government's confiscation of his Anglo-Irish wife's inheritance, because he had married her in contravention of the Statute of Kilkenny, was a source of grievance. He posed a threat sufficient to draw RICHARD II to Ireland in 1394. Although Art was forced to submit, relations with the English soon broke down again, and by 1399 not only was he claiming to be King of Ireland, but this time Richard was unable to break his resistance. Indeed Art, an outstanding military leader, remained a potent thorn in the flesh of the Lancastrian government until shortly before his death.

ARTGAL, SON OF DOMNAGUEL (?–872), King of the Strathclyde Britons. It is uncertain when Artgal became King of Strathclyde, but it may have been c. 849. His fortress at Dumbarton Rock was besieged and captured in 870 by the Vikings of Dublin led by OLAF THE WHITE and IVAR THE BONELESS, and he appears to have numbered among the many prisoners landed in Dublin the following year. The *Annals of Ulster* record that Artgal was killed in 872 on the advice of CONSTANTÍN I, King of the Scots, who appears to have followed a policy of trying alternately to resist and appease the invading Vikings.

ARTHUR, KING see essay on pages 32–3

ARTHUR (1486–1502), Prince of Wales. Eldest son of HENRY VII, he was created Prince, with a Council in the Marches of Wales administering the region in his name, in 1489; at the same time, a similar Council was set up in York with Arthur as titular Warden General. In March 1488 negotiations had begun for his marriage with CATHERINE OF ARAGON; the wedding, on 14 Nov. 1501, was accompanied by spectacular pageantry, a pioneering venture in Tudor court display, inspired by court ceremony of the Duchy of Burgundy. Arthur's early death at Ludlow (perhaps from plague) led to

Catherine's remarriage to his younger brother, the future HENRY VIII; the papal dispensations for this second marriage caused much dispute in Henry's efforts to secure annulment of his marriage. The question of whether Arthur's marriage was consummated (central to the annulment disputes) remains difficult. Against Catherine's firm insistence that she had remained a virgin, we can only range hearsay and reports of Arthur's adolescent sexual boasting.

ARTHUR OF BRITTANY (1187–1203), royal prince. Posthumous son and heir of GEOFFREY OF BRITTANY, he was nominated in 1190 by his uncle RICHARD I as his heir presumptive, but by 1199 JOHN, another uncle, was Richard's acknowledged successor. Some of the barons of Anjou revived Arthur's claim, but were rapidly outmanoeuvred. Arthur's opportunity came in 1202, when Philip II Augustus of France pronounced the confiscation of all of John's continental dominions and recognized Arthur as their lawful lord. When John captured Arthur at Mirebeau in Aug. 1202, he was never seen again; almost certainly he was killed on John's orders. Rumours of his fate were widespread by 1203 and did much to undermine John's authority in Anjou, Maine and Normandy.

ARUNDEL, EARL OF, 25TH see HOWARD, PHILIP; **26TH** see HOWARD, THOMAS

ARUNDEL, THOMAS (1353–1414), Archbishop of Canterbury (1396–7, 1399–1414). The combination of a high aristocratic birth (he was the third son of Richard FitzAlan, Earl of Arundel) and high ambition made him one of the most powerful of all English prelates. Beginning his ecclesiastical career as a youthful Bishop of Ely in 1374, he became Archbishop of York in 1388, then of Canterbury in 1396. His political connections led to his banishment by RICHARD II in 1397 and restoration by HENRY IV two years later. He had no fewer than five terms of office as Chancellor 1386–9, 1391–6, 1399, 1407–10, 1412–13, but his vigorous opposition to the Lollards showed that he cared about religious as well as secular affairs.

ARUP, SIR OVE (1895–1988), civil engineer and architect. Son of Danish parents but born in Newcastle-upon-Tyne, he studied philosophy and engineering and became involved in the structural design of such Modernist buildings as Highpoint flats in north London (1936–8) and the concrete ramps of the penguin pool at the London Zoo (1934). He was a builder of bridges, including Durham (1967), Runnymede (Surrey) (1978) and Kylesku (Lothian) (1984). Arup's company also acted as consultant to projects as diverse as the Sydney Opera House (1956–73) and the Eurostar railway terminal at Waterloo station in London.

ARWALD (?–687), King of the Isle of Wight. The last of three known kings of the Isle of Wight (*see also* STUF), Arwald was killed by CADWALLA, King of Wessex, who conquered the island and incorporated it into Wessex. Cadwalla entrusted its conversion to Christianity to St WILFRID.

ASAPH, ST (*fl.* late sixth century to early seventh century), churchman. Primarily known through the later medieval *Lives of Kentigern*, whose pupil he is stated to have been, Asaph is predominantly associated with north Wales, where his principal work took place. He is reputed to have been appointed Bishop of Llanelwy in the late-sixth century where several local churches are dedicated to him. The supposed association with KENTIGERN accounts for the traces of his cult in Scotland.

ASCHAM, ROGER (1515–68), scholar. Born in Yorks., he was one of the chief products of Sir Humphrey WINGFIELD's humanist school before St John's College, Cambridge. His Johnian connections (which included John CHEKE and William CECIL) secured him a place in royal education; he played some part in teaching EDWARD VI and in 1548 became tutor to Princess Elizabeth (the future ELIZABETH I). After disagreements, he spent time abroad before returning to serve successively Edward, MARY I (she esteemed his learning enough to pardon his Protestantism) and, once more, Elizabeth. Though a brilliant Greek scholar, he championed English as a language fit for intellectuals, and insisted on the value of sports in education; he wrote the first English treatise on archery, *Toxophilus* (1545).

ASHBEE, C(HARLES) R(OBERT) (1863–1942), craftsman. Born into an affluent Isleworth (Middx.) family, Ashbee declined to enter the family trading business, and, influenced by the writings of Edward CARPENTER, went in search of the simple life, moving to Whitechapel in London's East End in 1886 to work at Toynbee Hall. There he studied with the poor and unemployed, and formed the equivalent of medieval craft guilds to practice printing and bookbinding and the making of furniture and silverware. By 1898 this enterprise had become a limited company with Ashbee himself increasingly occupied with architectural design and conservation. In 1902 the guild moved to Glos., and Ashbee embraced the male communal life (with the reluctant acceptance of his wife) and published an inspirational tale for the guildsmen: *From Whitechapel to Camelot* (1892).

ASHBURTON, BARON, 1ST *see* DUNNING, JOHN; **1ST** and **3RD** *see* BARING FAMILY

ASHBY, DAME MARGERY (née Corbett) (1882–1981), campaigner for women's rights. Cambridge-educated, Corbett became secretary to the National Union of Women's Suffrage Societies (1906–7) and subsequently sat on the union's executive. A lifelong Liberal, she stood for Parliament several times, was twice President of the Women's Liberal Federation, and was a forceful speaker, a fluent linguist and an internationalist. She joined the International Alliance of Women when it was founded in Berlin in 1904, becoming its secretary in 1920 and its President in 1923, and edited the monthly *International Women's News*. Ashby represented the alliance at the Versailles peace conference in 1919; served as a British delegate to the disarmament conference at Geneva in 1932–4 and maintained a lifelong interest in the condition of women in the developing world.

ASHDOWN, SIR JOHN JEREMY ('PADDY') (1941–), politician. Known as 'Action Man' after his service in the Royal Marines, Ashdown entered the Commons in 1983 as Liberal MP for Yeovil (Som.). This was at the height of the success of the Social Democrats led by Roy JENKINS and then David OWEN. But the promised breaking of the mould of British politics never occurred, and after the union between the Liberals and the Social Democrats in 1987, Ashdown became one of the most vigorous front-bench spokesmen for the Liberal Democrats; in 1988 he succeeded Sir David STEEL as party leader. His closeness to Tony BLAIR and New Labour led to an agreement on electoral reform before the 1997 election, and to a place on a Cabinet committee thereafter. With the Liberal Democrats increasing their MPs to more than 40 in 1997, Ashdown, who resigned as leader in 1999, has been the most successful Liberal leader since LLOYD GEORGE.

ASHFORD, DAISY (MARGARET) (1881–1972), novelist. The daughter of a retired War Office official, Daisy Ashford was educated largely at home, where she wrote her comic novel about upper-middle-class Victorian social mores, *The Young Visiters, or Mr Salteena's Plan*, when she was nine years old. After her mother's death, she rediscovered the manuscript, which was published in 1919 with a foreword by J. M. BARRIE. Its ingenuous view of social pretensions, and its idiosyncratic spelling (which the publishers imaginatively left uncorrected) made it an instant and enduring success (the book was reprinted 18 times in the first year of publication), though doubts have occasionally been cast on its authenticity as the work of a child.

ARTHUR (*fl.* sixth century)
Legendary King of Britain

One of the most famous characters in British history, even though he may never have existed. Even if he did, his exploits are most unlikely to have resembled those attributed to him by later legends. The real Arthurian story is one of how successive ages have been fascinated by some extremely good romantic tales of knightly prowess and courtly love. Although they convey a very misleading impression of life in the Middle Ages, in more modern times they have been one of the most influential legacies of medieval civilization.

Although he supposedly lived in the sixth century, actual references to a historic Arthur are extremely rare before the twelfth century. The earliest mention is contained in a Welsh poem of *c.* 600, the *Gododdin*, supposedly written by ANEIRIN, which praises a named warrior's accomplishments, but says that he was 'no Arthur'. The name Arthur is Roman, and would therefore be appropriate to a member of the Romano–British aristocracy, struggling to stem the tide of the invading Angles and Saxons. An extraordinary range of stories has evolved out of this thin tissue of evidence, with the first mention of the idea of a legendary British champion appearing in the early ninth-century history attributed to NENNIUS, who, possibly on the basis of a lost seventh-century text, lists 12 battles that Arthur is supposed to have won against the invading Angles and Saxons as leader of the British. In the tenth century, the Welsh chronicle known as the *Annales Cambriae* assigned two of the battles to a date in the first half of the sixth century and, according to Nennius, one of the battles which Arthur is supposed to have won is the Battle of Mount Badon, known from other earlier and more reliable evidence to have been won by AMBROSIUS AURELIANUS. Scholars have not been able to identify the sites of most of the battles mentioned in Nennius; that one of them appears to have been located near Chester and another north of the Forth appears to indicate that Arthur's activities were extraordinarily, if not incredibly, wide-ranging. Information of this kind has of course fuelled the perennial debate as to whether the historic Arthur was Scottish or Welsh. There have been archaeological excavations at such places as South Cadbury (Som.) and Tintagel (Cornw.), both of which have for centuries been considered potential locations for Arthur's court, but all that can be proved is that they were places inhabited by a British prince who wielded local power in the immediate after-math of the departure of the Romans. South Cadbury has been shown to be an Iron Age hill fort refortified in the fifth and sixth centuries, and Tintagel, dramatically situated on a cliff-top, has been demonstrated to have strong Celtic connections. The recent surge of media interest which followed the discovery by a group of Glasgow University archaeologists at Tintagel of a stone engraved with the name Arthur is typical of the interest which these excavations of Arthurian sites still arouse. In this case, all that is certain is that a record of someone called Arthur has been preserved at Tintagel, but not necessarily of *the* Arthur. Ultimately, the only safe thing that can be said of the historic Arthur is that there may have existed a great soldier who temporarily halted the Anglo-Saxon assault, but that, the extensive range of supposed activity notwithstanding, it is doubtful whether he was a chieftain who united all the British against the invaders.

In subsequent history there are two very different *legendary* King Arthurs. One is the warrior champion who led the Britons in numerous battles against the invading Saxons – a distinctly Celtic hero. The other presided over a magnificent court, Camelot, and his deeds tended to be outshone by those of his followers, the Knights of the Round Table. This second Arthur is, quite simply, an ideal king – a model for any monarch of Britain, not necessarily one who was a Briton or a Celt. Any king who claimed lordship over the British Isles would be perfectly happy to look upon him as his predecessor. This second version also became the focus of chivalric literature, tales of magic and of knightly prowess.

By the early twelfth century, Arthur's story was clearly well known in Wales, Cornwall and Brittany, and one of its salient features was already established: the oppressed Britons dreamed of the day when King Arthur would return and restore to his people their rightful dominion over the island of Britain. This was the figure of Celtic legend whom GEOFFREY OF MONMOUTH transformed in the 1130s into the dominating personality of his historical fantasy, the *History of the Kings of Britain*. In Geoffrey's hands, Arthur was the British champion against the invaders, but he also became much more. As conqueror of Scotland, Ireland, Iceland, Norway, Denmark and Gaul, he was the equal of Alexander the Great and Charlemagne, and his court was a spectacular centre of international chivalry, courtliness and high fashion. Finally defeated and wounded, he was taken to Avalon and laid to rest. Geoffrey's history was a resounding success with his contemporaries, and when it was translated from its original Latin into Anglo-Norman, for example, by WACE, these new elements rapidly became even more prominent. On the one hand, from the 1170s and 1180s onwards they provided a courtly setting for the Arthurian romances of the authors who came after the Frenchman Chrétien of Troyes, who invented both the Round Table and Camelot, and brought the Arthurian stories conclusively to an international audience. On the other, they made it easier to overlook the specifically Celtic Arthur. The politically inspired 'discovery' of Arthur's body, still bearing terrible wounds, at Glastonbury in c. 1190 may have also helped to push into the background the image of a king being healed at Avalon so that he might return and drive out the English. In 1278 EDWARD I deliberately paid homage to Arthur's bones to demonstrate to the Welsh, whom he was then in the process of conquering, that the hope of delivery by a hero who would awaken in time of crisis was vain.

These literary developments cleared the way for the reconstruction of Arthur as primarily an English king, a process that was aided by the habit, common already in the twelfth century, of treating 'Britain' and 'England' as virtually interchangeable terms. Thus it seems that the earliest king of England to identify himself with Arthur was RICHARD I, a ruler who set off on the Third Crusade brandishing Excalibur; by the fourteenth century, EDWARD III was described as 'unmatched since the days of Arthur, one-time King of England'. His establishment of the Order of the Garter drew on Arthurian exemplars to establish a select chivalrous group. The Round Table which can still be seen at Winchester Castle was probably made for Edward I, although the surviving decoration was made on the orders of HENRY VIII.

Thanks to the fifteenth-century genius of Sir Thomas MALORY, whose Morte d'Arthur was subsequently printed by Thomas CAXTON, the cult of King Arthur survived into modern times, to be taken up and reworked in an extraordinary multiplicity of ways. Doubtless the Welsh blood of the Tudors allowed Edmund SPENSER to tell ELIZABETH I that her name, realm and race were all derived from 'this renowned prince'. But without any such association, Sir Richard Blackmore could make his Arthur represent William of Orange (the future WILLIAM III), while Alfred TENNYSON could equally well imagine ALBERT, VICTORIA's prince consort, finding in King Arthur 'some image of himself'. In general, however, the focus shifted away from King Arthur himself and developed instead into a great range of literary tales devoted to the members of the court, such as Lancelot, Gawain and Queen Guinevere. One of these, the search for the Holy Grail, which combined magic, love and religion in a single story, found its most moving and famous expression the late fourteenth-century Sir Gawain and the Green Knight.

Scepticism about the existence of the version of Arthur created in the twelfth century is almost as old as Geoffrey of Monmouth's History. Later in the twelfth century, for example, both WILLIAM OF NEWBURGH and Gerald de BARRI condemned Geoffrey's work as fiction. In the sixteenth century the Italian writer Polydore VERGIL launched an attack, which led to a defence of Arthur by John LELAND. None of this seriously stemmed the flow of literary production around the great Arthurian themes; they were taken up, for example, in Spenser's The Faerie Queene, although, interestingly, SHAKESPEARE left them alone. The development of scientific history from the nineteenth century onwards inevitably increased doubts about the tales' credibility. Yet, at the same time, the stories became even more popular with the Gothic revival, which was followed by a multitude of nineteenth-century and twentieth-century representations in, for example, Tennyson's poetry, pre-Raphaelite art, Elgar's music and several films. The continuing international appeal of the Arthurian image is indicated by the way in which, in the 1960s, the brilliant social scene associated with the Kennedy presidency led to its being described as a modern Camelot. It seems that, whatever happens, the Arthurian tales retain a place in popular imagination. Interestingly, however, their loss of a specifically Celtic identity has meant that Wales has looked to other past heroes to lead it to salvation from the English, most obviously Owain GLYN DWR. Scotland, in whose history Arthur has never been so prominent, has found its medieval heroes in William WALLACE and ROBERT BRUCE. Fifteen centuries have taken Arthur ever further away from the dimly perceived historical origins of one of the most renowned figures in British history.

Leslie Alcock, Arthur's Britain (1971)
Richard Barber, The Arthurian Legends (1979)

ASHLEY, LAURA (née Mountney) (1925–85), designer and retailer. The romantic Victorian floral fabrics, dress designs and furnishings that were central features of the Laura Ashley design and retail business struck a nostalgic chord with middle-class Britain in the 1970s, and from that an international retail company sprang. Trained as a secretary, Laura Mountney married Bernard Ashley in 1949, and the couple opened a mill to produce their own fabrics. By 1963 the still-small business moved to her native Wales; after just over 20 years the fashion group was floated, for £60 million, but Laura Ashley died in a fall. Her husband retained for the next eight years the controlling interest in a company that saw considerable difficulties emerge, especially in the North American market, in the course of the 1990s.

ASHLEY COOPER, ANTHONY see COOPER, ANTHONY ASHLEY

ASHMOLE, ELIAS (1617–92), antiquarian. Son of a wealthy saddler, he trained as a solicitor, fought for the Royalists in the Civil Wars, and as a student at Brasenose, Oxford, developed interests in astrology, science and mathematics. He was made Windsor Herald in 1660 and wrote or edited many works of antiquarian or hermetic interest. In 1677 he presented his extensive collections of curiosities, based around the Cabinet of Curiosities assembled by the Tradescant family (see TRADESCANT, JOHN), to Oxford University, where they formed the nucleus of the Ashmolean Museum. Its first curator was Robert PLOT, assisted by Edward LHUYD. Ashmole's principal intention had been to revitalize the teaching of natural sciences, but after 1860 scientific holdings were relocated in the new University Museum; the Ashmolean became and remains an art museum.

ASHTON, SIR FREDERICK (1904–88), dancer and choreographer. During a brief career in the City of London, he took ballet lessons in the evening with Dame Marie RAMBERT, who commissioned his first ballet, *A Tragedy of Fashion* (1926). Ashton was a founder of the Ballet Club (which became the Ballet Rambert and later the Rambert Dance Company), and worked with such ballerinas as Alicia MARKOVA. In 1935 he joined the Sadler's Wells Ballet (now the Royal Ballet) as a dancer and choreographer and in 1963 took over from Dame Ninette de VALOIS as Director. The creator of many ballets, including *La Fille Mal Gardée* (1960), *Marguérite and Armand* (1963) starring Margot FONTEYN and Rudolf Nureyev, Ashton also worked on the film *The Tales of Beatrix Potter* (1971) and choreographed the dance sequences for Benjamin BRITTEN's *Death in Venice* (1973).

ASKE, ROBERT (?–1537), rebel leader. A Yorks. gentleman and London lawyer who assumed leadership (in Oct. 1536), and co-ordinated rebel demands, in the series of northern risings against HENRY VIII's religious and social policies, collectively called the 'Pilgrimage of Grace for the Commonwealth' – a name which he may have created. He negotiated peace with Thomas HOWARD, Duke of Norfolk, at Doncaster on 6 Dec., and on disbanding his forces was given a personal assurance by the King in London that there would be redress of rebel grievances. He helped to suppress fresh disturbances at Scarborough and Hull in Jan. 1537, but the government seized on the excuse of a treasonable letter to him from Thomas Lord DARCY to imprison and interrogate him in the Tower of London. He was executed at York.

ASQUITH, H(ERBERT) H(ENRY) see essay on pages 36–7

ASQUITH, MARGOT (née Tennant) (Countess of Oxford and Asquith) (1864–1945), political hostess. Daughter of a wealthy Glasgow industrialist, she enjoyed an unrestricted Scottish childhood, and dazzling social success when she and her sister Laura were launched on London society in 1881, becoming part of a circle of clever young socialites known as 'the Souls', which included CURZON and Arthur BALFOUR. Many were surprised when, in 1894, she married the widower H. H. ASQUITH and became stepmother to his five children (and soon had two of her own). She did not prove a suitable wife for a Liberal Prime Minister though she was keenly interested in politics and had a generous and loyal nature. Her flamboyance and extravagance increased Asquith's financial problems and the perception that he was not an appropriate leader for a twentieth-century Liberal Party, and her often impetuous and ill-judged interventions in affairs of State gave him frequent political problems and little domestic respite.

ASSER (?–909 or 910), Welsh monk and author. Asser's *Life of Alfred* is thought by most scholars to have been composed in 893 during its subject's lifetime, though some believe it to be a late tenth-century or early eleventh-century forgery. He was a monk and priest at St David's (Dyfed), who first went to ALFRED THE GREAT's court in the mid 880s, and was made Bishop of Sherborne between the years 892 and 900. The *Life of Alfred* is modelled on Einhard's *Life of Charlemagne* and attempts to give a personal portrait of its subject. Some of its detail (if authentic) is fascinating, but its presentation of Alfred as a human and kingly paragon is the foundation of an often excessively uncritical approach to its subject.

ASTELL, MARY (1666–1731), writer. Born in Newcastle, she received no formal education but, on her arrival in Chelsea at the age of 20, became the central figure of a group of educated gentlewomen, including Lady Catherine Jones, Lady Elizabeth HASTINGS and subsequently Lady Mary Wortley MONTAGU. She published many controversial works, chiefly on religion and the role of women. Her best known, *A Serious Proposal to the Ladies for the Advancement of Their True and Greatest Interest* (1694–7), advocated religious retirement for women to undertake religious and secular study.

ASTLEY, PHILIP (1742–1814), circus pioneer. Astley's ability with horses was recognized whilst in the army and he was sent to study at the Earl of Pembroke's seat at Wilton under Pembroke's horse-trainer Domenico Angelo. On leaving the army in 1766 he opened an exhibition of horsemanship on the south side of the Thames. There he taught one horse to count, feign death, shoot a pistol, mind-read and spell out the name 'Astley'. In 1770 he built his Riding School, a wooden theatre for which he recruited a large company of entertainers, including clowns, acrobats and conjurers, alongside the performing animals. The company toured Britain during the winter, and Astley became a celebrity. His activities occasionally brought charges that he was breaching the theatre licensing laws and in Dec. 1782 he was imprisoned but was freed the next month by Lord Chancellor Thurlow who had employed him as riding-master to his daughter. In 1783 he opened the Amphitheatre Anglais in Paris, and in the following years toured Europe as far east as Belgrade. Although he did not introduce the Big Top, in other respects Astley established the essentials of the circus repertoire and his London and Paris establishments endured into the late nineteenth century.

ASTON, FRANCIS (1877–1945), physicist. Aston studied chemistry and physics at Mason College, Birmingham. From the late 1890s he developed vacuum pumps and studied electrical discharge. He continued this work at Birmingham University (1903–8) and, from 1910, at Cambridge University's Cavendish Laboratory, where he worked with J. J. THOMSON on the electromagnetic deflection of the 'positive rays' of electrical discharge and succeeded in analysing a beam of neon atoms into components of different atomic mass (later known as isotopes). After the First World War Aston returned to Cambridge and in 1919 completed a powerful apparatus for analysing atoms, the mass spectrograph. With this and more sensitive versions of the apparatus, he produced acclaimed evidence for the existence of the multiple isotopes of gaseous and metallic elements. His spectrograph revolutionized theories and practices in chemistry, and he won the 1922 Nobel Prize for Chemistry.

ASTON, SIR THOMAS (1600–46), politician. An Oxford-educated Ches. gentleman, he was created baronet in 1628. His prominent role in resisting Cheshire's levy for CHARLES I's Ship Money (despite having conscientiously collected it as Sheriff in 1634–5) earned him election to the Short Parliament (1640). Defeated, however, in standing for the Long Parliament later that year, he turned his energies to writing and campaigning in support of the Church of England's episcopal system and prayer book, though he was an opponent of Archbishop LAUD. He aroused nationwide support which was a significant factor in forming the Royalist Party on the outbreak of civil war in 1642. Captured by Parliamentary troops in a skirmish near Bridgnorth (1645), he died in prison from his wounds.

ASTOR, DAVID (1912–), newspaper editor. The son of Nancy ASTOR, he was foreign editor of the family-owned *Observer* newspaper from 1945, editor 1948–75 and the *de facto* owner of the paper after the death of his father in 1952. He transformed Britain's oldest Sunday newspaper from a very conservative one into the pre-eminent liberal journal of its day, campaigning on most of the fashionable post-war liberal causes, such as the abolition of capital punishment, prison reform and human rights. The paper was sold in 1975 after successive financial crises.

ASTOR, NANCY (née Langhorne) (Viscountess Astor) (1879–1964), politician. American-born Nancy Astor became the first woman to sit in the British Parliament when she took over the seat of her second husband. Waldorf Astor had to relinquish his role as Conservative MP for Plymouth Sutton when he inherited his father's viscountcy in 1919, but intended to resume his seat under a proposed Bill to allow peers to sit in the Commons. This was never enacted, however, and Nancy Astor held the seat for the next 25 years. Until 1921 she was the only woman MP. Never, in her own words, a 'party hack', Lady Astor was outspoken on matters affecting the family, women and children, and also on the evils of drink; she became a convert to Christian Science in 1914. She was a leading member of the notoriously pro-appeasement Cliveden set, centred on Astor's Berks. country house, but by the outbreak of war in 1939 she was deeply critical of German policy. Throughout the Second World War she served as Mayor of Plymouth as well as being the city's MP.

ATHELSTAN, KING *see* essay on page 38

ASQUITH, H(ERBERT) H(ENRY) (1st Earl of Oxford and Asquith) (1852–1928)
Politician and Prime Minister (1908–16)

The last Liberal Prime Minister to carry undivided support from his party and, until Margaret THATCHER, the longest serving premier of the twentieth century, Asquith's effortless patrician style effectively concealed his humble, Nonconformist, Yorks. origins.

After his father's death the responsibility for Asquith's education and upbringing passed to the family of his invalid mother, and it was his maternal grandfather who was responsible for saving the boy from life at Huddersfield College by sending him to the City of London school, where his scholarly abilities were recognized and from which he won a classical scholarship to Balliol College, Oxford.

It was at Balliol that he acquired the Oxford manner, that mixture of intellectual arrogance and effortless superiority, which was to be such a mark of the mature Asquith. In fact politicking at the Union and social life ensured that despite achieving a First his scholarly record was 'striking without being sensational'. But Asquith's interests lay in a political rather than a scholarly direction, and throughout his career the question of how to finance it would vex him. He was called to the Bar in 1875 but, unlike his later contemporary John SIMON, his earnings from that source were never phenomenal, and his early marriage and brood of four children all acted as a brake on his progress. Through his friend Richard HALDANE, Asquith was adopted for the Liberal seat of East Fife in 1885 and, thereafter, he and Haldane, along with Sir Edward GREY, were an uneasy triumvirate.

Of the three men, it was Asquith whose talents first attracted GLADSTONE's attention and it was a considerable coup to become Home Secretary in 1892, without ever having served in a government before. But three factors combined to hinder Asquith's meteoric progress: Liberal disunity, Conservative political dominance and a want of hard cash. After the death of his first wife in 1891 Asquith married Margot Tennant (see ASQUITH, MARGOT) in 1894. The daughter of an ambitious Glasgow industrialist of considerable fortune, Margot's comment on her predecessor, 'She was no wife for him. She lived in Hampstead and had no clothes', foreshadowed her own attempt to launch her husband in society; in Haldane's eyes Margot's influence corrupted Asquith but that was to ignore Asquith's willingness to be corrupted. Opposition after 1895 deprived Asquith of the chance of office but it was want of

finance that, in 1898, made him turn down the chance to lead his party, leaving the job instead to the unremarkable CAMPBELL-BANNERMAN.

During the Boer War and afterwards Asquith, Haldane and Grey were associated with the Liberal imperialist wing of their party but, once again, Asquith's outstanding talents marked him out as the coming man, and when the party took office in 1905 Bannerman played on his ambition by offering him any post he wanted. Despite the fact that he had made a pact with Grey and Haldane that they should take office together and force Bannerman to go to the Lords, Asquith immediately took the Exchequer and abandoned his friends to their own devices. As Chancellor of the Exchequer Asquith was clearly Bannerman's anointed successor, and he duly took over as Prime Minister on 8 April 1908.

The Liberal government elected to such acclaim in 1906 was already in trouble, since much of its legislative programme had been destroyed by the House of Lords. Asquith provided a new impetus, making LLOYD GEORGE his Chancellor and encouraging CHURCHILL's precocious talents at the Board of Trade. Asquith's promotion of the new, socially conscious Liberalism in place of the old Gladstonian variety, gave the Liberals a fresh lease of life and, despite the loss of seats in the two elections of 1910, most historians now believe that the Liberal Party's prospects in 1914 were by no means as bad as their later electoral performance suggested.

Asquith's talents as Prime Minister lay mainly in his ability to keep together a remarkable team of ministers and to drive them in the same direction. Lloyd George and Winston Churchill were responsible for introducing Old Age Pensions and National Insurance, thus laying the foundations for what would become known as the Welfare State. As Prime Minister, Asquith excelled in giving talented subordinates their head, although his critics alleged that in the case of Grey's francophile foreign policy he allowed this to go too far in an un-Gladstonian direction. The necessity of providing the finance for social reform and naval rearmament produced considerable tensions inside the government but Asquith's genius for finding compromises kept the ship afloat. After the two elections of 1910 Asquith held on to power by courtesy of the Irish Nationalists, and the Parliament that followed reflected this fact. But since the elections had been fought because of the rejection of Lloyd George's radical budget, the first act of the new Parliament was to curb the power of veto of the Upper House, limiting it to postponing legislation for two years. The Conservatives responded by stepping up the tone of their attacks on the government, particularly once it became clear that the way had been opened for a Home Rule Bill for Ireland which the Lords would not be able to throw out. The new Tory leader, Andrew Bonar LAW, came close to calling for armed resistance to the government and, by 1914, it seemed that not even Asquith could find a compromise settlement to the eternal Irish Question; the outbreak of the First World War provided a dramatic form of relief. The war also allowed Asquith to postpone two other pressing issues: female suffrage and how to deal with the growing power of the trades unions.

Asquith's detachment and intellectual superiority, which equipped him well to preside over a ministry replete with talented but difficult individuals, proved less suited to leadership in wartime. He was guilty of allowing Churchill too much rein to push his scheme for an attack on the Dardanelles, and of failing to deal with the problems of providing a sufficient supply of munitions to the Western Front. His answer to the political crisis which erupted because of these matters in May 1915 was characteristically a political one: he sought a coalition with the Tories and thus brought an end to the last Liberal government. Despite this Asquith was still unable to prevent a political coup by Lloyd George in Dec. 1916.

Unlike Neville CHAMBERLAIN in the Second World War, Asquith declined to serve under his successor and thus perpetuated a split in the Liberal Party which was to have disastrous effects. In 1918 those Liberals who owed allegiance to Lloyd George benefited from this fact in the General Election, while the 'Wee Frees' under Asquith were decimated, with Asquith himself losing his seat. The continuing Liberal disunion allowed the Labour Party to gain a foothold in Westminster politics which they were never to lose. It seemed as though the Edwardian Liberalism of Asquith had few answers to the problems of post-war Britain, and it transpired that Lloyd George was not much better equipped for the task, which led to the Tories deserting him in 1922. Thereafter the two Liberal leaders formed an alliance of convenience but failed to convince themselves, their party, or the electorate, that it was more than that. Asquith returned to Parliament in 1920 but made little impact. His one major achievement was to seal the doom of his own party. In 1923 the new Conservative leader, BALDWIN, called an election on Tariff Reform, which allowed the two wings of Liberalism to unite around this Gladstonian shibboleth. Following the election the Liberals were in third place, and Asquith took the decision to withdraw support from the Tories, thus allowing Labour's Ramsay MACDONALD to form a government; Labour never looked back and the Liberals never looked up. More conservative Liberals like Churchill defected to the Conservatives, while more radical ones like Haldane defected to Labour; there seemed little point in voting Liberal.

Asquith's final years were clouded by personal as well as political problems. Never a wealthy man, he found the strain of supporting a political career after the war too great for his purse, and without the largesse of Lord Beaverbrook (*see* AITKEN, MAXWELL) he would have struggled even more than he did. Elevated to the peerage in 1925 he outraged many Liberals by choosing the grandiose title of Lord Oxford and Asquith, which was, said one wag, like a suburban villa calling itself Versailles; despite the title, Oxford University declined to elect him as its Chancellor.

But Asquith always had his defenders, the most ardent being his daughter, Violet, who not only sought to conceal the romantic nature of his relationship with her friend, Venetia Stanley, but actively promoted the image of her father as 'the last of the Romans', a line adopted by Roy JENKINS, whom she selected as Asquith's biographer. Indeed, Jenkins himself, another Balliol man made good from humble origins, seemed to blur the line between himself and Asquith, seeing the latter as the political ancestor of social democracy. The feud between Asquith and Lloyd George was thus perpetuated long after the death of the former in 1928. But the continuing interest in Asquith and the last Liberal governments has established their succession in the line of reforming administrations begun by Grey in 1832 and continued by Gladstone in 1868 and ATTLEE in 1945; Lord Jenkins's support for BLAIR might imply that the torch has been passed on.

Roy Jenkins, Asquith (1964)
Stephen Koss, Asquith (1976)

ATHELSTAN (c. 895–939)
King of the English (924–39)

The eldest son of EDWARD THE ELDER, Athelstan was the first king ever to exercise control over all the English and have a quasi-imperial status among the British. Initially succeeding his father only in Mercia, he obtained Wessex when his half-brother Ælfweard died within a fortnight of his father. In 927 he took over the Viking kingdom of York by force after the death of SIHTRIC CAECH and in the same year he made a treaty at Penrith with CONSTANTÍN II, King of Scots. He also secured lordship over the rulers of Wales, including the very important HYWEL DDA. In 934 Athelstan became the first southern-based English king to lead an army into Scotland. In 937 he consolidated his dominance in one of the decisive battles in British history when he and his half-brother EDMUND defeated an invading army of Scots and Vikings led by King Constantín, OLAF GOTHFRITHSSON, King of Dublin, and YWAIN, SON OF DYFNWAL, King of Strathclyde, at the Battle of Brunanburh (site unknown, but probably in the East Midlands). He never married, perhaps because to have done so might have offended his many brothers and sisters and led, as often happened in the early Middle Ages, to conflict within the royal kindred. Although the massive power which Athelstan had accumulated disintegrated somewhat after his death, his immediate successors were in due course able to create a unified and stable kingdom of England on the basis of his achievements. He was succeeded by his half-brother Edmund.

In contrast to the reign of ALFRED THE GREAT, there are no detailed narrative sources for Athelstan's rule. Although much is uncertain, the accumulated weight of various types of evidence suggests the development of a new type of kingship and a prestige in continental Europe which probably exceeded that of even his greatest predecessors like OFFA and Alfred. Several of his sisters, such as EADGIFU, who married the Carolingian King of the West Franks, Charles the Simple, and Edith, who married the future German King and Emperor Otto I, had husbands from the most powerful of western Europe's ruling families. Not only this, Athelstan intervened in the politics of northern France, seeking, albeit unsuccessfully, to give military support to Eadgifu's son Louis IV, and successfully assisting in the establishment in Brittany of Count Alan 'Barbetorte' against Vikings based on the River Loire. He also maintained friendly relations with Rollo and William Longsword, the first rulers of what was to become the duchy of Normandy. Although his policy objectives were obviously no more than the limited ones of supporting his own kindred against their enemies and trying to reduce the Viking threat from the settlements in France, the scale and frequency of his involvement in cross-Channel politics were significantly greater than any of his predecessors. These contacts were also important in developing links with leading French monasteries, which were to have major consequences for the English Church; ODA, the future Archbishop of Canterbury, and an important pioneer of what has become known as the Tenth-Century Reform, was sent to France by Athelstan on a mission during which he became a monk at Fleury-sur-Loire.

Although the evidence for Athelstan's itinerary shows that his rule was mostly Wessex-based, he sought in a variety of ways to consolidate his kingship over the whole of England. He is known, for example, to have attempted to introduce a single coinage for the entire kingdom, something which was not actually accomplished until the time of his nephew EDGAR. After the manner of the most powerful predecessors, he issued five law-codes, which are primarily concerned with the punishment of crime and the maintenance of order. Although historians nowadays tend to see Anglo-Saxon codes such as Athelstan's as symbolic demonstrations of royal majesty as much as enforceable legislation, their importance to the development of kingly authority cannot be gainsaid. Charters were also produced in much larger numbers than previously to record royal confirmations of property; Athelstan is probably the first king to have a group of clerks at court specifically responsible for the production of documents in the king's name. The structure of local government was also changed. Prior to Athelstan's time, the chief local representative of the king, the ealdorman, had exercised authority within a single shire. Athelstan, however, instituted a pattern whereby the office became much more powerful, entailing control over several shires. The result was to establish some of the most important noble families of the tenth century, such as that of ATHELSTAN HALF KING, Ealdorman of East Anglia. This basic pattern of ealdormen (or, as their eleventh-century successors are normally styled, earls) lasted until after the Norman Conquest and is significant in all subsequent reigns, most notably those of CNUT and EDWARD THE CONFESSOR. Athelstan also has a reputation as a great patron of the Church. Not only did he encourage Oda, but St DUNSTAN, the future Archbishop of Canterbury, was at court during the last years of his reign. Superb manuscripts, such as the Athelstan Psalter, now in the British Library, were produced on his orders.

James Campbell (ed.), The Anglo-Saxons (1982)
Pauline Stafford, Unification and Conquest: A Political and Social History of England in the Tenth and Eleventh Centuries (1989)

ATHELSTAN, King of Kent (839–*c*. 852). Son of ETHELWULF, King of Wessex, and an older brother of ALFRED THE GREAT, he was installed as King in Kent by his father according to a practice initiated when EGBERT subjugated Kent to the power of the Wessex kings. Athelstan is known to have defeated Viking raiders near Sandwich in 851. The exact date of his death is unknown. He was succeeded in Kent by his brother ETHELBERT.

ATHELSTAN HALF KING (?–956), Ealdorman of East Anglia. One of the most powerful magnates of tenth-century England, as his nickname implies, he became Ealdorman of East Anglia in 932 as part of the policy whereby King ATHELSTAN extended an ealdorman's responsibilities to cover several shires. He was also guardian of the young King EDGAR. A supporter of the movement of religious change known as the Tenth-Century Reform, he became a monk of St DUNSTAN's Abbey of Glastonbury in 956 and was succeeded as Ealdorman in turn by his sons Ethelwold and ETHELWINE.

ATHOLL, EARL OF, **9TH** *see* STRATHBOGIE, JOHN OF; **19TH** *see* STEWART, WALTER

ATHOLL, KATHERINE STEWART-MURRAY (née Ramsay) (Duchess of Atholl) (1874–1960), politician and first female Conservative minister. Educated at the Royal College of Music, 'Kitty' married the Duke of Atholl's heir in 1899. Her background in voluntary work (she turned Blair Castle into a convalescent home for wounded soldiers during the First World War) and education made her an appropriate candidate for election as Conservative MP for Kinross and West Perthshire in 1923 and thus the first woman MP for Scotland. She was appointed Under-Secretary of State of the Board of Education, the first Conservative woman to hold ministerial office. Her appointment was not entirely successful in party terms, and, when the Conservatives lost the 1929 election, she never held office again. An opponent of women's suffrage, she was an outspoken and principled MP who twice resigned the party Whip and whose so-called 'masculine mind' was much admired by Harold MACMILLAN. By the mid 1930s Atholl had become an implacable opponent of the CHAMBERLAIN government's policies of appeasement towards Germany. Her opposition cost her her seat in 1938, and thereafter she returned to a life of voluntary service.

ATTERBURY, FRANCIS (1662–1732), Bishop of Rochester (1713–23). Atterbury, son of a clergyman, educated at Westminster and Christ Church, Oxford, attracted notice with his response to JAMES II's assault on the privileged position of the Church of England. His *Letter to a Convocation Man* (1697) argued that Convocation, as the Church's equivalent of Parliament, should meet more frequently and act more vigorously, as Parliament had come to do after the 1688 Revolution. During ANNE's reign, Atterbury distinguished himself as a forceful promoter of clerical claims and rights, becoming Anne's special adviser on Church matters. In 1713 he was made Bishop of Rochester. After GEORGE I's accession his anxiety that the Church was in danger from Whig one-party rule increased, he resented slurs on High Churchmen made in the 'Declaration of Confidence' after the 1715 rebellion and began plotting for a Jacobite restoration. After earlier plans to elicit men and funds from Sweden fell through, in 1722 Atterbury was at the centre of a plot to seize the Bank of England with 5,000 men. He asked the French Regent for support, but he instead alerted the British government. A Bill of Pains and Penalties was passed against Atterbury and he spent the rest of his life in exile.

ATTLEE, CLEMENT *see* essay on pages 40–1

ATTWOOD, THOMAS (1783–1856), economist and political campaigner. A passionate advocate of currency reform, in particular the use of paper money and flexible credit, he founded the Birmingham Political Union in 1830 to agitate for parliamentary reform. He was MP for Birmingham from the passing of the Reform Act 1832 until 1839, the year he presented the first Chartist petition which the Commons rejected.

AUBREY, JOHN (1626–97), antiquarian and biographer. Educated at Oxford and the Middle Temple, he acquired a reputation as an antiquarian, and was elected to the Royal Society in 1663. He was the first person to investigate in detail the prehistoric sites of Avebury and Stonehenge, and collaborated with Anthony Wood on the *Antiquities of Oxford* (1674). In 1680 he began to compile *Brief Lives*, the series of biographical sketches, mainly of contemporaries, for which he is now chiefly remembered. The copious manuscripts (among the many which he bequeathed to the Bodleian Library, Oxford) were edited and published in two nineteenth-century editions, but completely only in 1949. His *Miscellanies* of 1696 record myths, magical events, apparitions, comets and dreams. Also a pioneer in archaeology and local history, especially of his native Wilts., Aubrey has been criticized for his dilettantism and lack of critical rigour.

AUCHINLECK, SIR CLAUDE (1884–1981), soldier. Elder son of an artillery colonel, after

continued on page 42

ATTLEE, CLEMENT (1st Earl Attlee) (1883–1967)
Politician and Prime Minister (1945–51)

Once described by CHURCHILL as a 'modest little man with much to be modest about', Attlee was leader of the Labour Party for longer than anyone else. He presided over the most radical administration in British history, and retired at a time of his own choosing.

His background was untypical of Labour's early political leaders and, as a public schoolboy and an Oxford man, he was more characteristic of the generation which would succeed his own. He was called to the Bar in 1906 but in his spare time he did social work in the East End, demonstrating both the strong social conscience and the practical bent to his socialism which would characterize his later political career. Attlee had a 'good war', rising to the rank of Major. After the war, under the influence of the Fabians, he entered Labour politics, becoming Mayor of Stepney in 1920 and MP for Limehouse two years later; this solid background in East London Labour politics would serve him well in 1931.

Attlee made his mark early on and became private secretary to MACDONALD in 1922, a position he held until 1924 when he became Under-Secretary for War; he succeeded Oswald MOSLEY as Chancellor of the Duchy of Lancaster in 1930, becoming Postmaster General the following year; he did not follow MacDonald into the National Coalition, nor did he follow most of his fellow Labour MPs to defeat in the 1931 election. By the time of Labour's partial recovery in 1935 Attlee was the most senior figure available to replace the beloved but ineffectual George LANSBURY as leader of the party; no one expected him to retain that position for the next 20 years.

Attlee led the opposition to the National government until 1940, when his refusal to serve under Neville CHAMBERLAIN helped secure the premiership for Churchill. After Chamberlain's resignation in Oct. 1940 Attlee became not only Churchill's deputy but also chairman of all the influential Cabinet committees on domestic matters, a position from which he was able to ensure that Labour was well-represented in the formulation of post-war policies. He served successively as Lord Privy Seal (1940–2), Dominions Secretary (1942–3) and Lord President of the Council (1943–4). He would have been happy to have continued with the coalition but accepted the decision of the 1944 Labour conference that it should end with the war in Europe.

Attlee's own election campaign was as modest as the man himself and he spent most of it touring the country with his wife in his own car; he was as surprised as anyone to find that Churchill's massive prestige failed to deliver victory to the Conservatives and that, for the first time in its history, the Labour Party had power as well as office. There were those, particularly the new Home Secretary, Herbert MORRISON, who thought that Attlee should be swept aside in favour of a more dynamic figure, but since the Prime Minister enjoyed the support of the powerful and influential trade union leader, Ernest BEVIN, he was secure against such intrigues. Like ASQUITH before him, Attlee was skilful in steering a team of talented ministers and, although he did it unobtrusively, he exercised considerable authority. He knew that Labour had been elected to build a land that really would be fit for heroes and set about trying to fulfil the considerable popular expectations which the election and the end of the war had raised.

The circumstances were hardly propitious for the creation of a new Jerusalem, with Britain bankrupt and devastated by the effects of six years at war, but Attlee put together a strong team, with Bevin at the Foreign Office, Hugh DALTON at the Treasury, Morrison at the Home Office and, most daringly of all, Aneurin BEVAN at Health. Attlee's period in office saw the establishment of what some have described as a 'post-war consensus', although of late that term has become somewhat controversial.

The consensual elements of Attlee's programme owed their origin to initiatives taken by the Churchill coalition: the ideas of full employment and a National Health Service were also subscribed to by the Conservatives and the Liberals, as was the commitment to a US alliance and opposition to Soviet expansionism. The war had seen a massive extension of State control over the lives of individuals and it was natural for politicians to suppose that a system which had won the war would enable them to win the peace, although there were times when the 'Man in Whitehall knows best' syndrome seemed to amount to governmental claims to omniscience.

More controversial were Labour's measures to take control of the commanding heights of the economy. To those on the Left of the party the industries chosen for nationalization, coal, road haulage, the railways and (eventually) iron and steel, were a curious hodge-podge, while the form it took, control by government-nominated Boards of Control, was undemocratic and lacked proper worker participation. To the Conservatives the very idea of State confiscation of private property was anathema, and they fought a very successful campaign to ensure proper compensation for the coal and railway owners.

Attlee's greatest success was in encouraging the revival of a British export industry but the political costs of this were great; the consumer, who came in third place on Labour's list of priorities after the export market and investment, grumbled that the austerity of the post-war years was greater than during the war. Attlee was also beset by economic problems, and despite being bailed out by an American loan in 1946 and Marshall Aid a year later, found himself forced to devalue the pound, a humiliation which left a mark on one of Attlee's younger ministers, Harold WILSON. Labour narrowly scraped home at the 1951 election but, with many of the major figures in his Cabinet sick or on the verge of death (both Bevin and Stafford CRIPPS would die in 1951), Attlee struggled to hold his government together; 11 years in power left their mark even on the indestructible Attlee.

The 1951 government saw a conflict between those centrists like Morrison, who wanted to consolidate Labour's achievements, and leftists like Bevan who wanted to go further. Attlee attempted to satisfy both wings of the party but with little success. He allowed the nationalization of the iron and steel industries, which effectively cost him his small majority as two independent-minded Labour MPs, Desmond Donnelly and Woodrow Wyatt, defied the party Whip on the issue. But he also committed Britain to involvement as America's ally in the Korean War, which necessitated fresh sources of income to pay the costs of rearmament. The new Chancellor, Hugh GAITSKELL, demanded the introduction of charges for medical prescriptions which brought him into direct conflict with Bevan who resigned on the issue, joined by Harold Wilson and John Freeman. The government was now in as bad a way as most of its older figures and Morrison, who had replaced Bevin at the Foreign Office, cut a sorry figure there and was unable to provide the political ballast it needed. Attlee called another election in order to try to obtain a working majority but, despite getting more votes than Churchill, lost the election due to the vagaries of the British electoral system.

Attlee's administration long remained a landmark in Labour history and a yard-stick against which any successors would be measured (and found wanting). Historians of a certain generation would view it through spectacles tinted rose by nostalgia, which perhaps accounts in part for its favourable reputation. In this benign Whiggish historiography the one blot against Attlee's name is his government's refusal to join in the early stages of what would become the European Union. During the THATCHER years a different critique of the Attlee government would develop, concentrating upon the malign economic effects of nationalization, as well as the strains imposed by trying to create a Welfare State at the same time as spending heavily on armaments. What is not in doubt is the radical impact which Attlee's administration had on Britain: it created a National Health Service, introduced Keynesian demand management technique (*see* KEYNES, JOHN MAYNARD) as part of the function of the government and nationalised swathes of industry, creating such enduring institutions as British Gas, Electricity and Rail; it also presided over the creation of the North Atlantic Treaty Organization and the introduction of the British nuclear deterrent, as well as the loss of the Indian empire and the handing over of Palestine to the United Nations. In short it created much of what would be the fabric of British life for the next 30 years.

The man who had presided over this epoch-making government stayed on as Labour leader until 1955, when, judging that Morrison would be too old to win and Bevan too controversial, he retired, thus giving Gaitskell optimum conditions to succeed him, which he duly did. He took pride in becoming a member of the Order of Merit and an earl. His memoirs, *A Prime Minister Remembers*, were aptly characterized by A. J. P. TAYLOR as showing only how much he had forgotten – or cared not to retell. His last major public appearance was at Churchill's funeral in 1965 and, although he would never be the recipient of eulogies on the same scale, it is arguable that he did even more than that great man to shape modern Britain.

Kenneth Harris, Attlee (1983)

Sandhurst Auchinleck joined the Indian army and served in Egypt (1915) and Mesopotamia (1916–18). Promoted Major-General in 1936, Auchinleck recaptured Narvik (June 1940) but accused the government of incompetence and deeply offended CHURCHILL. Commanding anti-invasion forces, Auchinleck clashed with a new Corps Commander, MONTGOMERY, before he was appointed Commander-in-Chief in India. Ordered to replace WAVELL in the Middle East in June 1941, Auchinleck launched an offensive on 18 Nov. 1941 which drove Rommel out of Cyrenaica (Libya). But from Feb. to June 1942 8th Army suffered a succession of disasters, Auchinleck eventually managing to stop the Axis advance by a series of desperate and poorly co-ordinated counter-attacks at El Alamein. Replaced by Montgomery, Auchinleck again became Commander-in-Chief for India and was able to protect SLIM from Montgomery's protégé, General Oliver LEESE. Appearing in the late 1950s, Auchinleck's biography and Montgomery's memoirs gave different versions of key events, and continue to stimulate historical debate.

AUCKLAND, 1ST BARON see EDEN, WILLIAM; **1ST EARL OF** see EDEN, GEORGE

AUD THE DEEP-MINDED (*fl.* mid ninth century), wife of the Viking King of Dublin. Daughter of KETIL FLATNOSE, the Viking ruler of the Hebrides and the wife of OLAF THE WHITE, Aud is said to have set off for Iceland on hearing of the death of her son, THORSTEIN THE RED. She subsequently played a central role in the Scandinavian settlement of Iceland which took place between 870 and 930. Her career illustrates the extensive links which existed between the northern British Isles and the Viking colonies in the northern seas, as well as the matriarchal role which women often played in Viking society.

AUDEN, W(YSTAN) H(UGH) (1907–73), poet. Auden began to be taken seriously as a poet even before completing his degree at Oxford. After graduating in 1928, he lived in Berlin for a year. His early works, *Poems* (1928), *Poems* (1930) and his *tour de force*, *The Orators* (1932), are often associated with the writings of his contemporaries at Oxford, Cecil DAY-LEWIS, Stephen SPENDER and Louis MACNIECE. In 1929 he returned to England, where he became a schoolteacher: in reaction to the rise of Fascism in Europe Auden joined the GPO documentary film unit where he worked with the producer John GRIERSON. At the same time he was writing with Christopher ISHERWOOD *The Dog Beneath the Skin* (1935) and *The Ascent of F6* (1936) for the American experimental and socialist Group Theatre. In 1937 he went to Spain for two months to drive an ambulance for the Republican cause in the Spanish Civil War and wrote his most committed poem, 'Spain'. *Journey to a War,* which he co-wrote with Isherwood after their travels in China in 1938, contains some of Auden's greatest poetry. In 1939 the two left Europe for the USA, a 'defection' for which they were much criticized. (Auden became an American citizen in 1946.) He met the young poet Chester Kallman, who became his life-long companion. From this time, Auden's poetry became increasingly Christian in tone, rejecting utterly the view that poetry could influence politics. He was elected Professor of Poetry at Oxford University in 1956: they were not happy years. He died in a hotel in Vienna after a poetry reading.

AUDLEY, 7TH BARON see TUCHET, EDMUND

AUDLEY, THOMAS (1st Lord Audley of Walden) (1488–1544), Lord Chancellor. An Essex-born lawyer, he was already a royal administrator when chosen Speaker of the Commons in 1529 as a dependable agent of Crown policy. He steered the early stages of HENRY VIII's religious changes through Parliament and was rewarded with the Chancellorship in 1533; a peerage followed in 1538. Audley managed to serve all Henry's whims, playing a role in the deaths of Thomas MORE, John FISHER, ANNE BOLEYN, Thomas CROMWELL and CATHERINE HOWARD, and in the dissolution of the monasteries. He ploughed some of his gains back into the foundation of Magdalen College, Cambridge, from the former Buckingham College, and much into his home at the converted Essex monastery, Walden Abbey, which in the early seventeenth century became the spectacular mansion Audley End.

AUGUSTA (1719–72), Princess of Wales. The daughter of Frederick II, Duke of Saxe-Gotha, she came to Britain in 1736 to marry FREDERICK, Prince of Wales, whose court often served as a focus of opposition to the ministers of his father GEORGE II. After Frederick's death in 1751, Augusta secured her position as Regent should her eldest son (the future GEORGE III) still be a minor at the King's death (in the event he was of age). Whilst Augusta abandoned Frederick's overt support for the political opposition, she extended his legacy in other directions, such as at Kew Gardens where she commissioned ornamental buildings from Sir William CHAMBERS. After 1755 she engineered the ascendancy of the Earl of Bute (*see* STUART, JOHN) as tutor to her eldest son, thus ensuring that he would be reared in the reformist 'patriot' tradition supported by Frederick. Her opponents suspected the relationship between her and Bute to be sexual and, while this is unlikely, the rumours became a frequent subject for cartoonists in the early years of her son's reign, particularly when Bute was Prime Minister.

AUGUSTINE, ST (?–between 604 and 609). Missionary and first Archbishop of Canterbury (597–604 or 609). Sent in 597 as leader of the Roman mission to convert the English by Pope Gregory the Great, he successfully converted the kings of Kent and Essex and many of their people, thus establishing a foothold for the Roman Church in England. His career also demonstrates the considerable gap in understanding and ritual that separated Rome from the native British Christians, since his encounters with Britons were invariably unsuccessful. Augustine relied on an approach to a royal court and the conversion of a king and queen, in the expectation that their subjects would follow. His achievement was to begin the conversion of a small part of England, and to establish a connection with Rome, which ultimately played a crucial part in the development of the English Church. The strengths and limitations of his achievements are clearly evident in the difficulties faced by his successors LAURENTIUS and MELLITUS. The ambitious objectives of his mission were arguably not convincingly fulfilled until the time of THEODORE OF TARSUS.

AULUS PLAUTIUS (*fl.* AD 40s), Roman General. Commander of the successful invasion of much of lowland Britain which began in 43 in the time of the Emperor CLAUDIUS, he was subsequently the first Roman Governor of Britain until 47. He began his campaign by defeating British armies under the leadership of CARATACUS and Togodumnus at a battle on the River Medway and, by the end of his term of office, appears to have extended Roman power roughly to the line of the Fosse Way. On his return to Rome, he received the rare tribute of a triumphal ovation.

AURELIUS CANINUS (*fl.* early sixth century), British King. One of the 'five tyrants' condemned by GILDAS for laxity and corruption at the time of the Anglo-Saxon invasions, he is otherwise unknown. Although Gildas does not name his kingdom, it appears that he acquired it by deposing his father, as one of the sins he is accused of was parricide. It also appears that he controlled a powerful warband which was regularly employed in plundering raids against his neighbours.

AUSTEN, JANE (1775–1817), novelist. The seventh of eight children, Austen was born at Steventon (Hants), where her father was the rector. She started to write in her teens and her perceptive ironic wit and sense of the absurd are apparent even in her juvenilia. They included *A History of England*, which its young author ('a partial, prejudiced historian') boasted 'contains very few dates' and is a spirited vindication of MARY QUEEN OF SCOTS.

Always a careful writer of precise and measured prose, Austen redrafted her novels several times before they were published, often changing the title and sometimes the form. Before any were published, in 1801 her father removed his family to Bath, which Jane did not like but was to use as a setting for her novels. In 1809, after her father's death, Jane, her mother and sister Cassandra, who was her lifelong companion, correspondent and confidante, returned to Hants when her brother settled them in a modest house in the grounds of his estate at Chawton.

There Jane started to write again. Her brother Henry helped her to negotiate with publishers – he paid for the publication of *Sense and Sensibility* in 1811 – and Jane often stayed in Sloane Square (London) with him and his wife Eliza (widow of the Comte de Feuillide, who had been guillotined in the French Revolution), and was able to enjoy a metropolitan life of the theatre, exhibitions and parties. *Pride and Prejudice* (1813), her 'own darling child', received laudatory reviews, including one (unsigned) by Walter SCOTT in the *Quarterly Review*. *Mansfield Park* was published in May 1814; at the end of 1815 *Emma* appeared, dedicated to the Prince Regent, who had expressed his admiration of her books. But by the summer of 1816 she was suffering from Addison's disease, for which there was then no cure. *Persuasion* and *Northanger Abbey* were published posthumously in 1818, and she left an unfinished novel known as *Sanditon*.

Jane Austen declared that 'three or four families in a Country Village is the thing to work on', and her books might appear to reflect a tranquil English scene. But her society was changing: it was becoming secular and capitalist. Everyone has their place and their price, and her ironic observations are critical both of aristocratic neglect and *nouveau riche* pretensions. Her novels have an enduring appeal, partly for their 'heritage' aspect, but also for the cool sardonic eye which she casts on social mores, and in particular on women's constraints and strategies.

AUSTIN, ALFRED (1835–1913), poet. The son of a Leeds wool-stapler, Austin trained as a barrister before deciding to 'cast [his] bread in the precarious waters of literature'. An indisputably minor poet whose canvases were large – *The Human Tragedy* (1862–91), *England's*

Darling (1896), about Alfred the Great – and sentimental, he criticized his fellow poets, particularly TENNYSON, for not engaging with the dramatic sweep that was the proper subject of poetry. He was appointed Poet Laureate in 1896 because, it was rumoured, the Prime Minister, Lord Salisbury (*see* CECIL, ROBERT GASCOYNE), felt indebted to the support of the Tory *National Review* which Austin edited (1887–93), and anyway, Salisbury maintained, no one else had applied for the job.

AUSTIN, HERBERT (Baron Austin of Longbridge) (1866–1941), motor-car manufacturer. As a young man Austin left England to pursue an engineering career in Australia, where he went into business with Frederick Wolseley, a manufacturer of sheep-shearing equipment. Production was transferred to England, and in 1895 Austin moved to Aston, Birmingham. In the search for new engineering developments he turned to the internal combustion engine. His first motor car was built in 1895; after a short-lived partnership with Vickers, Austin's own company was formed in 1905 at Longbridge, Birmingham. Its success in the early years was due to Austin's inventive genius, but by 1921 the company had failed. A restructured company increased in strength thereafter, and with the success of the Austin 7 and other models the company became one of the Big Three in British motor manufacture.

AVELING, ELEANOR MARX (née Marx) (1855– 98), political activist and writer. The daughter of Karl MARX and his wife Jenny, Eleanor grew up in a Soho household peopled with intellectuals, political activists and revolutionary refugees. Well-educated, largely by her father, she translated *Histoire de la Commune de Paris de 1871* (1886) by the French radical journalist Lissagaray, with whom she had a long relationship. A teacher and actress, she also translated Flaubert and Ibsen, writing with Israel ZANGWILL *The Doll's House Repaired* (1891), a jokey version of Ibsen's play. In 1884 she became the common-law wife of Edward Aveling, a scientist and socialist whose unreliability, profligacy and sexual deceptions were to cause her much pain. Together they wrote several books on socialism and she edited a number of her father's works. She was deeply involved in trade-union agitation (including the 1889 dock strike and the formation of the Gasworkers' Union the same year), supported the first British May Day demonstration (1890) and helped organize the London International Congress of Socialists (1896). She died by her own hand, swallowing prussic acid supplied by Aveling.

AYER, SIR A(LFRED) J(ULES) (1910–89), philosopher. 'Freddie' Ayer went to Eton as a scholar and to Oxford. On the advice of the philosopher Gilbert RYLE, he spent the winter of 1932–3 in Vienna attending the lectures of the philosopher Moritz Schlick and meetings of the group of logical positivist philosophers, the Vienna circle, whose members included many Jewish and Marxist intellectuals. On his return to Oxford, Ayer took up a lectureship at Christ Church, to which he had been elected as an undergraduate. In 1936 he published *Language, Truth and Logic*. This lucidly written work remains the classic statement of English logical positivism, which asserts that only two sorts of cognitively meaningful statements exist, those which are in principle empirically verifiable (can be tested through observation) such as scientific statements, and those which are analytic (true by virtue of linguistic rules) such as statements of mathematics or logic; all other statements, such as those of metaphysics, ethics or religion, are nonsensical. The work was to have a profound impact on an entire generation of philosophers, including initially Ludwig WITTGENSTEIN. In 1940 Ayer published *The Foundations of Empirical Knowledge*, a rigorous and refined defence of empiricism. This defence was further refined in *The Problem of Knowledge* (1956), published during his time as Grote Professor of the Philosophy of Mind, University College, London. Three years later he returned to Oxford, as Wykeham Professor of Logic. Ayer believed that philosophy should be clear, simple and aim at generality, a view conveyed in his teaching and numerous publications. An outspoken advocate of many liberal and secular causes, he was a gregarious and charming man who loved the company of women and was married four times, twice to the same woman.

AYLWARD, GLADYS (1902–70), missionary. The child of Nonconformist parents, Gladys worked as a parlourmaid but never doubted that God had other plans for her. In 1930 she travelled to China where she joined an elderly Scottish missionary in establishing the 'Inn of the Sixth Happiness' in the remote outpost of Yangzheng in Shanxi province in order to convert the population to Christianity. Aylward worked in China until 1949, becoming a Chinese citizen in 1931, and was appointed a foot-inspector to enforce the recently introduced law which outlawed the ancient custom of female foot-binding. In 1940, she led 100 children from Shanxi, then occupied by the Japanese, across mountainous territory to safety, an act of bravery that was to be commemorated in the film *Inn of the Sixth Happiness* (1958).

AYSCOUGH, ANNE (1521–46), martyr. From a knightly family of Lincs., Ayscough (or Askew) was a devout Protestant who walked out of her unhappy marriage with Thomas Kyme, a religious conservative. Arrested in 1546, she refused to recant her condemnations of the Mass; she was personally tortured by Privy Councillors in an effort to gain evidence against prominent evangelicals at Court including Queen CATHERINE PARR. Refusing to yield or to recant, she was burnt at the stake. Her remarkable diary of her sufferings was published by an admiring John BALE.

B

BABBAGE, CHARLES (1792–1871), mathematician and pioneer of computing. Born in London, Babbage studied mathematics at Cambridge, where, with John HERSCHEL and George Peacock, he launched the Analytical Society, a forum for promoting continental methods of mathematical analysis. In 1815 he moved to London, where he delivered popular lectures on astronomy, published on the calculus of functions and helped found the Astronomical Society (1820). In the early 1820s he built a prototype model of his 'difference engine' for automatically calculating and printing accurate astronomical, nautical and mathematical tables, and secured government funds to realize a full-sized engine. Between 1828 and 1839 he was Cambridge University's Lucasian Professor of Mathematics, publishing *On the Economy of Machines and Manufactures* (1832), a penetrating study of British and continental industry and the division of labour. An active reformist, during the politically turbulent 1830s he attacked the organization of the Royal Society in *Reflections on the Decline of Science in England* (1830), tried unsuccessfully to become a Liberal MP and helped found the British Association for the Advancement of Science (1831). In 1833 he had completed part of his 'difference engine' but by this stage he was planning the more sophisticated 'analytical engine', a machine capable of any single mathematical computation and which, by use of punch cards, could be programmed to perform several different computations. In 1842, however, the government withdrew its financial support for his schemes. In the early 1840s Babbage formed a relationship with Ada Lovelace (*see* KING, AUGUSTA ADA), who helped him with his calculations and who wrote on the 'analytical engine'. Regarded as a pioneer of computing, he wrote on mathematical analysis and notation, computation, electromagnetism, political economy, the organization and funding of science, natural theology, cryptography, taxation, geology and optics.

BABINGTON, ANTHONY (1561–86), conspirator. A Derb. gentleman, he became a passionate partisan of MARY QUEEN OF SCOTS, who was imprisoned near his home; soon he was an active agent for her and for Jesuit clergy as they secretly travelled round England on mission. In 1586 WALSINGHAM discovered his conspiracy to murder ELIZABETH I and used it to bring about the final downfall of Mary. Babington's gruesome execution caused even Elizabeth to pause.

BACON, LADY ANNE (née Cooke) (1528–1610), translator. One of the highly talented daughters of the scholarly politician, Sir Anthony Cooke, and involved in the bringing–up of Prince Edward (the future EDWARD VI), she was the second wife of Sir Nicholas BACON (her sister Mildred married William CECIL), and mother of Anthony and Francis BACON. In Edward's reign she translated devotional works by the exiled Italian reformer Bernardino Ochino (1487–1564); Queen MARY I retained her in the royal household despite her strong Protestantism. Her most important translation was the English version of John JEWEL's semi-official *Apology of the Church of England* (1564). In later years she watched with frequent anxiety both the erratic careers of her sons and the Church of England's failure to move to further reformation, on which two subjects she wrote forcibly in numerous letters.

BACON, ANTHONY (1558–1601), spy *see* BACON, FRANCIS

BACON, FRANCIS *see* essay on page 47

BACON, FRANCIS (1909–92), artist. Born in Ireland, a descendant of Francis BACON, he came to London via Berlin and Paris in 1925 when he was thrown out of home by his military father for cross-dressing, and worked as an interior designer before starting to paint. He was a Soho habitué, promiscuous homosexual and an inveterate gambler, but by the end of his life he was regarded as one of the world's major contemporary artists. Bacon's primal, distorted, cadaverous portraits including his series of popes based on Velázquez's portrait of Pope Innocent X (1650) and his self-portraits, painted in oils directly onto unprimed canvas, seem mutilated screams in a private purgatory. His triptych, *Three Studies at the Base of the Crucifixion*, caused a sensation when it was exhibited in 1944. Bacon's work was

continued on page 48

BACON, FRANCIS (1st Baron Verulam, Viscount St Albans) (1561–1626)
Politician, writer and philosopher

Francis and his elder brother Anthony (1558–1601) were the two youngest sons of Lord Keeper Nicholas BACON by his second wife Anne Cooke (see BACON, LADY ANNE); they inherited her considerable scholarly talents, in contrast to their elder half-brothers, who grew up to be solid Puritan squires and who clearly came to detest the two restless homosexual intellectuals. Francis and Anthony were encouraged in their ambitions by inheriting only a meagre share of their father's wealth, and while Anthony embarked in the 1580s on a rather seedy career of espionage overseas, followed in the 1590s by intrigues on behalf of Robert DEVEREUX, Earl of Essex, Francis combined law and politics in an effort to outshine his father's achievements. He was ultimately successful in this, although both brothers were dogged in their careers by disastrous finances, persistent insinuations of sexual scandal and complex and often tense relationships with their powerful relatives William CECIL, Lord Burghley, and Robert CECIL, Earl of Salisbury. After studying at Cambridge and Gray's Inn, Francis was sent (1576) as secretary to the English Ambassador in Paris; on his return in 1579 he began on his energetic quest for advancement. The influence of relatives secured him his first parliamentary seat, Bossiney (Cornw., 1581); thereafter he sat in every Parliament up to the Addled Parliament of 1614, for seven different constituencies, ending with Cambridge University. Though a bencher of Gray's Inn from 1586, he took little interest in legal practice beyond advancing his career. ELIZABETH I, who had known him since his boyhood, was not enthused by his eager efforts to ingratiate himself, and she was furious when in the 1593 Parliament he obstructed Lord Burghley's proposal for unprecedently heavy subsidy payments to the Crown, with a speech opposing a speedy payment of the taxation. She never offered him any worthwhile or profitable office. The patronage of Robert Devereux, Earl of Essex, from 1588 did him little good, and he was humiliated in 1594 when defeated for the post of Attorney General by his rival Edward COKE, thereafter a lifelong enemy. From 1595 he grew increasingly worried by Essex's political antics, and after the Earl's 1601 rebellion he played a major part in the prosecution at his trial. Preferment came more readily from his fellow homosexual and intellectual JAMES I; he became Solicitor General in 1607, Attorney General at last in 1617 and Lord Chancellor in 1618, gaining his barony in 1618 and viscountcy in 1621. A combination of enemies brought impeachment on bribery charges in 1621 (only marginally justified), and his political career was ruined. The character of his marriage (1606) at the age of 45 to a wealthy 13-year-old heiress can be gauged from the fact that he disinherited her in his will.

Bacon's uninspiring political career, his talent for making enemies and the considerable evidence of his cold selfishness must be balanced by his important and prolific writings on science, philosophy, history and education; his political disgrace increased his literary output. His essays (successive enlargements from 1597 to meet public demand) contributed to English prose style, compensating for the certainty that he did not write Shakespeare's plays. The huge influence of his thought throughout Europe in the later seventeenth and eighteenth centuries rivalled only that of René Descartes (1596–1650). He despised Aristotle, considering his intellectual system a misguided tyranny, which had been further abused by the medieval Church. To replace Aristotle, whose works still dominated contemporary university teaching, he proposed a programme of intellectual renewal, a recovery and restoration ('instauration', hence his *Instauratio Magna*, 1620–3) of a wisdom yet more ancient: this theme dominates his fable about the discovery of an imaginary island, the *New Atlantis* (posthumously published, 1626). His ambition to classify all knowledge in his 'Great Instauration' inevitably meant that his project could never be completed, and despite his mystical fascination with archaic wisdom, the effect was to value original experiment above classical tradition. This emphasis on experimentation, presented in the *Advancement of Learning* (1605) and the *Novum Organum* (1620), was later an inspiration to the scientific investigations promoted by the Royal Society, which may itself have been modelled on the scientific institute portrayed in the *New Atlantis*. In reacting against Aristotle, Bacon underestimated the importance of abstract theorizing in scientific advance. His distinctive achievement, however, was explicitly to detach scientific investigation from theological concerns; science (a word thereafter increasingly used in its specialist modern sense) thus sidestepped the pessimistic biblical concept of the Fall so central to contemporary Christian theology. This development encouraged an optimism about the possibility of human progress which has been central to Western scientific advance. Bacon's own experimental research resulted in few particular scientific discoveries, but it led to his death from a chill caught while exploring how to refrigerate a chicken.

B. H. G. Wormald, Francis Bacon: History, Politics and Science, 1561–1626 (1993) the subject of two major retrospective exhibitions (1962 and 1985) and today commands phenomenally high prices though few stylistic imitators.

BACON, NATHANIEL (?–1622), administrator. Second son of Sir Nicholas BACON (and elder half-brother to Edward and Francis BACON), he went to Cambridge and Gray's Inn and from the 1570s was set up by his father as a Norfolk county gentleman. A zealous Puritan more respected than liked by his neighbours, he devoted his considerable energies to championing what he saw as honest and efficient government in his locality, usually in opposition to the intervention of courtiers and central officialdom. His private archive has survived in huge quantities, though dispersed, and is a remarkable window on all aspects of early modern life.

BACON, SIR NICHOLAS (1509–79), royal servant. Son of a Bury St Edmunds Abbey estate official, he pursued a legal and administrative career under HENRY VIII in the Court of Augmentations, acquiring much ex-monastic property through his work. Although a firm Protestant, he kept his job in the Court of Wards under MARY I through his wife's influence; ELIZABETH I made him Lord Keeper of the Great Seal in 1558. With his brother-in-law, William CECIL, he was the main architect and longterm guardian of the Elizabethan Settlement of Religion (1558–9); he shared with Cecil an energetic if fussy attention to detail and a keen interest in education. Francis BACON was one of his younger sons.

BACON, ROGER (?1214–94), philosopher. Educated at the universities of Oxford and Paris, he became a Franciscan friar. His scientific work particularly in the subject of optics was of considerable significance: his major work was the *Opus Maius* (1266). He possessed a remarkably speculative mind proposing flying machines and mechanically powered carriages while insisting on the importance of observation and experimentation. At the request of Pope Clement IV, he drew up an ambitious plan of educational reform, but his outspokenness on every subject that he touched deeply disturbed the religious hierarchy and he spent two long periods in confinement.

BADEN-POWELL, DAME OLAVE (née Soames) (1889–1977), founder of the Girl Guides. In 1912, the daughter of a wealthy brewer, 23-year-old Olave married 55-year-old Robert BADEN-POWELL, the hero of Mafeking, who in 1908 had published *Scouting for Boys*. The couple honeymooned under canvas in the Algerian desert, and on their return to Sussex Olave gradually took over from her sister-in-law Agnes the organization of a parallel scouting body for girls, the Girl Guides. In 1916 she became Chief Commissioner (renamed Chief Guide in 1918). In 1930 she was elected Chief Guide of the World and when she died there were more than six million Girl Guides and Girl Scouts throughout the world.

BADEN-POWELL, ROBERT (1st Baron Baden-Powell) (1857–1941), soldier and founder of the Boy Scout and Girl Guide movement. Commissioned into the cavalry in 1876, Baden-Powell became a national hero when he defended Mafeking against the Boers for 217 days in 1900. Concerned with the poor physical quality of recruits from cities, his *Scouting for Boys* (1908) urged the formation of boys' clubs dedicated to camping in the country and learning basic military skills. Massive support from the popular press transformed this idea into a vast international movement for both boys and girls, with Baden-Powell being declared Chief Scout in 1920 and being raised to the peerage in 1929. After his death in Kenya in 1941, his wife (*see* BADEN-POWELL, OLAVE) continued an active involvement in the movement. By the century's end more than 500 million boys and girls throughout the world had at some time been Scouts and Guides, making the social impact of the movement little less than that of a major religion.

BADENOCH, LORD OF *see* COMYN, JOHN; COMYN, JOHN THE ELDER

BADER, SIR DOUGLAS (1910–1983), airman. Bader, who studied at the RAF college Cranwell, lost both his legs in an air crash on 14 Dec. 1931. Teaching himself to walk unaided on artificial legs, Bader rejoined the RAF in Nov. 1939, and between May 1940 and 9 Aug. 1941, when he was shot down over northern France and captured, accounted for 23 enemy aircraft. Bader proved a difficult prisoner, his constant attempts to escape leading to his incarceration in Colditz Castle, from where he was liberated in April 1945. Bader's biography, *Reach for the Sky* (1958), and the subsequent film, based on his life, provided an inspiration for the generation which grew up in the immediate aftermath of the Second World War.

BAETÁN MAC CAIRILL, King of the Dál Fiatach (*c.* 572–81). In a short reign of nine years, Baetán restored the military power and prestige of the Ulaid to the extent of making his northern Irish kingdom the most powerful in Ireland. He was reputed to have exacted hostages from Munster, his most powerful rival, and taken tribute from the other provinces of Ireland. In the normal fashion of northern Irish kings of his time, his ambitions extended across the Irish Sea and in 577 he annexed the Isle of Man and, soon afterwards, forced the submission of AEDÁN MAC GABRÁIN of Dál Riata. The circumstances of his death are unknown.

BAGEHOT, WALTER (1826–77), journalist and political writer. Bagehot came from a Unitarian family of Somerset bankers and after attending University College, London, and initially studying law, he turned to banking and journalism. He wrote for the *National Review* and, from 1860, edited *The Economist*. His best-known work was *The English Constitution* (1867), which some see as a brilliant analysis of the subject – even the best introduction to its subject, as Richard Crossman opined in 1963 – others as a superficial, misleading and engagingly written but unoriginal text. At a point when both the monarchy was becoming unpopular and the question of parliamentary reform was once again on the agenda, the book was an attempt to define the nature of the political system and the political culture which underlay it. The constitution had evolved into one in which there was a distinction between the 'efficient' and 'dignified' parts of government. The efficient was the largely secret machinery of decision-making and especially the Cabinet, to which Bagehot gave considerable importance; the 'dignified' parts consisted of the monarchy and the House of Lords. Since the 1832 Reform Act, constitutional monarchy had given way to a 'disguised republic' in which the monarch had the right to be consulted, to encourage and to warn. While the 'dignified' had been preserved to both hide and secure loyalty to the power of the 'efficient', what bound the system together was culture: deference exercised by the ruled to the rulers and what Bagehot called the '*theatrical show* of society', the pomp and ceremonies of power. Through this matrix of cultural and political relations, the aristocracy enjoyed the display of power, the middle classes exercised 'despotic power', and the 'masses' were kept in check. Both here and in another major work, *Physics and Politics* (1872), Bagehot displayed both an optimism about the possibilities of social progress, strongly influenced by contemporary theories of social and natural evolution, and a pessimism about the prospects of 'the race' being dragged back into despotism by the barbarian hordes. This mixture of optimism and pessimism, of certainties and doubts, is highly characteristic of much mid Victorian cultural and social thought.

BAGNALL, SIR NIGEL (1927–) soldier. Son of an army officer, he served in a number of post-colonial campaigns, before a defence fellowship at Balliol College, Oxford, (1972–3) gave Bagnall the chance to study the problems of defending western Europe, which convinced him that NATO doctrine was deeply flawed. Subsequently as Commander 1st British Corps and Commander-in-Chief British Army of the Rhine (1980–5), Bagnall abandoned the doctrine of stopping a Soviet offensive through attritional firepower, and stressed instead the importance of out-manoeuvring the enemy, thus setting in motion the development of a new approach to war fighting.

BAILEY, DAVID (1938–), photographer. East End born, Bailey taught himself photography and emerged as a fashion photographer epitomizing the 'swinging 60s': he changed the emphasis of fashion away from depicting the clothes towards showing the women wearing them, and made these models – and himself – take their place among the celebrities of the time. Bailey's photographs (particularly of Jean Shrimpton) dominated magazines like *Vogue*, and his books *Box of Pin Ups* (1964) and *Goodbye Baby and Amen* (1969) are a stylish record of that ephemeral decade.

BAILLIE, DAME ISOBEL (1895–1983), singer. A Scottish-born soprano who made her debut with the Hallé Orchestra in 1921, she became a world-famous oratorio singer and sang in more than 1,000 productions of HANDEL's *Messiah*.

BAINBRIDGE, CHRISTOPHER (*c.* 1464–1514), diplomat. A Yorks. man and Cambridge-educated, he rose up the clerical career ladder to become Archbishop of York (1508) and Cardinal (1511). From 1509 he was resident in Rome as English Representative, and in 1511 led a papal army against Ferrara. He was poisoned in Rome by one of his chaplains.

BAIRD, JOHN LOGIE (1888–1946), pioneer of television. Baird studied electrical engineering at Glasgow University but ill health forced him to leave the electrical engineering business and earn money by commercial trading. In 1922, while living in Hastings (Sussex), he developed a mechanical apparatus for transmitting moving images over short distances and in 1926 gave the first public demonstration of 'television'. In 1929 his mechanically scanned 30-line apparatus was used by the BBC for its first television programmes. Baird's later transmissions for the BBC were daily half-hour programmes in which sound and pictures were synchronized. In 1937, however, Baird's apparatus fell into disuse when the BBC decided to adopt Marconi-EMI's electrically scanned 405-line television system. Baird also developed infra-red television and apparatus for transmitting three-dimensional and coloured images.

BAÍTHÉNE, Abbot of Iona (?–*c*. 600). One of COLUM CILLE's original companions when he arrived at Iona, Baíthéne succeeded the saint in the abbacy following the great Abbot's death in 597. During Colum Cille's lifetime, Baíthéne had held positions of authority in Iona, Hinba (?Jura) and Mag Luinge on Tiree, and so perhaps had been designated successor to Colum Cille by the saint himself, and was being provided with experience in wielding abbatial authority. However, he lived for only three years after Colum Cille's death.

BAKER, AUGUSTINE (1575–1641), mystic and writer. Born David Baker in Abergavenny (Gwent), he studied at Oxford and was later converted to Roman Catholicism. He became a Benedictine monk at Padua, worked in Cambrai and Douai, and then maintained a clandestine ministry in London. Part of his important research on the history of the English Benedictines was published in 1626 and his main writings on the contemplative life were gathered posthumously as *Sancta Sophia* (Holy Wisdom) (1657).

BAKER, GEOFFREY (*fl*. 1350), chronicler. Author of a lively chronicle of the years 1303–56, written for the Oxon. knight, Sir Thomas de la More, who was also one of his informants, it includes the most dramatic version of EDWARD II's death, as well as a patriotic account of the early stages of the Hundred Years War.

BAKER, SIR HERBERT (1862–1946), architect. He is associated particularly with the grandeur of late imperial Britain, his most prominent design in Britain being for the Bank of England under NORMAN (1925–39), which destroyed much of SOANE's great work. Baker's best remembered work was his design for public buildings in New Delhi, India (in an orientalized neo-baroque), in collaboration (and often in confrontation) with LUTYENS from 1912.

BAKER, KENNETH (Baron Baker of Dorking) (1934–), politician. Baker was representative of the new style of Conservative MP who came to power during the THATCHER years. The grandson of a docker who was asked by Keir HARDIE to stand for the new Labour Party, son of an upwardly mobile father, a civil servant, who sent him to St Paul's school, London, and Magdalen College, Oxford, the young Baker worked in management for Shell and other companies before entering the Commons as MP for Acton, London, in 1968.

Very much a product of the Heathite Conservative Party, thrusting, young, smooth and professional, Baker held junior office under Edward HEATH, becoming his Parliamentary Private Secretary in 1974 after the election defeats of that year. This positioned him badly for life under the new leader, Margaret Thatcher. Not until 1981 did Baker get a foot on the ladder of promotion, but thereafter his rise seemed irresistible, even if his unctuous manner irritated many observers. He specialized in making an immediate impact on a ministry before swiftly moving on, going from Minister of Information Technology (1981–4) to Local Government (1984–5) before becoming in swift succession Secretary of State for the Environment (1985–6), Education (1986–9) and the Home Office (1990–2). He is best remembered for his 1988 Education Act, which infuriated educationalists and teachers but established the successful national curriculum.

BAKER, VALENTINE (1827–87), soldier. Commissioned into the Ceylon Rifles in 1848, he transferred to the cavalry in 1852, saw active service in South Africa (1852–3) and the Crimea (1854–6), acted as an observer in the Austro-Prussian War (1866) and the Franco-Prussian War (1870–1), and gathered intelligence in Central Asia (1873). On 2 Aug. 1875 he was convicted of indecently assaulting a young lady in a railway carriage and sentenced to 12 months imprisonment, and was dismissed from the army. His career destroyed, Baker joined the Turkish army, distinguished himself in the Russo-Turkish War (1877–8), and was promoted to Lieutenant General. He then commanded the Egyptian gendarmerie, fighting alongside the British in the campaign of 1884–5. The quintessence of the dashing cavalry officer, Baker's life became the stuff of legends.

BAKEWELL, ROBERT (1725–94), animal breeder. A farmer's son from Dishley (Leics.), he gradually assumed management of his father's farm between 1755 and 1760, and set up as a specialist breeder: his fame was established by the New Leicester breed of sheep, which fattened rapidly and had a high proportion of saleable – although coarse – flesh to bone. He then turned to cattle, and bred New Longhorns. Despite the interest which Bakewell's claims (which were subsequently disputed) aroused, they had a limited impact on farming practice; not until the nineteenth century were improved animal breeds widely diffused.

BALD (*fl. c*. 900–*c*. 950), physician. Nothing is known about Bald, except that he was the author of his *Leechbook*, the earliest surviving medical book in the English language. This book contains descriptions of remedies sent from Jerusalem to ALFRED THE GREAT and draws on a great variety of classical and lost vernacular texts.

BALDWIN, Abbot of Bury St Edmunds (?–1098). A French monk and EDWARD THE CONFESSOR's doctor, Baldwin was part of the small foreign element introduced into the English Church under the Confessor. Abbot of Bury St Edmunds (Suffolk) from 1065, he remained in office after the Norman Conquest, rebuilt the Abbey church and greatly developed the cult of the English martyr, St EDMUND.

BALDWIN (?–1190), Archbishop of Canterbury (1184–90). Although described as gentle and guileless by his friend Gerald de BARRI, in 1184 he galloped up and saved Gilbert of Plumpton from the gallows, forbidding such hangman's work on a Sunday. Author of religious works, a Cistercian monk and Abbot of Ford, then Bishop of Worcester, he became Archbishop in 1184, and was soon caught up in endless squabbles with the wealthy and privileged monks of Christchurch, Canterbury. After the capture of Jerusalem by Saladin in 1187, he preached the crusade in Wales in 1188 and went on crusade himself in 1190. At Acre 200 of his knights fought under the banner of Thomas BECKET, but five weeks after his arrival there, he died.

BALDWIN, STANLEY see essay on pages 52–3

BALE, JOHN (1495–1563), Bishop of Ossory. A prominent Carmelite friar of humble Suffolk parentage, he was converted to evangelical reformism in the early 1530s by Thomas, 1st Lord Wentworth. He rejected his friar's vows by marrying, and was commissioned by Thomas CROMWELL to help his religious reform programme by writing exuberantly abusive anti-Catholic plays; from then on, he produced plays and a host of savagely penned tracts throughout his career. In 1540 he fled to Germany to avoid the consequences of HENRY VIII's swing to a more conservative religious policy, and while abroad began important collections on English history. Appointed as Bishop of Ossory (Co. Kilkenny) in 1552, he tried to introduce EDWARD VI's Reformation to this unpromising setting, fleeing to the Netherlands and then to Basel on MARY I's accession. ELIZABETH I secured him a comfortable retirement as a Prebendary of Canterbury Cathedral.

BALFOUR, A(RTHUR) J(AMES) see essay on page 54

BALFOUR, SIR JAMES (?–1583), lawyer. An early Protestant from Fife, he served as a French galley slave (1547–9) for his part in assassinating Cardinal David BEATON at St Andrews Castle in 1546. Changing sides adroitly and repeatedly, he presided over the court of John HAMILTON, the next

Archbishop, and also over its replacement after the national revolution of 1560. He was implicated in the murder (1567) of Henry STEWART, Lord Darnley, but his appointment through James HEPBURN, Earl of Bothwell, as governor of Edinburgh Castle did not prevent his subsequent promotion to be president of the Court of Session. He became Laird of Pittendreich (Lothian). He was the author of *Balfour's Practicks*, the most comprehensive early Scots legal textbook, reflecting his central part in the late sixteenth-century codification of Scots law.

BALL, JOHN (*fl.* 1360), priest and rebel. One of the leaders of the Peasants' Revolt of June 1381, and the only one of whom anything earlier is known, as early as 1366 he was banned from preaching but evidently did not stop. Contemporaries universally saw him as the inspirational man of egalitarian ideas behind the revolt. According to FROISSART he was 'a foolish priest' who for 'foolish words' was three times imprisoned by the Archbishop of Canterbury. When the revolt broke out the Kentish rebels marched on Maidstone jail and freed him. At Blackheath outside London he preached a sermon on the text 'When Adam delved and Eve span, Who was then the gentleman?' This sermon, known only from the hostile summary given by Froissart, would centuries later be read as a powerful plea for social equality. 'They have the velvet and furs, we are clothed in poor cloth; they have wine, spices and good bread, we have coarse bread and water; they dwell in fair houses, and we have the pain and the labour, rain and wind in the fields.' When, after Wat TYLER's death, the revolt collapsed, Ball was captured and on 15 June 1381 hanged, drawn and quartered.

BALLANTYNE, R(OBERT) M(ICHAEL) (1825–94), writer. Born and educated in Scotland he started his adventurous life young, working in remote regions for the Hudson's Bay Co. His first book, *The Young Fur Traders* (1856), based on this experience, was a best-seller, as was his second, *Coral Island* (1858). The adventures which he described were often his own – in a remote lighthouse, as a miner or a London fireman – and he wrote a couple of adventure stories every year for nearly 40 years.

BALMERINO, 2ND BARON see ELPHINSTONE, JOHN

BALOGH, THOMAS (1905–85), economist. Born in Budapest and frequently linked with Nicholas KALDOR, he was interested primarily in international economics. He was influential in the senior ranks of the Labour Party, having been a member of the party's Economic and Financial

continued on page 55

BALDWIN, STANLEY (1st Earl Baldwin of Bewdley) (1867–1947)
Politician and Prime Minister (1923–4, 1924–9, 1935–7)

Son and heir of a Worcs. iron-master, Stanley Baldwin entered the family business after a scholastic career which varied between the mediocre and the dire; this left him with a lasting prejudice in favour of character over intellect, something which was to leave its mark on his career.

After the death of his father, Alfred, in 1908, Stanley inherited both the family business and his parliamentary seat. His career on the back-benches was of such blameless mediocrity that by 1916 he was being spoken of as a possible Speaker of the House. A stolid-looking, pipe-smoking, tweed-suited, bucolic figure, Baldwin was the very image of the local worthy who made the backbone of the early twentieth-century House of Commons; this image went far in explaining his later success. He held minor office in the LLOYD GEORGE coalition, where his only action of note as Financial Secretary to the Treasury was to donate, anonymously, one-fifth of his fortune towards payment of Britain's war debt. It was not an action which was widely imitated in a House of Commons peopled by those who, in Baldwin's own words, were 'hard-faced men who had done well out of the war'. He became President of the Board of Trade in 1921, a post which seemed well beyond the peak of any possible career ambitions but which, to everyone's surprise, including Baldwin's, proved to be the stepping stone to greater things.

Baldwin belonged to that group of Conservatives who, by 1922, were seriously worried about the effects upon their party of Lloyd George's unsavoury reputation. No one doubted his brilliance or that of his cronies, CHURCHILL and Birkenhead (see SMITH, F. E.), but none of them could have been considered 'sound' by 'sound' men. Considering himself greatly daring, and convinced that he was bringing his career to an end, Baldwin spoke at the Carlton Club meeting of the Conservative Party in Oct. 1922, where he called Lloyd George a 'dynamic force' and appealed to his colleagues not to let him destroy their party as he had the Liberals. The majority of the Conservative leadership ignored Baldwin's advice; the majority of Conservative MPs ignored their leaders'; so, by default, Baldwin found himself one of the leading figures as Andrew Bonar LAW formed the first purely Conservative government since 1905.

It could not be said that Baldwin's period as Chancellor of the Exchequer (1922–3) was a great success, indeed he was heavily criticized by Cabinet colleagues for his conduct of the negotiations with the Americans over loan repayments, but his knack for being in the right place at the right time was once again shown when Bonar Law fell mortally ill with cancer in early 1923. The Foreign Secretary, Lord CURZON, was possessed of far greater political experience and intellect but Baldwin had character, and a seat in the Commons; with Austen CHAMBERLAIN and the other leading Conservative coalitionists still sulking Baldwin added the premiership and the leadership of the Conservative Party to his responsibilities. To everyone's stupefaction he called a General Election in Oct. 1923 on the issue of Tariff Reform. Historians, as puzzled as contemporaries, have attempted sophisticated explanations of this strange decision but the most likely explanation is the one Baldwin preferred, if only because no one would have invented it: he claimed that he was bound by the promise of his predecessor not to introduce tariffs without an election and that, since tariffs were his only answer to Britain's economic problems, he had to call an election. He managed the remarkable feat of reuniting the Liberals and letting Labour into office. Had he not only just been selected leader, the Conservatives would have dumped him.

Baldwin's refusal to go into coalition with the Liberals to keep Labour out was the product of his belief in the essential decency of the British working man. He feared that if the two old parties ganged up on Labour it would only strengthen the hands of the few revolutionaries on the Labour benches; he never made the mistake of Churchill and Birkenhead in seeing Ramsay MACDONALD and Philip SNOWDEN as the Danton and Robespierre of the English revolution, a task rendered all the easier by his greater acquaintanceship with the English working man. The fact that Asquith's backing for Labour was bound to split the Liberals no doubt also entered into Baldwin's calculations. The fall of MacDonald's government in 1924 played nicely into Baldwin's hands. MacDonald was accused of having suppressed the prosecution of the Communist newspaper the *Morning Star* for political reasons, and the appearance during the election of the so-called Zinoviev letter, which purported to reveal that the Russian Soviets were backing Labour, enabled the Conservatives to run the election on the 'Red scare' issue, which brought them a large majority.

As Prime Minister, Baldwin's first priority was to mend the wounds in his own party, and he brought back Chamberlain and Birkenhead as Foreign and Indian Secretary. His second priority was to consolidate the Conservatives as the party of the centre ground, and towards this end he astonished the political world by inviting Churchill, who was not even a Conservative, to become his Chancellor of the Exchequer. By appointing a Free Trade Liberal to this sensitive post Baldwin was simultaneously reassuring those Liberals who had voted for him and encouraging them, and others of their persuasion, to look to the Conservatives. English decency, common-sense and pragmatic 'One Nation' Conservatism became, under Baldwin, the bulwark against revolutionary socialism. But important though image and mood-music were, by themselves they would not have sustained the Conservatives; Baldwin's Disraelian rhetoric (see DISRAELI, BENJAMIN) was accompanied by the Peelite efficiency (see PEEL, SIR ROBERT) of the Minister of Health, Neville CHAMBERLAIN, whose programme of social reform provided the backbone of the government's achievement.

As leader Baldwin operated best when in the last ditch; indeed it sometimes seemed that only a serious threat would galvanize him. During the General Strike (1926) he tried to restrain his own right wing, while ensuring that trade union militants were defeated. After that he subsided into exhaustion and, in 1929, the Conservatives went down to their second defeat in three elections under Baldwin's leadership. He faced serious challenges to his leadership from tariff reformers and rebels (led by Churchill) against his Liberal policy on home rule for India but his luck held in so far as his opponents proved unable to combine against him. His last-ditch fighting qualities were shown at the St George's by-election in early 1931 when, in mounting an attack on his enemies in the press, he accused Lords Beaverbrook (see AITKEN, MAXWELL) and Rothermere (see HARMSWORTH, HAROLD) of wanting 'power without responsibility – the prerogative of the harlot down the ages'. His own candidate, Duff COOPER, easily won the contest and Baldwin's leadership was safe – at least for the moment.

Baldwin's consensual style and lack of *amour propre* made him the ideal Conservative leader to take his party into the National government in Aug. 1931, although he was content to let MacDonald be Prime Minister while, as Lord President of the Council, he concentrated on doing what he did best – nothing. The establishment of a vast parliamentary majority for the National government in the election in Oct. 1931 allowed Baldwin to sponsor moderate legislation such as the India Bill, which a purely Conservative administration would never have permitted. He became Prime Minister just before the election in May 1935, mainly because MacDonald was by this point virtually senile.

His major achievement in this last phase of his career was to steer the country through the abdication of King EDWARD VIII in 1936, the handling of which won him general plaudits. He took the opportunity of the coronation of GEORGE VI to retire in early 1937, becoming the first Conservative leader to lay down the office of Prime Minister and party leader at a moment of his own choosing. After a brief period under the unfamiliar appellation of Sir Stanley Baldwin, he became an earl.

Although Baldwin's career had been a triumph of good timing, his retirement brought a terrible nemesis. By the time of Dunkirk in 1940 he and his administration had become scapegoats for the country's supposed unreadiness to fight Hitler's Germany, and Baldwin became as universally execrated as he had been beloved. It was a sad end to a career which had been marked by an eagerness to heal social and political divisions.

During the long reign of the Churchillian version of the 1930s as the 'years which the locusts have eaten', Baldwin's reputation remained low and, despite the fact that at least three of the leading figures in the post-war Conservative Party, EDEN, BUTLER and Lord Home (see DOUGLAS-HOME, ALEC), had all owed their preferment to him, his name all but vanished from Conservative Party literature. As the post-1945 economic boom faded in the 1960s, historians came to have more sympathy for a government faced with seemingly intractable economic problems, and the rise of a revisionist school on the subject of appeasement also helped Baldwin's reputation.

Historians now have a better sense of Baldwin as the first politician of the modern media age, appreciating his skills as a communicator on the radio, as well as a recognition of his achievement in reconciling the Conservative Party to the rise of Labour, and the Labour Party to the virtues of parliamentary democracy.

Keith Middlemas, Baldwin: A Biography (1969)

BALFOUR, A(RTHUR) J(AMES) (1st Earl of Balfour) (1848–1930)
Politician and Prime Minister (1902–5)

Balfour was one of the most intellectual yet ineffectual of Conservative leaders and one of the few politicians whose career continued long after his premiership.

Balfour owed his political career to his uncle, the 3rd Marquess of Salisbury (*see* CECIL, ROBERT GASCOYNE), whose private secretary he was between 1878 and 1880. The possessor of an ample private fortune, Balfour entered the Commons in 1874, and after 1880 acted as the link between Salisbury and the 'Fourth Party' led by Lord Randolph CHURCHILL. The publication of his major philosophical work, *A Defence of Philosophic Doubt* (1879), confirmed him in the parliamentary mind as an intellectual unfitted for the rough and tumble of real politics, and his appointment to the exacting post of Chief Secretary for Ireland (1887–91) occasioned a sense of surprise surpassed only by that occasioned by his efficient and ruthless conduct in office. One of the few English politicians to gain credit from association with Ireland, 'Bloody Balfour' had established himself as his uncle's political heir. From 1891 to 1892, and again from 1895 until 1902, Balfour combined the posts of First Lord of the Treasury and the leadership of the Commons, and as Salisbury's heir apparent he exercised considerable influence, especially in the field of foreign affairs where he often acted as his uncle's deputy. Balfour was a proponent of a German alliance in the late 1890s, and he opposed the move in 1901 towards an alliance with Japan.

When he became Prime Minister following Salisbury's retirement in July 1902, Balfour had two main preoccupations but was soon provided with a third by Joseph CHAMBERLAIN. Concern over the provision of education above elementary level led to the Balfour Education Act of 1902 which provided State and Church schools with financial aid from the rates (thus arousing the ire of Chamberlain and other Nonconformists who did not want Anglican schools to receive such help); the Act modernized the education system but at considerable political cost to the Conservative government. Balfour had been greatly concerned about the deficiencies in British defence planning and co-ordination exposed by the Boer War and, in 1902, established the Committee of Imperial Defence to meet this need. But his attempts in 1902 and 1903 to reorganize the army caused further rifts in his party. Then, in 1903, Chamberlain dropped the bombshell of Tariff Reform.

Politically, the effects of Chamberlain's announcement were damaging to Balfour in two ways: in the first place Chamberlain himself, the most prominent figure in the government, resigned to campaign for his controversial policy; in the second place, by proposing to abandon the Free Trade policies which Britain had pursued since the 1840s, Chamberlain managed to split the Conservative Party and unite the Liberals. 'Free food' Conservatives such as Winston CHURCHILL moved towards the Liberals, and Balfour found himself unsuccessfully trying to find a compromise upon which all Conservatives could agree; philosophy was, if anything, a hindrance here, since only Balfour could actually find such a position. The final 18 months of the administration were an unhappy time for Balfour and the Conservatives, marked only by the successful negotiation of an *entente* with France by Lord Lansdowne (*see* PETTY-FITZMAURICE, HENRY).

Balfour sought to take advantage of rumours of splits in the Liberal Party by resigning in Dec. 1905 but, in the ensuing General Election, he lost his seat and the Conservatives went down to their worst defeat until that of 1997; only Chamberlain's stroke prevented a Chamberlainite take-over of the party. Balfour soldiered on until 1911 when, after two elections at which the Conservatives failed to turn out the Liberals, he gave way to Bonar LAW.

The First World War and the wartime coalitions resurrected Balfour's career, and as LLOYD GEORGE's Foreign Secretary he was responsible, in 1917, for the declaration which bears his name, promising the creation of a Jewish homeland in Palestine. As Foreign Secretary he was a leading advocate of co-operation with the USA and one of the main proponents of the Conservatives remaining within the Lloyd George coalition. After the 1922 Carlton Club revolt against the coalition Balfour went into retirement, having gone to the Lords in May 1922 after half a century in the Commons.

Balfour played some part in advising the King against appointing CURZON as Prime Minister in 1923 and, as Chairman of the 1926 Imperial Conference, composed the famously complex formula which defined the nature of the relationship between Britain and her Dominions: 'co-operation without jealousy' was, he remarked, the 'motto of the British Empire'. He died in 1930. Balfour's career spanned the transition to mass politics and the passing of the *Pax Britannica*; his remote and aristocratic style prevented him from dealing effectively with either phenomenon.

Max Egremont, Balfour: A Life of Arthur James Balfour (1980)

Committee (1943–64). He was economic adviser to Harold WILSON's government after 1964 and became a life peer in 1968. He was a consistent critic of neoclassical economics, which he regarded as simplistic, particularly as applied to international trade. Hence he advocated dirigiste economic policies, including the use of import controls and incomes policy. His well-known antipathy to devaluation may have reinforced Wilson's decision to avoid that policy option in 1964 and to impose a 15 per cent tariff on manufactured goods in the face of international objections. As Minister of State for Energy in 1974–5 Balogh was responsible for reshaping policy on the exploitation of North Sea oil. He was Deputy Chairman of the British National Oil Corporation from 1976 to 1979.

BALTHILD, ST (?–680), Queen of the Franks (c. 648–57). Reputedly an English slave, she married the Merovingian Clovis II, King of the Franks, and, after his death in 657, was Regent for their son until forced into a nunnery in 664. The information about her low birth is the sort of slander frequently spread around in the Middle Ages to defame the character of a powerful woman. Balthild was a great religious patron, founding two important abbeys at Chelles and Corbie.

BALTIMORE, BARON, 1ST see CALVERT, SIR GEORGE; **2ND** see CALVERT, CECIL

BANCROFT, RICHARD (1544–1610), Archbishop of Canterbury (1604–10). Cambridge-educated, he developed a lifelong detestation of Puritans probably while chaplain to Bishop COX of Ely. Later, devoted to Archbishop WHITGIFT and Sir Christopher HATTON, he made his name exposing Puritan activity. In 1589 he preached a sensational sermon at Paul's Cross (outside St Paul's Cathedral) attacking Puritans and Presbyterians, and his efforts culminated in 1591 in the prosecution of the leaders of the clandestine Presbyterian organization within the Church known as the Classical Movement. Bishop of London from 1597, he continued Whitgift's drive for conformity, revising the Church's code of canon law in 1604, the year he became Archbishop.

BANDA, HASTINGS (1898–1997), Malawi politician. The son of subsistence farmers from northern Nyasaland, Banda was educated by missionaries and took the name Hastings from his Scottish teacher. As a medical practitioner in Britain he became active in Labour and pan-African politics, but with the formation of the Central African Federation in 1953 his pro-British sympathies were shattered and he moved to the Gold Coast before returning to Nyasaland in 1958, where he was greeted as a saviour. He led a campaign of non-violent non-co-operation and was deported. In negotiations in 1960 Banda (with KAUNDA and NKOMO) argued for independence and led his new Malawi Congress Party to electoral victory in 1961. The federation was dissolved in 1963. Nysaland's independence followed in 1964; it was renamed Malawi. Dr Banda became an increasingly despotic ruler, making Malawi a one-party state, assuming the title of Life President in 1971, while encouraging a traditional emphasis on agriculture.

BANKS, SIR JOSEPH (1743–1820), botanist. Born to a wealthy Lincs. family, Banks was educated at Eton and Oxford. In 1764 he inherited his father's estate, where he developed his interests in botany. In 1766 he worked as a naturalist on an expedition to Newfoundland and brought back specimens which won him scientific acclaim. In 1769 he paid for himself to join James COOK's famous expedition on the *Endeavour* to the southern hemisphere. He returned to England in 1772 with over 800 hitherto unknown botanical specimens and thereafter became a national celebrity and was taken up by GEORGE III and other powerful figures. In 1778 he was elected President of the Royal Society. In his 41 years in this position, he established himself as one of the most powerful and, to some, autocratic figures in British science. He made his London residence the centre of scientific life, sustained connections between English and continental science and sought to control other scientific societies. Through his friendship with the King, he helped establish the Royal Botanic Gardens at Kew, a world centre for studying plants. Research at Kew enabled species such as the bread-fruit plant of Tahiti and the Chinese tea plant to be established in other colonies. Banks was also a leading figure in the establishment and maintenance of a convict settlement colony at Botany Bay in 1788.

BANNATYNE, GEORGE (?1545–1608), anthologist. A lawyer's son who became an Edinburgh merchant, he used the leisure afforded by an outbreak of plague, which shut down the burgh's normal life in 1568, to compile a massive collection of Scots poetry from the previous hundred years. The manuscripts remain a vital source of knowledge about early Scots literature.

BARBAULD, ANNA LETITIA (née Aikin) (1743–1825), author. She was educated by her father, John Aikin, who in 1758 became a tutor at Warrington Academy, enabling her to come into contact with scholars. A collection of her poems was published to great acclaim in 1773. Many of her works were educational, in particular *Hymns in Prose for Children* and *The Female Speaker*.

Elizabeth MONTAGU wanted her to be involved in her projected Ladies' Academy but Mrs Barbauld was not enthusiastic. She edited a 50-volume edition of *The English Novelists* (from 1808), and in 1811 wrote the poem 'Eighteen Hundred and Eleven', forecasting the collapse of Great Britain through war. She was painted as one of the *Nine English Muses* in 1779.

BARBER, ANTHONY (Baron Barber of Wentbridge) (1920–), politician. A barrister, he became an MP in 1951, rising to become Minister of Health under DOUGLAS-HOME (1963–4). He served as Chairman of the Conservative Party (1967–70) and was involved in the early negotiations to join the European Economic Community (EEC, known subsequently as the European Community, and now as the European Union). As Chancellor of the Exchequer in Edward HEATH'S government from July 1970, following the sudden death of MACLEOD, he pursued what came to be regarded as inappropriately expansionist tax-cutting policies, thus creating the 'Barber boom'. A consequent run on sterling in the foreign exchanges forced him to 'float' the pound in June 1972. In the autumn, in order to control inflation, he introduced a statutory prices and incomes policy. With the economy further weakened by the oil crisis, in Dec. 1973, when following the Arab–Israeli war the Organization of Petroleum Exporting Countries (OPEC) quadrupled the price of oil, he introduced large-scale spending cuts, credit controls and tax surcharges. Although he achieved high growth rates and a surge in output, the consequent inflation and pay policy precipitated industrial conflict, particularly with the miners, which was to bring down the government in Feb. 1974.

BARBON, NICHOLAS (?–1698), insurance pioneer and property developer. His father was Praise-god BARBON, the Puritan MP for whom the Barebones Parliament was named. He studied medicine at Leiden and Utrecht before returning to London to practise. Following the Great Fire of 1666 he emerged as one of the great buyers and redevelopers of property. By 1681 he had founded the Phoenix Fire Office: the possibility of establishing insurance companies had been a talking point for some decades, but only after the Great Fire of 1666 were any such schemes launched, Barbon's being one of the earliest. Barbon's conversions of old buildings caused controversy, as did his *Discourse Concerning Coining the New Money Lighter* (1696) which challenged LOCKE'S argument that there was an intrinsic value in metals other than that representing the goods for which they were traded.

BARBON, PRAISE-GOD (c. 1596–1679), politician. Barbon (or Barebone), a London merchant and leader of a radical congregation, achieved fame by the satirical appropriation of his name to describe the 'Barebones' Parliament of 1653, of which he was a member. The assembly, nominated by the Council of Officers of the army, was the first in British history to claim representatives from the entire British Isles; it functioned for only six months before a faction of its members withdrew in Dec. and surrendered power to Oliver CROMWELL. Outspoken in his opposition to CHARLES II's restoration, Barbon was imprisoned in the Tower of London for some years from 1661.

BARBOUR, JOHN (?–1395), royal servant. He was clerk of the Scottish royal household and Archdeacon of Aberdeen. In the 1370s, he wrote the Scottish national epic, *The Bruce*, the story in verse of the careers of ROBERT BRUCE and his companion-in-arms James DOUGLAS.

BARCLAY, ALEXANDER (?1475–1552), poet. Possibly Scots by birth, he travelled in Europe, became a secular priest in Devon, then a Benedictine monk, then a Franciscan friar until the dissolution of the order (1538), preaching widely in defence of traditional religion. He subsequently became a household chaplain to Princess Mary (the future MARY I), but in 1551 was persuaded to abandon her and accept Protestantism, under the influence of Archbishop CRANMER. He made a free translation into English of Sebastian Brant's *Ship of Fools* (1508), wrote English eclogues (pastoral poems) during his Benedictine years, and undertook various translations from Latin and Italian.

BARCLAY, DAVID (1682–1769) and his son **DAVID** (1729–1809), merchants and bankers. A Quaker son of Robert BARCLAY, David was apprenticed to a London merchant and became a highly successful linen-draper, exporting cloth to Philadelphia, New York and the West Indies. His son David took over the business in 1769 but, with Atlantic trade threatened by growing tensions between Britain and America, concentrated on banking and brewing. He sponsored an attempt to settle Anglo-American differences by negotiations between NORTH and Benjamin FRANKLIN in 1774–5; later he encouraged Quaker businessmen to take a leading role in the anti-slavery campaign. The modern Barclay's Bank traces its origins to their firm.

BARCLAY, ROBERT (1648–90), Quaker activist. From a family of minor Scottish landowners, he became a Quaker in 1667 (*see also* FOX, GEORGE) and was quickly established as the leading advocate of the movement in Scotland. His book *The Apology* (1676) was seen as a definitive statement of Quaker beliefs, rejecting the primacy of scripture over personal revelation. Barclay found an ally in James, Duke of York, the future JAMES II, who secured him baronial jurisdiction over his estates and a share in the patent of East New Jersey, intended as a haven for Quakers (1683).

BARHAM, SIR GEORGE (1836–1913), businessman. Both a barrister's clerk and a carpenter, Barham used his spare time to work in the London milk trade, balancing surpluses and shortfalls of supply. Buying his own retail dairy on the edge of the City of London in 1858, he exploited the growing demand for milk in the metropolis by transporting it on the railways, changing both railway freight and the rural economy of many areas in southern and central England. His retail company, Express Country Milk, became Express Dairies in 1881. He was succeeded by his sons Arthur (1869–1952) and Titus (1860–1937), who took the wholesaling and retailing businesses in different directions.

BARING, SIR EVELYN (1st Earl of Cromer) (1841–1917), *de facto* governor of Egypt. A member of the BARING FAMILY, Evelyn served in the Royal Artillery before becoming secretary to the Viceroy of India (his cousin) in 1872. For the next 11 years his public appointments alternated between India and Egypt; named British agent in Cairo in 1883, he was instructed to prepare for the evacuation of the British army of occupation, until the Mahdi's revolt in the Sudan obliged the British to delay withdrawal. His new role was to reform the precarious finances of the Egyptian government. Ultimately he managed to balance the state budget and oversaw land and irrigation reforms that increased both agricultural output and tax revenues. With British withdrawal further delayed, and desire for a naval base at Alexandria, Baring as Consul General extended British influence over the Khedive, Egypt's ruler. When Abbas Hilmi II succeeded as Khedive in 1892, *de jure* and *de facto* rulers clashed; Britain supported Baring, and his reforms and control continued. The addition of Sudan to his responsibilities in 1898 increased his power. He resigned from Egypt in 1907, having seemed impervious to rising Egyptian resistance to British rule until the Dinshaway Incident of 1906 (reprisals against peasants accused of assaulting British officers) brought international condemnation.

BARING FAMILY *see* essay on page 58

BARING, GEORGE (3rd Earl of Cromer) (1918–91), banker. As a senior member of the BARING FAMILY, he worked in the City of London as chairman or director of a string of financial, commercial and industrial organizations, also serving on various government committees and international commissions. He made a substantial impact on the post-war economy of Britain during his period as Governor of the Bank of England and Director of the Bank for International Settlements (1961–6). In this capacity he encouraged the development of the eurodollar and eurobond markets, which were instrumental in making London the most important international financial centre in the world.

BARING, THOMAS GEORGE (2nd Baron Northbrook) (1826–1904), Viceroy of India *see* BARING FAMILY, essay on page 57.

BARLOW, WILLIAM (?–1568), churchman. An Augustinian canon in Essex, he was probably the author of early reformist tracts in the 1520s, but was forced by Sir Thomas MORE to write a condemnation of European reformers (1531). Through Thomas CROMWELL's patronage he became prominent in his Order, followed by the bishopric of St Asaph, then St David's (both 1536), actively promoting religious reform in south Wales; Bishop of Bath and Wells during EDWARD VI's reign, he fled to the continent under Mary. ELIZABETH I made him Bishop of Chichester. His career, notoriously difficult to reconstruct, is important because of his part in consecrating Matthew PARKER as Archbishop of Canterbury (1559); he was the only bishop present to have been consecrated under traditional forms, a material consideration to some later High Churchmen. He is also a distinguished father of the Church, as all his five daughters married bishops.

BARNARDISTON, SIR SAMUEL (1620–1707), politician. Barnardiston (or Barnadiston) was a younger son from a Suffolk Puritan knightly family. As an apprentice in London, in 1641 he took part in a demonstration petitioning for peace. Queen HENRIETTA MARIA is said to have noticed him and commented 'See what a handsome round head is there.' These words soon became current as the nickname for the Parliamentarians in the English Civil Wars. Samuel became wealthy on trade in the Levant and India, was made baronet in 1663 and became a long-serving MP. He gained a popular reputation for his part against the House of Lords in the dispute over Thomas Skinner's case. He was tried by Judge George JEFFREYS for protesting about government action in the Rye House Plot (1683) (*see* RUSSELL, WILLIAM; SIDNEY, ALGERNON), and was imprisoned for refusing to pay a fine; he was released by the crumbling regime of JAMES II in 1688.

BARNARDO, THOMAS (1845–1905), philanthropist. He moved to the London Hospital from
continued on page 59

BARING FAMILY
Bankers and politicians

The London financial house of Baring was established by Sir Francis Baring (1740–1810) in 1762, and his direct descendants continued to run the establishment until the 1990s. Francis's father John (1697–1748) had moved into the Exeter wool trade in 1717 from Germany. In the London world of international shipping, Francis became a middleman for bills of exchange. His merchant bank established a name for reliability: by the 1780s Francis was the confidant and adviser of leading politicians, becoming an MP in 1790, while his bank secured a number of lucrative government contracts. His three sons Sir Thomas (1772–1848), Alexander, 1st Baron Ashburton of the second creation (1774–1848), and Henry (1776–1848) took the business over in 1803, changing the name four years later to Baring Bros. By the end of the Napoleonic Wars in 1815 Baring Bros was the most important of the City's merchant banks, established as an essential means by which governments could finance and manage operations overseas. Barings entered the market in France, together with longterm Amsterdam partner Hope & Co., to raise government loans, actions that aggrieved the emerging ROTHSCHILD house.

Now hugely wealthy, the Barings were busy acquiring landed estates; the banking tradition was that eldest sons did not go into the counting house. Alexander's nephews, Thomas (1799–1873) and John (1801–88), sons of Sir Thomas, were destined to lead the next generation of Barings in the bank, following the investment disasters of Alexander's son Francis, later 3rd Baron Ashburton (1800–68), in Mexico in 1826, while Alexander had entered politics (first as a Whig and later as a Tory). Francis, later 1st Baron Northbrook (1796–1866), Sir Thomas's eldest son, continued to adhere to the Whig cause; he was Chancellor of the Exchequer in 1839, but seems to have been scrupulous in financial dealings with his family. Times were tighter for Barings, while Rothschilds established themselves as much the larger merchant bank. Yet new blood was being brought in, notably the American Joshua Bates, and the foundations were being laid for investments in South America, especially Argentina, that together with Russian loans would be a mainstay of Barings business. Thomas Baring and Joshua Bates led the business from 1848 (the year that three of the older generation died) until Bates's death in 1864.

Railway financing had become an important area of business in both Russia and South America. From Thomas Baring's death in 1873, the finance house was to be piloted by his cousin's son Edward, and then by John, 2nd Baron Revelstoke (1863–1929). Edward, 1st Baron Revelstoke (1828–97), was, at least until 1890, a lucky gambler in finance. Although the banking branch of the family no longer involved itself in politics, many within the wide cousinage entered public life. Thomas, 2nd Baron Northbrook and 1st Earl of Northbrook (1826–1904), was appointed Viceroy of India in 1872 and then to the Admiralty in 1880; Evelyn, Lord Revelstoke's younger brother, became benevolent ruler of Egypt (see BARING, EVELYN). The bank, meanwhile, although it made huge profits out of the frenzied public flotation of the Guinness brewing company in 1886, was making commitments in the Americas far greater than its assets. The crash came in 1890: the end of the railway-building mania in South America, especially in Argentina, exposed Barings to an extent that shocked the City to its core. The Bank of England under its governor William Lidderdale effected a rescue of Barings, if only for fear that the whole of the City would collapse, while the wider family also rallied round. Revelstoke was forced to resign, and the family business was transferred to a new limited liability company.

By 1914 the bank and family had recovered their former power in the City, doing much to finance transport, especially in London, but had lost ground to newcomers, mainly of German origin, such as Kleinwort. Under Edward Peacock (not a family member), Barings became involved in British corporate investment in the 1930s, while changes in the traditional business accelerated after 1945, in the sterling market, corporate finance and bond trading. The firm was reorganized in 1985 as Barings plc, with many family members still in charge.

The second Baring crisis came in February 1995 when, as the result of 'rogue trading' in the new derivatives market by Singapore-based trader Nick Leeson (1967–), the bank was left with losses in excess of £1 billion. Unlike the 1890 crisis, the bank was not rescued by the City 'club' and went into receivership. It was taken over by the Dutch bank ING. Leeson, who fled to Germany, was extradited and subsequently jailed in Singapore for six and a half years (released in 1999), while the Baring family was forced to withdraw gracefully after more than two centuries at the heart of the City.

Philip Ziegler, The Sixth Great Power: Barings 1762–1929 (1988)

Ireland to prepare for a career as a medical missionary, but found the needs of East London more pressing. The first of more than 90 'Dr Barnardo's Homes' for destitute children, with their policy of unlimited admittance, was opened in Stepney in 1870. The charity bearing his name continues his work to this day.

BARNATO, BARNEY (originally Barnett Isaacs) (1852–97), financier. A diamond magnate who rivalled RHODES in the struggle for control of South African mining, he was the son of an East End Jewish shopkeeper. Barnett Isaacs and his brother Henry went to Kimberley in South Africa in 1873 in the diamond rush; they had been vaudeville entertainers in London as the Barnato Brothers, and they adopted that name for their diamond brokerage. Barnato began to speculate boldly in mining claims in 1876, in direct competition with Rhodes and De Beers. Rhodes, backed by ROTHSCHILDS, won the ensuing contest, and the two companies finally merged in 1888 as De Beers Consolidated Mines with Barnato as a life governor.

BARNETT, DAME HENRIETTA (née Rowland) (1851–1936), social reformer. She worked with Octavia HILL amongst the poor of Marylebone where she met and married a Christian Socialist curate, Samuel BARNETT; together they founded Toynbee Hall, a university settlement in Whitechapel. Henrietta Barnett was the first woman guardian responsible for poor law relief and was a member of the committee to inquire into poor law schools; she was closely associated with the Whitechapel Art Gallery which opened in 1901. Inspired by the discrepancy between housing in the East End where she worked and her own comfortable London home, she instigated a social housing project, Hampstead Garden Suburb in north London, which she intended would 'provide a bridge between poverty and privilege' with integrated housing for young and old and provision for community activity.

BARNETT, SAMUEL (1844–1913), social reformer. In 1873 he married Henrietta Rowland (see BARNETT, DAME HENRIETTA) and together they founded Toynbee Hall in 1884, while he was vicar of St Jude's, Whitechapel. He played a leading role in the development of the East End Dwellings Co., which replaced slum buildings near the Royal Mint with model dwellings for the working classes. Within his parish he employed visitors, including Katherine, Teresa and Beatrice Potter (see WEBB, BEATRICE), who adopted the approach to individualized work with the poor advocated by Octavia HILL. He became a canon of Westminster in 1906.

BARO, PETER (1534–99), theologian. French-born, he became one of CALVIN's ministers in Geneva. After returning to France he fled to England (1574) and William CECIL secured him the Lady Margaret chair at Cambridge. He began expressing his doubts about Calvin's theology on predestination, in defiance of the general Reformed orthodoxy in the English Church. When a young Cambridge don, William Barrett, championed his views in 1595, there was a major university row which led to Archbishop WHITGIFT formulating the moderate Calvinist Lambeth Articles as a statement of belief on predestination. Baro felt compelled to leave Cambridge for London in 1596. He was a pioneer of the anti-Calvinist movement which later, as Arminianism, found leadership in William LAUD.

BARRETT BROWNING, ELIZABETH (née Barrett) (1806–61), poet. The oldest of 11 children, she was precociously gifted, sharing her brothers' lessons in Greek and Latin, teaching herself Hebrew and reading voraciously in her father's library. Her first book of poems was privately published when she was 14. An illness that mysteriously struck in her teens meant that she was regarded as 'delicate' and dependent. Her seclusion was complete when her mother and favourite brother died and, with the abolition of slavery, her possessive father lost the fortune made in Jamaica's sugar plantations. As a reclusive semi-invalid, Barrett kept up a stream of poetry production, much of it challenging female stereotypes to which she herself seemed so perfectly to conform. Her *Poems* published in 1844 brought her fame and resulted in a correspondence with and eventual clandestine marriage to the considerably younger poet Robert BROWNING. The couple fled her father's house and settled in Florence. In Italy she gradually recovered her strength sufficiently to travel throughout Europe and bear a son. She was an admirer of the Italian liberation movement, the *Risorgimento*. Among her finest poems are the flirtatious poems written to her husband-to-be, 'Sonnets from the Portuguese' (published as part of *Poems*, 1850), and *Aurora Leigh* (1857), a nine-volume novel in verse about the role of women, which established her fame and is an inspiration to feminists still.

BARRI, GERALD DE see essay on page 60

BARRIE, SIR J(AMES) M(ATTHEW) (1860–1937), writer. Born into a humble household in Kirriemuir (Forfars.), immortalized as 'Thrums' in his writings, Barrie achieved great success and huge wealth from his writing. First a journalist, he started to write vignettes about Scotland. *Auld Licht Idylls* (1888) and *A Widow in Thrums*

continued on page 61

BARRI, GERALD DE (c. 1146–1223)
Author

The youngest son of William de Barri, Lord of Manorbier on the south Pembs. coast, he portrayed himself in his autobiography as a boy building sand churches on the beach rather than the sand castles which his older brothers preferred. Destined for an ecclesiastical career and educated at Gloucester and Paris, he was appointed Archdeacon of Brecon (c. 1175) by his uncle David Fitzgerald, Bishop of St David's. Disappointed not to become bishop when his uncle died in 1176, he returned to Paris and to advanced studies in law and theology. The decisive moment in his life came when he entered the service of HENRY II (c. 1184); for the next 10 years he served Henry and RICHARD I as an expert on the affairs of Wales and Ireland. Through his mother he had family ties with the Fitzgeralds (who were colonizing Ireland) and with native Welsh princes; his maternal grandmother was NEST, so he was a kinsman of RHYS AP GRUFFUDD, the greatest Welsh ruler of the day. He accompanied the future King JOHN to Ireland in 1185 and Archbishop BALDWIN of Canterbury on a tour around Wales, preaching the crusade in 1188.

It was in this busy period that he wrote his earliest and most original works, those for which he is best remembered today: *The History and Topography of Ireland, The Conquest of Ireland, The Journey through Wales* and the *Description of Wales*. He re-invented the ethnographic monograph, a genre not seen since classical antiquity, writing about language, dress, music as well as about such details of everyday life as how the Welsh looked after babies or cleaned their teeth. He saw that the pastoral economy of the Welsh and Irish created a different kind of society from that of more agrarian and urbanized England, and explained this in terms of a ladder of evolution of human societies and the persistence of primitive survivals from an earlier stage. The two books on Ireland are written from the point of view of the colonists. They provide a detailed narrative of the English invasion, powerfully and vividly reinforcing the stereotype of the barbarous Irish. His works on the Welsh are more balanced. The *Description* included chapters advising the English how to conquer and govern Wales, and advising the Welsh on how best to resist. Indeed it ended on a note of Welsh patriotism.

His service to the Crown led him to hope for promotion to an English bishopric but he was disappointed. His contemporary *Life* of Archbishop GEOFFREY OF YORK shows that in the struggle of court faction during Richard I's absence he supported the side that lost in the end. He retired to Lincoln and devoted himself to more conventional forms of literature, saints' lives and criticisms of clerical shortcomings. In 1199 the canons of St David's elected him as Bishop on the understanding that he would revive St David's old claim to be the metropolitan see of Wales, independent of Canterbury. Inevitably this guaranteed that his election would be opposed by Archbishop Hubert WALTER. According to Gerald, Hubert argued that Gerald was too Welsh to be a politically safe choice. In his attempt to win the see Gerald increasingly identified himself with his Welsh kindred, writing 'we Welsh' where once he had written 'we English'. Gerald de Barri became Giraldus Cambrensis or Gerald of Wales, and correspondingly critical of the English. He received financial support from LLYWELYN AP IORWERTH and letters on his behalf from many Welsh princes, but King John supported Hubert Walter; under heavy political pressure the canons backed down and Pope Innocent III ordered a new election. Gerald resigned his archdeaconry in favour of his nephew, with whom he then quarrelled fiercely. From now on he was a bitter man. In his subsequent polemical writings, *The Invectives, On the Rights and Status of St David's* as well as his *Autobiography* he went over and over his struggles, proving to his own satisfaction that he was right both morally and in law, and that others were wrong and corrupt. Now, disillusioned with the Welsh, he instead idealized France, the country in which he had been a student. The attempt by the Capetian prince, Louis of France, to overthrow John in 1216 won Gerald's enthusiastic support and he completed his book, *On the Instruction of Princes*, in a mood of violent hostility to the Plantagenet kings, damning them as tyrants in contrast to serene and peace-loving kings of France. Despite his failures, Gerald's genius as a writer, his gift for stylish pen portraits and lively anecdotes, and the originality of much of his subject matter (doubtless related to his own confused identities and ambitions) ensured that he achieved at least one of the goals he set himself, undying fame.

Robert Bartlett, Gerald of Wales (1982)

(1889) were published to both critical and public acclaim. His first successful play was a jointly authored satire on the current Ibsen cult (1891), followed by a full-length comedy, *Walker, London* (1892), which played more than 1,000 performances, and *The Professor's Love Story* (1892), a comparable success. Other plays, *The Admirable Crichton* (1902), *Dear Brutus* (1917) and of course *Peter Pan, or The Boy Who Wouldn't Grow Up* (1904), were phenomenal commercial if not always critical successes. He was a complex figure, and his later reputation as possibly a pederast with an intense mother fixation cannot detract from his extreme generosity: during the First World War he funded a hospital for displaced children, and in 1929 he gifted the 'Peter Pan Wing' to London's Great Ormond Street Hospital for Sick Children and assigned all future royalties to the hospital. In 1988 a special Act of Parliament honoured Barrie's bequest by extending the hospital's copyright into perpetuity.

BARRINGTON, GEORGE (1755–?), thief and colonial administrator. Originally from Maynooth in Ireland, where he was born George Waldron, he ran away from school in 1771 and joined a group of petty criminals. He subsequently travelled to England where he posed as a clergyman in order to rob members of the aristocracy. He was arrested and sentenced to hard labour in 1777 and again in 1778, but was swiftly released on account of his good behaviour. Eventually, in 1790, he was sentenced to seven years transportation to Botany Bay. During the voyage he helped foil a plot by the conspirators to seize the ship; he was rewarded with money and the first warrant of emancipation to be awarded to a convict in New South Wales. Barrington settled in Australia where he became superintendent of convicts and High Constable of Paramatta, and wrote books about the country and his experiences.

BARRINGTON, SHUTE (1734–1826), moralist, Bishop of Llandaff (1769–82), Salisbury (1782–91) and Durham (1791–1826). He was the younger brother of the second Viscount Barrington, a Whig statesman, who arranged for him to become chaplain to GEORGE III in 1760. Barrington was close ideologically and personally to George III, and was a canon of Windsor from 1776. Along with Beilby Porteus, who was Bishop of Chester, then of London, he was the most evangelically inclined of later eighteenth-century bishops. He advocated measures to restore public morality, including Bills in 1771 and 1779 to prevent the guilty party in a divorce from remarrying, which passed the Lords but not the Commons. He was a prominent supporter of Sunday schools and other forms of popular educa-

tion, and was President of the Society for Bettering the Condition of the Poor, instigated by Sir Thomas BERNARD, which WILBERFORCE also supported. Barrington saw the French Revolution as arising from the immoral climate of Catholic countries.

BARROW, HENRY (*c.* 1550–93), martyr. One of several Cambridge Puritans who became radicalized into Separatism, i.e. the belief that the Church should be independent of secular authority. In 1587 (not 1586 as often stated) he was seized by order of Archbishop WHITGIFT while visiting John GREENWOOD in prison, and never released. He and Greenwood were hanged for seditious writings attacking the established Church and advocating Congregationalism (i.e. Church government devolved to each individual congregation).

BARROW, SIR JOHN (1764–1848), promoter of exploration. A member of the staff of George MACARTNEY on the 1793 mission to China, and then in the Cape of Good Hope when it was taken over by Britain, Barrow used his subsequent career from 1806 as second secretary at the Admiralty to promote exploration and discovery. Parts of West Africa and the north polar regions were first charted by 'Barrow's Boys', in official and semi-official expeditions which he supervised. He was a founder member of the Royal Geographical Society (1830), the backbone of Victorian exploration.

BARRY, SIR CHARLES (1795–1860), architect. Designer of one of the best-known buildings in the world, he beat 96 other contenders to rebuild the Houses of Parliament after they had largely been destroyed by fire in 1834. Barry's detailed draughtsmanship (with assistance from William PUGIN in the perpendicular detail and much of the interior) convinced the Commissioners that he could follow the brief for a quintessential British building in the Gothic or Tudor vernacular, which he did up to a point. The £2 million building was opened in 1852, though work continued for some seven years after his death.

BARRY, ELIZABETH (*c.* 1658–1713), actor. The daughter of a Royalist barrister, her guardian was Sir William DAVENANT, who first put her on stage in 1675, at a time when actresses were still something of a novelty. She became the protégé and lover of Rochester (*see* WILMOT, JOHN), despite the advances of Thomas OTWAY, who wrote many of her best parts. She became the leading actress in the United Company formed in 1682, and was one of the leaders of the secession from Drury Lane to Lincoln's Inn Fields in 1695 (*see also* BETTERTON,

RICH, CHRISTOPHER and JOHN). She was often attacked by her enemies for avarice and sexual promiscuity, but this did not damage her reputation as the greatest actress of her generation.

BARRY, JAMES (1795–1865), military doctor. A woman who successfully passed herself off as a man, Barry joined the army in 1813 as a hospital assistant, and rose to the rank of Inspector General of the Army Medical Department. Barry, who saw extensive service in the Mediterranean and in South Africa, was generally regarded as one of the finest surgeons in the army, a profession she could not have followed if her sex had become widely known. She was protected by a small group of sympathizers, among whom was an erstwhile lover, Lord Charles Somerset, Governor of the Cape and brother of the Military Secretary Lord Fitzroy SOMERSET, the future Lord Raglan.

BARTHOLOMEW (?–1184), bishop. A respected canon lawyer, he was elected Bishop of Exeter in 1161. Although courted by both parties, he steered an unwavering middle line in the dispute between HENRY II and Archbishop BECKET, but after Becket's murder maintained that King Henry was responsible. He preached the first sermon when Canterbury Cathedral reopened a year after Becket's death.

BARTLETT, SIR FREDERIC (1886–1969), psychologist. Bartlett studied philosophy in London and worked at Cambridge under W. H. R. Rivers and C.S. Myers at the newly opened laboratory of experimental psychology. In 1922 he was appointed Director of the laboratory and in 1931 became Cambridge's first Professor of Experimental Psychology. He made his laboratory a leading centre, where he taught many leading British psychologists. His most famous work, *Remembering* (1932), showed that remembering and perceiving were not direct acts but constructive, selective and transformative processes tied to an individual's interests, experiences and attitudes. The book remains one of the most influential psychological works of the twentieth century.

BARTON, ELIZABETH (?1506–34), visionary. A Kentish servant girl who began uttering prophecies in 1525, she was declared a genuine visionary after a diocesan investigation. She was installed in St Sepulchre's nunnery, Canterbury, under the care of leading monks of Canterbury Cathedral and, as 'the Nun [or Maid] of Kent', she much impressed leading figures in Church and State such as Cardinal WOLSEY, John FISHER, Archbishop WARHAM and Thomas MORE. Her prophecies quickly developed a political slant amid the crisis caused by HENRY VIII's campaign to secure annulment of his marriage to CATHERINE OF ARAGON and England's subsequent separation from the Papacy: she eventually declared in 1533 that the King was deposed. She and her clerical backers, led by Edward Bocking, were arrested. Under interrogation she was forced to say that her trances were faked, and she was executed with her associates on 20 April.

BASKERVILLE, JOHN (1706–75), printer. Of humble background, he went to Birmingham to work as a teacher, and had begun to make a success in business as a practitioner of the new craft of 'japanning' (finishing metalwares with an imitation of Japanese laquerwork) before becoming interested in type-founding in 1750. Baskerville successfully sold a new Greek typeface to Oxford University in 1758, the same year that he was elected printer to Cambridge University, where he produced editions of Juvenal, CONGREVE and ADDISON. He was not commercially successful. The universities cut their links with him, although Baskerville continued to publish editions of classical texts until his death. He was only later hailed as the 'finest typographer of his age'. A revived version of his typeface, named Baskerville, is still in use.

BASSENDYNE, THOMAS (?–1577), printer. Based in Edinburgh, he produced a major edition of Sir David LINDSAY's works and the earliest Bible published in Scotland; he was given a licence to print it in 1575, although the Old Testament was not finished until after his death in 1579.

BASTWICK, JOHN (1593–1654), churchman. An Essex-born Puritan educated at Emmanuel College, Cambridge, he took a medical degree at Padua. He gained celebrity when William LAUD persecuted him for his controversial writing and had him fined and imprisoned. Eventually in 1637 he had his ears cropped (with Henry BURTON and William PRYNNE). He was released by the Long Parliament in 1640 and later served in Parliamentarian forces. As a Presbyterian he wrote bitterly against the Independents.

BATESON, WILLIAM (1861–1926), biologist. A zoologist with strong interests in evolution and heredity, Bateson studied the fauna of salt lakes in Africa, Asia and Europe. This research formed the basis of his *Materials for the Study of Variation* (1894), in which he proposed the controversial theory that species do not evolve by a series of gradual changes, as most evolutionists believed, but rather by a series of discontinuous jumps. He sought to produce evidence for this theory from extensive breeding experiments on plants and animals. From 1900, partly to support his theory, he championed the work of Gregor Mendel, an Austrian monk who, from his research in the 1860s on plant hybridization, had formulated principles governing the inheritance of character- istics: Mendel's experiments on successive generations of peas had shown how height and colour, for example, are inherited. In his *Mendel's Principles of Heredity* (1908), however, Bateson showed, in contradiction to Mendel, that some traits are not inherited independently, and explained this in terms of interactions between two 'genes', a word which he coined along with 'genetics'. He was the first Professor of Genetics at Cambridge University (1908–10) and Director of the John Innes Horticultural Institution in Surrey (1910–26).

BATH, 10TH EARL OF *see* PULTENEY, WILLIAM; **1ST MARQUESS OF** *see* THYNNE, THOMAS

BATTIE, WILLIAM (1704–76), medical pioneer. A clergyman's son, he was educated at Eton and King's College, Cambridge, where he began prac- tising medicine while still an undergraduate. He moved to London and he built up a highly successful practice, specializing in mental illness and establishing a private lunatic asylum. In 1751 he became physician to St Luke's Hospital for the insane, set up to relieve the Bethlehem Hospital and also compete with it by adopting a modern administrative structure where subscribers could become governors and the inmates were not shown to the public as entertainment. Battie's private asylum influenced the 1774 Act regulating hospitals for the insane.

BAUTHUMLEY (OR BOTTOMLEY), JACOB (1613–*c*. 1685), writer. Bauthumley was the son of a Leicester shoemaker. His father was already being harassed by the authorities for his involve- ment in a separatist 'gathered church', when Jacob was a boy. Bauthumley fought for Parliament and, self-taught, wrote a compelling mystical tract *The Light and Dark Sides of God*. This led to savage punishment: his tongue was bored through with a hot iron and he was dismissed from the army. George FOX, antagonized by his influence among Quakers, called him a Ranter, though he has no traceable links with other Ranter activists. He later held minor offices in Leicester and published an abbreviation of John FOXE's *Book of Martyrs* (1676).

BAX, ARNOLD (1883–1953), composer. Bax studied in composition at the Royal Academy of Music (1900–5). After discovering the writings of YEATS in 1902, he became obsessed with Irish culture and his music is strongly influenced by his fascination with Ireland and Celtic folklore. His first symphony (1921), written in the aftermath of the First World War and the Dublin Easter Rising, is one of the most intense and fiercely passionate of all his works.

BAXTER, RICHARD (1615–91), churchman. A distinguished example of the clergy of the old established Church excluded from office by the post-1660 Church Settlement, Baxter rose from humble beginnings to ordination in 1638, and began a devoted ministry at Kidderminster (Worcs.) in 1641. Hostile to the high view of Episcopacy and the ceremonialist and sacramen- talist theology of Arminian leaders like LAUD, he was also unenthusiastic about some of the alterna- tives on offer on the collapse of the old Church, including doctrinaire Presbyterianism, strict Calvinism and the religious Independency favoured by Oliver CROMWELL. During the 1650s, he sought to heal Protestant divisions, bringing diverse local clergy together in the Worcestershire Association. He turned down a bishopric in 1660 and, in negotiations over the future of the Church, was out-manoeuvred by the Anglican leadership. Despite frequent persecution, he then devoted himself to ministering to Dissenters. Of his many writings on theology and philosophy, some hymns and his autobiography are outstanding.

BAYLEY, JOHN (1925–), literary critic *see* MURDOCH, DAME IRIS

BAYLIS, LILLIAN (1874–1937), theatre manager. The daughter of musicians, Baylis spent the period from her late teens in South Africa as a music teacher before returning to London in 1898 to help manage the temperance music hall oper- ated by her aunt, the philanthropist Emma Kons, on the site of the present Old Vic near Waterloo station. She assumed the management on her aunt's death in 1912 and produced SHAKESPEARE and opera at prices working people could afford. The Old Vic became a national success; in 1931 she reopened Sadlers Wells Theatre in Islington, which concentrated on opera and ballet while the Old Vic remained a centre for drama. Some thought her an inefficient tyrant yet she commanded enormous respect as a saviour and guardian of the traditions of British theatre.

BAYNTON, SIR EDWARD (*c*. 1490–1544), courtier. From a Wilts. gentry family, from the 1520s he was prominent in HENRY VIII's entourage, which enabled him to build a formidable West- Country power base. He was a strong partisan of ANNE BOLEYN, but also contrived to remain in the service of all Henry's later wives. His powers of survival make him an important figure in the early

English Reformation because, from the early 1530s, he was a strong partisan for religious reform, and used his considerable influence to promote and protect evangelicals.

BAZALGETTE, SIR JOSEPH (1819–91), engineer. Bazalgette was faced with the mounting problems of London's sewage when he was appointed chief engineer to the Metropolitan Board of Works in 1855. The growing use of water closets meant that the city's drains, which had been designed to deal only with rainwater, were becoming blocked and contaminated; huge cesspools by the Thames threatened the capital's drinking water and in July 1858 such was the 'great stink' that Parliament's sitting had to be suspended. Within less than a decade he had built 83 miles of main sewers, which discharged more than 400 million gallons each day into the Thames downstream at Barking and Plumstead. In 1862 the board was charged with building an embankment along the Thames from Blackfriars to Chelsea. Bazalgette also modernized most of the bridges that span the Thames, built new ones at Putney and Battersea and put in train a plan for the Blackwell tunnel to run under the Thames.

BEACONSFIELD, 1ST EARL OF see DISRAELI, BENJAMIN, essay on pages 250–51

BEALE, DOROTHEA (1831–1906), educationalist. In 1858 she became Principal of Cheltenham Ladies' College and in 1893 founded St Hilda's College, Oxford. Authoritarian, energetic and deeply religious, she exemplified a conservative tradition of feminist social reform.

BEALE, ROBERT (1541–1601), royal servant. Son of a London merchant and possibly educated at Cambridge, he revealed his Protestant sympathies by leaving MARY I'S England for Strasbourg to live with his uncle Sir Richard Morison, and he later studied at Zürich. In 1564 he was at the Embassy at Paris, which began a long association with his fellow Puritan Francis WALSINGHAM. From 1572 Clerk of the Privy Council and several times an MP, he frequently annoyed ELIZABETH I by his sharp criticism of the Church establishment, which eventually resulted in his suspension from office from 1593 to 1597. His MS collections in the British Library, drawing on his years at the centre of government, are of major significance.

BEALES, EDMOND (1803–81), radical. Son of a Cambridgeshire corn merchant and radical, Samuel Pickering Beales, he was educated at Eton and Trinity College, Cambridge, and became a barrister. Through his advocacy of international causes from the 1830s onwards he was drawn closer to working-class radicalism. Initially a supporter of Polish independence, he became a keen advocate of the radical cause of Italian nationalism, helping to organize the reception committee in 1864 to welcome the hugely popular Garibaldi to Britain and supporting the North during the US Civil War (1861–5). From the early 1860s he spoke on behalf of parliamentary reform and was leader of the Reform League (1865–9), though he was unsuccessful when he stood for Tower Hamlets as a League candidate in 1868.

BEARDSLEY, AUBREY (1872–98), artist. Born in Brighton, Beardsley was ill with debilitating tuberculosis from childhood and achieved only six fevered years of professional artistic productivity before his death at 25, yet his name is synonymous with the *fin de siècle* revolt against rectitude. A clerk, encouraged by BURNE-JONES, he took evening art classes and realized that the new technologies of magazine and book illustration offered a way of living as an artist. Beardsley produced more than 550 drawings for a new edition of Thomas MALORY's *Morte d'Arthur* (1892). His sketch of *Salome with the Head of St John the Baptist,* inspired by reading the French text of Oscar WILDE's play *Salome,* appeared in a new monthly art magazine, *The Studio* (1893). Wilde persuaded his publisher to commission Beardsley to illustrate the English version. 'The naughty scribbles' of eunuchs, hermaphrodites and sexually explicit licentiousness brought Beardsley notoriety and the art editorship of another new magazine, *The Yellow Book*, published by John LANE, in which Beardsley's anatomically grotesque, almost foetal, obsessively sexual drawings leavened the more sonorous contributions of such dignitaries as the President of the Royal Academy, Frederic LEIGHTON. But with the imprisonment of Wilde for 'acts of gross indecency' in 1895, the climate grew more cautious (though Wilde had never contributed to *The Yellow Book*) and Beardsley was sacked only to be taken up by the opportunistic Leonard Smithers for a magazine with which he planned to outdo *The Yellow Book*. Booksellers' caution meant that *The Savoy* failed, but Smithers commissioned Beardsley to illustrate Alexander POPE's *The Rape of the Lock* and Aristophanes' comedy *Lysistrata* (both 1896).

BEATON, SIR CECIL (1904–80), photographer. Educated at Harrow and Oxford, Beaton soon established himself as a fashion photographer with a theatrical flair, a fastidious and stylish presence behind the camera, and became famous in the 1930s for his photographs of celebrities in his work for *Vogue*. During the Second World War he worked in various theatres of war for the Ministry of Information: his images were published as *Air of Glory* (1941) and *Winged Squadrons* (1942).

After the war, he turned to the theatre, designing costumes and sets including those for the film *My Fair Lady* (1965), for which he won an Oscar, though he also continued to portray members of the royal family in flattering and often-reproduced portraits, and was the official photographer at the wedding of Princess MARGARET to another photographer, Anthony ARMSTRONG-JONES.

BEATON, DAVID *see* essay on page 66

BEATTIE, JAMES (1735–1803), poet and philosopher. Son of a shopkeeper, he went to Marischal College, Aberdeen. He set up as a schoolteacher, and began contributing poems to the *Scots Magazine*, which he continued to do when he became Professor of Moral Philosophy and Logic at Marischal College. He was strongly critical of David HUME's philosophy and atheistical religious views, and devoted himself to providing an alternative, associating himself with the 'common-sense' school of philosophy being developed by Thomas REID. His principal philosophical work was the *Essay on the Nature and Immutability of Truth in Opposition to Sophistry and Scepticism* (1770). His lectures to students proceeded from the premise that abstract analysis too often led inquirers into a morass; sound religious and moral principles were better derived from a study of ancient and modern literature. Beattie's poetry was extremely popular, particularly *The Minstrel*, published in two volumes in 1771 and 1774. Written in Spenserian stanzas (*see* SPENSER, EDMUND), it reflected both Beattie's disillusion with eighteenth-century commercial culture and growing public interest in the medieval world.

BEATTY, DAVID (1st Earl Beatty) (1871–1936), sailor. From an Anglo-Irish family, he joined the navy in 1886, and as a result of his exploits commanding gunboats on the Nile (1896–8) was appointed to the Distinguished Service Order (DSO). Promoted to Commander over 395 more senior officers, Beatty was wounded in China in July 1900, and then promoted Captain, aged only 30. In 1901 he married Ethel Tree, a wealthy American divorcee, whose social connections helped further accelerate his career. An Admiral by 1910, Beatty commanded the battle-cruiser squadron in 1913. Youthful, handsome and aggressive, Beatty captured the public imagination on 28 Aug. 1914 when he sank two German cruisers after a thrilling chase into Heligoland Bight, and his repute survived a less successful action off the Dogger Bank on 24 Jan. 1915. On 31 May 1916 Beatty lost two battle-cruisers to superior German gunnery off Jutland, but demonstrated his sang-froid with the comment 'There seems to be something wrong with our bloody ships today, Chatfield.' Luring the Germans north to within range of JELLICOE's Grand Fleet, Beatty's ships took enormous punishment, and when, despite this sacrifice, Jellicoe subsequently failed to annihilate the enemy, recriminations were bitter. Appointed to command the Grand Fleet at the end of 1916, Beatty became First Sea Lord in 1919.

'BEAU' NASH *see* NASH, RICHARD

BEAUCHAMP, 8TH VISCOUNT *see* SEYMOUR, EDWARD

BEAUCHAMP, GUY (10th [2nd Beauchamp] Earl of Warwick) (*c.* 1273–1315), royal servant. After distinguished and loyal service in EDWARD I's war against the Scots, he became a fierce critic of EDWARD II's government, notably the King's reliance on Piers GAVESTON, who called Warwick the 'black dog of Arden'. In 1310 he became one of the Ordainers appointed to reform the realm. His capture of Gaveston in controversial circumstances in 1312 led to the favourite's summary beheading, an event which overshadowed the rest of the reign. He refused to serve in the Bannockburn campaign (1314). His death was followed by rumours of poison.

BEAUCHAMP, RICHARD (13th [5th Beauchamp] Earl of Warwick) (1382–1439), soldier. He succeeded his father Thomas in 1401. A famously chivalrous warrior, he fought GLYN DWR and the Percies in 1403. He went on a pilgrimage to Rome and Jerusalem, returning in 1410 through Russia. He was instrumental in suppressing OLDCASTLE's rising in 1414. He was the Chief Commander of the forces of HENRY V in France between 1416 and 1421, and was a Deputy of Calais, becoming Lieutenant of France in 1437. On Henry V's death in 1422 he was entrusted with the care of the young HENRY VI. He endowed the magnificent Beauchamp Chapel in St Mary's, Warwick.

BEAUFORT, EDMUND (4th Earl and 2nd Duke of Somerset) (*c.* 1406–55), soldier. Earl from 1444 and Duke from 1448, his feud with RICHARD OF YORK precipitated the outbreak of the Wars of the Roses. After 20 years of military experience and high command in France, his supine conduct of the defence of Normandy in 1449 came as a shock. The surrender of Rouen, widely held to be dishonourable, led to York's launching a series of personal attacks on him from late 1450 onwards. Yet he retained HENRY VI's confidence, was appointed Captain of Calais in 1451, and continued to accumulate the Crown offices and pensions which he wanted to supplement a relatively small landed

continued on page 67

BEATON, DAVID (c. 1494–1546)
Archbishop of St Andrews and Cardinal

Third son of John Beaton of Balfour (Fife), he was an unusually talented and cosmopolitan specimen of the Scots gentry who regarded the late medieval Church as a meal-ticket for life. After study at St Andrews, Glasgow and Orleans universities (possibly also Paris), in 1522 he began service with the new governor of the realm, John STEWART, Duke of Albany, accompanying him as Ambassador to France in 1524. Patronage from his uncle James Beaton, who became Archbishop of St Andrews, brought a variety of ecclesiastical plum offices including the abbacy of Arbroath (1524). He devoted the next few years to building up his career in Scotland, consistently aligning himself with Albany against the pro-English interests of James HAMILTON, 2nd Earl of Arran, and his affinity; he was made Keeper of the Privy Seal for life in 1529.

From 1533 Beaton made seven journeys into France in 10 years on diplomatic missions, including the negotiations which led to JAMES V's marriage to the French Princess Madeleine (1537). Her sudden death led to his return to negotiate a new marriage for James (against furious English opposition) to MARY OF GUISE; in Dec. 1537, during the successful culmination of this mission, he was made Bishop of Mirepoix, and in Dec. 1538 he received a Cardinal's hat. This marked the real beginning of his activity as a clergyman. He nevertheless continued to live with his mistress, Marion Ogilvie, as if he were a married layman, with a family of at least eight children; these had all been born before he was finally ordained to the priesthood, which apparently occurred around the time that he was consecrated Bishop of Mirepoix.

Consistently pro-French and an opponent of HENRY VIII and the Reformation, Beaton was a close ally of Mary of Guise in urging James V to remain loyal to the traditional Church against the Anglophile party. In 1539 he succeeded his uncle as Archbishop of St Andrews, and even before James Beaton's death he initiated the burning of five heretics. In subsequent persecutions he showed himself wary of offending powerful noble or gentry interests, and most of those prosecuted were from humble backgrounds. He was influential in passing parliamentary legislation against heresy in 1541, although for the moment it remained ineffectual. On James's death (1542) Beaton was involved in a power struggle with the Anglophile James HAMILTON, 3rd Earl of Arran,

and was briefly imprisoned; on his release, he bitterly and successfully opposed the Treaty of Greenwich (1543) which promised MARY QUEEN OF SCOTS in marriage to Henry's son, the future EDWARD VI, and he backed parliamentary legislation renewing the struggle against heresy. Seeing the weight of support for Beaton, Arran now changed sides, allying with his former enemy; Beaton became Chancellor in Dec. 1543. He also gathered at St Andrews Castle a collection of hostages from among the Scots nobility which helped to ensure his continuing power. The Pope made him Legate *a latere* (special resident papal representative) in Jan. 1544; now Beaton had a concentration of secular and ecclesiastical power unprecedented in Scotland, and resembling that of Thomas WOLSEY in England 20 years before. He continued to face opposition to his nationwide jurisdiction from Gavin Dunbar, Archbishop of Glasgow, which undermined the Church authorities' efforts to contain the growth of reformist religion. He nevertheless resumed his campaign against heresy, the chief victim being George WISHART (1546). At the same time he convoked a Provincial Council which seems to have made some cautious moves towards ecclesiastical reform. There was hardly any time to develop this initiative before a group of Protestant conspirators seized St Andrews Castle, where they murdered Beaton in his bedroom, in revenge for his burning of Wishart. His body was hung over the castle ramparts, and the assassins held out against a siege for the next year.

Beaton was a charismatic personality who was able to dominate those around him: a lay politician who very belatedly completed his formal qualifications as a clergyman to justify his concentration of offices in the Church. His potential importance in defeating the Reformation in Scotland is attested by the depth of viciousness in subsequent Protestant descriptions of him (particularly those of John KNOX, who described him as that 'bloody wolf'). His patriotism, which led him to champion the Auld Alliance with France against English encroachments, was discounted after Protestant Scotland had entered its long alliance with England, while his reputation has not been helped by his refusal to see that his happy and faithful family life was incongruous in a priest leading the defence of the old religion.

Margaret H. B. Sanderson, Cardinal of Scotland: David Beaton c. 1494–1546 (1986) inheritance in England. Inevitably this exploitation of his dominance over a feeble King, combined with the catastrophic ending of the Hundred Years War, made him intensely unpopular. Arrested when York became Protector in 1454, he was released as soon as the King recovered his sanity. In May 1455 York and his allies took up arms and, at the first Battle of St Albans, made sure that Somerset was killed.

BEAUFORT, SIR FRANCIS (1774–1857), hydrographer. Born in Ireland, Beaufort entered the navy in 1787 and saw active service in the wars against Spain. By 1800 he had reached the rank of Commander and devoted much of his time to surveying. In 1805 he developed the 'Beaufort scale' of wind force, a scale ranging from 0 to 12, in which Force 12 is defined as wind 'that no canvas can withstand'. He also invented a notation for describing weather. In 1812 he was badly wounded by Turkish pirates whilst surveying the coast of Asia Minor and on returning to England constructed charts of his survey. He was appointed hydrographer to the Royal Navy in 1829 and retired in 1855 with the rank of Rear Admiral.

BEAUFORT, HENRY (1377–1447), Cardinal. Son of JOHN OF GAUNT and Catherine Swynford, he became Bishop of Lincoln in 1398 and was translated to Winchester in 1404; his influence in Church matters extended well beyond England. In 1417, in recognition of his services at the Council of Constance, Pope Martin V wanted to make him a Cardinal; in 1427, he led an unsuccessful crusade against the Hussites of Bohemia. Ultimately, however, his interests and loyalties were English. Thus, he bowed to HENRY V's refusal to allow him to accept the Cardinal's hat (he finally achieved it in 1426) and, in 1429, after preaching another anti-Hussite crusade, he used the resulting army to prop up the English cause in France.

His ability, his great wealth, which he used to make substantial loans to the Crown, and his royal connections enabled him to play a prominent political role during the reigns of his kinsmen, not only Henry V but also HENRY IV and HENRY VI. Three times he served as Chancellor (1403–5, 1413–17, 1424–6). In later years, his more conciliatory attitude towards France added fuel to the flames of his long-standing rivalry with his nephew Duke HUMPHREY OF GLOUCESTER.

BEAUFORT, LADY MARGARET *see* essay on page 68

BEAUFORT, THOMAS (2nd [1st Beaufort] Duke of Exeter) (*c.* 1375–1427), Admiral of the Northern Fleet for life. Youngest son of JOHN OF GAUNT and

Catherine Swynford, he was a commander of the forces of HENRY V and HENRY VI in France from 1413 to 1427, and was made Duke of Exeter and Lieutenant of Normandy in 1416, and Count of Harcourt in 1418. He died at his manor of Greenwich in 1427.

BEAUMONT, FRANCIS (1584–1616), playwright. Son of a prominent judge (also Francis), he studied at Oxford and the Inner Temple and entered the circle of Michael DRAYTON and Ben JONSON (writing introductory verses for several of his plays); with John FLETCHER, he wrote a series of plays between 1606 and 1616, a collected edition of which appeared in 1647.

BEAVERBROOK, 1ST BARON *see* AITKEN, MAXWELL

BECKER, LYDIA (1827–90), suffragist. The daughter of a Manchester chemical manufacturer of German descent, Becker was educated mainly at home in England and (for a year) in Germany. In 1866 she heard Barbara Leigh BODICHON's paper at the meeting of the National Association for the Promotion of Social Science in Manchester, which converted her to the cause of women's suffrage. She then became a leading national figure in the movement, though sometimes a controversial one within it, mainly through her founding of the *Women's Suffrage Journal*, which she edited from 1870 to 1890.

BECKET, THOMAS, ST *see* essay on page 69

BECKETT, SAMUEL (1896–1989), playwright. Born a Dublin Protestant, Beckett settled permanently in Paris in 1935, where he wrote, in French, a number of novels which he usually translated into English himself. But it was his plays that revolutionized dramatic form, and were to define the Theatre of the Absurd, a critique dramatizing modern man in an inhuman universe, asking always 'what has one thing to do with another?' They had a transforming influence on the British theatre through the writing of Harold PINTER and Tom Stoppard. Beckett's plays include *Waiting for Godot* (1955), *Krapp's Last Tape* (1958) and *Happy Days* (1961), culminating in *Breath* (1969), which lasts for 30 seconds, *Not I* (1973), a brief monologue in which only 'the Mouth' is seen, and *Footfalls* (1976), where only the feet appear. He was awarded the Nobel Prize for Literature in 1969.

BECKFORD, WILLIAM (1709–70), merchant and politician. Born in Jamaica, son of a wealthy planter who was Speaker to the colonial assembly, he was sent to England to be educated. He
continued on page 70

BEAUFORT, LADY MARGARET (1443–1509)
Countess of Richmond and Derby

Daughter of John Beaufort, Duke of Somerset, Margaret devoted her career to the successful promotion of her son Henry Tudor to the English throne as HENRY VII, against considerable odds which included a parliamentary Act barring the Beauforts from the royal succession. Of her four marriages, Henry was the product of her second, to Edmund TUDOR, Earl of Richmond (her first, to John de la Pole, having been dissolved). She was 12 years old when she married Edmund (1455), and by the time that her son was born she was a 13-year-old widow. The birth is likely to have been traumatic and physically damaging; certainly she had no more children, and had every incentive to concentrate her formidable energies on the future of her only child, despite the fact that they can rarely have met during his childhood spent in Wales with William, Lord Herbert, and his many years abroad. She married twice again, to Henry, Lord Stafford (1458), and fourthly to Thomas STANLEY, Earl of Derby (1471). When Herbert was killed at Edgecote (1469), she began taking responsibility for her son's security. Stafford ended up supporting EDWARD IV in his victory over the Lancastrians who had restored HENRY VI in the 'Readeption' (1470–1); Margaret feared, however, that Edward would eliminate Henry Tudor, who with his uncle Jasper Tudor continued to hold Pembroke Castle for the Lancastrians, and she arranged for his escape to Brittany. She negotiated a reconciliation between the King and her son in 1482, but Edward's death transformed the situation. After making initial overtures to RICHARD III, even taking part in his coronation ceremonies, she abruptly changed sides and supported a failed plot to rescue EDWARD V and his brother from the Tower. When the princes disappeared, she developed a new strategy, uniting with the relatives of Edward IV's widow ELIZABETH WOODVILLE to promote her son's claim to the throne, with the promise of a marriage alliance to Edward's daughter Elizabeth of York. She was spared from the worst consequences of her involvement in the unsuccessful revolt (1483) of Henry STAFFORD, Duke of Buckingham, by Derby's public loyalty to King Richard; with Derby's connivance, she continued to liaise with Henry, who was now taking refuge in France.

In Sept. 1485 mother and son were at last reunited after the victory at Bosworth, at which Derby had played a crucial part by deserting Richard. From now on she worked in close concert with the new King. Her key role was recognized by the 1485 declaration enrolled in Parliament declaring her a *femme sole*: this was a privilege enjoyed by Queens of England, and meant that she could hold property as if she were a single woman, despite the fact that she was still married to Derby. During Henry's reign she was given extensive personal power, based on grants of estates concentrated in the Midlands. Several of her servants, most prominently Reynold BRAY, occupied key administrative positions at Westminster, while her former chaplain and fellow conspirator John MORTON became Archbishop of Canterbury (1486). In 1499 she set up her own household at Collyweston (Northants.), vowing chastity, though she and her husband seem to have remained on cordial terms up to his death in 1504; also in 1499 she changed her normal signature from 'M. Richmond' to 'Margaret R.' (probably to stand for 'Regina', to emphasize her quasi-regal status). All this probably formed part of a strategy agreed with her son for strengthening royal control. Her private council played an increasingly important part in governing central England, and she also sponsored large-scale drainage schemes in the eastern Fens.

Margaret came to display an intense personal piety, and she received a papal grant making her patroness of the cult of the Holy Name of Jesus in England. A well-educated woman with her own collection of books, she made translations from French, including a contribution to a new version of Thomas à Kempis's *Imitation of Christ* (1504); she gave patronage to a series of printers, including William CAXTON and Wynkyn de Worde. She was encouraged by her confessor John FISHER to extend her piety to humanist learning: she endowed professorships of divinity at Oxford and Cambridge, but her chief interest was shown towards Cambridge, the nearer university to her Collyweston Palace. There she refounded God's House as Christ's College, began the foundation of St John's College and played a major part in establishing Jesus College. She lived to see her grandson, HENRY VIII, ascend peacefully to the throne. Her pious activism and her extrovert weeping over the vanity of human endeavour have obscured her worldly skills: she has a strong claim to be the most successful English politician of the fifteenth century.

Michael K. Jones and Malcolm G. Underwood, *The King's Mother: Lady Margaret Beaufort, Countess of Richmond and Derby* (1992)

BECKET, THOMAS, ST (?1120–70)
Archbishop of Canterbury (1162–70) and Saint

He was elected Archbishop because he was the King's good servant, then murdered in his own cathedral at the instigation of that same King, a life that is one of the most puzzling and dramatic – hence most dramatized – in English history.

Son of a Norman merchant settled in London, he was educated at Merton Priory (Surrey) and Paris. He worked as an accounts clerk to a banker (his cousin) before entering the service of Archbishop THEOBALD of Canterbury in 1145. He became the Archbishop's confidential agent and was rewarded with the rich archdeaconry of Canterbury. In 1155 he attracted HENRY II's attention and was appointed Chancellor. In this office he displayed a wide range of talents, administrative, diplomatic and military. He also enjoyed a lifestyle more ostentatiously lavish than the King's. His zeal in the King's interests, even where they seemed to conflict with the Church's, led Henry to believe that Thomas was his loyal friend. He decided to make Thomas Theobald's successor, despite the Canterbury tradition that the archbishop ought to be a monk. Reluctantly the monks of Canterbury Cathedral Priory bowed to royal pressure and elected Becket. On 2 June 1162 he was ordained priest, and the next day consecrated Archbishop.

Once Archbishop, Becket opposed the King at almost every opportunity, even on routine matters which raised issues of principle only for someone who was determined to find them. He began a campaign for the canonization of ANSELM, a monk-archbishop who had defied kings. Henry was bewildered by Becket's abrupt volte-face; in this he has been followed by historians ever since. Many more or less creative attempts have been made to explain the mystery but, without good evidence for the state of Thomas's mind in 1162, they necessarily remain highly speculative. The earliest lives of Becket, in Latin by JOHN OF SALISBURY and William Fitzstephen for example, and in French by Guernes of Pont-Sainte-Maxence, do little to unravel the puzzle. Written after his murder and as part of the campaign to secure his canonization, they present him as a martyred saint.

In 1163 Becket found a cause in the matter of Benefit of Clergy, the Church's claim that the clergy belonged to a privileged order, exempt from the jurisdiction or sentence of ordinary courts of law, which meant that they could be tried only in ecclesiastical courts. Since Church courts could not impose the death penalty, this certainly bene-fited clerics accused of serious crimes. In Jan. 1164 Henry tried to deal with the problem of 'criminous clerks', the conventional term for such clerics, and other issues by having a written statement of what he saw as the King's customary rights over the English Church drawn up as the Constitutions of Clarendon. Becket reluctantly but publicly accepted these constitutions. Immediately afterwards he infuriated the King and confused his fellow bishops by trying to wriggle out of this commitment. Henry therefore brought him to trial at the Council of Northampton (Oct. 1164); Becket, seeing that the King was determined to break him, fled in disguise to France. He remained in exile until 1170, studying canon law, leading a life of ascetic severity and claiming to be defending not only the rights of the Archbishop of Canterbury but also the liberties of the Church as a whole. Both Louis VII of France and Pope Alexander III urged reconciliation but neither Henry nor Thomas trusted the other. The coronation of HENRY THE YOUNG KING in June 1170 by the Archbishop of York brought matters to a head. In Thomas's eyes, crowning the King was one of the privileges of Canterbury. He swiftly agreed terms with Henry. This enabled him to return to England with the intention of punishing those who had infringed that privilege. In Nov. 1170 he excommunicated three bishops, York, London and Salisbury. They complained to the King in Normandy. Henry's angry words prompted four knights to cross the Channel and kill Becket on 29 Dec. 1170. The murder shocked Christendom. In Feb. 1173 Thomas was formally canonized by Alexander III.

During his life few churchmen believed that Becket's truculence did much to help the cause of the English Church; fewer still, probably none, thought him saintly. He had chosen to resurrect troublesome issues which nearly everyone, even popes, preferred to shelve, for 50 years earlier the career of Anselm had shown that, when raised to the level of high principle, the differences between Church and State were insoluble. Becket's murder, however, put Henry in the wrong and caused him to make some concessions, although none of much significance. But the Church of Canterbury undoubtedly profited. As CHAUCER's *Canterbury Tales* attest, Becket's tomb became the greatest pilgrimage shrine in England. In 1538 HENRY VIII declared Becket a traitor and destroyed the shrine, but the cult survived.

Frank Barlow, Thomas Becket (1986)

inherited the family estates on his brother's death, and also prospered as a West India merchant. An MP from 1747, from 1754 he represented the City of London, which he also twice served as Lord Mayor, playing an important part in mobilizing City support for PITT THE ELDER, and sponsoring an influential political-essay paper, *The Monitor*. A statue in Guildhall still commemorates the occasion when, presenting a City remonstrance to GEORGE III in 1770 against the misdeeds of the NORTH ministry, he seized the opportunity to deliver a political speech to the indignant King.

BECKFORD, WILLIAM (1760–1844), connoisseur. The son of Alderman William BECKFORD, he was educated at home, then sent on a Grand Tour. His bizarre novel *Vathek* (written in French *c.* 1781–2, published in English 1786) is a pioneering venture in sham-oriental fiction. He used his wealth to finance his taste for fine art and architecture, creating the pseudo-Gothic Fonthill Abbey (Wilts.), the most extravagant fantasy-house in England until it was ruined by major structural collapse in 1825; the architectural follies which he created at Bath survive. Evidence for his sexuality is ambiguous, but since the nineteenth century he has often been dubbed homosexual. He was also an MP, from 1784 to 1793.

BECON, THOMAS (*c.* 1511–67), writer. Born in Norfolk and Cambridge-educated, he was in trouble in the 1540s for advocating religious reform in his books, but under EDWARD VI he entered the service of Archbishop CRANMER, helping to compile the Prayer Book. Losing his promotions under MARY I, he fled abroad, returning in 1559 to be given a canonry of Canterbury Cathedral. His numerous devotional writings were best-sellers in his lifetime and throughout ELIZABETH I's reign.

BEDE, ST *see* essay on pages 72–3

BEDFORD, EARL OF, 3RD *see* RUSSELL, JOHN; **6TH** *see* RUSSELL, FRANCIS; **DUKE OF, 1ST** *see* JOHN OF LANCASTER; **3RD** *see* TUDOR, JASPER; **7TH** *see* RUSSELL, JOHN

BEECHAM, THOMAS (1820–1907) and **SIR JOSEPH** (1848–1916), entrepreneurs. As a young farm-worker Thomas acquired both herbal knowledge and a reputation for curing human and animal ailments with his home-made pills. 'Dr' Beecham (as he thenceforth styled himself) moved to north-west England in 1847 and both manufactured and sold his own brands of laxative and cough pills. He swiftly became the dominant force in the nation's fast-growing patent medicine business, especially in wholesaling. His son Joseph, who took control in 1881, instigated publicity and advertising drives at home and abroad to increase the firm's fortunes. Joseph was knighted in 1912 for his services to philanthropy; his elder son was the orchestral conductor Thomas BEECHAM. The family's involvement in the pharmaceutical business dwindled after the First World War.

BEECHAM, SIR THOMAS (1879–1961), conductor. Son of the successful manufacturing chemist Sir Joseph BEECHAM, he studied composition privately in London and Paris but as a conductor was self-taught. Beecham's access to a private fortune enabled him to found several orchestras and an opera company, the Beecham Symphony Orchestra (1909), the Beecham Opera Company (1915), London Philharmonic Orchestra (1932) and the Royal Philharmonic Orchestra (1946). Described as 'the most gifted executive musician England has ever produced', Beecham introduced a number of new operas to Britain, works by Russian composers, and new compositions by Joseph Holbrooke, Dame Ethel SMYTH, Charles Stanford and his friend Frederick DELIUS. He was responsible for the first London performances in 1911 of Diaghilev's *Ballets Russes*, and did more than any earlier English conductor to promote the music of Mozart and Haydn. A champion of Richard Strauss, he conducted the first British performances of many of his operas, including *Elektra* (1908) and *Der Rosenkavalier* (1913). As Artistic Director at Covent Garden (1932–9) he conducted several parts of Wagner's *Ring* cycle. He toured widely in America (1940–4), conducting the Seattle Symphony Orchestra, the Metropolitan Opera and the New York Philharmonic. A conductor of genius who directed mostly from memory, his wit and portentous pronouncements were memorable.

BEECHING, RICHARD (Baron Beeching) (1913–85), public servant. Beeching trained as a physicist at Imperial College, London, and joined ICI in 1948, becoming a technical director in 1957. His fame or notoriety rests on his period as Chairman of British Railways from 1963 to 1965: his report, *The Reshaping of British Railways*, arguing for the rationalization of the rail system, the closure of 2,000 stations and the loss of 70,000 jobs, caused national furore. 'Beeching's axe', as it became known, did not fall everywhere as he had proposed, but sweeping reforms were implemented.

BEERBOHM, SIR HENRY MAXIMILIAN (MAX) (1872–1956), writer. The son of an immigrant Lithuanian corn merchant and half-brother of the actor-manager Herbert Beerbohm TREE, Beerbohm left Oxford without taking a degree but found that his dandyism and lack of respect for bourgeois convention flourished in the exuberant artistic and literary circle of the metropolis. He contributed to *The Yellow Book*, in which he wrote a fable about the downfall of Oscar WILDE, 'The Happy Hypocrite' (1896), and to *The Savoy* and the *Daily Mail*. In 1898 he succeeded George Bernard SHAW as theatre critic of the *Saturday Review*, where he worked until 1910, when he married and retired to the Italian Riviera. His novel *Zuleika Dobson* (1910) is an imaginative reconstruction of his undergraduate days, while *Seven Men* (1919), a pastiche of the literati of *fin de siècle* London, mingled real with imaginary characters. His enduringly vivid caricatures of his contemporaries including Wilde, BEARDSLEY, H. G. WELLS, Shaw, CONRAD, KIPLING and Henry James display a comparably sharp eye.

BEESLY, EDWARD (1831–1915), positivist. Son of a clergyman, Beesly was educated at Wadham College, Oxford, taught at Marlborough College from 1854 and became Professor of History and Principal of University College, London, in 1860. Greatly influenced by the work of the French positivist Auguste Comte, his vision was of a moralistic, capitalist Utopia. He drew increasingly close to trade unionism in the 1860s, becoming a close associate of the 'Junta' (*see* APPLEGARTH, ROBERT), a frequent contributor to *The Beehive*, the most important labour newspaper of the period, and an activist in the Reform League. From the 1860s he also sought to foster international contacts between British trade unionists and their European counterparts.

BEETON, ISABELLA (née Mayson) (1836–65), writer. One of a family of 17 children and stepchildren of the clerk to Epsom race course, she was 19 when she married Sam Beeton, the publisher of the *English-Woman's Domestic Magazine*, the first popular woman's magazine. Isabella was appointed assistant editor with particular responsibility for fashion. The book she edited and largely wrote, *Mrs Beeton's Book of Household Management* (1861), appeared first as a monthly part-work comprising more than 3,000 recipes, many sent in by readers, as well as household hints and articles on legal, medical and others matters commissioned from experts. Its intention was to avert 'family discontent' as a result of household mismanagement and it proved a *vade mecum* for the middle-class housewife whom Mrs Beeton likened to the commander of a domestic army. It was an immediate best-seller which has been in print (though heavily revised) ever since. Isabella died from puerperal fever, the scourge of Victorian childbearing women, shortly after the birth of her fourth child when she was only 28.

BEHAN, BRENDAN (1923–64), playwright. From a Dublin Republican family, he left school at 14 to become a house-painter. He joined the Irish Republic Army (IRA), was arrested in Britain, and was sent to a young offenders' prison later described in his memoir *Borstal Boy* (1958). In 1941 he was arrested for shooting at a policeman in Dublin; his experiences in Mountjoy prison inspired his play *The Quare Fella* (1954) which attacks capital punishment. His last major work was *The Hostage* (adapted for Joan LITTLEWOOD's theatre company from an Irish-language play *An Giall*); though his reputation was now well established, the quality of his work was affected by alcoholism and ill health, leading to his premature death.

BEHN, APHRA (née Johnson) (1640–89), playwright. She came from Kent but according to her own account, disputed by some scholars, spent part of her youth in Surinam. She married a Dutch merchant in London in 1664, but he died in 1666 and after an unprofitable period in espionage Behn turned to writing. Her first play, *The Forced Marriage,* was performed in 1670 and was followed by many others. Behn's alleged experiences in South America contributed to her novel *Oroonoko, or the History of the Royal Slave* (1688), which attacked slavery; this was adapted for the stage by Thomas SOUTHERNE in 1695. Behn and her works were much criticized for their profanity, deemed inappropriate for a woman, not least by Whig writers, critical of her Tory sympathies, but she was an extremely able and successful writer.

BEIT, ALFRED (1853–1906), financier. Born in Hamburg and trained in the diamond trade in Amsterdam, Beit moved to Kimberley in 1875 where he flourished in South African diamond trading and mining. In 1887, already wealthy in his own right, he joined Cecil RHODES in the establishment of De Beers Consolidated Mines. In the meantime, in concert with Julius Wernher, Beit bought up claims in the newly discovered Transvaal gold fields and floated many mining companies. In the years that followed his move to England in 1889 the various Wernher–Beit companies were the largest and wealthiest mining finance group of South Africa. In 1895 Beit joined Rhodes and Leander JAMESON in the abortive conspiracy to overthrow the Boer republic; he was a major equipper of the imperial armies in the Boer War, and a powerful advocate for mining interests in the post-war colonial administration of Lord MILNER.

BEDE, ST ('THE VENERABLE') (672 or 673–735)
Monk and scholar

The greatest scholar of his day and a man who has profoundly influenced many aspects of British and European history, Bede was presented to BENE-DICT BISCOP as a child oblate at the age of seven, and lived almost all of his life in the twin monasteries of Monkwearmouth and Jarrow (Northumb.). He was educated under the tutelage of Abbot CEOLFRITH and subsequently became a deacon and a priest. Although he is known to have visited Lindisfarne and York, all Bede's learning came from the study of the Bible and from the magnificent library which Benedict Biscop had assembled. *The Ecclesiastical History of the English People* is the most famous and accessible of Bede's works, but his contribution also included biblical exegesis, mathematics, science, hagiography, homiletic writing and moral criticism. His skill, which can only be truly appreciated by reading his works, was to transform his profound learning into meaningful scholarship and into literature which his contemporaries could identify with and understand. To say that he was the greatest historian between the heyday of classical historical writing and the twelfth century minimizes his achievement. Both the universality of his concerns and his rational application of learning place him far above all his contemporaries. All his works have his original personal imprint on them; all reflect a man determined to leave the world a better place than he had found it.

Bede's primary interest was in biblical exegesis as a means to understand the Christian faith. Fundamentally this required an accurate knowledge of Latin and constant reflection on the Christian texts. The need for instruction and education were themes which ran through his life. The Latin grammars which he composed to educate a people whose first language was the very different Old English were carefully laid out and full of examples which would have had contemporary meaning. His biblical exegesis was typical of his day, namely based on the painstaking collection of authorities and their compilation into a meaningful whole. For eighth-century scholars the biblical text was not just a source to be read literally, but one with numerous allegorical and relevant meanings which had to be teased out by assiduous reading. It was this approach which informed Bede's compilation of the *Ecclesiastical History* and much else that he wrote. Thus, when he praised St AIDAN's and St CUTHBERT's manner of life he did so partly because their poverty and simple manner of life were close to the biblical

example, and partly because he wished to draw contemporaries' attention to them as models of the best Christian behaviour. It was an approach which also led Bede in, for example, his famous letter to Archbishop EGBERT of York, to criticize scathingly the behaviour and morals of contemporary churchmen because he saw it as his duty to give a warning after the manner of an Old Testament prophet.

As a part of his exegetical work, Bede developed a special interest in chronology and the critical examination of texts. It is this side of his work which makes the preface to the *Ecclesiastical History*, with its emphasis on the accurate presentation of material and the assessment of oral and written testimony, sound like a modern work of historical scholarship. The sense of chronology also gives the *Ecclesiastical History* a narrative dimension which makes it very appealing. His interest in dates led him to write chronicles which supplied the raw material for the *Ecclesiastical History* and his fascination with numbers, and in particular with the *computus*, that is, the science of understanding the ecclesiastical calendar, gave him a particular concern about the calculation of the date of Easter, an issue which divided the Roman missionaries from the Celtic. Bede's personal interest in the subject, which surfaces on a number of occasions in his writings, may well have created a misleading impression that the argument was more heated than it actually was; as far as the kingdom of Northumbria was concerned, the matter was settled at the Synod of Whitby called by King OSWY in 664, but the Roman dating was not accepted at Iona until the time of Abbot DÚNCHAD. Two treatises on the Christian calendar survive (*De Temporibus* and *De Temporum Ratione*). Bede's studies in chronology, combined with the extensive dissemination of his works, popularized the division of time into BC and AD, thereby leading to the adoption of the system which is still in use today.

The *Ecclesiastical History* is our main source for the history of the conversion of the English to Christianity from the time of St AUGUSTINE through to the early eighth century. Not only this, because of Bede's range of interests it is inevitably quarried for the history of early medieval society and for all manner of subjects related to the history of Britain. Its power and influence are such that it pays occasionally to imagine how different (and indeed how slender) our understanding of early British history would be if it had not been written. Completed in 731 and therefore written towards the end of his life, the *Ecclesiastical History* was consciously intended as the culmination of a lifetime's work. Its ultimate purpose was probably to present the heroic past of early Christianity in England both to provide a coherent record and to act as an example to eighth-century contemporaries. Since it was dedicated to King CEOLWULF of Northumbria, its audience was always intended to be more than Bede's fellow monks. Like all that Bede did, it drew on earlier exemplars, in this case Eusebius' *History of the Church*, but Bede's personality was such that it inevitably acquired an original character.

Some of the story-telling is extraordinarily vivid and some of the incidents remarkably poignant. The tale of the conversion of the pagan high-priest COIFI, with his destruction of his own temple and his analogy between the brief span of human life and a sparrow passing through a nobleman's hall into darkness, is one of the best known and beautiful explanations of Christianity ever written. The amusing tale of how King REDWALD of East Anglia constructed a building with a Christian altar at one end and a pagan one at the other is a superb example of the impact of conflicting belief-systems, and the long saga of King EDWIN's conversion shows how slowly the Christian message permeated seventh-century society. While such marvellous stories, selected from many, give us an illustration of the complexity of the times, it is important to recognize that for Bede they demonstrated God's power; Redwald's incomprehension was justly punished and the overcoming of Edwin's resistance to dreams, miracles, papal letters and his wife's persuasion were signs of the ultimate strength of Christianity. As a historian, Bede was true to the conventions of his times, putting great stress on accuracy, but making no pretence of objectivity and omitting what did not suit his purpose – we learn very little about Anglo-Saxon paganism from him! For all this, Bede's history is a magnificent amalgamation of the values of Christianity and of a violent warrior society. Thus, while Bede set before his readers the good lives of the likes of Aidan, COLUM CILLE and King OSWALD, he frequently made a direct link between a good Christian life and success in war. Coifi's conversion takes us directly amongst the beer-drinking and feasting in a king's hall of the kind recorded in the *Beowulf* poem. The *Ecclesiastical History*'s

references to the likes of St ÆLTHELFRYTH, St ÆLFFLÆD and St HILDA also show the important role which women played in the establishment of the Christian Church in England. Bede's best known other historical works are the *Historia Abbatum* (History of the Abbots of Monkwearmouth and Jarrow) and his *Life of St Cuthbert*.

Bede's life and work must ultimately be placed in the context of the so-called Northumbrian Renaissance, a great flowering of early Christian culture in northern England in the seventh and eighth centuries. Although Bede was without doubt its greatest figure, its achievements were also due to the efforts of many others, such as CÆDMON, St Cuthbert, St EGBERT OF IONA, St WILFRID, to the founders of great libraries such as Benedict Biscop, to the important cathedral school founded at York by Egbert, and to the creators of such superb manuscripts as the *Codex Amiatinus* and the *Lindisfarne Gospels*. The renaissance also drew strength from Northumbria's proximity to other areas of cultural activity such as Iona and, through Iona, to Irish monasticism. In turn, it influenced the development of the Christian Church within the Carolingian empire, through the careers of Anglo-Saxon missionaries such as St WILLIBRORD and St BONIFACE, and through ALCUIN OF YORK, who was called to Charlemagne's court to act as a cultural and educational adviser. It was brought to an end by the arrival in 865 of the Viking 'Great Army' of HALFDAN and IVAR THE BONELESS. Bede's writings were immensely popular and influential. Not only did they spread to Europe, but they exercised a powerful influence on English ethnic identity. For instance, both OFFA and ALFRED THE GREAT adopted to great effect the idea which Bede had first expressed – that the English were a single people who could be united under a single ruler – and used it to buttress their claims to rule over more than one kingdom. Bede is known to have died in 735. Although Monkwearmouth and Jarrow were devastated by Vikings in the eighth century, remains which were thought to be Bede's were discovered in the eleventh century and moved to Durham Cathedral. What purports to be his tomb can still be seen in the Gallilee Chapel of that great church.

Bertram Colgrave and R. A. B. Mynors (eds), *Bede's Ecclesiastical History of the English People (1969)*
James Campbell, *Bede (1968)*

BEK, ANTONY (?–1311), Bishop. He was the King's nominee as Bishop of Durham in 1283, at a time of conflict between the see and the Archbishop of York. Although a showman with a retinue of 140 knights, he was also famously temperate and chaste. He was used as an adviser, an ambassador and military commander by EDWARD I, leading his own horsemen on two royal expeditions against Scotland, but fell out of favour in 1300. Under EDWARD II he returned to favour and wreaked vengeance on his past adversaries.

BELL, ALEXANDER GRAHAM (1847–1922), pioneer of the telephone. Educated in his native Edinburgh and in London, Bell initially worked as an assistant to his father, a celebrated teacher of elocution. In 1870 he moved with his family to Canada and a year later settled in Boston (Mass.), where he concentrated on teaching the deaf and where in 1873 he became the university's Professor of Vocal Physiology. His deep interest in his father's system of 'visible speech' and in the conversion of sound into other forms of vibration led to his invention in 1875 of a device for turning speech into fluctuating electric currents and vice-versa – the telephone. He secured a patent for the instrument in 1876 but had to defend it against rivals such as Thomas Alva Edison. He launched the Bell Telephone Company (now AT&T) in 1877 and later in his career invented instruments such as the photophone and gramophone, and studied aeronautics.

BELL, SIR CHARLES (1774–1842), anatomist and surgeon. Bell studied medicine with his brother, an eminent surgeon, and at Edinburgh University. In 1806 he established himself as a surgeon and medical lecturer in London and subsequently held a number of positions including surgeon at the Middlesex Hospital (1812), Professor of Anatomy and Surgery at the Royal College of Surgeons (1824) and Professor of Surgery at Edinburgh University (1836). He is best known for his pioneering work on the nerves: from 1811 he showed that each nerve consists of a 'bundle' of different nerves and that there are separate nerves for sensory and motor functions (in other words, nerves can transmit impulses only in one direction). He also identified a type of paralysis of the facial nerve now known as Bell's Palsy. A devotee of William PALEY's natural theology, he attacked French materialistic science and believed that the evidence of design in the human body is evidence of a divine designer.

BELL, GERTRUDE (1868–1926), archaeologist and traveller. Educated at Lady Margaret Hall, Oxford, she became fluent in Arabic and Persian. She spent most of her life exploring the desert regions of the Middle East, publishing both scholarly and popular accounts of her travels and finds. She was appointed to the Arab Bureau in Cairo during the First World War, and subsequently Oriental Secretary to the British Military High Command in Iraq. She later became the first Director of Antiquities in Iraq, and through a bequest in her will helped to create the British Institute of Archaeology in Iraq. She was imperialist in outlook, intensely patriotic and strongly independent, while deeply against the assertion of sexual equality.

BELL, JOHN (1745–1831), printer. In 1777 he began publishing 'Bell's edition' of *The Poets of Great Britain complete from Chaucer to Churchill*. The 109 volumes anticipated the edition of English poets planned by a cartel of major London booksellers, accompanied with the *Lives* by Samuel JOHNSON, which were published from 1779, but Bell's books, largely reprints from Edinburgh editions produced by the Martin brothers, for whom Bell was the London agent, were cheaper and sold well, successfully demonstrating the limits of the booksellers' power and also growing popular appetite for literature.

BELL, PATRICK (1799–1869), inventor. Son of a Forfarshire farmer with engineering interests, Bell trained for the ministry but in the late 1820s explored the possibility of mechanizing the reaping process. In 1827 he exhibited a mechanical reaper to the Highland and Agricultural Society and won the society's patronage for his work. Although his machines proved successful in America, Bell did not patent his invention, and he devoted the rest of his life to his ministerial duties. In mid Victorian Britain, Bell was seen as the inventor of the first efficient reaping machine, a precursor to the American inventor Cyrus McCormick's celebrated harvester.

BELL, VANESSA (née Stephen) (1879–1961), painter. Daughter of Leslie STEPHEN and older sister of Virginia WOOLF, Vanessa Bell studied at the Royal Academy Schools. In 1905 she founded the Friday Club on the lines of the literary circle that her brother Thoby was gathering at Gordon Square, the house in Bloomsbury where the Stephen children had moved on the death of their father in 1904. Vanessa married the art historian Clive Bell in 1907 and had two sons. From 1913 to 1919 she was the co-director with Roger FRY of the Omega Workshops, which was devoted to improving contemporary design. She exhibited her bold abstract paintings, which were influenced by Cézanne and Matisse, at Fry's notorious second Post-Impressionist exhibition in London (1912), and designed textiles, ceramics and book-jackets for the Woolfs' Hogarth Press. In 1916 she moved to Charleston (Sussex), where she was to live for the next 50 years with the painter Duncan GRANT and where some of her decorative work remains.

BELL BURNELL, SUSAN (née Bell) (1943–), radio astronomer. Born in Belfast, Bell Burnell studied mathematics and astronomy at Glasgow and Cambridge and later worked at the Royal Observatory, Edinburgh. In 1967, whilst pursuing doctoral research on radio astronomy under Anthony Hewish at Cambridge, she, Hewish and others detected strange and rapidly pulsating radio signals from the sky. The astronomer Thomas Gold proposed the now accepted theory that such radiation emanated from rapidly spinning neutron stars or 'pulsars'. Since the late 1960s Bell Burnell has conducted extensive research on the gamma-ray, X-ray, infra-red and optical sources in the cosmos.

BELLOC, HILAIRE (1870–1953), poet and novelist. He was born in France (*see* PARKES, BESSIE RAYNER), and his family came to England during the Franco-Prussian War. Belloc took British citizenship in 1902. He was a Liberal MP for Salford (1906–10), but, impatient with the party system, left politics and published *The Party System* (1911) and *The Servile State* (1912), in which he called for a return to the medieval guild system. Best known for his children's books, which include *The Bad Child's Book of Beasts* (1896) and *Cautionary Tales* (1907), he also wrote history books, notably *The French Revolution* (1911) and *A History of England* (1915), biographies, travel books, apologias for Catholicism and satirical novels, many of which were illustrated by his friend G. K. CHESTERTON, with whom he wrote anti-imperialist articles during the Boer War.

BENEDICT BISCOP (?628–89), monk. The chief historical importance of this Northumbrian nobleman, who underwent a religious conversion in 653, is as the founder and first Abbot of the monastic community of Monkwearmouth and Jarrow, where BEDE spent most of his life. His pilgrimages to Rome, his association with WILFRID and his insistence on large buildings and an excellent library are all indications of the Roman and Mediterranean influences on the early Christian Church in England. This was in contrast to the more ascetic character of the form of monasticism associated with Ireland and Iona (*see* AIDAN; COLUM CILLE). His work was continued by Abbot CEOLFRITH.

BENEZET, ANTHONY (1713–84), anti-slavery campaigner. He was born in France, but left as a child when his father converted to Protestantism. The family became Quakers in London and then emigrated to Philadelphia where Anthony became a schoolmaster. He founded schools for girls and for slaves and became one of the leaders of anti-slavery agitation, publishing *A Caution and Warning to Great Britain* in 1767, which inspired abolitionists across the British territories.

BENN, ANTHONY WEDGWOOD (TONY) (1925–), politician. Educated at Westminster school and New College, Oxford, in 1950 he was elected Labour MP for Bristol South-East. He was barred from sitting in the Commons in 1961 following succession to his father's title (Viscount Stansgate), which he fought for three years for the right to renounce. The passing of the Peerage Act 1963 enabled him to relinquish the title and he was re-elected to his Bristol seat. Tony Benn (who abandoned other parts of his name in a sometimes sneered-at populist move) served as Postmaster General (1964–6), Minister of Technology (1966–70) and of Power (1969–70) and as Secretary of State for Industry (1974–5) and for Energy (1975–9). He was seen as the archetypal exponent of the 'white heat of technological revolution' of the Harold WILSON era. As Minister for Technology he championed the Concorde programme, and as Industry Secretary he was responsible in 1965 for setting up the National Enterprise Board, seen as a major instrument in the State direction of industry, and for obtaining funding for workers' co-operatives. He was a leading opponent of Britain's entry into the EEC (the European Economic Community, now the European Union) and continues to be so.

As a backbench MP following Labour's defeat in the 1979 General Election, his move to the Left intensified, and in the fierce internal party battles that followed the 'Bennite left' became the focus of attempts to widen the selection procedure for the party leadership, force the reselection of sitting MPs and impose greater control by the National Executive Committee over the party manifesto. His influence in the party reached a peak in 1981 when, by the narrowest margin, he was defeated for the deputy leadership by HEALEY. A compelling orator of acknowledged principles, integrity and enthusiasm, Benn has nevertheless become an increasingly isolated figure as the Labour Party has sought to present a moderate 'modernizing' image.

BENNELONG (*c.* 1764–1813), Australian aboriginal. In 1789 Bennelong was captured on the orders of Arthur Phillip, Governor of the penal colony of New South Wales, with the intention of teaching him British customs, as an experiment in civilizing the native inhabitants, and so that he might serve as an intermediary between the two cultures. Brought to London when Phillip returned there in 1792, he was presented to GEORGE III, but soon ceased to be a curiosity and spent most of 1794 on a ship in the Thames. He returned to New South Wales with Phillip's successor John Hunter in 1795, but was culturally isolated between two societies that were becoming increasingly antagonistic, and was eventually disowned by the colonizers after he demonstrated his incomplete conversion to British ways by intervening to stop British soldiers suppressing a tribal punishment.

BENNET, HENRY (1st Earl of Arlington) (1616–85), politician. He fought on the Royalist side in the Civil Wars and served CHARLES II in exile, during which time antagonism developed between him and Edward HYDE, Earl of Clarendon. Appointed Secretary of State in 1662, he used his influence among court supporters in the House of Commons to undermine Clarendon's position and, in 1667, promoted his impeachment and dismissal. A leading figure in the Cabal ministry of 1667 to 1673 (*see also* CLIF-FORD, THOMAS; VILLIERS, GEORGE; COOPER, ANTHONY ASHLEY; MAITLAND, JOHN), he was among the inner group who in 1670 negotiated the secret Treaty of Dover between Charles II and Louis XIV of France. He did not favour rigid Anglican religious policies, and backed the Declaration of Indulgence (1672) suspending the penal laws against Dissenters and Roman Catholics. He did, however, support the Test Act (1673) which was designed to exclude all non-Anglicans from civil and military office; his support was possibly a manoeuvre against his former ally, Clifford. The following year, he survived an impeachment attempt but exchanged the secretaryship for the post of Lord Chamberlain. Opposing Danby (*see* OSBORNE, THOMAS) in 1678, he favoured his impeachment. On his deathbed he declared himself a Roman Catholic.

BENNETT, ARNOLD (1867–1931), novelist and journalist, best known for his stories of people living ordinary lives, most of them set in the Staffs. potteries of his childhood. *Anna of the Five Towns* (1902) was followed by *The Old Wives' Tale* (1908) and *Clayhanger* (1910). In 1918 he became Director of Propaganda in the Ministry of Information.

BENNETT, AIR VICE-MARSHAL DONALD (1910–86), airman. Son of a wealthy Australian grazier, he was educated at Brisbane grammar school, joined the Royal Australian Air Force, and later transferred to the Royal Air Force. In 1935 he resigned to become a pilot for Imperial Airways, for

which he established a number of records for long-range flights. Rejoining the RAF in Aug. 1941, Bennett, a skilled navigator, formed a Pathfinder Force from amongst the most competent pilots and navigators. From 1943 onwards Bennett's Path-finders, equipped with the most advanced radars and blind-bombing devices, led streams of bombers to their targets, dramatically improving the effectiveness of Bomber Command's attacks, service for which he was appointed to the Distinguished Service Order (DSO).

BENSON, A(RTHUR) C(HRISTOPHER) (1862–1925), writer. Son of Edward White Benson, headmaster of Wellington College (where A. C. Benson was educated) before being appointed Archbishop of Canterbury in 1883. Of the six children, none married, and Benson, who taught at Eton before becoming Fellow (1904) and then Master (1915) of Magdalene College, Cambridge, suffered from bouts of depressive illness all his life. He managed to achieve a prodigious amount of writing, homely philosophical observations, *belles lettres* and a two-volume life of his overshadowing father (1899). His verses to commemorate the coronation of EDWARD VII, 'Land of Hope and Glory', enjoyed as the words for ELGAR's first *Pomp and Circumstance* march a patriotic status second only to the national anthem. His brother E. F. Benson was also a prolific writer, best remembered for his 'Mapp' and 'Lucia' series, while his sister Margaret (Maggie) was an economist, philosopher and archaeologist.

BENSON, E(DWARD) F(REDERICK) (1867–1940), writer *see* BENSON, A.C.

BENSON, MARGARET (MAGGIE) (1865–1916), economist *see* BENSON, A.C.

BENTHAM, GEORGE (1800–84), botanist *see* HOOKER, SIR JOSEPH DALTON

BENTHAM, JEREMY (1748–1832), philosopher and jurist. Son of an attorney, he was educated at Westminster and Oxford, neither of which he enjoyed. He then began to read for the Bar. He devoted most of his life to voluminous schemes for the rationalization of English law, paralleling the work of the law reformers of the continental Enlightenment. His works include: *A Fragment on Government* (1776), questioning BLACKSTONE's celebration of the English legal system; *Introduction to the Principles of Morals and Legislation* (1789); and *Constitutional Code* (1827–30). He advocated the 'greatest happiness' principle, that government should promote the greatest good of the greatest number, and is seen as one of the progenitors of

Utilitarianism. In the 1790s he made strenuous efforts to interest governments in his plans for a new model prison, the Panopticon; disappointment in this and other things helped to persuade him of the need for parliamentary reform. His thought was disseminated by a small circle of disciples, including RICARDO and James and John Stuart MILL. Numerous reforming administrators, most notably Sir Edwin CHADWICK, sought to give practical effect to his ideas, which also attracted enthusiastic interest in the newly independent South American states. University College, London, was founded under the influence of his educational ideas.

BENTINCK, LORD GEORGE (1802–48), politician and racehorse-owner. Son of the Duke of Portland, Bentinck was a famously successful racehorse-owner whose horses won all the major events except the Derby, but who in 1846 sold his entire stud for £10,000 in order to lead the Tory Protectionists in the House of Commons after the party split over PEEL's repeal of the Corn Laws. Bentinck was a loyal supporter of DISRAELI, whom he both helped financially and made respectable to the Tory landed interest. Protection, however, was an eroding cause, and when Bentinck was deserted by his supporters after he voted to allow Jews to sit in Parliament, he resigned and died within a year, but not before he had watched one of the horses he had sold win the Derby.

BENTINCK, HANS WILLEM (5th [1st Bentinck] Earl of Portland) (1649–1709), politician. A Dutch courtier of WILLIAM III, Bentinck was closely involved in preparations for the 1688 invasion, and was subsequently given an English title and large estates, acquiring the unpopular reputation of a 'favourite'. He was appointed Ambassador to France in 1697 and signed the first Partition Treaty in 1698, providing for the division of the domains of the childless King Charles II of Spain between Bavaria and the French Dauphin. Although he resigned in 1699, the following year he was blamed for the second Partition Treaty, which substituted Austria for Bavaria, but enlarged the portion assigned to France, and was criticized for giving the French too much power in the Mediterranean. He was impeached by the Commons but acquitted by the Lords.

BENTINCK, WILLIAM CAVENDISH (3rd Duke of Portland) (1738–1809), politician and Prime Minister (1783, 1807–9). Occupying a key place within the kinship network of Whig magnates, and loyal to the Whig dissidents who formed a distinct grouping under Rockingham (see WATSON-WENTWORTH, CHARLES) in the 1760s, Portland was assigned a variety of senior posts. Appointed Lord Chamberlain when the Rockinghamite Whigs took

office in 1765, he resigned with them in 1766; Lord Lieutenant of Ireland 1782–3, in 1783 he became First Lord of the Treasury and as such nominal head of the FOX–NORTH administration. Selectively supportive of PITT THE YOUNGER's government from 1792, he led a group of Whigs into formal alliance with Pitt in 1794. He became Home Secretary, and Lord President of the Council under ADDINGTON in 1802. In 1807, although largely incapacitated by age, he became nominal head of a Pittite ministry effectively dominated by CANNING and Castlereagh (see STEWART, ROBERT), resigning in their wake in 1809.

BENTLEY, DEREK (1933–53), judicial victim. Bentley and his accomplice, Christopher Craig, were apprehended on the roof of a Croydon (Surrey) warehouse on 2 Nov. 1952. Craig shot and killed a policeman. Bentley, who was held by the police at the time, is alleged to have shouted, 'Let him have it, Chris.' Whether he meant hand over or discharge the gun was disputed, as was Bentley's mental age (estimated at about 10). Nevertheless he was hanged on 28 Jan. 1953 aged 19; Craig then aged 16, below the age for capital punishment, was released in 1963. A 40-year campaign to clear Bentley's name was conducted by his family with strong public support. In 1993 the Home Secretary announced a posthumous, limited pardon.

BENTLEY, RICHARD (1662–1742), scholar. On leaving Cambridge University he became tutor to Edward STILLINGFLEET's son James, and was made Stillingfleet's chaplain in 1690 and in 1694 Keeper of the Royal Libraries. Bentley had an extensive knowledge of ancient texts which laid the foundations of modern classical scholarship in England but led him into controversy. Particularly provocative was his *Dissertation on the Letters of Phalaris* (1699), seen at the time as a pedantic attack on Charles Boyle's edition of the *Letters*, but which conclusively showed that 'Phalaris' lived 1,100 years after his supposed date of 600 BC. Boyle had championed Phalaris as part of an argument about the superiority of ancient to modern learning; paradoxically Bentley's use of refined scholarly techniques illustrated the indispensability of 'modern' learning for a just appreciation of the ancient world. A friend of NEWTON, Christopher WREN and John LOCKE, he delivered the first Boyle lectures (see BOYLE, ROBERT) in 1692, using Newton's law of gravity to prove the existence of an omnipotent creator.

BEORHTRIC, King of Wessex (786–802). He succeeded CYNEWULF as King of the West Saxons in 786, defeating his main rival EGBERT with the aid of King OFFA of Mercia, whose daughter

EADBURH he married. Beorthric may well have responded to the first known Viking raid on Wessex, which took place in 789, by emulating Offa in imposing general obligations to military service on his kingdom, an important preliminary to Wessex's successful resistance to the Vikings in the time of ALFRED THE GREAT. He was succeeded by Egbert.

BEORNWULF, King of Mercia (823–6). The successor of the deposed King CEOLWULF II, Beornwulf was decisively defeated by King EGBERT of Wessex at the Battle of Ellendun in 825. He was killed fighting rebels in 826. His defeat at Ellendun marks the end of the Mercian hegemony south of the Humber which had reached its apogee in the time of King OFFA. His successor WIGLAF was even temporarily expelled from his kingdom.

BERENGARIA (?–c. 1230), Queen of England (1191–9). Although she was Queen of England (and gave her name to a Cunard liner) she never set foot in England. To RICHARD I, a King going on crusade, she and her father, King Sancho VI of Navarrre, represented so useful an alliance that he married her in May 1191 in highly controversial circumstances, and in a place where queens of England are rarely married, Limassol in Cyprus. After the crusade, however, she and Richard spent little time together; certainly they had no children. After Richard's death his successor, King JOHN, refused to give her the lands and revenues to which she was legally entitled. King Philip II of France was more generous and she ended her days as 'lady of Le Mans'. Her tomb is in the neighbouring Cistercian abbey of L'Epau, her own foundation.

BERGER, JOHN (1926–), novelist, essayist and art critic. Berger first worked as an artist and teacher but soon turned to art criticism. He was a Marxist and his column in the *New Statesman* defended socialist realist painting against the fashionable abstract art from the USA. *Ways of Seeing* (1972) (a television series and a book) was influential in showing the material basis of art production and argued for a re-evaluation of great works of art. He won the Booker Prize in 1972 with his novel *G* and has collaborated on works with a United Nations photographer, Jean Mohr, including *A Fortunate Man* (1967), the study of the life of a country doctor.

BERHTWALD (?–731), Archbishop of Canterbury (692–731). The successor of THEODORE OF TARSUS and the first Archbishop of Canterbury of English birth. Although his early years were probably overshadowed by St WILFRID's pretensions to the arch-

bishopric, Berhtwald eventually mediated Wilfrid's return from exile in 705. His career is notable for continuing Theodore's policy of dividing the large English dioceses and for his collaboration in law-making with King WIHTRED of Kent.

BERINGTON, JOSEPH (1746–1827), campaigner for Catholic Emancipation. He came from a Catholic gentry family; his brother Charles held the honorary bishopric of Hierocaesaria (*de facto* operating as an English bishop). Ordained in France, Berington established himself as a moderate English Catholic, seeking emancipation on the grounds that, although a Catholic priest, he was a 'man and Englishman' and entitled to the same rights as other Englishmen. He was less forthright in arguing that since Catholicism was declining it was no longer a threat, and his rejection of the authority over English Catholics of the Pope's representative, the Vicar Apostolic, led to his suspension as a heretic in 1792, but he was reinstated after a token retraction. He represented a strand in English Catholic thought against which a more papalist, cisalpine reaction began to develop at the end of the century.

BERKELEY, GEORGE (1685–1753), philosopher, educationalist and Bishop of Cloyne (1734–53). Educated at Trinity College, Dublin, he published his key philosophical work, the *Principles of Human Knowledge*, in 1710. In it he argued that 'we live, move, and have our being' in a divine mind that perceives everything in the universe; our own ideas and perceptions of experience are merely imperfect apprehensions of a fuller reality. He came to England in 1713, where he met Joseph ADDISON, Sir Richard STEELE and SWIFT but, on GEORGE I's accession, was unable to gain preferment and left for Europe. On his return to Britain in 1721 he called for a return to a simpler way of living and restrictions on expenditure to avoid another catastrophe of speculative finance like the South Sea Bubble, which had burst the previous year. He saw salvation for civilization in America and lived in Rhode Island, New England (1729–32), eventually settling his property there on Yale University to provide scholarships. He spent most of the rest of his life as Bishop of Cloyne in Ireland.

BERKELEY, SIR JOHN (1st Baron Berkeley) (*c.* 1606–78), soldier and diplomat. Ambassador to Sweden in 1637, he was commander for CHARLES I in the Bishop's Wars against the Scots (1639–40) and prominent in the English Civil Wars in the West Country, surrendering Exeter to Fairfax in 1646. The following year, he unsuccessfully tried to negotiate between the King and Parliament, and retired to France, becoming governor to the Duke of York (the future JAMES II) and obtaining his peerage in 1658. He resumed his military career in 1660, becoming Lord Lieutenant of Ireland (1670–2) and life Lord President of Connaught from 1661. In 1676–7, during the Franco-Dutch wars, he was one of the ambassadors extraordinary at the multilateral negotiations between European powers at Nijmegen. This worthy career was probably of less enduring significance than his highly informative memoirs.

BERLIN, SIR ISAIAH (1909–97), historian of ideas. Chichele Professor of Social and Political Theory (1957–67), first President of Wolfson College, Oxford (1966–75) and President of the British Academy (1974–8), Berlin was born into a Russian Jewish family in Riga, Latvia, and as a child in St Petersburg witnessed the Russian Revolution. The memories of this event later marked his political and philosophical orientation. At 11 he came to England, and was the first Jew to be elected as a Fellow of All Souls, Oxford (1932). On the outbreak of the Second World War, Berlin served at the British embassy in Washington, when he became a close friend of the Zionist leader and first President of Israel, Chaim Weizmann, and Berlin influenced the British government in favour of the creation of a Jewish State. After a brief secondment to the British embassy in Moscow, he returned to Oxford. He began work on the history of ideas; his *Two Concepts of Liberty* (1958) was a robust defence of individual liberty, demonstrating an agonistic liberalism that was the hallmark of Berlin's philosophy.

BERMINGHAM, JOHN (Earl of Louth) (?–1329), soldier. In 1318 when commander-in-chief of the English forces in Ireland he routed EDWARD BRUCE, the Scottish claimant to kingship in Ireland, at the Battle of Faughart, and was created Earl of Louth by EDWARD II. He was described in the *Annals of the Four Masters* as the 'most vigorous, puissant and hospitable of the English in Ireland'. He was treacherously killed in an Anglo-Irish squabble, along with his Irish bard O'Carroll.

BERNAL, J(OHN) D(ESMOND) (1901–71), crystallographer. Born in Ireland, Bernal developed interests in crystallography and Marxism while studying natural sciences at Cambridge. As a lecturer at Cambridge (1927–37) he rose to become a leading expert in X-ray crystallography: he devised a powerful method of indexing crystal planes and used X-ray crystallography to make pioneering studies of the structure of water and of crystalline organic molecules such as proteins.

During the Second World War he was scientific adviser to Combined Operations where his work included testing bombs and the problems of the D-Day landings. He held chairs in physics and then crystallography at Birkbeck College, London (1938–68), where he continued his crystallographic work, and published on the importance of Marxism to science and on the social functions, organization and history of science. He was a notable self-publicist and active campaigner for international peace.

BERNARD, SIR THOMAS (1750–1818), philanthropist. The second son of an American colonial governor, Sir Francis Bernard, he studied law in London and made large sums as a conveyancer, complementing the inheritance of his wife Margaret Adair. He was able to retire in his thirties and then involved himself in good works. In 1796 he founded, with Shute BARRINGTON and WILBERFORCE, the Society for Bettering the Condition of the Poor, which aimed to suggest to well-placed supporters ideas as to how they might best help the poor, and help the poor to help themselves. It focused especially on the provision of cheap food and other necessaries and on effective domestic management, as well as promoting friendly societies and education for poor children. In 1808 Bernard helped to found the first teacher-training college in England, in Bishop Auckland (Co. Durham). He also played a part in founding the Royal Institution, to promote scientific experiment and public lectures, and the British Institution, a connoisseurs' association for the promotion of British art.

BERNSTEIN, SIDNEY (Baron Bernstein of Leigh) (1899–1993), entrepreneur. Bernstein inherited his father's cinema business on the eve of the sound age. He developed the initial group of four cinemas into the Granada chain, and from 1930 built vast cinemas in towns and cities. During the Second World War he was film adviser to the Ministry of Information and, from 1944, head of psychological warfare for the Allied expeditionary force. He brought Alfred HITCHCOCK back from Hollywood and the two later collaborated on film productions. Initially opposed to the advent of commercial television, he formed Granada Television which in 1956 acquired and still holds the franchise for north-west England. Even before the decline of its cinema business the Granada group had diversified, into bingo, television rental, catering and hotels.

BERNSTORFF, ANDREAS GOTTLIEB VON (1649–1726), German minister to GEORGE I. The most senior of the advisers who accompanied George from Hanover in 1714, his influence remained high until 1719, when George I supported STANHOPE's peace plan at the end of the Great Northern War against the advice of Bernstorff, who feared the eventual Prussian conquest of all northern Germany. In 1721 he returned to Germany, but continued to advise George I from semi-retirement.

BERRY, WILLIAM EWART (BILL) (1st Viscount Camrose) (1879–1954) and **JAMES GOMER** (1st Viscount Kemsley) (1883–1968), newspaper proprietors. The Berry brothers were the second and third sons of John Berry, a Merthyr Tydfil (Glam.) estate agent. With a loan from their elder brother Henry Seymour Berry, later Baron Buckland of Bwlch (1877–1928), William established a weekly trade paper, *Advertising World*, in 1901; its success was so immediate that Gomer had to be drafted in and the brothers enjoyed a 35-year partnership. They acquired the *Sunday Times* in 1915, the *Financial Times* in 1919, *Kelly's Directories* in 1920 (a deal that brought Sir Edward Iliffe into their partnership), many papers and businesses from the HARMSWORTH stable and in 1927 the *Daily Telegraph*. The partnership was dissolved amicably in 1937, Gomer taking Allied Newspapers, one of the great chains of provincial newspapers, Bill the *Daily Telegraph* and *Financial Times*. Although they exercised considerable political influence over the newspapers under their control, the brothers were not as interventionist as their rival proprietors. The family lost control of the *Daily Telegraph* in 1986; by then the bulk of the titles held by Lord Kemsley had been sold to Roy THOMSON in 1959. The Berry press empire was relatively short-lived, but at its peak the brothers, together with Beaverbrook (*see* AITKEN, MAXWELL) and the HARMSWORTHs, dominated the industry.

BERTHA (?–after 601), Queen of Kent. A Christian Frankish princess, she was married to King ETHELBERT of Kent. Although, like most medieval women, she remained very much in the background, her religion and contacts with the already-Christian Franks are likely to have proved extremely important in enabling the acceptance of St AUGUSTINE's mission of conversion. *See* LIUDHARD, St.

BERTHELET, THOMAS (*c.* 1490–1535), printer. First in the service of the printer John Rastell, and later working with Richard Pynson, he used the surname 'Bercula' in his earlier career; in 1524 he settled in Fleet Street, London, publishing works ranging from legal textbooks to several of ERASMUS' writings, some in English translation (one by Margaret ROPER, one his own). From 1529 to 1547 he printed the parliamentary statutes and many of the official publications of HENRY VIII, but the accession of Protestant EDWARD VI appears to have prompted his retirement.

BERTIE, PEREGRINE (13th Baron Willoughby of Eresby) (1555–1601), soldier. Son of Catherine WILLOUGHBY, Duchess of Suffolk, and her second husband, Richard Bertie, he was born in Cleves while his parents were in Marian exile (hence his given name 'wanderer'). Back in England from 1559, he was among the boys educated by William CECIL and in 1580 inherited his mother's baronial title. In 1582 and 1585 he led diplomatic missions to Denmark, then served in the wars in the Low Countries, eventually succeeding Robert DUDLEY, Earl of Leicester, as English commander (1587); he gained lasting celebrity for obstructing the Spanish advance. But infuriated here and in the English expedition to France in 1589–90 by shortage of funds and government indecision, he retired to travel in Europe. From 1597 he served as Governor of Berwick-on-Tweed.

BERTIE, ROBERT (1st Earl of Lindsey) (*c.* 1582–1642), soldier. He followed his father, the distinguished Elizabethan soldier, Peregrine BERTIE, in many varied military and naval assignments from the late 1590s, becoming Earl of Lindsey in 1626, Lord High Admiral in 1636 and Governor of Berwick-on-Tweed in 1638. He was also active in fen drainage in his native Lincs. Having raised forces there and in Notts. for CHARLES I in 1642, he became the first commander of the Royalist field army. He died, much lamented, from wounds which he received during the Royalist defeat at Edgehill on 23 Oct.

BESANT, ANNIE *see* essay on page 81

BESANT, SIR WALTER (1836–1901), novelist and social investigator. After graduating from King's College, London, and Christ's College, Cambridge, Besant embarked on a career as an educationalist and explorer in Palestine but became primarily a novelist. He collaborated (1871–81) in a number of novels with James Rice and then wrote *All Sorts and Conditions of Men* (1882) and *Children of Gibeon* (1886). In these he contributed to the re-discovery and investigation of poverty in the East End of London. The great popularity of *All Sorts and Conditions of Men* inspired the Beaumont Trust to fund the People's Palace in Mile End, opened in 1887 and envisaged as a means of bringing the 'refinements' of West End bourgeois culture to the masses of the East End. A prolific author himself, Besant was also concerned with the conditions of the writer: in 1884 he helped to establish the Society of Authors and founded and edited *The Author* in 1890.

BESANT, ANNIE (1847–1933)
Social reformer

Her long, active and highly effective life spanned two continents and a spectrum of religious and political beliefs. Of Anglo-Irish descent, she was born in London; her businessman father died when she was five, and the family's straitened circumstances meant that Annie was brought up largely by an Evangelical aunt. She was a pious, rather naïve girl of 18 when, in 1865, she married a clergyman, the Rev. Frank Besant. But after eight years of marriage the Rev. Mr Besant insisted on a legal separation when his wife's religious convictions faltered so much that she felt unable to attend Communion. Always a free thinker and now, temporarily, an atheist (her book *The Gospel of Atheism* was published in 1877), she was to form close friendships with a number of other free thinkers, including Charles BRADLAUGH, Edward Aveling (who left her for Karl MARX's daughter) and George Bernard SHAW, who called her 'the greatest orator in England'. In 1874 she joined Bradlaugh's National Secular Society, becoming its vice-president and editing his journal, *The National Reformer*.

In 1877 she and Bradlaugh were convicted of obscenity when they republished (largely at Besant's initiative) a 40-year-old pamphlet explaining methods of birth control, and sentenced to six months' imprisonment and a fine of £200. The conviction was quashed on appeal, but, as a result of the case, Besant lost the custody of her daughter. Later that year, Besant's own book on the subject, *The Laws of Population*, was published: it sold 110,000 copies over the next decade. By 1885, partly influenced by Aveling and Shaw, Besant had joined both the Fabian Society and the Social Democratic Federation, which estranged her from Bradlaugh and his radical individualism. She supported a number of workers' demonstrations, and became the chief organizer of the 'match girls' strike' by poorly paid women working in dangerous conditions at Bryant & May's factory in the East End of London in 1888. That same year Besant was elected to the London School Board, where she managed to persuade the guardians to waive school fees for poor children, provide free school meals and pay their employees trade-union rates.

But dramatically in 1889, after reviewing Helena BLAVATSKY's book, *A Secret Doctrine*, and having begun to despair of the likelihood of social reform permanently improving the human condition, Besant was converted to theosophy. Theosophy seemed to offer a link between the spiritualism of her youth and the 'brotherhood' of socialism. She immersed herself in the study of the occult and employed her great oratorical gifts to promote her new-found beliefs. In 1893 Besant visited India, where the international headquarters of the Theosophical Society were located, and, deciding that India was her motherland, settled there for the rest of her life. She learned Sanskrit, studied the Hindu scriptures and translated the *Bhagavad Gita* (1895). Seeing Hinduism as the expression of theosophy's ancient tenets she was determined to raise Hindu self-esteem in the face of British imperialism. Convinced that an educational system supportive of Hinduism was essential to counteract the effects of British missionary schools, she founded the Central Hindu College in 1898, which was to become Benares Hindu University, and eventually a network of schools throughout India administered by the Theo-sophical Educational Trust. In 1907 Besant was elected President of the Theosophical Society.

After 1913 she began to extend the scope of her activities, taking part in the politics of her adopted subcontinent by supporting the cause of Indian *swaraj* (self-government) within the British Empire. Initially a moderate, she became increasingly frustrated with the Indian National Congress, leading her to launch the league for home rule for India with B. G. Tilak, which was able to extract reforms from London. In 1917 the Governor of Madras panicked and interned Besant at a hill station. After more than three months she was released to a hero's welcome, a martyr to the cause of Indian independence, and in Dec. 1917 was appointed the fifth President of Congress. But after the First World War Besant began to lose nationalist support and was eclipsed as Mahatma GANDHI began to emerge as the focus of Indian nationalism. After her presidency ended in 1923, Besant worked on the drafting of a constitution for a self-governing India and collaborated with Srinivasa Sastri to form the National Constitutional Convention in 1924. The next year she won the backing of the Labour Party for the Commonwealth of India Bill. Still a spiritual zealot she travelled widely throughout India promoting Krishnamurti, her adopted son, as the World Teacher in the theosophical cosmology, the new Messiah.

Besant died near Madras, 14 years before her hope for an independent India was realized, but having encompassed a range of causes that were questioning, courageous and prescient.

Annie Besant, An Autobiography (1893)
Arthur H. Nethercott, The First Five Lives of Annie Besant (1960); The Last Four Lives of Annie Besant (1963)

BESSEMER, SIR HENRY (1813–98), inventor. Bessemer was self-taught and developed engineering expertise in his father's type-foundry, where he made several inventions and ran a profitable business manufacturing metallic goods. Between 1854 and 1869 he secured patents for a highly economical and efficient process for making steel and, in particular, stronger rifle barrels for the army, the celebrated 'Bessemer process'. In this process, the carbon, silicon and manganese impurities in cast iron (which make it brittle) are oxidized and then removed by blowing air through molten cast iron in a reverberatory furnace. The molten iron is then transformed in a 'Bessemer converter', a tiltable vessel with holes in its base for the air blast. The presence of phosphorous impurities in his steel forced him to refine his process (exploiting techniques developed by Sidney Gilchrist THOMAS and others), and subsequently he launched what would become an extremely successful steelworks in Sheffield. Although the process was not initially accepted by many English steelmasters, it was eventually exploited in all the major steel-making countries, particularly the USA. It revolutionized steel-making and engineering, and made its inventor a millionaire.

BETJEMAN, SIR JOHN (1906–84), poet and broadcaster. Betjeman studied divinity at Oxford but left without a degree. After working briefly as a schoolmaster, he became assistant editor of the *Architectural Review* (1930) and film critic for the *Evening Standard* (1933). Betjeman's first poem, 'Death in Leamington', was published in the *London Mercury* in 1930 and his first collection of verse, *Mount Zion*, was published a year later. His poems did not receive the kind of immediate attention that was given to his *Ghastly Good Taste or the Depressing Story of the Rise and Fall of English Architecture* (1933), in which he attacked Modernist, conventional and unthinking antiquarian trends in architecture. His love of Victorian architecture and his writings on the subject prompted a revival of interest in the period and the eventual founding of the Victorian Society. Betjeman's career as a poet flourished in the 1940s and 1950s, the first edition of his *Collected Poems* (1958) selling over 100,000 copies. The popularity of his work owes much to his ability to portray what Philip LARKIN described as 'a gaiety, a sense of the ridiculous, and affection for human beings and how and where they live, a vivid and vivacious portrait of mid-twentieth-century English social life'. He was appointed Poet Laureate in 1972.

BETTERTON, THOMAS (*c.* 1635–1710), actor and playwright. His father, under-cook to CHARLES I, apprenticed him to a bookseller. At the Restoration he became part of William DAVENANT's Duke's Company of actors and was sent by CHARLES II on the first of several missions to study the French theatre. In 1671 he became joint manager of the company when it moved to the new Dorset Garden Theatre, off Fleet Street, and continued after its amalgamation with the King's Company at Drury Lane. His greatest role was Hamlet. In 1692 Betterton lost £8,000 in a merchant venture that fell prey to the French; he continued acting, taking the leading players from Drury Lane to Lincoln's Inn Fields in 1695 when the management refused to pay their salaries, and then in 1705 to the Haymarket, but died in 1710 in poverty.

BEUNO, ST (*fl.* seventh century), cleric. He was one of the most popular of the early Welsh saints, with churches dedicated to him in Powys and Gwynedd as well as Ireland. Reputedly an Abbot, little is known about him. The surviving life of him was written in the fourteenth century.

BEVAN, ANEURIN *see* essay on page 83

BEVERIDGE, WILLIAM *see* essay on page 84

BEVIN, ERNEST *see* essay on page 85

BEWICK, THOMAS (1753–1828), engraver. The son of a farm worker from Northumb., he was apprenticed to a Newcastle engraver in 1767, and supplied book illustrations for Newcastle's large printing trade. Becoming a partner in the business in 1777, he demonstrated the versatility of wood as a medium for cheap, high-quality prints rather than simply for crude woodcuts. His first great achievement was the *General History of Quadrupeds* (1790, and reissued seven more times in Bewick's lifetime, his engravings becoming more sophisticated with each edition). It was surpassed by the two-volume *History of British Birds* (1797–1804), for which he also wrote much of the text on the basis of his own research and observations. WORDSWORTH praised his 'truest feeling for nature'. His importance lies not only in his technical skill as a pioneer of wood-engraving, but also in his exemplification of the thriving cultural life of provincial England in the later eighteenth century.

BHOWNAGGREE (1851–1933), Indian nationalist politician and Westminster MP *see* NAOROJI, DADABHAI

BIGGS, RONALD (1929–), robber. A member of the armed gang that carried out what became known as the Great Train Robbery of the night mail train from Glasgow to London on 8 Aug.

continued on page 86

BEVAN, ANEURIN ('NYE') (1897–1960)
Politician

Born in the small coal-mining community of Tredegar (Mon.), the son of a miner and a miner himself from the age of 13, he was active in the South Wales Miners' Federation: at 19 he was already chairman of his union lodge. In 1919 he won a scholarship to the Central Labour College and left the valleys for London, where his studies fused his fierce anger at the condition of the working classes and hatred of capitalism with a honed Marxist theoretical confidence in the inevitability of the socialist organization of society which was to be his lifetime's fight.

The south Wales to which Bevan returned was a changed place: the boom which wartime requirements had brought to mining burst, with a rapid decline into lowered wages, unemployment and idle pits. It was a bitter time for Bevan, convinced of the power of industrial action, and himself only fitfully employed. This lesson was driven home by the defeat of the miners in the 1926 General Strike: 'the defeat ended a phase', he later wrote in *In Place of Fear* (1952), 'and from then on the pendulum swung to political action'. In 1929 he was elected Labour MP for the mining seat of Ebbw Vale. He was soon noticed as a powerful, apocalyptic orator and an eloquent critic of the 1931 National government with its Tory majority and unwillingness or inability to tackle the pressing issues of poverty and unemployment. Yet he also garnered a reputation as someone who was rapidly shaking the coal dust from his boots, a 'Bollinger Bolshevik … [a] lounge-lizard Lenin', taken up by the likes of Lord Beaverbrook (*see* AITKEN, MAXWELL).

During the Second World War Bevan's star rose: from being an unregarded, maverick socialist agitator (an impression strengthened by his marriage in 1934 to a fellow MP, Jennie LEE, a protégée of James MAXTON), he emerged as a public figure, a biting and effective critic of the wartime government. In 1945 with the Labour victory, ATTLEE boldly appointed the rebel Bevan Minister of Health with responsibility for housing too. It was an indication of Labour's commitment to genuine social change, but the backlog of slum clearance and the destruction of the housing stock during the war, and the nation's expectations for health raised by the BEVERIDGE report, made it a daunting portfolio. Bevan rashly promised 'five million houses in quick time': he did creditably to achieve one million by 1951, 82 per cent of them for local authorities in line with his intention to provide high-quality social housing for the British people.

But it was the creation of the National Health Service (NHS) that was to be Bevan's finest achievement: a plan that built on earlier schemes but took his radical approach, pragmatic flexibility and dogged determination to achieve. The rows with the British Medical Association (BMA) made the Act seem a more socialist measure than in fact it was (consultants could still treat private patients and pay beds remained in the nationalized hospitals), but in July 1948 the NHS which was universal and free (for a short time) at the point of delivery came into being, and Bevan was able to boast that 93.1 per cent of the population had enrolled under its care.

The 1950 election savagely slashed the Labour majority, and Bevan was blamed by the Labour right for frightening off the moderate voter with what he had described as his 'burning hatred' for the Conservatives as being 'lower than vermin' in a 1948 speech. He was ready to move from Health but was left to 'clear up the mess' that the gross underestimate of the cost of the NHS had created for an economically embattled government until Jan. 1951 when he was moved sideways to the unenviable job of Minister of Labour. Passed over again for higher political rank, on 22 April Bevan resigned, ostensibly over the decision of the new Chancellor, Hugh GAITSKELL, to charge for spectacles and dentures as part of government welfare cuts to meet the cost of rearmament for the Korean War. Correct that the rearmament budget was militarily unnecessary and economically unrealizable ('the arithmetic of Bedlam') Bevan left what he perceived as the rightward-drifting Labour Party: his departure contributed to split the party for the next 13 years, spent out of office. In 1957 he and Gaitskell struck an uneasy truce, with Bevan appointed shadow Foreign Secretary and later that year deputy Party leader. But he rowed with former left-wing colleagues, the climax being at the 1957 Labour Conference when he rounded on the unilateralists, insisting that Britain should retain an independent nuclear deterrent. The dismal bickering continued until his untimely death on 6 July 1960. A crusader whose passing even the *Daily Express* mourned: 'unmanageable, incalculable, adored – and hated, Bevan *was* the history of socialism'.

Michael Foot, Aneurin Bevan (2 vols, 1962, 1973; abridged edn 1997)

BEVERIDGE, WILLIAM (Baron Beveridge of Tuggal) (1879–1963)
Social reformer and administrator

Author of the Beveridge Report, the blueprint for Britain's Welfare State, Beveridge had a monumental public career. The son of a judge in the Indian Civil Service, he was educated at Charterhouse and Balliol College, Oxford, achieving firsts in mathematics and Classical Moderations followed by Greats. He then took a degree in civil law in 1903 and was awarded a civil law fellowship at Oxford, which he held until 1909. By then he had decided that he was more concerned with social matters than with legal, and in 1903 went to work at Toynbee Hall, a university settlement in the East End of London. His father did not approve, charging his son with 'sentimental philanthropy', but, though Beveridge was to grow impatient with purely voluntary forms of social welfare, he used his time to provide empirical evidence to demonstrate that poverty and unemployment were structural, not individual issues, and as such were remediable by limited State intervention. His next job was as a leader writer on the *Morning Post* (1906–8) after which he became a civil servant, working first as personal assistant to Winston CHURCHILL, who was then at the Board of Trade. During this time Beveridge was closely associated with the introduction of labour exchanges (1909–10) and the National Insurance Act (1911). Soon after the outbreak of the First World War he was drafted to the Ministry of Munitions and subsequently worked in the newly created Ministry of Food, becoming Permanent Secretary in 1919, the year in which he resigned from the Civil Service.

At the invitation of Sidney WEBB he became director (1919–37) of the London School of Economics, making it a world-class centre for the study of the social sciences, and later became Master of University College, Oxford (1937–44). He remained active in public life, serving on the Samuel Commission on the Coal Industry (1925–6), and chairing the Unemployment Insurance Statutory Committee for 10 years from 1934. In Dec. 1940 Beveridge was appointed to the Ministry of Labour to oversee manpower requirements in wartime. An erudite polymath himself, he could seem abrasive and arrogant to others, and the minister, Ernest BEVIN, was relieved to recommend him as chair of an interdepartmental committee of civil servants charged with surveying various social insurance provisions and making recommendations. With his experience in social insurance Beveridge already had a clear outline view of what was required and, though he consulted, interviewed and took evidence, he dominated the committee, and the report issued in 1942 is rightly known as the Beveridge Report.

The recommendations went far beyond what the government had anticipated and pulled together existing piecemeal provision to provide a comprehensive Welfare State which would care for its citizens 'from the cradle to the grave' by slaying the 'five giants of want, disease, ignorance, squalor, and idleness'. The report was the work of a 'scientific economist' convinced that social security and economic growth were mutually reinforcing. Beveridge sought to ensure an acceptable standard of living for all citizens through a free National Health Service, family allowances and a universal subsistence level of social insurance, but not to make them dependent on the State: it was a contributory system supported by government-maintained full employment. Indeed Beveridge disliked the term 'welfare state', arguing that it suggested an over-munificent State. To a nation at war, but with a strong sense that victory would have to bring a fairer peace, the statistically dense Beveridge Report was an optimistic sensation, selling well over half a million copies. Churchill's coalition government was reluctant to commit itself to implementing the report, and there was a backbench revolt.

Beveridge entered the Commons briefly as Liberal MP for Berwick-on-Tweed in 1944, in the cause of his report, but lost his seat in the Labour landslide the next year and went to the Lords in 1946, where he continued to chair committees (including those on new town development and the BBC) as well as writing books, essays and pamphlets, more than 1,000 in his lifetime, all concerned with social welfare and academic issues. The most significant of these, apart from the Beveridge Report, was *Full Employment in a Free Society* (1944), though his first work, *Unemployment: A Problem in Industry* (1909), was also hugely influential.

Beveridge was a complex figure, and his firmly grounded vision of the interpendence of State and society and his ability to rationalize both the existing and a considerable amount of already planned legislation into a comprehensive and comprehensible whole earn him the accolade of the architect of the Welfare State. By no means all the report's recommendations were put into practice after the Labour government came to power in 1945, and Beveridge's admixture of collectivism laced with self-help has been gradually eroded ever since.

José Harris, William Beveridge (1977)

BEVIN, ERNEST (1881–1951)
Politician and trade union leader

Like many of the early Labour leaders, including Ramsay MACDONALD, Bevin was illegitimate, and he liked to say in later life that he could have held only two positions at the Foreign Office, janitor or Foreign Secretary; it was the rise of the Labour movement which ensured that it would be as the latter that he would make his name.

Bevin left school before the age of 12 and worked at a series of casual jobs, including that of carter, before he became in 1911 a full-time official in the dockers' union. His combative nature and sharp intelligence led him to become a leading figure in the National Transport Workers' Federation, and his presentation of the workers' case to the 1920 Shaw Inquiry into the conditions of dock labour led to the nickname 'the dockers' KC'. Bevin distrusted Communists, Marxists and other manifestations of middle-class or cosmopolitan influences on the labour movement, and he opposed attempts to use the unions for political purposes in the early 1920s; no syndicalist he. In 1922 he was one of the founders of the Transport and General Workers' Union (TGWU), which became Britain's largest union; Bevin was its General Secretary from 1922 to 1940.

After the 1926 General Strike Bevin joined the other moderate union leader, Walter CITRINE, in strengthening the links between the unions and the party and, through the General Council of the Labour Party, he played an influential role in the party, particularly after the 1931 electoral disaster. Bevin fiercely opposed attempts to forge links with the Communists in the late 1930s, and it was his reputation in the labour movement which led CHURCHILL to ask him, in 1940, to become Minister of Labour. A parliamentary seat was soon found for Bevin and from 1940 to 1945 he was virtually dictator of the home front. His experience and trade union contacts were invaluable in maintaining production during the war, and, despite his poor parliamentary performances (Bevin never did feel at home there), he was one of the key figures in Churchill's Coalition government. When Labour won the 1945 election it was generally expected that Bevin would go to the Exchequer but to general surprise ATTLEE appointed him Foreign Secretary. To some extent this was due to domestic political considerations, since the mutual detestation between Bevin and Herbert MORRISON, the Home Secretary, meant that the less the two men had to do with each other the better; the King's

veto on Hugh DALTON may also have influenced Attlee. Bevin turned out to be an inspired appointment. The fears of the professional diplomats were soon dispelled by the realization that Bevin shared their mistrust of the Soviet Union, and by the knowledge that he was such a powerful figure in Cabinet that the Foreign Office view was usually bound to prevail over Labour Party dogma. Bevin's trade union background made him a loyal supporter of Attlee whom he could have supplanted, had he so wanted, at any time; in return Attlee deferred to Bevin's judgement that Stalin's Russia was an expansionist power which threatened British interests.

Bevin was an instinctive Palmerstonian (*see* TEMPLE, HENRY) in foreign affairs, and he viewed British weakness at the end of the war as temporary, so his main concern was to ensure that others did not take advantage of this situation. He shared Churchill's predilection for the Atlantic Alliance with the USA but realized that the latter needed time to come round to his view of Russia. In the meantime he concentrated on trying to forge a Western European Defence Union, with the 1947 Dunkirk Treaty with France as the first move in that direction. He also liquidated the British commitment in Palestine, arousing in the process considerable hostility from pro-Zionist members of the Labour Party by his lack of solicitude for Jewish interests. The Marshall Aid programme of 1947 was largely the product of Bevin's own initiative, and he played a major role in the creation of the North Atlantic Treaty Organization in 1948 by which, for the first time, America committed itself to an alliance in peacetime. Bevin was also one of the architects of Britain's nuclear defence policy, and a staunch defender of Britain's position in the Middle and Far East. His opponents underlined the lack of difference between Bevin's policies and those of his predecessor by commenting, 'My, hasn't Eden grown fat!'

Bevin was one of the mainstays of the Attlee government, and the post-war Atlanticist consensus in foreign affairs owed much to his influence. He struggled on until 1951 despite increasing ill health. Attlee reluctantly moved him to the office of Lord Privy Seal after the 1951 election but Bevin died a few weeks later. He was Labour's greatest Foreign Secretary.

Alan Bullock, Ernest Bevin (3 vols, 1960–83)

1963, Biggs was sentenced to 25 years for conspiracy and 30 years for armed robbery. Escaping from gaol in 1965, he fled first to Australia and finally to Brazil, where extradition attempts failed. He became something of a celebrity, always willing to grant interviews to the world's press, while films about the robbery and his life have accorded him legendary status. Less than a quarter of the £2.5 million stolen in the robbery was ever recovered.

BIGOD, ROGER (4th Earl of Norfolk) (*c.* 1213–70), royal servant. He succeeded his father Hugh in 1225, and became a ward first of the Earl of Salisbury, then of ALEXANDER II of Scotland. He fought bravely for HENRY III in France in 1242, and was made Earl Marshal in 1246. He represented the barons at the introduction of the Reforms of Oxford in 1258 but returned to the King's side in opposition to Simon de MONTFORT in 1259. When de Montfort won the Battle of Lewes in 1264, he reappeared on the barons' side.

BIGOD, ROGER (5th Earl of Norfolk) (1245–1306), courtier. He succeeded his uncle Roger BIGOD in 1270. With EDWARD I threatening their power, he and Humphrey de BOHUN, Earl of Hereford, led the barons' refusal to go to war in 1297. When the King left for Flanders, he and Bohun enlisted the support of the citizens of London, attended a meeting with an armed force, and forced the Regent (later EDWARD II) to confirm charters renouncing the right to exact arbitrary taxation. The King himself confirmed these in 1301. Having attained his object, Bigod gave up his marshal's baton, made the King his heir and disappeared from public view.

BILLINGTON-GREIG, TERESA (1877–1964), suffragette. Daughter of a shipping clerk, she attended Manchester University extension classes and undertook teaching and social work. A prominent member of the Women's Social and Political Union (WSPU), she was twice imprisoned in Holloway but, critical of their focus and tactics, broke with the suffragettes after 1911 and became rather less prominent thereafter.

BILNEY, THOMAS (*c.* 1495–1531), martyr. A Cambridge don converted to religious reform by reading ERASMUS' translation of the New Testament, in preaching campaigns he denounced religious images and pilgrimages. He was arrested, and recanted in 1527 but, when he repeated his denunciations four years later, he was burned at the stake. His execution created a national furore. With his Norfolk and possibly Lollard origins, he may be a rare link between Lollardy, the medieval movement of religious protest, and the new intelligentsia of the Reformation.

BINGHAM, GEORGE CHARLES (3rd Earl Lucan) (1800–88), soldier. Educated at Westminster school, and bought a commission in the 6th Foot in 1816, by the time he succeeded to his father's title in 1839, Lucan had purchased his way to the lieutenant-colonelcy of the 17th Lancers. Twelve years later he was appointed General, though he had never been in a battle. In 1854 Lucan commanded the cavalry division in the Crimea, and quarrelled with the commander of the Light Brigade, his brother-in-law, the Earl of Cardigan (*see* BRUDENELL, JAMES), whom he detested. On 25 Oct. a garbled message from Lucan sent Cardigan and the Light Brigade charging against a mass of Russian guns. Although Lucan was lionized by later generations, the charge was regarded at the time as a catastrophe (the Light Brigade was virtually wiped out) and Lucan was sent back to England.

BINNS, JOHN (1772–1860), radical. Son of a Dublin ironmonger, he came to London in 1794 to work as a plumber, and joined Thomas HARDY's London Corresponding Society. In 1797 he hired a large room in the Strand to hold political debates, and established links with the United Irishmen (*see* TONE, WOLFE). His activities were monitored by government agents and in Feb. 1798 he was arrested at Margate (Kent) on his way to France. He was acquitted of the charge of treason but again arrested and released in 1801. Binns then emigrated to the United States, where he became a successful journalist and politician.

BIRD, ISABELLA (1831–1904), traveller and writer. From an Evangelical family (William WILBERFORCE was a relation) and with a missionary zeal herself, Bird started to travel in her early twenties. Her notes and letters from her trip to the USA, *The Englishwoman in America* (1864), became an instant best-seller. Plagued by back trouble, she travelled to the Sandwich Islands and Australia seeking a cure, and from there to Malaysia, Japan, Saigon and Singapore. *A Lady's Life in the Rocky Mountains* (1879) chronicled her second American adventure ('no place for women or tourists'). In 1881 she married Dr Bishop who had cared for her dying sister, but within five years he too had died and she threw herself into nursing studies, travelled to the Middle East to establish a hospital in her husband's memory and journeyed on to Tibet, Central Asia, Persia and India. On her return she published accounts of these expeditions, addressed the House of Commons on Armenian and Syrian issues and then set off again as a missionary for the Baptist Church Missionary

Society, trekking all over China, establishing orphanages and a hospital financed by selling the silver plate which she had packed for the purpose. She was elected the first female Fellow of the Royal Geographical Society in 1892.

BIRDWOOD, WILLIAM RIDDELL (1865–1951), soldier. Son of an Indian government official, educated at Sandhurst, he returned to India to serve with the Bengal Lancers. A series of staff appointments with KITCHENER, beginning with the Boer War, ensured rapid promotion. In the spring of 1915 Birdwood, now a Major-General, distinguished himself as commander of the Australian and New Zealand Army Corps at Gallipoli. He subsequently commanded the Australian Corps in France until May 1918, and then commanded 5th Army for the offensives which broke the German army. Birdwood emerged from the war with an enhanced reputation, a tribute more to the quality of the men he commanded than to his own military prowess.

BIRINUS, ST (?–*c.* 648), churchman. Although less well known than other early participants in the conversion of the peoples of England to Christianity, such as St AIDAN, St AUGUSTINE and PAULINUS, Birinus, as the missionary responsible for the conversion of the kingdom of Wessex and the baptism of King CYNEGILS, is an important figure. Probably a Frank like his contemporary St FELIX, he set up a single bishopric for the entire kingdom at Dorchester-on-Thames. He was Bishop (?–*c.* 648) and was succeeded by another Frank, St AGILBERT.

BIRKBECK, GEORGE (1776–1841), educationalist. A physician from Yorks., he was a tireless advocate of educational improvement for the working classes. As Professor of Natural Philosophy at Anderson's College, Glasgow, he offered free lectures to working people, and in 1824 founded the London Mechanics' Institution, now Birkbeck College, University of London, to promote adult education.

BIRKENHEAD, 1ST EARL OF *see* SMITH, F. E.

BIRT, SIR JOHN (1944–), broadcaster. Director General of the BBC from 1992 to 2000, having been deputy since 1987, Birt brought a new management style to the public-service ethos of the corporation. At Granada and subsequently at London Weekend Television, where he rose to become director of programmes, he was in the forefront of informative documentary and factual programming. He brought that 'mission to inform' to the BBC, as well as a belief (much-contested) that the enlightened ways of management and the market needed to be introduced.

BIRTWISTLE, SIR HARRISON (1934–), composer. While studying the clarinet at the Royal Manchester College of Music, Birtwistle founded the New Music Manchester Group in 1953, which was devoted to performances of the Second Viennese School and avant-garde. The impact of Boulez and Stockhausen prompted him to take up composition in 1957, and the 1965 premiere of *Tragoedia* established him as one of Britain's leading young composers. His first opera, *Punch and Judy*, was performed in 1968 and the 'dramatic pastoral' *Down by the Greenwood Side* in 1969. Appointed Musical Director of the National Theatre (1975), he wrote incidental music for numerous productions, including Peter HALL's *The Oresteia* (1981). His large-scale operatic works include *Nenia: the Death of Orpheus* (1970), *The Mask of Orpheus*, which was first performed to critical acclaim in 1986, and the monumental *Gawain* (1991).

BLACK, CLEMENTINA (1854–1922), social investigator. Born in Brighton, the daughter of a solicitor, she is best known as an advocate of women's trade unionism and of improvements in women's working conditions. Through her great friendship with Amy Levy, a friend of Eleanor Marx AVELING, she was drawn into the Women's Protective and Provident League, later the Women's Trade Union League. Between 1886 and 1889 she was its Honorary Secretary. Disgruntled, however, with the results of the WTUL, she helped to establish the Women's Trade Union Association, which merged in 1897 with the Women's Industrial Council, a body of mainly middle-class women whose aim was the investigation of women's work and the improvement of women's skills. Through her work on the council she undertook many important investigations on sweating and edited the book *Married Women's Work* (published in 1915), in which she advocated the right of married women to paid work.

BLACK, CONRAD (1944–) newspaper proprietor. Canadian-born Black became one of Britain's most important 'press barons' when he purchased the Telegraph group of newspapers in 1985. Like Lord Beaverbrook (*see* AITKEN, MAXWELL) and Lord Roy THOMSON before him, he established his fortune in Canada before buying into Fleet Street. He bought the ailing, right-wing *Daily* and *Sunday Telegraph* titles from the Berry family (*see* BERRY, WILLIAM), thus establishing himself at the centre of Conservative Party politics in the country. He also bought *The Spectator* magazine in 1988.

'BLACK DOUGLAS' *see* DOUGLAS, ARCHIBALD

BLACK, JOSEPH (1728–99), chemist. He studied medicine and chemistry at Glasgow and Edinburgh. In experiments summarized in 1756 and 1757 he identified 'fixed air', now known as carbon dioxide, and showed that it was exhaled in respiration and was a by-product of fermentation and the burning of charcoal. He has been called the 'father of modern chemistry', but left much work to be pursued by others. His study of melting ice could not successfully explain what Black called 'latent heat' but it did lay the grounds for the science of thermodynamics. He experimented with steam and influenced the work of James WATT.

BLACKBURN, HELEN (1842–1905), suffragist. Daughter of a civil engineer, she was Secretary of the National Society for Women's Suffrage (1874–95) and editor of the *Englishwoman's Review* (1881–90). She wrote important studies of women in industry and a pioneering history of the women's suffrage movement.

BLACKBURNE, FRANCIS (1705–87), cleric and religious writer. For most of his life rector of Richmond (Yorks.), where he was born, Blackburne is best known for his contribution to the subscription controversy, the debate as to whether Anglican clergy (among others) should be required to swear to their belief in the Thirty-Nine Articles officially defining the doctrine of the Church of England. In *The Confessional* (1766), Blackburne proposed that a profession of belief in the Scriptures should be all that was required of a Protestant minister. The work inspired liberal Anglicans to present the Feathers Tavern petition to Parliament in 1772, requesting that the Anglican clergy, civil lawyers and physicians should not be required to subscribe to the Thirty-Nine Articles. Supporters included Edmund LAW, Theophilus LINDSEY, John JEBB and John DISNEY. Parliament voted to reject it, and also a second petition presented in 1774. The rejection of the petition caused several of its supporters to leave the Church of England.

BLACKETT, PATRICK (Baron Blackett) (1897–1974), physicist. Blackett served in the navy during the First World War and subsequently studied physics at Cambridge and Göttingen. He worked under Ernest RUTHERFORD at Cambridge University's Cavendish Laboratory, where he took the first cloud-chamber photographs of nuclear disintegration and in 1932, independently of the physicist Carl Anderson, produced evidence for the electron's 'anti-particle', the positron. He and Anderson shared the 1948 Nobel Prize for Physics. In the 1930s he made acclaimed studies of cosmic rays, and in the Second World War he pioneered operational research methods and worked on radar and the atomic bomb. He was Professor of Physics at Birkbeck College, London (1933–7), Manchester University (1937–53) and Imperial College, London (1953–65). After the war he supported international controls on atomic weapons and campaigned to improve Britain's scientific and technological standing, advising the Ministry of Technology introduced by the 1964 Labour government.

BLACKSTONE, SIR WILLIAM (1723–80), judge and jurist. The posthumous son of a London silkman, he was brought up by his brother, a surgeon, and educated at Oxford, then the Middle Temple. Elected to a fellowship of All Souls, in 1758 he became the first Vinerian Professor of English Law at Oxford, a subject which had previously not been taught there. An MP from 1761, he was never a skilled or successful politician. Solicitor General to Queen CHARLOTTE in 1763, from 1770 he was a Justice of Common Pleas, then briefly of King's Bench before returning to Common Pleas as Lord Chief Justice. His lasting achievement was the publication of his Oxford lectures as *Commentaries on the Laws of England* (1765–9); the admiring picture which it promulgated of the English constitution as a carefully regulated system of checks and balances was disseminated throughout Europe in translations of his works, and influenced the creators of the constitution of the United States of America.

BLACKWELL, ELIZABETH (1821–1910), doctor. Born in Bristol and educated in the USA, she became the first woman to obtain a medical degree there. She subsequently returned to England, and became Professor of Gynaecology at the London School of Medicine for Women. *See also* BLACKWELL, EMILY.

BLACKWELL, EMILY (1826–1910), doctor. Younger sister of the better-known Elizabeth BLACKWELL, she was the first woman doctor involved extensively in major surgery and was also the administrator of many of her sister's projects. Rejected by 10 medical schools because she was a woman, Emily Blackwell finally graduated in 1854 in the USA. She worked in Europe assisting in obstetric surgery and, with Elizabeth, subsequently founded the New York Infirmary and became Dean and Professor of Obstetrics and Diseases of Women at the Women's Medical College in New York.

BLACKWELL, GEORGE (1547–1613), churchman. London-born, he resigned his Oxford fellowship after adopting Roman Catholicism and in 1574 was ordained in Douai. He worked in

England from 1576, suffering imprisonment (1578). In 1598 Pope Clement VIII made him Archpriest of the secular (non–monastic) Catholic clergy in England, trying to provide some central authority to end internal squabbles with the Jesuits, but Blackwell was widely regarded as favouring Jesuits against seculars, and quarrels continued, with appeals (by the 'Appellants') to the Pope against his authority. Rome turned against him when in 1606 he advised his clergy to accept the English government's Oath of Allegiance; he was deprived of his office.

BLAIR, ANTHONY (TONY) (1953–), politician and Prime Minister (1997–). A barrister educated at Fettes College, Edinburgh and Oxford, Blair was elected as MP for Sedgefield (Co. Durham) in a by-election in 1983. He quickly established himself as a modernizer, building on the work of Neil KINNOCK, prepared to shed left-wing shibboleths in a drive to make the Labour Party electable after nearly two decades in opposition. As Shadow Home Secretary Blair's slogan that Labour would be 'tough on crime and tough on the causes of crime' summed up both the spirit and the tone of what would become New Labour. John SMITH's unexpected death in 1994 suddenly opened the leadership to the new generation; it was said that Blair and Gordon BROWN decided which one of them would run over dinner in an Islington restaurant, although the latter would never forgive his more telegenic rival. On being elected leader, Blair continued the recasting of the Labour Party, dropping Clause Four (which committed the party to nationalization) and unofficially renaming the party as New Labour in an attempt to further distance it from its past. He also made an election pledge not to raise income tax levels, aware that during the THATCHER years this had become a touchstone for the electorate.

Blair was fortunate in his timing. After four successive election victories the Conservative Party had grown stale and complacent, and John MAJOR, although liked, was not respected. A series of scandals involving bribery and sex rocked the government, which was also badly divided on the subject of further European integration. Blair was able to present New Labour as the antidote to Tory 'sleaze', emphasizing that his party would not take away the gains made under Thatcherism but would provide the more human and 'caring' approach.

During the longest General Election campaign in modern times (Feb. to 1 May 1997) Blair's revamped and technologically sophisticated publicity machine comprehensively out-classed and out-performed the Conservatives but even the media pundits were taken aback by the scale of Blair's victory which left him with a majority of 179 over all other parties – more seats than the Conservatives retained. Blair promised that 'things could only get better' and that having campaigned as 'New Labour, we will govern as New Labour'. It was the biggest Labour victory ever, after a century in which the Conservatives had dominated British politics. For its first 18 months the government remained almost preternaturally popular, something reflecting the lack of alternatives and the general desire for it to succeed; Blair's own popularity ratings remained at all-time highs, allowing him to use his personal prestige to guide the government over a few rough places. The end of 1998 saw the end of the honeymoon period when, after the resignation of the Welsh Secretary in lurid circumstances, Peter MANDELSON, the architect of New Labour, had to resign over the appearance of financial irregularity; more recently, Ken LIVINGSTONE made a mockery of the Labour selection process for the Mayor of London.

By 2000, the persistence of problems in the health service and education began to raise questions about the substance of some of Labour's policies, and to chip away at Blair's previously unassailable position.

BLAKE, GEORGE (1922–), spy. A dangerously successful double agent who worked for MI6 and the USSR and is alleged to have betrayed more than 40 British agents, he was convicted in 1960, but was sprung from prison six years later and fled to the Soviet bloc.

BLAKE, PETER (1932–), painter. From the Royal College of Art and a figurative painter, he came to define 'pop art' in Britain with his fusion of high art practice and low art taste in badges, toys, comics, Elvis Presley fan-club magazines and other ephemera of popular consumer culture. His best-known work is probably the sleeve for the Beatles (see LENNON, JOHN) record *Sergeant Pepper's Lonely Hearts Club Band* (1967). In 1971 he was a founder member of the seven-strong Brotherhood of Ruralists (modelled on the pre-Raphaelites) in a community near Bath, where his paintings were inspired by 'the spirit of the countryside'. He returned to urban culture in 1979.

BLAKE, ROBERT (1599–1657), naval commander. A merchant before the Civil Wars, Blake was elected to the Long Parliament and gained prominence in Parliamentary warfare in the West Country, coming to see the Parliamentary cause in millenarian terms: it was a crusade against all monarchy which would usher in the thousand-year rule of the saints under Jesus Christ. Appointed Admiral and General at Sea in 1649, he spent the next two years removing the remaining Royalist island strongholds and shattering Prince RUPERT's fleet. He led the successful naval campaigns in the First Dutch War in 1652–4, destroyed a Turkish pirate fleet in 1655 and the Spanish West Indies fleet at Santa Cruz in 1657. While returning to England, he died of fever. Although he was the outstanding British naval commander of the century, his body was ejected from Westminster Abbey at the restoration of CHARLES II.

BLAKE, WILLIAM (1757–1827), artist and poet. Son of a prosperous London hosier, he was sent to drawing school and apprenticed to an engraver. Later he studied at the Royal Academy, but did not take to the academic mode, preferring to draw from his imagination rather than from life. He initially made a living by selling illustrations to booksellers, but in 1784 opened a print shop. He wrote poetry from boyhood and developed a unique style of intaglio (relief etching) to illustrate his verse. Although his *Songs of Innocence* (1789) and *Songs of Experience* (1794) employ simple verse forms, they offer serious moral comment, showing the corruption of innocence by an oppressive political and religious regime. He was influenced by unorthodox religious ideas, including Swedenborgianism. *The Book of Thel* (1789–94) was the first of a series of visionary and prophetic works, in which he challenged conventional morality. In 1791 the bookseller Joseph Johnson employed him to illustrate some of Mary WOLLSTONECRAFT's writings for children. Through Johnson, Blake met such radical figures as Richard PRICE, Joseph PRIESTLEY, GODWIN and Thomas PAINE. He spent three years in Norfolk on the invitation of William Hayley, whose life of COWPER Blake was illustrating. Among outstanding illustrative work of his final years were his 'Inventions to the Book of Job'. Blake's engravings, and the profundity of his warnings against a mechanized, inhuman post-industrial world, ensured his growing reputation into the twentieth century.

BLANE, SIR GILBERT (1749–1834), physician. Blane studied medicine at Edinburgh before becoming a physician in London. One of his patients, Admiral RODNEY, appointed him physician to the fleet in 1779. Blane studied shipboard mortality and introduced wine and fruit into sailors' diet, resulting in fewer deaths and a reduction in cases of scurvy. Returning to shore in 1783, Blane worked at St Thomas's Hospital and became physician to the future GEORGE IV. As commissioner for sick and wounded seamen from 1795 to 1802, he persuaded the navy to include citrus fruit juice on ships as a scurvy preventative and also advised the government on the Quarantine Act of 1799, guarding against the spread of plague from the Mediterranean.

BLATCHFORD, ROBERT (1851–1943), socialist and journalist. Born in Kent in 1851 to a travelling comedian father and an actress mother, he was in his early thirties when he first turned to journalism. In 1884 he joined *Toby*, a satirical paper in Leeds, and in 1885 he began working for Edward HULTON's *Bell's Life* and *Sunday Chronicle*. Observing the Manchester slums while also encountering socialist ideas, Blatchford converted to socialism in 1889. From then through the 1890s he had close, if sometimes difficult, relations with socialist organizations including the Social Democratic Federation, the Fabians and the Independent Labour Party (from 1893). Above all, Blatchford became the defining force in the growth of *The Clarion* newspaper (from 1891) and the Clarion movement in the 1890s. At the heart of this was the building of educational and cultural organizations embracing women as well as men, children as well as adults, with the purpose of creating a socialist 'fellowship'. Blatchford's writing, in the paper and in books and pamphlets, was outstanding in its social comment: his *Merrie England* (1894) was a brilliantly successful piece of socialist propaganda selling more than two million copies. Blatchford's socialism was strongly inflected by both his jingoism and his imperialism: he supported both the Boer War (1899–1902) and the First World War. As a propagandist for socialist ideas in the 1890s he was without equal.

BLATHMAC (?–825), monk of Iona. A monk at the famous early medieval Abbey of Iona, Blathmac remained on Iona at a time when it was suffering heavily from Viking attacks. Although most of the community transferred to Kells, in the Irish midlands, Iona was never abandoned and Blathmac appears to have been the senior figure on the island. When it was subjected to a further Viking assault in 825, he was martyred for refusing to reveal the whereabouts of the reliquary of COLUM CILLE. An indication of the European importance of this event is that the account of Blathmac's martyrdom was preserved by the Carolingian scholar, Walafrid Strabo, in the monastery of Reichenau.

BLATHWAYT, WILLIAM (*c.* 1648–1717), royal servant. Brought up by his uncle, Thomas Povey, treasurer to the Duke of York (later JAMES II), in 1668 he became secretary to Sir William TEMPLE at the Hague. He was sent on a number of diplomatic missions, and in 1675 became a clerk at the Plantation Office, thus inaugurating a long period of involvement with colonial affairs. In 1683 he purchased the post of Secretary at War (an essentially administrative post), and three years later became Clerk to the Privy Council. He was the star witness against the seven bishops, who, under the leadership of Archbishop SANCROFT, led resistance to James II's 1687 Declaration of Indulgence. Although he was not unsympathetic to the aims of those who displaced James, his loyalty led him to continue to regulate army business for the King during the Revolution of 1688. He remained Secretary at War until 1704, accompanying WILLIAM III abroad, and was a Commissioner of Trade (1696–1706). As an MP (1685–7 and 1692–1710) Blathwayt was a consistent government supporter and has been seen as a prototype of the professional civil servant.

BLAVATSKY, HELENA (1831–91), mystic. A teenage bride, she left her husband, a Russian general, and arrived in the USA in 1873, having travelled widely in the Near East and the Orient. In 1875 she founded the Theosophical Society, a popular Hindu-inspired occultist movement that influenced Annie BESANT among others. Branded a fraud by the Society for Psychical Research in 1885, she nevertheless retained a large following in Britain and elsewhere.

BLEDDYN AP CYNFYN (?–1075), King. One of the kings installed in Wales by Earl Harold of Wessex (the future HAROLD II) and EDWARD THE CONFESSOR after the defeat of GRUFFUDD AP LLYWELYN in 1063. He is normally associated with the kingdom of Powys but may also have ruled in Gwynedd. Despite his early client status, he was well regarded by Welsh chroniclers, and followed the traditional policy of his predecessors. He assisted Earl EDWIN of Mercia in a fruitless rebellion against WILLIAM I THE CONQUEROR.

BLESSINGTON, MARGUERITE (neé Power) (Countess of Blessington) (1789–1849), society lady. She led a dazzlingly extravagant lifestyle, was painted by Thomas Lawrence, and took to writing after her aristocrat husband lost his fortune. Her *Journal of Conversations with Lord Byron* (1832) is still valuable for the light it sheds on the poet's personality and ideas.

BLIGH, WILLIAM (1754–1817), naval officer. Bligh served as master of HMS *Resolution* on James COOK's last voyage of exploration (1775–9). In 1787 he was given command of the armed transport *Bounty*, for a voyage to transport breadfruit plants from Tahiti to the West Indies. The crew mutinied, led by Bligh's second-in-command Fletcher Christian, and Bligh and 18 men were set adrift in an open boat. By outstanding seamanship, he reached the Dutch

colony of Coupang, 4,000 miles distant. After service at Camperdown and Copenhagen, he was sent as Governor to New South Wales. Christian's friends portrayed him as brutal to the point of sadism; it has been argued that it was as much his violence of speech as of behaviour that alienated his men.

BLISS, SIR ARTHUR (1891–1975), composer. After studying at the Royal College of Music under Gustav HOLST, Charles Stanford and Ralph VAUGHAN WILLIAMS, Bliss began his compositional career in the 1920s by rejecting traditional forms and allying himself to the musical idioms of Modernists such as Stravinsky and Schoenberg. Within a short time, however, he moved to an overtly romantic style inspired by the works of Edward ELGAR. In close co-operation with H. G. WELLS, he composed the film music to Wells's and Alexander KORDA's *Things to Come*, and later composed two ballets, *Checkmate* (1937) and *Miracle in the Gorbals* (1944). Director of Music at the BBC (1942–4), Bliss was appointed Master of the Queen's Music in 1953. His later works include several orchestral compositions, cantatas and an opera for television, *Tobias and the Angel* (1960).

BLOUNT, CHARLES (8th Baron Mountjoy, 1st Earl of Devonshire) (1563–1606), courtier and soldier. From *c.* 1583, he became a favourite of ELIZABETH I. Then, after initial explosive jealousy, he allied with Robert DEVEREUX, Earl of Essex, whose sister Penelope Rich became Mountjoy's mistress. Much naval and military service made him an obvious choice for command in Ireland, but he was appointed Lord Deputy only in Feb. 1600 after Essex's military disaster there. He prevented Hugh O'NEILL, Earl of Tyrone, from liaising with the Spanish expeditionary force at Kinsale (1601), and eventually brought him to England to be pardoned by JAMES I; an earldom was Blount's reward in 1603. His last months were clouded by royal anger at his irregular marriage to Penelope after her divorce from Lord Rich.

BLOUNT, WILLIAM (4th Baron Mountjoy) (*c.* 1478–1534), scholarly patron. Still a boy when he succeeded to his peerage in 1485, he studied in Paris in 1496, forming a lasting friendship with ERASMUS. In England he served in the army which defeated the Western rebellion (1497) and became one of the future HENRY VIII's tutors. He remained in royal service at court, in Calais and in the 1523 invasion of France but retired in distress in 1533 at the treatment of CATHERINE OF ARAGON. Not only Erasmus but many distinguished English humanists (e.g. Roger ASCHAM, John COLET, William GROCYN and Thomas MORE) enjoyed his patronage or friendship.

BLUNDEN, EDMUND (1896–1974), poet and critic. Blunden fought in the trenches in the First World War and the poems he wrote about it 'Third Ypres' and 'Report on Experience', are regarded as among the finest of that war; he also wrote an autobiographical account, *Undertones of War* (1928), and, after the Second World War, the reflective volume of poems *After the Bombing* (1950). Besides his mainly rural Georgian poetry, he edited the work of the Northampton poet John CLARE (1920), whom he rescued from obscurity, and published editions of the war poets Wilfred OWEN (1931) and the then virtually unknown Ivor GURNEY (1954).

BLUNT, ANTHONY (1907–83), art historian and spy. An art historian of international reputation, Blunt was Director of the Courtauld Institute of Art (1947–72) and Surveyor of the King's and then the Queen's Pictures (1945–72). At Cambridge University he had been recruited by Guy BURGESS as a Soviet spy and, as a member of the British Secret Service, passed information to the Russians during the Second World War; he helped Burgess and MACLEAN defect to the Soviet Union in 1951 when it became clear that MI6 was aware of Maclean's espionage activities. He consistently denied accusations about his own espionage until an American who had been a friend of Blunt at Cambridge gave evidence to the FBI in 1964. He confessed and was given immunity from prosecution in exchange for information but, following allegations published in 1979, Prime Minister THATCHER informed the House of Commons that Blunt had been a Soviet spy.

BLUNT, WILFRED SCAWEN (1840–1922), poet, diplomat and Arabist. Born into a landed Catholic family, he entered the Diplomatic Service at 18, married BYRON's granddaughter, wrote in defence of Egyptian, Indian and Irish independence, and was imprisoned in 1888 for being active in the Irish Land League. A prominent literary figure whose friends included William MORRIS, Oscar WILDE, Ezra Pound and YEATS, his poetry was both polemical and romantic.

BLYTON, ENID (1897–1968), writer. Suburban born and educated, a teacher and governess before she took to writing, in the late 1930s she began her prodigious output of children's fiction which was to result in more than 400 books translated into more than 20 languages or dialects, often producing a full-length book in a five-day working week. Her 'Malory Towers' school stories for girls, her 'Famous Five' and 'Secret Seven' adventures, and her *Little Noddy in Toyland* (1949) made her the best-selling children's writer of the twentieth century. By the 1960s her books had come to be regarded as classist, sexist, racist and of impoverishing imagination and limited vocabulary for children, and many public librarians banned them. But 10 years after her death, Blyton's English-language sales alone topped 200 million a year.

BOADICEA *see* BOUDICCA, essay on page 98

BOCHER, JOAN (?–1550), martyr. 'Joan of Kent' embarrassed less forthright evangelical Church leaders like CRANMER by her outspoken advocacy of religious reform under Henry VIII; she had contacts with evangelicals at court and with Anne AYSCOUGH. Under EDWARD VI she began attacking the orthodox account of the Trinity, and in 1549 was arrested and tried for heresy. Despite hesitations, the Edwardian authorities eventually burned her as an Anabaptist; she died defiant, having resisted strenuous efforts to persuade her to recant.

BOCKING, EDWARD (?–1534), conspirator *see* BARTON, ELIZABETH

BODICHON, BARBARA (née Leigh Smith) (1827–91), campaigner for women's rights. Bodichon was fortunate in a father who believed that his daughters should have the same opportunities and financial independence as his sons. Benjamin Leigh Smith, a radical MP and Unitarian minister, settled £300 a year on her when she came of age, enabling her to establish a non-denominational, co-educational school where she herself taught. She was active in promoting the Married Women's Property Bill in 1856, and her most important publication, *Women and Work* (1857), argued for the necessity of paid work for women. That same year she married an Algerian medical reformer, Dr Eugène Bodichon, and thenceforth wintered in Algiers with him, spending the rest of the year pressing for women's rights in Britain. She financed *The Englishwoman's Journal*, the major feminist voice of the nineteenth century, and supported the first suffrage petition in 1866 and the founding that year of the Women's Suffrage Committee. In conjunction with Emily DAVIES, Bodichon established what became Girton College, Cambridge. A talented artist, Bodichon, who was a great beauty, is supposed to have been the model for George ELIOT's *Romola* (1863).

BODLEY, THOMAS (1545–1613), library founder. Exeter-born; his parents fled MARY I's persecution, and his experience of Geneva shaped his later Puritanism. He returned to Oxford (1559–76), but then left to travel in Europe; an MP in 1584 and 1586, from 1585 he became a diplomat, and was Ambassador to the Dutch

United Provinces from 1588 to 1596. Retiring thereafter, he devoted himself to a refoundation of Oxford University's library, wrecked in EDWARD VI's reign; the first large donation, in 1600, was of books captured by Robert DEVEREUX, Earl of Essex, in the 1596 sack of Cadiz. The library was formally opened in 1602, and was given his name in 1604.

BOECE, HECTOR (?1465–1536), Scottish historian. First Principal of King's College, Aberdeen, in 1526 he published a Latin history of Scotland. Its legendary account of Scottish origins made it popular enough to be translated into English 10 years later. Its importance lies in the self-confident image of Scottish sovereignty which Boece's myth-making provided for JAMES V, and for its lurid picture of the reign of MACBETH, which was used by SHAKESPEARE.

BOEHM, SIR JOSEPH (1834–90), sculptor. Born in Vienna but educated in England, where he settled in 1862, he is known for Queen VICTORIA's head on the coinage, taken from one of his busts, the statue of the Duke of Wellington on his horse (1888) at Hyde Park Corner, a stern statue of Thomas CARLYLE on Chelsea Embankment (1875), busts of Prince ALBERT, commissioned by his inconsolable widow, and a statue at Balmoral of John BROWN, also commissioned by a grieving Queen.

BOHUN, HUMPHREY VII DE (7th [3rd Bohun] Earl of Hereford, 8th [2nd Bohun] Earl of Essex) (c. 1249–98), soldier. He succeeded his grandfather Humphrey V in 1274 and held the high office of Constable of England. In 1292 he was imprisoned for levying private war against the Earl of Gloucester. In 1296 he escorted John, Count of Holland, and his 14-year-old wife, the English Princess Elizabeth, back to Holland, and she later married his son Humphrey VIII de BOHUN. In his last years he was involved with Roger BIGOD, Earl of Norfolk, in compelling EDWARD I to renounce the right to arbitrary taxation.

BOHUN, HUMPHREY VIII DE (8th [4th Bohun] Earl of Hereford, 9th [3rd Bohun] Earl of Essex) (c. 1276–1322), soldier. He succeeded his father Humphrey VII de BOHUN in 1298. He was Constable of England. In 1302 he married Elizabeth, daughter of EDWARD I. He was one of the Ordainers appointed in 1310 to reform the government of EDWARD II. He was captured at the Battle of Bannockburn in 1314 and exchanged for the wife of ROBERT BRUCE. In 1321, at the head of an armed force, he denounced the King's favourite, Hugh DESPENSER, but was driven north

by the King and killed at the Battle of Boroughbridge.

BOHUN, MARY DE (Countess of Derby) (?–1394), heiress. Daughter and co-heiress of the last Earl of Hereford, in c. 1380, while they were both still children, she married Henry Bolingbroke, then Earl of Derby, but died five years before her husband deposed RICHARD II and became King as HENRY IV. She was the mother of HENRY V.

BOLEYN, GEORGE (Baron Rochford) (?–1536), politician. Son of Thomas BOLEYN, Earl of Wiltshire, brother of ANNE BOLEYN and a competent poet, he was active in his sister's cause, and shared her reformist religious outlook (translating at least two French evangelical treatises). He was active in the royal campaign to establish the royal supremacy in the Church from 1531 to 1533 and undertook negotiations with France. He then shared in Anne's disaster, being executed on charges of incest with her.

BOLEYN, SIR THOMAS (1st Viscount Rochford, 12th [1st Boleyn] Earl of Wiltshire, 8th [1st Boleyn] Earl of Ormond) (1477–1539), courtier. From a leading Norfolk family, Boleyn became an accomplished courtier and diplomat under HENRY VII and HENRY VIII. His grooming for courtly life of his children George (see BOLEYN, GEORGE), ANNE BOLEYN and Mary (Henry's mistress before Anne) paid rich dividends, with a viscountcy in 1525 and, after Anne's rise to favour, his two earldoms in 1529. He was the first major patron of Thomas CRANMER from 1529. Boleyn's career was permanently ruined by Anne's fall.

BOLINGBROKE, 1ST VISCOUNT see ST JOHN, HENRY

BOLINGBROKE, HENRY see HENRY IV

BONAR LAW, ANDREW see LAW, ANDREW BONAR

BONDFIELD, MARGARET (1873–1953), trade unionist and politician. She began work as a shop assistant, aged 11, and in 1898 became an official in the Shop Assistants' Union. At the TUC conference the following year, she supported the setting up of the Labour Representation Committee, the forerunner of the Labour Party, to ensure parliamentary representation for smaller unions. She was National Officer of the National Union of General and Municipal Workers (1908–38) and served on the TUC General Council 1918–24 (chair, 1923) and 1926–9. The most prominent woman in the labour movement in the inter-war years, she became an MP (1923–4, 1926–31) and was the first woman to take a seat in Cabinet as Minister of Labour (1929–31). She was also active in the National Council of Social Service and in women's training and employment.

BONHAM-CARTER, MARK (Lord Bonham-Carter) (1922–94), politician. A scion of a great Liberal family (his grandfather was the Prime Minister Herbert ASQUITH), educated at Winchester and Oxford, his own parliamentary career was brief, as Liberal MP for Torrington (Devon) in 1958–9. He made a greater contribution to public affairs than most backbenchers could have hoped as Chairman of the new Race Relations Board, set up in 1966 by Harold WILSON's Labour government, and as Chairman of the Community Relations Commission (1971–7). His name became synonymous with the search for better race relations in the 1960s, when immigration from new Commonwealth countries was the subject of heated political controversy and social unrest.

BONIFACE, ST *see* essay on page 95

BONNER, EDMUND (*c.* 1500–69), churchman. Possibly the illegitimate son of a Ches. parson, he studied at Oxford and entered WOLSEY's service, then from 1530 was busy in HENRY VIII's efforts to secure the annulment of his marriage to CATHERINE OF ARAGON. Becoming a client of Thomas CROMWELL, he was a notably undiplomatic Ambassador to France (1538–40); made Bishop of London in 1540, he abandoned his previous commitment to reformist religious policies and pursued heretics. Deprived as Bishop and imprisoned in 1549, he was reinstated by MARY I in 1553 and became notorious for renewed vigour in attacking heresy. His deprivation and renewed rigorous imprisonment in 1559 was inevitable, and as 'bloody Bonner' he became one of the chief villains in John FOXE's story of the Marian martyrs.

'BONNIE DUNDEE' *see* GRAHAM, JOHN

BOOLE, GEORGE (1815–64), mathematician. Born in Lincoln, Boole taught himself mathematics and spent his early years as a schoolteacher. He started building his reputation as a mathematician in the late 1830s with papers on analytical transformations and algebraic forms. In his most celebrated work, *An Investigation of the Laws of Thought* (1854), he showed how abstract logic could be reduced to algebraic operations. Boolean algebra is of major importance in computers. He was Professor of Mathematics at Queen's College, Cork (1849–64).

BOOT, JESSE (1st Baron Trent of Nottingham) (1850–1931), retail chemist. The son of a medical herbalist and Evangelical Nonconformist, born in Nottingham where the business bearing his name is still based, Boot decided to expand his herbalist business in 1874 by retailing patent medicines. From the outset, he relied on popular press advertising, undercutting prices, fast turnover and manufacturing his own medicines. When the law permitted limited companies to employ pharmacists in the mid 1880s, Boot moved into dispensing, opening new branches in other Midland towns. His wife Florence was prime mover behind new business lines: bookselling, stationery and fancy goods. The greatest expansion came in the 1890s and again in 1901 when Boot acquired rival chains of drug stores, in Lancs. and then in London and the south-east, bringing salesmanship, cheaper drugs, lending libraries and tearooms to ever wider numbers of customers. In 1920 Boot sold a controlling interest to American business. (British control was regained in the 1930s.) Much of his vast wealth was then used to rebuild University College Nottingham, for which munificence he was ennobled in 1928.

BOOTH, CATHERINE (née Mumford) (1829–90), co-founder of the Salvation Army. Of deeply religious parentage, she joined a Brixton Wesleyan Methodist church where, at a prayer meeting, she met her future husband William BOOTH. It was she who persuaded him to undertake the street evangelism for which they became famous, and with him she established the Salvation Army. An effective speaker, she was convinced of women's mission to preach the gospel.

BOOTH, CHARLES (1840–1916), social reformer. A wealthy businessman drawn into social research, he was responsible for the first scientific estimates of poverty and the development of survey methods in social investigation. His *magnum opus, Life and Labour of the People in London*, with its memorable series of coloured maps of poverty, was begun in 1886 and completed 17 years later. Among other factors, he identified old age as a major source of poverty, and campaigned for old age pensions with some success.

BOOTH, SIR GEORGE (1st Baron Delamere) (1622–84), conspirator. A Ches. gentleman who fought for Parliament in the English Civil Wars and supported Oliver CROMWELL, he nevertheless became disillusioned and in 1659 led an unsuccessful Ches. rising for CHARLES II, being defeated at Nantwich by John LAMBERT. He was rewarded with a peerage at the Restoration.

BOOTH, WILLIAM (1829–1912), co-founder of the Salvation Army. Born in Nottingham of
continued on page 96

BONIFACE, ST (c. 675–754)
Missionary

The greatest of the eighth-century Anglo-Saxon missionaries to the continent, Boniface played a central role in the conversion to Christianity of what we now call Germany. As the trusted confidant and emissary of the Carolingian kings of the Franks and of the Papacy, he was responsible for extending the authority of both and may well have taken an important part in consolidating the alliance between them which was to culminate eventually in Charlemagne's coronation as Emperor by the Pope on 25 Dec. 800. A native of Devon and educated initially at Exeter, Boniface was Archbishop of Mainz up until almost the end of his life. Beyond any question, he played a significant role in the history of early medieval Europe.

Originally named Wynfrith, he adopted the name of one of the early Christian martyrs with the Pope's permission shortly after leaving England in 718. Abandoning the possibility of promotion as either abbot or bishop in England, he set out on a path already followed by other Anglo-Saxons such as St WILLIBRORD, whom Boniface initially joined, and whose chief achievement was the conversion of Frisia. In due course Boniface undertook to complete the conversion of modern-day Hesse and Thuringia, a task which occupied him for approximately 20 years. He did so with the support both of the Papacy and of the Carolingian mayor of the palace, Charles Martel. His missionary work involved him in the extirpation of paganism in a region where Christianity was still weak and in the development of ecclesiastical organization. He was joined by a number of his compatriots, some of whom, such as St LEOBA, St LUL and St WILLIBALD, were promoted to high ecclesiastical office. In the late 730s he was involved in the establishment of new bishoprics in Bavaria, again with the backing of Charles Martel and the Papacy. Boniface's period of great political eminence came in the 740s after his major work of conversion had been completed, when he initiated councils of the Frankish Church under the auspices of Charles's sons, Carloman and Pippin the Short. These councils are normally seen as laying the foundations for the great Church reforms of Pippin's reign and of his much more famous son Charlemagne. Boniface may even have anointed Pippin when he took over the kingship from the Merovingians in 751.

We know more about Boniface than about most personalities of the early Middle Ages because of the survival of a considerable number of his letters. It is clear from some of his early writings that he benefited from the great educational traditions of western England associated with St ALDHELM and his disciples. Much more remarkably, his career and contacts illuminate just how extensive were the connections between seventh-century and eighth-century Britain and Europe. Not only was Boniface able to recruit compatriots to join in his organizational and missionary work, he also kept in touch with numerous ecclesiastics in Britain; a letter to Archbishop EGBERT of York requesting copies of the works of his older contemporary BEDE shows that he was in contact with the so-called Northumbrian Renaissance and that he was responsible for disseminating Bede's works on the continent. His reforming zeal also had an impact on the Church in England, since it was in part at his insistence that Archbishop CUTHBERT of Canterbury and King ETHELBALD of Mercia called a reforming council in 747.

Boniface's career exemplifies much about the early history of the Christian Church in Britain and Europe. It is important to keep in mind that he was born within a century of St AUGUSTINE's mission which had brought Christianity back to England and that older contemporaries included St THEODORE OF TARSUS and St WILFRID as well as Bede; he grew up in a world in which paganism was still a very real threat, but also one where organization and education were on the agenda of leading churchmen. Not only did he recruit disciples from England, but he established a pattern whereby others found their way after him to the Carolingian court; the most renowned is of course ALCUIN OF YORK, Charlemagne's close adviser. Boniface is said to have regretted that he had achieved so little in his lifetime and that he had been so heavily involved in politics. In particular, he wished that he had taken on the task of converting the Saxons, an intractable business which Charlemagne accomplished only through the most savage repression. In 753 he resigned the archbishopric of Mainz and returned to missionary work in Frisia, where he was killed by pirates in 754. The book with which he tried to protect himself is preserved at the Abbey of Fulda which Boniface himself had founded. His greatest achievement was arguably his contribution to what later became the Carolingian Renaissance, a movement which in due course impacted back on the English Church through the so-called Tenth-Century Reform associated with St DUNSTAN, St ETHELWOLD and St OSWALD.

Timothy Reuter (ed), The Greatest Englishman: Essays on St Boniface and the Church at Crediton (1980) humble parentage, he was converted to active Christianity in 1844 and joined the Methodist New Connexion. His book *In Darkest England* (1890) helped galvanize opinion with its shocking indictment of conditions in London. The Salvation Army, which he founded with his wife (*see* BOOTH, CATHERINE) and which emerged out of his missionary work in London's East End, gave institutional expression to the view that traditional Christianity could not succeed in the face of widespread poverty.

BOOTHBY, SIR ROBERT (1st Baron Boothby of Buchan and Rattray Head) (1900–86), politician and author. Born in Edinburgh, educated at Eton and Oxford, he was strictly speaking a political failure. As a Conservative MP for a Scottish farming and fishing seat (East Aberdeenshire), which he struggled gamely for 32 years to understand, he was something of a star in his early years at Westminster. His fruity-voiced eloquence and high society charm totally ensnared Lady Dorothy, the wife of the future Prime Minister, Harold MACMILLAN, while his political abilities caused Winston CHURCHILL to appoint him his Parliamentary Private Secretary (1926–9). When Churchill replaced Neville CHAMBERLAIN (whose policies of appeasement Boothby had bitterly opposed) he gave Boothby the job of Parliamentary Secretary at the Ministry of Food, but later the same year Boothby resigned, allegedly enmeshed in some dubious dealings over the Czech gold reserve. He never held office again, remaining a trenchant critic of the government on many occasions, a sparkling and incisive columnist, broadcaster and television commentator and a moving spirit behind the 1967 Sexual Offences Act, which decriminalized homosexual acts for consenting adults.

BORROW, GEORGE (1803–81), writer. 'Few have equalled him in the art of transporting the reader's spirit into the wilderness whilst his body sits by the fireplace', wrote HAZLITT of the Norfolk-born writer, who boasted of his facility for picking up languages and whose 'only study [was] man' as he took his famous 'walks', often lasting several months, all over Britain as well as on the continent. *The Bible in Spain* (1843), written after he had been sent there by the British and Foreign Bible Society, established his reputation, but his greatest success came with his episodic, autobiographical accounts of his life on the road and encounters with gypsy culture, *Lavengro* (1851) ('lavengro' being the gypsy name for a philologist), *Romany Rye* (1857) and *Wild Wales* (1857).

BORU, BORUMA, BRIAN *see* BRIAN BORUMA

BOSANQUET, BERNARD (1848–1923), philosopher *see* BOSANQUET, HELEN

BOSANQUET, HELEN (née Dandy) (1860–1925), social reformer. Born in Manchester to a Nonconformist family and one of the first two women to gain first-class honours in moral sciences at Cambridge University in 1889, Bosanquet then began work for the Charity Organization Society. There and as editor, from 1909, of the *Charity Organisation Review*, she was a major influence on the theory and practice of social work. Believing that charitable work should encourage the 'rational wills' of individuals rather than merely relieve poverty, she held that social workers should have both professional training in the skills needed to encourage rational behaviour and education in economics, history and sociology. She was married to Bernard Bosanquet, the liberal-Hegelian philosopher, from 1895 until his death in 1923.

BOSE, SUBHAS CHANDRA (later known as Netaji) (1897–1945), Indian nationalist. Bose was educated in India and at Cambridge before coming under the political influence of GANDHI. After a period as Chief Executive of Calcutta Corporation, he was arrested as a suspected terrorist and detained (1924–7). His health collapsed in repeated imprisonment and Bose became disillusioned with Gandhi. By the late 1930s, when he had already begun courting Adolf Hitler, he advocated violence against the British. Politically disowned by Gandhi and the Congress Party in 1940, he was arrested, disappeared and resurfaced in Nov. 1941 in Berlin; 18 months later he returned to Asia under the name of Netaji to lead a collaborationist army, Azad Hind Fauj, fighting alongside the Japanese. Early victories were soon reversed and Bose fell back to Bangkok, where he died.

BOSWELL, JAMES (1740–95), biographer and diarist. Son of the Scots judge Alexander Boswell, Lord Auchinleck, he studied at Glasgow and Edinburgh. Visiting London in 1762–3, he was introduced to Samuel JOHNSON, and they became close friends. A sociable man, Boswell cultivated the acquaintance of eminent contemporaries, including BURKE and Joshua REYNOLDS. In 1773, he toured the Highlands and Western Islands of Scotland with Johnson, but published his account of the trip only after the latter's death. His monumental biography of his friend and mentor, the *Life of Johnson* (1791), was an instant success, although some criticized it as gossipy and indiscreet. His journals, first published in the twentieth century, record his personal, social and professional life, and are full of acute and extraordinarily candid observations.

BOTHMER, JOHANN KASPAR VON (1656–1732), Hanoverian diplomat. He first came into contact with large numbers of British politicians when Hanoverian minister at the Hague (1702–11). In 1711 Elector George Louis (later GEORGE I) made him his envoy extraordinary to London to prepare the ground for the Hanoverian succession. With the Archbishop of Canterbury and the Lord Chancellor, Bothmer possessed one of the three lists of Lords Justices nominated to govern Britain in the name of George I between ANNE's death and the new King's arrival in 1714. Bothmer was often accused by British ministers and historians of having too great an influence over George I but he interfered little in specifically British affairs and in any case was inferior in office to BERNSTORFF.

BOTHWELL, EARL OF, 3RD see HEPBURN, PATRICK; **4TH** see HEPBURN, JAMES

BOTTOMLEY, HORATIO (1860–1933), financier and politician. An orphan from London's East End, Bottomley started a newspaper, the *Hackney Hansard*, when he was only 24, and by 1900 was a multi-millionaire businessman. He was charged with fraud in 1891 and 1909 but was acquitted; as few shareholders from the numerous companies which he promoted ever received their money, numerous bankruptcy petitions were filed against him. Founder of the magazine *John Bull* (1906), he was elected MP for South Hackney the same year, but petitioned for bankruptcy and in 1912 applied for the Chiltern Hundreds (a nominal office of profit under the Crown for which MPs apply if they wish to leave the Commons, since they cannot resign). In 1918 he was able to discharge his bankruptcy, having raised some £900,000 in subscriptions for various patriotic causes during the First World War, and was elected to Parliament again as an independent, but in 1922 he was sent to prison for five years for fraud.

BOTULF, ST (?–680), Abbot. Very little is known about Botulf, an East Anglian saint still commemorated at Boston (Lincs.) and Colchester (Essex). He was evidently a very important influence on the development of early Christian monasticism in England, since the abbey he founded at Icanho (site unknown) was very well regarded by St WILFRID and exercised influence over the organization of the great Northumbrian abbeys of Monkwearmouth and Jarrow, where BEDE was a monk.

BOUCHERETT, EMILIA (JESSIE) (1825–1905), campaigner for women's rights. Daughter of the High Sheriff of Lincs., she went to London in 1859 and immediately became a women's rights activist, joining the Langham Place Group and working with Barbara Leigh BODICHON and Adelaide PROCTOR to found the Society for the Promotion of Employment for Women, which also ran a school to teach women arithmetic and bookkeeping. Despite her belief in women's suffrage and her financial support for the *Englishwoman's Review* (of which she was the first editor, 1866–70), her primary concern was the employment of women, since she regarded the ability of a woman to earn her own living as the most important (and achievable) emancipation. She wrote several articles and books, including *The Condition of Working Women and the Factory Acts* (1896) with Helen BLACKBURN.

BOUDICCA, QUEEN *see* essay on page 98

BOULTON, MATTHEW (1728–1809), engineer and industrialist. He expanded his father's silver-stamping business in Birmingham, building his 'Soho' factory in 1762. He was a founder-member of the Lunar Society, a largely Dissenting scientific group whose other members included Erasmus DARWIN, Thomas DAY, Richard Lovell EDGEWORTH, Joseph PRIESTLEY, James WATT and Josiah WEDGWOOD; the society met in Boulton's house (now a museum). He experimented with steam-driven pumps and, in 1775, entered into partnership with James Watt, patenting a double-action steam engine in 1782. Boulton introduced steam-powered coining presses in 1788 and, in 1797, produced the new British copper coinage. (His improved coining machine was in service in the Mint until 1882.) Boulton and Watt engines were installed in many of the earliest steam-powered factories in Britain. They were often sold on a form of 'hire-purchase', the firm providing supervisors to ensure the machines continued to function. One of these managers was William MURDOCK, whose discoveries led Boulton and Watt into the field of gas lighting. In his array of interests and activities, Boulton typified an important sector of the late eighteenth-century industrial elite.

BOURCHIER, THOMAS (1403–86), Archbishop of Canterbury (1455–86). Bourchier was made Bishop of Ely in 1443, Archbishop in 1455 and Cardinal in 1473. He was Chancellor of England from 1455 to 1456, during an illness of HENRY VI and while RICHARD OF YORK was Protector. In the pursuit of peace he mediated successfully between MARGARET OF ANJOU and Humphrey STAFFORD, Duke of Buckingham, in 1458; in the same cause he persuaded ELIZABETH WOODVILLE to allow her younger son, Richard, to be removed from sanctuary in 1483.

BOUDICCA (*fl.* AD 60s)
Queen of the Iceni

Boudicca (also known as Boadicea, a Victorian corruption normally rejected by the specialists) was the widow of Prasutagus, King of the Iceni, and led a famous rebellion against the Romans in AD 61. Her dramatic and ultimately tragic attack on the Roman conquerors of Britain has achieved a legendary status in the history of the British Isles, epitomized by countless representations of a fearsome woman driving a huge war-chariot with scythes attached to the wheels. Boudicca was actually unknown to British historians before the sixteenth century, when the only contemporary written source, TACITUS, became known to English scholars. The legendary Boudicca is more than anything a creation of the nineteenth century and undeniably has resonances with the rule of another great queen, VICTORIA. Aspects of the popular image are certainly false – the British war-chariot, for example, was light and highly maneuvrable – but the revolt was undoubtedly an important event which shook Roman rule in Britain to its foundations.

Although JULIUS CAESAR had twice invaded Britain in 55 and 54 BC, Roman power only became established after the invasion by the armies of the Emperor CLAUDIUS in AD 43. The earliest stages of conquest, led by AULUS PLAUTIUS and OSTORIUS SCAPULA, were distinguished by the defeat and subjugation of the tribes of south-east England, such as the Catuvellauni, Trinovantes, Durotriges and Dobunni, who inhabited regions centred respectively in modern Herts., Essex, Wilts. and Glos. Other tribes, such as the Iceni, whose territory approximated to modern Norfolk and northern Suffolk, were forced to accept the status of what historians call client kingdoms which, while retaining a considerable measure of independence, recognized that the Romans had the right to intervene when they wished. The death of Boudicca's husband was followed by an attempt to impose direct rule on the Iceni. The Romans seem to have gone about their task in a very provocative way, physically mistreating Boudicca and her daughters and provoking a violent backlash among their discontented new subjects which soon became an extensive revolt. The Iceni were joined by the Trinovantes and others and set out on a violent campaign of destruction, which included the sack of the Roman towns of Colchester, London and Verulamium (now St Albans) and the defeat of part of the Roman 9th Legion under PETILLIUS CERIALIS. Large numbers of Romans were slaughtered. These early successes must, however, have owed a great deal to the absence of the Roman Governor SUETONIUS PAULINUS on campaign in north Wales. Suetonius' return was followed by a great battle at an unidentified site somewhere in the Midlands at which Boudicca and her forces were eventually defeated. Boudicca died shortly afterwards, possibly from taking poison.

Boudicca's rebellion undoubtedly had the effect of slowing the Roman advance into Britain at least for a time. In the aftermath of the revolt, Suetonius Paulinus, who had favoured harsh repression, was recalled to Rome, and more conciliatory policies were followed during the next decade. Boudicca's resistance, like that of other British leaders such as CASSIVELLAUNUS and her near-contemporary CARATACUS, ultimately demonstrated the massive military superiority which Romans could bring to bear when required. Four legions had taken part in the initial conquest, supported by an equivalent number of auxiliary troops – around 40,000 men in all. Their victory had been followed by settlement which accorded with a long-established formula. In Britain, most former tribal territories became self-governing units known as *civitates,* each focused on an urban centre which was either an existing British town or a new Roman one. These centres comprised all the typical features of a Roman town and were intended to accustom the natives to Roman civilization; there were about 15 by the time that the Roman conquest was complete – examples are Canterbury, Cirencester and Colchester, as well as the lost town of Silchester. In Britain, the career of COGIDUBNUS, whose main residence may have been the magnificent palace recently excavated at Fishbourne (Sussex), may well provide an illustration of a native client-king who flourished under Roman rule and adopted Roman ways.

While the popular image of Boudicca owes a great deal to Victorian embellishment, the dramatic last year or so of her life remains a significant episode in the history of Roman Britain because it shows the unpopularity and instability of early Roman rule and the vigour of British survival. Her life has left traces not only in the literary sources, but also in the archaeological record, since excavations at London, Colchester and Verulamium have all produced evidence of destruction at what looks to be the appropriate historical period. Within a decade of her death, however, the advance was resumed and Roman armies crushed the native British in Wales and northern England. The governorship of AGRICOLA witnessed a determined attempt to conquer the whole of the British Isles, which was ultimately abandoned.

Graham Webster, Boudicca: The British Revolt against Rome AD 60 (1978)

BOURKE, RICHARD (6th Earl of Mayo) (1822–72), Viceroy of India. Dublin-born and educated, Mayo was appointed Chief Secretary for Ireland in 1852, and in 1869 was made Viceroy of India. Having travelled extensively in Russia as a young man he was better disposed to Russia than many who held that office, pursuing a more friendly policy towards Afghanistan and other peripheral states, while he continued the reforming policy of his predecessor John LAWRENCE. His mission was to 'civilize' Indians, and various lower official positions were opened to them. Ignoring growing internal unrest, Mayo was killed by a Wahabi dissident while on a visit to a penal settlement.

BOWDEN, SIR HAROLD (1880–1960), manufacturer. Bowden's father, Frank, had founded the Raleigh Cycle Co. in Notts. in the late 1880s, transforming a hitherto small engineering concern as the bicycling craze swept society. The bicycle offered mobility at small cost, and was taken up by both men and women and at every social level. Bowden was also a pioneer in worker relations, introducing profit-sharing schemes.

BOWER, WALTER (c. 1385–1449), historian. Abbot of Inchcolm (Fife), he was the author of the *Scotichronicon*, a long narrative amplifying and continuing JOHN OF FORDUN's, and offering an intensely patriotic account of Scottish history from its legendary beginnings until 1437.

BOWLBY, JOHN (1907–90), psychiatrist. A psychologist for the London Child Guidance Clinic (1937–40), between 1946 and 1972 Bowlby was based at the Tavistock Clinic, where he ran the department for children and parents. He is best known for his work on the effects of maternal deprivation on the behaviour and mental health of children. His *Forty-Four Juvenile Thieves* (1946) linked juvenile delinquency to maternal deprivation, and in later works he argued that the mother should give her child prolonged attention and love during the formative stages of its life because that is how the child develops emotional bonds. Several feminists attacked him for provoking maternal guilt but his ideas have informed psychoanalysis and medical practices.

BOWMAN, SIR WILLIAM (1816–92), physician and ophthalmic surgeon. Bowman learned surgical skills in Birmingham, in London and at several European universities. He qualified as a surgeon in 1839 and spent most of his distinguished career developing ophthalmic surgery at King's College Hospital, London. He was one of the first British surgeons to use the ophthalmoscope and to treat glaucomas with the iridectomy operation. In the 1840s he published major research on the anatomy of the eye and the kidney (notably a membranous sac now known as 'Bowman's capsule').

BOWYER, ROBERT (c. 1560–1621), parliamentarian. Son of the Keeper of Records in the Tower of London, he studied at Oxford and the Middle Temple and entered the service of Thomas SACKVILLE, Lord Buckhurst, who secured him his first parliamentary seat (Steyning) in 1601. He became Clerk of the Parliaments in 1610 and devoted himself to conserving and arranging the archives of Parliament (having also succeeded to his father's office in the Tower). His diary of Parliament during 1606–7 is of great importance.

BOYCE, WILLIAM (1711–79), composer and music historian. A chorister at St Paul's and then an organist at several London churches, as well as writing music for the theatres and pleasure gardens. In 1736 he became composer to the Chapel Royal and studied under PEPUSCH, who encouraged his interest in music history. From 1737 he was conductor to the Three Choirs Festival in Hereford, Worcester and Gloucester. Master of the King's Musick from 1757, he inherited the collection of his predecessor Maurice Greene and from this and his own books and manuscripts researched *Cathedral Music* (three vols, 1760–73). Boyce emphasized the importance of seventeenth-century composers, such as GIBBONS and PURCELL, and established what would become the dominant musical taste of nineteenth-century Anglicanism.

BOYCOTT, CHARLES (1832–97), estate manager. The agent of a large landowner in Co. Mayo, he was the first victim of Charles PARNELL's anti-eviction campaign of 1880. Boycott was subjected to social and commercial ostracism and his crops were only saved by a specially recruited workforce of Orangemen, working under the protection of more than 1,000 troops. On 13 Dec. 1880, the *Daily Mail* coined the word 'boycott' to describe the new weapon of the Irish Land League, and it entered general usage thereafter.

BOYD, ROBERT (1st Baron Boyd) (?–1469), politician. Created Lord Boyd by JAMES II in 1454, he was a regent of Scotland during the minority of JAMES III, gaining control of the kingdom in 1464. He negotiated the marriage of the King with MARGARET OF DENMARK, thereby obtaining Orkney for Scotland. When his son Thomas married the King's sister Mary, the Scottish nobles, jealous of his supremacy, arraigned him and his brother Alexander for treason. Alexander lost his head, while Robert fled to Alnwick (Northumb.), where he died.

BOYD, THOMAS (1st Earl of Arran) (?–*c*. 1473), royal servant. The eldest son of Robert BOYD, he married Mary, sister of JAMES III of Scotland. In 1469 he was sent by his father to bring back MARGARET OF DENMARK as the bride for the young King. When he returned he was told that his father and uncle were on trial for treason. He landed the princess but did not set foot on land himself. He and his wife then sought protection in exile with the Duke of Burgundy, and he is reported to have died at Antwerp.

BOYD-ORR, JOHN (1st Baron Boyd-Orr) (1880–1971), nutritionist. His report *Food, Health and Income* (1936), which revealed dietary deficiencies in up to half of the British population, stimulated widespread debate on the state of the nation's health. His broadly based approach to nutrition, including proteins and vitamins as well as calories, was influential in the planning of rationing during the Second World War. As first Director General of the Food and Agriculture Organization of the United Nations, he was involved in unrealized schemes for a World Food Board to counter global shortages. He was awarded the Nobel Peace Prize in 1949.

BOYLE, SIR EDWARD (Baron Boyle of Handsworth) (1923–81), politician. Elected as MP for Handsworth in 1950, Boyle was always on the liberal wing of the Conservative Party, resigning as Economic Secretary to the Treasury in 1956 in opposition to the Suez adventure. He returned to office under Harold MACMILLAN in 1957 and two years later became Financial Secretary to the Treasury. In 1962 he became Minister of Education, a post which he held until 1964. In 1966 he lost his seat. As one of the leading liberal Conservatives Boyle protested against Enoch POWELL's 'rivers of blood' speech in 1968. Increasingly out of sympathy with modern Conservatism he left politics in 1970 to become Vice-Chancellor of the University of Leeds.

BOYLE, HENRY (1st Earl of Shannon) (1682–1764), Irish politician. A member of the Irish Parliament from 1705, he enjoyed a large landed base as the manager of the Irish estates of his kinsman Richard BOYLE. In the 1729 Parliament he successfully led the resistance to a government Bill seeking supply for 21 years (which would effectively have dispensed with the need for a parliament during that time). WALPOLE dubbed him 'King of the Irish Commons' and in 1733 this status was confirmed when he became Speaker of the House and Chancellor of the Irish Exchequer. As the chief manager or 'undertaker' for the ministry in Ireland, he gained the ability to ensure that Ireland was governed on his terms, but he had

rivals, such as Archbishop George STONE. A major showdown occurred in 1753, between the Irish 'undertakers' and the British ministry, as Boyle and his 'Patriot' allies opposed the government's appropriation of the surplus on the Irish revenue (arguing that it should be at the disposal of Parliament). Stone then succeeded in having him dismissed. When Hartington (*see* CAVENDISH, WILLIAM, 4th Duke of Devonshire) became Lord Lieutenant in 1755 he strove to accommodate Boyle and his party. Boyle's acceptance of a pension and an earldom in 1756 was bitterly attacked by many of his radical supporters, such as Charles LUCAS, as a betrayal of principles.

BOYLE, RICHARD (2nd [1st Boyle] Earl of Cork) (1566–1643), politician. Having arrived in Ireland in 1588 as a Crown official, in 1602 he bought Sir Walter Raleigh's Irish possessions, the foundation of his huge fortune. Despite frequent accusations of embezzlement, his honours grew from a knighthood in 1603 to an earldom in 1620; he also became, in 1631, Lord Treasurer of Ireland. He invested lavishly in the various plantation schemes to bring English and Scots Protestant settlers to Ireland. He was a consistent opponent of Thomas WENTWORTH, undermining his position in Ireland, and he was probably influential in Wentworth's impeachment by the English Parliament in 1641.

BOYLE, RICHARD (3rd Earl of Burlington, 5th [4th Boyle] Earl of Cork) (1695–1753), patron of the arts. He succeeded to the peerage at the age of nine in 1704, and 10 years later became a Privy Councillor. He spent several years of his youth in Italy, and emerged as the foremost English champion of Palladianism (a form of classicism developed by the Italian Renaissance architect Andrea Palladio) – initially particularly associated with the Whigs, partly through his influence. In 1716 he commissioned Colen CAMPBELL to rebuild Burlington House, Piccadilly (now rebuilt as the Royal Academy), and in 1730–6 he built Chiswick House, London, derived from Palladio's Villa Rotonda; he also designed the Assembly Rooms at York and built them at his own expense. He published editions of the works of Inigo JONES and Palladio, and was a patron of William KENT; POPE addressed his moral essay, 'On the Use of Riches' to him and praised his disinterested devotion to the arts.

BOYLE, ROBERT (1627–91), natural philosopher. Son of Richard BOYLE, Earl of Cork, he travelled on the continent with a tutor, then went to Oxford in 1654, where he became a leading member of the 'Invisible College' which preceded the Royal Society, and played a leading part in rethinking the objects and procedures of scientific study. With his assistant, Robert HOOKE, he devised an improved air pump and established experimentally the relationship between the pressure and volume of gases: Boyle's Law gives abstract expression to his findings. Gases formed the subject of several of his published books; he also wrote treatises on alchemy, to which he applied experimental methods. A pious Christian, he endowed by will the Boyle Lectures for the defence of Christianity against atheists, Jews and Muslims, and used his position as a director of the East India Company to encourage missionary activity in the East.

BOYLE, ROGER (1st Baron Broghill, 1st Earl of Orrery) (1621–79), politician. Brilliant and devious younger son of Richard BOYLE, Earl of Cork, he served first in the Irish Royalist army during the war in Ireland against the Confederate forces, then, in 1644, in the Parliament's army. Despite plotting for CHARLES II in 1649 he became a loyal ally of Oliver CROMWELL, serving in Ireland and Scotland, gaining a peerage from him and urging him to become King. He backed Richard CROMWELL until support for Charles II's restoration became a realistic option; an earldom followed, with the presidency of Munster from 1660 to 1672, and he survived an attempt at impeachment in 1669. He was a minor playwright.

BRABOURNE, THEOPHILUS (1590–*c*. 1661), writer. A Norfolk clergyman, he was imprisoned in 1631 after writing two pamphlets maintaining that Saturday, not Sunday, should be the Lord's Day for Christians; the controversy contributed to CHARLES I reissuing JAMES I's *Book of Sports* about lawful Sunday recreation in 1633. Brabourne was again advocating his sabbatarian views in the 1650s but, after CHARLES II's restoration, concentrated on literary attacks on the Quakers.

BRACKEN, BRENDAN (1st Viscount Bracken) (1901–58), politician. The career of Bracken, who was described as Winston CHURCHILL's 'faithful chela', rose and fell with his mentor. With a great mop of uncontrollable red hair and thick 'gig-lamp' spectacles, Bracken was a striking figure; to some he seemed little more than a charlatan, whose presence in Churchill's entourage confirmed the latter's poor judgement of character. Bracken deliberately made a mystery of his origins, doing nothing to discourage the rumour that he was Churchill's illegitimate son; not unnaturally this failed to endear him to Mrs Churchill. In fact he came of Irish stock, had spent time in Australia, and had lied about his age in order to attend Sedburgh public school in order to provide himself with some sort of educational pedigree. As a financial jour-

nalist, his love of fantasy and ability to convince others of his abilities stood him in good stead. At the age of 29 he was elected MP for Paddington North and attached himself to Churchill's fading star. Throughout Churchill's wilderness years Bracken could be counted upon, providing not just political but also financial and emotional help. His finest hour came in 1941 when Churchill made him Minister of Information, a post which had already finished off Sir John REITH and Duff COOPER. But an extrovert fantasist was just what the job of 'Minister of Propaganda' required, and Bracken's journalistic background made him a successful choice. Churchill made him First Lord of the Admiralty in 1945 and when he lost his seat that year helped him find one in Bournemouth. But whether the ill health which would eventually kill him was already taking its toll, or whether he had simply tired of the political life, he played little part in opposition politics up to 1951 and refused office when Churchill returned to power in that year. Founder of the *Financial Times*, Bracken spent his final years in business. He ordered all his papers to be destroyed after his death, an action which ensured that an air of mystery would continue to surround him.

BRACKLEY, 1ST VISCOUNT *see* EGERTON, THOMAS

BRACTON, HENRY (?–1268), churchman and judge. He was for many years considered to be the author of a comprehensive treatise on English common law, *On the Laws and Customs of England*; it is commonly and conveniently still called 'Bracton' even though he probably only made some additions to a work written by a judge or judge's clerk from the previous generation.

BRADDOCK, ELIZABETH (BESSIE) (née Bamber) (1899–1970), politician. Born, brought up in and forever associated with Liverpool, she came from a family of political radicals: her socialist mother Mary was acclaimed by Sylvia PANKHURST as 'the finest fighting platform speaker in the country'. Bessie worked for the Co-operative Movement and joined the Independent Labour Party. In 1922 she married Jack Braddock, and the couple dominated Merseyside politics, in a city with the highest rates of poverty and infant mortality in Britain, for more than three decades. In 1945 Bessie Braddock was elected MP for Liverpool Exchange, a seat which she held for Labour until 1970. But Liverpool was her manor. Jack was leader of the City Council, and Bessie was a council member (1930–61) and served as an alderman (1955–61), as well as being a vociferous MP at Westminster. 'Battling Bessie Braddock' remained on the back benches, fighting for better housing and educational opportunities for the poor of Merseyside, and beyond, abrasive not only to her political opponents but also increasingly to the left wing of her own party.

BRADDON, MARY (1835–1915), novelist. Braddon started acting and writing when young in order to help the family finances. Her most famous novel, *Lady Audley's Secret* (1862), was first published as a serial in the *Sixpenny Magazine,* a tale of murder, arson and bigamy which was one of the first 'sensation novels' of the 1860s. It sold nearly a million copies and made its author and publisher rich. Braddon's own life had a sensational quality too: she was unable to marry her Irish lover, John Maxwell, the publisher of the *Sixpenny Magazine*, to whom she bore a child, as he was already married to a wife incarcerated in a lunatic asylum. They finally married in 1874 and had six further children. Braddon, acclaimed as 'Queen of the Circulating Libraries' was one of the best-selling of all Victorian women novelists.

BRADFORD, JOHN (*c.* 1510–55), martyr. He became a leading Protestant preacher after a 1548 sermon of Hugh LATIMER had caused him to feel remorse for his part in military embezzlement. After playing a prominent role in establishing early Protestantism in his native south Lancs., he was imprisoned in 1553 (despite having saved the Catholic Gilbert Bourne from lynching after Bourne's sermon at Paul's Cross in London) and he was burned at the stake on 1 July 1555. During imprisonment he wrote much, and was energetic in maintaining Protestant morale; he championed the doctrine of predestination against the radical group known as Freewillers (several of whose leaders were imprisoned with him) who wanted to assert humanity's role in its own salvation.

BRADFORD, WILLIAM (1590–1657), colonist. Born in Yorks., Bradford joined the exiled separatist congregation at Amsterdam in 1607, and was one of the group which sailed in the *Mayflower* and came to settle at Plymouth, New England, in 1620; he succeeded John CARVER as Governor of Plymouth (later part of the colony of Massachusetts) in 1621. His historical writings are a major source for knowledge of the New England settlement.

BRADLAUGH, CHARLES (1833–91), politician. A charismatic figure, he edited the *National Reformer* in which radical, republican and secularist ideas were voiced. In 1880 he was elected MP for Northampton; a professed atheist, he claimed the right to affirm his allegiance instead of taking the oath in the House of Commons, a stand which led to his being thrice re-elected before he was finally allowed to take his seat, in

1886. He was also a propagandist for birth control, for advocacy of which he and his close friend Annie BESANT were prosecuted in 1877.

BRADLEY, HERBERT (1846–1924), philosopher. A Fellow of Merton College, Oxford, from 1870, he was influenced by Kant and Hegel and became the most important British Idealist philosopher of the period. His chief works were *Ethical Studies* (1876), *Principles of Logic* (1883) and *Appearances and Reality* (1883). His writings drew attention in England to Hegelianism and continental thought in general.

BRADSHAW, GEORGE (1801–53), printer. Salford-born, apprenticed to an engraver, Bradshaw set up his own printing and engraving business in Manchester in the 1820s. In addition to maps, he published the first railway timetable in 1839, *Bradshaw's Railway Companion*. By the time he died, from cholera, his guides had become a regular publication.

BRADSHAW, JOHN (1602–59), lawyer. A Ches. barrister, he presided over the High Court of Justice which condemned CHARLES I to death in Jan. 1649. He was President of the Council of State (the executive body of the Commonwealth regime) from 1649 to 1652, but opposed Oliver CROMWELL's establishment of the Protectorate as a betrayal of the republic; he returned to political life only after the collapse of Richard CROMWELL's regime in 1659, but died soon after. Buried in Westminster Abbey, his body was dug up and 'executed' for treason in 1660 after the restoration of CHARLES II.

BRADWARDINE, THOMAS (*c.* 1290–1349), Archbishop of Canterbury (1349). A Fellow of Merton College, Oxford, an eminent mathematician and theologian, he was one of the most learned men ever to be Archbishop of Canterbury, although this was a reward for his diplomatic services to the King. A royal chaplain, he accompanied EDWARD III to Flanders in 1338, where he was one of the commissioners who negotiated with Philip of France after the Battle of Crécy in 1346. He was elected Archbishop while in France in 1348, but fell to the Black Death only days after his return to England.

BRADY, IAN (1938–), murderer *see* HINDLEY, MYRA

BRAGG, SIR WILLIAM HENRY (1862–1942), physicist. Born in Cumberland, Bragg studied mathematics at Cambridge and subsequently held professorships at Adelaide (1886–1908), Leeds (1909–15) and London (1915–23). In 1904

he began his lifelong research into the nature of X-, beta- and gamma-rays. In 1912 he and his son William Lawrence BRAGG exploited the pioneering X-ray diffraction work of Max von Laue and others, and began developing powerful practical and theoretical tools for using X-ray diffraction in the determination of the atomic structures of simple crystals. In 1913 he invented the first X-ray spectrometer and used it to study the atomic structure of various substances. He shared the 1915 Nobel Prize for Physics with his son.

BRAGG, SIR WILLIAM LAWRENCE (1890–1971), physicist. Son of William Henry BRAGG, he developed an important mathematical law of X-ray diffraction and, with his father, pioneered the further use of X-ray diffraction. As Professor of Physics at Manchester (1919–38) he developed powerful quantitative techniques of X-ray analysis. As Cavendish Professor of Experimental Physics at Cambridge (1938–54) he promoted crystallographic studies of proteins, radio astronomy and the physics of metals. As Fullerian Professor at the Royal Institution, London (1954–66), he led a research group on the X-ray analysis of proteins.

BRAILSFORD, H(ENRY) N(OEL) (1873–1958), writer. His father was a Yorks. Methodist minister. Brailsford's novel *The Broom of the War-God* (1898), based on his experiences fighting with the Greeks against the Ottoman empire, caught the attention of C. P. SCOTT, editor of the *Manchester Guardian*, who employed him. Brailsford led a relief mission to Macedonia in 1903 and published his authoritative analysis of the Balkan situation in 1906. Leaving the Liberal Party in 1907 partly over the Boer War, he joined the Independent Labour Party (ILP) but continued to write in Liberal periodicals, railing against British imperialism: *The War of Steel and Gold* (1914) denounced the link between capitalism and arms. During the First World War he was in the forefront of calls for international government, publishing *A League of Nations* (1917). After the war he travelled through war-torn Europe reporting on the devastation, and in 1920 visited the Soviet Union, whose socialist economic planning impressed him, but not its repressive politics. Appointed editor of the ILP weekly *New Leader* (1922), he transformed it into an opinion-forming periodical until he was removed, after which he travelled extensively and continued to write campaigning articles. *The Levellers and the English Revolution* was published posthumously (1961).

BRAINE, JOHN (1922–86), novelist. Educated at St Bede's grammar school, Bradford, Braine was for many years a librarian in Yorks. and Northumb. His early novels, *Room at the Top* (1957) and *Life at the Top* (1962), were immediate successes. They portrayed ruthlessness and opportunism, their central character, Joe Lampton, being singled out by critics as one of the provincial 'angry young men' of the 1950s.

BRAMAH, JOSEPH (1748–1814), inventor. The son of a farmer, he was a cabinetmaker by trade but quickly distinguished himself by a gift for invention, beginning with an improved water-closet. Other inventions included a beer machine for use in public houses, a safety lock, a hydraulic press (patented 1795, for moulding large pieces of iron and steel and thus enabling the manufacture of giant iron ships and bridges) and a press for printing bank notes. The application of the screw propeller was the most notable of his many ingenious proposals. His work pointed the way towards the standardization of machine parts and screw threads.

BRAMHALL, JOHN (1594–1663), churchman. Born in Yorks., he studied at Cambridge, and in 1633 accompanied Lord Deputy Thomas WENTWORTH to Ireland as his chaplain. Made Bishop of Derry in 1634, he was vigorous in harnessing the Irish Church to the policies of Wentworth and William LAUD and reorganizing Church finance. In 1642 he left Ireland for England, and was in continental exile (except for a brief return to Ireland in 1648) until CHARLES II's restoration, when in 1661 he was made Archbishop of Armagh. He wrote extensively defending a High Church view of Episcopacy, and from 1655 made successive attacks on Thomas HOBBES's materialist philosophy. Passionately seeking the reunion of Christian Churches, his writings had a lasting effect in shaping a Catholic Anglican theology.

BRAND, JOHN (1744–1806), antiquarian. Brought up in Newcastle by a cordwainer uncle to whom he was apprenticed, his former master at the Newcastle Royal grammar school helped him to go to Oxford, after which he was ordained. He spent most of his clerical career in Newcastle where in 1777 he published *Observations on Popular Antiquities*. This revised and expanded a work by an earlier Tyneside antiquarian, Henry Bourne, and catalogued and commented upon the customs of ordinary people in northern England. Brand's priority was to identify harmful Romish superstitions that corrupted the lower class, but it established a reference point for future students of folklore, as well as alerting readers to the detrimental effect of commercial society on folk customs. Brand was appointed resident Secretary of the Society of Antiquaries of London (1784), and was working on a revised edition of *Observations* at the time of his death.

BRANDON, CHARLES (4th [1st Brandon] Duke of Suffolk) (*c.* 1484–1545), courtier and soldier. Starting as a minor courtier, Brandon built his career on his jousting prowess, which won him HENRY VIII's friendship, military advancement and a dukedom on the third of his four marriages, to Mary Tudor, sister of the King. In 1515 Mary had been provided with a suitable dynastic marriage to Louis XII of France, but Louis died within the year and, when Suffolk was sent to France with official greetings for the new King FRANCIS, he secretly married his old love. Henry's subsequent fury was bought off at great expense, and Suffolk survived thereafter by devoted servility, although in the early 1530s he suffered temporary eclipse for his coolness towards ANNE BOLEYN. After Mary's death in 1533, Suffolk married his young ward Catherine WILLOUGHBY, who influenced him towards religious reformism, but ideas were never his strong suit. In 1538, at Henry's and CROMWELL's bidding, he uprooted himself and his power-base from his native East Anglia to become a magnate in Lincs., in an attempt to control the area after its religious rising of 1536. His lifetime of undistinguished but costly military campaigns was crowned with the capture of Boulogne in 1544.

BRANSON, SIR RICHARD (1950–), entrepreneur. A flair for publicity, casual dress and marriage of worthy causes with profit-seeking within his 'Virgin' retail and communications companies made Branson one of the quintessential new business figures of the 1980s and 1990s. His first commercial successes came at the age of 18 when, having left Stowe (Bucks.) public school with three O levels, he set up *Student* magazine, a contraceptive advice bureau and the first Virgin enterprise, a mail order record business. From that followed in 1971 the first of a chain of Virgin record shops; in 1973 the Virgin record label was started. The fewer frills Virgin Atlantic airline went into business in 1984; the Virgin music interests were sold to Thorn EMI in 1992, partly to finance expansion of the airline business (which was then to be the victim of unprofessional competitive activity from British Airways). By that time Branson was Britain's youngest billionaire. In 1996 he became one of the post-privatization railway entrepreneurs.

BRAY, SIR REYNOLD (?–1503), administrator. A Worcs. gentleman, Bray entered HENRY VII's service through office in Lady Margaret BEAUFORT's household; a trusted companion of Henry's exile, he was swiftly appointed a Councillor and Chancellor of the Duchy of Lancaster in 1485. From 1492 he masterminded the development of the Chamber as the centre of royal finance and administration, enabling Henry to keep close personal control of his revenues using this department of the Royal Household. By 1500 he had developed the Council Learned in the Law, a sub-committee of the King's Council, as an agency for enforcing royal demands. Claims that he designed the Henry VII Chapel at Westminster Abbey have no foundation.

BRAY, THOMAS (1656–1730), founder of the SPCK and SPG. A Warws. clergyman, he attracted notice through his popular religious writings. In 1695 he was given the task of organizing Maryland into parishes. As only impoverished clergy would emigrate, Bray successfully lobbied the bishops for the funds to buy libraries for the new parishes; he extended the scheme into England and Wales. In 1698, with the help of sympathizers including Simon PATRICK, he set up the Society for the Promotion of Christian Knowledge in order to carry out and extend these tasks. Bray stayed in Maryland for only a few months in 1699–1700 and returned to England to win a royal charter (1701) for the Society for the Propagation of the Gospel, intended to promote Anglicanism in the colonies. Bray also supported the education of slaves and in 1722 founded a society to continue that work.

BREAUTÉ, FALKES DE (?–1226), soldier. His loyal service to the Crown, notably in the civil war at the end of JOHN's reign, enabled de Breauté to rise from humble origins as the illegitimate son of a Norman knight to become one of the most powerful men in England, *de facto* ruler of the Midlands. He acquired an aristocratic wife, but his rivals always regarded him as an upstart, and in 1224 they pushed him to the point of revolt against the government of Hubert de BURGH. His career ended with the siege of Bedford; his wife divorced him and he died in exile.

BRECON, LORD OF *see* BRIOUZE, WILLIAM DE

BREMBRE, SIR NICHOLAS (?–1388), politician. Lord Mayor of London four times between 1377 and 1384, he was a leading supporter of RICHARD II and an opponent of JOHN OF NORTHAMPTON and the party of JOHN OF GAUNT. He was a collector of customs for the port of London, with Geoffrey CHAUCER as his controller,1379–86. He ensured being re-elected as Lord Mayor the fourth time by filling Guildhall with armed men. He effected the ruin of John of Northampton for treason, but was himself charged with treason and with beheading 22 Newgate prisoners without trial, and was executed at Tyburn.

BRENTFORD, 1ST VISCOUNT *see* HICKS, WILLIAM JOYNSON

BRESSAL (?–801), Abbot of Iona. Although Bressal died in his 31st year as Abbot, little is known of his rule over the famous early-medieval Abbey of Iona. Relations between the Abbots of Iona and the Clann Cholmáin, the ruling dynasty of the southern Uí Néill, forged during the 740s and 750s, were maintained during Bressal's abbacy, for in 778 the 'Law of COLUM CILLE' was enforced in Ireland by Bressal and Donnchad Midi, King of Tara. The law's contents are unknown, but must surely have originated in Iona, bringing prestige both to the Uí Néill kings and to the abbey.

BRETT, REGINALD (2nd Viscount Esher) (1852–1930), military reformer. Educated at Eton and Cambridge, he served (1878–85) as private secretary to the Marquess of Hartington (*see* CAVENDISH, SPENCER), the last three years at the War Office. Immensely wealthy and well connected, personal friend of both Queen VICTORIA and EDWARD VII, Esher dabbled in public life as the mood took him, organizing the Diamond Jubilee (1897) and Victoria's funeral (1901) with exemplary efficiency. In 1902 Esher served on the commission investigating the Boer War, the first in a long association with military committees. He collaborated with Lord ROBERTS in establishing a modern General Staff (1906), helped Richard HALDANE secure acceptance for the Territorial Army (1908) and during the First World War played the role of *éminence grise* in negotiations between the British and French.

BREWSTER, SIR DAVID (1781–1868), physicist. Educated privately and at Edinburgh University, he trained as a Presbyterian minister but abandoned a clerical career for journalism and natural philosophy. He was the editor of the *Edinburgh Magazine* (founded 1802) and *Edinburgh Philosophical Journal* (founded 1819) and in the 1810s began publishing his research on optics, notably the polarization of light. He is celebrated for showing that, when light strikes a glass surface, the polarization of reflected light is at a maximum when the tangent of the angle of the incident light (the 'Brewster angle') is equal to the refractive index of the reflecting medium. His optical research also includes optical mineralogy and the invention of the kaleidoscope in 1816. Through his books and journalism he became a leading popularizer of science. He was a founder of the British Association for the Advancement of Science (1831) and in 1837 was appointed Principal of St Andrews University.

BRIAN BORUMA (BORU) (?–1014), King of Munster (976–1014) and Irish High-King. A member of the powerful Dál Cais family, he emerged after the murder of his brother MATHGA-MAIN from the dynastic politics of Munster during the 960s to dominate that kingdom. Over the next 30 years he gradually asserted his control over Dublin and the other coastal Viking settlements and over other Irish kings. Notable landmarks in his rise to power include: the Battle of Belach Lechta (978), which established his power in Munster; the submission of Leinster in 983; the capture of Dublin in 999; and the submission of the Uí Néill High-King MAEL SECHNAILL II MAC DOMNAILL in 1002. Brian's successes always rested on a fragile military basis, and in 1014 he was killed fighting against an alliance of Vikings and Irish at the Battle of Clontarf (Co. Dublin). His achievements were somewhat misleadingly elevated to heroic status by the twelfth-century biography, *Wars of the Gaedhil against the Gaill*.

BRIDEI, SON OF BELI, King of the Picts (*c.* 672–93). Controversy surrounds the manner by which Bridei acquired kingship over the southern Picts. The latest theory suggests that his kingship represented a resurgence of the lordship of the Strathclyde Britons over the southern Picts after the death of the previous overlord, OSWY of Northumbria, in 670, as Bridei appears to have been a younger brother of YWAIN, SON OF BELI, King of Strathclyde. Whatever the case, Bridei's reign is especially important because his victory over ECGFRITH of Northumbria at Nechtanesmere in 685 ensured that Northumbrian power was henceforth confined to south of the Forth.

BRIDEI, SON OF DERILE, King of the Picts (?–706). Perhaps King in 695, he was certainly King by 697, as he ratified ADOMNÁN's *Lex Innocentium*, promulgated in that year. BEDE relates the defeat and death of Berctred, *dux* of the Northumbrians, at the hands of the Picts in 698, which would have occurred during Bridei's reign; the comparative silence, however, of the sources concerning Bridei suggests his reign was one of stability and was relatively peaceful.

BRIDEI, SON OF MAILCON, King of the Picts (?–584). An undoubtedly powerful and influential King, the Pictish king-lists give Bridei a reign of 30 years, indicating his accession in *c.* 554. In 559 he defeated the Scots of Dál Riata and it may have been the threat to Dál Riata that prompted COLUM CILLE to visit Bridei's court soon after his arrival from Ireland. ADOMNÁN's *Vita Columbae* is an important source of information for Bridei, the only King of the northern Picts about whom such information survives. His stronghold was located by the River Ness and Adomnán relates that he had hostages from the King of Orkney, implying a system of sub-kings under his control and also a fleet sufficient to control the Northern Isles. Latterly his reign may have been preoccupied with the southern Picts, as his death is recorded in battle in Circinn, the region just north of the Tay.

BRIDEI, SON OF UURGUST, King of the Picts (?–763). Given a reign of two years in the *Chronicle of the Kings of the Picts*, nothing is recorded in the sources concerning Bridei other than a simple obituary in the *Irish Annals* in 763. He was the brother and successor of the powerful OENGUS, SON OF FERGUS.

BRIDGEMAN, CHARLES (?–1738), landscape gardener. He worked under WILLIAM III's gardener Henry Wise on the gardens of Blenheim (*see* CHURCHILL, JOHN) from 1709, and was also involved with the development of Stowe (Bucks.) for Richard TEMPLE from 1711. In 1728 he was made master gardener to GEORGE II. He enclosed Kensington Gardens at the request of the King, and also developed the gardens at Richmond, complementing KENT's buildings. His importance lies in the role he played in moving from the formal French tradition to the natural landscape garden, echoed on the continent in the *jardin anglais*.

BRIDGEMAN, SIR ORLANDO (*c.* 1606–74), statesman and lawyer. A clergyman's son, he built up a great reputation for his legal expertise during the reign of CHARLES I. A keen Royalist, he was knighted in 1643, but after the King's death he retired into private practice, chiefly conveyancing. Emerging from retirement at the Restoration in 1660, he presided over the trial of the regicides in 1660 and was then made Lord Chief Justice of the Common Pleas. After Clarendon's fall (*see* HYDE, EDWARD) in 1667 he was appointed Lord Keeper and CHARLES II's chief spokesman in the Lords but he obstructed the passage of grants which the King wished to make to his mistresses, attacked the commission for martial law and opposed the 'stop of the Exchequer' (which allowed Charles II to default on Crown debts), leading to his dismissal in 1672.

BRIDGET (BRIGID OR BRIDE), ST (*c.* 450–523). Although tradition has it that she was baptized by St PATRICK, the patron saint of Ireland, and became Abbess of Kildare, she is also the embodiment of the pre-Christian Celtic fertility goddess, Brigid. Many miracles and stories associated with her are probably survivals of pre-Christian myth.

BRIDGEWATER, 3RD DUKE OF *see* EGERTON, FRANCIS

BRIGGS, HENRY (1556–1630), mathematician. A Cambridge don who became first Professor of Geometry at Gresham College (1596–1620); in 1619 he became Sir Henry SAVILE's Professor of Astronomy. He made modifications to John NAPIER's system of logarithms, consulting with Napier in Edinburgh and publishing (among much else) logarithmic tables in 1624 and 1633. He also published on American exploration and left important mathematical works in manuscript.

BRIGHT, JACOB (1821–99), politician. Like his brother John BRIGHT, he was educated as a Quaker and worked for the mill-owning family firm in Rochdale. While active in the Anti-Corn Law League in the 1840s, he had links to local Chartist groups in Rochdale and supported Joseph Sturge's Complete Suffrage Union, which attempted to link the two movements. Liberal MP for Manchester (1867–74 and 1876–85) and for Manchester South (1886–95), he was a leading campaigner for women's suffrage alongside his wife Ursula (née Mellor).

BRIGHT, JOHN *see* essay on page 107

BRINDLEY, JAMES (1716–72), engineer. Son of a cottar (a very small farmer) he was apprenticed to a millwright. Living in Staffs., for most of his career he repaired and designed machinery, including equipment for the WEDGWOOD potteries. He is most famous as the first large-scale canal builder, beginning in 1759 when he was commissioned to build a canal from Manchester to coalmines at Worsley owned by the Duke of Bridgwater (*see* EGERTON, FRANCIS). Brindley's methods of puddling clay to reinforce the canal banks and his use of subterranean channels and aqueducts, including the 12-metre high Barton aqueduct over the River Irwell, established him as pre-eminent in his field, despite his lack of education. Brindley continued to work for Bridgwater on projects including the Bridgwater canal from Manchester to Liverpool and the Trent and Mersey canal, supervising the construction of nearly 600 kilometres of waterway.

BRIOUZE, MATILDA DE (?–1211), noblewoman. When King JOHN doubted the loyalty of her husband William de BRIOUZE, she refused to give her sons as hostages to a man who had, she said, murdered his nephew. John pursued her relentlessly, first to Ireland, then to Galloway, where she was captured in 1210. She and her eldest son were imprisoned, probably in Windsor Castle, and were never seen again. According to common report they were starved to death.

BRIOUZE, WILLIAM DE (Lord of Brecon) (?–1211), nobleman. He was one of King JOHN's

continued on page 108

BRIGHT, JOHN (1811–89)
Politician

He was born in Rochdale (Lancs.), in the heartland of the rapidly expanding cotton manufacturing trade. His father was a textile manufacturer and a Quaker: economics and religion were to be central to Bright's formation as a leading radical and spokesman for the 'industrial interest' in mid nineteenth-century Britain. His earliest political concerns, advocating temperance in 1830 and taking part in the campaign against church rates in 1834, were very typical of the concerns of the Nonconformist Lancashire middle classes. Even more so, his involvement in the Anti-Corn Law League (1838–46), the greatest middle-class campaign of its day, saw Bright emerge as a leading figure of radicalism, alongside Richard COBDEN. Their variety of liberal radicalism was distinguished by a strong belief in Free Trade, not only as an economic principle but as a source of moral virtue – men should be free to pursue their interests unhindered by State 'restraint' – and also as the foundation of a world order in which peace would reign. At the same time, the movement against the Corn Laws, which was successful to the extent that the Corn Laws were repealed in 1846 (though only partly through the work of the Anti-Corn Law League), was a major public, 'out-of-doors' campaign, which provided for Bright the platform on which he exercised his gifts as a public speaker. Bright's radicalism, however, left him a more marginal figure than might have been expected: radicalism was, in many ways, a fragmented phenomenon after 1846 and Bright's pacifism meant that he was not only marginal to the liberalism of Palmerston (see TEMPLE, HENRY), the dominant political figure of the 1850s, but also at odds with some of his fellow radicals and the middle-class social base which sustained radicalism. His opposition to the Crimean War (1853–6) on pacifist and anti-aristocratic grounds cost him in 1857 the support of the commercial interests of Manchester and his seat as an MP, which he had held since 1847. (He had previously been elected MP for Durham in 1843.) He was also opposed by many of the working-class non-electors of Lancs. for his history of opposition to factory legislation restricting the working hours of women, young people and children in textiles.

Within a year of his defeat at Manchester, Bright's political standing and effectiveness were to change decisively. Elected for Birmingham in 1857, he announced his conversion to parliamentary reform in the sense of some extension of the franchise to hitherto unrepresented and mainly working-class voters. Radicals like Bright had, for some years, advocated parliamentary reform but essentially for a redistribution of seats to give greater weight to middle-class voters in boroughs. Bright's declaration that he was in favour of a (modest) enlargement of the franchise helped to make possible a rapprochement with an emerging popular working-class movement for the vote. His intervention in the reform question became of major importance for the creation of a popular movement, partly because he displayed a moral passion and style which appeared to speak both to and for his audience. At the same time, he could rhetorically evoke 'the nation' as being grounded in the morally pure, disinterested populace. His brilliance in this regard was also to link parliamentary reform to the economic interests of the people: those who were without votes were also, he argued, those who bore excessive tax burdens on articles of consumption, particularly tobacco and paper. Reform aristocratic government and economic benefits would follow. Bright was never a democrat: he wished to restrict the vote to male household heads only and was strongly opposed to including the 'residuum' of the poor, a term which, in its political meanings, he invented. But he was unquestionably popular and he was a major figure in the debates on reform, within and without Parliament, until the Reform Act of 1867. This also made him a major presence within the Liberal Party as it emerged as the great popular constellation of Gladstonian Liberalism. GLADSTONE could not afford to ignore Bright and made him President of the Board of Trade in 1868, a post which he held until 1870. Gladstone had offered him the secretaryship of state for India in 1868 but Bright refused it because of the military responsibilities involved. Subsequently he was Chancellor of the Duchy of Lancaster 1873–4 and again 1880–2. Bright's Nonconformist conscience put him at odds with Gladstone in the 1880s: he resigned his post in 1882 in protest against the naval bombardment of Alexandria. Bright was not, fundamentally, an anti-imperialist: generally opposed to colonies, like most Liberals of his era, he nonetheless had advocated the retention of India and opposed Gladstone's moves to Home Rule for Ireland in 1885–6. Bright was one of the dominant political figures of his era and for many represented, then and since, the force of Victorian Nonconformity in politics.

Keith Robbins, John Bright (1979)

favourites in the early part of his reign. The King suddenly turned against him in 1208, probably because he knew too much about the fate of ARTHUR OF BRITTANY, but officially for non-payment of debt 'in accordance with the law of the Exchequer'. When his estates in Wales were harried he and his family fled to their lands in Ireland. In 1210 his wife Matilda de BRIOUZE was captured but he managed to escape to France where he died. Archbishop Stephen LANGTON, another victim of John's tyranny, conducted his funeral.

BRISTOL, EARL OF, 1ST see DIGBY, JOHN; **2ND** see DIGBY, GEORGE; **4TH** see HERVEY, FREDERICK

BRITTAIN, VERA (1893–1970), writer and lecturer. Educated at Somerville College, Oxford, Brittain served as a VAD nurse during the First World War. Her only brother and her (unofficial) fiancé were both killed in action on the Western Front, and her poignant autobiographical account of the 'lost generation' of the Great War, *Testament of Youth* (1933), brought her acclaim for having written 'the real war book of the women of England'. Thereafter Brittain dedicated her life to peace, becoming a sponsor of the Peace Pledge Union in 1937, and wrote numerous pamphlets, one of which was a denunciation of saturation bombing, *Seeds of Chaos* (1944); she chaired the board of *Peace News* (1958–64) and actively supported non-violent direct action for the Campaign for Nuclear Disarmament (CND), travelling all over the world to lecture on pacifism and feminism. Her sequel to *Testament of Youth, Testament of Experience* (1957), continues the story of her life from 1925 to 1950 and is an auto-biography of pacifism; *Testament of Friendship* (1940) tells of her relationship with the writer Winifred HOLTBY. In 1925 Brittain married the political philosopher George Caitlin: her daughter is the politician Shirley WILLIAMS.

BRITTEN, BENJAMIN (Baron Britten of Aldeburgh) (1913–76), composer, pianist and conductor. A leading figure in the revival of British music's reputation in the twentieth century, he was born at Lowestoft (Suffolk), and studied at the Royal College of Music (1930–3). A large part of his reputation rests on his operas and song cycles, which belong to the international main-stream of modern music while building on English choral and folk traditions. His opera *Peter Grimes* (1945) established Britten as the first native operatic composer of stature since PURCELL. His *War Requiem* (1961), commis-sioned for the opening of Coventry Cathedral, is widely performed. In 1948 he co-founded (with his partner the tenor Peter Pears (1910–86)) the Aldeburgh Festival (Suffolk), where many of his works were premièred.

BROAD, SIR CHARLES (1882–1976), soldier. Son of an army officer, he was educated at Cambridge, served in the Boer War as a private, and was commissioned in the Royal Artillery in 1905. During the First World War, Broad proved a gifted gunner, was appointed to the Distinguished Service Order (DSO) in 1917, but in 1923 trans-ferred to the Royal Tank Corps (RTC). Unlike Giffard MARTEL, John FULLER and others, Broad's *Mechanized and Armoured Formations* (1929) recognized the importance of other arms, an approach which marked his command of the experimental 1st brigade RTC in 1931. Starved of funds during the Depression, Broad quarrelled bitterly with the Chief of the Imperial General Staff, Lord Gort (*see* VEREKER, JOHN), which led to his being sidelined into a series of dead-end jobs until his retirement in 1942.

BROCKWAY, FENNER (1888–1988), politician. The son of a long line of missionaries to India, Brockway grew up with a determination to see the end of the British Empire: his long life and tireless campaigning meant that he almost did so. He joined the Independent Labour Party (ILP) in 1907 and at 24 was editor of the ILP paper *Labour Leader*. A founder member of the No-Conscription Fellowship in 1914, he was jailed for over two years in terrible conditions as a conscien-tious objector, which he wrote about in *English Prisons Today* (1922). In 1926 he replaced H. N. BRAILSFORD as editor of the renamed ILP paper *New Leader* and supported the ILP break with the Labour Party in 1932 though he had been Labour MP for Leyton (1929–31). He organized support for GANDHI in Britain and was involved in anti-Fascist activity. Having finally broken with the ILP, he came back to the Commons as Labour MP for Eton and Slough in 1950, and he founded the Movement for Colonial Freedom with Tony BENN (1954), protested against the war in Vietnam and was in the forefront of the Campaign for Nuclear Disarmament (CND), attending demonstrations until the very end of his long life.

BRODIE, SIR BENJAMIN (1783–1862), physi-ologist and surgeon. Born in Wilts., Brodie was educated at Oxford and served an apprenticeship at St George's Hospital, London, where he became surgeon in 1822. In the 1810s he published researches on the influence of the brain on animal heat, and he made important studies of diseases of the joints and pioneered the subcuta-neous operation. One of the most distinguished medical figures of the nineteenth century, he was surgeon to GEORGE IV, serjeant-surgeon to

WILLIAM IV and Queen VICTORIA and President of the Royal College of Surgeons in 1844.

BROGHILL, 1ST BARON see BOYLE, ROGER

BROMLEY, WILLIAM (1664–1732), politician. From an old Midlands family, he went after Oxford on a Grand Tour, of which he published an account. An MP from 1690, representing Oxford University from 1701 until his death, he gained a reputation as an effective parliamentarian. He was an ardent High Churchman and prominent in the attempt to secure a Bill against occasional conformity (1702–4): that is, to stop Dissenters qualifying themselves for public office by taking Anglican communion only a minimal number of times for that purpose. In 1705 he was a candidate for Speaker, but was discredited by the selective highlighting of passages in his account of his Grand Tour, in which, for instance, he described kissing the Pope's slipper. In 1710, in the wake of the SACHEVERELL affair, he was returned as Speaker without opposition; 1713 he became Secretary of State, but lost office on the death of ANNE.

BRONOWSKI, JACOB (1908–74), mathematician and broadcaster. Bronowski was born in Poland and, after emigrating to England in 1920, studied mathematics at Cambridge. He lectured at Hull University (1934–42) and during the Second World War invented 'operational research' methods for increasing the effectiveness of bombing. He remained in government service until 1963 but established himself as a leading writer on science. He upheld the importance of the imagination in science as well as in poetry, and identified the dangers of regarding science as a value-free, non-imaginative enterprise. His works include *A Poet's Defence* (1939), *The Common Sense of Science* (1951) and *Science and Human Values* (1956). He is best known for his appearances on the radio programme *The Brain's Trust* and as the author and presenter of the television series *The Ascent of Man* (1973).

BRONTË, ANNE (1820–49), novelist. The youngest of the six children of the Rev. Patrick Brontë (*see* BRONTË, CHARLOTTE and EMILY), as a child Anne was educated largely at home at Haworth Parsonage (Yorks.), where with her sisters she obsessively wrote stories about imaginary lands and peoples, in her case Gondal, which she invented with her sister Emily. In 1839 Anne, like her sisters, embarked on a career as a governess: of the three sisters, Anne was the best able to cope with life outside the parsonage, though her unhappiness with the place of a governess was evidenced in her semi-autobiographical first novel *Agnes Grey* (1846), published

under the pseudonym Acton Bell. *The Tenant of Wildfell Hall* (1848) was a more ambitious work and received greater acclaim. Some 20 of Anne's poems were included in *The Poems of Currer, Ellis and Acton Bell* (1846). She died of tuberculosis aged 29.

BRONTË, CHARLOTTE see essay on page 110

BRONTË, EMILY (1818–49), novelist. The most hermetic of an intensely reclusive family (*see* BRONTË, CHARLOTTE), Emily joined with her siblings in obsessively chronicling a make-believe world, drawing on her prodigious reading: she created (with Anne) the Gondal saga which she continued to write for almost the rest of her life. In 1846 a collection of the sisters' poems was published. Emily's poems were singled out for admiration in reviews, and in 1847 *Wuthering Heights* was published (under the name of Ellis Bell). The vivid sexual passion and power of its language and imagery impressed, bewildered and appalled reviewers, and to this day the contrast between the narrow boundaries of Emily's life and the tempestuous, savage passionate sweep of the physical and human landscape of her wild moorlands ensures that this unique classic of English literature remains an endless subject of fascination. Her poetry achieved increasing critical attention in the twentieth century. Refusing all medical treatment, she died of tuberculosis aged 31.

BROOK, PETER (1925–), theatre director. One of the most accomplished and innovative of the generation of theatre directors that revolutionized British theatre from the mid 1950s Brook directed many productions for the Royal Shakespeare Company, including several ground-breaking performances of SHAKESPEARE's plays, most notably *A Midsummer Night's Dream* (1970). From the mid 1960s he worked increasingly abroad and found a particularly receptive audience in France, where he remains one of the very few English artists and intellectuals to have been taken seriously. He became Director of the Paris-based International Centre of Theatre Research and won an international reputation for his productions of world theatre, culminating in *The Mahabharta*, performed in Avignon, Paris and Glasgow in the mid 1980s. His book, *The Empty Space* (1968), remains a seminal text in theatrical studies.

BROOKE, 1ST BARON see GREVILLE, FULKE

BROOKE, SIR ALAN (1st Viscount Alanbrooke) (1883–1963), soldier. Ninth child of Anglo-Irish gentry, he grew up in France speaking French and German. Delicate, introspective, bad at sport, and
continued on page 111

BRONTË, CHARLOTTE (1816–55)
Novelist

Charlotte's father was the Rev. Patrick Brontë, an Irishman; her mother died when she was five. In 1824 the four oldest Brontë children were sent to a school for the 'daughters of poor clergy' near Kirkby Lonsdale (Lancs.). She immortalized the school some 20 years later as Lowood, to which Jane Eyre, the eponymous heroine of Charlotte's novel, is sent. Charlotte and Emily BRONTË were removed from 'that hateful place' after their two older sisters, Maria and Elizabeth, died from tuberculosis, to continue their education at home with their younger sister (*see* BRONTË, ANNE). The children read in their father's library and borrowed books from the Mechanics' Institute in Keighley (Yorks.), and Patrick would discuss current affairs with them.

In 1831 Charlotte was again sent away to school, where she made friends with Ellen Nussey (her letters to Nussey are the most fertile source for Charlotte's life) and taught at the school herself until 1838, when her sense of isolation and alienation brought her close to a breakdown, and she returned home to her father's parsonage at Haworth (Yorks.). The next year she went as a governess to the Sidgwick family near Skipton (Yorks.). Again it was a disaster: 'a private governess has no existence, is not considered as a living and rational being except as connected with the wearisome duties she has to fulfil', she wrote to Emily, and was home again after only two months. Rendered despondent by her experiences as a governess but aware that she must earn an income, she hit upon the idea of starting a school at the parsonage with her sisters. In order to be able to teach the foreign languages required by paying pupils, in Feb. 1842 Charlotte and Emily set off for Brussels to improve their French and German. To their fellow pupils, the sisters seemed odd, almost monosyllabic in conversation and fearfully old-fashioned. But Charlotte had fallen in love, unstated at the time and unrequited, with the owner of the Pension Heger and on her return to England wrote such frequent and impassioned letters that M. Heger forbade her to write more than twice a year.

The parsonage was now an even bleaker place. Branwell, 'the family genius' on whom high hopes had been pinned, had come to nothing: his career as an artist had never progressed beyond a few portrait commissions, he was sacked from his position as a railway clerk in 1843, was summarily dismissed from his post as a tutor amidst rumours of impropriety with his employer's wife, was drinking heavily and smoking opium. Charlotte found his behaviour mortifying, and certainly totally inimical to any scheme of opening a school for young ladies at Haworth.

Then a new possibility presented itself: at Charlotte's instigation a collection of the sisters' poetry under the pseudonyms Currer, Ellis and Acton Bell was published in May 1846 and it received admiring notices. Emboldened, Charlotte sent off a novel by each of the androgynously named writers. Although the work of 'Ellis' and 'Acton' found a press, *The Professor* (based on Charlotte's experiences in Brussels) was rejected by every publisher to which it was sent (it did not appear until two years after her death). Smith & Elder wrote an encouraging letter, however, so Charlotte submitted another novel: *Jane Eyre: An Autobiography* by Currer Bell was published in Oct. 1847. It was an instant success: THACKERAY found it so interesting 'that I lost (or won if you liked) a whole day reading it'.

A year after the publication of *Jane Eyre*, Branwell died 'without knowing that his sister had published a word'; in Dec. Emily died of tuberculosis, and in May 1849 Anne succumbed to the pernicious disease too. In her grief Charlotte continued to write: *Shirley*, her novel based partly on the experiences which her father had recounted of the Luddite machine-wrecking disturbances of 1811–12 in the town where he had been a curate, was published in Oct. 1849.

Her identity by now established, Charlotte paid five visits to London, 'this big Babylon', visiting the Great Exhibition in 1851, and meeting such luminaries as Thackeray and Harriet MARTINEAU. In 1850 Charlotte was introduced to a fellow Yorks. author, Elizabeth GASKELL, and they became friends, visiting each other's homes and keeping up a correspondence. *Villette* (1853) (a reworking of *The Professor* with Brussels renamed and M. Heger the model for Paul Emmanuel) was hailed as 'the confirmation of Currer Bell's genius' and G. H. Lewes, the partner of George ELIOT, thought it 'a still more wonderful book than *Jane Eyre*. There is something preternatural in its power.' On 29 June 1854, Charlotte married her father's curate (whom Mrs Gaskell thought 'very stern and bigoted'). The marriage, which, Charlotte reflected, meant that she had 'not so much time for thinking: I am obliged to be more practical' lasted less than a year. She too died of tuberculosis, aged 38.

Elizabeth Gaskell, The Life of Charlotte Brontë (1857)
Juliet Barker, The Brontës (1994)

already an enthusiastic bird-watcher, Brooke was educated at Woolwich, commissioned into the Royal Artillery and, after service in Ireland and India, was posted as an artillery staff officer to the Western Front, where he provided MAXSE's 18th Division and Sir Julian BYNG's Canadian Corps with innovative and effective fire support; subsequently both generals made sure Brooke's career prospered. A Major-General by 1935, he commanded anti-aircraft defences in 1938, commanded II Corps in France in 1940, and in Nov. 1941 succeeded Sir John DILL as Chief of the Imperial General Staff. With Charles PORTAL and Dudley POUND, and assisted mightily by 'Pug' ISMAY, Brooke managed to canalize CHURCHILL's enormous energies away from schemes of dubious practicability towards more profitable projects.

BROOKE, BASIL (1st Viscount Brookeborough) (1888–1973), Prime Minister of Northern Ireland. From a Fermanagh gentry family, Brooke was active in the Ulster campaign against Home Rule before 1914 and served in the First World War. He helped to organize the Ulster Special Constabulary as a loyalist self-defence force during the Anglo-Irish War of 1919–21. He represented the Lisnaskea division of Fermanagh in the Northern Ireland Parliament (1929–65). As a fairly successful Minister for Agriculture (1933–41) he acquired notoriety for speeches advising employers to hire only Protestants. Minister for Commerce (1941–3), in 1943 Brooke displaced John ANDREWS as Prime Minster of Northern Ireland.

As Prime Minister (1943–63), he benefited from the post-war economic boom, increased British sympathy for Northern Ireland because of its strategic role in the Second World War, and from the extension of the post-war Welfare State to the province. His failure to take advantage of these developments to try to reconcile the Catholic minority is seen as a missed opportunity. His amateurish gentlemanly style of government was unsuited to the renewed problems of the late 1950s, as Northern Ireland's shipbuilding and textile industries resumed their decline.

BROOKE, FRANCES (née Moore) (1724–89), writer. The daughter of a Lincolns. clergyman, she married a military chaplain, John Brooke. Her travels with him took her to Canada, where her experiences provided a source for her novel *Emily Montague* (1769). Frances Brooke was also a journalist, writing as 'Mary Singleton' in *The Old Maid* (1755–6); she also wrote several sentimental novels and operas, and was co-manager of the Haymarket Theatre (1773–8).

BROOKE, HENRY (11th Baron Cobham) (1564–1619), conspirator. His scheme of 1603 to replace JAMES I with his cousin Arabella STEWART (the Main Plot) was quickly betrayed to the government. Walter RALEIGH was among those convicted thanks to Brooke's abject accusations at his trial, but all the leaders escaped execution, unlike those of the Bye Plot, a contemporary Roman Catholic scheme to kidnap James and extort a promise of toleration from him, which the government tendentiously linked to the Main Plot. Official manipulation of both plots remains obscure but likely. Brooke spent nearly all his life thereafter imprisoned in the Tower of London.

BROOKE, SIR JAMES (1803–68), Raja of Sarawak. One of the most colourful administrators in Britain's expanding sphere of nineteenth-century quasi-colonies, Brooke was the son of an East India Co. civil servant. He ran away at age 16 to join the company's army; by the age of 30 he was exploring the Indonesian archipelago in search of adventure and commerce. In Sarawak in 1840 he was instrumental in suppressing revolts against the Sultan of Brunei and was rewarded with its governorship. Formally installed as Raja in 1842, and made British Commissioner in Borneo and Governor of Labuan in 1847, he was an able administrator and a scourge of piracy. An official investigation (1849) into allegations of excessive force against pirates cleared Brooke but suspicions remained. Escaping a Chinese murder plot in 1857, he left Sarawak in 1863 shortly before it was recognized as a separate state, and his nephew succeeded him.

BROOKE, RUPERT (1887–1915), poet. He became famous for such poems as 'The Old Vicarage, Grantchester' and 'The Soldier' ('If I should die, think only this of me . . .'). The latter was published early in 1915, shortly before he died on active service *en route* to the Dardanelles; he was buried on the island of Skyros. Brooke was more than just a young Apollo; he was witty and scholarly with marked left-wing sympathies.

BROOKE-POPHAM, SIR HENRY (1878–1953), airman. From a Suffolk gentry family, educated at Sandhurst, he volunteered for the Royal Flying Corps in 1912. He spent the First World War in charge of technical support for the squadrons on the Western Front, rising to the rank of Brigadier General. Transferring to the RAF, Brooke-Popham was the first Commandant of the RAF Staff College, the first RAF officer to head the Imperial Defence College and in 1940 was the first RAF officer to become Commander-in-Chief of all British forces in the Far East. But when the Japanese attacked on 8 Dec. he was comprehensively defeated. Removed from his post on 27 Dec. 1941, Brooke-Popham returned to Britain to become President of NAAFI (Navy, Army and Air Force Institutes).

BROOKEBOROUGH, 1ST VISCOUNT *see* BROOKE, BASIL

BROTHERS, RICHARD (1757–1824), prophet. Born in Newfoundland, he entered the navy at 14 but resigned in 1790 on conscientious and religious grounds. After spells in a workhouse and a debtors' prison, he began his religious mission in 1792, publishing pamphlets announcing the fulfilment of biblical prophecies. His claims that he would be revealed as Prince of the Hebrews, and that GEORGE III would give up his crown for him, attracted wide public notice. Arrested for treasonable practices in March 1795, he was examined by the Privy Council, judged a lunatic and committed to a private asylum in Islington, London, where he wrote further pamphlets. He was released in 1806, when Lord GRENVILLE withdrew the warrant of high treason against him.

BROUGHAM, HENRY (1st Baron Brougham and Vaux) (1778–1868), lawyer and politician. A man of wide intellectual interests and enormous energy, he was a founder and regular contributor to the *Edinburgh Review*, a fervent opponent of the slave trade, a great educationalist and an outstanding legal reformer. He held office as Lord Chancellor from 1830 to 1834 and played an important role in the Reform Act debates. But he is best remembered for his defence of Queen CAROLINE in 1820 and for the type of horse-drawn carriage that bears his name. His radicalism, practical rather than visionary, made a significant contribution to the campaign for a more humane and democratic society.

BROUGHTON, 1ST BARON *see* HOBHOUSE, JOHN CAM

BROWN, SIR ARTHUR (1886–1948), aviator. Glasgow-born, he was the navigator on the first non-stop crossing of the Atlantic in a Vickers biplane on 14 June 1919, and with his fellow aviator, John ALCOCK, was knighted for the achievement.

BROWN, GEORGE (Baron George-Brown) (1914–85), politician. A Londoner, whose first job at age 15 was selling fur coats, he was an active member of the Transport Workers' Union before being elected to Parliament as Labour MP for Belper (Derb.) in 1945. He had a rapid rise at Westminster and in 1960 succeeded BEVAN as deputy leader of the Labour Party, a position he held until 1970. He was Harold WILSON's main rival for the party leadership in Feb. 1963 on the death of GAITSKELL. When Labour came to power in 1964, a special Cabinet title of First Secretary, effectively with the role of Deputy Prime Minister, was invented for him in recognition of his political weight, and he was placed at the head of a new Department of Economic Affairs (DEA). This department was intended as a counterweight in Whitehall to the central position of the Treasury and as the engine for strategic policies of economic and industrial expansion. Brown's National Economic Plan, published in Sept. 1965, envisaged a 25 per cent increase in national output by 1970. The plan was, however, indicative rather than instrumental and was rapidly pushed to one side by reality, allowing the Treasury to re-establish its primacy in matters of economic management. Brown became Foreign Secretary in 1966 and played a significant role in the Wilson government's decision to apply for membership of the European Economic Community (later European Union). His political position, weakened by the failure of the DEA and by the devaluation of sterling in 1967, was further undermined by his own maverick behaviour and drinking. He resigned from the government in 1968, lost his seat in the 1970 election and was created a life peer. He resigned from the Labour Party over the second Wilson government's trade-union legislation.

BROWN, GORDON (1951–), politician. Typecast as the dour son of the manse, that is exactly what he was before going on to be a brilliant student at Edinburgh University. He worked as a journalist before becoming Labour MP for Dunfermline East in 1983, the same year as his friend and rival Tony BLAIR entered Parliament. It was ironic but also crucial that both men should have come into the Commons at the low point of Labour's fortunes; 1983 provided them with an example of what Labour must avoid at all costs. Brown and Blair both got their chance to shine under John SMITH, whom Brown in particular much admired. As Labour spokesman for Trade and Industry under Smith, Brown established himself as one of the leading politicians of the younger generation, but Smith's sudden death in 1994 created a vacancy for the leadership. Brown or Blair were the obvious successors, but Blair's greater charisma, engaging personality and the early endorsement of colleagues led to Brown reluctantly agreeing to stand aside. It was a decision Brown never entirely came to terms with, creating tension between the two. After Labour's massive 1997 election victory Brown went to the Exchequer, where his identification with the New Labour project and his 'business-friendly' approach soon won him respect as an 'Iron Chancellor'.

Brown was devoted to establishing Labour as a party of financial prudence, and his promise to stay within the spending limits set by the Conservatives in their last year in power enabled him to resist cries from 'old Labour' to 'tax and spend'. There was, however, a decisive redistribution of wealth in his budgets, with health and education also being given priority for new spending. Handing over the power to control interest rates to the Bank of England was a further sign of fiscal orthodoxy which endeared him and New Labour to the business community. As Chancellor, Brown was the most politically cautious of his cabinet colleagues towards adopting the Euro, the currency of the European Union.

BROWN, JOHN ('ESTIMATE') (1715–66), social commentator. Son of a clergyman, he took orders himself. After writing several poems and two plays, and also an essay (later praised by J. S. MILL for its clear exposition of Utilitarian principles) on Shaftesbury's *Charac-teristicks* (*see* COOPER, ANTHONY ASHLEY, 3rd Earl), Brown published *An Estimate of the Manners and Principles of the Time* (1757), followed by *Thoughts on Civil Liberty, on Licentiousness, and on Faction* (1765). He argued that the country was sinking into social and moral decline through the development of a commercial society which shattered traditional hierarchies, and that there were now two nations, the propertied and unpropertied. Increasingly prey to depression, Brown, after 1761 vicar of St Nicholas's, Newcastle, committed suicide in 1766.

BROWN, JOHN (1826–83), royal servant. The son of a crofter, Brown was appointed to the royal household by Prince ALBERT in 1849. After Albert's death, he was summoned to Osborne in Oct. 1864 in the hope that he could revive the spirits of the grieving VICTORIA by encouraging her to ride again. He soon became a close companion of the reclusive monarch, so much so that rumours of an affair circulated, the Queen was lampooned as 'Mrs John Brown', those inclined to republicanism fanned the flames and Victoria's children, while denying any sexual impropriety, expressed disquiet at their mother's dependence on her gillie. The facts remain uncertain, but it seems likely that most of the public were more censorious of Victoria's dereliction of her public duties than of any possible liaison.

BROWN, LANCELOT ('CAPABILITY') (1716–83), landscape gardener. He gained early experience under William KENT at Stowe (Bucks.), completing the work there after Kent's death. The designer of more than 140 estates, he earned his nickname 'Capability' from his habit of telling clients that their gardens had 'capabilities of improvement'. He replaced formal gardens with 'natural' park landscapes, com-prising extensive grazing, serpentine lakes and scattered clumps of trees, continuing the trend away from the formal French or Dutch garden begun during the ascendancy of BRIDGEMAN towards a style that was seen as distinctively English. Examples of his designs survive at Blenheim, Claremont, Longleat, Petworth and Warwick Castle.

BROWNE, GEORGE (?–*c*. 1556), Archbishop of Dublin (1536–54). As English Provincial of the Augustinian friars, he administered their Oath of Royal Supremacy in 1534. Imported to Ireland as Archbishop two years later, he became a willing tool of HENRY VIII's and EDWARD VI's Reformation. He was made Primate of all Ireland in 1552, in place of the Archbishop of Armagh who had traditionally been Primate, but Armagh regained the primacy under MARY I and in 1554 Browne was forced to resign Dublin as a married priest: he was compensated with lesser livings. He was a man who made enemies easily.

BROWNE, NOEL (1915–97), Irish politician. A doctor from an extremely poor family, he became involved in the Clann na Poblachta Party, founded by Sean MACBRIDE in 1946, which advocated republicanism and social reform. In 1948, when Clann na Poblachta entered a coalition government, Browne became Minister for Health (1948–51) and established a reputation as a forceful administrator through a campaign to improve the treatment of tuberculosis. His proposals, however, for free medical care for mothers and children under 16 antagonized the medical profession and the Catholic bishops, who feared the growth of State welfare implied State control of the medical profession and might encourage un-Catholic attitudes on such matters as contraception. Browne had failed to secure support from his Cabinet colleagues, who disowned him, and he was forced to resign; he published the correspondence surrounding his departure, causing a sensation by revealing the nature of the bishops' involvement. Clann na Poblachta was irretrievably split and virtually disappeared, while Browne and three sympathizers were re-elected as independent members of the Dáil. Browne's subsequent career saw several changes of party, during which he sat in the Dáil (1951–65, 1969–73, 1977–82) as an Independent, and a member of Fianna Fáil, the short-lived National Progressive Democrats, the Labour Party, and of the Socialist Labour Party. While some were alienated by his increasingly ultra-leftist views and brusque manner (exacerbated by ill health and a period of financial hardship) and he was widely criticized for his inability to work with others, he retained immense symbolic power through his political martyrdom.

BROWNE, ROBERT (?1550–1633), Separatist. A relative of William CECIL, he was influenced by the prominent Puritan, Thomas CARTWRIGHT, at Cambridge, but as a parish minister in Norwich diocese he developed radical ideas of separating from the established Church. After he founded an independent congregation at Norwich with Robert HARRISON in 1581, the name 'Brownist' was often applied to religious separatists, although he did not originate Separatism. After Cecil had got him released from prison in 1581, he led his flock to Middelburg (Netherlands) and wrote propaganda tracts, including *A Treatise of Reformation without Tarrying for Any* (1582). His travels in Scotland and England were marked by imprisonment and frequent quarrels with fellow independents; in 1591 reconciliation with the establishment led to ordination by a bishop and 40 quieter years as a Northants parson.

BROWNING, SIR FREDERICK ('BOY') (1896–1965), soldier. Son of a London businessman, educated at Eton and Sandhurst, he served on the Western Front with the Grenadier Guards and, a company commander at age 20, was nicknamed 'Boy', a name he was stuck with thereafter. In the inter-war years 'Boy' Browning cut a glamorous figure as Colonel of the Grenadier Guards and husband of Daphne DU MAURIER. Commanding the new airborne forces in 1940, Browning designed the Pegasus badge and did much to make paratroopers acceptable to the military establishment. As Deputy Commander of First Allied Airborne Army, Browning jumped with his men in the ill-fated Arnhem operation in Sept. 1944, and is credited with coining the phrase 'a bridge too far.' Browning was a fine battalion commander, but lacked the ability to perform effectively at higher levels.

BROWNING, ROBERT (1812–69), poet. Self-taught son of a Bank of England clerk, he wrote poetry from an early age, was influenced by Percy SHELLEY and admired by J. S. MILL, who remarked that Browning's work developed 'a more intense and morbid self-consciousness than I ever knew in any sane being' and directed the poet towards the dramatic adaptation of *personae* that is evident in *Men and Women* (1855) and in *The Ring and the Book* (four vols, 1868–9). He began corresponding with Elizabeth Barrett (*see* BROWNING, ELIZABETH BARRETT) in 1845 after admiring her work, and they were secretly married the following year. In addition to its philosophical depth and spiritual insight, Browning's poetry was innovatory in the development of a new kind of narrative structure to replace the epic and the pastoral. Notwithstanding repeated complaints about the obscurity of his writing, he was a major influence on RUSKIN and Christina ROSETTI, achieved enormous popularity and was buried in Westminster Abbey.

BROWNRIGG, ELIZABETH (?–1767), murderess. Brownrigg was appointed midwife at the workhouse in the parish of St Dunstan's in the City of London in 1765. In Aug. 1767 one of her apprentices, Mary Clifford, was found dying at Brownrigg's home. Her husband James, a house-painter, was arrested but suspicion soon fell on Elizabeth, who was found guilty of murder on 12 Sept. 1767 and executed two days later. The cruelty with which she was charged attracted much public notice. Before her death she repented and urged employers to treat their young dependents well.

BRUCE, SIR DAVID (1855–1931), microbiologist and physician. Born in Australia, he studied medicine at Edinburgh and joined the Army Medical Corps in 1883. In the late 1880s, while stationed in Malta, he and his wife used the novel techniques of bacteriology to identify the bacterium (later named *Brucella*) responsible for Malta fever. Between 1894 and 1903, while based in South Africa, he showed how both nagana, a cattle disease, and sleeping-sickness in humans were caused by a protozoal parasite (*Trypanasoma brucei*) transmitted by the tsetse fly. The importance of his work was widely recognized. He was Commandant of the Royal Army Medical Corps 1914–19.

BRUCE, EDWARD *see* EDWARD BRUCE, essay on page 283

BRUCE, ROBERT (ROBERT I) *see* ROBERT BRUCE, essay on pages 688–89

BRUCE, ROBERT (3rd Earl of Carrick) (?–1304), nobleman. Son of Robert BRUCE the Competitor, he became Earl by Scottish custom on his marriage to the Countess of Carrick in 1271, but resigned the earldom to his eldest son ROBERT BRUCE, King of Scots, in 1292. He inherited his father's claim to the Scottish throne. In 1296 he asked EDWARD I if he could have the throne which JOHN BALLIOL had forfeited. 'Have I nothing better to do than win thrones for you?' was Edward's withering reply.

BRUCE, ROBERT THE COMPETITOR (Lord of Annandale) (1210–95), nobleman. He was a claimant to the throne of Scotland in 1238, and a regent for the boy-king, ALEXANDER III, in 1255. On Alexander's death in 1286 he revived his claim to the Scottish throne, but at the famous competition at Norham (Northumb.) in 1291–2, EDWARD I decided in favour of JOHN BALLIOL. The aged

Bruce never accepted the decision, passing his claim to his son Robert BRUCE, Earl of Carrick.

BRUDENELL, JAMES (7th Earl of Cardigan) (1797–1868), soldier. Only boy of eight children, privately educated and turned into a spoiled brat by his doting mother and seven sisters, he bought a commission in the 8th Hussars in 1824, and by 1832 had purchased the lieutentant-colonelcy of the 15th Hussars. A difficult quarrelsome man, he achieved immortality during the Crimean War by leading the Light Brigade to its destruction at Balaclava in 1854. The type of knitted woollen jacket he wore in the Crimea is called a cardigan after him.

BRUMMELL, GEORGE ('BEAU') (1778–1840), man of fashion. Son of the private secretary of Lord North (see NORTH, FREDERICK), who died in 1794 leaving him some £30,000, he was renowned for his wit and fashionably studied moderation in dress. He was popular with the Prince Regent (the future GEORGE IV), whom he had first met at Eton, and with other members of Regency high society. In matters of taste in dress, his word was law. In 1818 he retired to Calais, having quarrelled with the Prince, and being overburdened with gambling debts. He was imprisoned for debt in 1835 and died in an asylum.

BRUNEL, ISAMBARD KINGDOM (1806–59), engineer. Son of Marc Isambard Brunel, a French–English engineer celebrated for his machinery for making ship's blocks, he was educated in Paris and subsequently joined his father's engineering firm, where he was involved in the unsuccessful project to build a tunnel beneath the Thames (1825–31). Operating independently, he designed the Clifton suspension bridge in Bristol between 1829 and 1831 (completed in 1864) and was appointed engineer to the Great Western Railway in 1833, surveying the proposed London to Bristol line and adopting a broad gauge which was eventually altered in favour of the narrow gauge of George STEPHENSON. For the Great Western Railway, he built the Paddington and Bristol termini and all the bridges, viaducts and tunnels, including the Saltash bridge near Plymouth and the two-mile tunnel at Box near Bath. He also built the Hungerford suspension bridge in London (1845) and an atmospheric railway in south Devon.

Brunel was also famed as a shipbuilder. By 1838 he had launched the *Great Western* and the *Sirius*, steamships designed to 'extend' the Great Western line from Bristol to New York. In 1843 he launched the *Great Britain*, an iron-hulled, screw-driven ship, and in 1853 began planning the *Great Eastern*, a 680-foot-long vessel with a double-skinned iron hull and steam-driven paddle wheels

that, until 1899, was the largest ship ever constructed. Despite engineering and financial problems, the ship was finally launched on 13 Jan. 1858, seven days after Brunel collapsed on board from overwork and poor health. The *Great Eastern* proved too costly to run as a passenger ship and in the late 1860s was used to lay Atlantic telegraph cables. The restored *Great Britain* survives in Bristol as an exhibit and a memorial of Brunel.

BRUNO, GIORDANO (1548–1600), philosopher. An outstanding Renaissance mind: astronomer, mystic, atheist and a renegade Dominican friar, he spent March 1583 to Nov. 1585 at the French embassy in London, writing some of his most celebrated works. Befriended by Philip SIDNEY and Robert DUDLEY, Earl of Leicester, he gave lectures at Oxford University on philosophy and astronomy, which the authorities there stopped when he was accused of plagiarism. The historian, John Bossy, has made a good case for suggesting that he was the embassy spy 'Henry Fagot', who was recruited by Francis WALSINGHAM and who played a vital role in unmasking Francis THROCKMORTON's plot. He was burnt at the stake as a heretic in Rome in 1600.

BRUTON, JOHN (1947–), politician and Taoiseach (Irish Prime Minister). Associated with the conservative wing of the Fine Gael Party rather than the social democrats around Garrett FITZGERALD, his stringent budget as Minister of Finance (1981) brought down the coalition of Fine Gael and Labour, and as Minister for Industry and Energy in the 1983–7 coalition his support for financial discipline produced tension with Labour ministers (and Fitzgerald). He was defeated by Fitzgerald's protégé Alan Dukes when Fitzgerald retired in 1987, but Dukes's support for the HAUGHEY government's harsh fiscal measures led to his eclipse by Dick SPRING and deposition in favour of Bruton in 1990. The collapse of Albert REYNOLDS's government in 1994 allowed Bruton to serve as Taoiseach (1994–7), heading a 'rainbow coalition' of Fine Gael, Labour and the ex-Marxist Democratic Left. A competent Taoiseach, Bruton believed it was his duty to pay equal attention to Unionist and nationalist concerns. Critics argued that he was over-sympathetic to the Northern Unionists and should act as leader of nationalist Ireland. The coalition was defeated by the coalition of Fianna Fáil and Progressive Democrats in 1997; Bruton remained leader of the opposition.

BRYAN, SIR FRANCIS (?–1550), courtier. A courtier's son, his jousting skill, love of a dissolute good time and poetic skill (little of his verse survives) made him a favourite of HENRY VIII, who nicknamed him 'the vicar of Hell'. Partisan for his cousin ANNE BOLEYN, he had already cynically distanced himself before her fall (1536). He was active in suppressing the Pilgrimage of Grace but, as a religious conservative, fell from favour through CROMWELL's hostility in 1538. He served in the 1547 Scottish war, and in 1548 obliged the English government by marrying the widow of James Butler, 9th Earl of Ormond, preventing her proposed marriage to Gerald FITZGERALD, uniting the powerful earldoms of Ormond and Desmond. His reward was the lord marshalship and lord justiceship of Ireland but he died suddenly soon afterwards.

BRYDGES, JAMES (1673–1744) (9th Baron and 1st Duke of Chandos), patron of the arts. From 1707 to 1712 he enjoyed the lucrative post of Paymaster General, earning sums which he increased to half a million pounds by speculation. He acquired the estate of Canons, near Edgware (Middx.), from his first wife's uncle in 1712, and spent vast sums building a great house there, employing an array of designers, including THORN-HILL, William KENT and Grinling GIBBONS. GEORGE I rewarded him for his Whiggism with an earldom in 1714 and a dukedom in 1719. Chandos became notorious for his opulent lifestyle: he was the only British nobleman to employ a whole choir, for which HANDEL composed anthems. There was also a music academy at Canons, with PEPUSCH as Director. Chandos's wealth was damaged by the collapse of the South Sea Co. and a series of failed business ventures, and on his death his house was auctioned off for its materials.

BUC, SIR GEORGE (1562 or 1563–1622), writer. From an East Anglian gentry family, Buc (or Buck) followed the family tradition of service with the Howard family, served with Charles, Lord HOWARD of Effingham, on the expedition to sack Cadiz in 1596, and was knighted in 1603. Master of the Revels and licenser of plays (1608–22), he wrote poetry and various historical works, notably a sympathetic biography of RICHARD III (1619, published 1647). He went insane in his last year of life.

BUCER, MARTIN (1491–1551), religious reformer. A former Dominican friar who, after basing himself in Strasbourg, became a leading figure in the Reformed (i.e. the non-Lutheran) Churches of Switzerland and South Germany after the death of Huldrych ZWINGLI in 1531. At that time, he began a cordial correspondence with Thomas CRANMER which developed into a friendship significant for the future of the English Reformation. He wrote voluminously and not always with clarity on theology and biblical commentary (Martin LUTHER called him 'the

chatterbox'). Opposing the religious conservatism of the Interim imposed in the Holy Roman Empire by CHARLES V, he took refuge in England in 1549 and was made Regius Professor in Cambridge, where he made a great impact in a short time. He was extremely influential on Archbishop Cranmer's liturgical and theological development. He was given an official university funeral in Cambridge; six years later, under MARY I, his body was dug up and publicly burned for heresy by the university authorities led by Andrew PERNE. An equally solemn Cambridge ceremony in 1560 (also with Perne presiding) announced his rehabilitation as one of the most celebrated of reformers.

BUCHAN, EARL OF, 5TH see COMYN, WILLIAM; **6TH** see COMYN, ALEXANDER; **7TH** see COMYN, JOHN; **9TH** see STEWART, ALEXANDER; **11TH** see STEWART, JOHN

BUCHAN, JOHN (1st Baron Tweedsmuir) (1875–1940), writer. A son of the manse, Buchan worked with MILNER on the reconstruction of South Africa after the Boer War, served as Governor General of Canada (1935–40) and wrote his histories, biographies, short stories and adventure novels (which he called 'yarns'), of which there were 100, in his 'spare' time. It is for his five 'Richard Hannay' thrillers that he is best known, particularly *The Thirty Nine Steps* (1915), which was filmed by HITCHCOCK (1935).

BUCHANAN, GEORGE (1506–82), scholar and writer. A brilliant man of multiple accomplishments, he was born in Stirlings. and persisted, despite poverty, in studies at Paris and St Andrews. He eventually gained a teaching position in Paris and built a reputation as an exponent of humanist Latin. There he tutored Gilbert Kennedy, 3rd Earl of Cassillis, and returned with him in 1536 to Scotland, where JAMES V made him tutor to his bastard son James STEWART (future Earl of Moray). Forced to flee to England in 1539 and charged with heresy after writing a satirical poem about the Franciscans, he taught mostly in France (though briefly in Portugal before three years' imprisonment by the Inquisition), and returned to Scotland only in 1561. Now rejecting his Catholic ordination and declaring his Protestant faith, he became Principal of St Leonard's College, St Andrews (1566), and court poet. He came to loathe MARY QUEEN OF SCOTS and, in the case against her for the murder of Henry STEWART, Lord Darnley, witnessed that she had written the 'Casket Letters'. He was appointed tutor to JAMES VI, who grew to detest him, and he played little part in politics after resigning as Lord Privy Seal in 1578. His political writings included *De Jure*

Regni (1579), influential in Scotland for its emphasis on popular consent in government and the right to resist tyranny. He wrote a standard history of Scotland; as a Gaelic speaker with a sympathy for the Highlands unusual among Scots intellectuals, he was the first scholar to recognize the common origins of all Celtic languages.

BUCKHURST, 1ST BARON *see* SACKVILLE, THOMAS

BUCKINGHAM, 4TH EARL OF *see* THOMAS OF WOODSTOCK; **1ST MARQUESS OF** *see* TEMPLE-NUGENT-GRENVILLE, GEORGE; **DUKE OF, 1ST** *see* STAFFORD, HUMPHREY; **2ND** *see* STAFFORD, HENRY; **3RD** *see* STAFFORD, EDWARD; **4TH** and **5TH** *see* VILLIERS, GEORGE; **6TH** *see* SHEFFIELD, JOHN

BUCKLAND, WILLIAM (1784–1856), geologist and palaeontologist. Born in Devon, Buckland was educated at Oxford and was ordained in 1809. Long interested in geology and fossil-hunting, he conducted geological field-work during tours of south-west England (1808–15). Professor of Mineralogy (1813) then Reader in Geology (1819) at Oxford, he established himself as the leading teacher and practitioner of geology and palaeontology. In 1845 he became Dean of Westminster: a devotee of natural theology (which regards evidence of design in nature as evidence of the Divine designer), he spent much of his career attempting to reconcile geology and Scripture. His celebrated *Reliquiae Diluvianae* (1823) upheld the idea that the earth's geology had been shaped by a series of catastrophes and presented geological and palaeontological evidence of one such catastrophe, the Universal Flood. He is also noted for his work on the stratigraphy of the British Isles and his 1824 announcement of fossil evidence for what he called the Megalosaurus – later regarded as the first description of a dinosaur.

BUCKLE, HENRY (1821–62), historian. A scholar gentleman from Kent, he was self-educated, isolated yet proficient in 18 foreign languages. He is best remembered for his two-volume *History of Civilization in England* (1857–61), which sought to demonstrate the possibilities of a positivist history, but actually showed how limited these were.

BUCKTON, RAY(MOND) (1922–95), trade-union leader. Buckton started his working life as a groundsman before moving to work on the railways in 1940: he was for a time a fireman on the *Flying Scotsman*. A Labour councillor in York, he was the youngest alderman in the country aged 33. As a full-time Associated Society of Locomotive Engineers and Firemen (ASLEF) official by 1960, Assistant General Secretary (1963) and General Secretary (1970–87), he saw his union's membership fall from 77,000 to 25,000 with the introduction of the single driver train and became the rail commuter's hate-figure as a result of a series of strikes between 1973 and 1982. The most serious was the dispute over the introduction of flexible rostering to replace the eight-hour day in 1982. Charged with seeming to imagine that the railways were still in the 'age of steam', Buckton's response was always that his members' wages still were.

BULL, JOHN (?1562–1628), composer. A chorister and later organist in the Chapel Royal, with doctorates in music from both Oxford and Cambridge, he became first Professor of Music at the newly founded Gresham College, London, from 1596 to 1607. From 1601, his Catholic sympathies led to increasingly extensive stays on the continent, which became permanent in 1613; he was appointed Antwerp Cathedral's organist in 1617. One of the best keyboard players of his day, Bull influenced the continental keyboard tradition leading to J. S. Bach. With Orlando GIBBONS and William BYRD he published the important collection of keyboard music entitled *Parthenia* (1613).

BULLER, SIR HENRY REDVERS (1839–1908), soldier. Educated at Eton and commissioned into the 60th Kings Royal Rifle Corps, Buller joined the Red River expedition in 1870, and became a key member of the emerging Wolseley circle, serving with Sir Garnet WOLSELEY in Zululand (1879), where he won the Victoria Cross, Egypt (1882) and the Sudan (1884). Rising to Adjutant General in 1890, Buller's luck changed in 1899, when, appointed to command British forces at the outbreak of the Second Boer War, he presided over a series of disasters. Replaced by Frederick ROBERTS, Buller gave an after-dinner speech in Oct. 1901 in which he launched into a drunken harangue against the government. Roberts, now Commander-in-Chief, dismissed Buller from the army. Relations between the officers of the Wolseley and Roberts 'rings' remained permanently embittered.

BULLOCK, ALAN (Baron Bullock of Leafield) (1914–), historian. The author of two major works of twentieth-century European history, *Hitler: A Study in Tyranny* (1952) and *Hitler and Stalin: Parallel Lives* (1991), Bullock has also made a significant contribution to British academic life as Founding Master of St Catherine's College, Oxford (1960–80), and Vice-Chancellor of Oxford University (1969–73), and to cultural life as chairman of the Committee on Reading and Other Uses of the English Language (1972–4). His report, published in 1975, rebutted the notion that standards of literacy were falling but offered practical advice on attaining skills. He was also the instigator and joint editor of the *Dictionary of Modern Thought* (1977).

BULWER-LYTTON, EDWARD see LYTTON, EDWARD BULWER

BUNYAN, JOHN (1628–88), religious writer. A Bedfordshire tinsmith who served during the English Civil Wars as a Parliamentarian soldier (1644–6), he became fired by religious zeal through the influence of his wife and the prophecies of the approaching rule of Christ made by the Fifth Monarchist sect. In *c*. 1653 he joined an Independent congregation in Bedford, becoming a strict Calvinist believer in predestination and an enthusiastic prophet of the coming early rule of Christ and his saints (millenarianism). He began to preach and write, especially against the newly emerging Quaker movement; persecuted by Presbyterian clergy in 1658, he suffered more seriously after CHARLES II's restoration, spending most of the period from 1660 to 1672 in prison for violating the new legislation against Separatist congregations (conventicles). Thereafter he travelled, preaching and writing his masterpiece *Pilgrim's Progress* (1678, 2nd expanded edn 1684). An immediately outstanding and enduringly successful work, it became a centrepiece of English Protestant literature, especially for evangelicals and nonconformists, and was said to be one of the few books commonly found in the cottages of the barely literate.

BURBAGE, RICHARD (?1567–1619), actor-manager. Son of the actor James Burbage (*c*. 1530–97), his entire life was spent in the theatre, in a brilliant acting career (from *c*. 1594 in association with SHAKESPEARE) and later in management. Having inherited his father's theatres at Blackfriars and Shoreditch in 1597, he re-erected the Shoreditch Theatre as the Globe at Southwark two years later, rebuilding it after a fire in 1613. He was also a talented artist, credited with one surviving portrait at Dulwich Picture Gallery. *See also* ALLEYN, EDWARD.

BURDETT, SIR FRANCIS (1770–1844), politician. Younger son of the 4th baronet, he lived in Paris during the early part of the French Revolution, returning to England in 1793. In 1796 he was elected an MP; he opposed the French Revolutionary war and supported parliamentary reform. He campaigned successfully for an inquiry into the mismanagement of Coldbath Fields prison, a showpiece of prison reform, where several radicals were held.

In 1802 he was elected MP for Middlesex in the first of a series of hard-fought battles in popular constituencies. When this election was declared void he fought again but lost; he won the seat in 1805, lost it in 1806 and then was elected for Westminster. He opposed corporal punishment in the army and in 1809 campaigned for an inquiry into a scandal over the sale of army commissions which implicated the Duke of York (*see* FREDERICK AUGUSTUS). He was imprisoned in 1810 for breach of parliamentary privilege, and again in 1819 for criticizing repression at Peterloo. He successfully promoted the Catholic Emancipation (Relief) Act, which was passed in 1829. He remained an MP until his death, latterly supporting Robert PEEL. Representing himself as a champion of ('traditional') English liberty rather than as an innovator, he interpreted this cause in radical ways and won a devoted popular following. His secure social background gave him the opportunity to emerge as one of the most prominent and effective early nineteenth-century radical spokesmen.

BURDETT-COUTTS, ANGELA (1814–1906), philanthropist. The granddaughter of banker Thomas Coutts and daughter of Sir Francis BURDETT, she was the richest heiress in Europe, a great society figure and the friend of artists and actors, most notably Charles DICKENS. She was known as the 'queen of the poor' and gave £3 million to housing projects and other charities during her lifetime.

BURGES, WILLIAM (1827–81), architect and designer. Son of an engineer, Burges was a leading exponent of the Gothic revival in Britain. In 1865 he acquired a wealthy patron, the 18-year-old Marquess of Bute who was 20 years his junior, and the unlikely pair worked together for the rest of Burges's life, creating Gothic palaces including Cardiff Castle and Castell Coch, designing the interiors, fittings and furniture as well as the fairytale turreted exteriors. Burges designed a home for himself in Melbury Road, Kensington. It was, said W. R. LETHABY, 'barbarously splendid'.

BURGESS, GUY (1911–63), spy. Burgess became a member of the Communist Party whilst at Cambridge University from 1931 and was recruited as a Soviet agent. During the war he worked for the BBC and allegedly also for British intelligence. In 1944 he joined the Foreign Office and was sent to Washington in 1950, where he was a colleague of Kim PHILBY. On 25 May 1951 Burgess, who had returned to London, was alerted by Philby of an impending MI5 investigation of MACLEAN and fled across the Channel with his fellow spy. Burgess did not find life in Moscow much to his liking and died there of acute alcoholic poisoning and kidney failure at the age of 52.

BURGH, HUBERT DE (2nd Earl of Kent) (*c.* 1175–1243), soldier and administrator. The younger son of a family of Norfolk gentry, he rose to govern England and become brother-in-law to the King of Scotland. In the 1190s he entered JOHN's service and made his name by his determined defence of Chinon in 1205. He was Seneschal of Poitou from 1212 to 1215; appointed Justiciar in 1215, he remained in that office, with overall responsibility for the administration of England, until 1232. He played a key role in the civil war of 1215–17, first as defender of Dover (1216–17), then as commander of the victorious fleet at the Battle of Sandwich (Kent). From 1219 he was the most influential figure in HENRY III's government, successfully presenting himself as a moderate and patriotic Englishman opposed to the arbitrary excesses of such foreigners as de BREAUTÉ and Peter des ROCHES. In 1221 he married, as his third wife, Margaret, sister of ALEXANDER II, and four years later he was created Earl of Kent. In 1232 de Burgh's rival des Roches persuaded the King to dismiss and imprison him. Although he made a dramatic escape in 1233 and was reconciled to Henry in 1234, he never recovered his former position.

BURGH, JAMES (1714–75), writer. The son of a Perths. Presbyterian minister, throughout his life he had an urgent sense of the need to reform abuse. In the 1740s he moved to London, seeking work as a schoolmaster. He came to public notice with the publication of *Britain's Remembrancer, or The Danger not Over* (1746), in which he argued that the Jacobite rebellion represented God's punishment for English luxury and corruption. Probably as a result of his friendship with Stephen HALES, he was introduced to the Leicester House circle around the future GEORGE III, becoming Clerk to the Closet to the dowager Princess AUGUSTA. In 1754 he tried to launch a 'Grand Association' of 'persons conspicuous for their character and stations' to improve public morals, but this foundered through lack of support. He became friendly with neighbouring cleric Richard PRICE, and under his influence moved towards Arianism. He initially had high hopes of the new King, George III, but lost faith in him and began instead to pin his hopes on a popular reform movement, moving in Wilkite circles (*see* WILKES, JOHN). His *Political Disquisitions* (1774–5), advocating a Grand National Association to remedy the nation's constitutional ills, provided inspiration to later eighteenth-century and early nineteenth-century reformers.

BURGH, RICHARD DE (3rd (2nd de Burgh) Earl of Ulster) (*c.* 1259–1326), courtier. He succeeded his father Walter in 1271, when he was about 12. The most powerful English noble in Ireland, known as the Red Earl, from 1286 he constantly intervened, usually with success, in native Irish dynastic politics, placing his own nominees on the thrones, and taking tribute from them. In the 1290s, however, his feud with John Fitzthomas destabilized the English colony. He served with EDWARD I in Scotland in 1296 and 1304, was Lieutenant of Ireland in 1308 and fought against the invading EDWARD BRUCE in 1315–17.

BURGH, WILLIAM DE (?–1205), soldier. One of the leaders of the English conquest of Ireland, and the first to make substantial inroads into the lands west of the Shannon. He accompanied JOHN's expedition to Ireland in 1185 and was well rewarded with grants of Irish land. He married a daughter of DOMNAL MÓR UA BRIAIN. In the 1190s John granted him the whole of Connacht, and his invasion, exploiting quarrels between Irish claimants to the kingship of Connacht, was so successful that it alarmed King John, who reversed his policy and recognized Cathal Croibhdhearg as King of Connacht in 1204. But by this time William was known as 'the Conqueror'. It was said of him that he was the destroyer of all Erin and that he died of a singular disease too shameful to be described.

BURGH, WILLIAM DE (4th [3rd de Burgh] Earl of Ulster, the Brown Earl) (1312–33), soldier. A boy in England when his grandfather Richard de BURGH died in 1326, he arrived in Ireland in 1328 determined to assert himself. This rapidly led to quarrels with his tenants and other de Burghs, notably his cousin Walter, whom he allegedly starved to death at Greencastle (Co. Donegal). The upshot was his own murder at the hands of some Ulster lords when he was just 20. His death marked the end of de Burgh dominance in the north of Ireland.

BURGOYNE, JOHN (1723–92), soldier. He gained a reputation for decisive action in the Seven Years War; in 1761 he was elected to Parliament. Sent to North America in 1774 to reinforce GAGE, his campaigns lacked the whole-hearted support of his superiors, were poorly supplied with troops and equipment, and underestimated American resistance. In 1777 Burgoyne intended to march from Quebec to meet forces coming from New York but these failed to arrive and Burgoyne was captured by the Americans at Saratoga. He negotiated the Convention of Saratoga, by which the British troops were to be disarmed and deported by WASHINGTON. On his return GEORGE III and NORTH rejected his account of Britain's shambolic conduct of the war. Having supported the war in Parliament, Burgoyne now joined the opposition and advocated American independence. After the fall of North he was a conciliatory Commander-in-Chief in Ireland during the constitutional agitation, associated especially with Henry GRATTAN, of 1782–3.

BURGOYNE, SIR JOHN FOX (1782–1871), soldier. Commissioned in the Royal Engineers in 1798, Burgoyne served throughout the Peninsular War (1809–14), and subsequently he commanded engineers in the assault on New Orleans (1815). In 1845 Burgoyne was appointed Inspector General of Fortifications, accompanied the expeditionary force to the Crimea in 1854, and was blamed for the failure to capture Sebastapol immediately after the Battle of the Alma. Burgoyne's more lasting influence was in Britain, where he dominated the debate over national defences in the 1840s, 1850s and 1860s and provided the intellectual and technical justification for massive schemes of fortification, which still dot the Channel coast.

BURGRED, King of Mercia (852–74). The penultimate king of independent Mercia, he left his kingdom when the struggle against the Viking armies of HALFDAN and IVAR THE BONELESS was becoming impossible. Little is known about him, but it appears that he attempted to defend his kingdom against the Viking 'Great Army' in close alliance with the kings of Wessex from ETHELWULF to ALFRED THE GREAT before capitulating to overwhelming force and leaving Mercia to a rival, CEOLWULF II. He married Ethelwulf's daughter ETHELSWITH.

BURKE, EDMUND see essay on page 121

BURKE, WILLIAM (1792–1829), murderer see KNOX, ROBERT

BURLINGTON, 3RD EARL OF see BOYLE, RICHARD

BURNE-JONES, SIR EDWARD (1813–98), artist. Born in Birmingham, from the appearance and industrial values of which he was to recoil, he was a contemporary of William MORRIS at Oxford University. Burne-Jones too abandoned his intention to enter the Church and resolved to become an artist, a job he conceived as 'remoulding [the world] nearer to the heart's desire'. A pupil of Dante Gabriel ROSSETTI from 1855, he followed the style of the founder of the Pre-Raphaelite Brotherhood, but interpreted it in distinct ways that drew on the work of Botticelli. Taking inspiration from legend and from the poetry of CHAUCER, TENNYSON, SWINBURNE and KEATS, from the revival of Gothic architecture and most significantly from the Arthurian legends (see ARTHUR, KING) in their recounting in Thomas MALORY's Morte d'Arthur, Burne-Jones's pale, ethereal beauties in rich garments and settings grace tapestries that were woven by Morris's Arts and Crafts company, including the six-panel Holy Grail (1891–4), stained glass for churches, decoration for books published by Morris's Kelmscott Press, including The Works of Geoffrey Chaucer, and paintings of his 'romantic dream' such as the Briar Rose series (1890), The Beguiling of Merlin (1884), The Wheel of Fortune (1891) and The Sleep of Arthur at Avalon (c. 1891).

BURNELL, ROBERT (?–1292), cleric and royal servant. A clerk of the future King EDWARD I, together with Walter GIFFARD, Archbishop of York, and Edward Mortimer, he was Regent (1272–4) when Edward was returning from his crusade and Lord Chancellor (1274–92). Elected Bishop of Bath and Wells in 1275, he was constantly in attendance on the King. In 1283 Parliament met in his hall at Acton Burnell near Shrewsbury. A skilful politician, his moderating influence tempered the harsher proposals of the King. Edward twice proposed him as Archbishop of Canterbury but his personal wealth and illegitimate children stood in the way of further ecclesiastical advancement.

BURNET, GILBERT (1643–1715), cleric and historian. He took a master's degree at Marischal College, Aberdeen, at 14, then studied divinity, learning Hebrew in Amsterdam, where he was impressed by Dutch religious tolerance. His willingness to support an Episcopal system, at a time when support for Presbyterianism was strong in Scotland, was influenced by his conviction that religion should be above party; this conviction worked unevenly in his favour in Restoration Britain. After he had served a period as tutor to the young Andrew FLETCHER of Saltoun, the patronage of Lauderdale (see MAITLAND, JOHN) helped him to the position of Professor of Divinity at Glasgow in 1669, where he was active in negotiations for accommodation with the Covenanters, which earned him disfavour, and he left for London; he was later a witness at Lauderdale's impeachment. In 1679 he began to publish a History of the Reformation. When Titus OATES's accusations helped to touch off the Popish-Plot scare this subject acquired a new resonance.

After some of his friends were executed for complicity in the Rye House Plot (1683) (see RUSSELL, WILLIAM; SIDNEY, ALGERNON), Burnet left for the continent and in 1686 took up a post in the entourage of the Prince of Orange, the future WILLIAM III. He wrote the text of William's 1688

continued on page 122

BURKE, EDMUND (1729–97)
Writer and politician

His father was a Dublin attorney, his mother daughter of an impoverished Irish Catholic gentry family. Career and social restrictions made it attractive to bring up middle-class boys as Protestants. Edmund was educated at a Quaker school, then at 14 entered Trinity College, Dublin.

In 1750, he went to London to study law at the Middle Temple. His first book, *A Vindication of Natural Society* (1756), attacked the deistic writings of Henry ST JOHN, Lord Bolingbroke, by parodically extending Bolingbroke's notion of 'natural religion' to society. To Burke, the idea that there could be a just and virtuous 'natural society' was ridiculous: artificial societies, with all their disadvantages, offered the only basis for civilized life. More ambitious was *A Philosophical Enquiry into the Origins of Our Ideas of the Sublime and the Beautiful* (1757). Building on John LOCKE's ideas about the mind to explain aesthetic responses, it attracted much attention.

With his prospects as a writer developing, Burke in 1757 married a Catholic doctor's daughter. They were to live happily together for 40 years. To secure his family's finances, Burke took on two jobs: as secretary to a politician, William Gerard Hamilton, and as editor of the *Annual Register*, a review of the year's events. He made many friends in London cultural circles, including Samuel JOHNSON, Oliver GOLDSMITH and Joshua REYNOLDS. In 1761 Hamilton was appointed Irish Chief Secretary, requiring attendance in Ireland during biennial parliamentary sessions. Burke accompanied him, and renewed his own concern for Irish Catholic peasants, oppressed, as he saw it, by grasping landlords.

Burke broke with Hamilton in 1765, and entered the service of Lord Rockingham (*see* WATSON-WENTWORTH, CHARLES), then about to head his first ministry. He was also offered a parliamentary seat. His efforts to make his way in the world by talent and industry were paying off. He quickly made a name as a speaker, and became a key member of the Rockingham team. The ministry did not last, but Burke was to remain Rockingham's secretary until Rockingham's death.

In opposition, Burke emerged as in effect the ideologist of the Rockingham Whigs. He came to share their suspicion of GEORGE III and the ministers preferred by him, kept in power, as they thought, by 'secret influence'. Burke set out the group's paranoid views in *Thoughts on the Cause of the Present Discontents* (1770).

Burke had long believed that society was best governed by a benevolent aristocracy. For him, the aristocratic Rockingham Whigs (for all their sometimes frustrating inattentiveness to public duty) represented the germ of an ideal ruling class. He was as wary as any of the more radical ideologies favoured by some outside Parliament, on whose discontent the Rockinghamites yet had somehow to capitalize. In 1780, when Christopher WYVILL presided over the rise of a movement for parliamentary reform, receiving some support from such Rockinghamite allies as Charles LENNOX, Duke of Richmond, and Charles James FOX, Burke argued the case for leaving Parliament as it was, and instead implementing 'economical reform' to reduce Crown and ministerial influence. When he lost his Bristol seat at the general election that year, partly for not having paid enough attention to his constituents' views, his *Address to the Electors of Bristol* provided a classic statement of the view that an MP is no mere delegate, but must exercise independent judgement.

Most deeply engaging his passions were the causes of religious toleration, especially for Catholics, and proper treatment of the various peoples on whom British government impinged, especially the Irish, Americans and Indians. The impact of the American Revolutionary War, and growing criticism of the East India Company's proceedings, made these issues topical.

Even in opposition, Burke was able to help promote extensions of religious toleration. During two brief Whig ministries in the early 1780s – the second Rockingham ministry (1782) and Fox–NORTH ministry (1783) – he promoted economical reform; he saw America granted independence, and Ireland legislative independence. In 1783 he drew up a reforming India Bill, but, to his outrage, the King made this the pretext for dismissing the ministry. Not believing that PITT THE YOUNGER cared about the welfare of Indians, Burke dedicated himself to publicizing and punishing abuse by trying to impeach former Indian governor Warren HASTINGS.

His obsessive pursuit of this issue weakened his influence. When he denounced the French Revolution in its early, moderate days in his *Reflections on the Revolution in France* (1790), many were unpersuaded, though soon his warnings seemed prophetic. He helped persuade some Whigs to transfer their support to Pitt in 1794, under the leadership of the Duke of Portland (*see* BENTINCK, WILLIAM CAVENDISH).

Subsequently acclaimed as a father of conservative thought, Burke was evidently a more complex figure, combining a consistent horror of oppressive and exploitative styles of government with an equally consistent distrust of any form of social levelling.

Conor Cruise O'Brien, *The Great Melody* (1992)
F. P. Lock, *Edmund Burke* (2 vols, 1998–)

Declaration on invading England, and accompanied him to England. Appointed Bishop of Salisbury under the new regime, he favoured the inclusion of Dissenters within the Church, and his sermons contributed to the popularization of a new, Latitudinarian preaching style, emphasizing the moral teaching of the Church rather than theological argument. His informative but partisan *History of My Own Time* was published posthumously (1723–34).

BURNETT, JAMES (Lord Monboddo) (1714–99), judge and intellectual. Educated at the universities of Aberdeen, Groningen and Edinburgh, he became an advocate in 1737 and rapidly established a commanding reputation as a lawyer. He was appointed a Lord of Session in 1767 when he became known as Lord Monboddo. He is remembered for his contributions to Scottish Enlightenment thought through his *On the Origin and Progress of Language* (six vols, 1773–92) and *Antient Metaphysics* (six vols, 1779–99) which defended the superiority of ancient Greek philosophy and literature. The first work expanded the boundaries of debate by denying that language or the State were natural to human society, and attracted ridicule by claiming the orang-utan as part of mankind. Monboddo also held regular 'learned suppers' which acted as social foci for Scottish Enlightenment thinkers.

BURNEY, CHARLES (1726–1814), musician and music historian. The son of a dancer, violinist and painter from Shrewsbury, in 1744 he met ARNE in Chester and became his pupil; although badly treated, he mixed with the leading musical personalities of the day, including HANDEL, associations that continued when he worked (1747–9) for the leader of fashion Fulke Greville. After a decade's retreat in King's Lynn he returned to London as a music teacher in 1760. Despite his relatively lowly social status Burney mixed with members of the nobility and leading literary figures such as Samuel JOHNSON, Hester THRALE, BURKE, Joshua REYNOLDS, GARRICK and Mary DELANY. In 1770 and 1772–3 he toured Europe researching his *History of Music* (four vols, 1776–89). The work's popularity was based on its literary skill and deployment of anecdote, as well as its display of technical knowledge and historical research, but has suffered because Burney saw pre-eighteenth-century music as 'barbarous', in contrast to his more antiquarian rival Sir John HAWKINS. His daughter was the novelist Frances BURNEY.

BURNEY, FRANCES (FANNY) (1752–1840), novelist and diarist. She was the daughter of the musicologist Charles BURNEY. Largely self-educated, she wrote copiously during childhood but destroyed all her manuscripts when she was 15. Eventually *Evelina, or a Young Lady's Entrance into the World* was published in 1778, followed by *Cecilia* in 1782. Through Mary DELANY, in 1785 she was appointed Second Keeper of the Robes to Queen CHARLOTTE, but found the environment of the backstairs court stultifying and in 1791 she was allowed to retire. Two years later she married a French émigré general, Alexandre D'Arblay. The couple supported themselves through Fanny's writing, principally through the success of *Camilla* in 1796. The D'Arblays lived in France for most of the Napoleonic period and Fanny's last and unsuccessful novel *The Wanderer* (1814) reflects her sense of dislocation during that time. Her niece edited her diaries after her death and despite substantial omissions these remain a valuable source of observations about late eighteenth-century literature and women's place in society. A new edition of the diaries was published in the twentieth century, reinstating much material excised by Fanny herself, her niece and later editors.

BURNS, JOHN (1858–1943), trade unionist and politician. An engineer by trade, he became interested in socialism, made his name in the unemployment agitations of 1886–7 and the London dock strike (1889) and was elected to the first London County Council in 1889 and to Parliament as MP for Battersea in 1892. Thereafter he moved to the Right and was appointed President of the Local Government Board in 1905 and of the Board of Trade in 1914, the first working man to become a Cabinet minister. Content to follow the advice of his officials rather than initiate new policies, he opposed the reforming recommendations of the Royal Commission on the Poor Laws (1909), which would have made significant advances in health service provision. He left public life in 1914, believing that war was avoidable.

BURNS, ROBERT (1759–96), poet. A 'heaven-taught ploughman' in the words of a contemporary writer, Burns was one of the seven children of a Scottish Calvinist cottar (small farmer) with a determination to see his sons as well educated as possible. A voracious reader, Burns farmed, wrote poetry and capitalized on his strikingly good looks. In 1786 a collection of his poetry written over the years, *Poems, Chiefly in the Scottish Dialect*, was published to immediate critical acclaim and he was lionized by the Edinburgh literati. Burns returned unsuccessfully to farming, and also worked for the excise. His major narrative poem *Tam O'Shanter* was published in 1791. He died at the age of 37 of rheumatic heart disease, having written hundreds of songs, including *O My Luve's Like a Red, Red Rose, Ye Banks and Braes* and *Auld Lang Syne*. A writer fluent in both 'standard' English and his native Scots, he was much admired by his contemporaries and his birthday, 25 Jan., is still celebrated by his fellow countrymen and women all over the world.

BURT, SIR CYRIL (1883–1971), psychologist. Born in London, Burt was educated at Christ's Hospital and Oxford and developed his interests in psychology at Würzburg. He was lecturer in psychology at Liverpool University (1908–13), educational psychologist to the London County Council (1913–32), Professor of Educational Psychology at the London Day Training College (1924–32) and Professor of Psychology at University College, London (1932–50). His broad-ranging activities included the linking of intelligence to hereditary factors, the invention of highly influential tests for intelligence and aptitude, the development of factor analysis (a statistical technique used in evaluating intelligence) and the study of the causes of delinquent and 'backward' children. After retiring in 1950 he continued to publish on psychological subjects including consciousness, psychical research and the multifactorial theory of inheritance. His posthumous reputation has declined rapidly owing to evidence that he faked some of the data on which his findings are based.

BURT, THOMAS (1837–1922), trade unionist and politician. The first working man to be elected to Parliament, he began as a coal hewer, becoming Secretary of the Northumb. Miners' Association in 1865. He sat as Lib-Lab MP (one of a group of pre-First World War MPs who represented the labour interest but were elected with the support of the Liberal Party) for Morpeth from 1874 and held junior office under GLADSTONE. He was a staunch trade unionist and active in the co-operative movement, and was hostile to independent labour representation in Parliament.

BURTON, HENRY (1578–1648), churchman. Born in Yorks.; his early employment as tutor to Sir Robert Carey's sons and as Clerk of the Closet, first to Prince HENRY FREDERICK and then the future CHARLES I from 1612 to 1625, suggests a career cleric, but his outspoken detestation of the sacramental and clericalist churchmanship of the circle of William LAUD led to his dismissal by Charles. He was presented to a London parish, was imprisoned for attacks on the bishops in 1629 and was tried for sedition in Star Chamber with William PRYNNE and John BASTWICK in 1636. The case resulted in a huge fine, loss of his ears and condemnation to perpetual imprisonment. He became a popular hero and, on the collapse of Charles's regime, was released in 1641. The following year he began using his parish as the basis for an Independent congregation.

BURTON, SIR MONTAGUE (originally Ossinsky) (1885–1952), businessman. Born in Lithuania, and moving to England in 1900 as many Jews did to escape persecution, Burton opened his first clothing shop in 1904 and by 1910 had five shops in northern towns selling ready-made men's clothing. Based in Leeds (Yorks), the firm cemented its success by expansion to provide uniforms for the troops in the First World War. A successful combination of bespoke tailoring and large-scale production fuelled post-war growth, and Burtons became a familiar shop on high streets across the country. The company produced about a quarter of all the armed forces' uniforms during the Second World War and a third of demobilization clothing. Hence the saying, it is sometimes alleged, 'gone for a Burton'. By the time of his death, Burton had transformed the nation's clothing, especially that of working-class men.

BURTON, SIR RICHARD (1821–90), explorer, translator and orientalist. Of Irish descent and erratic education, Burton spent much of his life travelling in Africa, the Middle East and North and South America, acquiring fluency in many languages and dialects. In 1852 he was sent by the National Geographic Society to explore Arabia where, disguised as an Indian Pathan, he made the pilgrimage to the forbidden city of Mecca. The following year he was the first white man to enter the city of Harvat in Somalia. In 1857–8, on an expedition commissioned to discover the source of the Nile, he discovered Lake Tanganyika. Burton produced an unexpurgated 16-volume translation of a huge number of oriental stories collected under the title of *The Arabian Nights* in which the anthropological footnotes outran the text, and he also anonymously translated the *Kama Sutra* (1883) and *The Perfumed Garden* (1886).

BURY, RICHARD DE (1288–1345), cleric. Born at Bury St Edmunds (Suffolk) and educated at Oxford, he became a Benedictine monk, and tutor to the future EDWARD III, who secured his appointment as Bishop of Durham in 1333. He served Edward as diplomat and ambassador (1334), as Treasurer and as Chancellor (1334–5), but is most famous as a scholar and book collector, author of the *Philobiblon* (The Love of Books).

BUSS, FRANCES MARY (1827–94), educationalist. Daughter of an impecunious artist, she taught at the school which her practical mother ran to support the family. In 1853 she founded the North London Collegiate School for Girls, education being for her an instrument of women's independence and professional advancement.

BUTE, 3RD EARL OF see STUART, JOHN

BUTLER, ELIZABETH (née Thompson) (1846–1933), painter. Educated at South Kensington School of Art, and in Florence and Rome, she witnessed in 1872 the autumn manoeuvres at Chobham and was inspired to paint *Calling the Roll after an Engagement, Crimea* (1874), which captured soldiers' exhaustion in the snows of the Crimea. In 1877 she married Major (afterwards Lieutenant General Sir) William Butler, who provided her with technical assistance, and sometimes with soldiers to act as models. The result was a series of military paintings which refused to glamorize war but captured the nobility of sometimes frightened, wounded or dying soldiers. Enormously popular, Butler's paintings helped change the public's image of the British soldier from a brutal and licentious 'lobster' to Tommy Atkins.

BUTLER, JAMES, (4th Earl of Ormond, the White Earl) (*c.* 1390–1452), nobleman. He succeeded his father in 1405 while still a minor. His unusually good relations with the Irish chiefs gave him a dominant position in Tipperary and Kilkenny but the appointment of John TALBOT, later Earl of Shrewsbury, as Lieutenant of Ireland in 1414 curtailed his power. After attending HENRY V in the French wars, he was made Lieutenant in 1420. From then until the 1440s the long-running feud between them led to alternating Butler and Talbot governorships.

BUTLER, JAMES (12th Earl and 1st Duke of Ormond) (1610–88), politician. Although a leading nobleman from the Old English elite, descendants of medieval Anglo-Norman settlers who mostly remained Roman Catholic in sympathy after the Reformation, he was brought up a Protestant in England in the household of Archbishop George ABBOT before returning to Ireland in 1633. A loyal servant of the Stuarts, he was Lord Lieutenant for two periods, 1643–7 and 1649–50. He first fought the Catholic Confederation of Kilkenny in the name of the King, then concluded a series of truces with Confederate forces to free him to help the King against Parliament; the most wide-ranging coalition (comprising nearly all the various Irish factions) was completed in Jan. 1649. In Aug., Oliver CROMWELL defeated this shaky grand alliance, and Ormond went into exile with CHARLES II (1651–9). Prominent in negotiations for Charles's restoration, he was brought back as Irish Lord Lieutenant and reinstated the Protestant

episcopal hierarchy in the Irish Church; he was awarded his dukedom in 1661. Involvement in English court politics led to periods of recall from the lieutenancy (1669–71 and 1675–7) until his replacement in 1684. His lifelong Protestant constitutionalism made him disapprove of JAMES II's policies but, much distressed by his wife's death in 1684, he took little further part in politics.

BUTLER, JAMES (13th Earl and 2nd Duke of Ormond) (1665–1746), soldier and statesman. Descended from an Old English family he was grandson of the first Duke of Ormond (see BUTLER, JAMES), but had a Dutch mother; family ties and indignation at JAMES II's offhand treatment of his family perhaps combined to persuade him to rally to the cause of WILLIAM III. Having done so, he was included in the Act of Attainder passed by the Irish Jacobite Parliament, so had a personal interest in William's victory. He was present at the Battle of the Boyne (1690), and later served under William in the Netherlands. Lord Lieutenant of Ireland from 1703, in 1711 he replaced Marlborough (see CHURCHILL, JOHN) as Commander-in-Chief against Spain and France. Having followed Bolingbroke (see ST JOHN, HENRY) in dallying with the Stuarts, he found himself facing impeachment at the hands of the Whigs after the accession of GEORGE I, and fled into exile. He helped the Old Pretender (see STUART, JAMES EDWARD) organize the Spanish invasion attempt on Britain in 1719, and spent his latter years at his court in Avignon.

BUTLER, JOHN (1717–1802), churchman and propagandist. He lacked a university education, but after taking orders became a popular preacher in London and by 1754 was chaplain to the dowager Princess of Wales. His ecclesiastical career relied on his progress as a political writer; having first been close to Bute (see STUART, JOHN) he wrote a pamphlet attacking him in 1763, addressed 'to the Cocoa Tree' (impugning Bute's adherence to Whig principles by implying that his natural habitat was the traditionally Tory coffee house of that name). In the 1770s he was paid to write propaganda for NORTH. Increasingly reactionary, he was made Bishop of Oxford in 1777 and Bishop of Hereford in 1788, where he milked the dioceses of funds and defended the slave trade.

BUTLER, JOSEPH (1692–1752), theologian. Son of a draper, he was sent to a Dissenting academy, but went to Oxford University in 1714–15, was ordained, and appointed to livings in Yorks. He published sermons in 1726; his most famous work, the *Analogy* (1736), argued against proponents of Deism that God was more than just a God of nature. Drawing on but developing the ideas of Shaftesbury (*see* COOPER, ANTHONY ASHLEY, 3rd Earl) as to the congruence of virtue and happiness, he argued that men experienced themselves as having consciences; the universe therefore must have a moral governor, revealed through conscience, and human life must be understood as a probationary state, a process of striving for virtue, which also brought psychological satisfaction. Butler became Bishop of Bristol in 1738, Dean of St Paul's in 1740 and Bishop of Durham in 1750. His belief in the importance of outward forms in strengthening belief and his fondness for lives of the saints led some to accuse him of Romanist tendencies. Intellectual interests dominated his career: according to Horace WALPOLE, he was wafted to his see 'in a cloud of metaphysics, and remained absorbed in it'.

BUTLER, JOSEPHINE *see* essay on page 126

BUTLER, PIERS (8th Earl of Ormond, 1st Earl of Ossory) (*c.* 1467–1539), politician. A protégé of HENRY VII's powerful lieutenant Gerald FITZGERALD, 8th Earl of Kildare, Butler succeeded as Earl of Ormond in 1515. He helped suppress Irish rebellions and was made Lord Deputy in 1521, then Lord Treasurer in 1524; he was created Earl of Ossory as compensation for surrendering the Ormond earldom to Sir Thomas BOLEYN (although he regained it after Boleyn's death). By now building his own power base against the Kildares, he supported the English administrators of the Pale of Dublin up to his death, sharing in their successful factional campaign to destroy the Kildares' ally, Lord Deputy Lord Leonard GREY. He encouraged textile and tapestry craftsmen to settle at his head-town of Kilkenny and he endowed an important school there.

BUTLER, R(ICHARD) A(USTEN) *see* essay on page 127

BUTLER, SAMUEL (1612–80), writer. The son of a Worcs. farmer and educated at Cambridge, Butler served several noble and gentle families in a secretarial capacity. Between 1663 and 1678 he published a verse satire named *Hudibras* after its anti-hero, thought to be based on Sir Samuel Luke, a Beds. Presbyterian and Parliamentarian army commander during the English Civil Wars. Modelled on *Don Quixote*, it ridiculed the hypocrisy of both Presbyterians and Independents (Congregationalists) and, in the prevailing national mood of revulsion against the Interregnum regimes, it was an instant success. CHARLES II rewarded Butler with £300 and a pension, and he was later employed by George VILLIERS, 5th Duke of Buckingham, helping him to write his satirical play, *The Rehearsal* (1671).

BUTLER, SAMUEL (1774–1839), educationalist. He was Headmaster of Shrewsbury school from 1798 to 1836, during which time he abandoned rote learning and reformed the school's teaching methods. The prefectorial system, introduced to encourage responsibility and self-discipline, helped to make his a model for other public schools.

BUTLER, SAMUEL (1835–1902), writer. Son of a distinguished Anglican family and educated at Cambridge, he declined to take holy orders and instead emigrated to New Zealand where he became a sheep farmer. He returned to England in 1864 and pursued a career as a painter. His utopian satire *Erewhon* (anagram of nowhere) was published in 1872 and was an immediate bestseller. For the rest of his life Butler wrote on a variety of topics in a variety of forms. He also edited *The Life and Letters of Dr Samuel Butler* (his grandfather, a bishop), which was published in 1896; translated the *Iliad* (1898) and the *Odyssey* (1900), having advanced the theory in 1897 that the author of the *Odyssey* was a woman; and in *Shakespeare's Sonnets Reconsidered* (1899) he suggested that the bard had penned his poems to a plebeian lover. In 1901 he published *Erewhon Revisited* (this time struggling with the origins of religious belief) and he managed to continue a life of prodigious polymathic endeavour beyond the grave with the posthumous publication in 1903 of his still much-read autobiographical novel, *The Way of All Flesh*.

BUTLER, THOMAS (10th Earl of Ormond) (1532–1614), politician. He succeeded as Earl on his father's poisoning in 1546, developing in his years spent at HENRY VIII's court a sympathy with England and with the cause of religious reform. He arrived in Ireland in 1554 seeking to be a conciliator in Irish politics, but was driven to respond to attacks by Gerald Fitzjames FITZGERALD, 14th Earl of Desmond, after which they were both summoned to London in 1565. During the five years which he spent at court, Desmond remained persistently aggressive and Butler's brothers became increasingly rebellious against English rule; on his return, Butler supported English colonial enterprises, which led to Desmond's defeat and murder in 1583. Five years later, he helped to massacre stragglers from the Spanish Armada of 1588, and from 1598 to 1599 he fought against Hugh O'NEILL's rebellion. He was made Lord Treasurer of Ireland in 1599 and Vice-Admiral in 1612. An effective administrator and the most consistent loyalist of all Elizabethan Irish noblemen, he has been left with the nickname 'the Black Earl', as a symbol of the betrayal of Catholic and autonomous Ireland.

BUTLER, JOSEPHINE (née Grey) (1828–1906)
Feminist

She was born to a wealthy Whig family in Northumberland. Her mother Hannah was a devout Moravian; her father John Grey was a political agent for the Whigs and a staunch opponent of slavery. The commitment to social reform, which Josephine inherited from her family, was shared by the educationalist, later Dean of Winchester, George Butler, whom she married in 1852. Josephine undertook charitable work and both she and her husband maintained their social reforming views, particularly in opposition to slavery and the south during the American Civil War (1861–5); when they moved to Liverpool, where George had been appointed Principal of Liverpool College (1866), Josephine's public work increased, partly as a means of dealing with the grief which she felt at the death of her only daughter in 1863. Initially she undertook workhouse visiting, then turned to working with prostitutes, first through taking them into her own home and then by establishing a refuge for them.

At the same time she was concerned with expanding the educational and employment opportunities for women. In 1867 she became President of the North of England Council for the Higher Education of Women and in 1868 she was chosen to petition Cambridge University for the setting of special examinations for women, part of the opening up of the university to women: Girton College was established in 1869, Newnham in 1871. In 1868 she published a pamphlet, *The Education and Employment of Women*, which she followed by editing *Woman's Work and Woman's Culture* (1869), to which many women and men active in contemporary feminism and the women's suffrage movement contributed. While arguing for the expansion of women's possibilities, Butler's feminism grew out of Christian philanthropy and Victorian conceptions of gender roles which meant that she only partially challenged the dominant assumptions of a separate sphere for women. While men and women were complementary, woman's particular strength lay in her moral pre-eminence, the nurturing and protection of the weak and the defence of the family, home and a single standard of chastity as against the double standard which allowed men sexual freedom.

The Contagious Diseases Acts were introduced between 1866 and 1869. Originally intended to reduce the incidence of venereal disease in garrison towns, the legislation was an attempt by the State to regulate prostitution by subjecting those believed to be prostitutes to compulsory, regular and humiliating medical examination. Women found to be diseased were to be incarcerated in special hospitals. It was in response to the attempt to extend the Acts in the late 1860s that a large public campaign against them got under way. The campaign was initially spearheaded by an association which excluded women. The Ladies' National Association (LNA) was founded in 1869 in opposition to that exclusion; it soon came to be the dominant force in the agitation and Butler emerged as its major voice. The LNA's work was conducted by a substantial membership, large public meetings and demonstrations, the *Shield* newspaper and political work in both by-elections and drawing-room lobbying, while its social base was drawn particularly from middle-class women in alliance with respectable working men. Within this agitation Butler had a major impact: she was a gifted public speaker and forceful leader who inspired immense loyalty.

Illness caused her to relinquish her role as the major figure of the campaign in 1874. (It was then led through Parliament by James STANSFELD until the Acts were repealed in 1885–6.) But the campaign had pushed her feminism in a new direction: she moved from being conscious of the ways in which the Acts denied women civil and legal rights to becoming much more aware of the manner in which the 'diabolical triple power' of police, magistrates and doctors who administered the Acts were part of a network of men engaged in the oppression and surveillance of women. At the same time, her Evangelical Christian roots led her in a conservative direction, seeing prostitutes as victims of the double standard of sexual morality. Rescue would be achieved by restoring the victimized woman to her natural role as home-maker and carer for others. It was in this spirit that she was drawn into the later 'social purity' campaigns, above all that associated with W. T. STEAD's campaign through his National Vigilance Association against 'white slavery' and child prostitution in 1885. After her husband's death she largely withdrew from public life, devoting herself mainly to the writing of *Recollections* of him (1892) and her own *Reminiscences of a Great Crusade* (1896).

Barbara Caine, Victorian Feminists (1992)

BUTLER, R(ICHARD) A(USTEN) ('RAB')
(Baron Butler of Saffron Walden) (1902–82)
Politician

Rab (as he was always known) came from a family with a long tradition of public service in education and the Indian Civil Service, and the Conservative Party was his natural political home; his earliest ambition was to be Viceroy of India, one which, like others, was to remain unfulfilled.

Rab entered the Commons in 1929 as MP for Saffron Walden, defying the general trend in that election. His formative political influence was Stanley BALDWIN, whose liberal brand of Conservatism he admired, adopted and continued. After the 1931 election Rab became Parliamentary Private Secretary to Samuel HOARE at the India Office, becoming his Under-Secretary in 1932, thus beginning a career on the front benches which would endure until 1964. Rab was naturally a 'party' man, loyal to his leadership and suspicious of rebels. His support for the India Bill which would create a federal India with greater self-government won him the hostility of those Tory imperialists like CHURCHILL who saw in it the first steps towards leaving India. After a short period at the Ministry of Labour (1937–8) he went to the Foreign Office as deputy to Lord Halifax (see WOOD, EDWARD) in Feb. 1938, where his enthusiastic support of appeasement once again earned him Churchill's enmity.

Despite later attempts to muddy the water, Butler was one of the leading proponents of appeasement and, as late as July 1939, he was still searching for ways of negotiating with Hitler; he would have preferred Britain to have allowed Germany to expand eastwards until it came into conflict with the Soviet Union. He was a CHAMBER-LAIN loyalist until the end and resented Churchill's accession to the premiership in 1940, regarding him as a half-American adventurer who would gamble the Empire away. But, as ever, Rab swallowed his own views and worked for the common good. Despite their previous difference Churchill offered Rab promotion in 1940, although he was surprised that he preferred to go to the Board of Education rather than to the War Office.

As a progressive Conservative Rab recognized that unless the party showed itself sensitive to the needs of the people after the war it would have little future. He was a keen supporter of the 1942 Beveridge Report, and at the Board of Education pioneered the 1944 Education Act which bore his name and which set the framework of education in Britain for the next three decades. When the Conservatives lost power in 1945 he was the major figure in the reorganization of the party and the rethinking of party policy. Rab himself propagated the myth that there was a 'new Conservatism' after about 1947 but most modern commentators see a continuity between the liberal, welfarist Conservatism of Baldwin and that promoted by Rab; but as a shrewd politician Rab realized that presentation was, if not all, then an awful lot, and he successfully rebranded the Conservatives as a party that could work with the Welfare State and the post-war consensus. So much was he identified personally with this line that when he became Chancellor in 1951 journalists coined the name 'Butskellism' to emphasize the continuity between his policies and those of his Labour predecessor, Hugh GAITSKELL.

The Conservative recovery after 1945 and the eventual victory in 1951 owed much to Rab, whose position was recognized by promotion to the Exchequer. But Rab was no economist, and happily went along with the advice of his officials, something which triggered off an economic crisis in 1955. Under Churchill he was one of the leading figures in the government but he felt nothing but contempt for the heir apparent, EDEN, and when the latter became Prime Minister in 1955 he was conspicuously lukewarm in his support, declaring on one occasion that Eden was 'the best Prime Minister we have'.

Rab's 1955 budget was widely held to have been an electioneering one, a suspicion confirmed by a post-election budget designed to damp down inflation. He allowed himself to be moved to the office of Lord President of the Council in 1955, a position which ensured that he lost influence during 1956 at a time when he would need it most. The Suez fiasco led to Eden's resignation in Jan. 1957. It was widely supposed that Rab was his natural successor but he swallowed his disappointment when MACMILLAN got the job, and served him loyally in a variety of positions until 1963. The loyalty was not returned and, when Macmillan suddenly resigned in 1963, he did his utmost to ensure that Rab did not succeed him. In an excess of loyalty, Rab became Foreign Secretary under Alec DOUGLAS-HOME but his heart was not in it. In 1964 he accepted the mastership of Trinity College, Cambridge, and a peerage. A liberal to the end, Rab disapproved of Margaret THATCHER.

Anthony Howard, RAB: The Life of R. A. Butler (1987)

BUTLIN, SIR WILLIAM (BILLY) (1899–1980), businessman. The product of a dislocated childhood, Butlin returned to England from Canada and at the age of 22 joined his mother's fairground relatives, soon finding ways to make money on his hoop-la stalls. With the increased accessibility of seaside resorts for day trips, Butlin set up a fixed fairground business in Skegness (Lincs.) in 1927, introducing new attractions from the USA such as dodgems. The amusement park business grew and in 1936 Butlin opened the first purpose-built holiday camp, again at Skegness. The 1938 legislation giving workers entitlement to holiday with pay helped make the holiday camp business a success. Butlin was the market leader until the late 1950s when cheap air travel offered other possibilities and families rebelled against the over-regimented camp life.

BUTT, ISAAC (1813–79), Irish politician. Son of a Protestant rector, he was called to the Irish Bar in 1835. He was associated with Irish Tory intellectuals who presented themselves as defenders of traditional Irish institutions against centralizing British reformers and the Catholic populism of Daniel O'CONNELL; Butt became prominent in the Orange Order. His attitude to the Union was altered by the official response to the Great Famine in the 1840s; he complained that a similar famine in Britain would have been treated more generously and the Union was interpreted to make Ireland share burdens but not benefits equally. He acted as defence counsel to Young Ireland leaders after the abortive rising of 1848. After a distinguished legal career (offset by financial carelessness and the need to support numerous legitimate and illegitimate children) and an undistinguished career as a Tory backbencher, Butt returned to prominence by defending Fenian prisoners. In 1870 he founded the Home Government Association (renamed the Home Rule League in 1873) to advocate a federal solution to the Irish demand for self-government. As MP for Limerick he led the 58-strong Irish Home Rule group in the Commons in 1874, but failed to convince Parliament of the need for serious consideration of the Irish Question. He was seen as ineffective and excessively sympathetic to the Conservative government; though nominal leader until his death his authority was undermined by the rising popularity of Charles Stewart PARNELL, whose policy of obstruction he opposed. Recent scholarship emphasizes longterm continuities in Butt's attitudes, derived from an older Protestant 'patriot' tradition.

BUTTERFIELD, HERBERT (1900–79), historian. Educated at Keighley grammar school and at Peterhouse, Cambridge, where he spent most of his adult years, Butterfield retained his commitment to the Methodist faith of his Yorks. childhood. Concern to establish how historians might understand the role of God in history informed one of his later books, *Christianity and the Historian* (1955). He made most impact through early polemical works. *The Whig Interpretation of History* (1931) attacked attempts by such historians as ACTON and TREVELYAN to understand the past as a highroad to the present. In *George III and the Historians* (1937) he attacked Sir Lewis NAMIER's brand of structural political history, calling it desiccated. His only substantial historical, as opposed to historiographical, study was *George III, Lord North and the People* (1949), a study of Britain around 1780. Here he emphasized the convulsing effect of the War of American Independence, which he saw as having brought about a quasi-revolutionary situation in both Britain and Ireland. Writing before Lord Rockingham's papers (*see* WATSON-WENTWORTH, CHARLES) had been made available to historians, Butterfield underestimated the part politicians played in stirring up popular discontent for their own purposes. Arguably, historians subsequently veered too far the other way, however, underestimating the spontaneity and depth of popular discontent in this period.

BUTTERFIELD, WILLIAM (1814–1900), architect. A High Anglican, Butterfield designed several London churches, reviving the Gothic style. He used bricks of many different colours set in a variety of geometric patterns on the outside and a rich excess of decoration within; All Saints, Margaret Street, London (built 1849–59), remains the finest example of the exuberant work of this austere bachelor.

BUTTS, SIR WILLIAM (?–1545), doctor. Norfolk-born and Cambridge-educated, he was a court physician from the 1520s. His importance lies in the influence he exercised in bringing Protestant reformers from Cambridge University to HENRY VIII's notice, and securing them favour and patronage, in alliance with other Protestant courtiers such as Sir Anthony DENNY.

BUXTON, SIR THOMAS (1786–1845), brewer and social reformer. MP for Weymouth from 1813 to 1837, he worked for criminal law and prison reform and the abolition of the slave trade, succeeding William WILBERFORCE as head of the anti-slavery party in 1823. The abolition of slavery in Aug. 1833 marked the high point of his career.

BYNG, GEORGE (1st Viscount Torrington) (1663–1733), naval commander and diplomat. His father, a Kentish landowner, fell into financial diffi-

continued on page 132

BYRD, WILLIAM (c. 1539–1623)
Composer

One of the greatest composers of his age, both for voices and instruments, Byrd dominates the most distinguished period in English musical composition before the twentieth century, representative of a generation when England led musical creativity throughout Europe. His early life and his year of birth are obscure, but he may have been a choirboy at Westminster Abbey, and his brothers were in the choir at St Paul's Cathedral during the 1550s. He is likely to have been a pupil of Thomas TALLIS in the Chapel Royal, and he was appointed organist of Lincoln Cathedral in 1563; in 1569 he was given a joint appointment with Tallis as honorary organist of the Chapel Royal, a post which he retained despite his increasingly open adherence to the Roman Catholic Church (by contrast, Tallis showed no signs of nonconformity to the new religious settlement). He was fined for his recusancy (refusal to take Communion in the established Church), and was closely linked to the community of recusant gentry in East Anglia, in whose houses much of his music was first performed. ELIZABETH I's continuing employment of him in the Chapel Royal is a measure of her recognition of his exceptional talent.

Byrd set himself up as an Essex country gentleman at Stondon Massey, where he died, and it is his prolific musical composition which filled a life otherwise uneventful apart from the common gentry pursuit of fighting lawsuits. His continuing co-operation with Tallis resulted in 1575 in the grant of a royal monopoly on issuing printed music and music-paper (1575); in that year they published *Cantiones Sacrae* – a collection of motets (short unaccompanied choral pieces for sacred use), dedicated to the Queen. Byrd followed this with two further volumes of *Cantiones Sacrae* (1589, 1591) and *Gradualia* (1605, 1607) devoted entirely to his own Latin sacred choral music. He wrote liturgical music both for the established Protestant Church and for the Catholic recusant community. Among his works for choirs to sing at morning and evening prayer in the Church of England, his 'Great Service' is the most sumptuous. In these compositions, he made an innovation which became distinctive in English liturgical music: a solo voice takes certain parts of the text and forms a dialogue with its organ accompaniment, as if voice and instrument together form a choir singing polyphony, and these sections are used in alternation with sections of text set for full choir. This form became the basis for the 'verse anthems' composed by Byrd and his successors for use in the services of the Established Church.

Byrd's liturgical music is at its most heartfelt, however, in his three Latin mass settings, for three, four and five voices; these were intended for use by recusants, and they noticeably stress the phrase *Catholicam Ecclesiam* (the Catholic Church) in their treatment of the text of the Creed. They were the last significant masses to be written in England until the twentieth century. His *Songs of Sundrie Natures* (1589) contained some of the first English madrigals, the secular equivalent of the motet, and he also wrote songs for the stage and other solo songs. His music for strings (the family of instruments known as viols) set fashions for compositions of 'fancies' (fantasias). He also popularized the peculiar English musical fashion started by John TAVERNER (c. 1495–1545) for writing variations on one particular fragment of plainsong chant set to the text *In Nomine Domini* (In the Name of the Lord); such a composition is entitled an *In Nomine*.

Byrd's interest in keyboard music led him to elaborate a variation style of composition which not only set the agenda for English composers until the late seventeenth century but greatly influenced contemporaries in the rest of Europe. His keyboard works are preserved partly in a major compilation of contemporary keyboard music (c. 1609–c. 1619) by a recusant gentleman, Francis Tregian, now known as the 'Fitzwilliam Virginal Book', since it became one of the foundation bequests of Cambridge University's Fitzwilliam Museum. Byrd also published jointly a number of keyboard compositions with Orlando GIBBONS and John BULL which formed a wedding present for Elizabeth, daughter of JAMES I, when she married the Elector Palatine Frederick V (1613). It was called *Parthenia*, a punning title at several levels (from the Greek word for virgin), since this was a book of virginal music presented to a virginal bride-to-be, and it was also the first book in which an English publisher had tried to produce music from engraved copper plates. For half a century it remained the only English keyboard music in print, and it became the standard starter-book for those learning the keyboard.

John Harley, William Byrd: Gentleman of the Chapel Royal (1997)

BYRON, GEORGE GORDON (6th Baron Byron of Rochdale) (1788–1824)
Poet

Descended from JAMES I through his mother, Catherine Stewart, a Scottish heiress, his father was 'Mad Jack' Byron, who squandered his wife's inheritance and his own. When his father fled abroad to escape his creditors, Byron's mother went home to her family in Aberdeenshire to raise her son in straitened circumstances. In 1799 he inherited the title and the family seat of Newstead Abbey (Notts.) but almost no money for the upkeep of his dilapidated new home, or indeed himself. Educated at Harrow and even there beginning to cultivate a persona of profligacy and excessive behaviour, Byron went up to Trinity College, Cambridge, in 1805.

Despite the dissipated image which he cultivated, he was a productive student: his first slim volume of 'warmly drawn' poetry, *Fugitive Pieces*, was privately published when he was 19. The self-censored (and expanded) volume, *Poems on Various Occasions* (1807), was '*vastly* correct and miraculously chaste'. Two months later another collection, *Hours of Idleness*, was published to Byron's great delight: 'in every bookseller's I see my *own name* and *say nothing*, but enjoy my *fame in secret*'. But not everyone was so enthusiastic: one critic compared the poems to 'school exercises' while in the influential *Edinburgh Review* Henry BROUGHAM likened the poems to 'so much stagnant water'. Byron was devastated and morose. But he rallied to revise a satire, *The Bards*, attacking the 'establishment' of SOUTHEY, COLERIDGE, WORDSWORTH and Sir Walter SCOTT.

In 1809 Byron, who was deeply in debt, partly from gambling and high living but also from reckless generosity to friends and people whose plight touched him, left England with his great friend John Cam HOBHOUSE (whose expenses he paid) for a 'grand tour' of Europe. Byron's letters and observations from his travels through France, Spain and the eastern Mediterranean were published in 1811 as *Hints from Horace* and, after his return to England, he finished the first two cantos of a poem begun in Albania, *Childe Harold's Pilgrimage*, which was published by John Murray in March 1812, a month after he had made his maiden speech in the House of Lords in favour of measures to alleviate the distress of the stocking-weavers of Nottingham and against a repressive Bill to make Luddite tactics of machine-breaking a capital offence. 'I spoke with a modest impudence', he wrote, 'abused every thing and every body ... I was born for opposition.' Though clearly a compelling orator, Byron was too volatile for a party political career:

Parliament provided too narrow a stage for his protest.

The year 1812 was to be a turning-point in his life. *Childe Harold* was acclaimed as a masterpiece and Byron as a literary lion, a must-have guest for every hostess, especially the great Whig hostesses. Lady Caroline LAMB, wife of the man who would, as Lord Melbourne (see LAMB, WILLIAM), become Prime Minister in 1834, read the book, and noting that anyone who wrote such a work must be 'mad – bad – and dangerous to know' urged Lady Holland to introduce them. They found each other irresistible and embarked on an intense, entirely indiscreet affair. Eventually worn out by the passions, histrionics and near madness of his 'wild antelope' Byron ended the relationship and in 1815 married Annabella Milbanke, a woman who thought she could reform the raffish, by now heavy-drinking poet and remove him from the febrile society that surrounded him in the metropolis. The marriage, which produced a daughter (*see* KING, AUGUSTA ADA), lasted less than a year.

By now Byron was even more deeply in debt than ever despite his literary success. He published *The Curse of Minerva* (1812), *The Giaour* and *The Bride of Abydos* (1813), *The Corsair, Lara* and *Jacqueline* (1814), *Hebrew Melodies* (1815), and *The Siege of Corinth* and *Parisina* (1816), all of which, particularly *The Corsair*, fuelled the growing legend of a Byronic hero who was dashing, debonair, dissolute and touched with melancholy. The poet refused (at present) to take royalties for his literary work while John Murray was becoming one of the most commercially astute of a new breed of publishers selling, to his amazement, 10, 000 copies of *The Corsair* on the first day of publication. But London society, seized by 'one of its periodic fits of morality' (in the words of MACAULAY), had turned against the poet, choosing to believe Lady Byron's accusations of her husband's incestuous relationship with his half-sister, Augusta Leigh. On 23 April 1816 Byron, accompanied by his friend Polidori, left England never to return.

After visiting the battlefield at Waterloo, which to Byron represented not a patriotic victory but was 'a place of skulls', a lost opportunity to rid Europe of tyrannical oppression, he sailed up the Rhine and thence to Switzerland. There he met for the first time Mary SHELLEY and 'that wonderful boy' Percy Bysshe SHELLEY who had also fled England's inhospitable shores, and the party, which included Mary's sister Claire

Clairmont, who was pregnant with Byron's child, spent that 'year without a summer' on the shores of Lake Geneva, where Byron wrote the third canto of *Childe Harold* and *The Prisoner of Chillon*. In Aug. the Shelley party left for England and Byron set off for Venice.

In Venice Byron wrote *The Lament of Tasso* and *Manfred* (1817), the fourth canto of *Childe Harold* and *Beppo* (1818), and *Mazeppa* (1819) as well as the first canto of his satirical, emotional autobiographical masterpiece, *Don Juan*. He also began a long-lasting liaison with the 19-year-old Teresa, Countess Guiccioli, in April 1819; later that year he moved to Ravenna to be nearer to Teresa, who had separated from her husband and was living in the house of her brother, Pietro, Count Gamba. Influenced by Teresa, who was the inspiration for *The Prophecy of Dante* (1821), Byron began to take an active interest in Italian nationalism, supporting the militant nationalist movement (the Carbonari led by Count Gamba, which was struggling to throw off Austrian domination and unite Italy) with money and also with influence, since by now he was a figure of commanding literary stature throughout Europe. Goethe started a correspondence with him, and included Byron in the second part of *Faust*, where he appears as Faust's child, Euphorion; Byron dedicated *Sardanapalus* (1821) to Goethe. But as a result of the Count's revolutionary activities, his properties were confiscated, the Carbonari seemed in danger of collapse and in Sept. 1821 Byron joined him and his sister in a flight to Pisa, where the Shelleys were also living.

By now Byron, no longer the dashing corsair of his youth, was running to fat, his luxuriant dark hair was thinning, his deformed foot, which had been such an embarrassment to him when he was younger, caused him to limp and use a cane, but he was at least more comfortably off. The sale of Newstead Abbey had at last gone through, a complicated marriage settlement meant that he received a generous annuity and he had begun to accept payment for his writing. He even toyed with thoughts of returning to England, which was in the grip of a repressive Tory administration. Yet, unwilling to identify with the actions of the 'rabble', such as those who had been killed or injured at the Peterloo Massacre in Manchester in 1819, Byron still held the Whig attitude of *noblesse oblige*, believing that the freedom of the people needed its guarantor in an aristocratic leader.

So for the time being he contented himself with writing a satiric parody of the eulogy on the death of GEORGE III penned by the Poet Laureate, Southey, whom Byron regarded with particular spleen as a 'turncoat' since Southey's rejection of his early radical views. *The Vision of Judgement* was published in Leigh HUNT's paper, *The Liberal*, in 1822, thus ending Byron's association with John Murray and causing Hunt (who published the subsequent cantos of *Don Juan* and, unlike the more conservative Murray, foregrounded their social and political commentaries) to be prosecuted for 'calumniating the late King and wounding the feelings of his present Majesty'. Southey retaliated, naming Byron the leader of the 'Satanic' school of poets.

In July 1823, deeply shaken by the death of Shelley, drowned in the Gulf of Spezia the previous summer, Byron had resolved on a cause. Leaving the distraught Teresa Guiccioli he sailed for Greece, his poetic alma mater, with a group of followers wearing helmets emblazoned with the message 'Crede Byron' (trust Byron), to take charge of the fight for freedom in the Greek War of Independence against Turkish rule on behalf of the London Greek committee. The situation which he discovered was confused, with internecine Greek fighting and not much clarity as to the 'cause'. 'I did not come here to join a faction, but a nation,' he wrote. He established himself in the mud-sodden, rain-swept small port of Missolonghi, intent on taking the Turkish stronghold at Lepanto. But he was already weak and ill. On 19 April 1824, bled almost dry by the doctor's leeches, Byron, who had contracted rheumatic fever, died aged 36. His lungs were donated to the people of Missolonghi; the rest of his body was transported back to England where, while radicals and literary men bowed their heads as they walked behind his black-plumed hearse followed by 47 carriages, respectable London society stayed at home, and he was refused burial in Westminster Abbey.

The Byronic legend far outlived its source, the guarantee of all that was most romantic in romanticism, of all that was most inspiring in fighting for freedom, as well as the scourge of official cant, cruelty and social hypocrisy. Lines of his poems are so familiar that they are often unattributed, and his great satire *Don Juan* is in the Augustan tradition of the poets whom he so admired, DRYDEN and POPE.

Leslie A. Marchand, Byron's Letters and Journals, (12 vols, 1973–82); Byron: A Portrait (1979)
Phyllis Grosskurth, Byron: The Flawed Angel (1997)

culties. He entered the navy aged 15. During the War of the Spanish Succession he assisted in the capture of Gibraltar, and defeated the French–Jacobite force in the Forth in 1708. Byng was rewarded with a place on the Admiralty Board in 1709 which continued under GEORGE I. Byng's action in 1715 separated the Jacobites from their supply lines in the North Sea. In 1718 he was sent to the Mediterranean to stop the Spanish conquest of Sicily, and successfully defeated the Spanish fleet off Cape Passaro, protecting the interests of Britain's ally the Emperor Charles VI, who hoped to secure Sicily for himself. Byng was British representative at the conference in 1720 which sought to preserve the peace of Europe against the ambitions of revisionist powers (those, such as Spain, who had done badly at the 1713 Treaty of Utrecht) by giving Sicily to the Emperor in exchange for Sardinia, which went to the Duke of Savoy.

BYNG, JOHN (1704–57), naval commander. A younger son of 1st Viscount Torrington (*see* BYNG, GEORGE), Byng had the misfortune of being in command of an ill-prepared and inadequate fleet sent at the outbreak of the Seven Years War to prevent a French attack on Minorca. Too late to prevent a French landing, he allowed a council of war to persuade him to leave the besieged garrison to its fate. The subsequent political row caused the resignation of Newcastle (*see* PELHAM-HOLLES, THOMAS). Byng was court-martialled and sentenced to be shot for neglect of duty. His execution on 14 March 1757 caused Voltaire's famous remark in *Candide* that 'the English thought it good to kill an Admiral from time to time to encourage the others' (*pour encourager les autres*).

BYNG, JULIAN (1st Viscount Byng of Vimy) (1862–1935), soldier. Youngest son of the Earl of Strafford, educated at Eton, commissioned from the militia into the cavalry, Byng served on the North West Frontier, in the Sudan in 1884, and in the Boer War, where Winston CHURCHILL briefly served as his dispatch rider. Promoted Major-General in 1910, Byng commanded a division at Ypres in 1915 and helped organize the evacuation of the Gallipoli peninsula. In May 1916 he returned to France to command the Canadian Corps, one of the crack corps of the British Empire, which managed to capture Vimy Ridge in April 1917. Appointed to command 3rd Army in June 1917, Byng organized the first mass tank attack which penetrated the German line at Cambrai in Nov. and successfully resisted and then counter-attacked the German offensive of 21 March 1918. A voracious reader of military history, Byng used his knowledge and intellectual flexibility to adapt to the conditions of the Western Front, his attack at Cambrai becoming a model for future armoured operations.

BYRD, WILLIAM *see* essay on page 129

BYRHTFERTH (*fl. c.* 1015), monk of Ramsey. Described by Sir Frank Stenton as 'the most eminent man of science produced by the English Church since the death of BEDE', Byrhtferth's particular scientific interests lay in what we would now call mathematics and astronomy. His manual on the *Computus* is a typical product of the Tenth-Century Reform, since it was written in both Latin and English in order to educate parish priests. A protégé of ABBO OF FLEURY, he also wrote historical works, such as a *Life of St* OSWALD.

BYRHTNOTH (?–991), Ealdorman of Essex. He achieved immortality because his heroic death in battle against the Danes during the reign of ETHELRED II THE UNREADY was recorded in the famous Old English poem describing the Battle of Maldon (Essex). He became Ealdorman of Essex in 956, was a strong supporter of the Tenth-Century Reform of the English Church associated with St DUNSTAN and St ETHELWOLD and had extensive land throughout eastern England. The bravery and self-sacrifice of Byrhtnoth and his men contrasts sharply with the conduct of many of their contemporaries.

BYRON, GEORGE *see* essay on pages 130–1

C

CABOT, JOHN (*c.* 1450–*c.* 1498), explorer. Born Giovanni Caboto in Genoa, he became a citizen of Venice (1476) and traded in the Middle East. He was seized by the idea that the precious Far-Eastern commodities which he was buying might be brought directly from Asia to Europe across the Atlantic Ocean and, in the late 1480s or early 1490s, moved to London to seek backing for his quest for a north-west passage. Christopher Columbus's voyage of 1492 spurred Cabot to get backing from Bristol merchants already involved in Atlantic exploration, and also to secure a charter from HENRY VII for a westwards expedition (1496). His second venture in 1497 made a landfall on a now unidentifiable part of the north American coastline, and in 1498 Cabot set off again. He may have died at sea; his enterprise was continued by his son, Sebastian CABOT.

CABOT, SEBASTIAN (1474–1557). A Bristol merchant, who sailed with his father John CABOT in 1497 to Newfoundland and Nova Scotia, in 1499 returning to explore the eastern coastline of north America southwards from Labrador to what are now the Carolinas. The exploration laid the foundation for the exploitation of the cod-fishing banks of Newfoundland. Further explorations of the coast with the backing of Bristolians in *c.* 1508 and 1521 were designed to find a short route to Asian trade, a north-west passage around the American continent. Cabot entered the service of the King of Spain until 1548, when he was invited back to England and was made life governor of Bristol's Society of Merchant Venturers when it was chartered in 1551.

CADAFAEL AP CYNFEDW (*fl.* mid seventh century), King of Gwynedd. Little is known of Cadafael. He is called King of Gwynedd in the *Historia Brittonum* where he is stated to have accompanied PENDA, King of Mercia, on his campaign against OSWY of Northumbria in 655, but is recorded as having withdrawn his troops on the eve of the Battle of Winwæd, in which Penda was subsequently defeated. In the *Trioedd Ynys Prydain* his lineage is described as 'sprung from villeins', suggesting that he was unconnected with the main Gwynedd dynasty of CADWALLON and CADWALADR, and may have emerged to fill a power vacuum.

CADBURY, GEORGE (1839–1922) and **LAURENCE** (1889–1982), manufacturers. The family's Birmingham cocoa and chocolate business had been established in 1831 by John Cadbury, but by 1861 it was near collapse. His sons George and Richard took over the business, and achieved a breakthrough in 1866 by marketing the first unadulterated cocoa in Britain, using new Dutch technology. Surplus cocoa butter from making cocoa essence was used to increase the quality and taste of eating chocolate. Needing new premises, the Cadbury brothers moved to a greenfield site just outside the city at Bournville, where workers' welfare, workers' rights and good housing were among their objectives. Business increased, and by 1908 Cadbury's profits were outstripping those of its rivals and fellow Quakers, FRYS of Bristol. George Cadbury's political support for the Liberal Party was underwritten by his ownership of the loss-making *Daily News* newspaper. His son Laurence carried on those interests in philanthropy and politics while overseeing further business expansion, from the merger of Cadbury and Fry in 1919 to guiding the new company's emergence by the 1950s and 1960s as an international public company.

CADE, JACK (?–1450), rebel leader. He was the otherwise unknown leader of a Kentish rebellion which brought the government of HENRY VI to its knees in 1450 and produced in its manifesto, *The Complaint of the Commons of Kent*, a telling diagnosis of the ills which beset the realm in the aftermath of humiliating defeat in the Hundred Years War. Cade himself took the name Mortimer, presumably as a reminder of the Mortimer–York claim to the throne and perhaps in the hope of winning the support of RICHARD OF YORK. Henry's courtiers blamed the people of Kent for the murder of the King's principal councillor, William de la POLE, Duke of Suffolk, in May 1450 and threatened to take reprisals against them. Kent's response was to rebel, and for some weeks the government seemed helpless in the face of a large army, including many gentry, drawn up on

Blackheath (Kent). When Cade's men ambushed an advance guard of the army sent against them, Henry retreated to Kenilworth (Warws.), allowing the rebels to enter London on 4 July and execute unpopular courtiers. When Cade proved unable to discipline his men, the Londoners turned against him. He was promised a free pardon and disbanded his troops, but was then hunted down and killed on 12 July 1450.

CADELL (*fl.* fifth century), 'King' of Powys. A legendary figure mentioned in the *Historia Brittonum* of NENNIUS, Cadell is said there to have taken over kingship in Powys from VORTIGERN. As such he should be regarded as the founder of the ruling family of Powys, although it is quite possible that he simply did not exist. That his name appears in the later ruling family of Powys (*see* CYNGEN AP CADELL) may suggest that he was a historical figure, but it is not decisive proof.

CADOG, ST (*fl.* sixth century), monk. He was one of the most renowned of the early Welsh saints. Details of his career and some relevant charters are preserved in a life written in the late eleventh or early twelfth century. He is believed to have lived in the sixth century, to have been Abbot of Llancarfan in the Vale of Glamorgan, and to have presided over a monastic confederation that stretched throughout south-east Wales. He was also venerated as a saint in Ireland.

CADWALADR AP CADWALLON (*fl.* mid seventh century), King of Gwynedd. Cadwaladr succeeded his father as King in *c.* 634. He vigorously continued CADWALLON's policies and tried for some time to recover the pre-eminent position held by the British kingdoms against the emergent kingdoms of Anglo-Saxon England. He may have continued Cadwallon's alliance with PENDA of Mercia, whom he may possibly have supported against OSWALD of Northumbria at the Battle of Oswestry in 642. The *Historia Brittonum* records his death from plague in 664, but the same source records CADAFAEL AP CYNFEDW as King of Gwynedd in 655, suggesting Cadwaladr's death before this date. Following his death, the *Brut y Tywysogion* laments that 'thenceforth the Britons lost the crown of the kingdom and the Saxons gained it'.

CADWALLA (?–689), King of Wessex (685–8). He succeeded his kinsman CENTWINE. His reign is notable for his conquest of the Jutes on the Isle of Wight (*see* ARWALD) and the establishment of a temporary hegemony over Sussex and Surrey. He occasionally called himself 'King of the Saxons', indicating that his reign marked a significant stage, based on steady military expansion under his predecessors, in the evolution of his family's rule towards kingship over the larger region, which was eventually controlled by his ninth-century and tenth-century successors, such as EGBERT and ALFRED THE GREAT. In 688 he resigned his kingdom and went to Rome on pilgrimage and was succeeded by INE.

CADWALLON (?–634), King of Gwynedd (*c.* 625–34). One of the most powerful of the early kings of Gwynedd, he appears to have reacted violently to the advance of Northumbria's power in northern Britain and in 633, in alliance with PENDA of Mercia, he defeated and killed King EDWIN. His career ended a year later with his death in battle against St OSWALD of Northumbria. Cadwallon is the only British ruler known to have overthrown an English king. His life illustrates the violent and fluid politics of the period when the early kingdoms were formed, as well as the impossibility of separating its 'Welsh', 'English' and 'Scottish' elements.

CADWGAN AP BLEDDYN (?–*c.* 1112), Welsh prince. In 1094 with Gruffud ap Cynan he demolished the Norman castles in Gwynned and overran Herefs., Glos. and Worcs., but was forced to flee to Ireland in 1099. He returned and joined ROBERT OF BELLÊME in fighting against HENRY I. As he was unable to control his son Owain, who had abducted NEST, wife of Gerald of Windsor, he was required to remain at the King's court. His land was restored in 1112, but on his return he was killed by his nephew Madog.

CÆDMON (?–680), monk. The subject of one of BEDE's miracle stories, in his later years, he was a monk of Whitby in the time of abbesses St HILDA, St ÆLFFLÆD and St EANFLÆD. Although little of Cædmon's work survives, we know from Bede (whose story tells how the monk miraculously acquired the ability to sing) that his great accomplishment was turning Bible stories into Old English verse. Although he was one of the lesser figures of the Northumbrian Renaissance, his activities show how Christian and vernacular cultures were assimilated.

CAESAR, SIR JULIUS (1558–1636), lawyer. Son of an Italian physician who settled in London and served MARY I and ELIZABETH I, Caesar studied at Oxford and the Inner Temple; he was the most prominent civil lawyer of his generation, also practising in Chancery, and frequently becoming an MP. Chancellor of the Exchequer (1606), then Master of the Rolls from 1614, he wrote on legal matters and extensive papers of his survive in the British Library.

CAIRD, JAMES (1816–92), agricultural specialist. An advocate of improved methods of husbandry, his booklet *High Farming: The Best Substitute for Protection* (1849) presented a strategy for survival in the more competitive environment created by the repeal of the Corn Laws. Better education, improved drainage, the application of chemical fertilizers and the use of machinery, he argued, would all enable British farmers to remain profitable. Subsequent publications included *English Agriculture* (1851) and *The Landed Interest and the Supply of Food* (1874), in which insecure tenancies, poor estate management and the State's *laissez-faire* attitude were identified as serious problems for the long-term health and vitality of British agriculture.

CAIRNCROSS, SIR ALEXANDER (ALEC) (1911–98), economist. Cairncross was born in Scotland and was a graduate of Glasgow (1933) and Cambridge (1936) universities. He was one of the academic members of the Radcliffe Committee on the Monetary System (1957–9). His powers of analysis and exposition resulted in his taking on the role of adviser to the Conservative government (1961–4) and he served as head of the government economic service (1964–9) under the Labour administration. He reorganized the service, which resulted in changes in training and recruitment and an influx of professional economists to departments other than the Treasury. His major publications, *Home and Foreign Investment 1870–1913* (1953) and *Factors in Economic Development* (1962) focused on empirical experience of investment and growth. Later work dealt with issues of monetary policy and problems of forecasting and planning.

CAITHNESS, 20TH EARL OF *see* SINCLAIR, WILLIAM

CAIUS, JOHN (1510–73), doctor. Norfolk-born, he studied at Cambridge and Padua and travelled extensively in Europe before returning in 1544 to lecture in anatomy in London. He was physician to EDWARD VI and MARY I, but was dismissed by ELIZABETH I in 1568 for his Roman Catholicism. In 1557 he re-endowed and refounded his old Cambridge college, Gonville Hall, as Gonville and Caius College, building its three extraordinary Renaissance gateways and becoming its first Master. He wrote on medicine (including pioneering observations on sweating sickness) and on Greek pronunciation, together with a book which predated the origins of Cambridge University in order to prove it older than Oxford: an Oxford rival, Thomas Key or Caius, then asserted Oxford's foundation by King ALFRED at the latest.

CALAMY, EDMUND (1671–1732), historian. His father and grandfather, also both Edmund,

were Puritan ministers: he gathered important collections on the lives of ministers ejected from the established Church in 1662, first published in 1702. His work provoked the High Church Anglican clergyman, John WALKER to perform a similar biographical task for Episcopalian clergy who suffered from 1640 to 1660 (published 1714).

CALDERWOOD, DAVID (1575–1650), historian. A minister educated at Edinburgh, he fiercely opposed attempts by JAMES VI to Anglicize the Scottish Church, suffering exile in 1617 and not returning until 1641, after which he helped to draw up the Directory of Public Worship (1645) to replace the English and Scottish Prayer Books. He wrote a standard official history of the Scottish Reformation: highly polemical but extremely informative.

CALGACUS (*fl.* AD 84), Caledonian war leader. According to TACITUS, Calgacus attempted to hinder AGRICOLA's advance beyond the Forth–Clyde isthmus into Caledonia by means of guerrilla warfare, but was ultimately forced to make a stand at the unidentified site of Mons Graupius, from which the Grampian mountains take their name. Described as a man of 'outstanding valour and nobility' by Tacitus, he appears to have escaped the rout with the bulk of his army and is subsequently unknown to history.

CALLAGHAN, JAMES *see* essay on page 136

CALLIL, CARMEN (1938–), publisher. Born and educated in Australia, Callil set up an independent feminist publishing house, Virago, in London in 1975, which excavated and reprinted long-forgotten (and out-of-copyright) women's writing and published it with distinction and style. It enjoyed great success in the 1970s and 1980s, though it was sometimes criticized for insufficiently encouraging new writing by women, a tendency that was rectified. After a series of publishing vicissitudes Virago was taken over by Little Brown in 1994, but by then Callil had severed her connection and had become a literary critic and writer.

CALVERT, CECIL (2nd Baron Baltimore) (1606–75), colonial proprietor. Son of Sir George CALVERT, he converted to Roman Catholicism a year before his father, and was the first grantee of Maryland in 1632, though he was never able to visit it in person. He urged discretion on the Roman Catholic settlers, and restricted the role of Jesuits working with them, while also persuading disaffected Puritans from Virginia to settle in the colony. In 1649 his sponsoring of a Maryland Act concerning religion produced the first English

continued on page 137

CALLAGHAN, JAMES (Baron Callaghan of Cardiff) (1912–)
Politician and Prime Minister (1976–9)

The only politician to hold all three major offices of State (Chancellor of the Exchequer, Home Secretary and Foreign Secretary) as well as the premiership, Callaghan represented the last remnants of the ATTLEE consensus and paved the way for Thatcherism.

Callaghan harked back to the early days of Labour and was the last Labour leader not to have attended a university, starting off his working life with the Inland Revenue in 1929 and working as a trade union official before the war, in which he served in the navy. He joined the Labour Party in its year of disaster (1931), and became MP for South Cardiff in its year of triumph (1945); but he held only minor office under Attlee. He was a Labour stalwart during the opposition years (1951–64) and challenged, unsuccessfully, for the Labour leadership after GAITSKELL's death in 1962. In recognition of his place in the party, Harold WILSON made Callaghan his Chancellor in 1964, confirming him in that post after 1966.

Like many of his Labour predecessors at the Exchequer, Callaghan was an instinctive fiscal conservative and he went along happily with Treasury advice and Wilson's desire to maintain the position of sterling, refusing to countenance any devaluation; but, like DALTON in 1947, Callaghan was unable to sustain this policy in the face of pressure from the money markets and he became the scapegoat for the devaluation of Nov. 1967. But, with his trade union background and bluff manner, Callaghan was a vital counterweight for Wilson to the influence of his own deputy, George BROWN, and so he found himself sent to the Home Office where he proved a conservative minister, particularly on the vexed question of immigration from the Commonwealth, which he restricted. After Brown resigned in 1968 Callaghan became the second most powerful man in the government, a position which he used in 1969 to block proposals from Wilson and Barbara CASTLE to limit the powers of trade unions.

When Labour returned to power in 1974, Callaghan went to the Foreign Office, where he had to handle the difficult issue of renegotiating Britain's terms of membership of the European Economic Community, a largely cosmetic act for which his own gift for fudging issues made him ideal. He was moved from the Foreign Office to Overseas Development in 1975, a move which was widely seen as heralding the end of his political career but the sudden resignation of Wilson in 1976 gave Callaghan's career an unexpected boost. Although older than Wilson, Callaghan was seen as a safer pair of hands than either the tough but unpredictable Denis HEALEY or the pro-European Roy JENKINS. Callaghan inherited a difficult economic position, with the British economy in such a parlous state that he had to call in the International Monetary Fund (IMF) to negotiate a loan; rising unemployment and rising inflation created a climate of political and social unrest which Callaghan's traditional Labour policies were unable to dispel; the word 'stagflation' was coined to describe the situation of the British economy.

Under the impact of the IMF, Callaghan and his Chancellor, Healey, began a process of imposing tight monetary controls which foreshadowed what would later be called 'monetarism'. In Sept. 1976 Callaghan signalled the end for traditional Labour policies when he told the party conference that the option of solving Britain's problems by increasing taxes and public spending 'no longer exists'. In return for $3.9 billion of credits in 1977 the Callaghan government had to impose cuts on public spending, including the jewel in Labour's political crown, the National Health Service. These cuts created problems with the trade union movement which resulted in the breakdown of the so-called social contract between it and the government in 1977. After 1977 the government's position depended upon support from the Liberals, the 'Lib–Lab' pact. Callaghan's natural talents as a political fixer suited him for the role of leader of a *de facto* coalition.

Callaghan was expected to hold a snap election in late 1978 but, to general amazement, chose not to do so; it was a fatal mistake. The crisis between the government and unions reached its peak during the 'winter of discontent' in 1978–9 when the dead were not buried and rubbish piled up, uncollected, in the streets. Labour appeared to have no answers to the problems facing the country and, when Callaghan was forced to call an election in May 1979 after losing a vote of confidence in the House of Commons, he relied upon his own popularity and the unpopularity of Margaret THATCHER to carry him through; they did not. Callaghan stood down as leader in 1980; Labour did not return to office until 1997.

Kenneth O. Morgan, Callaghan: A Life (1996)

legal guarantee of toleration to all Christians. From 1652 to 1657 he lost his proprietary rights to parliamentary commissioners, and thereafter continued to face problems in asserting his authority against the settlers.

CALVERT, SIR GEORGE (1st Baron Baltimore) (?1579–1632), colonial founder. Secretary to Robert CECIL, he became clerk of the Council in Ireland in 1608 and held the office of English Secretary of State from 1619 to 1625, resigning when he became a Roman Catholic. Having received grants of land in Ireland (from which his title derived), he unsuccessfully turned his attentions to Newfoundland (1621–3). When from 1629 to 1631 he attempted a new North American settlement in the jurisdiction of the Virginia Company, the company refused to allow this because of his Catholicism, so in 1632 he founded Maryland (named after CHARLES I's queen HENRIETTA MARIA) north of the Potomac River (the Virginian boundary) in 1632, with the intention of giving limited toleration to his fellow Catholics. His name lives on there in Calvert County and the city of Baltimore.

CALVERT, MICHAEL (1913–98), soldier. Son of an Indian government civil servant, educated at Woolwich and Cambridge, in 1941 he was an instructor in jungle warfare. A close friend of Orde WINGATE, Calvert led columns in the Chindit operations (1943–4), and then commanded SAS operations in Holland (1944–5). With the outbreak of the Communist insurgency in Malaya, Calvert organized the Malayan Scouts (1950–1), which formed the nucleus of the post-war SAS. His military career was cut short in 1952 when he was court-martialled for homosexual liaisons with German youths and cashiered. Increasingly dependent on alcohol, Calvert nevertheless kept up a stream of books and articles in which he preserved the memory of Wingate and attacked the generalship of SLIM.

CALVIN, JOHN (1509–64), religious reformer. This French-born Protestant theologian settled in Geneva between 1536 and 1538 and, from 1541 to 1564, came to dominate its Reformation and, from the 1550s, he had a European-wide influence. His theology (much affected by Martin BUCER) is expounded in his *Christianae Religionis Institutio* (the *Institutes*: successive editions from 1536), and became central to those Churches collectively labelled 'Reformed' (as opposed to those northern Protestant Churches loyal to the theological system developed from the thought of Martin LUTHER). It was elaborated by his successor at Geneva, Theodore Beza, and others in Heidelberg, the Netherlands, Cambridge and elsewhere, particularly in its assertion of God's predestination of souls either to salvation or damnation. Calvin also strongly argued that there should be equality within the clerical ministry rather than an episcopal hierarchy, and that decisions should be made in the Church by consensus within committees: the system which came to be known as Presbyterianism, which he claimed to be the biblical pattern of Church government. Argument continues about his influence on the Church of England: Calvinism came too late to play much part in shaping its official doctrines (formulated under EDWARD VI), but was very important in the thinking of Elizabethan churchmen, and only gradually lost its hold during the seventeenth century. In Scotland, Calvinism shaped the thought and institutions of the Church, thanks largely to the work of John KNOX, and it also proved very influential in the Church of Ireland as it was remodelled as the Church of the Protestant Ascendancy in the late sixteenth and early seventeenth century.

CAMBRIDGE, EARL OF, 2ND *see* HAMILTON, JAMES; LANGLEY, EDMUND; **3RD** *see* RICHARD OF CAMBRIDGE

CAMDEN, 1ST EARL *see* PRATT, CHARLES

CAMDEN, WILLIAM (1551–1623), historian and pioneer of archaeological research. Educated at Oxford, he was first usher then headmaster of Westminster school from 1575, where his anti-Puritan views were influential on many of his pupils, including Ben JONSON. He was appointed Clarenceux King of Arms in 1597. He was involved in the foundation of the first Society of Antiquaries *c.* 1585. Encouraged by Dean Gabriel Goodman of Westminster, from 1571 to 1600 he travelled throughout England gathering material on antiquity. The first version of his *Britannia* (a nationwide survey arranged ostensibly by classical tribes but in reality by county) came out in 1586; he published many historical collections, including (part-posthumously) the *Annals* of ELIZABETH I's reign.

CAMERON, JAMES (1911–85), journalist. A radical journalist whose left-wing opinions often put him at odds with a newspaper industry heavily dominated by right-wing proprietors, Cameron worked for the Beaverbrook press (*see* AITKEN, MAXWELL) from 1939 to 1950, but he found his journalistic voice on the photo-journalistic weekly *Picture Post*, owned by Edward Hulton. His association with the magazine ended in controversy in 1950 when he resigned in sympathy with the editor, Tom HOPKINSON, who had been sacked for trying to run Cameron's account of the treatment of prisoners in the Korean War against the wishes of Hulton. Cameron then worked for the Liberal *News Chronicle*, before that paper was forced to close in 1960. He was one of the first Western journalists to film in Hanoi at the start of the Vietnam War in 1965. Cameron's name became a byword for fearless, honest reporting, and he enjoyed an Indian summer as a writer on the *Guardian* in the 1980s.

CAMERON, JOHN (*c.* 1579–1625), theologian. After studies at Glasgow, he toured the Calvinist world, teaching at Sedan, Paris, Geneva, Heidelberg and Saumur, with an interval (1608–18) as a minister in Bordeaux. Escaping France's worsening religious situation in 1620, he became Principal of Glasgow University (1622); his absolutist political sympathies forced a return to France the following year, but in Montauban they also provoked an angry assault which hastened his death. His theological writings moderated the rigour of the Calvinist view of salvation and had wide influence on European Calvinist theologians.

CAMERON, JULIA MARGARET (née Pattle) (1815–79), photographer. One of the seven beautiful Pattle sisters, related to the Stephen family (*see* STEPHEN, LESLIE; BELL, VANESSA and WOOLF, VIRGINIA), she grew up in Calcutta and married a lawyer, Charles Cameron. It was not until she was 48 and living on the Isle of Wight that Cameron was given a camera and taught herself photography. Never particularly technically proficient, and so criticized by the clique of male professionals, she saw herself as an artist. She photographed her friends, neighbours and visitors, who, fortunately, were such people as TENNYSON, Charles DARWIN and HERSCHEL, and posed the family servants in front of her lens. Despite their technical imperfections Cameron's photographs have a perception that anticipated the great potential of the medium.

CAMERON, RICHARD (?–1680), Presbyterian. An Episcopalian schoolmaster, he was converted to advanced Presbyterianism by field preachers who rejected the Declarations of Indulgence issued by Lauderdale (*see* MAITLAND, JOHN). He was active in south-west Scotland, around Clydesdale and in Ayrshire. He issued the Sanquhar Declaration in June 1680, declaring CHARLES II and the Duke of York (the future JAMES II) enemies of God. Cameron was killed in July but his supporters continued; their campaigns were violent and were put down savagely. The name 'Cameronian' is often applied to those who rejected the non-Episcopal settlement of 1690 and in 1743 became the Reformed Presbytery and continued to reject union with the Church of Scotland.

CAMERON, VERNEY (1844–94), explorer. The first European to cross Africa from coast to coast, he went to the continent to relieve David LIVINGSTONE in 1873 and followed the course of the River Congo from Lake Tanganyika to the west coast. In 1878 he travelled to India to investigate the feasibility of a Constantinople (Istanbul) to Baghdad railway, and in 1882 joined Richard BURTON's expedition to the Gold Coast.

CAMPBELL, ARCHIBALD (4th Earl of Argyll) (?–1558), politician. He succeeded as Earl and was appointed Justiciar of Scotland and Master of the Household in 1529, but lost his offices two years later for misusing them in feuds with the Macdonalds. Later, he became an ally of Cardinal BEATON against the pro-English James HAMILTON, Earl of Arran, and until 1548 he played a leading role fighting the English. Then he was converted by a mixture of English gold and John Knox's evangelism to the Protestant, pro-English cause. In 1557 he became one of the Protestant Lords of the Congregation who successfully opposed the rule of the Regent MARY OF GUISE. His political skill, strong Protestant commitment and wide territorial control in Scotland were vital to the establishment of the Scottish Reformation.

CAMPBELL, ARCHIBALD (5th Earl of Argyll) (1530–73), politician. Son of the 4th Earl, as Lord Lorne he shared his father's Protestant conversion and was among those Lords of the Congregation inviting John KNOX back from his exile in Geneva in 1557. Although he helped MARY OF GUISE to suppress Protestant mob destruction of church interiors at Perth in May 1559, Argyll (who succeeded to the title in 1558) turned against her, and in 1559–60 obtained ELIZABETH I's military assistance against the Catholic forces, promising reciprocal help for the English against Gaelic armies in Ulster. He dutifully took part in government as a leading nobleman under MARY QUEEN OF SCOTS until her marriage to Henry STEWART, Lord Darnley, in 1565. He knew about the plot to murder Darnley in 1567, but soon repented of his hasty assent to Mary's marriage to James HEPBURN, Lord Bothwell; thereafter, with Bothwell out of Scotland, Argyll's participation in the civil wars was marked by his hesitant support for Mary, which wavered crucially at her defeat at the Battle of Langside in 1568, up to his submission to James STEWART, the Regent Moray, the following year. After further intrigue for Mary's return, he submitted to JAMES VI's supporters in 1571 and was made Lord High Chancellor a year later. Like his father, he was a major force in establishing Protestantism in the Church in the western Highlands.

CAMPBELL, ARCHIBALD (8th Earl and 1st Marquess of Argyll) (1607–1661), politician. Losing faith in CHARLES I after discovering that he had sponsored the plans of Randal MACDONNELL, Earl of Antrim, to invade Kintyre (1638), he joined the invasion of England in 1639 and, despite being made Marquess (1641), remained bitterly opposed to the Scottish Royalists led by James GRAHAM, Marquess of Montrose. Between 1644 and 1645 Montrose repeatedly defeated his forces until the Royalist defeat at Philiphaugh. Thereafter he was prominent in Scots government; in outrage at Charles's execution he backed CHARLES II's attempt to regain the throne (1650). Relations, however, remained cool, especially after he made his peace with Oliver CROMWELL's regime and, despite his journey to London to welcome back Charles in 1660, he was executed in Edinburgh for high treason.

CAMPBELL, ARCHIBALD (9th Earl of Argyll) (1629–85), politician. Unlike his father, executed in 1661, he fought on the Royalist side in the Civil Wars; in 1656–7 he refused to take a new oath for the Scottish nobility and was imprisoned in Edinburgh Castle. Favoured by Lauderdale (*see* MAITLAND, JOHN), he was made a member of the Scottish Privy Council in 1664 and employed in various capacities. The Argylls had long been one of the most powerful Scottish families and his independent power in the Highlands, combined with his staunch Protestantism, worried the Duke of York (later JAMES II), Lord High Commissioner of Scotland from 1680. In 1681 Argyll was prosecuted for expressing doubts about whether the Scottish Test Act, which ordered Scots to recognize the supremacy of the King in spiritual matters, was consistent with the Confession of 1560, which the Act also purported to enshrine. He was sentenced to death and his estates were confiscated. He escaped, and the fear of the political embarrassment that might result probably saved him from re-arrest. He was implicated in the Rye House Plot of 1683 (*see also* FERGUSON, ROBERT); fleeing to Holland, he plotted with Monmouth (*see* SCOTT, JAMES). He took a force to Scotland in 1685, and at Campbeltown in Argyll proclaimed Monmouth the rightful King. Invading the Lowlands, but unable to overcome royal troops, he was captured in June and executed at Edinburgh without fresh trial, being still under sentence of death.

CAMPBELL, ARCHIBALD (1st Earl of Ilay, 3rd Duke of Argyll) (1682–1761), politician. Younger son of the 1st Duke, as Lord High Treasurer of Scotland from 1705 he helped secure the passage of the Act of Union, and was rewarded with an earldom. Strongly committed to the Hanoverians, he raised the Argyllshire Highlanders against the Jacobites in 1715 and crucially secured the western Highlands for the government. His loyalty secured him the task of enforcing the Malt Tax in the face of hostile riots in 1721; his success led Robert WALPOLE to make him chief manager in Scotland. Assisted by Duncan FORBES and Andrew FLETCHER, Ilay influenced elections and distributed patronage; in 1736 he broke with his brother the 2nd Duke of Argyll (*see* CAMPBELL, JOHN) and remained loyal to Walpole. His inheritance of the Argyll dukedom made it difficult for the PELHAMS to displace him, and he died with his influence on Scottish politics largely intact.

CAMPBELL, COLEN (1676–1729), architect. Initially an advocate in Edinburgh, he was increasingly drawn to architecture and in particular the works of the Venetian architect, Palladio, whose merits had been championed in the previous century by Inigo JONES. He secured his fame by writing *Vitruvius Britannicus* (three vols in 1715, 1717 and 1725), praising Palladio and Jones while attacking the Baroque as degenerate. He also furthered the reputation of Palladio in England by publishing two editions of Palladio's *First Book of Architecture*. His ascendancy was confirmed when Sir Robert WALPOLE commissioned him to design his country seat at Houghton. His roles as architect to the Prince of Wales (later GEORGE II) and as Surveyor of Greenwich Hospital (from 1726), provided him with useful platforms with which to promote the Palladian cause.

CAMPBELL, COLIN (1st Earl of Argyll) (?–1493), royal servant. Son of Lord Archibald Campbell, taking the title of earl in 1457, he was a negotiator of the truce in 1463 and the treaty in 1474 with EDWARD IV of England. In 1483 he became Lord High Chancellor of Scotland, joined the conspiracy against JAMES III, but was conveniently in England when the King was murdered. He was restored to his office by JAMES IV in 1488.

CAMPBELL, SIR COLIN (Baron Clyde) (1792–1865), soldier. Son of a Glasgow carpenter, he was brought up and educated by his maternal uncle, Colonel John Campbell, who secured a commission for him in the 9th regiment in 1808. He fought at Rolica, Vimeiro and Corunna in the first Peninsula campaign, almost succumbed to fever in the Walcheren campaign in 1809, and then returned to Spain to fight at Barossa, Tarifa, Vittoria and San Sebastian. Twice badly wounded, he was promoted Captain without purchase in 1813. Campbell borrowed money to purchase the rank of Major in 1825, then served in China (1842–6) and India (1846–53), capturing the public imagination as the commander of the

Highland Brigade, 'the thin red line tipped with steel' which stopped the Russian attack at Balaclava in the Crimea. Appointed Commander-in-Chief in India in 1857 to quell the Mutiny, Campbell led a force of fewer than 5,000 European and loyal Indian soldiers to relieve Lucknow and destroy the mutineers' main armies, for which he was promoted General and elevated to the peerage.

CAMPBELL, DANIEL (1672–1753), merchant and MP. His political career was guided by his membership of the Duke of Argyll's clan, and illustrates the conflicting pressures on Scottish politicians after the Union. A successful merchant, he failed to be elected MP for Glasgow Burghs in 1708 when he was accused of using his position as Collector of Customs to buy votes, but Argyll and Ilay (*see* CAMPBELL, JOHN and ARCHIBALD) saw that he was elected in 1716. In the 1720s he lost the confidence of some Glasgow citizens after he was identified with measures preventing Glasgow tobacco merchants from undercutting English rivals, and then in 1725 his house at Shawfield was burnt down by a mob because he was said to have voted for the Malt Tax, much resented in Scotland and argued by some to be contrary to the terms of the Union (*see also* OGILVY, JAMES). Order had to be restored by troops under WADE; Campbell had difficulty recovering his credibility and retired in 1734.

CAMPBELL, JOHN (1st Earl of Loudon) (1598–1662), politician. CHARLES I stopped his creation as Earl in 1633 because of his furious opposition to royal religious policy in Scotland. He was prominent in the leadership which created the National Covenant in 1638 and waged war on England in 1639 and 1640, finally becoming Earl and Scottish Lord Chancellor in 1641. Between 1640 and 1647 he was repeatedly Scottish envoy to Charles; he rallied to CHARLES II, being present at his Scottish coronation (1650) and in the royal army defeated by Oliver CROMWELL at Dunbar (1650). He was involved in the unsuccessful Highland rising of 1653. Charles heavily fined him in 1662 for opposing the execution of his friend Archibald CAMPBELL, Marquess of Argyll.

CAMPBELL, JOHN (2nd Duke of Argyll, 1st Duke of Greenwich) (1678–1743), soldier and statesman. Head of the Presbyterian and therefore traditionally Whiggish clan, his social standing helped secure him high political office at an early age, and he remained a key figure for any government seeking influence in Scotland. As Lord High Commissioner for Scotland, he promoted the union of the English and Scottish Parliaments in 1707. A successful general in the War of the

Spanish Succession, he was hostile to Marlborough (*see* CHURCHILL, JOHN) and therefore associated with Robert HARLEY and the Tories, who made him Commander-in-Chief in Spain in 1711 and, at the end of the war, Commander of the Forces in Scotland. His opposition to Jacobitism won him the favour of GEORGE I, who retained him in post to suppress the 1715 rebellion. Deprived of office for a few years during a period of Whig backlash against ANNE's later ministries, he held a series of official positions from 1718. He and his brother Archibald CAMPBELL, Earl of Ilay, established themselves as the principal managers of patronage in Scotland, and as such indispensable to Robert WALPOLE. Made Field-Marshal in 1736, Argyll was responsible for repressing the PORTEOUS riots, but soon afterwards broke with Walpole. He used his electoral influence in Scotland to help topple Walpole, but retired from politics after the latter's fall.

CAMPBELL-BANNERMAN, SIR HENRY (1836–1908), politician and Prime Minister (1905–8). Born in Glasgow and educated at Cambridge University, he worked for the family drapery firm before entering Parliament in 1868 as Liberal MP for Stirling, a seat he represented for 40 years until his death. 'C-B' was a committed supporter of Irish Home Rule and held office as Chief Secretary for Ireland during GLADSTONE's third administration (Jan.–June 1886) and then as Secretary of State for War (1892–5). In June 1895, after a vote of censure was narrowly passed on him by the Commons for not having provided the army with sufficient cordite, a new smokeless explosive, the Cabinet resigned and lost the ensuing General Election.

When Rosebery (*see* PRIMROSE, ARCHIBALD) resigned as leader the following year the Liberal Party was in further disarray, particularly over social reform, the conduct of the Boer War and the tensions between Liberalism and imperialism. In 1898 Sir William HARCOURT, unable to contain the factions, also resigned and almost by default Campbell-Bannerman was elected to lead the Liberals in the Commons. His conciliatory temperament and steadfast insistence that the Liberal Party mattered more than a Liberal political agenda paid dividends: on BALFOUR's resignation in 1905 he was invited by EDWARD VII to form a government, and in the ensuing election in 1906 the Liberals had a landslide victory and 'C-B' formed a new 'Ministry of all the Talents' which included ASQUITH, GREY, LLOYD GEORGE and MORLEY. It was to be a 'splendid sunset of his career', as a colleague put it, and laid the basis for the reform of the House of Lords, the Union of South Africa and trade-union recognition. 'C-B' died in office, a stalwart Gladstonian Liberal to the end: he was respected by many as a practical, undidactic premier and applauded by others for the idealism which led him to condemn the 'barbarities' of the Boer War and for his belief in arbitration to settle international disputes.

CAMPION, EDMUND (1540–81), writer and martyr. A London bookseller's son, Campion was set on a brilliant career at Oxford. He was ordained deacon in the Church of England in 1568, but then converted to Roman Catholicism, left for Dublin in 1569 and, after an interval in London, escaped arrest by fleeing to the Catholic college at Douai in the Low Countries in 1571. He joined the Jesuits at Rome in 1573 and, in June 1580, reached England for a new Jesuit mission with Robert PARSONS, causing great government alarm. He was arrested in Berks. in July 1581, was tortured and, on 1 Dec., executed. He wrote poetry, a history of Ireland and Catholic propaganda.

CAMROSE, 1ST VISCOUNT *see* BERRY, WILLIAM EWART

CANNING, CHARLES ('CLEMENCY') (1st Earl Canning) (1812–62), diplomat. The third son of George CANNING, after a career in diplomacy and originally service with the East India Co., Canning was made Governor General of India in 1856 (and from 1858 first Viceroy). He was immediately confronted by a host of military and administrative difficulties, notably the war with Persia to restore the Afghan ruler, and the settlement of Oudh, which had been annexed in Feb., the very month he arrived. Within a year the Indian Mutiny broke out. Giving full freedom of action to Sir Henry Lawrence and John LAWRENCE in Oudh and the Punjab respectively, Canning was steadfast in his support for British actions in the Mutiny. Created an Earl in 1859, he spent the three years that remained to him reorganizing India's administrative, legal and financial systems, his skill earning him the name 'Clemency'.

CANNING, GEORGE *see* essay on page 142

CANTILUPE, ST THOMAS (*c.* 1218–82), royal servant. As a younger son of baronial stock destined for a clerical career, he was sent to Oxford, Paris and Orléans universities. His sympathies with Simon de MONTFORT led to his appointment as Chancellor of England in 1265, but after the Battle of Evesham he retired to Paris and the study of theology. Following EDWARD I's accession, he became a member of the King's Council, and in 1275 was elected Bishop of Hereford. A conscientious diocesan, his insistence on his rights as well as his duties involved him in litigation at the papal curia, where he died.

His bones were returned to his cathedral and became the focus of a flourishing cult that led to his canonization in 1320.

CAPEL, ARTHUR (21st [1st Capel] Earl of Essex) (1631–83), politician. His father was Lord Capel, executed in 1649 for his fidelity to CHARLES I. Made an earl at the Restoration, Essex became a critic of CHARLES II who nonetheless appointed him Lord Lieutenant of Ireland in 1672. Capel's rule in Ireland was conscientious, seeking to balance the interests of Presbyterians, Anglicans and Catholics, but Charles II dismissed him in 1677 for failing to raise revenues equivalent to those promised by Richard JONES, Lord Ranelagh. From April to Nov. 1679 Essex was First Lord of the Treasury in the short-lived government of Country politicians formed by Charles II to defuse the crisis associated with attempts to exclude the Duke of York (the future JAMES II) from the line of succession (*see* COOPER, ANTHONY ASHLEY). When this failed, Essex became a prominent Exclusionist sympathetic to Monmouth (*see* SCOTT, JAMES). Although he, like William RUSSELL and Algernon SIDNEY, was probably ignorant of the Rye House Plot of 1683 to assassinate Charles II and the Duke of York (*see also* FERGUSON, ROBERT), Essex was arrested and committed suicide at the start of Russell's trial.

CARATACUS (*fl.* AD 40s), British resistance leader. He has acquired semi-heroic status as the leader of British resistance to the Roman Conquest that began in 43. The son of CUNOBELIN, King of the Catuvellauni, he was defeated by AULUS PLAUTIUS during the initial invasion. He reappeared in 47 leading first the Silures, then the Ordovices, in unsuccessful resistance. After his defeat at the Battle of Caer Caradog (site unknown, but possibly at Church Stretton or Llanymynech, Salop.) by OSTORIUS SCAPULA, he was handed over to the Romans by CARTIMANDUA, Queen of the Brigantes, in 51 and taken to Rome. There, according to TACITUS, he made a speech that so impressed the Emperor CLAUDIUS that he was granted his freedom.

CARAUSIUS, Roman 'Emperor' (287–93). A Menapian (i.e. a member of a tribe inhabiting what is now modern Belgium), he was given the responsibility early in the reign of the Emperor Diocletian (284–305) of defending the English Channel against barbarian raids. In 287 he revolted and declared himself Emperor, 'ruling' apparently successfully in Britain and parts of northern France until he was assassinated by one of his followers. His murderer, Allectus, subsequently maintained himself as Emperor until 296, when he was defeated and killed by an invading

continued on page 143

CANNING, GEORGE (1770–1827)
Politician and Prime Minister (1827)

In oratorical ability, controversy and brilliance, Canning was the Winston CHURCHILL of the early nineteenth century but unlike Churchill he was not granted the time and opportunity to leave a decisive mark on British history.

In an age of aristocratic politicians, Canning's background aroused distrust. His father's early death left his mother to fend for herself and her children, and she took up the disreputable occupation of actress as the means of so doing, a circumstance Canning's opponents would always use against him. Canning ensured that there would be plenty of adversaries throughout his career by the unrestrained use of his talent for satire against duller wits than his own. A brilliant career at Oxford provided him with entrée to PITT THE YOUNGER, under whose auspices he entered the Commons in 1794. He was one of the main contributors to the Conservative and patriotic journal, *The Anti-Jacobin*, which established him as a leading Pittite. His marriage to an heiress in 1800 gave Canning the financial security to play the political game for the highest stakes but Pitt's hopes that he would succeed him as Prime Minister in the near future were disappointed by a combination of political bad luck and self-inflicted misfortunes. Like Churchill a century later, Canning's evident ambition did not endear him to contemporaries; he did not suffer fools gladly, and his definition of who came into that category was a wide one; the many recipients of his sarcasm may have been too tongue-tied to respond verbally but they helped contribute to the reputation which Canning gained of being superficial and light-weight.

Personal loyalty to Pitt prompted Canning to resign with him in 1801, an event from which his career never recovered. Canning resented Pitt's action as much as he resented his successor, ADDINGTON, and his constant attempts over the next few years to unseat the latter and to restore the former (despite Pitt's own support for Addington) gained for him the reputation of being an unprincipled intriguer inspired mainly by self-interest; this dogged him for the rest of his career. When Pitt formed his final administration in 1804 Canning was mortified to see contemporaries such as Lord Hawkesbury, the future Lord Liverpool (*see* JENKINSON, CHARLES), and Castlereagh (*see* STEWART, ROBERT) promoted ahead of him into the Cabinet.

After Pitt's death in 1806 Canning went into opposition before becoming Foreign Secretary in the Portland (*see* BENTINCK, WILLIAM CAVENDISH) administration (1807–9). He energetically supported Swedish, Portuguese and Spanish resistance against Napoleon. His attempts in 1809 to have Castlereagh removed from the War Office were, thanks to Portland's incompetence, easily construed as a personal intrigue and resulted in his fighting a duel with Castlereagh on 16 Sept. 1809, in which Canning was wounded. This led to the collapse of Portland's administration, and Canning was not included in the subsequent PERCEVAL government. His refusal to serve with Castlereagh in 1812 when the Liverpool administration was formed was a mistake which was to leave him in the political wilderness until the 1820s.

It was Castlereagh's unexpected death in 1822 which prevented Canning from going to India as Governor General and provided him with the opportunity to begin finally to fulfil his promise, when he once again accepted the Foreign Office. His accession to the Foreign Office coincided with PEEL's acceptance of the Home Office, and together the two men helped to give a more liberal tone to the Liverpool government. Canning gladly accepted what Castlereagh had sadly acknowledged, that co-operation with the autocratic powers was not possible. Canning quickly established himself as a champion of liberalism, at least rhetorically, and his strength on the floor of the Commons and in the country at large more than compensated for the distrust of many of his Cabinet colleagues. His support for the independence of Spain's Latin American colonies and for the Greek revolt against the Turks, along with his championing of the Portuguese liberals, made him at once the bogeyman of European conservatives and the darling of patriotic English public opinion. By the time of Liverpool's stroke in 1827 Canning was both the most obvious successor and the main cause of political division.

High Tories and those around Wellington (*see* WELLESLEY, ARTHUR) objected to Canning's liberalism on the question of Catholic Emancipation, and refused to serve with him, forcing him back on Whig support. He became Prime Minister on 12 April 1827 but died on 8 Aug., leaving Metternich to comment: 'It is an immense event, for the man was a whole revolution in himself alone.' Canning left disarray in politics, a great reputation and, in his courting of public opinion at home and liberalism abroad, an example which Palmerston (*see* TEMPLE, HENRY) would follow.

Wendy Hinde, George Canning (1973)

Roman army led by CONSTANTIUS I Chlorus. Britain was then rejoined to the Roman empire. The Britons' complacent acceptance of this brief secession is best explained in terms that also explain the Gallic empire (*Imperium Galliarum*), the term used to describe the period from 260 to 273 when the provinces of Gaul, Spain, Germany and Britain briefly seceded from the Roman empire. Having become one of the most peaceful provinces of the Roman empire, the British were content with arrangements that removed them from direct involvement in the turbulence elsewhere.

CARDEN, SIR SACKVILLE (1857–1930), sailor. Carden joined the Royal Navy in 1870. After small-boat service in Egypt, the Sudan and Benin, Carden rose steadily to the rank of Rear Admiral. In 1914 Carden, now commanding British naval forces in the Mediterranean, attempted to destroy Turkish fortifications along the Dardanelles, using purely naval forces. The bombardment began on 19 Feb. 1915 but by 16 March, with no Turkish collapse in evidence, Carden, realizing that he had compromised any other means of passing through the straits, suffered a nervous breakdown, and relinquished command.

CARDIGAN, 7TH EARL OF *see* BRUDENELL, JAMES

CARDWELL, EDWARD (1813–86), politician and military reformer. Son of a Liverpool merchant, Cardwell was educated at Winchester and Oxford, and after studying law was elected to Parliament for a Lancs. constituency in 1842. A Peelite Free Trader (*see* PEEL, ROBERT), he refused office under Lord John RUSSELL and Lord Derby (*see* STANLEY, EDWARD) but joined the Aberdeen (*see* GORDON, GEORGE) coalition government in 1852. As GLADSTONE's Secretary of State for War (1868–74), he introduced the short-service principle as the basis of enlistment, created a reserve, and abolished the purchase of commissions. The latter reform, designed to open the army to middle-class officers, had the ironic effect of making it more aristocratic.

CAREW, RICHARD (1555–1620), historian. A Cornish gentleman and MP who studied at Oxford; his writings included translations of Italian epic poetry by Tasso and the engaging and pioneering antiquarian *Survey of Cornwall* (1602).

CAREY, GEORGE (1930–), Archbishop of Canterbury (1991–). An unusual archbishop in several respects, Carey was educated at Bifrons secondary school in Barking (Essex), and came from the Evangelical tradition within the Church of England, in contrast to his Anglo-Catholic predecessor Robert RUNCIE. He was Principal of Trinity Theological College in Bristol (1982–7) and Bishop of Bath and Wells (1987–91). As Archbishop, his most difficult task was to oversee the introduction of the ordination of women as priests, an issue that threatened to divide the Church. Despite several high-profile defections to the Roman Catholic Church in protest (including some MPs), the General Synod eventually passed the necessary legislation in 1994. The Church of England remained relatively intact. Notwithstanding his support for the ordination of women, Carey disappointed those who expected him to take up the cause of homosexuals and lesbians within the Church.

CAREY, LUCIUS (2nd Viscount Falkland) (*c.* 1610–43), politician and scholar. During the 1630s, Carey (or Cary) opened his home at Great Tew, Oxon., to a remarkable array of thinkers and writers sympathetic to Christian humanism, a broad and inclusive approach to religion informed by the Renaissance engagement with classical literature (*see* CHILLINGWORTH, WILLIAM; HALES, JOHN; HOBBES, THOMAS; HYDE, EDWARD – the future Earl of Clarendon; JONSON, BEN; SELDEN, JOHN; SHELDON, GILBERT; WALLER, EDMUND). This Great Tew circle discussed issues of the day as rationally and openly as possible. Loth to choose sides in the gathering political crisis, Falkland first supported Parliament against CHARLES I but, in the effort to avoid war, was in 1642 made Privy Councillor and Secretary of State. His death fighting for the King at the First Battle of Newbury in September 1643 left his great ally Edward Hyde isolated against Royalist extremists.

CARLETON, DUDLEY (1st Viscount Dorchester) (1573–1632). Worthy early Stuart diplomat, and Secretary of State from 1628, his chief importance to historians is the survival of a huge quantity of his official papers in the Public Record Office and other collections.

CARLETON, GEORGE (1529–90), Puritan. Son of a Westminster Abbey estate official and Oxford-educated, he fought at the victory against the French at St Quentin (1557) and later in Ireland (1573); he accumulated large Midland and eastern estates, sponsoring innovative fen drainage schemes in Lincs. He was in charge of the Catholic clergy imprisoned at Wisbech Castle (1580–90). In Parliament, sitting through patronage by the Puritan Francis Russell, Earl of Bedford (1527–85), he fervently supported various proposals for drastic Church reform; some of the 'Martin Marprelate' Tracts were printed at his East Molesey house, and he may have had a hand in writing them. *See also* THROCKMORTON, JOB; COOPER, THOMAS.

CARLILE, RICHARD (1790–1843), radical journalist and free-thinker. Carlile was important in the dissemination of radical ideas, especially between 1817 and 1832. Through journalism, especially in association with William T. Sherwin on *Sherwin's Weekly Political Register* (1817–19) and with the reprinting of radical works like PAINE's *Age of Reason*, he became a major publicist in London for radical opposition to the monarchy, aristocracy and established religion, an advocate of free thought, women's rights and birth control. Dogged by trials for seditious libel and blasphemy and periods of imprisonment, he moved away from mainstream working-class radicalism after 1832 and into a millennialism in which he drew on atheism and extreme rationalism but also on Christianity.

CARLISLE, EARL OF, 1ST *see* HARCLAY, ANDREW; **6TH** *see* HOWARD, CHARLES

CARLYLE, THOMAS *see* essay on page 145

CARMARTHEN, 1ST MARQUESS OF *see* OSBORNE, SIR THOMAS

CARNARVON, 10TH EARL OF *see* HERBERT, GEORGE

CAROLINE (1683–1737), Queen of Great Britain and Ireland. The daughter of John Frederick, ruler of the Protestant principality of Brandenburg-Ansbach, she was raised at the Prussian court, where her mentor was the scholar and philosopher Leibniz. In marrying the future GEORGE II in 1705 she provided supporters of the Protestant succession in Great Britain with valuable propaganda, as she had chosen on religious grounds to ally with a Protestant prince rather than accept a marriage with the future Habsburg Emperor Charles VI, which would have given her a higher status but entailed conversion to Catholicism. She arrived in Britain with her husband in 1714. Her intelligence and social ease, especially with literary figures not normally inclined towards the Whig ascendancy, such as POPE, made her court a relatively glamorous one. Sir Robert WALPOLE sought her aid to ensure that he retained office after the accession of George II; on other occasions too she smoothed relations between George II and his ministers. She also instigated alterations to Hampton Court and St James's Palace and expanded Kensington Gardens. Her death in 1737 was a blow from which George II never recovered. Much of the detail of their relationship was recorded waspishly by John HERVEY.

CAROLINE (1768–1821), Queen of Great Britain and Ireland. Daughter of Charles, Duke of Brunswick, she married her first cousin George, then Prince of Wales (*see* GEORGE IV), on 8 April 1795. The marriage was a disaster from the start and the couple separated in 1796, a few months after the birth of their daughter Charlotte (who died in 1817). Caroline's subsequent behaviour at home and abroad was unconventional and indiscreet although she was exonerated from charges of adultery by a 'Delicate Investigation' in 1806. When her husband succeeded to the throne in 1820 she determined to return to England and take her place as Queen. She landed at Dover in June, having spurned a government annuity of £50,000 to relinquish her title and stay in exile. The next month, a Bill of Pains and Penalties was introduced by the government in the House of Lords to divorce her from the King and strip her of her queenship. The combination of her popularity in the country (she was taken up by radicals and Whigs) and her incisive defence by BROUGHAM led to the withdrawal of the Bill. Nevertheless she was forcibly excluded from her husband's coronation in July 1821 and died at Hammersmith a few weeks later.

CARPENTER, EDWARD (1844–1929), libertarian. After education and ordination at Cambridge University, where he became chaplain to F. D. MAURICE, Carpenter renounced his orders in 1874. He became first a university extension lecturer and then established himself at Millthorpe (Derb.) as a progressive socialist thinker. His life of open-air communal fellowship was deeply influenced by the American writers Ralph Waldo Emerson, Henry Thoreau and Walt Whitman, as well as by RUSKIN and William MORRIS. Carpenter was a leading exponent of causes which became commonplace in the twentieth century but were seen as alien and dangerous in the late nineteenth: sexual reform, women's rights, clean air, vegetarianism, wearing few or no clothes and overt homosexuality. On the margin of society and a thorn in the flesh of middle-class convention in his lifetime, Carpenter has since been hailed (or reviled) as a prophet of modern thinking.

CARPENTER, MARY (1807–77), philanthropist. Brought up in a strict Unitarian household, she remained a deeply religious woman. She opened her first ragged school in 1846, wrote extensively on the need for reformatories and industrial schools, and exerted some influence on the resultant legislation.

CARPENTER, WILLIAM BENJAMIN (1813–85), physiologist. Born in Bristol to a family of staunch Unitarians, he studied medicine in

continued on page 146

CARLYLE, THOMAS (1795–1881)
Writer and social critic

Born in Ecclefechan (Dumfries.), he was the eldest of nine children of a mason and his second wife; the family were members of the Burgher Secession Church, a strict Calvinist sect formed in rebellion against the established Kirk in eighteenth-century Scotland. Carlyle entered Edinburgh University in 1809 at the not unusual age of 13. He did not take his degree, but in 1813 he began to study divinity part-time, financed by school teaching. Then in 1817–18 he abandoned both teaching and the notion of entering the Church and turned to writing, although the passage to becoming a man of letters was accompanied by great stress and considerable poverty.

Two developments were decisive for Carlyle: his assimilation of German romanticism and his meeting in 1821 with Jane Welsh, whom he married in 1826. Their marriage has been the source of endless speculation. While Jane was intellectually brilliant and in many ways the centre of their social life – their home in Chelsea, London, to which they moved in 1834 became the meeting place for a sparkling coterie of writers and intellectuals – her life within the marriage became an increasingly constricted and tormented one, evident in the vast quantity of letters which she, like her husband, poured forth throughout her life. Probably sexless from the 1840s, certainly childless, the marriage caused Jane endless distress. Yet Carlyle inscribed on her tombstone in 1866 that the light of his life had been extinguished.

From 1819 Carlyle immersed himself in German literature and thought, and especially in the works of Goethe from whom he took a disposition towards the world and an eclectic sifting of some of his ideas rather than a systematic philosophy. Mixed with the legacy of discipline and asceticism inherited from his religious upbringing, which remained a deeply important shaping force in his life even when he rejected the theology of the Church, what emerged was a belief in a spiritual order which lay beneath the visible world and gave reality to it. The function of men of letters like himself was to act as prophets who would bring others to awareness of the spiritual order. This constellation of ideas was central to the stream of essays and books on historical, social and cultural themes which Carlyle was to write from the later 1820s, initially in the pages of the *Edinburgh Review*.

In essays such as 'Signs of the Times' (1829) and books such as *Sartor Resartus* (1838) Carlyle showed that he was both devoted to the values of hard work, the ultimate justification of a man's existence, and yet was highly critical of the evils of unfettered capitalism, the worship of mammon and the dependence upon the cash nexus. His solution was the elevation of the heroic figure of the kind celebrated in *On Heroes, Hero-Worship and the Heroic in History* (1841). He looked to captains of industry, heroes and the values of hard work within essentially autocratic and authoritarian rule to rescue civilization from the social consequences of unrestrained commercialism. At the same time, he also warned of the dangers of revolution and democracy, as in *The French Revolution* (1837), his essay on Chartism (1839) and *Past and Present* (1843).

For Carlyle, these issues were also intimately connected to questions of race. Influenced and influencing the developing discourse of racial difference and superiority which was becoming more pervasive in the Britain of the 1840s and beyond, Carlyle published anonymously his 'Occasional Discourse on the Negro Question' (1849), which argued that black men were born to be mastered. The essay was republished in 1853 with the more inflammatory title of 'Occasional Discourse on the Nigger Question'. After the rebellion at Morant Bay, Jamaica, in 1865, Carlyle led the support for Governor Eyre, the Governor who had brutally suppressed the rising, and celebrated him as a hero. In his 'Shooting Niagara: and After?' (1867), occasioned by both the Jamaica question and the controversies surrounding the extension of the franchise, Carlyle's fear and hatred of democracy were linked to his contempt for black people and their white supporters. In this vitriolic text, Carlyle argued for the maintenance of a social order in which white ruled over black, men over women, the whole to be governed by an aristocratic elite.

One of the most prominent intellectuals of his time, Carlyle's subsequent influence has been substantial if baneful, partly because of his contribution to the continuing romantic strain within British thought, echoed on the political Left as well as on the Right, but also because he helped to place racism within the mainstream of cultural and political thought.

Fred Kaplan, Thomas Carlyle: A Biography (1983)

London and Edinburgh, and subsequently lectured on physiology at the Bristol Medical School, and became Professor of Physiology at the Royal Institution, Professor of Forensic Medicine at University College, London (both in 1845), and Registrar of London University (1856). He published on a wide range of subjects including marine zoology, botany, marine physics and temperance, but is best known for his work on physiology. From the mid 1830s he began to publish researches on the nervous system and these informed his highly influential *Principles of General and Comparative Physiology* (1839). A psychological materialist, he believed that mental phenomena were consequences of physiological processes in the brain, and worked hard to show that certain human beliefs and actions, notably those associated with such 'irrational' activities as mesmerism and spiritualism, were caused by the unconscious reflex actions of the brain.

CARR (OR KER), ROBERT (6th [1st Carr] Earl of Somerset) (*c.* 1587–1645), courtier. Carr was a Roxburghs. gentleman who travelled south with James VI and, *c.* 1607, became his homosexual favourite; an earldom followed in 1613, despite a sensational scandal involving the murder in the Tower of London of his friend Sir Thomas OVERBURY, who had opposed his planned marriage to Frances HOWARD, the divorced wife of Robert DEVEREUX, 20th Earl of Essex. Carr joined with his new wife's family, the Howards, to back a Spanish alliance, but was displaced as James's favourite in 1614–15 by George VILLIERS, Duke of Buckingham, who was to attract far more popular hatred than Carr. The way was then clear for a long unravelling of the Overbury affair, which made plain Carr's wife's guilt and ruined his career.

CARRICK, 3RD EARL OF *see* BRUCE, ROBERT

CARRINGTON, DORA (1893–1932), artist. 'Carrington', as she was always known, was a student at the Slade School of Art in London (1910–13): her contemporaries included Stanley SPENCER, Augustus JOHN and Mark GERTLER. With W. Gertler she formed an attachment but refused to marry him. Drawn into the Bloomsbury set by Virginia and Leonard WOOLF, she fell in love with the writer Lytton STRACHEY and from 1917 lived with him. In 1921 Strachey, a homosexual, encouraged her to marry Ralph Partridge, whom he also loved, and the three set up a *ménage à trois* at Ham Spray (Wilts.) in 1924: this neither inhibited Carrington from having other affairs and entanglements, nor diminished her deep love for, and devotion to, Strachey. Six weeks after he died, she shot herself. Carrington's artistic production was

small: she had a disabling diffidence about her work, and her memorial is in her craft work and her insightful and moving letters and diaries.

CARRINGTON, PETER (6th Baron Carrington) (1919–), politician. Carrington was the last hereditary peer to hold the Foreign Office, and the fact that he should have done so under the meritocratic Margaret THATCHER says much about the nature of the modern Conservative Party. Carrington never served in the Commons, succeeding his father in the Lords in 1938. He entered politics in 1951, holding a variety of minor offices under Winston CHURCHILL, Anthony EDEN and Harold MACMILLAN, before becoming First Lord of the Admiralty in 1959. In opposition under Edward HEATH, Carrington led the attempt to reform the House of Lords by eliminating the influence of hereditary peers in 1968, which was defeated by Enoch POWELL and Michael FOOT. He was Secretary of State for Defence in the Heath Administration, moving to the Department of Energy in 1974 just in time to fail to deal with the miners' strike.

Thatcher made him Foreign Secretary in 1979, where his Whiggish tone reassured those alarmed by her more strident ones, but the two worked well together, notably in settling the Rhodesian question in 1980. It was typical of Carrington's old-world manner that despite the fact that he was not personally to blame for the failure to anticipate the Argentinian invasion of the Falkland Islands in 1982 he should have chosen to resign. He went on to become Secretary General of NATO (1984–8) and chaired the European Community conference on the former Yugoslavia (1991–2). Carrington's career covered the period of Britain's transition from pretensions of Great Power status to the realization of the realities of diplomacy. He realized that Britain's effectiveness in the international area in the late twentieth century depended upon close relations with the USA and upon the state of her relations with the other countries of the EEC.

CARROLL, LEWIS (originally Charles Lutwidge Dodgson) (1832–98), mathematician and writer. A mathematics don at Christ Church, Oxford, in July 1862 Dodgson promised Alice Liddell and her sisters that he would write down the stories which he had been telling them on their river trip that afternoon. Under the name Lewis Carroll, *Alice's Adventures in Wonderland* was published in 1865, and *Through the Looking Glass* in 1871, both illustrated by John Tenniel. The brilliant inverted logic and unforgettable characters of the stories make them as irresistibly quotable by adults as readable to children. Dodgson's attraction to the innocence of childhood, which was also expressed in the many photographs which he took, has caused unease in a later, more sexually interrogative age.

CARSON, EDWARD (1st Baron Carson of Duncairn) (1854–1935), Irish politician. A Dublin lawyer, he came to prominence through his role in helping Arthur BALFOUR to suppress land agitation in the late 1880s. Elected Unionist MP for Trinity College, Dublin, in 1892, he moved to England to become a leading figure of the English Bar, noted for skill in cross-examination. As defence counsel for the Marquess of Queensberry (*see* DOUGLAS, JOHN SHOLTO) in the libel action brought by Oscar WILDE (Carson's contemporary at Trinity College), it was Carson whose cross-examination destroyed Wilde's case and led to his prosecution for homosexual acts. He served as Solicitor General (1900–5). In 1910 he became leader of the Irish Unionist MPs, and oversaw the organization of the Ulster Volunteer Force to resist Home Rule. His uncompromising declarations that Ulster would fight helped to bring about the partition of Ireland and creation of Northern Ireland, while a personality cult, propagated by the Unionist publicity machine, made him a symbol of Ulster identity. Ironically, Carson's attitude towards Catholics was more tolerant than that of many of his Ulster followers, and as a Southern Unionist his feelings about partition were mixed. In 1915 he became Attorney General; he played a crucial role in bringing down ASQUITH in 1916, but proved an ineffective administrator as First Lord of the Admiralty (1916–17) and as a member of the War Cabinet (1917–18). Elected MP for the Belfast constituency of Duncairn in 1918, he became a law lord in 1921 after turning down the post of Prime Minister of Northern Ireland. He opposed the Anglo-Irish Treaty, and in his last years lamented the 'betrayal' of the Southern Unionists, for which he was partly responsible. For many contemporary Unionists Carson remains a symbol of strong, uncompromising leadership; this iconic representation, based on contemporary political publicity, disguises the complexities of his career.

CARSWELL, JOHN (?–1572), churchman. A priest educated at St Andrews who became one of the first ministers of the Scottish Reformation, he was chaplain to the strongly Protestant Archibald CAMPBELL, 5th Earl of Argyll, who arranged his appointment as Superintendent of Argyll in 1561 and lavishly endowed his work; MARY QUEEN OF SCOTS was prevailed on to make him Dean of the Chapel Royal, Bishop of the Isles and titular Abbot of Iona in 1566. He made a free Gaelic translation of the Kirk's *Book of Common Order* (1567): the first Gaelic book to be printed. *See also* KEARNY, JOHN.

CARTE, RICHARD D'OYLY (1844–1901), impresario. Son of a musical instrument-maker for whom he worked, he later became a concert agent and from 1875 began to produce the light operettas of W. S. GILBERT and Arthur SULLIVAN with great success. The Savoy Theatre (1881) where the performances were held was built by D'Oyly Carte and was the first public building to be lit by electricity. The D'Oyly Carte Company continued to stage Gilbert and Sullivan's work until the 1980s.

CARTER, ELIZABETH (1717–1806), writer. Her father, Nicholas Carter, curate of Deal, taught her nine languages, ancient and modern history, geography and music. From 1734 she was a regular contributor to the *Gentleman's Magazine*, and Edward CAVE published her *Poems on Particular Occasions* in 1734. *Poems on Several Occasions* followed many years later in 1762. In the intervening years Carter translated Epictetus, which proved a huge commercial success, and became part of the 'bluestocking' circle of Elizabeth MONTAGU.

CARTER, HOWARD (1874–1939), Egyptologist. In 1891 he went to Thebes as a draughtsman with Flinders PETRIE's archaeological survey and was later appointed inspector general of the Egyptian antiquities department. The patronage of George HERBERT, 5th Earl of Carnarvon, enabled him to make such notable discoveries as the tombs of various pharaohs, most significantly the almost intact burial chamber of King Tut'ankamun who had died aged 18 *c*. 1340 BC. The work of excavating, cataloguing and dispatching these matchless treasures occupied Carter for the rest of his life.

CARTERET, JOHN (2nd Baron Carteret, 2nd Earl Granville) (1690–1763), politician. Appointed a Gentleman of the Bedchamber to the new King GEORGE I in 1714, five years later he was sent as Ambassador to Sweden. His knowledge of German endeared him to the Hanoverian kings, and with Sunderland's (*see* SPENCER, CHARLES) backing, he was made southern Secretary of State in 1721, but lost office the following year on his patron's death. He served as Lord Lieutenant of Ireland (1724–30), where he was immediately confronted with the furore provoked by William WOOD's patent. The ministry calmed the storm by rescinding the patent (1725); subsequently, Carteret was on good terms with SWIFT, who had played a prominent part in the agitation. After Robert WALPOLE's fall in 1742 royal favour aided Carteret's career once again: he became northern Secretary of State and worked closely with GEORGE II in the diplomacy attending the War of the Austrian Succession, but was accused of sacrificing British interests to Hanoverian ones and forced to resign in 1744. Although he was invited by the King to form a government with Lord Bath (*see* PULTENEY, WILLIAM) in 1746, lack of support forced him to decline. He was Lord President of the Council from 1751, but had little effective power. Carteret's career illustrates the insufficiency of royal favour for the highest political success in an era of parliamentary government.

CARTIMANDUA (*fl.* AD 50s), Queen of the Brigantes. She maintained the independence of the Brigantes (an important British tribe occupying a territory approximately equivalent to modern England north of the Humber) during the early stages of the Roman Conquest by allying herself with the invaders. In this role, she handed over to them the British resistance leader CARATACUS in 51. After a quarrel with her husband Venutius, she had to be rescued by the Romans, an event that opened up northern England for conquest.

CARTON DE WIART, SIR ADRIAN (1880–1963), soldier. Son of a lawyer, educated at Oxford, he served with the Imperial Yeomanry in South Africa (1900–2). He lost an eye fighting in Somaliland in 1904, lost his left hand and suffered seven other severe wounds in fighting on the Western Front (1914–18) and was awarded the Victoria Cross. Retiring to an estate in Poland's Pripet marshes, in 1939 Carton De Wiart escaped the German invasion by way of Romania, fought in and escaped from Norway, was shot down on a mission to Yugoslavia and taken prisoner by the Italians (April 1941), who subsequently used him to negotiate an armistice with the Allies (Aug. 1943). Larger than life, Carton De Wiart was immortalized as Brigadier Ritchie Hook by Evelyn WAUGH in the *Sword of Honour* trilogy.

CARTLAND, DAME BARBARA (1901–2000), novelist. A romantic novelist and, officially, the world's most prolific writer, Cartland published her first novel at the age of 21 and was still turning them out at the rate of at least three or four a year in her nineties. Her formulaic novels of love and romance gained an early national and international following and she set the standard for a generic type of popular romantic fiction. She produced an average of 23 books a year for 18 years in succession: in France alone she sold over 25 million books. Her daughter Raine married Earl Spencer, the father of DIANA, Princess of Wales.

CARTWRIGHT, EDMUND (1743–1822), inventor. Brother of the political reformer John CARTWRIGHT, he was educated at Oxford and took holy orders. In 1784, having visited ARKWRIGHT's spinning factory, he began work on machinery to improve weaving, taking out a patent for a power-loom in 1785, but his invention needed much

refinement. In 1787 he set up a factory in Doncaster (Yorks.) but fell into debt and went to London to pursue further inventions. In 1809, having discovered that a modified form of his loom was in wide use, he applied to Parliament for a reward and was given £10,000.

CARTWRIGHT, JOHN (1740–1824), political reformer. Descended from an old Notts. family, he served in the navy (1758–70) and subsequently became a major in the Notts. militia. He first attracted public notice with the publication of the pamphlet *Take Your Choice!* (1776), which advocated annual Parliaments and electoral reform. A persistent supporter of parliamentary reform thereafter, he was one of the founders of the Society for Constitutional Information (1780), which printed and reprinted tracts for distribution in London and the provinces, and he played a prominent part in the radical movement which grew after the French Revolution. He was fined £100 for sedition in 1820. He also wrote in favour of abolishing slavery and the emancipation of Greece.

CARTWRIGHT, THOMAS (1535–1603), churchman. The Cambridge career of the Herts.-born Cartwright, already interrupted by MARY I's reign, was ended in 1570 when, as the newly appointed Lady Margaret Professor, he gave lectures attacking the government of the Church of England by bishops and promoting the idea of Presbyterian Church government (*see* CALVIN, JOHN); this was the first major challenge to the episcopal system of government which ELIZABETH I's religious settlement had left in place. After visiting Geneva, the intellectual powerhouse of Calvinism, he became embroiled in the *Admonition* controversy (1572–6), a battle of the books with the defender of the Church's status quo, John WHITGIFT, and fled again. From 1585 he was back but, although arrested in 1590, he benefited from patronage and protection by Robert DUDLEY, Earl of Leicester, and his brother Ambrose DUDLEY, Earl of Warwick. He therefore escaped the harsh treatment meted out to other leading Presbyterians by the government in the early 1590s.

CARVER, JOHN (*c.* 1575–1621), colonial pioneer. A Puritan who joined the Separatist exiles in the Netherlands in 1608 and, as deacon in the Leyden congregation, crossed the Atlantic with the Pilgrim Fathers in the *Mayflower* (1620). Elected first Governor of Massachusetts, he signed a treaty with local native Americans in 1621, but soon after died of heatstroke.

CARVER, MICHAEL (1st Baron Carver) (1915–), soldier and military historian. A descendent of the Duke of Wellington (*see* WELLESLEY, ARTHUR), educated at Winchester and Sandhurst, Carver was commissioned into the Royal Tank Corps in 1935. In the Second World War he fought in the North African campaign, landed at Salerno, fought from Normandy to the Elbe, was awarded the Military Cross and twice appointed to the Distinguished Service Order (DSO). Carver conducted counter-insurgency campaigns in Kenya and Cyprus in the 1950s and early 1960s, commanded British forces which defeated the Indonesian confrontation of Malaysia in 1966 and as Chief of the General Staff (1971–3) dealt with the most violent period of the 'troubles' in Northern Ireland. As Chief of the Defence Staff (1973–6), Carver opposed Labour's reductions in the defence budget though he also supported the abolition of nuclear weapons. Carver developed a subsidiary career as a writer in the early 1950s, and over the next half century produced more than a dozen highly regarded works on military history and theory.

CARVER, ROBERT (*c*. 1490–*c*. 1550), composer. Nothing is known of this brilliant Scots musician apart from the masses and motets contained in the Edinburgh MS, the 'Scone Antiphonary', although continental style-traits and Flemish compositions also present in the MS suggest that he may have studied abroad. One mass is associated with the Scottish Chapel Royal; the latest motet, much simpler in style, is dated 1546. Carver is also called 'Arnat' in the MS.

CARY, JOHN (?–*c*. 1720), writer. Son of a Bristol vicar, he traded in West Indian sugar and was Warden of the Bristol Merchant Venturers' Company (1683–4). He attracted notice with his *Essay on Trade* (1695) and corresponded with LOCKE. His ideas influenced the instructions to the newly founded Board of Trade in 1696, especially his urging that customs duties be manipulated to encourage the export of manufactures. He favoured the establishment of workhouses for the poor and in 1697 helped found one in Bristol that was widely imitated.

CASAUBON, ISAAC (1559–1614), classical scholar. A Genevan-born Protestant academic who settled in France and became librarian to Henri IV (1604). He was as suspicious of extreme Calvinism as of Roman Catholicism and when Henri was assassinated (1610) he migrated to England, and spent his last few years there much honoured, with a prebend at Canterbury Cathedral and burial in Westminster Abbey. He produced outstanding editions of various classical authors and wrote defending the Church of England.

CASEMENT, SIR ROGER (1864–1916), Irish nationalist. Born and educated in Ireland, Casement joined the British Colonial Service in 1892. He won an international reputation as a humane administrator, exposing the harsh treatment of rubber plantation workers in the Belgian Congo and Peru. While serving the British government, however, he harboured strong Irish nationalist sympathies and joined the Irish Volunteers in 1913 after retiring from the Colonial Service. He saw the First World War as an opportunity to elicit support from Germany for the cause of Irish nationalism and opened negotiations with the German government to this end. He was caught by the British smuggling a small number of German weapons into Ireland on Good Friday 1916, just before the Easter Rising in Dublin. Together with other nationalists involved in the aborted rebellion, Casement was tried and sentenced to death. Because of his reputation an international campaign was mounted to save his life, but this was fatally undermined by the British government's publication of diaries alleged to be his which showed details of homosexual activities. Although never proved, the imputation alienated him to Irish Catholic and English public opinion and he was hanged on 3 Aug. 1916.

CASSELL, SIR ERNEST (1852–1921), financier. A man who penetrated society with the same determination and guile with which he achieved success in business, Cassell was an intimate member of the circle surrounding EDWARD VII. A self-made man of German Jewish origins, he was never entirely accepted and his star waned after the King's death in 1910. Born in Cologne into a small-scale banking family, he moved to Liverpool in 1869, and swiftly displayed his flair in banking with a series of deals in Constantinople. Investment in Swedish iron and steel laid the foundations of his own fortune. By the turn of the century his investment activities included electricity supply and shipbuilding, but also involved South Africa and Egypt. There he financed dam and irrigation companies and established the National Bank of Egypt and other loan companies before repeating these successes in Morocco. In Turkey, where his financial activities were encouraged after the Young Turk Revolution of 1908, he was ultimately less successful, especially in the face of French opposition.

CASSIVELLAUNUS (*fl*. 50s BC), British war leader. He was chosen in 54 by a confederacy of the tribes of southern Britain to head the resistance to the Roman invasion led by JULIUS CAESAR. Other than his military exploits and that he may have been King of the most powerful tribe in southern Britain in the first century BC, the Catuvellauni, nothing is known about him. Although he lost a pitched battle, had his base camp captured and was eventually forced to make an apparently disadvantageous peace, his tenacious resistance obstructed Caesar's advance and contributed much to undermining the Romans' plans for conquest.

CASSON, SIR HUGH (1910–99), architect. Educated at Cambridge University, Casson was Director of Architecture for the Festival of Britain (1951), Professor of Environmental Design (1953–75) and then Provost (1980–6) of the Royal College of Art, President of the Royal Academy (1976–84), planning adviser to a number of new town developments, and the author of several books including *Homes by the Million* (1947). He played a notable part in the transformation of the post-war built environment of Britain.

CASTLE, BARBARA (Baroness Castle of Blackburn) (1910–), politician. She was a fiery redhead who helped establish that women politicians could operate at the first rank. Elected to the Commons in the Labour landslide of 1945, she soon attracted attention, as much by her determination and oratory as by her striking appearance. A devoted Bevanite during the 1950s (*see* BEVAN, ANEURIN), she was brought into government by Harold WILSON as Minister for Overseas Development (1964–5). But it was as Minister of Transport (1965–9) that she made her mark, introducing the breathalyser and traffic wardens. At the Department of Employment in 1969 she worked with Wilson, who was convinced that Labour's economic policy could not succeed without a thorough-going reform of industrial relations, to reform legislation covering trade unions. Her White Paper, *In Place of Strife*, proposed the introduction of compulsory strike ballots and a 'cooling off' period for unofficial strikes, but was defeated in Cabinet thanks largely to Jim CALLAGHAN and the trade unions. Castle's reputation was damaged and the Labour governemnt seemed weakened by this reverse

She was, however, appointed Secretary of State for Social Services in the Wilson government (1974–6), where she abolished private beds in National Health hospitals but was sacked when her old adversary Callaghan became Prime Minister in 1976. A long-standing opponent of the European Common Market, she resigned her Blackburn seat in 1979 to become a member of the European Parliament. She published her political diaries in the 1980s, following the fashion set by Richard CROSSMAN but, apart from revealing the backbiting in the Wilson Cabinet, they contributed little to our understanding of Labour's failure under Wilson. Even in retirement her fiery nature can be ignited by acts of social injustice and she showed what she thought of New Labour by her opposition to its cuts in welfare spending for single mothers, and by her advocacy of increases in the old age pension.

CASTLEHAVEN, 2ND EARL OF *see* TUCHET, MERVYN

CASTLEMAINE, COUNTESS OF *see* VILLIERS, BARBARA

CASTLEREAGH, 1ST VISCOUNT *see* STEWART, ROBERT

CAT, CHRISTOPHER (*fl.* 1703–33), club host. He was proprietor of the Cat and Fiddle Tavern in Shire Lane near Temple Bar, where leading Whigs met from 1703. In his honour, the group became known as the Kit-Cat Club. Its 39 (later 48) members included such outstanding literary and political figures as Joseph ADDISON, Richard STEELE, Marlborough (*see* CHURCHILL, JOHN), SOMERS, Halifax (*see* MONTAGU, CHARLES) and Robert WALPOLE. Some of the three-quarter-length portraits of members commissioned to hang in the club room (probably at one of its other meeting places, Jacob Tonson's house at Barn Elms), the so-called Kit-Cat portraits, survive in the National Portrait Gallery.

CATESBY, ROBERT (1573–1605), conspirator. Son of a Roman Catholic Warws. knight and Oxford-educated, he was forced to sell his Oxon. home, Chastleton House, after his involvement in Robert DEVEREUX, Earl of Essex's failed coup of 1601, and retired to Northants. A charismatic figure, he became the major force in the conspiracy of Guy FAWKES to destroy JAMES I in Parliament. Fleeing from London when Fawkes was arrested, he was killed when cornered by government forces in Staffs.

CATHAL MAC FINGUINE (?–742), King of Munster. Cathal mac Finguine was one of the few kings of Munster before the reign of BRIAN BORUMA to cut a figure on a broader Irish stage. His career of military expansion, begun in 721, was characterized by a mixture of successes and failures. Later legend extravagantly suggested that he had been King of all Ireland.

CATHAL Ó CONCHOBHAIR ('THE REDHAND') (1152–1224), King of Connacht (1189–1224). Known from a birthmark as *croibhdhearg* (the Redhand), he was the youngest son of TAIRDELBACH UA CONCHOBAIR. He became King of Connacht in 1189 and set out to save Ireland from the English. After defeats in 1200–2 he became more accommodating, and agreed to hold Connacht as a fief of the English Crown. Throughout his reign he had to face rivals for kingship from within his own family. According to his obituary in the *Annals of Connacht* he was 'the King whom of all Kings in Ireland God made most perfect in every good quality . . . the fiercest and harshest to his enemies, the King who most blinded, killed and mutilated rebels'.

CATHERINE HOWARD (1521–42), Queen of England. Niece of Thomas HOWARD, 8th Duke of Norfolk, she was promoted by the conservative faction at court to console HENRY VIII for his disappointment over ANNE OF CLEVES. She was a racy young lady who did not have the sense to see her danger when she continued amorous dalliances after her royal marriage in 1540. Unsurprisingly, it was a Protestant courtier who uncovered the evidence of her indiscretions, and Archbishop CRANMER who passed it to the King. Henry, humiliated and grief-stricken, had her and her lovers executed.

CATHERINE OF ARAGON (1485–1536), Queen of England. Daughter of Ferdinand and Isabella of Aragon and Castile, she was married in her teens to Prince ARTHUR and, after his death, to his younger brother HENRY VIII on 24 June 1509. The marriage was at first successful, Catherine proving to be an able Regent of England in Henry's absence in France in 1513. She produced only one child, however, to survive infancy, Mary (the future MARY I) in 1516, and the relationship cooled. Henry, desperate for a male heir, had already, in 1514, mooted an annulment (a declaration of the non-existence of his marriage) in order to secure a fertile wife; from 1526, with the incentive of his love for ANNE BOLEYN, he obsessively pursued this course, attacking the papal dispensations which had been required for his marriage to Catherine because she was his brother's widow. In 1527 and 1529, with the backing of her nephew CHARLES V, particularly in the form of pressure on Pope Clement VII, Catherine put up fierce resistance to successive attempts to declare her marriage invalid, but when the King embarked on a unilateral course in 1532–3, she could only refuse to recognize CRANMER's annulment sentence (May 1533) and the declaration that her daughter was illegitimate. Attracting much public sympathy, especially from fellow religious conservatives, she lived her last years in dignified misery, although punctiliously surrounded by the comforts appropriate to a Princess Dowager. Her death delighted Henry, who did not attend her funeral in Peterborough Abbey.

CATHERINE OF BRAGANZA (1638–1705), Queen Consort. Her father, King John IV of Portugal, had ended Spanish rule there in 1640 but was recognized by very few European powers. Her marriage to CHARLES II in 1662 was partly an attempt to strengthen the position of her father and the Braganza dynasty. Her position at court was weakened by her failure to have a full-term pregnancy and the pre-eminence enjoyed by her husband's mistresses, particularly Barbara VILLIERS and Louise de KÉROUALLE. Her Catholicism was also a liability. English Catholics were prohibited from using her court as a centre. In 1678, echoing the accusations by OATES, an address passed the Commons accusing her of planning her husband's murder, but Charles II rejected it as he did the frequent suggestions that he divorce her. After the Glorious Revolution, Catherine left for Portugal, where she helped John and Paul METHUEN gain support for their treaty.

CATHERINE OF VALOIS (1401–37), Queen of England. Daughter of Charles VI of France, in 1420 she was married to HENRY V in accordance with the terms of the Treaty of Troyes, and bore him a son, the future HENRY VI. Widowed in 1422, she secretly (c. 1431–2) married Owen TUDOR and bore Edmund TUDOR (later Earl of Richmond and father of HENRY VII) and Jasper TUDOR. Buried in Westminster Abbey, her remains were there kissed by Samuel PEPYS as a tribute to her legendary beauty.

CATHERINE PARR (1512–48), Queen of England. Daughter of Sir Thomas Parr, a royal official, she had been twice widowed when HENRY VIII chose to marry her in 1543. Her warmth, tact and openness to her assorted royal stepchildren made the marriage a success. She developed Protestant sympathies, promoting reformist interests at court, but conservative attempts to discredit her with Henry (and even destroy her) backfired. On Henry's death she married an earlier love, Lord Thomas SEYMOUR, published a reformist pious tract, *The Lamentations of a Sinner* (1547), and encouraged the publication of ERASMUS' *Paraphrases* of the New Testament in translation. She died in childbirth.

CATROE, ST (c. 900–c. 971), Abbot of Metz. A notable figure in the European monastic changes of the tenth century and the subject of a *vita* compiled on the continent within a few years of his death, Catroe was described as a kinsman of DYFNWAL, SON OF YWAIN, King of the Cumbrians (Strathclyde), but may possibly have been of Pictish descent, given his early association with the Ionian community at Dunkeld. Leaving Scotland as a pilgrim in c. 941, Catroe became involved in the important monastic reforms of Adalbero, Bishop of Metz, being appointed firstly Prior, then Abbot, of Waulsort, then ultimately as Abbot of Metz.

CATTO, THOMAS (1st Baron Catto of Cairncatto) (1879–1959), Governor of the Bank of

England. Catto was the son of a Newcastle ship-wright, but his business acumen took him from a clerkship in a Tyneside shipping company to commercial success in the Baltic, the USA, Turkey and India, a peerage and ultimately governorship of the Bank of England. His greatest success was as Calcutta head of the Anglo-Indian merchants Andrew Yule (1919–31). A considerable figure both in India and in the City, he became Managing Director of Morgan Grenfell in 1928. In the summer of 1940 he took an advisory post in the Treasury, where he was intellectually close to KEYNES: Catto and Doggo were their nicknames. Appointed Governor in 1944, he represented the Bank of England in negotiations (to which many of his City colleagues were hostile) before its nationalization by the Labour government in March 1946.

CAULFIELD, JAMES (4th Viscount and 1st Earl of Charlemont) (1728–99), Irish politician. His high-ranking Protestant family had been established in Ireland under ELIZABETH I. Made an earl in 1763 after helping to calm rural disturbances in Ulster, in 1768 he helped to force FLOOD's Octennial Bill through the Irish Lords, requiring general elections at least every eight years. He spent long periods in London where he was associated with the opposition to NORTH; in Ireland, he established himself as a critic of British administration. As patron to Henry GRATTAN he was at the forefront of the moves towards Irish legislative independence, becoming first Commander-in-Chief of the Irish Volunteers in July 1780. In 1782 he co-authored the resolutions demanding 'legislative independence', to which the British capitulated. His opposition to Catholic Emancipation, however, contributed towards the failure of the Volunteers to endure as a political force.

CAVE, EDWARD (1691–1754), printer and editor. Educated at Rugby grammar school, he worked as a printer on several London and local papers and in 1731 founded the *Gentleman's Magazine*. Initially containing almost entirely extracts from newspapers and periodicals, it soon attracted its own writers. In the late 1730s and early 1740s, when JOHNSON was its parliamentary correspondent, circulation exceeded 12,000: its format was widely imitated and established the 'magazine' as a concept in periodical literature, although Cave's publication was itself inspired by an earlier journal published by Motteux. Cave's success earned the enmity of the booksellers but he was able to prosper because his position in the Post Office allowed him to distribute the title across the country under frank. The magazine endured until 1914; later publishers included John NICHOLS.

CAVELL, EDITH (1865–1915), nurse. Daughter of a Norfolk rector, Cavell entered the London Hospital as a probationer in 1895, and in 1907 was appointed matron of Berkendael Medical Institute in Brussels. Permitted to continue her work by the German army after the occupation of Brussels in Aug. 1914, Cavell set up an escape route to neutral Holland for Allied soldiers cut off by the German advance. She was betrayed and arrested in Aug. 1915, tried by court-martial and shot. She became a national martyr, commemorated for her courage and defiance of German militarism.

CAVELLUS, HUGO *see* MACCAGHWELL, HUGH

CAVENDISH, LORD FREDERICK (1836–82), politician. Younger brother of the Liberal politician Lord Hartington (later Duke of Devonshire, *see* CAVENDISH, SPENCER) and a Liberal MP (1865–82), he was a protégé of GLADSTONE, whose niece Lucy he married. Cavendish held junior office (1872–4 and 1880–2). After the 1882 Kilmainham Treaty, an agreement between Gladstone and Charles Stewart PARNELL that ensured Parnell's release from gaol on condition that he and his supporters accepted the 1881 Land Act, he was appointed Chief Secretary for Ireland in succession to W. E. FORSTER. But on 6 May 1882, hours after taking office, he was killed with Under-Secretary T. H. Burke in Phoenix Park, Dublin, by a Fenian splinter group, the Invincibles. The 'Phoenix Park murders' were presented by Unionists as proof of the lawlessness and treachery of Irish nationalists and hence the folly of Gladstone's post-1886 attempt to conciliate them through Home Rule. Parnell was falsely accused of complicity in the murders on the basis of documents forged by Richard PIGOTT. Hartington led the Liberal Unionist opponents of Home Rule, while Lucy Cavendish's support for her uncle's policy was seen by Home Rulers as symbolizing Anglo-Irish reconciliation.

CAVENDISH, GEORGIANA (née Spencer) (Duchess of Devonshire) (1752–1806), political hostess. Daughter of the pious Georgina SPENCER (whose anomalous love of gambling she shared), Georgiana married the 5th Duke of Devonshire in 1774 and became a leader of aristocratic fashion. She was a politically active Whig and an ally of Charles James FOX; historians are divided as to whether they were lovers. Both her private life and her public actions aroused controversy. Her public activities included organizing an auxiliary corps of noblewomen to defend the country against a French invasion in 1778. Her canvassing in the Westminster election of 1784 attracted the satirical attention of caricaturists. She exerted her considerable political influence in an attempt to bring Fox into the ADDINGTON ministry after the fall of PITT THE YOUNGER in 1801, and helped assemble William GRENVILLE's coalition of 1806.

CAVENDISH, HENRY (1731–1810), chemist. Grandson of the 2nd Duke of Devonshire. Possessed by a driving scientific curiosity, he was unusual among his generation of scientists in his mathematical mastery. His first paper to the Royal Society, in 1766, won him the Copley Medal; it analysed 'factitious airs' and identified the specific gravity of what are now known as hydrogen and carbon dioxide compared to atmospheric air. His 1784 paper 'Experiments on Air' included the discovery that water was a compound of hydrogen and oxygen. Cavendish also made one of the most accurate estimates of the density of the earth and his work on electricity, had it been published, would have greatly facilitated the work of later scientists such as FARADAY. His research was supported by family money; this, combined with his refusal to publish anything with which he was not personally satisfied and the priority he gave to results that contributed towards a unified theory of the universe that would succeed NEWTON's work, led to most of his work being unknown until his papers were edited by James Clerk MAXWELL in 1879.

CAVENDISH, SPENCER (Marquess of Hartington, 8th Duke of Devonshire) (1833–1908), politician. Known by the courtesy title of the Marquess of Hartington from 1858 to 1891, when he succeeded as Duke, he entered Parliament in 1857, a Liberal in the Whig tradition who was to sit in the Commons for 34 years (1857–68 and 1869–91). He held high office in various administrations between 1863 and 1874, being Secretary for War (1866) and Postmaster General (1868–74) in GLADSTONE's first ministry. During Gladstone's temporary abdication from 1875 to 1880, Hart-ington replaced him as party leader in opposition. Subsequently he served as Secretary of State for India (1880–2) and for War (1882–5), during which time he was partly responsible for sending General Charles GORDON to the Sudan and failing to rescue him from Khartoum. Hartington opposed Irish Home Rule in 1886 and joined with Joseph CHAMBERLAIN to form a new party of Liberal Unionists who combined with the Conservatives under Lord Salisbury (*see* CECIL, ROBERT GASCOYNE) to drive Gladstone from office. He subsequently served as Lord President of the Council in both Salisbury's and BALFOUR's Cabinets between 1895 and 1903. He made an important contribution to the 1902 Education Act and, after the same uncertainty that he had initially shown in his attitude towards Home Rule in 1886, offered firm leadership to the supporters of Free Trade during the Tariff Reform controversy in 1903. A business-like, somewhat uninspiring politician of moderate pragmatism rather than an embracer of ideological positions, and with rather too much self-disengagement for success, Hartington was realistic in his assessment of the support for Gladstone when he declined the premiership in April 1880 after Gladstone had refused to serve under him. He was equally realistic about his own supporters' preparedness finally to abandon Liberalism when he reluctantly declined Salisbury's suggestion of the premiership in both July and Dec. 1886.

CAVENDISH, THOMAS (1560–92), seafarer. A Suffolk gentleman, in 1586–8 he successfully imitated Francis Drake's circumnavigation of the world. Delighted by his sudden national fame, he squandered the wealth he had gained by setting sail again in 1591; he died on board ship in the Atlantic.

CAVENDISH, WILLIAM (9th Baron and 1st Earl of Ogle, 1st Duke of Newcastle) (1592–1676), soldier, patron and playwright. Tutor of the future CHARLES II from 1638 to 1641, he served the King through the 'Bishops' Wars' in Scotland (1639–40) and the English Civil Wars from 1642, particularly useful as a magnate who could still readily command tenantries for raising military forces. In 1644 he was sent unsuccessfully against the Scots and, after fighting in the Royalist defeat at Marston Moor, left in high dudgeon for a long and often penurious continental exile. At the restoration of CHARLES II he did not regain all his estates despite his huge expenditure in royal service, Charles instead giving him a dukedom in 1665; he retired from public life. Patron of Ben JONSON and later of John DRYDEN, he was himself a playwright and writer, like Margaret LUCAS, his second wife (who wrote his biography, published in 1667).

CAVENDISH, WILLIAM (4th Earl and 1st Duke of Devonshire) (1640–1707), politician. Born to a Derbys. Royalist family, he had an irregular education owing to the Civil Wars. Elected an MP in 1661, from the mid 1670s he acted with the parliamentary opposition. He played a prominent part in the investigation into the Popish-Plot stories of Titus OATES, and after the fall of Danby (*see* OSBORNE, THOMAS) was made a member of the reformed Privy Council under the presidency of Shaftesbury (*see* COOPER, ANTHONY ASHLEY). Although a keen proponent of the exclusion of CHARLES II's brother James (later JAMES II) from the line of succession he backed away when Shaftesbury and others seemed set on increasingly desperate measures, and was reconciled with the King in 1681, although he remained sufficiently faithful to his former loyalties to testify in William RUSSELL's favour at his trial in 1683. Soon after the accession of James II he distanced himself from the court and seemed to concentrate on the building of his country house in Chatsworth (Derbys.), largely designed by TALMAN. He maintained communication with the Prince of Orange (the future WILLIAM III) and was one of the 'Immortal Seven' who invited the Prince to England in 1688. He was William III's Lord Steward and accompanied him on several military and diplomatic expeditions. In ANNE's reign he was a commissioner for the Union with Scotland.

CAVENDISH, WILLIAM (4th Duke of Devonshire) (1720–64), politician and Prime Minister (1756–7). Scion of one of the great 'Revolution' Whig families, he entered the Commons as Whig MP for Derbys. in 1741. His marriage to Lord Burlington's (see BOYLE, RICHARD) daughter seven years later brought him further powerful Whig connections. Appointed Lord Lieutenant of Ireland in 1754, he returned to serve as First Lord of the Treasury upon Newcastle's (see PELHAM-HOLLES) resignation in 1756, in what was effectively PITT THE ELDER's administration. Resigning in the latter's wake in 1757, he became Lord Chamberlain of the Household. Like other Old Corps Whigs, including Newcastle and Hardwicke (see YORKE, PHILIP), he was both distrustful of and distrusted by GEORGE III; when he resigned office in 1762, the King struck his name from the list of Privy Councillors with his own hand.

CAWARDEN, SIR THOMAS (c. 1510–59), Master of the Revels. Son of a London clothworker, he contrived to be appointed as a gentleman of HENRY VIII's Privy Chamber in 1540, was prominent in administering the capture of Boulogne in 1544 and became Master of the Revels in 1545. He much expanded the post's activities and set himself up as a county magnate in Surrey. He contrived to remain in charge of court entertainment under EDWARD VI, MARY I and (briefly) ELIZABETH I.

CAXTON, WILLIAM see essay on page 155

CAYLEY, ARTHUR (1821–95), mathematician. Cayley studied mathematics at Cambridge University, where, after a career practising law (1849–63), he became Sadlerian Professor of Pure Mathematics (1863–95). One of the most prolific British mathematicians of the nineteenth century, Cayley's most important work includes his contributions to the theories of matrices and periodic functions, his invention of n-dimensional geometry and, with the distinguished Cambridge mathematician, James Joseph Sylvester, his construction of the theory of algebraic invariants and covariants.

CAYLEY, SIR GEORGE (1773–1857), aeronautical pioneer. Born to a wealthy family, Cayley acquired skills in mathematics and mechanics privately and at school in York. In the 1780s he began his lifelong pursuit of aeronautical machines: he built a toy helicopter (1784), wrote pioneering studies of the forces of flight (from 1799) and built what is regarded as the first successful unmanned glider (1809). He also designed airships, experimented with fixed-wing and flapping-wing machines and launched numerous other inventions including a hot-air engine (1807) and manned gliders (1849–53).

CEARL, King of Mercia (?–c. 626). The predecessor of the much more famous PENDA, Cearl's friendly relations with King EDWIN of Northumbria suggest that he and Penda were rivals for Mercian kingship. Penda subsequently persecuted Cearl's descendants, suggesting a typical Dark Age family conflict for power.

CEAWLIN (?–593), King of Wessex (?–593). Possibly a grandson of CERDIC, Ceawlin is the earliest King of Wessex for whom there is certain historical information. One of the seven kings named by BEDE as having been sufficiently powerful to exercise overlordship over all the English peoples south of the Humber, a status later described by the term Bretwalda, Ceawlin is chiefly known as a war leader based on the upper Thames, who fought several battles, including Dyrham (Glos.) in 577, against his British and English neighbours. Although not always successful in warfare, it appears that, during his time, there was a resumption in the English advance after the long peace which had followed the British victory under AMBROSIUS AURELIANUS at the Battle of Mount Badon (site unknown). The succession is unclear after his death; the next well attested King is CYNEGILS.

CECIL, ROBERT (15th Earl of Salisbury) see essay on page 156

CECIL, ROBERT (5th Marquess of Salisbury) (1893–1972), politician. The grandson of the great 3rd Marquess (see CECIL, ROBERT GASCOYNE), three times Prime Minister in the late nineteenth century, 'Bobbety' (as he was known and appears in so many contemporary diaries) was a close friend of Anthony EDEN and a notable figure in Tory politics.

Lord Cranborne (as he was known before succeeding to the title in 1947) became Conservative

continued on page 157

CAXTON, WILLIAM (c. 1420–91)
Printer and publisher

In 1475 Caxton produced the first book printed in English. No matter how small early editions may have been, averaging perhaps only 250 copies, this was a staggering advance when compared with the productivity of the scribe. By the end of the year he had published five more titles. But Caxton's first press was in Bruges, not in England. Bruges was then the commercial capital of northern Europe, one of the flourishing Flemish towns which sustained the flamboyant court culture of the dukes of Burgundy. Caxton was a leading representative of the English business community there and it was as such that four years earlier he had gone on a trade mission to Cologne. While there he took the momentous decision to learn the new craft of printing. Printing with movable type, a revolutionary method of reproducing script, had been perfected by Johann Gutenberg of Mainz in the 1450s. So complete was Gutenberg's technological breakthrough that there was to be no significant further advance for another 300 years. But at first printing spread slowly, and in 1471 was still confined to the Rhineland and Italy, which were the most developed regions in fifteenth-century Europe. It took time to master the new combination of technical, managerial and marketing skills required if overproduction and bankruptcy were to be avoided. By 1471 three printers were in business in Cologne, and with one of these Caxton studied for a year or so before moving back to Bruges and setting up his own press. Until then he had been a successful businessman. We know little about his personal life but he was a member of the London Mercers Company and almost certainly belonged to a family which had long been active in the company, involved in the import and export of goods, selling English cloth at Bruges and Antwerp and buying manufactured goods and luxury articles for the English market. He seems to have been good at it. In 1471 when he decided to leave familiar ground and learn, at his own expense, this new and risky trade, he was about 50 years old.

He clearly loved reading and writing, and translated over two million words. His first book, the *Recuyell of the Histories of Troy*, was his own translation of a French work written by a chaplain at the Burgundian court. He had begun it in 1469, the year after EDWARD IV's sister Margaret married Duke Charles of Burgundy and had been encouraged by her. In his early works, choice of type and layout was designed to reproduce in print the style of Burgundian luxury manuscripts. His second book, *The Game and Playe of the Chesse*, also printed in 1475, was dedicated to George, Duke of Clarence (*see* PLANTAGENET, GEORGE). In 1476 he moved to England and set up shop on the path which led from Westminster Abbey across Palace Yard to the Palace itself. Using court patronage, his intention was to make the latest Burgundian best-sellers available to the English reading public. A patron commissioned a work, took a large number of copies himself and distributed them to friends and clients. But the more experience he gained, the less he needed commissions. Major works such as *The Canterbury Tales* (1478) and *Chronicles of England* (1480) followed and he quickly broadened his range of titles: school books, devotional works and service books, most importantly the Sarum Missal, of which every church or chapel in the country was supposed to have a copy. Money was also to be made from printing ephemera: pamphlets, poems, news sheets, indulgences. Often printed on single sheets, only a tiny proportion survive; this kind of jobbing work must have been more important than the evidence allows us to see.

Printing was to be a major factor in the gradual standardization of the language. In his first prologue Caxton wrote, 'I was born and learned mine English in Kent in the Weald.' One of his most famous stories tells how a London mercer asked a Kentish housewife for eggs – for which the Kentish word was 'eyren'. 'And the good wife answered that she could speak no French.' It also helped to preserve ideas for posterity. While works circulated in manuscript only, they could all too easily get lost, and with them the ideas which they contained. Caxton's own longest work of translation, the *Golden Legend*, was produced in ignorance of the existence of one made c. 1430. He had a wife and daughter but probably no son to succeed him in the business. This was taken over by his former assistant Wynkyn de Worde. According to Wynkyn, Caxton finished his last translation, the 350,000 word *Vitas patrum*, in 1491 'at the last day of his life'. By then this book-loving workaholic had set in train a massive transformation of English culture and society.

George Duncan Painter, William Caxton: A Biography (1976)

CECIL, ROBERT (1st Viscount Cranborne, 15th [1st Cecil] Earl of Salisbury) (1563–1612)
Politician

Younger and much-cherished son of William CECIL, Lord Burghley, by his second wife Mildred (one of the daughters of Sir Anthony COOKE): despite lifelong ill health, Robert amply rewarded careful nurture, equalling his father's abilities in politics and administration and working closely with him. He studied at Gray's Inn, Cambridge and the Sorbonne, and in 1584 his father arranged for his education to include his election to Parliament for the family seat of Westminster; he sat in the Commons in all ELIZABETH I's subsequent Parliaments, latterly as knight of the shire for the Cecils' county, Hertfordshire. Elizabeth soon realized his worth and in 1586, at her request, he wrote a pamphlet defending her attempt to avoid executing MARY QUEEN OF SCOTS; she also characteristically signalled her affection by giving him a nickname as her 'pygmy', later substituting the less hurtful 'elf'. He was sent as part of the team to discuss peace with the Spaniards in the Netherlands in 1588. His marriage to Elizabeth Brooke (1589) was an effort by his father to ally the Cecil family line to ancient nobility, but it turned into a love match, and Robert bitterly mourned his wife's death in 1596. After Sir Francis WALSINGHAM's death (1590), he acted as informal assistant to his father, taking over the Secretary's duties, and he was knighted and became a Privy Councillor in 1591. He gradually took over his ageing father's role in late-Elizabethan government, and the Queen finally formalized his position as Secretary of State in 1596. Robert DEVEREUX, Earl of Essex (his father's former ward), increasingly resented his power and spitefully ridiculed his physical deformity and small stature; this feud created out of a personality clash became much more open after Burghley's death (1598). Essex became a rallying point for those who wished to see England pursue a policy of Protestant aggression; Cecil sought to end the war with Spain. While Essex brought about his own downfall (1601), Cecil pursued his prosecution with grim relish and ensured that he was executed. Cecil's dominance now seemed unchallengeable; he took over the contacts which Essex had established with JAMES VI and succeeded in securing a smooth succession for him to the English throne in 1603. James rewarded him with a barony. Despite James's esteem, Cecil faced hostility from a variety of courtiers and politicians, some former partisans of Essex, but also members of the Howard family, particularly Henry HOWARD, Earl of Northampton; they did their best to undermine his position, while his work was complicated by the Crown's financial problems and the failure of his efforts to remedy them. Nevertheless, he negotiated peace with Spain in 1604, and was first made a Viscount and then in 1605 an Earl. He was now in a position to indulge his passion for building, chiefly a vast new mansion at Hatfield (Herts.) alongside an old royal hunting lodge obtained from James by exchange for his palatial home at Theobalds. Becoming Lord Treasurer in 1608, he had high hopes for the 'Great Contract', a deal between Parliament and the King which would end royal feudal rights in return for payment of royal debts and a regular annual parliamentary income, but in 1610 Parliament failed to accept it and James became lukewarm to the proposal. Despite this disaster for his policy and the growing rival ascendancy of James's new love Robert CARR, the King needed his energy and efficiency, particularly to direct vital foreign diplomacy, and he would no doubt have regained his commanding position if he had not developed a fatal stomach cancer. He died in serious debt despite the huge wealth which he had accumulated, and still subject to a chorus of malicious publicity.

Cecil combined workaholism with broad and informed cultural interests, delighting in art, books, music, building and garden design. He began collecting paintings from all over Europe in the 1590s, and pioneered artistic patronage in England, later shaping the artistic taste of James's heir Prince HENRY. Hatfield House, the largest of his ambitious building projects, became the principal home of an enduring political dynasty, and it was also notable for the rich decoration of its new chapel, one of the first after the English Reformation to revive uninhibited religious imagery. This reflected the shift in Cecil's Protestantism to a more sacramental and ceremonial religious outlook; from the 1590s, his patronage of anti-Calvinist clergy like Lancelot ANDREWES and Richard NEILE was significant in establishing them in positions of influence in the Church, for the first time challenging the Reformed consensus which dominated it during Elizabeth's reign, and preparing the way for later Arminianism. His archive at Hatfield House, in continuity with his father's papers, is a central source for understanding the period.

J. Hurstfield, 'Robert, Earl of Salisbury', History Today 7 (1957)

MP for the family seat of South Dorset in 1929. He was Eden's junior at the Foreign Office (1936–8), when he resigned over appeasement of Italy: his resignation speech was notable for being the only real attack on Neville CHAMBERLAIN's foreign policy. He returned to office in Winston CHURCHILL's wartime coalition as Secretary of State for the Dominions, becoming Leader of the Lords and Colonial Secretary in 1941. After the war Salisbury's voice was an influential one on the Right, and Eden would have appointed him to the Foreign Office in 1955 but for the fact of his peerage. Happy to serve Churchill and Eden, Salisbury disliked and distrusted Harold MACMILLAN and in 1957 resigned from the government over the issue of how to deal with Cyprus.

CECIL, ROBERT GASCOYNE (3rd Marquess of Salisbury) *see* essay on pages 158–59

CECIL, WILLIAM *see* essay on page 160

CEDD, ST (?–664), Bishop of the East Saxons. Brother of St CHAD and a monk of Lindisfarne under St AIDAN, Cedd was sent in 663 to do missionary work in the recalcitrant kingdom of Essex, which was then ruled by King SIGEBERT SANCTUS. He also acted as interpreter between the Roman and Irish churchmen at the Synod of Whitby (*see* BEDE; COLMAN; WILFRID). He was the first bishop to be able to preach Christianity in Essex since the time of St MELLITUS. The surviving church at Bradwell-on-Sea (Essex) was probably built for the monastery that Cedd founded there.

CELLACH (?–815), Abbot of Iona. Following the third Viking attack on Iona in 806 in which 68 monks were killed, Cellach went to Ireland and began the construction of the monastery at Kells, in the Irish midlands, in the following year. The new monastery was completed in 814, following which Cellach resigned the abbacy and returned to Iona. Although the monastic centre of the Ionian confederation founded by COLUM CILLE was moved to Kells, Iona was never abandoned, and maintained a small community where Cellach remained until his death the following year.

CENRED, King of Mercia (704–9). A son of King WULFHERE and a descendant of King PENDA of Mercia. Little is known of his reign except that in 709 he dramatically renounced his kingship and went to Rome to become a monk. He was succeeded by his cousin CEOLRED.

CENRED (?–718), King of Northumbria (716–18). A briefly reigned king, who succeeded to the kingship after the murder of OSRED, and who claimed

descent from the first King of Bernicia, IDA. His brother CEOLWULF was King of Northumbria from 729 to 737.

CENTWINE (?–*c.* 685), King of Wessex (676–85). He was probably the son of King CYNEGILS and the brother of King CENWEALH. He succeeded after the brief rule of Cenwealh's widow SEAXBURH and a short intervening reign. His reign is notable for continuing the expansion of the kingdom into Devon at the expense of the Britons, although he seems also to have lost some power to Mercia around Dorchester-on-Thames. He resigned his kingdom to become a monk at Glastonbury and was succeeded by CADWALLA.

CENWEALH (?–672), King of Wessex (643–72). The son of King CYNEGILS, after an initial period of difficulty when he was driven from his kingdom by King PENDA of Mercia, Cenwealh became a powerful and successful king. He continued the expansion of the territory of the kings of Wessex at the expense of the Britons, which had been resumed in the time of King CEAWLIN, by taking control of what is now Somerset. After initially reverting to paganism, he became a strong supporter of Christianity, introducing St WILFRID to King ALHFRITH of Deira. He appointed St AGILBERT to his kingdom's bishopric, which was located at Dorchester-on-Thames, and subsequently created a second diocese at Winchester. He was succeeded briefly by his wife SEAXBURH and, after a period of warfare, by his brother CENTWINE.

CENWULF (?–821), King of Mercia. The last Mercian king to exercise the supremacy over the kingdoms of southern Britain which had been characteristic of the reigns of great predecessors such as ETHELBALD and OFFA. His defeat of the Kentish King EADBERT PRÆN in 798 and installation in Kent of his brother CUTHRED represents a typical reassertion of Mercian power but, in general, he seems never to have possessed the assured domination exercised by previous Mercian rulers; in particular he was obliged to abandon the claims of HYGEBERHT of Lichfield to rule an archbishopric and he was never able to subdue the ruler who finally destroyed Mercian pre-eminence in 825, King EGBERT of Wessex. He did, however, campaign successfully against the Welsh, and is the only English king before the tenth century whose power throughout Britain was great enough for him to be referred to as an emperor in contemporary sources. *See also* CWENTHRYTH; CYNEHELM.

CEOLFRITH (642–716), cleric. He was a monk and subsequently Abbot of Monkwearmouth and Jarrow (688–716) during much of BEDE's lifetime,

continued on page 161

CECIL, ROBERT GASCOYNE (3rd Marquess of Salisbury) (1830–1903)
Politician and Prime Minister (1885, 1886–92, 1895–1902)

As the second surviving son of the 2nd Marquess of Salisbury, Lord Robert Cecil was born to uncertain prospects. His elder brother, Lord Cranborne, suffered from a debilitating illness which made it unlikely that he would produce an heir to the title but, since he lived into his forties, Lord Robert grew to maturity without the assured position of being heir to the Cecil fortune. A delicate youth himself, he loathed Eton and did not care much for Oxford, which he left after two years with a nobleman's honorary fourth-class degree. A trip to Australia (1851–2) enabled him to recover his health but left him with a confirmed distrust of democracy. He showed something of his academic prowess by winning an All Souls fellowship and, in 1854, he entered the Commons for the 'pocket borough' of Stamford, which was controlled by his relative Lord Exeter.

The 2nd Marquess, who had married Lady Mary De La Warr in 1848 and was by 1857 the father of 10 children, was displeased with Lord Robert's intention of marrying Lady Georgina Alderson, who brought with her no dowry. It was this marriage in 1857 that sparked off young Cecil's career: it gave him a secure home environment and constant emotional support; it also forced him into journalism in order to support his growing family. With a natural bent for polemic, his articles in the *Saturday Review*, and later in the *Quarterly Review*, established him as an intelligent and articulate reactionary who scarified the Derby (*see* STANLEY, EDWARD) government of 1858–9, much to the distress of his father who was a member of it. The main target of his scorn was DISRAELI, whose utter lack of principle disgusted the high-principled Cecil. He earned the sobriquet which MACAULAY had bestowed upon GLADSTONE, 'the rising hope of those stern unbending Tories'. The financial concerns which almost drove him from politics in 1859 sharpened his pen, and he defended himself to his father by declaring that he had to write in a style which would sell newspapers.

His journalism decreased after he became Lord Cranborne in 1865 and, in 1866, he accepted office in Lord Derby's government as Secretary of State for India. However, alarmed by Disraeli's Reform Bill in 1866, he resigned from the government along with Lord Carnarvon and PEEL's youngest brother, General Jonathan Peel. Upon succeeding to the marquessate in 1867 he quit the Commons without regret and seemed to settle into the role of the philosopher-king of High Tory reaction.

Despite the bitterness of Salisbury's assaults on him, Disraeli offered him the India Office in 1874 when he formed his administration and, under pressure from his former step-mother (now Lady Derby) and her husband, the 15th Earl, who was Disraeli's Foreign Secretary, Salisbury took office – but with a view, as he put it, to 'keeping an eye on the captain'. Within months the two men clashed over the Public Worship Regulation Act, which Salisbury, as a High Anglican, disapproved of; but with the help of the Derbys the matter was smoothed over. In Dec. 1876 Salisbury was chosen to be the British representative at the Constantinople Conference to discuss the future of the Ottoman empire; Disraeli told him that he was being groomed for greater things. In the short term it led to nothing, save sea-sickness and a first meeting with Bismarck. Over the next year Salisbury was, along with Carnarvon and Derby, one of the chief opponents of Disraeli's jingoism over the Eastern Question but in early 1878 he changed tack, and when Derby resigned in March he became Foreign Secretary. The Congress of Berlin (1878) was a great triumph for his diplomacy and marked him out as the eventual successor to Disraeli.

When Disraeli died in 1881, the Conservatives were in opposition and Salisbury, as leader in the Lords, formed a duumvirate with Sir Stafford NORTHCOTE in the Commons. But Salisbury's assured handling of the issue of parliamentary reform in 1884 ensured that he was sent for by the Queen when the Conservatives formed a minority government in 1885. Despite his reputation as a diehard Salisbury was an acute tactician. Over the course of the Home Rule crisis of 1885–6 he manoeuvred his party into a position where it was able to benefit from the split in the Liberal Party, and between 1886 and 1892 he was Prime Minister at the head of an administration supported by the Liberal Unionists.

It was ironic that a man with such a distrust of democracy should have had an electoral appeal unequalled for a Conservative leader until Margaret THATCHER. On the home front Salisbury's main concerns were to contain the Irish problem by a combination of firm government and reform and to deal with social problems as they arose. The 'Tory Democracy' espoused by his Chancellor, Lord Randolph CHURCHILL, aroused Salisbury's distrust and, following his impulsive resignation in Dec. 1886, Salisbury took care to keep him at arm's length.

In 1885, and again from Jan. 1887, Salisbury was Foreign Secretary, a post he valued more than the premiership, having offered to serve under the Liberal Unionist Lord Hartington (*see* CAVENDISH, SPENCER) in 1886. As Foreign Secretary he has often been identified with the policy of 'splendid isolation' but this is a misreading of his diplomacy. Salisbury's diplomacy was, like his domestic policy, greatly influenced by the advent of democracy. It was his view that, since no British government could say in advance what the reaction of public opinion would be in hypothetical circumstances, no British government could pledge itself to an alliance. Despite the fact that he regularly used this to avoid continental alliances, he nevertheless hated the prospect of isolation. He had come to office in 1885 with Europe united against Britain thanks to Gladstone's diplomacy, and he spent much of his time in 1886–7 looking for a way out of isolation. The Mediterranean agreements of 1887 with Austria and Italy were typical of his diplomacy. He would have liked to have been able to win the friendship of France, which Gladstone had lost by his occupation of Egypt in 1882, but Salisbury knew that public opinion would not accept any sacrifice of British interests at Suez. He therefore aligned Britain with Austrian conservatism and Italian fearfulness in agreements which guaranteed the *status quo* in the Mediterranean, against French ambitions in the west and Russian expansionism in the east. Since Austria and Italy were Bismarck's partners in the Triple Alliance, this allowed Salisbury some claim on Bismarck's diplomatic support without any reciprocal commitment.

Salisbury's diplomacy had a rougher ride in the period after 1895. The development of the Franco-Russian alliance by 1894 gave the appearance of having split Europe into two armed camps from which Britain was isolated. Diplomatic incidents in 1896, such as the crisis over Venezuela with America and the Kruger telegram from the Kaiser, created the impression that isolation was dangerous, something reinforced by Russian expansionism in the Far East. Some of his colleagues, led by the energetic Colonial Secretary, the Liberal Unionist Joseph CHAMBERLAIN, wanted a move out of isolation and grew increasingly discontented with Salisbury's diplomacy.

Salisbury's social Darwinian view of international relations was best expressed in his 'dying nations' speech of 8 May 1898 in which he divided the world into 'dying' and 'living' nations; Chamberlain feared that 'splendid isolation' would mean that Britain ended up in the first category and advocated a German alliance as the solution to Britain's problems. Salisbury did not believe those problems were as severe as Chamberlain claimed and, having outfaced the French in the Fashoda crisis in late 1898 and survived the Boer War (1899–1902) without mishaps, he rejected the call for a German alliance.

Salisbury won an unprecedented (for a Conservative) second consecutive term of office in the 1900 election but, soon afterwards, relinquished the office of Foreign Secretary to Lord Lansdowne (*see* PETTY-FITZMAURICE, HENRY). He remained as Prime Minister until the end of the Boer War in 1902, after which he retired in favour of his nephew, BALFOUR. He died the following year.

Salisbury was a mass of paradoxes: a pessimistic anti-democrat, he was, electorally, the most successful Conservative leader until Margaret Thatcher; opposed to the extension of the franchise, he and his party profited most from it; bitterly critical of Disraeli, he became his right-hand man and anointed successor; despising jingoism and imperialism, he presided over an expansion of British territory in Africa and the Far East; anxious to avoid isolation in foreign policy, he became identified with a policy of 'splendid isolation'; the very personification of aristocratic, Anglican High Toryism, under Salisbury the Conservatives became the party of middle-class 'villa Toryism'; opposed to adventurism in foreign affairs, his government was responsible for the Boer War. Despite his success, Salisbury left no great name or heritage to his party. There was about him an air of *après moi, la deluge* and, within three years of his death, his party had indeed gone down to its greatest defeat since 1832. His reputation underwent a revival during the Thatcher era, when he became the icon of right-wing Conservatives, who admired his 'tough-minded' reactionary stance, and this has led to a re-evaluation of his reputation. He now stands high in the pantheon of Conservative leaders.

Andrew Roberts, Salisbury: Victorian Titan (1999)

CECIL, WILLIAM (1st Baron Burghley) (1520–98)
Politician

Cecil's family (Seisyllt) was from the Welsh Borders, and first rose from obscurity through the service of his grandfather David to a minor Welsh courtier of HENRY VII, Sir David Philip, who moved to Lincs., where the Cecils established themselves in Stamford. Educated at Grantham and Stamford schools and St John's College, Cambridge, he made lifelong friends at university who would later be significant in promoting the Reformation, notably his tutors Thomas SMITH and John CHEKE. He married first Cheke's daughter Mary (1541), despite the opposition of his father Richard, and second (1545) Mildred, one of the formidably intelligent and well-educated daughters of the prominent Evangelical Sir Anthony COOKE, another of whose daughters married Sir Nicholas BACON. Leaving Cambridge without a degree, he embarked like Bacon on a legal career at Gray's Inn, and may have first sat in the House of Commons in 1542. He entered the service of the Protector, Edward SEYMOUR, Duke of Somerset, after whose fall and a short spell of imprisonment he became one of the Secretaries of State (1550). One of a circle of cultivated evangelicals in Edwardian government, he sponsored formal debates between reformists and conservatives on the Eucharist at his house, and he enjoyed the esteem of both Archbishop CRANMER and John DUDLEY, Duke of Northumberland, despite their growing mutual distrust. He escaped serious consequences for his (hesitant) involvement in Lady JANE GREY's usurpation, and quietly conformed during MARY I's reign, being spared from serious inquiry into his religious beliefs by his genuine friendship with Cardinal Reginald POLE. His career as Principal Secretary (1558–72) resumed on ELIZABETH I's accession, when with his brother-in-law Bacon he was the chief architect of the Elizabethan settlement of religion; he was later (1572–98) Lord Treasurer. During the 1560s he faced opposition, particularly from noblemen who were religious conservatives, but also from Robert DUDLEY, Earl Leicester. This came to a head in intrigues against his position in 1568–9, but he emerged from the crisis with Elizabeth's confidence in him strengthened; in one of her few peerage creations, Elizabeth granted him his barony in 1571. From then on his life was synonymous with the story of Elizabethan government at home and abroad. He encouraged the creation of an intelligence-gathering service directed by Sir Francis WALSINGHAM. He enthusiastically backed the successful aid to the Protestant rebels of Scotland (1559–60), against Elizabeth's misgivings, but thereafter, acutely aware of England's precarious financial position, he was suspicious of the foreign military adventures for which some of his fervent Protestant colleagues such as Leicester and Walsingham showed enthusiasm, such as the disastrous expedition to France in 1562–3 and the increasing confrontation with Spain in the 1580s. Nevertheless, he was left with prime responsibility for managing the war effort once war had been declared. Only once did a serious breach develop between him and Elizabeth, when in 1587 he finally persuaded her to sign a death warrant for MARY QUEEN OF SCOTS and acted on it while she was still hesitating about the decision for execution; she banished him from her presence for some months. As his health began to fail in the 1590s, he began preparing the succession to his power for his younger son Robert CECIL (his eldest son Thomas did not share their exceptional talent). He was frequently at odds with Archbishop WHITGIFT over the latter's stern disciplinarian line against Puritans, but after a lifetime of gingerly patronage of the more moderate Puritan clergy he began sympathizing with anti-Calvinist clergy in his last years, as did Robert. In his last illness Elizabeth visited him and personally nursed him.

Cecil acquired a handsome fortune, building enormous mansions at Burghley House (Cambs.) near Stamford and Theobalds (Herts.). Particularly profitable for him was his office as Master of the Court of Wards, but he also used it to educate some favoured wards in his own household, not always with the results for which he had hoped (see DE VERE, EDWARD, Earl of Oxford). He was also active as Chancellor of Cambridge University, and as High Steward of Westminster he enjoyed unrivalled influence in the vill of Westminster and in the Abbey and School; with Robert, he was a major commercial developer in the area. Cecil was a brilliant and meticulous administrator, whose voluminous surviving papers, scattered in collections in the Public Record Office, family archives and the British Library (part of the Lansdowne MSS), form a central resource for understanding the period. He can be criticized for running a decaying administrative system efficiently rather than finding bold solutions to problems left by early Tudor reforms in government. Once he had supervised the long-projected restoration of the silver content in the coinage (1562) very little structural reform took place during his long years in power, and it was Robert who was left with the task of rationalizing government finance, a burden which eventually defeated him.

Conyers Read, Mr Secretary Cecil and Queen Elizabeth; Lord Burghley and Queen Elizabeth (2 vols, 1955, 1960) and must take much credit for encouraging the great scholar in his work. Before moving to Monkwearmouth–Jarrow, Ceolfrith had been a monk at St BOTULF's Abbey of Icanho. He built on the important work of his predecessor BENEDICT BISCOP and it was during his rule that the twin abbeys achieved material and intellectual prosperity. At the time of his death there were about 600 monks at the two abbeys. The magnificent illuminated manuscript, the *Codex Amiatinus*, the earliest surviving complete text of the Latin Bible, which is preserved in a library in Florence, illustrates the outstanding quality of his abbeys' achievements.

CEOLNOTH (?–870), Archbishop of Canterbury (833–70). A long-reigned Archbishop who successfully maintained Canterbury's pre-eminence within the Church in England at a time of considerable political turmoil by forming a close relationship with the rising power of Kings EGBERT and ETHELWULF of Wessex in the later 830s, and abandoning the more pro-Mercian policies of his immediate predecessors.

CEOLRED, King of Mercia (709–16). The last direct descendant of PENDA to rule in Mercia, Ceolred succeeded his cousin CENRED. Little is known about his rule, except that St BONIFACE described him to his successor ETHELBALD as an example of immoral kingship.

CEOLWULF (?–737), King of Northumbria (729–37). A patron of learning and the king to whom BEDE's *Ecclesiastical History* is dedicated. He seems not to have been a successful ruler, being temporarily deposed after two years of his reign in 731 and then retiring to the Abbey of Lindisfarne in 737. He was succeeded by his cousin EADBERHT.

CEOLWULF I, King of Mercia (821–3). The brother of King CENWULF, he ruled Mercia briefly before being expelled for reasons which are unclear. His reign coincided with the advance of King EGBERT of Wessex to domination over the kingdoms of southern Britain.

CEOLWULF II (?–879), King of Mercia (874–9). The last King of independent Mercia, Ceolwulf appears largely to have reigned as a puppet of the leaders of the Viking 'Great Army', GUTHRUM and HALFDAN. After his death the parts of Mercia not conquered by the Danes came increasingly under the sway of King ALFRED THE GREAT of Wessex. His successor, the Ealdorman ETHELRED, was never given the title of king.

CERDIC (?–c. 530), King of Wessex. Sources such as the late ninth-century *Anglo-Saxon Chronicle* name Cerdic as the first King of Wessex and state that he was a (possibly Saxon) war leader who landed in England in 495. He may well be a legendary figure, invented by later ages to impose a pattern on the obscure process whereby the English arrived in Britain. The likely location of the earliest lands of the Wessex dynasty (ultimately to be the most successful of all the kingly families of Anglo-Saxon England) is in the Upper Thames valley. The first King of Wessex about whom we have secure historical knowledge is a supposed grandson of Cerdic, CEAWLIN.

CEREDIG (*fl.* mid–late fifth century), King of the Strathclyde Britons. Recorded in early genealogical literature as the first of the kings of the Strathclyde Britons, Ceredig was a contemporary of St PATRICK, by whom he was denounced, in one of his surviving letters, as an ally of the Picts and Scots. On the evidence of Patrick's letter, Ceredig must have controlled substantial military and naval resources and his attested epithet *guledig* (wealthy) suggests a successful piratical career.

CETEWAYO (OR CESHWAYO) (*c.* 1826–84), Zulu warrior king. Last of the great Zulu kings, ruling from 1872 to 1879, he restored Zulu power and prestige until the Zulu War. Cetewayo began attacking the British in southern Africa even as a boy, yet when proclaimed King he was crowned by the British Secretary for Native Affairs in Natal. After the 1877 annexation of the Transvaal, official policy became pro-Boer; meanwhile Zulu military strength was growing. The High Commissioner for South Africa, Sir Bartle Frere, issued an ultimatum for the Zulu military to disband, and Zululand was invaded. Cetewayo led his people to victory against the British at Isandhlwana, then to defeat at Ulundi. Allowed to plead his case in London, where he made a great impression, he was restored as ruler in 1883 but was rejected by his people and died in exile.

CHAD, ST (?–672), churchman. The brother of St CEDD, Chad briefly held the bishopric of York, before giving way to the claims of the formidable St WILFRID. Educated in Ireland and at Lindisfarne, and a protégé of St AIDAN, Chad's emphasis on personal austerity, as recounted by BEDE, was typical of the Irish element among early churchmen active in England. He received the Mercian bishopric of Lichfield from St THEODORE OF TARSUS, Archbishop of Canterbury.

CHADWICK, SIR EDWIN (1800–90), social reformer. Son of a Lancs. businessman, and a barrister by profession, he was a writer on economics and associate of James MILL, Jeremy

BENTHAM and other leading Utilitarians. He played an important role as a reformer and administrator of the Poor Laws, but achieved lasting fame as the author of the *Report on the Sanitary Condition of the Labouring Population of Great Britain* (1842), which was eventually to lead to improved sanitation and public health. As Secretary of the Poor Law Commissioners and then, from 1848 to 1854, head of the Board of Health, his energy and drive led to conflicts as well as success, notably over the implementation of the New Poor Law in northern counties.

CHADWICK, SIR JAMES (1891–1974), physicist. Chadwick was educated in Manchester, Berlin and Cambridge, and researched radioactivity under Ernest RUTHERFORD at Manchester (1911–13). After the First World War, he resumed his work with Rutherford, both at Manchester and, from 1919, at Cambridge University's Cavendish Laboratory. At the Cavendish he investigated the scattering of alpha particles by nuclei and the artificial disintegration of light elements. This research led to his 1932 experimental evidence for the sub-atomic particle, the neutron, work which won him the 1935 Nobel Prize for Physics. He helped construct Britain's first cyclotron at Liverpool University (where he was Professor of Physics (1935–48)) and worked on the Allied atomic bomb during the Second World War. He was a leading figure in Britain's post-war nuclear energy programme.

CHAIN, SIR ERNST (1906–79), biochemist. Chain studied physiology and chemistry in his native Berlin and in 1933 fled from Nazi Germany to Britain. He studied biochemistry under Frederick Gowland HOPKINS at Cambridge and, between 1935 and 1948, collaborated with Howard FLOREY and others at Oxford on the isolation, production and medical use of penicillin. He shared the 1945 Nobel Prize for Medicine with Florey and Alexander FLEMING and was Scientific Director of the International Research Centre for Chemical Microbiology in Rome (1948–61). From the mid 1940s he was heavily involved in attempts to mass-produce penicillin and in 1961 became Professor of Biochemistry at Imperial College, London.

CHALMERS, THOMAS (1780–1847), divine and reformer. Scholar, preacher and prolific writer, he was the leading theologian of his day. His principal achievements were the enhancement of a voluntary poor relief system, which laid the basis for modern social casework, and the founding of the Free Church of Scotland. In 1843 he led the Disruption, the secession from the Church of Scotland of those who could not abide the political control of the Anglican establishment.

CHAMBERLAIN, SIR AUSTEN (1863–1937), politician. The only Conservative leader of the twentieth century never to become Prime Minister, it was said of Austen that 'he always played the game and always lost it'. Austen lived most of his life in the shadow of his forceful father, Joseph CHAMBERLAIN, the founder of the family's financial and political fortunes. He was the repository of the dynastic hopes of the Chamberlains, and, after receiving the education appropriate for a rising young politician (Rugby and Cambridge), he went straight into the Commons in 1892 for a safe Unionist seat. With his father the dominant figure in the Salisbury (*see* CECIL, ROBERT GASCOYNE) government, Austen enjoyed swift promotion, and, when Joseph resigned in 1903 to campaign for Tariff Reform, he became Chancellor of the Exchequer. After Joseph's stroke in 1906 Austen became the standard-bearer for the family cause.

He affected Joe's monocle and orchid in the button-hole, but there was no real resemblance between the two men. Where Joseph was a tough, even under-hand, operator Austen was a gentleman, even to the extent of agreeing to stand down rather than fight a contest to succeed Arthur BALFOUR in 1911. He served loyally under both ASQUITH and LLOYD GEORGE during the First World War, enhancing his reputation as a man of honour when he resigned in 1917 from the India Office after a report criticizing the conduct of the campaign in Mesopotamia, even though he had not been Secretary of State for India at the time. His reward was the Conservative leadership in 1921 when Bonar LAW stood down. Austen's loyalty to Lloyd George after the Conservatives voted against the coalition at the Carlton Club in Oct. 1922 ensured that it would be Bonar Law and not he who became Prime Minister. Austen's consolation prize came in 1924 when Stanley BALDWIN made him Foreign Secretary.

His career at the Foreign Office has been overshadowed by the disasters which overtook his brother Neville CHAMBERLAIN's policy of appeasement in the 1930s but it is notable for two things: first, the reassertion by the Foreign Office of its independence from prime ministerial control; and secondly for the Locarno Pact of 1925 which marked the end of the period of diplomatic unrest which had followed the 1919 Versailles settlement, and for which Austen was awarded the Nobel Peace Prize and made a Knight of the Garter. (He was the only Chamberlain ever to accept an honour.) His Francophile tendencies did not prevent him from getting on good terms with Germany. He was briefly First Lord of the Admiralty in Ramsay MACDONALD's National government of 1931. Thereafter he found a fresh lease of life as a senior backbencher, whose warnings against the dangers of Hitler went largely unheeded. He was widely expected to become Foreign Secretary in 1936 when Samuel HOARE resigned over his pact with Laval, but the young Anthony EDEN was appointed; as ever, Austen lost the game.

CHAMBERLAIN, JOSEPH *see* essay on page 164

CHAMBERLAIN, NEVILLE *see* essay on page 165

CHAMBERLAYNE, EDWARD (1616–1703) and his son **JOHN** (1666–1723), writers. The compilers of *Angliae Notitia, or The Present State of England*, which started publication in 1669 and was published regularly until 1755. Its name changed to *Magnae Britanniae Notitia, or The Present State of Great Britain* in 1708. A handbook to English, and later British, political life, it was inspired by *L'Etat Nouveau de la France*, first published there in 1661. Edward Chamberlayne came from a courtier family and fled his Oxford fellowship for the continent during the Civil War, returning at the Restoration: early editions plainly display his Cavalier and Anglican prejudices, although the tone softened as times changed. John Chamberlayne knew 16 languages and like his father held a number of administrative appointments; he was also associated with the SPCK (*see* BRAY, THOMAS). After John Chamberlayne's death, reprinting was taken over by booksellers as a commercial enterprise, but they showed less vigour and imagination in updating the work.

CHAMBERLEN, PETER (1601–83), physician *see* SHAW, HESTER

CHAMBERS, SIR WILLIAM (1723–96), architect. The son of a Scottish merchant based in Gothenburg, Sweden, Chambers began his career in the Swedish East India Co., travelling to the Far East and observing Chinese architecture. In 1749 he left trade and studied architecture in Paris and Italy. Returning to London in 1755 he gained attention as the only architect familiar with oriental buildings, and was appointed architecture tutor to the future GEORGE III. At the request of the dowager Princess AUGUSTA he laid out Kew Gardens with a mixture of oriental and classical ornamental buildings, and in 1761 was appointed an architect to the Crown, eventually becoming Comptroller of Works in 1769. Chambers's work at Kew and associated publications popularized the *jardin anglo-chinois* across Europe. His greatest architectural achievement was Somerset House, providing offices for government departments and learned societies within a neoclassical

structure which asserted British confidence after the Seven Years War. He also designed the imperial state coach still used by the British monarch.

CHAMPION, HENRY (1859–1928), socialist publisher. His father was a Major-General in India and Champion followed him into the army in 1876. By 1882 he was a socialist, joining the Democratic Federation (the Social Democratic Federation from 1884). With J. C. Foulger he ran the Modern Press, publishing a wide range of socialist literature, including the SDF paper *Justice* (1884–7). Resigning from the SDF in 1888, after bitter conflicts with H. M. HYNDMAN, he remained important as a socialist publisher and activist. Between 1888 and 1894, when he emigrated to Australia, he was preoccupied with working more closely with trade unionists, as in the London dock strike of 1889, and with developing a political stratcgy which would embrace a wide range of socialists: he actively supported Keir HARDIE in the mid-Lanark by-election of 1888. But these years were dogged by allegations that he had received 'Tory gold' to support his paper, the *Labour Elector*.

CHANCELLOR, RICHARD (?–1556), explorer. He sailed to the eastern Mediterranean in 1550 and in 1553 was put in charge of Sir Hugh WILLOUGHBY's voyage attempting to discover a north-east passage to Asia. He got as far as Archangel and travelled south to Moscow, to be received by the Muscovite court, returning to England via Archangel in 1554. He left a detailed account of his experiences. His second voyage to Russia (1555) ended in shipwreck on the Aberdeens. coast on the journey back.

CHANDLER, SAMUEL (1693–1766), Presbyterian minister. Son of a Presbyterian minister, he was educated at a Dissenting academy at Gloucester (where his fellow pupils included future Anglican Bishops Joseph BUTLER and Thomas Secker) and at Leiden. He acquired his first congregation in 1716, and gained an outstanding reputation through his sermons and writings. Throughout his life he pursued unification with the Established Church. In 1735 he preached a series of sermons in favour of a joint anti-Catholic programme and in 1748 was involved in negotiations with leading Anglican clergymen, including Archbishop HERRING, about reconciliation. Herring and Chandler broadly agreed the replacement of the Thirty-Nine Articles and the Athanasian Creed but this went too far for most Anglicans.

CHANDOS, 9TH BARON AND 1ST DUKE OF see BRYDGES, JAMES

CHAMBERLAIN, JOSEPH (1836–1914)
Politician

Chamberlain was the first unambiguously middle-class politician to reach the first rank of British politics, building on the legacy of COBDEN and BRIGHT but providing his own brand of dynamism.

He was the quintessential entrepreneur in politics. Born in London, Chamberlain made his fortune as a screw manufacturer, and entered politics at a local level in Birmingham in his late thirties. Chamberlain's early reputation was as a radical reformer and, as Mayor of Birmingham (1873, 1876), he took advantage of the permissive social legislation of DISRAELI's government to acquire land and public utilities which helped make the city a model of a modern municipality. Chamberlain's 'gas and water' socialism firmly established his local position, and he took the opportunity in 1876 to offer a by-election in 1876 to become MP for Birmingham. Chamberlain found a natural home on the extreme radical wing of the Liberal Party, his 'constructionist' ideas of State intervention making him an object of distrust as much to GLADSTONE as to Disraeli. Through his tight organization of local associations in Birmingham known as the 'caucus', Chamberlain provided himself with a personal fiefdom and an example of how to organize a mass electorate; the success of the caucus gave him a powerful political position.

Gladstone, while disapproving of Chamberlain's ideas, could not ignore him totally, although he did his best to do so by offering him the Board of Trade (April 1880) in a Cabinet dominated by Whigs. Chamberlain's hopes that as the leading radical in the Cabinet and as the power behind the National Liberal Federation he would have a decisive voice in policy-making were disappointed, and by 1885 a considerable gap had opened between himself and Gladstone. Where the latter clung to the liberalism of the early Victorian period, Chamberlain held that the challenge from socialism and Marxism could only be met by progressive radicalism. Where his Conservative opponents saw him as a dangerous socialist, Chamberlain wanted to preserve private enterprise and private property by getting the ruling classes to moderate the unacceptable face of late-Victorian capitalism. His 'Radical' or 'Unauthorized programme' (July 1885) argued for free elementary education, the provision by local authorities of smallholdings for agricultural and other workers, higher tax rates for large landowners, and a progressive taxation system. To many of his Whig colleagues and to Gladstone, all of this was dangerously uncomfortable but the great political crisis of 1885 and 1886 over Ireland

provided them with an unexpected way out of the dilemma of what to do about Chamberlain's ideas, as well as having a profound effect on Chamberlain's career.

Chamberlain was a convinced imperialist, and he was also unwilling to allow Gladstone's obsession with Ireland to dominate the political agenda on the Left, two reasons why he resigned from the Home Rule Cabinet in March 1885. As the leading Liberal Unionist in the Commons, Chamberlain found himself incongruously yoked with the Whig grandee, Lord Hartington (see CAVENDISH, SPENCER), in supporting Salisbury's minority (see CECIL, ROBERT GASCOYNE) Conservative government between 1887 and 1892. Although Chamberlain carried Birmingham with him, his apostasy gained him undying hatred in many parts of the Liberal Party. When Salisbury won the 1895 election, Chamberlain could no longer avoid choosing between joining him in formal coalition or settling for political impotence; no one was surprised when Chamberlain chose the former, although his choice of the Colonial Office surprised everyone.

Chamberlain saw Britain's colonial empire as a great undeveloped estate in need of modernization, and he set out to do it. He found himself at odds with Salisbury's cautious approach to diplomacy, most notably in the late 1890s when he argued publicly for an alliance with Germany. A proponent of closer links with America and Germany, Chamberlain's activism was a prime cause of the Boer War, and his fierce electioneering during the 1900 Khaki Election disgusted his opponents as much as it delighted his partisans. Having helped break the Liberal Party in 1886, he proceeded to help break up the Conservatives in 1903 when he decided to abandon Free Trade and declared for Tariff Reform. Chamberlain saw the latter as a means of unifying the Empire but in fact it served only to unite the Liberals in defence of their shibboleth of Free Trade. Chamberlain was now an old man in a hurry, and after the Conservative defeat in 1906 moved to take control of the party, a process halted only by a stroke in Feb. 1906 from which he never recovered. He died on the eve of the First World War, and he remained, for a generation afterwards, the idol of the imperialists.

A dominating and controversial personality, Chamberlain was the first but not the last politician to wish to modernize Britain in the face of foreign competition; his successors enjoyed no more success.

Peter T. Marsh, Joseph Chamberlain: Entrepreneur in Politics (1992)

CHAMBERLAIN, NEVILLE (1869–1940)
Politician and Prime Minister (1937–40)

The son of Joseph CHAMBERLAIN and half-brother of Austen CHAMBERLAIN, Neville was brought up to go into business and considered himself the 'least of the Chamberlain dynasty'.

Spared the Cambridge education which so inhibited Austen, Neville went off to restore the family fortunes by trying (and failing) to grow sisal in the Bahamas. Neville continued his father's tradition of participation in local politics, becoming Lord Mayor of Birmingham in 1915. His first taste of national politics came in 1917 when LLOYD GEORGE asked him to become Director General of National Service dealing with conscription, munitions and all matters relating to the military but the experiment was not a success; it left Chamberlain with an abiding mistrust of Lloyd George.

Neville entered the Commons on the coat-tails of the Lloyd George coalition in Dec. 1918 as MP for Birmingham Ladywood and, like his father, depended much upon his local base. His political mettle was shown early on when in 1922 he refused to back his brother Austen who, as Conservative Party leader, wished to maintain the Lloyd George coalition. Neville was a major beneficiary of the split in the party which took so many senior figures into the political wilderness in 1922, becoming Postmaster General in the Bonar LAW government (1922–3) and Paymaster General under BALDWIN (1923). It was a mark of his impact that Baldwin should have offered Neville the Exchequer in 1924, and a mark of his own character that he should have declined the office, preferring instead to go to the Ministry of Health (1924–9). Neville was never a traditional Conservative and, at the Ministry of Health, he was active in reforming local government and in overhauling the antiquated poor law system. With Winston CHURCHILL, he provided what dynamism the Baldwin government could muster and, in opposition after 1929, showed himself a reform-minded party chairman who sponsored the Conservative Research Department. During the economic crisis of 1931 it was Neville who led the Conservative team that negotiated with Ramsay MACDONALD and the Liberals to form the National government, in which he duly became Chancellor of the Exchequer.

As Chancellor from 1931 until 1937, Chamberlain was responsible for steering the British economy off the rocks and the experience left a profound mark upon him; unlike some of the government's critics in the late 1930s he would never underestimate the possible effect on the economy of rearmament. Chamberlain's stewardship of the economy was orthodox and successful, with one of his own proudest hours coming in 1932 when the Ottawa agreement on empire tariffs realized some part of his father's dream of Tariff Reform. When Baldwin retired in 1937 after the coronation of GEORGE VI, Neville was the obvious choice for leader of the party, a post to which he was seconded by Winston Churchill.

Chamberlain intended his government to be dominated by domestic reforms but Hitler made this impossible. Chamberlain's policy of appeasement has been the object of much controversy but in reality it was composed of two parts: in the first place to try to reduce international tensions by removing their main cause, German revisionism; and, in the second, to ensure that Britain would be adequately prepared militarily if diplomacy should fail. Chamberlain's name will be for ever associated with the Munich Settlement (1938). At the time his series of three dramatic flights to Germany to avert the possibility of a war over the future of the Sudeten regions of Czechoslovakia, and his arrival back in London with Hitler's promise not to go to war, were considered a great triumph and his declaration that he had brought back 'peace with honour' was acclaimed. But Hitler's failure to keep his word and his invasion of Czechoslovakia in March 1939 left Chamberlain looking like a dupe. Subsequent British guarantees to Poland on 31 March were designed to restore his own political position and to deter Hitler but they did neither and, on 3 Sept. 1939, Britain declared war on Germany.

With hindsight, Chamberlain's policy had not been the total failure it is sometimes considered to be. He had been successful in ensuring that neither Italy nor Japan would join with Hitler at the outbreak of war and the Germans were facing an Anglo-French alliance which was, on paper, strong enough to contain them. Chamberlain was not an inspiring war leader and, after the Norway campaign, was replaced by Churchill in May 1940, although he remained leader of the Conservative Party. He loyally stayed on as Lord President to support Churchill but had to retire through ill health in Oct. He died on 9 Nov. 1940.

Chamberlain's reputation was blasted by the failure of appeasement but it has proved easier to condemn him than to suggest how a declining empire could have successfully resisted Hitler by itself.

Keith Feiling, The Life of Neville Chamberlain (1946)

CHANDOS, SIR JOHN (?–1370), soldier. As companion-in-arms and adviser to EDWARD THE BLACK PRINCE, he fought at Crécy and Poitiers, became one of the heroes of FROISSART's chronicles and one of the first knights of the garter, and thanks to the profits of war a very wealthy man. During 1361–2 he supervised the transfer of territory to the English Crown under the terms of the Treaty of Brétigny. In 1364 he was the victorious commander at the Battle of Auray; he was mortally wounded in a skirmish at Lussac six years later.

CHANNON, SIR HENRY ('CHIPS') (1897–1958), diarist. Universally known by his nickname 'Chips', Channon was a Conservative MP; American-born, rich and glamorous in his own right, he established himself at the centre of English high society by marrying into the Guinness family in 1933. His social and political position gave him a ringside seat at most of the important social and political events of the 1930s and 1940s, and he served briefly as a junior minister in the Foreign Office in Neville CHAMBERLAIN's government. But it is for his remarkable diaries, published after his death, that he is known: full of candid observation, they started a trend for a greater degree of disclosure in later political memoirs and diaries.

CHAPLIN, SIR CHARLES (CHARLIE) (1889–1977), film star. At the peak of his career Chaplin had so many imitators that he had to preface his films with 'None genuine without his signature'. Born in a working-class area of London, he first appeared on stage at the age of five. In 1913 he was recruited to the Keystone Studio in Hollywood, where he made 35 silent slapstick comedies, most of them featuring him as the Tramp, a moustachioed, bowler-hatted dandy who waddled and sported a walking cane and enormous shoes. In 1919 he gained greater control over his work by joining D. W. Griffith, Mary Pickford and Douglas Fairbanks to form United Artists, where he made *The Gold Rush* (1925), *The Circus* (1928), which won him a special Oscar, and *City Lights* (1931). One of his greatest films, *Modern Times* (1936), was followed by his satirical caricature of Adolf Hitler in *The Great Dictator* (1940). Beset by scandals, when on a promotional tour in Europe for his film *Limelight* in 1952, he was warned that if he returned to America he would be charged with 'moral turpitude and Communist sympathies'. An incorrigible womanizer but never a Communist, Chaplin settled in Switzerland with his fourth wife and was awarded a special Oscar in 1972.

CHAPONE, HESTER (née Mulso) (1727–1801), author. She came from a Northants. gentry family. Despite little encouragement at home, she learned French, Italian, Latin, music and drawing. Her first essays were published by Samuel JOHNSON in *The Rambler* in 1750, and she became friendly with literary figures such as Elizabeth CARTER (for whose Epictetus she composed a dedicatory ode) and Samuel RICHARDSON. Many of her writings were devoted to the improvement of women, although within the traditional social framework; these included *Letters on the Improvement of the Mind*, written in 1772 for her niece and in print well into the nineteenth century.

CHAPPLE, FRANK (Baron Chapple of Hoxton) (1921–), trade-union leader. The son of a shoe repairer who could neither read nor write, Chapple left school at 14 and worked as a hotel page boy before becoming an apprentice electrician. An organizer for the Young Communist League and a member of the Electrical Trades Union (ETU), Chapple left the Communist Party in 1958 and in 1961 he and John Byrne brought a civil action against their union for alleged ballot-rigging by the communist-dominated executive. The 42-day action succeeded. In 1963 Chapple was elected Assistant General Secretary of the ETU (it became the EETPU by merging with the Electronics, Telecommunications and Plumbers Union) and General Secretary from 1966 to 1984. In this capacity he opted for 'realism' which in his view meant pushing the union to the Right. A member of the General Council of the Trades Union Congress (TUC) (1971–82), he was Chairman in his final year.

CHAPUYS, EUSTACE (1499–1556), diplomat. The Savoy-born Chapuys, Ambassador of the Holy Roman Emperor CHARLES V in London for most of the period from 1529 to 1545, was a passionate supporter of CATHERINE OF ARAGON's cause, and brazenly intrigued with religious conservatives against HENRY VIII. He retired to Leuven in the Low Countries. Historians have made much use of his despatches home, but Chapuys was often successfully fed false information even by English politicians whom he detested, and his own wishful thinking also needs to be taken into account.

CHARKE, CHARLOTTE (née Cibber) (1713–c. 1760), actress. She was the daughter of Colley CIBBER and after an early, failed marriage to a violinist she joined her father's company at Drury Lane. In 1733 she defected to join Henry FIELDING at the Haymarket until he was closed down by the 1737 Licensing Act. She was known for portraying men and actually lived as a man at times, allegedly becoming engaged to a young woman before revealing her true gender. She published her *Memoirs* in 1755, followed by several novels, but they did not cover her expenditure and she died in poverty and obscurity.

CHARLEMONT, 4TH VISCOUNT AND 1ST EARL OF *see* CAULFIELD, JAMES

CHARLES I *see* essay on pages 168–69

CHARLES II *see* essay on pages 170–71

CHARLES V (1500–58), Holy Roman Emperor. Son of Philip the Handsome and Joanna the Mad, Charles became King of Spain in 1516 and Holy Roman Emperor in 1519 (crowned by Pope Clement VII in 1530). Through his inheritance of Habsburg, Burgundian and Spanish territories, with a vast and expanding New World empire, he was the most powerful European of his time, and was preoccupied until his retirement in 1556 with defending his impossible dominion. He remained the chief support of his aunt CATHERINE OF ARAGON through her marriage crisis with HENRY VIII, and later was a mainstay for her daughter MARY, particularly in her refusal to abandon Catholicism under EDWARD VI. After Mary came to the throne, he arranged her marriage to his son PHILIP II in 1554. He opposed the growing Lutheranism in his German dominions and, after many struggles culminating in the Schmalkaldic War (1546), his defeat of Protestant princes of Germany at the Battle of Mühlberg on 24 April 1547 allowed him to impose the Interim of Augsburg in 1548; this was a temporary compromise which made minimum concessions to Protestants. Many Protestants who could not accept the Interim took refuge in England and contributed significantly to the Reformation in England. *See* BUCER, MARTIN; MARTYR, PETER.

CHARLES (1948–), Prince of Wales. Prince Charles seems likely to emulate the achievement of his great-great-grandfather, Albert Edward (later EDWARD VII), in waiting half-a-century for the throne; he also resembles him in having married one of the most glamorous women of the age, but there the resemblance stops. Where the future Edward VII was self-indulgent, sensual and frivolous, Prince Charles possesses the opposite qualities. Hard-working, conscientious and concerned for the welfare of others, he has constantly sought to carve out a role for himself during his prolonged apprenticeship.

Lacking the forcefulness of his sister Anne, Charles has always given the air of a man upon whom the shadow of the Crown has fallen. By nature a quiet and introverted youth, his position has constantly forced him to act against his nature. His investiture as Prince of Wales at Caernarvon Castle on 1 July 1969 was watched by a television audience of more than 200 million people, inaugurating a lifetime under such scrutiny. At Trinity College, Cambridge, as an undergraduate, he was counselled by the Master, R. A. BUTLER, and he has shown himself to be a caring, if conservative figure concerned with the environment, the young and architecture.

After more than a decade of blameless public service and speculation about a possible royal bride, Charles married the youthful Lady DIANA Spencer at St Paul's Cathedral on 29 July 1981 before a television audience of more than 750 million viewers. Bored with a generation of relatively colourless royals to whom they had become accustomed, the British public took 'shy Di' to their hearts and the tabloids took her to their headlines, where she remained for the rest of her life. The birth of Prince William on 21 June 1982 and Prince Harry on 15 Sept. 1984 meant that she had provided the heir and the spare but, away from the headlines, the marriage was not, it transpired, the 'fairy tale' the pubic had thought. By the early 1990s the rumours that all was not well had become unstoppable, and in 1992 the royal couple separated, to be divorced in 1996. Charles came in for the lion's share of public blame, and his affair with Camilla Parker-Bowles did nothing to help his public reputation. All the work which he had put in through the Prince's Trust helping deprived youngsters counted for nothing with the public compared to the more meretricious activities of the glamorous Diana; her sudden death in 1997 sent his reputation to a new low, not helped by his previous public admission of adultery.

Since Diana's death his obvious affection for his children and his tireless record of public service have, to some extent, redeemed him in the eyes of the tabloid press. His mother's announcement in her Christmas broadcast in 1991, on the eve of the fortieth anniversary of her accession, that she hoped to serve the nation for 'some years to come' has not been revised, and Charles's years in limbo seem to have no end in sight, although talk of the succession bypassing him to his older son, William, has largely subsided.

CHARLOTTE (1744–1818), Queen Consort. The niece of Adolphus Frederick III, Duke of Meckenburg-Strelitz, she came to England in 1761 to marry King GEORGE III. She had little interest or influence in State affairs but, at George III's insistence, the 1765 Regency Act stated that she would be Regent if the King died while his heir was a minor. She devoted her time to bringing up her 15 children and to charities,

continued on page 172

CHARLES I (1600–49)
King of England, Scotland and Ireland (1625–49)

Heir apparent to JAMES VI AND I after his elder brother Prince HENRY's death in 1612. At first there was an expectation that he would follow Henry in championing a militant Protestant foreign policy against his father's efforts to produce universal peace by conciliating the Roman Catholic powers of Europe. However from 1617 James involved him in marriage negotiations for the Spanish Infanta Maria which caused much anti-Catholic national anxiety, particularly when, accompanied by James's favourite George VILLIERS, Duke of Buckingham, he travelled in person (thinly disguised) to Madrid in 1623. English joy at the end of these negotiations was tempered when in the following year he was betrothed to the French Princess HENRIETTA MARIA, likewise a Roman Catholic. Charles also escaped from the dominance of the Calvinist chaplains and Scots courtiers whom he had inherited from Prince Henry, and gathered round him a set of Arminian or Laudian chaplains, who had already begun to enjoy favour from his father; he became an enthusiast for their sacramentalist and ceremonialist piety.

He succeeded to the throne and married in 1625; his continuing dependence on Buckingham caused much ill-will nationwide up to the Duke's assassination in 1629. Thereafter Charles turned for companionship to Henrietta Maria, and they became a model of marital devotion, although he got little credit for this from a political nation suspicious of Catholic subversion. Popular worries accumulated because of his consistent favour to the Arminian clergy, especially William LAUD, and also as a result of his difficult relationships with successive English Parliaments over a combination of financial, religious and political issues. The background to this was Charles's pursuit of war against Spain (begun, with Buckingham's encouragement, as part of the French marriage alliance in 1624), to which in 1626 he added war on a second front with France. Both brought a series of disasters widely blamed, with some justice, on Buckingham's incompetent administration. The 1625 Parliament proved grudging in revenue grants and unprecedentedly offered tonnage and poundage (import and export duties) for a year only, as a gesture of protest against government policy. The 1626 Parliament attempted to impeach Buckingham. Although peace was made with France and Spain in 1630, the wars aggravated a mass of debt which Charles tried to solve with a variety of expedients, some of dubious legality: for instance he persisted in collecting tonnage and poundage. In 1627 he tried to raise money through a forced loan, provoking an indecisive legal clash with a group of gentlemen (the 'Five Knights') who refused to pay and suffered a year's imprisonment, becoming national heroes. The 1628 Parliament presented the King with a Petition of Right outlining a series of grievances about the use of the royal prerogative; Charles grudgingly accepted it, published a doctored version and then ignored it. After the 1629 Parliament degenerated into chaos, he dissolved it, and showed every sign that he did not intend to meet Parliament again.

Charles's personal rule 1629–40 (the 'Eleven Years' Tyranny' or 'Thorough') made a fitfully energetic effort to sort out the very real problems in national and local administration; it rode out opposition, for instance to the levy of Ship Money to rebuild the navy, though it was peppered by a series of public relations disasters in persecuting opponents such as John BASTWICK and William PRYNNE, and Charles's former chaplain Henry BURTON. In 1633 he reissued the *Book of Sports*, issued by James I in 1618 to authorize certain Sunday pastimes, which proved bitterly divisive, offending widespread sabbatarianism; opposition to it became a symbol of opposition to Arminianism. He also alarmed many English gentry by permitting Thomas WENTWORTH, his Lord Deputy in Ireland, ruthlessly to recover lands for the Crown and the Established Church, both from long-established Anglo-Irish gentry and nobility and recently arrived New English landowners like Richard BOYLE. Equally insensitive to public opinion in his other kingdom of Scotland, Charles showed no comprehension of Scottish national pride despite his ancestry: his first visit to Scotland for his coronation in 1633 did not improve the atmosphere, and in particular he provoked fury among the Scots because of the English-style religious ceremonial with which he worshipped. The situation became critical in 1637 when he tried to impose an English-style Prayer Book on Scotland without any formal consultation with the Scots Parliament or the General Assembly of the Kirk. This provoked resistance which in 1638 was formalized in the Scottish National Covenant. In 1639 and 1640 the covenanted Scots twice defeated English armies in the 'Bishops' Wars' and Charles was forced to recall the English Parliament; it met only from 13 April to 5 May 1640, when he dissolved it, unnerved by its barrage of criticism. But the continuing crisis meant that he could not avoid meeting Parliament again, and what became the Long Parliament opened on 3 Nov. 1640. Now Charles made sweeping political concessions, which in effect redressed all the grievances which had built up against him and his advisers over the previous years. He also agreed to the execution of Wentworth (May 1641), though thereafter he always regarded this as the chief stain on his conscience.

What is remarkable after this apparent settlement of the kingdom's worries was that within two years, Charles managed to throw away any goodwill thus gained and trigger the Civil Wars in England. His determination to seize back power on his own terms and his consistent betrayal of compromise (including his unsuccessful personal appearance in the Commons on 4 Jan. 1642, to arrest five MPs who had prudently left) destroyed the trust of many MPs. Confrontation over who would control an army to suppress the Irish rebellion of 1641 became civil war in 1642, when Charles retreated from Westminster and raised his standard at Nottingham. Natural loyalty to the monarch among gentry and aristocracy, and widespread fear of what the radicals in the Westminster Parliament were intending, now created for him a constituency of Royalist support, and he set up his capital and Parliament at Oxford. The first Battle of Edgehill (Warws.) on 23 Oct. 1642 was indecisive, but Marston Moor (Yorks.) on 2 July 1644, the largest-scale battle of the war, lost Charles control of northern England. After the creation of the New Model Army for the Westminster Parliament by Oliver CROMWELL, a series of Royalist defeats, notably Naseby (14 June 1645), left Charles facing defeat. In May 1646 he surrendered to the Scots, reluctantly abandoning his previous commitment to the system of episcopal government in the Church in the hope of winning their support. The negotiations were abortive and the Scots handed him over to the Westminster Parliament; he was imprisoned successively at Holdenby House (Northants.), Hampton Court and Carisbrooke Castle (Isle of Wight). These years were filled with futile attempts at constructing a lasting settlement. Renewed Royalist risings in summer 1648 persuaded army leaders that he must be destroyed. He won much sympathy by his dignity at his trial and execution (30 Jan. 1649), and a martyr's cult quickly developed. This was encouraged by the ghost-written account of his meditations in his last months, *Eikon Basilike*, which became a major samizdat best-seller, provoking a huge pamphlet literature including an attempt at comprehensive refutation by John MILTON, *Eikonoclastes*. Charles's martyr status, much exploited at CHARLES II's restoration, resulted in a commemorative service in the Book of Common Prayer, removed only in 1859, and one or two churches were dedicated to him, notably at the Royalist spa of Tunbridge Wells (Kent).

Charles has always provoked sharply contrasting assessments. He was hard-working, personally impressive and charming, with an informed interest in art, building up one of Europe's most distinguished collections of paintings (dispersed by government sales in the Interregnum). His visual image has been fixed by Anthony VAN DYCK, whose heroic portraits managed to conceal the King's diminutive stature. In combination with his posthumous image as defender of the Church of England (in reality tarnished by his Scottish negotiations of the late 1640s), material has always been on hand for a sympathetic and even admiring interpretation of his career. In recent years some revisionist historians have challenged the negative view of Charles in different ways; detailed studies such as those of D. L. Smith and R. M. Smuts have pointed out that the Eleven Years' Tyranny was not a monolithic regime, and that it accommodated several different viewpoints among leading politicians, as well as exhibiting tensions between leading figures such as Laud and Henrietta Maria. Other historians (notably Kevin Sharpe and Julian Davies) have seen Charles's religious policy as a quest for consensus directed by the King, with Archbishop Laud merely as an agent of policies deriving from the King himself. Sharpe has also argued that opposition to royal religious and financial policies in the 1630s was less widespread than previously thought, and that the collapse of the regime in 1640 can therefore be blamed mainly on the immediate disaster of defeat in Scotland. What is difficult to escape is the atmosphere of isolation and confrontation which existed in Charles's immediate court circle against the wider political nation before the Civil Wars. He found it difficult to convey his intentions to the public, or even to see that there was a need to do so. He had a firm belief that his conscience was ordained by God to act as the conscience of the realm, and he was inclined to dismiss conscientious opposition as dishonest posturing. The most likely verdict on Charles is that, whatever his private virtues and admirable aesthetic sense, in public life he was egocentric, inept and devious.

Charles Carlton, Charles I: The Personal Monarch (1983)

CHARLES II (1630–85)
King of England, Scotland and Ireland (1649–85)

Son of CHARLES I and HENRIETTA MARIA of France, his early adolescence was overshadowed by political crisis: at 11, he was sent to the Lords to plead for the life of Strafford (see WENTWORTH, THOMAS), at 14, he was made nominal commander of Royalist forces in the south west (where his advisers included the young Chancellor of the Exchequer, Sir Edward HYDE). In 1646 his troops were overwhelmed, and he fled, joining his mother in exile near Paris. In 1648, he moved to the Hague, where he joined his sister Mary, wife of William of Orange (mother of the future WILLIAM III) and brother James (later JAMES II).

When in 1649 his father was executed, Charles was proclaimed King in Edinburgh and Dublin. In 1650 he reached agreement with the Scots, promising to support their two 'covenants' (requiring the establishment of Presbyterianism in Scotland and England). The negotiations had been difficult, however, and when he landed in Scotland tensions were evident. English forces meanwhile pressed hard on Scotland. In 1651 Charles tried to save the situation by invading, but his forces were trapped at Worcester, and he was one of the few to escape, famously taking refuge briefly in the 'royal oak' at Boscobel (Salop.).

Disabused of hope in the Presbyterian option, Charles henceforth placed his greatest trust in Royalists, notably Hyde, qualified by his lifelong habit of playing advisers off against each other. Within a few years Royalist activity revived in the British Isles (some gentry forming the 'Sealed Knot' to work for his restoration). Neither French nor Dutch, however, were prepared to help exploit this discontent; on the contrary, the trend was for European powers to come to terms with the new English regime under Oliver CROMWELL. In 1655 new prospects opened when the Protectorate alienated the Spanish by seizing Jamaica; Charles moved to the Spanish Netherlands and began to build an army. The Spanish, however, judged an invasion too much of a gamble.

These were frustrating years for Charles, somewhat mitigated by bouts of pleasure involving travel, hunting and swimming, and relationships with women. His first affair, with Lucy Walter, had begun in Holland: she bore him a son, James SCOTT, later Duke of Monmouth. The censorious Hyde more than once reprimanded the young King for inattention to business.

Cromwell's death did not immediately bring the revulsion against the Protectorate for which the exiles had hoped, but by 1659 the new regime looked shaky. Charles opened secret negotiations with MONCK, and in his Declaration of Breda (April 1660) promised a free parliament and religious liberty (to be confirmed by Parliament after mature deliberation). Other matters, such as the precise terms of an amnesty and policy on sequestered estates, were to be referred to Parliament.

A new 'Convention Parliament' voted to restore the monarchy. Charles returned in May 1660 and was proclaimed King, his accession being formally backdated to 1649. Hyde was confirmed in the post of Lord Chancellor, but the Privy Council was composed in eclectic fashion. Lauderdale (see MAITLAND, JOHN) was made Secretary of State for Scotland, Monck, Lord Lieutenant for Ireland (soon to be replaced by Ormond, see BUTLER, JAMES). Local office was bestowed on a mix of Royalists and old republicans. This conciliatory course upset some old Royalists.

Charles's propensity for debauchery attracted unfavourable notice from the start. He introduced actresses to the English stage, and was to make one, Nell GWYNN, his mistress. Other mistresses included Barbara VILLIERS, Duchess of Cleveland and Countess of Castlemaine, and Louise de KÉROUALLE, Duchess of Portsmouth. His court was also noted for gaming, one focus for which was horse-racing at Newmarket, promoted by Charles from the mid 1660s.

The most pressing issue was the need to determine the shape of the Restoration settlement. What constitutions would operate in the three kingdoms? What would happen to lands that had changed hands since 1640? And what would the religious settlement be? The political classes proved unwilling to restore monarchical power as of old: Star Chamber and the Court of High Commission were abolished, the Triennial Act, requiring new elections every three years, initially retained. In other respects the terms agreed were more conservative than Charles might have opted for. Crown and Church lands were handed back. The three kingdoms each recovered their own Privy Councils and Parliaments, but Episcopacy was everywhere restored (though most parish clergy were initially able to remain in place). The English 'Cavalier Parliament', elected in 1661, ordered the burning of the Solemn League and Covenant, refused to repeal penal laws against Catholics, and passed two Acts, the Corporation Act 1661 and Act of Uniformity 1662, both limiting the religious and the political opportunities of non-Anglicans. Charles's so-called Declaration of Indulgence of 1662, asking Parliament to extend religious liberty, fell on stony ground.

Four major issues dominated the politics of the remainder of his reign. First, the religious settlement proved unstable. It proved impossible to establish a sustainable consensus as to how much religious liberty should be given to Protestant dissenters on the one hand, Catholics on the other. Charles was not temperamentally sympathetic to hardline Anglicans, but accepted that religious dissent, of any kind, might provide an ideological basis for rebellion.

A second, irresoluble issue was a foreign-policy conundrum. The challenge for the British was to position themselves to advantage amidst three major powers: the Dutch, French and Spanish. Whether Dutch commercial rivalry, Spanish-American commercial opportunity and French military might were best tackled by seeking alliances or confrontation was always moot. In the 1660s, for a spell, the British seemed to have the worst of all worlds, having alienated the Spanish by Charles's marriage to CATHERINE OF BRAGANZA, daughter of the Portuguese rebel 'King', and being at war with Dutch (1665–7), French (1666–7), and Danes to boot! In the late 1660s they managed better, forming a Triple Alliance with the Dutch and Swedes, then in 1670 also coming to terms with the French (an agreement prefaced, as few knew, by a secret Treaty of Dover, in which Charles promised to convert to Catholicism and to promote the Catholic cause in England in return for French financial aid – though the pragmatic King probably had no intention of fulfilling this promise). Statesmen seem to have approached foreign-policy issues primarily with an eye to practical advantage – but the issues were complicated by religion: some sections of opinion favoured Dutch or French alliances for ideological reasons.

A third continuing source of difficulty was constitutional. Parliament and King recurrently tussled over religious, foreign-policy and related fiscal issues (the last exacerbated by the King's dissolute reputation). There were also recurrent clashes over the respective rights of Lords and Commons.

A fourth issue, the question of the succession, brought several of the others together in a particularly explosive way. Charles fathered no legitimate children and when in the early 1670s his brother James was revealed to be a Catholic convert some argued that he should therefore be 'excluded' from the line of succession. Possible consequential policies included moving on to James's children, legitimizing the Duke of Monmouth, and allowing Charles to divorce and remarry. Charles,

however, regarded all such schemes as affronts to monarchical power, and was never prepared to go further than suggesting that James's rule might be subject to limitations.

The politics of Charles's reign fell into five main phases. Up to 1667 Hyde (created Earl of Clarendon after his daughter had secretly married James) dominated politics but his overbearing and didactic style grated on Charles. In 1667 he was sacrificed to appease anger at the reverses of the Second Dutch War. Charles was not eager to replace him with another 'Prime Minister'. Although the years from 1667 to 1673 are conventionally dubbed the era of the 'Cabal administration', from the initials of some of its leading lights, Thomas CLIFFORD, Arlington (see BENNET, HENRY), Buckingham (see VILLIERS, GEORGE), Ashley (see COOPER, ANTHONY ASHLEY) and Lauderdale, historians argue that this convenient term is misleading: the disparate group never operated as a team. They agreed on the merits of engaging the Dutch in a third war (1672–4) but split deeply in the fracas that resulted from James's conversion. The staunchly Anglican Danby (see OSBORNE, THOMAS) offered a *via media* acceptable to public opinion from 1673 to 1679 but himself proved unable to cope with the passions aroused by Titus OATES's allegations of a Popish Plot. From 1679 to 1681, the political scene was convulsed by the Exclusion Crisis beginning with the first general election since 1661. Ashley, now Earl of Shaftesbury, emerged as the leader of the anti-court Country Party. Characteristically, Charles first tried to deal with Shaftesbury by giving him a central role in a new ministry, but dismissed him when he remained ungovernable. When court attempts to contain the wider agitation by changing the personnel of local government and campaigning to affect the outcomes of two general elections met with limited success, Charles dispensed with Parliament for the remainder of his reign. In fact, many members of the political classes seem to have felt that Shaftesbury had pushed his challenge too far: they were no more anxious to fall prey to a Presbyterian than to a Popish plot. Discredited Whigs (a new coinage arising from the crisis) fled abroad: a Tory reaction that was partly natural, if partly also engineered, saw Charles through the last years of his reign, and secured James a relatively smooth succession (marred only by the easily extinguished Monmouth's rising).

Ronald Hutton, Charles II: King of England, Scotland and Ireland (1989) including the Magdalen Hospital for Penitent Prostitutes and, from 1800, what became Queen Charlotte's Maternity Hospital. During her husband's illnesses from 1788–9 onwards she took the advice of doctors that she should not see him, and at first acquiesced in the repressive methods of the Willis family (*see* WILLIS, THOMAS), although in 1805 she turned against them. The 1811 Regency Act awarded her the care of the King's person and responsibility for the maintenance of the royal dignity.

CHARNLEY, SIR JOHN (1911–82), orthopaedic surgeon. Charnley studied medicine at Manchester University. After the Second World War he was assistant orthopaedic surgeon and then a consultant at the Manchester Royal Infirmary, where he worked on osteoarthritis of the hip-joint. He began to explore materials and designs for an artificial hip-joint in his private workshop and, from 1961, at the hip-surgery centre which he founded at Wrightington Hospital, Wigan. In 1963 he settled on the design, a polyethylene hip-socket and steel femur-head attached to the bone with acrylic cement. Charnley's hip-surgery has brought increased mobility to thousands of patients.

CHATHAM, 1ST EARL OF *see* PITT, WILLIAM THE ELDER, essay on page 652–53.

CHATTERTON, THOMAS (1752–70), poet. The posthumous son of a Bristol schoolmaster, as a boy he became fascinated by medieval English and in 1764 began to forge the works of several 'antique poets', chief among whom was 'Thomas Rowley', supposedly a fifteenth-century Bristol monk. Chatterton also wrote in contemporary styles but it is as a pseudo-medievalist that he is best remembered. In 1770, after a correspondence with Horace WALPOLE who for a time was convinced by the Rowley poems, Chatterton was released from his apprenticeship at an attorney's and moved to London; some poems were accepted for publication but his financial position quickly became desperate and he committed suicide. Chatterton was mythologized as an unappreciated genius by the Romantic poets, who saw him as a representative of a primitive sensibility neglected by his materialist contemporaries.

CHAUCER, GEOFFREY *see* essay on page 173

CHEKE, SIR JOHN (1514–57), scholar. Cambridge-born and educated, Cheke became England's foremost Greek scholar and, in 1540, first Regius Professor of Greek at Cambridge. His strong evangelical reformism influenced the future EDWARD VI, to whom he was tutor from 1544,

and pupil showed much favour to teacher in his reign, including the provostship of King's College, Cambridge. Briefly imprisoned by MARY I in 1553, he went into continental exile, but was kidnapped in 1556 and brought to the Tower of London, where he recanted. Shame about this hastened his early death.

CHELMSFORD, 2ND BARON and **1ST VISCOUNT** *see* THESIGER, FREDERICK

CHEPMAN, WALTER (?1474–?1538), patron of printing. A royal servant and Edinburgh merchant who financed the printing enterprise of Andrew MILLAR, the first in Scotland. It was given a royal monopoly in 1507. Early products of the press included poetry by William DUNBAR and Robert HENRYSON and an accomplished edition of the breviary following the use of Aberdeen Cathedral. *See* ELPHINSTONE, WILLIAM.

CHERWELL, 1ST VISCOUNT *see* LINDEMANN, FREDERICK

CHESELDEN, WILLIAM (1688–1752), surgeon and anatomist. He began to practise medicine in 1711, when he was already teaching comparative anatomy to medical students in London, the first course of its kind. In 1713 he published *The Anatomy of the Human Body,* which remained a definitive textbook until the end of the century. Cheselden built up a fashionable practice and in 1727 was appointed surgeon to Queen CAROLINE, although they soon quarrelled. He came to specialize in removing kidney stones, and published details of his operation in 1723. He also experimented in ophthalmic surgery in an attempt to relieve certain forms of blindness, but had to be stopped from perforating a convict's eardrum in order to study hearing loss.

CHESTERFIELD, 4TH EARL OF *see* STANHOPE, PHILIP

CHESTERTON, G(ILBERT) K(EITH) (1874–1936), writer. His talents as a journalist and polemicist emerged as a young man, at the same time as he became closely associated with Liberal Party politics. Chesterton was a fervent anti-imperialist, one of the themes of his fantasy novel, *The Napoleon of Notting Hill* (1904). He wrote the first of his 'Father Brown' books in 1911, but as well as his more frivolous fiction he produced a stream of books on virtually every topic of contemporary political, philosophical and social interest. None has stood the test of time, but of his writings on Catholicism (he converted in 1922) his studies of *St Francis of Assisi* (1923) and *St Thomas Aquinas* (1933) were best-sellers.

CHAUCER, GEOFFREY (c. 1340–1400)
Poet

His poems, especially his immediately popular masterpiece, *The Canterbury Tales*, unsurpassed in its fluency, grace and wit, are amongst the finest ever produced in England. Even before they were printed by CAXTON, they helped to establish English as the main language of the nation's literature in place of French or Latin. Hence his younger contemporary Thomas HOCCLEVE described him as 'the first finder of our fair language'.

Chaucer's life is much better known than that of most early English authors, yet what we know about him throws little light on the poet. He was the first poet to be buried in Westminster Abbey, but this was because he was a royal servant who had leased a house in the Abbey precincts, not because he was a poet; Poets' corner is a much later creation. He was born into a family of wealthy London wine merchants with court connections, and these were to be central throughout his life. From 1357, when we first hear of him, until 1391 he was in the service of the royal family, first as a page to Elizabeth, Countess of Ulster, wife of LIONEL, Duke of Clarence, and then in the service of the Black Prince (*see* EDWARD THE BLACK PRINCE), of JOHN OF GAUNT and, from 1373, EDWARD III. He saw military service in France in 1359 (when he was captured and ransomed) and 1369; between 1365 and 1378 he was often on diplomatic missions, some highly confidential, to France, Flanders, Navarre and Italy. His wife, Philippa, with whom he had two sons, was also in royal service and may have been sister to Katherine de Roet (later Swinford), Gaunt's mistress and then wife. From 1374 to 1386 he was Controller of the Custom and Subsidy of Wool in the Port of London, responsible for supervising the collection of customs duties which comprised about one quarter of the total annual revenue of the Crown. He was an MP for Kent (1386) and a Justice of the Peace in the late 1380s. From 1389 to 1391 he was RICHARD II's Clerk of Works responsible for the maintenance of various royal lodges and palaces, including the Palace of Westminster. After 1391 he lived in semi-retirement in Kent, writing *The Canterbury Tales* and still enjoying the patronage of the great.

He spoke the English and French of the cultivated Londoner of the day, the first great age of English literature. As well as a host of lesser poets his contemporaries included LANGLAND, John GOWER and the unknown author of *Sir Gawain and the Green Knight*. Richard II's was the first English-speaking royal court since 1066. Chaucer's active career at the heart of government means that when,

as in *Troilus and Cressida*, he takes us into the world of court intrigue and international politics, he knows what he is talking about; similarly with the world of big business, banks and exchange rates as in *The Shipman's Tale*. In his *House of Fame*, one of his characters upbraids him for always having his nose in a book:

> Dumb as any stone
> Thou sittest at another book
> Till fully dazed is thy look
> And so being oblivious to what was
>   happening not only in the wider world
> But of thy very neighbours
> That dwell almost at thy doors
> Thou hearest neither that nor this

As usual in his references to himself, we are clearly faced with one of his mocking half-truths.

Already famous as a writer of love songs in the 1360s, his first major poem was *The Book of the Duchess* (c. 1369), written to console Gaunt after the death of his wife Blanche, and based on French models. Chaucer's travels gave him an unprecedented familiarity both with contemporary French poets such as Machaut and Deschamps and with the great Italians, Dante, Petrarch and Boccaccio. Their influence on him was great but, into everything he read and learned from them, he breathed a new life of his own which often made his models look stilted. Much of his masterpiece, *The Canterbury Tales*, was based on familiar stories too. As one of the pilgrims put it:

> I can't recall a pithy tale just now.
> But Chaucer, clumsy as he is at times
> In metre and the cunning use of rhymes
> Has told them in such English, I suppose
> As he commands; for everybody knows
> That if he has not told them, my dear
>   brother,
> In one book, he has told them in another.

The link-passages to *The Canterbury Tales* and the vivid pen-portraits of the pilgrims in the prologue are highly original but, even when dealing with stock figures of anti-clerical satire, what Chaucer produced seemed fresh, as he knew well:

> For out of old fields, as men seyth,
> Cometh all this new corn, from year to year.

Derek Pearsall, The Life of Geoffrey Chaucer (1992)
Geoffrey Chaucer, The Canterbury Tales, trans. N. Coghill (1951)

CHEW, ADA (née Nield) (1870–1945), suffragist and trade unionist. In 1894, a tailoress in Crewe and largely self-educated, she published a series of letters in the *Crewe Chronicle* advocating the vote and trade unionism for women. The letters cost her her job, and she was drawn into the Independent Labour Party for which she became a travelling organizer. After marriage to George Chew in 1897 and the birth of her daughter in 1898 she recommenced her work for the Women's Trade Union League and, from 1912, as an organizer for the National Union of Women Suffragists. Her main distinction was in her advocacy of economic independence for all women, and collective childcare and improved domestic organization to support them, although she did not believe in men being more involved in childcare or housework. From 1915 she ran a mail-order business and largely withdrew from public life.

CHICHELE, HENRY (?1362–1443), Archbishop of Canterbury (1414–43). A lawyer, diplomat and administrator, he was made Bishop of St David's in 1408, then in 1414 was HENRY V's choice as Archbishop of Canterbury. He helped to finance the war against France, organized the fight against Lollardy and founded All Souls College, Oxford.

CHICHESTER, ARTHUR (1st Baron Chichester) (1563–1625), soldier and administrator. While at Oxford *c.* 1583 he assaulted a royal purveyor (revenue official) and fled to Ireland. He served against the 1588 Spanish Armada and later on the continent, returning to Ireland to fight under Robert DEVEREUX, Earl of Essex, in 1598. Appointed Lord Deputy (1604–14), he was eventually recalled because of his reluctance to carry out the government's policy of repression against Roman Catholics, which he saw as impractical. Nevertheless, he was energetic in disarming the Gaelic Irish and seeking to break down the clan system, and he was prominent in promoting the settlement of Scots Protestants in Ulster. From 1616 to 1625 he was Lord Treasurer of Ireland.

CHICHESTER-CLARK, JAMES (Baron Moyola of Castledowson) (1923–), Prime Minister of North-ern Ireland. A country gentleman from South Derry, cousin of Terence O'NEILL, he was Minister for Agriculture (1967–9); a carefully timed resignation enabled him to defeat Brian FAULKNER in the leadership election after O'Neill's resignation. As Prime Minister (1969–71) Chichester-Clark experienced widespread sectarian rioting, which forced the Northern Ireland government to call in British troops and turned Stormont (the Northern Ireland Parliament) into a political liability for the British government. Widely ridiculed as remote and ineffective, he resigned in protest at the developing situation and was succeeded by Brian Faulkner.

CHIDLEY, KATHERINE (?–*c.* 1653), writer. Wife of a Shrewsbury tailor, Daniel Chidley, she and her family had to leave for London *c.* 1629 because of their prominent role in a Separatist congregation; they continued in protests against the religious policies of William LAUD. In 1641 and 1645 she published pamphlets defending Separatists from the Presbyterian Thomas EDWARDS, also asserting (against his abusive fury) women's rights of conscience. In 1646 she moved to Bury St Edmunds and encouraged her son, Samuel, in his polemical pamphleteering. From 1649 she was a leader of the Levellers, organizing mass demonstrations outside Parliament against persecution of her comrades.

CHILD, SIR FRANCIS THE ELDER (1642–1713) and **SIR FRANCIS THE YOUNGER** (*c.* 1684–1740), bankers. The elder Child was the son of a Wilts. clothier and in 1656 was apprenticed to a goldsmith in London. In 1671 he married Elizabeth Wheeler, heiress of a family who had been goldsmiths with banking interests since the sixteenth century, whose business he took over. In the 1680s he administered public loans, leading in 1690 to his being the first to abandon goldsmithing to concentrate on banking. He assisted in the support of government expenditure under WILLIAM III and ANNE, and amassed a fortune that enabled him to buy the Middx. estate of Osterley Park. His second son Francis became head of the business in 1721; he was a prominent Tory MP from 1727 to 1740, a connection which increased the bank's aristocratic profile. In 1729 he introduced the first pictorial banknote.

CHILD, SIR JOSIAH (1630–99), merchant and writer on economics. Having started in business as a naval supplier, he became Mayor of Portsmouth, from 1659 was an MP, and was made a baronet in 1678. A Director of the East India Co. and, later, Governor (1681–3, 1686–8), he is best known for his short *New Discourse on Trade* (1663), in which he advocated the reduction of interest rates, to encourage trade and industry, and relief schemes involving the employment of the poor. Such proposals typified what subsequent commentators have termed the last stages of mercantilist thought.

CHILDERS, ERSKINE (1870–1922), novelist and Irish politician. Though born in London, he was raised in Ireland. He served in the British army in the Boer War and in 1903 published *The Riddle of the Sands*, a widely read thriller warning against a possible German invasion, which influenced public attitudes towards naval re-armament. A strong supporter of Irish Home Rule, in 1914 he smuggled a cargo of guns to the Irish Volunteers in his yacht *Asgard*. He served in the British forces during the First World War, but after the failure of attempts at a compromise settlement between Home Rulers and Unionists his views grew more radical, and during the Anglo-Irish War he played a major role in Sinn Féin publicity and propaganda. Childers advised the delegation which negotiated the Anglo-Irish Treaty, but rejected the final document and was one of its most articulate opponents. Many supporters of the treaty held exaggerated views about his responsibility for the Civil War (1922–3); he was court martialled and executed in questionable circumstances. His son Erskine Childers (1905–74) was a Fianna Fáil member of the Dáil (1938–73), Cabinet minister (1951–4 and 1957–73) and President of Ireland (1973–4).

CHILLINGWORTH, WILLIAM (1602–44), scholar. An Oxford don (one of Lucius CAREY's Great Tew circle), he converted to Roman Catholicism while debating with the Jesuit John Percy (alias Fisher the Jesuit), but by 1634 had returned to the Church of England and, thereafter, made classic defences of it as best placed to allow reasoned exploration of religion. His broad tolerance was based on the assertion that 'the Bible only is the religion of Protestants'. Chaplain in the Royalist army in 1643, he was already incapacitated by his last illness when captured at the Parliamentary siege of Arundel Castle.

CHIPPENDALE, THOMAS (*c*. 1718–79), furniture designer and manufacturer. The son of a joiner from Otley (Yorks.) he was probably trained by the cabinetmaker, Richard Ward. Established as a cabinetmaker in London by 1749, he published his *The Gentleman and Cabinet Maker's Director* in 1754, sealing his reputation as an authority on furniture design and manufacture, which he maintained despite business difficulties. Chippendale is primarily associated with the popularization of the originally French Rococo style in English furniture, but some critics consider his best work to have been in the neoclassical tradition. By the 1790s he was considered outdated, but his work was rediscovered in the early twentieth century.

CHRISTIAN, FLETCHER (1764–93), mutineer. The younger son of a minor Cumbs. gentleman, he joined the navy in 1782. Appointed master's mate of the *Bounty* in 1787, he served under William BLIGH on his expedition to the South Pacific. In late April 1789, following the *Bounty*'s departure from Tahiti, Christian led a mutiny, overthrowing Bligh and allowing the men to claim their lovers from Tahiti. The mutineers and their wives, with some Tahitian men, settled on the remote Pitcairn Island, under Christian's leadership, but disputes between the men led to Christian's death in Sept. 1793. The islanders eventually came under the government of the surviving mutineer, John Adams, who turned to Evangelical Christianity; Pitcairn and Norfolk Islands are still largely inhabited by the descendants of the mutineers.

CHRISTIE, DAME AGATHA (née Miller) (1891–1976), detective fiction writer. Born in Torquay (Devon) of a wealthy American father, and educated at home and in Paris (where she studied singing), she worked as a VAD nurse in the First World War, and started to write detective fiction: *The Mysterious Affair at Styles* was finally published in 1920. *The Murder of Roger Ackroyd* (1926) is considered a classic of detective fiction and by far Christie's best book. The mistress of the traditional 'who dunnit' with a cast of usually upper middle-class suspects and a littering of red herrings, her output was prodigious, more than 70 books translated into 103 languages. With a run of nearly 50 years, her play *The Mousetrap* (1952) continues to attract coach parties to the West End.

CHRISTIE, JOHN (1898–1953), murderer. Hanged for the murder of his wife at what was then 10 Rillington Place, Notting Hill, London, Christie had confessed to strangling Mrs Evans who, with her husband Timothy and infant daughter, had been lodgers in Christie's house, as well as five other women. Evans had been hanged for the murder of his daughter in 1950 and charged with killing his wife. He was granted a free pardon in 1966 and this horrific miscarriage of justice fuelled the debate over capital punishment, which was finally abolished in 1965.

CHRISTINA OF MARKYATE (*c*. 1097–*c*. 1160), visionary. Born to a wealthy Huntingdon family, she was forced into marriage by her parents. She escaped and went into hiding in a hermitage; eventually her unconsummated marriage was annulled. She changed her name to Christina (from Theodora) and was formally admitted into the religious life, becoming the Prioress of the small community of Markyate (Herts.) and spiritual adviser to the Abbot of St Albans. A life of her, written by an anonymous monk of St Albans, reflects her own account of her struggles against sexual desire, in herself and others.

CHRISTOPHERSON, JOHN (?–1558), churchman. His killing of a fellow pupil at Sir Humphrey

WINGFIELD's school did not harm his Cambridge career, but his traditionalist religious views made him leave England under EDWARD VI. He returned to become chaplain to MARY I, Master of Trinity College, Cambridge, Dean of Norwich (1554), then Bishop of Chichester (1557). His fierce opposition to ELIZABETH I's Reformation brought imprisonment. He wrote effectively defending Mary's government (1554), translated many Greek Church historians into Latin, and bequeathed to Trinity important MSS.

CHUBB, THOMAS (1679–1747), religious writer. An assistant tallow-chandler from Salisbury (Wilts.), he was released from this labour when William WHISTON helped him to get *Supremacy of the Father Asserted* published in 1715, and thereafter he concentrated on writing and learned activities. Inclined towards Arian, and increasingly Deist, views, his supporters among both clergy and educated laity tended to be men of similar persuasions: Samuel CLARKE and Benjamin HOADLY were among their number. Although self-educated, Chubb was able to popularize ideas of Christian morality and faith as reliant on rational inquiry in a way that more socially elevated Deists could not.

CHUDLEIGH, ELIZABETH (1720–88), society hostess and bigamist. Her father had been Lieutenant Governor of Chelsea Hospital, but he died when she was a child and she grew up in the country. In 1743 through the patronage of William PULTENEY, Earl of Bath, she was appointed maid of honour to AUGUSTA, Princess of Wales. The next year she met and married Augustus John Hervey, second son of John, Lord HERVEY; neither he nor she could afford to lose their careers so the marriage remained secret. A child was born in 1747 but died soon afterwards; the relationship dissolved and Elizabeth Chudleigh built a reputation as an independent fashionable lady, notoriously appearing semi-naked at a masked ball in 1749. She became the mistress of the Duke of Kingston, and hosted several glittering balls, such as that on the birthday of the Prince of Wales (the future GEORGE III) in 1760. Hervey tried to negotiate a divorce but Chudleigh denied in court in 1769 that she had ever been married to Hervey; that year she married Kingston. After the Duke's death in 1773 both Hervey (3rd Earl of Bristol from 1775) and Kingston's family pressed for a trial; she was found guilty of bigamy by the House of Lords in 1776, but fled to the continent to avoid further proceedings, eventually dying in Paris.

CHURCHILL, CHARLES (1731–64), poet. A clergyman's son, he was educated at Westminster where he was a friend of COWPER. His early

marriage in 1748 precluded his taking up a place at Cambridge. He entered the Church and made a meagre living until 1761, when his first published poem, the *Rosciad*, praising and insulting by turns many of the personalities of the day, earned him instant notoriety. Churchill continued to write satires, leaving his wife, debts and clerical career behind. *The Prophecy of Famine* in 1763 ridiculed Bute (*see* STUART, JOHN) and the Scots and he narrowly avoided being arrested with his friend WILKES.

CHURCHILL, JOHN (1st Duke of Marlborough) *see* essay on page 177

CHURCHILL, LORD RANDOLPH (1849–95), politician. Third son of the 7th Duke of Marlborough (and father of Winston CHURCHILL), in 1874 he married Jennie Jerome, daughter of a wealthy American businessman, and entered Parliament. He became the leader of the 'fourth party', a Conservative backbench ginger group, who saw him as a future leader of Tory democracy. Rash, impetuous and fond of threatening resignation, he did so once too often in Dec. 1886 when as Chancellor of the Exchequer he left Salisbury's Cabinet (*see* CECIL, ROBERT GASCOYNE) and terminated a promising career at 37. His alleged death from syphilis has been the subject of enduring curiosity.

CHURCHILL, SARAH (Duchess of Marlborough) (née Jenyns or Jennings) (1660–1744), politician and courtier. Coming from an impoverished gentry family, she became a maid of honour to MARY OF MODENA in 1673 and met and married John CHURCHILL. In 1683 she was appointed Lady of the Bedchamber to the future Queen ANNE, who treated her as a confidante despite the difference in their ranks. After the Glorious Revolution, Sarah became a lobbyist for Anne's interest, attempting to prevent WILLIAM III being granted the throne for life and straining her subsequent relations with the court. In 1691 Sarah and Anne began to write to each other as 'Mrs Freeman' and 'Mrs Morley', terms which emphasized their intimacy but were also intended to confuse spies. On Anne's accession she became her Groom of the Stole, but relations were strained. Sarah took an active political role, becoming the defender of the Whig interest at court and brokering political appointments, but Anne was uncomfortable with the Whig Junto, and eventually turned to her bedchamber woman, Abigail MASHAM, who helped her build up a relationship with Robert HARLEY. Sarah was finally dismissed from court in Jan. 1712 and joined her husband in exile the next year. Sarah had poor relations with the Hanoverians; Princess CAROLINE (later Queen) ignored her

continued on page 178

CHURCHILL, JOHN (1st Duke of Marlborough) (1650–1722)
Military commander and diplomat

Son of a Dorset Royalist, he had been page to the Duke of York (the future JAMES II); his sister Arabella was James's mistress by 1667. He remained always very much the courtier: charming, but inclined to dissemble. As an adolescent he joined the Foot Guards; during the Third Dutch War, his activities with an English regiment in French service earned praise from the brilliant Marshal Turenne. Showing a taste for strong-willed women he began, aged 20, an affair with the Duchess of Cleveland (*see* VILLIERS, Barbara), recently discarded as the King's mistress. In 1677 he married another strong character, Sarah Jennings (*see* CHURCHILL, Sarah).

In 1678 Churchill and Sidney GODOLPHIN were sent to negotiate with William of Orange (the future WILLIAM III). The Stuarts were then playing off the Dutch against the French. Anti-French and anti-Catholic feeling was rising in England. When in 1679 CHARLES II sent James into exile in the hope of dampening opposition, Churchill accompanied him.

In 1683 the Churchills shifted their allegiance, taking posts in the household of James's daughter ANNE. When Charles's illegitimate son Monmouth (*see* SCOTT, JAMES) rebelled upon James's accession in 1685, Churchill helped defeat him at Sedgemoor. He was, however, unsympathetic to James's pro-Catholic coterie, and, with Bishop Henry COMPTON, helped defend Anne from pressure to convert. He stirred up military opposition to James and, though appointed Lieutenant General when William's invasion fleet approached, defected. In the power vacuum after James's flight, he did not help shape the political settlement but concentrated on reconstructing the army.

Though wary of his ambition, William made him an earl, and put him in charge first of the campaign in the Netherlands, then of resisting French invasion, then against Jacobite forces in Ireland. There were nonetheless tensions between him and William's core (especially Dutch) entourage. In 1692 he was dismissed from both military and civil office and accused of Jacobite plotting. He responded by allying himself with the Tory opposition in Parliament and attacking the use of foreign troops.

Relations between Marlborough and William thawed after the death of Queen MARY; the King in 1698 made him governor to the Duke of Gloucester, Anne's son and heir, realizing that of Anne's circle he was most inclined to a forward military policy. Gloucester's death in 1700 coincided with a European crisis, as Louis XIV accepted the Spanish throne for his second grandson. Marlborough was charged with forging an anti-French alliance and commanding British forces in the Netherlands.

On the accession of Anne he was made not only a duke but Captain General and commander of all the allied forces, a position which he held for most of the War of the Spanish Succession. His diplomatic skills were crucial in holding the Grand Alliance together; he drew even the cautious Dutch into supporting offensive strategies. As commander, his achievement lay in developing offensive tactics, a series of feints preparing the way for a devastating assault, enabling him to achieve notable victories at Blenheim (1704), Ramillies (1706) and Oudenarde (1708). Malplaquet (1709) was more equivocal, and the single decisive victory he sought eluded him. He concentrated on attacking French forces where they were strongest, resisting Whig pressures to undertake a major offensive in Spain.

Though never as Whiggish as his wife, he increasingly depended on Whig backing for the war, and was insufficiently sensitive to ebbing support for its human and financial cost. He was in jeopardy once the Tories gained ascendancy in 1710. Though Robert HARLEY was initially keen to keep him in post, as a *quid pro quo* Sarah, at odds with the Queen since 1708, was dismissed from her place at court in Jan. 1711. Peace preliminaries agreed at the end of the year made Marlborough dispensable. He was attacked by SWIFT in his *Conduct of the Allies* for sacrificing the national interest to self-aggrandizement. Dismissed, he was threatened with prosecution for corruption. He remained on the continent in voluntary exile from 1712 to 1714, when the Elector of Hanover (soon to be GEORGE I) asked him to defend England in the event of Jacobite invasion; as King, George reinstated him as Captain General. He oversaw but did not actively command the forces which put down the 1715 Jacobite rebellion. In 1716 he suffered a disabling stroke.

Marlborough was exceptional as an Englishman in achieving European standing: the German Emperor more than once offered him the post of Governor of the Spanish Netherlands, though political considerations precluded this. Public moneys funded his grandiose palace, built by VANBRUGH, at Woodstock near Oxford (named Blenheim, after his early victory). His descendants rose to political prominence again in the late nineteenth century (*see* CHURCHILL, RANDOLPH); his most famous descendant, Sir Winston CHURCHILL, used some conclusions he had drawn from studying his ancestor's life in devising his own wartime strategies.

Winston Churchill, Marlborough: His Life and Times (4 vols, 1933–8)
J. R. Jones, Marlborough (1993)

advice and insulted her intelligence. She inherited Blenheim from her husband in 1722 and attempted intrigues against Robert WALPOLE but 'Cobham's cubs' (*see* TEMPLE, RICHARD) proved a more effective political grouping than her Rumpsteak Club. Although her family continued to wield local political influence, she died having failed to establish it as a leading political dynasty.

CHURCHILL, SIR WINSTON SPENCER *see* essay on pages 180–81

CHURCHYARD, THOMAS (?1520–1604), writer. After serving Henry HOWARD, Earl of Surrey, he lived as a mercenary soldier in Europe and served various noblemen; his first pamphlets were published before the death of EDWARD VI, and a stream of short works and broadsheets followed, both prose and poetry, many of which are commentaries on current events.

CIBBER, COLLEY (1671–1757), actor and playwright. He was the son of the Dutch-born sculptor Caius Gabriel Cibber, and the founder of a theatrical dynasty. He joined the Theatre Royal, Drury Lane, in 1690, and became one of its leading players after BETTERTON and others defected to Lincoln's Inn Fields. His first play, *Love's Last Shift,* appeared in 1696 with Cibber himself as Sir Novelty Fashion; he reprised the part, promoted to Lord Foppington, in VANBRUGH's sequel *The Relapse*. He continued to combine acting and writing, particularly with adaptations such as *Richard III* from SHAKESPEARE (1700) and *The Non-Juror* from Molière's *Tartuffe* (1718). His quarrelsome nature made enemies of many other literary figures and his appointment and works as Poet Laureate from 1730 were widely derided, but his *Apology for the Life of Colley Cibber* (1740) displayed a capacity for self-mockery as well as providing much information about the stage of his era.

CILLÉNE DROICHTECH (?–752), Abbot of Iona. The description in his obituary as an anchorite and, in the Martyrology of Gorman, as 'Cillein of constant virginity' indicates that Cilléne was closely involved with the *Céli Dé*, the 'Servants of God', a rigorous ascetic movement which emerged in the mid eighth century, perhaps even as a founding member. Like all abbots of the great Abbey of Iona, Cilléne was involved in politics on both sides of the Irish Sea. His by-name *Droichtech* (bridge-builder), is an apparent reference to the peace he forged between the two northern Uí Néill kindreds of the Cenél Conaill and the Cenél nEógain.

CINAED II, King of the Scots (971–95). Son of MAEL COLUIM I, he took over the Scottish kingship

from the collateral line of Kings INDULF and CUILÉN. His raid on Stainmore on the border of Cumbria and Yorks. shows how far south his power extended. He also attended the famous meeting with King EDGAR at Chester in 973. Otherwise his reign is notable for the way in which he sought to settle kingship on his son (the future MAEL COLUIM II) to the detriment of the descendants of Kings Indulf and DUB. This exacerbated tensions within the ruling kindred and began a feud that lasted for almost a century.

CINAED III, King of the Scots (997–1005). A son of DUB, Cinaed killed his predecessor, CONSTANTÍN III, son of CUILÉN, and seized the kingship, thereby continuing the feud over the kingship which had begun when his father was killed by Cuilén. Nothing is otherwise known of his reign, which appears to have been one of turbulent upheaval as rival factions strove for supremacy. He appears to have attempted to exclude rival segments by introducing his son, Giric II, as a joint King to ensure the succession; both Cinaed and Giric, however, were defeated and killed by MAEL COLUIM II, son of CINAED II, in 1005.

CINAED MAC ALPÍN, King of the Scots and Picts (840–58). His origins are obscure; all that is clear is that, by *c*. 847, he had managed to impose himself by violence on the kingdoms of both the Picts and the Scots at a time when they were threatened by Viking assaults from the north, west and south. It is probable that he received indirect assistance from the Vikings, since they appear to have inflicted a great military defeat on the Picts in 839. There had been previous temporary unions of the two kingdoms, but Cinaed's conquest of the Picts was converted by his successors into a lasting one. Although much of his reign is shrouded in obscurity, it is recorded that he 'died of a tumour, ultimately, on the Ides of February, the third day of the week, in the Palace of Forteviot'.

CINIOD, SON OF FERADACH (?–775), King of the Picts. He was the successor of BRIDEI, SON OF UURGUST. Little is known of Ciniod's reign. In 768 his lands were invaded by AED FIND THE FAIR, King of Dál Riata, in what appears to have been a major raid rather than a serious attempt at conquest. The twelfth-century writer Symeon of Durham records that ALHRED, deposed as King of Northumbria in 774, sought refuge at Ciniod's court.

CITRINE, WALTER (1st Baron Citrine of Wembley) (1887–1983), trade-union leader. As General Secretary of the Trades Union Congress (TUC) (1926–46), he played a crucial role in establishing trade-union influence within the

Labour Party. In Aug. 1931 he opposed cuts proposed by Ramsay MACDONALD's Cabinet, precipitating the fall of the second Labour government. He was then responsible, with BEVIN, for rallying the bulk of the Labour Party to oppose the National government and securing Macdonald's expulsion. From 1931 he increasingly asserted control of the trade-union movement over Labour Party policy via the TUC-dominated National Joint Council. Having, with Bevin, pursued a strong anti-communist stance and opposition to Fascism, he wholly supported the war effort and chaired a committee that led, in 1942, to the setting up of national and local production boards. Under the post-war Labour government, he presided over the nationalization of the electricity industry, serving on the National Coal Board and becoming Chairman of the Central Electricity Authority (1947–57).

CLAPHAM, SIR JOHN (1873–1946), historian. He read history at Cambridge and took up the study of British economic history at the suggestion of Alfred MARSHALL, and was appointed Fellow of King's College and later Professor at the universities of Leeds (1902–8) and Cambridge (1928–46). He had a profound influence on the development of economic history with his major surveys, *The Economic Development of France and Germany* (1921), *An Economic History of Modern Britain* (three vols, 1938–52) and *The Bank of England* (two vols, 1944). His interest in the development of institutions and their impact on economic circumstances became unfashionable with economists but has recently come back into prominence.

CLARE, GILBERT DE (4th Earl of Gloucester) (*c*. 1180–1230), nobleman. He inherited his title from his mother in 1217. In 1215 he and his father Richard de CLARE were among the barons confronting King JOHN at Runnymede (Surrey). He became one of the 25 appointed to ensure that John kept to the terms of Magna Carta. Fighting on behalf of Louis of France, later LOUIS VIII, he was captured by William MARSHAL at the Battle of Lincoln (1217); soon afterwards he married William's daughter Isabella. His military career included several campaigns in Wales and finally one with HENRY III in Brittany, where he died.

CLARE, GILBERT DE (6th Earl of Gloucester, the Red Earl) (1243–95), military commander. Initially, he supported Simon de MONTFORT, fighting for him at Lewes (Sussex) (1264) but then quarrelled and fought against him at Evesham (Worcs.) (1265). In 1268 he occupied London in order to bring pressure on HENRY III and Edward (later EDWARD I) to restore the estates of the 'disinherited' – those who had suffered forfeiture for being on the losing side in the recent civil war. He finally won the point in 1271. He built Caerphilly Castle (Glam.) as a check to LLYWELYN AP GRUFFUDD and became one of Edward's chief commanders in the wars against the Welsh. In 1290 he married, as his second wife, Edward I's daughter Joan.

CLARE, GILBERT DE (7th Earl of Gloucester) (1291–1314), royal servant. He succeeded to the title after the death of his mother Joan, daughter of EDWARD I, in 1307. During the banishments and recalls of EDWARD II's favourite Piers GAVESTON, who was his brother-in-law, he remained marginally the King's man. Although still only 22, he was Regent during the King's absence in 1311 and again in 1313. He was killed fighting bravely against the Scots at the Battle of Bannockburn (1314), possibly to counter being accused of cowardice.

CLARE, JOHN (1793–1864), poet. Born in Northants, Clare worked on the land and wrote about the rural poor. His anthology *Poems Descriptive of Rural Life* was published in 1820, *The Village Minstrel* in 1821, *The Rural Muse* in 1835 and *The Midsummer Calendar* posthumously. Clare's sense of melancholy loss (of his first love Mary Joyce, of the open fields enclosed during his lifetime and of his own intimate sense of place when he moved 3 miles away from his village of Helpston in 1832) suffuses his poems; in 1837 he became mentally ill and was eventually committed to Northampton General Asylum, from where he continued to write poetry in his own dialect and idiosyncratic syntax. As the rare authentic poetic voice of the agricultural labourer, Clare was briefly lionized in London, but the public taste for pastoral poetry declined in his lifetime and it was not until the twentieth century that his songs of alienation struck a chord and his poems, rescued from his publisher's editorial attempts at 'standardization', were again valued.

CLARE, RICHARD DE ('STRONGBOW') (2nd Earl of Pembroke) (*c*. 1130–76), soldier. He inherited his father's earldom of Pembroke in 1148 but, as STEPHEN's man, forfeited it when HENRY II came to the throne, the King allowing him to keep little more than the lordship of Striguil (Chepstow, Mon.). In *c*. 1166, still out of favour at court, he accepted DIARMAIT MAC MURCHADHA's offer of marriage to his daughter Aífe and succession to the kingdom of Leinster in return for military assistance. In 1170 he went to Ireland, occupied Dublin and Waterford, married Aífe and in 1171 succeeded Diarmait. He then beat off RUAIDRÍ UA CONCHOBAIR's siege of Dublin. At this

continued on page 182

CHURCHILL, SIR WINSTON SPENCER (1874–1965)
Politician and Prime Minister (1940–5, 1951–5)

Described by A. J. P. TAYLOR as the 'greatest Englishman of all time', Churchill was half-American, one of many products of what had been called the 'gilded prostitution' of the 1860s and 1870s when large numbers of American heiresses married into British society; his mother, Jennie Jerome, was a noted beauty; his father, Lord Randolph CHURCHILL, second son of the 7th Duke of Marlborough, was a maverick and ultimately self-destructive Conservative politician. Young Winston was always his father's son.

Showing little scholastic promise at Harrow, Winston was packed off to Sandhurst. His father's premature death in 1894 sparked off an ambition to emulate and vindicate him, and Lady Randolph Churchill used her extensive social and political contacts to secure postings for her son which would allow him to achieve fame as an author and journalist. Such activities did not appeal to Winston's military superiors but they did succeed in their objective. His escape from Boer captivity in 1900 made him into a newspaper celebrity, a status he was to maintain for the next 65 years. Slight, with receding red hair and a slight lisp, Churchill was not a natural public speaker, and his impulsiveness and obsessive personality seemed to fit him badly for political life, but by sheer force of will Churchill overcame these handicaps to make himself an accomplished orator. Oratory would be the main pillar of his career as a politician, making it difficult for his enemies to ignore him.

Churchill entered Parliament in the 1900 General Election as MP for Oldham but he was not the stuff of which loyal backbenchers were made. His vocal disagreements with the army reorganization of the BALFOUR government in 1902 led to calls to withdraw the Whip from him, and his own dissatisfaction with the 'old gang' of the house of Cecil led Churchill to speculate with Rosebery (see PRIMROSE, ARCHIBALD) and other Liberal imperialists upon the virtues and possibilities of a centre party; this chimera, which would haunt Churchill's political dreams for the rest of his life, represented his own political position better than any party label he would ever wear. In 1904 he ceased to sit on the Conservative benches, and he stood in Manchester with Liberal support in the 1905–6 election. He was given junior office under CAMPBELL-BANNERMAN, who felt that young men should win their spurs; he was the object of execration from his former Conservative

colleagues, and many Tories would never quite forgive his apostasy. ASQUITH, who succeeded Bannerman in 1908, was Churchill's political patron and appointed the young man in a hurry to the Board of Trade in 1908, where he formed a radical partnership with LLOYD GEORGE in which the two men helped lay the foundations of the Welfare State.

It was typical of Churchill's ability to absorb himself in his department that, during this period, he should have poured scorn on the notion of a military threat to Britain from Germany and that he should have opposed increases in expenditure on the navy; neither position would be regarded by his admirers as characteristic. What was characteristic was his total volte-face on both positions when he became First Lord of the Admiralty in 1911, after a brief period as Home Secretary. Churchill owed his preferment to Asquith. Although he demonstrated great gifts both as orator and administrator, his manner had won him many political enemies and few friends. Tories found the radical attacks on the peerage in the 1910 elections far harder to take from the scion of the house of Marlborough than they did from Lloyd George, while his navalist attitudes at the Admiralty soured his relations with the radical wing of the Liberal Party. These things came to matter greatly when the war broke out in 1914.

Ostensibly Churchill seemed ideally placed to benefit from the war: he was one of the few Liberals with any idea about the rudiments of military matters, he was a man of overwhelming energy and decision and he was in charge of Britain's weapons of war, but he lacked patience and prudence. Britain's early naval set-backs prompted Churchill to advocate the assault on the straits at the Dardanelles, which led to yet another failure and a long and costly campaign with which Churchill's name would always be linked. Instead of ascending the 'greasy pole', Churchill slid down it with even more rapidity than he had climbed it. Unionists demanded his removal from the Admiralty as their price for entering into coalition with Asquith in May 1915. Churchill found his humiliating demotion to the chancellorship of the Duchy of Lancaster bearable only as long as it seemed to give him some influence on government strategy; by late 1915 it was clear this was not the case, and he resigned from the government and joined the army.

After a brief period of military service, Churchill was rescued from the political wilderness by a new political patron, his old radical friend Lloyd George, who wanted his debating power on his rather than Asquith's side of the Liberal divide, and who managed to convince highly sceptical Conservatives that Churchill's energies were just what were wanted at the Ministry of Munitions. For once, Churchill confined himself to his job and he played a notable part in ensuring the smooth running of the demobilization process in 1919. But after his appointment as Secretary of State for War and Air in 1919, Churchill once more showed his capacity for self-destructive behaviour by his reckless championing of the cause of the White Russian Generals against the Bolsheviks; as Lloyd George put it, 'his ducal blood revolts at the wholesale slaughter of Grand Dukes'. This reinforced the image of Churchill as an enemy of Labour, which he had originally acquired as Home Secretary in 1910. During his final period of office under Lloyd George, as Colonial Secretary, Churchill was active in trying to secure a settlement of the situation in the Middle East. He lost his seat in the 1922 General Election.

Churchill was fortunate that the next three years were such volatile ones in British politics, as this allowed him to survive the decline of the Liberal Party and to draw closer to the Conservatives on the issue of opposition to Labour. After the 1923 election victory BALDWIN, to universal surprise, made him Chancellor of the Exchequer. Of all the offices he held, the Exchequer was the one in which Churchill was least happy, and his responsibility for restoring Britain to the gold standard in 1925 led some to blame him for Britain's subsequent economic problems. But by 1929 he had established a claim to succeed Baldwin. His attempt to press this claim during the period when the Conservatives entered opposition in 1929 led to his subsequent exclusion from the party's front bench on the issue of dominion status for India. When the National government was formed in late 1931 there was no place for him.

In the Churchill legend the 1930s were the 'wilderness years' but, for most of this period, he seemed a dated and out-of-touch figure. His opposition to Hitler after 1933 and his criticism of Neville CHAMBERLAIN's appeasement policy revived his career, and after 1939 made him appear (not least in his own eyes) as the prophet of truth. Churchill entered the War Cabinet as First Lord of the Admiralty in Sept. 1939 and, despite his responsibility for the fiasco of the invasion of Norway in April 1940, became Prime Minister in May 1940 after the fall of Chamberlain. The speeches he made that summer established the policy of 'no surrender' and his subsequent reputation; they gave him enormous political capital, which not even a series of military reverses could quite destroy. His faith in the Americans seemed to be rewarded after Pearl Harbor in 1941, and he paid much attention to wooing the US President F. D. Roosevelt. Churchill also attempted to get on good personal terms with the Soviet dictator, Stalin; he was a great believer in personal diplomacy.

Despite his own later claims to be worried about growing Russian influence, Churchill's eyes remained fixed firmly on the defeat of Nazi Germany. His own preference for a Mediterranean strategy may not have helped this cause as much as he believed but his interest in and influence upon allied strategy was immense. He paid less attention to the home front but his liberal instincts allowed the development of a consensus in favour of a Welfare State and a managed economy. Churchill was shattered by losing the 1945 election but soon made a political come-back. His speech at Fulton, Missouri, in March 1946 warning about the 'Iron Curtain' falling across Europe, is generally held to have heralded the start of the Cold War. He was also active, in opposition, in championing European unity.

Many colleagues thought that he would retire when he reached 80 but after winning the 1951 election he proved difficult to remove from power. Although increasingly deaf and prone to strokes, Churchill remained active, particularly in foreign affairs, where his last great crusade after Stalin's death in 1952 was to try to bring about an end to the Cold War. By 1955 with no success on this front, his health failing and an election due, Churchill finally resigned as Prime Minister, leaving the way open to his chosen successor, Anthony EDEN. Churchill did not resign from the Commons until 1964. He died in Jan. 1965 and his State funeral marked, in the eyes of many, the passing of Britain's greatness.

Martin Gilbert, Churchill: A Life (1995)
John Charmley, Churchill: The End of Glory (1993)

stage, alarmed by the prospect of seeing Strongbow as the independent ruler of an Irish kingdom from which he could threaten to occupy Pembroke, Henry II at last decided to take up his long considered project of taking over Ireland. In the meantime he confiscated Richard's English and Welsh estates. Strongbow took the hint, submitted to Henry and handed Dublin and Waterford over to him. In return he was at last recognized as Earl and then, on Henry's departure, as his representative in Ireland. The 1173–4 rebellion against Henry was exploited by both Welsh and Irish; in consequence Strongbow suffered setbacks both in Wales and Ireland, notably at the hands of DOMNALL MÓR UA BRIAIN and Ruaidrí Ua Conchobair. Despite this there can be no doubt that his gamble had succeeded; and the English conquest of Ireland had begun.

CLARE, RICHARD DE (5th Earl of Gloucester) (1222–62), royal servant. He succeeded his father Gilbert de CLARE in 1230 at the age of eight; through his mother he inherited a share of William MARSHAL's estates, including Kilkenny in Ireland. Matthew PARIS criticized his 'base avarice' but praised his eloquence and knowledge of law. His rank, wealth and ability meant he was often employed on embassies abroad, perhaps the most delicate being when sent to Edinburgh in 1255 to free HENRY III's daughter MARGARET and her husband, the young King ALEXANDER III, from the control of a Scottish court faction. After 1258 he picked his own way in the quarrels between King and Simon de MONTFORT, dying before they degenerated into civil war.

CLARENCE, DUKE OF, **1ST** see LIONEL OF CLARENCE; **2ND** see THOMAS OF CLARENCE; **3RD** see PLANTAGENET, GEORGE

CLARENDON, 1ST EARL OF see HYDE, EDWARD, essay on page 443

CLARK, ALAN (1929–99), historian and politician. He was the son of the art historian Kenneth CLARK. His indictment of British military leadership in the First World War, *The Donkeys* (1961), influenced Joan LITTLEWOOD to produce *Oh! What a Lovely War!* Conservative MP for Plymouth Sutton from 1974, he served as Minister of State for Defence (1989–92) and in 1992, as a former Minister at the Department of Trade, was found by the inquiry into the Matrix Churchill affair to be deeply involved in the sale of arms to Iraq. His diaries (1993) are an indiscreet, personal view of the Thatcher government and his admiration for 'the lady'. Having resigned his seat in 1992, Clark returned to politics as MP for Kensington and Chelsea in 1997.

CLARK, KENNETH (Baron Clark) (1903–83), art historian. The only child of wealthy parents, Clark read history at Oxford. In 1925 he was introduced to the art historian Bernard Berenson, with whom he collaborated on the revision of Berenson's work on Florentine drawings at I Tatti in the Florentine hills. Clark's *The Gothic Revival* was published in 1928. The next year he was appointed to catalogue the Leonardo da Vinci drawings at Windsor Castle (Berks.), and a series of prestigious appointments followed, Keeper of the Department of Fine Art at the Ashmolean Museum, Oxford (1931), Director of the National Gallery (1934–45), Surveyor of the King's Pictures (1934–35) and Slade Professor of Fine Art at Oxford (1946–50). He established the Council for the Encouragement of Music and the Arts and was instrumental in supporting the work of struggling artists, notably Henry MOORE. From his lectures there emerged two highly regarded books, *The Nude* (1956) and *Rembrandt and the Italian Renaissance* (1966). His flair for writing and lecturing, his handsome features, and his elegant and urbane manner made him an ideal candidate for the BBC television series *Civilisation*. The programmes, broadcast in 1969, achieved an unparalleled success, becoming for millions of people a source of aesthetic inspiration.

CLARKE, ALURED (1696–1742), churchman. Son of a Hunts. gentleman, he became a royal chaplain in 1720 and entered the circle of CAROLINE, Princess of Wales. With support from Caroline and GEORGE II Clarke was one of the founders of the first county hospital in 1736, at Winchester where he was a Prebendary. He was also Dean of Exeter from 1731 and co-founded the Devon and Exeter Hospital 10 years later.

CLARKE, JEREMIAH (*c.* 1674–1707), composer. Possibly a member of the Clarke family who were involved with music for many generations at St George's chapel, Windsor, he became organist and vicar choral of St Paul's Cathedral in 1699. Around this time he probably wrote his most famous work, *Trumpet Voluntary*. There is no contemporary score but it is very similar to *The Prince of Denmark's March*, contributed to an anthology in 1700. Clarke also wrote church and theatre music, songs and an anthem for the coronation of Queen ANNE in 1702. Depressed, possibly over a love affair, he committed suicide in 1707.

CLARKE, KENNETH (1940–), politician. Another product of the Cambridge and Bow group nexus which produced politicians such as Geoffrey HOWE. He was elected as MP for Rushcliffe (Notts.) in 1970 and a Whip by 1972; he willingly did Edward HEATH's business for him but in the process acquired credentials on Europe which would return to haunt him. Margaret THATCHER's long tenure of office was a blessing for Clarke; it allowed him to live down his Heathite past and to move steadily upwards; indeed he was the only MP who could claim to have been a member of the government from 1979 (Parliamentary Secretary at Transport) through to 1997. He entered the Cabinet in 1985 as Paymaster General and Minister for Employment, in which capacity he first showed his abilities as a communicator on television. A relaxed, genial man with a love of jazz, he was a deceptive interviewee; underneath the surface there was a shrewd mind at work. His period as Health Secretary (1988–90) was marked by controversy over money for the NHS but Clarke's robust presentation of the government's case won him a considerable reputation. At Education (1990–2) he found himself at odds with the teaching unions but he also presided over the abolition of the so-called binary divide in higher education between polytechnics and universities. After John MAJOR's 1992 election victory Clarke became Home Secretary before moving to the Exchequer in 1993 after the sacking of Norman LAMONT following the fiasco over Britain's membership of the European Monetary System and the Exchange Rate Mechanism. Under Clarke's robust stewardship the Conservatives began to regain a little of their reputation for financial competence, but his pro-Europe attitude meant that he was often at odds with those such as John REDWOOD who wished to halt the move towards greater European integration.

After the great defeat in the 1997 election Clarke was the Europhile choice for leader of the party but there were not enough of that group to elect him. A last-minute pact with his arch-opponent, Redwood, did nothing to help either man, and William HAGUE became leader. Clarke retired to the back benches to bide his time.

CLARKE, SAMUEL (1675–1729), philosopher and controversialist. A follower of NEWTON, whose *Opticks* he translated in 1706, he made his reputation with his Boyle lectures (*see* BOYLE, ROBERT) in 1704–5, and was considered the foremost English metaphysician after LOCKE. Rejecting Lockean scepticism, he founded the 'intellectual' school, which deduced moral law from logical necessity. He was criticized for promoting a disguised Deism; his *Scripture Doctrine of the Trinity* (1712) was attacked for Arianism, and he was widely thought to share his friend WHISTON's heretical views. The subject of a complaint to Convocation in 1714, he was forced to affirm his orthodoxy and promise to teach no more.

CLARKSON, THOMAS (1760–1846), anti-slavery campaigner. One of the first effective publicists in Britain against slavery and the slave trade, Clarkson began his campaign in 1785. He allied himself with William WILBERFORCE and amassed the information that was the backbone of the latter's parliamentary campaign. In 1807 the Abolition Act was finally passed and the following year Clarkson published his two-volume history of the slave trade. His efforts continued until 1815 when international condemnation of the slave trade was agreed at the close of the Napoleonic Wars.

CLAUDIUS (Tiberius Claudius Caesar Augustus Germanicus) (10 BC–AD 54), Roman Emperor (AD 41–54). He launched the second successful Roman invasion of Britain (*see also* JULIUS CAESAR). His motives have been much discussed by scholars; his need to establish his personal prestige after the assassination of his predecessor Caligula and the threat to Roman power in Gaul posed by the developing power of the Catuvellauni are likely to have been the predominant ones.

Claudius took part in the invasion himself, arriving when his army had reached the Thames and leading the triumphal entry into the Catuvellaunian capital of Colchester. He appointed good generals, e.g. AULUS PLAUTIUS and OSTORIUS SCAPULA, and presumably contributed to the plans for the organization of the new Roman province.

CLAYTON, JOHN (1709–73), churchman. Educated at Manchester grammar school, Clayton imbibed certain High Church notions of piety from Manchester Non-juring circles (*see also* DEACON, THOMAS). At Oxford, he befriended the WESLEYS and other Methodists, before moving to take up a series of church appointments around Manchester. He welcomed Charles Edward STUART to Manchester in 1745 and offered prayers for his success at Manchester collegiate church, where he was chaplain. He was suspended from his post but reinstated in the general amnesty. He also founded a grammar school in Salford to rival that at Manchester, and in 1755 wrote *Friendly Advice to the Poor*, which denounced the poor as idle and feckless and in need of moral guidance.

CLAYTON, SIR ROBERT (1629–1707), entrepreneur, politician and philanthropist. The son of a small farmer, he was apprenticed to a London scrivener (a specialist in placing loans), and became wealthy through involvement in implementing the Restoration land settlement. He also owned an ironworks in Ireland. An alderman of London between 1670 and 1683, he was MP for the City in 1679 and 1681; closely associated with Anthony Ashley COOPER, 1st Earl of Shaftesbury, and very active in the Exclusion Parliaments.

Prominent in trying to defend the City's charter against JAMES II, he was ejected when it was withdrawn. A member of the City delegation sent to meet William of Orange (the future WILLIAM III) in 1688, he became an active member of the Convention Parliament of 1689 and the succeeding Parliaments of William's reign, and subsequently a Commissioner of Customs and a Director of the Bank of England. Sustaining a tradition of civic charity, he secured the foundation of the Royal Mathematical school at Christ's Hospital in 1673, to train boys for navigation; he was Vice-President of the London Workhouse, President of St Thomas's Hospital and Governor of Christ's Hospital, contributing to the cost of rebuilding the last two institutions.

CLELAND, JOHN (1709–82), writer. He was employed by the East India Co. (1728–40). His pornographic novel *Fanny Hill, or Memoirs of a Woman of Pleasure* (1748–9) brought him a summons before the Privy Council and the resulting suppression of the unexpurgated text for over 200 years. He produced further novels and wrote government propaganda and philology, in which he pointed out similarities between Sanskrit and the Celtic languages many decades before Sir William JONES.

CLENNOCK, MAURICE see CLYNOG, MORYS

CLERKE, SIR PHILIP JENNINGS (1722–88), parliamentary reformer. His election to the Commons in 1768 followed an undistinguished military career. After 1777 he consistently voted with the opposition to NORTH, and in 1778 introduced for the first time a Bill to exclude from the House of Commons government contractors, except those who held their posts as the result of an auction. The object of the Bill was to reduce ministerial influence in the Commons, at a time when, according to the opposition, only such influence was keeping in power a ministry that was disastrously mismanaging national affairs. The Bill was defeated but was reintroduced annually, passing the Commons but being rejected by the Lords in 1780. It was finally passed in 1782, under the brief second Rockingham (see WATSON-WENTWORTH, CHARLES) administration.

CLEVELAND, DUCHESS OF see VILLIERS, BARBARA

CLIFFORD, LADY ANN (1590–1676) (Countess of Dorset, Pembroke and Montgomery), builder. Heiress of George Clifford, 3rd Earl of Cumberland, she survived unhappy marriages to Richard Sackville (later Earl of Dorset) and Philip Herbert, Earl of Pembroke and Montgomery. Meanwhile she fought bitter battles to claim her inherited estates, but triumphed only on the death of her cousin and rival the 5th Earl of Cumberland in 1643. Once the Civil Wars had ended, she enjoyed the life of a great northern magnate, and commemorated her success by a spectacular orgy of building, restoring her castles to medieval splendour, rebuilding several churches and founding almshouses. She wrote an autobiography.

CLIFFORD, THOMAS (1st Baron Clifford of Chudleigh) (1630–74), politician. Son of an army officer, he was elected MP in 1660, and became prominent among Arlington's (see BENNET, HENRY) Court party and a promoter of war with the Netherlands. A Commissioner of the Treasury in the 1667–73 Cabal ministry, so-called from the initials of its leading members (see CHARLES II), Clifford had a reputation for incorruptibility but was also close to the Duke of York (later JAMES II) and, with Arlington, carried out the secret preparations for the Treaty of Dover, in which Charles II promised Louis XIV that he would work for the restoration of Catholicism in England. Principal promoter of the Declaration of Indulgence, suspending laws against religious dissent (1672), he was made Lord Treasurer but the following year the passage of the Test Act, barring Catholics from office, obliged him to resign. His death soon after was reputed to be suicide.

CLITHEROW, MARGARET (née Middleton) (*c*. 1556–86), martyr. A York merchant's daughter, she converted to Roman Catholicism and became central to the support network for priests in Yorks. Arrested for her activities in 1586, she insisted on refusing to plead in court in order to save her family the ordeal of testifying against her, and to preserve their property from confiscation. This brought her the horrifying prescribed penalty of being crushed to death with heavy weights. Her life was written by her somewhat intimidated admirer, the priest John Mush.

CLIVE, ROBERT (1st Baron Clive of Plassey) (1725–74), military commander and administrator. Son of a small Salop. landowner of ancient family, he joined the East India Co. in 1742. He spent three periods in India, each time returning with a larger fortune to cut a bigger figure on the English social and political scene.

From 1746 to 1753 he took part in fighting against the French in India; on his return, he was elected MP. From 1756 he led a successful offensive against the French and the Nawab of Bengal. On 23 June 1757, after the Nawab had captured and sacked the company settlement at Calcutta, Clive led company troops against him at Plassey, and won despite the superior numbers of the

Bengali forces. He was able to impose a pro-company nawab on Bengal and himself became Governor of the company's Bengal presidency. In England, he was elected MP for Salop. in 1761 and given an Irish barony. He returned to India in 1763 as Governor and Commander-in-Chief, arriving after a crucial victory at Buxar. The Mughal Emperor granted the company responsibility for civil administration in Bengal, including the right to collect revenue.

When Clive came back to England for the final time in 1767, he used his by then fabulous wealth to build up a parliamentary interest, and in 1772 was made Lord Lieutenant of Shropshire. Much of his later career was spent justifying his position. After defending his financial integrity to a parliamentary inquiry (1772–3) he committed suicide in Nov. 1774 even though his conduct had been vindicated. A man of energy and courage, although often criticized for his ruthless ambition, he was the most successful of the so-called 'nabobs', men who amassed fortunes in India that made it possible for them to live in the manner of Indian princes ('nabobs' or in modern usage 'nawabs'). His great collection of treasures from India is on show at Powis Castle, Powys.

CLODIUS ALBINUS (Decimus Clodius Albinus) (?–197), Roman Governor of Britain. He proclaimed himself Emperor in 193, after the Emperors Commodus, Pertinax and Didius Julianus had all been murdered during the period 192–3. He took a large army from Britain to the continent, but was defeated near Lyons by rival Emperor SEPTIMIUS SEVERUS in 197.

CLORE, SIR CHARLES (1904–79), businessman. The son of a textile manufacturer in London's East End, Clore worked for his father before moving to South Africa in 1924, where he became interested in land opportunities. Returning to England in 1927, he began a series of property transactions, managing entertainment venues and building offices and hotels on land which he had acquired. After the Second World War his interests switched to buying moribund trading businesses and revitalizing them, textiles, shipbuilding and a range of footwear businesses that by the 1960s, as the British Shoe Corporation, had a quarter of the footwear industry's retail trade. His purchase of Sears, the foundation of his footwear empire, in 1953 was a turning-point in British business practice: using an aggressively contested takeover, he realized assets by selling freeholds and leasing them back to a holding company. In the 1960s Clore continued in property; ultimately his property partnership with Jack COTTON merged with Land Securities in 1968, forming the UK's largest property company. Clore

then withdrew from active business, concentrating on his philanthropic interests.

CLOUGH, ARTHUR HUGH (1819–61), poet. The exemplar of Victorian 'critical pessimism', Clough, a pupil of Thomas ARNOLD at Rugby and subsequently a Fellow of Oriel College, Oxford, wrestled throughout his life with matters spiritual and intellectual (he was active in the Oxford Movement representing a revival of Anglo-Catholicism), as also with persistent ill health. Much of his poetry remained unpublished in his lifetime, but by 1900 *The Collected Poems* had been reprinted 16 times, and, in one of Britain's darkest wartime hours, it was Clough whom Winston CHURCHILL quoted when he declaimed 'Westward look, the land is bright.'

CLYNNOG (OR CLENNOCK), MORYS (*c.* 1525–81), churchman. Oxford-educated, Clynnog was enthusiastic for Roman Catholic renewal and became chaplain to Reginald POLE, but his nomination as Bishop of Bangor was blocked by MARY I's death. He left for Rome in 1559 and in 1567 was appointed officer for the hospital for English pilgrims; this became the basis for the English College, training priests for the English mission, and he was made first rector in 1578. Disagreements (partly over supposed favouritism shown to Welsh students) continued after his removal in favour of Jesuit leadership in 1579. He drowned while travelling to Spain.

CNUT, KING *see* essay on page 186

COBBE, FRANCES (1822–1904), women's rights advocate. Born into an Anglo-Irish landowning family, Cobbe sought independence from it following the death of her father in 1857. Initially she worked with delinquent children but from the early 1860s her main work was as a writer and journalist concerned with women's rights, especially those of married women. Her article 'Criminals, Idiots, Women and Minors' (1868) argued for women's legal right to divorce, child custody and economic independence; *Wife Torture* (1878) proposed that wife assault be grounds for legal separation and was some influence on the Matrimonial Causes Act 1878, which gave a wife the right to separation with maintenance and custody of the children under the age of 10. From 1870, she was also a leading campaigner against vivisection.

COBBETT, WILLIAM *see* essay on page 187

COBDEN, RICHARD (1804–65), politician. The son of a Sussex farmer, he became a Manchester-based calico-printer, an ardent advocate of Free

continued on page 188

CNUT (*c.* 994–1035)
King of the English (1016–35)

The younger son of SVEIN FORKBEARD, King of Denmark, Cnut succeeded to the English kingdom after he and his father, who died in 1013, had defeated King ETHELRED II THE UNREADY (978–1016) and he had overcome the subsequent resistance of Ethelred's son EDMUND IRONSIDE. Cnut's conquest should be seen as part of a long-standing Scandinavian interest in making conquests in the British Isles, which went back at least to the time of ALFRED THE GREAT and continued until long after the Norman Conquest. His reign in England is nonetheless an exceptional episode in that for a short period the kingdom became part of a large North Sea empire when Cnut succeeded his brother as King of Denmark in 1018–19 and annexed Norway in 1028 by driving out the Norwegian King St OLAF.

After an initial period of turbulence during which Cnut imposed his regime by violence, killing, for example, the slippery EADRIC STREONA in 1017, and taking exceptionally heavy tributes and taxation from his new subjects, his rule in England was largely a peaceful one which emphasized continuity from previous kings. He secured his regime further by marrying EMMA, Ethelred the Unready's widow, in 1017, a union which isolated Emma's exiled sons, EDWARD THE CONFESSOR and ALFRED, and left them without a clear base for intervention in England. The exceptionally detailed law-codes of his reign owed a great deal to the work of Archbishop WULFSTAN II of York and represent both a continuation of the law-giving of earlier English kings and a remarkably wide-ranging manifestation of those activities. Cnut, who had been a pagan in his youth, converted to Christianity some considerable time before becoming King of the English and, for much of his life, was an ostentatious and generous patron of the Church; the history of the Church in England during his reign was by and large one of prosperity and continuity. The composition of England's ruling aristocracy was, however, significantly changed. In his early years he replaced several Anglo-Saxon ealdormen with his military commanders, who, although often called earls by his historians, exercised authority over one or more shires like their predecessors. While new Danish landholders were given possessions in almost every shire in England, it is, nonetheless, generally believed that the aristocracy remained more Anglo-Saxon than Anglo-Scandinavian. By the end of the reign the two most powerful men in the kingdom after the King were GODWINE, Earl of Wessex, and LEOFRIC, Earl of Mercia, both English in origin. It should be noted, however, that

Godwine, who was to play a fateful role in the politics of eleventh-century England, although of English descent, owed his prominence entirely to Cnut.

As the ruler of two – and, briefly, three – kingdoms, Cnut was a king of European stature. He demonstrated his eminence by attending the coronation of the Emperor Conrad II in Rome in 1027 and, at the end of his life, he arranged for his daughter GUNNHILDA to marry Conrad's son, the future Henry III. Cnut's control of his extensive territories was, however, never entirely secure. Norway was especially problematic; his power there was crumbling by the time of his death and his son was easily supplanted. Denmark too required regular military intervention to maintain his authority. The loyalty of some of Cnut's associates in the conquest of England, such as THORKELL THE TALL, proved questionable. Cnut's domestic circumstances were also complex, since alongside his marriage to Emma, he also maintained ÆLFGIFU OF NORTHAMPTON, a woman of Mercian origin, by whom he had had children; this overt *ménage à trois*, seemingly managed during Cnut's lifetime by despatching Ælfgifu and her offspring to distant parts of his territories, such as, after 1028, the kingdom of Norway to act as Cnut's regent, suggests that certain aspects of Cnut's Christianity were only skin-deep. The result was that after his death his sons by his two wives, HAROLD I HAREFOOT and HARTHACNUT, disputed rule over his kingdoms and, with their respective deaths in 1040 and 1042, Cnut's great Danish North Sea empire fell apart. The restoration of the Anglo-Saxon line in 1042 in the person of Edward the Confessor meant that Danish rule over England was only a short episode.

In England, Cnut's achievement was the preservation of the strong monarchy created by the tenth-century kings. There can be no doubt that he personally was a strong and effective ruler. The brevity of his empire was the result of the turbulent dynastic politics typical of the early medieval period and of the early deaths of his sons. The (possibly apocryphal) story telling how he demonstrated to his courtiers that he could not hold back the sea first appeared about a century after his death (*see* HENRY OF HUNTINGDON), its purpose being to show the humility of the former pagan and his awareness that the power of a king was limited. Historians no longer use the Anglicized form of his name, Canute.

M. K. Lawson, *Cnut: The Danes in England in the Early Eleventh Century* (1993)
Frank Barlow, *The English Church, 1000–1066* (1979)

COBBETT, WILLIAM (1763–1835)
Radical journalist

He was born in Farnham (Surrey), where his father was a small farmer. He joined the army in 1784, served in Nova Scotia, and became a sergeant-major. In 1791, on returning to England, he sought in vain to expose corruption in the army and was forced to take refuge in France and then America. Essentially an old Tory patriot, he was fierce in his defence of Britain against the French Revolution while living in Philadelphia (1792–9) and returned to Britain in 1800 still a Tory. During these years he had taught himself journalism. On his return to England he began to publish transcripts of State trials and parliamentary debates and, from 1802, edited his great newspaper, the *Weekly Political Register*. Initially adopting a strongly conservative anti-French nationalism Cobbett moved by 1806 to advocacy of parliamentary reform. By 1810 his reputation for radicalism was sealed by his being sentenced to two years in Newgate for seditious libel. In 1816 the influence of the *Political Register* was greatly extended when he introduced a cheap edition, the 'Twopenny Trash'. In a flourishing radical 'pauper press' – cheap newspapers aimed at a popular audience and engaged in constant struggles against the restrictions imposed by the State through libel laws and stamp duties – the *Political Register* emerged as the most important. At its height in the years 1816–20 it sold up to 44,000 copies a week, giving it a probable readership of 10–15 times as many.

In the *Political Register* Cobbett constantly railed against 'Old Corruption', the system of sinecures, placemen and privilege which radicals identified as the centre of corrupt aristocratic power. Cobbett added little that was new to formal radical argument: Tom PAINE's *Rights of Man* (1791–2) had brilliantly put the radical critique of aristocratic government. But Cobbett's genius was to speak plainly in emphatic and angry terms and provide a means of communication for a movement for parliamentary reform which, after 1815, was both becoming increasingly national in its spread and working-class in social base. The paper could not only be read but read aloud to audiences with variable standards of literacy. It also carried a radicalism which spoke from within a traditional framework. It was to the 'free-born' Englishman that he spoke, to those whose 'independence' and 'rights' were being destroyed by industrialization and the new ideologies of 'progress' like utilitarianism. Industrial labour, be it of men and women or of children, was 'unnatural'. Against this Cobbett celebrated the 'virtues' of an idealized past in which the 'little man' – the small farmer or the independent artisan – had enjoyed a robust independence and individualism. At the centre of his moral and political outlook was labour. As he wrote in his 'Address to the Journeymen and Labourers' (*Political Register*, 2 November 1816): 'the real strength and all the resources of a country spring from the labour of its people'. The condition of the labourer, especially the agricultural labourer, was the standard by which a society must be measured. The labourer's social rights – to make an honest living in exchange for his labour, to be supported in times of distress, to live in the country of his birth – had been stolen by the ravages of a bloated aristocracy, especially through the expropriation of medieval Church lands at the time of the Reformation. Political reform would restore such rights. Yet if there was much in Cobbett which suggested a possible restoration of the old ways of a mythologized social compact of medieval duty and obligation between the Church and landowners on the one side, the common people on the other, he also recognized the need for labourers as a class to organize in political associations and in trade unionism to defend and extend the rights of labour. That is, Cobbett was at the cusp of two traditions: one, looking backwards, modelled itself on the preservation of a predominantly rural and traditional world; the other looked forward to welcome and encourage the formation of a labour movement. Yet that which predominates in him is the conservative vision, embodied in not only the *Political Register* but also in his prolific other works like *A Grammar of the English Language* (1818) and, most famous of all, *Rural Rides* (1830). That book, written in 1821, after he had fled England once more in 1817 and returned in 1819 to take up farming again, describes his travels around England. It continued the attack on corruption and the aristocracy and extolled the values and ways of life of the countryside. It was also a vision which contributed not only to anti-industrialism but also to conservative 'Englishness' which have been such important cultural themes since.

Raymond Williams, Cobbett (Past Masters Series) (1983)

Trade and a founder member of the Anti-Corn Law League. Elected to Parliament in 1841, he played a key role in the campaign for the abolition of the Corn Laws. The Cobden–Chevalier Treaty, a reciprocal trade agreement by which France would admit British machinery, coal, textiles and iron on a reduced tariff, and in return Britain would reduce the duty on French wines, brandy and silk, a further step towards Free Trade, was another success. Cobden himself was a failure as a businessman and was rescued from ruin only by public subscription.

COBHAM, BARON, 4TH *see* OLDCASTLE, SIR JOHN; **11TH** *see* BROOKE, HENRY; **1ST VISCOUNT** *see* TEMPLE, RICHARD; **2ND EARL** *see* GRENVILLE-TEMPLE, RICHARD

COBHAM, ELEANOR (Duchess of Gloucester) (?–1452). Widely perceived as an ambitious adventuress when HUMPHREY OF GLOUCESTER repudiated his first wife in order to marry her in 1428, she became one of the most notorious women of the century. Her dabbling in the occult was used by her husband's political enemies to discredit him, and in 1441 she was tried on charges of sorcery, necromancy and treason (as wife of the heir presumptive to the throne, she was accused of conspiring to be queen). On being found guilty, she was divorced, forced to submit to a humiliating public penance and imprisoned for life.

COCHRANE, THOMAS (10th Earl of Dundonald) (1775–1860), sailor, politician and adventurer. First going to sea in his uncle's frigate in 1793, Cochrane, now commanding a brig, captured a large Spanish frigate on 6 May 1801. Commanding frigates after 1803, and leading a fireship attack against the French fleet in 1811, Cochrane's exploits made him a national hero. He then had a turbulent political career as a radical MP but in 1814 went to prison for stock exchange fraud. Abandoning Britain, Cochrane commanded Chile's fleet against the Spanish, and Brazil's ships against the Portuguese, and commanded the Greek squadron in the war against Turkey, participating in the Battle of Navarino in Oct. 1827. Reinstated in the navy in 1832, he was disappointed when, at the age of 80, he was refused a command in the Crimean War and had to content himself with developing and urging (unsuccessfully) the use of poison gas against Sebastopol.

COCKBURN, CLAUD (1904–81), journalist. After leaving Oxford, he worked for *The Times* and could have followed a conventional career in journalism, but in 1932 Cockburn set up his own rudimentary 'newsletter', *The Week*. With an approach new in British journalism, he published all the gossip, innuendo and speculation that the rest of the staid, pre-tabloid conservative-minded British press deemed unfit to print. Sometimes he was very wide of the mark, and sometimes he was proved gloriously right. He invented the term 'the Cliveden set' to describe those in government and Fleet Street who supported the appeasement of Hitler in the late 1930s. *The Week* became essential reading in the corridors of power throughout Europe, and it acquired a reputation out of all proportion to its circulation. It also inspired a new generation of journalists and satirists to found *Private Eye* with which he was involved from the start, and in 1963 he was guest editor of that magazine during the famous PROFUMO scandal. A member of the Communist Party, during the 1930s he was on the staff of the party newspaper, the *Daily Worker.*

COCKCROFT, SIR JOHN (1897–1967), physicist. Cockcroft studied mathematics at Manchester University, served in the army during the First World War and developed engineering skills at Metropolitan Vickers and Manchester's College of Technology. He studied mathematics at Cambridge University and, in 1924, started researching atomic nuclei under RUTHERFORD at the Cavendish Laboratory. In 1932 he and Ernest Walton split lithium and boron nuclei with a beam of protons accelerated in a high-voltage particle accelerator of their own design. They were hailed as the first scientists to split the atomic nucleus and won the 1951 Nobel Prize for Physics. Their work paved the way for particle physics. During the Second World War Cockcroft was Chief Superintendent of the Air Defence and Research Establishment and participated in the atomic bomb programme. He was Jacksonian Professor of Natural Philosophy at Cambridge (1939–46) and head of the Atomic Energy Research Establishment at Harwell (1946–59), where he helped build Britain's first nuclear reactors and worked on nuclear fusion.

COGIDUBNUS (*fl.* AD 40s). Known only from one literary reference and an inscription found at Chichester in 1723, he appears to have been either a Briton or a Gaul to whom the Romans gave authority in part of southern Britain soon after AD 43, and who may have continued in that role until the time of AGRICOLA. The magnificent villa at Fishbourne in Sussex may well have been his main residence.

COHEN, SIR JOHN (JACK) (originally Jacob Kohen) (1898–1979), entrepreneur. Cohen, whose Tesco shopping empire has been one of the retailing and commercial successes of modern

Britain, came from an East End tailoring family. He escaped from the confines of the sweatshop in 1915 to join the Royal Flying Corps; he turned to street trading after the war, and became known as the quintessential costermonger, self-confident, cheeky and loud. Through his wife's influence he subsequently moved into wholesaling, first of soap and then of tea. The Tesco brand name was born. Through the 1930s Cohen brought his street-trading techniques into retailing, piling the goods high and selling them cheap in outlets acquired in the new shopping arcades being built throughout London. He responded to wartime food shortages by entering farming and food-processing; then in 1947, after a visit to the USA, he introduced self-service shopping. The abolition of food rationing sped up his retail revolution; a decade later, the abolition of retail price maintenance against which Cohen had fought for so long promoted national expansion. Much growth was achieved by takeover, culminating in the absorption in 1968 of Tesco's great rival Victor Value.

COIFI (early seventh century). A pagan high priest at the court of King EDWIN of Northumbria, made famous in BEDE's *Ecclesiastical History* because of his ritual desecration of a pagan shrine. His explanation that the gods had failed to bring him material prosperity is an interesting comment on the way in which England was converted to Christianity, because it shows how (Bede believed) early converts saw wealth and success in warfare as indications of the Christian God's superiority.

COKAYNE, SIR WILLIAM (?–1626), entrepreneur. A London merchant, he became Governor of the City-sponsored colonization project in Ulster in 1612. In 1614 he enlisted government aid to break the Merchant Adventurers' monopoly in cloth export and to stimulate the English finishing industry by banning unfinished cloth exports. Corrupt and under-capitalized, his new company could not cope with reorganizing the trade and, after a trade crisis, the Merchant Adventurers regained their privileges in 1616; the affair generated much public anger. Cockayne nevertheless went on to be knighted and made Lord Mayor, cushioned by his huge wealth and by six sons-in-law who were peers.

COKE, SIR EDWARD (1552–1634), lawyer. Coke's family connections with the East Anglian Catholic recusant community gave him much employment early in his legal career, before he entered a wider world as Solicitor General in 1592, Speaker of the Commons in 1593, and Attorney General in 1594; his advancement earned him the jealous hatred of Francis BACON. Continuing to combine frequent Commons service with legal eminence, he began publishing law reports in 1600 and became Chief Justice of the Common Pleas in 1606. His feud with Bacon and his independent attitude to JAMES I's government culminated in his dismissal in 1616. Fiercely opposing James's pro-Spanish policies, he was sent temporarily to the Tower in 1622, but continued to personify legalistic opposition. Publication of his monumental *Institutes of the Laws of England* was completed only in 1644. This and his other writings decisively shaped the legal profession's view of its past and hence its priorities for the future, notably its sense of its own importance.

COKE, THOMAS (1st Earl of Leicester of Holkham) (1752–1842), agricultural improver. Inheriting a large Norfolk estate, Holkham Hall, from his father, he was elected MP in 1776. A persistent Foxite Whig (*see* FOX, CHARLES JAMES), he sat until the Reform Act 1832, by which time he was the 'father of the House'. Between 1778 and 1821 he held annual meetings at Holkham to demonstrate progressive farming methods, expending vast sums in the improvement of his estate. He encouraged good farming practice among his tenants, giving them security in the form of long leases, and publicized the merits of 'Norfolk husbandry', in particular the use of marls and clover, new grasses and artificial feeds. Although challenged by some of his political critics, his achievements (which he himself exaggerated) were celebrated, and he is believed to have increased the annual rental on his estate from £2,200 to £20,000.

COLE, G(EORGE) D(OUGLAS) H(OWARD) (1889–1958), socialist intellectual and historian. He produced over 50 works in the fields of economics, socialist theory and labour history, notably *Practical Economics* (1937), *The Common People* (with R. W. Postgate, 1938), *Chartist Portraits* (1941) and *A History of Socialist Thought* (1953–8); a number of his works were co-authored with his wife Margaret COLE. In his early years he promoted the idea of small-scale co-operation (guild socialism), and as a member of the New Fabian Research Bureau (1931–5) he influenced Labour Party policy through his advocacy of a socialist planned economy. As well as teaching at Oxford University (1925–57) he was a leading exponent of adult education through the Workers' Educational Association.

COLE, HENRY (1808–82), designer. A moving spirit behind the Great Exhibition of 1851, mounted to demonstrate Britain's manufacturing prowess, Cole supported the design of Joseph Paxton's great glass edifice in Hyde Park against critics and jeremiads. The exhibition was a notable popular success, and with the surplus raised from the sale of tickets Cole, who had been appointed Secretary to the Department of Science and Art, was able to realize his dream of a complex of museums on the South Kensington estate which now houses the Science, Natural History and Victoria and Albert museums, as well as the Imperial College of Science, the Royal Colleges of Art, Music and Organists and the Albert Hall. Criticized by those of more delicate sensibilities, like RUSKIN, for vulgar commercialism at the expense of art, Cole's mission was to ensure a high standard of design of mass-produced goods for an industrial age.

COLE, DAME MARGARET (née Postgate) (1893–1980), socialist. From a family of liberal intellectuals, she was educated at Girton College, Cambridge. Her brother's imprisonment as a conscientious objector during the First World War drew her to socialist politics: she left teaching to join the Fabian research department at a time when Labour politics were in a period of formation and intense discussion. By 1918, with her husband (*see* COLE, G. D. H.), she had come to oppose the Webbs' form of State socialism (*see* WEBB, BEATRICE and WEBB, SIDNEY), instead advocating a form of industrial democracy and political pluralism known as guild socialism. The Coles rejoined the Fabian Society by the end of the 1920s (Margaret Cole served as its President from 1962–80), and the research which they undertook in the 1930s was to form the statistical underpinning of the post-war Labour government's social reform programme.

COLERIDGE, SAMUEL TAYLOR (1772–1834), poet and philosopher. Youngest of the 13 children of a Devon clergyman, Coleridge was educated at Cambridge University. Together with Robert SOUTHEY, he planned (but never established) a 'Pantisocracy', an ideal community to be established in America. He produced *The Watchman*, a political and literary journal, in 1796, and preached for Unitarian congregations. His literary partnership with William WORDSWORTH produced the *Lyrical Ballads* (1798), which included the poem for which Coleridge is best known, *The Rime of the Ancient Mariner*, and laid the foundations for English Romanticism. His early radicalism gave way to a philosophical conservatism, founded on a critique of the soulless materialism of developing industrial society. He published *Biographia Literaria* in 1817, the theological *Aids to Reflection* in 1825 and *On the Constitution of Church and State* in 1830. His idea of a 'clerisy' of teachers, priests, scientists and philosophers as an independent estate of the realm has appealed

to intellectuals ever since it was first proposed in 1833.

COLET, JOHN (?1466–1519), churchman. From a wealthy London family, Colet studied at Oxford and on the continent; after ordination in 1496 he lectured at Oxford on the Pauline Epistles, establishing himself as a leading English exponent of the humanist fascination with ancient Greek and Latin literature. He became Dean of St Paul's in 1505; his outspokenness on Church reform (e.g. in his speech to the Convocation of Canterbury in 1512) led to frequent serious confrontations with Bishop Richard Fitzjames of London. In 1518 he founded St Paul's school which, because of its statutes, remained distinctively free from clerical control.

COLLEGE, STEPHEN (?1635–1681), carpenter and anti-papist. Known as 'the Protestant joiner', College was a London carpenter whose skill in joinery brought him into contact with powerful patrons, such as William, Lord RUSSELL, who, at the time of the Popish-Plot scare set off by the accusations of Titus OATES, encouraged him to denounce the superstitions of popery in speeches and broadsides. College played a part in the trial of Lord Stafford (*see* HOWARD, WILLIAM), testifying to the respectability of one of the witnesses against him. When CHARLES II, battling against those who wished to exclude his Catholic brother (the future JAMES II) from the line of succession (*see* COOPER, ANTHONY ASHLEY), convened Parliament in Oxford in 1681 (which some parliamentarians feared might be a means of strong-arming Parliament) College went there on horseback, wearing armour, carrying weapons and advocating resistance. In June he was arrested in London and charged with seditious words, but a grand jury impanelled by Whig sheriffs dismissed the charges. The government then had him tried in Oxford. Some of the witnesses against him had previously given evidence against 'popish' conspirators, which it was argued made them credible. Amidst much controversy, College was found guilty of treason, hanged and quartered.

COLLEY, SIR GEORGE (1835–81), soldier. Second in his year at Sandhurst, Colley was commissioned without purchase into the 2nd Foot (1852), with whom he served in South Africa (1854–60) and China (1860). One of the finest military intellects of his day, Colley, after coming head of his year at Staff College, was chosen by WOLSELEY to command logistics for the Ashanti expedition. Now a part of Wolseley's circle, Colley was promoted Major-General in 1880. Early in 1881, to suppress a newly proclaimed Boer republic, Colley took a brigade into the Transvaal, occupying Majuba Hill, which overlooked Boer positions. Early on 27 Feb. Boer marksmen attacked up the hill, routing the British and killing Colley. Majuba Hill stirred an officers' debate, still raging, as to the relative merits of intellectual attainment and tactical competence in education.

COLLIER, JEREMY (1650–1725), religious writer and historian. Son of a cleric and schoolmaster, educated at Cambridge and later ordained, in 1688 he published a pamphlet arguing that JAMES II's flight did not constitute abdication and therefore the throne was not vacant; he was imprisoned but released without trial. After refusing to take oaths recognizing the legitimacy of WILLIAM III and MARY II as sovereigns, thus becoming a Non-juror (see also SANCROFT, WILLIAM), he wrote pamphlets on related subjects; his 1695 *Short View of the Immorality and Profaneness of the English Stage* was well received, receiving praise from William III and several Presbyterians, chiming as it did with contemporary interest in the reformation of manners. In 1696 Collier administered absolution to those to be executed for their involvement in a plot to assassinate William III; refusing to surrender for trial, he was outlawed. Consecrated Bishop by the Non-juring Bishop Hickes in 1713, he led the movement from 1715, adopting a separate liturgy for Non-jurors based on the 1549 rather than the 1552 Prayer Book. The intellectual integrity behind his polemic and his refusal to contemplate reconciliation with mainstream Anglicanism helped the Non-jurors endure well into the eighteenth century (see also DEACON, THOMAS).

COLLIER, MARY (c. 1689–c. 1762), poet. The first published working-class woman poet in England, she came from Hants., where her parents taught her to read. Collier worked as a laundress and in other manual tasks, and in 1739 published *The Woman's Labour* in reply to DUCK's *The Thresher's Labour*, criticizing male prejudices about working women as well as further exploring agricultural and domestic labour as subject matter. Her collected poems were published with an autobiographical preface in 1762.

COLLINS, ANTHONY (1676–1729), philosopher. From a wealthy family, he married into the banking CHILDs. After his friend LOCKE's death he began to publish books building on his ideas, particularly regarding religion, where he emerged as a leading Deist. Several of his works rejected priestly authority, and others attacked both the literal and allegorical interpretations of the Bible as nonsensical, leading to criticism from such contrasting figures as WHISTON and WARBURTON.

COLLINS, JOHN (also known as Canon Collins) 1905– 82), anti-nuclear campaigner. Educated at Sidney Sussex College and Westcott House, Cambridge, Collins was curate of Whitstable (Kent) in 1928–9 and chaplain of Sidney Sussex College. He was Dean of Oriel College, Oxford (1938–48) and canon of St Paul's Cathedral, London (1948–81), where he gained attention for his controversial sermons. Actively involved in numerous political crusades, he was one of the founders of the Campaign for Nuclear Disarmament (CND) in 1958 and later acted as its Chairman. A vociferous campaigner against apartheid, Collins was awarded a Gold Medal from the UN Special Committee against Apartheid in 1978.

COLLINS, MICHAEL (1890–1922), Irish politician and soldier. The son of a farmer from west Cork, he returned to Ireland after a period in London to join the Easter Rising of 1916. After release from internment in Dec. 1916, he became Secretary to the reformed Irish Republican Brotherhood and assumed its presidency in 1917. He was a member of the first Dáil Eireann (the Irish Parliament, made up of Sinn Féin MPs returned in the 1918 Westminster election) and Minister for Finance in its underground government, but also organized and led attacks on British forces, including the killing of 11 British intelligence officers in Dublin in Nov. 1920. Collins proved a capable administrator (he organized a successful 'Dáil loan' campaign, financing the underground government through public subscriptions repayable after independence), a ruthless and energetic guerrilla commander, and a skilful negotiator in the Dáil's delegation to the London conference of Oct. 1921. He signed the Anglo-Irish Treaty of Dec. 1921 which established the Irish Free State with dominion status. When DE VALERA resigned after the Dáil ratified the treaty, Collins headed a provisional government recognized by the British to implement the treaty (though in Irish eyes he remained nominally subordinate to Arthur GRIFFITH, head of the Dáil government which continued to exist until elections were held, after which the two governments merged under Griffith). At the same time, Collins sponsored clandestine operations aimed at destabilizing the government of Northern Ireland. During the Irish Civil War (1922–3) between pro- and anti-treaty forces, he became the Free State's Commander-in-Chief. On Griffith's death on 12 Aug. 1922 his dominance was unquestionable, but he died on 20 Aug. in an ambush in Co. Cork. Widely admired as a courageous and romantic leader, he was known as 'the Big Fellow'; those dissatisfied with the subsequent development of Irish society often speculate that things might have been better had he survived.

COLLINS, WILKIE (1824–89), novelist. Son of a landscape painter, and a friend and collaborator of Charles DICKENS, he was a prolific writer but secured recognition only with *The Woman in White* (1860), acclaimed as one of the finest examples of sensation fiction, and *The Moonstone* (1868), often called the first detective novel. His popularity, principally as a writer of mystery and suspense, was exceeded only by that of Dickens.

COLMÁN, ST (?–676), Bishop of Lindisfarne. Colmán was sent from Iona to Lindisfarne following the death of FÍNÁN in 661. During his episcopate, OSWY, King of Northumbria, convened the Synod of Whitby in 664 to resolve the disparity between the Irish and Roman methods of calculating the date of Easter (*see* BEDE). The decision in favour of St WILFRID and Rome may have been as much a political one as ecclesiastical. Colmán returned first to Iona, then to Ireland, with those who wished to continue the Irish observance, ultimately establishing a new monastery, Mayo of the Saxons, on the west coast of Ireland. He maintained good relations with Oswy, who accepted his recommendation of Eata, Abbot of Melrose, as his successor as Bishop of Lindisfarne.

COLQUHOUN, PATRICK (1745–1820), magistrate and pamphleteer. His father was registrar of the records of Dumbarton, and he was educated at the grammar school there. Having gone to Virginia at the age of 15, he returned in 1766 and became a Glasgow merchant. Prominent in commercial lobbying and in local improvement schemes, he was elected Lord Provost of the city (1782–3). In 1783 he founded the Glasgow Chamber of Commerce and was its first Chairman. In 1789 Colquhoun moved to London and, three years later, was appointed one of the new metropolitan police magistrates through DUNDAS's patronage. In numerous pamphlets he attempted to estimate the extent of London's vice and crime, and suggested schemes for improving public institutions and policies. His works included *Treatise on the Police of the Metropolis* (1795), *A Treatise on Indigence* (1806) and *Treatise on the Wealth, Power and Resources of the British Empire* (1814), which historians frequently use as a basis for estimating the distribution of wealth across the early nineteenth-century social structure.

COLSTON, EDWARD (1636–1721), slave-trader and philanthropist. The son of a Bristol Royalist merchant, he began his career in his father's wine importing business, and built his first fortune expanding its market from Spain to other parts of the western Mediterranean. In 1680 he became a member of the Royal African Co., which controlled the trade between England, her American colonies and the West African coast. Colston's manufactured trading beads that were exchanged with other goods for slaves, who were then transported in densely packed holds to the West Indies and mainland North America. Bristol and Liverpool were among the English ports that benefited most from the trade. Although a High Churchman and often in conflict with the Whig corporation of Bristol, Colston transferred a large segment of his original shareholding to WILLIAM III at the beginning of 1689, securing the new regime's favour for the African Co. The value of Colston's shares increased and being without heirs he began to donate large sums to charities, principally educational ones including Christ's Hospital in London and Queen Elizabeth's school in Bristol. He withdrew from the African Co. in 1692 but continued trading in slaves privately. In 1708 he founded Colston's school in Bristol, and a further school, Temple, for his own Bristol parish in 1712. Colston was MP for Bristol (1710–13). His life demonstrates how it was possible for the morally righteous to play leading roles in the slave trade while elsewhere pursuing good works.

COLUM CILLE, ST *see* essay on page 193

COLUMBA, ST *see* COLUM CILLE

COLUMBANUS (530 or 545–612), monastic reformer. He was one of the great figures of early western European monasticism. Born in Leinster, Columbanus began his monastic life in St Comgall's foundation at Bangor. Although almost nothing is known of most of his lifetime, he set out on pilgrimage to Europe in *c.* 590 with 12 companions. After visiting the Burgundian court, he established the monasteries of Annegray, Luxeuil and Fontaine. Disciples flocked to these new establishments, which quickly became involved in the ecclesiastical and political life of Merovingian Gaul. Following his enforced departure from Gaul, he crossed the Alps into Lombardy and founded the monastery of Bobbio, where he died in 612. Columbanus provided an extraordinary impetus and direction to the growth of monasticism in Europe, as many religious houses founded in seventh-century Gaul were inspired by his work at Luxeuil. His *Rule* was widely adopted, while his penitential and introduction of frequent, private confession wrought a revolution in the penance-discipline of continental Europe. A confidant of kings, his surviving letters to the Pope of *c.* 604 provide the only record of the justification for the Irish dating of Easter prior to the adoption of the Roman calculation.

COMBE, GEORGE (1788–1858), phrenologist. Combe was educated in his native Edinburgh and

continued on page 194

COLUM CILLE (OR COLUMBA), ST (*c.* 521–97)
Abbot

Founder of Iona, Columba is one of the great figures of early British Christianity. Born of royal blood in Ireland as Crimthainn mac Feidlimid into the ruling Cenél Conaill dynasty of the Uí Néill, his close kinsmen in the later sixth century were kings of Tara. He appears to have been given the name Colum Cille (literally, 'the dove of the church') as a baptismal name and to have been committed to the Church at an early age. In spite of the missionary efforts of the likes of St PATRICK and PALLADIUS, Ireland was still essentially pagan at this time, and it may be that the adoption of Christianity by such a prominent figure as Colum Cille provided the new religion with respectability among the nobility of Ireland.

Colum Cille was fostered by a priest called Cruithnechán and studied first in Leinster and then under a bishop who was probably Finnian of Clonard. In 561 the Cenél Conaill fought the ruling Southern Uí Néill at Cul Drebene, 'and prevailed through the prayers of Colum Cille', following which, as ADOMNÁN (on whose life of Colum Cille we rely for a great deal of our information) relates that he was excommunicated by a synod held in Southern Uí Néill territory. Other than this tantalizing glimpse of what must have been a significant political event which seems to have provoked a personal crisis, little is known of his life prior to his departure for the Western Isles of Scotland two years later. Colum Cille arrived in Dál Riata in 563 and was granted the island of Iona by its King, CONALL MAC COMGAILL. Although this journey may well have been a penance for his excommunication, it is important to bear in mind that peoples from what we now call Ireland and Scotland moved regularly across the North Channel during this period. Colum Cille was taking a route that many had taken before him.

It is uncertain precisely when he founded the monastery of Iona, for he seems to have visited the court of the Pictish King, BRIDEI, SON OF MÁILCON, beforehand and other churches are associated with him in Dál Riata. He is known to have travelled in Pictland and returned several times to Ireland, establishing a network both of churches and of political connections. In time, however, the remote island of Iona became his base and because of the links which Colum Cille established it became a place of immense renown in the early history of Christian Britain. He had a reputation for wisdom and holiness and was a celebrated scholar. In the century following his death, several *vitae* were written about him, although only that written by Adomnán has survived. He has acquired a reputation as the evangelist of the Picts, but this may not be historically accurate since no mention is made of such work by Adomnán. His achievements at Iona were certainly the basis for the later conversion of the Picts and for St AIDAN's foundation of the community at Lindisfarne and for his missionary work in Northumbria during the abbacy at Iona of SÉGÉNE. In his last years, Colum Cille founded abbeys in Ireland, which gave him great influence there. His political achievements included presiding over the so-called Convention of Drumcett (Co. Derry) in 575 between AEDÁN MAC GABRÁIN, King of Dál Riata, and the Irish High-King Aed mac Ainmerech, which settled the terms on which the kings of Scots Dál Riata ruled their Irish lands. A life-style of travel, prayer and political mediation was the norm for an exceptionally holy man at this time.

The community on Iona remained famous as a spiritual and missionary centre until Viking raids forced its inmates to leave in the ninth century. Subsequently refounded, its prestige was never as great as it had been in the time of Colum Cille and the abbots who succeeded him. The confederation of monasteries established by Colum Cille stretched from Durrow and Derry in Ireland, to Tiree and Hinba off the west coast of Scotland, to Lindisfarne off the north-east coast of England. It proved to be a major force in propagating Irish and Celtic values of personal austerity and humility during the period of the conversion of the English to Christianity in the seventh century. It was also a network which produced religious manuscripts of extraordinarily high quality. The famous *Book of Kells*, for example, which is now preserved in the library of Trinity College, Dublin, may well have been written and illuminated at Kells in the eighth century or early ninth century. Another of the confederation's products is the Lindisfarne Gospels. Colum Cille died on 9 June 597 in the chapel at Iona and was buried there. When Iona became an insecure resting-place due to the increasing menace from the Vikings, the relics were moved first to Dunkeld (Perths.) and subsequently to Kells in Ireland.

Alan Orr Anderson and Majorie Ogilvie Anderson (eds), *Adomnan's Life of Columba (1961)*
Alfred P. Smyth, *Warlords and Holy Men: Scotland*, AD *800–1000 (1984)*

subsequently worked as a lawyer. Initially sceptical of phrenology, a practice in which judgements of human character and mental powers are based on an external study of the cranium, he was converted to it in 1817 after attending lectures by the phrenologist Johann Gaspar Spurzheim. Subsequently he became the leading British champion and developer of phrenology: he lectured on it throughout the country, and founded, with his brother Andrew, a physician, the Edinburgh Phrenological Society (1820). He published numerous works on phrenology, notably the best-selling *Constitution of Man* (1828), expressing his fundamental belief that phrenology was a credible science of human nature that offered self-knowledge and which was open to all educated people. In conservative sections of society his phrenological claims were attacked as scientifically dubious, materialist and atheistic, but by the late 1820s he was enjoying a considerable following throughout Britain, not least because phrenology harmonized with existing values of self-improvement and moral earnestness.

COMENIUS, JAN (1592–1670), writer and educationist. Born in Bohemia, Comenius (or Komensky) became a pastor of the Bohemian Brethren (the Moravian Church). In 1628 he fled the Bohemian political crisis and travelled widely in Europe, spending time in England on the invitation of John PYM and others in the Long Parliament in the 1640s. His numerous writings on education advocated tolerance and persuasion, to hasten what he saw as a dawning peaceful new age of rational Christianity; he also wrote widely on science. Though the Civil Wars in the British Isles strained his optimism and made him leave England, he remained much admired in British intellectual circles.

COMPTON, HENRY (1632–1713), churchman. The younger son of the Earl of Northampton, and thus of a strongly Royalist family, he was ordained in 1666 and promoted rapidly through family connections and his friendship with Thomas OSBORNE, Earl of Danby, becoming Bishop of Oxford in 1674 and of London in 1675. In 1676 he oversaw the 'Compton census' on behalf of Danby, who hoped to gather statistics on religious adherence that would prove to CHARLES II that the Dissenters were not a substantial force and could be crushed through rigorous enforcement of the penal laws. (The census suggested that only one in 22 adults was a Nonconformist, although some conformists probably also attended Dissenting meetings.)

Although he had opposed the campaign to exclude the future JAMES II from succeeding to the throne, Compton did take issue with his Catholicizing policies. He was dismissed from the Privy Council for opposing James's claim to be able to use his power to dispense Catholics from the Test Act (that is, remove the bar to their holding public office); in 1686 he was suspended from his see for refusing to discipline a clergyman for anti-papal sermons. He was the only cleric to sign the invitation to William of Orange (the future WILLIAM III), and played a prominent part in the Glorious Revolution, at one point acting as colonel of a regiment. Reinstated as Bishop of London and as Privy Councillor, he crowned William III and MARY II in 1689.

COMPTON, SPENCER (1st Earl of Wilmington) (*c.* 1673–1743), Whig politician. Commanding trust, but of no great ability, Compton was elected Speaker of the Commons in 1715. He served as Treasurer to the Household of the Prince of Wales, whose intention on succeeding as GEORGE II was to make him first minister. Once faced with the realities of administration Compton felt inadequate to the task and asked Sir Robert WALPOLE for advice; he did not resist when, with the help of Queen CAROLINE, Walpole secured his hold on office. In 1728 Compton became Earl of Wilmington; in 1730 he became Lord President of the Council. In 1742, when Walpole fell, the King turned to the elderly Wilmington to head the ministry, but CARTERET, PULTENEY and PELHAM were the dominant figures, the latter succeeding when Wilmington died.

COMYN, ALEXANDER (6th [2nd Comyn] Earl of Buchan) (?–1289), politician and soldier. Son of the Justiciar of Scotland, William Comyn, from the time of his father's death in 1233 he played an important part in Scottish politics. During the minority of ALEXANDER III he led one of the parties contending for control of the Council. In 1264 he harried the Western Isles to punish them for supporting the King of Norway's side in his great campaign of the previous year. From 1286 to his death he was one of the six guardians of the realm on behalf of the child Queen, MARGARET, MAID OF NORWAY.

COMYN, JOHN THE ELDER (Lord of Badenoch) (?–1303), nobleman. Known to contemporaries as the 'Red Comyn' (the usual sobriquet for the head of the family), and to some historians as the 'Black Comyn', he was chosen in 1286 as one of the six guardians of the realm of Scotland for the child Queen, MARGARET, THE MAID OF NORWAY. After her death he became the most powerful supporter of the claim to the throne of his brother-in-law JOHN BALLIOL, who was made King in 1292. In 1296 he submitted to EDWARD I but by 1298 had joined the resistance movement led by William WALLACE.

COMYN, JOHN (7th [3rd Comyn] Earl of Buchan) (*c.* 1255–1308), soldier. He succeeded his father Alexander COMYN and, like the rest of the Comyns, he supported JOHN BALLIOL as King of Scots but was forced to submit to EDWARD I in 1296. Sent by Edward to suppress William WALLACE, he disappointed the King by fighting against him at the Battle of Falkirk (1297). Despite the Scottish defeat there he continued the struggle for independence until 1304, by which time it seemed hopeless. ROBERT BRUCE'S murder of his cousin John COMYN in 1306 ensured that he remained on the English side until he died, unlike his wife Isabella, who went to assist at Bruce's inauguration as King (and, according to English chroniclers, to become Bruce's mistress), for which offence Edward had her confined in a cage in Berwick Castle (where she stayed until 1310). Her husband was defeated by Bruce at Inverurie, and fled to England, where he died.

COMYN, JOHN (Lord of Badenoch, the Red Comyn) (?–1306), soldier. Head of the senior branch, the Red Comyns, the most powerful of the Scottish baronial families, from 1298 he was one of the leaders of Scottish resistance to EDWARD I until he submitted in 1304. As JOHN BALLIOL'S nephew, he stood close to the Scottish throne, and it was presumably this that lay behind his long-standing rivalry with ROBERT BRUCE, which culminated in his murder at Bruce's hands in the Greyfriars kirk of Dumfries on 10 Feb. 1306.

COMYN, WILLIAM (5th [1st Comyn] Earl of Buchan) (?–1233), royal servant. He obtained the title by marriage to Countess Margaret. His role in Anglo-Scottish relations during the reigns of WILLIAM I THE LION and ALEXANDER II helped to make the Comyns the most powerful baronial family in thirteenth-century Scotland. His second son Walter, Earl of Menteith, became virtual ruler of the realm during the minority of ALEXANDER III. He was buried in the Cistercian Abbey of Deer in Aberdeen, which he had founded in 1218.

CONALL CRANDOMNA (?–660), King of Dál Riata. A son of EOCHAID BUIDE and brother of DOMNALL BRECC, whom he succeeded as King in *c.* 642. About 655 some at least of Dál Riata was made subject to OSWY, King of Northumbria, and would remain tributary for the remainder of Conall's lifetime. His death is recorded in 659 in the *Annals of Tigernach*, but in 660 in the *Annals of Ulster*.

CONALL MAC COMGAILL (?–574), King of Dál Riata. The *Annals of Ulster* record 'the death in the sixteenth year of his reign of Conall son of

Comgall who granted the island of Iae (Iona) to COLUM CILLE' in 574. In 568 he is recorded raiding the Cenél nOengusa of Islay taking 'many spoils'. Following his death, Conall's son, Donnchad, 'and many others of the allies of the sons of Gabran, fell at the Battle of Delgu', in Kintyre, possibly indicating a power struggle over the succession, which passed to Conall's cousin, AEDÁN MAC GABRÁIN, later that year.

CONALL, SON OF TADG (?–807), King of the Picts and, later, of Dál Riata. Conall ruled over the Picts in *c.* 784–9, before being deposed by CONSTANTÍN, SON OF FERGUS in 789. The *Annals of Ulster* record Conall's death in Kintyre at the hands of Conall mac Aedáin in 807, when, according to the *Duan Albannach*, he had been King of Dál Riata for two years. His predecessor, according to the *Duan*, had been Domnall (*c.* 781–*c.* 805), who appears to have been the son of the rival who deposed him in 789. The history of Dál Riata, and its status as a subject kingdom to Pictland, is far from clear at this time and Conall's career illustrates well the obscurities of the period and the violence of inter-family feuds.

CONAMAIL, SON OF FAILBE (?–710), Abbot of Iona. He succeeded ADOMNÁN as Abbot in 704. Conamail's abbacy appears to have been one of upheaval due to the controversy over the differences between the Irish and Roman methods of calculating the date of Easter (*see* BEDE), which was a subject of violent controversy between the British and Anglo-Saxon churches and which seems to have come to a head in the famous abbey at Iona at this time. Conamail is recorded as Abbot at his death in 710, but DÚNCHAD was recorded as Abbot of Iona 707–17; this suggests that Conamail resigned the abbacy in 707 and was succeeded by Dúnchad.

CONCHOBAR MAC DONNCHADA (?–833), King of Meath and Tara. One of the two sons of Donnchad Midi between whom AED OIRDNIDE had divided Meath, Conchobar slew his brother to reunite the kingdom. His accession to the kingship of Tara in 819, in succession to Aed Oirdnide, preserved the alternation to the kingship between the northern and southern Uí Néill. From 827 he seems to have acted for a time in alliance with FEIDLIMID MAC CRIMTHAINN, King of Munster, the other great kingdom of early medieval Ireland. But the alliance subsequently collapsed and shortly before his death he is known to have raided into southern Ireland. He was succeeded by the more formidable NIALL CAILLE MAC AEDA.

CONGREVE, WILLIAM (1670–1729), playwright. Born in Yorks., he grew up in Ireland where his father was agent for the Earl of Cork. His first play, *The Old Bachelor*, was performed in London in 1693. It was followed by four others, most famously *Love for Love* (1695). Congreve's style of wit-led Restoration comedy was going out of fashion and when *The Way of the World* (1700) was poorly received he retired from the stage and earned a living from posts in civil administration, although he was still esteemed by his Augustan contemporaries, in particular his friend from youth, SWIFT.

CONINGHAM, SIR ARTHUR (1895–1948), airman. Born in Brisbane, the son of an Australian cricketer, he fought at Gallipoli in 1915 with the Australian and New Zealand Army Corps (ANZAC). Coningham (his nickname 'Maori' was soon corrupted to 'Mary') joined the Royal Flying Corps and, electing to stay in the new RAF after the war, pioneered the aerial policing of Iraq in the 1920s. Selected to command the Desert Air Force in 1941, Coningham developed techniques of air–ground co-operation in North Africa superior to those of the Axis and took these with him to north-west Europe where he commanded 2nd Tactical Airforce. Having established the essential principles of air–ground co-operation, Coningham was killed in an air crash in Jan. 1948.

CONNACHTACH (?–802), Abbot of Iona. Connachtach succeeded BRESSAL as Abbot of Iona, but his abbacy lasted less than a year before his own death. He had a reputation as a distinguished scribe which makes him a candidate to be the artist of illuminations of the great Dark Age manuscript, the *Book of Kells*, now preserved at Trinity College, Dublin.

CONNAD CERR (?–629), King of Dál Riata. A son of CONALL MAC COMGAILL, Connad is referred to as King of Dál Riata by the *Annals of Tigernach* in 627 and 629. EOCHAID BUIDE is known to have also been King of Dál Riata at this time, but since Connad defeated the Dál nAraidne in 627 and was himself killed in battle by them in 629, it may be possible that, under Eochaid's overlordship, Connad was Sub-King over those Dál Riata territories in Ireland subsequently lost by DOMNALL BRECC.

CONNAUGHTON, RICHARD (1942–), soldier and military theorist. Educated at Sandhurst, commissioned into the Royal Army Service Corps in 1961, and, as Colonel, Head of the British Army's Defence Studies in 1990, he founded the Strategic and Combat Studies Institute, which brought academics, senior civil servants, businessmen and military officers into close co-operation. A Cambridge (1989) fellowship allowed

Connaughton to study the collapse of the Soviet empire, and he began to develop new doctrines for peace-keeping in the 'new world disorder', ideas which he developed in *Military Intervention in the 1990s, A New Logic for War* (1992) and *The Nature of Future Conflict* (1995). He also helped establish the Permanent Joint Force Headquarters, an organization designed to control and direct military force in increasingly complex environments. Connaughton's influence on the development of peace support operations in the 1990s has been compared to that of John FULLER on the development of armoured warfare in the 1920s and 1930s.

CONNERY, SIR SEAN (1930–), actor. A Glasgow-born film actor (and before that a body builder), he became an international star through his portrayal of the secret agent James Bond in the film versions of Ian FLEMING's novels in the 1960s. Altogether he played the role six times, from *Dr No* (1963) to *Diamonds are Forever* (1971). Despite fears that he would be typecast Connery re-invented himself as a character actor in a number of successful films such as *The Man who would be King* (1975); for *The Untouchables* (1987) he won an Oscar. Although resident in Spain, Connery became prominent in Scotland for his support of Scottish nationalism in 1998.

CONNOLLY, CYRIL (1903–74), writer and journalist. Educated at Eton and Oxford, and a self-declared 'bright young thing' of the immediate post-war generation, his only book of note was *Enemies of Promise* (1938), an amusing, part-autobiographical dissection of the perils of trying to lead a life of letters. It was as a literary journalist that he found his true vocation, although it was one that he himself always belittled. His greatest achievement was co-founding and editing the literary magazine *Horizon* (1940–50), which was influential in introducing an embattled and culturally deprived wartime readership to the latest currents of continental and American Modernism. Literary reviewer for the *Sunday Times* from the 1950s, he attracted a large readership for his concise and elegant literary judgements and exercised considerable power over the shape of contemporary fiction.

CONNOLLY, JAMES (1868–1916), trade-union leader and socialist. Born in Edinburgh of Irish parents, Connolly served in the British army before settling in Dublin as a labourer and socialist activist. Poverty and a growing family led him to emigrate to the United States in 1903, where he remained active in socialist circles. In 1910 he returned to Ireland as Belfast organizer of James LARKIN's Irish Transport and General

Workers' Union (ITGWU). He was briefly imprisoned for his role in the 1913 Dublin lock-out and in 1914 moved to Dublin as acting General Secretary of the ITGWU during Larkin's absence in America. Connolly was shocked by the failure of the international socialist movement to organize effective opposition to the First World War. He joined the insurrectionary plans of the nationalist Irish Republican Brotherhood, although he had previously criticized non-socialist nationalists and advised socialists against co-operation with them. In 1916 he led the socialist Citizen Army to join the Easter Rising, and was one of the seven leaders who signed the rebels' proclamation. He was severely wounded during the fighting, and after the surrender was court-martialled and shot.

Apart from his martyrdom, Connolly's importance lies in the corpus of writing on the relationship between Irish nationalism and socialism and on the nature of class conflict in Irish history which makes him Ireland's foremost Marxist theorist (*see* MARX, KARL), a remarkable achievement for a self-educated man living in poverty with a large family.

CONRAD, JOSEPH (originally Teodor Jozef Konrad Korzeniowski) (1857–1924), novelist. Born of Polish parents in the Ukraine, because of his father's radicalism he spent his childhood in exile in northern Russia. Conrad gained much of his raw material for his novels and stories from 20 years spent at sea in the merchant marine before settling in England in 1894, having become a British subject in 1886. It was then that he began to write. His major works include *The Nigger of the Narcissus* (1897), *Lord Jim* (1900), *Nostromo* (1904), *The Secret Agent* (1907) and, what is probably his best-regarded work today, *Heart of Darkness* (1902), a study of the human psyche and corruptibility set on the Congo. All his published work was in English, his third language, which he mastered to great literary effect. By the time of his death he was regarded as among the leading Modernists, and his critical star has risen greatly since the 1940s.

CONRAN, SIR TERENCE (1931–), designer. He is credited with almost singlehandedly bringing good and affordable design into modern British homes, especially with the chain of Habitat stores which he founded in 1964. In the 1950s he had opened a series of cheap restaurants in London. His retail empire grew, with the acquisition of Mothercare in 1982 and the merger with British Home Stores in 1986. The combine was not a success, in part because of wider economic malaise, and Conran resigned in 1990 to return to design and restaurant ownership. His flamboyant personality, retailing skill and championship of design have made him a seminal influence on lifestyle in Britain since the 1960s.

CONSTABLE, JOHN (1776–1837), landscape painter. Probably the most consistently popular English artist, Constable was born the son of a miller, at East Bergholt (Suffolk), and most of his best-known work relates to his native Stour valley. Rural landscapes and the transient effects of light are the principal characteristics of his painting, and in his feeling for nature's simplicity and the power of the landscape he has obvious affinities with William WORDSWORTH and the other Romantic poets. Paintings such as *The Haywain* (1821) or *Dedham Vale* (1828) are imprinted upon the national consciousness, although their apparent documentary quality is artifice.

CONSTANTÍN I, King of the Scots (862–77). A son of CINAED MAC ALPÍN, he ruled during a period when northern Britain was attacked by powerful Viking armies. He appears to have tried to maintain an alliance with some of the Viking war bands while the land of the Picts and the kingdom of the Strathclyde Britons were ravaged (*see* ARTGAL, SON OF DOMNAGUEL). Eventually he was himself defeated by a war band led by HALFDAN in 875, and was killed two years later.

CONSTANTÍN II (?–952), King of the Scots (900–43). A recent commentator, Professor Alfred Smyth, has remarked that Constantín's reign was the time when 'the medieval kingdom of Scotland came of age'. It is clear from the fragmentary evidence that Constantín finally secured the kingdom against the Vikings and, having built on the domination gained by his predecessors over the Picts and Strathclyde Britons, consolidated the territory which they had won (*see* CINAED MAC ALPÍN; DOMNALL II MAC CONSTANTÍN).

He first fought against the Vikings when RAGNALL was establishing his rule over the kingdom of York, apparently suffering defeats in battle at Corbridge (Northumb.) in 919. He later supported the Norseman against the northwards advance of the kings of Wessex, fighting alongside OLAF GOTHFRITHSSON, King of Dublin, against King ATHELSTAN of Wessex at the Battle of Brunanburh (937). The evidence suggests that he manipulated the rulers of Wessex and Dublin to his advantage, and his treaties with Athelstan demonstrate that, by the 930s, he was securely established as the strongest ruler in northern Britain. In 906 he had sworn to uphold the rights of the Scottish Church, another sign of the expanding notions of the duties of kingship. He retired to the monastery at St Andrews in 943, and died in 952.

CONSTANTÍN III THE BALD, King of the Scots (*c*. 995–7). Constantín inherited the feud caused by his father CUILÉN's killing of his cousin DUB to seize the kingship. According to the chronicler Fordun, Constantín had plotted against CINAED II, Dub's brother, who had striven to monopolize the kingship within his own line of descent, the descendants of MAEL COLUIM I. In 995 Cinaed II was killed by treachery and Constantín succeeded to the kingship. His reign lasted only 18 months, however, before he in turn was defeated and killed by CINAED III, son of Dub.

CONSTANTÍN, SON OF FERGUS (?–820),
King of the Picts and Dál Riata. Apparently belonging to the Dál Riata kindred of the Cenél nGabráin, Constantín defeated CONALL, SON OF TADG, King of the Picts, in 789, and thus he became the first known King of Pictland of Gaelic origin. While the history of both Pictland and Dál Riata is far from certain at this time, it appears that Constantín's rival Conall defeated and deposed his son Domnall from the kingship of Dál Riata in *c.* 805, ruling until 807. Constantín himself subsequently took the kingship of Dál Riata in 811, ruling both kingdoms jointly until his death in 820. The *Chronicle of the Picts* states that it was Constantín who built the church at Dunkeld.

CONSTANTINE (*fl.* early sixth century), King of Dumnonia. One of the 'five tyrants' condemned by GILDAS for laxity and corruption at the time of the invasion of Britain by the Angles and Saxons, Constantine appears to have formerly been an abbot, since he was stated to have murdered two 'royal youths' and their guardians in a church while wearing the mantle of an abbot; it is, however, possible that he committed the act while so disguised. The episode may reflect a typical Dark Age attempt to secure a monopoly in the line of succession by removing rival claimants.

CONSTANTINE I THE GREAT (*c.* 274–337), Roman Emperor (306–37). Proclaimed at York on the death of his father CONSTANTIUS I during the latter's campaign that had taken him north of HADRIAN's Wall, he is generally regarded as one of the greatest of the Roman emperors, making Christianity the empire's favoured religion and building the new capital at Constantinople. The notion that his mother was British is a myth invented in the Middle Ages.

Because of his many concerns elsewhere, he may not have revisited Britain after 314. The manner in which he was proclaimed Emperor, while showing the power of the Roman army in Britain to influence the imperial succession, also contributed to the longterm disruption of the empire by causing civil war and demonstrating how a strong man could use local troops to support personal ambition. *See also* CARAUSIUS; MAGNUS MAXIMUS; CONSTANTINE III.

CONSTANTINE III, Roman Emperor (407–11).
He was the last of the many Roman emperors to be proclaimed by the army in Britain (*see* CARAUSIUS; CONSTANTINE I THE GREAT; MAGNUS MAXIMUS). By removing most of the remains of the Roman army in Britain to fight on his behalf against his rivals, he effectively left the Britons to fend for themselves. His activities were one of the chief causes of the declaration in 410 by the Emperor HONORIUS that Britain should henceforth look after itself.

CONSTANTINE, ST (*fl. c.* 600). It is uncertain precisely who Constantine was, but he had two important cult centres, at Kilchousland, in Kintyre, and at Govan in modern Glasgow. Jocelin of Furness believed he was a son of RHYDDERCH HAEL, King of Strathclyde, but the *Aberdeen Breviary* states that he was related to the ruling British dynasty of Cornwall, became a monk in Ireland, then a missionary to Scotland, where he was martyred in Kintyre.

CONSTANTIUS I (Constantius Chlorus), Roman Emperor (305–6). From 293 he was 'Caesar' (in this case the term signifies 'co-emperor') with special responsibility for the western provinces of the empire. He visited Britain on two occasions: in 296 to defeat the followers of CARAUSIUS, and in 305–6 to campaign north of HADRIAN's Wall against the Picts. He is also credited with the military reorganization of northern England after a period of weakness. In 306 he died at York, where his son was immediately proclaimed as Emperor CONSTANTINE I.

COOK, A(RTHUR) J(AMES) (1885–1931), trade unionist. Born in Som., as a boy he was a Baptist preacher and farmhand; then, from 1905, he became a miner in south Wales and an active syndicalist (*see* MANN, TOM). After the First World War he led the Miners' Federation of Great Britain. His militant leadership contributed to the series of conflicts that resulted in the General Strike of 1926; a brilliant orator, he kept the miners out on strike for months before accepting defeat. He gave his support to the Labour Party in 1929 but, before his death two years later, flirted with the New Party of MOSLEY.

COOK, JAMES (1728–79), navigator and explorer. The son of a farm labourer, he was apprenticed to a shopkeeper, but preferred a life at sea. In 1755 he joined the navy and became an officer through his skill in navigation. He was responsible for the successful piloting of the fleet which took Quebec (1759) and taught himself surveying techniques. He was so successful that he was selected to command the *Endeavour* on

her voyage on behalf of the Royal Society to make astronomical observations from Tahiti. On the same voyage he successfully charted New Zealand and the eastern coast of Australia (already known to Dutch voyagers as 'New Holland') where the expedition's naturalist, Joseph BANKS, gathered a multitude of specimens at a place he named 'Botany Bay'. Cook's second Pacific and circumpolar voyage successfully disproved the rumoured existence of an undiscovered Great Southern Continent and charted part of Antarctica. His third voyage took him to the North Pacific, where he discovered Hawaii among what he termed the Sandwich Islands, where he was surprised to find the natives talking the language of Tahiti. He charted the north-western coast of North America in the search for a north-west passage. On the way back, his usually sure touch with the local inhabitants finally deserted him and he was killed in a skirmish with Hawaiians. Cook's voyages among the Polynesians caught the popular imagination, but he was chiefly celebrated for his contributions to knowledge.

COOK, ROBIN (1946–), politician. Cook was a Labour activist from his days as a student at Edinburgh in the 1960s. He began his political career a generation before his two New Labour rivals, Tony BLAIR and Gordon BROWN, becoming MP for Edinburgh Central in 1974, a seat which he held until 1983 when he became MP for Livingston. He was the opposite of photogenic but, despite New Labour's obsession with the media and appearance, he forced his way into contention through sheer intellectual power and oratorical force. As Shadow spokesman on trade and industry after 1992, he successfully harried the MAJOR government over successive diplomatic fiascos, most notably the so-called 'arms to Iraq' issue which resulted into an inquiry by Mr Justice Scott into whether the government had known about illegal arms supplies to Iraq. But despite his performance in the Commons it was clear that Blair would be a far more media-friendly leader of the Commons after John SMITH's sudden death in 1994.

Cook became Foreign Secretary after the Labour victory in 1997, announcing that his main priority was to establish an ethical dimension to foreign policy. Despite being such a strong performer in opposition, Cook has never looked comfortable in government. A messy divorce further undermined his position. From being sceptical towards the single currency, Cook has repositioned himself as its greatest champion in government.

COOK, THOMAS (1808–92), travel-company founder. The son of a Derbys. couple who could neither read nor write, Cook realized the potential of railway travel with the success of his first venture, an all-in shilling-a-head (including food, speeches and a brass band) temperance excursion from Leicester to Loughborough in July 1841, organized originally to provide a counter-attraction to the alehouse or horse-racing track, and turned to organizing travel full time. His excursions to Scotland, which he first ran in 1848, were the most popular, but he was topical too, arranging an excursion to London to see Wellington (see WELLESLEY, ARTHUR) lying in state in Westminster Hall in 1852 and a trip across the newly opened Saltash bridge (Devon), designed by Isambard Kingdom BRUNEL, in 1859. A Free-Trader with faith in the benefits of travel to promote world peace, dubbed 'the 'Napoleon of excursions', he was soon leading his parties to Italy for culture and to Switzerland for Alpine walking tours and 20,000 visitors to the Paris Exhibition in 1887 (where he also organized the accommodation for half that number with vouchers that would one day develop into the concept of the package holiday). When the Civil War was over, he organized excursions to America, to Egypt and Palestine and, in 1872, Around the World – in 222 days. Thomas Cook and Son included John (1834–99) from 1864 who was more of a businessman, and increasingly the firm moved into the luxury end of the travel market, sending royalty on holiday, organizing steamer trips on the Nile but also providing the transport for the troops sent to relieve General GORDON at Khartoum (1884).

COOKE, SIR ANTHONY (c. 1505–76), politician. From an Essex landed family, and an early enthusiast for Protestantism, he became a tutor to EDWARD VI, and two of his five brilliantly talented daughters married Nicholas BACON (see BACON, ANNE) and William CECIL. Bacon's and Cecil's continuing government office under MARY I meant that his exile for his religion was not too uncomfortable, and they also gave him a position of influence on his return in 1559 as the new religious settlement was being pushed through Parliament. Thereafter he retired from national politics.

COOKE, HENRY (1788–1868), Irish Presbyterian minister. Though in favour of Catholic Emancipation, Cooke was hostile to Daniel O'CONNELL's repeal movement and in the 1830s tried to persuade Irish Presbyterians to join their traditional Tory opponents in a pan-Protestant alliance to oppose disestablishment of the Church of Ireland. Only a minority followed Cooke's advice and the alliance foundered on renewed disputes between the Church of Ireland and Presbyterians in the 1840s, but it anticipated the pan-Protestant Unionist alliance created in the 1880s. Protestant fundamentalist Unionists like Ian PAISLEY see Cooke as exemplifying religious and political orthodoxy, while nationalists blame him for turning nineteenth-century Ulster Presbyterians away from the attitudes of the United Irishmen.

COOPER, ANTHONY ASHLEY (1st Earl of Shaftesbury) *see* essay on pages 202–03

COOPER, ANTHONY ASHLEY (3rd Earl of Shaftesbury) (1671–1713), moral philosopher. His education was supervised by John LOCKE, against whose conviction that ideas were derived from experience he was later to react. He published *An Inquiry Concerning Virtue* (1699); his best-known work, *Characteristicks of Men, Manners and Times*, was published in 1711. Probably influenced by the Cambridge Platonists (*see* WHICHCOTE, BENJAMIN), he believed in a moral order implicit in human nature, finding expression not only in actions and moral judgements but also in aesthetic tastes. True to his Whig inheritance, he argued that parliamentary monarchy was most conducive to cultural development. Although he remained an ardent Whig throughout his life, shyness and ill health prevented him from playing an active part in Parliament.

COOPER, ANTHONY ASHLEY (7th Earl of Shaftesbury) (1801–85), social reformer. An Evangelical Christian, he led the 'ten hour movement' to limit working hours in factories by statute. The Factory Acts 1833–50, which restricted hours worked in factories by women and children and thus effectively for many men, came into law largely as a result of his legislative campaigns; and the Mines Act 1842, which forbade women and girls and boys under the age of 10 from working underground, was also his Bill.

COOPER, LADY DIANA (née Manners) (1892–1986), socialite. The grandniece of the Earl of Crawford, though probably not the daughter of the Duke of Rutland, her mother's husband, but of Harry Cust, 'the Rupert BROOKE of his day', she was stunningly beautiful and adored by such well-known men as H. H. ASQUITH and Lord Beaverbrook (*see* AITKEN, MAXWELL), while she was immortalized in prose by Evelyn WAUGH, Arnold BENNETT and D. H. LAWRENCE. Cooper acted: her most memorable performance was as the Madonna in Reinhardt's *The Miracle*, and she starred in the first British colour films. She married the diplomat and statesman Duff COOPER in 1919. He adored her too (though he was serially unfaithful). She accompanied him to Paris when he went there as British Ambassador in 1944 (a delicate posting at the time), and when a Labour government took office in 1945 it was rumoured that it was only because the Foreign Secretary, Ernest BEVIN, was so enchanted with Diana that Cooper was allowed to remain in post until 1947.

COOPER, (ALFRED) DUFF (1st Viscount Norwich) (1892–1954), politician and diplomat. After an Oxford career marked by intellectual brilliance and personal dissoluteness, Cooper found himself a niche in the Foreign Office, which he left in 1917 to fight on the Western Front where, showing great courage, he won the Distinguished Service Order; the life of a professional diplomat lacked excitement after that. Cooper's desire for a political career was hampered by lack of money, which was provided by his beautiful wife (*see* COOPER, LADY DIANA). Her earnings from the stage enabled him to stand as the Conservative candidate for Oldham (Lancs.) in the 1924 election. He made steady progress under Stanley BALDWIN's patronage but could never overtake Anthony EDEN whose expertise on foreign affairs deprived Cooper of the opportunity to shine in that field.

Cooper lost his seat in 1929 but made a spectacular return to politics in early 1931 as the official Conservative candidate for the St George's division of Mayfair, London, where he fought Beaverbrook's (*see* AITKEN, MAXWELL) Empire Free Trade candidate and won a famous victory. After junior office at the Treasury, Cooper became Secretary of State for War in 1935 and First Lord of the Admiralty in 1937. His finest hour was his resignation from the Cabinet over Neville CHAMBERLAIN's Munich agreement with Hitler. Winston CHURCHILL made him his first Minister of Information in 1940 but it was not until his appointment as Ambassador to France in late 1944 that Cooper found his *métier*. Cooper argued for a Western European Union, and his most notable achievement was the 1947 Treaty of Dunkirk. Diplomat, lover, politician and author, Cooper was a Regency buck out of his time.

COOPER, THOMAS (*c.* 1511–94), writer and churchman. Fellow of Magdalen College, Oxford, he postponed ordination until the death of MARY I, but then rapid promotion in the Church eventually led to the bishopric of Winchester. He was a prolific writer, producing a Latin dictionary (1548), a popular chronicle (successive enlargements from 1548) and polemical works both against Roman Catholics and the 'Martin Marprelate' satirists. *See also* THROCKMORTON, JOB.

COOPER, THOMAS (*fl.* 1626), writer. An Oxford-educated Puritan, he became a parish clergyman and was preacher to the navy in 1626. He wrote moralizing pamphlets on the

Gunpowder Plot and on current events, but also wrote attacking witchcraft, magic and astrology (1617), drawing on his own experience of witchcraft accusations.

COOPER, THOMAS (1805–92), Chartist. Born in Leicester, he was an apprentice shoemaker and autodidact, teaching himself Latin, Greek, Hebrew and French before turning to teaching others, preaching and politics. He was leader of the Leicester Chartists in the early 1840s and something of a firebrand prior to a brief spell of imprisonment. This led him to reject the utility of 'physical force' Chartism which he had previously espoused, in favour of the more moderate 'moral force' Chartism of LOVETT, with its emphasis on knowledge, temperance and self-respect. His autobiography, published in 1872, is a classic account of the Victorian self-educated working man, his political passions and literary leanings.

COOTE, SIR EYRE (1726–83), soldier. The son of an Irish gentleman cleric, he was a member of the first British regiment to embark for India in 1754 and two years later persuaded CLIVE to fight the Nawab of Bengal at Plassey rather than wait for reinforcements, thus winning the battle before the Nawab's French allies could arrive. His victory over the French at Pondicherry in 1761 sealed the end of their influence in India. In 1779 he returned to India as Commander-in-Chief to take on HYDER ALI, ruler of Mysore. He led a successful campaign against much larger forces but in 1782 fell seriously ill and had to retire, dying in Madras the next year.

COPPE, ABIEZER (1619–72), writer. From humble origins, his early brilliance won him Puritan support for his education, but he left Oxford without a degree on the outbreak of the Civil Wars (1642) to become a travelling Anabaptist preacher and briefly (1646) an army chaplain. From 1649 his writings, including *A Fiery Flying Roll* (1650), provoked scandal and imprisonment, with their emphasis on a religion based on an inner light within all humans; he was one of the group of radical activists nicknamed Ranters. Though he recanted and was released in 1651, he returned to radical preaching, publishing another pamphlet in 1657, but after CHARLES II's restoration (1660) he took the name Higham and began a quiet career as a doctor in Surrey.

CORAM, THOMAS (*c.* 1668–1751), philanthropist. Originally from Lyme Regis (Dorset), he trained as a shipwright in London before emigrating to Mass. in 1693. Convinced that England needed to exploit her colonies' resources, he succeeded in obtaining an Act of Parliament rewarding importers of colonial tar (1704), which helped develop tar production in North America and reduce the navy's dependence on Baltic imports. In 1719 he settled in London and began a lengthy campaign to establish a charitable foundation to look after abandoned children and teach them skills useful to the development of the British Empire. With the help of Thomas BRAY and petitions from 21 noblewomen and 51 noblemen and gentlemen, Coram obtained a royal charter for the Foundling Hospital in 1739. A permanent site was found in Lambs Conduit Fields and the hospital, which was supported by endowments and subscriptions, became a centre for cultural display exhibiting the works of HOGARTH, a major benefactor, and other artists; HANDEL (who left the hospital the rights to the *Messiah*) gave fund-raising concerts in the chapel. The hospital moved from London in the 1920s, but the founder is remembered in Coram Fields and the Thomas Coram Foundation, a children's charity.

CORBET, SIR JOHN (1594–1662), politician. A Salop. knight made baronet in 1627, he was one of 'five knights' (with Thomas DARNELL, Walter ERLE, Edmund HAMPDEN and John HEVENINGHAM) who refused to pay a forced loan demanded by CHARLES I, and were imprisoned. They appealed for a writ of *Habeas Corpus* to King's Bench, which returned them to prison, but avoided making a final decision in their case, and they were released in 1628. Corbet was twice more imprisoned for his opposition to royal policies, was elected to the 1640 Long Parliament, and fought for Parliament in the 1642–6 Civil War.

CORBETT, SIR JULIAN (1854–1922), naval historian and strategist. Educated at Cambridge, he worked as a travel-writer and novelist before Sir John Knox LAUGHTON persuaded him to try naval history. Appointed to a lectureship in history at the Royal Naval War College, Greenwich, in 1902, Corbett wrote *Some Principles of Maritime Strategy* (1911), an outline of the British 'Blue Water school' of maritime strategy. Corbett argued that Britain's interests could best be served by controlling the sea lanes, rather than by sending forces to the continent. After the First World War military writers like Liddell HART, appalled by the slaughter of the Western Front, returned to Corbett's writings for inspiration.

CORELLI, MARIE (originally Mary Mills) (1855–1924), novelist. She was the illegitimate daughter of Charles Mackay, a Scottish poet, who eventually did marry her mother who had been his servant. She took the stage name Marie Corelli when she embarked on a musical career in 1885,

continued on page 204

COOPER, ANTHONY ASHLEY (1st Earl of Shaftesbury) (1621–83)
Politician

Born of West Country gentry stock, he was educated by private tutors, and briefly at Oxford and Lincoln's Inn. In 1640 Cooper became one of the youngest members of the Short Parliament, but failed to gain election to the Long Parliament. He hesitated to commit himself in the Civil Wars, siding first with CHARLES I, then with Parliament, changing because he thought the King's aims 'destructive to religion and the State'. He became prominent in local government. When his first wife died, he married the sister of the Earl of Exeter (see CAPEL, ARTHUR), a member of the republican Council of State.

From 1652 his star rose: he served on a law reform commission, as a nominated member of Barebone's (see BARBON, PRAISE-GOD) Parliament and its Council of State, then on the Council of State which made Oliver CROMWELL Lord Protector, and in the Protectorate Parliament. He emerged as a moderate reformer, not one of the dogmatic godly party, a man of growing practical experience, whom Cromwell trusted. By 1655, objecting to Cromwell's dictatorial conduct, he went into opposition. His third wife was connected with Royalist families, though Cooper did not respond when the future CHARLES II wrote inviting a declaration of loyalty.

After Cromwell's death in 1658, Cooper took a leading role among those pushing Parliament's claims against the army. He negotiated with agents of MONCK, who saw him as a vital recruit to the Royal cause, which he finally espoused in May 1660, claiming that he had long been so inclined. He was immediately made a Privy Councillor: the only republican other than Monck. He demonstrated his loyalty to the new regime by sitting on a commission to try regicides and, in 1661, was made Lord Ashley and Chancellor of the Exchequer. He clashed with Clarendon (see HYDE, EDWARD), over religious toleration, which Ashley favoured and Hyde did not. He was not, however, among the most virulent critics who brought Hyde down in 1667.

In 1668 Ashley became dangerously ill from a cyst on his liver, which was removed in an operation supervised by John LOCKE. Once well again, Ashley resumed his place in the ill-assorted post-Clarendonian team sometimes termed the Cabal ministry, from the initials of leading members (see CHARLES II). Not trusting him, the King did not inform him of the secret clauses of the Treaty of Dover (1670), which promised French subsidies in return for Charles declaring himself a Catholic and making war on the Dutch. There were, however, commercial reasons for such a war, and Ashley helped with its finance. He supported the Declaration of Indulgence issued as war started in 1672, favouring its grant of toleration to Dissenters, and not being too concerned that it gave lesser liberties to Catholics. He was created Earl of Shaftesbury and made Lord Chancellor.

His experience up to this point had mainly been that of loyal public servant, his years of opposition in the final years of the Protectorate the exception. Now, however, he reverted to oppositional mode. Crucial to this change was turbulence in the country, as antipathy to the government's pro-French war policy linked with distrust of Charles's Catholic brother James (later JAMES II). Shaftesbury shared those feelings, and when rumours of his disaffection prompted the King to dismiss him he began to seek out ways to force a settlement to his liking.

To this end he joined others promoting Bills designed to limit both the threat of popery and royal power. The King's response was to prorogue Parliament and promote Danby (see OSBORNE, THOMAS). Shaftesbury argued that only a general election (not held for some 15 years) would allow a fresh start and, with this in view, published anonymously a *Letter from a Person of Quality to his Friend in the Country* (1675), claiming that a plot had existed since the Restoration (indeed, the days of LAUD) to put the country in the hands of 'the high Episcopal Men, and of the old Cavaliers'. Once again, the King prorogued Parliament, now for 15 months.

Shaftesbury's prominence made him a magnet for the discontented, including both MPs, some of whom had long identified themselves with the Country as opposed to the Court party, and London merchants. In 1676 he moved to a new house in the City, conveniently placing himself for his links with City and mercantile opinion to develop. Contemporaries noted people in the streets wearing green ribbons, Leveller colours (see LILBURNE, JOHN), and identified them as 'Shaftesbury's party'. His cultivation of public opinion prompted the government to counter-attack, decrying him as an unpredictable turncoat. When Parliament reassembled, it was plain that he lacked enough support to get his way. He was required to ask pardon, and sent to the Tower, where he remained for a year, until he apologized for his 'ill-advised action'.

A revival of opposition followed the Popish Plot touched off by the allegations of Titus OATES in 1678. Shaftesbury was given a prominent place in the committees investigating the plot, and did his best to turn the spotlight upon James. The King dissolved Parliament and finally called an election but the new Parliament proved if anything even more ungovernable. The King then sent James abroad, dismissed Danby, and reconstructed the Privy Council, making Shaftesbury president and bringing in both other critics, such as Essex (see CAPEL, ARTHUR) and Halifax (see SAVILE, GEORGE), and members expected to be more amenable, such as Sunderland (see SPENCER, CHARLES).

These men began to discuss means of controlling the threat that James was said to represent, whether by limitations to the power of the Crown or by James's exclusion from the succession. Shaftesbury emerged as the chief proponent of exclusion, an option well supported by the Commons and in the City. Among exclusionists, some, like Essex and Sunderland, favoured substituting for James his daughter MARY, wife of William of Orange (later WILLIAM III), while others inclined to Charles's illegitimate son Monmouth (see SCOTT, JAMES). Shaftesbury's own preference may have been for the King to divorce and remarry, in the hope of begetting a son, though failing that he was prepared to back Monmouth.

Having failed to contain Shaftesbury, and calculating that French subsidies would allow him to do without Parliament for a while, the King dismissed him in the autumn. The rest of Shaftesbury's life was to be spent in opposition. The battle between Court and Country was fought out through another Parliament, a further set of elections, and the brief meeting, at Oxford, of a third Exclusion Parliament.

During this period Shaftesbury and his associates used various techniques to mobilize public opinion and keep up pressure on government and Parliament to proceed with exclusion, including the publication of newspapers and pamphlets, ceremonial pope-burnings, the collection of signatures for petitions, and the issuing of electors' instructions to MPs. The Court party responded in kind – substituting for petitions addresses expressing 'abhorrence' of the state's proceedings. These efforts drew on and developed agitational techniques employed earlier in the century; such devices would continue to provide the means of political conflict down to the 1830s and beyond; just as the names Whig and Tory, first bestowed in the course of this conflict upon Court and Country sides respectively (from Whiggamore, a Scots Presbyterian rebel, and Tòraidhe, an Irish bandit) would have a long after-life as terms for two opposing views of politics.

The conflict was more ferocious and unscrupulous than emphasis on such prefigurings of the future might suggest. It was fought against a background of continuing allegations of Popish and Presbyterian plots, and of the trials and executions of alleged conspirators. Shaftesbury and his friends feared that the King might turn the army against Parliament; meanwhile, they contemplated insurrection as a last resort.

As the King held firm, and prorogued or dissolved one Parliament after another, fear that the cause was lost, of civil war and of royal vengeance began to erode support for the exclusionists' cause. Some who had given evidence of Popish plots began to claim that Whigs had suborned them. In July 1681 Shaftesbury was arrested on a charge of high treason.

Though the King delayed the trial, hoping to find some way of overcoming the likely sympathies of a City jury, in the end he gave in: at the trial in November, the grand jury threw the charges out. The final struggle was for control of the City. When the Court party managed to secure the election of Tory sheriffs and lord mayor, Shaftesbury went into hiding. Shortly afterward he escaped to the Netherlands, where his health failed. He died within a few weeks.

Supporters of the Court party vilified Shaftesbury, accusing him of inconstancy and ambition. Critics often fastened upon his small size, calling him, for example, 'the little toad'. DRYDEN's Absalom and Achitophel, composed in 1681, contained the most famous hostile portrait. Though charges of Presbyterianism and republicanism need qualifying for his later years, they did point up certain consistencies in his views: notably suspicion of episcopal tyranny, and overweening monarchical or dictatorial power. These attitudes lay at the heart of the Whig tradition, which he helped to found.

Kenneth D. H. Haley, The First Earl of Shaftesbury (1968)

but within months had a self-described 'psychic experience' and turned to writing instead. Her third published book *Thelma: A Society Novel* (1887) was her breakthrough, and with the publication of *The Story of a Dead Self* (1889) she could even count GLADSTONE among her hordes of admirers, though the critics were less enamoured of her sensationalist romances awash with swoons, psychic experiences and ecstatic visions. By the time *The Sorrows of Satan* was published in 1895 Corelli was rumoured to be earning £10,000 for each book and for over a decade thereafter could claim to be Britain's best-selling novelist.

CORK, EARL OF, 2ND and **5TH** *see* BOYLE, RICHARD

CORMAC MAC CUILENNÁIN (?–908), Bishop and King of Cashel. An ecclesiastic and a renowned scholar, Cormac was elected to the kingdom of Munster, along with Tára, one of the strongest kingdoms of early medieval Ireland. Possibly a stop-gap, like other ecclesiastics known to have been elevated to kingship in early Ireland, Cormac proved himself an able soldier, challenging for the overlordship of all Ireland. He was defeated and killed, however, by FLANN SINNA MAC MAÍL SHECHNAILL, King of Tára, at the Battle of Belach Mugna (Co. Carlow) in 908. His challenge was the last attempt by the Eoganachta of Munster to maintain their status and his defeat, together with a resurgence in Viking activity in Munster following his death, destroyed their prestige and led to a period of weakness for the kingdom. The kingdom was revived by the Dál Cais dynasty (*see* MATHGAMAIN; BRIAN BORUMA).

CORMAC UA LIATHÁIN (?–*c*. 590), monk of Iona, Prior of Durrow. ADOMNÁN, in his *Life of Colum Cille*, relates that Cormac attempted three ocean voyages to seek out a hermitage. The first failed; the second saw his arrival in Orkney, when COLUM CILLE requested his safe passage from BRIDEI, SON OF MÁILCON, the overlord of Orkney; while his third voyage took him as far as the Arctic Ocean. The incidental mention of such voyages is an indication of the perilous endeavours which were frequently undertaken by Irish monks. Cormac was ultimately appointed Colum Cille's successor at Durrow.

CORNELYS, THERESA (1723–97), impresario. A Venetian, she performed in many parts of Europe under various names, eventually settling on the Dutch Cornelys. While still enjoying a career as a singer and actress, she bought Carlisle House in Soho Square in 1760, which became the location of a 'society' for public assemblies, successfully reintroducing the masquerade as a fashionable entertainment in London. Admittance to the society was regulated by a committee of fashionable women. Assemblies began with concerts, which later became separate entertainments under the direction of J. C. Bach and C. F. Abel. Carlisle House remained fashionable for a decade but their defection, the launch of the Pantheon on Oxford Street and legal action forced Cornelys into bankruptcy in 1772, and she died in the Fleet prison.

CORNWALL, EARL OF, 2ND *see* RICHARD OF CORNWALL; **4TH** *see* GAVESTON, PIERS

CORNWALLIS, CHARLES (1st Marquess Cornwallis) (1738–1805), soldier. He joined the army in 1756, and in 1760 became an MP, moving to the Lords on the death of his father, the 1st Earl Cornwallis, later the same year. He was a commander in the War of American Independence, with successes at Camden, New Jersey, in 1780 and Guilford courthouse in North Carolina in March 1781, but in Oct. was trapped at Yorktown, Virginia, by co-ordinated moves by the French and American armies; the British fleet at the same time withdrew from the Battle of the Chesapeake, having failed to draw off the French. Cornwallis had no option but to surrender unconditionally to General George WASHINGTON.

Cornwallis was appointed Governor-General of India in 1786. In the wake of major controversy concerning the East India Co. role in the country, and PITT THE YOUNGER's India Bill (1784) establishing the Board of Control to supervise the company's administrative role, he carried out administrative reforms, and in 1792 defeated TIPU, Sultan of Mysore, in the Third Mysore War. His successes helped to give retrospective credibility to Pitt's India legislation. As Lord Lieutenant of Ireland, Cornwallis organized the suppression of the 1798 Irish rebellion (intended to draw upon support from revolutionary France to overthrow British rule); four years later he helped negotiate the Peace of Amiens, temporarily ending the Franco-British hostilities. He returned to India in 1804 to serve again as Governor General, but died the following year.

CORT, HENRY (1740–1800), ironmaster and inventor. The son of a mason, he was acting as a navy agent by 1765. In 1775, determined to improve the quality of British iron with British military and naval needs in mind, he set up a forge near Fareham (Hants.). Between 1783 and 1785 he took out patents for puddling and rolling, processes which allowed the conversion of large quantities of pig iron into refined bar iron. Whereas open-hearth refining required the use of charcoal, puddling could be coal-fuelled, an advantage when timber supplies were limited but coal mining was developing. It involved the decarbonizing of pig iron in a reverbatory furnace: carbon from the iron combined with oxygen from clinker rich in iron oxide (the chemistry underlying these operations was not understood until the nineteenth century). The technique complemented the work of Dud DUDLEY and DARBY, and improved the iron industry's output. Cort set up works near Gosport to supply the navy, in company with a deputy paymaster who financed the enterprise by borrowing from naval funds in his hands. When this was discovered Cort was ruined, but the merits of his invention were recognized, and he was given a pension in 1794.

COSGRAVE, LIAM (1920–), politician and Taoiseach (Irish Prime Minister). Son of W. T. COSGRAVE, he was member of the Dáil for south Dublin constituencies (1943–81), junior minister in the 1948–51 coalition, and minister in the 1954–7 coalition. He stood for the Fine Gael leadership against James DILLON (1958) and succeeded him as leader in 1965. Between 1973 and 1977 he was Taoiseach as head of a Fine Gael and Labour coalition. He negotiated the Sunningdale agreement with Edward HEATH in 1973 to establish a power-sharing executive in Northern Ireland, but after its collapse concentrated on defending the Republic against destabilization from the North. His government was weakened by harsh security measures, the resignation of President O Dalaigh after he was insulted by a minister, tensions with colleagues over Cosgrave's conservative Catholic views, and the economic effects of the post-1973 oil crisis. In 1977 the coalition was crushingly defeated by Fianna Fáil under Jack LYNCH. Cosgrave resigned the Fine Gael leadership and was succeeded by Garrett FITZGERALD.

COSGRAVE, W(ILLIAM) T(HOMAS) (1880–1965), Prime Minister of the Irish Free State. A Sinn Féin member of Dublin Corporation from 1909, Cosgrave was sentenced to death after the 1916 Easter Rising, but had his sentence commuted. MP and member of the Dáil for Kilkenny (1917–27) and Cork City (1927–44), he served as Minister for Local Government in the underground Dáil government (1919–22) and was a supporter of the Anglo-Irish Treaty. After the deaths of Arthur GRIFFITH and Michael COLLINS he led the pro-Treaty Sinn Féin faction which became Cumann na nGaedheal in 1923. As head of the Free State government (1922–32) Cosgrave was competent but uncharismatic. Ruthless security measures (especially during the 1922–3 Civil War) were widely criticized and the social conservatism of his government undermined its political base; nonetheless he played a crucial role in consolidating Irish democracy, not least by his willingness to give up power to Fianna Fáil after electoral defeat in 1932. On the formation of Fine Gael in 1933 he yielded the leadership to Eoin O'DUFFY, but replaced him in 1934 and remained leader until 1943, presiding over a massive decline in support.

COSIN, JOHN (1594–1662), churchman. From a Norwich mercantile family and Cambridge-educated, he made his clerical career in Durham diocese and was an enthusiast for the sacramental religion championed by William LAUD; his *Collection of Private Devotions* (1627) was an attempt to provide a Church of England alternative to Roman Catholic devotional works at court. He went into exile with HENRIETTA MARIA, doing his best to keep the Anglicans in her household from Catholic conversion. After CHARLES II's restoration he was made Bishop of Durham (1661), did much to restore the principal churches of the diocese and was influential in revising the Book of Common Prayer (1662).

COSTELLO, JOHN (1891–1976), Taoiseach (Irish Prime Minister). One of the most successful Irish barristers of his day, he was Attorney General in W. T. COSGRAVE's government (1926–32) and Fine Gael member of the Dáil for south Dublin constituencies (1933–69). He was chosen as Taoiseach of the 1948 coalition, the leader of Fine Gael, Richard Mulcahy, being unacceptable to the Republicans of Clann na Poblachta (one of the five other parties) because of his role in the summary executions of Republicans during the Irish Civil War (1922–3). The new government declared the state to be a republic (a point left ambiguous by the 1937 constitution) though it did this in a maladroit manner, causing severe tension with the British government. Costello declared that this would 'take the gun out of Irish politics' but, when the British government guaranteed that Northern Ireland would not cease to be part of the United Kingdom without the consent of its Parliament, the Irish state launched an all-party anti-partition campaign. This strengthened the Unionist government in Northern Ireland by helping it to present opposition as endangering the state, later being seen as encouraging the revival of the IRA.

The Costello government proved reasonably competent but was brought down in 1951 by internal divisions, particularly opposition to Noel BROWNE's proposal for a state scheme of maternity health care. Costello opposed his Health Minister on the issue and declared that his Catholicism transcended all other allegiances. The subsequent election saw significant gains for Fine Gael (which had seemed on the verge of extinction) and showed that an alternative government to Fianna Fáil was possible, preparing the way for the 'two-and-a-half party system' which dominated Irish politics until the 1980s.

In 1954 Costello returned to power as head of a three-party coalition (Fine Gael, Labour, Clann na Talmhan): lacking an overall majority and suffering from economic problems, it fell in 1957 over security legislation against the IRA's 1956–62 border campaign. Costello retired after defeat in the ensuing General Election.

COTMAN, JOHN SELL (1782–1842), painter. A Norfolk man, he settled first in Norwich where he was a leading member of the Norwich School, and then in Yarmouth (1811–23). His mentor was J. M. W. TURNER, who secured him a position at King's College, London. Like Turner his subject was landscape, in Cotman's case spare and reminiscent of Japanese calligraphic paintings. *Greta Bridge* (versions *c*. 1805 and 1810) is a celebrated example.

COTTINGTON, FRANCIS (Baron Cottington) (?1579–1652), politician. A diplomat with much experience in Spain, he became secretary to the future CHARLES I in 1622 and secretly converted to Roman Catholicism in 1623. After the assassination of his enemy George VILLIERS, Duke of Buckingham (1628), he was made Chancellor of the Exchequer (1629–42), allying with his fellow-Catholic Richard WESTON against William LAUD. Lord High Treasurer from 1643 in Charles's regime based at Oxford, he went into continental exile in 1646 and eventually settled in Spain.

COTTON, JACK (1903–64), property developer. First opening an estate agency in his native Birmingham in 1924, Cotton subsequently set up an architectural practice as middleman between farmers selling land and speculative builders developing the suburbs around Birmingham and other cities. He acquired an ever greater hold on the central Birmingham property market, becoming a property developer himself in the late 1930s. In post-war Britain, he became an adventurer in the redevelopment of war-torn cities, moving into the London property market, exploiting shortages of government office space through building and leasing schemes, and pioneering joint partnerships with insurance companies for large property developments. In 1960 his company, City Centre Properties, merged with City & Central Investments headed by Charles CLORE. The uneasy relationship between the two was compounded by internal power struggles, and Cotton was removed as Chairman in a boardroom coup in 1963. The supreme ugliness of most of his building projects that changed so radically the face of post-war Britain remains.

COTTON, SIR JOHN HYNDE (*c*. 1688–1752), Jacobite politician. He entered the Commons in 1708, held minor office under Robert HARLEY, and became a noted Tory leader under GEORGE I and GEORGE II. After WYNDHAM's death in 1740 he was the main leader of the party and in 1743 was one of those who invited Charles Edward STUART to invade Britain. Nonetheless, with some of his colleagues, Cotton accepted office as Treasurer of the Chamber in the Broad-Bottom Ministry in 1744. Caricaturists used his physical girth to give point to the nickname. Comfortable in office, Cotton chose not to support the 1745 rebellion, but in 1746 he was dismissed, to spend the rest of his career as a supporter of FREDERICK, Prince of Wales.

COTTON, ROBERT BRUCE (1571–1631), antiquary. A Hunts. gentleman who devotedly collected manuscripts and antiquities, which he made available to a wide circle. He contributed to historical publications by William CAMDEN and others; JAMES I made him first a knight (1603, at which point he adopted the extra surname Bruce, to mark his descent from ROBERT BRUCE), and a baronet in 1611. Elected to Parliament several times, he became critical of CHARLES I's policies and was excluded from his own library from 1629. His manuscript collection, though terribly damaged by fire in 1731, is one of the treasures of the British Library.

COURCY, JOHN DE (?–*c*. 1219), soldier and diplomat. A minor landowner from Cumbria who, in five years (1177–82) of audacious soldiering, castle building and diplomacy, married a daughter of the King of Man and conquered the northern Irish kingdom of Uladh, carving out a virtually independent principality of Ulster for himself and even issuing his own coinage. None of this was to the liking of King JOHN, who employed Hugh de Lacy II (1201–5) to eject him from Ulster. In 1210 he helped the King to bring de Lacy down, but was not rewarded by being restored to Ulster.

COURTAULD, SAMUEL, IV (1876–1947), manufacturer and arts patron. The great-nephew of Samuel Courtauld III (1793–1881), who had established the Huguenot family's wealth in silk manufacture in Essex, he spent his life in the family textile business. When he came to prominence the company was poised to enter huge profitability through making viscose rayon. Courtaulds magnificently survived the boom and bust of rayon manufacture in the 1920s and 1930s under Samuel's steady and serious-minded chairmanship, while the arts in Britain profited considerably from his patronage. The Courtauld Institute of Art, founded in 1931, was created and endowed by him.

COURTENAY, EDWARD (20th Earl of Devon) (1526–57), dynast. Dangerously close to the royal succession, he was confined in the Tower of London by HENRY VIII after the execution of his father Henry COURTENAY, Marquess of Exeter, in 1539. Released by MARY I in 1553, he was mooted as a husband for her, but was plainly unsuitable after his long captivity; he frittered away his freedom dabbling in treasonous schemes and died at Padua (possibly poisoned) during his continental travels.

COURTENAY, HENRY (19th Earl of Devon, 1st Marquess of Exeter) (c. 1498–1539), dynast. Their Plantagenet descent and West Country power earned this family the suspicion of HENRY VII and, fatally after years of favour (including Henry Courtenay's marquessate in 1525), of HENRY VIII. Courtenay supported the annulment of Henry's marriage to CATHERINE OF ARAGON and helped defeat the Pilgrimage of Grace (1536), but thereafter he drifted into conspiracy with Thomas CROMWELL's opponents, leading to his execution with Cardinal POLE's brother Henry, Baron Montague (c. 1492–1539), and their uncle Sir Edward Neville.

COURTENAY, WILLIAM (c. 1341–96), Archbishop of Canterbury (1381–96). As Bishop of London (1375) and then Archbishop of Canterbury, he led the opposition within the English Church to WYCLIF and the Lollards. He was particularly influential in driving them out of Oxford, the university at which he had been a student and became Chancellor.

COUSINS, FRANK (1904–86), trade-union leader and politician. A former miner and lorry driver who became a full-time official of the Transport and General Workers' Union (TGWU) in 1938, Cousins was appointed national secretary of the road transport commercial group within the TGWU in 1948 and General Secretary in 1956. This marked a more militant role for the TGWU than under its previous leaders Ernest BEVIN and Arthur DEAKIN, espousing a confrontational approach to the Conservative government that culminated in the 1958 bus strike. Cousins promulgated an internationalist political position for his union and led it to prominent advocacy of nuclear disarmament. Despite Labour Party criticism that his militancy was making the party unelectable, the strength and influence of the TGWU grew, and in 1964 Cousins accepted Harold WILSON's offer of the new post of Minister of Technology in the Labour government. His two years in office were not successful and in 1966 he mobilized the TGWU in opposition to Labour's wage policies and the trade-union reform proposals of *In Place of Strife* (1969). He retired from the TGWU in 1969 to head the Community Relations Commission, another unsatisfactory role from which he resigned in 1970. In the 1950s and 1960s it had looked as if Cousins was defining the role of the trade-union movement as a dynamic political as well as industrial force, but the accommodation between the Labour Party and the unions was never to be the forceful, innovative political partnership he envisaged.

COVENTRY, THOMAS (1st Baron Coventry) (1578–1640), royal servant. From a Worcs. gentry family and Oxford-educated, he followed his father's legal career to become Solicitor General (1617–21), Attorney General (1621–5) and Lord Keeper of the Great Seal until his death; he was made Baron in 1628. He was generally respected for his honesty, and while scrupulously carrying out royal wishes attempted to mediate in the confrontations between CHARLES I and leading politicians.

COVENTRY, SIR WILLIAM (c. 1626–86), royal servant. Younger son of Thomas COVENTRY, he was educated at Oxford and fought for CHARLES I in the 1642–6 Civil War. Immediately before CHARLES II's restoration, he offered his services to James, Duke of York (the future JAMES II), and was made his secretary. Chiefly employed in naval matters, he proved an industrious and efficient administrator. He was elected an MP in 1661 and rapidly rose to the fore in the House of Commons, playing a part in precipitating the Second Dutch War (1665–7). A vigorous critic of Edward HYDE Earl of Clarendon's ascendancy, he nevertheless did not support attempts to impeach him. In 1667 he was appointed to the reforming Treasury Commission with Thomas CLIFFORD and Sir George DOWNING, but in March 1669 he fell from power over a quarrel with George VILLIERS, Duke of Buckingham, who had planned to caricature him on stage. He was intensely disliked by Charles II, for reasons which are obscure. Though he had achieved a great reputation as a shrewd and constructive parliamentarian, he never held office again.

COVERDALE, MILES (?1488–1568), Bible translator. An Augustinian friar already associated with reformers at Cambridge in the 1520s, he left for the continent in 1529 to help William TYNDALE, whose incomplete biblical translation work he continued, publishing his English Bible in 1535. In 1537 the first officially authorized English Bible, edited by John ROGERS under the pseudonym 'Thomas Matthew', used mainly the Tyndale/Coverdale text; the 1539 Great Bible, issued officially, was a Coverdale revision, with a new preface written by Thomas CRANMER in 1540.

Vulnerable as a Protestant writer, Coverdale fled to the continent once more after the fall of his patron Thomas CROMWELL in 1540; he found favour under EDWARD VI, who made him Bishop of Exeter (1551). After exile in Denmark and Germany during the reign of MARY I, he refused to resume his bishopric under ELIZABETH, but remained a star preacher. The Church of England's Book of Common Prayer still uses his psalm translations.

COWARD, SIR NOEL (1899–1973), writer and actor. Coward's first stage success was *The Vortex*, produced in 1924, followed by a string of West End hits which confirmed his place as Britain's most bankable inter-war playwright: *Easy Virtue* (1925), *Bitter Sweet* (1929), *Private Lives* (1930), *Design for Living* (1932) and *Blithe Spirit* (1941) all enjoyed long runs. His plays, in which he occasionally acted himself starred many of the leading actors of the day such as Laurence OLIVIER. Coward's own most famous role was as a naval officer in the wartime film *In Which We Serve* (1942), based on the exploits of his friend Louis MOUNTBATTEN's destroyer HMS *Kelly*. A self-taught lyricist and songwriter of such numbers as 'Mad Dogs and Englishmen', Coward was witty, debonair and observant of the high society to which his charm had gained him an entry and, although some of his work treated controversial subjects, such as drug addiction in *The Vortex*, his *métier* was essentially light comedy.

COWEN, JOSEPH (1829–1900), politican and newspaper proprietor. Born in Blaydon Burn (Co. Durham), the son of Joseph Cowen, Liberal MP and brick manufacturer, he was a close friend of Mazzini and Kossuth and one of the most important advocates of liberal internationalism of the mid nineteenth century, especially in his support of Italian, Polish and Hungarian nationalisms. In the 1860s he became the proprietor of the *Newcastle Daily Chronicle* and the *Newcastle Weekly Chronicle*, the latter becoming one of the most widely read provincial papers. Partly through the paper he became the chief Liberal middle-class supporter in the north-east of working-class interests, notably the struggle for the vote in 1866–7. A leading republican from the 1850s to the 1870s, he was Liberal MP for Newcastle 1874–86 and supported Irish Home Rule in 1886.

COWLING, MAURICE (1926–), historian. A journalist and politician *manqué* before falling into history in the 1960s, Cowling became a Fellow of Peterhouse, Cambridge, in 1963, and over the next three decades established himself and the college as a bastion against leftist thinking and socialist assumptions.

He was not an exponent of disinterested historical truth but he was a rigorous archival historian whose achievement in his three main books, *1867: Gladstone, Disraeli and Revolution* (1967), *The Impact of Labour* (1971) and *The Impact of Hitler* (1975), was to establish the autonomy of 'high politics'. His working assumption was that politics at Westminster consisted of the sayings, doings and ambitions of several dozen leading politicians, and his books provided a minute examination of how that solipsistic world of Westminster worked. While his influence as a historian influenced the study of British political history, his own actions as one of the founders of the Salisbury group in 1978 helped lay the intellectual foundations of the 'new Right' of the 1980s.

COWPER, WILLIAM (1st Earl Cowper) (*c.* 1665–1723), lawyer and Whig politician. Son of a Whig politician and associate of Shaftesbury (*see* COOPER, ANTHONY ASHLEY), his support for the future WILLIAM III in 1688 helped his successful legal and political career. Lord Keeper from 1705, and from 1707 to 1710 Lord Chancellor, he overruled objections about the non-specific nature of the charges at the trial of the provocative Tory clergyman SACHEVERELL and voted for his impeachment. When the Whigs came to power again on GEORGE I's accession, he again became Lord Chancellor. He wrote *A Brief History of Parties* for the King, a recent history of British politics subtly arguing for Whig supremacy which his second wife Mary translated into French (probably to make it more easily accessible for the King and his courtiers). Faced with attacks on dissenting meeting-houses during the 1715 rebellion, Cowper introduced the Riot Act 1715, which made it a felony for members of a crowd of 12 or more to refuse to disperse within an hour of being ordered to do so by a magistrate. He left office in 1718 (following Robert WALPOLE and TOWNSHEND into opposition) over a Bill supplying an additional £100,000 a year to George I without reserving some of it for the Prince of Wales (later GEORGE II). In opposition, he allied himself with the Tories to such an extent that he was named as a Jacobite by Christopher LAYER, although the charge was probably false.

COWPER, WILLIAM (1731–1800), poet. A clergyman's son, he trained first as a solicitor and then as a barrister. His legal career was effectively halted by a suicide attempt in 1763 shortly before he was to be examined for a position at the House of Lords. Converted to Evangelical Christianity by his cousin Martin MADAN, Cowper moved first to Huntingdon and then to Olney (Bucks.) where he undertook charitable work between periods of depression. In collaboration with the curate of

Olney, John Newton, Cowper produced *Olney Hymns* in 1779. He was encouraged by his sometime fiancée Mary Unwin to write poetry, eventually collected in book form in 1782. Further verse followed, most notably *John Gilpin* (1782), the six-book *The Task* (1785) and *Castaway* (1794), written following Mary Unwin's death.

COX, RICHARD (*c.* 1500–81), churchman. Cambridge-educated, he was one of the secretly reformist academics unwittingly imported by Cardinal WOLSEY to his ambitious Oxford college (1525); he later became its first Dean when HENRY VIII refounded it as Christ Church (1546), having been tutor to Prince Edward (the future EDWARD VI). As Chancellor of Oxford, he was an aggressive Protestant, responsible for destroying the medieval university library and much else (earning the nickname 'Cancellor'). In exile under MARY I at Frankfurt, he successfully led opposition to John KNOX, particularly in defence of the Edwardian Prayer Book (having been involved in its compilation). He returned to be Bishop of Ely from 1559, but endured harassment from influential local Puritans.

CRABBE, GEORGE (1754–1832), poet. Born in Aldeburgh (Suffolk), the setting of many of his poems, he was apprenticed to a surgeon. He published *Inebriety* in 1775, a poem in the style of POPE warning against the iniquities of drink, and in 1780, resolving to be a writer, went to London. There he was saved from destitution by BURKE, who introduced him to the London literati, encouraged him to enter the Church (he became chaplain to the Duke of Rutland between 1782 and 1785, which gave him leisure to write), and advised him to publish *The Village* (1783) (as did Samuel JOHNSON); this poem, in heroic couplets, established Crabbe's reputation as a realist poet of rural life, 'Nature's sternest painter yet the best', as BYRON called him. *The Borough* (1810) contained the story of Peter Grimes on which BRITTEN based his opera of the same name.

CRAIG, JAMES (1st Viscount Craigavon) (1871–1940), Prime Minister of Northern Ireland. A stockbroker and Boer War veteran, Craig was a Westminster MP for East Down (1906–18) and Mid-Down (1918–21), and a junior minister (1916–18 and 1919–21). As representative of a more populist generation of professional and business Unionists reacting against the aristocratic amateurism of older Unionists like Edward SAUNDERSON, he played a leading role in founding the Ulster Unionist Council in 1905 and organizing the Ulster Volunteer Force to resist Home Rule after 1910. Generally recognized as Edward CARSON's right-hand man, he made skilful use of publicity to bolster Carson's image as a heroic and uncompromising leader. In 1921, after Carson refused the position, he became the first Prime Minister of Northern Ireland. Craig made effective use of harsh security measures and British contacts to avert the threat of IRA attacks and British concessions to the new Irish Free State at Northern Ireland's expense. He was less successful as a peacetime premier, given to reckless promises of public funds in order to retain support; his Cabinet, dominated by ageing businessmen, was unimaginative in dealing with the inter-war depression and the decline of Northern Ireland's traditional industries. His sanction of anti-Catholic discrimination and refusal (despite conciliatory statements in his earlier years as premier) to address the concerns of moderate nationalists such as Joseph DEVLIN stored up problems for his successors.

CRAIG, SIR THOMAS (1538–1608), lawyer. Educated at St Andrews and Paris, he was admitted as an advocate in 1563, was Justice Depute from 1564 to 1573 and then Sheriff Depute for Edinburgh. He became Laird of Riccarton (Lothian); knighted in 1603, he accompanied JAMES VI to England and was a commissioner for the unsuccessful scheme to unite the two kingdoms. In 1603 he published *Jus Feudale*, a pioneering discussion of Scots feudal law, and also wrote a major work (unpublished at the time) in favour of union, considering its potential implications for the Scots and English legal systems.

CRAIG, WILLIAM (1924–), politician *see* TRIMBLE, DAVID

CRAIGAVON, 1ST VISCOUNT *see* CRAIG, JAMES

CRANBORNE, 1ST VISCOUNT *see* CECIL, ROBERT, essay on page 158

CRANBROOK, 1ST EARL OF *see* HARDY, GATHORNE

CRANE, WALTER (1845–1914), illustrator. Son of a Manchester portrait painter, Crane became well known for his high-quality illustrations of children's books, the most famous of which was *The Baby's Opera* (1877). He also illustrated SPENSER's *Faerie Queen* (1894–6). A strong supporter of the aims of William MORRIS, for whose company he designed wallpapers and friezes, he was the first President of the Arts and Crafts Exhibition Society, published *The Claims of Decorative Art* (1892) and, a convert to socialism, produced many graphics in promotion of the cause.

CRANFIELD, LIONEL (1st Earl of Middlesex) (1575–1645), royal servant. A London mercer who gained the favour of Henry HOWARD, Earl of Northampton, under JAMES I, becoming Surveyor General of Customs 1613, he filled many other offices rising to Lord Treasurer in 1621; he gained his earldom in 1622. An able minister, he tried to reform government and avoid war and wasteful expenditure, but was careless enough to make a wide range of enemies, including those sworn foes, Francis BACON and Edward COKE. Coke engineered his impeachment on corruption charges in 1624, and his career was ruined.

CRANMER, THOMAS *see* essay on page 211

CREAGH, RICHARD (?1525–85), Archbishop of Armagh. He studied at Leuven and was made Roman Catholic Archbishop of Armagh in 1564. Confined in the Tower of London in 1565, he was tried for treason in Dublin in 1567 and although acquitted remained a prisoner and died in the Tower. He wrote on the Irish language, a history of Ireland, lives of saints, and polemical religious works.

CREWE, JOHN (1st Baron Crewe) (1742–1829), politician, and his wife **FRANCES ANNE** (née Greville) (?–1818), political hostess. Crewe became an MP in 1765. A close friend of Charles James FOX, he spent large sums supporting Fox's debts. His only significant contribution to politics came in 1782 when he piloted Crewe's Act through the Commons, disenfranchising customs and excise officers from voting in elections. He was promised a peerage by Fox, but was not rewarded until 1806. His wife, a noted beauty, was a well-known hostess with a circle of distinguished literary and political friends.

CREWE-MILNES, ROBERT (2nd Baron Houghton, 1st Marquess of Crewe) (1858–1945), politician. He was the son of the Victorian man-of-letters and politician, Richard Monckton-Milnes, and inherited great estates from his mother Annabel, heiress of the last Lord Crewe. One of the few young Whigs who stuck with GLADSTONE, Crewe became Viceroy of Ireland in 1892 at the age of 34; two years later he inherited the Crewe estates and became Earl of Crewe. In the last Liberal government he became successively Colonial Secretary, Secretary of State for India and Lord President of the Council and Leader of the Lords. In 1911 he was given the Garter and a marquessate. From 1922 to 1928 he was British Ambassador in Paris where he presided in Whiggish splendour.

CRICHTON, JAMES (1560–?1585), scholar. Son of a prominent Scots lawyer, he was educated at St Andrews and Paris, where he is reputed to have held academic disputations in 12 languages. He served as a soldier in France, travelled in Italy, was much acclaimed for his learning, but was killed in a brawl in Mantua. What survives of his writings are poems and dedications to prominent Italians. Sir Thomas Urquhart wrote a highly coloured life of him in 1652, and bestowed on him the nickname 'the admirable Crichton'.

CRICK, FRANCIS (1916–), molecular biologist. Crick studied physics at University College, London, and during the Second World War worked for the Admiralty. By 1949 he had joined the Medical Research Council's molecular biology department in the Cavendish Laboratory, Cambridge, and worked with Max PERUTZ, John KENDREW and others on X-ray crystallographic techniques of determining the structure of large biological molecules. In 1951 he met James Watson, an American zoologist who shared Crick's belief that the nature of the gene could be best probed by determining, by X-ray crystallographic and other methods, the molecular structure of deoxyribonucleic acid (DNA). Crick and Watson drew extensively on the work of others in what was to become a celebrated collaborative research project; notably Oswald Avery's demonstration that genes consist of DNA, Erwin Chagraff and Alexander TODD's work on DNA's chemical composition, Maurice Wilkins's work on DNA's double-helical structure and Rosalind FRANKLIN's evidence that phosphate groups are positioned on the outside of the DNA helix. By 1953 they had worked out a molecular structure of DNA that consisted of two intertwined helical chains of sugar-phosphate groups linked horizontally at regular intervals by organic bases. Their structure explained how the cell's hereditary material replicated itself and how DNA encoded the structure and function of each cell. Thus, Crick played a crucial part in one of the twentieth century's most celebrated scientific accomplishments, the determination of the structure of the gene. He shared the 1962 Nobel Prize for Medicine or Physiology with Watson and Wilkins and subsequently worked on the ways in which DNA encodes, translates and transfers genetic information. In 1977 Crick left Cambridge for the Salk Institute in California, where he worked on molecular genetics.

CRÍNÁN (?–1045), Abbot of Dunkeld. Crínán may also have been the ruler of the province of Atholl and his abbacy of Dunkeld may well have been a hereditary, laicized office, for his career is anything but that normally associated with a churchman. Married to a daughter of MAEL COLUIM II, Crínán ensured the succession of his son, DONNCHAD I, as King following his father-in-law's death in 1034. Following Donnchad's death

continued on page 212

CRANMER, THOMAS (1489–1556)
Archbishop of Canterbury (1533–56)

From a minor Notts. gentry family, characterized by strong traditional piety; his sister Alice became a nun and his brother Edmund followed him to Jesus College, Cambridge. In the mid 1510s he surrendered his Jesus College fellowship in order to marry, but this first wife died in childbirth, and Cranmer was then ordained and returned to Jesus. Like many Cambridge dons, he was recruited by Cardinal WOLSEY for diplomatic service and served on a mission to the court of CHARLES V in Spain in 1527, meeting HENRY VIII on his return. This initial contact bore fruit in 1529, when in the middle of deadlock over Henry's attempts to force the Pope to agree an annulment of his marriage to CATHERINE OF ARAGON, Cranmer suggested fresh consultations with European university theology faculties. He was sent on a mission to Italy in 1530, and while in Rome was granted the benefice of Bredon (Worcs.) by the absentee Italian Bishop of Worcester, Jerome Ghinucci. Over the next year, it is likely that his work on Henry's case destroyed his faith in the Papacy and encouraged him to abandon traditionalist piety. On a further diplomatic mission to the Lutheran city of Nuremberg in 1532, he gave a dramatic demonstration of this by marrying Margarethe, niece of the German Lutheran theologian Andreas Osiander, an illegal act for a priest. To his embarrassment, Henry then engineered his appointment as Archbishop of Canterbury after the death of William WARHAM (1532). Consecrated with reluctant papal approval in 1533, he soon pronounced the King's first marriage annulled and cleared the way for a marriage to ANNE BOLEYN. This was the beginning of a pursuit of reform in the Church in close co-operation with Thomas CROMWELL. Anne was also his religious ally, but, when she and Cromwell quarrelled and Henry was convinced of her adultery, Cranmer granted the King a further annulment (1536).

Cranmer continued to work closely with Cromwell to further reform, but acquiesced in Henry's conservative Act of Six Articles (1539), which meant that his wife had to leave England. He survived Cromwell's fall (1540) due to the favour of CATHERINE HOWARD (he had opposed Cromwell's advocacy of the marriage to ANNE OF CLEVES), but in 1541 he was the only person at court capable of breaking the news to Henry of Catherine's adultery. Henry's trust in him enabled him to survive conservative attempts in 1543 to brand him a heretic, and he remained in

the King's favour through the turbulent last years of the reign. In EDWARD VI's reign, he was a chief architect of the Edwardian religious changes, constructing the two Prayer Books (1549, 1552), the second of which was more radical than the first and better expressed his evangelical outlook. He also drew up an Ordinal (the order of service in which bishops, priests and deacons are ordained) in 1550, and wrote two books vigorously defending against Stephen GARDINER his belief that the Eucharist did not bring a physical presence of Jesus Christ to the elements of bread and wine. He presided over the compilation of a doctrinal statement for the Church of England, the Forty-Two Articles (issued 1553), the basis for the 1563 Thirty-Nine Articles which are still the Church's doctrinal standard; he also vigorously forwarded a complete recasting of the Church's canon law (later called by John FOXE the *Reformatio Legum*), which was however prevented from becoming law in 1553 by the hostility of John DUDLEY, Duke of Northumberland.

Despite Cranmer's strained relations with the Duke, he reluctantly agreed to the unsuccessful attempt to sidestep the succession of MARY I by making JANE GREY Queen. Convicted of treason (1553) and of heresy (1554), he was imprisoned with Hugh LATIMER and Nicholas RIDLEY. Demoralized by imprisonment, he signed six recantations, some of which were signed after it was clear that he would still be condemned to burn at the stake. He made a final bold statement of his Protestant faith, publicly repudiating his recantations before his burning, and made a point of thrusting the right hand which had signed them into the flames. Cranmer's devotion to Henry VIII (amounting to a single-minded belief in the central theological importance of the royal supremacy in the Church) led him into compromises which now seem difficult to excuse, and his hesitations before his death render him far from a ready-made hero in Reformation disputes. Yet he showed a forgiving spirit, unusual in that age, towards his enemies (apart from Observant Franciscan Friars, whom he detested as the most effective champions of the old religion), and he did not shrink from arguing with Henry about theology. He was an impressively learned if unoriginal scholar, and his genius for formal prose has left a lasting mark not merely on Anglican liturgy but on the speech-patterns of the English language.

Diarmaid MacCulloch, Thomas Cranmer: A Life (1996)

at the hands of MACBETH in 1040, Crínán led a short-lived uprising against Macbeth in 1045, which collapsed following his defeat and death in battle.

CRIPPS, SIR STAFFORD (1889–1952), politician. After a highly successful career at the Bar, becoming the youngest KC in 1927, Cripps was drawn into Labour Party politics in 1929. His uncle by marriage, Sidney WEBB, and his father were both Cabinet ministers in Ramsay MACDONALD's government, and in 1930 Cripps became Solicitor General. He declined the invitation to continue in that post in the National government of 1931, and threw himself with zeal into militantly socialist politics. His willingness to work with communists led both to his expulsion from the Labour Party and to his election to the National Executive at the 1937 party conference. Readmitted to the party, he was expelled again in Jan. 1939 for advocating a cross-party Popular Front to oust Neville CHAMBERLAIN's government. Party and public opinion were divided about him; sent as Ambassador to Moscow in 1940, Cripps was convinced of the need to persuade Stalin away from the Nazi–Soviet Pact of 1939. After Hitler attacked the Soviet Union in June 1941, Cripps's role in furthering the Anglo-Russian accord was significant. As a member of the War Cabinet, he was sent to India to gain Indian support for the war effort; he failed, and left the Cabinet to become Minister of Aircraft Production until 1945.

Cripps became President of the Board of Trade in the 1945 ATTLEE government, and so prime mover of the difficult post-war economic reconstruction strategy and its accompanying austerity measures including higher taxation, even stricter rationing than in wartime and the diversion of domestic production to exports. Becoming Chancellor of the Exchequer in 1947 after Hugh DALTON's resignation, Cripps had the difficult task of implementing wage and dividend freezes, but in Sept. 1949 was forced into a devaluation of the pound. He resigned due to ill health in Oct. 1950. The mixture of wealthy grandee and ardent socialist, combined with the force of personality which allowed an unpalatable economic policy to be maintained for so long, made Cripps an important figure in Labour politics through the 1930s and 1940s. Yet his legacy gave opponents of subsequent Labour governments the ready charge that theirs was the devaluing party, and with his departure the general resentment in the country at his economic measures became only too apparent.

CROMER, EARL OF, 1ST see BARING, EVELYN; **3RD** see BARING, GEORGE

CROMPTON, SAMUEL (1753–1827), inventor. Born in Lancs., Crompton learnt weaving and mechanical skills at home, later working in a spinning mill where he became acquainted with James HARGREAVES's spinning jenny. Dissatisfied with the quality of yarn produced by Hargreaves's machine, he sought to improve it and in 1779 completed his famous 'spinning mule', a cross between Hargreaves's jenny and Richard ARKWRIGHT's spinning machine. Crompton's invention stretched and twisted the yarn and made it both stronger and of finer quality. By the early 1800s it was by far the most widely used spinning machine and had caused a boom in the British cotton trade. For several reasons, Crompton did not patent his invention and sold it for £67. Subsequently he tried unsuccessfully to make a career in manufacturing and, despite receiving a £5,000 government award for his invention in 1812, he spent his last years in dire financial straits.

CROMWELL, OLIVER see essay on pages 214–5

CROMWELL, RALPH (3rd Baron Cromwell) (?1394–1456), royal servant. He was a prominent member of the Council that ruled England during HENRY VI's minority. As Treasurer of England (1433–43), he was responsible for the survey of government finance presented to Parliament in 1433. Involvement in local feuds led to a notorious attempt to murder him at Westminster in 1449 and so to his own active role in helping to bring down William de la POLE, Duke of Suffolk, in 1450. He built Tattershall Castle (Lincs.) with the profits of a lifetime in government.

CROMWELL, RICHARD (1626–1712), politician. Son of Oliver CROMWELL, he found himself Lord Protector for want of an alternative on his father's death in 1658, having previously served conscientiously in second-rank offices. His regime at first looked stable, but was undermined by financial chaos and confrontation between government and army. The army forced him to dissolve Parliament in April 1659 and he was overthrown in May. He later lived in retirement unmolested, first in Paris, then in London and Hampshire: an amiable, hard-working man thrust into power at the most difficult of times.

CROMWELL, THOMAS see essay on pages 216–7

CROOKES, SIR WILLIAM (1832–1919), chemist and journalist. Crookes studied chemistry in his native London and subsequently plied his skills in photography, analytical chemistry, meteorology, and journalism. He was the editor of several major scientific periodicals (notably the *Chemical News*) and is celebrated as the discoverer, in 1861, of the element thallium. In 1869 he began his lifelong interest in spiritual phenomena and two years later began seriously to investigate radiation forces. This latter work led to his invention of such spectacular instruments as the radiometer and X-ray tubes. Later he explored electrical discharge in rarefied gases, spectroscopy, radioactivity and chemical periodicity. He was President of the Society for Psychical Research (1896–9). He was an indefatigable entrepreneur, his commercial schemes including gold extraction, antiseptic spray, sewage recycling and electric lighting.

CROSBY, BRASS (1723–93), politician. Born in Stockton-on-Tees, he became an attorney in London, involving himself in City and national politics as an ally of John WILKES. An MP for Honiton (Devon) from 1768, he was elected Lord Mayor of London in 1770 and set himself on a collision course with government and Parliament. He ordered constables to prevent press gangs operating in the City and the arrest of King's messengers sent by order of Parliament to arrest printers who were publishing parliamentary debates. He and a fellow City magistrate, Oliver, were sent to the Tower after the Commons resolved that this breached the privileges of the House (March 1771), but were released at the end of the session (May) to wild popular acclaim.

CROSLAND, ANTHONY (1918–77), politician and theorist. An economics lecturer at Oxford University before becoming an MP in 1950, his highly influential work *The Future of Socialism* (1956) advocated improved economic performance to advance socialist policies of welfare provision. This emphasis on economic competence was seen as setting the agenda for Harold WILSON'S governments of the 1960s, though he was seen by the right of the Labour Party as GAITSKELL'S political heir and Wilson kept him out of the Treasury. He served as Minister of State for Economic Affairs in 1964–5. As Secretary of State for Education and Science (1965–7), he played a major role in promoting comprehensive schools, becoming President of the Board of Trade (1967–70) after devaluation (for which he had argued). As Environment Minister (1974–6) in the second Wilson government, he called a halt to local authority spending in the face of unresolved economic difficulties. Appointed Foreign Secretary by CALLAGHAN in 1976, he died in office the following year, depriving Labour of one of its intellectual heavyweights.

CROSS, CHARLES FREDERICK (1855–1935), chemist. Cross studied chemistry in London, Zürich and Manchester. With Edward Bevan he formed an analytical chemistry firm and explored the chemistry and technology of wood- and paper-making. In 1892 Cross, Bevan and Clayton Beadle took out a patent on the 'viscose' process, a technique for extracting cellulose and then converting it into spinnable fibres of 'viscose' rayon. This patent has been seen as the origin of the artificial fibre industry, although Cross and his collaborators took more than 10 years to make their product commercially successful.

CROSSMAN, RICHARD (1907–74), politician. A philosophy don who became a journalist, politician and, in 1970, editor of the *New Statesman*, Crossman was leader of the Labour group on Oxford City Council (1936–40) before entering Parliament as Labour member for Coventry in 1945. A 'Bevanite' in the 1950s (*see* BEVAN, ANEURIN), he did not achieve office until 1964 when he was Minister of Housing in Harold WILSON'S government; subsequently he became Leader of the House of Commons, in which capacity he tried to reform the procedures of Parliament in line with his principles of democracy and accountability. In 1968 Crossman became the first head of the new Department of Health and Social Security, where he was disappointed at the failure of his controversial attempt to introduce a national superannuation scheme. After the defeat of the Labour government in 1970 he began work on the political diaries he had kept assiduously whilst in office. He died before the legal wrangle, in which the Labour Attorney General sought to prevent publication, was resolved but the publication of *The Diaries of a Cabinet Minister* (1975–7), in which he recorded the workings of the British political system and the 'mumbo jumbo' of office, provide an invaluable record of both the Wilson years and the decision-making processes of a supposed democracy.

CROWE, SIR EYRE (1864–1925), diplomat. Born and educated in Germany, he joined the Foreign Office (1885), where his 'Memorandum on the present state of British relations with France and Germany' (1907), a sober assessment of the balance of power in Europe, was an impetus to war in 1914 in as much as it suggested that if German expansion in Europe, Africa and Asia was not contained it would threaten Britain's position. As Assistant Under-Secretary of State for Foreign Affairs his advice was that the terms of the *Entente Cordiale* (1904) committed Britain to support France in the case of German aggression.

CROWLEY, ALEISTER (originally Alexander) (1875–1947), mystic. Innovative about his origins, claiming that he was the direct descendant of Genghis Khan, descended from CHARLES II, the reincarnation of John DEE'S 'scryer' with a variety of other magicians or charlatans as antecedents, Crowley was in fact the son of a wealthy alehouse owner and his wife, both Plymouth Brethren, so

continued on page 218

CROMWELL, OLIVER (1599–1658)
Soldier and statesman

Oliver's Welsh great-grandfather had changed his surname of Williams to Cromwell in compliment to his cousin and patron Thomas CROMWELL. He came from a very minor gentry background in Huntingdon; his father was the younger son of a knight, but also a townsman with no land and a very modest income. He studied law and, through the influence of the Montagu family of Hinchingbrooke, was returned as an MP for Huntingdon in 1628. After public humiliation in a quarrel with his Montagu patrons, he seems to have had a nervous breakdown in the early 1630s, followed by a conversion to an activist Puritan faith, and through various family connections he became closely linked to the network of leading Puritan families of Essex, particularly that of Robert RICH, Earl of Warwick. It may have been this influence which led to election for Cambridge in the Short and the Long Parliaments (1640); after the outbreak of war with the King (1642), it probably also promoted his increasing prominence in the Eastern Association, East Anglia's military organization commanded by Edward MONTAGU, Earl of Manchester. As the Westminster Parliament's war effort fell into increasing disarray, Cromwell became steadily more critical of the High Command, which he regarded (with some justice) as defeatist: his discontent produced a serious quarrel with Manchester after the indecisive second Battle of Newbury (27 Oct. 1644). He was already displaying suspicion of the Presbyterian Scottish allies of Parliament, who backed Manchester, and revealing a commitment to a much more decentralized ideal for reorganizing the Church (Independency). In order to remove Manchester and like-minded commanders like Robert DEVEREUX, Earl of Essex, Cromwell secured Parliament's adoption of the Self-Denying Ordinance, which disqualified members of both houses from military or naval field commands; this should be combined with the formation of a New Model Army, for the first time a national force free of restrictions imposed by the regional organizations. Manchester and Essex complied with ill grace, and resigned their military commands; Cromwell and others were reinstated where convenient. He backed Thomas FAIRFAX's command of the New Model Army, emerging as the most powerful military commander with Independent sympathies manoeuvring against the Presbyterian group in Parliament. His first great success, though fairly close-run, was his victory over Prince RUPERT at Naseby (June 1645). After

CHARLES I's surrender (1646) Cromwell and his son-in-law IRETON were the army's most active representatives in the prolonged and futile negotiations to find some permanent political settlement, increasingly suspicious that Presbyterians would make too many concessions to the King, but also worried by the radical social views expressed by the Levellers within the army. He and his fellow officers engaged in a series of debates with the radicals in Putney parish church during 1647–8; these produced little result. He was shocked by the outbreak of Royalist uprisings leading to the Second Civil War (summer 1648) and, after playing a major part in putting it down, became convinced that no deal could be made with Charles. After the army had ejected the Presbyterian party from Parliament in PRIDE's Purge (6 Dec. 1648), leaving the Rump Parliament, Cromwell superintended Charles's trial and execution in 1649 and was the first chairman of the Council of State set up by the Rump on 17 Feb. 1649. He was also instrumental in confronting and ruthlessly suppressing Leveller leadership in the army. In Aug. 1649 he faced the formidable challenge offered by an Irish coalition led by James BUTLER, Earl of Ormond; landing at Ringsend (Dublin) and marching north to Drogheda, he treated the town ruthlessly after capturing it, and behaved equally savagely in his southern campaign at Wexford. Both these atrocities may later have been exaggerated, but they were real; Cromwell had no hesitation in regarding them as God's judgement on a bloodthirsty and barbarous enemy. By Dec. he held the whole east coast of Ireland, and by the time that he left Ireland to face a new threat from Scotland in May 1650 the English forces held the advantage. Cromwell defeated a Scots Presbyterian army fighting for CHARLES II, first at Dunbar (3 Sept. 1650) and then at Worcester (3 Sept. 1651), after which Charles fled abroad.

From now on, Cromwell was the most significant person in the republican government, but he did not as yet control decision-making, and his relations with the Rump Parliament were increasingly strained. When the Rump seemed to be legislating to choose its successors, Cromwell yielded to army pressure and dissolved it, with theatrical relish (20 April 1653), though he had little idea about how to replace it. Nevertheless, as Commander-in-Chief of the army, he was the only authority left to rule the British Isles and to find a lasting balance of army power against civilian longing for peace and proper representation in government. His first attempt was to create a nominated assembly (swiftly and contemptuously nicknamed Barebone's Parliament (*see* BARBON, PRAISE-GOD) but his high hopes were soon dashed; the measures of social radicalism proposed by some members alarmed him, and he accepted a surrender of power by a group of more conservative members (11 Dec. 1653). The disappointment left him with a lasting pessimism about reforming England, and the settlement which he now accepted from John LAMBERT in the Instrument of Government was essentially a defence of a commonwealth run by landed gentry. Radicals in Church and army regarded it as betraying their revolution. Cromwell was now declared Lord Protector, a title giving him supreme legislative and executive power in association with Parliament (now elected, on a new franchise) and the Council of State. In 1654 he ended the war against the Dutch begun by the Rump in 1652, with little gained after an indecisive conflict. The campaigns launched against Tunisian piracy in 1655 and the Spaniards (1655–8) were successful, the Spanish war resulting in the conquest of Jamaica. His national Church Settlement effected a comprehensive and tolerant Protestantism, alongside which strict adherents of the pre-war Church (Laudian Episcopalians) maintained semi-open worship, and Roman Catholics were paradoxically less molested than they had been for a century. He was responsible for readmitting Jews into England in 1655; following a mission by Manasseh ben Israel of Amsterdam, Cromwell tacitly rescinded the expulsion order of 1290, and a test case at law in 1656 confirmed Jewish property rights. Although this may seem like modern liberalism, it was a mix of pragmatism and excitable theology characteristic of the Interregnum and of Cromwell in particular. One of the biblical signs to announce the coming of Christ in the last days would be the conversion of the Jews, but an obstacle to this was that there were apparently no Jews to convert in England: hence the need to readmit them.

Cromwell, faced by renewed threats of Royalist and radical conspiracy, and by the task of keeping the resentful components of the British Isles under English rule, needed to expand the army, whose maintenance already caused acute financial difficulties. He therefore instituted the rule of the major-generals, originally to supervise financial exactions on Royalists and organize a new local militia; the new institution also aroused fresh government hopes that old ideals of Puritan reform of national morality could be imposed by official

action. The experiment was disastrously unpopular and led to demands from Cromwell's second Parliament (1656) for further constitutional change. Central to this Humble Petition and Advice was the proposal that he become King. He eventually refused, since the army loathed the idea, but he allowed legislation to make the Protectorate hereditary in his family and to restore an Upper House to Parliament. Some of his advisers were former Royalists, and he lived in increasingly monarchical splendour, with his court providing significant patronage for music (of which he was extremely fond). On the night of one of the century's greatest storms, he died, 'people not much minding it', in the diarist Ralph JOSSELIN's unkind phrase. His son Richard lacked either the charisma or the determination to maintain the Protectorate, and the ensuing political chaos led to Charles II's restoration. Cromwell's body, buried in Westminster Abbey, was dug up and ceremonially executed in 1660; his head is buried in Sidney Sussex College Chapel, Cambridge.

Cromwell remains one of England's most symbolically controversial figures: a hero to those believing that Britain's problems stem from excessive deference and persistent social inequality, a villain to those seeing him as overturning a settled constitution and wantonly killing a king, and equally a villain to those remembering his summary executions of Leveller leaders. A great military commander and religious idealist, he lacked personal ambition. His strong streak of humility and self-doubt, most apparent in his political leadership, makes it inappropriate to see him as anticipating modern dictatorships, although many reading the portrait of a God-sent hero presented by Thomas CARLYLE have interpreted him in this way. His complex career, destroying both hereditary monarchy and aspirations for radical democracy, and bearing responsibility for some of the worst English triumphalism towards the other peoples of the British Isles, is marked by his unhappy attempts to balance two irreconcilables. Like so many Puritans, he wished to make the world safe for landowning gentry (an anxiety no doubt heightened by the social insecurity of his early life), but he also wished to transform society in the cause of godly reformation. He was acutely aware of his failure to resolve this; yet one can forgive much to a man who when writing to the General Assembly of the Church of Scotland (1650) could 'beseech you, in the bowels of Christ, [to] think it possible you may be mistaken'.

Christopher Hill, God's Englishman: Oliver Cromwell and the English Revolution (1970

CROMWELL, THOMAS (16th [1st Cromwell] Earl of Essex) (?1485–1540)
Royal servant

Son of a tradesman from Putney or Wimbledon (Surrey), Cromwell gained an all-round education through a colourful if obscure early career in continental travel and commerce. He may have served as a soldier in the Franco-Italian wars; without spending any time at university, he acquired Latin, French and Italian. From *c.* 1514 he was back in England, entering the service of Thomas WOLSEY in 1516; in 1517 and 1518 he made two further ventures to Rome on business for the town of Boston (Lincs.). He combined his work for Wolsey with an extensive private practice as an attorney (again, apparently despite having had no formal legal training), but by the early 1520s he was becoming Wolsey's chief man of affairs. He was particularly concerned with the dissolution of small religious houses in order to endow Wolsey's deluxe school, Cardinal College, Ipswich, and the Oxford college to which it was linked (Cardinal College, the nucleus of the later Christ Church); this provided useful experience for HENRY VIII's later dissolutions. Elected MP in 1523, he opposed royal expenditure on war with France, possibly as Wolsey's mouthpiece. Admirably loyal to Wolsey when he fell from power 1529, and defending his fallen master against attacks in the House of Commons, he transferred to royal service with quiet efficiency after Wolsey's death in 1530 and rapidly gained Henry VIII's trust, becoming a member of the Royal Council in 1531 and Master of the Jewels and Master of the Wards in 1532. He succeeded his rival Stephen GARDINER, another former Wolsey servant, as the King's secretary in 1534. Opinions differ on how far he originated the idea of breaking with the Papacy in order to solve Henry's marriage problem; although it is likely that the concept was the King's, Cromwell supervised the detailed working out of the scheme which reflected his own experience of the House of Commons – until then an unusual background for a senior royal adviser. The breach with Rome was effected by a series of Acts in the Reformation Parliament (1529–36): first in 1532 legislation to intimidate Rome, the Conditional Restraint of Annates (i.e. clerical taxation owed to the Papacy), next in 1533 a declaration that England was an 'empire' without any superior on earth in the Act in Restraint of Appeals, and then the explicit recognition of the royal supremacy over the Church in the Act of Supremacy (1534). Noteworthy in this and other legislation of the 1530s were the preambles or prefaces to the Acts, setting out the reasons for their enactment. These were part of an awareness of the need to explain the religious revolution, which also saw Cromwell sponsoring the first large-scale English propaganda campaign to use the printing industry, in imitation of the flood of pamphlets which spread LUTHER's reformation in Germany. He encouraged authors to write for the King, and many of them were increasingly open in their advocacy of further evangelical reformation.

Cromwell quickly formed an alliance with the like-minded evangelical Archbishop Thomas CRANMER, and together they sponsored a large-scale campaign during 1534 to make the clergy acknowledge the royal supremacy. This formed part of a visitation of the province of Canterbury by Cranmer (a 'metropolitical' visitation), but Cranmer's officials found themselves running into grave problems about jurisdiction in relation to the newly proclaimed royal supremacy; Cromwell became convinced that some other means of asserting royal authority in the Church was needed. Accordingly in early 1535 he secured his own appointment as Vicar General, giving him power to carry out a visitation of religious houses, and also as Vicegerent in Spirituals: this was a new title which, as its powers expanded, effectively gave him the same sweeping powers over the Church in the King's name which Wolsey had exercised as Papal Legate *a latere*. During 1535 he acted as Vicar General to carry out a general visitation of the monasteries, one aim of which was to gather discreditable material which could be used as propaganda for the suppression of smaller religious houses by Act of Parliament in 1536. He instituted a survey of the wealth of the entire Church, the *Valor Ecclesiasticus*, which reported with a speed and accuracy remarkable for the period. He also set up courts of Augmentations and of First Fruits and Tenths to deal respectively with former monastic property and with the taxes formerly paid to the Pope, and he applied his reforming zeal to the prerogative courts of Star Chamber and of Requests.

By now conservative politicians saw Cromwell as a dangerous threat, all the more when he adroitly abandoned his embattled former ally Queen ANNE BOLEYN and successfully worked for her downfall in May 1536, emerging from this crisis with his own power strengthened and the cause of evangelical reform intact. During summer 1536 he presided as Vicegerent over the province of Canterbury's Convocation (assembly) despite being a layman, and issued injunctions for the whole Church, which began to dismantle traditional devotion and tried (with limited success) to ensure that every parish should obtain a Bible in Latin and English. One of the chief demands of the northern rising known as the Pilgrimage of Grace (1536–7) was his removal, and it was noticeable that in the aftermath of its defeat a newly select Privy Council took shape, whose purpose was probably to ensure that rival politicians could have a guaranteed say in advising the King. Nevertheless he pursued his reformist policies during 1538. He issued further injunctions, a notable provision of which was the order for every parish to keep a register of births, marriages and deaths, a crucial source thereafter for many aspects of English history. He masterminded the rapid dissolution of all friaries, and secured the full authorization for the first time of an English Bible, while at the end of the year he ruthlessly secured the destruction of his traditionalist enemies centred on the COURTENAY and POLE families, remnants of the Yorkist royal line. Busying himself with an accelerated programme of dissolving all remaining monasteries, he survived the enactment of the Six Articles (1539) which emphasized the conservative side of Henry VIII's religious settlement. Thereafter his fatal blunder came with the fiasco of the marriage which he had negotiated for Henry to ANNE OF CLEVES (1540), an attempt to align Henry with the princes of north Germany, who were mostly supporters of the Reformation. Henry, agonized because he was unable readily to extract himself from this sexually incompatible relationship, became receptive to insinuations from conservative politicians that Cromwell was a dangerous heretic. After a spring of wildly varying political signals, during which he was granted one of England's most ancient earldoms, he was suddenly arrested on charges which now appear absurd. He lived only long enough to provide Henry with the evidence which the King needed to end the Anne of Cleves marriage (*see also* CATHERINE HOWARD), after which he was beheaded in the Tower of London.

Cromwell generally had a poor press from history, despite the early admiration of John FOXE for his contribution to the Reformation, even from his one significant biographer, R. B. Merriman.

He found a redoubtable champion, however, in Sir Geoffrey ELTON, who made him the central figure of a 'Tudor Revolution in Government' designed to take administration and decision-making out of the royal household and create formal bureaucratic structures. In later years Elton accepted criticisms that Cromwell did not have the freedom of action to create a coherent system, but he still saw him as making his changes according to a preconceived vision of routinization and centralization. It is certainly true that Cromwell was behind the legislation which united the administrative institutions of Wales to England, and that he initiated major moves to tie Irish government more closely to Westminster. His centralizing drive, however, can be seen as following patterns initiated and carried through less single-mindedly by his old master Wolsey.

Elton also reacted against the traditional picture of a cold bureaucrat (perhaps fostered by the celebrated HOLBEIN portrait of Cromwell), stressing his loyalty to his friends and his ability to form networks of personal contacts. Against earlier historians who had seen Cromwell as an agent of royal tyranny, he emphasized that the Reformation under Cromwell became enshrined in parliamentary legislation, giving Parliament an importance which helped to secure its future; he pointed out that the alternative, less formal means of national consultation, the Great Council, ceased to be summoned after the 1530s (apart from a brief revival in CHARLES I's crisis of 1640). Elton also explored Cromwell's commitment to evangelical religious reform and to planned change in society, trade and industry: while in power, Cromwell encouraged discussion of a variety of such schemes, which would be the basis of a 'commonwealth' ideology of improvement during the mid century, involving such figures as John HALES and Thomas SMITH. Many such protégés went on to play a major part in the religious changes and the political life of EDWARD VI and ELIZABETH I. The battleground for continuing debate remains the rich archive of Cromwell's papers (preserved by confiscation at his arrest), which although containing more of his incoming than his outgoing correspondence, are rich in his memoranda detailing matters for action, a fascinating window on the omnivorous concerns of one of Tudor England's greatest and most creative politicians.

R. B. Merriman, Life and Letters of Thomas Cromwell (2 vols, 1902) the young Crowley had a strict upbringing. Expelled from both his public schools, he went up to Cambridge in 1895, where he wrote erotic verse, and had his first 'mystic' experience in Sweden. For the next few years Crowley travelled widely throughout Britain, Europe, India, Ceylon and Mexico in search of spiritual truths, mystical sects, magic lore and sexual adventure, and acquired a home on the shores of Loch Ness.

In 1904 when he was in Cairo the 'Angel Alwass' dictated *The Book of the Law* to him and this was to be the basis of a 'religion', 'Crowleyanity', that would succeed Christianity, and of which he was the Antichrist, the Great Beast 666 of the Apocalypse. In 1923, following a series of rumours of infant sacrifice, sexual depravity and unexplained deaths, he was evicted by Mussolini from the abbey of Thelema which he had founded in Sicily. Forced by the Second World War to return to Britain, the man who liked to be known as 'the wickedest man alive' published *The Book of Thoth* (1944), which came with set of tarot cards.

CROWLEY, SIR AMBROSE (1658–1713), industrialist. Son of a Quaker nail manufacturer (although he became a member of the Church of England), Crowley acquired three major iron manufactories near Newcastle and had a chain of distribution warehouses. A major supplier to the navy, he prospered in the wars of 1689–1713. A Director of the South Sea Co., Sheriff of London (1706–7), he was knighted, and elected an MP. The Law Book of his ironworks laid down rules for the running of what was at that time an exceptionally large industrial organization and has interested historians for the insight it provides into early industrial management. Crowley's nephew was Sampson LLOYD, the banker.

CROWTHER, SAMUEL (*c.* 1807–91), bishop. Sold into slavery at the age of 12 from the land that is now Nigeria, he was taken from the slave ship by the Royal Navy and brought to Sierra Leone and freedom. Converted to Christianity, he went to Britain, was ordained an Anglican priest in 1843 and returned to Yorubaland. In 1857 he was sent to the Niger and was made Bishop in 1864. As agent of the Church Missionary Society he led the way in codifying and translating many West African languages but was accused of laxity in tolerating heathen practices and forced to resign in 1891. He was seen by many in Africa as a victim of racial prejudice, and schism along racial lines in the Christian missionary movement followed.

CRUICKSHANK, GEORGE (1792–1878), caricaturist. A prolific political caricaturist, he established himself as the successor to GILLRAY with his cartoons on the private life of the Prince Regent (later GEORGE IV) and such works as *The Scourge* (1811–16) and *The Meteor* (1813–14). He also illustrated Grimm's stories, Charles DICKENS's *Oliver Twist* (he is supposed to have used himself as the model for Fagin) and *Sketches by Boz*, William COWPER's *John Gilpin*, DEFOE's *Robinson Crusoe* and Walter SCOTT's *Waverley*, among others. From 1835 he was editor of *The Comic Almanack*, one of the precursors of *Punch*, but much of his later life was devoted to proselytizing against the evils of drink: *The Bottle* (1847) and *The Drunkard's Children* (1848) are examples.

CRUISE O'BRIEN, CONOR (1917–), politician and controversialist. Born into a celebrated nationalist political dynasty (Hanna SHEEHY-SKEFFINGTON was an aunt), he was marked by its political and religious divisions. A civil servant, he also established a reputation as a literary critic and historian, writing a pioneering work on Charles Stewart PARNELL and his party. As an Irish representative at the United Nations in the 1950s he advanced a non-aligned Irish foreign policy, but resigned amidst international controversy in 1961 over his role as UN representative in suppressing the attempted secession of Katanga from the newly independent Congo. He returned to Ireland to serve as Labour member of the Dáil for Dublin North-East (1969–77) and Minister for Posts and Telegraphs (1973–7). Despite earlier anti-partition activities and support for the Civil Rights movement, he reacted to the emergence of the Provisional IRA by becoming the foremost critic of the official Irish view that the North should be reintegrated into the Republic against the will of the majority, expressing his criticism in his influential book *States of Ireland* (1973), and during the 1973–7 coalition government he became particularly associated with support for restrictive security legislation. He was also highly critical of the influence of the Catholic Church. After losing his Dáil seat in 1977 Cruise O'Brien was elected to the Irish Senate but resigned in 1978 to edit the *Observer* (1978–81). He remained a prolific journalist and writer but his influence gradually declined. In 1996 he joined the UK Unionist Party and represented them at the inter-party talks which led to the Good Friday Agreement (1998); he opposed the agreement (as did his party), arguing that its appeasement of paramilitaries undermined Irish democracy. His increasing marginalization tends to obscure his earlier intellectual and political impact, but he remains one of the most prominent intellectuals of twentieth-century Ireland.

CÚ CHUIMNE THE WISE (?–747), monk of Iona. Together with Rubin of Dairinis (d. 725), Cú Chuimne compiled the *Collectio Canonum*

Hibernensis, an extremely important compilation of biblical and patristic teaching and church decrees governing every aspect of Church life, together with tracts on law and secular and ecclesiastical government. Compiled against a background of emergent ascetic reform in Ireland, the work, like much literary work produced by early Irish monasticism, exercised considerable influence throughout Europe for the next four centuries.

CUBITT, THOMAS (1788–1855), builder. A Norfolk builder who revolutionized the trade, he was responsible as a speculative builder for large swathes of Belgravia as well as the east façade of Buckingham Palace and an ambitious sewerage scheme.

CUDLIPP, HUGH (Baron Cudlipp) (1913–98), journalist. Cudlipp worked on provincial papers before arriving in Fleet Street in his early twenties, first as features editor on the *Daily Mirror* and then on its stablemate the *Sunday Pictorial* in the late 1930s. At that time Beaverbrook's *Daily Express* (*see* AITKEN, MAXWELL) dominated the mass circulation newspaper market, but Cudlipp, together with Cecil KING, imported modern tabloid methods from America, including strip cartoons and bold headlines, giving the *Daily Mirror* a populist, irreverent and anti-Establishment flavour that laid the groundwork for its post-war success. As editorial director of the Mirror group (1952–63), he oversaw the steady increase in circulation that made the *Mirror* the country's best-selling paper by the late 1950s, selling over 3 million copies a day. The *Daily Mirror* always supported the Labour Party, and Cudlipp's own politics reflected this link, but the paper never merely followed the party line, positioning itself as the independent voice of the working class.

CUDWORTH, RALPH (1617–88), theologian. Cudworth went to Emmanuel College, Cambridge, where he was contemporary with Benjamin WHICHCOTE, becoming a Fellow in 1639. Like Whichcote and other Cambridge Platonists (*see also* MORE, HENRY), he supported the Parliamentarians in the Civil Wars. They appointed him Master of Clare Hall in 1645, and then of Christ's College in 1654, a post in which he was confirmed by CHARLES II. Cudworth's most important work, *The True Intellectual System of the Universe* (1678), argued that the thought of the ancient philosophers implied a primitive monotheism rather than the atheism often claimed, and thus prepared the way for Christianity.

CUFFAY, WILLIAM (1788–1870), Chartist. Grandson of an African sold into slavery and son of a slave from St Kitts who worked as a ship's cook, he worked as a tailor in London, became a Chartist in 1839 and soon became a leading and militant figure in the movement. He is best known for his part during the spring and summer of 1848 in a secret revolutionary committee planning an uprising of Chartists in London in August. He was sentenced to transportation for life in 1849 and spent the rest of his life in Tasmania. There he continued to be active as a political radical and trade unionist.

CUÍLÉN, King of the Scots (966–71). A son of King INDULF, he seized the kingdom from King DUB, possibly because he had been excluded from the sub-kingdom of Strathclyde contrary to a succession pattern that had existed for much of the ninth century. Cuílén's usurpation began a feud which lasted for a century until the time of MACBETH and MAEL COLUIM III CENN MÓR. He was himself killed by a RHYDDERCH, whose daughter he had abducted.

CULLEN, PAUL (1803–78), Irish Archbishop and Church reformer. Educated in Rome, where he was rector of the Irish College (1832–49), he brought back to Ireland as Archbishop of Armagh (1849–52) and Dublin (1852–78) a determination to implement Roman standards of discipline and devotional practices; his (largely successful) attempts to remodel the hierarchy brought him into conflict with Archbishop John MACHALE of Tuam. In 1866 he became the first resident Irish Cardinal. Cullen is associated with the displacement of folk-Catholic practices by continental-style devotions, though this 'devotional revolution' was well advanced by his arrival. Suspicious of lay-led nationalist movements as potential seedbeds for anti-clerical revolutionaries such as those he witnessed in Italy, he was often accused of putting the interests of the Church (and the clergy) before those of the country as a whole, and strongly opposed the Fenians. Cullen also clashed with John Henry NEWMAN over the running of the Catholic University established in Dublin (with Newman as rector) as a rival to the non-denominational Queen's Colleges. The most prominent leader of the Irish Catholic Church in the nineteenth century, Cullen is seen as the main architect of the form of Irish Catholicism which prevailed until the aftermath of the Second Vatican Council in the 1960s.

CULLEN, WILLIAM (1710–90), physician and chemist. His father was factor to the Duke of Hamilton. He learned medical theory at Glasgow and practised on a merchant ship in the West Indies before inheriting money which enabled him to attend Edinburgh University from 1733. After a few years practising in Hamilton, where he was supported by the Duke, he went to Glasgow in 1744 to found the medical school, where his pupils included Joseph BLACK. In 1756 he moved to Edinburgh to become Professor of Chemistry. He gave innovative lectures on clinical medicine, concentrating on common diseases and also speaking in English rather than Latin. In 1766 he became Professor of Theoretical Medicine, and in 1773 of Practice. His most successful book was the four-volume *First Lines of the Practice of Physic* (1776–84), which gave priority to the nervous system.

CULLWICK, HANNAH (1833–1909), domestic servant. Born in Salop., the daughter of a housemaid and a saddler, Cullwick entered service at eight years old. In 1854 she met Arthur Munby, author and poet, and for the following 18 years the two conducted a secret relationship. Throughout this period she kept diaries (since published in extensive selection) at Munby's command, recording in rich detail the life of a servant. The diaries were also framed by the bizarre liaison of Munby and Cullwick, suggestive of a master–slave and sado-masochistic relationship. They ceased at the point of their marriage in 1873. Their relationship remained largely secret even after Hannah stopped working as a servant in 1888.

CULPEPER, NICHOLAS (1616–54), writer. Having practised medicine and astrology in pre–Civil War London, he was badly wounded serving in Parliamentary armies, but resumed his medical practice and devoted himself to publishing in English on medical themes, earning fury from the Royal College of Physicians for publishing in 1649 a translation of their Latin *Pharmacopeia* (Catalogue of Medicines). His *English Physician Enlarged* (known as 'Culpeper's Herbal', 1653) was a huge publishing success. He left many works in manuscript.

CUMBERLAND, DUKE OF, 2ND *see* GEORGE (CONSORT OF QUEEN ANNE); **3RD** *see* WILLIAM AUGUSTUS

CUMMÉNE FIND (?–669), Abbot of Iona. A nephew of SÉGÉNE, Abbot of Iona, Cumméne himself aquired the abbacy in 657. During his tenure, however, there was a decline in the great abbey's political influence throughout Ireland and northern Britain, as the kingship of the Uí Néill passed from the COLUM CILLE's Cenél Conaill kindred to the southern branches of the dynasty; while the Synod of Whitby, held by King OSWY in 664, weakened relations with Northumbria. A renowned scholar; one of the sources for ADOMNÁN's *Vita Columbae* was Cumméne's (now lost) *Liber de Virtutibus Sancti Columbae*.

CUNARD, NANCY (1896–1965), socialite. Daughter of the society hostess Lady Emerald Cunard, she founded the Hours Press in 1928, publishing the work of such writers as Ezra Pound, Robert GRAVES and Samuel BECKETT. Her cohabitation with a black jazz musician, Henry Crowder, with whom she edited an anthology of black art, *Negro* (1934), caused a major scandal and the couple fled to Australia, from where Cunard penned a pamphlet, *Black Man and White Ladyship,* condemning British racism in general and that of her mother in particular. She became a political activist organizing support for black youths condemned to death in Alabama for allegedly assaulting white prostitutes in 1934. She covered the Spanish Civil War (1936) and wrote anti-Fascist articles for the *Manchester Guardian* and the Associated Negro Free Press. After the war Cunard continued to support various causes such as Spanish refugees, prisoners of Franco and Venetian gondoliers.

CUNARD, SIR SAMUEL (1787–1865), shipowner. Founder of the first regular Atlantic steamship line, Cunard was a Nova Scotia merchant's son. He devised a plan in 1830 for a mail service across the Atlantic and arrived in England in 1838, forming, in partnership with merchants in Glasgow and Liverpool, the British and North America Royal Mail Steam Packet Co., known as the Cunard Line. This was the basis of one of the great shipping companies and its heyday was the 'liner age' of the 1920s and 1930s.

CUNEDDA (*fl. c.* 400), founder of the first dynasty of Gwynedd. According to the ninth-century *Historia Brittonum*, Cunedda, together with eight sons and one grandson, came from Manaw Gododdin (the area around Stirling) to Gwynedd and 'expelled the Irish for ever from these lands'. This occurred, it is stated, 146 years before the reign of MAELGWYN, King of Gwynedd (?–549), who was himself stated to be a descendant of Cunedda. While the historical background to the migration is uncertain, several northern and western Welsh dynasties claimed descent from the sons of Cunedda.

CUNEGLASUS (*fl.* early sixth century), British king. One of the 'five tyrants' condemned for laxity and corruption by GILDAS at the time of the invasions of Britain by the Angles and Saxons, the territory over which Cuneglasus ruled is unknown, although Gildas infers that he was a frequent raider upon his neighbours. The fragmentary reference to such petty rulers and their raids gives a glimpse of the transitory nature of the emergent British kingdoms in post-Roman Britain.

CUNNINGHAM, SIR ALAN GORDON (1887–1983), soldier. Brother of the future Admiral (*see* CUNNINGHAM, ANDREW), he served on the Western Front (1915–18), and was awarded the Military Cross and appointed to the Distinguished Service Order (DSO). In the spring of 1941 Cunningham, now commanding British forces in Kenya, overran Italian East Africa. Appointed to lead the 8th Army against Rommel, Cunningham was out-manoeuvered, suffered a nervous breakdown, and requested to be relieved. Excellent in the static conditions of the First World War and in colonial campaigning, Cunningham never acclimatized himself to the use of armour, fighter bombers and radio on the battlefield.

CUNNINGHAM, ANDREW (1st Viscount Cunningham) (1883–1963), sailor. Son of the Professor of Anatomy at Trinity College, Dublin, and brother of Lieutenant General Alan CUNNINGHAM, he served ashore during the Boer War with the Naval Brigade, took part in the Dardanelles landing in 1915 and in the Zeebrugge raid of 1918 and then served in the Baltic in semi-clandestine operations against Bolshevik Russia in 1919. In Nov. 1940 Cunningham, now commanding the Mediterranean Fleet, launched the first major aircraft-carrier operation in history against the Italian Fleet in Taranto harbour, badly damaging three battleships, while in a night action off Cape Matapan the following March his battleships sank three Italian heavy cruisers. Cunningham's ships also evacuated British forces from Greece and Crete, supplied garrisons in Tobruk and Malta, and later supported Allied landings in North Africa, Sicily and Italy. Following the death of Sir Dudley POUND in Oct. 1943, Cunningham became First Lord and Chief of the Naval Staff, and spent the rest of the war with Sir Alan BROOKE and Charles PORTAL, devising British grand strategy.

CUNNINGHAM, WILLIAM (9th Earl of Glencairn) (?1610–64), politician. A Scottish Privy Councillor in 1641, he was one of the few Royalist Scottish noblemen at the outbreak of the English Civil War in 1642, but was later made Lord Justice General by Parliament, a post which he held until 1648, when his involvement in the attempted rescue of CHARLES I was discovered. CHARLES II commissioned him to lead a renewed Scottish rebellion in 1653; he was defeated at Dunkeld the following year and arrested by George MONCK in 1655. Honours bestowed on him at Charles II's restoration included the Lord Chancellorship of Scotland in 1661.

CUNOBELIN (*fl.* AD first century), King of the Catuvellauni. The historical basis of SHAKESPEARE's Cymbeline, he ruled the Catuvellauni from about 5 to 41, during which time he made them the dominant power in south-eastern England. The extent to which he did this can be seen in his coinage, which shows that he had taken over Colchester, the chief town of the Trinovantes. There are signs that he developed his rule along Roman lines, but there is no evidence either of direct relations with the empire or that he in any way provoked CLAUDIUS' invasion in 43.

CUNOMOR (MARK) (*fl. c.* 560), British ruler in Cornwall. Best known as the cuckolded king in *Tristan and Iseult*, the earliest written versions of which date from the middle of the twelfth century, Cunomor's historical existence is attested by an inscription near Fowey (Cornw.), which reads *Drustanus hic iacit Cunomori* and is dated to the mid sixth century. He also appears to have ruled over the territory of Cornouaille in Brittany, as he seems to have supported a rebellion against Clothair, King of the Franks, during the course of which both Cunomor and Clothair were killed.

CURETAN (OR KIRITINUS), ST (*fl.* early eighth century), Bishop of Rosemarkie. In common with his possible contemporary, SERF, Curetan's later *vita* provides him with an exotic Near Eastern origin. This is unlikely and probably derives from the fact that little was known about him even in the early Middle Ages. He is associated with the foundation at Rosemarkie, in the Black Isle (Ross), and, possibly, with foundations in Orkney. He is said in his *vita* to have founded 150 churches in Pictland. His alternative name, Boniface, suggests his adherence to the Roman rather than to the Irish rite and so it may be the case that, encouraged by King NECHTÁN, he sought to establish the authority of the Roman Church in the far north following the expulsion of the monks of Iona from Pictland in 717.

CURZON, GEORGE (1st Marquess Curzon of Kedleston) (1859–1925), Viceroy of India (1898–1905). Curzon was one of the most brilliant products of late Victorian Oxford. An aristocrat who could trace his ancestry back to the Norman Conquest, he was an ardent imperialist who believed that the British had a duty to civilize backward nations. In his youth Curzon was a great traveller, making himself an expert on Persia and on the Middle East, but he never wore his learning lightly, and a reputation for pomposity would always dog him.

As Salisbury's (*see* CECIL, ROBERT GASCOYNE) junior at the Foreign Office (1895–8), Curzon favoured a much more aggressive line of diplomacy than his superior, and his promotion to India in 1898 was a relief in some quarters. As Viceroy, he continued to warn of the Russian menace and wanted to take active precautions against the Russians by pursuing a forward policy in Tibet, Afghanistan and the Persian Gulf, which led to conflict with Arthur BALFOUR after 1902 and to Curzon's resignation in 1905. For the next decade Curzon's career languished, and it was not until 1919 that he achieved his ambition of becoming Foreign Secretary. Ironically, the limitations on British power after 1919 meant that he could not pursue the sort of policy that he had advocated to Salisbury. His failure to become Conservative leader in 1923 was the final disappointment to what had once seemed a brilliant career.

CUTHBERT (?–760), Archbishop of Canterbury (740–60). An archbishop notable for holding the important Synod of the English Church at *Clofesho* (location unknown) in response to criticisms of the Church in England and to recent reforming legislation in the kingdom of the Franks sent to him by St BONIFACE. Cuthbert's archiepiscopate illustrates the importance for eighth-century England of the careers of the Anglo-Saxon missionaries abroad.

CUTHBERT (?–after 764), Abbot of Monkwearmouth and Jarrow. A disciple of BEDE, he composed a well-known account of his master's death. Records of Cuthbert's abbacy reveal connections with the English missionaries in Germany, such as St LUL, and a significant role in the dissemination on the continent of Northumbrian manuscripts and ideas, in a way which clearly prepared the ground for ALCUIN OF YORK's career within the Carolingian empire.

CUTHBERT, ST (*c*. 635–87), churchman. His life as a monk, hermit and, briefly, bishop, mainly at Melrose and Lindisfarne (685–7), seems to be typical of many religious men trained in the traditions of early Irish Christianity (*see* AIDAN; COLUM CILLE). As two surviving early lives, one of which was written by BEDE, attest, his was a personality of quite extraordinary power. Miracles were claimed to have been performed at his tomb from 698, and in 995 his body reached its current resting place in Durham Cathedral. He became a sort of patron saint of the far north of England, and his remains subsequently defied the attentions of the Vikings, WILLIAM I THE CONQUEROR's followers, and HENRY VIII's commissioners.

CUTHRED (?–807), King of Kent (798–807). Brother of King CENWULF of Mercia, Cuthred was installed in Kent after the expulsion of EADBERT PRÆN, the last independent King of Kent. Cenwulf and Cuthred are known to have tried to conciliate Kentish interests, but hegemony over Kent nonetheless passed permanently to Wessex in the time of King EGBERT.

CWENTHRYTH (?–after 827), Abbess of Winchcombe. Daughter of King CENWULF of Mercia, Cwenthryth's career illustrates very well how the political power of early medieval kings relied on making use of both family and the Church. Installed as Abbess at the family monastery of Winchcombe, she was also made Abbess of Minster-in-Thanet and Reculver in Kent to consolidate Cenwulf's disputed hold on that kingdom. This involved her in a dispute over control of the Kentish churches which was eventually settled in favour of Archbishop WULFRED of Canterbury in 825. There is generally thought to be no truth in the later story that she murdered her brother St CYNEHELM.

CYNAN AP BROCHFAEL (*fl. c*. 600), King of Powys. The subject of a praise poem by TALIESIN, nothing is known of Cynan other than the information contained within the elegy. If this is at all reliable, he is represented as a potent war leader with substantial military resources which were employed regularly against his neighbours.

CYNDDYLAN AP CYNDRWYN (*fl*. mid seventh century), King of Powys. It is uncertain whether Cynddylan was King of Powys, but he was certainly a powerful ruler over Pengwern, in eastern Powys. One line of the ninth-century *Canu Llywarch Hen* gives Cynddylan as one of the British rulers who supported PENDA at the defeat of OSWALD in 642. At some point subsequent to this, however, Cynddylan and his brothers lost much of their power in eastern Wales and the west Midlands before they were killed in a raid, recounted in ninth-century Welsh verse. The fall of Cynddylan's dynasty allowed English expansion into modern Salop. and Herefs.

CYNEGILS (?–643), King of Wessex (611–43). A military defeat at the hands of the redoubtable PENDA, King of Mercia, seems to have cost Cynegils some of the territory in modern Glos. and Worcs. gained in the time of King CEAWLIN. Cynegils's chief historical significance, however, lies in his being the first King of Wessex to accept Christianity and in the establishment of BIRINUS in the bishopric of Dorchester-on-Thames. He was succeeded by his son CENWEALH.

CYNEHELM, ST (?–812). A son of King CENWULF of Mercia buried at the family monastery of Winchcombe, Cynehelm came to be venerated as a saint in the west Midlands. Almost nothing is known of his life, and the surviving account written in the eleventh century, which includes mention of his murder by his sister CWENTHRYTH, is regarded as a fabrication. His posthumous reputation (which may have little basis in fact) parallels that of other Anglo-Saxon royal kindred who died young, such as St EDWARD THE MARTYR and St WYSTAN.

CYNEWULF (?–786), King of Wessex (757–86). The first King of Wessex about whom much is known since INE, Cynewulf was initially successful in recovering lands taken from his kingdom by King ETHELBALD of Mercia. Cynewulf was defeated, however, at the Battle of Bensington in 679 by the greatest of the kings of Mercia, OFFA, and, although never entirely submissive to Offa, he was very much overshadowed by him. Cynewulf was killed by his kinsman Cyneheard in a famous incident described at length in the *Anglo-Saxon Chronicle*. He was succeeded by BEORHTRIC.

CYNEWULF (*fl.* early ninth century), poet. His name was included in runic symbols in the texts of his poems, allowing him to be one of the few Anglo-Saxon poets to be identified. He probably lived in Mercia, but nothing is known of his life. Of his poems, devoted to religious themes, over 2,000 lines survive.

CYNGEN AP CADELL (?–*c.* 855), King of Powys. The last king of the old royal line of Powys which claimed descent from VORTIGERN, it was Cyngen who set up the famous Eliseg's Pillar, near Llangollen. Besides the problems of Danish incursions in England, Cyngen still faced the threat of assault from Mercia, particularly the attempt by BURGRED of Mercia to conquer Powys in 853. His sister, Nest, married MERFYN FRYCH AP GWRIAD, King of Gwynedd, who twice went on pilgrimage to Rome, and a copy of a letter sent from Merfyn to Cyngen, preserved in Bamberg, Bavaria, is the earliest surviving 'Welsh' document of its kind.

D

DACRE, THOMAS (2nd Baron Dacre of Gilsland) (1467–1525), dynast. After succeeding his father Humphrey in 1485, he built on his family's prominence to become dominant on the Anglo-Scottish Borders. In July 1524 Cardinal WOLSEY instituted a commission of inquiry into his conduct as Warden of all the Marches. Dacre was imprisoned for corrupt administration and admitted his offences in the Court of Star Chamber in Sept. 1525. Because he was killed soon afterwards in a riding accident, the significance of his fall has been obscured, but it was a major victory for centralizing Henrician government over traditional aristocratic power.

DADD, RICHARD (1819–87), painter. In 1843 Dadd, a promising artist, suffered a mental breakdown and murdered his father. He was committed to the Bethlehem asylum and later to Broadmoor. There he spent his time executing minutely detailed paintings of fairies, of which *The Fairy-Feller's Master Stroke* (1855–64) is an example. His strange fantasies have been the subject of revived interest and exhibition since the 1970s.

DAFYDD AP GRUFFUDD (?–1283), youngest, ablest and most ambitious of the siblings of LLYWELYN AP GRUFFUDD, Prince of Wales. His readiness to seek English aid against his brother was one of Llywelyn's most intractable problems in the 1260s and 1270s. Although EDWARD I provided for Dafydd out of conquered territory in 1277, five years later English oppression pushed him into joining Llywelyn in a war of national liberation. After the Prince's death in 1282, Dafydd became leader of the Welsh cause, but he was captured in June 1283, convicted of treason and hanged.

DAFYDD AP GWILYM (*fl.* 1320–80), poet. Although he was of aristocratic Welsh stock virtually nothing is known about his life, but the sheer gusto, combined with irony, with which he wrote about the love of nature and women and about his own, allegedly, comic adventures has made him generally acknowledged as the greatest poet ever to write in the Welsh language. The innovative verse forms with which he experimented remained basic to Welsh poetry for centuries to come. When he died is unknown, although a contemporary poet observed that given the frequency with which he was dying of love in his poems his death must have been a fairly common occurrence.

DAFYDD AP LLYWELYN (*c.* 1208–46), Prince of Gwynedd. During his father LLYWELYN AP IORWERTH's lifetime he was generally recognized as heir to Gwynedd and to all his father's authority over native Wales. But after Llywelyn's death in 1240, HENRY III's government, posing as the guardian of Welsh tradition, set out to undermine the embryonic principality. By supporting all of Dafydd's rivals, other princes as well as his half-brother Gruffudd, it forced him to accept humiliating terms in 1241. By 1244 English high-handedness had provoked a Welsh rebellion, which Dafydd was leading when he died.

DAFYDD AP OWAIN (?–1203), Prince of Gwynedd. He was a son of OWAIN OF GWYNEDD, and married Emma of Anjou, half-sister of HENRY II. When Owain and his son Iorwerth died in 1170, Dafydd and his brother Rhodri killed their half-brother Hywel and divided Gwynedd between them. After Rhodri died in 1195, LLYWELYN AP IORWERTH took control, imprisoned Dafydd in 1197, and forced him into exile at his English manor of Ellesmere (Salop.).

DALHOUSIE, 10TH EARL AND 1ST MARQUESS OF *see* RAMSAY, JAMES

DALLAM, THOMAS (*c.* 1570–*c.* 1630), organ-builder. Founder of a distinguished organ-building family, his unique achievement was to ship across the Mediterranean in kit form an extraordinary novelty pipe-organ as a present from ELIZABETH I to the Ottoman Sultan, 1599–1600. His account of this adventure vividly recounts the hazards, including storms and the prospect of being detained in Turkey with his own harem.

DALRYMPLE, SIR JAMES (1st Viscount Stair) (1619–95), lawyer and politician. The son of a minor Scots laird, he was educated at Glasgow

University. He went to Breda to negotiate with CHARLES II in 1650 and after Oliver CROMWELL's conquest of Scotland successfully led the Scottish Bar in its refusal to abjure Charles in favour of the Commonwealth. After the Restoration he opposed the extension of the royal prerogative attempted by Lauderdale (*see* MAITLAND, JAMES) and refused to renounce the National Covenant, for which he temporarily lost his place as a judge. His independence was protected by his indispensibilty to the Crown, but when his amendments to the 1681 Test Act were rejected he was dismissed from the presidency of the Court of Session (which he had held since 1670) and fled to Holland. In exile, he wrote *The Institutions of the Law of Scotland*, the first authoritative treatise on Scots law. This emphasized reason over precedent, and showed how Roman, French and Dutch civil law had influenced justice in Scotland. Treason proceedings were abandoned in 1687 when his son Sir John DALRYMPLE made peace with JAMES II. Dalrymple landed at Torbay with William of Orange (the future WILLIAM III) in 1688 and was restored as President of the Court of Session and made Viscount of Stair (1690).

DALRYMPLE, SIR JOHN (1st Earl of Stair) (1640–1707), politician. Son of Sir James DALRYMPLE, he was knighted by CHARLES II. He became an advocate at the Scottish Bar, showing early promise. He defended Argyll (*see* CAMPBELL, ARCHIBALD) against a charge of treason in 1681. Persecuted for several years, in 1685 he made his peace with JAMES II, coming to his aid by recognizing his claim to have the power to dispense Catholics from the restriction on their holding public office imposed by the Test Acts. His father's engagement in the cause of William of Orange (the future WILLIAM III) helped him to keep abreast of the political crisis which developed in 1688. Elected to the Scottish Convention Parliament, he moved that James had forfeited the throne, and was one of three commissioners sent to offer the Crown to William and MARY II. William appointed him Lord Advocate, with responsibility for representing the government in the Scottish Parliament, although his record as an erstwhile supporter of James II (if a pragmatic one) ensured that he was a focus for the hostility of MPs who continued to identify with the Covenanting cause. In 1690 Dalrymple moved the establishment of the Presbyterian, in place of the Episcopal, Church in Scotland. As Secretary of State he helped shape policy in pacifying the Scottish Highlands; most notoriously, he ensured that the Act of Loyalty imposed on Highland chiefs would isolate a few recalcitrant tribes, who might be punished to make an example. From this policy resulted the Massacre of Glencoe (*see* MAC-

DONALD, ALEXANDER) although, when Stair's enemies tried to use this against him in 1695, he was granted a royal pardon stating that he had had no foreknowledge of the means that were employed. Nonetheless, he resigned and, when he succeeded to the peerage on the death of his father, initially refrained from taking his seat. After the accession of ANNE, he was made a Privy Councillor, created Earl of Stair and served as the government's chief adviser on Scottish affairs. He supported plans for Anglo-Scottish parliamentary union in 1707, but the rigours of debate on the measure brought on an attack of apoplexy, of which he died.

DALRYMPLE, JOHN (2nd Earl of Stair) (1673–1747), soldier and diplomat. Brought up by his grandfather Sir James DALRYMPLE in Holland, he was educated at Leiden and fought under WILLIAM III in Flanders. During the War of the Spanish Succession he was aide-de-camp to Marlborough (*see* CHURCHILL, JOHN) and earned a high military reputation, particularly at the Battle of Oudenarde in 1708. GEORGE I appointed him British representative in Paris, where he befriended the Duke of Orléans, Regent from 1715, and was instrumental in negotiating the Triple Alliance with France and the United Provinces. Stair introduced Orléans to John LAW but came to oppose Law's ascendancy in 1719–20, and when this threatened Franco-British relations he was recalled. In the late 1730s he worked with Argyll (*see* CAMPBELL, JOHN) in the opposition to Robert WALPOLE and in 1742 was made Field Marshal and Commander-in-Chief of the British army in the War of the Austrian Succession, taking John PRINGLE with him as his physician, but he was no match for his French counterpart Noailles and resigned in 1743.

DALTON, HUGH (Baron Dalton of Forest and Frith) (1887–1962), politician. Son of the domestic chaplain to Queen VICTORIA, EDWARD VII and GEORGE V, Dalton was brought up at court and educated at Eton and Cambridge, where he became part of a circle that included J. M. KEYNES and Rupert BROOKE. He first served as a Labour MP from 1924 to 1931; when he lost his seat he taught at the London School of Economics, published works on public finance and planning and was closely involved in rewriting Labour's domestic policy. *Practical Socialism* (1935) served as a blueprint for ATTLEE's post-war government policy. Having returned to Parliament in 1935, he joined the War Cabinet in 1940 as Minister of Economic Warfare; as President of the Board of Trade from 1942, he advocated nationalization of coal and power. Appointed Chancellor of the Exchequer in Attlee's Cabinet in 1945 (not Foreign Secretary as he had hoped), his policies were intended to bring about an economy run on socialist principles: he oversaw the nationalization of the Bank of England and worked to lower interest rates, a policy that ran into great difficulties during the severe financial and fuel crisis of 1947. He was forced to resign later that year because of a premature leak of Budget information; although he returned to the Cabinet as Chancellor of the Duchy of Lancaster (1948) and Minister for Town and Country Planning (1950–1), he never regained his former influence on the shaping of Labour policy.

DALTON, JOHN (1766–1844), chemist. Born to a humble Cumb. Quaker family, he attended a Quaker school, of which he assumed control in 1778. Between 1781 and 1793 he and his brother ran a Quaker school in Kendal, where he developed his mathematical and natural philosophical skills and his deep interest in meteorology. In 1793 he began teaching mathematics and natural philosophy at Manchester Academy, a dissenting college, but after resigning this position in 1799 he earned a living as a private tutor, conducted private scientific research and participated in the activities of the Manchester Literary and Philosophical Society. His studies of the weather informed his interest in atmospheric gases and, subsequently, his celebrated work on mixtures of gases. In 1801 he constructed what is now known as the law of partial pressures: that the pressure of a mixture of gases is the sum of the pressures which each component would exert if it alone occupied the same space. He also formulated the law of the thermal expansion of gases and worked on the solubility of gases. This work led to his famous atomic theory, enunciated in his *A New System of Chemical Philosophy* (1808–27), which proposed that matter consisted of tiny, spherical, incompressible and indivisible atoms, that atoms of a given element have identical physical and chemical properties, that each atom has a definite relative atomic weight and that compounds formed from atoms combine in simple arithmetical ratios. Dalton also invented a symbolic language for his theory and produced tables of the atomic weights of the elements measured relative to hydrogen. Dalton's theory transformed chemistry, not least because it fostered the idea of the chemical atom and paved the way for quantitative chemistry. Although much of his theory was challenged, refined and rejected, it remains central to modern concepts of matter.

DAMIEN DE FALCUSIS, JOHN (?–c. 1516), failed aviator. An Italian alchemist who gained JAMES IV's favour and was made Abbot of Tongland (Galloway), in 1507 he attempted to impress departing French ambassadors by flying from Stirling Castle battlements equipped with wings made of eagles' feathers. He survived a rapid descent onto a rubbish heap, and blamed his failure on the adulteration of his costume with the feathers of hens. The attempt was described in a satirical poem by William DUNBAR.

DANBY, 1ST EARL OF *see* OSBORNE, SIR THOMAS

DANCE, GEORGE, THE ELDER (1695–1768) and **GEORGE, THE YOUNGER** (1741–1825), architects. Dance the Elder became Clerk of Works to the City of London in 1735 and designed the Mansion House and several London churches. His younger son succeeded him in 1768, having studied architecture in Italy, where he learned neoclassicism. He introduced new forms of street topography to London, notably the circus and the crescent, which had for most of the eighteenth century been associated with the WOODS in Bath, and replanned several areas of the City, although many of his plans were never realized or were slow to reach fruition. He also helped obtain the Building Act 1774, which regulated new construction in the capital.

DANCE, SIR NATHANIEL (1748–1827), East India Co. commander. Dance was commodore of the fleet dispatched from China by the East India Co. in Jan. 1804, conservatively valued with its cargoes at upwards of £8,000,000. The expected Royal Navy escorts had failed to arrive, and the Indiamen, although armed and impressive in appearance, were woefully inadequate for a serious fight. Intercepted by a French squadron near the Straits of Malacca, Dance counterattacked vigorously, and the French broke off the action after 40 minutes. The China fleet reached England triumphant.

DANGERFIELD, THOMAS (*c.* 1650–85), conspirator and perjurer. Imprisoned several times both as a coiner and as a debtor, Dangerfield posed as a wronged Catholic and attracted the attention of leading Catholic ladies such Elizabeth Cellier and the Countess of Powis (whose husband had been imprisoned for alleged involvement in the Popish Plot). They secured his release and employed him to take notes at trials of those accused during the anti-Catholic hysteria precipitated by the accusations of Titus OATES in 1678–9. Dangerfield claimed to have information of a Presbyterian plot to assassinate CHARLES II and the Duke of York (the future JAMES II): the plot has come to be known as the Meal-Tub Plot. Dangerfield presented a list of supposed Presbyterian meetings where conspirators led by the Duke of Monmouth (*see* SCOTT, JAMES) had been plotting the assassination of the King and his brother and the establishment of a

Commonwealth. When he produced further documents, supposedly found in a tub of meal, he was recognized as a former convict and his credibility collapsed. He tried to implicate Lady Powis and Mrs Cellier in the plot but failed; he was eventually, in 1685, found guilty of perjury, pilloried, whipped and fined £500, before being assassinated by a barrister.

D'ARBLAY, MADAME *see* BURNEY, FRANCES

DARBY, ABRAHAM (1677–1717), industrialist. Son of a Quaker farmer, he was apprenticed to a malt-mill maker. In 1704 he visited Holland, returning to England with some Dutch brass-founders, with whom he established the Baptist Mills brassworks at Bristol. In 1708 he patented the use of sand-cast iron instead of brass for making cheaper utensils for the poor. He leased an old furnace at Coalbrookdale (Salop.), and developed a technique for smelting iron ore with coke rather than charcoal. The Coalbrookdale works flourished and expanded under his namesake son (1711–63) and grandson (1750–91). The latter constructed the world's first cast-iron bridge there (1776–9), which gave its name to the Ironbridge valley, often dubbed the birthplace of the industrial revolution.

DARCY, THOMAS (1st Baron Darcy of Templehurst) (*c.* 1467–1537), soldier and politician. A career of faithful service, mostly in the north, under HENRY VII and HENRY VIII, led to his peerage (1529), but he came to oppose the annulment of Henry's marriage to CATHERINE OF ARAGON and the dissolution of the monasteries. Accordingly, in 1536, he joined the Pilgrimage of Grace after the rebellion had broken out in Yorks. Despite a royal pardon in Jan. 1537, he was arrested and beheaded on Tower Hill after a treasonable letter which he had written to Robert ASKE had been intercepted.

DARLING, GRACE (1815–42), heroine. She was the quiet, submissive seventh child of the overbearing lighthouse-keeper on the Farne Islands (Northumb.). On 7 Sept. 1838 the steamboat *Forfarshire* was wrecked in a gale and she and her father courageously set out in a small fishing boat and managed to rescue five survivors. She became the immediate focus of media attention, and was painted and hymned; £1,700 was raised by subscription, and she was awarded a gold medal by the Royal Humane Society. She died of consumption four years later.

DARNELL, SIR THOMAS (?–*c.* 1640), politician. A Lincs. knight made baronet in 1621, he was one of 'five knights' (with John CORBET, Walter ERLE, Edmund HAMPDEN and John

HEVENINGHAM) who in 1627 refused to pay a forced loan demanded by CHARLES I and were imprisoned. They appealed for a writ of *Habeas Corpus* to King's Bench, which returned them to prison, but avoided making a final decision in their case, and they were released in 1628.

DARNLEY, LORD *see* STEWART, HENRY

DARTMOUTH, 2ND EARL OF *see* LEGGE, WILLIAM

DARWIN, CHARLES *see* essay on pages 228–29

DARWIN, ERASMUS (1731–1802), physician, botanist and poet. Erasmus Darwin studied medicine at Cambridge, London and Edinburgh, and in 1756 moved to Lichfield, where he established a celebrated medical practice, promulgated radical social and political views, wrote poetry, created a small botanic garden and founded a botanical society. In 1766 he, Matthew BOULTON and others founded the Lunar Society of Birmingham, a leading centre of intellectual and political debate. In 1783 he published translations of Carl Linnaeus's (1707–78) great natural history works, *Systema Naturae* and *Genera Plantarum*, and moved his medical and botanical practices to Derby, where he founded the Derby Philosophical Society and built several mechanical inventions. He expressed his passion for natural philosophy, invention and plant classification in his famous long poem, *The Botanic Garden* (1789). He is best known for *Zoonomia, or the Laws of Organic Life* (1794–6), a treatise on pathology presenting his potent evolutionary argument that species adapt themselves to their environment in their struggle for existence. For many, Erasmus Darwin thus anticipated the ideas of his grandson, Charles DARWIN, and other nineteenth-century evolutionists.

DASHWOOD, SIR FRANCIS (15th Baron le Despencer) (1708–81), politician. Renowned throughout his life and afterwards for debauchery, Dashwood presided over the order of 'Monks of Medmenham Abbey', which he founded in 1755. The 'monks' allegedly indulged in pseudo-Satanic and profane rituals in artificially constructed underground grottoes, which can still be visited, as can Dashwood's house in High Wycombe (Bucks.). Stories of the group's activities (often confused with those of Philip WHARTON's Hellfire Club) are probably exaggerated. Politically, Dashwood was fiercely independent, until won over by the accession of the 'patriot' King GEORGE III. He was involved in drafting the militia Bills (envisaged as reviving national patriotism crushed by Hanoverian preference for a professional army) in the 1750s. He

continued on page 230

DARWIN, CHARLES ROBERT (1809–82)
Naturalist

He was born in Shrewsbury (Salop.), the son of Robert Waring Darwin, a wealthy physician, Whig and free-thinker, and of Susannah Wedgwood, daughter of the pottery industrialist, Josiah WEDGWOOD. His grandfather was the botanist, poet and evolutionary theorist, Erasmus DARWIN. He studied medicine at Edinburgh University (1825–7) but, disgusted by anatomy and surgery, spent much of his time collecting sea creatures under the guidance of Robert Edmond Grant, a naturalist who taught Darwin continental-style invertebrate anatomy and supported such subversive doctrines as materialism, democracy and the evolutionary theory of the French naturalist Jean-Baptiste Lamarck. Sent to study theology at Cambridge in 1827, Darwin spent much of his time there shooting birds, collecting beetles and learning safe science from Anglican teachers – natural history from the Rev. John Stevens Henslow and geology from the Rev. Adam SEDGWICK. They upheld the prevailing view, most widely known through William PALEY's *Natural Theology* (1802), that every species had been separately created through divine fiat and had remained fixed since their creation. Darwin initially shared this view although by the late 1830s he, like many political radicals and reforming Whigs, would hold that nature was ruled by divine law rather than isolated miracles.

After Darwin graduated in 1831, Henslow secured him a position as an unpaid companion and naturalist to Captain Robert Fitzroy, commander of HMS *Beagle* on a scientific survey of the southern hemisphere. For the next five hard years of his life Darwin explored among other places Tenerife, the Cape Verde Islands, the South American coasts, the Galapágos, Tahiti, New Zealand, Tasmania, Australia and Mauritius, making geological observations, collecting animal and plant specimens, and acquiring an immense knowledge of geology and natural history. He also produced striking geological evidence for Charles LYELL's argument that the earth's surface had been shaped continuously by natural causes acting over vast periods of time. Darwin would soon apply this to the organic world.

Soon after his return, Darwin settled in London, became active in the Geological Society of London and worked on publications that would establish him in scientific circles, notably his papers on the cleavage and foliation of rocks, and his famous *Journal of Researches into the Geology and Natural History of the Various Countries Visited by H. M. S. 'Beagle'* (1839). He also began to suffer lassitude, digestive disorders and vomiting, symptoms of an illness which plagued him for the rest of his life and obliged him to live a reclusive existence.

In early 1837 Darwin reached the momentous conclusion that species evolved, or originated by descent with modification, from other species, and were neither fixed nor created by miracles. He based this conclusion partly on four key observations made during his *Beagle* voyage: species inhabiting an island of Galapágos were related but detectably different (in terms of habits) from species inhabiting another island; species inhabiting adjacent geographical areas were replaced by different but related species; several species found on the isolated Galapágos islands resembled those found on the nearby South American continent; fossil animals were similar to related living animals in the same continent. This theory also enabled Darwin to deal with the extinction, adaptation and limited life-spans of species, among several other unaccountable observations in comparative anatomy, embryology and palaeontology. He needed to find causes for the adaptive change and diversification of species and in September 1838 he found the beginnings of an answer in Thomas MALTHUS's *An Essay on the Principle of Population* (1798), which argued that human populations always grow faster than their food supplies, thus resulting in a struggle for existence and the death of the weakest. Malthus's work was highly topical in a period when the poor were sent to workhouses on such principles, and Darwin recognized that the Malthusian principle operated in nature: since animal and plant populations outstrip their food supplies they are forced into fierce competition and only species which are best adapted to survive the competition are 'selected' by nature. More specifically, in any species, those which have a chance variation that makes them better adapted to their environment will survive and pass on that variation to their offspring, so that in time the whole species will be changed adaptively by a process of natural selection. Darwin continued to work on the origin of species but did not publish for over 20 years. He was painfully aware that evolutionary theories were seen as atheistic and a threat to the Established Church and Anglican society. As a gentleman who moved in respectable Anglican circles, publishing an evolutionary theory would, as he later remarked, be like 'confessing to a murder'.

In January 1839 he married his wealthy cousin Emma Wedgwood and in 1842 they moved to Down House in Kent, where he was able to live as a country gentleman and pursue scientific interests in a study, laboratory and glass-houses.

During his first 16 years at Down House, Darwin wrestled with the problem of the origin of species and published on other aspects of his *Beagle* voyage: he presented a theory of how coral atolls originated in *The Structure and Distribution of Coral Reefs* (1842), linked major elevations of land to earthquakes and volcanic eruptions in *Geological Observations on the Volcanic Islands* (1844), and published his extensive research on barnacles, which he regarded as a key case study for his evolutionary theory. He discussed his work with his colleagues and supporters, Lyell and Joseph Dalton HOOKER, experimented on the way seeds colonized islands (1855), and explored plant- and pigeon-breeding (1855–8) which helped him understand how new pigeon varieties are artificially produced. Darwin was also preoccupied with the death of his father (1848) and 10-year-old daughter Annie (1851), events which greatly weakened his Christian faith, and with heterodox medical therapies for relieving his stomach pains, greatly exacerbated by anxieties over evolution.

In 1856, on Lyell's and Hooker's advice, Darwin started preparing a large work on 'natural selection' for publication. Two years later he was shocked to receive a paper from the naturalist Alfred Russel WALLACE presenting an evolutionary theory similar to his own. This prompted Darwin to hasten the completion of a shorter book on evolution and led to the famous presentation in July 1858 of Darwin's and Wallace's joint paper on evolution at the Linnaean Society in London. Darwin's epoch-making book, *On the Origin of Species by Means of Natural Selection*, was finally published in November 1859. It was a cautious work: he based his argument on a wealth of evidence drawn from palaeontology, the distribution of species, morphology and embryology; he dealt with possible objections to his theory (notably the lack of the fossil evidence for intermediate varieties of species); and he avoided the crucial question of the origin of man. The book received a mixed reception. Several praised it as the most important scientific work of the time, while others argued that Darwin had not supported his theory with satisfactory evidence. Many strongly objected to the fact that Darwin's work rejected the biblical account of Creation and made species the product of chance rather than design, while others sought to reconcile Darwin's evolutionary theory with orthodox religious dogma. Darwin remained aloof from the controversy, but others (notably T. H. HUXLEY and the German zoologist Ernst Haeckel) championed and aggressively defended his work. Indeed, for most Victorians Huxley was the most conspicuous representative of Darwinism while Darwin himself managed to cultivate an image of the quiet and respectable sage.

Darwin incorporated his responses to his critics in the five subsequent editions of the *Origin* and from the early 1860s produced a series of books which expanded various aspects of the work. In *On the Various Contrivances by Which British and Foreign Orchids are Fertilized by Insects* (1862) he sought to show how the beautiful features of plants followed from his theory; in *The Variation of Animals and Plants under Domestication* (1868) his aim was to explain the phenomena of heredity with his theory of 'pangenesis'; in his controversial *The Descent of Man, and Selection in Relation to Sex* (1871) he tackled the thorny question of man – marshalling evidence for man's descent from anthropoid apes – and detailed his theory of 'sexual selection' to explain those attributes of species that could not be explained by natural selection. From the 1870s he published a series of works focusing on the botanical evidence for his evolutionary theory. In *Insectivorous Plants* (1875) he showed how plants acquired adaptations which allow them to feed on insects; in *Climbing Plants* (1875) he described how plants acquired adaptations that maximize their exposure to air and sunlight; in *The Effects of Cross and Self Fertilization in the Vegetable Kingdom* (1876) he presented experimental evidence for the argument that vegetable species resulting from cross-fertilization are greater in number, size, weight and vigour than those resulting from self-fertilization. In his last work, *The Formation of Vegetable Mould, through the Action of Worms* (1881), he explored how worms fortify and aerate soil.

Darwin was showered with academic distinctions throughout his life and, though his work had challenged Victorian religious beliefs, was buried in Westminster Abbey, an honour owing much to the contemporary perception of him as a major but moderate and respectable intellectual.

Darwin's work transformed the disciplines of biology, palaeontology, anthropology and sociology, and paved the way for such ground-breaking twentieth-century scientific enterprises as genetics and microbiology. Although his work continues to be debated, supported and attacked, he revolutionized the way in which humans think about themselves and their relation to the natural world.

Francis Darwin (ed.), *The Life and Letters of Charles Darwin* (3 vols, 1887)
Adrian Desmond and James Moore, *Darwin: The Life of a Tormented Evolutionist* (1991)

supported WILKES early in his career but denounced him in 1763 over the *Essay on Woman*. In 1762 he had become Chancellor of the Exchequer to Bute (*see* STUART, JOHN), but was much criticized for attempting to impose unpopular excise duty on cider and perry and subsequently only held minor offices.

DAUBENEY, GILES (1451 or 52–1508), nobleman *see* JOSEPH AN GOF, MICHAEL

DAVENANT, CHARLES (1656–1714), political economist. Son of the playwright Sir William DAVENANT. As Commissioner of Excise from 1683–9, he was able to collect statistics and observe the strengths and weaknesses of government finance. Out of favour after the Revolution, he warned in his *Essay upon Ways and Means of Supplying the War* (1695) that the economy would not meet the stress of the Nine Years War unless WILLIAM III had less recourse to direct taxation and instead relied more on the excise. He wrote several other economic commentaries and from 1705 acquired the post of Inspector General of Imports and Exports, collecting trade statistics for official and parliamentary use.

DAVENANT, SIR WILLIAM (1606–68), author and theatrical manager. Unsubstantiated theatrical tradition makes him the illegitimate son of SHAKESPEARE. His first play, *The Cruell Brother*, was performed at Blackfriars in about 1629. A friend of young lawyers including Bulstrode WHITELOCKE and Edward HYDE, Davenant gained the patronage of CHARLES I, for whom he wrote masques. In 1638 he succeeded JONSON as Poet Laureate, and in 1639 was granted a patent to build a theatre. In the later years of Charles I he commanded Royalist ships, seizing Parliamentary supplies and carrying messages for Royalists, and was knighted by the King for his services. During the Interregnum he was imprisoned but emerged to slowly revive public theatre. At the Restoration he successfully renewed his 1639 patent and formed the Duke's Company, performing at Lincoln's Inn Fields, in competition with the King's Company of KILLIGREW. His protégés included Thomas BETTERTON and Elizabeth BARRY.

DAVENPORT, CHRISTOPHER (*c.* 1595–1680), theologian. Converted to Roman Catholicism while at Oxford, he became a Franciscan at Ypres in 1617 (taking the name Franciscus a Sancta Clara) and was later chaplain to HENRIETTA MARIA and CATHERINE OF BRAGANZA. Ecumenically minded, he had many friends in the established Church, and in 1634 wrote a tract designed to show that it would be possible to understand the Church's Thirty-Nine Articles in a manner acceptable to Roman Catholics. He also wrote attacking astrology.

DAVENPORT, JOHN (1597–1670), churchman. Uncle of Christopher DAVENPORT, his religious path from Oxford was very different: his prominence as a Puritan parish minister in London brought conflict with the Bishop, William LAUD, particularly because of his involvement with the Feoffees for Impropriations, a Puritan consortium of trustees (feoffees) who bought up alienated parish revenues (impropriations) to endow preaching. When Laud had their corporation dissolved in 1633, Davenport left to minister in Amsterdam, and in 1637 sailed for Boston (Massachusetts), the following year founding New Haven (a colony now part of Connecticut). He died as minister of Boston's First Church. A prolific writer, he was much involved in controversies about how rigorously Congregational Church membership should be restricted.

DAVID I *see* essay on page 231

DAVID II (1324–71), King of Scots (1329–71). As the only surviving legitimate son of ROBERT BRUCE, he succeeded his father in 1329, by which date he was already married to EDWARD III's sister JOAN. In 1331 he became the first Scottish king to be crowned and anointed. Whether he would be able to keep his throne was another matter. Any Bruce kingship was bound to be faced by the combined hostility of Edward III, EDWARD BALLIOL and the 'Disinherited', the Scottish landowners whom Robert Bruce had disinherited after his victory at Bannockburn (1314) and who for the next few decades, as advocates of war against Scotland, remained an influential group at the English court. While David was a child the outlook was bleak, particularly after Balliol and the Disinherited defeated an army loyal to David at the Battle of Dupplin Moor (Perths.) (12 Aug. 1332). Two years later another invasion led to his being sent to France for safe-keeping, while others such as Andrew MORAY fought off the English. Fortunately for David, in the late 1330s Edward III's military ambitions turned to France, permitting him to return to his kingdom in 1341, a committed supporter of alliance with France, the 'Auld Alliance'. In 1346 he invaded England while Edward was engaged at the siege of Calais, but his army was intercepted at Neville's Cross near Durham by a force raised by the Archbishop of York. In the battle (17 Oct.) David was wounded and captured. By the Treaty of Berwick (1357) he agreed to pay a ransom of 100,000 marks. During the negotiations he considered making Edward III, with whom he shared a taste for chivalrous and amorous pursuits, his heir presumptive, a reflection of the recurrent tension between him and Robert the Steward (later ROBERT

continued on page 232

DAVID I (c. 1081–1153)
King of Scots (1124–53)

He was a consciously modernizing King some-times credited with transforming his kingdom through a 'Davidian revolution', although it seems likely that his predecessor and older brother ALEXANDER I anticipated at least some of the things for which David is justly celebrated. Youngest son of a Scottish King, MAEL COLUIM III CENN MÓR and his English wife, St MARGARET, he was taken to England after his parents' deaths in 1093. He helped his older brother EDGAR recover the Scottish throne in 1097 and became a familiar, trusted and handsomely rewarded figure at the English court after his sister MATILDA married HENRY I in 1100. He acquired an estate in Normandy, and the earldom of Huntingdon and Northampton when he married Maud, the former Earl's widow in 1113. Moreover it was at Henry's insistence that Alexander gave David a huge prin-cipality in southern Scotland. Even when he became King after Alexander's death in 1124, David seems to have spent as much time at Henry's court as he did in Scotland. It was, wrote his English contemporary WILLIAM OF MALMES-BURY, 'his upbringing amongst us that polished away the rust of his native barbarism'. (One of the problems of interpreting David's achievement is the absence of any contemporary Scottish history.)

He adopted a style of kingship that he had learned in England. He was the first Scottish king to issue his own coin (silver pennies modelled on Henry I's), to establish new-style sheriffdoms, to found chartered burghs and to promote the devel-opment of towns at Edinburgh, Dunfermline, Perth, Stirling, Inverness and Aberdeen. Urban law was based on the legal customs of Newcastle-upon-Tyne. By ordering the payment of a teind (tithe) from all living in the area served by a local church he in effect founded the Scottish parish system. He welcomed English, Flemings and French to his court; a new French-speaking aristocracy was established in Lothian. The Bruce, Stewart, Morville, Montgomery and Lindsay families all owed their wealth and power in Scotland to his encouragement. His charters were addressed to his subjects 'French, English, Scots' – and sometimes 'Galwegian' as well. According to William of Malmesbury, he promised tax rebates to those of his subjects who adopted a civilized lifestyle and so brought a measure of refinement to a previously barbarous people. He founded and promoted monasteries such as Selkirk, Melrose and Holyrood in keeping with fashionable English and European ideas on religious observance; in much of this he continued the work of Anglicization begun by his mother. Hence he was enormously admired by Cistercian authors such as St Bernard of Clairvaux and ÆLRED OF RIEVAULX. The war waged by Angus of Moray (a grandson of LULACH) may reflect the hostility of traditionalists to so many new-fangled and foreign ways. But in 1130 Angus was defeated and killed, and the new ways imposed on Moray.

The accession of STEPHEN to the throne in 1135 instead of David's niece, the Empress MATILDA, meant that for the first time David was excluded from the English court; in consequence he pressed his wife's claim (as daughter of Earl WALTHEOF) to Northumbria. He launched inva-sions of England in 1136, 1137 and 1138. The 'native' Galwegians and Highlanders in his armies treated these expeditions as slave raids and committed atrocities which outraged the English, who were shocked too that so 'well-brought up' a King allowed such things to happen. When finally forced to stand and fight at the Battle of the Standard, near Northallerton (Yorks.), in 1138 by an army organized by THURSTAN, Archbishop of York, David was convincingly defeated. His army was no match for the English in terms of armour and ammunition. Despite this, the Empress's arrival in England next year tied Stephen's hands and allowed David to negotiate the Treaty of Durham by which he secured the recognition of his son, significantly named HENRY, as Earl of Northumbria. Since he also acquired Cumbria this meant that, for once in British history, a Scottish king, now in possession of Newcastle and Carlisle, was almost as rich and powerful as the king of England. The Yorks. historian, WILLIAM OF NEWBURGH, felt that by the good peace which he brought to the government of northern England as well as by his more conventionally pious good works, David made up for the slaughter of inno-cent women and children by his troops in the 1130s. Henry died, however, in 1152 and David's decision to designate his young grandson, the future MAEL COLUIM IV, as his heir was to put much of his remarkable achievement at risk. Even so Scotland was to be ruled by his descendants, and they ensured that by the thirteenth century he had attained mythical status; the 'Laws of King David' may have been largely fictitious but for Scots they represented 'good, old law'.

G. W. S. Barrow, David I of Scotland (1984)

II) which led to the abortive rising of 1363. About half of the sum due under the ransom was in fact paid; raising the money meant developing direct and indirect taxation as well as a general overhaul of government and the extension of its authority in the Highlands and Islands. David still had no heir when he died unexpectedly while trying to divorce Margaret Logie (his second wife) in order to marry his latest mistress, Agnes Dunbar.

DAVID, ELIZABETH (née Gwynne) (1913–92), writer. The woman who revolutionized the British nation's palate first developed her interest in French cooking when, as student at the Sorbonne, she lodged with a French family. Married and living in Ross-on-Wye (Herefs.), she taught herself French cookery and in 1950, when Britain was still in the grip of post-war austerity and rationing, enured to spam and snoek, she published *Mediterranean Cookery,* followed the next year by *French Country Cooking* and *French Provincial Cooking.* More than recipe books, they are an evocative and discursive meander into French life and habits, and have proved enduringly successful, influencing a generation of cooks and cookery writers. In later years David was prepared to sample her native culinary tradition, publishing *Spices, Salts and Aromatics in the English Kitchen* (1970) and *English Bread and Yeast Cookery* (1974).

DAVID (OR DEWI), ST (*fl.* sixth century). Little is known about the historical St David. Although the first life of him was written only in the late eleventh or early twelfth century, it is clear from the combined evidence of church dedications in Wales and early sources in Ireland and Brittany that, from at least the seventh century, David was the most popular Welsh saint. His fame accelerated in the twelfth century during the failed attempt to elevate the church of St David's into an archbishopric (*see* BARRI, GERALD DE), which was to provide the basis for his status as the patron saint of Wales.

DAVIES, CLEMENT (1884–1962), politician and party leader. A successful barrister, he was Liberal MP for Montgom. (1929–62). In 1945 he accepted the party leadership after Sinclair's defeat in the General Election. In 1951 he considered but declined Winston CHURCHILL's offer of a Cabinet post, choosing to maintain the Liberals as an independent force. He saw the party through the nadir of its fortunes when reduced to only six MPs in the 1951 and 1955 elections, and witnessed the first signs of a Liberal revival when the leadership passed to GRIMOND in 1956.

DAVIES, DAVID (?–*c.* 1819), statistician. As vicar of Barkham (Berks.) in the 1780s and 1790s,

he was stimulated by Parliament's collection of data on poor-relief expenditure to investigate the spending habits of agricultural labourers in his parish and beyond, publishing his findings in *The Case of the Labourers in Husbandry Stated and Considered* (1795). The book was influential both as a source of statistical information and for its illustration of the state of the working poor in the late eighteenth century.

DAVIES, LADY ELEANOR (?–1652), prophet. Daughter of George Tuchet, 11th Baron Audley, she married Sir John DAVIES, and later Sir Archibald Douglas, both of whom were alarmed by and unsympathetic to her often baffling ecstatic utterances. Her numerous published works of prophecy and frequent public demonstrations (including her capture of the bishop's throne in Lichfield Cathedral) brought repeated imprisonment and the unkind anagram 'Never so mad a ladie', but she had many supporters, particularly those who approved of her gloomy and eventually justified predictions for CHARLES I and William LAUD.

DAVIES, EMILY (1830–1921), educational reformer. The daughter of an Evangelical clergyman, Davies developed a strong social conscience and interest in women's rights from an early age. Influenced by the work of Barbara BODICHON and Elizabeth Garrett ANDERSON, her main crusade was for improved educational opportunities for girls. She campaigned for girls' education to be included in the remit of the 1865 Schools Inquiry Commission and was herself a powerful witness, and in 1866 formed the London Schoolmistresses' Association, of which she was Secretary until 1888. She had already pressed for the admission of women to degrees at London University and in 1869 was involved in the establishment of a college for women in Hitchin (Herts.), which moved to Cambridge in 1873 as Girton College. Davies's belief in equal educational opportunities led her to insist that women should be admitted to Cambridge degrees on the same terms as men. This did not happen until 27 years after her death. A supporter of women's suffrage since the petition of 1866, Davies was fiercely critical of militant tactics. She lived long enough to vote in 1918 in the first election in which it was possible for women to do so.

DAVIES, JOHN (*c.* 1567–1644), writer. An Oxford-educated Puritan, he became rector of Mallwyd (Clwyd) and Prebendary of St Asaph Cathedral. Perhaps the greatest Welsh scholar of his time, he was co-author with Bishop Richard Parry of St Asaph (1560–1623) of the Welsh translation of the Authorized Version of the Bible, and a revised version of the Book of Common Prayer in Welsh. He organized the copying of Welsh manuscripts, which he used in the preparation of his dictionary and grammar of Welsh (1632), and published devotional writings and poetry.

DAVIES, SIR JOHN (1569–1626), lawyer. Born in Wilts., and having studied at Oxford, he became a barrister. He was energetic as Solicitor General for Ireland from 1603, and Irish Attorney General (1606–19); he was also, in 1613, Speaker of the Irish Parliament, despite Catholic opposition. Concerned for the wretched state of Ireland, his remedies were to dismantle what remained of the traditional Celtic legal system, secure the banishment of Roman Catholic clergy and promote plantations (settlements of English or Scots immigrants). He was appointed Lord Chief Justice of the King's Bench (England) as a reward for maintaining the legality of CHARLES I's forced loans in 1626, but died before entering office. He published poetry and a discussion of the condition of Ireland.

DAVIES, RICHARD (?1501–81), writer. Son of a parish priest, he went to Oxford and was a Protestant exile at Frankfurt under MARY I. He was made Bishop of St Asaph (1560) and St David's (1561). As well as working on the Bishops' Bible (the official translation of 1568 ordered by ELIZABETH I), he co-operated with William SALESBURY in translating the New Testament into Welsh (1565–7), and was a leading patron of Welsh bards.

DAVIS, THOMAS (1814–45), journalist. From a Protestant professional background, Davis joined Daniel O'CONNELL's Repeal Association in 1841 and was one of the founders of *The Nation*. His vigorous didactic ballads and advocacy of a systematic programme of intellectual nation-building made him the outstanding figure of the Young Ireland group, while his commitment and high moral tone exerted immense personal influence over his contemporaries. He saw O'Connell as over-inclined to compromise with British Whigs for the sake of patronage and unwilling to convert his rhetorical denunciations of the Union into action, while O'Connell saw Davis and his associates as irresponsible and insensitive towards Catholic grievances. In 1845 the two factions quarrelled over the newly introduced non-denominational Queen's Colleges; O'Connell endorsed Catholic episcopal denunciations of 'Godless colleges' while Davis and the Young Irelanders argued that mixed education would help to bridge religious divisions. Davis's writings were highly influential for later generations of nationalists.

DAVISON, EMILY (1872–1913), suffragette. Involved in the Women's Social and Political Union since 1906, Davison was one of its most prominent militants who received eight prison sentences for pillar-box arson, window-breaking and assault, and was forcibly fed 49 times. She became a martyr to the cause when, wrapped in a Women's Social and Political Union flag, she ran on to the racecourse and was mortally injured as she tried to seize the reins of King GEORGE V's horse as it rounded Tattenham Corner during the 1913 Epsom Derby. Her funeral was attended by members of trade-union organizations as well as by representatives of all the suffrage societies.

DAVISON, WILLIAM (?1541–1608), royal servant. After diplomatic service in the Netherlands and Scotland, he became a Privy Councillor and second Council Secretary in 1586. A trial commissioner against MARY QUEEN OF SCOTS in 1586, he was made scapegoat for ELIZABETH I's sense of guilt at signing her death-warrant on 1 Feb. 1587, being fined and imprisoned in the Tower for implementing the signature. Burghley (*see* CECIL, WILLIAM) secured his release and further appointments, but his career never fully recovered.

DAVITT, MICHAEL (1846–1906), Irish politician. The son of an evicted Co. Mayo smallholder and brought up in Lancs., Davitt lost an arm in a factory accident as a child. He became a Fenian and in 1870 was imprisoned for gun-running. On his release in 1877 he helped to bring about the 'new departure' (an alliance between local land agitators in Ireland, the Parnellite section of the Home Rule Party (*see* PARNELL, CHARLES STEWART) and Irish-American Fenians led by John DEVOY) and took a leading role in the Land League on its foundation in 1879. He later came to see the Land League as dominated by larger farmers, and while imprisoned again in 1881–2 became an advocate of Henry GEORGE's model of land nationalization rather than land purchase. Though marginalized by Parnell, Davitt continued to support the Home Rule movement and see its alliance with Liberals after 1886 as confirming his view that the British and Irish masses were natural allies in the struggle against class privilege. One of Parnell's fiercest opponents in the split, Davitt served as anti-Parnellite MP for Meath South (1892–3), where he was unseated on petition due to clerical intimidation, and for South Mayo (1895–9), when he resigned in protest at the Boer War. He remained active in nationalist agitation in Ireland and supported radical movements in Britain. Towards the end of his life he quarrelled with the Irish Catholic bishops over his support for State control of education.

DAVY, SIR HUMPHRY (1778–1829), chemist. The son of a Cornish wood-carver, in 1795 Davy was apprenticed to an apothecary-surgeon. Subsequently he studied chemistry privately and in 1798 became an assistant at the Pneumatic Institution in Bristol. There Davy synthesized various oxides of nitrogen (notably nitrous oxide or laughing gas) and explored their physiological effects. His *Researches . . . Concerning Nitrous Oxide* (1800) made his reputation and led to his appointment in 1801 as lecturer at the fledgling Royal Institution, London. By 1802 he was the institution's Professor of Chemistry and fast becoming one of the most popular lecturers of the day. Having lectured on the institution's key research areas of agricultural chemistry and tanning, he explored his strong electrochemical interests and in 1806 showed that electric currents decompose water into hydrogen and oxygen, and presented theories of electrolysis and voltaic action and chemical reactions. His reputation rests largely on his work of 1807–12: in 1807 he used electrolytic techniques to produce evidence for the elements potassium and sodium; in 1808 he used similar techniques to isolate barium, calcium, magnesium and strontium; and in 1812 he presented evidence for the elemental nature of muriatic acid (later called chlorine). Davy consolidated this research in *Elements of Chemistry* (1812) and tackled the problem of mine explosions which led to his invention, in 1816, of the famous safety lamp. He was President of the Royal Society (1820–7).

DAVYS (OR DAVIS), JOHN (*c*. 1550–1605), explorer. Enthusiastically seeking a north-west passage to Asia, Davys sailed to Greenland in 1585, and in 1587 explored the Davis Strait into Baffin Bay in northern Canada. He was a commander against the 1588 Spanish Armada. In 1591–3 he was one of the leaders of Thomas CAVENDISH's unsuccessful attempt at world circumnavigation, during which he was the first recorded Englishman to encounter the Falkland Islands. Turning to east Asian voyages after 1598, he was murdered by Japanese pirates off Singapore. He wrote valuable accounts of his experiences and a pioneering work on navigation.

DAWKINS, RICHARD (1941–), biologist and popularizer of science. Dawkins was educated at Oxford where he was appointed Reader in Zoology (1989) and Professor for the Public Understanding of Science (1996). He won acclaim for his researches on the evolution of animal behaviour but he is best known for his popular and often controversial expositions of Charles DARWIN's theory of evolution by natural selection. In his best-selling *The Selfish Gene* (1976) he argued that evolution was driven by self-preserving genes rather than individuals or species. He also held that ideas (including, controversially, that of God) are transmitted in human societies along Darwinian lines

and described the unit of transmission as 'memes' by analogy with genes. He is an outspoken science propagandist and critic of astrology, parapsychology and other so-called pseudo-sciences.

DAWSON, CHARLES (1864–1945), antiquary. A Sussex solicitor whose hobby was geology, Dawson either discovered or planted the remains of what came to be known as 'Piltdown man', accepted by anthropologists as the so-called 'missing link' in Charles DARWIN's theory of the chain of evolution. It was not until 1953 that the fragments of cranium and the jaw-bone which he 'found' in a chalk pit at Piltdown (Sussex) in 1912 were shown to be a deliberate hoax – a human cranium spatched onto an orang-utan's jaw – though not necessarily by the man after whom it was named *Eoanthropus dawsoni*.

DAWSON, GEOFFREY (1874–1944), newspaper editor. Educated at Eton and Oxford, he entered the Colonial Office in 1899 and served under MILNER in South Africa (1901–5). He went on to edit the *Johannesburg Star* (1905–10) and joined *The Times* in London in 1911, becoming its editor under Alfred HARMSWORTH, Viscount Northcliffe (1912–19), and again under Astor (1924–41). He was a close friend of BALDWIN, supporting his India Bill and foreign policy. A member of the Cliveden set (*see* ASTOR, NANCY), Dawson was a supporter of appeasement, reflecting the opinions of Neville CHAMBERLAIN and his colleagues.

DAY, LUCIENNE (née Conradi) (1917–) and **ROBIN** (1915–), designers. The impact of the Days' designs on post-war austerity in Britain made his furniture and her textiles into twentieth-century classics. Robin Day, whose plastic stacking chairs brought elegance to mass-production in seating, was also responsible for the interiors of the Super VC10 airplane as well as of numerous concert halls, theatres and stadia, while Lucienne Day's textiles (most notably Calyx for Heals (*see* HEAL, AMBROSE), produced for the Festival of Britain in 1951) are now collectors' items.

DAY, SIR ROBIN (1923–), broadcaster. Day pioneered a new style of television journalism which was less deferential and more aggressive than had been the style of earlier television journalists such as Richard DIMBLEBY. With his trademark polka-dot bow tie and halting delivery, he was the BBC's chief political interrogator throughout the 1970s and 1980s. His televisual jousts with Mrs THATCHER were particularly memorable. Many found his style abrasive and arrogant, but by the time he retired in the late

1980s every self-respecting television journalist to some extent emulated Day's approach.

DAY, THOMAS (1748–89), author. When a student at Oxford in the 1760s Day became a follower of Rousseau, and his subsequent career was guided by the idea that society should return to the 'simplicity of nature'. His first published poem, *The Dying Negro* (1773), attacked the American colonists as hypocrites for keeping slaves while praising liberty; he was unsympathetic to the War of American Independence, and mourned the destruction which it caused in *The Desolation of America* (1777). His children's novel *Sandford and Merton* (three vols, 1783–9) remained highly regarded throughout the nineteenth century for its moral lessons.

DAYE, JOHN (1522–84), publisher. Suffolk-born, he established his printing business in London *c*. 1546 and became a leading publisher of Protestant literature, the most famous product (after his return from Marian exile) being John FOXE's *Book of Martyrs*, from 1563. He experimented, with the encouragement of Archbishop Matthew PARKER, with printing in Greek and Anglo-Saxon typefaces, published musical settings of the Psalms by Thomas TALLIS, and was prompted by John DEE into mathematical publishing, including the first English use of many mathematical signs. He fathered 26 children.

DE DOMINIS, MARCO ANTONIO (*c*. 1560–1624), churchman. An Italian academic, he was a Jesuit before becoming Archbishop of Spalato (Split, in Croatia). He caused a sensation in 1616 when, after quarrels with his clergy, he quit his diocese and joined the Church of England. As a star convert, he was made Dean of Windsor and wrote bitterly attacking Rome. Renewed quarrels, however, and his fears for his position if negotiations for a Spanish marriage for the Prince of Wales (the future CHARLES I) were successful, prompted his return to Roman Catholicism, and he wrote equally savagely against Anglicanism. In 1624 the Inquisition arrested him, and he died a prisoner in Rome.

DE GUINGAND, SIR FRANCIS (1900–79), soldier. Son of a tobacco pipe manufacturer, educated at Ampleforth and Sandhurst, De Guingand served in Ireland (1921) under MONTGOMERY. After serving in staff appointments, in Aug. 1942 he was appointed by Montgomery as his Chief of Staff. The irascible Montgomery never totally appreciated De Guingand's charm and diplomacy. When he was appointed Chief of the Imperial General Staff in 1946 he discarded De Guingand – a cause of lasting bitterness.

DE HAVILLAND, SIR GEOFFREY (1882–1965), aircraft designer. De Havilland studied engineering and subsequently worked in engineering and motor-car firms. Between 1908 and 1910 he built and flew his first aeroplanes and then worked at the Royal Aircraft Factory, Farnborough (Hants). During the First World War he designed and flew military aircraft and in 1920 started the De Havilland Aircraft Co., which launched some of the most celebrated aeroplanes of the twentieth century including the *Tiger Moth* (1930), a civilian biplane, the *Mosquito* (1941), a fast bomber, the *Vampire* (1943), the first British jet-powered aeroplane and the *Comet* (1949), the first jet airliner.

DE LA BILLIÈRE, SIR PETER (1934–), soldier. Son of a naval surgeon, educated at Harrow, he joined the army as a private soldier, but was soon commissioned and joined the SAS, with whom he saw extensive service in the Middle East. Appointed Director of the SAS in 1978, de la Billière oversaw operations in the siege of the Iranian embassy at Prince's Gate in 1980 and in the Falklands campaign of April to June 1982. In 1990 he was appointed to command British forces in Saudi Arabia, and as a skilled Arabist acted as a *de facto* second-in-command to General Norman Schwarzkopf. On his retirement, De la Billière became embroiled in a serious dispute with the Ministry of Defence over the publication of his memoirs.

DE LA FLÉCHÈRE, JOHN see FLETCHER, JOHN

DE LA POLE *see* POLE, DE LA

DE MONTACUTE *see* MONTAGU

DE QUINCEY, THOMAS (1785–1859), essayist and critic. Son of a Manchester linen merchant, and a promising classicist, De Quincey had a self-inflicted intermittent education, ending up at Worcester College, Oxford, in 1803, though he left without taking a degree. In 1807 he travelled to the Lake District to meet his hero, William WORDSWORTH, to whom he was introduced by COLERIDGE, and he rented Wordsworth's former home, Dove Cottage at Grasmere, for several years. By 1813 he was a confirmed opium addict, and to sustain his habit and his family (eventually of eight children) he turned to journalism. His notorious *Confessions of an English Opium Eater* (1822) was first published in the *London Magazine*, for which he wrote numerous other articles, and after its demise he moved to Edinburgh and started publishing in *Blackwood's Magazine* in 1826. His many distinguished articles, produced over more than 20 years, include his masterpiece, 'On Murder Considered as One of the Fine Arts'. Despite his prodigious and brilliant output, his life was precarious, hounded by creditors, estranged from the Lakeland poets, an estrangement that was made final by the publication of *Recollections of the Lakes and the Lake Poets* (1834–9). His use of symbolism and imagery influenced subsequent writers like Poe and Baudelaire, and has some echo in twentieth-century hallucinogenic literature.

DE ROBECK, SIR JOHN (1862–1928), sailor. Born into Anglo-Irish gentry, he joined the navy in 1875, and by the First World War was regarded as one of the finest training officers in the service. Having specialized in small-boat operations De Robeck was appointed deputy to, then subsequently replaced, Admiral CARDEN in the attempt to push a passage through the Dardanelles in the spring of 1915, taking over when Carden suffered a nervous breakdown on 16 March. Two days later, when six Allied battleships were either sunk or badly damaged by Turkish mines, De Robeck cancelled the operation. Knowing that only a combined operation would suffice, he was not surprised that the military landings on 25 April also failed. At the end of 1915 De Robeck conducted an efficient evacuation of the peninsula, and was one of the few senior officers to emerge from the campaign with his reputation enhanced.

DE VALERA, EAMON *see* essay on page 237

DE VALOIS, DAME NINETTE (originally Edris Stannus) (1898–), dancer and choreographer. Born in Co.Wicklow, she studied under Cecchetti and in 1923 became a soloist with Diaghilev's Ballets Russes. In 1926 she opened an Academy of Choreographic Art in London and persuaded Lilian BAYLIS to let her choreograph ballets at the Old Vic. In 1931 De Valois and Baylis formed the Vic-Wells Ballet, later the Sadler's Wells Theatre Ballet, and, at last in 1956 after the grant of a charter in 1956, the Royal Ballet. *Job* (1931), *The Rake's Progress* (1935) and *Checkmate* (1937) were among the ballets she created; she worked with the young choreographer Frederick ASHTON and with the dancers Margot FONTEYN and Robert Helpmann.

DE VERE, EDWARD (17th Earl of Oxford) (1550–1604), courtier. His father, the 16th Earl, was a patron of drama and literature, and Edward's education continued as a ward of William CECIL before studies in Oxford. He travelled abroad (according to John AUBREY, out of chagrin at farting in the presence of ELIZABETH I), flirted with Roman Catholicism and, despite being dogged by debt thanks to personal extrava-

gance, maintained a company of actors, for whom he is said to have written plays. His charm and poetic talents were coupled with a violent temper which probably resulted in the killing of one of Cecil's servants. The lost plays have helped inspire the fantasy that he was the true author (or at least co-author) of William SHAKESPEARE's drama and poetry.

DE VERE, JOHN (13th Earl of Oxford) (1443–1513), politician. One of the most consistent supporters of the Lancastrian cause. Succeeding his father as Earl in 1462, he played a prominent role at the coronation of ELIZABETH WOODVILLE (1465) but was imprisoned in the Tower three years later on suspicion of plotting with Lancastrians. Pardoned in 1469, he joined Warwick the Kingmaker's conspiracy (*see* NEVILLE, RICHARD), fled abroad and returned with the restored HENRY VI. Exiled again on EDWARD IV's return, he seized St Michael's Mount (Cornw.) in 1473, and thereafter spent 11 years in prison in Hammes (Calais) before escaping to join Henry Tudor, Earl of Richmond, later HENRY VII, commanding his archers at Bosworth (1485). Thereafter he was one of the few leading noblemen completely trusted by Henry, who gave him wide discretion in ruling East Anglia.

DEACON, THOMAS (1697–1753), churchman. He was a member of the much diminished second generation of Non-jurors, churchmen who rejected the oath of loyalty imposed on clergy after the Glorious Revolution. (*See also* SANCROFT, WILLIAM; COLLIER, JEREMY.) A Jacobite agent in 1715, he wrote declarations for condemned rebels to make from the scaffold before their execution. A Non-juring bishop from 1733, he combined his activities as leader of the True British Catholic Church with a successful medical practice in Manchester, and supported the 1745 rebellion. Three of his sons died for the cause. Deacon's work ensured that Manchester remained the centre of later eighteenth-century Non-juring Anglicanism, after the London Non-jurors followed the Scottish Episcopalians in recognizing the Hanoverian succession in 1788; the succession of Manchester bishops continued until the death of the last of the line some time after 1805.

DEAKIN, ARTHUR (1890–1955), trade-union leader. The son of a domestic servant, Deakin began his working life in the steel mills of south Wales. By 1919 he had become a full-time union official with the local branch of the General Workers' Union, the forerunner of the Transport and General Workers' Union (TGWU). His rise in the union hierarchy was expedited by the patronage of the TGWU's founder and formidable

continued on page 238

DE VALERA, EAMON (1882–1975)
Irish politician

Born in New York of Irish-Spanish parents, de Valera was brought up in Ireland by relatives after his father's death and his mother's remarriage. He became a teacher of mathematics and was active in the Gaelic League. In 1913 he joined the Irish Volunteers and commanded a battalion in Dublin during the Easter Rising of 1916. He was sentenced to death, but his sentence was commuted and he was released in 1917. That year de Valera was elected a Sinn Féin MP (for Clare, which he represented until 1959) and leader of the movement.

Interned in Lincoln gaol in 1918–19, he escaped to the USA, where he raised funds for the Anglo-Irish War. In 1919 he was appointed President of Sinn Féin's provisional government. He opposed the Anglo-Irish Treaty of 1921, lending his support to the anti-Treaty forces in the Irish Civil War and refusing to recognize the legitimacy of the new state. De Valera's opposition to the treaty (though based on legitimate concerns) was couched in highly legalistic and hair-splitting terms, as were many of his policies throughout his career. Opponents attributed his actions to ambition and jealousy of Michael COLLINS and held him personally responsible for the Civil War; while attracting remarkable devotion from his followers throughout his career, he could also arouse passionate hatred. He broke with the most hardline Republicans (who kept the title Sinn Féin) in 1926, founding his own party, Fianna Fáil (Warriors of Ireland). Fianna Fáil entered the Dáil (Parliament) in 1927 when faced with the choice between taking an oath of fidelity to the State or forfeiting their seats. In opposition, they won over many former treaty supporters antagonized by the failure of W. T. COSGRAVE's free-trade policies, based on support for large-scale beef-farming, to deliver economic development. Fianna Fáil argued that this reflected the Irish Free State's subservience to British interests and that they could bring prosperity by implementing measures advocated by earlier economic nationalists, developing Irish industries through protective tariffs and encouraging agriculture based on labour-intensive tillage. Fianna Fáil also founded the *Irish Press* daily newspaper in 1931 to counter the hostility of most existing newspapers. It became de Valera's personal property (under controversial circumstances), and for the rest of his life was the most popular newspaper in Ireland.

De Valera's victory in the election of 1932 began a 16-year period as Taoiseach (Prime Minister), during which he promoted Irish independence through a trade war with Britain and the enactment of a new constitution in 1937, which largely dismantled the treaty settlement. It also embodied Catholic values, though to a lesser extent than some zealots wished. Bans on divorce and contraception, and a rigid form of literary censorship, introduced by the Cosgrave government, were at their strictest under de Valera.

De Valera used the Irish Republican Army (IRA) to help him fight off the quasi-fascist Blueshirt movement under Eoin O'DUFFY, then suppressed it when it refused to accept his constitution as granting real independence. The IRA caused further problems for de Valera by 'declaring war' on Britain in 1939, sending its members (including the young Brendan BEHAN) to plant bombs in British cities, and trying to establish contact with Nazi Germany as a potential ally against Britain. During the Second World War de Valera repressed it more severely than even the Northern Ireland government, executing several IRA men after summary courts martial and interning large numbers of Republican suspects. He maintained Irish neutrality, resented in Britain, but in fact engaged in low-profile co-operation with the British war effort. Neutrality also asserted Irish independence and helped to unite old political opponents. De Valera lost office in 1948, but returned as Taoiseach 1951–4 and 1957–9. These latter terms of office were disappointing; he was aged and ill, and the economic policies instituted in the 1930s had failed to prevent massive emigration and economic stagnation. He was President from 1959 until his retirement, aged 90, in 1973. Two of his grandchildren were Fianna Fáil ministers.

De Valera was a skilful politician and negotiator, but his tortuous and legalistic attempts to justify the contrast between his image as a man of unbending principle and his relative pragmatism in power exposed him to charges of hypocrisy and self-deception. As Ireland has changed, his reputation has been diminished by his association with economic stagnation (rural nostalgia in a 1943 speech is often used misleadingly to present him as revelling in backwardness) and a Catholic puritanism which was widely shared at the time. He remains, however, one of the defining figures of twentieth-century Ireland, who played a vital role in consolidating Irish democracy.

T. P. O'Connor and Lord Longford, De Valera (1970)
Tim Pat Coogan, De Valera: Long Fellow, Long Shadow (1993)

General Secretary, Ernest BEVIN. When Bevin joined the wartime Coalition government in 1940, Deakin took over as acting General Secretary of the TGWU. In 1946 he was elected in his own right, a position which he held until his death. Like his mentor, Deakin was a robust right-winger. He was loyal to the leadership of the Labour Party during the ATTLEE governments of 1945–51, giving them full support even when it meant accepting wage restraint coupled with increasing productivity. He was notoriously intolerant of left-wing opposition to his leadership of the TGWU: in 1949 he succeeded in having Communists banned from holding office in the union. Deakin typified the solid, patriotic, common-sense trade unionism of the 1940s and 1950s, when for the first time in British history the trade-union movement occupied a central role in the economic decision-making of government.

DEARBHFHORGHAILL (DEVORGILLA) (?–1290), college founder. Daughter of Alan of Galloway, she married John Balliol, the Lord of Barnard Castle (Co. Durham), who established bursaries for scholars at Oxford before he died in 1269. In his memory, Dearbhfhorghaill established the Cistercian Abbey of Sweetheart (Kirkudbrights.) on the River Nith, and further endowed the college at Oxford which bears his name. Her son JOHN BALLIOL became King of Scotland in 1292.

DEE, JOHN (1527–1608), scientist. Born in London, he studied and lectured at Cambridge (where his ingenious theatre sets triggered his lifetime reputation as a magician), then at Leuven and Paris. He survived a Star Chamber prosecution for sorcery against MARY I in 1553, and unsuccessfully urged her in 1556 to found a royal manuscript library. Scientific and medical consultant to ELIZABETH I, he made many friendships during numerous overseas research trips. In 1583, while he was on an extended European tour, his Mortlake (Surrey) home and superb library were wrecked by a mob fearful of his magic. His wardenship of Manchester College (1595–1604) was rather meagre official recognition. An outstanding geographer, astronomer and mathematician, also influential in Sir Philip SIDNEY's circle, Dee has subsequently been unfairly marginalized for backing scientific and mystical lost causes such as astrology, alchemy, crystal divination and the mystical cult of Rosicrucianism.

DEFOE, DANIEL (c. 1660–1733), writer. Son of a London butcher, educated at a Dissenting academy at Newington Green, London, he took part in Monmouth's (see SCOTT, JAMES) rebellion in 1685, but escaped after its defeat at Sedgemoor (Som.).

By that time established as a merchant, he went bankrupt in 1692 and took to pamphleteering. A prolific writer, he probably did not write all that has been attributed to him. His satirical *Shortest Way with Dissenters* (1702) led to his imprisonment for libel. Robert HARLEY helped to secure his release in 1703, subsequently employing him to gather political intelligence; Defoe was his chief agent in Scotland during the negotiations for the union of English and Scottish Parliaments, which resulted in the Act of Union of 1707.

Defoe edited the *Review of the Affairs of France* (1704–13) in the Tory interest, sometimes going against his own beliefs in the process. When the Whigs came to power in 1714, they demanded as the price for not prosecuting Defoe that he continue to write for the Tory press but 'soften' it to help the Whig cause; he was thus employed on the Tory *News Letter* from 1715 and the Jacobite *Mist's Journal* from 1717. He also started writing novels, publishing *The Life and Surprising Adventures of Robinson Crusoe* (1719), a lasting success, and one of the few eighteenth-century novels to appear in chapbook form. Other well-known works include *Moll Flanders* (1722), *Journal of the Plague Year* (1723) and *Tour of the Whole Island of Great Britain* (1724–7).

DEINIOL, ST (fl. sixth century), one of the more important of the early Welsh saints, venerated in both north Wales and Ireland, of whom little is known. The centre of his cult was at Bangor and at Bangor-on-Dee.

DEKKER, THOMAS (c. 1570–1641), dramatist. The theatrical manager Philip Henslowe commissioned him to write plays in collaboration with many leading writers, including Michael DRAYTON and Ben JONSON, although many are now lost; during 1601–2 he was involved in a pamphlet war with Jonson. His principal plays include *The Shoemaker's Holiday* (1600), *The Honest Whore* (1604, 1630) and *The Witch of Edmonton* (1623), written with John Ford and William Rowley). Despite persistent financial troubles including imprisonment for debt, he left a reputation for cheerfulness, and his writings are notable for their sympathetic portrayal of people on the margins of society.

DELANE, JOHN (1817–79), editor. Joining *The Times* straight from Oxford in 1838, he was appointed its editor three years later. It was to be the period of the newspaper's greatest pre-eminence: protected from competition to an extent by the tax on paper and on advertising, which did not start to be lifted until 1853.

At the time *The Times* promulgated the views of its editor. A sociable and hardworking man,

Delane gleaned stories, often scoops, at the dinner table or on the hunting field. He decided the subject for the leaders, selected the news stories, chose the correspondence for the letters page and the books for review. *The Times* supported Britain's entry into the Crimean War (indeed readers were able to read the text of the British ultimatum to Russia before the Tsar had seen it) but was first to condemn the grievous mismanagement of the war in W. H. RUSSELL's despatches from the front. Like Lancs. cotton workers, and many of the British aristocracy, Delane supported the South in the American Civil War, and his paper came out in support of the contentious Bill that permitted Jews to sit in Parliament (1858–60). When he retired in 1877, he could claim that the circulation of *The Times* had all but doubled, to just under 60,000.

DELANY, MARY (née Granville) (1700–88), diarist and artist. From a long-established noble family, she was married in 1718 to an elderly Cornish landowner. When he died in 1725 Mary went to live in London where she was a friend of Samuel JOHNSON among others. She was married again in 1743, to Patrick Delany, Dean of Down, and went to live with him in Ireland; after his death in 1768 she returned to England, to live first with her friend the Duchess of Portland and then in a house provided for her at Windsor by GEORGE III. Her talents were multiple. She produced many representations of flowers in a form of collage or 'paper mosaic': their naturalism attracted the praise of Erasmus DARWIN. Throughout her life she wrote detailed letters to her sister Ann Dewes, her niece Mary Port and her great-niece Georgina. These were published in the nineteenth century and provide a valuable source for the social and cultural life of the upper social strata in eighteenth-century Britain.

DELFONT, BERNARD (Baron Delfont of Stepney) (1909–94) impresario. Having moved to Britain from Russia with his family in 1912, he went into theatrical management in 1941 and over the next 20 years acquired property, notably the Hippodrome in London's Leicester Square, which he turned into the famous Talk of the Town restaurant in 1958. Delfont owned 30 companies covering everything from theatre, film and television to music and property. His main vehicle was the EMI Film and Theatre Corporation, and he staged the Royal Variety Performance every year from 1961 to 1978.

DELIUS, FREDERICK (1862–1934), composer. Born into a mercantile family, Delius studied at the Leipzig Conservatory, where he was befriended by Edvard Grieg whose influence was lasting. He finally established himself as an important composer with his opera *A Village Romeo and Juliet* (1901). It was followed by *Appalachia* (1903), *Sea Drift* (1904) and his greatest and grandest work, *A Mass of Life* (1905), a setting of Friedrich Nietzsche's *Also Sprach Zarathustra*. As a result of syphilis contracted in his youth, Delius became blind and paralyzed in 1923, after composing the choral and orchestral work *Hassan* and his second violin sonata. With the assistance of his amanuensis, Eric Fenby, he continued to compose for nine more years. The works from this last period include the sublime *Songs of Farewell* (1930), settings of Walt Whitman, and *Idyll* (1932).

DELMER, 1ST BARON see BOOTH, GEORGE

DEMPSEY, SIR MILES (1896–1969), soldier. Educated at Shrewsbury and Sandhurst, Dempsey was wounded on the Western Front and awarded the Military Cross. In 1940 he served as a battalion commander at Dunkirk, and two years later, now a Lieutenant General, commanded the 8th Army's XIII Corps in Tunisia, Sicily and Italy. In Jan. 1944 MONTGOMERY chose Dempsey to command the 2nd Army in the invasion of northwest Europe. It was an inspired choice. Hating publicity, Dempsey allowed Montgomery to secure credit for many successful operations for which he (Dempsey) was in fact responsible. Leaving very few papers, Dempsey remains the least well known of senior British commanders of the Second World War.

DENMAN, LADY GERTRUDE (née Pearson) (1884–1954), administrator. Gertrude Pearson (whose father was created Viscount Cowdray) married when she was 19. She accompanied her husband to Australia when he was appointed Governor General, and, on her return to England in 1916, chaired a sub-group of the Agricultural Organization Society which promoted Women's Institutes (WI) with the aim of improving the quality of rural life. From 24 branches that year, the WI Federation grew to its peak in the 1950s with 8,000 branches and a membership of 450,000. Gertrude Denman was Chairman from 1917 to 1946. In the First World War, she worked with the Women's Bureau of Food Production, and in the Second she brought her knowledge of food and farming to her role as organizer of the Women's Land Army until she resigned in 1946, when 'land girls' were denied the same pension rights as those accorded to other women in the services and civil defence.

DENNING, ALFRED THOMPSON (Baron Denning of Whitchurch) (1899–1999), judge.

Probably the best-known judge of the twentieth century, Denning, a Hants. draper's son, won 'firsts' in mathematics and jurisprudence at Oxford. He was called to the Bar in 1923, and his rise was meteoric. By the time he was 40 he was a King's Counsellor. He was made a Justice of the High Court in 1944, Lord Justice of Appeal in 1948 and Lord of Appeal in Ordinary in 1957. Reputed to find the Lords dull, he returned to more active forensic law when he was appointed Master of the Rolls in 1962, a post which entailed his presiding also over the Civil Division of the Court of Appeal from 1962 to 1982, and it was during these years that his most noteworthy judgements were made. Complaining that many of his colleagues were 'timorous souls', 'Tom' Denning refused to be bound by precedent, and was prepared to stretch points of law to obtain the result that he thought right.

His crusades were in defence of individual rights in the modern State, against government, bureaucracy, big business and trade unions. Denning chaired the inquiry into the PROFUMO affair and any possible breaches of national security. His report (1963) was a best-seller. But in later years 'the people's judge' seemed to be increasingly out of touch, dismissing, for example, the possibility of police malpractice in the cases of the Birmingham Six and the Guildford Four (both IRA bomb attacks), and occasioning complaints of racism. He reluctantly retired in 1982, aged 83, and continued to pronounce on a range of legal issues.

DENNY, SIR ANTHONY (1501–49), royal servant. Son of a senior Exchequer official, Denny was a brilliant scholar at St Paul's and Cambridge and remained keenly interested in education; his career success, however, was in HENRY VIII's Privy Chamber, in which he became Chief Gentleman in 1539. This position in the monarch's private and domestic apartments gave him privileged access to the King. Formerly one of Thomas CROMWELL's circle, he played a vital role for the evangelical (Protestant) group in the power struggles around Henry, wielding great financial power and, on 31 Aug. 1546, taking control of the 'dry stamp' signature matrix which substituted on official documents for the royal signature.

DENT, J(OSEPH) M(ALLABY) (1849–1926), publisher. Born in Yorks., Dent was apprenticed to a printer at the age of 13, but switched to book-binding. In 1872 he opened a bindery in London and in 1885 started his own publishing company. Principally concerned with the reprint market, in 1904 he established (with Ernest Rhys) the Everyman Library with the aim of publishing 1,000 volumes in a 'working library of the world's literature, within the means of every book buyer, to be sold at a shilling a volume'. Dent never achieved this ambitious figure, but, much imitated, the series continues in attenuated form today.

DERBFORGAILL (DEVORGILLA) (?–1172), royal princess. Wife of TIGERNÁN UA RUAIRC, King of Bréifne, she was abducted by DIARMAIT MAC MURCHADHA in 1152. This so enraged her husband that when, 14 years later, he had the opportunity, he drove Diarmait out of Ireland, triggering the sequence of events which led to the English invasion of Ireland. Hence the so-called 'rape of Devorgilla' came to have a significant part in traditional Irish historiography, and with good reason.

DERBY, EARL OF, 10TH see STANLEY, THOMAS; **16TH** see STANLEY, JAMES; **23RD** and **26TH** see STANLEY, EDWARD; **COUNTESS OF** see BOHUN, MARY; BEAUFORT, LADY MARGARET

DERBY OR FERRERS, 6TH EARL OF see FERRERS, ROBERT

DERHAM, WILLIAM (1657–1735), scientist and clergyman. Educated at Oxford, he became vicar of Upminster (Essex) in 1689. Derham studied natural history and mechanics and was an exponent of the view that scientific rationalism and religion were not merely compatible but mutually reinforcing. His work *The Artificial Clockmaker* (1696), on the science of calculation, was followed by his Boyle lectures of 1712 (see BOYLE, ROBERT), *Physico-Theology: or A Demonstration of the Being and Attributes of God from the Works of Creation* and by *Astro-Theology: or A Demonstration of the Being and Attributes of God from a Survey of the Heavens* (1715). Derham saw the deity as a 'divine clockmaker' superintending a rationally ordered universe; his arguments were later developed by William PALEY. The popularity of such 'natural theology' arguments created an intellectual climate in which some came to insist on the role of God as divine architect at the expense of more traditional views and of the notion of Christ's special role as sacrifice and redeemer, the development known as Deism.

DERING, EDWARD (1540–1576), clergyman *see* LOCKE, ANNE

DERMOT MAC MURROUGH see DIARMAIT MAC MURCHADHA, essay on pages 246–47

DESAGULIERS, JOHN THEOPHILUS (1683–1744), scientist. The son of a French Protestant minister, he came to England with his father in 1685 after the revocation of the Edict of

Nantes. Educated at Oxford, in 1712 he began lecturing in Westminster, making his lectures more accessible to the general public by re-staging his experiments. In 1714 Desaguliers was appointed curator and demonstrator to the Royal Society. He later received clerical preferment from GEORGE I and GEORGE II and was chaplain to Prince FREDERICK. Besides contributing towards the public understanding of science Desaguliers built a ventilator for the House of Lords and invented the 'planetarium', which measured the exact distances of heavenly bodies by both the Newtonian (see NEWTON, ISAAC) and Copernican systems.

DESBOROUGH, JOHN (1608–80), soldier. Oliver CROMWELL's brother in law, Desborough (or Disbrowe) fought for Parliament, notably at the capture of Bristol in 1645 and the defeat of CHARLES II's Scots army at the Battle of Worcester in 1651. He was energetic as one of the major-generals chosen by Oliver Cromwell to regulate local government (1655–7) but, as a firm oppo-nent of all monarchy, he led with Charles FLEET-WOOD the military opposition which brought down Richard CROMWELL in 1659. Cashiered by the Rump Parliament when it was put back in power in 1659, in 1660 he was imprisoned on the eve of Charles II's restoration, again later in the year and, after intrigues in the Netherlands, in 1666–7.

DESMOND, EARL OF, 3RD see FITZGERALD, GERALD; **8TH** see FITZGERALD, THOMAS FITZ-JAMES; **14TH** see FITZGERALD, GERALD FITZJAMES; **15TH** see FITZGERALD, JAMES

DESPENCER, 15TH BARON LE see DASH-WOOD, FRANCIS

DESPENSER, HENRY (c. 1340–1406), prelate. Bishop of Norwich from 1370, he acquired a mili-tary reputation by his vigorous suppression of the Norfolk sector of the Peasants' Revolt in 1381. Two years later, he led the 'Norwich crusade', an expe-dition to fight the French supposedly as adherents of the 'anti-pope' in Flanders. Its failure resulted in his impeachment and the forfeit of the secular possessions of his see. These were restored two years later, and his subsequent loyalty to RICHARD II meant that, although he never openly rebelled against HENRY IV, he barely recognized the latter as King.

DESPENSER, HUGH (c. 1287–1326), courtier. Known as 'the younger' to distinguish him from his father, like whom he was a leading figure at EDWARD II's court, he was clearly the King's favourite by 1321. His acquisitiveness, especially in the Welsh Marches, led to the formation of an

anti-Despenser coalition; after this was defeated at Boroughbridge (Yorks.) in 1322, his greed and arrogance reached new heights. He alienated public opinion to such an extent that, when Roger MORTIMER and ISABELLA OF FRANCE invaded in 1326, no one raised a finger to help him, and he and his father were executed by the new regime.

DEVEREUX, ROBERT (20th [3rd Devereux] Earl of Essex) (1591–1646), soldier and courtier. Granted the forfeited family earldom in 1604, he was a rather more convincing model of a Puritan soldier-nobleman than his father (see Robert DEVEREUX, 19th Earl of Essex), although divorce from his wife, Frances HOWARD (mistress of Robert CARR, Earl of Somerset), in 1613 brought him misery and public humiliation. Horror at his father's fate may have combined with resentment at CHARLES I's neglect of his service; in 1628 he voted for the Petition of Right which criticized royal conduct of government, and, although second in command of the army sent north to fight the Scots in 1639, he became a leader of the aristocratic group seeking curbs on the King. Parliamentary Lord General from July 1642, he worked closely with John PYM, helping to save London from Royalist attack in Nov. 1642. Increasing military reverses discredited his lead-ership, especially defeat by the Royalists at Lostwithiel (Cornw.) in Sept. 1644. He resigned in April 1645, pre-empting the Self-Denying Ordinance which removed members of the two Houses of Parliament from military command. His death soon after the Parliamentary victory over Charles meant the loss of an important bridge-figure between the army and the Parlia-mentary leaders who sought a Presbyterian Church settlement and close alliance with the Scottish army.

DEVEREUX, ROBERT (19th Earl of Essex) see essay on page 242

DEVLIN, BERNADETTE see **MCALISKEY, BERNADETTE**

DEVLIN, JOSEPH (1871–1934), Ulster politi-cian. A former bar-tender who rose to prominence as a nationalist organizer in West Belfast from the 1890s, he was MP for Kilkenny North (1904–6), for West Belfast (1906–22) and for Fermanagh-Tyrone (1929–34). He combined nationalism with populist appeals for social reform; this won him respect among Protestant as well as Catholic workers but was limited by his Catholic middle-class support and by the sectarianism implicit in his use of the Ancient Order of Hibernians (Catholic equivalent of the Orange Order) as a power-base. Devlin was the only younger nationalist to be admitted to the

continued on page 243

DEVEREUX, ROBERT (19th [2nd Devereux] Earl of Essex) (1566–1601)
Soldier and courtier

Devereux was the great-nephew of ANNE BOLEYN and thus a cousin of ELIZABETH I. At the age of nine he inherited the earldom from his father Walter Devereux, together with heavy debts; his mother, Lettice Knollys, married Robert DUDLEY, Earl of Leicester, while he became ward to Lord Burghley (see CECIL, WILLIAM). He studied at Cambridge, and in 1584 Leicester brought him to court, perhaps with the motive of providing a new royal favourite within his own family circle. In 1586 Leicester took Essex with him on the Netherlands campaign; there his cousin Philip SIDNEY's death left Essex under the delusion that he should bear Sidney's legacy of Puritan chivalric virtue (he did marry Sidney's widow Frances Walsingham in 1590). From 1587 his good looks and charm fascinated Elizabeth; he distracted her from fears of growing old, and she allowed him considerable latitude in displays of temper and arrogance, though she had the sense never entirely to trust his judgement in politics or war. Throughout the 1590s he exploited her affection to act as a loose cannon in politics, seeking glory and power to the exclusion of all rivals, both similar glamour-boys like Walter RALEIGH and the very different Robert CECIL, son of his former guardian, Burghley; relations between Essex and Robert would seriously deteriorate after Burghley's death (1598). Essex was also concerned to finance his extravagance by improving his shaky personal fortunes, and in 1590 Elizabeth granted him the right to levy duty on sweet wines (the 'farm' of sweet wines), a profitable right previously enjoyed by Leicester.

Essex was convinced that his destiny lay in military glory. Elizabeth reluctantly granted him the command of an expedition to help Henri IV of France in 1591; he commemorated his moderate success by knighting a batch of his commanders (to Elizabeth's annoyance), and he was recalled after the unsuccessful siege of Rouen. On his return he diversified his quest for glory by taking an interest in government, particularly foreign affairs and overseas intelligence, to the increasing alarm of the Cecils; he became a Privy Councillor in 1593 and put much energy into cultivating JAMES VI of Scotland, who was becoming increasingly anxious to confirm his status as heir to the English Crown. Essex gained cheap popularity by uncovering a supposed plot by Roderigo LOPEZ to murder the Queen (1594); the Cecils were horrified at what was almost certainly a fiction, and Elizabeth was unimpressed. He was given command of one of the five squadrons to attack Spain in 1596. Ignoring his infuriated superior the Lord Admiral Charles HOWARD, Lord Howard of Effingham, he pressed ahead with a landing in Cadiz, which his men sacked, a spectacular achievement which brought a useful haul of plunder, a fresh crop of controversial knighthoods, and a wave of orchestrated publicity; for the rest of his life, he ostentatiously maintained his beard in the spade-shape which he had cultivated on the Cadiz expedition. He tried again in 1597, with an expedition intended to confront a further Spanish Armada and then capture the Spanish treasure fleet in the Azores; nothing was achieved, and he quarrelled bitterly with his fellow commander Raleigh. On his return he was furious when Lord Howard was made Earl of Nottingham and Lord Steward, and was not placated until he was given an office, Earl Marshal, to outrank Nottingham's. His problem was that the Cecils were entrenched in the political establishment; he was more prepared than Robert Cecil to build up a partisan faction. This cultivation of support and his military and chivalric rhetoric looked like disruptive opposition to the status quo, and he attracted into his circle discontented gentlemen and younger nobility who felt excluded from government, besides numerous admiring intellectuals eager to lend their scholarship to justify his bid for power. Essex might have redeemed himself by displaying competence, and in 1599, after bitter arguments, Elizabeth granted him the lord lieutenancy of Ireland, to fight Hugh O'NEILL. Essex squandered the best equipped English army yet sent to Ireland on minor campaigns, then rushed back to court in Sept. 1600 to explain his initiative in signing a truce with O'Neill. An embarrassing early-morning confrontation with Elizabeth at Nonsuch Palace led to house arrest. Faced with financial ruin when Elizabeth refused to renew his farm of sweet wines, convinced that his enemies were intent on destroying him and surrounded by young would-be heroes, Essex staged a pathetic attempt at a *coup d'état* in the city of London in Feb. 1601. After trial, in which his former client, Francis BACON, played an important part in the prosecution, he was executed.

Robert Lacey, Robert, Earl of Essex: An Elizabethan Icarus (1970) core leadership of the Irish Parliamentary Party, and was widely seen as eventual heir apparent, but his prospects were shattered by partition and the downfall of the Irish Party. Devlin retained a personal base in Belfast, but his attempts to represent nationalist interests within the Northern Ireland Parliament (of which he was a member (1921–34), though virtually abstentionist except in 1926–9) were stymied by Sinn Féin hostility and Unionist intransigence. He was the most prominent Ulster nationalist of the twentieth century before John HUME.

DEVON, EARL OF, 19TH see COURTENAY HENRY; **20TH** see COURTENAY, EDWARD

DEVONSHIRE, EARL OF, 1ST see BLOUNT, CHARLES; **DUKE OF, 1ST AND 4TH** see CAVENDISH, WILLIAM; **8TH** see CAVENDISH, SPENCER; **DUCHESS OF** see CAVENDISH, GEORGIANA

DEVORGILLA see DEARBHFHORGHAILL; DERB-FORGAILL

DEVOY, JOHN (1842–1928), Irish politician. His role in recruiting for the Fenians among Irish soldiers in the British army led to his imprisonment (1866–71), after which he emigrated to America. He became the most prominent American Fenian leader and leading figure of the secret Clann na nGael, though smaller groups were led by rivals such as O'DONOVAN ROSSA, and the Irish-based wing of the organization remained outside his control. In 1879 he supported Charles Stewart PARNELL and DAVITT in the New Departure, but a few years later backed a bombing campaign in Britain. The Clann na nGael was weakened from the mid 1880s by a split between the followers of Devoy and those of Alexander Sullivan, but reunited in 1900 under Devoy and Daniel Cohalan. Devoy and his newspaper, the *Gaelic American,* played a vital role in obtaining US support for new separatist movements in Ireland; his co-operation with German agents in preparing for the Easter Rising and opposing American entry into the First World War led to harassment by the American government. In 1919–20 Devoy and Cohalan quarrelled with Irish envoys led by DE VALERA about the tactics to be used in securing American support, leading to another split in the American organization; the Devoy–Cohalan group supported the Anglo-Irish Treaty (largely because De Valera opposed it) and when Devoy revisited Ireland shortly before his death he was received by the Free State government as a national hero.

DEWAR, DONALD (1937–), politician. As MP for Aberdeen South (1966–70), Glasgow Garscadden (1978–97) and Glasgow Anniesland from 1997, the tall dour figure of Donald Dewar has come to represent the future of Scottish Labour. Chosen as Secretary of State for Scotland in 1997 by Tony BLAIR following Labour's landslide victory, it was Dewar's job to preside over the legislation introducing devolution for Scotland. His quiet but shrewd handling of the issue ensured that he was chosen as Scotland's First Minister after the elections for the Scottish Assembly in May 1999.

D'EWES, SIR SIMONDS (1602–50), historian. Grandson of a Flemish immigrant, a lawyer and one of the antiquarian circle that included Sir Robert COTTON and John SELDEN; he was elected to the Long Parliament in 1640 and was a vociferous conservative Presbyterian until expelled from the Commons in the army coup, PRIDE's PURGE, in Dec. 1648. A self-important snob, he left published and unpublished papers and historical works of great value.

DIANA (née Spencer) (1961–97), Princess of Wales. It seems unlikely that a future age will be able to grasp either her glamour or her secular canonization at the time of her death, but she will remain a phenomenon which will tell historians much about the age in which she lived.

She was the third daughter of the 8th Earl Spencer and his wife, Frances, who divorced when she was only eight years old. Showing no sign of scholarly or any other attainments, she seemed destined to follow the lifestyle of her fellow 'Sloane Rangers', but it happened that, young and virginal, she was seen as an ideal bride for CHARLES, Prince of Wales, and on 24 Feb. 1981 their engagement was announced. Their wedding on 29 July 1981 was watched by more than 750 million people world-wide; it was the fairy-tale wedding and she was the fairy-tale princess.

She swiftly became the most glamorous and most photographed person in the world; the public could not, the tabloids said, get enough of her. Her spontaneous and loving relationship with her two children, Prince William (1982) and Prince Harry (1984) contrasted favourably with the stuffy ways of her in-laws and her husband, and she quickly found herself the idol of young women everywhere; when it transpired that her marriage was far from perfect, this admiration increased as she became Everywoman who had ever been deceived, scorned or victimized.

There were those who thought that she might have contributed something to the breakdown of her marriage, but her own skilful use of the admiring media challenged such heresy. The publication of *Diana: Her True Story* by Andrew Morton in 1992 fixed in the public mind the image of her as the helpless victim; this was further reinforced by a remarkable interview for the BBC's *Panorama* programme in Nov. 1995 when more than 20 million viewers witnessed her baring her soul in public. Her divorce in 1996 freed her but it was not clear which direction she would move in. Speculation about her relationship with the son of the Egyptian tycoon, Mohammed Al-Fayed, flared up in Aug. 1997 when they were photographed on holiday in the Mediterranean. But this was cut short by the news of their deaths in a car crash in Paris on 31 Aug. 1997. The Prime Minister, Tony BLAIR, mourned the passing of the 'people's princess'. The week which followed saw an outbreak of public mourning without precedent, and on the day of her funeral, 6 Sept. 1997, the whole of Britain seemed to come to a standstill. The carpet of flowers outside her London home at Kensington Palace resembled a tidal wave, while the queues of visitors stretched for miles and people waited for hours to sign the books of remembrance. Then, as suddenly as it had come, the 'cult of Saint Diana' which had raised more than £30 million for an appeal in her name, came to an end. She had, however, left an indelible mark on her age, although the effect on the British monarchy seemed short lived; the planned public memorial for Diana had not been realized by the second anniversary of the death, when some newspaper headlines spoke of the 'forgotten' princess.

DIARMIT MAC MAÍL NA MBÓ (?–1072), King of the Uí Néill Chennselaig and Leinster (1046–66). Diarmit Mac Maíl na mBó was a member of the Uí Chennselaig, one of the dynasties of Leinster. In a career that began in the 1030s, he seized the kingdom of Leinster by force in 1046, took over the Viking kingdom of Dublin in 1052 and then assisted decisively in the efforts of his protégé, TURLOCH O BRIEN, to become King of Munster. He also gave succour and military assistance to the sons of the English King HAROLD II after 1066. Until his death in battle, he was undoubtedly the strongest king in Ireland.

DIARMAIT MAC MURCHADHA *see* essay on pages 246–47

DICETO, RALPH (*c.* 1125–*c.* 1200), historian. His name suggests that he came from Diss (Norfolk). His erudite *Epitome of Chronicles* covers the period from the Creation to 1148, his *Images of History* that from 1148 to 1200. As Dean of St Paul's he felt himself to be close to the court (he officiated at the coronation of RICHARD I) and was the nearest that any medieval author came to being an official historian of the English Crown. He worked hard to absolve HENRY II from responsibility for BECKET's murder. His history increasingly became a record of his own correspondence with a wide circle of patrons and friends in powerful places, notably WALTER OF COUTANCES. They kept him well informed, relying on his sympathy and discretion.

DICK-READ, GRANTLEY (1890–1959), gynaecologist. Publication of his *Natural Childbirth* (1933), with its rejection of the medicalization of childbirth and particularly the use of anaesthetics, caused controversy on publication, and set a daunting standard for women, but modifications of his approach have informed much later thinking on parturition.

DICKENS, A(RTHUR) G(EOFFREY) (1910–), historian. Yorks.-born, he held chairs in the universities of Hull and London and served as Director of the Institute of Historical Research 1967–77. A pioneer of research on religion in the localities (particularly northern England), his most celebrated work is *The English Reformation* (1964), an account of the Reformation to 1558 notable for its emphasis on the popular support enjoyed by religious reform. His interpretation was challenged by a series of 'revisionist' historians in the 1980s, who have preferred to explore the strength of traditional religion in England.

DICKENS, CHARLES *see* essay on page 248

DIGBY, GEORGE (2nd Earl of Bristol) (1612–77), courtier. Digby was born in Madrid during the embassy of his father John DIGBY the 1st Earl; as an MP, he supported the opposition to CHARLES I until the impeachment of Thomas WENTWORTH, Earl of Strafford, in 1641, when he began working for peace. He also encouraged Charles, however, to attempt the seizure of the 'five members' (John HAMPDEN, Arthur HASELRIG, Denzil HOLLES, John PYM and William STRODE). He became a passionate Royalist, fought for Charles I at his defeat at Edgehill on 23 Oct. 1642 and bitterly quarrelled with both moderate politicians and Prince RUPERT. After his northern military commands ended in defeat in 1645, he undertook military service in France. He became Secretary of State to the exiled CHARLES II (1657), but was dismissed on becoming a Roman Catholic. He intrigued unsuccessfully in 1663 against Edward HYDE, Earl of Clarendon. His many talents did not include a sense of proportion.

DIGBY, JOHN (1st Earl of Bristol) (1580–1653), diplomat. He was repeatedly Ambassador in the fruitless quest for Spanish marriages for Princes HENRY and Charles (the future CHARLES I) (1611–17, 1622–23), latterly earning Charles's hostility, which led most unjustly to his disgrace.

Thoroughly alienated, he refused to support the King against the Petition of Right by which, in 1628, Parliament criticized royal government, but in 1640, he felt that his hour had come as an aristocratic mediator. In fact, he lost the trust of both sides, particularly because of his son George DIGBY's maverick Royalist role. After years of ineffectual advice to the King, he went into exile in 1646, dying in Paris.

DIGBY, SIR KENELM (1603–65), politician and scholar. Son of Sir Everard Digby, a Catholic convert and associate of the Gunpowder plotters executed in 1606, Digby was sent to Oxford and afterwards toured extensively in Europe, accompanying Prince Charles (the future CHARLES I) and George VILLIERS, Duke of Buckingham, to Madrid in 1623. In 1628 he commanded a Mediterranean privateering fleet which defeated the French and Venetian ships gathered in Scanderoon harbour. Only briefly wavering from Roman Catholicism, he became Chancellor to HENRIETTA MARIA in her French exile from 1644, unsuccessfully appealed to Pope Innocent X for help for the royal cause, but later combined his royal service with work for Oliver CROMWELL. He was prominent in the Royal Society from its foundation (1663) and experimented with the respiration of plants.

DIGGES, LEONARD (c. 1510–?1557), mathematician. From a Kentish gentry family and Oxford-educated, he had official surveying responsibilities at Calais; he was involved in the 1554 rising of Sir Thomas WYATT the younger, and was twice attainted (declared legally dead) in MARY I's reign. He wrote treatises on mathematics, and his observations on optics provided the theory which foreshadowed the invention of the telescope. Much of his work was published posthumously by his equally distinguished mathematician son, Thomas DIGGES, whose education he had entrusted to John DEE.

DIGGES, THOMAS (?–1595), mathematician. Son of Leonard DIGGES, he was educated at Cambridge. He was a friend of John DEE and a client of Robert DUDLEY, Earl of Leicester, and was twice MP as well as holding the important military office of Muster Master General in 1586–7 and 1590–94. In 1572 he published a pioneering description of a supernova; the support which this gave to the new astronomical system proposed by Nicolaus Copernicus was reinforced in 1576 by a combined edition of his own and his father's work, which proved a publishing success; he was much praised by the Danish astronomer Tycho Brahe. He was among those appointed to prepare an abortive expedition to explore the Far East and the Antarctic in 1590.

DILKE, SIR CHARLES (1843–1911), politician. Son of a lawyer who became a Liberal MP, he too was called to the Bar and represented the Liberals in Parliament. A radical, imperialist and republican, he held office under GLADSTONE and might even have succeeded him had he not been ruined by a divorce scandal in 1886. He returned to political life in 1892 and remained an active back-bench campaigner for women's suffrage, minimum wage legislation and women's property rights. The first Wages Board legislation of 1909 was passed largely as a result of his efforts.

DILKE, LADY EMILY (1840–1904), trade unionist. She was influenced by Emma PATERSON in the 1870s and became involved in the women's movement. She married Sir Charles DILKE in 1885 after an unhappy marriage with Mark Pattison was ended by his death the previous year, and she supported Dilke in the political scandal that ensued when he was cited in a divorce case the following year. Her importance as a feminist derives from the commanding position she came to occupy in the Women's Trade Union League, of which she became President in 1902. She campaigned for equal pay, better conditions and the effective organization of women workers.

DILL, SIR JOHN (1881–1944), soldier. Educated at Sandhurst, Dill saw active service in South Africa (1901), and, clearly destined for high rank, served in a variety of staff appointments during the First World War. In the inter-war years he rose steadily until in May 1940 he was appointed Chief of the Imperial General Staff, a promotion which set him on a collision course with CHURCHILL, particularly over Dill's objections to sending an expeditionary force to Greece (March 1941). Replaced by Alan BROOKE in Nov. 1941, Dill became head of the British military mission in Washington until his death.

DILLON, JAMES (1902–86), Irish politician. Son of John DILLON, he was member of the Dáil for Donegal (1932–8), and for Monaghan (1938–69). Originally elected as an independent, a founder and deputy leader of the National Centre Party which merged with Cumann na nGaedhael and the Blueshirts in 1933 to form Fine Gael, he called, as deputy leader of Fine Gael, for Ireland to enter the Second World War on the Allied side; this led to his expulsion from the party in 1942, but he held his seat as an independent, rejoining Fine Gael in 1950. Minister for Agriculture (1948–51 and 1954–7), leader of Fine Gael (1958–66), he was a colourful orator and representative of an older style of politics.

DIARMAIT MAC MURCHADHA (DERMOT MAC MURROUGH) (?–1171)
King of Leinster (1132–66, 1170–1)

In 1169 three ships carrying 30 knights, 60 men-at-arms and 300 archers commanded by Robert Fitzstephen and Maurice Fitzgerald landed at Bannow Bay on the south coast of Ireland. They had come at the invitation of Diarmait Mac Murchadha, who had sought their military help in recovering his kingdom of Leinster. They attacked and captured Wexford and he, as he had promised, gave them the town.

The capture of Wexford was the first English conquest in Ireland, the beginning of a process which an annalist in the *Book of Leinster* summed up as: 'The English came into Ireland and Ireland was destroyed by them.' As these words make clear, the Irish King who invited the 'Saxons' in, VORTIGERN of Ireland, was not going to be treated kindly by Irish historians. It was his fault, according to the seventeenth-century *Annals of the Four Masters*, that 'all Ireland was made a trembling sod', and it was only right that, 'having brought over the Saxons, having inflicted great injuries on the Irish, having plundered many churches, he should die of an insufferable and unknown disease, for he became putrid while living and he died without penance, without the body of Christ, without unction, as his evil deeds deserved'.

Diarmait owed his notoriety solely to the actions of the last five years of his life, and to their aftermath. The story of these dramatic events is told in two near-contemporary narratives, one a history written by Gerald de BARRI, a nephew of Robert Fitzstephen, and the other an anonymous *Chanson de geste*, now known as *The Song of Dermot and the Earl*.

But for much the greater part of his life Diarmait was a highly successful and fairly conventional Irish king, twelfth-century style. Ireland was a land of many kings, in the words of *The Song* 'as many kings as counts elsewhere'. According to the theory of the law tracts there were three grades of kings: king (*rí*), over-king (*ruiri*) and king of overkings (*rí ruirech*). These last were the 'province-kings', those who ruled the principal regions or provinces (Connacht, Leinster, Munster, Meath and Ulster), and they were the only ones who really counted. In the twelfth century the lesser 'kings' were increasingly called lord (*tigerna*) or leader (*toísech*) rather than king. If one of the province-kings forced some or all the others to recognize him as their lord, he might be called, or think of himself as, a high-king, king of Ireland (*rí Érenn*). All the kings were involved in struggles for power and wealth, principally in the form of cattle, and in practice it was men who proved themselves in this competitive world who were chosen as kings. Struggles for kingship within dynasties tended to be as fierce as conflicts between dynasties, since every male of every branch of a royal, or once royal, family had the chance to be a king; and since successful kings commonly had several wives (Irish marriage customs being different from those which now applied in twelfth-century England and France) they often had many sons, all with claims to kingship. Children were given to other families, to be fostered by them, and a man's ties with his foster-family were often closer than with his own family.

Diarmait belonged to the Síl nOnchon branch of the Uí Chennsalaig dynasty in south Leinster; it was there in the south-east, around Ferns, that his family's lands lay. He was fostered among the Uí Caellaide, and it was with their help that by 1132 he had succeeded in ousting his many rivals and making himself King of all Leinster. He had faced stiff opposition, especially in north Leinster where a member of the leading local dynasty, the Uí Faeláin, was supported by TAIRDELBACH UA CONCHOBAIR, a high-king in the making. It had taken a dramatic act to impose himself on north Leinster, the capture of the richest church in the region, the nunnery of Kildare, and the ritual violation of the abbess. It was probably a revolt of north Leinster dynasts which lay behind Diarmait's killing and blinding of 17 of them in 1141.

With north Leinster came the opportunity to control the Ostmen (the Hiberno-Norse) of Dublin, with their expanding commerce and their fleet. As early as 1137 Diarmait used the fleets of Wexford and Dublin to lay siege to Waterford. But so rich a prize as Dublin attracted the attention of greater kings than Diarmait, and he generally had to recognize the overlordship first of Tairdelbach Ua Conchobair (until 1149) and then of MUIRCHERTACH MAC LOCHLAINN as high-kings.

In 1144 Tairdelbach rewarded him with a grant of part of east Meath; the other part went to TIGERNÁN UA RUAIRC, King of Bréifne. Between the two of them a struggle for control of the region led, in 1152, to Diarmait's abduction of Tigernán's wife, DERBFORGAILL, the so-called 'rape of Devorguilla'. This, in the historian Geoffrey Keating's opinion, was the crime that brought about Diarmait's downfall. Undoubtedly it was an outrage which Tigernán never forgot, but while Diarmait was protected by the power of Muirchertach there was little he could do about it. Muirchertach's death in battle in 1166 was swiftly followed by the total failure of Diarmait's own bid for the high-kingship.

Muirchertach's great rival RUAIDRÍ UA CONCHOBAIR captured Dublin with the help of his Ua Ruairc ally. Ruaidrí was content with Diarmait's submission but Tigernán was not. With the help of the Ostmen of Dublin, Leinster rebels and treachery from within Diarmait's own retinue, Tigernán's forces penetrated as far as Ferns itself. Driven from his capital Diarmait with his wife and daughter took ship for Bristol on 1 Aug. 1166. He went to HENRY II, did homage to him and received permission to recruit what help he could from within Henry's dominions. According to *The Song of Dermot* he offered land as well as money: 'whoever shall ask for soil or sod, richly shall I enfeoff them'. In 1167 Diarmait returned with a small band of soldiers from Pembroke, and did well enough to be recognized, in return for handing over hostages to Ruaidrí, as King of Uí Chennsallaig. He also had give Tigernán 100 ounces of gold in reparation for the blow to his honour suffered 15 years earlier.

But Diarmait wanted all of Leinster back. In 1169 and 1170 he persuaded many more mercenaries to sail across the Irish Sea. Among them was Raymond FITZGERALD and, by far the most important, Strongbow (*see* CLARE, RICHARD DE). To him Diarmait promised the hand of Aífe, his daughter by his most recent marriage, and with Aífe, in flagrant breach of Irish law, the succession to the kingdom of Leinster. Strongbow arrived in Aug. 1170. He captured Waterford and there married Aífe.

In Sept. Diarmait and the English outflanked Ruaidrí's army and took Dublin. Diarmait died in the spring of 1171, leaving Strongbow as *de facto* King of Leinster. This was a political development so alarming to Henry II that he arrived later that year with a massive English army. Most Irish kings decided to submit and he assumed the title Lord of Ireland. Diarmait's ambition had set in motion the train of events which led, in the words of the contemporary English historian, WILLIAM OF NEWBURGH, to 'the conquest of the Irish by the English', which he described as 'the end of freedom for people who had hitherto been free since time immemorial, unconquered even by the Romans'.

So far as Diarmait's reputation was concerned this was to overshadow everything else. For decades he had been a successful King, issuing charters, building in stone, endowing and founding churches (especially in Dublin). He co-operated with the papal reorganization of the Irish Church when he attended the Council of Clane, at which a Papal Legate confirmed the appointment of his brother-in-law LORCÁN as Archbishop of Dublin in 1162. He promoted monastic reform when, *c.* 1148, he established a Cistercian abbey at Baltinglass (Co. Wicklow). For this he received a congratulatory letter from the greatest of all Cistercians, St Bernard of Clairvaux, who wrote: 'in our opinion it is truly a great miracle that a King at the end of the earth, ruling over barbarous peoples, should undertake with great generosity such works of mercy'. In 1171–2 many of the leading Irish churchmen welcomed Henry II's presence in Ireland as a means of pressing on with modernization and reform. Letters from them led Pope Alexander III to express his joy at the news that vice was decreasing now that 'a barbarous and uncivilized people has been made subject to the noble King of the English'.

A King as alert as Diarmait to recent European ideas and fashions must have been aware of these views; and his own association with the cause of reform may have made it all the easier for him to turn to outside help. It was his great misfortune that the perception of Ireland as a backward land of incest and adultery coincided with a time of European demographic growth, when younger sons and others were encouraged to travel to 'the end of the earth'. Many thousands of English colonists and settlers followed where Strongbow and Henry II led, believing that by taking other men's lands they were advancing the cause of civilization. So it was that Diarmait's invitation led to what the twelfth-century *Annals of Tigernach* called 'the start of Ireland's woe'. In traditional Irish historiography 1169 remains the year of destiny.

No biography. An introduction in Sean Duffy, Ireland in the Middle Ages (1997)

DICKENS, CHARLES (1812–70)
Writer

Incomparably the most widely read of all Victorian novelists, the son of a feckless naval petty officer and his wife, Dickens was born in Portsmouth, moved to Chatham, then London, where his father was imprisoned for debt in the Marshalsea. Charles was sent, aged 12, to work in Warren's blacking warehouse. It was a desolate period for the child: 'my whole nature ... was penetrated by grief and humiliation'. Though it lasted only a few months, and on his father's release from prison he was sent to Wellington House Academy to complete his neglected education, the experience scarred him. It drove him to work compulsively and inspired much of his early fiction, including *David Copperfield* and *Little Dorrit*. At 15 he went to work in a solicitor's office, teaching himself shorthand and rising to become a court reporter. In 1832 he started to work for the *Mirror of Parliament* and was in the press gallery when the first Reform Bill debates raged.

From there he joined the *Morning Chronicle* as its parliamentary reporter, and also contributed articles to various journals including the *Monthly Magazine*, edited by his friend George Hogarth whose daughter, Catherine, Dickens married in 1836. These articles, 'Illustrative of Every-Day Life and Every-Day People' of the London of WILLIAM IV, were republished in 1836–7 as *Sketches by Boz* (from a childhood name for one of his brothers) with illustrations by George CRUICKSHANK. The *Sketches* attracted the attention of the publishers Chapman Hall, who commissioned Dickens to write 12,000 words a month of *The Posthumous Papers of the Pickwick Club*, which started to appear in 1836.

Though largely ignored at first, when in the fourth episode Sam Weller was introduced as a character and Phiz (Hablot Knight Browne) took over the illustrations, the success of *The Pickwick Papers* was assured, being published in volume form in 1837 when Dickens was just 25 years old. Simultaneously *Oliver Twist*, which satirized the cruel effects of the 'reformed' Poor Law of 1834, began to come out in serial form in a new publication, *Bentley's Miscellany*, of which Dickens was the first editor, and monthly episodes of *Nicholas Nickleby* followed. In 1840, backed by Chapman Hall, he started the periodical *Master Humphrey's Clock*, and although the journal's formula was not a success, Dickens's long stories in it were, and they continued to appear as *The Old Curiosity Shop* (1840–1) and *Barnaby Rudge* (1841).

In 1841 Dickens paid his first visit to America, where there was great enthusiasm for his work, a feeling that he at first reciprocated, but his later disillusion is recorded in *American Notes* (1842) and *Martin Chuzzlewit* (1843–4). By now father of a growing family, and with *Martin Chuzzlewit* not enjoying the success of earlier works, he turned to writing what he hoped would prove lucrative Christmas books, of which the first and most enduringly popular was *A Christmas Carol* (1843). Still contributing journalistic articles as well as writing serialized books (*Dombey and Son* was published 1846–8), he briefly edited the *Daily News*, a radical paper which he had started in 1846, and in 1850 founded and edited *Household Words*, which was incorporated into *All the Year Round* in 1859. Most of his subsequent work appeared in the pages of these journals: *David Copperfield* (1849–50), *Bleak House* (1852–3), *A Child's History of England* (the heroes of which are Oliver CROMWELL and King ALFRED) (1851–3), *Hard Times* (1854), *Little Dorrit* (1855–7), *A Tale of Two Cities* (1859), *Great Expectations* (1860–1) and *Our Mutual Friend* (1864–5).

Dickens did not just novelize the condition of Victorian England (George Bernard SHAW was to opine that *Little Dorrit* was 'a more seditious book than *Das Kapital*'); he engaged actively with social issues too. While in America he had been vociferous in his condemnation of slavery and in favour of international copyright for authors; he worked for the reform of prostitution and for building model dwellings in the East End of London, and he helped arrange theatrical entertainments, often for the benefit of impecunious authors and playwrights.

He fell in love with a young actress, 16-year-old Ellen Ternan, and separated from his wife, the mother of his 10 children, after publishing 'Some domestic troubles of mine of long-standing' in *Household Notes*, in 1858. His restless energies took him all over the country giving dramatic public readings from his work, and in 1867 he returned to America for another successful tour. Dickens died suddenly at Gad's Hill, his beloved home in Kent, aged 58, leaving an unfinished novel, *The Mystery of Edwin Drood*, and an immense fund of sentimental portrayals, memorable caricatures and sensationalist stories, and a panorama of English social history which remains many people's main picture of that period.

Fred Kaplan, Charles Dickens (1988)
Peter Akroyd, Charles Dickens (1990)

DILLON, JOHN (1851–1927), Irish politician. Son of the Young Ireland leader John Blake Dillon, he came to prominence as a radical land agitator and one of Charles Stewart PARNELL's lieutenants, though his personal relations with Parnell were distant. MP for Tipperary (1880–3) and for East Mayo (1885–1918), he took a leading role in the Plan of Campaign in the late 1880s, opposing Parnell in the split. He became the principal figure in the main anti-Parnellite faction (which he led from 1896), trying to maintain its centralized structure and its alliance with the Liberal Party despite opposition from the clericalist HEALY. When the Nationalist Party reunited Dillon ceded the leadership to John REDMOND, but after the secession of William O'BRIEN in 1903 he was established as its second most important figure. Highly suspicious of new trends in Irish nationalism as distractions from the central task of winning Home Rule (he was violently hostile to Horace PLUNKETT's co-operative movement and criticized some aspects of Gaelic League policy), he was less committed to the Liberal government's foreign policy and more suspicious of its war policy than Redmond. After the 1916 Easter Rising he publicly criticized the treatment of the captured rebels. He succeeded Redmond as party leader in 1918 but presided over the party's destruction by Sinn Féin and lost his own seat in the 1918 General Election.

DIMBLEBY, RICHARD (1913–65), broadcaster. Dimbleby began his journalistic career on the family newspaper, the *Richmond and Twickenham Times*. In 1936 he invented a job for himself at the BBC as the corporation's first proper news reporter, and it was his news reports during the Second World War that made his reputation. He was the first BBC correspondent to fly with Bomber Command and report on the raids over Germany, and he was the first reporter into the Belsen concentration camp when it was liberated in 1945. After the war Dimbleby became the BBC's principal 'anchor-man' on the new and quickly expanding medium of television. With an authoritative voice and a physical presence to match, Dimbleby became the quintessential presenter on the most important current affairs and political programmes such as *Panorama* and a household name (and voice) for his commentaries on such State occasions as the coronation of ELIZABETH II in 1953 (an event which gained a television audience of 20 million viewers) and the funeral of Winston CHURCHILL in 1965. His sons David and Jonathan followed him into television journalism.

DINGLEY, ROBERT (1710–81), philanthropist. The son of a London jeweller, he made a fortune in the Russia trade and was a Director of the Bank of England (1757–67). An active governor of Thomas CORAM's Foundling Hospital, in 1758 Dingley founded the Magdalen Hospital for Penitent Prostitutes. He offered to stand against WILKES in the Middx. parliamentary election and in 1769 promoted an anti-Wilkes loyal address from the City.

DIRAC, PAUL (1902–84), physicist. Dirac studied electrical engineering and mathematics at Bristol University, and during doctoral research at Cambridge University developed a form of quantum mechanics that differed from the matrix and wave forms of Werner Heisenberg and Erwin Schrödinger respectively. From 1927 he taught mathematics at Cambridge and rapidly gained an international reputation as a leading architect of quantum mechanics. In the same year he applied quantum mechanics to the electromagnetic field, thus founding the widely used Quantum Field Theory. He is best known for his formulation, in 1928, of the relativistic wave equation for the electron. From this equation he predicted that the electron had an intrinsic 'spin' and a magnetic moment, and deduced the existence of the anti-electron (later called the positron) and the anti-proton. Evidence for these anti-particles has since been produced by Patrick BLACKETT and others. During the 1930s he published his influential *Principles of Quantum Mechanics* (1930), became Lucasian Professor of Mathematics at Cambridge (1932) and shared the 1933 Nobel Prize for Physics with Schrödinger.

DISNEY, JOHN (1746–1816), religious leader. Grandson of a pious layman of the same name who had supported the early eighteenth-century 'reformation of manners' movement (*see* STEPHENS, EDWARD) and become a cleric in middle age, he had planned a career in law, but when his health broke down he entered the Anglican ministry, serving as chaplain to Edmund LAW. In 1771 he was active in the campaign to repeal the requirement that Anglican clergy subscribe to the Thirty-Nine Articles. In 1774 he married the daughter of the campaign's leader, Francis BLACKBURNE. After its failure he at first remained an Anglican, unlike his friend Theophilus LINDSEY, but in 1782 he joined Lindsey as a Unitarian, taking over his church at Essex Street in London in 1793. Disney had been involved in the parliamentary reform movement of 1780 and now campaigned for Parliament to end the penalties on those who spoke or wrote against the doctrine of the Trinity, a campaign that succeeded in 1813.

DISRAELI, BENJAMIN *see* essay on pages 250–51

DISRAELI, BENJAMIN (1st Earl of Beaconsfield) (1804–81)
Politician and Prime Minister (1868, 1874–80)

Quite the oddest figure ever to lead any British political party, the spectacle of this Jewish, literary dandy leading the Anglican squires of the mid Victorian Conservative Party has an enduring fascination. Had his father, Isaac, not quarrelled with his local synagogue while Ben was a youngster, the most colourful career in Victorian politics would not have been possible, since Jews were not allowed to sit in the Commons until 1857. Baptized a Christian at the age of 12, D'Israeli the Younger (as he was known) first sought fame as a writer but his early literary ventures, like his financial ones, simply made him notorious. By the time he was 22 he had published his first novel *Vivian Grey* (1826) and had run up huge debts which were to dog him throughout his career.

After several unsuccessful attempts to enter Parliament as an independent radical, Disraeli managed, partly through the aid of the former Lord Chancellor, Lyndhurst, to get a seat at Folkestone, an event which finally relieved him from the threat of arrest for debt. His rackety personal life reached some sort of equilibrium in 1839 when he married the widow of his former colleague, Wyndham Lewis, Mary-Ann. As he later admitted, he married her for her money but it was characteristic of his ability to charm older women that he should have added to this the caveat that if he had to do it again he would do it for love.

Disraeli was not the sort of figure to be offered even minor office by Sir Robert PEEL and, although he had no claims on Peel, he resented being passed over and soon made himself a nuisance in a variety of ways. As the leading light in the 'Young England' movement, Disraeli stimulated criticism of Peel from younger, paternalistic aristocrats who took objection to their leader's utilitarian liberalism and argued, along Disraelian lines, for a more paternalistic vision of Conservatism. Disraeli himself pursued this line in a tryptich of famous novels, *Coningsby* (1844), *Sybil* (1845) and *Tancred* (1847), in which he also held up Peel to ridicule, a device he used to some effect in the Commons after 1845.

One central problem with Disraeli was summed up in the words of his 'Young England' colleague, Lord John MANNERS, who described Disraeli's thoughts as his own 'but does he believe them?' Historians, like contemporaries, have never quite agreed on this. His admiring early twentieth-century biographers, Moneypenny and BUCKLE, saw his actions over the repeal of the Corn Laws

as a natural attack on a Prime Minister who had betrayed his party, and as an essential step in the creation of the modern Conservative Party, which he then proceeded to educate over the 1867 Reform Act and during his final term as Prime Minister. Modern historians, in particular Lord BLAKE in his influential biography published in 1966, have preferred to stress the contingent, not to say opportunist, element in Disraeli's thoughts and actions.

Certainly his criticism of Peel in 1845 and 1846 over the repeal of the Corn Laws was not the product of his own belief in them and, as early as 1847, he was arguing that the party had to move away from Protectionism. Nonetheless, Disraeli had a point in criticizing Peel for neglecting the essential basis of his parliamentary position, his own party; in this sense he was one of the first politicians to recognize the importance of party. But his own party loved him not and, while the Protectionist leader Lord Derby (*see* STANLEY, EDWARD) agreed to work with him, Disraeli was only one of a triumvirate of leaders in the Commons. His stoutest ally was CANNING's former private secretary, Lord George BENTINCK, more noted for his interest in the Turf than the Blue Book. Along with his brother, the Duke of Portland, Bentinck helped provide the money to set up Disraeli as a country gentleman by buying the estate of Hughenden (Bucks.) which became his base from the late 1840s. But although this gave him a country house, it did not make him any more acceptable to many of the country gentlemen of England.

As the only Conservative of oratorical talent in the Commons, Disraeli was Lord Stanley's 'necessity' but, as the man most hated by the Peelites, he was also the greatest obstacle to Conservative reunion. As Chancellor of the Exchequer in Derby's government in 1852, he cut an incongruous figure but was generally felt to have made a decent stab at a budget in Dec. 1852 before GLADSTONE destroyed both it and the government; thenceforth there was no love lost between the two men.

The 1850s and 1860s were largely ones of frustration for Disraeli. The Conservatives were the largest single party but were never able to command a parliamentary majority, having to settle for minority governments in 1851–2, 1858–9 and 1866–8. The Earl of Derby was the party leader and, despite the concentration historians have lavished on the more colourful Disraeli, it was Derby who set the tone for the Conservatives and he was content to keep Palmerston (*see* TEMPLE, HENRY) in office to provide a check on reform. Palmerston's death in 1865 put an end to this option, and John RUSSELL and Gladstone's mismanagement of the reform issue brought Derby and Disraeli in for another term.

The older view that the passing of the Second Reform Act had anything to do with 'Tory Democracy' and 'educating' the Conservative Party has failed to survive the scrutiny of modern historians, who have convincingly demonstrated the elements of opportunism and party political advantage that shaped Disraeli's tactics. His aims were twofold: to ensure that it was the Conservatives and not the Liberals who would get the credit for passing the Act, and to ensure Conservative control over the redistribution of seats which would accompany it. Thus he established himself as Derby's inevitable successor in 1868. It was characteristic that he should have declared that he had at last 'climbed to the top of the greasy pole'. But he did not stay there for long: finding himself trapped by Gladstone into a defence of the Church of Ireland, Disraeli went down to defeat in 1868.

As leader of the opposition he was largely quiescent before 1872, his main activity being to write another novel, *Lothair* (1870). Despite murmurings against him, Disraeli reminded his colleagues of his formidable power in 1872, when in speeches in Manchester and the Crystal Palace he established a devastating critique of Gladstone's domestic and foreign policies; although his rhetoric about 'empire' and 'social reform' was just that, he recognized that men are not to be ruled by reason alone. His success in harnessing symbolism and 'image' made him, in many ways, a curiously modern politician. His depiction of the Gladstone front bench as a 'range of extinct volcanoes' caught to perfection the exhausted nature of the great Liberal reforming government by 1872.

In Feb. 1874 Disraeli became the first Conservative leader since Peel in 1841 to win a parliamentary majority; one sign of his surprise at this was the fact that he had no legislation to propose. This meant that the first session was dominated by the Public Worship Regulation Act, designed to suppress 'Popish practices' in the Anglican Church, which brought him into conflict with his Secretary of State for India, Robert CECIL, 3rd Marquess of Salisbury, whom he called a 'master of gibes and flouts and jeers'. The social reforms that his administration did pass, in the regulation of food and drugs and the area of public housing, were largely the work of his Home Secretary, Richard Cross.

Disraeli was fascinated by what he called *haut politique*, and the romantic in him responded to the twin stimuli of managing the British Empire and the widowed Queen Victoria. It was a sign of his flair and showmanship that he should have promoted the Imperial Titles Act of 1876 which made the Queen the Empress of India; his opponents attributed the purchase of the Khedive's shares in the Suez Canal for £4 million to much the same instincts but Disraeli's geopolitical vision of British interests suggested that the canal was the hinge of empire, and he wanted to ensure it was not in the hands of a potential enemy.

It was the same concern for British pride and interests which led Disraeli to try to break the League of the Three Emperors when the Eastern Question reared its head in 1875–6. He refused to adhere to Bismarck's plans to deal with the Ottoman empire which he feared would lead to its destruction and the expansion of Russian power. This led to Disraeli being accused of condoning Turkish massacres in Bulgaria but he held to his position, convinced that public opinion would turn in his favour once the extent of Russian ambitions became clear. This was indeed the case in early 1878 when the music halls rang to the song whose chorus, 'We don't want to fight but by jingo if we do', added a new word to the English language. Harnessing what became known as jingoism, Disraeli was able to stand up to Russia and return triumphantly from the Congress of Berlin in June 1878 declaring that he was bringing 'peace with honour'.

A martyr to bronchial problems, Disraeli retired to the Lords in 1876, taking the title he thought Edmund BURKE would have taken, Earl of Beaconsfield. But the last years of his government were clouded by imperial difficulties in Afghanistan and South Africa, which gave Gladstone the excuse for mounting his Midlothian 'pilgrimages of passion' condemning the excesses of 'Beaconsfieldism'. Even more effective in eroding support for the Conservatives was the onset of hard times in the form of the great agricultural depression and, in 1880, the government was defeated at the General Election. Increasingly infirm, Disraeli lingered on until 1881. After his death his legend grew apace and, as late as the 1980s, his name was used to symbolize the 'One Nation' Tory opposition to Margaret THATCHER.

Robert Blake, Disraeli (1966)

DIXIE, LADY FLORENCE (née Douglas) (1857–1905), writer and traveller. A member of the eccentric QUEENSBERRY family (whose brother John Sholto DOUGLAS, 9th Marquess of Queensberry, prosecuted Oscar WILDE), she married Sir Beaumont Dixie in 1875 and had two sons. An expert horsewoman, efficient whisky drinker and crack shot, she was sent by the *Morning Post* to cover the First Boer War (1880–1) and on her return to Britain campaigned for the release of King CETEWAYO and the independence of Zululand. She travelled all her life, big-game hunting in Africa and trekking across Patagonia, and wrote about her travels as well as publishing novels and poetry. In favour of the rights of woman (her novel *Gloriana, or The Revolution of 1900* (1890) depicts a feminist Utopia, where a woman disguised as a man enters Parliament and engineers an ideal state) and, latterly, against blood sports, publishing *Horrors of Sport* in 1891, Dixie epitomizes a tradition of aristocratic Victorian women who sought and encountered thrilling adventures but also displayed considerable ability and achievement.

DOBSON, WILLIAM (1610–46), artist *see* VAN DYCK, ANTHONY

DOD, JOHN (?1549–1645), churchman. A Cambridge don who became a prominent Puritan clergyman, suspended from his Oxon. parish for nonconformity in 1604. Later he ministered at Fawsley (Northants.) to the leading Puritan family of Knightley. Witty as well as a Puritan, he is said to have been kidnapped by undergraduates enraged at his preaching against their drunkenness, but to have disarmed them by his adroit sermon on the text 'malt'. He gained the nickname 'Decalogue Dod' from his best-selling exposition of the Ten Commandments, among numerous other devotional works.

DODD, WILLIAM (1729–77), preacher and forger. A clergyman's son, he became a successful preacher in London, particularly as chaplain to the Magdalen Hospital for Penitent Prostitutes (from 1758), where he stirred the imaginations of visitors to the chapel with pathetic invocations. His equally successful journalism included editing the *Christian Magazine* published by John NEWBERY (1760–7). He was appointed chaplain to GEORGE III in 1763, took a country house in Ealing, and tutored aristocratic boys. Despite his success his extravagant lifestyle exceeded his income and in 1774 after his wife tried to buy a London living for him he lost his royal chaplaincy. In 1776 he sold the proprietary chapel where he preached and the next year signed a bond for £4,200 with the name of his patron and former pupil Lord Chesterfield

(*see* STANHOPE, PHILIP). He was convicted of forgery and, despite appeals from his society friends, was hanged.

DODDRIDGE, PHILIP (1702–51), churchman. His grandfather was a minister ejected at the Restoration for Nonconformity and Doddridge studied at the Dissenting academy at Kibworth (Leics.). Never a stickler for orthodoxy, he had difficulty winning the favour of a congregation, and from 1723 served as minister to several Leics. and Northants. groups. In 1725 he became the first tutor at a new academy at Market Harborough (Leics.), which soon moved to Northampton. His willingness to allow debate on religious matters provoked local Anglican clergy to try to have the academy closed, but Doddridge was sympathetically regarded by various leading Whigs and GEORGE II intervened in his favour. He sought to overcome divisions between various forms of Dissent, and took part in the discussions that sought to include Nonconformists within the Church of England, initiated by Archbishop Thomas HERRING and Samuel CHANDLER. His best-known works were *On the Rise and Progress of Religion in the Soul* (1745) and the *Family Expositor* (1723–56), written to assist domestic religious study and worship; he also wrote hymns.

DODSLEY, ROBERT (1703–64), bookseller and poet. Apprenticed to a Notts. stocking-weaver, he ran away and entered service as a footman. His first published poem, *Servitude*, appeared in the opposition journal *The Craftsman* (1729). Praised by DEFOE and POPE, and with the support of his employer and her friends, Dodsley was able in 1735 to set up a bookshop and have a play, *The Toyshop*, performed at Covent Garden. He became Pope's publisher and continued to write poems, plays and educational works. He commissioned Samuel JOHNSON's *Dictionary* and founded the *Annual Register* (1758), a political and literary review, with Edmund BURKE as editor.

DODWELL, HENRY (1641–1711), churchman. Born in Dublin of English parents, he was educated at the free school at York and at Trinity College, Dublin. He declined to seek ordination from a conviction of his own mean abilities. In 1688 he was appointed Camden Professor of History at Oxford, but was dismissed in 1691 on refusing to take the oath of allegiance to WILLIAM III and MARY, thus becoming a Non-juror (*see also* SANCROFT, WILLIAM). Dodwell wrote a number of works attacking Catholicism and Nonconformism and had a lengthy dispute with Richard BAXTER. Following the death of the last of the original Non-juring bishops in 1710, Dodwell's *The Case in View, Now in Fact* successfully persuaded many to return to the Church of England rather than perpetuate a schism.

DOMANGART MAC DOMNAILL (?–673), King of Dál Riata. A son of DOMNALL BRECC, Domangart apparently succeeded his uncle CONALL CRANDOMNA as King in c. 660. Little is known about him except that Dál Riata remained tributary to Kings OSWY and ECGFRITH of Northumbria for the entire length of his reign. His killing is recorded in the *Annals of Ulster* in 673, but the circumstances behind his death are unknown.

DOMANGART MAC FERGUSA (?–507), King of Dál Riata. According to the source known as *Senchus Fern Alban*, Domangart was the only son of the King traditionally regarded as the founder of Dál Riata, FERGUS MÓR MAC EIRC, and succeeded his father, ruling for 'five ever-turbulent years'. His sons, Comgall and GABRÁN, SON OF DOMANGART, founded two of the three main dynasties of Dál Riata who competed for power there until the beginning of the ninth century. The *Annals of Ulster* record his death, in his thirty-fifth year, in 507.

DOMNALL Ó NÉILL (*fl.* 1283–1325), King of Tír Eoghain. Although he claimed to be 'true heir to the whole of Ireland' he resigned his claim to the high-kingship in favour of EDWARD BRUCE. In 1317 he sent the famous Remonstrance of the Irish Princes to Pope John XXII, lamenting the sufferings of his people under the oppression of the English and seeking papal recognition for Edward as King of Ireland.

DOMNAGUAL, SON OF TEWDWR (?–c. 760), King of the Strathclyde Britons. Domnagual appears to have slain his predecessor, Rhodri, who seized the kingship following the death of Domnagual's father, TEWDWR, SON OF BILI, in c. 752. Nothing is known of his reign other than his submission to a joint Northumbrian–Pictish army in August 756, recorded by the twelfth-century writer Symeon of Durham.

DOMNALL I MAC ALPÍN (?–862), King of the Scots and Picts (858–62). The brother and successor of CINAED MAC ALPÍN, he continued the latter's conquest of the Picts by imposing the laws of Dál Riata on them, a significant step towards unification. Little else is known about his reign, and later events suggest that Scottish hegemony over the Picts remained unstable (*see* CONSTANTÍN I). It is possible that Domnall was assassinated.

DOMNALL II MAC CONSTANTÍN (?–900), King of the Scots and Picts (889–900). A son of

CONSTANTÍN I, Domnall II was the first Scottish ruler to be called 'King of Scotland' (by the *Annals of Ulster*). This territorial title acknowledged the hegemony which predecessors since CINEAD MAC ALPÍN had established over other northern British tribes such as the Picts and the Strathclyde Britons. It suggested the possibility of the territorial unification in northern Britain which became more substantial in the tenth century. Very little is known of his actual life. Although his rule was apparently little disrupted by the Vikings, this was the time when the earldom of Orkney became securely established (*see also* ROGNVALD OF MOER and TORF EINAR).

DOMNALL BRECC, King of Dál Riata (629–42). His reign was a time of major reverses for Dál Riata after the earlier successes of AEDÁN MAC GABRAÍN, and his defeat at the Battle of Mag Rath in 637 effectively brought to an end the kingdom's power in Ireland. He also suffered setbacks against his neighbours, the Picts and the Strathclyde Britons. He was finally defeated and killed by YWAIN, SON OF BILI, King of Strathclyde, at Strathcarron in c. 642.

DOMNALL MIDI MAC MURCHADA (?–763), King of Meath and Tara. Defeating and killing AED ALLÁN MAC FERGAILE and seizing the kingship of Tara in 743, Domnall was the first of the southern Uí Néill kings of Clann Cholmáin to hold the kingship of Tara, which would henceforth alternate between the two branches of the Uí Néill until the mid tenth century. Despite his violent accession, his 20-year reign was unusually peaceful and Domnall himself appears to have been devoutly religious, being a major patron to the monastery of Durrow, where he was to be buried. He was succeeded in the kingship of Tara by Aed Allán's brother, NIALL FROSSACH MAC FERGAILE.

DOMNALL MÓR UA BRIAIN (?–1194), King of Thomond (1168–94). Domnall became, in Gerald de BARRI's words, one of the main bulwarks of the ancient liberty of the Irish in their struggle against English colonization. Although he decided to submit to HENRY II in 1171, at a time when he was hampered by the enmity of RUAIDRÍ UA CONCHOBAIR, he defeated Strongbow (*see* CLARE, RICHARD DE) in battle at Thurles in 1174; although he lost Limerick, his fortified capital on the Shannon, to Raymond le Gros (*see* FITZGERALD, RAYMOND) in 1175, he recovered it next year. From then on he dominated the politics of Thomond and not until after his death did Limerick finally fall to the invaders.

DOMNALL UA NÉILL (?–980), King of Ailech and Tara. In common with several predecessors,

Domnall is referred to as 'King of Ireland' in the *Annals of Ulster* at his death, but his is the earliest contemporary record of the usage 'High-King of Ireland'. Succeeding to the kingship of Tara in 956, he was a particularly able soldier who introduced several military innovations which contributed to his domination in Ireland. He also harboured ambitions to secure a dynastic monopoly over the kingship of Tara, to the exclusion of the southern Uí Néill kindred of the Clann Cholmáin, between whom the kingship alternated with Domnall's Cenél nEógain kindred. While the fulfilment of these ambitions looked assured during his lifetime, the Cenél nEógain were unable to prevent the accession of MAEL SECHNAILL II MAC DOMNAILL of the Clann Cholmáin to the kingship of Tara following Domnall's death in 980.

DONALD *see also* DOMNALL; DYFNWAL

DONALD III BAN (*c.* 1033–1100), King of Scots (1093–4, 1094–7). Son of DONNCHAD I, he seized the throne of his brother MAEL COLUIM III CENN MÓR in 1093 and promptly reversed Mael Coluim's policy of welcoming Englishmen to court. He was defeated and dethroned by his nephew DUNCAN II in May 1094, but before the year was out he had recovered power and procured Duncan's death. Three years later, another nephew, EDGAR, captured and blinded him. As champion of the native cause against growing Anglo-Norman immigration and influence, it is appropriate that Donald should be the last Scottish king whose bones were claimed by the Gaelic monastic community of Iona.

DONNÁN, ST (?–617), Abbot of Eigg. A younger contemporary of COLUM CILLE of Iona, Donnán's origins are obscure. Several church dedications to him in Strathclyde may reflect earlier missions, but his main activity centred on north-west Pictland. His chief centre was his foundation on Eigg, but he is also associated with eastern Sutherland and Caithness. The *Annals of Ulster* record 'the burning of Donnán of Eigg with 150 martyrs' on Sunday 17 April, apparently at the hands of pagan Picts.

DONNCHAD I (*c.* 1010–40), King of the Scots (1034–40). Donnchad held the kingship of Strathclyde under his grandfather, MAEL COLUIM II, whom he succeeded as King of the Scots. He led an invasion of northern England and besieged Durham in 1039. The long-standing blood feud, however, between rival segments of the Scottish ruling dynasty, and his grandfather's recent destruction of the descendants of CINAED III, whose granddaughter GRUOCH was married to MACBETH of Moray, provoked Donnchad's invasion

of Moray in 1040, where he was defeated and killed by Macbeth who, in turn, assumed the kingship.

DONNCHADH CAIRBRECH Ó BRIAIN (?–1242), King of Thomond (1194–1242). A son of DOMNALL MÓR UA BRIAIN, he became a King of Thomond on his father's death, at first in association with his brothers but from *c.* 1208 on his own. Unusually open to new ideas, he was an early patron of the Franciscans in Ireland and one of the very few Irish kings to be knighted, by King JOHN in 1210. He generally relied on English military aid in his conflicts with neighbouring rulers in Desmond and Connacht as well as against internal rivals, acquiescing in the loss of Limerick in return for their support.

DONNE, JOHN (1571–1631), poet and churchman. Son of a London merchant; his background was strongly influenced by Catholic recusancy, his mother being of the family of Sir Thomas MORE but, during studies at Oxford (possibly also Cambridge) and the Inns of Court, he was, by 1598, drawn to the Church of England. A secular career seemed to prosper, after his participation in the military expeditions (1596–7) of Robert DEVEREUX, Earl of Essex, and then his entry into the service of Thomas EGERTON, Lord Ellesmere.

Ellesmere, however, dismissed Donne in 1601 for marrying Ann More, a favourite relative, and Donne then had to support his wife and children through years of poverty. Part of his living was made through commissioned writing, including works of controversy with Roman Catholics, and he gained favour from JAMES I, who was among those persuading him to become ordained (1615). His advancement to the deanery of St Paul's Cathedral came soon (1621), and he became one of the most renowned preachers of the day, producing prose which has an enduring force beyond most of his contemporaries' pulpit oratory. Some of his poetry is secular in subject (although not all of his love-lyrics predate his ordination) and some sacred or devotional, most of the latter dating from the years of struggle before he turned his energies to preaching. His verse is at the heart of the 'metaphysical' tradition, combining intensely spiritual, physical and even textually visual imagery. His extraordinary funeral monument, showing him standing in his shroud, was one of the few in St Paul's to survive the Great Fire of 1666.

DORCHESTER, 1ST VISCOUNT *see* CARLETON, DUDLEY

DORMAN-SMITH, ERIC ('CHINK') (1895–1969), soldier. Son of an army officer, educated at Sandhurst, he was commissioned into the

Northumberland Fusiliers who nicknamed him 'Chink' because of his resemblance to the regimental mascot, an Indian Chinkara antelope. Wounded three times on the Western Front, awarded the Military Cross, and afflicted twice by shell-shock, Dorman-Smith was transferred to Italy, where he became friends with Ernest Hemingway, subsequently inspiring such Hemingway characters as Wilson-Harris in *The Sun Also Rises*. After fighting the IRA in the early 1920s, Dorman-Smith's advocacy of mechanized infantry led him into conflict with both traditionalists and armoured warfare radicals. As Commander of the new Staff College in Haifa in 1940, Dorman-Smith helped WAVELL plan the offensive which drove the Italians from Egypt, and then became *éminence grise* to AUCHINLECK, producing ideas of great originality but of dubious practicability. Dismissed in Aug. 1942 after the first Battle of El Alamein, Dorman-Smith eventually managed to secure command of a brigade in Italy, but was again dismissed when his battalion commanders complained of his want of leadership in battle. Dorman-Smith was arrogant, and as his career waned he slid into paranoia. Retiring to his estate on the Eire–Northern Ireland border, a bitter Dorman-Smith changed his name to O'Gowan and actively supported the IRA (he is the model for the turncoat Nick Barry in Daphne DU MAURIER's *A Border-Line Case*).

DORMER, JANE (1538–1612), courtier. From an Oxon. knightly family, she was sent to Princess Mary's (later MARY I) household, became a playfellow of Prince Edward (the future EDWARD VI), and one of Mary's close friends, attending her deathbed. When PHILIP II of Spain came to marry Mary (1554), one of his household, Don Gomez Suarez de Figueroa, Count of Feria, fell in love with Dormer, and they hastily married after Mary's death, Dormer becoming Countess, then Duchess, of Feria. The marriage was one major exception to the generally cold relations between Philip's entourage and the English nobility. The couple went abroad with a number of English Catholics; Dormer visited MARY QUEEN OF SCOTS in France (1560) and they maintained a lifelong correspondence. She spent the rest of her life in Spain, and was a major force in financing and encouraging English Catholic activism.

DORSET, EARL OF, **4TH** *see* SACKVILLE, THOMAS; **6TH** *see* SACKVILLE, CHARLES; **COUNTESS OF** *see* CLIFFORD, ANNE

DOUGLAS, LORD ALFRED (1870–1945), poet. The third son of the erratic John Sholto DOUGLAS, 9th Marquess of Queensberry, 'Bosie' (a familial name derived from a childhood mispronunciation) edited an undergraduate magazine, *The Spirit Lamp*, at Oxford, to which he also contributed a homo-erotic poem. In 1892 he met Oscar WILDE, who was ensnared by his golden good looks, and they embarked on a passionate and often tempestuous friendship, which was to bring about Wilde's downfall. After a series of legal disputes, Douglas was jailed for six months in 1923 for a false accusation against Winston CHURCHILL.

DOUGLAS, SIR ARCHIBALD (*c*. 1296–1333), soldier. The son of Sir William Douglas, 'the Hardy', he defeated EDWARD BALLIOL at Annan (Dumfries.) just after he had been crowned in 1332, and became one of the regents of Scotland during the minority of DAVID II. He was probably too impetuous a military leader and was killed when defeated by EDWARD III at the Battle of Halidon Hill (Northumb.). His second son William became 1st Earl of Douglas.

DOUGLAS, ARCHIBALD (also known as Archibald the Grim or the Black) (3rd Earl of Douglas) (*c*. 1328–*c*. 1400), soldier and Lord of Galloway. Illegitimate son and successor in 1388 of the 2nd Earl, James, he was a firm and rigorous administrator who became Constable and Sheriff of Edinburgh in 1361. He was Warden of the Western Marches in 1364, from where he led the largest part of the Scottish forces for the invasion of England in 1388. An energetic border chief, he was renowned for his prowess with the two-handed sword.

DOUGLAS, ARCHIBALD (4th Earl of Douglas) (*c*. 1369–1424), nobleman. He succeeded his father Archibald the Grim (*see* DOUGLAS, ARCHIBALD, 3rd Earl of Douglas) in *c*. 1400 and married Margaret Stewart, daughter of ROBERT III, in 1390. Known as 'Tyneman' (the Loser) for his notably unsuccessful military leadership, he led raids into England, losing an eye and being captured by Hotspur (*see* PERCY, HENRY), then joined the Percy rebellion, fighting at Shrewsbury, and again being captured. He led the Scottish force in France in 1423 and was created Duke of Touraine. He was killed in the Battle of Verneuil against John, Duke of Bedford (*see* JOHN OF LANCASTER).

DOUGLAS, ARCHIBALD (5th Earl of Douglas) (*c*. 1391–1439), nobleman. As Earl of Wigtown he was one of the leaders of the Scots army in France after 1419, defeating THOMAS OF CLARENCE at Baugé in 1421. He inherited the title when his father died at the Battle of Verneuil in 1424, which he missed due to illness. Back in Scotland he managed to defend family interests without quarrelling too violently with JAMES I; after the latter's murder (1437) he was appointed Lieutenant General of the realm, but died soon after.

DOUGLAS, ARCHIBALD (also known as 'the Great Earl') (22nd Earl of Angus) (1453–1514), royal servant. He gained the alternative nickname 'Bell the Cat' after a group of noblemen in 1483 decided to curb JAMES III in his rampant favouritism, but could not summon up the courage to act. Angus, referring to the fable of the mice and the cat, declared that he would bell the cat to warn the mice of its approach. The eventual result was James's murder in 1488. Becoming a favourite of JAMES IV, Angus was High Chancellor 1493–98. Furious when James ignored his advice to avoid the Battle of Flodden (1513), he left before the battle, though two of his sons were among the large numbers of Scots nobility killed.

DOUGLAS, ARCHIBALD (23rd Earl of Angus) (c. 1490–1557), courtier. He succeeded his grandfather Archibald DOUGLAS, 'the Great Earl', in 1514, and married MARGARET TUDOR, sister of HENRY VIII and widow of JAMES IV; they were eventually estranged, and their marriage was annulled in 1527. He was a member of the Council of Regency for JAMES V (1517–21, 1525–26), and latterly all-powerful. Much hated by James, he fled to England in 1529, not to return until 1542, with a group of pro-English noblemen. He kept the peace with England until Henry VIII's invasion of Scotland in 1544, which transformed his stance. He led the Scots to victory at Ancrum Moor (1545) and to defeat at Pinkie (1547).

DOUGLAS, GAVIN (?1474–1522); poet. Son of 'Bell-the-Cat' (see DOUGLAS, ARCHIBALD), he studied at St Andrews, but found his clerical career disrupted after his father's death (1514), when he lost his promotions as Abbot of Arbroath and Archbishop of St Andrews. Queen MARGARET nominated him bishop of Dunkeld in 1515, but the pro-French John STEWART, Duke of Albany, had him temporarily arrested for receiving his bulls of office from the Pope, and in 1521 he was deprived of the bishopric as punishment for his mission to England on behalf of Albany's enemy, Archibald DOUGLAS, the 23rd Earl of Angus. He died of the plague. He wrote allegorical poetry, and made a pioneering translation of Virgil's *Aeneid* into Scots.

DOUGLAS, JAMES (also known as James the Good or the Black) (Lord of Douglas) (c. 1286–1330), nobleman. He joined ROBERT BRUCE in 1306, became commander of his forces and was knighted on the field of Bannockburn in 1314. An excellent military tactician, a specialist in surprise attacks such as that by which he captured Roxburgh Castle, he led highly successful raids deep into England. His career and its rewards established the Douglases as one of Scotland's leading families. After Bruce's death in 1329, he took the King's heart with him on a campaign against the Muslims in Spain, where he was killed.

DOUGLAS, JAMES (2nd Earl of Douglas) (c. 1358–88), nobleman. He inherited the title from his father William in 1384. Before then, in 1371, in order to secure the loyalty of his family to the new royal dynasty (Stewart), he had been betrothed to Isabel, daughter of ROBERT II. In 1388 he led a raiding party into England. Intercepted at Otterburn (Northumb.) by Hotspur (see PERCY, HENRY) the Scots won the battle but he, the 'doughty Douglas' of the *Ballad of Chevy Chase*, was killed.

DOUGLAS, JAMES (also known as James the Gross) (7th Earl of Douglas) (c. 1372–1443), nobleman. Second son of Archibald the Grim, the 3rd Earl, he was known as 'the Gross' for the 'four stone of tallow' he carried. As Sir James Douglas of Balvenie he supported the regency of the Duke of Albany (see STEWART, JOHN); despite this he won JAMES I's friendship. He inherited the title after the arrest and summary execution of his great-nephew William at the notorious 'black dinner' of 1440 and, rather than seek revenge, concentrated on re-uniting and consolidating the vast Douglas estates.

DOUGLAS, JAMES (9th Earl of Douglas) (1426–91), nobleman. After JAMES II's killing (the Scots Parliament declared it 'no murder') of his brother William in 1452, he took over his brother's title, his widow Margaret, the Fair Maid of Galloway, and his feud with the King. After he sacked the royal burgh of Stirling an apparent peace was made (Jan. 1453) but, two years later, his castles were destroyed and he was forced to flee to England. Not until 1484, with the help of Albany (see STEWART, ALEXANDER), did the exile attempt to return in force, only to be captured and to die in prison.

DOUGLAS, JAMES (4th Earl of Morton) (?1516–81), politician. After becoming Earl (in right of his wife) in 1553, he supported the anti-French and pro-Protestant cause by subscribing the first bond of the Lords of the Congregation in 1557, but withdrew his support from them in 1559; he was Lord Chancellor in 1562. Having reluctantly supported MARY QUEEN OF SCOTS's marriage to Henry STEWART, Lord Darnley, he was one of RIZZIO's murderers in collaboration with Darnley in 1566. Darnley hypocritically denounced him for the murder, but he returned from his flight to England when pardoned by Mary. He seized Edinburgh in revolt against James HEPBURN, Earl of Bothwell, and was again Lord Chancellor in the regime which proclaimed JAMES VI in 1567. Furious at the murder of the Regent James STEWART, Earl of Moray, he induced ELIZABETH I to recognize James as King in 1570.

As Regent himself from 1572, he reformed justice, secured peace on the borders with England and strengthened Protestantism, beginning to rebuild an episcopal system in the Church. Losing the regency when James VI was persuaded to assume government in 1578, he was rapidly reinstated by Parliament. With James's connivance, however, he was (probably unjustly) accused of procuring Darnley's murder; he was executed on 'the Maiden', the guillotine which he himself had reputedly introduced.

DOUGLAS, JAMES (2nd Duke of Queensberry and 1st Duke of Dover) (1662–1711), politician. Commissioned in Dundee's (*see* GRAHAM, JOHN) regiment, he was the first Scottish nobleman to join William of Orange (the future WILLIAM III), and commanded a regiment against Dundee in 1689. Lord High Treasurer of Scotland (1693) and Lord Privy Seal (1695), he became Commissioner to the Scottish Parliament in 1700, where he and the Earl of Argyll (later the first Duke) were able to persuade Parliament to abandon plans to set up a new Scots colony on the isthmus of Darien (later Panama), with the object of acquiring a share of England's entrepot trade, in return for promises of trading concessions with England. He remained commissioner under ANNE but had to resign in 1704 after his own agents were revealed to include Jacobites. His followers, however, still enjoyed an ascendancy in Parliament, and restored to all his offices by 1706, he helped engineer the passage of the Act of Union, for which he was rewarded with a British dukedom.

DOUGLAS, JOHN SHOLTO (9th Marquess of Queensberry) (1844–1900), aristocrat and sportsman. A natural athlete in his youth, he gave his name to the rules which he formulated to regulate boxing. In 1895, by now acrimoniously divorced from one wife, his marriage to the next annulled and hopelessly trying to play the stern Victorian pater to his children, he objected to his son Bosie's (*see* DOUGLAS, ALFRED) public friendship with Oscar WILDE and accused the playwright of being a 'somdomite' [*sic*]. In the ensuing trial for libel, Queensberry was vindicated.

DOUGLAS, LADY MARGARET (*c.* 1515–1578), royal princess. Daughter of MARGARET TUDOR (sister of HENRY VIII), and Archibald DOUGLAS, 23rd Earl of Angus, her royal descent led to prolonged exiles in England. Anne BOLEYN's execution in 1536 temporarily left her the likely heir to the English throne. Romantic escapades with Lord Thomas HOWARD (1536) and Sir

Charles HOWARD (1541) led to Henry marrying her off safely to Matthew STEWART, Earl of Lennox, in 1544. Becoming an increasingly strong Catholic, she was in disgrace under Henry, EDWARD VI and ELIZABETH I, but favoured by MARY I. Her position was made worse under Elizabeth by her intrigues to marry her son, Henry STEWART, Lord Darnley, to MARY QUEEN OF SCOTS, and by her engineering of her second son's marriage to Bess of HARDWICK's daughter. Her scheming was posthumously rewarded when her grandson by Darnley, JAMES VI, succeeded Elizabeth on the throne of England.

DOUGLAS, WILLIAM (8th Earl of Douglas) (*c.* 1425–52), nobleman. Succeeding his father James in 1443, the next year he married his cousin Margaret, the Fair Maid of Galloway, and became Lieutenant General for the young JAMES II. For a few years he and his brothers dominated Scottish politics. When earlier friendship with the King turned sour, he went on a pilgrimage to Rome (1450). On his return a reconciliation of sorts was arranged, but it ended when he went, under safe-conduct, to Stirling Castle and was stabbed 26 times, perhaps in hot blood, by James and his followers.

DOUGLAS, WILLIAM SHOLTO (1893–1969), airman. Douglas joined the Royal Flying Corps in 1915 and, after a distinguished career as a fighter pilot, joined the RAF in 1920. As Deputy Chief of the Air Staff in 1940 he clashed with Hugh DOWDING over the conduct of the Battle of Britain, eventually succeeding him and organizing offensive sweeps over northern France. In 1944, as Commander-in-Chief of Coastal Command, he helped create the conditions which made Operation Overlord (the Normandy landings in June 1944) possible.

DOUGLAS-HOME, ALEC (13th Earl of Home, Baron Home of the Hirsel) (1903–95), politician and Prime Minister (1963–4). He was Parliamentary Private Secretary to Neville CHAMBERLAIN (1937–40), whom he accompanied to Munich in 1938. After the war he was a junior minister at the Scottish Office (1951–5), and then Secretary of State for Commonwealth Relations (1955–60) and Leader of the House of Lords (1959–60). He was Foreign Secretary under MACMILLAN (1960–3), securing the Nassau agreement, by which the USA agreed to sell Britain its submarine-launched Polaris missile (which called into question the 'independent' British nuclear deterrent) and the partial test-ban treaty (1963) banning nuclear tests in the atmosphere, under water and in space, following the Cuban missile crisis. Invited unexpectedly by the Queen to become Prime Minister in succession to Macmillan in 1963, after the traditionally obscure consultation procedures, he renounced his peerages and returned to the House of Commons via a by-election. His aristocratic demeanour and career were in stark contrast to Harold WILSON's modern and technocratic image; but despite this, and the fact that the Conservatives were beset by scandal and had been in office for 13 years, he only lost the 1964 election by four seats. He resigned as leader in 1965 and MPs chose Edward HEATH as his successor, using for the first time a formal voting system put in place on his initiative. He was Foreign Secretary again (1970–4).

DOVER, 1ST DUKE OF see DOUGLAS, JAMES

DOVER, ROBERT (1582–1652), promoter. A wealthy lawyer in Warws., of Catholic sympathies, *c*. 1611 he founded (claiming to have refounded) the Whitsuntide Cotswold Games, staged in a natural amphitheatre near Chipping Camden (Glos.), uniting all sections of society in a variety of sports, in a deliberate riposte to the rise of Puritanism. The games became celebrated, were commemorated by a group of poets in 1636 but were brought to an end by the Civil Wars.

DOWDING, HUGH ('STUFFY') (1st Baron Dowding) (1882–1970), airman. Educated at Winchester and Woolwich, he was commissioned into the Royal Garrison Artillery, transferred to a mountain battery serving on India's North West Frontier and learned to fly when he was at Army Staff College in 1913. During the First World War Dowding commanded a squadron on the Western Front, rose to the rank of Brigadier General, and earned the reputation (and nickname 'Stuffy') as a humourless stickler for detail. Transferring to the RAF after the war, Dowding served in Iraq and Palestine, and in 1936 was chosen to head the new Fighter Command. By 1940 Dowding had created a fully integrated air defence system, but had also upset many vested interests and created enemies, notably on 15 May 1940 when he persuaded the Cabinet not to send air reinforcements to France. Dowding managed to give Fighter Command the narrow margin it needed to achieve victory in the Battle of Britain, but he also earned the hostility of LEIGH-MALLORY. By Nov. 1940 his formidable array of enemies was sufficiently strong to secure Dowding's dismissal from Fighter Command. Subsequent offers of employment were so insulting that Dowding requested his own retirement in July 1942. The loneliness of a bitter retirement was relieved only at the very end, when he was given a standing ovation by his veterans at the première of the film *The Battle of Britain* (1969).

DOWLAND, JOHN (1563–1626), composer and lutenist. One of the finest songwriters of his or any age, Dowland frequently travelled abroad between 1594 and 1606, having failed to secure positions at court, during which time he brought out four major collections of songs. His most famous song, *Flow my Teares* (1600), was known throughout Europe. Many of his works embody the melancholia fashionable at the time. In his later years, he finally secured a court appointment, but wrote little more.

DOWNING, GEORGE (1623–84), royal servant. Son of a London Puritan attorney who emigrated to Massachusetts in 1638, he was one of the first graduates of Harvard University. On his return to England, he became preacher to a regiment in the New Model Army (1646–7), and in 1649 Oliver CROMWELL made him Scoutmaster General (i.e. director of military intelligence). He was MP in the two Parliaments of Cromwell's protectorate (1654, 1656), and in 1657 he was sent as resident (English representative) to the United Provinces of the Netherlands at the Hague.

He was active in the Convention Parliament of 1660 which invited back CHARLES II, and served as an MP throughout Charles's reign. Made Secretary to the Treasury Commissioners in 1667, he played a crucial part in reshaping and extending their role, systematizing office procedures and organizing a regular system of payments to those whose loans to government were secured on ordinary revenue. He tried to make government loans attractive to small investors, but failed to compete with private bankers; after the 1672 Stop of the Exchequer, when the Crown partially repudiated its debts, he was replaced as Secretary, but was given a seat on the Customs Board. Towards the end of his life, he developed Downing Street (off Whitehall in London), where the Prime Minister and Chancellor of the Exchequer now have their official residences. He was a man with a talent for unpopularity: after his devious part in the capture (after the Restoration) of three of those who had signed CHARLES I's death warrant, 'an arrant George Downing' became a term describing a treacherous figure.

DOWNSHIRE, 1ST MARQUESS OF see HILL, WILLS

DOWSING, WILLIAM (1596–1668), iconoclast. A Suffolk yeoman, he was an enthusiastic Puritan and book-collector, and in 1643 gained a unique Parliamentary commission under their commander Edward MONTAGU, Earl of Manchester, to destroy 'monuments of idolatry' in East Anglian churches. Much of his extraordinary diary of his activities survives, detailing his precise approach to wrecking Church furnishings. His activities ceased when Manchester lost his military command.

DOWSON, ERNEST (1867–1900), poet. Born to comfortably-off though somewhat rootless parents, Dowson epitomized the paradox of the decadent *fin de siècle* with his search for beauty in his art and the tragic depravity of his life. He left Oxford without taking a degree and fell deeply in love with a 12-year-old waitress. The finale of this protracted courtship, coupled with the suicide of both his parents, intensified Dowson's already restless wanderings, across England and the continent, and he died almost on the streets.

DOYLE, SIR ARTHUR CONAN (1859–1930), writer. Born in Edinburgh, where he qualified as a doctor, Conan Doyle made extensive use of his medical knowledge in his first Sherlock Holmes novel, *A Study in Scarlet* (1887), and Holmes is supposed to have been based on an eminent Edinburgh surgeon, Dr Joseph Bell. The novels originally appeared in instalments in *Strand Magazine* and were instant successes. Holmes's popularity, however, became a burden to Doyle, who wanted to write other books, and so he killed off Holmes in a famous hand-to-hand struggle in 1893. The public was outraged, and Doyle was prevailed upon to concede that Holmes had, after all, escaped with his life. More books followed, including his best-known adventure, *The Hound of the Baskervilles* (1901). Doyle was interested in spiritualism, and wrote a *History of Spiritualism* (two vols, 1926) as well as works of history. An ardent patriot and imperialist, he twice stood unsuccessfully for Parliament.

DRAKE, SIR FRANCIS *see* essay on page 260

DRAYTON, MICHAEL (1563–1631), poet. He began publishing his poetry in 1593, and wrote very extensively, much of his verse being on historical themes, also including a tribute to the beauties of English landscape, *Poly-Olbion* (1613–22). He wrote plays in collaboration with Thomas DEKKER and John WEBSTER, and was a friend of William SHAKESPEARE and William DRUMMOND of Hawthornden.

DRENNAN, WILLIAM (1754–1820), poet and radical. The son of a Presbyterian minister in Belfast, he studied medicine and philosophy at Glasgow, where his friends included Dugald STEWART. His interest in politics emerged in 1784 when he wrote a series of letters on the under-representation of the northern counties in the Irish Parliament, using the pseudonym 'Orellana,

the Irish Helot'. In June 1791 he wrote the prospectus for the reforming association, the 'United Irishmen', and was its Chairman in 1792 and 1793 (see TONE, WOLFE). He was tried for sedition for issuing the *Address of the United Irishmen to the Volunteers of Ireland* in 1794 but was acquitted. Withdrawing from active involvement in the increasingly radical movement, he wrote poems about Irish liberty; these included *When Erin First Rose* (1795) in which he was the first to call Ireland 'the Emerald Isle'.

DRIBERG, THOMAS (TOM) (Baron Bradwell) (1905–76), journalist and politician. A Labour Party politician, a gossip columnist, a flamboyant homosexual at a time when homosexual acts were still a crime, a writer and dedicated Bohemian, Driberg had a comfortable middle-class upbringing against which he rebelled at every opportunity. He left Oxford University without a degree, and moved into upper middle-class literary Bohemia in London. Politicized by the General Strike of 1926 and the mass unemployment of the 1930s, he joined the Communist Party, but at the same time made use of his connections to become a journalist. Lord Beaverbrook (*see* AITKEN, MAXWELL) gave him the British press's first modern 'gossip column' in the *Daily Express* under the pseudonym William Hickey in 1928. Driberg was later to write one of the best studies of the controversial press baron, *Beaverbrook – A Study in Power and Frustration* (1946). Ever a mass of social and political contradictions, Driberg acted as an agent for MI5 within the Communist Party in the late 1930s. In 1942 he was elected as a Labour MP and remained in the House of Commons, with only a brief break, until 1974. A conscientious backbencher and one of the darlings of the left wing, he was considered too much of a security risk to attain Cabinet rank and was constantly overlooked in favour of less talented but 'safer' men. Acutely conscious of this fact, he married in 1951 to acquire some much needed respectability. But the marriage collapsed and by the 1960s he had become a marginal political figure.

DRUMMOND, THOMAS (1797–1840), inventor and administrator. A Scot who went to Ireland to work on the Ordnance Survey (where he used his invention of limelight as a signalling device) he became Under-Secretary for Ireland in Lord Melbourne's (*see* LAMB, WILLIAM) government and the key figure in administering reforms required by O'CONNELL as the price of his support. Drummond repressed the Orange Order, appointed more Catholics to the magistracy and administration, and responded to calls from landlords for coercive legislation by reminding them

continued on page 261

DRAKE, SIR FRANCIS (c. 1540–96)
Seafarer

Drake came from a Devon farming family already fiercely Protestant when he was a boy. After leaving Devon to live near the naval dockyard at Chatham, his father was ordained in 1560 and became a Kentish parish clergyman, while two of Francis's brothers took up a career at sea. Drake was apprenticed to a Thames captain in the 1550s, and in 1563 and 1566 he joined his distant cousin John HAWKINS's voyages to Africa, some of the earliest ventures in the English slave trade. His first command came under Hawkins in a large-scale but none-too-successful voyage attacking the Spanish in the Atlantic during 1567–9, ending with a bad defeat by Spanish ships in the port of San Juan de Ulua (Honduras). By this time the longstanding Burgundian alliance between England and Spain was breaking down because of religious differences and maritime rivalry, and with both religious and financial considerations to motivate him Drake came to see himself as an instrument of God in crusading against the Spanish empire. He was soon planning to remedy his earlier setbacks by his own voyages against Spain; after voyages to the West Indies in 1570 and 1571, he achieved spectacular success in seizing gold and silver in America and the Atlantic in 1572–3, although his wounds in the fighting at Nombre de Dios (Panama) prevented his squadron from seizing the central Spanish store for South American bullion. By now he was being quietly encouraged by ELIZABETH I, who regarded his activities as a useful way of distracting the Spaniards from following up their military successes in curbing the Dutch rebellion in the Netherlands; yet his growing reputation throughout Europe as 'el draque' (the dragon) and Spanish fury at his activities made the English government cautious in fully acknowledging or honouring what he had done.

Drake, remembering his sight of the Pacific Ocean when he had travelled in Panama, now planned his most spectacular exploit, circumnavigating the globe between 1577 and 1580. He was backed by various courtiers, including Sir Francis WALSINGHAM and Sir Christopher HATTON, but he also had secret instructions from the Queen to attack the Spanish colonies of the Pacific coast. Although he lost two of his fleet of five before he rounded the Straits of Magellan, this was the first time that English ships had sailed in the Pacific Ocean, and it anticipated England's later trading and colonial involvement in the East Indies. The voyage, led by Drake's ship the *Pelican* (later renamed the *Golden Hind*), included in June 1579 a landfall in what is now California, which Drake declared annexed to the English Crown. The expedition brought him great wealth, much of which he used to establish himself as a country gentleman by buying a former monastery, Buckland Abbey (Devon); the house still survives. In 1581 Elizabeth, after some hesitation, decided to ignore furious Spanish protests, ostentatiously knighting him on the *Golden Hind* (subsequently preserved at Deptford as a tourist attraction). He now entered Parliament at a by-election in 1581, and sat again in the 1584 Parliament through the influence of his family's long-standing patrons the Russells (see RUSSELL, FRANCIS, EARL OF BEDFORD); he would again be MP, for Plymouth (of which he had previously been mayor), in 1593. He continued his feud with Spain, now openly backed by Elizabeth: he carried out destructive raids in the Spanish Caribbean in 1584–5, which also involved the rescue of the remaining English colonists in Virginia, returning to Portsmouth in 1586. He led the expedition which wrecked the Spanish fleet at Cadiz in 1587; this delayed by a year Spanish plans to invade England. He then took a major part in the English naval campaign which repelled the 1588 Armada. He captured the galleon *Rosario* and also successfully urged the use of fireships, which was a major contribution to breaking up the Spanish fleet while it was lying off Calais; the following day his ship came into close combat with the flagship of the Spanish commander, the Duke of Medina Sidonia, in the Battle of Gravelines (29 July 1588) which forced the Spanish fleet north in its fatal attempt to sail home around the Scottish and Irish coasts. He was one of the consortium which set up a fund for injured sailors in 1590 – the 'Chatham Chest'. His career after the Armada nevertheless went downhill. He was responsible for a disastrous attack on Portugal in 1589, a fiasco in part caused by his quarrels with his fellow commander Sir John Norris. His last expedition to the Caribbean in 1595 was equally catastrophic; there were no successes against the Spaniards, and after John Hawkins died at sea Drake himself was killed by dysentery off Porto Bello (Panama). Despite this sad coda to his career, his achievements were astonishing, and his personal role in the denting of Spanish overseas prestige was unique.

John G. Cummins, Francis Drake: The Lives of a Hero (1995) that 'property has its duties as well as its rights'. Drummond was held up by contemporary and subsequent constitutional nationalists and Liberal reformers as showing what could be achieved by British reformers addressing Irish grievances.

DRUMMOND, WILLIAM (1585–1649), writer. Having studied at Edinburgh, Bourges and Paris, he succeeded as Laird of Hawthornden (Lothian) in 1610. He designed various measuring instruments and weapons, and wrote accomplished and innovative poetry (in southern English rather than Scots), a history of Scotland and tracts designed to seek peace in the Civil Wars of the 1640s. He protested against the Covenants of 1638 and 1643, made against the regime of CHARLES I, and advocated negotiations with Charles after his defeat in 1646. His death was reportedly hastened by the King's execution.

DRUST (?–729), King of the Picts. During the 720s, Drust contended with NECHTAN, ALPÍN, SON OF EOCHAID and OENGUS, SON OF FERGUS for Pictish overlordship. The tortuous events of the conflict can be followed in the scarce sources. Having defeated Nechtan, he was at one point temporarily expelled by Alpín and was finally defeated and killed by Oengus.

DRUST, SON OF DOMNALL (?–678), King of the Picts. Following the death of TALORCAN, SON OF EANFRITH, King of the Picts, in 657, it appears that OSWY, King of Northumbria, launched an offensive against the Picts which resulted in an interregnum until the emergence of Drust as King in 665–6. In 672 Drust was expelled after being defeated by Oswy's successor ECGFRITH. He may have attempted to return in 676, when many Picts 'were drowned in Land-Abae'. He appears to have died in exile in Ireland in 678.

DRYDEN, JOHN (1631–1700), poet. The son of a Northants. clergyman, Dryden was educated at Cambridge, and became a government clerk. He wrote *Heroick Stanzas* on CROMWELL's death and *Astrea Redux* at the restoration of CHARLES II. From 1663 he wrote numerous plays for the revived theatre. Created Poet Laureate in 1670, he wrote several verse satires: *MacFlecknoe* (1682), a satire on his fellow poet and playwright Thomas SHADWELL; *Absalom and Achitophel* (1681), an allegory on the state of Restoration England; and *The Hind and the Panther* (1686), which dealt with religious themes. He also collaborated with PURCELL, for example on the semi-opera *King Arthur* (1691). He converted to Catholicism in 1686, and was dismissed as Poet Laureate after the Glorious Revolution of 1688–9, probably because he refused

to reconvert. Perhaps the most celebrated poet of his age, Dryden was also a pioneering dramatic critic and literary historian; his later work includes a translation of Virgil.

DU MAURIER, DAPHNE (1907–89), novelist. Granddaughter of George du Maurier, *Punch* cartoonist and author of *Trilby*, and daughter of the actor-manager Gerald, she married Lieutenant Colonel (later General) Frederick BROWNING in 1932. *Jamaica Inn* (1936) and *Rebecca* (1938) were by far the most successful of her many novels. Alfred HITCHCOCK's film *The Birds* was based on Du Maurier's short story. A long-time resident of Cornwall (where most of her novels are set), Du Maurier's *Vanishing Cornwall* was published in 1967.

DUB (?–966), King of the Scots (962–6). A son of MAEL COLUIM I, he was challenged and overthrown by CUILÉN, a son of King INDULF, a usurpation that began a violent blood feud lasting many years. The outbreak of this feud within the Scottish royal family occurred when the threat from the Viking war bands had died away. In this time of apparently increased security, the Scottish rulers reembarked on the kind of family warfare that was typical of many early societies in an attempt to monopolize the kingship within their own immediate successors.

DUBLIN, 1ST MARQUESS OF *see* DE VERE, ROBERT

DUCK, STEPHEN (1705–56), poet. He was an agricultural labourer in Wilts. until his poetry, first published in 1730 and running into 10 editions that year, brought him fame and patronage from Queen CAROLINE. Nicknamed 'the thresher poet', his poems, the best known of which was *The Thresher's Labour* (1730), were derided by other writers of higher social status or education who lacked court patronage. His impressions of working-class women were criticized by 'the washerwoman poet' Mary COLLIER. Duck tried to rationalize his anomalous social position by entering the Church but although he continued to write he fell from favour after Queen Caroline's death and he eventually committed suicide.

DUDLEY, AMBROSE (21st [3rd Dudley] Earl of Warwick) (*c.* 1528–90), politician. Eldest son of John DUDLEY, Duke of Northumberland, he escaped a traitor's death for his part in the attempt to put JANE GREY on the throne, and was a commander at the English victory over the French at St Quentin (1557). Benefiting from his younger brother ROBERT's favour with ELIZABETH I, he was granted the earldom in 1561, was prominent in the disastrous campaign in Normandy (1562–3) and served against the rebellious northern earls (1569). He was a major force in supporting Puritanism in the Midlands.

DUDLEY, DUD (1599–1684), ironmaster and inventor. An illegitimate son of Edward, 5th Earl of Dudley, he was educated at Oxford but in 1619 was summoned to manage his father's ironworks. He experimented with smelting iron (to produce pig iron) in a blast furnace fuelled not with charcoal but with coal (probably in the form of coke). He obtained patents from JAMES I and CHARLES I to protect his processes, but was denied another by CHARLES II. In 1665 he published a rather vague account of his invention in *Metallum Martis* (Metal of War). The coke-smelting process was subsequently perfected by Abraham DARBY.

DUDLEY, EDMUND (?1462–1510), royal servant. After studies at Oxford, he became a lawyer. As Councillor from *c.* 1485, and later as one of the Council Learned in the Law (the law-enforcing sub-committee of the Royal Council), he rapidly became one of HENRY VII's chief agents in ruthless financial exactions. With Richard EMPSON, he was made a scapegoat for the old regime's unpopularity on HENRY VIII's accession and was executed in 1510, having left a frank record of the old King's excesses. In prison he wrote a tract on government, *The Tree of Commonwealth*, which emphasized the absolute power of the monarch, but appears to have had negligible contemporary impact.

DUDLEY, JOHN (1st Duke of Northumberland) *see* essay on page 263

DUDLEY, ROBERT (14th Earl of Leicester) *see* essay on page 264

DUKES, ALAN (1945–), Irish politician *see* BRUTON, JOHN

DUNBAR, 11TH EARL OF *see* HUME, GEORGE

DUNBAR, WILLIAM (?1485–?1530), poet. For some time a Franciscan friar, he was given a pension at the Scots court in 1500. His verse gives a lively and often sour picture of contemporary Scots society, especially of court life under JAMES IV, but also includes religious poetry of great power.

DUNCAN *see also* DONNCHAD

DUNCAN II (*c.* 1060–94), King of Scots (1094). Son of MAEL COLUIM III CENN MÓR and his first wife Ingiborg, he was sent in 1072 as a hostage to the court of WILLIAM I THE CONQUEROR, where he remained until after his father's death. With the help of an army supplied by WILLIAM II RUFUS, he defeated his uncle DONALD III BAN in May 1094. His foreign supporters were detested and, although he promised to introduce no more Englishmen or Normans into Scotland, this was not enough to save him: Donald engineered his murder on 12 Nov. 1094. Duncan II's brief reign graphically illustrates the dynastic and ethnic tensions in late eleventh-century Scotland.

DUNCAN, ADAM (1st Viscount Duncan) (1731–1804), sailor. A Scot, he entered the navy in 1746, under the care of an uncle. His career advanced in wartime, stagnated in years of peace. He became an admiral in 1795. A man of great presence, his reputation for humanity and fairness was an important factor in his crews' return to duty after the mutinies of 1797 had spread to his command at Yarmouth. The loyalty of his men contributed to his decisive defeat of the Dutch fleet at the Battle of Camperdown in 1797, for which he is chiefly remembered, and which demonstrated to France that the mutinies had not inflicted significant damage on Britain's fighting capacity. This, together with his imagination and courage in bluffing the Dutch into remaining in port when only two ships were maintaining the blockade at the height of the crisis, make him one of the leading figures of the French Revolutionary Wars.

DÚNCHAD (?–717), Abbot of Iona. Although it has been suggested that Dúnchad was appointed Abbot at the head of a faction in Iona opposed to Abbot CONAMAIL's continued support for the older 84-year cycle for the calculation for the date of Easter (*see* BEDE; EGBERT OF IONA; OSWY), it seems more likely that Dúnchad simply succeeded to the abbacy following his predecessor's resignation in 707. While little else is known of his tenure, the Roman calculation was indeed adopted during his abbacy, but not until 716, a significant moment in the history of British Christianity.

DUNDAS, HENRY (1st Baron Dunira, 1st Viscount Melville) (1742–1811), politician. A Scottish lawyer who held office under Frederick NORTH, Rockingham (*see* WATSON-WENTWORTH, CHARLES) and PITT THE YOUNGER, he played a key part in the political management of Scotland for several decades. He also dominated the Indian political scene as the practical manager of the affairs of the East India Co. from 1784 to 1801. He was the supreme authority on Indian matters and with his encyclopaedic knowledge guided the Governor General's policies. To some he was wise, to others 'active and meddling'. In 1805,

continued on page 265

DUDLEY, JOHN (7th [1st Dudley] Baron and Viscount Lisle, 19th [1st Dudley] Earl of Warwick, 1st Duke of Northumberland) (c. 1504–54)
Politician

Son of HENRY VII's executed minister, Edmund DUDLEY. His mother remarried Arthur PLANTA-GENET, Viscount Lisle, while his wardship was granted to Sir Edward Guildford, who was responsible in 1512 for securing the reversal of the effects of his father's attainder. Thereafter he married Guildford's daughter and Guildford obtained his entry to court; he accompanied Sir Edward on Charles BRANDON's French campaign (1523). As a successful courtier and supporter of ANNE BOLEYN, he was a natural choice as county MP in Parliaments of the 1530s (for Kent) and 1542 (for Staffs.). It took him some time to build up his own estate in the Midlands, with the lands of his impoverished cousin Lord Dudley as a nucleus; he gained his viscountcy when the title became available on his imprisoned Plantagenet stepfather's death (1542). After service from 1542 in Scotland and France he was prominent in peace negotiations with France (1546), returning to strengthen the evangelical party at court, although his assault on Stephen GARDINER in the Council chamber temporarily removed him from politics. He acquiesced when Edward SEYMOUR, Duke of Somerset, seized power as Protector in 1547, being granted the earldom of Warwick as part of the share-out of rewards, but is said to have encouraged Thomas SEYMOUR's fruitless intrigues against the Protector. Appointment in early 1549 as Lord President of the Council in the Marches of Wales was quickly superseded by his summons to remedy military setbacks in Scotland and then to defeat Robert KETT's rebellion in Norfolk in Aug. 1549. Somerset now quarrelled with him, a fatal mistake, since Dudley's military success was the perfect rallying-point for Councillors furious at the Protector's flamboyant social policies and military strategy. After Somerset's overthrow in Oct., he adroitly outmanoeuvred conservative nobility to dominate the Council, a triumph sealed by his appointment as Lord President of the Council in 1550. The title was a deliberate symbol that he would not seek to monopolize power like Somerset, and he also gave the young King EDWARD VI a sense of playing a proper part in government. His reconciliation with Somerset was fragile; at the same time that Dudley was made Duke (Oct. 1551) Somerset was arrested on treason charges, and although these charges were clearly exaggerated, Northumberland pressed ahead with his execution in Jan. 1552 – the crisis marked by a fresh hand-out of lands and wealth to his collaborators. When the King became fatally ill in the winter of 1552–3, he and Northumberland decided to divert the succession

from the future MARY I and ELIZABETH I to JANE GREY (original responsibility for the idea is not certain, but the boldness of the scheme does not suggest the Duke's habitual caution). The Privy Council was persuaded and Jane married Northumberland's own son Guildford Dudley. Now the Duke's ruthless sureness of political touch faltered as his own health deteriorated; plans were disrupted by the regime's desperate shortage of money and the King's rapid collapse in health, and Mary was, disastrously, left a free agent in her Herts. house. On Edward's death (6 July) the plan nevertheless seemed to have succeeded until a wholly unanticipated popular revulsion in favour of Mary intervened. Northumberland led an army to confront her forces in East Anglia, but at Bury St Edmunds he lost his nerve and turned back to Cambridge, where he proclaimed Mary Queen. At his execution on 22 Aug. he affirmed his Catholicism, to Jane's disgust; his family were once more attainted.

Dudley remains a controversial and mysterious figure. He has not aided interpretation by his curious inarticulacy on paper, and at key stages in his later political career he lapsed into serious illness. In the Protestant interpretation of Edward's reign pioneered by John PONET, Somerset was the idealistic 'Good Duke', betrayed by political villains of whom Dudley was the worst, an amoral power-seeker whom Ponet styled 'the Alcibiades of England'. As Somerset has been reassessed, so Northumberland's stock has risen, and the elements of consolidation and reconstruction in his post-1549 regime have been given more credit. He recognized that the French and Scots wars were ruining the country, and patiently extricated England, unflinchingly courting unpopularity when he sealed peace with France by handing back Boulogne, Henry VIII's only substantial war-prize. He hesitantly started to restore a fine silver standard to the coinage after a decade of ruinous debasement, although the piecemeal character of this reform won him further unpopularity; he also began to sort out chaos in government finances and administration, an effort which Mary's government continued after his fall. He seems to have been a sincere evangelical from the 1530s up to his final abject surrender to Mary, and he carried on the dynamic of Protestant reforms launched by Somerset's regime, while continuing to line his own and his supporters' pockets.

Barrett L. Beer, Northumberland: The Political Career of John Dudley, Earl of Warwick and Duke of Northumberland (1973)

DUDLEY, ROBERT (14th [1st Dudley] Earl of Leicester) (1532 or 1533–88)
Courtier and politician

Fifth son of John DUDLEY, Duke of Northumberland, he grew up in the courts of HENRY VIII and EDWARD VI, and from an early age he knew the future ELIZABETH I. In 1550 he became a member of Edward's Privy Chamber, and also married Amy Robsart; his likely future was as a landed gentleman of Norfolk. He tried strenuously to hold Norfolk for Lady JANE GREY against MARY in 1553, but after his trial for treason and attainder, he was pardoned and released by PHILIP II; thereafter he lived obscurely until he was allowed to fight for Philip against France in 1557, resulting in the reversal of the attainder. Immediate favour and appointment as Master of the Horse came with Elizabeth I's accession. It was difficult for scandal not to attach to the mysterious death of Amy at Cumnor Place (Oxon.) in Sept. 1560, but the likelihood is that she was killed by an accidental fall in an advanced stage of cancer. The Queen's continuing affection led to widespread speculation about imminent marriage, and Dudley (possibly with Elizabeth's encouragement) even sounded out Philip II as to whether or not he would support the match. He now began an active involvement in policy-making, particularly in relation to Scotland, where he cultivated close relations with William MAITLAND of Lethington, secretary to MARY QUEEN OF SCOTS, and James STEWART, Earl of Moray; he became a Privy Councillor in 1562. Elizabeth granted him Kenilworth Castle and extensive north Wales estates in 1563 and made him Earl in 1564; although she came to realize that marriage to him was politically impossible, she tried to persuade him to marry Mary Queen of Scots, in association with her own proposal to marry an Austrian Habsburg. Leicester opposed both schemes, and now began to emerge as a champion of militant Protestantism both at home and overseas – the most prominent standard-bearer for the dynamic religion of the Edwardian Reformation in Elizabeth's rather more ambiguous Church Settlement. Through the 1560s, Leicester's relations with William CECIL were sometimes tense, but the often-told story of his part in a noblemen's plot to overthrow Cecil in 1569 can now be shown to be false. Thereafter the two Protestant statesmen worked on the Privy Council in general harmony, though Leicester was more inclined to urge aggressive moves to support Protestantism abroad.

His place at court, dependent on his intimate relationship with the Queen, was put in jeopardy by love affairs – he was desperate for an heir – and a son, Robert, was born to him and Douglas Sheffield in 1574; controversy remains as to whether he married Douglas. His urgent need to keep Elizabeth happy was spectacularly expressed in the lavish entertainment which he created for her at Kenilworth on her progress of 1575. Elizabeth was infuriated by his eventual marriage to Lettice Knollys, the Earl of Essex's widow (1578, but probably earlier in secret); their son died in 1584. At the same time, Leicester showed the power that he had now accumulated when he led the successful opposition to Elizabeth's marrying FRANCIS OF VALOIS. He pushed for command of an expeditionary force to help the rebel Dutch against Spain. Reluctantly Elizabeth agreed in 1585, but was furious when he accepted the Dutch offer that he become Governor General of the Netherlands. By 1587 the expedition had become a fiasco; Leicester had little understanding of Dutch politics, his last personal experience of military command was back in 1557 (since Elizabeth had always insisted that he remain in England) and his health was increasingly frail. He was recalled; he was beginning to regain favour with energetic preparations to fight the Armada at his death from a malarial infection in 1588. The Queen mourned him deeply.

Leicester's reputation has suffered from a brilliantly malicious Roman Catholic portrait of him, *Leycester's Commonwealth* (1584, possibly by Charles Arundell), which gained its effectiveness from being based on a good deal of accurate detail; equally, one of the chief contemporary Protestant commentators, William CAMDEN, presented an unsympathetic picture of him in his *Annals*. The problem has been compounded by the wide dispersal of his archive, which in fact largely survives and is now being assessed and exploited. Leicester came to command the loyalty and love of many outstanding contemporaries apart from the Queen, including his nephew Philip SIDNEY, Francis DRAKE and Edmund SPENSER. Perhaps the way to understand his fascinating combination of roles as Puritan patron and flamboyant, cultured courtier is to see his ambitions as twofold: both to become a Calvinist magnate of international stature, and to restore the fortunes of his family, claiming a medieval inheritance in line to the Beauchamp earls of Warwick.

Derek Wilson, Sweet Robin: A Biography of Robert Dudley Earl of Leicester (1981) having returned to office with Pitt, he was impeached for financial abuses for which he accepted formal responsibility as treasurer of the navy. The last British minister to have been thus indicted, he was, however, acquitted in the Lords.

DUNDEE, 1ST VISCOUNT see GRAHAM, JOHN

DUNDONALD, 10TH EARL see COCHRANE, THOMAS

DUNFERMLINE, 1ST EARL OF see SETON, ALEXANDER

DÚNGAL MAC SELBAIG (?–?736), King of Dál Riata. Dúngal appears to have become King in 723, when his father entered into monastic life, but he was deposed by Eochaid, great-grandson of DOMNALL BRECC, in 726. Like all kings of Dál Riata, Dúngal's political interests encompassed events in Ireland and in 733 he raided in Donegal, where he seized Bridei, son of the Pictish king OENGUS, SON OF FERGUS. On Eochaid's death in the same year, Dúngal returned to Dál Riata, only to be driven out by Oengus in the following year. In 736 Oengus again attacked Dál Riata, capturing both Dúngal and his brother, whose subsequent fates are unknown.

DUNIRA, 1ST BARON see DUNDAS, HENRY

DUNK, GEORGE MONTAGU (2nd [Montagu] Earl of Halifax) (1716–71), politician. Chiefly remembered for his tenure as President of the Board of Trade (1748–61), where assisted by his secretary Pownall, he reformed mercantile and colonial policy, treating the colonies far more systematically than before as assets that should directly benefit Britain. Halifax's administrative and legislative reforms had far-reaching consequences, contributing eventually to the War of American Independence. Newcastle (see PELHAM-HOLLES, THOMAS) regarded him as a threat to the power of the secretaries of state but after Newcastle's fall Halifax was admitted to the Cabinet. As Secretary of State to Bute (see STUART, JOHN) in 1763, Halifax signed the general warrant under which WILKES was arrested. Halifax in Nova Scotia is named after him.

DUNLOP, JOHN (1840–1921), inventor. A veterinary surgeon working in Belfast, Dunlop developed one of the most beneficial innovations in wheeled transport. The story goes that his invention of the pneumatic tyre was a response to his son's plea to make his solid-tyred bicycle go faster; the patent which Dunlop registered in March 1889 was swiftly taken up. The Pneumatic Tyre Co. was set up in Belfast, but ran into difficulties when an earlier patent, essentially identical, was found to have been registered by Robert William Thompson in 1845. The Dunlop patent was declared invalid and the company continued without him, but the name stuck. The new company established in England in 1896 by a former partner was called Dunlop.

DUNNING, JOHN (1st Baron Ashburton) (1731–83), lawyer and politician. Son of an attorney, he was articled to his father, but being judged promising went to read at the Middle Temple. Appointed Solicitor General in 1768, Dunning distanced himself from the government's proceedings against WILKES, and joined the opposition in 1770. In 1780, with mounting opposition to the NORTH ministry associated with the War of American Independence (see BURKE, EDMUND; WYVILL, CHRISTOPHER), he moved his famous Commons resolutions, that 'the influence of the Crown has increased, is increasing and ought to be diminished' and that 'it is competent to this House to examine into and correct abuses in the expenditure of the civil list revenues, as well as in every other branch of the public revenue' as it wished. Both resolutions were carried resoundingly against North's wishes, although enthusiasm for supporting reform in practice quickly ebbed. Moving to the Lords, Dunning sat in the Cabinets of both Rockingham (see WATSON-WENTWORTH, CHARLES) and Shelburne (see PETTY, HENRY) as Chancellor to the Duchy of Lancaster, but he never achieved the lord chancellorship to which he aspired.

DUNS SCOTUS, JOHN (?1266–1308), philosopher. A Scottish-born Franciscan, he studied and taught at Oxford, Paris and Cologne. Known as 'Doctor Subtilis', his ability to make new distinctions and invent new terms won many adherents to his critique of Aquinas's theory of knowledge. With time, these disciples also came to be regarded as archetypal hair-splitting schoolmen, denounced as 'dunces' by those sixteenth-century humanists who cherished the belief that philosophy could be kept free of technical jargon.

DUNSTABLE, JOHN (c. 1390–1453), composer. A prolific composer, whose motets were much admired by contemporaries in France and Italy as well as in England. The best known is the fourpart *Veni Sancte Spiritus*. He served John, Duke of Bedford (see JOHN OF LANCASTER), as musician at his court in Paris in the 1420s and 1430s, probably returning to England to serve HUMPHREY OF GLOUCESTER. According to a Burgundian poet, it was by following the 'English method' exemplified by Dunstable that other composers learned how to make their music joyous and bright. His epitaph in St Stephen's church, Walbrook, implies that he was buried there.

DUNSTAN, ST (*c*. 909–88), Archbishop of Canterbury (959–88). Dunstan and the younger St ETHELWOLD and St OSWALD were leaders of the so-called Tenth-Century Reform in Anglo-Saxon England, the basic principles of which began to be developed during ATHELSTAN's reign and which Dunstan developed further following his appointment as Abbot of Glastonbury in 940. The central principle of the Tenth-Century Reform, implemented through the *Regularis Concordia* (*see* ETHELWOLD for more detail) was to introduce the Rule of St Benedict to English monasteries and to use these monasteries as the spearhead to improve the moral, organizational and spiritual standards of the Church. Although Dunstan's historical reputation rests on his achievements as an ecclesiastical reformer, he was also a profoundly political figure. He had family ties with the highest levels of the aristocracy, acted as chief adviser to Kings EDMUND and EADRED, and was exiled by EADWIG. After EDGAR's accession, he was almost immediately appointed Archbishop of Canterbury: the partnership between him, the other reformers and Edgar was of decisive importance.

DURHAM, 1ST EARL OF *see* LAMBTON, JOHN

DURY, JOHN (1596–1680) churchman. A Scots minister's son, Dury (or Durie) was appointed minister to the English congregation at Elbing (Prussia) in 1625; he travelled extensively trying to interest leading churchmen in uniting all Protestant Churches. He was ordained in the Church of England in 1634 and was tutor to Princess Mary in exile, but in 1645 returned to London to join Presbyterian discussions for reconstructing the Church. He was a prominent advocate for the return of Jews to England, believing that it would hasten the last days of the world. Further travels in unsuccessful efforts at ecumenical progress led to his quitting England permanently for Cassel after CHARLES II's restoration.

DYER, REGINALD (1864–1927), soldier. Son of a brewer, commissioned from Sandhurst in 1885, he spent the next 30 years soldiering in India, Burma and Iran. In the spring of 1919, Dyer, now a Brigadier General, was faced with what he believed was the beginning of an insurrection among the Sikhs. On 13 April Dyer, commanding only 50 men, ordered his troops to open fire on a crowd of thousands who had assembled in the central square in Amritsar. Firing a total of 1,650 rounds at point-blank range, Dyer's men killed at least 400 and wounded another 1,200. At the subsequent inquiry, though Dyer had numerous defenders (the *Morning Post* raised £26,000 for his defence), the Commander-in-Chief of India ordered him to resign. Dyer went to his grave believing he had saved the Raj; in reality he had hastened its end.

DYFNWAL, SON OF YWAIN (?–975), King of the Strathclyde Britons (*c*. 943–before 973). King before 943, Dyfnwal appears to have abdicated before 973, for the King of the Cumbrians who rowed King EDGAR on the Dee was named as Mael Coluim. Dyfnwal is known to have gone on pilgrimage to Rome and to have become a monk, dying abroad in 975. If, as is thought probable, the ruling dynasty of Strathclyde had been expelled in the late ninth century by DOMNALL II MAC CONSTANTÍN, the re-emergence of the British names such as Ywain and Dyfnwal in the tenth and eleventh centuries suggests the resurgence of a native ruling dynasty, perhaps in the aftermath of CONSTANTÍN II's defeat at the Battle of Brunanburh (937).

E

EADBALD (?–640), King of Kent (616 or 618–40). When he succeeded his father ETHEL-BERT, Eadbald briefly abandoned the latter's support for Christianity before being converted by Archbishop LAURENTIUS. Also, following pagan custom, he married his father's widow (presumably not his mother). Such evidence as there is suggests that, during Eadbald's rule, the kingdom of Kent declined from the high point of the previous reign. For one thing, he did not follow Ethelbert in the list of kings, later described as *Bretwalda*, said by BEDE to have exercised overlordship over the other early English kingdoms.

EADBERHT (?–768), King of Northumbria (737–58). An able and effective king, Eadberht followed his less successful cousin CEOLWULF. His reign is the first from which coins minted in the name of a Northumbrian king survive on any scale, an indication of the kingdom's prosperity. Although his rule was disturbed by Mercian invasions of Northumbria and conflicts with rivals, it was in relative terms a stable period in the generally turbulent history of the kingdom of Northumbria. It is noted for the collaboration with his brother Archbishop EGBERT of York which made York one of the great schools of eighth-century Europe. In 758 Eadberht abdicated to become a monk in his brother's monastery. His retirement was followed by a long and turbulent feud for control over the Northumbrian kingship, which began with the murder of his son King OSWULF in 759 and his replacement by ETHELWOLD MOLL.

EADBERT PRÆN (?–c. 811), King of Kent (796–8). A member of the Kentish royal house exiled in Francia, Eadbert seized the kingdom of Kent after the death of King OFFA of Mercia in 796 and expelled the pro-Mercian St ETHELHEARD, Archbishop of Canterbury, from his see. Eadbert was subsequently captured by King CENWULF of Mercia, badly mutilated and shut up in a monastery for most of the rest of his life. His brief dramatic career illustrates how the lesser English kingdoms were subjugated to the strong powers of Wessex and Mercia. The last member of the Kentish royal house to rule the kingdom, he was succeeded by Cenwulf's brother CUTHRED.

EADBURH (?–c. 814), Queen of Wessex (789–802). Daughter of King OFFA of Mercia and wife of King BEORHTRIC of Wessex, her marriage symbolized contemporary Mercian supremacy over Wessex. ALFRED THE GREAT's biographer ASSER, writing almost a century later, presents her as a villainous, scheming woman who poisoned her husband's rivals, fled to the continent after the succession of her husband's rival EGBERT and who, after becoming an abbess, was expelled from her monastery for debauchery. Much of this story could reflect the normal anti-female prejudice of a medieval cleric against a woman whose career was not ultimately successful.

EADBURH, ST (?–751), Abbess of Minster-in-Thanet. She illustrates the high level of learning achieved by the eighth-century Church in Kent and also its contacts with the great Anglo-Saxon missionaries in Germany such as St BONIFACE. The teacher of St LEOBA, Eadburh was also a very distinguished manuscript illuminator, receiving a commission from Boniface and producing a splendid copy of the *Acts of the Apostles* which survives in the Bodleian Library in Oxford.

EADFRITH (?–721), Bishop of Lindisfarne (698–721). Eadfrith was most probably the scribe of the famous manuscript known as the *Lindisfarne Gospels*, which can now be seen in the British Museum. While the script of the *Gospels* is Irish, the manuscript also displays a great deal of Mediterranean and Germanic influence, demonstrating what a cosmopolitan world eighth-century Northumbria must have been. Eadfrith was also involved in developing the cult of St CUTHBERT by commissioning a life of the saint from his contemporary BEDE.

EADGIFU (?–951), Queen of the Franks. A daughter of EDWARD THE ELDER and St ÆLFFLÆD, Eadgifu was married to the Carolingian King of the West Franks, Charles the Simple, and was Queen from 918 to 923. When Charles was deposed by rivals, Eadgifu used her English connections and, with the assistance of her half-brother King ATHELSTAN, her son Louis IV (d'Outremer) regained his father's kingdom in

936. Eadgifu's career illustrates a common pattern of marriage alliances made between England and France in the ninth and tenth centuries to sustain co-operation against the Vikings (*see* JUDITH), as well as the power which early medieval women could wield through family connections.

EADGIFU (?–after 966), Queen of Wessex (*c*. 920–4). She was the third wife of King EDWARD THE ELDER. Her marriage to the King from *c*. 920 to 924, took place during the lifetime of his second wife St ÆLFFLÆD; it is possible that Edward's need for allies in Kent against the Viking threat led to an urgent political marriage. Eadgifu long outlived her husband and was extremely influential during the reigns of her sons EDMUND and EADRED and her grandson EDGAR. An ally at court of St DUNSTAN and a strong supporter of the movement which developed into the so-called Tenth-Century Reform, Eadgifu, along with Queens EMMA and EDITH, is an example of an Anglo-Saxon queen who wielded great power because of her position in the family.

EADMER (*c*. 1060–*c*. 1130), historian. A Canterbury monk, he was briefly (1120–1) Bishop of St Andrew's but his claim to fame is as Archbishop ANSELM's disciple and historian. In his *History of Recent Events in England* the main theme was Anselm's public career as Archbishop; in his strikingly original *Life of Anselm*, he reconstructed his master's conversations in order to shed light on his character. These two books were based on detailed notes which Eadmer kept from the time of his entry into Anselm's household in 1093. In exile with the Archbishop from 1097 to 1100 he wrote up his notes. What happened when Anselm discovered what he was doing is best left in Eadmer's own words. 'He ordered me to destroy the quires on which I had put together the whole work. I was utterly confounded. I did not disobey him, but I could not face the destruction of a work on which I had spent so much time. So I obeyed him in the letter by destroying those quires having first transcribed their contents on to other quires.'

EADRED (?–955), King of the English (946–55). Son of EDWARD THE ELDER and EADGIFU, he succeeded his brother EDMUND after the latter's premature death. He maintained the military pressure on the Scandinavian kingdom of York, being elected as King of York (probably in the year 952), and finally expelling the last Scandinavian King of York, ERIC BLOODAXE, in 954. This completed the absorption by the kings of Wessex of the lands conquered by the Vikings from the time of the 'Great Army' of HALFDAN and IVAR THE BONELESS onwards. Eadred also advanced the careers of both St DUNSTAN and St ETHELWOLD, thereby greatly assisting the development of the Tenth-Century Reform. Despite his successes, he left money in his will to pay the Vikings not to attack in the future, an indication of perennial tenth-century English anxiety which was once more realized in the time of ETHELRED II THE UNREADY. Eadred was succeeded in turn by his nephews EADWIG and EDGAR.

EADRIC (?–686), King of Kent (684–6). A short-reigned king, notable for the way in which he used force to make his brother HLOTHERE share the kingdom with him and for producing one of the earliest Anglo-Saxon law-codes, thereby maintaining a tradition set by his predecessor ETHELBERT. The next King of Kent of note was WIHTRED.

EADRIC STREONA (?–1017), Ealdorman of Mercia. After 1007 he became ETHELRED II THE UNREADY's chief counsellor and Ealdorman of Mercia, but his role in the military disasters that followed earned him a contemporary reputation for cowardice and treachery. In 1015, having been in command of King Ethelred's army, he changed sides and joined CNUT. He subsequently changed sides twice, in 1016 joining first EDMUND IRONSIDE and then deserting him at the Battle of Ashingdon to rejoin Cnut, who afterwards had him killed. The nickname 'Streona' means 'acquisitor', and modern analysis suggests that he grew rich out of the proceeds of royal taxation.

EADULF (?–1041), Ealdorman of Bamburgh (1038–41). He succeeded to Bamburgh after the murder of his brother EALDRED in 1038. He fought off an attack from DONNCHAD I, King of the Scots, but was subsequently killed in 1041 by Earl SIWARD who then added Bamburgh to his enlarged earldom of Northumbria. Eadulf was the last member of the long-enduring house of Bamburgh to hold an earldom in northern England.

EADULF CADEL (?–*c*. 1018), Ealdorman of Bamburgh. Briefly Ealdorman of Bamburgh after the murder of his brother UHTRED in 1016, but, because King CNUT gave Yorkshire to ERIC OF HLATHIR, lord of much less territory than his brother. He was seemingly replaced by his nephew EALDRED after his defeat at the Battle of Carham (1018) by MAEL COLUIM II, King of the Scots.

EADULF OF BAMBURGH (?–913). Although little is known of his life, Eadulf appears to have sustained himself as independent ruler in the former kingdom of Bernicia after the defeat of the kingdom of Northumbria (*see* ÆLLE) and the establishment of the Scandinavian kingdom of

York by HALFDAN. He appears to have made some sort of alliance with his Wessex contemporary ALFRED THE GREAT. He was succeeded by his son EALDRED OF BAMBURGH.

EADWIG (c. 940–59), King of the English (955–9). Eldest son of EDMUND, he was about 15 when he succeeded his uncle EADRED as King. There appears to have been a succession dispute with his younger brother EDGAR and conflict at court. In 956 Eadwig exiled St DUNSTAN and the dowager Queen EADGIFU, but after 957 his authority was reduced to control over Wessex as a result of the rebellion launched on Edgar's behalf. He was forced to divorce his wife ÆLFGIFU. Eadwig's reputation was posthumously vilified (perhaps unfairly) by Edgar's supporters, who included Dunstan.

EADWIG THE ÆTHELING (?–after 1017). A younger son of ETHELRED II THE UNREADY's first marriage, he was its last surviving male offspring after the death of King EDMUND IRONSIDE in 1016. He apparently left England after CNUT's accession to the kingdom. On his return he was murdered on Cnut's orders.

EADWULF, King of Northumbria (705). Possibly a son of ETHELWOLD, King of Deira, Eadwulf disputed the succession to Northumbria with the supporters of the young OSRED, son of King ALDFRITH. Defeated at Bamburgh by an extensive coalition of Northumbrian nobles, he was expelled from the kingdom.

EALDHUN (?–1018), Bishop of Chester le Street, Co. Durham. Became Bishop of Chester-le-Street in 990 and therefore the protector of the relics of St CUTHBERT. He is notable for moving his bishopric and the remains of the saint to what proved to be their permanent location at Durham in 995, and for starting a new cathedral on the site where Durham's cathedral still stands.

EALDRED (?–1038), Ealdorman of Bamburgh. The son of UHTRED of Bamburgh, he succeeded his uncle EADULF CADEL in 1018. He avenged his father's murder by killing THURBRAND THE HOLD in 1019, an event which started a long period of hostility in the north between the two families. He was himself killed by Thurbrand's son in 1038 and was succeeded by his brother EADULF.

EALDRED (?–1069), Archbishop of York (1060–69). He typifies the extravagant display of the late Anglo-Saxon state, as well as the co-operation between churchmen and secular authority. At one stage in the 1050s, he held three bishoprics, attended papal councils in Rome and, in 1054, led the diplomatic mission to Germany that negotiated the return to England of EDWARD THE EXILE. He was, in addition, a great church builder and collector of valuable books. He appears to have quickly appreciated the decisiveness of the Norman victory in 1066, since he crowned WILLIAM I THE CONQUEROR in Westminster Abbey on Christmas Day 1066, and was well regarded by the Normans.

EALDRED OF BAMBURGH (?–c. 930). After succeeding his father EADULF OF BAMBURGH in the lordship of Bamburgh, Ealdred was driven out by RAGNALL, the Viking King of York. After his expulsion, Ealdred sought support from CONSTANTÍN II, King of the Scots. From 920, however, he had to acknowledge the overlordship of Kings EDWARD THE ELDER and ATHELSTAN as they drove English power north. He was succeeded by his brother UHTRED OF BAMBURGH. His whole career illustrates the increasing pressures imposed on lesser nobles by the emergent kingdoms of tenth-century Britain and by Scandinavian settlement.

EALHHELM (?–951), Ealdorman (940–51). Possibly a kinsman of the kings of Wessex, he was appointed Ealdorman of part of Mercia by King EDMUND, thereby illustrating the process whereby the descendants of EDWARD THE ELDER and ATHELSTAN consolidated their hold over England outside Wessex. Among Ealhhelm's sons was ÆLFHERE, Ealdorman of Mercia.

EALHSWITH (?–902), wife of ALFRED THE GREAT. Although a woman of Mercian stock, very little is known about the historical Ealhswith, whose marriage to Alfred in 868 presumably epitomizes another facet of the Wessex–Mercian alliance against the Viking 'Great Army' of HALFDAN and IVAR THE BONELESS. In conformity with ninth-century practice, Ealhswith was never formally crowned as queen, a custom at the time changed only in exceptional circumstances (see JUDITH), but abandoned in favour of regular coronation in the tenth century.

EANFLÆD, ST (626–c. 704), Queen and Abbess. A daughter of King EDWIN of Northumbria, who is said by BEDE to have been the first Northumbrian to have been baptized by PAULINUS, Eanflæd's long life epitomizes several key aspects of early medieval politics and religion. Married from 642 to 670 to King OSWY of Northumbria , the great dynastic rival of her paternal family's descendants such as OSWINE, King of Deira, she was ultimately unsuccessful in resolving this inter-familial conflict. As joint Abbess of Whitby (670–c. 704) with her daughter St ÆLFFLÆD after her husband's death, she personifies the well-established prominence of royal women in North umbrian religious life. She also presided over a productive literary and cultural phase in her monastery's history.

EANFRITH (?–*c.* 674), King of the Hwicce. He was the first known King of the Hwicce, an Anglo-Saxon kingdom in the Severn valley, roughly coterminous with the modern dioceses of Worcester and Gloucester, generally assumed to have been formed on the basis of a distinct Anglo-Saxon settlement by King PENDA of Mercia. Very little is known about Eanfrith and the other kings. The kingdom was reintegrated into Mercia by OFFA.

EANRED (?–?841), King of Northumbria (?810–?841). Very little is known about Eanred's long reign. Given that his father St EARDWULF had established the family's kingship through slaughtering a number of rivals after a lengthy period of feuds, the longevity of Eanred's reign is remarkable. In 829, for a period of one year, he temporarily acknowledged the overlordship of EGBERT of Wessex.

EARDWULF (854–99), churchman. As Bishop of Lindisfarne, he was responsible for moving the monastery and its precious relics of St CUTHBERT from Lindisfarne to Chester-le-Street after the monastery had again been attacked by Vikings in 875. The community was eventually moved to Durham in 995 by EALDHUN; that it survived at all suggests that Viking kings of York from HALFDAN onwards protected it.

EARDWULF, ST (?–?810), King of Northumbria (?796 –?810). An able and energetic ruler, whose ruthlessness and skill enabled him to survive the turbulent dynastic politics of the kingdom of Northumbria and die peacefully. A nobleman, apparently from outside the two main kindreds feuding for control over the Northumbrian kingship, he was chosen as King after the murder of King ETHELRED and the brief reign of King OSBALD. He maintained his rule by slaughtering potential and actual rivals (*see* St ALHMUND), but was sufficiently resourceful to pursue his enemies by launching an attack on King CENWULF of Mercia and, when he was himself driven out, returning with the assistance of the great King of the Franks, the Emperor Charlemagne (768–814). After ECGFRITH of Mercia, he was the second English king known to have been formally consecrated to his office by bishops. He was succeeded by his son EANRED and buried at Breedon-on-the-Hill (Leics.) where a cult developed.

EARLE, JOHN (?1601–65), writer. Oxford-educated, he wrote a popular series of character studies, *Microcosmography* (1628), and became tutor to Prince Charles (the future CHARLES II). Losing his Church preferment after the Civil Wars, he went into exile with Charles II and was rewarded at the Restoration with the deanery of Westminster, then the bishoprics, first of Worcester, second Salisbury. He opposed repressive measures against Dissenters.

ECGFRITH (?–685), King of Northumbria (670–85). The son of King OSWY, Ecgrith was a notably warlike king who briefly extended Northumbrian power to its furthest limits. His ambitions in the south were thwarted by ETHELRED of Mercia in 679, but in the north he crushed the Picts in *c.* 672 and established a bishopric at Abercorn on the Firth of Forth in 681. Four years later he set out to invade Ireland, but was defeated and killed at Nechtanesmere in the kingdom of the Picts. His first wife was ÆTHELTHRYTH, founder of Ely Abbey. Although Ecgfrith's reputation for piety has remained intact, he was involved in a spectacular quarrel with Bishop WILFRID, which seems to have been caused by the encouragement Wilfrid gave to Æthelthryth to leave her husband. He was succeeded by his brother ALDFRITH.

ECGFRITH (?–796), King of Mercia (July–Dec. 796). Son of the mighty King OFFA of Mercia, Ecgfrith is notable as the first English king ever to be anointed and crowned during his father's lifetime. This imitation of practices followed by Offa's very successful Carolingian contemporaries such as the Emperor Charlemagne involved the creation of an archbishopric of Lichfield (*see* HYGEBERHT), and was intended to consolidate Offa's fragile hegemony over England south of the Humber. Ecgfrith's early death ended schemes to sustain this extensive Mercian domination. He was succeeded by a distant kinsman CENWULF.

EDDIUS STEPHANUS (?–*c.* 720), scholar. Between 709 and 720 he wrote a biography of St WILFRID, which provides invaluable material on the early Christian Church in England. Little else is known about Eddius.

EDEN, SIR ANTHONY *see* essay on page 271

EDEN, SIR FREDERICK MORTON (1766–1809), social commentator. The son of a Governor of Maryland, he was co-founder and Chairman of an insurance company. In 1794–5 he responded to complaints about the rising poor rates by organizing visits to several parishes across the country. The resulting three-volume work, *The State of the Poor; or an History of the Labouring Classes in England from the Conquest to the Present Period*

continued on page 272

EDEN, ANTHONY (1st Earl of Avon) (1897–1977)
Politician and Prime Minister (1955–7)

Son of a beautiful mother and an eccentric baronet, Eden inherited characteristics from both parents which marked his political career. He belonged to that generation of British politicians who were shaped by their experiences of the First World War.

Eden's own war record was exemplary and included the award of the Military Cross for outstanding bravery. After the war he read oriental languages at Oxford, obtaining a First before going into politics, where his handsome appearance and Military Cross stood him in good stead. He was fortunate enough to find the safe seat of Warwick and Leamington, which carried him through his whole career (in striking contrast to his near contemporaries, Duff COOPER and Harold MACMILLAN, whose careers were interrupted by losing marginal seats).

Eden was given his first political post at the Foreign Office under Austen CHAMBERLAIN and he quickly acquired a reputation as an expert on foreign affairs; exceptionally he was to spend most of his career in that area, serving for only two short periods on the domestic front. His meteoric rise continued under BALDWIN who, after the HOARE–Laval pact of 1935, brought him to the Foreign Office in an effort to salvage the government's reputation; at 38 he was the youngest Foreign Secretary since 1807, a fact which failed to win him favour in the eyes of either his contemporary rivals or among his seniors. Eden's record as a champion of the League of Nations placed him firmly on the liberal wing of the Conservative Party, an organization for which he had little time or sympathy.

Tensions swiftly arose between him and Neville CHAMBERLAIN after Baldwin's resignation in 1937. Although Eden later chose to portray the conflict as one over the nature of appeasement, it was actually over the much smaller issue of whether or not to recognize the Italian conquest of Abyssinia and it was a mark of Eden's defects as a politician that, when he resigned in Feb. 1938, only his closest friend, Lord Cranborne (see CECIL, ROBERT), went with him; his resignation speech was notable for its lack of rancour. There was a general feeling by the end of the year that Eden wanted to work his way back into office, a line of action supported by his successor at the Foreign Office, Lord Halifax (see WOOD, EDWARD).

Eden's gentlemanly opposition meant that he was overtaken as chief rebel by CHURCHILL and it was the latter who was appointed to the Cabinet on the outbreak of war in 1939; Eden had to wait until Churchill became Prime Minister before being appointed to the War Office, and he owed his return to the Foreign Office in Dec. 1940 to the same patron. This set the tone of the Churchill–Eden relationship and for the next 15 years Eden would imagine that he was about to replace Churchill as Prime Minster, an illusion which was fostered by Churchill, who found it made Eden easier to manage.

Eden found being Foreign Secretary in wartime a frustrating experience. Churchill insisted on dominating the most important field, Anglo-American relations, so it was not surprising that Eden should have made Anglo-Soviet relations his own sphere; but his hopes for future co-operation were blasted by the nature of Stalinism and the onset of the Cold War. Back at the Foreign Office in 1951, Eden found it difficult to adapt to Britain's reduced circumstances and he resented American attempts to replace British influence in the Middle East. The 1954 Geneva Conference at which he mediated between the Americans and the Soviets over Vietnam and Laos was his finest hour, and in 1955 he finally replaced Churchill, going on to win an election in May 1955.

But Eden failed to put his own stamp on the government and unfavourable comparisons with Churchill were quickly being drawn. It was partly in an attempt to shore up his own domestic position that Eden responded so firmly to Nasser's seizure of the Suez Canal in 1956. Already suffering from ill health, Eden threw away his reputation for integrity by colluding with Israel and France to attack Egypt in Nov. 1956, lying to the Commons and to posterity about this to the end of his life. The Americans, furious at not having been consulted, put economic and diplomatic pressure on Britain to pull out of the Suez campaign, imposing an immense humiliation on their old wartime ally. Eden's own reputation could hardly recover, and he was fortunate to be able to use the excuse of his health to retire in 1957, his reputation, like that of Neville Chamberlain, blasted by one disastrous episode at the end of his career.

Robert Rhodes James, Anthony Eden: A Biography (1987)

(1797), was critical of most eighteenth-century poor-law reforms as neither saving money nor respecting the moral obligations of the prosperous to their dependants. Eden's work has been drawn on by many social analysts, including Karl MARX.

EDEN, GEORGE (1st Earl of Auckland) (1784–1849), Governor General of India. A Whig politician, elected to the Commons in 1810 and sitting in the Lords from 1814, Auckland served as President of the Board of Trade under Charles GREY (1830–2), as First Lord of the Admiralty (1834), and the following year was appointed Governor General of India. Responsible for the First Afghan War, part of his policy of pursuing British interests beyond India and against Russian encroachment, he enjoyed early successes in 1838–40 (for which he earned his earldom) followed by dismal failure in the winter of 1841–2. Only one survivor returned from 16,000 men; Auckland was recalled in disgrace, but briefly served again as First Lord of the Admiralty before ill health forced his retirement.

EDEN, WILLIAM (1st Baron Auckland) (1744–1814), politician. A younger son of a Co. Durham landowning family, Eden became a successful barrister. Appointed an Under-Secretary of State in 1772, he published his *Principles of Penal Law* in the same year, the first English treatise on a subject that was exciting the attention of enlightened thinkers across Europe. An MP from 1774, he became an authority on economic issues and between 1776 and 1782 held posts at the Board of Trade, with the commissioners who attempted to negotiate with the American colonists, and as Chief Secretary to Ireland. In 1783 PITT THE YOUNGER made him responsible for negotiating a commercial treaty with France. The treaty, agreed in Sept. 1786, provided for reciprocal customs duties on a 'most favoured nation' basis, replacing the heavy duties that had been previously paid on French exports to Britain. Eden agreed a similar arrangement with the Dutch but the Spanish were unreceptive. He returned to Britain in 1793 but Pitt distrusted his ambitions and recalled him to office only in 1798 as Postmaster General; he resigned in 1801 when Pitt resigned.

EDGAR (944–75), King of the English (959–75). He was the youngest son of King EDMUND. After seizing Northumbria and Mercia from his brother EADWIG, and then succeeding him as King of the English two years later, Edgar's reign was apparently largely peaceful and successful. The most famous event was his 'second coronation' at Bath in 973, followed by a meeting at Chester with a large number of British kings, including CINAED II, King of the Scots, and DYFNWAL, SON OF YWAIN, King of the

Strathclyde Britons, who rowed him on the River Dee to demonstrate their subjection. All the evidence suggests that these dramatic and unusual incidents allowed Edgar to consolidate the claims of his tenth-century predecessors such as ATHELSTAN to imperial domination over Britain, claims which were sustained by all his successors up until the time of EDWARD I and beyond. A strong supporter of the religious movement known as the Tenth-Century Reform, he appointed St DUNSTAN to the archbishopric of Canterbury soon after his accession and he advanced his former tutor St ETHELWOLD to the bishopric of Winchester. He is also important for his extensive law-codes and for his important reform of the coinage in 973, which ensured that thereafter coins of high silver quality were regularly reminted at mints controlled by the king.

Edgar's reign marks a high-point in the theory and practice of Anglo-Saxon kingship, with its emphasis on the king's direct responsibility to God for the performance of his duties. Many of its governmental achievements endured and were the foundations of the strong monarchy of the Norman and Angevin kings. The conflicts, however, that began during the reign of his son EDWARD THE MARTYR, demonstrate the personal nature and fragility of kingly power at this period. Somewhat surprisingly for a man of his religious sensibilities, his marital relationships were confused and unstable. A daughter, St EDITH OF WILTON, came to be regarded as a saint.

EDGAR (c. 1074–1107), King of the Scots (1097–1107). The eldest son of MAEL COLUIM III CENN MÓR and St MARGARET, he took refuge in England when his parents died in Nov. 1093. After the death of his half-brother DUNCAN II the following year, he became the Anglo-Norman candidate for the Scottish throne, which he won in 1097 with the aid of an army supplied by WILLIAM II RUFUS, overthrowing DONALD III BAN. In 1098 he recognized the King of Norway's lordship over the Western Isles. His reign was an unusually peaceful one, probably thanks to substantial Anglo-Norman support. In 1100 he gave his sister MATILDA in marriage to HENRY I. He died unmarried and was buried in Dunfermline Priory (Fife).

EDGAR THE ÆTHELING (c. 1052–c. 1125), royal prince. The word Ætheling signifies a prince of royal blood, and was used regularly in the tenth and eleventh centuries. As son of EDWARD THE EXILE he was proclaimed King in London in 1066 after HAROLD II's death, but was almost at once forced to submit to WILLIAM I THE CONQUEROR. Deeply involved in the abortive revolts of 1069–70, he went into exile. Even after his reconciliation with William in 1074, his status as a potential English candidate for the throne made for an awkward time at court, and he travelled, taking part in the First Crusade. He generally supported ROBERT II Curthose and consequently was taken prisoner at the Battle of Tinchebrai in 1106; after his release, he settled for a quiet life in the country.

EDGEWORTH, MARIA (1767–1849), novelist and educationist. One of 20 siblings and stepsiblings, Maria Edgeworth worked with her father to improve the agricultural productivity of the family home, Edgeworthstown (Co. Longford). Her first novel, *Letters from Literary Ladies*, was published in 1795 and *The Parent's Assistant* (two vols, 1796 and 1801) and *Moral Tales* (1801) were among the first books written specifically for children, as was the textbook she wrote with her father, *Practical Education* (1798). Her best-known novel, a portrait of Irish life, *Castle Rackrent*, was published in 1800. Edgeworth enjoyed both commercial success, earning more from her books than Walter SCOTT or Jane AUSTEN, and a literary reputation unequalled until George ELIOT.

EDGEWORTH, RICHARD LOVELL (1744–1817), author and inventor. The son of an Irish barrister and landlord, he studied law but spent more of his time inventing suitably gentlemanly machines such as a land-measuring device and a carriage which won him a medal from the Society of Arts (he also experimented with a velocipede). An admirer of Erasmus DARWIN and a close friend of Thomas DAY, he shared many of their ideas and when in Paris visited Rousseau, whose educational teachings they both followed. Edgeworth invested much time and money in the improvement of his Irish estates and was an ally of Charlemont (*see* CAULFIELD, JAMES) during the agitation for 'legislative independence' in 1783. His concern for Ireland and for rational reform was inherited by his daughter, the novelist Maria EDGEWORTH.

EDINGTON, WILLIAM (?–1366), royal servant. Efficient and a reformer, he became Treasurer (1344–56) and Chancellor (1356–63). He did much to restore public confidence in EDWARD III's government. When appointed Treasurer, he inherited a legacy of debt and financial chaos; his innovations in Exchequer procedure and record-keeping allowed ministers to obtain a clear overview of the state of royal finances. By taking the increasingly lucrative wool subsidy into direct government control, he tapped the resources that enabled Edward to mount some of the major campaigns of the Hundred Years War. As Bishop of Winchester (1346–66), he began rebuilding the nave of the cathedral.

EDITH (1020 or 1030–75), Queen of the English and wife of EDWARD THE CONFESSOR. A daughter of Earl GODWINE of Wessex and sister of King HAROLD II, her marriage to King Edward was intended to consolidate the alliance between her father and the recently restored King. She shared in the vicissitudes and triumphs of her family and in 1065–7 was the patron of the *Vita Ædwardi Regis*, which, at first intended to celebrate her family's achievements, turned into a lament for their deaths and a eulogy of her husband's sanctity. The *Vita* is the far from trustworthy foundation on which the image of the Confessor as a saintly king was constructed. Edith lived on under Norman rule.

EDITH OF WILTON, ST (961–84), a daughter of King EDGAR (possibly by a concubine). Edith during her lifetime acquired a great reputation for skills as an embroiderer and illuminator of manuscripts and by 997 at the latest she had acquired a reputation as a saint. The development of her reputation in many respects parallels that of young Anglo-Saxon male royal kindred, such as St CYNE-HELM, St WYSTAN and her half-brother St EDWARD THE MARTYR, who were also canonized.

EDMUND (c. 921–46), King of the English (939–46). The son of EDWARD THE ELDER and his third wife EADGIFU, he assisted his half-brother ATHELSTAN at the Battle of Brunanburh and succeeded him as King. Although his brother's death was followed by the revival of Scandinavian power in northern England by OLAF GOTHFRITHSSON and OLAF SIHTRICSSON, he was able to continue successful military campaigns against them. He also continued his predecessor's support for his nephew, the Carolingian King Louis IV, in his wars in France. He maintained the Anglo-Saxon kingly practice of issuing law-codes and patronized the Church. When he was about 25, he was killed while trying to protect his steward from an attack by an outlaw. His sons by his first marriage, EADWIG and EDGAR, were presumably considered too young to become kings; he was succeeded by his brother EADRED.

EDMUND IRONSIDE (c. 981–1016), King of the English (1016). A son of ETHELRED II THE UNREADY by his first wife Ælfgifu, he rebelled against his father in 1015 in all probability because he feared that his claims to the succession would be set aside in favour of Ethelred's sons by his second wife EMMA. He was subsequently reconciled and succeeded Ethelred in 1016. He was briefly successful in resisting the Danish armies of King CNUT, with whom he made a short-lived partition of the English kingdom in 1016 after the Battle of Ashingdon (Essex). His subsequent death from wounds inflicted during the battle enabled Cnut to take the entire kingdom.

continued on page 276

EDWARD I (1239–1307)
King of England (1272–1307)

A domineering personality and a dominating figure who stood head and shoulders above the other men of his time: when his tomb in Westminster Abbey was opened in 1774 his body was measured at 6 feet 2 inches. In contrast to his peace-loving father HENRY III, he turned quickly and confidently to war (at which he was a notably efficient practitioner) as a favoured method of tackling problems. Not until the seventeenth century did a ruler of England raise armies larger than those which Edward led against the Scots. In consequence no King of England has left so great a mark on England's relations with Wales and Scotland.

He was only 15 when, in 1254, some of his responsibilities as eldest son and heir to the throne were thrust upon him; in that year he married ELEANOR OF CASTILE and was made Lord of Ireland (which he never visited) and of Aquitaine, and received the earldom of Chester as well as other castles and estates in England and Wales, where the policies of his officials provoked LLYWELYN AP GRUFFUDD's rebellion in 1256.

In 1256 he took part in the first of his many tournaments. During the turbulent years 1258–65 he found himself torn between his position as heir to the throne and his sympathy for some of the reforms proposed by the baronial opposition. Because he changed sides several times, a contemporary poet compared him to a leopard, regarded as the most devious and untrustworthy of beasts. In the end he became his father's most energetic champion, but was defeated by Simon de MONTFORT at the Battle of Lewes (1264) and made a hostage. Next year he escaped and cleverly organized the campaign which trapped de Montfort at Evesham.

Out of sympathy with a policy of reconciliation after civil war, he and Eleanor went on crusade (1270–2). At Acre he was wounded by an assassin's knife; much later the story of how his wife sucked poison from the wound would be told. On his way home he heard of his father's death (Nov. 1272), but he stayed on the continent until 1274, detained by the affairs of Aquitaine; he was the last reigning King of England to visit the duchy as its ruler.

He returned from crusade with an enhanced reputation and deeply conscious of the need for reform to improve the efficiency and reputation of royal justice. A massive inquiry into the workings of local government resulted in the first Statute of Westminster (1275). Further statutes were issued in 1278, 1279, 1283, 1285 (the second Statute of Westminster) and 1290. They covered almost every aspect of law, criminal, commercial, property, and did much to regulate the Crown's relationships with both secular and ecclesiastical landowners. This was the unprecedented volume of legislation that led nineteenth-century historians to label him the English Justinian. Some of the statutes were promulgated in Parliament, which at this stage of his reign Edward primarily saw as a mechanism through which he could both consult his subjects and publicize the achievements of his government. He instituted a customs duty on wool exports in 1275. This brought in useful revenue and transformed royal finance by providing the security on which the Crown could borrow vast sums from international bankers such as the Riccardi of Lucca.

No English King made greater efforts to rule the whole of Britain. In two campaigns (1276–7 and 1282–3) he defeated Llywelyn and conquered the principality of Wales. By the Statute of Wales (1284), he reorganized Welsh law and government, creating English-style shires in the north (Flint, Anglesey, Merioneth and Caernarfon) and establishing chartered boroughs for English settlers from which the Welsh were excluded. Great castles such as Flint, Rhuddlan, Caernarfon, Conwy and Beaumaris defended these new towns. In 1301 he made his eldest son (later EDWARD II) Prince of Wales, a precedent followed by every subsequent English monarch who could.

In confident mood after the conquest of Wales he took the Cross for a second time in 1287 and raised taxation from the English Church in order to finance his crusade, only to disappoint the expectation that he would be the Holy Land's saviour. Acre, the capital of the crusader kingdom of Jerusalem, fell in 1291, exactly 100 years (as contemporaries noticed) after RICHARD I had captured it, and Edward spent the money on his other wars.

The succession dispute that followed the death of MARGARET, MAID OF NORWAY, in 1290 meant that he was increasingly drawn to intervene in the politics of Scotland. The 13 claimants to the Scottish throne all recognized his overlordship and agreed to abide by his arbitration. In 1292 he awarded the throne to JOHN BALLIOL (who probably had the best claim) and then treated him not as the king of another country but as though he were an English baron. He referred to Scotland not as a kingdom but as a land.

When the Scots turned for help to Philip IV of France, making the treaty of mutual assistance which marks the beginning of the Auld Alliance between France and Scotland, Edward invaded, captured Berwick (then the largest town in Scotland) in 1296, took Balliol prisoner and carried off the Scottish crown jewels and the Stone of Scone, on which Scottish kings had been enthroned. Yet, despite his victories in the battles of Dunbar (1296) and Falkirk (1298), the heroic resistance of leaders such as William WALLACE and Andrew MORAY prolonged the War of Scottish Independence far longer than Edward had imagined possible. Although poor in material resources the Highlands of Scotland were far too extensive to be ringed around with castles like north Wales. Even so, by 1305 it seemed that Edward had won and was in the process of reorganizing Scotland under English administration as he had Wales. According to Peter LANGTOFT: 'Now are the islanders all joined together / And Scotland re-united to the realm / Of which King Edward is proclaimed Lord.'

But ROBERT BRUCE had other ideas. Surprised and infuriated by Bruce's bid for the Scottish throne, Edward reacted ferociously. He treated Bruce's supporters not as foreign enemies but as rebels and punished them brutally, although on balance this strengthened rather than weakened their patriotism and resolve.

Although modern historians have liked to think that a turning-point in his reign came with the sense of personal loss which he felt when Eleanor died in 1290, the moment when things turned sour came in 1294. In that year Philip IV of France declared Aquitaine confiscated and invaded the duchy. The immense costs of a war against France in defence of Aquitaine, including diversionary campaigns in Flanders, meant that from then on he taxed all his subjects ruthlessly. Pope Boniface VIII tried to protect the churches in England and France from the financial demands of their kings, but in 1297 he was forced by Philip (for on this subject the two Kings were at one) to concede that in emergencies national churches could be required to contribute to the needs of their rulers, and that it would be the Kings who determined whether or not a state of emergency existed.

By 1297 the weight of taxation in England provoked a protest movement which, while Edward was in Flanders, forced his ministers to make tax concessions and confirm Magna Carta. After 1297 his tax revenues declined but he continued to spend huge sums on war in Aquitaine and Scotland and on building castles in Wales.

By the end of the reign the strain of fighting on three fronts, against French, Scots and Welsh rebels, was beginning to tell. When he died, at Burgh-by-Sands (Cumb.) in 1307 leading his army on yet another invasion of Scotland, Crown finances were in a sorry state. He had shown himself to be distrustful of his heir's political judgement, on one occasion even attacking him and tearing his hair out, yet he had left him a difficult legacy: a heavy burden of debt and an unwinnable war in Scotland. Towards his other children (in all he had at least 15 by two wives, Eleanor of Castile and MARGARET OF FRANCE) he showed himself to be a fond if sometimes hot-tempered father. In 1297 he had to pay for repairs to his daughter Elizabeth's coronet after he had thrown it into the fire.

His reign left a deep imprint on English government and society. In 1290 he expelled the Jews, a measure which reflected his own religious convictions and was applauded by the anti-Semitic majority of his subjects.

To meet the escalating costs of war in the latter part of his reign he turned increasingly to Parliament. By now the idea had grown up that even the most powerful individuals – earls and barons – had no right to commit ordinary subjects to pay the king's taxes. Thus more frequently and more systematically than any king before him he summoned representatives of shires and boroughs to join the Lords in Parliament in the expectation that they would consent to taxation. He made sure that MPs had the authority to commit their constituents to pay.

The years from 1294 were a crucial period in the development of the principle of representation and in the emergence of the House of Commons as an integral part of Parliament. Other profound legacies of his rule were the expulsion of the Jews, the destruction of the last independent Welsh principality and an enduring hostility between English and Scots. In the sixteenth century the words 'Hammer of the Scots' were inscribed on his tomb in Westminster Abbey.

Michael Prestwich, Edward I (1988)

Edmund was nicknamed 'Ironside' (probably by contemporaries) as a tribute to his courage. After 1016 his young sons were taken abroad for safety; one, EDWARD THE EXILE, who had made a career in Hungary, was brought back to England as a possible successor to EDWARD THE CONFESSOR.

EDMUND OF ABINGDON, ST *see* RICH, EDMUND

EDMUND OF LANGLEY, (2nd Earl of Cambridge, 1st Duke of York) (1342–1402), soldier and royal servant. The fourth surviving son of EDWARD III, he fought in France and Spain alongside his brother JOHN OF GAUNT, and in 1372 he married Isabella of Castile, daughter of Pedro the Cruel. Created Earl of Cambridge (1362) and Duke of York (1385), his lack of ambition led his nephew RICHARD II to appoint him Regent during his absences in Ireland; on the second occasion (1399) his lack of action allowed Henry Bolingbroke, later HENRY IV, to overthrow the King.

EDMUND, ST (*c*. 841–70), King of East Anglia (*c*. 855–70). The last king of an independent kingdom of East Anglia, Edmund was killed after being defeated by the Viking 'Great Army' led by HALFDAN and IVAR THE BONELESS. Although the evidence is slender, Edmund may have died in a ritual sacrifice to Scandinavian gods. By the year 900, he was already regarded as a saint, and in *c*. 1020 the monastery of Bury St Edmunds was founded to house his tomb. Although very little is known about the historical Edmund, his cult developed in such a way that later ages regarded him as the epitome of a good king. His shrine at Bury was destroyed in 1538, but a group of bones formerly preserved at Toulouse and now at Arundel (Sussex) is claimed to be his.

EDWARD (1453–71), Prince of Wales. The only child of HENRY VI and MARGARET OF ANJOU, after his father's defeat and capture at Northampton, he was disinherited by the Parliament of Oct. 1460 in favour of RICHARD OF YORK. From then on, he was kept at his mother's side, accompanying her into exile in Scotland and France. In July 1470 he was betrothed to Warwick's (*see* NEVILLE, RICHARD) daughter ANNE NEVILLE, but his involvement in the campaign to restore the Lancastrian dynasty ended with his death at the Battle of Tewkesbury.

EDWARD I *see* essay on pages 274–75

EDWARD II *see* essay on page 277

EDWARD III *see* essay on pages 278–79

EDWARD IV *see* essay on page 280

EDWARD V (1470–?83), King of England (1483). Son of EDWARD IV and ELIZABETH WOODVILLE, he was at Ludlow (Salop.), where his household as Prince of Wales was based, when he succeeded to the throne on 9 April 1483. The Council, dominated by his mother's relatives, fixed his coronation for 4 May, and he was on his way to London in the care of Anthony WOODVILLE, Earl Rivers, when, on 30 April, his uncle Richard of Gloucester (*see* RICHARD III) arrested Rivers and took the 13-year-old boy into custody. Richard then made himself Protector and postponed the coronation until 22 June.

Government business continued to be transacted in Edward V's name until 16 June when another postponement of the coronation (until Nov.) made it plain that the Protector had something else in mind. From 22 June Richard's adherents put forward the argument that all the children of Edward IV and Elizabeth Woodville were illegitimate, although hitherto their legitimacy had been taken for granted, and on 26 June Edward was dethroned and Richard III proclaimed King. Despite at least one scheme to rescue them, Edward and his younger brother Richard, Duke of York, remained in the Tower of London. During the autumn of 1483, while rumours of their deaths circulated, King Richard made no attempt to prove that the boys were alive, most probably because he had by then disposed of them.

In 1674 two skeletons discovered in the Tower were identified as being those of Edward and Richard, the 'princes in the Tower', and were buried in Westminster Abbey. Although a forensic examination carried out in 1933 claimed to confirm this finding, scientists since then have generally remained sceptical.

EDWARD VI *see* essay on page 281

EDWARD VII (1841–1910), King of Great Britain and Ireland (1901–10). The second child of Queen VICTORIA (who was inclined to blame the scandal associated with his wayward behaviour on his father ALBERT's untimely death), Edward was Prince of Wales from the age of one month to 60 years. Largely excluded from royal duties during his near lifetime as heir apparent to the throne, he devoted his attention to society, being cited in two divorce cases, but also encouraged his mother to return to public life after her long withdrawal following the death of Albert.

Coming to the throne on Victoria's death in 1901, Edward proved to be an effective and popular monarch. He was an excellent linguist who was interested in and well informed on foreign affairs. His pro-French sympathies accorded well with Edward GREY's foreign policy. However, contrary to received opinion, the King was not the architect of the Anglo-French *entente*

continued on page 282

EDWARD II (1284–1327)
King of England (1307–27)

His was a tragic reign which proved to be a disastrous turning-point in the history of English politics. Born at Caernarfon, the 11th and youngest child of EDWARD I and ELEANOR OF CASTILE, in 1301 he became the first heir to the throne to bear the title Prince of Wales. A contemporary chronicler described him as 'fair of body and great of strength'; sadly he was also little of brain. Even before his accession in 1307 his indiscretions were causing concern; during his reign these same failings led to new levels of political savagery; in the end they brought about his own downfall and death.

His father left him a difficult legacy, a large debt and a war against a formidable enemy, ROBERT BRUCE. As a new king Edward had the opportunity to achieve a new political consensus and make a fresh start in tackling these problems. Instead he quickly allowed his early years to be bedevilled by quarrels with the barons, who were disturbed, as his father had been, by his (possibly homosexual) infatuation with Piers GAVESTON. In 1311, in an attempt to check his excessive generosity towards his favourite, the baronage drew up a series of reforms, known as the Ordinances, which as well as exiling Gaveston and his associates called for stringent controls on royal appointments and policy. When Edward welcomed Gaveston back civil war broke out, leading, in 1312, to Gaveston's murder. The Scottish victory at Bannockburn two years later added to Edward's humiliations, forcing him to acquiesce in the *de facto* take-over of government by his cousin, THOMAS OF LANCASTER, the man whom he held responsible for Gaveston's death. During the next few years (1315–17) Edward showed himself capable of politic behaviour, gradually forming a group of allies amongst the aristocracy. By 1318 he was in a position to re-assert his own authority. In 1319, however, his inadequacy as a military leader was demonstrated again at the siege of Berwick and, in the following years, he showed himself still susceptible to the blandishments of an avaricious favourite, this time Hugh DESPENSER. By 1321 a widespread anti-Despenser movement had led to renewed civil war. Andrew HARCLAY, fighting for the King, defeated Thomas of Lancaster at the Battle of Boroughbridge (1322). Thomas was beheaded and two dozen nobles were hanged, a judicial bloodbath of unprecedented proportions and Edward's revenge for Gaveston's death. The Scottish war continued to go badly and in 1323 Harclay was himself executed for dealing directly with Robert Bruce.

After destroying their principal opponents, Edward and the Despensers set about enriching themselves with scant regard for law or justice. In 1324 disputes in Gascony led to war with France. ISABELLA OF FRANCE (to whom Edward had been married since Jan. 1308) was sent to Paris to discuss peace terms with her brother, King Charles IV. When she refused to return to England, it became clear that the Despensers' ascendancy had led to the complete alienation of the Queen. In Sept. 1326 she and her lover Roger MORTIMER invaded England. They had only a small force, but since virtually no one would obey Edward's orders it was more than sufficient. The fact that royal finances were now in a 'healthy' state did the King no good at all. The Despensers and some of their associates were either lynched or brutally executed. Edward fled but was captured and taken to Kenilworth (Warws.). In Jan. 1327 Parliament accepted a damning, and largely accurate, indictment of his rule, concluding that, since he was 'incorrigible without hope of amendment', he should be deposed. Edward then abdicated in favour of his 14-year-old son, EDWARD III. He was imprisoned in Berkeley Castle (Glos.), but while alive he remained a potential threat to the government of Mortimer and Isabella. Attempts to rescue him sealed his fate and it was later announced that he had died at Berkeley on 21 Sept. Almost certainly he was murdered, perhaps in gruesome fashion. Some, notably his son's foreign enemies, preferred the story that he had escaped and was living incognito as a hermit. Although stories of the tragic fate of an anointed King led to his tomb in Gloucester Cathedral becoming the focus of a short-lived cult, his reign had, in fact, brought the prestige of monarchy to a new low; before 1485 three more kings of England would be deposed and murdered (nothing like this had happened since Anglo-Saxon times). From now on, moreover, it was not just kings whose lives were in danger. The killings of 1312, 1322 and 1326 ushered in three centuries ('the centuries of blood', F. W. MAITLAND called them) when, in sharp contrast to the previous 200 years, politically active nobles risked ending their lives on the scaffold.

Natalie Fryde, The Tyranny and Fall of Edward II, 1321–1326 (1979)

EDWARD III (1312–77)
King of England (1327–77)

Edward's long reign witnessed both the early stages of a great war, the struggles with France known as the Hundred Years War, and the onset of a great catastrophe, bubonic plague, beginning with the Great Pestilence of 1348–50 which was later known as the Black Death. But no one held the King responsible for bringing plague-carrying rats to England and for centuries after his death people looked back on Edward's reign as a golden age.

They believed that they saw a unified realm basking in the glory of military victories: Crécy, Calais, Poitiers. For them he was a valiant and chivalrous King in whose time England was 'the realm of realms, which won so many victories, captured so many kings and conquered so many lordships'. Many centuries later these were felt to be the wrong criteria and he was judged more harshly. In William STUBBS's opinion he lacked statesmanship, and was ambitious, ostentatious and extravagant. In the second half of the twentieth century the pendulum swung back again and now more weight tends to be given to contemporary opinion.

Since HENRY II's time the kings of England had also been dukes of Aquitaine, but whenever possible they avoided doing to the king of France the homage owed for the duchy. In 1325 EDWARD II sent his 12-year-old heir to Paris to do homage on his behalf. There the boy was used by his mother, ISABELLA OF FRANCE, and her lover Roger MORTIMER to legitimize the coup which they were plotting against the King. In order to raise troops they betrothed him to PHILIPPA OF HAINAULT.

When their invasion succeeded they had him acclaimed King in London in Jan. 1327, when he was just 14. Later that year the young Edward was notionally in command of an army which was outmanoeuvred by the Scots at Stanhope Park (Co. Durham), an experience which reduced the young King to tears of frustration. The 'shameful peace' (Treaty of Northampton) with the Scots in 1328 and the execution of his uncle Edmund of Lancaster in 1330 completed Edward's education. In 1330 he organized the coup that sent Mortimer to the scaffold and took the reins of power into his own hands. Determined to erase the memory of recent humiliations at the hands of the Scots, he espoused the cause of EDWARD BALLIOL. This prompted Philip VI of France to assist the Scots by adopting a more aggressive policy towards Gascony. Thus from 1337 it was the war with

France, rather than with Scotland, that chiefly engaged Edward's attention.

In 1340, primarily to please his Flemish allies (who were technically French subjects), he assumed the title King of France. Despite a naval victory in the Battle of Sluys (24 June 1340), the first stage of the Hundred Years War achieved little and the coalition of allies which he built up turned out to be phenomenally expensive, precipitating the crisis of 1340-1. Lords and Commons in Parliament combined against misrule and heavy taxation; Edward blamed his ministers, chiefly Archbishop John STRATFORD.

Lessons were learned, and although Edward persisted with the war he adopted a less expensive strategy of smaller, shorter campaigns, exploiting divisions within France. The fortunes of war swung in his favour at Crécy (24 Aug. 1346), Calais (1347) and Neville's Cross (17 Oct. 1346) where DAVID II of Scotland was captured. Celebratory tournaments and the foundation of the Order of the Garter (1348–49) asserted Edward's claim to be at the pinnacle of European chivalry, a claim that was widely recognized, and was re-inforced when his son EDWARD THE BLACK PRINCE captured King John of France at the Battle of Poitiers (19 Sept. 1356).

Although peace negotiations revealed that Edward was prepared to drop his claim to the French throne, the territorial gains (Calais, Guines, Ponthieu and Poitou) registered in the Treaty of Brétigny ratified in Oct. 1360 gave him everything that his ancestors had been fighting for since 1259, as well as the promise of a 3 million écu ransom for the French King. Victory brought a more compliant Parliament; the Commons granted him the war-taxes which he wanted, above all the wool subsidy, a tax on wool exported to the continent via Calais, which rapidly became the backbone of Crown finance. Between 1360 and 1371 his subjects enjoyed the longest respite from direct taxation for more than a century, yet the revenues from the export tax on wool and the profits of war enabled Edward to embark on a major building programme (notably the palatial rebuilding of Windsor Castle). In return for the compliance of their representatives, the MPs, Edward allowed the gentry a greater say in affairs, both centrally and, through Justices of the Peace, in the shires. This combination of vested interests created the political and financial system which had to face the shattering demographic and economic crisis triggered by the Black Death.

The epidemic arrived in England in 1348, and by 1350 it had probably carried off about 40 per cent of the population. Henry Knighton observed that crops perished in the fields for lack of harvesters and that even livestock wandered freely in the absence of anyone watching over them. The sudden drop in the supply of labour resulted in a demand for higher wages. King, lords and gentry, landlords and employers all, were alarmed.

While the pestilence still raged it was thought to be too dangerous to assemble in Parliament, but Edward III's Council responded to the economic crisis by issuing the Ordinance of Labourers in June 1349. This was chiefly intended to peg wages at pre-plague levels although it also ordered innkeepers and others not to charge exorbitant prices for food and drink. According to Knighton, 'the workmen were so arrogant and obstinate that they did not heed the King's mandate'. When Parliament finally met in Feb. 1351 it converted the ordinance into a statute and for many years the authorities, in particular the Justices of the Peace, worked vigorously to enforce these Acts. Until 1362 the government even allowed the amount collected in fines for excess wages to be set against a county's tax assessment.

It seems that in 1348 England had been an over-populated country and in the decade after 1350 population levels rose quite quickly, so for a while these measures had some effect. But the plague struck again in 1361–2, 1368–9 and 1374–5 and these recurring visitations inhibited longer-term demographic recovery. A sudden price rise in 1362–3 was allegedly caused by a combination of guild monopoly and the aspirations of people who wanted to enjoy a lifestyle above their station. The government responded by passing sumptuary laws (designed to limit personal expenditure to 'appropriate' levels), but reversed its policy a year later, again in response to lobbying in the Commons.

Like all governments Edward III's was fairly helpless against economic forces which it barely understood. Crown and ruling classes were just as united against the wage demands of their poorer compatriots as they were against the French. Nonetheless, by the end of Edward's reign the economic climate in England favoured workers rather than employers and did so at a time when government legislation and its enforcement had heightened class tension. In Parliament speakers were beginning to worry about a peasants' revolt.

In the meantime the French, now led by the astute Charles V, had renewed the war in 1369 and were recovering lost territory. Aged 55 in 1369, the easy-going Edward wished, not surprisingly, to leave campaigning to his sons. The Black Prince's illness meant, however, that he was no longer an inspirational commander. Moreover 1369 had seen the death of the popular Queen Philippa and her replacement in the King's bed by Alice PERRERS, a mistress with political ambitions. The dominance that she and a clique of courtiers eventually obtained over a senile King provoked an explosion of criticism in the Good Parliament of 1376. Edward died on 21 June 1377, comforted by a single priest, abandoned even by Alice (so, at least, a monkish author would have us believe).

It was unfortunate for his reputation that Edward lived as long as he did. War had been his driving ambition, and he had got on supremely well with those, lords and gentry, who had shared in the enterprise. He owed much of his success and his popularity with patriotic Englishmen to his own enthusiastic participation in the theatre of war, deeds of arms and courtly spectacles. But by 1377 he was no longer vigorous and the glory years were long since past.

Some modern historians, out of sympathy with a warrior-king who went light-heartedly to war, have dwelt on the rural unrest and the scandals which overshadowed the end of his reign. They have also argued that his apparent successes were bought at the price of concessions to both lords and gentry which undermined the longterm future of monarchy.

But Parliament was not the Crown's enemy and the rights of royal lordship were still being exploited by the Tudors; they had not been given away. Edward had shared, embodied and projected the values and ideals which held sway in his own day. His long reign had produced a sense of stability, and when he died it was his achievements which were remembered, both his military triumphs and a long period of domestic peace which was all the more remarkable given the low ebb to which events at home and abroad between 1307 and 1330 had brought the English Crown.

W. M. Ormrod, The Reign of Edward III: Crown and Political Society in England, 1327–1377 (1990)
Scott L. Waugh, England in the Reign of Edward III (1991)

EDWARD IV (1442–83)
King of England (1461–83)

As the eldest son (with the title Earl of March) of RICHARD OF YORK and Cecily Neville, he was only 17 when he began to play an adult's part in his father's armed struggle against the Lancastrian regime. In every respect he was well equipped for the role. Intelligent and brave, his skeleton shows him to have been 6 feet 3 inches tall, and powerfully built; clad in high-quality armour, he was a force to be reckoned with on the battlefields of the Wars of the Roses, an inspirational leader. But his earliest experience of war was a humiliating one; in Oct. 1459 the Yorkists fled from Ludford Bridge (Salop.) rather than fight against King HENRY VI. While his father escaped to Ireland, Edward found sanctuary with his cousin Warwick (*see* NEVILLE, RICHARD) in Calais. From there he helped the Nevilles to launch the invasion of England which culminated in their capture of the King at the Battle of Northampton in July 1460. A Yorkist Parliament decided in Oct. that after Henry's death he should be succeeded by Richard of York and his heirs. Two months later, in Dec. 1460, Richard was killed at Wakefield (Yorks.) and Edward became the Yorkist heir to Henry VI's Crown. In Feb. 1461 Warwick's defeat at St Albans meant that the Yorkists lost possession of King Henry and were forced into a hasty assertion of Edward's kingship, a momentous step facilitated by the young man's recent victory, in his first independent command, over Jasper TUDOR in the Battle of Mortimer's Cross (Herefs.). No sooner had he been proclaimed King (March 1461) than he marched north and crushed the Lancastrians at the Battle of Towton (Yorks.).

The crisis over, he relaxed and enjoyed the pleasures of being King, although he always remained the guiding hand behind major issues of policy (somewhat to the chagrin of Warwick who felt it should be his). Since Edward possessed the natural politician's gift of never forgetting name and face, he probably had too much faith in his own ability to keep friends and charm former enemies; at least this meant that he rarely felt the need to be unforgiving. The only foolish thing he did, in political terms, was to marry for love. The fact that for four months he kept his May 1464 marriage to ELIZABETH WOODVILLE a secret even from his closest advisers shows that he foresaw some of the political consequences that would flow from marrying a widow with two children,

five brothers and seven unmarried sisters. The clandestine marriage contributed to the breakdown in trust between Edward and Warwick which precipitated the second crisis of the reign. In July 1469 Warwick, conspiring with Clarence (*see* PLANTAGENET, GEORGE), took Edward prisoner, only to be forced by public opinion to release him two months later. In March 1470 Edward's prompt and ruthless response to the Lincolnshire rising forced Warwick and Clarence to escape to France, where they joined forces with MARGARET OF ANJOU. In Sept. it was Edward's turn to flee when taken by surprise by Warwick's hitherto loyal brother, John Neville, Marquess of Montagu. But with naval support from Duke Charles of Burgundy he was able to return to England in March 1471. Within two nerve-wracking months he had recovered the throne, acting first deviously to disarm opposition, then diplomatically, to win over Clarence, and finally with such speed and determination that he was able to bring his enemies to battle separately, at Barnet (Herts.) and Tewkesbury (Glos.). Henry VI, whom he had captured in 1465 and allowed to live, was now murdered on his orders. Clarence, after continuing to intrigue against his brother, finally met the same fate in 1478. In 1475 Edward invaded France in alliance with Burgundy, but allowed himself to be bought off by the Treaty of Picquigny. In 1480 he resurrected English claims to lordship over Scotland, setting up the Duke of Albany (*see* STEWART, ALEXANDER) as a puppet king against his brother JAMES III, and in 1482 his troops recaptured Berwick. His death came suddenly in April 1483, the result of an illness which some historians blame on his own excesses.

Unexpectedly propelled to the throne at the age of 18 in the midst of one of the most tumultuous periods of the Wars of the Roses, he had seized every opportunity with courage and aplomb. In the crises of his reign he demonstrated political intelligence and leadership of the highest order. But his promiscuous lifestyle offended puritans both then and since and this has sometimes led to unrealistic denunciations of him as a lazy and pleasure-loving King who failed to foresee that the consequence of over-indulgence would be his own early death and the tragic circumstances in which his brother, RICHARD III, would ascend the throne.

Charles Ross, Edward IV (1974)

EDWARD VI (1537–53)
King of England and Ireland (1547–53)

HENRY VIII's longed-for son by JANE SEYMOUR, who died 12 days after his birth, became King on 28 Jan. 1547. Edward's tutors (perhaps thanks to his godfather Archbishop CRANMER) were of reformist religious outlook, particularly John CHEKE, Richard COX and Anthony COOKE. Henry arranged in his will for a Council of Regency weighted towards Evangelical (Protestant) sympathizers, including Edward's uncle, Edward SEYMOUR: Seymour manoeuvred his colleagues into recognizing him as Lord Protector of the Realm, and took the title Duke of Somerset. Somerset's efforts to monopolize access to the King were challenged unsuccessfully by Thomas SEYMOUR in 1548–9 and successfully by John DUDLEY, Duke of Northumberland, in Oct. 1549. In this crisis Somerset tried to exploit his possession of Edward by taking him from Hampton Court to Windsor Castle ostensibly to defend him against the other Councillors, but Cranmer and William PAGET persuaded the Protector to abandon resistance. In the aftermath, it may well have been Edward's own insistence on being surrounded by reformist gentlemen in his Privy Chamber that prevented religious conservatives from exploiting Somerset's overthrow to regain political power. He seems to have resented the Protector, and the evidence suggests that he reacted without much emotion to Somerset's execution (1551). By contrast, he liked John Dudley, who made a point of respecting his growing wish for power and punctiliously brought him into political decision-making. From 1550, the growing teenager was never a negligible factor in politics, being always ready to endorse the radical religious changes being put through by the government, though he showed a grasp of political detail which sometimes disconcerted his adult political advisers. From 1551 he played a major personal role in confronting his half-sister the future MARY I over her refusal to conform to the new liturgy, and in winter 1553 he was beginning to take a direct role in government expenditure. By now, however, his previously robust health was giving way. Commonly it has been suggested that he had tuberculosis, but his symptoms suggest complications developing from pneumonia. Edward was appalled at the thought of Mary's succession, and it may have been he rather than Northumberland who made the initial move to divert the succession from both his half-sisters to his cousin JANE GREY. His death came more quickly than expected, which may account for Northumberland's inept failure to round up Mary from her country residence and neutralize her bid for the throne.

Edward's considerable body of surviving papers, a remarkable archive of a Tudor deluxe education, witnesses to a lively mind quick to learn, with a passionate commitment to thoroughgoing religious reformation, and a delight in sport and military display; his personal 'Chronicle' (journal) is a document of major historical importance. His one close friend in his generation, Barnaby Fitzpatrick, an Irish nobleman's son, later returned home as Baron of Upper Ossory, and witnessed to the enduring memory of his friendship by being one of the very few completely reliable loyalists to the English government in Ireland.

Edward's brief reign had major consequences for the future of the British Isles. In religion, the Church structures, reformed liturgy and doctrinal statement formulated under Thomas Cranmer's guidance were restored with little modification by ELIZABETH I, and are still normative for the Church of England today. Official religious policy would never again be so radical except in the Interregnum of 1649–60, and there was systematic destruction of Church art, together with a thoroughgoing plunder of Church assets which has left the impression of a greedy and secular-minded political elite intent on turning Reformation to its own profit. There is truth in this image, though it must also be remembered that the government was desperately short of resources after the wars begun by Henry VIII in the 1540s, and the Church provided a convenient source of cash. Edward's reign saw the first officially backed moves to turn English maritime strength to ventures of world exploration (*see* WILLOUGHBY, HUGH and CHANCELLOR, RICHARD); there was also a spirited attempt to unite the whole British archipelago under English rule. Somerset's government invaded Scotland in order to secure the marriage of Edward and MARY QUEEN OF SCOTS, but it also sought to charm the Scots into a union, using newly coined propaganda stressing common British identity. The effort was inept and in the short term a failure, but by 1603 a union of crowns seemed a natural outgrowth of the religious links set up in the Edwardian era, instead of the bizarre mismatch of opposed peoples which it would have been a century before. In Ireland it was Edward's government which planned the fatal policy of planting settlers from overseas in colonies. In Wales evangelicals made the first efforts to establish a native Protestant culture which later became central to Welsh identity. *See also* SALESBURY, WILLIAM.

Jennifer Loach, Edward VI (1999)

(the *Entente Cordiale*) of 1904 nor the Anglo-Russian agreement of 1907. He was an enthusiastic supporter and European contacts man rather than an instigator. Although, as during the build-up to the Parliament Act 1911, he revealed that he could occasionally be heir to his mother's tradition of political intervention, in general he played the role of a twentieth-century constitutional monarch, who, though he enjoyed and understood the role of monarchical pomp and circumstance, also understood the limits of royal authority.

EDWARD VIII (Duke of Windsor) (1894–1972), King of Great Britain and Ireland and Emperor of India (1936). The eldest son of GEORGE V and Queen Mary, strict parents much concerned to instil correct regal ways into the heir to the throne, he was educated, briefly, at Oxford and during the First World War had a non-combatant role with the British Expeditionary Force in France. Invested as Prince of Wales in 1911, in 1919 he embarked on the first of a series of tours of the British Empire, which were a great personal success, showing not only the British monarchy's imperial commitment but also the Prince's easy-going charm.

More akin to his grandfather, EDWARD VII, than to his harsh, disciplinarian father, as shown in his relations with women, he fell in love, after a series of flirtations and dalliances, with a married American divorcée from Baltimore, Mrs Wallis SIMPSON. Unlike his grandfather, he wished to regularize the union. Though the press kept the liaison secret, the Conservative government knew about it only too well, and was appalled. Edward was already regarded as unsound on political matters because, in his self-appointed role as the 'people's prince', he was given to visiting areas of Britain hit hardest by the Depression, where he talked sympathetically to the unemployed. And in 1926, after the collapse of the General Strike, he had contributed £10 to the miners' relief fund, suggesting in the accompanying note that the miners had been obliged to 'give in on account of the sufferings of their dependants'.

George V died in Jan. 1936, and it looked as if Edward as King would prove unsound also on constitutional matters and bring the monarchy into disrepute, since in Oct. 1936 Ernest Simpson divorced his wife and Edward intended to marry her. 'The King's matter' dominated politics: he suggested a morganatic marriage by which he would have a wife but no Queen. The Prime Minister, Stanley BALDWIN (further incensed by what could be construed as an attack on the Conservatives' economic policies when, in Nov. 1936 while on a visit to the unemployment black spot of south Wales, the King had pronounced 'something must be done to find them work')

would not countenance this, neither would the Labour leader, ATTLEE, nor those Dominion leaders who were consulted. On 10 Dec. 1936 Edward signed the instrument of abdication and the following day, no longer king, travelled to France where he and Wallis Simpson were married on 3 June 1937. The new King, his brother GEORGE VI, bestowed the title Duke and Duchess of Windsor on the newly-weds but the Duchess was forbidden to style herself 'Her Royal Highness'.

The bitterness between the Windsors and the British monarchy and government continued. Edward was groundlessly feared as a possible 'king over the water', and suspected of pro-Fascist sympathies: he visited Hitler in Oct. 1937, and after France fell in 1940 the Windsors fled to Fascist Spain, from where CHURCHILL dispatched them to the Bahamas for the Duke to take up the post of Governor. It was not until 1967 that the Windsors were invited to Britain for an official function, though some sort of royal pardon was forthcoming, since after his death in Paris the Duke's body was brought back for burial in the royal mausoleum at Frogmore, Windsor.

EDWARD BALLIOL (*c.* 1283–1364), King of Scots (1332–56). On the death of ROBERT BRUCE in 1328, Edward, son of JOHN BALLIOL, was encouraged to claim the Scottish throne. In Sept. 1332, after the victory at Dupplin Moor (Perths.), he was crowned at Scone (Perths.). His hold on his kingdom was always precarious, and his dependence on English arms led him to do homage to EDWARD III in 1333. Three years later, he was forced to retire to the English court, and in 1356, he surrendered all claim to the Scottish Crown to Edward III.

EDWARD BRUCE *see* essay on page 283

EDWARD OF YORK (1st Duke of Aumale, 1st Earl of Rutland, 2nd Duke of York) (*c.* 1373–1415), courtier. He succeeded his father EDMUND OF LANGLEY in 1402. A favourite of RICHARD II, who made him Earl of Rutland and then, in 1397, Duke of Aumale, he was variously suspected of murdering THOMAS OF WOODSTOCK in 1397, abandoning Richard II in 1399 and plotting against HENRY IV in 1405. He survived all these accusations and eventually met an honourable death at the Battle of Agincourt. He founded, and was buried in, the collegiate church of Fotheringhay (Northants.).

EDWARD THE BLACK PRINCE (1330–76), Prince of Wales. The name Black Prince was given (for unknown reasons) to EDWARD III's eldest son in the sixteenth century. His semi-legendary fame is chiefly due to FROISSART's romanticized and unreliable story of the rise and fall of a chivalric hero.

continued on page 284

EDWARD BRUCE (?–1318)
King of Ireland (1315–18)

He was the younger brother of ROBERT BRUCE and the key figure in the Bruces' campaign to create a pan-Celtic alliance against the English. Had his bid to be King of Ireland succeeded, the political history of these islands might well have taken a very different course.

A vigorous and bold soldier, Edward was one of his brother's chief lieutenants in the war that won Scotland. By 1309 Robert had made him Lord of Galloway, and Earl of Carrick in 1313. In this year he laid siege to Stirling Castle and, according to the doubtful evidence of John BARBOUR, it was his rash decision to grant the garrison a year's respite which forced the more prudent Robert to risk battle against EDWARD II's relieving army. However that may be, the Battle at Bannockburn (Aug. 1314), where Edward Bruce commanded the leading Scottish brigade, ended in the most humiliating defeat ever suffered by English arms and allowed the Bruces to take the initiative. In May 1315 Edward landed on the Antrim coast with a large army, including many veterans of Bannockburn, and at once blockaded Carrickfergus. He took the title King of Ireland with the support of a number of Irish kings, notably DOMNALL UA NÉILL, King of Tír Eógain. In a famous letter, the Remonstrance of the Irish Princes (1317), Domnall explained to the Pope that the Irish had turned to Bruce 'to throw off the harsh and intolerable yoke of servitude' which they suffered under the English, 'who say that it is no more sin to kill an Irishman than a dog'. As early as 1307 the Bruces had looked to the Irish for support, appealing to the 'common language and common custom' which linked Scots and Irish and expressing the hope that their one nation would be able to recover its ancient liberty. By 1316 it was rumoured that if Bruce succeeded in Ireland, he would raise the Welsh in rebellion, 'for these two peoples curse English domination and resent the yoke to which they are subjected'. The whole future shape of the British Isles was at stake.

Playing the pan-Celtic card made it very unlikely that the English of Ireland would support Bruce, but he and his Irish allies won some early successes in battle, notably against the most powerful magnate in Ireland, Richard de BURGH, 2nd Earl of Ulster and Lord of Connacht. When Carrickfergus fell in 1316 Bruce made it his capital, held court and summoned Parliaments. Twice Robert Bruce came over to Ireland and in Feb. 1317 the brothers came within a few miles of Dublin, only to decide against a siege. Instead they marched south and west, trying as in 1315–16 to make Edward's kingship a reality in the manner of earlier Irish 'high-kings', touring the island and taking tribute and hostages. But the fierce rivalry within native dynasties meant that for every Irish ally they won they also made an enemy or two. Moreover, a series of harvest failures in 1315–17 made the presence of an army even more burdensome than usual. When at last a good harvest allowed Edward Bruce to take the initiative again he was unexpectedly killed at the Battle of Fochart (near Dundalk) on 14 Oct. 1318.

It had been a major crisis in the history of the British Isles. By 1300 the English king's lordship of Ireland was producing a fair profit for the Crown, perhaps as much as 15 per cent of total royal revenue. Despite some signs of strain at its end, the thirteenth century had witnessed a continuing expansion of English control and administration, through castles, towns, sheriffs and judges, on the back of a substantial movement of English settlers into Ireland. In his attempt to complete the English conquest of Britain, EDWARD I deployed Irish resources in Wales and Scotland. This was the process which the Bruces set out to reverse, to deprive the English of Irish resources and place them instead at the disposal of the Scots. Indeed Edward Bruce might have become King of both Scots and Irish since in 1315 Robert had no sons and he made his brother his heir. Although the Scottish King of Ireland was defeated, the English colony in Ireland suffered a blow from which it would not recover for centuries. The area under Dublin control contracted: Crown revenue fell away, and the island became a drain on English royal resources. Although much of this might have happened without Edward Bruce, the fact remains that he gave dramatically added impetus to the Gaelic revival. He came close to conquering Ireland and might have done so, had it not been for the wet summers of 1315–17.

Colm McNamee, The Wars of the Bruces: Scotland, England and Ireland 1306–1328 (1997)

Having been entrusted by his father with nominal command of the van at Crécy so that (in Froissart's phrase) 'the boy might win his spurs', he went on to become one of the outstanding English leaders in the Hundred Years War. In 1355 he conducted a destructive and profitable expedition through Languedoc; the raid of 1356 culminated in the Battle of Poitiers, where he plucked triumph out of near disaster. Having married JOAN OF KENT (presumably for love) in 1361, he intervened in Spain on behalf of Peter I of Castile, winning the Battle of Najera in 1367 but also contracting the disease (possibly a form of dysentery) that was to dog the last 10 years of his life. He expected the population of Aquitaine, of which he had been made Prince in 1362, to meet the costs of the Spanish campaign. His tax demands provided some of the more independent French lords, already hostile to a regime that took little account of regional tradition, with the perfect opportunity to challenge English lordship. In the war that followed, he took the city of Limoges by assault (1370) and, according to Froissart, ordered the massacre of its inhabitants. The following year he returned to England where, although he enjoyed tremendous prestige, his illness kept him in the background until his death.

EDWARD THE CONFESSOR, ST *see* essay on pages 286–87

EDWARD THE ELDER (*c*. 870–924), King of Wessex (899–924) and King of Mercia (*c*. 918–24). A son of ALFRED THE GREAT, Edward's great achievement was to subdue, in alliance with his sister ETHELFLÆD, Lady of the Mercians, all the Danes south of the Humber. After overcoming a challenge to his succession from his cousin ETHELWOLD, Edward campaigned regularly against the Danes, gaining a notable victory over the settlers in the kingdom of York, which had been established by HALFDAN, at the Battle of Tettenhall (Staffs.) in 910. His acquisitions were consolidated by the construction of planned towns which are called 'burhs'; he also issued law-codes and patronized the Church. After the deaths of Ethelflæd and her daughter, ÆLFWYNN, in 918 and 919 respectively, he became effective ruler of both Wessex and Mercia, as well as overlord of the kingdom of York. These developments represent a significant, if possibly accidental, step in the unification of England into a single kingdom. Edward himself may well not have actually intended to combine the kingdoms, since he was succeeded in Wessex by Ælfweard, a son of his second marriage to ÆLFFLÆD, and in Mercia by ATHELSTAN, a son of his first marriage; Ælfweard's death, two weeks after his father, allowed Athelstan to take the whole inheritance for himself. The revival of the kingdom of York under RAGNALL meant that Edward's successors had to conduct a long series of campaigns. He was outlived by his third wife, the formidable EADGIFU.

EDWARD THE EXILE (?–1057), a son of King EDMUND IRONSIDE. In exile after CNUT's triumph in 1016, he eventually became domiciled in Hungary, but was recalled to England in 1057, presumably as a likely successor to the childless EDWARD THE CONFESSOR. He died soon after reaching England, but there is no serious evidence to indicate that his death was not a natural one. His son EDGAR THE ÆTHELING was briefly proclaimed King of England in London in 1066.

EDWARD THE MARTYR, ST (*c*. 963–78), King of the English (975–8). He was about 12 at the time of his accession, and the sparse evidence suggests that his reign was typified by conditions approximating to civil war. He was murdered on 18 March 978 by retainers serving his younger half-brother ETHELRED II THE UNREADY, who then became King. By 1000 Edward was widely regarded as a saint and miracles were recorded at his tomb in Shaftesbury Abbey. There can be little doubt that his posthumous reputation was enhanced by the disasters that befell England during Ethelred's reign.

EDWARDES, SIR MICHAEL (1930–), industrialist. Born in South Africa, he initially worked in his father's Cape Battery Co. He moved to Britain to work for Chloride in 1951; he was taken onto its board aged 39, when he had already shown the skill in rationalizing businesses. Chairman of Chloride (1974–7) when profits soared he was then appointed to the National Enterprise Board before becoming Chairman and Chief Executive of troubled British Leyland (1977–82). He rapidly instituted a 'survival plan' and sought a deal with the long-militant trade unions. During his time there, the workforce was almost halved, management styles were radically altered and labour relations improved.

EDWARDS, ROBERT (1925–), physiologist. Edwards studied medicine at Edinburgh University, where, in the 1950s, he successfully replanted embryos in mice. In 1963 he moved to the physiology department at Cambridge University, where he sought to apply this technique to human embryos and to tackle the problem of female infertility. His attempts were not successful, but in 1968 he met Patrick Steptoe, a distinguished English gynaecologist who had invented an instrument (a 'laparascope') for extracting mature eggs from the uterus, and collaborated with him on a method for fertilizing extracted mature eggs in a culture outside the uterus and then replanting the embryo in the uterus for natural development (*in vitro* fertilization). After 10 years of unsuccessful trials, Edwards and Steptoe had refined their technique and managed successfully to replant a fertilized embryo. In July 1978 the first child to be conceived by their method was born and became the first of many 'test-tube' babies.

EDWARDS, THOMAS (1599–1647), churchman. A Cambridge don turned London preacher who was disciplined by Archbishop LAUD for his attacks on Arminian ceremonialist theology and practice in the Church. During the arguments about the future shape of Church government during the English Civil War (1642–6) he became an aggressive Presbyterian, pouring his energy into attacks on Independents (Separatists) and the more radical sects, notably in his exceptionally vicious and informative book *Gangraena* (1646).

EDWIN (?–633), King of Northumbria (616–33). The son of a king of Deira, he was driven into exile by ETHELFRITH, the first King of the united Northumbria, and spent his youth at the court of REDWALD of East Anglia. In 616, he and Redwald defeated and killed Ethelfrith in battle, and Edwin succeeded to the Northumbrian throne. He had a Christian wife, St ETHELBURH, and also allowed the missionary PAULINUS to come into his kingdom (*see also* COIFI); his own conversion, accomplished by Paulinus and described by BEDE, seems to have taken a long time. He was a great warrior, who was included in Bede's list of what were later termed Bretwaldas and was said by him to have been more powerful than any previous English king. He died in battle at Hatfield Chase near Doncaster, defeated by PENDA of Mercia and the British King CADWALLON of Gwynedd. His death was followed by a period of civil war before Ethelfrith's son, St OSWALD, established himself as King over the single kingdom of Northumbria.

EDWIN (?–1071), Earl of Mercia (*c.* 1062–71) The son and successor of Earl Ælfgar of Mercia, he supported HAROLD II in 1066, but was afterwards able to come to terms with WILLIAM I THE CONQUEROR. He was taken to Normandy as an honoured 'guest' in 1067 and, despite retaining his earldom, complained that he was being treated dishonourably. He rebelled on two occasions, and was ultimately killed by his own men.

EGBERT (?–673), King of Kent (664–73). Son of King EORCONBERHT, Egbert's murder of his two cousins led to the foundation of the two important minsters at Sheppey-in-Thanet and Reculver, the latter of whose Anglo-Saxon churches stood until it was substantially demolished in 1809. Egbert's

control over Surrey and his co-operation with King OSWY of Northumbria indicate the continuing political importance of the kings of Kent at this period.

EGBERT (?–766), Archbishop of York (732–66). An active churchman and correspondent of BEDE, Egbert obtained papal permission to make York an archbishopric in accordance with Pope Gregory the Great's plan. He also made the school at York possibly the most distinguished in Europe; its most famous pupil, ALCUIN OF YORK, became Charlemagne's spiritual adviser. His co-operation with his brother King EADBERHT of Northumbria was a notably fruitful one. He was succeeded by his relative, the distinguished teacher and churchman, ÆLBERHT.

EGBERT (?–839), King of Wessex (802–39). A great warrior king, who briefly dominated all the other kingdoms of England after he had defeated King BEORNWULF of Mercia at the Battle of Ellendun (Wroughton, Wilts.) in 825. This achievement should not be seen as a true unification of England, since its character was as personal and ephemeral as the supremacy of the Mercian Kings ETHELBALD and OFFA. Mercia under King WIGLAF and Northumbria under King EANRED threw off Wessex's control in 830. Egbert's permanent achievement was the incorporation into Wessex of south-west England, after the Battle of Hingston Down in 838, and of the former kingdom of Kent. He thereby created the kingdom that would eventually form the basis for the unification of England that began under ALFRED THE GREAT. He was succeeded by his son ETHELWULF.

EGBERT OF IONA, ST ('THE ENGLISHMAN'), (639–729), monk. A Northumbrian who spent most of his life among the Irish and Scots, Egbert became a monk at Iona in 716 after a long period as a monk in Ireland. He was, like other monks of his age and kind, an adviser of kings, and is also said to have finally persuaded the community of Iona (*see* DÚNCHAD) to accept the Roman date of Easter. He was also a teacher, and under his influence one of his pupils, St WILLIBRORD, undertook missionary work among the Frisians. Our main informant for his life is BEDE.

EGERTON, FRANCIS (3rd Duke of Bridgwater) (1736–1803), investor in canals. Succeeding to the title at the age of 12, he had little formal education. He withdrew from London society in 1759 following an unhappy love affair, and concentrated on developing his considerable estates in Lancs. Intending to build a canal to convey coal from his collieries at Worsley to Manchester, he approached

continued on page 288

EDWARD THE CONFESSOR, ST (c. 1005–66)
King of the English (1042–66)

The eldest son of ETHELRED II THE UNREADY and his second wife EMMA, Edward was driven into exile in Normandy in 1013 by the invading armies of the Danish King, SVEIN FORKBEARD, and his son CNUT. Cnut's succession to the English kingdom and his marriage to Emma in 1017 created a complex personal and political network which initially removed all prospect of Edward returning to England. He therefore remained in Normandy under the protection of his uncle, Duke RICHARD II (996–1026), his cousin, Duke ROBERT I (1027–35), and his nephew, the young WILLIAM I THE CONQUEROR, and developed strong personal bonds with his Norman relatives. After Cnut's death in 1035, both Edward and his brother ALFRED visited England in 1036, having apparently been encouraged to do so by their mother, with Alfred dying a violent death as the result of a betrayal to which GODWINE, Earl of Wessex, may have been an accomplice. In 1041 Edward was summoned back to England by the sickly and childless King HARTHACNUT (1040–2), a son of Cnut's by Emma, who designated him as his successor. In 1042 Edward succeeded peacefully to the English kingdom.

As King, Edward was thrust into a political situation which was largely an inheritance from Cnut's reign, and within which his room for manoeuvre was limited. The kingdom's politics were dominated by the three great families of Godwine, Earl of Wessex, LEOFRIC, Earl of Mercia, and SIWARD, Earl of Northumbria; of the three, Godwine was unquestionably the most powerful. In addition, Cnut's Danish kindred retained an interest in the English succession, and early in his reign Edward, probably in order to acquire breathing space, appears to have promised Cnut's grandson, SVEIN ESTRITHSSON, King of Denmark, that he would be his successor. In these early years, Edward's sense of obligation to Godwine seems to have been a very strong one, and in 1043–44 the Earl's eldest sons, SVEIN and the future King HAROLD II, were advanced to earldoms, while in 1045 he married the Earl's daughter EDITH. Towards 1050, however, Edward was able to advance some relatives and protégés from France, of whom his nephew RALPH, who became Earl of Hereford, and the churchman ROBERT OF JUMIÈGES were the most important.

Edward's reign up until c. 1050 was largely peaceful and prosperous. In 1051, however, he moved against Godwine and his family, an attack which was probably fuelled by a long build-up of resentment and represents a bid for greater political freedom on Edward's part. The available near-contemporary sources present differing versions of events and all have their own particular bias. The various versions of the *Anglo-Saxon Chronicle* mention a quarrel between Edward and Godwine about the latter's supposed failure to punish a riot which occurred at Dover during a visit to England by the King's brother-in-law, Count Eustace of Boulogne. The *Vita Ædwardi Regis*, written between 1065 and 1067 for Queen Edith, refers to the intrigues of Edward's Norman protégé, Robert of Jumièges, who had been appointed to the archbishopric of Canterbury against the claims of a relative of Godwine; Robert apparently reminded Edward of his brother Alfred's death and suggested that Godwine was now plotting against him. A third element, deducible from the main Norman sources, is that Edward had conveyed some sort of promise of succession to the English kingdom to the young Duke of Normandy (later William I the Conqueror) through the intermediacy of Robert of Jumièges in the spring of 1051 before the outbreak of hostilities with Godwine; this promise, which is unlikely to have been popular with the Earl, appears to have been guaranteed by the dispatch to Normandy of hostages from the Earl's family, including his youngest son WULFNOTH. With the acquiescence of Leofric and Siward, Godwine and his sons were forced into exile and Queen Edith was shut away in a nunnery. Duke William visited England shortly afterwards, presumably to confirm the agreement made earlier with Robert of Jumièges. A number of Edward's personal favourites were in the meantime advanced to earldoms and other positions of power. Edward's triumph was, however, short-lived. Godwine and his sons invaded England in the summer of 1052 to secure their reinstatement. The English nobility, said to have been unwilling to start a civil war, refused to fight against them. Edith was reinstated and although Godwine died in 1053, the succeeding years witnessed the rise of his sons to unrivalled dominance within the kingdom; alongside Harold, TOSTIG, GYRTH and LEOFWINE also received earldoms during the 1050s. The probability that negotiations began around 1054 for the return to England of EDWARD THE EXILE, a grandson of Ethelred the Unready's first marriage, suggests that the childless Edward was also forced, at least publicly, to abandon his plans for Duke William's succession.

With Godwine's progeny securely in control, the English kingdom was largely at peace from 1052 until 1065, in spite of minor internal political turbulence involving quarrels between Godwine's sons and Leofric's son, Earl ÆLFGAR of Mercia. The English were able to intervene successfully in Scotland and Wales, with Edward supporting Earl Siward's expedition to Scotland in 1054 which led to the overthrow of King MACBETH and the installation of the English protégé MAEL COLUIM III CENN MÓR. In Wales the great power built up by GRUFFUDD AP LLYWELYN was destroyed by Harold's 1063 campaign. Edward the Exile's death, however, in 1057 shortly after his return to England ensured that the succession remained a live issue. In 1064 or 1065 Edward ordered Harold to visit Normandy. Whatever the motives for the visit – Norman sources say that it was made to reaffirm the promise of the succession whereas English suggest that it was merely a diplomatic mission, or even an accident – its outcome was an oath by Harold to support William's claim to be the next King of the English. Soon afterwards, in the autumn of 1065, the Northumbrian nobility revolted against Tostig's rule and marched south. Edward's response was to seek to make war on the rebels, but he received insufficient support and had ultimately to agree to peace terms negotiated by Harold, which involved the removal from office and exile of Tostig. At some point during these negotiations, the King suffered the first of a series of strokes. As he lay dying over Christmas at Westminster, he bequeathed the English kingdom to Harold. The main source for Edward's last days, the *Vita Ædwardi Regis*, tells us that the King experienced visions on his deathbed which were interpreted as prophecies of catastrophes to come. He died on 5 Jan. and Harold was crowned the next day.

Edward's government of England continued the well-organized regime of his predecessors. Particular attention can be drawn to a silver coinage which was regularly reminted to a high standard and the increasing extensive use of the writ to make known royal confirmations of property transactions and, occasionally, royal administrative instructions. The Church in England was for the most part in good condition during the reign. Although Archbishop STIGAND of Canterbury was in some respects disreputable, there were many churchmen within the kingdom of high quality; Edward himself was probably personally responsible for some improvements through his sponsorship of episcopal appointments such as LEOFRIC of Exeter, and others like him, who had been educated on the continent. Edward's rule sustained England's predominance

within the British Isles. The reign could undoubtedly be judged a success, but for the dramatic events which followed the King's death, and for which the extent of his direct responsibility has been hotly debated. In this context, the King's personality and motives have been a source of considerable debate. The *Vita Ædwardi Regis* presents an image of a saintly, unworldly King who left the day-to-day running of the kingdom to Godwine and later to Harold and his brothers. It is also the earliest source for Edward's chastity. Although the *Vita*'s evidence was taken by later ages as indicating that the King and Queen abstained from sexual relations out of personal piety, it should probably not be read in that way. Written as it was on Edith's behalf against the background of the succession crisis which followed Edward's death, it very much suited her interests to explain a childless marriage in terms of her husband's sanctity. Given the numerous references to Edward's vigour and activity, the *Vita*'s portrayal of a passive personality is also probably false.

The crucial background to Edward's rule and the Norman Conquest was the sequence of succession disputes which had afflicted the English kingdom since the tenth century. The Scandinavian interest in the succession created by Cnut's conquest served only to deepen the crisis. Edward's personal contribution was to add William of Normandy to the cast-list of claimants; in the face of persistent opposition in England, his loyalty to the family which had given him succour during his years of exile can be seen as stubbornness verging on perversity. It exemplifies the kind of occasional obduracy such as the attack on Godwine's family in 1051–2. The events of 1066 demonstrated beyond any doubt that, in the circumstances which followed Edward's death, Harold was a generally acceptable choice and, in contrast to EDGAR THE ÆTHELING, an able and effective adult with a chance of riding the storms to come. Edward's deathbed designation of Harold was a final act of pragmatism by a man who had for most of his life taken the line of least resistance when the going got tough. It was the sort of accommodation to circumstances which had enabled Edward to survive and prosper throughout his life. In 1066, in the context of the rivalries which had built up over previous years, and which Edward's perverse streak had encouraged, it led to a blood-bath.

Frank Barlow, Edward the Confessor (1970)
Robin Fleming, Kings and Lords in Conquest England (1991)

the engineer James BRINDLEY, who persuaded him to build one including a massive aqueduct. The resulting canal halved the cost of Worsley coal at Manchester, and encouraged Bridgwater to pursue further schemes, the greatest of which was the Bridgwater canal between Manchester and Liverpool, completed in 1772. Bridgwater spent more than £220,000 on canals, and a further £170,000 expanding his coal interests; the investment proved financially rewarding.

EGERTON, SIR THOMAS (Baron Ellesmere, 1st Viscount Brackley) (1540–1617), lawyer. A barrister who rose to become Lord Keeper of the Great Seal in 1596 and Lord Chancellor in 1603. He took a hostile view of the House of Commons' assertions of privileges against the Crown, and understandably resisted claims of lawyers like Sir Edward COKE for the primacy of the common law's jurisdiction against that of his own Court of Chancery. A conservative Elizabethan in outlook, he opposed the Great Contract, Robert CECIL's proposed deal for royal finances (1610), and, after Cecil's death, he sided against the Howard family's faction at JAMES I's court (*see* HOWARD, CHARLES, Earl of Nottingham; HOWARD, HENRY, Earl of Northampton; HOWARD, THOMAS, Earl of Suffolk). His valuable official papers and historical manuscripts survive.

EILAF (?–*c.* 1035), nobleman. His life provides a notable example of the sort of career which was made possible by CNUT's North Sea 'empire'. A Scandinavian who first came to England in 1009 in the army of THORKELL THE TALL, Eilaf was appointed in 1018 by the King to an earldom which centred on Glos. Having quarrelled with Cnut, he fought against him in Denmark in either 1025 or 1026, but was later reconciled with him. He was brother-in-law to both Cnut and GODWINE, Earl of Wessex.

EINAR FALSEMOUTH, Earl of Orkney (1014–20). Son of SIGURD THE STOUT, his harsh and unpopular rule was eventually challenged by his youngest brother THORFINN THE MIGHTY. Einar was subsequently killed in his own hall at Sandwick by one of Thorfinn's supporters; Thorfinn then succeeded him.

EINION AP OWAIN (?–984), Prince of Deheubarth. A son of OWAIN AP HYWEL DDA, King of Deheubarth, and elder brother of MAREDUDD AP OWAIN, later King of Deheubarth and Gwynedd, Einion was sent by his father in 969 and again in 977 to assault Gwyr (Gower), which had been held by HYWEL DDA, Einion's grandfather. He was certainly able to extend the family territories into south-east Wales, but his overlordship seems to

have been resented and he was killed by enemies in Gwent.

ELDER, JOHN (1824–69), engineer. Elder's father John was an engineer at Robert NAPIER's Glasgow shipbuilding firm and constructed the first marine engine. The son was an apprentice, then a draughtsman, to Napier and in 1852 joined what would become the famous Randolph, Elder & Co. engineering firm. There he exploited his knowledge of thermodynamics and the expertise of the Glasgow engineering professor William Rankine in the development of the first successful compound marine steam engine (1854). Because it used steam twice in a cycle, Elder's invention allowed considerable savings on fuel. Later in his career Elder built even more economical compound engines and thus enabled steamships to carry less fuel and more cargo.

ELEANOR OF AQUITAINE *see* essay on page 289

ELEANOR OF CASTILE (1242–90), Queen of England. Daughter of Ferdinand III of Castile, she married Prince Edward (later EDWARD I) in 1254, becoming her husband's constant companion and accompanying him on crusade, as well as to Gascony and Wales. According to a story, first written down 100 years later, when he was wounded by an assassin's knife at Acre in June 1272, she sucked poison out of the wound. She probably bore 14 children, the last of them, the future EDWARD II, at Caernarfon. She was reputed to be a grasping woman. 'The King he wants to get our gold, the Queen would like our lands to hold' ran a contemporary rhyme. Nonetheless, historians have sometimes argued that Edward became a harsher ruler after her death. She died at Harby (Notts.), and Edward ordered the construction of a commemorative cross at each stopping place of the cortège on its way to Westminster Abbey. Now known as Eleanor Crosses, 12 were built, the last being at Charing Cross, London.

ELEANOR OF PROVENCE (1223–91), Queen of England. Daughter of Raymond Berenguer, Count of Provence, and Beatrice of Savoy, she married HENRY III in 1236; five of their children, including the future EDWARD I, survived infancy. Henry was devoted to Eleanor, and his generosity to her uncles the Savoyards provoked criticism. A lady of strong opinions, including anti-Semitic ones, she remained an influential figure during the reigns of both her husband and her son, until she became a nun at Amesbury (Wilts.) in 1286.

ELFODDW (?–809), Archbishop of Gwynedd. It is generally believed that Elfoddw was based in

continued on page 290

ELEANOR OF AQUITAINE (1122–1204)
Queen of France (1137–52), Queen of England (1154–89)

A vast inheritance (the duchy of Aquitaine), a formidable personality and a long life made her the most powerful woman of her age. Her ancestors had governed Poitou since the tenth century; her grandfather, Duke William IX, was the first named lyric poet composing in Occitan, the *langue d'oc* (or Provençal) of the troubadours. There is no evidence that she championed women's rights or courtly love, or even that (as some of her admirers have believed) she was an unusually influential patron of troubadours.

William X's sudden death in 1137 left her, as his elder daughter, with a claim to the duchy, and she was at once snapped up by King Louis VII of France. She accompanied her husband on a crusade 10 years later (1147–9), which ended badly and during which their relationship came under increasing strain. At Antioch her friendship with her uncle Raymond, Prince of Antioch, gave rise to rumours which pursued her to the end of her life. On their return she and Louis visited Pope Eugenius III; he prepared a magnificent bed for them to sleep in. This resulted in the birth of their second child, another daughter. But Louis wanted a son, and so the marriage, despite the enormous increase in wealth and standing it brought him, was annulled on grounds of consanguinity in 1152.

A few months later she married Henry of Anjou (later HENRY II), to whom she was also related within the prohibited degrees. She had inherited a claim to Toulouse from William IX, and in 1159 Henry (as Louis had done in 1141) attacked Toulouse in support of her claim. In the first 15 years of their marriage they had eight children, including five boys. Despite the frequent pregnancies she played an active part in the government of England and Aquitaine, where, as is shown by RICHARD I's later trust in her political judgement, she must have guided her second son's earliest steps as Duke of her duchy. When her eldest surviving son, HENRY THE YOUNG KING, rebelled against Henry II in 1173 she and the barons of Poitou joined the war against her husband; she sent Richard and Geoffrey to the safety of her ex-husband's court, but was herself arrested while she was making her way there, disguised, claimed one shocked contemporary, GERVASE OF CANTERBURY, in male clothing. These events generated immense controversy then and in subsequent centuries.

Probably she was fighting for the rights of the Duchess of Aquitaine (in particular for her claim to Toulouse which Henry had recently abandoned) rather than for the rights of women; nonetheless what she did was extraordinary. It was perceived as a subversive attempt to overthrow the proper relationship between the sexes, and hence as a threat to all political and social order. While Henry forgave his rebel sons, his wife remained his prisoner for at least 10 years and did not recover her former lands and revenues until he died.

On Richard I's accession (1189) she was released, aged 67, and from then on played a very important part in politics, particularly during his absences on crusade and in prison (1192–4). She escorted his prospective bride, BERENGARIA, to Sicily. She visited him in Germany. A contemporary insider, ROGER OF HOWDEN, states that it was on her advice that Richard did homage to the Emperor Henry VI and treated his untrustworthy younger brother JOHN with notable generosity; in return she had some slight success in curbing John's treacherous instincts.

On Richard's death in 1199 she helped John (now her only surviving son) win the allegiance of Anjou against ARTHUR OF BRITTANY. Early next year, in pursuit of peace with her ex-husband's son, King Philip II of France, she travelled to Castile and brought back a niece as a bride for his son, the future Louis VIII. War, however, broke out again in 1202 and it was while Arthur was besieging her in Mirebeau that he fell into his uncle's hands. Towards the end she retired to the nunnery of Fontevraud. After her death (31 March 1204) she was buried there, near to the bodies of Henry II and Richard I. Throughout her life she remained the lawful ruler of Aquitaine and when she died, a crucial moment in the collapse of the Angevin empire, her subjects immediately transferred their allegiance to the King of France. The real scandals of her life – on crusade, the divorce, her rebellion against Henry II – soon provided fertile ground for the propagation of many a good story: she and the great lyrical poet, Bernard de Ventadour, were lovers; she and her eldest daughter, Marie de Champagne, presided over 'courts of love'; she murdered the 'Fair Rosamund'. All of these may well be myths; her life was extraordinary enough.

D. D. R. Owen, Eleanor of Aquitaine: Queen and Legend (1993)

Bangor, although this is not stated in any early source. He is the first of only two Welsh churchmen mentioned in pre-eleventh-century sources to be referred to as archbishop at his death. Elfoddw was the instigator of the synod which adopted the Roman calculation of the date of Easter (*see* BEDE) in the Welsh Church in 768.

ELGAR, SIR EDWARD (1857–1934), composer.

Elgar was the most important composer in Britain since HANDEL, and the forerunner of a distinguished series of twentieth-century British composers. His style, especially in a great series of orchestral and choral works, combined romanticism with an English sensibility, exemplified in the works which made his name: the symphonies and violin and cello concertos, the orchestral suite *Enigma Variations* (1899) and the oratorio *The Dream of Gerontius*, a setting of NEWMAN's poem, which was first performed in 1900. The sensitivity of Elgar's work, his Roman Catholicism and attachment to his native Malvern Hills (Worcs.) belie the popular imperialist image of him sometimes conveyed by the *Pomp and Circumstance* marches, to one of which A. C. BENSON added the words 'Land of Hope and Glory', now widely familiar for being sung annually at the Last Night of the Proms.

ELIOT, GEORGE *see* essay on page 291

ELIOT, SIR JOHN (1592–1632), politician. MP

for Cornish seats between 1614 and 1628, his oratory repeatedly dramatized opposition concerns. He was knighted in 1618. Initially in 1624 he supported George VILLIERS, Duke of Buckingham, in his war policy against Spain, but his horror at the subsequent strategic blunders led him into bitter attacks, and he was imprisoned in 1627. He championed the Petition of Right (1628) asserting the subject's rights against arbitrary government, furiously denounced the ceremonialist innovations of Arminian clergy in the Church of England and led the opposition to the collection of tonnage and poundage without parliamentary sanction. Imprisoned on a variety of charges in 1629 and fined £2,000, he died in prison. He left behind manuscripts discussing the issues involved which show how remote the opposition was from thoughts of rebellion at this stage. Even so, Eliot's intransigence had done much to wreck parliamentary and royal co-operation by putting CHARLES I on the defensive.

ELIOT, T(HOMAS) S(TEARNS) (1888–1965),

poet, critic and playwright. Born in Missouri, educated at Harvard, the Sorbonne and Oxford, Eliot arrived in England in 1915 and took British citizenship. Later describing himself as 'classicist in literature, royalist in politics, and Anglo-Catholic in religion', his first major poem 'The Love Song of J. Alfred Prufrock', written with the encouragement of Ezra Pound, was published in 1915; and in 1922 'The Waste Land' appeared in the inaugural issue of *The Criterion* and achieved immediate critical acclaim as a central text of Modernism. The religiosity of Eliot's work became more pronounced in the inter-war years with the publication of such poems as *The Hollow Men*, *The Journey of the Magi* and *Ash Wednesday*, and culminating in his *Four Quartets* (*Burnt Norton* 1935, *East Coker* 1940, *The Dry Salvages* 1941, and *Little Gidding* 1942, which evokes the blitz as purgatory and contains the line 'History is now and is England'). A conservative, pessimistic observer, his best-known work of criticism is *Towards a Definition of Culture* published in 1948, the year he was awarded both the Order of Merit and the Nobel Prize for Literature and the year before his play *The Cocktail Party* was a West End hit. A Director of the publishing house of Faber & Faber from 1925, Eliot developed an impressive poetry list and his book of light verse *Old Possum's Book of Practical Cats* (1939) has helped to provide for Faber's material prosperity through the transmogrification of that volume in the hugely successful musical *Cats*.

ELISEG AP GWYLOG (*fl.* mid eighth century),

King of Powys. Perhaps a contemporary of OFFA, King of Mercia. Little is known about Eliseg or his reign. The ninth-century monument, Eliseg's Pillar, built by Eliseg's grandson, CYNGEN AP CADELL, states that he managed to retake 'the heritage of Powys ... from the power of the Saxon', which, if this does not merely mean that he consolidated the lands of Powys west of Offa's Dyke, may indicate that he managed to regain that lost part of Powys, to the east of the dyke. If so, this was to be only a temporary reassertion of the sovereignty of Powys there.

ELIZABETH (née Bowes-Lyon) (1900–), Queen

Consort. Brought up largely at Glamis Castle in Scotland, the daughter of the 14th Earl of Strathmore, she married the Duke of York, second son of GEORGE V in 1923. They had two daughters, Princess Elizabeth (1926) and Princess MARGARET (1930).

In 1936 the abdication of her brother-in-law EDWARD VIII brought her husband to the throne as GEORGE VI. The monarchy, discredited by the abdication, earned respect during the Second World War through the work of the royal couple, who stayed in London during the blitz, sharing the same dangers as their subjects. A widow since George VI's premature death, her daughter ascended to the throne as ELIZABETH II in 1952.

continued on page 292

ELIOT, GEORGE (originally Mary Ann Evans) (1819–80)
Novelist

Evans was one of five children and spent her childhood at Arbury Hall near Coventry where her father was estate manager; many incidents and people from those days figure in her novels. In 1841 she met Charles Bray, a philanthropist and free thinker, and his wife Caroline. Influenced by the Brays and by Caroline's brother, Charles Hennell, and his wife Sarah, both progressive intellectuals, Evans's strongly held religious faith began to waver, much to the distress of her father. Sarah Hennell had begun to translate the rationalist David Friedrich Strauss's controversial *Das Leben Jesu*, and in 1844 Evans took over the translation published in 1846 as *The Life of Jesus, Critically Examined*. She then embarked on a translation of Spinoza's *Tractatus theologico-politicus*. After the death of her father and with a small annuity Evans went to London in 1852, where she became effectively the editor of John Chapman's radical *Westminster Review*. To it she also contributed a number of articles, as to other periodicals, several of which constitute her manifesto on the nature of fiction.

In 1854 she met George Henry Lewes, a fellow contributor to the *Westminster Review*. Lewes, a philosopher, scientist, critic and journalist, was married. He had condoned the adultery of his wife with his friend Thornton Hunt, and continued to support her and her three children by Hunt. This condonation meant that Lewes was unable to obtain a divorce. After much agonized thought Evans (by now known as Marian) and he decided to defy Victorian convention and live together as man and wife. This estranged Evans from her family, including her beloved brother Isaac, and there were many who would not risk their own reputation by being seen either to invite or to visit the couple. As her fame grew, however, many of these social scruples gradually became diluted, and the Sunday salons at the Regent's Park house to which the couple moved in 1863 became a noted feature of London literary life.

Given her relationship with Lewes (and her diffidence, which persisted regardless of her growing reputation as a writer), it was imperative that Evans publish under a pseudonym: she chose 'George Eliot'. *Scenes from Clerical Life*, a collection of stories, was published in January 1858. *Scenes*, often drawn from Eliot's own life, were well received and encouraged her to persist with *Adam Bede* (1859), another narrative of rural life in which she largely followed her own prescription for portraying characters that were 'more or less commonplace and vulgar', also dealing with sexual double standards. 'The Lifted Veil', a sombre study of clairvoyance, appeared in *Blackwood's Magazine*, and the novel that established her reputation, *The Mill on the Floss*, was published in 1860. Again with a rural setting, and drawing on her life with her own nature and aspirations grafted onto the unruly, perceptive Maggie Tulliver, it received instant acclaim, and Eliot found herself described as 'a writer without rival'. In 1860 Eliot and Lewes visited Florence, which was to be the setting for *Romola* (1863), a historical novel dealing with the life of the fifteenth-century political figure Savonarola. It did not enjoy the success of her English novels, and she returned to the setting of her childhood. *Felix Holt, the Radical* (1866), Eliot's only 'political novel', appeared a year before the passing of the Second Reform Act, and takes as its focus the 1832 Act, though its canvas is broader, taking in incest, illegitimacy and inheritance as well. *Middlemarch: A Story of Provincial Life*, set in the same period as *Felix Holt*, started appearing in *Blackwood's Magazine* in 1871: apart from being a rich and often humorous panorama of English life, it is an indictment of the narrow opportunities open to nineteenth-century women. The milieu of Eliot's last book, *Daniel Deronda* (1876), was contemporary London, the metropolitan upper-middle class rather than the rural peasantry, and its theme was Anglo-Jewish society.

In 1878 Lewes died, and Eliot turned to edit the remaining volumes of his *Problems of Life and Mind*, on which he had been working at the time of his sudden death. In 1880 she accepted a marriage proposal from the persistent John Walter Cross, a friend and business adviser to both her and Lewes, who was 20 years her junior. The marriage served to reconcile Isaac and other members of her family from whom she had been estranged for some 25 years, before her death within a year.

Part of F. R. LEAVIS's *The Great Tradition* (1948), Eliot has been endorsed as one of the major Victorian novelists, while feminists find in her novels persuasive evidence of the restricted opportunities and sexual stereotyping of nineteenth-century women, and in her life an inspiration for scholarship, courage and unconventionality.

Jenny Uglow, George Eliot (1987)

Her Majesty Queen Elizabeth the Queen Mother has continued to perform a public role, as the first woman Lord Warden of the Cinque Ports (1958) and Chancellor of the University of London (1955–80) among others, as well as pursuing her private interests in fishing, horse-racing and her Scottish home, the Castle of Mey. Her century longevity has further increased the popularity of the Queen Mother, a gracious figure with a distinctively personal style and an undiminished enthusiasm for the royal walk-about.

ELIZABETH I *see* essay on pages 294–95

ELIZABETH II (1926–), Queen of Great Britain and Northern Ireland and Head of the Commonwealth (1952–). The abdication of EDWARD VIII placed his brother Albert on the throne as GEORGE VI, making his 10-year-old-daughter Elizabeth heir apparent. In 1947 she married her cousin, Prince PHILIP of Greece, who became a British citizen on the eve of the wedding, taking the title Duke of Edinburgh. She succeeded to the throne on 6 Feb. 1952 following the premature death of her father; with a glamorous 26-year-old Queen the pundits predicted the opening of a 'new Elizabethan age'. The reality was otherwise.

Elizabeth II succeeded to a country which, ravaged by the Second World War, had neither the will nor the ability to hang on to its Empire. Her own enthusiasm for the Commonwealth helped cushion the ending of Empire abroad, while at home she and her consort attempted to pioneer a new style of monarchy in the 1960s. Conscious that the monarchy looked stuffy and out of date in the 'swinging sixties', the royal couple accepted the advice of Philip's uncle Lord MOUNTBATTEN that they should 'let in some fresh air' through the medium of television. The resulting programme on the royal family certainly produced a favourable press but it whetted the appetite for further 'royal' stories and proved the precursor to press intrusion which, by the 1990s, would become intolerable.

The Queen continued to play the role established by her grandfather, GEORGE V, in which the monarchy presented itself to the nation as a family which set an example to all. She also followed her father's example in the role of constitutional monarch. It proved easier to accomplish the latter role than the former, although there were those who thought that in 1963 and again in 1997 she allowed herself to be used for political purposes by Prime Ministers Harold MACMILLAN and Tony BLAIR, while her dislike of Margaret THATCHER became mysteriously well known. It was, however, the marital strife of her sister MARGARET and her children, CHARLES, Anne and Andrew that caused most problems for the monarch in the 1990s.

The breakdown of the fairy-tale marriage between Charles, Prince of Wales, and his wife, DIANA, focused the media spotlight on the royal family in an unprecedented way. As the tabloids speculated on the reasons for their estrangement attention was drawn to the shortcomings of the Queen as a mother and the monarchy as an institution. With the divorce of Charles and Diana, finalized in 1992, and the fire at Windsor Castle, along with public furore about the fact that the Queen paid no income tax, it was easy to see why she described that year as an *annus horribilis*, but there was worse to come.

In 1997, following the death of Diana in a car crash, there was unprecedented personal criticism of the Queen for her failure to join in the national tide of emotion, and under pressure she gave an extraordinary broadcast to show that she shared the feelings of her subjects. For a time the criticism grew in volume until there were even those who wondered whether the monarchy could survive for much longer. It was under this pressure and these impulses that the Queen took advice about how to reposition the monarchy in a less deferential age. There followed a series of informal royal visits and even an incongruous trip to a public house, all as part of a campaign to make the royal family more 'relevant'. The ultimate success of these efforts remains to be seen but once again the monarchy has shown the resilience and willingness to adapt which have enabled its survival.

ELIZABETH WOODVILLE (?1437–92), Queen of England. Daughter of Richard Woodville, when she married EDWARD IV there were few precedents for a Queen of England who was both English herself and had numerous English relatives. Edward IV married her for love and proceeded to make her family powerful.

Her first husband, Sir John Grey, was killed at St Albans (Herts.) in 1461. By marrying her in May 1464 Edward IV took on responsibility for providing for her many brothers and sisters, as well as for her two sons by her previous marriage. The apparent Woodville monopoly of royal patronage led to deep resentment.

When Edward was driven into exile in 1470, Elizabeth took sanctuary at Westminster Abbey, where she gave birth to their first son (the future EDWARD V). In April 1483 she was forced into sanctuary again by the coup that followed her husband's death, but in June she was persuaded to release her younger son to the care of the Archbishop of Canterbury. RICHARD III then seized the throne, claiming that Edward had already been married when he married her and that their children were therefore bastards although, hitherto, they had been universally accepted as legitimate.

By the autumn of 1483, probably realizing that her sons were dead, she was contemplating a marriage between her daughter, Elizabeth of York, and Henry Tudor (*see* HENRY VII), but after the collapse of Buckingham's (*see* STAFFORD, HENRY) rebellion, she came to terms with Richard, leaving sanctuary in return for his promise to provide for her and her daughters. In 1486, following Richard's fall and with her daughter wed to the new King, she was granted all her rights as Queen Dowager and, the next year, retired to the convent of Bermondsey (Surrey).

ELLENBOROUGH, 1ST BARON AND 1ST EARL OF *see* LAW, EDWARD

ELLERMAN, SIR JOHN (1862–1933), ship owner and financier. The son of a Hull shipbroker, of German extraction, Ellerman went into accountancy. At the age of 29 he and two other young financiers acquired the shipping business of Frederick Leyland, who had died suddenly; despite their inexperience the company prospered. He acquired company after company, taking shipping businesses that had gone into decline and revitalizing them under his close personal scrutiny, before selling to the American J. P. Morgan for cash in 1901 and starting afresh. His new list of companies, combined as Ellerman Lines (from 1916 Ellerman Wilson Lines), gave him a major presence in all the main shipping routes. As a profit-maximizing financier Ellerman invested widely in other industries, from collieries to newspapers. By 1910 he was the richest man in Britain. Indeed, during the First World War he may have become, in real terms, the richest ever man in Britain.

ELLES, SIR HUGH (1880–1945), soldier. Son of an Indian army officer, born in India, educated at Woolwich, commissioned into the Royal Engineers in 1899, Elles went immediately to South Africa. Serving on the staff of 4th division in 1914, he took part in the retreat from Mons, was wounded in April 1915 and was subsequently asked to report on the operational employment of a still secret weapon, the tank. Promoted to Brigadier General, Elles commanded the new Tank Corps in 1917 and 1918. Commander of the Tank Corps training centre (1919–23), he ended his military career as Master General of Ordnance (1934–8), pushing through a massive re-armament programme. Afterwards he served as Director of Civil Defence for south-west England, overseeing the arrival, accommodation and training of more than 1.5 million American servicemen between 1942 and 1945. Elles was the quintessence of the twentieth-century scientific soldier; excessively modest, he let others like John FULLER and Basil

Liddell HART claim credit for much that he had achieved.

ELLESMERE, 1ST BARON see EGERTON, THOMAS

ELLIOT, EBENEZER (1781–1849), industrialist and poet. Born in Rotherham (Yorks.) he was a radical who turned to poetry to vent his anger at the Corn Laws, which he blamed for the bankruptcy of his father's iron foundry. His volume *Corn Law Rhymes* (1831), which attacked the 'bread tax', established his reputation as a social critic. Hostility to the Corn Laws led him into other radical movements: he was an early supporter of Chartism and a delegate to the Chartist Convention, but broke with it when it turned to physical force and socialism.

ELLIOT, GILBERT (1st Earl of Minto) (1751–1814), Governor General of India. Educated in Paris under David HUME and at Oxford, Elliot entered Parliament in 1776 as a Whig. He took an early interest in Indian affairs and was an associate of Edmund BURKE and an opponent of Warren HASTINGS. Made Governor of Corsica in 1794 and envoy to Vienna (1799–1801), he was appointed President of the East India Co.'s Board of Control in 1805 and thereafter Governor General. Under him during the Napoleonic Wars, British rule was reinforced in India, the Sikh kingdom was temporarily quietened and French and Dutch possessions in south-east Asia, including Java, were seized.

ELLIOT, GILBERT (4th Earl of Minto) (1845–1914), Viceroy of India. From a line of successful soldiers, Minto stood in a distinguished tradition in India. After military service in many campaigns, periods spent as a newspaper war correspondent, as a daredevil racehorse rider and in county politics, he was made Governor General of Canada in 1898, where he coped with the Klondyke gold rush and settled the Alaskan boundary dispute. He succeeded CURZON as Viceroy of India in 1905. During his tenure he co-operated with John MORLEY at the India Office in constitutional reforms that allowed some elected representation in India's government. Relations with the radically tinged Morley were strained because of Minto's deep conservatism, while the Minto–Morley reforms also stored up problems for the future by establishing separate spheres for Hindu and Muslim electorates.

ELLIOTSON, JOHN (1791–1868), physician. Trained as a physician in Edinburgh, Cambridge and London, Elliotson became Professor of the Practice of Medicine at London University in 1831 and helped found University College Hospital, London. He was a distinguished medical lecturer and text-book writer, and enjoyed a lucrative

continued on page 296

ELIZABETH I (1533–1603)
Queen of England and Ireland (1558–1603)

Daughter of HENRY VIII and ANNE BOLEYN, she was declared illegitimate after her mother's execution in 1536, but in an Act of Parliament of 1544 she was once more included in the succession, and was given a royal humanist education at court with the encouragement of Queen CATHERINE PARR. Thomas SEYMOUR tried to win her love in 1547–9, and the traumatic effect of these overtures from a man nearly three times her age on a teenage girl may have had a bearing on her later emotional difficulties over marriage; the scandal certainly encouraged her to keep a low profile in the reign of EDWARD VI. Her position during MARY I's reign was sometimes dangerous; although nothing was ever proved to link her with Protestant conspiracies against the Queen, she was in prison from 1554 to 1555, at first briefly in the Tower of London, then at Woodstock (Oxon.), before being released into a circumscribed retirement at Hatfield (Herts.). As it became apparent that Mary's illness was terminal, Elizabeth's friends, particularly William CECIL and Nicholas BACON, quietly prepared the ground, and her accession on 17 Nov. 1558 was trouble-free. Immediately she sanctioned steps towards a religious settlement that restored the Protestant Church in a form left unfinished at Edward VI's death, with substantially the same Prayer Book. (For differing views of the settlement, *see* NEALE, JOHN.) She carefully chose her new senior clergy to accommodate her own prejudices against Calvinists, aggravated by her fury at John KNOX's injudicious condemnation of female monarchs in his *First Blast of the Trumpet against the Monstrous Regiment of Women*. She and her ministers devoted much energy to restoring a proper silver content to the coinage after two decades of reckless debasement and frequent changes of monetary policy; she was particularly proud of this achievement, which was completed in 1562. The prospect of marriage was a long-standing problem; while it quickly became clear that her preference for Robert DUDLEY, later Earl of Leicester, was politically unacceptable, a queue of foreign suitors included a somewhat unenthusiastic PHILIP II of Spain (1559), the Austrian Archduke Charles (1564), Henry, Duke of Anjou (1571), and FRANCIS OF VALOIS (1572–81). Much negotiation was diplomatic play-acting, much reflected her ministers' nervousness (she nearly died of smallpox in 1562) and some came near to persuading her. The thought of a Catholic consort was increasingly unacceptable to the Protestant governing group, and the opponents of the Valois

negotiations in the late 1570s began to emphasize the advantages to England of being ruled by a virgin Queen. That was an image which Elizabeth, overcoming her initial feelings of fury and disappointment at the end of the Valois wooing, came to see as one to be exploited in propaganda, though it had originally been imposed on her against her will.

Partly by their manipulation of these foreign marital possibilities, Elizabeth and her ministers preserved the regime, in its fragile first decade, from hostile Roman Catholic intervention in English affairs, and they kept an increasingly uneasy peace with English Catholic sympathizers. By 1568, however, domestic and foreign tensions began to accumulate, especially after the flight to England of the Catholic heir to the throne, the much-married MARY QUEEN OF SCOTS, who became Elizabeth's prisoner. In 1569 ill-prepared Catholic uprisings by northern noblemen were defeated with relative ease (*see* NEVILLE, CHARLES, Earl of Westmorland), but the rebellion resulted in Elizabeth being declared excommunicate by the Pope and in consequence deposed, in his bull *Regnans in Excelsis* (1570). This presented acute dilemmas of conscience for those of her subjects trying to remain loyal to the Pope, but few supported such conspiracies aimed at her life as those of Roberto RIDOLFI (1570) and Anthony BABINGTON (1586). Her relationship with the captive Mary was tense, and she hesitated until 1587 before agreeing to Mary's execution. Still agonizing about having destroyed a monarch chosen by God, she vented her feelings of guilt and fury at those who had persuaded her to sign the death warrant, temporarily dismissing Cecil from court and ruining the career of her secretary William DAVISON.

Elizabeth's caution in overseas military adventures brought conflict with those of her advisers like Leicester who were enthusiasts for a forward foreign policy to help fellow Protestants abroad. Reluctantly she sanctioned military aid to the Scots Protestants against the Catholic regime of MARY OF GUISE and Mary Queen of Scots in 1559–60; this proved a success, but her caution was justified by the disastrous outcome of efforts to help the French Protestants (Huguenots) in 1562–4. Nevertheless, growing tensions with Spain and the revolt of the Netherlands, England's chief trading partner, against Spanish rule, forced her hand. From 1585 she found herself presiding over an undeclared but increasingly expensive and complicated world war. Faced by the threat of Spanish invasion with the Armada expedition of 1588, she reviewed her assembled troops at Tilbury (Essex) on 9–10 Aug. 1588 and personally enthused them with a dramatic speech, although the text may not have been that later credited to her. The Armada's dispersal was not a turning-point in the war, for further Armadas were launched against England, and Elizabeth frequently hampered the operations of her motley armies in France, the Netherlands and Iberia by her indecision in giving orders and her financial cheeseparing. In the late 1590s her commitments were extended to an all-out attack on the Gaelic noblemen in Ireland who had rebelled against English rule and who sought to rally Spain and the Pope to their cause (*see* O'NEILL, HUGH). Yet the aggressive foreign policy which Elizabeth loathed met with longterm success in asserting England's place in the world, and its dominance of her other kingdom of Ireland; ironically, it left her most lasting image as a founder of empire. As a result of worldwide seaborne operations in her reign, partly building on her father's investment in the navy, England became a major force in maritime warfare and trade.

In Elizabeth's last years, death successively robbed her of many politicians who had been her faithful if occasionally exasperated servants since the 1550s, Leicester, Francis WALSINGHAM, Christopher HATTON and William Cecil. Her choice of men with first class political talent and her dominance of court quarrels now faltered, particularly in combination with the inept selfishness of Robert DEVEREUX, Earl of Essex, until he brought ruin on himself in 1601. Her neurotic refusal to name an heir to the throne added to the atmosphere of insecurity in the 1590s and much alarmed the obvious candidate, JAMES VI of Scotland, but capable senior politicians, particularly Robert CECIL, managed the transition on her death with exemplary efficiency.

Although documentation about her is abundant, Elizabeth has guarded her privacy from subsequent scrutiny. In particular, her religious views remain opaque; Francis BACON famously said of her (in a remark often misattributed to the Queen herself) that she did not choose to make windows into men's souls. There is no question that she was Protestant in outlook, but her variety of Evangelical religion had hardly moved on from her happy teenage years at Henry VIII's court in Catherine Parr's time. She was irritated by what she regarded as an excessive reverence for preaching among many of her subjects, and came into direct conflict with Archbishop GRINDAL when he refused to take responsibility for suppressing the sermon-training gatherings known as 'prophesyings'; as punishment for his defiance, she ended his active career (1577). She had a taste for ceremonial worship, scandalizing many clergy by retaining a silver cross and candlesticks on the communion table in her Chapels Royal, and she employed the composer William BYRD despite his open Catholicism. Equally, she does not seem to have been worried by the discovery in the 1580s that various members of her personal guard were members of the secretive mystic sect called the Family of Love, leading some to the daring speculation that she may herself have been a Familist sympathizer.

Elizabeth's reign witnessed a flowering of literature and music which made England for the first time a cultural centre of international significance, although much that is described as Elizabethan, such as most plays by William SHAKESPEARE, was in fact the product of the years after her death. Highly self-conscious, the Queen was a brilliant self-fashioner, exploiting her indispensability for the Protestant cause in England and genuine popular affection and loyalty, for instance in the official encouragement of spontaneous celebrations of her accession day and in the use of her progresses throughout the country. She was much more assiduous than her father in going widely through the realm, and from early in her reign she extracted the most lavish expenditure from her hosts. This culminated in the architectural fashion for 'prodigy houses', built by leading gentry and aristocracy not simply for their own use but to accommodate the needs of a visiting court and drawing on every architectural device in a reckless display of grandeur. Elizabeth herself did not spend heavily on building, and her one major project at Windsor Castle has largely been destroyed. Her personal sense of theatre encouraged the creation of her image as patriotic, Protestant and classical heroine, fostered by ceremony and painting; often her rhetorical skills needed to be employed to mend fences broken by her own ill-tempered defence of her prerogative against parliamentary interference especially in foreign and religious policy. Yet as a woman in a political world ordered by men she succeeded in remaining dominant in a situation full of potential dangers.

John E. Neale, Elizabeth I (1934)

private practice, with patients including Charles DICKENS and William Makepeace THACKERAY. He introduced several novel devices and techniques into his hospital practice, including the stethoscope, acupuncture and mesmerism. The last was a controversial technique, promulgated by the eighteenth-century Austrian physician, Franz Anton von Mesmer (1734–1815), in which a patient was induced into a state of trance and, typically, anaesthetized by mesmeric 'operators' controlling the patient's will. At a period when anaesthetics were unavailable, Elliotson worked hard to display the surgical value of mesmerism, but in 1838 he was forced to resign his professorship following a fierce medical campaign against mesmerism. The word 'hypnotism' was coined in the 1840s by the physician James Braid to distinguish the physical effects of mesmerism on the human body from the 'magnetic fluid' theories which mesmerists used to explain these effects. In 1843 Elliotson launched *The Zoist,* a periodical dedicated to mesmerism and phrenology, and in 1849 founded the London Mesmeric Infirmary.

ELLIS, HAVELOCK (1859–1939), sexologist. After a private education in Surrey and teaching in New South Wales (1875–9) Ellis trained in medicine at St Thomas's Hospital, London (1881–9). A polymath – he wrote on art, literature, criminology, social policy and much else – his major work was on sexuality and he became the most influential British writer on the subject in the first half of the twentieth century. He was also important in introducing the ideas of Freud and others into British discussions of sex and sexualities. His own work, such as *Studies in the Psychology of Sex* (seven vols, 1897–1928), was distinguished by regarding the immense varieties of sexual behaviour, including homosexuality, without prejudice, at the same time seeing sexual behaviour as having a fundamental biological basis in which men sexually conquered women. There remained an unresolved tension in his work between the psychological and the biological. Thus for example he came to believe by the 1930s that monogamy had fundamentally biological roots: the purpose of marriage was to consolidate monogamy while providing the stability necessary for the family which, in turn, became central to social policy.

ELLIS, RUTH (née Neilson) (1926–55), murderess. A nightclub hostess who shot dead her unfaithful and abusing lover, she was the last woman to be hanged in Britain. Her execution gave impetus to the growing campaign for the abolition of capital punishment.

ELPHINSTONE, JAMES (1st Baron Balmerino) (1557–1612), politician. Successively a Lord of Session (1587), one of the 'Octavians' or eight Treasury Commissioners (1596) reforming Scots royal finances (*see also* HAMILTON, THOMAS; SETON, ALEXANDER), Secretary of State (1598) and President of the Court of Session (1605); he was created Baron in 1606. He was later condemned to death for forging the content of a letter to Pope Clement VIII unwittingly signed by JAMES VI in 1599, and commending Roman Catholicism. Although reprieved and released, he died while still under attainder.

ELPHINSTONE, JOHN (2nd Baron Balmerino) (?–1649), politician. Restored in blood in 1613, a year after his father, James ELPHINSTONE, had died under sentence of attainder for treasonous contacts with the Pope; he was sentenced to death in 1635 merely for possession of a parliamentary petition against CHARLES I's Scottish ecclesiastical policy, but was pardoned after a national outcry. Prominent among the sponsors of the National Covenant (1638), he advised appealing to France for help. He was chosen President of the Scottish Parliament in 1641 and a Commissioner to the Westminster Parliament in England in 1644.

ELPHINSTONE, WILLIAM (1431–1514), educational patron. After studies at Glasgow and Paris, he served as Ambassador and Councillor and was Bishop of Ross (1481) and Aberdeen (1483). Despite his strong support for JAMES III, JAMES IV made him Lord High Chancellor (1488) and Keeper of the Privy Seal (1492). Besides rebuilding the choir of Aberdeen Cathedral, he obtained a royal charter to found King's College, Aberdeen, intended primarily to train lawyers, in 1498. He was the first patron of Scots printers (*see* CHEPMAN, WALTER; MILLAR, ANDREW) and promoted revised versions of the Church's liturgy with a new emphasis on Scottish saints. His death is said to have been hastened by grief at the Scots defeat at Flodden.

ELPHINSTONE, WILLIAM (1782–1842), soldier. His father, a Director of the East India Co., bought him a commission in the 41st regiment in 1804. By 1813 Elphinstone had managed to rise to Lieutenant Colonel without once being in action, though in 1815 he commanded the 33rd regiment at Waterloo, reportedly with considerable bravery. In 1839, now a Major-General, he was sent to India, and two years later his father's influential East India Co. friends helped him secure command of British forces in Afghanistan. When the Afghans rose against the British in late 1841, Elphinstone made an inept attempt to withdraw his army from Kabul through the mountains. The entire command was wiped out and he died of dysentery while captive. One of the greatest disasters suffered by British forces in the nineteenth century, it fuelled the attack on corruption and nepotism in military appointments.

ELSTOB, ELIZABETH (1683–1756), scholar. The daughter of a Northumb. clergyman, she may have accompanied her brother William to Oxford. When William became rector of Stone (Staffs.) Elizabeth joined him. She and her brother embarked on an edition of the 80 Anglo-Saxon homilies of Aelfric Grammaticus with parallel modern English text. William praised her scholarship in a preface to the first volume and Elizabeth defended the project against the attacks of SWIFT. In 1715 William Elstob died and Elizabeth lost the financial support she needed to continue the project. She worked for many years as a schoolmistress until she was rediscovered by a group including Mary DELANY, who first obtained for her a pension from Queen CAROLINE, and then a post as governess to the daughters of Margaret, Duchess of Portland. Despite this support she was unable to finish her academic projects.

ELTON, SIR GEOFFREY (1921–94), historian. Born in Tübingen, son of the classical historian Victor Ehrenberg, he escaped Nazi persecution in 1938 and spent his academic career in London and Cambridge universities. An eminent parliamentary historian, he made the study of the 1530s his own. His book *The Tudor Revolution in Government* (1953) sparked a long-running debate, arguing that Thomas CROMWELL consciously weakened the Royal Household's role in government and finance, building a central bureaucratic administration. Some medievalists pointed out that medieval England already had the most complex bureaucracy in Europe, while Stuart historians showed that government finance and policy-making became personalized once more under the early Stuarts. Other work has reassessed the Tudor court, emphasizing its continuing importance in government, and many Cromwellian reforms had precedents in Thomas WOLSEY's ascendancy. Nevertheless, historians constantly rediscover the 1530s as crucial in bringing major change in English politics and central and local government – let alone the revolution in the English Church, which was not Elton's prime concern.

ELYOT, THOMAS (before 1490–1546), writer. Son of a judge, his legal education led on to his formidable learning as a scholar of Renaissance humanism; Cardinal WOLSEY's interest in him diverted his career to the clerkship of the King's Council in 1523. His public advance was then checked, first by Wolsey's fall and then by his own associations with the party loyal to the cause of CATHERINE OF ARAGON in her struggle to resist the annulment of her marriage to HENRY VIII; he was nevertheless knighted in 1530, and to test his loyalty he was sent as Ambassador (1531–2) to the Emperor CHARLES V. Later he was despatched to flush out William TYNDALE from his exile in the Low Countries.

In 1531, Elyot published *The Boke Named the Governour*, an influential treatise on education for government. Later he published the first English translations of several Greek classics (notably Platonic dialogues), a pioneering Latin dictionary and a medical treatise.

EMECHETA, BUCHI (1944–), writer. Born and educated in Nigeria, Emecheta came to England in 1962. Separated from her husband, she brought up her five children while working as a librarian. She studied sociology at the University of London and became a community worker. Her first books were partly autobiographical, such as *Adah's Story* (1983). In 1977 she won the Jock Campbell Award for Britain's most promising writer, for *Slave Girl*, which drew on the experiences of her grandmother and mother. She also writes books for children, radio plays and reviews and has been a member of the Arts Council and of the Home Secretary's advisory council on race.

EMMA (c. 985–1052), Queen of the English. Daughter of Count Richard I of the Normans, wife (in turn) of ETHELRED II THE UNREADY and his supplanter, CNUT, and mother (by Ethelred) of EDWARD THE CONFESSOR and (by Cnut) of HARTHACNUT. A strong personality and a manipulative politician, she schemed incessantly to retain her place at the centre of events and to advance the (often incompatible) careers of her children. The *Encomium Emmae Reginae* was written on her behalf in 1041/2, when Harthcnut was King and Edward his designated successor, to celebrate and justify her career and her family's achievements.

EMMET, ROBERT (1778–1803), Irish nationalist. His father was physician to the Lord Lieutenant of Ireland. As a student at Trinity College, Dublin, Emmet became involved in revolutionary politics and joined the United Irishmen in 1798, fleeing to France when their rebellion collapsed (*see also* FITZGERALD, LORD EDWARD; LAKE, GERARD). He was led by Napoleon to believe that a French invasion of England was imminent. The resumption of war between Britain and France (1803) suggested the possibility of a successful rising. The plan went wrong and the rising collapsed within an afternoon. Emmet was tried on 19 Sept. 1803 and hanged the next day. His speech from the dock became renowned as a patriotic declaration from which future generations of both British radicals and Irish nationalists drew sustenance.

EMPSON, RICHARD (?–1510), politician. A Yorkist official and barrister, he was Speaker of the House of Commons (1491–2) and, as a member of the Council Learned in the Law (the law-enforcing sub-committee of the Royal Council), became one of HENRY VII's chief agents in ruthless financial exactions; he was Chancellor of the Duchy of Lancaster from 1504. With Edmund DUDLEY, he was made scapegoat for the old regime's unpopularity on HENRY VIII's accession, and was executed in 1510.

ENGELS, FRIEDRICH (1820–95), German socialist, economist and co-author of *The Communist Manifesto* (1848). Son of a cotton manufacturer, he spent most of his adult life as an agent for the family firm in Manchester and used the profits to subsidize the activities of Karl MARX, with whom he had collaborated since 1844. He was a prolific writer: *The Condition of the Working Classes in England in 1844* (1845), an analysis of the social impact of industrialization, is now regarded as a pioneering study in urban geography and sociology, while *The Origin of the Family, Private Property and the State* (1884) put sexual and production relationships into a historical perspective. After Marx's death in 1883, Engels devoted the remainder of his life to editing and translating his works. A man with a formidable intellect and generous personality, Engels as much as Marx was the father of 'scientific socialism'.

ENGLISH, SIR DAVID (1931–98), journalist. English went straight into Fleet Street journalism on leaving school, working successively for the *Daily Mirror, Daily Sketch* and *Daily Express*. Appointed editor of the *Daily Sketch* in 1969, he became editor of the *Daily Mail* in 1971, a position which he held until 1992. The *Daily Mail* had been founded in 1896 as the first daily newspaper for a mass readership, but by the 1960s it was languishing well behind its mid-market rivals the *Daily Express* and *Daily Mirror*. It was also the only national paper that remained in the hands of its founding family, the HARMSWORTHs. English rescued the *Mail* and, recognizing that Britain had sociologically become more 'middle class', converted it into the journal of right-wing 'middle England'. He targeted the paper particularly at women, used tabloid-type headlines and layout and paid top Fleet Street rates to revive the paper's fortunes. Before his departure as editor, the *Mail* had overtaken the *Express* in circulation and in 1998, just after his death, the paper also overtook the *Mirror*.

EOCHAID BUIDE (?–629), King of Dál Riata. According to ADOMNÁN, when AEDÁN MAC GABRÁIN questioned COLUM CILLE about which of his sons would succeed him, Eochaid Buide was the prophesied beneficiary while he was still very young. He is given a reign-length of 15 or 16 years, so he appears not to have immediately succeeded his father. Little is known of Eochaid's reign; he is, however, called 'King of the Picts' (*rex Pictorum*) in his obituary in the *Annals of Ulster*. If correct, this suggests that he had annexed some part of Pictish territory to tributary status, which he ruled directly, in addition to his Dál Riata territories on both sides of the Irish Sea.

EOCHAID, SON OF RHUN (*fl. c.* 878–89), King of the Strathclyde Britons (?and the Scots). Son of the King of Strathclyde and grandson of CINAED MAC ALPÍN, Eochaid is named in *Berchan's Prophecy* as 'the first Briton to rule over the Gael'. His reign over the Scots is obscure; he may have ruled jointly with GIRIC I, King of the Scots, or accepted client status under him. In 889 Giric and, perhaps, Eochaid were expelled by DOMNALL II MAC CONSTANTÍN, a significant moment in the development of a single kingdom in Scotland. It is uncertain whether Eochaid survived this defeat.

EÓGANÁN, SON OF OENGUS, King of the Picts and Scots (834–9). Succeeding his father, Eóganán's accession consolidated the continuity in the ruling dynasty established over both kingdoms by his father and uncle, CONSTANTÍN, SON OF FERGUS, and further encouraged the concept of the unification of both kingdoms under a stable dynasty. In 839, however, Eóganán and his brother were killed in battle by the Vikings, leaving the way open for CINAED MAC ALPÍN to take the kingship.

EORCENBERHT (?–664), King of Kent (640–64). The son of King EADBALD and husband of SEAXBURH, daughter of King ANNA of East Anglia, Eorcenberht is said by BEDE to have ordered the destruction of all pagan idols within his kingdom. His rule therefore marks a significant stage in the consolidation of Christianity in what was then an important Anglo-Saxon kingdom and part of the foundation from which an Archbishop of Canterbury such as St THEODORE OF TARSUS was able to give a stronger lead to the Church in England. Eorcenberht was succeeded by his son EGBERT.

EORCENWALD, ST, Bishop of London (675–93). The founder of monasteries at Barking and Chertsey, he was consecrated as Bishop of London by St THEODORE OF TARSUS, Archbishop of Canterbury. Relatively little is known about his life, but he came to be regarded as a saint who remained popularly honoured at St Paul's throughout the Middle Ages.

EPSTEIN, JACOB (1880–1959), sculptor. The son of Polish–Jewish immigrants, Epstein was born in New York and, after working in a bronze foundry and studying in Paris where his interest in primitive and ethnographic sculpture was aroused, he came to London, becoming a British citizen in 1907. One of the outstanding sculptors of the twentieth century he was controversial and often derided: his frieze of 18 naked carved figures for the British Medical Association (1907–8) was later mutilated; *Rock Drill* (1913–15), which he said 'symbolized the terrible Frankenstein monster we have turned ourselves into' has been destroyed; there was a petition (Conan DOYLE was one of the signatories) for the removal of his monument to the naturalist W. H. Hudson in Hyde Park; his Assyrian-like tomb for Oscar WILDE in the Père Lachaise cemetery in Paris (1911) aroused furious debate, as did his monumental works on religious subjects, *Risen Christ* (1919), *Genesis* (1931), *Ecce Homo* (1935) and *Jacob and the Angel* (1940–2). Even his *Night and Day* figures (1928–9) for London Transport's headquarters in St James's had to be genitally edited in response to public outrage. In the face of such hostility Epstein turned to modelling portrait busts, but after the Second World War he began to receive due recognition, with *Lazarus* (New College Chapel, Oxford, 1947–8), and the memorial to the trade union war dead on the TUC headquarters in Great Russell Street, London (1956–7). His final public work, *St Michael and the Devil*, for the façade of Coventry Cathedral, was unveiled posthumously.

EQUIANO, OLAUDAH (also known as Gustavus Vassa) (*c.* 1745–97), writer, traveller and abolitionist. He was probably born at Iseke in the kingdom of Benin (now in Nigeria) to an aristocratic African slave-owning family. Kidnapped in 1756, he was sold into slavery. An English naval officer, Michael Pascal, whom he accompanied during the Seven Years War (1757–63), gave him the name of Gustavus Vassa after the sixteenth-century Swedish King. Pascal allowed him to be educated but in 1762 sold him on without warning. Equiano spent the next few years in the West Indies, where he saved enough money to buy his freedom. He worked on commercial vessels, and in 1773 served on the expedition to the Arctic to find a north-west passage. At this time he became interested in Methodism. He agreed with a former owner, now a friend, to help him set up a plantation on the Mosquito coast in Central America, where Equiano himself was to oversee slaves but, dismayed by the harsh way in which the slaves were treated in his absence, he resigned and returned to England, where in the 1780s he became a leading campaigner for the abolition of slavery and assisted Granville SHARP, alerting him to atrocities such as the mass murder of slaves on the ship *Zong*. In 1787 he was appointed Commissioner for Stores to the project to resettle former slaves in Sierra Leone, but was dismissed when he sided with the colonists against the senior administrators. His *Interesting Narrative of the Life of Olaudah Equiano, or Gustavus Vassa, the African* (1789) was written to help the anti-slavery cause; it shows the ambiguous feelings of a West African who had adopted British ways but also condemned the values of the country that had enslaved him. The book was translated into Dutch, Russian and German. He married an Englishwoman in 1792; their surviving daughter inherited an estate of £950, largely arising from profits on the sale of the book.

ERASMUS, DESIDERIUS (?1469–1536), Humanist. Erasmus, Dutch-born, became the leader of the movement of scholarship known as humanism. Their fascination with ancient Latin and Greek literature led the humanists to apply their learning to contemporary concerns; it had taken hold in Italy in the fourteenth century and, during the fifteenth and sixteenth centuries, developed into a Europe-wide Renaissance. He made extended English visits on his perennial search for wealthy patrons, and for learned company to fill his personal loneliness. His 1499 visit to court and Oxford University was at the invitation of his pupil William BLOUNT, Lord Mountjoy, and was important in turning his attention from Latin classical literature towards theology and the study of Greek (encouraged by John COLET); it also impelled him to begin *Adagia* (a collection of proverbs, the first best-seller in print) as a money-spinner after Dover Customs officers confiscated all his English currency. His 1505 visit brought him patronage from Archbishop William WARHAM, and most of his 1509–14 extended stay was spent at Cambridge University. Thereafter his huge correspondence included many English scholars and would-be humanists. His edition of the Greek text of the New Testament (1516, and later revisions), with his own translation into humanist (i.e. properly classical) Latin, had Europe-wide influence, providing a new view of the biblical text for many future Protestant reformers.

There is a lazy tendency to term all Tudor humanism 'Erasmian'; nevertheless his influence was very great, although his vision of a tolerant Christianity minimizing the power of the clergy was much retarded by the ideological struggles of the Reformation.

ERBURY, WILLIAM (1604–54), radical mystic. Oxford-educated, William was vicar of Cardiff

(1623–38) until the Bishop of Llandaff forced his resignation for Puritan preaching. He became a Parliamentary army chaplain, then travelled preaching. He scandalized Calvinists by proclaiming that all people would be saved, then denied Christ's divinity, and later said that the Holy Spirit had left the world in the first century AD (therefore all existing churches were valueless). His widow Dorcas became a leading proclaimer of the messianic Quaker James NAYLER (*see also* SIMMONDS, MARTHA), and was briefly imprisoned for her part in Nayler's demonstrations.

ERIC BLOODAXE (?–954), the last Viking King of York. His blood-soaked career fully justifies his nickname. A member of the family of the kings of Norway, he was briefly King before his expulsion in 946. In 947 he was invited from Orkney by the inhabitants of York to take over a kingdom whose political life had been constantly disrupted by interventions by English and Viking armies. He controlled York in 947–8 and 952–4 against the opposition of a Scandinavian rival OLAF SIHTRIC-SSON and the English King EADRED. Abandoned by Archbishop WULFSTAN I of York, who had supported him, and finally expelled as the English armies of King Eadred marched north, he was betrayed and killed by his enemies near Carlisle. His violent lifestyle earned him a prominent place among the heroes of Viking saga literature. His daughter RAGNHILD lived out an almost equally turbulent life in the earldom of Orkney.

ERIC OF HLATHIR (?–*c*. 1023), Earl of Northumbria. A beneficiary of the conquest of England by SVEIN FORKBEARD and CNUT, Eric was given the earldom of Northumbria after Earl UHTRED's murder in 1016. Originally from Norway, he had consistently supported the Danish kings in their wars against the Norwegian King OLAF TRYGGVASON. The earldom and his marriage to Svein's daughter were undoubtedly rewards for political support. His son HAKON also prospered under Cnut's regime.

ERLE, SIR WALTER (1586–1665), politician. A leading Dorset Puritan gentleman and MP knighted in 1616, Erle (or Earle) was one of 'five knights' (*see* CORBET, JOHN; DARNELL, THOMAS; HAMPDEN, EDMUND; HEVENINGHAM, JOHN) imprisoned for not paying CHARLES I's forced loan in 1627–8. Erle was prominent in Puritan North American colonial projects, and was a notably unsuccessful commander of Dorset's Parliamentarian forces during the 1642–6 Civil War. He was sequestered from Parliament in PRIDE's purge of Presbyterian sympathizers (1648), but became active in the politics of Oliver CROMWELL's protectorate; he retired after CHARLES II's restoration.

ERMENGARDE (?–1233), Queen of Scots. She was the daughter of the Vicomte de Beaumont and a cousin of HENRY II, who arranged her marriage in 1186 to the 43-year-old WILLIAM I THE LION, King of Scots, strengthening the influence of French culture on her husband's court. As a wedding present Henry restored Edinburgh to William.

ERSKINE, JOHN (18th [1st Erskine] Earl of Mar, 6th Baron Erskine) (?–1572), courtier. Intended for a Church career until he became the heir to the barony, Erskine signed the nobles' invitation to John KNOX to return to Scotland in 1557, but thereafter avoided religious partisanship. After MARY QUEEN OF SCOTS restored his dormant earldom in 1565, he supported her marriage to Henry STEWART, Lord Darnley, and defeated James STEWART Earl of Moray's rebellion; guardian of the infant JAMES VI from 1566, he became consistently devoted to the King's cause, helping to force Mary's abdication in 1567. He was chosen Regent in 1571 as a respected mediating figure after Moray's murder, but before his last fatal illness he had made little effort to curb the rise to power of James DOUGLAS, Earl of Morton.

ERSKINE, JOHN (19th [2nd Erskine] Earl of Mar) (1562–1634), courtier. Educated with JAMES VI; their longterm friendship survived some abrupt reversals. In 1578 James DOUGLAS, Earl of Morton, encouraged him to claim the guardianship and custody of the teenage James, as previously held by his father John ERSKINE, 18th Earl of Mar; his hostility to the Catholic influence on James of Esmé STUART, Duke of Lennox, lost him office once Morton was destroyed in 1581. His part in the Ruthven Raid (*see* RUTHVEN, WILLIAM), which seized control of James in 1582, regained him power, but consequent struggles and the ascendancy of James STEWART, Earl of Arran, brought kaleidoscopic changes in 1584: banishment, a short-lived seizure of Stirling Castle for the Presbyterian party who sought to banish Episcopacy from the Scottish Church, followed by flight to England. From 1585 Arran's fall ended Erskine's troubles; he became Prince HENRY FREDERICK's guardian in 1595, aided James against the 'Gowrie Conspiracy' (*see* RUTHVEN, ALEXANDER) which in 1600 supposedly threatened the King and, as Scots Ambassador in London, smoothed James's path to the English throne on the death of ELIZABETH I. He was made an English Privy Councillor and, as Lord High Treasurer of Scotland (1616–30), he was one of the group keeping the kingdom quiescent in James's absence.

ERSKINE, JOHN (23rd [6th Erskine] Earl of Mar) (1675–1732), politician. When he succeeded to the title as a young man, the family fortunes were at a low ebb. Initially he mainly associated with the Court party under Queensberry (*see* DOUGLAS, JAMES), and served as a Commissioner for the Union of Scottish and English Parliaments (effected by the Act of Union 1707) and as Secretary of State for Scotland. He was made a Scots representative peer in the enlarged House of Lords but by 1713 favoured repeal of the Union. Appointed a Secretary of State in the Tory ministry of 1712, he was dismissed when GEORGE I constructed his first ministry. Returning to Scotland, he proclaimed James STUART, the Old Pretender, King at Braemar on 8 Sept. 1715, and took command of the Jacobite forces. An indecisive commander, he repulsed the 35,000-strong government forces of John CAMPBELL, Duke of Argyll, with only 10,000 Highlanders behind him, but lacked the skill to press home his advantage and saw his army disintegrate. Mar left Scotland with James in Feb. 1716. In exile with the Pretender, he both sought ties with the Hanoverian government and fostered Jacobite plots. Distrusted by his fellow Jacobites, he went into retirement in 1725.

ERSKINE OF DUN, JOHN (1509–90), churchman. An Angus laird, educated at King's College, Aberdeen, he sponsored Scotland's first teaching of Greek, and befriended the reformer George WISHART. From the 1557 invitation to John KNOX to return from Geneva, he was prominent in the Protestant national revolution; from 1560 he was the new Church's Superintendent for Angus and the Mearns, sponsoring in 1568–9 one of Scotland's first major witch-hunts. He was among those drawing up the second Book of Discipline (Church order) in 1578, joined the Royal Council in 1579 and was Superintendent of the Kirk's General Assembly in 1589.

ESSEX, EARL OF, 1ST *see* MANDEVILLE, GEOFFREY DE; **4TH** *see* FITZPETER, GEOFFREY; **8TH** *see* BOHUN, HUMPHREY VII DE; **9TH** *see* BOHUN, HUMPHREY VIII DE; **16TH** *see* CROMWELL, THOMAS, essay on page 218–19; **19TH** *see* DEVEREUX, ROBERT, essay on page 242; **20TH** *see* DEVEREUX, ROBERT; **21ST** see CAPEL, ARTHUR

ETHELBALD (?–757), King of Mercia (716–57). In succession to PENDA and WULFHERE, he was one of a series of powerful kings of Mercia from the seventh and eighth centuries, and the first Mercian king to exercise domination over all the English kingdoms south of the Humber. Like most early medieval kings, he emerged from among the available royal kindred by violence and force of personality. Little is known in detail about his reign, but it is probable that several characteristic features of the period of Mercian hegemony which became much clearer during the reign of

his better known successor OFFA, such as the proliferation of the obligation on all landholders to do military service and repair bridges and fortifications, date from his time. His treatment of the Church and his sexual *mores* were criticized by St BONIFACE, but he was looked on with favour by St GUTHLAC and there is evidence of support for the Church. The fact that he was murdered by his own war-band points to serious political divisions and emphasizes how much Mercian domination depended on the personality of the king. His death was followed by a civil war from which Offa emerged as his successor.

ETHELBALD, King of Wessex (855–60). The son of King ETHELWULF of Wessex, Ethelbald succeeded his brother ATHELSTAN as King of Kent and was installed as King of Wessex when his father and his younger brother ALFRED THE GREAT set off on pilgrimage to Rome in 855. Although Ethelbald rebelled and refused to hand Wessex back to his father when he returned from his pilgrimage, he did eventually succeed him peacefully. He subsequently married his step-mother JUDITH, presumably because, as a crowned queen, her children by any husband would have been considered heirs to the kingdom. After a short reign, he was succeeded by his brother ETHELBERT.

ETHELBERT (*c.* 552–*c.* 616), King of Kent (*c.* 560–*c.* 616). The first English king to convert to Christianity and the first to issue a law-code; in 597 he welcomed St AUGUSTINE's mission to Kent, persuaded to do so probably by the great advances that Christianity was making elsewhere in western Europe and by the influence of his Frankish Christian wife BERTHA. According to BEDE, he was prepared to meet the Christians only in the open air for fear of their magic. Third on Bede's list of what were later termed Bretwaldas, that is rulers who exercised some sort of predominance over the rulers of the other early Anglo-Saxon kingdoms, he used his power to assist the spread of Christianity to Essex and East Anglia, and, through his daughter ETHELBURH, to Northumbria. Although the security of the Christian mission in Kent and elsewhere was threatened in the time of kings such as Ethelbert's son EADBALD and REDWALD of East Anglia, his reign can ultimately be seen as establishing the powerful connection in England between kingship and the Church, which was to remain a significant feature of the country's history for centuries.

ETHELBERT (?–*c.* 762), King of Kent (725–*c.* 762). Very little is known about the long reign of Ethelbert, who was a son of King WIHTRED. A correspondence with St BONIFACE shows that he maintained the continental contacts typical of the kings of Kent. At various stages of his reign he is known to have ruled in co-operation with his brothers. He also accepted the overlordship of King ETHELBALD of Mercia, an arrangement which seems at the time to have been undefined and undemanding, but which led in due course to a much harsher subjugation, as in the time of OFFA and EADBERT PRÆN.

ETHELBERT, King of Wessex (860–5). One of the five recorded sons of King ETHELWULF of Wessex, Ethelbert was installed as King of Kent by his father when the latter set off on pilgrimage for Rome in 855. Ethelbert succeeded his brother ETHELBALD as King of Wessex in 860 and apparently reached an agreement with his two younger brothers, the future Kings ETHELRED I and ALFRED THE GREAT, by which the kingdom of Kent was suppressed in return for a promise that they would succeed him; the disappearance of a distinct kingdom of Kent marks a small, but significant, step towards the creation of a single kingdom of the English which occurred under Alfred's successors. Like his predecessors and successors, Ethelbert was involved in fighting against Viking raids.

ETHELBERT, ST (?–794), King of East Anglia. Very little is known about Ethelbert beyond his murder on the orders of King OFFA of Mercia for reasons which are unknown. His death presumably fits into the pattern whereby Offa imposed his power on all the kingdoms of southern Britain. A cult of sanctity subsequently developed.

ETHELBURH, ST (?–647), Queen. The daughter of the Christian ETHELBERT, King of Kent, Ethelburh was sent north to become the wife and queen (625–33) of the pagan EDWIN, King of Northumbria. Her career illustrates the role played by women in the conversion of the early Anglo-Saxon kingdoms to Christianity since, by taking the Roman missionary PAULINUS north with her, she effectively began the conversion of Northumbria (*see also* COIFI). She returned to Kent in 633 after her husband had been killed, founding a monastery at Lyminge (Kent) of which she became Abbess.

ETHELBURH, ST (?–664), Abbess of Faremoutiers-en-Brie. A daughter of ANNA, King of East Anglia, and sister of St ÆTHELTHRYTH and of SEAXBURH, her religious life is typical of that of many Anglo-Saxon noblewomen. Her entry to a religious community in France illustrates the strong connections between southern Britain and the Frankish Church during the early conversion period.

ETHELBURH (?–after 726), Queen of Wessex (c. 688–726). Wife of King INE, Ethelburh is

known to have led a military campaign on her husband's behalf when he was away in another part of his kingdom and to have persuaded him to abandon kingship to live in Rome. Although very little is known about her, she clearly exemplified the traditional supportive virtues of early medieval queenship.

ETHELFLÆD (also known as Lady of the Mercians) (?–918), daughter of ALFRED THE GREAT and EALHSWITH. Ethelflæd was married to Ealdorman ETHELRED of Mercia between 883 and 888. The marriage was the last of a series between the rulers of Mercia and Wessex which cemented their collaboration against the Viking threat. Effective ruler of Mercia during her husband's illness-ridden last years and after his death in 911, in co-operation with her brother EDWARD THE ELDER, she devoted her principal efforts to meeting the threat from Scandinavian settlers in north-west England (*see* INGIMUND) and from the kingdoms of Dublin and York (*see* RAGNALL), leading extensive military campaigns and extending the system of burhs developed by Alfred into the west and north-west of Mercia. A figure of heroic proportions with massive achievements to her name, she was effectively the last ruler of independent Mercia. Her daughter ÆLFWYNN was dispossessed by Edward the Elder.

ETHELFRITH (?–616), King of Bernicia and of Northumbria (603–16). A grandson of IDA, first King of Bernicia, Ethelfrith was a pagan whose aggressive wars enabled him to impose his authority over both Bernicia and Deira, thereby becoming the first king to rule Northumbria, and to drive back his British neighbours. His greatest victories were the defeat of the British of Rheged (*see* URIEN) over AEDÁN MAC GABRÁIN, King of Dál Riata, at *Degsastan* (location unknown) in 603, and over a British army near Chester in *c*. 613. He was eventually defeated and killed by REDWALD, King of East Anglia, and EDWIN, a member of the Deiran dynasty whom he had exiled. Ethelfrith's sons OSWALD and OSWY were driven into exile, but subsequently returned to be outstandingly important kings of Northumbria. His daughter ÆBBE was later Abbess of Coldingham.

ETHELHEARD, ST (?–805), Archbishop of Canterbury (792–805). A protégé of King OFFA of Mercia, chosen as a part of his schemes to make Lichfield into the premier archbishopric in England, Ethelheard eventually, and somewhat unwittingly, succeeded in reinstating Canterbury's superiority when King CENWULF of Mercia defeated King EABERT PRÆN of Kent, who had expelled Ethelheard from Canterbury. When Cenwulf failed to persuade the Papacy to transfer

Canterbury's archiepiscopal status to London, he reinstalled Ethelheard in Canterbury and removed his support from Archbishop HYGEBERHT of Lichfield, thereby reinstating Canterbury's traditional pre-eminence.

ETHELHERE (?–655), King of East Anglia. He succeeded his brother ANNA as King after the latter had been killed in battle by PENDA, King of Mercia. For reasons which are entirely obscure, Ethelhere became an ally of Penda and died fighting with him against King OSWY of Northumbria at the Battle of the River *Winwæd* (in Yorks., precise location unknown). His successor was called Ethelwold, but very little is known of the history of the kingdom of East Anglia at this period.

ETHELMÆR (?–1014), Ealdorman of the Western Provinces. He succeeded to his father ETHELWEARD's office in *c*. 998. He was a generous patron of the Church, like his father. He retired to the abbey of Eynsham in 1005 but was recalled in 1013 to lead the unsuccessful resistance in the West Country to SVEIN FORKBEARD's invasion. He appears to have avoided involvement in the more lurid political events of ETHELRED II THE UNREADY's rule.

ETHELNOTH (?–1038), Archbishop of Canterbury. One of the most distinguished of the later Anglo-Saxon archbishops of Canterbury. The first monk of the Canterbury Cathedral monastery to be elected Archbishop, his rule is notable for the production of some magnificent manuscripts at Canterbury. He supported HARTHACNUT against HAROLD I HAREFOOT, and refused to crown the latter.

ETHELRED (?–704), King of Mercia (675–704). A son of King PENDA, whose victory over ECGFRITH of Northumbria in 679 ended that kingdom's supremacy in England and paved the way for the Mercian supremacy of the reigns of ETHELBALD and OFFA.

ETHELRED (?–796), King of Northumbria (774–9 and 790–6). The son of King ETHELWOLD MOLL, Ethelred was a participant in the violent feuds for control of the Northumbrian kingship in the second half of the eighth century. Having driven out his father's supplanter, ALHRED, he was in turn ousted by St ÆLFWALD in 779. After Ælfwald's murder, Ethelred drove out his successor Osred, killing both him and Ælfwald's sons. He was himself murdered in 796, to be succeeded briefly by OSBALD and then by St EARDWULF. The famous sack of the monastery of Lindisfarne by a band of pagan Vikings took place during Ethelred's reign in 793; it marks the start of regular interventions by Scandinavian warriors in the politics of the English kingdoms.

ETHELRED (?–911), Ealdorman of Mercia. He was chosen as ruler of Mercia after the death of the Danish puppet-king CEOLWULF II. Although in certain respects he ruled Mercia in the manner of a king, he was never given the title and in 883 he submitted himself to the overlordship of the King of Wessex ALFRED THE GREAT, marrying his daughter ETHELFLÆD at a date between 883 and 888. Thereafter Ethelred consistently co-operated with Alfred and EDWARD THE ELDER in their wars against the Vikings and was also willing to allow Alfred to take over Mercia's traditional overlordship of the King of Gwynedd (*see* ANARAWD AP RHODRI). Ethelred and Ethelflæd's co operation with the kings of Wessex was a crucial factor both in the defeat of the Viking invasion and, unintentionally, in the eventual unification of England under the kings of Wessex.

ETHELRED I, King of Wessex (865–71). The fourth son of King ETHELWULF of Wessex and the elder brother of ALFRED THE GREAT, Ethelred succeeded his brother ETHELBERT as King. His entire reign was overshadowed by the arrival in northern England in 865 of the Viking 'Great Army', led by HALFDAN and IVAR THE BONELESS, which proceeded to destroy the ancient kingdoms of Northumbria (*see* ÆLLE) and East Anglia (*see* EDMUND, ST). Ethelred and Alfred provided military support to King BURGRED of Mercia. The 'Great Army' launched a direct assault on Wessex in 870, with Ethelred dying in the next year as a result of wounds sustained in battle. In conformity with the agreement reached with their brother Ethelbert, Ethelred, despite having two sons (*see* ETHELWOLD), was succeeded by Alfred.

ETHELRED II THE UNREADY *see* essay on page 304

ETHELSWITH (?–888), Queen of Mercia. Daughter of ETHELWULF, King of Wessex, and sister of ALFRED THE GREAT, her marriage to King BURGRED of Mercia in 853 was a typical medieval statement of close alliance between the two kingdoms, in this case against the mounting Viking threat. When Burgred fled his kingdom in 874, Ethelswith went with him as a pilgrim to Rome, outliving her husband and dying at Pavia in 888. What is generally believed to be her finger-ring can be seen in the British Museum.

ETHELWALH (?–*c*. 685), King of Sussex. The first King of Sussex of whom anything is known since ÆLLE, Ethelwalh apparently ruled under the overlordship of King WULFHERE of Mercia. His

continued on page 305

ETHELRED II THE UNREADY (966–1016)
King of the English (978–1016)

Ethelred became King at the age of 12 after the murder of his half-brother, King EDWARD THE MARTYR, and died when his realm had been almost completely conquered by the Danish King CNUT. He married first an English noblewoman named Ælfgifu and in 1002 EMMA, the sister of RICHARD II, duke of Normandy. The raids from Denmark began in 980 at first on coastal districts for the exaction of plunder and tribute. In 991 Ethelred and his advisers decided to pay Danegeld, a well-established tactic of his more successful predecessors, including ALFRED THE GREAT. In this case, however, the payment of tribute provided only a temporary respite from the attacks, since the Danes and their allies kept coming back for more. From 1009 onwards, large armies led by SVEIN FORKBEARD and THORKELL THE TALL arrived, bent on exacting massive wealth and, ultimately, on conquest. By Christmas 1013 the English people had accepted Svein as their King and Ethelred had fled to Normandy, taking with him Queen Emma and his young children by her, Edward (later to be known as EDWARD THE CONFESSOR), ALFRED and GODGIFU. Called back after Svein's death in Feb. 1014, Ethelred successfully drove Svein's son, the future King Cnut (1016–35), out of England, but then quarrelled disastrously in 1015 with his own son by his first marriage, EDMUND IRONSIDE. At the time of Ethelred's death on 23 April 1016, his divided kingdom was again at the mercy of Cnut's armies.

Historians debating the extent of Ethelred's personal responsibility for the disasters that befell his kingdom have pointed out that the main narrative source for the reign, the *Anglo-Saxon Chronicle*, which is sharply critical of the King and tells a story redolent of misjudgement and incompetence, was largely compiled with the benefit of hindsight after his death. Its damning verdict needs to be set in the context of the size of the invading armies, which were undeniably very large and well-organized by the standards of the times. The Danes' fleets gave them mobility and the capacity to make surprise attacks, and their bases in Ireland and Normandy were strategically helpful. It is important too to bear in mind that the Viking kingdom of York had been finally extinguished only in 954 and that the loyalties of the many Scandinavian settlers in the north and east of England must have been divided.

Ethelred's responses to the Danish threat were praiseworthy in many ways: he had a large fleet built; some of his campaigns were well-conceived; by marrying the Norman Princess Emma he sought to neutralize the duchy; and the collection of Danegeld involved a complex and extensive administrative effort. The reign is also notable for the production of law-codes, the later ones of which were composed by the great homilist and legal scholar, Archbishop WULFSTAN II of York. Much of Ethelred's industriousness, however, was tainted in some way or another. Although he was probably too young to have been personally involved, the murder of his half-brother Edward the Martyr may well have been carried out by members of the household of his mother Queen ÆLFTHRYTH. His policy between 984 and 993 of plundering Church lands represents a reversal of the sponsorship of the so-called Tenth-Century Reform; it was associated with the prominence of a particular noble faction at court. His second marriage, although politically astute, had the disadvantage of threatening the prospects of his sons by his first wife Ælfgifu; the disruptive quarrels with Edmund Ironside are likely to have been a consequence of this. The St Brice's Day Massacre of 13 Nov. 1002, whose target was all the Danes settled in England, must have undermined the loyalty of many peaceful settlers. Ethelred's reign is also littered with a series of political murders, such as that of ÆLFHELM, Ealdorman of Northumbria, in 1006, some of which are associated with EADRIC STREONA, the King's closest adviser and the kingdom's most prominent noble during the last decade of the reign. It is clear too that Eadric and others were lining their pockets with the proceeds of Danegeld. Ethelred's reign is notable for feats of individual heroism, the most famous of which are the defiant death in 991 of BYRHTNOTH, Ealdorman of Essex, at the Battle of Maldon and the martyrdom in 1012 of St ÆLFEAH, Archbishop of Canterbury, by followers of Thorkell the Tall. In general, however, it looks as though Ethelred's attempts at effective resistance were undermined by corruption, disunity and incompetence. Ethelred's well-known nickname 'Unræd' (no counsel) was a play on words originating in the twelfth century, signifying that he took no advice or bad advice. Although not the whole story of a disastrous reign, it is in many ways apt.

M. K. Lawson, *Cnut: The Danes in England in the Early Eleventh Century* (1993)
Simon Keynes, *The Diplomas of King Æthelred 'The Unready', 978–1016* (1980)

reign is notable for the very late conversion of Sussex to Christianity supervised by St WILFRID. Encouraged by WULFHERE to make military incursions against the kingdom of Wessex, Ethelwalh was killed by the future king of Wessex, CADWALLA. The kingdom of Sussex reached the end of its obscure history when it was suppressed by King OFFA of Mercia.

ETHELWEARD (?–c. 998), Ealdorman. A prominent adviser of ETHELRED II THE UNREADY during the early years of his reign, Ethelweard is remarkable as the first English author of a Latin chronicle and as the patron of leading writers of the Tenth-Century Reform. His literacy and learning are notable testimony to the cultural accomplishments of the aristocracy of later Anglo-Saxon England. He was succeeded by his son ETHELMÆR. His sister ÆLFGIFU was briefly Queen of the English.

ETHELWINE (?–992), Ealdorman of East Anglia. The youngest son of ATHELSTAN HALF-KING, he succeeded an elder brother in his father's office of Ealdorman of East Anglia. A close friend and adviser of King EDGAR and St OSWALD, like his father, he was a noted supporter of the Tenth-Century Reform. His political rivalry with ÆLFHERE, Ealdorman of Mercia, included taking different sides in the disputed succession between St EDWARD THE MARTYR and ETHELRED II THE UNREADY, as well as to religious reformers such as Oswald.

ETHELWOLD (?–655), King of Deira (?651–5). Son of King OSWALD of Northumbria and nephew of King OSWY, Ethelwold was installed in Deira by Oswy after King OSWINE's murder. He appears to have tried to free himself from Oswy's tutelage by making an alliance with PENDA, King of Mercia, but, along with Penda, he was killed in battle against Oswy at the Battle of the River Winwæd in 655. He was succeeded as King of Deira by Oswy's son ALHFRITH.

ETHELWOLD (?–902), the son of ETHELRED I of Wessex. One of ALFRED THE GREAT's elder brothers, Ethelwold contested the succession of Alfred's chosen heir, EDWARD THE ELDER, and died in battle in 902. His willingness to ally himself with the Vikings shows the depth of the division which the succession caused within the Wessex family, and in turn emphasizes how even this outstandingly successful kin-group resembled all contemporary royal families. Edward closed off the dynastic claims of Ethelwold's kindred by marrying his niece ÆLFFÆD.

ETHELWOLD MOLL (?–765), King of Northumbria (759–65). Probably the leading nobleman of the Northumbrian kingdom, Ethelwold became King after King Oswulf (758–9) had been murdered by his own followers. His accession marks the effective beginning of the feud which followed the abdication in 758 of King EADBERHT. Ethelwold was, in due course, killed by Oswulf's kinsman AHLRED, who was in turn driven out by Ethelwold's son ETHELRED.

ETHELWOLD, ST see essay on page 306

ETHELWULF (?–858), King of Wessex (839–58). King of Kent under the overlordship of his father King EGBERT until the latter's death, Ethelwulf himself had five known sons, of whom two, ATHELSTAN and ETHELBALD, were also kings of Kent during their father's lifetime. Ethelbald and his three brothers, ETHELBERT, ETHELRED and ALFRED THE GREAT, were subsequently kings of Wessex. A monarch notable for his personal magnificence and for his firm resistance to the Viking attacks which preceded the arrival of the 'Great Army' of HALFDAN and IVAR THE BONELESS in 865, he cooperated against them with King BURGRED of Mercia (see ETHELWULF, Ealdorman). Ethelwulf and his youngest son Alfred went on pilgrimage to Rome in 855 and returned to find that his son Ethelbald, his eventual successor, had usurped the kingship of Wessex. He married firstly OSBURH and secondly, when around 50 years of age, the 12-year-old JUDITH.

ETHELWULF (?–870), Ealdorman of Berkshire. A Mercian who was responsible for Berkshire under the last kings of Mercia, Ethelwulf retained office when his shire was transferred from Mercia into the kingdom of Wessex by Kings BURGRED and ETHELWULF. Subsequent evidence shows him leading the local levies of Berks. against the Vikings. He was killed in battle in 870. His career illustrates our increased knowledge in the ninth century of local government. The office of ealdorman, which was generally restricted to a single shire at this time, was reformed by King ATHELSTAN.

ETHEREDGE, SIR GEORGE (c. 1635–c. 1691), playwright. An Oxon. gentleman, his first play, *Love in a Tub* (1664), was a great success and earned £1,000 for the Lincoln's Inn Fields Company as well as making Etheredge a court favourite. *She Wou'd if She Cou'd* (1668) was less successful and Etheredge accepted a diplomatic posting to Constantinople. On his return he produced his most successful and last play, *The Man of Mode* (1676), satirizing Rochester (see HYDE, LAURENCE) in the shape of the misogynist but charming Dorimant. He was Ambassador at Ratisbon under JAMES II, whom he joined in Paris after the Revolution (1688–9), dying there in poverty.

ETHELWOLD, ST (?–984)
Bishop of Winchester (963–84)

He was one of the great figures in the so-called Tenth-Century Reform of the English Church. Along with St DUNSTAN and St OSWALD, he was at the centre of a set of changes which completed the revival of the English Church after the Viking invasions and established a framework which, with significant modifications in the twelfth century, endured until the Reformation.

Born in Winchester, Ethelwold was a member of the household of Bishop ÆLFHEAH THE BALD of Winchester and, like Dunstan, of a group of young churchman at the court of King ATHELSTAN. He became a monk at Glastonbury when Dunstan became Abbot there in 940 and in the early 950s he was made Abbot of the deserted Abbey of Abingdon. The revival of monasticism in southern England was a shared aim of the reformers, as also was the importation of up-to-date monastic customs from French monasteries such as Fleury-sur-Loire. Unlike Oswald, Ethelwold is not known to have travelled abroad, but monks from his monastery certainly did. Like the other reformers, Ethelwold was also in regular contact with the royal court; EADGIFU, the widow of EDWARD THE ELDER, was, for example, partly responsible for sponsoring his appointment to Abingdon and the future King EDGAR, who was to be a strong supporter of the monastic revival, was educated there.

Ethelwold's episcopate is notable for the installation of monks in the cathedral chapter at Winchester, for his remarkable patronage of art and learning there, and for his supervision of the compilation of the Regularis Concordia (970). The first of these, which involved the expulsion of the incumbent clerks, was the first of these reorganizations to be undertaken. It was followed by the creation of monastic chapters at Canterbury and Worcester and, much later, by the installation of monks after the Norman Conquest at Durham and Norwich. Monastic chapters of this kind were unique to the English Church. It is clear that Ethelwold and his colleagues believed that monks and monasticism should be to the forefront of the Church; he was himself also responsible for the foundation or re-establishment of monasteries at, for example, Peterborough, St Albans and Ely. These monasteries fulfilled the role of schools for future bishops and abbots, with the longterm result that English bishops for the next century until after the Norman Conquest were chosen primarily from the monastic order. Important literary figures such as ÆLFRIC OF EYNSHAM also owed their education to Ethelwold, whose patronage encompassed a great range of activities, including building, manuscript production, metal-working and art. He is known to have rebuilt the cathedral at Winchester and rehoused the shrine of St SWITHUN; the scope of his work is now much better known from the archaeological excavations of the 1970s. Manuscript illumination is superbly represented by the famous Benedictional of St Ethelwold, now preserved in the British Library. He is generally regarded as being the individual most directly responsible for the widespread dissemination in England of the script known as Caroline Minuscule, the official script of the Carolingian empire from the eighth century, first introduced into England in the time of ALFRED THE GREAT; its letter-forms were later adopted for printing and are essentially those still in use today. The Regularis Concordia was a supplement to the Rule of St Benedict. Its objective was to make all monasteries in England follow a common pattern of observance. It drew extensively on the customs of the reformed monasteries of northern France.

The activities of Ethelwold and his colleagues had implications which reached out far beyond the Church. Their collaboration with King Edgar is of exceptional importance for a considerable number of reasons. Above all, the reformed monasteries through their liturgy and ritual enhanced the dignity and prestige of kingship. The Regularis Concordia, for example, required monks to pray for the King's welfare seven times a day. New rituals such as Edgar's second coronation of 973 were undoubtedly inspired by the reformers. Grants of property and local jurisdiction to the new monasteries reinforced royal power by taking it away from established aristocratic kindreds. In Edgar's reign, the alliance of King and reforming churchmen was a very powerful force indeed. Its strength is well illustrated by the disorder and the reactive attempts to regain monastic property which characterized the short reign of EDWARD THE MARTYR and the first years of ETHELRED II THE UNREADY's. Ethelwold lived on through the early years of these fraught times, his influence probably mitigating their worst excesses. The long-term influence of his and his colleagues' efforts can still be seen in the great monastic remains from medieval England, in the writings of his successors such as Archbishop WULFSTAN II of York, and in a political and monastic culture which endured beyond the Conquest.

Barbara Yorke (ed.), Bishop Æthelwold: His Career and Influence (1988)
James Campbell (ed.), The Anglo-Saxons (1982)

ETTY, WILLIAM (1787–1849), painter. The son of a baker, he studied under Lawrence at the Royal Academy Schools and in Venice before becoming a renowned painter of voluptuous Victorian nudes, 'too luscious for the public eye', *The Times* warned, which he regarded as a tribute to 'God's most glorious work ... woman'. He also painted historical and classical subjects.

EUSTACE (*c.* 1128–53), English Prince. Had he not died unexpectedly in Aug. 1153, this young man, a notably energetic soldier, would either have succeeded his father STEPHEN as King of England or, at the least, have made life very difficult for HENRY II. Although in April 1152 Archbishop THEOBALD and the English bishops refused to anoint Eustace as Stephen's successor, he had long been groomed as heir. By arranging his marriage in 1140 to Constance, sister of King Louis VII of France, his mother MATILDA OF BOULOGNE had created a vital ally, and one who was all the keener to help Stephen and Eustace when the future Henry II married Louis's divorced wife ELEANOR OF AQUITAINE in 1152. Eustace's sudden death led his father to give up the struggle to keep the throne of England for the house of Blois.

EVANS, SIR ARTHUR (1851–1941), archaeologist. The son of Sir John Evans, an eminent industrialist and archaeologist, Arthur Evans was educated at Harrow and Oxford. In the 1870s and 1880s he travelled extensively in Europe, conducting minor excavations and collecting ancient artefacts. He was curator of the Ashmolean Museum, Oxford (1883–1908), where he began to study the coinage of ancient Crete. He is best known for his excavations at the Bronze Age city of Knossos in Crete (begun in 1899). In 1904 he announced evidence of what he called the Minoan civilization, which he believed vastly predated the ancient Greeks. The excavation revealed a palace (dated at 1700–1400 BC), clay tablets inscribed in linear script and sophisticated pottery and frescoes. He reconstructed parts of the palace and published his findings in *Scripta Minoa* (1909) and *The Palace of Minos at Knossos* (1921–35).

EVANS, ARTHUR MOSTYN ('MOSS') (1925–) trade-union leader. He was prominent during the 'winter of discontent' of 1978–9, which led to the downfall of James CALLAGHAN's Labour government. From a poor Welsh family, Evans moved to Birmingham at an early age and became involved with the trade union movement in the west Midlands. Rising through the ranks of the Transport and General Workers' Union (TGWU), he eventually replaced Jack JONES as General Secretary in 1978. It quickly became clear, however, that he lacked Jones's political nous; he publicly repudiated his predecessor's calls for wage restraint in 1978, with disastrous results, and when TGWU members (notably petrol tanker and lorry drivers) embarked upon some of the bitterest strikes of the winter he appeared to lose control of the union, though he remained at the head of the TGWU until 1985.

EVANS, SIR GEORGE DE LACY (1787–1870), soldier and army reformer. Third son of impoverished Anglo-Irish gentry, educated at Woolwich, in 1807 he joined the 22nd Foot in India. The years 1808 to 1815 saw Evans campaign and fight in more than 40 battles on three continents, India (1808), Mauritius (1810), the Peninsula and southern France (1813–14), Washington and New Orleans (1814–15) and at Waterloo (June 1815). Wounded four times, he had five horses shot from under him, and in 1815 in recognition of his service was promoted Lieutenant Colonel by brevet. In 1835 Evans took command of the British Legion in Spain. He commanded a division in the Crimea (1854–5), and was once more badly wounded. He entered Parliament on his third attempt in 1833 as a campaigner for military reform, including abolition of purchase and the introduction of promotion by merit. Always at odds with the military hierarchy, Evans's record meant that his views had to be listened to. Purchase was abolished a year after his death.

EVANS-PRITCHARD, SIR EDWARD (1902–73), social anthropologist. Evans-Pritchard studied history at Oxford and then social anthropology at the London School of Economics, where his ideas where shaped by Bronislaw MALINOWSKI and C. G. Seligman. His doctoral research involved a field-study of the Azande of East Africa. Between 1928 and 1940 he held several academic positions in England and Egypt and conducted field-work among the Azande, Nuer and Anuak tribes of Africa. As RADCLIFFE-BROWN's successor to the chair of social anthropology at Oxford in 1946, he created one of the world's leading departments of social anthropology. His books, notably *Witchcraft, Oracles, and Magic among the Azande* (1937) and *The Nuer* (1937), are classic ethnographic studies of tribal cultures. *Witchcraft* explored the exotic beliefs of the Azande and argued that such beliefs were part of a single, internally coherent and plausible system of thought. *Nuer* showed how stateless societies could be ordered on the basis of a single belief or value, specifically an 'interest in cattle'. Later he held that social anthropology was an historical, interpretative and artistic enterprise rather than the scientific project envisioned by Radcliffe-Brown.

EVELYN, JOHN (1620–1706), diarist. After fighting in the Royalist army in the First Civil War, in 1646 he travelled in France and Italy studying art and antiquities, of which he made sketches and engravings. Among those who planned the Royal Society, he was named a member of the council in the society's charter (1662). Evelyn was frequently at court after the Restoration and held various minor offices. A collector, patron of musicians and artists, including the woodcarver Grinling GIBBONS, and a garden enthusiast, he published many translations, as well as *Sylva, or a Discourse on Forest Trees* (1664). He is best known for his diary, which provides a detailed account of his life from 1641; it was first published in 1818–19.

EVESHAM, EPIPHANIUS (1570–*c*. 1634), sculptor. From a Herefs. family of Roman Catholic sympathies, he established a workshop in Southwark in the 1590s specializing in tomb sculpture, and after a decade working in Paris returned to London in 1614. Many of his monumental brasses and sculpted monuments survive, demonstrating his distinctive interest in sculpting scenes.

EWING, WINIFRED (1929–), politician. Ewing's election to Parliament at a by-election in Hamilton (Strathclyde) in 1967 indicated the emergence of the Scottish National Party (SNP) as a serious electoral force. Glasgow-born and educated, a practising solicitor with three children, she became overnight a media sensation (the SNP had not even fielded a candidate at Hamilton in the 1966 General Election). Her election was thought to indicate widespread nationalist fervour and to presage possible independence for Scotland, and Ewing was its only spokesperson at Westminster. But a recession in SNP support meant that Labour regained Hamilton at the 1970 election. In 1974 Ewing captured Moray and Nairn, but lost it again to the Conservatives five years later. A Member of the European Parliament for the Highlands and Islands since 1979, Ewing has increased her share of the vote at every election. In 1999 she was elected a member of the newly devolved Scottish Parliament.

EXETER, 1ST MARQUESS OF *see* COURTENAY, HENRY; **DUKE OF, 1ST** *see* HOLLAND, JOHN; **2ND** *see* BEAUFORT, THOMAS; **3RD** *see* HOLLAND, JOHN

EYRE, EDWARD (1815–1901), explorer and colonial official. An emigrant to Australia in 1833, Eyre became a pioneer sheep farmer and explorer: Lake Eyre and the Eyre Peninsula in South Australia are named for him. A magistrate and an early protector of the aboriginal rights, Eyre then entered colonial administration, serving as Lieutenant Governor of New Zealand (1846–53), and of the Caribbean island of St Vincent (1854–60) and as Governor of Jamaica. On 11 Oct. 1865 revolt broke out on the island at Morant Bay, followed on Eyre's orders by repression and more than 400 executions. He then forced the legislature to abolish itself and the constitution, making Jamaica a Crown colony. Both praised and censured, he was recalled in July 1866 amid calls for his trial for murder. Prosecutions followed but none was successful.

EYSENCK, HANS (1916–97), psychologist. Eysenck was born in Berlin and studied in France and in Britain. In 1934 he fled from Nazi Germany and settled in Britain where he studied psychology under Cyril BURT. In 1946 he became Director of the new Psychological Department at the Maudsley Hospital, London, where he developed his influential psychometric and other laboratory-based techniques for studying human intelligence and personality. He was a notorious critic of Freudian psychoanalysis and other psychological theories and techniques resting on apparently unsatisfactory evidence. In the 1950s he pioneered 'behaviour therapy', a technique that, unlike Freudian psychotherapy, treats the symptoms rather than the unconscious causes of mental illness and conditions patients into socially more acceptable forms of behaviour. For much of his career he produced experimental evidence for the genetic basis of intelligence and personality. In *Race, Intelligence and Education* (1971) he claimed that intelligence depended on racial type and therefore on genetic factors, a conclusion sparking controversy and claims that Eysenck's methods were culturally biased. He was Professor of Psychology at London University's Institute of Psychiatry (1955–83). A prolific writer of such best-selling books as *Uses and Abuses of Psychology* (1953), *Know your Own IQ* (1962), he was one of the most conspicuous figures in British psychology.

EZRA, DEREK (Baron Ezra of Horsham) (1919–), manager of nationalized coal industry. After army service (1939–47), Ezra's career spanned most of the history of the National Coal Board, of which he was Chairman (1971–82). His passionate belief in the potential for expansion in the coal industry, to be achieved largely through replacing obsolescent plant while retaining a large workforce, was supported by Labour governments but was never realized. Following his chairmanship, the ailing coal industry was to be racked by industrial action, led by Arthur SCARGILL, and near terminal decline.

F

FAGEL, GASPAR (1629–88), Dutch politician. In the 1660s he was one of the leaders of the 'middle party' between the De Wits and the Orangeists; his preference for the latter helped bring William of Orange (the future WILLIAM III) to power in 1672. As Grand Pensionary of Holland, he was a valuable ally and supported William in his designs on the English succession. In early 1688 a letter which he had written was published and circulated to strengthen William's position in England. The original recipient was James Stewart, a Scots Presbyterian lawyer who had returned to Britain following JAMES II's Declaration of Indulgence. James was seeking the support of Dissenters for his pro-Catholic policies, but Fagel condemned him for allowing Catholics to acquire political power. At the same time, Fagel identified William and MARY II with the view that no Christian should be persecuted for his conscience. James II responded by recalling all English soldiers serving with the Dutch army. Fagel assisted William in winning support for his invasion of England but died before he could see the policy bear fruit.

FAILBE (?–679), Abbot of Iona. Following the death of CUMMÉNE FIND, the abbacy passed to his cousin, Failbe, in 669. He is recorded travelling extensively in Ireland between 673 and 676, most likely visiting the Irish foundations of the Ionian confederation of monasteries. Little is known of his abbacy itself, although it appears to have been a period of peaceful stability for the great monastery. It also appears that Failbe had designated ADOMNÁN as his successor before his death in 679.

FAIRBAIRN, ANDREW (1838–1912), theologian. Principal of Mansfield College, Oxford, from 1888 to 1909, he was an elegant essayist and distinguished scholar. His books advocating liberal Congregational theology, especially *Studies in the Philosophy of Religion and History* (1876) and *Christ in Modern Theology* (1884), were highly regarded by contemporaries, but are now read only by specialists.

FAIRBAIRN, SIR WILLIAM (1789–1874), engineer. Born in Kelso (Roxburghs.), Fairbairn was apprenticed to a millwright in a Northumb. colliery and he taught himself scientific and literary subjects. By 1817 he had settled in Manchester, where with James Lillie he established an engineering firm which by 1830 had moved into shipbuilding and boiler-making. In 1832 he split with Lillie and continued on his own as a consultant shipbuilder. Three years later he set up shipbuilding works in Millwall, although this did not prove as successful as his Manchester business. One of the most distinguished engineers of iron structures, he designed and built hundreds of iron bridges, as well as iron ships, boilers and drainage works, and helped George STEPHENSON to build the tubular bridge across the Menai Straits.

FAIRFAX, FERDINANDO (2nd Baron Fairfax of Cameron) (1584–1652), soldier. From Yorks., he was frequently MP between 1614 and his death. He was General of Parliament's northern army against CHARLES I 1642–5, commanding the infantry at Charles's defeat at Marston Moor (1644). Resigning his command in the Self-Denying Ordinance of 1645 (*see* CROMWELL, OLIVER), he remained Governor of York until his death in an accident. He was succeeded as Baron by his son, Thomas FAIRFAX.

FAIRFAX, THOMAS (3rd Baron Fairfax of Cameron) (1612–71), soldier. A professional soldier who, though knighted by CHARLES I (1641), became General of Horse for the army of the Westminster Parliament when civil war broke out the following year. He proved an outstanding commander, outshining his father Ferdinando FAIRFAX, who also fought for Parliament. He shared in Parliament's victory at Marston Moor (1644) and as Lord General of Parliament's reconstituted forces, the New Model Army, commanded at the victories at Naseby and Langport (1645). He recaptured Colchester from Royalists in the renewed Civil War of 1648 but, increasingly unhappy at army militancy, took no part in the King's trial later that year. Though he relished suppressing the Leveller radical groups in the army, he resigned his command rather than invade Scotland in 1650. He was returned as a member for Oliver CROMWELL's Protectorate

Parliaments of 1654–5 and 1656–8, but boycotted both, and, though he played a part in recalling CHARLES II, he thereafter retired to Yorks., shunning active involvement in politics.

FAITHFULL, EMILY (1835–95), feminist. Daughter of a Surrey clergyman, Emily joined the Langham Place group (*see* BODICHON, BARBARA) and in 1860, concerned about lack of work opportunities for women, established the Victoria Press, employing 16 women compositors to print such periodicals as the *Englishwoman's Review* and the *Law Magazine,* an innovation that was regarded with much hostility by male printers. Appointed Printer and Publisher in Ordinary to Queen VICTORIA in 1862, Faithfull founded the *Victoria Magazine* (of which she was also editor until 1880), and in 1865 *Women and Work.* Cited in a messy and highly publicized divorce case in 1864, which did not endear her to colleagues in the Women's Suffrage Society in which she was briefly involved at the time, she founded the Women's Printing Society with Emma PATERSON.

FALKLAND, 2ND VISCOUNT *see* CAREY, LUCIUS

FANTOSME, JORDAN (*fl.* 1170), poet. A Winchester clerk, he was the author of an Anglo-Norman historical poem describing the 1173–4 revolt against HENRY II, including by far the most detailed account of WILLIAM I THE LION's invasions of the north of England.

FARADAY, MICHAEL *see* essay on page 311

FARMAN, JOSEPH (1930–), atmospheric scientist. Farman studied mathematics and natural sciences at Cambridge and in 1956 began researching atmospheric science for the British Antarctic Survey. In 1984 he and his colleagues produced startling evidence for the significant depletion of the ozone gases in the stratosphere above the Antarctic. Farman's evidence for this ecologically catastrophic ozone-hole has been widely accepted and linked to the artificial manufacture of chloroflurocarbons (CFCs), a gas used as an aerosol propellant. He continues to campaign for the reduction of chlorofluorocarbon production.

FARNABY, GILES (*c.* 1566–1640), composer. Cornish-born, he graduated from Oxford. Little is known of his life, but many of his keyboard pieces are found in the Fitzwilliam Virginal Book (*see* BYRD, WILLIAM), and he also wrote music for metrical psalms. His son Richard also composed keyboard music.

FARQUHAR, GEORGE (1678–1707), playwright. Said to have been the son of a poor cler-gymen, he left Trinity College, Dublin, to become an actor but, after accidentally injuring a colleague on stage, turned to writing. His first play, *Love and a Bottle*, was performed in London in 1698. His plays gradually moved from the cynicism of Restoration comedy, through the moralistic *The Constant Couple* (1699) and its sequel *Sir Harry Wildair* (1701), inspired by Jeremy COLLIER's criticisms of the stage, to his later and more good-natured plays, set in the provinces rather than tainted London society, including *The Recruiting Officer* (1706) and *The Beaux's Stratagem* (1707), the latter written when he was dying.

FARRER-HOCKLEY, SIR ANTHONY (1924–), soldier. While still under age he enlisted as a private in the Gloucestershire Regiment and in 1942 was commissioned into the airborne forces, with which he fought in Italy and Greece. After the war Farrer-Hockley saw extensive active service, including Palestine (1945–6), Korea (1950–3), Cyprus and Port Said (1956), Jordan (1958), Radfan (1962–5), Borneo (1965–6) and Northern Ireland (1970–1). A defence fellowship at Exeter College, Oxford, gave him the time to reflect on an extraordinary career and Farrer-Hockley subsequently became a notable military historian and a leading commentator on military affairs.

FASTOLF, SIR JOHN (1378–1459), soldier. An English commander in the Hundred Years War, he fought at Agincourt (1415), became Lieutenant of Normandy in 1423, and Governor of Maine and Anjou 1423–6. Victor at the 1429 'battle of her-rings', when he successfully defended a convoy of supplies, he was soon afterwards accused of cowardice when he retreated before Joan of Arc at Patay. From then on, he concentrated on his English estates, having entered the property market on the profits he had made out of the war. His dealings are unusually well documented: he employed William WORCESTER as his secretary, and much of his business correspondence survives in the PASTON letters. He built Caister Castle (Norfolk). His London property included the Boar's Head Tavern but, this apart, there is nothing to support the view that he was the model for SHAKESPEARE's Falstaff.

FATEH ALI TIPU *see* TIPU SULTAN

FAUCONBERG, THOMAS (?–1471), naval commander. An illegitimate son of William Neville, Lord Fauconberg, and known as the 'bastard of Fauconberg', he was employed as a naval commander by his cousin, Richard NEVILLE, Earl of Warwick (1470–1). As self-proclaimed 'captain of the navy of England' and 'leader of our liege lord King Henry's people in Kent', he raised

continued on page 312

FARADAY, MICHAEL (1791–1867)
Natural philosopher

Born in Newington (Surrey), a blacksmith's son, he was a member of a small dissenting religious sect, the Sandemanians. His fundamental belief in the unity of natural phenomena and his aversion to rash scientific speculation owed much to Sandemanian doctrines. After a rudimentary education, he was apprenticed in 1804 to a London bookbinder and developed his knowledge of natural philosophy by intense reading and attending public lectures on science. In 1813 he was appointed Humphry DAVY's assistant at the Royal Institution, where he remained for the rest of his life. Under Davy, he gained considerable expertise in analytical chemistry, with which he achieved such important chemical results as the liquefaction of chlorine and many other gases and the isolation of carbon chloride compounds (1820) and benzene (1825). In 1821, following the discovery by the Danish philosopher Christian Oersted that electricity produces magnetic fields, he built an apparatus which demonstrated that current-carrying wires are surrounded by circular magnetic lines of force. It is regarded as the first electric motor. In 1825 Faraday began the Royal Institution's Friday Evening Discourses, which helped him establish himself as the foremost scientific lecturer of his day, and in 1826 he succeeded Davy as director of the Royal Institution, where he launched the famous Christmas lectures for children. He also taught chemistry at the Royal Military Academy, Woolwich (1829–53), and investigated such issues as lighthouse illumination, the condition of mines and spiritualism.

In 1831 Faraday produced evidence for 'electromagnetic induction' – the induction of an electric current in a wire when it moves relative to the lines of magnetic force surrounding a magnet. The instrument which he used to display this phenomenon is regarded as the first transformer. He followed this with the construction of a machine for generating electricity from the rotation of a copper disc in a magnetic field (later seen as the first dynamo) and a series of other ground-breaking results. In 1833 he proposed his famous laws of electrolysis, which state that the mass of a chemical substance produced by electrolysis is proportional to the quantity of electricity passed through a solution, and that for a given quantity of electricity, the mass of a chemical product of electrolysis is proportional to its chemical equivalent (its atomic mass divided by its valence). A year later Faraday observed that when a current-carrying conductor is broken the magnetic field produced by the current induces a current in the same conductor ('self-induction') – an observation made independently by the American physi-

cist Joseph Henry in 1832.

By this time Faraday had developed the notion that the transmission of electromagnetic forces between inducing and induced bodies was due to a state of electrical tension (the 'electrotonic state') in the space between those bodies and not, as commonly held, action-at-a-distance forces between positive and negative imponderable electrical fluids. Faraday attributed the electrotonic state to the action between the contiguous polarized molecules constituting the 'dielectric' between inducing and induced bodies. Grave difficulties with this explanation prompted Faraday to explore the nature of matter and to reject, after a period of mental exhaustion (1839–43), the traditional doctrine that matter consisted of discrete atoms. Particularly during the mid 1840s he upheld the alternative and radical view that matter was merely a plenum of forces filling space. In 1845 he produced sensational evidence for the rotation of a ray of plane-polarized light by a strong magnetic field and for 'diamagnetism' – the susceptibility of all matter to magnetism. Faraday used this work to reinforce his long-held belief in the ontological primacy of the lines of force and to show that the phenomena of light, heat and gravitation were vibrations in those lines of force. During the 1850s Faraday promoted his sophisticated theory of magnetism (where he defined the concept of the 'magnetic field') and sought to demonstrate, often with specially designed instruments, the geometrical and quantitative connections between electrical and magnetic lines of forces. This latter project reflected his lifelong concern to show that the putatively distinct forces of electricity, magnetism, heat, chemical affinity and light were in fact unified.

Few of Faraday's scientific contemporaries grasped or accepted his work on lines of force, but through the work of James Clerk MAXWELL and others it reached wider audiences and Faraday himself was hailed as the founding architect of electromagnetic field theory. In 1862 he retired from the Royal Institution and spent his last years at Hampton Court.

Faraday is widely regarded as the greatest experimenter in the physical sciences. Although hailed as the 'father of the electrical industry', he was less directly concerned with the useful applications of his work on physical forces than with using it to develop the understanding of the natural world.

H. Bence Jones, *The Life and Letters of Faraday* (2 vols, 1870)
David Gooding and Frank A. J. L. James (eds), *Faraday Rediscovered: Essays on the Life and Work of Michael Faraday, 1791–1867* (1989)

the fleet and army that besieged London for three days in May 1471; the city held out. After surrendering to EDWARD IV, Fauconberg was executed.

FAULKNER, BRIAN (Baron Faulkner of Downpatrick) (1921–77), Prime Minister of Northern Ireland. He rose to prominence as a capable administrator and Cabinet minister under Brookeborough (*see* BROOKE, BASIL) and Terence O'NEILL, becoming a focus for Unionists who thought O'Neill's reforms went too far, and was seen as an opportunist by O'Neillites and hard-liners who disliked his reluctance to oppose O'Neill openly. He was defeated by one vote in the leadership contest after O'Neill's resignation in 1969, but succeeded CHICHESTER-CLARKE as Unionist Party leader and Prime Minister in 1971. He made some conciliatory gestures towards opponents, but these were offset by repressive and ill-judged security policies (such as internment for suspected terrorists) in response to growing political violence. In 1972 Stormont (the Northern Ireland Parliament) was suspended by the British government. In 1974, after elections to a new assembly, Faulkner negotiated the establishment of a power-sharing executive backed by the British government and including representatives of the centrist Alliance Party and the moderate nationalist Social Democratic and Labour Party (SDLP). Faulkner's electoral mandate was unclear; a large minority of assembly members supported more extreme Unionist parties, and the Feb. 1974 Westminster General Election showed that a majority of Unionist voters, constituting a narrow majority of the Northern Ireland electorate, opposed the agreement. Faulkner resigned as Unionist Party leader but remained head of the power-sharing executive until it was brought down by the Ulster Workers' Council strike. From 1974 to 1976 Faulkner led the Unionist Party of Northern Ireland, but this splinter group made little electoral impact and had disappeared by 1980.

FAWCETT, HENRY (1833–84), academic and politician. He lost his eyesight in a shooting accident when a young man. Professor of Political Economy at Cambridge from 1863, he became a Liberal MP for Brighton two years later. An advocate of women's rights and the husband of Millicent FAWCETT, he was as Postmaster General responsible for introducing the parcel post, postal orders and sixpenny telegrams.

FAWCETT, DAME MILLICENT (née Garrett) (1847–1929), women's suffrage leader. The younger sister of Elizabeth Garrett ANDERSON and friend of Emily DAVIES, she married Henry FAWCETT in 1867. His blindness led her to work as his political secretary and gave her access to the world of politics. She published *Political Economy*

for Beginners in 1870 and was active in campaigning for university education for girls and married women's property rights, but it was the cause of women's suffrage that was her lifetime crusade. She became President of the National Union of Women's Suffrage Societies in 1897, as well as speaking out against Home Rule in Ireland and being sent on a delegation to investigate concentration camps in South Africa during the Boer War. With the rise of the Pankhursts' militant suffrage movement, the Women's Social and Political Union (*see* PANKHURST, CHRISTABEL, EMMELINE and SYLVIA), Fawcett continued to recruit women who sought the vote through constitutional means and to strengthen party political alliances to this end. A conservative and patriot, she linked enfranchisement with social purity and hoped that when women had the vote domestic values would become the standard in public life. On the outbreak of the First World War she, like Mrs Pankhurst, urged her fellow suffragists to prosecute the war with vigour, but in 1916 she again petitioned for women's suffrage, which was passed by both Houses of Parliament in 1918.

FAWKES, GUIDO (OR GUY) (1570–1605), conspirator. Son of a Church lawyer from York, he converted to Roman Catholicism and from 1593 served in Spanish armies. A few desperate Catholic gentry led by Robert CATESBY decided to destroy their community's persecutors by blowing up JAMES I, Lords and Commons at Parliament's formal opening on 5 November 1605; Fawkes was chosen as agent for the actual explosion. Catholics reluctant to see friends killed betrayed the plans; the government may have allowed the plot to go forward. Fawkes was caught in the cellar below Parliament and under torture revealed the conspirators' names before his execution. The anniversary merged with earlier Protestant November celebrations as a permanent commemoration, featuring his burning in effigy.

FAYRFAX, ROBERT (*c.* 1464–1521), composer. From Lincs., he worked at Cambridge and Oxford and in the Chapel Royal (in which capacity he attended HENRY VIII at the Field of the Cloth of Gold in 1520), and was organist of St Albans Abbey, where he is buried. He composed much vocal music, including masses and motets.

FEATHER, VIC(TOR) (Baron Feather of Bradford) (1908–76), trade-union leader. Yorks.-born, Feather left school at 14 to work in a Co-operative grocery and was a shop steward for the Shopworkers Union by the time he was 15. He joined the staff of the Trades Union Congress (TUC) in 1937, rising to be General Secretary in succession to George WOODCOCK in 1969, and led the union opposition to the Labour government's White Paper 'In Place of Strife', which proposed legal restrictions on trade unions' right to strike. Faced with such forceful dissension, the government substituted a 'solemn and binding obligation' on the trade unions not to call unofficial strikes, and, though this had no legal force, Feather, a popular leader, worked to enforce it. When the incoming Conservative government, committed to curbing union power, passed an Industrial Relations Act (1971), Feather kept the unions united in skilful nullifying tactics. In 1974 the Labour government repealed the legislation, thus underlining the links between the unions and the government at that time.

FEIDLIMID MAC CRIMTHAINN (?–847), King of Munster (820–47). One of the most powerful kings of Munster before the time of BRIAN BORUMA, Feidlimid mac Crimthainn was able to impose his superiority over neighbouring kingdoms such as Leinster, and even claimed domination over the most powerful kingly family of early medieval Ireland, the Uí Néill, who ruled in the north. He was also a monk and interfered directly in ecclesiastical as well as secular politics. His readiness to burn monasteries founded by rival families made him notorious.

FELIX, ST (?–647), churchman. Invited to the kingdom of East Anglia by King SIGEBERHT, Felix was the first Bishop of East Anglia (c. 630–47). His career illustrates the diverse origins of the earliest missionaries to England, since, like St BIRINUS, he was a Frank, although possibly from a monastery founded by the Irish St COLUMBANUS. His successful collaboration with Sigeberht, like St AUGUSTINE's with ETHELBERT, illustrates the importance of royal–episcopal co-operation in the first stages of the conversion.

FELL, MARGARET (née Askew) (1614–1702), Quaker pioneer. Daughter of a Lancs. gentleman, in 1632 she married Thomas Fell, a lawyer, and they had nine children. In 1652 she was converted to Quakerism by George FOX while he was staying with the Fells at Swarthmoor Hall (Lancs.). She corresponded with Oliver CROMWELL, urging toleration for Quakers, was prominent in encouraging Jews to return to England to hasten the world's last days and led female protests against tithe payment. After CHARLES II's restoration (1660) she travelled organizing women's meetings, wrote numerous pamphlets arguing that women could experience divine revelation in the same way as men and so could play an equal part in worship, and suffered imprisonments, although she also successfully negotiated the release of thousands of Quakers in 1661; in 1669 she married Fox. She wrote an autobiography in 1690.

FENNER, DUDLEY (?1558–87), theologian. A brilliant Cambridge scholar, he was expelled for his Puritan views and, after travel abroad with Thomas CARTWRIGHT, returned as curate at Cranbrook (Kent) in 1583, clashing with Archbishop WHITGIFT over subscription to articles swearing religious conformity. Among his writings, mostly posthumously published, was *Sacra Theologia* (1585) the first work of English Protestant systematic theology. It was notable for expounding covenant theology, thereafter much developed among English and North American Puritans – also known as federal theology (*foedus* means treaty, covenant). This drew on the Old Testament idea of a covenant (agreement or treaty) between God and his people, to answer a problem posed by the Protestant doctrine that salvation is a free gift of God's grace: free grace might seem to destroy the importance of moral law in human affairs. Fenner therefore contrasted two different covenants: an unconditional covenant of grace, made by God only with true Christian believers, and a conditional covenant of works, binding on everyone, and dependent on observing God's moral code.

FENTON, ROGER (1819–69), photographer. The world's first accredited war photographer, Fenton, who had studied painting and exhibited at the Royal Academy, was helped by Queen VICTORIA and Prince ALBERT, whom he had photographed several times at Windsor and Balmoral, to go to the Crimea in 1855. The photographs which he took of the campaign conditions and the soldiers provide an incomparable historical source for the battles.

FENWICK, SIR JOHN (c. 1645–97), conspirator. Descended from an old Northumb. family, he was an MP under CHARLES II and JAMES II. A keen supporter of James II, he emerged after the Glorious Revolution of 1688–9 as a flamboyant and provocative Jacobite. Arrested in June 1696 for involvement in an assassination plot against WILLIAM III, he set out to cause more trouble by implicating GODOLPHIN, Marlborough (see CHURCHILL, JOHN), Shrewsbury (see TALBOT, CHARLES) and Edward RUSSELL in negotiations with James, provoking Godolphin's resignation. The Commons voted his accusations false and scandalous. Fearful of lack of sufficient evidence to convict, and of the embarrassment of further airing the accusations at a public trial, the ministry decided to proceed by bringing a Bill of Attainder in Parliament, where normal common-law trial rules would not apply. Many MPs and others were unhappy that the government was evading recent legislation passed to protect the rights of defendants in treason trials. After fierce debate, the Act was passed, and Fenwick was executed in Jan. 1697.

FERGUS MÓR MAC EIRC (?–?501), King of
Dál Riata. Traditionally the founder of Dál Riata,
although Gaelic settlement in the area is known to
date from before the late fifth century. It is more
likely that he was the first of the Dál Riata royal
dynasty to migrate to the colony from Ireland,
apparently under pressure from the eastwards
expansion of the Uí Néill; *The King-list of the
Kings of Dál Riata* states that he 'was the first of
the descendants of Conaire to receive the
kingdom of Scotland'. He may well have been
killed by his own followers.

FERGUSON, ADAM (1723–1816), moral
philosopher. A minister's son, he studied at St
Andrews and Edinburgh. He was made chaplain
of the Black Watch and was present at Fontenoy
(1745), a French victory in the War of the
Austrian Succession. He acted as tutor to the
sons of John STUART, Earl of Bute, and was
Professor of Modern Philosophy at Edinburgh
(1759), and Professor of Mathematics (1785). In
1778 he accompanied the British commissioners
on an unsuccessful attempt to negotiate peace
with the American colonies. The best received of
his works was his *Essay on the History of Civil
Society* (1766): this asserted the importance of
property for the evolution of manners and
customs that had accompanied the course of
economic development, culminating in the polite
and commercial society of the eighteenth
century, but urged that such a society risked
degenerating if not kept vigorous by military
endeavour.

FERGUSON, HENRY (HARRY) (1884–1960),
tractor manufacturer. The designer and producer
of the Little Fergie tractor which, with its cheap-
ness and mobility, was one of the great farming
successes of the 1940s and 1950s, Harry Ferguson
embodied both Anglo-American co-operation and
rivalry in the agricultural machinery market. A
farmer's son from Co. Down, he established a
motor-car business in Belfast in 1911. During the
First World War he supervised tractor deployment
in Irish agriculture and, recognizing the tractor's
potential and American superiority in production,
made the first of many approaches to Henry Ford
before setting up a manufacturing business in the
USA with the Sherman brothers. He established
the first of his UK tractor businesses with David
Brown of Huddersfield (Yorks.) and in 1938 struck
a manufacturing deal with Ford. Over 300,000 of
his 9N and 2N tractors were produced in the USA
between 1939 and 1947; when Henry Ford II
reneged on the production deal, Ferguson won
substantial damages in a patent application
lawsuit. In Britain his Little Fergie went into
production in Coventry in 1946; in 1953 his

company was merged with the Canadian
machinery firm of Massey-Harris.

FERGUSON, ROBERT (c. 1637–1714), conspirator. A Scot, he became a minister, but was expelled
from his living in Kent when he refused to conform
after the Restoration. He became a prominent religious controversialist, and wrote many pamphlets
in the context of the crisis associated with attempts
to exclude CHARLES II's brother James (the future
JAMES II) from the line of succession. He is thought
to have been one of the chief contrivers of the Rye
House Plot (1683), for which Algernon SIDNEY and
William RUSSELL were executed. Ferguson also
advised Argyll (*see* CAMPBELL, ARCHIBALD, 9th Earl)
and Monmouth (*see* SCOTT, JAMES); he served as
chaplain to the latter's army and in 1685 wrote the
manifesto circulated for him. Although he accompanied the invasion of William of Orange (the
future WILLIAM III) and was made Housekeeper to
the Excise, he felt insufficiently rewarded and
became a leading Jacobite agent. He was arrested
after an attempted Jacobite landing in 1692, and
again for involvement in an assassination plot in
1696. His *History of the Revolution* (1706) alleged
that the Glorious Revolution was a papal plot to
advance Cath-olicism. His last book, published in
1715, was appropriately enough a history of
conspiracies against governments from the reign of
WILLIAM I onwards.

FERRAR, NICHOLAS (1592–1637), religious
leader. A Cambridge academic, influential on
George HERBERT, he rejected a promising political
career in 1625 to retire to Little Gidding (Hunts.),
a tiny neglected parish. Having been ordained
deacon, he founded the Church of England's first
post-Reformation religious community there: an
idiosyncratic sanctified gentry household. Its
High Church ceremonialist and sacramentalist
devotion led to its destruction by Parliament's
soldiers in 1647, but its reputation lived on
(notably in T. S. ELIOT's *Four Quartets*, 1943) and,
recently, the community has been revived.

FERRAR, ROBERT (c. 1500–55), martyr. Yorks.-
born, he studied in Cambridge and Oxford, where
he converted to religious reformism. Thomas
CROMWELL's client, in 1535 he undertook (with
William BARLOW) a secret mission to JAMES V, advocating religious reforms like HENRY VIII's. In 1536
he became Prior of Nostell (Yorks.) and in 1548 he
succeeded Barlow as Bishop of St David's. Here
he became embroiled in disputes with senior
clergy, although several shared his Protestantism;
the documentation throws light on the early
Reformation in Wales. In 1553 MARY I imprisoned
him; he was one of very few Protestants to be
burned in Wales.

FERRERS, 4TH EARL OF *see* SHIRLEY, LAURENCE

FERRERS, ROBERT (6th Earl of Derby or Ferrers) (*c.* 1239–*c.* 1279), nobleman. A feud with Prince Edward (later EDWARD I) made him a supporter of Simon de MONTFORT's cause. He took up arms again in 1266 but was defeated at Chesterfield (Derb.) and imprisoned. He was released three years later but only after he had, in effect, allowed himself to be defrauded of his lands. They were given to HENRY III's son Edmund of Lancaster.

FERRIER, SIR DAVID (1843–1928), neurosurgeon. Ferrier studied philosophy in his native Aberdeen, psychology at Heidelberg, and medicine at Edinburgh and in Suffolk. He spent his early career as a physician and neuropathologist at King's College, London, and became a consultant to the National Hospital for Nervous Diseases. In 1873 Ferrier began to study the electrical excitation of the brain in invertebrates and subsequently produced evidence in support of the localization of the cerebral functions, notably the motor and sensory regions, using this work to develop powerful techniques in brain-surgery. Anti-vivisectionists bitterly opposed his experimental methods but many physicians regard him as the founder of neurosurgery.

FERRIER, KATHLEEN. (1912–53), singer. As a teacher of the piano, Ferrier entered a singing competition at the Carlisle Festival in 1937, and having won the contralto class she embarked on a singing career, touring the country and singing with the Bach Choir in London and recording songs with the accompanist Gerard Moore. An accomplished performer of *lieder*, particularly those of Brahms, she made her opera début in the premiere of BRITTEN's *The Rape of Lucretia* at Glyndebourne (Sussex) in 1946. She achieved critical acclaim on the continent and in the USA with her performances of Gustav Mahler's *Das Lied von der Erde*, her recordings of which are legendary, as are hers of ELGAR's *The Dream of Gerontius* under Sir John Barbirolli. Much loved by audiences and performers, she was awarded a CBE for her services to music just months before her premature death.

FIELD, JOHN (1545–88), clergyman. Oxford-educated, he spent his clerical career in London, harassed by Church authorities as a Puritan, particularly for his part in writing the fierce critique of the ecclesiastical status quo, the *Admonition to Parliament* (1572). Even so, he always had powerful patrons, chiefly Robert DUDLEY, Earl of Leicester. In the 1580s he became secretary and organizing genius of the group of clergy which set up a Presbyterian organization in the Church (the Classical Movement); this did not long survive his death.

FIELDEN, JOHN (1784–1849), politician. Inheriting with his brothers the family cotton-spinning business in Todmorden (Lancs.), against type Fielden became a principal promoter of the legislation to protect factory labour. He was elected a radical MP in the first reformed House of Commons of 1832, alongside COBBETT. He backed radical measures throughout his career and was a vigorous opponent of the 1834 New Poor Law. Author of the influential 1836 pamphlet *Curse of the Factory System*, he fought for the 10-hour factory working day and successfully sponsored the 1847 Ten Hours Act but lost his seat in that year's election. His family's influence in Todmorden, which became a hotbed of Chartism, was immense.

FIELDING, HENRY (1707–54), magistrate, dramatist and novelist. The son of an army officer, he was educated at Eton. Needing to make a living, he became a prolific writer of comedies and farces with a political edge, including *Pasquin* (1736) and *The Historical Register for the Year 1736*. Fielding helped provoke Robert WALPOLE's government into passing the 1737 Licensing Act, restricting performances to the theatres with royal patents or others with licences in special circumstances, and forcing all plays to be approved by the Lord Chamberlain before performance. Abandoning the theatre, Fielding undertook legal training at the Middle Temple, but continued to make his living chiefly by writing. After parodying Samuel RICHARDSON's enormously successful novel *Pamela* with his own *Shamela*, he produced several further 'comic epics', including his masterpiece *Tom Jones* (1749). Political connections led to his appointment as a Westminster magistrate in 1748; he became chairman the following year. In 1750 he commented on the background to the post-war crime wave in his *Inquiry into the Causes of the Late Increase in Robbers*. With his half-brother Sir John FIELDING, he tried to improve the standards of magisterial competence in London; the most remembered innovation is the Bow Street Runners, initially recruited from the ranks of freelance 'thief-takers', who investigated crimes and arrested offenders under Fielding's direction. They, and the similar teams attached to the Middx. justices by Parliament in 1792, were integrated by Robert PEEL into the Metropolitan Police in 1828.

FIELDING, SIR JOHN (?–1780), pioneer of policing. The half-brother of Henry FIELDING and Sarah FIELDING, blind from birth, he succeeded his brother as magistrate at Bow Street in 1755 and impressed contemporaries by building up a detailed knowledge of the criminal underworld, and was recognized as a key figure in the policing of the metropolis. In 1763 he obtained government funding for the establishment of horse patrols. Fielding's great advance in promoting a national criminal investigation network came in 1772, when he sent circulars to the clerks of the peace in England and Wales asking them to send him descriptions of escapees and suspects. In 1773 he founded the *Hue and Cry*, which contained these descriptions and was sent to all magistrates for them to reproduce; the cost was later undertaken by the government.

FIELDING, SARAH (1710–68), novelist. A sister of Henry and half-sister of John FIELDING, she published *The Adventures of David Simple* (1744), the story of a young idealist travelling through a corrupt world. Several more novels, including two more David Simple books and the moral tale for girls *The Governess* (1749), and a translation of Xenophon followed. She was a friend of Samuel RICHARDSON, who rated her abilities higher than those of her brother Henry.

FIELDS, DAME GRACIE (1898–1979), singer. A precocious child performer who sang in music halls from the age of 12, Gracie Fields was born in Rochdale (Lancs.). She remained associated with a down-to-earth North Country warmth and direct humour that battled the Depression, despite the facts that she lived half her life abroad and by 1938 was the highest-paid singer in the world. Best known for her comic songs such as 'The Biggest Aspidistra in the World' and her greatest hit, the sentimental 'Sally in Our Alley', she starred in a number of British comedy films. When her second husband, the Italian-born actor-director Monty Banks, whom she married in 1940, was declared an undesirable alien, the couple left for Hollywood. There Fields made more films and she toured the theatres of war entertaining British troops, who did not always appreciate her 'desertion' of Britain despite her fund-raising activities for the war effort. She settled in Capri, but made return visits to Britain: it was 'Our Gracie' who in 1951 closed the Festival of Britain, which King GEORGE VI had opened.

FIENNES, CELIA (1662–1744), traveller and diarist. Granddaughter of William FIENNES, 1st Viscount Saye and Sele, she married a merchant. A Whig and a Dissenter, she is best known for her travel journals, written in unpunctuated prose during several tours of England (*c*. 1687–1701). Her account, frequently cited by social and economic historians, chronicles urban improvement, the building and enhancement of country houses, and manufacturing and agricultural projects. Large parts of the text were published in 1888 and the whole in 1947.

FIENNES, NATHANIEL (*c*. 1608–69), politician. Son of William FIENNES, Lord Say and Sele, and a friend of Oliver CROMWELL, he was one of the leading members of the Long Parliament to favour an Independent rather than Presbyterian restructuring of the Church. In 1643 he escaped execution by Parliament for surrendering Bristol to Prince RUPERT, and, five years later, was a member of the Committee of Safety removed at PRIDE's Purge for their willingness to negotiate with CHARLES I. He was a member of the Council of State 1654–9, until Richard CROMWELL's fall; he sat in Oliver's House of Lords and tried to persuade him to take the Crown.

FIENNES, WILLIAM (1st Viscount Say and Sele) (1582–1662), politician. Although he gained his title through the influence of George VILLIERS, Duke of Buckingham, in 1624, Fiennes still resisted Buckingham and CHARLES I when they proposed new devices for raising royal revenue. He became involved in various schemes for New World colonies with Puritan and anti-Spanish aims, including the Providence Island Company (*see also* RICH, ROBERT, Earl of Warwick; RUSSELL, FRANCIS, Earl of Bedford), though his suggestion for establishing hereditary aristocracy in New England was not well received. These schemes kept opponents of Charles in contact. He refused Charles's military oath during the 'Bishops' Wars' (1639–40), and thereafter played a leading part with John PYM in the moves leading to the English Civil War in 1642. He sat in the Westminster Assembly which, from 1643, decided on the future shape of the Church, and he helped engineer the Self-Denying Ordinance which from 1644 to 1645 removed most of Parliament's senior commanders in favour of Oliver CROMWELL and his colleagues. His exact significance in Civil War politics is still controversial, particularly in formulating the Heads of the Proposals (the peace terms offered to Charles in 1647) – not surprisingly, given his nickname 'Old Subtlety'. Having spent much of the years after the King's execution brooding on Lundy Island, he was made Privy Councillor and Lord Privy Seal at CHARLES II's restoration in 1660.

FIFE, 13TH EARL OF *see* STEWART, MURDAC

FILMER, SIR ROBERT (?–1653), political writer. A strong Royalist, he lost much property during the Civil Wars, and was imprisoned in 1644. His treatise *Patriarcha*, which traced the rights of monarchs from Adam's rights as a father, was first published in 1680, along with other works useful to the Tories in the Exclusion Crisis. His *Freeholders' Grand Inquest* (1648) was also reissued in the 1680s: in its attack on the increasing claims of the Commons, it argued that Parliament and laws owed their origins to royal concessions, and had no independent title to exist. LOCKE criticized *Patriarcha* at length in his two *Treatises on Government* (1690).

FÍNÁN (?–661), churchman. A significant figure in the spread of Christianity to northern England, Fínán was sent from Iona in 651 as successor to St AIDAN, Bishop of Lindisfarne. BEDE relates that he built a new church on Lindisfarne, which was subsequently dedicated to St Peter, and that, following the death of PENDA, King of Mercia (d. 655), Fínán consecrated a priest called Diuma as Bishop of the Mercians. Despite condemning him for his observance of the date of Easter, Bede concedes that Fínán was remembered for his faith and piety.

FINCH, ANNE (née Kingsmill) (Countess of Winchilsea) (1661–1720), poet. A maid of honour to MARY OF MODENA, she married Heneage Finch, one of the Duke of York's (later JAMES II) Gentlemen of the Bedchamber. Her husband refused to take the oaths to WILLIAM III and MARY II in 1689 and they moved to the home of his nephew the Earl of Winchilsea, upon whose death he succeeded to the title in 1712. Anne Finch contributed anonymously to several anthologies in the 1690s and 1700s, including religious poems and many which observed contemporary manners and the social constraints faced by women. These included *The Spleen* (1701) which distinguished real from affected depression. Her best-known poem is, however, the naturalistic 'A Nocturnal Reverie' (1713), describing the sensations of a moonlit night.

FINCH, DANIEL (14th [2nd Finch] Earl of Nottingham) (1647–1730), politician. Nicknamed 'Dismal' for his lugubrious appearance, he was first elected an MP in 1673. A moderate High Churchman with a powerful following in the Commons, he usually supported the court, notably in the Exclusion Crisis, when he opposed moves to exclude the Catholic Duke of York (later JAMES II) from the succession. He unsuccessfully promoted a scheme for a regency in 1688–9, but was close to Queen MARY II and was made Secretary of State. In 1689 he introduced the Toleration Act, which provided that those who took the oaths of allegiance and supremacy and subscribed to a declaration against transubstantiation would escape the penalties for not attending church and for Dissenting worship. He hoped to accompany this with a Comprehension Act widening the parameters of the Anglican Church, but the Bill failed to pass. Forced to resign in 1693, he returned to office with GODOLPHIN and John CHURCHILL (later Duke of Marlborough) in 1702 as leader of the anti-Jacobite, High-Church Tories. His support, however, for an Occasional Conformity Bill (disqualifying for public office those who conformed occasionally but attended Dissenting services) and a 'bluewater' policy (avoiding military effort on the continent and concentrating on the navy, colonial expansion and overseas trade) embarrassed the ministry, and he resigned in 1704. Disliking the moderate Robert HARLEY, from 1711 he co-operated with the Whig Junto lords, opposing a peace in return for their support for an Occasional Conformity Bill. He took office in the Whig government of 1715, but was soon dismissed for advocating clemency for Jacobite peers involved in the rising.

FINDLAECH MAC RUAIDRÍ (?–1020), Mormaer of Moray. The father of MACBETH, Findlaech is reported in Scandinavian sources to have been defeated by SIGURD THE STOUT, Jarl of Orkney, at Skidmoor, in Caithness, at some point prior to 995. His career, otherwise, is unknown, although the circumstances of his death indicate that he was involved in a bitter family feud, being killed by his brother's sons, Mael Coluim and Gille Comgáin, the latter succeeding as Mormaer of Moray.

FINDLATER, 4TH EARL OF *see* OGILVY, JAMES

FÍNGHEN MAC CARTHAIGH (?–1261), King of Desmond. He succeeded in 1252 after the murder of his father Domnall by John Fitzthomas of Shanid. Fínghen ended the peace and went on the rampage, making a point of destroying English castles, finally overwhelming the English army at Callan (Co. Kilkenny) and killing Fitzthomas and his son Maurice. He was killed during a raid on Kinsale (Co. Cork) later the same year.

FIRMIN, THOMAS (1632–97), philanthropist. A London mercer, he was interested in philosophical and religious questions. His friends, who included Benjamin WHICHCOTE, John WILKINS and Thomas TILLOTSON, encouraged him to investigate social grievances and find solutions. Among his schemes was a clothing factory which employed those left destitute by the Great Plague of 1665 and a larger enterprise in which the poor manufactured linen. This was never profitable and Firmin supported it from his own wealth. His entrepreneurial approach to charity and his efforts as a publicist for such projects, however, set a pattern that many were to follow in the next two centuries and more. His other causes included

Protestant refugees from Poland and, in 1688–9, from Ireland, the dethronement of JAMES II and Socinianism. His protégé Stephen Nye was the first to coin the term 'Unitarian' for those Christians who rejected the doctrine of the Trinity as unscriptural, in a book sponsored by Firmin. In 1691 he was among the founders of the Society for the Reformation of Manners, which raised funds to finance prosecutions of those guilty of such 'moral' offences as prostitution and swearing.

FISH, SIMON (?–1531), writer. A Gray's Inn lawyer, he was one of a group of London religious reformists who had to flee to the Low Countries in the 1520s; abroad, he wrote the anti-clerical *Supplication of the Beggars* (1529), which infuriated Thomas MORE and is said to have delighted HENRY VIII when ANNE BOLEYN showed him a copy. His widow married an early reformist martyr, James Bainham.

FISHER, EDWARD (?–1650), writer. A London barber-surgeon, he published in 1645 (as 'E.F.') *The Marrow of Modern Divinity*, an extreme version of Calvinism, emphasizing God's absolute predestination to salvation and damnation. When the hard-line minister, James Hog of Carnock (Fife) (*c*. 1658–1734), republished the book in 1718, it was condemned by the Church of Scotland's General Assembly; they claimed that it implied that the saved are exempt from keeping laws, since they are elect to salvation (the doctrine of antinomianism: *see* FENNER, DUDLEY). The condemnation, much disputed, led to the prolonged 'Marrow Controversy' in the Kirk.

FISHER, GEOFFREY (Baron Fisher of Lambeth) (1887–1972), Archbishop of Canterbury (1945–61). Son of a clergyman, Fisher was ordained priest in 1913 and appointed Bishop of London in 1939. As Archbishop of Canterbury he fulfilled his spiritual and political duties with great skill and enthusiasm. He officiated at the coronation of Queen ELIZABETH II, with whom he cultivated a close personal friendship, as he did with successive prime ministers. He is best remembered for his ecumenical work, in particular his enthusiasm for closer ties between Rome and Canterbury. His efforts culminated in his meeting with Pope John XXIII in the Vatican in 1960, the first such meeting since Thomas ARUNDEL's visit to the Holy See in 1397.

FISHER, JOHN (1469–1535), Bishop of Rochester. A Cambridge humanist scholar of international reputation, he became confessor to Lady Margaret BEAUFORT, persuading her to benefit Cambridge with a divinity chair (to which he was appointed in 1503) and with the foundation of colleges. He was made Bishop in 1504 and did not seek a wealthier diocese; he became a renowned preacher. He brought ERASMUS to Cambridge in 1511, and they became lifelong friends. In the 1520s Fisher wrote important defences of Catholic theology, and pleased HENRY VIII by defending the King's orthodox tract *Assertio Septem Sacramentorum* (1521) following attacks from Martin LUTHER. From *c*. 1526, however, he threw his considerable moral influence against Henry's search for a marriage annulment, and bitterly opposed the break with Rome. He was arrested with Thomas MORE in 1534 (provocatively, the Pope gave Fisher a cardinal's hat); their execution the following year for refusing to swear to Henry's royal supremacy over the Church horrified European monarchs and scholars.

FISHER, JOHN (1st Baron Fisher of Kilverstone) (1841–1920), sailor. The son of a captain in a Highland regiment stationed in Ceylon, his Asiatic features earned him the nickname 'the Chink'. Entering the navy in 1854, Fisher served in the Baltic in the Crimean War, fought in China in 1860, and in 1863 was appointed to the *Warrior*, Britain's first steam-powered ironclad frigate. Fisher, an advocate of new naval technology and soon the navy's leading technocrat, devoted the 1870s to the development of torpedoes; retaining his interest in big-gun ships, he was appointed to command *Inflexible*, Britain's largest battleship, for the bombardment of Alexandria in 1882. In 1902 Fisher was appointed Second Sea Lord with responsibility for personnel. He immediately supported Lord Selborne's unpopular reforms of naval education, designed to give all officers a degree of technical competence. Promoted First Sea Lord in 1904, Fisher designed the first turbine-powered all big-gun ship, *Dreadnought*, which rendered all existing battleships obsolete and fuelled a naval construction race with Germany. Resigning in 1910, Fisher was called back to the navy in 1914 by his friend Winston CHURCHILL, but they quickly clashed over strategy. Fisher resigned again in 1915, and spent the remainder of the war as Chairman of the Admiralty Invention Board.

FISHER, SIR RONALD (1890–1962), statistician and biometrist. Fisher became interested in genetics while studying mathematics at Cambridge. Graduating in 1912, he worked as a statistician and a schoolteacher, and studied the correlation of human inheritance statistics and Mendelian genetics (*see* BATESON, WILLIAM). In 1919 he was appointed statistician to the Rothamsted Experimental Station, St Albans (Herts.), where he analysed data on agricultural field trials, conducted experiments on animal breeding and developed highly influential statistical techniques for designing and analysing experiments. In 1929 he published the celebrated embodiment of his statistical work, *Statistical Methods for Research Workers*, and a year later published *The Genetical Theory of Natural Selection*, a classic attempt to reconcile Darwinian evolution and Mendelian genetics which explained natural selection in terms of the mutations of genes in populations. *The Genetical Theory* also warned that selection in civilized communities would foster increasing dysgenic effects on human ability, which Fisher sought to reverse with eugenics. As GALTON Professor of Eugenics at University College, London (1933–43), he worked on the genetics of blood groups. He was also Professor of Genetics at Cambridge (1943–57).

FITT, GERRARD (GERRY) (Baron Fitt of Bell's Hill) (1926–), politician. A former merchant seaman who in the early 1960s emerged as the dominant nationalist politician in West Belfast (previously dominated by competing labour–nationalist splinter groups) and leader of the Republican Labour Party. As Westminster MP for West Belfast from 1966, he voiced Catholic grievances and built links with sympathetic Labour MPs. He was prominent in the Civil Rights movement of the 1960s. In 1970 he became the first leader of the Social Democratic and Labour Party (SDLP), and was Deputy Chief Executive of the power-sharing executive in 1974. In 1979 Fitt helped to bring down the CALLAGHAN government by abstaining in a vote of confidence in protest at its handling of Northern Ireland. Soon after the 1979 election he resigned from the SDLP leadership and the party itself after members opposed him by supporting John HUME's view that any future settlement must include a role for the government of the Republic of Ireland. Fitt's vocal opposition to the H-Block agitation and the 1981 hunger strike (*see* SANDS, BOBBY) eroded his support in West Belfast; his family home was regularly attacked and had to be abandoned. In 1983 he lost his West Belfast seat to Gerry ADAMS.

FITZALAN, HENRY (1512–90), nobleman *see* LLWYD, HUMPHREY; LUMLEY, JOHN

FITZGERALD, LORD EDWARD (1763–98), revolutionary. Younger son of the Duke of Leinster and a cousin of Charles James FOX, Fitzgerald received a Whiggish and reformist upbringing on his family's Irish estate (his mother's educational ideas were influenced by Rousseau). He joined the British army but was cashiered in 1792 for having attended a revolutionary banquet in Paris, where he was hailed as Citizen Fitzgerald. Elected to the Irish Commons, he was almost expelled in 1793 for derogatory remarks about the Lord Lieutenant. In 1796 he joined the revolutionary United Irishmen, rose speedily in their hierarchy, and became their military commander. In March 1798, in an attempt to forestall a rising, the Irish administration ordered the arrest of members of the Leinster Directory of the United Irishmen. Fitzgerald escaped, but in May was mortally wounded evading arrest and died in prison, securing for himself a place in the canon of Irish 'patriot' martyrs.

FITZGERALD, EDWARD (1809–83), poet. Fitzgerald was born and lived most of his life in Suffolk, where he sailed, penned lengthy, elegant letters to his many friends – including THACKERAY, TENNYSON and CARLYLE (which have greatly aided their subsequent biographers) – wrote books and translated a number of poems, the most celebrated being his free translation of *The Rubáiyát of Omar Khayyám*, from the Persian (1859).

FITZGERALD, GARRETT (1926–), Irish politician. A civil servant and academic before entering politics, Fine Gael Senator (1965–9) and member of the Dáil for Dublin South-East (1969–89), Fitzgerald became leader of the social democratic wing of the party (as distinct from the conservatives associated with party leader Liam COSGRAVE). Foreign Minister in the 1973–7 coalition, during which he oversaw the country's adjustment to EEC membership, he became party leader after the massive electoral defeat of 1977. Fitzgerald led a short-lived Fine Gael and Labour coalition government in 1981–2, and after a brief Fianna Fáil minority government returned to power in another coalition (1983–7). Fitzgerald's record as government leader was mixed: a proposal to legalize divorce was defeated by referendum in 1986, and a constitutional amendment aimed at further restricting abortion was carried despite his opposition, while he contained but did not reverse massive financial deficits deriving from the irresponsible fiscal policies of previous governments. His major success, the 1985 Anglo-Irish Agreement, gave the Irish Republic a say in the running of Northern Ireland and helped to shore up the moderate Social Democratic and Labour Party (SDLP) against Sinn Féin, but further alienated Ulster Unionists and had little impact on the political fortunes of his government. The coalition broke up in 1987 and after an election defeat Fitzgerald stepped down as party leader.

FITZGERALD, GERALD (3rd Earl of Desmond) (*c.* 1338–98), nobleman. Son of Maurice Fitzthomas, 1st Earl of Desmond, he held the office of Justiciar of Ireland (1367–9). Despite the official policy (as in the Statute of Kilkenny, 1366) to put a stop to the Gaelicization of the English colony, this prominent Englishman is famous above all as a Gaelic poet. He was held prisoner (1370–1) by Brian Ó Briain, King of Thomond, one of the episodes in his life about which he wrote verse, and in 1388 he sent a son to be fostered, Irish fashion, by the Uí Briains.

FITZGERALD, GERALD (8th Earl of Kildare) (c. 1456–1513), Irish leader. Known as 'the Great Earl', from his succession to the title in 1477 he was effectively ruler of Ireland (officially Lord Deputy from 1480). Pardoned for supporting Lambert SIMNEL's imposture in 1487, in 1494 he was attainted on suspicion of supporting Perkin WARBECK and imprisoned in the Tower of London. Nevertheless HENRY VII recognized his usefulness in sustaining fragile English power in Ireland and, as Lord Deputy again from 1496, Kildare remained loyal against Warbeck and reigned supreme. A skirmish with a rival led to his death from wounds.

FITZGERALD, GERALD (9th Earl of Kildare) (1487–1534), politician. Known in Ireland as Garret Og (young Gerald), he was son of the 8th Earl, and a hostage in England from 1497 to 1503. He was appointed High Treasurer of Ireland (1503–13), then succeeded his father as Lord Deputy (1513–18, 1524–5, 1532–34). His career, which saw the decay of the Geraldine ascendancy, was a curious mixture: royal service in Ireland and at the English court (both his wives were English); feuding particularly with his brother-in-law, Piers BUTLER, Earl of Ormond; repeated recalls to England on suspicion of treason, during the last of which he died in the Tower.

FITZGERALD, GERALD (11th Earl of Kildare) (1525–85), politician. After the execution of his brother, Thomas FITZGERALD, the 10th Earl, in 1536, he was taken to Flanders and Rome for safety, returning after HENRY VIII's death to regain, in 1552, his forfeited estates; he won further favour from MARY I for his part in helping to suppress the Kentish rebellion of Sir Thomas WYATT the younger (1554), and he forwarded her Irish colonization plans. A pattern familiar to great Irish lords followed under ELIZABETH I: partly because of his continuing Catholicism, he was alternately favoured and harassed for suspected disloyalty.

FITZGERALD, GERALD FITZJAMES (14th Earl of Desmond) (c. 1533–83), Irish leader. One of the most powerful men in Ireland and a constant problem for ELIZABETH I, he was imprisoned in London from 1567 to 1573 for feuding with his stepson James BUTLER, Earl of Ormond. Thereafter he intrigued with Catholic overseas powers until openly rebelling in Munster in 1579. The rebellion was gradually beaten back, and he was in hiding, his family's power destroyed, when he was treacherously murdered by his own followers.

FITZGERALD, JAMES (15th Earl of Desmond) (c. 1570–1601), politician. Born in England, all his life he was a political pawn. He was sent to Ireland in 1579 when his father rebelled and was imprisoned in Dublin Castle before being returned to the Tower of London (1584). In 1600, with Ireland convulsed by Hugh O'NEILL's war of independence, he was restored to the earldom and sent to Ireland to rally Fitzgeralds to Crown loyalty away from his cousin James Fitzthomas Fitzgerald (?–1607; derisively known by loyalists as 'the súgán [straw rope] Earl'). As a Protestant outsider, he made no impact. He returned to London and died suddenly.

FITZGERALD, JAMES FITZMAURICE (?–1579), politician. In 1569 he rebelled in Desmond (south-west Ireland) against the imposition of Protestantism but, after a stalemate, submitted to Sir John PERROTT in 1573. Thereafter he travelled widely on the continent, planning with Pope Gregory XIII and the maverick English soldier Sir Thomas STUCLEY an invasion of Ireland which was backed by a papal indulgence and was proclaimed both as a papal crusade and as an Irish war of liberation from English rule: a new combination of ideas which had a lasting effect on Irish relations with England. Soon after landing at Dingle (Kerry) with the invasion force, he was killed by his cousin Theobald Burke.

FITZGERALD, JAMES FITZTHOMAS, (?–1607), soldier see FITZGERALD, JAMES

FITZGERALD, MAURICE FITZTHOMAS (?–1356), soldier. In 1312 he married Catherine, daughter of Richard de BURGH, Earl of Ulster. This stopped, albeit temporarily, a long-standing family feud. He was created 1st Earl of Desmond in 1329. In 1346, championing the cause of the English born in Ireland, he was imprisoned for refusing to attend the Parliament. He was released in 1349, became loyal to EDWARD III, and for the last year of his life was Viceroy of Ireland.

FITZGERALD, RAYMOND (also known as Raymond le Gros) (?–1182), soldier. He first went to Ireland as Strongbow's (see CLARE, RICHARD DE) representative in 1170, when he took Waterford. He became Constable of Leinster, and in 1175 Governor of Ireland, before handing over to

William Fitzaldhelm a year later. He moved south, where he pacified the area and became master of Cork. His character and military exploits were admiringly described by his cousin, Gerald de BARRI.

FITZGERALD, THOMAS (Baron Offaly, 10th Earl of Kildare) (1513–36), Irish leader. Known as 'Silken Thomas', he was the son of the 9th Earl. Told (wrongly) that his father had been executed, and angry at government attempts to curb his family's power by promoting rivals, he rebelled in 1534 (the Kildare rebellion), murdering John ALLEN, Archbishop of Dublin, on 28 July and appealing for support from the Pope and the Emperor CHARLES V. After surrendering to Lord Leonard GREY in 1535, the promise of a pardon was betrayed and he was executed as a traitor, with five of his uncles.

FITZGERALD, THOMAS FITZJAMES (8th Earl of Desmond, the Great Earl of Desmond) (c. 1426–68), soldier. A Yorkist supporter, who pursued a feud against the pro-Lancastrian Butlers (earls of Ormonde), defeating them in battle at Pilltown (Co. Kilkenny) in 1462, the year he succeeded his father as Earl. He governed English Ireland as Clarence's (see PLANTAGENET, GEORGE) deputy until 1467, when his friendships with the Irish led to him being replaced by John TIPTOFT, Earl of Worcester, and convicted of treason and executed. The rebellion of the Geraldines of Munster that followed meant that the English government lost control of south-west Ireland.

FITZGERALD, THOMAS FITZMAURICE (7th Earl of Kildare) (?–1478), royal servant. Between 1455 and 1475 he several times governed English Ireland as a Yorkist Deputy Lieutenant. Like his brother-in-law, Thomas FITZGERALD, Earl of Desmond, he was accused of fostering alliances with the Irish and convicted of treason in 1468, but escaped to England and secured the reversal of the verdict. The events of 1468 and their aftermath left the earls of Kildare as the only Anglo-Irish magnates of sufficient stature to govern the dwindling colony.

FITZGIBBON, JOHN (1st [Irish] Earl of Clare) (1749–1802), politician. The second son of a landowning barrister, he was called to the Irish Bar in 1772, where he built up a successful practice. Elected MP in the Irish Parliament in 1778, he was a supporter of cautious reform although not of full legislative independence. Nonetheless, GRATTAN supported his appointment as Attorney General in 1783. Fitzgibbon used the post to block further radical reform and introduce repressive measures against potential rebellion. He opposed Catholic enfranchisement but advocated voluntary land reform to end the power of 'rapacious agents' over poor tenants. In 1789 he was made Lord Chancellor of Ireland as a reward for his steadfast support of PITT THE YOUNGER's ministry during the Regency crisis, and in 1795 his ascendancy over Irish politics was demonstrated when he forced the Lord Lieutenant, Earl Fitzwilliam, from office over his mildly pro-Catholic policy, and was himself made an earl. Fitzgibbon supported the Union of 1801 on the grounds that it preserved the connection with Great Britain and guaranteed stable finances, but his antipathy towards Catholicism contributed to his failure to make a mark at Westminster.

FITZHAMON, ROBERT (?–1107), royal servant. His loyalty to WILLIAM II was rewarded with great estates on the Welsh frontier, a position that was buttressed by his marriage to Sybil, daughter of Roger of Montgomery, and extended by an aggressive policy which ensured that later tradition would see him as the conqueror of Glamorgan and builder of Cardiff Castle. Fighting for HENRY I at Falaise in Normandy in 1106 he was fatally wounded by a spear thrust through the head. His lands went to his daughter Mabel and her husband ROBERT OF GLOUCESTER.

FITZHERBERT, MARIA (née Smythe) (1756–1837), 'wife' of King GEORGE IV when Prince of Wales. From the Catholic gentry, she was widowed twice as a young woman, and moved in fashionable society. The Prince of Wales fell in love with her but she refused to become his mistress. Despite the provisions of the Royal Marriages Act of 1772, which required such marriages to have the monarch's consent, and the Act of Settlement of 1701, which would have barred the Prince from the throne had he legally married a Catholic, a marriage ceremony took place in Dec. 1785. George concealed the ceremony from his political allies, leading in April 1787 to embarrassment for Charles James FOX after he denied in the Commons that any such event had taken place. The couple grew apart in 1793–4 over the Prince's rakish existence and his infidelities, but after the failure of his legal marriage to CAROLINE of Brunswick they were reconciled, Pope Pius VI assuring Maria that her marriage was valid in the eyes of the Church. A final separation took place in 1809 after the Prince fell in love with the Marchioness of Hertford, but Maria remained the residual legatee of his will and after his death received £10,000 a year from the government in return for releasing her claims on his property.

FITZHERBERT, WILLIAM (also known as St William of York) (?–1154), Archbishop of York

(1141–7, 1153–7). He was an aristocratic, affable and generous cleric, and his first election as Archbishop of York (1141) was bitterly opposed by the Cistercians. In 1147 they secured his deposition on grounds of simony (the buying and selling of ecclesiastical offices) by the Cistercian Pope, Eugenius III. In 1153 the new Pope, Anastasius IV, restored Fitzherbert to his see, but his death, probably of a fever, very soon after his return to York resulted in the rumours of poisoning that contributed to a popular view of him as a martyred saint. He was canonized in 1226.

FITZNIGEL, RICHARD (*c*. 1130–98), royal servant. Like his father Nigel, Bishop of Ely, before him, Richard was an active servant of the Crown (Treasurer from *c*. 1158; judge from the 1170s) and was rewarded with the bishopric of London in 1189. He is the author of the *Dialogue of the Exchequer* (*Dialogus de Scaccario*), an account of Exchequer procedure written in the late 1170s and the earliest administrative handbook in English history.

FITZOSBERN, WILLIAM (1st Earl of Hereford) (?–1071), soldier. A friend of William of Normandy (later WILLIAM I THE CONQUEROR), and one of the planners of the Norman Conquest, he fought at the Battle of Hastings in 1066, was created Earl in 1067 (traditionally of Hereford, but probably with far wider authority) and shared control of England with Bishop ODO of Bayeux when William returned home. Normans admired him; the English thought his rule severe. He built the early stone castle at Chepstow (Mon.). He was killed at the Battle of Cassel while intervening in a disputed succession to the county of Flanders.

FITZPATRICK, BARNABY (*c*. 1535–81), nobleman *see* EDWARD VI, essay on page 281.

FITZPETER, GEOFFREY (4th [1st Fitzpeter] Earl of Essex) (?–1213), royal servant. From relatively modest origins, he rose through administrative service as Sheriff, Baron of the Exchequer and judge, was appointed Chief Justiciar by RICHARD I in 1198 and was created Earl of Essex in 1199. Although relations between him and JOHN were at times tense, he remained the chief minister until his death. He may have been the author of the lawbook known as *Glanvill*.

FITZROY, AUGUSTUS HENRY (3rd Duke of Grafton) (1735–1811), politician and Prime Minister (1767–70). Elected MP in 1756, he moved to the Lords on succeeding his grandfather the following year. One of several well-born young men who came to the fore in the 1760s, he was made northern Secretary of State in Rockingham's (*see* WATSON-WENTWORTH, CHARLES) 1765–6 ministry, and First Lord of the Treasury in Chatham's (*see* PITT THE ELDER) ministry of 1766. When Chatham fell ill, Grafton became head of the administration, but his ministry lacked cohesion and incurred unpopularity over the WILKES affair, and he resigned in 1770. He served as Lord Privy Seal under NORTH (1771–5), resigning over American policy. He was again Lord Privy Seal under Rockingham and Shelburne (*see* PETTY, WILLIAM) in 1782–3, then retired from political life. A rake as a young man, he subsequently reformed and wrote several religious tracts.

FITZROY, HENRY (1st Duke of Richmond) (1519–36). HENRY VIII's only acknowledged illegitimate son, by Elizabeth Blount, was made Duke in 1525 to provide a possible male heir to the throne. He was showered with various nominal administrative titles, including the lieutenancy of Ireland (1529). He married Mary, the daughter of Thomas HOWARD, 3rd Duke of Norfolk, and his brother-in-law Henry HOWARD, Earl of Surrey, educated with him, became a close friend. He died of tuberculosis; his widow long survived him and became an enthusiastic Protestant.

FITZROY, ROBERT (1805–65), explorer. As commander of HMS *Beagle*, sailing round the world (1831–6) with Charles DARWIN on board as naturalist, Fitzroy made his name as an explorer, publishing two volumes of narrative accounts of the *Beagle* voyages in 1839. Darwin published the third volume. Fitzroy was elected MP for Durham in 1841, and was Governor of New Zealand (1843–5). He was recalled because of his support for Maori land rights. Retiring from public service in 1850, he became a meteorologist, and invented the storm warning system.

FITZWILLIAM, 2ND EARL OF *see* WENTWORTH-FITZWILLIAM, WILLIAM

FITZWILLIAM, SIR WILLIAM (1526–99), administrator. He was Vice-Treasurer for Ireland (1559–73), Lord Justice (1571) and Lord Deputy (1572–5 and 1588–99). In 1587, as Governor of Fotheringhay Castle, he presided over MARY QUEEN OF SCOTS's execution. Primarily a financial expert whom circumstances propelled into military action, in 1561 he played a crucial part under Thomas RADCLIFFE, Earl of Sussex, against Shane O'NEILL. Until he left Ireland in 1594, Fitzwilliam remained reluctantly active in colonial warfare.

FLAMANK, THOMAS (?–1479), rebel *see* JOSEPH AN GOF, MICHAEL

FLAMBARD, RANULF (?–1128), bishop. His

role as WILLIAM II RUFUS's financial expert and chief agent of that King's notoriously extortionate government guaranteed Flambard's unpopularity, especially in monastic circles. In 1097 he was managing for his own and the King's profit no fewer than 16 vacant abbeys and bishoprics. In 1100 the new King, HENRY I, in a gesture calculated to win applause, threw him into the Tower, but he escaped and made his way to the court of ROBERT II Curthose. After Henry's conquest of Normandy in 1106, he restored him to Durham, the bishopric which he had bought in 1099. There, although his worldly lifestyle scandalized the monks, he was to be largely responsible for building the great nave of Durham Cathedral.

FLAMSTEED, JOHN (1646–1719), astronomer. The son of a Derby businessman, he studied astronomy while working for his father. His discoveries were rewarded in 1675 when he was chosen as the first Astronomer Royal. With the help of friends at court, and later his own inheritance, he equipped the Royal Observatory at Greenwich and by 1689 had made over 20,000 observations. His achievements included establishing the latitude of Greenwich and methods of calculating the co-ordinates of heavenly bodies, as well as valuable work on the sun and moon. His insistence on witholding his work until he was sure that it was correct hindered the research of NEWTON and HALLEY, and his great star catalogues, *Historia Coelestis Britannica* and *Atlas Coelestis,* were not published until after his death.

FLANN SINNA MAC MAÍL SHECHINALL (?–916), King of Meath and Tara (879–916). As head of the Clann Cholmáin, Flann Sinna succeeded AED FINDLAITH MAC NÉILL as King of Tara in 879, thus maintaining the alternation of the kingship between that southern Uí Néill dynasty and the Cenél nEógain of the northern Uí Néill. For much of his long reign, Flann Sinna had to contend with a renewed challenge to the supremacy in Ireland of the Uí Néill kings of Tara from the Munster kings of Cashel. The challenge from Munster, however, was crushed by the defeat and death of CORMAC MAC CUILENNÁIN, King of Cashel, at the Battle of Belach Mugna in 908.

FLAXMAN, JOHN (1755–1826), sculptor and illustrator. His father, the plaster modeller John Flaxman (1726–91), worked for SCHEEMAKERS, ROUBILIAC and WEDGWOOD among others. The younger Flaxman won several prizes from the Society of Arts when very young, and began designing for Wedgwood in 1775, also working as an independent sculptor. From 1787 he was based in Italy, where he received commissions to illustrate the works of Dante, Homer and Aeschylus which won him fame throughout Europe. From 1810 he was Professor of Sculpture at the Royal Academy. GEORGE IV commissioned a statue of Britannia from him for Marble Arch, but it was eventually placed as Minerva on the portico of the National Gallery.

FLEETWOOD, CHARLES (1618–92), soldier. A colonel in Parliament's New Model Army created in 1645, he was prominent in the army's 1647 confrontation with Parliament over pay and the direction of future policy, though himself an MP. He became son-in-law to Oliver CROMWELL in 1652, and succeeded him as Commander-in-Chief in Ireland. Later (1654–7) he was Lord Deputy in Ireland, but his reform schemes there were abortive and from 1655 he was more active in England as one of the major-generals instituted to levy taxes and impose discipline in the regions. He was influential in resisting the proposal that Cromwell take the Crown in 1657 and, as Commander-in-Chief in England in 1659, he helped remove Richard CROMWELL, but was ousted by the restored Rump Parliament before the recall of CHARLES II.

FLEMING, SIR ALEXANDER (1881–1955), bacteriologist. Born in Ayrshire, Fleming studied medicine at St Mary's Hospital, Paddington, where, after graduating, he worked under Almoth Wright on immunization and was one of the first to use Salvarsan to treat syphilis sufferers. During the First World War he served in the Royal Army Medical Corps and linked infection to the presence of streptococcus in wounds and observed the antibacterial powers of substances occurring naturally in the human body. After the war he developed this work at St Mary's and in 1922 announced the existence of 'lysosome', an antibacterial enzyme found in mucus, saliva and tears. In 1928, he was appointed Professor of Bacteriology at St Mary's, he made what many regard as a revolutionary scientific discovery: he observed that a culture of staphylococcus microbes had become contaminated with a mould that had stopped the growth of the microbes. After isolating and growing the mould, which he called penicillin, he observed that it had very powerful antibacterial powers and did not harm healthy tissue or antibacterial cells. Fleming anticipated the considerable medical uses of penicillin, but abandoned clinical trials owing to difficulties purifying and producing a stable form of the substance. Howard FLOREY, Ernest CHAIN and others working in Oxford successfully completed Fleming's work over 10 years later. Fleming shared the 1945 Nobel Prize for Medicine with Florey and Chain.

FLEMING, IAN (1908–64), writer. Educated at Eton and the military academy at Sandhurst,

Fleming went into journalism, working for Reuters, as foreign manager of Kemsley newspapers and as the columnist 'Atticus' in the *Sunday Times*. During the Second World War he worked in naval intelligence in Whitehall. This, and his experiences as a foreign correspondent, gave him much of the background for his 'James Bond' books, the first of which was *Casino Royale* (1953). The novels were an instant success and he wrote them at the rate of rather more than one a year until his death. The best-known, *Goldfinger* (1959), *From Russia with Love* (1957) and *Dr No* (1957), were made into highly successful films in the 1960s starring Sean CONNERY. Bond was a hero for the Cold War era, though criticized for violence, sadism and sexism, and the formula of the romantic hero taking on a selection of exotic master-criminals usually intent on world destruction proved remarkably enduring.

FLETCHER, ANDREW (1653–1716), political thinker. The son of an East Lothian landowner who employed Gilbert BURNET to tutor him, he spent most of the period 1665–78 being educated on the continent. On his return Fletcher was elected MP for East Lothian, where he became a leading spokesman of the opposition to Lauderdale (*see* MAITLAND, JOHN), attempting to frustrate the introduction and collection of new taxes to support the army. He went into exile in 1683, eventually joining the court of the Duke of Monmouth (*see* SCOTT, JAMES), whom he accompanied to England in 1685 despite his misgivings about rebellion. Fletcher broke with Monmouth before the rebellion's failure and travelled across Europe, returning with William of Orange (the future WILLIAM III) and initially supporting a parliamentary union of England and Scotland, but he came to see William's ambitions as no different from those of Louis XIV and other would-be 'universal monarchs'. Fletcher now became the champion of Scottish self-determination, investing £1,000 in the Darien venture (1699), a scheme to set up a company to trade with South America; in 1703 he returned to the Scottish Parliament and forced through the Act of Security. This provided that if ANNE's successor in Scotland also succeeded her in England, Scotland should be governed by a committee appointed by annual Parliaments. Fletcher thought that he had successfully guaranteed Scottish independence, but his actions made London more determined to seek an incorporating union and he was unable to stop its passage. Although regarded as a Scottish patriot, he lived at least half his life outside Scotland and saw the country as a model for the government of small states in an age of empires.

FLETCHER, ANDREW (Lord Milton) (1692–1766), administrator. The nephew of Andrew FLETCHER of Saltoun, he became an advocate in 1717 and a Lord of Session in 1724 with the title of Lord Milton. In 1735 he became Lord Justice Clerk, having impressed the Earl of Ilay (*see* CAMPBELL, ARCHIBALD) with his legal knowledge and ability, and assumed the management of Scottish patronage and elections. After the 1745–6 Jacobite rebellion, Milton took the lead in reforming the Highlands, devising the means to abolish heritable jurisdictions and measures to integrate the Highlands with the wider economy.

FLETCHER, JOHN (1579–1625), playwright. Son of Richard Fletcher, a leading clergyman who became Bishop of London, *c.* 1606 he began co-writing with Francis BEAUMONT, producing a series of plays, a collected edition of which appeared in 1647. He also wrote plays without collaborators, and additionally worked with Philip Massinger (1583–1640), with William Rowley (?1585–?1642) and probably with William SHAKESPEARE on *Henry VIII* (1617).

FLETCHER (OR DE LA FLÉCHÈRE), JOHN (1729–85), Methodist. He came to England from Switzerland in 1752 as tutor to the sons of a Salop. gentleman, Thomas Hill, a relative of Richard and Rowland HILL. Fletcher became an Anglican priest in 1757 with the aim of assisting John WESLEY. Hill gave him a Salop. parish, Madeley, in 1760, where he became well known for his measures to maximize the numbers of his congregation. Selina HASTINGS, Countess of Huntingdon, appointed him Superintendent of the ministerial college at Trevecca in 1768, but he resigned in 1771 when he sided with Wesley over the Calvinistic controversy.

FLINDERS, MATTHEW (1774–1814), map-maker and explorer. The son of a Lincs. surgeon, he joined the navy in 1790. One of his early missions was, with William BLIGH on the *Providence*, to bring breadfruit from the Pacific to the West Indies. Bligh recognized his abilities and gave him responsibility for navigation. In 1795 he went to New South Wales with Governor John Hunter and devoted his spare time to the exploration of Australia, helped by naval surgeon George Bass, who in 1798 discovered Bass Strait between the mainland and Tasmania, a discovery confirmed by Flinders in 1799. In 1801 he was appointed Commander of the *Investigator*, charged with mapping the coast of Australia; he covered most of the coast but his ship needed repairs and when seeking help in Mauritius he was arrested as a spy. Imprisonment from 1803 to 1810 broke his health and he died before he could complete an account of his discoveries.

FLITCROFT, HENRY (1697–1769), architect. The son of a labourer, he was working as a journeyman carpenter at Burlington House in 1719 when he fell from the scaffolding and broke his leg. Lord Burlington (*see* BOYLE, RICHARD) paid for his treatment and on visiting him saw his drawings and engaged him as his architectural assistant. Although he was not as imaginative as KENT or CHAMBERS, Flitcroft's work combined a devotion to Palladian architecture with personal experience of the construction process. He joined the Office of Works in 1726, rising to be Comptroller in 1758. His most enduring works are the Pantheon and Alfred's Tower at Stourhead (Wilts.), commissioned by Henry HOARE, and a folly for the Marquess of Rockingham (*see* WATSON-WENTWORTH, CHARLES), Hooker's Stand, at Wentworth Woodhouse (Yorks.).

FLOOD, HENRY (1732–91), politician. Illegitimate son of the Chief Justice of the Irish King's Bench, he studied both at Trinity College, Dublin, and at Oxford, was admitted to the Inner Temple, and for some years practised law in England before returning to Ireland and entering Parliament as an opposition member in 1759. A prominent 'patriot' during the late 1760s and early 1770s, he piloted the Octennial Act through the Irish Commons in 1768 and became for a while an ally of the Lord Lieutenant, Viscount TOWNSHEND. He accepted office in 1775, but soon found himself outshone by a new generation of 'patriots'. The late 1770s and early 1780s saw Flood and GRATTAN vying to outdo each other as champions of the causes of the day, the removal of British restrictions on Irish trade and the independence of the Irish Parliament both from oversight by the British Privy Council and from any attempt by the British Parliament to legislate for Ireland. Once the independence of the Irish Parliament had been conceded in 1782, and further confirmed by the British Parliament's 'renunciation' of any claim to legislative competence in Ireland, Flood championed the cause of parliamentary reform. He introduced a Bill whose provisions included triennial Parliaments and the addition of neighbouring rural electors to decayed boroughs (but remained silent on the controversial issue of removing the bar on Catholic voting); it was voted down by more than two to one.

FLOREY, SIR HOWARD (Baron Florey) (1898–1968), pathologist. Florey studied medicine in his native Adelaide, physiology at Oxford, pathology at Cambridge and surgery in the United States. He was Professor of Pathology at Sheffield (1931–4) and at Oxford (1935–62), where he conducted his celebrated work on penicillin, the antibacterial substance discovered by Alexander FLEMING in 1928. By 1941 he and the chemists Ernest CHAIN and Norman Heatley had isolated, purified and conducted successful clinical trials on penicillin. Subsequently they persuaded American drug companies to mass-produce penicillin, which enabled the drug to be used for the casualties of the D-Day landings. Florey, Fleming and Chain shared the 1945 Nobel Prize for Medicine.

FLORIO, JOHN (?1553–?1625 or 1626), writer. Son of an Italian Protestant refugee who settled in London, Florio studied and taught at Oxford and, with encouragement from aristocratic patrons including Robert DUDLEY, Earl of Leicester and Henry WRIOTHESLEY, Earl of Southampton, specialized in introducing Italian and French texts to England. He produced an Italian–English dictionary (1598), and in 1603 published the first English translation of the essays of Michel Eyquem de Montaigne (1533–92). From 1603 he held offices at the royal court.

FLUDD, ROBERT (1574–1637), scientist. He studied at Oxford and abroad, and became prominent in the Royal College of Physicians. In pursuing magical wisdom, he took a vow of chastity. He became a leading advocate for pseudo-Egyptian mystical writings attributed to the god Hermes Trismegistus (the *Corpus Hermeticum*), and wrote (sometimes pseudonymously) championing the Rosicrucians (exponents of occult wisdom and science), publishing mostly abroad and in Latin. He wrote defending his scientific mysticism against the Danish astronomer Johann Kepler and the French philosopher Pierre Gassendi. Despite considerable influence in promoting astrology, he was already coming under attack in his last years.

FOLEY, PAUL (*c*. 1645–99), politician. The son of Thomas Foley, Dissenting owner of ironworks at Stourbridge (Worcs.), he was influenced by his father's friend Richard BAXTER, gaining a reputation for personal piety and honesty. An MP in 1679, he played an active part, on the Whig side, in the Exclusion Parliament (*see* COOPER, ANTHONY ASHLEY). JAMES II tried to win him over, and made him a magistrate. Nonetheless, Foley supported the accession of WILLIAM III and MARY II in 1689, and again played an active part in the Convention Parliament. He emerged as leader with Robert HARLEY of a group, at first staunch Whigs, who later opposed the Whig Junto. Elected Speaker in 1695, from the Chair he opposed the attainder of FENWICK in 1696, and with his kinsman Harley proposed a National Land Bank to offer an alternative to the Bank of England. He opposed foreign trade and William III's foreign ministers, seeing both as a threat to parliamentary government.

FOLIOT, GILBERT (?–1188), cleric. A Cluniac monk, he became Abbot of Gloucester and, in 1148, Bishop of Hereford. Accepted by all as a man of great ability and asceticism, he was a trusted Councillor of HENRY II and antagonist of BECKET, refusing to give an oath of obedience to Canterbury when made Bishop of London in 1163. Becket excommunicated him in 1169; Foliot was not absolved until after the Archbishop's death.

FONTEYN, DAME MARGOT (née Peggy Hookham) (1919–91), ballerina. The first ballerina trained in Britain to achieve international status, she joined the Vic-Wells Ballet School in 1934 (her first performance was as a snowflake in the *Nutcracker Suite*) and a year later was a soloist. Over the next three decades she established a career interpreting classical roles, including Odette/Odile in *Swan Lake* and Coppèlia, as well as working with new choreographers such as Frederick ASHTON. In 1962, when she was 43, she began a memorable partnership with the Russian dancer Rudolf Nureyev, which lasted for the next 10 years.

FOOT, MICHAEL (1913–), politician. Foot's youthful radicalism impelled him away from the liberalism of his father Isaac, a Liberal MP, into socialism. He worked as a journalist and editor of the left-wing *Tribune* newspaper and, incongruously, he also worked for Lord BEAVERBROOK (*see* AITKEN, MAXWELL), who also supported *Tribune* financially. Elected MP for Plymouth in 1945, during the ATTLEE years Foot positioned himself on the extreme left of the Labour Party, finding a mentor in Aneurin BEVAN, to whom he hitched his star. He lost his seat in 1955 and returned to the Commons only in 1960 when he took over Bevan's constituency of Ebbw Vale. A leading figure in the Campaign for Nuclear Disarmament, during the 1960s he devoted himself to this cause, writing a hagiographical account of Bevan's biography and opposing the defence and foreign policies of Harold WILSON's government.

Foot's entry into the Shadow Cabinet when Labour went into opposition in 1970 was an early sign of the leftward shift of the party, and the fact that Wilson made him Secretary of State for Employment in 1974 was a clear signal that the government intended to give the striking miners their full demands for more pay. Thereafter Foot was seen as the best hope of the Labour left. In 1976 he challenged CALLAGHAN for the leadership and, although he did not win, he did well enough to ensure that he would play a leading role in the new government. As Leader of the Commons (1976–9) he acted as mediator between the Cabinet and the increasingly left-wing parliamentary party, and, after Callaghan's resignation

following the 1979 election defeat, he beat Denis HEALEY for the party leadership in 1980.

Socialism now had a suitably radical leader and, in Margaret THATCHER, a suitably reactionary opponent, and under Foot the party turned sharply left. The 1983 election manifesto was the most left-wing in Labour's history, calling for wholesale nationalization, the scrapping of all the Thatcher trade union laws and unilateral disarmament. Labour lost and Foot resigned.

FORBES, ARCHIBALD (1838–1900), war correspondent. Son of a Scottish minister of religion, educated at Aberdeen University, he was inspired to become a war correspondent after attending a lecture series given by William Howard RUSSELL. Forbes covered the siege of Metz in 1870 for the *Daily News*, pioneering the transmission of lengthy, instantaneous reports of action by the telegraph. Forbes's emphasis was always on the speed at which the story could be filed rather than its accuracy. A fine horseman, his rides from battlefronts to telegraph offices became legendary, the most famous being a 280-mile round trip in Zululand in 1879 which he accomplished in just 55 hours. Forbes's dispatches were invariably the way the British public first learned the details of campaigns in the far-flung corners of the Empire.

FORBES, DUNCAN (1685–1747), lawyer and administrator. Forbes became an advocate in 1709 and was appointed manager of the estates of the Duke of Argyll (*see* CAMPBELL, JOHN). A propagandist for Argyll and against the management of Scotland by Roxburghe (*see* KER, JOHN), he was elected an MP in 1721. As Lord Advocate (1725–37) he handled most of the business that would have been undertaken by a Secretary of State before the suspension of the office. He then became President of the Court of Session. Forbes had a reputation for even-handedness. His repression of Glasgow after the Malt Tax riots of 1725 was balanced by his concern for difficulties of Scottish products in competing with English imports, and in 1726 he successfully allocated the £20,000 raised by the Malt Tax to the development of Scottish manufacturing. During the 1745 rebellion, Forbes was the only representative of the government in northern Scotland, the Battle of Culloden being fought on his estate; his protests against Cumberland's treatment of the Highlanders failed to have a direct influence.

FORBES, JAMES (1821–74), sailor. A hard-driving captain of Liverpool's Black Ball Line of emigrant ships to Australia, he became known as 'Bully' Forbes. He made his reputation in 1852, taking the ship *Marco Polo* to Melbourne in the then phenomenal time of 68 days out (at a time when the average passage was 120 days) and 76 days back. This was achieved using a gruelling 'Great Circle' route, based on the work of Matthew Fontaine Maury and John Towson, going deep into the southern latitudes. Forbes made a series of successful voyages in the *Marco Polo* and *Lightning* before the wreck of the *Schomberg* near Cape Otway, Victoria, in 1855 also made a shipwreck of his reputation.

FORD, ISABELLA (1860–1924), social reformer. Daughter of a prosperous Quaker who ran evening classes for mill girls, Ford was active in the trade-union movement, organizing tailoresses and in 1890 supporting a mill girls' strike in Bradford (Yorks.). Elected to the Leeds Trades and Labour Council, she was the Independent Labour Party (ILP) delegate to the annual conference of the Labour Representative Committee (which became the Labour Party) and was the first woman to address conference when she spoke in 1903. She declined to stand as a Labour Party candidate at the end of the First World War and instead devoted herself to the Quaker cause of alleviating German post-war suffering.

FOREST, JOHN (*c.* 1470–1538), martyr. An Observant Franciscan friar and a formidable preacher, he opposed HENRY VIII's annulment proceedings against CATHERINE OF ARAGON. Imprisoned briefly at first, he was re-arrested on heresy charges (apparently, counselling in the confessional, he denied that Henry was supreme head of the Church). He was hung in chains over a fire; Hugh LATIMER preached vindictively beforehand. The flames were fuelled by a wooden image from north Wales, Derfel Gadarn; there was said to be a prophecy that it would set fire to a forest. The punishment may have been Henry VIII's idea of a joke.

FORMAN, SIMON (1552–1611), doctor and astrologer. A Wilts. yeoman, he was schooled at Salisbury, where (1564) he started the diary which combines with his medical case-books as an extraordinary window on Elizabethan society. In 1580 he began unorthodox medical practice, settling permanently in London in 1588 and gaining a reputation after effectively combating a plague outbreak in 1592–3 (despite jealous disapproval from the Royal College of Physicians). His medical business included casting horoscopes; his papers (now in the Bodleian Library) confirm the contemporary popularity glimpsed in Ben JONSON's caricature of him in *The Alchemist*.

FORSTER, E(DWARD) M(ORGAN) (1879–1970), novelist and essayist. He was an undergrad-uate at Cambridge and a member of the Apostles, an exclusive intellectual society through which he met members of what would become the Bloomsbury group. Forster's first novel, *Where Angels Fear to Tread*, was published in 1905, *The Longest Journey* in 1907, *A Room with a View* in 1908, and his 'condition of England' novel *Howards End*, which established his reputation, in 1910. In 1912 Forster visited India and his intense dislike of imperialism led him to start writing his most acclaimed novel, *A Passage to India*, which he did not finish until 1924. It was the last novel he was to write: he spent the last 46 years of his life lecturing (he became a lifetime fellow of King's College, Cambridge, in 1945) and writing (*Aspects of the Novel* was published in 1927, *Two Cheers for Democracy* in 1954, and he co-wrote the libretto for Benjamin BRITTEN's opera *Billy Budd* in 1949). Forster was strongly opposed to censorship: he argued in favour of the publication of the unexpurgated version of *Lady Chatterley's Lover* in 1960. He became the first Chairman of the National Council for Civil Liberties in 1934. *Maurice*, his novel about a homosexual relationship, written in 1917 for private circulation, was not published until 1971, a year after his death.

FORSTER, REINHOLD (1729–98) **and GEORGE** (1754–94), naturalists. Originally from Prussia, the father taught in Russia and later in England, where with his son he translated the work of the French explorer Bougainville. They went on James COOK's second expedition expecting to write the official account of the journey; when it became clear on their return that Cook intended to do so himself, Reinhold Forster was prohibited by the Admiralty from writing his own account. No such restriction applied to George, who published the Forsters' version of the expedition in 1777, concentrating on their botanical discoveries.

FORSTER, W(ILLIAM) E(DWARD) (1819–86), politician. A Quaker, he married the daughter of Thomas ARNOLD in 1850, entered Parliament in 1861 and as Vice-President of the Council created the first national system of elementary education in England, through the Education Act 1870 (sometimes known as the Forster Education Act). He resigned office after an unhappy spell as Chief Secretary for Ireland (1880–2): having pursued a coercive policy, he could not accept the government's subsequent shift towards conciliation involving Charles PARNELL.

FORTE, CHARLES (Baron Forte of Ripley) (1908–91), hotelier. His Italian father Rocco moved to Scotland in 1911 to open a café and the family followed in 1913. Charles opened his first catering establishment, a milk bar in London's West End, in 1935 and after the Second World War expanded into hotels. In 1970 his company merged with Trust Houses and the resulting combine became Britain's largest caterer and hotel provider. Chief Executive of Trust House Forte from 1971, and Chairman from 1978, he adhered to the gospel of work and self-advancement, making him a firm admirer and financial supporter of Margaret THATCHER.

FORTESCUE, JOHN (?1394–1479), writer. A lawyer of Lincoln's Inn (London), he was eight times an MP between 1421 and 1437 and Chief Justice of King's Bench from 1442, but as a prominent Lancastrian he was dismissed and attainted by EDWARD IV in 1461. He followed the Lancastrian royal family into exile in Scotland and Flanders as their titular Chancellor, and returned with MARGARET OF ANJOU in 1471. Captured at the Battle of Tewkesbury (1471), he agreed to recognize Edward as King in 1473 and lived in retirement on his estates until his death.

His works included several defences of the title of the house of Lancaster to the throne, and (in 1473, to seal his change of allegiance) one defending Edward's title; but of more permanent influence were two treatises about the nature of English government, written during his exile in the 1460s. *On the Governance of the Kingdom of England* remained in manuscript until 1714. *De Laudibus Legum Angliae* (Praises of the Laws of England, first printed 1537) compared English and French law, and expressed the idea that judges were loyal to the common law and an impersonal entity called the Crown (the King in Parliament) as much as to the physical person of a particular monarch. Fortescue claimed that England, unlike exclusively 'regal' France, was a mixed monarchy (*regnum politicum et regale*), where the 'politic' element was based on the consent of the monarch's subjects. He took a very high view of the legislative powers of Parliament, which he expressed both in his legal judgements and in his writings, reflecting ideas for a refoundation of trust in the monarchy which had been expressed in Parliament during the 1450s. Fortescue is not generally considered an original thinker, which makes his expression of such ideas all the more interesting as evidence for the commonplaces of legal thought in fifteenth-century England.

FOSTER, JOHN (1st Baron Oriel) (1740–1828), politician. His father was Lord Chief Baron of the Irish Exchequer; he was educated at Trinity College, Dublin, became an Irish MP in 1761 and a barrister in 1766. In 1784 he became Chancellor of the Exchequer and was responsible for the passing of the Irish Corn Law, which rewarded corn exporters with large bounties and raised high tariffs against imports, measures which were to have fatal consequences during the Irish Famine but in the short term gave a boost to Irish agriculture. In 1785 he was elected Speaker of the House of Commons. From the Chair, he opposed pro-Catholic measures and also union with Britain; his refusal to talk to Catholic anti-unionists until very late in the day helped seal the fate of the old Irish Parliament, which was absorbed into a new Westminster-based Imperial Parliament in 1801. He became a Westminster MP and served in several ministries, continuing to oppose any measure of Catholic Emancipation.

FOSTER, NORMAN (Baron Foster of Thameside) (1935–), architect. Trained at Manchester and Yale universities, Foster initially worked with another masterly exponent of 'high tech' architecture, Richard ROGERS, together with their (then) wives, as 'Team 4' (1963–7). He set up his own practice in 1967 in London, and it now has projects all over the world. His most notable buildings include the Sainsbury Centre for the Visual Arts at the University of East Anglia (1976–8), the Hong Kong and Shanghai Bank (1978–9) (described as the most expensive office building ever constructed), the Stansted Airport terminal (1980–90) and Chek Lap Kok airport, Hong Kong (1998). He was awarded the Order of Merit in 1997. A recent project is the rebuilt Reichstag in Berlin (1992–9), a material symbol of German reunification, and he is the architect in charge of the rebuilding of that potent symbol of British sporting achievement, Wembley Football Stadium, as well as of the controversial Millennium Bridge over the Thames.

FOWLER, HENRY (1858–1933), lexicographer. Educated at Rugby and Oxford, Fowler produced a four-volume translation of Lucian (1906) and a concise abridgement of the *Oxford English Dictionary* (1911) with his brother, but his name is known for his eponymous *Modern English Usage* (1926, subsequently revised), the authoritative source of English grammar and word usage.

FOX, CHARLES JAMES see essay on page 329

FOX, DAME EVELYN (1874–1955), mental health pioneer. A descendant of the Whig leader Charles James FOX, she was educated at Somerville College, Oxford, and was involved in the Women's University Settlement, working among the poor of East London. Fox worked to introduce the Mental Deficiency Act 1913 and the setting up of the Central Association for Mental Welfare, a voluntary organization that lobbied for improvements in the care of the mentally handicapped in the years before the introduction of the National Health Service in 1946.

FOX, CHARLES JAMES (1749–1806)
Politician

Fox was the younger son of Henry FOX, to whom he was devoted. His belief that his father had been badly treated by Bedford (*see* RUSSELL, JOHN) and other Old Corps Whigs helped shape his early allegiances. Educated at Eton and Oxford, he acquired expensive tastes: he liked showy clothes and gambling, and ran up notoriously large debts.

At the age of 19 he became MP for Midhurst in 1768, although technically too young to stand, and quickly distinguished himself in debate. He supported the ministry of Augustus FITZROY, Duke of Grafton, taking part in attacks on WILKES. NORTH made him a junior Lord of the Admiralty but in 1772 he resigned in outrage against the Royal Marriages Act, which gave GEORGE III power to control the marriages of his adult children (Henry Fox had eloped, and bequeathed to his son antipathy to parental dictation in such matters). Speedily reappointed, he was dismissed two years later for disrespect for North's authority in the Commons.

He then changed his political colours, associating with BURKE and the Rockinghamite Whigs (*see* WATSON-WENTWORTH, CHARLES) and opposing North's American policy. Profound distrust of the King was the leading theme of his later politics. When WYVILL's 'Association' put parliamentary reform on the agenda, Fox indicated support. In 1781 he was elected MP for Westminster and, when Rockingham came to power the following year, made Secretary of State. Personal and political differences with Shelburne (*see* PETTY, WILLIAM), caused him to resign immediately on Rockingham's death and team up with his old enemy North, an unprincipled alliance in the opinion of some observers.

Together they came to power in April 1783, under the nominal leadership of Portland (*see* BENTINCK, WILLIAM CAVENDISH). George III did his best to make life difficult for them. His antipathy to what he saw as Fox's unbridled ambition was deepened by Fox's friendship with his son (later GEORGE IV), whom he led into dissolute ways. When Fox introduced an ambitious Bill to reform the East India Company, the King used it as a pretext to force him from power.

The new minister, PITT THE YOUNGER, initially had reforming credentials as good or better than Fox's. From 1788 to 1791, however, Pitt opposed and Fox supported the Dissenters' campaign to repeal the Test and Corporation Acts (restricting their access to public office). Fox also welcomed the French Revolution more eagerly than Pitt. From the onset of the Terror in 1792, some Whigs began to vote with Pitt; in 1794 a group led by Portland formally joined the ministry. Fox retained a following among some old Whig families and some younger men such as Charles GREY, but his political prospects appeared to be nil. He was able to make some capital out of opposing Pitt's more repressive measures – following on the success of his Libel Act of 1792, which declared the right of a jury rather than the judge to decide whether a libel was seditious; also from attacking what he portrayed as an unnecessary and damaging war. After 1795 some who had become disillusioned with Pitt rallied to him, including even his old rival Shelburne, but, despairing of significantly affecting public policy, he encouraged his followers to withdraw from public life from 1797.

Pitt's resignation in 1801 reanimated Fox's interest. He supported the Peace of Amiens of 1802; he blamed the resumption of war on ADDINGTON's bungling. In 1803 he drew closer to the GRENVILLE party, sharing their belief that the admission of Catholics to Parliament was a necessary part of policy towards Ireland. In 1804 he helped to force Addington out and rejected advances from Pitt. Despite the King's opposition, he was made Foreign Secretary in Grenville's 1806 'ministry of all the talents'– only to find the King immovably opposed to Catholic emancipation and the French not ready to come to terms. Sinking deeper into an illness that had troubled him for some time, he died in Sept.

Fox's lack of respect for conventional morality (his late marriage to his mistress, Elizabeth Armistead, did little to mollify moral rigorists) and his tolerance for radical politics caused many to mistrust him but he was beloved by a small circle of Whig aristocrats, and earned qualified respect from more radical figures. His defence of civil liberties in the face of counter-revolutionary panic, his support for Catholic emancipation and his opposition to the slave trade played an important part in defining the character of early nineteenth-century Whiggery. His admirers founded 'Fox clubs' to perpetuate his memory.

L. G. Mitchell, Charles James Fox (1991)

FOX, GEORGE (1624–91), founder of the Quakers. Son of a Leics. weaver, he was apprenticed to a shoemaker and general merchant, but in 1643 he began travelling to seek enlightenment and in 1646 experienced 'inner light', a conviction that knowledge of truth comes from a voice within the soul. He abandoned church attendance, adopted simple dress, speech and manner and, in 1647, he started preaching his message, travelling as far as Ireland (1669), the Caribbean and North America (1671–2) and the Netherlands (1677, 1684). He married Margaret FELL of Swarthmore Hall (Cumbria), which became the centre of his movement. It caused much alarm, but it took permanent shape through Fox's combination of charisma and an organizing ability not shared by many radical leaders. He called his followers 'Friends of the Truth', soon nicknamed Quakers, after Fox told a judge to tremble in the sight of the Lord (the sect itself adopted the name 'Religious Society of Friends' in the late eighteenth century). He was several times imprisoned. His *Journal* is a fascinating insight both on a remarkable personality and on the religious turbulence of his age.

FOX, HENRY (1st Baron Holland) (1705–74), politician. His father Stephen was a courtier and administrator, who made a fortune from the profits of public office; Henry, a child of his old age, was to be among the more ambitious Whig politicians of his time, and to acquire a reputation for greed and unscrupulousness. He was educated at Eton with PITT THE ELDER. As a young man, he gambled away much of his money. He entered Parliament in 1735 and attached himself to Robert WALPOLE, who rewarded his loyalty with the post of Surveyor General of Works. On Walpole's fall he resigned but was re-appointed by the PELHAM administration, becoming a junior Lord of the Treasury and then Secretary at War. In 1755 both he and Pitt, although members of the administration, launched a parliamentary attack upon it; Fox allowed himself to be bought off by being made Secretary of State and Leader of the Commons. Paymaster of the Forces (1757–65), he profited from the opportunities which that post notoriously provided to enhance his personal fortune. He led the Commons during the unpopular Bute (*see* STUART, JOHN) ministry, thus alienating the Old Corps Whigs, his former colleagues, many of whom had lost office when Newcastle (*see* PELHAM-HOLLES, THOMAS) was dismissed. Fox can be charitably assessed as having displayed a form of political pragmatism characteristic of much mid-century Whiggery, but was increasingly superseded, among a younger generation of self-proclaimed Whigs, by a new self-consciously principled style, popularized by the elder Pitt.

FOX, RICHARD (?1448–1528), royal servant. A distinguished example of the late medieval royal servant clergyman; Winchester in 1501 was his last step on the bishops' ladder of preferment, accompanying service to HENRY VII both before and after his accession. The ablest survivor of the old Council in HENRY VIII's first government, he put forward Thomas WOLSEY as royal almoner in an effort to counterbalance war-hungry secular noblemen. Going blind, in 1516 he retired from politics to attend to his episcopal duties and to give lavishly to education, including the foundation of Corpus Christi College, Oxford.

FOXE, EDWARD (?1496–1538), propagandist. Cambridge-educated, he became secretary to Thomas WOLSEY. As leading members of the team trying to secure the annulment of HENRY VIII's marriage to CATHERINE OF ARAGON, in 1529 Foxe and Stephen GARDINER recruited Thomas CRANMER. With Cranmer, who shared his reformist outlook, he compiled the manuscript collections now known from their heading as the *Collectanea Satis Copiosa* (Complete Enough Collections), which were ready in autumn 1530. These formed the basis for defining the royal supremacy over the English Church, thus justifying the break with Rome. Foxe's reward was more work writing on the royal supremacy, particularly the book *De Vera Differentia* (1534), embassies in Germany, and the bishopric of Hereford in 1535.

FOXE, JOHN see essay on page 331

FRANCIS I (1494–1547), King of France (1515–47). Francis was too similar to HENRY VIII in age, physical prowess and cultural pretensions for either's comfort. Their relationship was one of elaborate courtesy (notably their meeting at the Field of the Cloth of Gold in 1520) alternating with open and costly warfare, plus continual jealous imitation of Francis by Henry. During the 1530s Henry particularly cultivated Francis since England's traditional 'Burgundian' alliance with the rulers of the Low Countries had been disrupted by CHARLES V's fury at Henry's repudiation of his marriage to CATHERINE OF ARAGON and at the break with Rome. From 1534 Francis ended previous hesitations and began persecuting religious reformers, but he was never as committed a Catholic as Charles V.

FRANCIS II (1544–60), King of France (1559–60) and of Scotland (1558–60). Son of King Henry II of France; by the Treaty of Haddington (July 1548) he was betrothed to the infant MARY QUEEN OF SCOTS and they married in April 1558. They assumed the English royal arms in addition

continued on page 332

FOXE, JOHN (1517–87)
Writer

Foxe was born in Boston (Lincs.) and went to Brasenose College, Oxford (c. 1534–8), then to Magdalen College, which he had to leave in 1545 because of his uncompromising evangelical religion. He became a tutor to the Lucy family of Charlecote (Warws.) until he got married. Then he became tutor to the children of the recently executed Henry HOWARD, Earl of Surrey, including Thomas HOWARD, the future 9th Duke of Norfolk; now living in Edwardian London at the centre of events, he got to know many leading reformers, including John BALE, whose view of history as a detailed unfolding of God's purpose would have a great influence on his own writings. Among his other contacts was the Unitarian activist Joan BOCHER, for whom Foxe seems to have had much personal sympathy, and whose burning (1550) he deplored; he was left with an abhorrence of burning people for heresy, regardless of whether or not he approved of their views, which was an unusual attitude in the sixteenth century. He was ordained deacon in 1550 and was responsible for suppressing one of the last shrines in England, a Marian cult near Reigate (Surrey). He fled to Frankfurt and Strasbourg under MARY I and developed Bale's scheme of collecting the history of anti-papal martyrs, producing his first works in Latin (1554 and 1559).

Foxe returned from exile in 1559 to welcomes and hospitality from his old student the Duke of Norfolk and John Parkhurst, Bishop of Norwich, his fellow exile; he eventually set up house in London to carry on his work. The first English edition of his work, entitled *Acts and Monuments*, was published in 1563. Preoccupied with the labour of researching and producing the *Acts* and other writings, he did not seek high office in the Elizabethan Church, which he increasingly regarded as unsatisfactory and only half-reformed, and his only significant preferment was a canonry of Salisbury Cathedral. His stand in the Vestiarian controversy (1565–6) against the wearing of traditional clerical dress brought tensions with his former friend Archbishop Matthew PARKER, who also disapproved of his flourishing practice as an exorcist of the mentally disturbed. He attended the Duke of Norfolk at his execution (1572).

Produced in association with an enthusiastic and talented Protestant printer, John DAYE, the *Acts* was enriched with grisly pictures (all the more effective for being rare in English Protestant literature), and a famous title-page which depicted in graphic detail the Protestant view of the true and the false Church. Quickly nicknamed 'Foxe's Book of Martyrs', it was a huge publishing success, running to several enlarged editions, in which Foxe reworked and extended his material, partly in response to fierce criticism from Roman Catholic polemicists. The book was given almost biblical status when in 1571 all cathedrals and senior clergy were ordered to have a copy available for public consultation; by the reign of CHARLES I, however, it was regarded as a rallying-point for opposition to the Church policy promoted by William LAUD, and no further edition was printed until the collapse of royal power in 1641. By the time of the final edition in Foxe's lifetime in 1583, the book had expanded from an account of the Marian years to take in the sufferings of the godly across the whole sweep of Church history; Foxe developed a scheme of historical periods which reflected the struggle between God and Antichrist, featuring the progressive corruption of the Church, which was only reversed in his own time. This providential view of history gave a comforting sense of England's importance in God's battle-plan, and the volumes (often in more manageable abridgements) had a profound impact on the English Protestant outlook, providing abundant documentation and a rationale for national hatred and fear of Roman Catholics. It is still invaluable for the information it has preserved, for despite his obvious bias Foxe did his best to be a careful scholar, as well as reporting events from eye-witnesses.

Foxe wrote many other devotional and polemical works besides the 'Book of Martyrs'. In 1571 he published the manuscript of an official codification of canon law prepared in 1551–3 but never issued (which he entitled the *Reformatio Legum Ecclesiasticarum*); this was his contribution to the wider Puritan campaign to secure change in the Church, and his preface to it guardedly criticized the Book of Common Prayer. The memoir of Foxe by his son Simeon (1568–1630), first published in the 1641 edition of the *Acts*, succeeded in promoting the image of a conformist clergyman, rather at odds with the reality of a combative champion of the English Reformation. His papers, from which he used only selections for his printed text, survive in the British Library, and are a source of exceptional importance.

J. F. Mozley, John Foxe and His Book (1940)

to their own after MARY I's death and in July 1559, after Henry's death from tournament injuries, became King and Queen of France. Francis died without ever seeing Scotland.

FRANCIS OF VALOIS (Duke of Alençon, then of Anjou) (1554–84), youngest surviving son of Henry II of France. Duke of Alençon until 1574, when he succeeded his brother Henry as Duke of Anjou, Henry became King Henry III of France 1574–89). Both Henry and Francis were put forward by their mother Catherine de Medici as suitors for ELIZABETH I, but Francis was the more serious contender, in 1572 and from 1579 to 1581. On the second occasion, his diplomatic importance was considerable as he was playing a leading role in the Netherlands revolt against Spain. Elizabeth was genuinely fond of him, calling him her 'Frog', and she may have seen him as a last chance to marry; she showed real grief when it became obvious that Francis's Roman Catholicism would be widely unpopular, making marriage impossible.

FRANKLIN, BENJAMIN (1706–90), American founding father. Franklin is remembered both for helping to draft the American Declaration of Independence in 1776, which justified the war, and as a seemingly eccentric experimenter and inventor. Born in Boston, Mass., he became a printer, working in London (1724–6) before returning to Philadelphia, where he ran the influential *Pennsylvania Gazette* and published almanacs every year between 1733 and 1758. His practical experiments in natural philosophy, especially the one using a kite to demonstrate that lightning was electricity, contributed to his fame. In 1757, as agent for the colonies, he returned to England, where he mixed in intellectual circles and joined in the controversies which would ultimately bring about the split between Britain and its North American possessions; he returned to America in 1774. During the War of American Independence he was Ambassador to France, helping secure that nation's assistance in the war with Britain. He returned to the new United States of America in 1785, and was a signatory to the federal constitution.

FRANKLIN, SIR JOHN (1786–1847), explorer. Franklin entered the navy at the age of 14 and served in the battles of Copenhagen, Trafalgar and New Orleans. In 1818 he participated in an unsuccessful expedition to reach the North Pole and between 1819 and 1829 commanded expeditions that followed the Coppermine River and the Canadian Arctic coast and which explored the Mackenzie River region. He is best known for his attempt to find the Northwest Passage, the sea route along the northern Canadian coast believed to connect the Atlantic and Pacific oceans. His ships, the *Erebus* and *Terror*, departed in May 1845 and were last seen in Baffin Bay in late July 1845. By 1847 there was still no trace of Franklin's expedition and several relief expeditions tried unsuccessfully to find it. In 1854 evidence came to light that Franklin's ships had sunk, and five years later the Arctic explorer Leopold McClintock found the remains of the crew and ships of Franklin's expedition, including a cairn revealing that Franklin had died in 1847 and that he had found the Northwest Passage.

FRANKLIN, ROSALIND (1920–58), X-ray crystallographer. Franklin studied chemistry at Cambridge (1938–41) and X-ray diffraction methods in Paris (1947–50). In 1950 she moved to King's College, London, where she developed Maurice Wilkins's X-ray diffraction studies of deoxyribonucleic acid (DNA). Subsequently she produced high-quality X-ray diffraction photographs of DNA which confirmed DNA's helical structure and its existence in two crystalline forms. Francis CRICK and James Watson exploited her X-ray photographs in their celebrated double-helix model of DNA.

FRASER, BRUCE (1888–1981), sailor. The younger son of a general, Fraser saw active service in 1916 as gunnery officer aboard the cruiser *Minerva* in the Dardanelles. In 1920, commanding gunboats transported overland to the Caspian Sea he was captured and held by the Soviets for eight months. Fraser then became proficient in both aircraft-carrier operations and gunnery. Commanding the British Home Fleet in Dec. 1943, he sent *Scharnhorst* to the bottom off North Cape. Eighteen months later, as Commander of the British Pacific Fleet, he proved equally adept at operating his carriers off Japan.

FRASER, HUGH (1st Baron Fraser of Allander) (1903–66), retailer. The third generation of Glasgow department-store owners, Fraser entered the family business and was appointed Chief Executive in 1924 and Chairman in 1927. Determined to keep English firms out of Scotland, he expanded the scale of the enterprise and the company went public as House of Fraser in 1947, after which it moved its sights south of the border. The new series of acquisitions culminated with the purchase of Harrods in 1959.

FRASER, SIMON (12th Baron Lovat) (c. 1667–1747), conspirator. His father, a younger son, had opposed the Revolution of 1688. After leaving King's College, Aberdeen, Fraser took a commission in Lord Moray's Jacobite regiment.

To secure the Lovat title and estates, he tried and failed to kidnap his cousin's daughter, then forcibly married the cousin's widow. Convicted of treason, he fled to Skye and was outlawed. Although pardoned in 1700, he maintained ties with James Edward STUART, the Old Pretender, and in 1703 went to the Highlands to try to raise support for a rising, but was mistrusted. Thought to have betrayed Moray, he was imprisoned on his return to France. Escaping to Scotland, he supported the Hanoverians in 1715, and was made Sheriff of Inverness and Commander of the Highland Regiment. He renewed his contacts with the Jacobites in 1737, was made Duke of Fraser by the Pretender in 1742 and was thereupon removed from his public offices. Initially keeping a low profile in 1745, he declared openly for the Stuarts only after the victory of Prestonpans. He went into hiding after Culloden, but was captured, convicted of high treason and beheaded in 1747.

FRASER, WILLIAM (1st Baron Strathalmond of Pumpherston) (1888–1970), entrepreneur. The son of the founder of the Pumpherston Oil Co., Scotland's leading shale-oil concern, Fraser joined the company in 1909 and succeeded as Chairman in 1915. After the First World War his oil businesses were bought by Anglo-Persian Oil. Founded in 1909 to exploit oil concessions in Persia, this company had been largely acquired by the Admiralty in 1914 because of its strategic importance. Fraser and Sir John Cadman, whom he eventually succeeded as Chairman in 1941, won many agreements in the fast-growing oil industry, notably the joint marketing arrangements negotiated between 1928 and 1934 with Royal Dutch Shell, the secret 1928 agreement to reduce oil supply and keep prices up, and the 1944 Anglo-American Oil Treaty. After the Shah nationalized the Persian oil industry in 1951, Fraser helped create the new consortium to exploit Iranian oil, in which Anglo-Iranian Oil (since 1955 known as British Petroleum) had the largest share.

FRAZER, SIR JAMES (1854–1941), anthropologist and folklorist. Born in Glasgow, Frazer studied but never practised law and in 1879 embarked on an academic career at Cambridge in classics and social anthropology, the latter interest owed to Edward TYLOR's *Primitive Culture* (1871) and contact with William Robertson Smith, a theologian and orientalist. He is celebrated as the author of the magisterial *The Golden Bough: A Study in Comparative Religion* (12 vols, 1890–1915). Drawing on a vast and exotic range of secondary ethnographic evidence, and written in a florid prose style, the work upheld the nineteenth-century idea that human civilization progresses from the magical to the religious and then to scientific stages. Although the conclusions of the work are now regarded as doubtful, it raised the profile of anthropology and informed the work of several twentieth-century writers including A. E. Housman and T. S. ELIOT.

FREDERICK (1707–51), Prince of Wales. Father of GEORGE III, he was often at odds with his own father GEORGE II. Kept in Germany during the reign of his grandfather GEORGE I, he arrived in Britain in 1728, and hurriedly worked to establish himself, building links with the opposition to Robert WALPOLE. These connections became most active after 1737, when he removed his wife AUGUSTA from Hampton Court to St James's so that her first child, also Augusta, was born outside his parents' authority. George II responded to this calculated insult by barring Frederick from the royal palaces. Frederick set up a rival court at Leicester House, which became a centre of opposition to Walpole, including both 'patriot' Whigs such as PULTENEY and Tories who may have been inspired by the writings of Bolingbroke (*see* ST JOHN, HENRY) to see in Frederick the model of a 'patriot' King, who would rescue the nation from the grip of a self-seeking Whig clique. Walpole's fall in 1742 brought about a partial reconciliation between father and son, but Frederick, not allowed to take up arms, felt marginalized during the War of the Austrian Succession and by the end of the decade was once more intriguing with Tories and Whigs opposed to PELHAM. In 1750, anticipating his father's death, Frederick prepared a plan for taking up the reins of government and appointing his friends to office, but he died unexpectedly the next year.

FREDERICK AUGUSTUS (Duke of York and Albany) (1763–1827), Royal Prince. The second son of GEORGE III and Queen CHARLOTTE, he received a thorough military education in Hanover, and in 1784 was gazetted Colonel of the Coldstream Guards. Appointed to command British expeditionary forces to Flanders in 1793, the Duke proved brave but incapable, his marching and counter-marching giving rise to the popular nursery rhyme *The Grand Old Duke of York*. Despite this the King insisted in 1795 that the Duke be appointed Commander-in-Chief and he again led an expedition to the continent with equally disastrous results in 1799. He proved a much better administrator than operational commander; between 1795 and 1815 he oversaw a massive expansion in the army, and between 1816 and 1827 worked hard to minimize the impact of swingeing cuts.

FRENCH, JOHN (1st Earl of Ypres) (1852–1925), soldier. Son of a naval officer, he initially followed his father into the navy (1866–70), but, a poor sailor, he enlisted in the Suffolk Artillery Militia and four years later transferred into the cavalry. In 1884 French commanded WOLSELEY's mounted forces in the dash up the Nile to rescue General Charles GORDON, and in 1899 commanded the cavalry in South Africa, relieving Kimberley in Feb. 1900, and then waging a two-year campaign against Boer commandos. Appointed Chief of the Imperial General Staff in 1912, French resigned in the Curragh 'mutiny' in 1914, when 57 officers of the 3rd Cavalry Brigade threatened to resign their commissions rather than impose Home Rule on Ulster. French was almost immediately reinstated and appointed as Commander of the British Expeditionary Force (BEF). The BEF's safe retreat from Mons owed more to good luck than competent generalship. His heavy drinking increased after the bloody repulse of the BEF's attack at Loos in Sept. 1915. A cabal of senior officers, led by HAIG and RAWLINSON, engineered his resignation on 4 Dec. 1915, Haig replacing French as Commander-in-Chief. Appointed to command Home Forces, French suppressed the Dublin uprising of April 1916, narrowly avoided an IRA assassination attempt in Dec. 1919, and wrote *1914*, a transparently mendacious attempt to vindicate his generalship, which initiated a host of post-war memoirs.

FREUD, ANNA (1895–1982), psychoanalyst. Daughter of the pioneer of psychoanalysis, Sigmund Freud, she was born and educated in Vienna and was taught psychoanalysis and psychoanalysed by her father. By the mid 1920s she was pioneering the psychoanalytical treatment of childhood neuroses. She held that a child's neuroses could be best understood by analysing its dreams and play. Like her father, she believed that emotions develop sequentially via several distinct sexual phases, and accordingly argued that a gentle treatment of a child's neuroses was the most effective. In 1936 she published *The Ego and the Mechanisms of Defence*, an acclaimed analysis of the ways in which the ego rationalizes and represses, and thus acts as a defence against, threatening emotions. In 1938 the Freuds fled from Nazi Austria to London, and during the Second World War Anna founded the Hampstead war nurseries for children. Shortly after the war she launched the celebrated Hampstead child therapy course and clinic.

FREUD, LUCIAN (1922–), painter. Grandson of the psychoanalyst Sigmund Freud, Lucian escaped from Nazi Germany and settled in London in 1933, studying at the Central School and Goldsmiths' College. His early work was abstract touched with surrealism, but by the late 1940s his chosen subject was the human figure in a bare environment; he is now regarded as one of the most significant British figurative painters with his probingly, pitilessly hyper-realistic nudes and analytical portraits '*of* people, not *like* them', in his own words.

FRIDESWIDE, ST (?–727). Patron saint of the University of Oxford. Very little is known of her actual life, although it is clear that she was venerated as a saint from a relatively early date, since a church dedicated to her existed by 1002, when the Danes of Oxford took refuge in it during the St Brice's Day massacre of ETHELRED II THE UNREADY's reign. She was possibly related to the kings of Wessex.

FRITH, JOHN (*c.* 1503–33), martyr. A Cambridge don who transferred to Cardinal WOLSEY's new Oxford College (now Christ Church), he was imprisoned for heresy in 1528, escaped and joined William TYNDALE in the Low Countries to translate the Bible. He returned to England in 1532 and was arrested after Thomas MORE had discovered his MS treatise denying Christ's bodily presence in the Eucharist. He died on charges of rejecting the doctrines of purgatory and transubstantiation. His views were claimed by John FOXE as influential on the eucharistic thought of later English reformers.

FRITH, WILLIAM (1819–1909), painter. Son of a Harrogate (Yorks.) innkeeper who sent him to the Royal Academy Schools, Frith exhibited *Malvolio, Cross-gartered before the Countess Olivia* at the Royal Academy when he was 21. So admired were his paintings of literary and historical scenes that in 1853 he was elected to the academy to fill the vacancy left by J. M. W. TURNER's death. But it was his teeming social panoramas, the visual equivalent of DICKENS's novels, that brought him a huge popular following and enduring fame as a Victorian genre painter. *Life at the Seaside (Ramsgate Sands)* (1854) was bought by Queen VICTORIA. *The Derby Day* (1858), which was nearly eight feet long, had to be protected from the crowds by policemen, and *The Railway Station* (1862) was equally popular, as was *The Private View at the Royal Academy in 1881* (1882), particularly with those celebrities who could spot themselves in the crowd. Photography made Frith's detailed work possible: it never detracted from the popularity of his intensely representational art.

FROBISHER, SIR MARTIN (1539–94), explorer. Despite family wealth in Yorks. and a Master of the Mint as grandfather, Frobisher began sailing, at the age of 14, on expeditions to West Africa, graduating to piracy and dubious intrigue with the Spanish. In the 1570s he became fascinated by the prospect of a north-west passage to Asia, and in 1576 he led an expedition as far as what is now Baffin Island in the Canadian Arctic. Convinced that he had found gold, he set out again in 1577 and 1578. After these fruitless attempts, the public lost faith in him. He redeemed himself by his brilliant seamanship against the 1588 Spanish Armada, was given a knighthood and then joined in the subsequent harassment of Spanish treasure-fleets. This won him one spectacular capture in 1592, but he died from fatal injuries fighting off the Britanny coast in 1594.

FROISSART, JEAN (*c.* 1335–*c.* 1407), historian. Born at Valenciennes (Hainault, in the Low Countries), he may have been educated at the English court; he spent the years 1360–6 in England and visited Scotland in 1365, working in the service of first PHILIPPA OF HAINAULT and then of her brother-in-law Robert of Namur; his later patrons were Wenceslas, Duke of Brabant, and Guy II of Châtillon, Count of Blois. He began his French prose *Chroniques* in Queen Philippa's service and, as the work grew, adapted it to the interests and entertainment of his successive patrons. The chronicle provides an account of the history of Europe from 1327 to 1400, based up to 1361 on the work of the earlier Hainault chronicler Jean le Bel; it contains generous treatment of England's involvement in the opening phases of the Hundred Years War but is also very informative of the reign of RICHARD II, after Froissart had left England. Most surviving manuscripts are copies of the earlier version, which was more pro-English than the later work produced for Guy of Châtillon; Froissart's final English visit, in 1395, seems to have dampened his enthusiasm for the country. His style is vivid and he is intensely readable, although sometimes his information has the value of high-class gossip.

FROMANTEEL, AHASUERUS (1607–93), clockmaker. From a family of Dutch Protestant refugees settled in Norwich, he worked in London from 1629, though for many years in conflict with the Worshipful Company of Clockmakers. Soon, before 1658, he introduced the first pendulum-regulated (and long-case) clocks to England, drawing on Dutch models. From 1668 to 1676 he lived in the Hague. His sons carried on his business.

FROST, JOHN (1784–1877), Chartist. A draper and Justice of the Peace in Newport, South Wales, he helped to establish a Chartist association in the town in 1838. In Nov. 1839 he and Zephaniah Williams and William Jones led 3,000 colliers in a march to rescue Chartist prisoners held in Newport (Mon.), fuelled by protests at the impris-

onment of a leading Chartist, Henry Vincent, in Monmouth. The crowds were scattered by soldiers; 24 were killed or died from injuries; 125 were arrested; and 21, including Frost, Jones and Williams, were charged with high treason. Condemned to death in Jan. 1840, Frost had his sentence commuted to transportation for life. Controversy continues to surround the 'Newport rising' and the extent to which it was merely a local mass demonstration or was intended as a trigger for a more general, even national, uprising.

FROUDE, J(AMES) A(NTHONY) (1818–94), historian. His loss of faith cost him his Oxford fellowship, after which he wrote history to earn a living. His best-selling 12-volume *History of England from the Fall of Wolsey to the Defeat of the Spanish Armada*, published between 1856 and 1870, is a compelling account, surpassed only by MACAULAY, and went to seven editions within his own lifetime. He worked (albeit sloppily) from manuscript sources, and presented his arguments, from a Protestant perspective, in a disciplined and coherent way, ensuring that his work still remains valuable to cultural and religious historians.

FROUDE, RICHARD (1803–36), Tractarian. The brother of J. A. FROUDE, he was a Fellow of Oriel College, Oxford, and active in the Oxford Movement, which sought to revive the Church of England by emphasizing its Catholic inheritance. He wrote *Lyra Apostolica* with his close friend Henry NEWMAN (1832–3) and contributed three of the *Tracts for the Times* published to demonstrate the Church's unique authority to pronounce on matters spiritual.

FRY, ELIZABETH (1780–1845), philanthropist. A banker's daughter and a Quaker, she founded hostels for the homeless as well as sundry charities, but is best remembered for her selfless devotion to the cause of prison reform. In 1813 she became aware of conditions in Newgate prison (London) and particularly the degradation of women and child inmates. She campaigned to improve their lot, creating a prisoners' aid society, touring the country's prisons to expose abuses and founding pressure groups to sustain the agitation. Her energy and example helped to arouse the nation's conscience and bring about the more humane treatment of offenders introduced by PEEL in the 1820s.

FRY, JOSEPH, II (1826–1913), manufacturer. From the fourth generation of Bristol-based chocolate makers, he joined the family firm in 1846, became a partner in 1855 and took full control in 1886. During his time the firm expanded greatly, partly through the success of its famous chocolate cream bar introduced in 1866. Like their competitors, the CADBURYs of Birmingham and ROWNTREEs of York, the Frys were active Quakers concerned with the welfare of their workers and their home town. For all its success, by the end of his life Fry's business was weak and vulnerable, and it was swiftly taken over by its Cadbury rivals.

FRY, ROGER (1866–1934), art critic. Son of an eminent Quaker judge, destined for a career in science, after studying at Cambridge he took painting classes and visited Italy to study the Renaissance painters, publishing *Giovanni Bellini* (1899). In 1901 he was appointed art critic for the influential *Athenaeum* and in 1904 was invited to become Director of the Metropolitan Museum in New York. Returning to England in 1910, he organized a 'Post-Impressionist' exhibition, having coined the term to describe painters such as Cézanne, Gauguin and Van Gogh. It caused a sensation, and an even greater furore was caused by his 1912 exhibition with works by Matisse and Picasso. Fry paved the way for the acceptance of abstract art in Britain in lectures which drew large audiences and in articles in the *Burlington Magazine* (collected as *Vision and Design,* 1920), as well as in studies of Cézanne (1927) and Matisse (1930). Fry encouraged the work of young artists through the Omega Workshops in Fitzroy Square (*see* GRANT, DUNCAN), a co-operative that employed them to decorate everyday artefacts, furniture, pottery and textiles, applying 'art' to 'craft'. Fry was part of the Bloomsbury group which shaped much of the English cultural agenda until the Second World War. The art historian Kenneth CLARK opined that 'if taste can be changed by one man, it was changed by Roger Fry'.

FUCHS, KLAUS (1912–88), spy. Born in Germany, Fuchs fled Nazi persecution and came to Britain in 1933. He was interned at the start of the Second World War, then received British citizenship in 1942. In 1943 he went to the USA to work on the atom bomb project in Los Alamos, returning to Britain in 1946 to head the theoretical physics division at the Atomic Energy Research Establishment at Harwell (Berks.). In 1950 he was imprisoned for 14 years for passing nuclear secrets to the Russians, information which, it was estimated at the time, saved the USSR 10 years' research lag in the arms race. Released nine years later, Fuchs continued to work on nuclear research in East Germany.

FULKE, WILLIAM (1538–89), churchman and astronomer. A Cambridge don, he was a prominent Puritan in various confrontations with ELIZABETH I's Church Settlement but, as a formidable theologian, was also an obvious choice to dispute with the imprisoned Edmund CAMPION in 1581. His best-selling attack on the 'Rheims Bible', the Roman Catholic English version of the New Testament (*see* MARTIN, GREGORY), paradoxically publicized its suggestions for translation, which influenced the 1611 'Authorized' version. An accomplished astronomer, he wrote attacking astrology in *Antiprognosticon* (1560).

FULLER, JOHN ('BONEY') (1878–1966), soldier and military thinker. Son of an Anglican clergyman, he was educated at Sandhurst and commissioned into the Oxfordshire Light Infantry in 1898. After service in South Africa and India, Fuller spent the first two years of the First World War on the staff of various headquarters, until at the end of 1916 he was appointed to the new Tank Corps. Fuller planned the successful mass tank attack at Cambrai in Nov. 1917, and in July 1918 drew up 'Plan 1919', a proposal to use shock action to disrupt German command and control, and then use mechanized forces to break the German line. At the Staff College and then as military assistant to the Chief of the Imperial General Staff in the 1920s, Fuller advocated a completely mechanized army, but, increasingly frustrated by the return to imperial policing, became ever more extreme in his opinions. Retiring in 1933, Fuller flirted with the British Union of Fascists and devoted himself to the study of military history. Fuller had a small but dedicated following in Britain, and much larger ones in Hitler's Germany and Stalin's USSR.

FULLER, THOMAS (1608–61), historian. A Cambridge-educated clergyman, he managed to retain a parish in the aftermath of the Civil Wars, despite official suspicion of his service with Royalist armies, and despite his strong affection for the pre-war Church of England. His *Church-History of Britain* (1655) is an important early work of synthesis, and his *Worthies of England* (1662) is an engaging source of anecdotal information; his numerous writings are characterized by their quirkily and genially pungent style.

FURNIVALL, FREDERICK (1825–1910), philologist and educator. Somewhat of a polymath, who read mathematics at Cambridge, Furnivall practised as a barrister, though his real interest was English studies. He joined the London Philological Society in 1847 and was the editor (1861–79) of the society's dictionary, which became *The Oxford English Dictionary* (*see* MURRAY, JAMES). He also founded the Early English Text Society (1864), one of the most important scholarly societies of the late nineteenth century, which published some 250 volumes, many of them transcriptions of original manuscript. Furnivale converted to Christian Socialism (though later rejecting its religious persuasion), he worked tirelessly to promote adult education and in 1854 helped found the Working Men's College in London, where he taught grammar and literature for many years.

FURSA, ST (?–*c.* 650), Irish monk. He undertook missionary work in East Anglia during the 630s. An ascetic in the Irish monastic tradition and representative of its highly individualistic evangelism, Fursa travelled to East Anglia in the aftermath of its king's conversion through the influence of EDWIN of Northumbria. St Fursa subsequently founded a monastery near Paris.

FURSE, DAME KATHERINE (née Symonds) (1875–1952), first Director of the Women's Royal Naval Service (WRNS). Daughter of the historian John Addington Symonds, she married the artist Charles Wellington Furse (for whom she was the model for *Diana of the Uplands,* now in the Tate Gallery). But after four years of marriage Furse was widowed in 1900, having borne two sons. A woman of prodigious energy, she joined the Red Cross in 1912 and was its Commandant by the outbreak of war in 1914. Infuriated by the organization's attitude to women, Furse resigned in 1917 but was immediately charged with setting up 'a naval organization of women'. She was appointed Director of the WRNS (or 'Wrens') in 1918 and by the end of the First World War in Nov. that year there were 5,000 women naval ratings and more than 400 officers. The WRNS was disbanded in 1919, but was re-formed to serve in the Second World War, after which it remained as a permanent service.

G

GABOR, DENNIS (1900–79), physicist. Gabor studied engineering in his native Budapest and in Berlin. In 1933, while working for the Siemens and Halske electrical engineering firm, he fled from Nazi Germany to Britain, where he worked at the Thomson-Houston electrical company (1934–48). There, in 1947–8, he developed holography, a technique for producing three-dimensional holograms by the interference of beams of monochromatic light. As Professor of Applied Electron Physics at Imperial College, London (1949–58), he invented a microscope for producing three-dimensional images. He won the 1971 Nobel Prize for Physics for his work on holography.

GABRÁN, SON OF DOMANGART (?–*c.* 560), King of Dál Riata. The eponymous ancestor of the Cenél nGabráin, the largest of the Dál Riata kindreds who competed for the kingship until the beginning of the ninth century (*see* DOMANGART MAC FERGUSA). Nothing more is known either of him or of his reign, other than the attribution of a reign of 22 years.

GAGE, THOMAS (1721–87), soldier and colonial administrator. He served under Cumberland (*see* WILLIAM AUGUSTUS) in the War of the Austrian Succession and was based in America for the duration of the Seven Years War. From 1763 to 1772 he was Commander-in-Chief, North America, based in New York. In 1774 he became Governor of Massachusetts Bay, intending to make the increasingly refractory colonists accept government from Westminster, but his combination of conciliatory measures with the suppression of unlicensed town meetings, the seizure of arms and the imposition of a new council only further antagonized them. After the destruction of the militia weaponry stores at Concord on 18 April 1775, Gage's troops were forced to fight colonial forces at Lexington, the first battle of the War of American Independence. Within months he was beseiged in Boston by WASHINGTON. He was appointed Commander-in-Chief despite the failure of his tactics, but resigned soon afterwards and was replaced by William HOWE.

GAIMAR, GEOFFREY, historian. The author of the Anglo-Norman *L'Estoire des Engles* (*c.* 1140), the earliest extant historical work written in French. Conceived as a continuation of GEOFFREY OF MONMOUTH's *History of the Kings of Britain*, it covers the period from the Anglo-Saxon settlements to the reign of WILLIAM II RUFUS in a romantic and courtly manner intended to appeal to the Anglo-Norman aristocracy.

GAINSBOROUGH, THOMAS (1727–88), artist. Son of a Suffolk woollen manufacturer, he showed an early talent for drawing. Sent to London to work with a silversmith, he was tutored by the French engraver Gravelot. Marrying at the age of 19, he moved to Ipswich, and set up as a portrait-painter, developing a distinctive portrait style within landscape settings, before moving to fashionable Bath in 1760. There he developed a new style derived from VAN DYCK, often using deliberate archaism in costume. When he moved to London in 1774, Gainsborough became the most sought-after portrait-painter; there he developed a more fluid and impressionistic painting style and an interest in the early romantic themes of rugged scenery and peasant life.

GAITSKELL, HUGH (1906–63), politician. The son of an Indian civil servant, Gaitskell was educated at Winchester and Oxford and was appointed a lecturer in economics at University College, London, in 1928. He had joined the Labour Party during the General Strike while still at Oxford, was Hugh DALTON's private secretary during the Second World War and became MP for Leeds South in 1945. In 1947 he was made a junior minister and was appointed Chancellor of the Exchequer in 1950. A rising star on the right wing of the party, he came into conflict with the Left over the need to finance increased defence expenditure because of the Korean War and over the introduction of some National Health Service charges. In opposition over the following decade, Gaitskell and BEVAN were the main protagonists on the opposing wings of the party. When ATTLEE resigned as party leader after losing the 1955 General Election, Gaitskell defeated both Bevan and MORRISON for the succession.

Tested almost at once by the Suez crisis, he showed skill in opposing the government's policy as a matter of principle without seeming unpatriotic. After Labour's third consecutive election defeat in 1959, he initiated a basic review of Labour's policies and machinery, seeking unsuccessfully to persuade the party to drop Clause 4 of its constitution, which committed Labour to the common ownership of the means of production and distribution. He bitterly contested the vote for unilateral nuclear disarmament at the 1960 party conference, and by diligent work with trade-union leaders behind the scenes he secured its reversal the following year. Between then and his death as a result of an unidentified virus, his prestige and control of the party were at their height. He is considered by many to be the outstanding representative of the social democratic tradition within the Labour Party and joins the small pantheon of Labour leaders who, in the words of his biographer, 'might have been the great political leader that twentieth-century Britain has badly needed'.

GALLACHER, WILLIAM (WILLIE) (1881–1966), politician. Born in Paisley, Scotland, he worked first as a grocer's delivery boy and then in a brass foundry, and in 1906 joined the Social Democratic Federation. As Chairman of the Clyde Workers' Committee during the First World War, Gallacher was imprisoned for sedition and for rioting. He met Lenin in Russia and, returning to Britain convinced that workers should participate in parliamentary politics, formed the British Communist Party (1920–1). MP for West Fifeshire (1935–51), he was the longest-serving Communist MP at Westminster.

GALSWORTHY, JOHN (1867–1933), writer. Galsworthy's interest in writing began with a chance meeting with Joseph CONRAD, but it was his long association with the professional reader and publisher's talent spotter, Edward Garnett, that assured his success. Galsworthy's preoccupation with the problem of poverty and his fascination with social mores and the constraints of convention are revealed throughout his plays and novels. His sequence of novels chronicling three generations of a prosperous London family, published collectively as The Forsyte Saga (1922), the second Forsyte collection A Modern Comedy (1929) and On Forsyte Change (1931) offered a critical examination of Victorian respectability. The works were extremely successful in their day and later became a popular television series (1967). Galsworthy was honoured with numerous awards, including the Nobel Prize for Literature (1932), but he refused a knighthood.

GALTON, SIR FRANCIS (1822–1911), founder of eugenics. A cousin of Charles DARWIN, Galton studied medicine in Birmingham and London, and read mathematics at Cambridge, although he failed to complete his courses of study. He inherited a considerable fortune when his father died in 1844, which enabled him to concentrate on his scientific interests. In 1850 he began exploring south-west Africa and subsequently wrote works which made his scientific reputation, Tropical South Africa (1853) and The Art of Travel (1855). From the 1860s he was involved in meteorology and later developed the concept of anticyclones, invented pioneering weather-mapping techniques and helped establish the Meteorological Office. Following the publication of Darwin's Origin of Species (1859), he began his lifelong study of the inheritance of physical and mental attributes in the human population. In his Hereditary Genius (1869) he argued that mental attributes such as intelligence are inherited in the same way as physical attributes and that inherited attributes, rather than environmental factors, determine character. He measured the physical and mental abilities of over 9,000 people in an anthropometric laboratory founded in 1884–5. Much of this research was presented in Inquiries into the Human Faculty and its Development (1883). A pioneer of the empirical analytical approach to human abilities, he developed such widely used statistical tools as the correlation coefficient and the method of classifying individuals by fingerprints. Controversially, Galton believed that the physical and mental ability of the human race could be improved by selective breeding. He called this project eugenics and promoted it by founding eugenic societies and a professorial chair and laboratory in eugenics at University College, London.

GANDHI, MOHANDAS KARAMCHAND (later known as Mahatma, 'great soul') (1869– 1948), pioneer of Indian independence. Born in Gujarat in western India, to a merchant caste family, Gandhi studied law in England and practised from 1893 in South Africa. There he devoted himself to the welfare of the Indian population, and instituted satyagraha, campaigns of passive resistance against discriminatory legislation. After an accord was reached with SMUTS in 1914, his South African campaign ended. Gandhi returned to India in 1915 and swiftly established his ascendancy over the Indian National Congress Party. The principles laid down in his 1909 tract Hind Swaraj, home rule for India, became the basis of his personal and political life: self-control, passive resistance, self-sufficiency, a duty to resist the British and their civilization. By 1920, after the massacre at Amritsar carried out under DYER, he persuaded the Congress Party to adopt these principles. The Non-Cooperation movement began in that year, followed by the Civil Disobedience movements, with the great marches against the salt tax, in 1930–1 and again in 1932–4, and finally the Quit India movement of 1942. Imprisoned by the British on numerous occasions, but only tried once (1922), and often using fasting as a weapon to force change, Gandhi became a political martyr to the cause of independence.

Gandhi protested against the import of cloth and advocated the making and wearing of home-spun, adopting a simple white loincloth and shawl, which he wore throughout his 1931 visit to Britain, including to a reception at Buckingham Palace. He preached *ahimsa*, non-violence, and when not in prison he lived in an *ashram*, an ascetic religious community. Although many of his political goals may be described as vague, the India that he hoped for would be regenerated along traditional lines, small village communities held together by the freely accepted obligations of their members to one another and largely self-sufficient.

Gandhi severed formal links with Congress in 1934, but he still held considerable sway, notably when he frustrated the efforts of BOSE to take over the party in 1938. The Second World War provided a new platform for Gandhi's call to the British to leave India: he was imprisoned together with the whole Congress Party leadership. His influence waned after 1945; opposed to the idea of partition and the creation of a Muslim state, and distressed at the rising tide of violence, he embarked on a final series of fasts to try to achieve his goals. India was born in 1947 amid hideous bloodshed; Gandhi was murdered in Delhi, when on his way to prayers, by a Hindu extremist on 30 Jan. 1948. His tenets of non-violent activism were to have adherents in many subsequent protest movements.

GARDINER, SIR GERALD (1900–90), lawyer. Called to the Bar in 1925, he successfully acted for the defence in the prosecution of Penguin Books for an alleged offence under the Obscene Publications Act in publishing the unexpurgated version of *Lady Chatterley's Lover* in 1960. Joint chairman with Victor GOLLANCZ of the campaign for the abolition of capital punishment, during his six-year term of office as Lord Chancellor in Harold WILSON's Labour government, he oversaw the end of hanging as well as reform of the laws on abortion and homosexuality. He appointed the first woman judge (Mrs Justice LANE) and introduced compulsory training for magistrates.

GARDINER, STEPHEN (*c*. 1497–1555), politician. A Suffolk clothmaker's son whose kinship with Richard Eden, clerk of HENRY VIII's Council, encouraged his legal career and the beginning of a lifelong association with Cambridge. As Cardinal WOLSEY's secretary (1525) he was drawn into the negotiations for the annulment of Henry's

marriage to CATHERINE OF ARAGON; he energetically promoted the King's cause without sharing colleagues' religious reformism, and his book *De Vera Obedientia*, ably supporting the royal supremacy in the English Church (1535), would later be an embarrassment. Bishop of Winchester from 1531, he missed the archbishopric, which went to Thomas CRANMER, and Henry never fully trusted him or allowed him and his allies to destroy Cranmer. As a rallying-figure for conservatism, he spent most of EDWARD VI's reign in prison, but MARY I made him Lord Chancellor. He reluctantly accepted Mary's marriage to King PHILIP II of Spain, and initially promoted the campaign of burning heretics. His reputation as 'wily Winchester' may have exaggerated his conspiratorial skills and ignored his frequently self-destructive temper, but he consistently used his attention to detail and brilliant command of sarcastic English as the arch-defender of conservative religion.

GARNET, HENRY (1555–1606), churchman. A youthful convert to Roman Catholicism, he studied in Rome and became a Jesuit before returning to England as a missionary in 1586; the following year he became Superior of the English Jesuit Mission. After the Gunpowder Plot (*see* FAWKES, GUY), he was arrested and executed as an accomplice; he may have known about it only through secrets told him in the confessional.

GARRICK, DAVID (1717–79), actor-manager. The son of an army captain, he studied at Samuel JOHNSON's academy at Lichfield (Staffs.), but left for London with Johnson in 1737. Originally a wine merchant, he was drawn into acting through amateur theatricals, first performing publicly in 1741, and became the leading actor of his generation. He was famous for the naturalism of his performances and for the variety and strength of the emotions which he displayed, rejecting the exaggerated declamatory style of his great rival QUIN. He wrote several farces, and was a proprietor of the Drury Lane Theatre (1747–76); he engaged in extravagant competition with Covent Garden, managed by John RICH.

GASKELL, ELIZABETH (née Stevenson) (1810–65), writer. Brought up by her aunt in Knutsford (Ches.), after her mother died, she married the Rev. William Gaskell, minister of a Manchester Unitarian chapel, in 1832. It was a particularly happy and companionable marriage, bearing six children of whom four daughters survived.

She helped her husband in his ministry and started writing her 'condition of England' novels after the death of her son from scarlet fever in

1844. DICKENS so admired *Mary Barton, A Tale of Manchester Life* (1848) that he serialized some of her subsequent work in his periodical, *Household Words. Cranford* (1853) is based on life in genteel Knutsford, and *North and South* (1855) deals with northern industrial unrest, while *Ruth* (1853), a less enduring novel, is a plea for a more humane attitude towards unmarried mothers, which caused an outcry, coming as it did from the pen of the wife of a man of God. In 1850 Gaskell met Charlotte BRONTË, they became friends and on Charlotte's death her father asked Mrs Gaskell (as she is invariably known) to write her biography. *The Life of Charlotte Brontë* (1857) was greatly admired as a work of literary biography although it attracted threats of litigation from several of those who featured in it.

GAUDEN, JOHN (1605–62), writer, churchman. He attended Oxford and Cambridge before becoming a Cambs. parson. Initially sympathizing enough with Parliament to join the Westminster Assembly (planning a new Presbyterian national Church) in 1643, he developed Royalist sympathies, and was probably the real author of the devotional narrative of CHARLES I's sufferings supposedly written by the King: *Eikon Basilike* (1649), one of the most influential books in later seventeenth-century England for its ultra-divine right message. Despite keeping his parish during the 1650s, he wrote extensively defending Anglicanism, and, after CHARLES II's restoration, was rewarded with bishoprics of Exeter (1660) and Worcester (1662).

GAVAN DUFFY, SIR CHARLES (1816–1903), Irish politician. Born in Monaghan of a middle-class Catholic family, Duffy became a journalist and co-founded *The Nation* with Thomas DAVIS and John DILLON. Like other Young Irelanders, he was critical of O'CONNELL and seceded from the Repeal Association in 1846. In 1848 he supported a rising, but though briefly imprisoned managed to escape conviction and remained politically active. He joined with tenant-right groups north and south to found a Tenant League and independent Irish Party at Westminster, but the party split when some members took office under the Aberdeen (*see* GORDON, GEORGE) government, and Duffy clashed with Archbishop Paul CULLEN over the political role of the Church. After serving as MP for New Ross (1852–5) he emigrated to Australia, where he served as Prime Minister of Victoria (1871–2). After his political retirement he returned to Europe, and wrote his memoirs and works on Irish history (including a biography of Davis) which did much to shape subsequent generations' perceptions of O'Connell and Young Ireland. His son, George Gavan Duffy, was a

signatory of the Anglo-Irish Treaty, served briefly as Foreign Minister of the Irish Free State and became a High Court judge and prominent jurist.

GAVESTON, PIERS (4th Earl of Cornwall) (?–1312), royal favourite. Son of a Gascon noble in EDWARD I's service, his close, possibly homosexual, relationship with EDWARD II ended in personal and political disaster. The extent of Edward's infatuation became clear when in 1307 he asked his father to make Gaveston Count of Ponthieu, which resulted in the first of Gaveston's short-lived banishments.

Immediately after Edward II's accession in July, Gaveston was recalled, created Earl of Cornwall and given a dominant place at court. This so disconcerted the other earls that, in 1308, they combined to compel Edward to send Gaveston to Ireland. His return to court a year later led, in 1310, to the earls' forcing Edward to appoint the Ordainers. To many contemporaries, including the King, the most important Ordinance issued by these men was the clause expelling Gaveston yet again but, by Christmas 1311, he was back with Edward. The earls took up arms, besieged Gaveston at Scarborough (Yorks.) and captured him. Then a group of them, headed by THOMAS OF LANCASTER, used the dubious authority of the Ordinances to sentence him to death for treason. Edward II never forgave those whom he held responsible for his friend's execution, and he took his revenge after his victory at Boroughbridge (Yorks.).

GAY, JOHN (1685–1732), dramatist and poet. A member of the literary Scriblerus Club (founded 1713) with John ARBUTHNOT, Bolingbroke (*see* ST JOHN, HENRY), Thomas PARNELL, POPE and SWIFT, he wrote a variety of satirical poems and plays, as well as the libretto for HANDEL's *Acis and Galatea* (1732). His own *Beggar's Opera* (1728) was an immediate hit, and remained exceptionally popular until the end of the century. It pioneered the 'ballad opera', in which dialogue was interspersed with songs set to popular tunes arranged by PEPUSCH, and introduced characters, such as Macheath and Jemmy Twitcher, who became stock types (*see* MONTAGU, JOHN). The play exposed the moral degradation of English society, and was received by contemporaries as a comment upon the corrupting effects of Robert WALPOLE's rule, but its satire is broadly conceived and it continues to amuse modern audiences.

GEDDES, SIR ERIC (1875–1937), politician. Geddes gained experience in the railway industry in India and Britain before being appointed Deputy Director General of Munitions Supply in the First World War. LLOYD GEORGE promoted him to Director General of Transportation for the British army in France and later Controller of the navy in 1917, the year that he was elected Unionist MP for Cambridge in a by-election. He held the offices of First Lord of the Admiralty (1917–18) and Minister of Transport (1919–21), in Lloyd George's Coalition governments, but became best known for his chairmanship of the Committee on National Expenditure, set up to look at ways of cutting back the bloated government budget immediately after the war. In 1921 the committee proposed public expenditure cuts of almost £100 million, which came to be known as the 'Geddes axe'. The cuts caused widespread bitterness and resentment among those who had placed great hope in Lloyd George's promise to build a 'land fit for heroes' after the end of the war.

GEDDES, JENNY (*fl.* 1637), demonstrator. Supposedly an Edinburgh vegetable-seller, she was reputed to have sparked a riot in St Giles's Cathedral, Edinburgh, by hurling her folding stool at Bishop David Lindsay, when in 1637 he was conducting the inaugural service from the new Prayer Book ordered for Scotland by CHARLES I. The riot led to a Scottish national insurrection opening more than two decades of civil war and constitutional disturbance in the British Isles. She is first recorded in 1670, as then still alive, and the putative stool remains in the National Museum of Scotland.

GEDDES, SIR PATRICK (1854–1932), town planner. A Scot who studied under T. H. HUXLEY, becoming Professor of Botany at the University of Dundee (1889–1914), in 1892 he established the world's first 'sociological laboratory' in Edinburgh. He believed that the concept of evolution could be applied to societies as to species, and wrote *City Development* (1904) in which he stressed the importance of sociological research 'diagnoses before treatment' in urban planning.

GELDOF, BOB (1954–), singer and fund raiser. Dublin-born, Jesuit-educated, after a rebellious youth Geldof helped to form and was the lead singer of the Boomtown Rats, a highly successful punk rock band in the 1970s. In 1984 he wrote and organized the recording of a single to raise money for Ethiopian famine relief, *Do They Know It's Christmas?*, performed by an all-star rock group, Band Aid, assembled for the purpose. The record raised £8 million and inspired the Live Aid project, a marathon rock concert organized and publicized by Geldof, which performed simultaneously in London and Philadelphia on 13 July 1985 and was broadcast worldwide, raising more than £50 million for famine relief. Geldof remains involved in the Band Aid Trust and its various projects as well as heading his own television production company.

GEOFFREY (*c.* 1153–1212), Archbishop of York (1189–1212). An illegitimate son of HENRY II, his father obtained his election as Bishop of Lincoln in 1173, but he had no wish to be a priest and in 1182 he resigned rather than be consecrated. Henry then appointed him Chancellor and he served his father faithfully, even when the King's legitimate sons rebelled. 'The others are the bastards, this is my true son', the dying King is alleged to have said, and he promised him the vacant archbishopric of York, even though Geoffrey notoriously preferred dogs and horses to books and priests, and gossip said that he had hopes of being king himself one day. RICHARD I forced the canons of York to elect him in 1189, but made him promise to stay out of England while Richard was on crusade. In 1191 he landed at Dover, took sanctuary to avoid arrest, but was dragged from the altar. This scandal allowed JOHN to bring down the government of William LONGCHAMP and Geoffrey to go to York in the heroic guise of a persecuted churchman; as such his life to this point was written by Gerald de BARRI. He spent the rest of his life quarrelling with both Kings and the canons of York and he died in exile.

GEOFFREY OF BRITTANY (1158–86), royal prince. Third son of HENRY II and ELEANOR OF AQUITAINE, he was given the title Duke of Brittany in 1166 when Henry forced Duke Conan to resign and betrothed Conan's daughter Constance to Geoffrey. From 1173 onwards, when he joined his mother's rebellion against his father, he was in the thick of every family quarrel. He was conspiring with King Philip II of France when he was killed in a tournament at Paris. According to Gerald de BARRI, he was 'smooth as oil, a hypocrite in everything, capable by his syrupy eloquence of corrupting two kingdoms with his tongue'. Constance, whom he had married in 1181, was pregnant with ARTHUR OF BRITTANY when he died.

GEOFFREY OF MONMOUTH *see* essay on page 343

GEORGE (1653–1708), (Prince of Denmark, Duke of Cumberland), Consort of Queen ANNE. The son of King Frederick III of Denmark, he came to England to marry Anne in 1683. He supported William of Orange (the future WILLIAM III) in 1688 and was made a duke but his position remained ambiguous. In 1702 Anne attempted to have him made King and Captain General of the Netherlands but was defeated. He was given the largely honorific title of Generalissimo of the

continued on page 344

GEOFFREY OF MONMOUTH (?–1155)
Historian

He wrote the Latin prose *History of the Kings of Britain* (which included *The Prophecies of Merlin*) and a *Life of Merlin* in Latin verse. These works were chiefly responsible for taking two figures, King ARTHUR and MERLIN, from the world of Celtic legend and launching them on to the wider stage of European culture, where they have remained ever since. Geoffrey referred to himself as 'of Monmouth' and he was almost certainly a Welshman (although some people have suggested he was a Breton). Between *c.* 1130 and *c.* 1150 he was based at Oxford, probably a canon of the collegiate church of St George. In 1152 he was consecrated Bishop of St Asaph, but he died soon afterwards.

The *History* records the reigns of no fewer than 99 British kings from Brutus, the great-grandson of Aeneas of Troy, down to CADWALADR, who died in 689. To present almost 2,000 years of British history in one majestic sweep was a stunning achievement; it certainly stunned its earliest known reader, HENRY OF HUNTINGDON, who saw a copy of it in 1139. Before Geoffrey set to work in the 1130s there was no such thing as a British history. Apart from oral tradition, there was just the account of fifth-century Britain written by GILDAS in the sixth and an early ninth-century compilation known as the *History of the Britons*. The author of the last had only the most fragmentary sources at his disposal, and his compilation is, in consequence, itself piecemeal and disjointed. Geoffrey faced precisely the same problem as the anonymous ninth-century compiler (usually known as NENNIUS), but he solved it in an entirely different way, creating a coherent and powerful artistic whole, one of the supreme achievements of the historical imagination, and almost entirely a work of fiction, the first great work of the Oxford school of history. He invented British history.

The *History* was completed by 1139 and primarily dedicated to ROBERT OF GLOUCESTER. It became an instant best-seller, its readers sharply divided between those (such as WILLIAM OF NEWBURGH) who dismissed it as a tissue of lies, and those who saw it as genuine history. There have always been sceptics, men like those who, as CAXTON reported, 'hold opinion that there was no such Arthur'. But from the thirteenth to the sixteenth century believers outnumbered sceptics; as late as the nineteenth century there were still some willing to take it seriously. Even today there are those who cannot bring themselves to renounce their belief in the towering figure of King Arthur. In his preface Geoffrey claimed that all he did was to translate into Latin 'a certain very ancient book written in the British language' (by which he meant Welsh). But the book has not yet been found and it was then common practice for authors wishing to add a spurious air of authority to their own work to claim that they were 'merely' following an ancient text. Moreover, the whole structure of the *History* is well calculated to give an appearance of authority since it is only in the second half of the book that the figures of King Arthur and Merlin appear and, with them, that combination of magic, romance and heroism which gives the history so wide an appeal. In the first half the reader is offered a chronicle of events. A skilful mixture of the familiar, such as JULIUS CAESAR's British campaign, and the unfamiliar, such as the sad story of Cordelia and King Lear (who, Geoffrey explains, gave his name to Leicester), or the capture of Rome by the British King Belinus (hence Billingsgate), was all narrated in a lucid and fairly sober style. Geoffrey, in other words, delays Merlin's entry until the reader is predisposed to take him seriously.

Geoffrey's purposes in writing fiction masquerading as history have been much debated. At one level he was teasing the leading English historians of his day, WILLIAM OF MALMESBURY and Henry of Huntingdon. But he was also providing his own people, the twelfth-century descendants of the Britons, with a splendid and civilized past and doing so at a time when the English were beginning to look down on the Welsh as simple and immoral savages. After HENRY I's death (1135) the Welsh fought back against the French and English who had been invading and colonizing their land since the 1090s, turning it, as one contemporary put it, into 'a second England'. One of the Welsh triumphs was the 1136 capture of Caerleon by MORGAN AP OWAIN; it is striking how much interest Geoffrey takes in this small town (in Wales near Monmouth), making it the seat both of Arthur's court and of the (equally legendary) primate of all Britain.

Geoffrey of Monmouth, The History of the Kings of Britain, trans. L. Thorpe (1966) armed forces and Lord High Admiral, advised by a committee. He was subject to sustained criticism from those who wanted to reform naval administration or free his post for a politician, but George undertook his duties conscientiously. Although he fathered large numbers of children upon Anne, all miscarried or died young. His death was a blow to Anne's confidence.

GEORGE (2nd Duke of Cambridge) (1819–1904), soldier. The grandson of GEORGE III, he was educated by military tutors and joined the 12th Lancers. On the death of his father in 1850 George became Duke of Cambridge. In 1854, now a general, he commanded a division at the Battle of Inkerman (5 Nov. 1854), during which more than half the Duke's division were killed or wounded and the Duke suffered a complete physical and psychological breakdown. Wracked with guilt over what he believed was his desertion of his men, the Duke was nevertheless treated as a hero and appointed Commander-in-Chief in June 1856. He subsequently played a major role in the creation of the Army Staff College at Camberley (Surrey), in the provision of educational opportunities for other ranks, and in the establishment of Aldershot (Hants) as a virtual military city, with libraries, sporting facilities and theatres. He also managed to secure a modest increase in soldiers' pay. It was not for nothing that the Duke became known as 'the soldier's friend'.

The arrival of Edward CARDWELL in the War Office in 1868 forced the Duke into ever increasing conservatism. In 1888 a commission chaired by Lord Hartington (*see* CAVENDISH, SPENCER) recommended the abolition of the post of Commander-in-Chief once the Duke retired. Deeply offended, Cambridge clung on until 1895 when even his loyal cousin, Queen VICTORIA, told him it was time to go.

GEORGE I *see* essay on page 345

GEORGE II *see* essay on page 346

GEORGE III *see* essay on page 347

GEORGE IV (1762–1830), King of Great Britain and Ireland, and King of Hanover (1820–30). Eldest son of GEORGE III, he became Prince Regent in 1811 because of his father's incapacity and succeeded him in 1820. Like most of the Hanoverians, his relationship with his father was oppositional and antagonistic, which had a considerable effect on his morals. Clever, indolent, a dandy when young and, in later life, obese (he was known in some circles as 'Prince of Whales'), George 'married' Mrs FITZHERBERT, a Catholic, in 1785 and the invalid union continued

until 1811, although the King legally married CAROLINE of Brunswick in 1795 and they had a daughter, Charlotte (1796–1817). The scandal surrounding his attempt to divorce Caroline and have her excluded from his coronation further damaged a monarchy already held in low esteem and some ridicule. However, for all his excesses, George IV was a man of culture, a patron of the arts and admirer of fine architecture. He is particularly associated with the seaside resort of Brighton where he built an elaborate dome- and minaret-encrusted pavilion for Mrs Fitzherbert.

GEORGE V (1865–1936), King of the United Kingdom and Emperor of India (1910–36). Second son of EDWARD VII and Queen ALEXANDRA, he served in the navy from 1877 to 1892, marrying Princess Mary of Teck (1867–1953) in 1893. He became heir following the death of his elder brother Clarence in 1901, and acceded to the throne in 1910, holding a memorable coronation durbar in India the following year. Initially showing little zest for kingship, he nevertheless proved a dutiful and conscientious monarch, attempting to assist in the reconciliation of the Irish Home Rule crisis at a conference at Buckingham Palace in 1914 and providing leadership during the First World War. In 1917 he changed the royal family's name from Saxe-Coburg to Windsor. He played a role in politics through his choice of BALDWIN as Prime Minister in 1923 and in persuading Ramsay MACDONALD to form a National government in 1931. He began the tradition of Christmas broadcasts to the country and Empire in 1932, and his Silver Jubilee in 1935 was genuinely popular. He was succeeded by his eldest son, EDWARD VIII.

GEORGE VI (1895–1952), King of the United Kingdom (1936–52) and Emperor of India (1936–47). The second son of GEORGE V and Queen Mary, as Prince Albert he served in the Royal Navy (1909–17), being present at the Battle of Jutland, and then for a year in the Royal Air Force. Created Duke of York in 1920, he married Lady ELIZABETH Bowes-Lyon in 1923. Long in the shadow of his more outgoing elder brother David, who became EDWARD VIII, he came to the throne as a result of the abdication crisis of 1936. Overcoming both shyness and a stammer, he did much to restore the credibility of the monarchy, especially during the Second World War by maintaining residence in Buckingham Palace during the blitz and visiting bombed areas with the Queen. He was succeeded by his daughter ELIZABETH II.

GEORGE, EDWARD (EDDIE) (1938–), banker. A graduate in economics from Emmanuel College, Cambridge, he joined the Bank of

continued on page 348

GEORGE I (1660–1727)
King of Great Britain and Ireland (1714–27) and Elector of Hanover

His father was Ernst August of Brunswick-Lüneburg and his mother SOPHIA, granddaughter of JAMES VI AND I. Ernt August was the youngest of four sons and started without significant territory or title. When he became Duke of Hanover in 1679, George was 19.

Although, perhaps because, his destiny was originally uncertain, he was trained to cope with the complexities of European affairs after the Thirty Years War, learning German, French, Latin and some Dutch and Italian. He fought his first military campaign aged 15: on the Dutch side against the French. In 1682 it was agreed that he should marry Sophia Dorothea, daughter of his uncle the Duke of Celle, thus securing the future unity of the duchies, and bolstering Hanover's claim to be an imperial electorate.

His first child, Georg August (later GEORGE II), was born 1683. By 1691 his marriage was on the rocks. George had a mistress, Melusine von der SCHULENBURG, but when his wife openly took a lover the lover was secretly murdered, and she divorced and kept a virtual prisoner to stop her becoming a pawn in international politics. In 1698 George succeeded as Duke of Hanover. The death of ANNE's sole surviving son made his succession to the English throne a real prospect; the Act of Settlement 1701 named first his mother then him as nearest Protestant heirs. In 1705 George inherited Celle from his uncle, along with skilled advisers, BERNSTORFF and his protégé Robethon. In 1708 he was appointed Field Marshal of the German imperial army in the War of the Spanish Succession, but soon resigned. Hanover was nonetheless made an imperial electorate in 1708.

George kept in contact with English ministers. He welcomed Charles TOWNSHEND's Anglo-Dutch Treaty of Barrier and Succession of 1709, binding Dutch troops to protect Hanoverian interests. When GODOLPHIN was replaced by Robert HARLEY, in a ministry dependent on Tory support, he worried about their commitment to European affairs.

His mother's death in 1714 was quickly followed by Anne's. The Hanoverian representative in London, BOTHMER, collaborated with those ministers who, after Anne's last-minute dismissal of Harley (now Earl of Oxford), ensured that the Treasury went to the safe hands of Shrewsbury (see TALBOT, CHARLES). George came speedily to England and, though professing to choose ministers on their merits, in fact appointed mostly Whigs, among whom James STANHOPE and Sunderland (see SPENCER, CHARLES) gained ascendancy. The provisions of the Act of Settlement, prompted by dislike of WILLIAM III's promotion of Dutch favourites, precluded him from giving office or reward to Hanoverians, though some of his advisers became objects of jealousy nonetheless.

Though George may have wished to balance the parties, the Whigs insisted on extending their power. Their marginalization of Tories and pressing of impeachment charges drove Bolingbroke (see ST JOHN, HENRY) and Ormonde (see BUTLER, JAMES) abroad, and made others sympathize with the Jacobite rebellion led by the Earl of Mar (see ERSKINE, JOHN). The rebels were defeated, and Toryism destroyed as a political force.

George had difficulty in carrying all the ascendant Whigs along with him. Absent in Hanover in 1716, he became impatient with Robert WALPOLE and Townshend, who seemed reluctant to complete a post-war alliance with France and the Dutch and unsympathetic to his Baltic ambitions; in 1717 they went into opposition. George also fell out with his son, whom he refused to make regent during his absences in Hanover. Expelled from court, the prince set up his own household at Leicester House, which became a focus of opposition. Developing a mastery of the political game, George sought reconciliation with his son in 1720; Walpole and Townshend were also reconciled. Later that year speculative fever, associated with government attempts to reduce interest payments on war debt via a complicated deal with the South Sea Company, climaxed with the bursting of the 'South Sea Bubble' (in which the King, like many of his subjects, lost a substantial sum). Stanhope and Sunderland both died soon after; Walpole and Townshend achieved a mastery which they were to retain for the rest of the reign.

George's background and German interests led him to focus on achieving a European balance of power favouring his concerns: Britain was always only one of these. London became his main base of operations, and his grasp of British politics should not be underestimated. His uncertain command of English was not crippling; French served for most political business. He attended formal Cabinet meetings and though Walpole and Townshend's cohesion and strong power-base in the Commons reduced his room for manoeuvre, that might have happened to any monarch. Judged cold and dull by some English observers, George was a cultured man and a shrewd and pragmatic ruler. He responded with restraint to anti-Hanoverian sentiment in Britain, and supported religious toleration.

Ragnild Hatton, George I: Elector and King (1978)

GEORGE II (1683–1760)
King of Great Britain and Ireland (1727–60) and Elector of Hanover

The only son of GEORGE I, who imprisoned his mother for life in 1694 on a charge of adultery, he was raised as a German prince, with a grounding in European history and languages, though he showed most interest in military matters. His prospects widened after 1701, when the English Act of Settlement placed him in the line of succession after his father and grandmother SOPHIA.

With family support, in 1705 he married CAROLINE of Ansbach. Told that he could not join Hanoverian forces in the War of the Spanish Succession until he had an heir, he tried to oblige: his son FREDERICK was born in 1707. He was then allowed to fight one campaign as a cavalry commander under Marlborough (*see* CHURCHILL, JOHN). Returning to the electoral court, he took an English mistress, Mrs Howard, whom Caroline accepted without fuss (his grandmother said it might at least improve his English).

In 1714 on Anne's death, he accompanied his father to England, and was made Prince of Wales. His stormy and difficult temperament was already evident. He was often on bad terms with his father, in part because he was not trusted with much power: thus, when the King first returned to Hanover in 1716, he refused to make George Regent. These tensions were exacerbated by intrigues between rival groups in the ministry. In 1717 the quarrel came to a head, and the Prince established a rival court at Leicester House (in summer, at Richmond Lodge), among whose attendants were Robert WALPOLE and Charles TOWNSHEND, Whigs out of office. Father and son were reconciled in 1720, and the Whig split healed. For the next few years Prince George accepted a place on the political margin.

In June 1727 his father died and George succeeded to the throne. He asked Spencer COMPTON, a leading figure at his court, to form a ministry, but, impressed by Walpole's greater political acumen, especially his ability to obtain from Parliament a generous financial settlement, decided to continue him in office. Caroline favoured Walpole: her charm and good sense were to ease and guide the King's early dealings with politicians, though George resented suggestions that she ruled rather than he.

His difficulties with his father were replicated with his own son. Frederick had been kept in Hanover, and came to England only in 1728; George proved reluctant to trust him, the more so when he began dallying with Bolingbroke (*see* ST JOHN, HENRY) and the Old Corps opposition to Walpole. As that opposition grew stronger, family relations worsened. In 1737 a serious quarrel prompted Frederick to establish a rival court at Leicester House. Caroline died the same year. The King's mistress, Baroness von WALLMODEN, henceforth the most powerful woman at court, played some part in politics but manifested no particular sympathies.

The War of the Austrian Succession (1739–48) made the King especially concerned about Hanover; widespread suspicion that the war was waged more in Hanoverian than in British interests troubled successive ministries. PITT THE ELDER attracted the King's special dislike by his vigour in voicing such criticisms. George played an active part in the war, commanding the allied army in the Low Countries, and leading them to victory at Dettingen in 1742, the last occasion on which a reigning British monarch commanded in battle. War constrained the King's political freedom; in 1742 he was forced to accept Walpole's resignation; in 1744, to dismiss Granville (*see* CARTERET, JOHN), whose broad European vision had appealed to him but had proved impracticable; in 1746, to accept Pitt as Paymaster of the Forces. To forestall this last, he entreated Granville and Bath (*see* PULTENEY, WILLIAM) to form a ministry, but they could not rally support. PELHAM and subsequently his brother Newcastle (*see* PELHAM-HOLLES, THOMAS) were to the fore for the rest of the reign, although from 1754 Pitt became a contender for power in his own right. The Seven Years War (1757–63) was less problematic for the King than the Austrian conflict. New imperial acquisitions were acclaimed in Britain, and although complaints of Hanoverian bias were once again heard, Pitt, now Secretary of State, headed them off with flamboyant patriotic gestures.

Opinionated and assertive, George was always a force to be reckoned with. Recognizing that his ministers needed parliamentary support, and that this limited his freedom of action, he yet resented being a 'King in toils'. He oversaw a broadening in the political basis of the regime: he had flirted with the Tories in his youth, and in 1744 they were admitted to minor positions in Pelham's Broad-Bottom ministry; Pitt also cultivated their support. By and large, however, George accepted that the leading ministries should come from among Old Corps Whigs, a convention that his grandson and successor GEORGE III thought was a mistake.

John Van Der Kiste, King George II and Queen Caroline (1997)

GEORGE III (1738–1820)
King of Great Britain and Ireland (1760–1820) and Elector of Hanover

Grandson of GEORGE II, he was the first of the Hanoverian kings to be born and bred in Britain. Because of this, his leading ministers could not plausibly argue (as his grandfather's sometimes had) that they knew the constitution better than the King. Pious, chaste and conscientious, George maintained throughout his life a firm conviction of his own rectitude.

His father, FREDERICK, died when George was 12. The boy was raised by his mother, AUGUSTA, dowager Princess of Wales, and by a series of controversial tutors. In 1752 his governor, Lord Harcourt, complained that the Prince's current tutors were crypto-Jacobites. In 1755, John STUART, Lord Bute took charge of George's education, and won his affection. George learned about the history and government of Britain and Europe, geography, agriculture and commerce. He was taught to revere Britain's balanced constitution, and was encouraged to strive to embody an ideal form of British kingship.

When he came to the throne in 1760, he hoped to inaugurate a new era in politics, above all by ending the exclusion of the Tories from royal favour, court and other office. The gestures which he made to this end did win him the loyalty of many former Tories and certain independents, but a section of the Old Corps Whigs, those later to be known as the Rockingham Whigs (see WATSON-WENTWORTH, CHARLES) took offence. This group, who were to spend most of the King's reign out of office, did much to blacken his reputation. They accused him of unconstitutionally relying on the influence of Bute, a favourite behind the curtain, and of plotting to enhance the power of the Crown; he, in turn, believed them to be motivated by self-serving ambition.

The first five decades of the reign were troubled by the growth of extra-parliamentary radicalism, the extraordinarily destructive Gordon Riots (see GORDON, LORD GEORGE) of 1780, and war with the North American colonies which resulted in American independence, as well as troubled relations with Ireland and India and a prolonged and taxing war with France. In the early 1780s the King more than once contemplated abdication.

As George saw it, successive crises revealed that not merely the more obviously (from his point of view) 'unreliable' public figures of the day but also those apparently more trustworthy could not in the end be trusted to stand firm. Thus in the Gordon Riots metropolitan magistrates proved unwilling to stand up to the rioters and George himself had to order in troops. In the concluding stages of the American War of Independence even NORTH, his trusted minister for 12 years, became convinced, contrary to the King's own judgement, that it was necessary to accede to American demands and resorted to resignation to force the King's hand, delivering him into the hands of the Whig opposition, whom the King found it difficult to respect or trust. In 1801 PITT THE YOUNGER, who in 1783 had rescued him from the hands of that group, resigned because the King would not agree to his wish for a further measure of Catholic emancipation.

Throughout his reign George showed himself willing to go behind the backs of his leading ministers, if necessary, in search of figures whom he felt he could trust – a propensity which encouraged the perception that he showed an unconstitutional predilection for favourites. He did initially continue to consult Bute despite Bute's inability to maintain himself in high political office, though he acceded to politicians' demands by ceasing to consult him from 1765. In the later stages of North's ministry George made a confidant of the Secretary of War, Charles JENKINSON, who became, and remained, a focus for similar suspicions.

George married Princess CHARLOTTE of Mecklenburg Strelitz in 1761. A devoted husband and father to his 15 children, George attempted to restrict his children's personal lives, and above all their marital choices, in ways which many of them found oppressive. Like his grandfather and great-grandfather, he had a stormy relationship with his eldest son (later GEORGE IV), whose taste for high living and loose company his father blamed in large part on the influence of the Whig Charles James FOX and his cronies.

He also suffered recurrent outbreaks of 'madness' (retrospectively diagnosed as a symptom of the kidney disorder, porphyria) giving rise to regency crises in 1765 and 1788. In 1811 he became permanently incapable, and his eldest son was made regent. Yet, curiously, in the later decades of his reign, when he had entered his final descent into insanity, the King's personal popularity within Britain, which had never been inconsiderable, blossomed, in part as a result of loyalist rallying in response to the French Revolutionary and Napoleonic Wars.

John Brooke, King George III (1972)

England in 1962, where he has spent nearly all of his working life. In his early years he worked mainly on the international aspects of the bank's activities and became chairman of the deputies of the International Monetary Fund's Committee of Twenty on international monetary reform in the 1970s and adviser on international monetary issues until 1977. Until 1997 the bank was subservient to the Treasury, but it was then given a more significant policy-making role, deciding rates of interest. Hence it acquired a greater degree of independence than at any time since the days of Montague NORMAN. The sobriquet 'Steady Eddie', given to George by the Conservative Chancellor Kenneth CLARKE, illustrated the developing partnership with the Treasury and the growing emphasis on stability.

GEORGE, HENRY (1839–97), economist and social critic. An American journalist, he became a major influence on radicalism and early socialism in Britain in the 1880s. His *Progress and Poverty* (1879), a best-seller in both the USA and Britain, argued that the remedy for all economic problems, especially poverty, was a single tax levied on the value of property exclusive of improvements. The book's message, extended by George's tours of the depressed agricultural areas of Scotland and Ireland, became immensely popular at a time when economic depression was severe and the problems of poverty and inequality were once more becoming major issues.

GEORGE-BROWN, BARON *see* BROWN, GEORGE

GERALD OF WALES *see* BARRI, GERALD DE, essay on page 60

GERALDINES, THE The name for the early sixteenth-century Irish following and sphere of influence of the FITZGERALD earls of Kildare.

GERARD (*fl.* 1166), heretic. Leader of a group of heretics, who because of their practices were assumed to be not English but Cathars from Germany, he was condemned at Oxford, branded on brow and chin, stripped and publicly flogged, and driven out naked into the icy winter to perish.

GERARD, JOHN (1545–1612), herbalist. A barber-surgeon, he travelled abroad and for 20 years acted as William CECIL's gardener. In 1596 he published a catalogue of his own garden in Holborn. The following year saw the publication of his illustrated *Herball*, which contains the first English-language reference to the potato. Although it was not entirely original, this compendium of plants and their medical uses continued to have Europe-wide influence for more than a century, and in recent years has enjoyed renewed popularity.

GERMAIN, LORD GEORGE (1st Viscount Sackville) (1716–85), soldier and politician. The third son of the 1st Duke of Dorset, Germain, formerly Sackville, was educated at Westminster and Trinity College, Dublin (his father then being Lord Lieutenant of Ireland). An MP from 1741, he fought in the War of the Austrian Succession. In the Seven Years War he fought at Minden as Commander-in-Chief on the Rhine; he overruled Granby's (*see* MANNERS, JOHN) wish to pursue the French and was dismissed. A court martial in 1760 found him unfit to serve in a military capacity. A wealthy widow, Lady Betty Germain, left him her estates in 1769, and he took her surname. His career revived under GEORGE III, who had disagreed with the original sentence. He was Secretary of State for the Colonies (1775–82), advocating harsh measures against the Americans, and was rewarded with a peerage when he fell with NORTH.

GERMANUS (?–*c.* 437), Bishop of Auxerre. The record of Germanus' two visits to Britain in the early fifth century is one of the few documentary sources for conditions in Britain after the end of Roman rule. Since the purpose of his journeys was to combat the heresy of PELAGIUS, it can be presumed that Britain was still largely Christian. The story of Germanus' part in a military victory over the Picts and Saxons demonstrates a British community still successfully resisting its invaders in the period between HONORIUS' recall of the Roman legions from Britain in 410 and AMBROSIUS AURELIANUS' great victory at Mount Badon.

GERMANUS (?–?1013), Abbot. Like the much more distinguished St ABBO OF FLEURY, Germanus was a monk from the renowned French monastery of Fleury-sur-Loire, called to England by St OSWALD. Abbot of Winchcombe from 970 to 975, he returned to Fleury in 975. He may be identical with the Germanus who was Abbot of Ramsey (992–3) and Abbot of Cholsey (993–1013).

GERRALD, JOSEPH (1763–96), radical. He came from an Irish family in the West Indies but was educated in London. In 1788 he returned to Britain from a legal career in Pennsylvania to secure some family property, and joined the radical London Corresponding Society. He and Maurice Margarot were elected delegates from the LCS to the British Convention of the Delegates of the People, which met in Edinburgh in 1793 to explore applying the principles of the French Revolution to Britain. They were arrested for sedition, found guilty and transported to Australia. Gerrald died in Sydney in 1796, one year into his sentence.

GERVASE OF CANTERBURY (*c.* 1145–*c.* 1210), chronicler. A monk of Christ Church, Canterbury, he was led by his devotion to his abbey to its archives and then to writing historical works in which the affairs and especially the litigation of Christ Church were central. Of inestimable value to architectural historians is his detailed description of the rebuilding of Canterbury Cathedral after the fire of 1174.

GIBBON, EDWARD (1737–94), historian. His father, heir to a large fortune, was briefly an MP. Ill health meant Gibbon's education was irregular: a voracious reader when left to himself, he notoriously regarded the 14 months he spent at Oxford as 'idle and unprofitable'. The writing of Conyers MIDDLETON gave him an inclination towards Catholicism, but his family sent him to Lausanne to be cured. During the Seven Years War (1757–63) he served in the Hampshire militia and developed an interest in military history. He conceived the idea for his massive *History of the Decline and Fall of the Roman Empire* while touring Italy in 1763–4. The first volume appeared in 1778 and was well received, although his pessimistic assessment of the effects of Christianity attracted criticism, which he answered in *A Vindication* (1779). In 1772 he settled in London, where he mixed in fashionable and literary circles, and was a member of Samuel JOHNSON's literary club. An MP from 1774, he served as a Commissioner of Trade and Plantations to 1782, and consistently supported NORTH's ministry on the War of American Independence. The final volumes of the *Decline and Fall* were completed in 1788: it is remarkable chiefly as a literary and semi-philosophical exploration of cultural and political change.

GIBBONS, GRINLING (1648–1720), woodcarver and sculptor. The son of English parents living in Holland, he probably trained in stonework in Amsterdam before coming to England as a ship carver in 1667. In 1671 he was 'discovered' by John EVELYN in his home at Deptford carving a copy of Tintoretto's *Crucifixion*. Evelyn presented him at court, and helped him win commissions for his work, particularly his celebrated intricate reproductions of flowers. These included decorations at Windsor Castle for CHARLES II, the choir stalls at St Paul's and ornaments at other London churches for WREN, as well as work for several noblemen including William CAVENDISH, 1st Duke of Devonshire, at Chatsworth (Derb.). His finest work, 'Attributes of the Arts', was commissioned by Charles II as a gift for Grand Duke Cosimo III of Tuscany, presented in 1682. WILLIAM III appointed him master-carver to the Crown in 1693.

GIBBONS, ORLANDO (1583–1625), composer. Organist of the Jacobean Chapel Royal, he had degrees from both Oxford and Cambridge. His music ranged widely in style and form: keyboard pieces, madrigals, fantasias for viol consort, variations based on street cries and choral writing for the English liturgy. With John BULL and William BYRD he published the important collection of keyboard music entitled *Parthenia* (1613). The fact that he was writing in the reigns of both ELIZABETH and JAMES I is a reminder of the artificiality of the cultural labels 'Tudor' or 'Elizabethan' in music as in literature or architecture.

GIBBS, JAMES (1682–1754), architect. A Catholic Tory, son of a merchant at Aberdeen, he was educated at Marischal College, Aberdeen, and at the Pontifical Scots College in Rome, where he studied with the leading Baroque architect, Carlo Fontana. He was appointed surveyor to the commission for building new churches in London in 1711; St Martin-in-the-Fields, London, innovative in its placing of a steeple behind the west portico, was his most influential design. The Fellows' Building of King's College and the Senate House in Cambridge and the circular Radcliffe Camera in Oxford were also designed by him; his later work (when he was taken up by Whig patrons) followed the neo-Palladian style popularized by Colen CAMPBELL. His *Book of Architecture* (1728) was one of the most widely used pattern books of the eighteenth century.

GIBSON, EDMUND (1669–1748), cleric and religious writer. Ordained and elected a Fellow of Queen's College, Oxford, in 1694, he edited several historical works, including the *Anglo-Saxon Chronicle* (1692) and CAMDEN's *Britannia* (1695), and published several pamphlets in the controversy over the rights of Convocation (1701–2). His best-known work, *Codex Iuris Ecclesiae Anglicanae* (Book of the Laws of the Church of England) (1712) was long the standard authority on ecclesiastical law, earning him the nickname 'Dr Codex'. He became Bishop of Lincoln (1716) and then of London (1720). As Robert WALPOLE's chief adviser on ecclesiastical matters, he was called 'Walpole's Pope'; they split in 1736 when Gibson opposed the Quaker Relief Bill (designed to protect from legal harassment Quakers who refused to pay tithes for conscientious reasons), and he was passed over when the archbishopric of Canterbury fell vacant the following year. Offered the post in 1747, he declined on grounds of ill health.

GIDDENS, ANTHONY (1938–), sociologist. Possibly the best-known academic sociologist presently at work in Britain, especially for his influence on the political thinking of Tony BLAIR and New Labour by advocating a Third Way between conservatism and old-style socialism. From 1969 his career was largely spent at Cambridge, but, he was made Director of the London School of Economics in 1998. His principal publications have been on class and political theory.

GIDEON, SAMPSON (1699–1762), banker. The son of a Portuguese–Jewish merchant who had settled in London, Gideon's financial expertise brought him a large fortune. He was virtually the sole financial adviser and fund manager for the British government during and after the War of the Austrian Succession, arranging loans and devising financial instruments by which the fiscal system could be tided over the strains of wartime.

GIELGUD, SIR JOHN (1904–2000), actor. The great-nephew of the actress Ellen TERRY, Gielgud made his London début at the Old Vic in 1921, after graduating from the Royal Academy of Dramatic Arts. Quickly establishing himself as a superb Shakespearean actor (*see* SHAKESPEARE, WILLIAM), he went on to play Hamlet in 1930, a role he was to perform over 500 times during his career. He also performed and directed plays by contemporary playwrights Terence Rattigan and Graham GREENE in the 1950s, and is considered to have made a major contribution towards the acceptance of Chekhov's works on the English-speaking stage with his performances in *The Seagull* (1936) and *The Three Sisters* (1937). Gielgud's stage reputation has overshadowed his film and television career, but he has appeared in some very successful parts, often as the quintessential Englishman, in *Brideshead Revisited* (1981) and *Chariots of Fire*, while more recently appearing as Prospero, a part he has played many times on stage, in Peter Greenaway's film *Prospero's Books* (1988). In 1994 he was honoured by the renaming of the Globe Theatre in London's Shaftesbury Avenue as the Gielgud Theatre, to celebrate his 90th birthday.

GIFFARD, WALTER (?–1279), Archbishop of York. A papal chaplain and Archdeacon of Wells, he was elected Bishop of Bath and Wells in 1264, made Chancellor in 1265, and translated to York in 1266, where he was a strict and fearless reformer of abuses, although a rich and liberal entertainer. He was one of the regents (1272–4) after the death of HENRY III. He continued the long-standing dispute with Canterbury over his right as Archbishop to have his cross carried upright within the province of Canterbury.

GIFFORD, BONAVENTURE (1642–1734), Catholic churchman. The son of a Catholic landowner, he was educated at Douai and the Sorbonne. In 1677 he was appointed missionary priest to England and, in 1685, chaplain to JAMES II. In Jan. 1688 he became a bishop and Vicar Apostolic of the Midland district in the provisional Catholic hierarchy arranged by James II. In March he succeeded Samuel Parker as President of Magdalen, Oxford. He quarrelled with the fellows and expelled those who rejected his authority in Aug., but under growing political pressure James concurred in Gifford's ejection from Magdalen in Oct. Arrested in Nov. and imprisoned until 1690, he subsequently lived in London, his security endangered by his status as an outlaw, but he remained an active Catholic bishop.

GILBERT, SIR ALFRED (1854–1934), sculptor. The creator of one of London's most famous landmarks, the statue of Eros in Piccadilly Circus (1886–93), Gilbert sculpted other notable monuments in metals, notably his bronze *Icarus* at the National Museum of Wales in Cardiff and the elaborate tomb of the Duke of Clarence at Windsor (1892–1926).

GILBERT, ELIZABETH (1824–85), pioneer of work for the blind. The daughter of the Principal of Brasenose College, Oxford, who resolved that his daughter should receive as normal an education as possible after she was left blind from an attack of scarlet fever when she was three, Gilbert learned to read using the newly invented Braille system and devoted her life to helping the blind to lead useful and productive lives. She lobbied to have provision for blind children inserted into the 1870 Education Act.

GILBERT, HUMPHREY (?1539–83), explorer. From a Devon gentry family long interested in seafaring, Gilbert studied at Oxford and was briefly a page to Princess Elizabeth (the future ELIZABETH I). After military service in France (1562–3), he devoted one of his numerous pamphlets to the supposed north-west sea-passage to Asia and pursued another family interest: colonization of Ireland. This led him to think of imitating Spanish settlement in America. His first expedition intended for North America in 1578 got no further than the Cape Verde Islands, but after further frenzied fundraising he set out in 1583 and formally annexed St John's in Newfoundland (long visited seasonally by whaling and fishing fleets), without persuading his expedition to leave a permanent presence. On the home voyage he went down with his ship in a storm.

GILBERT OF LIMERICK (?–1140), reformer. First Bishop of Limerick from 1107, his treatise *De Statu Ecclesie* served as a blueprint for the diocesan restructuring of the Irish Church, over which he, as Papal Legate, presided at the Council of Rathbreasail of 1111.

GILBERT OF SEMPRINGHAM (1087?–1189), founder of a religious order. Destined by physical deformity to a clerical career, he became rector of Sempringham (Lincs.), a church under his father's patronage. His interest in teaching the boys and girls of the parish led to the foundation, at Sempringham c. 1130, of a nunnery for seven girl pupils. Other benefactors followed his example and Gilbert soon found himself supervising several communities and, under Cistercian influence, extending them by bringing in lay sisters and brothers as the nuns' servants. In 1147 he tried to transfer them to the Cistercians but the Pope ordered him to stay on as master of a new order, the Gilbertines, to which he added regular canons as priests and estate managers. Sexual scandal and a revolt of the lay brethren in 1166–7 resulted in an investigation which did much to establish his reputation for sanctity. Miracles at his tomb at Sempringham were reported; in 1202 he was canonized.

GILBERT, THOMAS (c. 1719–98), politician and social reformer. Dependent for his seat in the Commons on Earl Gower (see LEVESON-GOWER, GRANVILLE) whose estates he helped develop, he was for most of his career a member of the 'Bloomsbury gang' of followers of John RUSSELL, Duke of Beford. He is best remembered for his attempts to reform the poor law, the only successful measure being Gilbert's Act of 1782. This empowered groups of parishes to unite and establish a common workhouse, in which children and the aged poor (but not the able-bodied) might be confined. Because these workhouses could not be used to deter the able-bodied poor from claiming poor relief, it has been described as a humanitarian measure but at the time its policy of even limited confinement was controversial. Its effects were limited: by 1830 only 927 parishes had adopted it, forming 67 unions.

GILBERT, WILLIAM (1540–1603), scientist. From a prosperous Colchester family, Gilbert became a Cambridge don and a distinguished doctor and, as President of the Royal College of Physicians from 1599, he attended ELIZABETH I as she was dying. He was an outstanding pioneering scientist who rejected the dominance of Aristotle's writings and investigated magnetism; he expounded his findings in De Magnete (1600), and in De Mundo (not published until 1651) supported Copernican theories about the rotation of the earth and discussed planetary motion.

GILBERT, SIR W(ILLIAM) S(CHWENK) (1836–1911), librettist. He is best known for his series of Savoy operas which he produced in partnership with the composer Arthur SULLIVAN for performance in the Savoy Theatre, London. The operas of Gilbert and Sullivan have seemed for generations to be quintessentially British: light-hearted, eclectic in their music, clever with words, romantic and often totally improbable in their plots. From Trial by Jury (1875) to The Grand Duke (1896), by way of The Pirates of Penzance (1880) and The Mikado (1885), the sequence of operas has proved of enduring appeal.

GILDAS (c. 516–c. 570), monk and scholar. A highly respected churchman and scholar, Gildas is credited with the compilation of a penitential which greatly influenced early monasticism in Britain and Ireland. The author of the early-Irish Penitential of Uinniau was stated by COLUMBANUS to have consulted Gildas on a question of discipline, and Gildas seems to have spent some time in Ireland helping to organize the fledgling Irish Church.

Gildas's best-known work is De Excidio et Conquestu Britanniae (The Ruin of Britain), the earliest literary source of native origin for the history of Britain, which provides an important record of the English invasions of the fifth and sixth centuries. The Battle of Mount Badon (see AMBROSIUS AURELIANUS), which Gildas states to have occurred in the year of his birth, is recorded in the Annales Cambriae to have taken place in 516. Frequently scorned by modern scholars, the De Excidio was intended primarily as a denunciation of contemporary kings and clergy, rather than as an account of the Anglo-Saxon expansion into Britain for which it is now studied, and it may therefore relate to events of a more localized character than its famous invective against debauched rulers and its prediction of consequential disasters. Gildas's death is recorded in the Annals of Ulster in 570. Interestingly, the De Excidio makes no mention of King ARTHUR.

GILL, ERIC (1882–1940), sculptor, engraver and typographer. A Roman Catholic convert, he produced Stations of the Cross for Westminster Cathedral (1913–18) and formed the Guild of St Joseph and St Dominic, a semi-religious community of craftsmen. His many sculptural commissions included the BBC's Broadcasting House (1929–31) and the League of Nations building in Geneva (1935). These and much of his figurative work in stone, wood and woodcut combine religious expression with overt sexuality, as did his unconventional private life. His printing typefaces, especially Perpetua (1927) and Gill Sanserif (1928), continue to be widely used.

GILLRAY, JAMES (1757–1815), caricaturist and engraver. Briefly apprenticed to a letter engraver, Gillray joined a group of strolling players, then studied at the Royal Academy Schools. He illustrated books before turning to the caricatures for which he is best known; these he produced in association with a series of specialist print-sellers. After 1782 he devoted himself almost entirely to topical and political subjects, savagely satirizing both the radical fervour aroused by the French Revolution and the folly and greed of leading politicians and the royal family. From 1811 he was confined to his room as insane.

GILPIN, BERNARD (1517–84), churchman. His career was founded on being great-nephew to Bishop Cuthbert TUNSTALL, and in the 1540s and 1550s he had an uneasy and ambiguous relationship with evangelical Church reforms. Although rejecting ELIZABETH I's offers of promotion, he devoted himself to revitalizing parish life in northern England by hospitality and itinerant preaching, winning admirers who included Puritans, and leaving a reputation as 'Apostle of the North'. His earliest biography (1628) by George Carleton, Bishop of Chichester, refashioned him as a firm Protestant.

GILPIN, WILLIAM (1724–1804), travel writer. Educated at Oxford, he was ordained, and worked as a schoolmaster. His accounts of his travels in Cumb., Westmld. and the Scottish Highlands (1789) and in western England and the Isle of Wight (1798) contributed towards the late eighteenth-century cult of the picturesque. The books were illustrated with his own aquatints.

GIRALDUS CAMBRIENSIS see BARRI, GERALD DE, essay on page 60

GIRIC I (?–889), King of the Scots. Assisted by EOCHAID, SON OF RHUN, King of Strathclyde, Giric defeated and killed his predecessor, AED THE FURIOUS, to become King in 878. Taking advantage of the temporary collapse of the kingdom of York, following the expulsion of HALFDAN, Giric appears to have filled the power vacuum by subduing Bernicia and temporarily holding sway there. He is also recorded as being 'the first to give liberty to the Scottish Church', although it is uncertain in precisely what way. In 889 both Giric and Eochaid were deposed by Domnall mac Cinaeda, who succeeded as DOMNALL II MAC CONSTANTÍN.

GISSING, GEORGE (1857–1903), novelist. In his own words 'well-educated, fairly bred, but *without money*', Gissing spent a life of seemingly self-inflicted adversity, yet it provided some of the most insightful social novels of the late nineteenth century. He studied at Owen's College (later the University of Manchester), but was expelled and sent to prison when it was discovered that he had stolen from fellow students in order to support a 'fallen woman' whom he sought to redeem. Sent to America to make a fresh start, he wrote for the *Chicago Tribune* before returning to London in 1877, where he took odd jobs and wrote. His pessimistic novels of 'the unclassed', the title of his second novel (1884), did not have many readers among the subscribers of the circulating libraries, and, after the death of his first wife from syphilis and alcohol, he married another unsuitable partner. From 1897 Gissing's lot briefly improved: he turned to short-story writing and found a ready market in the burgeoning field of magazines, and he left his second wife, settling in the Pyrenees with a French woman who was more of an intellectual companion. Of his novels, Gissing's masterpiece is *New Grub Street* (1891), a topical story of the commercialization of literature and the price which 'art' extracts from its practitioners. *The Odd Woman* (1893) is an affecting view of the 'woman question'.

GLADSTONE, W(ILLIAM) E(WART) *see* essay on pages 354–55

GLANVILL (OR GLANVILLE), RANULF (?–1190), Justiciar. Younger son of a Suffolk baron, he served HENRY II as sheriff, soldier (in 1174 he captured WILLIAM I THE LION), judge, Chief Justiciar and educator of the future King JOHN. Although he is no longer regarded as the author of the law-book known as *Glanvill*, 'By his wisdom', wrote ROGER OF HOWDEN, 'the laws which we call English were established'. But his reputation for corruption led to his dismissal by RICHARD I. He died on crusade at the siege of Acre.

GLEIG, GEORGE (1796–1888), Chaplain General of the Forces and military reformer. He was educated at Glasgow and Oxford universities, commissioned into the 85th regiment (1812) and fought in Spain, southern France and in both the Washington and New Orleans campaigns, was wounded six times before returning to Oxford in 1816 and was ordained in 1820. He began to write in order to supplement his curate's stipend and for 68 years he wrote books on his own experiences, on military history, and on army reform. Appointed Chaplain General of the Forces in 1844, he developed a doctrine of Christian militarism, which argued that the profession of arms was a higher and more moral calling than any other. This belief was well entrenched in the British school system by the time of his death, through his training schools for teachers and his school textbooks. Inspector General of Military

Schools (1846), he established an Army Corps of Schoolmasters, which evolved into the Royal Army Education Corps.

GLENCAIRN, 9TH EARL OF see CUNNINGHAM, WILLIAM

GLENDOWER, OWEN see GLYN DWR, OWAIN

GLOAG, ANN HERON (née Souter) (1942–), entrepreneur. A nurse, Ann Gloag moved into the bus and passenger business in 1980 in partnership with her brother, Brian Souter. Their company, Gloagtrotter, soon renamed Stagecoach, grew in strength through the 1980s and 1990s, especially by taking advantage of the deregulation and privatization of the bus industry and thereafter of the railways. Stagecoach has become one of the prime providers of public transport in Britain.

GLOUCESTER, EARL OF, 4TH, 6TH and 7TH see CLARE, GILBERT DE; **5TH** see CLARE, RICHARD DE; **DUKE OF, 1ST** see THOMAS OF WOODSTOCK; **2ND** see HUMPHREY OF GLOUCESTER; **DUCHESS OF** see COBHAM, ELEANOR

GLUBB, SIR JOHN (also known as Glubb Pasha) (1896–1986), soldier. Glubb attained fame as the Commander of the Arab Legion (1939–56), a tribesmen army in Transjordan (subsequently Jordan). An army officer's son himself, he rose in the army ranks before volunteering to serve in Iraq, then resigned from the army in 1926 to become administrator there. In 1930 he was made a Brigadier in the Arab Legion, and transformed it into a disciplined army, supporting the Allies in the Second World War, and then in 1951 raising a national guard to defend Jordan's borders against Israeli raids. With Arab pressure to end British influence in the region, Glubb Pasha was dismissed, and retired to England.

GLYN, ELINOR (née Sutherland) (1864–1943), writer. A romantic on the page and in her life, Elinor was brought up in Jersey and Canada. A notable beauty, she showed a tendency to become infatuated with public figures, including Lord CURZON, Lord MILNER and F. D. MAURICE. In 1892 she married a wealthy but profligate English landowner. *Three Weeks* (1907), her second novel, was a torrid tale of passion between a young English aristocrat and an older woman, the Queen of the Balkans, involving the famous tiger rug (a gift from Curzon) episode. It caused a sensation and Glyn followed its success with a number of other cliff-hanging romances full of tempestuous emotions, frustration and snobbishness; they went some way towards paying off her husband's

mounting debts. By now she had become an 'expert' on affairs of the heart, acted as a counsellor and published *The Philosophy of Love* in 1923, as well as trying her hand at scriptwriting in Hollywood.

GLYN DWR, OWAIN see essay on page 356

GODDARD, RAYNER (Baron Goddard of Aldbourne) (1877–1971), judge. Goddard was called to the Bar in 1899 and specialized in commercial law. He was promoted to the Court of Appeal in 1938 and created a Law Lord six years later before being appointed Lord Chief Justice in 1946, a post which he held until he retired aged 81. Throughout his career, he was a vocal advocate of both corporal and capital punishment, earning a reputation as a harsh judge. He was particularly criticized for his handling of the trial of Derek BENTLEY (1952), during which he is alleged to have prejudiced the jury in favour of the police and against Bentley.

GODFRAID CRÓBÁN (GODRED CROVAN) (?–1095), Lord of Man. He conquered the Isle of Man (*c.* 1079) and founded a dynasty that, nominally as dependents of the Norse kings, ruled over the sea-borne empire of Man and the Isles (the Western Isles of Scotland), in whole or in part, for the next two centuries. For three years his naval power enabled him to rule Dublin as well, until driven out by MUIRCHERTACH UA BRIAIN in 1094.

GODFREY, SIR EDMUND BERRY (1621–78), supposed murder victim of the Popish Plot. The younger son of a Kentish gentry family, he gave up his legal training because of poor hearing and entered the timber trade. A well-liked Justice of the Peace for Westminster, he was knighted in 1666 for his efforts to relieve suffering and keep order during the Great Plague. In Sept. 1678 Titus OATES reported the Popish Plot to Godfrey, and swore depositions before him; a few weeks later Godfrey was found murdered in a ditch on Primrose Hill. He had been stabbed with his own sword but some doctors thought he had been strangled beforehand. Three men connected with the Queen's Chapel in Somerset House were hanged for the murder, more on the basis of anti-Catholic hysteria than convincing evidence.

GODGIFU see GODIVA

GODGIFU (?–*c.* 1049), sister of EDWARD THE CONFESSOR. She went into exile with her brothers Edward and ALFRED in 1013 and, shortly afterwards, married Drogo, Count of the Vexin, a friend of the dukes of Normandy. Her son RALPH came to England with Edward and was advanced by him to

continued on page 357

GLADSTONE, W(ILLIAM) E(WART) (1809–98)
Politician and Prime Minister (1868–74, 1880–5, 1886, 1892–4)

The only Prime Minister to have a lectureship at Oxford devoted to him, 'Gladstone studies' have been one of the most vigorous areas of scholarship in recent years. Matthew's two volumes of *Gladstone*, along with the monumental 14 volumes of the Gladstone diaries, have carried the subject to new levels of complexity. These make the old view, based upon John MORLEY's official biography, of Gladstone moving from the darkness of early Tory reaction to later Liberal light seem inadequate.

What modern scholarship has done is to restore to the study of Gladstone's career the religious dimension which he always held was central to it; this has helped produce a picture of the 'Grand Old Man' with more light and shade than either the eulogies of his admirers or the execrations of his opponents.

Gladstone's early career resembled that of his great mentor PEEL, with a period at Eton and Christ Church being followed by entry into the Commons for a pocket borough, in this case Newark (Notts.), a seat owned by the extreme Evangelical, the 4th Duke of Newcastle (see PELHAM-HOLLES, THOMAS), who appreciated Gladstone's verdict that he saw 'something of the anti-Christ' in the First Reform Act. Gladstone's first parliamentary speech was a defence of slave-owning and his first book a defence of the principle of the notion of the confessional state; MACAULAY accurately described him as 'the rising hope of those stern unbending Tories' who distrusted Peel. Gladstone's early vision, of a moral state working hand-in-hand with a purified Anglican Church, was always unrealizable in the context of the politics of his time but the processes by which he came to this knowledge himself helped shape his career.

The greatest influence upon him as a politician was Peel, who steered the promising young man away from the religious obsessions which threatened to curtail his career. By making him successively Vice-President (1842–3) and then President (1843–5) of the Board of Trade, Peel placed Gladstone at the heart of his project of liberalizing and modernizing the financial and fiscal systems of the United Kingdom. From that experience Gladstone carried away a reputation as a formidable administrator and executive politician, as well as a growing belief that freedom, as a concept, applied to more than trade.

The decade and a half after Peel's downfall in 1846 were difficult politically and personally for Gladstone. As the most conservative of the Peelites, he was regularly approached by the Protectionists under Lord Derby (*see* STANLEY, EDWARD), and DISRAELI even offered to stand aside for him if he would join a Conservative Cabinet. Gladstone's aversion to Disraeli ran too deep for that, although he did accept a post as High Commissioner in the Ionian Islands from Derby in 1858. But his destruction of Disraeli's budget in 1852, which marked him out as Peel's natural successor, was a better indication of where his political future lay. On a personal level the conversion to Roman Catholicism of friends like Henry MANNING and Hope-Scott saw the wreckage of his hopes for the purification of the Anglican Church. The near-bankruptcy of his wife's family in financial schemes which he had favoured saw Gladstone plunged into a task of financial rescue which would occupy him for much of the 1850s and 1860s. It was also during this period that he embarked upon the other rescue work which would preoccupy him for so long – his mission to rescue prostitutes by accosting them in the street and trying to convert them from their life of shame; his more worldly colleagues despaired of ever convincing him of the effect which this work had upon his reputation in the eyes of his distinctly cynical opponents.

The same volcanic energy which allowed Gladstone to spread himself over so many areas of work also made him a formidable politician and, by the 1850s, he had acquired another belief which pushed him away from his Conservative roots. Gladstone's attachment to the cause of freedom gave him a sympathy with Italian nationalism which was deepened and reinforced by his own love of Italian culture so, when the Liberal Party came together in June 1859 over the cause of Italian unity, it made it impossible for Gladstone to refuse the offer of the Exchequer under Palmerston (see TEMPLE, HENRY) – much as he disapproved of him personally.

The next seven years made Gladstone's career. Although his relations with Palmerston were never cordial and he came near to resignation on several occasions, Gladstone remained at the Exchequer until 1866. As Chancellor he created the Treasury in its modern form as the vital engine of the modern state. He set out to complete Peel's Free Trade programme, reducing public spending, abolishing the paper duties which restricted the growth of the press and cutting taxes. Despite his own High Churchmanship, Gladstone forged a vital alliance with Nonconformity, based on his side on an admiration for the moral seriousness which Dissent promulgated among the lower orders. Always an out-and-out inegalitarian,

Gladstone nevertheless recognized that the central problem of modern politics was how to govern the 'millions of hard hands'; firm leadership, a high moral tone, and the promulgation of religious equality were the tools which Gladstone utilized.

By the time of Palmerston's death in 1865, Gladstone was widely recognized as the greatest force in the Liberal Party but his mishandling of the reform issue meant that Disraeli and the Conservatives got the opportunity to pass the Second Reform Act in 1867 and confound the Liberals. Always terrible on the rebound, however, Gladstone seized the moral and political highground in 1868 by taking up the issue of the disestablishment of the Church of Ireland. This reunited the ranks of fissiparous Liberalism while simultaneously nailing Disraeli firmly to the defence of a cause that had few supporters outside the ranks of extreme Protestantism.

As Prime Minister from 1868 to 1874 Gladstone led the greatest reforming administration of the nineteenth century after that of Peel. The characteristics of his Liberalism can be seen by the fact that he was largely concerned with administrative reform and with scrapping barriers to freedom and personal advancement: he established the army, Civil Service, local government and the law as careers open to talent. But he abhorred what he called constructivist legislation, and refused to use the power of the State to compel people. His Education Act of 1870, which created for the first time a network of Board Schools to provide elementary education for all, upset his Nonconformist allies and helped to destabilize his government. In 1874 he lost the General Election to Disraeli and retired from the leadership of his party the following year. Without a virtuous passion to which to appeal, Gladstone felt himself to be a spent force.

The popular agitation of 1876, against the massacres in Bulgaria, convinced Gladstone that there was still a moral conscience to which he could appeal and provided him with a route back into active politics through the medium of criticizing the popular imperialism (or jingoism) of Disraeli's foreign policy. His famous 'pilgrimages of passion in Midlothian' in 1879 and 1880 made him an irresistible choice as Prime Minister when the Liberals won the 1880 General Election. He was the first Prime Minister to take it for granted that a central part of his duty was to speak directly to the people.

But the high moral passion which won the election proved less suited to the task of governing. Gladstone's second administration suffered a series of set-backs in foreign policy, where it proved impossible to implement Midlothian principles in an era dominated by Bismarck. The conflict between the Whigs who dominated his Cabinet and younger Liberals like Joseph CHAMBERLAIN, who wanted what Gladstone considered quasi-socialist legislation, made the government less fertile in legislation than his first and helped lead to its collapse in 1885.

Gladstone's espousal of the cause of Irish Home Rule in late 1885 was certainly in line with his developing views on nationalism but it also served the twin causes of forcing his opponents within the party to accept his political agenda and style or leave; Hartington (see CAVENDISH, SPENCER) and the Whigs, then Chamberlain and his followers, all chose the latter course, leaving a purified Gladstonian Liberal Party. But Gladstone failed to get his Home Rule Bill through the Lords in 1886. His final period in office from 1892 to 1893 marked an anti-climax to perhaps the greatest political career of the nineteenth century.

Gladstone's Liberalism wanted to free the individual from restrictions which prevented him from fulfilling his potential but it provided no solution to the problems of how to provide for the elderly, the sick and the unemployed. This left the way open for those who advocated statist remedies. Abroad, Gladstone's Liberalism believed in the Concert of Europe and the rule of law but, since Bismarck's European system was founded upon assumptions of *Realpolitik*, it meant that Britain lacked influence in the international arena under Gladstone. However, following the nemesis of Bismarckianism in the First World War, Gladstone's ideals of internationalism and co-operation helped inspire the League of Nations.

Gladstone was the towering figure of Victorian Liberalism and his virtues and defects were identical with those of his creed: a deep moral seriousness, a commitment to personal freedom accompanied by a sense of responsibility and a belief in the power of man to ameliorate his own condition, all made Liberalism a creed which appealed to the respectable working classes. But a relentless high-mindedness, a tendency to sanctimony, and unrealistic hopes in the perfectibility of human nature provided an Achilles' heel.

H. C. G. Matthew, Gladstone (2 vols, 1986, 1990

GLYN DWR, OWAIN (c. 1355–c. 1416)
Welsh rebel leader

The leader of the last major Welsh revolt against English rule, and in subsequent centuries a national legend, he served the English Crown during the 1380s in campaigns against the Scots and French; in the Earl of Arundel's retinue he was listed among 127 esquires, below four bannerets and 32 knights. The fact that for more than a decade a mere Welsh esquire could mount so great a challenge to English rule is a measure of the strength which he drew from his fellow-countrymen. In part this was due to his descent from the Welsh princes of Powys and Deheubarth; after the murder of Owain LAWGOCH, legitimist Welsh hopes centred on him. In part it was due to his inspirational leadership. In part it was because all sections of Welsh society had justified grievances. Laws passed in the wake of EDWARD I's suppression of the Welsh rebellion of 1295 had reduced the Welsh to the level of second-class citizens in a land where all the centres of power and wealth (castles, of which there were at least 100, and towns) were in the hands of the English; the Welsh were not permitted to live in the towns or to trade outside them. Although these regulations were often ignored, their mere existence reveals underlying assumptions about the Welsh which ensured that all senior posts in the government of Wales went to Englishmen. Since all the owners of great estates were English, this meant that in Wales there was an ethnic edge to the kinds of tension between landlords, tenants and labourers which, in England, led to the Peasants' Revolt. All it needed was the political turmoil in England in 1399–1400 associated with the dethronement of RICHARD II for the Welsh to snatch the opportunity to take up arms against the arrogant and oppressive nature of English rule.

On 16 Sept. 1400 Owain was proclaimed Prince of Wales and in the next few days attacks were launched on the English towns of north-east Wales. This rising was quickly suppressed but when the English Parliament of 1401 reacted by sharpening and extending anti-Welsh legislation the revolt flared up again, and spread more widely. In 1402 Owain won the Battle of Bryn Glas (Radnors.), capturing Edmund MORTIMER, a potential rival for HENRY IV's throne, and then drawing him over to the Welsh cause. Next year there were risings all over Wales. Even Cardiff was besieged. Each further Welsh success produced another panicky and draconian response from the English. In Parliament it was alleged that Welsh labourers in England were streaming back to join the national revolt and that Welsh students at Oxford and Cambridge were conspiring against the State. By 1403 any Welshman caught within Chester city walls after sunset was liable to the death penalty. Although Henry IV went to Wales four times between 1400 and 1403, he never stayed there for more than a month. He faced too many threats to be able to give Wales the same high priority that Edward I had. When his son, the English Prince of Wales (the future HENRY V), was wounded in 1403 English policy in Wales lacked all co-ordination. The collapse of landlord control accelerated the end of serfdom and allowed tenants to obtain more favourable terms.

From 1403 on Owain's revolt found friends outside Wales: from the French who sent military aid in 1403 and 1405; from the Avignon Papacy which liberated the Welsh Church by accepting its allegiance in 1406; and from the Percy family in England, culminating in the Tripartite Indenture of 1405, whereby Glyn Dwr, Mortimer and Henry PERCY, Earl of Northumberland, agreed to divide England and Wales between them, Owain's share being an enlarged Wales. In the event the capture of Harlech (Merion.) and Aberystwyth (Card.) in 1404 and the holding of Welsh Parliaments, at Machynlleth (Montgom.) (1404) and at Harlech (1405), were to mark the summit of his achievements. Once Henry IV had survived the financial and political difficulties of his early years, the much greater English resources were bound to tell. In 1408 the Percy rebellion was crushed at Bramham Moor (Yorks.); English cannon enforced the recapture of both Harlech and Aberystwyth. From then on the Welsh cause was hopeless. By and large the *ancien régime* was reinstated, and although resentment fuelled by poetry and prophecy burned bright there was to be no further revolt. The lesson of defeat had been learned. But Owain himself never submitted. His extraordinary ability to inspire loyalty from his close associates meant that he was still at large when he died, place and date unknown to mere historians. In the words of the Welsh annalist, 'Very many say he died; the prophets insist he did not.' He had joined the select band of heroes, like CADWALADR and ARTHUR, whose time had been but was also to be.

R. R. Davies, *The Revolt of Owain Glyn Dwr (1995)*

an earldom. Her second husband, Count Eustace of Boulogne, also played a role in the politics of the English succession.

GODIVA, LADY (?–*c*. 1080), wife of Earl LEOFRIC of Mercia. Little is known about the historical Godiva (Godgifu), except that she and her husband were generous patrons of several churches. She is now famous for her legendary ride, naked, through the streets of Coventry in an attempt to persuade her stubborn husband to reduce the taxation on the people of the town. The story of the ride originated in the thirteenth century.

GODOLPHIN, SIDNEY (1st Earl of Godolphin) (1645–1712), politician. A courtier of CHARLES II, an MP from 1668 and a Lord of the Treasury from 1679, he remained in favour during and after the crisis which accompanied attempts to exclude James, Duke of York (the future JAMES II) from the line of succession, despite having urged that concessions be made to the Whigs. In 1684 he became Secretary of State, then succeeded Rochester (*see* HYDE, LAURENCE) as Lord High Treasurer.

He was removed from office on the accession of James II, but was entrusted with secret negotiations with Louis XIV; in 1687 he again became a Lord of the Treasury. Among the last ministers to remain loyal to James, he was sent to negotiate with William of Orange (the future WILLIAM III) in Dec. 1688. He voted for William to be Regent rather than King, but agreed to head the Treasury (1690–6) while continuing to correspond with James and Jacobite agents; when this was exposed, he resigned.

He returned to the Treasury in 1700–1, and under ANNE served as Lord Treasurer (1702–10), grappling effectively with the demanding task of financing the War of the Spanish Succession, and working closely with Marlborough (*see* CHURCHILL, JOHN). He became increasingly dependent on the support of the Whigs, and in 1710 he favoured the impeachment of SACHEVERELL, after which the Queen asked him to resign. Charles II said of Godolphin that he was never 'in the way or out of the way': his reliability as an administrator was the key to his success.

GODRED II (?–1187), King of Man and the Isles (1152–87). Son of Olaf I, he became King in 1152, but was soon at odds with powerful enemies, MUIRCHERTACH MAC LOCHLAINN, with whom he disputed rule over Dublin, and SOMERLED. Somerled first forced him to share the Isles with him and then, in 1158, to flee to Norway. After Somerled's death in 1164 he returned with Norwegian support, mutilated a

rival – his own brother – and from then on reigned in relative peace. His daughter Affreca married John de COURCY, Lord of Ulster.

GODRED CROVAN *see* GODFRAID CRÓBÁN

GODRIC OF FINCHALE (?–1170), recluse. A merchant, shipowner and widely travelled pilgrim, in *c*. 1110 he acquired a little book-learning at Durham before becoming, for almost 60 years, a hermit at nearby Finchale. Such was his reputation for holiness and wisdom that two lives of him were written during his lifetime, the one by Reginald, Prior of Durham, being presented to him on his deathbed.

GODWIN, WILLIAM (1756–1836), writer. Trained like his father for the Dissenting ministry, he made connections with radical Whigs, and abandoning the ministry in 1782 turned to making a living by journalism and other writing. He was enthusiastic about the French Revolution, and came to prominence in 1793 for his *Inquiry Concerning the Principles of Political Justice*, in which he set out his ideas on the perfectibility of man and the worthlessness of existing institutions. Similar concerns inform his novels, the first of which was *Caleb Williams* (1794). He was also interested in 'sensibility', that is, in ideas about the natural basis of human emotional response, and explored these in his novel *Fleetwood, or the New Man of Feeling* (a title which evoked Henry MACKENZIE's earlier *Man of Feeling*). In 1796 he married Mary WOLLSTONECRAFT, who died the following year, shortly after the birth of their daughter, the future Mary SHELLEY. In later years, he struggled to support himself by writing and editing. After his death excerpts from *Political Justice* were printed in Chartist newspapers, but the complete book was not reprinted until 1946.

GODWINE (?–1053), Earl of Wessex. He was the most powerful man in England (after the king) during the reigns of CNUT, HAROLD I HAREFOOT, HARTHACNUT and EDWARD THE CONFESSOR. The father of HAROLD II, he was an adroit survivor in the dynastic and political crises that shook the Anglo-Saxon State in the eleventh century.

An Englishman of relatively obscure origins, he was created Earl of Wessex in 1018 by Cnut and married into the Danish royal family. In the time of Harold Harefoot, he organized the capture of Edward the Confessor's brother ALFRED and was therefore an accomplice to the blundered gouging out of his eyes which was probably the cause of his death. He so ingratiated himself, however, with Edward that the latter married his daughter EDITH in 1045. His eldest sons, SVEIN and Harold (the future king), were created earls in 1043–4. A complex quarrel broke out between Godwine and Edward in 1051, which resulted in the Earl's exile until the autumn of the following year, when he secured his reinstatement with the backing of an overwhelming military force.

Godwine must have been an able man, who may well have come close to dominating King Edward and the kingdom in the 1040s. He has a reputation for being somewhat irreligious and, although of English origin, his links with Scandinavia were typical of the upper aristocracy of late Anglo-Saxon England. Other sons, TOSTIG, LEOFWINE and GYRTH, were all advanced to earldoms after his death.

GOLDING, ARTHUR (1536–1606), translator. From an East Anglian gentry family, Golding was well connected in Tudor literary circles through his relationship to Edward DE VERE, Earl of Oxford; he became a friend of Sir Philip SIDNEY. Though his original works were minor, he devoted himself to translation, notably many of John CALVIN's works, Julius Caesar and (despite his strong Puritanism) his English verse rendering of Ovid's *Metamorphoses* (1565–7).

GOLDING, WILLIAM (1911–93), novelist. Born in Cornwall, Golding was educated at Oxford, and became a schoolteacher in Salisbury (Wilts.) in 1939. During the Second World War he served in the Royal Navy, seeing action, including the D-Day landings. His wartime experiences influenced much of his writing, with the theme of human cruelty at the core of many of his works. After the war Golding returned to teaching, writing in his spare time. His first and best-known novel *Lord of the Flies,* the story of schoolboys who, when stranded on an island, revert to savagery and human brutality, appeared in 1954. A spate of novels followed, including *The Inheritors* (1956), *Pincher Martin* (1956), *Free Fall* (1959) and *Rites of Passage* (1980). In 1983 Golding was awarded the Nobel Prize for Literature.

GOLDSMITH, SIR JAMES (1933–98), businessman. The son of Frank Goldsmith (originally Goldschmidt), a former MP who left Britain during the First World War to escape anti-German hysteria and became a well-known French hotelier, Goldsmith showed his ability to make money as a schoolboy: he left Eton having won £8,000 betting on horses. Throughout the 1960s his business empire grew through acquisitions in foods, then in banking and investment. By the early 1970s he was Britain's largest grocer. Selling out of Britain after the 1973 crash, by the early 1980s he was the third largest retailer in the world and the best-known of the 'corporate raiders', especially in the USA, buying and selling companies at high speed before anticipating the 1987 stock market collapse and selling out at the market's peak. In 1989 he attempted to take over British American Tobacco in a hotly contested corporate fight and in 1990 he acquired significant interests in mining concerns owned by Lord HANSON. His business career largely over, he turned to ecology and finally, in the 1997 General Election, funded the anti-Europe Referendum Party. It failed to make any significant electoral showing and Goldsmith died suddenly the following year. He had never been far from the gossip columns, because of his business ventures, his gambling and his attentions to women.

GOLDSMITH, OLIVER (1730–74), writer. Son of an Anglo-Irish curate, he was rejected for ordination and became a physician. He produced many biographies, translations and other literary hackwork, edited *The Bee* and the *Lady's Magazine* and joined Samuel JOHNSON's literary club. Although he had to struggle to remain solvent, Goldsmith was a relatively successful example of the professional litterateur in a period that saw the emergence of that species. His best-known works include *The Citizen of the World* (1762), a series of satirical letters supposedly by a Chinese visitor to London, the novel *The Vicar of Wakefield* (1766), the poem 'The Deserted Village' (1770) and the play *She Stoops to Conquer* (1774).

GOLDWELL, THOMAS (*c.* 1500–85), churchman. From a Kent gentry family including Canterbury Cathedral's last prior, after Oxford he studied at Padua and Leuven, staying on the continent in the 1530s because of his hostility to HENRY VIII's break with Rome. Closely associated with Reginald POLE, he joined the Theatine order at Naples. Accompanying Pole to England in 1554, as Bishop of St Asaph (1555) he revived traditional devotion, escaping abroad after ELIZABETH I's accession. The only English bishop at the Council of Trent (1561–3), he remained an active and revered figure among English Roman Catholics, the last survivor of the old episcopate.

GOLLANCZ, VICTOR (1893–1967), publisher. Of Polish extraction, born in London, he read classics at Oxford and was dismissed from his first teaching post at Repton school (1916–18) for stirring up political dissent. After a brief spell in publishing, Gollancz set up his own firm in 1927; it proved an almost immediate success, making best-sellers of such authors as A. J. Cronin and Dorothy L. SAYERS. A convert to socialism, he saw publishing primarily as the dissemination of political ideas and used his commercially successful list to subsidize the Left Book Club (1936), which soon established itself as a potent voice of the Left (*see* ORWELL, GEORGE).

GOMBRICH, SIR ERNST (1909–), art historian. Born in Vienna, Gombrich emigrated to England and joined the Warburg Institute, University of London, in 1936 and became its Director and Professor of History of the Classical Tradition (1959–76). After working for the BBC monitoring service during the Second World War, he completed his *The Story of Art* (1950). Interested in the theory of art and the psychology of pictorial representation, particularly in his influential *Art and Illusion* (1960), Gombrich, considered one of the foremost art historians of the Renaissance, was awarded the Order of Merit in 1988.

GOMME, SIR GEORGE LAURENCE (1853–1916), folklorist. A pioneer in regarding folklore as worthy of serious scientific study, Gomme believed that it did not consist simply of myths and stories but constituted the vestiges of 'archaic social existence'. A founder member and subsequently President (1890–4) of the Folklore Society, his publications include *Primitive Folk Moots: or Open Air Assemblies in Britain* (1880), *Folklore as an Historical Science* (1908) and a *Handbook of Folklore* (1890). The first clerk of the London County Council, he was one of the initiators of the Victoria County History, the great encyclopaedia of English county history, begun in 1899 as a fitting commemoration of Queen VICTORIA's diamond jubilee.

GONNE, MAUD (1865–1953), revolutionary. The daughter of a British army officer of Irish descent, she became active in Irish nationalist politics in the 1880s in support of land agitation and evicted tenants. She went on to campaign on behalf of Irish Republicans and anti-British French nationalists (she had two children by the French journalist Lucien Millevoye). In 1900 she founded a women's Republican organization, *Inghinidhe na h-Eireann* (Daughters of Ireland). The poet YEATS developed an unrequited passion for her which inspired much of his verse, but they disagreed over the relative importance of poetry and politics. In 1903 she married Major John MacBride, who had fought for the Boers in an 'Irish Brigade' during the Boer War, but the marriage broke down and disputes over the custody of their son, Sean MACBRIDE, caused her to live in France until after MacBride's execution in 1916 for his role in the Easter Rising. She was active in support of Irish prisoners during the Anglo-Irish War, and remained a prominent Republican activist until the 1930s.

GOODMAN, ARNOLD (Baron Goodman) (1913–95), government adviser. Goodman became known in Labour Party circles as formidable defence solicitor for Aneurin BEVAN in a libel action by *The Spectator* in 1957, and in 1964 George WIGG asked him to negotiate in a particularly intractable strike in the TV industry. Harold WILSON was impressed by his skills, and Goodman became his 'Mr Fixit', a role he played for subsequent prime ministers. He was used as an intermediary between the British government and the renegade leader of Rhodesia, Ian SMITH, by both Wilson and his successor Edward HEATH. A very successful Chairman of the Arts Council (1965–73), Goodman was also involved in the reform of the legal profession and the defence of press freedom in the 1970s. He was Master of University College, Oxford (1976–86).

GOODMAN, CHRISTOPHER (?1521–1603), writer. Son of a wealthy merchant, his Oxford teaching ended with flight from the unsympathetic Catholic regime of MARY I to Strasbourg, Frankfurt and Geneva. He wrote against Mary's government in a commentary on Amos and in pamphlets including *How Superior Powers Ought to be Obeyed* (1558), saying that to kill tyrants was legitimate and (echoing his fellow-Geneva exile John KNOX) that women had no right to be monarchs. ELIZABETH I shared Mary's low opinion of these ideas, and for a decade Goodman had to minister in Scotland and Ireland. His later career as Archdeacon of Richmond and Puritan activist was stormy and precarious.

GOODMAN, GODFREY (1583–1656), churchman. Nephew of Dean Gabriel Goodman of Westminster, a rare early High Church Anglican, Godfrey was Bishop of Gloucester from 1625 until Parliament forced him to retire in 1643. His main claim to fame is as the only early Anglican bishop to have converted to Roman Catholicism. William LAUD detested him: an interesting indication of the anti-Roman character of Laud's Arminian theology.

GOODWIN, JOHN (c. 1594–1665), religious leader. A Cambridge don, from 1633 he was vicar of St Stephen's, Coleman Street, London, and in the English Civil War (1642–6) set up an Independent congregation there. His theology became quasi-Arminian (i.e. he rejected the high Calvinist belief in strict predestination to salvation or damnation), and he was an early advocate of religious toleration, though he wrote pamphlets against a variety of contemporary religious groups including Presbyterians, Baptists and Fifth Monarchy Men, besides attacks on Royalists and on the Interregnum committees which attempted to regulate English clergy, the Triers and Ejectors. Having defended CHARLES I's execution, he was arrested at CHARLES II's restoration but later released.

GORDON, CHARLES (1833–85), soldier. Son of a general, he was educated at Woolwich, commissioned into the Royal Engineers (1852) and posted to the Crimea where he was wounded in June 1855. After survey work in Asia Minor, in 1860 Gordon took part in the expedition against China, and was appointed commander of the force that ultimately suppressed in 1864 the Taiping rebellion, which was destabilizing both the Chinese rulers and European influence. Subsequently known as 'Chinese Gordon', he entered the service of the Khedive in Egypt, administering the Sudan (1874–80) and helping stamp out the slave trade there. Sent back to Sudan in 1884 to rescue garrisons isolated by the Mahdi's revolt, he was cut off in Khartoum, where he died after a 10-month siege. His death unleashed public indignation in Britain against GLADSTONE that a relief force had not been dispatched, and he became a hero of Empire. His heroic status was reduced by his inclusion in Lytton STRACHEY's scathing series of portraits in *Eminent Victorians* (1918).

GORDON, GEORGE (4th Earl of Huntly, 15th Earl of Moray) (1513–62), politician. With a formidable power-base in northern Scotland, he was Regent in 1536, High Chancellor in 1546–9 and 1561–2. He supported Cardinal David BEATON against the pro-English James HAMILTON, Earl of Arran. After defeating the English at Halidon Hill (1542), he suffered defeat at Pinkie (1547); he christened this defeat 'the Rough Wooing', a *bon mot* later applied to the whole series of English campaigns of 1544–5 and 1547–50. Although Catholic, he was loth to choose between the factions under MARY QUEEN OF SCOTS, and rebelled against Mary when she deprived him of the earldom of Moray in 1562; James STEWART, the new Earl, defeated him in battle, and he died probably of a heart attack (he was extremely overweight) the same day.

GORDON, GEORGE (5th Earl of Huntly) (?–1576), politician. A Protestant, unlike his father George GORDON, the 4th Earl, he escaped execution to be restored to favour as Chancellor (1564–7) and abetted the murder of Henry STEWART, Lord Darnley, and the marriage of James HEPBURN, Earl of Bothwell, to MARY QUEEN OF SCOTS. His backing for her abdication (1567) proved temporary, and he was only persuaded to end his support for Mary in 1572, after prolonged negotiations. He died of a seizure after a game of football.

GORDON, GEORGE (6th Earl and 1st Marquess of Huntly) (*c.* 1563–1636), courtier. After a youth spent in France, he devoted his northern Scottish power to restoring Catholicism,

despite lip-service to Protestantism. While captain of the Scottish Royal Guard, in 1588–9 he raised a rebellion after correspondence with Spain. He tried again in 1594, having meanwhile continued three generations of family feud in the murder of James STEWART, 'the bonny Earl' of Moray (1592). None of this deterred JAMES VI from holding Huntly in similar esteem to his former favourite Esmé STEWART, Duke of Lennox (Huntly's father-in-law); he conferred the marquessate in 1599. CHARLES I tried to tame Huntly by removing his hereditary shrievalties of Aberdeen and Inverness.

GORDON, LORD GEORGE (1751–93), politician and agitator. A son of the Duke of Gordon, he was elected an MP in 1774 and gained a reputation for making biting but eccentric interventions. In 1780, a time when almost all MPs were prepared to support the removal of certain legal restrictions on Catholics, Gordon accepted the presidency of a newly formed Protestant Association. Inspired by the riots in Edinburgh and Glasgow which had persuaded the government not to extend the 1778 Catholic Relief Act to Scotland, the Protestant Association organized a petition to Parliament to request repeal, even though most civil and religious restrictions on Catholics remained in force. Anti-Catholics made the traditional equation between Catholicism, superstition and tyranny; supporters of relief argued that anti-popery was itself superstitious and tyrannical.

On 2 June 1780 Gordon led a march on Parliament to present the petition; the march was followed by attacks on Catholic chapels in London and fighting between crowds and authorities. This was followed by 10 days of violence, in which the houses of Catholics and supposed sympathizers (including WILLIAM MURRAY, Earl of Mansfield) were attacked, as well as prisons and other public buildings, and many were destroyed; 12,000 troops, summoned by GEORGE III, fired on the crowds. About 700 people were killed during the riots; 450 were arrested, 160 indicted and 25 executed. Gordon was tried for high treason, but was acquitted; the Lord Mayor of London was fined £1,000 for criminal negligence. Gordon subsequently converted to Judaism; in 1787 he was imprisoned for a libel on Marie Antoinette, and died in Newgate prison.

GORDON, GEORGE (4th Earl of Aberdeen) (1784–1860), Prime Minister (1852–5). The mirror-opposite of Palmerston (*see* TEMPLE, HENRY), Aberdeen was a dour Scottish peer who came into political life under PITT THE YOUNGER. The formative influence of his career was being sent in 1813 by Castlereagh (*see* STEWART, ROBERT) to negotiate the treaty of alliance between Britain and Austria and Russia (Teplitz). He witnessed the bloodiest battle of the Napoleonic Wars, Leipzig (16 Oct. 1813), which left him with a permanent repugnance for war. By temperament and experience, he was a conservative, and he agreed with Castlereagh's policy of aligning Britain with Austria after the Vienna settlement (1815); like his mentor he came under suspicion of being autocratic in his sympathies.

Foreign Secretary in the Wellington (*see* WELLESLEY, ARTHUR) government (May 1828), Aberdeen returned to the Foreign Office in 1841. He had long criticized Palmerston's conduct of British diplomacy as headstrong, and he set out to improve Britain's relations with those powers which his predecessor had offended, most notably France and America. Aberdeen was largely responsible for the 1842 Webster–Ashburton Treaty which settled most of the border disputes between the USA and what would become Canada, and also for the *entente cordiale* between Britain and France. His policy came in for criticsm from those, particularly Palmerston, who alleged that it stemmed from weakness and a want of nerve. But Aberdeen was firm in taking the view that war was an evil to be avoided at almost any cost, a line of thinking which would influence his youthful admirer, GLADSTONE.

After Robert PEEL's death in 1850 Aberdeen became the leader of the Peelite faction, and when a coalition government was formed in 1852 he was the obvious choice for Prime Minister, having played little part in the fierce arguments over the Corn Laws which had destroyed Peel's career.

It was the supreme irony of his career that it should have been under his premiership that Britain became involved in the Crimean War. The problem was that, with Palmerston and Aberdeen in the same Cabinet, British foreign policy lacked a firm direction; the series of diplomatic blunders which preceded the war could probably have been avoided had either man had sole direction of policy. After criticism from the Commons, Aberdeen resigned in 1855, haunted by his failure to avoid war. A mixture of the old eighteenth-century diplomatic style with some of the moral concerns which would later mark Gladstonian Liberalism, Aberdeen was a transitional figure in British foreign policy.

GORDON, THOMAS (?–1750), political writer *see* TRENCHAND, JOHN

GORE, CHARLES (1853–1932), churchman. A lifelong Anglo-Catholic, as Fellow of Trinity College, Oxford, Vice-Principal (1880–3) of Cuddesdon College and principal librarian (1884–93) at Pusey House, Gore wielded strong influence on the theological life of Oxford. He contributed a controversial essay to *Lux Mundi* (1889), was a member of the celibate Community of the Resurrection (1898–1901), canon of Westminster (1894) and Bishop of Worcester (1902) and of the new diocese of Birmingham (1905), a post he funded almost entirely from his own private income. In 1911 he was appointed to the bishopric of Oxford, but resigned in 1919 after several controversies, to become Dean of the theological faculty at King's College, London. His many influential works include *Christ and Society* (1928), reflecting the social beliefs that led him to support the Working Men's Association and vote in favour of LLOYD GEORGE's 'People's Budget' in 1909.

GORE-BOOTH, EVA (1870–1926), suffragist. Sister of Constance (later Countess MARKIEWICZ), the two founded a Women's Suffrage Society in Co. Sligo, where they were born and brought up, the daughters of a wealthy landowner. In 1896 Eva met Esther Roper, the Secretary of the North of England Society for Women's Suffrage and joined her in Manchester to campaign for the rights of working women, serving as Joint Secretary of Manchester and Salford Women's Trade Union Council, editing *Women's Labour News* and, with Roper, working to organize Manchester women textile workers and barmaids whose livelihood was put in jeopardy by the 1906 Licensing Act. During the First World War she worked tirelessly in the cause of pacifism.

GORING, GEORGE (2nd Baron Goring) (1608–57), soldier. Son of a popular courtier under JAMES I and CHARLES I, he became a professional soldier, first abroad and then, from 1638, for Charles. Although very equivocal in support for the King in 1641–2, from Dec. 1642 he came to have increasing prominence in the Royalist command. Imprisoned in the Tower of London in 1643–4, on his release he fought at Charles's defeat at Marston Moor (July 1644) and took command in the West Country. Despite personal bravery, his generalship was disastrous, marked by his own drunken quarrelsomeness and popular ill will stirred by his troops' indiscipline. Finally defeated at Langport (July 1645), he fled abroad. After service for both the United Provinces of the Netherlands and Spain, he died in Madrid.

GORMLEY, JOSEPH (Baron Gormley of Ashton-in-Makerfield) (1917–93), trade-union leader. Gormley worked in the pits for 26 years before his election to the National Union of Miners (NUM) National Executive Committee in 1957, and four years later began working full-time for the union as its General Secretary in the north west. Always considered a moderate, Gormley beat Mick

MCGAHEY, the left-wing leader of the Scottish miners, in the ballot for the NUM's presidency in 1971, and the following year reluctantly led the union into its first confrontation with Edward HEATH's Conservative government, the first national miners' strike since 1926. Using flying pickets (since made illegal) to prevent the movement of emergency fuel supplies, the miners forced the government to accede to their demands after seven weeks. Two years later, faced with rising oil prices and further demands for improvement in pay and conditions from the NUM, Heath called an election largely focused on the issue of trade union power, demanding 'Who governs Britain?'. The miners renewed their strike, and when Labour was returned to power in 1974 Harold WILSON ended the stoppage by granting most of the union's demands. A confrontation with Margaret THATCHER's government in 1981 over proposed pit closures (settled when the government granted the industry extra subsidy) proved to be Gormley's last victory, and he retired in 1982, being succeeded, against his wishes, by the militant left-winger Arthur SCARGILL.

GORT, 6TH VISCOUNT *see* VEREKER, JOHN

GOSCELIN OF SAINT-BERTIN (?–after 1107), writer. A Flemish monk living in England from *c*. 1060 and surviving into the early twelfth century, he wrote lives of numerous English saints and, through his writings, is responsible for the preservation of many English traditions threatened with destruction by the Normans. He is possibly the author of the *Vita Ædwardi Regis*.

GOSCHEN, GEORGE (1st Viscount Goschen) (1831–1907), politician. A self-described 'violent moderate', he was a Liberal MP from 1863: he proved a cautious yet financially adroit Chancellor of the Exchequer (1887–92) but, disturbed by the Liberals' increasing radicalism, declined to join GLADSTONE's second ministry, and, after the failure of the first Irish Home Rule Bill in 1886, was joint leader with Hartington (*see* CAVENDISH, SPENCER) of the Liberal Unionists, the group which effectively maintained Salisbury's (*see* CECIL, ROBERT GASCOYNE) government in power, and which fused with the Conservatives in 1912.

GOSSE, SIR EDMUND (1849–1928), critic and essayist. Translator of Ibsen's *Hedda Gabler* (1891) and *The Master Builder* (1893), librarian at the British Museum (1867) and the House of Lords (1904), lecturer in English literature at Trinity College, Cambridge (1884), and book reviewer and essayist for the *Sunday Times*, Gosse also published plays, poems and critical studies, but is remembered today for *Father and Son* (1907). Published anonymously, and sub-

titled 'A Study of Two Temperaments', it generously recounts his austere childhood with his widower father, a distinguished zoologist and strict member of the Plymouth Brethren.

GOTHFRITH (?–934), King of Dublin (921–34). Brother of SIHTRIC CAECH, he became King of Dublin when Sihtric took over the kingdom of York. After his brother's death in 927, he tried to sustain the well-established Dublin interest in York, but was defeated by the English King ATHELSTAN. He was succeeded in Dublin by his son OLAF GOTHFRITHSSON who also involved himself in the politics of the kingdom of York.

GOTT, BENJAMIN (1762–1840), industrialist and factory pioneer. His woollen manufacturing works at Bean Ing, Leeds (Yorks.), established in 1793, was at that time amongst the largest in the world. Interestingly, many of the processes were hand-powered, suggesting that a major motive and accomplishment of the factory system was the organization and disciplining of labour rather than the introduction of new technologies.

GOUGE, WILLIAM (1578–1653), writer. A Cambridge don who as a London incumbent became a leading Puritan, prominent in the 'Feoffees for Impropriations' scheme (*see* DAVENPORT, JOHN). He bitterly opposed the royal *Book of Sports* (1618, 1633) and sat in the Presbyterian Westminster Assembly (*see* GAUDEN, JOHN) from 1643. Among numerous devotional writings, the most generally interesting is his *Domestical Duties* (1620), a best-seller at the time: a useful window into conventional contemporary attitudes to marriage, the family and the household.

GOUGH, SIR HUBERT (1870–1963), soldier. Son of an army officer, educated at Eton and Sandhurst, he served with the cavalry in South Africa, acquiring a reputation as a dashing 'Prince Rupert' thanks to his relief of Ladysmith in 1900. In March 1914 Gough, now a Brigadier General, orchestrated resistance to an attempt by the government to use the army to impose Irish Home Rule on Ulster. Saved from the consequences of the so-called Curragh mutiny by the outbreak of the First World War, Gough proved an effective brigade leader and reasonably competent divisional commander, but in 1916 he was promoted to command an army. Soon out of his depth, Gough's problems were compounded by personal arrogance and abysmal staff work by semi-competent subordinates. Protected for a time by his fellow cavalry officer Douglas HAIG, the catastrophic collapse of Gough's 5th Army in the face of the German offensive of 21 March 1918 led to his immediate dismissal.

GOUGH, RICHARD (1635–1723), antiquarian. A yeoman farmer, like his father, Gough is remembered for his history of his native Salop. parish of Myddle, north of Shrewsbury, composed *c.* 1700. It is a remarkable local history, organized on the basis of family histories and engaging anecdotes concerning the occupiers of the pews in the parish church, and hence the properties to which those pews were allocated.

GOWER, 2ND EARL OF *see* LEVESON-GOWER, GRANVILLE

GOWER, GRANVILLE (2nd Earl Granville) (1815–91), politician. He was born to diplomacy (his father was British Ambassador in Paris in the 1830s), and he was part of the Whig cousinhood assured of an early place in British political life; even so his arrival at the Foreign Office at the age of only 37 was remarkable, but it was evidence more of the weakness of the Whigs after Palmerston's (*see* TEMPLE, HENRY) dismissal in 1851 than of Granville's talents. Asked by Queen VICTORIA to state the principles of British foreign policy, he said that they were to encourage 'progress' abroad, avoid interference in the affairs of other countries by force, and to carry on a policy marked by 'justice, moderation and self-respect'; it was the classic statement of British self-confidence and superiority at the height of the *Pax Britannica* before the Crimean War and the rise of Bismarck's Germany helped undermine it.

When Granville returned to the Foreign Office after the death of Clarendon (*see* HYDE, EDWARD) in 1870, Bismarck was on the verge of war with France, and the creation of Germany in 1871 overshadowed Granville's subsequent career. GLADSTONE wanted to apply Liberal ideals and the notion of the rule of law to foreign affairs; Granville was sceptical about this but lacked the force of personality or political weight to influence his leader.

Granville might have become Prime Minister in 1880 but stood aside in favour of Gladstone. Neither could cope with Bismarck's determined efforts to strike at their Liberal idealism. After the occupation of Egypt in 1882, Granville and Gladstone found themselves at Bismarck's mercy and made substantial colonial concessions to him in 1884 and 1885. By the time the Liberal government collapsed in 1885, Britain was isolated in Europe and on the verge of war with Russia over Afghanistan. Granville's own powers were declining even faster than those of his country, and although he was briefly Colonial Secretary in 1886, 'Pussy' (as he was known because of his caressing manner) was a spent force politically. When he died in 1891 it was revealed that he was bankrupt, and the last act of Whig solidarity was to pay off his debts.

GOWER, JOHN (?1325–1408), poet. Writing with equal facility in three languages, this courtly English poet composed a total of some 80,000 lines of mostly moralizing verse. His principal works were *Mirour de l'Homme* in French, *Vox Clamantis* in Latin and *Confessio Amantis* in English. He obtained the patronage of Bolingbroke (the future HENRY IV) and became increasingly Lancastrian in his sympathies.

GOWRIE, 2ND EARL OF *see* RUTHVEN, WILLIAM

GRADE, LEW (originally Louis Winogradsky) (Baron Grade of Elstree) (1906–91), entrepreneur. Born in Russia, Grade moved to London's East End in 1912 with his family to escape anti-Jewish persecution. Working in clothing, embroidery and professional dancing, he became a theatrical agent in 1934, in partnership first with Joe Collins and from 1943 with his brother Leslie. Theirs became Europe's largest theatrical agency; in 1954 they made two attempts to break into the new market of commercial television, succeeding with Associated Television (ATV). From 1954 until 1968 ATV held the lucrative London weekend and Midlands weekday franchises; Lew Grade relinquished most of his theatrical business to concentrate on television, and he framed an important part of British commercial television's success with generally lowbrow, variety-led mass entertainment.

GRAFTON, 3RD DUKE OF *see* FITZROY, AUGUSTUS HENRY

GRAFTON, RICHARD (*c.* 1507–73), printer and historian. An evangelical London merchant who financed the first printing in Antwerp of the 'Matthew Bible' (*see* ROGERS, JOHN) – the first authorized Bible in England (1537). With Edward WHITCHURCH, he went on to publish the officially sponsored Great Bible (1539) and continued to print important works such as the official Homilies (1547) and the 1549 and 1552 Books of Common Prayer. Though in religious disgrace under MARY I, he was MP for London (1554, 1558), then for Coventry (1563). His popular *Chronicle* (1568) brought conflict with the much more conservative historian, John STOW.

GRAHAM, JAMES (5th Earl and 1st Marquess of Montrose) (1612–50), soldier. He initially fought for the Scots alliance championing the Scottish National Covenant of 1638 against the English armies in the 'Bishops' Wars' (1639–40), but he was alienated from the Covenanting cause by his suspicion of the Argyll Campbells. In 1641 he was imprisoned for communicating with CHARLES I, and in 1643 joined him at Oxford. From autumn

1644 he led a Royalist campaign in the Highlands, using Highland and Irish forces with spectacular success against the Covenanters, and he was made Captain General of the King's Scottish forces in May 1645. In the Lowlands, however, his troops began to desert, and he was defeated by superior forces at Philiphaugh (Sept. 1645). After foreign service, he fought for CHARLES II in northern Scotland (1650). Betrayed after defeat in battle, he was executed in Edinburgh. His poetic skill helps to make a convincing picture of a romantic hero.

GRAHAM, JAMES (1745–94), quack physician. He studied medicine at Edinburgh but probably never qualified. Undeterred, he set up in practice at first as an oculist but later specialized in improving the physical appearance and, at the height of his notoriety in the early 1780s, the sexual health of his patients. After a few years in Yorks. and America he arrived in Pall Mall, London, in 1775, gaining Georgiana CAVENDISH, Duchess of Devonshire, as a patient and, with her, swathes of fashionable society. In 1780 he converted Schomberg House on Pall Mall into the Temple of Health and Hymen, hiring beautiful young women to act as 'priestesses' and the 'goddess', who read to and attended female patients receiving Graham's beauty treatments. Graham became increasingly eccentric and propagated his own brand of Evangelical Christianity, declaring himself 'the Servant of the Lord of Wonderful Love'. He moved to Edinburgh for financial reasons and continued to practise despite being confined to his own house for some time as a lunatic.

GRAHAM, SIR JAMES (1792–1861), politician. He entered Parliament in 1826, supported Catholic Emancipation and parliamentary reform, and held office under Charles GREY and Robert PEEL. As Home Secretary (1841–6), he was responsible for public order during the Chartist disturbances, but his most solid achievement was as a naval reformer. His tenure as First Lord of the Admiralty under Grey ensured that administration of the navy was overhauled, which may help to explain why, unlike the army, the Royal Navy performed tolerably well during the Crimean War.

GRAHAM, JOHN (3rd Earl of Montrose) (1548–1608), politician. He supported the Reformation, fighting against MARY QUEEN OF SCOTS at Langside in 1568, and succeeded his grandfather as Earl in 1571. Privy Councillor from 1578, he led opposition to the Regent Morton (James DOUGLAS) and was prominent at Morton's trial (1581). Though involved in the Raid of Ruthven (1583; *see* RUTHVEN, WILLIAM) he adroitly

changed sides when JAMES VI regained freedom of action. High Treasurer 1584–5, High Chancellor 1598–1605, he headed the Scots commission in unsuccessful Anglo-Scottish union negotiations; Viceroy of Scotland in 1604, he backed royal moves to strengthen Episcopacy.

GRAHAM, THOMAS (1st Baron Lynedoch) (1748–1843), soldier. A Scottish aristocrat, Graham had shown no interest in soldiering until the summer of 1791, when his attempt to bring the body of his beloved wife Catherine, who had died on a Mediterranean cruise, home through France was thwarted by the revolutionary National Guard. Developing an almost obsessive hatred for the French, Graham raised a regiment at his own expense and led it in raids against the Brittany coast and in the capture of Minorca and Malta. He went on to serve in the Peninsula, rising to the rank of General, and defeated the French at Barossa in 1811. Lynedoch's (he had been raised to the peerage in 1814) lasting contribution to the army was the founding in 1817 of the United Services Club in Pall Mall. As its critics feared, the club quickly became a military pressure group, a function it continues to perform.

GRAHAM OF CLAVERHOUSE, JOHN ('BONNIE DUNDEE') (1st Viscount Dundee) (*c.* 1649–89), soldier and rebel. A relative of JAMES GRAHAM, Marquess of Montrose, whom he admired, he spent some years in military service abroad under William of Orange (the future WILLIAM III) among others. From 1677 he was employed in Scotland under the Duke of York (the future JAMES II), repressing Presbyterian Covenanters dissatisfied with the restoration of Episcopacy which had accompanied the restoration of the Stuart dynasty, a task which he performed with notorious rigour. In 1688, when William of Orange landed with Dutch forces, Dundee took Scottish forces to join James II at Salisbury, and was made a viscount; after James fled the country, Dundee was allowed to return to Scotland. He attended the Scots Convention Parliament, but withdrew, alleging a plot to kill him. When he refused an order to return he was proclaimed a traitor. He assumed the leadership of Highland clans loyal to James and led them to victory at Killiecrankie in July 1689, but died in action. Without Dundee's leadership the Jacobite cause in Scotland effectively collapsed and his forces, lacking his inspiring command, were defeated at Dunkeld in Aug.

GRAHAME, KENNETH (1859–1932), children's author. The stories about three bachelor animals – a toad, a mole and a water rat – who live the life of Edwardian country gentlemen that

Grahame, who worked for the Bank of England, told to his son, were published as *The Wind in the Willows* (1908). The subsequent addition of illustrations by E. H. Sheppard and later Arthur Rackham made the book a twentieth-century children's classic, as did its adaptation as a stage play, *Toad of Toad Hall* (1929) by A. A. MILNE. The son committed suicide aged 19.

GRAND, MADAME SARAH (originally Frances Elizabeth McFall) (née Clarke) (1854–1943), writer and feminist. Poorly educated in comparison to her brothers, in 1870, aged 16, she married a surgeon who worked in an institution for prostitutes who had contracted venereal disease, and the couple travelled to Hong Kong, Japan and the Far East. Her first novel, *Ideala* (1888), entwined discussion of contemporary women's issues with a traditional story of romance and domestic matters, and earned her sufficient money to leave her husband and move with her son to London, taking the name Madame Sarah Grand as her pseudonym to suggest feminist pride.

She worked with Josephine BUTLER's campaign to have the Contagious Diseases Act repealed and this work informed her next book, *The Heavenly Twins* (1893), which was a sensational success, selling more than 20,000 copies in its first year of publication. *The Beth Book* (1897), the final volume of the trilogy, was largely autobiographical. Grand was an active supporter of 'votes for women and purity for men'. Credited with giving currency to the term 'the new woman' in 1894, Grand moved to Bath where she became a civic dignitary, serving as mayoress for six terms.

GRANE, 1ST VISCOUNT see GREY, LEONARD

GRANT, DUNCAN (1885–1978), artist. A cousin of Lytton STRACHEY, Grant studied art in London and Paris, and his paintings were included in the second of Roger FRY's Post-Impressionist exhibitions held in London in 1912. The following year he was the co-founder with Fry of the Omega Workshops. In 1916 he moved with Vanessa BELL to Charleston (Sussex); their daughter was born in 1918. Though a practising homosexual, many of his paintings portray their happy life together with other members of the Bloomsbury group such as Strachey, J. M. KEYNES and Virginia WOOLF: much of his decoration of Charleston survives, as do the murals which he painted with Vanessa and her son Quentin for nearby Berwick church (1940–2) and Lincoln Cathedral in 1956.

GRANVILLE, EARL, 1ST *see* CARTERET, JOHN; **2ND** *see* GOWER, GRANVILLE GEORGE

GRATTAN, HENRY *see* essay on page 366

GRAUNT, JOHN (1620–74), pioneer of social statistics. A wealthy London haberdasher, he compiled *Natural and Political Observations, made upon the Bills of Mortality*, first published in 1662 and revised several times. This was the first attempt to analyse what data there were on births, marriages and deaths in England, collected by parish clerks. Graunt learned that there were more boys born than girls and that urban mortality was higher than rural, but that the information on the cause of death was meagre and generalized. From 1665 publication of the *Observations* was taken over by the Royal Society, of which Graunt was one of the first fellows, and after his death further revisions were made by his friend and protégé William PETTY.

GRAVES, ROBERT (1895–1985), poet. From a comfortable upbringing and after a public school education, he joined the army in 1914 and, still in his teens, was left for dead on the battlefield. As a result of his experiences in the trenches he suffered from shell-shock for more than a decade. After the end of the war, and still ill, he went to Oxford to study literature. Graves was the youngest member of that group of young, middle-class British war poets (including Siegfried SASSOON) whose poetry increasingly reflected the horrors and futility of war. His first major success was the memoir *Goodbye to All That* (1929), a best-seller which condemned the narrow-minded, philistine English middle-class system of upbringing and education for the grievous waste of life of his own generation. Although he regarded himself principally as a poet, and wrote an examination of the poetic muse, *The White Goddess* (1948), he turned to prose to make money and his novels proved his most enduring works. *I Claudius* and *Claudius the God* (1934) were both best-sellers (and subsequently very successful television adaptations). Graves spent his later life turning down honours and guarding his privacy on the island of Majorca, where he lived from 1929 to 36 and again from 1946, but he did serve as Professor of Poetry at Oxford University (1961–6).

GRAY, THOMAS (1716–71), poet. Son of a London scrivener, he was sent to Eton, where he became friendly with Horace WALPOLE, then to Cambridge, after which he accompanied Walpole on a Grand Tour. Although always dismissive of the pettiness of university life, he spent most of his adult years in Cambridge, enjoying access to its libraries. He began to publish poetry in the 1740s. His *Elegy Written in a Country Churchyard* (1751), composed over a 10-year period, was his most successful work, being much reprinted and pirated.

GRATTAN, HENRY (1746–1820)
Irish politician

Son of the Recorder and MP for Dublin, Grattan went to Trinity College, Dublin, then in 1767 to the Middle Temple, London. He was impressed by the parliamentary opposition, then riding high on the back of the WILKES affair, and especially by the oratory of BURKE.

In Ireland for the vacation, he attacked the Lord Lieutenant, George TOWNSHEND, in the *Freeman's Journal*, and attracted the attention of Henry FLOOD. Back permanently from 1772, he turned to politics. Many in Ireland supported the Americans in their conflict with Britain. In this context, in 1775, Grattan was offered a parliamentary seat by opposition luminary Lord Charlemont (*see* CAULFIELD, JAMES), and distinguished himself by his 'spontaneous flow of native eloquence'.

Noting the issue of the deleterious effect of the American War of Independence on the Irish economy, Grattan denounced British economic policy as selfish, and took the lead among 'patriots' in the Commons. When France allied with America (1778), oppositionists organized military Volunteer corps to protect Ireland from attack and Grattan became an officer. In 1779 Grattan followed the King's speech with a motion calling for 'free trade' (Ireland's admission to Britain's protected trading system). Even office-holders such as Flood supported this: government was losing control over the Irish Parliament. British economic concessions came too late to stem demands for more self-government. In April 1780 Grattan moved 'that the people of Ireland are of right an independent nation and ought only to be bound by laws made by the King, Lords and Commons of Ireland'. Though this was not carried, it was strongly supported by a Volunteer convention at Dungannon.

When NORTH's administration fell in 1782, Grattan and Charlemont pressed the case for constitutional change on the new Rockingham (*see* WATSON-WENTWORTH, CHARLES) administration, to which many Irish grandees were linked by kinship and friendship. Though reluctant to dismantle existing arrangements without a ratified alternative, they were bounced into agreeing. Relevant clauses of Poynings' Law 1495 (providing that all legislation of the Irish Parliament needed the approval of both Irish and British Privy Councils), and the 1720 Declaratory Act (establishing the supremacy of the British over the Irish Parliament) were repealed. (No one challenged the right of the Crown, in effect the British ministry, to nominate the Lord Lieutenant.) Grattan was hailed as a national hero, and Parliament gave him £50,000 to buy an estate. He saw his mission thereafter as providing an independent voice in politics, and did not seek office.

His patriotic eminence was quickly challenged by Flood, keen to reinstate his former reputation. He argued that repeal was not enough; Britain must *renounce* the right to legislate for Ireland (which she did in 1783). Relations between the two men were permanently soured.

Until the end of the decade, Grattan offered qualified support to successive Irish administrations while distancing himself from Flood's continuing interest in using Volunteers to force the pace of change. He opposed PITT THE YOUNGER's 1785 attempt to bind Ireland more closely in return for further trade concessions. Unlike his old schoolmate FITZGIBBON, now Lord Chancellor, he did not favour simple repression as a response to increasing violent agitation by Irish peasant farmers; he thought this should be coupled with the substitution of a county tax for tithes (taxes on crops, for the support of the Protestant Church of Ireland). At the end of the decade Grattan more fiercely criticized what he saw as Lord Lieutenant Buckingham's (*see* TEMPLE-NUGENT-GRENVILLE, GEORGE) government by corruption, and allied with Charlemont and other Irish Whigs to ensure, on the occasion of GEORGE III's illness, that as much power as possible went to the pro-Whig Prince of Wales (later GEORGE IV). In 1790 he was elected MP for Dublin.

In the early 1790s, contrary to the wishes of the Dublin corporation, Grattan welcomed Pitt's wish to extend the rights of Irish Catholics, arguing that the Protestant ascendancy could best gain strength from 'the progressive adoption of the Catholic body'. He gave friendly advice to Wolfe TONE and his Catholic committee. As tension between conservative Protestants and Catholics influenced by the French Revolution increased, Grattan strove to hold a middle ground, promoting his own ideal, a reformed Parliament legislating for Ireland under the British Crown. After the collapse of Fitzwilliam's (*see* WENTWORTH-FITZWILLIAM, WILLIAM) reforming ministry, despairing and in poor health, he advised his followers to withdraw from Parliament and himself declined to stand in 1797. He was absent for the 1798 Irish Rebellion, as he was in England to give evidence against United Irishman Arthur O'Connor.

He re-entered Parliament in 1800 to oppose Union (the incorporation of the Irish into the British Parliament). This battle lost, in 1805 he agreed to stand for the new Imperial Parliament to support Catholic emancipation. Though his oratory was admired, his cause did not prevail. As he lay dying, Parliament voted that he be buried in Westminster Abbey.

Stephen L. Gwynn, Henry Grattan and his Times (1939)

GRAY OF HETON, THOMAS (?–*c*. 1370), writer. Constable of Norham Castle (Northumb.) from 1345, he was captured by the Scots in 1355 and imprisoned in Edinburgh Castle until 1359. Reading in the library there spurred him to write his own history, an Anglo-Norman prose chronicle of England, from the earliest times to 1363, the *Scalacronica*. It includes many an old soldier's tale of the Anglo-Scottish wars.

GREEN, J(OHN) R(ICHARD) (1837–83), historian. Born and educated at Oxford, he became vicar of an East London parish but turned to history after contracting tuberculosis. His *Short History of the English People* (1874) was a path-breaking attempt to write social history for a popular audience. A literary and commercial success, it remains a landmark in the development of a people's history.

GREEN, T(HOMAS) H(ILL) (1836–82), philosopher. Based at Oxford and influenced by Hegel, he tried to formulate a concept of citizenship that would unite men of different social classes, imbuing them with a purpose (borrowed from German Idealistic metaphysics) that could be realized through concrete measures of social reform. Toynbee Hall (*see* BARNETT, DAME HENRIETTA and BARNETT, SAMUEL) and the New Liberalism were inspired by his thinking.

GREENAWAY, CATHERINE (KATE) (1846–1901), children's book illustrator. A commercially successful woman artist, the daughter of a wood-engraver and a prize-winning student at the Slade, Greenaway started her career designing greetings cards and sketching for the *Illustrated London News*. A new colour-engraving process opened possibilities for her work, and *Under the Window: Pictures and Rhymes for Children* (1878), written and illustrated by her, was an immediate success. Admired and helped by RUSKIN, who spoke of the 'radiance and innocence of reinstated infant divinity', undogmatically religious, resolutely old-fashioned in her depiction of idealized sunlit rural children in eighteenth-century dress, Greenaway became an enduring household name with such publications as the *Kate Greenaway Birthday Book for Children* (1880).

GREENE, GRAHAM (1904–91), novelist. He was educated at Berkhamsted (Herts.) school, where his father was Headmaster, and while still a student at Oxford he published his first book of verse, an 'unwise publication', *Babbling April* (1925). The success of his first novel, *The Man Within* (1929), galvanized him into leaving *The Times,* where he had been working as a sub-editor, and becoming a full-time writer. His publishing triumphs came with *Brighton Rock* (1938), *The Confidential Agent* (1939) and *The Power and the Glory* (1940). His skill at using popular forms, including the thriller or the detective story, and his ability to evoke the atmosphere of exotic or seedy locations, encountered during his lengthy and frequent journeys in Central and South America, Africa and South-East Asia, gave his many books colour and flavour. He had become a Roman Catholic in 1926 and the moral dilemma faced by his characters added depth to his writing.

GREENHAM, RICHARD (*c*. 1543–94), churchman. A Cambridge don who left Pembroke College for parish ministry at nearby Dry Drayton (1570–91). His ministry and formation of ordinands set standards for godly pastoral care. Though he refused to wear the surplice, Bishop Richard COX used him against religious radicals (the Family of Love) and Roman Catholics. He opposed Thomas CARTWRIGHT as a threat to Church unity and preached furiously against the Marprelate Tracts (*see* THROCKMORTON, JOB). His last years were spent in a London lectureship. Most of the published works attributed to him appeared posthumously.

GREENWICH, 1ST DUKE OF *see* CAMPBELL, JOHN.

GREENWOOD, ARTHUR (1880–1954), politician. Elected as a Labour MP in 1922, during his time as Secretary to the Labour Research Department (1920–43) he was instrumental in uniting the disparate intellectual and trade-union wings of the party and for planning Labour social policy strategy. Minister of Health (1929–31), he introduced the Widows', Orphans' and Old Age Contributory Pensions Act 1929, and appointed the BEVERIDGE committee to inquire into social welfare provision. As deputy leader of the Parliamentary Labour Party (1935), he was implacably opposed to Neville CHAMBERLAIN's appeasement policy.

GREENWOOD, JOHN (*c*. 1560–93), Separatist. Like several Elizabethan Separatist leaders, a Cambridge-educated Puritan converted through activism to the more radical position that it was sinful for the Church to be linked with secular government. He was imprisoned for gathering a conventicle (an Independent congregation) in 1587, but persisted on release, and was hanged with Henry BARROW for publishing seditious books.

GREER, GERMAINE *see* essay on page 368.

GREG, WILLIAM (1809–81), social commentator. From a prominent family of cotton-mill

continued on page 369

GREER, GERMAINE (1939–)
Feminist, critic and writer

Australian born and convent educated, she went to Newnham College, Cambridge, in 1964 to write a PhD thesis on 'The Ethics of Love and Marriage in Shakespeare's Early Comedies', in which one of the plays she discussed was *The Taming of the Shrew*. She performed with the undergraduate company Footlights and contributed articles to the counter-culture hippie magazine *Oz* published by her compatriot Richard Neville. Her first academic job was teaching English at Warwick University, but she continued her journalism, writing for *Rolling Stone* as well as *Oz*, co-founding and contributing to the 'sex paper' *Suck* (which was produced in Amsterdam to avoid British censorship laws) and appearing in the Granada television series *Nice Time*. She also contracted a short-lived marriage. The late 1960s were years of protest – anger at the prosecution of the Vietnam War, student unrest and demands for civil rights for Blacks – but there seemed to be no new place for women or their demands in these revolutionary times.

In 1963 Betty Friedan's critique of middle-class women's lot, *The Feminine Mystique*, was published in the USA. The 'woman question' was beginning to be raised in Britain too in small discussion groups and in the workplace, with calls for equal pay. In Oct. 1970 Greer's 'advocacy of delinquency' among women, *The Female Eunuch*, was published. With its powerful cover of a suspended fibreglass female torso, this potent manifesto of sexual liberation and pleasure heralding the end of the psychological and physical repression of women that made them society's castrates became a best-seller translated into 12 languages. Its analysis of sexist representations of women in society and its call to women to stop colluding in their own patriarchal repression ('what will you do?' demands the book's final sentence) reached a much wider audience than the still-small women's movement. But its popularity was never high among the activists of the movement, for though it succeeded in raising the profile of the feminist agenda and Greer's own media profile in particular, its message of redemptive individualism did not accord with the collective action for women's rights that was seen as the way forward.

An American tour followed when *The Female Eunuch* was published there in April 1971, culminating in the notorious New York Town Hall debate chaired by Norman Mailer. In 1972 Greer resigned her post at Warwick University and for the next two decades earned her living as a columnist for the *Sunday Times* and later the *Guardian*, writing for the *Spectator* and *Harpers* as well as for the alternative press and appearing as a panellist and commentator on radio and television (she was a regular fixture on Channel Four's *The Late Show* and notable as a discussant on the annual Booker Prize award programmes).

From her Tuscan farmhouse, Greer continued to attract media attention and interviews in such unlikely publications as *Playboy* where, in order to achieve 'my life's work … to make the feminist position more and more comprehensible to more and more people', she insisted that it was necessary 'to preach to the unconverted … exposing myself to the worst kinds of prejudice and antagonism and doing my best to discredit them'. In Italy, and later at her farmhouse in Essex, Greer gardened and wrote a series of columns under the pseudonym 'Rose Blight' for *Private Eye* and later *The Oldie*. In 1981, 11 years after the publication of *The Female Eunuch*, she published *The Obstacle Race: The Fortunes of Women Painters and their Work*. This erudite study of the constraints on women artists, starting with the early Renaissance, included the career of Artemisia Gentileschi, with whose 'aggressive independence' Greer empathized. *Slip-shod Sibyls: Recognition, Rejection and the Woman Poet* took up the same theme for wordsmiths in 1985. *Sex and Destiny: The Politics of Human Fertility* (1984) railed against the export of Western attitudes to sexuality, marriage and children to the Third World, though it has been criticized for sentimentalizing peasant society and endorsing the extended family as a desirable model for our times. Probing her own family traumas, *Daddy, We Hardly Knew You* (1990) details Greer's painstaking search for her father's identity. *The Change: Women, Ageing and the Menopause* (1992) is a challenge to older women to recognize that they had been 'junked by consumer culture' and could achieve a new potency. *The Whole Woman* (1999) is a stock-taking of the position of women 20 years on from the 'second wave' of feminism, for which Greer had given a clarion call in 1980: 'it's time to get angry again'. Combining a powerful critical media presence with academic concerns (Greer holds fellowships at both Cambridge and Warwick universities, and has founded a press to publish scholarly editions of Restoration women writers), she remains a high-profile, unfailingly controversial feminist icon.

Ian Britain, Once an Australian: Journeys with Barry Humphries, Clive James, Germaine Greer and Robert Hughes (1997) owners of Styal (Lancs.), he was an influential writer on social and political questions and an important contributor to the public debates on factory reform, especially in 1831–3. His *Essays on Political and Social Science* (1853) furnish an example of 'rational dissent' (he was brought up as a Unitarian) and liberal opinion on issues such as the need for moral reform of the working class. A later essay, 'Why are Women Redundant?' (1862), commenting on the increasing number of single women, argued that 'redundant spinsters' should be encouraged to emigrate. Expressive of much mid Victorian male thinking on the position of women, it drew much criticism from contemporary feminists.

GREGORY, LADY AUGUSTA (née Persse) (1852–1932), playwright and folklorist. Born to a Galway landed family of Evangelical tendencies, in 1880 she married Sir Robert Gregory, a 63-year-old neighbouring landlord and former Governor of Ceylon, who died in 1892. During the 1890s she adopted an increasingly fervent Irish nationalism, and after befriending YEATS established herself as his patron and literary collaborator. Her Co. Galway home, Coole, became one of the centres of the Irish literary revival. Yeats and Gregory collaborated in collecting folklore from the local people. From 1903 Gregory became in her own right a prolific and popular playwright. She also published popularized versions of early Irish sagas (written, like her plays, in a stylized adaptation of local dialect). Her autobiography and journals are major sources for the history of the literary revival.

GRENVILLE, GEORGE (1712–70), politician and Prime Minister (1763–5). Born to a landed Bucks. family and educated at Eton and Oxford, Grenville was called to the Bar in 1735 and elected MP in 1741. He was made a Lord of the Admiralty in 1744 and then Treasurer of the Navy under Newcastle (*see* PELHAM-HOLLES, THOMAS). Closely associated with his brother-in-law, PITT THE ELDER, he was dismissed in 1755 for criticizing the ministry's foreign policy, but returned to office in Pitt's two administrations nominally led by Devonshire (*see* CAVENDISH, WILLIAM) and Newcastle. On Pitt's resignation in 1761 he remained in the ministry and became First Lord of the Admiralty. A conscientious man, with a taste for the technical work of administration, he was made First Lord of the Treasury on the resignation of Bute (*see* STUART, JOHN) in 1763, and turned his attention to the rebuilding of resources drained by the Seven Years War and to the rationalization of imperial administration. He devised the Stamp Act 1765, which introduced taxes on official and legal papers, newspapers, pamphlets, playing cards and dice in North America and the West Indies (along the lines of taxes already existing in Britain). This met unexpected resistance and set in motion the chain of events that would lead to the War of American Independence. GEORGE III found Grenville tedious and didactic, and continued to consult Bute; in 1765 he replaced him with Rockingham (*see* WATSON-WENTWORTH, CHARLES). Reunited with Pitt (now Chatham) Grenville played a part in the opposition to Grafton (*see* FITZROY, AUGUSTUS). He successfully put forward the Election Act 1770, which reformed the procedure which the Commons used to determine elections where the results were contested.

GRENVILLE, SIR RICHARD (*c.* 1542–91), seafarer. Unruly heir to West Country estates, he fought against the Turks in Hungary (1566) and took part in unsuccessful Irish colonial projects (1568–9) before becoming interested in overseas voyaging and harassment of the Spanish colonies. He commanded the fleet taking settlers to his cousin Walter RALEIGH's abortive English colony at Roanoke in 1585, plundered Spanish shipping, and served in the home defence against the Spanish Armada in 1588. He died on his ship the *Revenge*, fighting against impossible odds in the Azores expedition of Thomas HOWARD, later Earl of Suffolk.

GRENVILLE, WILLIAM (1st Baron Grenville) (1759–1834), politician and Prime Minister (1806–7). The youngest son of George GRENVILLE, he entered the Commons in 1782 and was Foreign Secretary for 10 years during PITT THE YOUNGER's first ministry. Coming under the influence of Charles James FOX, he refused office in Pitt's second ministry but, after Pitt's death, returned to lead the Ministry of All the Talents, which abolished the slave trade. After Fox's death in Sept. 1806, however, he was unable to control the coalition and resigned in 1807 rather than promise GEORGE III not to raise the question of a further extension of civil rights to Catholics. He never held office again. The Grenvilles remained a relatively conservative element of the Whig opposition until the 1820s.

GRENVILLE-TEMPLE, RICHARD (5th Baron and 3rd Viscount Cobham, 2nd Earl Temple) (1711–79), politician. Heir to the title and fortunes of a Bucks. landed family, and an MP from 1734 until he succeeded to the earldom in 1752, Temple was PITT THE ELDER's brother-in-law, financial backer and close political ally, moving in and out of office with him in the 1750s and early 1760s. He was a vigorous opponent of Bute (*see* STUART, JOHN), backed John WILKES's weekly paper the *North Briton* and paid his legal expenses. With his brother George GRENVILLE he opposed the Rockingham (*see* WATSON-WENT-WORTH, CHARLES) ministry. He split with Pitt in 1767 when the latter took office as Earl of Chatham, but was reconciled after Chatham's resignation in 1768 and played a leading part in opposition in 1769–70. After his brother's death at the end of that year he retired from politics.

GRESHAM, SIR THOMAS (1519–79), financier. From a wealthy London merchant family, Gresham became England's leading operator in the international money market and cloth trade, doing much to reduce royal debt abroad under both EDWARD VI and MARY I. Ambassador in the Netherlands (1560–3), he keenly observed the deteriorating political situation there. Left childless, he devoted his huge wealth to founding a London bourse as the Royal Exchange (from 1566); his endowment of a university college in London was squandered in later years. Gresham was also responsible for the idea of Gresham's Law: the notion that 'bad money drives out good', people preferring, in a system where the precious-metal content gave the coinage an intrinsic value, to pass on coins that had been clipped or contained an incorrect proportion of base metal, while holding on to coins that had not been clipped or debased.

GREVILLE, CHARLES (1794–1865), diarist. He was Clerk to the Council and, with his cousin Lord George BENTINCK, manager of the Duke of York's stud. Greville's diaries, which he wrote from 1817 to 1860, reveal much about mid-nineteenth century politics and particularly about Wellington (*see* WELLESLEY, SIR ARTHUR) and Palmerston (*see* TEMPLE, HENRY).

GREVILLE, FULKE (1st Baron Brooke) (1554–1628), courtier and diplomat of ELIZABETH I and JAMES I. He was active in Welsh and navy administration, and was Chancellor of the Exchequer from 1614–21. Hero-worshipping Sir Philip SIDNEY from their Shrewsbury schooldays together, he wrote Sidney's biography, as well as plays and poems, and became patron to many intellectuals. Spending his last years restoring Warwick Castle, he died after an attack by a servant convinced that Greville had treated him shabbily in his will.

GREY, LADY CATHERINE (1540–68), younger sister of Lady JANE GREY. She married Henry Herbert, the future Earl of Pembroke, but they were later divorced. In 1560 she secretly married Edward Seymour, 9th Earl of Hertford (1539–1621), son of Edward SEYMOUR, Duke of Somerset, and nephew of Queen JANE SEYMOUR.

For treasonably marrying without her consent, ELIZABETH I imprisoned the pair separately in the Tower of London, but they contrived to have two children there. Their marriage was declared invalid in 1562. Catherine died under house arrest at Cockfield Hall, Yoxford (Suffolk), and Hertford later remarried.

GREY, CHARLES (2nd Earl Grey) (1764–1845), politician and Prime Minister (1830–4). A conservative Whig, Grey was nevertheless a long-time campaigner for parliamentary reform. He was a founder member of the Society of the Friends of the People in April 1792, a group committed to 'more equal representation of the people in parliament', and introduced an unsuccessful franchise Bill in 1797. Grey was also a strong opponent of PITT THE YOUNGER's foreign and domestic policies during the 1790s (as a friend of Charles James FOX he was closely involved in the move to impeach Warren HASTINGS). First Lord of the Admiralty in 1806, Grey succeeded Fox as Foreign Secretary but resigned in protest at GEORGE III's demand for a pledge not to introduce Catholic Emancipation. In opposition from 1807 (having succeeded to the earldom in that year), Grey was invited to form a ministry in 1830 and the following year made another attempt at parliamentary reform. The Bill was defeated: Grey called an election on the issue of reform and when returned introduced a new Bill which passed through the Commons but was defeated by the Lords. Grey resigned but, having secured a commitment from WILLIAM IV that he would create a sufficient number of peers sympathetic to reform to secure the passage of the Bill through the Lords, returned to office a few days later in May 1832. Although Grey intended that the Reform Act would settle the question of parliamentary reform, the 1832 Act proved only the beginning of the near century-long process of enfranchising the adult British population. Grey resigned in 1834 on account of Cabinet disagreements over his Irish policies, and retired from political life.

GREY, SIR EDWARD *see* essay on page 371

GREY, LORD LEONARD (1st Viscount Grane) (*c.* 1490–1541), administrator. A courtier who became Marshal of the English forces in Ireland in 1535 and in the following year Lord Deputy. Although he achieved much in pacifying the country and defeated a joint Scottish–Irish force at Bellahoe in 1539, his conciliatory attitude to religious conservatism and to his GERALDINE in-laws aroused royal suspicion; on returning to England in 1540 he was arrested, then executed. Sir Anthony ST LEGER, his successor as Lord Deputy, continued his reconciliation policy.

GREY, SIR EDWARD (1st Viscount Grey of Falloden) (1862–1933)
Politician and Foreign Secretary

Stigmatized by his former colleague, LLOYD GEORGE, as 'one of the two men most responsible for the war', Sir Edward Grey has generally received a favourable press from historians who have seen his period at the Foreign Office as one marked by a continental commitment which enabled Britain to intervene successfully in the First World War against the hegemonic ambitions of Germany.

Grey was the quintessence of the English country gentleman: well-bred (he was descended from the Greys of Howick) and well-educated, he loved the gentler country pursuits, particularly birdwatching, on which subject he wrote a best-seller, *The Charm of Birds,* in 1925; a man of character rather than of intellect, Grey represented the sort of statesmen the English admire most, something which has continued to protect his posthumous reputation.

Grey came into Parliament for Berwick-on-Tweed in 1885, the same year as his friend ASQUITH with whom his career was to be so closely linked. As an hereditary Liberal rather than one by conviction of intellect, Grey was one of the few politicians untroubled by the Home Rule crisis, and his loyalty was eventually rewarded when he was made Under-Secretary at the Foreign Office by Rosebery (*see* PRIMROSE, ARCHIBALD) in 1894. In that position he gained some notoriety in 1895 when he declared the Nile valley a British sphere of influence, much to the annoyance of the French. He remained firmly on the imperialist wing of the Liberal Party during the Boer War and after and, during his years in opposition, came to very gloomy views as to Germany's intentions and Britain's diplomatic position. In this he was at one with many contemporaries and when he came to the Foreign Office he found that many diplomats shared his views.

Grey was not CAMPBELL-BANNERMAN's first choice as Foreign Secretary but he was Asquith's and, despite the failure of the latter to abide by an agreement he had made with Grey and HALDANE before the election of 1906, Grey did become Foreign Secretary, a post he was to retain until 1916, the longest continuous tenure of that office in British history. Grey came to the office with clear-cut views which experience did nothing to shake. He thought that Germany was bent on securing the mastery of Europe and that it would fall to Britain to stop her. This he managed to combine with the view that England was militarily weak and therefore needed allies. In his eyes the Anglo-French *entente* of 1904 marked a turning-point in British diplomacy and it became the first principle of his policy to do nothing to imperil it; the second principle was to supplement it by an *entente* with Russia to secure Europe against any possible German aggression.

Grey came to office during the first Moroccan crisis and, without consulting the Cabinet, he committed Britain to offering the French full support in the event of German aggression. He saw nothing incompatible between such a declaration and his repeated assurances to the Commons that Britain still possessed a 'free hand'. His colleagues were unable to question him on this, or on the military conversations which were opened with France in 1906, since they were not informed on such matters; Grey liked to keep foreign affairs away from the Gladstonian and Lloyd George wings of his own party. Contemporary accusations of excessive secrecy were fully justified. Grey saw his policy as an attempt to contain Germany and consistently scouted German accusations that Britain had abandoned her neutrality; Grey may have had peaceful intentions but the same was not necessarily true of his French and Russian partners.

Despite Grey's hopes, Anglo-Russian relations never gained any warmth but Britain's support for France in the second Moroccan crisis (1911) and her naval agreement with France (1912) marked, at least in French eyes, a moral commitment by Britain.

That this was not how Grey saw things became clear in 1914 during the crisis which followed the assassination of the Archduke Franz Ferdinand. French requests for Britain to honour her commitments were met by bland statements from Grey denying any commitments. In Cabinet, however, Grey argued fiercely for a British declaration of war. His declaration on the eve of war that, 'The lamps are going out all over Europe, we shall not see them lit again in our lifetime', proved prescient. Singularly ineffectual in wartime, Grey left office with Asquith in Dec. 1916. After 1919 he devoted his career to sponsoring the League of Nations and to birdwatching, the latter of which enjoyed most success. His memoirs, *Twenty-Five Years* (1928), were an eloquent, if misleading, apologia for his diplomacy.

Keith Robbins, Sir Edward Grey: A Biography of Lord Grey of Falloden (1971)

GREY, MARIA (née Shirreff) (1816–1906), educational reformer. The founder of the Girls' Public Day School Trust (GPDST), which set out to provide relatively inexpensive education for girls, Grey also initiated the Teacher Training and Regeneration Society (1877), which trained the teachers to staff the GPDST schools.

GREY, LADY MARY (after 1540–78), youngest sister of Lady JANE GREY. As with her elder sisters, JANE GREY and Catherine GREY, her life was ruined by her royal blood. The uncompleted schemes of John DUDLEY, Duke of Northumberland, included in 1553 her betrothal to her cousin the son of Arthur, Lord Grey of Wilton. Under ELIZABETH I her secret love match (1565) with Thomas Keyes, a royal serjeant-porter as tall as she was short, effectively excluded her from the succession, but still led to years of imprisonment.

GRIERSON, JOHN (1898–1972), documentary film maker. Grierson's first film, *Drifters* (1929), about North Sea herring fishermen, was original in technique and conception. As films officer and later producer to the Empire Marketing Board (EMB), he encouraged young and talented directors, who made over 100 films between 1930 and 1933 about the lives of working people; the films were both idealistic in their conception and realistic in their portrayal. In 1933 the EMB was dissolved and Grierson's unit moved to the GPO documentary film unit, where increased budgets and improved working conditions enabled the team to create masterpieces such as *The Song of Ceylon* (1935), *Coal Face* (1935) and *Night Mail* (1936). Grierson recruited W. H. AUDEN and Benjamin BRITTEN to make propaganda films during the war, and he helped the Canadian government create the National Film Board of Canada, of which he became Director in 1939. Though frequently considered more of a teacher than an artist, he was one of the greatest documentary and propaganda film directors of the century.

GRIFFITH, ARTHUR (1871–1922), journalist and Irish politician. From a Dublin working-class background, he came to prominence from 1899 as editor of a separatist weekly, the *United Irishman* (*Sinn Féin* from 1906). Initially a Republican, he came to advocate a dual monarchy based on GRATTAN's Parliament as a compromise designed to attract supporters of the Irish Parliamentary Party and moderate Unionists. Griffith argued that Irish MPs should leave Westminster and set up a shadow parliament and administration while disrupting the British administration by non-co-operation and nationwide agitation. In 1905 he established Sinn Féin as a political organization to propagate this policy and challenge the Irish Parliamentary Party. At first it had only limited success, but after the 1916 Easter Rising the opposition to the Irish Party regrouped under the Sinn Féin title. Griffith became MP for Cavan East in 1918, but was seen as excessively moderate by many new Sinn Féiners; he was displaced as party President by Eamon DE VALERA and his role in the Anglo-Irish War was largely confined to publicity, though he served as acting President between De Valera's departure to America and his own arrest in 1920. He headed the delegation which negotiated the Anglo-Irish Treaty in 1921, and succeeded De Valera as head of the Dáil government, but died a few days after the outbreak of the Civil War in 1922. His reputation as 'the father of Sinn Féin' suffered because of some illiberal views (including anti-Semitism and attacks on James LARKIN for ruining Irish businesses by irresponsible strikes), and his contribution to the foundation of the modern Irish State is currently undervalued.

GRIMBALD OF SAINT-BERTIN (?–901), Flemish monk. He was recruited by ALFRED THE GREAT in *c.* 886 to help with his programme of educational reform. Alfred's letter to the Archbishop of Rheims seeking to recruit Grimbald sets out explicitly the King's belief that raising religious standards was crucial to successfully resisting the Vikings. Grimbald played a central role in the reforms, both as Alfred's mass-priest and in organizing the restocking of English libraries with continental manuscripts. *See also* JOHN THE OLD SAXON.

GRIMOND, JO(SEPH) (Baron Grimond of Firth in the County of Orkney) (1913–93), politician. Married to ASQUITH's granddaughter, Grimond trained as a barrister before becoming Liberal MP for Orkney and Shetland from 1950 to 1983. In 1956, at the nadir of his party's fortunes, he took over the leadership from Clement DAVIES and gave the party fresh vision and drive, making particularly good use of the new medium of television. In 1958 the Liberals achieved their first by-election success since 1928 at Torrington (Devon); Orpington (Kent) followed in 1962, and in the decade leading up to 1966 the number of Liberal MPs doubled to 12. Grimond's political beliefs were in individual liberty, decentralization (he supported Home Rule for Scotland and Wales) and participatory democracy made possible by electoral reform. If the precise implementation of these beliefs was not clear after the Orpington by-election, when he rallied his party to 'march towards the sound of gunfire', his overall aims were to create an effective radical non-socialist party of the Left, an electable alternative to the

Conservative Party. This had only been partially achieved by the time he resigned in 1967, with the Liberals still a minority force in Parliament.

GRIMSTON, SIR HARBOTTLE (1603–85), politician. A lawyer and MP in 1628 and from 1640 in the Long Parliament, in which he joined the Parliamentarian cause and was a prominent moderate Presbyterian. Active in negotiations with CHARLES I in 1648, he was excluded from Parliament by the army in PRIDE's Purge, and only re-entered politics in 1660 on Richard CROMWELL's fall as Speaker of the Convention Parliament which issued the invitation to CHARLES II to return. Charles knighted him and gave him a life appointment as Master of the Rolls.

GRINDAL, EDMUND (?1519–83), Archbishop of Canterbury. His Cambridge career was interrupted by his exile under MARY I because of his Protestantism, but this made him an obvious high-flyer in the Church of ELIZABETH I; he became Bishop of London in 1559, Archbishop of York in 1570, then of Canterbury in 1575. There a distinguished ministry foundered when Elizabeth ordered him to suppress the clerical preaching seminars known as 'exercises of preaching' or 'prophesyings'. His defiance of her led to his suspension in 1577 under house arrest, and he had not recovered favour at his death. He is often seen as a lost hope of official rapprochement with Puritan activists in the Church. Nevertheless, exercises of preaching were later quietly revived, apparently without the Queen noticing.

GRIVAS, GEORGIOS (also called Dighenis) (1898–1974), Cypriot guerrilla leader. Although his actions helped bring about the independence of Cyprus in 1960, Grivas never achieved his true goal of *enosis,* or union with Greece, and he remained a fugitive until his death. After leading right-wing wartime resistance movements during the German occupation of Greece, he formed EOKA (National Organization of Cypriot Struggle) on his native island. A guerrilla campaign was waged against the British, alongside the political campaign, and with the ready connivance of his then ally, Archbishop MAKARIOS III. When Makarios accepted British terms for independence without *enosis,* Grivas turned against him. In 1971 he returned to revitalize the anti-Makarios terrorist movement. He died as the attempted coup promoted by the Greek junta failed and Turkey invaded Cyprus, partitioning its northern region.

GROCYN, WILLIAM (?1449–1519), scholar. An Oxford academic, he was the first major English Greek scholar, becoming acquainted at first hand

with the Italian Renaissance in his travels *c.* 1488–90. His learning impressed even foreign humanists like ERASMUS.

GROSSETESTE, ROBERT (*c.* 1170–1253), scholar and prelate. Despite his name, he was no 'fathead' but a dominating figure of thirteenth-century English intellectual and religious life. Very little is known about his first 50 years, only that, as an author of scientific treatises, he composed works particularly on light and optics of such quality that one twentieth-century scholar chose to title his book *Robert Grosseteste and the Origins of Experimental Science*.

In later years, Grosseteste turned more to philosophy and theology for which he learned Greek, and after 10 years lecturing at Oxford he was consecrated Bishop of Lincoln in 1235. Within a year he had quarrelled with his cathedral canons and deposed 11 heads of religious houses. 'A heartless tyrant,' observed Matthew PARIS. Grosseteste's intense concern for pastoral care led him to welcome the friars; it also meant that no one, Pope, King or ordinary parishioner, was immune from his starkly expressed views (often delivered in person) on how they could do better. By the time he came to write the Bishop's epitaph, Paris had found much to praise.

GROSSMITH, GEORGE (1847–1912) and **WEEDON** (1854–1919), authors. After working as a court reporter for *The Times*, George became a full-time entertainer performing comic songs and readings from material which he largely wrote himself, and (1877–89) appearing in GILBERT and SULLIVAN's operettas. Meanwhile Weedon, who had studied at the Royal Academy Schools and the Slade, exhibited his paintings before taking up professional acting (1885). In 1892 the brothers combined their talents to produce illustrated extracts from the diaries of Charles Pooter, a fictional City clerk, for *Punch*. Their ironic minor masterpiece *Diary of a Nobody* was published in book form in 1891, and, despite its topical origins, continues to amuse today.

GROTE, GEORGE (1794–1871), historian and politician. MP for the City of London from 1832, of the same reforming persuasion as Jeremy BENTHAM and James MILL, Grote had started to write the *History of Greece* in the 1820s, and when he retired from Parliament (1841) and the family banking firm (1843) completed his Utilitarian view of the ancient world, published in eight volumes (1845–6).

GRUFFUDD AP CYNAN (*c.* 1055–1137), Prince of Gwynedd. The only Welsh ruler to be the subject of a surviving near-contemporary biography, the anonymous *Historia Gruffudd vab Kenan*, he made his first bid for power in 1075. It took three turbulent decades, one of them spent in a Norman prison, before he finally established himself on the throne of Gwynedd, for much of the time as client of HENRY I. Although he was constantly at war with rival princes, his biographer gives him credit for an economic revival. He was succeeded by his son OWAIN OF GWYNEDD.

GRUFFUDD AP GWENWYNWYN (?–*c.* 1286), Lord of Cyfeiliog in Powys. In 1241 he regained the estates of his father, becoming effectively a baron of HENRY III; old rivalry with Gwynedd kept him loyal to the King during the revolt of DAFYDD AP LLYWELYN, and in 1257 LLYWELYN AP GRUFFUDD seized his lands. So well did the Welsh cause prosper that in 1263 he recognized Llywelyn as Prince of Wales. But old rivalries resurfaced in 1273–4 and again in 1278 (the dispute with Llywelyn over Arwystli). He ended his days as he had begun them, a client of the King of England; he had little choice.

GRUFFUDD AP LLEWELYN *see* essay on page 375

GRUFFUDD AP RHYDDERCH (?–1055), King of Deheubarth. A rival to GRUFFUDD AP LLYWELYN, King of Gwynedd, who had briefly annexed Deheubarth in 1044, Gruffudd waged a war against his northern rival for two years, finally securing the undisputed mastery of Deheubarth in 1047. He employed Scandinavian mercenaries in campaigns in south-east Wales and against Glos. to consolidate his power. He was killed in 1055 by Gruffudd ap Llywelyn, who subsequently became nominal ruler of all Wales.

GRUFFUDD AP RHYS (?–1137), Prince of Deheubarth. The son of RHYS AP TEWDWR, he went into exile in Ireland when his father died in 1093, returning in 1113 to begin a fight which for many years had little prospect of success, and became leader of Welsh resistance against the invaders. The death of HENRY I in 1135 was the signal for a great revolt, in which the most striking victories were those won by Gruffudd ap Rhys and his wife GWENLLIAN, daughter of GRUFFUDD AP CYNAN of Gwynedd; she was killed in battle in 1136. He died in 1137, allegedly killed by the treachery of his second wife, but his sons continued the struggle and the alliance with Gwynedd on which it was based.

GRUNFELD, HENRY (1904–99), merchant banker *see* WARBURG, SIEGMUND

GRUOCH, Queen of the Scots (1040–57). The historical 'Lady Macbeth', she was a grand-daughter of CINAED III and married to Gille Comgáin, Mormaer of Moray (d. 1032). Following his death, she married Gille Comgáin's cousin, MACBETH, who succeeded to his position. Through Gruoch, the Moray dynasty inherited both a claim to the kingship and the long-standing feud between the rival branches of the Scottish royal house to control the kingdom. Her reputation as a ruthlessly ambitious woman who pushed her husband into a succession of murders is SHAKESPEARE's invention.

GUEST, LADY CHARLOTTE (née Bertie) (1812–98), writer and businesswoman. Daughter of the 9th Earl of Lindsey who died when she was six, Charlotte managed, despite her clergyman stepfather's disapproval of education for girls, to read widely in the classics and learn modern European languages as well as Hebrew, Persian and Welsh. In 1849 a definitive edition of four-teenth-century Celtic tales, *The Mabinogion*, which she had translated and edited, was published, and in her enthusiasm for the Welsh language she promoted the revival of Welsh festivals and eisteddfods. In 1833 Charlotte had married an iron-master, (Sir) Josiah John Guest, and bore 10 children. When he died (1852) she took over the running of his large industrial concern at Dowlais (Glam.), until she married her eldest son's tutor, Charles Schreiber, in 1855, and subsequently led a more leisured Victorian life of travel and collecting.

GUEST, EDMUND (1518–77), churchman. A Cambridge don, he wrote against the Mass in 1548, disappeared into obscurity under MARY I, and emerged to become Bishop of Rochester (1560), then of Salisbury (1571). He was important in finalizing the text of the Church of England's doctrinal statement, the Thirty-Nine Articles (1563), formulating a clause saying that the body of Christ is taken by communicants 'only after an heavenly and spiritual manner', although he was uneasy about the Reformed (Calvinist) views of the Eucharist increasingly prevailing in the English Church over Lutheran ideas (*see* ZWINGLI, HULDRYCH).

GUILFORD, 1ST BARON *see* NORTH, FRANCIS; **8TH BARON AND 4TH EARL OF** *see* NORTH, FREDERICK.

GUINNESS, EDWARD (1st Earl of Iveagh) (1847–1927), brewer. The man who took the Dublin-based family brewing business from a local to an international concern, Guinness joined the management on his father's death in 1868. Over the course of the next 20 years, as tastes changed, his firm took over almost all the UK's

continued on page 376

GRUFFUDD AP LLYWELYN
King of Gwynedd (1039–63)

The first and last native King of all Wales, Gruffudd imposed his power temporarily over all the other kingdoms of eleventh-century Wales. His life, which consisted of relentless military campaigning against other Welsh kings and against the English, was played out in the midst of the complex family and territorial rivalries which were typical of the politics of early medieval Wales, and against a wider background of English and Scandinavian intervention, the latter coming from the Norse settlements in Ireland and elsewhere in western Britain. His period of domination over all Wales, which lasted from 1055 to 1063, was the result of the violent subjugation of the other Welsh kingdoms. His power was eventually destroyed by an invasion from England, after which Wales reverted politically to its previous fragmented condition as all the kingdoms which he had defeated re-emerged.

The son of LLYWELYN AP SEISYLL, who had briefly controlled the two kingdoms of Deheubarth and Gwynedd until his death in 1023, Gruffudd emerged from Dyfed in 1039 to seize Gwynedd by killing its King, IAGO AP IDWAL. He took over Deheubarth in 1044 when he killed its King, Hywel ap Edwin, in battle in 1044, but he was then himself defeated by the formidable GRUFFUDD AP RHYDDERCH in 1045. Gruffudd finally defeated Gruffudd ap Rydderch in 1055, thereby taking over Deheubarth, as well as dominating south Wales and the kingdom of Morgannwg from the same date. Although his power was finally destroyed by outside intervention from England, Gruffudd for a long time manipulated potential enemies with great skill. His power was such as to put a stop temporarily to Viking raids on Wales from Ireland, which had been a cause of considerable disruption as late as the 1040s, and he made use of Viking warriors in his wars. Soon after becoming King, Gruffudd had killed a brother of Earl LEOFRIC of Mercia and during the 1050s he was able to annex territory from the English as a result of raids across the River Wye. As the ally of Leofric's son, Earl ÆLFGAR of Mercia, he played a significant role in English politics supporting Ælfgar against the mounting power of the sons of Earl GODWINE. Nemesis came, however, after Ælfgar's death when, in 1062–3, he was crushed by a two-pronged assault by sea and land led by Godwine's sons, the future HAROLD II and TOSTIG. After his defeat, he was killed by his own men, most probably as a result of a Welsh dynastic feud.

Gruffudd's rise and fall fits in a lot of respects into a pattern which had characterized the politics of the Welsh kingdoms from the ninth century onwards. Gwynedd, supposedly founded by CUNEDDA in the fourth century, was usually the most powerful of the Welsh kingdoms. In a society where the principle attributes of kingship were gift-giving and leadership in war, warrior-kings such as MAELGWYN and CADWALLON had consolidated Gwynedd's pre-eminence. However, with succession to kingship following no clear-cut lineal pattern and all family members having an interest, conflicts and instability were frequent. From the time of RHODRI MAWR in the ninth century onwards, the chief families of Gwynedd and Deheubarth possessed claims to both kingdoms; as a result HYWEL DDA had temporarily added Gwynedd to Deheubarth in the mid tenth century and kings such as MAREDUDD AP OWAIN and Llywelyn ap Seisyll had subsequently for a time controlled both. Welsh kings had always had to take account of their more powerful English neighbours and, from the ninth century onwards, even kings like Hywel Dda found it necessary to acknowledge a theoretical English supremacy. Arguably Gruffud, while pursuing policies within Wales which were typical of his predecessors as kings of Gwynedd, over-reached himself as far as the English were concerned.

While it is, of course, wrong to see Gruffudd as a King who achieved a unification which fulfilled proto-nationalist aspirations, it is important to recognize the role of conquest in the creation of the nations of Britain: England, for example, was the result of the wars of aggression from the time of ALFRED THE GREAT onwards. Gruffudd's kingship could have pushed forward a similar process in Wales but, with the re-emergence of local dynasties after his death, the prospects of unification were aborted. It is somewhat ironic that Harold's defeat of Gruffudd removed the one Welsh ruler who might have put up effective resistance to the Normans; the most notable of his immediate successors were BLEDDYN AP CYNFYN of Powys and GRUFFUDD AP CYNAN of Gwynedd. After 1066 Welsh rulers bowed to superior force and gradually ceased to call themselves kings. Gwynedd, however, remained the most powerful Welsh kingdom or principality until the time of LLYWELYN AP GRUFFUDD's defeat by EDWARD I.

Wendy Davies, Wales in the Early Middle Ages (1982)

market in dark beer, porter and stout. Output rose from 350,000 barrels in 1868 to 1.2 million barrels in 1886, largely through explosive growth in England. In 1886 the business was offered for sale to the public and the flotation was a runaway success. He retired as Managing Director in 1889, and as Chairman in 1914, when professional managers replaced family as prime figures in the business. Guinness was created successively baronet, Baron Iveagh, Viscount Elveden and in 1919 Earl of Iveagh. He saved Kenwood House (London) for the nation in 1925, bequeathing with it his priceless picture collection.

GUNDULF (?–1108), architect. A Norman monk of Bec, Prior of St Stephen's, Caen, and, from 1077, Bishop of Rochester, he was renowned as the greatest architect of his day. In England, the White Tower of the Tower of London is his main achievement, but he also worked on the castles and cathedrals of Canterbury and Rochester.

GUNNHILDA (?–1038), wife of the Emperor Henry III. A daughter of King CNUT and Queen EMMA, she married the future Henry III (1039–56) in 1036. The marriage illustrates Cnut's role as a political figure of European importance. Gunnhilda died within two years of the marriage.

GURNEY, IVOR (1890–1937), composer and poet. Born in Glos., Gurney, who studied at the Royal College of Music, was gassed and wounded at Passchendaele in Sept. 1917. He published two volumes of poetry, *Severn and Somme* (1917) and *War's Embers* (1919), but the impact of his wartime experience on an already fragile mental state was so severe that he was committed in 1922 and spent the rest of his life in a mental hospital in Kent. But he continued to compose music and poetry, which was later collected and published.

GUSTAVUS VASSA *see* EQUIANO, OLAUDAH

GUTHFRITH (?–895), Scandinavian King of York (*c.* 883–95). The second known Scandinavian King of York after HALFDAN. What we know about Guthfrith's kingship suggests assimilation into a British and Christian political framework; he is known, for example, to have minted coins in an English style, to have confirmed the possessions of the church of Lindisfarne and to have been buried in York Minster. The establishment of a major Viking settlement at York led to the town's expansion to become, after London, the second largest town in England. The recent archaeological excavations show it to have been a great centre of trade.

GUTHLAC, ST (*c.* 675–714), hermit. The surviving near-contemporary *Life of Guthlac*, written by the otherwise unknown monk Felix, is an important source for early Anglo-Saxon lay and ecclesiastical society, describing as it does his military career and his eventual retirement to become a hermit at Crowland in the Fenland. It shows, for example, how Guthlac as a young warrior pillaged the countryside and had little to do with the royal court, and also the way in which a hermit acted as a counsellor to many people, including kings. He was a relative of King ETHELBALD of Mercia.

GUTHRIE, JAMES (*c.* 1612–61), churchman. He was a student at St Andrews; Samuel RUTHERFORD inspired him to become a fierce defender of the Presbyterian system of Church government, and he was ordained in 1642, thereafter playing a prominent part in Scottish ecclesiastical politics, always championing the National Covenant (1638) which set out a pure Calvinist separation between the jurisdictions of the State and of the national Church. In 1654 he became one of the 'Triers' who vetted candidates for ordination. Arrested for treason by the restored royal government in 1661, he was hanged in Edinburgh.

GUTHRUM (?–890), Viking chieftain and Danish King of East Anglia. After initially joining forces in 871 with HALFDAN and IVAR THE BONELESS, Guthrum was the leader of the 'Great Army' which in 875 made a spectacular attack on the kingdom of Wessex, penetrating as far as Exeter, and almost defeating ALFRED THE GREAT. After his defeat by Alfred at the Battle of Edington in 878, Guthrum accepted terms and converted to Christianity. In 880 he set himself up as King of East Anglia and made a treaty with Alfred to define a common frontier. Despite subsequent tensions, he appears to have ruled constructively.

GUY, THOMAS (*c.* 1645–1724), philanthropist. He became a bookseller in London in 1668 and built his fortune by successfully challenging the monopoly of the King's printers in Bible production, and then investing the money in government securities. MP for Tamworth (1695–1707), where he had grown up and where he built an almshouse and town hall, in 1704 he became a Governor of St Thomas's Hospital, to which he added three new wards. In 1720 he sold what had been £45,000 of South Sea stock at £270,000 and, guided by his friend Richard MEAD, devoted it to the building of a new hospital opposite St Thomas's. Guy left £200,000, the largest sum in a will full of substantial legacies, to the governors of the hospital, which still functions as Guy's Hospital.

GWENLLIAN (?–1136), Welsh heroine. She was described by Gerald de BARRI as 'queen of the

Amazons' for her role in the great Welsh rebellion which followed the death of HENRY I. While her husband GRUFFUDD AP RHYS of Deheubarth went north to seek help from her father GRUFFUDD AP CYNAN of Gwynedd, she rode to war at the head of his troops. Defeated in battle by Maurice of London, she was killed and decapitated.

GWENWYNWYN (?–1216), Prince of Powys. He was one of the most ambitious of the princes of Powys, but his career showed that Powys, of all the ancient Welsh kingdoms, was the most vulnerable to English power. Succeeding his father OWAIN AP GRUFFUDD as ruler of southern Powys in 1197, he at once took the role of national deliverer but was rapidly defeated in battle at Painscastle (Radnors.) in 1198. He tried again whenever opportunity offered, but was humiliated by King JOHN in 1208, allowing LLYWELYN AP IORWERTH to step in, to seize both territory and national leadership. In 1216 he was evicted by Llywelyn and died in exile.

GWYNN, NELL (c. 1642–87), actor and royal mistress. She began her theatrical career selling oranges at the Theatre Royal, Drury Lane, and made her stage début there in 1665, soon playing lead roles in comedies. By 1669 she had become CHARLES II's mistress and was to bear him two sons. She continued to perform as a member of the King's Company, although her appearances declined through the 1670s as she concentrated on maintaining her position at court, threatened by mistresses of higher rank such as Louise de KÉROUALLE. Her status as a performer continued to be recognized; Aphra BEHN dedicated a play to her and she made frequent visits to Oxford and Cambridge. Charles treated her more casually than he did his other mistresses and she never received a peerage, although her eldest son became Duke of St Albans.

GYRTH (c. 1025 66), Earl of East Anglia. Son of GODWINE, Earl of Wessex, he was brother of, among others, King HAROLD II and Queen EDITH, wife of EDWARD THE CONFESSOR. He received the earldom of East Anglia soon after 1057 as part of the process which advanced several of his kin to political prominence. His death in Harold's army at Hastings is portrayed on the Bayeux Tapestry. *See also* LEOFWINE; SVEIN; TOSTIG; WULFNOTH.

H

HACKET, WILLIAM (?–1591), messiah. Sad fanatic who was proclaimed 'King of Europe' in London's Cheapside by two Puritan gentlemen, Edmund Copinger and Henry Arthington. Hacket was executed within a fortnight. His antics discredited beleaguered Puritan activists who had no connection with him, and made it easier for the government to justify repression of Protestant religious nonconformity.

HACKETT, SIR JOHN (1910–), soldier and academic. Son of an Australian lawyer, educated at Geelong grammar school and Oxford, Hackett joined the army and served in Palestine and Trans-Jordan in the 1930s, and in the invasion of Vichy French Syria in the summer of 1941. Volunteering for the new airborne force, he fought in Italy and at Arnhem, before taking command of the Trans-Jordan Frontier Force after the war, finishing his career as Commander-in-Chief British Army of the Rhine (1966–8). A fine classicist, Hackett became Principal of King's College, University of London (1968–75). He wrote widely on military history but is best remembered for *The Third World War* (1978), which warned of increasing Soviet strength and increasing NATO weakness, and which had a considerable influence on the policies of the governments of both THATCHER and the US President Reagan in the 1980s.

HADDINGTON, 1ST EARL OF see HAMILTON, THOMAS.

HADRIAN (AD 76–138), Roman Emperor (117–38). The decision to build what has come to be known as Hadrian's Wall was undoubtedly taken during his visit to Britain in 122. His reign marks an important stage in the evolution both of the Roman empire and of Roman Britain, since it was from this time that the empire effectively ceased to expand. Coming after AGRICOLA's campaigns in Scotland, Hadrian's policies demonstrate a more cautious approach to controlling the British province. Hadrian's Wall, one of the most elaborate building projects ever undertaken by the Romans, is a magnificent reminder of their capabilities. It was briefly abandoned when the Emperor ANTONINUS PIUS attempted to place the frontier further north by ordering the construction of the Antonine Wall, but after 160 it remained the northern limit of Roman Britain until HONORIUS ordered the departure of the Roman armies in the early fifth century.

HADRIAN (?–709 or 710), Abbot of St Augustine's, Canterbury (c. 668–709 or 710). A native of North Africa, Hadrian joined the Archbishop St THEODORE OF TARSUS at Canterbury. He is reputed to have been a great teacher, his pupils included St ALDHELM, and he and Theodore together made Canterbury into an important intellectual centre of vital importance to the development of Christianity in southern Britain.

HAGGARD, SIR H(ENRY) RIDER (1856–1925), author. The son of a prosperous Norfolk squire, Haggard went as aide to the Lieutenant General of Natal, South Africa, in 1875 and two years later joined Theophilus Shepstone's party to annex the Transvaal. Returning to England, he was called to the Bar in 1885, but the success of his novels *King Solomon's Mines*, published that year, and *She: A History of Adventure* (1887) decided him on a literary career. His powerful, sometimes eroticized 'lost world' narratives, drawing on his fascination with Zulu culture, were regarded as a robust literary innovation to match the imperial adventure, and with Robert Louis STEVENSON he was hailed as co-founder of a new 'school of romance'. Though his portrayal of the primitive has been condemned as racist, it is a complex view, informed by history and an understanding of the role of myth. In 1880 he married the heiress to a Norfolk estate and his interests turned to farming and the problems of agricultural decline.

HAGUE, WILLIAM (1961–), politician. He sprang to public notice when, at the age of 16, he delivered an amazingly self-confident speech at the Conservative Party conference which had Margaret THATCHER and the party leadership applauding loudly.

As a Yorkshireman from Rotherham who went to a comprehensive school followed by Oxford and a period as a management consultant, he was well placed to epitomize the success of Thatcherism. In Feb. 1989 he became MP for Richmond (Yorks.), the last by-election the Conservatives would win before 1997. He entered the Cabinet in 1995 when John REDWOOD resigned to challenge John MAJOR for the Conservative leadership; Hague replaced him as Secretary of State for Wales. It was the devastating Conservative defeat in 1997 which propelled Hague above the heads of his seniors into the party leadership. Michael PORTILLO, the most charismatic figure of the Right, had lost his seat, the Europhiles would not vote for Redwood at any cost, while the Eurosceptics (now a majority of the party) would not vote for the vastly experienced and popular former Chancellor, Kenneth CLARKE. In the circumstances, and with none of the other candidates for the post making a good showing, Hague's youthful enthusiasm, oratorical talents and lack of political baggage made him the ideal compromise candidate.

At the age of 36 he was the youngest leader of any major political party since PITT THE YOUNGER. With the task of trying to restore the Conservatives to office ahead of him, Hague set about reforming the party to make it more democratic and accountable. He regularly bested Tony BLAIR in the Commons, but making headway with the electorate was much more difficult.

HAIG, DOUGLAS (1st Earl Haig) (1861–1928), soldier. Son of the Scottish whisky-distilling dynasty, educated at Oxford and Sandhurst, he was commissioned into the 7th Hussars in 1885. Strongly influenced by the military historian G. F. R. Henderson at Staff College, Haig served under KITCHENER in the Sudan in 1898, and in South Africa in 1899, campaigns which seemed to confirm Henderson's contention that manoeuvre was the key to success. Now close to Kitchener, in 1905 Haig married a lady-in-waiting to Queen ALEXANDRA; both connections facilitated a rapid rise. A Corps Commander (1914–15), he supported moves to force Commander-in-Chief Sir John FRENCH's retirement, and succeeded him. Convinced that manoeuvre was possible once the German front was pierced, Haig's attempts to break through on the Somme and at Passchendaele were repulsed with huge casualties. Protected by the royal family, and by loyal friends like Sir William ROBERTSON, from the attempts of an increasingly hostile LLOYD GEORGE to dismiss him, Haig's army won crushing victories in the 'Hundred Days' (8 Aug.–11 Nov. 1918), but the memoirs of politicians made certain he got no credit. Portrayed as a horse-loving technophobe, in reality Haig wanted more tanks and aircraft, and even supported experiments to irradiate German positions with beams from powerful X-ray machines, in effect a primitive neutron bomb. Portrayed, too, as an insensitive butcher, Haig's belief in an after-life, confirmed by contact with dead friends in seances, gave him the psychological strength to order yet more attacks, while making him repellent to the modern mind.

HAILES, BARON *see* HEPBURN, JAMES

HAILSHAM, 2ND VISCOUNT *see* HOGG, QUINTIN

HAKEWILL, WILLIAM (1574–1655), legal scholar. A lawyer, frequently elected to the Commons between 1601 and 1628 and an habitual commentator on constitutional conflict with the Crown; he was a member of a commission on legal reform from 1614–20. Hakewill's important works on personal liberty and parliamentary procedure were both published in 1641. They added to Parliament's appeal to a generally mythical early constitutional history against CHARLES I's assertions of royal power.

HAKLUYT, RICHARD (1552–1616), publicist for exploration. *The Principal Navigations, Voiages and Discoveries of the English Nation* (1589, much expanded 1598–1600), narratives of sixteenth-century English explorers and voyagers, crowned the life's work of Hakluyt. Inspired by his uncle of the same name, Hakluyt (a clergyman) collected and published accounts of England's increasing prowess at sea, helping to give impetus to further exploration and colonization. Between 1583 and 1590 he was closely associated with Walter RALEIGH, whose colony at Roanoke failed ignominiously, and he wrote memoranda exhorting ELIZABETH I to establish colonies in North America, an undertaking which finally came about in Virginia in 1607. Samuel PURCHAS continued Hakluyt's work of collecting and publishing, while the Hakluyt Society, founded in 1846, publishes scholarly editions of exploration narratives.

HAKON (?–1030), Earl of Worcestershire. Son of ERIC OF HLATHIR and a nephew of King CNUT, he was another of the Scandinavians who prospered in England under Cnut. Created Earl of Worcestershire in 1018, he subsequently acted as Cnut's regent in Norway from 1028. He apparently died in a shipwreck.

HALDANE, J(OHN) B(URDON) S(ANDERSON) (1892–1964), geneticist. The son of John Scott Haldane (1860–1936), an eminent physiologist and philosopher, he was educated at Eton and studied mathematics, biology and classics at Oxford. Later he worked on genetics and during the First World War served in the army and became an atheist. After the war he researched human physiology at Oxford and biochemistry at Cambridge and held London University's chairs of genetics (1933–7) and biometry (1937–57). From the late 1920s he published ground-breaking papers on human genetics, notably his statistical and quantitative evidence showing the complex effects of selection on the genetic constitution of populations. Together with Ronald FISHER, he played a leading part in reconciling the Darwinian theory of evolution (*see* DARWIN, CHARLES) and Mendelian genetics. In the 1930s he became a communist, contributing to the *Daily Worker* and publishing influential works on Marxism and science, but left the party in 1956 over Soviet policy on genetics. In 1957 he emigrated to India, where he worked for the Indian Statistical Institute, Calcutta. A key figure in the biological sciences, his scientific writings combined a phenomenal knowledge of genetics, biochemistry and mathematics. He was a leading twentieth-century synthesizer and popularizer of scientific and other intellectual ideas.

HALDANE, RICHARD (1st Viscount Haldane) (1856–1928), politician and army reformer. Born into a prominent Scottish legal family, educated at Edinburgh and Göttingen universities, a barrister, he was elected MP for East Lothian in 1885. Haldane was a Liberal Imperialist, who on the formation of the Liberal government in 1905 became Secretary of State for War. A man of considerable administrative genius, Haldane recognized that the British army, which had developed almost organically to police an ever-expanding Empire, needed to be reorganized to meet the conditions of modern warfare. He combined hitherto scattered units into divisions, creating a small army which could be used as an expeditionary force, converted the Volunteers and Yeomanry into a Territorial Army which could reinforce the regular army, created an Officer Training Corps so that an expansion could take place very rapidly and formed an Imperial General Staff so that forces from the Dominions could be integrated quickly with British forces. A regular visitor to Germany, in part to observe army manoeuvres, in 1914 Haldane was subjected to a virulent press campaign and eventually driven from office. Free to concentrate his energies on administrative reform and education, Haldane helped reorganize the Civil Service, served as first President of the Institute of Public Administration, helped establish the London School of Economics and accepted the presidency of Birkbeck College. Breaking with the Liberals, he became Chancellor of the Exchequer in the first Labour government of 1924.

HALE, MATTHEW (1609–76), lawyer. During the Civil Wars of the 1640s he acted as defence counsel for several Royalists, but he was prepared to serve the Commonwealth; from 1652 he presided over the Rump Parliament's major commission on law reform, in 1654 becoming Chief Justice of the Court of Common Pleas. He was prominent in the Convention Parliament which in 1660 invited CHARLES II to return, and he was Chief Justice of the Court of King's Bench from 1671; his broad sympathies led him to friendships with John SELDEN, Richard BAXTER and leading clergy who represented the tolerant latitudinarian grouping within the Church. He is chiefly important for his extensive writings on the Common Law, although he also wrote on theological and scientific matters; his legal histories – principally *The History of the Common Law* (1713) and *The History of the Pleas of the Crown* (1736) – were published only after his death, and his opinions are still cited by lawyers.

HALES, SIR EDWARD (?–1695), soldier. Hales converted to Catholicism in 1685, and received a dispensation from JAMES II to continue as colonel of a regiment even though he was no longer an Anglican communicant as required by the Test Act of 1673. Hales's coachman, Arthur Godden, was instructed to bring an action against his employer in order to test the legality of the Crown's dispensing power. Kent assizes found against Hales but he appealed to King's Bench; James removed six judges whom he thought would oppose the dispensation. Of the 12 judges who heard the case, 11 voted in Hales's favour and Lord Chief Justice Herbert ruled that the King had sole discretion regarding dispensation from the penal laws. Hales later went into exile with James II.

HALES, JOHN (*c.* 1516–72), writer. Not to be confused with various Tudor namesakes who were lawyers or MPs, Hales came from a Kentish family including many lawyers, and profited from working for Thomas CROMWELL. A royal servant and MP under EDWARD VI, he was a prominent exponent of the 'commonwealth' programme which Cromwell had encouraged: a fusion of enthusiasm for evangelical reform in the Church with plans for improvement in all aspects of national life. With the encouragement of the Lord Protector, Edward SEYMOUR, Duke of Somerset, he led an official campaign against enclosure of commons and arable land for pastoral farming. Somerset's fall sent him from 1551 into prolonged continental residence, which continued through the dangerous years of MARY I's reign. He was never slow to publish on various topics (although *The Discourse of the Common Weal* formerly attributed to him is now known to be the work of Sir Thomas SMITH); his pamphleteering on the royal succession won him further trouble under ELIZABETH I.

HALES, JOHN (1584–1656), writer. From Bath, he became an Oxford don and a noted Greek scholar, and was a fellow of Eton from 1613 until dismissed by Parliament in 1649. In 1616 he was chaplain to Sir Dudley CARLETON's Netherlands embassy and attended the Dutch Church's doctrinally decisive Synod of Dort or Dordrecht (1618–19), acquiring a distaste for strict Calvinism because of its repression of anti-Calvinist Arminians (*see also* HALL, JOSEPH). Archbishop LAUD made him his chaplain in 1639. He spent his last years in retirement. Nicknamed 'the ever-memorable' for his learning, much admired by Lucius CAREY, Viscount Falkland, he championed moderation, tolerance and Christian reunion.

HALES, STEPHEN (1677–1761), biologist. He spent most of his life as curate at Teddington (Middx.), and his great scientific work was the identification of the basis of what is now called the transpiration stream. Hales rejected the theory that sap circulated like blood and instead showed that water flowed within the plant from root to stem to leaf, and that water pressure was greatest when the plant was exposed to light, but he continued to believe that the plant fed through its leaves on light and air. Hales experimented with animal physiology and theorized that muscles were operated by electric charges; he also invented the artificial ventilator, which injected air through bellows into confined spaces. A friend of FREDERICK, Prince of Wales, and a supporter of William SHIPLEY in the Society for the Encouragement of Arts, Manufactures and Commerce, he also took an interest in social issues, supporting the work of the SPCK (*see* BRAY, THOMAS). Hales drew on his scientific knowledge to promote the campaign against gin-drinking and the cause of better ventilation in prisons, securing the erection of a windmill venti-lator on top of Newgate prison.

HALEY, SIR WILLIAM (1901–87), journalist. Haley joined *The Times* immediately after the First World War and worked his way up to be managing editor by 1930. Editor-in-chief at the BBC (1943–4) and Director General (1944–52), he was appointed editor of *The Times* in 1952. An austere and high-minded figure, he was perfectly in tune with the mood of a serious and war-weary nation during the 1940s and 1950s, when he led

the country's two pre-eminent media institutions. His leading articles in *The Times* were famous for urging his fellow citizens to new heights of sobriety and hard work, especially when the coronation of 1953 threatened to bring a little gaiety into people's lives. *The Times* was very much still the paper of the 'Establishment' and the leader of informed opinion in the country, but the close (often too-close) relationship that the paper had enjoyed with successive governments was shattered by the Suez crisis of 1956. In the tradition of treating *The Times* as an instrument of State, Haley was briefed on Anthony EDEN's secret collusion with France and Israel to invade Egypt; he was so appalled by the dishonesty of the plan that he withdrew his paper's support for the government, and *The Times* became a much more independent voice. Haley resigned as editor when *The Times* was sold to Roy THOMSON in 1966: he was succeeded by William Rees-Mogg.

HALFDAN (?–877), Viking chieftain. Along with his brother IVAR THE BONELESS, Halfdan was leader of the Viking 'Great Army' of 865, which by the late 870s had destroyed all the English kingdoms except the Wessex of ALFRED THE GREAT. A spectacular sequence of campaigns throughout England ended the independent histories of the kingdoms of Northumbria in 866/7 (*see* ÆLLE), East Anglia in 870 (*see* EDMUND, St) and Mercia during the 870s (*see* BURGRED; CEOLWULF II) and gravely threatened Wessex's survival. In 875 Halfdan appears to have abandoned the attempt to conquer Wessex, and the following year is said to have 'shared out the land of the Northumbrians' among his followers, thereby establishing the foundations of the Viking kingdom of York consolidated by GUTHFRITH. Leadership of the 'Great Army' passed to GUTHRUM. Halfdan was killed in Ireland in a sea battle fought at Strangford Lough in an attempt to regain his brother Ivar's former kingdom of Dublin.

HALIFAX, EARL OF, 1ST (AND 3RD VISCOUNT) *see* WOOD, EDWARD; **2ND** *see* DUNK, GEORGE MONTAGU; **3RD** *see* MONTAGU, CHARLES; **1ST MARQUESS OF** *see* SAVILE, GEORGE;

HALL, EDWARD (1496 or 1497–1547), historian. A Cambridge-educated lawyer and veteran MP with reformist religious sympathies; his major historical work, *The Union of the Two Noble and Illustre Families of Lancaster and York* (1548, enlarged by Richard GRAFTON, 1550), was much used by William SHAKESPEARE in his history plays, and is still of major value for eye-witness (if ultra-loyal) accounts of central politics under HENRY VIII.

HALL, JOSEPH (1574–1656), Bishop of Norwich. A Cambridge scholar whose ability as poet and devotional writer won aristocratic patronage and Church preferment under JAMES I. He was an English representative at the Dutch Reformed Church's Synod of Dort (1618–19; see HALES, JOHN) and became Bishop of Exeter in 1627. His moderate Calvinism was not to William LAUD's liking, but he vigorously defended Episcopacy (government of the Church by bishops) and was promoted to Norwich in 1641. Immediately caught up in the general storm of anger against bishops which was part of the crisis precipitating the English Civil Wars, he died in poverty-stricken retirement.

HALL, MARSHALL (1790–1857), physician. Born in Notts., Hall studied medicine in Edinburgh and on the continent, and between 1826 and 1853 ran a private medical practice and taught medicine in London. He published on the circulation of the blood and respiration, but is best known for his experiments on the reflex action of the spinal system. In the 1830s he showed that a frog's body responded to stimuli to the nerves even when the spinal cord had been severed from the brain. Identifying this response as involuntary or reflex action, he argued that reflexes are controlled by the spinal cord rather than consciousness and that the nervous system consists of a chain of independently functioning 'reflex arcs'. Hall's reduction of reflexes to mere mechanism was championed by radical and continental physicians but attacked by the medical establishment, which regarded it as a threat to cherished notions of the soul.

HALL, SIR PETER (1930–), theatre manager and director. Educated at Cambridge, where he directed a number of student productions, Hall directed the first British production of Samuel BECKETT's *Waiting for Godot* at the Arts Theatre in 1955. Subsequently he has occupied the key role in major British theatrical companies, the Royal Shakespeare Company (1960–5), the National Theatre (1973–88) and Glyndebourne Festival (1984–90), and in 1988 he founded his own company.

HALL, RADCLYFFE (MARGUERITE) (1880–1943), writer. The daughter of a dilettante known as 'Rat' who left her American mother within weeks of her birth, she grew up, a neglected child, fitfully educated. She always dressed in tailored clothes and was known in private as 'John'. In 1915 she met Una Vincent Troubridge, who was very unhappily the wife of an admiral, and they lived together for many years. Dropping the hyphen from her name (having discarded 'Marguerite' earlier), she published poetry, and the second of her five volumes contains the poem 'Ode to Sappho'; many poems were set to music. She began to publish novels, *The Unlit Lamp* (1924), and *Adam's Breed* (1926), which was awarded both the prestigious *Prix Femina* and the James Tait Black Memorial Prize (a feat matched only by E. M. FORSTER with *A Passage to India*). In 1928 *The Well of Loneliness,* the largely autobiographical though romanticized story of the 'congenital invert' Stephen Gordon, was published with an introduction by Havelock ELLIS. It caused outrage and Hall and the publisher were prosecuted. Despite the willingness of Virginia WOOLF and Forster to testify to its literary merit, it was withdrawn from sale in England, though it was published in Paris.

HALL, STUART (1932–), cultural theorist and socialist. From the 1960s Hall became an immense influence on the development of cultural studies and of socialist politics. Born in Jamaica, he came to England in 1951 as a Rhodes Scholar at Oxford University, where he studied literature. A founding editor of *Universities and Left Review* (1957–9), with Raphael SAMUEL and others, he became the first editor of *New Left Review* (1960–2). The New Left was distinguished by a search for a path between social democracy and communism. It also took the question of culture as politically and intellectually central. In his work at the Centre for Contemporary Cultural Studies at the University of Birmingham (1964–79), Hall brought together the concern with culture and politics and extended it in new ways. At the heart of this was a critique of Marxist notions of 'base' and 'superstructure' (*see* MARX, KARL) and the reformulation of social and cultural theory inspired both by British writers including Raymond WILLIAMS and E. P. THOMPSON, and by continental European Marxists including Gramsci and Althusser. At the Open University, where he was Professor of Sociology (1979–97), Hall's work continued to be characterized by a continual dialogue with many intellectual traditions; his own 'double location' in relation to Jamaica and England, with its origins in colonialism, has been of decisive importance in Hall's work. He also became the most acute critic of Thatcherism (*see* THATCHER, MARGARET) and the limits of Labourism while arguing for a socialism which is open to 'identity politics'.

HALLÉ, SIR CHARLES (originally Carl Halle) (1819–95), pianist and conductor. Founder of the Manchester-based orchestra that bears his name, Halle was born in Westphalia and was trained in Germany. He fled from Paris at the time of the 1848 Revolution, and settled in Manchester. His promotion of concert series led to the formation of an orchestra with a formidable reputation, which he conducted throughout the rest of his life. In 1893 the Royal Manchester (subsequently

Northern) College of Music was founded largely through his efforts.

HALLEY, EDMUND (1656–1742), astronomer. Son of a wealthy London soapboiler, he was already making advanced astronomical observations while at school at St Paul's and later at Queen's College, Oxford, and was made a Fellow of the Royal Society at the age of 22. Halley's research was advanced by the calculations of NEWTON in the *Principia*, whose publication he funded. During this period Halley discovered that the density of the atmosphere correlated to its distance from the earth's surface. Suspicion that his religious views were unorthodox contributed to his failure to secure election to the post of Savilian Professor of Astronomy at Oxford in 1691. From 1698 to 1702 he took a naval command so that he could undertake various enterprises, including an attempt to discover a southern continent, a study of compass variation and a survey of the tides and coasts of the English Channel and the Adriatic. In 1703 Halley returned to Oxford as Savilian Professor of Geometry; while there he published his most famous discovery, that the comets of 1531, 1607 and 1682 were appearances of the same body, which would return in 1758. When this proved the case Halley's posthumous fame was assured. Halley also published new editions of ancient scientific texts, and his study of Ptolemy led him to realize that the positions of stars change over time. Astronomer Royal from 1721, he renewed the instruments and added new devices, helped after 1729 by the patronage of Queen CAROLINE. Halley will always be remembered for his comet, but his achievements were manifold, including the compilation (with Caspar Neumann of Breslau) of the first modern lifetable (allowing the calculation of life expectancies at various ages) from Breslau data, work on terrestrial magnetism, planetary motion, tides, the determination of longitude, eclipses, conic sections and diving bells.

HAMILTON, CICELY (1872–1952), writer and actress. She had always had to earn her own living and she regarded women's economic subordination as central to their struggle for equality: her polemic *Marriage as a Trade* (1909) remains a biting satire on the cash nexus in relationships. Her play *Diana of Dobsons* (1908) made her reputation as a dramatist, and she wrote some 20 further plays, including two about the suffrage movement, *How the Vote was Won* (1909) and *A Pageant of Great Women* (1910), in which she was active as a member of the Women's Freedom League and a founder member of the Women Writer's Suffrage League. She organized entertainment for British troops during the First World War, and thereafter was preoccupied with what she regarded as man's naturally warlike tendencies and the terrible destructive potential of science, themes that she explored in her inter-war plays, *William, An Englishman* (1919) (which won the *Prix Femina*), *Theodore Savage* (1922) and *The Old Adam* (1924).

HAMILTON, CLAUD (1st Baron Paisley) (?1546–1621), politician. Youngest son of James HAMILTON, Duke of Châtellerault, he supported MARY QUEEN OF SCOTS, fighting at her defeat at Langside in 1568 and taking part in the murder of Matthew STEWART, Earl of Lennox, in 1571. Despite repeated political disgrace, he continued to intrigue energetically for Mary and, after her death, for Spain, until in 1590 his growing religious mania ended his political career.

HAMILTON, GAVIN (1721–98), painter. The son of a country gentleman, he spent most of his life in Italy, although he made occasional brief visits to Britain and remained in close contact with British painters and patrons. He was strongly influenced both by the work of HOGARTH and by the neoclassical theorist Winckelmann. In his six-part *The Wrath of Achilles* (1759–75) Hamilton blended reverence for the ancients of Hogarth's series. Many of his subjects, such as *The Oath of Brutus* (1766) and *Agrippina with the Ashes of Germanicus* (1772), were interpreted as attacks on tyranny and his admirers included the French Revolutionary painter David.

HAMILTON, SIR IAN (1853–1947), soldier. Born in Corfu, the son of a captain in the Gordon Highlanders, educated at Sandhurst, Hamilton was commissioned in the Gordons in 1873, saw action in Afghanistan in 1879, and attracted the attention of Frederick ROBERTS, who wanted him as an aide-de-camp. With Roberts's support, Hamilton's rise was assured. Badly wounded at Majuba in 1881, on the staffs of both Roberts and KITCHENER during the Boer War, he was appointed chief of a military mission to Japan during the Russo-Japanese War (1904–5) and Commander-in-Chief in the Mediterranean in 1910. Hamilton was the logical choice to command the Gallipoli landings of 25 April 1915, the largest and most complex amphibious operation yet undertaken, which ended in humiliating failure. Replaced by MONRO in Oct. 1915, he never again had an active command, though the operational failure owed more to the primitive nature of ship-to-shore communications and the lack of specialized landing craft than to Hamilton's conduct.

HAMILTON, JAMES (2nd [1st Hamilton] Earl of Arran) (*c*. 1475–1529), politician. Son of JAMES

III's sister Mary, he was created Earl after completing the marriage negotiations between JAMES IV and MARGARET TUDOR, the sister of HENRY VIII, in 1503. As Scottish Lieutenant General from 1504 he finally re-established royal control over the Western Isles and helped to restore the King of Denmark to his throne, but his command of a costly naval expedition in 1513 achieved few results against the English. The politics of JAMES V's youth were dominated by struggles between Arran, Archibald DOUGLAS, Earl of Angus, and John STEWART, Duke of Albany; Arran repeatedly opposed English influence. His tangled divorce from his first wife complicated the claim to the throne of his son by a second marriage, James HAMILTON, the 3rd Earl.

HAMILTON, JAMES (3rd [2nd Hamilton] Earl of Arran, Duke of Châtellerault (*c.* 1515–75), politician. On JAMES V's death in 1542, he engineered his recognition as Regent of Scotland and heir presumptive, briefly embracing Anglophile and reformist religious policies before recoiling to his family's traditionally anti-English and conservative stance. His lifelong political irresolution was encouraged by his precarious but genuine prospects of the Scottish throne if MARY QUEEN OF SCOTS died childless. He was conciliated with a French dukedom in 1549 after accompanying the infant Queen to France, but in 1554 he was forced to yield the regency to MARY OF GUISE, widow of James V. In 1559 he returned from abroad to join the Protestant Lords of the Congregation against the Regent, and vainly pressed for a marriage between ELIZABETH I and his eldest son James HAMILTON (later the 4th Earl). Queen Mary's marriage to Henry STEWART, Lord Darnley, in 1565 drove him into open opposition together with James STEWART, Earl of Moray; later, reluctant to accept JAMES VI, he was reconciled to Mary and opposed the regencies of Moray and his longterm rival Matthew STEWART, Earl of Lennox, but he submitted to the Regent, James DOUGLAS, Earl of Morton, in 1573.

HAMILTON, JAMES (4th [3rd Hamilton] Earl of Arran) (*c.* 1537–1609), dynast. Son of James HAMILTON, 3rd Earl of Arran: his royal claim led to marriage proposals for ELIZABETH I in 1543 and 1559–60, alternating with similar attempts on MARY QUEEN OF SCOTS in 1543–7 and 1561–2. These increasingly desperate family efforts at dynastic engineering were curtailed by his going insane in 1562; his political significance (which had always depended on his genealogy rather than his personal capacity) ended.

HAMILTON, JAMES (2nd Earl of Cambridge, 7th Baron, 3rd Marquess and 1st Duke of Hamilton)
(1606–49), courtier. Hamilton's career as politician and soldier was marked by indecisiveness and a talent for exciting mistrust. His command (1631–4) of British forces fighting on the continent for Protestantism in the Thirty Years War was undistinguished. In 1638 CHARLES I used him as a mediator in the crisis in Scotland over royal liturgical innovations, vainly hoping that Hamilton's power and prestige would end protest. Despite giving up his royal commission in Scotland in 1639, Hamilton continued to work to avoid further war, but Charles interpreted his fumbling policy as criminal negligence and imprisoned him (1644–6). On his release Hamilton tried further mediation between Charles and the Scots; finally in Dec. 1647 securing an 'Engagement', a royal agreement to an interim Presbyterian Church Settlement in England, he led a Scots Royalist army south, only to be defeated by Oliver CROMWELL and John LAMBERT at Preston. The following year, he was beheaded for invading England, his English earldom providing a pretext for a treason charge under English law. His papers survive, a rich historical source.

HAMILTON, JOHN (1511–71), Archbishop of St Andrews. Illegitimate son of James HAMILTON, 2nd Earl of Arran, his predictably rapid Church career included the abbacy of Paisley from 1525, the bishopric of Dunkeld and the ultimate prize, the archbishopric of St Andrews in 1547 (effective tenure from 1549). He showed far greater talent and commitment to Catholicism than his half-brother James HAMILTON, the Regent Arran. His efforts at Church reform included the sponsoring of a Scots catechism for lay instruction; during the 1560s he resisted the Reformation and faithfully supported MARY QUEEN OF SCOTS (even though she connived in his imprisonment, 1563–6), baptizing her son, the future JAMES VI. After Mary's flight, he was hanged for complicity in the murder of James STEWART, the Regent Moray (1570); his knowledge of the murder of Henry STEWART, Lord Darnley, is more doubtful, although he encouraged Mary's marriage to James HEPBURN, Earl of Bothwell, in 1567.

HAMILTON, PATRICK (*c.* 1504–28), martyr. A Scots gentleman given the income of the abbey of Fern while still a boy, he became enthusiastic for Martin LUTHER while studying in Paris and St Andrews, and visited Wittenberg in 1527. He wrote *Patrick's Places* (1527), one of the earliest Scots summaries of reformed belief. When he returned to Scotland, he was burned at the stake, after converting Alexander ALESIUS, who had been assigned to persuade him to recant.

HAMILTON, THOMAS (1st Earl of Haddington, 1st Earl of Melrose) (1563–1637), politician. Son of a prominent Lothian lawyer, he studied at Paris, was a Lord of Session from 1592, and among the treasury 'Octavians' (1596; *see also* ELPHINSTONE, JAMES; SETON, ALEXANDER). After 1603 he remained in Scotland in the team of competent administrators ruling the kingdom, and benefited from becoming brother-in-law to the royal favourite Robert CARR. From 1616 he was Lord President of Session, made Earl in 1619. Although his power diminished on CHARLES I's accession, he died immensely wealthy by Scots standards, partly through mining enterprises on his estates.

HAMILTON, SIR WILLIAM ROWAN (1805–65), mathematician. Born in Dublin, Hamilton mastered mathematical techniques and 13 languages in his youth. He was educated at Trinity College, Dublin, and in 1827 was appointed Professor of Astronomy at Trinity College and Astronomer Royal for Ireland. He is celebrated for his work on caustics and for inventing sophisticated mathematical techniques for describing the behaviour of a particle or a system of particles. These techniques have proved highly significant in the formulation of quantum mechanics. He is also famous for inventing, in the 1840s, quarternions, complex numbers that describe rotations in three dimensions. Quarternions have played a crucial part in the development of vector analysis and matrices.

HAMMOND, ERIC (1929–), trade-union leader. Elected General Secretary of the Electrical, Electronics, Telecommunications and Plumbing Union (EETPU) in 1984, Hammond concluded a single union 'no strike' agreement with employers. This was in opposition to Trades Union Congress (TUC) policy and the EETPU was expelled from the TUC in 1988. Four years later Hammond resigned, and the EETPU joined with the Amalgamated Engineering Union (adding 'Electrical' to the new nomenclature).

HAMMOND, J(OHN) L(AWRENCE) (1872–1949) and **L(UCY) B(ARBARA)** (1873–1961), economic and social historians. Married in 1901, they wrote influential works on the industrial and agricultural revolutions, which drew on their political views and those of the Liberal circles in which they moved. These were an indictment of the policies of government and landowners and were a broadly pessimistic view of pre-industrial Britain. Their trilogy *The Village Labourer, 1760–1832* (1911), *The Town Labourer, 1760–1832* (1917) and *The Skilled Labourer, 1760–1832* (1919) were important landmarks in British social history, complemented by *The Rise of Modern Industry* (1925) and *The Age of the Chartists* (1930). Their work has been criticized by left-wing historians for its 'Whiggism' and by Conservative commentators for its sentimental approach to pre-industrial society, but their meticulously researched and documented histories were extensively used as texts in schools in the post-war education movement. *The Village Labourer* is still studied today.

HAMPDEN, SIR EDMUND (?–1628), politician. From Bucks. and a cousin of John HAMPDEN, he was one of 'five knights' (*see also* CORBET, JOHN; DARNELL, THOMAS; ERLE, WALTER; HEVENINGHAM, JOHN) imprisoned by CHARLES I in 1627–8 for refusing to pay a forced loan. He died in prison before the King decided to release the accused.

HAMPDEN, JOHN (1594–1643), politician. A member of an old Bucks. family with an extensive cousinage he combined Puritanism with increasing suspicion of CHARLES I's political intentions. Repeatedly elected to Parliament from 1621, he sprang to prominence in 1627 for refusing to pay the forced loan, Charles's attempt to evade Parliament's refusal to grant taxes; the consequent year's imprisonment did not prevent his resisting, from 1635, the imposition of Ship Money, the renewed royal attempt to raise extra-parliamentary revenue. A natural Commons hero in 1640, he collaborated closely with John PYM in pressing for strong curbs on Charles's power and was one of the 'five members' who escaped the King's attempt at arrest in 1642. On the outbreak of war in 1642 he was an active commander, urging vigorous attack against the royal armies; his death from wounds after a skirmish at Chalgrove Field (Oxon.) was a severe blow to the preservation of consensus on the Parliamentarian side.

HANCOCK, DAME FLORENCE (1893–1974), trade-union leader. One of 14 children of a Wilts. weaver, she went to work in a café when she was 12 for three shillings a week for a 12-hour day. Hancock joined the newly established Workers' Union when she was 14. By then working in a condensed-milk factory, she was appointed its district officer for Wilts. (1917) and Glos. (1918). When the union merged with the Transport and General Workers' Union (TGWU) in 1929 she became women's officer in Bristol, and in 1942 was appointed chief woman officer of the TGWU, campaigning for better pay, better working conditions and childcare facilities for the 200,000 women members, most of whom were unskilled. A member of the General Council of the Trades Union Congress (TUC), she became its third woman President in 1947, having advised the Ministry of Labour during the Second World War.

HANCOCK, THOMAS (1786–1865), inventor. Brother of Walter Hancock, a steam locomotive pioneer, in 1820 he patented india-rubber springs for making clothes more elastic, and a rubber 'masticator', which enabled rubber to be turned into blocks and sheets and thus into convenient shapes for making rubber articles. In the 1830s he collaborated with Charles Macintosh in the manufacture of rubberized waterproof fabrics. The best-known development of this patent was the mackintosh coat. Hancock's rubber patents, including those for cutting rubber and for making vulcanized or hardened rubber, transformed the Victorian rubber industry.

HANCOCK, TONY (1924–68), comedian. After working as a stand-up comic while in the RAF during the Second World War, he made his professional stage début in *Wings* (1946), and his popularity grew with regular appearances in cabaret and pantomime. He moved to radio with the comedy *Educating Archie* (1951), and in 1954 was given his own radio show, *Hancock's Half Hour*, written by Alan Simpson and Ray Galton. The show was an immediate success, making the character of Anthony Aloysius Hancock, the lugubrious pedantic ponderer from Railway Cuttings, East Cheam, Britain's number one comic. In 1961 the series transferred to ITV, but it was never as successful on television. His final years were spent battling against chronic alcoholism, and in 1968 he committed suicide while in Australia attempting a comeback.

HANDEL, GEORGE FREDERICK (GEORG FRIEDRICH) (1685–1759), composer. A native of Halle in Lower Saxony, he had already gained an international reputation through his work in Germany and Italy when, in 1709, he was appointed *Kapellmeister* to the Elector of Hanover, the future GEORGE I. Following his arrival in England in 1711, in advance of his master, he wrote 35 operas in the conventions of Italian *opera seria*, and dominated London opera until the late 1720s. From 1732, with interest in opera waning, he turned to oratorios, usually on biblical and classical themes, among them the *Messiah* (1742). His two major orchestral works, the *Water Music* (*c*. 1717) and *Music for the Royal Fireworks* (1749), were both written for the royal court. He was an active supporter of the Foundling Hospital (*see* CORAM, THOMAS) and staged annual concerts there for its benefit. Unusually for a composer of the period, his work continued to be performed after his death; a series of Handel Commemorations in Westminster Abbey, first staged in 1785, became a musical institution in their own right.

HANDLEY, THOMAS (TOMMY) (1892–1949), comedian. A Liverpool-born entertainer, Handley found his *métier* in radio comedy and achieved fame with ITMA (It's That Man Again), which was broadcast during the Second World War to raise morale: with its stock characters, catch-phrases (e.g. 'Can I do you now, Sir?') and lampooning of the country's wartime bureaucracy with such inventions as the Ministry of Aggravation, it succeeded spectacularly.

HANKEY, SIR MAURICE (1st Baron Hankey) (1877–1963), Royal Marine officer and civil servant. Son of a wealthy Australian grazier, he was educated at the Royal Naval College. After service in the Royal Marine Artillery, in 1903 Hankey transferred to the Naval Intelligence Department, where his carefully reasoned memoranda became models for future generations. An outstanding analyst, Hankey's ability to see defence problems in an imperial context was helped by his Australian antecedents and by his marriage in 1903 to Adeline Smid, a South African. In 1908 Hankey was appointed Assistant Secretary in the Committee of Imperial Defence (CID), and in 1912 was promoted to Secretary. On the outbreak of war in 1914 he was co-opted onto several important committees, inevitably becoming a *de facto* co-ordinator of governmental activity. In the teeth of Treasury and Foreign Office opposition, he was able to formalize his position in 1916 with the formation of the Cabinet secretariat, becoming virtual Chief of Staff to the Prime Minister. By the time he retired in 1938, Hankey's office had become the lynch-pin of the Whitehall administrative system. Brought back into government by Neville CHAMBERLAIN in 1939, Hankey was given a seat in Cabinet by CHURCHILL in 1941, but his support for the use of Bomber Command aircraft to hunt U-boats and his opposition to strategic bombing, led the Prime Minister to remove him in 1942.

HANMER, SIR THOMAS (1677–1746), politician. An MP from 1701, he refused office under Robert HARLEY but became a leading backbencher as Chairman of the Committee on the State of the Nation in 1712. He was among the 'whimsical Tories' of 1713–14, who voted down a commercial treaty with France and for pro-Hanoverian measures. In 1714 he was elected Speaker. Hanmer was offered the Exchequer on the accession of GEORGE I, and again declined office. His sense of independence prevented him from making the most of his opportunities to lead the Tories in George I's reign and in 1727 he retired to his Suffolk estate.

HANNINGTON, WALTER (1896–1966), trade-union official and political activist. Born in London and trained as a toolmaker, this self-taught Marxist became active in the shop stewards' movement during the First World War. He joined the Amalgamated Engineering Union (AEU) and was a founder member of the Communist Party of Great Britain in 1920. In 1921 he set up the National Unemployed Workers' Movement (NUWM) and led a series of demonstrations throughout the early 1920s, being imprisoned for his activities in 1922, 1925–6 and 1932. He organized national 'hunger marches' in 1932, 1934 and 1936 to campaign for improved treatment of the unemployed, and led the opposition to the means test of 1931 (introduced as an emergency measure by which those in receipt of unemployment insurance beyond the statutory six months had to undergo a 'household means test': by the end of 1932 180,000 had been denied unemployment insurance) and the Unemployment Assistance Board legislation of 1935. Although he failed in his larger purpose of politicizing the unemployed on behalf of the Communist Party, he did achieve widespread publicity for their plight. After the NUWM suspended activities in 1939, Hannington returned to trade-union work as a national organizer for the AEU from 1942 to 1951, only retiring in 1961. He wrote *Unemployed Struggles, 1919–1936* (1936), *Ten Lean Years* (1940) and an unfinished autobiography, *Never on Our Knees* (1967).

HANRATTY, JAMES (*c.* 1936–62), judicial victim. Convicted of killing Michael Gregsten, who was with his lover Valerie Storie in a parked car by the A6 (Beds.) in Aug. 1961, Hanratty, a petty criminal of low intelligence, was identified by Storie, who had been raped and shot too: he was hanged in April 1962. Subsequently several people came forward to verify his alibi and after a 30-year fight by his family a police inquiry in 1997 found that he had been wrongly convicted.

HANSARD, THOMAS (1776–1833), parliamentary reporter. Son of Luke Hansard, who had printed House of Commons *Journals* from 1774, he started to print parliamentary debates (the official proceedings of Parliament still bear his name today) from 1803. In 1810 he was imprisoned for libel as the printer of COBBETT's *Parliamentary Debates*.

HANSOM, JOSEPH (1803–82), inventor and architect. He designed Birmingham Town Hall and the Roman Catholic cathedral at Plymouth, but is best remembered for the 'Patent Safety (Hansom) Cab' (a two-wheeled horse-drawn cab accommodating two passengers, with the driver seated behind), which he invented in 1834.

HANSON, JAMES (Baron Hanson of Edgerton) (1922–), entrepreneur. Leaving school early to run his Yorks. family's haulage businesses, Hanson inherited much of the £3 million compensation paid after they were nationalized in 1948 and

emigrated to Canada to set up his own haulage business. In partnership with Gordon WHITE he ran a greetings-card business and then a commercial-vehicle sales and distribution company. This was taken over by the Wiles group in 1965, of which Hanson took control and became Chairman in 1965, renaming it Hanson Trust four years later. His business then concentrated on acquiring, rationalizing and disposing of companies on both sides of the Atlantic, so-called corporate raiding, with Hanson the deal-maker in the UK and White in the USA. Hanson Trust was one of Britain's biggest companies by the end of the 1980s, when its £3.5 billion acquisition of Consolidated Goldfields was the largest takeover in British industrial history. The Hanson star waned in the 1990s, as recession bit and the break-up of large conglomerates became fashionable.

HANWAY, JONAS (1712–86), philanthropist. His father, a victualler for the navy, died when he was a boy. At the age of 19 he went to work for a merchant in Lisbon. Returning to London, he worked for the merchant Robert DINGLEY, for whom he travelled to Persia, publishing an account of his journey. From the 1750s he wrote prolifically on public issues of the day, initially in connection with the crisis surrounding the Jew Bill of 1753, when Tories whipped up public hostility to proposals to ease the naturalization of Jewish immigrants. A number of Russia Co. merchants, including Dingley, interested themselves in social policy questions. Hanway became both a philanthropic activist and a publicist for these concerns. In 1756 he helped to found the Marine Society, designed to apprentice poor boys as sailors, with the object both of providing them with a living and maintaining the stock of seamen. In 1758 he became a Governor of CORAM's Foundling Hospital and helped to found the Magdalen Hospital for Penitent Prostitutes. He campaigned for measures to increase the survival chances of poor children consigned to the care of parish wet-nurses and to protect child chimney-sweeps, the plight of the latter being described in *The Sentimental History of the Chimney Sweepers in London and Westminster* (1785). Other causes included prison reform and the foundation of Sunday schools.

HARALD HARDRAADA (also known as 'The Ruthless') (1015–66), King of Norway (1047–66). A great Scandinavian warrior who set himself up as King of Norway in 1047 after a life of exile and freelance violence. Claiming the English kingdom on the basis of a promise supposedly made by King HARTHACNUT to Harald's predecessor Magnus, he invaded England in 1066. He was defeated by HAROLD II and killed at the Battle of Stamfordbridge.

HARCLAY, ANDREW (1st Earl of Carlisle) (?–1323), soldier. He made his reputation fighting the Scots. On 16 March 1322 he commanded an army loyal to EDWARD II which intercepted rebels led by THOMAS OF LANCASTER crossing the River Ure and defeated them in the Battle of Boroughbridge (Yorks.). On 25 March he was created Earl of Carlisle. Less than a year later, on 3 March 1323, he was executed for treason, the fate which had befallen many of those whom he had beaten at Boroughbridge. Despairing of the King's ability to defend the north he had entered into direct negotiations with ROBERT BRUCE.

HARCOURT, SIR WILLIAM (1827–1904), politician. A Cambridge-educated lawyer by profession, he held office under GLADSTONE as Solicitor General (1873–4), Home Secretary (1880–5) and Chancellor of the Exchequer (1886, 1892–5). Gladstone's natural successor as Liberal Party leader, he would have been Prime Minister but for Queen VICTORIA's preference for Archibald PRIMROSE, Earl of Rosebery. Harcourt's Budget of 1894, which introduced the principle of graduated taxation, indicated the way forward in the financing of social reform.

HARDIE, KEIR (1856–1915), politician. Born illegitimate and in conditions of great poverty in Lanarkshire, Hardie began working in the mines at the age of 10. He attended evening classes, was an avid reader and began to write as a journalist. From 1878 he also became involved in trade unionism and was a major figure in the organization of the Lanarkshire and Ayrshire miners. In 1886 he became Secretary of the Scottish Miners' Federation, in 1887 Chairman of the Scottish Labour Party, and in 1888 contested the mid-Lanark by-election. In 1892 he was elected for West Ham South (London) to become one of the few working-class MPs. He was a major figure in the foundation of the Independent Labour Party in 1893. Although a class-conscious socialist – his cloth cap and tweed coat were important symbols of both his class and his politics – Hardie was anxious to build a political movement with the generally non-socialist (in some cases anti-socialist) trade unions. In 1900 he was instrumental in forming the Labour Representation Committee (LRC) to represent their interests and in 1906 became the Chairman and leader of the Parliamentary Labour Party which succeeded the LRC. Although the Labour Party was not a socialist body it had an important place for the ethical socialism of men like Hardie whose credo was heavily inflected by an austere Christianity, pacifism, devotion to moral respectability (he was characteristically a staunch temperance advocate) and a belief that socialism was ultimately the creed of the whole people bound together in the nation.

HARDING, ALLAN ('JOHN') (1st Baron Harding of Petherton) (1896–1989), soldier. Employed initially as a clerk in the Post Office Savings Bank, Harding volunteered in 1914, was wounded at Gallipoli, and awarded the Military Cross in Palestine. Reluctant to return to his previous life, he secured a regular commission and spent much of the inter-war period in India. Finally promoted to Lieutenant Colonel in July 1939, Harding spent two years in staff appointments in Egypt before he was given command of 7th Armoured Division in Sept. 1942. Badly wounded in Jan. 1943, Harding served as Chief of Staff to ALEXANDER until in March 1945 he commanded XIII Corps in fighting in northern Italy. Harding had just ended a distinguished post-war career as Chief of the Imperial General Staff (1952–5) when he was appointed Governor of Cyprus (1955–8).

HARDING, STEPHEN (?–1134), monk. An Englishman, revered as a saint, he was elected Abbot of Cîteaux in Burgundy in 1108, and played a key role in the formation and initial expansion of the Cistercian order; indeed, he probably wrote the earliest history of the new foundation. More important, he composed the first version of the order's distinctive and influential constitution: the Charter of Charity (*Carta Caritatis*).

HARDINGE, HENRY (1st Viscount Hardinge of Lahore) (1785–1856) Governor General of India. Having spent his career from 1799 in the army, Hardinge was elected to Parliament in 1820 and served as Secretary of State for War under both Wellington (*see* WELLESLEY, ARTHUR) and PEEL. In 1845 he was appointed to India, where he actively promoted expansion into Sikh lands, culminating in the First Sikh War (1845–6). Rather than annexing the Punjab, he engineered a palace coup with effective political control placed in the hands of the British Resident. Elsewhere in India he acted firmly against *suttee* and other offending ritual practices. Retiring in 1848, he had a succession of military appointments. As Commander-in-Chief in succession to Wellington from 1852, he was widely blamed for lack of readiness for the Crimean War.

HARDWICK, ELIZABETH (Countess of Shrewsbury) (*c.* 1520–1608). 'Bess of Hardwick', a Derb. squire's daughter, triumphantly conquered a man's world, acquiring four successively wealthier husbands (Robert Barlow, Sir William Cavendish, Sir William St Loe and George TALBOT, Earl of Shrewsbury), but she met her match in

ELIZABETH I, who frustrated her dynastic plans for her daughter-in-law Arabella STEWART. She outlived Shrewsbury (d. 1590) after an epically quarrelsome marriage, during which she had accused him of adultery with MARY QUEEN OF SCOTS. Besides her husbands' rebuilding of the houses at Chatsworth and Worksop, she transformed the ancestral Hardwick home in Derb., then built an even more spectacular house directly beside it which survives remarkably unchanged. Her talents as sexual politician, estate manager and speculator, industrial investor, loan shark and architectural patron are easier to admire from a safe chronological distance.

HARDWICKE, 1ST BARON AND 1ST EARL OF see YORKE, PHILIP

HARDY, GATHORNE (1st Earl of Cranbrook) (1814–1906), politician. Born in Bradford and educated at Shrewsbury and Oriel College, Oxford, he was called to the Bar in 1840 and elected to Parliament in 1856. He held senior office under DISRAELI, including the Home Office (1867–8) and the War Office (1874–8), where he completed CARDWELL's army reforms. He was also a formidable debater, who gave the Tory front bench weight and bite.

HARDY, OLIVER (originally Hardy Newell Jr) (1892–1957), comedian see LAUREL, STAN

HARDY, THOMAS (1752–1832), radical. Trained as a shoemaker by his grandfather in Stirlings. and having moved to London in 1774, by 1792 he was a prosperous bootmaker in Piccadilly. That year he founded the London Corresponding Society to promote parliamentary reform. The LCS, whose members were largely artisans and working men, was soon communicating with every reform organization in the country and sent a congratulatory address to the French National Convention on the establishment of a republic. The LCS supported the Edinburgh Convention of 1793 and sent Joseph GERRALD and Maurice Margarot as representatives. When the Edinburgh Convention was dissolved the LCS and the similar Society for Constitutional Information planned a London convention to replace it, but Hardy was arrested with HORNE TOOKE and THELWALL and tried for high treason in Oct.–Nov. 1794. Hardy and his comrades were acquitted; he returned to business and after his retirement received an annuity from wealthy radicals.

HARDY, THOMAS (1840–1928), novelist and poet. Born into a stonemason's family, Hardy trained as an architect in Dorchester and London. He published his first novel in 1871. Over the following 24 years Hardy wrote a series of novels in which his characters, based in his native Dorset and adjoining counties, struggle against the indifference of fate. Among the most enduring in the language, they include *Far from the Madding Crowd* (1874), *Tess of the D'Urbervilles* (1891) and *Jude the Obscure* (1894). After the hostile reaction to the latter, Hardy returned to poetry, which some critics now consider his greater achievement. In his fiction he had created a world rooted in the everyday and in observation, often ironic, sometimes symbolic, of his native region, reviving the name Wessex which has since passed back into wide usage.

HARDYNG, JOHN (1378–*c*. 1465), chronicler. After war service against the Scots and French, he was in Scotland (1418–21) on HENRY V's behalf, collecting evidence on English claims over Scotland (and using his considerable antiquarian knowledge to forge supporting documents) as well as information on the best way to invade the country. He wrote a chronicle in English verse, which, in 1457, he presented to HENRY VI and then, six years later, suitably revised in the Yorkist interest, to EDWARD IV. As his invasion maps show, one of the purposes of the chronicle was to urge the Kings to conquer Scotland.

HARE, WILLIAM (*fl.* 1829), murderer see KNOX, ROBERT

HARGREAVES, JAMES (?–1778), inventor. A weaver-carpenter from Blackburn (Lancs.), whose inventive skill encouraged Robert PEEL to employ him to construct an improved carding machine, he devised in the mid 1770s the spinning jenny, which enabled a spinner to produce several threads at once, so beginning the sequence of spinning improvements of the early industrial revolution. Because he had made and sold several before he took out a patent in 1770, the patent was later held by the courts to be invalid. The original jenny was too small for woollen yarn, so John KAY developed an improved model in the 1770s in the factory of his partner Thomas James, in Hockley (Notts.).

HARINGTON, JOHN (1540–1613), nobleman see STUART, LUDOVICK

HARINGTON, JOHN (1561–1612), writer. Cambridge-educated, a wit and favourite godson of ELIZABETH I, who ordered him to translate all Ariosto's *Orlando Furioso* to punish him for translating one lewd tale from it. In 1596 he published pseudonymously *The Metamorphosis of Ajax*, which portentously announced his invention of the water-closet (a jakes); the Queen had to pretend annoyance at its scatalogical satire on various courtiers including Robert DEVEREUX, Earl of Essex. He ingratiated himself with JAMES VI by a tract (1602) supporting his succession, but neither monarch took Harington seriously enough to give him the high office which he craved.

HARLAND, SIR EDWARD (1831–95) and **WOOLF, GUSTAV** (1834–1913), shipbuilders. Born in Scarborough (Yorks.), where his family were friends of George STEPHENSON, Harland began as an engineering apprentice with Robert STEPHENSON & Co. in Newcastle in 1846. He moved to Belfast at the end of 1854 in pursuit of a shipbuilding career. After a few years as manager, Harland bought Hickson's yard with the financial assistance of G. C. Schwabe, whose nephew, the Hamburg-born and Lancs.-trained engineer Gustav Woolf, had recently become Harland's assistant. Schwabe was also instrumental in securing customers for the yard, notably orders from the Bibby and White Star Lines for iron ships. Harland & Woolf, as the firm was known, developed new, more robust shapes for their iron ships; the *Oceanic*, launched in 1870, was the first modern ocean liner. Harland withdrew from active participation in the firm by 1880, but Woolf did not retire until 1906. The firm's great growth in ship-building and engine-making came after 1889, under the control of new partners, William Pirrie and Walter Wilson. Harland & Woolf became one of the dominant employers in Belfast; with the advent of the Civil Rights movement in the 1960s the company's sectarian employment policies were a frequent source of bitterness.

HARLEY, BRILLIANA (née Conway) (?1600–43), letter writer. Third wife of Sir Robert HARLEY, she shared his strong Puritanism; while defending their home, Brampton Bryan Castle (Herefords.), against a Royalist siege in the First English Civil War, she fell ill and died. Her surviving correspondence with her family reveals a fascinating picture of a strong-minded, meticulous and affectionate woman.

HARLEY, EDWARD (2nd Earl of Oxford and Mortimer) (1689–1741), connoisseur. The son of Robert HARLEY, he married Henrietta, heiress of the CAVENDISH dukes of Newcastle, and spent most of the inheritance building up a vast library of books, manuscripts, pictures, medals and curiosities which he opened to his literary and antiquarian friends including POPE, SWIFT and VERTUE. Financial difficulties forced him to sell the Harley estate of Wimpole and place his wife's estates in trust. Most of the library was sold in 1745. His widow employed Vertue to catalogue the manuscript collection, which was sold to the British Museum in 1753. His librarian, William

Oldys, had already copied extracts from the manuscripts and library, which were published as the *Harleian Miscellany*.

HARLEY, EDWARD (3rd Earl of Oxford and Mortimer) (*c.* 1699–1755), politician. The nephew of Robert HARLEY, he inherited his Tory father's latterly High Church sympathies. An MP for Herefs. in 1727, he emerged as one of the most active proponents of reform of legal and other abuses in his party. He founded a Tory club which met at the Cocoa Tree coffee-house in Pall Mall and usually consisted of about 25 senior parliamentary Tories. It appealed to a broader number of MPs than the quasi-Jacobite Loyal Brotherhood of the Duke of Beaufort and came to represent the interests of Country MPs suspicious of the court but loyal to the Hanoverians, organizing them when particular measures or electoral contests demanded. Although not a leader, Harley was good at coalition-building and negotiated with Whigs, including the allies of Prince FREDERICK. In 1741 he succeeded to the title and moved to the Lords, where he remained an exceptionally diligent parliamentarian.

HARLEY, ROBERT (1st Earl of Oxford and Mortimer) *see* essay on page 391

HARMSWORTH, ALFRED (1st Viscount Northcliffe) (1865–1922), newspaper proprietor. Born in Ireland, Harmsworth moved to London as a child and enjoyed a rapid rise in journalism. In 1888, together with his brother Harold HARMSWORTH, he founded his first newspaper, *Answers to Correspondents*, a popular weekly not unlike the trivia and quiz-filled publications of more recent years. Its success prompted the launch of the *Evening News* in 1894 and then the mass market *Daily Mail* in 1896, priced at a halfpenny. That venture led to the launch of the *Daily Mirror* in 1903, with equally rewarding results. Alfred provided the journalistic flair in the partnership, Harold the business sense. Ennobled in 1905, Harmsworth was the first of the 'press barons'. When Associated Newspapers Ltd was incorporated, Harmsworth's next move was to acquire the *Observer* for his stable of titles and finally in 1907 he succeeded in the battle for acquisition of *The Times*. He vehemently attacked ASQUITH and KITCHENER in the First World War in his newspapers; LLOYD GEORGE employed those skills of propaganda in the closing years of the war. Harmsworth was rewarded with a viscountcy for his leadership of the war mission to the USA in 1917. His final years were clouded by heightened megalomania and illness, but he was the greatest newspaperman of the decade around 1900.

HARLEY, ROBERT (1st Earl of Oxford and Mortimer) (1661–1724)
Politician

His grandfather and father were Herefs. gentry, MPs and Puritans. His father conformed to the Anglican Church at the Restoration, but opposed persecuting dissent and distrusted Catholics. Robert was educated by dissenting teachers. He spent his career opposing overweening power in Church and State: this left him uneasily poised between political camps.

The Harleys supported the 1688 Revolution. In 1689 Robert was elected MP, joining his father and their kinsmen the Foleys in a small Whig grouping. Branded a 'Commonwealth's man' and enemy of the Church, his father lost his seat in 1690; Robert survived. In the early 1690s tensions grew between Whigs supportive of the growing power of the post-Revolutionary government, arguably crucial to war against France, and critics who thought the regime overmighty and corrupt. Harley, though no great orator, emerged as leader of the small but fiery group of Country (as against Court) Whigs. He worked with more numerous Country Tories on 'commissions of public accounts' scrutinizing public expenditure, and helped secure the Triennial Act 1694, ensuring elections at least every three years.

In 1696, the dominant Junto Whigs exploited an assassination attempt on WILLIAM III to strengthen their position. Tory loyalties were questioned and they lost local offices; the Commission of Public Accounts was disbanded. The 1698 elections and the ending of the war strengthened the Junto's critics. Harley secured larger-scale army demobilization than the King had wished, and obstructed government fiscal plans.

Accepting the need for concessions, William made Rochester (see HYDE, LAURENCE) and GODOLPHIN ministers, and in 1701 backed Harley as Speaker of the Commons. As such, Harley upheld government on his own terms. He saw through the Act of Settlement, which identified the Hanoverians, as closest Protestant heirs, as next in the line of succession after ANNE but as part of a package which also included provisions for the eventual exclusion of officeholders, including ministers, from the Commons, an attempt to increase the independence of the Commons which would have transformed English government had it been implemented. Though he blocked reviving the Commission of Public Accounts, he encouraged the attack on the Partition Treaties, promoted by William as part of a plan to redistribute power in Europe on the death of the moribund, heirless Spanish King.

Harley was helped by the accession of Anne, who opposed the Junto. Promoting Marlborough (see CHURCHILL, JOHN) and Godolphin, she backed Harley to continue as speaker, recognizing his ability to deliver Commons support, and in 1704 made him Secretary of State. The revival of an aggressive Church Toryism, not to his taste, posed problems of management, though he managed to stop efforts to prevent Dissenters qualifying for public office by 'occasional conformity'. He also blocked attempts to add 'country' provisos to the 1705–6 Regency Bill, a Whig measure, designed to ease Hanoverian accession. His formidable intelligence network (Daniel DEFOE was one agent) helped him secure support for Anglo-Scottish union in 1707. He was aided by a growing Junto Whig element in the ministry, yet he feared their power, and they his. When one of his clerks was shown to be a French spy, he resigned; Henry ST JOHN and other moderate Tories followed him into opposition.

The Junto's miscalculation in persecuting the Tory cleric SACHEVERELL opened the way for his return: in 1710 he became Chancellor of the Exchequer and effective head of the ministry. Prolonged war had drained the government's resources. Harley managed to win financiers' confidence; he also established the South Sea Company, to complement the Bank of England in holding the National Debt. An attempt to assassinate him (1711) prompted the Queen to show confidence by making him Earl of Oxford and Lord Treasurer. When his attempts to secure peace with France alienated the Junto and looked set to capsize in the Lords, she dismissed Marlborough and created new peers to support the measure.

As Lord Treasurer, uncomfortably heavily dependent on Tory support, Oxford had to cope both with Whig recovery and with tensions in Tory ranks. 'Whimsical Tories', pro-Hanoverian and sympathetic to Whig European policies, increasingly voted with the Whigs. He had some success in taming discontented backbench Toryism, and his tentative feelers towards the Pretender, James STUART, have been explained as a strategy for managing Jacobite Tories. Most threatening was the rivalry of St John, put out among other things at having gained no greater a title than Viscount Bolingbroke. Oxford fell when, in July 1714, Anne backed the younger man.

The Hanoverian accession brought vengeful Whigs to power. Oxford was impeached for his part in obtaining the Peace of Utrecht and imprisoned for two years, but finally acquitted. In retirement he began the collection of books and manuscripts now in the British Library, continued by his son (see HARLEY, EDWARD).

Brian W. Hill, Robert Harley, Speaker, Secretary of State and Prime Minister (1988)

HARMSWORTH, HAROLD (1st Viscount Rothermere of Hemsted) (1868–1940), newspaper proprietor. The younger brother of Alfred HARMSWORTH, Harold became the business manager in the partnership which the two founded: his close financial control was legendary. Although Alfred reserved the pick of the journalistic jobs for himself and Harold was initially given responsibility for the firm's papermaking in Newfoundland, Harold also launched his own newspaper in Scotland, the *Daily Record*, then bought out his brother's interest in the *Daily Mail* and finally founded the *Sunday Pictorial*. He controlled the Associated Newspapers group from Alfred's death in 1922 until 1932, but was not a great success as a newspaper executive. Beaverbrook's (*see* AITKEN, MAXWELL) *Daily Express* outstripped the *Mail* after 1933. Rothermere (who had been made a viscount in 1919 for his wartime services) bought the Hulton newspapers from Beaverbrook before selling them on to the BERRY brothers, while he and Beaverbrook had other joint interests. One of the most important press barons of the early twentieth century, Rothermere's support for right-wing causes and his admiration for Hitler and Mussolini made him a figure of notoriety by the end of his life.

HARNEY, GEORGE (1817–97), Chartist and internationalist. Born in Deptford, London, to a working-class family, Harney was radicalized by involvement in the agitation for parliamentary reform (1831–2) and by working as a shop boy for Henry Hetherington, the publisher of the *Poor Man's Guardian* and a leading figure in the 'war of the unstamped' (1830–4), when radicals fought for the freedom of the press from government taxes. As a Chartist, Harney was strongly influenced by James Bronterre O'BRIEN and a strong advocate of armed action against the government. From the mid 1840s he became a key figure in the development of working-class internationalism through the Society of Fraternal Democrats. At the same time a leading socialist, he was close to MARX and Friedrich ENGELS, whom he had known since the mid 1840s. In 1850 his *Red Republican* published the first English translation of the *Communist Manifesto*. By 1852–3, however, Chartism was collapsing as a movement, Harney became estranged from Marx and Engels and own most recent paper, the *Star of Freedom*, closed. Moving to Newcastle in 1853, he was an active advocate of republicanism and internationalism with Joseph COWEN, but by 1855 he went into virtual exile in Jersey (1855–63) and then in the USA (1863–88), returning to England in 1888.

HAROLD I HAREFOOT, King of the English (1037–40). The son of King CNUT and ÆLFGIFU OF NORTHAMPTON, he was initially regent for his brother HARTHACNUT after Cnut's death in 1035. In 1036 he was involved in the killing of the ætheling ALFRED, brother of EDWARD THE CONFESSOR. In 1037, he seized the throne with the aid of his mother and a party of nobles. Little is known about his reign, and he apparently had a colourless or weak character.

HAROLD II GODWINSON (?1020–66), King of the English (1066). The last Anglo-Saxon King of the English and second son of GODWINE, Earl of Wessex. Made Earl of East Anglia in 1043–4, he became undoubtedly the most powerful man in England after King EDWARD THE CONFESSOR when he succeeded to his father's earldom in 1053.

His route to the throne is not clear, since nothing is known of his personal motives. He appears to have been involved in the schemes to bring EDWARD THE EXILE back to England, and in 1064 or 1065 he went (or was sent by King Edward) to Normandy, where he was made to swear an oath in support of the claim to England of Duke William, the future WILLIAM I THE CONQUEROR. In 1065 he acquired the bitter enmity of his brother TOSTIG, Earl of Northumbria, for failing to support him against a rebellion within his earldom. The split within the family was a disastrous one with significant consequences in 1066. The dying King Edward chose Harold as his heir, and he was crowned on 6 Jan. 1066, the day after the Confessor's death.

Government continued to function effectively during Harold's brief reign, but inevitably his chief preoccupations were to unite the nobility and to counter invasion. A judicious marriage gained him the alliance of EDWIN, Earl of Mercia, and of the latter's brother MORCAR, Earl of Northumbria. On 25 Sept. Harold defeated the army of HARALD HARDRAADA, King of Norway, and his brother Tostig at Stamfordbridge (Yorks.), but on 14 Oct. he was himself defeated by Duke William of Normandy at the Battle of Hastings.

Harold's generalship, although courageous and skilful, is open to criticism. After Stamfordbridge he rushed south in an attempt to take William by surprise, leaving some of his army behind, and was himself caught off-guard and forced to fight a long defensive battle with tired troops. The manner of his death towards the end of a bitterly and closely contested engagement, although not a matter of any great historical importance, remains controversial. Was he killed by an arrow through the eye? Interpretations of the crucial scene on the Bayeux Tapestry will always differ.

HARRINGTON, JAMES (1611–77), political writer. Educated at Oxford, he went to the Netherlands and joined the army of Frederick, the exiled Elector Palatine; during the English Civil

Wars, he was Groom of the Bedchamber to CHARLES I. In 1656 he published *The Commonwealth of Oceana*, in which he set out an ideal republican constitution based on limited landholding, much influenced by the writings of Macchiavelli and the example of the Venetian Republic. In 1659, he formed the Rota, a club to discuss the implementation of this scheme (so named because among other proposals it advocated the holding of public offices by rotation). Two years later CHARLES II imprisoned him for sedition.

HARRIOT, THOMAS (1560–1621), mathematician. Oxford-educated, he became a client of Walter RALEIGH working on mathematical problems bearing on navigation, and sailed on the voyage to Raleigh's projected colony of Roanoke (Virginia), writing a detailed account of his observations later published by Richard HAKLUYT (1600). The association with Raleigh cast a cloud over his career under JAMES I, but he continued investigating algebra, astrology and astronomy, his astronomical observations paralleling those of Galileo Galilei.

HARRIS, SIR ARTHUR ('BOMBER') (1892–1984), airman. From an Indian civil service family, in 1909 he went to farm in Rhodesia. After joining the 1st Rhodesian Regiment and taking part in the occupation of German South-West Africa, Harris returned to England (where he had been educated) to join the Royal Flying Corps, flying in anti-Zeppelin patrols and on the Western Front. Joining the RAF in 1919, Harris pioneered the use of air power to control hostile populations on India's North West Frontier and in Iraq, and in 1939 used a more sophisticated version of these tactics to suppress insurgents in Palestine. Appointed Deputy Chief of Staff to PORTAL in 1940, he spent a year in the United States purchasing aircraft and supplies, before returning in 1942 to lead Bomber Command. Harris did not introduce the policy of area bombardment (that had been introduced by Portal in late 1940) but it was under Harris that Bomber Command became strong enough to launch 1,000-bomber raids, to create firestorms in German cities and to kill tens of thousands of civilians in a single night. Believing aerial bombardment alone would defeat Germany, Harris resisted efforts to divert his aircraft to other purposes like maritime reconnaissance or the tactical support of armies and he also sabotaged Portal's efforts to reintroduce precision bombing. Nor did Harris doubt the morality of the systematic destruction of enemy cities, but in 1945 he was the only senior commander not to get a peerage.

HARRIS, FRANK (1856–1931), writer and editor. A Protestant from Co. Galway, Harris travelled to America as a teenager taking a variety of jobs including that of cowboy. On his return to Britain he worked as a journalist, then as editor of a number of publications, the *Evening News* (1882–6), which he made a sensational success, the *Fortnightly Review* (1886–94) and the *Saturday Review* (1894–8), which became one of the most brilliant of London's literary reviews, publishing among others G. B. SHAW (whom Harris advised to turn to drama criticism), WELLS, BEERBOHM and SWINBURNE. He wrote short stories, novels, two plays and biographies of Shaw (1931) and of WILDE (1916), to whom he was a friend and adviser, but he is best known for his scandalous *My Life and Loves* (four volumes, 1922–7), a braggart's view of his own intellectual and sexual prowess.

HARRIS, HOWEL (1714–73), Evangelical. Younger son of a prosperous Brecons. farmer, Harris, a schoolteacher, regularly conducted worship at the family home, Trevecca. He built up a local reputation and attracted followers from elsewhere, whom he organized into Evangelical societies, in effect founding Welsh Calvinistic Methodism. According to WHITFIELD, by 1739 Harris had already founded 30 such societies. In 1751 he quarrelled with his principal colleague Daniel ROWLANDS, dividing Welsh Methodists into two parties. Harris withdrew to Trevecca, preaching daily and in 1752 founding a religious community or 'family' of about 100 members. In later life he was closely allied with Selina HASTINGS, Countess of Huntingdon, who founded her own school for ministers at Lower Trevecca.

HARRISON, FREDERIC (1831–1923), positivist. Educated at Wadham College, Oxford, and a Fellow there from 1854 until he married in 1870, he was called to the Bar in 1858. Originally a High Church Anglican, he was strongly influenced by Richard Congreve at Wadham and became a follower of the positivist doctrines of Auguste Comte. During the 1850s Harrison and E. S. BEESLY and other English positivists became increasingly critical of the worship of Mammon and *laissez-faire* and in this were strongly influenced by the writings of Thomas CARLYLE and John RUSKIN. The hostility to contemporary political economy and the moral values associated with it, together with the prolonged building workers' disputes in London (especially those of 1861–2), drew Harrison and the other positivists towards the organized working class. From the early 1860s Harrison was a regular contributor to labour and radical periodicals, achieving prominence as the prime middle-class intellectual advocate of trade unionism, which he saw not only as the instrument for improving the wages and conditions of labour but also as embodying the highest ideals and purposes of the working class. He was a member of the Royal Commission on Trade Unions (1867–9). With Thomas HUGHES he wrote the minority report, which defended the principles of trade unionism and provided the basis for the trade unions' campaign for full legal recognition of unionism (1871–5). Harrison was also a consistent critic of imperialism and a strong supporter of internationalism. He and Beesly were among the most prominent and eloquent defenders of the Paris Commune (1871). Besides his energetic involvement in social and political affairs, he was also active in legal education and was a prolific writer on historical, literary and political subjects, with a very wide range of friendships within the networks of Victorian cultural and intellectual life.

HARRISON, GEORGE (1943–), musician *see* LENNON, JOHN

HARRISON, JANE (1850–1928), classical scholar. A Fellow of Newnham College, Cambridge, she was Vice-President of the Hellenic Society (1889–96) and later Director of the British School of Archaeology in Rome. She is noted for her original and innovatory application of archaeology and anthropology to the interpretation of Greek religion, a subject formerly confined to literary studies.

HARRISON, JOHN (1693–1776), inventor. Harrison grew up in Lincs. where he trained as a carpenter but taught himself mathematics and became renowned as a clockmaker. The Longitude Act 1714 had provided for a prize of £20,000 to be paid to the person who discovered a means of calculating longitude. Harrison's work on the problem was supported by Edmund HALLEY, but after Halley's death advocates of a purely astronomical method for calculating longitude gained ground and Harrison had trouble claiming his prize, despite the effectiveness of four successive versions of his clocks on board ships. He received half the prize in 1765 but on the condition that he surrendered his clocks and original plans to his chief rival, the Astronomer Royal, Nevil MASKELYNE, who was compiling his *Nautical Almanack* of astronomical calculations. Harrison's method was eventually endorsed by James COOK.

HARRISON, ROBERT (?–?1585), Separatist. A Cambridge-educated Norfolk Puritan, who joined Robert BROWNE in forming a Separatist congregation at Norwich in 1581 and fled with him to the Netherlands the following year. After a quarrel in 1583, they pursued their ideas independently. Harrison produced some Separatist writings, but remains obscure.

HARRISON, THOMAS (1606–60), soldier and politician. He fought for Parliament throughout the First and Second Civil Wars (1642–6, 1648) and in 1646 was elected to the Long Parliament as MP for Wendover; he quickly emerged as a zealous radical, opposing negotiations with CHARLES I and urging his trial. He commanded home forces while Oliver CROMWELL fought in Scotland in 1650–1, and was elected to the Council of State in 1651; he presided over an official commission for missionary work in Wales. He helped Cromwell disperse the Rump Parliament in April 1653 and sat in the 'Barebones' Parliament (*see* BARBON, PRAISE-GOD). His millenarian Fifth Monarchist passions led, however, to a breach with Cromwell and he was cashiered in 1653 and imprisoned in 1655–6 and 1658–9. An obvious target for Royalist anger at CHARLES II's restoration, he refused to flee, and faced his execution for his part in Charles I's death with great courage.

HARRISON, TONY (1937–), poet. He was born and educated in Leeds. His verse translations and adaptations for the theatre and television include *The Oresteia* (1981) and other Greek tragedies and the York Mystery Plays. His rich, vernacular poetry, concerned with the condition of England and class conflict in particular, includes *Earthworks* (1964), *V* (1985), *The Gaze of the Gorgon* (1992) and *Permanently Bard* (1995). A Fellow of the Royal Society of Literature since 1985, he was canvassed as 'the people's' Poet Laureate on the death of Ted HUGHES, though this was not an aspiration which he professed.

HARRISON, WILLIAM (1535–93), historian. A Puritan and millenarian-minded scholar, rector of Radwinter (Essex) from 1559 and Canon of Windsor from 1586. His *Description of England* and translation of a description of Scotland were published in HOLINSHED's *Chronicles* (1577); more ambitious was his attempt to trace the Church of England's role in God's providence through a universal chronology of the world, tracing the fulfilment of biblical prophecy. This formidable work remains in manuscript.

HARRISSON, TOM (1911–76), social anthropologist. Cambridge-educated, Harrisson did fieldwork in Borneo and returned there during the Second World War to assist the resistance to the Japanese invasion. In 1937 he had turned his trained eye on the British way of life, and, with Charles Madge and Humphry Jennings, established a project, Mass Observation, with the aim of bridging the gap between the 'Establishment' view and the opinion of the 'people'. Mass Observation's most famous survey was of Bolton ('Worktown'), and this and the detailed reports which it collected of citizen morale during the Second World War for the Ministry of Information are an unmatchable source for historians of the period.

HARROD, SIR ROY (1900–78), economist. He was a great admirer of KEYNES and wrote a comprehensive if somewhat hagiographic biography. In 1939 he extended Keynes's theoretical framework to investigate the longer-term, dynamic implications of *The General Theory of Employment, Interest and Money*. He developed one of the earliest and most influential models of how economic growth may proceed in advanced capitalist societies. This work had much in common with, but was published independently of, that of the American economist Evsey Domar, and after the Second World War the so-called Harrod–Domar model of growth switched the focus of economics. The model gave primacy to the accumulation of capital and offered a framework for investigating the growth performance of different economies.

HARSNET, SAMUEL (1561–1631), writer and churchman. A Cambridge don, he began rebelling against the Church of England's Calvinist consensus on predestination in the 1590s, and was ordered by Archbishop WHITGIFT not to comment further on the subject after a sermon in 1594. He became chaplain to Richard BANCROFT, however, and went on to be Bishop of Chichester (1609–19) and of Norwich (1619–28) and Archbishop of York (1629–31). His attack on both the Puritan exorcist John Darrell and Roman Catholic exorcists (1603) satirically listed the names of spirits, subsequently borrowed by William SHAKESPEARE in *King Lear*.

HART, SIR BASIL LIDDELL (1895–1970), military strategist. Son of a Methodist minister, educated at Cambridge, he was commissioned in 1914 into the King's Own Yorkshire Light Infantry. After suffering shell-shock and gas poisoning on the Western Front, Liddell Hart, while serving as a training officer, attracted the attention of MAXSE, who employed him to write a new infantry manual. After a short period in the Army Education Corps, Liddell Hart was appointed military correspondent for the *Daily Telegraph* (1925–35) and *The Times* (1935–9), at first giving wide exposure to John FULLER's theories of armoured warfare, but increasingly developing his own ideas, particularly in relation to 'lightning war' and the 'indirect approach'. Closely allied to the unpopular War Minister Hoare Belisha at the outbreak of the Second World War, Liddell Hart lost much influence when the latter left office early in 1940, a loss which he

compounded by his opposition to total war and by his advocacy of a compromise peace with Germany. Inter-viewing and editing the papers of German generals after the war, Liddell Hart quickly recovered his reputation, as masters of armoured operations like Heinz Guderian credited him with influencing the development of 'Blitzkrieg'. An internationally famous military 'guru' by the 1960s, he received from the Israelis title 'the captain who teaches generals', following their use of his theories to achieve victory in the Six Day War in 1967.

HART, H(ERBERT) L(IONEL) A(DOLPHUS) (1907–92), jurist. A barrister who had practised at the Chancery Bar before returning to Oxford to teach philosophy in 1945, he became, with J. L. Austin, central to the development of analytical philosophy there. As Professor of Jurisprudence (1952–68), he wrote a number of works transforming the philosophy of law by its association with social, political and moral theory. Of these the most influential was *The Concept of Law* (1961), which defined law as a nexus of rules that create obligations supported by social pressure required for the maintenance of society.

HARTE, HENRY (?–1557), religious radical. From Kent, he was already singled out as involved in radical (Anabaptist) religious dissent in the 1530s, and by 1550 led a group called 'Freewillers', who opposed mainstream Protestantism's trend towards strict theories of predestination (*see* CALVIN, JOHN) and who generally deplored theological dogmatism. He published two theological works during EDWARD VI's reign, and was imprisoned by MARY I, arguing bitterly with Protestant leaders in gaol, but by the time of his death he had been released.

HARTHACNUT (?1019–42), King of the Danes (1028–42) and of the English (1040–2). Son of King CNUT and his second wife EMMA, he was clearly intended to be Cnut's successor in both Denmark and England after the latter died in 1035. The military threat to Denmark from King Magnus of Norway, however, prevented him from establishing himself in England, and allowed HAROLD I HAREFOOT to seize the kingdom. Harthacnut's plans to invade England in 1040 were rendered unnecessary by King Harold's death. Harthacnut's own short reign was notable only for a number of brutal acts and for the invitation made to return to England to his half-brother EDWARD THE CONFESSOR, which led in 1042 to the restoration of a descendant of the Wessex dynasty.

HARTINGTON, MARQUESS OF *see* CAVENDISH, SPENCER

HARTLEY, DAVID (1705–57), philosopher. The son of a poor Yorks. vicar, he was educated at Cambridge but resigned his fellowship at Jesus on doctrinal grounds, taking up medicine as a career. In 1749 he published *Observations on Man, his Frame, his Duty and his Expectations*. Hartley saw the mind and body as a co-ordinated system where each could influence the other. He followed LOCKE in placing emphasis on individual human experience as the principal means of discovering knowledge but placed Locke's ideas in a Christian context. Hartley's study of the nervous system identified seven classes of pleasures and pains: sensation, imagination, ambition, self-interest, sympathy, theopathy (the contemplation of God) and the moral sense. The first four were unworthy in themselves but were constrained by the latter three.

HARTLIB, SAMUEL (*c*. 1599–*c*. 1670), writer. An energetic Anglo-German scholar whose optimistic millenarianism (the belief in a thousand-year rule of Christ with his saints on earth) fuelled his scientific and statistical interests. He sought refuge in England *c*. 1628 but, unlike Jan COMENIUS, whose writings he promoted, he stayed throughout the Civil Wars of the 1640s and prospered. His intellectual circle included John MILTON, and Oliver CROMWELL granted him an official pension. His proposals for agricultural, welfare and educational reforms and a nationwide news service were largely unoriginal and had little immediate effect, but they aroused much interest.

HARTNELL, NORMAN (1901–79), couturier. The son of a grocer, Hartnell left Cambridge to work in the fashion business. In 1923 he opened his own showroom in Mayfair and in 1927 had his first Paris show. Overcoming the disbelief that the British could make a contribution to the world of fashion, Hartnell was a success in the USA, designed glittering dresses for stars and in 1947 was invited to make the wedding dress for Princess Elizabeth and the robes which she wore at her coronation as Queen ELIZABETH II in 1953.

HARVEY, WILLIAM (1578–1657), medical writer. After gaining his Cambridge BA in 1597, he studied at Padua, Europe's foremost medical faculty, where he became interested in the problem of the circulation of the blood. He acquired a Cambridge MD in 1602, then practised in London. Seven years later he became physician to St Bartholomew's Hospital and in 1615 began anatomical lectures, during which, for the first time in medical history, he outlined the true circulation of the blood, illustrated by dissections. He quickly gained a Europe-wide reputation, which earned him honour under the various regimes of the 1650s despite his position as physician-in-ordinary to CHARLES I while Oxford was the royal capital during the First Civil War (1642–5). He had previously been physician extraordinary to JAMES I. He also made important investigations in embryology.

HARVEY-JONES, SIR JOHN (1924–), businessman and pundit. Harvey-Jones went into the navy at the age of 13, and stayed there until 1956, specializing in submarines and intelligence work. Thereafter he joined ICI as a work study officer. Chairman of the petrochemicals division by 1970, he was appointed Chairman of the whole company in 1982. The traumatic losses of the previous years were turned into £1 billion profits by 1984–5. Harvey-Jones retired in 1987, having radically restructured the company by dividing it in two, the traditional bulk commodities and the specialized growth areas. He then became a well-known business pundit through publications and television appearances: his outspoken views, untidy hair and loud ties have made him a familiar figure of modern business.

HASILRIG (OR HESILRIGE), ARTHUR (?–1661), politician. Baronet and fierce opponent of William LAUD and Thomas WENTWORTH, Earl of Strafford, he was one of the 'five members' whom CHARLES I attempted to arrest (1642), and he became a distinguished Parliamentary military commander. Resigning his commission under the provisions of the Self-Denying Ordinance in 1645, he emerged as a leading Independent (supporter of the army and opponent of the Presbyterian peace party) in the Commons. Despite avoiding sitting as a judge at Charles I's trial (Jan. 1649) he took up military commands once more and was a constant member of the successively remodelled Council of State, the executive body in the Republic's government. Angered by Oliver CROMWELL's dissolution of the Rump Parliament in 1653, he opposed Cromwell becoming Lord Protector, and helped to engineer the fall of Richard CROMWELL in 1659. His habitual political clumsiness proved no match for George MONCK and, after the restoration of CHARLES II, he was arrested; he died in the Tower of London after being reprieved from execution.

HASLETT, DAME CAROLINE (1895–1957), engineer. Daughter of a Sussex railway-signal fitter, Haslett worked as a secretary in an engineering firm, transferred to the works side and, during the First World War, was able to gain sufficient experience to qualify as an engineer and then as an electrical engineer. She founded the Women's Engineering Society in 1919 and was for many years its secretary. She edited *The Electrical*

Handbook for Women and *Household Electricity*, and in 1924 founded the Electrical Association for Women, which grew to be a national organization. Haslett was in the vanguard of persuading employers and professional institutions that women engineers were worth the same opportunities as men.

HASTINGS, LADY ELIZABETH (1682–1739), intellectual and philanthropist. The daughter of the 24th (7th Hastings) Earl of Huntingdon and Elizabeth Lewis, heiress of the Ledstone estate (Yorks.), she inherited the estate when her brother died in 1708 and lived there unmarried, supervising the upbringing of her stepsisters. Lady Elizabeth used her wealth to promote the scheme of her friend Mary ASTELL for a religious and intellectual retreat for women. Her educational charities included George BERKELEY's proposed college in Bermuda. She also helped provide an environment for the development of Methodism through her support for the young John WESLEY and for her half-sister Margaret's marriage to the Methodist Benjamin Ingham. These contacts helped to set the scene for the Evangelical conversion of her stepbrother's wife Selina HASTINGS, Countess of Huntingdon.

HASTINGS, LADY FLORA (1807–39), courtier. Appointed in 1832 to the household of the Duchess of Kent, mother of the future Queen VICTORIA, she soon found herself at the heart of the battle between the Duchess and her daughter. A Tory, mistrusted by Victoria as by her Prime Minister, Lord Melbourne (*see* LAMB, WILLIAM), she was by Jan. 1839 clearly unwell. Pregnancy was suspected and the father was rumoured to be the most scheming member of the Kent entourage, Sir John Conroy. Hastings finally agreed to be medically examined by the royal physician, who pronounced her a virgin and not with child. The Hastings family were outraged at the slur on their kinswoman's reputation: but the rumours persisted and the 'Flora Hastings affair' got into the press. On 5 July 1839 she died: the post-mortem revealed a tumour on the liver. Public opinion was outraged at the Queen's callous treatment and Victoria herself felt remorse about the partisan speed with which she had judged the morals of her mother's 'amiable lady'.

HASTINGS, FRANCIS (4th Baron Moira and 1st Marquess of Hastings) (1754–1826), Governor General of India. Distinguished in his military service during the War of American Independence, Hastings was active in politics from 1781 as an MP and subsequently a peer; at first an ally of PITT THE YOUNGER, he joined the Whig opposition after 1783. Appointed as both Governor General and army Commander-in-Chief in India (1812), his aim was 'to render the British paramount in effect, if not declaredly so'. His forward policy was pursued through agreement with the Maratha chiefs, war with Nepal and the Pindari War. The first Governor General to refuse to recognize the Mughal emperor's authority, he saw the East India Co. achieve control of two-thirds of India. Censured by the company for his expansionist policies, he continued to promote British trade and security: Ceylon was occupied in 1819, trade was opened with Thailand in 1822. Hastings left in 1823 for his final post as Commander of Armed Forces in Malta.

HASTINGS, HENRY (20th [3rd Hastings] Earl of Huntingdon) (*c.* 1536–95), politician. Earl from 1560; his position as trusted cousin of and possible heir to ELIZABETH I made him an appropriate guardian for MARY QUEEN OF SCOTS (1569–70). From 1572 to his death he was Lord President of the Council of the North, proving an effective royal agent as a Midlands outsider to northern affairs, and doing much to break the power of northern Catholic landowners. A strong Puritan, he promoted radically minded clergy wherever he had influence.

HASTINGS, SELINA (née Shirley) (Countess of Huntingdon) (1707–91), Evangelical. A younger daughter of the 2nd Earl Ferrers, she married Theophilus Hastings, 26th Earl of Huntingdon, in 1728, and was converted to Methodism by her sister-in-law, Lady Margaret Hastings (*see* HASTINGS, LADY ELIZABETH), but she leaned towards Calvinism rather than the Arminianism of the WESLEY brothers. She played an important part in spreading Evangelical ideas in aristocratic circles. As a peeress, she could appoint as many chaplains as she wished (WHITEFIELD became one in 1747), and in this way was able to shield many clergy whose beliefs might otherwise have made their position difficult. Her 'Connexion' grew gradually from her first chapel in Brighton in 1761; others followed, e.g. in Bath, Tonbridge and London, all registered as Dissenting chapels. In 1768 Trevecca House, near Howel HARRIS's religious community, was set up as a seminary for her ministers. After her death, the Connexion was directed by Lady Anne Erskine, and it still exists as a small independent Church.

HASTINGS, WARREN *see* essay on page 398

HASTINGS, WILLIAM (1st Baron Hastings) (*c.* 1430–83), royal servant. He was EDWARD IV's most trusted political adviser and Lord Chamberlain throughout his reign, whose support was crucial

continued on page 399

HASTINGS, WARREN (1732–1818)
First Governor General of British India

Of old gentry stock (a source of pride), he was educated at Westminster, then found a place as a 'writer' in the East India Co. In 1750 Hastings set sail for Calcutta, like Bombay and Madras a company trading base. The company depended on co-operation from the Mughal administration and Indian businessmen for its trade. Hastings learnt both Persian and Urdu.

The Mughal empire was fragmenting into warring successor states. Hastings witnessed the struggle between successive nabobs (local rulers) of Bengal and the British, initiated by one nabob's attack on Calcutta, where British residents were imprisoned in the notorious Black Hole. CLIVE's victory at Plassey and the removal of the nabob resolved the matter until the British fell out with and overthrew the next nabob. Hastings acquired military and diplomatic experience, and married a Black Hole victim's widow.

Clive believed that British success in India depended on threats and force. In 1757 he left, however, and when the new nabob came in for criticism, Clive's more conciliatory successor, Vansittart, and Hastings both took the nabob's side; conflict reignited, the British restored the former nabob, and Clive returned to sort things out. Hastings resigned and returned to England, where he stayed until 1769. When asked to join the Council in Madras, then in conflict with HYDER ALI in nearby Mysore, he accepted. There, as he saw it, the British were again undermining Indian authority, while London-based directors showed undue 'partiality to the military'.

In 1771 his supporters on an increasingly politicized Court of Directors secured him the job of Governor of Bengal. In London, tales of abuse in India were gaining ground; Hastings was charged to investigate company staff misdeeds. In his view the British should take more power but construct a system conformable to 'the original constitution of the Mogul empire', improving on what Indian government had become. Hastings reordered the nabob's household, tried to reduce tax burdens on peasants, lengthened leases, rationalized and reduced tolls and constructed a new system of civil and criminal courts. Hastings wished to restore much of the administration that had fallen into British hands to Indians when suitable men had been trained. Meanwhile, he set Brahmin pundits to work codifying traditional law as a basis for legal practice.

In 1773, NORTH's Regulating Act created the new post of Governor General of the disparate territories of British India. Hastings was appointed; his new colleagues followed in 1774.

Ironically, they shared his ideals – respect for Indian ways, government without corruption, no unnecessary force – yet claimed that he contravened these. In 1776 their critical reports persuaded the Directors to recall him, but the shareholders countermanded the order.

From 1777 Hastings was drawn into major fighting. He first allied with other Indian states against the Mahrattas, a warrior group in western and central India, threatening Bombay. News that the French had allied with American rebels necessitated an attack on their Indian bases. The situation worsened when Hyder Ali again turned on the British in the south. Remarriage, to a German divorcée, brought Hastings private happiness, but critical colleagues and the demands of war made him increasingly autocratic, reckless in using power yet self-righteous, blaming the war on other British presidencies. He was open to charges of war-mongering, coercion of footdragging Indian allies and connivance at corruption. The fall of the North ministry and end of the American War of Independence freed Parliament to consider Indian affairs. These especially engaged Edmund BURKE, whose chief informants were among Hastings's critics. Burke's reforming 1783 India Bill embodied a swingeing indictment of Hastings's rule.

Finding his authority undermined, and his wife depressed, Hastings resigned and came home. Hoping that the loss of Burke's Bill, and rise of PITT THE YOUNGER would safeguard his reputation, he was dismayed to find Pitt also critical. In 1786 Burke launched a campaign to impeach him. Staunch in his own defence, Hastings came across as arrogant, tainted by the despotic ways of the Orient. To his mortification, the impeachment went through, supported by Pitt. Trial in the Lords began in 1788, lasting seven years. Some testified to his character: his generally critical successor CORNWALLIS reported that he was esteemed and respected by Indians. Acquitted in 1795, Hastings thenceforth lived quietly in the Cotswolds.

The charges against him had some substance, but are generally agreed to have been overdrawn. He was unfortunate to hold power at a time of rising public expectations: conceiving himself to be a reformer, he seemed to his critics to be still stuck in old barbaric ways. He was also to some extent a victim of Burke's obsession with establishing the superior virtue of the Whigs. In the last years of his life, enthusiasm for Wellington's (see WELLESLEY, ARTHUR) efforts in India led to a re-evaluation of Hastings's achievements

Keith Feiling, Warren Hastings (1966)

in helping Edward to recover the throne in 1471. In 1483, after Edward's death, Hastings took an active part in the anti-Woodville movement (see ELIZABETH WOODVILLE) but on 13 June he was arrested and summarily executed on the orders of Richard of Gloucester (the future RICHARD III), presumably because he had (or would have) opposed the plan to depose EDWARD V.

HATTERSLEY, ROY (Baron Hattersley) (1932–), politician. He was elected MP for the Sparkbrook division of Birmingham in 1964 and remained the constituency's MP until his retirement from the House of Commons in 1997. A junior minister during Harold WILSON's government in the late 1960s, he was Secretary of State for Prices and Consumer Protection (1976 9). He played a vital role in ensuring the continuity of the social democratic tradition within the Labour Party during the 1980s after much of the right wing of the party split off to form the breakaway Social Democratic Party in 1981. At the time the left, under Tony BENN, was in the ascendancy in the party and Hattersley's staunch support for institutions such as NATO and the EEC was unfashionable. But he stuck to his principles, and after the electoral defeat in the 1983 election on a Bennite programme of unadulterated 'socialism' the tide began to turn. That autumn, Neil KINNOCK was elected leader and Hattersley his deputy on what was called the 'dream ticket'. Hattersley thereafter played a vital but often understated role in the gradual overhaul of Labour's policies and presentation that would transform the party into New Labour by the mid 1990s. His hopes of gaining office again were dashed by the election defeat of 1992 and both he and Kinnock resigned as leaders. Thereafter, Hattersley increasingly turned to writing and produced a series of acclaimed memoirs, novels and articles. Remaining remarkably consistent in his political views, he has become a critic from the left of New Labour.

HATTON, SIR CHRISTOPHER (c. 1540–91), politician. Son of a Northants. gentleman, Hatton won ELIZABETH I's favour after being made a gentleman pensioner in 1564; in 1577 he was knighted and made Vice-Chamberlain of the Household and Privy Councillor. His relations with rival favourites were never easy, particularly with Walter RALEIGH, although he and Robert DUDLEY, Earl of Leicester, contrived to remain friends despite differences of outlook on policy and religion. He urged punishment of MARY QUEEN OF SCOTS after investigating Anthony BABINGTON's plot, and he was among those nerving the Secretary, William DAVISON, to dispatch her death warrant (1587). Elizabeth's anger at this abrupt end to her hesitations over the execution was diverted to Davison and, soon afterwards, Hatton

became Lord Chancellor. The appointment was based on his courtly career, but his nickname 'the Dancing Chancellor' has obscured the reality of a highly astute politician, particularly important for backing Archbishop John WHITGIFT's drive for conformity in the Church, and for patronizing conformist clerics such as Richard BANCROFT.

HAUGHEY, CHARLES (1925–), Irish politician. As Fianna Fáil member of the Dáil for North Dublin, Haughey served as Minister for Justice (1961–4), Agriculture (1964–6) and Finance (1966 70), and was seen as one of a new generation of young Fianna Fáil leaders. He was one of several contenders to succeed Sean LEMASS (his father-in-law), but stood down in favour of a compromise candidate, Jack LYNCH. In 1970 he was forced to resign from the Cabinet, and was subsequently tried but acquitted on charges of smuggling arms to nationalists in Northern Ireland. Haughey remained within Fianna Fáil and became a focus for discontent with Lynch and his deputy, George Colley. Minister for Health (1977–9), when Lynch resigned in 1979, Haughey defeated Colley for the leadership, but a large minority within the party continued to see Haughey as untrustworthy. While talking of austerity to meet the growing financial crisis he engaged in further public spending, but was narrowly defeated in the 1981 General Election. When Garrett FITZGERALD's coalition fell early in 1982 Haughey headed a minority Fianna Fáil government, but this fell in Nov. 1982 after a series of scandals and internal party rows, and a Fine Gael and Labour coalition was returned to office. In opposition Haughey pursued a populist line, attacking financial cutbacks, allying with Catholic groups to oppose Fitzgerald's 'constitutional crusade' and denouncing the Anglo-Irish Agreement as a betrayal of republicanism; this led to the secession of five Fianna Fáil deputies, led by Desmond O'Malley, who formed the Progressive Democrats as a free-enterprise party committed to social liberalism. In 1987 Haughey regained power but failed to win an overall majority; he implemented spending cutbacks more stringent than those which he had attacked in opposition, and continued to operate the Anglo-Irish Agreement and security policies which he had branded as anti-Republican. In 1989 he tried to win an overall majority but was forced to enter a coalition with the Progressive Democrats in order to retain power. This breach with long-standing Fianna Fáil hostility to coalitions alienated many of his supporters, and after further scandals and concessions to the Progressive Democrats he was forced to resign early in 1992. Haughey attracted passionate loyalty from supporters, while opponents hated him intensely; admirers praised his flair for the grand gesture and gave him credit for the economic recovery of the 1990s, while critics claimed that these policies were forced on him and that his irresponsible behaviour was the cause of many of the original problems. In 1998–9 long-standing rumours about his financial dealings were confirmed by revelations that he had received large sums of money from prominent businessmen.

HAVELOCK, SIR HENRY (1795–1857), soldier. Following the collapse of his father's fortune and consequently his own plans for studying law, Havelock was commissioned into the 95th regiment in 1815. He transferred to India, where he fought in the Burmese War (1824–6), the campaigns in Afghanistan (1839–42), the First Sikh War (1845–7) and the Persian War (1856–7). Becoming a Baptist in 1829, Havelock set up army Bible-reading and temperance societies, and encouraged soldier education: his men became known as 'Havelock's Saints'. Promotion remained slow: he eventually got a majority without purchase in 1843 and a lieutenant colonelcy in 1854. In 1857 the 62-year-old Havelock was preparing to retire when mutiny broke out in the Bengal army. On 7 July, taking command of only 1,000 men, among whom were the 78th Highlanders, Havelock fought his way through central India to reach besieged Lucknow on 25 Aug. As news of Havelock's march reached Britain he became a national hero, *in absentia* was promoted Major-General and created a baronet with a pension of £1,000 a year. He died of cholera four days after Lucknow was relieved by Sir Colin CAMPBELL, and became a potent symbol in the struggle to reform the army's system of promotion.

HAW HAW, LORD *see* JOYCE, WILLIAM

HAWKE, EDWARD (1st Baron Hawke) (1705–81), admiral. Son of a barrister, he entered the navy aged about 15. At the Battle of La Rochelle in 1747 he captured 10 of the 12 French ships, and was knighted. An Admiral from 1757, he mounted several successful campaigns in the Seven Years War. Hawke's greatest victory was at Quiberon Bay, where during 20 and 21 Nov. 1759 an entire French fleet was destroyed or damaged, ending France's pretensions to naval supremacy. He received a pension of £1,500 a year. The jealousy of his colleagues and politicians precluded further triumphs, but he was First Lord of the Admiralty (1766–71).

HAWKESBURY, BARON, 1ST *see* JENKINSON, CHARLES; **2ND** *see* JENKINSON, ROBERT

HAWKING, STEPHEN (1942–), theoretical physicist. Hawking studied physics at Oxford and researched the general theory of relativity at Cambridge, where he was appointed Lucasian Professor of Mathematics in 1980. Since 1962 he has suffered from a rare and progressive motor neuron disease but has risen to become one of the world's leading theoretical physicists. His research on Einstein's general theory of relativity led to his work on space-time 'singularities' (infinitely small and dense regions of space-time where the laws of classical physics break down), frequently pursued in collaboration with Roger PENROSE. In the early 1970s he showed that black holes and the universe at the time of the Big Bang are singularities, and, paradoxically, that black holes, regions from which light cannot escape, can emit electromagnetic radiation. Hawking's monumental project to produce a quantum theory of gravity, a theory that would incorporate all the fundamental forces of nature, is ongoing. He is most widely known for *A Brief History of Time* (1988), a best-selling account of the origins and fate of the universe.

HAWKINS, SIR JOHN (1532–95), sailor. Son of a Plymouth merchant, from the 1560s Hawkins was voyaging to Africa. In 1562–3 he first began capturing or purchasing people in Sierra Leone to sell them as slaves across the Atlantic in the Spanish Caribbean settlements. He soon clashed with the Spanish and Portuguese colonial authorities, since foreigners were forbidden to trade with their colonies, and in 1568 a fierce skirmish with Spanish forces at San Juan de Ullua (Honduras) marked an early step in the breakdown of Anglo-Spanish relations. Soon he was co-operating with his younger cousin, Francis DRAKE, in anti-Spanish schemes. From 1577 he was a naval administrator, and seems to have been responsible for introducing a new type of warship and for other reforms. He was second-in-command against the 1588 Spanish Armada and was knighted as a result. His 1590s voyages were less successful and both he and Drake died during the course of the last, an attempted attack on the West Indies. His personal bravery, honesty and competence, and his practical steps to help sick and aged sailors, can never efface his part in initiating the English slave trade.

HAWKINS, SIR JOHN (1719–89), music historian and lawyer. The son of a London carpenter, he was largely self-educated, qualifying as an attorney in 1742. He also studied music and played as an amateur in several concerts. His friends included HANDEL, PEPUSCH and BOYCE, and he accumulated a large library including a number of musical works. He retired from legal practice in 1759 (although he served as a Justice of Peace, for which he was knighted), devoting much of his time to researching his *General History of* *the Science and Practice of Music* (five vols, 1776). Although praised for its erudition, the work lacked formal structure and its emphasis on sixteenth-century and seventeenth-century composers offended believers in progress and was diametrically opposed to the views of Charles BURNEY, whose own history came out in the same year. Burney began a campaign against Hawkins, whose sales declined, although from a historian's point of view the strengths of the two authors complement each other.

HAWKSMOOR, NICHOLAS (1661–1736), architect. As clerk to Christopher WREN from the age of 18, Hawksmoor became intimately associated with the official style and Baroque architecture of the later seventeenth century. He worked on Chelsea and Greenwich hospitals, and helped Wren rebuild St Paul's. After Wren died, Hawksmoor became a major architect in his own right and a collaborator-cum-assistant to VANBRUGH, notably on projects like Castle Howard and Blenheim Palace. Hawksmoor's feeling for the grandeur of ancient Rome, and his often idiosyncratic amalgamation of features into a powerful whole, is seen to great effect in the churches which he designed as part of the plan to build 50 new churches in London (1711). In the event only 12 were built, of which Hawksmoor, as surveyor to the Commissioners, designed six himself, including St George's, Bloomsbury (1716–30), and Christ Church, Spitalfields (1714–29).

HAWKWOOD, SIR JOHN (?–1394), mercenary. He was commander of a company of professional soldiers, the White Company, most of whom were (like him) English veterans of the Hundred Years War. From 1361 they fought for whichever Italian power had them under contract (*condotta*), but, more than most *condottieri*, Hawkwood enjoyed a reputation for honesty and reliability. From 1380 he fought almost exclusively for Florence: Uccello's equestrian memorial to him can still be seen in the cathedral there.

HAWORTH, SIR WALTER NORMAN (1883–1950), chemist. Haworth began research into carbohydrates at St Andrews University in 1912 and continued this work as Professor of Chemistry at the universities of Durham (1920–5) and Birmingham (1925–48), where he and his co-workers conducted chemical investigations into the molecular structure of polysaccharides such as cellulose and starch. In 1932 they announced that they had determined the structure of and synthesized vitamin C, which made possible the mass-production of vitamin C and led to Haworth sharing the 1937 Nobel Prize for Chemistry with Paul Karrer.

HAWTREY, SIR RALPH (1879–1971), economist. He read mathematics at Cambridge. Between 1904 and 1945 he worked at the Treasury and was Price Professor of International Economics at the Royal Institute for International Affairs (1947–52). One of the group of British economists who wrote extensively on monetary theory in the 1920s and improved understanding of the interaction of money, the banking system and interest rates, he also made major contributions to clarifying the operation of central banks in his *The Art of Central Banking* (1932). Originally he was wedded to the pre-Keynesian 'Treasury view' of fiscal policy; it suggested that any increases in public spending would simply drive up the rate of interest and crowd out private spending, so that public works were dismissed as self defeating as a way of dealing with unemployment. Later he changed his ideas but always remained a critical Keynesian (*see* KEYNES, J. M.).

HAY, JOHN (2nd Marquess of Tweeddale) (1645–1713), politician. Having supported the 1688–9 Revolution, he became one of the leaders, along with Roxburghe (*see* KER, JOHN) of the Squadrone Volante group of politicians in the Scottish Parliament during ANNE's' reign and was Queen Anne's Commissioner to Parliament when Andrew FLETCHER's Act of Security 1704 was passed. Tweeddale persuaded Anne to accept the Act because without it Parliament would not grant the 'cess' or land tax. With Roxburghe, Tweeddale led the Squadrone into voting for the Anglo-Scottish Parliamentary Union of 1707 as the best way of preserving the Scottish Church and State while gaining the needed access to English markets.

HAY, JOHN (4th Marquess of Tweeddale) (?–1762), politician. He was a grandson of John HAY, 2nd Marquess, and an ally of CARTERET. The office of Secretary of State for Scotland was revived for him in 1742 in an attempt to provide a counterweight to the 'management' of Scotland by the CAMPBELL brothers, the Duke of Argyll and the Earl of Ilay. But he proved ineffective and was unable to organize resistance to the Jacobite rebellion in 1745, leading to the permanent suspension of the Scottish secretaryship. There would be no Cabinet minister to deal with exclusively Scottish affairs until the 1880s, and no Secretary of State until the 1920s.

HAYEK, FRIEDRICH VON (1899–1992), economist. One of the founders of the Austrian school of economics, over a period of more than 60 years he propounded his belief in the efficacy of capitalism, individualism and free markets. His ideas were important in the thinking of the New Right in Britain in the 1970s and he was sometimes referred to as one of Margaret THATCHER's 'gurus'. He became Professor of Economics at the London School of Economics in the 1930s but emigrated to America in the late 1940s. He was awarded the Nobel Prize for Economic Science in 1974.

HAYMAN, FRANCIS (1708–76), painter. He won acclaim in the 1730s for his naturalistic theatrical scene-paintings in London. His first major commission came from Jonathan TYERS, for whom in 1741–2 he executed paintings for the booths at Vauxhall Gardens depicting country festivals and children's games as well as theatrical scenes. A friend of HOGARTH and an active promoter of British art, in 1746 he instituted the annual dinner at the Foundling Hospital, on the anniversary of the landing of WILLIAM III, to celebrate the union of liberty and the arts. After the Seven Years War he painted a further series for Vauxhall Gardens celebrating Britain's triumphs. He was one of the first 40 Royal Academicians when they seceded from the Society of Artists in 1768, and served as librarian from 1771 until his death.

HAYS, MARY (1760–1843), writer. She was educated at the Dissenting academy in Hackney and wrote a pamphlet defending freedom of worship which brought her into contact with Mary WOLLSTONECRAFT and William GODWIN. Her radical novel *Emma Courtney* (1796) was notorious in its depiction of a heroine who actively pursues the man she loves. Hays continued to write on behalf of women and compiled a six-volume *Female Biography* (1803) with entries for 300 distinguished historical women; her career then declined and she turned to writing moral works for the poor.

HAYWOOD, ELIZA (née Fowler) (1693–1756), novelist. Daughter of a London tradesman, she was by far the most prolific woman novelist of the early eighteenth century. Her first novel, *Love in Excess* (1719), which went into four editions in five years, recounted the amorous adventures of a rake. She and her clergyman husband separated in 1720 and she turned to writing for and performing on the stage. After POPE attacked her in the *Dunciad*, she wrote anonymously between 1728 and 1744, concentrating on accessible popular romantic fiction, but also political satire such as the *Adventures of Eovaii, Princess of Ijaveo* (1736) which denounced Robert WALPOLE and the political and social settlement. From 1744 to 1746 Haywood edited the *Female Spectator*, a periodical dealing with issues of interest to women.

HAZLITT, WILLIAM (1778–1830), essayist. One of the most influential essayists and critics of the early nineteenth century, in terms of both literary style and thought, Hazlitt acquired strong liberal views from his Unitarian upbringing. His first writings were largely political, including support for both the French Revolution and Napoleon, critiques of MALTHUS and other political economists, and character studies of BURKE, Charles James FOX and others in *The Eloquence of the British Senate* (1807). Thereafter he turned increasingly to literary essays and criticism, contributing to periodicals such as the *Edinburgh Review* and publishing collections of essays in *Table Talk* (1821–2) and *The Spirit of the Age* (1825). He had a tempestuous personal life, with two failed marriages separated by a period of obsessive love that threatened his sanity and his livelihood.

HEAL, SIR AMBROSE (1872–1959), designer. He studied at the Slade School of Art and was apprenticed to a cabinet-maker before joining the family firm in 1893. Initially influenced by, and contributing to, the arts and crafts design idiom, by the 1930s Heal's work was to be in the forefront of simple modern design which offered the British public an alternative to the reproduction furniture to which it seemed wedded.

HEALEY, DENIS (Baron Healey of Riddlesden) (1917–), politician. The best leader Labour never had, Healey's natural political home was the ATTLEE government of 1945–51, with its mixture of state intervention at home and support for NATO abroad; his robust defence of these positions would win him many enemies at a crucial time in his career. He entered the Commons at a by-election in 1952, gravitating naturally to the Gaitskellite (*see* GAITSKELL, HUGH) rather than the Bevanite (*see* BEVAN, ANEURIN) wing of the party; his vocal support for the British nuclear deterrent made him a natural enemy of the Labour left, a position he enjoyed. As Defence Secretary in Harold WILSON's government (1964–70) he found himself faced with the realities of Britain's position as a world power in sharp decline and with an economic crisis. His instinct, like Wilson's, was to preserve Britain's commitments east of Suez but after 1967 he presided over Britain's withdrawal from the Persian Gulf, Aden and its other eastern bases.

He was Chancellor of the Exchequer under Wilson and then CALLAGHAN (1974–9), where he once again had to face the harsh realities of Britain's economic decline and the inability of Labour's economic policies to deal with it. Attempts to devise incomes policies to restrain inflation led to conflicts with the trade unions and his own left wing in the Commons, and his naturally combative style won him many enemies. The collapse of sterling in 1976 led to an application to the International Monetary Fund for a loan of $3.9 billion, which led in turn to savage cuts in public spending which, with hindsight, foreshadowed Thatcherism (see THATCHER, MARGARET).

Healey failed to win the leadership of his party in 1976, when MPs preferred the emollient style of Callaghan. When Callaghan stood down in 1980 it was widely thought that Healey would win, but the sharp move of the party to the left resulted in victory for Michael FOOT, under whose weak leadership the party lost the 1983 election. A Labour loyalist, Healey despised those MPs who left to form the Social Democratic Party, and he stayed to help KINNOCK and the Labour moderates to regain control of the party.

HEALY, TIMOTHY (1855–1931), Irish journalist, lawyer and politician. MP for Wexford (1880–4), Monaghan (1884–5), South Tyrone (1885–6), North Longford (1887–92), North Louth (1892–1910) and North-East Cork (1911–18), Healy came to prominence as PARNELL's secretary but fell out with him and in 1890–1 played a crucial role in defeating him by unremitting ridicule and denunciation; many held him personally responsible for Parnell's death, and his lasting reputation rests on his role in the destruction of Parnell. In the 1890s he led a minority anti-Parnellite faction which relied on clerical support and favoured a looser party structure, where power rested with constituency organizations rather than a central leadership. In 1900 his followers were purged after the reunion of the party: he remained a thorn in the party's side, especially after he formed an alliance with the other major dissident, William O'BRIEN. Healy was a successful barrister and wit and was fond of high political intrigue, a pursuit at which he greatly exaggerated his own talents. After 1916 he drew closer to Sinn Féin, and when the Free State was founded he became its first Governor General (1922–8).

HEANEY, SEAMUS (1939–), Irish poet. From a small south Derry farming family, a graduate from Queen's University, Belfast, he was one of the first generation of Northern Ireland Catholics to benefit from the post-war extension of educational opportunities, and much of his work is marked by tension between his role as an inheritor of the English literary tradition, aware of its connections with colonial exploitation and oppression, and nostalgia for the experiences and loyalties of childhood qualified by knowledge of their limitations. His first collection of poems appeared in 1966. In 1972 he moved to teach in the Republic. His response to the Northern conflict aroused controversy; some Republican commentators accuse him of evading his responsibility to speak for his own people, while others claim that his poetry of the early 1970s (especially the collection *North*, 1975) aestheticizes violence by presenting it as an immemorial ritual. In the 1980s he was a leading member of the Derry-based 'Field Day' group of artists and intellectuals which tried to explore and redefine Irish identity. Long recognized as the most significant Irish poet of the later twentieth century, Heaney was awarded the Nobel Prize for Literature in 1995.

HEATH, SIR EDWARD see essay on page 404

HEATH, SIR ROBERT (1574–1649), lawyer. Appointed Solicitor General and knighted in 1621, and Attorney General in 1625, under CHARLES I he took a lead in formulating the Crown case (sometimes unscrupulously) in legal confrontations on constitutional principles. Although William LAUD engineered his dismissal as Chief Justice of Common Pleas for supposed Puritan sympathies in 1634, Charles made him Chief Justice of King's Bench in 1642, after he had presided at the trial of royal opponents. Parliament ignored his title and in 1645 impeached him, declaring his office vacant.

HEATHCOTE, SIR GILBERT (c. 1651–1733), financier. He made his fortune in trade with Spain and the West Indies, amassing £7,000,000 by the time of his death. He was one of the founders of the Bank of England in 1694, and subsequently a Governor. As a substantial Whig businessman, he was one of the nine who loaned a total of £250,000 to the government in 1710 so that it could continue the war with France.

HEAVISIDE, OLIVER (1850–1925), physicist. Born in London, Heaviside developed scientific interests as a telegraph operator in Newcastle. In 1876, owing to deafness, he moved to London and studied James Clerk MAXWELL's and William THOMSON's writings on electromagnetism. His concern to improve signalling through long telegraph cables informed his construction of powerful and much-exploited theoretical tools for understanding electromagnetic phenomena. He designed new apparatus for telegraphic signalling, predicted the existence of what is now known as the Heaviside layer or ionosphere and introduced important electrical engineering terms such as self-induction and impedance.

HEILBRON, DAME ROSE (1914–), lawyer. Called to the Bar in 1939, she became a QC and in 1956 the first woman recorder. In 1974 she was appointed a High Court judge on the northern circuit (only the second woman to hold this position), and presiding judge in 1979. In 1975 Heilbron was chair of the Home Secretary's advisory committee on rape.

HEATH, SIR EDWARD (1916–)
Politician and Prime Minister (1970–4)

By his own estimation Heath was a far-sighted statesman whose achievement in taking Britain into the Common Market in 1973 will make his name live in history; to his many enemies that will happen for other reasons. In many ways Heath was the bridge between the old Conservative Party of CHURCHILL and MACMILLAN and the new Conservative Party of the 1960s and after. In the first Heath could rise to be Chief Whip, in the second he could become leader; temperamentally he came to prefer the former but could never forget he owed his achievements to the latter.

Born in Broadstairs (Kent), the son of a builder and a lady's maid, Heath was a bright grammar school boy who won an organ scholarship to Oxford (Balliol) and who, after a good war, worked for the Conservative Central Office before becoming an MP in 1950 – a position he was to retain for the next half century. His initial political progress was through the Whips' Office, and he made his name in those circles by his handling of the Suez crisis under EDEN. He was Chief Whip from 1955 to 1959 before going on to become Minister of Labour and then Lord Privy Seal under Macmillan. In this last capacity he led the British team negotiating entry into the Common Market; the veto by General de Gaulle in 1963 devastated Heath. He was Secretary of State for Trade and Industry under DOUGLAS-HOME.

After Harold WILSON's election victory in 1964, it was widely felt that the Conservatives needed a 'modern' and 'dynamic' leader in the 'classless' mould of Wilson, and the choice fell on Heath. As it turned out, Heath was a notoriously bad performer on television (where his strangulated vowel sounds revealed the attempt to turn himself into an upper-class Tory) and he was regularly bested by Wilson in the Commons. Heath's woes were increased by backbench rebellions on the issue of Rhodesia, where Tory imperialists tended to support Ian Smith and the Rhodesian whites against attempts to impose majority black rule. Enoch POWELL's famous 'rivers of blood' speech in 1968 led Heath to sack him but created a permanent problem with those in the party who supported Powell. In 1969 at a meeting at Selsdon Park, Heath committed the party to a radical agenda, including union reform and control over the money supply along with cuts in government spending. Few expected the Conservatives to win in 1970 but they did.

Heath's period in office was one of the most traumatic and controversial in recent history and it helped form the attitudes of the next generation of Conservative leaders. His major achievement was undoubtedly Britain's entry into the Common Market but many in his own party were deeply unhappy about the policy and the manner in which this was achieved, and the legacy of this division dogged the party for the rest of the century. In Northern Ireland Heath had to abolish Stormont and resort to direct rule, which led to the withdrawal of support by the Ulster Unionists, something which had fateful results in 1974 when Heath lost his majority. But it was on the economic and industrial front that the government had most trouble.

Heath proved unable to control the money supply and, after 1972, resorted to a Wilson-like policy of trying to control prices and incomes; but the trades unions would not co-operate with him. His attempts to legislate against unofficial strikes simply led to more trouble with the unions and, by late 1973, the country was crippled by the effects of the miners' work-to-rule which led to a three-day working week and regular power cuts. With the worsening world economic situation following the oil crisis caused by the Yom Kippur War in 1973, Heath found himself being held to ransom by the miners and the TUC. He tried to break this deadlock by calling an election in 1974 on the issue of 'who rules?' As it turned out the electorate had no more idea than Heath himself and a hung Parliament followed. But Heath lacked support from the Ulster Unionists, and the Liberals under Jeremy THORPE eventually declined to join a coalition.

Heath was not an effective opposition leader in 1974, spending much of his time calling for a government of national unity. He lost his third election out of four in Oct. 1974 but declined to resign. In early 1975 Margaret THATCHER decided to stand against him and, to his amazement, she won. For much of the next 15 years Heath kept up steady sniper fire on his successor, giving the impression of being in a perpetual sulk, although he denied such allegations.

John Campbell, Edward Heath: A Biography (1993)

HELWYS, THOMAS (*c.* 1550–*c.* 1616), religious leader. From a Notts. gentry family, in 1608 he accompanied John SMYTH into exile in the Netherlands because of his wish to worship in a Separatist church, and, after joining an English congregation in Amsterdam, joined Smyth in rejecting infant baptism; Smyth rebaptized him in 1609. They founded the first English Baptist Church, and in 1612 Helwys set up the first congregation in England at Pinners' Hall in London. His one published work argued that the State has no right to interfere in religious practice.

HENDERSON, ALEXANDER (*c.* 1583–1646), churchman. A minister in Fife from 1611, he opposed the Anglicization of the Scottish Church, and led the drafting of the National Covenant of the Kirk in 1638, becoming moderator of the 1638 General Assembly. Thereafter he was so dominant that CHARLES I was forced to make him Dean of the Scots Chapel Royal in 1641. His Oxford negotiations for peace with Charles in 1643 were futile, but he drafted the Solemn League and Covenant for the two kingdoms (1643) and the 1644 replacement for the Book of Common Prayer, the *Directory of Public Worship*.

HENDERSON, ARTHUR (1863–1935), politician. A Wesleyan (*see* WESLEY, JOHN) lay preacher and trade-union official who believed in the necessity of the Labour Party as the means of representing working-class interests, he served as Labour Chief Whip (1906–14), President of the Board of Education (1915–16), Minister for Labour (1916) and member of the War Cabinet (1916–17). His moderation was reinforced by his revulsion towards the Soviet system, which he had seen for himself in 1917. As party Secretary, he was an architect of the 1918 Labour Party constitution and of the party's organizational development. He served as Home Secretary under Ramsay MACDONALD in 1924, Foreign Secretary (1929–31) and interim leader (1931–2) when Labour disowned Macdonald's National government. Much of his later career was devoted to work for the World Disarmament Conference.

HENGIST (?–?488), King (?) of Kent. Later traditions (of which the earliest is recorded by BEDE) identify Hengist as the first King of Kent. The story is that, in the mid fifth century, he and his brother Horsa were invited into Kent to serve as mercenaries by the Romano-British ruler VORTIGERN, whom Hengist subsequently overthrew. His historical existence is unverifiable, but archaeological evidence does at least show English settlement in Kent at a time when Hengist might have been leading English warriors into the region.

HENLEY, JOHN (also known as Orator Henley) (1692–1756), controversialist. The son of a Leics. clergyman, after Cambridge he entered the Church. Known for unorthodox opinions, he was denied advancement. He left the Church and in 1729 set up an 'oratory' in Lincoln's Inn Fields where he gave lectures on theology and other subjects. He offered his services to Robert WALPOLE and between 1730 and 1739 published *The Hyp-Doctor,* a ministerial reply to the *Craftsman*. His later career involved accusations of Jacobitism and disputations in the theatre with Samuel FOOTE.

HENRIETTA MARIA (1609–69), Queen of England. Youngest daughter of Henry IV of France, she married CHARLES I in 1625. Their initially cool relations turned to devoted love after the murder of George VILLIERS, Duke of Buckingham, in 1628. She never liked William LAUD or Thomas WENTWORTH, forming a curious alliance in the 1630s with Puritan courtiers to obstruct a diplomatic rapprochement with Spain; her Catholicism, however, fuelled public fears about Catholic influence on Charles. After civil war broke out in 1642, her schemes and her fundraising from Catholics were both a help and a hindrance to Charles's war effort; though often politically inept, she did her best to persuade him to be flexible in negotiations after his defeat. Having moved to France in 1644, she was left poverty-stricken after Charles's execution, and angered exiled Anglican courtiers by her efforts to convert her children to Rome. She returned to England from 1660 to 1665, but then went back to France.

HENRY I *see* essay on page 406

HENRY II *see* essay on page 407

HENRY III (1207–72), King of England (1216–72). Eldest son of JOHN and ISABELLA OF ANGOULÊME, he succeeded on 28 Oct. 1216, aged nine, to a realm torn apart by the civil war provoked by his father's misrule. While he was a minor the government was headed in turn by William MARSHAL, Peter des ROCHES and Hubert de BURGH, who coped well with the immense military, financial and political problems facing the Crown. Only in Poitou, overrun by LOUIS VIII in 1224, did Henry suffer a permanent loss of rights.

He declared himself to be of age in 1227, but not until after his marriage to ELEANOR OF PROVENCE in 1236 did he take personal control of government. The delay was entirely characteristic of a King who occasionally made ambitious policy pronouncements, on both foreign and domestic affairs, but lacked the drive and determination to

continued on page 408

HENRY I (1068–1135)
King of England (1100–35)

WILLIAM I THE CONQUEROR's third surviving son Henry was well educated, hence his subsequent nickname Beauclerk. In 1087 his father left him a huge sum of money but his prospects remained uncertain until 2 Aug. 1100. On that day, whether by chance or by design, the King, WILLIAM II RUFUS, was killed. Henry, who was nearby, rode to Winchester, where he took possession of the Treasury, and then to Westminster where, on 5 Aug., he had himself crowned. Anticipating that his older brother ROBERT II, Duke of Normandy, would dispute his right to the throne, he issued a coronation charter renouncing some of the oppressive practices of Rufus's reign and promising good government.

In Nov. 1100 by marrying MATILDA, descendant of Anglo-Saxon kings and sister of King EDGAR of Scotland, Henry strengthened his claim to the throne and secured his northern border. Robert had strong support, however, from powerful Anglo-Norman magnates such as ROBERT OF BELLÊME, and the inevitable war of succession lasted until 1106, when Henry won the Battle of Tinchebrai, captured his brother and conquered Normandy. Now that he held both parts of the Anglo-Norman realm his hold on England was much more secure. He kept his brother in prison for the rest of his life, but released Robert's young son, William Clito (1102–28), who grew up to be a thorn in his uncle's flesh. The King of France and the Count of Anjou, alarmed by Henry's power, recognized Clito's claim. While England stayed peaceful throughout the remainder of Henry's long reign, in Normandy he constantly had to fight hard.

The King's need for money to fund the defence of Normandy led to administrative developments in England and the rise of ROGER OF SALISBURY. Henry has been credited with the centralization of royal power and the employment of 'new men' of relatively humble origins, 'raised from the dust', in government service. But, although the earliest extant references to the Exchequer date from his reign, the centralized auditing of royal revenues (under whatever name) must have pre-dated it. Moreover, although Henry, like all kings, employed some 'new men', he depended much more on the greater, and better rewarded, services that magnates could give him.

Early in his reign royal authority had faced an unprecedented challenge. ANSELM, as Archbishop of Canterbury ultimately loyal to a militant and reforming Papacy, brought the prohibition of lay investiture to England, thereby threatening one of the customary powers of the English king, his control of ecclesiastical appointments. This was a serious matter when prelates were great landowners and men of political weight. Eventually in a series of agreements made between 1105 and 1107 Henry was able to retain the reality of control while renouncing the traditional ritual of investiture. By giving up investiture, Henry was acknowledging the fundamentally secular nature of kingship. Diplomatic, realistic and secular-minded, Henry's ecclesiastical policy was entirely characteristic of the man. Morally dubious although many of his actions were thought to be, he was always able to justify them as necessary for the well-being of the State. Even the sex drive which resulted in his acknowledging more than 20 bastards, more than any other English king so far, was justified in political terms: he used his illegitimate children as diplomatic pawns to construct marriage alliances. Once his hold on the throne was secure, the promises made in the coronation charter were increasingly revealed as hollow.

Yet for all his fertility of brain and body Henry had only one legitimate son, William, drowned in the White Ship disaster in 1120. From then on the succession problem dominated the reign. Queen Matilda had died in 1118 and, less than three months after William's death, Henry took a second wife, ADELA OF LOUVAIN. But the male heir desperately hoped for was never born. In 1127 Henry made his barons swear to recognize his only legitimate daughter, the Empress MATILDA, as heir, and the following year he married her to GEOFFREY PLANTAGENET, Count of Anjou. But Henry was reluctant to part with any of the power that he had exercised for so long. The chronicler, HENRY OF HUNTINGDON, portrayed him as a man made permanently miserable by anxiety. 'Each of his triumphs only made him worry lest he lose what he had gained.' At the time of his death (Dec. 1135), supposedly as a result of eating too much of a favourite dish, 'a surfeit of lampreys', he was quarrelling violently with Geoffrey and Matilda. This quarrel re-opened old divisions within the Anglo-Norman baronage and allowed his nephew STEPHEN to snatch the Crown from the hands of Henry's designated heirs. During the civil wars which followed, men who had feared his cunning and ruthless exercise of power came to see his stern rule as an age of peace under a 'lion of justice'.

Judith A. Green, The Government of England under Henry I (1986)

HENRY II (1133–89)
King of England (1154–89)

Eldest son of GEOFFREY PLANTAGENET, Count of Anjou, and of the Empress MATILDA, by the time he was 14 he was already taking an active part in the campaign to wrest control of his mother's inheritance, the Anglo-Norman realm, from STEPHEN. In 1151 his father died and Henry took over rule of Anjou and Normandy; reluctantly he also took an oath on his father's body to hand Anjou to his younger brother Geoffrey when he acquired England. In 1152 he married ELEANOR OF AQUITAINE, and began to rule her duchy in her name. The 19-year-old now held greater territories in France than even its King, Louis VII, Eleanor's ex-husband, but could he hold them? In England his supporters were hard pressed by Stephen; an angry King of France was invading Aquitaine and Normandy, while in Anjou, Henry's brother Geoffrey was in revolt. In these circumstances his decision to sail to England in Jan. 1153 staggered contemporaries by its audacity. Henry's luck held. Stephen's elder son EUSTACE died in Aug. and Stephen reluctantly acknowledged Henry as his heir. When Stephen died in Oct. 1154, Henry, in Normandy, had no need to return in haste to England. His succession represented the restoration of peace after many years of civil war and he could afford to take his time. Not until 19 Dec. 1154 was he crowned at Westminster. He was now Henry II of England, ruler, and in large part creator, of the Angevin empire. He did not give Anjou to Geoffrey, but made him Count of Nantes instead. After Geoffrey's death in 1158 he was unchallenged; as contemporaries observed, in extent of his dominions he was a greater King than any of his predecessors.

During the first 20 years of his reign Henry was a belligerent ruler, chiefly interested in territorial expansion at the expense of his neighbours. He took Northumbria from MAEL COLUIM IV and, after the capture of WILLIAM I THE LION, installed English garrisons in Scottish towns such as Edinburgh and Berwick; he launched attacks on the leading Welsh princes, OWAIN OF GWYNEDD and RHYS AP GRUFFUDD. He invaded Brittany again and again, forcing its Duke Conan to betroth his daughter to his own son, Geoffrey (see GEOFFREY OF BRITTANY). In 1171 he invaded Ireland in order to impose his will on both Strongbow (see CLARE, RICHARD DE) and the native Irish kings of Ireland. In view of his overwhelming strength he was recognized as lord by nearly all the Irish kings, eventually including even RUAIDRÍ UA CONCHOBAIR. Although the acquisition of the Quercy was regarded as a disappointing outcome of his massive 1159 invasion of Toulouse, in 1173 the Count of Toulouse was persuaded to do homage. During this period, with the exception of his appointment of BECKET as Archbishop of Canterbury, Henry suffered few serious setbacks. But the rebellion of his wife and three oldest sons, HENRY THE YOUNG KING, Richard (later RICHARD I) and Geoffrey, in 1173–4 marked a major turning-point. From then on he was mainly on the defensive, concentrating on holding what he had won.

To the end Henry remained a man of boundless energy, always on the move, either hunting or riding from one part of his dominions to another. The sheer size of his empire inevitably stimulated the growth, especially in England, a country where a bureaucratic tradition was already strong, of localized administrations which dealt with routine matters of justice and finance in his absence. Thanks largely to ROGER OF HOWDEN's Chronicles, the texts of many of Henry's assizes (sets of instructions given to the King's judges) survive, and together with treatises on royal finance and law written by, or attributed to, Richard FITZNIGEL and Ranulf GLANVILL, these reveal the rapid development, at the King's command, of English common law, a law uniformly applied throughout the kingdom, administered by a network of courts, county courts and central courts sitting at Westminster, the seat of the Exchequer, and linked with each other by the routine use of written documents known as writs. Since the eighteenth century the 'making of the common law' has been regarded as the most significant aspect of the reign and in consequence Henry has been seen as a King with a genius for law and government, but that is not how his contemporaries viewed him.

Despite urgent pleas he failed to go to Jerusalem. To most people it seemed that his only contribution to the crusade was to lay a massive tax, the Saladin Tithe, on his subjects. By the end of his reign he was an unpopular King who appointed corrupt judges, oppressed the Church and had failed to manage his family: there were further rebellions of his sons in 1183 and 1188–9, and he died defeated by an alliance between Richard and Louis VII's son, Philip. His accession had been warmly welcomed; so was his death.

Wilfrid Lewis Warren, Henry II (1973

see them through. After the humiliating failure of the campaign in Guyenne (1242), he made little effort to recover the continental dominions lost in John's reign; indeed, in the Treaty of Paris (1259) he renounced them. As a good family man, he promoted the interests of his foreign relatives, first the Savoyards, then the Lusignans, but in ways that alienated an aristocracy that was increasingly conscious of its Englishness.

From 1244 onwards those who doubted his capacity to rule were advocating reforms that were, in effect, reversions to the practice of his minority government by ministers accountable to great councils (assemblies of lay and ecclesiastical magnates) rather than to the King. In 1258 his financial predicament, the result of his misguided Sicilian ambitions and his failure to keep the court faction within bounds, made it impossible for him to avoid one such reform scheme, the Provisions of Oxford. He tried to escape their constraints as soon as he could, and the outcome was years of tense political manoeuvring, culminating in the Barons' War. After being defeated and captured at Lewes (Sussex) in 1264, he was effectively dethroned by Simon de MONTFORT. The following year he was restored thanks to the victory won at Evesham by his eldest son, the future EDWARD I.

By now, Henry was head of the family in name only and could safely leave politics to others while he concentrated on rebuilding Westminster Abbey. At the end of a very long reign, he was at least still King of England. Naïve, pious and well-meaning, he loved quiet as well as peace, and generally let events take their course. His claim that he had given his subjects peace would have been justified had it not been for the drift into civil war in the 1260s.

HENRY IV ('BOLINGBROKE') (1366–1413), King of England (1399–1413). He was born at Bolingbroke (Lincs.), hence the name by which he is commonly known. As JOHN OF GAUNT's son he was heir apparent to the richest estate in England, and his prospects improved still further when in 1380 he married Mary de BOHUN, co-heiress of the earldom of Hereford. In consequence he was styled Earl of Derby from 1377 and Earl of Hereford from 1384. In 1387 he became one of the Appellants (the leaders of the aristocratic opposition to RICHARD II) and he defeated the King's favourite, Robert de VERE, at the Battle of Radcot Bridge (Oxon.) (20 Dec. 1387), but at this date he may have argued against deposing the King. During the early 1390s his knightly reputation was enhanced by crusades with the Teutonic knights and a pilgrimage to Jerusalem. In the tense political climate created by Richard, a quarrel with Thomas MOWBRAY, Duke of Norfolk, leading to charges and counter-charges of treason

ended with Henry's exile in 1398. His father died while he was abroad and the King seized his duchy of Lancaster. In 1399 with just a few hundred men Henry returned to England, seeking the restoration of his inheritance and posing as a champion of the rule of law against a tyrannous King. It was soon clear that the throne was there for the taking and, with decisive support from Henry PERCY, he took it, asserting in justification a non-existent hereditary right. Richard was deposed and imprisoned in Sept. 1399 and, the following Feb., after a failed rescue attempt, Henry had him murdered.

The new King's denunciations of Richard's extravagance made him vulnerable on the same score. The Parliaments of 1401 to 1406 complained angrily of the costs of the royal household, of excessive annuities and of taxes misspent. On several occasions he had to accede to the Commons' demands. Cash shortages crippled his response to GLYN DWR's revolt and meant that he treated the Percies, especially Thomas PERCY, less well than they expected. They allied with Glyn Dwr with the intention of putting Edmund MORTIMER on the English throne. Henry's swift reaction prevented them from combining forces and saved his son (see HENRY V) from falling into their hands. At Shrewsbury (23 July 1403) father and son defeated Hotspur (see PERCY, HENRY) in pitched battle. But it was not until 1408, with the recapture of Harlech and Aberystwyth (Cardign.) from the Welsh and the death of Henry Percy in battle at Bramham Moor (Yorks.), that he clearly won the upper hand against his enemies. This eased his money problems and consequently his relations with Parliament, but by this time he had a new enemy, ill health, brought on, according to later chroniclers, by his execution of Richard SCROPE, Archbishop of York, in 1405. After this date a king who had come to the throne with a reputation for prowess was hardly ever capable of leading his troops in person. He died aged 46 after a number of temporarily incapacitating, if unidentifiable, illnesses, which forced him at least once, in 1411, to ward off an attempt to make him abdicate in favour of his eldest son. In his last two years he hardly left London except to go to BECKET's shrine at Canterbury, where he opted to be buried, and where his second wife, JOAN OF NAVARRE, was to join him.

HENRY V *see* essay on page 409

HENRY VI (1421–71), King of England (1422–61, 1470–1). He became King in Sept. 1422 at the age of nine months, following the early death of his father HENRY V. In Oct., after the death of his maternal grandfather, Charles VI of France, and in accordance with the Treaty of Troyes, he was proclaimed King of France. The governments
continued on page 410

HENRY V (1387–1422)
King of England (1413–22)

Son of Henry Bolingbroke (*see* HENRY IV) and Mary BOHUN, he was born at Monmouth (and sometimes called Henry of Monmouth). His expectations were dramatically transformed when his father seized the throne in 1399. Created Prince of Wales, he was soon faced by the prospect of losing his principality in Owain GLYN DWR's revolt. From 1400 until 1406 he was preoccupied with Wales. In these formative years he learned how to cope with the harsh realities of waging war with little money and over difficult terrain. The tales of Prince Hal's misspent youth were not written down until he was already a figure from the heroic past. The sign which dominated his early life was not that of the Boar's Head Tavern but the Red Dragon of Wales. In 1403 at the Battle of Shrewsbury he was wounded in the face by an arrow, but refused to leave the field until Hotspur (*see* PERCY, HENRY) had been killed and the Percies defeated. From Dec. 1406 he took to attending council meetings assiduously. Henry IV's uncertain health meant that domestic politics were complex and factious, in which an ambitious prince had to tread warily. In 1410–11 it sometimes seemed that the Prince and his friends were the real rulers of the country and the makers of a foreign policy that exploited the division in France between Burgundian and Armagnac parties. In Nov. 1411 Henry IV, fearing that he was being pushed towards abdication, re-asserted himself, with the result that his eldest son was excluded from power until March 1413 when the King died. The tale of the Prince trying on his sleeping father's crown reflects a very real frustration.

As King he initiated a policy of reconciliation with the Welsh, but in 1414 faced a new form of opposition in the shape of the Lollard rising led by Sir John OLDCASTLE. As a sincere champion of religious orthodoxy he felt that he deserved divine support; it was in this mood that he decided to vindicate his right, if necessary via trial by battle, to the Crown of France. On the eve of his embarkation at Southampton he learned that plotters led by his cousin RICHARD, EARL OF CAMBRIDGE, intended to put Edmund MORTIMER, Earl of March, on the throne. He had the plotters executed (Aug. 1415). The invasion of 1415 was meticulously prepared but the decision, taken after the capture of Harfleur, to march through Normandy was a gamble which nearly ended in disaster. The English were strategically outmanoeuvred and began to lose heart. Fortunately for Henry on 25 Oct. the over-confident French launched a frontal assault on his position at Agincourt and suffered appalling losses at the hands of the English archers. The victory made Henry a hero overnight. 'No King of England ever achieved so much in so short a time and returned home with so great and glorious a triumph. To God alone be the honour and glory, for ever and ever. Amen.' These words, written soon afterwards by a royal chaplain, encapsulated the desired tone. The English were a nation blessed by God, and favoured because their deeply pious King was favoured. For five years enthusiastic Parliaments voted him all the money he needed, and never again did a French army dare to stand in his way. He built up a navy, clearing the Channel of enemy shipping, and using his ships for trading to meet part of the cost. He led a second army to France in 1417 and methodically and ruthlessly conquered Normandy. By the Treaty of Troyes, Charles VI of France recognized him as his heir. In June 1420 he married CATHERINE OF VALOIS, and next day marched off to continue the conquest of his kingdom, only to die of dysentery a few months before his father-in-law.

The Englishness of his government was emphasized by a policy of having official documents written in English and encouraging the celebration of English saints. A self-disciplined and obsessively efficient ruler, he conformed so effectively to the model of an ideal king that, as SHAKESPEARE's *Henry V* makes plain, for centuries posterity regarded him as the perfect King of England. Indeed some historians still do. In his short reign he impressed foreign enemies as well as loyal subjects. Yet doubts remain. Some historians have wondered whether, finally, his ambitions did not exceed those of his subjects (at the end of his reign ADAM OF USK wrote of 'the smothered curses of the tax-payers') or whether his brilliant exploitation of opportunities was not leading him into conquests which, in the longer term, would have proved impossible to maintain. Contemporaries, however, had no doubts on this score and the English position in France would remain tenable and profitable for another 20 years at least.

Christopher Allmand, Henry V (1992)

of his minority in both kingdoms were remarkably effective; problems multiplied after he was declared of age in 1437.

His love of peace may have been genuine, but it went hand-in-hand with inertia: in his entire reign, he visited his continental kingdom only once, when he was taken there as a boy (1430–2). When he married MARGARET OF ANJOU in 1445, he promised to surrender Maine to her uncle, Charles VII (who, as Dauphin, had declared himself King of France within two weeks of Henry being proclaimed), a promise that had to be kept secret from his advisers and was not fulfilled until 1448. The humiliating military defeats (1449–53) in the closing stages of the Hundred Years War shocked his subjects, precipitating CADE's rebellion at home and culminating in the final loss of Normandy and Aquitaine. In Aug. 1453, a few days after the news of the defeat at Castillon, he suffered a total breakdown. Although he recovered what passed for his right mind in 1455, he played an increasingly passive role thereafter.

Loyalty to his person still counted for something, as was apparent when he relieved RICHARD OF YORK of the second protectorship in 1455 and when he confronted the Yorkists at Ludlow in 1459, but he became little more than a symbolic parcel of monarchical authority, passed from hand to hand as the fortunes of the Wars of the Roses swayed from one to the other at St Albans (Herts.), Northampton and St Albans again. After EDWARD IV's crushing victory at Towton (Yorks.) in March 1461, Margaret took Henry to Scotland.

His occasional appearances in Northumbria failed to revive the Lancastrian cause, and when deprived of Scottish aid by Edward's truce with the Scots in 1463, after the last Lancastrian strongholds in Northumbria had been captured, he became a King in hiding. Discovered by the Yorkists in 1465, he was imprisoned in the Tower. There he might have lived out his days had he not been restored to the throne in Oct. 1470 (after Edward's flight to Holland), and then deposed again in April 1471 after Edward's return. The killing of his only child, Prince EDWARD, at the Battle of Tewkesbury (Glos.) sealed Henry's fate. He was now the last obvious representative of the Lancastrian dynasty, and Edward judged that he could no longer allow him to live: Henry VI was murdered on 21 April 1471.

After 1485 it became politically convenient to present Henry as a pious King, pure and blameless, an innocent unjustly dethroned, and even to press for his canonization. Undoubtedly his life had been tragic, but for his subjects, his reign had been calamitous. He had stood helplessly by as England slid into the Wars of the Roses, and as well as losing the throne of England twice he witnessed from afar the loss of all his dominions in France except Calais.

HENRY VII see essay on pages 412–13

HENRY VIII *see* essay on pages 414–15

HENRY FREDERICK (1594–1612), Prince of Wales. The elder son of JAMES I, he admired Walter RALEIGH and imitated the cultured soldier role of Sir Philip SIDNEY. Seen after his death from typhoid as a lost leader, his military interests and patronage of Puritans contrasted markedly with both his father and the later interests of his younger brother, the future CHARLES I, but it is difficult to know how this would have developed.

HENRY OF BLOIS (?–1171), churchman. Son of Count Stephen of Blois, he was brought up as a monk in the abbey of Cluny. In 1126 his uncle HENRY I gave him the abbey of Glastonbury and, three years later, the bishopric of Winchester. Since he contrived to hold both for over 40 years, he was the richest prelate in England and in 1135 helped his brother STEPHEN to obtain the throne.

Although he failed either to become Archbishop of Canterbury or to convert Winchester into a metropolitan see, he played an extraordinarily prominent political and even military role throughout Stephen's reign, particularly during the years 1139–43, when the struggle between the King and the Empress MATILDA was at its most intense and he used his authority as Papal Legate to hold councils in highly publicized, if largely unsuccessful, attempts to settle the affairs of the kingdom. At HENRY II's accession in 1154, he withdrew to Cluny, but returned four years later to play the part of elder statesman. As a builder of castles and palaces (notably Wolvesey at Winchester), and as a connoisseur who acquired pagan statues from Rome because he appreciated them as works of art, he provoked the wrath of the austere St Bernard of Clairvaux, who called him the 'old wizard' and the 'whore of Winchester'.

HENRY OF HUNTINGDON (?–*c.* 1160), historian. Archdeacon of Huntingdon, he wrote a *History of the English*, written in Latin, covering the period from Caesar's invasion of Britain to his own day, initially up to 1129, then in subsequent editions to 1154. His systematic analysis of Anglo-Saxon history was to prove influential: for example, he introduced the notion of the heptarchy. He also gives the earliest known version of the story of King CNUT and the waves, though in his version it illustrates a sensible king's scorn for the flattery of courtiers.

HENRY OF LANCASTER (also known as Henry of Grosmont) (4th Earl and 1st Duke of Lancaster) (*c.* 1310–61), soldier. He succeeded his father as Earl of Lancaster in 1345 and was created Duke (with palatine powers) in 1351. He was EDWARD III's most successful aide during the early stages of the Hundred Years War, and the marriage of his daughter Blanche to JOHN OF GAUNT strengthened his ties with the royal family. As Lieutenant in Aquitaine (1345–7), he won famous victories at Bergerac and Auberoche, and in the 1350s he commanded in Brittany and Normandy. With the spoils of war, he built the Savoy Palace in London, yet he was also the author of a spiritual handbook, *Le Livre de Saintz Médecines*.

HENRY OF NORTHUMBRIA (1st Earl of Northumbria, 4th Earl of Huntingdon, 3rd Earl of Northampton) (*c.* 1114–52), nobleman. Son of DAVID I, King of Scots, and MATILDA, Countess of Huntingdon and Northampton, and grandson of Earl WALTHEOF of Northumbria, he received from King STEPHEN his mother's earldom but not his grandfather's, so he joined his father's 1138 invasion of England and fought at the Battle of the Standard on 22 Aug. Next year Stephen gave him both the Northumbrian earldom and Ada de Warenne's hand in marriage. In 1144 he was recognized as heir to Scotland but died before his father.

HENRY THE YOUNG KING (1155–83), son of HENRY II and ELEANOR OF AQUITAINE. For reasons that are obscure, in 1170 he was crowned by the Archbishop of York (*see* BECKET, THOMAS) and was called both Henry III and the Young King. He initiated the great rebellion of 1173–4 against Henry II, and he was again in revolt against his father when he died in 1183. This turbulent history may explain why he remains the only heir to the English throne to be crowned during his father's lifetime. Contemporary chroniclers describe him as a charming but feckless playboy; he was doubtless frustrated by the fact that his father had no intention of relinquishing control over the territory which he had given to the young Henry.

HENRYSON, ROBERT (?1430–1506), poet. A schoolmaster associated with Dunfermline Abbey after studies at Glasgow University, his *Tale Of Orpheus* was printed in 1508 by Walter CHEPMAN, and his *Testament of Cresseid* (not published until 1593) was long attributed to his model Geoffrey CHAUCER. Writing with a strong consciousness of the wider European literary scene, he is often regarded as the greatest Scots poet of his age.

HENTY, G(EORGE) A(LFRED) (1832–1902), children's author. The son of a stockbroker, Henty left Cambridge to fight in the Crimean War and subsequently worked as a war correspondent. His first successful boy's adventure story, *The Young Buglers*, set in the Peninsular War, was published in 1880. His stories of empire, war, adventure and rigid racial and class hierarchies guaranteed him a phenomenal success: 150,000 copies of his books were published every year. But immediately after his death unease grew that this xenophobic belief in British superiority could encourage pugilistic tendencies in his readers.

HEPBURN, JAMES (Baron Hailes, 4th Earl of Bothwell) (*c.* 1535–78), Scottish nobleman. In 1556 he succeeded to the power wielded in the Scottish Borders by his father Patrick HEPBURN, the 3rd Earl. Although (unlike his father) a Protestant, he opposed the reforming programme of the Lords of the Congregation, endearing him to MARY QUEEN OF SCOTS. At her entreaty for help against the rebellion of James STEWART, Earl of Moray, he returned from exile in 1565. As she increasingly turned her affections to him, he determined to supplant Henry STEWART, Lord Darnley, as royal consort. After the latter's murder in 1567, a farcical trial acquitted BOTHWELL of any involvement; he then seized the Queen, probably raping her at Dunbar, and secured a hasty annulment of his first marriage from John HAMILTON, Archbishop of St Andrews. He and Mary were rapidly married at Holyrood Palace. Immediately national anger combined against them, resulting in their defeat at Carberry Hill (15 June); by the end of the year Bothwell was stripped of his honours and a fugitive. He sailed to Norway, where creditors and relatives of a wronged former mistress seized him and took him to prison in Denmark. Never released, he died in chains, stark mad. Occasional modern efforts at rehabilitating him are doomed to failure.

HEPBURN, PATRICK (3rd Earl of Bothwell) (*c.* 1511–56), politician. Less than two years old when his father was killed at Flodden (1513), he was persistently at odds with JAMES V and in English exile in the 1530s; after James's death (1542) he unsuccessfully wooed MARY OF GUISE, fiercely opposing the projected marriage of MARY QUEEN OF SCOTS and the future EDWARD VI. By 1545, however, he had changed sides back to the English, nevertheless handing over George WISHART to Cardinal BEATON for burning (1546). After 1553 he made his peace with Mary of Guise and became Lieutenant of the Border.

HEPPLEWHITE, GEORGE (?–1786), furniture-maker and designer. Little is known about his life, which seems to have been spent in London, and none of his pieces has survived. After his death and the sale of his stock, his widow Alice compiled *The Cabinet-maker and Upholsterer's Guide* (1788)

continued on page 416

HENRY VII (1457–1509)
King of England, Lord of Ireland (1485–1509)

Son of Edmund TUDOR, Earl of Richmond, Henry was born at Pembroke Castle and brought up as a minor member of the royal family by William HERBERT at Raglan Castle (Gwent). His only certain experience of seeing England before he came to the throne was a traumatic one: the Battle of Edgecote (26 July 1469), where Lord Herbert, defending EDWARD IV against Edward's own brother George PLANTAGENET, Duke of Clarence, was defeated and executed. This was a lesson in the untrustworthiness of great noblemen which Henry seems to have taken to heart in later life. In June 1471, after the failure of the 1470–1 'Readeption' of HENRY VI, Henry was left dangerously exposed as the most senior Lancastrian claimant to the throne. The plan was to take him to safety in France, but storms drove him to land in Brittany. This proved a lucky accident, since France would later have proved dangerous when Edward IV and Louis XI were reconciled; he spent the next 13 years in Brittany. His highly shaky royal claim through his mother Margaret BEAUFORT only gained real significance after Edward V's murder and the unsuccessful rebellion of Henry STAFFORD, Duke of Buckingham (1483); now he became the focus not just for the Lancastrian remnant but also for Yorkists alienated from RICHARD III. Despite the fiasco of an attempt to invade England in Oct. 1483, on Christmas Day 1483 he took an oath in Rennes Cathedral to marry Elizabeth of York, Edward IV's daughter, and to rule jointly with her. Now threatened by betrayal in Brittany, he fled to France, where he was joined by a few remaining Lancastrians. He landed at Milford Haven in 1485, defeating and killing Richard III at Bosworth (22 Aug. 1485). In 1486 he honoured his pledge to marry Elizabeth of York, though not his pledge to rule jointly with her.

Henry found it difficult to establish his authority. His predecessor's power-base had been in the north: a rising there in autumn 1486 was followed by a dynastic challenge from Lambert SIMNEL (impersonating Edward PLANTAGENET, Earl of Warwick) in 1487, whom Henry defeated at the Battle of Stoke (near Newark, Notts.). Though this is sometimes seen as the last battle of the Wars of the Roses, there was renewed popular unrest in Yorkshire in 1489, and Henry's main asset in gradually winning goodwill in the north lay in his opponents' alliance with the Scots, traditional enemies of northern Englishmen. After Simnel, Henry faced another pretender, Perkin WARBECK, and in 1497 there was a popular rebellion in Cornw. against excessive taxation, which gained widespread support in the West Country and which reached Blackheath (Kent) before it was defeated. He secured his rule in Ireland only in 1494. He made some patchy efforts to please the Welsh by stressing his ancestry, displaying the red dragon banner, removing discriminatory legal status from some areas of Wales and granting favourable charters to them; above all, recalling the British past by naming his eldest son ARTHUR. This policy seems to have worked; throughout the sixteenth century, Wales was the least troublesome part of the Tudors' realms.

Henry had little acquaintance among English noblemen and good reason to suspect their loyalty. He therefore shared government sparingly, trusting only his small personal circle: Lady Margaret BEAUFORT, Archbishop John MORTON, his uncle Jasper TUDOR, Duke of Bedford, John DE VERE, Earl of Oxford. In Ireland, he came to rely on Thomas BUTLER, Earl of Ormond, as a counterweight to the long-standing ascendancy of the GERALDINES. It was noticeable that none of these close allies had a son and heir who might be a rival focus to royal loyalty. Otherwise he conducted government through a group of efficient bureaucrats who owed their careers to him, such as Reynold BRAY, Richard EMPSON and Edmund DUDLEY. He created very few new peers, and the peerage's numbers dwindled during his reign.

Henry made the central aim of his reign the restoration of central authority and government credibility, after some initial floundering as he came to grips with an unfamiliar country. Knowing nothing of English government, he tried to restore the traditional central role of the Exchequer in gathering revenue, but soon reverted to using Yorkist Chamber methods of controlling royal finance through local receivers reporting to royal servants under the King's personal supervision. He also exploited his feudal financial rights to the full, partly for the profit which could be made, and partly as a means of asserting control over royal tenants-in-chief. He revived the Council in the Marches of Wales set up by Edward IV to administer the estates of the infant Prince of Wales, using it as a way of controlling the Welsh Borders and the activities of the Marcher Lords; in 1489 he set up a similar council at York, nominally to assist Arthur as titular Warden General in the north. His Royal Council was a large body which did its work mainly through various smaller groups. Most important was the sub-committee 'the Council Learned in the Law', set up about 1498; this body included most leading lawyers and, under Bray and later Dudley and Empson, it played the chief part in Henry's government. So closely was it associated with Henry's cold efficiency that it disappeared on his death. He also manipulated the legal system to intimidate local magnates and curb private lawlessness. He forced many to enter bonds (legal documents binding the subject to observe conditions on pain of forfeiting money) or recognizances (bonds acknowledging a debt, often to be released on good behaviour). The great advantage of these was that Henry could keep close personal control over their use, since it was his private decision, rather than that of a judge sitting openly in a law-court, as to whether the conditions had been broken. Former opponents, like Thomas HOWARD, Earl of Surrey, were restored to positions of honour and influence, but characteristically with their estates curtailed; the incentive for good behaviour was that greater restorations would follow.

Henry's foreign policy was aimed at creating stability by avoiding war and at gaining recognition and alliance for his dynasty. The Treaty of Étaples (1492) brought profitable peace with France, and although Edward IV's sister Margaret, Duchess of Burgundy, backed the successive pretenders to the English throne, a commercial treaty, the *Intercursus Magnus* (1496), stabilized trade with the Low Countries. Likewise, a treaty of perpetual peace with Scotland (1502) led to the marriage of Henry's daughter MARGARET TUDOR to JAMES IV, King of Scots. The other fruit of much convoluted marital diplomacy was the alliance with Aragon and Castile bringing Princess CATHERINE OF ARAGON to England, first as bride for Prince Arthur, in 1501; Henry kept her as a prospective bride for his surviving son Henry. Despite these achievements, Henry's later years seem to have been characterized by growing suspicion and insecurity. Although recent research overturns the earlier finding of K. B. Mcfarlane and J. R. Lander that there was a significant increase in bonds and recognizances imposed on nobility and gentry, there was a crop of executions in 1499, including Warbeck and Edward, Earl of Warwick, while Edmund de la POLE, Earl of Suffolk, was forced to flee into exile. This reflects Henry's continuing worry about his dynastic security, perhaps associated with his negotiations for the Spanish

marriage, but the deaths of Prince Arthur (1502) and Queen Elizabeth (1503) may have added to his sense of the fragility of his achievement. His death was concealed even from the new King for two days, reflecting murderous court tensions in which the older nobility reasserted their position in government. The new regime ostentatiously broke with its predecessor, cancelling many bonds and saying that many had been levied unjustly, and Empson and Dudley, arrested after the announcement of Henry's death, were executed as symbols of the change of direction.

Henry is often seen as cold and calculating, but his family relations were close and affectionate, particularly with his wife and his mother. His intimate circle was small, and he had good reason to distrust most prominent noblemen. He balanced his private style of government with a recognition of the need to impress his subjects by magnificence at his court; its model was the standard of ceremony perfected by the dukes of Burgundy, who had a similar need to stabilize a newly arrived regime with the aid of solemn court ritual. At the heart of his court was a suite of private apartments, the Privy Chamber, deliberately staffed by people without major political importance, so that he could withdraw from the pressures of powerful politicians; the Privy Chamber took on a very different character, and assumed a major political role, during his son's reign. Some of the peculiarities of his reign may be seen as the product of his brief time at the French court, where as a newly credible candidate for the English throne he was for the first time close to government. From this experience may have come his readiness to sell offices under the Crown, not previously an English custom, and his preference for calling meetings of informal Great Councils rather than Parliaments when he wished to sound out opinion or transact major business: this parallels the French institution of the *Grand Conseil*. One feels, however, that the chief hallmark of his regime, the constant personal supervision of every aspect of government, was the unique product of a compulsively energetic personality. Henry was, since the Norman Conquest, the least likely candidate for the English throne to achieve his ambition, yet he left a peaceful and united realm, ending fifteenth-century instability and securely establishing a dynasty of remarkable talent and creativity.

S. B. *Chrimes, Henry VII (1972)*

HENRY VIII (1491–1547)
King of England (1509–47) and Lord, then King, of Ireland

There is a reliable tradition that as the second son, Henry was intended by his father HENRY VII for a senior position in the Church before he became heir to the throne on the death of his elder brother ARTHUR in 1502. At his accession, his ebullience, sporting prowess and genuine if fitful interest in humanist learning were a welcome contrast with his introvert father, and he soon completed long-drawn-out negotiations for marriage with Arthur's widow CATHERINE OF ARAGON. Bored by detailed administration, he found the ideal bureaucrat minister in Thomas WOLSEY, who like many of Henry's former tutors had been associated with Magdalen College, Oxford. By 1511 Wolsey was supplanting the council of cautious aristocrats and bishops who had initially dominated government. Henry rapidly turned to a traditional source of English royal glory in the first (1512–13) of several expensive wars with France; he fought (ironically, as it now seems), as a crusader for the Pope, with whom the French King was then at war. This campaign brought him temporary control of the city of Tournai, and simultaneously an army under Thomas HOWARD, 7th Duke of Norfolk, inflicted a crushing defeat on the Scots at Flodden (1513). Otherwise, Henry's campaigning brought little permanent result at any stage of his reign, although at huge expense he captured Boulogne in 1544. His successive ministers were constantly forced to devise new sources of revenue to finance war, including a cynical and damaging debasement of the coinage in the 1540s.

Henry used Wolsey's talents in complex and often contradictory diplomacy designed to secure an equal place with the much more powerful Holy Roman Emperor and the French King FRANCIS I; the confusing and wasteful character of his foreign policy was symbolized in 1520 when he staged an immensely lavish meeting to establish close friendship with Francis at the Field of the Cloth of Gold, only a few weeks before making a secret agreement with the Emperor not to ally with France. His marital troubles further complicated matters. His marriage to Catherine of Aragon was ruined by his obsession with securing a male heir, since she had produced only one surviving daughter, the future MARY I, in 1516. From early 1527 his love for ANNE BOLEYN made matters worse, but his quest to have his marriage declared invalid (soon tactfully known as the King's 'Great Matter') was made harder by his insistence that it was a theological issue, in which the Pope must acknowledge that the Papacy had made a fundamental mistake when it had granted a papal dispensation for the marriage to take place. He ignored any easier approach.

In 1529 the resulting inevitable deadlock made Henry jettison Wolsey, after the papal envoy Campeggio sitting with Wolsey in a hearing of the case at Blackfriars (London) had adjourned the hearing and thus given Catherine the chance to lodge an appeal in Rome. Henry's fury at this manoeuvre destroyed his earlier extravagant papal loyalty, which in 1521 had won him the title Defender of the Faith for writing (or taking the credit for) the anti-Lutheran *Assertio Septem Sacramentorum* (Defence of the Seven Sacraments). Instead, he built on his equally long-standing conviction of his own God-given place at the head of the English Church. Out of this, a committee of clerical academics created a theory of royal sovereignty, by which Henry was recognized as subject under God to no other earthly ruler (and therefore an imperial monarch); consequently he was Supreme Head of the Church in England. The means to put this theory into effect was created by Thomas CROMWELL in the Parliaments of the 1530s, and Henry granted Cromwell much of his newly found power by making him Vicegerent in Spirituals – in effect allowing Cromwell to exercise the powers over the Church which Wolsey had exercised on behalf of the Pope. The supremacy was used to sanction the dissolution of all monasteries, nunneries and friaries by 1540 (legislation followed in 1545 to begin dissolving the chantries); this conveniently released a large revenue to the Crown, though it was mostly soon dissipated for immediate gain as the Crown sold off the bulk of monastic lands to pay for the wars of the 1540s. Henry authorized the reading of the Bible in English in 1537, following this by allowing Cromwell to sponsor a new official translation (the Great Bible) in 1539.

Henry's marital misfortunes continued; marriage to Anne Boleyn (1533) produced only a daughter, later ELIZABETH I, and another miscarriage. This suggested to Henry that God was still angry with his marriage, and Anne's enemies were thus given the opportunity to persuade him of her adultery; after her execution (1536), a new wife, JANE SEYMOUR, at last provided him with his son, later EDWARD VI, but died of illness as a result (1537). Genuinely heartbroken, Henry nevertheless entered fresh matrimonial adventures. His decision to follow Cromwell's advice and seek a bride who would symbolize alliance with the Lutheran princes of Germany led to his betrothal to ANNE OF CLEVES. This proved a disaster when Henry found her physically repulsive, and the fiasco undermined his faith in Cromwell. A hasty annulment of the marriage (1540) was followed by a love-match with CATHERINE HOWARD, a disaster in its turn when she was revealed without question as unfaithful. Catherine was executed (1542), and only with CATHERINE PARR (1543) did Henry find a contented partnership for his last years. Meanwhile he kept a cruelly careful balance between religious reformists and conservatives at court, using their murderous struggles to sanction the destruction of Thomas MORE and John FISHER (1535), Henry COURTENAY, Earl of Devon (1538), Cromwell (1540), Thomas HOWARD, 8th Duke of Norfolk, and his son Henry HOWARD, Earl of Surrey (1546–7) – besides numerous figures across the spectrum of belief who died for not conforming to his religious blueprint. A further consequence of the break with Rome was that Henry decided that he must replace his title Lord of Ireland, since it was widely believed that it was derived from the supposed twelfth-century papal grant by Adrian IV, *Laudabiliter*. He was therefore declared King of Ireland by the Irish Parliament in 1541 and by the English Parliament in 1542.

Henry's last years were dogged by ill health, especially recurrent ulcers on his legs, probably the result of old tournament injuries. This meant that access to the King became much more restricted, as he was increasingly confined to his private apartments and gave up active participation in sport. There were political consequences: those staffing his Privy Chamber were mainly evangelical (reformist or Protestant) in sympathy, and were able to use their intimate relationship to the King to negate the advantage gained by conservative politicians at Cromwell's death, and biasing the future in favour of religious change. Henry's part in these changes is complicated, for he shifted his beliefs, creating his own theological mixture to puzzle both contemporaries and modern observers. He lost any strong belief in a middle state of the afterlife (purgatory), a central component of late medieval piety. Besides a strong dose of aristocratic anti-clericalism, he remained proud of his part in sponsoring an English Bible and curbing the cult of images and destruction of shrines. He entrusted his son's education to Cambridge reformists rather than traditionalist scholars. Even so, he never accepted the reformers' Protestant emphasis on justification by faith alone; despite some late hesitations, he maintained the provisions of the savagely Catholic Act of Six Articles (1539) including traditional definitions of the Mass and the retention of compulsory celibacy for clergy, ex-monks and ex-nuns. His most enduring conviction was that, next to God, he knew best.

Henry's place in folk-memory has been assured by his eccentric marital history and by enduringly vivid visual images of himself and his court provided by the drawings and paintings of Hans HOLBEIN the younger. His reign was genuinely of great significance in British history, not merely for the religious break with Rome. It marked an important stage in the assertion of Westminster government within England, and of England's dominance over the Celtic lands of the British Isles. Within England, patterns of medieval government which had fully operated only in the south-eastern and Midlands heartland were now made effective also in the north and west, with administration through justices of the peace and the twice-yearly progresses of judges from central courts around assize circuits. From 1536 Wales was also assimilated to English administrative institutions, and relations between Anglophone and Gaelic culture in Ireland were permanently altered as the English government determined on more aggressive policies. Henry also reasserted claims over the Scottish kingdom which were ironically to be fulfilled in reverse in 1603 when JAMES VI and I, a Scots descendant of his sister MARGARET the wife of JAMES IV, assumed the English Crown. He took a keen personal interest in the navy, investing much money in new ships. Much debate has raged over how far Henry can be given credit for developments in the reign; the ultimate reaction against seeing him as an all-powerful, all-controlling tyrant came in the work of Geoffrey ELTON, who saw the changes which he styled a 'Tudor Revolution in Government' as resulting from the conscious strategy of Thomas Cromwell. Recent research tends to restore credit to Henry, even if he was shrewd enough to delegate hard detailed work (and frequently also blame for unpopular policies) to talented ministers. One can admire his achievements without admiring the man, though many will not admire the achievements.

J. J. Scarisbrick, Henry VIII (1968)

including several examples of her husband's designs. It was eagerly received as the first pattern-book since the increasingly outdated work of Chippendale. Although he was for a time influential in both North America and northern Europe, Hepplewhite was soon overtaken by Thomas SHERATON as the principal promoter of the ADAM style in furniture.

HEPWORTH, DAME BARBARA (1903–75), sculptor. Trained at Leeds School of Art and the Royal College of Art, Hepworth travelled on a scholarship to Italy and was a member of the Seven and Five Society of radical artists, exhibiting at the Beaux Arts Gallery in London in 1928 with her first husband, the sculptor John Skeaping, and at Tooth's Galley (*Madonna and Child*) in 1930 before moving to St Ives in Cornwall in 1939 with her second husband, the sculptor Ben Nicholson, and their triplets. From the mid 1930s Hepworth's sculptures were increasingly abstract, using pierced forms, often strung with string or wire, and were worked in stone or cast in metal and later bronze. Her sculpture was a feature of the 1951 Festival of Britain, and examples can be seen today on John Lewis's Oxford Street store in London (*Winged Figure*, 1963), on the UN building in New York and in the shopping centres of post-war new towns, such as Harlow (Essex) and Hatfield (Herts.). Hepworth bequeathed her St Ives studio, where she was to die in a fire, to the nation as a museum of her work.

HERBERT, A(LAN) P(ATRICK) (1890–1971), writer. With versatility and wit, Herbert wrote for the satirical magazine *Punch* for many years. His first important book, *Secret Battle* (1919), is a moving account of the horrors and inhumanity of war. Independent MP for Oxford University (1935–50), he campaigned vigorously for a number of reformist causes, notably changes to the divorce laws and improving authors' rights. His time as an MP is recounted in *Independent Member* (1950). His best-known novel is *The Water Gipsies* (1930).

HERBERT, EDWARD (1st Baron Herbert of Chirbury) (1583–1648), politician and writer. Herbert of Chirbury (often misspelled Cherbury) was the son of a Montgomerys. gentleman; after a brilliant Oxford career, he travelled extensively in Europe for pleasure and on military and diplomatic service (1608–24), and was created Baron in 1629. Imprisoned for a Royalist speech in 1642, he tried to remain neutral in the English Civil Wars after 1642, but on surrendering Montgomery Castle to Parliament in 1644 he was granted a pension and administrative office. Highly esteemed among European and British intellec-

tuals, his writings range from history and philosophy to poetry and an autobiography. His inquiring tolerance, rooted in Renaissance mysticism and sceptical of Christian orthodoxy, contributed much to the later movement of thought known as deism, which sought to seek universal beliefs in God without appealing to dogma claiming to be divinely revealed.

HERBERT, GEORGE (1593–1633), poet. Brother of Edward HERBERT, Lord Herbert of Chirbury; his pious fellow-Cambridge don, Nicholas FERRAR, persuaded him to become a clergyman. After predictable first steps up the ladder of comfortable preferment, he took an obscure parish, Bemerton (Wilts.), in 1630. A gentleman becoming a clergyman was rare enough at the time, but Herbert's work in his parish provided an ideal for sacramentally and ceremonially minded High Churchmen thereafter, particularly as presented in the biography by Izaak WALTON; his devotional poetry and prose have never ceased to win admirers, beginning with William LAUD and CHARLES I.

HERBERT, GEORGE (10th [5th Herbert] Earl of Carnarvon) (1866–1923), amateur Egyptologist. He sponsored Howard CARTER's excavations of royal tombs at Thebes and died (some say mysteriously, since there was a rumour that there was a curse on anyone who disturbed the royal burial place) shortly after the 1922 discovery of Tutankhamun's tomb in the Valley of the Kings.

HERBERT, HENRY (20th [1st Herbert, 2nd creation] Earl of Pembroke) (*c*. 1506–70), politician. From Herefs., his father was the illegitimate son of the last Herbert, Earl of Pembroke, and was in HENRY VII's service. He began a military career after involvement in a murderous fight in Bristol; his prowess led him to the royal guard. HENRY VIII married his wife's sister CATHERINE PARR (1543). From 1544 he lavishly rebuilt the former nunnery at Wilton (Wilts.). He remained in government under EDWARD VI, MARY I (after some athletic back-tracking from support of JANE GREY) and ELIZABETH I; this political skill was not hindered by an apparent inability to write.

HERBERT, MARY (née Sidney) (Countess of Pembroke) (1561–1621), poet. Sister of Sir Philip SIDNEY (who wrote the first version of his *Arcadia* for her while staying at Wilton), she married in 1563 (as his second wife) Henry Herbert, 21st Earl of Pembroke. They entertained ELIZABETH I at Wilton (Wilts.) in 1574, and made it a major centre of literary and dramatic patronage. The high quality of her own verse and verse translations, long obscured by their complex and dispersed manuscript history, is now becoming appreciated.

HERBERT, SIDNEY (1st Baron Herbert of Lea) (1810–61), politician and army reformer. Second son of the Earl of Pembroke, he was educated at Harrow and Oxford, and was MP for South Wilts. from 1832 until his elevation to the peerage in 1860. Well acquainted with the defects of the army thanks to his father, who had fought in the Revolutionary Wars, Herbert used his first period in the War Office (1845–56), to push through reforms, including limited enlistment, soldier education and a reduction in corporal punishment. In his second period (1852–5), he began the concentration of the army in a vast new camp at Aldershot (Hants). With the outbreak of the Crimean War Herbert threw himself into the reform of logistic and medical services, sending Florence NIGHTINGALE and her volunteer nurses to Scutari. Though desperately ill, Herbert returned to the War Office in 1859 and laboured assiduously until his death to restructure the Volunteer Rifle Movement and the Militia and to secure a larger share of the budget for defence from the Chancellor of the Exchequer.

HERBERT, WILLIAM (22nd [3rd Herbert, 2nd creation] Earl of Pembroke) (1580–1630), politician and literary patron. He was a courtier to ELIZABETH I, JAMES I and CHARLES I, with a consequent clutch of offices including (from 1617) the chancellorship of Oxford University (Pembroke College being named after him). He took an active interest in worldwide voyaging and colonies in Virginia and Bermuda. Becoming the greatest patron of a war policy against Spain, he was rival, first, to Henry HOWARD, Earl of Northampton, then (until he was bought off) to George VILLIERS, Duke of Buckingham. He continued his family's literary interests as a poet and artistic patron (he was joint dedicatee of SHAKESPEARE's First Folio) but his love of a lavish good time combined with calculated political oppositionism probably did more for his general popularity.

HEREFORD, EARL OF, 1ST *see* FITZOSBERN, WILLIAM; **7TH** *see* BOHUN, HUMPHREY VII DE

HEREWARD (*fl. c.* 1070), rebel. The most celebrated leader of English resistance to the Norman conquest, in 1070 he plundered Peterborough Abbey to finance the revolt in the Fenlands; a year later, when other leaders surrendered to WILLIAM I THE CONQUEROR, he and his followers escaped from the Isle of Ely. After that, nothing certain is known of his career, only that, by fighting on, he became, by the mid twelfth century, a legendary figure, called (for unknown reasons) Hereward the Wake from the thirteenth century onwards.

HERKOMER, SIR HUBERT VON (1849–1914), artist. Born in Bavaria, he studied in Southampton, where his family settled in 1857, and at art schools in Munich and in London (South Kensington). Success came early: *The Last Muster* won a gold medal at the Paris Exhibition in 1878, while his social realist paintings, such as *On Strike* (1891), were innovative. He was also a composer, singer, actor, engraver, a pioneer of (silent) British films and a popular water-colourist and portraitist: his subjects included John RUSKIN, whom he succeeded as Slade Professor of Fine Arts at Oxford (1885).

HERLEVA (?–*c.* 1050), mother of WILLIAM I THE CONQUEROR. ROBERT I, Duke of Normandy's mistress, she was mother of his son, the future William I the Conqueror. She is usually thought to have been the daughter of a tanner or embalmer from the Norman town of Falaise, although her origins are not clearly recorded in sources written before the twelfth century.

HERRING, THOMAS (1693–1757), Archbishop of York (1743–7) and Canterbury (1747–57). A clergyman's son and a strong Whig, he is most famous for organizing the first 'county association' with the aim of financially supporting GEORGE II and the PELHAM ministry against the Jacobite rebellion in 1745. Herring himself gave £200 and Yorks. as a whole raised almost £33,000, but the association's chief value was in gathering support for the ministry and in propaganda through a series of loyal addresses. Rewarded with the archbishopric of Canterbury, Herring made unsuccessful efforts towards reincorporating the Dissenters into the Church of England. In 1748 he was involved in negotiations with Samuel CHANDLER, a leading Dissenter, reaching broad agreement on the need for the replacement of the Thirty-Nine Articles and the Athanasian Creed, but this went too far for most Anglicans.

HERSCHEL, CAROLINE (1750–1848), astronomer. Born in Hanover, the sister of William HERSCHEL, she was educated at home and spent her youth caring for her brothers. In 1772 she joined William in Bath where she tried unsuccessfully to build a career as an oratorio singer. By the late 1770s Caroline had become a key figure in William's astronomical project, assisting in the construction of his telescope mirrors, recording his observations and helping to write his publications. Her independent observation of hitherto unidentified nebulae and comets won her a reputation as one of the world's foremost women astronomers. She published a revision of John FLAMSTEED's star catalogue in 1798 and returned to Hanover in 1822. In 1835 she became one of the first two female honorary fellows of the Royal Astronomical Society.

HERSCHEL, SIR JOHN (1792–1871), astronomer and natural philosopher. Son of William HERSCHEL, he studied mathematics at Cambridge, where, with Charles BABBAGE and others, he promoted continental methods of mathematical analysis. After Cambridge he studied law but then devoted himself to natural philosophy and astronomy. From about 1816 he was actively involved in his father's work and by the early 1830s had catalogued the positions of thousands of double stars and nebulae. He conducted a celebrated survey of the skies of the southern hemisphere from the Cape of Good Hope, observing thousands of previously uncharted double stars, nebulae and clusters (1834–8). He also proposed that the Milky Way was annular-shaped and researched solar photometry. Returning to England, he worked on geophysics and meteorology, and began publishing his Cape observations. A prolific and influential writer on astronomy and natural philosophy, his works include *A Preliminary Discourse on the Study of Natural Philosophy* (1830) and *Outlines of Astronomy* (1849). He was also a skilled chemist and a pioneer of photography: he coined the word photography, produced the first photographic image on a glass plate, devised the cyanotype process, and introduced the notion of positive and negative images.

HERSCHEL, SIR WILLIAM (1738–1822), astronomer. A musician in the Hanoverian Guards before moving to England in 1757, Herschel developed strong interests in astronomy and mathematics. By 1774 he had constructed a reflecting telescope with which he observed, in 1781, what was later identified as the planet Uranus. This brought him fame and a position as GEORGE III's court astronomer. He later built an observatory at Slough, where, with the considerable help of his sister Caroline HERSCHEL, he constructed increasingly powerful telescopes and made vast contributions to astronomical knowledge: for example, he observed the sun's motion through space, satellites of Uranus and Saturn and the rotation of Saturn's rings; he catalogued the positions of over 2,000 nebulae and located over 800 double stars; and he proposed influential accounts of the structure and dimensions of the Milky Way. He is also credited with the discovery, in 1800, of infra-red radiation.

HERTFORD, 8TH EARL OF *see* SEYMOUR, EDWARD

HERVEY, FREDERICK (also known as Earl-Bishop of Derry) (4th Earl of Bristol) (1730–1803), churchman and politician. Frederick Hervey was the third son of the courtier John, Lord HERVEY. After studying at Westminster and Cambridge he took holy orders. In 1767 his brother George, 2nd Earl of Bristol, Lord Lieutenant of Ireland, nominated him Bishop of Cloyne; he was made an Irish Privy Councillor, then in 1768 Bishop of Derry. Derry was already a wealthy see but Hervey almost trebled its revenues, from £7,000 to £20,000 a year, through agricultural reform. He also built roads to improve communications and in the early years of his tenure visited every parish in the diocese, something almost unheard of. He travelled widely outside the British Isles and was a friend of Voltaire and Jeremy BENTHAM. He campaigned in the Irish Parliament for the relaxation of laws against Catholics. In 1779 he succeeded as 4th Earl of Bristol and returned to Ireland in 1782 to play a leading role among the Volunteers, then pressing for an extension of Irish political rights (*see* GRATTAN, HENRY). His flamboyant style earned him the distrust of Charlemont (*see* CAULFIELD, JAMES) as indeed did his support for the extension of the franchise to Catholics. After 1783 he effectively retired from politics.

HERVEY, JOHN (1696–1743), courtier and memoirist. Predeceasing his father, the 1st Earl of Bristol, he never inherited the title; he was known by the courtesy title Lord Hervey. He is best remembered for his *Memoirs of the Reign of King George II* (1848). These told of life at court in the 1730s when Hervey was Vice-Chamberlain, in which post he enjoyed friendly relations with Queen CAROLINE and acted as an intermediary between the royal couple and Robert WALPOLE. Hervey judged GEORGE II of narrow intellect and dull tastes, dominated by his wife and the Prime Minister. He lost his place soon after Walpole's fall. He was reputed for androgyny and was dubbed by his enemy POPE 'Lord Fanny'.

HESELTINE, MICHAEL (1933–), politician. As a dynamic entrepreneurial figure whose business interests made him a multimillionaire, Heseltine was at once characteristic and uncharacteristic of the HEATH and THATCHER Conservative Party. He became MP for Tavistock in 1966, holding minor office in the early 1970s when he was identified as a 'Heathman'; in fact he was always a Heseltine man, as events showed. With his striking mane of blonde hair and his charismatic style, he became the darling of the Tory conference, and was rewarded with the office of Secretary of State for the Environment by Thatcher in 1979.

A high-profile minister with a natural talent for grabbing the headlines, particularly as the so-called minister for Merseyside after the riots in that area in 1981, his interventionist instincts put him at odds with Thatcher, as did his pro-European stance. In 1986 the tension erupted over the minor question of a West Country helicopter firm, Westland. Heseltine wanted the company to get an important defence contract, Thatcher wanted it to go to the Americans. In the most spectacular resignation of the 1980s Heseltine stormed out of Cabinet and gave a press conference denouncing the Prime Minister. For the next four years Heseltine kept up a steady sniper fire from the back benches while making sure that he kept closely in touch with constituency MPs who much valued his ability as a crowd-pleaser. After Sir Anthony Meyer's unsuccessful bid for the leadership in 1989 revealed the doubts which existed in the party about Thatcher, Heseltine was encouraged to stand against her in 1990 after the resignation of Sir Geoffrey HOWE. Although he gained enough votes to force her resignation, Heseltine lost the ensuing leadership contest to John MAJOR, under whom he was President of the Board of Trade (1992–5). His loyalty in not standing against Major in 1995 was rewarded by his being made deputy Prime Minister, a post which he held until the 1997 election defeat. Hopes of becoming leader were dashed by recurring heart problems after the election.

HESS, DAME MYRA (1890–1965), pianist. Hess made her concert début in 1907 playing Beethoven's Fourth Piano Concerto at the Queen's Hall in London, conducted by Thomas BEECHAM. This was a work with which she became particularly associated, as with her arrangement of Bach's *Jesu Joy of Man's Desiring*, though her range was catholic, from Debussy and Mozart to Scarlatti and Schumann, and she sometimes included contemporary music in her repertoire. During the blitz, when all concert halls were closed, she organized a series of lunchtime concerts at the National Gallery in London, where office workers could go to eat their sandwiches as they listened to some of Britain's finest musicians.

HEVENINGHAM, SIR JOHN (1577–1633), politican. From a Norfolk knightly family and knighted in 1603, he was one of 'five knights' (*see also* CORBET, JOHN; DARNELL, THOMAS; ERLE, WALTER; HAMPDEN, EDMUND) imprisoned by CHARLES I in 1627–8 for refusing to pay a forced loan. His son and heir, William (1604–78), was one of the judges at CHARLES I's trial (1648–9), although he did not sign the death warrant and was pardoned in 1660.

HEWISH, ANTHONY (1924–), radio astronomer *see* BELL BURNELL, SUSAN

HEY, JAMES (1909–), radio astronomer. Hey studied physics in Manchester and from the outbreak of the Second World War worked on radar anti-jamming techniques at the Army Operational Research Group (AORG). In 1942 he linked mysterious jamming of British anti-aircraft radar systems with the existence of radio waves emitted by the sun. Three years later his use of radar to track German V2 rockets led to exploitation of radio waves in the day-time and night-time location of meteor streams. After the war he continued his work at the AORG and there collaborated on producing evidence for a strong discrete stellar radio source in the constellation of Cygnus.

HEYLYN, PETER (1600–62), historian. An Oxford don, he became a scourge of establishment Calvinists like the Regius Professor John Prideaux, and thus gained William LAUD's patronage. Laud's chief propagandist for Arminian innovations in the 1630s, he gleefully pursued Bishop John WILLIAMS to humiliation in Star Chamber. Predictably victimized after CHARLES I's defeat, he kept a low profile until the late 1650s, when he resumed violently polemical writing for High Church Anglicanism, including an attack on Thomas FULLER. He wrote a learned but partisan history of the English Reformation (1661) and an admiring life of Laud, published 1668.

HICKS, AMIE (1839–1917), trade unionist. Of Chartist parentage, and a ropemaker by trade, she joined the Social Democratic Federation in 1883, was Secretary of the East London Ropemakers' Union (1889–99), and a founder member of the Women's Industrial Council. An energetic campaigner on behalf of women and labour, she was a direct and effective speaker.

HICKS, SIR JOHN (1904–89), economist. After graduating from Oxford he taught at the London School of Economics, Cambridge and Manchester before returning to Oxford as a Fellow of All Souls and Professor of Economics in 1952. He became the first British Nobel Laureate in Economics in 1972. The prize was shared with the American economist Kenneth Arrow for their respective contributions to the theory of general equilibrium and welfare economics. Hicks's *magnum opus* was *Value and Capital* (1939), later complemented by his *Capital and Growth* (1965). Other major contributions were in fields as diverse as wage theory, social accounting, consumer theory and international trade. He showed how KEYNES's ideas on the role of money in the determination of interest rates could be reconciled with neoclassical ideas, which give primacy to savings and investment.

HICKS, WILLIAM JOYNSON (1st Viscount Brentford) (1865–1932), politician. He served short periods as Conservative Postmaster General, Financial Secretary to the Treasury (with a seat in Cabinet) and Minister of Health before becoming

Home Secretary in Nov. 1924. He acted against suspected communist subversion by authorizing the Arcos raid (on the London headquarters of a Soviet trading company), and took a strong line against the Trades Union Congress (TUC) during the General Strike, mobilizing troops, police and special constables to maintain government control. A staunch Low Churchman, he was prominent in the defeat of the Revised Prayer Book in 1927–8.

HIGBALD, Bishop of Lindisfarne (781–802). He was Bishop at the time of the famous surprise Viking attack on the island in 793 when the famous scholar ALCUIN OF YORK recorded that 'the church of St CUTHBERT was splattered with the blood of the priests of God'. Despite the rhetoric, the attack appears to have been an isolated one and the monks continued to live on Lindisfarne until forced to move in 875 in the time of EARD-WULF after the arrival of the 'Great Army' of HALFDAN and IVAR THE BONELESS.

HIGDEN, RANULF (?–c. 1364), historian. A Benedictine monk of St Werburgh's, Chester and author of treatises on preaching, he is now best known for his Latin history of the world, the *Polychronicon*, which was translated into English by John TREVISA and remained the most popular account of world history available in England until Walter RALEIGH's in the early seventeenth century.

HILDA (OR HILD), ST (614–80), Northumbrian princess. She became Abbess of the 'double monastery'(i.e. for men and women) of Whitby in 657. Her career resembles that of other early Anglo-Saxon aristocratic women such as St ÆTHELTHRYTH, demonstrating the major role that women played in the development of the conversion of the early-English kingdoms to Christianity. During her life Whitby became an important religious centre, hosting the famous Synod of Whitby in 664 (*see* St COLMAN, OSWY, St WILFRID) and receiving kinswomen such as St ÆLFFLAED and St EANFLÆD as nuns. The poet CÆDMON was a monk at Whitby during her abbacy.

HILL, CHARLES (Baron Hill of Luton) (1904–89), doctor and broadcaster. The son of a labourer, Hill is remembered above all as the 'Radio Doctor', who projected his reassuring personality into people's homes in the darkest days of the Second World War. Snoek, pulses, 'black-coated workers' (prunes) and healthy exercise were among his enthusiasms. Hill had qualified in medicine but his ambitions were in public service. As Secretary of the British Medical Association for six years, during which the National Health Service was introduced, he was the middleman who brokered agreement between doctors and

government. Elected to Parliament in 1950, Hill held a succession of Cabinet offices until becoming a victim of the purge by Harold MACMILLAN in 1962. A life peer and Chairman of the Independent Television Authority in 1963, three years later he became Chairman of the BBC.

HILL, OCTAVIA (1838–1912), housing reformer. The granddaughter of the public health reformer Thomas Southwood Smith, she was influenced by her reform-minded father and the Christian Socialism of MAURICE and RUSKIN. Her emphasis on personal responsibility and the moral reformation of the tenant made her see the housing question as one that lay in individual character formation and which could be solved without state assistance. She undertook the management of slum properties owned by the Ecclesiastical Commissioners and others and, by means of the careful selection of tenants, refusal to allow arrears and eviction of 'undesirables', claimed that such properties could become a profitable investment. She also campaigned for the preservation of open spaces and recreation areas, founded the Kyrle Society (1875), to encourage the poor to enjoy art, literature and open-air recreation, and co-founded the National Trust 'to preserve places of historic interest and natural beauty' in 1895.

HILL, SIR RICHARD (1732–1808) and **ROWLAND** (1744–1833), Evangelicals. From a major landowning family in Salop. the brothers were notable for their support for Evangelical preachers and Methodists such as WHITEFIELD. Both were prolific writers of religious works. Richard, as MP for Salop. (1780–1806), drew attention to moral and spiritual issues, at a time before WILBERFORCE and his friends had given the cause wide currency. Rowland, meanwhile, had sought ordination but after rejection by six bishops, as he would not end his unlicensed preaching, he succeeded only in being made a deacon. In 1783 he gained his own chapel in London from which he supervised 13 Sunday schools. The brothers were among the founders of the British and Foreign Bible Society.

HILL, ROWLAND (1st Viscount Hill) (1772–1842), soldier. The fourth of 16 children of a Salop. gentry family, Hill was bought a commission in the 38th regiment in 1790. He managed to secure further promotion by raising recruits for his regiment. Following extensive service in the Mediterranean and in Ireland, Hill served in the campaigns in the Peninsula and southern France (1808–14) and at Waterloo (1815). At times it seemed that Hill could intuit Wellington's intentions (*see* WELLESLEY, ARTHUR), and as a consequence Wellington frequently trusted him with independent corps commands. When Wellington became Prime Minister in 1828, he appointed Hill as Commander-in-Chief of the army. Although often regarded as a cipher for his former chief, 'Daddy Hill' evinced a much greater concern for the rank and file than did Wellington and he ensured that the army usually avoided excessive force in domestic policing during this volatile period.

HILL, SIR ROWLAND (1795–1879), inventor of the penny post. Brought up by his Birmingham schoolmaster father to follow him into teaching, Hill developed radical new teaching skills and philosophies, incorporating honour codes but abolishing corporal punishment, which excited the admiration of BENTHAM and others. The school moved to the northern fringe of London in 1827 but Hill, whose health was poor, left it to his brothers to run. He formed societies for furthering inventions, was active in the colonization of south Australia, and from 1835 began planning the penny post, with adhesive postage stamps as the medium for prepayment. After considerable struggle, the simple practicality of the scheme carried it through Parliament, and the system was inaugurated in 1840. Hill suffered various tribulations at the hands of governments, but finally in Nov. 1846 he was made Secretary to the Postmaster General, a post he held until 1864, promoting reform throughout the Post Office. He was also heavily involved in the promotion of railways.

HILL, WILLS (1st Earl of Hillsborough, 1st Marquess of Downshire) (1718–93), politician. Heir to an Irish title, he entered the Commons in 1741, attracting attention as a young man of honour and merit. He intermittently held senior public offices between the 1760s and 1780s, ultimately as Secretary of State in the final years of the NORTH ministry. Noted for his hardline views on parliamentary sovereignty over the American colonies, he was identified by colonists with the enforcement of the unpopular sections of the Treaty of Paris (1763). These restricted settlement in the territory east of the Ohio which had been acquired from France, so as not to enrage either Spain (which had acquired Louisiana) or the native population.

HILLIARD, NICHOLAS (?1547–1619), miniaturist. He followed his father as a goldsmith, and became the first Englishman to distinguish himself in the Renaissance craze for 'limning' (miniature painting). He was limner and goldsmith to ELIZABETH I (re-engraving her great seal) and to JAMES I. His work provides us with many familiar visual images of the period, and he wrote a treatise on his art (c. 1597–1603).

HILLSBOROUGH, 1ST EARL OF see HILL, WILLS

HINDLEY, MYRA (1942–), murderer. Born in Gorton near Manchester, Hindley, and her lover Ian Brady, murdered several children. The press nicknamed them the Moors murderers, as two bodies were discovered on Saddleworth Moor. Hindley was convicted on two counts of murder in 1965 and sentenced to life imprisonment, and in 1986 she confessed to three other killings. The horrific nature of the crimes deeply shocked the public and, despite a campaign led by the Labour peer Lord LONGFORD for her parole or release after repeated claims of reform and repentance, successive home secretaries of every political hue have continued to block any such action.

HINTON, CHRISTOPHER (Baron Hinton of Bankside) (1901–83), scientist. An apprentice in what had been at the cutting edge of the previous century's technology, the Great Western Railway at Swindon (Wilts.), Hinton studied at evening classes before taking a first class degree in mechanical sciences at Cambridge, then joined Brunner MOND (soon to be ICI). By the outbreak of the Second World War he had become chief engineer there. During the war he was Deputy Director General of explosives factories. In 1945 he took charge of the UK atomic energy project that gave Britain its first atomic bomb and in 1956, with the opening of Calder Hall, a world lead in civil nuclear power. The first Chairman of the Central Electricity Generating Board (1956–64), he continued to use his influence to promote nuclear energy.

HIRST, DAMIEN (originally Damien Brennan) (1965–), artist. Trained at Goldsmiths' College of Art, Hirst achieved fame and sustained controversy of the 'is it dead meat or is it art?' variety with installations featuring such objects as a 12-foot tiger shark suspended in formaldehyde *The Physical Impossibility of Death in the Mind of Someone Living* (1991), a cow and calf sawn into four sections (*Mother and Child Divided* at the Venice Biennale, 1993), maggots, flies and displays of pharmaceutical bottles filled with controlled substances. Many of his works explored his 'obsession with trying to make the dead live or the living live forever', as well as with house paint flung onto spinning canvas, and spot paintings. He won the Turner Prize in 1995.

HITCHCOCK, SIR ALFRED (1899–1980), film director. After a Jesuit education and a short time in advertising and minor cinema jobs, Hitchcock directed his first film *The Lodger* (1927), about a family who suspect their lodger of being a latter-day JACK THE RIPPER. A shortage of extras obliged Hitchcock to appear himself; the momentary appearance became his trademark, a feature of almost all his subsequent films. Throughout the 1930s he established himself as a master of the thriller genre with films such as *The Man Who Knew Too Much* (1934), *The Thirty-Nine Steps* (1935) and *The Lady Vanishes* (1938). His adaptation of Daphne DU MAURIER's *Rebecca* won the Academy Award for best picture (1940). *Suspicion* (1941) starred Cary Grant, the first of his many successful appearances in Hitchcock films, culminating in the classics *To Catch a Thief* (1955) and *North by Northwest* (1959). Best remembered for his two horror films *Psycho* (1960) and *The Birds* (1963), Hitchcock is considered to have perfected the suspense thriller with his imaginative use of technique and sense of the visually dramatic.

HLOTHERE, King of Kent (673–85). A son of EORCENBERHT and the successor to his brother EGBERT, Hlothere is notable because of his continuation of the tradition of law-giving established in Kent by ETHELBERT. In 684 Hlothere was defeated by his brother EADRIC and, after a family feud typical of these early centuries, was forced to share the kingdom.

HOADLY, BENJAMIN (1676–1761), churchman. Educated at Catherine Hall, Cambridge, where he was elected a Fellow in 1699, he suffered a crippling illness, such that thereafter he had to preach kneeling. As a lecturer in London after 1701, he became one of the most prominent and aggressive Latitudinarian clerics (*see also* STILLINGFLEET, EDWARD; TILLOTSON, JOHN; TENISON, THOMAS), and in 1709 was attacked by Francis ATTERBURY for a sermon on the right of resistance to rulers. The controversy brought Hoadly into favour with the Whigs, and after the accession of GEORGE I he was made a royal chaplain, and later Bishop of Bangor. Hoadly is remembered for provoking the Bangorian controversy, which led to the dissolution of Convocation, the Church's representative assembly of the lower clergy (it was to remain inactive until 1852). His 1716 pamphlet, *A Preservative against the Principles and Practices of the Non-Jurors, both in Church and State*, and a 1717 sermon, in which he denied that Jesus had conferred special authority on any vicegerents, interpreters or judges, aroused alarm. Although Hoadly argued for State power over the Church, his ideas were suggested to be dangerously anti–authoritarian. A committee appointed by Convocation reported that such concepts threatened all government and discipline in the Church, as well as royal supremacy in ecclesiastical matters. The ministry, fearing that his doctrine might be formally condemned, had Convocation prorogued in Nov. 1717. The issue generated a voluminous pamphlet debate. Hoadly's role in the crisis did not harm his career; in 1721 he became Bishop of Hereford, in 1723 of Salisbury and in 1734 of Winchester.

HOARE, HENRY (1705–85), banker. Grandson of Sir Richard HOARE, he became a partner in the family bank in 1726 and in 1742 moved to Stourhead (Wilts.), bought by his father Henry in 1717. There he dammed the River Stour to create a lake and commissioned temples to surround it from FLITCROFT, with statues and busts by RYSBRACK. Hoare's will separated the house from the bank as he was convinced that an economic collapse would arise from the size of the national debt (further swollen by the War of American Independence) and did not want the Stourhead estate to leave the family; he was succeeded at Stourhead by his grandson Sir Richard Colt HOARE.

HOARE, SIR RICHARD (1648–1718), banker. The son of a London horse-dealer, he became a goldsmith in 1672, in partnership with his cousin James from 1674. The Hoares added banking to their business and their customers included PEPYS. In the 1690s and during the War of the Spanish Succession, Hoare's Bank acted as agent for government loans and with the firm of CHILD dominated the banking business: Hoare and Sir Francis Child denied in 1707 that they organized a damaging run on the Bank of England fuelled by rumours of an invasion by the Pretender, James Edward STUART.

HOARE, SIR RICHARD COLT (1758–1838), antiquarian. The grandson of Henry HOARE of Stourhead (Wilts.), he succeeded him there in 1785. Excluded from participation in the bank, he concentrated on the improvement of Stourhead and, until the Revolutionary Wars began, travelled extensively through Europe. He made detailed illustrations of the places and objects that he saw, which led to his role as illustrator of Coxe's *History of Monmouthshire* (1801). His two-volume *History of Wiltshire* (1812–21) was dominated by the study of the neolithic monuments at Stonehenge and Avebury, illustrated by several detailed plates, and paved the way for detailed scholarly examination of these and other ancient sites.

HOARE, SAMUEL (1st Viscount Templewood) (1880–1959), politician. A leading minister of the inter-war years, he served as Secretary of State for Air (1922–4, 1924–9), founding Imperial Airways in 1924, and as Secretary of State for India, steering the India Bill (which introduced a federal structure for India with fully responsible provincial governments) through the Commons against Winston CHURCHILL's fierce opposition. Appointed Foreign Secretary in June 1935, he devised the secret Hoare–Laval Pact with the French Prime Minister Pierre Laval, effectively to consolidate Italian gains in Abyssinia after the Italian invasion of Oct. 1935, but was forced to resign when its details were made public and the agreement was repudiated by the Cabinet. Hoare resumed his ministerial career as First Lord of the Admiralty (1936–7) and Home Secretary (1937–9). A supporter of Neville CHAMBERLAIN, he defended the Munich agreement with Hitler and joined the War Cabinet in 1939 as Lord Privy Seal, again becoming Secretary for Air in 1940. With Churchill's accession as Prime Minister in May, he became Ambassador to Spain, serving until 1944.

HOBART, SIR PERCY (1885–1959), soldier. Son of an officer in the Indian civil service, educated at Woolwich, Hobart was commissioned into the Royal Engineers and saw active service in France and Mesopotamia, where, not for the last time, he refused to carry out orders he knew to be unsound. Convinced that armies of the future would be armoured, Hobart became an enthusiast for tanks, and in Egypt in 1938 created the force which would become 7th Armoured Division. Fighting bitterly with WAVELL, Hobart was retired from the army, and in 1940 joined the Home Guard as a corporal. Reinstated as Major-General in 1941 at the insistence of an incredulous CHURCHILL, Hobart went on to raise and command 79th Armoured Division, a formation of specialized engineering assault vehicles which much reduced British casualties in Normandy.

HOBBES, THOMAS (1588–1679), philosopher. Oxford-educated, he became contemptuous of the Aristotelian and scholastic curriculum which still dominated teaching in the University. He became a longterm tutor, secretary and friend to the Cavendish family, earls of Devonshire, he was one of the Great Tew circle (*see* CAREY, LUCIUS) and was a friend of the aged Francis BACON. Having already travelled widely on the continent with his noble patrons (meeting, among others, Galileo), from 1641 he sat out the British Civil Wars in Paris as a Royalist, at one stage tutoring CHARLES II. He returned to England in 1652 to make peace with the regime, and published his masterpiece, *Leviathan*. At the Restoration in 1660, Charles gave him a pension and protection from churchmen infuriated by his writings, and in the later 1660s he produced a flood of further writing, which was refused publication during his lifetime.

Hobbes was a mild man horrified by the violence around him caused by civil war: he therefore emphasized humanity's search for peace, which he saw as dependent on the establishment of a civil power absolute in its authority, dominating both Church and State. His vision of a social contract between ruler and ruled is one of the earliest in political theory. His, however, is very different from the later liberal accounts of social contract by John LOCKE and his successors, given his bleakly pessimistic view of a humanity inclined by nature to selfishness and struggle, and needing the restraint of power from above to make settled society possible: his famous description of human life in the state of nature (very different from that of the biblical picture of the Garden of Eden) was that it was 'solitary, poor, nasty, brutish and short'. His state authority needed no supernatural claims to govern; it owed everything to the will to take and maintain power, making self-appointed tyrants as legitimate as any other ruler. Given Hobbes's radical scepticism about the claims of organized religion and traditional legitimacy, there is controversy about how far his work falls within the Christian tradition; he wrote much on Christian theology, yet his views of God are expressed in very material terms, giving the deity a virtually physical substance, and he abhorred the mystery which he saw as the cornerstone of power for priestly castes. From the moment of the publication of *Leviathan*, his writings aroused a storm of hostility. Nevertheless, his influence is often perceptible even in the thought of some later Stuart divines and writers who publicly denounced him for his scepticism and cynical view of human nature: some Anglican writers found congenial his arguments against the magistrate's allowing freedom of conscience. Hobbes also wrote an autobiography. His writings on law, society and philosophy have ultimately had a profound effect on political thought.

HOBHOUSE, JOHN CAM (1st Baron Broughton) (1786–1869), politician. Best known for his friendship with BYRON – his account of their journey through Albania was published in 1813 – and as a radical MP who coined the phrase 'His Majesty's Opposition'.

HOBSBAWM, ERIC (1917–), historian. One of the most cosmopolitan of British intellectuals, and perhaps better known internationally than any other British historian, Hobsbawm was born in Alexandria in 1917, the son of Anglo-Austrian parents. After a childhood and early adolescence in Vienna and Berlin, with his family he escaped Nazism and settled in London. Following his degree at Cambridge he taught at Birkbeck College, University of London (1949–82). The author of more than 500 books, articles and reviews in numerous languages, whose thought has been shaped above all by Marxism (*see* MARX, KARL), he has addressed and sparked debate on a wide range of major historical problems. These have included the transition from feudalism to capitalism and its social consequences such as the phenomenon of social banditry (*Primitive Rebels*, 1959; *Bandits*, 1969), the nature of labour movements and socialist and radical thought (*Labouring Men*, 1964) and the growth of European capitalism and its worldwide social and political consequences 1789–1991 in the best-known of his writings, the four 'Age of' books,

Revolutions 1789–1848, Capital 1848–1875, Empire 1875–1914 and *Extremes 1914–1991* (1962–94). He became, particularly from the late 1970s, an influential and frequently pessimistic commentator on the future of socialist and Labour politics in Britain. He was also for some years a distinguished jazz critic (under the name Francis Newton).

HOBSON, J(OHN) A(TKINSON) (1858–1940), economist. Remembered today principally for his 1902 work *Imperialism: A Study*, Hobson argued that militaristic imperial expansion was the result of the need to exploit surplus goods and capital produced by *laissez-faire* economic policies. This analysis formed the basis for Lenin's subsequent theories of imperialism. Hobson's unconventional views held him back from academic appointments but he was a prolific writer on economic and political affairs. His heretical attacks on *laissez-faire* principles, first advanced in *The Physiology of Industry*, co-authored with A. F. Mummery (1889), were to be an important influence on KEYNES.

HOBSON, THOMAS (?1544–1631), carrier. An innkeeper who dominated Cambridge's transport links with London, and who became proverbial for his strict rotation of his horses available for hire: 'Hobson's choice'. He was a major benefactor to the town in providing a public running-water system and a site for a workhouse. John MILTON wrote satirical epitaphs on him.

HOBY, LADY MARGARET (née Dakins) (1571–1633), diarist. A Yorks. gentlewoman educated in the Puritan household of Henry HASTINGS, Earl of Huntingdon, she married Walter Devereux (brother of Robert DEVEREUX, 19th Earl of Essex). After his death at the siege of Rouen (1591) she soon married Sir Thomas Posthumus Hoby (posthumously-born son of Thomas HOBY), who moved to her Yorks. estates, and they sought to impose their religious outlook on the neighbourhood. Her diary, the earliest surviving from an Englishwoman, vividly evokes the disciplined life of a Puritan household.

HOBY, SIR THOMAS (1530–66), translator. Cambridge-educated and an enthusiastic evangelical, he and his brother Philip were employed on diplomatic missions under EDWARD VI. He translated a Protestant propaganda work by Martin BUCER (1547) and, in 1561, Baldassare Castiglione's dialogue *Il Cortegiano* (1528), which as *The Courtier*, had a major effect on English upper-class manners and on Tudor literature. He married Elizabeth (1528–1609), herself a translator of a devotional work, and one of the brilliant daughters of Sir Anthony COOKE (*see also* BACON, ANNE; CECIL, WILLIAM).

HOCCLEVE, THOMAS (*c.* 1369–*c.* 1426), royal servant. His political and semi-autobiographical verse gives a lively impression of the daily life and outlook of a man who, as a Clerk of the Privy Seal, was employed close to the centre of Lancastrian government. He compiled a handbook of 900 standard letters sent out under the Privy Seal, but this never achieved the popularity of his *Regement of Princes*, a work of commonplace political advice completed in 1411 and dedicated to the future HENRY V, to whom he acted as a court poet, under-rewarded, as he said.

HOCKNEY, DAVID (1937–), artist. Bradford-born, Hockney went to the Royal College of Art in 1959 after studying at his local art school. Of the new 1960s generation of 'pop artists', he became an iconic artist-celebrity, with his dyed blond hair and gold lamé jacket. His figurative paintings won almost instant acclaim, including his 'homosexual propaganda' work, *We Two Boys Together Clinging* (1961) (referencing Walt Whitman) and *Mr and Mrs Clark and Percy* (1971–2). Since 1964 he has lived mainly in California. His flat-rendered acrylic paintings of azure swimming pools and manicured lawns, among them *A Bigger Splash* (1967), form his best-known *oeuvre*, though he has also produced etchings such as *The Rake's Progress* (1961–3), opera design, photo-collages, pictures of his dogs, his local Yorks. landscape and a panorama of the Grand Canyon exhibited in 1999 at the Royal Academy, of which he was elected an associate in 1985.

HODGKIN, DOROTHY (née Crowfoot) (1910–94), crystallographer. Hodgkin studied chemistry at Oxford and subsequently worked under J. D. BERNAL at the Cavendish Laboratory, Cambridge. There she used X-ray crystallography to explore the three-dimensional structure of large biological molecules. In 1934 she returned to Oxford, where she taught chemistry and continued her research. Her refinement of X-ray crystallographic techniques and skill in analysing the resulting data enabled her and her colleagues to determine the molecular structures of some of the most important biological molecules: penicillin (1949), vitamin B12 (1957) and insulin (1969). In 1964 she won the Nobel Prize for Chemistry.

HOECHSTETTER, DANIEL (1515–81), industrialist. From Augsburg, he gained experience in mining in the Tyrol. In 1563 he was licensed to search for minerals in England and began prospecting in Cumberland; with partners from Augsburg and England, he financed the Society of Mines Royal, incorporated in 1568, as one of the first two English joint-stock companies. The mines near Keswick, producing copper and some silver, survived in the hands of his family until *c.* 1634.

HOG, JAMES (*c.* 1658–1734), clergyman *see* FISHER, EDWARD

HOGARDE, MILES *see* HUGGARDE, MILES

HOGARTH, WILLIAM (1697–1764), painter and engraver. The first eighteenth-century British artist to gain an international reputation, he championed contemporary British artists against the vogue for old masters and persistently challenged the notions of the artistic establishment. Apprenticed to a goldsmith and silversmith, he set up in business as a copper engraver, becoming famous through his own engraved reproductions of his satirical and moral paintings, notably the *Harlot's Progress* (1732), the *Rake's Progress* (1733–5) and *Marriage à la Mode* (1743–5). His work was widely pirated, but he lobbied successfully for the Engravers' Copyright Act 1735. He donated works to CORAM's Foundling Hospital; others, such as HAYMAN and Joseph Highmore, followed his example, and the meetings of painters there led ultimately to the foundation of the Royal Academy in 1768. Hogarth's championing of the 'patriot' cause led him to celebrate the Rococo style over the dominant neo-Palladianism. His theoretical work on aesthetics, *The Analysis of Beauty* (1753), was, ironically given his own pugnacious Britishness, scorned in Britain but well received on the continent.

HOGG, JAMES (1770–1835), poet and writer. Son of a poor Selkirk farmer, Hogg received hardly any education but, when in 1790 he went to work as a shepherd in Yarrow (Selkirks.), his employer encouraged him to read and he published a collection of *Scottish Pastorals, Poems, Songs etc.* from oral tradition known to himself and his mother. Impressed by these, Walter SCOTT drew on them for *Minstrelsy of the Scottish Border*, while Hogg's own compositions were published as *The Mountain Bard* (1807). Giving up attempts to be a sheep-farmer, he moved to Edinburgh, where *The Queen's Wake* (1813) attracted the critical attention of such established poets as WORDSWORTH and BYRON, and he contributed articles to *Blackwood's Magazine*, writing as the 'Ettrick Shepherd'. His prose work, *The Private Memoirs and Confessions of a Justified Sinner*, which received its full appreciation only in the twentieth century, was published in 1824.

HOGG, QUINTIN McGAREL (2nd Viscount Hailsham, later Baron Hailsham of Saint Marylebone) (1907–), politician. His father, Douglas, was three times Lord Chancellor under Stanley BALDWIN. After a brilliant career at Oxford, he came to prominence in 1938 when he won a famous by-election for Oxford as the pro-CHAMBERLAIN candidate; he remained an MP until 1950, when his father's death took him to the Lords.

He was First Lord of the Admiralty during the Suez crisis (1956–7), and became Secretary of State for Education under Harold MACMILLAN before becoming party chairman. His undoubted talents were flawed by what his opponents took to be a lack of judgement and a vulgar taste for publicity. His appearance at the Conservative conference in Brighton in 1957 ringing a hand-bell to 'wake up' the country was appreciated by the party faithful but even some of them thought there was something vulgar about it. The passing of the Peerage Act 1963 (*see* BENN, ANTHONY) allowed existing peers to disclaim their peerages and Macmillan's sudden illness and resignation opened Hailsham's way to the premiership. In a dramatic gesture at the party conference, he disclaimed his peerage and announced his candidacy.

Although Hailsham was initially Macmillan's choice for leader, reaction to his blatant electioneering at the party conference meant that he could not command enough support; nor could his main rival, R. A. BUTLER, and the premiership went to Lord Home (*see* DOUGLAS-HOME, ALEC) who was also able to disclaim his peerage. Quintin Hogg, as he once more became, served under HEATH as Shadow spokesman in a variety of posts, and he was one of those who demanded the sacking of Enoch POWELL after his 'rivers of blood' speech in 1968. In 1970 he accepted the office of Lord Chancellor from Heath, along with a life peerage, which meant he once more went to the Lords. He served two further terms as Lord Chancellor under Margaret THATCHER between 1979 and 1987, making him the longest-serving Lord Chancellor of modern times. His son, Douglas, was a Cabinet minister under John MAJOR.

HOGGART, RICHARD (1918–), academic and writer. Born in working-class Leeds and educated at Leeds University, Hoggart taught at the universities of Hull and Leicester before becoming the first Director of the influential Centre for Contemporary Cultural Studies at the University of Birmingham 1964–73. He established his international reputation with *The Uses of Literacy* (1957). Together with left-wing academics of his generation such as E. P. THOMPSON and Raymond WILLIAMS, Hoggart established 'culture' as a defining political and social consideration in the history of the British working class and a legitimate and important area of serious academic inquiry, though one normally ignored by historians interested only in 'high culture'. But, as Hoggart feared, even as the book came out the rising tide of post-war affluence and 'Americanization' was already changing for ever the working-class environment which he had so faithfully described.

HOLBEIN, HANS ('THE YOUNGER') (?1497–1543), artist. Son of the artist Hans

Holbein of Augsburg, he moved to Switzerland, establishing wide acquaintance among leading humanists including ERASMUS. His first visit to England was in 1526 and after 1532 he rarely left except for royal commissions, including an ill-fated portrait of ANNE OF CLEVES. His official work included architectual decoration, glass and jewellery, but it is his superb portraits, unrivalled as a record of an early modern court, which shape our visual knowledge of HENRY VIII's political world.

HOLINSHED, RAPHAEL (?–c. 1580), historian. A London printer, in 1577 he completed a collaborative project, the *Chronicles of England, Scotland and Ireland*, which was entirely dependent on others' research (*see* HARRISON, WILLIAM), but proved a great publishing success. This and later enlarged editions attracted government censorship. SHAKESPEARE's history plays are indebted to Holinshed.

HOLLAND, 1ST BARON *see* FOX, HENRY

HOLLAND, JOHN (1st Duke of Exeter, 13th Earl of Huntingdon) (c. 1352–1400), soldier. Son of Thomas Holland, Earl of Kent, he married Elizabeth, daughter of JOHN OF GAUNT. He was created Earl of Huntingdon in 1387 for his military skills but was a man of violent temper, charged more than once with unlawful killing. He was created Duke in 1397 but, at RICHARD II's deposition, he was deprived of his ducal title and soon afterwards died as violently as he had lived, lynched by the people of Pleshey (Essex) for conspiring against HENRY IV.

HOLLAND, JOHN (3rd [2nd Holland] Duke of Exeter, 14th Earl of Huntingdon) (1395–1447), military commander. Son of John HOLLAND, the 1st Duke, in 1443 he regained the title lost by his father, having had the earldom of Huntingdon restored in 1413. He fought with conspicuous bravery at Harfleur and Agincourt, and was for most of his life a leader of the armies of HENRY V and HENRY VI in France. He held the offices of Constable of the Tower of London, Admiral of England and Governor of Aquitaine.

HOLLAND, SIR JOHN (1603–1701), politician. From a Norfolk knightly family and Cambridge-educated, from 1640 he sat in the Short and Long Parliaments. After unsuccessful efforts at conciliation between CHARLES I and Westminster, suspect to many because of his Roman Catholic wife, he spent much time abroad to 1660, when he was involved in negotiations for CHARLES II's restoration. A voice for moderation in the Cavalier Parliament (1661–79), he nevertheless voted for the future JAMES II's exclusion from succession. At his death, he was the last surviving member of the

Long Parliament, for which his surviving papers are a significant source.

HOLLES, DENZIL (1st Baron Holles) (1599–1680), politician. Second son of John Holles, 1st Earl of Clare, and from 1624, an indefatigable MP, Holles was a noisy opponent of George VILLIERS, Duke of Buckingham, and William LAUD. He was one of the five MPs whom CHARLES I unsuccessfully targeted for arrest in Jan. 1642. Though he fought for Parliament at Edgehill (23 Oct. 1642), he soon advocated a compromise settlement. His hour seemed to have come with CHARLES I's defeat (1646), but his Presbyterian Parliamentary group and alliance with City of London wealth failed to outface the increasingly assertive army leaders, and he was forced to flee in July 1647. Parliament's efforts to rehabilitate him were crushed with PRIDE's Purge (Dec. 1648), and after that he spent 11 years in the political wilderness. On Richard CROMWELL's fall, he helped prepare the restoration of CHARLES II, and was rewarded with a barony, privy councillorship and the Paris Embassy (1662–7). His closing years, however, found him once more at odds with the court, and he played a leading role in the House of Lords in the mid 1670s and late 1670s in opposition to Thomas OSBORNE, Earl of Danby.

HOLMES, ARTHUR (1890–1965), geologist. Educated at Imperial College, London, Holmes researched and taught geology there (1912–20). He was chief geologist at the Yornah Oil Co., Burma (1920–4), and later held professorial chairs at Durham and Edinburgh. In the 1910s Holmes developed a widely used technique for determining the age of rocks from the amount of radioactive constituents, which he used to determine the absolute ages of fossils and to claim that the earth was 4.55 billion years old.

HOLMES, RICHARD (1946–), military historian and senior officer of the Territorial Army. Educated at the universities of Cambridge, Northern Illinois and Reading, he joined the academic staff at Sandhurst in 1969, where he became a leading proponent of operational military history, an approach to the study of war he developed most fully in *Firing Line* (1985). An incisive lecturer, a professor at Cranfield University since 1987, in his television programmes like *War Walks* (1996) he introduced operational military history to a mass audience. Alongside his academic career, Holmes rose to command a Territorial Army unit, the 2nd Battalion the Wessex Regiment, and in the mid 1980s played a major role in establishing the Higher Command and Staff Course for officers of all three services selected for promotion to senior rank. Promoted Brigadier in 1994, three years later he became tri-service Director of Reserve Forces and Cadets dealing with swingeing cuts in the defence review of 1997–8. Reductions were made, but Holmes was able to save most of the Territorial Army by emphasizing the role specialist units would have in supporting the regulars in peace-keeping operations, a partial victory in the latest round of the battle between Britain's regular and part-time forces.

HOLMES, SIR ROBERT (1622–92), sailor. The son of a landowner from Co. Cork, he served in the Royalist and then the French army, and after the Restoration became a senior English naval officer. His missions to defend English trade in West Africa led to skirmishes with the Dutch there and in North America where in Aug. 1664 he captured New Amsterdam, which he renamed New York. He took a leading role in the Second Dutch War (1665–7). The English suffered heavy losses in the Four Days Battle of June 1666, including Holmes's ship, but Holmes survived and retaliated in Aug. by setting fire to 250 merchantmen and warehouses on the Dutch shore in 'Sir Robert Holmes, his bonfire'. After peace in 1667 Holmes became MP for Winchester (1670) and played a minor part in the Third Dutch War (1672–4).

HOLST, GUSTAV (1873–1934), composer. Involved together with VAUGHAN WILLIAMS in the folksong movement, Holst was a slow developer musically but became a great exponent of the traditions of English music, rediscovering sixteenth- and seventeenth-century works and styles. His best-known work, the orchestral suite *The Planets* (1917), represents the culmination of his initial phase of composition. He later completed many major choral works, from the *Hymn of Jesus* (also 1917) to the *Choral Fantasia* (1930).

HOLYOAKE, GEORGE (1817–1906), secularist, co-operator and journalist. Born in Birmingham, he followed his father's trade as a whitesmith. Influenced by Owenism (*see* OWEN, ROBERT), Chartism and free thought, Holyoake became the leading national figure of secularism (a movement which included John Stuart MILL and George ELIOT among its sympathizers), founding and editing its chief paper, *The Reasoner*, from 1846 to 1861. (Charles BRADLAUGH's more militant *National Reformer* then became secularism's national organ.) Holyoake was also a staunch advocate of co-operatives, becoming the best-known national and international representative of the co-operative movement between the 1850s and 1880s, an active supporter of Italian and other nationalisms and a devoted Gladstonian Liberal (*see* GLADSTONE, W. E.).

HOME, GEORGE *see* HUME, GEORGE

HOME, HENRY (Lord Kames from 1752 as a Lord of Session) (1692–1782), judge and intellectual. Son of a minor gentleman, he was bound a writer to the signet, a standard beginning for a Scottish legal career. He drew attention to himself by his writings, had a successful career in Scottish public life and became one of the leading figures of the Scottish Enlightenment. His *Historical Law Tracts* (1757) broke new ground by examining legal principles and anomalies through the development of justice in former societies. Kames further applied his interest in comparative historical analysis to literature in *Elements of Criticism* (1762); it brought him European fame particularly through his examination of the disturbing psychological power of the imagination. He also advocated agrarian reform in Scotland in *The Gentleman Farmer* (1776), which recorded the practices introduced on his wife's Perths. estates.

HOME, JOHN (1722–1808), playwright. Son of the town clerk of Leith, educated at Edinburgh University, he took a part against the Jacobite rebellion in 1745–6, then was inducted a minister. His friends included William ROBERTSON and David HUME. He had literary ambitions, but GARRICK rejected his first play, *Agis*, and also his second, *Douglas*, which was nevertheless performed to great acclaim in Edinburgh in 1756. Fiercely criticized as a minister writing for the stage, he left the Kirk. *Douglas* was picked up for Covent Garden by John RICH and played successfully during 1757. Home's career blossomed while London was receptive to Scottish culture but in the 1760s his position as secretary to the unpopular royal favourite Bute (*see* STUART, JOHN) did him no favours. His last successful play was *Alonzo* (1773).

HONE, WILIAM (1780–1842), publisher. His acquittal in 1817 for publishing material calculated to injure public morals and bring the Prayer Book into disrepute marked a turning-point in the campaign for the freedom of the press.

HONORIUS, Roman Emperor (395–423). He is famous as the Emperor who, in 410, instructed the people of Britain 'to look to their own safety', a declaration that marked the effective end of Roman rule in Britain. At the time, however, the order was probably intended to be a temporary measure enabling Honorius to cope better with the usurper CONSTANTÍN III as well as the invaders who were attacking Gaul and Italy. In practice, Rome never again possessed the resources to restore its authority in Britain.

HONORIUS, ST, Archbishop of Canterbury (627–53). The last of the group of Roman missionaries who had accompanied St AUGUSTINE to England to become Archbishop of Canterbury. Honorius' archiepiscopate appears in most respects undistinguished. His rule did, however, coincide with the development of the Church in Kent under King EORCENBERHT. Canterbury did not assume the clear leadership of the Church in England plannned by Gregory the Great and Augustine until the time of St THEODORE OF TARSUS. Honorius was succeeded by Deusdedit (655–64), the first Archbishop of English birth.

HOOD, ROBIN, outlaw. If he ever existed, he probably waylaid travellers going through Barnsdale (Yorks.) on the Great North Road, rather than Sherwood Forest (Notts.). Many attempts have been made to identify him and his great enemy, the Sheriff of Nottingham, without success.

The dating that places him in RICHARD I's reign was first made by the Scottish historian John Major in 1521, but it is likely that his was a name to conjure with as early as the thirteenth century since the surname 'Robinhood' has been found in documents dating from that period. The earliest surviving ballads date from the fifteenth century, but LANGLAND, writing in the late 1300s, refers to tales about him. A yeoman in the earliest ballads, by the sixteenth century he had acquired noble status and an association with Maid Marian. In other ways, the legends came to reflect the hopes and fears of later ages: after the Reformation he became more hostile to rich prelates, and for the eighteenth-century radical, Joseph Ritson, editor of the first systematic collection of Robin Hood tales and ballads, he was the egalitarian hero who robbed the rich to give to the poor. The notion that he led Anglo-Saxon resistance to Norman oppression goes back no further than Walter SCOTT's *Ivanhoe*.

HOOD, THOMAS (1799–1845), poet. Primarily a humorous poet with penchant for puns, he wrote (with J. H. Reynolds) *Odes and Addresses to Great People* (1825). But it was *Whims and Oddities* (1826–7), which included the ballad 'Faithless Nelly Gray', that established his reputation. Editor of the *Germ* (which published TENNYSON), he started the *Comic Annual* (1830) and edited the *New Monthly Magazine* (1841). In 1843 his 'Song of the Shirt', a powerful indictment of exploitation in the workplace, was published anonymously in *Punch*, reprinted by *The Times*, translated into French, German, Italian and Russian, dramatized as *The Seamstress* and reproduced in a variety of popular forms – including on handkerchiefs.

HOOKE, ROBERT (1635–1703), scientist, architect. Oxford-educated, he assisted Robert BOYLE in experiments; he was made curator of experiments for the Royal Society (1662), then

Secretary (1677–82). He wrote on the nature of combustion (1665) and on gravity, anticipating much of Isaac NEWTON's work. Rejecting the discipline of astrology, he modified and improved the telescope and used it in important astronomical observations, enabling for instance calculations of the rotation of Jupiter. He also realised the possibilities of the microscope, and invented several instruments including the marine barometer. His building designs included Bethlehem Hospital and the College of Physicians.

HOOKER, JOHN (pen name Vowell) (*c.* 1517–81), historian. From Exeter and a student at Oxford, Cologne and Strasbourg (where he lodged with Peter MARTYR VERMIGLI), his career was spent in the service of his native city, for which he twice served as MP, and about which he lovingly collected information, notably on the siege by traditionalist rebels in 1549. He also left a journal of the 1571 Parliament and of the Irish Parliament of 1568, in which he sat as a business agent of the Devon magnate Sir Peter Carew.

HOOKER, SIR JOSEPH DALTON (1817–1911), botanist. Son of the distinguished botanist, William Jackson Hooker, he studied medicine at Glasgow and later worked as a surgeon and naturalist on James Clark ROSS's Antarctic expedition (1839–43), classifying the vast number of botanical observations in *Flora Antarctica* (1844–7), *Flora Novae-Zelandiae* (1853–5) and *Flora Tasmaniae* (1855–60). Appointed botanist to the Geological Survey in 1845, he studied the flora, fauna and ethnography of India, eastern Nepal and Tibet. His interest in India resulted in numerous works including the *Flora of British India* (1872–97). He became assistant director (1855) then, in succession to his father, Director (1865) at the Royal Botanic Gardens, Kew, where, with the eminent botanist George Bentham, he wrote the great taxonomic work, *Genera Plantarum* (1862–83). At Kew he oversaw the construction of such buildings as the Jodrell Laboratory for plant anatomy and physiology (1876), which he turned into a world-centre of botanical research. A close friend of Charles DARWIN since 1839, he was a major figure in the construction, presentation and championing of the naturalist's theory of evolution by natural selection. From 1860 he embarked on further botanical expeditions, including those to Syria (1860), Morocco (1871) and the USA (1877). He retired from Kew in 1885.

HOOKER, RICHARD (*c.* 1554–1600), writer. An Exeter-born Oxford academic who, on his marriage in 1584, resigned his fellowship for a series of Church appointments, notably from 1585 the mastership (chaplaincy) of the Temple

Church, where he found himself drawn into clashes with his Puritan colleague Walter TRAVERS. His great work *On the Laws of Ecclesiastical Polity* was published in sections between 1594 and 1662; though its majestic language has earned Hooker a reputation as 'judicious', it was an all-out attack on Puritan doctrine and a passionate defence of the Elizabethan settlement of religion on philosophical grounds. Hooker played a great part in the formation of Anglican theology, with its respect for tradition within the framework of the Reformation, and its insistence on the importance of reason in the discussion of sacred subjects. His image was creatively reworked to stress a precocious Anglican identity in the biography by Izaak WALTON.

HOOKER, WILLIAM (1785–1865), botanist *see* HOOKER, SIR JOSEPH DALTON

HOOPER, JOHN (*c.* 1500–55), Bishop of Gloucester. A former Cistercian monk, he fled England in 1540 because of his reformist religious views; experience of Zürich (1547–9) made him more radical still. Edward SEYMOUR, Duke of Somerset, made him his chaplain on his return. In 1550–1 he provoked a stir by refusing to accept the bishopric of Gloucester if he had to swear to the royal supremacy using a traditionalist form of oath mentioning the saints, or wear certain traditional vestments at his consecration. His climb-down on the latter point was an important indication of the limits to radical change in EDWARD VI's Church. Proving a model Protestant bishop, he was an obvious target for MARY I; his death at the stake in Gloucester was unusually agonizing.

HOPE, VICTOR (2nd Marquess of Linlithgow) (1887–1952), Viceroy of India. Chairman of the Royal Commission on Indian agriculture in 1928 and of the joint select committee on Indian constitutional reform which resulted in the Government of India Act 1935, Linlithgow was made Viceroy the following year. Although his task was to introduce provincial autonomy and superintend Burma's separation, he was an unbending imperialist and acted to repress the mass appeal of the Indian National Congress. Responding harshly to the Quit India movement, he intensified anti-British sentiment, although he intended to maximize the war effort. He refused to visit Bengal, stricken by famine in 1943, and resigned that year after the longest and arguably the least enlightened viceregal tenure of the twentieth century.

HOPKINS, SIR FREDERICK GOWLAND (1861–1947), biochemist. In 1898 Hopkins was appointed lecturer in chemical physiology at Cambridge, where he established a leading centre of biochemistry and a reputation as the 'father of British biochemistry'. By the 1900s he was exploring the existence of 'accessory food factors' (later called vitamins), trace substances that, along with proteins, minerals, carbohydrates and fats, were essential animal nutrients. He became the first Professor of Biochemistry at Cambridge in 1914 and, for his work on vitamins, shared the 1929 Nobel Prize for Medicine with Christiaan Eijkman.

HOPKINS, GERARD MANLEY (1844–89), poet. Known as 'the star of Balliol' for his brilliance as a classics scholar at Oxford, Hopkins was received into the Roman Catholic Church by Cardinal NEWMAN in 1866. Anguished about his ability to combine the sensuate requirements of writing poetry with his religious vocation, he burned all his early work; his vow of poetic silence persisted until 1875 when he was encouraged to write a poem commemorating five Franciscan nuns who perished when their ship, the *Deutschland*, sank in the Thames estuary in Dec. that year. The poem was rejected for publication and, though Hopkins continued to write what he called 'sprung rhythm' poetry largely about his spiritual relation to God and his pantheistic rejoicing in nature (the best known being 'The Windhover'), none of his poetry was published in his lifetime. It was not until his close friend, the poet Edward Bridges, edited his poems (1918) that his work came to public attention.

HOPKINS, JOHN (?–1570), clergyman *see* STERNHOLD, THOMAS

HOPKINS, MATTHEW (?–1647), witch-finder. A loathsome conman who took advantage of the heightened public anxiety about witches during the English Civil Wars to procure himself a parliamentary commission to seek out witches (1645); he published an account of his work. About 200 people, mostly women, died in East Anglia before he himself was denounced and hanged as a sorcerer. His brief career as witch-finder general marked the last peak of the witch craze in England.

HOPKINSON, SIR THOMAS (TOM) (1905–90), journalist. In 1938 Hopkinson was appointed assistant editor to set up a new photo-journalism magazine, *Picture Post*, with a Hungarian journalist, Stefan Lorant, from whom he took over as editor in 1940. Within six months the magazine was selling a million and a half copies weekly. Its object was to show that the lives of 'ordinary' people were remarkable: during the Munich crisis it featured the people waiting anxiously on the pavement outside 10 Downing Street, rather than the politicians within. But by 1950 Hopkinson was at odds with the proprietor, Edward Hulton, and when that year, against Hopkinson's expressed wishes, Hulton pulled a story by James CAMERON (with photographs by Bert Hardy) on the brutal treatment of political prisoners by the South Korean regime which the United Nations was supporting, Hopkinson resigned. *Picture Post* ceased publication in 1957. Hopkinson went on to edit the South African magazine *Drum* and subsequently to give academic training to journalists, first at Sussex and then at Cardiff University.

HOPTON, RALPH (1st Baron Hopton) (1596–1652), soldier. A veteran soldier for the Protestant cause in the Thirty Years War, as an MP during the 1620s he showed his hostility to CHARLES I by presenting the Commons' Grand Remonstrance to him in 1641, but suddenly and mysteriously he became a passionate supporter of the King in 1642. Initially he won victories in command of western troops (and was made Baron in 1643). Later commanding the disintegrating Royalist army, he surrendered at Truro in 1646, and died in exile at Bruges.

HORAN, ALICE (1895–1971), trade-union leader. During the First World War 2,000 of the women at the factory where Horan worked making service equipment went on strike over piece-work rates: it was her introduction to trade-union activity and after serving as a shop steward she became a student at Ruskin College, Oxford. In 1926 she went to work as the women's district organizer for Lancs. of the recently established National Union of General and Municipal Workers. The union's membership increased seven-fold over the next two decades and in 1946 Horan was appointed national women's officer. During the Second World War she was involved in the regulation of women's earnings in war production.

HORNE, GEORGE (1730–92), theologian. The son of a Kentish clergyman, he was educated at Oxford, where he developed an interest in the ideas of John HUTCHINSON, which he was to champion as preferable to NEWTON's. He was elected to a fellowship at Magdalen, became President in 1768, and Vice-Chancellor of the university in 1776, where he came to the notice of Lord NORTH, then both Chancellor of the university and Prime Minister. His career developed apace: he was made Dean of Canterbury, and in 1792 Bishop of Norwich. He helped to keep the High Church tradition alive within the upper reaches of the establishment; unlike the next generation of High Churchmen, he was sympathetic to the variant of the High Church tradition represented by John WESLEY.

HORNE TOOKE, JOHN (1736–1812), radical. The son of a wealthy London poulterer, John Horne (as he was originally named) was ordained in 1760 and escorted several young men on the Grand Tour, meeting WILKES, STERNE and Voltaire. He campaigned for Wilkes in 1768, and was a founder of the Society of Supporters of the Bill of Rights, which raised money to pay Wilkes's legal costs and for parliamentary reform, but left after disagreements in 1771. His abrasively radical posture and connections repeatedly caused him trouble: he was imprisoned for a year in 1775 for raising a subscription for the families of Americans killed at Lexington; in 1794 he was tried for high treason but acquitted. In 1782 he added the surname of his friend William Tooke to his own, probably in the expectation that he would be Tooke's heir; when Tooke left his money elsewhere, Horne Tooke sued for a share. His philological interests were expressed in *The Diversions of Purley* (1786), which emphasized the importance of studying Anglo-Saxon. His election as MP for Old Sarum in 1801 was declared void because he was a clergyman.

HORNIMAN, ANNIE (1860–1937), theatre manager. Daughter of the Liberal MP and tea merchant who founded the Horniman Museum in south London, she studied at the Slade School and travelled widely, pursuing her growing interest in the theatre. Horniman financed George Bernard SHAW's first publicly performed play, *Arms and the Man*, in 1894. Convinced from her travels in Germany of the need for subsidized theatre, she offered a theatre which she had acquired in Abbey Street, Dublin, to the National Theatre of Ireland in 1904: it became the dramatic heart of the Irish renaissance, staging plays by W. B. YEATS, J. M. SYNGE and Lady Augusta GREGORY. In 1907 she bought and revived the Gaiety Theatre in Manchester as the country's first repertory theatre, alternating new plays with the classics.

HORROCKS, SIR BRIAN (1895–1985), soldier. Son of an army doctor, educated at Sandhurst, Horrocks was captured at Ypres in Oct. 1914 and was a prisoner of war in Germany until Nov. 1918. Dispatched to Russia to serve on Admiral Kolchek's staff, Horrocks was captured by the Soviets, who held him for 18 months. He had better luck in the Second World War. Chosen by MONTGOMERY to command XIII Corps at El Alamein, Horrocks fought through to Tunis, where he was badly wounded. In July 1944 he took command of XXX Corps in Normandy, a command he held until the end of the war. He subsequently became a television personality, his lucid account of battles setting a style for a host of latter-day imitators.

HORSBURGH, FLORENCE (1889–1969), politician. Elected Conservative MP for Dundee in 1931, Horsburgh was appointed Parliamentary Secretary to the Ministry of Health with responsibility for arranging the evacuation of children from the cities on the outbreak of the Second World War. She lost her seat in the 1945 election, but was finally returned to the Commons for Manchester Moss Side in 1950. In CHURCHILL's 1951 government she was appointed Minister of Education, a post which made her the first woman Conservative Cabinet minister when Education was brought into the Cabinet in 1953.

HORSLEY, SAMUEL (1733–1806), scientist. He studied astronomy at Cambridge as well as preparing for the priesthood. He was made a Fellow of the Royal Society in 1769, becoming one of its secretaries in 1773, but quarrelled with BANKS and resigned in 1784. He belonged to a tradition which held that scientific observation contributed towards a fuller understanding of the divine universe, and completed an edition of NEWTON's works in 1785. He was bitterly critical of the innovative thinking of Joseph PRIESTLEY in both science and theology. Horsley defined himself as a High Churchman, and became one of the most articulate representatives of that renascent element within the Church. Favoured by PITT THE YOUNGER, he became Bishop successively of St David's (1788), Rochester (1793) and St Asaph (1802).

HOTHAM, JOHN (?–1645), soldier. Hotham fought for Frederick the Elector Palatine's Protestant cause in the opening stages of the Thirty Years War and was made a baronet in 1622. Furious at removal as Governor of Hull in 1639, he withdrew earlier compliance with CHARLES I's extraparliamentary levy of Ship Money, and further revenged himself by refusing to admit Charles to Hull in 1642. He recaptured Scarborough for Parliament (1643) but soon afterwards his increasing jealousy of rivals, particularly Oliver CROMWELL, led him and his son John to intrigue with the Royalists. Parliament executed them.

HOTSPUR *see* PERCY, HENRY

HOUGHTON, 1ST BARON *see* MILNES, RICHARD MONKTON

HOUGHTON, JOHN (?1488–1535), monk. From 1531, he was Prior of the Carthusian priory in London (the Charterhouse), where most of the monks were among the few people actively to oppose HENRY VIII's break with Rome. Houghton was executed for refusing the Oath of Royal Supremacy; he is now a saint of the Roman Catholic Church.

HOUNSFIELD, SIR GODFREY NEWBOLD (1919–), electrical engineer. Hounsfield studied electrical engineering in London, lectured on radar during the Second World War and in 1951 began his lifelong career with Thorn-EMI's medical research group. He developed the technique of X-ray computer-assisted tomography (CAT) for building up images of soft-body tissues, and embodied his work in the CAT scanner which has greatly aided the detection of tumours in the body. In 1979 he shared the Nobel Prize for Medicine with fellow CAT-scan pioneer Allan Cormack, and subsequently explored nuclear magnetic resonance as a tool for imaging soft tissues.

HOWARD, CHARLES (2nd Baron Howard of Effingham, 10th [1st Howard] Earl of Nottingham) (c. 1536–1624), admiral and politician. After naval and military commands, in 1585 he became both Lord Chamberlain and Lord Admiral and directed operations against the 1588 Spanish Armada. His inharmonious joint command with Robert DEVEREUX, Earl of Essex, in the raid on Cadiz (1596) provoked a long feud, fuelled by Howard's creation as Earl (1597); Essex insisted on upstaging him with a grant of the earl marshalship, and Nottingham supervised the suppression of Essex's 1601 rebellion. He led Anglo-Spanish peace negotiations in 1604–5, a turning-point in English diplomacy, after half a century of alliance with the United Provinces of the Netherlands. He bitterly resented the growing influence on JAMES I of his cousin, Henry HOWARD, Earl of Northampton. In 1619 he was at last persuaded to retire as Lord Admiral, leaving a spectacular administrative mess for his successor George VILLIERS, Duke of Buckingham.

HOWARD, CHARLES (6th [3rd Howard] Earl of Carlisle) (1669–1738), politician. The grandson of a Parliamentarian ennobled at the Restoration, he succeeded his father in 1692. In the mid 1690s he developed Whig political ambitions, and rose with remarkable speed. In 1698–9 he bought land in North Yorks. and employed VANBRUGH to build Castle Howard. He was made a Privy Councillor in June 1701 and accompanied WILLIAM III on a visit to Holland. In Dec. 1701 he was made First Lord of the Treasury. He campaigned vigorously to reduce the influence of Tories unwilling to support an expensive continental war, but lost office on the King's death. Thenceforth he was a minor figure among the Junto Whigs.

HOWARD, SIR EBENEZER (1850–1928), town planner. A parliamentary shorthand-writer by profession, his book *Tomorrow: A Peaceful Path to Real Reform* (1898), which outlined a programme of self-contained communities with rural and urban facilities surmounted by 'green belts', became the Bible of the garden city movement with which he was long associated.

HOWARD, FRANCES (1592 or 1593–1632), accessory to murder. Daughter of Thomas HOWARD, 11th Earl of Suffolk, at 13 she married 14-year-old Robert DEVEREUX, 20th Earl of Essex, in a grand design to manufacture aristocratic family ties, but husband and wife loathed each other. Three months after divorce in 1613, Frances married JAMES I's boyfriend, Robert CARR, but in 1616 a series of trials climaxed in Frances confessing complicity in murdering Carr's friend, Sir Thomas OVERBURY, for opposing their marriage. Spared execution, Carr and Frances were released from the Tower to live obscurely.

HOWARD, HENRY (styled Earl of Surrey) (1516 or 1518–47), poet. In youth a friend of HENRY VIII's bastard son Henry FITZROY, Duke of Richmond (d. 1536), who married Howard's sister, he grew up a brilliant and cultured Renaissance nobleman with a European reputation, and was an accomplished and original poet. He served under his father, Thomas, 3rd HOWARD Duke of Norfolk, in Scotland in 1542 and in France in 1544, becoming Governor of captured Boulogne the following year. By now his pride in his exalted ancestry and his indifference to whom he offended had reached danger-point; court enemies of the Howard family, mostly Protestants like Sir Anthony DENNY, seized on his use of the royal arms quartered with his family coat. Nothing was more likely to raise the King's fears. Surrey was swiftly arrested and executed. His fall was a fatal blow to the Catholic court party in the King's dying months, even though Surrey did not share his family's religious traditionalism.

HOWARD, HENRY (9th [1st Howard] Earl of Northampton) (1540–1614), politician. The execution of his elder brother, Thomas 4th HOWARD, Duke of Norfolk, (1572) left him poverty-stricken, and his lifelong semi-secret attachment to Catholicism led to repeated investigations and imprisonments. He began to revive the family fortunes in the 1590s, allying himself with Robert DEVEREUX, Earl of Essex, against Robert and William CECIL, but full rehabilitation came only in the reign of his fellow intellectual and homosexual JAMES I, who made him Earl in 1604. After Robert Cecil's death, he consolidated his position, backing a policy of reconciliation with Spain and co-operating with his nephew, Thomas HOWARD, Earl of Suffolk, in wrecking an attempt to solve royal financial problems in the Addled Parliament (1614). A fascinating if unlikeable man, he was one of the most clever and devious politicians of his day; his numerous writings on politics, philosophy, liturgy and religion await full investigation.

HOWARD, JOHN (6th [1st Howard] Duke of Norfolk) (*c*. 1430–85), nobleman. He was knighted in 1461 on the accession of EDWARD IV and remained much in his favour. Although created a baron by HENRY VI on his restoration in 1471, he remained a Yorkist and fought that year at both Barnet and Tewkesbury. He was created Duke and Earl Marshal by RICHARD III in 1483. At Bosworth, where he was killed in the vanguard, he was the only major English peer to fight for Richard.

HOWARD, JOHN (1726–90), prison reformer. A Dissenter who inherited his prosperous upholsterer father's wealth, he spent part of the Seven Years War as a prisoner of war. As Sheriff of Bedfordshire in 1773, he had some responsibility for the state of county prisons. Concern to set local administrative shortcomings in context led him to undertake the first in a series of prison tours, subsequently extended to the continent. His travels and campaigns were subsidized by his cousin, the wealthy brewer and MP Samuel WHITBREAD the elder. His *State of the Prisons in England and Wales* (1777) attracted notice in Britain and Europe and helped to boost a nascent prison-reform movement. He is commemorated by a statue in St Paul's and in the name of the Howard League for Penal Reform.

HOWARD, PHILIP (25th [1st Howard] Earl of Arundel) (1557–95), Catholic convert. Despite the execution of his father, Thomas 4th HOWARD Duke of Norfolk, in 1572, he enjoyed a playboy life around the court until converted to Roman Catholicism in 1584. By 1585 he could conceal his feelings no longer and tried unsuccessfully to flee abroad. A conversion by the heir of England's former premier peer was politically very serious; he was captured, tried and imprisoned. Although the government mismanaged a second trial for treason in 1589, he was not released, and he died in the Tower. He is now a saint of the Roman Catholic Church.

HOWARD, THOMAS (13th Earl of Surrey, 7th [2nd Howard] Duke of Norfolk) (1443–1524), soldier and politician. He and his father John HOWARD fought for EDWARD IV at Barnet (1471) and for RICHARD III at Bosworth (1485). Released from the Tower of London by HENRY VII, he resumed a career of royal service principally in the north, resulting in gradual regrant of his confiscated estates. Earl Marshal for life from 1510, after commanding the victorious English against the Scots at Flodden (1513), he regained the dukedom (1514). As Thomas WOLSEY gained power, he went into semi-retirement, although he presided over the trial of his cousin, Edward STAFFORD, Duke of Buckingham (1521).

HOWARD, THOMAS (14th [2nd Howard] Earl of Surrey, 8th [3rd Howard] Duke of Norfolk) (1473–1554), royal servant and soldier. Son of Thomas 2nd HOWARD, Duke of Norfolk, he was created Earl in 1514 when his father was restored to the ducal title, for his part in the victory over the Scots at Flodden (1513). His long life was spent in royal service: Lieutenant in Ireland (1520–22), Lord High Treasurer (from 1522), general against the Scots (1542) and in France (1545). At court he represented traditionalist aristocratic Catholicism with no liking for clerical or Renaissance humanist reform. His relations with Thomas WOLSEY and Thomas CROMWELL were characterized by jealousy coloured by bluff friendship until the time seemed ripe to attack them; his investments in successive nieces, ANNE BOLEYN and CATHERINE HOWARD, as royal wives, did not pay off, but he adroitly abandoned them. His skills in political escapology were not equalled in his son, Henry HOWARD, Earl of Surrey, and a bewildered Norfolk found himself in the Tower in Dec. 1546; only HENRY VIII's death saved him from execution. Released and restored to his honours only on MARY I's accession, his geriatric last military command against Sir Thomas WYATT's rebellion (1554) was a humiliating failure. His second marriage to the spirited daughter of Edward STAFFORD, Duke of Buckingham, had ended in a spectacular and messy separation in 1533.

HOWARD, THOMAS (15th [3rd Howard] Earl of Surrey, 9th [4th Howard] Duke of Norfolk) (1538–72), politician. Son of the executed Henry HOWARD, Earl of Surrey, he dutifully acted his role as England's senior peer with his military command in Scotland (1559–60), but in the crisis of the late 1560s caused by MARY QUEEN OF SCOTS' flight to England he became a leading candidate for her hand. By then, grief at the death of successive wives had left him unable to cope with the strain of high politics; he was arrested in 1569 after he fled to his East Anglian estates. Evidence of continuing involvement with the plots around Mary (see RIDOLFI, ROBERTO) led to his execution in 1572. Though central to Catholic hopes and a patron of religious conservatives, he died proclaiming his Protestantism, still valuing the friendship of his old tutor John FOXE.

HOWARD, THOMAS (1st Baron Howard de Walden, 11th [1st Howard] Earl of Suffolk) (1561–1626), seafarer and politician. Second son of the executed Thomas 4th HOWARD, Duke of Norfolk, his rehabilitation began in the 1580s and was encouraged by his energetic naval service against the 1588 Spanish Armada and later, though his 1591 Azores expedition against Spain was marred by Sir Richard GRENVILLE's death. JAMES I gave him his earldom; with his uncle, Henry HOWARD, Earl of Northampton, he formed a pro-Spanish and Catholic-tinged faction in government, increasingly influential after Robert CECIL's death (1612). After co-operating with Northampton in wrecking an attempt to solve royal financial problems in the Addled Parliament (1614), he became Lord High Treasurer. Enmity from George VILLIERS, Duke of Buckingham, led to his dismissal for embezzlement in 1618; he was imprisoned and heavily fined, and his career was ruined. His profiteering in government had, however, enabled him to build a monstrously large mansion at Audley End (Essex) (see also AUDLEY, THOMAS).

HOWARD, THOMAS (26th [2nd Howard] Earl of Arundel, 16th [4th Howard] Earl of Surrey, 16th [1st Howard] Earl of Norfolk) (1585–1646), royal servant and art collector. In 1604 he regained the Arundel earldom forfeited by his father Philip HOWARD, and devoted his life to restoring his family's greatness. He abandoned Roman Catholicism and became involved in politics as part of the Howard faction opposing George VILLIERS, Duke of Buckingham; he made an unhappy commander against the Scots in the First Bishops' War of 1639, and presided at the trial of his enemy, Thomas WENTWORTH, Earl of Strafford, (1641) before escaping the wars to escort HENRIETTA MARIA into continental exile in 1644. He took up residence at Padua, where he died, having contributed handsomely to the Royalist cause from his fortune. More distinguished culturally than as a politician, he was one of the first English art collectors to equal continental connoisseurs, and from 1609 his tours abroad yielded a magnificent array of paintings and ancient sculpture. His manuscript collection substantially survives.

HOWARD, WILLIAM (15th Baron and 1st Viscount Stafford) (1614–80), victim of the Popish-Plot agitation. Younger son of the head of the powerful Catholic family, he made an advantageous marriage with the heiress of the Staffords. He often opposed the policies of CHARLES II in Parliament, but this did not spare him from the attentions of Titus OATES who in 1678 accused him, with Lords Arundell, Powis, Petre and

Belasyse, of intending to mount a Catholic coup. Stafford was tried first, found guilty (despite the absence of evidence of anything beyond support for religious toleration) and sentenced to be hanged, drawn and quartered. Charles II commuted the sentence to beheading.

HOWE, GEOFFREY (Baron Howe of Aberavon) (1926–), politician. Denis HEALEY described being attacked by Howe as akin to 'being savaged by a dead sheep', but in the most dramatic moment of his career Howe showed how damaging that could be. He was a product of the Cambridge University and Bow group nexus, which fitted him perfectly to rise in the Heathite Conservative Party during the decade (1964–74); mildly progressive in his social views, mildly conservative in his belief in the virtues of the mixed economy, he was almost the very model of a modern Tory. MP for Bebington (Ches.) (1964–6); and for Reigate (Surrey) in 1970, he migrated to Surrey East in 1974. Most of his career was spent on the front bench as the party's most reliable, if unexciting, work-horse. During HEATH'S premiership he was Solicitor General (1970–2) and then Minister for Trade and Consumer Affairs (1972–4). When Margaret THATCHER came to power in 1979, he was appointed Chancellor of the Exchequer.

Despite his quiet and self-effacing manner, Howe was a crucial component in the Thatcher revolution. After 1974 he had gradually become convinced that control over the money supply was the key to breaking the inflationary cycle which had afflicted Britain since the mid 1960s, and from his first dramatic budget, in which he nearly doubled Value Added Tax and cut income tax, he showed himself to be a radical Chancellor. During the period 1980–2, when unemployment rose and there were calls for a 'U-turn', Howe stood firmly beside Thatcher.

After the 1983 election victory Howe went to the Foreign Office, where his most notable achievements were the agreement to sign over Hong Kong to the Chinese (1984) and the Single European Market Act (1985). It was on this last subject that his differences with Thatcher began to become acute, particularly after 1987 when he aligned himself increasingly with Nigel LAWSON, his successor at the Exchequer, and in July 1989 Howe was demoted to Leader of the House of Commons and Deputy Prime Minister and was consistently marginalized by Thatcher for his opposition to her European stance. Although Howe stayed in office when Lawson resigned in Oct. 1989, his own resignation a year later set the fuse which would explode Thatcher's premiership. His resignation speech on 13 Nov. revealed how divided the Thatcher Cabinet had been over Europe and the depth of discontent over the

Prime Minister's leadership style encouraged HESELTINE to mount his leadership challenge.

HOWE, JOHN (1630–1705), churchman. An Oxford don during the 1650s, he became domestic chaplain to Oliver CROMWELL, then to Richard CROMWELL, and in 1662 was ejected from his Devon parish. Later he was chaplain to Lord Massereene in Antrim and led a Presbyterian congregation in London (1676); he was prominent in negotiating for Dissenters with JAMES II and WILLIAM III. Unlike most Dissenters he was Latitudinarian in sympathy, remained on friendly terms with leading Anglicans and worked unsuccessfully to unite Congregationalists and Presbyterians.

HOWE, RICHARD (4th Viscount and 1st Earl Howe) (1726–99), sailor. He entered the navy in his teens and was brother of William HOWE, with whom he had joint command in North America (1775–8). Howe commanded the Channel Fleet in 1782 during the War of American Independence and then again at the beginning of the French Revolutionary War, when he won the victory of the Glorious First of June (1794). He came back from retirement in 1797 to mediate between the Spithead mutineers (*see also* PARKER, RICHARD) and the Admiralty.

HOWE, WILLIAM (5th Viscount Howe) (1729–1814), soldier. Son of an Irish peer, he served under WOLFE at Quebec in 1759, and played a leading part in the War of American Independence. Although he disapproved of NORTH'S policies, he became commander of British forces in America in Oct. 1775 in place of GAGE. He launched the offensive that captured New York, and took Philadelphia in 1777. In May 1778, following BURGOYNE's defeat at Saratoga, he resigned, left America and, together with his brother, secured a parliamentary inquiry into the conduct of the war. Under the second Rockingham (*see* WATSON-WENTWORTH, CHARLES) ministry Howe became Lieutenant General of the Ordnance, and was given command of the home military districts in the French Revolutionary Wars.

HOWELL, GEORGE (1833–1910), trade-union leader. Born in Som. the son of a mason and builder, he was variously employed before settling as a bricklayer in 1853. A voracious reader, increasingly within the secular and religious literature of radicalism, he became a Chartist in 1848 and also converted from Anglicanism to Wesleyan Methodism, becoming a Sunday School teacher and a proselytizing teetotaller. Moving to London in 1855, he joined the London Order of the Operative Bricklayers' Society in 1859. Although rapidly gaining prominence in it and helping to reshape it on New Model lines, he consistently failed in his attempts to become General Secretary. He was elected to the London Trades Council in 1861, and was its Secretary (1861–2). His most important role was as Secretary of the Reform League from 1865, the chief instrument of the renewed agitation for votes for working men in the 1860s. When the Reform Act was passed in 1867 he also became the administrator of a special fund, gathered by the Liberal Party, to mobilize working-class votes in marginal constituencies. As such he helped to build the alliance between the Liberal Party and labour, a role he continued to play as Secretary of the Parliamentary Committee of the Trades Union Congress (1871–6). Howell's own ambitions to become an MP were thwarted until 1885, when he was elected as Liberal MP, with backing from both Liberal and radical organizations, for Bethnal Green, London.

HOWLETT, JOHN (1731–1804), demographer and social scientist. He studied at both Oxford and Cambridge and served 20 years as a curate in Kent before being presented to the living of Great Dunmow (Essex). He first became interested in statistics through the population controversy, publishing *An Examination of Dr Price's Essay on the Population of England and Wales* (1781) to challenge Price's argument that the population was in decline by exposing the failings of oft-quoted statistics such as tax returns and the Bills of Mortality. A few years later he similarly drew on empirical evidence to challenge prevailing views, arguing that enclosures did not cause depopulation. By the late 1780s he was showing increasing concern about the living conditions of the poorer classes, suggesting for example that expenditure on the poor, far from being over-generous, was not keeping pace with rising population and inflation.

HOYLE, SIR FRED (1915–), astronomer. Hoyle was educated at Cambridge, where he taught mathematics (1948–58) and was Plumian Professor of Astronomy and Natural Philosophy (1958–72). In 1948, with Hermann Bondi and Thomas Gold, he proposed the controversial 'steady-state' theory of the universe: this claimed that, since the universe is of uniform density, is expanding and appears the same everywhere and at all times, matter must be created continuously. Since the 1950s he has attempted to deal with new astronomical evidence that casts doubt on the theory. In 1957 he collaborated with William Fowler and Geoffrey and Margaret Burbidge on the influential nucleosynthesis theory of chemical-element formation inside stars. He has written numerous popular works on astronomy as well as science fiction.

HUDDLESTON, TREVOR (1913–98), churchman. Huddleston was a tireless campaigner against apartheid. 'A Christian', he once said, 'is always an agitator if he is true to his calling.' Educated at Oxford, ordained in 1937, he entered the Anglican Community of the Resurrection at Mirfield (Yorks.) and was professed as a monk in 1941. Between 1943 and 1956 he served in Johannesburg and on his return published the best-seller *Naught for your Comfort* denouncing the evils of racial segregation. As Bishop of Masai (south-east Tanganyika) (1960–8), he worked with Julius NYERERE to help the nation (renamed Tanzania) respond to independence. Suffragan Bishop of Stepney (1968–78), he was elected Bishop of Mauritius and Archbishop of the Indian Ocean (1978–83) and, after he retired, Chairman of the Anti-Apartheid Movement.

HUDSON, GEORGE (1800–1871), railway speculator. A York linen-draper and close friend of George STEPHENSON, he invested a legacy in local railways and made a fortune from speculation in railway company shares, becoming known as the 'Railway King'. Sharp and shady (he was found guilty of dishonesty in 1849), he did much to rationalize the unplanned and chaotic rail network through a series of mergers and amalgamations and the introduction of collaborative railway clearing-house arrangements. He went into land and politics, representing Sunderland as a Conservative MP (1849–51); although financially ruined in the railway mania which he did much to create, he still retained electoral support.

HUE DE ROTELANDE (*fl.* 1180), poet. He was the author of *Ipomedon* and *Protheselaus*, two romances composed in Anglo-Norman octosyllabic verse couplets, which appear to be sending-up the whole genre, so light-heartedly and flippantly are they written. He claims, for example, to be no more of a liar than Walter MAP. Little is known about this entertaining versifier, although the allusion to Map, together with his name, suggesting that he was born at Rhuddlan, and the fact that he had a patron who was Lord of Monmouth, indicates that he probably came from the Anglo-Welsh border.

HUGGARDE (OR HOGARDE), MILES (?–*c.* 1561), controversialist. A London tradesman, from the 1540s Huggarde was a prominent champion of traditional religion, and under MARY I wrote a series of tracts defending her restoration of Roman Catholicism. His writings, unusual as being from a layman without university education, are marked by lively humour, vigorous language and acute observation.

HUGGINS, MARGARET (née Murray) (1848–1915), astronomer. Born in Monkstown (Co. Dublin), Margaret Murray received instruction in astronomy from her grandfather. Later she built astronomical instruments and developed skills in painting, music and writing. Through the distinguished telescope-maker, Howard Grubb, she became acquainted with William HUGGINS, and in 1875 they married. She was a close collaborator on her husband's pioneering work on the spectra of stars, nebulae, planets and comets. Her considerable reputation as an astronomer was recognized in her honorary membership of the Royal Astronomical Society (1903) and in the terms of her husband's knighthood of 1897.

HUGGINS, SIR WILLIAM (1824–1910), astronomer. Huggins developed an interest in astronomy while working for his family's drapery firm. In 1856 he built a private observatory in London and, using telescopic and photographic instruments, made important new observations of celestial bodies. A pioneering astro-spectroscopist, from the early 1860s he began using spectroscopes to analyse the light of celestial bodies (notably the sun, nebulae and comets) and to construct evidence of the physical nature of such bodies. He also used spectroscopy to establish the speed of stars and pioneered spectroscopic photography. In 1875 he married Margaret Murray (*see* HUGGINS, MARGARET).

HUGH OF LINCOLN, ST (also known as Hugh of Avalon) (*c.* 1135–1200), bishop. Brought to England from Burgundy in *c.* 1180 to become Prior of HENRY II's Charterhouse at Witham (Som.), he was made Bishop of Lincoln in 1186, the only Carthusian monk to become an English prelate. His care for the sick, his personal charm to which both children and animals succumbed and the serene self-confidence and quick wit that enabled him to outface kings won him a great reputation as a saintly defender of ecclesiastical privileges. With the help of biographies written by Gerald de BARRI and his own chaplain, Adam of Eynsham, he was canonized in 1220. The Angel Choir in Lincoln Cathedral was built to accommodate his shrine.

HUGH OF LINCOLN, ST (also known as Little St Hugh) (*c.* 1246–55), child 'martyr'. His body was found in a well and, following the pattern of the WILLIAM OF NORWICH case, the Jews of Lincoln were blamed for his death: 18 were hanged. His tomb in Lincoln Cathedral was for a century a flourishing cult centre; in the 1920s visitors were charged 3d. to view the well.

HUGHES, TED (1930–98), poet. Hughes was educated at Cambridge, where he met the American poet Sylvia Plath, whom he married in 1956. His upbringing in the Yorks. Pennines, his close association with nature as a boy and frequent hunting and fishing expeditions, came to influence much of his writing, particularly his prize-winning first volume of poems, *Hawk in the Rain* (1957). His fascination with the animism of primitive cultures and his study of the role of poetry in these societies inspired his second collection of poems, *Lupercal* (1960); there followed two children's books, *Meet My Folks* (1961) and *Earth Owl* (1963). In Feb. 1963 Plath, from whom Hughes had separated, committed suicide. Six years later Hughes was beset by further tragedy when his subsequent partner took her own life and that of their daughter. These tragedies marked his best-known book of poems, *Crow* (1970), a dark and foreboding work. His extremely successful children's book *The Iron Man* (1968) was followed after an interval by a collaboration with Seamus HEANEY in editing two highly successful anthologies *The Rattle-Bag* (1982) and *The School Bag* (1997). Hughes was appointed Poet Laureate in 1984. His last two volumes were the best-selling *Birthday Letters* (1998), which recounted his years with Plath, and *Tales from Ovid* (1998).

HUGHES, THOMAS (1822–96), author and social reformer. Son of the classical scholar John Hughes, he was educated at Rugby and Oxford and called to the Bar in 1848. Strongly influenced by Christian Socialism, Hughes was an energetic supporter of producers' co-operatives. Influential in the foundation of the Working Men's College, London, he was its Principal (1872–83). As MP for Lambeth (1865–8) and then Frome (1868–74) he gained a reputation as a supporter of trade unionism. With Frederic HARRISON he wrote the minority report of the Royal Commission on Trade Unions, arguing for the recognition of trade-union rights. While that was his most important work, he is chiefly known for his authorship of *Tom Brown's Schooldays* (1857).

HULANICKI, BARBARA (1936–), designer. A fashion illustrator trained at Brighton School of Art, she and her husband Stephen Fitz-Simon opened Biba in a Kensington (London) back street in 1964. In its various black and gold Art Deco style Kensington incarnations Biba, with its bruised colours, skinny dresses, feather boas, suede boots and huge hats, was the fashion vernacular of 'swinging London' in the 1960s, a mecca that ended up taking over the department store of Derry and Toms to sell style in everything from paint and cosmetics to cat food. Acquired by a retail corporation, Biba was closed in 1976.

HUME, BASIL (originally George) (1923–99), cardinal. Son of a Scottish Protestant father and a French Catholic mother, he was educated at Ampleforth (Yorks.), becoming a Benedictine monk at the age of 18, as many of his contemporaries were conscripted for war. Hume taught at Ampleforth and was appointed Abbot in 1963. In 1976 he became Cardinal Archbishop of Westminster, the first Benedictine to hold the office since the Reformation. A supporter of Pope John Paul II, whom he persuaded to visit Britain in 1982, Hume managed the difficult balancing act between conservative and liberal Catholics during the aftermath of the Second Vatican Council. A mostly Left-leaning prelate, he campaigned on behalf of the Guildford Four, established a centre for the young homeless, and lobbied for overseas aid and the cancellation of Third World debt and, though he toed the official Vatican line, told homosexuals that they were 'precious in the eyes of God'. During his episcopacy the Roman Catholic Church in Britain moved centre-stage in public life, receiving some 600 converts a year including a member of the royal family, the Duchess of Kent, and several high-profile converts from Anglicanism distressed by the admittance of women priests.

HUME, DAVID (1711–76), philosopher. A native of Edinburgh, who spent some time at the university in his early teens, Hume passed his career on the fringes of the legal and governmental world, finally becoming Under-Secretary of State (1767–8). His philosophical works, including the *Treatise of Human Nature* (1739–40) and the *Enquiry concerning Human Understanding* (1748), which followed LOCKE'S example in linking a study of the human mind and emotions with an assessment of the nature and limits of human knowledge, were better regarded on the continent than in Britain. His political and economic essays and his *History of England* (1754–62) enjoyed greater success. A sceptical critic of simple moral and political postures, he also attracted notice for his atheism: BOSWELL noted with fascination his serene acceptance of death. Hume is today regarded as one of the most powerful thinkers of the Scottish Enlightenment.

HUME, GEORGE (11th [1st Hume] Earl of Dunbar) (*c*. 1555–1611), politician. Hume, son of a Lothian gentleman, was at JAMES VI's court from 1585 and Master of the Great Wardrobe from 1590, gaining the same office in England in 1603 (he was Scots High Treasurer from 1601). From then until his death he was James's closest adviser, becoming Earl in 1605. Returning in 1606 to head administration in Scotland, he frequently travelled to England. He ruthlessly improved Scottish tax revenues and established unprecedented permanent peace on the English–Scottish border. His collateral descendants did not take up his earldom.

HUME, JOHN (1937–), Northern Ireland politician. He was active in 1960s Civil Rights protests against anti-Catholic discrimination, and was elected to the Northern Ireland Parliament for the Foyle constituency in 1969, defeating the leader of the moribund Nationalist Party; he played a prominent role in the formation of the moderate nationalist Social Democratic and Labour Party, and became its deputy leader. He served in the power-sharing executive of 1974, and after its collapse (which left him with the abiding belief that no internal solution was possible and the Republic of Ireland must be involved as guarantor) he spent some time working on the Brussels staff of the Republic of Ireland's European Commissioner. In 1979 he replaced Gerry FITT as party leader and was elected to one of the three Northern Ireland seats in the European Parliament (which he has held ever since). From 1983 he was Westminster MP for Foyle. He proved highly effective at putting the Northern nationalist case across at international level (in contrast to the maladroit and inarticulate Unionists) and worked with the Republic's government to persuade Britain to make concessions to anti-nationalist feeling to stave off the Sinn Féin threat, playing a significant role in preparing the ground for the Anglo-Irish Agreement. By the late 1980s he was regarded with awe and veneration in the Republic. In 1988 he began a controversial series of contacts with Gerry ADAMS which helped to draw Sinn Féin into the peace process and bring about the 1994 ceasefires and the 1998 Good Friday Agreement. After the ratification of the agreement by referendum Hume stood aside and let his deputy Seamus Mallon become Deputy First Minister. Joint recipient of the 1998 Nobel Peace Prize with David TRIMBLE, Hume is the most impressive nationalist leader to have emerged from Northern Ireland in this century, though critics accuse him of showing insufficient understanding of Ulster Unionists and of acquiescing in the eclipse of his ageing party by Sinn Féin.

HUMPHREY OF GLOUCESTER (2nd Duke of Gloucester) (1390–1447), Royal Prince. Youngest son of HENRY IV, he was created Duke in 1414. He fought at Agincourt (1415) and was prominent in HENRY V's conquest of Normandy. A man of wide intellectual interests, founder of Duke Humphrey's Library at Oxford and a notable patron of scholars, he was an erratic politician who never quite held the power to which he aspired.

He was Protector of England only during Bedford's (*see* JOHN OF LANCASTER) absences and Regent only when HENRY VI was in France (1430–2). His marriage to Jacqueline of Hainault in 1422 and his subsequent pursuit of her inheritance threatened to undermine the vital Anglo-Burgundian alliance. In 1428 his marriage was annulled and he married his mistress, Eleanor COBHAM, from whom he was divorced when she was convicted of treason.

After 1435, as Henry V's sole surviving brother, he saw himself as the executor of the policy of conquest and was bitterly opposed to all peacemaking; this resulted in renewed quarrels with Cardinal Henry BEAUFORT and then with the dominant Suffolk (*see* POLE, WILLIAM DE LA) faction. In 1447 Suffolk planned to put Gloucester on trial on charges of treason but five days after his arrest he died, probably of a stroke. He became a political martyr, the 'good duke' to whose memory all those who opposed either the court or peace with France would appeal.

HUNEBERC (*fl.* eighth century), nun. An English nun, she was one of many women from England who took part in the missionary activity in Germany associated above all with St BONIFACE. Huneberc kept a record of the lives of some of her colleagues, including writing an account of the life of St WILLIBALD.

HUNGERFORD, WALTER (Baron Hungerford) (*c.* 1502–40), subject of a scandal. His stepmother Agnes was hanged (1524) for murdering her previous husband John Cotell (1518) at his father Sir Edward Hungerford's castle at Farleigh Hungerford (Wilts.). A courtier client of Thomas CROMWELL, made Baron in 1536, Hungerford was executed on Tower Hill beside Cromwell, on charges of sodomy, incest and sorcery. Although the charges may have been intended further to discredit Cromwell, Hungerford's third wife had in 1536 complained to Cromwell of long imprisonment at Farleigh and of his attempts to poison her. Hungerford was said to be deranged at his execution.

HUNNE, RICHARD (?–1514), suicide or murder victim. A London merchant whose quarrel with his parish priest over his son's burial led to his arrest on a heresy charge. He was found dead either by suicide or (more likely) murder in the Lollards' Tower, the Bishop of London's prison; the ensuing row involved the entire political establishment and dramatized tensions between the laity and Church authorities.

HUNT, HENRY (1773–1835), politician. An agitator and radical propagandist, he was the best-known platform performer of his day, garnering the nickname 'Orator' Hunt: his reputation was established at the anti-government Spa Fields demonstrations in London (1816–17). He was arrested for his part in the Peterloo Massacre in Manchester (16 Aug. 1819), when 11 people were killed and over 400 injured, and served over two years in jail. Hunt entered Parliament in 1830 as radical member for Preston, but was too vain and erratic to provide effective political leadership. His abrasiveness and demagoguery left him increasingly isolated. His cause was parliamentary reform: he was the only radical to oppose consistently the terms of the Reform Act 1832, insisting on 'universal suffrage or nothing'. Always a folk hero and individualist, his white top hat (the 'symbol of the purity of his cause') became well known and he lived with his longterm mistress in Brighton, since this was where his fellow adulterer the Prince Regent (the future GEORGE IV) lived with Mrs FITZHERBERT.

HUNT, JAMES LEIGH (1784–1859), man of letters. From 1808 to 1821, he co-edited (with his brother John) *The Examiner*, a literary and social journal of radical outlook. BYRON and Charles Lamb were contributors, as were SHELLEY and KEATS, who were first introduced to the public through its columns. Caricatured by Charles DICKENS as Harold Skimpole in *Bleak House*, Hunt was notable not only for his own journalism but also for his skill in bringing writers together for the exchange of ideas.

HUNT, JOHN (Baron Hunt of Llanfairwaterdine) (1910–99), soldier and mountaineer. A professional soldier who was awarded the Military Cross in the Second World War, he went to SHAPE (Supreme Head Quarters, Allied Powers, Europe) in 1951, was director of the Duke of Edinburgh's Award Scheme (1956–66) and led the British government relief mission to Biafra. Hunt is best remembered for his leadership of the expedition which, in May 1953, was the first to reach the summit of Mount Everest.

HUNT, WILLIAM HOLMAN (1827–1910), artist. One of the founders of the Pre-Raphaelite Brotherhood (*see* ROSSETTI, DANTE GABRIEL), he was trained at the Royal Academy Schools and exhibited *The Eve of St Agnes* at the Royal Academy in 1848. His search for authentic religious settings led him to the Middle East (1854–6), where he camped by the Dead Sea in order to complete *The Scapegoat* (1856). *The Finding of the Saviour in the Temple* (1854–60) established his reputation, but the detail which he required in his paintings meant that his output was relatively limited. His most famous religious painting is *The Light of the World* (1854); his most explicitly moral one, *The Awakening Conscience*

(1854). His memoirs, *Pre-Raphaelitism and the Pre-Raphaelite Brotherhood* (two volumes, 1905) is a major source for the movement's history.

HUNTER, WILLIAM (1718–83) and **JOHN** (1728–93), anatomists. William Hunter left the family home in Lanarks. to study for the Church, but was persuaded by the physician William CULLEN to become his pupil. In 1741 he went to London to study at St George's Hospital, and was soon teaching anatomy himself. John Hunter joined his brother in 1748 and despite his lack of education showed a flair for dissection that soon rivalled his brother's. They made many joint observations and discoveries. William attracted fashionable women clients to his midwifery practice, including, in 1762, Queen CHARLOTTE. John served as a naval surgeon from 1760 to 1763 and studied the treatment of serious injuries, leading to his *Treatise on the Blood, Inflammation, and Gunshot Wounds*. He discovered the collateral circulation of the blood, contributing towards knowledge of the growth of bone. He also worked on comparative anatomy, including that of fossils, where he prepared the ground for DARWIN's evolutionary theory. Both had substantial museums; William's was the more populist, adding coins, shells and other curiosities to the core medical collection. Their rivalry developed until, in 1780, William claimed John Hunter's work on utero-placental circulation as his; historians think that John was in the right.

HUNTINGDON, EARL OF, 4TH *see* HENRY OF NORTHUMBRIA; **13TH** and **14TH** *see* HOLLAND, JOHN; **20TH** *see* HASTINGS, HENRY; **COUNTESS OF** *see* HASTINGS, SELINA

HUNTLY, EARL OF, 4TH and **5TH** *see* GORDON, GEORGE; **6TH AND 1ST MARQUESS OF** *see* GORDON, GEORGE

HUNTSMAN, BENJAMIN (1704–76), steelmaker. Of German parentage, he worked as a clockmaker in Doncaster from 1725 where he became disenchanted with the quality of tools available. In 1740 he moved to Handsworth, Sheffield, where he began to experiment with making steel in a crucible. By 1750 the process had resulted in a much harder steel, because of its uniform carbon content, with which the Sheffield cutlers refused to work; Huntsman exported his steel to France and finally gained the interest of his Sheffield competitors. One, Samuel Walker, managed to steal Huntsman's process but Huntsman maintained his dominance of the industry until his death.

HURD, DOUGLAS (Baron Hurd of Westwell) (1930–), politician. The son of a LLOYD GEORGE

peer, he went into the Diplomatic Service, serving in Peking (1954–6) and at the United Nations (1956–60). After leaving the Foreign Office in 1966 he joined the Conservative Research Department, becoming HEATH's private secretary. A different version of the 'Heathman' from HESELTINE, he nonetheless prospered under Heath, whose political secretary he was throughout Heath's premiership (1970–4); his published diary *An End to Promises* (1979) remains an invaluable source for historians of the Heath years. In Feb. 1974 he was elected as MP for Mid-Oxon. (Witney after 1983) and seemed set for rapid promotion, but the Conservatives lost the election and, in early 1975, Heath was replaced as party leader by Margaret THATCHER.

It was testimony to Hurd's talents that he should have found a berth on the Thatcher ship, although in opposition and in government until 1983 he held posts connected with his own expertise in foreign affairs. It was not until 1984 that he entered the Cabinet, and then with the poisoned chalice of Northern Ireland. From 1985 until 1989 he was Home Secretary. Never one of Thatcher's inner circle, Hurd stood for the leadership once she had stood down, but his Old Etonian background counted against him, and he lost to John MAJOR, who made him Foreign Secretary. Hurd brought stability and professionalism to the Foreign Office but his freedom to manoeuvre was limited. In Europe it was the Franco-German axis which made the running, in the Middle East, particularly on the question of Iraq, it was the Americans. Hurd's attempts to forge a common European foreign policy to deal with the break-up of Yugoslavia came to nothing. He retired in 1995.

HURST, MARGERY (née Berney) (1914–1989), businesswoman. After the Second World War Hurst began an agency to supply temporary secretaries on a daily basis, calling it the Brook Street Bureau after the street in Mayfair (London) where it was located. It was an immediate success and soon had branches all over Britain and in the USA, Australia and Hong Kong, and Hurst was a millionaire. The company went public in 1965 and five years later Hurst became one of the first women members of Lloyd's underwriters.

HUSKISSON, WILLIAM (1770–1830), politician. The son of a Staffs. gentleman he entered Parliament in 1796, holding junior office under PITT THE YOUNGER and Portland (*see* BENTINCK, WILLIAM CAVENDISH). In 1823, he was President of the Board of Trade and in 1827 Colonial Secretary and Leader of the Commons. Killed by STEPHENSON's *Rocket* at the opening of the Liverpool to Manchester railway in Sept. 1830, he is chiefly remembered for his work in opening up colonial trade to foreign competition, the reduction of import duties, the relaxation of navigation laws and for promoting Free Trade.

HUTCHESON, FRANCIS (1694–1746), philosopher. Son of a Presbyterian minister in Armagh, he was sent to Glasgow University in 1710. On his return to Ireland, he became a licensed preacher and started a private academy in Dublin. He published on philosophical and religious subjects, being among those who responded to the provocative writings of Bernard MANDEVILLE, and in 1729 was elected to the chair of moral philosophy at Glasgow. He adopted and developed the moral-sense philosophy of the 3rd Earl of Shaftesbury (*see* COOPER, ANTHONY ASHLEY) but envisioned men exerting themselves on the basis of rational calculations as to what would best promote human happiness. His work encouraged interest in the psychology of morals, which was to be taken further by David HUME and Adam SMITH.

HUTCHINSON, ANNE (née Marbury) (1591–1643), religious leader. From a Lincs. gentry family, she sailed with John Cotton (1584–1652) to Massachusetts in 1634. She refused to accept women's subordination, and led a group of antinomians (who believed that those whom God elects to salvation are released from observing moral law). Condemned to death by the Church, she was banished from Massachusetts in 1637. Settling in Providence (now Rhode Island), after her husband William's death she migrated westwards and was murdered by native Americans: many clergy felt this an appropriate divine punishment.

HUTCHINSON, JOHN (1674–1737), theologian and philosopher. Son of a small landowner in Yorks., he qualified as a land agent and worked for the Duke of Somerset. Through the Duke's physician, John Woodward, he became interested in fossils, which he thought could be used to prove the biblical account of Noah's flood. With the Duke's support he studied Hebrew and in 1724 published *Moses' Principia*, in which he argued that Hebrew was the primitive language of mankind, which, properly interpreted, provided the key to all knowledge, secular and religious. He also claimed that God had embodied in the writings of Moses means for the understanding of the natural world. On this basis he challenged NEWTON's theory of gravitation. Although his ideas had something in common with prevailing natural theology, according to which the hand of God could be discerned in the laws of nature, he disparaged its often rationalistic tone, stressing that the quest for understanding must be a spiritual one, and that submission to the will of God

was the one virtue necessary for salvation. His views attracted some well-placed followers, including George HORNE and William JONES, who came to be recognized as forming a Hutchinsonian party.

HUTCHINSON, LUCY (née Apsley) (1620–after 1675), writer. Daughter of Sir Allen Apsley, and given an exceptional education, she married John Hutchinson (1615–64), a prominent Parliamentary soldier in the English Civil Wars and a signatory of CHARLES I's death warrant. She became a Baptist. In 1660 she was active in saving her husband from execution and devotedly attended him through his continuing imprisonment. Her writings include translations of the Latin philosopher Lucretius and a life of her husband which is particularly informative about the Civil Wars.

HUTTON, JAMES (1715–95), religious leader. The Moravians had broken from the Papacy in 1467 after the Hussite wars of religion in Bohemia. They sought to recapture the spirit and practice of the Apostolic Church, practising puritanical discipline and emphasizing good works. Count Nicholas Ludwig von Zinzendorf turned the sect's attentions outward in the 1730s, making contact with John and Charles WESLEY and, through them, with James Hutton, a bookseller. In 1739 Hutton visited the Moravians on the continent and founded the Society for the Furtherance of the Gospel (1741). He planned a Moravian settlement in Labrador and worked to maintain good relations with the Methodists despite the differences between the two movements.

HUTTON, SIR THOMAS (1890–1981), soldier. Educated at Woolwich, Hutton served on the Western Front during the First World War, was wounded three times and was awarded the Military Cross. Regarded as one of the most proficient gunners of his generation, he was promoted Colonel in 1930, Major-General in 1938 and in 1941 was appointed Lieutenant General commanding in Burma. Faced with a Japanese invasion in Jan. 1942, Hutton attempted to conduct a fighting withdrawal from the frontier, while his rear echelon forces moved supplies north from Rangoon into central and northern Burma. Although this redeployment allowed SLIM to conduct his epic retreat two months later, Hutton was blamed for the loss of Burma, and was transferred to an administrative backwater.

HUXLEY, ALDOUS (1894–1963), writer. Best known for his chilling dystopian novel *Brave New World* (1932) and his literary accounts of his experiences under the influence of the psychotropic drugs mescaline and LSD in *The Doors of Perception* (1954) and *Heaven and Hell* (1956), Huxley was the grandson of T. H. HUXLEY and brother of Sir Julian HUXLEY. In 1911 he developed an eye condition which left him nearly blind; it prevented him from pursuing a scientific career like his grandfather and brother, and it troubled him for most of his life, but he made a sufficient recovery to read English at Oxford. He became a protégé of Lady Ottoline MORRELL, and met many leading political, intellectual and literary figures of his day. His early satirical novels, particularly *Crome Yellow* (1921), poked fun at many of these people. The 1920s and 1930s were a particularly productive time during which he wrote *Antic Hay* (1923), *Those Barren Leaves* (1925), *Point Counter Point* (1928), *Brave New World* (1932) and *Eyeless in Gaza* (1936). In 1937, troubled by his eye condition, disenchanted with European politics and the failures of the peace movement, and hoping to find new spiritual direction, he moved to California, where he became interested in mysticism and parapsychology; he was later adopted by the hippie generation as a modern-day guru.

HUXLEY, SIR JULIAN (1887–1975), zoologist and philosopher. Grandson of T. H. HUXLEY and brother of Aldous HUXLEY, he went to Eton and studied zoology at Oxford, where he became a lecturer in zoology (1908–12). He taught zoology there after the First World War and held professorial chairs at King's College, London (1925–7), and the Royal Institution (1927–31). A wide-ranging writer, his best-known scientific work, *Problems of Relative Growth* (1932), explored the relative growth rates of different organs. One of the foremost expositors of science of his day, Huxley wrote numerous popular works on the biological sciences and regularly appeared on the BBC's *Brain's Trust* programme. In much of his writing, he upheld the social and humanistic values of scientific research. He was an advocate of eugenics and was the first Director General of UNESCO (1946–8), concerning himself with the problems of population growth and environmental damage. He helped establish the International Union for the Conservation of Nature (1948) and the World Wildlife Fund (1961).

HUXLEY, T(HOMAS) H(ENRY) *see* essay on page 442

HYDE, ANNE (Duchess of York) (1637–71), first wife of the future JAMES II. Her father was CHARLES II's adviser Edward HYDE, Earl of Clarendon. In 1654 she became a maid of honour to Mary, Princess of Orange (daugher of CHARLES I), and met the Princess's brother, the Duke of York. They married secretly in London in 1660, despite the opposition of their families. Only two of her eight children lived, the future Queens MARY II and ANNE. She was a patron of Peter LELY and shared her husband's Catholic leanings, refusing reconciliation with the Established Church on her deathbed.

HYDE, DOUGLAS (1860–1949), first President of Ireland. Son of a Church of Ireland rector in Co. Roscommon, he developed an interest in the Irish language as a boy and became a Gaelic scholar, collecting and publishing folk-tales and folk-songs drawn on by Irish Revival writers such as YEATS. He also published some poetry and the first plays written in modern Irish. In 1893 he co-founded the Gaelic League and became its first President, attempting to keep the language revival above party politics (though the league, and Hyde himself, frequently appealed to nationalist sentiment to win support). In 1915 he resigned as President after separatists took over the league. After the passage of the 1937 constitution he was chosen by all-party consent as first President of Ireland (1938–45), in recognition of the role of the league in preparing for the foundation of the State, and as a gesture to the Protestant minority.

HYDE, EDWARD (1st Earl of Clarendon) *see* essay on page 443

HYDE, LAURENCE (4th [1st Hyde] Earl of Rochester) (1641–1711), politician. Second son of Edward HYDE, Earl of Clarendon, he returned to England at the Restoration and became an MP. His sister's children were to become Queens MARY II and ANNE. Rochester became a Lord Commissioner for the Treasury on Danby's (*see* OSBORNE, THOMAS) resignation in 1679, and First Lord after Shaftesbury's (*see* COOPER, ANTHONY ASHLEY) dismissal. He resisted attempts to recall Parliament after successive Parliaments' insistence on excluding the Duke of York (later JAMES II) from the throne had led CHARLES II to dissolve them. Riding high in royal favour, Hyde was made an earl in 1681 and under James II was made Lord High Treasurer. He took instruction in Catholicism, but refused to convert and was edged out by the more compliant Sunderland (*see* SPENCER, ROBERT). He was dismissed in 1687.

After the invasion of William of Orange (the future WILLIAM III), he proposed the calling of Parliament, where he argued for a regency in order to preserve the notion that James was rightful King. Later he became close to his niece Mary and was leader of the High Church party. During the first year of his niece Anne's reign he, Nottingham (*see* FINCH, DANIEL) and Edward SEYMOUR represented the High Tories in an administration headed by

continued on page 444

HUXLEY, T(HOMAS) H(ENRY) (1825–95)
Zoologist

He was largely self-educated but briefly attended Ealing school in London, where his father taught mathematics. He studied medicine at Charing Cross Hospital (1842–5), acquiring skills in physiology and comparative anatomy, and in 1848 published researches on a layer of cells in the root sheath of hair ('Huxley's layer'). In 1846 he was appointed assistant surgeon on board HMS *Rattlesnake* during its surveying voyage to the South Seas, where he conducted extensive private researches into marine animals. He made his reputation as a zoologist after sending to the Linnaean Society his morphological studies of marine invertebrates. After returning to England in 1850, he became a fellow of the Royal Society (1851), winning awards for his expertise in dissection and microscopy. He resigned from the Royal Navy and supported himself by science journalism and lecturing. His struggles to gain a respectable scientific position were eventually rewarded: he became lecturer in Natural History and Palaeontology at the Government School of Mines (1854), naturalist to the Geological Survey (1855), organizer of and lecturer at the Museum of Practical Geology (1855) and Fullerian Lecturer at the Royal Institution (1856). Huxley then began his campaign to turn academic science into a profession and to challenge the Anglican stronghold on British cultural and intellectual life.

Huxley made crucial contributions to a wide range of scientific fields, notably invertebrate and vertebrate anatomy, palaeontology, physiology, geology, botany and ethnology. He made major studies of the Medusae (jellyfish), Ascidians (sea squirts) and Cephalous Mollusca (squids), which established that each genus and species was a development of a basic structure or 'archetype' and he placed jellyfish in a sub-class which he called Coelenterata. His considerable taxonomic work established new classification systems for vertebrates, mammals, birds and other major groups of animals. In palaeontology, he published important work on the Devonian fishes and showed that fossil evidence for ancestral forms of the horse furnished powerful support for his friend Charles DARWIN's theory of evolution by natural selection.

Before the publication of Darwin's *Origin of Species* (1859), Huxley had rejected transmutation of species as speculation but by the early 1860s had become the leading champion of Darwin's theory. In 1860 he famously defended the evolutionary claim that man had descended from apes against Bishop Samuel WILBERFORCE and the comparative anatomist Richard OWEN. By 1857 he had rejected Owen's vertebral theory of the skull and implicitly questioned the reliability of Owen's methodology by using new embryological studies of vertebrates in comparative anatomy. Three years later he proclaimed that man differed less from apes than apes did from the lower primates, a view directly in conflict with Owen's belief that man was zoologically distinct from all other mammals. By 1863 he had practically defeated Owen, showing fundamental flaws in his opponent's evidence, and in the same year he published his controversial *Evidence as to Man's Place in Nature*, in which he buttressed his evolutionary views with anthropological studies.

Although Huxley is seen as 'Darwin's bulldog', he nonetheless regarded natural selection as an unproven, albeit the most probable, mechanism of evolution. This reflected his policy of scepticism towards theories in general and his commitment to strict empiricist methods in science. Inspired by the work of David HUME and John Stuart MILL, he believed that physical causes, as elucidated by scientific method, were the sole foundation of reliable knowledge. On this basis he made the controversial claim that life could be most reliably explained in terms of purely physical processes, and held that questions which could not be objectively resolved – notably the existence of God – were beyond human knowledge. Huxley coined the term 'agnosticism' to express his reticence on religious questions.

From the mid 1850s he developed and promulgated techniques of teaching biology that were widely emulated, and produced a series of highly successful textbooks. His expertise as a writer and lecturer won him audiences with both specialist scientific and general (notably working-class) audiences. Through his frequent public lectures and his numerous contributions to general periodicals, he established himself as a leading scientist, a man of letters, and as the foremost promoter of the intellectual, moral and cultural importance of science. A key figure in the professionalization of science and spread of science teaching in Britain he was the president of several leading scientific societies including the Royal Society and British Association for the Advancement of Science, he sat on 10 royal commissions (including technical instruction) and was a founding member of the London School Board, a position in which he transformed elementary science teaching in the capital. He was the grandfather of Aldous and Julian HUXLEY.

Leonard Huxley (ed.), *Life and Letters of Thomas Henry Huxley* (2 vols, 1900)
Adrian Desmond, *Huxley: From Devil's Disciple to Evolution's High Priest* (1998)

HYDE, EDWARD (1st Earl of Clarendon) (1609–74)
Politician and historian

The son of a Wilts. gentleman, he was educated at Oxford and the Middle Temple, where he showed more interest in history than in law. His first marriage connected him with the powerful Villiers family (*see also* VILLIERS, GEORGE); his second, with a master of the Court of Requests, where he became a prominent practitioner. He was a member of the Great Tew circle of humanist and rationalist thinkers led by Lucius CAREY, 2nd Viscount Falkland. Disturbed by what he saw as the many violations of law during CHARLES I's personal rule, he secured election to Parliament (1640), and associated with the opposition, pressing especially for reforms in the administration of justice. In the Long Parliament he supported the impeachment of Strafford (*see* WENTWORTH, CHARLES), though he tried to prevent his execution.

Alienated especially by Parliamentarian hostility to the Church, Hyde shifted his allegiances, and in 1641 voted against the Grand Remonstrance proposed by PYM and others. Becoming an adviser to the King, he drafted several declarations for him, and was expelled from Parliament. He was made the King's Chancellor of the Exchequer in 1643, and advised summoning a Parliament at Oxford, to enhance the legitimacy of the royal cause; though it helped in raising money, the King resented it. Never a Cavalier extremist, Hyde was made Councillor to the Prince of Wales (later CHARLES II) from 1644, perhaps in part to distance him from the King's immediate circle; his basic trustworthiness was not in doubt. In 1646 he accompanied the Prince to Jersey, and began writing a *History of the Great Rebellion*. During the next few years he lived on the continent, from 1651 with Charles II. He became the exiled King's chief adviser and general co-ordinator of Royalist effort.

He was closely involved in drawing up the Declaration of Breda (1660), in which Charles offered a general pardon and an amnesty for all offences committed during the Civil Wars and Interregnum, and undertook to rely on the advice of a free Parliament and to provide a degree of religious liberty. In the same year he found to his consternation that his daughter Anne had been made pregnant by James, Duke of York (the future JAMES II); it was agreed that they should marry. The marriage produced future Queens, MARY II and ANNE. Accompanying Charles II on his return to London, Hyde was created Earl of Clarendon in 1661 and dominated the administration for the next few years, doing his best to hold the more extreme Cavaliers in check, and he favoured the restoration of moderate Episcopacy; he was prepared to see the Church's doctrines and practices so defined as to allow many Presbyterians to be reconciled to it (the policy termed 'comprehension'), but opposed the King's wish for measures of toleration for Dissenters. The four repressive measures known as the Clarendon Code in fact reflected a more unyielding position than his. These included the Corporation Act 1661, which excluded non-Royalists and non-Anglicans from municipal office, the Act of Uniformity 1662, establishing an Episcopal Church on the basis of the Book of Common Prayer, leading to the expulsion of 960 clergy, the Conventicle Act 1664, making it almost impossible for dissenting congregations to worship legally, and the Five Mile Act 1665, prohibiting expelled ministers from living within five miles of any place where they had served before the passage of the Act.

Clarendon was cautious and conservative in government and failed to see the need to conciliate and manage Parliament. He soon became vulnerable to his courtier enemies. In 1663 there was an abortive attempt to impeach him, while the unsuccessful Second Dutch War (1665–7), which he had tried to avoid, generated further criticism. His dismissal, engineered by Arlington (*see* BENNET, HENRY) in 1667, reflected the difficulty of holding the middle ground in the ideologically fragmented world of Restoration England, as well as the limits of his political skill. Fearing impeachment, he fled to France.

In exile he completed his *History of the Great Rebellion*, compiled out of what were originally distinct projects, a heavily documentary record of the rebellion and a more lively personal memoir. It was published (1702–4) after its author's death. It was an uneven production, but its breadth and tone of monumental impartiality made it an outstanding work for its time. Profits from its sale helped to finance the Oxford University Press's first purpose-built premises (the Clarendon Building); in the nineteenth century, profits from Clarendon's manuscripts, with which he had intended to endow a riding school in Oxford, were employed in a way thought more appropriate to a modern university, in financing a physics laboratory (the Clarendon Laboratory).

Brian Wormald, Clarendon: History, Politics and Religion (1951)

GODOLPHIN and Marlborough (*see* CHURCHILL, JOHN), but his vain insistence on such pro-Church measures as an occasional conformity bill led to his resignation in 1703. During these years he oversaw the publication of his father's *History of the Civil Wars* (1702–4). When the Tories returned to power with a vengeance in 1710, he was made Lord President of the Council, but died suddenly the following year.

HYDER ALI (1722–82), ruler of Mysore. Not of a princely family but displaying considerable military expertise from an early age, he took advantage of French interest in India to assemble the first brigade of troops under Indian command equipped with European weapons. In the 1750s he became Prime Minister to the Raja of Mysore and, in 1761, placed the Raja under house arrest and assumed sole authority. Hyder expanded the territory controlled by Mysore and rapidly became a threat to neighbouring powers, including the British East India Co. The company allied with the Marathas and the Nizam of Hyderabad in 1766 but Hyder successfully parted the allies and defeated the British. In 1769 he concluded a treaty with the British, but when the Marathas attacked him in 1771 the British refused to help. Hyder allied himself with the French and made war on Britain, seizing the pro-British city of Arcot, capital of the Carnatic, in 1780. The British under Sir Eyre COOTE won victories during 1781, but Hyder's son TIPU turned the tide against them at the Battle of Coleroon River early in 1782. The French sent Hyder reinforcements but the British, now led by Governor George MACARTNEY, retaliated by besieging Hyder and Tipu in their citadel at Arni, where Hyder died, urging Tipu to make peace with the British.

HYGEBERHT (?–803), Archbishop of Lichfield (787–99 or 801). The only Archbishop of Lichfield, Hygeberht's elevation was a result of King OFFA of Mercia's inability to overcome resistance by Archbishop JÆNBERHT of Canterbury to Mercian domination over Kent and to his plans to crown his son ECGFRITH during his lifetime. Hygeberht's usefulness was not acknowledged by King CENWULF of Mercia, and he seems to have been demoted to Bishop and then made an Abbot before papal approval for the Lichfield scheme was finally removed in 803.

HYNDMAN, H(ENRY) M(AYERS) (1842–1921), socialist. The son of a wealthy family whose money derived from Caribbean trade, he was a Tory democrat who became a socialist in the early 1880s. He was a founder of the Democratic Federation in 1881, which became the Social Democratic Federation (SDF) in 1884, an avowedly Marxist body. Hyndman's Marxism, like his personality, was dogmatic and imperious. Though committed to achieving socialism through parliamentary elections, the SDF was very hostile to trade unionism, which largely condemned it to a minority status in British labour politics. It played an important role, however, in the creation of a socialist current within Britain. Though an anti-imperialist for much of his life, Hyndman supported the First World War.

HYWEL AP IEUAF (?–985), King of Gwynedd. In 979 Hywel employed Norse mercenaries to depose his uncle IAGO AP IDWAL and secure the throne of Gwynedd. Initially Hywel faced a challenge from his cousin, Cystenin ap Iago, who had his own Scandinavian allies, but he defeated Cystenin in the following year and seems to have been subsequently untroubled by rival claimants. Little else is known of his reign or of the circumstances surrounding his death. The *Brut y Tywysogion* relates only that he was killed by the 'Saxons through treachery', making him one of a number of Welsh princes to perish at the hands of English enemies.

HYWEL DDA 'THE GOOD' (?–950), King of Dyfed. A grandson of RHODRI MAWR, he became King before the year 918. The English kings generally accorded him pre-eminence among the Welsh rulers and, after 942, he used his dynastic links to impose his rule on Gwynedd.

There are three reasons why he occupies a special place in the history of early Welsh kingship: his reputation as the instigator of the written collection of the customary laws of the Welsh, the so-called 'Laws of Hywel Dda', which, although they now survive in manuscripts which date from the thirteenth century and obviously contain a lot of later material, must at least contain some of the laws of Hywel's time; his pilgrimage to Rome in 928 or 929; and his status as the only pre-Norman Welsh ruler from whose reign a coin survives (a single penny minted at Chester). He seems to have been a powerful ruler inspired by the example of his tenth-century English contemporaries (*see* ATHELSTAN), but his involvement in Welsh dynastic politics in no way differed from that of his predecessors or successors.

I

IAGO AP IDWAL (?–after 979), King of Gwynedd. Iago and his brother, Ieuaf, were driven out of Gwynedd by HYWEL DDA soon after 942, but following Hywel's death in 950 Iago and Ieuaf defeated his sons, securing their hold over Gwynedd. Having thus secured Gwynedd's release from southern overlordship, the brothers fought amongst themselves. Iago captured and imprisoned his brother in 969 but was himself defeated by HYWEL AP IEUAF in 974 and again defeated, deposed and imprisoned by Hywel in 979. Iago's career is a good indication of the conflicts which make the history of Wales in the decades after the death of Hywel Dda so confused.

IDA (?–559), King of Bernicia (547–59). Very little is known about the historical Ida, the first recorded king in Bernicia. He and his followers are supposed to have occupied the fortress of Bamburgh (Northumb.) in 547. It is clear that he and his fellow Angles occupied only lands near the coast and remained under pressure from neighbouring British kings, such as URIEN of Rheged, up until the time of the great expansion of Bernicia under ETHELFRITH.

IDDESLEIGH, 1ST EARL OF see NORTHCOTE, SIR STAFFORD

IDWAL AP ANARWD (?–942), King of Gwynedd. Idwal appears to have succeeded his father ANARAWD AP RHODRI in 916 but little is known about his reign. In 922, when EDWARD THE ELDER had subdued all Mercia, Idwal, together with HYWEL DDA, did homage to him, as they were subsequently to do to ATHELSTAN in 926, to whom they rendered tribute. Both kings, together with MORGAN AP OWAIN, King of Gwent, were required in 934 to accompany Athelstan in his campaign against CONSTANTÍN II, King of the Scots, illustrating the dependency of many Welsh rulers on the English kings, which was a result of the tenth-century unification of England.

ILAY, 1ST EARL OF see CAMPBELL, ARCHIBALD

ILLTUD, ST (*fl.* early sixth century), monk. Founder of the famous monastic school of Llanilltud Fawr, Illtud was one of the principal pioneers of insular British monasticism as it developed before St AUGUSTINE's mission. One of the more important of the early Welsh saints, he was the reputed teacher of many subsequent saints, including St CADOG, St DAVID, St SAMSON OF DOL, and of GILDAS, although this may be the result of a subsequent linking of tradition. His *Vita* was written in the twelfth century.

INCHIQUIN, 6TH BARON AND 1ST EARL OF see O'BRIEN, MURROUGH

INDULF (?–962), King of the Scots (954–62). The son of CONSTANTÍN II, he had ruled the sub-kingdom of Strathclyde before his elevation to the kingdom of the Scots. His reign is notable for the expansion of the Scottish kings' power into Lothian, and specifically for the acquisition of Edinburgh. The collapse of the Scandinavian kingdom of York after the expulsion of ERIC BLOODAXE provided the opportunity for this advance.

INE (?–726), King of Wessex (688–726). Arguably one of the most significant of the early kings of Wessex, alongside CEAWLIN and EGBERT, Ine, having succeeded CENTWINE, proceeded to extend the domination of the Wessex kings as far as the borders of the still-independent British kingdom of Dumnonia, effectively reducing it to the region of modern Cornwall. A vigorous supporter of the Christian Church, Ine was also the first King of Wessex to issue a law-code. This, the only Wessex law-code before the time of ALFRED THE GREAT, is an invaluable source for the society of early Anglo-Saxon England. It also shows both the existence of a rudimentary structure of local royal administration and that payments to the Church such as 'church-scot', which over time evolved into tithes, were regarded as compulsory.

INGHAM, SIR BERNARD (1932–), journalist and spin doctor. As a Labour supporter and 'strong union man', from 1964 Ingham contributed a weekly column to the *Leeds Weekly Citizen*, an official Labour Party publication, in which he railed against the 'whole terrible Tory tribe [with] their feudal mentality'. Ingham left journalism in 1967 to work in the press office of several Labour government departments, and as a supporter of Harold WILSON, Ingham became gradually disillusioned both with the intellectuals in the Labour Party and with the unions.

In Sept. 1979 the newly elected Conservative Prime Minister Margaret THATCHER invited Ingham to be her chief press secretary. 'We're both radicals,' he explained. In this role his public profile increased, as did the dependence and protection of the Prime Minister, who spoke of him as 'indispensable' amid accusations that the press secretary's role was now one of partisan news management rather than information-giving, and one of media bullying. Said during the debate over the Westland affair in 1986 to be 'possibly the most important man in British politics', in 1989 he was promoted by the Prime Minister to be head of the government Information Service, with an advertising budget of £168 million a year. When Thatcher resigned on 21 Nov. 1990 he went too, after the longest partnership between an official and a prime minister in British history.

INGIMUND (*fl. c.* 910), Viking warrior. Based in Dublin he led the Scandinavian colonization of the Wirral in the early tenth century. The colony was prevented from expanding by a ring of encircling burhs constructed on the orders of Ealdorman ETHELRED and his wife ETHELFLÆD. His career is a less spectacular manifestation of the sort of Viking opportunism exemplified by IVAR THE BONELESS and RAGNALL.

INGLIS, ELSIE (1864–1917), doctor. Born in a Himalayan hill station, Inglis studied at the Edinburgh School of Medicine for Women founded in 1886 by Sophia JEX-BLAKE. But, appalled by Jex-Blake's high-handedness, she decamped to Glasgow where she set up the rival Medical College for Women and fought for women to be able to study surgery with men. In 1899 she was appointed lecturer in gynaecology at the Medical College for Women and also opened a small maternity hospital where poor women were for the first time given the benefits of anaesthesia in childbirth. When war broke out in 1914 Inglis volunteered for the Royal Army Medical Corps, which rejected her, so she raised £25,000 in a single month to establish the Scottish Women's Hospitals (SWH). Ignored by the British Foreign Office, units of the SWH served in France, Corsica, Salonika, Romania, Russia, Malta and Serbia, where Inglis was arrested and she and her colleagues, as prisoners, nursed in the military hospital.

INGOLD, SIR CHRISTOPHER (1893–1970), chemist. Ingold studied chemistry at Southampton and London. After working for a Glasgow-based chemical firm, he held academic positions at Imperial College, London (1920–4), and Leeds University (1924–30), and then became Professor of Chemistry at University College, London (1930–61). Ingold is beest known for his research on physical and chemical aspects of the reactions of organic molecules (notably benzene). This work informed his widely used electronic theory of chemical reactions, a theory that was fiercely challenged by his contemporary, Robert ROBINSON, but which has since revolutionized the nomenclature of organic chemistry.

INGRAMS, RICHARD (1937–), journalist and editor. Educated at Shrewsbury and Oxford, in 1962, with Peter Cook, William Rushton and others, he founded the weekly satirical lampoon *Private Eye* of which he was editor from 1963 to 1986. Subsequently a *Spectator* and *Observer* columnist and founder editor of *The Oldie* (1992), he is fearlessly irreverent while remaining deeply attached to such English traditions as cricket and Malcolm MUGGERIDGE, of whom he wrote a biography (1995).

IRELAND, 1ST DUKE OF *see* DE VERE, ROBERT

IRETON, HENRY (1611–51), soldier and politician. A lawyer, who fought for Parliament at CHARLES I's defeat at Edgehill (1642); despite being briefly captured during the further Royalist defeat at Naseby (1645), he became one of the most important army leaders. He married Oliver CROMWELL's daughter, Bridget, in 1646 and remained closely associated with him, especially in the army's attempts to negotiate with the King on the basis of the Heads of the Proposals in 1647–8, in Charles's trial and execution and in the discussions with radical army leaders in 1647–8, the Putney Debates. Lord Deputy of Ireland from 1650, he worked himself to death. His body was removed from Westminster Abbey at the restoration of CHARLES II and ritually humiliated.

IRVING, SIR HENRY (1836–1905), actor-manager. A transforming influence on the Victorian theatre, Irving contributed to the heightened sense of illusion on newly gas-lit stages, partly with technical innovations, using a front curtain to hide scene changes, introducing more flexible movable scenery and commissioning the leading artists of the day including ALMA TADEMA and BURNE-JONES to paint lavish sets, and partly with his dramatic (some said melodramatic) acting. He worked hard to achieve his success, slogging it out for 10 years and some 600 parts before his performance as the murderous villain Mathias in *The Bells* (1871) made him a star: he repeated the role some 800 times over the next 34 years. In 1878 Irving took over the Lyceum Theatre (London) and with a talented team (including his theatrical partner for 24 years, Ellen TERRY) staged the great Shakespearean tragedies, usually with himself in the lead. His revival of *Hamlet* (1874) was a triumph, playing for an exceptional 200 nights; his rendition of an ageing Romeo less so. In 1898 fire destroyed much of the Lyceum's expensive scenery; that, coupled with a loss-making production the same year, resulted in Irving's penury when he died in a Bradford (Yorks.) hotel after his performance in TENNYSON's play *Becket*. He was the first actor ever to be knighted.

ISAACS, SIR JEREMY (1932–), television and documentary film producer. Isaacs began as a television producer with *This Week* (1963) and *Panorama* (1965). He became director of programming at Thames Television, where he produced the acclaimed 26-part documentary series *The World at War* (1974). Appointed Chief Executive of the newly formed Channel Four Television in 1981, he revolutionized television in Britain. Channel Four produced programmes that reflected the views and experiences of minority ethnic groups, a young and sophisticated audience and individuals of different sexual orientation. After leaving Channel Four he became General Director of the Royal Opera House (ROH) from 1988–97, where falling ticket sales, cuts in government subsidies and controversy surrounding the expansion of the ROH's home at Covent Garden combined to make his job an uncomfortable one.

ISAACS, RUFUS (1st Marquess of Reading) (1860–1935), politician, Lord Chief Justice and Viceroy of India. The son of a Jewish fruit merchant in Spitalfields, London, he had such a meteoric rise that Lord Birkenhead (*see* SMITH, F. E.) said that the story of Dick Whittington 'fades into pale ineffectiveness' compared with the 'romance' of Lord Reading. He joined the family business at the age of 14, then worked as a jobber on the stock exchange and was 'hammered' when he could not pay his debts, before studying law and becoming a leading commercial advocate. As a Liberal MP (1903–13), he became Solicitor General, then Attorney General in 1910, and was a close friend of another outsider in British politics, LLOYD GEORGE. He was implicated but escaped formal censure in the MARCONI scandal of 1912–13, when the Marconi Co.'s successful tender for an 'imperial wireless chain' led to a huge rise in its share price and the accusation that government ministers had benefited corruptly from this. He and Herbert SAMUEL successfully sued for libel

and he became Lord Chief Justice (1913–21). During the First World War he was sent to the USA to negotiate a loan to finance the war, and served there as Ambassador (1918–19). As Viceroy of India (1921–6) he supervised the implementation of the Montagu–Chelmsford reforms (*see* THESIGER, FREDERICK) and generally adopted a conciliatory attitude to Indian concerns. His last political appointment was a brief spell as Foreign Secretary in the National government in 1931.

ISAACS, STELLA (née Charnaud) (Marchioness of Reading) (1894–1971), founder of the Women's Royal Voluntary Service. Of Huguenot descent, she married Rufus ISAACS, 1st Marquess of Reading, in 1931: he died four years later and in 1939 she responded to a Home Office appeal for assistance with air raid precautions. The Women's Voluntary Service (WVS) for Civil Defence was set up (it dropped 'Civil Defence' after the war and 'Royal' was added in 1966) with her as its chairman. The thousands of women who volunteered for this unpaid service worked throughout the war, helping in the evacuation of women and children from the cities, providing information and rest centres, canteens and welfare services for the troops at home and later overseas, as well as less 'womanly' tasks such as making camouflage nets (by 1945, 3,000 a week). After the war, the WVS made the transition to peace through filling the gaps left by State welfare provision: meals on wheels, 'home helps', clubs for the elderly, and support in national emergencies.

ISABEL OF GLOUCESTER (Countess of Gloucester) (?–1217), royal wife. An heiress who nearly became Queen of England, she was betrothed by HENRY II to his youngest son JOHN when her father, Earl William of Gloucester, died in 1183. Although the marriage was forbidden by BALDWIN, Archbishop of Canterbury, it went ahead on RICHARD I's orders in Aug. 1189 and she became Countess of Gloucester. As soon as he became King in 1199, John divorced her, but kept her in his custody until 1214 when Geoffrey de MANDEVILLE, Earl of Essex, agreed, presumably under pressure from the King, to pay him the incredible sum of 20,000 marks to marry her. After Geoffrey's death and a few days before her own death she was married again, such was the fate of great heiresses, to Hubert de BURGH.

ISABELLA OF ANGOULÊME (*c.* 1188–1246), Queen of England (1200–16). Daughter and heiress of Audemar, Count of Angoulême, she married King JOHN in Aug. 1200, despite already being betrothed to Hugh of Lusignan. The following year, angered at John making light of his protests, Hugh rebelled and appealed to Philip II

Augustus of France for justice, an action that was to lead directly to the collapse of the Angevin empire.

Isabella bore John five children. In 1218, two years after his death, she returned to Angoulême and married Hugh of Lusignan (the son of her former fiancé). Their nine children are known collectively in English history as 'the Lusignans'. In 1242 she encouraged HENRY III, her eldest son from her first marriage, to undertake the disastrous Taillebourg campaign. The following year, she retired to Fontevrault Abbey, where she was eventually buried.

ISABELLA OF FRANCE (1293–1358), Queen of England (1308–27). Daughter of Philip IV of France and reputed to be one of the most beautiful women of her time, she was married to EDWARD II in 1308. Tradition required the Queen to play the role of mediator, so her husband's alleged preference for Piers GAVESTON must have made her introduction to the English political scene a remarkably difficult one. Once Gaveston was dead, she bore the King four children (between 1312 and 1321). She clearly enjoyed widespread sympathy when, in 1325, she chose to disobey her husband and strike out on an extraordinary path of her own.

Having gone to France with her son, the future EDWARD III, to negotiate peace with her brother, Charles IV, she refused to return. In Paris, she became Roger MORTIMER's mistress, and together they planned and executed an invasion of England, landing in Sept. 1326. Virtually no one was prepared to fight for King Edward and his favourites, the DESPENSERS; within a matter of weeks Mortimer and Isabella were in control. In Jan. 1327 Edward III was proclaimed King as a 14-year-old; he still did what his mother told him and for the next three years she and her lover ruled England.

They were soon faced with gathering resentment of their ostentatious lifestyle and policies; Edward II's murder, the humiliating Treaty of Northampton and the execution for treason of the King's uncle, Edmund, Earl of Kent, were all laid at their door. On 18 Oct. 1330, the young King forced his way into his mother's chamber in Nottingham Castle and arrested Mortimer. Isabella was forced to forfeit her estates, but a substantial allowance of £3,000 a year enabled her to live very comfortably until, towards the end of her life, she took the habit of the Poor Clares. She has not enjoyed a favourable press since 1327, and is widely known by the nickname the 'she-wolf of France'.

ISABELLA OF FRANCE (1389–1409), Queen of England (1396–9). Daughter of Charles VI of France, she was married to RICHARD II just before her seventh birthday in 1396, a match that signalled Richard II's controversial policy of peace with France. She was confined at Sonning (Berks.) when Richard was deposed, but agreed to refrain from any intrigue, and was allowed to return to France in 1401. She married Charles of Orléans and, not yet 20, died in childbirth.

ISHERWOOD, CHRISTOPHER (1904–86), novel-ist. Having abandoned his history studies at Cambridge and dropped out of medical school in London, he went in 1930 to Berlin, where he taught English. His third novel was his first success, *Mr Norris Changes Trains* (1935). This was followed by *Goodbye to Berlin* (1939), later dramatized as *I am a Camera* (1951) and adapted as a musical, *Cabaret* (1968); both were filmed, and draw on his experiences in Weimar Germany with its sexual licence and its Nazi menace. On his return to London in 1933 he became part of a circle of left-wing intellectuals, including W. H. AUDEN, with whom he collaborated on two plays, *The Dog Beneath the Skin* (1935) and *The Ascent of F6* (1936). On the outbreak of the Second World War he and Auden emigrated to the USA, earning much opprobrium. Isherwood settled in California and, drawn to Indian philosophy, wrote on the subject, including a respected translation of the *Bhagavadgita* (with Swami Prabhavananda, 1944). Many of his books are lightly fictionalized autobiography, sometimes narrated by a character called Christopher Isherwood, while *Christopher and His Kind* (1972) is an *en clair* account of his own homosexuality.

ISLES, 4TH LORD OF THE *see* MACDONALD, JOHN

ISMAY, HASTINGS ('PUG') (1887–1965), soldier and *éminence grise*. Son of a senior civil servant in the government of India, Ismay was educated at Sandhurst. After a seemingly effortless passage through Staff College, he spent many years attached to the Committee of Imperial Defence. Promoted Major-General in 1939, Ismay was appointed CHURCHILL's Chief of Staff, from which position he wielded increasing influence in areas which were not his immediate concern. He said famously 'I spent the whole war in the middle of a web.' After the war Ismay worked with MOUNTBATTEN in India, oversaw the Festival of Britain (1951) and served as the first Secretary General of the North Atlantic Treaty Organization (NATO). The quintessential 'Whitehall warrior', Ismay was described as 'the man with the oil can'.

ISSIGONIS, SIR ALEXANDER (ALEC) (1906–88), automobile designer. Born in Turkey, he learned engineering from his father. In 1922 the family moved to London, where he studied engineering at Battersea Polytechnic and worked for car manufacturers. In 1936 he began working for Morris Motors and there designed front suspension mechanisms, a single-seater car and the Morris Minor (launched 1948), the first British car to sell more than one million. From 1955 he was technical director at the British Motor Corporation and, following the petrol shortage occasioned by the Suez crisis, was invited to design economical cars. This led to his development, in 1959, of the most successful car ever made in Britain, the Mini Minor.

IVAR THE BONELESS, King of Dublin. One of the great Viking warriors of the sagas, a literary creation of the twelfth and thirteenth centuries which glorified and mythologized the history of the Vikings. This superhuman figure may well have been based on Ingwaer, a son of RAGNAR LOTHBROK, who with his brother HALFDAN led the 'Great Army' which began a series of spectacular campaigns in northern England in 865. Ingwaer pursued a remarkable career of plunder and violence in Ireland, Scotland and England between 857 and 873, taking part in the overthrow of the kings of Northumbria (*see* ÆLLE) and, with OLAF THE WHITE, in the successful capture of Dumbarton Rock, the great fortress of the kings of Strathclyde in 870 (see ARTGAL SON OF DOMNAGUEL). Another possible exploit was the murder of St EDMUND, King of East Anglia.

IVEAGH, 1ST EARL OF *see* GUINNESS, EDWARD

J

'JACK THE RIPPER' (*fl.* nineteenth century), unidentified murderer. 'There is only one topic throughout all England', wrote W. T. STEAD in the *Pall Mall Gazette* in the autumn of 1888: it was the brutal murder of five prostitutes found stabbed to death in Whitechapel in the East End of London between Aug. and Nov. Media-induced panic spread through the metropolis: the police were accused of dereliction of duty, the dangers of 'outcast London' were exploited and speculation mounted as to the Ripper's identity. Whitechapel was a magnet to the 'young bloods' of the West End, as it was home to the poor and indigent who flocked to its teeming streets, and speculation about the murderer's identity was rife. Some gossip was anti-Semitic; other suggestions included a mad syphilitic doctor; the Duke of Clarence, the oldest son of the future EDWARD VII, was mentioned. No one was ever arrested and over a century later the affair continues to generate new and reworked old theories.

JÆNBERHT (?–792), Archbishop of Canterbury (765–92). A supporter of the Kentish kings' resistance to King OFFA of Mercia's domination, Jænberht by his obduracy eventually provoked Offa to obtain in 787 papal approval for the elevation of Lichfield into an archbishopric, thereby greatly reducing Canterbury's importance. This arrangement was not dismantled until 803 after Offa's death, in the time of Jænberht's successor St ETHELHEARD.

JAGGER, MICHAEL (MICK) (1943–), singer. The lead singer for the band the Rolling Stones, Jagger was educated at the London School of Economics. With the guitarist Keith Richards, whom he had met at primary school, he formed the band in 1963 together with bassist Bill Wyman, drummer Charlie Watts and guitarist Brian Jones. Although Jones died in 1969, the group were to perform together for over 30 years, a success that started in 1964 with the release of *It's All Over Now* which gave them their first number one in the record charts. The Stones cultivated a 'bad boy' image to distinguish them from the Beatles (*see* LENNON, JOHN), with whom they were often compared. The Stones's first British tour (1964)

caused hysteria and riots, but it was not until a year later that the group hit the big time internationally with the 'single' *Satisfaction*. Subsequent records (*Mother's Little Helper, Paint it Black, Under My Thumb*) tackled darker themes of drugs, sexuality and depression. Jagger, Richards and Jones were arrested on drugs charges in 1967 and a high-profile trial followed; the trio escaped with fines. The Rolling Stones continued to perform live into the 1990s, by which time most of their contemporary musicians were either retired or dead.

JAMES I (1394–1437), King of Scots (1406–37). In 1406, shortly after falling into English hands on his way to France for safety, he succeeded his father ROBERT III. He remained a captive until 1424. In his view, this was because the Duke of Albany, Scotland's governor and his uncle and heir presumptive, did nothing to secure his release, and it was only after agreeing to pay a ransom of 50,000 marks that he was freed. He used the enforced leisure to compose the greater part of a long, allegorical and romantic poem, the *Kingis Quair*, which includes a description of how he fell in love with JOAN BEAUFORT, whom he married in Feb. 1424.

On his return to Scotland, James initiated a flood of statutes. Very little escaped his paternalist and interventionist concern for law and order and the well-being of his subjects; for example, he forbade the playing of football. He also imposed taxes, ostensibly to raise the money for his ransom. He had other ways of filling his treasury: in 1425, he executed the leading members of the house of Albany and confiscated their estates and, by a similar treatment of other nobles, including Highland chiefs, he was able to treble the royal estates. Inevitably, some saw him as a tyrant. In 1437 a group of conspirators broke into his chamber at Perth and murdered him.

JAMES II (1430–60), King of Scots (1437–60). Although King since the murder of his father JAMES I in 1437, it was his 1449 marriage to MARY OF GUELDERS, niece of Duke Philip of Burgundy, that marked his assumption of power. By the marriage treaty, he was bound to pay her the immense dower of £5,000 a year.

His first moves were directed against the Livingstons, one of the families that had dominated Scottish politics during his minority. Between 1450 and 1455 he launched a series of attacks on the Black Douglases, including the murder of Earl William DOUGLAS in Feb. 1452 at Stirling Castle, a flagrant breach of his sworn word since the Earl had been under safe conduct. The ensuing confiscations and revocations of earlier grants meant that the Crown emerged much richer. In 1458 a compliant Parliament announced that 'all rebels and breakers of his justice are removed'.

An aggressive and warlike King, fascinated by guns, which were the latest weaponry, in his legislation James proclaimed his concern for justice, order, economic stability and royal authority. In 1460, intending to use the disarray south of the border to put an end to the English occupation of Teviotdale, he was besieging Roxburgh when one of his siege guns blew up and killed him.

JAMES III (1452–88), King of Scots (1460–88). Proclaimed King in 1460 after the death of his father JAMES II, six years later during one of the factional struggles that characterized his minority he suffered the indignity of being kidnapped. On taking over power in 1469, he had his abductors, the Boyds, punished as traitors. In the same year he married MARGARET OF DENMARK, whom, after her death in 1486, he tried to have canonized.

In 1479 he confiscated the estates of his brothers, the Duke of Albany and the Earl of Mar. The latter died in suspicious circumstances, and Albany fled to England. James attempted to make peace with England, betrothing his sister to Anthony WOODVILLE, Earl Rivers, but when she was found to be already pregnant, negotiations collapsed and in 1482 the English, accompanied by Albany, invaded Scotland. James mustered an army at Lauder (Berwicks.) only to be seized by a group of conspirators led by the Earl of Angus. He was held prisoner in Edinburgh Castle until the following year, when, by exploiting divisions between his various opponents, he was able to secure his restoration. His attempts to use the judicial process to punish his enemies, however, led only to a renewal of opposition, this time led by his own heir, the future JAMES IV.

James III was killed at, or after, the Battle of Sauchieburn (Stirlings.) on 11 June 1488. BOECE described him as the King who subdued the Highlands and brought peace to the whole of Scotland, but the prevailing image created by historians in the sixteenth and later centuries is of a king corrupted by low-born Councillors. Although many of the details of that image appear to be based on little more than legend, successive Parliaments in the 1470s and 1480s did criticize

his greed and laziness, and Lauder and Saucieburn bear witness to the degree of hostility felt by significant numbers of his more powerful subjects.

JAMES IV *see* essay on page 452

JAMES V *see* essay on page 453

JAMES VI AND I *see* essay on pages 454–55

JAMES VII AND II *see* essay on page 456

JAMES VIII AND III *see* STUART, JAMES

JAMES, C(YRIL) L(IONEL) R(OBERT) (1901–89), writer. A historian, novelist, polemicist, Marxist philosopher, cricket writer and prophet of pan-Africanism, James was born in Trinidad into a family of teachers, he moved to Britain in 1932 with his friend Learie (later Lord) Constantine, who was then beginning his cricket career. James started to write about cricket and published his first novel; both men were passionate about West Indian independence. James's masterwork as a historian was his study of the Haitian slave revolutionary Toussaint L'Ouverture (beginning as a London stage play for Paul Robeson in 1936). In 1939 he went to the USA, where he spent 15 years lecturing and pamphleteering; in 1945 he and other black leaders including the legendary W. E. B. duBois met leaders of emerging independence movements such as NYERERE and KENYATTA at the Pan-African conference in Manchester. Detained in the USA in 1953 during the McCarthyite anti-Communist terror, James was arrested again when he returned to Trinidad on the eve of its independence. The new Prime Minister, his former friend Eric Williams, feared James's influence and his promotion of a West Indian Federation. Sent to England, where he spent the remainder of his life, James gradually became a Grand Old Man of the Left, revered as a precursor of African liberation.

JAMES OF ST GEORGE (?–c. 1308), military architect. Originally from the town of St Georges d'Esperanche in Savoy, he was one of the greatest of all military architects. From 1278 to the end of the reign, he was in EDWARD I's service in Wales, Gascony and Scotland. As master of the King's works in Wales, he was responsible for the construction of the castles of Conwy, Caernarfon, Harlech, Beaumaris, Flint and Rhuddlan.

JAMESON, SIR LEANDER (1853–1917), South African politician. A close friend of Cecil RHODES and an administrator in his British South Africa Co., Jameson shared the vision of British rule from the Cape to Cairo. He was secretly commissioned

continued on page 457

JAMES IV (1473–1513)
King of Scots (1488–1513)

Son of JAMES III and MARGARET OF DENMARK, James grew up at Stirling Castle under the care of Margaret, who lived in virtual separation from her husband. The younger James gained the Crown aged 15 after the King's murder by a faction of the Scots nobility at the Battle of Sauchieburn. They had united behind the heir to the throne against his father's favouritism towards his second son (also called James), and the new King did penance on his coronation at Scone for his part in James III's death; all his life he wore an iron belt next to his skin as a symbol of penitence. His first years were spent in dealing with the political disruption, including defeats of a major rising in 1489 and of the rebellion of Archibald DOUGLAS, 22nd Earl of Angus, in 1491. James was determined to be conciliatory, placing supporters of James III in positions of authority, even making Angus Chancellor in 1492 and still more remarkably sharing a mistress with him in later years. In contrast with his father's concentration of power in a close-knit group of favourites, he made sure that his council represented the greatest families in the realm. Such measures undermined the efforts of HENRY VII to stir up trouble with potential opponents, and from the time that he obtained his majority in 1493, James maintained a general political harmony for the rest of his reign.

He was energetic in defending his frontiers, spending sums extraordinary for a small and poor kingdom on artillery and on his navy, including in 1511 the construction of the spectacular warship *Great Michael*, which spurred HENRY VIII to naval construction in jealous imitation. During the 1490s he led a series of expeditions into the Highlands to assert royal authority; he extended effective royal control to the Western Isles, declaring the Macdonald Lordship of the Isles forfeit in 1493. In 1492 he secured a grant from the Pope making the diocese of Glasgow into Scotland's second archbishopric. He developed Edinburgh's role as royal capital and seat of the law courts, establishing daily meetings of lawyers there. His relations with the newly established Tudor dynasty were turbulent despite the truce with Henry VII in 1491. James supported Perkin WARBECK in 1495–7, giving him hospitality at Stirling Castle in 1495 and providing military support for expeditions south. Their lack of success led to him concluding a further truce with Henry in 1497, and in 1502 he negotiated a treaty of perpetual peace which included his marriage to Henry's daughter MARGARET TUDOR in 1503. This formally concluded two centuries of warfare between the two kingdoms, and JAMES VI, the descendant of this marriage, would unite the two realms in 1603.

James's last years were increasingly coloured by his unrealistic determination to become a monarch of international stature. He mounted a naval expedition to help his cousin, the King of Denmark, against Swedish rebels in 1502. His relations with his brother-in-law Henry VIII deteriorated. After signing an alliance with France against England in 1512, part of a grand strategy to lead a Europe-wide crusade against the Turks, James invaded Northumberland in 1513, but he was defeated and killed by Thomas HOWARD, 13th Earl of Surrey, at Flodden; his lavish military spending had been completely wasted, and most of the leaders of Scottish society were killed with him. His body was taken to England and never returned, provoking many legends that he would return to claim his throne. He was succeeded by his infant son JAMES V.

James was a charismatic, intelligent and popular King, who revelled in his physical prowess both in the jousting-yard and in the bedroom. He made a particular point of meeting his subjects, particularly on frequent pilgrimages to notable Scottish shrines, and his ostentatious piety was also expressed in his support for the new Observant order of Franciscan Friars. Despite his love of conspicuous expenditure, he avoided making demands for taxation, mainly by raising revenue from Crown lands, creating new tenancies (feus) which were more secure and which therefore justified higher payments to the Crown. He was a great builder at his various palaces: notably Holyrood House, his new base near Edinburgh, and at Stirling the Chapel Royal and surviving great hall. He actively encouraged education, literature and the arts, giving an honoured place at his court to the poet William DUNBAR. He became patron of the new university college of King's, Aberdeen, in 1505, and in 1507 he licensed Scotland's first printing press. During his reign, the outlines of local power were laid down for the next century, as he ennobled a series of leading families, in contrast to the complete lack of creations of nobility during the reign of his son James V.

Norman MacDougall, James IV (1989)

JAMES V (1512–42)
King of Scots (1513–42)

James's long minority from his father JAMES IV's death at the Battle of Flodden in 1513 was dominated by struggles between his mother, MARGARET TUDOR, and noblemen ruling or seeking to rule in his name, principally John STEWART, Duke of Albany (1515–24), and Margaret's estranged second husband, Archibald DOUGLAS, 23rd Earl of Angus (1525–28); their conflicts were a confusing mixture of selfishness and genuine disagreement about whether England or France should be Scotland's ally. During these years James lived at Stirling Castle, and among his principal attendants were the poet and playwright, Sir David LINDSAY, and the historian and churchman, Gavin DOUGLAS. Although Margaret proclaimed James fit to rule in 1524, only in 1528 did he manage to escape the control of the Douglases, establish an independent position at Stirling and begin rebuilding the fragmented power and the shattered finances of the Crown. He expelled Angus from Scotland, and quickly showed himself adept in exploiting his kingdom's position as a balance among the competing powers in Europe, particularly as the Papacy looked for allies in northern Europe against the spread of the Reformation. In 1531 he secured a papal grant of three years' tenths of Church revenues in order to defend his realm.

In 1531 James also began planning a central court, the College of Justice, whose establishment was completed by parliamentary Act in 1541. This court incorporated the older procedure for appealing to the Crown in the Council of the Session, but it was based on the *Parlement* of Paris; its procedures were therefore those of civil law, derived from Roman law, and it was staffed mainly by lay rather than clerical lawyers. One of the main motives, however, of James's scheme was once more financial; he wished to enrich the monarchy at the expense of the Church. After hard-fought negotiations with the Church hierarchy, he secured a large endowment for the court out of Church revenues; this was the first time that the Scottish monarchy had sought major revenues in taxation. His demands forced many ecclesiastical landowners to rent out large proportions of their lands to lay tenants at fixed annual rents, for short-term financial gain in the form of initial down-payments ('grassums'), a form of tenure known as feuing. The long-term effect of feuing was to transfer ownership of land from the Church to laypeople, since the annual rents were usually inflexible and therefore vulnerable to inflation. Even in the short term, the effect was a process parallel to the English Reformation's plundering of Church lands; although James resisted HENRY VIII's suggestions that he dissolve Scottish monasteries, he also intruded his illegitimate sons as lay heads of major religious houses. James's determined search for money also embittered his relations with many noblemen, for when in 1537 he issued an Act revoking land grants made during the years of his minority, he broke with precedent by demanding large compositions (compensatory sums of money) in return for regrants. James used most of these newly gained revenues not for financing the College of Justice, but for grandiose building programmes, particularly at his palaces at Linlithgow, Stirling and Falkland.

James married successively two French princesses, Madeleine (1537–8) and MARY OF GUISE (1538), a symbol of his efforts to keep Scotland free from English domination by an alliance with England's traditional enemy. His strategy necessarily involved a rejection of the Reformation with which his cousin Henry VIII was flirting. Irritated by Henry's condescending advice on religious matters, he refused to follow him into a break with Rome; he sponsored three Acts of Parliament attacking heresy in 1541 and allowed the persecution of some heretics (*see* BEATON, David). At the same time he expressed his dissatisfaction with the state of the Church, and sponsored minor reforms. After James snubbed Henry VIII by not turning up at a scheduled meeting at York in 1541, Anglo-Scots relations descended once more into war, leading to a Scots defeat at Solway Moss (1542). James died in a state of nervous breakdown after hearing of this disaster. Since his two sons by Mary had died in 1541, he left as his heir the newborn MARY QUEEN OF SCOTS.

James's reign represents a new relationship between Crown and people in Scotland; he had more success than any previous king in asserting centralized control in the realm. In his adult reign, he kept great noblemen out of important positions in his government, relying on the administrative skills of lawyers. His premature death, however, led to 20 years of political instability; in particular, the quarrels and ambitions of his illegitimate offspring, such as the future Regent James STEWART, Earl of Moray, continued to complicate Scottish politics.

Caroline Bingham, James V, King of Scots, 1512–1542 (1971)

JAMES VI AND I (1566–1625)
King of Scotland (1567–1625) and of England and Ireland (1603–25)

Another royal victim of Scots political instability through a long minority, James became King aged only 13 months, on the deposition of his mother MARY QUEEN OF SCOTS. It is possible that he suffered from mild cerebral palsy, which would better account for some of his physical peculiarities than the hereditary disease porphyria often attributed to him. By his late teens he was turning his considerable intelligence and skill in devious diplomacy to establishing control of government, and he showed increasing political surefootedness. He began claiming real power in 1581, when he helped the first of many attractive male favourites, Esmé STUART, to overthrow the Regent, James DOUGLAS, Earl of Morton. Thereafter he endured temporary seizure by Protestant noblemen in the Ruthven Raid (1582); this trauma convinced him that he must curb the power-seeking aspirations of Presbyterians in Church and government. One important manoeuvre was to secure by 1592 a majority of Privy Councillors among the Lords of the Articles, the committee dealing with details of parliamentary legislation, and he also on occasion spoke and voted there himself; he thus gained a useful measure of control over a Parliament which had frequently been dominated by his opponents. His book *Basilikon Doron* (1599) provides a frank and practical exposition of his vision of personal kingship, which was demonstrated in a rather more brutal way in 1600 in the 'Gowrie conspiracy': James claimed that Alexander RUTHVEN, the Earl of Gowrie's brother, attempted to kidnap him at Gowrie House (Perths.). It was no coincidence that this brought the destruction of the Gowries, who had humiliated him in the Ruthven Raid and who were strong Presbyterian partisans. After moving to England he continued to exert control in Scotland, for instance forcing the Scots Kirk to accept a number of changes, including the Five Articles of Perth bringing Scotland more into line with the Church of England (1618, grudgingly passed by the Scots Parliament in 1621).

James married ANNE OF DENMARK in 1589 and in 1590, displaying an uncharacteristic heterosexual ardour, sailed the North Sea to collect her in person. His visit to Denmark introduced him to the European fascination with witchcraft; although James himself later became embarrassed about his intense if temporary interest (which had led him to write the treatise *Daemonologie* in 1597), his patronage of the witch-craze gave it a disastrous continuing popularity in Scotland.

Any grief felt by James at his mother's execution (1587) had been softened by the absence of personal memories of her, and by the prospect of succeeding to the English throne in right of his great-grandmother MARGARET TUDOR. After much anxious intrigue with anyone who might prove useful (particularly Robert DEVEREUX, 19th Earl of Essex, and, after his disgrace, Robert CECIL) he succeeded ELIZABETH I without fuss in 1603. Finding the English Church much to his liking, he disappointed Puritan hopes for further reform at the Hampton Court conference (1604), and showed much less favour for Roman Catholics than they anticipated, particularly after the Gunpowder Plot (1605). His delight at his new kingdom's comparative wealth was soon soured by the failure of its antiquated revenue system to provide enough money for normal government, let alone for his family's personal extravagance; successive ministers found no solutions, although the longterm significance of their conflicts with James's Parliaments has been exaggerated. His highly competent Secretary of State inherited from Elizabeth, Cecil (now Earl of Salisbury), tried to secure a parliamentary deal in 1604 to bring permanent security to royal finances. But both in this session and in 1606 James was embittered by obstruction of his pet project, full union between England and Scotland in a single kingdom of Great Britain. His anger in 1604 led to a Commons committee drawing up an Apology or defence of its discussion of royal finance, although since James (characteristically) soon became conciliatory, this document was never formally presented to him. Salisbury tried again in 1610, seeking a lump sum to clear debt and a permanent revenue settlement, in return for abolishing the court of Wards and Liveries and the payments for royal provisions called purveyance. Parliament raised an accumulation of grievances about central government, and James, encouraged by Cecil's opponents in his concern for the potential loss of his prerogative, was lukewarm to this Great Contract. Parliament was prorogued in Feb. 1611 with nothing achieved, and it was the end of efforts at major reform.

After his predecessor's reluctance to create peers, James redressed the balance with enthusiasm, both anxious to cement loyalties to his newly arrived dynasty and eager to profit from the revenue to be raised by selling titles; his expedients included the invention of baronetcies, a new hereditary title ranking above knighthood and below the younger sons of barons. These were first granted in 1611 supposedly to finance defence for the new plantations of Scots and

English in Ulster; a further colonial venture was marked by the inauguration of Nova Scotia baronetcies in 1624–5. If many saw this 'inflation of honours' as debasing nobility, it was senior noblemen who brought scandal, greater administrative corruption and factional division to government, particularly after Salisbury's death (1612). The Howard family (*see* HOWARD, CHARLES, Earl of Nottingham; HOWARD, HENRY, Earl of Northampton) became increasingly entrenched at court, allying with James's current favourite Robert CARR, through whom they were drawn into the sensational divorce case of Frances HOWARD and Robert DEVEREUX, 20th Earl of Essex. When James again called Parliament in April 1614 in an effort to solve the Crown's financial problems, it was wrecked by the factional intrigues of the Howards, who deliberately stirred up Commons suspicion of royal intentions. After a fierce dispute between Lords and Commons about privileges, James abruptly dissolved this Addled Parliament in June with nothing achieved. Aristocratic squabbles were exacerbated by the appearance of James's only English favourite, George VILLIERS (made Duke of Buckingham), introduced to James by enemies of the Howards; this shift of power brought the worst scandal yet as Carr and Frances Howard were tried for the murder of Sir Thomas OVERBURY. James pardoned them, probably to silence embarrassing personal revelations by Carr. Now Buckingham dominated government, and his extensive and rapacious family infuriated the nobility by monopolizing opportunities for money and favour.

Ironically, James's one major effort to economize brought further ill will: after the outbreak of the Thirty Years War (1618) and the Habsburgs' defeat of his son-in-law Frederick, King of Bohemia (1620), many of James's subjects wanted England to join the fight for the Protestant cause. James was reluctant to be pulled into warfare that his kingdoms could ill afford, and, to widespread disapproval, he pursued alliance with Spain, promoting a marriage for his son, the future CHARLES I, with the Spanish Infanta. The issue ruined the Parliament of 1621 (which also impeached Francis BACON as the chief symbol of corruption in administration): James abruptly dissolved the session in fury when the Commons demanded war with Spain and an end to the marriage negotiations. After a bizarre personal adventure to Spain by Charles and Buckingham, Spanish reluctance ended marriage prospects, to great rejoicing in England, and now James found that his son and his favourite added their voices to the call for war. His last Parliament settled some of his debts in return for a promise of war with Spain, and also (with Buckingham's encouragement) impeached his Lord Treasurer, Lionel CRANFIELD.

James's reputation has been curiously divided in relation to Scottish and English history. His successes in Scotland are obvious, building up royal power after the disasters of his mother's reign and routing the Presbyterian challenge to Episcopacy. In England, he has been the victim of a remarkably enduring negative presentation by a vengeful household servant, Anthony Weldon, who after being dismissed for anti-Scots abuse produced *The Court and Character of King James*, a grotesque picture of a slobbering, ineffective drunken coward (and the source of the put-down 'the wisest fool in Christendom'). A problem for James in England was his personal style, a breezy informality ideally suited to the openness of Scottish society but a shock to the English after more than a century of the fastidiously ceremonious Tudors. He was a foreigner, who had the bad taste to speak Scots and not English. Certainly he had little financial sense, a fault compounded by his lifelong eagerness to be generous to his friends. Nevertheless, his troubles with English Parliaments have obscured his other achievements. Although bored by the minutiae of government business, which he put aside for weeks on end for prolonged hunting expeditions, James was rightly proud of his peace-making activities: he curbed Scots aristocratic feuds and ended the centuries-old Anglo-Scots border war and the ruinously expensive Irish and Spanish wars, drawing away from the Elizabethan aggressive alliance with the Dutch United Provinces. He was interested in reunion schemes for the Western Church, expressing more goodwill towards the Roman Catholic Church than was common, and he kept a careful balance among the contending Calvinist and Arminian factions in the Church of England. Under his benevolent supervision, the English Church found security from the lay raids on its revenues allowed by Elizabeth, codified its canon law and matured into a self-confident body with an increasingly well-educated clergy. James's rather unconventional abilities, his broad wit (particularly handy against his opponents in the Church of Scotland) and his genuine talent as scholar and writer are generally held in high regard among modern historians.

Maurice Lee Jr, Great Britain's Solomon: James VI and I in His Three Kingdoms (1989)

JAMES VII AND II (1633–1701)
King of England, Ireland and Scotland (1685–8)

Second son of CHARLES I and brother of CHARLES II, James was created Duke of York in 1643. He was captured at the surrender of Oxford (1646) but escaped to Holland (1648) and served in the French and Spanish armies, returning to England at the Restoration. Like his brother a philanderer, he got the daughter of Lord Chancellor Clarendon (see HYDE, EDWARD), Anne Hyde, pregnant in 1660; it was agreed that they should marry. Of children born to this marriage only two daughters, Mary (the future MARY II) and ANNE, survived to adulthood.

Made Lord High Admiral, James was ordered by his brother to stay out of danger after a narrow escape in the Second Dutch War. Though reduced to a supervisory role, he took his responsibilities seriously. His conversion to Catholicism in the 1660s was widely rumoured, and aroused political controversy. The passage of the Test Act 1673, requiring office-holders to take Anglican communion, compelled him to resign. The same year, his first wife having died, he married the Catholic MARY OF MODENA, prompting parliamentary attempts to prevent consummation of the marriage, exclude him from the throne or compel future children to be brought up Protestant. In 1678 Titus OATES stirred up the Popish Plot crisis with his allegations of a conspiracy to place James on the throne; an Exclusion Bill to bar him from the succession precipitated the Exclusion Crisis. James went briefly into exile, but returned as Lord High Commissioner for Scotland (1680–2), when he reversed Lauderdale's (see MAITLAND, JOHN) policy of concessions to dissent. In 1684, after Charles had given up trying to work with Parliament, executed some Whig leaders and frightened others into flight, James was reappointed Lord High Admiral.

His succession to the throne (1685) was challenged by risings led by Charles's illegitimate son Monmouth (see SCOTT, JAMES) and Archibald CAMPBELL, 9th Earl of Argyll, but both were defeated. The Tory-dominated Parliament summoned at his accession voted a generous financial settlement, further enhanced by buoyant economic conditions. Devoutly committed to reviving Catholicism in Britain, and insensitive to national opinion, James promoted Catholics to civil and military posts, using the royal 'dispensing power' to nullify the Test Act. A Declaration of Indulgence (1687) gave relief to both Catholics and Dissenters. James began sounding out local elites to see if they would countenance the repeal of the Test Act, and set up a board of regulators to oversee the remodelling of corporations, to influence the next election. The Tory Anglicans who had originally supported him were alienated by these measures, as were politicians by pressure to convert. Only Sunderland (see SPENCER, ROBERT) stayed by him almost to the end. The bishops turned against him in 1688: seven among them, led by Archbishop SANCROFT, refused to read out a second Declaration of Indulgence (1688). They were tried for seditious libel but acquitted by a jury.

Matters came to a head when, in June 1688, the birth of a male heir (James Edward STUART) was announced. Thinking this too convenient to be likely, some claimed Mary's pregnancy had been faked, and the baby brought in a warming pan. Conspirators invited James's daughter Mary's husband, William of Orange (the future WILLIAM III), to intervene to ensure a 'free Parliament'. In Sept. 1688 James belatedly made concessions, abolishing the Commission for Ecclesiastical Causes, used to impose royal policy on the Church, and reinstating corporate charters. William invaded in Nov., and James fled London in early Dec. but was captured in Kent and returned. Later that month, William encouraged him to leave for France, opening his own way to the throne and precipitating the constitutional changes termed the Glorious Revolution.

James established a court in exile outside Paris with aid from Louis XIV. In 1689 he landed in Ireland with French military assistance, and summoned a largely Catholic 'Jacobite Parliament'. His forces were defeated at the Battle of the Boyne in July and he returned to France. By the Treaty of Ryswick of 1697, the French recognized William III as rightful King; a blow to James, but a transient gesture in European politics. James died at a time when Louis's ambitions were on the rise again; he then recognized James Edward as lawful King of Britain.

James strangely mixed the characteristics of military man, philandering courtier and devout Catholic. It is doubtful that he wanted 'absolutism', nor was he merely a pawn in the hands of France: in foreign policy he liked to keep his options open. But he dedicated himself to a religious mission unpalatable to most of his subjects, and treated opposition with a contempt which contrasted sharply with his brother's conciliatory approach. After the Revolution, many persisted in the belief that, since he was the natural heir and they had taken oaths to support him, he was the *rightful* King, but few in practice wanted him back.

John Miller, James II: A Study in Kingship (1978)

to lead a force of mounted men from Bechuanaland into the Transvaal in 1895 to promote a rising of the Uitlanders, non-Afrikaaner whites. The rising failed to materialize, the raiders were swiftly captured and the political fall-out was considerable: Joseph CHAMBERLAIN was supposed to have connived, Rhodes was forced to resign his premiership, a telegram from the Kaiser to Kruger congratulating him on repulsing the raid enraged British opinion and the Transvaal was pushed closer towards alliance with the Orange Free State. Tried in Britain, Jameson was sentenced to 15 months imprisonment, serving four. He became Prime Minister of the Cape Colony (1904–8), founded the Unionist Party in 1910 and led the opposition until ill health forced his retirement to England in 1912.

JANE GREY (1537–54), Queen of England (1553). Victim of her descent as great-granddaughter of HENRY VIII through her mother Frances Grey (née Brandon), Marchioness of Dorset and Duchess of Suffolk, Jane used learning and Protestant piety as a refuge from a bleak over regulated childhood. In 1553 she became a passive conspirator against MARY I's succession, when she was married to John DUDLEY Duke of Northumberland's son, Guildford Dudley, as part of a scheme concocted by Northumberland and EDWARD VI to defy the provisions of Henry VIII's will and divert the succession to the Grey line. Jane's recognition as Queen on Edward's death on 6 July at first seemed unstoppable, backed as it was by nearly all leading politicians, but a wide spectrum of English opinion was outraged at the exclusion of the Tudor daughters. Following provincial uprisings, the regime collapsed within a fortnight (Tudor propaganda soon fixed on the proverbial figure of nine days for her reign). Mary acceded to the throne on 19 July, and on 22 Aug. Northumberland was executed. Mary initially spared Jane, but executed her after the rebellion led in Jan. 1554 by Sir Thomas WYATT the younger.

JANE SEYMOUR (?1509–37), Queen of England. From a Wilts. knightly family and sister of Edward and Thomas SEYMOUR, she entered CATHERINE OF ARAGON's service in 1529, later serving ANNE BOLEYN. As the latter's marriage ran into trouble, Anne's conservative enemies brought Jane to HENRY VIII's attention; Henry rose to the carefully tutored bait and married Jane only two days after Anne's execution. Despite her brothers' later adherence to evangelical reformism, her religion was conventionally conservative; she argued for the retention of the monasteries, and even tried to get Mary, later MARY I, restored to the succession. She bore Henry's longed-for male heir, EDWARD VI, on 12 Oct. 1537, but died soon after, to Henry's intense grief.

JARDINE, WILLIAM (1784–1843) and **MATHESON, JAMES** (1796–1878), China trade merchants. Born in Dumfries, the area from which came in time 30 senior partners of the Asian trading firm that he founded, Jardine left Scotland aged 18 as a ship's surgeon's mate with the East India Co. He learned about trade on India and China voyages and became an independent merchant in 1817. In Bombay he first encountered a fellow Scot, James Matheson, and in 1825 the men became partners in Magniac & Co., an established firm in the China trade. The new firm of Jardine, Matheson & Co. was founded in 1832, on the eve of the abolition of the East India Co.'s China monopoly. A delegation under 8th Baron Napier, Chief Superintendent of Trade in China, to negotiate new trading conditions with the Chinese in Canton failed, but Jardine Matheson along with other agency houses began accepting cargoes sent to Canton, and came to control British financial dealings in the region, especially in the opium trade. Jardine (known to the Chinese as 'iron-headed old rat') and Matheson both returned to England, and advised Palmerston (*see* TEMPLE, HENRY) in the prosecution of the First Opium War in 1840. Matheson subsequently negotiated a satisfactory treaty with the Chinese, while Jardine stayed in England and was elected as a Whig MP for Ashburton (Devon) in 1841 but died two years later. Matheson succeeded him in the seat and later was elected as MP for Ross and Cromarty. He became Chairman of P&O as well as being a substantial landowner in his native Highlands. The firm that bears their joint names established itself in Hong Kong, ceded to Britain after the 1842 Treaty of Nanking, and subsequently until 1949 in Shanghai. Mainly managed by family members, early associates and their descendants, its power increased as the firm became a 'princely Hong' (leading light) of the colony.

JARMAN, DEREK (1942–94), artist and filmmaker. Son of an RAF officer, Jarman studied at the Slade School of Art (1963–7), where, he decided, 'decadence was the first sign of intelligence' and exhibited his paintings before turning to theatre and film design. His first feature film *Sebastiane* (1976) was about the martyred saint Sebastian. With Latin dialogue (subtitled), it was a minuscule budget production, as was much of his work, but his films remained painterly in their exploration of national decline, urban decay, punk violence and homo-eroticism: *Jubilee* (1978), *Caravaggio* (1986), *The Last of England* (1987), *Edward II* (1991) and finally *Blue* (1993), a compelling film about facing his own death from AIDS.

JARY, SYDNEY (1924–), soldier. He joined the army in 1942 as a private soldier, and from July

1944 until May 1945 Jary served as a Platoon Commander with the Somerset Light Infantry from Normandy to Bremerhaven. One of only a handful of junior infantry officers to have survived the entire campaign in command of the same unit, he was awarded the Military Cross. His account *Eighteen Platoon* (1987) turned out to be one of the finest books on the realities and problems of junior command ever written and became required reading in most military academies throughout the English-speaking world.

JAY, DOUGLAS (Baron Jay of Battersea) (1907–96), politician. Educated at Winchester and New College, Oxford, Jay was elected a Fellow of All Souls in 1930. A journalist on *The Times* and then the *Economist* before being appointed City editor of the *Daily Herald* in 1940, he was a civil servant during the Second World War, and attracted the attention of Clement ATTLEE who, after Labour's election victory in 1945, chose Jay as his personal assistant. A safe seat at Battersea (London) was found for him and he quickly moved through the junior ministerial ranks, serving first as Economic Secretary and then as Financial Secretary to the Treasury (1948–51). He earned a reputation as a central planner with his famous statement that 'The gentleman in Whitehall really does know better what is good for people than the people know themselves', but in fact he was never as much of an enthusiast for nationalization and State planning as this statement, which was often quoted against him, implies. During the 1950s, together with Roy JENKINS and Anthony CROSLAND, he formed the inner core of the 'Gaitskellites' (*see* GAITSKELL, HUGH), who attempted to reform and modernize Labour Party policy in the face of three successive electoral defeats. After Gaitskell's death in 1963, Jay was President of the Board of Trade under Harold WILSON (1964), but was sacked for his vocal anti-Europeanism in 1967, and until his retirement from the Commons in 1983 was one of Labour's most effective and sophisticated backbench opponents of British entry into the European Community.

JEBB, EGLANTYNE (1876–1928), philanthropist. The daughter of a Salop. landowner, because of poor health she retired early as a Froebel-trained elementary teacher. News in 1913 of the need for relief of the starving in Macedonia, victims of the Second Balkan War, precipitated her into fund-raising. After the 1918 armistice, 4.5 million children were starving as a result of Allied blockade in central and eastern Europe. Jebb founded Save the Children Fund as an emergency relief organization in 1919, raising £2 million in two years. The movement spread;

an International Union was set up in 1920 in Geneva.

JEBB, JOHN (1736–86), radical. Son of the Dean of Cashel, he studied both at Trinity College, Dublin, and at Peterhouse, Cambridge, where he was ordained, but his Unitarianism restricted his prospects there. He was an active campaigner for the Feathers Tavern petition in 1771–2 (*see* BLACKBURNE, FRANCIS). In 1775, following his failure to introduce annual public examinations at Cambridge, he resigned his clerical livings and went to study medicine at St Andrews. From 1778 he practised in London, where he became active in the reform movement, calling for a national assembly elected by universal suffrage and advocating prison reform.

JEFFREYS, SIR ALEC (1950–), geneticist. Jeffreys read biochemistry and biochemical genetics at Oxford University and in 1977 continued his genetics research at Leicester University. In 1984 he claimed that certain sections of a person's deoxyribonucleic acid (DNA) were highly characteristic of that particular individual and he subsequently proposed a technique for using a DNA profile for purposes of identification. Jeffreys's work, the basis of 'DNA fingerprinting', was first exploited in the USA in 1987 and subsequently adopted in criminal investigations across the globe.

JEFFREYS, GEORGE (1st Baron Jeffreys) (1648–89), judge. Of a Welsh family, he went to Cambridge and the Inner Temple. Appointed Recorder of London in 1677, he was actively involved in the prosecutions following the Popish-Plot scare (1678–9) stirred up by Titus OATES. He became Chief Justice of the King's Bench in 1683, and tried Oates, Algernon SIDNEY and Richard BAXTER. His ruthlessness when trying those who had participated in Monmouth's (*see* SCOTT, JAMES) rebellion earned the session the name of the 'Bloody Assizes': more than 300 were executed, and several hundred others were transported to the West Indies. Lord Chancellor from 1685, he was appointed to the Board of Regulators in 1687, alongside Sunderland (*see* SPENCER, ROBERT). Besides the task of remodelling the corporations initiated under CHARLES II, the board advised on remodelling commissions of the peace, replacing magistrates whose responses to three questions concerning the repeal of the Test Act were deemed unsatisfactory. Jeffreys was captured while trying to follow JAMES II into exile after the Glorious Revolution, and died in the Tower.

JEKYLL, GERTRUDE (1843–1932), garden designer. A transforming influence to whom much tribute is paid by today's new breed of gardeners, Jekyll was born into an intellectual and wealthy family and excelled at a variety of artistic production, embroidery, silverwork, painting and woodcarving. In her late thirties acute myopia led her to abandon such crafts and move to garden design. She worked closely with LUTYENS, whom she met in 1899, and designed more than 200 gardens. An advocate of the natural English garden, abloom with scented indigenous plants, Jekyll trailed plants through trees, encouraged wild flowers, designed white and silver gardens, planted herb gardens, championed the hardy annual and abandoned the formal beds of Victorian gardeners for today's massed herbaceous plantings. The author of several books and innumerable articles, she was briefly the editor of *Country Life* and the recipient of the Royal Horticultural Society's gold medal and other honours.

JELLICOE, JOHN (1st Earl Jellicoe) (1859–1935), sailor. Son of a captain in the merchant marine, he entered the navy from HMS *Britannia* (1874) and gained distinction in the Egyptian campaign (1882), by carrying dispatches through enemy positions while disguised as an Arab. Selected by John FISHER as his Chief of Staff, in 1891 Jellicoe was promoted Commander, and in 1893 was appointed Captain of *Victoria*. By a stroke of luck, on 22 June when Admiral TRYON contrived to sink *Victoria*, Jellicoe was in his bunk with fever, so that he emerged blameless from the navy's most embarrassing catastrophe. Serving in the Far East in 1900, Jellicoe was badly wounded while attempting to relieve the besieged legation in Peking, and after his recovery was chosen by Fisher to head the project to construct *Dreadnought*. Appointed to command the Grand Fleet in Aug. 1914, Jellicoe was widely expected to produce another Trafalgar, but he knew that Nelsonian (*see* NELSON, HORATIO) rashness in an age of mines, submarines and torpedoes would produce disaster. His characteristic caution made him unpopular and his failure to annihilate the German High Seas Fleet at Jutland on 31 May, the largest clash between battleships in history, compounded by his reluctance to introduce convoys to meet the threat of submarine attacks, led to his dismissal in Dec. 1917. Jellicoe is now regarded as one of the finest naval commanders in history, the man who was always conscious that 'he could lose the war in an afternoon'.

JENKINS, CLIVE (1923–99), trade-union leader. Jenkins left school at 14 to work in a metallurgy laboratory, and by the age of 20 had become the youngest union official in British history as a local branch secretary for the Association of Scientific Workers. In 1961 he became General Secretary of the Association of Supervisory Staffs, Executives and Technicians, later merged into the Association of Scientific, Technical and Managerial Staffs (ASTMS). As head of the ASTMS from 1970, he increased the union's white-collar membership (largely comprising bank and office workers) from 75,000 to 450,000 and won a reputation as one of the most articulate of the trade-union 'barons' of the 1970s. Despite his lifestyle, Jenkins remained a left-winger and was an important figure in framing Labour's 1981 constitution, giving the trade unions the largest say in choosing the party's leader.

JENKINS, ROBERT (*fl.* 1731–8), sea-captain. In 1731, when sailing from Jamaica, his ship the *Rebecca* was boarded and plundered by Spanish *guarda costa* who cut off one of his ears. He was allowed to state his case to GEORGE II, but little was done by the authorities until 1738 when, as a result of pressure from merchants aggrieved at the aggressive actions of the Spanish authorities, he was examined before a committee of the House of Commons, displaying his severed ear. The incident helped inflame demands for a war with Spain and, despite Robert WALPOLE's reluctance and the negotiations of the Convention of the Pardo in Jan. 1739, the War of Jenkins' Ear began that Oct.

JENKINS, ROY (Baron Jenkins of Hillhead) (1920–), politician. Jenkins was born into the Labour aristocracy. His father was a Welsh miner who was imprisoned for his part in the 1926 General Strike and entered Parliament for a mining seat. To his opponents on the Left Roy Jenkins betrayed this heritage. He appeared to be neither socialist nor Welsh, and turned himself into a model of effortless Balliol superiority, which is perhaps why his most satisfactory book was a biography of the Liberal leader, ASQUITH. Like Asquith, Jenkins took his colour from Oxford rather than from his Nonconformist roots and, like Asquith, he not only held a high opinion of his intellect, he also persuaded others to take the same view.

Jenkins entered the Commons in 1948, moving immediately into the orbit of the Prime Minister, ATTLEE, whose biography he wrote. In the internecine feuds that wrecked Labour in the late 1950s Jenkins was usually on the side of Hugh GAITSKELL and the modernizers, but he differed profoundly from his hero on the issue of Britain's membership of the Common Market.

Appointed Home Secretary in 1965, he proceeded, in the eyes of his opponents, to legalize the permissive society. It was a measure of his political courage, and personal self-confidence, that Jenkins was willing to tackle such controversial matters as abortion and homosexual law reform. In 1968, in the crisis following Labour's devaluation of the pound, Harold WILSON appointed him Chancellor of the Exchequer. Jenkins succeeded in producing a trade and revenue surplus but did not please Labour supporters by refusing to sponsor a 'give-away' budget to help the party's election prospects in 1970. This act of political courage and financial prudence was held against him by many Labour supporters when Labour lost the election. Jenkins's career never recovered the momentum it had had in the late 1960s. He became Home Secretary in Wilson's 1974 government but his Europhile views put him at odds with a majority of the party. During the 1975 referendum campaign he fought hard for the winning side, and in 1976 he resigned from the Commons to become President of the European Commission.

To judge from his diaries, Jenkins found the reality of Europe less alluring than the ideal. In Nov. 1979, six months after THATCHER's election victory, he called for the formation of a new centre party in a broadcast. To his old Labour opponents this was proof of what they had always maintained, that Jenkins was not one of them. 1979 was not the time to launch a new party but when Jenkins returned to Britain the moment was more oppor-tune, given Labour's lurch to the Left under Michael FOOT. In March 1981 Jenkins became one of the 'Gang of Four' along with David OWEN, Shirley WILLIAMS and William RODGERS, who founded the Social Democratic Party (SDP); whatever was true of the other members, the label of social democrat fitted Jenkins like a glove. As leader of the Social Democrats Jenkins fought a whirlwind campaign in Warrington (Lancs.), a safe Labour seat, and only narrowly lost. He returned to the Commons for Glasgow Hillhead in 1982 and master-minded the electoral pacts with the Liberals under David STEEL in 1983 and 1987. He lost his seat in 1987, after which the SDP was led by David Owen, with Jenkins going to the Lords. In 1987 he was elected Chancellor of the University of Oxford.

Rumoured to be the favoured elder statesman of the 'New Labour' leader, Tony BLAIR, Jenkins was appointed in 1998 to head the Independent Committee on Voting Systems which came out in favour of proportional representation. As yet, nothing has happened to implement the proposal but it may yet, like its progenitor, rise again.

JENKINSON, CHARLES (1st Baron Hawk-esbury, 1st Earl of Liverpool) (1727–1808), politi-cian. Scion of a minor gentry family, initially of independent political views, he admired the aspi-rations of the new King GEORGE III and his favourite Bute (*see* STUART, JOHN). In 1760 he became Bute's private secretary, in 1761 an MP and an Under-Secretary of State. Thereafter he habitually supported the same ministries as the King. He was reputed to wield 'secret influence' as a result of enjoying the King's favour, and was for several decades one of the favourite bogeymen of Whig politicians such as Edmund BURKE and Charles James FOX. A hard-working 'man of busi-ness', he became Secretary for War under NORTH, and President of the refounded Board of Trade under PITT THE YOUNGER.

JENKINSON, ROBERT (2nd Baron Hawkesbury, 2nd Earl of Liverpool) (1770–1828), politician and Prime Minister (1812–27). A Tory MP in the Commons from 1790, he was called to the Lords as Lord Hawkesbury (1803), and became 2nd Earl of Liverpool (1808). As Foreign Secretary (1801–3) he was responsible for the Treaty of Amiens with Napoleon in 1802; he was Home Secretary (1804–6, 1807–9) and Secretary for War and the Colonies (1809–12) during the Peninsular War. Liverpool succeeded PERCEVAL as Prime Minister in 1812. One of PITT THE YOUNGER's 'men of business', he was an able administrator who managed to consoli-date the disparate interests and abilities of his party to rally against the Napoleonic threat.

From 1815 his government was faced with a severe post-war fiscal crisis, the call for parlia-mentary reform and for Catholic Emancipation. Liverpool and his government ('a government of departments', claimed the Prince Regent, the future GEORGE IV) were ill equipped to co-ordi-nate a political strategy in the face of severe social unrest and demands for reform; they responded with a series of repressive measures, including the draconian Six Acts (1819). In 1822, after the suicide of Castlereagh (*see* STEWART, ROBERT), Liverpool moved to liberalize his administration by appointing George CANNING as Foreign Secretary, bringing in PEEL to replace Sidmouth (*see* ADDINGTON, HENRY) as Home Secretary, and appointing HUSKISSON at the Board of Trade and Frederick ROBINSON as Chancellor of the Exchequer in 1823. This period of 'liberal Toryism' introduced a series of domestic reforms to reduce the preposterous number of crimes that carried the death penalty, rationalize the system of criminal justice and advance the policies of moderate Free Trade and Tariff Reform. Liverpool resigned in 1827 after a stroke, his reputation still tainted for many of his contemporaries and subsequent historians by the years of political and social repression between 1815 and 1822.

JENNER, EDWARD (1749–1823), physician. Born in Berkeley (Glos.), Jenner was apprenticed to a surgeon in Sodbury (Glos.), and in 1770 began studying medicine in London under the great surgeon John Hunter. In 1773 he set up a medical practice in Berkeley, where he began to investigate the popular belief that cow-pox victims were immune to smallpox. Eventually he isolated the form of cow-pox pustules that appeared to give immunity and in 1796 inoculated a healthy boy with cow-pox and then smallpox matter, and subsequently observed that the boy had lasting immunity to smallpox. He published his investigations in *An Inquiry into the Causes and Effects of the Variolae Vaccinae* (1798), which introduced the term 'virus' to describe the material producing cow-pox. The practice of inoculation was fiercely resisted at first, but with support from medical figures and the use of humanized lymph it rapidly gained acceptance across Europe and America. By 1800 tens of thousands had been inoculated. Jenner spent the rest of his life practising, explicating and defending vaccination practices. For many, Jenner's work is the main reason for the dramatic decline in the death-rate between the end of the eighteenth century and the middle of the nineteenth century.

JENYNS, SOAME (1704–87), pamphleteer. A Cambs. country gentleman and an MP (1741–80) whose speeches as well as his essays generally supported the government of the day, he provided in his writings genuine insights on many subjects, including social and economic developments. Jenyns's most controversial work was his *View of the Internal Evidence of the Christian Religion* (1776), in which he defended Christianity but was held to have made too many concessions to its detractors. He opposed American independence, parliamentary reform and, perhaps surprisingly, the notion of principled opposition.

JERVIS, JOHN (Earl of St Vincent) (1735–1823), sailor. His father was Solicitor to the Admiralty and Treasurer of Greenwich Hospital, and Jervis entered the navy aged 13. At the beginning of the French Revolutionary War in 1793 he was appointed Commander-in-Chief in the West Indies and, with General Sir Charles Grey, took Guadeloupe and Martinique. He was made Admiral in 1795 and in 1796 became Commander-in-Chief in the Mediterranean. In Feb. 1797 he defeated the Spanish fleet off Cape St Vincent, with the help of NELSON, and was rewarded with an earldom. ADDINGTON made him First Lord of the Admiralty in 1801. St Vincent set up a royal commission to inquire into naval administration; extensive corruption was revealed and his predecessor Henry DUNDAS was impeached. Dundas's friend PITT THE YOUNGER objected to St Vincent's concentration on reform rather than rearmament and when Pitt returned to office St Vincent left the government.

JEVONS, W(ILLIAM) S(TANLEY) (1835–82), economist and logician. Born in Liverpool, he studied chemistry at University College, London (UCL), and was appointed assayer to the Mint in Sydney, Australia (1854–9). Jevons returned to UCL to study political economy and logic. He was appointed Professor of Logic at Owen's College, Manchester (now Manchester University) (1866) and Professor of Political Economy at London University (1876). His most influential work was his *Theory of Political Economy* (1872) which introduced the concept of utility rather than cost as the basis of value and was regarded by KEYNES as 'the first modern book on economics'. Jevons was drowned at sea.

JEWEL, JOHN (1522–71), writer. Oxford don whose Protestant views led him to flee abroad under MARY I, after initial wavering; he became a spokesman for moderation among the exiles. After ELIZABETH I's accession he was given the bishopric of Salisbury (1560), proving a model bishop. In 1562 he published his *Apologia* (defence) of the Church of England, primarily aimed against Roman Catholicism. One of the books to shape the future identity of the English Church, it much influenced Jewel's protégé, Richard HOOKER.

JEX-BLAKE, SOPHIA (1840–1912), physician. Jex-Blake was educated at Queen's College for Women, London, where she taught mathematics (1859–61). She studied medicine in New York under Lucy Sewall and Elizabeth BLACKWELL but her gender and the fact that her medical qualification had been obtained abroad barred her from continuing her studies in England. In 1869 she and five other women fought successfully to matriculate at Edinburgh University's medical school, but in 1873 she failed in her attempt to reverse the university's decision to prevent women from graduating in medicine. From 1869 she spearheaded a campaign for women's medical education. In 1874 she and Elizabeth Garrett ANDERSON founded the London School of Medicine for Women (where Anderson worked), and she was the driving force behind the 1876 Russell Gurney Enabling Act permitting medical examining bodies to open their tests to women. She eventually gained her medical licence through the King's and Queen's College of Physicians, Dublin, in 1877, founded a medical school in Edinburgh and lived to see Edinburgh University permit women to graduate in medicine (1894).

JINNAH, MOHAMMED ALI (1875–1948), founder of Pakistan. Born and educated in Karachi, and called to the Bar in England in 1896, Jinnah built up a lucrative legal practice in

Bombay while simultaneously establishing himself in politics through the Indian National Congress. On the Imperial Legislative Council from 1909 until he resigned in protest 10 years later, he joined the All India Muslim League in 1913 and the Home Rule movement under Annie BESANT in 1917. A widening gulf of opinion opened between Jinnah and GANDHI on questions of Hindu and Muslim rights and the Non-Cooperation movement; resigning from Congress in 1920, Jinnah became senior spokesman for the Muslim cause within India. When compromise failed he took a separatist line, notably when he returned in 1935 from a five-year stint practising law in London to head the Muslim League. In 1940 the League passed the Lahore Resolution calling for a separate Muslim state of Pakistan, and, when in the Second World War Congress leaders spurned the British, Jinnah reaped the political benefit. Talks between Gandhi and Jinnah in 1944 reached deadlock and Jinnah became the rock of intransigence upon which Pakistan was built. With independence in 1947 came partition and bloodshed.

JOAD, C(YRIL) E(DWIN) M(ITCHINSON) (1891–1953), philosopher. Oxford-educated, Joad worked as a civil servant for the Ministry of Labour from 1914 to 1930 before becoming head of the department of philosophy at Birkbeck College, London, in 1930. During the Second World War he took part in lunch-time open lectures at the college and appeared frequently on the BBC radio programme *The Brains Trust*. Imparting a great deal of liveliness to the programme, Joad was extremely popular with listeners and is well remembered for his catchphrase 'It all depends what you mean by . . .'. In 1948 his reputation as a sage and moralist suffered when he was convicted of travelling on a train without a ticket. A vivacious and highly personable individual with apparently limitless energy, he wrote some 47 books of which the best known are a *Guide to Philosophy* (1936), a *Guide to the Philosophy of Morals and Politics* (1938), *Decadence* (1948) and the autobiographical work *The Recovery of Belief* (1952).

JOAN (?–1237), Princess of North Wales. An illegitimate daughter of King JOHN, she was married to LLYWELYN AP IORWERTH in 1205, bringing with her the Salop. manor of Ellesmere. So important was her role as mother of Llywelyn's heir DAFYDD AP LLYWELYN and as mediator between her husband and the kings of England, that Llywelyn was reconciled to her after her adultery with William de Briouze was discovered in 1230, but he hanged William for it.

JOAN (1210–38), Queen of Scots (1221–38). Daughter of King JOHN and ISABELLA OF ANGOULÊME, she was betrothed to Hugh of Lusignan, but in 1220, when Hugh married her mother instead, her brother HENRY III promised her to ALEXANDER II of Scotland. They married in 1221. She attended the peace conference of 1237 at York, when the old Anglo-Scottish dispute over Northumbria was settled, and then went south with her brother, dying in England a few months later. She left no children.

JOAN (1321–62), Queen of Scots (1329–62). Daughter of EDWARD II, and known as Joan of the Tower, the place of her birth. In Scotland she was called Joan Make-Peace after the marriage of six-year-old Joan to four-year-old David (*see* DAVID II), son of ROBERT BRUCE, King of Scots, was part of the peace between England and Scotland. In 1357 she went south to discuss peace with her brother EDWARD III and stayed there until her death while her husband, as before, continued to enjoy a series of mistresses.

JOAN BEAUFORT (?–1445), Queen of Scots (1424–37). The daughter of John Beaufort, Earl of Somerset, she was seen by King JAMES I while he was a prisoner in England and they married in 1424. James wrote the story of their love in his *Kingis Quair*. Wounded when her husband was assassinated in 1437, she was formally appointed Regent for her young son JAMES II but exercised little real influence, losing even that when imprisoned as a consequence of marrying Sir James Stewart, 'the Black Knight of Lorne', in 1439.

JOAN OF KENT (also known as the Fair Maid of Kent) (1328–85), Princess of Wales. Reputedly one of the most beautiful women of her day. She was the daughter of EDWARD I's son Edmund, Earl of Kent, and in 1347 was married to William Montagu, Earl of Salisbury. The marriage was invalidated two years later on the grounds that she had earlier made a secret marriage with Sir Thomas Holland. Widowed in Dec. 1360, the following Oct. she married her son's godfather, EDWARD THE BLACK PRINCE, after obtaining the papal dispensations necessary to validate what would otherwise have been an incestuous marriage. As RICHARD II's mother, she played an important mediatory role in the early years of her son's reign. It was said that during the Peasants' Revolt (1381) some of the rebels asked her for a kiss.

JOAN OF NAVARRE (*c.* 1373–1437), Queen of England (1403–13). Daughter of the King of Navarre, she was the widowed Duchess of Brittany when she married HENRY IV in 1403. Widowed again 10 years later, in 1419 she was accused of attempting the death of her stepson, HENRY V, by sorcery and necromancy. Although never tried, she was held in custody for three years until Henry, on his deathbed, ordered that she be released and that her dower worth 10,000 marks a year be restored.

JOCELIN OF BRAKELOND (*fl. c.* 1200), historian. Author of a history of the Abbey of Bury St Edmunds (Suffolk) from 1180 to 1202, with his unrivalled account of life in the cloister and fine biographical portrait of a great Benedictine abbot (SAMSON, whose chaplain Jocelin was 1182–7), he inspired Thomas CARLYLE's *Past and Present* (1843).

JOHN, KING *see essay on page 464*

JOHN BALLIOL (*c.* 1250–1313), King of Scots (1292–6). Following the death of MARGARET, MAID OF NORWAY, in 1290 no one held the undisputed title to the kingdom of Scotland. No fewer than 13 more or less serious claimants (known as the Competitors) to the throne emerged. They agreed to recognize EDWARD I's overlordship and to abide by his arbitration. Balliol had a strong case both in law and in politics, in law because he was descended through his mother from the eldest of three daughters of WILLIAM I THE LION's brother, Earl David of Huntingdon, and in politics because the Balliols had lands in Galloway, as well as in northern England and France, and he enjoyed powerful support from his brother-in-law, John COMYN THE ELDER, of Badenoch. Edward decided in his favour, and he was enthroned in Nov. 1292. But Edward's subsequent overbearing treatment of him left John in an impossible position. Distrusting his capacity to resist Edward's demands, the Scottish nobles set up a Council of 12 in July 1295 and made a formal alliance with the King of France. Edward declared Balliol's throne forfeit and invaded. After being defeated at the Battle of Dunbar (April 1296), Balliol was captured (July 1296) and imprisoned in the Tower of London. Despite the fact that in 1298 he declared that on account of their malice and treachery he wanted nothing more to do with the Scots, those who opposed the King of England continued to do so in his name until 1304. In 1299 he was released into papal custody. Later he was handed over to the French; he spent the last decade of his life as a tool of French policy but at least living on his ancestral estates in Picardy. Had it not been for Edward's bullying use of English power he might have been a competent King of Scotland.

JOHN, AUGUSTUS (1878–1961), painter. Born at Tenby in Wales and trained at the Slade School, John became one of the leading artists of his day, becoming a member of the New English Art Club in 1903. A flamboyant and gruff man with an unorthodox domestic life, he rejected the kind of etiolated and ethereal aesthetic embodied in the work of the Pre-Raphaelites and created a robust and romantic style which owed much to symbolist painters. Though an official war artist in the First World War, John is best remembered as a portrait-painter whose subjects included politicians David LLOYD GEORGE, Winston CHURCHILL and Ramsay MACDONALD and writers W. B. YEATS, G. B. SHAW, James JOYCE, Dylan THOMAS and T. E. LAWRENCE. Gwen JOHN was his sister.

JOHN, GWEN(DOLEN) (1876–1939), painter. Older sister of the painter Augustus JOHN, she was born in Wales of a family with no previous artistic connection: their father was a solicitor. She followed Augustus to the Slade School where she studied figure drawing with Henry Tonks. In 1900 she held her first exhibition with the New England Art Club, but in 1903 returned to France where she had studied with WHISTLER. First the model, then the lover of the sculptor Rodin, she grew interested in mysticism and religion and in 1913 converted to Catholicism, spending much of her time with the Order of the Dominican Sisters. She exhibited on occasions at the Salon des Tuileries in Paris and Augustus John prophesied that posterity would know him as Gwen John's brother.

JOHN OF BEVERLEY, ST (?–721), Bishop of Hexham (688–705) and Bishop of York (705–21). The founder of Beverley Minster during his time as Bishop of York, John was a significant figure in the development of Christianity during the time of BEDE and St WILFRID. His miracles and personality were described by Bede, from whom we learn illuminating details about the pastoral and educational work of a bishop in the first century of the conversion of the English to Christianity.

JOHN OF FORDUN (*fl.* 1380s), historian. He wrote *c.* 1385 the earliest surviving full-scale history of Scotland, *Chronica Gentis Scotorum*. Since his purpose was the patriotic one of providing an ancient pedigree for an independent Scotland, his chronicle is naturally fairly scrappy on the relatively well-documented thirteenth and fourteenth centuries and much more detailed on the earlier centuries, about which so little was known that myth-making could run riot.

JOHN OF GAUNT (2nd Duke of Lancaster, King of Castile and Léon, Duke of Aquitaine) (1340–99), Royal Duke. Athough he is most familiar as the patriotic elder statesman who spoke for England in SHAKESPEARE's *Richard II*, his own concerns were both dynastic and international. A

continued on page 465

JOHN (1167–1216)
King of England (1199–1216)

During his reign Normandy and Anjou were lost – from then on kings of England stayed mainly in England – and Magna Carta was issued. The youngest son of HENRY II and ELEANOR OF AQUITAINE, he grew up fearing that everyone was against him and determined to outmanoeuvre them. Henry gave him the lordship of Ireland, but when he went there in 1185 he alienated both English colonists and Irish kings. Subsequent attempts to provide for John, already nicknamed Lackland, at the expense of the future RICHARD I provoked Richard to rebel; in 1189 John joined the revolt when he calculated that his dying father would lose. Respecting their father's wishes, Richard gave John a great estate in England (with control of six counties), Mortain in Normandy and a rich heiress, ISABEL OF GLOUCESTER, as wife. Despite this, when Richard left on crusade John first intrigued against the chief minister, William LONGCHAMP, and then rebelled in 1193 when he heard that Richard was a prisoner in Germany. Richard's subjects preferred, however, to pay a king's ransom and by Jan. 1194 John was so desperate that, in return for military help, he surrendered eastern Normandy to his brother's bitter enemy, Philip II Augustus of France. After Richard's release from captivity John begged forgiveness, which he obtained, although it was some time before his estates were restored. His record of treachery between 1189 and 1194 moved the judicious WILLIAM OF NEWBURGH to call him 'nature's enemy'.

For the next five years he stayed prudently in the background, gradually regaining Richard's trust. Despite doubts about his trustworthiness and competence, in 1199 he succeeded remarkably smoothly to the whole of the Angevin empire; only in Anjou itself did he have to overcome some armed opposition. But his marriage to ISABELLA OF ANGOULÊME and his maladroit handling of the Lusignan family provoked a rebellion in Poitou. The general belief that he murdered his nephew, ARTHUR OF BRITTANY (April 1203), meant that when Philip Augustus invaded Normandy and Anjou in 1203–4, very few people thought John was worth fighting for, especially since John himself retired to the safety of England. From then on he was known as Softsword. Recovery of the lost dominions was his first priority. He led an army to the continent in 1206 and was able to save something from the wreckage of his empire, but soon realized that he would have to build up a massive war-chest if he were ever to mount a serious challenge to King Philip.

For the next five years he concentrated on the government of England and on bullying the other rulers of the British Isles, Irish kings, LLYWELYN AP IORWERTH of Gwynedd and the ailing WILLIAM THE LION of Scotland. Annual royal income reached unprecedented heights, and by 1212 he had huge reserves of coin in his castle treasuries. All sources of revenue had been aggressively exploited, not only the politically weak such as churchmen, towns-people and Jews, but also powerful barons whom he treated with an alarmingly capricious mix of bribery and coercion. Hence by the time John was ready to return to the continent, he had so alienated his English subjects that the rest of his reign was one long crisis. When Philip responded to his threats by planning an invasion of England, John, who had quarrelled with the Papacy over the appointment of Stephen LANGTON as Archbishop of Canterbury, made England a papal fief (May 1213) in order to obtain Pope Innocent III's injunction against Philip. Only an English naval victory at Damme halted the French invasion. In 1214 John took an army to western France and sent his half-brother William LONGSWORD with another to join his dearly bought allies (Emperor Otto IV and the Counts of Flanders and Boulogne). But the grand strategy collapsed. On 2 July John retreated from La Roche-au-Moine; on 27 July his allies were over-whelmingly defeated at the Battle of Bouvines. Inevitably, baronial rebellion followed and John was forced to seal Magna Carta. Later seen as a funda-mental statement of English liberties, this was essentially a long critical commentary on his methods of government; he had no intention of implementing its terms. The reign ended with England torn in two by civil war and many of his former subjects giving their allegiance to Louis of France, King Philip's son.

Earlier this century the misconceived percep-tion of John as an essentially English King, combined with the systematic study of the volu-minous records of English government, led to John, after centuries of denigration, being regarded in a more positive light, a hard-working King who stayed 'at home' and presided over important administrative developments. But what historians came to see as administrative progress, contemporaries saw as oppressive government that only military and political success could have justified. In these spheres John's record was decisively poor.

S. D. Church (ed.), *King John: New Interpretations* (1999)
James C. Holt, Magna Carta (1992)

younger son of EDWARD III, born in Ghent (hence 'Gaunt'), his ancestry, wealth and ability (admired by FROISSART) made him a key figure in the European politics of the Hundred Years War. In 1359 he married Blanche, daughter of HENRY OF LANCASTER, and three years later inherited the entire Lancaster estate, becoming the greatest landowner in England, and was created Duke. His second wife, Constance of Castile, whom he married in 1371, brought him his royal title and a deep involvement in the affairs of south-western Europe, which was reinforced by his role first as Lieutenant (1370–1, 1373–4, 1388–9), then as Duke of Aquitaine from 1390.

Although a seasoned and competent soldier, prepared to fight for his rights (as in Spain, 1386–7), these interests made him quicker than most to see the advantages of a negotiated settlement with France. Since he was also deeply suspect in ecclesiastical eyes as an open adulterer and patron of WYCLIF, it is not surprising that in the 1370s, when the ill health of his father and older brother left him the most prominent member of the royal family, he should become the victim of rumours that he was plotting to kill the Bishop of London or usurp the throne. Although conventionally anti-clerical, he was a devout Catholic as well as loyal to his young nephew, RICHARD II. Yet these tales bore fruit in the violent hostility shown to him during the Peasants' Revolt (1381), notably the destruction of his London palace, the Savoy, and then in the increasingly tense relations between him and the adolescent King.

In 1386, after more than 10 years of defending royal authority in England, he sailed to pursue his claim to Castile and Léon. He conquered Galicia, but it soon became evident that, even in alliance with Portugal, his resources were inadequate. In 1387–8 he negotiated the Treaty of Bayonne, renouncing his claim to the Spanish thrones in return for £100,000 and an annual pension. His return to England in 1389, with his wealth greatly enhanced, marked the restoration of political stability after the Appellants crisis of 1387–8.

In 1396, to general astonishment, he married his long-term mistress, Catherine Swynford, and then secured the legitimization of their children, the Beauforts. In 1397–8, as his health became increasingly poor, he acquiesced in Richard's revenge on the Appellants, including the arrest of his brother THOMAS OF WOODSTOCK and the exile of his own son, Bolingbroke (the future HENRY IV). John of Gaunt's death in 1399 ushered in the last crisis of Richard's reign.

JOHN OF LANCASTER (1st Duke of Bedford) (1389–1435), Royal Duke. Created Duke in 1414, he served as Regent of England while his brother HENRY V was in France. During the minority of HENRY VI (1422–9) he acted as Protector of England, but he was chiefly responsible for pressing on with the conquest of France. He won the Battle of Verneuil in 1424, and was generally successful in maintaining the strategically vital alliance with the Duke of Burgundy, whose sister he married in 1422.

JOHN OF NORTHAMPTON (?–1397), politician. Twice Mayor of London, he was a controversial figure in London owing to his criticism of the domination of city politics by a small group of the richest businessmen. Elected mayor following the turmoil of the Peasants' Revolt, when the city had fallen to the rebels, his reputation suffered from association with WYCLIF and JOHN OF GAUNT. He imprisoned in the Tun, on Cornhill, those women guilty of breach of chastity, after shaving their heads. Charged with sedition by his successor as mayor, Sir Nicholas BREMBRE, his property was confiscated; 'the courtiers fell upon it like harpies', wrote Thomas WALSINGHAM.

JOHN OF SALISBURY (c. 1120–80), scholar. His letters and books reflect both the range of his scholarship and the vicissitudes of a remarkable ecclesiastical career. Born at Salisbury (Wilts.), he drew on his student days (1136–46) in the Paris of Abelard to defend, in his *Metalogicon*, the value of logic as an intellectual discipline. As political secretary 1147–61 to Archbishop THEOBALD OF BEC, he used his friendship with ADRIAN IV to promote Canterbury's interests at the papal curia, and then, in his *Policraticus*, his insider knowledge to discuss both contemporary history and the theory of relations between Church and State. He acted as an adviser to BECKET during his quarrel with HENRY II and, after Becket's murder, was active as a hagiographer promoting the cult of the martyred Archbishop. In 1176 he was elected Bishop of Chartres.

JOHN THE OLD SAXON (?–after 904), cleric. Like the Flemish GRIMBALD OF SAINT-BERTIN, John, a German, was recruited to England by ALFRED THE GREAT to help with the King's programme of educational reform. He is known to have helped with the translation of Gregory the Great's *Cura Pastoralis*. Appointed as Abbot of Alfred's new monastery at Athelney, he survived an assassination attempt organized by one of his monks, subsequently retiring to the abbey of Malmesbury.

JOHNSON, AMY (1903–41), aviator. Two years after gaining her pilot's licence in 1928, Amy Johnson was dubbed 'Queen of the Air' by the British press when she made a solo flight from London to Australia in 17 days in a converted De Havilland Moth. Her subsequent flights included solo trips to India and to Japan; she was the first woman to fly the Atlantic from east to west, and in 1932 she cut 10 hours off the flight from London to Cape Town, a record previously held by her husband Jim Mollison. She was killed while flying for the Women's Auxiliary Air Force during the Second World War.

JOHNSON, DR SAMUEL (1709–84), essayist and critic. Son of a Lichfield bookseller, he briefly kept a school there but left for London with David GARRICK, one of his pupils, in 1737. He wrote parliamentary reports for Edward CAVE's *Gentleman's Magazine* and in 1747 was commissioned by a consortium of booksellers to compile a new dictionary illustrated by quotations, which established his reputation when it appeared in 1755. Debt impelled him to recurrent spurts of productivity: his novel *Rasselas* (1759) was written in seven days. He also wrote essays collected as *The Rambler* (1750) and *The Idler* (1758), produced a new edition of SHAKESPEARE (1765) and wrote, for a consortium of booksellers headed by John BELL, the *Lives of the English Poets* (1777). He founded a literary club with BURKE, GIBBON, GOLDSMITH and REYNOLDS; Charles BURNEY was also a member. Other members of Johnson's circle included Hester THRALE and Mary DELANY. In his own day Johnson was both respected as a scholar and renowned as an eccentric personality. BOSWELL, who first met him in 1763, immortalized his character and conversation in his *Life* (1791).

JOHNSTON, ARCHIBALD (1st Baron Johnston of Warriston or Wariston) (1611–63), politican. Having helped to draw up the National Covenant in 1638, Johnston became one of the most uncompromising Scots Presbyterians dealing with England during the First Civil War (1642–6), sitting in the Westminster Assembly which met to decide on Church reform. He fiercely opposed the Scots reconciliation with CHARLES I proposed in the Engagement of 1647–8, but lost his legal offices after the collapse of the Scottish state in the wake of the Battle of Dunbar (1650). Oliver CROMWELL restored him as Lord Clerk Register (1657) and gave him a peerage (1658); he was prominent in the government cliques trying to preserve the Commonwealth in its last months after the deposition of Richard CROMWELL. Fleeing after the restoration of CHARLES II, he was arrested at Rouen and hanged in Edinburgh on flimsy charges of treason, more particularly because the King hated him (he had long before criticized Charles's sexual mores). His diary is a valuable historical source.

JOHNSTON, WILLIAM ('of Ballykilbeg') (1829–1902), politician. An eccentric Co. Down landlord, Johnston was active in the Orange Order and published an ultra-Protestant newspaper. In 1867 he achieved political fame (and six months imprisonment) by defying a law against party processions. The next year he was elected MP for Belfast in opposition to the official Tory candidate (and the aristocratic Orange leadership), advocating Orangeism and social reform. He pioneered a style of populist Protestant revolt against the perceived weaknesses of the Unionist establishment, a style imitated by malcontents down to Ian PAISLEY, while his defiance of the Party Processions Act made him a hero for future Orangemen insisting on the right to march.

JONES, BRIAN (1944–69), musician *see* JAGGER, MICK

JONES, CATHERINE (?–1790), intellectual *see* JONES, RICHARD

JONES, ERNEST (1819–69), Chartist and radical lawyer. Born in Berlin, the son of a Welsh army officer, Jones moved to England in 1838 and trained as a barrister. A Chartist from 1844, in the 1850s, following two years in prison (1848–50) for inflammatory speeches, he emerged as the leading figure of Chartist socialism. From 1857 he drew closer to middle-class radicalism while also resuming his legal career in Manchester from 1861. He became active in the Reform League and in the pro-North agitation during the US Civil War. He acted as one of the lawyers in defence of the Fenians in the Manchester bomb trials of 1867. Jones was also a supporter of women's suffrage and stood unsuccessfully as a Liberal candidate in Manchester in 1868.

JONES, HERBERT ('H') (1940–82), soldier. Educated at Eton and Sandhurst, he was commissioned into the Devon and Dorset Regiment in 1960, and in 1981, after service in Northern Ireland, was appointed to command the 2nd Parachute Regiment. Chosen to spearhead the liberation of the Falkland Islands following the Argentine invasion on 1 April 1982, Jones's battalion arrived on the night of 26 May at the north-eastern neck of the Darwin – Goose Green Peninsula where some 1,400 Argentinians, approximately three times the number of men in 2 Para, had dug in. Despite a BBC World Service announcement of Jones's position removing any chance of surprise, in the early hours of 27 May 2 Para attacked. Shortly after dawn, when the Paras' frontal assault on Darwin Hill was bloodily repelled, Jones attempted to rally his men by charging alone around the left flank of the Argentine position, but was cut down. His conduct of the battle has been subject to minute critical analysis, but he was undoubtedly a brave and gallant officer, qualities which were recognized in his award of a posthumous Victoria Cross.

JONES, INIGO (1573–1652), architect and artist. Son of a Catholic London clothworker; patronage from William, 3rd HERBERT Earl of Pembroke, and Thomas HOWARD, Earl of Arundel, enabled him to travel abroad and develop an understanding of classical architects' revival of ancient Roman and Greek styles, uniquely among his English contemporaries. Much of his work, principally for the royal family, was in the perishable form of scenery for masques (*see* JONSON, BEN) but from 1610 he turned to architecture, and, although there have been many other indiscriminate and unlikely attributions to him, several of his buildings survive, notably in London: St. Paul's, Covent Garden; JAMES I's Banqueting House at Whitehall; the Queen's House, Greenwich. Together with his brilliant drawings, they reveal a genius equal to any continental master. His classical alterations to old St Paul's Cathedral were (perhaps fortunately) destroyed in the great fire of London in 1666.

JONES, JAMES (JACK) (1913–), trade-union leader. The most influential trade unionist of the 1970s, at a time when trade-union power was at its height in Britain, he was regarded as the most powerful man in the country in a 1977 survey, more than double the number of those who opted for Prime Minister CALLAGHAN. Born in Liverpool, he worked in the city's docks and engineering industry from the 1920s, and was a City Councillor (1936–9). After serving as the Transport and General Workers' Union regional officer for the Midlands from 1955, Jones was elected General Secretary of the union in 1969. Although regarded as a left-winger, he proved moderate in office, calling for restraint in pay negotiations (a call rejected by his union's members in 1977), and was one of the trade-union movement's strongest advocates of industrial democracy. He attempted to democratize the TGWU, devolving power from full-time officials to shop stewards. He retired in 1978, refusing a peerage, and has devoted his energy to campaigning on behalf of pensioners.

JONES, RICHARD (3rd Viscount and 1st Earl of Ranelagh) (*c.* 1636–1712), profiteering administrator, and his daughter **CATHERINE** (?–1740), intellectual. Of an Irish family, he sat in the Irish Parliament, then came to England in 1670, attaching himself to the circle around Buckingham (*see* VILLIERS, GEORGE). An ingenious man, given to elaborate projects, he managed greatly to enrich himself, first when he persuaded the King to give him the management of the Irish revenues (1674–81), in the face of resistance from the Lord Lieutenant, Essex (*see* CAPEL, ARTHUR), and then as WILLIAM III's Paymaster General from 1691. He resigned in 1702 rather than face an inquiry into irregularities in his accounts. Much of his wealth was spent beautifying the gardens of his house in Chelsea, which became known as Ranelagh Gardens. Catherine Jones, a friend of Mary ASTELL, succeeded her father at Ranelagh Gardens and sold off furniture and rented out the house to pay her father's debts. The landlords, Chelsea Hospital, resumed control of the property in 1730 and it was converted into a pleasure garden to rival Vauxhall. The principal attraction was promenading in the Rotunda, a vast circular building lined with dining boxes and supplied with an orchestra. The house and rotunda were demolished in 1805. Ranelagh Gardens, replanned, still exists as part of the grounds of Chelsea Hospital.

JONES, ROBERT (1560–1615), Jesuit leader. Born on the Welsh Borders, he entered the Jesuit order in Rome in 1583 and became an influential teacher before returning to Britain in 1595: he created a clandestine structure for the Jesuit mission in Wales. From 1609 he was in charge of the entire English and Welsh Jesuit organization, and developed its effectiveness during a period of intensified persecution. He was killed in a fall while travelling at night to baptize a child.

JONES, WILLIAM (also known as William Jones of Nayland) (1726–1800), churchman and writer. As an undergraduate at Oxford he met George HORNE, who shared his admiration for John HUTCHINSON. Ordained in 1751, he gained a reputation as a writer of theological tracts, aimed mainly at the layman. In 1777 he became perpetual curate of Nayland (Suffolk), which became a centre for younger High Churchmen critical of Methodism and Unitarianism. In the 1790s he and William STEVENS launched the Society for the Reformation of Principles. Jones wrote loyalist tracts and argued that the French Revolution was a manifestation of the Antichrist. His ideas were perpetuated after his death by successive reprints of his works and helped influence the nineteenth-century conservative tradition in both Church and State.

JONES, SIR WILLIAM (1746–94), orientalist and jurist. For several years he was tutor to Lord Althorp, brother of Georgiana CAVENDISH, Duchess of Devonshire, through whom he was drawn into Whig patronage networks. He was a pioneering scholar of oriental law and language, publishing a Persian grammar in 1771 and translating poetry from several Asian languages, including Arabic and Sanskrit; he is credited with recognizing the links between Sanskrit and Indo-European languages. He read for the Bar from 1774 and published several legal studies. In 1783 the FOX–NORTH ministry appointed him judge to the Supreme Court of Calcutta, in British-dominated Bengal. On his arrival in India, he helped found the Asiatick Society, dedicated to the promotion of oriental studies, and published two digests of Indian law.

JONSON, BENJAMIN (BEN) (1572–1637), dramatist. Educated at Westminster, Jonson spent time as a soldier in Flanders before beginning to work for the Lord Admiral's theatre company as actor and playwright in 1597. Escaping death after killing a fellow actor by claiming benefit of clergy at his trial (i.e. reading the 'neck verse' of Latin scripture to show literacy and therefore the clerical status that gave immunity from hanging), he converted in gaol to Roman Catholicism for 12 years from 1598. Apart from his poetry and the series of great tragedies and comedies, such as *Every Man in his Humour* (1598), *Sejanus* (1603), *Volpone* (1605), *The Alchemist* (1610) and *Bartholomew Fair* (1614), he virtually created the court masque in close collaboration with Inigo JONES from 1605. They turned traditional court pageantry into a virtuoso theatrical and intellectual display – a distinctive English contribution to a Europe-wide flowering of Renaissance court spectacle. Masques combined drama, music, dance and art, presenting monarchy's divine majesty and usually featuring symbolic or abstract characters. Their literary quality declined when in 1632 Jonson abandoned masque-writing (1632), following a quarrel with Jones in 1630.

JOSEPH, SIR KEITH (Baron Joseph of Portsoken) (1918–1994), politician. Born into a wealthy Jewish family, Joseph was educated at Harrow and Magdalen College, Oxford. He served with distinction in the Royal Artillery in the Italian campaign in the Second World War, where he was wounded and mentioned in dispatches. Like many of his contemporaries he returned home to try to build a better world. A conservative figure, he found his first political niche in local London politics, where he served as an alderman (1946–49). An intellectual, Joseph was not a natural politician, and it took him longer than others of his generation to find a seat but he finally found his parliamentary base in Leeds North-East in 1956.

Joseph's obvious administrative and intellectual abilities ensured he did not languish on the back benches for long, and after brief spells at the Commonwealth Relations Office, the Board of Trade and Local Government, he was one of the major beneficiaries of Harold MACMILLAN's 'night of the long knives' in 1962 when the Prime Minister dramatically reshuffled his Cabinet to bring in new talent. As Minister for Housing and Local Government Joseph found himself responsible for one of the biggest spending departments in Whitehall, and he soon proved himself an adept

and capable minister, sponsoring the development of high-rise council estates, something he would later come to regret. When HEATH won the 1970 election Joseph was given the Department of Health and Social Security, an even bigger spender than Housing and Local Government. But it was during this period that he began to have doubts about whether governments should be consuming so much of the gross national product. In 1974, after the Conservative defeat, he founded and sponsored the Centre for Policy Studies, a radical Conservative think-tank presided over by Alfred Sherman and Ralph Harris, which spawned many of the ideas which would later go under the name of Thatcherism. Joseph's very public renunciation of his past as a great public spender did not make him popular with his former Cabinet colleagues, and only Margaret THATCHER was associated with his centre.

Given the dissatisfaction with Heath's many shortcomings as leader, it was natural that some Conservatives should have looked to Joseph as a successor. But he was cut out to be the intellect behind the throne, not its occupant. A widely publicized speech in which he seemed to be arguing a case for eugenics finished Joseph's chances of standing against Heath and he threw his support behind Thatcher. When she came to power in 1979 she appointed him Secretary of State for Industry, moving him to Education in 1981 where it was felt he would be more at home. She always felt a great fondness for 'Keith', paying handsome tributes to his influence on the development of Thatcherism, and it is indeed for that that he will be best remembered.

JOSEPH AN GOF, MICHAEL (?–1497), rebel. A blacksmith (*gof* in Cornish) from the Lizard, he raised a rebellion in 1497 against taxes destined for Scottish wars. He was joined in leadership by a Bodmin lawyer, Thomas Flamank, and at Wells (Soms.) by maverick nobleman James TUCHET, Lord Audley. Thousands marched eastward, killing a tax commissioner at Taunton and gaining support right across southern England, but were defeated on 13 June 1497 at Blackheath by Giles Daubeney, Lord Daubeney. Joseph, Flamank and Audley were executed.

JOSSELIN, RALPH (1616–83), diarist. Obscure Essex Puritan clergyman, vicar of Earl's Colne for most of his adult life, who has achieved posthumous fame by keeping a lively and detailed diary. Last edited by A. Macfarlane in 1976, it has been much used as a source for seventeenth-century cultural, economic and social history.

JOUBERT DE LA FERTÉ, SIR PHILIP (1887–1965), airman. The son of an officer in the

Indian medical service, educated at Woolwich, he joined the Royal Flying Corps and commanded squadrons in Egypt and Italy. Joining the RAF in 1918, Joubert pioneered the application of radar to aircraft. Promoted Air Chief Marshal and appointed Commander-in-Chief Coastal Command in 1941, Joubert improved air–sea co-operation, increased the rate at which submarines were being sunk but, incurring the hostility of the Admiralty, was relegated to a backwater in 1943. Snapped up by MOUNTBATTEN, Joubert finished the war as Deputy Chief of Staff for South East Asia Command.

JOULE, JAMES PRESCOTT (1818–89), physicist. Born in Salford (Lancs.), Joule was educated by private tutors, including John DALTON. From 1837 he worked in the family brewery and after 1854, when the brewery was sold, his independent wealth allowed him to devote himself to private scientific research. During the early 1840s he showed quantitatively that the heating powers of an electric current were proportional both to the square of the current and to the mechanical powers of the current. He also explored the more profound supposition that mechanical power was directly converted into heat. In 1843 he announced that 838 ft-lb of work was required to raise the temperature of 1 lb of water by 1° Fahrenheit. In 1849 he revised this quantity, the mechanical equivalent of heat, to 772 ft-lb. Poorly received at first, Joule's work gained currency in the 1850s. It established the interconversion of heat and work and underpinned nineteenth-century energy conservation laws. He is also known for his work on the kinetic theory of gases and for collaborating with William THOMSON on measuring the cooling of an expanding gas.

JOWETT, BENJAMIN (1817–93), Oxford don. Through his influence on such men as ASQUITH, CURZON and other politicians whom he taught as undergraduates, Jowett has been regarded as the father of Edwardian England. He was a legendary figure (especially for his monumental rudeness) in Oxford, where he was Professor of Greek from 1855 and Master of Balliol College from 1870. His published works, whether in the classics or theology, were polemical and divided critical and public opinion; but he held his life's work to be the development of the individual potential of each young man under his tutelage and the moulding of future statesmen.

JOYCE, JAMES (1882–1941), novelist. Joyce was one of the most revolutionary influences on the English-language novel and a pioneer of Modernism. His masterworks, *Ulysses* (1922) and *Finnegan's Wake* (1939), pushed linguistic experiment to extremes, developing the interior monologue or 'stream of consciousness' as a literary device, and were threatened with obscenity action which long delayed publication in Britain. Joyce was born at Rathgar, Dublin, and Dublin remained the focus of his writing even though he had left Ireland more or less for good in 1902, profoundly dissatisfied with what he saw as the narrowness and bigotry of Irish Catholicism. He never returned after 1912; most of his life after the First World War was spent in Paris.

JOYCE, WILLIAM (1906–46), propagandist. Known as 'Lord Haw Haw', he made propaganda broadcasts from Nazi Germany to Britain during the Second World War. His odd voice and often inaccurate predictions and war news made him a figure of derision. Despite his American citizenship (he had been born in New York of a naturalized American father who returned to Ireland in 1909), the British courts ruled in 1945 that he could be tried for treason. He was found guilty and hanged.

JUDITH (?–c. 870), Queen of Wessex. Judith's short life epitomizes the manner in which early medieval noblewomen were used as political pawns. Daughter of the Carolingian King Charles the Bald, she was married as a 12-year-old to the 50-year-old King ETHELWULF of Wessex in 856 to seal a political alliance. After Ethelwulf's death in 858, she was immediately married contrary to canon law by his son King ETHELBALD. Following Ethelbald's death in 860, she returned to her father's kingdom and was subsequently abducted by Baldwin 'Iron Arm', founder of the county of Flanders which was in due course to be so important in the history of medieval Europe. Contrary to the custom of ninth-century Wessex (*see* EALHSWITH), Judith, on her father's insistence, was formally crowned as queen; this status presumably made her politically irresistible to Ethelbald, who would otherwise have to fear any children she subsequently produced as potential rivals.

JULIANA OF NORWICH (*c.* 1342–*c.* 1416), mystic. Interest in Juliana has revived in the twentieth century, in part because of her conception of God as Mother. Despite her insistence that no one should regard her as a teacher since she was 'an ignorant, weak and frail woman', many did, including Margery KEMPE. A recluse enclosed in a cell belonging to Carrow Priory (Norfolk), Juliana stands out as the first English woman to be inspired by the long continental tradition of female visionaries and mystics. In her *Revelations of Divine Love* she described the visions of Christ received during a serious illness in 1373, and her subsequent meditations upon them, as well as further visions in 1388 and 1393. In the vision of

1388 she learned the meaning of her earlier visions. 'You would know our Lord's meaning in this thing? Know it well. Love was his meaning. Hold on to this and you will know and understand love more and more. But you will not know or learn anything else, ever.'

JULIUS CAESAR (Gaius Julius Caesar) (*c*. 102–44 BC), Roman statesman and General. His expeditions to Britain in 55 and 54 are well-known historical events, even though their actual results were small. The invasions took place during his conquest of Gaul and were probably intended both to stop the Britons assisting his Gaulish enemies and to enhance his personal prestige.

The first expedition appears to have been no more than a reconnaissance; the Romans left fairly rapidly after landing at Deal (Kent) and meeting stiff resistance. Caesar returned the following year at the head of a large army comprising five legions (around 27,000 men). Despite defeating the British under their leader CASSIVELLAUNUS and marching beyond the River Thames, Caesar soon made treaties with his opponents and returned to Gaul where his military position was still precarious.

Evidence of subsequent economic contact between southern Britain and Roman Gaul suggests that Caesar's expeditions brought Britain into closer touch with Roman power. His campaigns also provided lessons that assisted the later successful conquest begun by Emperor CLAUDIUS.

JULIUS FRONTINUS, SEXTUS (*fl*. AD 70s), Roman Governor. In office from 73 (or 74) to 77 (or 78), he continued the policy of aggressive campaigning that had been resumed by his prede-cessor PETILLIUS CERIALIS. His major successes were against the Silures, and he appears to have largely completed the subjugation of the tribes in Wales. He may also have been the founder of York. His governorship seems to be associated with major public building at, for example, Verulamium (St Albans) and Cirencester.

JUNIUS, pseudonymous political essayist. Junius's letters, bitingly critical of the ministers of the day, were published in the *Public Advertiser* (1768–72), and then in a collected edition. The trial, in 1770, of several newspaper editors for printing or reprinting a letter critical of the King was a *cause célèbre*, as successive juries refused to find the editors guilty of libel, despite judicial direction. The identity of Junius has been much debated over the centuries: Philip Francis, a vigorous Whig friend of Edmund BURKE, has long been a prime suspect.

JUXON, WILLIAM (1582–1663), Archbishop of Canterbury (1660–3). Oxford-educated and a friend of William LAUD, he was made Bishop of London in 1633. His appointment in 1636 as the first clergyman for more than a century to be Lord Treasurer was a mark of the triumph of the cere-monialist and clerical-minded Arminian party, although his personal kindness and tolerance prevented him attracting the hatred shown some of his fellow Arminians. He attended CHARLES I at his execution (1649), and spent the years until the restoration of CHARLES II in retirement. Juxon's appointment as Archbishop in 1660 was a predictable reward for a venerable symbol of the royal martyrdom.

K

KAHN, RICHARD (1905–89), economist. He was one of the circle of young economists regarded as highly influential in the development and promotion of Keynesian ideas in the later 1930s. His book *The Making of Keynes' General Theory* (1984) shows the evolution of KEYNES's work. Kahn was particularly associated with the development of the so-called 'multiplier', which demonstrates that the initial creation of employment as a result of extra spending gives rise to further rounds of spending and more employment. Keynes used a modified version of the idea, which contradicted the prevailing 'Treasury view' that nothing would come of extra public spending. Kahn's later work dealt with issues such as growth and inflation.

KALDOR, NICHOLAS (1908–86), economist. Born in Budapest, he was frequently bracketed with his compatriot Thomas BALOGH. Given their east European origins and the initials B and K, which coincided with those of Bulganin and Kruschev, the more xenophobic elements in Britain were less than pleased when they were both advisers to the Labour government in 1964–6. Kaldor came to Britain in the 1930s and taught at the London School of Economics. During the Second World War he was a major contributor to BEVERIDGE's influential *Full Employment in Free Society*, which informed post-war employment policy. He was extraordinarily prolific and made fruitful contributions to the development of economic theory, particularly in the analysis of growth and taxation. Never an ivory-tower academic, he was a member of the Royal Commission on Taxation of Profits and Income (1951–5) and adviser on fiscal policy to several governments. Left-wing politically, he was special adviser to Labour Chancellors of the Exchequer in 1964–8 and 1974–6. He is said to have been responsible for the notorious Selective Employment Tax, an attempt to divert labour to manufacturing by imposing a levy on employees in non-manufacturing sectors.

KAMES, LORD *see* HOME, HENRY

KARIM, ABDUL (THE 'MUNSHI') (1863–1909), royal servant. The son of a pharmacist at an Agra gaol (whom Karim was accused of misrepresenting as a Surgeon General), he came to England from India on the occasion of Queen VICTORIA's Golden Jubilee in 1887 and stayed on, first waiting at table but soon promoted as Victoria's 'Munshi' (teacher) to deal with royal correspondence relating to Indian matters, which created jealous murmuring from the rest of the royal household. In 1894 he was designated 'Indian secretary' with the title 'Hafiz' and a small staff of his own, and all photographs of him waiting at table were destroyed; Victoria defended him against the 'race prejudice' of court and politicians, provided for his large and rather irregular family, had his portrait painted by the Viennese artist von Angeli and pressed to include him on formal occasions and foreign travels. For his part the Munshi managed to teach the Queen sufficient Hindustani for her to greet Maharanees in their own tongue, and biased her in favour of Muslims during a period of increasing Hindu–Muslim riots, but it seems unlikely that he was the dangerous security risk that his enemies at court maintained.

KAUFFMANN, ANGELICA (1741–1807), painter. Born in Switzerland, she grew up working alongside her father, the painter Joseph Johann Kauffmann. In the 1760s she painted many English travellers in Italy and in 1766 came to London, where she was introduced at court. Her style appealed to the English fashion for neoclassicism and she won commissions including portraits of Christian VII of Denmark and Queen CHARLOTTE. She was elected a founder member of the Royal Academy in 1768, the only other woman member being Mary MOSER, and painted four ovals for the academy's entrance hall representing colour, design, composition and genius. Her success as a portraitist, despite her lack of formal training in life drawing, enabled her to command the resources and reputation to break the male monopoly on classical history painting. She married the Venetian painter Antonio Zucchi in 1781, and continued her career in Rome, although she maintained her connections with London, where she died.

KAUNDA, KENNETH (1924–), politician. Following in his parents' footsteps as a teacher, working in both Northern Rhodesia and Tanganyika, in 1949 Kaunda became active in the Northern Rhodesian African Congress, subsequently the African National Congress (ANC). He advanced rapidly, becoming the ANC Secretary General in 1953. A series of arrests and imprisonments for his political activities culminated in the forming of the breakaway Zambian African National Congress in 1958, with Kaunda as President (the name Zambia having been coined in 1953 as the land of the River Zambezi). Increasingly opposed to the colonial regime, the new Congress was banned in 1959 and Kaunda imprisoned. On his release the United National Independence Party was formed. The end of colonial rule in Northern Rhodesia was swift thereafter: Kaunda's walkout from talks precipitated the collapse of the Central African Federation of Nyasaland and the two Rhodesias. He won a sweeping electoral victory and became Prime Minister. Independence followed in Oct. 1964, with Kaunda as President.

KAY, JOHN (1704–after 1764), inventor. He managed a woollen manufactory for his father in Colchester (Essex), then returned to his birthplace, Bury (Lancs.), where he turned his hand to inventions. His patent of 1730 for a flying shuttle enabled broader cloths to be woven by one weaver instead of two. The shuttle was very widely adopted and hastened the expansion of the cotton and woollen industries; largely vain attempts to defend his patent involved him in litigation. He also tried to develop a power loom. It was another John Kay, a clockmaker of Warrington (Lancs.), who helped ARKWRIGHT produce his spinning frame.

KAY-SHUTTLEWORTH, SIR JAMES (originally James Kay) (1804–77), educational reformer. As secretary to the Privy Council's committee on education, he played the leading role in the creation of an official schools inspectorate. He instituted the pupil-teacher system, which apprenticed pupils over 13 to teachers to assist in the classroom during the day and pursue their own studies at night; after five years and success in an entrance examination, they were entitled to enrol in a teacher-training college with a queen's scholarship to finance further study. Pupil-teachers who failed the examination became assistant teachers. Kay, who married a Shuttleworth heiress in 1842 and added his name to hers, founded his own training college in London, which subsequently became St John's College, Battersea.

KEAN, EDMUND (1789–1833), actor. Son of an itinerant actress, his early life is obscure, but he appears to have moved between fairgrounds, provincial and London theatres, sometimes singing, dancing or tumbling, and sometimes playing roles from SHAKESPEARE. He married an actress in 1808, and in 1813 he was offered a three-year engagement at Drury Lane, making an immediate impression with his portrayal of Shylock. Despite an unimpressive physique, he had the gift of projecting powerful personalities and his fortunes changed abruptly for the better as his talents were recognized with gifts of money and shares in the theatre. After KEMBLE's retirement he was regarded as the foremost tragic actor, and his tours of the United States from 1820 aroused great excitement. His overbearing personality, hard drinking and affairs, however, caused offence and he was increasingly troubled by ill health and failures of memory. In 1833 he collapsed on the stage and died within a few weeks.

KEARNY, JOHN (O'CEARNAIGH, SEAN) (?–c. 1600), churchman. Cambridge-educated, he became treasurer of St Patrick's Cathedral, Dublin, and in 1571 published in Dublin a Protestant catechism and alphabet in Gaelic. This was the first Gaelic book published in Ireland, and its specialist typeface has remained a standard for Irish Gaelic printing (while in Scotland, following the model of John CARSWELL's pioneering text, Gaelic printing has adopted Roman characters). Kearny is said also to have translated the New Testament into Gaelic.

KEARTON, CHRISTOPHER (Baron Kearton of Whitchurch) (1911–92), industrialist. Kearton joined ICI's Billingham division in 1936, was seconded for a while to the new atomic energy programme and then in 1946 joined Courtaulds. He became its Chairman in 1964, transforming the old COURTAULD textile company's man-made fibres business with aggressive expansionist policies. Profits soared. Kearton was no corporate raider but was tireless in working to rationalize Courtaulds and other sectors of British industry. He was appointed to appropriate (if ultimately limited) positions in both of Harold WILSON's governments, as Chairman of the Industrial Reorganization Corporation (1966–8), formed to promote company mergers and help rationalize business, and Chairman and Chief Executive of the British National Oil Corporation (1976–9), an attempt at a nationalized North Sea oil industry.

KEATS, JOHN (1795–1821), poet. Son of the manager of a livery stables, he began a translation of the *Aeneid* whilst in his early teens. Apprenticed to an apothecary-surgeon, he abandoned this secure profession for the life of a fulltime poet in 1816, and in the same year his poem 'O Solitude' was published in Leigh HUNT's *The Examiner*. His first volume of poetry was published in 1817; 1818 and 1819 were his *anni mirabiles* in which his poetic output included the first version of 'Hyperion', 'The Eve of St Agnes', 'La Belle Dame sans Merci', 'Ode to a Nightingale' and probably 'Ode on a Grecian Urn' – all despite the fact that he was beset with financial problems and distracted by his intense love for Fanny Brawne. Keats died in Rome of tuberculosis aged 25. His reputation as one of the finest and most widely read of the English Romantic poets has increased ever since his death, as he himself suspected it would.

KEBLE, JOHN (1792–1866), churchman. From a High Church clerical family in Oxon., he went to Oxford University and became a Fellow of Oriel College in 1811; from 1836 until his death, he was vicar of Hursley (Hants). His contemporary reputation as a poet was great, winning him the Oxford chair of poetry (1831–41); it was initially based on *The Christian Year* (1827), once hugely popular but generally known now only in fragments as familiar hymns. His lasting significance was as an unwavering champion of the Oxford Movement: he is seen to have sparked this off with his Oxford Assize Sermon on 'National Apostasy' in 1833, in which he attacked the wider implications of the Whig government's plans for institutional reform in the Church of Ireland. Keble College, Oxford, was founded in his memory in 1869.

KEEGAN, SIR JOHN (1934–), military historian and journalist. Educated at Oxford, he was senior lecturer in war studies at Sandhurst (1960–86), during which time he taught and came to know most of the officers who were to hold senior rank in the British army. Inspired by such contacts, his *Face of Battle* (1976) was one of the finest works on the realities of war ever written and made Keegan internationally famous. As defence editor of the *Daily Telegraph* since 1986, Keegan has influenced the development of British and NATO military policy, and his columns have been used by senior Anglo-American commanders to send messages direct to the leaders of hostile states, such as Saddam Hussein in 1991 and Slobodan Milosevic in 1999.

KEELER, CHRISTINE (1942–), model *see* PROFUMO, JOHN

KEITH, GEORGE (4th Earl Marischal) (1553–1623), educational patron. After studies at Aberdeen, he had wide experience of study at continental universities, particularly Geneva, and returned in 1580 to become a favourite of the young JAMES VI, a Privy Councillor (1582) and leader of the embassy (1589) to arrange James's marriage to ANNE OF DENMARK, acting as royal proxy at the wedding at Kronborg. In 1593 he founded Marischal College, Aberdeen, as a university separate from the existing King's College (*see* ELPHINSTONE, WILLIAM), deliberately modelled on Lutheran and Calvinist universities abroad and with the best library in Scotland.

KEMBLE, FRANCES (FANNY) (1809–93), actress. Fanny Kemble saved the family fortunes (her father was Charles Kemble, the actor and part-owner of Covent Garden, her mother an actress and playwright) by her curtain-stopping stage debut in *Romeo and Juliet* in Oct. 1829. The niece of Sarah SIDDONS, she continued to star in tragedies as well as comedies until in 1832, on a tour of the USA, she met her future husband, Pierce Butler, who, she later discovered, owned a slave plantation in Georgia. Her efforts to improve the conditions of the slaves led to marital conflict and Butler forbade publication of her *Journal of a Residence on a Georgian Plantation* (which appeared only in 1863). The couple divorced in 1848. Kemble returned to the stage, but found her true *métier* in readings of Shakespeare, which she performed in Britain and the USA for 20 years.

KEMBLE, JOHN PHILIP (1757–1823), actor, manager and playwright. The younger brother of Sarah SIDDONS, he was sent to Douai to be trained for the priesthood, but in 1775 returned to England to become an actor. He toured extensively in northern England and gained a reputation as a performer of SHAKESPEARE, particularly *Hamlet*; his rejection of GARRICK's interpretation of this role initially divided critics. By 1785 he was established as the leading tragic actor in London, maintaining summer appearances in the provinces, often appearing with his sister. In autumn 1788 SHERIDAN appointed him manager at Drury Lane. Kemble staged a series of new productions including revivals of *Henry VIII* and *Coriolanus*, which attracted attention for their costumes and sets informed by historical research into the designs of the period. He revived Drury Lane's fortunes and in March 1794 opened a new theatre building, replacing that of 1674 (*see also* KILLIGREW, THOMAS). In 1803 he bought into Covent Garden and became manager there. The theatre became known for lavish productions but Kemble's intellectual approach to theatre was falling out of favour, audiences preferring the passion of Edmund KEAN.

KEMP, JOHN (?1380–1454), Archbishop of Canterbury (1452–4). Initially HENRY V's Keeper of the Privy Seal and Chancellor in Normandy, he became one of the longest-serving and most influential members of HENRY VI's Council, as well as serving two terms as Chancellor of England. Few English prelates have held such a string of bishoprics: Rochester (1419–21), Chichester (1421), London (1421–5), York (1425–52) and Canterbury. He also became a Cardinal in 1439.

KEMPE, MARGERY *see* essay on page 475

KEMSLEY, 1ST VISCOUNT *see* BERRY, JAMES GOMER

KEN, THOMAS (1637–1711), Non-juror. The son of an attorney he took holy orders in 1663, taught at Winchester and became known as a preacher in London. In 1679 he went to Holland as chaplain to Princess Mary, later MARY II. His High Church sensibility was offended by Dutch Presbyterianism and he had stormy relations with Mary's husband, the future WILLIAM III. He was appointed Bishop of Bath and Wells in 1684. At first an ally of JAMES II, he became alarmed at the King's pro-Catholic policies and called for an alliance with Dissent to outflank the King. In May 1688 he was one of the seven bishops, led by SANCROFT, who petitioned the King to excuse them from reading the second Declaration of Indulgence and was imprisoned in the Tower of London before being acquitted of seditious libel. Ken voted against the assumption of the throne by William and Mary and refused to take the oath of allegiance, thus becoming a Non-juror; he was deprived of his see in 1691. Ken opposed the consecration of further Non-juring bishops, alienating him from many of his colleagues. In 1710 he became the last surviving original Non-juring bishop and declared an end to the schism, but was not supported by activists such as Jeremy COLLIER.

KENDAL AND MUNSTER, DUCHESS OF *see* SCHULENBURG, MELUSINE VON DER

KENDREW, JOHN (1917–97), molecular biologist. Kendrew studied natural sciences at Cambridge and, after working on governmental radar research during the Second World War, returned there to research molecular biology and to found, with Max PERUTZ, the Medical Research Unit for Molecular Biology (1946). In the late 1940s he began working with Perutz on the structure of protein molecules. By 1960, having exploited the techniques of X-ray diffraction and electronic computer-processing, he elucidated the complex atomic structure of myoglobin, the oxygen-storing protein found in muscle fibres. For their work on proteins Kendrew and Perutz shared the 1962 Nobel Prize for Chemistry.

KENNEDY, JAMES (*c.* 1406–65), churchman. A grandson of ROBERT III, he was elected bishop in 1441, taking a reforming role in the Church and a leading part in politics. When Bishop of St Andrew's he founded St Salvator's College and the Grey Friars at St Andrews, and built a grandiose boat called the Saint Salvator, often used by his royal friends. He was one of seven regents during the minority of JAMES III in 1460.

KENNEDY, QUINTIN (1520–64), theologian. Son of Gilbert Kennedy, 2nd Earl of Cassillis, he studied at St Andrews and Paris and was made Abbot of Crossraguel (Galloway) in 1547. He held a disputation with John KNOX at Maybole College in 1562, wrote defending Roman Catholicism and was respected on all sides for his ability and integrity.

KENNETH *see* CINAED

KENNEY, ANNIE (1879–1953), suffragette. By the time she was 13 Kenney was working in a Lancs. textile mill. Inspired by the writings of Robert BLATCHFORD in *The Clarion*, she organized women workers in other mills to bargain for improved pay and conditions. In 1905 she started speaking on behalf of the Women's Social and Political Union (WSPU), appearing on platforms wearing clogs and a shawl. She was one of the first two suffragettes to serve a prison sentence when she and Christabel PANKHURST were arrested after unfurling a banner demanding the vote for women at a meeting in Manchester in 1905 addressed by Winston CHURCHILL and Edward GREY. Kenney was the only working-class woman to attain a key position in the WSPU and in 1912 took over its running when the leaders were imprisoned. In 1913 she was herself sentenced to 18 months in prison and suffered the indignities of the 'Cat and Mouse Act'. During the First World War she campaigned for women to be allowed to work in munitions factories.

KENT, EARL OF, 1ST *see* ODO OF BAYEUX; **2ND** *see* BURGH, HUBERT DE

KENT, BRUCE (1929–), peace campaigner. Ordained in 1958, a curate (1958–63) and later Catholic chaplain to the students at London University, he was elected General Secretary of the Campaign for Nuclear Disarmament in 1980, becoming chairman in 1987, the year he resigned his ministry. He was an unsuccessful Labour Party candidate for Parliament in 1992.

KENT, WILLIAM (1686–1748), architect. Apprenticed to a coach-painter at 14, he studied painting in Italy for 10 years, returning to England in 1719 with Richard BOYLE, Earl of Burlington, who became his major patron. Unsuccessful as a

continued on page 476

KEMPE, MARGERY (*c.* 1373–*c.* 1440)
Mystic

Author of the earliest known autobiography in the English language, *The Book of Margery Kempe*, between the ages of 20 and 40 she married, had a serious breakdown after the birth of her first child, bore 13 more children and set up and ran two businesses enterprises. All she wanted, or so it seemed to her later, was profit, pleasure, fashionable clothes and the applause of the world. When her second business, like the first, folded, she began a fundamental re-evaluation of her life. The outcome was a new career as celibate, pilgrim and visionary, a holy woman who spoke incessantly of God, of the 'mirth that is in heaven' and of the need for repentance. Her two careers show what a determined and energetic woman could do in the fifteenth century, at any rate if she had the good fortune to be born rich.

Her father, John Burnham, was five times mayor of King's Lynn (Norfolk). She married John Kempe in 1393, but clearly felt that he lacked ambition, so 'out of pure covetousness', as she put it, established her own brewery. All went well for a few years until her workers lost the knack of brewing ale with a good frothy head. When her corn-milling business failed equally mysteriously she decided that God must be punishing her for sin, principally for the sin of sexual desire. Eventually, in 1413, she managed to persuade her reluctant husband to join her in a celibacy vow. He was in debt so she used a legacy from her father to pay his bills in return for his agreeing to release her from what was called her 'marriage debt', the obligation to have marital sex. Later they lived apart but after he suffered a serious accident she took him back and nursed him at Christ's request: 'I pray you now look after him for love of me, for just as he once left your body free for me as you wanted and I wanted, so now I wish you to care for his body's needs in my name.' She came to see the 'much labour in washing and wringing' caused by his double incontinence as her atonement for having once too much desired him.

In 1414 she went on pilgrimage to Rome, where the canonization of St Bridget of Sweden (one of her role models) was being celebrated. She went on further pilgrimages to Compostella and the Holy Land, even, most unusually, to Stralsund on the Baltic coast. She gave away her money and visited the sick. But it was above all the manner in which she expressed the intensity of her religious experience which won her fame. Seeing a statue of Our Lady grieving for her crucified son, 'she wept so bitterly as though she would have died'. 'Woman,' a priest said, 'Jesus died a long time ago.' 'Sir, his death is as fresh to me as if he had died today – and so I think it ought to be to you.' Because she had 'so much feeling for the manhood of Christ', tears welled up at the sight of baby boys or handsome young men. The ceremonies and processions of the Church made her cry; so too did a good sermon. Her fits of loud weeping impressed, perplexed and irritated. Many people thought she was a hypocrite who could cry or stop crying at will, but she was encouraged by a visit to JULIANA OF NORWICH: 'the more contempt and shame you suffer in this world, the greater your merit in God's sight'. Although technically illiterate (her book was dictated to a priest), she was well versed in such devotional literature as the works of Walter Hilton and Richard ROLLE. 'Many a book of high contemplation', as she put it, was read to her by men in her circle. But not surprisingly some priests, perhaps exasperated by having their sermons interrupted by her noisy weeping, were hostile. Since Lollard theology allowed women much greater equality than did traditional Catholic teaching, she was often suspected of Lollardy, but she had powerful protectors. When she visited Lambeth, the Archbishop of Canterbury Thomas ARUNDEL gave her the privilege of choosing her own confessor and of taking communion every Sunday; once a year was the norm for the laity and 'frequent communion' was sometimes seen as a dangerously unorthodox demand. In 1438, having finished her book, extracts from which were later printed by Wynkyn de Worde (*see* CAXTON, WILLIAM), she was admitted to the most powerful club in Lynn, the guild of Holy Trinity. She had successfully insisted on her right to speak of God, to encourage people to follow her example 'and to have some little sorrow in their hearts for their sins'.

The Book of Margery Kempe, trans. B. A. Windeatt (1985)

painter, Kent became an architect and designer, popularizing neo-Palladian style in his work in London on, for example, Chiswick House, Kensington Palace and the Treasury buildings in Whitehall, and on Holkham Hall (Norfolk), as well as designing gardens at Rousham and Stowe. The last, designed for Richard TEMPLE, Viscount Cobham were the most famous gardens in eighteenth-century England; Kent's collaborators and successors included Charles BRIDGEMAN and Lancelot 'Capability' BROWN.

KENTIGERN, ST (?–612), monk. An ascetic monk, Kentigern, also known as Mungo, knew COLUM CILLE and travelled widely in both Scotland and Wales. The majority of his pastoral and missionary work was done with the Strathclyde Britons, among whom he had a status similar to that of St AIDAN in Northumbria. He is generally identified as the first Bishop of Glasgow.

KENYATTA, JOMO (1890–1978), Kenyan politician. Kenyatta is seen as a father of both Kenyan and African nationalism. Originally called Johnstone by Scottish missionaries, he took the name Jomo in 1938 when working and studying in Europe. After attending the 1945 Pan-African Congress in Manchester, he returned to lead the Kenya African National Union (KANU). In 1952, when a state of emergency was declared, he and others were arrested and charged with organizing the Mau Mau, the secret society killing both white settlers and Africans. The subsequent trial provoked international concern when Kenyatta and his co-defendants were found guilty. Finally in 1961 he was allowed to return home, emblematic of the struggle for independence that had been proceeding in his absence. He was given a place on the legislative council the following year and, after KANU swept to victory in the 1963 elections, became Prime Minister. Independence followed that Dec.; Kenyatta became the first President, re-elected in 1970 and 1974. After the political instability of the later colonial years, Kenya became remarkably stable. Kenyatta was a colourful leader, adopting a version of tribal dress as one element in reforging an independent identity.

KEPPEL, ALICE (née Edmonstone) (1869–1947), royal mistress. 'La Favorita' of Edwardian high society, the wife of George Keppel, third son of the 7th Earl of Albermarle, she was the mistress of Queen VICTORIA's oldest son, Bertie, when he was Prince of Wales and then EDWARD VII. It was a discreet affair conducted at country-house weekends, on trips to Biarritz, yachting at Cowes, racing at Ascot, at the bridge table. It brought 'Little Mrs George' status and considerable wealth and it lasted until Bertie's death, when Queen ALEXANDRA commended the mistress for the 'good influence' she had had over the King. 'Things were done much better in my day,' Mrs Keppel pronounced on hearing, in 1936, that EDWARD VIII had abdicated the throne in order to marry the divorcée Wallis SIMPSON. Mrs Keppel's daughter was Violet TREFUSIS; her great-granddaughter is Camilla Parker-Bowles, also the lover of a Prince of Wales.

KEPPEL, ARNOLD JOOST VAN (1st Earl of Albemarle) (1669–1718), politician. Born in Holland, he came to England with William of Orange (the future WILLIAM III) in 1688 as a page of honour. A constant and trusted companion of William, he fought in King William's War of 1689–98, was made an earl in 1696 and Major-General in 1697. After his rival Hans Willem BENTINCK retired (1697), he succeeded him as William's principal confidant and personal secretary. He returned to Holland on William's death and joined the allied forces fighting the War of the Spanish Succession under Marlborough (see CHURCHILL, JOHN). He established the Keppels as a leading Whig family.

KEPPEL, AUGUSTUS (1st Viscount Keppel) (1725–86), sailor. A younger son of the 2nd Earl of Albemarle, he entered the navy in 1735 and served on ANSON's circumnavigation of the world (1740–3); he also played a prominent part in the naval side of the Seven Years War. Elected MP for Windsor in 1761, he associated with the Rockinghamite Whigs (see WATSON-WENTWORTH, CHARLES). He was given command of the fleet during the War of American Independence despite his differences with John MONTAGU, Earl of Sandwich, First Lord of the Admiralty. An inconclusive engagement with the French fleet in 1779 caused public controversy: he faced a court martial for not pursuing the enemy, but was acquitted, an outcome celebrated by government opponents; he was then asked to resign. In Rockingham's second ministry and under the FOX–NORTH coalition he served as First Lord of the Admiralty, thereafter retiring from public life.

KER, JOHN (5th Earl and 1st Duke of Roxburghe) (?–1741), politician. Younger son of the 3rd Earl, he emerged as leader of the New Party in the Scottish Parliament in 1703. The party became known as the Flying Squadron or Squadrone Volante for their preference for impermanent political alliances. The Squadrone supported the Union as the best way to win economic concessions for Scotland, and their support was crucial in passing the Act, for which Roxburghe was awarded his dukedom. In 1716 he became Secretary of State for Scotland, but in 1725 he was dismissed on the grounds that he had encouraged riots protesting at the extension of the Malt Tax to Scotland. Roxburghe's position showed the difficulties of Scottish politicians (*see also* OGILVY, JAMES) in representing Scottish interests under the Union.

KÉROUALLE, LOUISE DE (Duchess of Portsmouth) (1649–1734), royal mistress. She came to England in 1670 as maid of honour to Henrietta Anne, Duchess of Orléans, sister of CHARLES II. Through intrigues at court, principally by French sympathizers, she became Charles II's mistress by Oct. 1671. More astute than Queen CATHERINE or MARY OF MODENA, she dismissed all her Catholic servants at the time of the Popish-Plot scare stirred up by the accusations of Titus OATES, and maintained good relations with the Duke of York (the future JAMES II) and the Prince of Orange (the future WILLIAM III), while hoping her own son, Charles LENNOX, later Duke of Richmond, would be a plausible candidate for the throne if the anti-Catholics succeeded in excluding the Duke of York. In Charles's later years she presided over the court like an alternative queen, but became financially and politically embarrassed after his death and eventually settled in France.

KERR, PHILIP (11th Marquess of Lothian) (1882–1940), politician and diplomat. Lothian never held elected office but contrived to 'be near the centre of power' from 1917, when he served as a member of LLOYD GEORGE's secretariat, to 1940 when he died while serving as Ambassador to the USA. A member of MILNER's kindergarten, he was a fervent believer in imperial federation, and when that seemed impossible after the First World War he became an advocate of world federation. A Lloyd George Liberal after 1917, he served as Under-Secretary at the India Office (1931–2) before resigning over the introduction of tariffs.

In the late 1930s he became identified with the so-called Cliveden set accused of sympathy with Hitler, although Lothian himself simply argued that German grievances stemming from the Versailles settlement had to be rectified. His appointment as Ambassador to Washington in 1939 allowed him to play an important part in furthering Anglo-American co-operation and in initiating what became known as Lend-Lease.

KETHE, WILLIAM (?–?1608), musician. A minister who was chaplain to Ambrose DUDLEY, Earl of Warwick, he is remembered for 'Kethe's Psalter', one of the first metrical psalm-books, compiled while he was a refugee from MARY I in Geneva and published in 1561. It contained the version of Psalm 100 set to a Dutch tune now known as the 'Old Hundredth'.

KETIL FLATNOSE (*fl.* 850s), ruler of the Western Isles. The best known of the early Scandinavian rulers of the Western Isles (Outer Hebrides), he either conquered the islands on behalf of the King of Norway, or did so independently and was then forced to submit to him. After Ketil's death, his family's influence quickly collapsed, and his daughter, AUD THE DEEP-MINDED, and her brothers became central figures in the early Scandinavian settlement of Iceland. The Scandinavian settlement of the Western Isles was included in the kingdom of Man and the Isles in 1079 and remained under the theoretical rule of the kings of Norway until 1266.

KETT, ROBERT (*c.* 1492–1549), rebel. A prosperous Norfolk yeoman who led popular demonstrations at Wymondham in July 1549. Trouble erupted suddenly in south-east England, East Anglia and the Thames Valley, suggesting co-ordination; the protesters seized prominent gentry and set up camps (producing the nickname 'the camping time'). Most dispersed after negotiation, except Kett's Norwich camp. There, government forces blundered into military confrontations; on 28 Aug. an army led by John DUDLEY, Earl of Warwick, massacred the protesters on Mousehold Heath. Robert and his brother William were among those subsequently executed.

KETTLE (OR KYTELER), DAME ALICE (*fl.* 1324), sorceress. The Bishop of Ossory, probably prompted by her great wealth, accused her, her son, William Outlaw, and Petronella of Meath of sorcery, of sacrificing living creatures and of holding nightly conference with a spirit called Robert Artisson. Petronella was flogged, confessed and was burnt alive. Alice was spirited home to England by her friends.

KEYES, ROGER (1st Baron Keyes of Zeebrugge) (1872–1945), sailor. Born into a military family, graduated from HMS *Britannia* in 1885, he saw extensive small-boat active service in the East African anti-slavery patrol in the 1890s and in the suppression of the Boxer rebellion in China (1900). A leading expert in coastal operations, in 1915 Keyes commanded the forces clearing mines in the Dardanelles, clashing bitterly with DE ROBECK. As Commander of the Dover Patrol in 1918 Keyes oversaw raids against German U-boat bases at Zeebrugge and Ostend, which raised British morale. In 1940 Winston CHURCHILL appointed Keyes as Director of Combined Operations, tasked to form commando units to raid the coasts of Europe. After bitter quarrels, Keyes relinquished his post to MOUNTBATTEN in 1941.

KEYNES, J(OHN) M(AYNARD) *see* essay on pages 480–81

KICKHAM, CHARLES (1828–82), Irish politician. Rendered almost deaf by an accident as a boy, Kickham was active in the Young Ireland movement in his native Tipperary and was a national leader of the Fenian movement. He was imprisoned in 1865–9, and his health was severely affected; but he remained an active Fenian, and was President of the Irish-based Supreme Council from the early 1870s until his death, opposing Fenian involvement in the Land League and Home Rule movement. He wrote several popular ballads and a number of novels and short stories; *Knocknagow, or the Homes of Tipperary* (1873), a sentimental portrayal of pre-Famine rural Tipperary and its destruction by eviction, was extremely popular with several generations of Irish nationalists.

KIDD, WILLIAM (?–1701), pirate. Possibly born at Greenock, he came to notice in Boston, Mass., where he operated a vessel trading with the West Indies; during King William's War (*see* WILLIAM III), he operated a privateer, a private ship licensed to harass enemy shipping. In 1695, on the recommendation of the Governor of Massachusetts, he was given a special commission to seize any pirates that he found on the coast of America or elsewhere. Three years later complaints reached the government that Kidd himself had engaged in piracy; arrested in 1699, he claimed that some of his actions had been legitimate, others forced on him by a mutinous crew. He alleged that he had left most of his treasure on Hispaniola (now Cuba), but it was never found. In 1701 he was sent to England for trial, where the opposition used the case to attack ministers, especially SOMERS, who had helped to finance the expedition. Kidd was found guilty of murder and piracy, and was hanged.

KIGGELL, SIR LAUNCELOT EDWARD (1862–1954), soldier. Born into an Anglo-Irish gentry family in reduced circumstances, commissioned from Sandhurst in 1882, Kiggell served on BULLER's staff in South Africa in 1899, and was appointed Chief of the General Staff to HAIG in Dec. 1915. An efficient bureaucrat, Kiggell lacked the flexibility and imagination the new post required, invariably agreeing with, instead of occasionally challenging, Haig's ideas. He suffered a mental breakdown early in 1918, after a visit to the Passchendaele battlefield exposed him to the reality of the fighting.

KILDARE, EARL OF, 7TH *see* FITZGERALD, THOMAS FITZMAURICE; **8TH, 9TH** and **11TH** *see* FITZGERALD, GERALD; **10TH** see FITZGERALD, THOMAS.

KILHAM, ALEXANDER (1762–98), Methodist leader. The son of Methodist parents, he began to preach at 21 and was appointed as an itinerant preacher in 1785. Following the death of John WESLEY, Kilham campaigned for a greater role for the laity in the administration of Methodism, attacking the Methodist Conference for imposing its organizational hierarchy on the movement and for not making a complete break with the Established Church. Kilham publicized his ideas in his journal, the *Methodist Monitor*, founded in 1796. In 1797 he and his supporters broke with Conference and founded the Methodist New Connexion at a chapel in Leeds. Kilham was accused of Jacobinism, and his followers were sometimes called Tom PAINE Methodists, but he denied a political motive. Kilham's movement continued until 1907 when it amalgamated with the Bible Christians and the United Methodist Free Churches to become the United Methodist Church.

KILLIGREW, JOHN (?–1584), pirate. From a Cornish family distinguished in Elizabethan diplomacy and seamanship and infamous in piracy, Killigrew was initially favoured for having aided Protestant emigrés under MARY I, but although a JP and military commander, became notorious for lawlessness, strengthened by appointment as a piracy commissioner (1577). Repeatedly MP for pliant Cornish boroughs, he died in debt. His son, also John (*c.* 1547–1605), was also an MP, but became more indebted, even less inclined to temper criminality with legality, and despite commanding Pendennis Castle offered no resistance to a destructive Spanish raid on west Cornwall (1595).

KILLIGREW, THOMAS (1612–83), playwright and theatrical manager. From a courtier family, he had already acted and written plays when in 1642 he was imprisoned by Parliament for taking up arms in the name of CHARLES I: later released, he fled to Oxford and then Paris where he became an adviser to the future CHARLES II. During the Commonwealth and Protectorate, Killigrew travelled Europe, writing and soliciting support for the Royalist cause, as dramatized in his *Thomaso: or, the Wanderer* (1664). In 1660 Charles II granted him a theatrical patent as head of the King's Company, which in 1663 moved to the new Theatre Royal, Drury Lane. He founded a school for actors at Hatton Garden (1672) and was Master of the Revels (1673–7), with responsibility for licensing theatres. He retired in favour of his son Charles, who merged the King's with the Duke's Company under BETTERTON.

KILVERT, FRANCIS (1840–79), diarist. As curate at Langley Burrell (Wilts.), Clyro (Radnors.) and then as vicar of Bredwardine (Radnors.), Kilvert kept a diary from 1870 until his early death from peritonitis. Selections from his diary, with its loving but unsentimental evocation of landscape and people, especially of the Welsh border and his vivid descriptions of young girls there, were published by William Plomer in 1938–40, and have become a classic of the Victorian countryside.

KILWARDBY, ROBERT (?–1279), Archbishop of Canterbury (1272–9). Educated at Paris, where he taught grammar and logic, he joined the Dominicans (c. 1240) and taught theology at Oxford, becoming a leading opponent of the ideas of Thomas Aquinas. He was Dominican provincial prior in England from 1261 until appointed Archbishop in 1272, the first English friar to hold such high office in the English Church. In 1278 he was created Cardinal Bishop of Porto and went to the papal curia.

KING, AUGUSTA ADA (née Byron) (Countess of Lovelace) (1815–52), mathematician. The only legitimate child of BYRON, Lovelace was encouraged in her mathematical abilities by her mother (herself known as the 'princess of parallelograms'), who arranged for her to be tutored in geometry and astronomy. In 1833 she met Charles BABBAGE and with him developed the 'Analytical Engine', a prototype computer. She translated mathematical papers and also demonstrated an impressive grasp of symbolic logic. She had three daughters, one of whom, Anna Blunt, became a famous traveller. Towards the end of her relatively short life her mathematical skills drew her to compute horse-racing odds, and back her calculations, with the result that she died persecuted by creditors. The computing language ADA is named in her honour.

KING, CECIL HARMSWORTH (1901–87), newspaper proprietor. Nephew of Alfred and Harold HARMSWORTH, King worked on a number of his uncles' newspapers after graduating from Oxford, joining the *Daily Mirror* in 1926. Together with Harry Bartholomew he transformed the *Mirror* from a middle-class picture paper into a brash working-class one. He subsequently (if temporarily) revived the fortunes of the *Sunday Pictorial* and by 1951 had become Chairman of the Mirror Group. Over the next 10 years, with the acquisition of Amalgamated Press from the BERRY family and of the Odhams Group, he built up International Publishing Corporation (IPC), the largest publishing company in Britain. King increasingly overplayed his hand, believing that he was to be the saviour of a declining British society, with visions of a polite coup led by Louis MOUNTBATTEN. When he signed a *Mirror* editorial

in May 1968 demanding that Harold WILSON should go, he was ousted by the board. He retired to Dublin, where he wrote memoirs and opinionated articles pondering on what might have been.

KING, GREGORY (1648–1712), statistician. One of the first practitioners of the science of political arithmetic (i.e. statistics used to shed light on the state of the nation), he used tax and other information to analyse population and the economy; his *Natural and Political Observations and Conclusions upon the State and Condition of England* (1696), with estimates of population size and income distribution and detailed consideration of London, was first printed in full by the statistician George Chalmers in 1801, and continues to be a basis for historians' understanding of elements of early modern demography and social structure.

KING, JOHN (Baron King of Wartnaby) (1917–), industrialist. After his only experience in motor-car engineering in Surrey, King established a successful ball-bearing manufacturing company in Yorks. In 1969 it was taken over by the Industrial Reorganization Corporation under KEARTON, and King ran a number of engineering companies before accepting the invitation from Margaret THATCHER to become Chairman of British Airways in 1981. He became one of her favourite industrialists, turning a loss-making warhorse into a sleeker and effective world airline. Privatization contributed to that process; competition from Freddie LAKER and Caledonian Airways was chased off or absorbed, King received a life peerage in 1983 and by 1993 British Airways had become the world's most profitable airline. It was also, however, the year that the so-called 'dirty tricks campaign' against upstart rival Virgin Atlantic, the airline set up by Richard BRANSON, was exposed.

KINGSLEY, CHARLES (1819–75), novelist, clergyman and reformer. Son of a vicar and educated at Cambridge, in 1842 Kingsley became curate and then vicar of Eversley (Hants) where he remained for the rest of his life, though he undertook many other activities and travels, including to the West Indies, the subject of his book *At Last* (1870). His writing reflected his growing interest in Christian Socialism and the influence of its leader MAURICE. Kingsley asked: 'What is the use of preaching about Heaven to hungry paupers?' *Alton Lock* (1850) depicted the conditions of agricultural and clothing workers, the appalling state of London sanitation, and Chartism – though Kingsley believed that it was not the agitation of working men but God's will that would bring about change on earth, and by the end of the novel his tailor hero comes to that

continued on page 482

KEYNES, J(OHN) M(AYNARD) (1st Baron Keynes of Tilton) (1883–1946)
Economist

Keynes was certainly the most famous and arguably the most influential economist of the twentieth century. Even his critics accept that his impact on the development of monetary theory and macro-economic policy were of major consequence. An academic, critic and periodic participant in public life, he also had a successful business career as chairman of the National Mutual Life Association (1921–38) and was the first chairman of the Arts Council in 1945. Keynes was born in 1883 into an impeccably middle-class background. His mother was Mayor of Cambridge in the 1930s. His father, John Neville Keynes, was Registrar of Cambridge University and as lecturer in logic and political economy was a highly respected authority in his subject. Keynes was to emulate and surpass his father in this respect. Whilst at Eton he won a scholarship to King's College, Cambridge, where he read mathematics. As a freshman at Cambridge he was approached by Lytton STRACHEY and Leonard WOOLF to become a member of the intellectually exclusive, secret society known as the Apostles. Strachey and Woolf were to figure later in his life when they were all members of the group of aesthetes which comprised the Bloomsbury set.

In 1905 Keynes was elected President of the Union and graduated as twelfth wrangler in the mathematical tripos. His interests were not confined to mathematics as he was also deeply influenced by the neoclassical economist Alfred MARSHALL, the mathematician philosopher Alfred WHITEHEAD and the philosopher G. E. MOORE. After coming second in the Civil Service entrance examination in 1906, Keynes chose to join the India Office partly on the grounds that, given the relatively smooth operation of the international gold standard, Indian currency questions represented more interesting monetary problems. He later published *Indian Currency and Finance* (1913). In the two years at the India Office, he completed a dissertation on probability, which won him a prize fellowship at King's College, Cambridge, and Marshall enticed him to return to Cambridge in 1909 by supplementing the meagre income the fellowship yielded. He lectured on money and was editor of the *Economic Journal* from 1911 until 1944. His interest in economics was not merely academic: he made himself and his college, of which he was bursar, very considerable sums of money speculating on the stock exchange and in commodity prices.

His expertise was also deployed in the wider public domain: after serving as a member of the Royal Commission on Indian Currency and Finance (1913–14) he joined the Treasury (1915–19) and became the Treasury's principal representative at the Paris Peace Conference after the First World War. He was deeply opposed to the economic terms of the Treaty of Versailles and as a consequence resigned his position. His trenchant criticism of the reparations burden imposed on Germany and the danger which they posed to the world economy was published in *The Economic Consequences of the Peace* (1919). While some have since disputed his analysis, the thrust of his criticism was vindicated in the continuing difficulties, which helped to undermine the Weimar republic and in the series of post-war conferences, which were required to deal with the tangle of war debts and reparations. He was again controversial in attacking the return to the gold standard at the pre-war rate of exchange by the British government in 1925. In his highly polemical *The Economic Consequences of Mr Churchill* (1925) he predicted that considerable unemployment would emerge as a result of sterling's overvaluation. Britain duly experienced a stagnant economy and bitter industrial strife for the rest of the decade.

Keynes was the inspiration behind LLOYD GEORGE's 1929 election programme for public spending to deal with large-scale unemployment; he was an influential member of the Macmillan Committee on Finance and Industry (1930) and published a two-volume work *A Treatise on Money* (1930). In that book he attempted to find a method to discover the 'dynamical laws governing the passage of a monetary system from one equilibrium to another' to explain why an economy is subject to periodic cycles of booms and slumps. Within six years, however, he had moved on from the framework of the *Treatise* to publish his best-known work, *The General Theory of Employment, Interest and Money* (1936). A highly controversial book, it rejected the prevailing orthodoxy that mass unemployment was a temporary aberration which could and would be solved by self-correcting market mechanisms. It also took issue with the so-called Treasury view that increased public spending would be ineffective as it would crowd out private spending. The essential core of the argument was that a contraction in the total level of demand for goods and services can occur, and hence large-scale unemployment emerge, if consumers or the business sector develop more pessimistic expectations about their future prospects and cease spending. The orthodox response to unemployment advocated a cut in the general level of real wages but Keynes argued that this would be extremely difficult to engineer and was uncertain in its effect. While he agreed that looser monetary policy and a fall in the rate of interest may be helpful, he thought that they were unlikely in the short run to reverse depressed expectations and prompt greater expenditure. Hence Keynes suggested that government should offset the fall in spending via its fiscal policy, that is by running a budget deficit. It has been suggested that Keynes's ideas were only about how to avoid depression but in *The General Theory* he described the inflationary difficulties that might arise as full employment was approached. He again used the framework of *The General Theory* in his *How to Pay for the War* (1940), which dealt with the inflationary problems posed by excess demand. It was this notion of active contra-cyclical policy which became the mark of post-war Keynesianism.

It is unlikely that Keynes's ideas would have been so readily taken up but for the Second World War, which had a radicalizing effect on political parties in Britain and elsewhere, resulting in an explicit commitment to full employment. In the latter stages of the war, Keynes began to focus on the post-war economic settlement. He was aware that a new framework for international co-operation was needed to reverse the breakdown and disintegration of the international economy which characterized the 1930s. In 1944 he was appointed head of the British delegation to the United Nations Monetary and Financial Conference at Bretton Woods, New Hampshire. The Bretton Woods Agreement produced the international financial order which prevailed until the 1970s. This coincided with the greatest period of expansion in the history of capitalism referred to by some economic historians as a 'golden age'. Keynes was a forceful advocate of the regime of fixed exchange rates but the International Monetary Fund (IMF) and the International Bank for Reconstruction and Development (the World Bank) were closer to the American view of post-war institutions. Keynes had argued, as early as 1943, for an International Clearing Union, which would operate in a more generous and symmetrical way than the IMF. Despite Keynes's denials, US negotiators were fearful that his scheme would be overly generous to deficit countries and, as the USA would be the main creditor for the foreseeable future, a conservative Congress would not agree. Over a period of three months in late 1945 Keynes was again the dominant figure in the British delegation in a series of debilitating negotiations held in Washington to obtain a substantial dollar loan. This was necessary to plug the gap which the abrupt cessation of Lend–Lease in September created in the UK balance of payments. Keynes had doubts about the terms of the final agreement, particularly the requirement to make sterling freely convertible in 1947, but given the parlous condition of the British economy he had to accept. The pressure of the negotiations undoubtedly imposed further strains on his health. He died as a result of a coronary heart attack in April 1946.

The influence of Keynesianism diminished in the late 1970s as a result of simultaneously accelerating inflation and rising unemployment. Followers of Keynes had hoped that active macroeconomic policy could fine-tune the economy to eliminate the business cycle, maintain full employment, keep prices stable and speed up economic growth. The attempt to achieve those objectives led to an encroaching corporatist approach to economic management. It is doubtful whether Keynes himself would have gone along with these ideas: he had never lost faith in the virtues of the liberal market economy. He instead focused on how macro-economic stability could be maintained and analysed the behaviour of the economy within a short-run framework: economic growth was not part of his purview. But in any case Keynesian policy prescriptions were widely criticized by monetarists and the neoclassical economists who advocated a form of policy passivism. It nevertheless remains clear that Keynes and his followers were responsible for the framework within which the discussion and analysis of modern economies is now cast. His emphasis on the key role of expectations in economic decisions is universally accepted, although the mechanism by which expectations are formed is a matter of continuing dispute. Finally, his integration of money into the determination of output levels is now taken for granted and vital concepts such as National Income and the consumption function are part of the tool-box of all economists.

Robert Skidelsky, John Maynard Keynes: A biography (2 vols, 1983, 1992) conclusion too. He wrote several historical novels: *Hypatia* (1843), *Westward Ho!* (1855) and his last completed novel *Hereward the Wake* (1866). The best known of his stories for children, *The Water Babies* (1863), the story of a cruelly treated chimney sweep, also had an instructive message overlaid with symbolic fantasy.

As well as his parish work, Kingsley was appointed chaplain to Queen VICTORIA in 1859, was Professor of Modern History at Cambridge between 1860 and 1869, and canon, first of Chester (1869) and then of Westminster (1873). A virulent anti-Catholic, his passionate altercations with the Catholic convert NEWMAN led the latter to write his autobiography *Apologia pro Vita Sua* (1864).

KINGSLEY, MARY (1862–1900), traveller. Mary Kingsley received no formal education (Virginia WOOLF used her in *Three Guineas,* as an example of a daughter's education sacrificed to that of her brothers) but read voraciously in her father's extensive scientific library. After the death of her parents in 1892, she travelled to West Africa in order to complete her father's project and collect zoological specimens from the previously uncharted terrain of the Congo Basin. In 1894 she made a year-long journey to the interior of West Africa, carrying out an extensive ethnographic survey of the indigenous peoples and adopting their way of life. An agnostic, vehemently opposed to what she regarded as intrusive missionary activities, she paid her way by trading in oil, rubber and ivory. *Travels in West Africa* (1897) was an immediate best-seller; *West African Studies* was published the same year and *The Story of West Africa* in 1899. The books fuelled debate about British imperial policy, and Kingsley lobbied the Colonial Secretary, Joseph CHAMBERLAIN, about the rights of the African people.

KINNOCK, NEIL (1942–), politician. Neil Kinnock will be remembered as the man who paved the way for Tony BLAIR and New Labour. He was cast in the mould of the Welsh firebrand, pioneered by LLOYD GEORGE and Aneurin BEVAN. A student activist at Cardiff in the 1960s, he became MP for Bedwellty (Mon.) in 1970, establishing himself on the far left of the party. In opposition in the early 1980s he was both anti-Europe and against the nuclear deterrent so, after the failure of Michael FOOT to deliver electoral success in 1983, Kinnock seemed the obvious candidate as leader.

Kinnock was a pragmatist, and during his time as leader fought a tough battle against the Militant Tendency to rid Labour of the 'loony left' which had cost it the 1983 and 1987 elections. Kinnock's oratorical skills were, however, those of the plat-form rather than the Commons, where his preference for long-winded questions often allowed THATCHER off the hook; he was known, not wholly affectionately, as 'the Welsh wind-bag'. But it was under Kinnock that Peter MANDELSON began the process of trying to rebrand the Labour Party, introducing the logo of the red rose, as well as the skills of the public relations consultant.

The 1992 election was expected to be Kinnock's finest hour but, despite a slick campaign, Labour lost narrowly to John MAJOR. Kinnock himself was felt to be part of the problem. His loquacity and unsoundness on defence issues were felt to be liabilities, and Kinnock generously stood down in favour of John SMITH. In an ironic twist of fate the former anti-European Union campaigner became European Commissioner for Transport in 1995 and in 1999 Vice-President for Administrative Reform.

KIPLING, RUDYARD (1865–1936), writer. The stories and verse that Kipling wrote at the turn of the century did much to shape public attitudes towards the British Empire and the worthiness of its purpose. Born in Bombay, the son of an art teacher and illustrator, he was educated in England (a miserable experience recaptured in some of his stories) before returning to India in 1882 as a newspaper reporter. Nine years later he came back to England with an emerging reputation as an author and poet for both adults and children. His works on Indian, imperial, military and patriotic themes enjoyed huge commercial and literary success, *Plain Tales from the Hills* (1888), *Barrack-Room Ballads* (1892), *The Jungle Book* (1894), *Just So Stories* (1902), *Stalky & Co.* (1899) and his generally acknowledged masterpiece *Kim* (1901) among them. Kipling won the Nobel Prize for Literature in 1907. For all the success and the seemingly jingoistic nature of the works, they were often double-edged in their depiction of the Raj and the British in India. Those in authority were often satirized, the ordinary soldier (his 'Tommy Atkins') was patronized, while those back in Britain were criticized for failing to comprehend the meaning and importance of Empire. Kipling subscribed to the gospels of hard work and progress as a remedy for these faults: therein lay much of his popular appeal and eventually the eclipse of his literary star. In 1892 he married and moved to Vermont, USA, for four years. He saw war at first hand only when visiting South Africa in 1900. Through his mother Kipling was related to the painter Sir Edward BURNE-JONES and the four-times Prime Minister Stanley BALDWIN, and he was friends with many of the public figures of the 1910s and 1920s. Yet he became increasingly disillusioned and dispirited: neither electors nor elected seemed capable of defending Empire or his idealized visions of England, encapsulated in *A School History of England* (1911) and the children's stories *Puck of Pook's Hill* (1906) inspired by his Sussex home, Bateman's, purchased in 1902. In spite of his warnings, he became convinced that the First World War, the Irish and the Indian questions all seemed to presage imperial decline, while personal sorrows crowded in. His only son John died in action in 1915 and his elder daughter Josephine had died of pneumonia in New York in 1899. In his latter years Kipling sought some solace in spiritualism, attempting to reach his loved ones. He was buried in Westminster Abbey as the Empire which he had celebrated was indeed entering its final phase.

KITCHENER, HERBERT *see* essay on page 484

KITCHIN, ANTHONY (*c.* 1477–1563), churchman. Oxford-educated, he was a Benedictine monk who after surrendering as Abbot of Eynsham (Oxon.) in 1539 was made Bishop of Llandaff in 1545. He distinguished himself by sitting out the reigns of HENRY VIII, EDWARD VI and MARY I in his diocese, being the only one of Mary's bishops to agree to continue serving under ELIZABETH I.

KITZINGER, SHEILA (née Webster) (1929–), childbirth educator. Kitzinger's pioneering psychosexual approach, which informed her book *The Experience of Childbirth* (1962), encouraged home births, and, with the aim of dispelling fear and minimizing pain, gave pregnant women full information and suggested relaxation techniques to achieve a 'natural' childbirth whenever possible. Kitzinger, a social anthropologist with five daughters of her own, developed her work in classes for the National Childbirth Trust, of whose advisory board she has been a member since 1960, and in subsequent books and lectures throughout the world.

KLEIN, MELANIE (née Reizes) (1882–1960), psychoanalyst. Educated in her native Vienna, in 1910 Klein moved to Budapest where she studied Freudian psychoanalysis. She began her pioneering work in child psychoanalysis while working at the Berlin Psychoanalytical Institute (1921–6). She moved to London in 1926, where she developed her techniques and participated in the British Psychoanalytical Society. From Freud's work on adult psychoanalysis she developed the now widely used technique in which a child's anxieties are understood and resolved by studying his or her play. She extended Freud's claims about the mental life of children to newly born infants, and thus illuminated the manifestation of early mental processes in child development. Many psychoanalysts challenged her claims while others, notably Anna FREUD, criticized her therapeutic methods.

Her work, however, has had a significant impact on psychoanalysis.

KNATCHBULL, MARY (1610–96), Abbess. From a Roman Catholic Kentish gentry family, she became a Benedictine nun in the Low Countries at Ghent (1628) and succeeded as Abbess in 1650. She used the nunnery's network of clandestine contacts to help exiled Royalists with finance and lines of communication central to CHARLES II's restoration plans. Her efforts produced little government gratitude after 1660. Although Charles gave her some financial support and apparently a verbal promise of royal status for a new monastery at Dunkirk, the town's handover by the English to the French (1662) ended what might have been a new initiative in official toleration of Catholicism.

KNELLER, SIR GODFREY (1646–1723), artist. Of German birth, he learned his craft in Amsterdam and Rome. In London he gained numerous commissions: CHARLES II asked for a portrait of Louis XIV; JAMES II is said to have been sitting for him when news came of the landing of William of Orange (the future WILLIAM III) at Torbay; and William and MARY patronized him. He delegated much routine work to his many assistants, and he left more than 500 portraits unfinished at his death. He founded an academy for artists in Great Queen Street, which taught several early eighteenth-century artists including Joseph Highmore.

KNIGHT, ROBERT (1675–1742), financier. The son of a London sugar-baker, he already had a reputation for unscrupulous financial ingenuity when appointed cashier to the South Sea Co. in 1711. Proposed by Robert HARLEY in 1710 and chartered in 1711 to trade with South America, the company was intended also to rival the Whig-dominated Bank of England and East India Co. as a source of loans to the government. Holders of short-term government securities were compelled to exchange them for shares at par in the new company, which was given a monopoly on trade with South America, the west coast of North America and all Spanish colonies. The company was guaranteed an annual payment from the Exchequer equivalent to 6 per cent of the stock it took over. In 1719 Knight began to massage the share price upwards, and to distribute stock illegally to prominent people, including GEORGE I and his mistress the Duchess of Kendal (*see* SCHULENBURG, MELUSINE), in order to ensure that Parliament approved the scheme by which government stock, with a low rate of interest, would be traded in for higher-yield company stock. New stock was issued on this basis in 1720 and instant profits were made, which drove the price up further. When the price of shares collapsed in the

continued on page 485

KITCHENER, HERBERT (1st Earl Kitchener of Khartoum) (1850–1916)
Soldier

Kitchener grew up on the family's estate in Ireland. At Woolwich (1868–70) he was commissioned into the Royal Engineers. The very antithesis of the young 'hearty', he was devoutly religious, quietly scholarly, hopeless at sport, and a collector of exotic *objets d'art*. Yet he thirsted after a life of adventure. In the autumn of 1870, with Prussian armies besieging Paris, Kitchener went to France, where he joined the army as a medical orderly, contracted a fever and was himself evacuated back to England.

Now determined to seize every opportunity to see action, in 1878 he visited the Turkish army, then heavily engaged in resisting a Russian advance in the Balkans, funding this completely unauthorized trip by writing of his experiences for *Blackwood's Magazine*. He next joined a military mission to Anatolia (1879–80), before returning to Cyprus (1880–3). Having failed in 1882 to secure a post with Garnet WOLSELEY's expedition to Egypt, Kitchener travelled to Alexandria disguised as a Levantine businessman, and carried out his own reconnaissance of Egyptian defences in the Nile delta, just prior to the British landings.

Severely admonished, in 1883 he nevertheless managed to engineer a transfer to Cairo to act as second-in-command of the Egyptian cavalry. In 1884–5 he commanded patrols of Bedouin irregulars on the Egyptian–Sudan border and attempted to maintain contact with General Charles GORDON, besieged in Khartoum by the Mahdi's Dervish armies. With the failure of Wolseley's expedition to rescue Gordon (Jan. 1885), Kitchener returned to Britain and was promoted lieutenant colonel by brevet.

Governor General of the Eastern Sudan, Adjutant General of the Egyptian army and Sirdar (virtual ruler) of Egypt (1892), in 1896 Kitchener with his reformed and revitalized Egyptian army, reinforced by a British Expeditionary Force, began the systematic reconquest of the Sudan, which culminated in the encounter at Omdurman on 2 Sept. 1898. It was a massacre rather than a battle: Kitchener lost fewer than 200 men, the Mahdi some 11,000. Pushing south, Kitchener overawed a small French force which had established itself at Fashoda, and persuaded it to withdraw from the upper Nile. The 'Fashoda Incident' brought Britain and France to the brink of war; but made Kitchener the hero of the hour. The following autumn, in an effort to recover from the early disasters of the Second Boer War (1899–1902), the War Office appointed Kitchener Chief-of-Staff to Lord ROBERTS, the new Commander-in-Chief in South Africa. Massive British reinforcements allowed Roberts to crush Boer armies in the field and he returned to Britain, leaving the 'mopping up' to Kitchener. When Boer commandos waged an increasingly effective guerrilla war, Kitchener's response was to burn the farms of the Free State and the Transvaal, to round up the civilian population and to concentrate them in camps on the coast, with lines of blockhouses and barbed wire fences which impeded the movement of Boer commandos. The system worked but it took 18 months, during which time 28,000 Afrikaaner and 15,000 Bantu women and children died in what were now called 'concentration camps'. Kitchener found himself at the centre of a storm: to Liberals he was a butcher; to Conservatives he was a hero.

During his period as Commander-in-Chief in India (1902–9) Kitchener modernized the Indian army and fought bitter battles over civil–military control with the Viceroy Lord CURZON. As British agent to Egypt he proved an able civil administrator and reformed the land tenure system.

In Aug. 1914, Kitchener replaced HALDANE as Secretary for War. He concluded that Germany and her allies could not be beaten in less than three years, and then only if Britain was willing to move towards almost total mobilization. Refusing to work through established recruiting mechanisms, Kitchener drove through a massive expansion of the army by voluntary means, from seven towards a projected 70 divisions. Simultaneously he laid the groundwork for a vast increase in munitions production, which would come to fruition in 1917. Unfortunately the setbacks of 1915 and early 1916 – the Dardanelles landings, the Battle of Loos and the shell crisis – began to weaken his political position. An erstwhile ally, Winston CHURCHILL, was forced to resign, and powerful elements led by LLOYD GEORGE began moving against Kitchener. The clash never came; on 3 June 1916 HMS *Hampshire*, the cruiser on which Kitchener was sailing on a mission to Russia, hit a mine. Kitchener was not among the survivors. His death was treated as a national calamity.

After the war a number of soldiers and politicians attacked Kitchener in their memoirs as a colonial soldier of dubious sexuality who was totally out of his depth in European warfare. In fact in 1914 Kitchener was virtually alone in understanding the effort and sacrifice which would be required to win a war against a modern industrial state.

George H. Cassar, Kitchener: Architect of Victory (1977)
Philip Magnus, Kitchener: Portrait of an Imperialist (1958)

autumn of 1720 Knight fled to Holland to escape investigation by Parliament, and eventually set up in Paris as a banker. He paid £10,000 for a pardon shortly before his death and returned to his estate in Essex.

KNOLLYS, SIR FRANCIS (by 1512–96), politician. Son of a courtier and reputedly Oxford-educated, he was a soldier under HENRY VIII, and an MP repeatedly between 1529 and 1593, with an interval under MARY I when his strong Protestantism exiled him in Germany. He was guardian of the fugitive MARY QUEEN OF SCOTS in 1568–9 and Treasurer of the Household 1572–96. He found difficulty in reconciling his close government links with sympathy for Puritan activists, but served as a useful bridge-figure between the two interests.

KNOX, JOHN see essay on page 486

KNOX, ROBERT (1791–1862), anatomist. Born in Edinburgh, Knox became the conservator of the museum of the Edinburgh College of Surgeons in 1824 and ran an anatomy school (1826–40). He achieved notoriety for obtaining subjects for anatomical dissection from William Burke and William Hare, who obtained the corpses by murder, rather than grave-robbing; this was also the subject of James Bridie's play, *The Anatomist*. He was also the author of *The Races of Men* (1850), an important influence in the development of racist thought in nineteenth-century Britain.

KNOX, RONALD (1888–1957), cleric. The son of a man who became Anglican Bishop of Manchester, Knox was a brilliant undergraduate at Oxford and President of the Union. He was elected to a fellowship of Trinity College in 1910, and to the college's chaplaincy two years later, where he influenced a generation of Oxford undergraduates including Evelyn WAUGH (who wrote his biography) and Harold MACMILLAN. In 1917, after Knox had vigorously attacked the modernist tendency within the Church of England, he was received into the Roman Catholic Church. He taught at St Edmund's College, Ware (Herts.), until returning to Oxford in 1926 as chaplain to the university's Catholic students. He resigned in 1939, to produce a new translation of the Bible; the New Testament was published in 1945, and the Old Testament four years later.

KNOX, VICESIMUS (1752–1821), educationalist. Knox combined a teaching career, as headmaster of Tonbridge school, with a prolific output of books, many of which were very successful, such as the *Elegant Extracts*, volumes of prose and poetry selected as model passages with which

schoolboys could improve their powers of thought and expression. He was devoted to the revival of classical teaching in grammar schools (at the expense of such modern subjects as geography and applied mathematics, which had recently been becoming more popular) as the best way of educating the professional and commercial male elite; his *Liberal Education* (1781) ran into 10 editions by 1790.

KOESTLER, ARTHUR (1905–83), writer. Born in Budapest and educated in Vienna, Koestler taught at the University of Vienna before working as a journalist in Germany, Spain, France and the Middle East. In 1931 he joined the German Communist Party and visited Soviet Russia. He reported on the Spanish Civil War (1936–7) for a number of French newspapers. Arrested by the Fascists in Malaga and condemned to death, he was saved by the International Red Cross, which organized an exchange of prisoners. His experiences in Spain are recounted in *Spanish Testament* (1937). He settled in England in 1940. *Darkness at Noon* (1940), a work considered on a par with George ORWELL's *Nineteen Eighty Four*, is based on the Stalinist purges of the 1930s. The theme of the terrors of totalitarian communism appeared again in his novel *Arrival and Departure* (1943) and in a collection of essays, *The Yogi and the Commissar* (1945). Koestler was deeply committed to the cause of Zionism, expressing his views in his novel *Thieves in the Night* (1946) and his history *Promise and Fulfilment* (1949). His numerous interests included parapsychology and the relation between artistic creation and scientific advances. An irascible misogynist, Koestler killed himself in a suicide pact with his wife after the onset of Parkinson's disease.

KORDA, SIR ALEXANDER (originally Sándor Laszlo Kellner) (1893–1956), film-producer. He was a journalist and film-maker in his native Hungary and in Vienna, Berlin and Hollywood before coming to Britain in 1932, where he set up London Film Productions and Denham Studios. Among his many films the most notable include *The Private Life of Henry VIII* (1933), one of the most commercially successful British films ever made, the coronation spectacular *Fire over England* (1936), *The Thief of Baghdad* (1940) and the great British film noir of the post-war black market during the Cold War, *The Third Man* (1949).

KRATZER, NICHOLAS (1487–?1550), astronomer. From Munich, he came to the English court in 1517, and lectured at Oxford. As royal horologer (clockmaker) he designed complex timepieces at court and elsewhere and was a close friend of

continued on page 487

KNOX, JOHN (c. 1513–72)
Religious leader

Knox was born in Haddington (Lothian) and studied at Glasgow University, where he was taught by John MAIR, and probably also at St Andrews. He was ordained and was made a notary apostolic (a Church lawyer) before becoming tutor to Lothian gentry, the Douglases and Cockburns; through them he met George WISHART and was converted to reformist views. When Wishart was burned at the stake (1546) Knox sought refuge with the Protestant garrison in St Andrews Castle; he now began his preaching career. Although he had not been involved in the garrison's murder of Cardinal BEATON, he was nevertheless made a galley-slave when the French captured the castle after a siege in July 1547. He was released in 1549 and went to England, where he actively promoted the government's Protestant changes. He was first active in the north, particularly at Berwick-upon-Tweed and Newcastle, inevitably coming into conflict with Bishop TUNSTALL; he also met his future wife, Marjory Bowes. In autumn 1551 he was made a royal chaplain, and John DUDLEY, Duke of Northumberland, brought him south, admiring his religious radicalism and probably hoping to use it in his plans to strip the Church of its wealth. Their relations deteriorated, however, and Knox was one of the leading clergy who in early 1553 denounced politicians' worldliness in a series of well-publicized sermons. He failed to persuade the Privy Council to modify the 1552 Book of Common Prayer to forbid kneeling at Holy Communion, although his protests prompted Archbishop CRANMER to insert a last-minute instruction (the 'black rubric') explaining that kneeling did not signify adoration of the bread and wine.

MARY I's accession interrupted his preaching ministry in Bucks. and he fled to the continent, where he championed thoroughgoing Calvinist reform among the English exiles; his efforts at Frankfurt resulted in his expulsion from the city (1555), so he returned to the more congenial atmosphere of CALVIN's Geneva, which he called 'the most perfect school of Christ on earth since the days of the Apostles'. In 1555–6 he made a large-scale clandestine preaching tour in Scotland, but resisted entreaties to stay longer and returned to Geneva; in 1556 he drew up a directory of worship for the English congregation which later became the basis of the Church of Scotland's Book of Common Order. After the bishops burned him in effigy in Edinburgh, he abandoned a planned return visit to Scotland in

1557. His attack on the two Catholic rulers Mary of England and MARY OF GUISE, *The First Blast of the Trumpet against the Monstrous Regiment of Women* (1558), asserted that it was monstrous (unnatural) for women to hold regiment (political power). Soon, unfortunately and accidentally, it applied to Protestant ELIZABETH I; furious, she scuppered his hopes of resuming his English career. Instead he turned back to Scotland; in 1559 he was appointed Minister of Edinburgh, and from then on became the most prominent clerical leader of the Protestant and anti-French revolution, leading the construction of a Calvinist Church Settlement, and successfully pressing William CECIL for English military support. In Aug. 1560 he was one of the team of ministers ('the six Johns') who drew up a Confession of Faith for the Kirk (the new national Protestant Church of Scotland); they also prepared a scheme to reorganize the Kirk on Calvinist lines, the first Book of Discipline, which through political uncertainty and lack of resources was not fully implemented. From 1561 he bitterly opposed MARY QUEEN OF SCOTS, who obligingly behaved badly enough to be deposed (1567); Knox preached at the coronation of her son JAMES VI. He also preached at the funeral of the murdered Regent, James STEWART, Earl of Moray (1570), but Moray's death and the resulting civil war lessened his influence. One of his last contributions to the Reformation cause was to overcome a debilitating stroke to preach one of his classic sermons on hearing of the St Bartholomew's Day massacre of French Protestants.

Knox has remained a potent and brooding symbol of the militant and uncompromisingly Presbyterian Scottish Reformation. He was indeed a crucial player in the Reformation, but was more flexible and Anglophile than either his detractors or his Presbyterian near-idolators have later recognized. His wife was English, and indeed the contemporary Roman Catholic controversialist Ninian WINZET accused him of 'knapping Suddron' (chattering in English) because his language was so Anglicized. Without the accidents of English politics, he might well have become the first of the long troop of Scotsmen to end up a bishop of the Church of England. His *History of the Reformation of Religion within the Realm of Scotland* (published 1587, but in full only in 1644) remains an essential if somewhat self-promoting witness to the Reformation.

Jasper Ridley, John Knox (1958)

ERASMUS and Hans HOLBEIN the younger, who painted his portrait and probably used his advice for the celebrated portrait of *The Ambassadors* (1533).

KRAY, RONALD (1933–95) and **REGINALD** (1933–), criminals. The Kray twins ran a criminal operation in London's East End, where they were born. With good connections and money, they became swinging London celebrities in the 1960s, and were even photographed by David BAILEY. They liked to think of themselves as 1930s-style Chicago gangsters, Ronnie giving himself the title 'Colonel'. They were convicted of murder, following an unsuccessful attempt years earlier, in 1969. They were both sentenced to imprisonment of not less than 30 years. Ronnie died in prison in 1995, after a campaign to free them failed in the late 1980s.

KYD, THOMAS (?1558–94), dramatist. A London scrivener's son, his play *The Spanish Tragedy* may date from the mid 1580s, but few other plays can be attributed to him. He wrote tragic verse and collaborated in many plays, being involved in the talented circle of writers which included Christopher MARLOWE. After Marlowe's death (1593) Kyd was tortured to provide evidence of the murdered dramatist's unorthodox opinions, and died in poverty not long after.

L

LACKINGTON, JAMES (1746–1815), bookseller. Apprenticed to a Taunton shoemaker, from whom he acquired his religious piety, he read widely and in 1774 started to sell books from his shop in London, helped by a £5 loan from a Methodist business fund, which he was rapidly able to repay. He abandoned the shoe trade and moved to much larger premises in Finsbury Square, known as the Temple of the Muses. He challenged traditional bookselling practice by selling at the lowest possible price and not destroying remaindered stock. By 1791, when he published his *Memoirs*, he claimed annual sales of 100,000 with profits of £4,000. He retired to the West Country in 1798 and later became a Methodist local preacher in Devon, building and endowing several chapels.

LACY, HUGH DE (?–1186), soldier. He played a key role in the early stages of the English conquest of Ireland. HENRY II granted him the entire Irish kingdom of Meath in 1172, and subsequently appointed him Governor of Ireland. His marriage to RUADRÍ UA CONCHOBAIR's daughter gave rise to rumours that he was planning to make himself King of Ireland; Henry is said to have been relieved when he was killed by the Irish. His younger son, Hugh de Lacy II, was created the first Earl of Ulster in 1205.

LAING, RONALD (1927–89), psychiatrist. Laing studied medicine in his native Glasgow and worked as a psychiatrist in the British army (1951–3) and at Glasgow University (1953–6). His radical views about mental illness developed while working at the Tavistock Clinic, London (1957–60), and at the Tavistock Institute of Human Relations, London (1960–7). In his first major work, *The Divided Self* (1960), he interpreted schizophrenia as a condition in which a person doubts the reality of himself and others and invents a false self 'in order to live in an unliveable situation'. In *Sanity, Madness and the Family* (1964), Laing linked madness not to biological factors but to disturbed family environments. At the Tavistock Clinic he sought to deal with the mentally ill by encouraging them to find themselves rather than by trying to cure them. His interpretations and practices were attacked by mainstream psychiatrists but still inform aspects of psychiatry.

LAKE, GERARD (1st Baron and 1st Viscount Lake) (1744–1808), soldier. A gentleman's son, he was appointed ensign in the Footguards at the age of 13, and rose through the ranks during the War of American Independence and French Revolutionary Wars. In Jan. 1797 he was sent to Ireland to suppress the United Irishmen. His proclamation requiring everyone except soldiers and officers of the peace to surrender their arms was condemned in both the Irish and British Houses of Commons. With a force of 13,000 he defeated the rebels under Father John MURPHY at Vinegar Hill in Jan. 1798, and in Sept. received the surrender of the French forces in Ireland. Lake later commanded in India, securing British supremacy with the capture of Delhi from the Marathas in 1803.

LAKER, SIR FREDERICK (FREDDIE) (1922–), entrepreneur. After a career in aircraft, both manufacture and operation, during which his airline freight business became part of British United Airways, Laker set up his own airline, Laker Airways, in 1966 as a charter company for the fast-growing package holiday trade. This was followed by a series of battles against the airline cartels for the right to run cut-price transatlantic charters, and in 1977 his famous Skytrain service was born. Within five years he was bankrupted, partly by the actions of his larger competitors, notably British Airways under its new Chairman, John KING. Although he won damages against his competitors, he was unable to get back into the airline business until 1992, but was remembered for his personality and giant-killer mentality.

LAMB, LADY CAROLINE (née Ponsonby) (1785–1828), novelist. Married at 16 to William LAMB, later Viscount Melbourne, in 1812 she conceived a passionate infatuation for the poet BYRON, whom she famously described as 'mad, bad and dangerous to know'. Byron discarded her in 1813 and she spent the rest of her life in a fragile and turbulent emotional state. Her first novel *Glenarvon* (1816), republished in 1865 as *The Fatal Passion*, caricatured Byron.

LAMB, WILLIAM (2nd Viscount Melbourne) (1779–1848), Prime Minister (1834, 1835–41). A

Whig MP, and follower of Charles James FOX from 1806 to 1812, he returned to the Commons in 1816 and was appointed Secretary of State for Ireland in CANNING's liberal Tory administration, a post which he held briefly under Wellington (*see* WELLESLEY, ARTHUR) in 1828. Home Secretary in GREY's Whig ministry, Melbourne (who had succeeded to the title in 1829) was an unexpectedly assiduous minister, ruthless in his control of radical dissent and agricultural unrest. After considerable hesitation he succeeded Grey as Prime Minister in 1834, but his government was weak and, when WILLIAM IV objected to the inclusion of the radical Whig Lord John RUSSELL as Chancellor, Melbourne was happy to offer his resignation, which was seized on by the King in Dec. He was Prime Minister again from 1835, when he proved unsympathetic to Chartist demands and growing pressure to repeal the Corn Laws in the face of deepening economic depression.

Melbourne is generally remembered as Prime Minister when VICTORIA came to the throne in 1837; he warmed to his role as mentor and paternal adviser on matters of State and politics to the 'girl queen'. His private life was turbulent: his wife, Lady Caroline LAMB, had a public infatuation for BYRON, and the Lambs had a judicial separation in 1825; and in 1836, while Prime Minister, he was cited in the divorce case that George Norton brought against his wife Caroline (*see* NORTON, CAROLINE), though their friendship was shown to be platonic. Melbourne resigned after the Whigs were defeated by one vote on a motion of no confidence in June 1841, and he suffered a severe stroke the following year.

LAMBARDE, WILLIAM (1536–1601), historian. Kentish gentleman and government archivist who in 1581 wrote *Eirenarcha* (Rule of Peace), a classic handbook for the increasingly busy Justices of the Peace, and also researched and published diligently on history. His deservedly popular *Perambulation of Kent* (1570) was one of the first substantial works on local history in Britain.

LAMBERT, JOHN (1619–83), soldier. Gaining a brilliant reputation and much popularity in the northern armies fighting CHARLES I during the First English Civil War (1642–6), he may have been involved in drawing up the Heads of the Proposals (the peace terms offered to Charles in 1647) and was active in the ultimately successful campaigns against the Scots (1648–51). Deputy Lord Lieutenant of Ireland from 1652, he was dominant in the army's Council of Officers from 1653, organizing the downfall of the 'Barebones' Parliament (Dec. 1653) and thereupon drawing up the Instrument of Government which was intended to structure the protectorate of Oliver CROMWELL. From 1655 he was active as one of the major-generals instituted to levy taxes and impose discipline in the regions. Increasingly at loggerheads with Cromwell, he became active in government again after the latter's death, but his career ended with his unsuccessful bid to oppose George MONCK's progress south in 1659 and arouse resistance to the restoration of CHARLES II in 1660. Spirited attempts to escape imprisonment ended in his life imprisonment on Guernsey from 1664.

LAMBTON, JOHN (1st Earl of Durham) (1792–1840), politician. One of the four people who drew up the Reform Bill of 1832, he served as Lord Privy Seal in the administration of his father-in-law Earl Grey (*see* GREY, CHARLES) but is best known for his dictatorial rule as Governor General of Canada (1837–8) and his report recommending self-governing status for that dominion in regard to internal affairs.

LAMONT, NORMAN (Baron Lamont of Lerwick) (1942–), politician. Lamont was one of that group of Cambridge Conservatives from the 1950s which included Kenneth CLARKE and Michael Howard and became prominent in the early 1990s after the downfall of Margaret THATCHER. MP for Kingston-upon-Thames from 1972, Lamont, as former chairman of the Bow group, found himself out of favour in the Thatcherite years. But as campaign manager for John MAJOR in the 1990 Conservative leadership contest he was rewarded with the Exchequer. As Chancellor at the depth of the recession of 1990–2 he was mocked for his readiness to discern the 'green shoots' of economic recovery at every opportunity. Following the economic crisis occasioned by Britain's entry into the European Exchange Rate Mechanism, Lamont was offered an alternative cabinet post in 1993 which he declined, leaving the government. Over the next few years he became Major's bitter enemy and a trenchant critic of further European union. He was defeated in the 1997 election and went to the Lords.

LANCASTER, EARL OF, 2ND *see* THOMAS OF LANCASTER; **4TH AND 1ST DUKE OF**, *see* HENRY OF LANCASTER; **2ND DUKE OF** *see* JOHN OF GAUNT

LANCASTER, SIR OSBERT (1908–86), cartoonist and writer. A student at the Slade School of Art, Lancaster worked as an illustrator on the *Architectural Review* and designed posters for London Transport before joining the *Daily Express* in 1939, where his Pocket Cartoons of upper-class mores seen through the eyes of Maudie Littlehampton and her circle were a daily delight.

LANCHESTER, FREDERICK (1868–1946), engineer. After several attempts in the 1890s and early 1900s to establish his own car company based on an advanced but ultimately uneconomic engine, in 1910 Lanchester became consultant engineer to the Daimler Motor Co. As early as 1909, however, he was studying the design and deployment of aircraft. His book *Aircraft in Warfare: The Dawn of the Fourth Arm* (1916) proved to be a seminal military text. It established mathematical formulae for assessing the mechanical and combat performance of aircraft, which provided the basis for the development of operations analysis for the rest of the century. Control of the air, Lanchester argued, would enable the victorious air fleet to cripple the industrial and transport infrastructure of its enemies. In effect, this meant the destruction of the enemy's cities. Lanchester's influence was profound; he provided an intellectual justification for independent air forces (the RAF was formed in April 1918) and foresaw the evolution of aerial warfare.

LANE, ALLEN (originally Williams) (1903–70), publisher. In 1935, Lane, then managing director of the Bodley Head (which had been the publishing house of his uncle John LANE, whose surname he took), launched a series of paperback versions of high-quality hardbacks, selling at a uniform price of 6d. He selected 10 titles with an appeal to the educated general reader, including Ernest Hemingway's *A Farewell to Arms*, books by Dorothy L. SAYERS and Agatha CHRISTIE, and *Ariel*, André Maurois's biography of SHELLEY: the agreement of Woolworth's to sell these books ensured the success of the Penguin 'paperback revolution'. During the Second World War, Lane was instrumental in the Armed Forces Book Club (1942), a government scheme providing books to soldiers serving all over the world and, later, to prisoners of war. Penguin Specials aimed to educate the public about political issues; Puffin Books (1940) were for children; Classics were launched in 1946 (the first was Homer's *Odyssey,* which sold well over a million copies). In 1960 Penguin was prosecuted under the Obscene Publications Act for publishing an unexpurgated version of D. H. LAWRENCE's *Lady Chatterley's Lover.* The prosecution failed: the publicity and subsequent sales justified Lane and his company's commercial acumen as well as its literary boldness.

LANE, DAME ELIZABETH (née Coulborn) (1905–88), lawyer. Called to the Bar in 1940, she was the third woman to be appointed a QC (1960), the first woman Circuit Court judge and the first woman High Court judge (1965). She was chair of the committee looking into the reform of the abortion laws (1971–3).

LANE, JOHN (1854–1925), publisher. A clerk who wanted to become an antiquarian book dealer, but without money or much education, he realized his ambition in 1877 when he was introduced to Charles Elkins Matthews, a rare-book dealer from Devon. Their shop was a success: the partnership was dissolved in 1894 and Lane took over the Bodley Head imprint which he soon developed into a major publishing house, starting the 30-volume 'Keynote' series of experimental fiction (many concerned with the 'woman question') and *The Yellow Book* (1894–7), of which Aubrey BEARDSLEY was the first art editor. He also published such notable *fin-de-siècle* authors as Oscar WILDE, Max BEERBOHM and Richard Le Gallienne.

LANFRANC (*c.* 1010–89), Archbishop of Canterbury (1070–89). A native of Italy, he left home *c.* 1030 to pursue his studies in France. He entered the poor and recently founded Norman monastery of Bec in 1042, becoming Prior about three years later; a biblical scholar of international repute notably in his defence of orthodoxy against the eucharistic heresy of Berengar of Tours his teaching did much to make Bec famous and wealthy. By 1063, when William of Normandy (*see* WILLIAM I THE CONQUEROR) appointed him Abbot of his foundation of St Stephen's, Caen, Lanfranc was evidently the Duke's man, and was probably responsible for presenting to the Papacy the case for William's claim to England.

Made Archbishop by William in 1070, he had the task of managing, reforming and reorganizing the English Church, and rebuilt Canterbury Cathedral on the model of St Stephen's. During the King's absences, he also took on wider responsibilities for the government of England. In return, William supported Canterbury's hotly disputed claim to primacy over York, the Conqueror seeing this as a means of bolstering his precarious authority over the north.

LANG, COSMO (1864–1945), Archbishop of Canterbury (1928–42). Educated at Glasgow and Oxford universities, he studied for the Bar. Although brought up as a Presbyterian, he was ordained into the Church of England in 1890. After a brief period as curate of Leeds parish church, he became vicar of St Mary's, university church of Oxford (1894–6), and of Portsea (1896–1901). He became Suffragan Bishop of Stepney (1901), then Archbishop of York (1908–28). As Archbishop of Canterbury he played an important role in the abdication crisis in Dec. 1936 (*see* EDWARD VIII). He retired in 1942.

LANGHAM, SIMON (?–1376), Archbishop of Canterbury (1366–8). Abbot of Westminster from 1349, he was elected Bishop of Ely in 1362 and appointed Chancellor in 1363. His opening speech to Parliament was the first to be given in English. He was created Archbishop in 1366, and was a stern administrator; EDWARD III forced him to resign in 1368, but his value as a Cardinal and diplomat at the papal curia led to his restoration to royal favour. In 1374 he was again elected Archbishop but the Pope would not let him go and he died at Avignon.

LANGLAND, WILLIAM (*fl. c.* 1380), poet. He wrote *Piers Plowman*, the visionary poem written in three different versions in the last three or four decades of the fourteenth century. Of his life nothing is known apart from what can be inferred from the poem: that he came from the West Midlands and lived on Cornhill in the City of London. His poetic ability to re-create people and places in vivid and concrete detail while shifting to and fro between religious allegory and ironic social criticism makes him an extraordinary witness to the world in which he lived.

LANGTOFT, PETER (*?–c.* 1307), rhyming chronicler. Probably born at Langtoft (Yorks.) he became a canon at the Augustinian priory at Bridlington (Yorks.). He wrote a history of England in French verse, making much use of GEOFFREY OF MONMOUTH. Historians have found his views on the reign of EDWARD I of interest. He criticized the King for getting up late in the mornings and for being too soft on the Scots.

LANGTON, STEPHEN (*c.* 1156–1228), Archbishop of Canterbury (1207–15, 1218–28). Educated at Paris, he stayed on to teach theology. He revised the order of the books of the Bible and their arrangement into chapters. Pope Innocent III made him a cardinal in 1206, and in 1207, consecrated him Archbishop of Canterbury. John's refusal to admit Langton into England led to a quarrel between King and Pope that lasted until John submitted in 1213.

Once in England, Langton's concern for lawful government made him an important mediator between the King and his baronial opponents, and he played a key role in negotiating Magna Carta. Once this had been sealed, he remained fully committed to its principles, a stance that brought him into conflict with a Pope now wholeheartedly on the side of a submissive King. Langton was suspended in Sept. 1215 and went to Rome. He returned to England in 1218, but it was only after he had paid another visit to the curia (1220–1), to secure the recall of an uncomfortably influential papal legate, that he was free to play an active role in English affairs. Until 1226 his moderating presence and co-operation with Hubert de BURGH did much to keep the peace during the minority of HENRY III.

LANGTON, WALTER (?–1321), royal servant. As EDWARD I's chief minister, from 1295 when the King's rule became increasingly unpopular, Langton became increasingly wealthy, being appointed Treasurer of England in 1295 and Bishop of Coventry and Lichfield in 1296. John Lovetot unsuccessfully accused him in 1301 of living in adultery with his step-mother. EDWARD II disliked him, and those who attacked him in 1307 had no difficulty in making their charges stick. His name became a by-word for corruption. Yet by 1312 Edward II, desperate for competent support, recalled him to office and to the Council, where he stayed until driven out again in 1315.

LANGTRY, LILLIE (née Le Breton) (1853–1929), actress. Daughter of the Dean of Jersey, she made a disastrous marriage to a wealthy yachtsman, Edward Langtry. A great beauty, she was painted by MILLAIS as 'the Jersey Lily'; Oscar WILDE adored her (in his fashion); King Leopold of the Belgians was infatuated by her and she was the first publicly acknowledged mistress of the Prince of Wales (*see* EDWARD VII). As an actress she was helped by another of the Prince's mistresses, the legendary Sarah Bernhardt, making her début in *She Stoops to Conquer*, and proved a particularly luminous star on the American stage. She had a succession of other wealthy lovers, was the first woman to be admitted to the Jockey Club when the colt given to her by an admirer won the Cesarewitch and died in Monte Carlo in the palatial home of her second husband. Unsympathetic to the demand of women for the vote to better their lot, she starred in an anti-suffragette satire, *Helping the Cause* (1912).

LANIER, EMILIA (née Bassano) (1569–1643), poet. Born in London, daughter of Giovanni Baptista Bassano, an Italian court musician, she was educated in the household of the dowager Countess of Kent and became mistress of Henry Carey, 1st Baron Hunsdon, before marrying a French court musician, Alphonse Lanier. Her religious verse was the first published in England (1611) by a woman. Her attempt to set up a London school to educate noblemen's children (1617) did not succeed. A. L. Rowse's attempt to identify her as the 'dark lady' of SHAKESPEARE's sonnets (published 1609) did not win universal acceptance.

LANSBURY, GEORGE (1859–1940), politician. Active in local government in East London from 1903, he became an MP in 1910 but resigned in 1912 to fight an unsuccessful by-election on a pro-women's suffrage manifesto. As an ex-mayor of Poplar he led the Poplarist campaign in 1921, as a result of which he and other Poplar Councillors were briefly jailed for refusing to increase the rates to raise necessary revenue, on the grounds that the people did not have the money to pay. He edited the *Daily Herald* (1919–22) and then his own *Lansbury's Labour Weekly* (1925–7). He again became an MP in 1922 and was Minister for Works (1929–31) in Ramsay MACDONALD's second Labour government. He became leader of the Labour Party (1932–5) after Macdonald had split it by forming the National government. A respected Christian socialist and pacifist, he resigned as leader when the party conference voted in favour of sanctions and possible military intervention in Abyssinia. He was succeeded as leader by ATTLEE.

LANSDOWNE, MARQUESS OF, 1ST *see* PETTY, WILLIAM; **5TH** *see* PETTY-FITZMAURICE, HENRY, essay on page 647

LARKIN, JAMES (1876–1947), trade-union leader. Brought up in Liverpool of Irish parents and a successful union organizer, Larkin led a strike in Belfast in 1907 which temporarily united sections of the Catholic and Protestant working classes, and later moved to Dublin. After quarrelling with the National Union of Dock Labourers he founded the Irish Transport and General Workers' Union (ITGWU) in 1909; it grew into the largest union in Ireland. He attracted attention for his passionate syndicalist views and denunciations of the living conditions of Dublin's poor. In 1913 attempts by Dublin employers, led by the newspaper and railway magnate William Martin Murphy, to exclude ITGWU members from their employment caused a strike and lock-out lasting from Sept. 1913 to Jan. 1914 and bringing severe hardship to workers and their families. Later in 1914 Larkin went to the United States to raise funds, leaving James CONNOLLY to run the union. In America he was sentenced to three years in gaol for involvement in radical and anti-war agitation. On his return to Ireland in 1923 he quarrelled with the interim leadership of the ITGWU and led the bulk of the Dublin membership into the breakaway Workers' Union of Ireland (WUI); the split damaged the trade-union movement for decades. Larkin also denounced the reformist Irish Labour Party and formed an Irish Workers' League affiliated to the Communist International; he was briefly a member of the Dáil for this movement in 1927 but failed to organize it efficiently, and the split weakened the Labour Party among the Dublin working class, to the benefit of Fianna Fáil. From the late 1920s his leadership was increasingly nominal, with the WUI run by his sons James and Denis. The Larkins rejoined the Labour Party and the Irish Trades Union Congress (ITUC) in the early 1940s, leading the ITGWU and some of its

affiliated members of the Dail to complain of communist infiltration and form the National Labour Party (which rejoined Labour in 1950) and the Congress of Irish Unions (reunited with the ITUC in 1959).

LARKIN, PHILIP (1922–85), poet. Born in Coventry, educated at Oxford, where he read English and developed an appreciation for jazz, he was unfit for military service because of bad eyesight, and was appointed local librarian in Wellington (Salop.) (1943). An 'inspired choice' of career, this was the first of a series of posts which he would hold until he was appointed librarian of the Brynmore Jones Library, University of Hull. An unworldly writer and something of a curmudgeon, Larkin liked living in Hull because 'it's so far away from everywhere else' and boasted of reading 'almost no poetry or little else except for novels and detective stories'. In 1944 he published his first anthology, *Poetry from Oxford in Wartime*. *The North Ship* was published in 1945 and his novel *Jill* (1946), set in wartime Oxford, describes the encounters of a working-class boy with the life of privilege. His second novel, *A Girl in Winter* (1947), recounts a day in the life of a librarian working in a drab provincial town. Larkin's work became associated with the Movement (a termed coined by the literary editor of *The Spectator* J. D. Scott to connote a style adopted by writers such as Kingsley AMIS, Robert Conquest, Donald Davie, D. J. Enright and John WAIN that was anti-romantic, sardonic and witty) and was published in *New Lines*. Larkin reviewed poetry and jazz (*All that Jazz* was published in 1970), and following the publication of his collection *The Whitsun Weddings* (1964), poems of social commentary and stoic wit, he was awarded the Queen's Gold Medal for Poetry. He edited *The Oxford Book of Twentieth Century English Verse* (1973).

LASDUN, SIR DENYS (1914–), architect. Trained at the Architectural Association, London, and an admirer of Le Corbusier, Lasdun was an advocate of the use of concrete. His best-known contributions to Britain's built environment are the Royal College of Physicians in Regent's Park, London (1958–64), the University of East Anglia (1962–8) and, most important, the innovative and controversial National Theatre (1967–76) on the South Bank of the Thames.

LASKI, HAROLD (1893–1950), political theorist. After graduating from Oxford in 1914, Laski spent two years lecturing in Canada before taking a post at Harvard in 1916. There, his support for striking policemen brought him under fire, and he returned to England in 1920, where he was appointed Professor of Political Science at the London School of Economics (1926) and he proved an inspirational teacher. He wrote voluminously on a variety of political topics, his best-known work being *A Grammar of Politics* (1925), a wide-ranging work in which he declared his ambition to 'construct a theory of the place of the State in the great society'. He served on the National Executive Committee of the Labour Party (1936–49) and provided rather erratic leadership for the intellectual Left within the party during this period. He frequently irritated the more middle-of-the-road Labour politicians who actually had to carry out policy in government with his extreme pronouncements (such as abolishing the monarchy), and during the 1945 election campaign he provided a handy left-wing bogeyman for the Conservative press. In 1946 he lost a libel action against two newspapers that had accused him of encouraging revolutionary violence.

ŁASKI, JAN (1499–1560), reformer. A Polish nobleman (latinizing his surname to à Lasco) who, nominated as Bishop of Veszprem (1529) and Archdeacon of Warsaw (1538), lost Church preferment when he married in 1540. He visited England in 1548 and settled there in 1550 to lead the London emigré congregations collectively known as the Stranger Church. Escaping MARY I in 1553, he eventually returned to lead the Reformed Church in southern Poland. A creative, independent-minded theologian whose relations with CALVIN were not warm, his scheme of Church government was widely influential in reformed churches.

LATIMER, HUGH (*c.* 1485–1555), preacher and martyr. Proud of his yeoman origins, as a Cambridge don during the 1520s he turned his exceptional preaching skills to passionate advocacy of Church reform. Support from HENRY VIII, ANNE BOLEYN and Thomas CRANMER preserved him through repeated harassment by conservative churchmen and, in 1535, brought the bishopric of Worcester, which he felt compelled to resign after Parliament passed the religiously conservative Act of Six Articles in 1539. He lived obscurely until EDWARD VI's accession, when he based himself in Westminster to conduct an influential preaching ministry, particularly at court. Although an old man by 1553, he was an obvious victim for MARY I, and was imprisoned, tried and burned at the stake in Oxford.

LAUD, WILLIAM *see* essay on page 494

LAUDER, HARRY (1870–1950), singer and comedian. Born in Portobello near Edinburgh, a factory worker and miner before becoming an entertainer, Lauder made his London debut at Gatti's Music Hall in 1900. A 'professional Scot', he always appeared in a kilt and glengarry. His songs, *I Love a Lassie, Roamin' in the Gloamin'*, *Stop Your Tickling Jock* and *The End of the Road*, brought him great success in Britain, the Empire and the USA, while his tours to entertain the troops in both world wars were equally popular.

LAUDERDALE, 2ND EARL AND 1ST DUKE OF *see* MAITLAND, JOHN

LAUGHTON, SIR JOHN KNOX (1830–1915), naval historian. Son of a Liverpool ship owner, educated at Cambridge, Laughton entered the navy in 1853 as a mathematics instructor. He saw extensive active service in the Baltic (1854–5) and on the China coast (1856–8) before teaching meteorology and marine surveying at Greenwich. Laughton, who began lecturing on naval history in 1876, started the systematic collection and study of primary material, founding the Navy Records Society in 1893. His pioneering work provided the foundation for Alfred Thayer Mahan's *Influence of Sea Power upon History*, published in 1890, and was quickly recognized as the naval equivalent of Clausewitz's *Vom Krieg* (On War).

LAUREL, ARTHUR STANLEY JEFFERSON (STAN) (1890–1965), comedian. Born in Lancs., he was understudy to Charlie CHAPLIN and so went to the USA in 1910. After his first film part in Hollywood in 1917, followed by unmemorable silent film comedies, he teamed up with Oliver Hardy, another slapstick comedian, from Atlanta (Georgia). Laurel and Hardy made over 100 films, including *Liberty* (1929), *The Music Box* (1932) and *Way Out West* (1937). Their catchphrase was Ollie's reproof to Stan, 'this is another fine mess you've got me into'.

LAURENCE OF LUDLOW (?–1294), wool merchant. He was the controversial head of the Shrewsbury-based firm founded by his brother Nicholas of Ludlow, the richest family business in England in the thirteenth century, when wool was the country's chief export. In 1281 he bought and subsequently extended Stokesay Castle (Salop.). In 1294 he allegedly persuaded the English wool merchants to agree to EDWARD I's demand that they pay a heavy export duty on wool, the notorious *maltote* (bad tax): it was thought no more than he deserved when he died in a shipwreck later that year.

LAURENTIUS (?–619), Archbishop of Canterbury (604/10–19). The second Archbishop of Canterbury and St AUGUSTINE's nominee as his successor. He lived through the great crisis for the

continued on page 495

LAUD, WILLIAM (1573–1645)
Archbishop of Canterbury (1633–45)

Laud was the son of a prosperous clothier of Reading (Berks.), and he went to St John's College, Oxford (1589), because of its link with Reading Grammar School. He had a deep affection for his college, spending 32 years there and becoming its President in 1611; his most lasting and beautiful memorial is the college's Canterbury Quad (1631–6). St John's was notorious as a college where Roman Catholic sympathizers were still quietly welcome, and this may have influenced Laud in developing his distinctively ceremonialist and sacramentalist faith, emphasizing the role of the priesthood and centrality of the Eucharist. He spent his career single-mindedly promoting this brand of Catholicism within the Church of England, and fiercely combating the Reformed Protestantism and the influence of CALVIN which had been dominant since 1559. He benefited from influential patrons, first Richard NEILE and later George VILLIERS, Duke of Buckingham (to whom he was devoted); he began his career in the wider Church when he was appointed Dean of Gloucester (1616). Straight away he plunged into controversy by restoring the cathedral communion table to the position of the medieval altar. In 1621 he finally left Oxford when Buckingham secured him the bishopric of St David's. In 1622 he held a confrontational discussion with the Jesuit evangelist John Percy (known as Fisher the Jesuit) in the presence of JAMES I and the future Prince CHARLES I, maintaining his opposition to the Church of Rome, but recognizing it alongside the Church of England as part of the universal Church (he published this 'Conference' in 1639). Charles was an enthusiastic admirer of his, finding a soulmate who believed in order, hierarchy and unquestioning obedience to royal authority; in 1626 Laud became Bishop of Bath and Wells, moving to London in 1628. He was appointed Chancellor of Oxford University in 1630, was a generous benefactor to the university and took a great interest in reforming its statutes. By now he had outstripped Neile as the leader of the Arminian party in the Church; his preferment culminated in the archbishopric in 1633, and from 1635 he was Charles's leading Councillor. He was determined to impose his brand of conformity on the Church, using Star Chamber and the ecclesiastical High Commission to impose often savage penalties on opponents (*see* BURTON, HENRY and PRYNNE, WILLIAM); he harassed reluctant older bishops into disciplinary campaigns, particularly to reorder church interiors to emphasize the place of the altar, and he vigorously sought to recover lost Church revenues, infuriating large numbers of landowners by his efforts. He encouraged a group of sympathizers among the Scottish bishops to compile the 1637 Scottish Prayer Book, a liturgy which reworked the English Book of Common Prayer in a Catholic direction; Scots fury sparked the two Bishops' Wars (1639–40) in which Charles's English armies were ignominiously defeated. Laud was widely blamed for the disaster, yet with Charles's encouragement he pressed ahead in the Convocation of Canterbury in 1640, enacting new canons (i.e. an ecclesiastical law-code) enforcing his beliefs and proclaiming the 'divine right of kings'. These also ordered clergy and graduates to swear that the Church hierarchy (listed, but suspiciously tailed with a vague 'etc.') accorded with the word of God. Amid acute national tension, the oath fuelled conspiracy theories of an Arminian plot to introduce the Pope. An obvious target for popular revenge when Charles's regime collapsed, in 1641 Laud was imprisoned in the Tower, although the House of Lords refused to accept an attempt to impeach him. He remained in prison, almost a forgotten figure, until he was put on trial in 1644; his old enemies hastened to repeat their grievances against him, the Westminster Parliament passed an act of attainder, and he was executed on charges of treason in 1645.

Laud remains a controversial figure, much revered by the nineteenth-century leaders of the Oxford Movement and still a hero to many High Church Anglicans. Some revisionist historians, notably Kevin Sharpe and Julian Davies, deny that he was the driving force behind the religious programme of the 1630s, and merely acted as a willing agent for the King's policies. This may be to take too seriously Laud's public affirmation of his secondary role in bringing about the radical change of direction in the Church. Personally kindly and austere, but also a hypersensitive and lonely bachelor (his innermost thoughts are rather embarrassingly revealed in his surviving private diary), he was never prepared to recognize that there might be other ways than his of viewing the Church of England, or that those who disagreed with him were anything else than enemies, usually to be dismissed with the abusive label 'Puritan'. He never appreciated the importance of conciliation or even of favourably publicizing his vision of a Catholic Church free from Roman Catholic error.

H. R. Trevor-Roper, Archbishop Laud, 1573–1645 (1940)

Christian mission when King ETHELBERT of Kent was succeeded by his pagan son EADBALD. Unlike his colleague St MELLITUS of London, Laurentius remained at his post; his miraculous conversion of Eadbald seemingly preserving the Roman mission in England.

LAVERY, JOHN (1856–1941), artist. Born in Belfast and orphaned young, Lavery was apprenticed to a Glasgow photographer in 1871, taking art classes in the evening. He moved to London, Paris (1881) and then the village community of Grez-sur-Loing where he met 'the Glasgow Boys', a group of artists excluded from their city's artistic establishment, who were to be important not only in revivifying Scottish art, but also as an influence on European painting, the Vienna Secessionists in particular. Returning to Glasgow in 1885, he turned to portraiture: in 1888 he was commissioned to paint *The State Visit of Queen Victoria to the Glasgow International Exhibition*. The success of the work established his career: he divided his time between studios in Britain and Tangiers, was elected Vice-President of the International Society of Painters, Gravers and Sculptors (WHISTLER was the president) and journeyed to the USA in the 1930s to paint Hollywood film stars.

LAW, ANDREW BONAR (1858–1923), politician and Prime Minister (1922–3). Born in Canada of an Ulster Presbyterian father and Scottish mother, he was brought to Scotland after his mother's death and at 16 started work in her family's ironwork business. He entered Parliament in 1900 when his strong pro-British Empire stand during the Boer War won Glasgow Blackfriars from the Liberals. In the sparse ranks of able Conservative MPs after the 1906 Liberal landslide, Bonar Law's support for Tariff Reform, the attempt to transform the Empire into a unified trading bloc, enlarging the market for industrial goods, earned him a reputation as a tough debater. When BALFOUR resigned in 1911, he succeeded to the leadership after the deadlock in the war of succession between Austen CHAMBERLAIN and Walter Long. As LLOYD GEORGE perceptively remarked, 'the fools have stumbled on the right man by accident'. As Conservative leader in opposition Bonar Law's task was to unite the party which meant supporting Ulster's resistance to Home Rule.

On the outbreak of the First World War the Irish Question was subsumed to that of winning the war with Germany, and Bonar Law agreed to suspend the usual parliamentary opposition for the duration. When a Liberal/Conservative coalition was formed under ASQUITH in May 1915, as Conservative leader he could have expected a senior post, such as Chancellor of the Exchequer or Minister of Munitions. In fact Asquith decided to offer him neither, but rather the second-rank post of Colonial Secretary, which was a personal slight to Bonar Law and meant that his party received only one major Cabinet post out of the six on offer (Balfour at the Admiralty). That this was a deliberate slight is undoubted, but the reason is less clear: it was partly to do with Asquith's low estimation of Bonar Law's abilities, partly to do with the taint that a firm with which he was involved had been trading in iron ore for armaments with Germany in Aug. 1914, partly because Asquith's own position in the wartime Cabinet would be strengthened if its Conservative members had no clear leader, and partly because Bonar Law's own party was less than totally enthusiastic about its leader. It was not until the fall of Asquith in Dec. 1916 that he moved to the political centre stage when he was appointed Chancellor of the Exchequer by the new Prime Minister, Lloyd George, and effectively his second-in-command. In this role he was an able manager of the wartime coalition, sustaining it into the peace until he resigned because of ill health in March 1921 and was replaced by Austen Chamberlain who was not able to restrain the growing tide of Conservative anti-coalitionists. At the Carlton Club meeting on 19 Oct. 1922 Bonar Law, fearful that if he did not act the Conservative Party would be irrevocably split, reluctantly put himself at the head of the Conservative revolt against the coalition, pledging a quiet political life for the country, and this ensured a second term in office. In May 1923 ill health again led to his resignation and he died seven months later. He was buried in Westminster Abbey, the grave of the 'unknown Prime Minister' close to that of the Unknown Warrior.

LAW, EDMUND (1703–87), theologian. Law's liberal theological views helped shape those of a reforming generation. His *Theory of Religion* (1745) argued that as humanity's knowledge progressed in other fields it advanced its understanding of religion, both natural and revealed enjoying 'divine education'. His other controversial beliefs included that the soul was immortal but slept between death and resurrection. At Cambridge Law was Master of Peterhouse and Professor of Moral Philosophy, and became Bishop of Carlisle in 1768. He supported Francis BLACKBURNE's petition of 1772, writing after the petition's rejection that it was unreasonable for the clergy to be expected to make any promise other than that they would observe the liturgy of the Church, without necessarily believing in its doctrines. Law's rational religion never led him to conclusions that forced him out of the Church, but he was an influence on others who did, such as Theophilus LINDSEY.

LAW, EDWARD (1st Baron Ellenborough) (1750–1818), lawyer. A Fellow of Peterhouse, Cambridge, where his father, Edmund LAW was Master in 1771, he was called to the Bar in 1780 and built up a large practice. Law was leading counsel for the defence of Warren HASTINGS, and won his acquittal in 1795 after a seven-year trial. He was assistant prosecutor in the trials of Thomas HARDY, HORNE TOOKE and several other radicals, establishing his conservative reputation, and in 1802 became Lord Chief Justice and a peer. He defended the suspension of *habeas corpus* and allied himself with GEORGE III as an opponent of Catholic relief, contributing to the end of William GRENVILLE's coalition in 1807. He was an advocate of the full range of corporal and capital punishments, particularly the pillory, but after sentencing Lord Cochrane to an hour in the pillory for defrauding the stock exchange in 1814 faced such an outcry that he could not oppose its abolition.

LAW, EDWARD (1st Earl of Ellenborough) (1790–1871), Governor General of India. Appointed Governor General in 1841 in succession to Auckland (*see* EDEN, GEORGE), Ellenborough had been a vocal and spirited Tory politician. Although he declared his objective to be peace, his brief tenure saw retribution against Afghanistan, Sind's annexation and a ferocious attack on Gwalior. The East India Co., incensed by his disdain for their instructions, recalled him in 1845 in defiance of the government's wishes. For all his military aggression, Ellenborough also pursued fiscal reforms and enlightened trade policies. In 1846 he was briefly First Lord of the Admiralty under Robert PEEL; as President of the East India Co.'s Board of Control, in the wake of the Mutiny (1857–8), he took the blame in the criticism led by DISRAELI of the annexation of Oudh under Charles CANNING and resigned.

LAW, JOHN (1671–1729), financier. The son of an Edinburgh goldsmith, he fled Scotland in 1694 to avoid punishment for murder. Apparently serving as secretary to the British resident in Amsterdam, he took a keen interest in the workings of the Bank of Amsterdam. He returned in 1701 to a Scotland reeling under the impact of the failure of the Darien scheme (*see* DOUGLAS, JAMES); he lobbied the Scots Parliament with proposals for financial reform, including a simplified taxation system, paper money representing not only gold and silver but land and other commodities, and a council of trade to co-ordinate investment in industry. Having failed to get his ideas adopted, he toured Europe as a gambler, until in 1716 the French Regent awarded him letters patent for the *Banque Générale*, with the power to issue paper money that was to be immune to the variations government brought about by manipulating the content of metallic currency. Law was able to advance loans at a low rate of interest and expanded the French economy; he supervised a series of mergers that between 1717 and 1720 amalgamated the *Banque* (nationalized as the *Banque Royale* in 1717), the Mint and the French overseas trading companies into one entity, known as the System. Law's abilities made him enemies, and his declared aim of breaking British dominance in trade aligned him with opponents of the Triple Alliance of 1716–17 (which had revolutionized international relations by bringing France, Britain and the United Provinces together). In 1719 Law undertook to pay off the national debt and was given control of government revenue, but the *Banque*'s notes were now subject to the same fluctuations as the metallic currency, and by early 1720 shareholders in the bank were converting their vastly inflated shareholdings back into coin. The System collapsed and Law left France, eventually dying in Venice.

LAW, WILLIAM (1686–1761), religious writer. Educated, ordained and elected a Fellow at Emmanuel College, Cambridge, and a devoted Tory, he was suspended from his degrees in 1713 for provocative allusions to the Old Pretender (*see* STUART, JAMES EDWARD) in a speech. On the accession of GEORGE I he refused to take the Oaths of Abjuration and Allegiance. He was also an active participant in the Bangorian controversy touched off by the writing and preaching of Benjamin HOADLY, attacking Hoadly's rationalistic position. Influenced by mystical writers, he published a practical treatise on Christian perfection in 1723 and, five years later, *A Serious Call to a Devout and Holy Life*, which achieved a high reputation as a devotional manual and was reprinted numerous times. On retirement in 1740 to his home at King's Cliffe (Northants.), he established a small religious community to live under a devotional regime of regular prayers and church attendance. He influenced Charles and John WESLEY and other early Evangelicals.

LAWES, SIR JOHN (1814–99), agricultural scientist. Educated at Eton and Oxford, in 1834 he inherited the family estate in Rothamsted, St Albans (Herts.), where he began his lifelong scientific research into agriculture. By 1843 he had opened a London-based company for manufacturing a superphosphate fertilizer (bones treated with sulphuric acid), a firm that eventually produced over 40,000 tons of the fertilizer each year. In 1843 he also established the renowned agricultural research station at Rothamsted, where he began working with Joseph H. Gilbert on detailed scientific experiments, notably the effect of fertilizers on crops and the economical feeding of domestic animals. From the sale of his lucrative fertilizer business Lawes endowed Rothamsted research which continues today.

LAWGOCH, OWAIN (also known as Owain of the Red Hand) (?–1378), Welsh chief. A great-nephew of LLYWELYN AP GRUFFUDD, he laid claim to the principality of Wales. During the Hundred Years War both the French and the Castilian governments were willing to support his cause. The English were sufficiently worried to have him assassinated.

LAWMAN (OR LAYAMON) (*fl.* 1200), poet. The first to write of King ARTHUR and the British past in English he was the first author of a long narrative poem in English since the Norman Conquest. His 16,000 line *Brut* was an amplified version of the *Roman de Brut* by WACE. Although nothing is known about him except what he cares to tell us in the poem (he was a priest with a living at Areley (Worcs.) 'at the lovely church by the Severn') he is significant for taking aristocratic literature in French to a wider audience.

LAWRENCE, D(AVID) H(ERBERT) (1885–1930), novelist and poet. Son of a coalminer from Eastwood (Notts.) and an ex-schoolmistress, he was influenced by his ambitious mother to gain a university education and become a teacher. His first novel *The White Peacock* was published in 1911; his most popular, *Sons and Lovers*, in 1913. In 1912 he met Frieda Weekley (née von Richthofen), the wife of his former professor. They eloped to Germany, married when Frieda was divorced and led a penurious, peripatetic life together. The sexual explicitness of *The Rainbow* (1915) led to a prosecution for indecency, and from 1919 Lawrence and Frieda lived in Italy, the USA and Mexico. *Women in Love* (1920) and *Lady Chatterley's Lover* (1928) were both published privately. It was only in 1960, following a new Obscenity Act, that a celebrated High Court judgement allowed Penguin Books to publish an unexpurgated edition of the latter. Lawrence died of tuberculosis in France aged 44. His short stories have always been highly regarded, while his novels have become part of the canon of English literature.

LAWRENCE, JOHN (1st Baron Lawrence) (1811–79), Viceroy of India. A distinguished Indian civil servant, joining the East India Co. in 1830, he laid the foundations for the so-called Punjab school of administration, identifying closely with the traditional interests of the peasantry. He was at odds in this policy with his brother and fellow commissioner in the Punjab, Sir Henry Lawrence (1806–57), who resigned in 1853 and was subsequently killed at Lucknow in the Mutiny. Yet in the Mutiny the Punjab stayed loyal to the Raj, a vindication of John Lawrence's policy, and in 1863 he was made Viceroy. Essentially an administrator, Lawrence's tenure (1863–9) was marked by improvements in irrigation, railways, urban sanitation, famine relief and defence.

LAWRENCE, STEPHEN (1974–93), murder victim. On the evening of 22 April 1993, Lawrence, a black British student, was stabbed to death at a bus stop in Eltham, south London, by a gang of white youths whom he did not know. Despite information received, no one was charged until finally Stephen's parents, Neville and Doreen Lawrence, instigated a private prosecution of five youths: the case failed. More than five years after Stephen's death, the report of an inquiry to the Home Secretary, Jack Straw, in Feb. 1999, was a damning indictment of more than police incompetence and lack of leadership: it drew attention to 'institutionalized racism' within the Metropolitan Police and other forces and institutions across the country. The 'Lawrence case' has become a defining moment in confronting Britain's history of race relations, and has led to calls for widespread reform.

LAWRENCE, T(HOMAS) E(DWARD) ('LAWRENCE OF ARABIA') (1888–1935), soldier and writer. He was born to well-off Anglo-Irish gentry and educated at Oxford. Working as an archaeologist in the Middle East at the outbreak of the First World War, Lawrence joined the Arab Bureau in Egypt in 1914 and, two years later, was assigned as an adviser to Prince Faisal, who was leading the Arab uprising against the Turks. He gained Faisal's confidence and helped him to weld the Arabs into the effective fighting force that seized the Red Sea port of Aqaba in 1917 and mounted an increasingly effective guerrilla war against Turkish communications on the British flank in Palestine. At the Versailles peace conference, Lawrence sought to secure pledges for Arab independence but was frustrated by the extension of imperial control over much of the former Turkish empire. His account of his campaigns *Seven Pillars of Wisdom* (private edition, 1926; abridged version published as *The Revolt in the Desert*, 1927) was hailed as a classic, but has been criticized by some for exaggerating his own role. A tortured individual, scarred by his wartime experiences, he joined the RAF in 1922 under an assumed name. He was killed in a motorcycle accident in 1935. He has remained an irresistibly complex subject for writers and a romantic, if little understood, hero to the public.

LAWSON, NIGEL (Baron Lawson of Blaby) (1932–), politician. Lawson was a key figure during the later years of THATCHER's government, being described by her at one stage as 'indispensable'. Lawson came late into political life, having spent his early career as a financial journalist, and his political career centred on economics. He was elected to the Commons in Feb. 1974. He spoke on Treasury matters in opposition, and became Financial Secretary to the Treasury under Geoffrey HOWE in 1979; the two men made a radical team and provided much of the thrust of Thatcherism in the form of monetarism and tax-cutting. As Secretary of State for Energy (1981–3), Lawson helped develop the idea of privatization as a way of de-nationalizing industries such as British Gas.

He made his greatest impact as Thatcher's Chancellor of the Exchequor after 1983 through a programme of income tax cuts and financial deregulation measures presiding over the so-called 'Lawson boom', in which the stock market and house prices rose to dizzy heights and 'popular capitalism' seemed, in the era of 'yuppies' (young, upwardly mobile professionals), to be thriving. It came to an end in Oct. 1987 when the stock market crashed. Lawson's tough financial restraints were later blamed for making the subsequent recession even worse than it need have been. His decision to peg sterling to the deutschmark in 1988 produced tension between him and Thatcher, which culminated in his resignation in Oct. 1989, citing Thatcher's reliance on the economist Alan Walters for advice, rather than her Chancellor.

LAYARD, SIR AUSTEN HENRY (1817–94), archaeologist. In Nov. 1845 Layard, who had no formal archaeological training, began excavating two huge mounds that stood between the Tigris and the Euphrates and by nightfall he had 'discovered' Nineveh, a six-and-a-half-acre Assyrian palace built in the seventh century BC. His books about this excavation, *Nineveh and its Remains* (1848–9) and *Nineveh and Babylon* (1853), caused a sensation.

LAYER, CHRISTOPHER (1683–1723), Jacobite conspirator. A barrister, he visited James Edward STUART in Rome in 1721 and with over-optimistic forecasts of support gained assent for his unrealistic plans to seize key public buildings in London, murder GEORGE I, his ministers and army officers and on this basis restore the Stuarts. The Pretender recognized the better-planned ATTERBURY Plot as the more credible and gave it more encouragement. Nonetheless, Layer continued to scheme until in Oct. 1722 he was arrested, tried, found guilty and hanged, drawn and quartered.

LE SUEUR, HUBERT (?1595–?1650), sculptor. Probably born in Paris, he arrived in England in 1628 and worked much at the court of CHARLES I. His bronze equestrian statue of Charles, commissioned in 1630 by Richard WESTON, Earl of Portland, was buried during the Interregnum and set up at Charing Cross only in 1674.

LEACH, BERNARD (1887–1979), potter. The son of a colonial judge, he spent his early life in the Far East. He was trained at the Slade School of Art (1903–8) and returned to Japan, where he was apprenticed to the sixth generation of Kenzen potters (1911). He established his pottery workshop in St Ives (Cornw.) in 1920 but continued to visit Japan and China, and his work combined both English and Eastern traditions. His *A Potter's Book* (1940) was a bible to a generation.

LEACH, SIR EDMUND (1910–80), social anthropologist. Leach, who read mathematics and engineering at Cambridge and worked for five years in China (1932–7), then studied anthropology at the London School of Economics (LSE) under MALINOWSKI, and in 1939 went to do fieldwork in Burma. After the Second World War (which he fought in Burma) he returned to teach anthropology at the LSE, moving to Cambridge in 1957 where he became Professor of Social Anthropology (1972–9) and Provost of King's College (1966–79). He destabilized anthropological orthodoxies about what societies are and how we need to think about them in *Rethinking Anthropology* (1961) and *Social Anthropology* (1982). His work on ritual and myth, *Genesis of Myth and Other Essays* (1969), and later on language and communication also criticized anthropologists who investigate the differences between societies rather than their underlying structures.

LEAKEY, LOUIS (1903–87), **MARY DOUGLAS** (née Nicol) (1913–96) and **RICHARD** (1944–), archaeologists. Louis Leakey was born and raised in a Kikuyu village in Kenya, where his parents were missionaries. He studied Kikuyu, anthropology, archaeology and palaeontology at Cambridge University (1923–6), led archaeological expeditions to East Africa (1926–35) and was curator of the Coryndon Memorial Museum, Nairobi (1945–61). He produced his best-known work with his wife Mary, a distinguished archaeologist. In 1942 they discovered the remains of one of the oldest-known apes on a site near Lake Victoria. Between 1959 and 1964 Louis and Mary discovered, in Olduvai Gorge, Tanganyika, the remains of *Australopithecus boisei*, a tool-making hominid dated at approximately 1.8 million years old, *Homo habilis*, a 1.7-million-year-old hominid, and *Homo erectus*, which Louis regarded as a direct ancestor of *Homo sapiens*. In 1967 Louis unearthed fossils of an ape 14 million years old, and nine years later Mary discovered hominid footprints which suggested that man's ancestors walked upright 3.75 million years ago. The Leakeys revolutionized our understanding of human origins, and their work showed that upright man originated in Africa and not Asia as originally believed and that he first appeared much earlier than previously thought. Their son Richard Leakey is a leading palaeo-anthropologist who in 1975 discovered the remains of the *Homo erectus*, dated at 1.6 million years old.

LEAN, DAVID (1908–91), film-maker. Lean started at the bottom in the film business in 1928 as a clapper-board boy with Gaumont Pictures and, working his way up the industry, in 1942 he co-directed (with Noel COWARD) *In Which We Serve*. A string of successes followed, including *Brief Encounter* (1946) and adaptations of DICKENS's *Great Expectations* (1946) and *Oliver Twist* (1948). He won Oscars for *The Bridge on the River Kwai* (starring Alec Guinness, 1957) and *Lawrence of Arabia* (starring Peter O'Toole, 1962); equally ambitious were *Dr Zhivago* (1965) and an adaptation of E. M. FORSTER's *A Passage to India* (1994).

LEAPOR, MARY (1722–46), poet. Her humble Northants. parents attempted to repress their daughter's literary ambitions, sending her out as a cook and then making her work as a seamstress. Her poems and plays circulated in manuscript and in 1745 the daughter of a former rector of Brackley, Bridget Freemantle, arranged for them to be published by subscription. They appeared in 1747 a few months after Mary's death; a second volume was published by Samuel RICHARDSON in 1751. Mary Leapor's short life and humble origins ensured her a place in eighteenth-century literary mythology as a 'natural' poet although she consciously followed the structural example of POPE.

LEAR, EDWARD (1812–88), writer and artist. The second youngest of 21 children, Lear was also an epileptic which, in Victorian times, was seen as shameful and meant that he led an isolated life with bouts of depression, nevertheless enchanting and amusing his readers both then and now with his comic verses. His drawings of the parrots in London's zoological gardens were published as *Illustrations of the Family of Psittacidae, or Parrots* when he was only 19. As a result, the Earl of Derby commissioned him to sketch the creatures in the menagerie at Knowsley Hall (Lancs.) and, while engaged in this task, Lear also wrote and illus-trated comic verse for the Earl's children, which was published as *The Book of Nonsense* (1846). Several more volumes appeared, containing such eternal childhood favourites as 'The Owl and the Pussycat', 'The Jumblies' and 'The Courtship of the Yongy-Bonghy-Bo'. Lear was also an accomplished artist: he took painting lessons from Holman HUNT, was engaged to teach Queen VICTORIA to draw and published a number of superbly illustrated books of his travels.

LEAVIS, F(RANK) R(AYMOND) (1895–1978), literary critic. Born and educated in Cambridge, Leavis was appointed lecturer at Downing College in 1935 and taught at Cambridge until 1964. In 1929 he married Queenie Roth, and as intellectual soul-mates their critical output was extensive, including the publication of his *New Bearings in English Poetry* (1932), the founding of the quarterly periodical *Scrutiny* and Queenie's *Fiction and the Reading Public*. A rigorous critic of the dilettante elitism characteristic of the Bloomsbury group, F. R. Leavis followed in the footsteps of nineteenth-century cultural critics like Matthew ARNOLD, and through his writings and editorship of *Scrutiny* sought to uphold high literary and cultural standards. In his early works, *Mass Civilization and Minority Culture* (1930) and *Education and the University* (1943) he argued for a critical intellectual elite whose task was to ensure the continuity and preservation of English culture and literature in the face of the levelling-down influences of mass media, advertising, mass production and standardization. In his most lasting work, *The Great Tradition* (1948), he sought to define the central canon of English literature.

LECKY, WILLIAM (1838–1903), historian. From a landed family in Carlow, Lecky contemplated taking Anglican orders before undergoing a crisis of faith. His first book, *Leaders of Public Opinion in Ireland* (1861, revised periodically throughout his career), looked back nostalgically to the aristocratic patriotism of Henry GRATTAN and lamented that the landed classes had ceded political influence to the Catholic priesthood. *The Rise of Rationalism in Europe* (1865) and *History of European Morals from Augustus to Charlemagne* (1869) were positivist-influenced attempts at sociological history, but Lecky's major achievement was the Irish section of his multi-volume *History of England in the Eighteenth Century* (1878–90), later published separately as *History of Ireland in the Eighteenth Century*. Despite his nostalgia for Grattan, Lecky fiercely opposed the Land League and Parnellite nationalism (*see* PARNELL, CHARLES STEWART) and served as Unionist MP for Trinity College, Dublin (1895–1902). His last work, *Democracy and Liberty* (1896), laments the eclipse of mid Victorian elite liberalism by the extension of the suffrage. While Lecky's history was criticized by later nationalists for concentrating on the Anglo-Irish elite and neglecting Gaelic culture, it marked a milestone in Irish professional history and set the framework through which eighteenth-century Ireland was viewed by scholars until very recently.

LEE, HENRY (1530–1610), courtier. After royal service in the armoury of HENRY VIII and EDWARD VI, he was knighted in 1553; he served ELIZABETH I as diplomat and courtier, becoming her Master of the Ordnance in 1580. From 1571 he organized her tournaments, acting as her personal champion up to 1590 particularly at her Accession Day tilts, promoting these into major theatrical spectacles. He thus played a crucial role in developing Elizabethan romantic chivalry.

LEE, JANET (JENNIE) (Baroness Lee of Asheridge) (1904–88), politician. The daughter of a Fifes. coal-miner, educated at Edinburgh University, Lee became in 1929 the youngest woman ever to enter the House of Commons, although she lost her North Lanark seat in 1931. She married Aneurin BEVAN in 1934 and temporarily forsook her own political career, but in 1945 she returned to the Commons as MP for Cannock. Lee was a member of Labour's National Executive Committee from 1958 to 1970.

After Bevan's death in 1960 she was Under-Secretary of State at the Department of Education (1965–7) and was instrumental in founding the Open University. She was appointed the first Minister of State with responsibility for the Arts (1967–70).

LEE KUAN YEW (1923–), politician. Born to a Straits Chinese family and educated at Raffles College (forerunner of the University of Malaya) and in Britain, Lee joined the Malayan Forum in London in 1949, founded to discuss Malaya's future. From that the People's Action Party was formed in 1954, with Lee its first Secretary General. Practising law in Singapore from 1950, he espoused labour causes and anti-colonial activism. Often regarded as a communist stooge, he brought the party to power in 1959 before breaking with the hard Left. With considerable reluctance, in the face of political difficulties with the alliance controlling the rest of what was becoming independent Malaysia, Lee led Singapore into political separation and then to great prosperity, promoting capitalism with a strong, sometimes domineering, State presence.

LEE, LAURIE (1914–98), poet and writer. Born in Slad (Glos.), where he attended the village school. The Cotswold people and countryside suffuse his

poet's evocation of his childhood, *Cider with Rosie* (1959). *As I Walked Out One Midsummer Morning* (1969) tells of his wanderings in London and on the continent, which culminated in his arrival in Spain during the Civil War.

LEE, ROWLAND (?–1543), administrator. From Northumberland and Cambridge-educated, he entered Thomas WOLSEY's service and was his agent alongside Thomas CROMWELL in suppressing smaller monasteries in 1528–9; becoming a royal chaplain, he was made Bishop of Coventry and Lichfield and also Lord President of the Council in the Marches of Wales in 1534. Granted unprecedented powers and lacking enthusiasm for the Welsh, he was energetic in suppressing lawlessness in Wales and left a fearsome reputation for judicial savagery.

LEEDS, 1ST DUKE OF *see* OSBORNE, SIR THOMAS

LEESE, SIR OLIVER (1894–1978), soldier. Commissioned directly into the Coldstream Guards, he was three times wounded on the Western Front during the First World War. In 1940 Leese was attached to the British Expeditionary Force (BEF) in France, helped plan the Dunkirk evacuation, and in 1941 raised and trained the Guards Armoured Division. Appointed to command XXX Corps at El Alamein in 1942, Leese played a pivotal role in the battle. In Oct. 1944 he was made Commander of Allied Land Forces in South East Asia. When he attempted to create jobs for his friends by sacking 14th Army Commander SLIM, a successful 'outsider' to the military establishment, Leese was himself sacked. The incident remains a *cause célèbre*.

LEFÈVRE D'ÉTAPLES, JACQUES (*c.* 1455–1536), scholar *see* ANNE BOLEYN

LEGGE, WILLIAM (2nd Earl of Dartmouth) (1731–1801), politician. He served as President of the Board of Trade under Rockingham (*see* WATSON-WENTWORTH, CHARLES); under his step-brother NORTH he combined this post with that of Secretary of State for the Colonies. In 1775 he became Lord Privy Seal, a post he retained until North's fall in 1782. Distinguished among the hardliners in the Cabinet for his relatively conciliatory attitude to America, he nonetheless supported the government's coercive policies. A pious man of Evangelical leanings, he was a friend of Selina HASTINGS, Countess of Huntingdon.

LEHMANN, JOHN (1907–87), magazine editor and publisher. He was the younger brother of the novelist Rosamond Lehmann. Although his poetry is largely forgotten today, his influence on

English writing is apparent. *Penguin New Writing* (1940–50) published 40 issues under his editorship, several of which sold 100,000 copies, and introduced the writing of Roy Fuller, Laurie LEE and Henry Reed among others. The publishing house of Lehmann (1946–51) brought Sartre's *Nausea* and Saul Bellow's *Dangling Man* to British readers.

LEICESTER, EARL OF, 8TH *see* THOMAS OF LANCASTER; **14TH** *see* DUDLEY, ROBERT

LEICESTER OF HOLKHAM, 1ST EARL *see* COKE, THOMAS

LEIGH-MALLORY, SIR TRAFFORD (1892–1944), airman. Son of an Anglican clergyman and older brother of George L. Mallory (lost on the Everest expedition of 1924), he was educated at Cambridge and fought with the Royal Flying Corps in France. Commanding No. 12 Fighter Group in the summer of 1940, Leigh-Mallory successfully challenged DOWDING's refusal to employ large fighter wings against the Germans. Mallory took over No. 11 Group, and in the spring of 1941 commenced large-scale offensive operations over north-eastern France. As Commander of the Allied Expeditionary Air Force for the liberation of Europe, Leigh-Mallory controlled more than 9,000 warplanes, and by 6 June 1944 had achieved total domination of the skies over northern France. He was killed in an air crash in Nov. 1944.

LEIGHTON, FREDERIC (1st Baron Leighton) (1830–96), artist. The gifted, privileged epitome of the Greek revivalists, Leighton spent much of his childhood travelling in Europe. His first major work, *Cimabue's Madonna Carried through the Streets of Florence* (1853–5), was exhibited at the Royal Academy and bought by Queen VICTORIA. The Victorian turn away from medievalism towards a fascination with the classical world brought Leighton pre-eminence with works like *Venus Disrobing* (1866–7), *Hercules Wrestling with Death for the Body of Alcestis* (c. 1867–71), his bronze sculpture of *An Athlete Struggling with a Python* (1874–7), *The Garden of the Hesperides* (1892) and the (then) hugely popular *Flaming June* (1895). He also painted more than 40 portraits and the frescos for the South Kensington Museum on the theme *The Arts of Industry as Applied to War and Peace* (1878–86). He was a towering president of the Royal Academy from 1878 until his death (he is the central figure in FRITH's painting *The Private View of the Royal Academy in 1881*), and was the first professional artist to be knighted. His exquisitely decorated home in Holland Park (London), an 'aesthete's palace' with its Moorish hall, is now open to the public.

LEIGHTON, ROBERT (1611–84), Archbishop of Glasgow. Ordained in 1641, he was Principal of Edinburgh University from 1653, and in 1661, in an effort to reconcile Presbyterians and Episcopalians, accepted the diocese of Dunblane, becoming Archbishop in 1670. Discouraged by the government's continuing repression of religious opponents, he resigned the archbishopric in 1674. A notable scholar of Stoic sympathies, he was an admirer both of John CALVIN and of medieval devotional writers, and left his splendid library to Dunblane.

LELAND, JOHN (c. 1502–52), historian. Born in London and a student at Cambridge, Oxford and Paris, he became a royal chaplain c. 1530, and in 1533–4 was given a royal order to search out antiquities throughout England. He spent six years travelling, describing the places which he visited and vainly urging comprehensive measures to save monastic libraries from the Dissolution. He wrote patriotic poetry and a treatise against the Pope (c. 1540); his admirer John BALE claimed that he spoke 10 languages. His labour in gathering his research material (much of which survives) led to mental collapse from 1550.

LELY, SIR PETER (1618–80), painter. Born in Germany of Dutch parentage, he came to England around 1643. Lely, formerly Pieter van der Faes, was employed by the Earl of Northumberland; other patrons included several Royalist families and Oliver CROMWELL. In 1661 he was appointed principal painter to CHARLES II. He maintained a busy portrait studio, where he himself painted the heads but usually left everything else to assistants. His most famous series was of the ladies of Charles II's court, known as the Hampton Court Beauties. He also amassed an unrivalled private collection of old masters. He was knighted in 1680. He was unchallenged as the premier portraitist of the day, but at his death KNELLER was emerging as a competitor.

LEMASS, SEAN (1899–1971), Taoiseach (Irish Prime Minister). He fought in the 1916 Easter Rising and Anglo-Irish War and for the anti-Treaty Republicans in the Irish Civil War (1922–3, during which his brother Noel was killed in police custody). Member of the Dáil for South Dublin (1924–69), Lemass played a leading role in building up the massively effective Fianna Fáil Party organization after 1926. A successful Minister for Industry and Commerce, he presided over a tariff-led policy of encouraging industrial development, and from the late 1940s was regarded as DE VALERA's heir apparent, though he did not become party leader (and Taoiseach) until 1959. In response to the economic failures of the late 1940s and 1950s he moved away from economic nationalism and fiscal conservatism to greater reliance on economic planning, dismantling tariff barriers and moving towards membership of the European Economic Community (not achieved until 1973). He and his principal adviser, WHITAKER, became associated with the economic boom and widening horizons of the 1960s. Lemass was seen as the symbol of Irish modernization and exalted at the expense of De Valera; recent historians, though less euphoric, still regard Lemass as outstandingly effective.

LENNON, JOHN (1940–80), musician. It would be difficult to over-estimate the importance of John Lennon and his group the Beatles to British pop music since the 1960s and to post-war popular culture in general. After a brief time at Liverpool Art College Lennon formed a band called the Quarry Men, which Paul MCCARTNEY and George Harrison joined. After playing in the clubs of Hamburg and Liverpool the band, renamed the Beatles (now joined by drummer Ringo Starr), released their first 'single', *Love Me Do*, in 1962. The album *Please Please Me* followed early in 1963: Lennon and McCartney wrote most of the album's songs themselves. The band achieved unprecedented popularity astonishingly quickly and 'Beatlemania' swept through Britain and America, dispelling the assumption that pop music was something best left to the Americans. The Prime Minister Harold WILSON capitalized on their popularity in 1965 by awarding the Beatles an MBE, ostensibly for the band's contribution to the export drive. (Lennon later returned his in protest again the Vietnam War.)

In 1964 Lennon published his first collection of stories, poems and sketches, *In His Own Write*, the same year as the release of the Beatles' first film, *A Hard Day's Night*. In the mid 1960s, the Beatles stopped playing live in order to devote more time to recording, and Lennon and McCartney started to compose songs more or less independently of each other. Lennon's output, both with the band and in his early solo recordings, became increasingly experimental, influenced by his relationship with the Japanese conceptual artist Yoko Ono, whom he married in 1969. The pair became politically active, staging a number of headline-grabbing stunts such as their famous 'love-ins' to promote causes like world peace and disarmament.

After the Beatles' split acrimoniously in 1970, Lennon continued his rather erratic solo recording career; his best-known single, *Imagine* (1970), was also the title of his most successful solo album. In Dec. 1980 Lennon was shot dead in New York (his home for most of the 1970s) by a deranged fan. The huge popularity of Lennon and the Beatles' music remains undiminished: the releases of the *Anthology* collections of rarities in 1995–6 returned the band to the top of the charts.

LENNOX, EARL OF, 13TH see STEWART, MATTHEW; **18TH AND 2ND DUKE OF** see STUART, LUDOVIC; **1ST DUKE OF** see STUART, ESMÉ

LENNOX, CAROLINE (1723–74), **EMILY** (1731–1814), **LOUISA** (1743–1821) and **SARAH** (1745–1826), aristocrats. Daughters of the 2nd Duke of Richmond, and thus born into the Whig elite, they lived through the period in which the Whigs changed from the natural party of government to more or less permanent opposition, a shift which left its mark on their own and their children's lives. Caroline eloped with up-and-coming young politician Henry FOX in 1744, and set up with him in Holland House. Her younger son, Charles James FOX, was to do much to imprint upon the Whig party the reforming character which it had in the early-nineteenth century. Emily, in another love match, married in 1747 James Fitzgerald, Earl of Kildare, later Duke of Leinster, member of the Irish Whig elite, whose estate lay near Dublin. On the death of her parents, she took charge of the upbringing of her two younger sisters. Louisa married a neighbouring wealthy Irishman, Thomas Conolly, in 1759. Sarah, sent to stay with her sister Caroline to be presented at court and find a husband, caught the eye of the Prince of Wales (the future GEORGE III), but he was sternly informed by his tutor, Lord Bute (*see* STUART, JOHN) that he must look outside Britain for a wife. In 1762 Sarah married the MP Charles Bunbury.

Two of the sisters subsequently embarked on rasher unions. By 1767 Sarah was having an affair with Lord William Gordon (older brother of Lord George GORDON), and bore his child. Thinking it the honest course to leave her husband, she did so; he divorced her (requiring an Act of Parliament, a rare event at the time) in 1776. Castigated by her older brother, Charles LENNOX, 3rd Duke of Richmond, Sarah lived for some years excluded from respectable society. Her second marriage, in 1781, to an army officer, George Napier, made her respectable once more. Emily meanwhile, most prolific mother of the sisters (in all she was to bear 22 children, of whom only half survived childhood), under the influence of Rousseau's notions of bringing up children, consigned her younger children to a 'bathing lodge' by the sea south of Dublin, under the care of a tutor, William Ogilvie, with whom she became romantically involved. After the death of her husband in 1773, she married Ogilvie. Both women did their best to advance their new husbands' fortunes, but were hampered by the King's distaste for the Whigs, although Ogilvie did become an Irish MP on the Duke of Leinster's interest.

Sarah's sons by Napier were to follow their father into the British army. Emily's son Lord Edward FITZGERALD, by contrast, threw in his fortunes with the United Irishmen (*see* TONE, WOLFE) and died in prison in 1798. After the death of her husband in 1803, Louisa responded to the challenges of the new era by setting up a day school, for Protestant and Catholic children, in which she strove to promote religious tolerance.

LENNOX, CHARLES (8th [3rd Lennox] Duke of Richmond and Lennox) (1735–1806), politician. Representative of that select but significant species, the 'radical dukes', he associated with Rockinghamite and Chathamite Whigs, and held office during their periods in power (*see* WATSON-WENTWORTH, CHARLES; PETTY, WILLIAM). In 1780, during the agitation by WYVILL's Association Movement, he laid before Parliament a proposal for annual Parliaments, manhood suffrage and equal electoral districts. He subsequently attached himself to PITT THE YOUNGER for whom he increasingly muted his reforming commitment.

LENNOX, CHARLOTTE (née Ramsay) (*c.* 1720–1804), novelist. Born in New York, she moved to England in 1735. To support herself and her dissolute husband, Alexander Lennox, she first acted and then wrote poems (published in 1747) and novels, the first of which was *Harriot Stuart* (1750). *The Female Quixote* (1752) is generally seen as her best work. Varying the theme of Cervantes's classic, it describes the misadventures of a young woman so steeped in traditional romances that she fails to understand the ways of the modern world. Winning enthusiastic praise from Samuel JOHNSON, Henry FIELDING and Samuel RICHARDSON, Lennox went on to produce a three-volume commentary on SHAKESPEARE's sources and to edit a women's magazine, the *Ladies' Museum* (1760–1).

LEOBA, ST (?–*c.* 780), Abbess of Tauberbischofsheim. An Englishwoman of aristocratic birth, she went to join St BONIFACE in Germany in *c.* 738. A great deal of information about her is contained in the life written 50 years after her death and in her letters. She appears to have been exceptionally learned and to have possessed an indomitable spirit. Her career illustrates the important role of women in the early Anglo-Saxon Church and, in this case, in its missionary activity.

LEOFRIC, Earl of Mercia (*c.* 1023–57). A member of a prominent English family, he succeeded his father LEOFWINE as Earl of Mercia and became one of the most powerful men in the kingdom under King CNUT. Thereafter he was at the forefront of English politics, favouring HAROLD I HAREFOOT against HARTHACNUT in 1037 and at times counter-balancing GODWINE under EDWARD THE CONFESSOR. He and his wife Godgifu (*see* GODIVA, LADY) were generous benefactors of the Church. Leofric was succeeded by his son ÆLFGAR.

LEOFRIC (?–1072), Bishop of Crediton/Exeter (1046–72). A Cornishman, educated in Lotharingia in the Rhineland, he returned to England in *c.* 1042 in the entourage of EDWARD THE CONFESSOR. An energetic reformer and typical of the continentally trained clerics whose work was slowly changing the late Anglo-Saxon Church, Leofric amalgamated the dioceses of Devon and Cornwall and transferred the cathedral church of the resulting new diocese to Exeter. He reformed the cathedral chapter and built up a good library, of which one important specimen, the *Exeter Book*, survives.

LEOFWINE, Ealdorman of the Hwicce and Ealdorman of the Mercians (?–1023/32). Appointed Ealdorman of the Hwicce in 994 by ETHELRED II THE UNREADY, Leofwine is a notable example of an Englishman who survived the Danish conquest and prospered further under CNUT, who appointed him Ealdorman of the Mercians in 1017 in succession to EADRIC STREONA. The reconciliation and promotion were, however, achieved at a price since a son and a grandson taken hostage by SVEIN FORKBEARD and Cnut were respectively killed and mutilated. Leofwine was succeeded as Ealdorman or Earl of Mercia by his son LEOFRIC.

LEOFWINE (*c.* 1025–66), nobleman. Son of GODWINE, Earl of Wessex, and brother of, among others, King HAROLD II and Queen EDITH, wife of King EDWARD THE CONFESSOR, Leofwine received an earldom comprising several counties in southeast England in the late 1050s or early 1060s as part of the process which advanced several of his kin to political prominence. His death in Harold's army at Hastings is portrayed on the Bayeux Tapestry. *See also* SVEIN, TOSTIG, GYRTH, WULFNOTH.

LESLIE, ALEXANDER (1st Earl of Leven) (*c.* 1580–1661), soldier. Thirty years' service in the Swedish army in its years of greatness prepared him for leadership in the victorious Scots forces supporting the National Covenant against English armies. He became Lord General in 1639, gaining his peerage from the defeated CHARLES I in 1641. He fought in Ireland and England against the Royalists, taking charge of Charles's captivity at Newcastle (1646–7). Breaking with Parliament to support CHARLES II, he was defeated by Oliver CROMWELL at Dunbar (1650). Although he was imprisoned from 1651 to 1653, his record and intervention by the Swedish government won him respectful treatment.

LESLIE, CHARLES (1650–1722), Non-juror. He was chancellor of the Irish diocese of Connor when he refused to take the oaths to WILLIAM III and MARY II, thus becoming a Non–juror (*see also* SANCROFT, WILLIAM). In 1693 he visited JAMES II in exile and was made his ecclesiastical representative with the right to nominate Non-juring bishops. He campaigned against William III in works such as *Gallienus Redivivus* (1695), which exposed William's complicity in the massacre of the Macdonalds by the Campbells at Glencoe in 1692 (*see* MACDONALD, ALEXANDER). He also wrote against Quakers, Deists, Judaism and Islam. In 1704 he launched *The Rehearsal*, a paper in which he attacked rationalist philosophers such as LOCKE and expounded divine right. In 1710 HOADLY accused Leslie of describing ANNE as a usurper in his *The Good Old Cause* (1710) and he fled to join the Pretender (*see* STUART, JAMES EDWARD) in France, spending much of the rest of his life at the Jacobite court with occasional visits to England and Ireland, where he died.

LESLIE, DAVID (1st Baron Newark) (*c.* 1600–82), soldier. A younger son of the 1st Earl of Lindores, after serving with Gustavus Adolphus of Sweden in the Thirty Years War, he returned in 1643 to fight for Parliament, and helped their victory at Marston Moor (1644). In 1645 he captured Carlisle, and defeated Montrose (*see* GRAHAM, JAMES) at Philiphaugh. From 1647 he was Lieutenant General of the Scots army and further defeated Montrose, but agreed to serve CHARLES II in 1650. Twice defeated, at Dunbar (1650) and Worcester (1651), he was imprisoned in the Tower of London until Charles's restoration, when he was rewarded with a peerage.

LESLIE, JOHN (1527–96), Bishop of Ross. After studying at Aberdeen, Paris and Poitiers, he strongly opposed the Scottish Reformation and was appointed to Ross in 1566. From 1569 he was agent and Ambassador for MARY QUEEN OF SCOTS, being imprisoned in England 1571–3 for his intrigues, and then remaining in exile until his death. His history of Scotland is important for its contemporary narrative.

LESSING, DORIS (1919–), writer. She was brought up on an isolated Rhodesian (now Zimbabwe) homestead, in some poverty and in 1949 came to England, divorced her husband and the next year published her first novel, *The Grass is Singing* (1950). About a white farmer's wife and her black servant, it was an instant success, and was followed by a collection of short stories and a five-volume series *Children of Violence* (1952–69), all of which concern personal and political loss and are set in England and Africa. Politically active, she left the Communist Party in 1956, but continued to support the Campaign for Nuclear Disarmament and was one of the founders of the *New Left Review* and, with Arnold WESKER, the radical theatre movement. *The Golden Notebook*, a series of fragments which chronicle and reconfigure 'what many women were thinking, feeling, experiencing' with some intimacy, was published in 1952. It became a feminists' bible, read by a succeeding generation of women. Subsequently Lessing became interested in Sufism and, experimenting with a number of literary forms including science fiction, published *Canopus in Argos: Archives* (1979–82), the dystopic *The Good Terrorist* (1985) and *The Fifth Child* (1988). A major prophetic writer, Lessing probes political issues from the standpoint of women.

L'ESTRANGE, ROGER (1616–1704), journalist and censor. Son of the Royalist Governor of King's Lynn during the First English Civil War, he served with the royal army; he was imprisoned, escaped, tried to stir up a Royalist rising in Kent in 1648, then fled to the Netherlands. In 1653 he returned to England. He published several tracts attacking army leaders (1659), favouring the restoration of CHARLES II (1660) and on the religious settlement (early 1660s). In 1663 he published a plan to regulate and supervise the press, and was appointed Surveyor of the Imprimery (a new office) and a licenser of the press, roles which he performed rigorously. In 1663–6 he published his own periodical, *The Intelligencer*, and he also published pamphlets trying to moderate anti-Catholic sentiment at the time of the Popish Plot (1678–9). Coming under suspicion himself, he took refuge briefly in the Netherlands but, on his return in 1681, he resumed pamphleteering, attacking Protestant Dissenters and defending the Duke of York (the future JAMES II). From 1681 to 1687 he published the polemical periodical *The Observator*. He was elected MP in 1685. He was removed from office as surveyor and as licenser of the press at the Glorious Revolution in 1688.

LETHABY, W(ILLIAM) R(ICHARD) (1857–1931), artist and designer. A pioneer of design and design education, Lethaby joined the practice of the architect Norman SHAW (1887) and was associated with the designer Ernest Gimson. A founder of the Art Workers' Guild (1884) and the Arts and Crafts Exhibition Society (*c.* 1886), Lethaby joined Philip WEBB and William MORRIS in the Society for the Protection of Ancient Buildings in 1891. Joint Principal and then Principal of the newly founded Central School of Arts and Crafts, London, he introduced workshop practice into art courses to train designers and craftsmen in the way specified by Morris.

LEVEN, 1ST EARL OF *see* LESLIE, ALEXANDER

LEVER, HAROLD (Baron Lever of Manchester) (1914–95), politician. After more than 20 years on the back benches, Lever, a barrister who was Labour MP for Manchester Central, was successively Under-Secretary in the Department of Economic Affairs (1967), Financial Secretary to the Treasury (1967–9) and finally Paymaster General (1969–70) in Harold WILSON's governments. Always on the right wing of the party, he made his greatest impact during Wilson's second spell in office when, despite his apparent sinecure post in the Cabinet as Chancellor of the Duchy of Lancaster, he became the Prime Minister's most valued economic adviser, frequently representing the government in negotiations with business, for example putting together the rescue package for the Chrysler car company (1976) and heading talks with petroleum companies about the exploitation of North Sea oil.

LEVER, WILLIAM (1st Viscount Lever of the Western Isles) (1851–1925), industrialist. The son of a Bolton (Lancs.) grocer, Lever expanded the family wholesale business and then from 1884 specialized in the marketing of soap. It bore the name 'Sunlight' and was an early and immensely successful example of brand-name promotion. From 1886 he and his brother James began to make the soap themselves in Warrington (Lancs.), using vegetable oils (instead of the commonplace tallow); as advertising swelled sales, the brothers decided to start a new factory enterprise with a model estate village attached, naming their Merseyside base Port Sunlight (Ches.). The factory was begun in 1888. The company acquired plantations for its raw materials in West Africa, Belgian Congo and the Solomon Islands. Failing to secure a monopoly in soap, Lever Bros diversified into margarine and food products in the twentieth century. Lever was an enlightened employer and was also responsible for many spectacular architectural and garden schemes; he was MP for Wirral (1906–9). In 1929 the firm merged with the Dutch company Jurgens to form Unilever.

LEVESON-GOWER, GRANVILLE (2nd Earl Gower, 1st Marquess of Stafford) (1721–1803),

politician. He came from a Tory family but after his sister married the Whig John RUSSELL, Duke of Bedford, in 1737 Leveson-Gower associated with Russell's faction in politics, holding several government offices in the 1750s and 1760s. Lord Privy Seal in 1767–9 he co-ordinated business in the Lords for Grafton (*see* FITZROY, AUGUSTUS HENRY) and NORTH, resigning when the War of American Independence, which he had supported, appeared to be going badly. He later played a part, with Temple (*see* TEMPLE-NUGENT-GRENVILLE, GEORGE), in putting together PITT THE YOUNGER's ministry, and was a member of it until 1796.

LEWIN, TERRANCE (Baron Lewin) (1920–99), sailor. Lewin joined the navy in 1939 and served in the destroyer *Ashanti* in hard-fought convoy actions to Malta and Murmansk. Appointed First Sea Lord in 1977, he became Chief of the Defence Staff in 1979, and was almost immediately embroiled in a battle with the Defence Secretary, John Nott, over planned cuts to the Royal Navy's surface fleet. When Argentina invaded the Falkland Islands in March 1982, Lewin masterminded Operation Corporate, a dangerous but successful plan to retake the islands, which won Prime Minister THATCHER enormous popularity. With the defeat of Argentina the reduction of the navy was quietly dropped.

LEWIS, C(LIVE) S(TAPLES) (1898–1963), theologian and writer. Born in Belfast and educated at Oxford, after being wounded at the Battle of Arras in the First World War, Lewis returned to Oxford as a Fellow of Magdalen College in 1925, where he became the centre of the 'Inklings', a circle of writers (including J. R. TOLKIEN). Lewis, who had lost his Christian faith during an unhappy childhood, regained it in 1931, as he recounts in *Surprised by Joy* (1955), and his Christian ethics inform all his subsequent work, his best-known scholarly work, *Allegory of Love* (1936), his science fiction trilogy (1938–45), his BBC wartime broadcasts, his *The Screwtape Letters* (1942) and his seven 'Narnia' stories for children beginning with *The Lion, the Witch and the Wardrobe* (1950). Appointed to the first chair of Medieval and Renaissance English at Cambridge in 1954, he married an American, Joy Gresham, in 1956; their brief love story before she died four years later is described in his *A Grief Observed* (1961) and is the subject of a popular stage play and film, *Shadowlands*.

LEWIS, DAVID (by 1520–84), administrator. Son of a Welsh parish priest, Lewis was an Oxford don and civil lawyer, twice MP under MARY I and President of the High Court of Admiralty from

1558. He was briefly the first Principal of the new Welsh foundation of Jesus College, Oxford (1571–2). He produced a notable analysis of Welsh government in 1576. His nephew and godson was David (Augustine) BAKER.

LEWIS, MATTHEW GREGORY ('MONK LEWIS') (1775–1819), novelist.

The son of a West Indian plantation-owner, as a young man he visited Goethe in Weimar, and after Oxford was posted as a diplomat to the Hague, where he wrote the sensational Gothic novel *The Monk* (1795). He followed its success with a long-running horror play, *Castle Spectre* (1798), and later became a friend of BYRON, Percy Bysshe SHELLEY and Polidori. He was an MP from 1796 to 1802. Although he did not free his slaves, he worked to improve their conditions in Jamaica.

LEWIS, WYNDHAM (1882–1957), artist,

novelist and critic. Born on a yacht off the coast of Nova Scotia to an American father and English mother, Lewis came to England as a child. He studied at the Slade School of Art and then in Paris (1901–8). A leading light of the Vorticist movement, with Ezra Pound, he edited *Blast, the Review of the Great English Vortex* (1914–15). Aggressive in outlook and stance, the movement attacked nineteenth-century sentimentality, considering it feeble, insular and ineffectual; owing much to Cubism and Futurism, it lauded violence, power and the machine. From 1916 to 1918 Lewis served as a bombardier, then as a war artist becoming increasingly disenchanted with the hollowness and loss of meaning within contemporary society. His fascination with power and order led him to a brief association with the British Union of Fascists and to praise of Hitler. Alienated and isolated in literary circles, he emigrated to Canada at the beginning of the Second World War, but returned to London in 1945. Lewis's writings, including the novels *Tarr* (1918), *The Childermass* (1928), *The Apes of God* (1930) and *The Revenge for Love* (1937) and the autobiographies *Blasting and Bombardiering* (1937) and *Rude Assignment* (1950), rank among the greatest of the twentieth century. His paintings, among the most experimental of the time, included portraits of Ezra Pound, Edith SITWELL and T. S. ELIOT.

LHUYD, EDWARD (1660–1709), scholar and

naturalist. Probably from Cardigans. (now Powys), he was educated at Oxford where he succeeded Robert PLOT as Keeper of the Ashmolean Museum in 1690. In 1697 he organized a public subscription to enable him to take a scholarly tour of the Celtic lands. By 1701 he had visited Wales, Scotland, Ireland, Cornwall and Brittany, copying manuscripts and inscriptions, collecting curiosi-ties and accumulating information on social customs as well as botanical, historical and linguistic data. The first volume of *Archaeologia Britannica* appeared in 1707 but subscribers were dismayed when it was dedicated entirely to comparative etymology; Lhuyd died before he could interest them in a second volume. Nonetheless he awakened scholarly interest in Celtic matters, providing them with a basis in scientific method rather than mythology.

LILBURNE, JOHN (?1614–57), political

reformer. Imprisoned by the Court of Star Chamber (1638–40) for printing unlicensed books, he fought for Parliament from 1642. Although he left the army in 1645, refusing to take the Solemn League and Covenant because of its doctrinaire Presbyterianism, he remained prominent in the radical Leveller contributions to army discussions about the future. He was repeatedly imprisoned, although his enemies generally respected his courageous straightforwardness; he was tried for sedition in 1649 but acquitted. During his last major imprisonment (1653–5) he joined the Quakers.

LILLY, SIR PETER *see* LELY, SIR PETER

LILLY, WILLIAM (1602–81), astrologer.

From a Leics. yeoman family, he published a study of the 1639 eclipse of the sun and from 1644 published an annual almanac. His work on astrology (1647) became a standard text, and, surviving an attempt at prosecution in 1654, he was seen as the foremost practitioner of astrological prediction, while also practising medicine and dabbling in magic. Publicly a sympathizer with Parliament, he tried to help CHARLES I in 1647–8, taking part in an unsuccessful escape attempt from Carisbrooke Castle. His MS autobiography and a substantial run of his astrological case-books survive in the Bodleian Library.

LILY, WILLIAM (?1468–1522), Humanist

scholar. After studying at Oxford, he made a pilgrimage to Jerusalem and studied Greek and Latin in Italy before returning to London to teach. John COLET made him first high master of St Paul's school (1512), and he wrote a pioneering Latin grammar for the school.

LINACRE, THOMAS (*c*. 1460–1524), doctor.

A distinguished Oxford don, he was one of the first English humanist scholars to experience the Italian Renaissance at first hand. He became physician to HENRY VII and HENRY VIII. He secured the foundation of the Royal College of Physicians in 1518 and founded chairs of medicine at Oxford and Cambridge.

LIND, JAMES (1716–94) and **LIND, JAMES** (1736–1812), physicians. Both Scots, but unrelated, and not to be confused, despite similarities in their careers and interests. The earlier James Lind was apprenticed as a surgeon, and practised in the navy. In 1754 he published *A Treatise on the Scurvy*, based on his experiments, calling for the use of citrus fruits, a practice eventually secured by Gilbert BLANE. In 1758 he was appointed surgeon to the naval hospital at Haslar (Hants.). He also published papers on typhus fever in ships and on the diseases of Europeans in hot climates. The later James Lind greatly extended the knowledge of Asian medical practice and oriental diseases in Britain. He gained his knowledge firsthand as a surgeon with the East India Co. in 1766, travelling to China. Lind was nominated by BANKS as a member of James COOK's second expedition, and though Cook turned him down Lind accompanied Banks on his voyage to Iceland later in the 1770s.

LINDEMANN, FREDERICK (1st Viscount Cherwell) (1886–1957), scientist, government adviser and politician. Born in Germany of an American mother and French–Alsatian father, he chose to serve Britain rather than his fatherland in the First World War, and worked at the Royal Aircraft Factory at Farnborough improving aircraft performance and safety. Elected to head Oxford's nearly defunct Clarendon Laboratory in 1919, Lindemann quickly turned it into one of the world's leading scientific institutions. By the mid 1930s, increasingly worried about the menace posed by the Luftwaffe, Lindemann pushed his way onto several Air Ministry committees, where he fought bitterly with his former colleague Henry TIZARD. His supporter Winston CHURCHILL appointed him as his personal scientific adviser and by 1941 Lindemann had been elevated to the peerage and had a seat in Cabinet. During the war Cherwell, as he was now known, wrote some 2,000 minutes for Churchill on scientific matters. He supported many important projects, including the development of proximity fuses (which revolutionized anti-aircraft fire), the electronic bending of German navigational radio beams, the H2S airborne radar and the atomic bomb. His most controversial contribution was his support for the policy of 'de-housing' Germany by area bombardment of German cities. On the extreme Right of British politics in the post-war years, he delighted in ridiculing those who would 'ban the bomb'. No single scientist had ever before (or since) enjoyed Cherwell's influence, and his contribution to the formulation of policy was immense.

LINDSAY (OR LYNDSAY), SIR DAVID (1490–1555), writer. A courtier and usher to the future JAMES V (1512–22), he was Lyon King of Arms (chief Scots herald) from 1529, led an embassy to CHARLES V in 1531 and wrote on heraldry. Among much other poetry, his play *Ane Satyre of the Three Estaits* was produced at Stirling Castle in 1540, combining brilliant writing with sharp social comment. His criticisms of the Church were echoed by Protestants, although he himself was a humanist loyal to the old Church.

LINDSAY, GEORGE MACKINTOSH (1880–1956), soldier. Son of an army officer, commissioned into the Monmouthshire Militia in 1898, he transferred to a regular commission in the Rifle Brigade while serving in South Africa in 1900. An early enthusiast of automatic weapons, Lindsay served with the Machine Gun Corps during the First World War, was appointed to the Distinguished Service Order (DSO) and in 1921 commanded an armoured car unit in Iraq which specialized in deep penetration operations supported only by aircraft. Appointed Inspector of the Royal Tank Corps (1925), Lindsay delivered an important series of lectures on firepower and mobility, and his command of a motorized infantry brigade in exercises in the early 1930s proved him equal to his German contemporaries. His advocacy of a new weapon system made him powerful enemies, and he was shifted into a series of minor administrative appointments.

LINDSEY, 1ST EARL OF *see* BERTIE, ROBERT

LINDSEY, THEOPHILUS (1723–1808), religious leader. Educated at Cambridge and ordained, Lindsey married the stepdaughter of his friend Francis BLACKBURNE in 1760, and followed him in questioning the requirement that the clergy subscribe to the Thirty-Nine Articles. Lindsey supported the Feathers Tavern petition, which asked Parliament to relax the subscription requirement, and on its rejection in 1773 resigned his living at Catterick (Yorks.) and set up a Unitarian chapel in Essex Street, London, with the help of Dissenters Richard PRICE and Joseph PRIESTLEY. This attracted occasional visits from many curious or sympathetic members of the nobility and gentry. Lindsey's *Apology* (1774) defended his action. He was joined by John DISNEY in 1783, allowing Lindsey to concentrate on writing and defining the Unitarian faith.

LINLEY, ELIZABETH ANN (1754–92), singer. Educated by her father, the fashionable Bath music-master and composer, Thomas Linley, she sang at his concerts and gained a reputation as a performer in London. Her hand was sought by many suitors. In March 1772 she eloped with SHERIDAN; they married in Calais but both were under age and the marriage was consequently invalid. The couple married officially in April 1773; Elizabeth's father was compensated with £1,200 for the loss of her earnings as neither of them wished her career to continue, although she did sing occasionally, usually to private audiences. Elizabeth assisted her husband with the business affairs of the Theatre Royal, Drury Lane, wrote poems and arranged songs for performance.

LINLITHGOW, 2ND MARQUESS OF *see* HOPE, VICTOR

LINTON, ELIZA LYNN (1822–98), novelist *see* LINTON, WILLIAM

LINTON, WILLIAM (1812–98), Chartist and republican. Apprenticed as a wood-engraver, Linton was a leading internationalist and republican and prominent English supporter of the Italian nationalist Mazzini. In 1847 they founded the Peoples' International League in 1847 to further the rights of every people to self-government and national self-determination. A 'moderate' Chartist, Linton became a keen supporter of Italian nationalism through the Friends of Italy (1851–5) and was a leading figure in the republican movement, mainly through his *English Republic* (1851–5). He married Eliza Lynn, novelist and woman of letters, in 1858; they subsequently separated. In 1866 Linton emigrated to New Haven (Connecticut), where he worked as a printer and engraver and published a number of works on engraving.

LIONEL OF CLARENCE (OR OF ANTWERP) (Styled 5th Earl of Ulster, 1st Duke of Clarence) (1338–68), royal prince. The third son of EDWARD III, born at Antwerp, he became Earl of Ulster by virtue of his marriage (1342) to the heiress Elizabeth de Burgh, and was created Duke of Clarence in 1362. He governed Ireland as his father's Lieutenant (1361–6): as Earl of Ulster he was the natural choice for the office once it had been decided that a member of the English royal family should be sent there, for the first time since King JOHN's reign, in an attempt to reverse the decline in fortune of the English colony in Ireland which had been all too evident since EDWARD BRUCE's invasion. Clarence was provided with an army funded from English resources but, since there was no united organized Irish enemy for him to find, let alone defeat, he could make little military impact. In 1366 he presided over a Parliament at Kilkenny. The Statutes of Kilkenny clearly reveal the processes by which the English in Ireland had long felt that their community was being undermined. The statutes range very widely, including matters such as the conduct of officials and the evils of hurling. Their most significant aspect has always been seen in the preamble's assertion that 'many English' now 'comport themselves according to the customs, fashion and language of the Irish enemies, and have entered into numerous marriages and alliances between themselves and the aforementioned Irish enemies'. The statutory prohibition of all such practices could not halt the continuing influence of Irish culture (*see* FITZGERALD, GERALD) and the development of an Anglo-Irish identity clearly distinct from that of the English of England. Although he was willing to experiment, as when he moved the seat of administration from Dublin to the 'more central' Carlow, Clarence's period as Lieutenant of Ireland achieved little, except perhaps to accustom the English government to giving, and the Anglo-Irish to receiving, financial assistance.

His wife had died in 1363, and he married their only child, Philippa, to Edmund MORTIMER, Earl of March, thereby creating the Mortimer claim to the throne. After Ireland, Clarence turned to Italy. He married the Duke of Milan's niece Violante Visconti in June 1368 in a ceremony of such magnificence that it generated rumours that he was about to become King of Italy. He died a few months later.

LIPTON, SIR THOMAS (1850–1931), businessman. A pioneer of the sale of wholesome and cheap food, Lipton was born into a poor shopkeeping family in Glasgow that had fled the Famine in Ireland. After five years in the USA, he returned to Glasgow with sufficient savings to open his first grocery shop in 1871. Shops were subsequently opened all over the country, with great success: they had standardized presentation of goods and well-groomed staff, gave no credit and were integrated with his suppliers, notably of tea. By 1898, when he sold the business for the vast sum of £2.5 million, he had 243 branch stores in Britain and 12 tea plantations in Ceylon; Lipton continued as Chairman until finally ousted by a shareholders' revolt in 1927. (The 615 Liptons shops were subsequently absorbed into the growing Van den Bergh retail empire.) Meanwhile in the late 1890s he had entered the circle of Edward Prince of Wales, subsequently EDWARD VII, with whom he took up the sport of ocean racing.

LISLE, 7TH BARON AND 1ST VISCOUNT OF *see* DUDLEY, JOHN; **6TH VISCOUNT** *see* PLANTAGENET, ARTHUR

LISTER, JOSEPH (1st Baron Lister) (1827–1912), surgeon and pioneer of antiseptics. Son of a microscopist, Lister studied medicine at University College, London. Qualifying in 1852, he continued his studies in Edinburgh under the surgeon James Syme and in 1860, having built a reputation in teaching and researches on inflammation, became Regius Professor of Surgery at Glasgow University. In this position he explored the fatal post-operative disease known as hospital gangrene. By 1865 he had rejected the common idea that sepsis was caused by the contact of an open wound with the air, and accepted the French chemist Louis Pasteur's theory that putrefaction was a fermentative process caused by organisms entering the wound. In 1867 he announced that his method of treating wounds with carbolic acid had stopped infection in the wounds of a high percentage of patients. His antiseptic techniques received a mixed reception among surgeons but were being widely adopted around the world by the 1890s. He built his fame and fortune developing his antiseptic technique and spent his later years challenging the rival aseptic technique of William MACEWEN and others. He was Professor of Surgery at King's College, London (1877–92).

LISTER, SAMUEL CUNLIFFE (1st Baron Masham) (1815–1906), inventor. Born in Bradford (Yorks.), Lister and his brother took charge of their father's worsted mill in Manningham (Yorks.) in 1837 and sought to improve textile manufacture. In the 1840s and 1850s he patented numerous textile inventions, including a swivel shuttle and in 1849, in collaboration with his business partner George Donisthorpe, a 'square-nip' mechanical comber. By the late 1850s he had gained control over all wool-combing patents (by purchasing all rival patents), built flourishing mills in Bradford and abroad, and was a wealthy man. Later he built a machine for spinning waste silk and a velvet loom, the latter further boosting his fortune. Lister used much of his wealth for philanthropic purposes, notably in Bradford.

LITTLEWOOD, JOAN (1914–1999), theatre director. After training at the Royal Academy of Dramatic Arts she founded with her then husband Ewen McColl a theatre group in Manchester which became the Theatre of Action, staging experimental and politically engaged work. During the Second World War Littlewood's politics ensured that she was banned by the BBC, and from appearing with the Entertainment National Service Association (ENSA). In 1953 she leased a run-down music hall, the Theatre Royal, Stratford East (London), as a permanent home for what were now called Theatre Workshop productions, started with Gerry Raffles in 1945. These included Brendan BEHAN's *The Quare Fellow* (1956) and *The Hostage* (1958), and Shelagh Delaney's *A Taste of Honey* (1958) and *Fings ain't what they used t'be* (1959). With the Royal Court, it was London's most exciting theatre in the 1950s

and many of its productions transferred from the East End to the West End, and all proved a nursery for sitcom stars, as did Littlewood's only film, *Sparrows Can't Sing* (1962). *Oh! What a Lovely War* (1963), an indictment of the General Staff in the First World War, in the form of an 'end of pier' musical entertainment, was a memorable success, transferring to the West End, being filmed (1969), and still retaining, in revival, the power to shock.

LIUDHARD, ST (?–*c.* 603), priest. Coming to England as chaplain of BERTHA, wife and Queen of King ETHELBERT of Kent, he was present in England before the arrival of St AUGUSTINE's mission, but he is not known to have played any part in the conversion of the English, beyond making arrangements for Bertha to worship in a pagan land.

LIVERPOOL, EARL OF, 1ST *see* JENKINSON, CHARLES; **2ND** *see* JENKINSON, ROBERT

LIVINGSTONE, DAVID (1813–73), explorer. Born in Lanarks., where he initially worked in a cotton mill alongside the rest of his impoverished family, Livingstone saved to study for a medical degree which he took in 1840. Thereafter his entire career was spent in Africa and he was a formative influence on Western attitudes towards 'the dark continent'. He was sent first to Bechuanaland by the London Missionary Society; for the next 15 years he was constantly on the move in the African interior, combining missionary zeal (principally by spreading the gospel through 'native agents'), medicine and exploration. Between 1849 and 1856 he discovered the Victoria Falls and Lake Ngami and explored the Zambezi. Returning to Britain a hero, star of print and speaking platform, he went back to Africa in 1858 on a better organized Zambezi expedition (including a paddle steamer). By 1864, despite great difficulties, he had explored the Zambezi's eastern tributaries and found Lake Nyasa. In 1866 he started on a third great expedition, to bring God and an anti-slavery message to eastern Africa and also to discover the Nile's source. By 1871, despite arguments with many in his party, he had penetrated further west than any previous European, but nothing had been heard of him and there were reports of his death. Livingstone was found in Oct. 1871 by Henry Morton STANLEY, who had been sent by the *New York Herald* to find him. They met on Lake Tanganyika, Stanley (according to tradition) greeting him with the words, 'Dr Livingstone, I presume?' Livingstone stayed on for two more years. Eventually he died at Chitambo (now in Zambia) in May 1873. His body was carried to the coast in an arduous nine-month journey, and he was buried in Westminster Abbey in 1874. Livingstone had made great medical, geographical and social discoveries; he was a Victorian paternalist yet also a firm believer in Africans' ability to move into the modern world.

LIVINGSTONE, KENNETH (KEN) (1945–), politician. Educated at Tulse Hill comprehensive school, he worked as a laboratory technician at the Chester Beatty Cancer Research Institute (1962–70). He entered London politics as a Labour Councillor for Lambeth (1971–8), where he served with the future Conservative Prime Minister John MAJOR on the Housing Committee, and then as a Camden Councillor (1978–82). In 1981 Livingstone was leader of the radical Left of the Labour Group of the Greater London Council (GLC) which ousted the moderate Labour leader, leaving Livingstone as leader of the GLC until 1986. There he was vilified by the Tory press as 'Red Ken'. As a product of the 1960s counterculture he had absorbed most of the politics of that era on issues such as gender, race and poverty, and during his tenure at the GLC he encouraged a range of fringe and often controversial groups, which put him at odds not only with the Conservative government of Margaret THATCHER at Westminster but with most of the older members of his own party. In 1981 his attempt to secure a massive cut in public transport fares throughout London was ruled illegal by the High Court. The fact that Livingstone was one of the few elected Labour politicians able to spend government money brought him permanently into conflict with the government and he thus became the most high-profile opposition leader of the era. To the Right he encapsulated all that was wrong with what was dubbed the 'loony left' by the press, and Mrs Thatcher's second government used its Commons majority to abolish the (Labour) Metropolitan Councils altogether; the GLC was abolished in March 1986. Livingstone was not unemployed for long: elected MP for Brent East in 1987, he became one of the most outspoken voices of the Left in the Commons and remained thoroughly out of tune with the politics of New Labour. He was voted onto the Labour National Executive Council (1987–9), and in 1998 he launched a campaign to secure the Labour nomination for the new position of elected Mayor of London against the wishes of the party leadership. When this failed, he stood as an independent candidate and was expelled from the Labour party. Livingstone was elected Mayor of London on 4 May 2000.

LLEWELYN DAVIES, MARGARET (1861–1943), co-operative lender. From a Christian socialist family, she was the niece of Emily DAVIES, who had founded Girton College, Cambridge, where Llewelyn Davies was a student. In 1911 she was appointed General Secretary of the Women's Co-operative Guild (founded in 1883) which, under her unpaid leadership, campaigned for improved working conditions and a minimum wage for women: by 1912 some 200 shops and the Co-operative Wholesale Society shops had introduced these. She went on to demand divorce for women on the same grounds as men, women's suffrage, maternity pay for working women, and improved ante- and post-natal care to lower rates of infant mortality. Testimonies of working women edited by her, *Maternity* (1915) and *Life as We have Known It* (1931) with an introduction by her close friend Virginia WOOLF, are a vivid historical source.

LLOYD, EDWARD (*fl.* 1688–1726), coffee-house keeper. In 1692 he relocated his coffee house from Tower Street to Lombard Street, in the City of London, where it became the recognized centre for ship-broking and marine insurance business. In 1696–7 he started a commercial and shipping chronicle called *Lloyd's News*: in 1726 a similar publication was restarted under the name of *Lloyd's Lists. Lloyd's Register of Shipping* is thought to have begun at about the same time, although the oldest surviving copies date from the 1760s. In 1770 ANGERSTEIN and others started an association of underwriters in Cornhill. Termed New Lloyds, it soon dropped the New, and relocated at the Royal Exchange. It was incorporated in 1871, and began to accept non-marine business from the 1880s. The organization survives to the present as the world's leading insurance market.

LLOYD, MARIE (originally Mathilda Wood) (1870–1922), music-hall star. The oldest of 11 children of a Hoxton (London) artificial flower-maker and part-time waiter, she worked at the Grecian Music Hall, first appearing aged 15 under the name Bella Delmere, which she soon changed to Marie Lloyd. In this guise she was an instant success, singing *The Boy I Love Sits up in the Gallery*. A Cockney triumph in music halls throughout Britain, Australia, South Africa and the USA with her risqué, sometimes poignant numbers, among the most popular being *My Old Man Said Follow the Van* and *Oh Mr Porter What shall I Do?*, she also appeared as principal boy in Drury Lane pantomimes with Dan Leno and Little Titch. The three-times-married Lloyd was a supporter of women's suffrage, appearing in *How the Vote was Won* (1909), and a generous benefactress of the East End poor.

LLOYD, SAMPSON (1699–1779), banker. His father was Sampson Lloyd, a Birmingham Quaker ironmonger who married the sister of Sir

Ambrose CROWLEY. Lloyd expanded his family business but, when demand for iron declined after the Seven Years War, he diverted his resources towards founding the first private bank in Birmingham, Taylors and Lloyds, in 1765. A London sister bank started in 1770. When Lloyd died he was succeeded by his four sons; the bank expanded and became a public company, precursor of the modern Lloyds Bank, in 1865.

LLOYD, SELWYN (Baron Selwyn-Lloyd) (1904–78), politician and barrister. Born in the Wirral (Ches.), he started his political life as a Liberal, then changed to Conservative in 1929 over the cause of protective tariffs. Made Foreign Secretary by Anthony EDEN in 1955, he helped frame the disastrous British policy over Suez in 1956, but emerged relatively unscathed. During MACMILLAN's premiership, Lloyd was again largely a tool for the leader's foreign policy; in 1960 he was made Chancellor of the Exchequer and introduced a modest wage freeze to curb inflation, which diminished his popularity. His major innovation was in economic planning, with the formation of the National Economic Development Council; his main legacy was the age of stop–go economics. His loyalty to Macmillan was rewarded by his summary dismissal in the 1962 'night of the long knives' in which a third of the Cabinet was removed. From 1971 he was Speaker of the Commons. Lloyd was one of the principal foot soldiers of post-war politics, never scaling the heights but an effective and diligent survivor.

LLOYD GEORGE, DAVID *see* essay on pages 512–13

LLOYD WEBBER, ANDREW (Baron Lloyd-Webber of Sydmonston) (1948–), composer. As an undergraduate at Oxford he teamed up with law student and budding lyricist Tim Rice, and worked on a musical entitled *Joseph and the Amazing Technicolour Dreamcoat*, which was loosely based on the Scriptures and influenced by the 1960s rock and pop music and lifestyle. A huge hit in 1968, it was followed by *Jesus Christ Superstar* (1970), a rock opera that provoked protest by religious groups for the blasphemous treatment of the Christmas story, but nevertheless proved so popular that it later transferred to Broadway. *Evita* (1978), a musical based loosely on the Eva Peron story, set Lloyd Webber on the way to becoming Britain's foremost musical theatre composer, commercially if not critically defining the genre which others were to follow. A host of internationally commercial successes followed: *Cats* (1981, based on T. S. ELIOT's *Old Possum's Book of Practical Cats*) became the longest running musical of all time in both

London and New York; others were *Starlight Express* (1984), *Phantom of the Opera* (1986) and *Aspects of Love* (1989).

LLWYD, HUMPHREY (1527–68), writer. Illegitimate son of a Denbighs. gentleman, he studied at Oxford and in 1553 became physician and librarian to Henry FitzAlan, 12th Earl of Arundel (1512–80); he was twice an MP. While collecting for Arundel's magnificent library, he pursued his own fascination with Welsh history, and among other collections his *Cronica Walliae* (1559) and his map of Wales prepared for the Dutch geographer Ortelius were milestones in the development of Welsh national consciousness.

LLWYD, MORGAN (1619–59), writer. From north Wales, he fought in Parliamentarian armies during the Civil War (1642–6) and founded an Independent church at Wrexham *c*. 1646. His mystical writings are among the greatest products of Welsh prose.

LLYWARCH HEN (*fl.* sixth century), British prince. As a historical figure, practically nothing is known of Llywach Hen, other than that his name occurs in northern genealogies and these show him to have been a cousin of URIEN of Rheged. He was in all probability a minor ruler in the late sixth century, but he has become better known through being the subject of a corpus of British poetry dating to the ninth century.

LLYWELYN AP GRUFFUDD *see* essay on pages 514–15

LLYWELYN AP IORWERTH *see* essay on page 516

LLYWELYN AP SEISYLL (?–1023), King of Deheubarth and Gwynedd. Llywelyn, in right of his wife, assumed the rule of Deheubarth following MAREDUDD AP OWAIN's death. In 1016 he defeated Aeddan ap Blegored and his sons, who appear to have usurped power in Gwynedd, to reunite temporarily Deheubarth and Gwynedd under his rule. The war between ETHELRED II THE UNREADY and SVEIN FORKBEARD in England, and the subsequent accession of CNUT to the English throne, appear to have relieved both English and Danish assaults on Wales and allowed the resurgence in the growth of power during Llywelyn's reign which would reach its peak under his son, GRUFFUDD AP LLYWELYN.

LLYWELYN DDU O FON *see* MORRIS, LEWIS

LOCKE, ANNE (née Vaughan) (*c*. 1533–95), writer. Daughter of Thomas CROMWELL's agent,

continued on page 517

LLOYD GEORGE, DAVID (1st Earl Lloyd George) (1863–1945)
Politician and Prime Minister (1916–22)

The most famous Welshman ever born in Manchester, Lloyd George enjoyed five types of reputation: first as a fiery Welsh radical who came to national prominence as an opponent of the Boer War; secondly as the radical, reforming President of the Board of Trade and Chancellor of the Exchequer in the Liberal governments of 1905–16; thirdly as the 'man of push and go' who 'won the war' between 1916 and 1918; fourthly as a presidential style Prime Minister before 1922; and finally as a flawed and increasingly marginal gadfly during his years in the wilderness. With the exception of CHURCHILL, no modern politician has been so studied, and none has been so successful in evading his biographers.

Monolingual historians have not always appreciated the importance of Lloyd George's Welshness. Welsh was his first language, and it was his Welsh background which both provided the context and the opportunity for his early political career. As a Nonconformist Lloyd George identified with the upsurge of Welsh national feeling against Anglican landlordism of the 1880s and 1890s and he was its direct beneficiary. Lloyd George had no sooner qualified as a solicitor than he was elected as Liberal MP for Caernarvon Boroughs in 1890 – a seat he would retain until 1945.

In his early years he followed the time-honoured path of seeking prominence as a radical opponent of both the Unionist government and his own front bench but the Boer War offered him the chance to move outside the purely Welsh arena. His vocal opposition to the war, which included a dangerous visit to the Birmingham fief of Joseph CHAMBERLAIN, made his name on the national stage and, when CAMPBELL-BANNERMAN formed his government in 1905, Lloyd George had an undeniable claim to Cabinet Office. As President of the Board of Trade (1905–8) and Chancellor (1908–15) he was the leading radical figure in the government, forming, after 1908, an alliance with Winston Churchill which made them the dynamo of Liberal reforms. With the Old Age Pensions Act (1908) and National Insurance Act (1910) to his credit, Lloyd George enhanced his reputation as the architect of Liberal social reform. His 1910 'People's Budget' consolidated his position as the man the Conservatives loved to hate and his radical rhetoric in the two elections of that year made him indisputably the second man in the government.

But Lloyd George, who was always vulnerable on the character issue, almost came to terminal political grief in 1912 with the MARCONI scandal. Lloyd George was a poor man by the standard of many of his fellow MPs and he was always on the look-out for money-making schemes. He had an unerring eye for bad investments, losing money early in his career in the Patagonian gold fields. In 1910 he invested money in the Marconi Wireless Company which, his opponents alleged, was an example of what would later be called 'insider dealing'. Although no crime could be proved, the affair damaged his reputation and would be held against him. It was at this time that the rumours began to circulate about his irregular private life. His wife, Margaret, declined to live or to bring up their family in the unhealthy environs of London and remained in north Wales where she was active in keeping Caernarvon Boroughs loyal to her husband, though he was not faithful to her. An attractive, vigorous and virile man, Lloyd George was not cut out for the life of a London bachelor and was fortunate on more than one occasion to escape being cited as co-respondent in a divorce case, something which in the moral climate of the time would have ended his career, as it had that of the great Irish leader, Charles Stewart PARNELL. It was Parnell's example that he used to his long-standing mistress, Frances Stevenson, to justify his refusal to leave his wife; after 1912 he virtually kept two households, one in London with Miss Stevenson, one in Wales with his wife. This created much controversy within the Lloyd George family but his press magnate friends were able to keep any mention of it out of the papers. Nevertheless, it contributed to the distrust in which he was held by many of his fellow politicians and, in time, would come to count against him.

Despite an initial reluctance to sanction Britain's entry into the First World War and despite his previous reputation as a pacifist, Lloyd George emerged as the one leading Liberal who seemed to be able to meet the challenges of war. Churchill destroyed his position through hyperactivity, ASQUITH achieved the same thing by the opposite means and, by 1916, even most Conservatives were willing to submit to Lloyd George's leadership if it would win the war. Lloyd George's performance as the first Minister of Munitions (1915–16) and as Minister of War

(1916) established him as the obvious successor to Asquith when the latter resigned in Dec. 1916 in an effort to prove his indispensability.

Lloyd George's premiership was indelibly marked by the circumstances in which he came to power. In the first place he was, as he remained, dependent upon a coalition of Conservatives and Liberals; in the second place the exigencies of war demanded from him a level of executive action unusual in a British Prime Minister and lent a presidential style to his period of office; and, finally, the war set his priorities.

As a war leader Lloyd George was bolder in his rhetoric than in deed. Much though he fulminated against the stupidity of some of the senior soldiers, he sanctioned their bloody offensives. But he was fortunate in his timing. With America's entry into the war, Germany's exhaustion and the successes enjoyed by British arms in 1918, he was able to preside over the defeat of the Central Powers. He immediately sought to reap the rewards which he felt were due to the man who won the war in an emotional General Election which was fought in an atmosphere of extreme bitterness; much of this was directed against Germany but, with Asquithian Liberals fighting Lloyd George Liberals in many seats, it was also a feature of the campaign in the constituencies.

With an overwhelming democratic mandate (the Conservative leader Bonar LAW said that 'the little man can be Prime Minister for life if he likes'), Lloyd George now had to win the peace, which meant creating a lasting peace settlement abroad, and dealing with the transition from war to peace at home. The requirements of vengeance were incompatible with those of a stable international order and the compromise agreed at the Versailles Peace Conference was compatible with neither, a failure which cost all the peacemakers dear with their respective electorates. Lloyd George's stock was further lowered by the failure to deliver the land fit for heroes which he had promised at the election. His reconstruction programme, designed to build more houses and to extend social insurance, fell victim to the 'axe' wielded by his Minister of Transport, Eric GEDDES, in 1921. His one constructive achievement, the Irish Partition of 1921, so alienated many members of the Conservative Party that it helped place his government in jeopardy. Rumours of corruption, fuelled by his selling of peerages to augment his own political 'fund', further helped undermine Lloyd George's position which was also weakened by his increasing remoteness from the Commons. In Oct. 1922 the Conservative Party voted at the Carlton Club meeting against remaining in the coalition, despite the wishes of its leadership.

In the ensuing election Lloyd George's few followers were routed. Thereafter, although his political fund and talents enabled him to play a part in the great political game, his reputation always ruled him out of contention for high office. The elections of 1923 and 1924 depleted Liberal funds, votes and seats which led to a death-bed reconciliation between Lloyd George and Asquith, the former providing the money, the latter the party machine and the votes. When Lloyd George became leader in 1926 it was of a party with only 40 seats.

Lloyd George's fund provided a fertile source of ideas in the Orange Book of the 1929 election, with its proposals for programmes of public works and expenditure; but the electoral system returned Ramsay MACDONALD and Labour. An untimely illness deprived Lloyd George of his chance of joining the National government in 1931 following the collapse of Labour. Thereafter, he was a powerful but isolated figure who devoted himself to refighting the political battles of the war years through the six volumes of his memoirs. Lloyd George was kept out of Churchill's coalition in May 1940 by his own reluctance to serve in a doomed cause and by Neville CHAMBERLAIN's refusal to serve with him. His defeatism kept him from office thereafter, although he was considered for the Washington Embassy in 1940. He married Frances Stevenson in 1945 and was elevated to the peerage in order to give him an opportunity to have his say in Parliament on the peace settlement; he died a few weeks later.

Lloyd George remains a hugely controversial figure: he laid the foundations of the Welfare State and provided inspirational leadership in the First World War; but he also failed to realize the hopes placed in him by progressives, and his own personal conduct in his private life would have ruined him in an age when the press was less deferential.

Bentley Brinkerhoff Gilbert, David Lloyd George: A Political Life (2 vols, 1990, 1992)

LLYWELYN AP GRUFFUDD (c. 1228–82)
Prince of Wales

The names by which he has long been popularly known, Llywelyn the Last or the Last Leader (Y Llyw Olaf), enshrine his place in British history as the Prince of Wales whose death in battle marked the end of the native principality of Wales. From that day to this – despite the Welsh Assembly – Wales has been governed from Westminster. The sense of a tragic fall was all the greater since it was Llywelyn who a few years earlier had taken the principality to a greater degree of coherence and independence than ever before. Much had been owed to his leadership. The Welsh followed him, as a contemporary put it, as though glued to him.

Much also was due to Welsh patriotism, a growing sense that the Welsh would have to put aside age-old rivalries if their independence and culture were to survive the growing power of the English State. Llywelyn's success led an English contemporary, Matthew PARIS, to note that, 'Such union between north and south Wales has never before been seen, for northerners and southerners have always been at loggerheads.' Yet Llywelyn was also, or so it has seemed to many, the leader whose flaws and ambitions brought about the dual tragedy of his own death and the extinction of the native principality.

In fact Llywelyn had many more divisions than that between north and south to contend with. Thirteenth-century 'Welsh' Wales was a land of many rival princelings claiming descent from rival kings. Although since the days of his grandfather, Llywelyn the Great (see LLYWELYN AP IORWERTH), Gwynedd had been the greatest of these principalities, there were still many reluctant to acknowledge Gwynedd's overlordship. Moreover there was no clear-cut rule of princely succession. Within each principality the death of the ruler was usually followed by a struggle for power; wars and partitions were the order of the day.

The kings of England had long been acknowledged as the overlords of the Welsh rulers and, in the expectation of fragmenting the Welsh polity further, they liked to press for division between sons on the dubious but convenient grounds that this was true Welsh custom. As the kings of England lost territory in France in this period so they tended to press harder in Wales. Although, as the young Lord of Dyffryn Clwyd, Llywelyn early showed talent for leadership, his involvement in the 1244–7 revolt against HENRY III meant that he soon had to learn how to endure defeat and humil-

iation. His father, Gruffudd ap Llywelyn, died while trying to escape from the Tower of London in 1244. When his uncle DAFYDD AP LLYWELYN died childless in 1246, the Welsh were already losing the war. Llywelyn and his brother Owain had to submit to the Treaty of Woodstock (April 1247). Henry III took possession of Gwynedd east of Conwy (Caern.), i.e. Perfeddwlad or the Four Cantrefs. The two brothers were left to share rule of the lands west of Conwy (Snowdonia and Anglesey) and they agreed, should disputes arise, to appear before the English King or his officials to adjudicate. According to Matthew Paris, 'Now Wales has been brought to nothing.'

By 1252 a third brother, DAFYDD, had obtained a share. Rather than see the process continue, for there was a fourth still to be provided for, Llywelyn decided to fight. In June 1255 he defeated Owain and Dafydd, took them prisoner and made himself sole ruler of west Gwynedd.

Next year, with the help of a Welsh rising against the oppressive rule of officials appointed by Edward (later EDWARD I), he recovered Perfeddwlad (the Four Cantrefs). In the words of the Welsh chronicle, the Brut Y Tywysogion, the Welsh there 'preferred to be killed fighting for their liberty rather than suffer themselves to be unjustly trampled over by foreigners'. Though the foreigners held on to the two big castles of Degannwy and Diserth, the tide of war continued to run in Llywelyn's favour throughout 1257–8. He drove southwards, pushing English Marcher lords out of Builth and Gwerthrynion. He was joined by Welsh rulers in Ceredigion, Powys and Deheubarth. GRUFFUDD AP GWENWYNWYN was driven out of southern Powys, but in general Llywelyn pursued a shrewd policy of restoring recovered lands to their original dynasties, 'keeping naught for himself save fame and honour', as the Brut proudly records.

At an assembly in 1258 all the Welsh made a pact to maintain unity and loyalty under his leadership. Henry III, troubled by serious domestic problems from 1258 on, had to agree to a series of truces which lasted until 1262. Then further disarray in England gave Llywelyn scope for more advances. In 1263 Diserth and Degannwy were captured and razed to the ground. Gruffudd ap Gwenwynwyn did homage.

Although Henry III was angered by Llywelyn's alliance with Simon de MONTFORT, the English government was eventually persuaded of the need to recognize him and his heirs as Princes of Wales

(Treaty of Montgomery, Sept. 1267). It accepted his conquests from English Marcher lords and agreed that, with the one exception of Maredudd ap Rhys of Ystrad Tywi, 'all the Welsh barons of Wales shall hold their lands from the Prince, and he shall have their fealty and homage'. This was a great triumph, rounded off in 1270 when Llywelyn bought the homage of Maredudd ap Rhys.

Could an independent Welsh principality have survived? 'Welsh' Wales produced no salt and not enough wheat, iron or cloth. Since it was economically dependent upon England, the principality would survive only if the King of England learned to accept it with good grace.

For this reason, in 1267, Llywelyn agreed to pay 25,000 marks (£16,666) in instalments in return for recognition. To raise this sum, which was about three times his annual income, he had to make unprecedented financial demands upon his subjects. Dispossessed but still powerful Marcher families such as the Mortimers and Bohuns were inevitably his enemies. It was important that Llywelyn avoid further disputes which gave scope for English intervention. Yet he continued to press forward.

On the grounds that he was protecting the Welsh of Senghennydd against the lord of Glamorgan, he destroyed Gilbert de CLARE's newly built castle at Caerphilly (Glam.). In 1273 he built the castle of Dolforwyn (Montgom.), threatening the security of his old enemy, Gruffudd ap Gwenwynwyn.

In 1274 Gruffudd and his own brother Dafydd fled to England. Above all it was important for Llywelyn to avoid disputes with the King of England. Yet after Christmas 1271 he paid no more instalments, and when Edward I came to the throne he pointedly avoided doing homage to him. In 1275 he arranged to marry Eleanor de Montfort, exasperating the English court with this reminder of his alliance with their arch-enemy. .

Llywelyn's argument that 'the rights of our principality are entirely separate from the rights of your kingdom' did not impress Edward who, in Nov. 1276, proclaimed him a rebel. Against England's vastly superior resources in money, arms and manpower, Llywelyn had no chance. In the autumn of 1277 the English landed on Anglesey and harvested the grain, and Llywelyn surrendered. The Treaty of Aberconwy allowed him to retain the title of prince, but drained it of all substance. The homage of the Welsh barons

was reserved to the King. The Four Cantrefs east of Conwy were surrendered to Edward, who gave two of them to Dafydd. Llywelyn kept only Gwynedd west of Conwy, out of which he had to provide for his two other brothers. In effect he was back where he had been in 1247, but now facing a much tougher King. In some respects Edward treated Llywelyn well.

He allowed him to marry Eleanor and, as a generous lord, he met the costs of the wedding in Worcester Cathedral in 1278. But in this, as in everything else, Edward was emphasizing Llywelyn's subordinate status. At Flint, Rhuddlan (Flints.), Aberystwyth (Card.) and Builth (Brecon), he started work on what was to be the great ring of Edwardian castles around Gwynedd. Although it was agreed that all disputes within Wales should be settled 'according to the laws and customs of those parts', it was Edward who appointed the judges. Moreover one of the underlying causes of tension was, as Archbishop PECKHAM expressed it in 1282, the English belief that Welsh law came from the devil, reinforcing the natural tendency of the Welsh to sin, sloth and barbarism.

Llywelyn was not the only one to be bullied by the new regime. Widespread resentment produced a well co-ordinated revolt in March 1282. Llywelyn claimed to have been kept in the dark, and he did not come out into the open until about the time (June 1282) of his wife's death giving birth to a daughter. Again an English army took the harvest of Anglesey but this time Llywelyn did not surrender. He tried to open up a new front in the Wye valley, and it was there, near Builth, that he was killed on 11 Dec. 1282 by a soldier who had no idea who he was.

By now Edward had decided that the time had come to put a permanent end 'to the malice of the Welsh'. In Jan. 1283 he crossed the Conwy and in an unprecedented winter campaign his troops overran Snowdonia. The principality of Wales was annexed to the English Crown. Llywelyn's head was sent to London to be jeered at by the crowd. His gold coronet and the jewel of King ARTHUR were taken to Westminster. He had no need of them now that his head was stuck on an iron spike in the Tower of London and crowned with ivy. 'Is it', asked a Welsh poet of the time, 'the end of the world?'

R. R. Davies, Age of Conquest: Wales 1063–1415 (1987)

LLYWELYN AP IORWERTH (c. 1173–1240)
Prince of North Wales (1199–1240)

Born into a society which, although united by culture, language and law, was divided into a number of independent and mutual hostile principalities, this Prince of Gwynedd, known as 'the great' soon after his death, dominated the history of Wales for 40 years. Though there had been little in the history of the previous 1,000 years to suggest that the rulers of Gwynedd would establish a lasting pre-eminence, this is what Llywelyn achieved. Despite the precious assets of the mountain pastures of Snowdonia and the corn of Anglesey (where Aberffro, Gwynedd's principal seat, lay), it was not the richest nor economically most developed of the ancient Welsh kingdoms. But it was, thanks to its tidal estuaries and mountains, the most defensible, and, with the growing pressure of English incursions and settlement, this came to be the critical factor.

Son of Iorwerth Drwyndwn (the Flatnosed), grandson of OWAIN GWYNEDD, Llywelyn's potential as a modern, English-style, ruler in Wales was recognized by Gerald de BARRI as early as 1189. The young man's rapid rise to power in the 1190s was likened by one of his court poets to 'the swirl of a great windstorm in a surly February'. As was traditional in Welsh politics his first rivals were his kindred. He defeated and exiled his uncle DAFYDD AP OWAIN, and by 1199 he had already assumed the title Prince of North Wales, although not until after the death of his cousin Gruffudd in 1200 did he become ruler of all Gwynedd. He was careful to recognize the overlordship of the English Crown, an inescapable fact of political life which had already made Welsh rulers increasingly think of themselves as princes rather than kings. In 1205 he married JOAN, King JOHN's illegitimate daughter. In 1208 he took advantage of turbulence caused by John's interventions in Wales to move against GWENWYNWYN OF POWYS, his main rival for leadership of the Welsh, seizing southern Powys and rebuilding the castle of Aberystwyth (Card.). But John turned against him and invaded Gwynedd twice in 1211, forcing Llywelyn to surrender Gwynedd east of Conwy (Caern.) and agree that the whole principality would revert to the Crown were he to die without an heir by Joan. Fortunately for Llywelyn, John's high-handed exploitation of this triumph united the Welsh people against him and catapulted Llywelyn into leadership of the revolt. In 1212, acting on behalf of 'all the princes of Wales', he made a treaty with King Philip II of France. A series of setbacks for John both in England and on the continent gave Llywelyn a free hand in Wales. In 1215 and 1216, as John's position collapsed, he captured Carmarthen, Cardigan and even the English town of Shrewsbury; he annexed southern Powys and presided over a partition of the southern Welsh principality of Deheubarth, both in 1216. In 1217 he captured Swansea. He pursued a highly successful policy of accommodation, including marriage alliances, with the English Marcher lords, Briouze, Lacy, MORTIMER and, above all, the earls of Chester. By the Treaty of Worcester (1218) HENRY III's minority council (of which Ranulf, Earl of Chester, was a prominent member) was brought to recognize many of his gains. Although he lost control of south-west Wales in 1223 and faced English expeditions against him in 1228 and 1231, Llywelyn never lost his position as protector and overlord of the other Welsh rulers, none of whom, after the fall of Gwenwynwyn, dared use the title prince. From now on they were merely lords and only the ruler of Gwynedd was prince. His own preferred title was Prince of Aberffro and Lord of Snowdon. In 1226 and again in 1238 he summoned all Welsh lords to swear allegiance to his son, DAFYDD AP LLYWELYN. In order to strengthen Dafydd's right of inheritance he got the Pope to declare Joan legitimate and sidelined the claims of his firstborn son Gruffudd by emphasizing his illegitimacy. As a modernizing ruler he built stone castles at Ewloe (Flints.), Castell y Bere (Merion.), Dolbardarn (Caern.) and Criccieth (Caern.). In Gwynedd he adopted a more English style of government, characterized by a preference for money rents over renders in kind and an increasing use of written documents authenticated by the Prince's seal. So too in politics; he preferred to exile or imprison rather than kill or mutilate his enemies, although he made an exception when he hanged William de Briouze for having an affair with his wife in 1230. More than any previous Welsh ruler he gave the Welsh a measure of political unity, not an amalgamation of principalities into a single State, but a federation under the presidency of Gwynedd. Whether it survived was to depend upon the attitude adopted by English kings, all the more so after the Crown's annexation of the earldom of Chester in 1237.

R. R. Davies, Age of Conquest: Wales 1063–1415 (1987)

Stephen Vaughan, she came from a circle of enthusiastic evangelicals which included her first
husband Henry Locke. In 1553 the Lockes entertained John KNOX, who began an intense correspondence with Anne; eventually she left MARY I's
England and her husband and travelled with her
children to Geneva (1557). She translated sermons
by CALVIN, and is the first woman known to have used
the sonnet form in any language. Back in London
(1559) she continued corresponding with Knox.
Her second husband of three was the outspoken
Puritan minister Edward Dering (?1540–76).

LOCKE, JOHN *see* essay on page 518

LOCKHART, SIR GEORGE (*c.* 1630–89),
Scottish judge. His father was a Scottish MP, a
Royalist, and later a judge. Trained in the law,
Lockhart served as Oliver CROMWELL's advocate
but was pardoned at the Restoration. Recognized
as the most able advocate of his generation, he
clashed with the government in 1674 when he
appealed to the Scottish Parliament over the heads
of the judges who had decided against his client.
Lockhart and his supporters were banished from
within 12 miles of Edinburgh by Lauderdale (*see*
MAITLAND, JOHN); they eventually yielded.
Lockhart continued to oppose the court, acting
for Argyll (*see* CAMPBELL, ARCHIBALD) in 1681
during his trial for treason. He became Lord
President of the Court of Session in 1685, and in
1686 was invited to London by JAMES II to advise on
Catholic toleration. He opposed James's policies
at meetings of the Lords of the Articles, but his
attitude to the arrival of WILLIAM III remains uncertain as he was assassinated in March 1689 by an
opponent's client in an alimony case.

LOCKYER, SIR JOSEPH NORMAN (1836–
1920), astronomer and journalist. Rugby-born
Lockyer developed an interest in astronomy as a
War Office clerk (1857–75). In the early 1860s he
began publishing observations of the planets and
the sun. He used spectroscopic observations of
solar eclipses to establish evidence for the
element helium in the sun (1868) and to
construct controversial theories of the sun and of
the genesis of the chemical elements. As
founder-editor of the best-selling science journal
Nature (first published in 1869) he crusaded for
science education and State endowment of scientific research. Professor of Astronomical Physics
at the Royal College of Science in South
Kensington (1890–1913), he published books on
solar physics and chemistry, science education
and ancient astronomical practices.

LODGE, SIR OLIVER JOSEPH (1851–1940),
physicist. Lodge worked in his father's Staffs.
pottery firm before studying physics in London
(1875–7). His early publications concerned electricity and heat and in 1881 he became Professor
of Physics at Liverpool College (later Liverpool
University). There, in collaboration with Oliver
HEAVISIDE and George Francis Fitzgerald, he
transformed James Clerk MAXWELL's work on
electromagnetism, sought empirical evidence for
the ether and began his lifelong researches into
psychical phenomena. In 1888 he produced
evidence for wireless telegraphic signals
(detected earlier that year by the German physicist Heinrich Hertz) and later built and marketed
what would be seen as the first radio receivers. As
Principal of Birmingham University (1900–19)
and after, he published numerous popular books
on physics, wireless telegraphy, psychical research
and Christianity.

LOEGAIRE MAC NÉILL (*fl. c.* mid to late fifth
century), legendary figure. The son of NIALL
NOÍGIALLACH. Nothing is known of the historical
Loegaire. He is, however, prominent in later
Patrician hagiography as the 'High-King of
Ireland' when St PATRICK arrived to undertake his
mission and is depicted as the inveterate enemy of
the saint. The embellished accounts of such
hagiographical traditions have little historical
basis and provide no certain evidence for him.

LOFTUS, ADAM (1st Viscount Loftus of Ely)
(1568–1647), politician. Nephew of Adam Loftus,
Archbishop of Dublin and Lord Chancellor of
Ireland, he was Archdeacon of Glendalough from
1594, but his career was in the law. He also
became Lord Chancellor in 1619, from which
office he was removed for corruption in 1638; he
was joint Lord Justice 1622–5, 1629–33 and in
1636. He was a consistent opponent of Richard
BOYLE, Earl of Cork. He fled the Irish rebellion in
1641 and died in Yorks.

LOMBARD, PETER (?–1625), theologian. From
an Old English family in Ireland, after studying and
teaching at Leuven, he became Provost of Cambrai
Cathedral. When in Rome, he was asked by Hugh
O'NEILL to be his advocate to the Pope; conse-
quently he wrote *De Regno Hiberniae, Sanctorum
Insula, Commentarius* (A Commentary on the
Kingdom of Ireland, Island of Saints, 1600,
published 1632), a major historical statement of
Catholic nationalism. In 1601 he was rewarded by
becoming head of the Roman Catholic Church in
Ireland as Archbishop of Armagh. He died in Rome.

LOMBE, SIR THOMAS (1685–1739), silk
manufacturer. The son of a weaver, he was
apprenticed to a London mercer, and was later
Alderman and Sheriff of London. In 1718 he

continued on page 519

LOCKE, JOHN (1632–1704)
Philosopher

Son of an attorney who fought as a Parliamentarian in the Civil Wars, Locke was educated at Westminster until 19, then went as a scholar to Christ Church, Oxford; in 1661 he was elected tutor in Greek. He complained later that he had been educated in nothing but 'peripatetic' (Aristotelian) philosophy, but in fact, alongside the formal curriculum, he took an interest in the new science, 'experimental philosophy', privately pursued by some scholars, among whom Robert BOYLE became a lasting friend. Uncertain what career to pursue, in 1665 Locke took a diplomatic post, as secretary on a mission to Brandenburg. Thereafter he fixed his sights on medicine and in 1667 began to collaborate with the medical researcher Thomas SYDENHAM. His scientific experience encouraged him to favour an inductive approach (reasoning from observations to generalizations). He was unpersuaded by the French philosopher Descartes's deductive method (reasoning from first principles to general laws), but Descartes's writings helped stimulate his interest in philosophy.

In 1667 Lord Ashley, later Earl of Shaftesbury (see COOPER, ANTHONY ASHLEY), invited Locke to live with him as his personal physician in London, then a centre of scientific activity. Locke was elected Fellow of the Royal Society in 1668. The fall of Clarendon (see HYDE, EDWARD) in 1667 improved Ashley's political standing: Locke was drawn into public affairs. His first substantial writings on religious toleration were composed then. He had written on this topic, illiberally, in 1661. Now he argued that purely speculative views should be tolerated: magistrates were obliged only to preserve the peace. Stimulated by Ashley's appointment as Chancellor of the Exchequer to consider economic questions, Locke also wrote on the rate of interest and value of money, in response to Sir Josiah CHILD's call for a lower rate of interest. He was also influenced by Ashley's enthusiasm for colonial ventures, becoming secretary to the Lords Proprietors of Carolina in 1668 and secretary to the Council of Trade and Plantations (1673). He was exposed to liberal religious currents: joining the congregation of the Latitudinarian Benjamin WHICHCOTE, and a friend of the Socinian Thomas FIRMIN. By the mid 1670s, Shaftesbury (as Ashley had become) was out of power. Locke now lived a more independent life. He returned to Oxford and secured a BMed, then travelled to France, perhaps for his health, living 15 months in Montpellier.

He returned in 1678 to find England in the midst of the Popish Plot scare touched off by the allegations of Titus OATES, and Shaftesbury's fortunes again in the ascendant. Locke's most influential political writings, the *Two Treatises on Government*, were composed during the ensuing Exclusion Crisis. The *Two Treatises* attacked the absolutist theories of Sir Robert FILMER, developed in the build-up to the Civil Wars but first published at this time. Locke argued that the basis of government was consent, and the powers of governors limited; if governors exceeded their powers, the people had a right to resist. Following Shaftesbury's death (1682), and the implication of Whig leaders Edward RUSSELL, Algernon SYDNEY and Lord Essex (see CAPEL, ARTHUR) in the Rye House Plot, Locke fled to Holland, where he moved in liberal religious Remonstrant circles and lived for two years in a Quaker household. There he composed his most influential work on toleration, the *Letter on Toleration*, published anonymously in Latin (1689, later in English translation). He also worked on an essay on 'human understanding', begun 1671, in which he tried to give inductivism systematic philosophical expression.

When William of Orange (later WILLIAM III) invaded England and JAMES II fled, Locke returned. A bookseller snapped up his *Two Treatises on Government*, though, probably because of their radicalism, Locke never publicly admitted authorship. By contrast, he sought maximum publicity for his *Essay Concerning Human Understanding*, which was very well received, though some thought it subversive of orthodox theology. He also published old and new economic writings, *Some Thoughts concerning Education*, and in 1695 (anonymously again) *The Reasonableness of Christianity*, a plainly unorthodox work which aroused controversy. He continued to take an interest in public affairs: his arguments in favour of liberty of the press, primarily on commercial grounds, helped persuade the Commons to resist the renewal of the Licensing Act 1695. In 1696 he accepted appointment as a Commissioner of the Board of Trade, and was one of its most active members until ill health led him to retire 1700.

During his last years, his writings, especially the *Essay on Human Understanding*, secured him a European reputation. He was to be a hero to Enlightened literati of the eighteenth century: the French Encyclopedists identifed him, along with Francis BACON and Isaac NEWTON, as one of the seminal thinkers of the age.

M. Cranston, John Locke (1957)

obtained a patent for mills for winding, spinning and twisting thread, technology based on industrial espionage carried out in Italy by his half-brother John, thus effectively founding the English silk industry. He set up a mill in Derby with water-powered throwing machines and in 1739 applied unsuccessfully to Parliament for an extension of his patent. By the late eighteenth century there were silk mills in some 20 counties.

LONDON, GEORGE (?–1714), landscape gardener. Encouraged by the gardener to whom he was first apprenticed, who sent him to France to study, he worked for Bishop Henry COMPTON at Fulham before founding Brompton nursery in 1681. By 1687 Henry WISE had joined him as partner and in 1689 the two were made joint Deputy Superintendents of the royal gardens. London let Wise concentrate on commissions in London while he toured the provinces, designing gardens at several great houses including Chatsworth (Derb.), Longleat (Wilts.), Wimpole (Cambs.) and Staunton Harold (Leics.). London's gardens were pragmatic as well as decorative, laid out in compartments around the house with kitchen gardens and mazes further out, and beyond them a wooded deer park whose trees might provide a timber crop.

LONDONDERRY, 2ND MARQUESS OF see STEWART, ROBERT

LONG, WALTER (1st Viscount Long of Wraxall) (1854–1924), politician. He was a bucolic, red-faced representative of what the 3rd Marquess of Salisbury (see CECIL, ROBERT) once described as 'pure squire Conservatism'. A lukewarm supporter of Tariff Reform, which he regarded as a squalid businessman's doctrine, and a rabid opponent of the reform of the Lords, he stood against Austen CHAMBERLAIN in 1911 for the Tory leadership. Both men stood down in favour of Bonar LAW. Long, regarded as the representative of the Tory agriculturalists, went on to serve in coalitions under ASQUITH and LLOYD GEORGE.

LONGCHAMP, WILLIAM (?–1197), royal servant. The Norman author of a treatise on civil law, he began his career in HENRY II's chancery. In 1189 he was made Bishop of Ely, then Papal Legate and head of the Regency Council which governed England while RICHARD I was absent on crusade. In consequence, Longchamp earned JOHN's enmity and was described in the latter's propaganda as lame, ape-like and excessively fond of boys. By ordering the arrest of GEOFFREY, ARCHBISHOP OF YORK, in Sept. 1191, he played into the hands of his enemies and within a month was forced into ignominious flight. Despite the collapse of his authority in England, he retained Richard's trust and remained Chancellor until his death.

LONGESPÉE, WILLIAM see LONGSWORD, WILLIAM

LONGFORD, 7TH EARL OF see PAKENHAM, FRANCIS

LONGSWORD (OR LONGESPÉE), WILLIAM (3rd Earl of Salisbury) (?–1226), diplomat and soldier. An illegitimate son of HENRY II, he gained the title through his wife Ela in 1198. By the time of his death he had been sheriff of eight counties, Lieutenant of Gascony, Constable of Dover and Warden of the Cinque Ports. In 1214 he commanded the English contingent at the Battle of Bouvines, when he was taken prisoner by the French. He was one of King JOHN's favourite gambling companions and most loyal servants; not until 1216 did he join the opposition to his half-brother. In 1220 he and his wife, who founded Laycock Abbey (Wilts.) laid foundation stones for the new cathedral at Salisbury, where he was buried.

LOPEZ, RODERIGO (?–1594), racial scapegoat. A Portuguese Jew, he settled in England in 1559 to practise medicine, and became a member of the Royal College of Physicians and chief physician to ELIZABETH I. Robert DEVEREUX, Earl of Essex, backed charges that he had plotted to murder the Queen and Antonio Perez, a Spanish refugee. Though almost certainly innocent, he was convicted and executed in a wave of anti-Semitism and anti-Spanish hysteria. One of very few Jews with a public profile in Tudor England, he may have inspired SHAKESPEARE's regrettable characterization of Shylock in *The Merchant of Venice*.

LORCÁN UA TUATHAIL, ST (ST LAWRENCE O TOOLE) (c. 1128–80), Archbishop of Dublin. Royal descent and royal connections as brother-in-law to DIARMAIT MAC MURCHADHA had brought him promotion, to Abbot of Glendalough (Co. Wicklow) in 1153, then to Archbishop of Dublin in 1162. He became deeply involved in the politics of the English invasion of Ireland and in 1179 incurred HENRY II's anger by accepting appointment as Papal Legate for Ireland and presiding over a reform synod at Clonfert (Co. Galway). His continuation of MALACHY's work reforming the Irish Church along continental lines and the austerity of his life secured his canonization as a saint in 1226.

LOTHIAN, 11TH MARQUESS OF see KERR, PHILIP

LOUDON, 1ST EARL OF see CAMPBELL, JOHN

LOUGHLIN, DAME ANNE (1894–1979), trade unionist. The oldest daughter of a Leeds-based Irish boot- and shoemaker, when her mother died the 12-year-old Loughlin was obliged to look after the family as well as working in a clothing factory. A shop steward in her teens and organizer of the 10,000-strong Tailor and Garment Workers' Union by the time she was 21, she worked particularly to combat the appalling 'sweatshop' conditions in the industry. In 1916 6,000 clothing workers went on strike at Hebden Bridge (Yorks.): Loughlin, a rousing speaker, was one of the organizers. She served on trade boards and travelled the country negotiating wage settlements in the 1920s and 1930s. In 1948 she was appointed General Secretary of the by now 100,000-strong union, the first time a woman had ever headed a mixed-sex union. In 1943 she was elected first woman president of the Trades Union Congress and the same year was the first trade unionist to be made DBE.

LOUIS VIII (1187–1226), King of France (1223–6). In late 1215, after the Concord of Runnymede (based on Magna Carta) had broken down, the rebel barons offered JOHN's throne to Louis, son of Philip Augustus, King of France. The following May, Louis arrived in England and soon won many supporters, but when John died in Oct. he faced the harder task of depriving the nine-year-old HENRY III of his natural inheritance. In 1217, after Louis's forces were defeated at the battles of Lincoln and Sandwich (Kent), he agreed, in the Treaty of Kingston (Surrey) (Sept. 1217), to abandon his claim. As King of France, he continued the process of dismembering the Angevin empire by his conquest (1224) of Poitou.

LOUTH, EARL OF see BERMINGHAM, JOHN

LOVAT, 12TH BARON see FRASER, SIMON

LOVELACE, COUNTESS OF see KING, AUGUSTA ADA

LOVELESS, GEORGE (1797–1874), leader of the Tolpuddle Martyrs. In Feb. 1834 the magistrates of Dorchester (Dorset) sentenced Loveless and five others, including his brothers John and James, to transportation for administering 'illegal oaths' in their union, the Friendly Society of Agricultural Labourers, which George had formed in Tolpuddle in Oct. 1833. The Whig government was fearful of a revival of the widespread rural unrest associated with 'Captain Swing' in 1830. Loveless's union had sought only to prevent wage reductions in one of the poorest-paid agricultural regions of Britain. After a campaign by the Grand National Consolidated Trades Union, established by Robert OWEN in 1833, and other sympathizers, the Tolpuddle Martyrs were pardoned in March 1836. Loveless, who was a moderate radical and had been a Methodist lay preacher, wrote an eloquent denunciation of the prosecutions in his *The Victims of Whiggery* (1837). In 1846 he migrated to Canada with his wife.

LOVELL, SIR BERNARD (1913–), astronomer. Lovell developed airborne radar systems during the Second World War and after the war returned to Manchester where he had previously taught physics, made observations of the sun and meteor showers using military radar equipment and began campaigning for the construction of a large radio telescope observatory at Jodrell Bank near Manchester. In 1947 he oversaw construction of a 218-ft diameter radio telescope, an instrument that he later used to observe radio signals from the Andromeda galaxy. In 1957 he completed at Jodrell Bank a hugely expensive 250-ft diameter steerable parabolic radio telescope. This telescope proved invaluable in tracking spacecraft and the detection of such novel astronomical phenomena as quasars and pulsars. He is a prolific writer on radio astronomy.

LOVETT, WILLIAM (1800–77), Chartist leader. One of the founders of the London Working Men's Association (1836), Lovett was also the chief drafter of the People's Charter (1838), which demanded annual parliaments, manhood suffrage, equal electoral districts, voting by ballot, abolition of property qualifications for MPs and payment for MPs. As a moderate 'moral force' Chartist he believed that it was necessary to make an alliance between 'the virtuous exceptions' among the middle classes and the 'reflecting part' of his own (working) class. He was appalled by the tactics of his more militant colleagues (Feargus O'CONNOR in particular), though he was himself imprisoned for a year in 1839 for publishing a pamphlet complaining about police methods.

LOWE, ROBERT (1st Viscount Sherbrooke) (1811–92), politician. Educated at Winchester and Oxford, he became a barrister and politician in Australia (1842–50). Back in Britain he was a Liberal MP from 1852; as Vice-President of the Board of Trade (1855–8) he extended limited liability through the Joint-Stock Companies Act 1856; as Vice-President of the Board of Education (1859–64), he introduced payment by results for teachers. In 1866 he became the leading opponent of franchise reform in the House of Commons and led the group of Liberals known as the Adullamites, the name, referring to the cave where David took refuge (1 Samuel 22), reflects the frequency of Biblical allusion in Victorian political discourse, who voted with the Conservatives to defeat his own Liberal Party. Despite this, he served under GLADSTONE as Chancellor of the Exchequer (1868–73). He served as the first MP for London University (1868–80).

LOWER, RICHARD (1631–91), physician. He studied chemistry and anatomy at Oxford, where he assisted Thomas WILLIS in his research on the nervous system. He pioneered blood transfusion, successfully transfusing blood from one dog into the vein of another at Oxford in 1665; he was unable to find a human subject until after Jean-Baptiste Denys had performed the experiment in Paris in 1667. Lower practised medicine in London and was pre-eminent in the late 1670s until embarrassed by his support for the Whigs during the Exclusion Crisis. *See also* COOPER, ANTHONY ASHLEY.

LOWNDES, WILLIAM (1652–1724), politician and administrator. Educated at the free school Buckingham, he first obtained a minor post at the Treasury in 1679, rising to become Chief Clerk and, in 1695, Secretary, and an MP. He was thus well placed to shape fiscal and economic policy, advising on the recoinage of 1696. He has been credited with the phrase 'ways and means', as in the House of Commons Committee of Ways and Means, one of its two main fiscal committees.

LOWRY, L(AURENCE) S(TEPHEN) (1887–1976), artist. Son of a Manchester estate agent, Lowry studied at art schools there and in Salford, where the family moved. These northern industrial landscapes are the scenes of his *faux naïve* paintings with their mass of busy-looking stick figures that seem to speak of urban alienation. His art became popular in the 1960s: a retrospective exhibition at the Royal Academy in 1976 demonstrated how Lowry had fulfilled his ambition 'to put the industrial scene on the map ... because nobody had done it seriously'.

LOWTHER, SIR JOHN (1582–1637), entrepreneur. From a knightly family of Cumb. and a barrister, he was county MP between 1623 and 1627, and became a client of George VILLIERS, Duke of Buckingham, serving on the Council in the North. He much expanded the family estates, and profited by money-lending, trading investments, collieries and saltpans, setting his family on its path to a notable industrial future. He kept parliamentary diaries and left an autobiography.

LUCAS, CHARLES (1713–71), doctor and politician. Apprenticed to an apothecary, he ran a shop in Dublin. In 1741 he attacked apothecaries' abusive practices, and gained a place on the Common Council, where he began to agitate for the reform of city government. In 1748 he stood for MP on the issue of Irish parliamentary corruption. He was associated with the outspoken *Freeman's Journal*, for which FLOOD later wrote, and was influential in encouraging extra-parliamentary opposition to the Lord Lieutenant during the struggle for ascendancy between the Crown party of Archbishop George STONE and the 'patriots' of Henry BOYLE. Parliament declared him an enemy of his country, and he fled to London. He returned and was elected MP for Dublin in 1760. Dubbed 'the Irish WILKES', he introduced an unsuccessful Bill for shorter Parliaments, opposed the augmentation of the army and favoured the establishment of a militia.

LUCAS, MARGARET (Duchess of Newcastle) (1617–74), writer. As maid of honour to HENRIETTA MARIA she followed her into exile in Paris and there married (as his second wife) William CAVENDISH, later Duke of Newcastle. Brilliant, unconventional and heedless of male chauvinist ridicule (e.g. from Samuel PEPYS), she was one of the most interesting and versatile writers of poetry, prose and drama in her day.

LUCRAFT, BENJAMIN (1809–97), radical. Born in Exeter, Lucraft was a cabinetmaker. Moving to London in the 1830s, he became a Chartist, remaining active until the last Chartist conference in 1858. That established the Political Reform Union, an important bridge between Chartism and the Reform League of 1865–8 in campaigning for votes for working men. By 1866 Lucraft was an 'ultra-radical' in the Reform League, holding weekly meetings in Clerkenwell to draw in the unorganized working class as well as the craft unionists, and urging, against the inclinations of the league's leadership, for an escalation of mass pressure on the government. But by the early 1870s he was becoming a typical 'lib-lab' (working-class radical associated with liberalism). He was elected for Finsbury to the London School Board in 1870 and was re-elected every three years until his retirement in 1890, and stood unsuccessfully as a parliamentary candidate for Finsbury in 1874 and Tower Hamlets in 1880.

LUCY, RICHARD DE (?–1179), Chief Justiciar. A loyal servant of HENRY II, and his Chief Justiciar for 25 years until he retired in 1178, he was the King's Councillor in the BECKET dispute and was twice excommunicated by the exiled Archbishop. During the war of 1173–4, while Henry stayed in France, Lucy held the fort in England, driving back the Scots in 1173 and defeating the rebel

Earls of Leicester and Norfolk at the Battle of Fornham (Suffolk) in 1174.

LUDFORD, NICHOLAS (*c.* 1490–1557), composer. By 1527 he was directing music in St Stephen's College in Westminster Palace, and after its dissolution in 1549 continued to live in Westminster. He was considered one of the leading English composers of his age, but his choral music, original and adventurous in its use of voices, has been rediscovered only in the last few decades and given its due importance.

LUDLOW, EDMUND (1617–92), soldier and writer. One of the chief army promoters of PRIDE's Purge of the Commons (Dec. 1648) and of CHARLES I's death, he regarded Oliver CROMWELL's assumption of the protectorate as a betrayal and retired. At the restoration of CHARLES II he escaped to Switzerland; he was astonished to find himself still unwelcome in England after the Glorious Revolution of 1688. His memoirs of his life, ruthlessly pruned and edited into urbanity by John TOLAND for publication in 1698–9, have recently re-emerged for publication from the original manuscript as the religiously charged *A Voyce from the Watch Tower*.

LUGARD, FREDERICK (1st Baron Lugard of Abinger) (1858–1945), colonial administrator. Born an army chaplain's son in Madras, he began his military career in 1878, distinguishing himself in the Sudan in 1885 and Burma in 1886. Seen by RHODES as a useful tool in the opening up of Africa, Lugard led intervention in Uganda in 1890 and was influential in establishing the protectorate there in 1894. Meanwhile his interest had shifted to West Africa, where he was appointed Commissioner for Nigeria in 1897, and High Commissioner of the new North Nigeria protectorate in 1900. Acquitting himself with skill, he crossed swords with the Colonial Office and resigned in 1906. After serving as Governor General of Hong Kong, he returned to Nigeria in 1912, governing the newly united north and south until 1919. The task of unification was difficult, but Lugard's lasting success is evident in the way in which Nigeria has striven to remain a single nation since. During his tenure he developed the so-called Lugard Rules, his legacy to colonial administration, controlling the different areas through their own native rulers and so combining co-operation with administrative economy.

LUL, ST (?–786), missionary. An eighth-century English missionary in Germany and a disciple of St BONIFACE, who continued the latter's work after his death, Lul was, like his predecessor, a confidant of the Carolingian kings, and is known to have been exceptionally active in the transmission of the works of BEDE and later scholars into Carolingian Europe.

LULACH, King of the Scots (1057–8). The son of Queen GRUOCH by her first marriage and the stepson of King MACBETH, he was briefly proclaimed King after the latter's death in battle against MAEL COLUIM III CENN MÓR. He was himself killed by Mael Coluim's forces at Essie (Aberdeens.).

LUMLEY, JOHN (6th Baron Lumley) (*c.* 1533–1609), artistic patron. Cambridge-educated, he was restored in blood in 1547 after his father George's execution (1537) following the Pilgrimage of Grace. From 1559 he was High Steward of Oxford University but, a Roman Catholic sympathizer, was imprisoned in the Tower from 1569 to 1573 for intrigues with his father-in-law Henry FitzAlan, 12th Earl of Arundel, and Thomas HOWARD, Duke of Norfolk. A keen antiquary, he made his home, Nonsuch Palace (Surrey), a centre of artistic patronage (*see* TALLIS, THOMAS); with Arundel (*see* LLWYD, HUMPHREY), he collected a superb library, a component of the royal collection, now in the British Library.

LUMLEY, RICHARD (2nd Viscount Lumley, 1st Earl of Scarbrough) (?–1721), soldier and politician. Grandson of a prominent Royalist, raised a Roman Catholic, he was a favourite of CHARLES II. He raised troops of horse to combat Monmouth's rebellion (*see* SCOTT, JAMES) in 1685 but later became disaffected with James II (*see* JAMES VII AND II), converted to Anglicanism and was one of the 'Immortal Seven' who in 1688 invited over the future WILLIAM III, for whom he fought in Ireland and Flanders. He was a Commissioner for the Union with Scotland, and held minor offices under GEORGE I.

LUTHER, MARTIN (1483–1546), reformer. Without Luther there might have been no Reformation in sixteenth-century Europe. His university career (principally at Wittenberg) forced him to doubt late medieval ideas on salvation, culminating in fury at a campaign promoting indulgences in 1517. He found himself leading a full-scale revolt against Roman authority and heading a new Lutheran Church, complete with doctrinal statements set out in the Augsburg Confession (1530, with revised text, the *Variata*, 1540, preferred in some Churches). Many princes of the Holy Roman Empire sponsored Lutheran reforms, and in 1531 formed the defensive league of Schmalkalden against potential attacks from CHARLES V. In England, Luther's ideas provoked official repression in the 1520s. HENRY VIII detested him after their literary clash (1521), and principled

Lutheran opposition to Henry's quest for annulment of his first marriage made matters worse; thereafter Henry encouraged dialogue with Lutherans only when diplomatic necessity demanded. Subsequently English Protestant theology diverged from Lutheranism, developing more personal contacts and sympathy with the Strasbourg reform of Martin BUCER and with Swiss Reformed Churches. Some Scots academics and clergy became interested in Lutheranism in the 1520s and also suffered repression (*see* HAMILTON, PATRICK; WISHART, GEORGE), but from the 1550s CALVIN was more important in the Scottish Reformation (*see* KNOX, JOHN; MELVILLE, ANDREW).

LUTYENS, SIR EDWIN (1869–1944), architect. He studied in London, and was strongly influenced by the Arts and Crafts movement (*see* MORRIS, WILLIAM; VOYSEY, C. F.), going on to design numerous country houses drawing on English vernacular style and neoclassical elements. Later, he worked on large official commissions, notably New Delhi (1912–31), the Cenotaph in London (1919) and a design (in the end abandoned) for a Roman Catholic cathedral in Liverpool (1929).

LYDGATE, JOHN (*c.* 1370–*c.* 1451), poet. A prolific and versatile English man of letters, a monk of Bury St Edmunds who wrote love poems as well as saints' lives to order, he is now generally regarded as a poet who made the mistake of trying to outdo Chaucer. His *Troy Book* was commissioned by HENRY V, and throughout the 1420s Lydgate remained close to HUMPHREY OF GLOUCESTER and the Lancastrian court.

LYELL, SIR CHARLES (1797–1875), geologist. Born in Scotland, the son of a landowner and botanist, Lyell read classics and developed his interest in geology and palaeontology at William BUCKLAND's geology lectures at Oxford. He went on geological tours of Scotland and the continent and in 1819 embarked on a legal career, but bad eyesight forced him to give it up for a career as a geologist. He was Professor of Geology at King's College, London (1831–3), and in 1832 married Mary Horner, his lifelong intellectual companion. His strongest institutional affiliation was the Geological Society, which he joined in 1819 and of which he was President (1835–7, 1849–51). He is chiefly remembered for his magisterial *Principles of Geology* (1830–3), in which the central argument was that 'causes now in operation' on the earth's surface, for example earthquakes, volcanoes and erosion, are sufficient to explain all geological changes, however ancient or dramatic, provided that an immense time scale is allowed for such causes to have had their accumulative effect. In Lyell's so-called 'uniformitarian' geology the

earth's landscape had evolved continuously, which contrasted to the prevailing view that the earth's geology had been shaped by catastrophes involving forces on a far greater scale than those known today. The *Principles* also sought to show that geology was a respectable, empirically based science, but, controversially, it upheld the great antiquity of the earth and rejected Divine intervention in nature. It made a deep impression on nineteenth-century science and literature, and informed the belief of Charles DARWIN, Herbert SPENCER and Thomas HUXLEY that organic features of the earth had evolved continuously from natural causes. Although Lyell promoted Darwin's theory of evolution, he maintained grave doubts about the idea that man had descended from apes, an equivocal view expressed in his *Antiquity of Man* (1863).

LYFING, Bishop of Crediton (1028–38) and Bishop of Worcester (1038–46). A politically minded English monk, appointed Abbot of Tavistock in 1009 by ETHELRED II THE UNREADY. Steadily advanced under CNUT, he was rewarded for his support with the bishopric of Worcester by HAROLD I HAREFOOT, only to be temporarily deprived under HARTHACNUT. He was subsequently able to ingratiate himself with EDWARD THE CONFESSOR. Like, for example, the younger Archbishop STIGAND, Lyfing represents the worldlier aspects of the pre-Conquest English Church.

LYNCH, JACK (1917–99), Taoiseach (Irish Prime Minster). Fianna Fáil member of the Dáil for Cork City (1948–81), Lynch was unusual among leading Fianna Fáilers of his generation in lacking any family link with the Anglo-Irish War. (He was originally chosen as a candidate on the basis of a successful amateur sporting career.) Minister for Education (1957–9), Industry and Commerce (1959–65), and Finance (1965–6), he was chosen as a compromise successor to Sean LEMASS to avoid a damaging contest between several prominent younger ministers (including Charles HAUGHEY, George Colley and Neil Blaney). His first period as Taoiseach (1966–73) was marked by tension between potential heirs, leading to the 1970 crisis when Haughey and Blaney were dismissed for trying to supply arms to Republican groups in the North. In the resulting trial the defendants were acquitted because of ambiguities about how far their activities were known to other members of the government. Lynch retained his leadership despite this setback; but Haughey survived as a focus for discontent. Lynch presided over Ireland's entry to the European Economic Community (1973). Narrowly defeated by a Fine Gael and Labour coalition under Liam COSGRAVE (1973), Lynch won a landslide victory (1977) on a reckless manifesto promising to bring the country out of recession by large-scale government spending. This policy (combined with the oil crisis of 1978–9) led to massive increases in unemployment and inflation, precipitating Lynch's retirement in 1979 and causing the defeat in the leadership election of his preferred successor, Colley, by Haughey. Many of Lynch's followers resented Haughey's succession, which contributed to the continuing factionalization of Fianna Fáil in the 1980s. Lynch's modest style of leadership was often contrasted with Haughey's Napoleonic pretensions.

LYNCH, JOHN (?1599–?1673), historian. From an Old English family of Galway and Jesuit-educated, he became Roman Catholic Archdeacon of Tuam, but was forced into exile by Oliver CROMWELL's invasion of Ireland and probably died at St Malo. He wrote in Latin on Irish history; he catalogued Irish bishops and bitterly attacked the twelfth-century Gerald de BARRI as a source of anti-Irish prejudice, although he also defended Old English Catholics against Old Irish partisans such as Richard O'FERRALL.

LYNEDOCH, BARON see GRAHAM, THOMAS

LYNN, DAME VERA (née Welch) (1917–), singer. Brought up in London's East End and a public performer with bands like those of Joe LOSS and Bert Ambrose from a young age, she went solo after being voted top singer in a *Daily Express* poll in 1939. During the war she was dubbed the 'forces' sweetheart', entertaining the troops with her own radio show *Sincerely Yours*, touring Britain and visiting Burma (1944), though there were official anxieties that her sentimental songs might make the boys 'soft'. Her most popular numbers were *The White Cliffs of Dover* and *We'll Meet Again*. In the 1950s her hit song *Auf Wiederseh'n*, which sold more than 12 million copies, made her the first British singer to top the US hit parade.

LYTHE, ROBERT (?–*c*. 1574), cartographer. He worked for the Crown in Calais in 1556 and in Ireland from 1567 to 1571, producing a complete map of the island, now lost, and several regional and local surveys which were incorporated into the work of John SPEED (1612) and thus gained wide and prolonged circulation.

LYTTELTON, HUMPHREY (1921–), musician. Even before beginning his formal schooling at Eton, where his father was a housemaster, Lyttelton demonstrated a precocious talent and as a teenager developed a passion for jazz. Teaching himself to play the trumpet, he formed his own band in 1948. Moving away from traditional New Orleans jazz towards swing, he contributed significantly to the development of British jazz by forming in 1951 the Humphrey Lyttelton Club, the longest running venue for jazz in London. By the 1960s he was a well-known figure in the international jazz scene. His BBC Radio 2 series, *The Best of Jazz*, ran for many years, and he continues to make frequent appearances on radio.

LYTTON, LADY CONSTANCE (1869–1923), suffragette. Constance joined the Women's Social and Political Union in 1908. Imprisoned for her militant protests, she was released rather than being forcibly fed when she went on hunger strike. Intent on exposing the preferential treatment of aristocratic women, Lady Constance disguised herself as a seamstress 'Jane Warton': she was arrested while protesting outside Walton gaol in Liverpool in 1911, and when she refused food was soon forcibly fed. The Home Secretary refused demands for a public inquiry into this unequal treatment of prisoners. *Prison and Prisoners: Some Personal Experiences* by C. Lytton and Jane Warton was published in 1914.

LYTTON, EDWARD BULWER (1st Earl of Lytton) (1831–91), Viceroy of India and poet. A successful diplomat and also a poet attached to the Brownings' circle (*see* BROWNING, ROBERT; BROWNING, ELIZABETH BARRETT), Lytton was offered the viceroyalty of India by DISRAELI in 1876. He used his flair for pageantry in organizing the great Durbar of 1877 in which Queen VICTORIA was proclaimed Empress of India; popular opposition to the Durbar caused him to repress criticism and dissidence, while in external relations his aggressive policies led to the Second Afghan War of 1878 and British occupation of Afghanistan. With a new government under GLADSTONE he was recalled; his successor Lord Ripon (*see* ROBINSON, GEORGE) sought peace.

M

MABBOTT, GILBERT (1622–*c.* 1670), journalist. A Nottingham tradesman's son, he became a member of the Westminster Parliament's clerical staff in 1643 and was thereafter throughout the 1640s and 1650s a major figure in writing, editing and distributing anti-Royalist newsletters, particularly associated with Ferdinando FAIRFAX and Thomas FAIRFAX, successive Lords Fairfax. He has been linked with the Leveller newsbook, *The Moderate*, but there is little evidence for this, and it seems out of character with his otherwise moderate parliamentary connections. From 1658 he lived in Ireland.

MACADAM, JOHN LOUDON (1756–1836), road-builder. Born in Ayr, from the age of 14 Macadam lived with his merchant uncle in New York, where he made a fortune as agent for the sale of prize properties. Returning to Scotland he became a magistrate and road trustee for Ayrs., when he began his experiments in building roads of compacted broken stone with a surface constructed for drainage. There, and later in the west of England, he put his designs into practice; macadamized roads transformed the countryside, providing better and longer-lasting surfaces and speeding mail coach communication. Macadam and his contemporary TELFORD built upon the achievements in road-building of their predecessors John METCALF, George WADE and William ROY. In 1827 Parliament appointed Macadam General Surveyor of Roads, with a substantial back payment for all his past efforts. The term 'tarmacadam' or 'tarmac' is derived from his name.

MAC AINGIL, AODH *see* MACCAGHWELL, HUGH

McALISKEY, BERNADETTE (née Devlin) (1947–), Irish politician. As a student in Queen's University, Belfast, she became involved in the left-wing People's Democracy movement and took a prominent role in civil rights demonstrations. Elected MP for Mid-Ulster in 1969, she drew international attention by her youth and articulateness. In Aug. 1969 she participated in the 'Battle of the Bogside', where demonstrators fought to keep the police out of the main Catholic area of Derry, triggering riots across Northern Ireland and forcing the Stormont (Northern Ireland Parliament) government to call on British troops to restore order; she was later briefly imprisoned for her role. She remained MP for Mid-Ulster until Feb. 1974 but was increasingly marginalized by her outspoken left-wing views. She was briefly associated with the Irish Republican Socialist Party and in the late 1970s campaigned on behalf of Republican prisoners' demands for political status; in 1981 she and her husband Michael McAliskey were shot and severely wounded by loyalist paramilitaries. She has remained active in Republican and women's groups, and has criticized the 1998 Good Friday Agreement.

MACARTNEY, GEORGE (1st Earl Macartney) (1737–1806), diplomat. Born and educated in Ireland, as a young man he made the acquaintance of the FOX family while on the Grand Tour. Through their influence he began his diplomatic career as envoy extraordinary to St Petersburg in 1764. In a long and adventurous life of public service, he was captured in the French attack on Grenada in 1779, served as Governor of Madras (1781–6), and was plenipotentiary to the Chinese imperial court in 1792–3. His refusal there to kowtow, to perform ritual homage to the Emperor, has been seen as a watershed in the increasing world dominance of Europe. Macartney was secret envoy to the exiled French King Louis XVIII at Verona in 1795–6 and ended his career as first Governor of Cape Colony.

MACAULAY, CATHERINE (née Sawbridge) (1731–91), radical historian and early feminist. Her father, a Kentish landowner, educated her alongside her brother. She began her *History of England from the Accession of James I to that of the Brunswick Line* soon after her wedding to George Macaulay, a physician at a lying-in hospital, in 1760. The first instalment appeared in 1763, to praise from all quarters including Horace WALPOLE and Thomas GRAY. Macaulay participated in many of the pamphlet debates of the day; she was a particular opponent of Edmund BURKE throughout his career. Her other writings included *Letters on Education* (1790) arguing for equality of the sexes in the classroom; she also paid extended visits to

France and North America, greeting Republicans. In 1778 she took as her second husband William, 21-year-old brother of Dr James GRAHAM; polite society was scandalized by the 26-year difference in their ages.

MACAULAY, THOMAS BABINGTON (1st Baron Macaulay) (1800–59), historian. He was the son of an anti-slavery campaigner and a member of the Clapham Sect, an Anglican Evangelical group centred round John VENN, rector of Holy Trinity church, Clapham, that engaged in philanthropic, missionary and other collective religious activities. Other sect members included William WILBERFORCE. A Cambridge-educated lawyer, Macaulay was a Whig MP who served as Secretary at War and Paymaster General, as well as drafting India's penal code and writing poetry and historical reviews. His *Lays of Ancient Rome* were published in 1842. He saw his *History of England* as 'eminently the history of physical, of moral and of intellectual improvement'. His ambition in writing it was to provide moral uplift, a permanent record (he believed his venture to be analogous to that of Thucydides), and to write such a compelling narrative that it would replace 'the last fashionable novel upon the table of young ladies'. His dramatic epic Whig version of history (five vols, 1849–61) was a best-seller, though he had only got as far as 1702 when he died. It remains a classic today.

MACBETH *see* essay on page 527

MACBRIDE, SEAN (1904–88), Irish politician. Son of Maud GONNE, he spent most of his childhood in France. On returning to Ireland he joined the IRA and fought in the Anglo-Irish War and the Civil War (on the Republican side). Chief of Staff of the IRA in the 1930s he moved towards constitutional politics in response to DE VALERA's dismantling of the Anglo-Irish Treaty. MacBride became a successful barrister and defended Republicans in several high-profile cases. In 1946 he founded Clann na Poblachta, a party combining former Republican associates with discontented Fianna Fáilers and young social reformists concerned about the social problems of post-war Ireland. Victories for MacBride and another candidate in by-elections led to a premature dissolution of the Dáil, and in the 1948 General Election the party won 13.2 per cent of the vote and 10 seats. It formed a coalition government with five other parties (including MacBride's former Civil War opponents in Fine Gael) to the derision of Fianna Fáil and the dismay of some more Republican supporters. MacBride became Minister for Foreign Affairs and another Clann na Poblachta member of the Dáil, Noel BROWNE, became Minister for Health. The party played a role (the extent of which remains unclear) in COSTELLO's decision

formally to declare Ireland a Republic, but found itself hampered by MacBride's aloof and authoritarian leadership, failure to establish a local government base, and the raised profile of Fine Gael. It was fatally split by MacBride's failure to support Browne over the Mother and Child Scheme, and was reduced to two seats at the following election. MacBride remained a member for the Dáil until 1961, but never again held Cabinet office; the party was wound up in 1965. He was awarded the 1974 Nobel Peace Prize, and campaigned for the withdrawal of American investment from Northern Ireland unless the 'MacBride principles' about fair employment were observed.

MACCAGHWELL, HUGH (1571–1626), poet and theologian. Known in Gaelic as Aodh Mac Aingil and in Latin as Hugo Cavellus, he taught theology at Salamanca, at the Irish Franciscan college at Leuven and in Rome. He died just after being chosen as Roman Catholic Archbishop of Armagh. He wrote Gaelic devotional and descriptive topographical poetry, and he was an outstanding philosophical theologian who besides his own writings contributed significantly to a European revival of interest in the theology of John DUNS SCOTUS with his editions of Scotus's work (*see also* WADDING, LUKE).

McCARTNEY, SIR PAUL (1942–), musician. Born in Liverpool, McCartney began playing the guitar at 13 and within a few months had joined John LENNON's band. He and Lennon collaborated in founding the Beatles, and as the song-writing partnership for the group they enjoyed a string of number-one hits between 1964 and 1970, including the Beatles' most famous album, *Sergeant Pepper's Lonely Hearts Club Band*, in 1967. The Beatles split up in 1970 and McCartney embarked on his highly successful composing career, in which he collaborated with his wife, the American photographer Linda Eastman, with whom he created the group Wings in 1971. Wings recorded the million-selling *My Love*, as well as the controversial singles *Give Ireland Back to the Irish* and *Hi Hi Hi* which were banned by the BBC, while *Mull of Kintyre* (1977) was the first single to sell over two million copies in Britain. With the dissolution of Wings in 1979, McCartney returned to solo performances and conceived and wrote the classical *Liverpool Oratorio* (1991) with the composer-conductor Carl Davis.

MACCLESFIELD, 5TH EARL OF *see* PARKER, THOMAS

McCULLOCH, JOHN RAMSEY (1789–1864), political economist. One of the great exponents of Ricardian economics (*see* RICARDO, DAVID), he was

continued on page 528

MACBETH
King of the Scots (1040–57)

He was immortalized by SHAKESPEARE as the epitome of evil, a scheming murderer who usurped power illegitimately and who met a thoroughly deserved death at the hands of his enemies. In view of this reputation, which was entirely the creation of the fourteenth-century and fifteenth-century chroniclers whose stories Shakespeare embellished, it is important to emphasize that Macbeth was regarded by all his contemporaries as a legitimate Scottish king. Although he did gain power by killing DONNCHAD I in 1040, this should be seen as the result of the kind of feud which was typical of early medieval Europe. In 1050 Macbeth became the first Scottish king ever to make a pilgrimage to Rome, where he apparently made a favourable impression, and appears to have been a successful and effective king during his 17-year reign.

Macbeth's career must be set in the context of contemporary early medieval British politics and society. Although a single kingship had by and large emerged in Scotland in the ninth and tenth centuries from the time of CINAED MAC ALPÍN, the effective power of these kings was mostly confined to the region between the Forth–Clyde line and the 'Mounth', that is, the southern limit of the great mountain range stretching from Ben Nevis to the North Sea coast near Stonehaven. In the early eleventh century MAEL COLUIM II (1005–34) had extended Scottish power southwards into Lothian and Cumbria as a result of the Battle of Carham (1018), bringing the emergent Scottish and English kingdoms into direct relations; as a result King CNUT had launched an expedition against the Scots to restrict further expansion. Effective control over northern Scotland was divided between the mormaers or kings of Moray, whose territory stretched from the eastern Highlands on the River Spey to Loch Alsh and Ross, and the Scandinavian earls of Orkney, who dominated most of the Isles and who intermittently acknowledged the overlordship of the kings of Norway. Macbeth was the son of FINDLAECH MAC RUAIDRÍ, Mormaer (great steward or *dux*) of Moray. He had gained control of Moray in 1032 by burning alive Gille Comgáin, who had usurped his father's power, and, in a typical attempt to resolve a feud, had married Gille Comgáin's widow GRUOCH, who was also a direct descendant of Mael Coluim II's predecesor, King CINAED III. As a result of this marriage Macbeth both possessed a claim to the kingship of the Scots and was the heir to a bitter feud between the two branches of the descendants of Cinaed mac Alpín. What is more, one of Macbeth's kinsmen and predecessors, another Gille Comgáin, had been killed by Mael Coluim II, who was Donnchad I's grandfather. In this context, it is unsurprising that war broke out between Macbeth and Donnchad.

After defeating Donnchad, Macbeth ruled the whole of Scotland until 1054. In 1045, he defeated CRÍNÁN, Abbot of Dunkeld, who was Donnchad's father, and at some stage he probably campaigned unsuccessfully against THORFINN THE MIGHTY, Earl of Orkney. In 1052, he received Norman exiles from EDWARD THE CONFESSOR's court, making him the first King of the Scots to make use of Norman mercenary soldiers. He also has a reputation as a generous patron of the Church. In 1054, however, he faced an invasion organized by Earl SIWARD of Northumbria in support of Donnchad's son, MAEL COLUIM III CENN MÓR, who had taken refuge in England. Macbeth had the worst of an indecisive battle fought at Dunsinnan near Scone (Perths.), thereafter losing control of Lothian and Strathclyde to Mael Coluim. Mael Coluim launched another English-sponsored attack in 1057, as a result of which Macbeth was killed at Lumphanan near Aberdeen. It is possible that Mael Coluim received support from Macbeth's stepson LULACH, who was briefly made King of the Scots after his stepfather's death before he too was defeated by Mael Coluim. It is possible that Macbeth was buried at Iona, the traditional resting-place of the kings of the Scots. His defeat allowed the more southerly based descendants of Cinaed mac Alpín to consolidate their grip on Scottish kingship during the long reigns of Mael Coluim Cenn Mór and subsequently of his son DAVID I. The decline in Macbeth's historical reputation can be seen as the fate of many losers in history. Representing as he did a branch of the Scottish royal family which was ultimately excluded from power, he came to be seen as the opponent of the rightful (that is, the successful) line of kings. The slaughter of his rivals, a practice which over time came to be seen as legitimate in the case of someone like Mael Coluim Cenn Mór, was portrayed as villainy, whereas, in truth, it was merely the normal stuff of British politics at this time. After Macbeth's death, kingship in Scotland did become the property of a single family. Another aspect of his reign, military intervention on the part of the kings of England, also became a regular feature of Anglo-Scottish relations.

Archibald A. M. Duncan, Scotland: The Making of the Kingdom (1975) also the author of numerous empirical studies. His book *A Discourse on the Rise, Progress, Peculiar Objects and Importance of Political Economy* (1824) was the first serious history of economic thought.

MACDIARMID, HUGH (originally Christopher Murray Grieve) (1892–1978), poet and Scottish nationalist. A major figure in the Scottish literary revival of the 1920s, he wrote lyric poetry in a synthetic Scots, drawing on dialect and oral traditions. He is best known for *A Drunk Man Looks at the Thistle* (1926), *First Hymn to Lenin* (1931) and his poem in English 'On a Raised Beach' (1934); he later worked on long, dense poetry about the Celtic consciousness. His Scottish identity increasingly took political shape, and in 1928 he founded the Scottish National Party (SNP). His writing took on a more Marxist tone after 1930, and four years later he was expelled from the SNP and joined the Communist Party.

MACDONALD, ALEXANDER (?–1692), Chief of the Macdonalds. He was chief of a sept of the Macdonalds who lived in Glencoe, and were renowned for cattle raiding and other lawlessness. He took part in risings against the 1688 Revolution under Dundee (*see* GRAHAM, JOHN) in Lochaber, and again in the northern Highlands. When the government required clan chiefs to swear an oath of loyalty by the end of Dec. 1691 he initially held out, but on learning that everyone else had complied presented himself at Fort William the day before the deadline. Finding no magistrate qualified to take his oath, he proceeded to Inverary, over snowy mountain passes, and took an oath before the Sheriff of Argylls. on 6 Jan. 1692. The Privy Council, however, decided to make an example of him, and quartered on him reliable pro-government troops, from the regiment of the Earl of Argyll, head of the pro-government clan Campbell. After a fortnight's reconnoitring, these troops were ordered to 'fall upon' the Macdonalds of Glencoe and 'put all to the sword under 70'. On 13 Sept., accordingly, 38 people were killed immediately; many others perished trying to escape. Macdonald was shot through the head, but two of his sons escaped. Subsequently, enemies of the Earl of Stair (*see* DALRYMPLE, JOHN) had an inquiry into the massacre convened, paying special attention to the Earl's part in ordering it: his instructions had talked about extirpating 'that sect of thieves'. The inquiry reported that the massacre was 'contrary to the laws of humanity and hospitality', but he was found guilty only of an 'excess of zeal'.

MACDONALD, ALEXANDER (1821–81), trade unionist. Having worked in the coalmines from the age of eight, he paid his way through Glasgow University and acquired a small fortune through commercial speculation. A capable organizer and lobbyist, he promoted mining unions and mining legislation and was one of the two working men elected to Parliament in 1875.

MACDONALD, FLORA (1722–1790), Jacobite heroine. Her father was Randal Macdonald of Milton, on South Uist in the Outer Hebrides, a 'tacksman', holding an estate from the chief with responsibility for raising his dependants as an armed force when necessary. South Uist was largely Catholic and Jacobite. In 1746 it was arranged that Flora should facilitate the escape of Prince Charles Edward STUART from government forces after they had crushed the Jacobite army at Culloden. She met him and his companions on 20 June and helped them to safety on Benbecula and then Skye, with the Prince in woman's clothes under the alias of Betty Burke, supposedly Flora's Irish maid. The Prince left her care on 1 July; on 12 July Flora was arrested. The escape was soon seen in a romantic light and, on her arrival in London in Oct. 1746, she became a celebrity, meeting social figures including FREDERICK Prince of Wales and having her portrait painted. She returned to Scotland after the general amnesty in 1747 but made a return visit to England in late 1748 where she collected money raised for her by supporters. She married a Skye landholder, Allen Macdonald, in 1750.

MACDONALD, JOHN (4th and last Lord of the Isles) (1434–1503), nobleman. He succeeded his father Alexander in 1449. Being so young, he found his huge and scattered inheritance, the earldom of Ross as well as the Western Isles, hard to defend against ambitious neighbours and a hostile Scottish Crown. He was on the losing side in the wars between JAMES II and Black Douglas (*see* DOUGLAS, ARCHIBALD) in the 1450s. In 1462 he made a pact with EDWARD IV of England, agreeing to the subjugation and partition of Scotland. Accused of treason in 1475, he lost Ross in 1476 and the lordship of the Isles in 1493.

MACDONALD, MALCOLM (1901–81), politician and diplomat. The son of Ramsay MACDONALD, Britain's first Labour Prime Minister, Malcolm achieved political eminence in his own right, as an MP from 1929 to 1945 and as a diplomat active in granting independence to former colonies. Elected to Parliament the year his father became Prime Minister, in 1934 he was given a Cabinet post by Stanley BALDWIN as Secretary of State for the Colonies. After surviving a Commons censure motion in 1940 when, after a visit to the Middle East, he proposed restricting the sale of land in Palestine to Jews, he went to Canada as High Commissioner in 1941. In 1946 he was made Governor General of the Malayan Union and Singapore, and subsequently Commissioner General in south-east Asia, a hot diplomatic posting with the Communist insurrection and the state of emergency declared in Malaya in 1948. After a term as High Commissioner of India, MacDonald went to Africa as Governor of Kenya, where he regarded KENYATTA with respect, staying on as High Commissioner after independence. He helped settle the military revolt in Tanganyika that threatened to topple NYERERE and ended his public career as Britain's roving Ambassador in Africa (1966–70).

MACDONALD, RAMSAY see essay on page 530

MACDONNELL, RANDAL (2nd Earl and 1st Marquess of Antrim) (1609–82), politician. Vain and ambitious, he was knighted by the Lord Deputy Thomas WENTWORTH (1639); he proposed raising Irish clansmen to unite with Scottish Macdonalds in crushing their Campbell enemies and fighting for the King. This abortive scheme rallied Archibald CAMPBELL, Earl of Argyll, to CHARLES I's opponents, and strengthened the impression that Charles was plotting with Roman Catholics. For (dubious) services to Charles, he was made Marquess in 1645. In 1647 he led the Catholic Irish Confederacy's fruitless embassy to the French and HENRIETTA MARIA. In 1662 the royal family intervened to exempt him from penalties for Roman Catholic rebels.

MACEWEN, SIR WILLIAM (1848–1924), surgeon. Born and educated in Glasgow, MacEwen built a medical career in his native city. As Joseph LISTER's student he practised and developed the novel techniques of antiseptic surgery, notably for operations on brain tumours. By the early 1880s he had rejected Lister's antiseptic techniques in favour of his own 'aseptic' method, in which surgical apparatus, gowns and dressings were sterilized by immersion in boiling water. He was a pioneer in brain surgery, and his contributions to the field of bone surgery include the development of a technique for rectifying the condition known as 'knock-knee' and the introduction of bone grafts.

McGAHEY, MICK (1925–99), trade-union leader. His father was a founding member of the British Communist Party and a pit union militant, and at 14 McGahey was already a pitboy and a member of the Young Communist League. Thereafter he worked his way up the hierarchy to become the President of the Scottish Miners in 1967. He suffered his first reverse when he lost

the battle to become President of the National Union of Mineworkers (NUM) in 1971, to the more moderate Joe GORMLEY. Austere, uncompromising and utterly dedicated to working-class politics, McGahey emerged as the Left's main strategist during the national coal strike in 1972 and the poll to strike in 1974 which helped to bring down the Conservative government of Edward HEATH. McGahey was explicit in that these actions were at least as much about politics as they were about securing wage increases, and their success saw the miners at the height of their power. Gormley ensured, however, that the militant McGahey would never succeed him as President of the NUM by changing the rules governing the succession, thus, ironically, paving the way for Arthur SCARGILL, who was more militant even than McGahey.

During the bitter miners' strike of 1984–5, McGahey was initially a determined advocate of the strike and a loyal lieutenant to Scargill. Rather sooner than Scargill, however, he realized that all the gains of previous years were at risk and privately argued for the strike to be called off six months before it actually was. By the time that Scargill ordered an end to the year-long strike, the miners had suffered a catastrophic defeat at the hands of the THATCHER government. It was then the Communist McGahey rather than Scargill who tried to heal the divisions within the working-class movement, urging reconciliation with the breakaway Union of Democratic Mineworkers.

McGONAGALL, WILLIAM (1830–1902), versifier. A Dundee weaver, of poetic ambition as a tragedian, McGonagall's doggerel verses on shipwrecks, battles and nature's marvels have earned him a persistent amused readership, particularly of 'The Tay Bridge Disaster' from *Poetic Gems* (1890).

MACGREGOR, SIR IAN (1912–98), industrialist. With a dour image and a reputation for ruthless job- and cost-cutting in the older industries, Sir Ian MacGregor embodied the objectives of the first governments of Margaret THATCHER. Born into a strict United Free Church family, MacGregor began his career in Scottish industry after graduating from Glasgow University in metallurgy, but after 1945 he based himself in the USA. He helped build Amax, a small molybdenum producer, into an industrial giant, and then joined New York merchant bank Lazard Frères. His reputation as a union-basher and cost-cutter brought him to the attention of the British government: as Chairman of the British Steel Corporation 1980–3, he halved the industrial workforce. Subsequently as chairman of the National Coal Board 1983–6 he confronted Arthur SCARGILL and the trade unions

continued on page 531

MACDONALD, RAMSAY (1866–1937)
Politician and Prime Minister (1923–4, 1929–31, 1931–5)

Born James MacDonald Ramsay, the illegitimate son of a Scottish servant in Lossiemouth (Moray), MacDonald's career was the stuff of which novels are (and were) made. On a personal level he went from outcast to Prime Minister and then back to outcast, at least in the eyes of the political movement which had taken him to Downing Street.

MacDonald's career was possible only in the context of his times. A bright lad in a country which valued education, MacDonald took the high road to Victorian London where he managed to find a series of jobs as a clerk before becoming secretary to a radical Liberal MP, Thomas Lough, through whose company he first came into contact with Sidney WEBB and the Fabians. Involvement with the Fabians and the Fellowship of the New Life brought MacDonald into company with many of the middle-class sponsors of the nascent labour movement and, in 1894, he joined the Independent Labour Party (ILP), which believed that Labour should seek power through its own means and not through alliance with the Liberals. His marriage in 1896 brought him a degree of financial independence unique in his generation of Labour leaders.

MacDonald played a leading part in the foundation of the Labour Representation Committee in 1900, which united the ILP with the Trades Union Congress and, at the age of 33, he was appointed secretary of the new organization. MacDonald's own brand of socialism, gradualist and moderate, suited the new movement as much as it suited him, and over the next decade he worked in harness with the Liberals, most notably through an agreement with the Liberals in 1903 over which seats each party should fight to establish a position for the new party. He became an MP in 1906.

With the outbreak of the war MacDonald's position changed. A bitter opponent of the war, he resigned the chairmanship of the Parliamentary Labour Party on 5 Aug. 1914 and, for the next six years, he was one of the most reviled men in British politics. In 1918 he fought hard to ensure that the Labour Party fought the election as an independent party, not as an adjunct to the Lloyd George coalition, and although he lost his own seat he laid the foundations for a political comeback in the early 1920s.

Unlike the extremists in the party, MacDonald was never tempted by the prospect of revolutionary action and he saw the future of progressive politics in Britain as lying in an alliance between organized labour and the radical wing of the Liberal Party; this had been his position in 1900 and would remain so until the end of his career, and it distanced him from some of the younger men who joined the party after the war. He returned to the Commons in 1922 and in 1923, thanks to BALDWIN calling an election on the issue of tariffs, MacDonald found himself as leader of the first Labour government, a post he combined with the foreign secretaryship. Neither in that government nor in the one formed in 1929 did MacDonald enjoy a parliamentary majority but his own centrist instincts would, in any event, have precluded anything like a socialist agenda.

Given both his character and his political instincts it was not altogether surprising that when in Aug. 1931 his government was hit by the severest economic crisis in British history MacDonald should have heeded the King's call to stay on as leader of a coalition government with Baldwin and the Liberals. This meant a complete break with his former 'comrades' and, after he led the National government to a crushing electoral victory in late 1931, MacDonald became the most reviled figure in the Labour movement; in Stalinist fashion, his name and reputation were expunged from the record of Labour's history.

MacDonald was an immensely vain man but to attribute his decision in 1931 simply to that was to misread both him and the history of the Labour Party. MacDonald, like GAITSKELL and BLAIR after him, saw Labour as a radical reforming party rather than a socialist one, and like both men found the Labour left and the old trade unionists unsympathetic; his personal tragedy was that circumstances required him to end his career by opposing the party to which he had devoted it. MacDonald was able to exercise little effect on what was, after 1931, a predominantly Conservative administration whose economic policies were dominated by the Chancellor of the Exchequer, Neville CHAMBERLAIN. By 1935 his mental faculties were failing and he swapped offices with Baldwin before the 1935 election; he remained as Lord President of the Council. He died at sea on 9 Nov. 1937.

David Marquand, Ramsay MacDonald (1977)

in the year-long miners' strike of 1984 that was one of the defining events of the Thatcher years. The most profound changes in the coal industry came under Sir Robert Haslam after MacGregor, by now knighted, had left his post and found new companies to which to apply his strong medicine.

McGUINESS, MARTIN (1950–), Northern Irish politician. From a working-class Derry City Catholic background, McGuiness became politically active at the outbreak of the Northern Ireland troubles in 1969; his alleged links to the Provisional IRA (Irish Republican Army) remain controversial. From the early 1980s he was second to Gerry ADAMS in the Sinn Féin leadership. His support was vital in the move from militarism to a political strategy centred on the peace process, where he was one of the principal negotiators. In 1997 he was elected Westminster MP for Mid-Ulster, and in 1999, despite Unionist indignation, became Minister for Education in the Northern Ireland executive established under the Good Friday Agreement.

MACHYN, HENRY (c. 1498–?1563), diarist. A London tradesman specializing in funerals, he kept a detailed diary of events from a London perspective from 1550 to 1563. It is marked by strong conservative religious sympathies.

MACINNES, COLIN (1914–76), journalist and novelist. Son of the novelist Angela Thirkell, descendant of Rudyard KIPLING, MacInnes grew up in Australia, but his 'London trilogy', *City of Spades* (1957), *Absolute Beginners* (1959) and the less successful *Mr Love and Justice* (1960), tellingly pinpoints the increasingly multicultural capital on the eve of the 'youth revolution' of the 1960s. A number of the perceptive essays he contributed to *New Society* were published in *England, Half English* (1961).

McKENNA, REGINALD (1863–1943), politician. McKenna practised law before becoming Liberal MP for North Monmouthshire in 1895. He fell under the tutelage of Sir Charles DILKE (*Punch* magazine caricatured the pair as Crusoe Dilke and Man Friday McKenna), and attracted attention as an effective opponent of the Conservative government's plans for Tariff Reform. In 1905 McKenna was appointed Financial Secretary to the Treasury in CAMPBELL-BANNERMAN's government, becoming First Lord of the Admiralty in 1908. Disagreements over whether Britain's response to German military aggression in 1911 ought to involve naval or land forces encouraged H. H. ASQUITH to move McKenna to the Home Office, where he remained until 1915, when he was appointed Chancellor of the Exchequer. At the Treasury he increased taxes and duties to pay for Britain's war effort, but after

clashes with the incoming Prime Minister LLOYD GEORGE he retired to the back benches in 1916.

MACKENZIE, SIR GEORGE (1636–91), lawyer and library founder. A student at St Andrews, Aberdeen and Bourges, he rose to legal prominence at the trial of Archibald CAMPBELL, Earl of Argyll in 1661 and became King's Advocate in 1677, being nicknamed 'Bluidy Mackenzie' for his vicious treatment of Covenanting Presbyterians. Disgraced by association with JAMES VII's regime, he retired to private life in 1688. In 1680 he founded Edinburgh's library of the Faculty of Advocates, now one of Britain's most important collections, the only Scottish library with the right to ask for all newly published British books.

MACKENZIE, HENRY (1745–1831), novelist and editor. An Edinburgh solicitor, he had immediate success with his first novel, *The Man of Feeling* (1771), epitomizing the concern of the era with 'sensibility'; its hero was an idealized sentimentalist whose virtues were expressed through his acutely felt emotions rather than worldly deeds and capabilities. Mackenzie's later novels and plays were less successful, but his work inspired many others including STERNE and GODWIN. He contributed to the Scottish literary enlightenment as editor of the first Scottish weekly literary periodical, *The Mirror* (1779–80), and chaired the investigation that established the Ossian poems as largely the creation of the eighteenth-century literary scholar James MACPHERSON.

MACKENZIE, KELVIN (1946–), journalist. Mackenzie worked on regional newspapers after leaving school before moving to Fleet Street as a sub-editor on the *Daily Express*. In 1981 Rupert MURDOCH appointed him editor of the *Sun*, which was already Britain's best-selling tabloid. Mackenzie on the *Sun*, became legendary for his abrasiveness, populist instincts and unerring eye for a memorable headline. The *Sun* captured the mood of the Thatcherite (*see* THATCHER, MARGARET) 1980s perfectly, and regularly sold over four million copies. Its headlines became the leitmotifs of an era, such as GOTCHA! over the picture of the sinking Argentinian cruiser during the Falklands War (1982).

MACKINTOSH, CHARLES (1760–1843), raincoat inventor *see* HANCOCK, THOMAS

MACKINTOSH, CHARLES RENNIE (1868–1928), architect and designer. Born in Glasgow, at the time a prosperous, expanding cosmopolitan city, he studied at the School of Art. The furniture and metalwork which he produced for the 1896 London Arts and Crafts Exhibition appeared in

The Studio, and this led to a commission to design a room for the Secession III exhibition in Vienna in 1900. He trained as an architect too, and in 1896 he was commissioned to design a new Glasgow School of Art: completed in two stages, 1897–9 and 1907–9, it is Mackintosh's masterpiece in architectural conception as in Art Nouveau decorative detail. Unable, however, to find sufficient work in Scotland, in 1913 he left Glasgow, settling in the south of France, where he painted landscapes. Famed in his lifetime mainly as a designer who drew on Celtic forms to modify his more sinuous early work, his architecture reinterpreted the Scottish vernacular in domestic as well as in public and commercial buildings (including a series of Glasgow tea rooms).

MACKWORTH, SIR HUMPHRY (1657–1727), philanthropist and industrialist. A barrister who acquired an estate in south Wales by marriage in 1686, which brought him more than £12,000 a year, he became known as a philanthropist, founding many charity schools on his estate and in 1698 was one of the founders of the SPCK (*see* BRAY, THOMAS). In 1695 he had bought the controlling shares in silver mines in Cardigans. and arranged for a lottery to fund a dramatic expansion of mining operations, into coal and copper, forming a new company, the Mine Adventurers of England, with himself as Deputy Governor for life and the Duke of Leeds (*see* OSBORNE, THOMAS) as Governor. The company appeared extremely successful; Mackworth's influence increased and in 1701 he was elected MP for Cardigans. He tried several times to steer a Bill through Parliament that would streamline poor relief, concentrating most of the poor in workhouses. His plans were twice passed in the House of Commons, but were blocked in the Lords. By this stage his business methods were being called into question; in March 1710 he was found guilty of frauds in violation of the Mine Adventurers Co. charter. He escaped punishment when the Whigs fell from power, but was unable to revive his business career.

McLAREN, MALCOLM (1946–), impresario. Famous as the inspiration behind the 'punk' movement of the mid 1970s, McLaren was involved in the late 1960s protest movements during his education at various London art colleges. His flirtation with subversion continued throughout his career and together with Vivienne WESTWOOD, the mother of his son, helped to establish punk as the rebellious movement of a generation. After opening a fashion shop with Westwood on the King's Road, London, in 1971, McLaren tried his hand at rock management with the band New York Dolls. This experience was to prove invaluable on his return to Britain with the creation and management of the band the Sex Pistols in 1976. McLaren instigated the group's anti-Establishment posturing and anarchic stage and media appearances.

MACLAURIN, COLIN (1698–1746), mathematician. The son of a minister, Maclaurin began studying for the Church at Glasgow but instead turned to mathematics and was appointed Professor at Marischal College, Aberdeen, when only 19. He met NEWTON in London in 1719 and the next year published *Geometrica Organica* which solved many of Newton's outstanding problems. Professor of Mathematics at Edinburgh from 1724, he founded the Philosophical Society in 1737, later the Royal Society of Edinburgh, and was an active secretary despite being engaged on writing his major work, the *Treatise on Fluxions* (1742), which refined and offered proofs for Newton's theories. His emphasis on Newtonian methods has been said by some to have harmed British mathematics as it isolated Britain from the growing use of calculus on the continent, but Maclaurin's letters show that he was interested in and informed on the subject. He also devised actuarial tables for insurance societies, proposed an expedition to find a north-east passage to the Pacific and supervised the defence of Edinburgh against the Jacobites in 1745.

MACLEAN, DONALD (1913–83), spy. Son of a Liberal MP, and a Marxist from his youth, Maclean was a brilliant undergraduate at Cambridge, where he met Guy BURGESS. He entered the Diplomatic Service in 1935 and was First Secretary at the British embassy in Washington in 1944–8. Maclean supplied the Russians with confidential information during the Second World War, and his position in the USA as joint Secretary of the new Combined Policy Committee on Nuclear Development made him particularly useful to them. He was recalled from his next posting as head of Chancery in Cairo in 1950 after his behaviour had become increasingly erratic, but his next job was on the American desk of the Foreign Office in London. Tipped off by his fellow spies PHILBY and BLUNT that MI5 suspected him, on 25 May 1951, with the help of Burgess, Maclean defected to Moscow.

MACLEOD, IAIN (1913–70), politician. One of BUTLER's leading lieutenants at the Conservative Research Department, redefining Conservatism after the 1945 General Election defeat, he became an MP in 1950 and a prominent member of the liberal Tory One Nation group. He was Minister of Health (1953–5) and Minister of Labour (1955–9). As Colonial Secretary (1959–61) under MACMILLAN, he was directly responsible for the rapid acceleration of the process of decolonization in Africa. He was Leader of the House of Commons (1961–3). The hostility towards him from those sections of the Conservative Party with links to white settlers in Kenya and elsewhere, and the feeling that he was 'too clever by half', combined to ensure that he was never a serious candidate for the leadership. A supporter of Butler in 1963, he refused to serve under DOUGLAS-HOME. Brought back into the Shadow Cabinet by Edward HEATH, he became Chancellor of the Exchequer in June 1970, but died within a month.

MACLISE, DANIEL (1806–70), artist. Born in Cork, he studied at the Royal Academy Schools, painted historical frescos for the House of Lords, *Wellington and Blücher at Waterloo* and *The Death of Nelson* (1857–66) and illustrated several of DICKENS's Christmas books and TENNYSON's poems.

MACMAHON, HEBER (1600–50), churchman and soldier. Known in Latin as Emerus Mattheus, he studied at Douai and Leuven and was ordained in 1625, becoming Roman Catholic Bishop of Clogher in 1643. He was much respected in the Catholic Irish Confederacy during the Civil Wars for his statesmanlike qualities, and rather inappropriately was chosen in 1650 to be general of the Ulster army. Defeated and captured by Oliver CROMWELL at Scariffhollis, he was executed.

MACMILLAN, HAROLD *see* essay on pages 534–35

McMILLAN, MARGARET (1860–1931), educationalist. Born in Scotland and educated at Inverness high school, McMillan became a teacher, a political activist and a leading figure in the Independent Labour Party in the 1890s. But her most important work was first in agitating through school boards and municipal councils for more local and national government provision for infants' health and, secondly, in establishing, with her sister Rachel, the Deptford clinic and nursery school in 1910. Privately funded, the clinic was the only one in operation in London schools before 1914. Strongly committed to encouraging imagination and self-expression in the children, McMillan sometimes ran into conflict with overworked working-class mothers over the best means of caring for children. The work which Margaret and Rachel pioneered, informed by the educational theories of the American John Dewey and the Italian Maria Montessori, was an important influence in the teaching of children and medical provision for children in the decades after the First World War.

McMILLAN, RACHEL (1859–1917), educationalist see MCMILLAN, MARGARET

McNAUGHTON, DANIEL (*fl.* 1843), murderer. The judgement at his trial for the murder of Sir Robert PEEL's private secretary has been codified as the 'McNaughton Rules', which define the criminal responsibility of the insane.

MACNEICE, LOUIS (1907–63), poet. Born in Carrickfergus, the son of a rector of the Church of Ireland (who became a bishop), MacNeice was educated at Marlborough and Oxford. A lecturer in classics who preferred to write, his poems include *Blind Fireworks* (1929), *Autumn Journal* (1939), a personal political view of the momentous events leading to the Second World War, and *Ten Burnt Offerings* (1952), usually regarded by critics, and by MacNeice himself, as his best work. He wrote novels (pseudonymously), criticism, including a study of YEATS (1941), plays, a much-acclaimed translation of *The Agamemnon of Aeschylus* (1936) (produced with music by BRITTEN) and *Letters from Iceland* (1937) with W. H. AUDEN, with whom he is often grouped as a junior member of the Auden–Isherwood–Spender 'literary axis'. In 1941 MacNeice joined the BBC where he worked for 20 years as a producer and scriptwriter: the fantasy inspired by the Second World War, *The Dark Tower* (1947), is a classic of this time. A poet of urban doings, deracination and loss, MacNeice's unfinished autobiography, *The Strings are False*, was published two years after his death from viral pneumonia following a chill caught while recording underground for the BBC.

MACNEILL, EOIN (1867–1945), scholar and politician. While working as a civil servant, MacNeill co-founded the Gaelic League and in its early years was deputy to Douglas HYDE: he was a pioneering scholar who revolutionized the study of early Irish history. In 1913 he called for the formation of a nationalist volunteer force in response to the Ulster Volunteers' threatened resistance to Home Rule, and became head of the Irish Volunteers, set up under separatist influence. After struggles for control between separatists and supporters of John REDMOND, the Volunteers split over Redmond's support for Britain in the First World War. The majority ('National Volunteers') followed Redmond, while MacNeill led the minority Irish Volunteers. He believed that the Volunteers should be kept in reserve to resist any attempt to impose conscription and remained ignorant of the intention of an Irish Republican Brotherhood faction, led by Padraic PEARSE, to mount a rising until almost the last moment and, on learning that a shipload of German guns had been intercepted by the Royal Navy, he published

continued on page 536

MACMILLAN, HAROLD (1st Earl of Stockton) (1894–1986)
Politician and Prime Minister (1957–63)

The progenitor of modern politics with its concentration upon image, Macmillan was the grandson of a Scottish crofter and one of the heirs to Macmillan and Company, the publishing house. Macmillan liked to project an image of himself as 'the last of the Edwardians', emphasizing his Oxford connections and his ducal marriage. By the end of his long life he had come to symbolize, in his own mind, a 'One Nation' Tory tradition which was under assault from Thatcherism (*see* THATCHER, MARGARET). This apotheosis could hardly have been predicted earlier in his career when he had seemed the very image of a reclusive and bookish young Conservative, noticeably out of his depth in the social circles into which his marriage to a daughter of the Duke of Devonshire had propelled him. The dominating influence upon his life was his American mother, who determined from his earliest years that the young Harold should be famous and who provided much of the thrust of his initial entry into politics.

A quiet academic career at Balliol was interrupted by the First World War, which was the other formative influence upon his career. Macmillan found himself leading men whose backgrounds were unimaginable to him but whose courage and patriotism made a permanent impression on him. His own courage was attested to by the variety and severity of the wounds which he sustained at the Front. It was while recuperating from his injuries during a spell as aide-de-camp to the Governor General of Canada, the Duke of Devonshire, that he met and married his younger daughter, Dorothy.

Macmillan's entry into politics was made smoother by his wife's family and his mother's money but, even so, he was only able to find a marginal seat at Stockton-on-Tees and was overshadowed during the next decade and a half by more prominent young men such as Oswald MOSLEY, Duff COOPER, Anthony EDEN and the flamboyant Bob BOOTHBY, whose long-standing affair with Lady Dorothy Macmillan added personal unhappiness to the political ones which assailed the young MP.

Macmillan's paternalistic sympathy was stirred by the plight of his own constituents who were particularly badly affected by the economic downturn of the late 1920s and 1930s. He lost his seat in 1929, only to regain it in 1931. During the depression years he became something of a back-bench rebel and his contacts with LLOYD GEORGE and KEYNES bore fruit in his 1938 book, *The Middle Way*, with its call for more government intervention in economic and social affairs. It was a short way from rebellion here to dissent over the National government's policy towards Italy and later Germany; for a brief period after 1936 the Conservative Whip was actually withdrawn from Macmillan. By 1939 his political career, like his private life, seemed characterized by failure and impotence.

Despite his later evocation of 'Winston', Macmillan was not a member of CHURCHILL's inner circle and was, indeed, involved in an abortive mini-rebellion against him in July 1940. What transformed Macmillan's career was his appointment as Minister Resident in North Africa in Nov. 1942. The post was offered as a consolation for not getting the domestic promotion for which he was angling but it tested him and showed what he could achieve when the opportunity presented itself; this would be the theme for the rest of his political career as, time and again, he surprised both himself and others by the way he rose to the challenges which he faced. As a cricket-lover he would have appreciated being called a natural player of fast bowling.

During this period he struck up good personal relations with two of the men who would play crucial roles in his later career, General Dwight D. Eisenhower and General Charles de Gaulle: Macmillan acted as political adviser to the first and helped the latter in the delicate negotiations that led to the union of the warring French factions in North Africa. Such was Macmillan's success in Algiers, and later in Italy and Greece, that he gained both the admiration of Churchill and the envy of Anthony Eden who was always alert to the emergence of potential rivals. An indication of the change in Macmillan's political fortunes is provided by his promotion to the Cabinet in Churchill's caretaker government of 1945.

Having correctly predicted the 1945 election result, Macmillan was one of the few Conservatives not to be surprised by it and his own ejection from Stockton was a foregone conclusion. But as one of the outer circle of Churchillians Macmillan was able to secure a safe Tory seat at Bromley later in 1945, from which time he was to occupy front-bench positions for the rest of his political career. The progress was painfully slow for a man already in his fifties. In 1951 Churchill made him Minister of Housing which was hardly one of the great offices of State. But again

Macmillan showed himself adept at grasping an opportunity, however unpromising it seemed. Housing was one of the great issues in the politics of the day and, by living up to the election pledge to build 300,000 houses, Macmillan trumped one of Labour's best cards and established himself as a minister with a populist touch. Later, historians would query the way in which the target was achieved and its effect on the rest of the economy; but Macmillan's short-term political success was what interested the minister. As Churchill's Minister of Defence in 1954–5, Macmillan was uneasy in the shadow of the great man but received his expected reward from Eden in April 1955, when he became Foreign Secretary.

But being Foreign Secretary to Eden was like being Defence Secretary to Churchill and, after a short and unhappy period, he was moved to the Exchequer. During the Suez crisis of 1956, he was one of the leading 'hawks' but having been one of the 'first in', he became, in Harold WILSON's telling phrase, 'first out' as things went wrong in Dec. This was not held against him and he became leader of the Conservative Party in Jan. 1957, expecting, he said, to hold the job for six weeks; he held it for six years.

Macmillan was fortunate, finally, in his timing. His premiership coincided with the great upturn in the world economy following the recovery from the devastation of the war and the period of affluence which it ushered into Britain produced an economic situation where it could truly be said that 'you've never had it so good'. These words, which Macmillan never quite uttered in this form, were held against him when things went sour but he was, in fact, well aware of the dangers of affluence. But his economic style remained Keynesian, his preferences remained expansionist and he was willing to see the resignation of his entire Treasury team (including Enoch POWELL) rather than restrict government expenditure; for Thatcherites looking back, this episode came to have a significance akin to that of Eve handing the apple to Adam.

Affluence at home was accompanied by imperial retreat abroad and by a strengthening of the Anglo-American connection, particularly in the area of nuclear co-operation, symbolized by the 1962 Nassau Agreement which gave Britain access to America's Polaris missiles. When Macmillan told the South African Parliament in 1960 that there was a 'wind of change' blowing through Africa, he was in typically dramatic fashion uttering a truism. One of the lessons of Suez was that the burdens of empire were no longer worth the bearing, and from 1957 onwards there was a headlong rush to grant independence to as many colonies as possible. But this did not mean that Britain was giving up her role as a world power. Macmillan aimed to achieve this by other means, specifically by joining the European Economic Community or Common Market.

This last object became the centrepiece of Macmillan's foreign policy after his election victory of 1959, and de Gaulle's veto on Britain's entry in 1962 came as a fatal blow to the government's prestige. By this stage Macmillan's luck was running out. The invincible 'Supermac' image fashioned by the cartoonist VICKY, which he had adopted as his own, concealed from the public gaze the shy and otherworldly inner man, who found himself ill-equipped to deal with the waves of scandal which engulfed his administration in 1962–3, culminating in the PROFUMO scandal of the latter year. Macmillan's handling of the affair seriously undermined confidence in him. Signs that he was losing his touch were plain to see in 1962 when, rattled by a series of by-election defeats, he had bungled a Cabinet reshuffle by turning it into what the newspapers called 'the knight of the long knives'. The Liberal leader, Jeremy THORPE, summed up the prevailing view with the epigram: 'Greater love hath no man than that he lay down his friends for his life.' Resignation came suddenly in Oct. 1963 when prostate trouble prompted Macmillan to surrender the leadership just before the party conference. He was widely, and correctly, suspected of rigging the selection process to ensure that Rab BUTLER did not succeed him. Ironically, in view of the satirical vogue for criticizing Macmillan's 'grouse-moor' image, his successor was Lord Home (see DOUGLAS-HOME, ALEC), to whom the adjective applied with even more force.

By dint of surviving into his nineties, Macmillan enjoyed a brief Indian summer as a critic of Thatcherism, most memorably criticizing her policy of privatization as 'selling the family silver'. Opinion remains deeply divided over whether he was an 'actor-manager' who was all pose and no action, or a 'One Nation' Tory who tried to adapt Britain to the realities of the post-war world.

Alistair Horne, Harold Macmillan (2 vols, 1988, 1989)

countermanding orders. The 1916 Easter Rising went ahead without his consent, but was postponed for a day and largely confined to Dublin. MacNeill's actions were criticized by many separatists, but he was accepted back into the Sinn Féin movement on release from prison in 1917 and became a leading member of its moderate wing. In 1918 he became MP for Derry City and the National University of Ireland, and served in the underground Dáil Cabinet. He supported the Anglo-Irish Treaty and was Minister for Education (1922–5), but resigned from the Cabinet after mishandling the Free State's case to the 1924–5 Northern Ireland Boundary Commission. After losing his Dáil seat in 1927 he returned to his scholarly pursuits.

MACPHERSON, JAMES (1736–96), writer. The son of a farmer, he confounded literary opinion with his production of *Fragments of Ancient Poetry collected in the Highlands* (1760), followed by the complete works, *Fingal* (1761) and *Temora* (1762), claiming them as translations of the works of a fifth-century Gaelic poet, Ossian. For some time most of the literary world accepted his story, and he won the patronage of Bute (*see* STUART, JOHN) and the endorsements of David HUME and Adam SMITH. Doubts arose after Macpherson refused to publish the putative Gaelic originals, and after his visit to the Western Isles Samuel JOHNSON denied the poems' authenticity. An investigation led by Henry MACKENZIE eventually concluded that Macpherson had taken fragments of Gaelic poetry and drastically expanded them to produce his own works.

McQUAID, JOHN CHARLES (1895–1973), Catholic Archbishop of Dublin. A friend of DE VALERA (who consulted him when drafting the 1937 constitution), McQuaid was a capable administrator and organizer of Church-run social services; he held extremely firm views about the role of the Church in society, the need to preserve it from State encroachment (this lay behind his opposition to Noel BROWNE's Mother and Child Scheme) and its doctrines from compromise. As Archbishop from 1940, he opposed attempts to extend interdenominational contacts and re-asserted the long-standing prohibition on Catholics attending Trinity College (seen as dominated by secular and Protestant influences). He found it hard to adapt to changes in Catholicism after the Second Vatican Council and criticisms of Church authority voiced in the 1960s by hitherto deferential media. When he retired in 1972 the confidence in Church authority which underpinned the early years of his episcopate had already been severely undermined, and he has been subjected to increasingly hostile retrospective criticism.

MACSWINEY, MARY (1872–1942), Irish politician. She brought up her younger siblings (including Terence MACSWINEY) after their father's death. A schoolteacher, she was active in the women's suffrage movement and became a Republican activist after the 1916 Easter Rising; MacSwiney was dismissed from the convent school where she worked because of her political activities and set up her own school. She came to national prominence as spokeswoman for the MacSwiney family during her brother's hunger strike, and was elected as member of the Dáil for Cork City (1920–7). An outspoken opponent of the Anglo-Irish Treaty and a leading member of Sinn Féin during and after the Irish Civil War, she was denounced by misogynists as proof that women were unsuited for politics. MacSwiney remained with the abstentionist rump after the secession of DE VALERA and his followers, and never regarded the Irish State as legitimate.

MACSWINEY, TERENCE (1879–1920), politician and hunger-striker. Active in separatist politics and literary societies in Cork from the turn of the century, MacSwiney was one of the Cork City commanders of the Irish Volunteers before the Easter Rising. After 1916 he alternated between periods of imprisonment and political activity on behalf of Sinn Féin. He was MP for Mid-Cork (1918–20) and became Lord Mayor of Cork after the assassination by Crown forces of his predecessor Tomas MacCurtain. He was arrested while presiding over an Irish Republican Army (IRA) staff meeting and sentenced by court martial; he refused to accept the legitimacy of the court and went on hunger-strike to demand his release. His 74-day fast, ending in his death in Brixton prison, London, in 1920, attracted worldwide attention and won sympathy for the Sinn Féin cause. Mary MACSWINEY was his sister.

MADAN, MARTIN (1726–90), Evangelical. A barrister until he heard John WESLEY preach, was converted and took orders. A leading member of Lady Huntingdon's (*see* HASTINGS, SELINA) nondenominational Evangelical 'Connexion', he became chaplain at the Lock Hospital and his sermons became highly fashionable, leading to a new chapel being built for him in 1762. Madan's calls for greater compassion to be shown to prostitutes won him praise, but in 1780 his concern with the reform of sexual relations led him to publish *Thelyphthoria*, advocating polygamy. Lady Huntingdon organized a petition of 3,000 signatories denouncing him and he was forced to retire to the country.

MADOG AP MAREDUDD (?–1160), Prince of Powys. He was the last great prince of a unified principality of Powys, which he ruled from 1132 until his death, and one of the leaders, both as a soldier and as a patron of Welsh poets, of the Welsh revival in the years after HENRY I's death in 1135. He fought on the winning side at the Battle of Lincoln (1141) and captured Oswestry (1149). But after 1150 he could check OWAIN OF GWYNEDD's expansionism only by allying with the English, and after his own death partition led to a more or less permanent division of his principality into northern and southern halves, Powys Fadog and Powys Wenwynwyn.

MADOG AP OWAIN OF GWYNEDD (*fl. c.* 1170), legendary sea-farer. There is no contemporary evidence of his activities but he is reputed to have gone to sea with 10 ships and 300 men, and to have disappeared. In the sixteenth century the discovery of America was attributed to his voyage; a tomb in the West Indies and descendants in a tribe of Welsh Indians in the Missouri valley have been added to his legend.

MAEL BRIGTE MAC TORNÁIN (?–927), Abbot of Armagh and Iona. Belonging to the Cenél Conaill, and thus the kindred from whom the greatest majority of the abbots of Iona, including COLUM CILLE himself, were drawn, Mael Brigte was, first of all, Abbot of Armagh, from *c.* 888. He also became Abbot of Iona in *c.* 891 and, since he thereafter based himself in Ireland, his dual office may be seen as a decisive moment in Iona's loss of its long-held religious predominance across Scotland and Ireland.

MAEL COLUIM I (?–954), King of the Scots (943–54). He consolidated the achievements of his predecessor, CONSTANTÍN II, and in 945 was recognized as controlling Strathclyde and Cumbria by the English King EDMUND. He nonetheless had to surmount a difficult crisis when ERIC BLOODAXE temporarily obtained control of Orkney and the kingdom of York; his reaction was to renew Constantín's alliance with the kings of Dublin. Mael Coluim was killed by the men of Moray in 954, a sign of the instability of the nascent kingdom of the Scots.

MAEL COLUIM II (*c.* 954–1034), King of the Scots (1005–34). A son of CINAED II, he acquired the throne by killing CINAED III (reigned 997–1005), the representative of a rival line. Mael Coluim's reign is notable for the way in which he tried to exploit the distracted English kingdom during the reign of ETHELRED II THE UNREADY to expand his power into Bernicia. In particular, he gained a notable victory at the Battle of Carham (Northumb.) in 1018, but was eventually forced to submit when King CNUT and his army marched

north in 1027. Mael Coluim's violent acquisition of the kingship and his determination to secure the succession for his grandson, the future DONNCHAD I, meant that the feuds that had typified Scottish history since the 970s continued. *See also* MACBETH.

MAEL COLUIM III CENN MÓR (*c.* 1031–93), King of the Scots (1058–93). He succeeded to the throne after killing his predecessor MACBETH and the latter's stepson LULACH – events that brought to an end the long-standing struggle for the Scottish kingdom. Mael Coluim's first marriage was to the daughter of THORFINN THE MIGHTY, Earl of Orkney; his second, to Margaret, sister of the English pretender EDGAR THE ÆTHELING, involved him in the politics of the Norman Conquest.

He launched several invasions of northern England, without acquiring more than booty and slaves. WILLIAM I THE CONQUEROR's invasion of Scotland in 1072 forced him to accept the Peace of Abernethy (Inverness) and become William's vassal; a similar settlement was made with WILLIAM II RUFUS in 1093.

MAEL COLUIM IV (1141–65), King of the Scots (1153–65). Son of HENRY OF NORTHUMBRIA, he was only 11 years old when his father died in 1152. Even so, his grandfather DAVID I persuaded the Scottish magnates to recognize him as the heir to the throne, and the next year the boy became King. In 1157 he agreed to surrender Cumbria and Northumb. to HENRY II, realizing, as WILLIAM OF NEWBURGH put it, 'that the King of England had the better of the argument by reason of his much greater power'. As compensation, Mael Coluim received the earldom of Huntingdon. His youth and what many Scots regarded as his subservience towards the King of England meant that his was a turbulent reign. But he had successfully overcome internal opposition notably in Galloway and from SOMERLED, King of Argyll, when he died in 1165, still unmarried and with a reputation for chastity (hence his nickname the Maiden).

MAELGWYN (?–549), King of Gwynedd. Described by GILDAS as the mightiest of the kings of the Britons, little is known about his actual career, except that he may once have been a monk and that he killed many of his relatives in the pursuit of power. His somewhat lurid prestige provides an early indication of the importance that the kingdom of Gwynedd was to have in Welsh and British history.

MAEL RUAIN (?–792), churchman. Mael Ruain was one of the chief instigators of the late eighth-century reform movement within Irish monasticism, which became known as the *Céli Dé*, the 'servants of God', and which aimed to revert to the austere asceticism of earlier times at the expense of pastoral care for the population at large. Although little is known of Mael Ruain, he certainly compiled a monastic rule which provided the impetus to reform and became a model for later rules. The arrival of the Vikings in Ireland just a few years after his death, and their subsequent permanent settlement in Dublin, seriously hindered the progress of reform.

MAEL RUBAI, ST, Abbot of Applecross (*c.* 642–722). A contemporary of ADOMNÁN of Iona, Mael Rubai's early ecclesiastical career began as a monk in St Comgall's foundation of Bangor. The *Annals of Ulster* relate that he went to Scotland in 671, founded the monastery of Applecross in 673, and died in 722 at the age of 80. Although both COLUM CILLE and St DONNÁN visited Skye, it is Mael Rubai who is credited with the permanent conversion of the island and neighbouring mainland. His career is a reminder that there was much Christian activity on the western seaboard of Scotland besides the better documented achievements of Iona.

MAEL SECHNAILL I (?–862), King of Tara. Mael Sechnaill became King of the southern Uí Néill, whose power was traditionally based at Tara (Co. Meath), in 846. His career included important victories over the Vikings, and his military success gave him domination over all the Irish kingdoms. The first northern Irish king to have his superiority acknowledged by Munster, he is therefore also the first who could be said to have been, in some sense, 'King of all Ireland'. His successors sustained this domination for a further two generations.

MAEL SECHNAILL II MAC DOMNAILL (?–1022), King of Tara. In 980, he became King over both the northern and southern Uí Néill, the two families who traditionally dominated kingship in the northern parts of early medieval Ireland. His reign was dominated by the struggle with BRIAN BORUMA of Munster for control over all the Irish kingdoms. A formidable warrior who defeated the Vikings of Dublin on three occasions, Mael Sechnaill was obliged to acknowledge Brian's superiority in 1002, but, after the latter's death at the Battle of Clontarf in 1014, he resumed his earlier role as the dominant Irish king.

MAGNUS (?–1265), last King of Man (1252–65). His submission to the King of Scotland in 1264 marked the end of an epoch in the history of the Hebrides and Irish Sea. A son of OLAF II, he seized the throne in 1252, acknowledging Man's allegiance to Norway in opposition to Scottish expansionism. He joined King Haakon IV of Norway's great Hebrides expedition of 1262–3, but when this failed he was left high and dry. In 1264 ALEXANDER III threatened to invade Man, compelling Magnus to do homage. When he died a year later, Alexander appointed bailiffs to rule Man.

MAGNUS MAXIMUS, Roman Emperor (383–8). A Roman General based in Britain who declared himself Emperor (*see also* CARAUSIUS, CLODIUS ALBINUS, CONSTANTINE I, CONSTANTINE III), he gained control of Gaul and Spain before his defeat by the Eastern Emperor Theodosius I. The extent to which he contributed to the eventual collapse of Roman power in Britain by removing troops is not clear: he is known to have defeated the Picts in 382, and Hadrian's Wall was still securely held at that time. The evidence, however, for a Roman withdrawal from Wales during his rule is much stronger.

MAGNUS OF ORKNEY, ST (*c.* 1080–c. 1116), Viking ruler. For some years, he and his cousin Haakon were co-rulers of the virtually autonomous earldom of Orkney. According to a later biography, his policy of taking cold baths whenever he was tempted meant that his wife remained a virgin throughout their 10-year marriage. This apart, both his life and the manner of his death, killed by his cousin in a struggle for power, seem to have been those of a typical Viking ruler. Yet a martyr's cult began to develop, which was institutionalized when his nephew Rognvald, Earl of Orkney, founded the cathedral of St Magnus at Kirkwall.

MAGUIRE (MÁG UIDHIR), HUGH (?–1600), clan leader. He succeeded to his lordship of Fermanagh in 1589 and found himself systematically harassed by the English; when the Lord Deputy Sir William FITZWILLIAM declared him traitor, he invaded Connaught in 1590, but was defeated by Sir Richard Bingham. Over the next decade, he was at the heart of resistance to English power. During his father-in-law Hugh O'NEILL's expedition into Munster and Leinster, he was killed in a small skirmish near Cork. His younger brother, Cuchonnacht Maguire, accompanied O'Neill in the 'Flight of the Earls' (1607) and died in Genoa in 1609.

MAGUIRE, MAIREAD (née Corrigan) (1944–), peace activist. She founded the Peace People with Betty Williams and the journalist Ciaran MacKeown in Aug. 1976 after her sister's three children were killed by a car which crashed after its IRA driver was shot by security forces. The Peace People held several large, cross-community peace rallies which attracted significant working-class support (previous peace movements tended to be middle-class dominated). This produced widespread hope of a breakthrough in the search for peace, culminating in the award of the 1976 Nobel Peace Prize to Corrigan and Williams, but the award was followed by internal squabbling and decline. Williams emigrated to America in 1982; Maguire, who married her brother-in-law, Gerry Maguire, in 1981 after the death of her sister, has remained active in Northern Ireland peace campaigns. The significance of the Peace People remains controversial. Critics see it as a flash-in-the-pan doomed by political naïvete and accuse it of ignoring State violence, while defenders argue that it reduced violence by making paramilitaries more aware of the constraints on public tolerance of their activities.

MAHDI, an influential Arab leader with powers akin to those of a Messiah. The term was applied from the 1880s to insurrectionary leaders in the Sudan who claimed to be the expected Mahdi. Claimants to the title caused the Victorians a great deal of difficulty, especially Mohammed Ahmed (1840–85) who in 1882 raised a revolt against Egyptian rule in the Sudan, defeated the Egyptian army and besieged and captured Khartoum in 1885, killing General Charles GORDON and his garrison. After the Mahdi's death, his successor ruled Sudan until he was defeated by KITCHENER at the Battle of Omdurman in 1898.

MAIR (OR MAJOR), JOHN (1469–1550), theologian. Lothian-born, after studies at Cambridge and Paris he taught in Paris (his pupils including John CALVIN) and St Andrews, becoming Provost of St Salvator's College there from 1533. He wrote philosophical works in the scholastic manner and a history of Britain (1520), which was notable for its unfashionably positive view of a union of Scotland and England; while defending ERASMUS against ultra-conservative Paris theologians, he also defended traditional theology against Protestantism.

MAITLAND, F(REDERIC) W(ILLIAM) (1850–1906), historian. Arguably the greatest of all historians of medieval England, he made a massive contribution to the history of English law through his writing and the editing of plea rolls. His most renowned works are *The History of English Law before the Time of Edward I* (1895) and *Domesday Book and Beyond* (1897), in which he proceeded from the 'known' (Domesday Book) to the 'unknown' (English society in the Anglo-Saxon period).

MAITLAND, JOHN (1st Baron Maitland of Thirlstane) (c. 1545–95), politician. Younger brother of William MAITLAND, he shared his loyalty to MARY QUEEN OF SCOTS; this brought him imprisonment and loss of legal office (Keeper of the Privy Seal from 1567, following his father). Regaining power as Privy Councillor (1583), Royal Secretary (1584) and Lord Chancellor (1587), he used his initially great influence over JAMES VI as far as he could to favour the Presbyterian party in the Church. James grew increasingly irritated by him, especially after being manoeuvred into accepting the 'Golden Act' of 1592 which restored Presbyterian Church organization.

MAITLAND, JOHN (2nd Earl and 1st Duke of Lauderdale) (1616–82), politician. Son of the 1st Earl of Lauderdale, he took the Covenant during the First Civil War and came to be regarded as one of the ultra-Covenanting party. From 1644 he was a member of the Committee of Both Kingdoms, but at the end of the decade favoured a settlement with CHARLES I and in the 1650s corresponded with Royalists in England. Appointed Scottish Secretary of State at the Restoration, he was the chief architect of British government policy in Scotland for the next two decades. Despite his Covenanting past, he helped to reimpose Episcopacy, and readily resorted to armed force to suppress religious and political opposition. He rose to dominance after the Pentland rising (1666), when nearly 1,000 Presbyterian Covenanters marched on Edinburgh, only to be defeated by government forces in the Pentland Hills. The climax to Lauderdale's rule in Scotland was the Battle of Bothwell Bridge (1679), where the royal army under the Duke of Monmouth (*see* SCOTT, JAMES) defeated a gathering of Covenanters. That such a conflict had taken place at all was judged to have exposed the bankruptcy of his approach, and resulted in his fall.

MAITLAND OF LETHINGTON, WILLIAM (c. 1528–73), politician. Son of a prominent lawyer and brother of John MAITLAND, he was appointed Secretary by MARY OF GUISE in 1558, but supported the Protestant Lords of the Congregation during the national revolution of 1559–60, and established close contact with William CECIL. As secretary to MARY QUEEN OF SCOTS he did his best to guide foreign policy into pro-English paths, and to restrain Protestant impatience with Mary. His compromise policy was imperilled by Mary's marriage to Henry STEWART, Lord Darnley, in 1565 and the latter's murder was not unwelcome to him. Obstinately loyal to Mary, Maitland vainly tried to engineer national reconciliation in 1570, and he held Edinburgh Castle, the last Marian stonghold, until 1573. His death in prison may have been suicide. Much of the archive of this understudied and brilliant politician remains, though sadly dispersed.

MAJOR, JOHN *see* essay on page 541

MAKARIOS III (originally Mikhail Khristodolou Mouskos) (1913–77), Cypriot Archbishop and politician. The leader in Cyprus's struggle for *enosis* (union with Greece) and independence from Britain, Mikhail Mouskos was a poor shepherd's son who rose through the ranks of the Church (taking the name of Makarios) to become Archbishop in 1950. In 1954 he gained Greek support for *enosis* and was then suspected of involvement with the EOKA (National Organization of Cypriot Struggle) terrorists under GRIVAS. He negotiated with the British in 1955–6, but his subsequent arrest and exile unleashed a wave of anti-British terror. Compromise was reached in 1959 and an independent Cyprus was born with Makarios elected President. Greek–Turkish rivalry and fighting intensified after 1963. Makarios worked for integration, Grivas turned against him. Successfully elected to a third term in 1973, in 1974 Makarios fled to London when the attempted coup masterminded by the Greek junta was followed by Turkish invasion and partition.

MALACHY, ST (MAEL MAEDÓC UA MORGAIR) (1094–1148), churchman. A priest from Armagh, as Bishop of Down (1128), Archbishop of Armagh (1132) and Papal Legate (1139), he pressed for changes intended to bring the Irish Church more into line with the norms of the Latin Church on the continent, in particular the establishment of a diocesan structure and the introduction of the Cistercian and Augustinian rules. In the face of fierce opposition from traditionalists, especially in Armagh, he looked to Rome for support but he died at Clairvaux while on one of his journeys to the papal curia.

The *Life of Malachy*, written in 1149 by his friend Bernard of Clairvaux, depicted him as the model of a reforming bishop, and, as such, he was canonized in 1190. St Bernard's vivid description of the difficulties encountered by Malachy helped to establish the new image of the Irish as barbarous.

MALINOWSKI, BRONISLAW (1884–1942), anthropologist. Educated in his native Poland, Malinowski studied under the eminent psychologist Wilhelm Wundt at Leipzig and studied anthropology at the London School of Economics. During the First World War he lived and worked with the inhabitants of the Trobriand Islands near New Guinea, developing what is known as the 'participant-observation' method of ethnographic field-work. In 1922 he published the *Argonauts of the Western Pacific*, the first of his many works on the Trobriand islanders, all of which illustrated what is now called the theory of 'functionalism'.

This argues that human actions, languages and material artefacts can be understood only in terms of their function in the whole culture, itself a complex and interconnected network of institutions which serve human biological and psychological needs. He became the first Professor of Social Anthropology at the LSE in 1927 before settling in the USA in 1938.

MALCOLM *see* MAEL COLUIM

MALLON, SEAMUS (1936–), Northern Irish politician *see* HUME, JOHN

MALORY, SIR THOMAS (*c.* 1416–*c.* 1471), writer. He was the author of one of the greatest, and in terms of its impact on subsequent Arthurian literature, most influential romances ever written in English, the *Morte d'Arthur*, completed by 1470. Of the several known mid fifteenth-century Thomas Malorys, the writer is generally identified with a knight of Newbold Revel (Warws.) who, in the 1450s, spent some years in prison facing charges (probably politically motivated) that included rape and theft, and who, released without trial, went on to play a minor role in the Wars of the Roses. If, however, as some literary scholars suggest, the author helped CAXTON revise the version printed in 1485, he was a different Malory. *See also* ARTHUR, King.

MALTHUS, THOMAS (1766–1834), economist and demographer. In his *Essay on the Principle of Population* (1798) Malthus advanced the notion that population had an inbuilt propensity to rise, and to outstrip any possible increase in food supply. The necessary conclusion was that population growth would be checked, either by the 'preventive' check of prudence or the 'positive' check of famine or calamity, which would reduce numbers to a proper level again. In later years he extended the analysis, and came to view the preventive check as being more possible than he had initially imagined. Malthus's name is erroneously linked for posterity with the idea that the positive check is inevitable. His ideas were important influences on the thought of Charles DARWIN, Alfred WALLACE, John Stuart MILL and Herbert SPENCER. His belief that indiscriminate charity encouraged population growth influenced the harsher nineteenth-century attitudes to the poor exemplified in the New Poor Law of 1834. Although he saw birth-control as wicked, the Malthusian (later Neo-Malthusian) League formed in 1861 openly advocated population control through contraception. (*See also* BESANT, WALTER; BRADLAUGH, CHARLES). Malthus is hailed as the founding father of modern demography, but he was also an important economist, engaging in lengthy dispute with David RICARDO about rent and

continued on page 542

MAJOR, JOHN (1943–)
Politician and Prime Minister (1990–7)

Next to Bonar LAW he was the most unexpected and colourless of Conservative leaders and Prime Ministers; but no one except Margaret THATCHER has served longer consecutive terms.

In the 1990 contest to succeed Thatcher, Major's background would turn out to be an advantage, which was not how it seemed during his childhood. His father was a one-time circus performer who later went into the gnome-making business without much success. Major's childhood was poor and he is the only Conservative leader this century except CHURCHILL not to have gone to university. After periods of unemployment, he went into banking in 1965 where he remained until 1979.

Major served his political apprenticeship on the Labour-dominated Lambeth Council, where he was Chairman of the Housing Committee (1970–1). He twice contested St Pancras North for the Conservatives in 1974 before getting the safe seat of Huntingdon in time for Thatcher's first election victory of 1979. Thereafter his rise was steady but unspectacular: Parliamentary Private Secretary at the Home Office (1981–3); Assistant Whip (1983–4); Government Whip (1984–5); Under-Secretary at the Department of Health and Social Security (1985–6); Minister of State at the DHSS (1986–7). But it was as a tough Chief Secretary to the Treasury between 1987 and 1989 that he first came to the attention of a wider public and, after the demotion of Geoffrey HOWE in 1989, he was promoted to be Foreign Secretary. This was more a recognition of him as a safe pair of hands than as a man of diplomatic flair. He was also to be the major beneficiary of the next stage in the crisis that afflicted the Thatcher government. When Nigel LAWSON spectacularly resigned from the Treasury in 1990 Major was moved in as his replacement. This gave him a political prominence that proved most useful later in the year when Thatcher herself resigned.

Faced with a choice between Thatcher's challenger, Michael HESELTINE, who was deeply unpopular with her supporters and Douglas HURD, who was widely seen as something of a 'toff', Major commanded the Thatcher vote as being her heir, and he was widely assumed to possess the common touch with his pledge to create a 'nation at ease with itself'. Initial popularity, boosted by the successful prosecution of the Gulf War, led to what was Major's finest hour – the 1992 election, which the Conservatives won, despite considerable anxieties in the party. His decision to speak out against devolution for Wales and Scotland, like his adoption of a soap-box for impromptu oratory, were decried by the commentators as the gambits of a doomed leader; instead Major came out with a majority of 17 seats.

The government was dogged by problems from the start. The divisions within the party over the question of further European integration, which had been containable before 1985, became less so after the Single European Act of that year and were exacerbated by anti-European negotiations at Maastricht. Thatcher's instincts had been against this new treaty from the start; speaking from the Lords and free of the restraints of office she was able to give vent to her real views on Europe. The government's decision to join the European Exchange Rate Mechanism (ERM) in 1990 back-fired disastrously as sterling came under heavy pressure on the world's money markets, and the enforced decision to withdraw from it in Sept. 1992 had three devastating effects: it destroyed the reputation which the Conservatives had always enjoyed for financial shrewdness; it broke the axis between Major and his Chancellor, Norman LAMONT; and it gave the Euro-sceptics a reason to stand up against further measures of integration.

Despite negotiating opt-out clauses at Maastricht in 1991 from various objectionable parts of the treaty which would lead to closer European union, it was a treaty too far for the Euro-sceptics, who came out in open revolt against Major; his inability to discipline them effectively further undermined a government which was already rocked by revelations of sexual misconduct and financial 'sleaze'. A small parliamentary majority limited the government's room to maneouvre over coal-pit closures, the introduction of VAT on fuel and the proposed privatization of the post office. In 1995, faced with increased sniping from within his own party, Major issued a challenge to his critics to 'put up or shut up', by resigning his leadership and standing for re-election. The decision by the Welsh Secretary, John REDWOOD, to stand against the Prime Minister, although he was defeated, indicated the strength and depth of opposition within the Conservative Party to Major.

Despite a booming economy, in 1997 Major led the Conservatives to the greatest defeat in their history. He resigned immediately, and in March 2000 announced that he would not stand at the next election.

Anthony Seldon, Major: A Political Life (1997)
John Major, The Autobiography (1999)

other topics. His economic views were re-evaluated in the twentieth century by KEYNES.

MANCHESTER, 2ND EARL OF see MONTAGU, EDWARD

MANDELSON, PETER (1953–), politician. Mandelson is the grandson of Herbert MORRISON but, despite being born into the Labour Party, it has not yet really loved him. Known as 'the Prince of Darkness' because of his legendary skills as a media manipulator or 'spin-doctor', he has been a vital part of the New Labour project of the 1990s. In 1985 Mandelson was brought in by Neil KINNOCK to be Labour's Director of Campaigns and Communications, during which time he rebranded and tried to modernize the image of the Labour Party replacing the red flag with the red rose. He lost favour under John SMITH in 1992 but was restored to it by the advent of his friend Tony BLAIR, under whom he enhanced his reputation as a master of 'spin'. With Labour's overwhelming victory in 1997, his future seemed assured, when he was made Minister without Portfolio, with the job of enforcing 'joined-up government' by overseeing the work of other departments and driving policy through.

To his disappointment he was not given a department to run but was left in charge of presentational issues as the Chancellor of the Duchy of Lancaster (1997–8), where he retained his responsibility for the Millennium Dome, which he saw as an up-dated version of the 1951 Festival of Britain for which his grandfather Morrison had been responsible and which others saw as symbolic of New Labour, image without substance. In the Cabinet reshuffle of 1998 he was promoted to the Department of Trade and Industry, but before he could make an impact was forced to resign after it was revealed that he had borrowed more than £250,000 from the controversial Paymaster General Geoffrey Robinson in order to buy a house in Notting Hill, west London. After a brief period on the back benches, he was brought back as Secretary of State for Northern Ireland in Oct. 1999 with the task of maintaining the Northern Ireland peace process.

MANDEVILLE, BERNARD (c. 1670–1733), writer. Born in Dordrecht, the Netherlands, Mandeville was educated at Leiden University, taking a doctorate in medicine. He moved to London, where he survived mainly by hack writing, in part in the Whig cause. His poem, *The Grumbling Hive* (1705), was republished with notes as *The Fable of the Bees, or Private Vices, Public Benefits* in 1714, and again in a further enlarged edition in 1724. It attacked various Christian charitable schemes of the day, arguing that the public good was best served when people acted from self-interest. Deliberately paradoxical, it was very successful, though it attracted much criticism (especially from the clergy), including its presentation as a public nuisance by the grand jury of Middx. in 1725. Moral philosopher Francis HUTCHESON was among Mandeville's critics. David HUME and Adam SMITH, though also dissenting from elements of Mandeville's analysis, found more to admire in it.

MANDEVILLE, GEOFFREY DE (1st Earl of Essex) (?–1144), rebel. An English baron, he was created Earl in 1140 and died of wounds suffered when he rebelled against STEPHEN (1143–4). His allegedly unscrupulous changes of allegiance during the civil war between Stephen and MATILDA led to him being represented as 'the great champion of anarchy' in J. H. Round's 1892 biography. Although Round's views no longer hold the field, interpretations of Mandeville's career continue to provide a controversial focus in studies of Stephen's reign.

MANDEVILLE, SIR JOHN. This is either the real name of, or the pseudonym adopted by, the author of *Mandeville's Travels* (1371 or earlier). Literary scholars continue to debate the matter. Either way the book describing the journeys which a fourteenth-century English knight from St Albans (Herts.) made through the Middle and Far East proved to be a resounding success, soon translated from the original French into English. Latin and many other languages. The author took the familiar genre of the narrative of pilgrimage to the Holy Land and transformed it into a work of fantasy, skilfully using scientific commonplaces like the circumnavigability of the earth in order to place his imaginative descriptions of marvels within an apparently realistic framework.

MANLEY, DELARIVIER (c. 1672–1724), writer. Daughter of Sir Roger Manley, Lieutenant Governor of Jersey (1667–72), she left her bigamist husband in 1694, initially with the support of Barbara VILLIERS, Duchess of Cleveland, and then lived by soliciting money from friends in different parts of the country. These experiences led to her first book, *Letters by Mrs Manley* (1696), imitating a French best-seller, *Travels into Spain*, by Baroness d'Aulnoy. Her most successful play was *The Royal Mischief*, with its daring sexual references and strong female lead. In ANNE's reign she became a political satirist with *The Secret History of Queen Zarah and the Zarazians* (1705) and *The New Atlantis* (1709), depicting the Whigs as a coterie of bestial debauchees centred on Sarah, Duchess of Marlborough (see CHURCHILL, SARAH). She also wrote seven numbers of SWIFT's *Examiner* (1711).

MANN, TOM (1856–1941), trade-union leader and socialist. Born near Coventry, Mann was an engineer and trade unionist in the Amalgamated Society of Engineers and in the 1880s was a leading figure in moving the union away from New Model Unionism (*see* ALLAN, WILLIAM). He also became an active socialist. In 1885 he joined the Social Democratic Federation (*see* HYNDMAN, H. M.). In 1889 he was a leader of the great dock strike in London, which inaugurated a new phase in trade-union history, became Secretary of the Independent Labour Party in 1893, and founded the Workers' Union in 1898, which was to become the largest union of its time. Between 1901 and 1910 he was active in Australia, where he founded the Socialist Party, and then, back in Britain, was a leading figure of syndicalism in the great wave of trade-union militancy between 1911 and 1913. A member of the British Socialist Party in 1916, he became the first Secretary of the Amalgamated Engineering Union in 1919, joined the Communist Party in 1921 and continued as a revolutionary and militant unionist into old age.

MANNERS, JOHN (styled Marquess of Granby) (1721–70), soldier. The eldest son of the 3rd Duke of Rutland and an MP, he began his military career in the Leicestershire Blues, a regiment raised by his father to oppose the 1745 rebellion. Granby led the regiment into Scotland with Cumberland (*see* WILLIAM AUGUSTUS), and then accompanied Cumberland to Flanders. His reputation for gambling and drunkenness restricted his advancement under GEORGE II. He went to Germany as Colonel of the Horse Guards in 1758 and gained a popular reputation as the best British military leader for his ferocity at Minden (1759), Warburg (1760), Gravenstein, Wilhelmstahl and Homburg (1761). Commander-in-Chief from 1763, he was attacked by JUNIUS for behaving in office as a 'broker in commissions'. He died in debt in 1770 before he could succeed to the dukedom.

MANNING, HENRY (1808–92), Cardinal. A fellow student of GLADSTONE at Balliol College, Oxford, in 1842 Manning published an exposition of Anglo-Catholic beliefs in *The Unity of the Church*. He was appointed Archdeacon of Chichester (1840) and in 1842 Select Preacher at Oxford, where on 5 November 1843 he preached an anti-papal sermon. However, in 1849 Manning paid a visit to Pope Pius IX and two years later resigned his archdeaconry and converted to Roman Catholicism. By 1865 he was Archbishop of Westminster and was appointed a Cardinal in 1875. A firm supporter of papal infallibility, he was doctrinally authoritarian and was much concerned with social questions and supported trade-union rights.

MANNING, ROBERT (also known as Robert of Brunne or Bourne in Lincs.) (*fl.* 1330), priest, chronicler and poet. In his *Handlyng Synne*, an amplification of the French *Manuel des Péchés* of William of Waddington, he was concerned with sin as a cause of social evil. The *Chronicle* which he completed in 1338 gave a patriotic rendering in English verse of the *Roman de Brut* of WACE and of Peter LANGTOFT's *Chronique*.

MANSBRIDGE, ALBERT (1876–1952), educator. A clerk, then cashier, with the Co-operative Building Society, after leaving Battersea grammar school at 14, Mansbridge attended extension classes at King's College, London, and in 1903 instituted a scheme of adult education, the Association to Promote the Higher Education of Working Men (which later became the Workers' Educational Association), becoming general secretary (1905–14). He established branches throughout the country and with the co-operation of universities organized tutorial classes for students at higher education level.

MANSEL (OR MAUNSELL), JOHN (?–1265), courtier. The son of a country priest, he rose to become Keeper of the Seal and Chief Councillor of HENRY III. He gained military distinction in French campaigns, and became very influential with the King, being sent as his emissary to Castile, Germany and Scotland. He was not popular, probably due to his continued loyalty to the King and his excessive accumulation of wealth. He was forced into exile by Simon de MONTFORT in 1263.

MANSFIELD, 1ST EARL OF *see* MURRAY, WILLIAM

MANSFIELD, KATHERINE (originally Kathleen Mansfield Beauchamp) (1888–1923), short-story writer and poet. Born in New Zealand, she was taken to London in 1903 to complete her education. Unhappily married, she met the writer John Middleton Murry: they lived together on and off from 1912, marrying in 1918. In 1917 Mansfield was diagnosed as having tuberculosis and most of the rest of her life was spent restlessly searching for a cure in France, Italy and Switzerland. Though she wrote poetry, it is for her short stories, many about her New Zealand childhood, that she is best known. She transformed the genre with *In a German Pension* (1911) and particularly her later work *Prelude* which was published in 1918 by the Hogarth Press, through which she met Virginia WOOLF (who acknowledged hers as 'the only writing I have ever been jealous of'); other books were *Bliss* (first published in 1918, generally regarded as her finest work), *Other Stories* (1920) and *The Garden Party and Other Stories* (1922). After her death, Murry, not always the most attentive or faithful of companions, was criticized for trying to inflate his wife's reputation: in recent years it has needed no such promotion and the unexpurgated publication of her journals and letters (1984) has served to enhance it further.

MANSON, SIR PATRICK (1844–1922), physician. Manson studied medicine at Aberdeen University and practised in the Far East. In the late 1870s and early 1880s, whilst running a hospital in Amoy (China), he confirmed that filarial infection in man was caused by a parasite transmitted by the common brown mosquito. In 1883 he moved to Hong Kong, where he set up a private practice and a school of medicine. Seven years later he returned to London, where he established a medical practice and began collaborating with Ronald ROSS on the life-cycle of the malaria parasite. He is best known for his theory, first announced in 1894, that the malaria parasite develops in and is transmitted by a mosquito. Giovanni Grassi and Ross later produced strong experimental evidence in support of Manson's theory. Through his friendship with Joseph CHAMBERLAIN he oversaw the reorganization of medical practice in the colonies and in 1899 helped found the London School of Tropical Medicine.

MAP, WALTER (*c.* 1135–1209 or 1210), Latin author and courtier. A raconteur and humorist whose masterpiece, *De Nugis Curialium* (Courtiers' Trifles), has amused readers from that day to this, although sometimes in bowdlerized translations, he was part English, part Welsh. Educated at Paris, he became Chancellor of Lincoln, then Archdeacon of Oxford, but was at his most prolific and satirical in the 1170s and 1180s when attached to HENRY II's court, of which he left a devastating portrait.

MAR, EARL OF, 14TH *see* STEWART, JOHN; **17TH** *see* STEWART, JAMES; **18TH, 19TH** and **23RD** *see* ERSKINE, JOHN

MARBECK (OR MERBECKE), JOHN (*c.* 1510–*c.* 1585), composer. While organist at St George's chapel, Windsor, he narrowly escaped execution as a heretic in 1543 for writing the first English attempt at a Bible concordance, published 1550. Also in 1550 he published his *Book of Common Prayer Noted*, whose simple musical settings for Holy Communion were enthusiastically revived for congregational Anglican use during the Oxford Movement in the nineteenth century.

MARCH, EARL OF, 1ST and **4TH** *see* MORTIMER, ROGER; **5TH** *see* MORTIMER, EDMUND

MARCONI, GUGLIELMO (1874–1937), radio pioneer. The 'father' of radio, Marconi developed a childhood interest in the newly discovered properties of radio waves in his family home in Bologna. Inspired by Heinrich Hertz's research, he conceived the idea of sending wireless messages in 1894. Travelling to Britain with his Scottish mother, he secured introductions and began large-scale experiments. He took out his first patent and founded the Marconi Co. in 1897, established his first permanent radio link and sent his first ship-to-shore message the following year, and by 1901 had transmitted the first radio message across the Atlantic. He was joint winner of the Nobel Prize for Physics in 1909, the year the first passenger ship was saved by sending an SOS radio message. He continued to experiment with ever-shorter radio waves; with its beam stations the Marconi Co. became a strong competitor to the submarine cable telegraph companies. In the slump, his company was merged in 1929 with the cable companies founded by Sir John PENDER to form Cable & Wireless.

MARE, SIR PETER DE LA (*fl.* 1370–7), politician. MP for Herefs. in the Parliament of April–June 1376, he impressed his fellow members by the eloquence with which he expressed the public mood of hostility to an allegedly corrupt clique of courtiers dominating the old and sick EDWARD III. The Commons chose him as their spokesman to present the outcome of their deliberations to the King's Council, which he did so effectively that he retained the role throughout that Parliament, becoming the first Speaker. Not only did the Commons refuse to make a grant of taxation, they also, for the first time in the history of representative institutions, led by de la Mare, used the procedure of impeachment to secure the dismissal of unpopular ministers, and the Parliament became known as the Good Parliament. De la Mare's connections with Edmund MORTIMER, Earl of March, may have helped him to take these unprecedented actions; if so, they did not prevent his imprisonment during the period of court reaction in the autumn of 1376. Released after Edward III's death (1377), he was again elected Speaker in the first Parliament of RICHARD II's reign.

MAREDUDD AP OWAIN (?–999), King of Deheubarth and Gwynedd. In 956–7, during the lifetime of his father OWAIN AP HYWEL DDA, Maredudd invaded Gwynedd killing Cadwallon ap Ieuaf, and succeeded in annexing the kingdom to reunite Gwynedd and Deheubarth. During the 13 years of his rule, he managed to hold both kingdoms together in face of internal enemies and against Viking attacks. He was succeeded by his son-in-law LLYWELYN AP SEISYLL.

MARGARET (1240–75), Queen of Scots (1251–75). Daughter of King HENRY III, she was married to the 10-year-old ALEXANDER III in 1251 but, until 1259, she and her husband were more or less helpless pawns in a game of power politics at the Scottish court. In letters to her father she complained of the bad weather and their cramped conditions. They visited England in 1260 and she stayed on to give birth outside Scotland (to the dismay of the Scots) to a daughter. She had two more children, but all three died before their father.

MARGARET (Countess of Snowdon) (1930–), Royal Princess. Younger daughter of King GEORGE VI and sister of Queen ELIZABETH II, in 1955 Princess Margaret gave the royal family the first of its 'soap opera' story lines by announcing that, 'mindful of the Church's teaching and conscious of my duty to the Commonwealth', she would not marry her father's divorced equerry, Group Captain Peter Townsend. She subsequently married the photographer Anthony ARMSTRONG-JONES (1960) and had two children. The marriage ended in divorce in 1978. Princess Margaret plays an ambivalent royal role, performing public duties while having a reputation as a restless socialite.

MARGARET LOGIE (?–1375), Queen of Scots (1363–9). Born Margaret Drummond, and widow of Sir John Logie (by whom she had a son), in 1363 she married DAVID II, who was desperate for a male heir and had fallen in love with her. When no child of the marriage had been born by 1369 he divorced her. Margaret, however, fled to the papal court at Avignon and there she appealed against the divorce, a suit still pending when she died.

MARGARET, MAID OF NORWAY (1283–90), Queen of Scots (1286–90). The only child of King Eric of Norway and Margaret, daughter of ALEXANDER III of Scotland, she was recognized in 1284, following the deaths of her mother (probably in giving birth to her) and her uncles as heir presumptive to the Scottish throne. When Alexander died two years later, she became Queen, in her absence, and was then betrothed to Edward, the eldest son of EDWARD I. But she saw neither husband nor kingdom, dying at the age of seven at Kirkwall on Orkney in Sept. 1290. Her death precipitated the most serious crisis in the history of Anglo-Scottish relations.

MARGARET OF ANJOU see essay on pages 546–47

MARGARET OF DENMARK (c. 1457–86), Queen of Scots (1469–86). Daughter of Christian I of Denmark–Norway, she married JAMES III in 1469, bringing to her husband all Norwegian rights over the Orkney and Shetland Islands, to be retained until a dowry of 60,000 florins had been paid in full. In the event this marriage treaty enabled Scotland to reach its modern borders.

MARGARET OF FRANCE (c. 1282–1318), Queen of England (1099–1307). Half-sister of Philip IV of France, she was married to EDWARD I (about 40 years her senior) in 1299. She bore him three children, but her chief role was the traditional queenly one of peacemaker between the Kings of France and England, and between her husband and her stepson, the future EDWARD II.

MARGARET, ST (c. 1046–93), Queen of Scots (1070–93). Although the 'royal saint' of Scotland, she was of English descent. Brought to Scotland when her brother EDGAR THE ÆTHELING fled from WILLIAM I THE CONQUEROR, her marriage (c. 1070) to MAEL COLUIM III CENN MÓR marked an important stage in the anglicization of the Scottish court. She and her husband had eight children, none of whom were given traditional Scottish names; three of their sons became king (see EDGAR; ALEXANDER I; DAVID I). According to the 'official' biography written by her chaplain, Turgot of St Andrews, she was exceptionally devout and charitable and did much to persuade her husband to bring the practices of the Scottish Church into line with the mainstream of Latin Christendom. She died on 16 Nov. 1093, on hearing of the deaths of her husband and eldest son at Norman hands. Her enduring memorial was the priory (later abbey) which she founded at Dunfermline, where she and her descendants were buried. She was canonized in 1250.

MARGARET TUDOR (1489–1541), Queen of Scotland. Her father HENRY VII's determination to marry her to JAMES IV of Scotland succeeded in 1503, ending two centuries of a formal state of Anglo-Scottish war. Her son, the future JAMES V, was born in 1512; after her husband's death at Flodden (1513), she disputed control of her son with John STEWART, Duke of Albany. Her remarriage to Archibald DOUGLAS, Earl of Angus, complicated his feud with James HAMILTON, Earl of Arran. In 1515 she fled to England; her daughter Margaret DOUGLAS, JAMES VI's grandmother, supplied James's claim to the English throne. Her estrangement from Douglas led to divorce and further factional intrigue; her attempts to divorce a third husband, Henry Stewart, Lord Methven, did not succeed.

MARGARET OF ANJOU (1430–82)
Queen of England (1445–71)

Margaret will always be remembered as SHAKE-SPEARE portrayed her, as the harridan of the Wars of the Roses, the she-wolf of France condemning RICHARD OF YORK to death while taunting him with a handkerchief soaked in his son's blood. (In reality he was killed in the Battle of Wakefield while she was in Scotland.) She was arrogant and impetuous but not peculiarly cruel. Although she is often visualized as a warrior queen, leading troops to war, her lavish expenditure on jewels, made even while royal finances were under strain, shows where her real interests lay. Her preoccupations were the usual ones for a lady of royal blood, display, piety, hunting, the well-being of her family and the marital prospects of her protégés.

She scarcely knew her father, Count Réné of Anjou, who was a prisoner in Burgundy during most of her youth. She was brought up in Anjou first by her mother Isabelle of Lorraine and then, when her mother left to pursue Réné's claim to the kingdom of Naples, by her grandmother Yolande of Aragon, both strong-minded women and keen literary patrons. She was to share many of their priorities. Negotiations for her marriage to HENRY VI began in 1444 as part of a policy of *détente* with France intended to end the Hundred Years War. This aroused suspicion in many Englishmen, who wanted to recapture the glories of HENRY V's reign. Lavish festivities accompanied her entry into London in 1445, but the atmosphere was soured when English troops withdrew from Maine and it was discovered that this concession to France had been secretly promised as part of the marriage agreement. The sudden collapse of the Lancastrian empire in France in 1449 bore out the warnings of those who had criticized *détente*. In May 1450 the chief architect of peace, Margaret's friend, the Duke of Suffolk (*see* POLE, WILLIAM DE LA), who had arranged her marriage, was impeached by Parliament and then murdered. Within weeks a major rebellion left London occupied by an army of Kentishmen led by Jack CADE, and the Queen, at Greenwich (Kent), in some danger, her husband having withdrawn to Berkhamsted (Herts.). She issued a general pardon, a strategy which helped to disperse the rebels, although (as so often) it is unclear how far she acted on her own initiative or merely rubber-stamped the recommendations of advisers.

More than most queens this young Frenchwoman needed friends, but finding them in the Suffolk–Beaufort faction (*see* BEAUFORT, EDMUND) meant that she made enemies of York and the Nevilles. Instead of performing the traditional queenly role of peacemaker she took sides in the party struggle. From the moment of her arrival in England Margaret found herself entangled in the hostilities which culminated in the Wars of the Roses.

Her only child, EDWARD, PRINCE OF WALES, was born in 1453, and the forceful, attractive Queen and her pusillanimous husband made such an unlikely couple that, when the child was eventually born, aspersions were cast on his legitimacy. Meanwhile the years of childlessness had encouraged the factionalism which scarred Henry VI's kingship. The most likely heir, Richard of York, fearing that his claim would be set aside in favour of the King's favoured cousins, the Beauforts, took up arms in 1452, only to back down immediately. News of Margaret's pregnancy in April 1453 completed his discomfiture. While the government launched a new French campaign, Margaret went to the shrine of the Virgin at Walsingham (Norfolk), bearing rich gifts as thanks for her pregnancy. On the way she tried to badger rich widows into marrying her retainers. Then disaster struck. The force sent to Gascony suffered a shattering defeat at Castillon (July 1453), and its commander, John TALBOT, was killed. In Aug. Henry completely lost his senses. Newly delivered of her son, Margaret tried to take control of the regime. Guided by a clique of her husband's advisers she made a desperate bid for the regency. In France this would have come to her as a matter of course but English custom dictated that York, rebellious but still the King's nearest adult male relative, was catapulted into power as Protector. Although great care was taken to provide properly for Margaret, she must have feared what might happen to her baby, particularly if Henry died. In fact Henry recovered at Christmas 1454. Steps were taken to bring York and his chief ally, Richard NEVILLE, Earl of Warwick, to book. But Henry's advisers underestimated their opponents. York and the Nevilles raised a force which attacked and defeated the King and his supporters in the streets of St Albans (Herts.) (May 1455). A head-wound compounded Henry's ill health, giving York an excuse to declare himself Protector once more.

Once Henry was well enough to end York's second protectorship in 1456, Margaret responded to her feeling of vulnerability by trying to establish an unbreakable hold on power. She took husband and son away from London into her territorial stronghold (the Midland castles of the duchy of Lancaster) and raised troops from Edward's earldom of Chester. Doctors, merchants and churchmen were set to work investigating alchemy as a means of improving both the King's health and his finances. None of this made war inevitable. Margaret and her allies, chiefly the heirs of those who had been singled out for slaughter at St Albans, cautiously attempted to intimidate their opponents into submission rather than confront them on the battlefield. But the Yorkists decided that the risks of being politically marginalized were greater than those of civil war. In the autumn of 1459 they took up arms. On 23 Sept. Margaret waited at Eccleshall Castle (Staffs.) while her army suffered defeat at nearby Blore Heath. But next month, when the royal army marched on York's stronghold at Ludlow (Salop.), the position was reversed. York, his sons and allies were forced to flee overseas. At a Parliament at Coventry they were declared traitors, their estates confiscated, and their heirs disinherited. But Margaret's triumph was brief. In the summer of 1460 a Yorkist army invaded and captured Henry at Northampton. Margaret took her son with her to find refuge first at Harlech (Merion.), losing some of her jewels on the way, and then in Scotland. She brought some Scottish troops across the border to join the Lancastrian captains who had defeated and killed York at Wakefield (Yorks.) (Dec. 1460), and then the whole 'northern' army marched south, reportedly spreading terror in its wake. She defeated Warwick at the second Battle of St Albans (Feb. 1461) and recaptured her husband. London now lay at her mercy, and, had she gone on to take it, she might have saved the Lancastrian, and her own, cause. Instead, conscious of her unpopularity in London, she withdrew north, leaving the capital for York's son to enter and be proclaimed EDWARD IV. A few weeks later the Lancastrians suffered a crushing defeat at Towton (Yorks.) (March 1461). She heard the news at York and fled north taking husband and son with her. In April in return for the hope of Scottish help she surrendered Berwick.

For the next 10 years she travelled the courts of Europe, a lonely figure seeking help, receiving little more than courtesy. In 1462 she sailed to France and back, surviving shipwreck on the Northumbrian coast. Next year she returned to France with Edward; she never saw her husband again. Her father Réné enabled her to nurture her son in a paltry court of exile at his castle of Koeur in Lorraine. She and Edward's tutor, the eminent judge Sir John FORTESCUE, corresponded tirelessly with supporters in England and with sympathetic crowned heads as far away as Portugal. But for years she got nowhere. Even the rump of Lancastrian peers who had gone into exile stayed away from Koeur. Only when Warwick quarrelled violently with Edward IV, fleeing to France in 1470 and taking Clarence (see PLANTAGENET, GEORGE) with him, did her prospects materially improve. Even then she had to pay a heavy psychological price, putting aside bitter enmity and agreeing that her Edward should marry Warwick's daughter, ANNE NEVILLE, in order to forge a common front for the restoration of Henry VI (whom Edward IV held in prison). By Oct. 1470 Warwick and Clarence had carried out their side of the bargain, but Margaret and her son stayed in France for six more months. Distrust of her new allies, indecision, contrary winds, all contributed to the delay. On 14 April 1471, the day she landed at Weymouth (Dorset), Warwick, was defeated and killed by Edward IV, returning from exile in Burgundy. Her army made for Wales, hoping to find fresh reserves of support there, but spring floods prevented her crossing the Severn. Edward IV caught up with her at Tewkesbury (Glos.) and, for the second time, inflicted a crushing defeat (4 May) on her forces. Her son was killed, she was captured, and a few days later Henry VI was murdered. The Battle of Tewkesbury and its murderous aftermath had effectively ended the Wars of the Roses with victory for York. Had the Yorkist dynasty not been brought down by RICHARD III's ambition in 1483 there could have been no Lancastrian come-back. But by then Margaret was dead. Kept a prisoner until 1475, when her father persuaded King Louis XI of France to ransom her, she was released in return for giving up all her claims, both in England and to her father's inheritance. She retired to Anjou and, after her father's death, was left destitute, dragging out the last two years of life in the Château of Dampierre, the forlorn guest of one of the lesser lights of the French nobility.

MARIE DE FRANCE (*fl.* 1180), poet. The earliest-known woman poet writing in French, the cultivated language of late twelfth-century English aristocracy, with whom her fables and verse tales, traditionally called lays (*lais*), were immensely popular. In one of the fables she identifies herself: 'my name is Marie and I come from France'. Many attempts have been made to pin her down more precisely, but none so far has been generally accepted.

MARISCHAL, 4TH EARL OF *see* KEITH, GEORGE

MARKHAM, GERVASE (?1568–1637), writer. From a Notts. knightly family, he fought in the Netherlands, like his brother and fellow author Francis (1565–1627). He used his restless intelligence to write on a variety of subjects, including horsemanship, veterinary science, military administration and agriculture, besides plays (in collaboration) and a life of Sir Richard Grenville. His household guide, *The English Housewife* (1631), was widely popular.

MARKIEVICZ, COUNTESS CONSTANCE (née Gore-Booth) (1868–1927), Irish revolutionary. Born in London but educated in Ireland, she married a Polish count while studying art in Paris. She was involved in the Dublin cultural milieu of the Abbey Theatre before joining Sinn Féin in 1908 and the following year founding Na Fianna, a paramilitary organization for boys. She was condemned to death for her part in the Easter Rising, though the sentence was commuted. Freed by an amnesty in 1917, she was elected a Sinn Féin MP in 1918, the first woman to be elected to the British Parliament, but refused to take her seat in accordance with the party's boycott of West-minster. The following year she became Minister of Labour in the provisional Sinn Féin government and was twice imprisoned during the Anglo-Irish War; because of her opposition to the Anglo-Irish Treaty, she was also imprisoned by pro-treaty forces. Joining Fianna Fáil in 1926, she was elected to the Dáil just before her death.

MARKOVA, DAME ALICIA (originally Lillian Alicia Marks) (1910–), ballerina. A classical ballerina, Markova was engaged by Diaghilev when she was 14. After his death she worked in New York, before becoming the prima ballerina of the Vic-Wells Ballet (1933–5) where she partnered Anton Dolin, with whom she formed a company (1935–8), the first to take ballet on extensive provincial tours. From 1938 she performed all over the world and in 1950 co-founded the London Festival Ballet. Retiring from the stage in 1953 Markova held a number of directorial posts in the ballet world, taught and gave a series of masterclasses on BBC television in 1980.

MARKS, SIMON (1st Baron Marks of Broughton) (1888–1964), entrepreneur. Joining the Leeds-based chain of 'penny bazaars' set up by his father Michael Marks in 1907, Simon Marks became the chairman of a company that emerged at the end of the First World War. With his brother-in-law Israel SIEFF he made Marks & Spencer, registered as a company in 1926, into one of the most consistently successful of twentieth-century British businesses, with high-quality merchandise, value for money and good working conditions; it had approaching 250 stores by the time Marks received a barony in 1961.

MARLBOROUGH, DUKE OF, 1ST *see* CHURCHILL, JOHN; **DUCHESS OF** *see* CHURCHILL, SARAH

MARLOWE, CHRISTOPHER (1564–93), dramatist. A Canterbury shoemaker's son, Marlowe went to Cambridge and became involved in espionage for Francis WALSINGHAM. At university he may already have written *Tamburlaine the Great*, the first of his brilliant plays and poems, showing a new mastery of blank verse. His success and flamboyant London pub-centred lifestyle brought both enemies and devoted friends (*see* NASH, Thomas); contacts with Walsingham shielded him from immediate punishment after allegations in 1593 of atheism and homosexuality. His death soon after in a Deptford pub brawl (*see also* KYD, Thomas) continues to provoke speculation, and so far remains without good explanation.

MAROT, DANIEL (1661–1752), designer and architect. Originally from Paris, the son of the architect Jean Marot, he worked at Versailles as an assistant until the Revocation of the Edict of Nantes in 1685, when he fled to Holland. There he met the future WILLIAM III and MARY II, whom he followed to England. He designed exterior and interior features at Hampton Court but, with Christopher WREN and TALMAN at work, he did not contribute substantially to royal projects in England. Instead he designed parts of the residences of the Duke of Montagu at Boughton (Northants.) and in London, and also Petworth in West Sussex for the Duchess of Somerset, the first English stately homes to incorporate aspects of the full flamboyant grandeur of the Baroque style of Versailles. Marot began to publish his drawings in 1687 and a collected edition was published in 1703. It became highly influential in England and the Netherlands.

MARQUIS, FREDERICK (1st Earl of Woolton) (1883–1964), businessman and politician. After a period in social work and as a schoolteacher, and membership of boards concerned with supplies during the First World War, he became Managing Director (1928) and Chairman (1936) of the Liverpool department store Lewis's. He was made Director General of the Ministry of Supply in 1939. Appointed Minister of Food by Winston CHURCHILL in 1940, he became the wartime face of rationing, forever associated with the austerity recipe for what was known as 'Woolton pie'; he then served as Minister of Reconstruction (1943–5), laying the foundations for much post-war reform legislation. Joining the Conservative Party in 1945, he became Chairman (1946–55) and was the critical figure in rebuilding the party's organization after the 1945 defeat.

MARRIOTT (OR MARRYOTT), MATTHEW (*fl.* 1700–30), workhouse contractor. He attracted attention by his economical management of a workhouse in his home parish of Olney (Bucks.) in the early eighteenth century. The Society for the Propagation of Christian Knowledge (SPCK) (*see also* BRAY, THOMAS), which was keen to promote the spread of these institutions, which had been gaining in popularity from the 1690s (*see also* CARY, JOHN), encouraged him to advise and train other workhouse masters. The Workhouse Act 1723, sometimes termed Marriott's Act (or alternatively Knatchbull's Act after its chief parliamentary promoter), allowed parishes to band together to set up workhouses and to make relief conditional on admission; while some parishes did apply the 'workhouse test', 'outdoor' relief through payments to the unemployed in their own homes remained predominant. A survey sponsored by Thomas GILBERT in 1776 revealed that there were then some 2,000 workhouses, with places for 90,000 poor people.

MARSHAL, WILLIAM *see* essay on page 550

MARSHALL, ALFRED (1842–1924), economist. Professor of Political Economy at Cambridge University (1885–1908), he was one of the most important figures in the development of neoclassical economics. He had the ability to synthesize and expound ideas with great clarity and was regarded as a superb teacher of economics. His *Principles of Economics* (1890) was still highly influential for most scholars until the advent of Keynesian (*see* KEYNES, JOHN MAYNARD) ideas in the 1930s. His debates and conflict with fellow-economist William Cunningham in particular mark the separation of academic economics from the broader-based political economy and economic history which the subject had once included.

MARSHALL, STEPHEN (?1594–1655), clergyman and politician. From a humble Hunts. background, he entered the 1640 political crisis with classic Puritan credentials – graduation from Emmanuel College, Cambridge, and a parish base in Puritan Essex. From 1640 he frequently preached before Parliament, taking a lead in discussions with the Scots about how to introduce Presbyterianism to the English Church, and in the consequent work of the Westminster Assembly after 1643. His ministrations to William LAUD before the Archbishop's execution and to CHARLES I in captivity were not received appreciatively. He deplored the drift from pure Presbyterianism during the 1650s, but served as a Trier (one of the committee examining candidates for the ministry) from 1654. Seen by Royalists as one of the chief forces behind Charles I's overthrow; his body was ejected from Westminster Abbey at the restoration of CHARLES II.

MARTEL, SIR GIFFARD LE QUESNE (1889–1958), soldier. Son of the Superintendent of Ordnance Factories, educated at Woolwich, commissioned into the Royal Engineers and serving in the Tank Corps (1917–18), Martel became a vociferous advocate of all-tank armies in the 1920s and 1930s. As Assistant Director of Mechanization after 1936 he was partly responsible for the British army's unbalanced tank-heavy formations. After the German onslaught in the west in May 1940, Martel's two-battalion counter-attack at Arras on 21 May, which caught the Germans by surprise, showed what could be achieved with a sudden armoured riposte. Appointed Commander of the Royal Armoured Corps in Dec. 1940, Martel soon clashed with HOBART, CHURCHILL's protégé, and in Sept. 1942 his post was abolished while he was in India on a tour of inspection.

MARTEN, HENRY (1602–80), politician. Son of a distinguished lawyer, he was elected MP in 1640, became a Parliamentarian commander in the Civil Wars (1642–8), and an active army political leader. Caring little for Puritan godliness, he frightened even his own side with his radicalism against CHARLES I, and took an enthusiastic part in Charles's condemnation in Jan. 1649. He saw Oliver CROMWELL as a threat to his republican ideals and left politics on the dissolution of the Rump Parliament (April 1653), returning only on its recall (1659). At the restoration of CHARLES II he bravely defended his conduct, and his death sentence was commuted to life imprisonment.

MARTIN, GREGORY (?–1582), biblical translator. Oxford-educated, he tutored the children of Thomas, 4th HOWARD Duke of Norfolk, but fled to Douai on the Duke's disgrace, and was ordained (1573). He devoted his life to producing an English Roman Catholic translation of the Bible,

continued on page 551

MARSHAL, WILLIAM (c. 1147–1219)
Soldier, courtier and Regent of England (1216–19)

Born in relative obscurity as the fourth son of John Marshal, a royal official and minor baron, he rose by his talents to the highest position in the land, governing England on behalf of the boy-king HENRY III. The remarkable story of his life was told in a remarkable poem, the *Histoire de Guillaume le Maréchal*, discovered in the late nineteenth century, the earliest known biography of a non-royal layman in British history. This poem of 19,214 lines in rhyming couplets, composed soon after his death by an otherwise unknown author named John, extols him as 'the best knight in the world'. It is written in French, the polite language of the aristocracy, and much of it is based on the old man's reminiscences. In it we can often hear William himself speaking, as when we are told that in his youth he was chiefly famous for eating and sleeping. It offers a unique window into the courtly and chivalrous milieu of the day.

In the 1170s William became a star of the tournament circuit of northern France, player manager of HENRY THE YOUNG KING's team, winning one mock-battle after another by a combination of physical strength, prowess with mace and sword as well as with lance, horsemanship, group discipline and cunning. Since, as in real war, victory generally went to the team which better maintained its cohesion, fighting in tournaments was an ideal form of training. As a tournament champion, moreover, William was able to win fortune as well as fame because, as in real war, captured knights had to pay ransoms to the victors. The young King's rebellions against his father, HENRY II, presented William with conflicting loyalties. To whom did he owe primary allegiance? The way he dealt with these awkward problems showed what an astute politician he was becoming. He stood by the young King against his father; after the former's death he stood by the old King against his son Richard, soon to be RICHARD I. By consistently remaining true to the losing side he won a great reputation for loyalty. In 1189, as soon as Richard became King, although William had fought against him a few days earlier, he rewarded him by giving him the hand of Isabel, heiress to the estates of Strongbow (*see* CLARE, RICHARD DE) in Normandy, England, Wales and Ireland. From now on the soldier-courtier was a great baron, who gradually won effective control of

more and more of Isabel's vast inheritance. In 1199 he was created Earl of Pembroke. In the 1190s he took on important governmental responsibilities, particularly in King Richard's absence.

From the 1180s until his death William acted as a hands-on general in the wars of the kings of England against King Philip II Augustus of France, but good though his advice always was (the *Histoire*, naturally, makes this clear) not even he could prevent JOHN from losing Normandy in 1204. Barons with lands on both sides of the Channel were now forced to choose between allegiance to the King of France (and losing their lands in England) or allegiance to the King of England (and losing their lands in Normandy). Only William pulled off the impossible trick of swearing allegiance to both, and keeping his lands on both sides of the sea. Inevitably he paid a price for this. John now distrusted him, so he judged it politic to retire to his wife's estates in Ireland. There he became an improving landlord, building and investing for the economic development of Leinster (and his own profit), founding, for example, the town of New Ross. He was also, in Matthew PARIS's opinion, a scourge of the native Irish. In 1212 he exploited John's deteriorating situation by proclaiming his loyalty to him; the more other men deserted, the higher he rose. In 1215 he was prominent among those who negotiated Magna Carta on John's behalf; when civil war broke out and the future Louis VIII of France invaded, he stood by the King. After John's death in Oct. 1216 he was chosen as Regent, as leader of those who supported the boy-king Henry III in the continuing civil war. When Louis divided his forces he seized the opportunity. At Lincoln (May 1217) the 70-year old rode into battle for the last time. After this victory he bought Louis off (Sept. 1217) and ruled the country in peace until his death 19 months later. Had he offered generous terms to the rebels in the interests of peace or, as his detractors said, in the interests of his French friends? Was he really as straightforwardly loyal as he seemed? The *Histoire de Guillaume le Maréchal* commissioned by his heir, William Marshal II, was written to prove that he was.

David Crouch, William Marshal: Court, Career and Chivalry in the Angevin Empire 1147–1219 (1990) and was the chief force in creating the Douai-Rheims version, of which the Old Testament was published in the year of his death and the New Testament in 1609–10; both these were influential on the language of JAMES I's Authorized version (1611).

MARTIN, KINGSLEY (1879–1969), journalist. An academic at the London School of Economics in 1924 before joining the staff of the *Manchester Guardian* in 1927, he was appointed editor of the *New Statesman and Nation* in 1928, a post which he held until 1960, a phenomenally long editorship. It was the *New Statesman*'s 'golden age': the circulation climbed from 14,000 copies a week in 1928 to over 80,000 during the 1950s. Martin's editorship coincided with the most constructive and successful period in the labour movement's history after the debacle of Ramsay MACDONALD's 1929–31 Labour government. As the intellectual organ of the movement, the *New Statesman* was at the forefront of the debate on the Left which paved Labour's long way back to power during the 1930s and the eventual success of ATTLEE's 1945–51 governments. Martin's own politics were extremely confused, but this had the advantage of enabling the magazine to eschew sectarianism and dogmatism, let alone become an uncritical supporter of the Labour Party.

MARTIN, VIOLET (1862–1915), novelist *see* SOMERVILLE, EDITH

MARTINDALE, ADAM (1623–86), writer. Son of a Lancs. yeoman, he became a schoolmaster then, during the Interregnum, a Presbyterian clergyman in Cheshire. Ejected from his living in 1662, he took refuge as a chaplain to Sir George BOOTH. Historians value the picture of ordinary life to be found in his painstakingly frank autobiography.

MARTINDALE, DAME HILDA (1875–1952), civil servant. Initially a social worker inspecting the workhouses of Paddington and travelling around the world to observe the treatment of children, she was appointed a lady factory inspector (*see* ANDERSON, ADELAIDE) for Ireland, rising by 1925 to be the sole woman Deputy Chief Inspector of Factories. In 1933 she was given in effect the top woman's job in the Civil Service: Director of Women's Establishments at the Treasury. In this role she sat on selection committees and various boards concerned with women, considering, for example, the question of admitting them to the Consular and Diplomatic Service. She worked generally for the greater equality of women in the Civil Service, a task that would long outlive her.

MARTINEAU, HARRIET (1802–76), novelist and political economist. Daughter of a Huguenot family, Martineau's first works were books of religious instruction but, in 1826 after the death of her Unitarian father, she decided that her financial independence was best secured by popularizing the principles of political economy, then a new discipline. *Illustrations of Political Economy* (1832–4), a series of stories based on the ideas of J. S. MILL and David RICARDO, was an immediate success, as were her subsequent similar books. As an established journalist she visited the USA and wrote on the anti-slavery movement, and when ill health confined her to home (1839–44) she turned to writing children's stories and adult novels, the best known of which is *Deerbrook* (1839). For the rest of her life she was an active and prescriptive writer on subjects as diverse as mesmerism, agriculture, prostitution, women's employment, rationalist thought and the philosophy of Comte. Martineau's dissemination of liberal ideas was an inspiration to reformers, and her *Autobiography* published posthumously in 1877 was a courageous comment on mid Victorian society and a vivid evocation of her own unhappy childhood.

MARTYR VERMIGLI, PETER (1499–1562), theologian. A leading Italian friar (Pietro Martire Vermigli) who fled to Switzerland after converting to Protestantism in 1542, on Thomas CRANMER's invitation he came to England (1547) and was made Oxford's Regius Professor of Divinity (1548). Cranmer gladly used his advice while compiling the 1552 Prayer Book, and he was one of the drafters of the abortive reform of the English Church's canon law later known as the *Reformatio Legum*. He fled abroad on MARY I's accession, and his deceased wife's body was disinterred and thrown on an Oxford dungheap. From Zürich he maintained a keen interest in and frequent correspondence on English developments.

MARVELL, ANDREW (1621–78), poet, writer and politician. Son of a respected Puritan preacher and schoolmaster, he acquired a reputation as a poet while still at Cambridge. Becoming an ardent republican and close friend of John MILTON, he managed to prosper under both Oliver CROMWELL and CHARLES II despite writing coolly brilliant assessments of them. After 1660 he turned to political and religious pamphleteering, vigorously attacking Edward HYDE, Earl of Clarendon, and the Church of England. He was MP for his home town of Hull in 1659, 1660 and 1661–78.

MARX, KARL *see* essay on page 552

MARY I *see* essay on page 553

MARX, KARL (1818–83)
Political theorist and revolutionary

Born in Trier, Germany, he read philosophy, law and history at the universities of Bonn and Berlin and then took a doctorate with a thesis on Greek philosophy at Jena in 1841. A radical Hegelian, left-wing and an atheist, Marx was unable to obtain a university post and instead earned a living as a journalist, primarily for a liberal Cologne paper, the *Rheinische Zeitung*, until its suppression in 1843. He then spent the rest of his life in exile, apart from a brief period back in Cologne editing the successor paper, the *Neue Rheinische Zeitung*, following the German revolution of 1848. As an exile in Paris, Brussels and, from 1849, London, he collaborated with Friedrich ENGELS, whose income from his family's cotton business in Manchester was a major source of support for Marx and his family throughout his life. Their first collaboration was *The Communist Manifesto* (1848), which embodied in highly schematic and rather abstract form their initial analysis of the dynamics of historical development and a programmatic statement of communism. At the heart of the analysis was an historical political economy which showed that the character of any particular kind of society derived from its economic structure. That economic structure was generally internally contradictory in that there were antagonistic interests between, say, capitalists and workers which were bound to give rise to class conflict and struggle as those who controlled the means of production wrestled to extract a surplus from the producers. Class struggle was also seen as crucial to the transformation of one kind of society into another (such as the transition from feudalism to capitalism). For Marx, however, capitalism had special characteristics. It generated constant technological and economic revolution, thus producing the means potentially to overcome scarcity; it created a world economy; and it produced diggers of its own grave in the form of the working class whose nature and interests as a class were international. The true interests of the working class lay in the creation of forms of co-operative economy and society which would both benefit humanity as a whole and usher in the era of communism, a form of society in which the means of production would be held in common and political life and institutions would be thoroughly democratic and participatory.

The voluminous writings of both Marx and Engels covered a huge range of subjects including historical and contemporary events and processes (like the French Revolution of 1848 and the history of the family) and highly theoretical reflections on the nature of money and capital. But while the economic structure was the key to the real movement of history, Marx's analysis by no means neglected the social and political. He sought to explain changes in political and legal institutions and in forms of social consciousness (including, for example, the arts) by showing how they were shaped (or 'determined') by the pressures exerted through class relations embedded in the economic structure. It was not expected that the proletariat would automatically respond to changes in its economic position and become socialist; rather only through the creation of its own political and cultural consciousness and organizations might it develop forms of class struggle which would lead to socialism and, eventually, communism.

Much of Marx's thought in these respects was shaped by his own experience of Britain. Although he was never very well known during his lifetime, *The Communist Manifesto* had first appeared in English in a Chartist newspaper in 1850 and both he and Engels had contact with the left wing of late Chartism in the 1850s; they were also to have contact with some leading trade unionists like Robert APPLEGARTH through the International Working Men's Association (1864–72). But Britain was the prime case of modern capitalism: it was there that capitalist industrialization had taken off in the late eighteenth century and that the best organized working-class movement was to develop before 1880. As such Britain had immense historical importance in the theoretical and political writing of both Marx and Engels, not least in Marx's greatest work, *Capital*, which remained unfinished in his lifetime. (The first volume was published in 1867; the third and final volume, edited by Engels, in 1894.) How far Marx and Engels made convincing sense of Britain's economic developments remains a matter of controversy. Britain for its part at the time disregarded Marx, as is shown by the fact of it being the Paris correspondent of *The Times* who reported his death in London. (He is buried in Highgate Cemetery, London.) Yet there can be no question of the sheer scale of Marx's subsequent importance: understanding the shape of modern culture and politics is inconceivable without reference to him.

David McLellan, Karl Marx: His Life and Thought (1973)

MARY I (1516–58)
Queen of England (1553–8)

Her early life was dominated by her dynastic importance as heir to her father HENRY VIII's throne, involving negotiations for betrothal first to the Dauphin (heir to the French throne) and then to her Habsburg cousin CHARLES V. Although Charles chose another prospective bride, this remained one of the most important relationships of her life. In 1525 she was created Princess of Wales, and Ludlow Castle (Salop.) became the setting for her princely court; from 1527, however, Henry's estrangement from her mother CATHERINE OF ARAGON undermined her position and destroyed her happiness. She was prevented from seeing her mother after 1531, and she was bastardized when the Aragon marriage was annulled (1533), being reduced to a lady-in-waiting to the new heir presumptive, later ELIZABETH I. The death of ANNE BOLEYN brought further humiliation, for after spirited resistance she was intimidated into a humble acknowledgement of her status in 1536. Her position thereafter improved, particularly after the King's final marriage to CATHERINE PARR (1543), and an Act of Parliament (1544) recognized her as second in line to the throne. During her half-brother EDWARD VI's reign (1547–53) she faced fresh troubles through her stubborn refusal to abandon the Catholic liturgy; in 1550 confused and unsuccessful efforts were made to arrange her escape to Habsburg territories. Edward's Privy Council tried to bypass her in placing JANE GREY on the throne in 1553, but with the aid of Catholic advisers she drew on popular provincial outrage at this insult to Henry VIII's blood-line and staged a brilliantly effective *coup d'état* based in East Anglia. She moved swiftly to restore not only traditional worship but also (to the surprise of most of her subjects) obedience to the Pope, although legal problems delayed England's reconciliation with Rome until Nov. 1554. She also brushed aside objections to marriage with her Habsburg cousin PHILIP II of Spain, including the challenge of Sir Thomas WYATT's rebellion (Jan. 1554); in the middle of general panic in London at the rebels' approach, she displayed firmness and courage and rallied support with a major speech at Guildhall. To her joy, Philip arrived to marry her at Winchester Cathedral on 25 July 1554. Once the old heresy laws were restored (1555) she became committed to persecution, which included almost 300 burnings. This was more intense than any previous English campaign to combat heresy, and was uncomfortably reminiscent of recent Habsburg persecution in the Netherlands; Protestant sufferings handed a propaganda asset to her opponents, but she obstinately persisted in encouraging the burnings. Her hopes for Catholicism were complicated when Cardinal Giampetro Caraffa was elected Pope PAUL IV (1555): he was not only bitterly anti-Spanish, but also an old enemy of her close ally and cousin the Papal Legate in England, Cardinal Reginald POLE. Mary, who wished to be the Papacy's most loyal daughter, found herself defying the Pope when Paul IV revoked Pole's legatine powers and tried to summon him to Rome on heresy charges.

Meanwhile her marriage did not produce an heir to secure the future of a Catholic revival. Her firm belief that she was pregnant caused national embarrassment and ridicule when the truth became plain in summer 1555, while Philip's good nature was strained by the lack of English enthusiasm for his presence; he returned in 1557 only in order to secure England's help for Spain in a war against France (and the Papacy). The war initially went well, but the loss of Calais (Jan. 1558) was a bitter blow, and illness in the summer proved not to be Mary's longed-for child but stomach cancer. She knew, in her prolonged terminal illness, that her half-sister Elizabeth would destroy everything that she had worked for: Pole died of influenza within hours of her.

Mary's swiftly curtailed reign still provokes widely differing assessments. Traditionally mainstream English historiography discussed it in terms of 'reaction', an unimaginative return to the pre-1529 past. So A. G. DICKENS stressed the vigour of Protestantism which rendered her task a losing battle, and both A. F. Pollard and Geoffrey ELTON were drawn to the metaphor of sterility to describe the reign. Recently Eamon Duffy has led reassessments of the potential in her religious programme, stressing the new elements which anticipated structural reforms of the Roman Catholic Church in the later stages of the Council of Trent (1545–63), for instance Pole's proposals for a network of clergy training colleges (seminaries) attached to the cathedrals. In secular government, much of the administrative and financial reorganization begun by Northumberland's (*see* DUDLEY, JOHN) government officials continued. There were major restructurings of customs revenue and of provision for national defence, neither of which were greatly modified for more than half a century. Philip also encouraged development of the navy, which ironically chiefly benefited Elizabeth and her later wars against him. However the reign is judged, Mary's blighted personal history can only attract sympathy.

D. M. Loades, Mary Tudor: A Life (1989)

MARY II (1662–94), Queen of England, Ireland and Scotland (1689–94). The eldest child of James, Duke of York, later JAMES II, and his first wife Anne Hyde. Her education, under Henry COMPTON, Bishop of London, was strictly Protestant. The death of her only surviving brother in 1671 left her as heir presumptive. In 1677 CHARLES II arranged her marriage to William of Orange (the future WILLIAM III) and she went to the Netherlands. During her father's reign she represented the hope of Protestant activists that James's Catholicizing policies would prove a brief interlude before the accession of a Protestant monarch, a hope that seemed dashed when her half-brother James Edward STUART was born in 1688.

Following William's invasion, she returned to England early in 1689 and influenced the form of the Revolution Settlement by refusing to contemplate serving as sole monarch. William and Mary were crowned joint sovereigns in April 1689. William exercised executive authority except when outside the realm, as in the case of his Irish campaign of 1690–1. Personally pious, Mary encouraged schemes for the reformation of manners. She died of smallpox.

MARY OF GUELDERS (?–1463), Queen of Scots (1449–60). A niece of Philip, Duke of Burgundy, she married JAMES II with great pomp at Holyrood (Edinburgh) in 1449. When she arrived at the siege of Roxburgh in 1460, James ordered his cannon to fire 'on account of joy at the arrival of the queen' and was killed when one exploded. Mary promptly took her infant son to the camp and inspired the men to capture the castle. For the last three years of her life she was Regent of Scotland for her son JAMES III.

MARY OF GUISE (1515–60), Queen of Scotland. A French princess spared a proposed marriage to HENRY VIII, she married JAMES V in 1538. She symbolized the French alliance and her political influence fluctuated in inverse proportion to that of the Anglophile party in Scotland; after the Scots defeat by Edward SEYMOUR, Duke of Somerset, at Pinkie (1547) she took power beside James HAMILTON, Earl of Arran, and replaced him as Regent for her daughter, MARY QUEEN OF SCOTS, in 1554. Reluctant at first to persecute Protestants, she was pressured into aggression by the French and by increasing Protestant militancy, facing full-scale confrontation from the Lords of the Congregation in 1559. She was driven out of Edinburgh and replaced as Regent by Arran (now Duke of Châtellerault); although determined to continue the fight, she was struck down by fatal illness. An able and resourceful woman determined to protect her daughter's interests, Mary was later unfairly demonized by Scots Protestant writers, beginning with John KNOX.

MARY OF MODENA (1658–1718), Queen Consort. The daughter of Alphonso IV, Duke of Modena, she put aside her original ambition of entering a convent to marry the future JAMES II, then Duke of York, in 1673. Viewed with suspicion by English Protestants because of her Catholicism, she escaped implication in the Popish-Plot scare, touched off by the accusations of Titus OATES, but was popularly identified with those who wanted a speedy and enforced conversion of England. Following the birth of her son James Edward STUART in 1688 her position became more exposed and she fled to France with her son in Dec. rather than be captured by William of Orange (the future WILLIAM III). The rest of her life was spent agitating for greater French support for the restoration of her husband and, after his death, her son, trying to secure the revenues due to her in England and doing charitable works.

MARY QUEEN OF SCOTS *see* essay on page 555

MASEFIELD, JOHN (1878–1967), poet. Masefield joined the merchant navy at 13 and, though he skipped ship in 1895 in New York, many of his poems are about the sea. *Salt-Water Ballads* (which contains the poem 'Sea Fever', beginning 'I must go down to the sea again') was published in 1902 and *Dauber* in 1913. Probably the best known of his works was *The Everlasting Mercy* (1911), but all were accessible. Although in recent years interest in him as a serious poet has not been great, he was a conscientious Poet Laureate for 37 years.

MASHAM, 1ST BARON *see* LISTER, SAMUEL CUNLIFFE

MASHAM, ABIGAIL (née Hill) (Lady Masham) (?–1734), courtier. Daughter of an impoverished merchant, she was nonetheless first cousin to Sarah CHURCHILL, Duchess of Marlborough, and second cousin to Robert HARLEY. Sarah arranged for her to become bedchamber woman to ANNE in 1704, but soon became convinced her cousin was plotting to oust her as the Queen's confidante. In reality, the Queen never saw Abigail as someone with whom she could be on familiar terms, as she had with Sarah, but did value her as a channel through which to establish and maintain good relations with Harley, with whose aid she was able to establish political independence from the Marlboroughs.

MASKELYNE, NEVIL (1732–1811), astronomer. He was drawn to astronomy while a student at

continued on page 556

MARY QUEEN OF SCOTS (1542–87)
Queen of Scots (1542–57)

Queen in her first days of life because of her father JAMES V's premature death, Mary was promised in marriage to HENRY VIII's son EDWARD by the Treaty of Greenwich (1543). The Scots' refusal to ratify this provoked Henry to invade in campaigns which were resumed in Edward's reign, and which included the Scots' defeat at Pinkie (1547), nicknamed the Rough Wooing. Mary was sent to France in 1548 while her mother MARY OF GUISE ruled Scotland, and in 1558 she married the future FRANCIS II, the Dauphin of France. Briefly Queen of France 1559–60 until Francis's early death, she reluctantly returned in 1561 to Scotland, where the Protestant grouping of noblemen known as the Lords of the Congregation had filled a political vacuum, and an alliance of Protestants continued to take the initiative against the Catholic Church authorities. Her advisers, who included highly talented politicians like her cousin James STEWART, Earl of Moray, and William MAITLAND of Lethington, helped her as a Catholic monarch to preside uneasily but with reasonable political success over a steady Protestant take-over.

By 1565, however, Mary determined to gain freedom of action; having rejected a series of proposals for arranged dynastic marriages, she married her cousin Henry STEWART, Lord Darnley, in July 1565. ELIZABETH I was furious at this union between two possible heirs to the English throne, while Moray fled to England. Apart from producing JAMES VI, the marriage was a catastrophe; Darnley's good looks and youthful charm concealed selfishness and vicious incompetence. Jealous of Mary's Italian favourite, her French secretary David RIZZIO, Darnley personally led the murder of Rizzio at Holyrood House, in Mary's horrified presence (9 March 1566). Desperate to maintain the legitimacy of her child against suggestions that it was Rizzio's, Mary co-operated with Darnley to escape imprisonment by the murderers, re-entered Edinburgh in triumph, and gave birth to James on 19 June 1566, but she now loathed her husband. She sought an ally in James HEPBURN, Earl of Bothwell, and this was followed (1567) by Darnley's murder at Kirk o'Field outside Edinburgh, the work of a widely based consortium including Bothwell. The ensuing marriage to Bothwell was a desperate attempt to regain the political initiative without returning to the influence of Moray, but it sealed the destruction of her reputation across Europe among Catholics and Protestants alike. The denunciations of her in the sermons of John KNOX now

seemed fully justified; the long-suffering Scots had had enough. Mary's supporters were defeated at Carbery Hill and she was deposed (July 1567). After escaping from prison she was defeated again at Langside (1568) and fled to England. This was yet another misjudgement; her absence steadily undermined the Marian loyalist party in Scotland, although it was only in 1573 that the last garrison surrendered Edinburgh Castle to a joint Anglo-Scottish army.

In England, Mary's arrival provoked an immediate political crisis and presented a longterm problem. A trial in 1568–9 decided that she was implicated in Darnley's murder (mainly on the strength of the 'Casket Letters', now lost and much debated), and she remained imprisoned, sparking various plans to get her married again, among others to Robert DUDLEY, Earl of Leicester, and Thomas HOWARD, 9th Duke of Norfolk. After the failure of the rebellion of the northern English earls in 1569–70, Mary continued to be associated with a series of Catholic plots; her English enemies, led by the intelligence-gathering of Francis WALSINGHAM, built up a body of evidence against her particularly in connection with the conspiracy to assassinate Elizabeth led by Anthony BABINGTON (1586). In Oct. 1584 a Bond of Association was designed by William CECIL and Walsingham to defend Elizabeth's life and pursue anyone who tried to harm her: Mary was the obvious target. Thousands joined this extra-legal vigilante group, which in modified form was given legality by Parliament. It nevertheless took two decades and great political pressure for Elizabeth I to overcome her qualms at ordering the execution of an anointed sovereign (see DAVISON, WILLIAM); Mary was beheaded at Fotheringhay (Northants). Her son, who had no personal memories of her, made merely formal noises of protest, conscious that he was now the most convincing successor to the English throne. When he was safely in England, he took pains in 1612 to exhume Mary's body from Peterborough Cathedral and rebury it in a place of honour in Westminster Abbey, at the same time pointedly rehousing Elizabeth in a rather less prominent tomb nearby.

Recipient of an astonishing amount of romantic historical attention, Mary impresses by her talent for wasting all the considerable assets which came her way. The ability to produce beautiful needlework is no basis for government.

Jenny Wormald, Mary Queen of Scots: A Study in Failure (1988)

Cambridge, and like many scientists of the age combined research with the Church. In 1761 he went to St Helena, principally to observe the transit of Venus for the Royal Society, but he also measured the tides and experimented in measuring longitude from lunar distances; this research led to the foundation of the *Nautical Almanac* in 1765, combining astronomical tables and navigational aids, probably Maskelyne's greatest work; his insistence on the superiority of the lunar distance method for measuring longitude made him a bitter rival of John HARRISON. From 1765 Maskelyne was also Astronomer Royal. He declared all observations made at the Royal Greenwich Observatory public property rather than that of the Astronomer Royal of the day, and allowed them to be published by the Royal Society.

MASON, SIR JOSIAH (1795–1881), manufacturer. A penmaker, Mason came up with the idea of inserting a steel nib with a slit in it in a cedarwood holder: despite the blotting and scratching involved in its use it was a huge improvement on quill pens, and by the mid 1870s it was said that Mason was producing about 250 million nibs made by more than 1,000 workers. He founded a College of Science in 1879, which was to become part of Birmingham University.

MASSIE, JOSEPH (?–1784), writer on economics. Possibly a factor or agent in the sugar trade, he published many works on economics and trade in the 1750s and early 1760s, implicitly defending PITT THE ELDER's policy in the Seven Years War. He aspired to write a history of the rise of British commerce, but failed to attract the official sponsorship for which he perhaps hoped. His calculations have been used as the basis of modern attempts to estimate income distribution in the mid eighteenth century.

MASSINGER, PHILIP (1583–1640), dramatist *see* FLETCHER, JOHN

MATHESON, JAMES (1796–1878), China trade merchant *see* JARDINE, WILLIAM

MATHEW, THEOBALD (1790–1856), temperance campaigner. A Capuchin friar from Cork, from 1838 he began a temperance crusade centred in Ireland which led to extraordinary scenes as large crowds pledged themselves against alcohol. The crusade drew international attention but disintegrated because of the Irish Famine, Mathew's failure to create a lasting organization and the suspicion of sections of the Catholic clergy who saw the crusade as hysterical and disliked his political conservatism and close association with Protestants.

MATHGAMAIN (?–976), King of the Dál Cais (964–76). He overthrew the Eóganacht kings of Munster and established his family's domination in southern Ireland. Seizing power in 964, he spent the subsequent years fighting neighbouring kings, dynastic rivals and the Vikings. Apparently secure by 974, he was defeated and murdered two years later in one of the recurrent feuds typical of early medieval Irish politics. He was succeeded by his brother BRIAN BORUMA.

MATILDA (?–1131), Queen of Scots (1124–31). Daughter of WALTHEOF, Earl of Northumbria, she was widowed from her first marriage to Simon de St Liz, Earl of Northampton. In 1113 she married David, Prince of Cumbria, later DAVID I. Through her the Scottish Crown inherited claims to the earldoms of Huntingdon and Northumbria, which were to have a major impact on Anglo-Scottish relations for the next 100 years.

MATILDA II (?–1118), Queen of England (1100–18). Daughter of MAEL COLUIM III CENN MÓR of Scotland and St MARGARET, she was married to HENRY I in 1100. Besides bearing two children, she was an important patron of music and literature (both Latin and Anglo-Norman) and often presided over the Council governing England while her husband was in Normandy.

MATILDA, EMPRESS *see* essay on page 557

MATILDA OF BOULOGNE (?–1152), Queen of England (1135–52). Married to STEPHEN in 1125, she had English estates strategically located around London, which facilitated her husband's seizure of the throne in 1135. She played a prominent role throughout the ensuing civil war, being much admired for her courage, sense of honour and diplomatic skill, an attractive contrast to the Empress MATILDA. Indeed, Stephen owed his throne to his wife's loyalty and leadership during the critical months of 1141, when he was imprisoned following his capture at the Battle of Lincoln. She bore him five children. His cause did not long survive her death in 1152.

MATILDA OF FLANDERS (?–1083), Queen of England (1068–83). Daughter of Baldwin V, Count of Flanders, she was married to Duke William of Normandy (the future WILLIAM I THE CONQUEROR) in 1050 or 1051. She was anointed Queen in May 1068. She generally stayed in Normandy, often presiding over the Council that governed the duchy during William's absences. Matilda is sometimes said to have been only 4 feet 2 inches tall but, since she successfully bore at least nine children, this is unlikely.

MATILDA (1102–67)
Royal princess and Empress

Daughter of HENRY I and MATILDA, she was sent to Germany in 1110 as an eight-year-old future bride for the German King and Holy Roman Emperor, Henry V. He entrusted her to Archbishop Bruno of Trier to be taught the language and customs of her new home; the marriage itself took place at Mainz in Jan. 1114. As a result she became known as the Empress (although, since she never received an imperial Crown from the hands of a Pope, formally her correct title remained Queen of the Romans). A description of the wedding feast dwells on her beauty, noble bearing and royal ancestry. In 1118 she accompanied her husband to his Italian kingdom and when he returned north again she stayed behind in charge of the imperial government in Italy until she rejoined Henry next year. These imperial years seem to have been the most triumphant and contented of her life. After the death of her brother William the Atheling in 1120 there was a distinct possibility that she and her German husband would be the next rulers of England and Normandy; in the event her husband died before her father. Since she had no children to nurture in Germany she returned to her father's court in 1125 soon after Henry V's death.

In 1127 the Anglo-Norman barons swore to accept her as their ruler if Henry I had no son. For as long as military leadership remained one of the principal obligations of a ruler, thrones were usually reserved for men, but there was no reason why, suitably married, Matilda should not rule jointly with a warrior husband. Next year she was married to Geoffrey PLANTAGENET, Count of Anjou. He was some 10 years her junior and at first relations between the two were troubled; she went back to her father in 1129 and stayed until 1131 when Geoffrey asked for her back. Between 1133 and 1136 they had three sons: Henry (later HENRY II), Geoffrey and William. But, although Henry I still regarded Maltilda and her husband as his heirs, he refused to allow them any sort of power base in England and Normandy; his quarrels with them meant that magnates loyal to him were driven into opposition to Matilda. For her this was a disastrous development since it meant that when Henry died there was a powerful faction only too ready, despite their oaths to Matilda, to give their support to her cousin STEPHEN. Naturally Matilda and Geoffrey refused to accept this. From their bases in Maine and Anjou they invaded Normandy in 1136, 1137 and 1138. In 1139, after her half-brother ROBERT OF GLOUCESTER had decided to throw in his lot with her, she crossed over to England. Thanks to Robert she had plenty of support in the West Country (Gloucester was her chief residence) but Stephen controlled London and the wealthier part of the kingdom. She ought to have triumphed after Stephen was captured at the Battle of Lincoln (Feb. 1141); for a while many of his supporters, including his brother HENRY OF BLOIS, were prepared to acknowledge her as Lady of England and Normandy. By midsummer 1141 she was at Westminster negotiating with the citizens of London for entry into the city, to be followed by a coronation, but in this, the crisis of her life, she lacked judgement and alienated potential supporters, above all the Londoners. She angrily rejected their request for a reduction in their financial burdens. On 24 June, as she prepared a ceremonial entry into the city, the bells of London rang out in a call to arms; she retreated in haste to Oxford, leaving the Londoners to plunder her lodgings and enjoy the banquet prepared for her. She then became embroiled in a struggle for Winchester and was almost captured, escaping only by riding away at full speed, sitting astride like a man. But Robert of Gloucester, who covered her retreat, was captured and had to be exchanged for Stephen. Matilda herself had another narrow escape in Dec. 1142 when besieged in Oxford Castle; wearing a white camouflage cloak she made her way through the snow and crossed the frozen Thames.

From then on her authority in England remained restricted to the West Country, so in 1148, realizing that she would never be accepted as Queen and that the future of the Angevin cause lay with her son Henry, she returned to Normandy, which her husband had conquered by 1145. Widowed in 1151, the last 15 years of her life were both peaceful and reputedly influential. Henry II was widely believed to respect his mother's advice; in his absence she often presided over the government of the duchy. It would be 400 years before a woman did what she came within an ace of doing in June 1141, and sat upon the throne of England as ruling queen.

Marjorie Chibnall, The Empress Matilda: Queen Consort, Queen Mother and Lady of the English (1991)

MATTHEUS, EMERUS *see* MACMAHON, HEBER

MAUDLING, REGINALD (1917–79), politician. On the liberal wing of the Conservative Party, he became an MP in 1950 and was President of the Board of Trade (1959–61), then Colonial Secretary (1961–2) under MACMILLAN, before becoming Chancellor of the Exchequer in 1962. Maudling attempted to defeat rising unemployment through a policy of 'expansion without inflation', involving tax cuts and concessions on investment spending, but by early 1964 he was faced by severe balance-of-payments difficulties, which were inherited by Harold WILSON's incoming Labour government. In 1965, after DOUGLAS-HOME stepped down, he stood for the Conservative leadership but was defeated by Edward HEATH. As Home Secretary (1970–2), he was increasingly involved with the security ramifications of Northern Ireland. He was forced to resign in July 1972 over unsubstantiated allegations that he had received money from John POULSON, an architect accused of corruption, thus ending his ministerial career.

MAUDSLAY, HENRY (1771–1831), engineer. Maudslay acquired engineering skills at the Woolwich Arsenal and at Joseph BRAMAH's lock-making factory where he invented a slide-rest lathe. In 1798 he set up his own business in London where he invented a screw-cutting lathe and a micrometer-based machine (dubbed the Lord Chancellor) capable of measuring to 1/10,000 of an inch. By the 1810s he had established himself as the foremost maker of precision tools and between 1800 and 1820 his firm produced numerous inventions including marine steam engines and machinery for making ships' blocks. As the teacher of James NASMYTH, Richard ROBERTS, Joseph WHITWORTH and many other celebrated engineers, Maudslay had an immense impact on Victorian engineering.

MAUDSLEY, HENRY (1835–1918), psychiatrist. Born in Yorks., Maudsley studied medicine in London and worked as a medical officer in several asylums. In 1859 he was appointed physician to the Manchester Royal Lunatic Asylum in Cheadle (Ches.), and four years later became joint editor of the *Journal of Mental Science*. He was lecturer on insanity at St Mary's Hospital (1868–81) and Professor of Medical Jurisprudence at University College, London (1869–79). He built up a lucrative private psychiatric practice and used his wealth to found in 1916 the Maudsley Hospital in London. His books on mental health, notably *The Physiology and Pathology of the Mind* (1867), *Body and Mind* (1870) and *Responsibility in Mental Disease* (1874), established him as the leading evolutionary psychiatrist of the late Victorian period. He believed that insanity had an observable biological and, in particular, hereditary basis. Linking insanity, poverty and criminality to biological and therefore inescapable causes, he dismissed the efficacy of the sympathetic treatment of society's 'degenerates'.

MAUGHAM, (WILLIAM) SOMERSET (1874–1965), novelist and playwright. He qualified as a physician at St Thomas's medical school (1897), where he had experience of the London slums. That informed Maugham's first book, *Lisa of Lambeth* (1897), which was such a success that he gave up medicine in favour of a literary career. *Of Human Bondage* (1915), the story of a club-footed aristocratic physician, is now thought to have been a *roman-à-clef* for Maugham's own suppressed homosexuality. All his books are in some way on the subject of being outside society: *The Moon and Sixpence* (1919) is acerbic about the painter Gauguin, *Cakes and Ale* (1930) a satire about the London literati. Many of his short stories, the form for which he is now best regarded, take the idea of the outsider into the colonial experience: *Rain* is an example. Maugham drove ambulances on the Western Front during the First World War: in 1915 he contracted a marriage of convenience which produced a son and ended in divorce in 1927, after which he went to live in Cap Ferrat in the south of France.

MAURICE, F(REDERICK) D(ENISON) (1805–72), Christian Socialist and educationalist. Raised a Unitarian, Maurice became an Anglican at Oxford and in 1834 was ordained. In 1840 he was appointed to the chair of English Literature and Modern History at King's College, London, and in the 1840s became friends with J. M. Ludlow, Charles KINGSLEY and Thomas HUGHES, who were to form the Christian Socialist movement. In 1848 he helped to establish Queen's College for the education of young women. In 1854 he founded the Working Men's College, which embodied both his preoccupations with education for the working class and the diffusion of 'manly' Christianity, and in 1866 he became Professor of Casuistry, Moral Theology and Moral Philosophy at Cambridge.

MAXIM, SIR HIRAM (1840–1916), inventor. Son of a farmer in Maine, USA, Maxim initially worked as a carriage-maker and engineer. In 1878 he became Chief Engineer at the United States Electric Lighting Co. and won fame for his incandescent electric lamps and electrical generators. During a European tour he decided to move into armaments and in 1881 settled in London where he established a workshop. In 1884 he completed the Maxim gun, an automatic rapid-firing machine gun greatly exploited by armies across the world until the 1930s. The Maxim Gun Co. marketed this weapon and, after joining with Vickers, produced the more refined and famous Vickers machine gun. Numerous other inventions are attributed to Maxim, including a flying machine and new forms of cordite.

MAXTON, JAMES (1885–1946), politician. The poverty and lack of educational opportunities Maxton witnessed in the Glasgow schools where he taught turned him to socialism. He joined the Independent Labour Party (ILP) in 1904 and represented the socially deprived Glasgow Bridgeton constituency as Labour MP from 1922. A forceful orator, a fearsome 'Red Clydesider' to many at Westminster, never afraid to take a vociferously principled stand, Maxton was imprisoned for sedition for his opposition to the First World War, and in 1923 was suspended from the Commons when he castigated as 'murderers' those on the Conservative benches prepared to support the Coalition government's proposal for cuts in health grants to local authorities.

But more than just a charismatic goad, Maxton, as Chairman of the ILP, the focus of left-wing opposition to Ramsay MACDONALD's Labour Party, propagandized a programme of 'Socialism in Our Time' in 1926, an analysis of unemployment and poverty, much influenced by the writings of J. A. HOBSON. The 1928 manifesto which Maxton produced with the miners' leader A. J. COOK took the ILP nearer to the Communist Party, and, in 1932, after bitter wrangling, the ILP disaffiliated from the Labour Party. Maxton, who opposed the Second World War as he had the First, was respected by those of a political persuasion very different from his own (including Winston CHURCHILL), not for his political judgement but for his principled humanitarianism.

MAXWELL, JAMES CLERK (1831–79), physicist. He published papers on oval curves and elastic solids during his teenage years and excelled in mathematics at Cambridge University. In 1856 he was appointed Professor of Natural Philosophy at Marischal College, Aberdeen, where he constructed a theory of Saturn's rings and worked on electromagnetism. In 1860 he became Professor of Natural Philosophy and Astronomy at King's College, London, where he worked on electrical standards and colour perception. He was the first Professor of Experimental Physics at Cambridge University (1871) and Director of the university's fledgling Cavendish Laboratory (1874).

Maxwell's reputation rests on his work on the electromagnetic field and the properties of gases. By the early 1860s, he had produced a model of the electromagnetic field in which magnetic fields arose from vortices in the hypothetical ether and electric fields from other distortions in the ether. Crucially, he traced electrical and magnetic phenomena to the field surrounding electric and magnetic sources and showed that light was an electromagnetic vibration in the ether. Maxwell embodied much of this work in *Treatise on Electricity and Magnetism* (1873). Late Victorian interpretations and reformulations of Maxwell's work on electromagnetism produced the monumental Maxwell's equations of the electromagnetic field and led to research on radio waves and the fundamental nature of electric conduction.

In the 1860s Maxwell developed a statistical interpretation of the kinetic theory of gases (which treats a gas as a population of randomly moving molecules undergoing elastic collisions with each other and the walls of a container). His interpretation of the kinetic theory of gases paved the way for the statistical mechanics of twentieth-century physics. In his last years he worked on the stresses in rarefied gases.

MAXWELL, ROBERT IAN *see* essay on page 560

MAYO, 6TH EARL OF *see* BOURKE, RICHARD SOUTHWELL

MAYOW, JOHN (1641–79), physician. Taught by Thomas WILLIS at Oxford before practising medicine, in 1668 he published his *Treatise on Respiration*, which rejected the theory of Descartes that blood fermented in the heart. Instead Mayow showed that the heart was a muscle driving blood around the body, and that the lungs exchanged the unwanted 'vapours' for the 'nitroaerian constituent' in the atmosphere that would be identified as oxygen by Joseph PRIESTLEY.

MAXSE, SIR IVOR (1862–1958), soldier. Educated at Sandhurst, commissioned into the Royal Fusiliers (1882), transferring to the Coldstream Guards in 1891, Maxse fought with KITCHENER in the Sudan in 1897, with Frederick ROBERTS in South Africa in 1899, and commanded the Guards Brigade in France in 1914. Maxse was among the first to accept that the Western Front was in reality a gigantic siege operation. The brilliant performance of his new command, the 18th division, on the Somme in 1916, proved the efficacy of his training troops like assault pioneers. In April 1918 Maxse was appointed Inspector General of training in France. The remarkable performance of the British army from Aug. to Nov. 1918 was, at least in part, the result of his now widespread influence.

MAYHEW, HENRY (1812–87), journalist and social investigator. The author of numerous

continued on page 561

MAXWELL, ROBERT IAN (originally Jan Ludvik Hoch) (1923–91)
Publisher, politician and media magnate

One of the most flamboyant, complex characters of post-war British business, he was of Czech origin and Jewish, and on the outbreak of the Second World War he fled Budapest where he had been working and came to the UK via France in 1940. Most of his family perished in the Holocaust. He joined the British army in 1943 using the name Du Maurier: on promotion to Second Lieutenant in 1944 he changed his name to Maxwell. He had a distinguished service record and was awarded the Military Cross. After the war he was part of the British Control Commission: his fluency in nine, mainly Central European, languages was extremely useful. It is thought that he became involved with the KGB at this time. Promoted to the rank of captain, he was nick-named Captain Bob.

In the 1950s Maxwell's business success was built on Pergamon Press, which published scientific and academic journals and books. In 1964 he was elected as Labour MP for North Bucks., remaining an MP until 1970. The flotation of Pergamon Press in 1964 gave him a vehicle through which the take-over of other publicly quoted companies could be launched. In the late 1960s he was involved in abortive take-over deals for the *News of the World* and the publishers Butterworths. This was followed by the failure to sell Pergamon to American interests in 1969; because of the complex relationship of the business to Maxwell's other private companies (as well as questionable accounting practices), his business activities were subject to a major Board of Trade inquiry, the outcome of which would have finished most men. Having reported a catalogue of commercial misdeeds the inspectors' judgement was unequivocal: 'he is not a person who can be relied upon to exercise proper stewardship of a publicly quoted company'. Despite this, Maxwell bounced back to resume control of Pergamon in 1973 and his business activities continued as before.

In 1981 he acquired the British Printing Corporation, which was on the brink of collapse, extending his interests into a considerable part of Britain's newspaper and publishing industry. In 1984 he became Chairman of the Mirror Group Newspapers which was dominated by the Labour-supporting tabloid *Daily Mirror*. It also gave him a platform from which he hoped to challenge his arch rival who had won the battle for the *News of the World*, the other media tycoon Rupert MURDOCH. In 1987 Maxwell sold BPC to a management group and in 1989 acquired the American publishers Macmillan along with several other publishing operations. He called this new conglomerate Maxwell Communications Corporation, and later strengthened his transatlantic media presence by purchasing the New York *Daily News*. He had also tried to establish newspapers *de novo*, setting up the *London Daily News* in 1988, which failed, and *The European* (1990). Maxwell also bought stakes in a number of football clubs: Reading, Derby County and particularly Oxford United, which became a vehicle for his self-publicizing activities. By 1990 Maxwell had established a global media empire which included TV and film production activities as well as US publishing houses. With the notable exception of the *Daily Mirror*, however, most of his business ventures were making a loss, hence he required substantial sums of borrowed money to keep the empire afloat. This was the least propitious time to be confronted with journalistic investigations and Maxwell, who was notoriously sensitive to public criticism, made frequent use of the libel laws to suppress a variety of stories about his more dubious financial activities.

In 1991 Maxwell disappeared from his luxury yacht off the Canary Islands. He was found five days later drowned. It is not certain but seems highly likely that he committed suicide as he was shortly afterwards shown to be at the centre of what proved to be a final and damning financial scandal. As chairman of the trustees for the Mirror Group Pension scheme he had simultaneously managed the scheme's assets via a financial management company for which he was also Chief Executive. As a result he was able to transfer these assets to his own private companies registered in Liechtenstein. He then used the shares and bonds as collateral to support borrowing from various City finance houses to cover losses being made elsewhere in his business empire. This operation could succeed only if the businesses became profitable again, and when they did not the scheme started to unravel. It was later revealed that Maxwell had embezzled £763 million in total, of which some £426 million had come from pension funds.

Thomas Bower, Maxwell: The Outsider (1992)

novels and plays of no particular distinction, he is best remembered for his multi-volumed *London Labour and the London Poor*, a pioneering and often affecting survey of the poor and trades of the metropolis. His status as a reliable social investigator, though, remains controversial.

MEAD, RICHARD (1673–1754), physician and public health reformer. The son of a Nonconformist minister from Stepney, he studied medicine at Leiden and began practising in 1696. A fellow of the Royal Society from 1703, Mead became the favourite physician of the future GEORGE II and Queen CAROLINE, who endorsed his scheme for widespread inoculation against smallpox. As Governor of St Thomas's Hospital from 1715, he encouraged Thomas GUY to found Guy's Hospital as a sister institution. His great contribution to public health came in his *Short Discourse concerning Pestilential Contagion*, written at the government's request in 1720 to avoid panic if the plague spread from Marseille. Mead advocated a council of health of public officials and medical men, to supervise preventive measures and collect statistics on the progress of the disease. His collection of books, manuscripts and curiosities was second only to that of SLOANE; much of it was preserved in a special museum in London until destroyed by bombing in 1940. Mead's house in Great Ormond Street remained a medical practice after his death and evolved into the Hospital for Sick Children.

MEAD, WILLIAM (1628–1713), Quaker. A wealthy London linen-draper who became a Quaker, in 1670 he was tried with William PENN in Bushell's case which established new conventions regarding the independence of juries. Penn and Mead were tried for tumultuous assembly and acquitted; the jurors, who had ignored the judge's guidance in their verdict, were fined by the Recorder of London and imprisoned until they paid. Edward Bushell, one of the jurors, obtained a writ of *habeas corpus* and obtained his discharge from the court of Common Pleas. Chief Justice Vaughan declared that jurors were the sole judges of fact in a trial; while the judge could advise a jury on matters of law, he could not direct it to deliver a particular verdict. Although the judgement was overturned on the grounds that Common Pleas had no jurisdiction in Bushell's case, Vaughan's principle was maintained.

MEDAWAR, SIR PETER (1915–87), immunologist. Medawar studied and researched zoology at Oxford and began his work on skin transplants treating burn victims during the Second World War. He held a succession of academic positions including professorships at Birmingham (1947–51) and London (1951–62). He worked on rabbit skin grafts and showed how recipient tissue possesses a natural and an acquired immunity to donor tissue and showed that an animal's tendency to reject donor tissue is not inherited but acquired during the foetal stage, and, having injected foreign tissue cells into foetal mice, demonstrated that mice develop an 'immunological tolerance' to foreign transplanted tissue. Medawar and Macfarlane Burnet shared the 1960 Nobel Prize for Medicine for this work. Their research led to techniques that would make organ transplants a success.

MEDE (OR MEADE), JOSEPH (1586–1638), writer. An Essex-born Cambridge don of encyclopaedic interests and knowledge, he was an eccentric High Churchman, maintaining that the Pope was Antichrist, while pleasing English Arminians with his devotional writings on the Eucharist. He was determined to show the validity of biblical prophecy, and his most influential work, *Clavis Apocalyptica* (1627), expounded the Book of Revelation, looking forward in millenarian style to a final thousand-year reign of the saints on earth. His ideas were much admired by John DURY and Samuel HARTLIB.

MEIKLE, ANDREW (1719–1811), inventor. Until Meikle's invention of the threshing machine the exhausting process of separating grain from straw had been carried out by armies of labourers. Meikle's machine, developed at the family millwright business in Scotland, fed corn stalks through cast-iron rollers driven at high speed by teams of horses, steam or water-power, beating grain from the ears. It was patented in 1785, and became popular in Scotland and northern England, where farmers feared that depopulation following industrialization would threaten their livelihoods. Farmers in southern England, where the economy remained heavily dependent on agriculture, remained hostile to the invention until well into the nineteenth century.

MEINERTZHAGEN, RICHARD (1878–1967), soldier and ornithologist. Educated at Harrow and commissioned from the Hampshire Yeomanry into the regular army, Meinertzhagen served as an intelligence officer in German East Africa (1914–16) before being appointed Chief Intelligence Officer in the Middle East. Brilliant if eccentric, he devised the deception plan which allowed ALLENBY's forces to break the Turkish line during the second Battle of Gaza in Oct. 1917, an exploit which led to his appointment to General Head Quarters in France. After attending the Versailles peace conference, Meinertzhagen served as an adviser to the Colonial Office with T. E. LAWRENCE, but resigned in 1924 to pursue ornithology as a career. Meinertzhagen last saw action in May 1940, when he was wounded on the beach at Dunkirk while helping to evacuate British troops across the Channel in his small river-cruiser.

MELBOURNE, 2ND VISCOUNT see LAMB, WILLIAM

MELCHETT, 1ST BARON see MOND, ALFRED

MELLITUS, ST (?–624), Bishop of London (604–19) and Archbishop of Canterbury (619–24). Third Archbishop of Canterbury after St AUGUSTINE and LAURENTIUS, Mellitus' career illustrates well the difficulties of the early Christian missionaries to England. Established within the kingdom of Essex as the first Bishop of London by King ETHELBERT of Kent, he was expelled from his see in 616 when King EADBALD of Kent lost control over London and the sons of King SÆBERHT of Essex reverted to paganism. It was almost another 30 years before St CEDD was successfully installed as Bishop of the East Saxons. BEDE, our chief source, tells us little about Mellitus' work in either of his churches; his supposedly miraculous role in saving Canterbury from fire illuminates a consistent theme of the miraculous in the early conversion.

MELROSE, 1ST EARL OF see HAMILTON, THOMAS

MELVILLE, 1ST VISCOUNT see DUNDAS, HENRY

MELVILLE, ANDREW (1545–1622), clerical politician. Studies at St Andrews, Paris and Poitiers culminated at Geneva (1569–74), which confirmed his enthusiasm for Calvinist Church reform. On his return to Scotland in 1574 he did much for university reform and development, and was the prime mover for the abolition of Episcopacy and a pure Presbyterian system in the Church. This provoked repeated clashes with JAMES VI which led in 1607 to imprisonment and four years later to French exile.

MELVILLE, SIR JAMES (1535–1617), diplomat. In the service of MARY QUEEN OF SCOTS in France during the 1550s, he was employed in embassies, for instance in an unsuccessful effort to win ELIZABETH I's goodwill towards Mary's marriage to Henry STEWART, Lord Darnley, and the offer of the regency to James STEWART, Earl of Moray, in 1567. He was made a Privy Councillor, and became Laird of Hallhill (Lanarks.). He left an autobiography in MS, which is a useful insider's view of Scottish court politics.

MENUHIN, YEHUDI (Baron Menuhin of Stoke d'Abernon) (1916–99), musician. Probably the greatest child prodigy of the twentieth century, Menuhin gave his first public performance of the Mendelssohn violin concerto at the age of seven and appeared professionally in San Francisco at the age of eight. In 1927 he became a world celebrity with his performance of the Beethoven concerto in the Carnegie Hall, New York. His belief that music, as a 'universal language', should be promoted in schools and be understood as playing a vital role in civilizing society (he had performed over 500 concerts to the Allied troops during the Second World War) led him to establish numerous festivals including Gstaad, Switzerland (1956), Bath (1958) and Windsor (Berks.) (1969), and he founded his own music school at Stoke d'Abernon (Surrey) (1962). A deeply spiritual man interested in Indian mysticism and devoted to yoga, he organized his daily timetable standing on his head and once conducted the Berlin Philharmonic thus.

MENZIES, SIR ROBERT (1894–1978), politician. Declaring himself to be 'British to his bootstraps', Menzies was Australia's longest-serving Prime Minister, 1939–41 and 1949–66. Coming from a political family, he worked his way up through the Melbourne and federal system. In Britain between 1941 and 1943, Menzies clashed with Winston CHURCHILL, and a small group of Conservatives favoured him as wartime leader. Returning to Australia, he formed the Liberal Party, which dominated politics for a generation. Advocate of a white Australia policy and an unabashed Anglophile (Menzies was made Warden of the Cinque Ports after Churchill's death and received many honours), he came to be seen by Australian posterity as embodiment of the 'cultural cringe'.

MERCATOR, NICHOLAS (c. 1620–87), mathematician. From Schleswig-Holstein, he latinized his surname from Kauffman, and studied and taught in the Netherlands and Denmark, coming to England briefly in 1654. From 1657 to 1682 he returned (probably on the suggestion of Samuel HARTLIB); teaching in London, he became a fellow of the Royal Society. Talent-scouted for French royal service by Jean-Baptiste Colbert, he died in France. He wrote extensively on mathematics and astronomy, developing the theory of logarithms (see NAPIER, John). He should not be confused with the Dutch Gerardus Mercator (1512–94), who developed Mercator's projection of the globe (see also RUDD, John).

MERCER, JOHN (1791–1866), chemist. Born in Lancs., Mercer received little early education and from the age of nine or ten worked as a bobbin-winder. After working as an independent dyer

(1807–9), he was employed as a weaver and chemist in the calico-printing works at Oakenshaw (Lancs.), improving his education, and inventing various dyes. He was a partner in the firm from 1825 until its collapse in 1848 but made enough money to finance independent research. He is best known for developing (*c.* 1844) the technique of mercerization in which cotton fibres are treated with caustic soda to give a silky texture. He patented his technique in 1850 but, owing to the high cost of caustic soda, it was not a commercial success until the 1890s.

MEREDITH, SIR WILLIAM (*c.* 1725–90) law reformer. MP (1754–80), first for Wigan, then for Liverpool, he was led by Enlightenment ideas about the proper character of penal codes to question the prevalance of capital punishment in England. His first, modest attempts to repeal certain obsolete capital statutes having been blocked on the grounds that his proposals were innovations, he returned to the attack with the claim that 'these hanging laws are themselves innovations', which he sought to demonstrate by totalling recent new capital statutes: according to him, 33 had been passed by the Parliaments of GEORGE II. Though the exercise was in many ways a misleading one, this was memorable propaganda. Subsequent penal reformers continued the tally, and many historians have cited such figures since.

MEREWALH (?–685), King of the Magonsæte. The first king of a people inhabiting modern Salop. and Herefords., it looks as though his kingdom was established by King PENDA of Mercia, whose son Merewalh may have been. Very little is known about Merewalh. His kingdom, a typical small kingdom of the Dark Age period, faded rapidly into obscurity.

MERFYN FRYCH AP GWRIAD (?–844), King of Gwynedd. Merfyn was the first of a new line on the throne of Gwynedd, succeeding Hywel ap Rhodri in 825. The change in dynastic line appears to have provoked a new vigour in the Gwynedd kingship, promoting the ideals of unification. Merfyn's court was a respected cultural centre, with the *Annales Cambriae* and the *Historia Brittonum* compiled during his reign. Both Merfyn and his son RHODRI MAWR were known and respected at the court of the Carolingian kings of the Franks. Merfyn is attributed with making two pilgrimages to Rome, during the course of the latter of which he died.

MERLIN (OR MYRDDIN), Arthurian figure. He first appeared as the wizard at the court of King ARTHUR in the twelfth-century writings of GEOFFREY OF MONMOUTH, although, in an interpolated text of the supposedly sixth-century poem *Gododdin* and in Welsh bardic tradition, there are references to a Myrddin who was an adviser to kings. Like Arthur, Merlin may be based on someone who actually lived in the sixth century, but the historical basis of Geoffrey's Merlin is flimsy and the modern Merlin of Camelot is pure legend.

MERTON, WALTER (?–1277), college founder. He rose from clerk in the Royal Chancery in 1237 to Chancellor in 1261–3. In 1264 he established the 'House of the Scholars of Merton' (Surrey), transferring it to Oxford 10 years later as Merton College. He was Chancellor again for two years (1272–4), and was elected Bishop of Rochester in 1274. He died after falling off his horse while fording the River Medway.

MERZ, CHARLES (1874–1940), electrical engineer. Educated in Newcastle, Merz developed electrical engineering expertise in electric supply, steam engine and electrical equipment firms. From 1897 he worked for an electrical apparatus firm, the British Thomson-Houston Co., running electric supply stations and building a tramway. In 1902 he formed an electrical engineering firm with William McLellan and together they patented electric supply apparatus and designed large-scale electric supply systems. They successfully implemented their ideas in north-eastern England, where they pioneered an integrated regional electrical supply and traction system using the most sophisticated and economical power stations of the period. Merz was later hired to reorganize electric supply systems across the world and became a prominent parliamentary witness in drafting Bills to regulate electrical power. He played a crucial role in the establishment of the Central Electricity Board and the National Grid.

MESTRELL, ELOYE (?–1578), minter. Born in Paris, he arrived in England *c.* 1560 and pioneered production of the English coinage by a mechanical mill or press instead of by hammer-striking (although milled issues of the Scots coinage in 1553 predated the English initiative). His method proved unreliable, and he was discredited by involvement in forgery in 1569; the experimental issues ceased in 1572 and milled English coins were not issued again until 1662. Mestrell was apparently hanged on further forgery charges.

METCALF, JOHN (1717–1810), engineer. Known as Blind Jack of Knaresborough, he lost his sight in childhood, but this did not hinder an adventurous career, in which he was active as a jockey, recruiting sergeant, horse-dealer, trader and smuggler. A spell in army transport inspired him to try to improve defective northern roads. The first road engineer of distinction, he constructed about 300 kilometres of turnpike road: the secret of his success was a foundation of heather and brushwood with provision for good surface drainage. His roads were solid and comparatively cheap to maintain.

METHUEN, SIR JOHN (c. 1650–1706) and **SIR PAUL** (1672–1757), diplomats. Son of a Wilts. clothier, John Methuen followed a distinguished legal career. He first became envoy to Portugal in 1691; in 1697 he became Lord Chancellor of Ireland, and was succeeded by his son Paul. In 1702 and again in 1703 the elder Methuen returned to Portugal, the second time as Ambassador, to conclude the two Methuen Treaties. The first brought Portugal into the Grand Alliance against France, Spain and Bavaria, effectively expanding the theatre of the War of the Spanish Succession within Spain itself. The second allowed English cloth free access to the Portuguese market; in return, Portuguese wines would bear significantly lower duties than those from France. This helped Britain maintain a balance of trade during the war and established British economic ascendancy in Portugal until the nineteenth century.

MEYNELL, ALICE (née Thompson) (1847–1922), poet and essayist. Her first volume of poetry, *Preludes*, was published in 1875 and two years later she married the journalist and critic Wilfred Meynell, who was among the literati who much admired it. A Catholic convert, she contributed to her husband's religious journals as well as writing for the *Pall Mall Gazette*, the *Spectator* and other periodicals to help support their family of eight children. A committed suffragist, Meynell published numerous collections of essays, as well as several volumes of mystical poetry which were so well regarded that she was canvassed as Poet Laureate on the death of TENNYSON.

MIDDLESEX, EARL OF, 1ST see CRANFIELD, LIONEL; **4TH** see SACKVILLE, CHARLES

MIDDLETON, CONYERS (1683–1750), theologian. First a student, then a Fellow of Trinity College, Cambridge, in 1721 he was made first *protobibliothecarius*, or university librarian. Middleton's rationalism led him to write *A Letter from Rome* (1729), one of the most lucidly argued versions of the popular Protestant charge that Catholicism was a veneer over enduring pagan beliefs. He also wrote many works challenging the literal historical accuracy of the Bible. His *Free Enquiry* (1749) argued that there had been no genuine miracles after the New Testament. Middleton was criticized by both Deists and traditional Christians, whose beliefs he had felt himself to be defending.

MIDDLETON, THOMAS (?1570–1627), dramatist. After studying at Gray's Inn, he became involved with the stage in 1592. Most of his numerous plays, mostly satirical comedies, were written in co-operation with others, including Thomas DEKKER, Michael DRAYTON, Ben JONSON and John WEBSTER; he was also employed by the City of London to write pageants and masques. His political play *A Game of Chess* (1624) was officially censured after protests from the Spanish Ambassador Gondomar.

MILDMAY, LADY GRACE (née Sharrington) (1552–1620), diarist. Daughter of Sir Henry Sharrington of Lacock (Wilts.), in 1566 she married Anthony Mildmay (c. 1549–1617, son of Walter MILDMAY). Their 50-year marriage was apparently very happy, after difficult early years when Anthony was at court or abroad enjoying himself. Grace, a stronger character than her husband, became a devout Puritan matriarch and also had a consuming and enlightened interest in medicine and the manufacture of medications. She left an illuminating diary, and her extensive household papers survive.

MILDMAY, SIR WALTER (before 1523–89), educational patron. An Essex merchant's son, Cambridge-educated, he entered government service in the 1530s, soon showing exceptional financial abilities and, after keeping a low profile under MARY I because of his Protestant enthusiasm, was Chancellor of the Exchequer from 1559. He was very frequently MP from 1545, and as a trusted member of ELIZABETH I's government, a useful mediator between Puritans and the Queen. Pursuing further gradual Church reform, he founded Emmanuel College, Cambridge, which down to the 1630s was a key centre of higher education for Puritan sympathizers.

MILES (OR MYLES), JOHN (1621–83), Baptist pioneer. An Oxford-educated Puritan, with Thomas Proud he founded the first Welsh Baptist church at Ilston (Glamorgan) in 1649; during the Interregnum he served the parish of Ilston but also directed a group of Welsh Baptist preachers. In 1663 he emigrated to New England and became a preacher in Massachusetts, dying at Swansea (Mass.)

MILL, JAMES (1773–1836), philosopher. A disciple of BENTHAM, he assimilated the ideas of MALTHUS and David RICARDO in the development of utilitarian economics, which came to dominate British social thought. Mill's initiative led to the formation of the group of Benthamites known as 'philosophic radicals'. His book *Analysis of the Phenomenon of the Human Mind* (1829) provided a psychological basis for utilitarianism. His belief in democracy was balanced by his distrust of both the aristocracy and the working classes, and he looked to the upcoming professional and commercial middle classes of early Victorian England to provide the balance. He also wrote the first English-language textbook of economics, contributed articles to the influential *Westminster Review*, and fathered J. S. MILL.

MILL, JOHN STUART *see* essay on page 566

MILLAIS, SIR JOHN EVERETT (1829–96), artist. A precociously talented painter, he was the youngest pupil that the Royal Academy Schools had ever admitted when he went there, aged 11, in 1840: he proved a stellar student exhibiting at the Academy when he was just 16. In 1848 the 19-year-old Millais was one of the seven who formed the Pre-Raphaelite Brotherhood (PRB) (*see*, ROSSETTI, DANTE GABRIEL). His first painting in this new reworking of the moral values of the Italian Renaissance (and its glowing pigments) was the banquet scene from KEATS's poem *Isabella*, for which he used his friends and family for models. His next, *Christ in the Carpenter's Shop* (1850), caused an outrage when it was exhibited at the Royal Academy: it offered 'the signal for a perfect crusade against the PRB' with condemnation of the artist's 'blasphemy' in 'associat[ing] the holy family with the meanest details of a carpenter's shop'. *Ophelia* (1851), the work for which Elizabeth SIDDAL modelled for the drowned Shakespearean heroine by lying for hours in a cold bath, and which exemplified the PRB intention 'to present on canvas what they saw in Nature' with its detailed rendition of a Kingston (Surrey) riverbank, established Millais's reputation, and historical subjects like *A Huguenot on St Bartholomew's Day Refusing to Shield Himself from Danger* (1852) and *The Order of Release* (1853), as also paintings that that have become a little saccharine for modern taste, such as *The Poor Blind Girl* (1856), consolidated his place in Victorian sentiment.

In 1855 he married Effie, after her marriage to RUSKIN had been annulled. With eight children to support, a market needed to be guaranteed and, with the PRB dissolving, Millais's later work, mainly historical narrative paintings, reached an apogee of commercialism with the painting of his grandchild *Bubbles* (1886), which the advertisement for Pears' soap ensured would be his best-known work ever (to the discomfiture of the

artist). In Feb. 1896 he was elected president of the Royal Academy in succession to LEIGHTON. It was short-lived dignification: by Aug. he was dead.

MILLAR (OR MYLLAR), ANDREW (*fl. c.* 1500–10), pioneer printer. A burgess of Edinburgh, he set up Scotland's first printing press with financial backing from Walter CHEPMAN; the first dateable book is from 1505, and they gained a royal monopoly in 1507.

MILLAR, JOHN (1735–1801), social theorist. Professor of Law at Glasgow University from 1761, whose writings included *Origin of the Distinction of Ranks* (1771) and *Historical View of the English Government* (1787), he was close to David HUME and admired the philosophy of Montesquieu. Millar argued that the ownership of property was an essential pre-condition for liberty. He regarded the rise of a prosperous commercial middle class with a mixture of admiration and apprehension, however, for although the liberty of this section of society was increasing, he feared that its very prosperity might prevent its social and economic inferiors from becoming property-owners themselves, thus permanently restricting their freedom.

MILLER, JONATHAN (1934–), physician and arts director. While studying medicine at Cambridge, Miller wrote for and appeared in a Footlights revue, *Beyond the Fringe*, which transferred to the London theatre and was the start of the anti-Establishment satiric boom of the early 1960s. Since 1962 he has directed plays, musicals and operas, notably *Rigoletto* (1982, 1985, 1995) for the English National Opera and *Così fan Tutti* (1995) for Covent Garden. He was editor and presenter of the influential BBC arts programme *Monitor* (1964–5) and a number of other television series including *The Body in Question* (1978, also a book) and *Madness* (1991).

MILLER, MAX (originally Thomas Sargent) (1895–1963), comedian. The 'Cheeky Chappie' was born in Brighton and after working as a motor mechanic joined Billy Smart's Circus as a comedian; after the First World War he was soon touring Britain. Four years after his début performance in London in 1922 he topped the bill with his brash and often blue comedy that audiences loved. He was essentially a throwback to the golden age of the music hall, in an era becoming dominated by the new media of film and later of television. Dressed in his trademark while trilby, kipper tie and plus fours, with his catchphrase 'Make something of that!', Miller was a household name.

MILLIGAN, TERENCE ALLAN ('SPIKE') (1918–), comedian and writer. Born in India, he

continued on page 567

MILL, JOHN STUART (1806–73)
Philosopher, economist and social theorist

He was one of the most influential thinkers and public intellectuals of his day, not least because the range of his writing was so extensive. His influence was felt in ethics, metaphysics, logic, political and social theory, economics and practical politics.

Born in London, he was subjected to an intensive education by his father, James MILL, historian and philosopher, aided and influenced by his friend, Jeremy BENTHAM, the founding figure of utilitarianism. John Stuart described his austere and emotionally barren education in his *Autobiography* (1873): he grew up 'with great inaptness in the common affairs of everyday life'. In 1823 Mill commenced work as a clerk for his father at India House, the office of the East India Co. But his life was thrown into turmoil in 1826 when he experienced a mental breakdown, memorably described in the *Autobiography*. He recovered and returned to work, and was in charge of the company's relations with the princely states of India until 1856.

He met Harriet TAYLOR in 1830. Theirs was an extraordinary relationship. Harriet was married and the mother of three children. From 1830 until her husband John's death in 1849, Harriet and Mill sustained an intense relationship with Taylor's knowledge yet it was only after Taylor's death that they were able to live together and, in 1851, marry. Harriet's emotional and intellectual influence on Mill was very considerable. She played a substantial part in the development of his major works and also extended the range of his ideas, centrally on the question of women's subjection and the prospects of emancipation, but also, for example, in leading him to a greater sympathy for co-operative socialism. Her death in Avignon in 1858 broke 'the spring of my life', as Mill was to write. After her death and the dissolution of the East India Co., Mill settled in Avignon, accompanied by his step-daughter, Helen TAYLOR, until he was elected as an MP for Westminster in 1865. When he was defeated in the General Election of 1868, he returned to France.

His writing covered a great range but he is perhaps best known outside strictly academic discussions for his ideas on political and moral philosophy. Central to his intellectual development was his modification of the main doctrines of utilitarianism, which, as developed by Bentham, espoused the notion of 'the greatest happiness of the greatest number': individuals sought to maximize their happiness; all conduct and institutions were to be judged by the extent to which their consequences achieved this end. Mill's critique, influenced by his reading of COLERIDGE and the Romantics and by the French philosopher Saint-Simon, retained the core doctrine but modified and extended it. He sought to distinguish qualitative differences between different kinds of happiness – 'better a Socrates dissatisfied than a pig satisfied' – and attempted to ground his ethics in a richer account of human nature.

A concern with individual self-development and fulfilment runs throughout Mill's political writings. He advocated the principles of *laissez-faire* in the *Principles of Political Economy* (1848) as a foundation of individual liberty. His essay *On Liberty* (1859) is celebrated for the principle that 'the only purpose for which power can be rightfully exercised over any member of a civilized community against his will, is to prevent harm to others'. Yet his concerns were not only with limiting the powers of the State and allowing free rein to the market. He was also anxious to preserve the political conditions of individualism through political participation. He was at one with an ancient strand of political theory which believed that engagement in civic life had an educative role. In Mill's case he believed that political argument and activity would advance individuals' 'intellect ... virtue ... and ... practical activity and efficiency' and would free the talent and creativity essential to enabling progress. Not the least of Mill's distinction in this regard was his advocacy of the rights of women to full participation in the community. He argued in *The Subjection of Women* (1869) that the oppression of women could and should be overcome, primarily through granting women full and equal civil and political rights with men. As an MP he presented the historic motion of women's suffrage in 1867 (although it was defeated heavily).

While Mill was committed to the extension of voting rights for men as well as women he drew limits: he advocated an extended suffrage but thought that the rights of minorities should be defended against the dangers of majority rule by allowing some, primarily intellectuals, plural votes.

As a public intellectual, whose books were widely read and whose views were discussed in many different social milieux, Mill's presence within mid Victorian society loomed large. He had a status which has rarely been matched by any single intellectual since.

William Stafford, John Stuart Mill (1998)

co-wrote and performed in the addictive BBC radio series *The Goon Show* (1951–60) with Peter Sellers, Harry Secombe and Michael Bentine. His sense of the absurd informed his work in many fields. He has acted on the stage, notably in *The Bed-Sitting Room* (1963, 1967), which he co-wrote, in films and on television. He has written comic novels, poems, children's stories, autobiography and the unclassifiable *Adolph Hitler, My Part in his Downfall* (1971) and *Peacework* (1991). He is a surrealist who is courageous in talking of the depressive underside of his zany humour.

MILLS, PETER (1598–1670), architect. Son of a Sussex tailor, he made a career in the London construction industry, becoming one of the supervisors for rebuilding the city after the 1666 fire. His main achievement was Thorpe Hall (near Peterborough) in 1654–8 for Oliver ST JOHN, a monument to cheerful English 'artisan mannerist' disregard of Inigo JONES's classical purity. Some of his buildings in London, Oxford and Cambridge also survive.

MILNE, A(LAN) A(LEXANDER) (1882–1956), children's writer. The son of a Scottish schoolmaster, Milne read mathematics at Cambridge but his humorous writing ability led to his appointment as assistant editor of *Punch*. After the First World War he published plays (and later adult novels and an indictment of war), but it was his writing for children that brought him fame. His verse included *When We Were Very Young* (1924) and *Now We Are Six* (1927); his books, *Winnie the Pooh* (1926) and *House at Pooh Corner* (1928), which feature Milne's own son Christopher Robin and his anthropomorphic animal toys, the hapless, honey-loving Pooh, the misanthropic Eeyore and the timid, squeaky Piglet, have had as much appeal to adults as children. The illustrations by E. H. Shepherd added to their enduring appeal.

MILNER, ALFRED (1st Viscount Milner) (1854–1925), imperial politician. Born in Germany of British descent, Milner was educated there and at Oxford, where he was one of those influenced by JOWETT. After an early career in the Civil Service he became High Commissioner in South Africa (1897–1905), Governor of Cape Colony (1897–1901) and then Governor of the Transvaal and Orange River Colony, administering Boer territories from 1901 to 1905. An advocate of 'enlightened imperial rule', he assembled what came to be known as a 'kindergarten' of able young Oxford men around him, several of whom went on to achieve high administrative office. Created a viscount in 1902 for his services in the Boer War, he returned to Britain in 1905 to become a vociferous critic of LLOYD GEORGE over

the People's Budget and Irish Home Rule, but in 1916 he became a key member of Lloyd George's War Cabinet. As Colonial Secretary (1919–21), he fostered the belief that the colonies should be shaped to assume the responsibilities of self-government. His sometimes rigid outlook nevertheless framed the later development of imperial policy.

MILNES, RICHARD MONKTON (1st Baron Houghton) (1809–95), writer and politician. From a wealthy Yorks. family, elected at Cambridge to the select group of Apostles (officially the Cambridge Conversazione Society, of which TENNYSON was also a member), he published five volumes of poetry and was MP for Pontefract from 1837, but it is for his patronage of young writers that he is gratefully remembered. He defended SWINBURNE's poetry against charges of decadence, he provided hospitality for a number of impecunious writers at his home, Fryston Hall (Yorks.) and his book *Life, Letters and Literary Remains of John Keats* (1848) secured the reputation of the Romantic poet. *See also* KEATS, JOHN.

MILTON, LORD see FLETCHER, ANDREW

MILTON, JOHN (1608–74), poet and writer. Son of a minor composer, he was already writing accomplished poetry while at Cambridge and in the 1630s wrote masques, including *Comus* (1634) for Philip Herbert, Earl of Pembroke. During the Civil Wars of the 1640s he wrote with increasing radicalism on politics and (not least as a result of personal circumstances) advocated the free availability of divorce; he published pamphlets defending free speech and attacking the instant cult of the executed CHARLES I. From 1649 to 1660 he was Latin Secretary to the Council of State, despite increasing blindness. Briefly imprisoned at the restoration of CHARLES II, he used his years of political disgrace to write some of his greatest poetry, including the final version of *Paradise Lost* (finished 1663) and *Samson Agonistes* (1671).

MINTO, EARL OF, 1ST and **4TH** *see* ELLIOT-MURRAY-KYNYMOUND, GILBERT

MINTON, THOMAS (1765–1836), chinamanufacturer. Born in Salop., he worked for the potter Josiah SPODE before setting up his own company in Stoke-on-Trent (Staffs.) in 1789, specializing in transfer-printing in blue underglaze. Credited with inventing the willow pattern, in 1793 he built a pottery at Stoke, producing fine, translucent porcelain by adding bone to the clay paste. His decorated tableware was and is much prized.

MITCHEL, JOHN (1815–75), Irish politician. The son of a Unitarian minister from Ulster, Mitchel came to prominence in 1845 after succeeding Thomas DAVIS as leader-writer for *The Nation*. He joined the Young Ireland secession from Daniel O'CONNELL's Repeal Association, but was in turn expelled from the Young Irelanders' Confederation in 1848 when he responded to the Great Famine by openly advocating a peasant uprising. (He later claimed that the Famine derived from a genocidal plot by the British government, a view widely held by later generations of nationalists.) In May 1848 he was convicted of treason felony and transported to Australia; his *Jail Journal* (1854) is one of the seminal works of nineteenth-century Irish nationalism. He escaped to America in 1853 and was active in Irish-American politics, defending slavery and supporting the Confederacy in the American Civil War. He returned to Ireland in 1875 and was elected abstentionist MP for Tipperary, though he was subsequently disqualified as an undischarged felon. Mitchel's influence on later generations of separatists can be traced in the writings of Arthur GRIFFITH, Eoin MACNEILL and Padraic PEARSE.

MITCHISON, NAOMI (Lady Mitchison) (née Haldane) (1897–1999), writer. From a distinguished intellectual lineage, daughter of the physiologist John Scott Haldane and sister of the biologist J. B. S. HALDANE, and a somewhat desultory student at St Anne's College, Oxford, she nursed as a VAD in the First World War and in 1916 married the Labour MP Richard Mitchison: they had seven children, five of whom survived. The first of her many historical novels, *The Conquered*, a tale of first-century Celts, was published in 1923, by which time she was involved in setting up birth-control clinics and travelling to Russia (1932) and Austria (1934), visits about which she wrote in a cautionary novel, *We Have Been Warned* (1935). During the Second World War, Mitchison was one of the correspondents for Mass Observation, recording the daily details of her wartime life where, with her husband in London working with BEVERIDGE on manpower surveys, she ran their Scottish estate Carradale on the Mull of Kintyre (Argylls.) and increased her involvement in Scottish nationalist politics. In the early 1960s she made the first of several trips to Botswana where the 30,000-strong Bakgatlas tribe made her their *Mmarona*, (tribal mother), and she wrote several books about her African experiences, two of which, *When We Become Men* and *African Heroes* (both 1965), were banned by the South African government. Fearless, unconventional, adventurous and opinionated in her writing as in her life, Mitchison wrote more than 80 books in a life that spanned 101 years.

MOIRA, 4TH BARON *see* HASTINGS, FRANCIS

MOLYNEAUX, JAMES (Baron Molyneaux) (1920–), Ulster politician. A farmer and Second World War veteran, Molyneaux was Westminster MP for South Antrim (1970–83) and Lagan Valley (1983–97). As leader of Ulster Unionist MPs at Westminster he grew in importance with the demise of Stormont (the Northern Ireland Parliament); he opposed the Sunningdale Agreement for a power-sharing executive in Northern Ireland, and in 1979 displaced Harry West as party leader. A taciturn figure who pursued minimalist tactics, Molyneaux was unenthusiastic about the re-creation of a devolved Parliament and his political career centred on Westminster. His tendency to overestimate the extent of British support for Ulster Unionism (encouraged by the influence of Enoch POWELL) was exposed by the implementation of the 1985 Anglo-Irish Agreement despite Unionist opposition. Molyneaux joined with Ian PAISLEY to oppose the agreement, but in the early 1990s he showed himself more willing than Paisley to negotiate with the government. By 1993 many Ulster Unionists felt they needed a younger and more vigorous leader. He retired in 1995 and became a life peer in 1997; in 1998 he supported the Ulster Unionist dissidents who opposed the Good Friday Agreement. Molyneaux represented an older kind of conservative Britishness associated with the wartime generation and eroded by later developments.

MOLYNEUX, WILLIAM (1656–98), scholar and writer. A philosopher, lawyer and astronomer, he was heir to a considerable fortune, so was able to indulge his intellectual interests. Educated at Trinity College, Dublin, and the Middle Temple, he was especially interested in mathematics, science and topography. He was elected to represent the university in Parliament in 1692, and published *The Case of Ireland's being bound by Acts of Parliament in England Stated* (1696), an attempt to establish Ireland's legislative independence. A correspondent and great admirer of John LOCKE, Molynuex evoked the authority of the *Two Treatises of Government* on the principle of consent and on the illegitimacy of deriving political right from the fact of conquest. The book crystallized a sense of Irish patriotism among the Protestant elite. It was declared 'of dangerous consequence' to the Crown and Parliament of England, though no action was taken against Molyneux himself. His work provided a text for eighteenth-century politicians seeking to reform the relationship between the English (later British) and Irish Parliaments, until success was achieved by Henry GRATTAN.

MONBODDO, LORD *see* BURNETT, JAMES

MONCK (OR MONK), GEORGE (1st Duke of Albemarle) (1608–70), soldier and politician. A professional soldier, Monck fought in the First Civil War for CHARLES I until captured in 1644. From 1647 he accepted Parliamentary commands, proving unbeatable in Ireland, Scotland and the 1652–4 Dutch War, and winning great trust from Oliver CROMWELL. In the mounting confusion of 1659, Monck's exasperated intervention with his northern garrison troops proved decisive; marching south in Nov. without making his purposes clear, he attracted a bewildering variety of future hopes. He ordered the reinstatement of the unpurged Long Parliament in its surviving membership of 1640; spurning offers of supreme power, he opened negotiations with CHARLES II and secured his restoration. Predictably loaded with honours, Monck retained military influence, playing a major role in the Second Dutch War of 1665–7, but he kept out of politics and did not let his Presbyterian sympathies interfere with the Anglican turn-around in the Church.

MONCKTON, WALTER (1st Viscount Monckton of Brenchley) (1891–1965), politician. President of the Oxford Union (1913), Monckton was a successful barrister in the 1920s and 1930s. He was appointed Attorney General to the Prince of Wales (an old Oxford friend) (see EDWARD VII) in 1932, and was deeply involved in the constitutional crisis which culminated in the abdication in Dec.1936. An intermediary between the King and the government, he was knighted the following year by the new King, GEORGE VI, as a reward for his discreet and deft handling of the affair. Elected Conservative MP for Bristol West in 1951, he had a controversial four-year stint as Minister of Labour, during which he was accused by right-wing Conservatives of 'appeasing' the unions, but this was the policy preferred by the Prime Minister Winston CHURCHILL. Monckton was Minister of Defence at the time of the Suez crisis (1956) and was an early opponent of Anthony EDEN's controversial plan to retake the Suez Canal by force in collusion with France and Israel. He resigned over the affair, though he did not express his opposition openly for fear of appearing disloyal while British armed forces were in action.

MOND, LUDWIG (1839–1909) and **ALFRED** (1st Baron Melchett of Landford) (1868–1930), manufacturers. Ludwig Mond, born in Cassel, Germany, left his chemistry studies in Heidelberg because he wanted to apply his knowledge to manufacturing problems, and indeed he introduced a new type of entrepreneurship. His breakthrough was the sulphur recovery process in soda manufacture, and he moved to Britain in 1862 to realize the potential of his discoveries. Development was fitful, and eventually the process was abandoned, but in 1870 Mond went into partnership with John Brunner from the Widnes (Lancs.) firm with which he had first been involved. Progress was slow but, based on the ammonia soda process that Mond had pioneered, profitable chemical production began in 1875. With Brunner Mond & Co. well on the road to success, Mond turned his attention to other chemical processes, the production of ammonia and gas and the purification of nickel. The Mond Nickel Co. was formed in 1900, and with it came scientific honours for him. His son Alfred followed into Brunner Mond; joining the board in 1895, he was soon Managing Director. He was also heavily involved with the Mond Nickel Co. A Liberal MP for a succession of seats between 1906 and 1928, he was the first Commissioner of Works (1916–21) and Minister of Health (1921–2). In 1923 he returned to the family firm of Brunner Mond, becoming Chairman in 1925. Then in 1926 he and Harry McGowan, later 1st Baron McGowan (1874–1961), masterminded the formation of ICI (Imperial Chemical Industries) through the union of Brunner Mond, United Alkali and British Dyestuffs. In the course of the 1920s Mond became an advocate of pure research, rationalization and Empire union, while also being an active Zionist. At his initiative the Mond–Turner talks on industrial co-operation with the Trades Union Congress (TUC) began in 1928, the year he was given his peerage. His grandson, Julian Mond, 3rd Baron Melchett (1925–73), became Chairman of the newly nationalized British Steel Corporation in 1967. His ambitious plans for dramatic expansion proved misguided: after his sudden death, when Sir Monty Finniston replaced him with the aim of carrying the expansion through, the world steel industry was hit by deep recession.

MONMOUTH, 1ST DUKE OF *see* SCOTT, JAMES

MONRO, SIR CHARLES (1860–1929), soldier. Educated at Sandhurst, commissioned into the 2nd Foot in 1879, Monro saw extensive colonial service, culminating in South Africa in 1900. Appointed Chief Instructor to the army's school of musketry at Hythe (Kent) in 1901, he spent the next six years applying the lessons learned in South Africa to improve the marksmanship of the British soldier, to the extent that the small British Expeditionary Force (BEF) in 1914 was able to engage and defeat very much larger German forces. In 1915 Monro, now a General commanding the newly raised 3rd Army, was sent to Gallipoli to replace Sir Ian HAMILTON but, realizing the situation was hopeless, organized a brilliant evacuation in which not a single man was lost. Appointed Commander-in-Chief in India in Oct. 1916, Monro instituted a four-fold expansion of the Indian army, simultaneously raising the quality of training, but proved unable to deal effectively with post-war disturbances. Appalled by the action of DYER at Amritsar in 1919, Monro insisted he should resign from the army, and also accepted responsibility himself and resigned as Commander-in-Chief.

MONTAGU, CHARLES (3rd [1st Montagu] Earl of Halifax) (1661–1715), politician. The son of a Northants. gentleman, he was one of the 'Immortal Seven' signatories of the letter of invitation to William of Orange (the future WILLIAM III) in 1688 and became a Whig member of the 1689 Convention Parliament and a leading figure in the Whig Junto. A Lord of the Treasury (1692), Chancellor of the Exchequer (1694) and First Lord of the Treasury (1697) he played a part in developing new financial devices to underwrite King William's War (1689–97), in the establishment of the Bank of England and in the recoinage of 1696. He resigned from the Treasury in 1699 in the face of allegations of corruption; he was impeached by the Commons in 1701 for his part in the Partition Treaty (promoted by William as part of a plan to redistribute power in Europe on the death of the heirless Spanish King), but the charge was dismissed by the Lords. Continuing the series of politically motivated accusations, the Tories charged him with neglect in his duties as auditor of the Exchequer, but no verdict was reached (1703–4). He continued in office throughout ANNE's reign, and was a Commissioner for the Union with Scotland in 1706. Appointed First Lord of the Treasury to GEORGE I, he died suddenly in May 1715. He was a friend of NEWTON, and patron of Joseph ADDISON, William CONGREVE and PRIOR; his vanity was satirized by POPE in his *Epistle to Dr Arbuthnot*.

MONTAGU, EDWARD (styled Viscount Mandeville, Baron Kimbolton, 2nd Earl of Manchester) (1602–71), soldier. Hostile to CHARLES I in the 1640 crisis, he was nearly arrested along with the 'five members' of the Commons in 1642 and, later that year, became one of the leading Parliamentary commanders when war broke out. He defeated Royalist forces at Marston Moor (1644) but in increasing defeatist gloom, and under pressure from his erstwhile subordinate Oliver CROMWELL, he resigned in 1645. He kept on the edge of Interregnum politics during the 1650s, but his part (as Speaker of the House of Lords) in hastening the restoration of CHARLES II brought him rehabilitation.

MONTAGU (OR MOUNTAGU), EDWARD (1st Earl of Sandwich) (1625–72), sailor. Montagu

fought for Parliament during the Civil Wars of the 1640s and was prominent in the government of Oliver CROMWELL's protectorate and in its naval campaigns. Richard CROMWELL's fall in 1659 drove him to Royalism, and he collaborated with George MONCK in bringing CHARLES II back to England. Rewarded with an earldom, he resumed his naval career, although his interest in quick profits through plunder rather than a broad strategy limited England's maritime success. In the Second Dutch War (1665–7) he commanded the fleet at the Battle of Lowestoft (1665), but was killed while in command in the Battle of Sole Bay at the beginning of the Third Dutch War. His journal, while lacking the universal appeal of his admiring subordinate Samuel PEPYS's diary, is an important historical source.

MONTAGU, EDWIN (1879–1924), politician. Montagu was the second son of a wealthy Jewish merchant banker who had been created Lord Swaythling in 1907 by CAMPBELL-BANNERMAN, and bequeathed Edwin a considerable sum of money on his marriage, provided that he married a Jewess. After Cambridge, where he was president of the Union, he became Liberal MP for the Chesterton division of Cambs. in 1906, a seat which he held until 1922.

He was ASQUITH's private secretary until 1910, with access to the inner circle when Asquith became Prime Minister in 1908. Asquith, who nicknamed him 'the Assyrian', had more regard for Montagu's wealth and contacts than he had for his character but made him successively Parliamentary Under-Secretary of State for India (1910–14) and Financial Secretary to the Treasury (1914–15), and regarded him as a dutiful follower. His marriage in 1915 to Asquith's confidante Venetia Stanley (who converted to Judaism to avoid the loss of her inheritance) came as a blow to the Prime Minister, as did his decision in 1917 to serve under LLOYD GEORGE.

From 1917 until 1922 Montagu was Secretary of State for India, where he proved himself a determined reformer. The so-called Montagu–Chelmsford reforms of 1919 which introduced a greater measure of self-government for India were, in fact, the product of Montagu's own fertile imagination. Montagu always attracted a certain amount of anti-Semitism, and his position rested largely upon Lloyd George's patronage. His disagreement with Lloyd George's policy towards Turkey in 1922 led to his resignation and the effective end of his political career.

MONTAGU, ELIZABETH (née Robinson) (1720–1800), intellectual and founder of bluestocking circle. Unusually well educated for a woman of her time, her early interest in literature was nurtured by her step-grandfather, Conyers MIDDLETON. She wrote vivacious irreverent letters (signed 'Fidget') to Lady Margaret Harley, the future Duchess of Portland, of whose literary circle she became a member, and continued to be a prodigious letter writer all her life. In 1742 she married Edward Montagu, grandson of the 1st Earl of Sandwich, a man nearly 30 years her senior and cousin of Lady Mary Wortley MONTAGU. Establishing her own literary salon, she permitted the wearing of blue stockings rather than the customary black silk. Her fellow 'bluestockings' included Elizabeth CARTER and Hester CHAPONE and the term came to apply in general to women with intellectual interests. After her wealthy husband's death in 1775 she became a patron of young writers and artists, and also a champion of the cause of child chimneysweeps. Her only published works comprise three dialogues in Lyttelton's *Dialogues of the Dead* (1760) and a spirited but anonymous repudiation of Voltaire's contempt in the *Writings and Genius of Shakespeare* (1769).

MONTAGU, JOHN (4th Earl of Sandwich) (1718–92), politician and naval administrator. Succeeding to his peerage at the age of 11, he was educated at Eton and Cambridge, then went on a prolonged Grand Tour. Returning to England, he became member of the 'Bedford gang' of politicians associated with John RUSSELL, Duke of Bedford, and served as a Lord of the Admiralty under PELHAM. He was dismissed with Bedford in 1751 and with him co-ordinated opposition to Pelham's Jewish Naturalization Bill in 1753, with an eye to influencing the imminent election. He was First Lord of the Admiralty and Secretary of State under George GRENVILLE, and re-appointed First Lord in 1771, serving throughout the War of American Independence. This saw embarrassing incidents such as the Battle of Ushant and the subsequent court martial of KEPPEL and the humiliating prospect of Britain losing command of the seas in the face of war with all the other major maritime powers. He is enduringly commemorated in the sandwich, a form of snack he favoured because it enabled him to continue playing cards while eating.

MONTAGU, LADY MARY WORTLEY (née Pierrepont) (1689–1762), traveller and writer. Eldest daughter of the Duke of Kingston, she taught herself Latin and became a friend of Mary ASTELL and a group of Whig writers including Joseph ADDISON and Richard STEELE, and later of POPE, and contributed to *The Spectator*. In 1716 she went to Turkey with her husband Edward, who had been appointed Ambassador; returning to England in 1718 she promoted the Turkish practice of inoculation against smallpox. From 1739

until 1758 she lived on the continent, largely in Italy. Her letters were published in 1763 and 1767; they were praised by Samuel JOHNSON and Voltaire for their lively and informal style and were widely read. Her collected works were first published in 1803.

MONTAGU (OR MOUNTAGUE), RICHARD (1577–1641), churchman. One of the Arminian clique of ceremonialist and sacramentalist clergy at Cambridge University, Montagu used his chaplaincy to JAMES I (from 1617) as protection, while infuriating the establishment with outspoken publications minimizing the difference between the Church of England and Roman Catholicism, attacking Puritans and exalting the monarchy. Ignoring successive Parliamentary calls for his punishment, in 1628 CHARLES I made him Bishop of Chichester and, 10 years later, of Norwich. His death saved him from Parliament's revenge.

MONTAGU (OR MONTACUTE), THOMAS DE (9th [4th Montagu] Earl of Salisbury) (1388–1428), courtier and soldier. He regained the title in 1421 that his father John had forfeited for treason in 1400. A popular commander, he fought in France from 1415, distinguishing himself at Harfleur and Agincourt and, after being created Lieutenant General of Normandy, at Meulan and Verneuil. He returned briefly to England in 1427 to arrange the back pay of his men, before returning to lay siege to Orléans, where he was killed by a shot from a cannon.

MONTEFIORE, SIR MOSES (1784–1885), Italian-born British philanthropist. The dominant figure in Anglo-Jewry in the nineteenth century, as President of the Board of Deputies of British Jews (1835–74) he played a leading role in the struggle to remove Jewish disabilities (Jews were admitted to Parliament in 1858) and was equally significant in promoting the claims of oppressed co-religionists in Poland, Russia, Romania and Damascus.

MONTFORT, SIMON DE *see* essay on pages 572–73

MONTGOMERIE, ALEXANDER (c. 1545–1610), poet. From an Ayrshire gentry family and at the Stewart court from 1578, he became poet laureate. While travelling in Europe in 1586 he was imprisoned, and spent many years fighting to retain his royal pension. He wrote courtly, allegorical and satirical verse.

MONTGOMERY, COUNTESS OF *see* CLIFFORD, ANNE

MONTFORT, SIMON DE (*c.* 1208–65)
Soldier and nobleman

Few men have provoked more hatred and more admiration from their contemporaries. In the name of justice he challenged the assumptions on which English royal government was based and led the country into civil war. In the end he and 30 of his friends were killed in the Battle of Evesham because his enemies decided that, in defiance of the chivalrous conventions which had governed warfare in England for the previous 200 years, they should be killed.

When the battle or, rather, as a contemporary historian, ROBERT OF GLOUCESTER, put it, 'the murder of Evesham, for battle it was none', was over, the victors mutilated Simon's body, cutting off his head, hands, feet and testicles. What was left of him was buried in Evesham Abbey and his tomb became the goal of a popular pilgrimage.

In songs he was compared with both Christ and Thomas BECKET for his readiness to sacrifice himself for the good of all. Authority tried in vain to suppress the cult. Before 1280 over 200 miracles had been credited to the posthumous power of a political saint. In 1266 a dinner party broke up as the guests quarrelled about Simon, and when one of them who was running him down suffered a stroke.

He had been the leader of the most fundamental attempt to redistribute power within the English State before the seventeenth century, a reform movement which subverted the royal prerogative by taking out of the King's hands the right to choose and appoint Councillors, distribute patronage and summon Parliament.

This remarkable trouble-maker was the third son of two remarkable parents, leaders of the crusade against the Albigensians which was launched in 1209. His father was Simon de Montfort senior (whose family seat was at Montfort l'Amaury, about 50 kilometres west of Paris); his mother was the equally devout and energetic Alice de Montmorency.

Because they chose to take their children with them on that pious and brutal campaign against heretics, it seems that Simon's earliest years were spent in an atmosphere of religious fervour and military excitement. He was present at the great siege of Toulouse where his father was killed in 1218. But virtually nothing is known of the 12 years of his life between that siege and 1230, when he left France for England.

As a son of Amicia, sister and co-heiress of Robert de Beaumont, Earl of Leicester, who died childless in 1204, Simon senior had had a claim to a share of the Leicester estates; Simon now hoped to succeed where both his father and elder brother had, in practice, failed. Thanks to the generosity of King HENRY III, and doubtless to his own persuasive charm, in 1231 he obtained the Leicester lands. One of his first decisions was to expel the Jews from Leicester, the act of an uncompromising and militant Christian.

Described by a contemporary as 'tall, handsome and full of energy', he either seduced or came close to seducing the King's sister Eleanor. Their quiet marriage in a chapel in the King's chamber in 1238 brought with it a dower which trebled his income. But the dower income was for the term of her life only, and could not be inherited by any of their six surviving children. Simon faced huge financial difficulties if he wanted to provide for them as befitted King JOHN's grandchildren.

Eloquent, highly educated and a fine soldier, the aristocratic virtue which Simon most conspicuously lacked was generosity. Throughout his political career his public idealism was to be hopelessly entangled with his private money problems. They began by undermining his friendship with Henry in 1239, which led to him going on crusade in 1240–1; they ended by triggering the collapse of his own autocratic rule in 1265. In 1248 he accepted the King's commission to pacify Gascony. When complaints about his arbitrary conduct poured in, Henry set up an investigation into his rule in 1252, and opened proceedings with a denunciation of his own.

But by now Simon had many friends in England, especially among leading churchmen, and they stood by him. Irritated by Henry's incompetence, Simon was one of the magnates who on 30 April 1258 went armed to Westminster Hall. 'Am I your prisoner?' asked Henry. Despite the re-assurances that he was given, so he was.

In June Henry and his heir (later to be EDWARD I) were forced to accept the Provisions of Oxford, which in the name of the community of England established a governing council of 15 which was required to consult at three specified times a year with a committee of 12 magnates in Parliament. Simon was appointed to the council of 15, and he like everyone else took an oath to observe the provisions. It was this oath that he always insisted must be kept, even after the Pope, in 1261, had declared it invalid. Those who did not keep it he called traitors.

In July 1258 Henry, sheltering from a thunderstorm, told Simon that much as he feared lightning 'by God's head I fear you more than all the thunder and lightning in the world'. Since Matthew PARIS, who reported these words, died in 1259 he could not know what Simon was to do in 1264–5.

For most of 1259 Simon was in France, involved in negotiations with Louis IX of France and resisting (although in the end in vain) any renunciation by his wife of her claim to the Angevin lands in France. Even so the further extension of the reform programme by which magnates agreed to place themselves under the same restraints as royal officials (Ordinance of Magnates in Feb. and Provisions of Westminster in Oct. 1259) owed much to Simon's recognition of the value of support from the gentry and others. But whereas most lords had been happy to see royal administration (both central and local) overhauled, many were disturbed by the prospect of interference with seigneurial (i.e. their own) administration.

Simon's reputation as a hard-liner was reinforced in 1260 when he insisted that Parliament should meet at the specified times whether or not the King was present. Henry III saw the opportunity to open up splits in the ranks of the aristocracy, and so to resume power in 1261. When other magnates acquiesced, Simon went abroad, for he was still at home in France as well as in England.

Two years later, with dissatisfaction with Henry's rule once more widespread, Simon's uncompromising record made him the obvious leader of the opposition. He rejected the arbitration settlement, the Mise of Amiens, made by Louis IX in Jan. 1264. Now at bay, his natural instinct was to fight rather than negotiate, and civil war soon broke out.

Against the odds, his aggressive generalship won the Battle of Lewes on 14 May 1264; as a result both Henry and Edward became his prisoners. The Parliament of June 1264, to which he summoned knights as representatives of the counties, confirmed a new scheme of government: three electors (Simon, Gilbert de CLARE, Earl of Gloucester, and Stephen Berksted, Bishop of Chichester) chose a Council of Nine which controlled the King. He became the *de facto* ruler of an England under constant threat of French-backed invasion from royalists who had fled abroad. To meet this he transferred many of the sheriffs' powers to keepers of the peace chosen by and responsible only to him.

In a further attempt to legitimize his regime and to give recognition to those who had sent forces to repel invasion in 1264, he summoned both knights of the shire and burgesses to a Parliament in Jan. 1265, hence the nineteenth-century view of him as the founder of the House of Commons. But his use of government patronage to enrich his family made him vulnerable to the charge that he was ultimately self-seeking, perhaps even aiming at the throne. This, together with his confidence in his own rectitude, exasperated many of his peers, most crucially Gilbert de Clare.

When Edward escaped from custody the fighting began again, to culminate at Evesham on the morning of 4 Aug. 1265. As Simon rode into battle wearing a hair shirt beneath his armour, a violent thunderstorm broke over the battlefield, and darkness fell.

The seventeenth-century Civil Wars between Crown and Parliament brought a renewed interest in the Earl; for some he prefigured Oliver CROMWELL but, not until the Victorian period, and the dominance of the Commons over the Lords, did Simon really come into his own as a visionary reformer and a founder of Parliament; as, in STUBBS's words, 'a buccaneering old GLADSTONE', a role which recent historians have increasingly denied him.

The later twentieth-century view that his 'political principles were a rationalization of his prejudices' and that his 'political leadership was a succession of blunders redeemed by a single battle' hardly does justice to his friendship with some of the most ardent moralists of the age, men such as Robert GROSSETESTE and the Franciscan Adam Marsh, nor to the qualities which in 1241 had led the barons of Jerusalem to ask for him as their governor.

Although Parliament as such was peripheral to his concerns, there is no doubt that two deeply entrenched political theories clashed in 1258 and after. One was the idea of sacred authoritarian monarchy, rather ineffectually represented by Henry III, pious but incompetent; the other was the notion of a limited monarchy within the community of the realm, an idea upheld by many in 1258 but, as time went by, more and more dependent upon the driving force, idealism and ambition of Simon de Montfort.

J. R. Maddicott, Simon de Montfort (1994)

MONTGOMERY, BERNARD LAW *see* essay on page 575

MONTROSE, 3RD EARL OF *see* GRAHAM, JOHN; **5TH EARL AND 1ST MARQUESS OF** *see* GRAHAM, JAMES

MOORE, FRANCIS (1657–1715), astrologer. A schoolmaster and physician in Lambeth, he first published his almanac in 1699, with the aim of helping farmers to predict the weather. Expanded, the pamphlet re-appeared as *Vox Stellarum* in 1700, containing predictions of the next year. It became known as *Old Moore's Almanack* and new editions appeared annually for the next three centuries.

MOORE, GEORGE (1852–1933), novelist and playwright. Born in Co. Mayo, the son of a race-horse-owning Irish MP, Moore studied art in Paris for 10 years before going to London in 1880. His realist novels, influenced by Zola but set in Victorian Britain, culminated in his finest book, *Esther Waters* (1894). In 1899, opposed to the British government's prosecution of the Boer War, he left his job as an art critic to return to Ireland where he converted from Catholicism to Protestantism. He was to be a major force in the Irish cultural revival, writing plays for the Abbey Theatre in Dublin (*see also* HORNIMAN, ANNIE).

MOORE, G(EORGE) E(DWARD) (1873–1958), philosopher. An outstanding student at Cambridge, Moore was a member of the invitation-only discussion group, the Apostles, at a time of intellectual effervescence (Lytton STRACHEY and KEYNES were contemporaries) and in 1898 was elected a Prize Fellow at Trinity. He returned to Cambridge as lecturer in moral science (1911–25) and then Professor of Philosophy (1925–39). Trained in the neo-Hegelian idealist tradition current at the time, Moore (with Bertrand RUSSELL) was in the forefront of the fight back to realism (a philosophy that fitted with the familiar world of 'tables and chairs') and a concentration on epistemology and ethics. The titles of his most celebrated papers track his route: 'The Refutation of Idealism' (1903), 'The Defence of Common Sense' (1925), 'A Proof of the External World' (1939). Solidly a Cambridge man of kindness and transparent integrity and an outstanding teacher, Moore's great work *Principia Ethica* (1903), his collected papers and his editorship of the philosophy journal *Mind* (1921–47) had a profound effect on philosophy. His insistence on clarity of language and precision of meaning paved the way for the development of linguistic philosophy. But his argument in *Principia Ethica* that 'personal affection and aesthetic enjoyments' are pre-eminently 'good' also proved fertile ground for his friends among the Bloomsbury group.

MOORE, HENRY (1898–1986), sculptor. The son of a Yorks. miner, Moore, who was gassed at Cambrai during the First World War, trained at Leeds School of Art on an ex-serviceman's grant and at the Royal College of Art, where he later taught, moving to Chelsea School of Art in 1930. The first of his many public commissions was *West Wind* (1928–9) for London Transport. Drawing inspiration from the vitality of the stone, wood and bronze with which he worked, from natural, organic forms, but also from Mexican and pre-Columbian art, Moore cast huge reclining female figures, the persistent idiom of his work. He was appointed an official war artist during the Second World War; his figures taking refuge in bomb shelters and underground stations are haunting evocations of a 'people's war'. From this time Moore began to receive international acclaim, winning honours at the Venice Biennale (1948), and contributing *Festival Reclining Figure* to the Festival of Britain (1951); his sculptures became ubiquitous in urban spaces throughout the world's buildings, for example, the UNESCO building in Paris (1956–7).

MOORE, JOHN (*c.* 1599–1650), politician. Son of a Liverpool gentleman, he was MP for the town in the Long Parliament (1640) and kept diaries of parliamentary proceedings; he served in Parliamentary armies during the Civil War of 1642–6, losing Liverpool to the Royalists in 1644–5 but campaigning effectively in Ireland from 1645 to 1648. He was active in PRIDE's Purge of Presbyterians from Parliament (1648) and was one of the signatories of CHARLES I's death warrant, but then returned to Ireland to further military success before dying of disease.

MOORE, SIR JOHN (1761–1809), soldier. On the outbreak of the American Revolution in 1776, his father, who had served as a military surgeon during the War of Austrian Succession, bought Moore a commission in the 51st Foot. He saw action against the Americans in Nova Scotia (1778), the French in Corsica (1793), guerrilla bands of escaped slaves on St Lucia (1797), Irish rebels at New Cross and Wexford (1798) and the French in Holland (1799) and in Egypt (1801). During this period he was severely wounded four times, survived two attacks of yellow fever, and rose to the rank of Colonel.

In 1803, with Britain facing invasion, Moore was appointed to command a brigade at Shorncliffe. He had developed radical ideas about tactics, training and discipline, which he now put into

continued on page 576

MONTGOMERY, BERNARD LAW (1st Viscount Montgomery of Alamein) (1887–1976)

Soldier

The fourth child of a vicar, Montgomery grew up in Hobart, Australia, and entered Sandhurst in Jan. 1907. He excelled in team sports, but was regarded (and regarded himself) as an outsider. Brought up strictly, Montgomery was terrified of his mother and hated her as a grown man. His biographers have sought the key to his personality – a combination of meticulous attention to detail, grotesque self-advertisement, and occasional reckless risk-taking – in this emotionally fraught relationship.

Commissioned into the 1st Battalion of the Warws. Regiment in 1908, Montgomery spent four years in India, before being posted back to Britain before the First World War. In August 1914 he displayed exemplary leadership and courage during fighting at Le Cateau; two months later he was severely wounded but on his recovery in the spring of 1915 returned to France. Reaching the rank of lieutenant colonel, he was involved in planning the operations of IX Corps, part of Herbert Plumer's 3rd Corps. In contrast to the slaughter of the early years of the war, by 1917 Plumer had perfected the tactics of 'bite and hold', in which infantry supported by armour advanced methodically behind a barrage. The objectives were limited but casualties were relatively light.

During the inter-war years, Montgomery held a variety of appointments: with the Army of the Rhine (1919), in Ireland (1921–2) and in Palestine (1930s) as well as the Army Staff colleges at Camberley and Quetta (1920, 1926 and 1934). The sudden death of his wife in 1937 left him emotionally bereft, and the Second World War for him was a godsend. Managing to secure command of 3rd Division in Sept. 1939, Montgomery was attached to Alan BROOKE's Corps in northern France. Montgomery's superb handling of his division in covering the retreat to Dunkirk in May 1940 convinced Brooke that he should be selected for high command. Promoted to Lieutenant General in July 1940, he quickly rose to head South Eastern Command, and in Aug. to commander of the Eighth Army which the German commander Rommel's smaller Axis forces had chased eastward to El Alamein, only 50 miles west of Alexandria. Knowing that his forces could not manoeuvre successfully against Rommel, Montgomery reverted to the methods of the First World War, remaining on the defensive, allowing Rommel to smash the Afrika Korps against Eighth Army defences on Alam Haifa ridge. A delighted Winston CHURCHILL urged an immediate offensive, but Montgomery refused until he had been substantially reinforced. The subsequent Battle of El Alamein, fought from 23 Oct. to 5 Nov., proved that he had been right, and the victory made him a national hero.

Montgomery displayed considerable skill in Tunisia, but his relations with his new American allies, particularly the flamboyant General Patton, became increasingly strained. Recalled to Britain in Dec. 1943, Montgomery directed the planning of the final stages of Operation Overlord, the Allied invasion of France, and commanded the land forces for the actual assault on 6 June 1944. Between 13 June and 26 July he expanded the beachhead at Normandy, but, unable to break out, was saved from dismissal only by Brooke's unwavering support. When the breakout came on 1 Aug. in the American sector, the slow British advance towards Falaise allowed tens of thousands of Germans to escape eastwards. Montgomery's relations with the Americans now spiralled downwards, a process accelerated by the ill grace with which he relinquished army group command to the inexperienced Eisenhower. In Sept. 1944, with Germany apparently on the verge of collapse, the normally cautious Montgomery secured US approval for a dash on a narrow front across the lower Rhine to encircle the Ruhr: the subsequent disaster left his American allies with little respect for his competence. Poised to cross the Rhine and advance on Berlin at the end of March 1945, Montgomery was ordered instead to advance north and leave the German capital to the Russians, an order which made little strategic sense (in later years Eisenhower came close to admitting that he had issued it to spite his difficult subordinate).

Britain bestowed honours and high office on Montgomery – he was appointed Field Marshal (1944), made a Viscount (1946) and Deputy Supreme Commander of NATO (1951–8). The publication of his *Memoirs* in 1958 upset many of his British colleagues as well as former American allies. Montgomery possessed enormous strengths: many British generals would have been defeated at Alamein and in Normandy, and he won these battles without squandering the lives of his men. But his corresponding arrogance and self-righteousness made him a hindrance in forging good relations with an increasingly powerful American ally. In an address to Sandhurst cadets shortly before his death Montgomery claimed: 'There have been three truly great generals in history – Alexander the Great, Napoleon … and me.' Nobody disagreed at the time but everyone in the audience knew he was wrong.

N. Hamilton, *Monty: The Battles of Field Marshal Bernard Montgomery* (1999) effect. Moore's brigade was trained as light infantry, which could either support a more conventionally trained army or, in the event of a massive French landing, break up into small units and act as guerrillas: emphasis was placed on the development of intelligence and individual initiative. The Shorncliffe experiment became the object of considerable interest and controversy, and the camp was visited by the Prime Minister and most senior military officers.

In 1808 Moore's reputation virtually assured his appointment as commander of the reconstituted expeditionary force in Portugal. Encouraged by reports of continued Spanish resistance to the French, in the autumn he advanced from Portugal to within a few days march of Madrid. On 23 Dec., however, after receiving reports that much larger French armies were closing in, he began a gruelling 250-mile retreat to the coast at Corunna. Here on 16 Jan. 1809 Moore was killed in a gallant rearguard action which enabled the bulk of his army to evacuate through the port. At first his march into Spain was severely criticized but it was soon learned that the incursion had so perturbed Napoleon that he had come to command French armies in the Peninsula himself. Moore's fame was assured when Napoleon praised him as a 'brave soldier, an excellent officer and a man of talent', and his work at Shorncliffe proved to be of enduring significance.

MOORE, PATRICK (1923–), astronomer and broadcaster. In 1952, after 12 years in the Royal Air Force, Moore combined his early interest in astronomy and his communication skills to start a career as a freelance author. Through his numerous popular books and, above all, his long-running television series, *The Sky at Night*, first broadcast in 1968, he has gained international fame and greatly promoted interest in astronomy.

MOORES, SIR JOHN (1896–1993), entrepreneur. After an elementary education and a period as a messenger boy and then as a cable telegraph operator, Moores began the Liverpool-based Littlewoods football pool in 1923, exploiting new freedoms in small-stake gambling. Within 10 years he was a millionaire and by the outbreak of war in 1939 he had also founded a Littlewoods mail-order business and retailing chain. By 1990 Littlewoods had become Britain's richest family business worth £1.6 billion. Moores retired in 1977 but, when transfer of control within the family proved difficult and profits fell, he returned as Chairman (1980–2). Life President of the company, he was a generous patron of education and the arts.

MORAY, EARL OF, 1ST *see* RANDOLPH, THOMAS; **4TH** and **15TH** *see* GORDON, GEORGE; **16TH** and **17TH** *see* STEWART, JAMES

MORAY OF BOTHWELL, ANDREW (?–1297), heir to great estates in Moray and Lanarkshire. He resisted the proposed capitulation of 1297 to EDWARD I, leading the rising in Scotland north of the Tay. He joined forces with William WALLACE and inflicted a humiliating defeat on the English at Stirling Bridge (11 Sept. 1297). Moray was mortally wounded in the battle.

MORAY OF BOTHWELL, ANDREW (1297–1338), Scottish leader. Posthumous son of Andrew MORAY (the hero of 1297), he married Christian, sister of ROBERT BRUCE. By copying his brother-in-law's military strategy he became the most successful leader of Scottish resistance to EDWARD III in the late 1330s. After some defeats, his St Andrews Day (30 Nov.) victory in the Battle of Culblean (Aberdeens.) (1335) was regarded as a turning-point in the war and led to his re-appointment as guardian of Scotland on behalf of the young DAVID II.

MORCAR (?–*c*. 1090), Earl of Northumbria (1065–8). The son of Earl ÆLFGAR of Mercia and the brother of Earl EDWIN of Mercia, Morcar was chosen as their Earl in 1065 by the Northumbrian rebels against TOSTIG. Acknowledged as Earl by EDWARD THE CONFESSOR and HAROLD II, he was initially accepted by WILLIAM I THE CONQUEROR, but subsequently rebelled in 1068. After his capture on the Isle of Ely with HEREWARD THE WAKE in 1071 he was kept in prison for almost all of the rest of his life.

MORE, HANNAH (1745–1833), writer on morals and religion. Daughter of an excise officer and schoolmaster, she was educated at home, then with her sisters ran a boarding school. On going to London in the 1770s she mixed with Elizabeth MONTAGU's bluestockings, and with Horace WALPOLE, Samuel JOHNSON and GARRICK. She published several poems and tragedies but, after Garrick's death, she turned against the theatre, and became increasingly concerned with the reformation of manners and Evangelical religion. She became a friend of WILBERFORCE and other members of the Clapham Sect. In response to the popular radicalism associated with the French Revolution, she published *Village Politics* (1792) and followed this with a series of conservative *Cheap Repository Tracts* (1795–8), circulated by voluntary committees. Settling with her sisters in Cheddar (Som.), she encouraged female friendly societies, and set up Sunday schools, one of which, at Blagdon, was attacked by the local clergyman as a conventicle or illegal Dissenting chapel under the terms of the Conventicle Act 1664, touching off a fierce controversy. A successful novel, *Coelebs in Search of a Wife*, appeared in 1809.

MORE, HENRY (1614–87), theologian. Son of a strong Calvinist, he was educated at Eton and Christ's College, Cambridge, where he became a Fellow in 1639. In the 1640s he had several poems published, which expressed his devotion to the ideas of Plato. He is commonly classed among the Cambridge Platonists, with Ralph CUDWORTH and Benjamin WHICHCOTE. His most enduring work was the *Divine Dialogues* (1668), which remained in print well into the eighteenth century, containing examinations of the nature and being of God as revealed in the created universe.

MORE, THOMAS *see essay on pages 578–79*

MORECAMBE, ERIC (originally Eric Bartholomew) (1926–84), comedian. Taking his stage name from his seaside home town, he began his career in variety theatre before the Second World War. He teamed up with Ernie Wise in 1941, and taking inspiration from the quick-fire repartee of Abbott and Costello and the visual humour of Laurel and Hardy (*see* LAUREL, STAN), the pair found success in the 1960s with *The Morecambe and Wise Show* starting on ITV and then switching to the BBC, where it stayed throughout the 1970s. The Christmas shows became almost a national institution, attracting an unprecedented 28 million viewers in 1977.

MORGAN AP OWAIN (?–974), King of Gwent and Glywsing. Under Morgan there were changes in the kingship of the small south Wales kingdoms of Gwent and Glywsing, as he, unlike his forebears over the preceding two centuries, did not share the kingship with other members of his family. Accompanying ATHELSTAN in his campaign into Scotland in 934 against CONSTANTÍN II, Morgan acted as witness in surviving West-Saxon charters, where he is described as Sub-King. Nevertheless, he appears to have been a formidable enough ruler, for the kingdom he ruled subsequently became known as Morgannwg, or Glamorgan, 'Morgan's land'.

MORGAN AP OWAIN (?–1158), Welsh King. By killing Richard de CLARE and capturing Caerleon and Usk (both Mon.) in 1136, Morgan, a descendant of the earlier Welsh kings of Glamorgan, ignited the great war of resistance which drew in other more powerful Welsh rulers such as GRUFFUDD AP RHYS and GRUFFUDD AP CYNAN and threatened to reverse the Anglicization of Wales which had gone on apace during the reign of HENRY I. These events caught the imagination of GEOFFREY OF MONMOUTH, who chose to set King ARTHUR's court at the otherwise little known Caerleon. Like other Welsh kings Morgan was drawn into the English civil war, fighting in support of ROBERT OF GLOUCESTER at the 1141 Battle of Lincoln when STEPHEN was captured. For two more generations Morgan's family held on to their 'native enclave' in south-east Wales.

MORGAN, SIR FREDERICK (1894–1967), soldier. Educated at Woolwich, he served with the artillery on the Western Front in the First World War. By 1940 he was in charge of the logistics of 1st Armoured Division in northern France, and organized the evacuation of much valuable equipment through Brest. Chief of Staff, Supreme Allied Command in 1943, he made the administrative arrangements for Operation Overlord, the landings in Normandy. With Eisenhower's appointment as Supreme Allied Commander in June 1944, Morgan became his Deputy Chief of Staff, in which capacity he clashed frequently with MONTGOMERY. In 1945–6 he ran the United Nations Relief and Rehabilitation Administration (UNRRA) in Germany until, clashing with Soviet and Zionist interests, he made too many powerful enemies, who engineered his dismissal. As Controller of Atomic Energy (1951–6), Morgan played a key role in Britain's nuclear weapons programme.

MORGAN, SIR HENRY (*c.* 1635–88), privateer and colonial administrator. A soldier in the army that in 1654 successfully captured Jamaica, he was given the rank of Captain in 1660 and authorized to take a non-commissioned 'private' vessel to defend Jamaica against the Spanish. Morgan was involved in a series of expeditions, and was appointed Commander-in-Chief of all Jamaican forces in 1669. He led an attack on Panama City, resulting in the town's destruction, in 1670, but he had violated an Anglo-Spanish treaty and was sent to London in chains. He nonetheless rapidly gained the friendship of CHARLES II, was knighted and in 1674 returned to Jamaica as Lieutenant Governor, but found his freedom of action limited. Morgan's notorious reputation came from a best-selling book by the Flemish author Oexemelin, published in the Netherlands, Spain and England in 1684, alleging horrific atrocities on Spanish civilians.

MORGAN, WILLIAM (1540?–1604), Bishop of St Asaph. After a Cambridge University career, he was an energetic parish clergyman at Llanrhaeadr-ym-Mochnant (Denbighs.) in 1578, and Llanfyllin (Montgomerys.) from 1579. He was appointed Bishop of Llandaff in 1595 and of St Asaph in 1601. Given enthusiastic support by Archbishop John WHITGIFT in his plan of translating the Bible into

continued on page 580

MORE, THOMAS (1477 or 1478–1535)
Politician and writer

More was educated at St Anthony's School, London, before becoming a page in the household of Cardinal John MORTON, Archbishop of Canterbury, in 1490; Morton provided him with a place at Canterbury College, Oxford. He did not take a university degree, but in 1494 returned to London and to legal study at New Inn and Lincoln's Inn, following his lawyer father's distinguished career; he soon developed a flourishing legal practice. He began building a circle of friends who shared an enthusiasm for the humanist rediscovery of ancient literature, notably Thomas LINACRE, William LILY and John COLET; in 1499 he first met Europe's greatest humanist scholar, Desiderius ERASMUS, and they began a long friendship which would cause Erasmus to pun on his name in one of his most influential secular writings, *The Praise of Folly (Moriae Encomium*, published 1509). He learnt Greek and began composing Latin verse, which took its cue and was in some cases a direct translation from the second-century AD Greek satirical poet Lucian. Yet complementing or warring with the aggressively sexual and physical humour of these writings was an austerity and distaste for his physicality which made him spend perhaps four years living at the London Charterhouse alongside the exceptionally rigorous monastic order of Carthusians; he even contemplated ordination to the priesthood. He lectured on Augustine of Hippo's classic analysis of the division between the earthly and the spiritual, *The City of God*, in the parish church of St Lawrence Jewry near his home.

In 1509 More was first elected to Parliament for the City of London, and throughout his life he showed a fascination with the city of his birth; when he bought a country house at Chelsea (*c.* 1525–6) he built a mound in the garden from which he could enjoy watching the city skyline. His first significant prose work (1513–14) was a history of the reign of RICHARD III, in Latin and an incomplete English version; in humanist style this has as one of its main models the writings of the ancient Roman historian Sallust. A commercial and diplomatic expedition to the Netherlands (1515) brought a friendship with Erasmus' Antwerp friend Peter Gilles, conversations with whom inspired his enigmatic fantasy *Utopia* (published in Latin 1516; translated into English 1551). It was a rapid Europe-wide success, establishing his reputation as one of the elite of humanist writers. The work falls into two parts, the first of which (probably written after the second) is a 'dialogue of counsel' debating the role which men of ideas might play in politics, a concern which then directly affected More himself at the moment of his entry into royal service. The second part, an account of an imaginary society (*Utopia* signifies 'nowhere'), is perhaps best understood as an exploration of the problem which fascinated humanists: how did their delight in the achievements and learning of pagan ancient Greece and Rome relate to their devout Christianity, and their sense that the only true knowledge was the Christian message revealed by God through the Bible and the Church? More's answer is to describe a society without Christianity to show the limits of human perfection when it is unaided by divine revelation; despite the rationality of its citizens and its many admirable features, the commonwealth of Utopia institutionalizes cruelty and slavery. Yet More uses his rhetorical power to disguise his own opinion of what he describes. This sardonically straight-faced distancing of himself from situations was a habit of mind with him, and it became a luxury which he could not afford only in the second half of his career.

In 1516 More joined the Royal Council, and soon grew close to HENRY VIII, undertaking a variety of diplomatic missions; in 1520 he accompanied the King to the meeting with the French King FRANCIS I at the Field of the Cloth of Gold, and in the same year he was knighted. In 1523 he was Speaker of Parliament and by 1525 he had risen to be Chancellor of the Duchy of Lancaster. In the early 1520s he became increasingly horrified at the effect of Martin LUTHER on the Western Church. He was involved in the editing of Henry's attack on Luther, the *Assertio Septem Sacramentorum* – ironically, in the light of later events, urging the King to tone down his proclamation of papal primacy. More himself wrote bitterly against Luther. His literary talents now turned to savage polemic, especially against William TYNDALE, beginning with the *Dialogue Concerning Heresies* (1528); it was now for the first time that he published in English. Henry's growing passion for ANNE BOLEYN, however, brought a serious personal dilemma; More strongly disapproved of Henry's wish to annul his marriage to CATHERINE OF ARAGON, but on the dismissal of

WOLSEY as Lord Chancellor (1529) the King insisted that More should succeed to his office. More made it clear that he could not support the royal quest for annulment, and he found himself increasingly isolated from Henry's inner circle of advisers as they worked on the proposal to break with papal authority. He concentrated on his legal duties and on combating heresy; he went on writing against Tyndale and he encouraged the burning of obstinate heretics, but his position at court grew increasingly unhappy. He resigned the chancellorship on 16 May 1532 after the Convocation of Canterbury had surrendered the English Church's rights to legislate for itself in the Submission of the Clergy; Henry's adulation of him was by now turning to hatred at his obstinate defiance.

More's prestige made him an obvious symbol of opposition, and he continued writing against the champion of royal supremacy, Christopher ST GERMAN, in the *Debellation of Salem and Byzance* (1533); he also wrote against the radical eucharistic views of John FRITH in *The Answer to a Poisoned Book*. He showed a cautious interest in Elizabeth BARTON's prophecies of the doom which would befall the King if he abandoned Catherine, and although he survived one examination by the King's Councillors without arrest, he could now see that disaster was drawing close. His writings shifted from the harsh polemic of the previous few years to devotional themes, first *A Treatise on the Passion*, in which his meditation on the sufferings of Christ were a reflection of his own situation. This was left incomplete because he was arrested in April 1534, examined once more by royal commissioners led by Thomas CROMWELL and taken to the Tower of London. His first work written in the Tower, *A Dialogue of Comfort against Tribulation*, allegorizes the situation of his beloved Catholic Church in the fictional setting of Hungary, recently devastated by Ottoman armies. His formidable discretion and legal acumen were now no defence against Henry's fury at his rejecting the royal supremacy; he consistently refused to swear the Act of Succession's oath of loyalty to the heirs of Henry and Anne Boleyn, and in Oct. he was attainted by Act of Parliament along with Bishop John FISHER. Now, in much more rigorous confinement, he began his last work, the Latin treatise *De Tristitia Christi*, returning to the theme of Christ's sufferings. On 1 July 1535, four days after Fisher was executed, he was tried under the provisions of the new Treason Act; his plea of not guilty could not save him from condemnation, the crucial evidence of a supposedly treasonous conversation in the Tower being supplied by his old acquaintance Richard RICH. He was beheaded five days later; the execution, like that of Fisher, shocked his admirers all over Europe. Any effort to create a martyr cult for the two men in the revived Catholic Church of MARY I was rendered very difficult by the fact that so many of their former enemies like Stephen GARDINER were then still in positions of power, but in a piece of private enterprise his family brought out a complete edition of his writings in English (1557). He was canonized by the Roman Catholic Church in May 1935.

More's image has been immortalized in portrait studies by HOLBEIN. Most symbolic was the painting of him amid his family (*c.* 1528), the completed version of which is now destroyed, but which in surviving sketches and copies symbolizes an essential dimension of his career, that his life was centred on the close and affectionate life of his household, presided over by his strong-minded second wife Alice Middleton. He remains a compelling and paradoxical figure: he was a master of humour, ranging from delicate irony to cheerful bawdy, who turned to contemplating the tragedy of human existence; a man of close and warm relationships who yet prized his solitariness, and who abandoned it only in the loneliness of prison in order to write of his own sense of pain and loss at the break-up of Christendom. His personal kindness and generosity faltered in his treatment of heresy, where his urgent sense of crisis made him feel that it was necessary to be cruel to individuals in order to avoid a greater cruelty to the whole company of Christendom. His career is an object lesson in the problems which faced Renaissance humanists when they put into effect their passionate belief that their scholarship and rhetorical skills should be applied to the business of government, and should form the basis of statecraft. In *Utopia* he created a work which has not ceased to provoke questions about the nature of social relations and the values of human society, yet which refuses to supply ready-made answers to those questions.

Richard Marius, Thomas More (1984)

Welsh, he published his translation in 1588 (the first complete one; *see also* SALESBURY, WILLIAM). Vigorous and direct, it played a crucial role in preserving the Welsh language and reconciling Welsh literary culture to the Protestant establishment.

MORGANWG, IOLO *see* WILLIAMS, EDWARD, essay on page 844

MORICE, RALPH (*c.* 1505–70), administrator. From a precociously Protestant Essex gentry family, he studied at Cambridge; here he may have formed the acquaintance with Thomas CRANMER which led him (through the intercession of George BOLEYN, Lord Rochford) to become the Archbishop's long-serving secretary from the early 1530s. He used his court contacts to save Cranmer from betrayal in the Prebendaries' Plot (1543) and supplied John FOXE with many stories which form a unique insight into court politics under HENRY VIII.

MORLAND, SIR SAMUEL (1625–95), inventor and diplomat. In 1653 he became secretary to Bulstrode WHITELOCKE and subsequently to John THURLOE (1654). While working for the Protectorate he secretly communicated with CHARLES II and was made a baronet at the Restoration. In financial difficulties as a result of trying to live up to the grandeur of the new court, he turned to engineering. In 1675 he acquired Vauxhall House in Kennington, which included a workshop. Among his inventions was a perpendicular-action pump used to supply water to Windsor Castle, as well as a plan for a steam engine similar to that later developed by WATT. He is often associated with the opening to the public of Vauxhall Gardens, longest-lived of the London pleasure gardens, but the gardens were attached to a Vauxhall inn rather than Morland's house and were already open to the public a decade before Morland moved there.

MORLEY, JOHN (1838–1923), biographer and politician. Defying his father's wish that he should enter the Church, Morley supported himself by writing penny-a-line articles on politics and literary and social matters for a number of periodicals: he was editor of the *Literary Gazette* (1860), the *Fortnightly Review* (1867–82), the *Pall Mall Gazette* (1880–3) and *Macmillan's Magazine* (1883–5). Under his editorship the *Fortnightly Review* became an opinion-forming journal and brought him into contact with most of the important politicians of the day. In 1883 he was elected a Liberal MP. Appointed Irish Secretary in 1886, and again from 1892–5, Morley was active with GLADSTONE in drafting and piloting through the Commons the Home Rule Bills (1886 and 1893)

which sought to solve the Irish problem, but in so doing fissured the Liberal Party. Morley perfected the Victorian genre of brief lives, including those of *Burke* (1879) (*see* BURKE, EDMUND) and *Walpole* (1889) (*see* WALPOLE, ROBERT), and edited the *English Men of Letters* series (1878–92). His monument is his exhaustive *Life of Gladstone* (1903), and his essay *On Compromise* (1874) proved to be a thoughtful contribution to the debate about where the Liberals should be heading.

MORLEY, SAMUEL (1809–86), businessman and politician. Born in Hackney (London), he was the son of a Nottingham hosiery manufacturer and was the sole owner of the business from 1860. He favoured the development of 'responsible' trade unionism in so far as it helped business stability. An active radical, he established the Administrative Reform Association in 1855, which sought open competitive examination for Civil Service entry. He became the main Liberal financial backer of the Reform League (1865–9) and an important conduit between the Liberal Party and working-class reformers. MP for Bristol (1868–85), he was in many ways typical of the Nonconformist radical Liberal in campaigning for the disestablishment of the Irish Church and the ending of religious tests in universities. He was a vigorous supporter of the London School Board (1870–6) and of Joseph ARCH's Agricultural Labourers' Union from 1872. He also owned the *Daily News*.

MORLEY, THOMAS (1557–1602), composer. A pupil of William BYRD, he was organist of St Paul's, London, *c.* 1589–92 and gentleman of the Chapel Royal from 1592. He wrote choral Church music (in English and Latin), instrumental and keyboard works and published *A Plaine and Easie Introduction to Practicall Musicke* (1597). His madrigals are considered outstanding, and he edited madrigals by various composers in *The Triumphs of Oriana* (1601) in honour of ELIZABETH I.

MORNINGTON, EARL OF *see* WELLESLEY, RICHARD

MORRELL, LADY OTTOLINE (née Cavendish-Bentinck) (1873–1938), hostess. Singular in every way, she was intellectual, unconventional and managed to be both gauche and exotic. She studied briefly at Somerville College, Oxford, became a close friend of ASQUITH, with whom she shared literary interests, and married a solicitor, Philip Morrell, who became Liberal MP for South Oxfordshire in 1906. She was a hostess of great literary and political command; guests at her regular 'at homes' in her London house in Bedford Square and, after 1913, at Garsington Manor

(Oxon.), included W. B. YEATS, Katherine MANSFIELD, Leonard and Virginia WOOLF, Lytton STRACHEY, KEYNES and other 'Bloomsberries'. Both the Morrells were pacifists, and during the First World War their home was a refuge for conscientious objectors. Ottoline was the mistress of several famous men, including Augustus JOHN and Bertrand RUSSELL; she was perceptive in spotting and encouraging literary talent in the young (T. S. ELIOT is an example) and was hurt and bewildered when those who had accepted her generous hospitality mocked her, as did Aldous HUXLEY in *Crome Yellow* (1921) and D. H. LAWRENCE in *Women in Love* (1921) and maybe in *Lady Chatterley's Lover* (expurgated edition, 1932).

MORRIS, LEWIS (LLYWELYN DDU O FON) (1700–65) and his brother **RICHARD** (?–1779), defenders of Welsh language and culture. Natives of Anglesey, they had no formal education but learned ancient and modern languages and mathematics from their parents. Lewis became a land surveyor and gained access to the manuscripts of the north Welsh gentry, who at this time were neglecting Welsh language and culture in favour of English and metropolitan society. To counter this, Lewis Morris set up the first printing press in north Wales in 1735 so as to make books available in Welsh (previously almost all Welsh literature had been printed in Shrewsbury). His own poems were his most successful output. An appointment as collector of customs at Holyhead was the first of the government posts that provided him with the time, money and connections to pursue his goal of completing Edward LHUYD's dictionary of Celtic culture, history and language, achieved in 1760, but not published until 1878. Richard Morris spent his career in the Navy Office in London and founded the Welsh literary society, the Cymmrodorion, there in 1751. He also supervised the translation of the Bible into Welsh. The 'Morris circle' of Welsh literati, whose correspondence is the largest collection to survive from eighteenth-century Wales, comprises over 1,100 letters, principally in Welsh. The brothers supported struggling poets and promoted their work in London, partly through the Cymmrodorion, but they considered south Welsh culture decadent and susceptible to 'fanatical' Methodism, inspiring Iolo Morganwg (*see* WILLIAMS, EDWARD) to counter-attack with his own version of Welsh literary tradition.

MORRIS, WILLIAM *see* essay on page 582

MORRIS, WILLIAM (1st Viscount Nuffield) (1877–1963), motor-car manufacturer and philanthropist. Starting work at the age of 16 in a bicycle shop, by 1914 he had set up his own repair business and then a car factory at Cowley, near Oxford. Use of mass-production techniques allowed him to market cheap Morris cars within financial reach of the middle classes, selling over a million vehicles by 1939 and making Morris Motors Ltd the largest British car manufacturer. In 1952 it merged with its rival, the Austin Motor Co., to form the British Motor Corporation, later British Leyland. One of the greatest British philanthropists, in 1937 Morris founded Nuffield College, Oxford, for postgraduate research and in 1943, with an initial grant of £10 million, he set up the Nuffield Foundation for medical and scientific research.

MORRISON, HERBERT (Baron Morrison) (1888–1965), politician. A journalist, he became Secretary of the London Labour Party in 1915 and Mayor of Hackney in 1919 before being elected to the London County Council (LCC) (1922–45), and then to the House of Commons (1923–4, 1929–31, 1935–59). He joined Ramsay MACDONALD's Labour government as Minister of Transport in 1929, and created the London Passenger Transport Board. London was always his political power base, and he oversaw the widespread development of the capital's housing, health, education and transport services. Appointed Minister of Supply in 1940 in the wartime coalition, he then became Home Secretary and Minister of Home Security (1940–5) with responsibility for air-raid precautions and emergency services (he created the National Fire Brigade to co-ordinate services during the blitz).

Morrison was primarily responsible for the manifesto commitments, including the blueprints for nationalized industries and for welfare programmes, that assisted Labour to victory in 1945. Deputy Prime Minister (1945–51), he served as Lord President of the Council (1945–7) and, as Leader of the Commons (1947–51), managed the passage of Labour's extensive legislative reforms, including the nationalization programme. Briefly Foreign Secretary in 1951, he was an unsuccessful rival to GAITSKELL for the leadership of the party in 1955, as he had been to ATTLEE in 1935. He took a life peerage in 1959, became President of the British Board of Film Censors and led the fight against the abolition of the LCC.

MORTIMER, EDMUND (1376–1409), nobleman. The youngest son of the 3rd Earl of March, he joined the cause of Henry Bolingbroke (*see* HENRY IV) in 1399 fighting alongside his brother-in-law Henry PERCY (Hotspur) against OWAIN GLYN DWR. Captured in 1402, he married Owain's daughter and was drawn into the revolt. In the Tripartite Indenture of 1405, Mortimer would have been given southern England. He was killed during the siege of Harlech Castle (Merioneths.).

MORRIS, WILLIAM (1834–96)
Designer, writer and socialist

One of seven children of a prosperous financier, Morris, was educated at the recently established Marlborough College and at Oxford, where he resolved to become an architect. He joined the Oxford practice of George Street, one of the most successful of the younger Gothic revivalists.

In 1857, now determined to be an artist, he and an Oxford friend, Edward BURNE-JONES were commissioned to decorate the walls of the Oxford Union. It was at this time that Morris met the 'stunner' Jane Burden, the ethereally beautiful daughter of a stable-hand, whom he persuaded to model for the frescos of scenes from *Morte D'Arthur* and for his painting 'La Belle Iseult', and, in 1859, to marry him.

He commissioned his former colleague Philip Webb to build the Red House at Bexleyheath (Kent) in 1859, a pioneer example of the Arts and Crafts movement, with gables, arches, casements, elaborate medieval decorations, allegorical embroideries, stained glass and purpose-built furniture; 'more a poem than a house' Dante Gabriel ROSSETTI rhapsodized. It exemplified Morris's dream of a society in which 'all ... were good handicraftsmen in some kind, and the dishonour of manual labour [was] done away with altogether', when commerce was made for man, rather than man for commerce. Morris and Co., 'Fine Art Workmen in Painting, Carving, Furniture and the Metals', started to trade in 1861.

Morris continued to write poetry, as he had done since his student days, despite the critical reception of *The Defence of Guenevere* (1858). *The Earthly Paradise*, a cycle of narrative poems (1868–70), proved a commercial if not entirely a critical success. But restless and spiritually dissatisfied, and with Janey involved in a passionate (though probably unconsummated) love affair with Rossetti, Morris journeyed to Iceland. He had previously worked with an Icelandic scholar on a transcription of Icelandic sagas and later published an epic poem, *The Story of Sigurd the Volsung and the Fall of the Nibelungs* (1877), drawing on Icelandic legends.

On his return Morris expanded the range of decorative commissions which his company undertook: in the 1890s the firm relocated to Merton Abbey (Surrey), with a showroom in London, and its reputation and orderbook were international. By now a successful capitalist entrepreneur, Morris ran his business on traditional hierarchical lines, albeit with above-average pay and aesthetically pleasing surroundings, producing high-quality goods much of which could no longer be individually crafted. A self-appointed architectural guardian, he protested against the vogue for the 'restoration' of public buildings and, determined to do more than 'mere constant private grumblings', started the Society for Protecting Ancient Buildings (SPAB), or 'anti scrape', in 1877, which attracted young architects and designers such as W. R. LETHABY, who would carry Morris's inspiration into the twentieth century.

But politically Morris was dissatisfied: the working classes appeared singularly uninterested in the social possibilities of design and history that he so passionately espoused. In 1883, in the hope of a 'constructive revolution', Morris joined the socialist Democratic Federation with the wholeheartedness with which he embraced all his causes. His socialism was eclectic, a fusion of MARX (read in French) and John Stuart MILL, John RUSKIN and Robert OWEN: he predicted revolution on the horizon and grew irritated with the leadership of what had become the Social Democratic Federation (SDF) under the leadership of H. M. HYNDMAN. In 1884 he broke away from the SDF to form the Socialist League and fought an uphill battle to gain working men's support for his visionary politics of rural Utopias and socialist communities, while trying to hold together a fissiparous collection of some 1,000 socialists with different agendas and strategies for radical change.

When the League finally broke asunder, Morris spent his time writing out his vision of a better, socialist world in works like *A Dream of John Ball* (1886–7) and *News from Nowhere* (1890), rather than in political campaigning and organizing. This, however, was a most productive time artistically; the products of his workshop were the realization of the artist craftsman. He designed wallpaper and fabrics that are still in production today, while tapestries on the Arthurian legend sketched by Burne-Jones were woven at Merton Abbey. Morris also started a printing press, the Kelmscott Press, designing new typefaces based on medieval fonts and ornamenting the text of some 53 finely produced books, including a compendious edition of Chaucer (1896), books that had influenced his intellectual and aesthetic life, as well as some of his own works.

When Morris died in 1896, the editor of the *Clarion*, Robert BLATCHFORD, wrote: 'he was our best man, and he is dead ... It is true that much of his work lives and still lives, and will live. But we have lost *him* and great as was his work, he himself was greater.'

Fiona MacCarthy, *William Morris: A Life for Our Time* (1994)
E. P. Thompson (ed), *William Morris: Romantic to Revolutionary* (1955)
Paul Thompson, *The Works of William Morris* (1991)

MORTIMER, EDMUND (5th Earl of March) (1391–1425), royal servant. He succeeded his father Roger MORTIMER in 1398. As his father had been presumptive heir to the throne of RICHARD II, he and his brother Roger were kept in custody by HENRY IV. He was released on the accession of HENRY V in 1413 and remained loyal to the King, serving in France until 1422. After the accession of the infant HENRY VI he was sent to be Lieutenant of Ireland, where he died of the plague shortly after his arrival.

MORTIMER, ROGER (Baron of Wigmore) (c. 1231–82), nobleman and rebel. An English Marcher lord and a grandson of LLYWELYN AP IORW-ERTH, initially on the side of the barons against HENRY III in 1258, he moved to the King's side in 1261, becoming a key figure in the defeat of Simon de MONTFORT in 1265. After the Battle of Evesham, Simon's head and testicles were sent to Mortimer's wife at Wigmore. He was permanently at odds with his kinsman, LLYWELYN AP GRUFFUDD, Prince of Wales, and was given an important command in EDWARD I's Welsh War of 1277.

MORTIMER, ROGER (1st Earl of March) (1287–1330), virtual King of England. As a great landowner in Ireland as well as heir to the Mortimer of Wigmore estates in the Welsh Marches, he was appointed Lieutenant of Ireland by EDWARD II and was responsible for its defence against EDWARD BRUCE's invasion (1316–18). By 1321, however, Edward II's new favourite, Hugh DESPENSER, was proving so dangerous and acquisitive a neighbour in the Marches that Mortimer joined a coalition of Marcher lords against him; their revolt was swiftly suppressed. Mortimer was condemned to life imprisonment but in 1324 escaped from the Tower and fled to the French court.

The next year he became the lover and political adviser of King Edward's queen, ISABELLA, and together they planned and carried out the deposition (and probably also the murder) of her husband. Mortimer now became king in all but name and exploited his position greedily, taking the bulk of Despenser's estates in south Wales and in 1328 giving himself the unprecedented title of Earl of March. Inevitably he had enemies, notably within the royal family; military failure against the Scots, leading to the unpopular Treaty of Northampton in 1328, tarnished his reputation further. The execution of the Earl of Kent on a charge of treason in 1330 showed all too clearly that his regime was no better than Despenser's had been. In Oct. 1330 the 17-year-old EDWARD III entered Nottingham Castle by a secret passage and had Mortimer arrested in his mother's chamber; he was executed the following month. He was survived by his wife Joan, by whom he had 11 children.

MORTIMER, ROGER (4th Earl of March and [7th Earl of] Ulster) (1374–98), nobleman. He succeeded his father Edmund in 1381 when aged seven, and was appointed Viceroy of Ireland a year later. In 1385 RICHARD II declared him presumptive heir to the throne. He accompanied Richard's expedition to Ireland in 1394, and was appointed Lieutenant, first of Ulster where he made a serious effort to challenge the Ó Néill supremacy, and then of Ireland. His forceful policy there ended when he was killed in battle by the Irish of Leinster.

MORTON, JOHN (c. 1420–1500), royal servant and Archbishop of Canterbury (1486–1500). An Oxford-trained canon lawyer; it was only in 1471 that he reconciled his loyalties to the Lancastrian royal house with EDWARD IV's regime; royal and diplomatic service followed. RICHARD III arrested him as a dangerous opponent; having encouraged the abortive rebellion of Henry STAFFORD, Duke of Buckingham, in 1483, he fled to Flanders and began intriguing for Henry Tudor (the future HENRY VII), who summoned him home on his victory at Bosworth in 1485 and made him Archbishop of Canterbury in 1486. He became Lord Chancellor in 1487 and was made Cardinal in 1493. He was prominent in Henry's ruthless financial exactions, giving his name to the 'Morton's fork' principle for tax assessment: ostentation is proof of wealth, while a poverty-stricken appearance is proof of hidden savings. Building and fen drainage also occupied his formidable energies.

MORYSON, FYNES (1566–1630), traveller. From Lincs., he studied and taught at Cambridge and from 1591 travelled extensively in Europe, reaching as far as Constantinople and the Holy Land; he also visited Scotland in 1598. In 1600 he went to Ireland as secretary to Charles BLOUNT, Lord Mountjoy, and took part in the campaigns defeating Hugh O'NEILL. In 1617 he published reminiscences of his travels and of the Irish wars.

MOSELEY, HENRY (1887–1915), physicist. Moseley studied physics at Oxford and worked under Ernest RUTHERFORD at Manchester University (1910–13), where he researched the X-ray photographic spectra of various elements. In 1913 he showed that the shortest wavelength of an X-ray line emitted by a chemical element was related to its nuclear charge or 'atomic number'. Later he used the X-ray spectra of metals to predict the existence of new elements, some of which have since been detected. His work transformed the understanding of chemical periodicity. He was killed in action during the First World War.

MOSER, MARY (?–1819), painter. The daughter of the enamel-painter George Moser, she became one of the founder members of the Royal Academy in 1768, with Angelica KAUFFMAN. She announced her retirement in 1793 when she married an army officer, Hugh Lloyd, but two years later undertook her most ambitious commission, the decoration of the flower room at Frogmore for Queen CHARLOTTE, and she began exhibiting regularly again in 1797. She was an active member of the Royal Academy; after her death no woman was elected a Royal Academician until Annie Louise Swynnerton became an Associate in 1922.

MOSLEY, SIR OSWALD *see* essay on page 585

MOTT, SIR NEVILL (1905–96), physicist. After studying physics at Cambridge, Mott taught at Manchester University and researched physics under Ernest RUTHERFORD in Cambridge and Niels Bohr in Copenhagen. In the 1920s he applied the new quantum theory to understand the scattering of atomic particles. In 1933 he became a Professor of Physics at Bristol University, where he researched the properties of metals and ionic crystals and established a major centre for solid-state physics. Whilst Cavendish Professor of Experimental Physics at Cambridge (1954–71) he worked on metal-insulator transitions ('Mott transitions') and transformed physics teaching. On 'retiring' from the Cavendish he explored the electronic properties of non-crystalline semiconductors, work for which he shared the 1977 Nobel Prize for Physics with Philip Anderson and Jon van Vleck.

MOUNTBATTEN, EDWINA (née Ashley) (Countess Mountbatten of Burma) (1901–60), public servant. Descended from the social reformer Lord Shaftesbury on her father's side and from Sir Edward CASSELL on her mother's, she was a rich woman on Cassell's death. She married a naval officer, Lord Louis MOUNT-BATTEN, in 1922: they had two daughters and Edwina Mountbatten led an active life of public service.

During the Second World War she was Superintendent-in-Chief of the St John's Ambulance Brigade, and when her husband became Chief of Combined Operations in 1942 and Supreme Allied Commander in South East Asia the following year, she took responsibility for organizing the welfare arrangements of these operations. When he was appointed the last Viceroy of India in 1946, she was at his side during the negotiations for the independence of India (and it was surmised that her intimate relationship with NEHRU at this time was an emollient) and helped co-ordinate the aid efforts of various voluntary bodies during the violence and mass population transfer before and after the partition of India and Pakistan. She died while on an arduous tour of inspection for the St John's Ambulance Brigade in north Borneo.

MOUNTBATTEN, LOUIS ('DICKIE') (1st Earl Mountbatten of Burma) (1900–79), naval officer and Viceroy of India. Son of Prince Louis of Battenberg, he was educated at Osborne and Dartmouth, and in 1916 was assigned to Admiral BEATTY's flagship. Anti-German hysteria had forced his father's resignation as First Sea Lord in 1914 and a change of the family name in 1917. Handsome, charming and well connected (particularly so after his marriage to millionairess Edwina Ashley, *see* MOUNTBATTEN, EDWINA), the young Mountbatten appeared the quintessential playboy but was also a diligent officer, driven by the idea that he too would be First Sea Lord. During the Second World War, while commanding the 5th Destroyer Flotilla in 1939, Mountbatten was mined, torpedoed and finally sunk by German dive-bombers, exploits immortalized in the Noel COWARD and David Lean film *In Which We Serve* (1942). Appointed chief adviser and then Chief of Combined Operations early in 1942, Mountbatten's performance was mixed, several successful raids balanced by the disaster at Dieppe. Diplomatically skilled and 'triphibious' in outlook, in the autumn of 1943 Mountbatten was appointed supremo of South East Asia Command, where he co-ordinated British, American and Chinese operations, and helped SLIM achieve victory in Burma. Openly sympathetic to Asian nationalism, between 1947 and 1948 he served as Viceroy and then Governor General of India, though his hope for an orderly British departure was marred by post-independence massacres. Returning to the navy, Mountbatten was promoted First Sea Lord (1954) and Chief of the Defence Staff (1959) and achieved his major ambition, the creation of a unified Ministry of Defence (1954). Retiring in 1965, Mountbatten worked to modernize the monarchy, was constantly in the public eye and while holidaying in Ireland in Aug. 1979 was murdered in an IRA bomb attack.

MOUNTJOY, BARON, 4TH *see* BLOUNT, WILLIAM; **8TH** *see* BLOUNT, CHARLES

MOWBRAY, JOHN (3rd Duke of Norfolk) (1415–61), hereditary Earl Marshal. He succeeded his father John in 1432 and went on pilgrimage to Rome in 1446. In the Wars of the Roses his family ties drew him to the Yorkist cause, and he fought on their side in the battles of 1460–1, including the particularly bloody affair at Towton (Yorks.).

MOWBRAY, THOMAS (2nd Earl of Nottingham, 1st Duke of Norfolk) (*c.* 1366–99), nobleman. He

continued on page 586

MOSLEY, SIR OSWALD (1896–1980)
Politician and Fascist leader

Born into a family of English landed gentry, Mosley made the only serious attempt between the wars to modernize English society and politics, and ended as the prototype 'lost leader'.

Mosley shared with Winston CHURCHILL the dubious distinction of being one of the few front-rank British politicians to have passed through Sandhurst rather than Oxford or Cambridge; this left both men with an impatience with the conventions of political life which, in Mosley's case, passed into contempt.

The formative experience of Mosley's life was the First World War, in which he served with the Royal Flying Corps. Flying, the epitome of modern technology, appealed to the technocrat in Mosley who throughout his life would be open to the appeal of the 'new' and the 'modern'; it was a microcosm of his later career that it should have been a flying accident which invalided him out of the service. Like his contemporary, Harold MACMILLAN, Mosley was attracted by the comradeship of the trenches, which left both men with a feeling of responsibility for those less well-situated in life than themselves; but the war also left Mosley with a burning contempt for the old men and old ways which had led to the war and to the mass slaughter it had involved.

Mosley, as a dashingly handsome war hero with wonderful natural powers of oratory and plenty of money, was much in demand by Conservative associations in 1918 and his marriage to Cimmie (Cynthia), the daughter of the Tory grandee Lord CURZON, was also politically (as well as financially) advantageous; he became MP for Harrow in 1918. Mosley showed his political courage early in his career by attacking LLOYD GEORGE's policy of repression in Ireland and, from 1922 to 1924, he sat for Harrow as an Independent. He found the dominance of the old men and old parties intolerable, and it was natural that he should have looked to the new Labour Party as the antidote to 'politics as usual'; it was equally natural that the Labour Party should have regarded its new recruit (1926) with a mixture of emotions. On the one hand, rich radical baronets were hardly common in the party and both his money and his personal electoral appeal were welcomed, particularly by the Labour leader Ramsay MACDONALD. Mosley's background, intellectual and personal arrogance, as well as his impatience with the traditions of the Labour movement, however, aroused deep suspicion in some quarters that he was buying his way into the party.

Mosley's impatience and conceit had blinded him to the reality of MacDonald's Labour Party, which was as wedded to the old ways as the other major parties. He became Chancellor of the Duchy of Lancaster in the 1929 MacDonald government, from which position he made the only serious attempt by Labour to come up with an answer to Britain's economic problems, particularly the growing scourge of unemployment. Mosley's attempt to deal with unemployment by a national plan that would galvanize the British economy through a programme of public works and government spending proved far too radical for the Labour Cabinet, which rejected it in early 1930, after which Mosley resigned (21 May 1930).

Mosley's instincts correctly told him that a major economic crisis was coming that would need radical measures to combat it, but the idea that he could form a new party which would implement such measures was an act of extreme hubris. In the crisis of 1931 the 'old gang' held together to form a National government, and Mosley and his wife both lost their seats. Their New Party was crushed as the electorate voted resoundingly for safety first.

Mosley was not deterred and, seeing the success of fascist movements in both Italy and Germany, decided to form his own British Union of Fascists in 1932; the death of Lady Cynthia in 1933 left Mosley free to follow his vision wherever it led. Fascism's fascination with the 'new' appealed to Mosley but its anti-Semitism and uniforms were what appealed to many of its supporters, particularly in working-class areas of east London, and Mosley quickly found himself in a dilemma he could never resolve: the 'high' way to power lay through the application of Keynesian-style economics (see KEYNES, J. M.) and national planning but the only way to win support seemed to be through the 'low' way of stimulating anti-Jewish and anti-Communist feeling. After the violence which attended the great fascist meeting at Olympia in June 1934, Mosley lost much of his respectable support and drifted to the margins of British politics.

He was interned in 1940 as a threat to national security. Despite his undoubted charisma, attempts to revive his career in the post-war years were unsuccessful.

Robert Skidelsky, Oswald Mosley (1975)

defeated a Franco-Spanish fleet off Margate (Kent) in 1386. In 1387 he joined the aristocratic opposition to RICHARD II, fought against the King's friends at Radcot Bridge (Oxon.) and was one of the Appellants in the Parliament of 1388. Won back to the King's side in the 1390s he became one of the Appellants of 1397, accusing three of his former allies of treason, and was probably responsible for the death of THOMAS OF WOODSTOCK, murdered while in his custody. He was then created Duke of Norfolk. But Bolingbroke (later HENRY IV) had followed the same path and the two were nervous. They quarrelled (his duel with Bolingbroke opens SHAKE-SPEARE's *Richard II*) and the King exiled him. He died in Venice.

MOWLAM, MARJORIE ('MO') (1949–), politician. Mowlam was elected Labour MP for Redcar (Yorks.) in 1987, entered the Shadow Cabinet in 1992, and became Shadow Secretary of State for Northern Ireland in 1994. In 1997 she was appointed Secretary of State for Northern Ireland, the first woman to hold the position. She brought a new style of leadership to the post, based on deliberate informality and links with community groups. She played a prominent role in the negotiations leading up to the Good Friday Agreement in 1998. Her decision to meet paramilitary prisoners when the loyalist ceasefire was under threat helped to preserve the peace, though criticized in some quarters as appeasement. Mowlam was enormously popular with nationalists and with British and Irish public opinion, which admired her commitment to her duties while recovering from serious surgery. Unionist politicians, however, saw her as biased towards nationalists, regarded her attitudes as deliberately insulting and preferred to negotiate directly with Prime Minister Tony BLAIR. In October 1999 she became Cabinet Office minister and was replaced as Northern Ireland Secretary by Peter MANDELSON, seen as more acceptable to Unionists and therefore better able to persuade them to further compromises.

MUDIE, CHARLES (1816–90), bookseller and founder of a popular circulating library. In 1847 he turned from selling to loaning books and created the commercial library that became an institution and strongly influenced the tastes of the Victorian reading public.

MUGABE, ROBERT (1924–), politician. Originally a schoolteacher in his native district of Makonde, Southern Rhodesia, Mugabe entered full-time politics in 1960, joining the National Democratic Party. After it was banned he became deputy to NKOMO in ZAPU (Zimbabwean African People's Union). Arrested several times, he fled to Tanganyika before breaking with Nkomo and joining Ndabaningi Sithole's Shona-dominated ZANU (Zimbabwean African National Union). Returning to Rhodesia in 1963 he was arrested again, spending the following 10 years in gaol. In 1974, regarded as a hardline Marxist, he replaced Sithole as leader of ZANU; backed by its military wing he became a serious contender to lead a new Zimbabwe. Realigning himself alongside Nkomo in the Patriotic Front, he led the liberation war against the SMITH regime from his base in Mozambique throughout the late 1970s. In the 1980 election following the Lancaster House agreement on independence, ZANU stood separately from Nkomo's followers and had the greater success; in the resulting coalition Mugabe became the first Prime Minister of the newly independent Zimbabwe. Ethnic divisions and violence have marred the nation's history.

MUGGERIDGE, MALCOLM (1903–90), writer and broadcaster. Brought up in a left-wing household and a dabbler in religion at Cambridge, Muggeridge made the first of many journeys to India before joining the *Manchester Guardian* in 1930. Posted to Moscow in 1932, he returned thoroughly disillusioned with Stalin's Soviet Union. He then wrote some of his most enduring prose, including *The Thirties* (1940), and saw war service as an MI6 spy in Africa. Made editor of *Punch* in 1953, he instituted radical changes before a series of outspoken remarks about the Establishment and the royal family pushed him out into the cold. In the USA he discovered a new career as a television pundit before a further volte-face at the end of the 1960s, when he became an outspoken critic of permissiveness. The nickname St Mug stuck; eventually, at the end of his see-sawing personal spiritual quest, he was received into the Roman Catholic Church.

MUGGLETON, LODOWICK (1609–98), religious leader. A London tailor, with his cousin John Reeve (1608–58) he founded in 1652 a sect which claimed to have had the final revelation from God; they were Unitarian in denying the doctrine of the Holy Trinity. Despite their estimable prohibition on seeking converts, Muggletonians survived as a quiet living link with the world of seventeenth-century radical religion until their last member died in 1979.

MUIRCHERTACH MAC LOCHLAINN (*fl. c.* 1160), King of Cenél nEógain. King from 1145, he soon dominated the north of Ireland. In 1149 he marched on Dublin, compelling DIARMAIT MAC MURCHADHA's submission; with the latter's support, he was able to win recognition as high-king after TAIRDELBACH UA CONCHOBAIR's death (1156). When he treacherously blinded one of his northern enemies at Easter 1166, widespread revulsion resulted in the sequence of violent events that, before the end of the year, had led to his own death in battle and to Diarmait fleeing for help to England.

MUIRCHERTACH MAC NÉILL (?–943), King of the Uí Néill. Muirchertach Mac Néill was one of the Irish kings who contributed most to containing the Viking conquests in Ireland. Defeated by them in 921, he subsequently achieved victories on sea and land, attacked Dublin in 938 and even launched sea-borne raids against the Norse-held Scottish islands. He also built up considerable power over other Irish kingdoms. His successes, and those of contemporary Irish kings, parallel the victories gained against the Vikings in England and Scotland by ATHELSTAN and CONSTANTÍN II.

MUIRCHERTACH Ó BRIAIN (?–1343), King of Thomond. His victory over Richard de Clare at the Battle of Dysart O'Dea (Co. Clare) (10 May 1318) was a significant turning-point in the history of the English in Ireland. EDWARD I's 1276 grant of the Ó Briain kingdom of Thomond to Richard's father Thomas de Clare had been part of that expansion of English colonization and settlement that had characterized the thirteenth century. In 1321 the Clare lordship (like so many in Ireland) was divided between heiresses, and this fragmentation of English control left the way clear for Muirchertach to engineer a restoration of Ó Briain power in Thomond which lasted until the early modern period.

MUIRCHERTACH UA BRIAIN (?–1119), King of Dublin and of Munster. Installed as King of Dublin by his father TAIRDELBACH UA BRIAIN in 1075, he became King of Munster on his father's death in 1086. By 1096 he dominated Leinster, Connacht and Meath. As a patron of ecclesiastical reform, he gave Cashel, the capital of the Uí Briains' ancestral enemies the Eóganachta, to the Church and presided over the synods of Cashel (1101) and Raith Bressail (1111). Although he was never able to bring the north, particularly the Meic Lochlainn of Cenél nEógain, to accept his high-kingship, his special status among Irish kings was recognized by the rulers of both England and Norway. In 1114 he fell seriously ill and never fully recovered.

MULGRAVE, 3RD EARL OF see SHEFFIELD, JOHN

MUN, THOMAS (1571–1641), economist. A merchant, and a director of the East India Co.

from 1615, he was one of the leading theorists of mercantilism, a complex collection of economic theories particularly dominant in English State policy in the seventeenth century, although based on the commonplaces of government since the fifteenth century. Mercantilists stressed the importance of the balance of external trade for a State's well-being. To achieve this balance, it was considered vital to regulate trade, the import and export of bullion and coin and the production of agricultural and industrial goods. Mun set out his ideas in several publications, notably *England's Treasure by Foraign Trade* (c. 1622, published 1664).

MUNDELLA, A(NTHONY) J(OHN) (1825–97), businessman and politician. A hosiery manufacturer in Nottingham, Mundella was a leading exponent of conciliation and arbitration in relations between employers and workers. Following a prolonged strike in the Nottingham hosiery industry in 1860 Mundella, Thomas Ashwell and J. H. Lee, the three largest employers, met with labour representatives to establish the Nottingham Board of Arbitration, a permanent body for negotiation which proved relatively successful. Mundella emerged as a leading national advocate for arbitration and conciliation. Radical MP for Sheffield (1868–85) and Sheffield Brightside (1885–97), he was important in the development of State education. As Vice-President of the Committee of Council on Education under GLADSTONE (1880–5) he introduced the Compulsory Education Act 1880, compelling school attendance. As President of the Board of Trade (1886) he created the Labour Department, establishing the first government department to deal specifically with labour affairs.

MUNGO, ST see KENTIGERN, ST

MUNSHI see KARIM, ABDUL

MURCHISON, SIR RODERICK (1792–1871), geologist. Born in Scotland, Murchison was educated at military college and after leaving the army in 1816 settled in Scotland where he led a gentlemanly existence. By the early 1820s he had developed an interest in geology and in 1824 moved to London to further it. By the late 1820s he had conducted, often with Charles LYELL and Adam SEDGWICK, geological explorations in Scotland, France and the Alps. He thus acquired beliefs that fossils were the best measure of geological age and that, in opposition to Lyell's 'uniformitarianism', the earth's crust had been subjected to occasional catastrophic changes, a belief which in later years informed his rejection of Charles DARWIN's theory of evolution. Following field-work conducted in south Wales during the early 1830s he identified the 'grauwacke' rocks underlying the Old Red Sandstone as the Silurian system, containing what he believed to be the oldest fossils. He presented his claims in his major work, *The Silurian System* (1839), which involved him in a fierce controversy with the geologist Henry De La Beche over the existence of coal plants in the 'grauwacke' of Devonshire. This resulted in Murchison and Sedgwick propounding the Devonian system, a stratum located between the Carboniferous and Silurian systems. In 1841 Murchison produced evidence for the Permian system. By the early 1840s he was well established in London scientific circles and notorious for his military-style campaigns against scientific opponents. In the 1840s he and Sedgwick were involved in a fierce controversy over the boundary between the younger Silurian system and the older underlying Cambrian system, which Sedgwick had identified. *Siluria* (1854) is an attack on opponents of organic progression of the fossil record. In 1855 Murchison became Director General of the Geological Survey, one of the most powerful positions in British geology. Both a distinguished geographer and an imperialist, he backed campaigns to explore and annex Africa.

MURDOCH, DAME IRIS (1919–99), novelist and philosopher. Born in Dublin to Anglo-Irish parents, Murdoch was educated at Somerville College, Oxford. After a brief period working at the Treasury and for the United Nations Rehabilitation and Relief Association in camps in Belgium (1944–6), she taught philosophy at Cambridge University and at St Anne's College, Oxford (1948–63). A leading specialist on French existentialist philosophy, she published her first major work, *Sartre, Romantic Rationalist*, in 1953 and her first novel, *Under the Net*, in 1954. Murdoch married the academic and literary critic John Bayley in 1956. It was an enduring marriage and Bayley wrote books about their relationship which were published before and after Murdoch's death. She published on Romanticism, reviewed extensively and wrote further novels. *The Bell* (1958), about a group of eccentrics living in a commune, dealt with mysticism and morality, issues featuring prominently in her later works. Fascinated by the relation between aesthetics and ethics, she believed that novels best show the nature and import of morality, though she never abandoned philosophical writing, publishing *The Sovereignty of Good* (1970) and *Metaphysics as a Guide to Morals* (1992). Murdoch's novels became increasingly dense in the 1970s and 1980s, and she won the Booker Prize in 1978 for *The Sea, The Sea*.

MURDOCH, RUPERT (1931–), media proprietor. Bringing a new brand of ruthlessness to British newspapers and broadcasting in the 1980s, he had already become one of Australia's media barons. The son of a distinguished war correspondent and newspaper owner, he inherited the *Adelaide News* in 1952. He established Cruden Investments, a family company that owns a substantial part of the media empire which he has since built up as News Corporation, with newspaper, magazine, book and satellite-based broadcasting interests in Australia, the UK, USA and Hong Kong. In the UK he acquired the *Sun* and *News of the World* in 1969, and has consistently led the tabloid newspaper agenda. When Murdoch acquired Times Newspapers in 1981 conflict with the Fleet Street trade unions followed and the 'stranglehold' of restrictive practices on newspaper production was broken. Since satellite broadcasting began in 1989, Murdoch's Sky Television (subsequently BSkyB) has become the leading provider, while purchase of William Collins the same year opened opportunities in book publishing. He became a US citizen in 1988 to allow him to own US newspaper and broadcasting interests.

MURDOCK, WILLIAM (1754–1839), inventor. The son of an Ayrs. millwright, he joined the staff of the engineers Matthew BOULTON and James WATT in Soho near Birmingham. From 1779 to 1799 he supervised their engines in Cornw. In 1792 he began experimenting with gas lighting and illuminated his house in Redruth, and in 1802 succeeded in lighting the whole Soho factory to celebrate the Peace of Amiens. Boulton and Watt received their first major order for gas lighting in 1804 from the Manchester cotton-spinner George Augustus Lee; Murdock completed that work by 1807.

MURPHY, JOHN (*c*. 1753–98), revolutionary. The son of a Wexford farmer, he trained for the priesthood at Seville, returning to his home area as an assistant priest in 1785. When the government 'proclaimed' the county to be in a state of disturbance in Nov. 1797, part of the long-standing pattern of protest against rural grievances, given a political edge by the ideas and hopes raised by the French Revolution, Murphy took the oath of allegiance and played a part in trying to preserve order. Incensed at the brutality of the army in May 1798, however, he took the part of the rebels (*see* TONE, WOLFE), raising the standard of revolt in Wexford, and gathering around him a force of 16,000. Murphy's force took several towns in the county, including Wexford itself, but attempts to raise Carlow and Kilkenny in revolt were less successful and Murphy retreated to his base on Vinegar Hill, where he was defeated by General LAKE.

MURPHY, WILLIAM (1844–1919), businessman. One of the most successful businessmen of late Victorian Ireland, he began as a building contractor and became a railway and newspaper magnate, owning the *Irish Independent* (which he made the most widely read nationalist newspaper), the Dublin trams and Clery's department store. Irish Party MP for the St Patrick's Division of Dublin (1885–92), he was an opponent of Charles Stewart PARNELL in the split and an associate of HEALY. Murphy's historical reputation was darkened by his leading role in the Dublin employers' attempt to break James LARKIN's union through the 1913–14 lock-out and by YEATS's denunciation of Murphy's opposition to a proposed municipal gallery.

MURRAY, SIR GEORGE (1772–1846), soldier. Son of a Lowland Scottish gentry family, Murray was bought a commission in the 71st regiment in 1789. A competent infantry officer, he demonstrated a flair for administration and logistics and in 1803 was appointed Assistant Quartermaster General at the Horse Guards. From 1808 to 1811 and from 1813 to 1814 Murray served as Quartermaster General in the Peninsula, at times performing near miracles in sustaining Wellington's army (*see* WELLESLEY, ARTHUR) without exploiting local resources, which would have alienated its Spanish allies. His post-war service as Governor of the Royal Military College, Sandhurst (1819–24), and Master General of Ordnance (1834–46) was an attritional struggle against Treasury-inspired cuts.

MURRAY, SIR JAMES (1837–1915), lexicographer. A Scottish schoolmaster whose *Dialects of the Southern Counties of Scotland* (1873) established his scholarly reputation, he began while still a teacher (1879) to edit the *New English Dictionary* for the Philological Society: this became the *Oxford English Dictionary*. Though Murray's editorial responsibilities stretched only from A–D, H–K, O–P and T, he moved to Oxford to complete this mammoth lexicographical task, which he achieved in 1928.

MURRAY, LIONEL (LEN) (Baron Murray of Epping Forest) (1922–), trade-union leader. General Secretary of the Trades Union Congress (TUC) (1973–84), Murray was instrumental in ensuring that the TUC had a role in planning government economic strategy, an arrangement that was formalized in the National Economic Development Council, a tripartite organization of employers, employees and unions. The Labour victory of 1974 gave him a powerful voice and he negotiated a social contract with the government, which agreed wage restraint in an attempt to reduce inflation in exchange for social measures

and had the effect of guaranteeing minimum wage increases for the lower paid. The so-called 'winter of discontent' (1978–9) of industrial disruption effectively tore up the contract when the Prime Minister, James CALLAGHAN, insisted on a further year of tight wage restraint. The incoming Conservative government under Margaret THATCHER gave short shrift to TU partnership hopes despite Murray's efforts, and in 1983 ill health, combined with the miners' strike in which the TUC seemed to have no role to play (*see* SCARGILL, ARTHUR) and the Conservative ban on union membership at Government Communications Headquarters (GCHQ) (the 'spy centre') which Murray thought questioned his members' national loyalty, led him to resign. In full health again, he became an active Labour spokesman in the Lords.

MURRAY, WILLIAM (1st Earl of Mansfield) (1705–93), judge and politician. A lawyer of Scots extraction, he wielded much influence as effective Leader of the Commons from 1747 and, as such, a rival and antagonist of PITT THE ELDER. His promotion to the position of Lord Chief Justice of King's Bench in 1756 brought him into the Lords, where he continued to be a powerful force. As a judge, he strove to develop systematic and rational bodies of legal precedent in, among other fields, commercial law and the law of settlement (which determined from which parish a poor person might claim relief). His pro-government decisions in various political cases of the 1760s and 1770s attracted criticism from radicals, who raked up his family's Jacobite connections and claimed that his reformist legal stance revealed contempt for the common law. His reputation among lawyers in general runs high to the present day, however. Many of his judgements set decisive precedents, and among these some of the most notable favoured the cause of liberty. These included the 1772 Somerset case, (SOMERSET *v.* Stewart), where he affirmed that black slaves in England might not forcefully be sold abroad by their masters. The decision received much press attention, and was widely regarded as ending slavery in England. He also defended the rights of Dissenters in the Mansion House case (in which he ruled that it was not appropriate for the City of London to raise funds for building a new house for the Mayor by fining Dissenters for refusing to hold offices they were legally barred from holding) and the rights of Catholics both in court and in Parliament. This last stance won him the hostility of the anti-Catholic Gordon rioters (*see* GORDON, LORD GEORGE), who burned down his town house at Bloomsbury Square, London, in 1780.

MUSGRAVE, SIR WILLIAM (*c.* 1506–44), politician. From a Westmoreland knightly family, he had entered royal service by 1529, giving him a power base on the northern English border which enabled him to pursue a family feud with William, 3rd Lord Dacre of Gilsland. His plots humiliated Dacre in 1534, but he was so unpopular in the north for his vigorous opposition to the Pilgrimage of Grace (1536–7) that he spent most of his last years in London. Nevertheless he was prominent in pursuing the war with Scotland after 1542 until his death.

MUSHET, ROBERT (1811–91), metallurgist. Born in Glos., Mushet developed skills in iron- and steel-making in his father's iron-works in the Forest of Dean. He used the ferro-manganese alloy *Spiegeleisen* to remove excess oxygen from the blown steel produced in the BESSEMER process, thus greatly improving the quality. Patented in 1856, his technique was crucial to the commercial success of the Bessemer process but Mushet, unlike Bessemer and many other steel-makers, made little profit from his technique since he lost his rights to the patent in 1859. Later, he was engaged in a fierce priority dispute with Bessemer following the latter's claims to have independently discovered the uses of *Spiegeleisen*. His greatest commercial success was his tungsten or Titanic steel, a self-hardening steel introduced in 1868 and widely exploited in machine tools.

MUSPRATT, JAMES (1793–1886), manufacturing chemist. Muspratt was apprenticed to a druggist in his native Dublin and, after fighting in the Peninsular War, set up a private chemical manufactory there. In 1823 he established in Liverpool the first English factory for mass-producing soda by Nicolas Leblanc's process. With growing demand for his product, he formed a short-lived partnership with the industrial chemist Josias Gamble and moved to larger factories in St Helens and Newton in Lancs. Between 1832 and 1850 Muspratt faced constant litigation from Newton landowners whose crops were allegedly damaged by the fumes produced by his factory. Subsequently he moved to what would become prosperous factories in Widnes (Lancs.) and Flint. Muspratt is regarded as the founder of the British alkali industry.

MUYBRIDGE, EADWEARD (1830–1904), photographer and inventor. Born in London, Muybridge emigrated to California in 1852 and by the late 1860s had become chief photographer to the US government. In 1872 he was invited to settle the problem of a horse's gait using photography. His initial attempts proved inconclusive but in the late 1870s he used a bank of cameras fitted with the new fast photographic plates to show that a trotting horse had all four feet off the ground simultaneously. He promoted his observations in *The Horse in Motion* (1882) and by animating drawings of the photographs in his 'zoopraxiscope', an instrument which he invented in 1881 and which is regarded as a forerunner of the cinematographic projector.

MYLNE, ROBERT (1733–1811), architect and civil engineer. His family had been distinguished masons and architects in Scotland for 300 years. He studied architecture at the Academy of St Luke in Rome. His first great work was Blackfriars bridge in London, completed in 1769. This gained him not only 12 other bridge commissions but a number of prestigious positions including engineer and architect to the City of London and surveyor to both Canterbury and St Paul's cathedrals. Mylne travelled extensively around Britain and worked on several country estates, particularly that of the Duke of Argyll at Inveraray. From 1767 he was engineer to the New River Co., and lived for most of his life at Islington to supervise the works on the canal from Herts. that supplied London with most of its water.

MYNNE, GEORGE (?–1648), industrialist. A clothier in Irish royal service by 1614, he became one of early Stuart England's leading industrialists through iron-smelting; from *c.* 1621 he was prominent in the Mineral and Battery Company, whose monopoly position resulted from its importance to government armaments. These activities and large-scale money-lending made him enemies, and he was prosecuted under CHARLES I's revived forest laws for destruction of timber for smelting. Despite a resulting huge fine in 1636, he was important in the English Civil Wars to the Royalist armaments supplies and was punitively fined by Parliament.

MYRDDIN *see* MERLIN

N

NAMIER, SIR LEWIS (1888–1960), historian. Born into a family of Polish landowners of Jewish extraction, Namier came to England in 1908 to study at the London School of Economics and Oxford, adopting British nationality and anglicizing his name. After the First World War he failed to find a permanent academic post at Oxford, mainly because of anti-Semitism but also because of a certain amount of anti-Namierism. Having made enough money to finance his studies for a while, Namier made himself an expert on British political history in the eighteenth century, demolishing single-handedly the widely held view that it had been a period of rigid party divisions. In his best-known book, *The Structure of Politics at the Accession of George III* (1929), he showed, by a minute examination of the backgrounds and political contacts of MPs, that personal rather than political motives were paramount.

In 1930 Namier was appointed Professor of History at Manchester University. During the next decade he devoted as much energy to his activities on behalf of Zionism as he did scholarship, and he was a fierce opponent of Hitler. In the late 1940s and early 1950s he became a dominant figure in British scholarship, partly through his role as one of those involved in the setting up of the History of Parliament Trust, which gave jobs to many young scholars. The word 'Namierism' was coined to denote his technique of minute examination of the material and social contexts within which MPs operated. He was accused of 'taking the mind out of history', which was ironic in view of his interest in psychoanalysis.

NAOROJI, DADABHAI (1825–1917), **BHOWNAGGREE, SIR MANCHERJEE** (1851–1933) and **SAKLATVALA, SHAPURJI** (1874–1936), politicians. Three times President of the Indian National Congress and a successful merchant in both India and Britain, Naoroji sat as a Liberal MP (for Central Finsbury in London, 1892–5), the first non-white to sit in the Commons. He took a generally conciliatory but fundamentally anti-British stand on the Raj. Such a direct attempt to have influence at the heart of the British Empire was rare, but he was to be succeeded by two more Indians. Sir Mancherjee Bhownaggree, a Conservative MP (1895–1906), advanced the cause of the disadvantaged Indians in South Africa, the cause in which GANDHI began his career of activism. Shapurji Saklatvala was elected in 1922 as Labour MP and in 1924 as Communist MP for North Battersea.

NAPIER, SIR CHARLES (1782–1853), soldier. Son of an Anglo-Irish army officer, he was bought a commission in 1794 and saw action with his brother William (*see* NAPIER, WILLIAM), defending their home against Irish rebels in 1798. Napier served in the Peninsula, in North America and in the Waterloo campaign, rising to command a regiment. Radicalized by his wartime experiences, as inspecting field officer in the Ionian Islands in the early 1820s Napier gave clandestine help to the Greek rebellion against the Turks, and as commander of the northern district of Britain after 1839 he handled Chartist disturbances with a mixture of firmness and compassion. Posted to India in 1843 he went on to conquer Sind, a success he announced in a witty one-word telegram to the British authorities: 'Peccavi' (I have sinned).

NAPIER, SIR CHARLES (1786– 1860), sailor. Son of a naval officer, Napier joined the navy in 1799 and as Commander of a brig, in Admiral COCHRANE's squadron, played a major role in the capture of a French 74–gun ship. After fighting the French in the Mediterranean and in the United States, Napier retired in 1815. He recouped initial financial loses from premature investment in steam-powered shipping by successfully commanding the Infanta's fleet in the Portuguese Civil War in 1833. Napier's capture of Beirut, Sidon and Acre from Mehemet Ali's forces in 1840 made him a national hero. Elected to Parliament in 1841, Napier devoted himself to naval reform. On the outbreak of war with Russia in 1854, Napier, aged 70, was chosen to command the British fleet in the Baltic, but his wooden warships could not engage modern Russian fortifications. His reputation plummeted. The ineffectiveness of Napier's ships propelled the navy towards the construction of ironclads, which in the next 10 years would revolutionize warship design.

NAPIER, JOHN (1550–1617), mathematician. Son of Sir Archibald Napier of Merchiston (Lothian), Treasurer-Depute of Scotland, he studied at St Andrews and possibly also in France. He invented a pumping device for mines, described a calculating machine, devised the modern system of notating decimal fractions and, with Henry BRIGGS, pioneered the use of logarithms. For an enthusiastic Protestant, however, these achievements were subsidiary to his speculations on the Book of Revelation (published 1593 and very frequently reprinted), which harnessed his mathematical ability and the analytical method of the French Calvinist philosopher Peter Ramus (1515–72) to explain biblical prophecy.

NAPIER, ROBERT (1791–1876), shipbuilder. Napier acquired mathematical and drawing skills privately and later worked as a blacksmith in Dumbarton and as an engineer in Edinburgh. In 1815 he began his own blacksmith's business in Glasgow, which he expanded into ironfounding and engineering, and turned into the leading manufactory of steamship engines. From the 1820s his firm began to produce high-powered engines for steamships including those operated by the East India Co. and the Royal Navy. In 1843 he constructed his first ship, the *Vanguard*, and later built steamships for Samuel CUNARD's transatlantic mail service (the origin of the Cunard Line). His booming business also built iron warships for British and foreign navies and established the Clyde as a leading centre of shipbuilding.

NAPIER, ROBERT (1st Baron Napier of Magdala) (1810–90), soldier. Educated at the East India Co.'s college, he was commissioned into the Bengal Sappers and Miners in 1828. During his service in India Napier constructed roads and canals in the Punjab, built cool, well-ventilated barracks and the new hill station at Darjeeling. He also commanded engineers in the First and Second Sikh Wars, acted as Chief of Staff to Sir James OUTRAM during the Indian Mutiny and in 1858–9 hunted down the last mutineers. In 1860 Napier commanded a division in the war against China, entering Peking on 24 Oct., and was promoted Major-General. In 1868 he led a force 420 miles from the coast into the mountains of Abyssinia, stormed Magdala, capital of the mad Ethiopian emperor, and freed British hostages, exploits which made him a national hero and earned him a peerage and appointment as Commander-in-Chief in India.

NAPIER, SIR WILLIAM (1785–1860), soldier and military historian. Brother of General Sir Charles NAPIER, he was commissioned in 1804 into a regiment serving under Sir John MOORE . He fought at Copenhagen in 1807 and was wounded during the Peninsular campaign. Unable to purchase command of a regiment, in 1819 Napier went on half pay and devoted himself to military history. His multi-volumed *History of the Peninsular War* (1828–40), a defence of the reputation of Moore and the Duke of Wellington (*see* WELLESLEY, ARTHUR), remains highly readable and a valuable source of information.

NASH, JOHN (1752–1835), architect. Of Welsh extraction, he was apprenticed to an architect, and later built up a substantial practice. He became a particular favourite of the Prince Regent (later GEORGE IV), for whom he planned the layout of Regent's Park, Regent Street, Carlton House Terrace, Trafalgar Square and St James's Park, London. He was also responsible for Marble Arch, the rebuilding of Brighton Pavilion and the transformation of Buckingham House into Buckingham Palace. His work is remarkable for its combination of neoclassical style with Gothic, Chinese, Egyptian and Indian influences.

NASH, PAUL (1889–1946), artist. Nash studied at the Slade School and his one-man show in his final year (1912) was of wooded places and bleak landscapes, themes of Englishness that would occur throughout his artistic life, culminating in *Landscape of the Vernal Equinox* (1944). He was a participant in the International Surrealist Exhibition in London in 1936. His landscapes were never photographic, but mysterious and strangely menacing. He was an official war artist in both world wars and powerfully depicted the grotesque destruction and detritus of war on the landscape, notably the lunar landscape of *The Menin Road* (1918–19) and *Totes Meer (Dead Sea)* (1940–1) in which aircraft that have been shot down appear like waves, while his huge *Battle of Britain* (1941) shows the RAF in action against the Luftwaffe.

NASH, RICHARD ('BEAU') (1674–1761), man of fashion. Son of a Swansea glass manufacturer, he left Oxford without taking a degree, purchased a commission in the army, resigned, then read for the Bar. He became known as a stylish dresser and extravagant gambler. In 1705 he moved to Bath and was elected master of ceremonies. He played an important part in making the city (then beginning its greatest period of growth) into a genteel resort, organizing subscription balls and assemblies, setting rules for dress and behaviour and regulating prices of lodgings. He deprecated 'ceremony', insisting that all admitted to polite society should stand on an equal footing. He took a commission on the proceeds of gaming in the Assembly Rooms;

stringent laws against gambling passed in 1740 and 1745 made his income uncertain.

NASH, THOMAS (1567–1601), writer. Son of a Suffolk minister, he studied at Cambridge, travelled in Europe and *c.* 1588 settled in London in the literary circle which included Christopher MARLOWE. Bitterly anti-Puritan, he zestfully wrote against the Marprelate Tracts (*see* THROCKMORTON, JOB), but had a knack of quarrelling with influential patrons, and from 1591 to 1599 conducted a savage literary warfare with the writer brothers Richard and William Harvey. His lost play *The Isle of Dogs* (1597) was indiscreet enough to result in a theatre being closed; his *The Unfortunate Traveller* (1594) ranks as one of the first English novels.

NASMYTH, JAMES (1808–90), engineer. Educated in his native Edinburgh, Nasmyth developed his mechanical and engineering expertise in Henry MAUDSLAY's London workshop. In 1834 he established his own workshop in Manchester for making tools and machines and two years later started building what would become the leading centre of machine-tool manufacture, the Bridgewater foundry. There, in 1839, he completed his steam hammer, an invention which enabled accurate forging of large materials, was exploited in the production of paddle-wheels for steamships and was used as a pile-driver; the originality of his invention was later challenged. His other inventions include railway steam locomotives, hydraulic presses and donkey pumps, and he devoted much time to astronomy.

NAYLER (OR NAYLOR), JAMES (?1617–60), Quaker. A Yorks. man, Nayler was serving in the Parliamentarian army during the Civil Wars of the 1640s when he discovered his preaching gift. In 1651 George FOX converted him from Independency (Congregationalism) to Quakerism. A West Country preaching tour five years later escalated into a triumphal approach to Bristol imitating Christ's entry into Jerusalem (*see* ERBURY, WILLIAM; SIMMONDS, MARTHA). Parliament, paranoid about religious extremism, voted vicious punishment including mutilation, although Oliver CROMWELL and government colleagues strongly disapproved. Belated parliamentary second thoughts brought the preacher's release in 1659.

NEALE, SIR JOHN (1890–1975), historian. Spending most of his career in the University of London, he was the leading parliamentary historian in his generation. In the early 1950s he suggested that ELIZABETH I wanted a semi-Catholic Church like that of HENRY VIII, but in 1558–9 was pushed into a more Protestant programme by House of Commons activists. His theory gained sway in text-books, but has no real basis. Hesitations in legislation which Neale noticed were caused by government politicking round Catholic bishops and peers until a Lords majority could be constructed to approve the religious settlement. Elizabeth had some conservative religious preferences, but little was allowed to influence the settlement – a barely modified fossilization of Protestantism at EDWARD VI's death.

NEAVE, AIREY (1916–79), politician. Neave became a national hero for his escape from the notorious Colditz Castle prison in 1942. Conservative MP for Abingdon in 1953, a seat which he held until his death, he held no office apart from a brief spell as a junior minister at the Ministry of Transport; he blamed the Conservative leader Edward HEATH for blocking his political advancement. His moment of revenge came in 1975 when, after the two successive election defeats of 1974, the Conservative Party had become increasingly dissatisfied with Heath's leadership. Neave was foremost amongst those who wanted Heath to go, and latched onto a comparative outsider, Margaret THATCHER. His historic contribution to British politics was transforming her leadership bid from a token effort into a serious campaign, skilful, secretive and efficient. Against expectation, she swept to victory in Feb. 1975, securing the leadership of the party for almost 16 years. Neave was rewarded with the post of head of her private office and was then appointed Shadow Secretary of State for Northern Ireland. He was set to attain Cabinet office, but at the beginning of the election campaign of 1979, which Mrs Thatcher went on to win, he was killed by a bomb which exploded under his car as he drove out of the House of Commons. It was planted by the Irish National Liberation Army, a splinter group of the IRA.

NECHTAN, King of the Picts (*c.* 706–24 and 728). By accepting the Roman calculation of the dating of Easter in *c.* 711, imposing it on his people and expelling the Irish monks in Pictland back to Iona in 717 (*see* DÚNCHAD), Nechtan played a significant part in the Romanizing of the Pictish Church. His reign is otherwise notable for the generally peaceful relations with his neighbours, although there was a major struggle for supremacy amongst the Picts themselves in its later years. Nechtan retired into a monastery, almost certainly coerced by DRUST in 724. This provoked a power struggle among four contenders, including Nechtan himself, who regained the kingship, briefly, in 728, before being defeated by OENGUS, SON OF FERGUS, who emerged with unchallenged supremacy the following year.

NEDHAM (OR NEEDHAM), MARCHMONT (1620–78), pioneer journalist. Having studied law and medicine, from 1643 Nedham led the production of Parliamentarian Civil War propagandist news in *Mercurius Britannicus*, but, after punishment for overstepping the mark in 1646, he turned to Royalist propaganda. He changed sides once more after CHARLES I's execution, editing the Republic's official journal from 1650 to 1660. Pardoned after CHARLES II's restoration, he played safe by combining medicine with a little pro-government writing. Journalists may admire his talent for survival.

NEEDHAM, JOSEPH (1900–95), biochemist, orientalist and historian of science. The son of a physician, Needham studied natural sciences at Cambridge, where he gained a doctorate in biochemistry (1925) and became Reader in biochemistry (1933–66) and Master of Gonville and Caius College (1966–76). He researched the biochemistry of embryonic development and in his *Chemical Embryology* (1931) argued that chemical mechanisms, rather than vital forces, controlled the development of a fertilized egg. At Cambridge he developed his lifelong support of left-wing politics and deep interest in Chinese science and culture. He headed the British scientific mission to China (1942–6) and throughout the Second World War advised the Chinese government on science, technology and medicine. These experiences informed his writings on the history of Chinese science, notably his magisterial *Science and Civilisation in China* (1954–). Director of the Department of Natural Sciences at UNESCO (1946–8), he was the founder and Director of the Needham Research Institute, Cambridge (established 1976), a centre for the study of East Asian history of science and technology.

NEHRU, JAWAHARLAL (1889–1964), Indian politician. India's first post-independence Prime Minister, Nehru was brought up in a rich Kashmiri household, the son of a leader of the Indian National Congress, and was introduced to the theosophical works of Annie BESANT as a child. Educated at Harrow and Cambridge, and called to the Bar in 1912, he returned to India, where Besant's arrest, the massacre at Amritsar and the rise of GANDHI changed his life's course. His daughter Indira, who as Indira Gandhi was herself to become India's Prime Minister, was born in 1918. Deeply involved in the Non-Cooperation movement, in and out of prison Nehru's political rise continued, especially given Gandhi's reticence. A popular orator, he was a principal negotiator with the British during the Second World War. Refusing to compromise with the Muslim League in the late 1930s, he cemented the intransigence of JINNAH that led to partition. Designated

Gandhi's political heir, Nehru was head of the 1946 interim government, and helped Louis MOUNTBATTEN pilot the last stages before independence. Undisputed choice as Prime Minister, he occupied that position until his death in 1964.

NEILE, RICHARD (1562–1640), churchman. Brought up in St Margaret's, Westminster, a parish unusual in the Elizabethan Church for its continuing ceremonialism, Neile provides a possible link between pre-Reformation religious conservatism and the later movement of ceremonialist and sacramentalist theology, Arminianism. From Cambridge, he returned to Westminster as Dean in 1605, moved swiftly up the episcopal ladder to Durham (1617) and acted as patron to William LAUD; he became the power behind the Arminian group (often called the Durham House set). As Archbishop of York (1631–40) he single-mindedly pressed Arminian policies.

NEILL, A(LEXANDER) S(UTHERLAND) (1883–1973), educationist. Son of a Scottish village schoolmaster, he too became a teacher. A graduate of Edinburgh University, he started a school in Germany, which he moved to Suffolk in 1927: Summerhill is a radically progressive, anti-authoritarian, co-educational school that prioritizes the social and emotional development of pupils, many of whom have experienced difficulties in education. Neill's educational philosophy is explained in his many books, including *Neill! Neill! Orange Peel!* (1973), and the school continues to wrestle with the often contemptuous media and sceptical Department of Education.

NELSON, HORATIO *see* essay on page 595

NENNIUS (*fl.* early ninth century), Welsh scholar. One of the few surviving histories of 'Dark Age' Britain, the *Historia Brittonum* (History of the Britons), has been attributed to him. It is now doubted that he was the actual author; rather, his name was probably appended to some of the surviving manuscripts of what was a complex editorial compilation. The *Historia* contains much material, a great deal of it the stuff of legends on characters such as AMBROSIUS AURELIANUS, VORTIGERN and ARTHUR.

NEST (*fl.* 1106–36), Welsh princess. Nest was the famously beautiful daughter of the Welsh King RHYS AP TEWDWR. After marrying Gerald of Windsor, Castellan of Pembroke, she was abducted by OWAIN AP CADWGAN and became mistress of, among others, Stephen, Constable of Cardigan, and HENRY I, by whom she had a son Henry. She was the grandmother of Gerald de BARRI.

NELSON, HORATIO (1st Viscount Nelson) (1758–1805)
Naval commander

Son of a Norfolk clergyman, he joined the navy aged 12 in 1770, serving first under an uncle. By 1773 he was a lieutenant, and a captain in 1778. During an expedition against a Spanish fort off the Mosquito Coast (Nicaragua), he showed the driving determination to overcome all obstacles that was to be his hallmark. Further service in the West Indies brought him into contact with Prince William (later WILLIAM IV), whom Nelson served as aide-de-camp.

He then served in the Caribbean, where his strict enforcement of the Navigation Laws, which forbade American ships to trade directly with the British West Indies, brought conflict with local officials inclined to wink at a practice hard to stop and locally desired. Questioned whether one so young should lay down the law, Nelson responded that he was 'as old as the Prime Minister of England' (then William PITT THE YOUNGER). In 1787 he married a young widow, whom he had met on the island of Nevis, and brought her back to Norfolk, where he waited out the peace. The trouble he had caused in the West Indies may have impeded his career, though he believed, 'Not being a man of fortune none of the Great care about me'.

On the eve of war in 1793, Nelson was finally found a ship and sent on diplomatic missions to Naples and Tunis. He commanded a squadron in an assault on Corsica, though injured and losing the sight in his right eye, then helped blockade Toulon. His boldness was beginning to give him a European reputation. In 1796 he was made Commodore. In 1797 he was to the fore in an attack on the Spanish fleet at Cape St Vincent, off the coast of Portugal, and was made rear-admiral and Knight of the Bath. He lost his right arm in an unsuccessful attack on Santa Cruz in Tenerife that year. Within a few months he was nonetheless back in the Mediterranean, tracking a French warfleet which carried Napoleon and an army to Egypt, only to be devastated by Nelson's smaller fleet at Aboukir Bay, in the Battle of the Nile, 1 and 2 Aug. 1798.

The victory was ecstatically received in Britain, where Nelson was accorded a barony (too small an honour, in his own judgement), and also in Naples, where he returned to celebrate his 40th birthday in style and begin an affair with Emma Hamilton, demonstrative wife of the ageing British envoy, Sir William Hamilton. He spent over a year there, evacuating the Hamiltons when the French attacked, then returning to wreak sanguinary justice on collaborators, for which he was awarded the Neapolitan title Duke of Bronte. His carryings-on with Emma attracted censure: according to his commanding officer, he cut 'the most absurd figure possible for folly and vanity'. Ignoring requests for his services elsewhere, he escorted the Hamiltons on a land journey to England, where his own marriage fell apart. Emma bore him a daughter in Jan. 1801.

Attached to the Baltic fleet, with the mission of keeping Denmark out of the League of Armed Neutrality, by diplomacy if possible, Nelson chafed at inaction. Finally authorized to attack Copenhagen, he disregarded orders to withdraw when the expedition ran into difficulties (raising his telescope to his blind eye and saying, 'I really do not see the signal'), and succeeded first in battling the Danes into a truce, then negotiating an agreement. For this he was made a viscount. He set up house with the Hamiltons in Surrey and, after the ending of hostilities, went with them on a triumphal tour through the West Country, to cheering crowds.

When war resumed, he was appointed to command in the Mediterranean, charged with keeping the French fleet bottled up. When the Toulon fleet broke out into the Atlantic, he pursued them round the West Indies. He was then urged to try to annihilate the combined French and Spanish fleets, gathered in Cadiz harbour. He planned to employ the tactic of 'breaking the line' of enemy ships, previously used to great effect in the Battle of the Saints (1782) and at St Vincent. Though the Battle of Trafalgar (21 Oct. 1805) was a spectacular success (18 French ships were destroyed or captured, without loss of one British ship) the flagship, the *Victory*, came under heavy fire, and Nelson, made conspicuous by the medals on his coat, was fatally injured by French sharp-shooters.

He was given the hero's burial in St Paul's Cathedral on which he had long set his sights. His extraordinarily bold and successful career, burgeoning British nationalism and the developing capacities of the media combined to ensure that his own exploits were celebrated on a scale and with an intensity unmatched by any previous British military or naval hero.

Christopher Hibbert, Nelson: A Personal History (1994)

NEUBERGER, JULIA (née Schwab) (1950–), rabbi. Educated at Cambridge and Leo Baeck College, she became Britain's first woman rabbi when she was appointed to the South London Liberal Synagogue (1977–89). Chancellor of two universities, Durham (1982) and Ulster (1993), she is a frequent broadcaster, commentator, member of advisory committees on ethical and human rights issues and, since 1997, Chief Executive of the King's Fund.

NEVILLE, CHARLES (6th Earl of Westmorland) (?1542–1601), rebel. Brother-in-law of Thomas 4th HOWARD Duke of Norfolk, he was one of the chief leaders in the unsuccessful rising of the northern earls against the Protestant government of ELIZABETH I in 1569–70 (*see also* PERCY, THOMAS, Earl of Northumberland). He fled to Scotland and from 1570 spent his life in the Spanish Netherlands in futile plotting.

NEVILLE, EDWARD (?–1538), conspirator *see* COURTENAY, HENRY

NEVILLE, RALPH (1st Earl of Westmorland, Baron of Raby) (1364–1425), royal servant. Throughout three reigns he was involved in negotiating with the Scots and guarding the Marches. He was created Earl in 1397 by RICHARD II. Since he was married to Joan Beaufort, Bolingbroke's half-sister, he helped first to put Bolingbroke on the throne as HENRY IV in 1399 and then to suppress rebellions led in 1403 and 1405 by his great northern rivals, the Percies. He and Joan took full advantage of their close association with the house of Lancaster to push the interests of their 12 children without scruple and to great effect.

NEVILLE, RICHARD (10th Earl of Salisbury) (1400–60), nobleman. Eldest son of Ralph NEVILLE, Earl of Westmorland, and Joan Beaufort, he gained the title in 1429 through his wife Alice, daughter of Thomas de MONTAGU. As a great northern landowner, he was continually concerned with control of the Scottish Marches. His rivalry with the PERCIES resulted in armed clashes in 1453 and led to the formation of the alliance with RICHARD OF YORK that precipitated the outbreak of the Wars of the Roses (first Battle of St Albans, 1455). With his son Richard NEVILLE, Earl of Warwick, Salisbury played a prominent part in the military struggle of 1459–60 until he was captured and decapitated after the Battle of Wakefield (Yorks.) in Dec. 1460.

NEVILLE, RICHARD (16th Earl of Warwick) *see* essay on page 597

NEVINSON, C(HRISTOPHER) R(ICHARD) W(YNNE) (1889–1946), artist. Nevinson studied at the Slade, and was (like Paul NASH) an official war artist in both world wars. Before the First, he painted in Paris, where he shared a studio with Modigliani and came under the influence of the Italian Futurists: he was the co-signatory with Marinetti of the *Vital English Art: Futurist Manifesto* (1914). Among his powerful First World War paintings (some of which were censored for their first-hand portrayal of the horror of war) were *Returning to the Trenches* (1914–15), *The Road from Arras to Bapaume* and *After a Push* (both 1917). In the 1920s and 1930s Nevinson enjoyed celebrity status as a practitioner of 'modern art' and concentrated mainly on themes of contemporary urban alienation, including his dystopian *The Twentieth Century* (1932–5).

NEWARK, 1ST BARON *see* LESLIE, DAVID

NEWBERY, JOHN (1713–67), publisher. Son of a Berks. farmer, Newbery was largely self-taught. He served as assistant on the *Reading Mercury*, married his master's widow and set up as a publisher, moving to London in 1745. He published newspapers and works by Samuel JOHNSON and Oliver GOLDSMITH; Dr Primrose in Goldsmith's *Vicar of Wakefield* was modelled on him. His 'juvenile library', including titles like *Goody Two Shoes*, pioneered children's book publishing. He also published a *Lilliputian Magazine*.

NEWCASTLE, DUKE OF, 1ST *see* CAVENDISH, WILLIAM; **4TH** *see* PELHAM-HOLLES, THOMAS; **DUCHESS OF** *see* LUCAS, MARGARET

NEWCOMEN, THOMAS (1663–1729), engineer. He invented the piston engine, which rapidly became popular in coal mines for pumping water out of the workings. It is uncertain whether he invented the engine before Thomas SAVERY received his patent in 1698; in any case Newcomen later worked in partnership with Savery, to whom he paid royalties. Newcomen's engine was greatly improved by the development of the plug rod, some time before 1712; this enabled the machine to be self-acting. The machine was expensive, as it was made of brass or iron, the latter version consuming far more coal; it was eventually superseded by the work of James WATT.

NEWLANDS, JOHN (1837–98), chemist. Newlands studied chemistry in London and worked as an analytical chemist and then as a chemist in a sugar refinery. In 1865 he argued that by arranging the 62 known chemical elements in order of increasing atomic weight, similar physical and chemical properties reappear at intervals of eight elements. This law of octaves was poorly received

continued on page 598

NEVILLE, RICHARD (16th [1st Neville] Earl of Warwick) (1428–71)
Nobleman

He has been known since the sixteenth century as the Kingmaker. Son of Richard NEVILLE, Earl of Salisbury, he married the nine-year-old Anne Beauchamp when he was six. When she inherited the earldom of Warwick in 1449 he became the richest of the English earls. He lived in a style that befitted his wealth, dispensing hospitality on a lavish scale and winning popularity: throughout his political career he was keenly aware of the importance of public opinion and adroit at manipulating it. Since he was by temperament inclined to seek violent solutions to most problems he inevitably came to play a dominating role in the Wars of the Roses but not as dominating as he wanted. According to the memorable *1066 and All That*, 'one of the rules in the Wars of the Roses was that any Baron who wished to be considered King was allowed to apply at Warwick the Kingmaker's'.

He and his father inherited the traditional hostility between Nevilles and Percies which in the early 1450s was allowed to escalate into private war by HENRY VI's demoralized government. Warwick's own property dispute with the King's leading Councillor, Edmund BEAUFORT, Duke of Somerset, made it all the easier for him and his father to support their kinsman RICHARD OF YORK when, against Somerset, he insisted that he should be appointed protector following the King's breakdown in 1453. But Henry's recovery at Christmas 1454 cut the ground from under the feet of York and the Nevilles, so they raised an army and attacked the royal court (first Battle of St Albans, Feb. 1455) where Warwick's aggressive leadership helped win the day. The King was captured and three Lancastrian nobles were killed, Somerset and two Percies. Warwick's reward was his appointment as Captain of Calais. After the end of the Hundred Years War this was all that remained of English possessions in France, and to defend it the Crown employed a permanent garrison, at the time England's only standing army. French raids on the south coast then led to Warwick being appointed admiral. He did little damage to the French but he made himself a popular hero (particularly in Kent and the south east) by plundering neutral shipping and defying the government, now under the control of the Queen, MARGARET OF ANJOU, when it reprimanded him. He was 'the most courageous and manliest knight living' wrote a London chronicler. When he and his friends were indicted, they once again appealed to arms. They mustered at Ludlow (Salop.), but were forced to flee when the troops brought by him from Calais refused to fight against the King. He retained control of Calais, and his popularity in the south east enabled him to enter London, gather a large army and then capture Henry at the Battle of Northampton (July 1460), allowing York to claim the throne. York, and Warwick's father, were killed at Wakefield (Yorks.) (1460), and Warwick himself was defeated at the second Battle of St Albans (Herts.) (Feb. 1461) when Margaret recovered possession of her husband. Following EDWARD IV's decisive victory at Towton (Yorks.), Warwick was given command of siege operations against Lancastrian strongholds in Northumbria (1462–4).

These were brought to a successful conclusion and Henry was captured. Had it not been for Warwick's ambition this would have marked the end of the dynastic struggle between Lancaster and York. But he increasingly felt denied the influence which he thought his due, and he began to plot with the equally dissatisfied Clarence (*see* PLANTAGENET, GEORGE), to whom he married his daughter Isabel. In July 1469 while playing the part of the King's loyal subject who sought only reform of the realm, he took up arms again. After his victory at Edgecote (Northants.) over the Earl of Pembroke, who was leading an army to the aid of a King whom he still recognized, Warwick had the Earl executed. He captured Edward, but after holding him in confinement for several weeks felt obliged to release him. He rebelled again in 1470, this time intending to put Clarence on the throne, but was forced to sail to France, capturing more shipping en route. He came to terms with his old enemy, Margaret of Anjou, and in Sept. invaded England. When his brother John Neville abandoned Edward, it was the King's turn to flee. Warwick rescued Henry VI from the Tower and swore allegiance to him but then, by adopting a cautious strategy, allowed Edward to recover control of both London and Henry. When, belatedly, he risked battle at Barnet (Easter Sunday, 1471) he was defeated and killed. Although this pirate Earl was admired by many, he was ruthless in his treatment of his enemies and it was he alone who was responsible for the renewal in 1469 of the Wars of the Roses.

Michael Hicks, Warwick the Kingmaker (1998)

by chemists at the time but by the late 1880s was being upheld as a major step in the classification of the elements.

NEWMAN, JOHN HENRY (1801–90), Cardinal. From a pious Evangelical background, he went to Oxford University and was elected a Fellow of Oriel College in 1822, becoming vicar of St Mary's, the university church, in 1828. Here he became celebrated as a compelling preacher, with as much influence among undergraduates as SIMEON had on a previous generation at Cambridge. By then his theology had moved away from his youthful Evangelicalism, and he was one of the circle of Oxford clerics who emerged as leaders of the Oxford Movement after the enthusiastic reception of KEBLE's Assize Sermon in 1833. He became one of the principal editors of the propaganda series *Tracts for the Times* and the journal the *British Critic*, but was astonished and shocked at the reaction (particularly from the Bishop of Oxford) to his Tract 90 (1841), an ingenious if perverse attempt to argue that the Thirty-Nine Articles of the Church of England were compatible with Catholic theology. This furore accentuated his growing doubts about the claims to Catholic continuity of his Church. After a period of agonized reflection, he renounced Anglicanism in 1842, being received into the Roman Catholic Church in 1845, a move which profoundly shocked many of his fellow Tractarians. After a period in Rome, he returned to England and founded the religious communities known as oratories at Birmingham (1847) and London (1850); he was principal founder and first rector of a new Catholic university in Dublin (1854). He was made a Cardinal in 1877, but was always regarded with suspicion as dangerously liberal by many Roman Catholics, especially his fellow-convert and Cardinal Henry MANNING. Among his voluminous writings, which include his sermons and some well-known hymns, outstanding is his account of his conversion to Rome, *Apologia pro Vita Sua* (1864), a riposte to Charles KINGSLEY.

NEWNES, SIR GEORGE (1851–1910), publisher. Son of a Congregational minister, he founded a string of popular journals including the *Strand Magazine* (1891) and *Country Life* (1897). *Tit-Bits* (1881), the first of his titles, was the forerunner of a new kind of sensational journalism. He was Liberal MP for Newmarket (1885–95) and for Swansea (1900–10); he was made a baronet in 1895.

NEWTON, SIR ISAAC *see* essay on page 599

NIALL CAILLE MAC AEDA (?–846), King of Ailech and Tara. The son of AED OIRDNIDE MAC NÉILL, Niall succeeded CONCHOBAR MAC DONNCHADA as King of Tara around 832, preserving the alternation of the kingship between the ruling dynasties of the northern and southern Uí Néill. He had earlier defeated Conchobar. In 838 he was temporarily overcome by FEIDLIMID MAC CRIMTHAINN, King of Munster, who achieved the upper hand in 840 by occupying Tara. But Niall's victory in the following year destroyed Munster hopes of the supreme kingship in Ireland until the time of CORMAC MAC CUILENNÁIN 60 years later.

NIALL FROSSACH MAC FERGAILE (?–778), King of Ailech and Tara. The younger brother of AED ALLAN MAC FERGAILE, one of the most warlike of the kings of Tara, Niall had a notably milder character. Succeeding DOMNALL MIDI MAC MURCHADA of the Clann Cholmáin as King of Tara in 763, his accession maintained the alternation of this symbolically significant kingship between the ruling dynasties of the northern and southern Uí Néill. In 770 he abdicated the kingship and entered the monastic life, dying in the monastery of Iona eight years later.

NIALL GARBH Ó DOMHNAILL (?–1439), Lord of Tír Conaill. Taking advantage of a succession dispute within the Ó Néill family after 1403, he took over from them the leadership of Gaelic Ulster and launched a series of profitable and eye-catching attacks on the English inhabitants of counties Louth and Meath. In 1434 he was captured by Sir Thomas Stanley and taken to the Isle of Man, where he died in captivity five years later.

NIALL GLUNDUB MAC AEDA (?–919), King of Ailech and Tara. A son of AED FINDLIATH MAC NÉILL, Niall succeeded FLANN SINNA MAC MAÍL SHECHNAILL of the Clann Cholmáin, to whose daughter Niall was married in 916, thus maintaining the alternation to the kingship of Tara by the ruling dynasties of the northern and southern Uí Néill. The following year, however, the annals record the arrival of Viking raiders in increasing numbers in the Irish Sea, and the subsequent years record bitter warfare between the Irish kings and these raiders. In 919 Niall and his allies attacked the raiders based on Dublin, but were defeated and Niall, together with five subordinate kings 'and many nobles', was killed.

NIALL NOÍGIALLACH, *(fl. c.* 450), ancestor of the Uí Néill and 'High-King of Ireland'. Though he is subject of many Irish legends, little is known for certain about him: tradition relates that his dynasty originated in Connacht. The source of Niall's power and influence appear to have been the result of a highly successful piratical career,

continued on page 600

NEWTON, SIR ISAAC (1642–1727)
Mathematician and natural philosopher

Son of a yeoman farmer in Lincs., he was educated at the grammar school, Grantham, then at Trinity College, Cambridge, graduating in 1665. As a boy he taught himself to make sundials and working models of corn mills. At university he developed an interest in mathematics, then marginal to the syllabus, and was especially stimulated by the mathematical, scientific and philosophical writings of Descartes.

Newton later identified 'the prime of my age for invention' as the plague years from 1665 to 1666, when Cambridge University was closed and he went home to Lincs. Building on the work of the mathematician John WALLIS, he began to develop the techniques of calculus. Newton conceived of the curves whose properties calculus deals with as moving points, and termed his theory a theory of 'fluxions'. He also conducted experiments in optics, building on the recent work of Robert BOYLE and Robert HOOKE, but interpreting their findings in terms of an idea he shared with Descartes, that light consisted of small particles, about whose properties Newton nonetheless had his own ideas. He also became interested in mechanics, building on the work of Galileo by trying to analyse and account for the motion of falling and rotating bodies, and in the application of this work to 'celestial mechanics', the movement of the moon and planets, though he did not pursue this far at the time.

Returning to Cambridge in 1667, he was elected to a fellowship. A manuscript on fluid mechanics from this period reveals his interest in the theological dimension of 'natural philosophy'. Against Descartes, he argued for God's omnipresence in the universe.

At this point Isaac Barrow, Lucasian Professor of Mathematics, drew his work to the attention of London scientific circles. Newton declined to make his writings available, but seized the chance to extend his acquaintanceships. Barrow probably selected Newton to succeed him in his chair in 1669. Newton spent most of the next 20 years in Cambridge, though in 1672, having been elected a Fellow of the Royal Society (in part, it seems, because he had presented them with a reflecting telescope), he read them a lecture on optics, which proved controversial. Persistent criticism from Boyle and others dissuaded him from publishing. His mathematical work was also still circulating only in manuscript. In 1676 he was put in touch with Leibniz, who had also been developing a theory of calculus; whose work had precedence was to become a matter of heated dispute.

In the late 1660s Newton began to undertake chemical experiments, perhaps initially in the fireplace in his college room. In the late 1670s and early 1680s he invested much time in these. He believed that ancient myths encoded chemical knowledge, and drew upon alchemical ideas for help in 'decoding' these. In 1679 Newton sent Boyle a paper speculating about the basic components of the physical world which reveals that he still attributed many effects to a pervasive 'aether'. He had not yet fully committed himself to modelling the universe on mathematical principles.

Correspondence with the astronomer FLAMSTEED helped reanimate his interest in celestial mechanics, though a more immediate impetus to the phase of work which culminated in the *Principia* was Edmund HALLEY's request that he develop a mathematical explanation for certain orbital patterns. After several years' hard work, Newton published his mathematical account of the universe, *Philosophiae Naturalis Principia Mathematica* (1687). When this was finished, he began work on his *Optics*, though that was not published until 1704.

Growing confidence associated with publication set the scene for Newton's emergence into public life. He stood out against JAMES II's attempt to force Catholics on the universities, and was elected a university MP to the Convention Parliament of 1689. (He was to serve once again, briefly, 1701–2.) He became acquainted with such diverse men of learning as John LOCKE, Gilbert BURNET and Richard BENTLEY. In 1696 Charles MONTAGU, a Cambridge friend, now Chancellor of the Exchequer, had him made Warden of the Royal Mint, later Master; he also acted *de facto* as scientific adviser to the Admiralty. In 1703 he was elected President of the Royal Society: the first scientific president for many years, he remained active in the post until his death. In 1705 he was knighted. At the same time he elaborated (in private manuscripts) his non-Trinitarian theology, worked on the interpretation of prophecy and tried to develop a chronology of ancient history, as well as revising his scientific writings.

Newton was working on a third edition of the *Principia* when he died. Though few understood his work, his fame had grown in his later years, and he was buried in Westminster Abbey, and acclaimed a national hero. Voltaire, who attended his funeral, helped to popularize his reputation as one of the seminal minds of the European Enlightenment.

A. Rupert Hall, Isaac Newton: Adventurer in Thought (1992) for early traditions relate that he raided Britain on seven occasions, during the course of the last of which he was killed. The expansion of the Uí Néill eastwards resulted in the pressure upon the population of eastern Ulster which gave rise to the migration of the royal dynasty of Dál Riata to Argyll.

NICHOLLS, JOSIAS (1553–1639), churchman. Son of a Canterbury merchant, he became a minister in Kent and exercised a remarkable sway over county clergy, leading opposition to Archbishop WHITGIFT's attempt to impose religious conformity, and lobbying Parliament in Puritan causes. His tract of 1602 addressed to JAMES VI has often been quoted as evidence of the variable fortunes of the Reformation in the countryside, and brought him official punishment. He left the established Church's ministry to work as a schoolmaster; his sons Suretonhie, Josias and Repentance were also nonconformist activists.

NICHOLS, JOHN (1745–1826), author and antiquarian. Son of a baker, he was apprenticed to the London printer, William Bowyer, becoming his partner in 1766, and taking over the entire business on his death in 1777. Nichols's first important literary work was the additional volumes and appendices to SWIFT's *Works*, published between 1775 and 1779. In 1778 he became manager and co-owner of the *Gentleman's Magazine*, and sole proprietor from 1792. He was a friend of Samuel JOHNSON and printed his *Lives of the English Poets*. Nichols's most successful work was probably his *Literary Anecdotes of the Eighteenth Century* (nine vols, 1812–15).

NICOLSON, SIR HAROLD (1886–1968), diplomat and writer. Nicolson flitted between a semi-bohemian world of literature on the edges of Bloomsbury and the establishment world of the Foreign Office, and was found not quite sound in either. Nicolson left the Civil Service in 1929 soon after the publication of *Some People* (1927), whose 'fictionalized' portraits were too near the bone for the mandarins. Thereafter a journalist, writing a gossip column for Lord Beaverbrook's (*see* AITKEN, MAXWELL) *Evening Standard* and editing the publications of Oswald MOSLEY's New Party (though he broke with Mosley when he realized he had become a fascist in the 1930s), and the official biographer of GEORGE V (1952), he was a prolific columnist, essayist and reviewer, an unsuccessful novelist and a frequent broadcaster; he was on television almost at its inception with a mission to redistribute the cultural capital of the (educated) upper classes, a longterm governor of the BBC, and National Labour MP for West Leicester (1935–45), a role which he took seriously. But today this appar-

ently quintessential Edwardian figure is remembered for his modern ways: his 'open' marriage with Vita SACKVILLE-WEST, his revealing diaries and the stream of letters that he wrote (an estimated 4,000 in 1938–9 as a sample). The letters and diaries are now to be found ornamenting a number of histories of the period.

NIGHTINGALE, FLORENCE *see* essay on page 601

NIKLAES, HENDRIK (1502–*c*. 1580), religious leader. A rich merchant ('H. N.' to his followers) who had revelations in visions, he spent his career largely in the Netherlands and probably never visited England; his disciples, however, brought the Family of Love, the only continental radicals or Anabaptists to make a lasting impression in England. Arriving under EDWARD VI, Familism persisted into the 1650s, when members may have joined the Quakers. Familists believed themselves pure and united with God, and entitled to lead a life of deception; they frequently denied Familism, and fitted without trouble into official churches. ELIZABETH I knowingly tolerated them among her personal servants; Puritans sought their persecution.

NINIAN, ST (*c*. 500–*c*. 550), missionary. Named by BEDE as the missionary who converted the southern Picts to Christianity, historically he is very obscure, and Bede's information may not be particularly reliable. He is known to have been a bishop who built a stone church at Whithorn in Galloway. His missionary work was probably among the Picts on the Firth of Forth or perhaps in Fife and Perths.

NKOMO, JOSHUA (1917–99), Zimbabwean politician. Born in Matabeland, Southern Rhodesia, of the Ndebele people, he became active in nationalist politics in the mid 1950s. Opposing federation with Nyasaland and Northern Rhodesia, he led a succession of organizations, each of which was then banned. The last of these, ZAPU (Zimbabwean African People's Union), he founded in 1961 together with Ndabaningi Sithole (1920–), but by 1963 Sithole led the breakaway ZANU (Zimbabwean African National Union), representing the numerically dominant Shona people. After Rhodesia's Unilateral Declaration of Independence in 1965 Nkomo and his ZANU rival Robert MUGABE were detained for 10 years; on his release Nkomo led the guerrilla struggle from Zambia. With Ian SMITH's regime progressively collapsing, he formed a new alliance with Mugabe. Differences were resolved at the 1978–9 Lancaster House conference, but after 1980's elections the coalition fell apart, split along ethnic lines. Having

continued on page 602

NIGHTINGALE, FLORENCE (1820–1910)
Nursing reformer

Florence Nightingale was named after the city of her birth; her father was a Whig landowner, her mother, the daughter of a well-known Abolitionist. She had a privileged English childhood, but despite the liberal education she received she found the stifling limitations and enforced idleness of Victorian womanhood insupportable. 'What is my business in this world, and what have I done this fortnight?' she agonized in 1846. Nightingale knew what she wanted to do with her life: nurse. But her father refused to allow it, since nursing at the time was a degraded profession and hospitals were seen as little better than brothels. Finally he relented and she set off for the Institute of Protestant Deaconesses in Germany, where she received some elementary training. In 1853 she took the unpaid post of superintendent of the Hospital for Invalid Gentlewomen in London and it was there that she proved to be an excellent administrator and skilful in orchestrating committees.

Britain had joined France in resisting Russian encroachments on the Ottoman empire in March 1854, and daily reports from the Crimea appeared in *The Times*, detailing the wretched conditions and high death rate among the soldiers. In the ensuing political outcry, the Secretary for War, Sidney HERBERT, asked Nightingale to lead a contingent of nurses to the battlefront. When they arrived in Scutari, they found that the 'hospital' was a barracks with no beds, just straw mats, and nowhere to prepare food, and, with polluted water and stinking sanitary conditions, vermin and dysentery were endemic. Through a combination of ruthless efficiency and Herculean hard work, and above all because she had the money to pay for medical stores and equipment on the open market in Constantinople, rather than petitioning for supplies through the incompetent, sometimes obstreperous official Purveyor-in-Chief, she appeared to work miracles: in a few months the death rate had dropped from 42 per cent to 2 per cent.

At Scutari Nightingale had to deal with all the hospital administration, writing reports to Herbert, soliciting and acknowledging donations and en-gaging in battles with Sir John Hall, the Chief of Medical Staff, whom she regarded as 'a fossil', incapable of dealing with the acute conditions of the Crimean War. But she saw her primary role as nursing; sitting with the dying ('her nerve is wonderful ... she had an utter disregard of contagion'), supervising medical procedures, administering medicines.

The relentless 18 months in the Crimea took their toll. In 1846 Nightingale was invalided home, a popular heroine whom Longfellow immortalized as the 'Lady with the Lamp' in the poem *Santa Filomena* (1857), an acclamatory legend that has persisted.

On her return to England she worked with Herbert on a Royal Commission on Army Medical Conditions, driving herself so hard that she collapsed. She recovered, but spent many of the ensuing 54 years confined to her room. But having found a cause, driving determination and a prodigious talent for getting things done against the odds, she lobbied tirelessly from her sickroom to improve the training and status of nurses and for medical reforms.

She and Herbert had packed the Commission with like-minded reformers and succeeded in drastically improving the life of soldiers. Statutory sanitary standards in barracks were set, and an Army Medical School was established to train doctors for the sort of conditions and for the injuries and diseases which they would encounter, with a statistical branch to quantify problems for future policy.

In 1860, with £45,000 raised by public subscription, Nightingale endowed a school for nursing at St Thomas's Hospital in London and planned every detail of the nurses' training: her *Notes on Nursing* (1859) and *Notes on Hospitals* (1863) explicate many of the rules of hygiene, technical competence and professionalism that were to raise nursing from its former menial status: within a couple of decades most of the voluntary and large workhouse hospitals were employing trained nurses, and several had set up their own nursing schools.

Rejecting the sentimental image of herself as the 'Lady of the Lamp', Nightingale insisted that her success owed much to the fact that she had wielded 'more political power than if I had been a borough returning two MPs'. She could be a bully, was often misguided and increasingly isolated, narrowly focused and self-dramatizing as a result of her long, self-imposed seclusion. But she was a heroine in her lifetime, the first woman to be awarded the Order of Merit, and although her theories of medical non-intervention, the originality of her ideas and the extent to which her achievements were hers alone, have subsequently been questioned, she remains the most famous British woman of the nineteenth century after Queen VICTORIA.

Cecil Woodham Smith, Florence Nightingale (1951)

fled in 1983 amid violence after accusations of plotting a coup, Nkomo returned in 1985. The two parties united in 1987, Nkomo becoming senior Vice-President, but his political role was over. The 'father of Zimbabwe', he had nevertheless been outmanoeuvred.

NKRUMAH, KWAME (1900–72), Ghanaian politician. Educated in his native Gold Coast, the USA and Britain, Nkrumah was active in African politics in London. Returning to the Gold Coast in 1947, he became General Secretary of the United Gold Coast Convention; imprisoned by the colonial authorities, he subsequently led a more vocal pro-independence campaign through the Convention People's Party, founded in 1949. Arrested by the British once more amid a widespread campaign of civil disobedience, Nkrumah was permitted to take his seat in the Legislative Assembly at the start of 1951, becoming leader of government business and then Prime Minister in 1952. He led the campaign for self-determination that culminated in independence, as Ghana, in 1957. His government swiftly took a dictatorial stand against political opponents and adopted pro-Soviet policies; Ghana was declared a republic in 1960, and a one-party state in 1964, before Nkrumah was overthrown in a coup in 1966.

NOLLEKENS, JOSEPH (1737–1823), sculptor. The son of the Dutch-born painter Joseph Francis Nollekens, he was apprenticed to SCHEEMAKERS before studying in Rome, where he gained his reputation by making portrait busts of British travellers. He returned to London in 1770 and two years later was elected to the Royal Academy. Nollekens's style was heavily influenced by classical sculpture, and he was most celebrated for his portraits, including Charles James FOX, sculpted in 1791, and the 5th Duke of Bedford in 1801. Copies of both were highly sought after. His Whig political loyalties prevented him from gaining many public commissions but he was widely respected as an artist.

NORFOLK, DUKE OF, 1ST see MOWBRAY, THOMAS; **3RD** see MOWBRAY, JOHN; **4TH** and **5TH** see BIGOD, ROGER; **6TH** see HOWARD, JOHN; **7TH, 8TH, 9TH** and **16TH** see HOWARD, THOMAS

NORMAN, MONTAGU (1871–1950), banker. In office between 1920 and 1944, he was the longest ever serving Governor of the Bank of England. Presiding over the bank during some of the most turbulent episodes in its history, he played a leading role in dealing with the problems caused by German reparations, Britain's return to gold in 1925, the collapse of the gold standard in 1931, monetary policy during the Depression and the financing of the Second World War. Despite his public image of a hard-nosed man of money dictating to politicians, it is now clear that power was shifting from the bank towards the Treasury throughout the period of his tenure. It was 50 years before the bank's independence over monetary policy was restored.

NORMANBY, 1ST MARQUESS OF see SHEFFIELD, JOHN

NORTH, SIR DUDLEY (1881–1961), sailor. North saw action at Heligoland Bight (1914), Dogger Bank (1915) and Jutland (1916). In 1939, now a Vice-Admiral, North was appointed to command at Gibraltar. He protested bitterly over the attacks on the French fleet on 3 July 1940 and in Sept. 1940 refused to open fire on a Vichy French squadron passing through the straits on its way to repel an Anglo-Free-French landing at Dakar. Sacked by the Admiralty, North returned to England and joined the Home Guard. His attempts to clear his name became a *cause célèbre* in the 1950s.

NORTH, FRANCIS (1st Baron Guilford) (1637–85), judge. The third son of the 4th Lord North, he studied at Cambridge and the Middle Temple, became an MP and Attorney General in 1673 and Lord Chief Justice from 1675. He was faithful to CHARLES II, doubted the claims of OATES concerning the existence of the Popish Plot, and opposed the Exclusionists (*see* COOPER, ANTHONY ASHLEY). In 1681 North tried the Protestant activist Stephen COLLEGE, who had arrived armed and mounted during the parliamentary session held that year at Oxford, calling for resistance to Charles II. North has been accused of undue bias against College, who was executed for treason. North was rewarded with the lord keepership, which he held until his death.

NORTH, FREDERICK *see* essay on pages 604–05

NORTHAMPTON, EARL OF, 3RD *see* HENRY OF NORTHUMBRIA; **9TH** *see* HOWARD, HENRY

NORTHBROOK, BARON, 1ST and **2ND** *see* BARING FAMILY; **1ST EARL OF** *see* BARING FAMILY

NORTHCLIFFE, 1ST VISCOUNT *see* HARMSWORTH, ALFRED

NORTHCOTE, SIR STAFFORD (1st Earl of Iddesleigh) (1818–87), politician. Private secretary to GLADSTONE and a barrister, Northcote was elected as a Conservative MP in 1855 and soon became a close confidant of DISRAELI. He served as

President of the Board of Trade (1866), Secretary for India (1867) and Chancellor of the Exchequer (1874–80). He was the first Chancellor to admit that income tax was not a temporary expedient, and he attempted to codify it in fiscal practice. He succeeded Disraeli as Conservative leader in the Commons during Gladstone's second ministry (1880–5) and used his political skills to achieve a compromise on the 1884 Reform Act, though in Disraeli's view his attachment to Gladstone in his youth inhibited his effectiveness in opposition. Northcote (who had been created an earl in 1885) was appointed Foreign Secretary in 1886, but resigned six months later and died the same day. A natural second-in-command, he was efficient, conscientious, pleasant, almost universally liked and always loyal.

NORTHUMBERLAND, EARL OF, 3RD *see* PUISET, HUGH DE; **4TH, 9TH** and **11TH** *see* PERCY, HENRY; **19TH** *see* PERCY, ALGERNON; **1ST DUKE OF** *see* DUDLEY, JOHN

NORTHUMBRIA, 1ST EARL OF *see* HENRY OF NORTHUMBRIA

NORTON, CAROLINE (née Sheridan) (1808–77), novelist and campaigner for the rights of women. Granddaughter of the playwright Richard Brinsley SHERIDAN, at 19 she married a failed barrister, who was to be jealous of her literary success. *The Sorrows of Rosalie* was published in 1829, though her most successful work, the sentimental poem *The Lady of La Garaye,* did not appear until 1861. The success of her poetry (which holds almost no appeal for contemporary taste) and her novels enabled Norton to earn her own living from writing.

In 1835 her Tory husband instigated divorce proceedings, citing the Whig Prime Minister, Lord Melbourne (*see* LAMB, WILLIAM), who had been a frequent visitor to Caroline Norton's literary gatherings, claiming damages of £10,000. Although he lost the case, his wife's reputation was irreparably damaged and her husband was granted custody of the children of the marriage after the couple legally separated, she being denied access to them, as was usual in such instances. She published *The Natural Claim of a Mother to the Custody of Her Children* in 1836, arguing that custody should be decided in Chancery on the basis of individual circumstances. Her writing influenced the framing of the Custody of Infants Act (1839), which gave mothers of 'unblemished character' access to their children in the event of separation and divorce. Her bitter marital experiences, when her husband tried to keep not only her children but also the copyright of her work from her, led her to write about how little protection the law accorded married women and their property in *English Laws for Women in the Nineteenth Century* (1854). The debate over the Divorce Act (finally passed in 1857) was greatly influenced by her arguments, particularly that divorced or separated women should have the sole right to their subsequent earnings. It was because Caroline Norton did not subscribe to the idea of women's equality with men that she sought the protection of their interests under law. Though her fourth novel, *Lost and Saved* (1863), deals with double standards for men and women, as between respectable and 'fallen' women, Norton continued to believe that marriage to a responsible man was a woman's best hope of happiness, and she embarked on the enterprise again in 1875 after her first husband died.

NOTTINGHAM, EARL OF, 3RD *see* MOWBRAY, THOMAS; **10TH** *see* HOWARD, CHARLES; **14TH** *see* FINCH, DANIEL

NOVELLO, IVOR (1893–1951), composer. His mother, a Cardiff singing teacher, encouraged his talent and Novello published his first song while still a chorister at Magdalen College school, Oxford: there were to be many more, among them *We'll Gather Lilacs* and (during the First World War, in which he served in the navy) *Keep the Home Fires Burning.* He also acted and wrote successful plays and films, but is best remembered for his romantic musicals, which include *The Dancing Years* (1939) and *King's Rhapsody* (1949).

NOWELL, ALEXANDER (*c.* 1507–1602), religious writer. Oxford-educated, he was in exile under MARY I and returned to be appointed Dean of St Paul's, London, in 1560. He published three catechisms (systems of religious instruction in question and answer form) which were widely used: he probably wrote the official catechism of 1549 also, since it is so like his small catechism: the differences were absorbed into the revised catechism printed with the Book of Common Prayer in 1604. *See* OVERALL, JOHN.

NOY, WILLIAM (1577–1634), lawyer. His enthusiastic attacks as a lawyer-MP on royal grants of monopolies and other fiscal excesses of the Crown were curbed when CHARLES I appointed him Attorney General in 1631. He led the prosecution of William PRYNNE, and used his knowledge of legal history to promote the financial antiquarian expedients of Charles's 1630s rule without Parliament, such as Ship Money to pay for the navy, and the forest laws, by which the government exploited the boundaries of ancient royal forests

continued on page 606

NORTH, FREDERICK (8th Baron North, 4th [2nd North] Earl of Guilford) (1732–92)
Politician and Prime Minister (1770–82)

He was born to a once Tory family turned Whig courtiers; his father was Lord of the Bedchamber to FREDERICK, Prince of Wales (father of GEORGE III). Some rumoured that the Prince had also fathered Frederick North, who looked like George.

Known as 'Lord North' by courtesy before his succession to the title late in life, he was educated at Eton and Oxford, then went on a Grand Tour with his stepbrother the Earl of Dartmouth (*see* LEGGE, William). On his return in 1754 he was elected MP, supporting the Whig ministry of Newcastle (*see* PELHAM-HOLLES, THOMAS) and establishing a reputation in debate. In 1759 he was appointed to the Treasury board. After the accession of George III, pressed by his father not to alienate the King by following other Whigs into opposition, he remained a government supporter. He took a leading part in proceedings against WILKES, declined to serve under Rockingham (*see* WATSON-WENTWORTH, CHARLES), but became Paymaster of the Forces under Chatham (*see* PITT THE ELDER), and Chancellor of the Exchequer and leader in the Commons in 1767. His parliamentary skills, grasp of finance and record of loyalty all helped to commend him to George III when Grafton (*see* FITZROY, AUGUSTUS) proved unable to cope with the storm brewed up by the Wilkes affair. In 1770 North was made First Lord of the Treasury and head of the administration.

In his first years in office, North calmed ruffled waters. He avoided previous ministers' error of standing intransigent in the face of popular opposition: when Wilkes's friends agitated against restrictions on press reporting of Parliament, North let them win. He soothed discontented American colonists, who had been protesting about overbearing British imperial rule since George GRENVILLE first attempted to impose stamp duties on them in 1763, by repealing duties imposed by the previous Chancellor, Charles TOWNSHEND, except that on tea. The calm proved temporary, however, for in 1773 tea duty became the focus for a campaign of direct action, the Boston Tea Party. Attempts to isolate and discipline the radicals of Massachussetts by a series of coercive measures (the Intolerable Acts) merely provoked the Americans to co-operate in a Continental Congress, which insisted that the British govern only with colonial consent. North and Dartmouth found themselves the most doveish members of a hawkish Cabinet. Last-ditch attempts to stem the drift to war in 1775, with an offer to let any co-operating colony help set the level of its financial contribution, should not be taken at face value, none the less. The object was less to conciliate the Americans than to divide them – a strategy central to British policy, political and military, through the first years of the war.

War began in April 1775 when British and American forces clashed at Lexington and Concord. In Aug. a general proclamation of rebellion was issued. American forces attacked Canada but were driven back; the British evacuated Boston. The Declaration of Independence was signed on 4 July 1776. In Sept., in a major amphibious assault, British forces under Richard and William HOWE captured New York city, but the following year William Howe failed to eliminate the Continental Army under WASHINGTON. A major turning-point came when the British attempted to divide New England from other colonies by sending forces under General John BURGOYNE from Canada to meet others coming north from New York. Burgoyne's forces were surrounded and he surrendered at Saratoga in Oct. This defeat induced the North administration to send a peace commission, under the Earl of Carlisle, offering to repeal all offensive Acts passed since 1763 and recognize the Continental Congress. But the French had moved first: a Franco-American treaty was signed in Feb. 1778.

France declared war on Britain in June; a series of more or less indecisive actions between French and British navies ensued. In Dec. 1778 a new campaign was opened in the south; British forces under Campbell subdued Georgia, and moved into South Carolina. In June 1779 Spain entered the war and a combined Franco-Spanish fleet threatened the invasion of Britain (disease aboard this fleet helped avert what could have been a disaster for the British). The Royal Navy was in an inferior, defensive position, worsened by the Dutch entry into the war a year later. Britain was then fighting all the other major naval powers. Gibraltar was besieged and most of Campbell's troops were withdrawn to protect Florida. It became clear that the French and Spanish were keen, above all, to make gains in the West Indies; they succeeded in seizing several British islands from 1778 to 1780, though their preoccupation with this task left the British relatively free to pursue war in the south.

Early in the war North had experienced relatively little difficulty in maintaining political ascendancy at home. Attempts by the main opposition groups under Rockingham and Chatham to convince the public that the Americans were victims of British abuse had not gone down well. As the war persisted, however, North's confidence began to falter. The Rockingham Whigs called for the recognition of American independence. Chatham fiercely opposed this, but collapsed in mid-denunciation, to die in May 1778. By 1779 North faced serious divisions within ministerial ranks: Gower and Weymouth, erstwhile followers of the 7th Duke of Bedford's (see RUSSELL, JOHN) hawkish faction, resigned. The King saw North as a bulwark against the opposition, and was keen to keep him on but, worried by his loss of confidence, worsened the situation himself by consulting other members of the ministry, behind North's back.

In 1780 public discontent with the war, and high taxes and the trade downturn associated with it, came to a head in WYVILL's Association, which mobilized public support for 'economical reform', intended both to cut costs and reduce ministerial patronage, and for parliamentary reform. Meanwhile, Irish discontent with the wartime collapse of trade had mounted; 1780 saw Irish counties petitioning for Irish legislative independence. This demand was the more formidable because of the support which it received from Irish Volunteers, first mobilized to maintain order in wartime and to repel French invasion, now emerging as an anti-government force. In April, the ministry was defeated over DUNNING's motion bewailing the increasing 'influence of the Crown'; North offered to resign, but was dissuaded by the King. In June London was devastated by the anti-Catholic Gordon Riots (see GORDON, LORD GEORGE). The King authorized sounding out the Rockinghamites about joining the ministry, but would not accept their conditions, including both economical reform and willingness to accept American independence.

North received a much-needed boost with the arrival of news of the capture of Charleston, South Carolina, which had followed the transfer of the main British army from New York to the south at the beginning of the year. A General Election brought him back to power, but with a reduced majority. Accepting the need for some reform, he appointed commissioners to audit the public accounts. Meanwhile the war continued to broaden. In Aug., Russia, Sweden and Denmark had inaugurated the League of Armed Neutrality. War had also broken out in southern India, where HYDER ALI gained ascendancy over British troops until in 1782 Sir Eyre COOTE reversed the position. North fell when the British position on the American mainland collapsed. CORNWALLIS succeeded in capturing Yorktown in Aug. 1781, but was surprised and trapped there by combined French and American forces. The French fleet held off a British one at the Battle of Chesapeake and Cornwallis was forced to surrender. In Feb. 1782 a motion that no further attempt be made to subdue the Americans by force was carried in Parliament. North resigned in March. The King was left to the mercies of the former opposition. Though the world war had not ended, the granting of American independence had become inevitable.

Initially keeping a low profile, North re-emerged as a political force in 1783, when the former opposition had split between the followers of Shelburne (see PETTY, WILLIAM), formerly the Chathamites, now forming the ministry, and the followers of Charles James FOX (formerly the Rockinghamites). Angered, it seems, by Shelburne's failure to protect the interests of American loyalists in the initial peace negotiations, and worried by the animosity towards him expressed by Shelburne's young lieutenant, PITT THE YOUNGER, North allied with Fox. Despite the King's preference for Shelburne, the 'unnatural coalition' of Fox and North forced its way to power in 1783, the leaders each taking a Secretaryship of State under the nominal lead of Portland (see BENTINCK, WILLIAM CAVENDISH). Thus ended North's only experience in active opposition in a career spent almost entirely in office. The coalition enjoyed overwhelming strength in the Commons, and North might have expected to end his career in power but, such was the King's dislike of Fox, that he seized upon the issue of East India Company reform (which could be portrayed as a ministerial power-grab) to force them out.

For a time, North opposed Pitt the Younger, but bad health and increasing blindness prompted his gradual withdrawal from Parliament. In 1790 he succeeded to his father's title, gaining a seat in the Lords. The fact that he had presided over the loss of most of Britain's American colonies inevitably tarnished his record at the time and since. He had been forced, however, by an intransigent King to persist with an unwinnable war, and his resilience over the longer term is impressive. Historians have questioned whether any other minister, even Chatham or the Rockinghams, who thought that they had all the answers, could have handled the crisis any better.

Peter D. G. Thomas, Lord North (1976)

in order to levy fines on those who had unwittingly encroached on them.

NUFFIELD, 1ST VISCOUNT *see* MORRIS, WILLIAM

NUN OF KENT *see* BARTON, ELIZABETH

NUTTING, SIR ANTHONY (1920–1999), politician. Nutting was elected Conservative MP for Melton (Leics.) in 1945. EDEN made him his Parliamentary Under-Secretary in 1951, and in 1954 he became Minister of State at the Foreign Office. His promising career came to an end in 1956 when he resigned in disgust over the Suez operation. His subsequent book, *No End of a Lesson* (1967), revealed the full story of the collusion between Britain and Israel but earned him further criticism from his former friends. He never held office again.

NYERERE, JULIUS (1922–99), Tanzanian politician. Son of a government chief, and educated in Tanganyika, in Uganda and at Edinburgh University, Nyerere returned to Tanganyika in 1952, becoming President of the Tanganyika Africa Association and then of the new Tanganyika African National Union (TANU). He resigned his schoolteaching post in 1955 to devote himself to politics, and embarked on a whirlwind recruitment drive that overwhelmed British attempts to stop TANU. He led a campaign to secure African majorities on all elective bodies; TANU then swept all before it in the elections of 1960. Nyerere was appointed Chief Minister. Independence followed in 1961. In the offshore British protectorate of Zanzibar, political independence was granted in 1963, but the Arab rulers were overthrown weeks later. Nyerere brokered the union of Tanganyika and Zanzibar as Tanzania. Under him, a single one-party socialist state swiftly emerged, unaligned but committed to African liberation.

O

OASTLER, RICHARD (1789–1861), social reformer. Known as 'the Factory King', he campaigned for the Ten Hours Act 1847 and opposed the New Poor Law, paving the way for the Chartist movement in the north. He also advocated the abolition of slavery. Oastler's stand against the introduction of the Poor Law led to his dismissal from his employment and subsequent imprisonment in the Fleet prison for debt (1840–4) where he wrote *Fleet Papers* in three volumes. For all that, he was a 'Tory radical', opposed to universal suffrage and a strong supporter of the Church (which led him to oppose Catholic Emancipation), the throne and a paternalistic social order.

OATES, LAURENCE (1880–1912), explorer. He fought in the Boer War, and in 1910 joined Robert Falcon SCOTT's expedition to Antarctica. He was in the party that reached the South Pole on 17 Jan. 1912, only to find that the Norwegian, Amundsen, had beaten them to it. On the way back fierce blizzards cut the team off, and Oates, suffering from severe frostbite, was convinced that he imperilled the survival of his companions, so he walked out into the snow to die, uttering the immortal words, 'I am just going outside and may be gone some time.'

OATES, TITUS *see* essay on page 608

O'BRIEN, CONOR CRUISE *see* CRUISE O'BRIEN, CONOR

O'BRIEN, JAMES (BRONTERRE) (1804–64), Irish radical. The 'schoolmaster of Chartism', he was the leading journalist, theorist and agitator in the campaigns for the unstamped press, parliamentary reform and social reform. Both the *Poor Man's Guardian* and the *Northern Star* owed their success to the quality of his writing. His understanding of the structural sources of inequality and his elaboration of a comprehensive social programme gave the democratic movement a direction that had hitherto been missing.

O'BRIEN, MURROUGH (6th Baron, 1st Earl of Inchiquin) (?1614–74), soldier. Munster's leading Protestant, he used his formidable and brutal military skill in Ireland's civil wars to fight the Catholic Confederates, first for CHARLES I, and from 1644 (in fury at Charles's negotiations with Catholics) for Parliament. With George MONCK, he won a crushing victory against the Royalist and Catholic forces at Mallow (Co. Cork) in 1647. Aggrieved at his lack of reward, in 1648 he returned to alliance with Charles and with the Catholics, but defeat by Oliver CROMWELL forced him into French exile (1650–60), with an earldom from the exiled Charles as empty consolation. He endured capture by Algerian pirates before returning to lavish honours and a quiet retirement as a Catholic convert in Ireland.

O'BRIEN, WILLIAM (1852–1928), journalist and politician. A former Fenian, O'Brien came to prominence as a journalist in the late 1870s by reporting on poverty among tenant farmers. Charles Stewart PARNELL made him editor of a weekly paper, *United Ireland*. He was MP for Mallow (1882–5), South Tyrone (1885–6), North-East Cork (1886–92) and Cork City (1892–6, 1900–3, 1904–9, 1910–18). A powerful if emotionally unstable and often scurrilous public speaker, he became one of Parnell's principal lieutenants. His leading role in the Plan of Campaign land agitation of the late 1880s and his refusal to wear prison uniform during a term of imprisonment made him a popular hero.

He opposed Parnell in the split of 1890 because he believed it necessary to maintain Gladstonian (*see* GLADSTONE, W. E.) Liberal support for Home Rule, and supported John DILLON against HEALY in the struggle for leadership of the anti-Parnellite faction. He retired temporarily from public life, but in 1898 organized a new land agitation, centred on the United Irish League, which became the vehicle for the reunion of the Home Rule Party in 1900. In 1903 he came to believe that Wyndham's Land Act, which took a major step towards solving the land question by providing government loans to allow tenants to buy their holdings from landlords, could lay the foundation for a rapprochement with moderate Unionists, leading to Home Rule by consent. When the party leadership rejected this view he broke away and

continued on page 609

OATES, TITUS (1649–1705)
Anti-Catholic agitator

Son of a New Model Army chaplain, Oates's life early assumed its characteristic pattern: he was expelled from school and college; though he took holy orders, he left one living charged with drunken blasphemy. Facing a perjury charge after he had accused a local gentleman of sodomy, he served as chaplain in a Tangier-bound ship (1675) but was dismissed for homosexual acts.

In 1677 Oates was received into the Catholic Church and sent to the Jesuit college at Valladolid but, found to know no Latin, was sent to a boarding school where his bawdy and blasphemous habits prompted his expulsion. He later claimed his conversion had been feigned, to gather information about Jesuits. His motives remain obscure.

Catholics were then widely feared, as were Popish influences at court: there was concern that CHARLES II's brother James (later JAMES II) was Catholic and anxiety about French influence on British policies. Some old Commonwealth men sought to exonerate themselves by blaming Jesuits for the Great Rebellion and execution of CHARLES I. Jesuits were widely believed to have started the Great Fire which destroyed much of London (1666). Oates turned to an old acquaintance, Israel Tonge, whose own church was destroyed in the fire and who nursed such fears. Oates regaled Tonge with a tale of Jesuit conspiracy to assassinate the King and raise rebellion in all three kingdoms, his acquaintance with Jesuit circles enabling him to speak with unnerving specificity.

Tonge began to spread the tale, gaining an audience with the King, who asked Danby (see OSBORNE, THOMAS) to investigate. Thus began the process whereby Oates's allegations were broadcast further and grew in the telling, as he responded to the fears and prompting of questioners by extending his charges from Jesuits to other religious orders, Catholic peers and gentlemen, and, on occasion, glancingly, to James, Duke of York, or the Queen, though he was generally cautious not to provoke the King by accusing those close to him. Initially supported by the Crown, he and Tonge were given Whitehall apartments and paid an allowance. Oates latterly developed close ties with the King's critics, especially Shaftesbury (see COOPER, ANTHONY ASHLEY): his fortunes rose and fell with theirs.

The next step towards widening the audience came in the autumn of 1678 when, apparently on James's urging, the Privy Council investigated; they ordered arrests and seizures of papers, some of which lent credibility to Oates's charges. On 17 Oct. 1678 the whole thing passed out of the government's hands when the magistrate before whom Oates had initially testified, Sir Edmund Berry GODFREY, was found mysteriously murdered. Opening Parliament a few days later Charles himself referred to a plot, happily foiled, against his life. Parliament asked for relevant papers, and the Commons summoned Oates to testify, and, as a result of his ever widening accusations, issued warrants for the arrest of several Catholic peers. In 1679 Jesuits and members of other religious orders were put on trial; there were also trials and executions in the provinces.

Charles spent several years struggling to contain what became a major political crisis by a mix of permitting, even encouraging, action against Catholics and trying to limit its extent. The court position was that there had been a plot, but it had been dealt with. The argument that conspiracy was still to be feared became the political opposition's. High-profile executions continued to 1681: Viscount Stafford (see HOWARD, WILLIAM) was executed in 1680, and Oliver PLUNKETT, Archbishop of Armagh, the next year. In some parts of the provinces fear of Catholic plotting peaked even later, but by summer 1681 Charles felt strong enough to turn the tables. Indeed, by this time there was much talk of 'Presbyterian plots', and anti-papists as well as papists found their way to the gallows.

Oates's allowance was discontinued in 1682. In 1684 he was charged with having referred to James as 'that traitor James, Duke of York'. Unable to pay damages of £100,000, he was imprisoned for debt. James also charged him with perjury. Those who had once believed Oates now impugned him. Though he fought his corner hard, he was convicted, unfrocked, pilloried, whipped and ordered to be imprisoned for life. James opined that 'now Oates was convicted the Popish Plot was dead', though Parliament's refusal to reverse Viscount Stafford's attainder showed that was not entirely true, and William of Orange's (later WILLIAM III) invasion a few years later demonstrated the evanescence of James's triumph.

The Revolution was good news for Oates: he was released from prison in Dec. 1688 and in Mar. 1689 petitioned Parliament for redress. The Lords refused to clear him of perjury, though they were prepared to try to close the matter by securing him a free pardon. He died in obscurity.

J. P. Kenyon, The Popish Plot (1972)

thereafter had little political influence, although he led a splinter group until 1918. His opposition to partition caused him to support Sinn Féin after 1916.

O'BRIEN, WILLIAM SMITH (1803–64), Irish politician. From a Protestant gentry background, he entered Parliament in 1828 and reacted to British neglect of Ireland by moving from Peelite (*see* PEEL, ROBERT) Toryism through independent Liberalism to nationalism. He joined the Repeal Association in 1843 and became O'CONNELL's second-in-command, but seceded from the association along with the Young Irelanders in 1846. In July 1848 he tried to raise a rebellion but made little impact, partly because of his ineffective leadership and respect for property rights. He was found guilty of treason and transported. Pardoned in 1854, he returned to Ireland in 1856, but took little further interest in politics. He was remembered as high-minded but ineffective, 'too much Smith and not enough O'Brien'.

ÓBRUADAIR, DÁIBHÍDH (*c.* 1625–98), poet. Little is known of his life or origins. Widely acknowledged as the finest Irish Gaelic poet of his age, he may have been trained in one of the poetic schools of Munster. His poetry illuminates the lives of the contemporary Munster gentry, and comments poignantly on the wreck of his country and of Roman Catholicism by successive English invaders during his lifetime.

O'CASEY, SEAN (1880–1964), playwright. Born into a clerk's family living in the Dublin slums, O'Casey moved from Orangeism to nationalism and socialism. In the early 1920s he revitalized Dublin's Abbey Theatre by his three best-known plays, using an urban setting and idioms, *The Shadow of a Gunman* (1923), *Juno and the Paycock* (1924) and *The Plough and the Stars* (1926). His critical treatment of recent nationalist movements created political controversy, and Republicans disrupted the *Plough* in protest at its portrayal of working-class participants in the 1916 Easter Rising as self-deluded. After the Abbey rejected his experimental play *The Silver Tassie*, O'Casey moved to England. O'Casey's political views were sometimes too Stalinist for comfort, his opinions on nationalism remain controversial and even the earlier plays on which his reputation rests have experienced a slight decline in estimation, but his achievement in establishing an idiom for the literary treatment of Dublin working-class life secured his place as one of the great figures of Irish theatre.

Ó CEARNAIGH, SEAN *see* KEARNEY, JOHN

O'CONNELL, DANIEL *see* essay on page 610

O'CONNELL, ROBERT (*c.* 1623–78), writer *see* O'FERRALL, RICHARD

O'CONNOR, FEARGUS (1794–1855), Chartist leader. Son of Roger O'Connor, a United Irishman, he gravitated from Irish radicalism to English Chartism to become the movement's best known and most popular leader. He established the influential weekly *Northern Star* in 1837, which advocated a 'land plan' for rural resettlement. Though identified with the use of physical force O'Connor was an agitator rather than a conspirator. He was elected MP for Nottingham in 1847, and introduced the 1848 Chartist petition to the Commons. A good mob orator, he was a poor organizer without the qualities necessary to create a working-class national party under his leadership. He was pronounced insane in 1852.

ODA, Archbishop of Canterbury (941–58). Oda is important for having advanced the careers of later and more important tenth-century reformers, his nephew St OSWALD and St DUNSTAN, and for having begun, with royal support, to hold councils of the entire English Church. In 936 he became a monk of the famous abbey of Fleury-sur-Loire, which was later to be very influential on the Tenth-Century Reform. Oda's career also demonstrates the integration of Scandinavians into English society, since he was the son of a pagan who had come to England in the Viking 'Great Army', and he also organized the reintroduction of a bishopric amid the Scandinavian settlements of East Anglia.

ODO OF BAYEUX (1st Earl of Kent) (*c.* 1036–97), churchman. Son of WILLIAM I THE CONQUEROR's mother, HERLEVA, by Herluin of Conteville (whom she married after the death of William's father), he was made Bishop of Bayeux in 1049 when still a very young man. For more than 30 years he was one of William's most powerful aides in both Normandy and England. The Bayeux Tapestry represents him as a principal architect of the 1066 campaign; when William returned to Normandy in Jan. 1067, Odo was one of those left behind to complete the conquest. In consequence by the 1070s he was Earl of Kent and, after the King, by far the richest landowner in England. In 1082, for reasons which are not clear, William had him arrested. According to one rumour he was planning to take an army to Rome and get himself elected Pope. Released when William died in 1087 he led the 1088 rebellion in England against WILLIAM II on behalf of the Duke of Normandy, ROBERT II Curthose; as a man with a stake in both England and Normandy, Odo wanted to see both under a single ruler. But his forces were defeated at Pevensey (Sussex) and Rochester (Kent) and he was driven to Normandy. In 1096 he accompanied

continued on page 611

O'CONNELL, DANIEL (1775–1847)
Irish nationalist, called 'The Liberator'

From a Catholic landowning family in Co. Kerry, O'Connell was at school in France during the French Revolution, which left him with an abiding horror of bloodshed. He developed radical political ideas as a law student in London, and for a time held heterodox religious beliefs; though he later returned to orthodox Catholicism, he maintained a general belief in religious liberty and political freedom almost unique among contemporary Catholics. This underpinned his support for causes such as the abolition of slavery and made him an inspiration to continental Catholics who wished to remain loyal to their Church while dissociating themselves from the *ancien régime*. He opposed the Irish rebellion of 1798, but spoke against the Union of 1800. He came to prominence as a barrister for his demotic (often highly insulting) courtroom style and use of the law as a weapon against the victimization of Catholics. Under his leadership the Catholic Association (founded 1824) replaced parliamentary campaigns for Catholic Emancipation waged by liberal Protestants like Henry GRATTAN and W. C. Plunket with mass agitation and organization of Catholic voters. The unrest was supported by the 'Catholic rent', a penny subscription organized by the Catholic clergy and paid by vast numbers of poor Catholics, while Catholic voters were encouraged to defy their landlords if necessary. The climax of this campaign, arguably the first European political mass movement, came in 1828 when O'Connell was elected MP for Clare and refused to take the anti-Catholic oaths required. Faced with the prospect of widespread disruption or massive repression, the Tory government conceded Catholic Emancipation. O'Connell's success not only reflected superb organizational and political skills, it also showed that the threat of violence, held in abeyance (brinkmanship, as we should now call it) could secure civil liberties.

O'Connell was MP for various Irish seats for the rest of his life and built up a parliamentary party of followers (centred on his own family) which co-operated with Whigs and radicals at Westminster to secure further Irish reforms. This alliance was strengthened when the Whigs became dependent on O'Connell's MPs to keep them in power after the 1835 general election; O'Connell was despised by British politicians, however, because of his Catholicism and demagogic tactics.

After the Tory victory of 1841 he launched a great campaign for repeal of the Union and restoration of an Irish Parliament, using the tactics which delivered Emancipation, but he found the British political establishment united against him. Only a small minority of Irish Protestants supported such a Parliament, which would inevitably be Catholic-dominated, while Robert PEEL detached conservative Catholic elements (including most bishops) by concessions. The repeal campaign collapsed when the government banned a mass meeting near Dublin in 1843 and O'Connell chose to submit rather than risk bloodshed. This intensified tensions between O'Connell and militant 'Young Ireland' supporters associated with the weekly newspaper *The Nation*. The Young Irelanders (several of whom were Protestants) accused O'Connell of equating nationalism with Catholicism, especially when he joined the Catholic bishops in opposing Peel's establishment of non-denominational Irish universities to accommodate Catholic and Presbyterian students. Young Ireland also accused him of seeking a renewed Whig alliance in order to get jobs for friends and supporters, and of promoting his son John as his political heir apparent at the expense of his deputy, William Smith O'BRIEN. In 1846 the Young Irelanders (including O'Brien) left the Repeal Association and set up a rival Irish Confederation after refusing to disown the use of force. O'Connell died in 1847, travelling to Rome after a speech in Parliament appealing for government aid for the Irish Famine; John O'Connell proved unable to keep his father's organization together.

O'Connell's reputation fluctuated over time. Although an Irish-speaker remembered in popular lore as the last great folk-hero of Gaelic Ireland, he accepted the extinction of the language as inevitable and even desirable; this was criticized by later cultural nationalists. In the late nineteenth and early twentieth centuries he was widely remembered in terms of the hostile criticisms made by Young Ireland writers, while positive images were centred on his role in Catholic Emancipation and produced an idealized picture of a specifically Catholic hero. In recent decades he has been rehabilitated as a great liberal and a pioneer of democracy of world significance.

Oliver MacDonagh, Daniel O'Connell (1991)

Robert on crusade and died at Palermo. The Bayeux Tapestry is first documented in Bayeux Cathedral in the fifteenth century and was probably commissioned for him, possibly for the dedication of his rebuilt cathedral in 1077.

O'DONNELL, HUGH ROE (AODH RUADH) (?1571–1602), 24th Chief of Tyrconnel. Grandson of Manus O'DONNELL; the English colonial government seized him as hostage for his father Sir Hugh's loyalty in 1587. After successive escapes and recaptures, he took over as Chief from his father in 1592 and, while pretending to submit, began aiding Hugh MAGUIRE in resistance, seeking Spanish help (the English styled him 'the arch-traitor'). His own military campaigns were allied to Hugh O'NEILL's after 1595, and his success faltered only in 1600. While appealing anew to the Spaniards, he was poisoned at Simancas.

O'DONNELL, MANUS (?–1564), 21st Chief of Tyrconnel. Becoming Chief in 1537, he allied with his family's traditional enemy Con Bacagh O'NEILL to invade the Pale of Dublin in 1539 but was soundly defeated, and in 1541 submitted to the Lord Deputy Anthony ST LEGER. His son Calvagh attacked him in 1548 and deposed him in 1555. He was a patron of scholarship, including a major life of COLUM CILLE.

O'DONNELL, RORY (OR RODERICK) (1st Earl of Tyrconnel) (1575–1608), clan leader. Brother of Hugh Roe O'DONNELL, he aided his brother in the 1590s wars until Hugh's death in Spain, when he submitted to Charles BLOUNT, Lord Mountjoy, at Athlone. He was then granted his earldom, a proposal first raised by the government in 1541 for Manus O'DONNELL. He grew apprehensive, however, of English intentions and in 1607 fled abroad with Hugh O'NEILL (the 'Flight of the Earls'); he died in Rome. His widow, who stayed in Ireland and married a loyalist Roman Catholic peer, survived until 1682.

O'DONOVAN ROSSA, JEREMIAH (1831–1915), Irish politician. A shopkeeper profoundly affected by memories of the Famine, he became active in the Fenian movement and was imprisoned in 1865–71. His maltreatment after refusing to conform to prison discipline won widespread attention, and he was elected MP for Tipperary in 1869 (his election was annulled). After release he went to America, where he headed a faction of the Irish Republican Brotherhood opposed to John DEVOY and organized a bombing campaign in Britain in the early 1880s. His burial in Dublin in 1915 became a great demonstration at which PEARSE delivered a notable speech invoking the Fenian tradition.

O'DUFFY, EOIN (1892–1944), Irish politician. An Irish Republican Army (IRA) man from Co. Monaghan, he was recruited to headquarters staff during the Anglo-Irish War by Michael COLLINS, who admired his administrative skills and may have seen him as a potential successor. As member of the Dáil for Monaghan (1921–2) he supported the Anglo-Irish Treaty. In 1924 he was briefly Chief-of-Staff of the Irish army. As first Commissioner of the Garda Siochana, the Irish police force (1922–33) he won great credit for successfully establishing it as an unarmed force. He was less popular with Republicans, who blamed him for their repression by gardai. O'Duffy's egotism was fuelled by his public image (which he carefully cultivated) and a growing drink problem. In 1932 he allegedly advocated a *coup* to prevent Fianna Fáil taking office. In 1933 he was dismissed; opponents of DE VALERA saw him as a political martyr, and he was chosen as head of the Army Comrades' Association or Blueshirts, a body of pro-Treaty veterans and sympathizers with fascist overtones who responded to what they saw as Fianna Fáil tolerance of Irish Republican Army (IRA) violence. After a Blueshirt march on Dublin was banned by De Valera, they merged with Cumann na nGaedheal and the conservative Centre Party to form Fine Gael. O'Duffy was chosen as leader in the hope that he would prove more charismatic than the former Cumann na nGaedheal ministers, but his unstable behaviour and increasingly violent clashes between government forces and Blueshirts led the conservative Fine Gael leaders to disown him. He resigned and formed a fascist splinter party, but attracted little support. In 1936 he led Irish volunteers to fight for Franco in the Spanish Civil War, but they were badly organized and returned to Ireland within six months. O'Duffy faded into obscurity, though shortly before his death he spoke of recruiting volunteers to fight for Nazi Germany on the Russian front.

OENGUS, SON OF FERGUS (?–761), King of the Picts and Dál Riata. One of the most powerful and warlike of the Pictish kings, Oengus emerged as the undisputed king in a four-way power struggle among the Picts during the 720s, following the abdication of NECHTAN in 724. In 740 he was in conflict with EADBERT, King of Northumbria, and in 741 he assumed the kingship of Dál Riata. In 744 the Picts attacked Strathclyde but in 750 TEWDWR, SON OF BELI, King of Strathclyde, decisively defeated the Picts at Mugdock, where two of Oengus's brothers were killed.

OENGUS, SON OF FERGUS (?–834), King of the Scots and Picts (820–34). Oengus succeeded his brother CONSTANTÍN II, establishing a continuity in the dynasty ruling jointly over Picts and Scots, which would continue in the succession of Oengus's son, EOGÁNÁN, SON OF OENGUS. In common with his brother, Oengus was a benefactor of the Church and was remembered for founding a church at Kilrimoneth, later St Andrews.

O'FERRALL, RICHARD (?–1663), writer. Educated at Lille and Douai, he became a Capuchin friar in 1634. With fellow Capuchin Robert O'Connell (*c.* 1623–78), he wrote the massively documented *Commentarius Rinuccinianus* (1661–6), to explain the proceedings of RINUCCINI while Papal Legate in Ireland (1645–9); it remains an invaluable source for the period, although (particularly thanks to O'Ferrall's aristocratic Gaelic prejudices) it is biased to the Old Irish position in the bitter wrangles with Old English Catholics which crippled the Catholic Confederacy's military and political effectiveness.

OFFA, KING *see* essay on page 613

OFFALY, BARON *see* FITZGERALD, THOMAS

OFFWOOD, STEPHEN (1564–*c.* 1635), Separatist. From a Suffolk yeoman family, he was drawn to separate from the official Church and moved in 1602 to Amsterdam, becoming a prosperous merchant as well as an influential member of its English Separatist Church. After splits in that congregation, he joined the Dutch Reformed Church before moving to its allied English congregation in Amsterdam. Quarrels in this Church in turn led him again to a pure Congregationalist position and rejection of strict Calvinism. Throughout these complicated moves, he was a leading publisher and editor of anti-Spanish and radical religious literature.

OGILVY, JAMES (4th Earl of Findlater and 1st Earl of Seafield) (1664–1730), Scottish politician. He became Secretary of State in 1692, and later supported proceedings against another holder of that office, DALRYMPLE. As President of Parliament in 1698, he opposed the formation of the African Co. and the subsequent Darien venture. Lord Chancellor of Scotland (1702–4 and 1705–7), he was an active supporter of the Union with England, commenting famously when signing the treaty, 'Now there's ane end of ane auld sang.' In 1713, reacting against the extension of the Malt Tax to Scotland, which he saw as an inappropriate extension of English policy, Ogilvy brought in a Bill to repeal the Union, on the grounds that the separate Scots Privy Council had been abolished, English treason laws applied and Scots peers were barred from taking their seats if also peers of Britain. The motion was lost by four votes. Ogilvy was often unpopular in Scotland but was an able

lawyer and a defender of what he saw as Scottish interests.

OGLE, 9TH BARON AND 1ST EARL OF *see* CAVENDISH, WILLIAM

OGLETHORPE, JAMES (1696–1785), colonist and philanthropist. As an MP from 1722, he brought conditions in debtors' prisons to Parliament's notice and was appointed to chair a committee of inquiry. Hopeful that colonization might remedy poverty and distress at home, he sought a charter for a new colony, Georgia, which was granted in 1732; as it bordered on Spanish territory, it also had an important military function. Having raised troops in England against Jacobite invasion in 1745, Oglethorpe faced a court martial for lingering in pursuit of the rebel army but was acquitted. His combination of philanthropy and an oppositional political stance not obviously motivated by a desire for office represents a significant strand in the public culture of the time, termed 'patriotism' by contemporaries.

O'HIGGINS, KEVIN (1892–1927), Irish politician. Active in Sinn Féin as a student, he became MP for Queen's County in 1918 and served as deputy to W. T. COSGRAVE in the underground Dáil Ministry of Local Government. He supported the Anglo-Irish Treaty and became Free State Minister for Home Affairs (1922–7). O'Higgins was associated with the uncompromising prosecution of the Civil War, and Republicans held him particularly responsible for such measures as the summary execution of prisoners under martial law. (His elderly father was murdered by Republicans in reprisal.) He earned a reputation as a stern but effective administrator concerned to uphold proper enforcement of the law, committed to economic conservatism and wishing to use Commonwealth membership to assert Free State sovereignty. He led a faction within the Cumann na nGaedheal government which saw the treaty and dominion status as good in themselves; those government supporters (led by Richard Mulcahy) who wished to emphasize continuity with the original Sinn Féin movement were marginalized, leaving a political space later occupied by Fianna Fáil. O'Higgins tried to end partition by offering an Anglo-Irish dual monarchy in return. He was seen as the 'strong man' of the Cosgrave government and his assassination by Republicans in July 1927 was a major blow to Cumann na nGaedheal. YEATS thought him the only post-independence Irish statesman worthy to join the pantheon of Anglo-Irish heroes.

OHTHERE (OR OTTAR) (*fl.* second half of ninth century), Norwegian merchant. A visitor to

continued on page 614

OFFA (?–796)
King of Mercia (757–96)

The greatest of the line of sixth-century and seventh-century kings of Mercia, of whom PENDA, WULFHERE, ETHELBALD and CENWULF are the most notable, Offa built up an effective, if often unstable, domination over the kingdoms of southern Britain. Offa's power was such that contemporary charters sometimes give him the title 'King of the English' rather than 'King of Mercia'. He was treated as an equal by his great near-contemporary Charlemagne and it was with Offa that the Papacy dealt when it wished to intervene directly in the affairs of the English Church.

There is much to show that Offa's kingship was both innovative and powerful. For instance, following the example of the Carolingian rulers, he organized in 787 the first coronation involving anointing with holy oil for his short-reigned son ECGFRITH. Similarly, again following Carolingian practices as well as local initiatives by the kings of East Anglia and Kent, he organized the first large-scale minting of silver pennies, a coinage which circulated throughout the territories under his control, and which initiated a stylistic pattern which lasted for centuries. The famous Offa's Dyke, which runs from Prestatyn (Clwyd) to Chepstow (Gwent), originally a continuous earthwork 192 kilometres in length intended to demarcate the boundary between Offa's kingdom and Wales, is the largest earthwork of its kind built anywhere in Europe. The deployment of resources required to make it is a massive testament to Offa's power. His power was also such that he was able to persuade the Papacy to change the traditional structure of the English Church established at the time of St AUGUSTINE's mission by creating an archbishopric of Lichfield in 787. He is also known to have issued a law-code, but its text has not survived.

Offa's power was nonetheless based fundamentally on violence. His accession after King Ethelbald had been killed by members of his own war-band was accomplished by defeating rivals. It is likely that during his reign several kinsmen were murdered to facilitate Ecgfrith's succession. There is also a lot of evidence to show that the expansion of Mercian rule throughout Britain south of the Humber was strenuously resisted. The kingdom of Kent, for example, was able to throw off his power for a period after the Battle of Otford (Kent) in 776. Subsequently Kentish resistance focused on Archbishop JÆNBERHT of Canterbury, who effectively forced Offa to develop the Lichfield scheme because Jænberht's refusal to crown Ecgfrith obstructed Offa's plans to consolidate his dynasty. ETHELBERT, King of East Anglia, was killed on Offa's orders, and Mercian power over Wessex was resisted with some success by King CYNEWULF, despite defeat in 779 at the Battle of Bensington (Oxon.), and, less successfully, by King BEORHTRIC.

Offa's rule undoubtedly marks a significant stage in the process which led to the unification of England into a single kingdom in the tenth century under the successors of King ALFRED THE GREAT. Some of the smaller English kingdoms, such as Sussex and Lindsey, were suppressed at this time and in others, such as Kent, local dynasties had to struggle to survive. The scale of Offa's interventions everywhere went much further than his predecessor Ethelbald's. Although the origins of the developments undoubtedly precedes Offa's time, his reign was also an important stage in the process whereby the so-called 'Common Burdens', that is, the obligation on all landholders to serve in the King's army, to repair fortifications and to repair bridges, were made universal throughout the kingdoms of southern Britain. Similarly, the document known as the *Tribal Hideage*, which appears to be a list for the levying of tribute from around 30 social groupings around Britain south of the Humber, may date from his reign. Despite all these achievements, however, like previous Mercian 'empires', Offa's fell apart shortly after his death and that of his son Ecgfrith in 796. Their successor Cenwulf was a distant kinsman who undoubtedly prevailed over rivals by violence in exactly the same manner as Offa himself had done. Cenwulf, however, faced reassertions of local independence in, for example, Kent and was never able to dominate Wessex as Offa had done. He speedily abandoned Offa's Archbishop of Lichfield, HYGEBERHT, and by 803 had allowed the revival of Canterbury's traditional pre-eminence over the Church in southern Britain. After 825 the period of Mercian hegemony came to an end and King EGBERT of Wessex initiated the era of Wessex domination which lasted throughout the ninth century. The kingdom of Mercia was itself destroyed by the Vikings in the 860s and 870s; its last King, CEOLWULF II, was no more than a puppet. Offa should undoubtedly be seen as the most important king to rule in England before Alfred the Great. His rule should, however, be seen as the high-point of the long-lasting Mercian hegemony, rather than a genuine unification of the English peoples.

James Campbell (ed.), The Anglo-Saxons (1982)
Nicholas P. Brooks, The Early History of the Church of Canterbury (1984)

the court of ALFRED THE GREAT, Ohthere supplied the King with stories about lands in the Arctic, which were incorporated into a translation of Orosius' *History of the Pagans*. Ohthere's visit illustrates the eclectic culture of Alfred's court and that contacts with Scandinavia were maintained despite Alfred's wars against the Vikings.

OLAF II (also known as Olaf the Black) (*c.* 1177–1238), King of Man and the Isles. Son of GODRED II, and his father's appointed heir, when Godred died in 1187 he was thrust aside by his brother REGINALD. After a turbulent and adventurous life he finally won his kingdom in 1226 and defeated Reginald in battle in 1229. He survived a Norwegian expedition sent to the Isles by his lord, King Haakon IV, in 1230, and with English help managed to rule until his death.

OLAF GOTHFRITHSSON (?–941 or 942), King of Dublin (933–41) and York (939–41). After establishing his power in Dublin, Olaf, who was the son of GOTHFRITH, King of Dublin, was prominent with CONSTANTÍN II, King of the Scots, and YWAIN, SON OF DYFNWAL, King of Strathclyde, in the coalition defeated in 937 by King ATHELSTAN at the Battle of Brunanburh. After Athelstan's death in 939 Olaf returned to England and, by 940, had achieved control over York and over Mercia as far south as Watling Street. His career illustrates the continuing interest in northern England of Dublin's Scandinavian rulers. He was succeeded by his cousin, OLAF SIHTRICSSON, but his conquests disintegrated after his death, and English domination in the north was temporarily restored by King EDMUND.

OLAF SIHTRICSSON (?–981), King of York (941–3 and 949–52) and King of Dublin (945–80). The son of SIHTRIC CAECH, King of Dublin and York, Olaf, like his predecessor OLAF GOTH-FRITHSSON, was a Viking warlord with interests on both sides of the Irish Sea. He was unable, however, to maintain himself in York, facing opposition from both the English Kings EDMUND and EADRED and from Scandinavian rivals. He was eventually expelled by ERIC BLOODAXE. He converted to Christianity in 944 and in 980 became a monk at Iona.

OLAF, ST (?–1030), King of Norway (1014 or 1015–30). A participant in the attacks on England in the later years of ETHELRED II THE UNREADY's reign, Olaf converted to Christianity in Normandy in *c.* 1013 under the sponsorship of Duke RICHARD II. He subsequently drove the pro-Danish regime which had supported SVEIN FORKBEARD and CNUT out of Norway and set himself up as King in 1014 or 1015. Driven out by Cnut in 1028, he was killed in 1030 attempting to return. He sought to continue the conversion to Christianity begun in Norway in the time of OLAF TRYGGVASSON. Many churches in England are dedicated to him.

OLAF THE WHITE (*fl.* 850s and 860s), King of Dublin. One of the great chieftains of the heroic Viking age associated with the conquests of the 'Great Army', he was active not only in Ireland but also in the far north of Britain. He was associated with KETIL FLATNOSE and ROGNVALD OF MOER in the conquest of the Hebrides and Orkney, and was with Ingwaer, King of Dublin (probably the historical IVAR THE BONELESS), at the siege of Dumbarton Rock.

OLAF TRYGGVASSON (?–1000), King of Norway (995–1000). A member of the Norwegian royal kindred and a participant in the attacks on England during ETHELRED II THE UNREADY's time, Olaf accepted Danegeld from ETHELRED in 994 and used the money to help set himself up for five years as King of Norway before being overthrown by his enemies. He was probably the leader of the Viking force which defeated Ealdorman BYRHT-NOTH at the Battle of Maldon.

OLD PRETENDER, THE *see* STUART, JAMES EDWARD

OLDCASTLE, SIR JOHN (4th Baron Cobham) (*c.* 1370–1417), rebel. A Herefs. knight, in 1414 he led a rising against HENRY V despite having been a long-time servant and friend of his. In 1413 it became clear that Oldcastle (Lord Cobham since 1409) had been leading a double life, and that his public political loyalty to the King mattered less to him than his secret religious loyalty to the Lollard heresy (*see* WYCLIF, JOHN). For years he had been employing unorthodox priests as his chaplains and using his manors as safe houses for heretics. Condemned to death for heresy, he was given 40 days' grace by the King – time to recant. Instead he escaped from the Tower and planned a coup. Conspirators disguised as mummers were to seize the royal family at Eltham Palace (Kent) while an army of Lollards took London. In the event, only 300 assembled at the place of muster (St Giles's Fields, London) and the revolt was easily suppressed. Oldcastle himself stayed on the run for three years, ignoring the offer of a general pardon. When captured and interrogated in Parliament his scorn for all earthly judges only served to confirm his fate. He was hanged and burned in Dec. 1417. Oldcastle's rising (as the fiasco of a revolt is generally known) reinforced the notion that heresy and treason were interlinked and so put an end to Lollard hopes of winning substantial upper-class support.

OLDFIELD, THOMAS (1755–1822), historian. His pioneering studies of parliamentary constituencies and elections, *The Entire and Complete History, Political and Personal, of the Boroughs of Great Britain* (1792) and the *History of the Original Constitution of Parliaments* (1797), were the result of an inquiry sponsored by the Society for Constitutional Information, an organization set up in 1780 to make the case for parliamentary and other reforms. While they served the ends of the reformers, the books were also the first substantive examinations of electoral history.

OLDKNOW, SAMUEL (1756–1828), cotton manufacturer. He joined his family muslin business in Lancs. in 1781, and saw the invention of the spinning jenny by HARGREAVES as an opportunity to use the high-quality cotton yarn it produced to compete with the Indian muslin trade: by 1789 he was selling over £80,000 worth of muslins a year. In 1790 the first steam-powered mill in the country was opened at Stockport, but Oldknow had overreached himself and in 1792, in order to try to clear his debts, chiefly to ARKWRIGHT, he divested himself of most of his business interests, spending most of the rest of his life at his model rural community of Mellor (Derb.).

OLIVIER, SIR LAURENCE (Baron Olivier of Brighton) (1907–89), actor and director. Son of a clergyman, he started his professional acting career at 17, establishing himself by 1939 as a powerful stage and screen performer. He directed and starred in highly successful film versions of SHAKESPEARE's *Henry V* (1943) and *Richard III* (1956). Founder-director of the National Theatre Co. (based at London's Old Vic Theatre, 1963–73), he was involved in planning the purpose-built National Theatre on the South Bank. Often seen as a latter-day representative of the great tradition of British actor-managers, he was knighted in 1947 and became in 1970 the first theatrical knight to be raised to the peerage.

O'MAHONY, JOHN (1816–77), Irish politician. A Gaelic scholar and exiled Young Irelander, O'Mahony founded the Fenian Brotherhood in 1858 as the American wing of the Irish Republican Brotherhood headed by James STEPHENS. Fenianism spread rapidly among Irish Americans (though disrupted by the involvement of many members in the American Civil War and by hostility from the hierarchy of the Catholic Church) and played a vital role in fund-raising for the Irish movement. With the end of the Civil War, however, members expected military action and grew impatient; a faction known as the Senate wing broke away from O'Mahony's control and argued that American Fenians, instead of waiting for action in Ireland, should attack Canada. Both factions mounted small-scale raids on Canada which attracted considerable attention but met with little success; they were badly prepared and over-confident of support from the American government, which gave limited toleration to Fenian activities for political purposes. The principal importance of the raids was their role in encouraging Canadian Confederation. On arriving in America in 1866 Stephens deposed O'Mahony as leader but was soon deposed himself, and the American organization sank into a chaos from which it recovered only after the arrival of DEVOY and O'DONOVAN ROSSA in the early 1870s.

OMAI (OR MAI) (*c.* 1753–*c.* 1780), Tahitian visitor to England. He was born on the island of Raiatea north-west of Tahiti. In 1773 he joined the crew of HMS *Adventure*, captained by Tobias Furneaux, which was accompanying James COOK on the *Resolution*. He came to Britain with the *Adventure* in July 1774, where he became a popular figure in London society and had his portrait painted by REYNOLDS. The idea that man in his 'natural' state was superior to 'civilized' man, associated with Rousseau, was then hotly debated. Nonetheless, the opportunity was taken to instill in him British culture. Cook returned him to Tahiti in 1777, where a house was built for him and he was given livestock, but he died within a few years and his house was destroyed.

Ó NÉILL, BRIAN (?–1260), Chief of the Uí Néills of Tír Eoghain (Tyrone). As chief from 1238 onwards, his protracted struggle against both the Meic Lochlainn and the English settlers for overlordship in northern Ireland eventually in 1258 drew him into alliance with the Uí Chonchobhair of Connacht and an attempted restoration of the high-kingship of Ireland. Although he was soon killed in battle against the colonists at Down, his career is often seen as an early manifestation of the Gaelic revival.

O'NEILL, CON BACAGH (1st Earl of Tyrone) (*c.* 1484–1559), clan leader. Descended from ancient chiefs of Tyrone, O'Neill exemplifies the constant tensions between aggression and compromise in early Tudor Anglo-Irish relations. He spent much of the 1520s and 1530s fighting the English and their allies, with occasional reconciliations. Staging a final devastation of the Dublin Pale in 1541, he submitted only after the Lord Deputy Anthony ST LEGER had three times invaded Tyrone. He went to England (1542), renounced his chieftainship and was created Earl, becoming a Privy Councillor of Ireland in 1543;

there seemed a good chance of the Gaelic north being reconciled with the Dublin government. In securing his grant of the earldom, however, he had passed over his legitimate son, Shane O'NEILL, in favour of his illegitimate son Matthew, and Shane began a bitter feud. Con was seen as a collaborator with English power; his prestige tarnished, he died as a refugee from Shane within the Pale, with English influence in Ulster destroyed.

O'NEILL, EOGHAN RUADH (OWEN ROE) (?1590–1649), soldier. A nephew of Hugh O'NEILL, and a veteran of 30 years' service in Spanish armies, in 1642 he returned to Ireland after the outbreak of the Irish rebellion, to lead the forces of the Catholic Confederacy in Ulster; his military skill won him epic status. In 1648 he opposed Confederate co-operation with the Royalist army of James BUTLER, Earl of Ormond, and continued leading purely Catholic and largely Gaelic forces. His death prevented a fruitful agreement with Ormond.

O'NEILL, HUGH (3rd Earl of Tyrone) *see* essay on page 617

O'NEILL, SHANE (SEÁN) (?1530–67), Gaelic leader. Eldest legitimate son and likely tanist (heir apparent) of Con Bacagh O'NEILL, 1st Earl of Tyrone; his bitter resentment at being passed over in the earldom for his bastard brother Matthew proved fatal to English plans to anglicize Ulster's paramount family. Family warfare culminated in Matthew's murder in 1558; shaky reconciliation with ELIZABETH I petered out in attacks on his family's rivals the O'Donnells and their Scots kinsmen the Macdonnells, and in intrigues with Spain and partisans of MARY QUEEN OF SCOTS. O'Neill's destructive rising in 1566 was beaten back from the Dublin Pale; when he over-trustingly took refuge with the Macdonnells. They murdered him, with English approval.

O'NEILL, TERENCE (Baron O'Neill) (1914–90), Prime Minister of Northern Ireland. A Unionist MP from 1946, as premier he sought to bridge the divide between the communities of Northern Ireland, visiting Catholic institutions and inviting Sean LEMASS and Jack LYNCH to visit Stormont (the Northern Ireland Parliament). O'Neill saw himself as a technocrat, bridging divisions through economic modernization, but gestures to the Catholic community were not followed up by concrete reforms, and annoyance at his failure to fulfil these expectations stimulated the Catholic Civil Rights movement. O'Neill was a remote leader, widely seen as arrogant and patronizing, and out of touch with back-bench opinion,

which exacerbated resistance to his initiatives, encouraged by hard-line Cabinet members such as Brian FAULKNER while Ian PAISLEY organized street demonstrations. His 1968 offer of local government reforms came too late to prevent growing polarization and violence. Having failed to strengthen his position after the election of Feb. 1969, which saw pro- and anti-O'Neill Unionist candidates standing against each other, he resigned in April in favour of James CHICHESTER-CLARKE. It is still debated how far he was a genuine reformer.

OPIE, PETER (1918–82) and **IONA** (née Archibald) (1923–), anthropologists. Painstaking and imaginative investigators and collectors of the culture of childhood, the Opies' first publication was a collection of the rhymes which children sing as they play skipping games, *I Saw Esau* (1947). This was followed by their compendious reference work, *The Oxford Dictionary of Nursery Rhymes* (1951), and collections of nursery rhymes (1955, 1963). *The Lore and Language of Schoolchildren* (1959) is a compilation of children's rhymes, chants and riddles collected from all over Britain, and the Opies also collected poems written about children in *The Oxford Book of Children's Verse* (1973), and *The Classic Fairy Tales* (1974) revives many and discusses their meaning, purpose and evolution.

ORDERIC VITALIS (1075–*c*. 1142), historian. The child of an English mother and a Norman father, he spent all but the first 10 years of his life in the Norman monastery of St Evroul, but his *Ecclesiastical History*, written between 1115 and 1141, ranges much more widely than its title suggests, offering a remarkably vivid portrait of Anglo-Norman society.

ORFORD, EARL OF, 1ST *see* RUSSELL, EDWARD; **2ND** *see* WALPOLE, ROBERT; **5TH** *see* WALPOLE, HORACE

ORIEL, 1ST BARON *see* FOSTER, JOHN

ORKNEY, 3RD EARL OF *see* SINCLAIR, WILLIAM

ORMOND, EARL OF, 4TH *see* BUTLER, JAMES; **8TH** *see* BUTLER, PIERS; BOLEYN THOMAS; **10TH** *see* BUTLER, THOMAS; **12TH AND 1ST DUKE OF** *see* BUTLER, JAMES; **13TH AND 2ND DUKE OF** *see* BUTLER, JAMES

ORPEN, WILLIAM (1878–1931), painter. A child prodigy who went to the Metropolitan School of Art aged 11 in his native Dublin, he studied under Henry Tonks at the Slade in 1895. Augustus JOHN was a fellow pupil, but Orpen's

continued on page 618

O'NEILL, HUGH (3rd Earl of Tyrone) (1550–1616)
Gaelic leader

O'Neill was the second son of Matthew O'Neill, Baron of Dungannon, who was the bastard son of Con Bacagh O'NEILL, Earl of Tyrone, and despite his illegitimacy, intended to succeed Con as Earl. Matthew was murdered by partisans of his half-brother Shane O'NEILL in 1558, and Hugh was taken to England for safety in 1559 (succeeding to the earldom when his elder brother Brien was in turn murdered by Shane's son Turlough Luineach O'Neill in 1562). He became a ward of ELIZABETH I, and lived in the households of Sir Henry SIDNEY and Robert DUDLEY, Earl of Leicester, for whom he retained a lifelong respect. English hopes that his English upbringing would make him useful in taming Gaelic Ulster at first seemed justified on his return to Ireland in 1568; he was placed in Tyrone to counterbalance the influence of Turlough. In the 1580s the Crown granted him wide powers in Ulster, together with substantial estates, and he attended the 1585 Parliament as Earl. Friction with the government, however, increasingly outweighed his long-standing feuds with relatives. A clash with the English in 1594 was patched up, but O'Neill now saw his best chance as alliance with England's enemies Spain and the Pope. In 1595 he seized and destroyed a strategic English fort on the River Blackwater (Armagh) and was proclaimed traitor. On the death of Turlough he succeeded to the ancient northern royal title of the O'Neill at a ceremony at Tullaghoge (Co. Tyrone), and he began extending the O'Neill's prerogatives in order to appoint lords in other parts of Ireland. In 1596 he made a formal demand to the Dublin government for liberty of conscience for Roman Catholics, and circularized leading landowners asking them to join a military alliance to defend Catholicism. He also drew on the rhetoric of liberation of Ireland from foreign (i.e. English) domination already used by James Fitzmaurice FITZGERALD in his 1579 rebellion, while the confederacy which he set up sought to transfer sovereignty of the Irish kingdom to a prince from the Habsburg family. A steadily more successful crusade culminated in his greatest victory (14 Aug. 1598) at the Yellow Ford on the River Blackwater near Armagh; he defeated and killed the English commander, Sir Henry Bagenal, who was the brother of his third wife and who had bitterly opposed their marriage. In 1599 he issued a political manifesto of 22 articles setting out his nationalist and religious demands (Sir Robert CECIL called it 'Utopia'), and he also encouraged the Irish theologian at Leuven, Peter LOMBARD, to present the Catholic nationalist case in 1600 to Pope Clement VIII in *De Regno Hiberniae, Sanctorum Insula, Commentarius* (A Commentary on the Kingdom of Ireland, Island of Saints). Clement, however, who was hostile to O'Neill's ally the King of Spain, offered no material help, and the Papal Nuncio (representative) appointed for Ireland was an Italian, Cardinal Mansoni, rather than O'Neill's preferred candidate, the Catholic Archbishop of Dublin, Matteo de Oviedo. Mansoni never arrived, and the Pope also omitted to respond to O'Neill's demands for a general excommunication of Catholics loyal to England. These were mostly Old English Catholics, who like the Pope remained suspicious of O'Neill's close links with the Spanish monarchy and were therefore reluctant to commit themselves wholeheartedly to his cause.

O'Neill was more than a match for the Royal Lieutenant, Robert DEVEREUX, Earl of Essex, and in 1599 manoeuvred him into signing a personal truce; he may have offered Essex help in his struggle to gain supremacy at the English court. He then faced the ruthless military talents of Lord Deputy Mountjoy (*see* BLOUNT, WILLIAM), and when a long-awaited Spanish intervention at Kinsale failed (1601), his power disintegrated; he submitted in 1603 at Mellifont, and was one of the peers who in Dublin signed the proclamation of JAMES I as King. Despite outward reconciliation, his distrust of English intentions led to the Flight of the Earls (1607), when together with the Earl of Tyrconnell, he left for France with his fourth wife, Catherine Magennis, and three of his sons. This was a turning-point in Irish history, representing the final end of Gaelic political power and the triumph of the English colonial initiative in Gaelic Ireland. The Irish Parliament declared Hugh attainted; his last years were spent in Rome, nearly blind, short of money and increasingly at odds with his wife. With his political and military skills and his intimate knowledge of his English opponents, he had represented the best hope of reversing the imposition of English rule in Ireland; Hiram Morgan's recent comparison of him to his Dutch contemporary as revolutionary leader, William the Silent, has much to commend it.

Hiram Morgan, Tyrone's Rebellion: The Outbreak of the Nine Years War in Tudor Ireland (1993)

Hamlet won the Slade summer prize in 1899. He was elected to the New English Art Club in 1900 and became an Associate of the Royal Academy in 1919. As an official war artist during the First World War, he painted *The Signing of the Peace in the Hall of Mirrors, Versailles, 28 June 1919*. He continued to paint Irish scenes, and his portraits came to be as well regarded as those of MILLAIS, WHISTLER and SARGENT had been, and commanded high prices.

ORRERY, 1ST EARL OF *see* BOYLE, ROGER

ORTON, JOE (1932–67), actor and playwright. Born in Leicester, Orton trained at RADA. His plays are full of 'in-your-face' bad taste, laced with *double entendres* and 'sauce': they were influenced by the work of Jean Genet, and aimed to disquieten the conventional. In *Loot* (1966), one of his two most successful, frequently revived plays, it is the mother's dead body that is stolen, while in *What the Butler Saw* (1969) farce tips over into incest and sadistic violence. In 1962 he was jailed for defacing Islington (London) library books with lewd annotations; his accomplice in this was his homosexual lover who, in 1967, bludgeoned Orton to death.

ORWELL, GEORGE *see* essay on page 619

OSBALD (?–799), King of Northumbria (796). A supporter of King ETHELRED of Northumbria against his dynastic rival St ÆLFWALD, he was made King after Ethelred's murder in 796 by a group of nobles, but he reigned for only 27 days. He fled to the kingdom of the Picts, but abandoned an attempt to gain reinstatement, becoming a monk. He was succeeded as King by another Northumbrian nobleman, St EARDWULF.

OSBORNE, DOROTHY (1627–95), letter writer. A descendant of the Royalist Osborne and Danvers families, she met the puritan lawyer William Temple in 1648, and they began to correspond. Her family disapproved of their marriage but it eventually took place at Christmas 1655. Osborne was a prolific letter writer but only her correspondence of 1652–4 has survived. It provides valuable information about the lives of wealthy women and Royalists in republican England.

OSBORNE, JOHN (1929–94), playwright. The archetypal 'angry young man' of the 'angry decade' of the 1950s, Osborne never lost his scatter-fire fury. Born to a Fulham barmaid and a commercial artist, he worked as a journalist, stage manager and actor before the Royal Court production of his *Look Back in Anger* (1956) brought him massive attention as a new voice in the British theatre currently dominated by drawing-room dramas which failed to engage with the social realities of the day. Jimmy Porter, the working-class anti-hero for whom 'there are no great causes left any more', became iconic for the angry young men's revulsion at what they saw as the moral bankruptcy of the Establishment. Though Osborne went on to write other angry plays, none achieved the defining fame of the first: *Inadmissible Evidence* (1964) is usually regarded as the finest, and *The Entertainer* (1957), which uses the death of the music hall as a metaphor for the decline of Britain, was acclaimed. In subsequent writing Osborne attacked the royal family, cricket, his mother, urban planning, Britain's nuclear policies, his ex-wives (sometimes, it seemed, women in general) and all politicians.

OSBORNE, SIR THOMAS (1st Earl of Danby, 1st Marquess of Carmarthen, 1st Duke of Leeds) (1631–1712), statesman. Son of a Yorks. Royalist, elected MP for York in 1665, he opposed Clarendon (*see* HYDE, EDWARD). He demonstrated his ability as Treasurer of the Navy from 1668; as Lord Treasurer from 1673 he improved the yield of hereditary Crown revenues. In 1675 he became the leading figure in a strongly Anglican ministry, but his ascendancy was always qualified: Shaftesbury (*see* COOPER, ANTHONY ASHLEY) hinted that his religious intolerance was popish in tendency, and in the Popish-Plot investigations Danby was revealed to have conducted secret negotiations with France. CHARLES II dissolved Parliament to prevent Danby's impeachment and provided him with a pardon, but Parliament ruled the latter illegal, and he was imprisoned. Released in 1685, he criticized JAMES II's Catholicizing policies and, in 1687, made contact with William of Orange (the future WILLIAM III), whose marriage to James's daughter Mary (later MARY II) he had arranged. He was one of the 'Immortal Seven' signatories to the invitation to William and secured the north for him at the time of the Glorious Revolution. Made Lord President of the Council, he was Chief Minister from 1690, but his appetite for wealth and honours attracted criticism. Though he was created a duke in 1694, his influence with William declined after he supported the Triennial Bill in that year, providing that no Parliament should last longer than three years; in 1695 he was impeached for accepting a bribe, but not convicted. Thereafter he had little influence.

OSBURH (?–*c*. 855), first wife of King ETHELWULF of Wessex. Osburh's Kentish origins indicate a political marriage intended to consolidate the Wessex kings' control over the kingdom of

continued on page 620

ORWELL, GEORGE (originally Eric Arthur Blair) (1903–50)
Writer

Born in Bengal, India, the son of a civil servant, he was sent back to preparatory school in Eastbourne (Sussex): his memories of his early schooldays, *Such, Such Were the Joys* was considered too libellous to be published in Britain until 1968.

A scholarship boy at Eton, he joined the Imperial Indian Police and served in Burma from 1922 to 1927. This experience, recounted in his first novel *Burmese Days* (1934), instilled in him a deep loathing of imperialism and he resigned his post, determined to earn his living as a writer. He took a series of menial jobs and generally lived in 'fairly severe poverty', as recounted in *Down and Out in Paris and London* (1933). In his early novels, his views on class surface in *A Clergyman's Daughter* (1935), while *Keep the Aspidistra Flying* (1936) is another 'experience reworked' novel, the story of a bookshop assistant and aspiring writer whose setbacks and humiliations were not dissimilar to those of Orwell himself.

In 1936 George Orwell (the pseudonym which Eric Blair had chosen) was commissioned to write an account of a pressing political issue, unemployment in the north of England. He lived in cheap lodgings and talked to working people wherever he found them. Published by Victor GOLLANCZ's Left Book Club in 1937, *The Road to Wigan Pier*, the book in which Orwell 'tried to make political writing into an art', proved a controversial bestseller, provoking middle-class unease with its description of working-class poverty and hardship and its attack on easy left-wing theoretical prescription.

At the end of 1936 Orwell, convinced of the justice of the Republican cause in the Spanish Civil War, went to fight for the Worker's Party of Marxist Unification (POUM), one of the small anti-Franco military groups. On his arrival at the front, he was appalled to witness the factional infighting, with POUM designated as Trotskyists by the official Communists and Soviet charges that it was 'Franco's fifth column'. When *Homage to Catalonia*, his attempt to make sense of the war, was published in 1938, it was to a howl of left-wing protest and its sales were pitifully small.

On the outbreak of the Second World War, Orwell was rejected as medically unfit for active service. Instead he joined the Home Guard, which he regarded as a people's militia, with all the potential which that implied for revolutionary action. He saw the war as the opportunity to work for a fairer peace, and his pamphlet *The Lion and the Unicorn: Socialism and the English Genius* (1941) hymned the steadfast English national character, but insisted that the country needed to be transformed along socialist lines if the people were to pull together to win the war. A review by V. S. Pritchett compared Orwell's 'subversive and non-conforming brand of patriotism' to that of COBBETT and DEFOE.

From 1941 to 1943 Orwell worked at the BBC while continuing a steady outpouring of politically engaged journalism. From 1943 he was literary editor of *Tribune*, the mouthpiece of the Bevanite (*see* BEVAN, ANEURIN) left wing of the Labour Party, while his own regular column, 'As I Please', ranged widely over political, social and cultural issues as did his other journalism and his essays: *Inside the Whale* (1940), *Critical Essays* (1946) and *Shooting an Elephant* (1950).

With Russia fighting on the Allied side from 1942, and with pro-Soviet support again strong on the Left, Orwell found it hard to find a publisher for *Animal Farm* (1945), a savage political satire on communism in the Soviet Union, but it proved a lasting success.

In 1947 Orwell, whose wife had died in 1945, took the child whom they had recently adopted to live on the remote Scottish Isle of Jura. It was there that he wrote the book that coined the word 'Orwellian' to signify a totalitarian nightmare: *Nineteen Eighty-Four* (1949), a dystopia that crystallized fears of a post-war world dominated by a Stalinist regime. Britain had become 'Airstrip One' in a world continually at war; the language so engineered as 'Newspeak' as to make opposition literally unthinkable; 'who controls the past, controls the future: and who controls the present controls the past', ran the party slogan; where 'Big Brother' was in control; and the 'thought police' were everywhere, including in your own family.

Orwell died of tuberculosis in 1950: he had married Sonia Brownwell almost on his deathbed, and for the next 18 years, under the hybrid name Sonia Orwell, she was to be the fierce literary guardian of a writer whose heterodox, unaligned politics had led, to his distress, to misappropriations by the Right, which did not always wish to understand the democratizing impulse that underlay the writing of that 'elastic brow'.

Sonia Orwell and Ian Angus (eds), George Orwell: Collected Essays, Journalism and Letters (4 vols, 1968)
Bernard Crick, George Orwell: A Biography (1980)
Michael Shelden, Orwell: The Authorised Biography (1991)

Kent first achieved by Ethelwulf's father EGBERT. ASSER praises her learning and her role in educating the most famous of her numerous progeny, ALFRED THE GREAT. Like all wives of the ninth-century kings of Wessex, with the exception of Ethelwulf's second wife JUDITH, Osburh was not crowned queen.

O'SHEA, CAPTAIN W. H. (1840–1905), Irish politician and **KATHERINE** (1845–1921), his wife see PARNELL, CHARLES STEWART, essay on page 632

OSLAC (?–after 975), Ealdorman of Northumbria (963–75). He was appointed Ealdorman by King EDGAR and appears eventually to have established domination over the whole of Northumbria. He was clearly instrumental in consolidating Edgar's power in the far north, but was driven from office soon after the King's death during the turbulent succession dispute involving EDWARD THE MARTYR and ETHELRED II THE UNREADY.

OSMUND OF SALISBURY, ST (?–1099), bishop. Nephew and Chancellor of WILLIAM I THE CONQUEROR, he was made Bishop in 1078 and completed the transfer of his see from Sherborne (Dorset) to Old Sarum (Salisbury, Wilts.), building a new cathedral and establishing a chapter of canons. He has been credited with introducing the Sarum Rite, which eventually became the standard ritual in the British Isles and the basis of the Book of Common Prayer. Since he was venerated as the founder of their church, a group of Salisbury residents began a campaign to have him canonized in 1228, a campaign which succeeded in 1457 (the last canonization of an 'English' saint until 1935).

OSRED (?697–716), King of Northumbria (705–16). The son of King ALDFRITH, Osred succeeded to the kingdom at the age of eight, against the opposition of EADWULF. Although initially benefiting from the support of a range of ecclesiastics, including BEDE, St WILFRID and his aunt St ÆLFFLÆD, his popularity declined drastically because of attempts to secure his rule by killing significant numbers of Northumbria's aristocracy. He was murdered in 716 and succeeded by CENRED.

OSRIC, King of the Hwicce (c. 675–85). As ruler of the small kingdom first recorded in the time of King PENDA of Mercia, Osric was responsible for establishing the Christian Church in Worcs. and Glos., setting up a bishopric at Worcester and an abbey at Pershore, with the agreement of his overlord King ETHELRED of Mercia.

OSSORY, 1ST EARL OF see BUTLER, PIERS

OSTORIUS SCAPULA (?–AD 52), Roman Governor. He succeeded AULUS PLAUTIUS as the second Governor of Britain in 47, remaining in that position until his death. He pushed Roman power westwards into Wales, and his achievements included the defeat and capture of CARATACUS. British revolts, which prefigured the great rebellion of BOUDICCA in 61, began during his rule, and the Roman hold on southern Britain, although secure, continued to be threatened by disturbances among the natives.

OSWALD, ST, King of Northumbria (634–42). A son of ETHELFRITH of Northumbria, he, along with his sister St ÆBBE and brother OSWY, spent years in exile among the Irish and the Picts during EDWIN's reign, before returning to establish himself not only in Northumbria, but as one of the small group of kings, described in later sources as Bretwaldas, who were said by BEDE to have exercised lordship over all the kings of the English. In order to establish his kingship, he defeated in 634 the formidable CADWALLON, King of Gwynedd, and he was also lord over some of the Irish and Picts. The longterm significance of his reign stems from his invitation to St AIDAN and monks from Iona to establish a community at Lindisfarne, from which they carried out the conversion of Northumbria to Christianity. A great warrior, he was eventually killed in battle against his greatest English rival, PENDA of Mercia. Oswald is something of a hero of Bede's *Ecclesiastical History* which records miracles performed by this notably Christian king.

OSWALD, ST, Bishop of Worcester (961–72) and Archbishop of York (972–92). Along with St DUNSTAN and St ETHELWOLD, Oswald was one of the three major figures of the English Tenth-Century Reform which sought to improve the moral and spiritual quality of the Church in England through monastic leadership. He spent much of the 950s at the famous reformed abbey of Fleury-sur-Loire in France. On his return to England, he advanced rapidly as a protégé of both Dunstan and King EDGAR. His career shows features typical of all the reformers: the encouragement of monasticism and learning and shrewd business management in the building up of the estates of the abbeys under his patronage. He was responsible for the construction of a new cathedral at Worcester, for the foundation of an abbey at Ramsey and for encouraging French monks such as St ABBO OF FLEURY and GERMANUS to visit England.

OSWINE (?–651), King of Deira (644–51). The last of the direct line of the kings of Deira, Oswine was a kinsman of King EDWIN of Northumbria. He went into exile during the period 634–42 when Northumbria was dominated by St OSWALD, but then returned to become King of Deira. With the growth in the power of Oswald's brother OSWY, Oswine's position became increasingly precarious, and he was eventually hunted down and killed by Oswy. The kingship of Deira was thereafter transferred to Oswy's nephew ETHELWOLD and then to his son ALHFRITH. Like many early murdered Anglo-Saxon kings, Oswine was subsequently proclaimed to be a saint.

OSWY (?–670), King of Northumbria (642–70). A younger brother of OSWALD, Oswy maintained the supremacy of the Northumbrian kings over the English and the Britons established by EDWIN and Oswald. His reign also saw the disappearance of the old kingdoms of Bernicia and Deira formed at the time of the Anglo-Saxon settlements, as a consequence of a succession of violent quarrels between Oswy and Kings OSWINE, ETHELWOLD and Oswy's son ALHFRITH. Oswy's greatest military success was his victory in 655 at the Battle of the River Winwæd (probably a tributary of the Humber) over King PENDA of Mercia, which was followed by the murder of Penda's son PEADA. The period in which Oswy exercised power over Mercia was an important one for the spread of Christianity to the Mercian kingdom, since that kingdom never reverted to paganism even though its independence of Northumbria was reasserted by WULFHERE. Oswy's reign is also notable for the expansion into Northumbria of Roman ideas on Church organization, associated principally with St WILFRID's arrival at Ripon in 660 and his appointment to the bishopric of York in 664. Oswy presided over the crucially important Synod of Whitby which decided that the Northumbrian Church should follow the Roman dating of Easter, rather than the Irish associated with Iona and Lindisfarne. *See also* BEDE, COLMAN.

O' TOOLE, LAWRENCE *see* LORCÁN UA TUATHAIL

OTWAY, THOMAS (1652–85), playwright. A clergyman's son, he left Oxford to become an actor, but was unsuccessful; Aphra BEHN encouraged him to write for the stage instead. His first play, *Alcibiades* (1675), was successful both for him and for Elizabeth BARRY, who made her début in the play. He won the patronage of Rochester (*see* WILMOT, JOHN), who became Barry's lover; Otway continued to write for her. Although his later plays were less successful commercially they included his most enduring works, *The Orphan* (1680), his first in blank verse, and the scathing satire on Shaftesbury (*see* COOPER, ANTHONY ASHLEY) and the Whigs, *Venice Preserv'd* (1682).

OUTRAM, SIR JAMES (1803–63), soldier. Outram joined the Indian army in 1819 after his father's early death. His early career was devoted to punitive expeditions and shooting animals, including at least 200 tigers. Service in Afghanistan (1839–42) brought him into conflict with the Commander-in-Chief Lord Ellenborough, but his heroic defence of the residency at Hyderabad in Sind in Feb. 1843 against 8,000 Baluchis earned him a lieutenant colonelcy. In 1844 Outram publicly opposed General Sir Charles NAPIER's annexation of Sind, and exposed corrupt practices amongst senior East India Co. officials. With his career effectively at an end, but protected from outright dismissal by the Governor General DALHOUSIE, in 1857 Outram commanded an expeditionary force against Persia. With the outbreak of the Indian Mutiny Outram hurried back, commanded the first relief force to Lucknow, and with only 5,000 men kept up constant pressure on some 120,000 mutineers until they could be destroyed by relief armies. Hailed as saviour of the Raj but with his health broken, Outram died a national hero, the very embodiment of the mid Victorian puritan soldier, the enemy of both British corruption and the sepoy's barbarism.

OVERALL, JOHN (1561–1619), theologian. A Cambridge don, Regius Professor of Divinity from 1595 to 1607, he was Dean of St Paul's, London, in 1602, Bishop of Coventry and Lichfield in 1614 and of Norwich in 1618. He expanded the catechism in the 1604 revision of the Book of Common Prayer (*see* NOWELL, ALEXANDER), and was an influential early voice against strict Calvinist views on predestination, protesting against John WHITGIFT's Lambeth Articles (1595).

OVERBURY, THOMAS (1581–1613), murder victim. Minor poet and diplomat who was knighted in 1608, he is chiefly important for his death. He opposed the marriage plans of his friend and employer, Robert CARR, to the divorced Frances HOWARD, Countess of Essex, so Carr engineered his imprisonment in the Tower of London, where he was poisoned, probably at the instance of the Countess. The scandal ruined Lady Essex and generally gave JAMES I's court a bad image.

OVIEDO, MATTEO DE (?–1610), clergyman *see* O'NEILL, HUGH

OWAIN AP CADWGAN (?–1116), Prince of Powys. Owain created a furore by abducting the beautiful NEST, wife of Gerald of Windsor, the Norman Castellan of Pembroke. He escaped to Ireland with her, returning later to recover his father's land from his cousin Madog, and he continued to harass the Normans. After his father CADWGAN AP BLEDDYN was murdered by Madog in 1112, HENRY I made Owain his successor. He was killed in a surprise attack by Gerald of Windsor.

OWAIN AP GRUFFUDD (?–1197), poet and Prince of southern Powys. Known as Owain Cyfeiliog (the name of the district which his uncle MADOG AP MAREDUDD gave him to rule in 1149). One of the claimants to Powys after Madog's death in 1160, he agreed in 1166 to a partition which resulted in the permanent division of the former kingdom. A patron of poets and a distinguished poet himself, in his ode *Hirlas Owain* (Owain's Long Blue Drinking Horn) he addressed his companions in arms, alive and dead, in the traditional tones of a lord of warriors. In politics he generally and sensibly bowed to the reality of English power.

OWAIN AP HYWEL DDA (?–988), King of Deheubarth. The unification of Wales achieved by HYWEL DDA disintegrated following his death in 950, and the course of Welsh history in the following decades is far from clear. Owain remained in control of Deheubarth, but made no further claims to Gwynedd after attacks in 952 and 954 had been defeated. In 955 both he and his rival IAGO AP IDWAL witnessed charters at the court of the English King EADRED. He also sent his son EINION AP OWAIN to campaign in Gwyr (Gower). In 986 his surviving son MAREDUDD AP OWAIN, increasingly controlling the affairs of Deheubarth because of Owain's age, invaded Gwynedd and succeeded in reuniting both kingdoms before Owain's death two years later.

OWAIN GLYN DWR *see* GLYN DWR, OWAIN, essay on page 356

OWAIN OF GWYNEDD (?–1170), Prince of Gwynedd. He succeeded his father GRUFFUDD AP CYNAN as ruler of Gwynedd in 1137 and took advantage of the troubles of STEPHEN's reign to make territorial gains, especially between the rivers Conwy and Dee. Although he was forced to submit to HENRY II in 1157 and 1163, his extraordinary success in leading united Welsh opposition to the English invasion of 1165 enabled him to reassert his independence and won for him a reputation as Owain the Great, King of Wales.

OWEN *see also* OWAIN; YWAIN

OWEN, DAVID (Baron Owen of the City of Plymouth) (1938–), politician. The son of a doctor, Owen began his professional life following in his father's footsteps. After Cambridge and medical school he became a neurological and psychiatric registrar at St Thomas's Hospital. Always intensely political, he was elected for the marginal seat of Plymouth Sutton in 1966 after failing to gain Torrington (Devon) at the 1964 election. He served in minor office in Harold WILSON's administration, under Denis HEALEY at the Ministry of Defence. In 1972 when Labour, then in opposition, decided to oppose British entry into the Common Market, Owen resigned from Shadow office, placing himself firmly on the social democratic wing of the party which looked to Roy JENKINS as its leader. When Labour returned to office in 1974 Owen went as a junior minister to the Department of Health and Social Security. Minister of State at the Foreign and Commonwealth Office in 1976 , he was unexpectedly appointed Foreign Secretary on the sudden death of Anthony CROSLAND the next year. The youngest Foreign Secretary since EDEN, he proved an energetic minister firmly in the Atlanticist and pro-European mould of his mentor Healey, and achieved notable success towards a solution of the Rhodesia situation.

After Labour's defeat in 1979, he was briefly opposition spokesman on energy, but in a Labour Party swinging ever to the Left he was not prepared to remain silent, or, as it turned out, to remain at all. In 1981 he became one of the founder members of the Social Democratic Party (SDP), along with Roy JENKINS, Shirley WILLIAMS and William RODGERS. Here too his high public profile and tremendous energy proved mixed blessings. On the one hand he was the party's greatest public asset, on the other he irritated fellow politicians who suspected him of hogging the limelight. After the Conservative victory in the 1983 election Owen became leader of the SDP and called for the mould of British politics to be broken.

Unfortunately for Owen his personality was not ideally suited to the compromises and 'fixing' required by the sort of coalition politics which his party pioneered along with David STEEL's Liberals. Steel was irritated by pubic perceptions that he was little more than Owen's puppet, while Owen was profoundly irritated by the woolly-minded anti-nuclear stance of the left wing of the Liberal Party. The 'Alliance', as the two parties were known at the 1987 election, failed to make the breakthrough needed, and Owen found himself faced with demands for a formal coalition with the Liberals. When most Social Democrats voted for this in 1987, Owen held aloof with his own much shrunken branch of the party. This was effectively the end of his political career. He did not stand in the 1992 election and accepted a peerage.

He returned to the international arena later in 1992 as co-chairman of the International Steering Committee on the former Yugoslavia, where he attempted to prevent civil war breaking out between the Bosnians and the Serbs. Despite two years of trying to bring the two sides together, Owen's work was not a success.

OWEN, GEORGE (1552–1613), writer. Son of a prominent lawyer of Henllys (Pembrokes.), he was

Vice-Admiral of Pembroke and Cardigan, and a notable antiquary who traced the history of his inherited lordship of Kemeys, wrote descriptions of Welsh topography, geology and government and supplied information for William CAMDEN's *Britannia*. His work epitomizes the enthusiastic reconciliation of the Welsh gentry with the Tudor monarchy. Not to be confused with his son George (d. 1665), a distinguished herald, or George Owen Harry, a Welsh clergyman and antiquary who also assisted Camden.

OWEN GLENDOWER *see* GLYN DWR, OWAIN, essay on page 356

OWEN, JOHN (1616–83), clergyman. A Puritan Oxford don ejected from his college fellowship by William LAUD in 1637, he served in private chaplaincies to Puritan gentry, then during the Civil Wars (from 1642) took parish livings. From 1648, however, he became a leading spokesman of the Independents (Congregationalists). Oliver CROMWELL much admired him, taking him on Irish and Scots military campaigns and restoring him to Oxford University, where he was made Dean of Christ Church. His public career ended at the restoration of CHARLES II, but his enemies respected him. Owen's voluminous writings against a variety of religious enemies, Arminianism, High Church Anglicanism, Presbyterianism, Quakers and Roman Catholicism, were marked by an unusual fair-mindedness. His writings are still esteemed by Calvinist theologians.

OWEN, SIR RICHARD (1804–92), comparative anatomist. Owen served an apprenticeship in surgery (1820–4) and studied medicine at Edinburgh University and at St Bartholomew's Hospital, London. He practised in London and in 1827 he was appointed assistant to the conservator of the Hunterian Museum at the Royal College of Surgeons, where he catalogued the museum's vast collections of zoological specimens, dissected vertebrates and cultivated a friendship with the eminent French naturalist, Georges Cuvier. As Hunterian Professor (1836–56), he gave annual lectures on the comparative anatomy and physiology of invertebrates and vertebrates and developed the morphological concept of 'archetypes', the ideal forms upon which all organisms of a given group were believed to have been constructed. In 1856 he was appointed superintendent of the natural history departments of the British Museum (later the Natural History Museum) and became Director when, 25 years later, the departments moved to South Kensington. The most celebrated British comparative anatomist and palaeontologist of his day, he was given a Civil List pension in 1842 and a residence by Queen VICTORIA in 1852.

Owen's reputation rests on the high quality of his zoological identification, description and taxonomy, and the several hundred publications on living and fossil invertebrates and vertebrates – notably those on the pearly nautilus, moas, monotremes and marsupials, extinct species of anteater, armadillo and llama, the giant flightless bird, *Dinornis*, and the Jurassic bird, *Archaeopteryx*. In 1841 he coined the word 'dinosauria', published one of the most comprehensive works in palaeontology, *A History of British Fossil Reptiles* (1849–84), and later helped design the dinosaur replicas at Crystal Palace.

Owen accepted that the fossil record showed an evolution of species and that new species may have appeared through the Creator working through secondary causes, but rejected DARWIN's theory of evolution. One of his principal objections was that Darwin, having convinced himself that man was distinct from anthropoid apes, could not explain the origin of man. Darwin's supporters fought a sustained campaign against Owen. Although he was generally recognized as a leading comparative anatomist, to Darwin and his allies he was a venal careerist.

OWEN, ROBERT (1771–1858), pioneer of the co-operative movement. A Welsh-born draper's assistant, he became a master spinner, and in 1800 he and others took over the New Lanark Mills in Scotland, originally founded by his father-in-law and ARKWRIGHT. In 1813 he published *A New View of Society*, in which he propounded the view that character was formed by environment, and claimed that the churches should recognize the evils of capitalism rather than castigate individuals as sinful. He improved working conditions, housing, sanitation and the education of children in the model community and village he established at Lanark, and his co-operative ideas were put into practice in such experimental communities as New Harmony (Ind., USA) (1825), Orbiston near Glasgow (1826), Ralakine (Co. Cork) (1831), and Queenswood (Hants) (1839). None survived nor did his Grand Consolidated National Trades Union founded in 1833, but his example influenced both the passage of the Factory Act 1819 and various co-operative movements and communities subsequently, and gives him a place as one of the founders of English socialism.

OWEN, WILFRED (1893–1918), poet. His writing matured after he joined the army in 1915; invalided back to Britain from the Somme in 1917, he began, with the encouragement of his fellow poet Siegfried SASSOON, to compose the poems that were to make him famous. He returned to France and was killed a week before the armistice. Only a handful of his poems were published in his lifetime, but he was posthumously recognized as one of the most effective and moving witnesses to the First World War. Some of his works were later set to music by BRITTEN in his *War Requiem*.

OXFORD, EARL OF, 9TH *see* DE VERE, ROBERT;

13TH *see* DE VERE, JOHN, **17TH** *see* DE VERE, EDWARD

OXFORD AND ASQUITH, 1ST EARL OF *see* ASQUITH, H(ERBERT) H(ENRY), essay on pages 36–37

OXFORD AND MORTIMER, EARL OF, 2ND and **3RD** *see* HARLEY, EDWARD

P

PAGET, SIR JAMES (1814–99), physician and pathologist. Educated at St Bartholomew's Hospital, London, where he taught anatomy and physiology and became full surgeon in 1861, Paget worked as sub-editor on the *Medical Gazette* (1837–42) and in 1853 published his *Lectures on Surgical Pathology*, now regarded as the pioneering work in modern pathology. He discovered the cause of trichinosis and of osteitis deformans (now known as Paget's disease). He was serjeant-surgeon to Queen VICTORIA and President of the Royal College of Surgeons.

PAGET, WILLIAM (1st Baron Paget) (?1505–63), politician. In deviousness, he outranked his early Cambridge patron, Stephen GARDINER. After diplomatic service, in 1543 he became a Royal Secretary, and in 1547 he openly abandoned Gardiner to mastermind Edward SEYMOUR's takeover as Lord Protector. A peerage followed two years later, but the Seymour link brought temporary disgrace during the ascendancy of John DUDLEY. Back in circulation by 1553, he was quick to leave JANE GREY, winning MARY I's grudging favour; despite fierce clashes with Gardiner and Mary's fury at his fomenting of opposition, his standing recovered and, by 1556, he was Lord Privy Seal. ELIZABETH I's accession prompted permanent retirement.

PAINE, THOMAS *see* essay on page 626

PAISLEY, 1ST BARON *see* HAMILTON, CLAUDE

PAISLEY, IAN (1926–), politician. A Protestant minister since 1946, founder and head since 1951 of the fundamentalist Free Presbyterian Church of Northern Ireland, Paisley comes from a tradition of working-class and rural fundamentalism which sees mainstream middle-class churches as betraying the gospel. In 1966 he established the ultra-loyalist Ulster Constitution Defence Committee to resist liberalizing influences in the Ulster Unionist Party. Paisley engaged in conspicuous protests against the liberal initiatives of Terence O'NEILL, but was seen as marginal until he polled strongly against O'Neill in the Northern Ireland parliamentary constituency of Bannside during the 1969 General Election, winning the seat when O'Neill resigned. In 1970 he became Westminster MP for North Antrim and in 1971 he founded the Democratic Unionist Party (DUP), supported by Ulster Unionist defectors. His demonstrations against Civil Rights marches, fiery language, extreme anti-Catholicism and Ballymena accent were seen internationally as symbols of Ulster bigotry. In response to the Sunningdale Agreement the DUP joined Vanguard (a hard-line Unionist movement) and anti-Sunningdale Ulster Unionists in the United Ulster Unionist Council, which won 11 of 12 Northern Ireland parliamentary seats in 1974. Paisley supported the Ulster Workers' Council strike of May 1974, which brought down the power-sharing executive set up by the Sunningdale agreement, and joined loyalist paramilitaries in a further unsuccessful strike in 1977. His relations with loyalist paramilitaries were ambiguous; he set up organizations with paramilitary overtones, but denied involvement in paramilitary activities. Paramilitaries accused him of stirring up trouble and leaving others to take the consequences.

The DUP grew throughout the 1970s, attracting effective young leaders and overtaking the Ulster Unionist Party (UUP) in the 1981 local elections. It won three Westminster seats in 1979, and topped the poll in the 1979 European elections. Many Unionists, however, were unwilling to endorse Paisley's extremism, deriving confidence from tough government security policies and seeing the impossibility of implementing DUP demands for the revival of Protestant hegemony. From 1981 the UUP vote stabilized.

Paisley formed an electoral pact with the UUP to oppose the Anglo-Irish Agreement of 1985; moderate Unionists, however, would not endorse the extreme non-co-operation advocated by the DUP. Paisley's unwillingness to make practical proposals or risk the extreme measures implied by his prophecies of doom, his autocratic leadership (which alienated prominent activists) and the damage done to Unionism by his antics weakened him, though he kept a determined core of support. In 1998 he joined the integrationist United Kingdom Unionist Party and UUP dissidents in opposing the Good Friday Agreement and secured about half the support of the Unionist community. The DUP, however, accepted seats on the execu-

continued on page 627

PAINE, THOMAS (1737–1809)
Writer and revolutionary

Born in Thetford (Norfolk), the son of a Quaker corsetmaker, he made his early career in the excise. Based in Lewes (Sussex), from 1766, Paine was active in the town debating society. In 1772 he was asked by disgruntled colleagues to write *The Case of the Officers of the Excise*, demanding higher pay, which he circulated to every MP; he was seen as ringleader and dismissed. Through the excise Paine had met George Lewis Scott, a senior official and fellow science-enthusiast who had been tutor to GEORGE III. Scott introduced him to Benjamin FRANKLIN. Paine resolved to start a new career in America and, armed with letters of recommendation from Franklin, left for Philadelphia in Oct. 1774.

There, he threw himself into the American crisis, supporting the colonists' claims and even attempting to find a safe way of making explosives in the home. After serving as editor of the *Pennsylvania Magazine* 1775, he wrote the first work to argue that the case of the American provinces pointed towards complete separation from Britain: *Common Sense*. He argued that government was a necessary evil, and monarchy a tyranny. George III had exposed the lauded separation of powers in Britain as a sham concealing an untrammelled executive. He argued for a republic, governed by provincial assemblies which would annually elect delegates to a Continental Congress. His plan was rejected as simplistic by practical administrators like John Adams, but *Common Sense* sold as many as 150,000 copies in North America (Paine calculated) and encouraged debate on the republican option. Late in 1776 Paine wrote his first essay on 'The Crisis', to boost morale during the harsh winter; others followed throughout the war, expounding the Americans' political creed and encouraging continued resistance. Paine was appointed secretary to the congressional committee on foreign affairs (1777), giving him official recognition as the revolution's chief ideologist.

He spent the mid 1780s at his farm at New Rochelle, a gift from the New York assembly, working on a plan for a single-arch iron bridge; in 1787 he went to England to begin construction. While there he wrote pamphlets for Charles James FOX on the crisis precipitated by George III's illness, and followed the French Revolution. As a friend of Lafayette and George WASHINGTON he hoped to have influence and returned to France in 1790. There, responding to BURKE's *Reflections on the Revolution in France*, he wrote *The Rights of Man*. He argued that civil rights were not based on precedent but on the natural right to act for one's own happiness when not in conflict with others' rights. Reason was the only possible basis for government; law should arise from the logic of justice in an equal society rather than from the dictates of royal judges. The work sold well in France, America and Britain. A second part, written in London in 1791, argued for the abolition of monarchy. Plans to circulate a subsidized edition among the poor gave the British government reason to prosecute Paine, but he left to take his seat in the French National Convention (1792).

In France, Paine opposed the authoritarian tendencies of Robespierre, argued for the exile rather than execution of Louis XVI and his family, and was imprisoned from Dec. 1793 until Nov. 1794 charged with conspiring against the French people. While he was in prison the first part of his third great work, *The Age of Reason*, was published. Paine argued that the religion revealed in nature was superior to all other revealed religion. The Bible was a secondary authority only and Christianity, in worshipping a man rather than God, was effectively a form of atheism. The second part, written after his release, further attacked Christianity and Judaism, rejecting the God of the Old Testament as the perpetrator of barbaric acts which no Deity would sanction, and the New Testament as inconsistent and hypocritical in its morality. Paine's arguments were not new, but he differed from the Anglican Deists of the early eighteenth century by writing in a way accessible to readers with little education.

Paine remained in France until 1802, when he returned to the United States disillusioned with Napoleon. In Washington he was welcomed by President Jefferson but his series of letters, *To the Citizens of the United States*, bore little relation to practical politics; many Americans were also offended by his outspoken Deism. Paine influenced Jefferson to purchase Louisiana from France in 1803, but was refused the government post he wanted.

Paine was considered little more than a hack writer in his later years, but in his heyday his status as a largely self-educated outsider and brilliant propagandist helped him convey unusually radical arguments, and he has continued to hold a high place in the echelons of radical thinkers.

John Keane, Thomas Paine: A Political Life (1995)

tive in Nov. 1999 while claiming that it did not recognize its Sinn Féin colleagues; it was widely accused of hypocrisy in accepting the benefits of the agreement while winning support by apocalyptic scaremongering against it. Paisley remains the best-known individual Unionist, but is clearly in decline; it is uncertain how far his church and party will survive him.

PAKENHAM, FRANCIS (7th Earl of Longford) (1905–), politician. Educated at Eton and Oxford and, invalided out of the army in 1940, he became personal assistant to William BEVERIDGE (1941–4). For the Labour Party he served as First Lord of the Admiralty, Secretary of State for the Colonies and Leader of the House of Lords (1964) but, a Catholic convert, it is as a moral crusader that Longford is best known, campaigning against sexual licence, for prison reform and for the release of Myra HINDLEY (sentenced to life imprisonment in 1966 for the Moors murders). His wife Lady Elizabeth Longford is a historical biographer, as is one of his daughters, Lady Antonia Fraser.

PALAVICINO, HORATIO (c. 1540–1600), financier. Genoese merchant whose business deals in the Netherlands led him, on Sir Thomas GRESHAM's death in 1579, to take over as chief English financial and diplomatic agent abroad. As an international financier, he was in a unique position to gather information. Loss of ELIZABETH I's favour brought retirement in the 1590s; he then used his staggering wealth to set himself up as an English country gentleman, as well as helping Robert CECIL in his struggles with Robert DEVEREUX, Earl of Essex.

PALEY, WILLIAM (1743–1805), philosophical writer. Paley was educated at Christ's College, Cambridge, where he was elected a Fellow. He was made Archdeacon of Carlisle (1782), later becoming a canon of St Paul's (1795). He was a leading exponent and popularizer of theological utilitarianism, arguing both that God had designed the natural and social order to effect his divine purposes and that human actions should be judged primarily by their consequences. His lectures, published as *The Principles of Moral and Political Philosophy* (1785), long served as a university textbook. In the view of GEORGE III, Paley's emphasis on the self-interested basis of morality made him unsuitable for the highest ecclesiastical offices.

PALLADIUS (*fl.* 431), churchman. Perhaps a member of the Gallo-Roman aristocracy from the region of Auxerre, Palladius seems to have represented the established elite of the Church hierarchy. Prosper of Aquitaine records that in 431 Pope Celestine appointed him as the first Bishop to 'the Irish believing in Christ'. That his mission to Ireland is subsequently invisible is due to the efforts of the later Armagh hagiographers in ascribing all such activity to St PATRICK, their patron, in their efforts to secure metropolitan control of the Church. Nevertheless, there can be little doubt that the organization of the earliest Irish Christian communities was due to Palladius.

PALMER, JOHN (1742–1818), postal innovator. He was a Bath brewer and theatre manager until he devised the mail-coach system, which, by the use of mail coaches instead of single riders or post boys, cut the three-day journey of a Bath–London letter to one day. PITT THE YOUNGER approved the plan in 1784, despite opposition from postmasters. In 1786 the system was extended to the London–Edinburgh route and Palmer was made Comptroller General of the Post Office. He succeeded in bringing more business to the Post Office despite the fact that Pitt saw his scheme as an opportunity to raise postal charges. Palmer was dismissed for his autocratic ways in 1792, but his scheme remained in place.

PALMER, SAMUEL (1805–81), painter. Precociously talented, Palmer exhibited at the Royal Academy at 14. He was a friend of William BLAKE, with whose visionary experiences and mystical style his own work has affinities. He set up an artists' commune, before its time, in Kent (1826–35); the group called themselves 'the Ancients'. After its collapse Palmer married and went to Italy and his painting style became more traditional. His work was in obscurity for nearly a century, but later such artists as Paul NASH and Graham SUTHERLAND drew inspiration from his other-worldly landscapes.

PALMER, SELBORNE ROUNDELL (1st Earl of Selborne) (1812–95), lawyer. Educated at Rugby, Winchester and Oxford, where he was President of the Union, he was called to the Bar in 1837 and was elected to Parliament as a Peelite (*see* PEEL, ROBERT) in 1847. He was Solicitor General (1861) in Palmerston's (*see* TEMPLE, HENRY) Liberal government and Attorney General (1863–6) but, opposed to GLADSTONE's disestablishment of the Irish Church (1869), he initially refused the lord chancellorship, then holding the office (1872–4 and again 1880–5). Created an earl in 1885, he despairingly left the Liberals in 1886 over Irish Home Rule and forthwith supported the Conservatives without joining their ranks. An outstandingly brilliant lawyer, his monument is the 1873 Judicature Act, which rationalized the courts of law in England and Wales, until then a mass of confusion, overlapping functions and intolerable delay. The separate courts were abolished and a Supreme Court of Judicature established, with a Court of Appeal for civil matters and a High Court with divisions corresponding to the previous separate courts. Selborne was also an expert on liturgical matters.

PALMERSTON, 3RD VISCOUNT *see* TEMPLE, HENRY, essay on pages 770–71

PANDULF (?–1226), Papal Legate. A clerk of the papal court, he was sent by Innocent III to England to demand the restoration of Stephen LANGTON as Archbishop. When JOHN submitted to the Pope, Pandulf became adviser to John and was elected Bishop of Norwich, and excommunicated the barons opposed to John. After the death of the Regent William MARSHAL in 1219, he became influential in the government of England, successfully calming the still smouldering factions. He returned to Rome in 1221.

PANKHURST, EMMELINE, CHRISTABEL and SYLVIA *see* essays on pages 630–31

PAOLI, PASQUALE (1724–1807), Corsican politician. The son of a Corsican chieftain, he was the supreme general of Corsica in the struggle against Genoese rule. In 1767 James BOSWELL visited Paoli; on returning to Britain he depicted him as an ideal 'enlightened' ruler. In May 1768 France bought Genoa's interest in Corsica and invaded; after a year of resistance Paoli fled to Britain where he failed to gain effective support from the government. He lived in exile for 22 years, becoming a familiar figure in society where his friends included Charles James FOX, BURKE and SHERIDAN as well as Boswell and Samuel JOHNSON. He returned to Corsica after the French Revolution, which he initially hailed as the fulfilment of his hopes, but was soon alienated by Jacobin excesses and official corruption and in 1793 sought British protection. In 1794 the French were driven out of Corsica and it became a kingdom associated with Britain on the model of Ireland, with its own Parliament and GEORGE III as King, but Paoli's aspirations were ill-tuned to the reactionary tendencies of the British government of the 1790s. In 1795 he again left, after which the French reconquered the island.

PARIS, MATTHEW (*c.* 1200–*c.* 1259), writer. A monk of St Albans (Herts.), he was a prolific author of historical and hagiographical works, often strikingly illustrated with his own line drawings. His Latin *Chronica Majora*, from the Creation to 1259, an extension of ROGER OF WENDOVER's chronicle and the most comprehensive history written in England up to that time, was so long that he produced several shorter versions as well. His informants included the most powerful figures in the realm, including HENRY III and RICHARD OF CORNWALL, but his opinions remained very much his own: xenophobic, often critical, always vividly expressed. He also wrote a history of his abbey and, for aristocratic ladies, a number of saints' lives in Anglo-Norman verse.

PARKER, MATTHEW (1504–75), Archbishop of Canterbury (1559–75). A distinguished Cambridge don and chaplain to ANNE BOLEYN, the Church preferments which he gained for his evangelical sympathies under EDWARD VI were all lost under MARY I. Emerging from rural obscurity in 1558, he found to his horror that ELIZABETH I had decided that her mother's old chaplain would make an ideal Archbishop of Canterbury. He did his gentle and conscientious best in the difficult opening years of the new religious settlement; with little support, he performed a balancing act between the Puritans and the Queen's demands for discipline, particularly in the Vestiarian Controversy of 1564–6, when he was constrained to enforce the Queen's requirements on uniform clerical dress. He also supervised an uninspired official translation of the Bible (the Bishops' Bible, 1568). Happiest in scholarship, he sponsored other historians, pioneering especially Anglo-Saxon studies, and he preserved many precious medieval manuscripts which are now in the library of Corpus Christi College, Cambridge.

PARKER, SIR PETER (1924–), public servant. Brought up in France and Shanghai, the son of an engineer, Parker took a distinguished degree at Oxford (interrupted by equally distinguished war service) and studied management in the USA before taking business responsibility in 1954 for the Duke of Edinburgh's Commonwealth Study Conferences. A series of senior executive posts in both the public and private sectors culminated in his chairmanship of British Rail (1976–83), where he launched a major programme of electrification, planned construction of the Channel Tunnel and did much to modernize the rail system. Since modernization involved job losses he was often at loggerheads with the unions; political and temperamental differences placed him at odds with the post-1979 Conservative government. It was a matter of some pride to Margaret THATCHER that she never used the railways, and Parker's articulate advocacy of government–union–industry co-operation found little favour.

PARKER, RICHARD (1767–97), mutineer. Having served in the navy, he returned to it as a volunteer in 1797 (when every effort was being made to recruit men for the war with revolutionary France) to escape imprisonment for debt. Dissatisfaction with conditions and pay was reaching its height. Parker joined the crew of the *Sandwich* at the Nore, off Southampton, on 31 March. The next month there was a mutiny among the

Channel Fleet at Spithead; the Admiralty responded with a number of concessions, and pardoned the leaders. A mutiny at Plymouth was settled with some violence in mid May. Parker's fellow sailors elected him president of a committee of delegates on 10 May and within a fortnight had mutinied, demanding that the terms agreed with the Channel Fleet should be extended to them, and that arrears of wages be paid before they set sail. The government was intransigent and stopped supplies; the mutineers responded by blockading London and threatening to sail to France. Parker was suspected of revolutionary sympathies; historians continue to dispute the extent and nature of Jacobin involvement. The *Sandwich* crew surrendered on 13 June and after a court martial Parker was executed on board ship on 30 June; at least 36 others were also executed.

PARKER, THOMAS (5th (1st Parker) Earl of Macclesfield) (*c.* 1666–1732), lawyer. The son of an attorney, he was educated at Cambridge and the Inner Temple, practised as a lawyer and became an MP. Admired by GEORGE I, he was made Lord Chancellor in 1718 and an earl in 1721. Although a fair-minded head of the judiciary, he came under investigation in 1724 for allowing Masters in Chancery to embezzle the funds they administered. He resigned in 1725 and was impeached. Found guilty of raising the entry fees paid by Masters in Chancery to such an extent that they had to use the money they were entrusted with, Macclesfield was fined £30,000, only a fraction of the £82,000 missing, and imprisoned in the Tower for six weeks, but was able to keep his remaining offices. The incident added to the reputation for corruption attending Robert WALPOLE's regime.

PARKES, BESSIE RAYNER (1829–1925), feminist. Daughter of Joseph Parkes, radical Whig and Unitarian, she was a close friend of Barbara Leigh BODICHON from the 1840s. Having published *Remarks on the Education of Girls* (1856), she became the editor of the *English Woman's Journal* in 1858 and was closely involved with the Langham Place group for the following nine years. In 1866 she published *Essays on Women's Work*, which were particularly concerned with women's employment. In 1864 she converted to Roman Catholicism. In 1867 in France she met and married Louis Belloc, and had two children, the writers Hilaire BELLOC and Marie Belloc Lowndes. She was never active in the campaign for women's suffrage but continued to show sympathy for feminist politics in her long later life.

PARKINSON, CECIL (Baron Parkinson of Carnforth) (1931–), politician. Parkinson will be remembered as the man who almost rose to the top but whose career was destroyed by a sex scandal. One of a large number of Conservatives from Cambridge University in the early 1950s, he came to politics after a business career in accountancy. As MP for Enfield West (London) (1970–4) he made little impact but as MP for Herts. West (1974–83) he gravitated into Margaret THATCHER's inner circle. His part, as Chairman of the Conservative Party, in helping win the 1983 election was expected to bring him to the Foreign Office but at this point he had to reveal to the Prime Minister that his secretary, Sara Keays, was pregnant with his child. In the ensuing scandal he resigned from the Department of Trade and Industry. His reputation as Thatcher's 'golden boy' was seriously tarnished, and his resignation was the first major blow to her government. He made a come-back as Secretary of State for Energy (1987–9) and Minister of Transport (1989–90) but went out with his patron in 1990. With the election of William HAGUE as Conservative leader, Parkinson was brought back as party Chairman (1997–8) to see through the reform of party structures.

PARKYN, ROBERT (*c.* 1510–69), diarist. A modestly prosperous conservative-minded country parson; for most of his career he was curate of Adwick-le-Street (Yorks.). He is notable for having copied and written much devotional literature in commonplace books, including a valuable if gloomy worm's-eye narrative of the changes brought by the Reformation.

PARNELL, ANNA (1852–1911), Irish politician. Sister of Charles Stewart PARNELL, she was introduced to the politics of social reform and women's rights by their American relatives (on their mother's side). Parnell and her sister Fanny founded the Ladies' Land League in Ireland and America to carry on the work of the Land League after the arrest of many leaders and activists. (The involvement of women in public agitation brought criticism from conservatives such as the Catholic Archbishop McCabe of Dublin.) After the Kilmainham Treaty in 1882 the Ladies' Land League was unilaterally wound up for being too radical and independent-minded. Anna never spoke to her brother again. Her memoir, *The Tale of a Great Sham* (1986) accuses the Land League of timidity.

PARNELL, CHARLES STEWART *see* essay on pages 632–33

PARNELL, FANNY (1849–82), co-founder of Ladies' Land League *see* PARNELL, ANNA

PARNELL, THOMAS (1679–1718), poet. A Dubliner, he went to Trinity College and entered the Irish Church. During his frequent visits to

continued on page 634

PANKHURST, DAME CHRISTABEL (1880–1958)
Suffragette

Born in Manchester, the oldest daughter of Richard and Emmeline PANKHURST, Christabel read law at Victoria University, Manchester, coming joint first in the LLB examinations in 1905. Nevertheless, on account of her sex she was denied admission to Lincoln's Inn, where her father had been a pupil; this incensed her and fuelled her militancy at the exclusion of women from the public sphere.

The Pankhurst home was a meeting place for radical politicians and intellectuals and Christabel was nurtured in feminist and political debate from an early age, sharing her mother's sympathy for the recently formed Independent Labour Party (ILP). But when the ILP refused to espouse the cause of votes for women, Christabel, who had been a member of the North of England Society for Women's Suffrage while still a student, founded with Emmeline the Women's Political and Social Union (WPSU) in 1903 to press for the extension of the franchise to women. Since no political party would commit itself to this, the WPSU remained politically unaligned, a single-aim pressure group with the unequivocal slogan 'Votes for Women'. For two years the WPSU campaigned peacefully, but in 1905 Christabel and Annie KENNEY took militant action, disrupting a Liberal election meeting at Manchester Free Trade Hall and getting arrested. The *Daily Mail* coined the term 'suffragette' (which the women adopted) and Christabel became famous as one of the first martyrs for the cause.

In 1907 she settled in London with the intention of making the WPSU a nationwide organization, acting as an organizer and an extraordinarily effective orator for the WPSU (as was Emmeline). Within two years a WPSU rally in Hyde Park drew a crowd of half a million. Continuing her militant campaign (smashing windows at the homes of politicians and Whitehall ministries was adopted as a suffragette tactic), Christabel was twice arrested and used her legal knowledge to argue her case, calling on one occasion the Home Secretary, Herbert Gladstone, and the Chancellor of the Exchequer, LLOYD GEORGE, as witnesses.

Fearing arrest on charges of conspiracy, Christabel fled to Paris in 1912, where she continued to edit the WPSU journal *The Suffragette*. To some her exile was the right course of action; to others it was an act of selfish betrayal leaving colleagues to take the risks and suffer the penalties. Her sister, Sylvia PANKHURST, criticized her on these grounds but the differences were also ideological. Sylvia wanted to extend the activities of the suffragettes to involve working-class women in a campaign for their rights. For Christabel this was unrealistic: to broaden the aims of the WPSU would be to diminish its force and chances of achieving that sole purpose for which it had been established, votes for women.

The outbreak of the First World War brought an end to the activities of the WPSU and division in its ranks in attitudes towards the war. In 1918, with the government at last having admitted the justice of the suffragettes' demand, Christabel stood, unsuccessfully, as a candidate for the Women's Party (the transformed WPSU) in support of the Coalition government. In 1920 she went to Canada and from there to California, where she lived for the rest of her life, embracing religion with a fervour that she had previously channelled into the suffragette movement, and prophesying a Second Coming.

Christabel Pankhurst, Unshackled: The Story of How We Won the Vote (1959)
David Mitchell, Queen Christabel (1977)

PANKHURST, EMMELINE (née Goulden) (1858–1928)
Suffragette

The oldest of the 10 children of a prosperous Manchester calico-printer, she was raised, as she was to raise her own five children, in an atmosphere of talk and radical politics. In 1879 she married Dr Richard Pankhurst, a barrister who was well known throughout Manchester for his reformist views. Their circle of friends included Annie BESANT, Keir HARDIE and William MORRIS. The Pankhursts served together on the Manchester Women's Suffrage Committee and on the Married Women's Property Committee. Both were members of the Liberal Party, until the 1884 Reform Act failed to extend the franchise to women, when they joined the Fabian Society, and then the recently established Independent Labour Party (ILP) in 1893.

After Richard's death in 1898 Emmeline worked as Registrar of Births and Deaths in Rusholme, a working-class suburb of Manchester, to support her family. Resigning from the ILP in 1903 for the same reason that she had left the Liberals, Emmeline and her daughter Christabel PANKHURST founded the Women's Political and Social Union (WPSU) to campaign for votes for women. As the WPSU grew more militant, and more nationally focused, Emmeline moved to London with Christabel where she organized petitions, demonstrations and, later, forays to shatter the windows of prominent politicians so as to draw attention to the cause. Though often domineering, autocratic and the cause of much dissension in the ranks of the WPSU, she was nevertheless a mesmerizing speaker who drew huge crowds to listen to her passionate rhetoric, and she embarked on fund-raising tours of the USA in 1909 and 1911.

She was arrested in 1911 and again in 1913 for incitement to commit a felony when LLOYD GEORGE's house was torched, and in 1913 was sentenced to three years' imprisonment. Since 1909 the suffragettes had often gone on hunger strike in prison, demanding that they should be treated as political prisoners, not criminals. Horrified at the thought of the political effect that numbers of respectable middle-class women dying might have, the Liberal government introduced forcible feeding and then in 1913 the despised 'Cat and Mouse Act', by which women were released from prison when their physical condition became critical, only to be re-arrested once they had

regained their strength. Emmeline Pankhurst endured 12 such re-arrests, but continued to campaign whenever she was at liberty, even to the extent of appearing on public platforms on a stretcher.

The WPSU ceased its activities on the outbreak of the First World War, and Emmeline embraced the war effort, urging enlistment and speaking with passion for this new great cause. In 1917 she went to Russia on behalf of the British government to try unsuccessfully to persuade the Bolsheviks to come back into the fighting. In 1920 she went to Canada campaigning for child welfare (she had herself adopted four illegitimate children) and social purity on behalf of the National Council for Combating Venereal Disease. She returned to England in 1926 and joined the Conservative Party, and was selected to fight as parliamentary candidate in Whitechapel in the East End of London, but she died before the election, just after women had at last been granted the vote on the same terms as men.

Emmeline Pankhurst, My Own Story (1914)
Sylvia Pankhurst, The Life of Emmeline Pankhurst (1935)

PANKHURST, SYLVIA (1882–1960)
Suffragette

The daughter of Richard and Emmeline PANKHURST, Sylvia was educated at Manchester High School for Girls and the Royal College of Art. Living in London, she supported herself as a freelance artist and was active in the Independent Labour Party (ILP), which she had first joined in Manchester. She was never to deviate from her socialist convictions and commitment to social justice. She worked as an organizer and speaker for the Women's Political and Social Union (WPSU), contributed articles to its journal, *The Suffragette*, and put her artistic talents at the service of the movement by designing the cover of the journal *Votes for Women*, suffragette banners, posters, murals and a 'Holloway Brooch', the proud badge of those suffragettes who had served time there.

From 1912, largely in opposition to the control of the WPSU by her sister Christabel PANKHURST, Sylvia set about establishing a mass movement which would also connect the emancipation of women to the emancipation of the working class in London's East End. She edited *The Worker's Dreadnought*, the journal of this offshoot (called the East London Federation of Suffragettes after the break with the WPSU) and was arrested and imprisoned 13 times under the terms of the notorious 'Cat and Mouse Act' (*see* PANKHURST, EMMELINE).

On the outbreak of war in 1914 Sylvia, a pacifist, was publicly critical of her mother's bellicose stance. She worked with the East London Federation to ameliorate social conditions there, setting up maternity and child welfare clinics, a factory to provide work for unemployed women, cost-price restaurants and a nursery school, as well as encouraging the wives of servicemen to demand improved allowances and pensions. She was a member of the Women's International League for Peace and Freedom and was fined for anti-war propaganda.

In 1920 Sylvia travelled to Russia as a stowaway to meet Lenin, published a somewhat disillusioned report, *Russia as I Saw It* (1921), and joined the British Communist Party for a period. She had a child at the age of 45 with an Italian socialist exile, Silvio Corio, with whom she lived, and called the child Richard Keir Pethwick Pankhurst, a litany of the people whose influence she most valued. In the 1930s Sylvia was active fighting fascism and supporting the struggle for independence in Abyssinia, where she edited newspapers and wrote books and pamphlets, and also an affecting second book of poetry. She died in Addis Ababa in 1960.

Sylvia Pankhurst, The Suffragette Movement: An Intimate Account of Persons and Ideals (1931)
Barbara Winslow, Sylvia Pankhurst: Feminist Politics and Political Activism (1996

PARNELL, CHARLES STEWART (1846–91)
Irish politician

A Protestant landowner, Parnell was seemingly an unusual exponent of Home Rule and opponent of landlordism. His great-grandfather, Sir John Parnell, opposed the Union and his grandfather, Henry Parnell, worked with O'CONNELL to achieve Catholic Emancipation, but his father was an undistinguished squire. His mother, Delia Stewart, was American (her father, a United States Admiral, distinguished himself against the British in the War of 1812–15). Some sources claim that she encouraged Charles to hate the English; others suggest her influence has been exaggerated. Entering Parliament in 1875 as MP for Meath, Parnell embarked upon obstruction of parliamentary business, which was disowned by Isaac BUTT but brought the Irish Question to the forefront of British parliamentary politics. Initially an unimpressive speaker, he developed an incisive style of oratory which contrasted with the reckless and flamboyant emotionalism favoured by many nationalists. In 1879 he formed a tacit alliance, known as the New Departure, with the land agitator Michael DAVITT and the American-based Fenian, John DEVOY. Parnell became president of the Irish Land League, demanding considerable rent reductions and resisting evictions by using boycotts (*see* BOYCOTT, CHARLES) in the face of continuing agricultural depression. In 1880 Parnell succeeded to the leadership of the Home Rule Party, and obtained funds from sympathetic Americans. He continually walked a political tightrope between advocating violence and following constitutional methods; many Land League activists and American supporters were Fenians, and he may have taken the Fenian oath. He also had to balance the radicalism of small farmers and agricultural labourers in the west of Ireland with the more conservative attitudes of larger Catholic farmers in the east and south and the Catholic bishops. Parnell did not confine his interest in Irish economic affairs to agrarian matters. He was interested in science and technology and devoted much time and money to speculative and generally unprofitable schemes for Irish industrial development, such as a sawmill on his estate at Avondale and a quarry near Arklow (both Co. Wicklow).

In 1881, after he had opposed GLADSTONE's Land Act as insufficient, the Land League was suppressed and Parnell was imprisoned with many of his lieutenants without trial. The Gladstone government claimed that the leaders' removal would allow the law-abiding majority to assert themselves; instead, violence continued, while the land agitation was directed by the Ladies' Land League under Parnell's sisters Fanny (1849–82) and Anna PARNELL (1852–1911). In 1882 Gladstone agreed to release Parnell and grant further minor concessions on the land question. One of the intermediaries who negotiated this Kilmainham Treaty was Captain W. H. O'Shea, MP for Clare (1874–85) and later Galway City (1885–6), whose wife Katherine was Parnell's mistress. After his release Parnell distanced himself from the radicals and disbanded the Ladies' Land League, while the Chief Secretary for Ireland W. E. FORSTER, associated with the coercion policy, resigned in protest at the concessions.

The Kilmainham Treaty was shaken though not overthrown by the assassination of the new Chief Secretary, Lord Frederick CAVENDISH, and a senior Dublin Castle official, T. H. Burke, by the Invincibles, a Fenian splinter group, in Phoenix Park, Dublin, a few days after Parnell's release in 1882. Several radical Land League officials with links to the Invincibles fled to America, strengthening Parnell's control of nationalist organization in Ireland. He replaced the Land League with the National League, which he kept under tight control. While lieutenants like T. M. HEALY and William O'BRIEN campaigned against the continuing use of coercion legislation by the Liberal Lord Lieutenant, Earl Spencer, Parnell consolidated his control of nationalist Ireland by purging the remaining Buttites from the Home Rule Party and forging an alliance with the Catholic Church. He promoted a personality cult based on delegating much day-to-day business to a select group of lieutenants and intervening only at decisive moments to reinforce his image as an austere figure of almost superhuman foresight and wisdom. The height of his power was reached in 1885 after the passing of the third Reform Act the preceding year, when he entered an opportunistic alliance with the Conservatives to bring down Gladstone. In the 1885 election Parnellites won 85 of the 103 Irish seats (the remainder – all in Ulster except for two university seats – were held by Unionists under Edward SAUNDERSON) and one Liverpool seat, but failed to hold the balance of power between Conservatives and Liberals.

It now became known that Gladstone had been converted to Home Rule and came into office in 1886 pledging to deliver it. His Home Rule Bill was defeated by the defection of 90 Liberal Unionist MPs led by Joseph CHAMBERLAIN and

Lord Hartington (*see* CAVENDISH, SPENCER), and the 1886 election led to the return of a Conservative government with Liberal Unionist support. Gladstone retained the support of the bulk of the Liberal Party, and mounted a nation-wide campaign on the Home Rule issue, presented as a moral crusade offering a historic opportunity for Anglo-Irish reconciliation. Gladstone became a popular hero for many Irish nationalists, though Parnell privately disliked him and regarded their alliance as purely tactical.

In Ireland, a new land agitation (the Plan of Campaign) was led by William O'Brien and John DILLON; it was partly a response to renewed agrarian discontent due to falling agricultural prices and poor harvests, partly an attempt to show that without Home Rule Ireland would be ungovernable. Their well-publicized (and reck-less) leadership was met by the stern tactics of Chief Secretary Arthur BALFOUR. Parnell took little part in the plan, believing it ill conceived.

In an attempt to discredit Gladstone *The Times*, with official support, claimed that Parnellism was not a bona fide political move-ment but a criminal organization; in particular, it claimed to possess proof that Parnell had connived at the Phoenix Park murders. An offi-cial commission was appointed to investigate the accusations; during its hearings it emerged that the 'proof' had been forged by Richard PIGOTT. Parnell was hailed by liberal opinion as the hero of the hour, and obtained libel damages from *The Times*; Unionists complained that the commission's wider findings about the ambiguous relationship between Land League activity and agrarian violence had been obscured by the issue of the Pigott forgeries.

Parnell's fall came swiftly in 1890 when he was named in the divorce case of Katherine O'Shea; his decision not to defend the case allowed Captain O'Shea to obscure his own collusion and present Parnell in the worst possible light. At first virtually all Parnell's Irish followers declared that his private life would not affect their support, but after Gladstone and the Liberals made it clear their Nonconformist followers would oppose Home Rule unless he resigned, a majority of the party (including most of his principal lieu-tenants) voted to depose him. Parnell refused to accept this, claiming that the Anti-Parnellites were corrupted by the Liberals. The split trau-matized Irish politics for a generation. Parnell presented himself as champion of uncompro-mising nationalism, and appealed to groups such as the Fenians, trade unionists and agricultural labourers who had been marginalized at the height of his political influence. Anti-Parnellites accused him of subordinating Ireland's cause to personal ambition; Catholic priests engaged in widespread spiritual and physical intimidation of Parnellites, while T. M. Healy subjected his former leader to devastating sexual ridicule. Each side blamed the other for the collapse of the Plan of Campaign and the sufferings of evicted tenants. Parnell was supported by about a third of the Irish electorate (especially in Dublin and the larger towns) and adroitly exploited divisions among his opponents, but his candidates were defeated in three hard-fought by-elections. Worn out, Parnell died in October 1891; his followers blamed his death on his opponents, kept up the split under the leadership of John REDMOND, and developed an elaborate culture of commemora-tion and remembrance to emphasize their faith-fulness to the fallen leader. The defeat of the Home Rule Bill in 1893 and the weaknesses and divisions which beset the Irish Party even after its reunification in 1900 further encouraged nostalgia for Parnell.

Parnell's dramatic downfall and death, after he had transformed Irish and British politics but without achieving his ultimate goals, combined with his deliberate ambiguity about the exact nature of his beliefs, has always attracted fasci-nation and speculation far excelling that provoked by his nearest counterparts, O'Connell and DE VALERA. For writers like JOYCE and YEATS he symbolized the heroic individual destroyed by envy and hypocrisy. Parnell weighed his words carefully and many of his public statements were ambiguous; even his famous declaration that 'no man can set bounds to the march of a nation', inscribed on his monument in Dublin, though often seen as a declaration of uncompromising nationalism, can be read in its original context as self-defence against advanced nationalists who criticized him for accepting restricted self-government. He has been seen as a crypto-sepa-ratist and as an enlightened conservative who wished his class to assume leadership of Irish nationalism to secure a place for itself. The displacement of the Home Rule Party by Sinn Féin led many in Britain as well as Ireland to see the Gladstone–Parnell alliance as a lost opportu-nity for national reconciliation; more recently, advocates of secularization in Ireland have adopted him as an icon. Every age imagines Parnell in its own image.

Alan O'Day, Charles Stewart Parnell (1998)

London he became a friend of writers on both sides of the political divide, contributing to *The Spectator* as well as dedicating his *Essay on the Different Styles of Poetry* (1713) to Bolingbroke (*see* ST JOHN, HENRY) and becoming a member of the Scriblerus Club, along with SWIFT, POPE and GAY. He gave his clerical career priority over his literary one, leading to his effective exclusion from the inner circle of Scriblerians. Anxious to reconcile England and Gaelic Ireland, he proposed schemes to print the Bible in Irish and introduce the language in Church of Ireland services, which never received government support. Among his poems, *The Hermit* (published posthumously, 1721) is sometimes cited as reflecting an Augustan preoccupation with the contrasting goals of retirement and involvement in the material world.

PARRY, SIR HUBERT (1848–1918), composer. One of the leading figures of Britain's musical revival in the last years of the nineteenth century, alongside his rival the Irish-born Charles Villiers Stanford (1852–1924), he was regarded less highly as a composer than as a teacher at the Royal College of Music and a promoter of talent, notably that of ELGAR. He is principally remembered for his anthems used on State occasions and his 1916 setting of William BLAKE's poem *Jerusalem*, swiftly adopted both by suffragettes and the Women's Institute but now almost a second national anthem.

PARSONS, SIR CHARLES (1854–1931), engineer. Born in London, the son of an astronomer, Parsons was educated in Dublin and at Cambridge. In 1884, after several engineering apprenticeships, he became a partner in a Gateshead engineering works. He is best known for inventing the high-speed steam turbine in which the steam expansion is divided into several pressure drops. In 1884 Parsons patented his first turbine and associated generator, and in 1888 launched a Newcastle-based company for producing turbo-dynamos of increasing power. By 1900 his firm was installing several-hundred-kilowatt turbo-dynamos in power stations across the country. In the 1890s he began developing the steam-turbine for marine use and in 1897 launched the first steam-turbine driven ship, the *Turbinia*. His firm went on to make some of the fastest ships in the world and his engines were widely adopted in civilian and military vessels.

PARSONS (OR PERSONS), ROBERT (1546–1610), churchman. A brilliant Oxford don, Parsons converted to Catholicism and fled to Leuven in 1574, becoming a Jesuit in 1575. Following his English mission with Edmund CAMPION in June 1580, he returned permanently to the continent, where he directed intrigues and propaganda against ELIZABETH I, and organized

Catholic educational institutions. Protestants detested him, but eagerly read his devotional treatise *The Christian Directory* (1582), usually without realizing the author's identity.

PASTON, MARGERY (*c.* 1445 –?), member of the Paston family. She was the most remarkable of the Pastons, the family of Norfolk farmers climbing into the gentry whose papers include the earliest surviving collection of private letters in English history, revealing for the first time how relatively 'ordinary' people, women as well as men, felt about each other and about the world in which they lived. Margery stunned the family in 1469 by disclosing, a few weeks after her brother Sir John Paston had announced his engagement to a cousin of the Queen of England (*see* ELIZABETH WOODVILLE), that a few years earlier she had secretly married the family's land agent, Richard Calle, the son of a shopkeeper. She and Richard had freely exchanged marriage vows and in law that made them man and wife. But there had been no public ceremony and no witnesses, so, if either she or Richard could be persuaded to deny what they had done, it would be as if the marriage had never been. Their love proved to be greater than all the pressures that were put upon them, particularly on her, and the family was forced to recognize the validity of the marriage. Although her husband continued to work for them, after 1470 she is never again mentioned in the Paston letters.

PATER, WALTER (1839–94), critic and essayist. An aesthete (who gave the word currency), Pater's dictum 'art for art's sake' seemed to give licence to writers like SWINBURNE and WILDE, who seized on his insistence that art should be appreciated for its qualities of aesthetic ecstasy, not for the good that it did, thus seeking to release it from Victorian moral and educational strictures. But Pater's essays *Studies in the History of the Renaissance* (1873), written while he was a Fellow of Brasenose College, Oxford, and later work, including *Marius the Epicurean* (1885), a philosophical romance set in Ancient Rome, his influential article 'Appreciations with an Essay on Style' (1889) and his lectures on Plato published as *Plato and Platonism* (1893) never wholly relinquished the ethical implications of the aesthetic, insisting on the intensity of the moment and the brevity of human life. An unlikely hedonist, Pater was a diffident bachelor who lived with his sisters mainly in Oxford, but in London society from 1885 to 1893. His output was prolific, his prose matchless. He declined to contribute to *The Yellow Book* in the 1890s, but the morbid aspects of his work were exploited to somewhat sinister effect in that decade and beyond, and it is only in recent years that a more careful evaluation of Pater has begun.

PATERSON, EMMA (1848–86), trade-union leader. Born in London, Paterson's major achievement was in establishing with Emily Pattison (*see* DILKE, LADY EMILY) the Women's Protective and Provident League in 1874 to encourage women's trade unionism. With Emily FAITHFULL she also founded the Women's Printing Society and the *Women's Union Journal* in 1876. In 1875 she became the first woman to attend the Trades Union Congress (TUC) and campaigned within it for women factory inspectors, an idea adopted by the TUC in 1878 and given legal effect by statute in 1893, and against the regulation of women's hours of labour where it applied only to women. She clashed with the patriarchal Henry Broadhurst, member of the parliamentary committee, who, like many male trade unionists, believed that a woman's proper place was within the home. She made a major contribution to establishing a place for women in the trade-union movement.

PATMORE, COVENTRY (1823–96), poet. Patmore worked as assistant librarian at the British Museum for nearly 20 years and contributed to the Pre-Raphaelite magazine *The Germ*. William MORRIS used a verse of Patmore as the text for one of his paintings. He was most popular in his day, and is mocked today, for his four-part poem *The Angel in the House* (1854–62), a hymn to married love and domestic bliss.

PATRICK, SIMON (1626–1707), churchman. Influenced by the Cambridge Platonist, John Smith (*see also* WHICHCOTE, BENJAMIN), he took Presbyterian orders before being secretly ordained by a dispossessed bishop (1654). In 1662 he became rector of St Paul's, Covent Garden, and rose to Bishop of Chichester (1689) and of Ely (1691). Patrick wrote prolifically, refuting Catholicism and encouraging education (like TILLOTSON, he founded a school in London in 1687) and promoting the study of the Bible. One of the five founders of the Society for the Promotion of Christian Knowledge (who included Thomas BRAY) he was also a supporter of the Society for the Propagation of the Gospel.

PATRICK, ST *see* essay on page 636

PATTEN, CHRISTOPHER (1944–), politician. Educated at Catholic schools and Balliol College, Oxford, Patten established a base for himself at the Conservative Research Department between 1966 and 1970, where he was seen as a moderate liberal Conservative in the Heathite (*see* HEATH, EDWARD) mould. After Margaret THATCHER's defeat of Heath in 1975 he found himself in the 'outer darkness'. After winning the marginal seat of Bath in 1979 he served in various junior posts before becoming a Minister of State at the Foreign Office (1986–9)

where he also served as one of Thatcher's speech-writers. His reward was promotion to the Cabinet in 1989 as Secretary of State for the Environment, where he was responsible for bringing in the Community Charge or 'poll tax' which caused immense controversy by replacing the domestic rates with a flat tax payable by every adult.

Between 1990 and 1992 Patten was Chairman of the Conservative Party and right-hand man to his close friend, John MAJOR, and his finest hour was helping to win the 1992 election; it was indicative of how he was regarded by many Thatcherites that there should have been cheers when he lost his seat at Bath in that election. He was appointed as the last British Governor of Hong Kong by Major in 1992. His period of office was notable for conflict with the Chinese and their supporters over the issues of democracy and human rights. On his return to Britain, Patten chaired a committee looking into the role of the police in Northern Ireland before being appointed European Commissioner for External Relations in 1999.

PAUL IV (1467–1559), Pope (1555–9). As a Neapolitan aristocrat, Giovanni Pietro Caraffa hated the Spanish colonial power in Naples, and devoted much energy in his pontificate to attacking Spain. This produced conflict with England, ruled by the Spanish King PHILIP and MARY I. After war broke out between Paul and Spain in 1556, Paul cancelled the English legatine powers of Cardinal Reginald POLE (an old enemy), recalling him in 1557 to face heresy charges. Mary refused to recognize a replacement legate, the aged Friar William Peto, or to let Pole submit: a major and ironical hindrance to English Catholic restoration.

PAULET, SIR WILLIAM (1st Baron St John, 13th [1st Paulet] Earl of Wiltshire, 1st Marquess of Winchester) (?1475 or ?1483–1572), politician. A discreet religious conservative who had a seemingly interminable government career from the 1520s (Lord Treasurer from 1550 until his death); he nimbly stepped through such minefields as the fall of Edward SEYMOUR, Duke of Somerset, and of JANE GREY, making himself indispensable with his experience of diplomacy and the intricacies of royal finance. From 1554 he presided over administrative and physical reconstruction of the Exchequer. His home at Basing (Hants.) was rebuilt as a fortress, probably in readiness to store government money, and later proved a formidable Royalist asset during the 1642–6 Civil War until destroyed in a fierce siege in 1645.

PAULINUS (?–644), Bishop of York. An Italian, in 601 he joined St AUGUSTINE's mission in Kent. In 619 he went to the court of the pagan EDWIN, King of Northumbria, in the entourage of the

continued on page 637

PATRICK, ST (*fl.* late fifth century)
British missionary and bishop

He is arguably the most famous character in Ireland's history. The evidence, however, for his life and career was so successfully manipulated, expanded and embellished by hagiographers in Armagh in the seventh and eighth centuries in its pursuit of the primacy of Ireland, that it is now next to impossible to separate the man from the myth. The only reliable information about him is found in his own writings, his *Confessio* and *Epistola*, which still survive in later manuscript copies. It is extremely difficult to establish the exact period when Patrick was active in Ireland or to assess the importance of his career in relation to that of other British missionaries such as PALLADIUS. Scholars can differ by as much as half a century on the dates of his mission and, while the weight of opinion probably now favours the second half of the fifth century, the scantiness of the evidence leaves room for debate. Likewise, it is now widely accepted not only that Palladius was the first Christian missionary to the Irish, but that the later history of Patrick appropriated details which actually belonged to Palladius' life.

A Briton from Strathclyde, Patrick was seized in a piratical raid when he was 16 years old and carried to Ireland where he was kept as a slave for several years. It has been suggested that the location of his captivity was Killala in Co. Mayo. According to the *Confessio*, his enslavement was also a time of spiritual crisis and, after a remarkable escape which is also described in the *Confessio*, he subsequently returned on a personal mission to preach, eventually becoming a bishop. The most likely date for his mission is the late fifth century, since the death of his disciple Mochta in 535 or 537 suggests that his master flourished a generation earlier. Although later tradition preserved at Armagh tells us that Patrick travelled widely on the continent after his escape, his own writings mention only that he returned to Britain. Since his written Latin shows no trace of continental influence, the balance of probability is that he never left Britain and Ireland. When he returned, his activities appear to have been centred in eastern Ulster, although the *Confessio* indicates that he travelled extensively throughout Ireland. It and the *Epistola*, which was written to the Irish chieftain Coroticus, suggest very strongly that he did take considerable risks by travelling among, and seeking to convert, the heathen Irish; the *Epistola* was indeed written after an attack on Patrick and his followers by Coroticus himself. The *Confessio*, which was composed partly to refute charges that Patrick was taking unnecessary risks and that he was ostentatious and extravagant, shows that he was in regular touch with contemporary churchmen in post-Roman Britain.

Patrick emerges from the *Confessio* as an intensely spiritual man who believed that his visions were divinely inspired and that it was his duty to act on them. His protestations of simplicity have until recently been taken at face value and, along with his rather basic Latin style, to indicate that he was largely uneducated. It has, however, been pointed out that, when his Latinity is set in its contemporary context, he emerges as much more learned than was once thought. Such reinterpretation again reinforces the idea that Patrick was less the isolated apostle that he was once thought to have been and more part of an organized mission with links across the Irish Sea. All this said, the scale and energy of Patrick's activities and the extent of the conversion which he achieved do both seem remarkable; it is important, for example, to note that Patrick was already seen as the key figure in the conversion of the Irish by the early seventh century, well before the traditions fostered in Armagh started to develop.

In spite of Armagh's later statements, the location of Patrick's death and burial are unknown. Tradition, based on seventh-century evidence, regards Downpatrick as the correct location, even though Armagh was advancing its own claims at the same time. The supposed close association of Patrick with Armagh was developed in a series of literary texts which used the saint to buttress a successful claim for primacy over all the churches of Ireland. It has led to the widely held view that Armagh was Patrick's church, an idea which most modern scholarship rejects as unlikely, and probably untrue; the site was after all still a major pagan sanctuary until the early sixth century. Ultimately, as with the unhistorical ARTHUR, it is crucial to acknowledge that the fifth century is the least well-documented century of British history and to assess scrupulously the evidence that is available. On this basis Patrick does appear as a very important historical figure, the founder of the greatness of the early medieval Irish Church exemplified by COLUM CILLE and others.

Charles C. Thomas, Christianity in Roman Britain to AD 500 (1981)
David N. Dumville (ed.), St Patrick, 493–1993 (1993)

latter's Christian bride, ETHELBURH, a Kentish princess. Paulinus eventually converted Edwin and many other Northumbrians, becoming the first Bishop of York. He returned south after Edwin's death in 633; thereafter the main agents of the conversion of Northumbria were St AIDAN and monks from Iona based on Lindisfarne.

PEACOCK, THOMAS LOVE (1785–1866), satirist. With little formal education, but formidably well read particularly in classical literature, Peacock enjoyed an unlikely close friendship with the poet SHELLEY. What they had in common was their radicalism, in Peacock's case manifest in his biting satires of current social and intellectual positions. *Headlong Hall* (1816), *Melincourt* (1817), *Nightmare Abbey* (1818), *Crochet Castle* (1831) and *Gryll Grange* (1860–1) are generally regarded as his finest books. It was one of his satirical attacks on art and literature that drew a response from Shelley in the form of *A Defence of Poetry*. Peacock also wrote poetry, including *The Paper Money Lyrics* (1837), a satire on political economy and the world of banking, the publication of which he suppressed while James MILL was alive, since Mill was his immediate superior at the East India Office.

PEADA (?–656), King of the Middle Angles (655–6). The son of the formidable King PENDA, Peada accepted Christianity after his father's defeat and death at the hands of King OSWY of Northumbria in 655. Oswy installed him as a dependent ruler in southern Mercia, but had him killed soon afterwards. Mercian power was revived by WULFHERE.

PEARCE, SIR EDWARD LOVETT (*c.* 1699–1733), architect. His father was a relative of VANBRUGH, who probably encouraged Pearce to give up his military career and study in Italy. He began practising architecture in Dublin in 1726 and was appointed Surveyor of Works and Fortifications in 1730. He designed several country houses and, most famously, the Parliament House, the largest Palladian public building in the British Isles at the time. Pearce's career was cut short by his early death, six years before the building (now the Bank of Ireland) was completed.

PEARS, SIR PETER (1910–86), singer. Pears's musical career began as an organ scholar at Oxford, and in 1933 he studied singing at the Royal College of Music. He had an extensive repertory, singing many leading tenor roles, and a deep understanding of and sympathy for modern works. This helped him in his musical collaboration and life partnership with Benjamin BRITTEN. Britten, who admired Pears's clear, flexible, forceful and expressive voice, composed many of his operas with Pears in mind, including *Peter Grimes* (1945), *The Rape of Lucretia* (1946) and *Billy Budd* (1951). Involved with Britten in the English Opera Group, composer and performer both became instrumental figures in promoting modern composition in Britain.

PEARSE, PADRAIC (1879–1916), Irish politician. Born in Dublin, he was a pioneering writer in Irish and a leading member of the Gaelic League, editing its journal for several years before resigning to found an experimental Irish-language school. He was a founder member in 1913 of the Irish Volunteers, and later joined the Irish Republican Brotherhood (IRB). In speeches and pamphlets he expressed an uncompromising separatism and denounced John REDMOND's support for the British war effort; at the same time, unknown to Irish Volunteer leader Eoin MACNEILL, he plotted what became the Easter Rising with his IRB colleagues. On 24 April 1916 he proclaimed the Irish Republic from the steps of Dublin's General Post Office and was named President of the provisional government; forced to surrender on 29 April, he was executed at Kilmainham gaol on 3 May. His death became a symbol of Irish resistance to Britain. Some commentators criticize his glorification of physical force and his contempt for compromise and majority opinion, but he remains a more complex and attractive figure than the two-dimensional icon of later official propaganda.

PEARSON, KARL (1857–1936), statistician and biologist. Born in London, Pearson studied mathematics at Cambridge and physics in Germany, and in 1882, after a brief legal career, devoted himself to mathematics. In 1884 he became Professor of Applied Mathematics and Mechanics at University College, London, where he met Francis GALTON and W. F. R. Weldon, whose pioneering applications of statistics to the study of heredity and evolution sparked Pearson's interest. From the 1890s he developed Galton's statistical methods to test the efficacy of natural selection as propounded by Charles DARWIN; that led him to construct some of the most important techniques in modern statistics, including theories of correlation and the chi-squared test (1900). In opposition to William BATESON and others he doubted that Mendel's laws of heredity could explain variability in natural populations and believed in gradual and continuous evolution rather than discontinuous variation. He published much of his work in *Biometrika*, a journal which he founded in 1901 and used, as its editor, to promote the use of statistics in the biological sciences and the biometrical school of Darwinism. In 1911 he was appointed as the first Galton Professor of Eugenics at University College, London.

PEASE, EDWARD (1857–1955), socialist. Writing of a number of Fabian marriages, Beatrice WEBB described Edward Pease and his wife as 'the utter essence of British bourgeois morality, comfort and enlightenment'. A colourless individual, Pease had founded the Fabian Society with Frank Podmore in 1884 and was its paid secretary (1890–1913) and its Honorary Secretary (1913–39). He is best remembered as its historian, publishing the *History of the Fabian Society* in 1916.

PECKHAM, JOHN (?–1292), Archbishop of Canterbury (1279–92). Educated at Oxford, he became a Franciscan friar and a highly respected theologian who taught at Paris and Rome. In 1279 he accepted papal nomination to Canterbury and immediately irritated EDWARD I by his zeal for reform and insistence on ecclesiastical privilege. In 1282 he tried in vain to reconcile Edward and LLYWELYN AP GRUFFUDD.

PECOCK, REGINALD (*c.* 1395–*c.* 1460), bishop. A priest in 1422, Bishop of St Asaph in 1444 and of Chichester in 1450, he tried to meet the challenge of the Lollards by reasoning with them rather than by burning them as heretics. But his own works, including *Repressor of Overmuch Blaming of the Clergy* (the first book of theology written in English since 1066), alienated conservative opinion and in 1457 he was charged with having set natural law above the scriptures. He was offered the choice 'recant or burn', and recanted at St Paul's Cross (London). His books were burnt. He resigned in 1459 and was confined to Thorney Abbey (Cambs.).

PEEL, SIR ROBERT *see* essay on pages 640–41

PEEL, SIR ROBERT (1750–1830), manufacturer and factory reformer. His family were well established in the Lancs. calico trade; his father had played a notable part in the development of printed calicoes. Having been educated at Blackburn and London, he became a partner in a calico-printing firm at 23. Peel was among those who prospered during the take-off in the cotton industry. By the turn of the century his firm had more factories spinning cotton with ARKWRIGHT's water frames than any other, though this was an old-fashioned technology; the newer and soon even larger firms used variants of CROMPTON's mule. Conflict with unionized calico-printers around Manchester persuaded Peel to remove his main centre of operations to Tamworth (Staffs.), well placed within the developing canal network, in 1790. He was elected MP for Tamworth; in Parliament he supported PITT THE YOUNGER, but was also quickly accepted as the spokesman for Manchester interests. A baronet in 1800, by 1802 he had taken up the cause of the factory apprentices whom he had once been accused of abusing, and succeeded in carrying the first Factory Act, the Health and Morals of Apprentices Act. In 1816 he introduced a revised Bill, extending regulation to 'free' child workers; though hotly opposed by many manufacturers, this passed into law in 1819.

PELAGIUS (?–*c.* 420), heretic. A Briton who travelled to Italy in the late fourth century, he developed a Christian heresy that denied the concept of original sin (the doctrine that human beings are born tainted with Adam's sin of disobedience to God). For unknown reasons, the heresy spread to Britain, and GERMANUS went there to combat it, both in 429 and shortly before 437. The heresy's strength in Britain shows the enduring nature of the latter's connections with the Roman empire, even after the removal of the army in the early fifth century.

PELHAM, HENRY (1696–1754), politician and Prime Minister (1743–54). Younger brother of Thomas PELHAM-HOLLES, Duke of Newcastle, he was educated at Westminster and Oxford, and served as a volunteer against Jacobite rebels in 1715. He entered Parliament in 1717. He was connected to both Charles TOWNSHEND and Robert WALPOLE by marriage, and consistently supported them. Appointed to various second-rank offices in the 1720s and 1730s, he took over the leadership of Walpole's parliamentary supporters, known as the Old Corps Whigs, after Walpole's fall; he gained office as First Lord of the Treasury in 1743. His position was strengthened after successfully obtaining the resignation of CARTERET, whose war policies were seen as too pro-Hanoverian and weakening the ministry, in 1744. From 1744 to 1746, Pelham governed as head of the Broad-Bottom Ministry, including usually disaffected elements such as John RUSSELL, Duke of Bedford, and his allies and Tories led by Sir John Hynde COTTON and Sir John PHILLIPS. After a showdown with the King in Feb. 1746 and the failure of Carteret to form an alternative ministry, the Pelham brothers held power largely on their own terms, retaining the Bedford Whigs (until 1751) but without the Tories. In Oct. 1748 the European war was temporarily halted by the Peace of Aix-la-Chapelle. Pelham was helped in managing fiscal aspects of the transition to peace by the banker Sampson GIDEON. When, partly to acknowledge the help which he had received from Jewish financiers, he promoted a Jewish Naturalization Bill, he failed to anticipate that he was arming the opposition with a powerful cry against him, one that could exploit latent Anglican anxieties about the safety of the religious establishment. Like Walpole in the Excise Crisis, Pelham saw no way of saving the situation but by withdrawing the measure. His ministry was brought to an end by his sudden death in 1754. He was succeeded by his brother, Thomas Pelham-Holles.

One of the longest-serving prime ministers of the eighteenth century, Pelham is now less renowned than Walpole, NORTH or PITT THE YOUNGER, perhaps partly because his emollient political style engendered less opposition. GLADSTONE admired his financial skill, and praised him as one of the few competent eighteenth-century statesmen.

PELHAM-HOLLES, THOMAS (4th [1st Pelham-Holles] Duke of Newcastle) (1693–1768), politician and Prime Minister (1754–6, 1757–62). One of the largest English landowners and a supporter of the Hanoverian succession, he was made a duke in 1715 and three years later married the granddaughter of Marlborough (see CHURCHILL, JOHN). Secretary of State from 1724, he went on to hold high office for longer than any other eighteenth-century politician. A keen manipulator of patronage, he played a crucial part in maintaining support for several ministries, but his garrulousness and emotional and demonstrative temperament excited derision. Normally content to play second fiddle to Robert WALPOLE, he nonetheless developed strong independent views about foreign policy which played a part in Walpole's downfall.

After the death of his brother Henry PELHAM in 1754, he succeeded him as First Lord of the Treasury but, faced by the rival ambitions of younger politicians such as PITT THE ELDER and Henry FOX, was unable to dominate politics. After an unsuccessful start to the Seven Years War led to the unpopular loss of Minorca (and the execution of Admiral John BYNG) Newcastle resigned in 1756. Pitt, however, needed Newcastle's carefully cultivated network of connections to keep the war financed, and they joined in a ministerial coalition the following year. Cornered into resigning by GEORGE III in 1762, he saw many of his followers dismissed from office; the episode was known as the Massacre of the Pelhamite Innocents and represented the largest removal of office-holders since the Hanoverian succession. It ended the long dominance of the Old Corps Whigs. Newcastle was associated with opposition Whiggery thereafter, and enjoyed a final spell in office as Lord Privy Seal in the first Rockingham (see WATSON-WENTWORTH, CHARLES) ministry of 1765.

PEMBROKE, EARL OF, 2ND see CLARE, RICHARD DE; **10TH** see VALENCE, AYMER DE; **16TH** see TUDOR, JASPER; **20TH** see HERBERT, HENRY; **22ND** see HERBERT, WILLIAM; **COUNTESS OF** see CLIFFORD ANNE; HERBERT, MARY

PENDA (?575–655), King of Mercia (626–55). The first of the formidable line of Mercian kings whose power reached its peak in the time of ETHELBALD and OFFA, he remained an unregenerate heathen at a time when many of the kingdoms of England were beginning to convert to Christianity. His numerous wars expanded Mercian territory, including the conquest of the much smaller kingdom of the Hwicce (see EANFRITH) which lay within modern Glos. and Worcs. The murder of several of the kindred of his predecessor CEARL was part of the process whereby he consolidated power in Mercia. In the northern part of what came to be called England, he disputed supremacy with the kings of Northumbria, and, after killing EDWIN and St OSWALD, he was eventually himself killed by King OSWY, probably at or after the Battle of the Winwaed. After his death, Mercia was briefly under Northumbrian domination until his son WULFHERE reasserted the kingdom's power. Penda's tolerance of Christianity assisted Mercia's conversion to Christianity under his successors.

PENDER, SIR JOHN (1816–96), entrepreneur. A successful cotton merchant in Glasgow and Manchester, Pender became involved in submarine telegraphy at the start of its history, with the London–Dublin cable company and then as a main backer of a proposed transatlantic cable. The fourth attempt to lay a cable was successful in 1866; two years later, when the inland telegraph companies were nationalized, he used his wealth to finance a grand scheme for linking the Empire to Britain by submarine cable. Between 1869 and 1879 a web of cables was laid to India, Africa, Australia, the Far East, South America and all points in between. The Pender companies, led by the Eastern Telegraph Co., formed the largest and most successful international telecommunications enterprise of the day. Pender enterprises were united with the MARCONI Co. in 1929 to form Cable & Wireless.

PENN, WILLIAM (1644–1718), founder of Pennsylvania. Son of an admiral, he was expelled from Oxford as a Dissenter in 1660. Sent to Ireland to manage the family estates, he regularly attended the Quaker meeting at Cork and, on his return to England, faced several trials including that in Bushell's case (see MEAD, WILLIAM). He was twice imprisoned for proselytizing, but nonetheless retained connections with the court. In 1681, CHARLES II repaid a debt owed to Penn's father by granting him a large province on the west bank of the Delaware River in North America. Penn drew up a framework for government to provide for religious toleration in the new colony, which he named Pennsylvania. After he had supervised the building of Philadelphia (1682–4), he returned to

continued on page 642

PEEL, SIR ROBERT (1788–1850)
Politician and Prime Minister (1834–5, 1841–6)

Peel's centrality to the history of the Conservative Party is clear; it is his exact place in it which makes him a controversial figure. Admirers, including his authoritative modern biographer, Professor Norman Gash, portray him as essentially a pragmatist who outgrew early prejudices to become the founder of the Conservative Party and the spiritual ancestor of liberal conservatism; to his critics he was the man who first betrayed and then split his party. More recently attempts have been made to transcend this dichotomy. Boyd Hilton has gone so far as to suggest that Peel might be read as a doctrinaire Liberal, and even as the godfather of the Gladstonian (see GLADSTONE, W. E.) Liberal Party.

He was the eldest son of a self-made cotton magnate; his background would later be held against him by his opponents but it was not unusual in the Tory Party which provided his first political home. Many of the peers in Lord Liverpool's (see JENKINSON, ROBERT) long administration (1812–27) were the first, or at best the second, holders of their title and most, like ADDINGTON, Eldon, ROBINSON and Wellington (see WELLESEY, ARTHUR) were self-made men; the old Tory Party offered a career open to talent in a way the more exclusive Whig Party did not.

The elder Sir Robert's fortune enabled the young Peel to be educated at Harrow and Christ Church, Oxford, the staff colleges of the ruling elite of late Hanoverian England, and it funded his early entry into the Commons in 1809, where he swiftly established himself as one of that small class of executive politicians whose primary duty was the governance of the nation; whatever else changed in his political career, he always remained loyal to this ethos. From 1812 to 1818 he was Chief Secretary for Ireland, where his stout defence of the Union and of Protestantism earned him the predictable sobriquet of 'Orange Peel'; thereafter he was Home Secretary from 1822 to 1827 and again between 1828 and 1830; he was briefly Prime Minister from 1834 to 1835, an office he held once more between 1841 and 1846; he held no office after that but was widely regarded as the most formidable figure in British political life. By the time of his death in 1850 opinion about his achievement and career was as polarized as it has tended to remain. The controversy which engulfed his political life and has subsequently dogged his reputation centred around the issues of Catholics, commerce and corn.

Despite the reputation he had gained in Ireland, Peel was intimately associated with the liberalizing tendencies which marked Liverpool's administration after 1822; his own role was to reform and modify the severity of the English judicial system. His name was associated with those of CANNING, HUSKISSON and Robinson and yet, when Liverpool was incapacitated by a stroke in 1827, Peel preferred to pass into opposition rather than join Canning's administration, an action which indelibly associated him with those ultra-Protestant Tories such as Lord Eldon, who refused to serve under a man whose liberal tendencies they had long distrusted.

If the 'ideologue' view of him is accepted, Peel was already in a false position, which was made worse by his joining Wellington's administration in 1828. On this line of argument, Peel's experience as Chairman of the Commission on the banking and financial system in 1819, which led to the setting up of the gold standard, was a formative one; impressed and convinced by the Free Trade arguments of Adam SMITH and David RICARDO, it was only Peel's past political associations, and his dislike of Canning, which kept him in the company of Wellington. The mistrust in which the latter was held can be gauged from the fact that many liberals interpreted Peel's introduction of the Metropolitan Police as part of an attempt to begin to set up an authoritarian government on the model of that then operating in France; the 'Peelers' or 'bobbies' outlived this unpromising start to become an integral part of British life.

Since the Wellington government's main claim to the support of its followers was its uncompromising defence of the Anglican State, its decisions to repeal the Test and Corporation Acts in 1828 and to pass the Catholic Emancipation Act a year later aroused fierce controversy and Peel, as the chief spokesman in the Commons, collected much of the blame. The 'pragmatist' school has seen these decisions as essentially acts of administrative expediency: the exclusion of Protestant Dissenters from the franchise was effective only in debarring those who were conscientiously scrupulous enough to refuse to take the Oath of Allegiance; the exclusion of Catholics was threatening to cause civil disorder in Ireland. But those who see Peel as essentially a liberal ideologue point out that he advanced neither claim at the time, explaining himself instead in terms which implied that he no longer believed in the intellectual case which his administration had been committed to defending.

Either way, Catholic Emancipation first revealed two features of Peel's character which would become more pronounced with the passing of time: his prickliness over his personal position and his honour which he insisted on putting at the forefront of his concerns; and his impatience with, and inability to manage, the Tory backbenchers. His attempt, along with that of his Prime Minister, to woo back support by rallying to the issue of the defence of the existing political order, actually helped finish off an already weakened administration, some of whose supporters thought that a more representative Parliament would not have passed the Catholic Emancipation Act.

The Whigs held power in 1830–4 and again from 1835–41 and it was during these years that the foundation of the modern Conservative Party was laid; beneath the success story were undercurrents which would come to the surface after 1841. Peel did not create the party, he established its tone and its organization. He held no formal position between 1832 and 1834. It was his prowess in debate and his status as the only major Tory figure left on the opposition front bench which led the scattered remnants of the opposition to the Whig reforms to rally to his side. It was the action of WILLIAM IV in sending for him after Wellington had declined to take office in 1834 which made him Prime Minister and leader of the 'Conservatives'. But it was Peel's own election address, named after his constituency, 'The Tamworth Manifesto', which established a judicious conserving of what was worth preserving as the main tenet of the opposition to the Whigs. But as MACAULAY recognized in 1838, the 'stern unbending Tories' murmured against Peel, whose opinions they distrusted but whose talent they could not do without. Between 1835 and 1841 Peel co-operated closely with the Whig premier, Melbourne (see LAMB, WILLIAM), as both men steered British politics towards the centre away from extremists on both sides.

This divide between Peel, his intimates and the backbenchers became one of the features of his great reforming administration of 1841 to 1846. Many ordinary MPs thought that the job of the Conservatives was done with the defeat of the reforming Whigs; Peel realized that the real job had only just begun. In a series of budgets and other financial measures after 1842, Peel lifted many of the restrictions on foreign trade, as well as the duties on imported food-stuffs: this was certainly in accord with the teachings of Adam Smith; but it also helped relieve the distress of the poorer urban classes by reducing the price of food. Peel saw this as a Conservative act because it helped attach the people to the aristocratic order; his backbenchers thought differently. By 1844 the latter had found their spokesman in DISRAELI, who baited Peel for pursuing a politics without principle and for betraying the men and the cause which had brought him to power.

Peel found such allegations from such a source peculiarly difficult to deal with. He ignored the prejudices of his followers once more in 1844 by granting aid to the Catholic seminary of Maynooth; when he did so again the following year by proposing the repeal of the Corn Laws, his party split. Peel's official excuse for repealing the duties on imported corn was the Irish famine but modern authorities agree in seeing this as the occasion for the Act rather than its cause. Peel resigned in Dec. 1845 but because the Whigs were unable to form an administration he came back in early 1846 and, retaining all bar one of his Cabinet, proceeded to carry repeal through the Commons – at the cost of his own party's unity. To a man of Peel's generation and temperament, carrying on the Queen's government was more important than the claims of party; he was almost the last British Prime Minister to take this view.

Thereafter he studiously refused to form or participate in any administration. His followers, the Peelites, constituted the cream of the Conservative Party, and condemned the Protectionist Conservatives to the title of 'the stupid party'. Peelite support kept the Whigs under Lord John RUSSELL in power until 1851. Sir Robert died on 2 July 1850 from serious injuries incurred three days earlier when he fell from his horse. Thereafter the Peelites attempted to hold the balance of power in the Commons but the fact that Peel's own chief disciple, Gladstone, went on to become one of the founders of the Liberal Party lends credence to the more recent view that, intellectually, Peel was more of a Liberal than a Conservative.

Norman Gash, Mr Secretary Peel
Sir Robert Peel (2 vols, 1962, 1972)

England and, on JAMES II's accession, secured the release of some 1,200 Quaker prisoners. Out of favour after the Glorious Revolution, he returned to America in 1699, but financial mismanagement forced him to mortgage his rights as proprietor of the colony.

PENNANT, THOMAS (1726–98), naturalist and writer. A member of the Welsh gentry, he began to study fossils while at Oxford. He travelled extensively, corresponded with Linnaeus and in 1766 published the first volume of *British Zoology*. Alongside his botanical works he published accounts of the journeys which he made through Britain during his research, which successfully met growing interest in the picturesque and a mythical vanishing rural world.

PENROSE, SIR ROGER (1931–), mathematician. Penrose was Professor of Mathematics at Birkbeck College, London (1966–73), before becoming Professor of Mathematics at Oxford University (1973). During the 1960s he and Stephen HAWKING developed Einstein's general theory of relativity and proposed that the centres of black holes consist of 'singularities', mathematical points where space and time are infinitely distorted and where the laws of physics break down. In 1970 they also claimed that the universe originated in a singularity and greatly expanded in the Big Bang. Penrose won international acclaim for this and later work on black holes, for his work on the geometry and topology of multidimensional spaces and for his ideas on the fundamental structure of the universe. His many popular scientific works include *The Emperor's New Mind* (1989) and *Shadows of the Mind* (1994).

PENROSE, SIR ROLAND (1900–84), painter and critic. A surrealist painter himself, he greatly contributed to British cultural life by his tireless promotion of British contemporary art, and surrealism in particular. He organized the 1936 Surrealist exhibition in London, and in 1947 co-founded (with Herbert READ) the Institute for Contemporary Arts, which continues to organize exhibitions, films, lectures and discussions on topics of contemporary culture.

PENRUDDOCK, JOHN (1619–55), Royalist rebel. A Wilts. gentleman, whose rising in 1655 was the only substantial fruit of a wider Royalist conspiracy. His minuscule force found little backing when they seized the Salisbury assize judges, and after marching westwards he was captured and executed at Exeter. The rising was the immediate cause of Oliver CROMWELL's instituting the major-generals as agents of central government to levy taxes and impose discipline in the regions.

PENRY, JOHN (1559–1603), evangelist. A talented Welsh Puritan educated at Cambridge and Oxford with a passion to evangelize Wales, his furious criticism of the Church authorities and his association with the group of satirical pamphleteers which produced the Martin Marprelate Tracts (*see* THROCKMORTON, JOB) forced his flight to Scotland (1590–2). On his return, he became a Separatist (i.e. he affirmed that any link between Church and State was unchristian), and he was executed for seditious writings.

PEPUSCH, JOHANN CHRISTOPH (1667–1752), composer. The son of a Protestant churchman from Berlin, he left Brandenburg in search of a more liberal political climate. In London by 1704, he wrote and produced masques at Drury Lane with Colley CIBBER. Between 1713 and 1730 he was musical director for James BRYDGES, Duke of Chandos, at Canons, where he organized the performances of works by the greatest composers and musicians of the day. He continued to write, producing over 100 violin sonatas alone and copious amounts of Church music for St Lawrence's at Canons. His most famous work was probably his overture and arrangements of ballads for GAY's *Beggar's Opera* in 1728; he also wrote music for the banned sequel, *Polly*. He was a founder member of the Academy of Ancient Music, which inherited much of his extensive library on his death.

PEPYS, SAMUEL (1633–1703), diarist and administrator. Secretary to the Admiralty (1672–9) under First Lord of the Admiralty Edward MONTAGU, Earl of Sandwich, he was dismissed because of his close attachment to the Duke of York (the future JAMES II) and attendant accusations of popery. Re-appointed from 1684 he served until the Glorious Revolution, presiding over a phase of naval expansion, and has since been celebrated as a naval reformer. He is best known for the diary in which he candidly chronicled his daily life, which he left with the rest of his library to Magdalene College, Cambridge: the surviving volumes in cipher date between 1660 and 1669, and were first deciphered and published in 1825. The marvellously vivid descriptions of his experiences in the Great Plague and the Great Fire of London have shaped our impressions of these events, but he has also endeared himself to his readers, and provided the archetype for diary writers, by his rueful accounts of his varying fortunes in marital and extra-marital relations.

PERCEVAL, SPENCER (1762–1812), politician and Prime Minister (1809–12). A barrister and Tory MP, Perceval served as Solicitor General in

1801 and Attorney General in 1802. He was Chancellor of the Exchequer (1807–9), and succeeded Portland (*see* BENTINCK, WILLIAM CAVENDISH) as Prime Minister in 1809. Faced with economic depression and Luddite agitation at home and the threat of Napoleon abroad, his administration was both divided and repressive. The only British Prime Minister ever to be assassinated, Perceval was shot in the lobby of the House of Commons on 11 May 1812 by a bankrupt who blamed the government for his troubles.

PERCIVAL, ARTHUR (1887–1966), soldier. Percival fought on the Western Front during the First World War, was awarded the Military Cross, and rose to the rank of acting Lieutenant Colonel. Taking a regular commission, Percival served in intervention operations in north Russia (1919), fought against the Irish Republican Army in Ireland (1920–2) and after promotion to Colonel helped plan the defence of Malaya (1936–7). A protégé of the Chief of the Imperial General Staff, Sir John DILL, in April 1941 Percival was promoted to Lieutenant General and appointed General Officer commanding Malaya. An excellent staff officer, when the Japanese invaded Malaya on 8 Dec. 1941 Percival proved unequal to the task. As disaster piled upon disaster Percival retreated to his underground command bunker in Fort Canning on Singapore Island, seemingly incapable of decisive action. Convinced that his situation was hopeless, on 14 Feb. 1942 he surrendered his 85,000 troops, who had almost unlimited quantities of ammunition, to 30,000 Japanese who were almost out of ammunition. Responsible for the single worst disaster in British military history, Percival attempted to exonerate himself after the war, but died a broken man.

PERCY, ALGERNON (19th [10th Percy] Earl of Northumberland) (1602–68), politician. Noblesse oblige led him into naval and military commands in the 1630s, but he was increasingly unhappy with CHARLES I's policies, and opposed the King's dissolution of the Short Parliament in 1640. Despite commanding the royal army against the Scots in the same year, he was soon supporting the Opposition in the House of Lords. He was prominent in various attempts to come to terms with Charles, and, horrified at the King's execution, he played no part in public life thereafter until the restoration of CHARLES II.

PERCY, HENRY (9th [1st Percy] Earl of Northumberland (1341–1408), nobleman. His creation as Earl in 1377 was a recognition of nearly 20 years of his military and political service to the English Crown and, above all, of the dominating position on the Scottish border held by the Percy

family, the result of their active participation in the war in the north throughout the fourteenth century. Angered by RICHARD II's 1398 attempt to undermine that position, Percy threw in his lot with Bolingbroke (the future HENRY IV); indeed it was he who in Aug. 1399, in a dramatic meeting in Conwy Castle (Caernarvons.), persuaded Richard to surrender by promising him that he would be allowed to keep his throne. He was rewarded by being made Constable of England and by recovering the wardenship of the West March based on Carlisle (of which Richard had deprived him). But Henry IV's reluctance to pay him and his son Henry PERCY (Hotspur) the huge sums owed to them fuelled their belief that they had deserved more from the man who, or so they alleged, had deceived them in 1399 by swearing that he had come to England seeking not the throne but only his lawful inheritance. In 1403 he, his son and his brother Thomas PERCY, Earl of Worcester, joined GLYN DWR in rebellion. But Hotspur published the rebel manifesto on 10 July, revealing his hand too early. The King reacted swiftly and at Shrewsbury (21 July), before either Northumberland or Glyn Dwr could intervene, the outcome was decided by Hotspur's death in battle, followed by Thomas Percy's execution. Next month Northumberland submitted to Henry IV and, although he lost the offices and estates received since 1399, was otherwise treated leniently, but the catastrophe which had overwhelmed the family at Shrewsbury made genuine reconciliation impossible.

Northumberland's discontent continued, spluttering into open rebellion again in 1405. He failed, however, to give his ally Archbishop Richard SCROPE the military support needed and instead fled to Scotland. The consequent loss of all his castles made him risk a raid into England in 1408, a desperate last throw which ended when he was killed in battle at Bramham Moor, near Tadcaster (Yorks.).

PERCY, HENRY ('HOTSPUR') (1364–1403), nobleman. Eldest son of Henry PERCY, Earl of Northumberland, he was appointed Warden of the East March based at Berwick in 1384 and soon won the reputation for daring and prowess against the Scots that led them to give him the name by which he is best known. In 1388 he brought a Scottish army commanded by James DOUGLAS to battle at Otterburn, but was himself captured – an incident recounted in the *Ballad of Chevy Chase*. Soon ransomed, he succeeded his father as Warden of the West March in 1396, retaining the post after helping HENRY IV to overthrow RICHARD II in 1399. In Sept. 1402 he defeated the Scots in battle at Homildon Hill (Northumb.), capturing many, including Archibald DOUGLAS. HENRY IV's refusal to let him and his father keep the ransoms for the prisoners taken at Homildon Hill embittered relations between him and the King. He was appointed Justiciar of North Wales with responsibility for suppressing OWAIN GLYN DWR's rebellion. But the wages due to him fell substantially into arrears and, as his dissatisfaction with Henry grew, so his negotiations with the Welsh developed into a conspiracy, one aim of which was to put Edmund MORTIMER, Earl of March (the nephew of Hotspur's wife) on the throne of England. On 10 July 1403 he impulsively and precipitately launched the Percy rebellion, poor timing that cost him his life when the King's rapid reaction brought him to battle at Shrewsbury (21 July) before his father and Glyn Dwr could join him.

PERCY, HENRY (11th [3rd Percy] Earl of Northumberland) (1421–61), soldier. The death of his father, the 2nd Percy Earl, at Neville hands in the first Battle of St Albans (Herts.) in 1455 ensured that, in the Wars of the Roses, he would be a committed supporter of Lancaster against York and the Nevilles. At the Battle of Wakefield (Yorks.) (1460) he avenged his father's death, but was himself killed at the Battle of Towton (Yorks.) next year.

PERCY, HENRY (13th [4th Percy] Earl of Northumberland) (1446–89), courtier and soldier. So strong was the feeling in the north of England that Northumberland should be held by a Percy that in 1470 EDWARD IV was compelled to release Henry Percy, the son of the 3rd Percy Earl, from prison and restore him to the earldom. RICHARD III took the throne in 1483 with Northumberland's support and he counted on it at Bosworth but, although the Earl went to the battlefield, he chose not to fight. He was soon restored to favour by HENRY VII, but was killed in an anti-tax riot.

PERCY, THOMAS (2nd Earl of Worcester) (c. 1344–1403), naval commander. Brother of HENRY, 1st Percy Earl of Northumberland, and a successful naval commander, he was created Earl by RICHARD II in 1397, but like all his family preferred Bolingbroke, the future HENRY IV, in 1399. Re-appointed admiral, he nonetheless joined his nephew Hotspur (see PERCY, HENRY) in rebellion in 1403, but the two of them were defeated in battle at Shrewsbury. He was captured and executed.

PERCY, THOMAS (16th [7th Percy] Earl of Northumberland) (1528–72), rebel. Restored in blood in 1549 after his father Sir Thomas's attainder for participation in the Pilgrimage of Grace (1537), he was regranted the Percy earldom in 1557. He disliked ELIZABETH I's religious settle-ment and in Nov. 1569 joined Charles NEVILLE, 6th Earl of Westmorland, in a northern rising designed to restore Catholicism. When the rebellion collapsed, he fled to Scotland, but was returned to England by the Regent James STEWART, Earl of Moray, for execution.

PERCY, THOMAS (1729–1811), folklorist. He entered the Church from Oxford and established himself in literary circles. In 1761 he translated (from the Portuguese) *Hau Kiou Chouan*, the first work of Chinese literature published in Britain. He then studied an old collection of poems and ballads which he had saved from destruction and added to it with documents received from friends and transcribed from libraries elsewhere in the country; *Reliques of Old English Poetry* was first published in three volumes in 1765. He made further studies of folklore and translation of the Icelandic *Edda* (1770). In 1783 he was made Bishop of Dromore, Co. Down, and his literary output declined.

PERKIN, SIR WILLIAM HENRY SR (1838–1907) and **WILLIAM HENRY JR** (1860–1929), chemists. Born to a family of chemists, the father studied under the German organic chemist August Wilhelm Hofmann at the Royal College of Chemistry in London. In 1856 he prepared the first aniline dye, a purple substance, from coal tar and subsequently, with his father's financial backing, launched a firm near London for manu-facturing his Aniline Purple. His dye proved immensely successful in Britain, where it was used in such items as the penny stamp, and in France, and led to Perkin's status as the founder of the synthetic dye industry. He later mass-produced other dyes based on coal tar (notably 'alizarin'), produced 'coumarin', the first synthetic perfume, and published widely on the synthesis of organic substances. He retired from business in 1874. His son was a distinguished chemist and teacher, and a leading figure in the early twentieth-century dyestuffs industry.

PERKINS, WILLIAM (1558–1602), theologian. A Cambridge don who, by the 1590s, became the most widely read Calvinist theologian in England, outselling even John CALVIN. His voluminous works were pioneering Protestant explorations of moral theology. He died apparently suffering from clinical depression.

PERNE, ANDREW (?1519–89), turncoat don. Master of Peterhouse from 1554, Dean of Ely from 1557, his Cambridge career conformed tidily to current official religion. Thus as Vice-Chancellor he presided first at the burning of the late Martin BUCER's bones for heresy (1557), then at a

Protestant service honouring Bucer (1560). Unsurprisingly anti-Puritan, he showed suspicious tolerance to Cambs. adherents of the Family of Love (*see* NIKLAES, HENDRIK). The satirical Puritan Marprelate Tracts (*see* THROCKMORTON, JOB) insinuated that Archbishop WHITGIFT had been his lover. He left a magnificent library to Peterhouse.

PERRERS, ALICE (?–1400), royal mistress. As EDWARD III's mistress, she procured promotion for her husband William de Windsor as Governor of Ireland. Her dominating presence at court after Queen PHILIPPA's death in 1369 led to her being blamed for the setbacks and financial scandals that dogged the last years of a King who was growing senile. The Good Parliament of 1376 sentenced her to banishment and forfeiture of her estates, a sentence that, by 1379, had been reversed, reconfirmed and finally, at her husband's request, reversed again.

PERROTT, SIR JOHN (?1527–92), administrator. Reputedly a bastard of HENRY VIII (certainly possessing his brusque temper), he made and ruined his career in Ireland, first as President of Munster (1571–3), then as Lord Deputy (1584–8). He sought to dismantle Gaelic institutions, defeated James Fitzmaurice FITZGERALD in 1573 and curbed Highland Scots intervention in Ulster. A feud with Adam LOFTUS, Archbishop of Dublin, led to disgrace and, with the connivance of William CECIL, Lord Burghley, a dubious treason conviction; he died in the Tower of London.

PERUTZ, MAX (1914–), molecular biologist. Perutz studied chemistry and biochemistry in his native Vienna and in 1936 began doctoral research on crystallography at Cambridge under J. D. BERNAL and W. L. BRAGG. The Second World War interrupted his project to determine the molecular structure of the haemoglobin protein by X-ray crystallography, but in 1947 he resumed his research and was appointed head of Cambridge's fledgling Molecular Biology Unit. Like KENDREW, his Cambridge student investigating the myoglobin protein, Perutz used computers to analyse X-ray photographs of protein molecules. Between 1958 and 1960 he published papers detailing haemoglobin's helical structure and shared the 1962 Nobel Prize for Chemistry with Kendrew. Later, Perutz explored the molecular mechanisms involved in haemoglobin's transport of oxygen in the blood.

PETHWICK-LAWRENCE, LADY EMMELINE (née Pethwick) (1867–1954), suffragette and social reformer. She exemplified her vision of a more equal life for women from her youth. With the Pankhursts, she organized the votes for women campaign which she described as 'the greatest bloodless revolution since history began'. Privately educated, she founded a Working Girls' Club with holiday hostels for members and their children and a co-operative dressmakers where the employees worked an eight-hour day with paid holidays (a great improvement on the lives of most working men). What would have been known as a 'fast' young woman, she smoked, ignored dress etiquette and, in 1901, when she married Frederick Lawrence, editor of the metropolitan evening newspaper *The Echo*, they hyphenated their names rather than losing hers in his.

In 1906 she was introduced by Keir HARDIE to Emmeline PANKHURST and agreed to become treasurer of the militant suffragette movement, the Women's Political and Social Union (WPSU), founded by Pankhurst and her daughter Christabel PANKHURST; both Pethwick-Lawrences devoted the years before the First World War to the suffragette cause, including raising and donating money and jointly editing the weekly paper *Votes for Women*. Both were imprisoned, Emmeline four times, including in 1906 for chaining herself to the railings of 10 Downing Street. But in 1912 they were expelled from the WPSU when Emmeline and Christabel Pankhurst espoused a more aggressively militant campaign from which they dissented: they subsequently joined the United Suffragists movement. During and after the First World War, Emmeline worked for peace and international causes, becoming president of the Women's Freedom League in succession to Charlotte DESPARD. In 1918 she was an unsuccessful Labour candidate in the first election in which women were allowed to stand for Parliament. Frederick was elected in 1923, and in 1945 was appointed Secretary of State for India in ATTLEE's Labour government.

PETHWICK-LAWRENCE, SIR FREDERICK (originally Lawrence) (1871–1961), social reformer and politician *see* PETHWICK-LAWRENCE, EMMELINE

PETILLIUS CERIALIS (Quintus Petillius Cerialis) (*fl.* AD 70s), Roman Governor. His governorship of Britain from 71 to 73 (or 74) is notable for the resumption of conquest after the period of consolidation that followed BOUDICCA's revolt in 61. The Roman armies in Britain were brought back up to their former strength of four legions, and Cerialis launched campaigns that are thought to have conquered the Brigantes and let his forces go as far north as Carlisle.

PETRE, SIR WILLIAM (1505 or 1506–72), politician *see* WADHAM, DOROTHY

PETRIE, SIR FLINDERS (1853–1912), archaeologist. His first archaeological survey was of Stonehenge: he then plunged into Egyptology, surveying the pyramids and the temples of Giza. A single-minded, aesthetically aware traveller with more than 100 books to his credit, Petrie was the first Professor of Archaeology at London University (1892–1933), where his magnificent collection remains.

PETTY, MAXIMILIAN (1617–62), Leveller. From an Oxon. gentry family, he became a London merchant, and by 1647 was prominent enough in the Leveller movement to be one of only two civilians allowed into the debates held with army leaders in Putney church. He was crucial in producing a compromise agreement between the two sides on a broad property-based franchise for future parliamentary elections, rather than the wider Leveller proposal. After the Levellers were suppressed in 1649 he ceased to be a significant political figure.

PETTY, SIR WILLIAM (1623–87), statistician. A Professor of Anatomy at Oxford, Petty was appointed Physician General to the army in Ireland: he reorganized the medical service there, and offered to undertake a survey of Irish estates as a preliminary to the redistribution of lands confiscated from the disaffected. A founder member of the Royal Society, he was knighted when the society was chartered. Petty was an enthusiastic proponent of the use of 'number, weight and measure' in political and social inquiry, and coined the term 'political arithmetic' to describe the application of arithmetical and mathematical analysis to the resources of the State. Other early 'political arithmeticians' were Charles DAVENANT and Gregory KING. Petty proposed the establishment of a statistical office to calculate population and revalue property for tax purposes. His publications included the later editions of *Natural and Political Observations . . . upon the Bills of Mortality,* compiled by his friend John GRAUNT until his death in 1674, *Political Arithmetic* (1690) and *The Political Anatomy of Ireland* (1691).

PETTY, WILLIAM (3rd Earl of Shelburne, 1st Marquess of Lansdowne) (1737–1805), politician and Prime Minister (1782–3). Born in Dublin, educated at Oxford, he fought in the Seven Years War and became aide-de-camp to GEORGE II. He entered the Lords on his father's death in 1761 and was employed as a mediator between Henry FOX and Bute (*see* STUART, JOHN). Fox judged him to have behaved duplicitously, an imputation he was repeatedly to attract. Much impressed by PITT THE ELDER, Shelburne resigned his post as President of the Board of Trade in 1763 to support him. In 1766 he became southern Secretary of State under Pitt (now Earl of Chatham).

In opposition throughout the 1770s, he was influenced in a radical direction by his association with Dissenters such as Joseph PRIESTLEY and Richard PRICE. Appointed Secretary of State in the Rockingham (*see* WATSON–WENTWORTH, CHARLES) administration of 1782, he had uneasy relations with the Rockinghamite Whigs. Favoured by the King, but distrusted by Charles James FOX, he replaced Rockingham on the latter's death that summer, but lost core Rockinghamite support. He was left with the difficult task of steering through Parliament preliminaries of the peace that was to end the War of American Independence, a task made more difficult by his espousal of Free Trade notions, making him unusually ready to dismantle empire. European powers restored to each other captured territory and Britain gained valuable concessions from the Dutch, but Shelburne failed to secure compensation for dispossessed American loyalists. The ministry was brought down in Feb. 1783 by an alliance between Fox and NORTH. Shelburne supported PITT THE YOUNGER in the 1780s but in the 1790s increasingly dissented from his policies of repression at home and belligerence abroad, and by 1796 was allied with Fox.

PETTY-FITZMAURICE, HENRY (5th Marquis of Lansdowne) *see* essay on page 647

PEVSNER, SIR NIKOLAUS (1902–83), architectural historian. Pevsner, whose doctoral dissertation was on German baroque architecture, left Germany for Britain in 1935 and started to write on contemporary industrial design. He was in the forefront of the rehabilitation of Victorian architecture and wrote an extensive re-examination of Norman SHAW in *Architectural Review* (1941); for 13 years he was Director of the Victorian Society, concerned with the conservation of nineteenth-century buildings. His work includes the *Dictionary of Architecture* (a joint author 1966) and *A History of Building Types* (1970). He was appointed Slade Professor of Art at Cambridge (1959) and was editor of the *Pelican History of Art* series (1953–). He is famous for his multi-volume guide, familiarly known as 'Pevsner', *The Buildings of England* (1951–), which he conceived, edited and largely wrote. With continuing systematic revision and updating, it provides an authoritative, detailed and committed exposition, county by county, of English architecture.

PHILBY, HAROLD ('KIM') (1912–88), spy. Son of an Arabist explorer, Philby won a scholarship to Trinity College, Cambridge, in 1929, where he joined the Socialist Society and met BURGESS,

continued on page 648

PETTY-FITZMAURICE, HENRY (5th Marquess of Lansdowne) (1845–1927)
Politician

One of the least remarked yet most remarkable of British foreign secretaries, Lansdowne could trace his ancestry on his father's side back to the Norman invaders of Ireland, while on his mother's side he was descended (albeit illegitimately) from the flexible and notorious French politician, Talleyrand.

Lansdowne's grandfather was a member of the Reform Bill Cabinet of 1832 and one of the leading Whig politicians for half a century, and his grandson seemed set to follow in his footsteps after inheriting the title in 1866 at the age of 21. As an undergraduate at Balliol in the JOWETT era, Lansdowne imbibed a proper sense of public duty, and soon after graduating was offered a junior lordship of the Treasury by GLADSTONE in 1868. He was appointed Under-Secretary at the War Office in 1872, and when the Liberals returned to power in 1880 he went as Under-Secretary to the India Office. In June 1880 he decided he could not stomach Gladstone's Irish policy and became the first of the Whigs to resign from the Liberal Cabinet. The ties of heredity were strong enough to induce him to become Governor General of Canada under Gladstone in 1883 but his new political orientation disposed him to accept from Salisbury (see CECIL, ROBERT GASCOYNE) the viceroyalty of India in 1887, a post he retained under the Liberals. In 1895 he became Secretary of State for War in Salisbury's government.

As Secretary of State Lansdowne had a rough ride during the Boer War when he could not avoid taking some of the blame for the poor performance of the British army, but it was a mark of the confidence reposed in him that Salisbury should have selected him as his successor at the Foreign Office in Oct. 1900. Salisbury had been Foreign Secretary in every Conservative administration since 1878 and he remained so as Prime Minister: Lansdowne's inheritance was far from easy on a personal level but the complications at a political level were also formidable. Traditionally Lansdowne's tenure of office has been treated as a postlude to Salisbury and a prelude to GREY, and the want of a modern study of his policy has rendered a considered verdict on it difficult. What is clear is that he inherited an unenviable diplomatic situation. Preoccupied by the Boer War, Britain faced hostility from her traditional imperial rivals, France and Russia, as well as from Kaiser Wilhelm's Germany; the 'splendid isolation' of which Salisbury had been proud seemed to his successor a source of possible danger. But while Lansdowne shared Joseph CHAMBERLAIN's view that Britain should escape from isolation, he took a more measured and pragmatic view about how this might be achieved, and his close collaboration with Salisbury until 1902 ensured a suitable degree of continuity.

Lansdowne was the first British Foreign Secretary to have to face the German naval challenge, and thus the first to tackle what later historians have called the problem of imperial overstretch; as a former imperial proconsul, he was well-placed to assess the diplomatic needs of a global power, and his foreign policy might best be categorized as an attempt to limit Britain's liabilities, rather than as a retreat from isolation. Some contemporaries and historians have read his 1902 alliance with Japan and 1904 *entente* with France as part of a turn from Salisburian isolationism, but they are better interpreted as part of a grand design which never quite came off.

Like Salisbury Lansdowne regarded Russia as the main threat to British power and he also shared his predecessor's desire to be on better terms with France; what he most emphatically did not share was his successor's obsession with the German threat. The Japanese alliance provided Britain with naval cover in the Far East against Russia, while the *entente* with France provided a diplomatic line to Russia. Throughout his period in office Lansdowne negotiated hard to secure an agreement with Russia but Tsarist ambitions in the Far East prevented a settlement of differences. But the French Foreign Minister, Delcassé, was willing to settle Anglo-French colonial disputes, and this led to the agreements of 4 April 1904. Under the terms of the *entente* Lansdowne felt obliged to offer the French diplomatic support against Germany in the first Moroccan crisis (1905–6) but, contrary to later reports, he never went as far as Grey would in offering the French armed assistance.

In opposition Lansdowne led the Conservative peers and, in 1916, took office in the LLOYD GEORGE coalition, only to resign in 1917 to argue for a negotiated peace in a gesture worthy of the last of the Whigs. He died in 1927.

MACLEAN and BLUNT. During visits to Vienna in 1933–4 he joined a Communist cell and was recruited as a Soviet agent. As an apparent pro-Fascist sympathizer he covered the Spanish Civil War from the Francoist side for *The Times*. In 1944 he entered British Secret Intelligence, working with the Special Operations Executive and then directing counter-espionage operations against the Soviet Union. From 1949 Philby was the liaison officer between MI6 and the CIA and FBI in Washington and from there was able to warn of Maclean's impending investigation as a Soviet spy. He was recalled to London, interrogated, and had to resign from MI6. Until 1963 Philby continued to pass information to both British and Soviet intelligence services from the Middle East where he worked as a journalist. After 12 years the net was closing in on the 'third man' and Philby defected to Moscow, where he was awarded Lenin's Order of the Red Banner and the honorary rank of Major-General in the KGB.

PHILIP II (1527–98), King of Spain (1556–98) and of England (1554–8). Son of the Holy Roman Emperor CHARLES V, who launched Philip on his dispiriting second marriage as King Consort to MARY I of England in 1554. Philip, a conscientious, deeply pious and courteous man, did his best on two English visits in 1554–5 and 1557, but he resented English politicians' concern to restrict his rights, and there was little warmth shown between his mainly Spanish entourage and the English nobility. He had much else to distract him, especially when in 1555–6 Charles retired and partitioned the Habsburg inheritance between his brother Ferdinand and Philip; Philip received Spain and its New World and Italian dominions and the Netherlands. The English efforts to colonize Irish territory which took shape during his years as King Consort may have been encouraged by the example of Spanish colonies in the New World; Leix and Offaly were renamed King's and Queen's County after Philip and Mary, and settlement began slowly and on a small scale.

England followed Philip into war with France in 1557, losing Calais in 1558. On Mary's death, which deprived him of all rights in England, Philip rather tepidly offered marriage to ELIZABETH I, but his third and fourth wives were French and Austrian. By the 1580s his relations with England deteriorated into undeclared but increasingly large-scale war, thanks to English involvement with the revolt of the Netherlands. In his unsuccessful efforts to curb English power, Philip launched armadas in 1588, 1596 and 1597.

PHILIP, PRINCE (Duke of Edinburgh) (1921–), Royal Consort. The son of Prince Andrew of Greece, great grandson of Queen VICTORIA,

Gordonstoun-educated and a naval officer, in 1947 he married another of Victoria's descendants, Princess Elizabeth, daughter of GEORGE VI. On the eve of the wedding Philip changed his name to that of his maternal grandfather, who had changed his name from Battenberg to Mountbatten during the First World War and took British nationality, and was created Duke of Edinburgh. In 1953 his wife was crowned Queen ELIZABETH II and as consort Prince Philip has fulfilled a difficult and undefined role with some success and considerable controversy. The Duke of Edinburgh's award for young people and his award for export have been sought after and high-profile; less welcome have been evaluations of him as a harshly authoritarian father and a forthright – sometimes insensitively so – public figure.

PHILIP, SIR JENNINGS *see* CLERKE, SIR PHILIP JENNINGS

PHILIPPA OF HAINAULT (?1314–69), Queen of England (1328–69). Daughter of William, Count of Holland and Hainault, she was betrothed to the heir to the English throne (the future EDWARD III) in 1326 when his mother ISABELLA OF FRANCE wanted the Count's naval resources to carry out the invasion of England that she and Roger MORTIMER were planning. The marriage took place in 1328. In 1347 Philippa successfully interceded for the lives of the six burghers of Calais whom Edward had wanted to execute when the town surrendered. Generally she seems to have been content with motherhood (she bore 12 children) and collecting fine clothes.

PHILIPPS, SIR JOHN (*c*. 1666–1737), philanthropist. Son of a Commonwealth Commissioner for the Propagation of the Gospel, he used his position as an MP to further religious and moral measures, including the Blasphemy Act of 1698. One of the first members of the Society for Promoting Christian Knowledge and the Society for the Propagation of the Gospel in Foreign Parts (*see also* BRAY, THOMAS), he campaigned against theatre and duelling and gave lavishly to educational causes. He established at least 22 charity schools in Pembs. (now part of Dyfed), where he was a major landowner. He was an early patron of Methodists including John and Charles WESLEY and George WHITEFIELD.

PHILIPPS, SIR JOHN (1700–64) politician. He shared his father Sir John PHILIPPS's religious leanings and, on entering Parliament in 1741, established himself as a leading Tory. He brought his followers to PITT THE ELDER's side in the 1750s in return for a promise to tighten the property qualification for parliamentary candidates and voters. He led his supporters away from opposition to subsidies and demands for parliamentary reform, which helped the assimilation of the Tories into the political establishment on GEORGE III's accession.

PHILLIP, ARTHUR (1738–1814), colonial administrator. Having joined the navy in 1755, Captain Phillip was entrusted in 1788 with the first convict settlement in Australia, named Sydney (after Thomas Townshend, Viscount Sydney). He carried the settlement through many early privations and as Governor of New South Wales ruled it with authoritarian benevolence, but returned to England in 1792 in bad health. He was promoted to Rear Admiral in 1801 and Vice-Admiral in 1810.

PHILLIPS, ALBAN (1914–75), economist. He came to economics late, having been an electrical engineer before taking his degree at the London School of Economics in 1949. Appointed Tooke Professor of Economic Science there, he built the Phillips machine, a physical model showing the behaviour of the macro-economy. His most notable contribution lay in the discovery of the Phillips curve in the 1950s, an idea that dominated economic policy for the next decade. This purported to demonstrate the existence of a negative relationship between unemployment and inflation since the nineteenth century. The stability of the relationship was discredited in the 1970s, when inflation and unemployment were rising together. When recast in a dynamic formulation, however, it allowed monetarists to argue that Keynesian (*see* KEYNES, J. M.) policies produce inflation without any permanent effect on unemployment.

PHILLIPS, SIR TOM (1888–1941), sailor. Son of an army officer, he saw active service in the Dardanelles in 1915, and by 1939 had risen to Deputy Chief of Naval Staff. A short man with an irascible temper (nicknamed 'Tom Thumb'), Phillips was not afraid to oppose CHURCHILL. As a result, in the autumn of 1941 Phillips was ordered to take the *Prince of Wales* and *Repulse* to Singapore, where it was imagined they would serve as a deterrent. On 9 Dec., one week after his arrival, Phillips took his ships north to intercept Japanese landing forces. Overwhelmed by Japanese air attacks three days later, Phillips went to the bottom with his command.

PICK, FRANK (1876–1941), administrator and arts patron. A subscriber to William MORRIS's vision of an 'earthly paradise', Pick, who worked for the London Underground from 1906, rising to be managing director in 1928, believed that an aesthetically pleasing, integrated transport system could create an appreciative civic community in the capital, and thus be profitable. To this end he commissioned leading contemporary architects for the buildings, and artists to design the lettering for stations, benches and litter bins. Jacob EPSTEIN and Henry MOORE were charged with providing Modernist sculptures for the Underground headquarters in 1929, and, such was the quality of the modern poster art that was subterraneanly displayed, that the Underground was known as the 'people's gallery' and Pick was hailed as a modern age patron of the arts, the industrial fulfilment of the Arts and Crafts concept of the role of aesthetics in everyday life.

PIGOTT, RICHARD (?–1890), journalist and forger. A former Young Irelander, Pigott published pro-Fenian newpapers between the 1860s and the early 1880s; he was chronically impecunious and allegedly engaged in various shady enterprises. After his papers were bought by the Parnellites (*see* PARNELL, CHARLES STEWART) he took money from the Dublin Castle administration to criticize the Land League. In 1886–7 he persuaded Unionist activists that his separatist contacts would enable him to obtain evidence implicating Parnell in the Phoenix Park murders (*see* CAVENDISH, LORD FREDERICK), and produced several letters, supposedly from Parnell, which were published by *The Times* to coincide with legislation on Irish coercion. Parnell denied the authenticity of the letters and demanded an inquiry. The Unionist government set up a Royal Commission, not only to investigate the authenticity of the letters but also the connection between the Land League, separatism and agrarian violence; Dublin Castle officials went to great lengths to help *The Times* accumulate evidence which might hurt the Irish Party. When called to the witness box Pigott broke down under cross-examination; he subsequently admitted that he had forged the letters and fled to Madrid, where he committed suicide.

PIGOU, ARTHUR CECIL (1877–1959), economist. Fellow of King's College and later Professor of Political Economy at Cambridge, he had wide interests, covering matters as diverse as public finance, industrial fluctuations, unemployment and welfare economics. His distinctive contribution lay in welfare economics and in his analysis of the problem of over-spill effects arising from particular economic activities. Such 'externalities' arise where social costs or benefits exceed private costs or benefits and create problems in a market economy. He advocated taxes and subsidies to rectify these disparities. Policies such as 'the polluter must pay' owe their origin to his early analysis of such problems. These ideas were also behind the kind of cost-benefit analysis used to assess major projects such as the London Underground's Victoria Line.

PILKINGTON, HENRY (HARRY) (Baron Pilkington of St Helens) (1905–83), industrialist. Born into the family glassmaking business founded in 1826 in St Helens (Lancs.), he rose partly through his analytical and mathematical abilities; although the company marked time in the 1930s, it had lucrative patents for making plate-glass. As Chairman from 1949, Pilkington oversaw the return to full profitability while also backing, at considerable expense, the revolutionary float process for making glass developed by Sir Alastair Pilkington (no relation), involving pouring molten glass over molten tin at 1000° C. Float glass gave Pilkington Bros the international edge that brought huge prosperity. The family company went public in 1970, just before Sir Harry stood down as Chairman. In the meantime he had also served on many public bodies, and chaired the Committee on Broadcasting (1960–2) that resulted in the establishment of BBC2.

PINTER, HAROLD (1930–), playwright. Educated at Hackney Downs school in east London, Pinter was first an actor. His first full-length play, *The Birthday Party*, was performed in 1958, but it was his second, *The Caretaker* (1960), that was a major success performed all over the world and frequently revived. He is one of Britain's most significant contemporary playwrights, the influence of Samuel BECKETT lingering over his plays with their enigmatic, unresolvable dramatic situations: to say that something is 'Pinteresque' is to mean it is redolent with pauses and silences. Since the mid 1980s Pinter's plays have increasingly reflected his frequently expressed left-wing political views, and the 'comedies of menace' have given way to parables on the abuse of political power world-wide, in works such as *Mountain Language* (1988) and *Ashes to Ashes* (1995). He has also scripted many successful films, including *The Servant* (1962), *The Go-Between* (1969), *The French Lieutenant's Woman* (1981) and *The Comfort of Strangers* (1989), and has directed several plays, including Simon Gray's *Butley* (1971), and continues to act.

PITMAN, SIR ISAAC (1813–97), inventor of a system of shorthand. A teacher who had been unsuccessful with his notions of a longer alphabet and a decimal system, he hit the jackpot with the invention of a shorthand based on sound, which proved to be much faster than any competing system. *Stenographic Soundhand* (1837) was a runaway success, being reprinted regularly and promoting Pitman shorthand world-wide.

PITT THE ELDER, WILLIAM *see* essay on pages 652–53

PITT THE YOUNGER, WILLIAM *see* essay on pages 654–55

PITT RIVERS, AUGUSTUS (1827–1900), soldier, anthropologist and archaeologist. Educated at Sandhurst, Pitt Rivers was commissioned into the Grenadier Guards (1845). His chief contribution to the army was in pioneering the scientific study of the development of firearms and in establishing an army school of musketry at Hythe (Kent). Pitt Rivers theorized from his anthropological research that human technology evolved in much the same way as biological mechanisms, an insight he tested by collecting boats, clothing, religious totems and many other human artefacts. In 1883 he presented his now enormous collection to the University of Oxford.

PLACE, FRANCIS (1771–1854), trade unionist and social reformer. Known as 'the radical tailor of Charing Cross', he was a working-class autodidact who favoured the extension of the franchise by the progressive means advocated by the philosophical radicals in whose circles he moved. His lobbying and research made possible the repeal of the Combination Acts and played a significant part in the Reform Bill agitation (1830–2). He drafted the petition that later became the People's Charter (1838) (*see* LOVETT, WILLIAM) but abhorred violence. He was a steady, industrious artisan, who thought that self-improvement was as important as the extension of the franchise.

PLANTAGENET, ARTHUR (6th Viscount Lisle) (*c.* 1480–1542), royal servant. Illegitimate son of EDWARD IV, he was Squire of the Body to HENRY VII, undertook military commands for HENRY VIII, and gained his title after marriage to Elizabeth Grey, Baroness Lisle, in 1523. He became Deputy of Calais in 1533. A religious conservative, he was arrested in 1540 as part of Thomas CROMWELL's rearguard action against his enemies, and accused of complicity in a Calais plot involving supporters of papal authority. He was imprisoned in the Tower of London, and reportedly died of excitement on hearing that he had been declared innocent. This inoffensive, undistinguished man has gained modern celebrity through his surviving correspondence, edited by Muriel St Clare Byrne, with his household and his formidable second wife Honor Grenville, widow of Sir John Basset.

PLANTAGENET, EDWARD (18th Earl of Warwick) (1475–99), dynast. HENRY VII feared the greater share of royal blood possessed by this son of George PLANTAGENET, Duke of Clarence, (and nephew of EDWARD IV), and from 1485 imprisoned him in the Tower. Lambert SIMNEL impersonated him in 1487, and Henry eventually had him executed on allegations of plotting with Perkin WARBECK.

PLANTAGENET, GEOFFREY (Count of Anjou, Duke of Normandy) (1113–51), soldier. Married young in 1128 to Empress MATILDA, he campaigned on her behalf (1135–44) against STEPHEN's forces in Normandy. His conquest of the duchy did much to weaken Stephen's position in England, and paved the way for the accession of their son, HENRY II, as ruler of England and Normandy as well as Anjou. The origin of one of Geoffrey's nicknames 'le Bel' (the handsome) seems obvious; why he was also called Plantagenet is unknown. In the nineteenth century it was suggested that he might have been in the habit of wearing a sprig of broom (*planta genista*) in his cap, and this explanation has been widely accepted. Although Plantagenet is now the name conventionally given to the English royal family descending from Henry II, it was not used as a dynastic label until adopted by RICHARD OF YORK.

PLANTAGENET, GEORGE (3rd Duke of Clarence) (1449–78), royal duke. He was created Duke in 1461 when his brother became King as EDWARD IV. In 1469 he married Isabel Neville and joined his father-in-law Richard NEVILLE, Earl of Warwick, in plotting against Edward. After the failure of the Lincs. rising and his abortive 1470 bid for the throne, Clarence fled to France. In Oct. he reluctantly acquiesced in the restoration of HENRY VI but, when Edward returned to England in force, he switched sides in time to fight at the battles of Barnet and Tewkesbury (both 1471). He remained discontented, all too inclined to oppose his brother and to become associated with treasonable proceedings, which inevitably caused his brother to distrust him. In 1477 Edward had Parliament convict him of treason, and he was executed in the Tower on 18 Feb. 1478; within a few years, the story (later used by SHAKESPEARE) that he had been drowned in a butt of Malmsey wine was in circulation. His son was the father of Edward PLANTAGENET.

PLANTAGENET, MARGARET (Countess of Salisbury) (1473–1541), dynast. Victim of HENRY VIII's dynastic paranoia as the last surviving member of the older royal line, she was daughter of George PLANTAGENET, 3rd Duke of Clarence. She married Sir Richard Pole. Henry restored her to Clarence's Salisbury title in 1513, but her known religious conservatism and the activities abroad of her son, Cardinal Reginald POLE, brought arrest in 1538. She was beheaded with unusual ineptitude.

PLAYFAIR, SIR LYON (1st Baron Playfair) (1818–98), chemist and politician. Born in India,

Playfair was educated at St Andrews, Edinburgh and London. He gained a doctorate in chemistry from Giessen (1839–40) and subsequently championed the work of the German chemist Justus von Liebig on agricultural chemistry. He held several academic positions in Britain including Professor of Chemistry at the Royal School of Mines, London (1845–58), and published important research in organic chemisty. He served on numerous official inquiries into areas such as agriculture, sanitation and education. His close connections with powerful figures, including Prince ALBERT, allowed him to advance his ideas for improving scientific and technical education in Britain. He was a leading figure in organizing the Great Exhibition of 1851, the Royal College of Science (now Imperial College) and the South Kensington Museum (now the Victoria and Albert Museum) and was a Liberal MP (1868–92).

PLAYFAIR, WILLIAM (1789–1898), architect. Nephew of the Scottish mathematician John Playfair, who provided an exegesis on Euclid, he was the leader of the Greek revival in Scottish architecture. Many of the great porticoed buildings in Edinburgh are his, including the completion of Edinburgh University (from 1817), the (unfinished) National Monument on Carlton Hill (1824–9), the Surgeons' Hall (begun 1829) and the National Gallery of Scotland (1850), at a time when the city was designated the Athens of the North.

PLAYFORD, JOHN (1623–*c.* 1686), bookseller and music publisher. In 1651 he issued *The English Dancing-Master*, the largest single source of traditional ballad airs. It continued to be published in revised and expanded forms until 1728.

PLEGMUND (?–923), Archbishop of Canterbury (890–923). Appointed to the archbishopric by ALFRED THE GREAT, he seems to have played an important role in the reigns of both Alfred and EDWARD THE ELDER. He advised Alfred on his translation of Gregory the Great's *Cura Pastoralis,* created new dioceses and appears to have been deeply involved in early efforts to convert the Danelaw to Christianity.

PLIMSOLL, SAMUEL (1824–98), politican and 'the sailor's friend'. From a Congregationalist family in Bristol, he set up as a coal merchant in London in 1853, having been the Honorary Secretary of the Great Exhibition of 1851. He obtained wide knowledge of shipping, which he put to use as radical MP for Derby (1868–80). He advocated a compulsory load-line on ships, successfully campaigned for a royal commission on the issue of shipping accidents in 1873 and was suspended from the Commons in 1875 for his

continued on page 656

PITT THE ELDER, WILLIAM (1st Earl of Chatham) (1708–78)
Politician and Prime Minister (1766–8)

Grandson of an East India Company merchant, 'Diamond' Pitt, and younger son of an MP, he was educated at Eton, Oxford and Utrecht. In 1731 his schoolfriend George Lyttelton helped him obtain a cornet's commission under Lyttelton's uncle Lord Cobham (*see* TEMPLE, RICHARD). In 1735 he was elected MP for Old Sarum (a notorious pocket borough) through the influence of his own uncle, Thomas Pitt. Cobham had recently joined the 'patriot' opposition to WALPOLE; Pitt followed. He, Lyttelton and Cobham's heir, Richard Grenville, became known as Cobham's Cubs.

Pitt had grown to adulthood in the Walpolean era of peace and prosperity, when religious and associated political animosities were losing their sharp edges. The survival of the Protestant regime, parliamentary government and religious toleration seemed probable. In that context, the rationale for Walpole's staunchly Whiggish, substantively conciliatory and in many respects cynical style of politics was not so evident. Pitt was to develop a style in public life that contrasted with Walpole's in almost every respect.

A ready speaker, Pitt rose to prominence in the late 1730s among critics of Walpole's pacific stance, attacking Walpole's conciliatory response to Spanish depredations on British trade, and calling for war with Spain, which broke out in 1739. When in 1740 Frederick the Great of Prussia seized Silesia from Britain's ally Austria, Britain was dragged into the larger War of the Austrian Succession. Walpole resigned in 1742, but otherwise only a minor Cabinet shuffle ensued, CARTERET being added. Pitt called in vain for Walpole's impeachment.

Carteret favoured significant British involvement in continental war. This appealed to GEORGE II, whose perspective was as much Hanoverian as British. Pitt, now among the foremost speakers in the Commons, claimed that this entailed the sacrifice of British to Hanoverian interests, of course antagonizing the King. In 1744, as Carteret's policy failed to deliver and became unpopular, PELHAM persuaded the King to dismiss him, and brought in former members of the Whig opposition, including followers of Cobham. But the King drew the line at Pitt.

For the next two years, Pitt concentrated on battering his way into power – on his terms: Britain should operate as no more than an auxiliary on the continent, he argued, and instead give priority to a 'maritime war'. When the 1745–6 Jacobite rising led by Prince Charles STUART was defeated, the ministry finally felt strong enough to bully the King. In 1746 Pitt was given the minor but potentially lucrative office of Paymaster of the Forces. His ostentatious refusal to profit from this post (in contrast to Walpole, among other previous holders) helped give credibility to his claim to be a man of principle.

The inconclusive ending of the war in 1748 was not expected by many to bring more than an interlude of peace. Pelham's broadly based Whig ministry faced little effective opposition in Parliament, especially after the death of FREDERICK, Prince of Wales, robbed opposition of a rallying point. Pelham's death in 1754, however, brought his less confident brother the Duke of Newcastle (*see* PELHAM-HOLLES, THOMAS) to power. Ambitious younger ministerialists Pitt, Henry FOX and William MURRAY (later Lord Mansfield) began to jockey for position, Pitt being aided by his small band of personal followers (his long-standing ties with the Grenville family were tightened when he married Hester Grenville in 1754). When Fox was made Secretary of State and Leader of the Commons, Pitt became obstreperous. He assailed Newcastle's foreign policy, which involved substantial subsidy payments to European allies, as both expensive and 'un-British', advocating instead more reliance on naval force and a shift of concern to North America, where a French and Indian war was rumbling on.

Dismissed from office, he found his criticisms fortuitously assisted by the French conquest of Minorca, which provoked a public outcry, and later the execution of the unfortunate Admiral John BYNG. Pitt refused to work with either Newcastle or Fox, and was allowed to form an administration with the 4th Duke of Devonshire (*see* CAVENDISH, WILLIAM) in Nov. 1756. Newcastle's efforts to protect Hanover had brought about a revolution in European alliances. Prussia had been drawn into Britain's orbit; Austria responded by turning to France. In Sept. Frederick of Prussia again precipitated war by invading Saxony. Pitt found himself faced with having to respond both to American troubles and to this European crisis. Annoyed by Pitt's attempts to obtain mercy for Byng, the King dismissed him in the spring, but shortly afterwards consented to bring him back in coalition with Newcastle. Newcastle, as First Lord of the Treasury, would fund the war; Pitt, as Secretary of State, would direct its conduct.

For Britain, the Seven Years War was to be the most successful of the century, the only one to bring major gains. The year of victories, 1759, was acclaimed an *annus mirabilis*: British and

German troops defeated the French at Minden; high points outside Europe were the capture of Guadeloupe from the French in May and of Quebec by WOLFE in Sept. In Nov. HAWKE's victory over the French fleet at Quiberon Bay gave the British complete command of the sea. In Jan. 1760 the British decisively defeated the French in southern India. War was waged on a more global scale than ever before. The results could be seen as a vindication of Pitt's maritime strategy. Certainly he was bathed in reflected glory. But the war also entailed substantial continental commitments, and there the record of success was more uneven. Pitt, however, largely managed to retain the loyalty of the various marginal groups on whose discontent he had capitalized when in opposition, merchants, independents and Tories, acceding to the long-standing demand that the militia be invigorated as a home-defence force alongside the regular army, thus enabling Tory squires long excluded from political influence to raise their local status by becoming militia officers. Pitt's principles were defended in print in the *The Monitor*, edited for him by a West Indian merchant friend, William BECKFORD.

Pitt's fortune changed with the accession of GEORGE III, who had been encouraged by his tutor Bute (*see* STUART, JOHN) to deprecate this 'bloody and expensive' war. In 1761 the King refused to extend the war to Spain, driving Pitt to resign. He was to spend most of the rest of his career in opposition. Pitt's dazzling record as a war-leader, and long-standing claim to be a politician of principle, a patriot in every sense of the word, impressed many younger politicians. He held himself aloof, however, from what became the main focus of Whig opposition, incorporating key elements of Old Corps Whiggery, organized first around Newcastle, then Rockingham (*see* WATSON-WENTWORTH, CHARLES). The milieu of high aristocratic Whiggery had never been one that he felt comfortable in, nor did he share their almost unqualified enthusiasm for parliamentary – as opposed to either royal or popular – power. He displayed no interest in joining the Rockingham Whigs when they briefly held office in 1766, and, though echoing their criticisms of his brother-in-law George GRENVILLE's American Stamp Act, refused to echo their insistence on Parliament's *right* to tax. When the King's relations with the Rockinghams deteriorated beyond saving, he turned to the once despised Pitt as a saviour, making him Earl of Chatham and First Lord of the Treasury. But ill health, perhaps a nervous breakdown, kept the new earl out of London and led him to resign in 1768.

When Chatham returned to politics it was as opposition leader once again, though both his prima-donna-ish temperament (not improved by advancing age) and differences of view continued to bedevil his relations with the Rockinghamites. His old mercantile connections, and greater willingness than the Rockinghams to contemplate making Parliament more accountable to the electorate, helped to give him a following among City radicals. Chatham and Rockingham tried to effect a union during the controversy associated with John WILKES and the Middx. election (1769–70), but NORTH's rise to power put paid to any hope of 'storming the closet'.

In the 1770s deteriorating relations with America dominated politics. Chatham was dismayed to see an empire that he had defended and extended jeopardized by ministerial bungling. In 1775 he proposed to try to mend relations by recognizing the Continental Congress and giving it a role in organizing the American contribution to imperial expenses but this conceded too much for most MPs. By 1778 hopes that the British army could speedily reduce the Americans to obedience had evaporated; on the contrary, American success was such that the French joined the war as their allies. The Rockinghams responded by urging the speedy grant of American independence. Chatham could not bring himself to contemplate this dismemberment of empire. While denouncing any such attempt with 'enthusiastic rapture' in the Lords in April, he collapsed, to die the following month.

His immediate political heirs were the small band of Chathamite Whigs who rallied round the Earl of Shelburne (*see* PETTY, WILLIAM), as their new leader, soon to be joined by Chatham's own talented younger son, PITT THE YOUNGER. For the next century and a half Chatham would be celebrated as a great war leader, and as an imperial statesman, until the winding down of empire robbed this part of his career of its appeal. He can also be seen as having helped to recast domestic politics. As a critic both of court politics and of aristocratic connection, little interested in outmoded political animosities, and as a (somewhat distant) patron of populist reformers, he helped to usher in a new era of reforming politics.

Marie Peters, The Elder Pitt (1998)

PITT THE YOUNGER, WILLIAM (1759–1806)
Politician and Prime Minister (1783–1801, 1804–6)

Younger son of PITT THE ELDER, he was a delicate child, educated at home until he was 14, when he was sent to Cambridge, where he remained off and on until 1779. His father had just died, and family fortunes were precarious. He qualified for the Bar, but kept his eye open for a parliamentary seat. His chance came at a by-election in 1781, when he was elected for Appleby (Westmld.).

The political scene was in flux. NORTH's administration was on its last legs, discredited by the failure of the American War of Independence. GEORGE III did not like the Rockingham Whigs (*see* WATSON-WENTWORTH, CHARLES). Pitt's father's followers had accepted the lead of the Earl of Shelburne (*see* PETTY, WILLIAM), whom the King preferred, but they were a small group. Pitt established himself as a ready speaker, sharply critical of North, supportive of parliamentary reform and other reforming policies to which many in opposition then inclined. When Rockingham's death in 1782 ended his short-lived administration and opened the way for Shelburne to take the lead, Pitt vaulted into office as Chancellor of the Exchequer. The following spring Shelburne himself fell before the combined forces of North and the new leader of the Rockinghamite Whigs, FOX. The King in desperation asked Pitt to head an administration. Pitt thought this too risky to attempt but, a few months later, he agreed, assured by expert calculations that suggested he could achieve majority support. The King then pressured the Lords to reject Fox's reforming India Bill, threw out the coalition and brought in Pitt – aged 24.

Many expected Pitt's 'mince-pie administration' to collapse before Christmas, but Fox and North failed in their bid to block essential fiscal measures. In 1784 the King agreed to an exceptionally early general election. The result was a great success for the government: not only small boroughs subject to influence but also a significant number of larger boroughs and counties supported Pittite candidates. Pitt was helped by the ambiguities of his position. He was on the one hand the King's man, but on the other hand, the son of a flamboyantly independent father, who had proclaimed himself a politician of principle; he himself had criticized the mismanagement of the American War of Independence, and was thought by WYVILL to be a more sincere friend to parliamentary reform than Fox.

For several years, Pitt was able to retain credibility both with the King and with many proponents of reform. The American War of Independence, and loosely associated crises in British relations both with Ireland and India, had left a legacy of serious policy problems. His success in dealing with these was mixed. He instigated a programme of fiscal recovery, involving reduced duties on tea coupled with increased efficiency in policing smuggling, a series of luxury taxes, and the establishment of a sinking fund to pay off the national debt. He also acceded to demands for economical reform, establishing a commission to explore the scope for economies in government. He was prepared to consider a liberal trade settlement with the independent United States, but was forced by the shipping lobby and advocates of protection to re-establish exclusive Navigation Acts. His attempt to liberalize trade relations with Ireland, as a *quid pro quo* for an agreement binding the Irish Parliament to follow Britain's lead in imperial affairs, foundered on a combination of opposition from the Irish and British manufacturers. He succeeded in getting an India Act through Parliament and in establishing a new framework for dealing with Indian affairs, involving the establishment of a Board of Control to supervise the East India Company; this was denounced by the Foxite Whigs as a half-baked measure, a sell-out of native Indians to corrupt East India Company interests.

In 1788 Pitt's mastery of the political scene was temporarily threatened when George III lapsed into insanity. The Foxite Whigs, being close to the Prince of Wales (the future GEORGE IV), hoped that he would obtain substantial powers as regent; Pitt opposed this. It has been suggested that had the King not recovered, and had the Foxites ended up in power when the French Revolution broke, Fox might have gone down in history as the conservative, Pitt as the reformer. The suggestion nicely conveys the continuing ambiguities of the political scene. In fact the King recovered and things proceeded otherwise.

Pitt's reforming credentials were first seriously tarnished when, between 1788 and 1791, the Dissenters three times brought to Parliament proposals, supported by a massive petitioning campaign, for the repeal of the Test and Corporation Acts, a hangover from the Restoration era, which restricted Dissenters' opportunities to hold public office. Pressed by the bishops not to weaken the position of the Anglican Church, Pitt opposed repeal, whereas Fox stood forth for the cause of religious toleration. Fox and some of his followers strengthened their credentials as reformers when they welcomed the French Revolution in 1789.

Pitt's response to the French Revolution was more guarded. By 1792, as it radicalized, and the

Terror reigned, he presided over a clamp-down on British popular radicalism, promoted by royal proclamation and semi-officially co-ordinated by John REEVES. By that time the British public was sufficiently scared of revolutionary excess for Fox's identification with it to be more a liability than an advantage. Pitt's reneging on his own former reforming commitments remained, however, something that could from time to time be turned against him: most notably in 1794, when Thomas HARDY, HORNE TOOKE and THELWALL were on trial for high treason, and defence counsel quoted Pitt's former reforming pronouncements to establish that the defendants had remained within the realm of legitimate political discourse.

In 1793 France invaded the Low Countries, tried to stir up revolutionary sentiment within Britain and declared war; Pitt found himself faced with the task of directing a war against a traditionally formidable enemy. French forces proved extremely effective on land. British effort came to focus on naval and colonial warfare, and the supply of subsidies to continental allies. Attempts to encourage Royalist risings in the Vendée met with disaster. In 1794 an Anglo-American treaty of commerce, the Jay Treaty, headed off the threat of a Franco-American alliance. In 1795 the British secured the trade route to India by seizing Capetown from the Dutch, as well as bases in Ceylon and West Indian islands. The advent of the more moderate Thermidorean regime in France helped to open up the prospect of peace, provoking debate in Britain about war aims.

Pitt had been tacitly supported from 1792 by a section of the former Whig opposition. In 1794 Portland (see BENTINCK, WILLIAM CAVENDISH) and other Whigs formally joined the ministry. Their attitudes were diverse. FITZWILLIAM, Rockingham's heir, who had been made Lord Lieutenant of Ireland, confused the situation there by promising to move ahead with further instalments of Catholic emancipation faster than Pitt thought wise. BURKE argued that the war should continue not merely until the French threat was contained but until the Bourbon monarchy was restored.

Hopes of peace foundered on French insistence that the British return all colonial conquests. From that point, the war turned against Britain. In Oct. 1796 Spain entered on the French side; the British fleet was forced to withdraw from the Mediterranean. The French threatened invasion, and tried to stir up rebellion in Ireland; rebellion did indeed break out in 1798 (see TONE, WOLFE), but ineffective French support left the rebels all but defenceless in the face of British troops. By 1797 the financial strains of war were such that Britain was forced off the gold standard. The Austrians made peace with France and the First Coalition collapsed. The situation was turned around by NELSON's victory in the Battle of the Nile in 1798, which stranded the Napoleonic army in Egypt and made possible the formation of a second anti-French coalition. At the end of the decade, however, Napoleonic victories in Italy and Russia's withdrawal from the war and promotion of a League of Armed Neutrality left Britain beleaguered once again. The institution of the first income tax meanwhile brought home the costs of war to taxpayers.

The pressures of war left Pitt with little energy or sympathy for reforming programmes. His Evangelical friend WILBERFORCE vainly urged the abolition of the slave trade, though immiseration at home associated with a bad harvest in 1795 did prompt Pitt to float a scheme for the reform of the poor laws (denounced as a farrago of impracticable proposals). In fact he continued to favour those reforms he thought compatible with the needs of the moment, and in 1801, when the King refused to accede to his desire to link a union of British and Irish Parliaments with the completion of Catholic emancipation, he resigned.

His successor ADDINGTON failed to drive a hard bargain at the Peace of Amiens in 1802 or to maintain Parliament's confidence. In the face of the renewed outbreak of war, Pitt returned to office in 1804 but his health worsened and he died in Jan. 1806.

A bachelor and a chaste man, though a hard drinker, Pitt was by no means as clubbable as Fox and his cronies. He had a good eye for hardworking and efficient young politicians, however, and nurtured the talents of George CANNING and Robert JENKINSON (the 2nd Lord Liverpool) among others. They became his devoted followers, striving to implement the merits of the 'Pitt system' as they saw it, dedicated commitment to sound government. Robert PEEL might be seen as the last politician who strove to embody this ideal. In the meantime, however, Pitt's legacy was also claimed by a younger breed of politicians with more passionate ideological commitments, notably to the defence of the 'Protestant Constitution' against Catholicism. Ironically, Pitt was idolized by these renascent Tories, who invoked his shade against that of Charles James Fox, and founded 'Pitt clubs' to promote a political creed quite different from Pitt's own.

John Ehrman, The Younger Pitt (3 vols, 1969–96)

protests against the shipowners' obstructions on the issue. In 1876 the Merchant Shipping Act legislated for the load-line, since known as the Plimsoll line. In 1890 he was made President of the Sailors' and Firemen's Union.

PLOT, ROBERT (1640–96), scientist and antiquarian. In 1670 he began research on a natural, geological and social history of England and Wales; only two volumes of his ambitious project were completed, those on the natural history of Oxon. (1677) and Staffs. (1686). Secretary to the Royal Society (1682–4), Plot presented several papers on chemistry. He was made first Professor of Chemistry at Oxford in 1683, as well as first Custodian of the Ashmolean Museum, formed from the collections of Elias ASHMOLE and the TRADESCANTs with the intention of revitalizing the teaching of natural sciences.

PLOWDEN, EDMUND (1519 or 1520–85), lawyer. A barrister educated at Cambridge and Oxford, he was repeatedly MP under MARY I. His legal career was hampered under ELIZABETH I by his Roman Catholicism: he defended other prominent Catholics in legal trouble such as Edmund BONNER. Considered the greatest lawyer of his day, his law reports became a standard text.

PLUNKETT, SIR HORACE (1854–1932), politician. A moderate Unionist, Plunkett worked to unite Ireland's feuding parties in the cause of Irish economic development. Unionist MP for South Dublin (1892–1900), he brought together nationalist and Unionist politicians on the Recess Committee, whose report led to the establishment of the Irish Department of Agriculture and Technical Instruction (DATI), which he headed. He was admired by many of the intellectuals of the Irish revival, who saw him as exemplifying practical patriotism. Plunkett found, however, that his politics were too moderate for many Unionists while he was opposed by nationalists who saw his activities as a distraction from Home Rule and a threat to shopkeeping interests. He lost his seat in 1900; in 1904 he stirred further controversy by criticizing the influence of the Catholic Church, and in 1907 he was dismissed from the DATI by the Liberal government. From 1910 Plunkett accepted Home Rule as inevitable and tried to negotiate a compromise guaranteeing minority rights while preventing partition. In 1917–18 he chaired the abortive Irish Convention, which tried to reach a settlement between moderate nationalists and Unionists. During the Anglo-Irish War (1919–21) he lobbied for dominion status. He was named to the Free State Senate in 1922, but retired to England after his house was burned by Republicans during the Civil War.

PLUNKETT, OLIVER (1629–81), martyr. From a prominent Old English family of Co. Meath, he trained for the priesthood in Rome and taught theology there until nominated Archbishop of Armagh (1669). He was energetic in organizing the Irish Roman Catholic Church and won even Protestant respect for his abilities. The government tolerated his presence until the passage of the Test Act, whereupon (1674) he went into hiding. Arrested in 1678 amid the hysteria surrounding the Popish Plot (*see* OATES, TITUS), he was tried in London for treason and executed. His body is enshrined at Downside Abbey (Som.), his head at Drogheda.

POCAHONTAS (1595–1617), native American heroine. Daughter of an Algonquin chief, Powhatan, she was supposedly responsible for saving the life of an English Virginian colonist, John Smith (1580–1631); thereafter from 1608 she began to visit the English colony at Jamestown but in 1612 she was kidnapped by the colonists as a hostage for good behaviour. In 1613 she converted to Christianity, took the name Rebecca and married another colonist, John Rolfe (1585–1622); travelling to England in 1616 she excited great interest, being presented to the royal family and in 1617 attending a court masque. In the same year she died at Gravesend (Kent), where she is buried. Her story became a model for the narration of many subsequent first encounters with England by visitors from the British Empire; it has often been used as a comforting diversion from the generally dismal tale of betrayal and exploitation which characterizes English relationships with native Americans. Interpretation in particular of John Smith's evidence remains controversial.

POLE, EDMUND DE LA (10th [6th de la Pole] Earl and 3rd Duke of Suffolk) (1471 or 1472–1513), dynast. HENRY VII's dynastic worries about Suffolk's royal blood (he was the son of EDWARD IV's sister) ruined his life, despite his surrendering the family dukedom in 1493 and serving loyally, e.g. in the defeat of the West Country rebels at Blackheath in 1497. He was forced by increasing government harassment to flee abroad temporarily in 1499 and permanently in 1501. In exile a diplomatic pawn, he was arrested and handed over to Henry in 1506, and he was eventually executed by HENRY VIII on the excuse that his brother was fighting in enemy French armies.

POLE, HENRY (Baron Montague) (*c.* 1492–1539), conspirator *see* COURTENAY, HENRY

POLE, MICHAEL DE LA (5th [1st de la Pole] Earl of Suffolk) (*c.* 1330–89), financier and royal servant. Son of William de la POLE, he pursued a military and political career, being appointed Chancellor in 1383 and created Earl of Suffolk in 1385. RICHARD II's mismanagement of the Parliament of 1386 led to his impeachment and conviction for embezzlement and negligence. The King almost immediately restored him to a position of trust, and in consequence he was accused of treason by the Appellants and forced to flee. Found guilty in his absence, he died in Paris.

POLE, REGINALD (1500–58), Archbishop of Canterbury (1556–8) and Cardinal. Grandson of George PLANTAGENET, Duke of Clarence; HENRY VIII chose to favour him and finance his extended education at Oxford and Padua which made him a respected humanist scholar. Pole's distaste for the proposed annulment of Henry's marriage to CATHERINE OF ARAGON increasingly estranged him from the King. Having received permission to leave England for Italy in 1532, he completed the breach by furious opposition to Henry's declaration of royal supremacy over the Church. The last straw came when Pope Paul III made Pole a Cardinal in 1536. The King had several of his family executed, including his aged mother, Margaret PLANTAGENET, Countess of Salisbury. In exile Pole courageously but vainly tried to reconcile Rome and Martin LUTHER's followers, earning enmity from more hard-line colleagues; his near miss in the 1549 papal election indicated his waning influence. His cousin MARY I's sudden accession in 1553 brought a new chance; he was chosen Papal Legate (representative) for England. CHARLES V's diplomacy delayed his arrival and reconciliation of England to Rome until the following year; he became Archbishop in 1556, doing his best to initiate Church reform, but he was hampered by lack of time and the cancellation of his legateship by his old enemy Pope PAUL IV. He died within a few hours of Mary in Nov. 1558.

POLE, WILLIAM DE LA (?–1366), financier. Son of a wool merchant from Kingston-upon-Hull, the new town on the Humber founded by EDWARD I, he became an immensely successful shipowner, property speculator and commodity dealer who traded in salt, wine, corn and metals as well as in wool. His great opportunity came in 1328 when the English attempt to conquer Scotland resulted in the royal administration moving from Westminster to York. He won lucrative government contracts and from then on played a central role in shaping Crown finances. When EDWARD III embarked on what became the Hundred Years War against France, he headed a consortium of English merchants which lent the King well over £100,000, a vast sum. In 1339 he was made a 'banneret', the first time this military rank was awarded for financial services. Next

year, when he was no longer willing or able to lend more money, he was arrested, convicted of smuggling and imprisoned. Later, when the great Italian banking houses also refused further war loans, Edward was forced to rely upon the domestic money market and de la Pole's financial expertise became indispensable. Formally rehabilitated in the Parliament of 1344, he set up a new company, the Company of the Staple, which was granted a monopoly of wool export and in return agreed to pay a customs duty of 40 shillings per sack, six times the former rate. This established the wool export duty as the backbone of English State finance; hence the Lord Chancellor in the House of Lords sits on a woolsack. De la Pole was granted possession of the lordship of Holderness and of 12 royal manors in Notts. and Yorks. His family (*see* POLE, MICHAEL DE LA) rose into the ranks of the aristocracy. Never before had an English businessman been accorded such public recognition.

POLE, WILLIAM DE LA (8th [4th de la Pole] Earl and 1st Duke of Suffolk) (1396–1450), royal servant. The grandson of Michael de la POLE, after active service in France under HENRY V and Bedford (*see* JOHN OF LANCASTER) he became Steward of the Royal Household in 1433 and by the mid 1440s was the leader of the dominant faction at HENRY VI's court. Although he disapproved of the King's decision to surrender Maine, he remained closely identified with the policy of peace with France during the closing stages of the Hundred Years War, and consequently many blamed him for the death of HUMPHREY OF GLOUCESTER in 1447.

By helping to plan the capture of Fougères in March 1449, which led to renewed hostilities, he was partly responsible for the collapse of English Normandy in 1450. Parliament sent him to the Tower on charges of treasonable dealings with the French, as well as of corruption and violence in his management of East Anglian politics (*see* CROMWELL, RALPH). To save him from a trial in which the verdict was a foregone conclusion, Henry declared his innocence but banished him for five years. As he left the realm, dissidents intercepted his ship off Dover, and he was dragged into a small boat and beheaded. Government threats of reprisals for his murder precipitated CADE's rebellion.

POLLITT, HARRY (1890–1960), political organizer. He joined the Independent Labour Party at 16, having left school at 12 to work in a cotton mill. Active in trade-union affairs through the Boiler Workers' Union, Pollitt was Secretary to the Communist Party of Great Britain (CPGB) from 1929 until 1956, when he became Chairman at the time of the Soviet suppression of the Hungarian uprising. During this period, though the membership of the party was low (around 6,000 in 1932) and its electoral impact minimal, its intellectual influence on the strategy of a 'united front' against Fascism prior to 1939 (when its membership peaked at 18,000) and was considerable, in organizations like the National Unemployed Workers' Movement, established in 1921 under the auspices of the CPGB to draw attention to the plight of the unemployed during the Depression, and if possible revolutionize them. Pollitt was also instrumental in forming the International Brigade to assist the Republican cause during the Spanish Civil War (1936–9).

PONET, JOHN (c. 1516–56), churchman. A Cambridge don, he became chaplain to Archbishop CRANMER, wrote vigorous Protestant sermons and pamphlets and was made Bishop of Rochester (1550); his translation to Winchester (1551) was marred by the discovery that his wife had a husband still alive, and he married instead a daughter of one of Cranmer's estate officials. Exiled under MARY I, he wrote *A Shorte Treatise of Politike Power* (1556), an important political tract which discussed the subject's right to rebel. A keen astronomer, he manufactured elaborate clock-dials.

PONSONBY, GEORGE (1755–1817), politician. Son of John PONSONBY, he was an Irish MP from 1776 and a barrister from 1780. His career changed direction in 1789 when he supported the address calling for the Prince of Wales (the future GEORGE IV) to be Regent without restrictions; as a result he lost his position as First Counsellor to the Revenue Board. Increasingly friendly to Catholic Emancipation, he joined GRATTAN in seceding from Parliament in 1797 and defended in court nationalists who took part in the 1798 rebellion. After the Act of Union, which he opposed, he led the Whig party in the Commons, succeeding Charles GREY, from 1807 to his death, but his Irish patriotism was viewed as anachronistic by O'CONNELL.

PONSONBY, JOHN (1713–89), politician. Second son of the 1st Earl of Bessborough, in 1743 he made a powerful alliance by marrying the sister of the 4th Duke of Devonshire (*see* CAVENDISH, WILLIAM), Lord Lieutenant of Ireland (1754–6). In 1756 this helped him to succeed Henry BOYLE as Speaker of the Irish Commons and as such become chief 'undertaker' (manager) in Parliament. He governed Ireland in partnership with Archbishop George STONE, and successfully fought off attempts to extend the power of the Lord Lieutenant. In 1767 newly appointed Lord Lieutenant TOWNSHEND arrived in Dublin intending permanently to reside there; after many struggles he forced Ponsonby's resignation in 1771.

PONSONBY, WILLIAM BRABAZON (Baron Ponsonby) (1744–1806), politician. The eldest son of John PONSONBY, like his brother George PONSONBY he was dismissed from office (joint Postmaster General) in 1789 for supporting the Regency. In 1789 he was one of the founders of the Irish Whig club, alongside James CAULFIELD, Lord Charlemont and in the 1790s advocated parliamentary reform. An opponent of the Union, he continued to sit in Westminster for Co. Kilkenny as a friend of Charles James FOX, who rewarded him with a peerage shortly before his death.

PONT, TIMOTHY (?1560–?1614), cartographer. Son of the minister Robert Pont (1524–1606), a major player in the Scottish Reformation, he studied at St Andrews and also became a minister. He was a skilled mathematician, and made detailed maps of Scotland which were the first attempt at a national atlas. In revised form they were published in 1654.

POPE, ALEXANDER (1688–1744), poet. Son of a Catholic wholesale linen merchant, at the age of 12 he contracted what is thought to have been tuberculosis of the spine, which stunted his growth and left him severely disabled as well as depressive. Educated at a variety of private schools, he became a voracious reader. His first verses were published in 1709; his *Essay on Criticism* (1711) in the style of Horace attracted wide notice, and he met ADDISON and STEELE. Later works include *The Rape of the Lock* (1712), an innovative mock epic; *The Dunciad* (1728), an attack on literary hackery; and the didactic *Essay on Man* (1733–4), which gained him an international reputation. His highly successful translations of the *Iliad* (1720) and *Odyssey* (1725–6) are estimated to have brought him the huge sum of £10,000: a careful manager of his literary output, Pope was highly unusual in the scale of his literary earnings. Together with ARBUTHNOT, Bolingbroke (*see* ST JOHN, HENRY), GAY, SWIFT and Thomas PARNELL, he formed the Scriblerus Club to write collaborative satires on false taste and learning associated especially, in their view, with the Whig establishment. Pope's support was courted by Whig opponents of Robert WALPOLE's ministry, including Cobham (*see* TEMPLE, RICHARD) and FREDERICK, Prince of Wales; his home at Twickenham, famed for its grotto, was the centre of a literary circle until his death.

POPE-HENNESSY, SIR JOHN (1913–94), art historian. An authority on Italian Renaissance art, publishing work on Italian sculpture (revised in three volumes, 1955–63), on Uccello (1950, 1972), Fra Angelico (1952, 1974) and other artists, Pope-Hennessy held curatorial and academic posts, the most significant of which were as director of the Victoria and Albert Museum (V&A) (1967–73) and of the British Museum (1974–6). A magisterial critic of the new regime at the V&A in the late 1980s, he railed against what he regarded as its vulgar commercialism and 'dumbing down' of scholarship in an effort to get visitors through the turnstiles.

POPPER, SIR KARL (1902–94), philosopher. A vociferous critic of Marxism (*see* MARX, KARL) and Fascism, Popper was born and educated in Vienna and early in his career associated with the Vienna circle. With Hitler's rise to power, he emigrated to New Zealand where he taught philosophy, and later to the London School of Economics in 1946 where he was Professor of Logic and Scientific Method. Unlike the logical positivists of the Vienna circle and WITTGENSTEIN, Popper, in his major work on scientific methodology, *Die Logik der Forschung* (1934, English trans. *The Logic of Scientific Discovery*, 1959), did not believe that an analysis of language enabled a distinction between science and other activities such as ethics or metaphysics, but argued that the distinction between science and non-science lay in the way scientific theories make testable predictions which, if they fail their tests, are then given up. His understanding of science was the foundation upon which his political philosophy rested. In *The Open Society and its Enemies* (1945) and in *The Poverty of Historicism* (1957), he demolished the belief that the course of human history has a discoverable pattern. Decrying human ignorance and championing the critical scrutiny of ideas, Popper attacked all forms of modern dogmatism.

PORRITT, SIR JONATHON (1950–), environmentalist. Best known as Director of Friends of the Earth (1984–90), he was educated at Eton and Oxford. After a time as a schoolteacher, he became a leading advocate of environmental politics, standing as a candidate for the Ecology Party and later the Green Party. Porritt wrote extensively on ecological issues, and his books, including *Seeing Green: the Politics of Ecology* (1984) and *The Coming of the Greens* (1988), were popular and highly influential. In 1991 he presented the BBC TV series *Where on Earth Are We Going?* and shortly after he was appointed a special adviser on ecological issues to CHARLES, Prince of Wales.

PORTAL, CHARLES (1st Viscount Portal of Hungerford) (1893–1971), airman. Educated at Winchester and Oxford, where he became a motor-cycle racing enthusiast, Portal volunteered for the army in 1914 as a dispatch rider, and was quickly commissioned. Transferring to the Royal Flying Corps, he won the Military Cross flying reconnaissance missions over the Western Front, and by 1918 had flown more than 900 operational sorties. In 1919 he joined the RAF, and by the late 1930s was involved in the construction of more than 30 new airfields, the creation of the Women's Auxiliary Airforce and the establishment of the Commonwealth Air Training Scheme. Appointed to head Bomber Command in April 1940, Portal quickly accepted that precision bombing was not possible, and pressed for the introduction of area bombing of cities. By late 1944 Portal was convinced that technical developments had at last made precision bombing possible, but had only limited success in convincing bomber supremo Arthur HARRIS to modify Bomber Command policy. Successfully distancing himself from Harris at the end of the war, Portal oversaw the development of Britain's atom bomb (1946–51), and then served as Chairman of the British Aircraft Corporation, pushing through the programme that produced Concorde.

PORTEOUS, JOHN (?–1736), soldier. The son of an Edinburgh tailor, he became Captain of the Edinburgh City Guard in 1715. After rioting followed the execution of a popular smuggler, Andrew Wilson, in 1736, Porteous ordered his men to fire into the crowd without authorization from the magistrates and several rioters were killed. Porteous was tried and sentenced to death but when the government pardoned him a mob broke into the gaol and lynched him. The incident became a focus for clashes between Robert WALPOLE and his opponents. The government, largely ignorant of Scotland, refused to believe that Porteous had been hanged without the co-operation of the local authorities and imposed penalties. Resentment at these encouraged Walpole's political ally in Scotland, John CAMPBELL, 2nd Duke of Argyll, to turn against him and return opposition candidates at the 1741 election, following which Walpole resigned.

PORTER, ENDYMION (1587–1645), royal servant. Brought up in Spain, and a page to the Count-Duke Olivares, on coming to England he entered the service first of George VILLIERS, Duke of Buckingham, then of CHARLES I. He was involved in their fruitless trip of 1623 to seek a Spanish royal marriage, and led unsuccessful negotiations for peace with Spain in 1628. A poet himself, he was associated with many other poets including Thomas DEKKER, and was a major agent in acquiring Charles's celebrated art collection. Expelled from Parliament for his royalism in 1643, he died in poverty-stricken exile.

PORTER, RODNEY (1917–85), biochemist. Porter researched proteins (1946–9) under the eminent Cambridge biochemist Frederick Sanger. Subsequently he became interested in the chemical structure of immunoglobulins (proteins that function as antibodies) and pursued this research at the London-based National Institute for Medical Research (1949–60) and St Mary's Hospital Medical School (1960–7). In the early 1960s he resolved the antibody molecule into two distinct protein chains and three distinct regions and later, exploiting the techniques of electron microscopy and the work of Gerald Edelman and others, proposed a four-protein chain structure of antibodies. He shared the 1972 Nobel Prize for Medicine with Edelman.

PORTILLO, MICHAEL (1953–), politician. A product of Peterhouse, Cambridge, where he was tutored by Maurice COWLING, Portillo worked at Conservative Central Office and as special adviser to a number of ministers before entering the Commons in 1984 as MP for Enfield Southgate (London). With a Spanish Republican father, a striking appearance and views as 'dry' as those of his heroine, Margaret THATCHER, Portillo soon made his mark, and as Chief Secretary to the Treasury under John MAJOR (1992–4) he made his political reputation as an astute champion of restraint on government spending. After a brief spell as Secretary of State for Employment (1994–5), he became a high-profile Secretary of State for Defence in 1995. There were rumours that he would stand against Major for the Conservative leadership in 1995 but, at some damage to his reputation for decisiveness, he left the job to John REDWOOD. He gained some notoriety for what was taken to be a bellicose and jingoistic speech at the Conservative Party conference in 1996, advocating a 'clear blue water' policy approach of staying true to right-wing principles, rather than trying to encamp on the centre ground with Labour. The loss of his seat on 1 May 1997 gave great joy to the political Left, and to some of his opponents in his own party, since it made him unable to be a candidate for the leadership. Had Portillo retained his seat, there is little doubt he would have been elected leader.

After the election Portillo devoted his considerable political skills to projecting a softer and more caring image of himself to the public through a series of television programmes. He remained the Thatcherite heir and was elected to Parliament as MP for Chelsea in late 1999, and within months was promoted to Shadow Chancellor of the Exchequer.

PORTLAND, EARL OF, 1ST see WESTON, RICHARD; **5TH** see BENTINCK, HANS WILLEM; **3RD DUKE OF** see BENTINCK, WILLIAM CAVENDISH

PORTSMOUTH AND CASTLEMAINE, DUCHESS OF see KÉROUALLE, LOUISE DE

POTTER, BEATRIX (1866–1943), writer and artist. Potter had a lonely, sickly though privileged childhood in London with a succession of governesses. She had already had some sketches accepted as Christmas card designs when in 1901 she published a story she had written and illustrated herself, *The Tale of Peter Rabbit*. It was subsequently taken up by the publisher Frederick Warne, who was to publish all her books. *Peter Rabbit* was an immediate success, selling more than 30,000 copies within a year of commercial publication, as were the rest of the series of uniform-size small books about anthropomorphized countryside, farmyard and domestic animals, with watercolour illustrations by Potter. They continue to sell in their millions in translation all over the world, and a full-length ballet based on the stories was filmed in 1971. Best known of the books include *The Tailor of Gloucester, The Tale of Squirrel Nutkin* (both 1903) and *The Tale of Mrs Tiggy Winkle* (1905). In 1913 Potter married the solicitor who dealt with her property in the Lake District, where she had bought a farm in 1905. Her later years were spent sheep farming, working for the preservation of the Lake District and campaigning against government agricultural policies.

POTTER, DENNIS (1935–94), television playwright. Son of a Forest of Dean (Glos.) mining family, Potter was educated at Oxford and became the foremost British television dramatist, using the medium not simply as a living-room version of the theatre or cinema but exploiting new technical and conceptual possibilities, with plays like *Vote, Vote, Vote for Nigel Barton* and its sequel *Stand Up for Nigel Barton* (both 1965), the memorable series *Pennies from Heaven* (1978) and *The Singing Detective* (1986), both using popular songs in innovative ways, *The Blue Remembered Hills* (1979), with adults cast as children, and *Treacle and Brimstone* (1978), which was initially banned by the BBC as blasphemous. His last plays, *Karaoke* and *Cold Lazarus*, were screened posthumously (1996) after Potter had expressed, in an interview with Melvyn Bragg filmed as Potter was in the final phase of dying from cancer, a wish that they should be shown both on the BBC and on Channel Four.

POTTER, GEORGE (1832–93), trade-union leader. Born in Kenilworth (Warws.), he was apprenticed as a cabinetmaker and joiner in Coventry. Moving to London in 1853, he became Chairman of the Progressive Society of Carpenters and Joiners in 1858. As Secretary to the Building Trades Conference he led the movement for the reduction of the working day to nine hours and won a partial victory over the employers in the builders' strike and lock-out of 1859–60. He established *The Beehive* in 1861, the most important labour newspaper of its time, and remained its driving force until 1876. At odds with the 'Junta' (*see* APPLEGARTH, ROBERT), and despite helping to establish the Reform League in 1865, he set up the rival London Working Men's Association in 1866, but it never achieved the pre-eminence of either the London Trades Council or the Reform League. By 1868–9 Potter was coming to terms with the Junta: he worked with Applegarth and others in the Labour Representation League and in campaigns over trade-union legislation until 1875. He was also active in other labour and radical campaigns in the 1870s, including the National Emigration League, and was an elected member of the Westminster School Board (1873–82).

POULSON, JOHN (1910–93), architect, and **SMITH, T. DAN** (1915–93), local authority leader. Corruption scandals that hit British politics at the end of the 1960s and into the 1970s had at their centre the architect and developer Poulson. At its peak his Newcastle architectural firm was one of the largest in Europe, but many contracts proved to have resulted from bribing councillors, local officials and politicians. Only when Poulson filed for bankruptcy in 1972, his funds exhausted by the bribery payments, did the truth emerge. Reginald MAUDLING, the Conservative Home Secretary, was forced to resign, five public officials were arrested, Poulson himself was jailed for five years, subsequently increased to seven. Among others jailed for their part in the affair was the former Labour leader of Newcastle Council, T. Dan Smith, a miner's son who became a city boss in the American style. His bravura made him a show-figure in Labour politics. Allegations of corruption forced him to relinquish most of his public appointments in 1970–1, and in 1973 he was arrested and convicted on corruption charges connected with Poulson. After release from prison he became active in the resettlement of offenders.

POUND, SIR DUDLEY (1877–1943), naval officer. Pound graduated from HMS *Britannia* in 1891, and rose to command the battleship *Colossus* at Jutland in 1916. He subsequently formed and commanded a naval plans division and in June 1939 was appointed First Sea Lord. Pound was invariably cautious and often clashed with CHURCHILL. He opposed the dispatch of battleships to the Far East in 1941 but was overruled. He had more success in organizing the Battle of the Atlantic, which was run from a new HQ at Liverpool, Western Approaches Command. Desperately overworked, Pound

resigned in 1943 and later that year died from a brain tumour.

POWELL, CECIL (1903–69), physicist. Powell studied the cloud-chamber technique for detecting charged atomic particles under Charles WILSON at the Cavendish Laboratory, Cambridge. He spent the rest of his career at Bristol University, becoming Professor of Physics (1948) and Director of the Physics Laboratory (1964). In the late 1930s he photographed the disintegration of nuclei and later helped develop important new photographic and microscopical techniques for measuring the key characteristics of particles involved in nuclear disintegration. In 1947 he used these techniques to produce new evidence for a new sub-atomic particle in cosmic rays striking the earth, the 'pi-meson'. For this discovery and the development of his influential photographic techniques, Powell won the 1950 Nobel Prize for Physics. He helped establish the European Centre for Nuclear Research (CERN) and promoted international co-operation in scientific matters.

POWELL, ENOCH (1912–98), politician. The son of schoolteachers, at Cambridge Powell showed himself a brilliant classical scholar, becoming Professor of Greek at Sydney University in Australia in 1938. Returning to Britain in 1939 to enlist as a private, by the end of the war he was a brigadier. Having, to his surprise, survived, he decided to enter politics. He was, in his own words, 'born a Tory', by which he meant 'a person who regards authority as immanent in institutions', perhaps explaining the ambivalence of his relationship with the Conservative Party. Powell was elected MP for Wolverhampton in 1950, a convinced imperialist, but after the shock of the Suez fiasco he concluded that the Empire was finished and looked for another political cause, finding it in English nationalism. For all his reputation as a fiercely intellectual politician Powell was a great romantic.

Powell was appointed Under-Secretary at Housing in 1955 under Anthony EDEN, and became Financial Secretary at the Treasury in 1957. But Harold MACMILLAN's natural expansionist and inflationary instincts in economic matters ran counter to Powell's desire for strict controls over the money supply and in 1958 he resigned. In Thatcherite mythology the resignation was a defining moment in the history of the Conservative Party, and THATCHER herself later acknowledged her debt to Powell. Powell returned to the Cabinet in 1960 as Minister of Health, where he proved himself both an able minister and a big spender. He refused to serve under DOUGLAS-HOME in 1963; he never held office again.

Powell stood for the party leadership in 1965 after Home's resignation but received only 15 votes to Edward HEATH's 150. He was made Shadow spokesman on defence, but found it impossible to restrict himself to just that topic. A turning-point in his career came on 20 April 1968 in a speech in Birmingham on race and immigration, in which he said that he was 'filled with foreboding' and 'like the Roman, I seem to see "the river Tiber flowing with much blood"'. He was the first front-rank politician to raise the sensitive issue of immigration from Asia and Africa. Heath and many of his Shadow Cabinet colleagues were horrified; Powell was immediately sacked, and there were demonstrations by dockers in favour of 'good old Enoch'.

In 1970 Powell's personal and political influence in the west Midlands helped Heath to a surprise victory but Powell soon turned against the government over Heath's decision to take Britain into the Common Market. As a fervent believer in English nationalism and the sovereignty of Parliament, Powell argued that entry into Europe would damage the former and compromise the latter. He led an active campaign against Europe and in the first election of 1974 dropped a political bombshell by resigning his seat and advising those who supported his views to vote Labour. He played a leading role in the 1975 referendum on Europe, speaking all over the country on the 'vote no' platform. He returned to the Commons in Oct. 1974 as Ulster Unionist MP for South Down. He opposed the 1985 Anglo-Irish Agreement because it gave Ireland a say in the affairs of the UK. Powell lost his seat in 1987.

POWELL, MICHAEL (1905–90), film-maker. Alexander KORDA, anxious to prove to the British government that the cinema was not a waste of valuable resources in wartime but a necessary morale-booster, made a documentary, *The Lion Has Wings* (1939), to prove the point; one of the contributors was Powell. With the government convinced, Powell was able to work with the Austrian scriptwriter Emeric Pressburger on propaganda feature films, to entertain but also to make clear that democratic values were worth fighting for. *The 49th Parallel* (1941) was followed by *One of Our Aircraft is Missing* (1942) and then the ambitious if surreal *Life and Death of Colonel Blimp* (1943). Post-war Powell and Pressburger collaborations included *Black Narcissus* (1946) and a film about ballet, *The Red Shoes* (1948). The partnership broke up, and Powell's *Peeping Tom* (1960), a voyeuristic murder story, produced alarm and hostility, though his erotic fantasies had often been implicit in his earlier work.

POWELL, VAVASOR (1617–70), churchman. A Puritan protégé of the Harleys of Brampton Bryan (*see* HARLEY, BRILLIANA), he became *c*. 1639 a travelling preacher in Wales (*see* WROTH, WILLIAM), and after fleeing to London on the outbreak of the Civil Wars (1642) returned to Wales in 1646, gathering a group of itinerant preachers whose activities anticipated George FOX and the Quakers. Hostile to Oliver CROMWELL's government, he modified his support of Independency to become a Baptist. After CHARLES II's restoration he spent most of his life in prison. *See also* TRAPNELL, ANNA.

POWER, EILEEN (1889–1940), historian. A medieval historian who held posts at Girton College, Cambridge, and the London School of Economics, she chose the wool trade and particularly women's economic position in the thirteenth and fourteenth centuries as the subjects of her research. The first woman invited to give the prestigious Ford lectures at Oxford (1938), she also worked with R. H. TAWNEY on *Tudor Economic Documents*, and she was involved in planning the medieval sections of the *Cambridge Economic History of Europe* and founded the *Economic History Review* (1927). She insisted that history is valuable 'only insofar as it lives', and aimed in her best-known work, *Medieval People* (1924), to present the past of so-called 'ordinary people' in ways that would interest the general reader . Her lectures on *Medieval Women*, edited by her husband, the economic historian Michael Postan, were published posthumously.

POWYS, JOHN COWPER (1872–1963), novelist. Born in Derb., one of three brothers who would all be writers, he spent much of his childhood in the West Country, which is the setting for a number of his books. An essayist before turning to novel writing, Cowper made his reputation by his extremely long novels, of which *Wolf Solent* (1929) was the first, followed by the best known, *A Glastonbury Romance* (1932) and *Weymouth Sand* (published originally as *Jobber Skald* in 1934). All of them blend folklore, the supernatural and an intense sense of landscape. They enjoyed a mixed critical reception, and there has been a revival of interest in his work among those of 'new age' persuasion.

POYNINGS, SIR EDWARD (1459–1521), administrator. From a knightly family of Kent, Poynings took part in the unsuccessful rebellion of Humphrey STAFFORD, Duke of Buckingham, in 1483, and returned to England with the expeditionary force which put HENRY VII on the throne in 1485. In 1494 Henry sent him to Ireland as Lord Deputy, as part of his effort to revive English administration and challenge the power of the GERALDINES in Ireland. Poynings forced the Irish Parliament of 1494–5 to enact that parliamentary sessions and proposed legislation must previously be approved in England. Ironically, the law was later used by Irish politicians to obstruct and delay the English administration in Dublin. It was repealed with much other restrictive legislation in 1782. *See also* GRATTAN, HENRY.

PRATT, CHARLES (1st Earl Camden) (1714–94), lawyer and politician. He was educated at Eton with PITT THE ELDER, who became a life-long friend. Called to the Bar, he defended the Jacobite, Alexander Murray, against a charge of seditious libel, arguing that the jury should be judges of law as well as fact, that is, they should judge whether what Murray had said was a libel, and not merely whether he had said it (a position argued for by John LILBURNE in 1653, later to be entrenched by Charles James FOX's Libel Act). In 1757 Pratt was made Attorney General by Pitt, with whose backing he drafted a Bill to extend *habeas corpus* to civil cases, but this was defeated by the Lords. He consolidated his popular reputation as Lord Chief Justice of Common Pleas during the WILKES affair, when he repeatedly ruled that general warrants, one of which had been used to arrest Wilkes, were illegal. After a three-year campaign the Commons ruled against general warrants in 1766. Lord Chancellor from 1766 to 1770, he was sacked for supporting Pitt's vote of censure against Parliament for its treatment of Wilkes and in opposition supported the American cause. Returning to the Cabinet as Lord President of the Council under Rockingham in 1782 (*see* WATSON-WENTWORTH, CHARLES), Shelburne (*see* PETTY, HENRY) and then PITT THE YOUNGER, he helped evade a regency during the insanity of GEORGE III in 1788–9, and thus the fall of the younger Pitt's administration, by suggesting the issue of letters patent under the great seal.

PRESTON, THOMAS (1st Viscount Tara) (*c.* 1585–1655), soldier. A younger son of the 4th Viscount Gormanston, he was educated at Douai and distinguished himself in Spanish armies in the Low Countries. In 1642 he returned to Ireland, now with French backing, and became a leading military commander for the Roman Catholic Confederacy, although his effectiveness was limited by alcoholism and rivalry with Eoghan Ruadh O'NEILL, who represented Gaelic interests against his Old English loyalties. CHARLES I made him Viscount in 1650. Finally defeated in Co. Galway by Henry IRETON in 1651, he escaped overseas and resumed his mercenary career.

PRICE, SIR JOHN (1502–1555), scholar and administrator. From a gentry family of Brecon, he studied at Oxford, was an early evangelical, and became a client of Thomas CROMWELL. With Sir Thomas Legh, he played a prominent role in visiting monasteries in 1535; after Cromwell's fall he became a key figure in Welsh administration and was repeatedly a Welsh MP. A keen and patriotic historian, he wrote defending the stories of King ARTHUR against Polydore VERGIL. He published one of the first Welsh printed books, *Yny Lhyvyr Hwnn* (1547), containing translations of the creed, commandments and Lord's Prayer.

PRICE, RICHARD (1723–91), radical. Son of a Glam. Dissenting minister, Price was educated at a series of Dissenting academies, then became a chaplain in Stoke Newington, London. He wrote two treatises on moral questions, but was best known for his financial and political writings, on the increase of population and the national debt. His *Observations on Civil Liberty and the Justice and Policy of War with America* (1775) was widely read. He favoured the French Revolution; his sermon *On the Love of our Country* (1789) provoked BURKE's *Reflections on the Revolution in France*.

PRICE, SIR UVEDALE (1747–1829), writer. He inherited the estate of Foxley (Herefs.) in 1761 and, after Eton, Oxford and a European tour with his friend Charles James FOX, returned there and began to redesign the gardens. He disagreed with the landscape gardening style of Lancelot 'Capability' BROWN believing that it obliterated nature instead of seeking to perfect it. Price sought the same effect in the countryside as could be found in a landscape painting, publishing his ideas in *Essay on the Picturesque* (1794). Though widely criticized, he influenced early nineteenth-century gardens such as Sir Walter SCOTT's at Abbotsford.

PRICHARD, RHYS (also known as Vicar Prichard) (*c.* 1579–1644), poet. From Llandovery (Dyfed) and Oxford-educated, he became vicar of Llandovery and eventually Chancellor of St David's Cathedral. He was an outspoken Royalist on the outbreak of the Civil War (1642). Energetic in preaching and evangelizing, he wrote simple religious verse which was widely circulated, although it was not put into print until after his death.

PRIDE, THOMAS (?–1658), soldier. Pride is remembered for Pride's Purge. Previously a prosperous brewer, he was a captain in the Parliamentary army during the First Civil War (1642–6), and after CHARLES I's defeat, having risen to the rank of colonel, he became active on behalf of the army in its trial of strength against the Presbyterian majority in Parliament. Increasing tension had included an attempted coup by Parliament against the army in summer

1647, and, in the wake of the army's crushing of a new Royalist coalition in the Second Civil War (summer 1648), the military leaders lost patience. In Dec. 1648 Pride's troops expelled from the Commons those MPs (mostly Presbyterians) who favoured further negotiations with Charles. After this purge, the remaining MPs (mainly Independents, i.e. Congregationalists) formed the Rump Parliament, which remained in session until 1653.

PRIESTLEY, J(OHN) B(OYNTON) (1894–1984), playwright, novelist and broadcaster. Succumbing at times to the role of the down-to-earth, pipe-smoking professional Yorks. man, Bradford-born Priestley was educated there and at Oxford and worked as a critic and journalist in London before the success of his novel of theatrical life, *The Good Companions* (1929). This was followed by *Angel Pavement* (1930), *Bright Day* (1946) and a stream of less memorable novels. He also wrote more than 50 plays and adaptations, the most enduring of which have proved the farce *When We Are Married* (1930) and the psychological mystery *An Inspector Calls* (1947), which enjoyed a massively successful revival in the 1990s. Much concerned with Englishness, Priestley also wrote social histories, and travelogues, ranging from *English Journey* (1934) to *Journey Down a Rainbow* (1955), which he wrote with his second wife, the archaeologist Jacquetta Hawkes, about their travels in Mexico. During the Second World War his regular broadcasts were influential in establishing a broadly progressive consensus, which assisted the Labour victory in 1951. As he had caught the mood of the 'common man' then, so his article in the *New Statesman*, 'Britain and Nuclear Bombs' on 2 Nov. 1957, which urged the British to take the moral lead in 'rejecting the evil [of nuclear warfare] for ever' drew an overwhelming response out of which was formed the Campaign for Nuclear Disarmament (CND), in which Priestley was to play a leading role. He was awarded the Order of Merit in 1977.

PRIESTLEY, JOSEPH (1733–1804), scientist and writer. Son of a Yorks. cloth-dresser, he was educated at the Daventry Dissenting academy, and was later a tutor at Warrington academy. He had a strong interest in experimental science and was elected to the Royal Society in 1766. The following year he published *The History and Present State of Electricity* and undertook chemical experiments leading to the identification of certain gases and the discovery of others, such as oxygen.

Always ready to support political reform projects, he questioned WILKES's sincerity. In *The Present State of Liberty in Great Britain and her*

Colonies (1769) he criticized public policy in Britain and America, and continued subsequently to support the cause of American independence. From 1772 he was employed by Shelburne (*see* PETTY, WILLIAM) as librarian and accompanied him to France.

His theological works include the controversial *Letters to a Philosophical Unbeliever* (1774), *History of the Corruptions of Christianity* (1782) and *History of Early Opinions Concerning Jesus Christ* (1786). His Unitarian theology alienated some orthodox Presbyterians but he was appointed Presbyterian minister at Birmingham in 1779.

Sympathetic to the French Revolution, he published a reply to BURKE's hostile *Reflections*; as a result of his views, his house, chapel and laboratory in Birmingham were destroyed in the Priestley riots of 14–18 July 1791. These followed a dinner commemorating the second anniversary of the fall of the Bastille. A 'Church and King' mob wrecked the tavern where the dinner had been held, as well as Dissenting chapels and the shops and houses of prominent Dissenters. Local authorities were criticized for their slow and ineffective response; it was suggested that they had colluded with or even incited the crowds. Priestley left for Philadelphia and died there 10 years later.

PRIMROSE, ARCHIBALD (5th Earl of Rosebery) (1847–1929), politician and Prime Minister (1894–5). An aristocrat who married a Rothschild heiress, Rosebery succeeded his grandfather as Earl in 1868. He first held office as Under-Secretary in the Home Office with responsibility for Scottish Affairs (1881–3) and was subsequently appointed Commissioner of Works and Lord Privy Seal, in which capacity he was largely responsible for the creation of the Scottish Office. He was the first Chairman of the London County Council (LCC) and served as Foreign Secretary in GLADSTONE's 1886 Liberal government, and again in 1892. He succeeded Gladstone as Prime Minister in March 1894, resigning in June 1895 after endless Cabinet disputes and defeat in the Commons. As Prime Minister he had failed to carry the Liberal legislative programme through the Lords – other than the Budget which introduced death duties for the first time. As Liberal leader he failed to give the party leadership in its internecine struggles, or a way forward as a credible party of the Left. He resigned from the leadership in 1896.

PRINCE REGENT *see* GEORGE IV

PRINGLE, SIR JOHN (1707–82), physician. He studied medicine at Edinburgh, Leiden and Paris and in 1742, during the War of the Austrian Succession, left his Edinburgh University post to take over the military hospital in Flanders; there he and John DALRYMPLE introduced the idea that hospitals on the battlefield are neutral territory. In 1744 Cumberland (*see* WILLIAM AUGUSTUS) appointed him Physician General to the forces, a post he retained after the war. He studied the sanitary conditions and health of the troops closely and his *Observations of the Diseases of the Army* (1752) set a standard for military hygiene that was followed throughout Europe. An innovative President of the Royal Society (1772–8), Pringle was the first for some time to be a scientific professional rather than a nobleman.

PRIOR, MATTHEW (1664–1721), poet and diplomat. He was probably from Dorset; his father's death interrupted his studies and he kept books for his uncle, a vintner, until he was discovered by the Earl of Dorset (*see* SACKVILLE, CHARLES) translating Horace. Sent to Westminster school, he became friendly with Charles MONTAGU, and obtained a scholarship enabling him to join the Montagu brothers at Cambridge. Thereafter he became a diplomat, highly regarded by WILLIAM III and then by ANNE. He helped negotiate the Treaty of Ryswick (1697) and in 1711 was responsible for the preliminaries to the Treaty of Utrecht, known as Matt's Peace. His humble origins prevented his taking credit for the final treaty. In 1715 he was impeached by the Whigs and imprisoned; released in 1717, he was near-destitute until friends including Edward HARLEY, GAY and ARBUTHNOT arranged the publication of his *Poems* in 1719. Praised for their combination of worldliness and refinement they earned Prior £4,000 and a lasting reputation.

PROCTOR, ADELAIDE (1825–64), poet and feminist. Queen VICTORIA's favourite poet, she wrote the verses of the *Lost Chord* and probably outsold all contemporary poets, TENNYSON excepted. Her feminism, an extension of her philanthropy, brought her into close involvement with the *Englishwoman's Journal* and the Society for the Employment of Women. She was among the small band of mid Victorian women who pioneered the movement to improve the civil and political status of women.

PROFUMO, JOHN (1915–), politician. Profumo entered the Commons in 1940 as one of the last defenders of Neville CHAMBERLAIN's record. After a good war in which he was awarded the OBE, he resumed his political career, rising to become Secretary of State for War in 1960. Married to an actress, Valerie Hobson, Profumo seemed to have it all, until in 1963 allegations were made that he had had an improper relationship with Christine Keeler, currently the mistress of a Soviet military attaché in London. His formal denial in the

Commons seemed to scotch the story, but evidence soon emerged that he had lied to the house, and, in an atmosphere electric with political tension and sleaze, Profumo resigned from the government, his seat and the Privy Council. The affair, and Harold MACMILLAN's handling of it, increased the impression in the country of a government that was out of touch with the people and contributed to the Tories' electoral defeat next year. Profumo subsequently worked at Toynbee Hall in London's East End, devoting his talents to the cause of the homeless for the next 25 years. In 1975 he was awarded the CBE for his charitable work.

PRYNNE, WILLIAM (?1602–69), polemicist. An Oxford-educated lawyer, he used his considerable learning to crusade against the cultural life of CHARLES I's court and the ceremonialist and sacramentalist Arminian party. For this he was savagely punished, including the successive cropping of his ears in 1634 and 1637. When royal power collapsed in 1641–2, he revenged himself by hounding William LAUD and defaming his memory. His pamphlets ecumenically expressed detestation of Catholicism, government of the Church by bishops, Independency and Presbyterian clerical power, and expressed his strong Erastian conviction that the State should control the Church. He managed to annoy the army and every government between 1647 and 1658, and was imprisoned from 1651 to 1653; similarly, his raucous welcome for the restoration of CHARLES II was soon qualified by criticism. He spent his last years harmlessly and enjoyably as royal archivist in the Tower of London.

PRYS, EDMWND (1544–1623), poet. From Maentwrog (Gwynedd) and Cambridge-educated, he became Archdeacon of Merioneth in 1576 and a canon of St Asaph in 1602. Anxious to promote humanist Protestant learning in Wales and despising the contemporary Welsh bardic tradition as decadent, from 1580 to 1587 he conducted a controversy in verse with the bard Wiliam Cynwal (*see* ROBERT, GRUFFUDD). His translation of the psalms into Welsh metrical poetry (first published in 1621, appended to the Welsh Book of Common Prayer) proved immensely successful.

PUGIN, AUGUSTUS WELSBY (1812–52), architect. Pugin was the principal theorist and publicist for the Gothic revival of the nineteenth century. His 1836 book *Contrasts* advanced the thesis that the Gothic style of the fourteenth and fifteenth centuries was the only true Christian architecture, and set the stage for the so-called 'battle of the styles' between Gothic and Classical in the succeeding generation. Pugin and some contemporaries combined a scholarly approach to the Gothic with architectural inventiveness, although few took the style to the decorative heights which Pugin attained at Scarisbrick Hall (Lancs.) and, most notably, in the interior decoration and fittings for Sir Charles BARRY's rebuilt Houses of Parliament. Pugin's medievalizing was part of a general trend at the beginning of VICTORIA's reign, and he had a significant influence upon RUSKIN and CARLYLE in the formation of their thought.

PUISET, HUGH DE (3rd Earl of Northumberland) (*c.* 1125–95), churchman. A nephew of King STEPHEN, he was created Bishop of Durham in 1153 and ruled the see in princely style for more than 40 years. A great builder, as both Durham Cathedral and the castle testify. The full extent of his ambitions was revealed in 1189 when he purchased the earldom of Northumberland and the justiciarship from RICHARD I, but he was outmanoeuvred by William LONGCHAMP and never recovered the King's favour.

PULTENEY, WILLIAM (10th [1st Pulteney] Earl of Bath) (1684–1764), politician. Son of a Leics. gentleman, he was elected MP in 1705. Secretary at War from 1714, he resigned with Robert WALPOLE and Charles TOWNSHEND in 1717, but was not given office when they came to power in 1720. Made Cofferer of the Household in 1723, he became increasingly critical of government, was dismissed in 1725, and thereafter emerged as perhaps the most vigorous opposition Whig, refusing to be bought off with office in 1730. He collaborated with Bolingbroke (*see* ST JOHN, HENRY) in various publications, including *The Craftsman*, took a leading part against the Excise Bill and from the mid 1730s was associated with the court of FREDERICK, Prince of Wales at Leicester House. He entered the Cabinet and, shortly afterwards, acquired a peerage following Walpole's fall but, when the new ministry failed to implement any programme of reform, he lost his 'patriot' reputation. After he and Granville (*see* CARTERET, JOHN) failed to secure parliamentary support for a ministry upon the King's invitation in 1746, Pulteney retired from public life.

PURCELL, HENRY (*c.* 1659–95), composer. Son of a gentleman of the Chapel Royal, which he joined as a choirboy in 1669, he benefited from court patronage of music. His career culminated in 1682, when he became an organist of the Chapel Royal; the following year, he was made Keeper of the King's Instruments in recognition to his outstanding talents. He wrote much Church music; his 1685 anthem *My Heart Is Inditing* was written for the coronation of JAMES II. In the 1680s

he was increasingly influenced by Italian musical styles and forms, and his *Dido and Aeneas* (1689) is the first undisputed masterpiece of English opera. Court patronage played a less important part in musical life after the Glorious Revolution and in his final years Purcell composed much music for the theatre, involving co-operation with DRYDEN.

PURCHAS, SAMUEL (?1575–1612), travel writer. A Cambridge-educated London clergyman, he produced a series of narratives of world history and overseas voyages: *Purchas his Pilgrimage* (1613), *Purchas his Pilgrim* (1619) and *Hakluytus Posthumus, or Purchas his Pilgrimes* (1625), which incorporated and continued the writings on voyaging of Richard HAKLUYT.

PUSEY, EDWARD BOUVERIE (1800–82), theologian. Appointed a Fellow of Oriel in 1823, the college of KEBLE and NEWMAN, he was ordained in 1828. When Keble in his Assize Sermon (1834) raised the question of the authority of the Church, Pusey wrote the first of his *Tracts for the Times* for the Oxford Movement, *Fasting* (1834), followed in 1835 by *Baptism* (which he signed, unusually for the Tractarians, thus giving the name Pusey as a generic for all those who sought to defend the Anglican Church while promoting Catholic principles in its worship and observance). Desolate after the death of his wife in 1839, he applied himself to theological scholarship (he was a Semitic scholar and Regius Professor of Hebrew), cataloguing all the Arabic manuscripts in the Bodleian library. In 1843 his sermon on the Real Presence led to a charge of heresy: not allowed to defend himself, Pusey was suspended from the office of university preacher for three years. But he did not waver, nor did he go over to Rome as Newman and MANNING had. He might have seemed a papist, he heard confessions and he wrote about possible union of the Church of England with Rome, but he could not tolerate Catholic doctrine on indulgences and purgatory. Pusey House in Oxford is his active memorial.

PYM, JOHN (?1584–1643), politician. An Oxford-educated Somerset man, he was, as an MP in the Parliaments of the 1620s, bitterly critical of royal government. In the Short Parliament (1640) he was a leading militant against CHARLES I, spearheading the impeachments of William LAUD and Thomas WENTWORTH, Earl of Strafford, and eventually rejecting conciliatory offers of the chancellorship of the Exchequer. He backed the Root and Branch Bill which in 1641 proposed the abolition of Episcopacy, and in the same year helped to draft the Grand Remonstrance of the Commons condemning Charles's government. Named first among the 'five members' whom the King tried to seize in 1642, he directed the setting-up of governmental, military and financial administration to support the war against Charles, and determinedly pursued alliance with the Scots before his early death from cancer.

PYTHEAS OF MARSEILLES (*fl. c.* 310 BC), Greek navigator. His account of a voyage from Greece to the coasts of Spain, France and Britain supplies the earliest written evidence of knowledge of the British Isles. His dramatic story of cold and fog may indicate that he sailed as far as the Arctic. The mysterious island of 'Thule', which he mentions finding to the north, was generally equated with Iceland during the Middle Ages, but it is possible that he travelled no further than the Shetlands.

Q

QUANT, MARY (1934–), designer. Welsh-born, Mary Quant studied art at Goldsmiths' College, where she met her husband Alexander Plunket-Greene. With a partner they opened a boutique, Bazaar, in Chelsea in 1955: it was a sensation, making the King's Road a 'happening' place and presaging the 'swinging sixties' in clothes (particularly the mini-skirt) and style, so much so that a Museum of London exhibition (1973) was entitled 'Mary Quant's London'.

QUEENSBERRY, 9TH MARQUESS OF *see* DOUGLAS, JOHN SHOLTO; **2ND DUKE OF** *see* DOUGLAS, JAMES

QUILLER-COUCH, SIR ARTHUR ('Q') (1863–1944), anthologist. A Cornishman, he was a true 'man of letters' with a prodigious corpus of work. Among his novels, he completed one that Robert Louis STEVENSON had left unfinished on his death, and wrote his own, including the well-regarded *The Ship of Stars* (1899). He wrote essays, criticism and verse, but his name is most associated with *The Oxford Book of Verse* (1899), which set the mainstream standard for poetry for the first half of the twentieth century and sold half a million copies in the lifetime of 'Q' (as he usually signed himself). Appointed to a professorship at Cambridge in 1912, he was in the forefront in establishing English as a discipline there, and his *On the Art of Writing* (1916) and *On the Art of Reading* (1920) enjoyed a wide readership.

QUIN, JAMES (1693–1766), actor. Illegitimate son of a barrister, he started acting in Dublin and made his London début in 1714. For most of his career he was associated with Drury Lane, of which he was for a time co-manager. His rivalry with GARRICK became part of theatre legend and their joint appearances at Covent Garden in 1746–7 drew huge audiences. Quin's formal acting style, however, came to seem old-fashioned compared with Garrick's and he retired to Bath. Greatly regarded as a wit in his lifetime, Quin appeared in several novels including SMOLLETT's *Humphry Clinker*.

R

RABY, BARON OF *see* NEVILLE, RALPH

RACHMAN, PETER (1919–62), property developer. A Polish-Jewish *émigré* who had fled from Nazi persecution and fought with the British army in the Middle East, by 1950 Rachman had become a London landlord, letting flats at extortionate rents to pimps, prostitutes and also to recently arrived West Indian immigrants whom many British landlords refused to accommodate. 'Rachmanism' was a term coined to signify the exploitation and terrorization of tenants without means or enforceable rights.

RADCLIFFE, ANN (née Ward) (1764–1823), novelist. Through Josiah WEDGWOOD's partner, Thomas Bentley, she mixed in literary circles from an early age, marrying a lawyer turned journalist, William Radcliffe. She began supplementing the family income by writing a series of lurid novels in which a heroine was placed in the midst of apparently supernatural occurrences in a location of poetical scenic beauty. They epitomized the Gothic style for a generation of readers; the most successful were *The Mysteries of Udolpho* (1794) and *The Italian* (1797), both of which earned her previously unprecedented advances. An influence upon Walter SCOTT, she was satirized by Jane AUSTEN in *Northanger Abbey*.

RADCLIFFE, THOMAS (8th [3rd Radcliffe] Earl of Sussex) (?1525–83), soldier and politician. His military career began in the 1540s, and despite supporting JANE GREY in 1553 he undertook MARY I's diplomatic missions to CHARLES V and Spain before becoming Lord Deputy (1556–60) and then Lord Lieutenant (1560–5) of Ireland. He supervised the policy of colonial plantation in Leix and Offaly from 1557, and energetically extended English control, although he had little success in campaigning against Shane O'NEILL. On his return to the court, he became the chief conservative opponent of Robert DUDLEY, Earl of Leicester, championing alternative marriage plans for ELIZABETH I with Catholic princes, first the Austrian Archduke Maximilian, and later the French Henry and FRANCIS of Anjou; he also opposed Leicester's interventionist policy of supporting the Netherlands' rebellion against Spanish rule. Nevertheless as Lord President of the Council of the North (1568–72) he defeated the 1569 rebellion of the northern earls (*see* NEVILLE, CHARLES; PERCY, THOMAS), pursuing the rebels into southern Scotland in 1570.

RADCLIFFE-BROWN, ALFRED (1881–1955), social anthropologist. Radcliffe-Brown was educated at Cambridge, where he was drawn to anthropological research by James FRAZER and W. H. R. Rivers. Subsequently he conducted field studies of the Andaman islanders (1906–8) and Western Australian tribes (1909–13). His academic positions included professorships at Sydney (1926–31), Chicago (1931–7) and Oxford (1937–46). With Bronislaw MALINOWSKI, he was a founder of modern social anthropology. He is remembered less for his ethnographic findings than for his theoretical writings, notably *Structure and Function in Primitive Society* (1952). A disciple of the French sociologist Emile Durkheim, he held that the goal of social anthropology was to understand, by a comparative study of primitive societies, the organization and functions of social structures: that with scientific methods social anthropology could become a proper theoretical science, distinguished from ethnologists' descriptive and conjectural method. His approach has been challenged by followers of Malinowski and others but still forms an important part of contemporary social anthropology.

RAEBURN, SIR HENRY (1756–1823), painter. Trained as a jeweller, Raeburn came to specialize in miniature painting. Following his marriage in 1780 to a prosperous widow, he studied first in London and then in Italy, learning from Joshua REYNOLDS, Allan RAMSAY and others. He returned to his home city of Edinburgh in 1787 and established himself as a portraitist. His 1792 portrait of Sir John and Lady Clerk of Penicuik is widely seen as his masterpiece. It departed from practice by emphasizing intimacy over display, showing his clients at ease with each other and with their surroundings. His paintings epitomized Scottish society in its golden age. He was active in several attempts to set up an exhibiting academy in Edinburgh, including what would become the Royal Scottish Academy, and was knighted by GEORGE IV on his 'jaunt' to Edinburgh in 1822.

RAFFLES, SIR STAMFORD (1781–1826), founder of Singapore. Having risen through the ranks of the East India Co., Raffles was sent to Penang in 1805. He was instrumental in the capture of Java from the Dutch in 1811 and was made Java's Lieutenant Governer. On the island's return to the Dutch in 1814, he was recalled to London to account for his administration there, since his sale of public lands had been much criticized. Partly exonerated, he was given further duties in the East Indies and was the leading voice behind the British purchase of Singapore. From 1819 Raffles and Singapore were synonymous and in his short period of rule there, until 1823, the foundations were laid for the colony's subsequent growth into the most important commercial trading base between Calcutta and Hong Kong, as well as a strategic military base.

RAGLAN, 1ST BARON *see* SOMERSET, FITZROY

RAGNALL (?–920), King of York (910/14–20). A grandson of IVAR THE BONELESS, who was expelled from the Scandinavian colony in Dublin in 902, Ragnall's career epitomizes Viking opportunism. Appearing in northern England following EDWARD THE ELDER's victory over the Vikings of York in 910, he defeated the Northumbrians and CONSTANTÍN II, King of the Scots, in two separate battles at Corbridge (Northumb.) to establish himself at York. He expanded his power further by driving out EALDRED OF BAMBURGH. Although he acknowledged the overlordship of EDWARD THE ELDER in 920, his whole career demonstrates the enduring capacity for renewal of the Viking colony of York. He was succeeded by his brother SIHTRIC CAECH.

RAGNAR LOTHBROK (?–850s), Viking warrior. A mixture of historical and legendary sources suggest that his piratical activities took him to Ireland, France and Northumbria, and that it was in the last that he was killed. He may well have established a pattern of activity followed by his sons HALFDAN and IVAR THE BONELESS who led the 'Great Army' of 865. He is reputed to have died after being thrown into a snake-pit by ÆLLE, later King of Northumbria.

RAGNHILD (?–*c*. 970), wife of several earls of Orkney. The daughter of ERIC BLOODAXE, the last Scandinavian King of York, Ragnhild is said to have dominated the politics of the Viking settlement of the Orkneys during her lifetime, marrying in turn three sons of THORFINN I SKULL-SPLITTER, and arranging for the deaths of the first two of them.

RAHMAN, TUNKU ABDUL (1903–90), politician. An unlikely leader of the independence movement, Tunku (meaning Prince) Abdul Rahman had led a playboy life, taking 25 years to qualify in law; his speaking and administrative skills were poor. Yet he steered Malaya from colony to independent nation. Taking control of the racially exclusive UMNO (United Malay National Organization) in 1952, he seized the initiative: the British under Malcolm MACDONALD had wanted gradual democracy and Malay–Chinese racial harmony. Rahman struck an electoral alliance with the Malayan Chinese Association and they had great success in 1955 when a majority of legislative seats were made elective. The guerrilla leader Chin Peng offered to disband his forces if the Communists were allowed into the political process. Rahman refused; Chin Peng's offensive continued until the 1980s but was ineffectual without superpower support. Meanwhile Rahman, with broad Indian and Chinese support, established a Malay-dominated state; Singapore's LEE KWAN YEW led his tiny country to separate independence. Communal riots in 1969 signalled the effective end of Rahman's political career.

RAIKES, ROBERT (1735–1811), philanthropist. Son of the printer who founded the *Gloucester Journal*, Raikes inherited the business in 1757. He took an active interest in such local institutions as the infirmary and model prison, and used his newspaper to promote good causes. In 1780 he tackled the problem of disorderly and idle children on the Sabbath by gathering a group together and teaching them in a Sunday school in church. Raikes's idea caught on, especially in industrial districts, where children worked through the week. Anglicans and Dissenters initially co-operated in setting them up, but from the 1790s they were increasingly founded on a sectarian basis.

RALEIGH, SIR WALTER *see* essay on page 671

RALPH (?–1057), Earl of Hereford. The son of Drogo, Count of the Vexin, and EDWARD THE CONFESSOR's sister GODGIFU, Ralph came to England with his uncle, and was created Earl of Hereford in *c*. 1050. Responsible for introducing French military techniques into his border earldom, he became notorious when, in 1055, an English cavalry force that he had trained ran away rather than fight the Welsh. His son Harold was able to regain a portion of his father's lands in the time of WILLIAM II RUFUS.

RALPH OF COGGESHALL (*fl*. 1207–24), chronicler. Abbot of the Cistercian abbey of Coggeshall (Essex) from 1207 until he resigned in 1218, he

continued on page 672

RALEIGH (or RALEGH), SIR WALTER (1554–1618)
Courtier, writer and colonial pioneer

From a minor gentry family of Devon, Raleigh studied at Oxford and fought in the French civil wars (1569–72); thereafter he embarked on a court career, with the advantage of a strategically placed relative, ELIZABETH I's old servant and friend Katherine Astley. The famous incident in which he threw down his cloak to give the Queen a dry path, first published in Thomas FULLER's *Worthies of England* (1662), is plausible enough, and he won her affection, despite the aggressive temperament which twice earned him imprisonment for affray and his fraught relationship with the more senior favourite Christopher HATTON. His first overseas venture was military service in Ireland in 1580–1, after which he returned to court to become Esquire of the Body. Raleigh was becoming increasingly preoccupied, however, with a world-wide role for England; although Elizabeth insisted that he remain near her, he backed Humphrey GILBERT's 1583 Newfoundland expedition, and was a major backer of the abortive 1584–6 attempts to colonize Roanoke on the coast of what is now North Carolina. He first entered Parliament in 1584 and thereafter sat in all Elizabeth's Parliaments except that of 1589, achieving a distinction unique among his contemporaries as knight of the shire for three different counties (Devon, Dorset and Cornw.), a tribute to his popular reputation, despite his many enemies in high political circles.

1587 was a high point in Raleigh's career, when he became Captain of the Guard in succession to Hatton, an office which kept him close to the Queen; he was granted major estates, partly confiscated from Anthony BABINGTON's fellow conspirators, partly subtracted from the Bishop of Salisbury's estates (Sherborne Castle, Dorset). He was also given extensive land in Ireland, which he visited in 1589 while avoiding trouble at court; while in Ireland he became friendly with Edmund SPENSER and sponsored the publication of *The Faerie Queene* (1590). He now faced the hatred of a younger rival at court, Robert DEVEREUX, Earl of Essex, who did his best to undercut his position. Far more damaging than Essex's crass manoeuvres, which the Queen fiercely resisted, was the exposure (1592) of Raleigh's secret marriage to the maid-of-honour Bess Throckmorton; this provoked Elizabeth to jealous rage, and she eventually sent him to the Tower of London. His career at court was ruined and the only possible means of reviving it was his commitment to maritime adventures; the government released him in order to sort out the chaos provoked at Dartmouth by the arrival of the enormously valuable cargo of the Portuguese ship the *Madre de Dios*, which had been captured by an expedition which he had organized in reprisal for the death at sea of Sir Richard GRENVILLE. Now that the Queen had banished him from court he was free to take part himself in a major expedition, a venture to Guiana, in the heart of the Spanish American empire, to search for Eldorado (the golden one). Setting out from Plymouth in 1595, he harassed the Spanish settlements in Trinidad before travelling into Guiana from the Orinoco River delta. Unusually among contemporary explorers, he made a good impression on the native Indians, but Elizabeth was not so impressed with his trophies of supposed gold ore and gems, despite the publishing success of his propaganda description of his exploits, *The Discoverie of the Large, Rich and Bewtiful Empyre of Guiana* (1596). A new opportunity came with the expedition to Cadiz (1596), in which he and Essex buried their differences; despite the meagre returns, his part in the spectacular exploit won him grudging royal reinstatement as Captain of the Guard from 1597. He shared in the failure of Essex's expedition against the Spaniards off the Azores, and his court position remained fragile; it was therefore particularly foolish of him after Essex's execution (1601) to alienate himself from the all-powerful Robert CECIL. JAMES I, pursuing peace with Spain, inflicted further humiliation by banning privateering expeditions, from which Raleigh was profiting. Raleigh became involved in the Main Plot (1603), a scheme of Henry BROOKE, Lord Cobham, to replace James I with his cousin Arabella STEWART. The plot was quickly betrayed to the government, who may have encouraged it to develop; Raleigh was among those convicted. His life spared for the time being, he lived in the Tower, occupying himself writing, including the unfinished *History of the World* (published 1614). The death of his new patron, Prince HENRY FREDERICK, dashed hopes of release and revival in his fortunes, but in 1616 James was persuaded to let him embark on another Guiana expedition. This proved a disaster, involving mutinies among his men and clashes with the Spaniards which led to Raleigh's long-postponed execution when he returned. His brilliant and varied talents never rescued a career of unfulfilled promise and unsuccessful playing of the courtly game.

Stephen W. May, Sir Walter Raleigh (1989)

wrote a lively account of events, chiefly in England but also on crusade between 1187 and 1224.

RAMBERT, DAME MARIE (originally Civia Rambam) (1888–1982), ballet teacher and director. Born in Warsaw, she studied eurhythmic dance, worked with Nijinsky and was a member of the *corps de ballet* of Diaghilev's Ballets Russes. In London, she married and started a ballet school, at which Frederick ASHTON was a pupil. In 1931 she founded what would become the Ballet Rambert, Britain's first permanent ballet company, and over the next half-century was to be a major influence on the success of British ballet, staging lunchtime ballet in factories during the Second World War, perfecting the company's classical repertoire and, once it was on a solid financial footing in the 1960s, encouraging experimental contemporary dance.

RAMSAY, ALLAN (1686–1758), poet and editor. Sent from Lanarks. to Edinburgh in 1701 to be apprenticed to a wigmaker, he became a successful tradesman and was one of the founders of the Jacobite Easy Club in 1712, where he developed his gift for poetry. In 1716 he became a bookseller and published his own edition of *Chrysts-Kirke on the Greene* from the sixteenth-century BANNANTYNE manuscript. This was followed by other collections, often mixing Ramsay's own verse with Scots literature of earlier centuries. The most influential of these was *The Ever Green* (two vols, 1724–7), an anthology of pre-1600 Middle Scots verse. Ramsay's work was praised by metropolitan writers including GAY, who travelled to Edinburgh to meet him, and POPE. After 1730 Ramsay wrote little but encouraged his son, the painter Allan RAMSAY.

RAMSAY, ALLAN (1713–84), painter. He was the son of the poet Allan RAMSAY. After periods of study in Edinburgh, London and Rome, in 1738 he began to practise as a commercial artist in London. He befriended HOGARTH and shared his belief that art should reflect experience. His *Dialogue on Taste* (1775) argued that art should require little sophistication to be understood and that abstract ideas of ideal human beauty were unrealistic. His ideas were rejected by REYNOLDS but Ramsay's success included becoming the King's painter (1761) and executing the coronation portrait of GEORGE III.

RAMSAY, SIR BERTRAM (1883–1945), sailor. Son of an army officer, he served in the Dover Patrol (1915–18), which culminated in the raid against Ostend. After a bitter clash with Commander-in-Chief of the Home Fleet (1935) Ramsay was forced to resign, but was recalled in Sept. 1939 to establish a modern version of the Dover Patrol. Ramsay organized the Dunkirk evacuation (May 1940), and subsequently oversaw the D-Day landings of 6 June 1944. He was killed in an air crash while on his way to take up a new appointment in the Far East in Jan. 1945.

RAMSAY, JAMES (10th Earl and 1st Marquess of Dalhousie) (1812–60), Governor General of India. Conservative in politics, he held office under Sir Robert PEEL and Lord John RUSSELL, but achieved lasting fame as Governor General of India during the Second Sikh War. Appointed in 1847, the youngest man to assume the reins of government in India, Dalhousie wanted above all to 'rationalize the map of India'. He acquired territory, developed the infrastructure of the subcontinent, repressed *suttee* and female infanticide and vastly improved administration. The post, railway, road and telegraph systems of India were reformed or implemented under him. He returned to England in 1856 to great acclaim, but the outbreak of the Indian Mutiny the following year called his policies of annexation and his faith in the local armies into question. His critics, however, were ill informed, and his record made him one of the most able governors of India.

RAMSAY, SIR WILLIAM (1852–1916), chemist. Ramsay studied chemistry in his native Glasgow and in Germany, taught and researched chemistry at Anderson's College, Glasgow (1872–80), and, as Professor of Chemistry at University College, Bristol (1880–7), conducted important work on the connection between the gaseous and liquid states. As Professor of Chemistry at University College, London (1887–1913), he explored the molecular structure of liquids and in 1895 announced, with Rayleigh (*see* STRUTT, JOHN WILLIAM), sensational evidence for a new inert element, argon. He also discovered neon, krypton, xenon and radon. In 1904 he became the first Briton to be awarded the Nobel Prize for Chemistry.

RAMSEY, MICHAEL (Baron Ramsey of Canterbury) (1904–88), Archbishop of Canterbury (1961–74). After leaving Cambridge, where he had been President of the Union, Ramsey entered the priesthood in 1928, working as a parish priest in Liverpool for 18 months. From 1930 until 1936 he was sub-warden of Lincoln Theological College (where he wrote *The Gospel and the Catholic Church*, his first and best-known theological work), and from 1940 to 1950 Professor of Divinity at Durham University and canon of Durham Cathedral. Subsequently Regius Professor of Divinity at Cambridge, he returned to Durham as Bishop only two years later, and was appointed Archbishop of Canterbury in 1961. Liberal on social issues and leaning towards the High-Church wing of Anglicanism, Ramsey tried to mend bridges with both Methodists (his proposals to reunify the Anglican and Methodist Churches were twice rejected by the General Synod) and Catholics (he visited Pope Paul VI in Rome in 1966). He presided over a transfer of power in the Church from Parliament to the General Synod, ending 300 years of direct parliamentary jurisdiction over the national Church.

RANDOLPH, THOMAS (1st Earl of Moray) (?–1332), nobleman. A nephew of ROBERT BRUCE, and later Regent for his son DAVID II, he was captured in 1306 and joined the English but was recaptured and rejoined the Scots. He was created Earl in 1312, captured Edinburgh Castle in a daring night attack, fought at Bannockburn (1314), campaigned in Ireland and won victories against the English in England at Myton (Yorks.) (1319), Byland (Yorks.) (1322) and Stanhope Park (Co. Durham) (1328).

RANELAGH, 3RD VISCOUNT AND 1ST EARL OF see JONES, RICHARD

RANK, J(OSEPH) ARTHUR (Baron Rank of Sutton Scotney) (1888–1972), businessman. J. Arthur Rank joined the successful Hull-based corn-milling business founded by his father in 1905 and became a mill manager in 1910. After the First World War, in which he served as an ambulance driver, he became joint Managing Director when the company went public. In the 1930s Rank entered the film business out of moral conviction, showing and making religious films; from that grew his film distribution and production empire. Pinewood Studios (Herts.) were built in 1935, Denham Studios (Bucks.) were acquired in 1938 and Elstree Studios (Herts.) in 1939, while the Gaumont group of companies and Odeon theatre chain were both bought in 1941. Rank emerged as the most powerful player in the British cinema industry and used his financial muscle to release creative talent. With a near monopolistic position, he was severely exposed to American competition in the late 1940s; in 1952 he surrendered his film interests to the Rank Organization and returned to the milling business. In 1962 he merged it with Hovis McDougall to form a giant diversified foodstuffs combine.

RANSOME, ARTHUR (1884–1967), writer. As a journalist for the *Manchester Guardian* Ransome was an eye-witness to the revolution in Russia in 1917: his account, *Six Weeks in Russia*, came out the same year. It was his second visit; after the first he had produced *Old Peter's Russian Tales* (1916); this time he married Trotsky's secretary. After travels in China he settled in the Lake District and wrote a series of highly successful adventure stories for children, the first of which was *Swallows and Amazons* (1931), all about being outdoors and messing about in boats – which is what he liked doing best himself.

RATHBONE, ELEANOR (1872–1946), social reformer. Born into a prosperous Nonconformist Lancs. family of shipowners and merchants, Rathbone became a committed feminist while at Somerville College, Oxford (1893–6). Her main concerns before the First World War were with the condition of poor widows and with women's suffrage. She was a member of the non-militant National Union of Women's Suffrage Societies (NUWSS) and like its leader, Millicent FAWCETT, supported the war. One of the issues arising from the war was that of women separated from their husbands and in 1917 Rathbone, with a number of others from the NUWSS and the socialist, Henry BRAILSFORD, produced a pamphlet on *Equal Pay and the Family*, which began the campaign for family allowances. The cause was strengthened when, in 1919, the NUWSS became the National Union of Societies for Equal Citizenship, and Rathbone succeeded Fawcett as President. In *The Disinherited Family* (1924) she argued that family allowances, paid directly to the wife, would end the dependence of women upon husbands. As independent MP for the Combined British Universities (1929–46) she carried the demand for family allowances into Parliament, but it was not until the end of the war that a scheme was adopted by government. In the 1930s she was a vigorous champion of Indian women's rights to the vote and of opposition to female circumcision in colonial Africa and the forced marriage of Arab girls in Palestine. She was also a strong advocate of the League of Nations and opponent of appeasement.

RATTLE, SIR SIMON (1955–), conductor. Rattle studied conducting at the Royal Academy of Music (1971–4), and in 1974, aged 19, won the first John Player International Conductors' Competition. He was then appointed as con-ductor of both the Bournemouth Symphony Orchestra and Bournemouth Sinfonietta. In 1975 he made his opera début with the Glyndebourne Touring Opera, conducting a performance of Igor Stravinsky's *The Rake's Progress*. From 1980 to 1991 he was principal conductor of the City of Birmingham Symphony Orchestra (CBSO) and from 1991 to 1998 its Music Director. Under him the CBSO flourished, turning Birmingham into a musical Mecca. Rattle has held the post of principal guest conductor with a number of the world's leading orchestras, including the Rotterdam Philharmonic (1981–4), the Los Angeles Philharmonic (1981–92), and the Orchestra of the Age of Enlightenment since 1992. He will take up the appointment as chief conductor and Artistic Director of the Berlin Philarmonic Orchestra in 2002.

RAVERAT, GWEN(DOLEN) (née Darwin) (1885–1957), wood-engraver. Granddaughter of Charles DARWIN, she was trained at the Slade School in London, where she met her husband, the artist Jacques Raverat, whose sister taught her to work in wood. She was a founder member of the Society of Wood-Engravers (1920), and Eric GILL considered her 'quite, or nearly quite' the best of all contemporary engravers. Her work illustrated several books, including the poems of her cousin, Francis Cornford, and her own still charming account of the 'intellectual aristocracy' at home, *Period Piece: A Cambridge Childhood* (1952).

RAVILLIOUS, ERIC (1903–42), painter and designer. A student of Paul NASH at the Royal College of Art, Ravillious used his artistic abilities in painting, wood-engraving, printmaking, book illustration (including work for the Golden Cockerel Press and the Curwen Press, both private presses which produced limited edition books illustrated by such artists as Eric GILL), textile, glass and ceramic design and he experimented with lithographs. He designed the official WEDGWOOD pottery commemorative mug for the coronation of EDWARD VIII, whose abdication made it redundant, but with revisions the design served to commemorate the coronations of GEORGE VI and ELIZABETH II. Appointed an official war artist in the Second World War, he painted naval scenes, including *Norway* (1940), but in Sept. 1942 the plane in which he was flying disappeared.

RAWLINSON, HENRY SEYMOUR (Baron Rawlinson of Trent) (1864–1925), soldier. Educated at Eton and Sandhurst, he was commissioned into the King's Royal Rifles in 1884. Rawlinson saw active service in Burma, the Sudan and South Africa, served as Commandant of the Staff College (1903–6) and was promoted Major-General in 1909. Commanding 4th division in 1914, he analysed correctly the situation on the Western Front and, as the Commander of IV Corps in 1915 and later of the 4th and 5th armies, pioneered the 'bite and hold' approach, in which infantry never advanced beyond effective artillery support, thus achieving only limited objectives but also reducing casualties.

RAYLEIGH, 3RD BARON *see* STRUTT, JOHN WILLIAM

RAYMOND LE GROS *see* FITZGERALD, RAYMOND

READ, SIR HERBERT (1893–1968), poet and critic. A highly effective promoter of Modernism in art (indeed known as 'the Pope of modern art'), Read was a poet who in 1922 was appointed assistant keeper of ceramics at the Victoria and Albert Museum (1922–31) and then Professor of Fine Art at Edinburgh University (1931–3). His publications include *The Meaning of Art* (1931), *Art Now* (1933), a comprehensive defence of contemporary art, *Art and Society* (1937) and *Education through Art* (1943), which suggests the teaching of art as a way to develop personality. He was editor of the influential *Burlington Magazine* (1933–9), one of the organizers of the 1936 Surrealist exhibition and a spokesman for the avant-garde collective of artists, architects and designers (including Burra, HEPWORTH, Paul NASH, Henry MOORE and the architect Wells Coates) who formed Unit One in 1934. In 1948 he co-founded (with Roland PENROSE) the Institute of Contemporary Arts in London that was intended to be 'an adult play centre … a source of vitality and daring experiment', which is what it remains.

READING, 1ST MARQUESS OF *see* ISAACS, RUFUS

RECORDE, ROBERT (*c.* 1510–58), mathematician. From Pembroke, he published *The Grounde of Artes* (1543) on arithmetic, *The Pathway to Knowledge* (1551) on geometry, *The Castle of Knowledge* (1556) on astronomy and *The Whetstone of Witte* (1557) on arithmetic and algebra. He was imprisoned (1556–7) under MARY I, probably because of his connections with Protestant intellectuals like Sir John CHEKE and Leonard DIGGES. His mathematical works remained standard textbooks for a century, and he formalized the mathematical use of the equals sign (=).

REDCLIFFE MAUD, JOHN (Baron Redcliffe-Maud of Bristol) (1906–82), public servant. A leading civil administrator of the post-war years, Redcliffe-Maud was an Oxford politics don, overtaken by political events. He worked in the Ministry of Food during the Second World War. As Permanent Secretary at the Ministry of Education between 1945 and 1952, he was one of the main implementers of the 1944 Education Act (*see* BUTLER, R. A.). His reputation was strengthened at the Ministry of Fuel and Power in the following seven years, with the conversion of the railways to diesel and the nuclear power programme. High Commissioner to South Africa, he became Ambassador when it left the Commonwealth; in 1963 he returned to Oxford as Master of University College. In 1966 he chaired the Royal Commission into the structure of local government in England. The report that bears his name urged root-and-branch change: the introduction of unitary authorities and metropolitan authorities and the reduction of inequality between urban and rural administrations. A watered-down version of his proposals was introduced by the Local Authorities Act 1972.

REDMOND, JOHN (1856–1918), Irish politician. Born of Catholic merchant gentry, Redmond was MP for New Ross (1880–5), North Wexford (1885–91) and Waterford City (1891–1918). Not in the first rank of Irish Party leaders until the split over Charles Stewart PARNELL, he emerged as Parnell's most outspoken defender and led the Parnellite minority after Parnell's death. When the Irish Party reunited in 1900 he became party leader, but his authority was circumscribed by continuing dissent and the influence of powerful lieutenants, notably John DILLON. He grew in stature after the nationalists obtained the balance of power at the General Elections of 1910 and his popularity reached its height when he forced the Liberals to introduce the third Home Rule Bill after the abolition of the House of Lords' veto, but Ulster Unionist threats of armed resistance and the emergence of the separatist-influenced Irish Volunteers called into question his reliance on parliamentary methods. On the outbreak of the First World War he supported the Allied war effort, but after initial enthusiasm the demands of war increased Irish nationalist mistrust, and after the 1916 Easter Rising the Irish Party was defeated in several by-elections by Sinn Féin. Redmond died in March 1918, just after the failure of an attempt at compromise with moderate Unionists and just before LLOYD GEORGE's attempt to impose conscription on Ireland completed the alienation of Irish nationalist opinion. Debate continues about whether the hesitant nature of Redmond's leadership reflected personal weakness or the difficulties of leading a factionalized party and the problems of accommodating the susceptibilities of British politicians and the Irish Unionist minority.

REDWALD (?–c. 627), King of East Anglia. Named by BEDE as one of the seven kings who had exercised lordship over the kingdoms south of the Humber, a position subsequently referred to as Bretwalda, his eminence presumably stemmed from his defeat of ETHELFRITH of Northumbria in 616 and the restoration of EDWIN that followed. He occupies a notably ambiguous place in the history of the conversion to Christianity, since he is said to have erected Christian and pagan altars in the same building. He is more likely than any other warrior to have been the body discovered in the tomb buried at Sutton Hoo in Suffolk, when it was excavated in 1939.

REDWOOD, JOHN (1951–), politician. A product of the intellectual dominance of the Right in the period which created Thatcherism, he was seen by many as THATCHER's true heir, a view opposed by those who cast Michael PORTILLO in that role. Redwood was academically brilliant (something for which the press would never forgive him), gaining a DPhil at Oxford for a thesis on seventeenth-century political thought, and a fellowship of All Souls. After working in investment banking (1977–87), during which time he also worked in Thatcher's policy unit (1983–5), he became MP for Woking (Surrey) in 1987. From 1989 until 1992 he worked at the Department of Trade and Industry, where he tried to push forward privatization. After the 1992 election he went to the Department of Employment before, in 1993, entering the Cabinet as Secretary of State for Wales, where he pursued a Thatcherite agenda.

Redwood was one of the leading opponents of further British integration into the European Community and was, on one famous occasion, described by John MAJOR as one of the 'bastards' in the Cabinet; others, noting his supposed resemblance to the *Star Trek* character Mr Spock, nicknamed him 'the Vulcan'. Major, tiring of the criticism from within, resigned his position in 1985 and called on his opponents to 'put up or shut up'; to general surprise Redwood, showing more political courage than his chief rival Portillo, 'put up'. He was defeated but made a respectable showing. During the final two years of the Major administration Redwood set himself to expounding his brand of Thatcherism and, retaining his seat in the 1997 debacle, stood once more for the leadership. In an attempt to prevent William HAGUE from becoming leader he made a pact with his chief ideological opponent, Kenneth CLARKE, but still failed to win. In opposition he proved one of the few Tory frontbench spokesmen capable of giving the BLAIR government a hard time in the Commons. He remained an important voice in the Conservative Party on European matters, but in Feb. 1999 was sacked from his post as Shadow Minister for Transport and the Environment by Hague.

REEVE, JOHN (1608–58), religious leader *see* MUGGLETON, LODOWICK

REEVES, JOHN (c. 1752–1829), loyalist entrepreneur. In 1783–4 he published *A History of English Law* and in 1791 was appointed Chief Justice of Newfoundland. On his return, he responded to growing radical fervour in the period of the French Revolution by organizing an Association for the Preservation of Liberty and Property against Republicans and Levellers (Nov. 1792): this circulated loyalist petitions and pamphlets, and local committees kept watch for seditious writings. Reeves solicited ministerial support but his relations with the government were never entirely easy. In *Thoughts on the English Government* (1795), which asserted the primacy of the Crown over Parliament, he was condemned by the Commons, PITT THE YOUNGER voting against him. Nevertheless, Reeves received preferment as Superintendent of Aliens and Law

Clerk to the Board of Trade and in 1800 he became the King's printer.

REGINALD I (?–1228), King of Man and the Isles. Son of GODRED II, he took the throne on his father's death in 1187, ousting his younger half-brother OLAF II. For 40 years he ruled vigorously, winning a formidable reputation as a commander of war-galleys, often in alliance with such great warriors as John de COURCY and Allan of Galloway. Deposed in favour of Olaf in 1226 he fought on until he met his death in battle at Tynwald (Isle of Man) in 1229.

REID, ROBERT (?–1558), Bishop of Orkney, scholar. A student at St Andrews, he became Abbot of Kinloss (Angus) in 1526 and followed the previous abbot in making his abbey a notable centre of schol-arship and education; he was made Bishop in 1541. He served as secretary to JAMES V and undertook embassies to England and France. Having arranged the marriage of MARY QUEEN OF SCOTS and the Dauphin (*see* FRANCIS II), he died travelling home. Part of his legacy for a college in Edinburgh was recovered (after legal wrangling) and used as foun-dation endowment for Edinburgh University.

REID, THOMAS (1710–96), philosopher. A minister's son, he attended Marischal College, Aberdeen, and began his career as a Church of Scotland minister. His 1748 *Essay upon Quantity* attracted attention by rejecting the argument of HUTCHESON that ethical questions could be explained in mathematical formulae, and in 1751 he was made Professor of Philosophy at King's College, Aberdeen. His *Inquiry into the Human Mind* (1764) attracted controversy by its rejection of HUME's empiricism, insisting that the mind already had a store of 'common sense' from which it provided perceptions relevant to sensual stimuli. The book helped win him the chair of moral philosophy at Glasgow, where he remained until his retirement in 1780. His pupils at Glasgow included Dugald STEWART.

REITH, JOHN (1st Baron Reith of Stonehaven) (1889–1971), Director General of the BBC. A dour, high-minded Scot whose early working experience was in munitions and engineering, in 1922 Reith became the first manager of the newly founded British Broadcasting Co. Released from private commercial concerns and exhilarated by the technical possibilities, Reith was determined to make the company a public service. That policy was underwritten when it became a corporation in 1927. Reith remained its Director General until 1938. He stamped his character on British 'public service' broadcasting, producing a mix of high-brow and light radio programmes intended to enlighten as well as entertain; resisting attempts by politicians to exert undue influence over the medium, he saw the BBC become a national insti-tution. Although sceptical about its significance, he presided over the first television service in 1936. After leaving the BBC he was Chairman of Imperial Airways and then of British Overseas Airways Corporation (1938–40) and served briefly in 1940 as Minister of Information and then of Transport, becoming Minister of Works (1940–2) before falling out with Winston CHURCHILL.

RENNIE, JOHN (1761–1821), civil engineer. Originally a millwright, both in his native Scotland and then in the 1780s at the Albion Mills in London for James WATT, Rennie subsequently became a civil engineer. He undertook the first trans-Pennine canal, the Rochdale Canal, completed in 1804, and the Kennet and Avon Canal, completed in 1810; he designed many bridges including Waterloo, Southwark and London bridges across the Thames and the great bridge at Berwick-on-Tweed; and he installed docks, harbours and urban water supply systems throughout the country. He was also instrumental in the harnessing of steam to shipping, for dredgers and tugs.

REPINGTON, CHARLES A'COURT (1858–1925), soldier and journalist. Of a Wilts. gentry family, Repington was educated at Eton and Sandhurst, and was commissioned into the Rifle Brigade in 1878. After fighting in Afghanistan, Burma, the Sudan and South Africa, and an academically distinguished time at Staff College, in 1902 his prospects of a glittering career were dashed when his affair with the wife of a British Colonial Office official achieved widespread noto-riety: his brother-in-law, General Henry Scobell, used his considerable influence to force Rep-ington's resignation from the army. He quickly developed an alternative career as a military jour-nalist, first for the *Morning Post*, then for *The Times*, and finally for the *Daily Telegraph*, coming to exert far more power than he could have as a soldier. In May 1915 he exposed the shell crisis on the Western Front, which was to prove instrumental in forcing the ASQUITH government into coalition.

REPTON, HUMPHRY (1752–1818), landscape gardener. Son of a Suffolk collector of the excise, he was intended to lead a commercial career, and spent part of his education in Holland learning the language. Having failed in various enterprises, he set up as a professional landscape gardener. Initially a follower of Lancelot 'Capability' BROWN, he developed his own, intentionally more natura-listic style, becoming a prime exponent of the new picturesque aesthetic that emphasized roughness and irregularity. His work for many country landowners and, in London, the laying out of

Russell Square in Bloomsbury and the redesigning of Kensington Gardens all attracted notice. He also published several books, including *An Inquiry into the Changes of Taste in Landscape Gardening* (1806). His later work was increasingly orientated towards the developing class of suburban clients.

REVELSTOKE, BARON, 1ST and **2ND** *see* BARING FAMILY

REVETT, NICHOLAS (1720–1804), antiquarian, painter and architect. The son of a Suffolk landowner, he did not have to earn his living as an architect, but he became one of the leading figures in the revival of Greek art and knowledge in Britain. In 1742 he travelled to Italy where he met James STUART and Gavin HAMILTON. Following the publication of their *Proposals for Publishing an Accurate Description of the Antiquities of Athens* (1748), which secured funding from wealthy dilettantes in Italy, Revett and Stuart spent 1751–4 in Athens measuring and making drawings of antiquities which resulted in *The Antiquities of Athens* (1762). From 1764 to 1766 Revett, with Richard Chandler and William Pars, was in Asia Minor making architectural drawings for the *Antiquities of Ionia* (two vols, 1769–97).

REYNOLDS, ALBERT (1932–), Irish politician. A self-made businessman and politician, he was elected Fianna Fáil member of the Dáil for Longford-Westmeath in 1977. Minister for Posts and Telegraphs (1979–81), he presided over the modernization of Ireland's communications system and was Minister for Industry and Commerce (1987–8), Finance (1988–91). From 1989 he was seen as leader of the 'country and western' wing of Fianna Fáil, traditional supporters of the Taoiseach (Irish Prime Minister) Charles HAUGHEY but alienated by his decision to enter coalition and subsequent concessions to the Progressive Democrats (PD). Ousted as Minister for Finance after attempting to depose Haughey, Reynolds emerged as successor when Haughey was forced to resign in 1992. The coalition broke up late that year over a clash of testimony between Reynolds and PD leader Desmond O'Malley at a tribunal investigating questionable practices in the beef industry. A maladroit election campaign produced the worst Fianna Fáil result since 1927. Reynolds remained Taoiseach by negotiating a new coalition with the Labour Party. His major achievements as Taoiseach were the negotiations which led to the Downing Street Declaration with John MAJOR in 1993 and the Irish Republican Army ceasefire in Aug. 1994. Tensions between Fianna Fáil and Labour over his style of leadership caused the break-up of the coalition. Reynolds resigned; a 'rainbow coalition' of Fine Gael, Labour and Democratic Left (1994–7) was formed under John BRUTON, and Bertie AHERN became leader of Fianna Fáil. Reynolds's departure was regretted by those who saw him as more successful in handling the Ulster situation than his successor, but reflected his reckless and single-minded style of leadership, which always involved significant risks.

REYNOLDS, EDWARD (1599–1676), churchman. Oxford-educated and of moderate Puritan sympathies, he became a member of the Westminster Assembly (1643), and returned to the university during the Interregnum. He was the only prominent Presbyterian to accept the offer of a bishopric at the restoration of CHARLES II, hoping to promote religious reconciliation. As Bishop of Norwich from 1661 he was conciliatory to Dissenters, and his devotional writings, moderately Calvinist and strongly sacramental, remained popular into the ninteenth century.

REYNOLDS, GEORGE (1814–76), journalist. Although Reynolds, the son of a Royal Navy Captain, was educated at Sandhurst he became a journalist and publisher. Joining the Chartists at a late stage in 1848 he became strongly anti-middle class and pro-physical force, although his involvement in the movement was heavily shaped by his business concerns. His great achievement was as the publisher of the radical Sunday newspaper *Reynolds's News* from 1850, part of the considerable growth of a popular Sunday press in the second half of the nineteenth century. The paper combined both radical democratic politics, strongly anti-aristocratic, supporting trade unionism and suffrage reform, with a heady mix of sensationalist news of crime and scandal, a combination characteristic of the other great Sunday paper of the day, *Lloyd's*. By 1875 his paper was selling around 300,000 copies (*Lloyd's* was around 500,000) but Reynolds himself largely abandoned radicalism shortly before his death.

REYNOLDS, SIR JOSHUA (1723–92), painter. Son of a Devon clergyman and schoolmaster, Reynolds was apprenticed to the London artist Thomas Hudson, successor in the practice of Jonathan RICHARDSON. He travelled to Italy in 1749, and spent three years in Rome. Returning in 1752, he quickly established himself as a fashionable portrait-painter, and became very wealthy. His friends included Samuel JOHNSON, GARRICK, BURKE and Oliver GOLDSMITH. Made first President of the Royal Academy in 1768 (although his authority in the institution was rivalled by GEORGE III's friend William CHAMBERS), he was knighted in 1769. He produced nearly 2,000 portraits. From 1768 to 1790 he delivered a series of *Discourses* to the academy criticized by dissidents, such as William BLAKE, as the dogma of the artistic establishment.

RHODES, CECIL (1853–1902), imperial entrepreneur and politician. Born into an East Anglian clergyman's family, Rhodes was sent to southern Africa because he suffered from a weak chest. His attempts at growing cotton in Natal failed, so he set off in 1871 for the Kimberley diamond fields then being exploited, where he made his fortune. He returned to England to study at Oxford, went back to southern Africa where he founded the De Beers diamond company in 1880. By the age of 30 he was one of the world's wealthiest men. He then moved into gold, founding Consolidated Gold Fields in 1887. His ambitions had become political and territorial; he had first stood for parliamentary election in the Cape Colony in 1880 and held that seat until his death in the closing stages of the Boer War. Wanting to secure a 'road to the north' for the Cape, he was instrumental in acquiring Bechuanaland in 1884 and in inducing the Matabele King to cede mineral rights, and in 1887 he founded the British South Africa Co., which received its royal charter in 1889. Its extensive territory, some of it acquired from African kings by dubious means, was to bear the name Rhodesia. In 1890 Rhodes became Prime Minister of the Cape Colony but was forced to resign in 1896 after being found guilty of complicity in the JAMESON raid. Much of his time of greatest influence was spent in promoting white European settlement of the region north of the Transvaal and outflanking the Transvaal under Kruger, not least with the construction of a railway north from Kimberley. His was the imperialism of Cape-based mining capital, of which he was the supreme embodiment. In his will he endowed the 170 scholarships which bear his name at Oxford, for students from the former colonies, the USA and Germany.

RHODRI MAWR (?–878) (also known as Rhodri the Great; Rhodri ap Merfyn), King of Gwynedd (844–78). One of the most powerful kings of Gwynedd, he was a member of a relatively new ruling family which brought new vigour to the kingdom. His military successes included the absorption of Ceredigion and Powys, and the defeat of a Viking war band in 856. He was driven from his kingdom by the Norsemen in 877 and, on his return, was killed by an alliance of Mercians and Vikings. His military achievements and dynastic marriages meant that his descendants had an interest in most of the other Welsh kingdoms, which in turn underpinned Gwynedd's predominance in pre-Norman Welsh political life. He was succeeded by his son ANARAWD AP RHODRI.

RHUN, SON OF ARTGAL (?–878), King of the Strathclyde Britons. Rhun married a daughter of CINAED MAC ALPÍN, despite the fact that his brother-in-law CONSTANTÍN I, King of the Scots, had given advice which had led to the death of his father, ARTGAL, SON OF DOMNAGUEL. The marriage further pulled Strathclyde into the sphere of influence of the kings of the Scots, upon whom the political fortunes of Strathclyde would become increasingly dependent up until the effective unification of the two kingdoms in the early eleventh century.

RHYDDERCH (*fl.* 971), ?King of the Strathclyde Britons. Named as 'son of Dyfnwal' in the *Chronicle of the Kings of Scotland*, Rhydderch was apparently a son of DYFNWAL, SON OF YWAIN, King of Strathclyde. It is not certain that Rhydderch himself was king, but he killed CUILÉN, King of the Scots, in 971 in revenge for the abduction and rape of his daughter. Cuilén's successor, CINAED II, plundered Strathclyde in revenge, but was defeated 'with very great slaughter'. If Rhydderch was indeed king, he can only have been so briefly. His fate is unknown.

RHYDDERCH AP IESTYN (?–1033), King of Deheubarth. Rhydderch appears to have attained power in Deheubarth following the death of LLYWELYN AP SEISYLL in 1023, probably after intruding himself into the kingdom by violence. He is recorded holding power, first of all, in south Wales in Gwent. He brought the political ambitions of south-east Wales into line with the rest of the country, but this undoubtedly contributed to the increasing political instability in the region. His family initially failed to hold on to kingship in Deheubarth, but their claims were later enforced by his formidable son, GRUFFUDD AP RHYDDERCH.

RHYDDERCH HAEL (?–*c.* 612), King of the Strathclyde Britons. ADOMNÁN states that Rhydderch was a friend and correspondent of COLUM CILLE. The *Historia Brittonum* of NENNIUS names Rhydderch as one of the confederation under URIEN of Rheged who besieged Lindisfarne in an attempt to halt the northwards expansion of the kingdom of Bernicia. Jocelin's *Vita* of St KENTIGERN relates that he was a contemporary and benefactor of the saint and that he died at his royal estate of Partick (near Glasgow) within a year of Kentigern's death, recorded under 612 in the *Annales Cambriae*.

RHYS AP GRUFFUDD (*c.* 1130–97), Welsh prince. Known as the Lord Rhys, ruler of Deheubarth, he led the resistance against HENRY II's invasions of Wales (1157–65), and was then able to acquire a 30-year ascendancy over all the Welsh princes of south Wales. In 1171–2 Henry accepted Rhys's territorial gains and in return Rhys recognized Henry's overlordship. During the relative peace that lasted until 1189, Rhys overhauled the government of Deheubarth, patronized churches and poets and was probably responsible for the compilation of the laws of HYWEL DDA. In the last years of his life diplomacy once more gave way to war, both between the Welsh and English and between members of Rhys's own family angling for the succession. After his death Deheubarth fragmented and was never reconstructed as the premier Welsh kingdom.

RHYS AP GRUFFYDD (?–1531), political victim. Grandson and heir to the Tudor loyalist Welsh magnate RHYS AP THOMAS, he was initially favoured by Thomas WOLSEY, but he and his clientage deeply resented his not being granted the elder Rhys's offices on his death. Conflicts with rival magnate Lord Ferrers led to his arrest and execution on flimsy treason charges, a pre-emptive strike much resented in Wales.

RHYS AP MAREDUDD of Dryslwyn (?–1292), Welsh prince. A Welsh princeling notable for his lack of opposition to EDWARD I; indeed, he fought on the English side in 1282–3. When ungenerously treated he rebelled in 1287, when the Welsh cause was already lost. His revolt was quickly suppressed and he remained a fugitive until 1292 when he was hanged, drawn and quartered.

RHYS AP TEWDWR (?–1093), King of Deheubarth. He secured his hold on the kingship by winning the Battle of Mynydd Carn (in or near Dyfed) in 1081, in alliance with GRUFFUDD AP CYNAN of Gwynedd, and by recognizing WILLIAM I THE CONQUEROR as his overlord. Exiled to Ireland in 1088 he clawed his way back to power in 1091 but was eventually killed fighting the Normans in Brecon. He was later known as Rhys the Great. Both Welsh and English chroniclers saw his death as marking the end of the truly royal Welsh kings.

RHYS AP THOMAS, SIR (1449–1525), politician. Of Dinefwr Castle (Dyfed), he was the leading gentleman of south-west Wales; his support for HENRY VII's 1485 Welsh invasion and at Bosworth (where he may have personally killed RICHARD III) brought him a knighthood and increasing dominance in Welsh government for the rest of his life.

RICARDO, DAVID (1772–1823), political economist. Apart from Adam SMITH, he was the dominant influence upon the aims and methods of nineteenth-century economics. Ricardo's law of rent, based on the observation that the differing fertility of land yielded unequal profits to the capital and labour applied to it, was his most notable formulation. His law of comparative cost, demonstrating the advantages of international specialization, lay at the heart of the Free Trade argument (see MALTHUS, THOMAS). Using what economists would now refer to as a model of the economic process, he demonstrated that the Corn Laws had the effect of increasing the price of corn and hence increasing the incomes of landowners and the aristocracy at the expense of the working class and the rising industrial class. Thus he argued for the abolition of the Corn Laws as this would help to distribute the national income towards the more productive and innovative group in society. Ricardo also developed the labour theory of value to explain the determination of prices, and this was a central idea in MARX's theories about the evolution of capitalism. His abstract deductive methods fell out of favour in the 1870s as the discrepancy between political economy and the real world became embarrassing and politically dangerous.

RICARDO, SIR HARRY (1885–1974), engineer. Born in London to a family of engineers, Ricardo built and researched petrol engines while studying engineering at Cambridge. From 1907 he worked in his grandfather's engineering firm and by 1916 he was designing engines for British tanks. In 1917 Ricardo launched his own company for developing internal combustion engines and researching the properties of fuels, devising the 'octane number' for rating the troublesome detonation or 'knocking' properties of fuel. He produced numerous pioneering engine designs, including sleeve-valve aero-engines and motorcycle engines, a widely used side-valve engine with improved combustion chamber and a sleeve-valve diesel engine that greatly reduced fuel consumption.

RICE, EDMUND (1762–1844), educationalist. A Catholic merchant from Waterford, Rice devoted himself to the education of the Catholic poor after his wife died, and from 1802 built up an association of Catholic teachers, formally recognized as a religious order, the Christian Brothers, in 1820. (A smaller breakaway group, the Presentation Brothers, also venerates Rice as its founder.) The Christian Brothers' school system, permeated with explicit Catholic observance, was unacceptable to the nominally non-denominational State-controlled National School system, from which it remained separate until after the establishment of the Irish Free State. This gave it some independence in choosing its curricula; it was seen as more nationalistic than the State system and many prominent Irish nationalists graduated from Christian Brothers' schools, which were regarded as catering to the lower middle classes and artisans and were disdained by Catholics with higher social pretensions. (James JOYCE's father referred to them and their pupils as 'Paddy Stink and Micky Muck'.) They also acquired a reputation for harsh discipline and extensive use of corporal punishment, though Rice himself opposed the use of physical punishment. At its height the order operated large numbers of schools and other institutions in Ireland and countries with large Irish-descended populations. In recent years vocations to the order decreased and it has suffered from scandals concerning large-scale maltreatment of children in its care, but it is recognized as having made a major contribution to Irish education. Rice has undergone the first stages of the Catholic Church's canonization process.

RICH, CHRISTOPHER (c. 1657–1714), theatrical manager. A lawyer by training, he managed the loans by which Alexander Davenant (son of Sir William and brother of Charles DAVENANT) maintained his control of the United Company at the Theatre Royal, Drury Lane, and gradually ousted the spendthrift Davenant. He introduced stringent financial measures and alienated the senior performers led by BETTERTON, who in 1695 left to form their own company at Lincoln's Inn Fields. Rich then promoted a new generation of actors including Colley CIBBER, who became his much-abused deputy. His domination of the theatre was practically ended in 1709 when the Lord Chamberlain ruled that he was wrong to take a third of actors' benefit fees and transferred Drury Lane to another manager. At his death Rich was preparing a new theatre at Lincoln's Inn Fields. He was succeeded by his son, the more artistically minded John RICH.

RICH, EDMUND, ST (also known as St Edmund of Abingdon) (c. 1170–1240), Archbishop of Canterbury (1233–40). Born at Abingdon (Oxon.) and educated at Oxford and Paris, he taught theology at Oxford before being elected Archbishop of Canterbury in 1233. A scholar and ascetic, he was the author of the widely read spiritual treatise *Speculum Ecclesie* (Mirror of the Church). Quarrels with HENRY III and the monks of Christ Church, Canterbury, took him to Rome but he died. He was canonized in 1246 after a campaign efficiently led by the Cistercian house of Pontigny (which possessed his body).

RICH, JOHN (1692–1761), actor–manager and actor. In 1714 he inherited his father Christopher RICH's theatrical patent and opened his new theatre at Lincoln's Inn Fields. To compete with the stronger company at Drury Lane, Rich introduced dancing, imported Italian and French performers and, most famously, pantomimes in which he appeared as Harlequin, using the name Lun. Rich gradually strengthened the company with performers such as QUIN. His biggest success was not a pantomime but John GAY's *The Beggars Opera* in 1728, which enjoyed an unprecedented run. In 1732 he moved to a new theatre in Covent Garden, where HANDEL produced and conducted his oratorios. Competition with Drury Lane intensified, particularly after GARRICK became its

manager in 1747, culminating in the rival productions of *Romeo and Juliet* in the 1750–1 season. Rich was accused of not developing good actors and claiming the authorship of unknown playwrights' works, but he was remembered for decades as a great dancer and Harlequin.

RICH, RICHARD (1st Baron Rich) (1496 or 1497–1567), politician. A Hants. lawyer, he was prominent in treason trials in the 1530s, notably of Elizabeth BARTON, John FISHER and Thomas MORE, who was convicted largely through his testimony (More denounced his perjury). He testified against Thomas CROMWELL in 1540. In 1536 he became Speaker of the Commons and Chancellor of the new Court of Augmentations, dealing with ex-monastic lands, a useful basis for his wealth and Essex estates. Though made Baron and Lord Chancellor in 1547, he was hostile to Protestantism, and was a notable persecutor under MARY I. He founded Felsted school (Essex).

RICH, ROBERT (23rd [2nd Rich] Earl of Warwick) (1587–1658), sailor and politician. Cambridge-educated, he was one of the leading Puritan peers before the Civil Wars of the 1640s; his pre-war privateering and colonizing experience in colonial enterprises and in privateering (licensed private warfare at sea) won him command of Parliament's navy 1642–5. He then retired under the provisions of the Self-Denying Ordinance of 1644–5 which created the New Model Army, but again took command in 1648–9. CHARLES I's execution made him quit politics, but he took a leading part in the inauguration ceremony for Oliver CROMWELL's protectorate in 1657.

RICHARD I COEUR DE LION *see* essay on page 681

RICHARD II *see* essay on page 682

RICHARD II (996–1026), Duke of Normandy. He is important in British history because of the asylum he gave in 1013 to his sister EMMA's children by ETHELRED II THE UNREADY, including the future King EDWARD THE CONFESSOR, when they fled from the conquering armies of SVEIN FORKBEARD and CNUT. Although Richard personally came to terms with Cnut in 1017, he continued to protect Edward, thereby consolidating the links which were to have such fateful consequences in 1066. His son ROBERT I and his grandson WILLIAM I THE CONQUEROR continued his patronage of the future English king.

RICHARD III *see* essay on page 683

RICHARD OF CAMBRIDGE (3rd Earl of Cambridge) (?–1415), noble conspirator. Second son of

continued on page 684

RICHARD I COEUR DE LION (1157–99)
King of England (1189–99)

Known as Richard the Lionheart, he played a more active role than any other English king on the world stage in the crusades, the struggle between Muslim and Christian for control of the Middle East. A legend in his own lifetime, his reputation as a crusader meant that for many centuries he was regarded as the greatest of all kings of England. But from the seventeenth century onwards that same reputation served to highlight the fact of his long absences from England, and led to the view that he was so negligent of his kingdom's welfare as to be the worst of kings.

Third son of HENRY II and ELEANOR OF AQUITAINE, from an early age it was intended that he should inherit his mother's duchy. In 1173–4 he joined the revolt against his father, but was pardoned and entrusted with Aquitaine, where he rapidly made a formidable reputation. In 1183 Henry helped him to put down a rebellion involving his elder brother. As his father became increasingly concerned to provide for JOHN, apparently at Richard's expense, so Richard turned to the King of France, Philip II Augustus. This alliance ensured Richard's undisputed succession, as a consequence of the earlier death of his two older brothers, to virtually the whole Angevin empire in 1189.

In 1187, in swift reaction to the news of Saladin's capture of Jerusalem, Richard had been the first prince north of the Alps to take the Cross, and he was determined to go on crusade. After his coronation (Sept. 1189), the first English coronation of which a detailed description survives, he concentrated on raising money to fund his crusade and on making arrangements for the government of all his lands (Anjou, Aquitaine and Normandy as well as England). In 1190 he set out, conquering Cyprus (May 1191) en route. At Limassol he married BERENGARIA, sealing the alliance with her father, Sancho VI of Navarre, which ensured the safety of his southern dominions during his absence. But the marriage also meant breaking with Philip, to whose sister he had been betrothed since 1169; it was widely believed that Henry II had seduced her while she was in his custody. The ensuing enmity between the two Kings was to overshadow the rest of his reign. Muslim Acre capitulated (July 1191) soon after Richard's arrival outside its walls, but Philip immediately left, leaving Richard with overall responsibility for subsequent events: the massacre of the prisoners of Acre, the victory over Saladin at Arsuf, the decision, taken largely on logistical grounds, not to besiege Jerusalem, the grant of Cyprus to Guy of Lusignan, and the selection of a new King of Jerusalem. Despite the failure to recover the Holy City itself, Richard negotiated terms with Saladin in Sept. 1192 that enabled the hard-pressed crusader states to survive for another century. His leadership, prowess and courage, notably at Jaffa in Aug. 1192, made him a legend throughout Europe and earned him the respect of his Muslim enemies.

Returning home he was seized (Dec. 1192) by Leopold of Austria, with whom he had quarrelled at Acre, and held to ransom by the Emperor Henry VI. His provisions for the government of England during his absence on crusade stood up well to this unforeseeable turn of events; John's rebellion was contained and the King's ransom raised. In Feb. 1194, after 100,000 marks had been sent to Germany, Richard was released. He returned to England, captured the last of John's castles and wore his crown in state at Winchester, before sailing to Normandy (May 1194) never to return, leaving the government of England in the capable hands of Hubert WALTER. By then Philip had taken possession of much of eastern Normandy and some vital Loire Valley castles. Richard devoted the remainder of his life to recovering lost ground. This task, which involved the creation of a formidable coalition of allies as well as building the great fortress of Château-Gaillard, was almost complete when he was fatally wounded at Châlus, a castle belonging to the rebellious Viscount of Limoges.

Richard was a song-writer, a highly educated man who understood the power of words, and he deliberately cultivated the King ARTHUR-like image of the Lionheart which has remained with him ever since. Other legends are later accretions. In the sixteenth century his story became entangled with that of Robin HOOD; in the twentieth century he was identified (without good evidence) as a homosexual. The most recent scholarship now recognizes that, far from neglecting England, he in fact ruled it masterfully – both during the few months when in England and when he was in his French dominions. He spent little time in England, but England was only one, and the least-threatened, of his dominions. He had much wider responsibilities, and in his own day he was admired for taking them seriously.

John Gillingham, Richard I (1999)

RICHARD II (1367–1400)
King of England (1377–99)

Son of EDWARD THE BLACK PRINCE and JOAN OF KENT, he was still a boy at his accession in 1377, a fact that evokes sympathy, even from historians. So too does the image of Richard grieving over the death of his first wife, ANNE OF BOHEMIA, in 1394. So too does the tragic finale portrayed in SHAKE-SPEARE's *Richard II*. But most, although not all, historians follow FROISSART in criticizing the King while sympathizing with the man.

In the first crisis of his reign, the Peasants' Revolt (June 1381), he displayed courage and coolness when seemingly at the mercy of rebel armies from Kent and Essex that had seized London and executed several government ministers and advisers. Fortunately for the young King he was, rightly, not held personally responsible for the military setbacks in the war against France, economic conditions and poll taxes which had precipitated that revolt. Moreover it was, wrongly, believed that as King, the fount of justice, he could be trusted to care for the welfare of his people. Many rebels went home when he agreed to their demand that serfdom should be abolished. Those who remained in London, still trusting him, allowed themselves to be dispersed at his command after one of their leaders, Wat TYLER, had been killed during a conference with the King at Smithfield (15 June). Once the revolt was over Richard revoked his concessions. 'Serfs ye are, and serfs ye shall remain.' In Nov. 1381 Richard asked Parliament whether he had been right to annul his promises. They answered 'as with one voice that it had been well done'.

Over the next few years he became difficult to deal with for those senior politicians around him, notably his uncle, JOHN OF GAUNT. He tended to think that anyone who criticized him was a traitor. His distribution of patronage, especially his generosity to Robert DE VERE, was ill judged. After Gaunt's departure for Spain, Richard became more reckless. In 1386 he tried to defy Parliament, but was forced to yield and watch while his minister Michael de la POLE was impeached and a commission was appointed to control the following year's expenditure and patronage. His response was to elicit from a panel of judges a definition of the royal prerogative in terms which declared that the 1386 proceedings were illegal and that those who promoted them should be punished as traitors. When the judges' opinions were leaked, a brief civil war followed, culminating in the Battle of Radcot Bridge (Oxon.) (Dec. 1387), where the troops which Robert de Vere hoped to bring to Richard's aid were scattered. In consequence Richard found himself at the mercy of his opponents, headed by the Appellants, and had to endure the humiliation of the Merciless Parliament (Feb. 1388), when a number of his friends, including Nicholas BREMBRE and Robert TRESILIAN, were convicted of treason and executed. But at least he avoided deposition. In 1389 he formally resumed control of government and with Gaunt's help ruled peacefully for eight years. Richard was the first English king since JOHN to lead an expedition to Ireland; indeed, he went twice, in 1395 and 1399. By contrast he showed little interest in following in the footsteps of his much admired father and grandfather (EDWARD III) in pursuing the Hundred Years War for the Crown of France. In 1396 he made a 28-year truce with France and married a seven-year-old French Princess, ISABELLA. The war effectively over, he set himself to make the Crown financially and hence politically independent of the Commons in Parliament; some historians see this as a progressive policy. But it went hand in hand with the pursuit of vengeance for 1388. By 1399 he was indeed a very wealthy King but he went nowhere without an armed guard. He had dispossessed one third of the upper nobility and had hounded his old enemies (including his uncle THOMAS OF WOODSTOCK) to death. At this stage, having alarmed all his subjects, he rashly chose to go to Ireland. In attempting to fashion a new and more exalted image of monarchy, which is visible in his portraits, he had lost touch with reality. When Bolingbroke (*see* HENRY IV) and Henry PERCY, 9th Earl of Northumberland, struck, no one lifted a finger to save him. He lost two armies in two weeks and surrendered at Conwy (Caern.), perhaps hoping for a repeat of 1387–9. Instead he was coerced into abdicating on 29 Sept. 1399, and was then imprisoned. A plot to rescue him in Jan. 1400 only revealed how little support he had and precipitated HENRY IV's decision to have him murdered. His body stayed at King's Langley (Herts.) until HENRY V had it reburied in Westminster Abbey, the church which in life Richard had tried to make the focal point of a cult of monarchy.

Nigel Saul, Richard II (1997)

RICHARD III (1452–85)
King of England (1483–5)

For SHAKESPEARE Richard was the evil genius whose malice and cunning overshadowed the Wars of the Roses from start to finish. In the first battle of the wars, St Albans (Herts.) (May 1455), we are shown Richard killing Somerset (*see* BEAUFORT, EDMUND) and speaking the words which establish his character: 'Heart, be wrathful still/ Priests pray for enemies, but princes kill.' (*Henry VI, Part 2* Act 5, Scene 2)

It is clear that Shakespeare was untroubled by mere fact, since Richard was only two years old at the time. The fourth son of RICHARD OF YORK and Cicely Neville, born on 2 Oct. 1452, he was created Duke of Gloucester in 1461 soon after his eldest brother, EDWARD IV, had won the throne for the house of York. Compared to another brother, George PLANTAGENET, Duke of Clarence, he remained conspicuously loyal, sharing Edward's exile in 1470 and the dangers and triumphs of the battles of Barnet (Herts.) and Tewkesbury (Glos.) in 1471. He was conspicuously well rewarded. To Clarence's chagrin, he married ANNE NEVILLE and, in consequence, obtained the northern half of the Warwick inheritance (*see* NEVILLE, RICHARD, Earl of Warwick). On this foundation he engineered a commanding position for himself as Edward's lieutenant in the north. In 1482 he commanded the invasion of Scotland, which resulted in the recapture of Berwick, and in Feb. 1483 he was given authority to keep whatever he could conquer in south-west Scotland.

Thus far his career had been, for a royal duke, fairly unremarkable. He had been overbearing and acquisitive, but not more so than many, and certainly not the murderer and schemer portrayed by Shakespeare. After EDWARD IV's death in April 1483, however, Richard's conduct was, to say the least, extraordinary. On 30 April, claiming that he was forestalling a Woodville conspiracy against him, he arrested Anthony WOODVILLE, Earl Rivers, took possession of young EDWARD V, and was subsequently appointed Protector. The Woodvilles were unpopular, and for this action he had widespread support. But his subsequent actions stunned contemporaries. On 26 June the boy was deposed and Richard proclaimed King. Richard's defenders incline to the belief that he took this step only after learning (*c.* 22 June) that Edward V and his brothers and sisters were illegitimate. Others believe he had made up his mind earlier and that the bastardization of his nephews and nieces was a political manoeuvre designed to clear his path to the throne. Undoubtedly other potential obstacles, for example, William HASTINGS and Rivers, were removed by the simple expedient of ordering their summary execution. By the autumn it was rumoured that the ex-King and his younger brother, the Princes in the Tower, had also been removed. Richard made no attempt to prove that they were still alive. In Oct.–Nov. 1483 many former servants of Edward IV risked life and property by joining the Duke of Buckingham (*see* STAFFORD, HENRY) in revolt against a King whom a few months earlier they had assisted in his programme of cutting the Woodvilles down to size. Richard suppressed the revolt, but grants of rebel property to his own loyal supporters reinforced the impression that his was a northern regime imposed upon a reluctant south. The Yorkists were now badly split, while the conviction that the princes were dead focused attention on a hitherto insignificant exile, Henry Tudor, the future HENRY VII.

Although Richard adopted a high moral tone in presenting himself as a God-fearing King opposed to the licentiousness which had, he proclaimed, characterized his brother's court, very little went right for him during the remainder of his short reign. His only legitimate son died in 1484. His wife died in March 1485 and he had to deny the story that he had caused her death in order to marry his niece. In Aug. 1485 he was able to muster enough troops to outnumber Henry's largely French army, but at Bosworth many of his followers either stood by or joined the invaders. He died fighting, believing he had been betrayed. A contemporary commented that in this battle the Red Rose (Henry VII) had avenged the White (the sons of Edward IV). By his murderous ambition Richard had restarted the Wars of the Roses and so brought down the House of York.

The instinct to leap to the defence of anyone whose character has been assassinated by Shakespeare has resulted in Richard's becoming the most controversial of English kings. Particularly in recent times, thanks to the work of the Richard III Society, he has found many admirers, and this despite his total failure to live up to a king's most basic responsibilities: to ensure the survival of himself, his dynasty and his followers.

A. J. Pollard, *Richard III and the Princes in the Tower* (1991)
John Gillingham (ed.), Richard III: A Medieval Kingship (1993)

EDMUND OF LANGLEY, Duke of York, he was created Earl by HENRY V in 1414. Despite this he became involved in a conspiracy (the 'Cambridge Plot') to place his brother-in-law Edmund MORTIMER, Earl of March, on the throne. Edmund revealed the plot to the King, and Richard and his fellow conspirators, Scrope and Grey, were executed.

RICHARD OF CORNWALL (2nd Earl of Cornwall) (1209–72), King of the Romans. Younger brother of HENRY III, he was created Earl in 1227. After early tensions between the brothers were resolved, Henry relied heavily on Richard's advice and financial support. In 1257 the Earl's reputation for prudence and his wealth helped to secure his election and coronation as King of the Romans, the formal title of the ruler of Germany until crowned Emperor (which Richard never was).

While he was in Germany (1257–9), Henry's authority crumbled. Richard returned to England, but his own responsibilities and ambitions in the Holy Roman Empire, where he had to face the problem of a rival candidate for the throne, took him out of England again in 1260 and 1262–3. In 1264 he was captured at the Battle of Lewes and held by de MONTFORT in custody until Sept. 1265. He visited Germany for the fourth time in 1268–9, and held a diet at Worms and married (as his third wife) Beatrice of Falkenburg but, as before, made little impression outside the Rhineland. In 1270–1, with the future EDWARD I on crusade and HENRY III ill, Richard enjoyed a brief period of authority in England, but it was overshadowed by the murder of his eldest son and ended when he suffered a stroke in Dec. 1271.

RICHARD OF YORK (also known as Richard Plantagenet) (3rd Duke of York) (1411–60), Royal Prince. He became Duke at the age of four when his uncle Edward was killed at Agincourt (1415). He served as HENRY VI's Lieutenant in France in 1436–7, then as Governor of France and Normandy (1440–5), but by the latter part of the 1440s the court regarded him with suspicion. As son of Anne Mortimer and RICHARD OF CAMBRIDGE (executed in 1415 for plotting against HENRY V), he was descended on both sides from EDWARD III, and, had Henry VI died childless, his claim to the English throne would have been virtually unassailable.

In 1447, instead of the command in France which he wanted, he was made Lieutenant of Ireland. His delay in taking up the appointment suggests that he shared the view that it was tantamount to exile. Although his estates in England, Ireland and Normandy made him the greatest of the King's tenants-in-chief, the Exchequer was slow in paying the wages due to him as Governor; in financial difficulties by 1450, he was forced to sell some of his manors. At the same time, the fall

of Normandy meant, in his case, the loss of valuable lordships as well as national humiliation.

In Sept. 1450 he returned from Ireland blaming Edmund BEAUFORT, Duke of Somerset, for the débâcle and determined to replace him in the King's counsels. But Henry, still reeling from the shock of CADE's rebellion with its Yorkist overtones, had no intention of allowing Richard to be foisted upon him. Nor was he mollified by a parliamentary Bill seeking Richard's recognition as heir presumptive. In an attempt to force Henry's hand, Richard took up arms in 1452 but soon had to back down. After the King's breakdown, the court found Richard's demands hard to resist and, in March 1454, he was appointed Protector. Henry's recovery led directly to the Wars of the Roses.

Deprived of authority, Richard resorted to force and with the support of Richard NEVILLE, Earl of Warwick (whose aunt Cecily Neville was his wife), he won the first Battle of St Albans (Herts.) (1455). In Nov. he was reappointed Protector, only for the King to relieve him of the office three months later.

By 1459 it was clear that the Queen, MARGARET OF ANJOU, was out to break anyone who appeared to threaten her son's prospects. Richard's response was to renew his appeal to arms but this ended at Ludlow (Salop.) in Oct. when he and the Nevilles failed to persuade their troops to fight against the King. Richard fled to Ireland but in 1460, after Warwick had captured Henry at Northampton, he returned and claimed the throne. Reluctantly the Oct. Parliament recognized him as Henry's heir and granted him the heir's estates, Wales, Cornwall and Chester. He marched to challenge the Lancastrian hold on the north, and was met at Wakefield by the sons of the men killed at St Albans. He was himself killed and his head displayed at York, embellished with a paper crown. The real crown would be worn by two of his sons, EDWARD IV and RICHARD III.

RICHARDS, KEITH (1943–), musician see JAGGER, MICK

RICHARDSON, DOROTHY (1873–1957), novelist. She is the writer for whose work the term 'stream of consciousness' (see also WOOLF, VIRGINIA) was coined by May SINCLAIR, though she dismissed it as 'a perfect imbecility'. Her lifetime's work was her 13-volume Pilgrimage (12 volumes, 1915–38); volume 13 was assembled from papers after her death and published in 1967. The work is a semi-autobiographical quest (H. G. WELLS, with whom Richardson had an affair, surfaces as 'Hypo G. Wilson') for 'the unchanging centre of being in our painfully evolving selves', and has been warily respected (particularly the first volume, Pointed Roofs) for its attempt to find a new form and language to explore a distinctive feminine consciousness.

RICHARDSON, JONATHAN, SR (1665–1745) and **JONATHAN, JR** (1694–1771), painters and critics. The elder Richardson was trained by John Riley, portrait-painter to WILLIAM III and MARY II, and married his niece. As a painter, Richardson attracted the same clientele as KNELLER. Assisted by his son, he elaborated the first systematic theory of art for English painters in *Essay on the Theory of Painting* (1715) and *Essay on the Whole Art of Criticism in Relation to Painting, and Argument in behalf of the Science of a Connoisseur* (1719). The Richardsons argued that history-painting stood at the apex of art and that the beauty of the Italian school was superior to the literalism of northern European painters. The father had a large art collection which was sold for £2,000 in 1747. The Richardson thesis was partly accepted by HOGARTH and more fully by Joshua REYNOLDS.

RICHARDSON, SAMUEL (1689–1761), novelist. Apprenticed to a London printer and stationer, he worked first as a compositor and proofreader, then as a publisher, gaining the lucrative new contract to print the *Journals of the House of Commons* in 1742. His epistolary novel *Pamela, or Virtue Rewarded* (1740) was praised for its realism and helped to give respectability to the new literary form, but its morals attracted mockery as well as praise: Henry FIELDING's *Shamela* was the most successful of several parodies. Richardson's *Clarissa: or The History of a Young Lady* (1747–8), much cited in JOHNSON's *Dictionary*, and *Sir Charles Grandison* (1753) were also avidly read and admired, by Jane AUSTEN among others.

RICHMOND, 13TH EARL OF *see* TUDOR, EDMUND; **2ND DUKE OF** *see* STUART, LUDOVIC; **COUNTESS OF** *see* BEAUFORT, LADY MARGARET

RICHMOND AND LENNOX, 8TH DUKE OF *see* LENNOX, CHARLES

RICKMAN, JOHN (1771–1840), statistician. He devised the methods used to take the first British census in 1801, and prepared reports on the four censuses between then and 1831. He also ushered in the civil registration of births, marriages and deaths in 1837, prepared annual abstracts of Poor Law returns (1818–36), and wrote two pamphlets on the Poor Laws. For most of his career, he was clerk assistant in the House of Commons, and dressed so carelessly that he was once pressganged as a tramp.

RIDLEY, NICHOLAS (?1500–55), churchman. Born in Northumb., he followed his uncle Robert, a celebrated conservative theologian, to Cambridge, becoming Master of Pembroke College in 1540, and he became Archbishop CRANMER's chaplain and confidant. Raised to Bishop of Rochester in 1547, then of London in 1550, he energetically promoted EDWARD VI's religious reforms, though he determinedly confronted John HOOPER's push for yet more speedy religious change. Outspoken preaching in support of JANE GREY sealed his fate under MARY I, leading to a show trial at Oxford with Cranmer and Hugh LATIMER (1554), and to his death at the stake for heresy.

RIDOLFI, ROBERTO DI (1531–1612), conspirator. Ridolfi, a Florentine banker resident in London since the reign of MARY I, co-ordinated plans in 1570 to depose ELIZABETH I with the aid of a Spanish invasion. Thomas 4th HOWARD Duke of Norfolk, was half-heartedly involved and as a result was executed in 1572. In 1571 Ridolfi escaped to Italy and had a prominent career in his native city.

RIGBY, RICHARD (1722–88), political manager. An MP from 1745, his political career took off in 1752 when he rescued the Duke of Bedford (*see* RUSSELL, JOHN) from a mob in Lichfield. He became his close friend, secretary and adviser and MP for the Bedford borough of Tavistock (1754–88), directing profits from offices which Bedford held to other members of the 'Bloomsbury gang'. Noted for his single-mindedness and insensitivity, he vigorously supported extreme measures against WILKES and his supporters in the 1760s and against the Americans in the 1770s. He awarded himself large sums as Paymaster General (1768–82) but on leaving office was unable to repay the money he had taken for his own use; his estate still owed £156,000 in 1791.

RILEY, BRIDGET (1931–), artist. Riley studied at Goldsmiths' College and the Royal College of Art. Her 'op art', black and white geometrically dazzling paintings which create three-dimensional optical effects, caused a sensation at the Young Contemporaries exhibition (1955). 'Op art' (associated with the work of the French painter Victor Vasarély), and 'pop art', developed by her RCA contemporary Peter BLAKE and others, became defining visual motifs of the 1960s.

RINUCCINI, GIOVANNI BATTISTA (1592–1653), diplomat. A Florentine born in Rome, he became Archbishop of Fermo in 1625 and was sent to Ireland as Papal Nuncio in 1645. Determined to secure complete freedom for Roman Catholicism, he opposed compromise between the Royalists and the Catholic Confederates, sabotaging agreements brokered by James BUTLER, Earl of Ormond; eventually Ormond made terms with the Parliamentarian forces instead. The ensuing military disasters led the Confederates to forbid him to meddle further, and he was recalled in 1649. His supporters, mainly Gaelic Old Irish, sought to vindicate him posthumously in the *Commentarius Rinuccinianus* (*see* O'FERRALL, Richard).

RIPON, 1ST EARL OF *see* ROBINSON, FREDERICK

RIVERS, 2ND EARL OF *see* WOODVILLE, ANTHONY

RIZZIO (OR RICCIO), DAVID (?1533–66), murder victim. An Italian musician born near Turin, in 1561 Rizzio charmed MARY QUEEN OF SCOTS after arriving in Scotland with the Savoy Ambassador; three years later he became her French Secretary. Her husband Henry STEWART, Lord Darnley, and other Scots nobles detested Rizzio's hold over the Queen, and a gang of them dragged him from Mary's presence at Holyrood Palace and murdered him.

ROBBINS, LIONEL (Baron Robbins) (1898–1984), economist. Robbins was educated at University College, London, and the London School of Economics (LSE), to which he returned as Professor of Economics (1929–61). As an academic economist, Robbins was not a great original thinker in the league of his near-contemporary J. M. KEYNES, rather, his strength lay as an expositor of other people's ideas and as an academic mandarin. In the 1930s, after a brief youthful flirtation with Fabian socialism, he became particularly associated with the economic school of 'economic liberalism' and was instrumental in making the LSE into a bastion of free-market and free-trade economics at a time when most other economics departments were becoming converted to the rival school of Keynesianism. The LSE (Robbins included) was to provide much of the intellectual ammunition for Thatcherism (*see* THATCHER, MARGARET) in the 1970s and 1980s, and it was Robbins who recruited F. A. HAYEK, the leading Austrian exponent of free-market economics, to the LSE in 1931. Robbins wrote one of the few contemporary free-market interpretations of the Depression of the 1930s, *The Great Depression* (1934). During the 1930s he was a member of the Economic Advisory Council chaired by Keynes, and from 1941 to 1945 he was director of the wartime economic section of the War Cabinet secretariat, playing an important role in formulating and drafting several landmark government decisions such as the White Paper on employment policy of 1944. After the war he served on several government bodies and commissions, chairing the Committee on Higher Education (1961–4). The Robbins Report recommended expansion of government-funded higher education, to the exasperation of many of his former free-market colleagues. The report was acted upon by successive Labour and Conservative governments.

ROBENS, ALFRED (Baron Robens of Woldingham) (1910–99), Chairman of the National Coal Board (1961–71). A trade-union official and Councillor in his native Manchester, elected Labour MP for Wansbeck in 1945, later for Blyth, Robens served as private secretary in the Transport and Power ministries, becoming Minister of Labour in 1951. His hopes of further political office dashed by Labour's seeming unelectability, he accepted Harold MACMILLAN's offer to run the coal industry and a life peerage. His task was to make coal more attractive to customers while reducing capacity, given declining demand and competition from oil. The number of mines was cut by more than half to 292 and miners' numbers were halved to 283,000, and the industry eventually made a modest profit. His chairmanship was tainted by what was seen as an official lack of compassion for the 1966 Aberfan disaster (when a school was engulfed by coal waste).

ROBERT I (*c*. 1010–35), Duke of Normandy (1027–35). The father of WILLIAM I THE CONQUEROR, he was the Norman duke who decided to give positive support to the exiled EDWARD THE CONFESSOR's claim to the English throne, in opposition to CNUT who had supplanted Edward's father ETHELRED II THE UNREADY. It is possible, although the matter is controversial, that Robert even attempted an invasion on Edward's behalf.

ROBERT II (also known as Robert Curthose [Short Boots]) (*c*. 1053–1134), Duke of Normandy. Eldest son of WILLIAM I THE CONQUEROR, he inherited Normandy after his father's death in 1087 and was expected by many to become King of England. In the event the Conqueror's choice for the throne, WILLIAM II RUFUS, defeated the rebellion raised on Robert's behalf by his father's half-brother, ODO OF BAYEUX. In 1096 Robert joined the First Crusade, mortgaging his duchy to William Rufus for 10,000 marks to finance the expedition; as one of the conquerors of Jerusalem, he returned with his reputation much enhanced. William Rufus's death in 1100 gave Robert a second opportunity to take the English throne, and the following year he invaded but withdrew rather than risk battle. At Tinchebrai in Normandy in 1106 he was captured by another brother, HENRY I, and remained his prisoner until he died in 1134. He is buried in Gloucester Cathedral.

ROBERT II (also known as Robert the Steward) (1316–90), King of Scots (1371–90). As son of Walter the Steward and of Marjory, daughter of ROBERT BRUCE, he was recognized as heir presumptive in 1318, but the birth of David Bruce (the future DAVID II) meant he had to wait more than 50 years before finally becoming the first Stewart king in 1371.

In the meantime he was made guardian of Scotland in David's absence in 1338 and again following the King's capture at the Battle of Neville's Cross (Co. Durham) in 1346, until he was freed in 1357. Not surprisingly, relations between King and heir presumptive, who had fled from Neville's Cross, remained troubled but, after the abortive rising of 1363, Robert bided his time.

After his succession at the age of 55, he proved to be a lax ruler, whose lack of interest in soldiering made him an ineffective leader once border warfare had been renewed on the death of EDWARD III in 1377. In 1384 he handed over responsibility for law and order to his eldest son John (later ROBERT III), but four years later he acquiesced in the appointment of his more energetic second son Robert, Earl of Fife, as guardian of the realm. He fathered at least 21 children, among them five legitimate sons.

ROBERT III (?1336–1406), King of Scots (1390–1406). When he succeeded to the throne, he took the name Robert in preference to his given name John. As King, he continued to play the prominent yet ineffective role which as the Earl of Carrick he had played during the reign of his father ROBERT II. In 1399 this led to the three-year appointment of his eldest son David, Duke of Rothesay, as King's Lieutenant and to quarrels between Rothesay and the King's uncle, Robert, Duke of Albany. Rothesay's arrest and death in 1402 resulted in rumours that Albany, who succeeded him as Lieutenant, had also been responsible for his murder. In 1406 the King decided to send his eldest surviving son (later JAMES I) to France but the boy was captured by the English and sent to the Tower. The following month Robert III died. According to BOWER, he asked that he be buried in a midden (dunghill) as 'the worst of kings and most wretched of men'.

ROBERT BRUCE, KING see essay on pages 688–89

ROBERT CURTHOSE see ROBERT II

ROBERT, GRUFFUDD (?–after 1585), writer. An energetic Archdeacon of Anglesey, he was deprived after ELIZABETH I's accession, went into exile, studied at Siena and served as a priest and theologian in Milan. In 1567 he published a pioneering treatise on Welsh grammar, with the aim of improving what he saw as the decadence of contemporary Welsh poets and writers (see Edmwnd PRYS). He also wrote a devotional manual in Welsh (1585). His prose style is much admired.

ROBERT OF BELLÊME (fl. 1077–1112). The most notorious of the Anglo-Norman magnates,

with a fearsome reputation for cruelty, he was the eldest son of Roger de Montgomery, Earl of Shrewsbury, and heir to his estates. Robert of Bellême was usually a loyal supporter of ROBERT II Curthose, Duke of Normandy, supporting him against WILLIAM I THE CONQUEROR in 1077, WILLIAM II RUFUS in 1087 and HENRY I in 1101–6. He did manage to co-operate with William Rufus after Robert Curthose's departure for the First Crusade but fell foul of Henry and was seized by him in 1112, remaining in prison until his death (date unknown).

ROBERT OF GLOUCESTER (1st Earl of Gloucester) (c. 1090–1147), illegitimate son of HENRY I. Created Earl in 1122, he became one of his father's most trusted advisers and the richest landowner in England. There is no evidence to support the theory that he was a candidate for the throne in 1135. Initially, he recognized STEPHEN, in 1138 transferring his allegiance to his half-sister, the Empress MATILDA; from then until his death he remained the mainstay of her party in England. His importance can be judged from the fact that Stephen was exchanged for him after they had both been captured in battle, Stephen at Lincoln (Feb. 1141), Robert a few months later at the rout of Winchester. A cultivated man, he was the patron of two of the greatest writers of twelfth-century Britain, GEOFFREY OF MONMOUTH and WILLIAM OF MALMESBURY.

ROBERT OF GLOUCESTER (fl. 1260–1300), historian. According to the opening lines of his verse Chronicle, completed c. 1300, 'England, I know, is a very fine land, the best of lands'. Written in English, they are the first lines of English (as opposed to Lawman's British) history written in that language since the ending (in the 1150s) of the Anglo-Saxon Chronicle. His account comments on the consequences of the Norman Conquest.

ROBERT OF JUMIÈGES (?–c. 1053), Bishop of London (1044–51) and Archbishop of Canterbury (1051–2). Robert of Jumièges was one of a small number of Normans who came to England with EDWARD THE CONFESSOR in 1041. An intimate counsellor of the King, his scheming and his elevation to Canterbury fuelled a civil war in 1051–2 between Edward and the family of EARL GODWINE of Wessex. Robert was the ambassador who promised the succession to Duke William of Normandy (the future WILLIAM I THE CONQUEROR) in 1051. He left England after Godwine's triumphant return, and died soon afterwards. Because he did not resign Canterbury before he departed, his successor STIGAND was perceived by the Papacy as a usurper.

ROBERT BRUCE (ROBERT I) (1274–1329)
King of Scots (1306–29)

On 10 Feb. 1306 Robert Bruce killed John COMYN of Badenoch, in the Greyfriars' church at Dumfries. With this act of sacrilege and murder, he catapulted himself to the forefront of the Scottish political stage at a time when EDWARD I had at last completed, or so it seemed then, the English conquest of Scotland.

Whatever he had hoped to gain by the meeting with John Comyn, the extent of the ambition long simmering within him was now revealed. If Edward would not protect him against the furious anger of the Comyns and their allies, Bruce would have to claim the throne of Scotland for himself.

Six weeks later, on the first available feast day, the feast of the Annunciation, 25 March 1306, Bruce was enthroned at Scone, a ceremony all the more telling as a symbol of national defiance because every Scot knew that Edward had removed the Stone of Scone. Few Scots would risk helping a murderer against the vastly superior power of the King of England.

At the Battle of Methven, in June 1306, Bruce's followers covered their heraldic devices with white cloth; not surprisingly, knights so afraid of being identified were routed by the English. More defeats followed, as Bruce withdrew westwards. In Aug. the last remnant of his army was scattered by Comyn's friends the MacDougalls of Argyll. Bruce and a few followers 'took to the heather'. He found his way by hill tracks and glens to the Castle of Dunaverty at the tip of the Mull of Kintyre. In Sept. the English Lords Percy and Clifford smashed their way into the castle but found that Bruce had gone. For the rest of that year the fugitive disappeared from view, entering the legendary world of caves and spiders.

The story of Robert's return to Scotland, of how he overcame each setback and won the initiative, of how by a mixture of patience and daring he recaptured nearly all the Scottish castles held by the English until at Bannockburn, in 1314, he at last felt strong enough to confront head-on the challenge of a full-scale invasion led by the King of England in person, is one of the great heroic romances of British history, all the more incredible for being true. And it is told as a romance in the earliest life of Bruce, John BARBOUR's epic poem, *The Bruce*.

In the end it became plain that Robert had fought not just for himself and his family, but for a greater cause, the survival of an independent Scotland, and it was this which lent dignity and grandeur to his own struggle. All this is summed up in the Declaration of Arbroath, the letter drafted in Bruce's chancery and sent to the Pope in 1320 in the name of the barons and free-holders of Scotland. 'Through God's grace we have been set free from countless evils by our most valiant Prince, King and Lord, the Lord Robert, who that his people and his heritage might be delivered out of the hands of enemies, bore cheerfully toil and fatigue, hunger and danger, like another Maccabeus or Joshua. We are bound to him for the maintaining of our freedom both by his right and his merits, as to him by whom salvation has been wrought unto our people, and by him, come what may, we mean to stand. Yet if he should give up what he has begun, seeking to make us or our kingdom subject to the King of England or the English, we would at once strive to drive him out as our enemy and a subverter of both his own right and ours, and we would make some other man who was able to defend us our King; for, as long as a hundred of us remain alive, we will never on any conditions be subjected to the lordship of the English. For we fight not for glory, nor riches, nor honours, but for freedom alone, which no good man gives up except for his life.' The total defeat of 1306 had marked the start of a personal and national recovery unparalleled in British history.

On his father's side Robert Bruce was, like his ancestors since the early twelfth century, a Lord of Annandale who also held lands in England, including a house in London and the pleasant suburban manor of Tottenham. His mother was Marjorie, heiress to the last Gaelic Earl of Carrick. His grandfather, Robert BRUCE the Competitor, had been a claimant to the Scottish throne in 1292 when Edward I first seriously threatened Scotland's traditional independence and asserted English overlordship, taking advantage of the fact that he had been asked to arbitrate the disputed succession, the so-called Great Cause.

Robert first joined the Scottish resistance movement in 1297, when Edward's own choice as King, JOHN BALLIOL, had been first humiliated and then comprehensively defeated by the English King. However, in 1301–2, when Balliol's fortunes seemed to be on the point of reviving, Bruce returned to the English allegiance, and was given a wife, Elizabeth, daughter of Richard de BURGH, Earl of Ulster, one of Edward I's strongest supporters.

Over the next few years Scottish independence became an increasingly lost cause: Stirling surrendered and WALLACE was captured. In this period Robert, who inherited his father's estates in 1304, seemed to be a loyal agent of the victorious English, employed as Sheriff of Lanark and Ayr. His bid for the throne in Feb. 1306 took everyone by surprise.

While in hiding he appealed for help to the Macdonalds and the Stewarts (enemies of the MacDougalls), and to the Irish. With men and galleys raised in the Western Isles he returned to mainland Scotland early in 1307.

Edward I's brutal and counter-productive policy of treating Scots not as honourable enemies but as rebels gave Bruce a chance, but his own family paid a terrible price; three brothers and three brothers-in-law were captured and put to death. By the summer he was once again a fugitive, hunted by MacDougall bloodhounds. His prospects still looked bleak when Edward I died in July 1307.

The succession of EDWARD II quickly reduced English political society to a state of disarray from which it would not begin to recover until after Robert's death. Still, English resources remained greater and the Scottish aristocracy remained bitterly divided. Bruce's future was far from assured. Everything depended upon his ability to wage war against Scots and English alike.

His usual strategy was the conventional one of plundering and burning rather than fighting battles. To save their lands from destruction many Scots were persuaded, or compelled, to join the murderer's cause. At Inverurie in 1308 he won his first important action, defeating the partisans of Comyn and Balliol and then using their confiscated estates to reward Thomas RANDOLPH and James DOUGLAS (who was to carry Bruce's heart into battle against the 'Saracens' of Granada).

In 1311 he launched the first of the great raids into northern England which turned the war of Scottish independence into a profitable enterprise. Shortage of fodder in Scotland meant that major English forces were sent there only in summer. When they arrived Bruce's adherents retreated into the Highlands or the forests of Selkirk and Ettrick.

To hold Scotland the English depended on castles and as early as 1306 Bruce had shown a crucial readiness to discard convention: rather than try to hold castles against superior English siege technology, he systematically demolished them, both his own and those captured, usually by stealth or surprise, from the English. By Nov. 1313 he felt strong enough to announce that his enemies had one year in which to acknowledge him or suffer perpetual disinheritance. This forced Edward II's hand. If his already disheartened Scottish supporters were not to defect *en masse* he had to make a major effort. Hence he led a great army to the relief of Stirling Castle. His captains expected the Scots to retreat as usual, and so on 23–4 June 1314 at Bannockburn they made crucial tactical mistakes which tempted Bruce to risk battle, a gamble which paid off handsomely. This was a huge triumph, the only time in history that an English army led by a King of England in person was defeated by the Scots.

This victory enabled him to open up another front with his brother EDWARD BRUCE's 1315–18 invasion of Ireland, appealing to pan-Gaelic patriotism.

Another gain from Bannockburn was the consequent exchange of prisoners, which enabled him to recover captives held since 1306, above all his wife, a matter of vital importance for the survival of an independent kingdom under his dynasty since in 1314 he still lacked a son. Further raids on England increased the pressure on the English; in 1318 he recaptured Berwick, at that time Scotland's largest town. Despite the fine words of the 1320 Declaration of Arbroath his position was still not unassailable; in the same year he faced and ferociously suppressed a conspiracy to put William de Soules on the throne. However by the time of the Cambuskenneth Parliament (1326), an innovative grant of taxation and the settlement of the succession on his long-awaited legitimate son, DAVID II, suggested that the new dynasty was at last firmly established.

One more attack across the border finally brought recognition of Bruce's kingship from an enfeebled English government. The Treaty of Northampton (1328) marked the re-establishment of an independent Scotland. Edward II's incompetence and Scottish patriotism had been brilliantly exploited by Bruce's active and shrewd leadership.

G. W. S. Barrow, Robert the Bruce (2nd edn, 1976)

ROBERT THE STEWARD *see* ROBERT II

ROBERTS, FREDERICK SLEIGH ('BOBS') (Earl Roberts of Kandahar, Pretoria and Waterford) (1832–1914), soldier. Son of an East India Co. general, educated at Eton, Sandhurst and Addiscombe, and commissioned into the Bengal Artillery in 1851, he fought in the Indian mutiny, winning the Victoria Cross in 1858, served on the North West Frontier in the early 1860s and was chief logistician for Robert NAPIER's expedition to Abyssinia in 1867. Widely regarded as an administrative genius, Roberts commanded the force sent to Afghanistan (1878–80), his march from Kabul to Kandahar making him as famous as Garnet WOLSELEY, with whom a fierce rivalry soon developed, as both men sought to promote the young officers who comprised their respective 'rings'. Roberts narrowly missed command in the First Boer War (1880–1) and was Commander-in-Chief in India (1885–93) and Ireland (1895). After 'Black Week' he took over command in the Second Boer War (1899–1900) and defeated Boer armies in the field before handing over to KITCHENER. Appointed Commander-in-Chief of the Army (1900–4). Roberts devoted his last years to campaigning for the introduction of national service, the continuation of compulsory military service for all males over 18.

ROBERTS, RICHARD (1789–1864), inventor. Born in Montgom., after an elementary education, Roberts was employed in quarries and as a pattern-maker and mechanic. In 1814 he began developing engineering skills under Henry MAUDSLAY in London and two years later founded an engineering firm in Manchester, where he excelled in the manufacture of machines for the textile industry and made an improved version of Maudslay's screw-cutting lathe and a metal-planing machine. He is known for patenting the self-acting spinning mule (1825), a machine that was regarded as an improvement on CROMPTON's spinning mule of 1779. In 1828 he went into partnership with Thomas Sharp and for the next 15 years built and sold spinning mules, textile machinery, locomotives and steam carriages.

ROBERTS, WILLIAM (1806–71), lawyer. Having qualified as a solicitor in 1828 and practised in Bath, Manchester and London, Roberts became involved in Chartism in Bath in 1838. He became legal adviser to Feargus O'CONNOR's land scheme and, in 1844, to the Miners' Association of Great Britain and Ireland, the first trade union to use the law courts systematically to defend its members' interests. It was largely as the miners' representative that Roberts stood, though unsuccessfully, as a parliamentary candidate for Blackburn (Lancs.) in 1847. Subsequently he continued his legal work and became an active radical lecturer in Manchester in the early 1860s, supporting the North in the US Civil War (1861–5) and the Reform League campaign for votes for working men (1865–7). He also assisted Ernest JONES in his defence of the Fenians in 1867.

ROBERTSON, SIR DENNIS (1890–1963), economist. He was a pupil and later a collaborator of KEYNES at Cambridge but became one of Keynes's foremost critics after the publication of *The General Theory of Employment, Interest and Money*, seeing Keynes's policy prescriptions as essentially inflationary. Like Keynes's, his field was monetary theory and he made a major contribution to the analysis of business cycles in *A Study of Industrial Fluctuation* (1915) and *Banking Policy and the Price Level* (1926). He was Professor of Economics at the University of London (1939–44) and returned to Cambridge as Professor in 1944. He served on the Royal Commission on Equal Pay (1944) and was one of the original 'three wise men' who constituted the Council on Prices, Productivity and Incomes (1957–9).

ROBERTSON, WILLIAM (1721–93), historian. A minister's son, he was educated at Edinburgh University before becoming a prominent Church of Scotland minister himself. From 1750 he was the leader of the 'moderate' party in the General Assembly. Robertson published the *History of Scotland during the Reigns of Queen Mary and of King James V* in 1759. The first edition sold out in a month and took the English literary scene by surprise with its elegant prose and non-partisan approach to the writing of history. Robertson's rewards included the positions of Principal of Edinburgh University (1762), Historiographer Royal, and Moderator of the General Assembly of the Church of Scotland (1763).

ROBERTSON, SIR WILLIAM (1860–1933), soldier. Son of a Lincs. tailor, he enlisted in the 16th Lancers in 1877, and quickly impressed his Colonel with his intelligence and leadership potential. In 1888 Robertson joined the 3rd Dragoons in India as a 2nd Lieutenant. Specializing in Indian languages, he distinguished himself in scouting operations on the North West Frontier, was seriously wounded, appointed to the Distinguished Service Order (DSO), and in 1896 became the first ranker to attend Staff College. Colonel George Henderson, the college's Professor of Military History, took Robertson to South Africa in 1900 as part of his intelligence unit. Appointed Commandant of Staff College in 1910, by 1914 Robertson was Quartermaster General to the British Expeditionary Force, and in Dec. 1915 was appointed Chief of the Imperial General Staff. He clashed with Prime Minister LLOYD GEORGE's plans to divert forces to secondary theatres away from the Western Front. Forced to resign early in 1918, Robertson was appointed to command the British Army of the Rhine in 1919, and in retirement wrote *Soldiers and Statesmen*, an account of his experience of civil–military relations which is still required reading in most Staff Colleges.

ROBEY, GEORGE (1869–1954), entertainer. Topping the bill as the King of Mirth, Robey made his music-hall début in 1891. After the First World War he started appearing in reviews, pantomime and straight plays, playing Falstaff in *Henry IV, part two* (1945) and appearing in the film version of *Henry V* with Laurence OLIVIER (1945), but it is as a music-hall star in a long frock-coat and bowler hat and with beetling eyebrows that he is best remembered.

ROBINSON, FREDERICK (Viscount Goderich, 1st Earl of Ripon) (1782–1859), politician and Prime Minister (1827–8). He entered Parliament in 1806 as a liberal Tory, and held office as Under-Secretary for the Colonies (1809), Vice-President of the Board of Trade (1819–22) and Chancellor of the Exchequer (1823–7). He served as Prime Minister following the death of George CANNING in Aug. 1827, but was indecisive and incapable of preserving the frail coalition of Canningite Tories and aristocratic Whigs. He resigned in Jan. 1828 after less than five months in office. He subsequently served under Charles GREY and Robert PEEL as Colonial Secretary, Lord Privy Seal and President of the Board of Trade.

ROBINSON, GEORGE (1st Marquess of Ripon) (1827–1909), Viceroy of India. The first viceroy to have served as both Under-Secretary and Secretary of State at the India Office (1861 and 1866–73), he resigned on converting to Roman Catholicism. Re-entering political life with GLADSTONE's 1880 electoral victory, he was appointed to rule India: it was hoped that he would mend the fences broken by his predecessor, LYTTON. Peace was negotiated in Afghanistan, while liberalizing measures were introduced in education, factory work and public health. These were only partially successful, given administrators' unwillingness to implement them; there was a political storm with the passage of the Ilbert Bill in 1883, giving to Indian judges criminal jurisdiction over Europeans. Ripon left the following year, given an emotional farewell by Indians and the cold shoulder by the white population.

ROBINSON, JOAN (1903–83), economist. A graduate of Girton College, Cambridge, she was one of the few females of her generation to make an impact on a notoriously male-dominated profession. She was a student and later a post-graduate collaborator of KEYNES in the 1930s and was Professor at Cambridge (1965–71). Politically left of centre: her *Essay in Marxian Economics* (1942) showed how Keynesian analysis could inform and improve on Marxist ideas on the instability of capitalism. She made original contributions to the development of economics in the *Theory of Imperfect Competition* (1933) and extended Keynesian theories to economic growth in *The Accumulation of Capital* (1956). Her *Economic Philosophy* (1963) remains one of the most accessible introductions to the methodology of economics.

ROBINSON, JOHN (c. 1575–1625), churchman. He seems to have studied at Cambridge; he left the ministry of the official Church to join a Separatist congregation at Scrooby (Notts.), which in 1608 went into Netherlands exile to avoid persecution. He taught in Leiden University, but when his exiled group objected to Leiden's prevailing hostility to strict Calvinism, he encouraged migration to the New World. These were the Pilgrim Fathers who sailed in the *Mayflower* in 1620. Robinson was unable to accompany them, but continued to encourage them; he died at Leiden.

ROBINSON, JOHN (1650–1723), diplomat and churchman. From a humble background, he left Oxford University in 1680 to become chaplain to the English embassy to Sweden, eventually becoming Ambassador himself. He was close to both Charles XI and Charles XII and in 1700 negotiated the renewal of the Treaty of the Hague which guaranteed free navigation in the North Sea. Dean of Windsor (1709) and Bishop of Bristol (1710), he became Lord Privy Seal in Robert HARLEY's ministry in 1711 with the task of negotiating the Treaty of Utrecht. Robinson successfully detached Britain from her allies and signed the treaty with the Bourbons in 1713, securing much of what is now Canada, with the exception of Quebec, for Britain, plus Gibraltar and Minorca. With the accession of GEORGE I his promotion prospects dwindled but he managed to evade the impeachment proceedings that ensnared Harley.

ROBINSON, JOHN (1727–1802), administrator. An attorney and Mayor of Appleby (Westmld.), he entered Gray's Inn in 1759. Marriage and inheritance made him wealthy; elected MP for the county in 1764, he later fell out with his patron, Sir James Lowther, but found an alternative seat in the Treasury borough of Harwich. Made Secretary to the Treasury by NORTH from 1770 to 1782, Robinson occupied a crucial place within the government's patronage machine. His elaborate lists, analysing the likely outcomes of General Elections, have shed light for modern historians on both the extent and limits of the political influence of eighteenth-century administrations. The phrase 'before you can say Jack Robinson' has its origins in a parliamentary joke at Robinson's expense: asked in debate to name the man whom he had charged with seducing opposition members into government ranks, the Whig SHERIDAN retorted that he could name the man 'as soon as I could say Jack Robinson'. Robinson can be seen as a proto-typical civil servant; he probably regarded himself as, above all, a loyal servant of the King.

ROBINSON, MARY ('PERDITA') (née Darby) (1758–1800), actress and writer. She moved to London from Bristol with her mother when quite young and gravitated towards the stage, but married a reckless lawyer when only 16. She published her first book of poems (1775) in an attempt to escape debtors' prison; she was released by the Duchess of Devonshire (see CAVENDISH, GEORGIANA) and GARRICK, who cast her as Ophelia and then as Perdita in *The Winter's Tale* (1779). She became the lover of the Prince of Wales (the future GEORGE IV) and then, in 1782, of Colonel Banastre Tarleton; he made her pregnant but a complicated miscarriage paralysed her from the waist down. Her stage career over, she turned to writing, bringing out more poems, several sentimental novels and calls for the social liberation of women.

ROBINSON, MARY (née Bourke) (1944–), President of Ireland and feminist. From a Catholic upper-class family, she became a law professor (1969–75) and Senator (1969–89) for Trinity College, Dublin, who was known for advocacy of constitutional change aimed at changing the legal status of women and diminishing the social role of the Catholic Church, promoting such causes as the legalization of contraception. A member of the Labour Party (1976–85), she resigned in protest at the imposition of the Anglo-Irish Agreement without Unionist consent. In 1990 she was put forward as presidential candidate by the Labour Party, and won an unexpected victory through effective campaigning and the blunders of the other candidates. The victory of a candidate associated with the 'liberal agenda' was presented as a symbol of the changing ethos of Irish society. Robinson was an extremely active President, who raised the profile of an office whose powers are largely symbolic, and maintained links with a wide variety of community groups: significant initiatives included visiting Somalia to draw international attention to its civil war, publicly shaking hands with Gerry ADAMS at a delicate point in the peace process and becoming the first Irish President to visit the Queen. In 1997 she became United Nations High Commissioner for Refugees.

ROBINSON, SIR ROBERT (1886–1975), organic chemist. Robinson studied and researched chemistry at Manchester University, researched natural dyes under William Henry PERKIN JR and taught chemistry under the eminent organic chemist Arthur Lapworth. Alongside Lapworth, he formulated an electronic theory of organic reaction mechanisms, a theory challenged by Christopher INGOLD. He held professorial chairs at Sydney and several British universities, became the foremost expert on the structure and artificial biochemical synthesis of plant pigments and other natural products, won the Nobel Prize for Chemistry in 1947 and for much of his career was a consultant to Imperial Chemical Industries and a prominent figure in the Shell Chemical Co.

ROCHES, PETER DES (*c.* 1175–1238), royal servant. A native of Touraine who entered royal service in the 1190s, he was rewarded with the bishopric of Winchester in 1205; throughout JOHN's quarrel with the Papacy he remained loyal to the King. As Justiciar (1213–15) he bore some responsibility for unpopular policies, but as guardian (1216–21) to HENRY III he became a key figure in the minority government, demonstrating his military expertise at the Battle of Lincoln in 1217. Ousted by Hubert DE BURGH in 1227, he went on crusade, played a prominent role in the Holy Land, reforming the Order of St Thomas, and on his return persuaded the King to dismiss de Burgh. From 1232 he and Peter des Rivaux (who was either his son or his nephew) dominated the government, but des Roches's severity, reminiscent of John's arbitrary rule, led to his own fall from power only two years later.

As crusader, pilgrim to Santiago (1221) and founder of a Cistercian house, he was certainly not indifferent to religion, but his lifestyle made him vulnerable to criticism, 'sharp at accounting, slack at scripture', as one satirist put it. As the most prominent of the foreigners active in English politics, labelled the Poitevins by their opponents, he was an easy target.

ROCHESTER, EARL OF, 2ND see WILMOT, JOHN; **4TH** see HYDE, LAURENCE

ROCHFORD, BARON see BOLEYN, GEORGE

ROCKINGHAM, 2ND MARQUESS OF see WATSON-WENTWORTH, CHARLES, essay on page 815

RODDICK, ANITA (née Perella) (1942–), entrepreneur. The first branch of her hugely successful Body Shop chain was opened in Brighton (Sussex)

in 1976, selling a small range of toiletries and cosmetics in refillable containers. Born in Littlehampton (Sussex) of Italian parents, Roddick originally worked as a teacher. She devised with her husband Gordon the formula of natural environmentally friendly products and a policy of franchising outlets. By 1992 there were over 750 Body Shops in 41 countries; success spawned imitations, and the concern has made a less powerful showing since, but its style and product range caught the spirit of an age.

RODGERS, WILLIAM (BILL) (Baron Rodgers of Quarry Bank) (1928–), politician. General Secretary of the Fabian Society from 1955, Rodgers was on the Labour Right, and was recruited by the nascent Campaign for Democratic Socialism as a full-time organizer in 1960. He achieved some success in mobilizing support in the constituencies for Gaitskellite (see GAITSKELL, HUGH) social democratic parliamentary candidates, and by the time the campaign was wound up in 1963 Rodgers was himself MP for Stockton-on-Tees (Co. Durham). He held several junior ministerial posts under Harold WILSON and was James CALLAGHAN's Secretary of State for Transport (1976). Following Labour's lurch to the Bennite Left (see BENN, ANTHONY WEDGWOOD) in the wake of the party's 1979 election defeat, Rodgers joined Roy JENKINS, David OWEN and Shirley WILLIAMS in launching the Social Democratic Party (SDP). Being the least well known of the 'gang of four', the loss of his Stockton seat in 1983 forced his retreat from active politics. In the wake of the 1987 election defeat he was a strong supporter of the merger between the SDP and Liberal Party which created the Liberal Democrats, and since 1998 he has been leader of the Liberal Democrats in the Lords.

RODNEY, GEORGE (1st Baron Rodney) (1719–92), naval officer. From a military family, he joined the navy in 1732. His varied career included a period as Governor of Newfoundland, several victories in the Caribbean during the Seven Years War, and 31 years as an MP. His greatest victory was the Battle of the Saints, fought off the Iles des Saintes between Guadeloupe and Dominica, on 12 April 1782. His French opponent, Admiral de Grasse, had captured St Kitts, Montserrat and Nevis, and was escorting an invasion convoy to join the Spanish in an attack on Jamaica. After the battle, in which the French flagship surrendered, British possessions in the West Indies were secured and the invasion cancelled. At a time when the American colonies had clearly been lost, this victory ensured that the global war which had ensued would not be a disaster for Britain. News of the victory came too late to save NORTH's

ministry and prevent Rodney's dismissal, but on his return Rodney was compensated with a pension of £2,000 a year and a peerage.

ROEBUCK, J(OHN) A(RTHUR) (1801–79), politician. An outstanding orator, he moved from a youthful Benthamite radicalism (see BENTHAM, JEREMY) to the more moderate opinions expected of one who became a Privy Councillor in a Tory government. In his prime, however, he had played a significant role in expounding the issues and policies of mid Victorian radicalism, and in 1855 had pressed for a committee of inquiry into the mismanagement of the Crimean War, which led to the downfall of ABERDEEN's government.

ROGER OF HOWDEN (?–c. 1202), historian. He was parson of Howden (Yorks.) and author of the *Gesta Regis Henrici Secundi et Richardi Primi*, formerly attributed to Benedict of Peterborough, as well as of the *Chronica*, which has always been recognized as Roger's work. The two histories cover the period from the eighth century onwards; from 1170 to 1201 they provide what is by far the most detailed extant narrative, the indispensable chronological framework for all subsequent historians of the reigns of HENRY II and RICHARD I. He became a royal clerk c. 1170 and although it was once thought that he left royal service in 1192 to work for Hugh de PUISET, Bishop of Durham, it is more probable that he continued to serve both Crown and Bishop until his death. His years in government service gave him access to many official letters. Without his habit of giving texts in full, very little would be known of English legislation and administration. His history covers much more than just England. He became an expert in Anglo-Scottish relations and a canon of Glasgow Cathedral. On crusade he went to Sicily and the Holy Land. Other diplomatic journeys took him to the papal curia, France, Scotland and (probably) Ireland, making him the most widely travelled of all medieval English historians, and one whose work reflects that range of interests.

ROGER OF SALISBURY (?–1139), royal servant. A Norman clerk in HENRY I's household, by 1101 he had become Chancellor and was nominated Bishop of Salisbury the following year. As an embryonic justiciar, he had general charge of financial and judicial business and, in the 1120s, headed the Council while Henry was in Normandy; he is often credited with the development of the Exchequer. He supported STEPHEN's succession but in 1139 the King suspected him of disloyalty and he and his family were arrested. He died a broken man, deprived of his wealth and castles.

ROGER OF WENDOVER (?–1236), historian. A monk of St Albans Abbey (Herts.), he founded the St Albans school of English history. After being dismissed from office as Prior of Belvoir (Leics.) for squandering the priory's resources, he concentrated on writing his *Flores Historiarum*, a chronicle of the period from the Creation to 1234. His work was continued by Matthew PARIS.

ROGERS, JOHN (*c.*1500–55), martyr. Cambridge-educated, while chaplain to the English community at Antwerp he met William TYNDALE and caught his evangelical enthusiasm. In 1537 he published the first entire English Bible, completing Tyndale's work, under the pseudonym Thomas Matthew. From 1548 he was in London as a parish minister until MARY I arrested him for defiantly preaching Protestant doctrine. He was the first Protestant whom Mary burned.

ROGERS, RICHARD (Baron Rogers of Riverside) (1933–), architect. Born in Florence and trained at the Architectural Association and Yale University, he was briefly in partnership with Norman FOSTER, and achieved international fame with his design, with Renzo Piano, for the *Centre National d'Art et de Culture Georges Pompidou* in Paris (1971–7), with its striking 'intestinal' aspect of structural and service functions enclosed in brightly painted exterior tubing; the exciting (though frequently criticized) building soon became a tourist attraction to rival the Eiffel Tower. With his next major commission, the headquarters of Lloyd's in the City of London (1978–86), he took a similar high-tech 'inside outside' approach to great effect. He also designed the European Court of Human Rights in Strasbourg (1989–95). A post-modern architect, not intimidated by traditional contexts, he has had a great influence on functionalism and the promotion of an industrial vernacular.

ROGET, PETER (1779–1869), lexicographer. An Edinburgh-trained doctor whose professional life was spent in medical and scientific research, Roget compiled *A Thesaurus of English Words and Phrases* (1852). A taxonomy of the vocabulary of its day by 'ideas', it went through 28 editions in his lifetime, and the editorship descended in the male line. It continues to be regarded by many today as an essential work of reference that fulfils its original brief. In the choice of synonyms, however, the *Thesaurus* reflects the cultural concerns of its age and current compilers, so inevitably each new edition causes controversy.

ROGNVALD BRÚASON (?–1047), Earl of Orkney (*c.* 1037–46). The son of Brúsi, Earl of Orkney, Rognvald spent many years fighting in the wars between CNUT and St OLAF for control of the kingdom of Norway. Returning to Orkney on his father's death, he shared power for about eight years with his uncle THORFINN THE MIGHTY before being driven out and eventually killed as a result of a quarrel. Rognvald's career was one of many classic Viking odysseys around the turbulent politics of northern Europe.

ROGNVALD OF MOER (*fl.* ninth century), Earl of Orkney. The saga tradition of the thirteenth century indicates that, in the second half of the ninth century, he received Orkney from the Norwegian King, Harold Finehair. Modern opinion, however, generally rejects this view, seeing it as a late tradition designed to demonstrate long-standing Norwegian authority over the islands. It is more plausible that Rognvald independently established his family's power there, perhaps in alliance with a Norse warrior from Dublin, such as OLAF THE WHITE. Rognvald's son Rollo founded what became the duchy of Normandy. The Scandinavian settlement on Orkney came to include parts of northern Scotland and sometimes lordship over the Western Isles. It remained subject to the kingdom of Norway until 1472. Rognvald was probably succeeded by his brother SIGURD THE MIGHTY.

ROLLE, RICHARD (also known as Rolle of Hampole) (*c.* 1300–49), writer. A Yorkshireman whose career is obscure, he probably studied at Oxford and possibly also in Paris at the Sorbonne. When he was 18 he decided to become a hermit and spent his later years near the Cistercian nunnery of Hampole (Yorks.). His writings were extensive and still influential during the sixteenth-century Reformation; they included biblical commentaries, English poetry and explorations of mystical experience.

ROLLS, CHARLES (1877–1910), manufacturer. Educated at Eton and Cambridge, he was wealthy enough to indulge in one of the new fads of the turn of the nineteenth century, the motor car. He opened a car agency in 1902 and set up business with Henry ROYCE in 1906. His driving exploits gave their hand-crafted cars a certain cachet but by 1908, the year production moved from Manchester to Derby, Rolls took up a new passion, flying. He resigned from Rolls Royce in 1910, and shortly after became the first Englishman to be killed in an aeroplane crash.

ROMILLY, SIR SAMUEL (1757–1818), law reformer. Son of a London Huguenot jeweller, Romilly was called to the Bar in 1783, and published pamphlets on the role of juries and need for criminal law reform in 1784 and 1786. Initially sympathetic to the French Revolution, he came to think that it had strengthened the cause of reaction more than that of reform. He was Solicitor General in the 'Ministry of All the Talents' in 1806–7. In opposition thereafter, he pursued the cause of law reform, and in 1808 and 1811 secured the passage of statutes removing the death penalty from particular offences. He published *Observations on the Criminal Law of England, as it Relates to Capital Punishment* in 1810–11. He also took part in the anti-slavery agitation and opposed the suspension of *habeas corpus*, the spy system and governmental repression. He committed suicide on the death of his wife in 1818.

ROMNEY, EARL OF *see* SIDNEY, HENRY

ROMNEY, GEORGE (1734–1802), painter. The son of a Lancs. builder and cabinetmaker and largely self-taught, he started practising in Kendal in 1757. Moving to London in 1762, he began to produce a series of portraits and conversation pieces in the neoclassical style. With Ozias HUMPHRY he travelled to Italy (1772–4), and on his return to London was able to deploy a more striking style to become the only serious rival to Joshua REYNOLDS as portrait-painter to fashionable society. By the late 1780s he was earning over £3,000 a year, despite his prices being lower than those of Reynolds or GAINSBOROUGH.

ROOTES, WILLIAM (1st Baron Rootes of Ramsbury) (1894–1964), manufacturer. Born into an engineering family in Kent, with his brother (later Sir) Reginald Rootes (1896–1977) he took joint managership of the family motor vehicle distribution business in 1919. Within 10 years the distributorship had grown into the largest in the country, by which time the brothers had also moved into manufacturing, acquiring the Humber, Hillman, Commer, Talbot and Sunbeam motor companies (1929–35). Reginald was the administrator, Billy Rootes the salesman. One of the Big Six British motor manufacturers, the firm tried to meet post-war American competition by introducing a new mass-market car, the Hillman Imp, that proved to be its undoing. Production began in 1963, but export difficulties and poor labour relations forced it to accept a progressive takeover by Chrysler from the USA that was under way at the time of its founder's death.

ROPER, MARGARET (née More) (1505–44), scholar. Eldest daughter of Sir Thomas MORE, her father was proud of her formidable learning, unequalled in a woman of her generation and cultivated by an exceptional educational programme; they maintained affectionate correspondence. She translated Eusebius and ERASMUS' *Treatise of the*

Paternoster, and wrote in Latin and Greek. She married the ecclesiastical lawyer William Roper *c.* 1525; he wrote a life of More which touchingly describes her interviews with her father while he was prisoner in the Tower.

RORY O'CONNOR *see* RUAIDRÍ UA CONCHOBAIR

ROSE, SIR MICHAEL (1940–), soldier. Born in India to a British military family, educated at Oxford, the Sorbonne and Sandhurst, Rose was commissioned into the Coldstream Guards in 1964. After service with the Special Air Service (SAS) in Malaya in the 1960s and Oman in the 1970s, he commanded the SAS regiment in the Iranian embassy siege in London in 1980 and in the Falkland Islands in 1982, where he masterminded a psychological operation which helped break the will of the Argentinian commander Brigadier General Menendez. Appointed to command the UN Protection Force in Bosnia in Jan. 1994, Rose soon mastered the complexities of Balkan politics, but the uneasy peace he brokered was wrecked by the United States' building up Croat and Muslim military forces. Criticized in the American media as pro-Serb, Rose's period in Bosnia threw into sharp relief the problems inherent in post-Cold War intervention operations.

ROSEBERY, 5TH EARL OF *see* PRIMROSE, ARCHIBALD

ROSENBERG, ISAAC (1890–1918), poet and artist. The son of Russian-Jewish *émigré* parents, Rosenberg grew up in Whitechapel in the East End of London where his father was a market trader. He was apprenticed to an engraver in 1911, but a wealthy Jewish family became his patrons and he studied art at the Slade School. Encouraged by Ezra Pound, he published two collections of poetry and a play at his own expense, but in 1915 joined the army (though he came from a pacifist family): he was killed in the Battle of Arras on the Somme in April 1918. His poetry written on the Western Front, including *Break of Day in the Trenches*, was published with his letters and other writings in 1937, with an introduction by Siegfried SASSOON and edited by Gordon Bottomley, a poet who had also encouraged the young Rosenberg to write.

ROSS, 1ST DUKE OF *see* STEWART, JAMES

ROSS, SIR JAMES (1800–62), explorer. A noted explorer in both the Arctic and the Antarctic, in 1819 Ross joined Sir William Parry's Arctic voyages that ended in 1827. In 1831 he set out again, on an expedition to find the north-west passage led by his uncle Sir John ROSS (1777–1856), and on that journey he located the north magnetic pole. In 1832, although their ship was crushed by ice, the explorers escaped to safety. Ross's Antarctic expeditions of 1839–43 were undertaken to match his earlier achievement and find the south magnetic pole. In the course of his voyages he discovered the Ross Sea and Victoria Land and charted the Graham Land coast, but the pole eluded him.

ROSS, SIR JOHN (1777–1856), Arctic explorer. He joined the navy aged nine, served in the Napoleonic Wars, surveyed the White Sea and Arctic, and in 1818 led an expedition in search of the north-west passage. He led a further expedition in 1829–33 during which he discovered Boothia Peninsula, King William Land and the Gulf of Boothia, so called after the wealthy distiller who financed the project.

ROSS, SIR RONALD (1857–1932), physician. Born in India, Ross studied medicine in London and worked for the Indian Medical Service (1881–99), where he began studying malaria. In 1894, having become acquainted with Patrick MANSON and his work on the causes of malaria, he began his laborious search for the malarial parasite in mosquitoes. By 1900 he had established that malaria was transmitted by the *Anopheles* mosquito and elucidated the life-cycle of the parasite of avian malaria (similar to human malaria) from development within a mosquito to transmission, via a mosquito bite, to a bird. In 1899 he returned to Britain, where he worked on the eradication of malaria, held several academic positions and was awarded the 1902 Nobel Prize for Physiology or Medicine (although who first discovered the causes of malaria was disputed). He founded the Ross Institute of Tropical Diseases in Putney in 1926.

ROSSETTI, CHRISTINA (1830–94), poet. For Edmund GOSSE, Rossetti was 'a wonderful woman who stands almost alone in the forefront of the world's female poets'; for her brother, the Pre-Raphaelite artist Dante Gabriel ROSSETTI, she was the model for his painting of the Virgin Mary, *Ecce Ancilla Domine* (1850). She was considered too frail to work as a governess. As an Evangelical Christian deeply attracted to Anglo-Catholicism, she declined to marry men who she felt did not share her precisely calibrated religious faith.

At first her poetry was privately printed and she contributed a number of poems under a pseudonym (Ellen Alleyne) to *The Germ*, the Pre-Raphaelite journal edited by her brother. *The Prince's Progress and other Poems* came out in 1866, and *Sing-Song: A Nursery Rhyme Book* in 1872. Her collection, *Goblin Market, Prince's Progress and Other Poems* (1875), which included 'Christmas Carol' (better known by its first line, 'In the bleak mid-winter'), made Rossetti briefly the toast of literary London, and critical interest in *Goblin Market*, an unnerving fairy story, has been reawakened in the twentieth century. For 10 years she was an associate of St Mary Magdalen's 'House of Charity', a refuge in Highgate for single mothers and prostitutes.

ROSSETTI, DANTE GABRIEL (1828–82), poet and painter. The son of an Italian political exile, he spent an unfulfilling time at the Antique School of the Royal Academy before, in the autumn of 1848 (the year of revolution in Europe), joining with six others (including his brother William, John Everett MILLAIS and William Holman HUNT) to found the Pre-Raphaelite Brotherhood (PRB). It was a revolt against the formalism that was endemic in English painting, seen as meretricious, stale and imitative, and exemplified by the 'grand paintings' of Sir Joshua ('Sir Sploshua') REYNOLDS. The members were devoted to authenticity, both in 'painting nature as it is around them' and in restoring to art its moral purpose and painting as it had been in the days before Italian Renaissance painter Raphael (1483–1520), with a visual brilliance and glowing colours. RUSKIN predicted that their art would be 'nobler than the world has seen for three hundred years'. Rossetti was generally recognized to be the guiding spirit, the 'planet' around which this gifted constellation spun.

His paintings included spiritual subjects such as *The Girlhood of Mary Virgin* (1849, the first painting which he exhibited) and the Annunciation, *Ecce Ancilla Domini,* and scenes from medieval myth and allegory, including frescos based on Thomas MALORY's *Morte d'Arthur* on the walls of the Oxford Union.

Rossetti's symbolic poem, *The Blessed Damozel* (for which he painted a companion picture), was published in the PRB magazine *The Germ*. In his anguish and remorse at the death from an overdose of laudanum of his wife, Lizzie (*see* SIDDAL, ELIZABETH), he had thrown his collected *Poems* into her coffin but, persuaded by his friends of their value, he disinterred them and they were published in 1870. He also translated work from the Italian, *The Early Italian Poets* (1861) and *Dante and His Circle* (1874). But it is for his sensuous, glowing paintings and sketches that Rossetti, who died attacked as a 'fleshly poet', ill, depressed and reclusive aged 54, is generally considered the most outstanding of the Pre-Raphaelites.

ROTHERMERE, 1ST VISCOUNT *see* HARMSWORTH, HAROLD

ROTHSCHILD FAMILY *see* essay on page 698

ROTTEN, JOHNNY (originally John Lydon) (1956–), singer. Lead singer of the Sex Pistols, the most notorious of the punk rock bands of the mid 1970s, Rotten was 'discovered' by the impresario Malcom MCLAREN and became vocalist and front man for the band, which also included Sid Vicious. The Sex Pistols were the quintessential punk band, and Rotten the archetypical punk singer, with his trademark snarl and sneering singing style. After being dropped by two major record companies, they were signed by the little-known label Virgin (owned by Richard BRANSON), which released their single *God Save the Queen* during the Silver Jubilee celebrations (1977). Banned by the BBC, it reached number two in the charts and secured success for their second album, *Never Mind the Bollocks – Here's the Sex Pistols*. The band's controversial US tour in 1978 saw the departure of Rotten, who left to form his own band, Public Image Ltd, which enjoyed considerable success in the early 1980s.

ROTZ, JEAN (*c.* 1505–*c.* 1560), cartographer and spy. His father was a Scotsman (surnamed Ross) who had migrated to Dieppe. He voyaged to West Africa, Brazil and perhaps the East Indies; in 1542 he entered HENRY VIII's service as royal hydrographer. He devised navigational instruments and presented Henry with a superb illustrated atlas which includes what may be a representation of Australia. In 1547 he became a spy for France, returning to Dieppe and supplying maps of Britain and military information to the French government.

ROUBILIAC, LOUIS FRANÇOIS (1695–1762), sculptor. Born in France, he studied at Lyon. He emigrated to England some time before 1738 when his statue of HANDEL was erected at Hyde Park Corner. Rapidly coming to rival RYSBRACK in popularity, his other works included a bust of POPE for Bolingbroke (*see* ST JOHN, HENRY), several busts and a statue of NEWTON for Trinity College, Cambridge, and a number of monuments at Westminster Abbey. Like HOGARTH and HAYMAN, he contributed to the decoration of Vauxhall Gardens, including a further and more famous statue of Handel.

ROWLAND, ROLAND ('TINY') (originally Roland Furhop) (1917–98), entrepreneur. Taking over a near defunct company, Lonrho (London & Rhodesian Mining & Land) in 1961, Tiny Rowland built it into one of the largest of the world's trading conglomerates over the course of the following 30 years. His business methods were not always approved – Edward HEATH described him in 1971 as 'the unacceptable face of capitalism' – but his success was evident. The son of a German trader father and a British mother, he was born in an internment camp in India. In the Second World War he served in the army before again being interned; he then established himself as a company fixer. Asked to take on Lonrho, he acquired assets (mostly in Africa by making partnerships with newly independent nations) and eventually built a massive trading company stretching from Caribbean resorts to the *Observer* newspaper. Heath's judgement on him arose from the revelation of Lonrho's business methods and the bribery of Duncan SANDYS, its Chairman and a Conservative politician; the board sacked Rowland but he regained control by engineering a shareholder revolt. His running battle with the al-Fayed brothers over their purchase of the House of Fraser (*see* FRASER, HUGH) and Harrods broke out into a public argument in the 1980s. By the early 1990s Lonrho's shine was tarnished: profits were falling and debts were mounting, and in 1992 Rowland sold a large stake to the hitherto little-known German property developer Dieter Bock, with whom he then shared the Chief Executive's role. Just before his death Rowland ended his quarrel with Mohammed al-Fayed.

ROWLANDS, DANIEL (1713–90), Methodist. The son of an Anglican clergyman from Cardigans. (now Dyfed), he turned to Evangelical preaching after he was ordained in 1735. In 1737 he met Howel HARRIS, who encouraged him to set up a society of converts. Rowlands became one of the leading figures in the Methodist Association founded in 1743 and originally centred around WHITEFIELD. His Calvinism led to a split from Harris in 1751. Rowlands continued to preach until the end of his life, despite his suspension from the Established Church in 1763.

ROWLANDSON, THOMAS (1756–1827), artist and caricaturist. Son of a failed merchant, he studied at the Royal Academy Schools and in Paris, as well as travelling widely elsewhere on the continent. His first exhibited works were history paintings, landscapes and portraits, but from 1784, needing money, he began to emulate the satirical drawings of his friend James GILLRAY and together they became the most effective popular graphic artists of the late eighteenth and early nineteenth centuries. Much of Rowlandson's output consisted of book-illustrations, including the topographical engravings that illustrate the *Microcosm of London* (1808) and the humorous drawings for William Combe's *Tours of Dr Syntax* (from 1798).

ROWLEY, WILLIAM (?1585–?1642), dramatist *see* FLETCHER, JOHN

ROTHSCHILD FAMILY
International bankers and art collectors

The great European Rothschild banking dynasty all descend from Mayer Amschel (1743–1812) of Frankfurt am Main and his wife Gutle (1753–1849). Mayer Amschel built up his banking fortune in the aftermath of the French Revolution. His five sons settled in the great financial centres of Europe (London, Paris, Vienna, Naples and Frankfurt) and each established banking houses that came to dominate international finance in the nineteenth century. A web of intermarriage and a firm commitment to Orthodox Jewry have maintained a strong sense of family identity to this day, while close communication between the various branches had always been a key to their success.

Of the five sons, the third, Nathan Meyer (1777–1836), struck out first on his own, moving to England c. 1798. He achieved swift success as a cotton textile trader in Manchester. Naturalized in 1806, he moved to London in 1810–11, where the firm of N. M. Rothschild & Bros (subsequently & Sons) became established as a leading merchant bank. The firm's earliest successes were in smuggling gold bullion into Europe and Nathan managed to get British government funds to Wellington (see WELLESLEY, ARTHUR) in 1814 and 1815. He had become 'the wonder of the City', bypassing BARING and other rivals, and principal financier to the British government. In the meantime, Nathan's four brothers were raised to the Austrian nobility. The English family had to wait for many years to receive similar recognition, even though Nathan saved the Bank of England in the midst of the 1825 banking crisis with a £10 million rescue operation. After Nathan's unexpected death in 1836, his eldest son Lionel (1808–79) succeeded him at the bank. Rothschilds became primary investors in railways and the family survived the 1848 revolutions in Europe: their financial resources were always pooled and no government could afford to let them go under.

Lionel and his English brothers long campaigned for political emancipation for Jews: in 1847 he and Mayer (1818–74) both stood for Parliament. Elected for the City of London Lionel was prevented from taking his seat because he refused to swear the oath as a Christian; only in 1858 through DISRAELI's brokering a compromise was Rothschild able to take his seat, though he took little active part in politics thereafter. The family also sought to gain recognition for Jews at the universities. Their fabled social life was underwritten by their establishment of a succession of country seats. Mayer built a grand house at Mentmore (Bucks.), to designs by Joseph Paxton in 1851; Anthony (1810–76) followed suit at Ascot (Berks.) in 1853; Lionel acquired Tring Park (Herts.) in 1872. Their cousin Baron Ferdinand

(1839–98), who had inherited the wealth of the Viennese branch, outdid them all with the treasure house he built at Waddesdon (Bucks.) after 1874.

When James (1792–1868), the last of the 'Frankfurt Five', died in France his generation had established itself as the wealthiest financial corporation the world had ever seen. The London bank's great coup was its financing of the British purchase of the Suez Canal shares in 1875. All the Rothschilds were avid collectors, and usually equally keen on blood sports, while a significant number became experts in zoology and horticulture. Nathan Mayer, or Natty, Lionel's son (1840–1915), was raised to the peerage as 1st Baron Rothschild in 1885 by GLADSTONE. He became one of the leading confidants of British politicians. In 1914 Natty's nephew Lionel (1882–1942) was personally refused permission to fight by GEORGE V, so great was the need felt for a Rothschild to continue in the government's financial service, but during the First World War the family's wealth was further increased through armaments investments and government loans.

Lionel and Anthony Gustav (1887–1961) led the bank in the somewhat complacent interwar years, although it was Anthony's tenacity that was to hold the bank together after 1940. Charles's son Victor (1910–90), 3rd Baron Rothschild in 1937, was expected to lead the bank, but he embarked instead on a great scientific and public career. He was infected by socialist ideas when at Cambridge along with BLUNT, BURGESS and others who subsequently became Russian agents. Speculation grew that Rothschild was the 'fifth man', the undiscovered Soviet traitor, but that speculation was ungraciously laid to rest by Margaret THATCHER in 1986. From 1971 Rothschild was the mainstay of the government think-tank, the Central Policy Review Staff, set up by HEATH.

With non-family blood brought into the bank by Anthony it had a considerable renaissance in the 1950s and thereafter (it was incorporated, and its partnership status was finally dissolved in 1970). Anthony's son, Sir Evelyn (1931–), and his cousin Jacob, 4th Baron Rothschild (1936–), have both enjoyed great success in the City. After tensions erupted between them, Jacob left in 1980 to expand the activities of the Rothschild Investment Trust. It became immensely successful in its own right, and eventually partnered the bid made by James GOLDSMITH for British American Tobacco. Jacob, Lord Rothschild since 1990, has also been a significant force in the world of the arts, as patron and administrator. Merger and acquisition business became the bank's bedrock, while in the 1980s and after Rothschilds have had considerable success in managing privatizations for the British and other governments.

Niall Ferguson, The House of Rothschild (2 vols, 1998)

ROWNTREE, JOSEPH (1836–1925), manufacturer, and **SEEBOHM** (1871–1954), manufacturer and social reformer. Rowntrees of York were, like their fellow Quakers the FRYS and CADBURYS, pioneers in indulging the British taste for chocolate. Joseph followed his father Joseph (1801–59) into the family grocery business, and in 1869 joined his brother Henry Isaac Rowntree (1838–83) in a cocoa and chocolate enterprise. The firm and their brand of cocoa became household names, while the brothers' Quaker principles made them pioneers in promoting labour welfare and education. Joseph's son Seebohm joined the family confectionery firm in 1889, became Chairman on his father's retirement in 1923 and remained on the board until 1941, by which time Rowntree was second only to Cadbury in the nation's chocolate sales. Seebohm was also a pioneer in social research. In 1897–8 in York he conducted one of the first scientific investigations of poverty, based on an estimation of nutritional requirements. This was followed by two further studies of York in 1936 and 1950 and other work. He was in charge of the welfare department of the Munitions Ministry (1915–18) and between the wars actively promoted family allowances and slum clearance.

ROXBURGHE, 5TH EARL AND 1ST DUKE OF see KER, JOHN

ROY, WILLIAM (1726–90), mapmaker. In 1746 he was appointed assistant to the Deputy Quartermaster General of Scotland to prepare a map of Scotland to assist in the extension of WADE's road-building projects and so strengthen government control of the Highlands. Roy's mapping, which was later applied to south-east England, was exceptionally detailed, with subtle but precise use of shading and symbols; his work led to the foundation of the Ordnance Survey in 1791. The Scottish maps are often used by historians in conjunction with Sir John SINCLAIR's *Statistical Account* and Alexander WEBSTER's population survey, as they depict Scotland on the verge of considerable economic change.

ROYCE, SIR HENRY (1863–1933), manufacturer. After a shaky beginning to his working life, caused partly by his farming father's failed business ventures in London, Royce formed a Manchester-based firm manufacturing electrical equipment and in 1904 switched to motor cars. The famous Rolls–Royce partnership followed in 1906, combining Royce's engineering skill with the salesmanship of Charles ROLLS. Royce had an obsession with quality and detail that he transferred into his cars and later his aero-engine designs. Rolls's untimely death had a great effect on him: Royce suffered a breakdown in 1911 and

although he continued to design he never visited the Derby factory again.

RUAIDRÍ UA CONCHOBAIR (RORY Ó CONNOR) (?–1198), High-King of Ireland (1166–83). In 1156 he succeeded his father TAIRD-ELBACH as King of Connacht and within 10 years was well enough established there to be able to exploit the sudden collapse of MUIRCHERTACH MAC LOCHLAINN's power. As the last high-king of an independent Ireland he drove DIARMAIT MAC MURCHADHA into exile, with the unforeseen consequence that he precipitated the English invasion of the island and the arrival of Strongbow (see CLARE, RICHARD DE), claiming to rule Leinster and Dublin as Diarmait's heir. In 1171 Ruaidrí brought together a large army and besieged Strongbow in Dublin but a surprise attack launched by the garrison, while Ruaidrí was bathing in the Liffey, drove his forces back in disarray. This was a decisive event. Not only was it a humiliating defeat for Ruaidrí, it was also sufficiently worrying to HENRY II to bring him to Ireland in 1171–2. On this occasion, from a safe distance in Connacht, Ruaidrí was one of the few Irish kings not to submit to the King of England. Soon, however, the turbulence of Irish politics (see DOMNALL MÓR UA BRIAIN) led him to see the advantages to be gained by coming to terms with the English. In the Treaty of Windsor (1175) Henry recognized Ruaidrí as King of Connacht and as overlord of all the Irish outside Henry's own acquisitions (Dublin and Waterford) and the English lordships of Leinster and Meath. To some extent this implied acceptance of Ruaidrí's high-kingship. Indeed Henry promised to help Ruaidrí against any Irish who would not obey him. In return Ruaidrí agreed to pay Henry one hide from every 10 rendered in tribute to him. The treaty was soon a dead letter, inevitably given the rapaciousness of the English newcomers and the fluctuations of native Irish politics. The marriage of Ruaidrí's daughter to Hugh de LACY (c. 1180) offered another way of coming to terms. In 1183 he retired to the monastery of Cong (Co. Galway) and his re-emergence two years later resulted only in a long power struggle in Connacht.

RUDD, JOHN (c. 1498–1579), cartographer. From Yorks., he became a Cambridge don and then Clerk of the Closet to HENRY VIII. His many Church benefices, in a career notable for conforming to every successive change of religion, financed his main activity, mapmaking; he may have been responsible for the map of the Holy Land in Miles COVERDALE's Bible (1535), and in 1561 he undertook a new map of England which is possibly the map of Britain in Gerardus Mercator's Dutch atlas of 1564. His assistant Christopher SAXTON produced England's first complete set of county maps in 1579.

RUGGLES-BRISE, SIR EVELYN (1857–1935), prison reformer. As Chairman of the government's Prison Commission from 1895 to 1921 Ruggles-Brise was a major force behind the reforms in prison conditions and penal methods which the Liberal governments of 1906–14 introduced. These included the development of the probation service in 1907, the extension of the period in which offenders could pay fines in 1914, thus helping to reduce the prison population, and he oversaw the reform of the conditions of prison labour and the training of prison staff. His most celebrated achievement was the Prevention of Crime Act 1908, which introduced the borstal system rather than prison for young offenders. It also introduced an extraordinary new principle into British penology: an offender sentenced to imprisonment after more than three previous convictions who was held to be 'persistently dishonest' was liable to between five and 10 years preventive detention, that is, could be imprisoned not for a crime already committed but for a crime which he *might* commit. The principle could not be effectively put into practice, and the Act was finally supplanted by the 1948 Criminal Justice Act.

RUNCIE, ROBERT (Baron Runcie of Cuddesdon) (1921–2000), Archbishop of Canterbury (1980–91). Educated at Oxford, Runcie served with the Scots Guards in the Second World War, winning the Military Cross. He was ordained at Westcott House, Cambridge, and became Principal of Cuddesdon College (Oxon.) (1960–9), and Bishop of St Albans (Herts.) from 1970 before being elevated to Canterbury in 1980. Runcie, who had a very academic manner, was essentially a conciliator when it came to the pressing questions of Church politics such as the ordination of women. He was a liberal Anglo-Catholic, although the Anglo-Catholics felt betrayed by his refusal to confront the ongoing liberalization of Church doctrine and practice. This resentment came to a head with the anonymous denunciation in *Crockford's Clerical Directory* in 1987, which accused Runcie of being an 'elitist liberal . . . taking the line of least resistance on each issue'. The author proved to be a former friend and Oxford academic, Dr Gary Bennett, who committed suicide over the furore that his article caused. Runcie's archbishopric will be remembered mainly for his frequent clashes with the Conservative governments of THATCHER, since Runcie supported the Church's right to speak out on social and economic issues; the Church's Commission on Urban Priority Areas (1985) argued that economic policies should be judged 'morally' and recommended a massive increase in public expenditure to alleviate poverty in the inner cities. Thatcher was also privately furious at Runcie's even-handed sermon at the service of thanksgiving for victory in the Falklands War in July 1982.

RUPERT OF THE RHINE (1619–82), prince and soldier. JAMES I's grandson, born in Prague while his father Frederick, the Elector Palatine, was briefly reigning as King of Bohemia. Homeless after Frederick was deposed by the Habsburgs, he began his military career in the Thirty Years War, but arrived in England in 1635. On the outbreak of the English Civil War in 1642, he was made Royalist General of the Horse, then Commander-in-Chief, also receiving the titles Earl of Holderness and Duke of Cumberland (1644). His military talents and experience gained in Europe were offset by his quarrelsomeness, and CHARLES I finally became disillusioned with him after the loss of Bristol, the last major Royalist stronghold, in 1645. Rupert then took command of the part of the navy which had come over to the Royalists, until it was dispersed by Robert BLAKE. He shared CHARLES II's exile, and after the Restoration undertook various naval and military commands. A man with an inquiring mind and artistic talent, he was an early member of the Royal Society founded in 1660 to promote investigations in the new science.

RUSHDIE, SALMAN (1947–), writer. Born to a Muslim family in Bombay and educated at Cambridge, Rushdie was engaged in various odd jobs before becoming a professional writer. He is considered among the leading exponents of Magical Realism. His attachment to India, and particularly Bombay, the strong sense of loss of country and city, informs all his writing, from his first novel *Grimus* (1975), a fantasy based on an ancient Sufi poem, through *Midnight's Children* (1981), winner of the Booker Prize, to *The Ground Beneath Her Feet* (1999). Rushdie's writings, grand in conception and scale, are embedded in a cosmopolitan and humanist tradition. This is particularly true of *The Satanic Verses* (1988), which was interpreted by Muslims as blasphemous. This brought upon him a *fatwa*, a sentence of death invoked by Ayatollah Khomeini in 1989. The book was burned in Muslim communities in Britain, and it provoked demonstrations in many Muslim countries. A number of the work's translators were killed, and Rushdie was forced into hiding under police protection. The *fatwa* was lifted in 1998.

RUSKIN, JOHN (1819–1900), art critic and social theorist. The only son of a well-to-do wine merchant family, Ruskin enjoyed extensive travel both before and after his time at Christ Church, Oxford, and acquired a lifelong love for French cathedrals, the Alps and northern Italy. In 1840 he first met J. M. W. TURNER, whom he defended vigorously in the first of his many books of art criticism, *Modern Painters, I* (1843). Ruskin singlemindedly developed a very personal brand of criticism, advocating a Venetian Gothic and the supremacy of medieval art, issuing a call for a return to medieval work values, and seeing art as a deep expression of morality. His best-known works remain *The Seven Lamps of Architecture* (1849) and *The Stones of Venice* (1851–3), which included the famous essay 'The Nature of Gothic'. He was a powerful supporter of the Pre-Raphaelites, while his diatribe against James WHISTLER, whose *Nocturne* he described in 1877 as 'flinging a pot of paint in the public's face' resulted in a celebrated libel suit. Ruskin had an unhappy and tempestuous love life; his first marriage to Effie Gray was annulled in 1854, and his passion for the young Rose La Touche went unrequited. After her death in 1875, Ruskin suffered increasing bouts of madness. For all the unhappiness of his private life, Ruskin was one of the most powerful artistic forces of the nineteenth century; he was himself a meticulous draughtsman of natural forms, and a critic who formed the sensibility of generations.

RUSSELL, BERTRAND (3rd Earl Russell) (1872–1970), philosopher. Grandson of Whig Prime Minister Lord John RUSSELL, he was orphaned as an infant and brought up by grandparents. Educated at home and at Cambridge, he produced thereafter a succession of important philosophical works. A lecturer at Trinity College, Cambridge, from 1910, his post was terminated in 1916 when he was convicted for his pacifist views. He was convicted again and jailed in 1918. Married four times (and with many lovers along the way), Russell's best-known marriage was to Dora Black in 1921: they founded an experimental school and although his involvement ended with the marriage in 1932 she continued the task alone. During the 1920s and 1930s Russell was a prolific, tireless advocate of progressive causes; his search to make ends meet bore fruit in a post at City College, New York, until the offer was overturned in a celebrated 1940 court case following vocal Catholic opposition. The lectures that he gave over the next two years at the Philadelphia college run by his rescuer, the maverick millionaire Albert Barnes, became his *History of Western Philosophy* (1945), the hugely successful book that solved his financial worries. He was awarded the Nobel Prize for Literature in 1950. In the new Cold War climate his outspoken disapproval of Soviet communism made him temporarily respectable, but his hatred for the system moderated after Stalin's death, while his condemnation of nuclear weapons increased. In 1958 he was a founder of the Campaign for Nuclear Disarmament, and then of the more radical direct action Committee of 100.

Russell's shock of white hair, his fame and his oratory gave him particular prominence: a last spell in gaol came in 1961, for inciting civil disobedience. He was politically active, notably against the war in Vietnam, up to his death.

RUSSELL, EDWARD (1st Earl of Orford) (1653–1727), politician. A nephew of John Russell, 1st Duke of Bedford, he followed a naval career. One of the 'Immortal Seven', he conspired with William of Orange (the future WILLIAM III), and accompanied him to England in 1688. He became a member of the Whig Junto, was made Treasurer of the Navy and Admiral in 1689 but by 1691 was hedging his bets by corresponding with JAMES II in exile. He was commander at the decisive victory over the French at La Hogue in May 1692, but was charged with having failed to take decisive measures to destroy the French fleet and dismissed. He was reinstated in 1693, and served as First Lord of the Admiralty in 1694–9, when his resignation, apparently because he was reluctant to labour on in the face of parliamentary criticism of ministerial policies, helped to bring down the Junto. He was among the Whig lords threatened with impeachment in 1701 over the partition treaties promoted by William as part of a plan to redistribute power in Europe on the death of the heirless Spanish King. The earldom became extinct upon his death but was revived for Robert WALPOLE, who had benefited in his youth from Orford's patronage.

RUSSELL, FRANCIS (6th [4th Russell] Earl of Bedford) (1593–1641), politician. A Puritan peer, he sponsored extensive fen drainage. He became one of the leading opponents of CHARLES I; in the 1640–1 crisis preceding the English Civil War, he worked closely with John PYM. His death lessened the chances of a compromise between Charles and his opponents.

RUSSELL, JOHN (3rd [1st Russell] Earl of Bedford) (?1485–1555), politician. A Dorset man, he entered court service after attending Philip of Burgundy and Joanna of Castile, who were wrecked off Weymouth in 1506 on their way to take the throne of Spain. Always on the winning side, Russell steadily rose through diplomatic, military and Household duties to become Lord Privy Seal (1542–55). On the way up, in 1550, he collected his earldom, as well as a staggering array of former Church lands.

RUSSELL, JOHN (7th [4th Russell] Duke of Bedford) (1710–71), politician. Scion of a great Whig family, he was educated at home, then went on a Grand Tour. He succeeded his brother as Duke in 1732. Rank and influence, the main basis of his claim to political power, allowed him to chart a semi-independent political course, to which his proud and obstinate character also inclined him. Having opposed Robert WALPOLE, and also CARTERET in 1744, he became First Lord of the Admiralty in PELHAM's Broad-Bottom Ministry. His supporters became known as the 'Bloomsbury gang' after Bedford's London estate; they included Gower (see LEVESON-GOWER, GRANVILLE), Weymouth (see THYNNE, THOMAS) and Sandwich (see MONTAGU, JOHN); from the 1750s their activities were co-ordinated by Richard RIGBY. In 1748 Russell became southern Secretary of State, allied himself with Cumberland (see WILLIAM, AUGUSTUS), and tussled with Newcastle (see PELHAM-HOLLES). He resigned in 1751 and with Alderman William Beckford started the essay paper, *The Protestor*. Made Lord Lieutenant of Ireland under PITT THE ELDER, he remained in office as Lord Privy Seal after Pitt's resignation (1761). He led the negotiations which resulted in the Treaty of Paris (1763), ending the Seven Years War. President of the Council under George GRENVILLE, he fell with that ministry in 1765. He opposed the Rockingham (see WATSON-WENTWORTH, CHARLES) ministry and its repeal of the Stamp Act. In 1766 negotiations designed to bring his supporters into the ministry of Chatham (as Pitt had become) were rebuffed by the King, but in Dec. 1767 they joined the Grafton (see FITZROY, AUGUSTUS) ministry without him. Failing sight and health limited his participation in public life thereafter.

RUSSELL, LORD JOHN (1st Earl Russell) (1792–1878), politician and Prime Minister (1846–52, 1865–6). A Whig MP from 1813, he represented the City of Westminster from 1843 to 1861, when he was created Earl Russell. A promoter of the abolition of the Test and Corporation Acts (1828) and an ardent advocate of parliamentary reform, he was largely responsible for drafting the 1832 Reform Act during his time as Paymaster General (1830–4), and he advocated further measures as a member of Aberdeen's (see GORDON, GEORGE) coalition government in 1852. He was Home and then Colonial Secretary before becoming Leader of the Commons in Melbourne's (see LAMB, WILLIAM) administration (1835–41). On PEEL's resignation in 1846 after the repeal of the Corn Laws, Russell became Prime Minister. Twice Foreign Secretary (under Aberdeen and Henry TEMPLE, Viscount Palmerston), he had an uneasy relationship with Palmerston, whom he had dismissed in 1852 over the latter's unauthorized recognition of Louis Napoleon's overthrow of the French Second Republic. Russell's record in foreign affairs, however, was chequered: he initially supported Britain's role in the Crimean War, but then resigned over its mismanagement; he was behind Piedmont in the struggle for Italian unification, aided COBDEN

in his efforts to conclude a Free Trade treaty with France, and introduced reforms in the foreign service in 1861. However, his handling, with Palmerston, of the *Alabama* affair during the American Civil War, when a British-built ship was allowed to fall into US Confederate hands, was potentially damaging to British–US relations. He became Prime Minister for a second time on Palmerston's death in 1865, but resigned in the same year when his government's proposals for further reform of the franchise were defeated by the revolt of the Adullamites led by Robert LOWE. A man of short stature and wide learning, 'Johnny Russell' was once reproved by his father, the 9th Duke of Bedford, for 'giving great offence to your followers in the House of Commons by not being courteous to them, by treating them superciliously, and *de haut en bas*, by not listening with sufficient patience to their solicitations or remonstrances'.

RUSSELL, RICHARD (1687–1759), physician. Best known for his support for Brighton as a spa resort, Russell's research centred on the use of sea water as a cure for glandular diseases: he advocated that it should ideally be drunk but that bathing in it was also beneficial. His writings helped to make visits to seaside resorts fashionable among the upper classes.

RUSSELL, WILLIAM (Baron Russell) (1639–83), politician. Son of John Russell, 1st Duke of Bedford, he was elected MP in 1660, and became associated with the Country opposition to the Catholicizing policies of the court. Married to a relative of the 1st Earl of Shaftesbury (see COOPER, ANTHONY ASHLEY), in 1675 he promoted an unsuccessful attempt to impeach Danby (see OSBORNE, THOMAS) and played a prominent part in the campaign for the exclusion of the Duke of York (later JAMES II) from the line of succession. In 1683 he was charged with complicity in the Rye House Plot (see FERGUSON, ROBERT) and, refusing to disavow a right of resistance, was convicted of treason and executed, along with Algernon SIDNEY.

RUSSELL, WILLIAM HOWARD (1820–1907), journalist. 'The first and greatest of war correspondents', reads the inscription on his memorial, and it was his reporting from the Crimean War (1853–6) for *The Times* that made his reputation and, in effect, brought down Aberdeen's (see GORDON, GEORGE) government. His twice-weekly despatches, which took 10 days to reach London, were a catalogue of indictments of the anachronistic army command structure and of military incompetence, with soldiers suffering and dying from the shortage of medical supplies. Russell subsequently reported on the Indian Mutiny, the American Civil War and the Zulu Wars. An Irishman he was a 'front-line'

continued on page 704

RUTHERFORD, SIR ERNEST (1st Baron Rutherford of Nelson) (1871–1937)
Physicist

The son of a New Zealand farmer and wheelwright, Rutherford graduated from Canterbury College, Christchurch, where he conducted research on the magnetization of iron by rapidly alternating electric currents, and on wireless waves. In 1895 he continued this research under J. J. THOMSON at the Cavendish Laboratory of Cambridge University, where in 1896 he began exploring the effect of the newly discovered X-rays on the discharge of electricity in gases. Shortly afterwards he studied the ionizing effects of the radioactive emanations or 'rays' recently discovered by Henri Becquerel and by Pierre and Marie Curie. This led to his distinction between 'alpha' and the less-powerfully ionizing but more penetrating 'beta' forms of radiation produced by uranium.

In 1898 Rutherford was appointed Professor of Physics at McGill University, Montreal, where he explored the radioactivity of thorium substances and by 1900 had identified a gaseous radioactive 'emanation' of thorium and 'active deposits' of thorium (thorium X) produced near the emanations. He also identified the highly energetic and penetrating 'gamma' form of radiation and showed that radioactive emanations, unlike the original elements, diminish in radioactivity over time. With the chemist Frederick SODDY he separated thorium X from thorium and found that, while thorium X lost its activity, thorium quickly regained its activity. This informed Rutherford and Soddy's sensational 1903 'disintegration' theory of radioactivity, which proposed that atoms in a radioactive element decay spontaneously into atoms of another element, and that the decay process is random and occurs in an average time-period unique to the decaying element. Their theory challenged the long-held idea that atoms are indestructible but was nonetheless rapidly and widely accepted by scientists. Later in 1903 Rutherford produced experimental evidence indicating that alpha particles are helium nuclei, a claim further supported by Soddy and W. RAMSAY's evidence that helium is produced when radium emits alpha particles during its radioactive decay. Between 1904 and 1907 Rutherford collaborated with Bertram Boltwood on the series of transformations undergone by radioactive elements and showed that decaying elements finish as lead.

In 1907 Rutherford was appointed Professor of Physics at Manchester University, where, shortly after arriving, he and the German physicist Hans Geiger developed sophisticated 'scintillation' apparatus for measuring the rate at which particles are emitted by radioactive material. With this apparatus and his own evidence that alpha particles generate helium, Rutherford confirmed that alpha particles are doubly charged helium ions. For this and his earlier work on disintegration, he was awarded the 1908 Nobel prize for chemistry. Subsequently he and his associates concentrated on the phenomenon of alpha-particle scattering in thin metal foils. In 1909 Geiger and Rutherford's student Ernest Marsden announced that some alpha particles had been deflected through an angle greater than 90°. Rutherford worked hard to explain this unexpected result and by 1911 believed he had done so with his revolutionary nuclear model of the atom, which proposed that an atom was mostly empty space and consisted of negatively charged electrons surrounding a tiny positively charged nucleus where most of the atom's mass was concentrated. His theory was coolly received at first but gained wide support after 1913. In this year the Danish physicist Niels Bohr showed that applying the new quantum mechanics to the theory enabled the correct prediction of the hydrogen spectrum, and one of Rutherford's students, Henry MOSELEY, showed that his own powerful experimental evidence for an 'atomic number' could be explained only by Rutherford's theory.

He continued to make decisive contributions to nuclear physics shortly before, during and after the First World War, when he worked on submarine detection for the Admiralty. In 1914 he showed that the positive rays of electrical discharge are hydrogen nuclei, and helped identify gamma rays as electromagnetic waves. More significantly, between 1917 and 1919, he showed that stable nitrogen nuclei disintegrate into hydrogen and oxygen nuclei when bombarded with alpha particles, which is regarded as the first artificial splitting of an atom. In 1919 he became director of the Cavendish Laboratory, which he transformed into the world centre of physics research and teaching and where he fostered some of the greatest scientific accomplishments of the twentieth century. For example, he predicted the existence of the neutron, for which his colleague James CHADWICK produced evidence in 1932, and he directed the construction of John COCKCROFT's and Ernest Walton's famous particle accelerator for disintegrating nuclei. His last researches at the Cavendish include his collaboration on the pioneering 'nuclear fusion' method of producing 'heavy water'. He was a prolific writer and his major works include *Radioactivity* (1904) and *Radioactive Substances and their Radiations* (1913). A towering figure in the history of science, Rutherford was rewarded for his research with a plethora of honours, including the presidency of the Royal Society (1925–30), the Order of Merit (1921) and a peerage (1931).

A. S. Eve, Rutherford (1939)
David Wilson, Rutherford: Simple Genius (1983)

man who earned the respect of those whose deeds he reported, and was injured in the line of duty; he also founded the *Army and Navy Gazette*, which he used to influence the defence policies of successive governments.

RUTHERFORD, DANIEL (1749–1819), scientist. Son of a physician, he studied medicine at Edinburgh under William CULLEN and Joseph BLACK. In 1772 he was the first to distinguish between carbon dioxide and nitrogen, although he believed the latter to be a compound of 'atmospheric air' and the supposed element 'phlogiston'. Rutherford's interests also included botany; he became Professor of Botany and Keeper of the Royal Botanic Gardens, Edinburgh, in 1786, while continuing to practise medicine.

RUTHERFORD, ERNEST *see* essay on page 703

RUTHERFORD, SAMUEL (*c.* 1600–1661), churchman. His university career at Edinburgh was interrupted in 1626 by sexual scandal, but soon afterwards an intense conversion experience took him into parish ministry. In 1636 he was punished by the High Commission for the extreme Calvinism expressed in his writings, but the revolution against CHARLES I brought renewed promotion. As a Scottish member of the Westminster Assembly (1643) he championed strict Presbyterianism, and wrote defending religious persecution against Jeremy TAYLOR (1649). Charged with treason in 1660 because of his attack on absolute monarchy in *Lex Rex* (1644), he died before a prosecution.

RUTHVEN, ALEXANDER (?1580–1600), alleged conspirator. Second son of William RUTHVEN, Earl of Gowrie, he studied at Edinburgh and became a Gentleman of the Bedchamber to JAMES VI and a favourite of ANNE OF DENMARK. In Aug. 1600 James claimed that Ruthven had attempted to kidnap him at Gowrie House; in the ensuing fight, Ruthven and his brother John, the 2nd Earl, had been killed. The details came from James himself; suspiciously, the affair brought destruction to the Ruthvens, strong supporters of the Presbyterian party which James was determined to curb, and his tormentors in the 1582 Ruthven Raid.

RUTHVEN, WILLIAM (2nd [1st Ruthven] Earl of Gowrie) (*c.* 1543–84), conspirator. He assisted his father Patrick, Lord Ruthven, in murdering RIZZIO and pursued the regime of MARY QUEEN OF SCOTS to destruction. Lord High Treasurer from 1571, he was prominent in the Regent Morton's government (*see* DOUGLAS, JAMES) and was made Earl in 1581. In Aug. 1582, he and John Erskine, 19th Earl of Mar, led Protestant noblemen in the Ruthven Raid, seizing JAMES VI to end the power of Esmé STUART, Duke of Lennox, and James STEWART, Earl of Arran. James escaped from Ruthven Castle in June 1583, his prejudice against Presbyterianism confirmed; Gowrie was executed.

RUTLAND, 9TH EARL AND 1ST DUKE OF *see* MANNERS, JOHN

RYLE, SIR MARTIN (1918–84), radio astronomer. Ryle studied physics at Oxford, and during the Second World War worked on radar. After the war he moved to the Cavendish Laboratory, Cambridge, where he built interferometers for studying solar and other astronomical radio emissions and established a world centre for radio astronomy. In 1960–1 he simulated from radio telescopes of large aperture by electronically synthesizing those from several small radio telescopes. Ryle's observations of radio galaxies challenged the accepted 'steady-state' theory of the universe propounded by HOYLE and others and supported the rival Big Bang theory. He shared the 1974 Nobel Prize for Physics with the radio astronomer Anthony Hewish.

RYSBRACK, JOHN MICHAEL (*c.* 1693–1770), sculptor. He came to England from Antwerp in 1720 and worked for designers such as William KENT and the architect James GIBBS before becoming independent. Responsible for several monuments in Westminster Abbey, including those for NEWTON, KNELLER, James STANHOPE and VERNON, he made sculptures of great architects for Chiswick House and of Hercules at Stourhead for Henry HOARE. With HOGARTH, Rysbrack was one of the first artists to establish a connection with CORAM and the Foundling Hospital. His eminence was challenged by SCHEEMAKERS and after the mid 1740s by ROUBILIAC, but he continued to produce statuary of significance, including a collaboration with the young Robert ADAM.

S

SAATCHI, CHARLES (1943–) and **MAURICE** (1946–), advertising agents. With their witty and adroit advertising campaigns, the Saatchi brothers took the firm which they had founded in 1970 to the heights of creative power and wealth before suffering badly in the stock market crash and recession of the late 1980s. Born in Baghdad, the sons of a Jewish Iraqi textile merchant who moved to London in 1947, they created the world's largest advertising agency, which achieved particular prominence with its work for the Conservative Party. In the mid 1980s Saatchi & Saatchi took over three major agencies in the USA and made unsuccessful bids for the Midland Bank and Hill Samuel, while Charles and his then wife Doris (née Lockhart) became two of the nation's greatest collectors of modern art. Narrowly escaping extinction, the firm clawed its way back before the brothers finally split in 1997.

SACHEVERELL, HENRY (c. 1674–1724), Anglican clergyman. Sacheverell's grandfather had been expelled from his living as a Presbyterian in 1662, but Sacheverell's father, a Wilts. rector, had conformed to the requirements of the Act of Uniformity, and Sacheverell himself became a passionate High Churchman and enemy of Dissent. A Fellow of Magdalen, Oxford, from 1701, Sacheverell gained a wider audience for his arguments after 1705 when he became chaplain at St Saviour's, Southwark. A sermon in Derby at the 1709 assizes, repeated on 5 Nov. 1709 before the Lord Mayor and aldermen of London, on 'the perils of false brethren in Church and State', provoked a crisis, claiming that the GODOLPHIN ministry was allowing Dissenters to weaken the Church of England. The government started impeachment proceedings but in doing so provoked riots in Sacheverell's favour, during which Dissenting meeting-houses were attacked. Sacheverell was suspended from preaching for three years but allowed to perform other clerical functions. He was hailed as a martyr; the ill-advised impeachment contributed to Queen ANNE's dismissal of Godolphin and his replacement with a Tory-oriented ministry led by Robert HARLEY. Harley and his allies distrusted Sacheverell's demagoguery but Anne granted him the lucrative living of St Andrew's, Holborn, in 1713 and with further gifts and legacies he died a wealthy man.

SACKVILLE, 1ST VISCOUNT *see* GERMAIN, GEORGE

SACKVILLE, CHARLES (6th Earl of Dorset and 4th [1st Sackville] Earl of Middlesex, known until 1675 as Lord Buckhurst) (1638–1706), courtier and poet. From a Royalist family, he returned from Italy in 1660, became an MP and fought in the Dutch wars. He was best known for his rakish lifestyle, being the lover of Nell GWYNN among others, and for being a patron of writers including DRYDEN, WYCHERLEY and PRIOR. His poems reflect the social and leisure concerns of Restoration high society.

SACKVILLE, THOMAS (1st Baron Buckhurst, 4th [1st Sackville] Earl of Dorset) (?1536–1608), politician and writer. Son of a royal administrator, he wrote poetry and co-authored the historical tragedy *Gorboduc*. Benefiting from kinship to ELIZABETH I, he was created Baron in 1567. He undertook various administrative and diplomatic duties (including announcing the sentence of death to MARY QUEEN OF SCOTS) before being appointed Lord Treasurer in 1599; JAMES I inherited him as a reliable servant, and gave him his earldom.

SACKVILLE-WEST, VITA (1892–1962), writer and gardener. Better known today as the creator of the garden at Sissinghurst (Kent), and the lover of women who also had a companionate 'open' marriage and two sons with the diplomat and writer Harold NICOLSON, Sackville-West was a novelist and poet. Born at Knole (Kent), a magnificent Tudor house reputed to have a bedroom for each of the 365 days of the year but which she was barred from inheriting because of her sex, she won the Hawthornden Prize for her epic poem *The Land* (1927), and the best of her novels were about the aristocracy, *The Edwardians* (1930) and *All Passion Spent* (1931); they were largely unread for several decades, but began to attract feminist interest in the 1980s. Her biographies included one of her grandmother, a flamenco dancer, *Pepita*

(1937). She contributed gardening notes to the *Observer* (1943–61). Her passionate relationship with Violet KEPPEL (Trefusis) is chronicled in *Portrait of a Marriage* (1973), by here son Nigel Nicolson; she also had a love affair with Virginia WOOLF, their letters have been published (1984) and Woolf's *Orlando* was in homage to Sackville-West.

SADLER, SIR RALPH (1507–87), politician and diplomat. From Middx., his career was founded on the patronage of his guardian, Thomas CROMWELL, who engineered his appointment as Gentleman of the Privy Chamber in 1536. He undertook important diplomatic missions to Scotland for HENRY VIII, as well as military service in the 1544 and 1547 campaigns against Scotland. His Protestantism brought withdrawal from politics under MARY I, but renewed service, especially in his Scottish diplomatic speciality, under ELIZABETH I.

SÆBERHT (?–616 or 617), King of Essex. He was the first King of Essex to receive Christianity, probably under the influence of his powerful uncle King ETHELBERT of Kent. However, his sons were pagans who drove out St MELLITUS, the bishop installed at London. Essex remained pagan until the time of SIGEBERHT SANCTUS. As the later events in the time of King SIGHERE demonstrate, the conversion of Essex was for some time uncertain.

SAINSBURY, JOHN (1844–1928), **JOHN** (Baron Sainsbury of Preston Candover) (1927–) and **DAVID** (Baron Sainsbury of Turville) (1940–), retailers. John Sainsbury, who established his dairy and grocery shop in 1869 in Drury Lane, London, founded a firm which became one of Britain's most successful food retailers. The career of his grandson, John, marched alongside the supermarket revolution: he joined the firm in 1950, the year it opened its first supermarket, becoming a director in 1958 and Chairman in 1969. During his chairmanship the number of Sainsbury supermarket stores rose from 82 to 313 and sales quadrupled. With substantial holdings in a firm that was floated publicly only in 1973, the Sainsbury clan are Britain's fourth richest family though by the late 1990s the chain was experiencing severe difficulties in the highly competitive food retailing sector and had been overtaken by Tesco at the top of the league. Many members are notable philanthropists in their own right. John Sainsbury's cousin David joined the company as Finance Director in 1963. Deputy Chairman in 1988 and Chairman in 1992, David became a wealthy backer of the Social Democratic Party at the start of the 1980s. He has since returned to the Labour fold, and was elevated to the House of Lords in 1997 by Tony BLAIR, who gave him a ministerial post in science.

ST ALBANS, 1ST VISCOUNT *see* BACON, FRANCIS, essay on page 47

ST GERMAN, CHRISTOPHER (1460–1541), legal writer. A Middle Temple lawyer, he retired to write the highly influential common-law textbook *Doctor and Student* (1528, 1530). His religious conservatism did not inhibit fierce attacks on clerical power and Church courts; advocating royal supremacy over the Church, anchored in co-operation with Parliament, he drew on older anti-clerical thought to provide ammunition for the religious changes of the 1530s.

ST JOHN, 1ST BARON *see* PAULET, WILLIAM

ST JOHN, HENRY (1st Viscount Bolingbroke) (1678–1751), politician. Although a notorious free thinker, he was a key figure in the (assertively Anglican) Tory party of ANNE's reign, and was made Secretary of State in 1710. He became increasingly jealous of his colleague and rival Robert HARLEY, Earl of Oxford, and worked to eclipse him by supporting extreme Tory measures such as the Schism Act of 1714, which provided severe penalties for teaching without a licence from a bishop. He was successful, but the death of Anne and the rise of the Whigs under GEORGE I limited his political options and in early 1715 he fled to France to join the Old Pretender (*see* STUART, JAMES). From 1715 to 1716 he was Jacobite Secretary of State, but gradually distanced himself from the Stuart cause after the failure of the 1715 Jacobite rebellion. Returning to England in 1723, he disclaimed his former Tory legitimism. Barred by the terms of his pardon from taking his seat in the Lords, he nonetheless threw himself into extra-parliamentary opposition to Robert WALPOLE, contributing to the influential journal *The Craftsman* and attempting to rally Tory and opposition Whig forces under the banner of Country ideology, a favourite strategy of opposition leaders since the days of Anthony Ashley COOPER, 1st Earl of Shaftesbury. In his later years he moved in the circle around FREDERICK, Prince of Wales. His pamphlet *The Idea of a Patriot King*, published in 1749 but written over a decade earlier, has been alleged to have shaped the future GEORGE III's political ideas.

ST JOHN, OLIVER (?1597–1673), politician and lawyer. He was associated with the Providence Island scheme of the 1630s in which a consortium of prominent Puritans promoted a Caribbean colony; he was counsel for John HAMPDEN against Crown prosecution in 1637. CHARLES I tried to buy him off with the solicitor generalship (1641), but St John remained a close ally of John PYM and continued in Parliament's service during the Civil Wars, accepting appointment as Chief Justice of Common Pleas in 1648. Although he refused to take part in Charles's trial, he stayed on to serve the Republic and supported the plan to make Oliver CROMWELL King. The restoration of CHARLES II ended his career.

ST LEGER, ANTHONY (?1496–1559), administrator. St Leger (pronounced 'Sellinger') was a Kentish gentleman who rose in Thomas CROMWELL's service to become Lord Deputy of Ireland (1540–8). He subdued much of Gaelic Ireland before implementing a policy of reconciliation and Anglicization, including HENRY VIII's recognition as King of Ireland in 1541. A second deputyship from 1550 ended after a year because of his increasingly open hostility to Protestant religious changes, and a third period in office (1553–5) ended with allegations of embezzlement, still being pursued at his death. His consistently conciliatory policies to the Gaelic lords were abandoned, with fateful longterm consequences.

ST VINCENT, EARL OF *see* JERVIS, JOHN

SAKLATVALA, SHAPURJI (1874–1936), Indian nationalist politician and Westminster MP *see* NAOROJI DADABHAI

SALESBURY (OR SALISBURY), WILLIAM (?1520–?1584), writer. Salesbury, a Denbighs. gentleman, studied at Oxford and the Inns of Court; his twin enthusiasms were Protestantism and the Welsh language. Among his many publications were a proverb collection and a Welsh–English dictionary (both 1547, among the first printed books in Welsh); in 1565–7 he produced a Welsh version of the Book of Common Prayer and a New Testament in collaboration with Richard DAVIES. Although his eccentric ideas for reforming Welsh spelling on classical lines were ignored by successors, his work was crucial for the survival of the language.

SALISBURY, EARL OF, 3RD *see* LONGSWORD, WILLIAM; **9TH** *see* MONTAGU, THOMAS; **10TH** *see* NEVILLE, RICHARD; **15TH** *see* CECIL, ROBERT; **COUNTESS OF** *see* PLANTAGENET, MARGARET; **MARQUESS OF, 3RD** *see* CECIL, ROBERT GASCOYNE; **5TH** *see* CECIL, ROBERT

SALMON, ROBERT (*fl.* 1800), agricultural inventor. The son of a carpenter and builder, he worked as clerk of works, then from 1794 resident architect, to the Duke of Bedford at Woburn, where he made alterations to the sowing machine

invented by Jethro TULL and refined by later inventors. He also invented a haymaking machine which was the forerunner of the modern rotary machine.

SALMOND, ALEXANDER (1954–), politician. Scottish Nationalist MP for Banff and Buchan since 1987, Alex Salmond became leader of his party in 1990 and was widely credited with making it a serious electoral force for the first time since the 1970s. Breaking with the old nationalist rhetoric about oil and independence, he stressed the idea of autonomy within the European Union, a line which played well in 1997 when the SNP became the second party in Scotland. But his lacklustre campaign in the 1999 election for the Scottish Assembly, plus his overt criticism of the government's military campaign in Kosovo, resulted in the loss of the SNP's lead in the opinion polls and their less impressive than expected showing in the election itself. Salmon resigned in 2000.

SALT, DAME BARBARA (1904–75), diplomat. She was the first woman to be appointed an ambassador (1962), but serious illness prevented her from taking up her position in Israel. She had previously held various diplomatic posts and was deputy head of the British delegation to the Geneva disarmament conference (1960) and at the UN in New York (1960–2). After 1962 she continued her distinguished career in the Diplomatic Service, despite her disabling illness, until her retirement 10 years later.

SALT, TITUS (1803–76), industrialist and philanthropist. Son of a wool-stapler, Salt made his fortune from new types of cloth, spinning alpaca yarn and mixing it with cotton, and making mohair from the wool of the Turkish angora goat. He used a large part of that fortune to improve the living conditions of his workers: in 1860 he moved all his five factories into one fine Italianate building on the River Aire just outside his home town of Bradford (Yorks.), constructed houses for his 850-strong workforce and provided them with modern sanitary facilities, public baths, a cricket pitch, a hospital, a library and a Congregational church, but no public houses or pawn shops. Saltaire stands today, reconstructed as a tourist centre, and remains a memorial to a paternalistic Victorian businessman whose funeral procession was respectfully watched by some 120,000 people, most of them workers, for the mills fell silent that day.

SAMSON (1135–1211), churchman. The hero of JOCELIN OF BRAKELOND's *Chronicle*, a Norfolk man educated in Paris, he became a monk in 1166 and was elected Abbot of Bury St Edmunds (Suffolk) in 1182, when the abbey finances were in a parlous state. It was a period when, with efficient management, great landlords could do well and Samson was the supreme businessman among medieval English abbots. A respected voice in local and national politics, he led the abbey knights to war when JOHN rebelled against RICHARD I in 1193.

SAMSON OF DOL, ST (*fl.* sixth century), Bishop of Dol. He is known mostly through a life written in the ninth century. From south Wales, he was educated at the monastery of Llanilltud Fawr (now Llanwit Major, South Glam.), and subsequently moved to Brittany where he founded a monastery and became a bishop. His career illustrates the religious aspects of British migration to Brittany as well as monastic life in early medieval Wales.

SAMUEL, HERBERT (1st Viscount Samuel) (1870–1963), politician and party leader. He entered Parliament in 1902, serving in minor posts until 1909 when he became Chancellor of the Duchy of Lancaster, then Postmaster General (1910). In 1916, he was Home Secretary in ASQUITH's coalition Cabinet, having to deal with the Easter Rising, but he resigned when LLOYD GEORGE supplanted Asquith in Dec., and lost his seat in the 1918 'coupon election'. He was then appointed the first High Commissioner in Palestine (1920–5), and headed the Royal Commission on the Coal Industry (1925–6), the report of which, recommending wage cuts for miners as the only hope of a profitable coal industry, both prompted, and formed the basis for the ending of, the General Strike. He returned to Parliament in 1929 and, as acting Liberal leader, supported the formation of the National government in 1931, again taking the post of Home Secretary. He resigned over the introduction of protectionist policies in 1932, heading the Liberal opposition known as the Samuelites until 1935. He took a peerage in 1937 and led the Liberals in the Lords (1944–55). A committed Liberal, he was gradually eclipsed by the decline in his party's influence between the wars.

SAMUEL, RAPHAEL (1934–96), historian. A widely influential socialist historian, Samuel was a guiding force behind the development of the History Workshop movement from 1967 and its journal, *History Workshop*, from 1976. History Workshop grew out of a combination of the focus of the historical research of students at Ruskin College, Oxford, where Samuel taught (1962–96), with a political commitment to the democratization of history, both in the sense of taking the 'ordinary' people and their history as the major object of study and in how the subject should be studied. The movement was strongly opposed to restricting the study of history to professional

historians. Samuel's upbringing in a communist family and later close involvement in the creation of the New Left (*see* HALL, STUART), after breaking with the Communist Party in 1956, were formative in shaping History Workshop and its subsequent development. His own historical work was marked by a combination of intense detail and immersion in a huge range of sources and a grasp of larger questions, be they about the nineteenth-century working class and poor or about the political and cultural representations and uses of history, a major theme of his later work, such as *Theatres of Memory* (1994).

SANCHO, IGNATIUS (1729–80), writer. He was born on a slave ship in mid Atlantic, the son of a woman kidnapped from West Africa. He was sold as a house-servant to three maiden ladies in Greenwich; they treated him badly but their neighbour, the 2nd Duke of Montagu, encouraged his education. In 1749 he escaped to become the widowed Duchess's butler, and later worked for her son-in-law, the 1st (Brudenell) Duke of Montagu. In 1766 he wrote to congratulate Lawrence STERNE on his depiction of slavery in *Tristram Shandy*; Sterne introduced him to the circle of Hester THRALE, and Sancho began to write novels himself. In his later years he had a grocer's shop in Westminster. His collected letters were first published in 1782, and depict the divided loyalties and uncertain position of the African, whether slave or free, in eighteenth-century England.

SANCROFT, WILLIAM (1617–93), Archbishop of Canterbury (1678–89). The son of a small landowner in Suffolk, he went to Emmanuel College, Cambridge, where his uncle was Master. He was elected a Fellow, but was ejected for refusing to take an oath of loyalty to the Commonwealth, and travelled on the continent. He was Dean of St Paul's (1664–77), and Archbishop from 1678. Following an unsuccessful attempt to convert JAMES II to Anglicanism, he and the King fell into open dispute in 1688, when Sancroft headed the seven bishops who defied royal orders by refusing to promulgate the King's Declaration of Indulgence for Dissenters and Catholics. He played no part in the Glorious Revolution, arguing that the oath he had taken to James precluded his taking another to WILLIAM III and MARY II. As a result, he was suspended from office in 1689, becoming the most eminent of the 'Non-jurors' (six other bishops, including all but one of the seven bishops, and about 400 clergy). Contemporaries agreed that Sancroft was a man of integrity noted for abstemiousness and charitable giving, but the staunch Whig, Gilbert BURNET, condemned him as cold and weak.

SANDERS (OR SANDER), NICHOLAS (*c.* 1530–81), controversialist historian. Oxford-educated, as a Roman Catholic he was exiled under ELIZABETH I; he was ordained in Rome, attended (1561) the Council of Trent and wrote against John JEWEL's defence of the Church of England, championing the Pope's monarchical rule. In 1579 he travelled to Ireland as papal agent to incite rebellion (*see* FITZGERALD, JAMES FITZMAURICE; STUCLEY, THOMAS), recruiting Gerald Fitzjames FITZGERALD, 14th Earl of Desmond, but died a fugitive. His history of the English Reformation, *De Origine et Progressu Schimatis Anglicani* (1585), is highly prejudiced but full of useful information.

SANDERSON, ROBERT (1587–1663), churchman. An Oxford don, he benefited from William LAUD's patronage and suffered accordingly during the 1640s Civil Wars; he regained preferment only on CHARLES II's restoration, becoming Bishop of Lincoln in 1660. A moderate Calvinist in his views on salvation, he wrote works of lasting significance on moral theology and casuistry (the study of cases of conscience and conflicting duties).

SANDES, FLORA (1876–1956), soldier. Daughter of a Co. Cork rector, Sandes went with a St John's Ambulance Association nursing unit to Serbia in 1914 and, joining the Serbian Red Cross, worked with a Serbian army ambulance crew. In a country where it was not unusual for peasant girls to fight, she had soon abandoned her Red Cross insignia to fight in the mountains and on the front line with the Serbian army. Seriously wounded, she was invalided home to England, but returned to her regiment a year later. By 1922 she was a lieutenant and by 1926, when the army was demobilized and she had been decorated for conspicuous bravery in the field, a captain. In 1927 she married a White Russian who had fled from the revolution. Interned by the Germans in Belgrade during the Second World War, she retired to Suffolk on her release.

SANDS, BOBBY (1954–81), hunger-striker. In 1972 his family were intimidated out of their North Belfast home by loyalists and moved to West Belfast, where Sands became active in the Irish Republican Army (IRA). While imprisoned (1973–6) he was associated with Gerry ADAMS. He was re-arrested in Oct. 1976 for terrorist activities and after conviction participated in what became known as the H-Block protest in the Maze prison, Belfast, a campaign for political status which involved non-co-operation, including refusal to wear prison uniform. On 1 March 1981 Sands began a hunger strike in support of the campaign, followed at intervals by other prisoners. On 10 April he became MP for Fermanagh-South Tyrone in a by-election, revealing an unexpected depth of sympathy for the prisoners among Northern Irish nationalists. This drew worldwide attention, but despite attempts by mediators to find a solution he died on 5 May, and nine other prisoners died before the strike ended in October. The electoral support shown for H-Block candidates and the favourable publicity which their cause received marked the breakdown of the policy, pursued since the mid 1970s, of treating paramilitaries as ordinary criminals, and encouraged Sinn Féin to move into electoral politics. In succeeding years most of the prisoners' demands were granted. Sands became an icon for Republicans, though in the late 1990s Republican opponents of the Good Friday Agreement (including Sands's relatives) disputed the claim of mainstream Sinn Féin to his political legacy.

SANDWICH, EARL OF, **1ST** *see* MONTAGU, EDWARD; **4TH** *see* MONTAGU, JOHN

SANDYS, DUNCAN (Baron Duncan-Sandys) (1908–87), politician and military reformer. Having held a variety of ministerial posts during and after the Second World War, he was, as Minister of Defence, responsible for the 1957 Defence Review which led to the ending of national service and the acquisition of an independent nuclear deterrent.

SANDYS, EDWIN (*c.* 1516–88), churchman. A Cambridge don, he was Vice-Chancellor at the time of JANE GREY's bid for the throne, and was imprisoned in the Tower of London for supporting her; in a narrative of his troubles, he seems to be the first to have used the phrase 'Bloody Mary' for MARY I. Later he escaped to Europe, returning under ELIZABETH I to become Bishop of Worcester (1559), London (1570) and York (1577). Sir Robert Stapleton's attempt in 1581 to blackmail him by planting a woman in his bedroom caused a national sensation.

SARGENT, JOHN SINGER (1856–1925), artist. The son of wealthy American parents, born in Florence, he studied in Paris and in 1884 exhibited the sensational *Madam X* at the Salon, but was particularly influenced by the work of Spanish painters like Velázquez. Sargent settled in London in 1885 but made frequent visits to the USA, where he became as greatly sought after as a portraitist of society beauties and celebrities as he was in London. His work is far from formulaic portraiture and his paintings, such as those of the SITWELLS and Robert Louis STEVENSON, can be revealing, even chilling. He came to regard his highly paid commissions as a 'profession for pimps' and after 1907 accepted fewer, preferring to execute landscapes, scenes from mythology and the shocking, haunting *Gassed* (1918), which he painted as an official war artist.

SARSFIELD, PATRICK (Jacobite Earl of Lucan) (?–1693), soldier. From Old English gentry of Lucan (Co. Dublin), he served as a soldier in France and England and in 1688 raised troops for JAMES II in Ireland. Made Earl, and in 1691 James's Commander-in-Chief until superseded by Charles Chalmont, Marquess de St Ruth, he defended Limerick in the 1690 siege and salvaged something from St Ruth's defeat at Aughrim (12 July 1691). His diplomatic skill mitigated the severity of terms in the Jacobite capitulation at Limerick (Oct. 1691). He returned to French service, and was killed on campaign.

SASSOON, SIEGFRIED (1886–1967), poet and novelist. Having failed to obtain a degree at Cambridge, Sassoon lived on a modest income as a country gentleman. He published nine small volumes of his poetry between 1906 and 1912. Serving with the Royal Welch Fusiliers in the First World War he acquired a reputation for bravery fighting in France. Nicknamed 'mad Jack', he was awarded the Military Cross and was recommended for the Victoria Cross. During his convalescence from shell shock, he reflected upon the horrors and brutality of war. As an act of protest he published *A Soldier's Declaration* (1917), which attacked 'the political errors and insincerities for which the fighting men are being sacrificed', and, in a widely publicized act, threw his MC in the River Mersey. This behaviour was attributed to shell-shock by the Home Secretary, and Sassoon was hospitalized. In 1919 *War Poems* was published; bitterly ironical, the poems were universally recognized as some of the greatest tragic poetry ever written. In 1928 he published *Memoirs of a Fox-Hunting Man,* the first of a series of autobiographical prose pieces. Lamenting the loss of values associated with English pastoral life, Sassoon attacked modern society in *Satirical Poems* (1926) and the inhumanity of war in *The Road to Ruin* (1933). *The Tasking* (1954) revealed a profound melancholy and an overwhelming desire for spiritual reassurance. The 1960 publication of *The Path to Peace* showed that Sassoon's conversion to Catholicism had granted him spiritual solace.

SAUNDERS, ERNEST (1935–), businessman. The son of Viennese Jews who fled to London in 1938, Saunders specialized in the emerging discipline of marketing after graduating from Cambridge. Crowning a successful career with a series of companies, he left the multinational Nestlé to become Chief Executive of the drinks company Guinness in 1981, and its Chairman in 1986. He transformed the business, stripping away all the diverse interests which it had been acquiring under the family's control, to concentrate on its core trade and brand. His strategy reached its peak with the successful take-over of the Bells and Distillers spirits groups, making Guinness the second most profitable beverage company in the world, but the acquisition of Distillers in 1986 was tainted by financial scandal. Saunders was accused of arranging an illegal share-support and at the subsequent trial, was found guilty and sent to gaol. Ill health, from which he made a surprisingly swift recovery, won him release from gaol after 10 months of a five-year sentence imposed in 1991; European courts have since held that elements of his trial were unfair.

SAUNDERSON, EDWARD (1837–1906), Ulster politician. The first leader of the Ulster Unionist Party, and member of a family prominent in Cavan politics since the eighteenth century, Saunderson was Liberal MP for Cavan (1865–74), until displaced by the new Home Rule Party. He was a vociferous opponent of the Land League, and returned to the Commons as Conservative MP for North Armagh (1885–1906). Though an effective campaigner against Home Rule, his extreme pro-landlord views and amateurish attitude to politics emerged as political liabilities when the Home Rule threat receded after 1895, and by his death he had been supplanted by more professional figures like James CRAIG.

SAVERY, THOMAS (*c*. 1650–1715), inventor. Born in Devon, he was a military engineer, who devised a number of inventions. In 1698 he obtained a patent for a pumping engine which used steam to raise water; he described this in *The Miner's Friend* (1702). Later he entered into partnership with a Dartmouth ironmonger, Thomas NEWCOMEN, who made vast improvements to Savery's engine, developing the first atmospheric, self-acting engine. A company was formed to market the improved engines by 1711; they were widely adopted, not only in mines, but also to supply drinking water and to feed canal reservoirs and locks.

SAVILE, GEORGE (1st Marquess of Halifax) (1633–95), politician. Son of the Royalist Governor of Civil War Sheffield and York, Halifax played a prominent part in political life in the 1660s and 1670s, being notable for his consistent efforts to maintain a moderate stance in those difficult times. Having been educated at home, and possibly having travelled abroad, he served in the Convention Parliament of 1660. He opposed Danby (*see* OSBORNE, THOMAS), and was a friend of Shaftesbury (*see* COOPER, ANTHONY ASHLEY); in

1679 he was given a position in the new Council of 30, set up to try to gain control of the escalating political crisis first touched off by Titus OATES's Popish-Plot accusations. He also opposed, however, the exclusion of the future JAMES II from the succession. Briefly Lord President of the Council under James II, he was dismissed for failing to support a plan to repeal the Test and Corporation Acts. He joined the moderate opposition and, in his *Character of a Trimmer* (privately circulated 1685), argued the cause of moderation. He remained neutral in the early stages of the Glorious Revolution, supporting William of Orange (the future WILLIAM III) only after James's flight. Having played a prominent part in debate in the Lords about the constitutional settlement, when he opposed the proposal for a regency, he was chosen to offer William and MARY II the Crown. Appointed Lord Privy Seal in Feb. 1689, he tried to form a broadly based government, but was unable to rally support from either side. Resigning in 1690, he remained in opposition thereafter.

SAVILE, SIR HENRY (1549–1622), scholar. An Oxford don and from 1596 Provost of Eton, knighted in 1604, he was one of the most distinguished scholars of his age, and was prominent in the creation of his friend Thomas BODLEY's library at Oxford. He is reputed to have tutored ELIZABETH I in Greek; he founded Oxford chairs in geometry and astronomy.

SAXTON, CHRISTOPHER (*c.* 1542–*c.* 1620), cartographer. Initially employed in 1570 by John RUDD, Saxton published in 1579 the first atlas of England and Wales, followed in 1583 by the first wall-map. His work was within a sixteenth-century tradition of map-making, often for military purposes, but Saxton brought a greater precision to his task than anyone before him. He was officially encouraged by William CECIL, Lord Burghley, for whom many of the maps were originally drawn as part of his information-gathering network. Saxton later had a successful estate-surveying career; his atlas achievement was built upon by John SPEED.

SAY AND SELE, 1ST VISCOUNT see FIENNES, WILLIAM

SAYERS, DOROTHY L(EIGH) (1893–1957), poet and novelist. The daughter of a clergyman, brought up in the Fens which are evoked in several of her books, Sayers was educated at Somerville College, Oxford, worked for an advertising agency (where she wrote the slogan 'My Goodness, My Guinness') and, to supplement her income, started to write detective fiction. This features the aristocratic sleuth Lord Peter Wimsey and, later,

Harriet Vane, Sayer's *alter ego* as a detective story writer, a character who enables Sayers to explore women's position in the 1930s. The first was *Whose Body?* (1923); the most successful were *The Nine Tailors* (1934) and *Gaudy Night* (1935). In middle age Sayers abandoned crime writing in favour of religious themes: *The Zeal of Thy House* (1957) is about WILLIAM OF SENS, who rebuilt Canterbury Cathedral, while *The Man Born to be King* (1941–2), a series of plays for the BBC on the life of Christ (originally commissioned for children), caused controversy with its everyday treatment of divine matters.

SCANLON, HUGH (Baron Scanlon of Davyhulme, Manchester) (1913–), trade-union leader. Apprenticed as an instrument-maker after an elementary school education, Scanlon joined the Association of Engineering Workers' Union. He was a shop steward (1947–63). President of the Amalgamated Union of Engineering Workers (1968–78), he was a member of the Trades Union Congress (TUC) General Council.

SCARBOROUGH, 1ST EARL OF see LUMLEY, RICHARD

SCARGILL, ARTHUR (1938–), trade-union leader. Scargill entered a Yorks. colliery aged 15, and quickly became an active member of both the National Union of Mineworkers (NUM) and the Young Communist League. From the latter organization, on whose National Executive he served around 1956, he acquired the belief in the inevitability of class struggle which would later motivate his trade-union activities. After the miners' successful strike in 1972, Scargill was elected President of the Yorkshire NUM, and in 1981 succeeded the moderate Joe GORMLEY as the union's national President. He led the NUM into its disastrous strike of 1984–5, during which his belligerence and refusal to compromise not only arguably prolonged the dispute and increased the THATCHER government's antipathy towards the miners but also distanced the union's militant leadership both from its more moderate followers (many of whom broke away to form the Union of Democratic Mineworkers) and from many erstwhile allies within the Labour Party. Scargill was held largely responsible for the failure of the strike, and in particular for making several tactical mistakes such as declining to have a national ballot at the start. This robbed the strike of an important degree of legitimacy in the eyes of many who would otherwise have supported the miners. Nonetheless, his prediction that the coal industry would be devastated proved to be largely accurate. Throughout the rest of the 1980s, pits were gradually closed down, with Scargill by then impotent to do anything about it. In 1996 he split from Tony BLAIR's New Labour to create a hard-left Socialist Labour Party, and stood unsuccessfully for Parliament in 1997.

SCARMAN, LESLIE (Baron Scarman of Quatt) (1911–), judge. Scarman was called to the Bar in 1936, became a QC in 1957 and a High Court judge in 1961. He was appointed the first chairman of the Law Commission, a standing body set up under a 1965 Act to undertake a systematic reform of the English law (Scotland has a separate commission). Promoted to the Court of Appeal (1973) and to the House of Lords as Lord of Appeal in Ordinary (1977–86), he headed the inquiries into the Red Lion Square events (1974) and the Brixton riots (1981). His report on the Brixton riots was an indictment of the neglect of inner-city problems and led to a fundamental government rethink. As President of the Senate of the Inns of Court and the Bar (1976–9), he achieved valuable reforms in legal education and with Lord Devlin he urged the reopening of the case of the Guildford Four, part of the campaign by the Provisional IRA to bring the Irish troubles to the British mainland. Three men and a woman convicted in 1974 for bombing pubs in Woolwich (London) and Guildford (Surrey) were released in Oct. 1989 when the government finally conceded that their convictions were no longer safe. Scarman is an advocate of a Bill of Rights for the UK as proposed by the European Convention of Human Rights in 1950.

SCHEEMAKERS, PETER (1691–1781), sculptor. Like his rival RYSBRACK he came from the Netherlands, working and studying in Denmark and Italy before coming to London. His most successful period began in 1735, after he returned from a journey to study Roman sculpture. He came to rival, if not exceed, Rysbrack in popularity. Most of his output took the form of church monuments. Scheemakers's most famous work was his SHAKE-SPEARE in Westminster Abbey; he also executed a series of busts of British worthies for FREDERICK, Prince of Wales which were given by the Prince to POPE. He retired to Antwerp in 1771.

SCHREINER, OLIVE (1855–1920), writer. The sixth of the 10 surviving children of a Methodist missionary working in Basutoland, Schreiner worked as a governess to various Boer farming families. In 1881 she went to England, taking with her the partly autobiographical manuscript of *The Story of an African Farm*, published under the pseudonym 'Ralph Iron' in 1883. It brought her immediate fame and attracted interest from 'free thinking' left-wing intellectuals in its anticipation of the 'new woman' fiction of the 1890s. Eleanor

Marx AVELING became a close friend as did Karl PEARSON, Havelock ELLIS (with both she became unhappily emotionally involved) and Edward CARPENTER.

In 1889 Schreiner returned to South Africa, where her brother was a minister in Cecil RHODES's government. A supporter of Rhodes, she became increasingly disillusioned particularly after the Jameson raid (1895): her allegory *Trooper Peter Halket of Mashonaland* (1897) is a polemic against the raid. In 1894 she married Samuel 'Cron' Cronwright, an ostrich-farmer and politician: their daughter died almost at birth, and they gradually became estranged though Cronwright (who added Schreiner to his name) was active in promoting her writing. Politicized by both her London circle and the political situation in South Africa, she was active in the women's rights movement from the 1890s, publishing an important analysis *Women and Labour* (1911). Seen as writing out of 'double colonialism' as a woman and a South African, she was a critic of apartheid, and an early supporter of the African National Congress. She was an important influence on such writers as Virginia WOOLF and Doris LESSING.

SCHULENBURG, MELUSINE VON DER (Duchess of Kendal and Munster) (1667–1743), royal mistress. From the region of Magdeburg in central Germany, she began her relationship with the future GEORGE I in 1691 and bore him three daughters, none of whom were acknowledged and who were officially described as her nieces. She acted as George's hostess in Hanover and accompanied him to Britain on his accession in 1714, where her height and thin physique gave her the nickname 'the maypole'. In Britain she acted as an intermediary for government ministers who were reluctant to approach the King directly with their ideas. Some of her conduct was controversial, such as her involvement in the sale of the contract for minting Irish coinage to William WOOD, and her receipt of free stock during the South Sea Bubble, but her behaviour was not unusual for the political elite of the era and she spent large amounts of money trying to support South Sea shares after their price collapsed. After George I's death she lived quietly in Twickenham.

SCHWEPPE, JACOB (1740–1821), inventor. He initially worked as a silversmith and jeweller in Geneva, developing his carbonation process as a hobby but turning it into a business in 1783. He transferred to London in 1792, where his artificial mineral waters became popular as a mixer for alcohol and fruit cordial, and were endorsed by Erasmus DARWIN. Schweppe retired from his London business in 1802 and returned to Geneva.

The Schweppes business continued to prosper, and in the 1960s was merged with the CADBURY confectionery empire.

SCOTT, C(HARLES) P(RESTWICH) (1846–1932), editor.

Appointed editor of the *Manchester Guardian* (which was owned by a relation) when he was only 25, Scott worked hard to make its northern voice a principled, Liberal national one. In the 1880s, following GLADSTONE's lead, he moved the paper leftwards to support a growing number of radical causes like women's suffrage, trade-union rights, Irish Home Rule and retrenchment on naval expenditure. A Liberal MP himself for a decade (1895–1905), Scott formed an important link with LLOYD GEORGE in opposition to the Boer War. In 1914 the *Manchester Guardian*, still under Scott's editorship, was behind ASQUITH's declaration of war on Germany, though it had been a hard decision: in 1916 the *Guardian* led the campaign to replace Asquith with Lloyd George in the interest of a more vigorous prosecution of the war, but in 1918 Scott was profoundly critical of Lloyd George's chauvinist 'coupon election' campaign. With the disintegration of the Liberal Party in the 1920s came a diminution of Scott's influence.

SCOTT, SIR GILBERT (1811–78), architect.

Many of Britain's distinctive, pointed, spidery buildings can be directly attributed to Scott or to his influence: from inauspicious beginnings designing workhouses, he grew to be rich and famous from the Gothic revival in the restoration of hundreds of churches, college chapels and public buildings. Influenced by PUGIN, he was opposed by William MORRIS, whose 'anti-scrape' movement, the Society for the Protection of Ancient Buildings, was formed to try to curb the thorough-going excesses of Scott's Anglo-French High Gothic style. Today it is necessary only to 'look around', as with WREN, to see his monument: the Martyrs' Memorial in Oxford, the central buildings of Glasgow University, the Albert Memorial, St Pancras station and hotel, the Albert Memorial in Hyde Park and dozens more.

SCOTT, JAMES (1st Duke of Monmouth) (1649–85), pretender.

The illegitimate son of CHARLES II and Lucy WALTER, he was recognized by the King and created Duke in 1663. In 1670 he was appointed Captain General of the royal forces, and participated in the Third Dutch War. He took the Whig side in the attempt to exclude the future JAMES II from the line of succession, yet in the same period put down the revolt of Scots Presbyterian Covenanters at Bothwell Bridge. Exiled to Holland to prevent him intriguing to be made heir to the throne, he returned in 1680 to popular acclaim. He was arrested, and in 1683 was exiled once more.

What came to be known as Monmouth's rebellion – the rising which took place at the death of Charles II in support of Monmouth in preference to the Catholic James II – had its roots in the abortive 1683 Rye House Plot (*see also* FERGUSON, ROBERT) and involved the same group of conspirators. A new scheme was already in hand when Charles's death brought James to the throne. Argyll (*see* CAMPBELL, ARCHIBALD) strove to stir up a rising in Scotland, but was defeated. Monmouth, having been expelled from Holland on James's accession, landed at Lyme Regis (Dorset) on 11 June 1685, and issued a proclamation asserting his own claim to the throne. He collected a following of between 3,000 and 4,000, apparently chiefly men of middling social status, some of them Dissenters and supposedly including Daniel DEFOE. They succeeded in capturing Taunton (Som.), but were defeated by royal troops at Sedgemoor on 5 July. Some 1,300 rebels were killed, and a similar number captured. Found in hiding after the defeat, Monmouth was taken to London and executed on 15 July.

SCOTT, SIR PERCY (1853–1924), sailor.

Educated at Eastman's Naval Academy and HMS *Britannia*, Scott helped direct the bombardment of Alexandria in 1882, and designed new fire control systems which greatly increased the effectiveness of naval gunnery. During the First World War he specialized in naval deception, anti-submarine warfare and anti-aircraft defences, first for the fleet and later for London. As early as June 1914 he predicted that the combination of the submarine and aircraft had rendered the battleship obsolete. The naval establishment worked hard to discredit Scott; he died in 1924, the centre of a doctrinal storm which was not settled until 10 Dec. 1941, when Japanese torpedo bombers sank the *Prince of Wales* and *Repulse*.

SCOTT (OR SCOT), REGINALD (*c.* 1537–99).

A Kentish gentleman, an MP in 1589, who was an enthusiast for the Neoplatonist mystical philosophy and scientific tradition which had been revived as part of the Renaissance enthusiasm for ancient wisdom. His interest in Neoplatonism's picture of the magical links between natural and supernatural worlds led him to deep scepticism about alternative cosmologies which stressed the existence of witchcraft; his book *The Discoverie of Witchcraft* (1584) was a notable demolition of contemporary neuroses about witchcraft and had much influence in Europe, despite JAMES I's order that it should be burned.

SCOTT, CAPTAIN ROBERT (1868–1912), Antarctic explorer.

Scott joined the Royal Navy in 1880

and commanded HMS *Discovery* on the National Antarctic Expedition (1901–4). The ship reached the Antarctic in 1902 and Scott's team located King Edward VII's Land and sounded the Ross Sea. Promoted Captain in 1904, he led another expedition in 1910 which aimed to be the first to reach the South Pole. Severe blizzards and low temperatures hampered the progress of the 11-man team and seven were forced to return to base camp at Cape Evans. Scott and four others persevered and on 18 Jan. 1912 reached their destination, but found that the Norwegian explorer Roald Amundsen had arrived there a month earlier. Scott and his colleagues perished on the return journey and their bodies were found in Nov. 1912. He was posthumously knighted.

SCOTT, SIR WALTER (1771–1832), poet, novelist and critic. A lawyer, born in Edinburgh, and the son of a writer, Walter Scott published several volumes of poetry between 1805 and 1817. He refused the laureateship in 1813 and ceased to write poems in favour of novels. His prodigious anonymous output included *Waverley* (1814), *The Antiquary* (1816), *Old Mortality* (1816), *Rob Roy* (1817), *The Heart of Midlothian* (1818) and *Ivanhoe* (1819). It was not until 1827 that Scott conceded authorship of the novels. A year earlier his involvement with a publishing firm had left debts of £114,000, for which he declared he would be solely responsible, ensuring that the creditors received payment in full after his death. Scott also wrote plays, penned and edited numerous works of literary, historical and antiquarian interest, and contributed to the influential *Edinburgh Review* until he objected to its Whiggish stance.

SCOUGALL, DAVID (*fl.* 1654–77), portrait-painter. Practically nothing is known about Scougall's life but he is recognized as the most influential portraitist in Scotland in the third quarter of the seventeenth century. His work is characterized by a richer appreciation of colour than shown by earlier painters. His style was continued, in a cruder form, by John Scougall (*c.* 1645–1737), who may have been his nephew.

SCROPE, RICHARD (*c.* 1350–1405), Archbishop of York (1398–1405) and rebel. Bishop of Coventry from 1386, he was translated to York in 1398. In 1405 he joined the PERCY rebellion, issuing a manifesto that criticized HENRY IV's taxation of the clergy and voiced fears of clerical disendowment. When the Percies failed to come to his aid he disbanded his army and surrendered. After an irregular trial, he was executed at York on 8 June, the only pre-Reformation English bishop to meet this fate. His tomb in York Minster rapidly became the focus of a popular cult; Henry IV's subsequent illnesses led many to believe that the King had been struck down with leprosy as a punishment for killing God's servant.

SCUDAMORE, SIR JOHN (1st Viscount Scudamore) (1601–71), Royalist. From a Herefs. knightly family, Oxford-educated, he was made Baronet in 1620 and was frequently county MP; he became a client of George VILLIERS, Duke of Buckingham, was made Viscount in 1628 and served as Ambassador in France 1635–9. Enthusiastic in Royalist campaigning from 1642, he was a prisoner in London from 1643 to 1646. Scholarly (and an expert on fruit trees), he was an extrovertly extreme supporter of William LAUD, snubbing French Protestants while on embassy in Paris: his chief memorial is his restoration of the lovely Cistercian Abbey Dore (Herefs.)

SEACOLE, MARY (née Grant) (*c.* 1815–81), nurse. Born in Kingston, Jamaica, the daughter of a Scottish army officer and a Jamaican boarding-house owner, she learned herbal medicine and folk remedies from her mother, who often treated British soldiers stationed in Jamaica. On hearing of the terrible conditions in the Crimean War, Seacole, convinced that her knowledge of tropical medicine would be of service, went to London in 1854 and applied for a position as a nurse. Despite her references from army doctors, the personal intervention of the wife of the Secretary of War, Mrs Sidney Herbert, and the shortage of trained nurses, Seacole was turned down but, undeterred, borrowed sufficient money to make the nearly 4,000-mile journey to the Crimea alone. Florence NIGHTINGALE set her to work helping with the embarkation of the sick and wounded. Noticed in the dispatches of William RUSSELL, the war correspondent of *The Times,* for her courage under fire and comforting presence to the wounded, Seacole was the first woman to enter Sebastopol when it fell after a long siege. When the peace was suddenly concluded she was left almost destitute, but the Commander-in-Chief of the British forces, Lord Rokeby, organized a benefit and William Russell wrote the introduction to the memoirs of a woman who succeeded despite the racial prejudice of influential sections of Victorian society.

SEAFIELD, 1ST EARL OF *see* OGILVY, JAMES

SEAXBURH (?–673), Queen of Wessex. She ruled as an independent Queen for a year after the death of her husband, King CENWEALH, despite the existence of at least one male kinsman, Cenwealh's brother CENTWINE. Another well-known example of a woman wielding independent power is ETHELFLÆD of Mercia in the tenth century, but such cases are extremely rare in the Middle Ages.

SEAXBURH (?–*c.* 700), Queen of Kent and Abbess of Minster-in-Thanet and Ely. Daughter of King ANNA of East Anglia and wife of King EORCENBERHT of Kent, Seaxburh's career followed a pattern very similar to that of many other early Anglo-Saxon royal women. A great religious benefactor, she founded a monastery at Minster-in-Sheppey, of which she became abbess after her husband's death. She then succeeded her sister St ÆTHELFRYTH as Abbess of Ely.

SEBBI, ST (?–693 or 694), King of Essex (663–693 or 694). Co-ruler of Essex with his brother SIGHERE, Sebbi is said by BEDE to have remained a Christian even though his brother and most of his people reverted to paganism. This episode illustrates the vulnerability of the early conversion of the English peoples to Christianity. Sebbi became a monk at the end of his life and was succeeded by his two sons Sigeheard and Swæfred.

SEDGWICK, ADAM (1785–1873), geologist. The son of a Cumb. vicar, Sedgwick was educated at Cambridge, where he spent the rest of his distinguished career. In 1818 he was ordained priest and a year later appointed Woodwardian Professor of Geology in which position he did much to shape nineteenth-century English ideas concerning geology and palaeontology. One of the foremost field geologists, he devoted much of his career to the geology of diverse areas of Britain. A leading figure in the Geological Society of London (President 1829–31), his best-known work was the establishment of a stratigraphic succession of fossiliferous rocks in north Wales, the oldest of which he named (in 1835) the Cambrian system. Roderick MURCHISON, a geologist with whom Sedgwick had evidenced the Devonian system of rocks, argued that Sedgwick's Upper Cambrian strata were actually identical with his own Lower Silurian strata. This prompted a fierce controversy between the two geologists. It was not until much later in the nineteenth century that this controversy was resolved and the Cambrian and Silurian systems were redefined and distinguished. A devout Christian and devotee of natural theology, Sedgwick criticized Charles LYELL's 'uniformitarian' geology and rejected the theories of Charles DARWIN and others on the evolution of species.

SEDLEY, SIR CHARLES (*c.* 1639–1701), courtier and poet. Son of a Kentish baronet, he went to Oxford, entered Parliament and gained a reputation as a rake. A friend of Rochester (*see* WILMOT, JOHN) and SACKVILLE, he was highly regarded as a poet and playwright in his own lifetime, although not greatly since. His daughter Catherine was a mistress of JAMES II.

SEELEY, SIR JOHN (1834–95), historian. An Evangelical and Professor of Modern History at Cambridge, he was influenced by positivism and hoped to create a science of history to improve both the training and performance of modern statesmen. He wrote a popular life of Christ, *Ecce Homo* (1866), while his *Expansion of England* (1883) captured the imperial mood. He was also an important figure in the professionalization of the study of history.

SÉGÉNE (?–652), Abbot of Iona. Ségéne's abbacy, from 623, was one of the most assertive of any abbot of Iona since COLUM CILLE himself, largely because it coincided with the return of the Cenél Conaill, Colum Cille's kindred, to the kingship of the Uí Néill, and because of a strong friendship with Northumbria, both of which gave Iona enormous political influence. During his abbacy several new monasteries were founded, including Lindisfarne, in Northumbria.

SELBACH (?–730), King of Dál Riata. A son of Fearchar Fota and brother of AINBCELLACH, who was deposed in 698, Selbach defeated and killed his brother's captor in 700, but then seized the kingship himself and defeated Ainbcellach in 719. The Cenél nGabráin, however, one of the three dynasties which competed for kingship in Dál Riata, attacked and defeated Selbach in a sea battle the following month. In 723 he was recorded as entering the monastic life, apparently relinquishing the kingdom to his son, DÚNGAL MAC SELBAIG.

SELBORNE, 1ST EARL OF *see* PALMER, ROUNDELL

SELDEN, JOHN (1584–1654), legal writer and politician. A brilliant Oxford-educated lawyer (bencher of the Inner Temple, 1612), historian and oriental scholar, he was a member of Lucius CAREY's Great Tew circle, and prominent as an experienced MP in the opposition to CHARLES I. His secular-minded *History of Tithes* (1617) much annoyed clergy. Though active in the Long Parliament throughout the 1640s, he left public life in 1649.

SELFRIDGE, GORDON (1858–1947), retailer. The man who began the Americanization of London's retailing, Selfridge was born in Wisconsin, USA, the son of a store owner, and he joined the retailing firm Marshall Field in Chicago. After 20 years as its successful general manager, in 1906 he set up his own business by opening a store in London's Oxford Street. His flamboyance won him instant recognition; after 20 years of growth the Gordon Selfridge Trust was founded in 1926, but the 1930s were lean years.

Forced to retire in 1939, Selfridge died without property.

SEN, AMARTYA (1933–), economist. Born in Bengal, a graduate of Calcutta and Cambridge universities, he has held many academic posts of distinction, and having been Professor of Economics at Delhi, the London School of Economics and All Souls College, Oxford, he became Master of Trinity College, Cambridge, in 1998. He was awarded the Nobel Prize in Economics in 1998. His prolific work covers a wide spectrum, dealing with matters such as third-world poverty, inequality and unemployment. He has focused on issues of welfare economics and social choice, in particular taking into account liberty and rights. Latterly he has developed an analytical framework to explain the causation of famines, which have previously been viewed as in essence an outcome of a decline in the availability of food. Sen, however, examined a number of major famines and showed that they were caused by problems of 'food acquirement'. He developed the concept of 'entitlements': famines rarely impact upon the whole population of a given country, rather they affect particular groups which are at risk because they do not have the economic political or social entitlements ('leverage') which enable them to acquire food even in circumstances where supply is plentiful. This approach produces interesting hypotheses: it explains the gender bias which characterizes famines and suggests that even in very poor societies famines are less likely to occur if there are democratic structures, adversarial politics or a free press.

SEPTIMIUS SEVERUS, Roman Emperor (193–211). In 208, 11 years after he became uncontested Emperor following his defeat of CLODIUS ALBINUS, Severus brought a large army to Britain. He campaigned far into Scotland against tribes such as the Maeatae and Caledonii, who seem to have been especially restive at this time. He died at York while preparing for another campaign with the possible aim of a complete conquest of Britain; civil war in Rome meant that his son Caracalla had to abandon the project.

SERF (OR SERVANUS), ST (*fl. c.* 700). During the later Middle Ages, various traditions concerning Serf emerged, which provide contradictory detail and widely differing dates for him. Several sources give an Israelite or Canaanite origin, but exotic origins are claimed for several Scottish saints and should most likely be discounted. He is claimed variously as a contemporary of St KENTIGERN, PALLADIUS and ADOMNÁN. Serf's sphere of influence was certainly Fife, with several foundations, particularly at Culross, Lochleven and Dysart, and it is therefore most likely he was of Pictish or, perhaps, British descent.

SETON, ALEXANDER (1st Earl of Dunfermline) (1555–1622), politician. A son of George, Lord Seton, Jesuit-educated at Rome, he was made titular Prior of Pluscarden; although proclaiming himself Protestant on returning to Scotland, he retained Roman Catholic sympathies. After legal training in France, he was the leading Scots lawyer of his generation. Privy Councillor from 1585 and in 1596 one of the Treasury 'Octavians' (*see* ELPHINSTONE, JAMES; HAMILTON, THOMAS), he was Chancellor of Scotland from 1604 to 1608, given his earldom in 1605, working closely with George HUME, Earl of Dunbar, to administer Scotland for the absentee JAMES VI.

SETTLE, ELKANAH (1648–1724), playwright. Abandoning his studies at Oxford when his first play, *Cambyses*, was performed at Lincoln's Inn Fields in 1666, Settle wrote a series of bombastic political allegories often set in African or Asian countries. His political allegiances shifted between the court and its opponents, and, perhaps even more intensely than SHADWELL, he enjoyed a long feud with DRYDEN. In 1690 he was appointed poet to the City of London, but his work became anachronistic and when he died he was a 'poor brother' of Charterhouse.

SEWARD, ANNA (1747–1809), poet. Her father was a canon of Lichfield, where she lived for most of her life. She was encouraged to write by Erasmus DARWIN, and benefited from the secure environment of the apartment which she first shared with and then inherited from her father. She rarely visited London but her friends included Hester THRALE and later Robert SOUTHEY and Walter SCOTT. Her first published works appeared in the *Batheaston Miscellany* (1775–81) edited by Lady Miller, and her 'poetical novel' *Louisa* (1782) went to five editions. She became known as the Swan of Lichfield. Seward described JOHNSON as 'the great Cham' of literature, writing against him in the *Gentleman's Magazine* under the pseudonym Benvolio, but advised BOSWELL when he wrote his biography.

SEYMOUR, EDWARD (5th Duke of Somerset) *see* essay on page 717

SEYMOUR, EDWARD (1539–1621), nobleman *see* GREY, LADY CATHERINE

SEYMOUR, SIR EDWARD (1633–1708), politician. The head of a powerful West Country family, the junior branch of which were Dukes of Somerset, he became an MP in 1661 and was

continued on page 718

SEYMOUR, EDWARD
(Viscount Beauchamp, 8th [1st Seymour] Earl of Hertford, 5th [1st Seymour] Duke of Somerset) (?1500–52)
Politician

Of Wolf Hall (Wilts.), he studied at Oxford, perhaps also at Cambridge, and was already serving at court in his teens; he first saw military service in Charles BRANDON's expedition to France in 1523, and became Master of the Horse to HENRY VIII's bastard son Henry, Duke of Richmond. His career blossomed when his sister JANE SEYMOUR married the King in 1536, and he was made a viscount. A year later he became Earl of Hertford, and from 1542 was prominent in Henry's Franco-Scottish wars. He served with notable success in Scotland in 1542 and 1544–5, then led a victory over the French in 1545 before returning to Scotland. A final tour of service in France in 1546 culminated in his role in peace negotiations.

By now Seymour and his formidable second wife, Anne Stanhope, were identified as in the evangelical or reformist religious grouping at court, and he increasingly aligned himself with his fellow soldier John DUDLEY. Tension grew with another military colleague, Henry HOWARD, Earl of Surrey, son of the veteran conservative politician Thomas HOWARD, 8th Duke of Norfolk, so it was a stroke of luck for Seymour and his fellow evangelicals in the delicate balance of politics in Henry VIII's last months that Surrey's indiscreet ambition made a charge of treason plausible. The Duke of Norfolk only escaped following his son to the scaffold because of the King's death (28 Jan. 1547). In the King's will, Seymour was named an executor, and with William PAGET's help he persuaded the Council of Regency to appoint him Protector of the Realm; he was promoted as Duke of Somerset and Earl Marshal of England, Paget claiming that this had been the wish of Henry VIII just before his death. Soon he removed Thomas WRIOTHESLEY, the only conservative Councillor likely to rally opposition to him. He monopolized power (in popular opinion, encouraged by his wife), frequently ignoring his fellow Councillors. To enforce marriage proposals between EDWARD VI and MARY QUEEN OF SCOTS he renewed war with Scotland, winning a victory at Pinkie (10 Sept. 1547); in an attempt to consolidate his success, he began planting English garrisons in Scots strongholds, which proved hugely expensive. He financed this by continuing disastrous debasement of the coinage, but also by attacking the old religion, which gave an excuse to complete the dissolution of the chantries and confiscation of their property. Genuinely enthusiastic for religious change, he began a step-by-step programme of reformation, organizing the destruction of Catholic church fittings and authorizing liturgies in English. In 1549 widespread unrest broke out, encouraged by his sponsorship of enclosure investigations (see KETT, ROBERT); Seymour showed open sympathy to popular grievances and prepared to make sweeping concessions to the demonstrators. Against a background of the bloodily suppressed Western Rebellion against religious change and France's renewal of war, his fellow Councillors led by Dudley decided that enough was enough; in Oct. 1549 they deprived Seymour of power, after a tense stand-off in which he nearly appealed to popular mob armies to maintain his position. Pardoned in 1550, he was released from the Tower and readmitted to the Council, but Dudley remained suspicious of his popularity and Seymour began intriguing to improve his position, in his increasing desperation making overtures to such unlikely allies as Stephen GARDINER and the Lady Mary, later MARY I. Arrested in Oct. 1551, he was executed on 22 Jan. 1552 on flimsy charges of treason.

He was an ambitious builder, demolishing St Mary-le-Strand and quarrying materials from other London churches to begin Somerset House, whose site is now occupied by eighteenth-century government buildings. His other projects at Berry Pomeroy Castle (Devon) and Great Bedwyn (Wilts.) are both now scanty ruins, but all were remarkable for being among the first pure Renaissance designs in England.

Somerset's reputation as a high-minded idealist and friend of the Reformation, 'the Good Duke', began as early as the writings of his contemporary admirer John PONET, and reached its apogee in A. F. Pollard's biography. M. L. Bush argued by contrast that he was a conventional-minded nobleman who was merely prepared to gesture towards reform in order to court popularity, and whose approach to politics was little different from that of his fellow Councillors; Bush interpreted Seymour's main concern as the securing of his successes in Scotland by his garrisoning policy. Recent discovery of some of his correspondence with the demonstrators of 1549, however, reveals the extraordinary degree to which he was prepared to listen to and even encourage their demands for reform. He was making a populist appeal beyond his colleagues in government, and he displayed a hyperactive concern for reform in all spheres of policy that gives his brief time in power an atmosphere unique in Tudor politics.

M. L. Bush, *The Government Policy of Protector Somerset* (1975) elected Speaker of the Commons in 1673. CHARLES II made him a Privy Councillor but Seymour demonstrated his independence from the court to such an extent that in 1679 the King vetoed his re-appointment as Speaker. Seymour opposed the Bill to exclude the future James II from the line of succession, but urged James to return to Anglicanism; later he suggested that the Prince of Orange (the future WILLIAM III) should become Regent if James was still a Catholic at his accession. He again advocated a regency in 1689, but accepted William and MARY II as joint monarchs. After a brief spell in government Seymour realigned himself with the Country opposition led by Robert HARLEY. When Louis XIV recognized James Edward STUART as James III in 1701 Seymour supported William's military plans as the lesser evil. ANNE made him Comptroller of the Royal Household, but his support for militarization and involvement in continental affairs was never wholehearted and he was dismissed by Marlborough (*see* CHURCHILL, JOHN) in 1704.

SEYMOUR, THOMAS (1st Baron Seymour of Sudeley) (?1508–49), soldier. Brother of Edward SEYMOUR, Duke of Somerset, and Queen JANE SEYMOUR, he gave diplomatic, military and naval service to HENRY VIII. On EDWARD VI's accession he was created Lord Admiral and Baron. He married the royal widow, CATHERINE PARR, an old love and, after her death in childbirth, made unsubtle overtures to the teenage Princess Elizabeth (*see* ELIZABETH I). His jealous intrigues against his brother, Edward SEYMOUR, the Lord Protector, led to his execution; although the charges of treasonous conspiracy were genuine enough, the Protector's reputation suffered.

SHACKLETON, SIR ERNEST (1874–1922), explorer. Serving in the merchant marine from 1890, and a sublieutenant in the Royal Naval Reserve from 1901, Shackleton joined the first *Discovery* expedition under Robert SCOTT but was invalided out. He returned to Antarctica in 1908 as an expeditionary leader and got to within 150 km of the South Pole, claiming Victoria Land for the Crown. He led a further Antarctic expedition in 1914–16, planning to be the first to cross Antarctica, but his ship was crushed in the ice. He and his colleagues drifted on ice floes for five months, and finally escaped in boats to South Georgia where they were the first to cross the island in their struggle to get help. Shackleton returned to Antarctica in 1922 but died on South Georgia.

SHADWELL, THOMAS (*c.* 1642–92), playwright. He came from Norfolk and was educated at Cambridge and the Middle Temple before abandoning law for theatre. He married an actress, Anne Gibbs, and after studying the French stage had his first play, *The Sullen Lovers*, performed in 1668. It was adapted from Molière, as was *The Miser* (1672). Shadwell's later plays included *The Virtuoso* (1680), a satire on the Royal Society, and his greatest success, *The Squire of Alsatia* (1688), based in the lawless district of Whitefriars. Shadwell quarrelled fiercely with his Tory rival DRYDEN, who satirized him as a dull writer although Shadwell's plays were just as vigorous as those of his contemporaries; in 1689 he supplanted Dryden as Poet Laureate.

SHAFTESBURY, EARL OF, **1ST, 3RD, 5TH** and **7TH** *see* COOPER, ANTHONY ASHLEY

SHAH, SELIM JEHANE ('EDDIE') (1944–), publisher. Known as the man who 'broke' the power of the print trade unions in the newspaper industry and publisher of Britain's first colour newspaper, Shah was born in Cambridge, the son of an authority on maritime law. His early years were spent in India. Experience on a free newspaper in Manchester gave him the confidence to launch his own newspaper, the *Sale and Altrincham Messenger,* in 1974. By 1983 his business was a success, and he came to national attention in his battle, ultimately victorious, with print unions over their closed shop. Flushed with victory, he established a national colour newspaper, *Today*. A financial disaster, the title was sold to Lonrho (*see* ROWLAND, ROLAND) and then to Rupert MURDOCH, who profited from the trail that Shah had blazed.

SHAKESPEARE, WILLIAM *see* essay on page 719

SHANNON, 1ST EARL OF *see* BOYLE, HENRY

SHARP, CECIL (1859–1927), folk-song and dance collector. A lawyer who turned to music, Sharp was Principal of the Hampstead Conservatory (1896–1905) and collected hundreds of English folk songs and dances. In 1911 he founded the English Folk-Dance Society.

SHARP, DAME EVELYN (1903–85), civil servant. The daughter of a vicar of Ealing and educated at Somerville College, Oxford, she entered the Civil Service in 1926, rising to be Permanent Secretary (the first woman to hold this position) to the Ministry of Housing and Local Government (1955–66). She worked to strengthen the links between central and local government and was particularly influential in the development of new towns in the post-war years.

SHAKESPEARE, WILLIAM (1564–1616)
Dramatist and poet

Notoriously, the undramatic and relatively ill-documented life of England's greatest dramatist has provoked fantasy and various snobbish reassignments of his work, the least deranged of which are to Francis BACON or Edward DE VERE, 17th Earl of Oxford. Shakespeare was born at Stratford-on-Avon (Warws.), and his education, the acquisition of what Ben JONSON patronizingly styled his 'small Latin and less Greek', was probably at the town's free grammar school. The school had a succession of masters who were Roman Catholic sympathizers. Similarly Shakespeare's father John, a wool dealer and glover, began refusing to attend his parish church in 1576, and a MS copy of the *Spiritual Testament* brought to England in the 1580s by Jesuit missioners from the Archbishop of Milan Carlo Borromeo, a work of intense Counter-Reformation devotion, was discovered hidden in John's former home in 1757. It is likely that Shakespeare's early acting career was spent in the network of recusant gentry families; he may have served as a resident player (under the variant surname 'Shakeshaft') with the Hoghton family at Lea Hall (Lancs.) in the late 1570s. He married Anne Hathaway in 1582. Probably at the end of the 1580s he began his theatrical career in London, where evidence of strong Catholic sympathies becomes difficult to trace in his work: he may have started writing plays *c*. 1588. He attracted patronage from Henry Wriothesley, 4th Earl of Southampton, to whom he dedicated much of his poetry: *Venus and Adonis* (1593) and *The Rape of Lucrece* (1594). It has been argued that Southampton was also the male subject of his sonnets, not published until 1609. Shakespeare spent his acting career from 1594 with the Lord Chamberlain's Company (renamed the King's Company after JAMES I's accession in 1603), of which Richard BURBAGE was the principal actor, and with Burbage and others he acquired interests in two theatres, the Globe (1599) and Blackfriars (1609). The chronology and scope of his drama remains less certain than standard editions pretend. Subsequent forgeries are easy to detect, but throughout his career he wrote some plays in collaboration with others, and in retirement at Stratford from *c*. 1613 (in the house New Place which, as a mark of his prosperity and success, he had bought in 1597), he revised many plays for publication. The first collected edition of his works (the First Folio) was published posthumously in 1623. A subsequent owner of New Place, infuriated at crowds of tourists, demolished it in 1759, but the house which was in all probability Shakespeare's birthplace survives, restored to a Tudor condition. Shakespeare's cultural influence both on the English language and on European culture has been immense. Soon after his death, his work was esteemed above that of his English contemporaries as dramatists, with three folio editions of his work between 1623 and 1664; thereafter his work was frequently edited during the seventeenth and eighteenth centuries in order to smooth down what was considered its unacceptable roughness and, in the nineteenth century, while the language was restored, many sexual and scatological elements in the plays were omitted from editions, notoriously in that of 1818 by Thomas Bowdler (1754–1825; hence 'bowdlerization'). Translations into major European languages (e.g. German 1762, French 1776, Italian 1814, Russian 1841) played a great part in the romantic movement and stimulated the search for similar symbolically dominant literary figures for other national cultures. Shakespeare's sonnets have captured the European imagination not simply for their literary merits but also for the tangled emotional story which seems to lie behind them, with their mysterious dedication to 'Mr. W. H.' and their evident focuses on both a male and a female beloved.

In the history plays, Shakespeare drew on the commonplace historical sources of his day, especially HOLINSHED's *Chronicle*, and this resulted in the triumphalist dynastic propaganda of the Tudors about themselves and their predecessors becoming deeply embedded in English consciousness; in particular this has distorted assessment of Shakespeare's arch-villain RICHARD III. The universality of Shakespeare's vision remains a major point for discussion: his espousal of the uninformed attitudes of his age to Jews in *The Merchant of Venice* offers problems for a post-Holocaust audience, and his complex portrayal of the figure of Caliban in *The Tempest* provokes questions about racial attitudes in the early encounters of Europe with the New World. Overall, his works, and phrases remembered from them, have shaped the development of English as decisively as the almost contemporary English translations of the Bible and CRANMER's Prayer Book. The widespread interest in the unearthing of the sites in Southwark of theatres associated with him, the Rose and the Globe (destroyed by fire in 1613), illustrates the continuing English fascination with Shakespeare as a national symbol.

Samuel Schoenbaum, Shakespeare's Lives (1970)

SHARP, GRANVILLE (1734–1813), anti-slavery activist, political and religious campaigner. Grandson of an Archbishop of York, and ninth son of the Archdeacon of Northumberland, Sharp was apprenticed to a London linen-draper, but joined the ordnance as a clerk in 1758. Having become concerned about the case of an abused slave, Jonathan Strong, he researched constitutional history and the laws of personal liberty, and published *A Representation of the Injustice . . . of Tolerating Slavery* (1769). His efforts prompted Lord Mansfield's (*see* MURRAY, WILLIAM) landmark judgement in the Somerset case. Having developed American contacts in this connection, he supported the American colonists against Britain in the War of American Independence, and resigned his post. He also supported the Irish campaign for legislative independence, and the cause of parliamentary reform. He became President of the Quaker-dominated Society for the Abolition of the Slave Trade in 1787, played a part in the establishment of a colony for freed slaves in Sierra Leone (1787), and was a founder of the African Institution (1807). His allies in the anti-slavery campaign included Josiah WEDGWOOD and both Samuel WHITBREADs. He worked with Archbishop SECKER to establish Episcopacy in the independent United States, and was prominent in the establishment of the British and Foreign Bible Society (1804) and the Society for the Conversion of the Jews (1808). He was first Chairman of the Protestant Union formed to oppose Catholic Emancipation. He established a rule or 'canon' for the translation of the New Testament from Greek, which became a crucial factor in the debate over Unitarianism, and published works to demonstrate the fulfilment of scriptural prophecies.

SHAW, GEORGE BERNARD (1856–1950), playwright, critic and political activist. After an unsatisfactory Dublin childhood as the son of a downwardly mobile Anglo-Irish family, he went to London in 1876, worked successfully as a journalist – he wrote about music under the name Corno di Bassetto for *The Star* (1888–90) and was drama critic of the *Saturday Review* (1895–8) – and set about educating himself, mainly in the reading room of the British Museum, where he read MARX's weighty *Das Kapital* in French as it had not yet been translated into English. A reforming and sometimes radical political activist all his life, in 1884 he joined the newly formed Fabian Society when he hoped it had a more urgent agenda than its name and later gradualism suggested: Shaw thought that two weeks was about the time needed to establish socialism in Britain. He persuaded his friends Beatrice and Sidney WEBB to join, edited *Fabian Tracts* (writing three himself) and put his considerable oratorical gifts at the service of the society. By the end of the 1880s, now convinced that Fabianism must be a constitutional, politically respectable movement, Shaw, following the policy of 'permeation', entered London politics, serving as a Councillor for St Pancras (1897–1903). In 1893 he was one of the two Fabian representatives at the inaugural conference of the Independent Labour Party and in 1904 stood, unsuccessfully, for election to the London County Council (LCC) as a Progressive.

By 1900 he had found another vehicle for his political energies: his career as a dramatist had taken off, though he continued to write and orate on behalf of the Fabians, as on a variety of other causes including vegetarianism, eugenics, reform of the marriage laws and even a reformed alphabet. His very long explanation, *The Intelligent Woman's Guide to Socialism and Capitalism* (1928), sold in its thousands and in 1937 was the first Pelican (*see* LANE, ALLEN) to be published. All his plays had a political purpose: they were intended to engage the audience in intelligent debate, though their elegance, wit and irony meant that only parts seemed like lectures; humour is 'my sword, my shield and my spear', he maintained. Several were performed only in private, and each had a long preface written by Shaw which gave more space to his views on social, political and moral matters: *Mrs Warren's Profession* (1893, though banned from performance until 1925) was about poverty and prostitution; *Arms and the Man* (1894), which inverts the traditional view of male gallantry, was the first to be permitted a public performance; *Man and Superman* (1903) reflects his interest in eugenics ('creative evolution') and advocates selective breeding; *John Bull's Other Island* (1904, his first real stage success) made an intervention into the 'Irish Question' of land reform and Home Rule; *Major Barbara* (1905) is about the arms trade; *The Doctor's Dilemma* (1906) is a prescient argument for the establishment of a national health service; while the extravaganza *The Apple Cart* (1929) takes an anti-democracy line advocating a government of enlightened despots. In 1925 Shaw received the Nobel Prize for Literature: other honours he eschewed. Of his more than 50 plays a number continue to be staged; a few have been filmed, and *Pygmalion* (1913) was made into the musical *My Fair Lady* (1964).

SHAW, HESTER (?1586–1660), midwife. From London, she was in practice from *c.* 1610 and in 1634 led a successful petition of midwives in protest against the scheme of the physician and man-midwife Peter Chamberlen (1601–83) to found a college of midwives under his direction. Evidence in a lawsuit resulting from the destruction of her London house in a gunpowder explosion in 1650 portrays a woman whose self-confidence, piety and education clearly intimidated her male contemporaries.

SHAW, NORMAN (1831–1912), architect. Trained in the Gothic style, Shaw became interested in the conservation and particularly the reproduction of an 'old English style' in building. He incorporated mullioned windows, gables and inglenooks into his buildings. Bedford Park, a speculative building development of Queen Anne style brick houses in west London built in the late 1870s as the first ever 'garden suburb', is most usually associated with Shaw's architecture. A number of his pupils, most notably W. R. LETHABY, were to be part of the Arts and Crafts movement but, by the 1890s, Shaw, who also designed a number of eclectic country houses, had changed his style again, as evidenced in the more classical New Scotland Yard (1890). He was involved in interminable discussions over the rebuilding of parts of central London, including Piccadilly Circus, but died before they came to fruition.

SHAW, SIR WILLIAM, NAPIER (1854–1945), meteorologist. Shaw studied natural sciences at Cambridge University and in 1877 became Assistant Director of the Cavendish Laboratory there, where he transformed physics teaching and researched hygrometry, evaporation and the behaviour of air currents. As Director of the Meteorological Office (1905–20), he built up a scientifically trained staff, pioneered balloon-based observations of the upper atmosphere and invented synoptic charts for representing North Atlantic pressure systems. He also introduced the millibar as a unit of pressure and developed Jacob Bjerknes's 'polar front' theory of cyclones. His *Manual of Meteorology* (1926–31) was an influential textbook.

SHAWCROSS, SIR HARTLEY (Baron Shawcross of Friston) (1902–), politician. A distinguished law student with a flourishing practice at the Bar in the 1920s and 1930s, Shawcross came to international attention as the UK's chief prosecutor at the Nuremberg war crimes tribunal. He retired from the Bar in 1958, but had long since entered politics: Labour MP for St Helens (Lancs.) (1945–58), he was Attorney General (1945–51), then President of the Board of Trade in ATTLEE's short-lived second government. Never perfectly adjusted to his party, he was caricatured as Sir Shortly Floor-cross. He was a member of many legal panels and company boards, for example the influential panel on takeovers and mergers (1969–80).

SHAXTON, NICHOLAS (c. 1485–1556), churchman. A Cambridge don who benefited from Anne BOLEYN's patronage to become Bishop of Salisbury in 1535, his evangelical enthusiasm impelled him to resign the see when the traditionalist Act of Six Articles was passed in 1539. After arrest in 1546 on heresy charges, however, the trauma forced him to recant his views, which he did publicly at the burning of Anne AYSCOUGH. He remained a Catholic for the rest of his life, alienated from his wife and children, and participating in the examination of Protestants under MARY I.

SHEEHY, NICHOLAS (1728–1766), Catholic priest. A native of Co. Tipperary, Sheehy was educated in Spain before returning to his home county to become a priest. In the 1760s his parish of Shanraghan and Templetenny became a centre for the 'Whiteboys', Irish small farmers protesting against tithes and other agrarian grievances, interpreted by some contemporaries as opponents of Protestant rule. Sheehy fell under suspicion. In 1764 soldiers escorting a prisoner to Clonmel gaol were attacked near his house. Sheehy agreed to be tried for high treason if he could appear before a court in Dublin rather than Clonmel. This was accepted and his alibi was proven before a Dublin court. He was immediately rearrested and tried at Clonmel in connection with the murder of an informer. He was found guilty and executed despite the absence of evidence to connect him to the killing.

SHEEHY SKEFFINGTON, FRANCIS (originally Skeffington) (1878–1916), politician. An agnostic and advocate of socialism, pacifism and women's suffrage, he was associated in campaigning for secular education with Michael DAVITT, whose biography he published in 1908. In 1915 Sheehy-Skeffington served a short term of imprisonment for making anti-war speeches, and during the 1916 Easter Rising he was arrested and shot by a British officer. The execution and subsequent cover-up were widely unpopular in Ireland, and he came to be revered as a nationalist martyr. He married Hanna Sheehy in 1903, and joined his name to hers; their son Owen was a prominent member of the Irish Senate.

SHEEHY SKEFFINGTON, HANNA (née Sheehy) (1877–1946), feminist. One of a new generation of professional women from Catholic middle-class backgrounds who entered the Irish suffrage movement (hitherto predominantly Protestant), a socialist and agnostic, she married Francis Skeffington in 1903; they added each other's surname as a symbol of equality. She was a militant suffragist, imprisoned at one point for her activities, and edited the Irish feminist journal, the *Irish Citizen*. After the killing of her husband in 1916 she became a Republican activist; opposing the Anglo-Irish Treaty, she was extremely critical of the position assigned to women by the first governments of the new State, and remained active in Republican and feminist groups for the rest of her life.

SHEFFIELD, JOHN (3rd Earl of Mulgrave, 1st Marquess of Normanby and 6th [1st Sheffield] Duke of Buckingham) (1648–1721), politician. Son of the 2nd Earl of Mulgrave, he took an active part in the Dutch wars and at court. He was a friend of JAMES II (eventually marrying his illegitimate daughter) but in 1689 submitted to WILLIAM III. In opposition for most of William's reign, he was made Lord Privy Seal and a duke by Anne. When forced out of office by the Whigs in 1706 Buckingham agitated for the bringing of the Electress SOPHIA to England but only embarrassed Anne and caused the Hanoverians to mistrust him. He was in office again from 1710 under Robert HARLEY but was excluded from the government by GEORGE I on his accession. Buckingham was also an accomplished poet and playwright and a patron of John DRYDEN.

SHELBURNE, 3RD EARL *see* PETTY, WILLIAM

SHELDON, GILBERT (1598–1677), Archbishop of Canterbury (1663–77). Educated at Oxford, ordained and appointed Warden of All Souls in 1626, he associated with the Great Tew circle (*see* CAREY, LUCIUS). He was confidential adviser to CHARLES I in 1646–7 and during the Isle of Wight Treaty negotiations. In 1648 he was ejected from his wardenship and imprisoned for a year. Reinstated in 1659, he was made Bishop of London the following year. He was prominent in royal favour, and was a member of the Privy Council. From April to July 1661 he presided over the Savoy conference, where Anglicans and Presbyterians tried to find a consensual basis for the Restoration religious settlement. His disinclination to allow variety in practice within the Church, despite the arguments of the Presbyterians led by Richard BAXTER, contributed to the thwarting of proposals for comprehension, and the climate which allowed the passing of the various laws against Dissenting worship and participation in public life, termed the Clarendon Code. In 1663 he was made Archbishop of Canterbury and oversaw much of the practical work of re-establishing the Church. Sheldon has been criticized for his narrowness of vision but must be given credit for the energy with which he achieved the re-establishment of a united and disciplined Church.

SHELLEY, MARY (née Godwin) (1797–1851), novelist. She was the only daughter of two radical writers, William GODWIN and Mary WOLL-

STONECRAFT; the latter died within days of her birth. She met the poet Percy Bysshe SHELLEY in 1812 and eloped with him to Europe in 1814, marrying him in Dec. 1816. In the summer of 1816 they stayed with BYRON on Lake Geneva and it was here that Mary, aged 19, started to write her Gothic novel *Frankenstein* (1818). After her husband's death in 1822, the deaths of two of their children and two miscarriages, Mary returned to England intent on supporting her only surviving child, Percy, by her writing, and preserving the reputation of Shelley. She edited his poetry, prose and letters as well as publishing several other novels, none of which achieved the fame of *Frankenstein*.

SHELLEY, PERCY BYSSHE (1792–1822), poet and radical. An atheist, radical, political pamphleteer and poet since his teens, Shelley was the son of the MP for Horsham (Sussex). For him, poetry and politics were inseparable, and his philosophy found expression in such works as *Queen Mab* (1813), *Alastor* (1816), *The Revolt of Islam* (1818), 'Julian and Maddalo' (1818, published 1824, an exploration of his friendship with BYRON), 'Ode to the West Wind' (1819), *The Mask of Anarchy* (1819, written on hearing of the Peterloo Massacre), *Prometheus Unbound* (1820) and 'To a Skylark' and 'The Cloud' (both 1820). His impecunious, nomadic life and his flouting of conventions – he eloped with the 16-year-old Harriet Westbrook in 1811 and in 1814 with Mary Godwin (*see* SHELLEY, MARY), whom he married in 1816 – led him to Italy, where he settled permanently in 1818 and where he was drowned in the Bay of Spezia in Aug. 1822.

SHELTON, JOHN (1797–1845), soldier. Commissioned in 1805, he served in the Peninsular War, losing his right arm in the storming of San Sebastian in 1813. Shelton exchanged into the 44th regiment in India, and in 1827 secured the lieutenant colonelcy. By 1840 he commanded a brigade, including the 44th, in Afghanistan. Cut off in Kabul by a popular uprising, he quarrelled openly with Sir William ELPHINSTONE, the overall commander. The subsequent retreat in early Jan. 1842 through the mountains to India, with Shelton commanding an ever-diminishing rearguard, turned into the British army's single greatest disaster of the nineteenth century. Of the 20,000 who began the retreat, only one man reached India, while Shelton himself, and 100 or so European women and wounded British officers, survived as prisoners of the Afghans until their release in Sept. Exonerated by a court martial, Shelton returned to England to rebuild the 44th, where his harsh training and irascible temper made him loathed by both officers and men. When he died on 13 Nov. 1845, the entire regiment paraded and gave three cheers.

SHERATON, THOMAS (?–1806), furniture designer. From Stockton-on-Tees, he was working in London by 1791, probably as a drawing-master and designer of furniture, although it is uncertain whether he actually had a workshop. His influence came from his books, which codified and disseminated ideas on taste in furniture at the end of the eighteenth century, overtaking the lingering influence of CHIPPENDALE. The first, *The Cabinet-maker and Upholsterer's Drawing-Book*, was completed in 1793. Like HEPPLEWHITE, Sheraton popularized furniture inspired by the work of the ADAM brothers, particularly that at the Prince Regent's (the future GEORGE IV) new residence of Carlton House. Sheraton's *Cabinet Directory* of 1803 heralded what became the Regency era in furniture; the next year he began an epic alphabetical part-work, *The Cabinet-maker, Upholsterer, and General Artists' Encyclopaedia,* but when he died he had only reached the letter C.

SHERBROOKE, 1ST VISCOUNT *see* LOWE, ROBERT

SHERIDAN, RICHARD BRINSLEY (1751–1816), playwright and politician. Son of an Irish actor and teacher of rhetoric, he moved to England with his parents in the 1760s, and finished his education at Harrow. He eloped with the singer Elizabeth LINLEY in 1772, a complex incident which landed him in a duel and gave him a romantic aura. He began writing for the theatre, making his name with a series of witty comedies, including *The Rivals* (1775) and *The School for Scandal* (1777). From 1776 he was a proprietor and manager of the Drury Lane Theatre in London's Covent Garden. Income from this gave him a basis for political activity; in 1779 he founded a short-lived opposition journal, *The Englishman,* and in 1780 he was elected MP. He was Under-Secretary of State in the 1782 Rockingham (*see* WATSON-WENTWORTH, CHARLES) administration, and Secretary of the Treasury in the FOX–NORTH coalition. A leading opponent of PITT THE YOUNGER, his views were not changed by the French Revolution, and in 1792 he and Charles GREY founded the Society of Friends of the People to recruit liberal Whig support for parliamentary reform; despite early misgivings it was endorsed by Fox. In later life he acquired a reputation for unreliability: the theatre was placed under the control of a committee, and he was later bought out, financial control passing to the younger Samuel WHITBREAD. In politics he was judged quixotic and calculating, but was nonetheless made Treasurer of the Navy in 1806–7.

SHERRINGTON, SIR CHARLES (1857–1952), neurophysiologist. Sherrington studied at Cam-bridge, London, Strasbourg and Berlin, and became lecturer in physiology at St Thomas's Hospital, London (1887–91), and Professor of Physiology at Liverpool (1895–1912) and at Oxford (1913–35). In the 1890s he mapped the connections between the muscular and nervous systems, made pioneering studies of knee-jerk reflex, and invented several new neurological concepts including 'synapse' (the connection between nerve cells). Later he determined the neurone connections in the spinal cord and brain-stem that are responsible for the reflex actions in vertebrates, mapped out the motor points of the cerebral cortex in apes and showed 'conditioned reflex' in certain nerve cells in the spinal cord. His researches culminated in his seminal *Integrative Action of the Nervous System* (1906). He shared the 1932 Nobel Prize for Medicine with Edgar ADRIAN.

SHINWELL, EMMANUEL (MANNY) (Baron Shinwell) (1884–1986), politician. Apprenticed at 11 to be a tailor's cutter, 'Manny' (as he was always known), a ferocious reader, took the autodidact's route into politics, joining the Independent Labour Party in 1903 and becoming involved in trade-union politics as a member of the Glasgow Trades Council and an organizer for the National Union of Seamen.

On 'Bloody Friday', 31 Jan. 1919, a demonstration in Glasgow in favour of a 40-hour working week was broken up by the police with great brutality and, as one of the strike leaders (though himself a moderate), he was jailed. It made him a local hero and in the 1922 General Election he was returned to Parliament as Labour member for Linlithgow. He held office in the 1924 Labour government and in 1931 was one of the handful of Labour MPs asked by Ramsay MACDONALD to join the National government. He refused, and was out of the House until 1935, when he ousted MacDonald from his constituency of Seaham (Co. Durham). He declined to join the wartime Coalition government, but in 1945 accepted ATTLEE's offer of the Ministry of Fuel and Power, charged with nationalizing the coal industry. His short-termist approach to politics made him a disaster in the job, and in 1947 his reputation reached a nadir with his handling of that year's fuel crisis. He lost his seat in Cabinet and became Minister for War, advocating the creation of NATO (North Atlantic Treaty Organization), and when he was appointed Minister of Defence in 1950 was a hardliner in pressing for increased expenditure on rearmament in the face of war in Korea and the escalating East–West Cold War. After Labour lost the 1951 election, trusted by neither wing of the party, he lost any power base which he had had, and was an unpopular chairman of the Parliamentary Labour Party (1964–7), forever at odds with Richard CROSSMAN, the Leader of the House. A bitter opponent of Labour's support for the EEC (European Economic Community), as of the party's leftward drift, Shinwell was essentially an opposition politician, more an orator than a policy maker.

SHIPLEY, WILLIAM (1714–1803), promoter of the arts and commerce. Shipley ran a school for drawing in Northampton for many years before moving it to London in 1750. He established the Society for the Encouragement of Arts, Manufactures and Commerce in 1754 in order to promote innovations that could be applied to economic development. It offered prizes in the polite and liberal arts; agriculture, dyeing and mineralogy; and trade and colonies. Prizes were given only to unpatented inventions, to encourage the diffusion of new ideas. The society provided drawing classes to improve the skills of British designers. It continues today as the Royal Society of Arts.

SHIPPEN, WILLIAM (1673–1743), politician. A barrister and MP, he came to prominence as a Tory spokesman during the reign of GEORGE I. An ostentatious Jacobite, Shippen was commended in a letter from ATTERBURY to James Edward STUART for his loyalty. He escaped implication in the Atterbury Plot, however, and continued to oppose the ministry, demanding vengeance on South Sea Co. directors for the bursting of the South Sea Bubble and the reduction of the Civil List, and opposing the excise and Hanoverian interests. Consistently shunning the court, he condemned erstwhile allies who entered the ministry after Robert WALPOLE's fall. He was unenthusiastic about Jacobite invasion schemes in the 1740s and his importance lies more in his principled and sustained opposition to Walpole within the Commons than in his loyalty to the Stuarts.

SHIPTON, MOTHER, fictitious prophet. She is first mentioned in a 1641 pamphlet as an early Tudor figure who prophesied the death of Cardinal WOLSEY; this inspired a genre of prophecy literature using her name, which lasted up to the nineteenth century, mirroring a variety of contemporary concerns. Her cave can be visited at Knaresborough (Yorks.).

SHIRLEY, LAURENCE (1720–60) (4th Earl Ferrers), murderer. After separation from his wife in 1758 on grounds of cruelty he quarrelled with his steward John Johnson, who had been appointed as receiver of rents, and, having failed to eject Johnson from a farm, shot him fatally. Found guilty of murder by the Lords, despite a plea of occasional insanity, he was hanged on 5 May 1760;

the use of a silken rope which he had prepared was forbidden; his body was dissected like that of other felons at Surgeons' Hall.

SHIRLEY, THOMAS (1638–78), litigant. Shirley, physician in ordinary to CHARLES II, in 1675 brought a suit in Chancery against Sir John Fagg (?–1701), a veteran of CROMWELL's army and MP for Steyning, in an attempt to regain his grandfather's estate, which he argued had been sold illegally. When he lost, he appealed to the Lords. The Commons voted this a breach of privilege, and had Fagg imprisoned when he appeared to answer the appeal. The constitutional dispute lapsed only when Charles II prorogued Parliament. Since the Commons did not again contest the Lords' right to act as the final court of appeal, even in cases involving MPs, the episode in effect established a constitutional principle.

SHRAPNEL, HENRY (1761–1842), soldier. Educated at Woolwich, commissioned into the Royal Artillery in July 1779, Shrapnel devoted his long periods in garrison duty to improving ordnance. In 1804 the most famous of his inventions, an exploding shell filled with musket balls, was used with devastating effect during the siege of Surinam. In the same year, Shrapnel, now a Lieutenant Colonel, was appointed First Assistant Inspector of Artillery. For the next 21 years he worked at improving artillery performance, devising range tables, parabolic chambers and a new recoil mechanism and perfecting his shell. During the Napoleonic Wars the British high command regarded Shrapnel's shells as a highly effective secret weapon. Shrapnel's name remains synonymous with all exploding shells.

SHREWSBURY, 4TH EARL OF see TALBOT, JOHN; **15TH EARL AND 1ST DUKE OF** see TALBOT, CHARLES; **COUNTESS OF** see HARDWICK, ELIZABETH

SICKERT, WALTER (1860–1942), artist. Born in Munich, the son of an artist, he went with his family to England in 1868. Sickert was briefly an actor, and theatre and music-hall scenes figure in much of his work. He studied at the Slade School of Art and in 1882 was an assistant to WHISTLER in London, and then to Degas in Paris, becoming one of the most influential proponents of French Impressionism. He lived in Dieppe (1898–1905), and on his return to London became a member of the Camden Town group (1911) and the London group (1913), urban realists who painted north London life in all its dingy vitality. *Ennui* (1914) is one of his best-known paintings from this time. His paintings from the 1930s were also topical, but were copied from photographs and newspaper images, rather than directly from life; his portrayal of EDWARD VII is an example. Sickert was regarded as a fine teacher; his most illustrious private pupil was Winston CHURCHILL.

SIDDAL, ELIZABETH (LIZZIE) (1829–62), artist and model. The delicate, haunting muse of the Pre-Raphaelite Brotherhood, Siddal, the daughter of an ironmonger and cutler, posed for William Holman HUNT and was the model for MILLAIS's *Ophelia*. In 1852 she became a pupil of Dante Gabriel ROSSETTI, whom she married in 1860: their daughter was stillborn in 1861 and she died of an overdose of laudanum the following year. John RUSKIN was her patron and some of her work was exhibited at the Pre-Raphaelite exhibition in 1857.

SIDDONS, SARAH (1755–1831), actress. The daughter of actor-manager Roger KEMBLE and his actress wife Sarah, she started acting as a child with her parents' company and then in various other provincial companies with her husband William. GARRICK recruited her in late 1775 for Drury Lane but her performances attracted derision and she was dismissed. She resumed touring the provinces, gained a huge reputation and returned to Drury Lane to great acclaim in 1782. She appeared in London every year until she retired in 1812. She first played Lady Macbeth in 1785 and her interpretation, particularly the sleepwalking scene, was followed for generations.

SIDGWICK, HENRY (1838–1900), philosopher. Educated at Rugby and Trinity College, Cambridge, graduating in 1859, Sidgwick spent the rest of his career within the university. Although he wrote extensively on moral philosophy and economics, work such as his *Methods of Ethics* (1874) and *Principles of Political Economy* (1883) were written largely in the shadow of John Stuart MILL. His main distinction was as a reformer of the university and supporter of women's rights within it. He was a strong advocate of the abolition of religious tests for university membership (a cause won in 1871) and a supporter of the provision of lectures for women, achieved by the opening of Newnham Hall in 1876. In 1881 he successfully advocated the admission of women to the university and examinations.

SIDGWICK, NEVIL (1873–1952), chemist. Sidgwick read sciences and classics at Oxford, where he built a distinguished academic career in organic chemistry. From 1914 he studied the electronic theory of atomic structure and later proposed the 'hydrogen bond' as an explanation of puzzling properties of certain organic compounds. He is best known for his work on valency, notably his influential *Electronic Theory of Valency* (1927), in which he developed the concept of the covalent bond.

SIDMOUTH, 1ST VISCOUNT *see* ADDINGTON, HENRY

SIDNEY, ALGERNON (1622–83), republican and conspirator. Second son of the 2nd Earl of Leicester, he initially fought for CHARLES I in the First Civil War, but in 1643 joined the Parliamentary side, distinguishing himself as both soldier and administrator. He was appointed to the commission to try the King, but did not take part in the trial or sign the death warrant. A member of the Council of State from 1652, he became increasingly critical of Oliver CROMWELL's tyrannical ways. He went into exile at the restoration of CHARLES II. Having been giving permission to return to England in 1677 to settle his affairs, he was caught up in the excitement associated with the Popish-Plot accusations of Titus OATES and the ensuing Exclusion Crisis (*see* COOPER, ANTHONY ASHLEY). He was accused of heading a rival Nonconformist plot: the Quaker William PENN had indeed aided him in his attempts to win election to the Exclusion Parliaments; Sidney was also a friend of John WILDMAN. He intrigued with the French Ambassador, and sought to persuade Louis XIV that French interests would be well served by the establishment of a republic in England. In 1682–3 he appears to have been among the Whig leaders who debated the merits of resorting to force to challenge the regime. Upon the discovery of the so-called Rye House Plot, to assassinate both the King and his brother (the future JAMES II), he was arrested and, despite flimsy evidence of his involvement, found guilty of high treason and executed, along with William RUSSELL (*see also* CAMPBELL, ARCHIBALD; CAPEL, ARTHUR; FERGUSON, ROBERT). His manuscript, *Discourses on Government*, which argued the case for tyrannicide, was cited in evidence against him. The *Discourses* were published in 1698. Radical Whigs of the eighteenth century honoured Sidney as a martyr to the cause of liberty.

SIDNEY, SIR HENRY (1529–86), administrator. As his father was a servant to the future EDWARD VI, Sidney grew up with the Prince, entering his service and being knighted in 1550. He was sent on diplomatic missions before his first service in Ireland in 1556 and, from 1559 to his death, he was a frequently absentee President of the Council in the Marches of Wales. Becoming Irish Lord Deputy in 1565, he declared his contempt for what he saw as the barbarity of the Irish and, to secure their submission, he continued the aggressive policies of Thomas RADCLIFFE, Earl of Sussex, together with more plantations of English settlers on confiscated land. Although Sidney resigned in frustration in 1571 at the lack of government support, he was reappointed four years later and continued his strategy. He was finally recalled in 1578 to his Welsh duties, after intrigues by his rival Thomas BUTLER, Earl of Ormond, who led resistance to his attempts to raise Irish taxation.

SIDNEY, HENRY (Earl of Romney) (1641–1704), statesman. A younger son of the 2nd (Sidney) Earl of Leicester, in 1679 he became CHARLES II's envoy to the Hague, and subsequently General of the English regiments in Dutch service. He established close ties with the Prince of Orange (later WILLIAM III) but was recalled in 1685 by JAMES II. In 1688 he carried the invitation of the 'Immortal Seven' to William at the Hague and returned to England with him. William made him Lord Lieutenant of Ireland in 1692 but he dissolved Parliament after six weeks when its exclusively Protestant membership refused to pass William's measures of Catholic toleration. Although he remained close to William, he never returned to senior office.

SIDNEY, SIR PHILIP (1554–86), soldier and writer. Son of Henry SIDNEY, he studied at Oxford and travelled abroad (1572–5); he served with his father in Ireland in 1576, and the following year undertook diplomacy in central Europe and the Low Countries. By then he dominated a literary circle, including Edmund SPENSER and Fulke GREVILLE, distinguished both by its Protestant fervour and its enthusiasm for the humanist learning of the Renaissance.

Sidney found that ELIZABETH I's affection for him was clouded by his vigorous espousal of the pet projects of Protestant activists, such as colonization in the New World, help for the Netherlands' rebellion against Spain and opposition to her marriage negotiations with the Catholic FRANCIS OF VALOIS. Made Governor of the Netherlands town of Flushing (Vlissingen) in 1585, he was wounded besieging Zutphen and died at Arnhem a month later. His poetry and prose works were published posthumously, mostly in the 1590s, adding to the near saint-like image of cultured Protestant chivalry which began at his lavish funeral at St Paul's Cathedral. *See also* DEVEREUX, ROBERT; HENRY FREDERICK.

SIEFF, ISRAEL (1st Baron Sieff of Brimpton) (1889–1972) and **MARCUS** (2nd Baron Sieff of Brimpton) (1913–), entrepreneurs. Israel Sieff together with his friend and brother-in-law Simon MARKS built the success of the British retailing chain Marks & Spencer. Born and educated in Manchester, Sieff worked in his father's cloth business before joining Marks & Spencer, becoming a full-time board member as Vice-Chairman in 1926. He was particularly influential in moulding the company's social outlook and benevolent employment policy and in forging direct links with manufacturers, as well as being a passionate and influential Zionist. Succeeding Marks as Chairman in 1964, Sieff retired in 1967. His son Marcus, who had joined the firm in 1935, became Chairman in 1972. He followed his father in many other ways, in promoting labour relations and in Zionism, but it was under his leadership that 'Britain's favourite retailer' extended its product range and its operation overseas.

SIEMENS, SIR CHARLES (1823–83), engineer. Born in Hanover, Siemens was educated in Göttingen and apprenticed in an engineering works. In 1843 he settled in Britain and in the 1850s started collaborating with his brothers, Werner and Friedrich, on his regenerative furnace in which the air supply was fed into a brick chamber pre-heated by waste gases from the furnace and then channelled into a second brick chamber where it mixed with burning fuel. This process enabled higher temperatures, greater fuel economies and increased production of iron and steel. By 1861 regenerative furnaces were being used to manufacture iron, glass and steel. To make his process more attractive to British steel-makers Siemens developed, with the French metallurgist Pierre Martin, the open-hearth regenerative steel furnace, which made steel by melting cast and wrought iron in the furnace. By 1900 Siemens's technique had become the most widely used steel-making process in the world. Siemens was also a leading manufacturer of telegraph cables and a prominent electrical engineer.

SIGEBERHT, King of East Anglia (630 or 631–*c*. 635). Son of King REDWALD of East Anglia, Sigeberht, in conjunction with the Burgundian monk St FELIX, was responsible for the establishment of a bishopric in East Anglia and, therefore, for the beginnings there of an organized Church. Choosing to resign his kingship in favour of his kinsman Ecgric in order to become a monk, he was subsequently obliged to join the East Anglian army when the kingdom was attacked at an unknown date by King PENDA of Mercia. Going into battle unarmed, he was unsurprisingly killed. He and Ecgric were succeeded by ANNA.

SIGEBERHT SANCTUS (?–*c*. 653), King of Essex. The first King of Essex to be Christian since the time of SÆBERHT, Sigeberht was persuaded to convert by the powerful OSWY, King of Northumbria. He installed St CEDD as Bishop of Essex, the first bishop since the departure of St MELLITUS. As later events in the reign of SIGHERE demonstrate, the early stages of the Christian conversion of Essex were especially precarious.

SIGERIC (?–995), Archbishop of Canterbury (990–5). Like all archbishops of Canterbury in ETHELRED II THE UNREADY's reign, Sigeric was a monk who was later promoted to a bishopric. He lacks the distinguished reputation of his contemporary at York, WULFSTAN II, and is personally associated with the policy of paying Danegeld to buy off Scandinavian attacks. This willingness to use Canterbury's resources to buy peace may have contributed unwittingly to the martyrdom of St ÆLFHEAH.

SIGHERE (?–688), King of Essex (663–88). Co-ruler of Essex with his brother SEBBI, Sighere led many of his people back to paganism during an outbreak of plague in 664. This episode shows the vulnerability of the early conversion of the English peoples to the impact of adverse events at a relatively late date. Sighere appears to have conquered Kent at some stage in his life.

SIGURD THE MIGHTY, Earl of Orkney (c. 850–70). He was the brother of ROGNVALD OF MOER who, it is said, established him in Orkney, although the sources relating to Sigurd's career are generally late ones, and even the dates of his activities are uncertain. It is known that, in alliance with THORSTEIN THE RED, he used the islands as a base from which to conquer Caithness and Sutherland, and it is likely that his wars established the earldom of Orkney. The next notable Earl of Orkney was TORF EINAR.

SIGURD THE STOUT, Earl of Orkney (c. 985–1014). One of the greatest of the earls of Orkney, he was successful not only in defending the mainland territories of the earldom against Scottish encroachments, but also in extending his authority to include overlordship of the Scandinavian settlements in the Hebrides. He was supposedly converted to Christianity by force by OLAF TRYGGVASSON, King of Norway, in 995. His great power involved him in the politics of western and northern Britain, and he died fighting alongside the Scandinavian King of Dublin at the Battle of Clontarf. He was succeeded by his son EINAR FALSEMOUTH.

SIHTRIC CAECH (?–927), King of Dublin (917–20) and York (921–7). A grandson of IVAR THE BONELESS, Sihtric was first established in Dublin with the assistance of his brother RAGNALL and then succeeded him as King of York. Despite the advance of English power northwards under EDWARD THE ELDER, Sihtric appears to have ruled York as an independent king and in 926 he made a treaty with ATHELSTAN, the new English King, by which he accepted Christianity and married one of the King's sisters. He speedily renounced both, but died soon afterwards. He was succeeded in Dublin by his brother GOTHFRITH and in York (temporarily) by the English King Athelstan.

SILLITOE, ALAN (1928–), novelist. Nottingham-born, Sillitoe began to write when, after serving in Malaya with the RAF, he was demobilized with TB and unable to work. *Saturday Night and Sunday Morning* (1958), about a working-class Nottingham bicycle factory anti-hero, Arthur Seaton, was akin to the provincial realist fiction being written by Stan Barstow – *A Kind of Loving* (1960) – and John BRAINE. The anarchistic figure in Sillitoe's second novel, *The Loneliness of the Long Distance Runner* (1959), is a Borstal boy who refuses to 'play the game' by deliberately losing races. Both books made successful films.

SILVERMAN, SIDNEY (1895–1968), politician. Son of an impoverished Manchester pedlar, Silverman was imprisoned as a conscientious objector during the First World War. He qualified as a solicitor in 1927: acting largely on behalf of the poor and exploited convinced him that their problems needed wider address and he entered politics, first as a councillor and then as MP for Nelson and Colne (Lancs.) in 1935, a seat which he retained until his death, always as a back-bencher. The Second World War brought tension between his views as a pacifist and as a Jew threatened by the policies of Nazi Germany, and after the war he was an advocate of Jewish rights in Palestine. A leading member of the Campaign for Nuclear Disarmament (CND), Silverman also led the parliamentary campaign for the abolition of the death penalty.

SIMEON, CHARLES (1759–1836), church reformer. A fellow of King's College, and incumbent of Holy Trinity, Cambridge, and a noted preacher, he was a leader of the Evangelical revival in the Church of England and a founder of the Church Missionary Society (1793). His contacts with Cambridge undergraduates gave him an unrivalled influence on the future clergy of the Church of England; one can compare his effect with that on the next generation of John Henry NEWMAN in the early stages of the Oxford Movement.

SIMMONDS, MARTHA (née Calvert) (1624–1665 or 1667), Quaker pioneer. From Somerset, she moved to London in the 1640s, marrying Thomas Simmonds, a printer who published much radical religious literature. With others in her family, she embraced radicalism and by 1655 was a travelling preacher, proclaiming the Last Days. Many male Quaker leaders (*see* FOX, GEORGE) were alarmed, but she fascinated James NAYLER and, with other women including William

ERBURY's widow Dorcas, she led his Messianic entry into Bristol (1656). Released and becoming nurse to Oliver CROMWELL's sister, she engineered Nayler's freedom. She later came to terms with the less apocalyptic Quakers.

SIMNEL, LAMBERT (?1475–1525), conspirator. This Oxford-born youth was taken to Ireland in 1487 and promoted by Yorkist plotters (including Gerald FITZGERALD, 8th Earl of Kildare, and Walter Fitzsimons, Archbishop of Dublin) as Edward, Earl of Warwick, the imprisoned nephew of EDWARD IV. Recognized by Queen MARGARET, he was crowned as Edward VI. His supporters invaded England; captured after the Battle of Stoke near Newark (Notts.) on 16 June 1487, he was pardoned as harmless and allowed to survive as a servant.

SIMPSON, WALLIS (née Warfield) (Duchess of Windsor) (1896–1986), consort of EDWARD VIII. A twice-married socialite from Baltimore, she first met Edward, Prince of Wales, in 1931. When in Jan. 1936 Edward (or David as he was known) succeeded to the throne on the death of his father, GEORGE V, he had for some time been besotted with Mrs Simpson, whose husband allowed her to divorce him in Oct. Although the case was reported in the foreign press, Beaverbrook (*see* AITKEN, MAXWELL) ensured that no mention was made of the affair in the British newspapers until shortly before the King, finally convinced that he would never be able to ascend the throne with Wallis as his Queen, abdicated on 10 Dec. 1936.

The couple were married in France in June 1937 and, after a wartime sojourn as Duke and Duchess of Windsor in the Bahamas, returned to Paris where the Duchess lived until she died, snubbed by the British royal family until 1967, forbidden to be addressed as 'Your Royal Highness' and subject to vilification as a shallow, grasping and manipulative woman who had condemned a weak king to a politically suspect and pointless existence in exile. Her memoirs, *The Heart Has its Reasons*, were published in 1956.

SIMON, SIR JOHN (1816–1904), pathologist and public-health pioneer. Simon built a distinguished medical career, first at King's College Hospital, London, and then at St Thomas's Hospital, London. He was a key figure in nineteenth-century sanitary reform and public health. Following the 1848 Medical Health Act, he was appointed the first medical officer of health for London and subsequently Chief Medical Officer to the General Board of Health (1855–8) and to the Privy Council (1858–71). He spent some 30 years collecting data on subjects such as sanitation, cholera and vaccination, data which led to numerous legislative enactments, notably the 1858 Medical Health Act.

Unlike the sanitary reformer Edwin CHADWICK, he believed that diseases could be traced to highly specific causes (rather than the diffuse clouds of poisonous 'miasma') and successfully promoted epidemiological and physiological research as a means of improving public health.

SIMON, SIR JOHN (1st Viscount Simon) (1873–1954), politician. Simon was a brilliant lawyer whose character ensured that he failed to go as far as his intellect would have allowed. A Fellow of All Souls, Oxford, Simon was called to the Bar in 1899, where he soon rivalled F. E. SMITH in his earning power. He entered the Commons as Liberal MP for Walthamstow, London, in 1906 and was made Attorney General by H. H. ASQUITH in 1910 at the age of 37. He strongly opposed Winston CHURCHILL's attempts to spend more money on naval re-armament in 1913–14, and almost resigned from the Cabinet in 1914 over the decision to enter the war. In May 1915 he declined the lord chancellorship, preferring the Home Office and an extension of his career in the Commons. But in Jan. 1916 he resigned rather than support conscription, and he lost his seat in 1918.

Simon's career was adversely affected by the decline of the Liberal Party after the war, although he returned to the Commons in 1922. He was Chairman of the Simon Commission appointed by Stanley BALDWIN to look into the future of India (1927–30), and of the inquiry into the R101 airship disaster. In 1931 he broke with LLOYD GEORGE and led his own Liberal National Party (Simonites) into Ramsay MACDONALD's National government, where he became Foreign Secretary after the election. Simon's period at the Foreign Office (1931–5) coincided with the increase of international instability, and the challenge from Japan in the Far East in the form of the 1931 Manchurian crisis, and was accompanied by the rise of Hitler in Germany, and by Mussolini's adventurism in Abyssinia: in none of these areas was Simon able to mount a satisfactory defence of British interests, and his 1935 Naval Agreement with Germany was later condemned as encouraging Hitler. Neither Simon's cold personal manner nor his unctuous liberal pronouncements on morality in foreign policy commended him to the majority of his fellow MPs.

Simon went back to the Home Office in 1935 and was Neville CHAMBERLAIN's Chancellor of the Exchequer (1937–40), where he was again heavily implicated in appeasement as one of the *Guilty Men* by Michael FOOT and Frank Owen (1940). In reality he worked hard with Chamberlain to bring Britain's defence policy into line with its financial resources. He was Lord Chancellor in the Churchill coalition until 1945, after which he never again held office.

SIMPSON, SIR JAMES (1811–70), physician. Simpson studied medicine at Edinburgh University and became Professor of Midwifery there in 1839. The leading Scottish obstetrician of his day, he became physician to the Queen in Scotland in 1847. He pioneered the use of ether as an anaesthetic in childbirth and in 1846–7 experimented with chloroform as an alternative to ether. His chloroform anaesthesia was fiercely attacked in religious and medical quarters but gained considerable legitimacy after he used it successfully on Queen VICTORIA during her pregnancy in 1853. He also pioneered the uterine sound and sponge tent methods in gynaecology.

SINCLAIR, ARCHIBALD (1st Viscount Thurso) (1890–1970), politician. Having trained as a soldier, he served as his friend Winston CHURCHILL's personal military secretary at the War Office (1919–21). An MP from 1922 to 1945, he joined the National government in 1931 as Secretary of State for Scotland, but resigned with Herbert SAMUEL in 1932. Becoming Liberal leader in 1935 in succession to Samuel, he oversaw the reorganization of the party. Opposed to appeasement, he declined to serve in Neville CHAMBERLAIN's War Cabinet in 1939, but joined Churchill's coalition as Secretary for Air (1940–5). He lost his seat in the 1945 election and was succeeded by Clement DAVIES as Liberal leader.

SINCLAIR, SIR CLIVE (1940–), inventor. Sinclair founded the first of his electronics companies, Sinclair Radionics, in 1962. Having established himself in miniature radio and hi-fi production, he achieved fame in 1972 for marketing the world's first pocket calculator. Sinclair Radionics was taken over by the National Enterprise Board in 1979, the year Sinclair Research was founded. Within a year the cheap ZX home computer range was launched, with over a million sold in two years. By 1986 intense competition and product failures (notably of the C5 mini electric car) led to the Sinclair Research rights being sold to Amstrad, the rival company formed by Alan SUGAR. Sinclair has continued to develop consumer products; his success as an inventor has been greater than as a businessman.

SINCLAIR, SIR JOHN (1754–1835), agricultural improver. He was born in Caithness, educated at the universities of Edinburgh, Glasgow and Oxford and was an MP from 1780. In 1782, horrified by the effects of famine on his estates in northern Scotland, he secured £15,000 in aid from the government and turned his attention to economic problems. In 1790 he began compiling *The Statistical Account of Scotland,* using information on population and produce supplied by parish ministers, following the example of Alexander WEBSTER. In 1793 he persuaded PITT THE YOUNGER to set up a Board of Agriculture, and became its first President. The board attempted to carry out a Statistical Account for England, but received little co-operation. Sinclair was a passionate encloser of land and one of the landlords behind the Highland clearances, encouraging sheep-farming, with drastic consequences for Highland communities.

SINCLAIR, WILLIAM (3rd Earl of Orkney, 20th [1st Sinclair] Earl of Caithness) (?1404–80), artistic patron. High Chancellor of Scotland 1454–8, he resigned the earldom of Orkney in 1470 to the Scottish Crown after Norway had ceded the islands to JAMES III. He resigned his Caithness earldom in 1476 to his son William. The memorials of his regally lavish lifestyle are the bizarrely elaborate Roslin Chapel (Lothian), a chantry college founded in 1446 which, although unfinished, remains one of Scotland's most memorably eccentric buildings and the equally individual if more fragmentary Roslin Castle.

SITWELL, DAME EDITH (1887–1964), poet. The eldest child of aristocrats severely deficient in parenting skills, the lonely, angular, clever Edith formed a close bond with her younger brothers Osbert and Sacheverell and developed a personality that was against convention in style and literary production. She claimed an affinity with the Tudor age, and wrote about ELIZABETH I in *Fanfare for Elizabeth* (1946) and *The Queen and the Hive* (1962), both of which had a considerable success, as did *The English Eccentrics* (1933).

She was primarily a poet: her first poem, 'Drowned Suns', was published in the *Daily Mirror* in 1913. With her brothers she launched a periodical anthology, *Wheels*, which, in opposition to the current common-sensical Georgian poetics, was modernist and opaque; it published work by Aldous HUXLEY, Nancy CUNARD and Wilfred OWEN.

Sitwell's interest in the relations between the senses and meaning found its most extraordinary expression in *Façade* (1923), when she spoke her technically innovative poems, 'abstract patterns in sound' often based on dance tunes, through a megaphone from behind a curtain to the music of the then unknown young composer, William WALTON. Her own work grew more sombre: 'Still Falls the Rain' (1942), perhaps her best-known poem, about the London blitz, was published in *Street Songs* (1942). The inspiration for *The Shadow of Cain* (1947) was eye-witness accounts of the bombing of Hiroshima. Sitwell was the first poet ever to be created a Dame of the British Empire (1954). She converted to Catholicism a year later.

SIWARD, Earl of Northumbria (*c*. 1032–55). A Danish follower of King CNUT, who was made Earl in Deira in *c*. 1032 and in Bernicia in *c*. 1042, his little-known career is notable mostly for its military exploits. He appears to have extended English rule into Cumbria, and in 1054 his victory (immortalized by SHAKESPEARE) over MACBETH, King of the Scots, led to the installation in Scotland of King MAEL COLUIM III CENN MÓR. His son WALTHEOF was too young to succeed him in 1055.

SKEFFINGTON, FRANCIS *see* SHEEHY SKEFF-INGTON, FRANCIS

SKEFFINGTON, SIR WILLIAM (by 1467–1535), administrator. A Leics. gentleman who was a professional soldier and Master of the Royal Ordnance 1515–34, he was appointed Lord Deputy of Ireland in 1530. Continually frustrated by financial difficulties and the jealous rivalry of Gerald FITZGERALD, 9th Earl of Kildare, who had married into the GREY family (Skeffington's Leics. patrons), he nevertheless effectively crushed the GERALDINE's rebellion (*see* FITZGERALD, Thomas). His son Leonard, lieutenant of Nottingham Castle, is said to have invented 'Skeffington's daughter', an instrument of torture which forcibly bent its victims double.

SKELTON, JOHN (?1460–1529), poet. He studied at Oxford and Cambridge and was made Poet Laureate by these universities and Leuven; court poet from 1489, he was a tutor to the future HENRY VIII, winning ERASMUS' admiration. He became rector of Diss (Norf.) in 1502. He wrote for various courtly patrons, including Lady Margaret BEAUFORT and Thomas HOWARD and his son Thomas, successively Dukes of Norfolk; his morality play *Magnyfycence* may have been written, together with other pageants, for Henry Percy, 10th Earl of Northumberland. Some of his vigorous satire was directed against Cardinal WOLSEY, although the extent of the reference remains controversial.

SLATER, JAMES (JIM) (1929–), financier. From his beginnings in business as general manager of a group of metal-finishing companies in the mid 1950s, and then in the car industry where he became Leyland Motors' deputy sales director, he set up in 1964 in partnership with the rising Conservative politician Peter WALKER. Slater Walker Securities was an investment company, specializing in asset-stripping take-overs, and it profited considerably through the 1960s, when Slater's word could make or break a share, and in the short boom enjoyed by many 'New Tories' associated with Edward HEATH's government,

until the stock market collapse of 1973. In the case of Slater Walker the whole venture collapsed along with many secondary banks that the Bank of England had to shore up. Slater resigned; Walker as an active politician had long distanced himself from involvement in the company. Slater, Chairman of Salar Properties since 1983 and a prolific author on stock market matters, has remained in demand as a stock analyst.

SLESSOR, SIR JOHN (1897–1979), airman. Left lame by an attack of poliomyelitis, in 1914 Slessor was rejected for military service, but managed to circumvent regulations by joining the Royal Flying Corps and saw extensive service in the Middle East and France. Convinced that the future of war lay in the air, Slessor's *Airpower and Armies* (1936) was a ringing endorsement of strategic bombing at the expense of air–ground co-operation. The subsequent failure of strategic bombing was a rude surprise. Slessor was more successful as Commander-in-Chief of Coastal Command, which he led during the most critical phase of the Battle of the Atlantic. Slessor ended his career as Chief of Air Staff (1950–3), when he oversaw the first steps to the creation of a British nuclear bomber force.

SLESSOR, MARY (1848–1919), missionary. Born in Aberdeen, the daughter of a shoemaker father and a weaver mother, Slessor worked in a Dundee linen mill and was an active church worker before sailing for West Africa in 1876 as a missionary with the United Presbyterian Church. She worked largely alone with the Okoyong peoples, aiming not so much to convert them to Christianity as to stamp out such practices as twin murder and ritual human sacrifice, and establishing schools and dispensaries. Appointed a vice-consul in 1892, she also set up missions to the Aro and Ibibio peoples, encouraging trade between coastal tribes and the interior.

SLIM, WILLIAM (1st Viscount Slim) (1891–1970), soldier. In 1914 Slim, a junior clerk in a Birmingham steel-tubing factory and part-time Territorial Army soldier, was commissioned as a Lieutenant in the Warws. Regiment. He saw service at Gallipoli and in Mesopotamia, surviving two severe wounds, winning the Military Cross and rising to the rank of Captain. In 1919 he transferred to the Indian army. Despite periods of teaching at the Staff College at Camberley and studying at the Imperial Defence College, Slim was promoted from Major to Lieutenant Colonel in 1938 only because of the threat of war.

During the first 30 months of the Second World War, as Slim's more rapidly promoted contemporaries went down to defeat, he rose from battalion to divisional command, fighting in the relative backwaters of Ethiopia, Syria and Iran. As Commander of Burcorps he withdrew British and Indian forces from Burma in the face of the rapidly advancing Japanese (March–May 1942). In the spring of 1943 he again saved British and Indian forces from disaster in the Arakan, an action which in Oct. 1943 won him command of the British Eastern Army.

Slim managed to galvanize this demoralized formation into the 14th Army, which destroyed an attempted Japanese invasion of India in the bloody attritional battles of the second Arakan and Imphal–Kohima (Jan.–June 1944). In Jan. 1945 Slim sent the 14th Army deep into central Burma, enveloping and dislodging large Japanese forces between Mandalay and Meiktila, leading to the Japanese evacuation of Rangoon on 29 April.

The most successful British General of the twentieth century, Slim's military skill was matched by his political astuteness. He maintained surprisingly cordial relations with American and Chinese allies, dealt ruthlessly with powerful and difficult subordinates like WINGATE, fought off three attempts by a hostile British military establishment to sack him, and then in 1947, in the teeth of opposition from MONTGOMERY, secured appointment as Chief of the Imperial General Staff. As Governor General of Australia (1953–60) he was equally effective, managing to stop a burgeoning republican movement in its tracks, at least for a generation.

Since his death in 1970 Slim's reputation has been steadily increasing. His account of the Burma campaign, *Defeat into Victory* (1956), is acknowledged as the finest work on the Second World War produced by a participant.

SLOANE, SIR HANS (1660–1753), physician and collector. He was born in Ireland and studied medicine in France. From 1685 to 1687 he was physician to the Duke of Albemarle, Governor of Jamaica, and brought 800 species of plants back to London with him. His study of Jamaica's flora was published in 1696, and a further work on the West Indies published in two volumes in 1707 and 1725. Sloane combined his research on the medicinal qualities of plants with a successful medical practice in Bloomsbury Square. Secretary to the Royal Society (1693–1712), he subsequently became its President and co-founded the College of Physicians (1696). His earnings enabled him to buy the manor of Chelsea in 1712, where in 1721 he established the Chelsea Physic Garden for the Society of Apothecaries, intended as a place where apothecaries and physicians could study botany and the medicinal uses of plants. GEORGE I made Sloane Physician General to the army in 1714 and a baronet in 1716. An early advocate of inoculation against smallpox, Sloane inoculated several members of the royal family. His wide circle of acquaintances and his growing fortune enabled him to build up a large correspondence and a collection of curiosities which became famous. Both were left to the nation on his death; combined with the manuscripts of Edward HARLEY and Robert COTTON, they became the core of the British Museum, established in 1754.

SMART, CHRISTOPHER (1722–71), poet. Smart spent his youth in Durham where his father was steward to the Vane family, who became his patrons. Elected and a Fellow of Pembroke Hall, Cambridge, he continued to write but fell into debt through drinking and left the university for London where he worked for John NEWBERY, editing (1751–3) *The Midwife, or the Old Woman's Magazine*, under the alias of the elderly Mary Midnight. Descending through religious mania into insanity, in 1759 he was confined to a private madhouse in Bethnal Green, where he wrote the poem *Jubilate Agno*, expressing an extraordinary range of spiritual and material concerns in antiphonal verse-form adapted from Hebrew literature, one section beginning 'For I will consider my cat Jeoffrey'. The surviving fragments were not published until 1939. On leaving Bethnal Green in 1763 he wrote his other best-known work, *A Song to David*.

SMEATON, JOHN (1724–92), engineer. An instrument-maker who became an authority on mechanics, a Fellow of the Royal Society (1753), Smeaton was proposed as the designer for a new Eddystone lighthouse, off Plymouth, the original having been destroyed by fire. Smeaton's lighthouse was completed in 1759 and was the first wave-swept lighthouse, made of Portland stone and Smeaton's own hydraulic cement. The lighthouse stood until it was dismantled in 1876, its upper portion being transferred to Plymouth Hoe. Smeaton also worked on improvements to NEWCOMEN's steam-engine, and constructed 44 windmills and watermills, accompanied by an exhaustive study of their design and efficiency.

SMELLIE, WILLIAM (1697–1763), obstetrician. From Lanark, he also practised there, probably after training at Glasgow. He moved to London in 1739 and set up a practice in Pall Mall. He visited Paris to attend lectures on midwifery, and began to teach the subject in London in 1741. He rejected customary practice and made his own observations of the movement of the foetus through the pelvis, and advanced understanding of the physiology of labour, publishing his *Treatise on the Theory and Practice of Midwifery* (three vols, 1751–63). Smellie failed to attract many noble clients and, although he had his followers in Scotland, Europe and North America, English medicine preferred the more traditional practice of William HUNTER well into the nineteenth century.

SMILES, SAMUEL (1812–1904), economic publicist. *Self-help*, published in 1859, was the title which made Samuel Smiles's name and came to sum up an age of Victorian bourgeois values. The son of a shopkeeper from Haddington (Lothian), Smiles had a varied career including stints as a surgeon, newspaper editor and railway company secretary. He advocated political, social and personal reform, along the *laissez-faire* lines of the Manchester school (*see* BRIGHT, JOHN and COBDEN, RICHARD) and wrote biographies of those who suited his outlook. In *Self-help* he preached industry, thrift and self-improvement as the path to progress, and attacked over-government. The work struck a significant chord, rapidly became immensely successful, and was translated into many languages. In 1861–2 *Lives of the Engineers* proved almost as great a success; his case studies were intended as an exemplar of what could be achieved by men with determination. Smiles's message has consistently been derided in the twentieth century, although it saw a revival in the selective espousal of traditional 'Victorian values' by THATCHER in the 1970s and 1980s. Studies of entrepreneurs have shown that successful nineteenth-century men usually had much greater initial advantages than Smiles ever allowed, and that the impact of self-help was considerably less than the publicity suggested.

SMITH, ADAM *see* essay on page 733

SMITH, DELIA (1941–), cookery writer. Her food-writing career started in 1969 with recipes for the *Daily Mirror* magazine and the *Evening Standard* (1972–85). *How to Cheat at Cooking* (1973) was the first of a regular production of books on English cookery, sales of which keep the book trade afloat at Christmas and allegedly clear supermarket shelves of the recommended ingredients. *How to Cook* (1998), published to accompany the television series of the same name, was not received uncritically, but nevertheless sold over one million copies in hardback. A committed Christian, Smith also writes on spiritual matters.

SMITH, FLORENCE ('STEVIE') (1903–71), poet. Born in Hull, she lived from the age of three in Palmer's Green, north London, where 'the absolute dearth of companionship drives one into writing'. Her first book, *Novel on Yellow Paper*, was published in 1936 and Smith, who worked for a publisher for 30 years, wrote two more melancholy/comic novels. In 1953 she gave up work to care for her elderly aunt (known as the 'Lion of Hull') who until then had kept house for her and features in her work. Smith's eight volumes of *faux naïf* poems illustrated with her own comic line drawings, of which *Not Waving but Drowning* (1957) is the best known, are funny, sad, affecting and deceptively profound; and although sometimes dismissed by 'serious' poets her recitations enjoyed great popular success, particularly on radio.

SMITH, F(REDERICK) E(DWIN) (1st Earl of Birkenhead) (1872–1930), politician. 'F. E.' (he was always known by his initials) was one of the most brilliant intellects of his day: after an outstanding academic career at Oxford, where he captured most of the 'glittering prizes' (a phrase of his own), he went on to a successful career at the Bar before turning to politics, where his natural powers as an orator made him an instant success. His background was more important to his political career than his pose as the typical Oxford swell might lead one to suppose: Protestantism of the Orange hue, and his brand of Tory democracy were both inherited from his Merseyside roots. His election to the Commons in 1906, the year of disaster for Arthur BALFOUR's government, gave F. E. the chance to make an immediate mark in the most famous maiden speech of the twentieth century, in which he defied the convention that such orations should be non-controversial. He played a leading role under Sir Edward CARSON in opposing H. H. ASQUITH's government's proposals to give Ireland Home Rule. As Attorney General, in 1916 he took the decision to prosecute Sir Roger CASEMENT for treason, and in 1918, at the age of 46, became the youngest Lord Chancellor since Judge JEFFRIES in the seventeenth century. During the LLOYD GEORGE coalition he alienated many of his own former supporters by backing the 1921 treaty of partition which led to the creation of the Irish Free State.

A charismatic and dominating figure, he was censured for his extravagant lifestyle and his heavy-drinking, and much of the distrust felt in certain parts of the Conservative Party for the Coalition derived from the prominence in it of men of the type of Birkenhead and Winston CHURCHILL. Birkenhead defended the Coalition at the notable Carlton Club meeting in Oct. 1922 but his arrogance only helped convince others to follow Stanley BALDWIN and Bonar LAW, who established a new tone for the party. By the early 1920s Birkenhead looked like a figure from a bygone age. The old, non-unionized working class upon which his Tory Democracy had been based was gone and, with the rise of the Labour Party and the disappearance of the Irish issue,

continued on page 734

SMITH, ADAM (1723–90)
Economist

Posthumous son of a customs officer at Kirkcaldy near Edinburgh, he was raised by his mother. Educated at the classical burgh school, he went to Glasgow University at 14, where he became interested in Newtonian physics and mathematics and in Stoic moral philosophy, which emphasized self-command. Francis HUTCHESON, his most inspiring teacher, helped interest him in economic phenomena. He was less impressed by Oxford, where he went at 17, though he did read widely in the classics and in modern European literature.

Smith worked as a freelance teacher in Edinburgh (1748–5) and became a friend of David HUME. He lectured on rhetoric and criticism, on the history of philosophy and on jurisprudence or 'the principles of the laws of nations', linked with a speculative history of the development of human societies. Such subjects, not favoured in English universities, helped to align Scots students with fashionable currents in continental thought and to make Scotland the home of what historians have termed the Scottish Enlightenment, characterized by ambitious theorizing about the nature of man and society. Luminaries of this intellectual efflorescence, such as Hume and Smith, had a European reputation such as no English intellectuals enjoyed between NEWTON and LOCKE in the seventeenth century and such figures as BENTHAM and DARWIN in the nineteenth.

Smith was elected Professor of Logic at Glasgow in 1751, of Moral Philosophy in 1752. In the latter post he lectured on natural (as opposed to revealed) religion, ethics, justice and 'political regulations … calculated to increase the riches, the power and the prosperity of the State'. His views attracted much attention, and were debated in the Political Economy Club, where he encountered merchants and manufacturers involved in such trades as tobacco and linen, then helping to make Glasgow a boom town. The publication of his ethics lectures as The Theory of Moral Sentiments (1759) won him a European reputation. The book built upon theories of Hutcheson and Hume, arguing that moral and aesthetic judgements are based on feelings. Smith gave 'sympathy', natural responsiveness to others' feelings, a vital role in his theory (akin, one reader suggested, to that of gravity in Newton's physics).

Hume promoted his work, drawing it to the attention of rising Whig politician Charles TOWNSHEND, who persuaded Smith to widen his experience and cultivate powerful connections, by accompanying Townshend's stepson the Duke of Buccleuch and his brother on a Grand Tour to France and Geneva. They visited Voltaire in Geneva and, through Hume, who had been secretary to the British embassy in Paris, Smith met philosophes such as d'Alembert, Diderot, d'Holbach and Helvétius. He also met physiocrats such as Quesnay and Turgot, who argued that prosperity rested on agriculture and that the economy should be left to take its natural course – laissez faire. When in 1766 his younger pupil died Smith returned to London, staying for a year to work on public finance for Townshend, then Chancellor of the Exchequer.

He returned to his mother in Kirkcaldy to write The Wealth of Nations (1767–73). This systematized his academic and recent experiences into an account of the workings of economies and the logic of economic development. Stressing man's natural propensity to 'truck and barter', Smith suggested that market society embodied an 'obvious and simple system of natural liberty'. Attempts to regulate economic activity might redistribute wealth, but commonly reduced its potential scale, though governments needed to supply infrastructural support. Smith however recognized political constraints on the dismantling of the 'mercantile system' (this name reflecting his conviction that merchants championed trade restrictions from a short-sighted vision of their interests). He returned to London in 1773 to finish his book, adding comment on growing tensions with the American colonies. Not believing that heavily regulated, colonial trade best served any nation's economic interests, he favoured giving colonists independence.

In 1778 Smith was appointed Commissioner of Customs for Scotland, entailing the supply to government of economic advice, and moved with his mother to Edinburgh. Other publishing projects ran aground, though he revised the Wealth of Nations with an eye especially to the crisis over the East India Company (1783–4). The 1790 edition of The Theory of Moral Sentiments added reflections on the remodelling of constitutions, recently attempted in America and being attempted in France. In 1790 his health deteriorated; before dying, he burnt his unfinished manuscripts.

The Wealth of Nations, his most enduringly famous book, was initially admired more for its range and coherence than for any particular theories which it propounded. It may, however, have helped to influence Britain's vigorous participation in bilateral negotiations to liberalize international trade in the 1780s and to inform debates over the regulation of the corn trade in the 1790s. It was rapidly translated into other European languages. In the nineteenth and twentieth centuries Smith's name has often been invoked by ideologues whose social vision in fact differs significantly from his.

Ian Simpson Ross, The Life of Adam Smith (1975)

could no longer be won to Conservatism by the old ways.

Birkenhead returned to office under Baldwin in 1924, where he was a noticeably reactionary Secretary of State for India. He retired in 1928 'to make some money' in the City but died two years later of the ravages of alcohol, a burnt-out case politically and personally.

SMITH, SIR HARRY (1787–1860), soldier and colonial governor. One of 13 children of a Cambs. surgeon, Smith bought a commission in the 95th regiment (the Rifle Brigade) in 1805. After training at Shorncliffe under Sir John MOORE, he saw action at Montevideo and Buenos Aries (1807), in the Corunna campaign (1808–9) and in the campaigns in the Peninsula and the south of France (1810–14). Between Aug. 1814 and June 1815 Smith took part in the sack of Washington and the Battle of New Orleans, and then returned to Europe to fight at Waterloo, a record unequalled in the army, which earned him promotion to Lieutenant Colonel by brevet. Smith's later career involved service in India, where in 1846 he was promoted Major-General for his role in defeating the Sikhs at Aliwal, and in South Africa, where as Governor of the Cape of Good Hope he campaigned against the Xhosas in the Eastern Cape and against the Boers across the Orange River.

SMITH, IAN (1919–), politician. The first native-born Prime Minister of Southern Rhodesia, Smith led his country in a unilateral declaration of independence (UDI). First elected to Southern Rhodesia's legislative assembly in 1948 and then to the assembly for the Federation of the Rhodesias and Nyasaland, Smith became chief government Whip under Sir Roy Welensky. In 1961 he formed the Rhodesian Front; ousting Winston Field as Prime Minister in April 1964, he pledged to secure independence under white rule. NKOMO and other black leaders were arrested; constitutional negotiations with Britain broke down and UDI followed on 11 Nov. 1965. Under an illegal regime, Rhodesia was subject to an international trade embargo but secured supplies from South Africa and commercial companies willing to 'bust' sanctions. Smith's stance softened in the 1970s, his hand forced by increasing violence against white residents from guerrilla forces, and in 1976 announced his willingness to negotiate African majority rule. Lacking international recognition, his new government set up with moderate black politicians was forced to accept the outcome of the 1979 Lancaster House conference, from which the new Zimbabwe was born. Smith remained leader of the white interest until many defected in 1983; leader of the Rhodesian Front (renamed the Conservative Alliance) until 1987, he was censured for exhorting

South Africa to maintain apartheid and retired from political life.

SMITH, JOHN (1938–94), politician. Educated at Glasgow University, Smith was called to the Scottish Bar in 1967 and, an outstanding advocate and public speaker, he was appointed a QC in 1983. A Labour MP from 1973, first for Lanarkshire and then for Monklands East, he was appointed Trade Secretary by James CALLAGHAN in 1978 and after Labour went into opposition in 1979 was front-bench spokesman on trade, energy, employment and economic affairs. He succeeded Neil KINNOCK as leader of the party after Labour's deep disappointment and frustration at losing the 1992 election.

Smith's career was cut tragically short by a massive second heart attack at age 56, and he was replaced as Labour leader by Tony BLAIR and his New Labour project. Smith was a humanitarian and principled politician; the 'what if' school of political speculation regrets the passing of his integrity to Labour values while wondering if he could ever have succeeded in making the party so massively electable as his successor did in 1997.

SMITH, SYDNEY (1771–1845), wit, essayist and clergyman. Ordained in 1796, Smith went as a tutor to Edinburgh where he became part of a circle that included Sir Walter SCOTT. In 1802 he founded the *Edinburgh Review*, one of the nineteenth century's most distinguished journals, and wrote for it for 28 years on a variety of subjects, including the harsh game laws, the oppression of Ireland and 'the enormous wickedness of the slave trade'. Returning to England in 1804, he became a prolific pamphlet writer, popular preacher and a lecturer on moral science at the Royal Institution. His wit brought him an *entrée* into the Whig circle of Holland House and in 1808 he was appointed to a living in Yorks., where he also farmed and continued to write. *The Letters of Peter Plymley*, an attack on the opposition of some of his Protestant colleagues to Catholic Emancipation, started to appear in 1807. Appointed prebendary of Bristol Cathedral in 1828, Smith took the living of Combe Florey (Som.) soon afterwards and was appointed canon residentiary at St Paul's in 1831.

SMITH, T. DAN (1915–93), local authority leader *see* POULSON, JOHN

SMITH, THOMAS (1513–77), administrator and writer. A polymath Cambridge don and civil lawyer, his evangelical views and enthusiasm for reform brought favour and diplomatic service under Edward SEYMOUR, Duke of Somerset, discreet retirement under MARY I and renewed eminence under ELIZABETH I. William CECIL esteemed him and he served two stints as Principal Secretary, 1548–9 and 1572–7. Among his varied writings, not yet all in print, are the *Discourse of the Common Weal* (written 1549, published 1581), often attributed to John HALES, and the political survey, *De Republica Anglorum* (posthumously published, 1584).

SMITH, WILLIAM (1769–1839), geologist. Born in Oxon., the son of a blacksmith, Smith gained knowledge of the diverse geology of England and Wales while working as a canal surveyor and mining prospector. His reputation as the 'father of stratigraphical geology' rests on his use of fossils to identify different beds of strata and his *Delineation of the Strata of England and Wales, with part of Scotland* (1815), the first large-scale stratigraphic map (5 miles to an inch) of England and Wales, and indeed of any country, in which Smith established a regular succession in geological strata across the country.

SMITH, W(ILLIAM) H(ENRY) (1825–91), newsagent and politician. Son of a prosperous London newsagent and bookseller, he became his father's partner in 1846. Three years later the firm secured the privilege of selling books and newspapers at railway stations. Smith entered Parliament in 1868 and held high office under DISRAELI and Salisbury (*see* CECIL, ROBERT GASCOYNE). His influence, though, was probably greater as a creator and supplier of the popular demand for good cheap literature. W. H. Smith remains a significant force in the retail market.

SMOLLETT, TOBIAS (1721–71), author. He studied medicine at Glasgow but pursued literary ambitions in addition to his medical career. Smollett's first important work was the poem *The Tears of Scotland* (1746), attacking Cumberland's (*see* WILLIAM AUGUSTUS) brutality in the Highlands. His first novel, *Roderick Random* (1748), established his grotesque style of picaresque satire, further developed in novels such as *Peregrine Pickle* (1751) and *Ferdinand Count Fathom* (1753). His income was supplemented by journalism, including the editorship of the *Critical Review* (1756–63) and popular non-fiction such as the *History of England* and the *Universal History*. He edited *The Briton*, a political paper putting the point of view of Lord Bute's (*see* STUART, JOHN) ministry. This provoked Lord Temple (*see* GRENVILLE-TEMPLE, RICHARD) to support John WILKES in producing the oppositional *North Briton*. Smollett's sensitivity to the anti-Scottish tone of Wilkite propaganda is reflected in his last novel, *Humphry Clinker* (1771), in which the decadence of England, especially the metropolis, is contrasted with the more promising state of other parts of the kingdom. Reflecting his increasing ill health, *Travels through France and Italy* (1766) is a splenetic report of Smollett's continental wanderings.

SMUTS, JAN (1870–1950), politician. Cape-born and Cambridge-educated, Smuts was at the forefront of South African politics for half a century. He led Boer guerrilla forces during the Boer War, negotiated the peace treaty of 1902 and was a key figure in the formation of the Union of South Africa in 1910 and in attempts to reconcile Boer and English interests. He served in the British War Cabinet (1917–18) and took part in the Paris peace conference before returning to South Africa to become Prime Minister (1919–24). He was premier again in 1939 when Hertzog resigned rather than take South Africa into the Second World War. A member of Winston CHURCHILL's War Cabinet (1940–5), Smuts found his pro-British stance and distaste for segregation increasingly at odds with resurgent Afrikaaner nationalism; his United Party was defeated in 1948 by the National Party. He was shocked by the scale of his defeat, and died shortly thereafter. He was arguably the only internationally regarded statesman produced by South Africa before Nelson Mandela.

SMYTH, DAME ETHEL (1858–1944), composer and suffragette. The daughter of a general and educated at Leipzig Conservatory, Ethel Smyth's formidable musical reputation was established with the performance of her *Mass in D* at the Albert Hall in 1893. Her opera *The Wreckers* was acclaimed in Leipzig and Prague before being performed in England in 1909, and Sir Thomas BEECHAM produced another of her operas, *The Boatswain's Mate*, in 1916. In the popular imagination, Smyth remains best known for her activities as a suffragette. On one occasion, when imprisoned in Holloway for throwing stones at a Cabinet minister's windows, she conducted her *March of the Women* (1911) by waving a toothbrush from the window of her cell.

SMYTH (OR SMITH), JOHN (*c.* 1554–1612), Baptist. A Puritan Cambridge don, he left the English Church's ministry for a Lincs. Separatist congregation, but *c.* 1608 led a group to join the English Separatists in Amsterdam. There, doubting the validity of infant baptism, he was led to baptize himself (hence his designation the 'Se-Baptist', 'self-baptizer') together with a number of sympathizers (*see* HELWYS, THOMAS); later he joined the Dutch (Anabaptist) Mennonites. After his death, Helwys and others returned to England to establish (in London) the first English Baptist church.

SMYTHSON, ROBERT (1534 or 1535–1614), architect. His major surviving works are Longleat House (Wilts., *c*. 1568–80), for the THYNNE family, Wollaton Hall (Notts., 1580–8), for Sir Francis Willoughby, and, most notably, Bess of HARDWICK's 'more glass than wall' house, the new Hardwick Hall (Derbys.). There is evidence for his work at several major houses, some now termed 'prodigy houses', designed for royal progresses, reflecting the needs of a visiting court grafted on to a normal household; every architectural device was used to express display and grandeur. Smythson combined unusual understanding of classical architecture with delight in post-Gothic fantasy. His son John (d. 1634) undertook major building at Bolsover Castle (Derbys.) for the CAVENDISH family, including romantic Gothic revival; John's son, Huntingdon Smythson (d. 1648), probably designed Bolsover's still operational 'artisan mannerist' riding school.

SNOW, C(HARLES) P(ERCY) (1st Baron Snow of Leicester) (1905–80), writer and scientist. Snow's second novel, *The Search* (1934), draws on his experience as a research scientist at Cambridge: his subsequent best-selling 11-book series, *Strangers and Brothers* (the first volume (1950) was so named and later retitled *George Passant*), follows his fictional near *alter ego* Lewis Eliot from provincial obscurity (in Snow's case Leicester) to the *Corridors of Power* (1964) and beyond. Snow was a Civil Service commissioner responsible for scientific recruitment (1945–60) and Parliamentary Secretary at the Ministry of Science and Technology (1964–6). His 1959 Rede lecture, published as *The Two Cultures and the Scientific Revolution*, drew a furious riposte from a fellow Cambridge don, F. R. LEAVIS, who regarded Snow's solution to the failure of communication between scientists and 'literary intellectuals' as philistine in its utilitarian concept of the humanities. In much the same groove, the debate continues in the public arena to this day.

SNOWDEN, PHILIP (1st Viscount Snowden of Ickornshaw) (1864–1937), politician. A Yorks. man who sat for Lancs. seats, Snowden was an autodidact, a doctrinaire ethical socialist of 'seagreen incorruptibility'. He represented the liberal radical side of the Labour Party, with its emphasis on temperance, pacifism and asceticism, and had little time for the party's other wing, the trade-union movement. As a young man he contracted spinal tuberculosis which left him severely crippled. Snowden was a founder member with Keir HARDIE of the Independent Labour Party (ILP), and from 1904 was an inspiring and implacable evangelist on its behalf. He entered Parliament in 1906 as MP for Blackburn and soon established himself as the new Labour Party's financial spokesman. A pacifist-inclined opponent of the First World War (unlike most of his party), he was an advocate of high taxation to pay for it, proposing the extension of 'the conscription of life to the conscription of wealth'; and into the immediate post-war years he was a critic of the Labour Party from the ethical stance of the ILP.

In the 1924 Labour government, Snowden (now sitting for Colne Valley) was appointed Chancellor of the Exchequer and introduced a Liberal-style Budget that advocated Free Trade, cut taxes and was designed to appeal to a broad sweep of 'progressive opinion'. He left the ILP in 1927 and was appointed Chancellor again in Ramsay MACDONALD's 1929 second Labour government. His fiscal policies were orthodox and redistributive, with an overriding commitment to Free Trade: he had no answer for the pressing issue of unemployment and no intention of increasing government intervention. When the Labour Cabinet split over a proposed cut in unemployment benefit, he accepted Macdonald's invitation to join his National government in 1931, and in the subsequent election lashed the Labour electoral programme as 'Bolshevism run mad'. He went to the Lords as Lord Privy Seal but resigned after nine months over the issue of protection, and spent his remaining years in righteous invective against his former leader and party, to the end a believer in the great Liberal tenet of Free Trade. Regarded with obloquy as a traitor by generations of Labour supporters, Snowden perfectly exemplified the early Labour Party mixture of liberal radicalism and moral socialism.

SNOWDON, 1ST EARL OF see ARMSTRONG-JONES, ANTHONY

SOAMES, CHRISTOPHER (Baron Soames) (1920–87), politician. An Old Etonian grandee, Soames's entry into the upper echelons of the Conservative Party was assured by his marriage in 1947 to Mary, daughter of Winston CHURCHILL. Soames was a genial, convivial man who established excellent relations with his father-in-law; his adoption as Conservative candidate for Bedford in 1950 was not hindered by the family connection. As Churchill's Parliamentary Private Secretary he exercised more power and influence than many ministers, not least because Churchill increasingly relied upon him. He held junior posts at the Air Ministry and Admiralty under Anthony EDEN and Harold MACMILLAN and was Minister of Agriculture under Macmillan and DOUGLAS-HOME.

Soames lost his seat in 1966 and in 1968 was made Ambassador in Paris by Harold WILSON as a prelude to trying to negotiate Britain's entry into the Common Market. From 1973 to 1977 he was the senior British EEC Commissioner. In 1979 he was appointed by Margaret THATCHER as the last British Governor of Rhodesia and given the task of presiding over the transfer of power to Robert MUGABE. From 1980 to 1981 he was Leader of the Lords but, identified as a 'wet' by Margaret Thatcher, was summarily dismissed. It was, she noted in her memoirs, no doubt a curious reversal of roles in his eyes that she should have sacked a grandee like Soames; it showed how much the Tory Party had changed since Churchill's day.

SOANE, SIR JOHN (1753–1837), architect. Son of a Reading stonemason, he worked for the architects George Dance the Younger and Henry Holland, studied at the Royal Academy Schools and spent three years in Italy on a travelling scholarship, returning to England in 1780. He made his reputation by designing country houses in a personalized variant of the neoclassical style. He was then retained by several public institutions, in an age when public building projects were becoming increasingly important among architectural enterprises: first by the Bank of England, which he rebuilt from 1788; and subsequently by Parliament and Chelsea Hospital. He became Professor of Architecture at the Royal Academy in 1806. Surviving works include the Dulwich Picture Gallery and Mausoleum, and his house in Lincoln's Inn Fields, London, which he left to the nation together with his collection of architectural drawings, books, antiquities and pictures, including important works by HOGARTH.

SODDY, FREDERICK (1877–1956), radiochemist. Soddy studied chemistry at Oxford and in 1900 began working with Ernest RUTHERFORD on radioactivity at McGill University in Canada. From 1900 they proposed the celebrated interpretation of radioactivity as the spontaneous disintegration of heavy elements into lighter ones. In 1903 he and William RAMSAY identified helium as a product of the decay of radium and, while teaching at Glasgow University (1904–14), Soddy introduced the concept of isotopes (elements with different atomic mass but identical chemical properties), formulated laws of radioactive decay and wrote on the uses of atomic energy. He won the Nobel Prize for Chemistry in 1921.

SOMERLED (?–1164), King of Argyll. Of Norse–Gaelic descent (Somerled means 'summer voyager' in Norse), he was a powerful figure in Scottish politics. Only rarely did he recognize the authority of MAEL COLUIM IV although, as the result of one short-lived reconciliation with him, he acquired the nickname 'Sit-by-the-King'. In the late 1150s he defeated the King of Man and conquered much of the Western Isles, becoming an important patron of Iona. He was killed in 1164 while leading an attack on Glasgow. His sons divided his territories between them, and it is from them that the numerous MacDougalls, MacRorys, Macdonnells and Macdonalds of the Isles claim descent.

SOMERS, JOHN (1st Baron Somers) (1651–1716), lawyer and politician. Son of an attorney who fought for Parliament in the Civil Wars, Somers was called to the Bar in 1676. He was junior counsel for the defence at the trial of the seven bishops who, led by Archbishop SANCROFT, had refused to promulgate JAMES II's Declaration of Indulgence for Dissenters and Catholics. Elected MP for Worcester in 1689, he played an active part in the Convention Parliament, and presided over the drafting of the Declaration of Rights. A firm Whig, he was also concerned to protect constitutional balance. Becoming Lord Keeper in 1693 and Lord Chancellor in 1697, he increased the efficiency of the House of Lords as a legal tribunal by compelling the judges to sit as assessors, and he played a key part in bringing about Anglo-Scottish union in 1707. Accumulated experience and dedication to public business and learning made him pre-eminent among the Junto Whigs; he was also noted for his charm, which won him many friends among MPs. State papers from his library were published in 1748 as the Somers Tracts.

SOMERSET, EARL OF, 6TH see CARR, ROBERT; **4TH AND 2ND DUKE OF** see BEAUFORT, EDMUND; **5TH DUKE OF** see SEYMOUR, EDWARD

SOMERSET, LORD FITZROY (1st Baron Raglan) (1788–1855), soldier and military administrator. Son of the 5th Duke of Beaufort, he bought a commission in the 4th Light Dragoons in 1804, accompanied Arthur WELLESLEY, Duke of Wellington as aide-de-camp in the Peninsular campaign and was subsequently wounded at Waterloo in 1815. Between 1827 and 1852 he served as secretary to the Horse Guards, then succeeded Wellington as Commander of the army. Raglan assumed command of the Crimean campaign in 1854, winning the Battle of Alma on 20 Sept. and through rash bravery the engagement at Inkerman on 5 Nov. After the disastrous Charge of the Light Brigade, the blame for which Raglan conveniently heaped on the head of Lord Lucan, Raglan was made the scapegoat for the reverses and privations of the terrible winter of 1854–5, compounded by the failure of the attack on Malakhoff and Redan on 18 June. He died only 10 days later.

SOMERSET, JAMES (fl. 1769–73), American slave, subject of landmark legal decision. Probably originally from Virginia, Somerset was brought to England by his master Charles Stewart from Boston in 1769. In late 1771 he left Stewart and refused to return to America. Stewart abducted him and sold him to a Jamaica-bound slave trader but a writ of *habeas corpus* was obtained to prevent Somerset from being taken out of England. The case of Somerset *v.* Stewart was brought before Lord Chief Justice Mansfield (*see* MURRAY, WILLIAM). Somerset was supported by opponents of slavery such as Granville SHARP: Mansfield ruled in June 1772 that once in England slaves could not be forcefully sold abroad by their masters, effectively ending slavery in England. The ruling was difficult to enforce and many black people continued to be kept in England as slaves until the abolition of slavery in 1833. A more robust measure was the ruling in the case of Knight *v.* Wedderburn in Scotland in 1778, where the relation of master and slave was declared contractually void.

SOMERVILLE, EDITH (1858–1949), writer and illustrator, and **MARTIN, VIOLET** (pen name Martin Ross) (1862–1915), novelist. Second cousins, close friends and collaborators, their jointly authored novels and correspondence chronicle the decline of the Anglo-Irish gentry of which they were part. Somerville, whose father was a colonel in the Buffs, grew up at the family seat in Co. Cork and attended art schools in Germany, Paris and London. Violet (who was always known by her surname Martin) came from Co. Galway. They met in 1885 and the first Somerville and Ross novels, *An Irish Cousin* (1889) and *The Real Charlotte* (1894), a powerful tale about class in Ireland, are distinguished by acutely heard dialogue. They also travelled together and published books about their trips, including *Through Connemara in a Governess Cart* (1892).

In 1903 Somerville became the first ever woman Master of the Hounds, and both worked for the cause of Irish suffrage, though rejecting the militancy of the English suffragettes. Though both Unionists, they differed on the question of the Irish Land League's tactics in the 1890s. After Ross's death, Somerville continued their collaboration, believing that Ross's spirit still guided their production. *The Big House at Inver* was published in 1925; the 'big house' came to stand as a symbol for Anglo-Irish decline, parts in ruin, and rented out, as in later works by Elizabeth Bowen and Molly Keane. Their very popular, though somewhat stereotypical, collections of short stories about a resident magistrate outwitted by wily Irish peasants, *Some Experiences of an Irish RM* (1889) and *Further Experiences of an Irish RM* (1908), have been broadcast as television drama.

SOMERVILLE, MARY (née Fairfax) (1780–1872), scientific writer. A native of Jedburgh (Scots Borders), Somerville began to study mathematics in the early 1790s and in 1807, following the death of her first husband, received private tuition from several Edinburgh intellectuals. In 1816 she moved with her second husband to London where she moved in the leading intellectual circles and began to publish her scientific writings, including her research on the effects of the sun's radiation. Her *Mechanism of the Heavens* (1831), a translation of the French mathematician Pierre Simon Laplace's *Mécanique Céleste*, her synthesis of sciences, *On the Connection of the Physical Sciences* (1834), and her *Physical Geography* (1849) enjoyed long-lasting scientific and general readerships. She was an active campaigner for women's suffrage and Somerville College, Oxford, is named after her.

SOPHIA (1630–1714), Electress of Hanover. The youngest daughter of Frederick V, Elector Palatine of the Rhine and 'Winter King' of Bohemia (1619–21) and his wife Elizabeth, daughter of JAMES VI AND I, she was brought up in exile in the Netherlands. In 1658 she married Ernst August, who in 1692 became Elector of Hanover. She was well educated and a friend of the philosopher Leibniz. As the senior Protestant descendant of James I after ANNE, she was named as heir to the English throne in the Act of Settlement (1701). In 1705 she allowed the Tories to propose a motion inviting her to England, which forced the pro-Hanoverian Whigs to vote it down, embarrassing her, her son the Elector George Louis (later GEORGE I) and Anne. She died in June 1714, seven weeks before Anne.

SOPWITH, SIR THOMAS (1888–1989), aircraft designer. Sopwith started a successful motor-car business in his teens and by 1910 was flying balloons and aeroplanes. In 1912 he started building aeroplanes for the Royal Navy and two years later launched the Sopwith Aviation Co., which built such major First World War military aircraft as the *Pup* and *Camel*. His firm collapsed in 1920 but he subsequently launched the Hawker Engineering Co., which built a series of powerful aeroplanes including the *Hurricane, Lancaster* and *Meteor*, as well as motor cars and bicycles. Sopwith retired from his company in 1963, a period when it was building the *Harrier* jump-jet.

SOUTHAMPTON, 5TH EARL OF *see* WRIOTHSLEY, THOMAS

SOUTHCOTT, JOANNA (1750–1814), prophetess. Daughter of a small farmer, she worked as a shop assistant and servant, and joined the

Methodists in 1791. The following year, while staying with her sister in Devon, she experienced 10 days of the 'power of darkness' and began to write prophecies, which she showed to local clergy. Her first published work was *The Strange Effects of Faith* (1801); many others followed. In 1802 she moved to London and began 'sealing' the faithful in preparation for the millennium. By 1805, when she opened a chapel in Southwark, she claimed to have 'sealed' 10,000: certainly she attracted a large following. Her theology was relatively orthodox, and she used the Anglican Book of Common Prayer. She died in 1814 of a brain tumour, shortly after having announced that she was to give birth to a second Prince of Peace. In 1851 there were more than 200 followers still awaiting her resurrection.

SOUTHERNE, THOMAS (1660–1746), playwright. He came to London from Dublin to study for the Bar but was drawn towards the theatre. An admirer of DRYDEN, his first play was a political allegory, *The Loyal Brother: or the Persian Prince* (1682), praising the Duke of York (the future JAMES II). He began a military career under James II but returned to the stage at the Revolution. His most successful works were collaborations or adaptations, such as his completion of Dryden's *Cleomenes* (1692) and his adaptations of Aphra BEHN's novels, *The Fatal Marriage* (1694) and *Oroonoko* (1695).

SOUTHEY, ROBERT (1774–1843), poet and critic. A distinctly radical youth, Southey was expelled from Westminster school for writing an article attacking corporal punishment. He wrote a poem in support of the French Revolution while at Oxford and a play about the Peasants' Revolt, *Wat Tyler* (1817) (*see* TYLER, WAT). He was a friend of COLERIDGE, with whom he wrote another play, *The Fall of Robespierre*, and planned to set up a 'pantisocratic community' in America based on William GODWIN's idea of human perfectibility.

By 1800 his views had turned distinctly Tory. He settled in the Lake District, and his own six children plus the responsibility which he assumed for the family abandoned by Coleridge meant that Southey had to keep up a continual stream of writing, articles and histories as well as poetry, and in 1808 he started writing regular political articles for the Tory *Quarterly Review*. In 1813 he was appointed Poet Laureate and turned out a number of poems on such public events as Waterloo (1816) as well as histories of NELSON (1813), Brazil (1810–19), WESLEY (1820) and the Peninsular War (1823–32), *Lives of British Admirals* (1833) and a Christian romance *Roderick the Last of the Goths* (1814). Lampooned by PEACOCK as Mr Feathernest in *Melincourt* (1817), despised as a turncoat in the politically volatile years after the Napoleonic Wars,

he savagely attacked BYRON in the introduction to his paean to the recently dead king, *George III, A Vision of Judgement* (1821) (*see* GEORGE III): Byron's satirical response *The Vision of Judgement* was a humiliatingly brilliant parody. For all this, Southey refused a baronetcy when it was offered by PEEL, while gratefully accepting a pension from the same source in 1835.

SPEED, JOHN (*c.* 1552–1629), cartographer and historian. A London merchant, Speed became fascinated by mapmaking and history, encouraged by Fulke GREVILLE. He published a series of county maps from 1607, collected together in *The Theatre of the Empire of Great Britain* in 1611. The influence of his *History of Great Britain*, published in the same year with the encouragement of William CAMDEN and Robert COTTON, has not lasted as well as has that of his detailed maps, which incorporate plans of prominent towns and a host of charming additional flourishes. He also wrote treatises on biblical history.

SPEKE, JOHN (1827–64), explorer. The first European to reach Lake Victoria, which he correctly identified as the source of the Nile, Speke had been commissioned in the British Indian Army in 1844. In 1855 he joined Richard BURTON to explore Somaliland. Severely wounded in an attack, he later rejoined Burton and they struggled inland from the coast to Lake Tanganyika in 1858. Speke then went northwards and found Lake Victoria. His conclusion that it was the Nile's source was vigorously disputed by Burton, but Speke was acclaimed. In a second expedition in 1860 with James Grant, Speke mapped Lake Victoria and found the Nile outlet. In February 1863 Speke and Grant reached southern Sudan. There they met Samuel Baker, who was led to Lake Albert by the information which they provided. Speke's Nile claims were again disputed by Burton, but on the day they were due to debate Speke was killed by his own gun while out hunting.

SPENCE, SIR BASIL (1907–76), architect. Spence started his career working with Edwin LUTYENS on his designs for government buildings in New Delhi (1929–30). He came to public attention with his designs for the Britain Can Make It exhibition (1946) and the Ships and Sea Pavilion for the Festival of Britain (1951). That same year he won the competition to redesign Coventry Cathedral (1951–62), razed by bombing in 1940. A team of artists worked with him, including John Piper and Graham SUTHERLAND. Coventry Cathedral, one of Britain's best-known twentieth-century buildings, is a potent symbol of post-war reconstruction, a phoenix from the ashes fusing an uncompromisingly modern building with the perpendicular ruins of the medieval original. Spence continued his post-war work of building a new Britain as architect of university buildings, including Southampton (1960–73), Liverpool (1959–60) and Sussex (1964–75), of housing for Basildon New Town, of the first major office building in London, Thorn House (1959), and of the barracks for the Household Cavalry in Knightsbridge (1970).

SPENCE, THOMAS (1750–1814), radical. His father was a netmaker and shoemaker, with 19 children, who taught his son to read. Spence, a schoolmaster in Newcastle, was inspired by a lawsuit between the freemen and corporation over the use of common land to develop 'Spencean philanthropy', outlined in *The Real Rights of Man* (1775), whereby all land would be held in common by each parish, profits from rents to be used to support administration and public libraries and schools; each parish would choose a representative for a national assembly and every adult male would be a member of the militia. Moving to London in the 1780s he was imprisoned without trial several times, but was eventually tried and jailed for writing and publishing a seditious libel, *The Restorer of Society to its Natural State* (1801). He also issued tokens bearing radical symbols during a period of coin shortage, many examples of which survive. After his death, the Society of Spencean Philanthropists advocated his reforms, some members being involved in the Cato Street conspiracy (*see* THISTLEWOOD, ARTHUR).

SPENCER, CHARLES (3rd Earl of Sunderland) (1674–1722), politician. He was educated by a tutor, in part in Holland, where his father the 2nd Earl had fled in 1688. He entered Parliament in 1695; his second marriage, to Marlborough's (*see* CHURCHILL, JOHN) daughter in 1700, brought him important Whig connections. Although disliked by Queen ANNE, he became Secretary of State in 1706 and was one of the Whig Junto that dominated the government from 1708 to 1710, when he was dismissed for his part in impeaching SACHEVERELL. His career revived after the accession of GEORGE I, and he rose to become First Lord of the Treasury in 1718, controlling internal affairs while James STANHOPE dealt with foreign policy. The South Sea Bubble, the runaway investment boom of 1720, had its origins in his schemes to reduce the burden of the national debt. After the bubble burst in the autumn, he ceded the effective headship of the Treasury to Robert WALPOLE (who ably defended him in the Commons). As Groom of the Stole, however, he retained personal access to George I, and only his

unexpected death forestalled a further bid for ascendancy at court.

SPENCER, GEORGIANA (née Poyntz) (Countess Spencer) (1737–1814), political hostess and philanthropist. Her father, Stephen Poyntz, was a courtier of humble origins; he ensured his children were well educated, and Georgiana was noted for her classical learning. In 1755 she married John Spencer, later Earl Spencer. She became a leading hostess among the Whig aristocracy; her circle also included cultural figures such as GARRICK and STERNE. Following the deaths of two of her children in infancy and her inability to cure her addiction to gambling, she turned increasingly to religion from the 1770s. She was a supporter of Sunday schools and William JONES of Nayland compared her appearances at fund-raising activities as akin to episcopal visitations.

SPENCER, HERBERT (1820–1903), philosopher and sociologist. He was educated in his native Derby and then in Somerset by his uncle, Thomas Spencer (1796–1853), a schoolmaster and radical writer on social issues such as slavery and the Corn Laws. Herbert was particularly interested in scientific and mathematical subjects and, after a brief stint as a schoolmaster in Derby, worked as a railway engineer (1837–41). Subsequently he made some mechanical inventions and began to develop and publish his radical political views. He moved to London in 1848, where he worked on *The Economist* (1848–53) and developed friendships with writers such as George ELIOT and G. H. Lewes. In 1851 he published his first major work, *Social Statics*, a fierce argument for individualism and *laissez-faire* government, and in 1853 dedicated himself to full-time writing. From 1856 he expounded his 'development hypothesis', which states that all forms of evolution involve a transition from a simpler to a more complex state. Holding that social development, like biological, is driven by competition for resources, he believed that the 'survival of the fittest' (his phrase) has natural and therefore moral sanction. His hypothesis, elaborated in such works as *First Principles* (1862), *The Principles of Biology* (1864–7) and *Principles of Sociology* (1876), became the most influential evolutionary theory of the late nineteenth century. The leading mid nineteenth-century theorist of psychology and sociology, he published *Descriptive Sociology* (1881), a foundation text of sociology, and *Principles of Psychology* (1855), an application of evolutionary theories to associationist psychology. Spencer's work has often been seen as the underpinning of an individualist non-revolutionary approach to society, in common with the theories of his French and German counterparts, Emile Durkheim and Max Weber.

SPENCER, ROBERT *see* essay on page 742

SPENCER, SIR STANLEY (1891–1959), artist. A painter of visionary though carnal spirituality, with affinity to William BLAKE in his everyday settings of the miraculous, Spencer, who has in recent years provoked biographical interest in his irregular and detritus-filled private life, was a gifted scholarship student at the Slade School of Art. He exhibited at Roger FRY's second Post-Impressionist exhibition in 1912, with *John Donne Arriving in Heaven*.

During the First World War he served in the medical corps and then, as an infantryman, in Macedonia. Appointed an official war artist in 1918, he represented his experience of war in his subsequent realist naïve paintings, many of which deal with religious subjects in familiar settings, like his large painting *Resurrection in Cookham* (1926), set in the churchyard of the Berks. village where he lived for much of his life. *The Resurrection of the Soldiers*, part of his series of murals for the Memorial Chapel at Burghclere (Hants.) (1932), evokes the frescos of Giotto, whom he admired. Spencer also painted a number of merciless portraits of himself and his second wife, Patricia Preece, which prefigure Lucian FREUD in their fleshy honesty. During the Second World War he was commissioned as an official war artist to paint the Clydeside ship industry, to show the massive effort needed to win the war.

SPENDER, SIR STEPHEN (1909–95), poet and critic. A member of the AUDEN (whom he met while a student at Oxford) generation which included Louis MACNEICE and Cecil Day Lewis, Spender was persuaded by Christopher ISHER-WOOD to go to Germany when he dropped out of university to write (1929). There he developed an anti-Fascist stance, which he mistook for Communism, and in 1936 went to Spain to file dispatches from the Civil War for the *Daily Worker*. Returning to London, he was joint editor with Cyril CONNOLLY of *Horizon* (1939–41), the most influential literary magazine of the Second World War, and co-editor of the magazine *Encounter* (1953–66), until a revelation about its possible CIA (US Central Intelligence Agency) funding caused him to withdraw. He taught in US universities and was Professor of English at University College, London (1970–5). Most of Spender's poetic output was between the wars: his best, his first *Poems* (1933). He also wrote criticism, but it is for his memoirs, with their poignant evocation of their time, that he is best known and they are most valuable for historians and critics: *World Within World* (1951), *The Thirties and After* (1978) and *Journals, 1939–1983* (1985).

SPENSER, EDMUND (?1552–99), poet. London-born, he began publishing poetry while at Cambridge and was introduced to the household of Robert DUDLEY, Earl of Leicester, there meeting Sir Philip SIDNEY. He went to Ireland in 1580 as secretary to the Lord Deputy, Arthur, Lord Grey de Wilton, making his home there until the 1598 upheavals caused by the success of Hugh O'NEILL's military campaigns; he died while taking dispatches to London. Spenser's reputation as the greatest Elizabethan poet centres on *The Faerie Queene*, begun *c*. 1579 and published 1590–6.

SPODE, JOSIAH (I) (1733–97) and **JOSIAH (II)** (1754–1827), pottery manufacturers. The older Josiah Spode set up a pottery business in Stoke (Staffs.) in 1762, and continued it alone or with partners until his death. He is usually credited with introducing the transfer printing process, a method for printing words or pictures on pottery, to the Staffs. potteries and thereby dramatically increasing the quality and range of designs. His son Josiah moved to London during the 1770s where he set up his own pottery besides acting as an agent for his father and other Staffs. manufacturers. With his partner, William Copeland, who had been one of the elder Spode's apprentices, Spode vigorously marketed his wares and was soon second only to WEDGWOOD as a supplier of fine china to fashionable London.

SPOONER, WILLIAM (1844–1930), Oxford don. A fellow of New College, Oxford, he had a tendency to methathesis (transposing the initial letters of two or more words) and such lapses are now popularly known as 'spoonerisms'. Examples abound – 'you have hissed all my mystery lessons, you have tasted your worm, you will leave town by the first town drain' – though sadly the most ingenious are now recognized to be apocryphal.

SPOTTISWOODE, JOHN (1565–1639), historian. Glasgow-educated, in 1603 he was made Archbishop of Glasgow (receiving consecration by English bishops in 1610, a significant theological point for High Church Anglicans); in 1615 he became Archbishop of St Andrews. He worked against Presbyterians in the Scottish Church, and was made Chancellor of Scotland in 1635, although he was unhappy about enforcing CHARLES I's new prayer book in 1637. He fled to England after the 1638 revolution and was deposed by the Kirk's General Assembly on absurd charges. His voluminous contemporary history of Scotland is invaluable, although inevitably partisan.

SPRING, RICHARD (DICK) (1950–), Irish politician. Member of the Dáil for Kerry North since 1981 and junior minister (1981–2), Spring was

continued on page 743

SPENCER, ROBERT (2nd Earl of Sunderland) (1641–1702)
Politician

Son of the 1st Earl (killed in the Civil War 1643), he married Lady Anne Digby, daughter of the Earl of Bristol (*see* DIGBY, GEORGE). Financial pressures turned him to public life. Having found a patron in the Earl of Arlington (*see* BENNET, HENRY), a friend of the Digbys, he was sent on diplomatic missions to Spain and France, but Arlington's fall in 1674 left him casting around for backers until Danby's fall in 1679 (*see* OSBORNE, THOMAS) opened up the political scene. Sunderland's diplomatic experience made him a possible Secretary of State; family links with the increasingly powerful Shaftesbury (*see* COOPER, ANTHONY ASHLEY) suggested he might mediate between factions. When the King appointed a new Privy Council combining 'Country' leaders with younger courtiers, Sunderland took a leading part.

The ripening of the Exclusion Crisis, as Parliament tried to force CHARLES II to exclude his Catholic brother James (later JAMES II) from the line of succession, left him exposed. Not a man of strong convictions, he was tossed by conflicting currents. In James's judgement 'he lacked that boldness so necessary in these difficult times'. As Shaftesbury grew more radical, however, Sunderland's hesitations made him seem loyal; in 1680 the King dismissed Shaftesbury in favour of Sunderland, GODOLPHIN and Laurence HYDE, dubbed 'the Chits'. Sunderland began to toughen up, developing the acerbic pragmatism that was to be his hallmark. He and Hyde purged exclusionists from local government. Meanwhile he began to put together a Europe-wide anti-French coalition, a bid at a popular foreign policy. Shaftesbury fought back, persuading the Middx. grand jury to try to present James as a Popish recusant; the dream of a Grand Alliance also began to founder. Sunderland cast around for another way out. He talked Charles into agreeing to James's exile but when he came out in favour of exclusion (substituting for James his children, in the first instance MARY, wife of William of Orange, later WILLIAM III, making a neat fit with his foreign-policy plans), the King dismissed him. His experience made him hard to dispense with for long, and in 1682 they were reconciled. Sunderland never again set his will against a king's; he immediately accepted direction to seek closer ties with France.

Not initially favoured by James II, who remembered his support for exclusion, Sunderland won him round by supporting his Catholicizing policies. His support for the repeal of the Test Act (which excluded Catholics from civil and military office) won him the lord presidency of the Council in place of the warier Halifax (*see* SAVILE, GEORGE). The only significant political figure to remain in James's inner circle to the end, he was appointed to the Ecclesiastical Commission, to enforce discipline on recalcitrant churchmen (1686), and to the Board of Regulators (1687), to co-ordinate appointments to local government, alongside JEFFREYS. He nonetheless hedged his bets, for example by not publicly declaring himself a Catholic until the birth of James's son in June 1688 suggested that his policies might endure.

Even then, he was more alive to the limits of the possible than James's other advisers. Thus he argued strenuously against trying the seven bishops who, under the leadership of SANCROFT, refused to promulgate the King's Declaration of Indulgence for Catholics and Dissenters, though, once overruled, he gave evidence against them. Once it became clear that William would invade, he urged concessions. James, complaining again of his want of 'firmness and courage', dismissed him, whereupon he fled to Rotterdam. Supported by his loyally Anglican wife, he reconverted. In 1689 he published a pamphlet justifying his conduct as an attempt to moderate James's policies. He was excluded from both the Indemnity Act 1689 and James's offer (1692) of a pardon in the event of his reinstatement as King.

In 1691 he nonetheless returned to England and reappeared in Parliament. By 1692 William III, who had worked with him during the Exclusion Crisis and who was determinedly eclectic in his choice of Councillors, regularly consulted him on ministerial changes. He functioned as 'minister behind the curtain', fearing parliamentary con-demnation if he took office. In 1697 William, wanting his advice as the peace-making process began, made him Lord Chamberlain, but he resigned later that year when attacked in the Commons.

The startling twists and turns in Sunderland's career made him an object of suspicion, even hatred. In turbulent times, what he had to offer to kings was, first, loyalty and experience and, second, daring and some nerve in coping with crises, even if at the height of a crisis that nerve sometimes broke. Ironically, perhaps, his chief political legacy lay in his boost to the fortunes of the young Whig party, though, inasmuch as he helped to make it into a party of government, that legacy reflected the concerns that had driven his own career.

John P. Kenyon, Robert Spencer, Earl of Sunderland, 1641–1702 (1958) unexpectedly chosen as Labour Party leader in 1982; he was Tanaiste (Deputy Prime Minister) and Minister for the Environment (1982–3) and Energy (1983–7). In 1987 Labour left the coalition govern- ment in protest at budgetary cutbacks, and losses at the ensuing election produced a strong challenge from the anti-coalition Left, which Spring eventu- ally contained. The decision of Fine Gael to support Fianna Fáil on economic reform enabled Spring to become the most prominent opposition leader, confirmed in 1990 when an effective campaign brought the Labour-backed presidential candidate, Mary ROBINSON, an unexpected victory. In 1990–2 he established himself as an excoriating critic of the scandals and controversies surrounding the Fianna Fáil government, and in 1992 Labour had its best ever election result, winning 33 seats. Expected to form a coalition with Fine Gael and the neo-liberal Progressive Democrats, it antagonized some supporters by its alliance with Fianna Fáil. Spring became Foreign Minister, and Labour won an unusually strong Cabinet representation. Personal tensions between Spring and Albert REYNOLDS culminated in the break-up of the coalition in 1994; a new coalition was formed in which Spring secured the Finance Ministry, as well as Foreign Affairs, for Labour and forced Fine Gael to accept the left-wing Democratic Left rather than the Progressive Democrats as the third coalition partner. Both coali- tions passed legislation liberalizing the law on social issues such as divorce. In policy concerning Northern Ireland Spring was seen as a safeguard against Reynolds's perceived Republican bias, and later as a check on John BRUTON's perceived sympathy for the Unionists. In 1997 Labour suffered severe losses in the General Election, and after the poor showing of the party's presidential candidate later that year Spring resigned from the party leadership. It remains unclear whether the gains made by Labour under Spring are the founda- tions for further growth or simply reflect electoral volatility, but he proved an effective leader who moved Irish politics in a more social democratic direction.

SPRY, CONSTANCE (1886–1960), cook and flower arranger. Spry started her venture in floristry in 1929 with a small shop in London's Victoria, later moving to South Audley Street where she started a school of floristry. By the 1950s her supremacy of the domestic arts was such that she was a joint Principal of the Cordon Bleu Cookery school in London, ran a 'finishing school' for girls in Berks. and was adviser to the Ministry of Works on the floral arrangements for the coronation of ELIZABETH II in 1953.

SPURGEON, CHARLES (1834–92), preacher. One of the greatest of Victorian Baptist preachers,

he expounded a simple fundamentalist faith in a riveting manner. The Metropolitan Tabernacle, seating 6,000, was built for him in 1859–61 and filled to capacity whenever he preached. His books of sermons and sayings were immensely popular.

STAFFORD, 15TH BARON AND 1ST VISCOUNT see HOWARD, WILLIAM; **1ST MARQUESS OF** see LEVESON-GOWER, GRANVILLE

STAFFORD, EDWARD (3rd Duke of Buckingham) (1478–1521), magnate. Restored in 1485 to the title and family honours forfeited by his father Henry STAFFORD, in his 1483 rebellion against RICHARD III, his ruthless preoccupation with rebuilding family power in south Wales and the West Country kept him from court. This, combined with his royal blood, attracted HENRY VIII's paranoia, and he was executed on nebulous treason charges.

STAFFORD, HENRY (2nd Duke of Buckingham) (?1454–83), nobleman. Grandson and heir of Humphrey STAFFORD, in April 1483 he emerged from relative (for a duke) obscurity to provide the support that was crucial to RICHARD III's seizure of the throne. He was handsomely rewarded with a massive grant of prestigious and profitable offices in Wales and in the Marches, yet by Oct. he was plotting to put Henry Tudor (the future HENRY VII) on the throne. His motives for joining a conspiracy which was led by former members of EDWARD IV's household but has since become known as Buckingham's rebellion are unknown. He may have held Richard responsible for murdering the Princes in the Tower (see EDWARD V), although some defenders of Richard's reputation have blamed him, and have even suggested that he may have been aiming at the throne himself. At all events so sudden a switch of allegiance was discon- certing and very few people trusted him enough to follow him into rebellion. His part in the revolt ended in fiasco and he was executed for treason on 2 Nov. 1483.

STAFFORD, HUMPHREY (1st Duke of Buck- ingham) (1402–60), politician. Created Duke in 1444, he was a politician of moderate views who generally tried to mediate between Yorkists and Lancastrians. But in the last resort, perhaps because he had a long-standing dispute with Warwick (see NEVILLE, RICHARD), he chose to fight for HENRY VI. He was wounded and captured at the first Battle of St Albans (Herts.) in 1455 and was later killed at Northampton.

STAFFORD, JOHN (?–1452), Archbishop of Canterbury (1443–52). Educated at Oxford, he held a series of great offices of state, being in turn

Treasurer, Keeper of the Privy Seal and Chancellor (1432–50). For his devoted administrative service he was appointed Bishop of Bath and Wells (1425) and Archbishop (1443). It was said of him if he had done little good he had done no harm.

STAFFORD, THOMAS (?1531–57), conspirator. Nephew of Cardinal Reginald POLE, he travelled in Italy after 1550, and sought foreign help to persuade MARY I to restore him to the title of his grandfather Edward STAFFORD, Duke of Buckingham. Angered by her lack of sympathy, he was imprisoned in 1554 for opposing her marriage to PHILIP II of Spain, but fled to France and intrigued for her overthrow. His expedition from Dieppe in 1557 was farcical, although he captured Scarborough Castle; he was executed at Tyburn.

STAIR, 1ST VISCOUNT *see* DALRYMPLE, SIR JAMES; **2ND EARL OF** *see* DALRYMPLE, JOHN

STANHOPE, LADY HESTER (1776–1839), traveller. Niece of PITT THE YOUNGER and mistress of his household, she left England after his death and travelled in the Levant. In 1814 she settled on Mount Lebanon where she established herself as an eccentric but influential prophetess-cum-political leader. She was buried there. She was an important figure in the transmission of orientalist ideas to Victorian Britain.

STANHOPE, JAMES (1st Earl Stanhope) (1673–1721), politician. Grandson of the 1st Earl of Chesterfield, he fought in the wars of the 1690s and early eighteenth century, ultimately becoming commander of the British forces in Spain. Elected MP in 1701, he was a strong Whig and played a major part in the impeachment of SACHEVERELL. He helped suppress the Jacobite rebellion of 1715, was made southern Secretary of State, served briefly as First Lord of the Treasury in 1717, but returned to the secretaryship. His main political achievements were in foreign policy, helping to secure the Treaty of Westminster (1716) and the Triple Alliance (1717). As a leading minister, he shared with Sunderland (*see* SPENCER, CHARLES) the blame for the bursting of the South Sea Bubble in 1720, which effectively ended his political career.

STANHOPE, PHILIP (4th Earl of Chesterfield) (1694–1773), politician and writer. Educated at home and at Cambridge, Chesterfield was elected MP in 1715, associated with the Prince of Wales (later GEORGE II) and opposed Robert WALPOLE as well as the PELHAM administration in its early years. On succeeding to his father's title in 1726, he became eligible for various posts usually reserved for men of rank. As a diplomat, he helped to negotiate the second Treaty of Vienna, and, after being reconciled with Pelham, was made Lord Lieutenant of Ireland in 1745. The following year he served as northern Secretary of State but resigned in 1748 when Newcastle (*see* PELHAM-HOLLES, THOMAS) opposed peace with France. In 1751 he persuaded Parliament to adopt the Gregorian calendar, bringing England into line with the continent. His circle of literary friends and correspondents included ADDISON, SWIFT, POPE, Montesquieu and Voltaire. His posthumously published *Letters* to his illegitimate son, advising him on manners and social duties, were criticized for their worldly values, JOHNSON famously describing them as teaching 'the morals of a whore, and the manners of a dancing master'.

STANIHURST, RICHARD (1547–1618), historian. From a Dublin Old English family, he studied at Oxford and contributed material on Ireland to Raphael HOLINSHED's chronicles. Travelling abroad, he converted to Roman Catholicism, was ordained, and became involved in Spanish intrigues against ELIZABETH I. He translated Virgil's *Aeneid*, wrote on Irish history (with little sympathy for Gaelic Irish culture) and engaged in Church controversy with his Protestant nephew James USSHER. He may have invented (in Latin) the phrase 'Anglo-Irish'.

STANLEY, ARTHUR (1815–81), theologian. He was a leading figure in the 'Broad Church' within the Church of England. Distinguished by a commitment to tolerance of a wide range of theological opinion and to the idea that the Church should be as inclusive as possible in membership, the Broad Church sat, often uneasily, between the Low, or Evangelical, and the High, or Anglo-Catholic, wings of Anglicanism. Stanley wrote widely on theological questions: his *Essays, Chiefly on Questions of Church and State* (1870) are representative. In 1861 he was one of many to defend *Essays and Reviews* (1860), a collection which called for a historical and critical approach to the Bible rather than a literalist reading of it, for recognition of religious traditions other than the Judaeo-Christian and for an acceptance of scientific finding on such matters as the age of the earth. The surrounding controversy was the most important theological dispute of the century. Despite his liberal views Stanley was accepted within the mainstream of the Church: he was Dean of Westminster (1864–81).

STANLEY, EDWARD (23rd [14th Stanley] Earl of Derby) (1799–1869), politician and Prime Minister (1852, 1858–9, 1866–8). His political loyalties were fluid in the early stage of his career.

Identified with the Whigs from 1820, he neverthe-less served in the liberal Tory administration of George CANNING and Goderich (*see* ROBINSON, FREDERICK). He established his reputation as an able parliamentary orator in Charles GREY's Whig ministry in which, as Secretary for Ireland, he carried the Irish Education Act of 1831, and, as Secretary for War and the Colonies (1833–4), brought about the abolition of slavery in the West Indies. In 1835 he resigned over Lord John RUSSELL's plan to use Irish Church revenues for secular purposes, and thereafter allied himself with PEEL, whom he served as Colonial Secretary (1844–5), resigning the following year over the repeal of the Corn Laws. During the 1850s and 1860s he led the Protectionist wing of the Conservatives and co-operated with DISRAELI in the rebuilding of the party. Thrice Prime Minister of minority governments, his principal aim was to establish the Conservatives as a credible party of government in a fast-growing democracy. The extension of the franchise in the provision of the 1867 reform in his final administration seems to have been prompted by this attempt to establish Conservative credibility.

STANLEY, EDWARD (26th [17th Stanley] Earl of Derby) (1865–1948), politician. He served as an MP and in government (1895–1905) before, in 1908, succeeding to the Derby title with its enor-mous wealth and local influence in north-west England (this was to earn him the nickname 'King of Lancashire'). He is today best known for his recruiting schemes during the First World War. He raised five battalions of volunteers in 1914, promoted the 'Pals Battalions', and after his appointment as Director of Recruiting in 1915 inaugurated the 'Derby scheme' by which men attested to their willingness to serve: a first step towards conscription. He was Secretary of State for War from 1916 to 1918, then Ambassador to Paris (1918–20), and attempted, unsuccessfully, to mediate in the Anglo-Irish War.

STANLEY, SIR HENRY MORTON (1841–1904), explorer and journalist. He joined the staff of the *New York Herald* in 1857 and established himself as a reporter of Britain's unfolding colo-nial mission in Africa. In the 1870s and 1880s he explored the African interior, notably around Lake Victoria and along the length of the River Congo. He is best remembered for his dramatic account of the successful search for Dr LIVINGSTONE, whom he found at Ujiji on 10 Nov. 1876.

STANLEY, JAMES (Baron Strange, 16th [7th Stanley] Earl of Derby) (1607–51). In 1642 he threw his power in the north-west behind CHARLES I and after the Royalist defeat at Marston Moor (July 1644) withdrew in defiance to the family lordship of the Isle of Man. His return in 1651 to rally Lancs. to CHARLES II was a failure; defeated at Wigan, he aided Charles in his flight, was captured and was summarily beheaded.

STANLEY, SIR JOHN (*c.* 1350–1414), Lord of Man. From a family of Cheshire gentry, he was appointed Lieutenant of Ireland by HENRY IV in 1400 and granted the Isle of Man in 1406. His death in 1414 was alleged to have been caused by the curses of the Irish poets. Man was to remain in his family until 1736.

STANLEY, OLIVER (1896–1950), politician. Second son of the 26th Earl of Derby, Stanley was elected as Conservative MP for Westmorland in 1924. During the 1930s he held many minor offices. As Minister of Labour during the Munich crisis of 1938 he was tempted to resign along with Duff COOPER in protest against the betrayal of the Czechs but decided not to do so. From Jan. to May 1940 he served as Secretary of State for War, where he had occasion to remonstrate with the new First Lord of the Admiralty, Winston CHURCHILL, over the conduct of the Norwegian campaign. This may have influenced Churchill's decision to remove him from that office in May 1940. After two years out of office Stanley accepted the post of Colonial Secretary in 1942. In opposi-tion after the war his devastating wit was used with great effect to attack the economic policies of the ATTLEE government. Had he lived he would have been Chancellor of the Exchequer in the 1951 Conservative government.

STANLEY, THOMAS (Baron Stanley, 10th [1st Stanley] Earl of Derby) (?1435–1504), nobleman. Despite being made Constable of England by RICHARD III, Stanley, a shrewd and cautious politi-cian, changed sides at Bosworth to support Henry Tudor (his stepson by marriage to Lady Margaret BEAUFORT and the future HENRY VII). This gained him the earldom, which still survives, and estab-lished his family's hegemony in Lancs.

STANSFELD, SIR JAMES (1820–98), politician. The son of a Halifax lawyer, and raised as a Unitarian, he was educated at University College, London, and was called to the Bar in 1849. A close friend of Mazzini, he was actively involved in support for national movements in Europe in the 1840s and 1850s. He was MP for Halifax (1859–95), held junior office in 1863–4, 1866 and 1868–9 and was President of the Poor Law Board and the Local Government Board (1871–4). His main distinction was as both a consistent supporter of women's suffrage and, above all, as the chief parliamentary leader of the campaign to repeal the Contagious Diseases Acts from 1874. He was knighted in 1895.

STANSGATE, VISCOUNT *see* BENN, ANTHONY WEDGWOOD

STARK, DAME FREYA (1893–1993), traveller. Born in Paris, brought up largely in Italy, she started her travels in 1929 with a visit to the Lebanon (she had learned Arabic) and from then went successively further east, travelling to the interior of Iran and Iraq and southern Arabia in search of nomadic tribes. These travels are described in such books as *The Valley of the Assassins* (1934) and *The Southern Gates of Arabia* (1938). During the Second World War her knowledge of the Middle East made her useful for British military propaganda work there. After the war she continued her travels, including to Turkey, India and Afghanistan, writing more travel books, contracting a brief marriage and publishing four volumes of autobiography (1950–61). In 1976, aged 83, she journeyed down the Euphrates.

STARKEY, THOMAS (?1499–1538), writer. An Oxford don and humanist scholar, he was caught unhappily between his wish for preferment and his loyalty to Reginald POLE and the Pole family, placed on the wrong side in Henrician politics. He travelled with Pole in Italy and wrote a treatise on possible ways of reforming English government, *A Dialogue between Pole and Lupset* (1529, completed *c.* 1535). Later tracts of his supported HENRY VIII's break with Rome.

STARR, RINGO (originally Richard Starkey) (1940–), musician *see* LENNON, JOHN

STEAD, W(ILLIAM) T(HOMAS) (1849–1912), crusading journalist. Editor of the *Pall Mall Gazette* (1883–90), he was largely responsible for the introduction of American 'yellow journalism' (journalism of a reckless and unscrupulously sensational character) into the respectable English press. His exposure of child prostitution, *The Maiden Tribute of Modern Babylon* (1885), in collaboration with Josephine BUTLER led to fame, imprisonment and the passage of the Criminal Law Amendment Act, raising the age of consent to 16. A spiritualist and pacifist, he died in the *Titanic* disaster.

STEARN (OR STERNE), JOHN (1624–69), doctor. Great-nephew of James USSHER, he studied at Dublin, Cambridge and Oxford, returning to Ireland in 1651; in 1656 he became lecturer in Hebrew at Trinity College, Dublin, and Professor of Medicine in 1662. He practised medi-

cine in Dublin and in 1660 was first President of the Irish College of Physicians.

STEARNE, JOHN (*fl.* 1644–8), witchfinder. An East Anglian Puritan and assistant to Matthew HOPKINS, he published a self-justifying book about his work in 1648, after Hopkins's ignominious death.

STEEL, SIR DAVID (Baron Steel) (1938–), politician. Steel was the youngest MP in the Commons when elected as a Liberal for Roxburgh, Selkirk and Peebles in 1965 and he achieved early fame (and notoriety) as sponsor of the 1967 Abortion Act. He became Liberal leader in 1976 following Jeremy THORPE's retirement and had to deal with the embarrassment caused by Thorpe's trial. From 1977 he supported the CALLAGHAN government in a formal parliamentary pact (the Lib–Lab pact) which allowed Labour to stay in power until 1979. Steel and the Liberals were challenged by the break-away from the Labour Party of David OWEN and the rest of the 'gang of four' to form the Social Democratic Party. The two parties both did well in 1983 but fatally split the left-of-centre vote with Labour, thus allowing Margaret THATCHER another term of office. After 1983 Steel worked in uneasy partnership with David Owen, who was always the more dynamic figure. After the failure of their Alliance at the 1987 election Steel proposed a merger of the two parties, which occasioned Owen's resignation and the formation in 1988 of the Liberal-Democratic Party. Steel stood down as leader in Paddy ASHDOWN's favour. In 1999 Steel was elected as an MSP (Member of the Scottish Parliament) for Lothian and was appointed Presiding Officer.

STEELE, SIR RICHARD (1672–1729), essayist. The son of a Dublin attorney, educated at Charterhouse, where he met his future collaborator Joseph ADDISON, and a soldier, he was moved to write an essay, *The Christian Hero* (1700), after wounding his opponent in a duel. Its success was crowned by praise from WILLIAM III; he then became a playwright, penning a succession of comedies. In 1709 he launched a thrice-weekly essay paper, *The Tatler*, helped by Addison; articles on different subjects were grouped together under the headings of separate coffee houses. In 1711 *The Tatler* was replaced by the more famous *Spectator*, revolving in part around a fictitious club whose members included a Tory squire, Sir Roger de Coverley, and a Whig merchant, Sir Andrew Freeport. Both publications tried to disseminate the values of a liberal 'polite' culture to a wide readership. From 1712 Steele concentrated on politics, becoming a Whig MP in 1713. He was expelled in 1714 for writing seditious libels but returned next year in GEORGE I's first Parliament.

He was also a patentee of the Theatre Royal, Drury Lane, and continued to issue pamphlets and periodicals, usually supporting the Whigs, although his opposition to James STANHOPE and his Peerage Bill (which would have prevented any net addition to the peerage, a proposal which split the Whigs) caused a break with Addison in 1718.

STEELE, TOMMY (originally Thomas Hicks) (1936–), singer. Britain's first rock'n'roll star, Steele, a merchant seaman, was plucked from obscurity by the impresario John Kennedy, who discovered him in a coffee bar in Soho, and made him a star overnight with his first single, *Rock with the Cavemen,* in 1956. The second single *Singin' the Blues* reached number one in Britain a year later, but by the beginning of the 1960s, his rock'n'roll image looked increasingly dated, with the rise of new groups like the Beatles (*see* LENNON, JOHN). Steele deftly restyled himself as a family entertainer, recording such songs as *Little White Bull* (1968) and appearing as Tony Lumpkin in Oliver Goldsmith's *She Stoops to Conquer* (1960), in variety shows and in musical films such as *Half a Sixpence* (1963).

STENTON, SIR FRANK (1880–1967), historian. Expert in Anglo-Saxon and early Norman history, his greatest books were *The First Century of English Feudalism* (1932) and *Anglo-Saxon England* (1943). The first formed the foundation for the modern study of the Anglo-Norman baronage, and the second, a general survey, brought many problems of interpretation securely into focus and advanced significantly the exploitation of placename and archaeological evidence.

STEPHEN (*c.* 1096–1154), King of England (1135–54). The younger son of Stephen, Count of Blois, and Adela, daughter of WILLIAM I THE CONQUEROR, he became, thanks to the generosity of his uncle HENRY I, the wealthiest Anglo-Norman magnate, and in 1125 he married MATILDA OF BOULOGNE, heiress to that French county. Although in 1127 he had sworn an oath recognizing his cousin the Empress MATILDA as her father's heir, when Henry died on 1 Dec. 1135, he wasted no time in getting himself crowned King at Westminster on 22 Dec. and then recognized as Duke of Normandy.

While the Empress Matilda and her husband, Geoffrey of Anjou, concentrated on invading Normandy, Stephen first dealt successfully with challenges to his authority in England. But from 1139, the year in which Matilda landed in England, he was in serious difficulties. Although the fact that his rival was a woman had allowed him to seize the throne in the first place, it also meant he now faced an opponent whom it was hard to eliminate without offending against

chivalry. In Feb. 1141 he was captured at the Battle of Lincoln and for several months his cause seemed lost. In Normandy, Geoffrey made crucial advances; in England, Stephen's brother, HENRY OF BLOIS, was prepared to accept the verdict of battle. But the Empress overplayed a winning hand, allowing Stephen's queen to organize a comeback. When the Empress's half-brother, ROBERT OF GLOUCESTER, was captured, an exchange of prisoners was agreed, Robert for Stephen. Stephen retained control of London and much of eastern England, but he never returned to Normandy and by 1145 Geoffrey had completed his conquest of the duchy.

From then on, Stephen's supporters with major connections in Normandy could give him, at best, half-hearted allegiance. He fought on, however, until disheartened by the deaths of his wife and his eldest son Eustace, both in 1153. By the Treaty of Winchester in Nov. of that year, he recognized Matilda's eldest son, later HENRY II, as his heir in return for life possession of the throne and a guarantee that his own second-born son, William, would be allowed to keep all his family lands in England and Normandy. After 14 years of civil war, no one was prepared to dispute Henry's right to the throne when Stephen died the following Oct.

Stephen has to take some responsibility for the troubles of his reign. Above all, the fact that he visited Normandy only once, in 1137, meant that he failed to take proper account of the cross-Channel structure of the Anglo-Norman realm. In addition, he was perhaps too chivalrous and gallant for his own good, for example, at Lincoln. On the other hand, these were the very qualities that had made him an attractive candidate for the throne and enabled his wife to campaign on his behalf in the crisis of 1141.

STEPHEN, SIR LESLIE (1832–1904), scholar and critic. Brought up in a strict Evangelical household, he took holy orders but subsequently became a celebrated exponent of agnosticism. His *History of English Thought in the Eighteenth Century* (1876), which attempted to relate intellectual development to social change, is still consulted, as is the *Dictionary of National Biography,* which he founded and edited. Nevertheless, he is probably best remembered as the father of Virginia WOOLF and Vanessa BELL.

STEPHENS, EDWARD (?–1706), pamphleteer and moral reformer. Stephens emerged as a pamphlet writer under CHARLES II. Among his early works were attacks on Catholicism and an account of measures by which apprentices could gain legal redress from their masters. He welcomed the Revolution of 1688 hoping that it would lead to a reformed moral climate at all levels in society. When the first 'reformation of manners' clubs, financing prosecutions for moral offences such as prostitution and swearing, began to appear in 1690, Stephens assumed a prominent role as organizer and propagandist. When in 1692 an over-enthusiastic reforming Justice of the Peace, Ralph Hartley, was prosecuted for summarily convicting moral offenders, Stephens publicized his case in a pamphlet and gained widespread support. A triumph for the reformers was the passing of a tightened Blasphemy Act in 1698. Although a fierce critic of Catholics, Dissenters and Quakers, Stephens advocated conciliatory measures to heal religious divisions, to some extent foreshadowing the Latitudinarian Anglicanism espoused by many of the founders of the Society for the Propagation of Christian Knowledge and Society for the Propagation of the Gospels (*see also* BRAY, THOMAS).

STEPHENS, JAMES (1824–1901), Irish politician. Stephens was a Young Irelander who went into exile in Paris after the failure of the 1848 Rising. In 1858, back in Ireland, he founded the Irish Republican Brotherhood (IRB), sometimes known as the Fenians, modelled on continental revolutionary secret societies. The new movement quickly established a mass following despite police surveillance and hostility from the Catholic Church, and started a newspaper, the *Irish People*, to raise funds and propagate its ideas. Stephens was an autocratic leader who believed that he should command the same unquestioned leadership as a general in the field. In 1865, fearing the arrival of large numbers of Irish American veterans of the American Civil War, the government arrested most of the Fenian leaders. Stephens escaped from prison, but disappointed his followers by refusing to call an insurrection on the grounds that there was no hope of military success. He went to America in 1866 and displaced John O'MAHONY as leader of the American Fenians but, after repeatedly predicting an imminent rising while refusing to give the order for one, Stephens was himself deposed by a military leadership under Thomas Kelly, which launched an unsuccessful rising in 1867. A minority within the IRB wished to restore Stephens as leader, but this was precluded by his insistence on nothing less than his old untrammelled authority. In 1891 he returned to Ireland, where a house was bought for him by public subscription; after endorsing Charles Stewart PARNELL in the split of 1890 he took no further role in public life.

STEPHENS, JOSEPH RAYNER (1805–79), social reformer. A Dissenting firebrand, he campaigned for the People's Charter, the Ten Hours Act, and against the New Poor Law. The three independent chapels which he created at Ashton-under-Lyne supplied a popular following for his Tory radicalism.

STEPHENSON, GEORGE *see* essay on page 749

STEPHENSON, ROBERT (1803–59), engineer. Son of George STEPHENSON, he served an apprenticeship at Killingworth colliery (Northumb.), helped his father survey the famous Stockton and Darlington railway, and studied briefly at Edinburgh University. In 1823 he became a managing partner in Robert Stephenson & Co., a steam-locomotive firm in Newcastle-upon-Tyne which he founded with his father and others. From 1827 the company began to build increasingly powerful locomotives, notably his father's *Rocket*. In 1838, after battling with engineering, political and commercial problems, he completed the construction of the 112-mile London to Birmingham railway. His greatest accomplishments, however, were his bridges, notably the tubular bridges over the Menai Straits (1850) and St Lawrence River (1859), the high level bridge in Newcastle (1849) and the Royal Border bridge at Berwick (1850). He was Conservative MP for Whitby (1847–59) and a major figure in the history of engineering.

STEPTOE, PATRICK (1913–88), gynaecologist *see* EDWARDS, ROBERT

STERNE, LAURENCE (1713–68), writer. Son of a soldier who was killed in a duel, he had an irregular early education, then went to Jesus College, Cambridge. Ordained in 1737 on the advice of an uncle who was a canon of York, he became a Prebendary at York in 1741. His innovative novel, *The Life and Opinions of Tristram Shandy, Gentleman* (1760–7), substituted digressive memoir for the narrative form that was then becoming established as the conventional novelistic mode. He celebrated emotional impulsiveness, and made this a key feature of his self-representation in *The Sermons of Mr Yorick* (1760–9) and *A Sentimental Journey through France and Italy* (1768), based on travels undertaken for his health. After his death, his body was 'resurrected' by grave robbers but recognized at a Cambridge anatomy lecture.

STERNHOLD, THOMAS (before 1517–49), musician. An enthusiastically Protestant court musician under HENRY VIII, he survived a Catholic crackdown in 1543 to become MP for Plymouth in 1544. He dedicated a pioneering collection of metrical psalms to EDWARD VI (whom he said delighted in listening to them) in 1549; a posthumous enlargement contained further psalms by 'J. H.' (John Hopkins, probably a Suffolk clergymen who d. 1570), and an entire psalter published by

continued on page 750

STEPHENSON, GEORGE (1781–1848)
Engineer

Stephenson was born near the horse-drawn tram road for Wylam colliery (Northumb.), where his father worked. As a child he was employed as a cowherd but by the age of 17 he was, like his father, a fireman on the Wylam colliery's pumping engine, and was teaching himself how to read and write. By 1801 he was a brakesman of the steam-driven winding engines at Black Collerton colliery and a year later worked on similar engines used to haul coal wagons from Willington Quay colliery (Northumb.). Following the death of his wife and daughter in 1805 he contemplated emigrating but the education of his son Robert STEPHENSON compelled him to remain in Britain. From 1804 he was employed on the engines at Killingworth colliery (Northumb.) and displayed such mechanical skill that by 1812 was in charge of the machinery in all the collieries owned by the 'Grand Allies', the partnership between the principal coal-mining families of Durham and Northumb. In 1815 he invented a safety lamp which embroiled him in controversy with Humphry DAVY. At Killingworth he constructed several stationary engines and replaced the horse-drawn coal sleds with coal wagons rolling on rails and pulled by the stationary steam engines. By this period, colliery owners were regarding the steam-driven locomotive running on rails as an economically attractive alternative to horse-power, not least because the steam locomotives designed by Richard TREVITHICK and others were then being used successfully to haul coal in a few collieries in the north east. In 1813 Stephenson was commissioned to build a locomotive for Killingworth colliery and in 1814 he successfully launched his *Blucher*, a locomotive which boasted flanged wheels running on edge rails and hauled 30 tons up an incline of 1 in 450 at a speed of 4 mph. From this time he devoted himself to making more powerful and comfortable railway locomotives and in 1822 completed, at the Hetton colliery (Co. Durham), the first railway to be operated solely by steam locomotives. In 1821 he persuaded promoters of the proposed Stockton and Darlington railway, a scheme that had just received parliamentary approval, to involve him in the construction of the line and to use his steam locomotives as a source of motive power. With the considerable assistance of his son, Robert Stephenson, he surveyed the line, oversaw the laying of wrought-iron rails and designed the railway's first locomotive, *Locomotion*, a machine built by Robert's new engineering firm in Newcastle-upon-Tyne. The railway was opened, with George Stephenson driving *Locomotion*, before large and jubilant crowds in September 1825. The resounding success of this railway informed Stephenson's later reputation as the 'father of the railways' and led to his appointment in 1826 as engineer to the proposed Liverpool and Manchester railway. He had already acted as surveyor to this line but the accuracy of his work was undermined by errors made by his assistants and Parliament consequently refused the application to build the railway. Later in 1826, after further political struggles, the railway gained parliamentary approval and Stephenson and his staff began the arduous task of laying a railway line through frequently treacherous terrain. Two years later the Liverpool and Manchester Railway Co. held a competition to test Stephenson's suggestion that steam locomotives would be the best source of motive power on the railway. Four locomotives were entered for the competition, but the clear winner was judged to be the *Rocket* of George and Robert Stephenson and Henry Booth, a fast (30 mph) locomotive with tubular boilers which had proved extremely difficult to construct. The *Rocket* demonstrated the practicality of long-distance railway travel by steam locomotives. In 1830 the Manchester and Liverpool railway was opened amid much public enthusiasm. It was the first railway to carry passengers and helped spread George Stephenson's fame even further.

During the rest of his life Stephenson was actively involved in the refinement of locomotives and the construction and extension of railways. He was chief engineer to most of the British lines laid in the 1830s including the Grand Junction line connecting Birmingham, Manchester and Liverpool. He also advised on the construction of the Belgian State railway, the first continental railway to be operated solely by steam. He was successful in the battle between the Stephensons' 'narrow gauge' and Isambard Kingdom BRUNEL's 'broad gauge' railway. In 1847 he founded the Institution of Mechanical Engineers and spent his last years in retirement in Chesterfield (Derby.). Although Stephenson cannot be considered the inventor of the steam locomotive he played the leading part in turning that invention into a practical means of hauling coal and transporting passengers over long distances.

Samuel Smiles, *The Lives of George and Robert Stephenson* (1874)
Lionel T. Rolt, *George and Robert Stephenson: The Railway Revolution* (1960)

John DAYE in 1562 became known as 'Sternhold and Hopkins', a standard collection into the late seventeenth century.

STEVENS, WILLIAM (1732–1807), lay theologian and philanthropist. Stevens's father was a Southwark businessman but his first cousin was George HORNE, and although Stevens entered the hosiery trade he shadowed his cousin's religious career. He taught himself Hebrew, Greek, Latin and French and participated in theological debates. His *Essay on the Nature and Constitution of the Christian Church* defending the Thirty-Nine Articles against the Unitarians, published in 1773, was reprinted regularly for 70 years. He became an active member of the Society for the Propagation of the Gospel, and in 1782 was made Treasurer of Queen Anne's Bounty, allowing him regular access to bishops and identification with Church patronage. With William JONES of Nayland he formed the Society for the Reformation of Principles in the 1790s to counter radicalism in Church and State and was associated with the High Church 'Hackney phalanx' in the early nineteenth century.

STEVENSON, ROBERT LOUIS (1850–94), novelist and essayist. Edinburgh-born, he was a frail man who left the law to write and travelled extensively, dying in the Pacific where the Samoans had dubbed him 'The Teller of Tales', Stevenson's most enduring tales are *Treasure Island* (1883), *The Strange Case of Dr Jekyll and Mr Hyde* (1886), *Kidnapped* (1886), *The Master of Ballantrae* (1889) and the posthumous *Weir of Hermiston* (1896). His essays and short stories were published in volume form as *Virginibus Puerisque* (1881).

STEWART, ALEXANDER (also known as the Wolf of Badenoch) (9th [1st Stewart] Earl of Buchan) (*c.* 1343–*c.* 1405), royal servant. The fourth son of ROBERT II , who appointed him Justiciar of Northern Scotland, he extorted protection money from many, including the Bishop of Moray. After losing office he sacked the bishop's burgh and cathedral at Elgin, earning his nickname. He held the lordship of Badenoch.

STEWART, ALEXANDER (3rd [1st Stewart] Duke of Albany) (*c.* 1454–85), Royal Prince. Second son of JAMES II, he opposed the pro-English policy of his brother JAMES III, was indicted for treason in 1479 and fled to France. In 1482 an English invasion led by the Duke of Gloucester (*see* RICHARD III) persuaded James to welcome him back and appoint him Lieutenant General, but he was soon in further trouble and by 1485 was back in Paris, where he was killed in a tournament.

STEWART, ARABELLA (1575–1625), dynast. As daughter of Charles Stewart, Earl of Lennox, younger brother of Henry STEWART, Lord Darnley, she was a close cousin of JAMES I, and was brought up mainly by her grandmother Bess of HARDWICK; she spent much time in the company of the imprisoned MARY QUEEN OF SCOTS. She was not allowed to succeed to the Lennox title, despite the best efforts of her family, who kept her closely guarded. In 1603 she became the hapless centre-piece of the Main Plot, a scheme of her cousin Henry BROOKE, Lord Cobham, to replace JAMES I with her. The plot was quickly betrayed to the government; RALEIGH was among those convicted, but the leaders escaped execution. The government tendentiously linked it with a contemporary Roman Catholic scheme to kidnap James and extort a promise of toleration from him (the Bye Plot); official manipulation of both plots remains obscure but likely. Arabella was treated leniently by James, but she was imprisoned in 1610 after secretly marrying William Seymour who, as grandson of Edward SEYMOUR, Duke of Somerset, and Catherine GREY had his own dose of royal blood. After briefly escaping from house arrest the following year, she spent the rest of her life in deep depression in the Tower of London.

STEWART, DUGALD (1753–1828), philosopher. Son of a Professor of Mathematics at Edinburgh, where he was educated, he was drawn by the presence of Thomas REID to Glasgow University. He returned to Edinburgh, initially to teach mathematics, and succeeded Adam FERGUSON as Professor of Moral Philosophy in 1785. He became the most prominent British philosopher of his day although his strength was more in teaching and disseminating others' ideas than in developing his own. He helped perpetuate the legacy of the Scottish Enlightenment, contributing among other works a five-volume edition of Adam SMITH, and Edinburgh's reputation as a centre of intellectual activity. His pupils included Henry BROUGHAM and many of the other writers of the influential Whig journal the *Edinburgh Review*, founded in 1802.

STEWART, HENRY (styled Lord Darnley) (1545–67), King of Scots. Born in Yorks. to Matthew STEWART, Earl of Lennox, and Lady Margaret DOUGLAS; his mother's incessant scheming for his dynastic advancement finally succeeded when, having been allowed to leave England in 1565 by an exasperated ELIZABETH I, he captivated MARY QUEEN OF SCOTS with his vacant good looks, and perhaps his Catholicism. Showering him with honours and a peerage title, Mary married him and pronounced him King of Scots in July 1565. Soon even she could see that he was utterly untrustworthy; Darnley, furious at her obvious affection for David RIZZIO, collaborated in the Italian's murder (1566). After Mary gave birth to Darnley's son (the future JAMES VI AND I) later the same year, the couple separated; by now Mary was involved with James HEPBURN, Earl of Bothwell. She persuaded Darnley to return to Edinburgh; he was found strangled after his lodging, Kirk o' Field, had been blown up. The murder proved the downfall of Mary and Bothwell.

STEWART, JAMES (1st Duke of Ross) (?1479–1504), younger son of JAMES III. He was made Duke in 1488; in 1497 his elder brother JAMES IV made him Archbishop of St Andrews, and in 1500 he became Papal Legate in Scotland. Neither he nor his successor as Archbishop (1504–13), James IV's 11-year-old illegitimate son, Alexander Stewart, inspire confidence in James's quality control of senior Church office in Scotland.

STEWART, JAMES (16th [1st Stewart] Earl of Moray, 17th Earl of Mar) (?1531–70), politician. A bastard son of JAMES V, he became an admirer of John KNOX, and in 1559 one of the Lords of the Congregation, henceforth championing pro-English and Protestant policies. He was associated with the murders of both David RIZZIO and Henry STEWART, Lord Darnley; the ascendancy of James HEPBURN, Earl of Bothwell, sent him into brief exile. He returned to become Regent for JAMES VI in 1567. His assassination by a Catholic sparked civil war.

STEWART, JAMES (17th [2nd Stewart] Earl of Moray) (?1568–92), courtier. Heir of James, Lord Doune, in 1581 he married Elizabeth, daughter of James STEWART, 16th Earl of Moray, and Countess in her own right, and was recognized as Earl. Known from his good looks as the 'bonny Earl of Moray' and a great favourite of ANNE OF DENMARK, he was murdered by the family enemy, George GORDON, 6th Earl of Huntly, after a spectacular feud which had disrupted north-east Scotland for a decade.

STEWART, JAMES (5th [1st Stewart] Earl of Arran) (?–1595), politician and soldier. Younger son of Andrew Stewart, Lord Ochiltree, he fought Spain in the Netherlands; back in Scotland (1579) JAMES VI showered him with favours including guardianship of semi-lunatic James HAMILTON, 4th Earl of Arran. Claiming the Hamilton line as illegitimate, he obtained Hamilton's earldom in 1581; as Chancellor (1584) he outraged Presbyterians by passing the pro-episcopal Black Acts. After a 1585 coup he fled Scotland, losing the earldom, returning to live quietly until rehabilitated at court in 1592. Sir James Douglas assassinated him, in revenge for the execution of James DOUGLAS, 4th Earl of Morton.

STEWART, JOHN (11th [3rd Stewart] Earl of Buchan) (c. 1381–1424), politician and soldier. As commander of the 6,000 Scottish troops that went to France in 1419 to help the Dauphin (later Charles VII) resist HENRY V, Buchan played an important role in the Hundred Years War. Victorious at the Battle of Baugé (1421), he was appointed Constable of France, but was killed in battle at Verneuil (1424). Nephew of Alexander STEWART, he was styled Earl of Buchan from 1412.

STEWART, JOHN (14th Earl of Mar) (c. 1457–80), courtier. The fourth son of JAMES II, he played little part in politics but his paranoid brother JAMES III saw him as a potential threat. He accused him of using magical arts and had him covertly put to death. Various, often lurid, accounts of this survive, some probably composed to justify the 1488 rebellion against James. In one version a vein was opened and he was made to bleed to death.

STEWART, JOHN (4th Duke of Albany) (1481–1536), politician. The grandson of JAMES II, in 1515 he came reluctantly from France to become Regent of Scotland for JAMES V, and maintained pro-French policy until he finally returned home permanently in 1524. His initially capable regency was undermined by vicious struggles with rivals, including the dowager Queen, MARGARET TUDOR, and by English intrigue and harassment.

STEWART, MATTHEW (13th Earl of Lennox) (1516–71), politician. Distinguished by descent rather than talent; service in France from 1532 to 1543 made him champion French interests in Scotland against James HAMILTON, Earl of Arran. HENRY VIII's offer of finance, however, and a dynastic bride (Lady Margaret DOUGLAS) turned him pro-English and sent him into English exile from 1544 to 1564. The couple's religious conservatism was a nuisance to EDWARD VI and ELIZABETH I; their eldest son was Henry STEWART, Lord Darnley. Elected Regent in 1571 for his grandson JAMES VI, Lennox was captured and killed by partisans of MARY QUEEN OF SCOTS.

STEWART, MICHAEL (Baron Stewart) (1906–90), politician. A Labour moderate, in 1964 he was appointed Minister of Education in Harold WILSON'S government, then replaced Patrick GORDON-WALKER as Foreign Secretary (1965–6), defending the government's support for US involvement in the Vietnam War. He served as First Secretary of State (1966–7), with responsibility for economic affairs, until the post's abolition in Aug. 1967, whereupon he returned to the Foreign Office (1968–70) and attempted mediation in the Nigerian civil war and the Rhodesian dispute. He supported Britain's entry into the EEC (now the European Union) and served as leader of the Labour group in the European Parliament (1975–6) before retiring from politics in 1979.

STEWART, MURDAC (2nd Duke of Albany, 13th Earl of Fife) (?–1425), Scottish nobleman. He succeeded his father Robert STEWART, both as duke and as Regent of Scotland in 1420. While still Earl of Fife he was captured by the English at the Battle of Homildon Hill (Northumb.) in 1402 and remained a prisoner in the Tower until 1415. When his fellow prisoner, JAMES I, returned to Scotland in 1424, he ordered the arrest of Albany and his son Alexander in the Parliament of March 1425 and they were swiftly beheaded.

STEWART, ROBERT (1st Duke of Albany) (c. 1340–1420), Royal Prince. Third son of ROBERT II, in 1388 he was made guardian for his ailing elder brother (who became ROBERT III in 1390) and in 1406 he was chosen Regent for the uncrowned boy-king JAMES I, who was held prisoner in England. Hence for 32 years he was *de facto* ruler of Scotland. In 1419 he sent John STEWART and a Scottish army to help the French in the Hundred Years War. He was created Duke in 1398.

STEWART, ROBERT (Viscount Castlereagh) *see* essay on page 753

STEWART, ROBERT A. (1949–), soldier. Educated at Sandhurst, commissioned into the Cheshire Regiment in 1969, Stewart studied international relations at Aberystwyth (1974–7). Service in Bahrain, Malaya and Germany was followed by a posting to Northern Ireland where in a bomb blast at Ballykelly on 6 Dec. 1982 the Cheshires lost 11 dead and scores wounded. Chosen to conduct a United Nations humanitarian mission to Bosnia in the winter of 1992–3, Stewart quickly discovered his regiment (the Cheshires) to be operating in a completely anarchic environment. With no clear directions, Stewart began creating his own policy, using unprecedented media exposure to influence decisions in London, in Washington and at the HQ in New York, simultaneously turning his regiment and himself into television stars in the attempt to use public opinion to force John MAJOR's government towards full-scale intervention.

STEWART, WALTER (19th [1st Stewart] Earl of Atholl) (c. 1360–1437), Royal Prince. The second son of ROBERT II by his second wife, he was created Earl of Atholl in 1404. He took a leading part in the movement for the return of JAMES I in 1424, giving his son David as a hostage in England. But after his son's death he turned against the King. With the help of his grandson Robert (whom he was supposedly intending to put on the throne) he had James murdered in Feb. 1437. But he failed to gain possession of the six-year-old JAMES II and was swiftly captured and beheaded, probably being spared the tortures which were inflicted on the assassins themselves.

STIGAND (?–1272), Archbishop of Canterbury (1052–70). A worldly and very wealthy prelate whose failings typify what were later perceived as the weaknesses of the English Church before 1066. Stigand was an unashamed careerist who held Canterbury and Winchester, the two richest dioceses in England, in plurality after 1052, as well as a large private estate. He was intruded into Canterbury after the expulsion of Archbishop ROBERT OF JUMIÈGES and, for this reason, his position was regarded as uncanonical by the Papacy. He was apparently at first accepted by WILLIAM I THE CONQUEROR, but in 1070 was abandoned and deposed by a Papal Legate.

STILLINGFLEET, EDWARD (1635–99), theologian. Educated at Cambridge, he took orders. In 1659 his *Irenicum* was published. It became one of the most influential statements of Latitudinarianism (a conciliatory, rationalistic form of churchmanship), arguing that the apostles had left the government of the Church undecided. While rejecting Nonconformity, the book urged that the Church should accommodate the beliefs of both Anglicans and Presbyterians. Under CHARLES II Stillingfleet became a popular preacher and eventually Dean of St Paul's in 1678, but he maintained his connections with Presbyterianism. WILLIAM III made him Bishop of Worcester in 1689. Stillingfleet amassed a large library; on his death his manuscript collection was bought by Robert HARLEY.

STIRLING, SIR DAVID (1915–90), soldier and adventurer. Son of an army officer, educated at Ampleforth and Cambridge, Stirling volunteered in 1941 for service with Edward Laycock's commandos in the Mediterranean. After their virtual destruction, Stirling formed a raiding group codenamed the Special Air Service (SAS) which, in combination with the Long Range Desert Group, was responsible for destroying more than 400 Axis aircraft in the summer of 1942. Promoted Lieutenant Colonel in July 1942, Stirling was captured in Tunisia six months later, and after four attempts at escape ended up in Colditz Castle. After the war Stirling settled in Southern Rhodesia, but returned to Britain in the early 1960s to found GB 75, an organization designed to keep essential services running in the

continued on page 754

STEWART, ROBERT (Viscount Castlereagh, 2nd Marquess of Londonderry) (1769–1822)
Politician

As a leading member of the Anglo-Irish Protestant ascendancy, Castlereagh was the chief promoter of PITT THE YOUNGER's Act of Union between England and Ireland; his reputation suffered from the controversy aroused by this measure and the means used to enact it. His long involvement in British politics as a member of the House of Commons included two other controversial areas which have also tarnished his reputation: his participation as Secretary of State for War in the disastrous military expedition to Walcheren in 1808; and his defence of the repressive measures passed by the Liverpool government (see JENKINSON, ROBERT) between 1816 and 1820 to ensure the maintenance of social order. The attempt by George CANNING to remove him from the War Office in 1808 led to a duel between the two men, despite the fact they were members of the same Cabinet.

Castlereagh's claim to historical significance is mainly the leading role he played as Foreign Secretary after 1812 in forming the coalition which defeated Napoleon and the part he played in the peace settlement and subsequent attempts to restore the balance of power in Europe. It was accurately said of him that although 'his talents were great', he 'owed his influence and authority as much to his character as to his abilities'. He was an affable and agreeable colleague in Cabinet and his counsel was much valued by his Prime Minister, Liverpool; he was an assiduous and painstaking Foreign Secretary, whose abilities were respected by his foreign counterparts such as Prince Metternich and Talleyrand; it was in the Commons that he was seen to least advantage. Those who knew him best were best placed to appreciate his qualities; but he was caviare to the general.

Castlereagh was a 'prolix' and 'monotonous' speaker and, despite the care he lavished on his speeches, he never succeeded in dominating the Commons in the way his great rival Canning did. But his own ability as a behind-the-scenes manager, and the weakness of the government front bench in debating power, meant that Castlereagh had to bear the burden of leading the House as well as being Foreign Secretary.

His enemies liked to link his reactionary domestic policy with what they took to be his preference for acting with the autocratic powers of Europe abroad. Those who thought that his 'head was turned by emperors, kings and congresses' ignored the realities of diplomacy. If Napoleon was to be defeated it could only be by a European coalition, and Castlereagh's willingness to assure Tsar Alexander I and the Austrian Chancellor,

Metternich, that Britain was fully committed to a continental campaign played an important part in paving the way for the Treaty of Chaumont (May, 1814) that cemented the final coalition against Napoleon. Castlereagh did not belong to that insular school of statesmanship which held that Britain could, with safety, now ignore what happened on the continent; having played a major role in creating the final coalition against Napoleon, Castlereagh determined to secure a peace settlement which gave Britain real security. At the Congress of Vienna (1814–15) he was instrumental in preventing the imposition of a vindictive peace on France and in limiting Prussian and Russian ambitions in alliance with Metternich. By Article VI of the Peace of Paris (1815) the Great Powers agreed to meet periodically to ensure the peace of Europe. To radical critics this meant that Britain became identified with the reactionary tendencies of the Tsar's 'Holy Alliance', but as Castlereagh showed in 1820 this was not so. Asked to join in a congress at Laibach to intervene against the liberal revolution in Naples, Castlereagh declined, drawing a distinction between interfering in the affairs of other countries, which Britain would not do, and intervening to prevent the spread of revolutionary disorder, which Britain would do.

After 1820 the diplomatic axis between London and Vienna began to weaken as Metternich's autocratic instincts pushed him towards Tsar Alexander's interventionist policies. This caused Castlereagh great anguish and he tried hard to find a middle way between the Tsar's policies and his own preferences. His Cabinet colleagues were less enamoured of the connection with the 'Holy Alliance' powers, and Castlereagh found little support there.

On 11 April 1821 Castlereagh succeeded his father as the 2nd Marquess of Londonderry but as an Irish peer he remained Leader of the Commons and Foreign Secretary. The burden of his two offices resulted in a nervous breakdown and, on 12 Aug. 1822, Castlereagh evaded his doctors' care for a moment and committed suicide. Castlereagh's role in defending the repressive policies of the Liverpool government in the years after the Napoleonic Wars had won him the hatred of the London mob who cheered at his funeral, and of radicals like BYRON, who wanted to urinate on his grave. More measured assessments have now prevailed, and Castlereagh is recognized as one of the most successful of British foreign secretaries.

C. J. Bartlett, Castlereagh (1963)

event of a general strike. He became a prominent figure in the Movement for True Industrial Democracy, dedicated to opposing possible communist take-overs of British unions.

STIRLING, JAMES (1926–92), architect. Born in Glasgow, an early exponent of high-tech design, Stirling designed university buildings, including the Engineering Department, Leicester (1959– 63) – which established his reputation – the History Faculty, Cambridge (1965–8), the Florey Building, Queen's College, Oxford (1966–71) and student accommodation at St Andrews (1968). He also designed art galleries in Stuttgart and Berlin and an extension to the Tate Gallery in London to house the TURNER collection, the CLORE Gallery (1987).

STOCKTON, 1ST EARL OF *see* MACMILLAN, HAROLD

STOCKWOOD, MERVYN (1913–80), churchman. The son of a rural solicitor, Stockwood was educated at Christ's College, Cambridge, and Westcott House. After 20 years in a working-class parish in Bristol, which radicalized him and revitalized the congregation, he was appointed to the university church of Great St Mary's in Cambridge in 1955 and then to the see of Southwark in south London, where Aneurin BEVAN was among the congregation at his enthronement in 1959. Always a controversial and charismatic figure, frequently accused of using his pulpit as a political soap-box, Stockwood was dismissive of the idea that the Church should be above politics, which in his view meant that the clergy should be Conservatives: his aim was to make the Church relevant to and responsible towards the problems of contemporary society. On his retirement in 1980 he hoped to continue to sit in the House of Lords, but the THATCHER government was disinclined to offer a continuing public platform to its Labour-supporting goad.

STOKES, DONALD (Baron Stokes of Leyland) (1914–), manufacturer. Born into an engineering family in Kent, Stokes joined the Leyland company, makers of buses and lorries, in 1930 as an apprentice. His true expertise lay in selling; he was given charge of the export division in 1946, and when later given overall sales responsibility he made Leyland more market-orientated and helped it move into car-making. Managing director from 1963, and Chairman from 1967, he was by now head of British Leyland, one of the world's largest vehicle manufacturers after the take-over of British Motor Holdings. He had difficulty in managing the unwieldy giant and solving its management and labour problems. After a government report in 1975 was critical of his control and

the decline of British Leyland, Stokes was effectively dismissed; but this was far from being the end of British Leyland's difficulties, which led the continuing decline of the British motor industry.

STOKES, SIR GEORGE GABRIEL (1819–1903), physicist. Educated in his native Ireland, Bristol and Cambridge, Stokes was Lucasian Professor of Mathematics at Cambridge (1849–1903) and Secretary of the Royal Society (1854–85). He discovered fluorescence in 1852 and worked on fluid dynamics, acoustics, spectroscopy, stellar aberration and geodesy and mathematical functions. Several late-Victorian physicists studied under him, including James Clerk MAXWELL. A lifelong Evangelical Anglican, he was a supporter of natural theology, an outspoken critic of materialism and Darwinian evolution (*see* DARWIN, Charles) and a Conservative MP (1887–91).

STONE, GEORGE (1708–64), churchman and politician, Archbishop of Armagh (1747–64). He went to Ireland as chaplain to the Duke of Dorset, the Lord Lieutenant, and from 1733 gained a rapid series of promotions in the Irish Church. Appointed Archbishop of Armagh, a Privy Councillor and a Lord Justice in 1747, Stone was suspicious of the 'undertakers' who managed business in the Irish Parliament as being insufficiently loyal to British interests, and built up his own Crown party in the Commons against the 'patriot' party of the Speaker, Henry BOYLE. Stone and Boyle clashed in 1751 over whether Irish surplus revenues could be appropriated without royal assent. Stone and the British government won in 1753 and Stone became master of Irish politics. The arrival of the Duke of Devonshire (*see* CAVENDISH, WILLIAM, 4th Duke) as Lord Lieutenant in 1755, however, led to the rehabilitation of Boyle and the rise of John PONSONBY. Stone lost many of his parliamentary supporters and never enjoyed total ascendancy again.

STONE, NICHOLAS (1586–1647), sculptor. Having worked in the Netherlands, he collaborated with Inigo JONES at court and undertook prominent architectural projects in Oxford; he was prolific in tomb sculpture of a quality exceptional in Jacobean England (including John DONNE's standing shrouded effigy at St Paul's, London). Among his sons employed in his business, Nicholas (also d. 1647) worked with Bernini in Italy.

STOPES, MARIE (1880–1958), birth-control pioneer. Edinburgh-born, the daughter of an archaeologist father and a suffragist mother who was also a Shakespearean scholar, Stopes became a paleobotanist, studying in London and Munich, and in 1904 was appointed lecturer in botany at the University of Manchester, the first woman in the science faculty. Her first marriage was unconsummated, and she immersed herself in the subject of sexual fulfilment in the reading room of the British Library. Her *Married Love* (1918) offered conjugal bliss and was such a huge popular success that Stopes, in response to a deluge of inquiries from readers who saw the likely consequences of such conjugality, published *Wise Parenthood* later that year: together the books sold over 700,000 copies in five years. An overnight authority on sexual matters, Stopes remarried (the pioneer aviator Humphrey Roe), published more books, edited *Birth Control News*, replied to sackfuls of letters every week requesting advice, opened a clinic in Holloway, north London, to give free contraceptive advice to poor mothers, pressured the Ministry of Health to provide such advice at prenatal and child welfare clinics and helped found the National Birth Control Association, which became the Family Planning Association in 1931. Though progressive and sometimes so anatomically explicit as to cause shock, and of course opposed by the Roman Catholic Church (she brought a highly publicized and eventually successful libel action against a Catholic doctor), Stopes always aimed to restrict sexual ecstasy strictly to the marital bed, and managed to reassure both those concerned about a decline in the middle-class birth rate and those concerned about an exponential increase in the working classes, as well as ignorant or confused married couples.

STORY, JOHN (*c.* 1504–71), lawyer. From Salisbury, after a stormy Oxford University career, he became a civil lawyer, frequent MP and outspoken conservative who left the country after a parliamentary attack on the 1549 Prayer Book. Chancellor of the London diocese under MARY I, he was a key figure in persecuting Protestants. In 1563, after fresh outspokenness, he avoided imprisonment by taking refuge in the Netherlands, but in 1570 was kidnapped by English sailors, tried for treason, and executed at Tyburn with more than customary brutality. The Roman Catholic Church beatified him in 1886.

STOW, JOHN (1525?–1605), historian. A self-educated London tailor of conservative religious sympathies, from the 1560s he devoted himself to gathering manuscripts and producing chronicles, activities which exposed him to the jealousy and attack of a rival and staunchly Protestant chronicler, the printer Richard GRAFTON. He escaped serious trouble for possession of Catholic writings after repeated official examinations between 1568 and 1570, and retained the friendship of his fellow historian Archbishop Matthew PARKER; his devotion to scholarship dispersed his commercial fortune, despite the success of many of his publications, and in his last years he was frequently dependent on the charity of admirers. His works include an edition of Geoffrey CHAUCER's poetry (1561), various medieval chronicles, his own *Chronicle of England* compilation (1580) and a revision of HOLINSHED's *Chronicle* (1585–7), but his lasting achievement is his *Survey of London* (1598), a loving and detailed account of his native city.

STRACHEY, JOHN (1901–63), politician. The son of the proprietor of *The Spectator*, educated at Eton and Oxford, Strachey joined the Labour Party in 1923. He was Labour MP for Aston (1929–31), Dundee (1945–50) and West Dundee (1953–60). Parliamentary Private Secretary to Oswald MOSLEY, who had special responsibility for unemployment policy in the second Labour government (1929), Strachey resigned with his minister when Mosley's expansionist plans for the economy were turned down. The two founded the short-lived New Party but within a year Strachey, discerning Mosley's Fascist tendencies, left and applied to join the British Communist Party. Regarded as an unsound intellectual, he was refused, but thought and wrote like a communist anyway. In 1936 he joined with Victor GOLLANCZ and Harold LASKI to start the New Left Book Club.

His own books, *The Theory and Practice of Socialism* (1936) and *Why You Should Be a Socialist* (1938), were both hugely influential, the latter selling over a quarter of a million copies in two months. The Communist Party's support for the Nazi–Soviet pact caused him to break with the party after the invasion of Norway in 1940. Appointed Minister of Food by ATTLEE in 1946, he was the scapegoat for the disastrous ground-nut scheme in East Africa; after the fall of the Labour government in 1951 he was a shadow minister until his death.

Strachey's major work was *Contemporary Capitalism* (1956), which attempted to integrate the ideas of KEYNES with those of MARX as a basis for democratic socialism. His reputation as Labour's post-war theorist was eclipsed by Anthony CROSLAND's *The Future of Socialism*, published the same year.

STRACHEY, LYTTON (1880–1932), biographer. A prominent member of the Bloomsbury group of intellectuals, writers and artists including Virginia WOOLF, J. M. KEYNES and E. M. FORSTER, many of whom he had met at Cambridge University, Strachey had an often tortured personal life, living in sexual triangles within the group (*see also* CARRINGTON, DORA). He began his writing career as an essayist, but the publication of *Eminent Victorians* (1918) was a landmark in biography. The essays, on Cardinal Henry MANNING, Florence NIGHTINGALE, Thomas ARNOLD and Charles GORDON, were witty and skilled exercises in the debunking of Victorianism. He followed it with *Queen Victoria* (1921) and *Elizabeth and Essex* (1928), which although often flawed in their historical accuracy (especially the latter) were early essays in the application of psychology to the art of biography.

STRAFFORD, 1ST EARL OF *see* WENTWORTH, THOMAS

STRANGE, BARON *see* STANLEY, JAMES

STRATFORD, JOHN (?–1348), Archbishop of Canterbury (1333–48). Educated in law at Oxford, he was appointed, to EDWARD II's irritation, Bishop of Winchester by the Pope in 1323. He became Chancellor in 1330 and Archbishop in 1333. He was EDWARD III's adviser and chief minister from 1330 until he and the King fell out in spectacular fashion in 1340. Active in negotiations with France and Scotland, he played a key diplomatic role in the onset of the Hundred Years War. The failure of Edward III's 1340 campaign resulted in a constitutional crisis when the King accused him of incompetence and Stratford appealed to Parliament. The right of peers to trial by their peers in Parliament was confirmed, but Stratford was never again so powerful a figure.

STRATFORD, JOHN (*c*. 1582–*c*. 1635), tobacco-grower. From a Gloucs. gentry family (and grandson of William TRACY), he became a London merchant. Concerned to find crops suited to stimulate rural employment, when his trade in flax declined he retired to his Gloucs. estates and in 1619 began large-scale tobacco-farming. Within a year the government, fearful of competition with the new North American colonies, banned English tobacco-growing; although Stratford put up a legal fight for some years, the ban was not rescinded. English cultivation of narcotic weeds has remained clandestine, despite the suitability of the climate.

STRATHALMOND OF PUMPHERSTON, 1ST BARON *see* FRASER, WILLIAM

STRATHBOGIE, JOHN OF (9th Earl of Atholl) (?–1306), Scottish noble. His shifting loyalties during the Wars of Scottish Independence ended with his distant cousin, EDWARD I, having him hanged, beheaded and burned in 1306, the first earl to be executed in England since WALTHEOF in 1076. He had fought for the Scots at the Battle of Dunbar in 1296, then for the English, and finally and fatally for his brother-in-law ROBERT BRUCE.

STRAW, JACK (also known as Rackstraw) (?–1381), rebel. He was a leader of the Peasants' Revolt and was summarily executed. His individual prominence during the violent events in London on 14 and 15 June 1381 (he is the only rebel whom CHAUCER names) persuaded some commentators, both then and since, that the name was no more than an alias for Wat TYLER. The chronicler Thomas WALSINGHAM used what he called 'Jack Straw's confession' to set out a melodramatic version of the rebels' aims.

STREET, G(EORGE) E(DMUND) (1824–81), architect. His architectural practice was a nursery for the Arts and Crafts movement in the 1850s, employing or training William MORRIS, Philip WEBB, Norman SHAW and others. Appointed as architect to the Oxford diocese, his practice soon grew to include ecclesiastical commissions all over the country, and he developed a strong English vernacular incorporating many elements of High Gothic design. In 1866 he won the competition to design the Law Courts in the Strand, the last major Gothic-revival building in London.

STRICKLAND, AGNES (1796–1874), historian and novelist. One of nine children of whom six became writers, she wrote poems, books for children and translated Petrarch before turning to writing history. As a woman she was denied access to State papers by Lord JOHN RUSSELL: it took the intervention of the Liberal statesman Lord Normanby for her to be allowed to use them as a source for her series of biographies, *The Lives of the Queens of England* (1840–8), which she wrote with her sister Elizabeth. She went on to write the *Lives* of the *Queens of Scotland* (1850–9), *Bachelor Kings of England* (1861), *Seven Bishops Committed to the Tower of London in 1688* (1866), *Tudor Princesses* (1868) and finally *The Lives of the Last Four Princesses of the Royal House of Stuart* (1872), as well as several historical novels. A Tory whose politics uncritically shaped her work, she was nevertheless an assiduous and imaginative researcher whose somewhat gossipy history reached a large popular audience.

STRODE, SIR WILLIAM (1562–1637), politician. From a Devon gentry family much involved in tin-mining, he was a friend of Francis DRAKE and Walter RALEIGH and was prominent in coastal defence from the 1588 Armada onwards. Frequently MP from 1597, he was a strong Puritan, though he became a leading client of George VILLIERS, Duke of Buckingham, standing out against parliamentary attempts to destroy Buckingham. He signed a protest against CHARLES I's attempt to levy Ship Money in 1637, and his son

William (?1599–1645) was one of the 'five members' whom Charles tried to arrest in 1642.

STRONG, SIR ROY (1935–), historian. Educated at the Warburg Institute, a sartorial aesthete, Strong was appointed assistant keeper (1959) and then Director of the National Portrait Gallery (1967) and Director of the Victoria and Albert Museum (1974–84), since which time he has written on art, pageantry, history, decoration and gardening, and published his social-gossip diaries, an illuminating source for contemporary historians.

STRONGBOW *see* CLARE, RICHARD DE

STRUTT, JEDEDIAH (1726–97), cotton spinner. One of the pioneers of the cotton industry from his base at Belper (Derb.), He made significant improvements to the stocking frame. He took out two valuable patents (with his brother-in-law William Woollatt) in 1758 and 1759. He subsequently became a partner with ARKWRIGHT, and Belper became one of the central locations of the early cotton industry.

STRUTT, JOHN WILLIAM (3rd Baron Rayleigh) (1842–1919), physicist. Born to a family of Tory aristocrats, Rayleigh studied mathematics at Cambridge, and his early publications embraced optics, acoustics and fluid dynamics. In the early 1870s he began exploring psychical phenomena and published the influential textbook, *The Theory of Sound* (1877–8). As Professor of Experimental Physics at Cambridge's Cavendish Laboratory (1879–84), he developed electrical standards and advanced the teaching of practical physics. Thereafter he made acclaimed studies of acoustics, electricity, optics and thermodynamics in his private laboratory, and discovered, with William RAMSAY, the element argon, in 1895. He helped found the National Physical Laboratory (1897) and in 1904 became the first Briton to win the Nobel Prize for Physics.

STUART, CHARLES EDWARD (also known as Charles III, Bonnie Prince Charlie, Young Pretender) (1720–88), royal pretender. Eldest son of the Old Pretender (STUART, JAMES FRANCIS EDWARD), he was born in exile in Rome. In 1744–5 Louis XV of France, then at war with the British, encouraged his attempt to retake the British throne for the Stuarts. Landing in the Hebrides in July 1745, he reached Edinburgh in Sept. He defeated government forces at Prestonpans (E. Lothian), and advanced southwards, but he turned back at Derby in Dec. and was defeated at Culloden on 16 April 1746. Thereafter he spent five months as a fugitive in the Highlands before escaping to France with the help of Flora MACDONALD.

The Treaty of Aix-la-Chapelle provided that he should be removed from France to Avignon (then a papal state). In 1750 he made a secret visit to London and converted to Anglicanism, but plans for another rising in 1752 came to nothing. When his father died in 1766, Pope Clement XIII, keen to improve relations with Britain, withheld recognition from Charles. He married Princess Louise of Stolberg in 1772, but produced no heirs; his brother Henry, Cardinal Duke of York, who survived him, made no formal claim to the throne.

Charles's youth, early success and ultimate failure in 1745 gave him an aura of romance that stirred contemporary imaginations, although to little or no serious political effect. In later life, jaded and drunken, he failed to impress.

STUART, ESMÉ (6th Seigneur d'Aubigny, 1st Duke of Lennox) (?1542–83), politician. This personable French gentleman was invited to Scotland in 1579 by his cousin JAMES VI, who quickly developed a teenage crush and showered him with honours. Stuart's Catholicism and obvious ambition alarmed Protestant Scots magnates and in 1582 James was forced to send him into exile after the Ruthven Raid (*see* RUTHVEN, WILLIAM).

STUART FAMILY. Conventions about the spelling of this important family name are not consistent. In general, representatives of the family, including the Scottish royal family, are styled 'Stewart' before JAMES VI also became James I of England in 1603 (apart from French Stuarts). Thereafter, and especially in an English context, the royal family's name is spelt 'Stuart'; other branches make their own decisions.

STUART, JAMES (also known as James VIII and III, Old Pretender) (1688–1766), royal pretender. The only surviving son of JAMES II, his birth provided the King with a presumptively Catholic heir, and helped to spark the Glorious Revolution. Some found his birth too convenient to the King to be plausible, and suggested that he had not, in fact, been born to the Queen but had been smuggled in in a warming pan.

Growing up in the Jacobite court at St Germain in France, he was excluded from the succession by the Act of Settlement but, on JAMES II's death in 1701, was acknowledged King by Louis XIV. Although he fought in the French army in the War of the Spanish Succession, he was exiled from France under the terms of the Treaty of Utrecht. He landed in Scotland in 1715, in the context of a Jacobite rising organized by John ERSKINE, Earl of Mar, but government forces impelled his troops to retreat, and James fled to France.

His court moved from St Germain to Rome, then in 1719 to Madrid, where another rising was planned with Spanish help. Bad weather drove back the bulk of the force; the remainder surrendered after a brief encounter at Galashiels (Selkirks.). When correspondence with Bishop ATTERBURY relating to plans for further risings was discovered by the British government, James dismissed Mar on suspicion of treachery. Hopes for a restoration increasingly focused on James's son Charles STUART, whose departure for Scotland in 1745 was kept from James until after the event. He died in Rome.

STUART, JAMES (1700–89), and his son **JOHN** (1743–1821), Scottish churchmen. The Scottish Society for Promoting Christian Knowledge proposed a Gaelic translation of the Bible as a means of pacifying the Highlands after the 1745 Jacobite rebellion. James Stuart, minister at Killin (Ross.), was the most prominent of those who translated the New Testament, published in 1767. His son John, minister at Luss (Perths.), revised the work of his father and his colleagues and supervised the translation of three of the seven volumes of the Scots Gaelic Old Testament, published in 1801.

STUART, JAMES (also known as Athenian Stuart) (1713–88), architect and antiquarian. Son of a Scottish sailor, he taught himself painting, geometry, Latin and Greek, and in 1742 went to Italy to work as a guide for British visitors, where he met Nicholas REVETT. They worked on the project that resulted in *The Antiquities of Athens*, Revett concentrating on the architectural drawings and Stuart on the text. Stuart's desire to refute the arguments of the French scholar Le Roy led to his buying out Revett in 1756. The *Antiquities* was published in 1762, and a further volume published in 1789 included a full survey of the Acropolis. Stuart practised as an architect but lacked the marketing skills of others, and the impact of his discoveries was eventually realized by Robert and John ADAM.

STUART, JOHN (3rd Earl of Bute) (1713–92), courtier, politician and Prime Minister (1762–3). He married the daughter of Lady Mary Wortley MONTAGU. Elected a Scottish representative peer in 1737, he became acquainted with FREDERICK, Prince of Wales, and was made Gentleman of the Bedchamber to him in 1750. After Frederick's death, he helped his widow AUGUSTA forge links with PITT THE ELDER, to balance the alliance between WILLIAM AUGUSTUS, Duke of Cumberland (her brother-in-law), and Henry FOX, which she feared. His friendship with the dowager Princess attracted scandalous gossip. He also served as tutor and companion to the young Prince George (later GEORGE III) and in 1756 Bute was made Groom of the Stole to the Prince, the leading post in his household; within six months' of George's accession, he was brought into the ministry as northern Secretary of State.

After first Pitt and then Newcastle (*see* PELHAM-HOLLES, THOMAS) resigned in 1762, Bute was made First Lord of the Treasury. His ministry concluded the widely unpopular Treaty of Paris in 1763; a new cider excise also attracted criticism. Bute was attacked by politicians and pamphleteers, including most notoriously John WILKES, and lampooned as a royal favourite; it was suggested that he was encouraging the King to extend monarchical power.

Bute resigned in 1763 but continued to advise the King against his successor, GRENVILLE's wishes; only in 1765 did George promise not to consult him. Although Bute opposed the repeal of the Stamp Act 1766, he had by then largely withdrawn from political life, although the Old Corps Whigs continued to attack him and to suggest that he was a power behind the throne.

STUART, LUDOVICK (18th Earl, 2nd Duke of Lennox, Earl of Newcastle-upon-Tyne, 2nd [1st Stuart] Duke of Richmond) (1574–1624). Son of Esmé STUART, he travelled from France in 1583 and was President of the Privy Council and joint Lieutenant of Scotland aged 15 or 16 during JAMES VI's absence in Denmark. Closely involved in negotiations for James's English throne, he went south in 1603 and was a leading courtier. In 1616 he took over the patent of John, Lord Harington (1540–1613), for minting copper farthings, a profit-making venture; as England's only base metal currency, it proved widely unpopular.

STUBBS, GEORGE (1724–1806), painter. He studied anatomy with his father, a currier in Liverpool, and as a young man lectured on anatomy to medical students while making a living as a portraitist. Following a stay in Italy (1754–6) he moved to Lincs. where he studied equine anatomy intensively. In 1758 he settled in London where his unprecedentedly detailed paintings of horses were eagerly bought by a wealthy clientele. *The Anatomy of a Horse* (1766) included 18 large plates engraved by Stubbs himself. His patrons included the Prince of Wales (later GEORGE IV), WEDGWOOD and the *Turf Review*, for whom he painted 16 leading racehorses; his works were also popular as engravings.

STUBBS, JOHN (*c.* 1542–90), controversialist. A Norfolk gentleman, Cambridge-educated and a strong Puritan (his sister married Thomas CARTWRIGHT; his wife was a Separatist), he caused a national sensation by publishing *The Discoverie of a Gaping Gulf Wherinto England is like to be Swallowed by Another French Marriage* (1579), denouncing ELIZABETH I's marriage negotiations with FRANCIS OF VALOIS. Besides the vaginal innuendo of the title, Elizabeth was infuriated at his meddling in foreign policy; Stubbs and his publisher had their right hands cut off, to widespread dismay. Stubbs went on protesting fervent loyalty to her, and was elected MP in 1589.

STUBBS, WILLIAM (1829–1901), historian. His importance for the study of English history rests primarily on three great scholarly achievements: his *Select Charters* (1860); his edition of 19 volumes for the massive late nineteenth-century project to edit the medieval chronicles of Britain (the Rolls Series); and his three-volume *Constitutional History* (1873–8).

The *Select Charters*, which identified what he regarded as key documents for the understanding of England's history, had a profound influence on the teaching of medieval history in British and American universities until the 1960s. In addition, his massive contribution to the Rolls Series did much to set the study of medieval chronicles on a modern footing.

The *Constitutional History*, nowadays rarely read but still regularly referred to, was an epoch-making book. Covering the period from the fifth to the sixteenth centuries, it sought to answer the question of why Britain's historical experience was different from continental Europe's. The answer for Stubbs lay in an unbroken tradition of Constitution and Parliament going back to the Germanic assemblies described by Tacitus, mediated through the Anglo-Saxons and stimulated by the Normans. Although this thesis is very widely rejected nowadays, the attention Stubbs gave to broad historical questions of national development and identity still provides food for thought. The idea that England's history was a long and continuous one of parliamentary and constitutional activity has profoundly influenced nineteenth- and twentieth-century perceptions of England's (and Britain's) 'special' place in the world.

STUCLEY, SIR THOMAS (*c.* 1525–78), adventurer. Reputedly HENRY VIII's bastard, he served Charles BRANDON, Duke of Suffolk, then Edward SEYMOUR, Duke of Somerset, fleeing to France on Somerset's fall. He became a double agent between France and England, spending most of MARY I's reign abroad escaping debts. Under ELIZABETH I he turned to piracy; in Ireland, supposedly fighting Scots marauders, he began plotting with Spain. He fought at Lepanto, the Spanish victory over the Turks (1571), and planned to invade Ireland. He hired his army (financed by the Pope)

to the King of Portugal invading Morocco, where he was killed in battle.

STUF (*fl.* early sixth century), King of the Isle of Wight. A possibly legendary figure who is said to have accompanied CERDIC to England and been given the Isle of Wight by him. BEDE suggests that the Isle of Wight, like Kent, was settled by a distinctive people, the Jutes. One of the small kingdoms typical of the earliest phase of the settlement of Angles, Saxons and other peoples in England, the Isle of Wight was incorporated into Wessex when King CADWALLA killed ARWALD. Bede's statement in confirmed by archaeological evidence.

STUKELEY, WILLIAM (1687–1765), antiquarian. The son of a Lincs. attorney, he went to Cambridge University before studying and then practising medicine in London. In 1718 he was one of the co-founders of the Society of Antiquaries. He became fascinated by ancient remains, travelling the length of HADRIAN's Wall in 1725, and in 1740 published his theories on Stonehenge, which he argued was the central temple of Druidism, which he thought of as a monotheistic rationalist religion not unlike early eighteenth-century Anglicanism. He gave up medicine to be ordained in 1729, as the clerical life better complemented his antiquarian studies. He was extremely unreliable as a historian and bears much of the credit for establishing the popular misconceptions surrounding prehistoric monuments such as Stonehenge and Avebury.

STUMPE, WILLIAM (*c.* 1497–1552), industrialist. A self-made man from Gloucs., he was frequently MP for Malmesbury (Wilts.), and after Malmesbury Abbey was dissolved (1539) took over the buildings for cloth manufacture on an unprecedented industrial scale, preserving much of the splendid church for parochial use and building his own mansion in the precincts. A similar scheme for Oxford at Osney Abbey did not materialize. His family became landed gentry.

STURDEE, SIR FREDERICK (1859–1925), sailor. Son of a naval officer, Sturdee graduated from HMS *Britannia* in 1871 and as a gunnery specialist took part in the bombardment of Alexandria in 1882. Appointed Commander-in-Chief in the South Atlantic and South Pacific, he encountered von Spee's squadron off the Falkland Islands on 8 Dec. 1914, his battle cruisers sinking seven of von Spee's eight ships, a victory which turned Sturdee into a national hero.

STURGEON, WILLIAM (1783–1850), electrician and inventor. Sturgeon began his career as a shoemaker and a soldier (1802–20). During his military service he started publishing researches on various scientific subjects. He started a Woolwich-based shoemaking business in 1820 but three years later began making his living as a lecturer in science. For his invention of a soft-core electromagnet (1823) and a magneto-electrical engine with a commutator (1832), he is celebrated as the inventor of the electric dynamo and motor. He ran the short-lived *Annals of Electricity* (1836–43) and died in relative poverty.

SUDBURY, SIMON (?–1381), Archbishop of Canterbury (1375–81). Having studied at Paris, he had entered the papal administration before becoming a capable diocesan. Bishop of London from 1361, he was raised 14 years later to Canterbury, where he paid for YEVELE's rebuilding of the nave.

He had the misfortune to have been recently appointed Chancellor of England at the time of the Peasants' Revolt and was consequently blamed for government mismanagement and unjust taxation. Although he resigned the Great Seal on 12 June 1381, two days later the rebels dragged him from the Tower and beheaded him. His mummified head is displayed in the vestry of St Gregory's church, Sudbury (Suffolk).

SUETONIUS PAULINUS (*fl.* AD 60s), Roman Governor. He was trying to extend the Roman Conquest in north Wales when BOUDICCA's revolt broke out in 61; he returned to defeat her army at an unknown site in the Midlands. His subsequent repressive policies led to clashes with other Roman officials, who favoured more conciliatory measures; later in the same year, he was recalled to Rome where he subsequently prospered.

SUFFOLK, EARL OF, 5TH *see* POLE, MICHAEL DE LA; **8TH AND 1ST DUKE OF** *see* POLE, WILLIAM DE LA **10TH** and **11TH** *see* HOWARD, THOMAS; **DUKE OF**, **3RD** *see* POLE, EDMUND DE LA; **4TH** *see* BRANDON, CHARLES; **DUCHESS OF** *see* WILLOUGHBY, CATHERINE

SUGAR, SIR ALAN (1947–), entrepreneur. A genuine East End barrow boy, Sugar began to buy and sell electrical goods in 1968, when he founded AMS Trading, soon known as Amstrad. His first product lines were hi-fi, and the company went public in 1980, but his principal contribution to modern life was his introduction in 1984 of one of the first cheap and easy personal computers. Amstrad's phenomenal profitability (turnover grew from £9 million in 1980 to £626 million in 1989) was hit hard by the subsequent recession, and Amstrad has been unable to repeat that success. Sugar tried and failed to buy back the company in 1992; he has become better known as the principal investor in Tottenham Hotspur football club.

SULLIVAN, SIR ARTHUR (1842–1900), composer. Remembered today largely for the musical accompaniment to GILBERT's librettos in the operettas that enjoyed such fame in Victorian times, and beyond, Sullivan, son of a band master, himself a child prodigy, and later a great society success, composed a huge corpus of music as well as that for *The Mikado, HMS Pinafore, Iolanthe* and so on, much of which was witty and allusive. It included an opera, *The Tempest* (1862), written when he was a young man, a cantata, *The Golden Legend* (1886), orchestral works, anthems, marches and the music for the hymn *Onward Christian Soldiers*.

SUNDERLAND, EARL OF, 2ND *see* SPENCER, ROBERT; **3RD** *see* SPENCER, CHARLES

SURREY, EARL OF, 7TH *see* WARENNE, JOHN DE; **9TH, 13TH, 14TH, 15TH** and **16TH** *see* HOWARD, THOMAS

SUSSEX, 8TH EARL OF *see* RADCLIFFE, THOMAS

SUTCLIFFE, FRANK (1853–1941), photographer. His natural-looking photographs of Whitby (Yorks.) fishermen, farmworkers and children, which won him awards in his lifetime, have subsequently been the focus for much nostalgia about Victorian life.

SUTCLIFFE, PETER (1946–), murderer. Found guilty of 13 murders and 7 attempted murders of women, Sutcliffe, a lorry driver, had been interviewed several times by police but released. During the search for the murderer, he became dubbed the 'Yorkshire Ripper' and, regarding himself as a man with a 'cleansing mission', a number of prostitutes were among his victims. He was given a life sentence on each charge.

SUTHERLAND, GRAHAM (1903–80), artist. Trained at Goldsmiths' College of Art (1927–39), Sutherland began his career as an engraver using innovative techniques to portray pastoral scenes. The bottom fell out of the print market after the 1929 Wall Street crash, and he turned to oils, painting the organic strangeness of nature: gnarled branches, mutated roots. He was appointed an official war artist in 1939, and his fascination with semi-abstract shapes found expression in paintings of twisted aircraft wreckage and bomb-ruined buildings. In the post-war years he produced an increasing number of works on a religious theme, including crucifixes for churches (he had converted to Catholicism in

1926), and his massive 'Christ in Majesty' tapestry for Coventry Cathedral (*see* SPENCE, BASIL) was unveiled in 1962. His pugilistic likeness of Winston CHURCHILL (1954), subscribed by a grateful House of Commons, was so disliked by its subject that Lady Churchill destroyed it.

SVEIN (?–1052), nobleman. The scandalous eldest son of Earl GODWINE of Wessex. Like his brother HAROLD II, he received an earldom in 1043–44, which consisted of several shires in the south-west Midlands. A thoroughly disruptive influence in the politics of EDWARD THE CONFESSOR's England, his exploits included the seduction of an abbess and the murder of a cousin. He eventually died on pilgrimage to Jerusalem.

SVEIN ESTRITHSSON, King of Denmark (1047–76). The son of a sister of King CNUT, he was eventually able to impose his authority on Denmark. He represented another strand of the Scandinavian interest in the English succession in 1066; Scandinavian sources claim that he was promised the English throne by EDWARD THE CONFESSOR. His eventual invasion of England in 1069–70 was defeated rather easily by WILLIAM I THE CONQUEROR.

SVEIN FORKBEARD, King of Denmark (988–1014). He displaced his father Harold Bluetooth as King in 988, and from 994 (at the latest) he devoted a great amount of time to attacking and exploiting ETHELRED II THE UNREADY's England. Archaeological exploration of great Scandinavian camps such as Trelleborg has shown that the Danish kingdom possessed a formidable military organization. In 1013 Svein launched a campaign to conquer England, which had largely succeeded at the time of his sudden death. His work was continued by his son CNUT.

SWAN, SIR JOSEPH (1828–1917), pioneer of electric lighting. Born in Sunderland, Swan worked in chemical manufacturing trades. In the late 1840s he tried unsuccessfully to build durable incandescent electric lamps with carbon filaments, and from the 1850s he explored photography, patenting the carbon process for making permanent prints, the rapid dry-plate process and bromide paper. In the 1860s he returned to electric lighting research, and used powerful new dynamos and vacuum pumps to invent, in 1878, a durable incandescent lamp with a carbon filament. By 1881 he was an established electrical manufacturer in Newcastle and he later patented lamps with long-lasting cotton filaments. In the early 1880s the American inventor Thomas Alva Edison fought him over infringement of electric lamp patents, but in 1883 the two inventors joined forces to form the prosperous Edison and Swan United Electric Light Co.

SWEET, HENRY (1845–1912), philologist. The model for Professor Henry Higgins in G. B. SHAW's *Pygmalion*, he wrote *History of English Sounds* (1874), a seminal textbook in the study of linguistics, along with his *Anglo-Saxon Reader* (1876) and *Handbook of Phonetics* (1877). He persuaded Oxford University Press to undertake publication of the dictionary compiled by the Philological Society (*see* FURNIVALL, FREDERICK), which evolved to become *The Oxford English Dictionary* (*see* MURRAY, JAMES).

SWIFT, JONATHAN *see* essay on page 762

SWINBURNE, ALGERNON (1837–1909), poet. The son of an admiral, he was a 'macaw among owls' at Oxford, and left without taking a degree, though he was prodigiously gifted in languages as in the mastery of poetic form. He fell among the Pre-Raphaelites (*see* ROSSETTI, DANTE GABRIEL), and, of independent means, was a poet. He wrote furiously and lived on the edge. To John MORLEY he was the 'libidinous laureate of a pack of satyrs' when *Poems and Ballads* was published in 1865: a collection of pagan, sexual, sadistic, politically rebellious verses which were in stark contrast to the lyricism and moral high ground to which Victorian readers were accustomed from poets such as TENNYSON and WORDSWORTH. By 1880 Swinburne was an alcoholic. He was 'saved' by the novelist and critic Theodore Watts-Dunton, who carted him back to his suburban home, where Swinburne meekly stayed for the next 30 years, continuing to publish poems, verse plays and criticism for the rest of his long, productive and, by now, distinctly unrackety life.

SWINTON, SIR ERNEST (1868–1951), soldier. Born in India, educated at Woolwich, Swinton was commissioned into the Royal Engineers in 1888. After service in South Africa (1899–1902), he wrote *Duffer's Drift*, an entertaining treatise which imparts lessons of minor tactics to a young officer in a series of dreams. One of the finest training manuals ever written, it was used by the British army until the middle of the twentieth century and is still used by the US army (providing the inspiration for the Hollywood film *Ground Hog Day* in 1993). In 1914 Swinton was appointed an official war correspondent. He became convinced that use of a track armoured vehicle would help secure victory, and produced many War Office papers on their development. When the first tanks were built he was put in charge of training their crews, but was bitterly disappointed when he was not allowed

continued on page 763

SWIFT, JONATHAN (1667–1745)
Irish cleric and writer

Son of an English lawyer who moved to Dublin, Swift was ambivalent about the land of his birth: members of the Anglo-Irish ascendancy then habitually termed themselves 'English'.

He was raised in the (Anglican) Church of Ireland. His family had favoured the Royalist side in the Civil Wars; he was taught the need to preserve the 'balance of the constitution' (originally a Royalist slogan) from various pressures. His mother returned to England in his infancy; he was raised by an uncle and went to Trinity College, Dublin.

After the 1688 Revolution, now 21, he went to England to seek a fortune through literary talent. He became secretary to Sir William TEMPLE, who encouraged his literary ambitions. His career not developing as he hoped, Swift returned to Ireland (1694) to be ordained. His first presentation, to the Prebend of Kilroot in the diocese of Connor and Down, showed him the hard position of the poorly endowed and supported Irish Church, and he returned to Temple's service. In 1700 he was appointed to a superior position as a Prebendary of St Patrick's Cathedral, Dublin.

For the next two decades, Swift shuttled between Ireland and England. He published his first political pamphlet in 1701, defending the power of the Crown against Tory attack, seen as threatening the balance of the constitution. This earned him favour from leading Whigs such as Gilbert BURNET, and Junto lords SOMERS, Halifax (*see* MONTAGU, CHARLES) and Sunderland (*see* SPENCER, CHARLES). Encouraged, he completed a satire on abuses in religion and learning, *The Tale of a Tub* (1704): this targeted both Catholicism and Presbyterianism.

After some years in Ireland, he returned to London in 1707, aiming to secure the extension to Ireland of Queen ANNE's Bounty, a fund to increase the value of the poorest Church livings in England, but achieved neither this nor personal advancement. The seeds of his alienation from the Whigs were sown, though he still frequented Whig literary circles. In 1708, he met Joseph ADDISON and Sir Richard STEELE; he would contribute to their periodicals *The Tatler* and *The Spectator*, but his writing increasingly concerned Church matters, sometimes ironically treated, as in *An Argument against Abolishing Christianity in England*. Back in Ireland he wrote against Whig proposals for repealing the Irish Test Act (intended to exclude non-Anglicans from civil and military office).

In 1710 the moderate Robert HARLEY replaced the Whigs. When next in London, Swift was cultivated by Harley (who helped him with Queen Anne's Bounty), and drawn into his inner circle. He edited the Harleyite *Examiner*, lambasting Junto Whigs. His 1711 *Conduct of the Allies*, a scathing exposé of the deficiencies of Britain's allies in waging the War of the Spanish Sucession, aimed to rally support for the controversial project of British withdrawal from the war. He had high hopes of reward but the Queen disliked his satirical writings, and gave him only the deanery of St Patrick's. In 1713, he returned to London for his last regular sojourn, founding a new literary circle in the Scriblerus Club, with POPE, GAY and ARBUTHNOT. In *The Publick Spirit of the Whigs* (1714) he attacked Steele for casting doubt on the ministry's loyalty to the Protestant succession.

On the death of Anne and fall of the Tories he returned to Ireland for 12 years. Originally seeing this as exile, he developed a circle of friends and an interest in Irish politics. He resented England's unsympathetic treatment of Ireland, especially in economic matters; this reached its height when WALPOLE granted an English businessman, WOOD, the right to coin copper coinage for Ireland, on terms profitable to himself, though seen as likely to disrupt the Irish economy. Swift's *Drapier's Letters* (1724) fuelled the campaign which led to the patent's withdrawal in 1725.

His most enduring work, the satirical novel *Gulliver's Travels* (1726), derived from these Irish years. His nephew characterized it as 'a direct and bitter satire against the innumerable follies and corruptions in law, politicks, learning, morals and religion'. It was an instant success. Swift then again visited England, where he aided Bolingbroke (*see* ST JOHN, HENRY) and other oppositionists, who hoped (in vain) for favour from the new King GEORGE II. This was his last visit.

Swift fought shy of marriage. His most enduring relationships were with Hester Johnson, once a girl in Temple's household, and Esther Vanhomrigh, daughter of a Dutch-Irish merchant, whom he met in London in 1710; both set up households in Ireland. Naming the first 'Stella', the second 'Vanessa', he compiled for each narratives of his experiences and feelings. He also encouraged women's literary ambitions.

In his later years, he was treated as a celebrity; the first edition of his collected *Works* was published in Dublin (1735). By this time his memory was deteriorating; in 1742 a commission of lunacy pronounced him incapable of conducting his affairs.

J. A. Downie, *Jonathan Swift: Political Writer* (1984)
Irvin Ehrenpreis, *Swift: The Man, His Works and the Age* (3 vols, 1962–)

to command them in action. After spending the rest of the war on propaganda tours of the USA, Swinton was elected in 1928 to the Chichele professorship of the History of War at Oxford, a position he held until his retirement in 1939, and from which he offered support to Liddell HART, John FULLER and other controversial military reformers of the inter-war years.

SWITHUN, ST (?–862), churchman. Almost nothing is known about Swithun's life. He became Bishop of Winchester in 852. There may have been a local cult of sanctity soon after his death, but his reputation as a saint was forcefully propagated only in the time of his successor St ETHELWOLD. The notion that rain on St Swithun's Day (15 July) will be followed by another 40 days of precipitation seems to have been invented in the sixteenth century.

SYDENHAM, THOMAS (1624–89), physician. The son of a Dorset gentleman, his studies at Oxford were interrupted by the Civil Wars, where he fought as a Parliamentarian, but he later returned to study medicine. In the late 1650s he combined medical practice with government office; losing the latter at the Restoration, he concentrated on medicine, studying London epidemics. His discoveries were published in *Observationes Medicae* (1676), which distinguished between diseases with similar symptoms that had previously been regarded as identical. Despite his republicanism, Sydenham had a large number of wealthy clients and was able to pay for the education of his great-nephew, the painter James THORNHILL.

SYLVESTER, JAMES (1814–97), mathematician *see* CAYLEY, ARTHUR

SYNGE, JOHN MILLINGTON (1871–1909), playwright. Synge reacted against his Evangelical family background and after attempting to become a musician visited the Aran Islands and studied their inhabitants; the distinctive language of his plays reflects the survival of Gaelic idioms in Irish dialects of English. His literary endeavours were encouraged by YEATS, and in 1902 Synge became established as a major playwright with the acceptance of two one-act plays, *Riders to the Sea* and *The Shadow of the Glen*, by the Abbey Theatre, Dublin; the Abbey produced *The Well of the Saints* in 1904, and from 1905 Synge served as one of three Abbey directors with Yeats and Lady GREGORY. His plays aroused controversy because of their implicit paganism; many nationalists saw the decision of a character in *The Shadow of the Glen* to leave her husband for a tramp as slandering the chastity of Irish women, and his masterpiece *The Playboy of the Western World* (1907) provoked riots because its portrayal of a community lionizing a man believed to have killed his father was unfairly seen as reflecting stereotypes of the Irish peasantry as amoral and crime-ridden. While the view of his plays as un-Irish persisted in some quarters, Synge has long been recognized as one of the greatest artists of the Irish cultural revival.

T

TACITUS (Cornelius Tacitus) (*c.* AD 55–120), historian. His account of the career of his father-in-law AGRICOLA, written in 97–8, is a source of fundamental importance for our knowledge of Britain's history in the first century AD. It covers the entire period from the invasion in 43 (*see* CLAUDIUS) to Agricola's recall to Rome in 84.

Tacitus is often biased in Agricola's favour, tendentiously maintaining, for example, that he completed the conquest of the whole of Britain and that his successors threw away his achievements. But he also supplies invaluable material on Britain's geography and the Romanization of its inhabitants. This latter can be summed up by his famous comment: 'The toga was often to be seen among them.'

TAIRDELBACH UA CONCHOBAIR (TURLOCH Ó CONNOR) (*c.* 1088–1156), King of Connacht. Installed in 1106 as King in the Ua Conchobair kingdom of Connacht, which he was to rule for 50 years, by MUIRCHERTACH UA BRIAIN, by 1114 he was ready to seize the opportunity presented by the collapse of the Ua Briain high-kingship. Famous as a commander of fleets and builder of castles and bridges, he fought and ruthlessly intrigued his way to predominance. After 1131, when his enemies began to combine more effectively against him, his fortunes fluctuated and from 1150 he had to recognize the greater power of MUIRCHERTACH MAC LOCHLAINN. Even so, the elevation of Tuam in Galway to an archbishopric (1152) was an acknowledgement of what his long reign had done for the Connacht kingship.

TAIT, ARCHIBALD (1811–82), Anglican prelate and Archbishop of Canterbury (1869–82). A vigorous opponent of the Oxford Movement, an early nineteenth-century religious movement, representing a revival of the Catholic outlook of the High Church party in the Church of England, and Thomas ARNOLD's successor as Headmaster at Rugby school, he became Bishop of London in 1856. Firm but tactful in relation to ritualism and the controversies raised by biblical criticism, he was transferred to Canterbury in 1869, where he did much to reduce the unrest caused by Irish Disestablishment and improve Church organization in the colonies.

TAIT, ROBERT LAWSON (1845–99), pioneering gynaecologist. Tait studied medicine in his native Edinburgh and gained a licence to practise in 1866. He performed operations to remove ovaries as house-surgeon in Wakefield (Yorks.) (1867–70) and subsequently became a surgeon and lecturer in physiology in Birmingham. In 1871 he began his long career as a surgeon to the Hospital for Diseases of Women, Birmingham, where he performed pioneering work on the surgery of the abdomen, performing operations to remove diseased ovaries, blocked Fallopian tubes, uterine tumours and gall bladders. He also successfully operated on 33 patients undergoing ectopic pregnancy and was a founder of the British Gynaecological Society (1887).

TALBOT, CHARLES (15th [12th Talbot] Earl and 1st Duke of Shrewsbury) (1660–1718), politician. His father was killed in a duel with Buckingham (*see* VILLIERS, GEORGE), who had been having an affair with his mother; his brother was also killed in a duel; the effect was said to be to make him timorous. Educated a Catholic, in 1679 he was persuaded by the hubbub provoked by the Popish-Plot accusations of Titus OATES to convert to Anglicanism. His rank and talent favoured his political career, but indifferent health and indecisiveness limited his accomplishments. One of the 'Immortal Seven' who signed the letter of invitation to William of Orange (the future WILLIAM III), he was briefly in office from 1689 to 1690, and again from 1694, when he became Secretary of State in the Junto ministry and was made a duke. He resigned in 1700, pleading ill health, and spent several years abroad, initially in Rome. Returning to England, he was appointed Lord Chamberlain and became involved in peace negotiations with France (1711–12); in 1713 he was made Lord Lieutenant of Ireland, then Lord Treasurer shortly before ANNE's death. He helped make arrangements for the beginning of GEORGE I's reign.

TALBOT, HENRY FOX (1800–77), pioneer of photography. Born to a wealthy Dorset family, educated at Harrow and Cambridge, Talbot began experimenting on ways of fixing the images of a *camera obscura* in the early 1830s. By 1835 he had captured images on silver chloride paper. Louis Daguerre's announcement, in 1839, of his daguerrotype prompted Talbot to publicize his 'photogenic drawing' technique in the same year. With the help of John HERSCHEL, Talbot invented the Calotype process (1841) which was the first process allowing positive prints to be made from paper negatives and allowed shorter exposure times. Talbot published his work in his lavish *The Pencil of Nature* (1844–6), the first book with photographic illustrations. In the 1850s he patented techniques of etching photographs on metal plates and of flash photography for rapidly moving objects, but had begun to lose out to rival photographic inventors.

TALBOT, JOHN (4th [1st Talbot] Earl of Shrewsbury) (*c.* 1384–1453), soldier. The most famous English commander in the later stages of the Hundred Years War, after Charles VII conquered Gascony in 1451, he was sent out to retrieve the situation. He recaptured Bordeaux in 1452 but was then killed at the Battle of Castillon.

TALBOT, RICHARD (3rd [1st Talbot] Earl of Tyrconnell) (1630–91), soldier and politician. Younger son of an Irish Catholic baronet, he fought in Ireland during the Civil Wars, fled to the continent, where he met the Duke of York (the future JAMES II), went to England as a Royalist agent, was imprisoned and escaped. Made a Gentleman of the Bedchamber to the Duke at the Restoration, he was imprisoned for involvement in the Popish-Plot accusations of Titus OATES in 1678. On James's accession, he was made an earl and given command of the army in Ireland, which he sought to Catholicize. Lord Deputy in 1687, he introduced dramatic changes: Catholics were admitted to office in courts of law and corporations; money from vacant Anglican benefices was channelled into the Catholic Church. The proceedings of the Jacobite Parliament of 1689 revealed divisions between Tyrconnell's followers and James's. His role in the Jacobite defeat at the Battle of the Boyne was controversial, since he appeared indecisive and lethargic. He returned to Ireland in 1691 as Lord Lieutenant and Commander-in-Chief, and died suddenly a month after the Jacobite defeat at Aughrim, which ended any hope for a Jacobite settlement in Ireland.

TALIESIN (*fl.* late sixth century), British poet. Among the heterogeneous compositions attributed to Taliesin in the thirteenth-century compilation called *The Book of Taliesin*, there is a small nucleus of about a dozen poems which are accepted by scholars as being authentic. These are fairly brief panegyric and elegiac poems addressed to historical figures who are contemporary with Taliesin: URIEN, King of Rheged, and his son, Owain; Gwallawg ap Lleenawg, who appears to have been King of Elmet, around modern-day Leeds; and to CYNAN AP BROCHFAEL, King of Powys. This latter appears to have been the earliest of his works and it has been suggested that Taliesin himself was a native of Powys. He is mentioned in the *Historia Brittonum* of NENNIUS and, along with ANEIRIN, is the earliest of the Welsh poets.

TALLIS, THOMAS (?1505–85), organist and composer. Possibly from Leics., his first known job was at Waltham Abbey, just before its dissolution in 1540, the last monastery to be dissolved in England. After a short period of service at Canterbury Cathedral, he began a lifelong association with the Chapel Royal, and was organist there by 1569. His partnership with the much younger William BYRD produced the *Cantiones Sacrae* (1575), which contained the bulk of the choral works which Tallis published in his lifetime. Unlike Byrd, Tallis showed no sign of unhappiness with the Protestant Church Settlement, and readily adapted to writing hymns and anthems for its simplified liturgy. He demonstrated his continuing versatility with his astonishing 40-part motet *Spem in Alium* (probably written in the 1560s for the connoisseur John, Lord LUMLEY, for use at Nonsuch Palace). His choral works, virtually all for Church use, are the foundation of the Anglican musical repertoire.

TALMAN, WILLIAM (1650–1719), architect. The first house he is known to have designed was Chatsworth for William CAVENDISH, Duke of Devonshire, begun in 1687. In 1689 he was made Comptroller of Works by WILLIAM III, and Deputy Superintendent of the royal gardens in charge of developments at Hampton Court. Talman was heavily in demand as an architect but quarrelled with most of his private clients, feuded with his fellow architects, particularly Christopher WREN, and was in 1702 replaced as Comptroller by VANBRUGH. Despite the inconsistencies in his designs he was the greatest country house designer of the late seventeenth century.

TALORCAN, SON OF EANFRITH (?–657), King of the Picts. A son of King Eanfrith of Bernicia by a Pictish princess, and born during his father's exile in Pictland throughout the reign of EDWIN of Northumbria, Talorcan had secured the Pictish throne by 653. Little is known of his reign, other than that he is stated to have defeated the Gaels of Dál Riata the following year. Northumbria appears to have been unwilling to relinquish its influence in Pictland for, following Talorcan's death, his uncle OSWY subdued a large area of southern Pictland.

TANSLEY, SIR ARTHUR (1871–1955), botanist and ecologist. Tansley developed his botanical interests at University College, London, and in 1902 became the founder-editor of the *New Phytologist*, a botanical journal which greatly encouraged the study of British ecology and helped transform the teaching of plant sciences. He continued his campaign for botany and ecology as a textbook writer, and as lecturer in botany at Cambridge (1907–23) and Professor of Botany at Oxford (1927–37), founding the British Ecological Society in 1913. His best-known work, *The British Islands and their Vegetation* (1939), was a detailed survey of Britain's uncultivated lands and flora. He spearheaded research into wild habitats and helped found Nature Conservancy (1949).

TARA, 1ST VISCOUNT *see* PRESTON, THOMAS

TATCHELL, PETER (1951–), gay activist. Born in Australia, he left for Britain when he was 20 and was soon involved in the gay rights campaign. In 1983 he stood as Labour candidate in a by-election in Bermondsey (London) but was defeated after a homophobic campaign, with accusations of links with Militant Tendency, the far left Labour faction, was waged in the tabloid press. Founder of the gay rights group Outrage! (1990), he has attracted publicity for 'outing' prominent public figures, protesting against the attitude of the Church of England to homosexuality, lobbying for a reduction in the age of consent for homosexuals, working for gay health education and civil rights as well as his more extreme demands for freedom of gay expression.

TATE, SIR HENRY (1819–99) and **GEORGE** (1890–1955), manufacturers. Henry Tate, who entered the sugar business in Liverpool, patented an invention for cutting sugar loaves in 1872. He moved to London in 1880 and made a fortune in cube sugar. With his wealth he gathered a great picture collection that hung at his Streatham (Surrey) home; he subsequently gave the collection to the nation, together with the art gallery named after him to house it, built by the Thames on the site of the Millbank prison (demolished in 1893). His firm was amalgamated with Lyle's, the principal sugar rival, in 1921, and two years later Henry's grandson George joined the board. Made Chairman in 1937 in succession to C. E. L. Lyle, Lord Lyle (1882–1954), George's principal tasks were reconstruction of the industry after wartime destruction and fending off the post-war threat of nationalization.

TATE, NAHUM (1652–1715), playwright and poet. A clergyman's son, educated at Trinity College, Dublin, he moved to London where he became a friend and collaborator of DRYDEN. His 1681 adaptation of *King Lear*, where the Fool is excised and Cordelia and Edgar survive to marry, pleased contemporaries and superseded SHAKESPEARE's text until 1840. He made further adaptations of Shakespeare and other Jacobean playwrights, wrote much of the second part of Dryden's *Absalom and Achitophel* (1682) and, from 1692 until shortly before his death, was Poet Laureate.

TAVERNER, JOHN (*c.* 1490–1545), composer. Master of the music at Tattershall College (Lincs.), and from 1526 choirmaster at Cardinal College (now Christ Church), Oxford, his conversion to evangelical reformism made him abandon Church music and he entered Thomas CROMWELL's service, retiring to Boston (Lincs.). One of the most accomplished composers of choral music of his age, he began the English custom of writing variants on the plainsong fragment *In Nomine* (see BYRD, WILLIAM).

TAVERNER, RICHARD (*c.* 1505–75), writer. From Norfolk, he studied at Cambridge and Oxford, and lectured at Cambridge in Greek until he entered Thomas CROMWELL's service. With Cromwell's encouragement, he produced a flood of evangelical propaganda; his Postils (sermons) on the Epistles and Gospels to be read at Mass (1540) provided much material for the second set of official homilies issued in 1563. After Cromwell's fall he probably continued to work for Thomas CRANMER, and was a travelling preacher under EDWARD VI. He built up substantial landed estates.

TAWNEY, R(ICHARD) H(ENRY) (1880–1962), historian. Born in Calcutta, he became inspired by socially radical Anglo-Catholicism while at Oxford, and after unexpectedly mediocre Finals results, abandoned university life for slum social work and outstanding pioneer work in adult education, returning to academia in his long career at the London School of Economics. He developed an interest in social and economic history, always with an eye on present-day inequalities, and became the leading authority on Tudor England in this new field. His work on sixteenth-century agricultural change emphasized its exploitative nature and was followed by his adaptation of the ideas of the German sociologist, Max Weber, on the relationship between Protestantism and the spirit of capitalism: Tawney maintained (reversing Weber) that capitalism existed prior to Protestantism, but had found a deplorably congenial partner in it. The theme of social exploitation also fuelled his work on 'the rise of the gentry' (1941; later to be reinterpreted by H. R. TREVOR-ROPER). Subsequently much criticized both for his faulty statistics and for his patent contemporary concerns in his view of the past (particularly by Geoffrey ELTON), he was nevertheless a formidably creative historian who opened up new forms of historical enquiry.

TAYLOR, A(LAN) J(OHN) P(ERCIVAL) (1906–90), historian. A. J. P. Taylor was the best-known twentieth-century English historian and, through his television programmes, brought history to the people. This was an appropriate ambition for a Lancs. radical son of a millionaire, who was briefly a member of the Communist Party and an early and lifelong member of the Labour Party: all these strands went to make up Taylor's nature as a historian. Educated at Oxford and Vienna, Taylor gravitated towards diplomatic history, drawn by the controversy over the origins of the First World War. From 1930 he taught at Manchester University, where he met Lewis NAMIER. Namier introduced him to the world of journalism, passing onto him reviews for the *Manchester Guardian*. A Fellow of Magdalen College, Oxford (1938–76), he played the role of radical critic of the Establishment and in the 1950s he began to appear on television, where his sharp intellect and quick tongue made an instant impact in the era when television first became a mass medium. Taylor was one of its first stars, with his characteristic device of lecturing straight to camera without a script.

Although he considered himself a rebel, he was a highly productive scholar, producing the first volume of the Oxford History of Europe series, *The Struggle for the Mastery of Europe*, in 1954 (the next volume did not appear for another 20 years). His failure to win the Regius Chair at Oxford in 1960 was followed a year later by the publication of his most controversial book, *The Origins of the Second World War*, in which he argued that Hitler was 'just another German statesman' and had not planned the war. The controversy continued until Taylor's death, and it opened the way to a reappraisal of the diplomacy of appeasement and the reputations in particular of Neville CHAMBERLAIN and Winston CHURCHILL. His second major survey, *English History, 1914–45* (1965), helped shape contemporary perceptions of British history.

TAYLOR, HARRIET (née Hardy) (1807–58), women's rights advocate. In 1825 Harriet married John Taylor, a wholesale druggist and Unitarian. Though initially happy and having three children together, in 1830 Harriet met John Stuart MILL. From 1833, following a temporary separation from her husband, there was no effective bar to her relationship with Mill, and they spent a good deal of time together. In 1849 her husband died and in 1851 she married Mill. She was a very large influence on Mill's thinking. 'The Enfranchisement of Women', published under Mill's name in the *Westminster Review* (1851), was largely written by her, and Mill acknowledged that she was the major source of inspiration for the *Subjection of Women* (1869). Influenced by Robert OWEN's writings in her political and feminist ideas and arguing for the reform of marriage laws and women's economic independence, Taylor also helped to shape Mill's sympathies for some elements of socialism.

TAYLOR, HELEN (1831–1907), women's rights advocate. The youngest child of Harriet TAYLOR, Helen became companion and aide to John Stuart MILL following her mother's death in France in 1858. In the early 1860s she joined the Kensington Society, and in 1866 was active with Barbara Leigh BODICHON in collecting signatures for the women's suffrage petition of June 1866. She was also a founder of the second London committee for women's suffrage and continued to work for the cause throughout the 1860s and 1870s. In 1876 she was elected to the London School Board and remained active in many radical causes through the 1880s.

TAYLOR, JEREMY (1613–67), religious writer. Educated at both Cambridge and Oxford (sent by William LAUD to the latter), he had a high reputation as a preacher. He joined the Royalist army in the First Civil War (1642–6). His *Rule and Exercises of Holy Living* (1650) and *Rule and Exercises of Holy Dying* (1651) were very popular and went through many editions. They reflected and encouraged a trend away from Calvinism, stressing not dramatic conversion but the need to live a pious and worthy life. At the restoration of CHARLES II he was made Bishop of Down and Connor with Dromore.

TAYLOR, PETER (1819–91), politician. A partner in the textile firm of Samuel Courtauld and Co. (*see* COURTAULD IV, SAMUEL), Taylor became a leading radical middle-class advocate of internationalism. Part of the network of radical Unitarians and other Dissenters, he was active in the Friends of Italy (1851–5) and later in the anti-slavery London Emancipation Society during the US Civil War; he also championed the cause of international arbitration. A member of the Jamaica Committee, he was one of the leaders of the campaign to impeach Governor EYRE in 1864. He was also a Vice-President of the Reform League (1865–8), and with his wife Clementia, was an early and committed supporter of women's suffrage. He was Liberal MP for Leicester (1862–84), but from 1885–6 he supported Liberal unionism.

TEBBIT, NORMAN (Baron Tebbit of Chingford) (1931–), politician. Described by Denis HEALEY as a 'semi house-trained polecat', and by others as 'the Chingford skinhead', Tebbit was the archetypical Thatcherite minister whom the Left loved to hate. Tebbit's father, as everyone knew in the early 1980s, was a poor man who suffered periods of unemployment but who, in his son's famous words, 'got on his bike' to seek work. Tebbit himself was a grammar-school boy for whom National Service provided a way to become upwardly mobile. He trained as a pilot and later made his career in the RAF and with civilian airlines, acting as a chief negotiator for the pilots' union. As a believer in the virtues of thrift, hard work and personal responsibility, Tebbit was a natural Thatcherite. As MP for Epping (Essex) (1970–4) under Edward HEATH he was unhappy with the performance of his own government but, after Margaret THATCHER became leader in 1975, he was in his element. He was MP for Chingford from 1974 to 1992, and his London suburban constituency became a hallmark of the upwardly mobile working-class people who helped keep Thatcher in power.

After a series of minor offices (1979–81) Tebbit became Secretary of State for Employment in 1981, in which capacity he made his famous remark about the unemployed needing to get on their 'bikes'. He moved to the Department of Trade and Industry in 1983 after his friend Cecil PARKINSON had to resign. He played an important role in helping to defeat Arthur SCARGILL and the miners in 1983–84. He and his wife Margaret were badly injured in 1984 when the IRA tried to murder the Cabinet by blowing up the Grand Hotel in Brighton during the party conference, and even his enemies admired his personal courage as he was pulled from the rubble; the care with which he subsequently looked after his crippled wife belied his image as the 'hard man' of British politics. Tebbit was Chairman of the Conservative Party (1985–87) when, along with Lord YOUNG, he master-minded Thatcher's third election victory. He retired from front-bench politics in the same year to help secure his wife's future, but he remained an active voice on the Thatcherite wing of the party, and could always be relied upon to support the Eurosceptic cause.

TEDDER, ARTHUR (1st Baron Tedder) (1890–1967), airman. Son of a civil servant, educated at Magdalene College, Cambridge, Tedder was rejected by the army in 1914 because of a knee injury. He joined the Royal Flying Corps, and fought on the Western Front. Transferring to the RAF in 1919, he served in educational and staff appointments, and in 1938 was Director General of Research and Development. Two years later, he clashed with both the Minister of Aircraft Production, Lord Beaverbrook (see AITKEN, MAXWELL), and, more dangerously, Winston CHURCHILL. Appointed to command the RAF in the Middle East in 1941, Tedder survived Churchill's attempts to dismiss him and oversaw the creation of CONINGHAM's Desert Air Force. Appointed to head the Mediterranean Air Command under Eisenhower in Feb. 1943, Tedder's unobtrusive, diplomatic style perfectly suited inter-Allied command. In Dec., with Churchill admitting that he had been wrong, Tedder was chosen as Deputy Supreme Commander for the Normandy Landings (Operation Overlord). Raised to the peerage in 1946, Tedder worked to create NATO, and in 1950 was appointed Chancellor of Cambridge University.

TEERLINCK, LAVINIA (née Bening) (c. 1515–76), painter. Daughter of Simon Bening, one of the leading illuminators of Bruges, she married George Teerlinck, and the couple came to England c. 1545, both entering court service. Her skill as a miniaturist (she made an annual gift of a miniature to the monarch) was much respected in England, although it is not now considered to be in the first rank.

TEILO, ST (fl. sixth century), early Welsh saint. Church dedications show that his cult was venerated throughout south Wales. He appears to have lived at the monastery of Llandeilo Fawr (Carmarthens.). A life of him was written in the twelfth century, but its historical contents are of little value.

TELFORD, THOMAS (1757–1834), engineer. Born in Westerkirk, Eskdale, the self-taught son of a shepherd, Telford was apprenticed to a stonemason when he was 13. By the mid 1780s he was superintending the construction of buildings and in 1787 was surveyor of public works for Salop., where he built several impressive bridges and churches. His reputation was made with the building of the Ellesmere canal (1793–1805), notably the Pont-y-Cysylltau and Chirk aqueducts (Denbighs.). In the 1790s he helped construct many canals in the west Midlands and in 1801 was hired by the government to survey and improve public works in Scotland, where he built the spectacular 119-mile-long Caledonian canal (1804–22), 920 miles of new road, 1,200 bridges, and docks. From 1811 he constructed the London– Shrewsbury mail-route (including its extension to Holyhead), and this project led to his famous iron suspension bridge across the Menai Straits (1819–26). His other constructions include St Katherine's docks, London (1825–8), and the Gotha canal (1808–32). His enormous national networks of roads and canals, and his bridges formed the backbone to the world's first industrial economy.

TEMPLE, EARL, 2ND see GRENVILLE-TEMPLE, RICHARD; **3RD** see TEMPLE-NUGENT-GRENVILLE, GEORGE

TEMPLE, FREDERICK (1821–1902), Archbishop of Canterbury (1896–1902). He was educated at Balliol College, Oxford, and after his ordination as priest in 1847 he taught for a while at Balliol, becoming an advocate of educational reform. He was Headmaster of Rugby from 1857 to 1869, doing much to increase the school's reputation and becoming prominent in the arena of education. As Bishop of Exeter (1869–85) he fostered Church schools and the work of the temperance movement. After he became Bishop of London in 1885 he played an important role in the 1887 Jubilee celebrations and in the Lincoln Judgement of 1892. He was in constant conflict with the High Church party and his translation to Canterbury in 1897 (which coincided with Queen VICTORIA's Diamond Jubilee) was a political statement, echoed by the Lambeth Conference (1897) and the Lambeth Opinions (1899–1900).

TEMPLE, HENRY (3rd Viscount Palmerston) *see* essay on pages 770–71

TEMPLE, RICHARD (1st Viscount Cobham) (*c.* 1669–1749), soldier and politician. Entering the army as a youth, he then studied at Cambridge, but returned to follow a distinguished military career including commands under Marlborough (*see* CHURCHILL, JOHN) in the War of the Spanish Succession. Created a peer by GEORGE I, he generally supported Robert WALPOLE, until he broke with him over the Excise in 1733. He retired to his estate at Stowe (Bucks.), where he was creating a garden full of politically allegorical monuments and features, and became the patron of the 'boy patriots' or 'Cobham's cubs', young Whig politicians opposed to Walpole. The group included Cobham's nephews George GRENVILLE and George Lyttelton and Grenville's brother-in-law PITT THE ELDER. Cobham returned to office on Walpole's fall but continued to make a stand on 'patriot' issues such as the subordination of British to Hanoverian interests on the continent.

TEMPLE, SIR WILLIAM (1628–99), diplomat. Son of the Irish Master of the Rolls, he was elected an Irish MP in 1661. Two years later, he moved to England and, from 1665, was sent on a series of diplomatic missions. In 1668 Temple negotiated the Triple Alliance with the United Provinces (the Netherlands) and Sweden, and went as Ambassador to the Hague, but was recalled in 1670. He retired from public life before the outbreak of the Third Dutch War in 1672, and devoted himself to writing, including his very popular *Observations upon the United Provinces* (1672).

Returning to the fray, he helped negotiate the Treaty of Westminster (1674), concluding the war, in which the Dutch agreed to salute English shipping in northern European waters and to return New York. He was associated with Danby (*see* OSBORNE, THOMAS) and his attempt to build up a Protestant alliance against France. On his return to the Hague, he arranged the marriage of Princess Mary (the future MARY II) to William of Orange (the future WILLIAM III) in 1677. Brought into the Privy Council by CHARLES II in 1679 in an attempt to restore public confidence in the aftermath of the Popish-Plot crisis (*see* OATES, TITUS), he was removed in 1681 for what the King saw as his excessively conciliatory stance in the face of attempts to exclude the King's brother, the future JAMES II, from the line of succession.

TEMPLE-NUGENT-GRENVILLE, GEORGE (3rd Earl Temple, 1st Marquess of Buckingham) (1753–1813), politician. The son of Prime Minister George GRENVILLE, he succeeded his uncle Richard GRENVILLE-TEMPLE as Earl Temple in 1779. Having been a minister under SHELBURNE, Temple advised GEORGE III on the removal of the FOX–NORTH coalition. Hesitant to use the royal veto (not employed since the reign of ANNE) on 11 Dec. 1783, George III authorized Temple to state in the Lords that those who voted for Fox's India Bill could consider themselves the King's enemies. The Lords having obediently voted the Bill down, George demanded his ministers' resignation. Temple became Secretary of State to their successor PITT THE YOUNGER, but, fearing he might be impeached for what the displaced ministers claimed was an unconstitutional interference with the proceedings of Parliament, resigned after three days.

TEMPLER, SIR GERALD (1898–1979), soldier. Son of an army officer, educated at Sandhurst, Templer served with the Royal Irish Fusiliers in France (1917–18), in counter-terrorism in Palestine (1935–6), as Corps Commander in Italy (1943–4), and as Director of Civil Affairs in the British occupied zone of Germany. Appointed High Commissioner and Commander-in-Chief in Malaya in Feb. 1952, he implemented a sophisticated counter-insurgency programme based partly on his experiences in Palestine and Germany, which when he left Malaya in 1954 had broken the back of the communist insurgency. Templer devoted his retirement to the establishment of the National Army Museum.

TEMPLEWOOD, 1ST VISCOUNT *see* HOARE, SAMUEL

TENISON, THOMAS (1636–1715), Archbishop of Canterbury (1694–1715). He rose to prominence in public life when rector of St Martin's-in-the-Fields, debating religion with Jesuits and attending

continued on page 772

TEMPLE, HENRY (3rd Viscount Palmerston) (1784–1865)
Politician and Prime Minister (1855–8, 1859–65)

Indelibly a product of the Regency England in which he came to maturity, Palmerston was a late developer politically. As the holder of an Irish peerage he sat in the Commons for 58 years. He first held office under Lord Liverpool (see JENKINSON, ROBERT) and from 1808 to 1827 was Secretary at War, a post which gave him plenty of time to indulge in the romantic escapades which earned him the sobriquet of 'Lord Cupid'. He consistently refused either promotion or an English peerage. The first signs that he was something beyond the usual aristocratic placeman came after CANNING's death in 1827, when Palmerston ostentatiously adopted his mantle as the champion of the Greek cause against the machinations of the Holy Alliance. This led to his appointment as Foreign Secretary in GREY's Reform Bill administration of 1830, a post which he held until 1841 except for PEEL's 100 days in 1834–5.

Although Grey appears to have appointed Palmerston to run the Foreign Office while he himself controlled the direction of foreign policy, it worked out otherwise. Because of his long tenure of office under Liverpool, Palmerston was by far the most experienced member of the Whig administration, and he quickly established his domination over the Foreign Office, much to the displeasure of some of the clerks, who disliked his bullying manner and autocratic personal style. Having observed the way in which Canning was able to impose his diplomatic priorities on a Cabinet generally suspicious of his liberalism, by a wider appeal to public and parliamentary opinion, Palmerston was not slow to adopt Canning's methods to get his way in a Whig Cabinet in which he was the cuckoo in the nest.

Palmerston's handling of the crisis caused by the Belgian revolt against Dutch rule in 1830 was technically proficient and politically brilliant and established him as a major political figure. His support for the liberal cause there, and also in Spain and Portugal in 1835 with the formation of the Quintuple Alliance (with France as the fifth partner), enabled him to win a European reputation as the champion of constitutionalism and nationalism; the fact that the Austrian Chancellor and personification of autocracy, Prince Metternich, detested him, only helped his popularity at home.

In fact, his diplomacy was always more cautious than his rhetoric, just as Canning's had been. It was Palmerston who coined the dictum that England had no eternal friends or enemies, just eternal interests. His flexibility was shown by the way in which, despite his distrust of the Russians, he was able to co-operate with them in the Near Eastern crisis of 1839–40 to prevent the French-backed Pasha of Egypt, Mehmet Ali, gaining control of the Ottoman empire. His Whig colleagues threatened to resign but Palmerston insisted on defying them and the French, and got his way. His taste for noisy diplomacy and striking bellicose attitudes worried staider souls but won him massive popular support. By 1841 he had firmly established himself as a formidable political force and no future Liberal leader could ignore him.

Palmerston's attitudes were as conservative on domestic issues as they were liberal on foreign affairs and this made him a figure wooed by all sides in the confused politics which followed the fall of Peel's government in 1846. Although the Whigs under Lord John RUSSELL distrusted him, and Queen Victoria positively wished to veto his appointment to the Foreign Office in 1846, the fear that he would lend his support to the Conservatives under Lord Edward STANLEY led Russell to offer him the Foreign Office. He suffered a diplomatic defeat in 1846 when the French engineered the marriage of one of Louis Philippe's sons to the sister of the Queen of Spain but Palmerston had the last laugh two years later when the Orléans monarchy was swept from the throne in the 'Year of Revolutions'. Palmerston's rhetorical support for European liberalism seemed to be vindicated by the 1848 revolutions in Europe, and his personal popularity enabled him to ride out censure from the Lords and from some of his colleagues over the Don Pacifico affair in 1850. Charged with behaving in a high-handed manner in blockading Athens over the debts of a Gibraltarian Jew of dubious character, Palmerston, who was no great orator, gave the speech of his life in his own defence, enunciating the doctrine that a British subject should, like the Roman of old, be free from hazard abroad if he declared that he was *Civis Britannicus* (British subject). This caught the note of popular patriotism and established Palmerston as the personification of 'John Bullishness'.

One of Palmerston's most remarkable characteristics was his luck. In 1851, when he unilaterally recognized the *coup d'état* of Louis Napoleon

Bonaparte, Lord John Russell was able to dismiss him for having gone too far. But within three months, Palmerston engineered the fall of Russell's already weak administration and, henceforth, played a pivotal role in British politics and Cabinet-making.

Barred from the Foreign Office by the Queen's disapproval, Palmerston was appointed Home Secretary in the Aberdeen (see GORDON, GEORGE) coalition (1852–5). Influenced by his stepson-in-law, the 7th Earl of Shaftesbury, Palmerston proved a reforming minister in the fields of the prison service and factory legislation but he drew the line at another electoral reform Bill, and preferred to resign in late 1853 rather than agree to Russell's proposals for one. Again his luck held and the coincidence of his resignation with the Russian attack on the Turkish fleet at Sinope created the popular impression that he had gone because Aberdeen's diplomacy was too weak; this led to his reinstatement. When Aberdeen's government resigned in 1854 after censure over its shortcomings in the Crimean War, Palmerston was in his own characteristic phrase 'the inevitable'.

Palmerston's wartime leadership was hardly inspired but he was fortunate in coming to office just as the war was entering its final stages; he was therefore able to claim credit for the final victory, which allowed him to stay in office until 1857, when he won a General Election which turned very largely on his personality. Palmerston's combination of rhetorical boldness and administrative caution enabled him to capture the middle ground of Victorian politics and, although always a child of the Regency era, he showed, from his use of 'speeches out of doors', an ability to command popular support that GLADSTONE would learn from. It was an example of his occasional insensitivity to the sources of his own support which led to his downfall in 1858. Complying with Napoleon III's demands for legislation against giving asylum to would-be terrorists after the Orsini attempt on his life, Palmerston outraged patriotic opinion. But, as ever, his luck held, and the short-lived Derby administration, through its support for the Austrian cause in 1859, united liberals of all persuasions in favour of the Italian war of independence.

The government which Palmerston formed in June 1859 was the first real Liberal government and, with Gladstone at the Exchequer, it provided an enduring answer to the political confusion which had persisted since 1846. With Palmerston himself offering the Conservatives no target at which to aim, the Liberal government completed Peel's task of reducing duties on foreign trade, promoting Free Trade and bringing order to the British financial system. Palmerston's view that 'there is really nothing to be done. We cannot go on adding to the Statute Book ad infinitum', sums up his own views on issues such as further parliamentary reform. Conservative at home and Liberal abroad, Palmerston embodied in himself the equilibrium of mid Victorian politics. He won the 1865 election with ease.

Although his private life entered a more regular phase after his marriage in 1839 to his long-time mistress, Lady Cowper, Palmerston remained the subject of rumour and the target of would-be blackmailers but he scorned the former and, when necessary, paid the latter. When he was cited as co-respondent in the divorce suit of a Mrs Cain when in his late seventies, the word went round the clubs, 'she is Cain but is he Abel?' DISRAELI declined to use such rumours against him wearily declaring that it would only make the old man even more popular than he was. Palmerston died suddenly in Oct. 1865 at the age of 81, hale and hearty to the end. His final period in power marked, however, a recession from the heights of success scaled at the time of the Don Pacifico affair. His attempt in 1864 to bluff Bismarck into climbing down over the Schleswig-Holstein affair with Denmark was a notable failure and can be seen as demonstrating Britain's increasing impotence in the face of changes in the European balance of power. Palmerston had been able to get his way for a long time because of a favourable European balance, in which Russia had always acted as a check on any change in the Vienna system created in 1815; after her defeat in the Crimean War Russia abandoned this position, with grave consequences for Europe, and for Britain.

Palmerston was also fortunate in the timing of his death. Had he continued in power he would have had to face the twin problems of Bismarck's Prussia and parliamentary reform; as it was, he was able to bequeath these intractable problems to his successors. Palmerston remains the personification of Victorian England's self-confidence at the height of the *Pax Britannica*.

Kenneth Bourne, Palmerston: The Early Years 1784–1841 (1982)
E. D. Steele, Palmerston and Liberalism 1855–1865 (1991)

Monmouth (*see* SCOTT, JAMES) on the scaffold. He attended the seven bishops when they drew up the protest against JAMES II's Declaration of Indulgence of 1688 which led to their imprisonment, and early on was in the confidence of those who invited William of Orange (the future WILLIAM III) to England in 1688. He was rewarded for his political inclinations with an archdeaconry. As Archbishop, he supported moves for stricter observance of morality (reproving WILLIAM III himself for adultery), helped to found the Society for the Propagation of the Gospel, and attempted to promote Episcopal Protestantism in North America and Prussia. He fell out of favour under ANNE and wielded little influence in Convocation, which was dominated by High Churchmen (*see also* ATTERBURY, Francis). His last major action as Archbishop was to issue a *Declaration* in 1715, warning of the threat to Anglicanism from a Stuart restoration.

TENNYSON, ALFRED *see* essay on page 773

TERRY, DAME ELLEN (1847–1928), actress. Born into a theatrical family of 11 children, Terry first appeared on the stage at the age of eight in *A Winter's Tale*. In 1864 she left the stage to marry the painter G. F. WATTS who was 30 years her senior. The marriage lasted less than a year and she subsequently lived with the architect Edward Godwin, by whom she had two children (one of whom, Gordon Craig, was to become a distinguished theatrical designer). She had two more short-lived marriages. Financial necessity drove her back to the theatre later, and in 1878 her role in *Olivia* brought her to the attention of the actor-manager Henry IRVING, whose leading lady she was for nearly 20 years, playing the major Shakespearean roles (Desdemona, Portia, Viola and Lady Macbeth) but also minor parts if that was what the autocratic Irving decreed. In 1903 she became a not very successful manager herself and she had parts written for her by both George Bernard SHAW (whose correspondence with her was published in 1929) and J. M. BARRIE.

TEWDWR, SON OF BILI, King of the Strathclyde Britons (*c.* 722–*c.* 752). He is likely to have been the King who, in 750, defeated and killed Talorcan, son of Fergus, brother of OENGUS, SON OF FERGUS, King of the Picts, at Mugdock (Stirlings.). Although Oengus's power declined after this set-back, EADBERT, King of Northumbria, annexed Kyle from Strathclyde in the same year; it may be that the Picts and Northumbrians had united in a concerted invasion of Strathclyde, just as they would against DOMNAGUAL, SON OF TEWDWR, in 756.

THACKERAY, WILLIAM MAKEPEACE (1811–63), novelist. Thackeray began a career in journalism in 1833, and was impoverished the same year when he lost the greater part of his inheritance with the Indian bank failure. He suffered further financial difficulties through the expense of arranging care for his wife after her mental collapse in 1840. Financial imperatives forced Thackeray to produce prolific amounts of writing. He wrote many reviews, parodies and satires for such magazines as *Punch* and *Fraser's Magazine*, often under the pseudonym of one of his characters. The novel *Barry Lyndon* was serialized in 1840 and his reputation was consolidated with *The Book of Snobs*, an analysis of early Victorian class consciousness, which appeared in *Punch* in 1846–7. The novel for which he is now best known, his panoramic social satire *Vanity Fair*, was first published in monthly parts in 1847–8, and was followed in quick succession by *Pendennis* (1848), *Henry Esmond* (1852) and *The Newcomes* (1853–5). He continued to write and lecture prodigiously and in 1859 became founding editor of a literary periodical, the *Cornhill Magazine*, in which most of his later work was first published.

THATCHER, MARGARET *see* essay on pages 774–75

THELWALL, JOHN (1764–1834), radical. Apprenticed to a tailor and then to an attorney before becoming a full-time writer, he developed a reputation as a public speaker at meetings of the Society for Free Debate, which met in Coachmakers' Hall. Inspired by the French Revolution, he abandoned his conservative stance and became a radical, assisting HORNE TOOKE in his Westminster election campaign in 1790. In 1792 he joined the London Corresponding Society and the Society of Friends of the People. Thelwall was arrested in May 1794 on the charge of seditiously proposing a revolution at a meeting in Chalk Farm, and was imprisoned alongside Horne Tooke and Thomas HARDY, but was acquitted when tried in Dec. Leaving London a year later when the Act prohibiting seditious meetings and assemblies was passed, Thelwall toured the country lecturing on Roman history, drawing parallels with contemporary events, and teaching elocution.

THEOBALD OF BEC (?–1161), Archbishop of Canterbury (1138–61). A monk at the Norman monastery of Bec for 45 years, Abbot in 1137, he was created Archbishop by STEPHEN in 1138, continuing the tradition of archbishops coming from Bec. Although he tried to avoid involvement in the civil war between the houses of Blois and Anjou, he eventually angered Stephen by attending a papal council (1148) against the King's wishes and then by refusing, in 1152, to crown his son EUSTACE. Life was simpler once

continued on page 776

TENNYSON, ALFRED (1ST BARON TENNYSON) (1809–92)
Poet

He was one of 12 (eight surviving) children of George Tennyson, Rector of Somersby (Lincs.), and his wife Elizabeth. Alfred's father had entered the Church only when disinherited by his own father; he was a resentful, melancholic man given to furious, alcoholic rages, and Alfred always feared that this 'black blood of the Tennysons' coursed through his own veins. He was educated at Louth grammar school, which he hated, and then somewhat erratically by his father, which allowed him leisure for his own reading and roaming the fenland countryside that surrounded the rectory.

He was also writing poetry, and preening himself as a poet. In 1824 he was inconsolable at the death of BYRON, whom he regarded as his muse, and between 1823 and 1824 he wrote *The Devil and the Lady*, a clever dramatic verse pastiche of the Elizabethan form (which was not published until 1930). He joined his two brothers at Trinity College, Cambridge, in Nov. 1827, and there won the Chancellor's Gold Medal for poetry with 'Timbuctoo', the first example of blank verse to be awarded that honour. At Cambridge he was elected to the fellowship of the Apostles (an intellectual brotherhood formed for formal discussion and friendship in 1820) and met Arthur Henry Hallam, who was to be his close spiritual and intellectual companion.

In 1831 George Tennyson died, and Alfred left Cambridge without taking a degree. By now he was already a published poet: in 1827 *Poems by Two Brothers* (which included work by his brothers Charles and Frederick) had been published by a Louth bookseller, and this was followed in 1831 by *Poems, Chiefly Lyrical*. In 1832 another volume, entitled simply *Poems* and containing 'The Lady of Shalott' and 'The Lotos Eaters' was published, but the cusp of success fell when the volume was savaged by John Wilson Crocker as 'trivial' in the *Quarterly Review* and the wounded Tennyson fell into 'the ten years silence' during which he refused to expose his work to attack. It was a painful time, rendered almost insupportable by the sudden death of Hallam in 1833, which prompted Tennyson to note down reflections on mortality, religion and a great panorama of Victorian thought that would eventually be published as the compendious *In Memoriam* (1850), which is Tennyson's own enduring memorial too.

In the next few years he fell in love with Rosa Baring, and then in 1836 fixed his intentions on Emily Sellwood, whose sister had married his brother Charles. It was to be a protracted courtship: her father forbade the relationship in 1840; 10 years later, Tennyson resumed the correspondence, they became engaged, and married when he was 41 and she 37. In 1837, with three brothers suffering mental illness, the family removed to Epping in Essex. But a self-imposed ban on publication did not mean any cessation in writing, and in 1842 Tennyson published two volumes of poems which contained some of his finest work: revised versions of 'The Lady of Shalott', 'The Lotos Eaters', as well as 'Locksley Hall', 'Morte d'Arthur' and 'Ulysses'. In 1847 *The Princess*, a polemic on the rights of women, was published, and three years later his career triumphed with the publication of *In Memoriam* and his appointment as Poet Laureate in succession to WORDSWORTH. In this official role, he composed an ode on the death of Wellington (*see* WELLESLEY, SIR ARTHUR) (1852) and his poem on the charge of the Light Brigade at Balaclava during the Crimean War (1854). His work continued to pour forth, *Maud* in 1855 and the first of his four *Idylls of the King*, which he finished in 1885 and dedicated 'To the Queen' (VICTORIA). In 1875 the first of several forgettable dramatic works was published (Ellen TERRY starred in *The Cup* in 1881) and a pessimistic prose work, *The Promise of Mary* (1882).

Having several times declined a baronetcy, he accepted a peerage in 1884. The Tennysons had moved to the Isle of Wight in 1853 (they also had a house at Aldworth (Surrey)) and it was while crossing the Solent that he penned the reflective 'Crossing the Bar' which was included in *Demeter and Other Poems* (1889), the final collection of poems published in his lifetime. Three further volumes were published after his death. Tennyson's funeral in Westminster Abbey was attended by ranks of veterans from the Light Brigade. A biography by his son, Hallam, who had always protected his deeply sensitive father from criticism in his lifetime, was published in 1897. A poet of appreciated lyrical skills, Tennyson's reputation has wavered since his death, but he remains the archetypal versifier of a potent version of middle-class Victorian England in its solemnity, patriotism, mawkishness and protean productivity.

Christopher Ricks, Tennyson (1972)
Robert B. Martin, Tennyson: The Unquiet Heart (1980)

THATCHER, MARGARET (née Roberts) (Baroness Thatcher of Kesteven) (1925–)
Politician and Prime Minister 1979–90

The dominating personality in post-Second World War British politics, Mrs Thatcher was, is and will remain a figure who arouses every emotion save apathy; nor do feelings about her divide simply along party political lines.

For many Conservatives she was one of the more worrying aspects of the advent of mass democracy. The youngest daughter of alderman Roberts of Grantham, who ran the local grocer's shop, she brought not only the economics but also the *mores* of the provincial grocer into the highest political circles. Her career was a triumph of will-power against circumstance and, if she remained defiantly impervious to feminist cries for special treatment for women, that was as much the product of her own experiences as it was of her prejudices.

Grocers' daughters were not a common sight at Oxford University in the 1940s; women studying chemistry were an equally rare breed; since Margaret Roberts belonged to both groups, she was unique. Unlike her male contemporaries who played politics at the Union, Miss Roberts was expected to work, and work she did: women at Oxford in that era were expected to prove themselves worthy of their places, and Miss Roberts fitted into that ethos perfectly. But she was always a political animal, and, although she worked for a while as a research chemist, she saw the legal profession as her way towards a career in politics.

Vivacious and attractive young women were not much sought after by local Tory associations and, after her marriage to a divorcé, Denis Thatcher, the young Mrs Thatcher went back to her legal career and, along the way, produced twins. It was a mark of her determination and persistence that she conquered the prejudices of Conservative associations against working mothers by getting herself adopted as candidate for Finchley in 1959. Thereafter she was generally the beneficiary of what would now be called 'tokenism'; she was the token junior woman minister in MACMILLAN's final government; the token woman in the Shadow Cabinet in the late 1960s and, finally, the token woman minister in the HEATH government of 1970–4 when she occupied the post of Secretary of State for Education, traditionally a 'woman's post'. Her moment of notoriety came when she was responsible for abolishing the provision of free milk to schoolchildren, thus earning herself the sobriquet of 'Thatcher milk-snatcher'. It was only in the aftermath of the disastrous 1974 General Elections

that Mrs Thatcher emerged as more than the token woman.

There was widespread discontent in Conservative ranks with Edward Heath but it was combined with an equal lack of desire to incur his wrath by challenging him for the leadership of the party; Mrs Thatcher broke this deadlock. Her candidacy aroused interest more on account of her sex than for any other reason and her eventual defeat of Heath brought fresh male challengers into the ring. But her courage had given her an edge over her rivals which she was not to lose for a decade and a half and Conservative MPs astonished everyone, including themselves, by selecting a woman as their leader.

Her opponents would come to regard her as an ideologue but 'Thatcherism' as a phenomenon owed as much to her personality as it did to the eclectic range of ideas upon which she drew. Her instinctive distrust of Keynesian economics (*see* KEYNES, J. M.) and socialist over-regulation led her to the ideas of the Chicago school of economists (in particular Milton Friedman) and to the libertarian ideas being propounded by the Centre for Policy Studies, presided over by her friend and mentor, Sir Keith JOSEPH. But the most notable feature of her early career as leader of the opposition was the furore she caused by her outspoken criticism of the Soviet Union, which not only cut across the prevailing mood of *détente* but which provoked the resignation of her Shadow Foreign Secretary, Reginald MAUDLING, and prompted *Pravda* to dub her 'the Iron Lady', a sobriquet in which she came to revel. Her attitude towards employment law, immigration and monetary policy also gave rise to discontent among her colleagues and defeated rivals in the Shadow Cabinet; when the election came in 1979 she knew that she would have only one chance.

Opposing the wily and somnolent Jim CALLAGHAN had not been an easy task, not least because his Labour government had been forced to adopt the sort of economic policies which she had been advocating. But the industrial unrest which these policies provoked in the so-called 'winter of discontent' in 1978–9 played into the hands of the Conservatives at the election and Mrs Thatcher became the country's first female Prime Minister in May 1979.

Her first premiership fell into two halves, bisected by the Falklands War of 1982. In the first period, hamstrung by what came to be called the 'wets' in the Cabinet, some thought she proceeded too cautiously on monetary policy, industrial relations and employment law, doing enough to provoke opposition but not enough to rally her own supporters; by her own later confession there were times when she could scarcely rely upon the support of two other ministers. Her 1981 declaration that 'the Lady's not for Turning' was widely supposed to be the prelude to another Heath-like 'U-turn'; but this was to underestimate her. She began to clear out the 'wets' and, with the Argentinean invasion of the Falkland Islands in April 1982, the defining moment of her premiership had come.

The advice to do nothing and to negotiate with the Argentineans came from many quarters but instinctively she rejected it, despite the fact that sending a Task Force to the South Atlantic to take back the islands by force was an operation fraught with risk. The successful completion of the campaign transformed her position in the opinion polls and, from that point on, the Conservatives never looked in danger of losing the next election. Further aid was provided in the form of the new Labour leader, Michael FOOT, whose commitment to unilateralism and inability to control his party's left wing ensured that, for the first time in half a century, Labour fought an election on a genuinely socialist programme. Mrs Thatcher increased her majority from 45 to 144 seats.

Her second administration resembled its predecessor in getting off to a slow start in terms of radical reforms and in being marked by a fierce struggle, this time an internal one with the National Union of Miners and its leader, Arthur SCARGILL. But the adoption of a policy of privatization, originally as a means of denationalizing industries but then as a means of spreading 'popular capitalism', gave the administration its most notable innovation, while the defeat of the socialist Scargill marked the end of syndicalist hopes of revolution from below; it was Mrs Thatcher who seemed to be leading the revolution, from the right. The economic boom of 1987 with the appearance of the 'Yuppies' (young, upwardly mobile professionals) provided the ideal climate in which to go to the polls and to win an unprecedented third term in office, albeit with a majority reduced to 102.

During her third term as Prime Minister Mrs Thatcher became successively the longest serving premier of the twentieth century, the longest serving Prime Minister since Lord Liverpool (*see* JENKINSON, ROBERT) in 1827 and, in the eyes of some Conservatives, the greatest impediment to a fourth Conservative victory. Her championing of the hugely unpopular 'community charge' (or poll-tax as it quickly became known) and her opposition to further measures of European integration gave her opponents causes round which they could rally support against her. The revival of the Labour Party under Neil KINNOCK, who strenuously rooted out the Trotskyist elements in his ranks, gave rise to concerns that Mrs Thatcher's longevity as leader was becoming a liability.

She had been renowned for her intolerance of dissent and her premierships had been marked by dramatic sackings and resignations, the most spectacular of the latter in 1985 when Michael HESELTINE walked out of the Cabinet over the Westland affair. By early 1990 the rumours that Heseltine would decide to challenge her gathered force, stoked up by the resignation of her Chancellor, Nigel LAWSON, and the demotion of her Foreign Secretary, Geoffrey HOWE; the latter's bitter resignation speech precipitated an electoral contest in which Mrs Thatcher failed, by three votes, to win the necessary two-thirds majority. On prime-time TV, live, she told the BBC that she would 'fight, and fight to win'; but with lack of support from her Cabinet colleagues she resigned the following day.

She remained an influential and indeed iconic figure in the Conservative Party, always sure of an ecstatic reception at the party conference. Her advocacy of the Anglo-American alliance, her electoral successes, and the ideological success of Thatcherism, all made her an object of emulation for the new Labour leader after 1993, Tony BLAIR. The Left hated her for what they saw as her divisive social and economic policies; many Conservatives shared these views; elsewhere she was admired for her toughness and courage. In retirement she continued to promote the cause of free-market economics and liberty and she was always sure of an appreciative welcome in the USA. Her views on Europe were always sought after by Euro-sceptic Tories and, when William HAGUE became leader of the party after the disastrous election defeat of 1997, he sought and gained her endorsement. Age diminished neither her energies, nor the controversies she aroused, and she remains a figure adored and loathed in equal measure.

Margaret Thatcher, The Downing Street Years (1993)

there was an undisputed king on the throne (HENRY II). He drew both Thomas BECKET and JOHN OF SALISBURY into his service.

THEODORE OF TARSUS, ST (*c.* 602–90), Archbishop of Canterbury (668–90). The Greek theologian Theodore must be given credit for three achievements. Beginning at the Synod of Hertford, he undertook a major reorganization of the English Church during which a diocesan structure was created that, in broad terms, lasted for the rest of the medieval period. With Abbot HADRIAN he established a school at Canterbury with pupils that included St ALDHELM, which did a great deal to raise the educational standards of the higher clergy in southern England. Finally, he asserted the authority of the archbishopric of Canterbury in such a way as to produce for the first time a unitary English Church. This undoubtedly acted as a stimulus to a sense of unity among the English peoples. Texts such as the *Penitential* reveal a great deal about Theodore's pastoral methods. Although he quarrelled for a time with St WILFRID, he is generally remembered for his tact. His success is all the more surprising since he was already in his sixties when he was sent to England by Pope Vitalian. Theodore's achievements consolidated the special place which the archbishopric of Canterbury had acquired within English Christianity during St AUGUSTINE's mission and contributed considerably to the pre-eminence which it has held over the centuries in British religious life. His policies were continued by his immediate successor BERHTWALD.

THESIGER, FREDERICK (2nd Baron Chelmsford) (1827–1905), soldier. Educated at Eton, he was bought a commission in 1844, and served in the Crimea (1855–6) and during the last stages of the Indian Mutiny (1858). In 1868 Deputy Adjutant General with NAPIER's expedition to Abyssinia, Thesiger was subsequently promoted Major-General and appointed to South Africa. In 1879 Chelmsford (he had inherited the title on his father's death) led an army of 13,000 in widely dispersed columns into Zululand and met with disaster on 22 Jan. when Zulu Impis annihilated one of the columns at Isandhiwana. Alarmed by a storm of public criticism, the British government appointed Garnet WOLSELEY to command but, before he could reach Natal, Chelmsford managed to defeat the Zulus at Ulundi on 4 July. The victory was marred by the death of Napoleon III's son, the Prince Imperial, who had been deserted by his escort on a reconnaissance patrol when attacked by Zulus. Chelmsford returned to Britain to a series of non-jobs, including many years as Lieutenant of the Tower of London.

THESIGER, FREDERICK (1st Viscount Chelmsford) (1868–1933), Viceroy of India. Appointed Governor General and Viceroy in 1916, Thesiger had served as Governor of Queensland (1905–9) and of New South Wales (1901–13), then went with his regiment to India once war broke out in 1914. A cautious man, he was the antithesis of CURZON. Chelmsford advocated Dominion Home Rule for India, but his slowness in policy was overtaken by increasing nationalist fervour. The arrival of Edwin MONTAGU as Secretary of State for India in 1917 presaged change: he removed the ban on Indians for regular army commissions and released Annie BESANT and others from detention, before visiting India himself. The so-called Montagu–Chelmsford reforms of 1919 resulted: partial self-government with a bicameral parliament. Yet Chelmsford, to restrain nationalist feeling, used draconian powers of arrest and detention; GANDHI appealed for resistance, and demonstrations and rioting resulted. Chelmsford left India in 1921 with constitutional reform in place but having caused many more problems than he had solved.

THESIGER, SIR WILFRED (1910–), explorer. Thesiger was born in Addis Ababa, the son of the British minister to Ethiopia, and during a conventional English education at Eton and Oxford retained a love for the Middle East and Africa where he lived, mainly in the desert and the mountains, for most of his life. He was the last of the breed of great Victorian explorers, and though most of his journeys were ostensibly for geographical and scientific purposes they provided the material for several best-selling travel books such as *Arabian Sands* (1959) and *The Marsh Arabs* (1964), recording a civilization that was almost entirely to disappear after the oil price rises of 1973.

THIRLBY, THOMAS (?1506–70), diplomat. A Cambridge don, from 1540 to 1550 he was first and only Bishop of Westminster, then transferred to Norwich and in 1554 to Ely. His 1530s enthusiasm for evangelical reform faded, but he remained in favour under EDWARD VI because of his continuing usefulness in overseas diplomacy. In 1556 he was much distressed to be co-president at the degradation ceremony of his old Cambridge friend Thomas CRANMER. Refusing to conform under ELIZABETH I, he was imprisoned.

THISTLEWOOD, ARTHUR (1774–1820), radical revolutionary. A member of the underground world of revolutionary extremists, he was identified by the Home Office as a dangerous subversive and watched closely. His planned destruction of the Cabinet, the Cato Street conspiracy (23 Feb. 1820), was known to the authorities and easily thwarted. Found guilty of high treason, he was publicly hanged and decapitated at Newgate on 1 May 1820.

THOMAS, DYLAN (1914–53), poet. A Swansea-born son of an English teacher, Thomas showed great poetic promise as a teenager, and after a brief spell as a journalist on a local paper left for London in 1934, where he became a fixture in Fitzrovia pubs, meeting literary figures and earning a wholly inadequate income as a poet. During the Second World War he worked for the BBC, wrote film and documentary scripts and published two collections of short stories, *The Map of Love* (1939) and *Portrait of the Artist as a Young Dog* (1940), as well as *New Poems* (1943), all of which were ecstatically received. In 1937 he married Caitlin Macnamara, and in 1949 they moved to live with their children in the Boat House at Laugharne (Carmarthens.) (now a memorial to Thomas). By then the debt-hounded Thomas was in great demand in the USA as well as Britain for his sometimes intoxicated, always charismatic poetry performances with their sonorous, lilting Welsh cadences, and in the spring of 1953 his radio 'play for voices' *Under Milk Wood* was performed in New York, with Thomas himself taking one of the voices. On a return visit later that year, he slipped into an alcoholic coma from which he never recovered.

THOMAS, JAMES HENRY (JIMMY) (1874–1949), trade-union leader and politician. Thomas, the illegitimate son of a domestic servant, was brought up by his washerwoman grandmother and, leaving school at 12, went to work on the railways. In 1906 he became a full-time official for the National Union of Railwaymen (NUR), rising to become General Secretary (1916–31). From 1914 the NUR, already a large union, increased its political power base in a Triple Industrial Alliance with the miners and transport workers. But Thomas was personally vilified when in 1921 he refused NUR support for the miners and in 1926 the Trades Union Congress called off the General Strike. Labour MP for Derby (1910–36), he held office during the first Labour government (1924) and was regarded as a possible successor to Ramsay MACDONALD. His reputation declined in the 1930s: he was seen to be ineffective in the face of escalating unemployment and when he joined MacDonald's National government as Colonial and Dominions Secretary (the post he had held in the 1924 government) his ties with the labour movement were severed. He was forced to resign in 1936 over a budget leak.

THOMAS, MARGARET HAIG (Viscountess Rhondda) (1883–1958), editor. Daughter of a mine owner who was created Viscount Rhondda in 1916. She attempted, on his death in 1918, to take his seat in the House of Lords but was frustrated by legal proceedings. Soon after her marriage in 1908 to (Sir) Humphrey Mackworth (the marriage was not a success) she had become involved in the suffragette movement, and was sent to prison for chemical bombing a letter box, but was released when she went on hunger strike. In 1915 she survived when the *Lusitania* was torpedoed by a German submarine in the Atlantic, with more than 1,000 lives lost. In 1920 Thomas started an 'Independent Non-Party Weekly Review', *Time and Tide*, to 'change the nation's habit of mind', becoming editor in 1926. Its views were liberally right-wing, with, certainly in the early years, a strong feminist agenda attracting such contributors as Winifred Holtby, Rebecca WEST, Katherine MANSFIELD, Vita SACKVILLE WEST and Dorothy L. SAYERS, and it published work, like George ORWELL's anti-Stalinist commentary on the Spanish Civil War, that could not find a home elsewhere.

THOMAS OF CLARENCE (2nd Duke of Clarence) (*c.* 1388–1421), Royal Prince. The second son of HENRY IV, he was made Lieutenant of Ireland in 1401 and in 1408–9 made a vain effort to stem the tide of Gaelic resurgence. He held other commands in Wales and at sea, but was principally engaged as assistant to his brother, HENRY V, in the continuation of the Hundred Years War in France and the conquest of Normandy. He was killed in battle with Scottish and French forces at Baugé, probably due to his impetuosity.

THOMAS OF LANCASTER (2nd Earl of Lancaster, 8th Earl of Leicester) (1278–1322), nobleman. By far the richest earl of the day, he was able to play a dominating political role, which, because of his consistent opposition to EDWARD II, was also highly controversial. His enormous wealth was based on the Lancaster, Leicester and Ferrers earldoms, which he inherited from his father Edmund of Lancaster (Edmund Crouchback) in 1296, and the inheritance of the earldom of Lincoln by his wife, Alice de Lacy, in 1311. He became an Ordainer in 1310 and, two years later, took a leading part in the quasi-judicial murder of GAVESTON. During 1315 and 1316, after Edward II's humiliation at Bannockburn (1314), Thomas dominated the King's Council, insisting that the ordinances be observed.

His personality gradually alienated some of his supporters and led his wife to leave him. In 1317 Edward recovered control, and only the rise of a new royal favourite Hugh DESPENSER enabled Thomas to re-form an opposition group in 1321. But his popularity was already waning again. He had made the political error of seeking Scottish aid when he was brought to battle and defeated at Boroughbridge (Yorks.). Six days later he was executed for treason. Not since the execution of WALTHEOF in 1076 had a man of his rank been put to death for rebellion, but Edward, determined to avenge Gaveston, would not be stopped. Whatever his flaws, Thomas's presentation of himself as another Simon de MONTFORT and Edward's continuing unpopularity led to a movement that sought the Earl's canonization, and his tomb in Pontefract Priory (Yorks.) became the focus of a short-lived cult.

THOMAS OF WOODSTOCK (4th Earl of Buckingham, 1st Duke of Gloucester) (1355–97), nobleman. Youngest son of EDWARD III, he married Eleanor de Bohun, co-heiress of the earldom of Hereford, and was created Earl of Buckingham in 1377, Duke of Gloucester in 1385. From 1386 he was his nephew RICHARD II's fiercest critic, and in 1387–8 the most obdurate of the Appellants; according to one account, the Commons wished to make him king. Richard never forgave him and in 1397 had him arrested and charged with treason. Before he was brought to trial he died in prison in Calais, possibly of natural causes. An inquiry set up in 1399 reported with some plausibility that he had been murdered on Richard's orders.

THOMAS, SIDNEY GILCHRIST (1850–85), metallurgist. Born in London, Thomas studied science at Birkbeck College while working as a clerk in a police court (1868–79). He became interested in developing a process for improving the steel-making processes of Henry BESSEMER and Charles SIEMENS, specifically to remove the phosphorous impurity in pig iron which was believed to make steel brittle. After much experimentation in his makeshift home laboratory, he decided that a calcined dolomite-lined steel furnace, rather than Bessemer's acid-lined furnace, would solve the problem. His process proved successful at the Blaenavon (Mon.) steelworks (where his cousin Percy Gilchrist was a chemist), and in 1879 he took out a joint patent for the process with Gilchrist and spent the rest of his life marketing his process and profiting from its international exploitation.

THOMAS, WILLIAM (?–1554), writer and conspirator. From Powys, he may have studied at Oxford and spent much time abroad, especially in Italy, on which he became an expert, publishing a history (1549) and an Italian grammar and dictionary (1550); he was an admirer of Macchiavelli. He became clerk of the Privy Council in 1550 and helped EDWARD VI with his political education. Losing all office on MARY I's accession, he took part in Thomas WYATT's rebellion, was imprisoned, tortured and executed.

THOMPSON, E(DWARD) P(ALMER) (1924–93), historian. He was one of the most influential historians of the post-war era, his thought profoundly shaped by political engagement. A member of the Communist Party from 1942, he was a major figure in leading the breakaway from the party in 1956 and founding the New Left, co-editing with the historian John Saville the journal *New Reasoner* (1957–9) and being involved with *New Left Review* (1960–2). Central to his historical work was the attempt to offer a Marxist history which escaped the mechanical formulations and political dogmas of Stalinism, in which an economic base determined social and political life. His first major book, *William Morris* (1955), shows him engaged in this attempt, while his most celebrated and influential work, *The Making of the English Working Class* (1963), was a profoundly anti-Stalinist text. It presented an interpretation of the development of the working class between 1790 and 1832 in which the formation of class consciousness – the sense of belonging to a class and of being antagonistic to other classes – was the result of an interplay between the experiences of industrial revolution and the politics and culture created by the working class. The book had a huge impact on the growth of 'history from below', opening up social history to new sources and problems in order to 'rescue' the poor and the 'ordinary people' from 'the enormous condescension of posterity'. Thompson's later work moved back into the eighteenth century and displayed a greater engagement both with the nature of the State and its cultural and political domination (*Whigs and Hunters*, 1975) and with the cultural structures of the common people in the period (*Customs in Common*, 1991). Throughout his life Thompson was a polemicist: always passionate, his polemics could be either overblown, as in *The Poverty of Theory* (1978), a diatribe against the French Marxist Althusser, or more successful in hitting their targets, as in his extensive writings on the dangers of nuclear proliferation in the 1980s.

THOMPSON, JULIAN (1934–), soldier. Son of an army officer, he was commissioned into the Royal Marines, and served in the Far and Middle East in the 1950s and 1960s. Appointed to command 3 Commando Brigade in 1981, in May 1982 Thompson was in charge of the initial operations to retake the Falkland Islands from Argentina. Facing a task of appalling difficulty, Thompson also had to deal with an indifferent naval command and a high command in Whitehall which placed party politics first. Though he blamed himself for sending Lieutenant Colonel JONES against strong Argentinian positions at Darwin-Goose Green with inadequate support, the general consensus was that Thompson had handled the operation with consummate skill. Promoted to Major-General, Thompson retired in 1988 to a fellowship at King's College, London, where he has researched and written widely on military history.

THOMSON, SIR GEORGE PAGET (1892–1975), physicist. Son of Joseph John THOMSON, George Thomson studied mathematics and natural sciences at Cambridge and served in the Royal Flying Corps during the First World War. Subsequently he worked on electrical discharge at Cambridge and at Aberdeen, where he was appointed Professor of Natural Philosophy in 1923. In 1927 he and his colleagues showed that electrons passing through a thin metal foil were diffracted, a conclusion supporting the French physicist Louis de Broglie's ground-breaking claim that particles behaved as waves. For this work he shared the 1937 Nobel Prize for Physics with Clinton Davisson. As Professor of Physics at Imperial College, London (1930), he was appointed chief adviser to the British government on the atomic bomb and after the Second World War worked on particle physics and nuclear fusion.

THOMSON, JAMES (1700–48), poet. A Scottish minister's son, he studied at Edinburgh University, but left for London in 1725, and published his first major poem, *Winter*, the following year. It was immediately successful and enduringly influential, helping to develop the vogue for the picturesque. Other seasons followed, the four being collected in 1730. A member of the 'patriot' court of FREDERICK, Prince of Wales, in the late 1730s, Thomson also wrote a 'patriotic' poem *Liberty*, and composed the words to *Rule Britannia*, set to music by Thomas ARNE in 1740.

THOMSON, SIR JOSEPH JOHN (1856–1940), physicist. Thomson studied physical sciences in his native Manchester and mathematics at Cambridge, where he conducted research under Lord Rayleigh (*see* STRUTT, JOHN WILLIAM) at the university's Cavendish Laboratory. From the early 1880s he explored James Clerk MAXWELL's theories of electrodynamics, developed the idea that atoms were 'vortex-rings' in the electromagnetic ether and worked on electrical discharge in gases. In 1884 he became Director of the Cavendish Laboratory and in 1895, following the physicist Wilhelm Röntgen's production of X-rays, began experiments on the controversial phenomena of cathode-rays. By 1897 he had amassed evidence in support of British physicists' claim that cathode-rays were negatively charged material 'corpuscles' (later called electrons). More sensationally, he had shown that the corpuscle was 1,800 times lighter than a hydrogen atom and was a constitutent part of all atoms. By 1900 he was celebrated as the discoverer of the electron. During the next decades, he researched the scattering of X-rays by electrons and the positive rays of electrical discharge, which led to evidence for two isotopes of neon. Thomson won the 1906 Nobel Prize for Physics, taught seven Nobel Prize winners and turned the Cavendish Laboratory into the world centre for physics research. His discovery of the electron shattered the idea of the indivisible atom and paved the way for modern atomic and nuclear physics.

THOMSON, ROY (1st Baron Thomson of Fleet) (1894–1976), newspaper proprietor. Like his compatriot and fellow press proprietor Lord Beaverbrook (*see* AITKEN, MAXWELL), Thomson made his fortune in Canada in the radio and newspaper industry before moving to Britain. His first acquisition was *The Scotsman* newspaper in 1951. He followed this by buying Scottish Television, capturing the first franchise to broadcast independent television in Scotland, which he described as 'a licence to print money'. In 1959 he moved into the first division of media ownership when he bought Lord Kemsley's (*see* BERRY, WILLIAM and JAMES) chain of newspapers, which included the *Sunday Times*. In 1967 he also bought the loss-making but prestigious newspaper *The Times*. As a proprietor he was unusually non-interventionist, leaving all the editorial policy to his editors, though he was active on the commercial side. In 1962, for instance, the *Sunday Times* brought out the first colour supplement, boosting sales and advertising revenue considerably. Despite using his considerable personal fortune to invest in the papers, he was never able to stem the losses at *The Times*. After his death in 1976, his son, Kenneth, managed no better, and the two titles were sold to Rupert MURDOCH in 1981.

THOMSON, SIR WILLIAM (1st Baron Kelvin of Largs) (1824–1907), physicist. The son of a Professor of Mathematics, Thomson was born in Belfast and raised in Glasgow. He studied at Glasgow and Cambridge, where he excelled in mathematics. In 1846, after studying experimental physics in Paris, he became Professor of Natural Philosophy at Glasgow, where he established one of the most prestigious physics laboratories in Britain.

In the early 1840s he used the French mathematician J. B. J. Fourier's theory of heat distribution in a solid to construct a mathematical theory of electrostatic phenomena, and this led to his important analogy (1847) between the mathematical description of the forces in an electrostatic field and the forces in an incompressible elastic solid. His work challenged 'action-at-a-distance' theories of electrical and magnetic forces and linked Michael FARADAY's qualitative conception of the field and James Clerk MAXWELL's mathematical theory of electromagnetism. From the mid 1850s, Thomson was involved in submarine telegraphy. His theories of telegraphic signalling, his high-precision telegraphic instruments (notably his mirror-galvanometer) and his work as a consultant to several telegraph companies played a crucial part in the success of the Atlantic telegraphs. He was also a major figure in the establishment of electrical standards such as the Ohm.

In the late 1840s he promulgated the term 'energy' in the modern sense and used the theory of the French physicist Sadi Carnot on reversible heat engines in the construction of his absolute or Kelvin scale of temperature. His reconciliation of Carnot's theory and the new mechanical theory of heat led him to formulate, in 1851, the second law of thermodynamics, which states that in a non-constrained system energy tends towards a state of maximum dissipation. Thomson drew extensively upon the work on thermodynamics of such physicists as James JOULE and Rudolf Clausius, who had independently formulated the second law in 1850. In the 1850s Thomson collaborated with Joule on many experiments concerning heat, notably the cooling of expanding gases (the 'Joule–Thomson effect'). From the 1850s Thomson's energy conceptions dominated his work and he sought to make the study of physics the study of energy and its transformations. He used his work on heat to predict the 'heat death' of the universe and to criticize Charles DARWIN's work: in the late 1860s he calculated the earth's age from a thermodynamic model of its cooling and concluded that it was far too young for evolution by natural selection to have taken place.

By the 1880s Thomson was recognized as the doyen of British physics, a leading expert in mathematics and engineering, and was making a fortune from his electrical and navigational instruments. He played a crucial role in forging the new nineteenth-century subject of physics.

THORFINN I SKULL-SPLITTER (?–960), Earl of Orkney (c. 950–60). A son of TORF EINAR, Thorfinn appears to have shared rule over the Orkneys with the family of the last Viking King of York, ERIC BLOODAXE. Little is known about his life. He was succeeded by three sons, each of whom married Eric's daughter RAGNHILD.

THORFINN THE MIGHTY, Earl of Orkney (c. 1020–65). A son of SIGURD THE STOUT, he eventually emerged as sole ruler over the Scandinavian settlement of Orkney having supplanted his brother EINAR FALSEMOUTH and shared power with various other relatives. Like his father, he was a conqueror, securing control over the Shetlands, re-establishing lordship over the Hebrides and, according to saga tradition, launching a raid against England. Having been brought up at the court of MAEL COLUIM II, King of the Scots, he was more cosmopolitan than his predecessors; he later converted to Christianity and went on a pilgrimage to Rome, during which he visited the courts of the kings of Germany and Norway. His reign also saw the establishment of a bishopric in Orkney and a rudimentary governmental administration. *See also* THOROLF.

THORKELL THE TALL (?–c. 1023), Viking war leader. He was active in England during the last years of ETHELRED II THE UNREADY's reign and the first years of CNUT's. His army caused extensive disruption from 1009 to 1012. He went over to Ethelred's side in 1013, then back to Cnut's, and was subsequently made Earl of East Anglia and regent in England and Denmark. He was briefly banished in 1021.

THORNE, WILLIAM JAMES (WILL) (1857–1946), trade-union leader. Born in Birmingham, Thorne started work aged six in a ropeworks. In 1881 he moved to London with his wife and children, settling on a job at the Beckton gasworks. Already a radical, Thorne joined the Social Democratic Federation in 1884. Through it not only did he meet most of the leading socialists of the day but Eleanor Marx AVELING helped to improve his ability to read and write. In 1889 he was a founder of the National Union of Gas Workers and General Labourers, becoming its paid General Secretary. The success of the union, not least in obtaining the eight-hour day, was a major impetus to the explosion of 'New Unionism' after 1889. The union grew to embrace unskilled and semi-skilled workers from many industries and, following a merger with two smaller unions, it became the National Union of General and Municipal Workers in 1924. Thorne remained General Secretary until 1934. He was also Labour MP for West Ham South (1906–18) and Plaistow (1918–45), but he had an undistinguished career as a politician and moved increasingly to the right of the party.

THORNHILL, SIR JAMES (1675–1734), painter. The only major English decorative painter at a time when the field was dominated by foreign craftsmen, Thornhill's education was paid for by his great-uncle, the physician Thomas SYDENHAM, who placed him as a pupil with the King's painter, Thomas Highmore, then sent him to travel on the continent. His style, in the Baroque *trompe l'oeil* tradition, was influenced by that of Antonio VERRIO. Thornhill was made history-painter to GEORGE I in 1718: his more prestigious commissions included work at St Paul's Cathedral, Hampton Court, Blenheim Palace and Greenwich Hospital. His work fell out of fashion in the 1720s. His daughter married William HOGARTH.

THORNTON, ALICE (née Wandesford) (1626–1707), autobiographer. From a Yorks. gentry family, her father was Christopher Wandesford (1592–1640); she was brought up in Ireland while he was Lord Deputy and close associate of Thomas WENTWORTH. The Irish rebellion (1641) made her family refugees, condemned to poverty for their Royalism, but Alice married William Thornton, a Parliamentarian Yorks. gentleman. She was a widow from 1668 and wrote an extensive autobiography, structured by her strong Anglican piety.

THORNTON, JOHN (1720–90) and his son **HENRY** (1760–1815), Evangelicals. John Thornton inherited a large fortune and while continuing his family's involvement in trade and banking spent over £2,000 a year on charitable works. He was opposed to Methodism but bought advowsons to reward deserving clergymen with no patrons and set up a charitable trust to continue the work after his death. With Jonas HANWAY, he helped to found the Marine Society, whose object was to help the poor and the nation simultaneously by recruiting poor boys for apprenticeship at sea. Henry Thornton had a successful career as a banker and was elected MP for Southwark in 1782 despite refusing to buy votes. He was a close friend of WILBERFORCE, who shared his house in Clapham for several years in the 1790s, giving rise to the name, the Clapham Sect, for this group of wealthy Evangelical Anglicans (*see also* VENN, HENRY and JOHN). Henry Thornton joined with Wilberforce in opposing the slave trade; he was to the fore in encouraging the development of a black colony in Sierra Leone, and served as President of the Sierra Leone Co. He was also among the founders of several missionary societies, including the British and Foreign Bible Society of which he was first Treasurer in 1804.

THOROLF (*fl.* mid eleventh century), Bishop of Orkney. The first bishop to be appointed by the earls of Orkney, Thorolf was made Bishop after THORFINN THE MIGHTY had visited Rome in *c.* 1050. The ruins of Thorolf's church have been located at the Brough of Birsay.

THORPE, JEREMY (1929–), politician and party leader. Oxford-educated, he served as MP for North Devon (1959–79), achieving the leadership, aged only 38, at a time when the first Liberal revival under GRIMOND appeared to have faltered in the 1966 General Election with a fall in the overall Liberal vote. Thorpe was unable to prevent a halving of the party's representation at the 1970 General Election, from 12 to 6 seats, but presided over another mini-revival in 1972–3 as Edward HEATH's government ran out of steam, securing five by-election victories. In the Feb. 1974 General Election under his leadership the party obtained its largest share of the vote since 1928 and 14 seats. Allegations of his relationship with a male model Norman Scott and other bizarre accusations forced his resignation as leader in May 1976. Although subsequently acquitted of any criminal activity, his political career never recovered.

THORSTEIN THE RED (*c.* 855–75), Scandinavian warrior. The son of OLAF THE WHITE, King of Dublin, and AUD THE DEEP-MINDED, daughter of KETIL FLATNOSE, he was associated with SIGURD THE MIGHTY, Earl of Orkney, in the conquest of Caithness and parts of Sutherland. When he was killed by the Scots in 875, his family's fortunes collapsed, and his mother and other relatives left Britain to play an important role in the colonization of Iceland.

THRALE, HESTER LYNCH (née Salusbury) (1741–1821), writer. A member of a Caernarvons. gentry family, she contributed to the *St James's Chronicle* as a girl and continued to write poems, diaries and letters, later collected as *Thraliana* (1942). In 1761 she made an arranged marriage with a wealthy brewer, Henry Thrale. The couple became friendly with Samuel JOHNSON, who went to live with them in Streatham. When Henry Thrale died in 1781 Mrs Thrale fell in love with an Italian musician, Gabriel Piozzi, and married him (1784), to the horror of Johnson and her eldest daughter. The Piozzis moved to Italy but later returned to London, where Mrs Thrale published her *Anecdotes of the late Samuel Johnson* (1786).

THRING, EDWARD (1821–87), educationalist. As Headmaster of Uppingham from 1853, he transformed it from a poorly run grammar school into a public school of the first rank. He was, along with Samuel BUTLER and Thomas ARNOLD, one of the small band of progressive headmasters whose work arrested the decline of the public schools and made them into distinctive institutions with the aim of preparing pupils for the political and industrial élites.

THROCKMORTON, FRANCIS (1554–84), conspirator. An Oxford-educated gentleman from Worcs., he became a zealous Roman Catholic and was then involved in plots to invade England and place MARY QUEEN OF SCOTS on the throne. Betrayed to the government (*see* BRUNO, GIORDANO), he was tortured and executed. The revelation of his plot was the final straw in the break-down of diplomatic relations between England and Spain.

THROCKMORTON, SIR GEORGE (before 1489–1552), politician. From a Warwicks. knightly family, he was one of the few MPs to oppose HENRY

VIII's efforts to have his marriage to CATHERINE OF ARAGON annulled, though he gathered others at the Queen's Head tavern, Fleet Street. He repeated forthright criticisms to Henry's face, and although twice arrested during the 1530s, the second time because his brother Michael was a servant of Reginald POLE, he survived and prospered. Some of his numerous descendants were fiercely Protestant (e.g. his son, Nicholas THROCKMORTON, and grandson, Job THROCKMORTON) while others (like his grandson, Francis THROCKMORTON) remained Catholics.

THROCKMORTON, JOB (1545–1601), writer. Grandson of Sir George THROCKMORTON, Oxford-educated and a talented and witty Puritan, he may have been the main author of the pseudonymously produced Puritan pamphlets by 'Martin Marprelate', which satirically attacked leading churchmen in 1588–9 (but *see also* CARLETON, GEORGE). Older Puritans were shocked, and investigations by a furious government incidentally provided much material for anti-Puritan repression. Throckmorton was arrested but, although it was clear that some pamphlets had been printed at his house, nothing could be proved.

THROCKMORTON, NICHOLAS (1515–71), politician and diplomat. Son of Sir George THROCKMORTON, he served Henry FITZROY, Duke of Richmond, and later Catherine PARR, and followed her fervent evangelicalism. He became a soldier. Although he alerted MARY I to EDWARD VI's death, he was involved in Thomas WYATT's rebellion (1554); he conducted such a vigorous defence that the jury acquitted him, to government fury. He fled to France after further involvement in conspiracy (1556). Under ELIZABETH I he was a successful Ambassador to France, vigorously supporting Huguenot interests, but was disgraced for intrigues around the marital future of MARY QUEEN OF SCOTS (1569).

THURBRAND THE HOLD (?–1019). A member of an Anglo-Danish family settled near York, Thurbrand killed Earl UHTRED of Northumbria in 1016, apparently with the agreement of King CNUT. Thurbrand was himself killed by Uhtred's son EALDRED in 1019. The feud between these two northern English families continued through most of the eleventh century.

THURFERTH (?–934), nobleman. A Scandinavian war leader who is known to have submitted to EDWARD THE ELDER in 917. He was able to retain his lands around Northampton and his title into the reign of King ATHELSTAN. His career illustrates the compromises with existing power structures which were made as the kings of Wessex advanced their power northwards.

THURLOE, JOHN (1616–68), administrator. A lawyer, he entered Parliamentary service in 1645 for peace negotiations with CHARLES I, and after diplomatic service became secretary to the Council of State (1652), also sitting repeatedly as an MP. His low public profile belied his importance in foreign and domestic policy and in intelligence-gathering; his career predictably ended with the Restoration. His papers remain an invaluable resource.

THURSO, 1ST VISCOUNT *see* SINCLAIR, ARCHIBALD

THURSTAN (?–1140), Archbishop of York. Many Archbishops of York championed the independence of their see against the claims of Canterbury to a primacy over the whole of Britain but none more successfully than Thurstan. Appointed Archbishop in 1114, chiefly thanks to his administrative work for HENRY I, he finally got the Pope to decide in York's favour in 1126. He inspired the Yorks. army that defeated DAVID I's invading army at the Battle of the Standard (near Northallerton, Yorks.) (1138). The abbeys of Fountains and Rievaulx (both Yorks.) testify to his role as an important patron of the Cistercians.

THYNNE, THOMAS (3rd Viscount Weymouth and 1st Marquess of Bath) (1734–96), politician. A grandson of Robert WALPOLE's opponent John CARTERET, he inherited the Longleat estate in Wilts. in 1751 and employed Lancelot 'Capability' BROWN to redesign the gardens. A member of the Bedford (*see* RUSSELL, JOHN) faction, he held several political posts including that of Secretary of State (1768–70), when he impressed GEORGE III with his repression of the WILKES riots. Wilkes planned to impeach him after Weymouth's letter ordering the use of force against the demonstrators gathered around the King's Bench prison, where Wilkes was then held, was intercepted (several people had been killed by troops, the so-called St George's Field massacre), but Weymouth had Wilkes expelled from the House on the grounds of seditious libel. He resigned from the government with Gower (*see* LEVESON-GOWER, GRANVILLE) in 1779.

TICHBORNE, CHIDIOCK (?1558–86), Catholic conspirator. From an ancient Hants. family, he was one of the principal actors in Anthony BABINGTON's plot to murder ELIZABETH I. Arrested, he was executed with a brutality which prompted Elizabeth to order speedier deaths in future. Some moving verses of his are said to have been written on his last night of life, together with a letter to his wife.

TIGERNÁN UA RUAIRC (O'ROURKE) (?–1172), King of Bréifne. He was DIARMAIT MAC

MURCHADHA's rival for control of Meath. In 1166 he drove Diarmait overseas in revenge for the abduction of his wife DERBFORGAILL 14 years earlier. This set off the train of events leading to the English invasion of Ireland. Still fighting for Meath, he was killed by Hugh de LACY, and his head sent to HENRY II.

TILLETT, BEN (1860–1943), trade-union leader and politician. Tillett, who was born in Bristol, spent his childhood in great poverty before joining the Royal Navy at 13 and then, at 16, the merchant marine. Hardly able to read and write until he was 17, he became a voracious reader when he moved to London as a young man, working in the East End docks as a casual labourer and as a warehouseman in a tea company. He also came into contact both with socialist ideas, especially those of the Social Democratic Federation, and with organized trade unionism. In 1887 he became Secretary of the Tea Operatives' and General Labourers' Association, a union with a precarious existence. In 1889 he led, alongside Tom MANN and John BURNS, the great dockers' strike for 6d. an hour basic rate. At its height, the strike involved 100,000 dockside workers and won widespread sympathy both in Britain and internationally. It also established Tillett, a powerful and effective orator, as a national figure within the labour movement and transformed the tea operatives' union into the Dock, Wharf, Riverside and General Labourers' Union of Great Britain and Ireland. Tillett became General Secretary, remaining so until 1922 when the union merged with others into the Transport and General Workers' Union. That was also the high point of Tillett's career. He continued as an active trade-union leader, and was associated with the militant and socialist wing of unionism in the 'great unrest' trade-union militancy of 1911–13. He swung behind supporting the First World War and was MP for North Salford (1917–24 and 1929–31).

TILLEY, VESTA (originally Matilda Alice Powles) (1864–1952), entertainer and male impersonator. The daughter of a Notts. music-hall manager, she first appeared in male costume at the age of four. As an adult performer she was known as 'the London Idol' and, because of her intense patriotism, 'England's greatest recruiting sergeant'. Her songs included *The Army of Today's All Right, Jolly Good Luck to the Girl Who Loves a Sailor* and *Burlington Bertie*. She appeared in the first Royal Command Performance in 1912 and, when she retired from the stage in 1920, took 17 curtain calls, and Ellen TERRY presented her with a tribute signed by two million. In 1890 she married a music-hall owner, (Sir) Walter de Frece, who later became an MP.

TILLOTSON, JOHN (1630–94), Archbishop of Canterbury (1691–4). Son of a prosperous clothworker, he was elected a fellow of Clare Hall, Cambridge, in 1651 but was ejected 10 years later as a Presbyterian following the Act of Uniformity. He was influenced by Cambridge Platonists, such as William CHILLINGWORTH and John WILKINS (*see also* WHICHCOTE, BENJAMIN), and became a leading Latitudinarian, a proponent of doctrinal flexibility and ecclesiastical broadmindedness. By 1675 he had been appointed Dean of Canterbury and a Prebendary of St Paul's. In 1691 he succeeded SANCROFT as Archbishop of Canterbury, having carried out the duties of the office since 1689, when Sancroft, as a Non-juror (one who had refused to take the oaths recognizing WILLIAM III and MARY II as rightful monarchs), was disabled from acting. Tillotson's 'His Commandments Are Not Grievous' is said to have remained the most popular sermon throughout the eighteenth century.

TINDAL, MATTHEW (1657–1733), theologian. He changed his religious position several times during his career, briefly converting to Catholicism in 1687, but caused most controversy for his attacks on High Church Anglicanism and defence of Deism. His work *The Rights of the Christian Church* (1706) denied that the priesthood had any divinely sanctioned authority, causing the government to burn the book alongside SACHEVERELL's sermon in 1710 in an attempt to show even-handedness. *Christianity as Old as the Creation* (1730) became the standard text of Deism. It argued that the true Christian faith rested on rationally discovered laws of the universe rather than on any particular revelation, leading to accusations of atheism.

TIPPETT, SIR MICHAEL (1905–98), composer. Having studied at the Royal College of Music, Tippett conducted and directed a number of small operatic societies throughout the 1930s, organizing music at a work-camp for unemployed miners in North Yorks. and becoming involved in communist and later pacifist politics. He completed his first major work, the oratorio *A Child of our Time,* in 1941, although it was not performed until 1944, a few months after his release from a spell in Wormwood Scrubs prison as a conscientious objector. His first symphony (1945) expressed his Jungian convictions and belief that music should symbolize a 'dramatic flow in the psyche'. And though he composed lighter pieces, particularly his *Suite for the Birthday of Prince Charles* (1948), the culmination of this dramatic genre came with the composition of his first and most popular opera *A Midsummer Marriage* (1952). Tippett's most remarkable work, *The Vision of St Augustine* (1965), is highly textured, a style that was further developed in his succeeding works, including the operas *The Knot Garden* (1970) and *The Ice Break* (1976) and his third and fourth symphonies, the third remarkable for its contrasting romantic ideals with twentieth-century nihilism and the threat of nuclear annihilation, in the idiom of the Blues.

TIPTOFT, JOHN (2nd Baron Tiptoft, 4th Earl of Worcester) (1427–70), politician and scholar. Unusually for an aristocrat of the time, he studied at Oxford and later at Padua University and built up a splendid library with real connoisseurship. He was created Earl of Worcester in 1449, becoming Treasurer of England in 1452 aged 24. From 1457 to 1461 he travelled abroad, initially with an embassy to the Pope and then going on pilgrimage to the Holy Land: this gave him an acquaintance with humanism quite exceptional among contemporary English politicians. He rallied to EDWARD IV's regime, earning great unpopularity for the severity with which he carried out his office of Constable of England (1462–7, 1470). He was Deputy Lieutenant of Ireland from 1465 and crossed there in 1467 to preside over Parliament, continuing his judicial savagery against the rebel earls of Kildare and Desmond and their followers. He was unable to escape with Edward IV in the readeption, and was tried and executed for high treason. He made translations from Latin, including Cicero's *De Amicitia*, and won high praise for his work and abilities from CAXTON.

TIPU SULTAN (Fateh Ali Tipu) (*c.* 1751–99), ruler and Sultan of Mysore in south central India. His father, HYDER ALI, ensured that his son was taught European military and administrative skills by French officers. Tipu took a leading part in his father's campaigns from the 1770s and in Feb. 1782 defeated the British at the Battle of Coleroon River, overwhelming enemy forces of 1,900 with just 400 French soldiers. On succeeding his father in Dec. 1782 he followed his wishes and negotiated a treaty with the British by which they recognized him as Sultan of Mysore. In 1789 Tipu attacked the adjacent British protectorate of Travancore; the resulting war ended in 1791 with humiliating defeat and the annexation by the East India Co. of half of Tipu's sultanate. Tipu sought revenge by allying himself with revolutionary France but he now faced the revitalized company army under CORNWALLIS and Arthur WELLESLEY and the last of the Mysore Wars ended with Tipu's death defending his capital of Seringapatam and the division of his territories between the East India Co. and its allies.

TITMUSS, RICHARD (1907–73), historian. Titmuss, who became 'the high priest of the welfare state', was the son of an unsuccessful farmer who later became an unsuccessful haulage contractor. He left school at 14 and worked as an office boy and insurance clerk for many years. Having never sat an examination or obtained a formal degree, Titmuss was an imaginative and tremendously hard-working self-educated man. Encouraged and stimulated by his wife, Kathleen Caston Miller, he gave form to his interest in social and political issues with his book *Poverty and Population* (1938), which caught the immediate attention of liberal intellectuals and politicians, including the ROWNTREES, the CADBURYS and Harold MACMILLAN. *Problems of Social Policy* (1950) proved influential as an official history of social policy in Britain and important as a defence of welfare and social justice. Titmuss was appointed to the chair of social administration at the London School of Economics in 1950 and his last book, *The Gift Relationship: From Human Blood to Social Policy* (1970), was a study of the role of altruism in modern society.

TIZARD, SIR HENRY (1885–1959), scientist and civil servant. Educated at Oxford, a pilot in the Royal Flying Corps (1915–17), Tizard joined the Ministry of Munitions, and this determined him on a career in the administration of applied science. He became Secretary of the Department of Scientific Industrial Research (1920–9) and then Rector of Imperial College (1929–42), a post he held in conjunction with the chairmanship of a number of important Air Ministry committees, encouraging the development of the jet engine, radar and research into the atomic bomb. In the 1930s Tizard quarrelled bitterly with LINDEMANN, Winston CHURCHILL's scientific adviser, over the control and direction of applied research, and when Churchill became Prime Minister in May 1940 Tizard resigned from his committees. His major contribution during the war was leading a special technical assistance mission to the United States in the summer of 1940, which allowed some areas of the American defence industry to leap an entire generation of research. With the election of a Labour government in 1945 Tizard returned to chair key scientific committees; he established the Woomera rocket range in Australia, and dispersed scientific effort throughout the British Commonwealth. Tizard's flair was not for original research; his genius lay in recognizing this quality in others and making sure Civil Service mandarins did not obstruct their schemes.

TOD, ISABELLA (1836–96) feminist. Scots-born but Belfast-based, she was active in the campaign against the Contagious Diseases Act (*see* BUTLER, JOSEPHINE) and a lifelong temperance advocate. She fought for women's education, establishing the Belfast Ladies' Institute to train middle-class women to earn a living, and was an active Liberal Unionist and anti-Home Rule campaigner.

TODD, ALEXANDER (Baron Todd) (1907–97), chemist. Todd studied chemistry in his native Glasgow and Frankfurt am Main and did research in Oxford. Between 1934 and 1944 he worked at the Lister Institute, London, and at Edinburgh and Manchester universities; during this period he researched vitamins B1 and E and began his wide-ranging research programme into the nucleotides, nucleosides and nucleic acids. As Cambridge University's Professor of Organic Chemistry (1944–71) he synthesized the nucleotides central to the body's energy storage processes, notably adenosine triphosphate (ATP), and helped determine the structures of deoxyribonucleic acid (DNA) and vitamin B12. Todd won the 1957 Nobel Prize for Chemistry.

TODD, RON (1927–), trade-union leader. Son of a market trader, Todd joined the Transport and General Workers' Union (TGWU) while working at the Ford Motor Co. His steady rise through the union's ranks culminated in his appointment as general secretary (1985–92). The TGWU was Britain's largest union and its support was vital to any Labour government; Todd was close to Neil KINNOCK on a number of social and economic policies, but diverged over unilateral nuclear disarmament, which he supported.

TOFTS, MARY (*c.* 1701–63), hoaxer. The wife of a clothier in Goldalming (Surrey), in 1726 she apparently gave birth to a litter of 15 rabbits and became known as 'the rabbit woman'. She claimed to have been frightened by a rabbit when working as a field-hand: it was popularly supposed that experiences women had in pregnancy might affect their unborn children, although this was an extreme case! Several leading surgeons visited her and apparently delivered more rabbits, until Sir Richard Manningham exposed the hoax. She confessed and was briefly imprisoned in Bridewell. Her claims were revived in 1752 by William WHISTON, who thought that her alleged rabbit offspring presaged the imminent millennium.

TOLAND, JOHN (1670–1722), free-thinker and editor. Rumoured to be the illegitimate son of an Irish priest, he was brought up as a Catholic, converting to Protestantism in adolescence. Educated at Glasgow, Edinburgh, Leiden and Oxford, his free thinking *Christianity not Mysterious* (1696) aroused great controversy. John LOCKE feared that Toland's rashness and excessively high opinion of himself would get him into

serious trouble but in fact he attracted the patronage, first of booksellers, then of leading Whigs. In 1698 he edited MILTON's prose works, also Algernon SIDNEY's *Discourses* and LUDLOW's *Memoirs*; in 1699 he worked on the *Memoirs* of Denzil HOLLES and the following year on HARRINGTON's *Oceana*. He defended the Act of Settlement of 1701 (which provided that upon the death of Queen ANNE, by then childless, the succession would pass to the next Protestant heir, SOPHIA, Electress of Hanover) and was one of the party sent to Hanover to present a copy of the Act to the Electress.

TOLKIEN, J(OHN) R(ONALD) R(EUEL) (1892–1973), scholar and writer. Born in South Africa, Tolkien was educated at Oxford, where he became part of the 'Inklings' literary circle (*see* LEWIS, C. S.) and was later Merton Professor of English (1945–59). In the 1920s he made his reputation as a scholar of Middle English with *A Middle-English Vocabulary* (1922) and an edition of *Sir Gawain and the Green Knight* (1925). In 1937 *The Hobbit*, based on his bedtime stories for his own children, was published. It tells of an imaginary land peopled by a reluctant hero-gnome, Bilbo Baggins, and his battle with the dragon; it was followed by the three-part *Lord of the Rings* (1954–5). The books draw on Germanic folklore and myth but also present a parable about the threat to rural England from the predator, industry, and for that reason remains a cult today.

TONE, WOLFE (THEOBALD) (1763–98), Irish rebel. He studied at Trinity College, Dublin, and the Middle Temple, London, qualifying as a barrister in Dublin in 1789. Although an Episcopalian, he supported Catholic Emancipation, publishing *An Argument on Behalf of the Catholics of Ireland* (1791). In the early 1790s he became convinced that British power in Ireland was so heavily bound up with the existing structures of privilege that Ireland could be reformed only by separation. One of the founders of the United Irishmen, when forced to leave Ireland after being detected in contact with a French agent, he visited Philadelphia and then France in 1795 to solicit an invasion of Ireland. He joined the French army and, in Dec. 1796, accompanied Hoche's abortive invasion expedition. After the failure of the Irish rebellion, he returned with a much smaller force in Sept. 1798 and was captured. He was tried before a British military court and sentenced to death for treason, but committed suicide before execution. His journals and papers were published by his wife and son and form the basis of his subsequent high reputation; they show a charming and articulate personality (though also something of an adventurer). Tone has been seen as the ideal Irish nationalist by many nationalists (some holding views far removed from Tone's Enlightenment scepticism) and his grave at Bodenstown (Co. Kildare) is a place of pilgrimage for numerous competing varieties of Irish republicanism.

TOPCLIFFE, RICHARD (1531–1604), persecutor. A Yorks. gentleman who entered the service of Princess Elizabeth (later ELIZABETH I) *c*. 1557, he was active against the northern earls' rebellion in 1569 (*see* NEVILLE, CHARLES; PERCY, THOMAS), and was three times an MP; his prominence came after 1581 legislation against Roman Catholic recusants. He embarked on an enthusiastic career of investigating recusants, displaying gratuitous sadism in interrogation which occasionally aroused official unease and earned him widespread dislike.

TORF EINAR (EINAR I) (?–*c*. 900), Earl of Orkney. A son of ROGNVALD OF MOER and the next historically significant earl after SIGURD THE MIGHTY, Torf appears to have spent most of his life fighting against further Viking attacks from Norway. The next important earl was THORFINN I SKULL-SPLITTER.

TORRINGTON, 1ST VISCOUNT *see* BYNG, GEORGE

TOSTIG (*c*. 1030–66), Earl of Northumbria (1055–66). The third son of Earl GODWINE of Wessex, his appointment to the earldom of Northumbria in 1055, in contravention of the claims of the family of Earl SIWARD, seemed to cement the dominance of Godwine's sons over the English kingdom. Tostig, however, was unpopular and provoked a rebellion within his earldom in 1065; when his brother HAROLD II did not support him militarily, he went into exile and joined Harold's enemies. Harold became King soon after; Tostig was killed alongside HARALD HARDRAADA, King of Norway, at the Battle of Stamfordbridge (Yorks.).

TOWNSHEND, CHARLES (2nd Viscount Townshend) (1675–1738), politician. A childhood friend of Robert WALPOLE, whose sister he married, he became the future Prime Minister's close ally. Taking his seat in the Lords in 1697, Townshend supported the Junto Whigs, and helped negotiate the parliamentary union with Scotland of 1707 and the Barrier Treaties of 1709–15, which provided the Dutch with protection against French attack and Britain with Dutch troops against a Jacobite rebellion. When Sunderland (*see* SPENCER, CHARLES) and James STANHOPE persuaded GEORGE I to dismiss him in 1717, Walpole also resigned, and the two harried the ministry. Returned to office in 1720 and becoming Secretary of State in 1721,

Townshend pursued an aggressive foreign policy; in 1725 he abandoned an agreement with Austria and Spain in favour of a new alliance system, the League of Hanover with France and Prussia. Having tried and failed to jettison the more pacific Newcastle (*see* PELHAM-HOLLES, THOMAS), he resigned in 1730. A keen agricultural improver, he was nicknamed Turnip Townshend.

TOWNSHEND, CHARLES (1725–67), politician. Scion of an influential Whig family, he held a series of second-rank offices under the PELHAMS, PITT THE ELDER, Bute (*see* STUART, JOHN) and George GRENVILLE. Chancellor of the Exchequer in the ministry of Chatham (as Pitt became) and its most powerful representative in the Commons, he had the task of reconciling the British desire to tax the American colonies with American opposition. He justified his proposed system of 'Townshend duties' in a 'champagne' speech (so called for its effervescent quality), earning himself the sobriquet Champagne Charlie Townshend. The legislation applied customs duties to a range of goods upon their importation into America, including lead, paper, glass, painters' colours and tea. It was expected that some £40,000 a year would be raised, which was to be used to pay royal governors and certain officials (previously dependent on colonial assemblies for their salaries) and to support the expense of troops. Seen as part of a plan to strengthen British authority, the duties provoked a colonial campaign of, first, non-importation and then non-exportation. By the time that American reaction was apparent, however, Townshend was dead; his early demise cut short a promising career.

TOWNSHEND, SIR CHARLES (1861–1924), soldier. Son of a railway official (though heir presumptive to a marquessate), Townshend was commissioned into the Royal Marines in 1881. Forced by his relative poverty to transfer to the Indian army, he served in the Sudan (1896–8) and in South Africa (1899–1900). Returning to India in 1915 Townshend, now a Major-General, commanded the spearhead of the British advance into Mesopotamia against the Turks but was cut off in Kut on the Tigris and on 29 April 1916 was forced to surrender his 11,000 troops. Though the numbers involved were relatively small, the defeat was regarded as a major humiliation. Townshend destroyed what was left of his reputation by accepting preferential treatment from the Turks, while his men died in their thousands from starvation and disease.

TOWNSHEND, GEORGE (4th Viscount and 1st Marquess Townshend) (1724–1807), politician. In 1767 his brother Charles TOWNSHEND engineered his appointment at Lord Lieutenant of Ireland. He moved to Ireland with the mission of breaking the power of the 'undertakers', the group of Irish politicians then led by John PONSONBY who had traditionally managed the Irish Parliament for the ministry, but on their own terms (*see also* BOYLE, HENRY). Townshend initially intended to reduce the pension list, grant *habeas corpus* and establish a militia, all measures designed to appeal to Irish public opinion. He supported FLOOD's successful Octennial Act 1768, shortening the duration of Parliaments, which had until that point been required to dissolve only upon the death of the monarch, but as his drive against the practices of the Irish political elite continued he lost support. He next attempted to outmanoeuvre the 'undertakers' by creating new peerages and awarding many more pensions. In response, the Irish Commons voted their own supply Bill, rejecting the money Bill sent over by the British Privy Council. Townshend prorogued Parliament until the Commons succumbed, forcing John Ponsonby's resignation. NORTH recalled Townshend in 1772 rather than risk further antagonizing Irish politicians.

TOYNBEE, ARNOLD (1889–1975), historian. He came from a Lincs. farming family and his uncle founded the philanthropic foundation in London's East End still known as Toynbee Hall. Educated at Oxford and a tutor there until the First World War demanded his services, Toynbee was a member of the British delegation to the Paris peace conference in 1919. After briefly holding a chair in Greek at London University, he became Director of the Royal Institute of International Affairs (more usually known as Chatham House). His *A Study of History* (12 vols, 1931–51) portrayed the past as a series of repeated cycles of historical development of 'challenge and response', 'withdrawal and return'. His work is usually regarded as being rather too schematic for today's taste.

TRACY, WILLIAM (?–1530), heretic. Leading Gloucs. gentleman, an early Reformation convert, he made a will forbidding any commemoration of his soul. Amid acute political tension, conservative churchmen took this as a challenge, and the Convocation of Canterbury declared the will heretical in 1531; the Chancellor of Worcester diocese exhumed Tracy's corpse and burnt it at the stake. The Church looked foolish; Tracy's will was published as evangelical propaganda and subsequently in John FOXE's *Book of Martyrs*; many enthusiastic Protestants modelled their own wills on it. Tracy's son Richard (d. 1569) was also a Protestant activist and pamphleteer.

TRADESCANT, JOHN SENIOR and **JUNIOR**, gardeners and collectors. The elder John Tradescant (?–*c*. 1637) acted as gardener to a succession of leading figures, ending up in the service of CHARLES I; in extensive travels which included journeys to Russia and Algeria, he collected plants for study and for introduction to England, and he established a physic garden at Lambeth. His work was continued by his son John (1608–62), also royal gardener, who journeyed to Virginia looking for plants. The younger John built up a collection of natural and historical curiosities which was acquired by Elias ASHMOLE, forming the nucleus of Oxford's pioneer museum, the rather unjustly named Ashmolean. Lambeth old parish church now forms a garden museum as memorial to the Tradescants, with a re-creation of their physic garden.

TRAHERNE, THOMAS (?1637–74), writer. From humble beginnings in Herefs., he went to Oxford and became a Herefs. minister in 1657, subsequently conforming with enthusiasm to Anglicanism. He became chaplain to the prominent lawyer, Sir Orlando BRIDGEMAN in Middlesex. This uneventful career, and one publication of a controversial work in his lifetime, concealed an astonishing output of sublimely mystical prose and verse, whose piecemeal and coincidental rediscovery (one MS rescued from a burning Lancs. rubbish tip in 1967) has been one of the nineteenth century's most remarkable literary revivals.

TRAPNELL, ANNA (?–1660), prophet. Daughter of a London shipwright, she suffered Puritan spiritual turmoil before a revelation in a Baptist congregation in 1642; by 1652 she had joined the millenarian Fifth Monarchy Men. From 1654, when she supported Vavasor POWELL when he was being interrogated by the government, she publicly prophesied, her words being recorded in numerous pamphlets. Outspoken in criticizing both Oliver CROMWELL and Quakers, she was imprisoned for her itinerant preaching, but her charisma frequently preserved her from more severe persecution.

TRAVERS, WALTER (?1548–1635), churchman. Son of a Nottingham goldsmith, he was a Cambridge don until leaving for Geneva (1572). A strong admirer of the Genevan Church and consistent in refusing to conform in England, he wrote a blueprint for English Church reform, *Ecclesiasticae Disciplinae* (1574, translated by Thomas CARTWRIGHT). From 1580 he benefited from William CECIL's patronage to become lecturer at the Temple Church, London, where he clashed with Richard HOOKER. Later he taught at St Andrews, and thanks to Cecil became Provost of Trinity College, Dublin, before retiring to London.

TREE, SIR HERBERT (1853–1917), actor-manager. An acclaimed character actor (among his best-remembered parts were Falstaff, Shylock and Svengali) and half-brother of Max BEERBOHM, he took over the management of the Haymarket Theatre in 1887. With the profits from *Trilby* (1894) he built Her Majesty's Theatre, where his wife, the actress Maud Holt, was the director, and in 1904 he founded the Royal Academy of Dramatic Art (RADA) which staged the first performance of G. B. SHAW's *Pygmalion* in 1914.

TRENCHARD, HUGH ('BOOM') (1st Viscount Trenchard) (1873–1956), soldier and airman. Son of a bankrupt provincial lawyer, he received a patchy education, failed entrance exams for the navy and Woolwich and eventually secured a commission via the militia in a regiment in India. After soldiering on the North West Frontier (1893–9), Trenchard commanded a flying column in the Boer War, survived a serious wound, and served in the Southern Nigeria Regiment (1903–10) until invalided home with a serious tropical illness. Learning to fly in 1912, he transferred to the new Royal Flying Corps, where his seniority and natural authority (his voice was so loud he was nicknamed 'Boom') helped him rise rapidly to command No. 1 Wing RFC in France in 1914 and. to become Commander of the RFC in Aug. 1915 with the rank of Brigadier General. After overseeing a massive expansion in the RFC, Trenchard was appointed Chief of Air Staff, but disagreeing violently with government air policy resigned in Jan. 1918, returning to France to command the new Independent Bombing Force. Brought back as Chief of Air Staff by Winston CHURCHILL in Feb. 1919, Trenchard fought off attempts by the older services to strangle the new Royal Air Force at birth by demonstrating the utility of air power in policing parts of the Empire and in helping to prevent another war through the threat of mass bombing. Retiring from the RAF in 1929, he served as Commissioner for the Metropolitan Police (1931–5), and managed to reform the promotion system, creating an 'officer class' trained at a new police college.

TRENCHARD, JOHN (1662–1723) and **GORDON, THOMAS** (?–1750), political writers. A barrister and MP for Taunton, in his controversial *Short History of Standing Armies in England* (1698) Trenchard argued that these were incompatible with free government; in 1709 he wrote a *Natural History of Superstition*. Gordon, probably a Scot in origin, taught languages in London and took part in the Bangorian controversy, precipitated by the writings and preaching of Benjamin HOADLY, which brought him to the notice of Trenchard, whose secretary he became. From 1719 the two collaborated in producing the periodical, the *Independent Whig*, and in writing *Cato's Letters* (1720–3), which expressed 'patriot' views and were influential in America as well as Britain.

TRENT OF NOTTINGHAM, 1ST BARON *see* BOOT, JESSE

TRESHAM, SIR THOMAS (?1543–1605), architectural patron. Tresham, from an old Northants. family, was son of Sir Thomas Tresham, the last Grand Master of the English Hospitallers, and although brought up a Protestant was converted to Roman Catholicism by the Jesuits, spending seven years in gaol from 1581 for harbouring Edmund CAMPION. He was nevertheless strongly anti-Spanish, and was considered the representative figure among English Catholics by JAMES I's government. Despite imprisonment and heavy fines he remained wealthy and delighted in eccentric building, notably a triangular lodge at Rushton (Northants.), an architectural fantasy on the Trinity.

TRESILIAN, ROBERT (?–1388), royal servant. A Cornishman, he was Steward of Cornwall and was appointed a judge in 1377, becoming Chief Justice of the King's Bench in 1381. He tried and condemned the leaders of the Peasants' Revolt. As a convinced supporter of RICHARD II, he provided a very royalist definition of treason, and in consequence was charged with treason by the King's enemies (the Appellants) in 1388. He went into hiding but was caught and hanged at Tyburn.

TRESSELL, ROBERT (originally Robert Noonan) (1870–1911), author. Born in Dublin, the illegitimate son of Sir Samuel Croker, an inspector in the Royal Irish Constabulary and then magistrate, and Mary Noonan, he used the pseudonym Tressel as author of *The Ragged Trousered Philanthropists*. Between about 1890 and 1901 he lived in South Africa where he married (his wife died in 1895 of typhoid after four years of marriage), worked as a decorator and was involved with anti-British, pro-Boer Irish groups in Johannesburg. In 1901 he migrated with his infant daughter, his sister and nephew to Hastings (Sussex). It was his experiences as a skilled decorator in the building trades there and his socialist convictions that informed his novel. Probably written between 1906 and 1909, the book represents working-class life and class conflict. It was rejected by publishers in Tressell's lifetime. In increasing ill health and poverty by 1910–11, he died of bronchial pneumonia. After a number of abridged editions, the novel was finally published in full in 1955.

TREVELYAN, G(EORGE) M(ACAULAY) (1876–1962), historian. Son of historian George

Otto Trevelyan and nephew of Lord MACAULAY, he was Regius Professor at Cambridge from 1927. He published widely on British history and on the Italian Risorgimento, and also wrote the widely acclaimed *History of England* (1926), which offered the famous definition of social history as 'history with the politics left out', and *English Social History* (1944). Often seen as part of the Whig tradition of his forebears, he had a strong sense of the continuities of British history and a concern for the growth of liberal values.

TREVISA, JOHN (*c.* 1342–1402), translator. Vicar of Berkeley (Glos.), he contributed to the revival of English as a literary language with translations from Latin. Among his most successful was the translation of HIGDEN's *Polychronicon*, subsequently printed by CAXTON.

TREVITHICK, RICHARD (1771–1833), engineer. The son of a Cornish tin-mine manager, Trevithick gained experience of engineering and particularly steam engines in the local mining industry. In 1800 he built a new double-acting steam engine which, unlike James WATT's engine of 1782, used high-pressure steam (produced in his special cylindrical boiler) and eliminated the condenser, and was consequently more powerful and efficient. His engine was soon being exploited in mines, mills and ironworks and led to his invention of a compact steam engine/boiler which he used in his steam-powered vehicles. In 1801 he completed what is regarded as the first steam-powered passenger-carrying vehicle and subsequently built a steam road-carriage that carried passengers through London (1803), and a steam-powered locomotive that is considered the first successful railway locomotive (1804). Few of Trevithick's steam-powered vehicles were commercially successful, although he continued to develop his steam engine as a means of driving pumps, boats and agricultural machinery. His business went bankrupt in 1811 and he later gained and lost a fortune working his engines in Peruvian silver mines. He is seen as the 'father of railway locomotives', not least because his inventions showed that smooth iron-wheeled vehicles could be driven on iron rails.

TREVOR-ROPER, H(UGH) R(EDWALD) (Baron Dacre of Glanton) (1914–), historian. Spending all his academic career in Oxford, Trevor-Roper returned from military service to write a classic account of the last days of Hitler before he turned in 1951 to an attack on R. H. TAWNEY's account of the rise of the English gentry during the sixteenth century. His initial fire was turned on Lawrence Stone's account of the financial folly of many Tudor noblemen, which had given support to Tawney's thesis that their social inferiors had risen at their expense. Trevor-Roper went on to question Tawney's statistics, and argued that, in fact, lesser gentry and those reliant solely on agriculture suffered severely from Tudor economic fluctuations; if anyone profited, it was that section of gentry and nobility who had access to the profits of government office. His writings continued to emphasize the importance of the growing bureaucracy of European government in the sixteenth century, a time of 'general crisis', and he made an important pioneering contribution to the study of witchcraft in the period. Much of his work has been presented in the form of essays of striking elegance and wit. He was Regius Professor at Oxford from 1957, then Master of Peterhouse, Cambridge, from 1980–7, he was granted his peerage in 1979.

TRIMBLE, DAVID (1944–), Ulster politician. In the early 1970s he was prominent in Vanguard, a hard-line Unionist movement (led by former minister William Craig) which advocated an independent Protestant-dominated Northern Ireland. Part of the United Ulster Unionist Coalition's successful opposition to the Sunningdale Agreement for a power-sharing executive in Northern Ireland, Vanguard was fatally split in 1975 when Craig suggested an emergency government with the Social Democratic and Labour Party (SDLP). Trimble sided with Craig and was briefly deputy leader of his faction of Vanguard. He rejoined the Ulster Unionist Party but was relatively inactive while building up a career as a university law lecturer. In 1990 Trimble became Westminster MP for Upper Bann. He became known as a clever and articulate spokesman for a party notoriously lacking such figures. In July 1995 he supported the successful resistance of Portadown Orangemen to attempts to prevent them from marching through a Catholic area, and this contributed to his election as Ulster Unionist leader a few months later by delegates seeking a change from the passive leadership of James MOLYNEAUX. In April 1998 Trimble signed the Good Friday Agreement, despite criticism from Ian PAISLEY and sections of his own party, and after its ratification by referendum he became First Minister designate of the Northern Ireland executive. Trimble was awarded the 1998 Nobel Peace Prize jointly with John HUME; the formation of the executive was delayed, however, by Sinn Féin demands that it should receive ministerial positions without prior decommissioning of arms by the Irish Republican Army (IRA). Trimble did become First Minister but he continued to face dissent within his own party in the delicate negotiatons over the decommissioning of IRA arms.

TRIMMER, SARAH (née Kirby) (1741–1810), writer and pioneer of Sunday schools. The daughter of an artist who was appointed to teach perspective to the young GEORGE III, Sarah received a pious and bookish upbringing. At 21 she married James Trimmer, who owned several brickfields, and had 12 children. Encouraged by the example of Mrs BARBAULD, she began to publish writing for children. Her five-volume *Sacred History* (1782–4) was intended to instruct children in Christianity. She also wrote the series *New and Comprehensive Lessons*, which aimed to educate very young children by combining pictures with minimal text. Her *History of the Robins*, much reprinted into the twentieth century, was intended to discourage cruelty to animals. She pioneered Sunday schools in Brentford (her efforts being recognized by a visit from the King and Queen), and published an account of these schools and other charities which women might foster in her *Oeconomy of Charity* (1787). Her periodical, the *Family Magazine* (1788–9), aimed to encourage thrift and decency among the working classes.

TROLLOPE, ANTHONY (1815–82), novelist. Alhough remembered today for his novels, Trollope was a successful senior civil servant in the Post Office, responsible for the institution of the pillar box. He retired in 1867, stood unsuccessfully for Parliament as a Liberal and edited the *St Paul's Magazine* in which several of his novels were serialized. He wrote 47 novels and 16 other books, with sales sometimes in excess of 100,000. He is best remembered for his portrayal of the lives of the professional and landed classes in the six *Chronicles of Barsetshire* (1855–67) and the six 'Palliser' novels (1864–80). Although modest in his literary claims, regarding himself more as a craftsman than an artist, he was a great realist, a master of humour and pathos, and a penetrating observer of the Victorian class system.

TUCHET, JAMES (7th Baron Audley) (1462 or 1463–97), rebel. An impoverished nobleman, he joined the tax rebellion begun in Cornwall by Michael JOSEPH AN GOF and Thomas Flamank. The rebels were defeated on 13 June 1497 at Blackheath by Giles, Lord Daubeney. Joseph, Flamank and Audley were executed.

TUCHET, MERVYN (2nd Earl of Castlehaven) (1585–1631), subject of scandal. He was beheaded for homosexual acts and for raping his second wife. The charges, which caused a major sensation, may have been fabricated by the malice of his wife, who herself had an evil reputation, and judicial prejudice may have been aroused by his Roman Catholicism.

TUCKER, JOSIAH (1712–99), writer on economics. Son of a farmer and educated at Oxford, he became successively a curate in Bristol, domestic chaplain to Bishop Joseph BUTLER, Prebendary of Bristol (1756) and Dean of Gloucester (1758). He wrote essays on controversial topics such as gin and naturalization and *Elements of Commerce* (1755) for the instruction of the Prince of Wales (the future GEORGE III). In the 1770s he advocated allowing the American colonists their independence, on the ground that no special commercial advantage derived from their colonial status.

TUCKWELL, GERTRUDE (1861–1951), trade-union leader. Daughter of Christian socialist parents and niece of Emma PATERSON, she was brought up in a radical feminist family, followed her aunt into the Women's Trade Union League and succeeded her as President in 1905. She was a firm Labour Party supporter and a tireless activist for the improvement of women's wages and working conditions.

TUDOR, EDMUND (13th [1st Tudor] Earl of Richmond) (*c.* 1430–56), dynast. Eldest son of Owen TUDOR and CATHERINE OF VALOIS. He was created Earl of Richmond in 1452, when he was formally declared legitimate. He spent most of his short career in Wales, dying at Carmarthen, but is chiefly important for his marriage to Lady Margaret BEAUFORT in 1455, which gave their son (the future HENRY VII) a mother with limitless ambition and a significant amount of royal blood.

TUDOR, JASPER (16th [1st Tudor] Earl of Pembroke, 3rd [1st Tudor] Duke of Bedford) (*c.* 1431–95), nobleman. Younger son of Owen TUDOR and CATHERINE OF VALOIS, created Earl of Pembroke in 1452. He was a firm supporter of the Lancastrian cause throughout the Wars of the Roses, first in Wales until his defeat at Mortimer's Cross (Herefs.) in 1461, and subsequently as the companion-in-exile of his nephew, Henry Tudor (*see* HENRY VII). In 1485 he was rewarded for his loyal service by being made Duke of Bedford. Henry's esteem for him was no doubt increased by the fact that he had no legitimate children who might be competitors for the throne.

TUDOR, OWEN (OWAIN AP MAREDUDD AP TEWDWR) (?–1461), courtier. A Welshman attached to the household of HENRY V's widowed Queen, CATHERINE OF VALOIS, he married her, in secret, in *c.* 1428. In the end HENRY VI accepted his mother's shockingly low-born husband, who in the Wars of the Roses became a loyal Lancastrian. He was captured at the Battle of Mortimer's Cross and beheaded on the orders of the Earl of March (later EDWARD IV). According to a contemporary chronicle 'when the collar of his red velvet doublet was ripped off, he said, "This head shall lay upon the stock [i.e. block] that once lay in Queen Catherine's lap."' As father of Edmund TUDOR and grandfather of HENRY VII he was the real founder of the Tudor claims to political power in England.

TULL, JETHRO (1674–1741), agricultural improver. Educated at Oxford and Gray's Inn, he turned to farming in Berks. and Oxon., and *c*. 1701 invented a seed drill. In 1714, building on his observations on the continent, he developed a horse-drawn hoe to pulverize the soil. In 1733 he publicized his inventions and ideas in *Horse-Hoeing Husbandry*. He opposed the use of manures and crop rotations, believing that plants could be nourished only by tiny particles, which he called atoms. Seed drills were only slowly adopted until improvements were made to the early designs in the 1780s. At one time hailed as a hero of the agricultural revolution, Tull's contribution is now seen as marginal.

TUNSTALL, CUTHBERT (1474–1559), churchman and mathematician. A noted humanist who studied at Cambridge and Padua, he became Bishop of London in 1522 (in which capacity he snubbed William TYNDALE's proposal for biblical translation) and of Durham in 1530. Within the limits of safety he championed religious conservatism, but found it impossible to sustain his position under EDWARD VI, being imprisoned from 1551 (using the time to write a book on the Eucharist). Restored to Durham by MARY I, he stayed aloof from persecution; he was deprived once more by ELIZABETH I. He wrote a textbook on mathematics (1522).

TURGESIUS (?–845), Viking chieftain. Along with IVAR THE BONELESS and OLAF THE WHITE, he was one of the most prominent chieftains in the early Viking raids on Ireland. A twelfth-century source credits him not only with the founding of Dublin but also with seeking to conquer all Ireland. Early documents record only his defeat and death at the hands of the King of the Uí Néill.

TURING, ALAN (1912–54), computer pioneer. Turing studied mathematics at Cambridge and by the late 1930s had developed the concept of the 'Turing machine', an idealized computer which could be programmed to equal human beings in handling intelligent operations and which suggested that certain mathematical problems were insoluble by automatic machines. During the Second World War he worked on cracking the German naval Enigma code at Bletchley Park (Bucks.). He implemented his pioneering theoretical ideas on computing in the Automatic Computing Engine at the National Physical Laboratory (1945–8) and on the Manchester Automatic Digital Machine (1950–4). He devoted much of his career to the problem of whether machines can think. He committed suicide following a prosecution for homosexuality.

TURLOCH O BRIEN (TOIRRDELBACH UA BRIAIN) (?–1086), King of Munster. A member of the ruling kindred of Munster descended from BRIAN BORUMA, he was politically active from 1031, and fought a long war against his uncle, King Donchadd, eventually gaining control of Munster in 1063 with the aid of DIARMIT MAC MAÍL NA MBÓ of Leinster. After Diarmit's death in 1072, he forcibly established his own domination over Leinster, Connacht, Meath and Dublin. The divisions among the northern Irish rulers made him effectively King of all Ireland until his death.

TURNER, J(OSEPH) M(ALLORD) W(ILLIAM) (1775–1851), landscape painter. The son of a Covent Garden barber, Turner's precocious artistic talent gave him admittance to the Royal Academy Schools at the age of 14. His early work was mainly in watercolour; he moved to oil painting in 1796. While on his extensive travels, both on the continent and in Britain, he sketched incessantly. Turner's topographical and landscape style had many different aspects, but he came to be associated particularly with the romantic grandeur of nature and with historical events within grand settings. His work became ever more concerned with light, often acquiring an almost abstract quality, for example, *Snowstorm: Hannibal Crossing the Alps* (1812) or the late *Rain, Steam and Speed* (1844). He moved in and out of favour during his lifetime, especially when the detailed, studied style of the Pre-Raphaelites came to prominence; RUSKIN, however, championed him in *Modern Painters* (1843). Turner bequeathed most of his works to the nation, but they were often scandalously treated and only received their permanent home in 1987. By then his reputation had stabilized as probably the greatest native British artist.

TURNER, WILLIAM (*c*. 1520–68), botanist and churchman. Studying at Cambridge, his medical interests led to a book on plants and their medicinal uses (1538); in the 1540s his strong evangelicalism took him into European exile, bringing useful scientific contacts. Predictably he was promoted under EDWARD VI to become Dean of Wells (1550, although he was not ordained until 1552), before renewed travels in Europe under MARY I. He was restored as Dean under ELIZABETH I, but deprived in 1564 for nonconformity. His writings included Protestant polemic, a pioneering ornithological treatise (1544) and a large-scale herbal (1551–68).

TURPIN, RICHARD (DICK) (1705–39), highwayman. An Essex butcher turned thief, smuggler and a member of 'Gregory's gang' of housebreakers, he became a highwayman of legendary effrontery, working around the south of London. Escaping arrest for the theft of a horse, he fled to York, where he was captured, tried and executed. In subsequent retellings, his flight was conflated with the ride of 'Swift Nick' from London to York in 1676 to establish an alibi for robbery. The romanticization of Turpin's story included the naming of his horse Black Bess.

TUSSER, THOMAS (?1524–80), agricultural writer. From Essex, he was a chorister before going to Cambridge and serving as a musician to William Paget, Lord PAGET. He became a farmer in Suffolk, where he experimented with crop innovations and turned his experiences into verse in *A Hundreth Good Pointes of Husbandrie* (1557). Its mixture of advice on domestic and agricultural matters and good manners was a great success, and as *Five Hundreth Points of Good Husbandrie* (1574) it became a best-seller. His later careers as a Norwich choirman, then Essex farmer, were marred by ill health and debt.

TWEEDDALE, MARQUESS OF, 2ND and **4TH** *see* HAY, JOHN

TWEEDSMUIR, 1ST BARON *see* BUCHAN, JOHN

TYE, CHRISTOPHER (*c.* 1500–73), composer. He worked in music in Cambridge and Ely as well as in royal service, and from 1561 became a country parson in Cambs. He moved on from Latin choral music to writing for the Protestant liturgy, including a rather improbable verse version of the Book of Acts (1553), which has spawned various hymn-tunes, including the best-known tune to *While Shepherds Watched their Flocks by Night*, 'Winchester Old'.

TYERS, JONATHAN (?–1767), impresario. In 1728 he leased Spring Gardens in Vauxhall, which had been open to the public since the Restoration, refashioning the gardens and opening them to paying visitors in 1732. FREDERICK, Prince of Wales, attended the opening of Vauxhall Gardens as a fashionable place of entertainment; HOGARTH advised on decoration and designed the silver tickets given to regular visitors. Tyers introduced orchestral music in 1735 and singers in 1745. Despite its many imitators, principally RANELAGH Gardens in Chelsea, Tyers succeeded in retaining Vauxhall Gardens' attraction for an upmarket clientele. His family continued to own and manage the gardens until 1821. Vauxhall was finally closed, and the land sold for building, in 1859.

TYLER, WAT *see* essay on page 793

TYLOR, SIR EDWARD (1832–1917), anthropologist. Tylor worked in his father's foundry for several years before touring America, where he developed interests in archaeology and anthropology. His reputation as a founder of British anthropology rests on his *Researches into the Early History of Mankind* (1865) and *Primitive Culture* (1871), in which he argued that human culture develops along evolutionary principles. He held that primitive beliefs (for example, magic) which lingered on in modern culture were survivals of earlier phases in the development of mankind. He also believed that all religions were based on animism, a primitive belief in supernatural entities, and that religions progressed from this stage to polytheism and then to monotheism. He spent his later years at Oxford University where he was appointed Keeper of the University Museum (1883) and first Professor of Anthropology (1896).

TYNAN, KENNETH PEACOCK (1927–80), drama critic. The illegitimate son of a wealthy Warrington (Lancs.) businessman, Tynan lived up to his middle name, loving to shock, but his passion for the theatre was substantial and influential. Appointed theatre critic of the *Observer* in 1954 after a brief spell as an actor and director, he was part of the revival of English drama, promoting work by such playwrights as John OSBORNE, John Arden and Arnold WESKER. It was Tynan who effectively established Brecht's reputation in Britain, and, returning from the USA in 1960 where he had been drama critic of the *New Yorker*, he rejoined the *Observer*, became literary manager of the National Theatre company (1963–9) and led the campaign for the reform of British censorship laws. He celebrated this victory in *Oh Calcutta!* (1969 New York, 1970 London), when the ending of the Lord Chamberlain's powers meant that the nudes *did* move. Tynan also achieved notoriety as the first person to say 'fuck' on British television. His book on bullfighting, *Bull Fever* (1955), is considered very fine by that spectacle's *aficionados*.

TYNDALE, WILLIAM (?1494–1536), Bible translator. Oxford-educated, he taught in his native Gloucs. before embarking on the first large-scale English biblical translation since the Lollard translation of the 1390s. His unauthorized initiative quickly earned disapproval and suspicion from the Church hierarchy, recently thrown on the defensive by Martin LUTHER's revolt, so Tyndale settled in Germany and began publishing his work in 1525. In 1535 he was arrested by the imperial authorities and executed near Brussels. His incomplete translation lies behind all subsequent English biblical texts.

TYLER, WAT (?–1381)
Rebel

A man of unknown and humble origin who for five days, as leader of the Kentish section of the Peasants' Revolt, the most significant popular rebellion in English history, terrified the ruling class. His eloquence and intelligence were acknowledged in the words of those who feared him, but no other words than those written by his enemies survive. For Thomas WALSINGHAM he was 'the idol of the peasants'.

The poor resented the government's attempts (see EDWARD III) to hold down wages and prevent them from exploiting the post Black Death labour shortage. When the Hundred Years War went badly the government was accused of inefficiency and corruption. The last straw came with the unjust poll tax of 1380, levied at a flat rate per head ('poll' meaning 'head'), and with the stringent measures taken during the early summer of 1381 to enforce its collection, particularly in south-east England. Riots and demonstrations turned into revolt. On 10 June the Kentish rebels, led by Tyler, captured Canterbury, seized the sheriff and made a bonfire of all his records. Then Essex and Kentish rebels marched on London. According to John GOWER, 'savage hordes approached the city like waves of the sea and entered it by violence ... at their head a peasant captain urged the madmen on. With cruel eagerness for slaughter, he shouted in the ears of the rabble, "Burn! kill!".'

The young King RICHARD II took shelter in the Tower of London with his advisers. On 13 June the Kentishmen crossed London Bridge. Property belonging to the men whom they blamed for government failure and injustice, 'the traitors' as they called them, was attacked; JOHN OF GAUNT's Savoy Palace was burned down. On 14 June Richard met the rebels at Mile End, hoping that this would give those in the Tower a chance to escape. According to the anonymous eye-witness account of the *Anonimalle Chronicle*, Wat petitioned the King for the abolition of serfdom, for fair rents and for permission to deal with traitors. Having been given authority to seize all who could be proved to be traitors, and with the King in effect a hostage, Wat led his men to the Tower. They dragged out chief ministers, the Chancellor, Simon SUDBURY, and the treasurer, Sir Robert Hales, and cut off their heads. Relying on the King's promises, many of the rebels went home, but others continued with killing and looting, foreigners suffering especially badly. Next day Richard announced that all should meet him at Smithfield. According to the *Anonimalle Chronicle*, Tyler 'approached the King with great confidence mounted on a little horse so that the people could see him. Holding in his hand a dagger he dismounted, half bent his knee and took the King by the hand, shaking his arm forcefully and roughly, and saying, "Brother be of good cheer for in the next fortnight you will have 40,000 more of the common people with you and we shall be good companions".' When the King asked why they would not go home, Tyler 'answered with a great oath that neither he nor his fellows would leave until they had got the charter they wanted'. He then spelt out the terms: no outlawry, no lordship, the surplus wealth of the Church to be divided among parishioners. When Richard replied soothingly, Wat 'sent for a jug of water to rinse his mouth, because of the great heat he felt. He rinsed out his mouth in a very rude and villainous manner before the King.' Angry words with a member of the King's household who called him 'the greatest thief and robber in all Kent' led to a scuffle with William WALWORTH, the lord mayor, in which Wat was badly wounded. 'His horse carried him some fourscore paces while he called upon the people to avenge him, then he fell to the ground half dead.' At this moment, as some of the rebels began to bend their bows, Richard rode forward and commanded the people to meet him at Clerkenwell. While they obeyed the King whom they trusted, Tyler was carried to the nearby hospital of St Bartholomew's. Walworth had him removed, beheaded and his head put on a pole. 'And when the King saw the head he had it brought near him to subdue the commons, and thanked the lord mayor. And when the commons saw that their leader, Wat Tyler, was dead in this fashion they fell to the ground like beaten men, imploring the King for mercy for their misdeeds. And the King benevolently granted them mercy.' According to Jack STRAW's confession, Tyler had aimed at being King of Kent. Others said he had planned to kill all lawyers or kill the King and burn London to the ground. All that is sure is that with his death the revolt collapsed.

R. B. Dobson, The Peasants' Revolt of 1381 (1983)

TYNDALL, JOHN (1820–93), physicist. Born in Ireland, Tyndall worked as a civil engineer and surveyor before teaching mathematics in England and pursuing doctoral research in physics and mathematics in Germany. He was lecturer in physics (1853–67) at and Superintendent (1867–87) of the Royal Institution, London, where he became a leading expositor, through lectures, articles in periodicals and textbooks, of natural philosophy. His diverse scientific researches included diamagnetism, the absorption and transmission of radiation, the theory of glaciers, acoustics and the evidence for the spontaneous generation of life. A close friend of Thomas HUXLEY, he was a supporter of Charles DARWIN's theory of natural selection, a campaigner for scientific and technical education and a firm believer in the scientist as a preeminent intellectual and cultural authority. His apparent support for materialism and pantheism, his attack on the evidence for miracles and his views on the conservation of energy provoked fierce controversies.

TYRCONNEL, EARL OF, 1ST see O'DONNELL, RORY; **3RD** *see* TALBOT, RICHARD

TYRONE, EARL OF, 1ST *see* O'NEILL, CON BACAGH; **3RD** see O'NEILL, HUGH

TYRRELL, SIR JAMES (?–1502), royal servant. From a Suffolk gentry family, he was a loyal Yorkist said to have been employed to murder the Princes in the Tower (*see* EDWARD V; RICHARD III). HENRY VII retained him in royal service, making him Lieutenant of Guisnes Castle (Calais), but in 1501 arrested him on suspicion of conspiring with Edmund de la POLE, Earl of Suffolk, who had fled to Guisnes in 1499, and who now fled abroad again. Before Tyrrell's execution he is supposed to have confessed; the story is recounted in Sir Thomas MORE's *History of Richard III*.

U

UDALL (OR UVEDALE), JOHN (*c.* 1540–92), writer and scholar. Udall was a Puritan Cambridge don who wrote bitterly against episcopal government, was suspected of involvement in the Marprelate Tracts (*see* THROCKMORTON, JOB) and died in prison just after a sentence of death for seditious writing had been commuted. He published sermons, and there appeared posthumously a biblical commentary and a respected Hebrew grammar and dictionary.

UDALL, NICHOLAS (*c.* 1505–56), writer and dramatist. From Hants., he became first an Oxford don and then a schoolmaster, becoming headmaster of Eton (until dismissed in 1541 on charges of embezzlement and sex with a pupil; his notorious penchant for flogging did not form part of the indictment). He wrote interludes for court ceremony, regularly produced classical plays and published translations of classical works; of his own plays only the comedy *Ralph Roister Doister* survives. An officially sponsored diatribe against the Catholic western rebels of 1549 is now attributed to the Devon evangelical activist, Philip Nichols.

UHTRED (?–1016), Earl of Northumbria (*c.* 1006–16). A member of the house of Bamburgh and a great warrior, notable for his military achievements against the Scots, but most renowned for the way in which his murder by another Northumbrian nobleman, THURBRAND THE HOLD, whom Uhtred himself had vowed to kill, began a feud that lasted until after 1066. The feud, an exceptionally bloody one, is described in a source written at Durham in *c.* 1100, and starkly illustrates the role of family and local rivalry in medieval politics. King CNUT replaced him as Earl in Yorkshire with ERIC OF HLATHIR. Uhtred's brother EADULF CADEL gained Bamburgh.

UHTRED OF BAMBURGH (?–*c.* 949), Ealdorman. The son of EADULF OF BAMBURGH, Uhtred succeeded his brother EALDRED OF BAMBURGH in 930. Having for a time been driven out with Ealdred after 910 by the Scandinavian King of York RAGNALL, Uhtred, like his brother before him, subsequently acknowledged the overlordship of King ATHELSTAN. His acquisition of land in the Midlands shows how this previously independent Northumbrian noble family was sucked in by the growing power of the southern-based English kings.

ULSTER, EARL OF, 1ST *see* DE LACEY II, HUGH; **3RD** *see* BURGH, RICHARD DE; **4TH** *see* BURGH, WILLIAM DE; **5TH** *see* LIONEL OF ANTWERP; **7TH** *see* MORTIMER, ROGER

UNTON, HENRY (*c.* 1558–96), administrator. An Oxon. gentleman whose career was advanced by family friendships with Robert DUDLEY, Earl of Leicester, Francis WALSINGHAM and Sir Christopher HATTON, he was Ambassador to France 1591–2 and 1595–6, becoming a friend of King Henry IV. Clumsy parliamentary speeches in 1593 about proposed taxation earned him the Queen's fury, and he was lucky to get a second embassy; he died of illness in Henri's camp. His narrative memorial portrait in the National Portrait Gallery has a unique depiction of a wedding masque.

URIEN (*fl.* late sixth century), King of Rheged. An important and powerful King, Urien's kingdom of Rheged was most likely centred on modern-day Carlisle (Cumb.). According to the *Historia Brittonum* of NENNIUS, Urien led a successful British coalition against expansion by the Angles based in Bernicia.

USSHER, JAMES (1581–1656), churchman and historian. From the small Protestant Old English gentry community in the Pale of Dublin, he was one of the first graduates of Trinity College, Dublin, and rapidly became the leading figure in the Church of Ireland (Bishop of Meath in 1620 and Archbishop of Armagh from 1625), championing strict Calvinism and discreetly obstructing interference in the Irish Church from Archbishop LAUD. Stranded in England by the 1641 Irish rebellion, he was much respected by Puritans and honoured during the Interregnum. His formidable historical scholarship is perhaps unfairly remembered for his calculation of the date of Creation as about 9.00 a.m. on 26 October 4004 BC; his chronology is still to be found in some conservative editions of the Bible.

UVEDALE, JOHN *see* UDALL, JOHN

V

VALENCE, AYMER DE (10th Earl of Pembroke) (?–1324), royal servant and soldier. A son of HENRY III's half-brother, he became one of EDWARD I's most trusted captains against both Welsh and Scots, and was recognized as Earl in 1307. His quarrel with EDWARD II's favourite, Piers GAVESTON, caused him to lead the Ordainers but, when Gaveston was executed by Warwick (*see* BEAUCHAMP, GUY) in 1312 (in breach of promises given by Pembroke), he returned to the King's service, mostly taking a moderate line in the ensuing political struggles; in consequence historians used to credit him with the leadership of a construct which they called the 'middle party'.

VALERA, CIPRIANO DE (*c.* 1632–*c.* 1606), writer. A Spanish Observant friar, he converted to Protestantism and fled to Geneva in 1557, then to England in 1558. He became a Cambridge don and then a preacher and schoolmaster in London. From 1588 he was engaged in producing a stream of Protestant literature for the Spanish market, including an entire Bible in Spanish, Calvin's *Institutes* and Calvin's 1559 catechism (*see* CALVIN, JOHN).

VALOIS, DAME NINETTE DE *see* DE VALOIS, NINETTE

VAN DER FAES, PIETER *see* LELY, SIR PETER

VAN DYCK, SIR ANTHONY (1599–1641), artist. Born in Antwerp, where he worked in Rubens's studio, he lived briefly in England (1620–1) and then in Italy (1621–5), moving back to England as court painter to CHARLES I in 1632. He was immensely successful there. His works defined the magnificence (and inward-looking nature) of the King's court on the eve of the Civil Wars, and managed tactfully to disguise the shortness of the King's stature; they also introduced a new poetic, almost melancholic, portrait style and aesthetic, able to show, in Edmund WALLER's words, 'the art and power of a face'. Van Dyck's pupil William Dobson (1610–46) continued the style of portraiture to document the court at the King's capital of Oxford during the First Civil War (1642–6), and the look and dress of Van Dyck's sitters were revived as elements in Thomas GAINSBOROUGH's style a century later.

VANBRUGH, SIR JOHN (1664–1726), playwright and architect. The son of a sugar baker, he was a man of diverse talents: employed as an army officer in the 1680s, he began to write for the theatre. His earliest play, *The Relapse* (1696), which memorably caricatured the fashionable fop in the character of Lord Foppington, was also one of his most successful: throughout the eighteenth century, it was frequently rewritten for up-to-the-minute effect, once by David GARRICK. This play and Vanbrugh's *The Provok'd Wife* (1697) were among those attacked in 1698 by Jeremy COLLIER in his *Short View of the Immorality and Profaneness of the English Stage*.

Vanbrugh had earlier travelled to France to study architecture and, in an age when this was in transition from being a gentlemanly accomplishment to something more like a profession, was also employed to design several buildings. Sometimes characterized as Baroque, these were notable for their flamboyant magnificence. Castle Howard (1700) and Blenheim Palace (1705) were his most ambitious designs. He may also have trained his cousin, the Irish architect Edward Lovett PEARCE. He also built, owned and managed the Queen's Theatre in the Haymarket, London, Britain's first opera house, which opened in 1705.

VANE, HENRY (1613–62), politician and writer. 'The younger', in distinction to his father Sir Henry Vane (1589–1655), a Parliamentarian politician, he was Oxford-educated and travelled in Europe before emigrating to Massachusetts to escape England's episcopal Church and monarchical government. Though made Governor in 1636, he returned to be elected to the Long Parliament. He opposed doctrinaire Presbyterianism but also objected to Oliver CROMWELL's authoritarianism. CHARLES II arrested him and executed him for treason. His mystical writings are deliberately, almost pathologically, obscure.

VANSITTART, SIR ROBERT (1881–1957), diplomat. From a distinguished though latterly financially embarrassed family, Vansittart abandoned his original idea of a literary career and entered the Diplomatic Service, though he never stopped writing. Before the First World War, he worked under Eyre CROWE, whose prescience he greatly admired, and in 1919 attended the Paris peace conference. Private secretary in sequence to Lord CURZON, Stanley BALDWIN and Ramsay MACDONALD, he got the top job at the Foreign Office, Permanent Under-Secretary, in 1930.

For the following nine years he prophesied war and was prepared to consider any course that would avoid what he feared most: a German knock-out blow on an unprepared Britain. He encouraged the Hoare–Laval Pact (1935), a secret agreement that in effect carved up Abyssinia to appease Italy. When the details were known the pact was repudiated by both French and British governments, and Laval and Hoare both resigned. Vansittart's days were numbered: already unpopular for his lavish lifestyle and his tortuous literary memoranda, the appointment of Neville CHAMBERLAIN signalled that his Cassandra-like warnings of German aggression and barbarism would not be considered helpful in the search for a new initiative with (or appeasement of) Germany, and he was effectively kicked upstairs to be Chief Diplomatic Adviser (1939–41). After the war he called for a harsh peace for Germany, and ended his days warning of the dangers of the Soviet Union and encouraging the creation of the (western) European Community as a bulwark against Soviet expansion.

VAUGHAN, HENRY (1622–95), poet. From an old Welsh family of Powys, hence his proudly chosen nickname 'the Silurist', he was Oxford-educated and became a doctor in Wales. A spiritual crisis led to his series of mystical poems, some being translations from other writers, beginning with *Silex Scintillans* (1650, 1655).

VAUGHAN, HERBERT (1832–1903), Roman Catholic prelate and Cardinal. He entered the priesthood in 1854, became Bishop of Salford in 1872, succeeded Henry MANNING as Archbishop of Westminster in 1892, and received a cardinal's hat the year after. He founded St Joseph's College, Mill Hill, was owner of the periodicals *The Tablet* and the *Dublin Review*, and commissioned the building of Westminster Cathedral in 1895.

VAUGHAN WILLIAMS, RALPH (1872–1958), composer. A leading figure in the twentieth-century revival of English music, Vaughan Williams began to compose when he was only six. Though he was powerfully influenced by foreign composers, particularly Bruch and Ravel, with whom he studied (1897 and 1908), he rejected imitation and sought rather to renew native sources: this led him to English folksong, and Elizabethan and Jacobean music, as shown in his *Fantasia on a Theme by Thomas Tallis* (*see* TALLIS,

THOMAS). An assiduous archivist, he collected over 800 songs and variants and selected the tunes for *The English Hymnal* (1906). He was also a dedicated teacher of composition at the Royal College of Music and a gifted conductor of the Bach Choir.

VENN, HENRY (1725–97) and his son **JOHN** (1759–1813), Evangelical ministers. Henry, a clergyman's son, became a friend of John THORNTON when curate at Clapham and gained a large personal following. His work as vicar of Huddersfield (1759–71) and rector of Yelling (Hunts.) (1771–97) was characterized by particular attention to the poor of his parishes. John was also curate of Clapham, from 1792, where his church became the focus of the Clapham Sect, which included WILBERFORCE. John was a prominent campaigner against slavery and was also involved in founding missionary societies with Henry THORNTON.

VENNER, THOMAS (?–1661), radical millenarian. Venner was a wine cooper by trade but after the Restoration led a Fifth Monarchist congregation, believing that the Saints must seize civil power so that Christ might return. On 6 Jan. 1661, he led Venner's rising, a group of about 50, to recover the regicides' heads on display at Westminster Hall and on London bridge. Two days skirmishing with the militia led to about 20 losses on each side; Venner and 16 others were executed for murder and high treason on 19 Jan. Although less radical Dissenters condemned the uprising, the affair precipitated a variety of repressive moves. About 100 Fifth Monarchists and 4,000 Quakers were imprisoned, and the Crown argued that the incident demonstrated the need for a permanent military force and for new legislation restricting Dissenting activity. These needs were met in part by the establishment of the Guards and subsequently by the passage of the Clarendon Code (*see* HYDE, CHARLES, 1st Earl of Clarendon).

VERE, ROBERT DE (9th Earl of Oxford, 1st Marquess of Dublin, 1st Duke of Ireland) (1362–92), courtier. The friendship of this feckless young man with RICHARD II alarmed many, particularly when the adolescent King extravagantly created him Marquess of Dublin in 1385, then Duke of Ireland in 1386, titles held by no one else before or since. De Vere commanded the army with which Richard hoped to resist the Appellants but was defeated at the Battle of Radcot Bridge (Oxon.) on 20 Dec. 1387 and was forced to flee the country. In his absence, he was condemned to death for treason; four years later he died in exile.

VEREKER, JOHN (6th Viscount Gort) (1886–1946), soldier. Eldest son of an aristocratic Irish family, he was educated at Harrow and

Sandhurst, and was commissioned into the Grenadier Guards. Serving on the Western Front in the First World War, Gort frequently displayed near suicidal bravery, rose to command a brigade, and was appointed to the Distinguished Service Order (DSO) and awarded the Military Cross and Victoria Cross. By 1937 Gort was the youngest ever Chief of the Imperial General Staff but lacked the requisite experience and maturity. Appointed to command the British Expeditionary Force in 1939, Gort clashed bitterly with Secretary for War Leslie Hoare Belisha, devoting precious time to an elaborate plot that secured Belisha's dismissal in Jan. 1940. Ignoring his Corps Commanders' misgivings, on 10 May 1940 Gort responded to the German assault by advancing into Belgium, and, when cut off by the German advance through the Ardennes, rapidly lost control of the battle, suffered a nervous collapse and on 31 May was ordered back to England. Gort was subsequently kept out of operations and given command first of Gibraltar and then of Malta, where his physical courage and obsession with minutiae could be put to good use.

VERGIL (OR VIRGIL), POLYDORE (?1470–?1555), historian. An Italian, Vergil gained royal favour after coming to England as a papal tax collector in 1502; he stayed until 1551. His humanist scholarship had produced a pioneering work on human discoveries (1499) but HENRY VII now encouraged him to write his *Anglica Historia* (English History) (1513; published 1534, 1555). This aroused nationalist fury for dismissing the legend that Britain had been settled by Brutus, a refugee from Troy (*see* GEOFFREY OF MONMOUTH). The theory still had defenders in the seventeenth century, but common sense and Vergil eventually prevailed.

VERNEY, SIR RALPH (1613–96), letter writer. From a Bucks. knightly family, his father and brother (both Sir Edmund) were killed fighting for CHARLES I in the Civil Wars. He was married to 13-year-old Mary Blacknall in 1629 while still studying at Oxford: the marriage proved a great success, though its complexities are revealed in their correspondence, which is particularly intense during the separation caused by Ralph's exile for his Royalism (1646–8). Mary died in 1650; grief-stricken, he never remarried.

VERNON, EDWARD (1684–1757), sailor. Son of one of WILLIAM III's Secretaries of State, he entered the navy in 1700. Elected an MP in 1722, he was very much a political sailor, and active in opposition. By 1739, when the war with Spain which he had urged broke out (following accusations of Spanish atrocities made by Captain Edward JENKINS and others), Vernon was a Vice-Admiral and was given the West Indian command. His attack on Spanish settlements was initially very successful: his capture of Porto Bello 'with six ships only' was immensely popular in Britain, but a subsequent attempt on Cartagena foundered in quarrels with the army commander. He later commanded the Channel Fleet, and successfully prevented French reinforcements reaching the Jacobite forces during the 1745 rebellion. His fiery and controversial nature was a hindrance to achieving further command. Vernon was nicknamed Grog from the grogram cloth cloak he wore; the name was also applied to the watered-down rum ration that he introduced.

VERRIO, ANTONIO (*c.* 1639–1707), painter. Born in Italy, he came to England from France in 1671. CHARLES II commissioned him to decorate the interiors of the State rooms at Windsor Castle, co-ordinating with the carvings of Grinling GIBBONS. Verrio painted a series of illusionistic vistas on the walls and ceilings but most of his work at Windsor was destroyed by GEORGE III. Verrio opposed the 1688 Revolution and subsequently his main patron was the Earl of Exeter, for whom he worked at Burghley House near Stamford (Lincs.). He reconciled himself to working for WILLIAM III about 1700 when he painted the King's Staircase at Hampton Court with an allegory of the Protestant succession. His most significant protégé was THORNHILL.

VERTUE, GEORGE (1684–1756), engraver and antiquarian. The son of a tailor, he established a reputation as a portrait engraver, particularly of the works of KNELLER, and engraved plates for over 500 books including Rapin's *History of England*. Elected to the Society of Antiquaries in 1717 he was made its official engraver, reinforcing his existing interest in engraving items of historical interest found on travels with aristocratic patrons such as Edward HARLEY, 2nd Earl of Oxford. Vertue's other employers included FREDERICK, Prince of Wales, who commissioned him to catalogue his and other royal collections and who purchased many of his works. Frederick and Vertue planned an academy and drawing school together but the scheme was abandoned when Frederick died. Over the last 40 years of his life Vertue made notes for *Musaeum*, a history of the fine arts in England. After his death his notes were purchased and used for *Anecdotes of Painting in England* by Horace WALPOLE, although Walpole's work bore little relation to Vertue's plan.

VERTUE, WILLIAM (*c.* 1465–1527), mason and architect. From a family of master masons, he worked on completing their project at Westminster Abbey, the Henry VII Chapel, and St George's

Chapel, Windsor; he was also involved in completing King's College Chapel, Cambridge (*but see also* WASTELL, WILLIAM). From 1510 he was royal master mason, and designed Corpus Christi College, Oxford, St Peter's Chapel in the Tower of London and work at Eton College; several other major contemporary buildings appear also to be his.

VERULAM, 1ST BARON *see* BACON, FRANCIS, essay on page 47

VICIOUS, SID (1957–79), musician *see* ROTTEN, JOHNNY

VICKERS, THOMAS (1833–1915) and **ALBERT** (1838–1919), manufacturers. Born in Sheffield (Yorks.), where their father Edward (1804–97) established his own steel-making business, the Vickers brothers had a technical education in Germany. Both joined the business in 1854, with Tom the technologist and Albert the business strategist, and under their guidance Vickers became one of Sheffield's leading steel-makers. By the end of the century they had steered the firm towards the profitable trade of armaments manufacture, its success ranking them alongside Armstrong as Britain's leading arsenal makers. Tom resigned as Chairman in 1909, succeeded by Albert, who retired in 1918 when Vickers was Britain's fourth largest company in capital size. The difficulties of the 1920s demonstrated that over-reliance on armaments was a dangerous strategy, and the company eventually merged with its rival Armstrongs. It has however remained at the centre of Britian's heavy and defence industries.

VICKY *see* WEISZ, VICTOR

VICTORIA *see* essay on pages 800–01

VILLIERS, BARBARA (Countess of Castlemaine and Duchess of Cleveland) (1641–1709), royal mistress. The niece of George VILLIERS, Duke of Buckingham, and married to Roger Palmer, she met CHARLES II in exile and accompanied him back to London in 1660, where she was established as his mistress for most of the 1660s. She caused controversy because of the 'rents' which the King authorized her to collect from Irish office-holders, and for her conversion to Catholicism. Her influence waned after 1669 but the King gave her the royal palace of Nonsuch (Surrey), which she dismantled and sold off. Increasingly marginalized following affairs with John CHURCHILL and William WYCHERLEY, she moved to France in 1677, returning to England shortly before Charles's death.

VILLIERS, GEORGE (4th Duke of Buckingham) *see* essay on page 802

VILLIERS, GEORGE (5th [2nd Villiers] Duke of Buckingham) (1628–87), politician. Brought up in the royal family after the assassination of his father George VILLIERS, 4th Duke of Buckingham, he served in the Royalist army during the First English Civil War (1642–6) and in CHARLES II's council in exile. He married the daughter of General Thomas FAIRFAX, to whom Villiers's confiscated estates had been assigned. Recovering these at the Restoration in 1660, he became one of the richest men in England (though he was to die in debt), a prominent courtier and Privy Councillor. However, he also maintained throughout his career radical connections apparently first contracted in the 1650s, e.g. with John WILDMAN. He helped secure the downfall of Edward HYDE, Earl of Clarendon, and was a leading figure in the Cabal ministry (*see also* BENNET, HENRY; CLIFFORD, THOMAS; COOPER, ANTHONY ASHLEY; MAITLAND, JOHN). Although not informed of the secret clauses in the Treaty of Dover in 1670 by which Charles II undertook to Louis XIV of France to restore Catholicism, he came under attack as pro-French, and was dismissed at the Commons' request. Allying himself with Anthony Ashley Cooper, Earl of Shaftesbury, he joined in the furore over the Popish Plot (1678–9), and served as patron of a radical club during the Exclusion Crisis (1679–81), although he avoided voting on the Bill which sought to exclude the Duke of York (the future JAMES II) from the royal succession. His 1671 play *The Rehearsal* satirized John DRYDEN's heroic drama; he also wrote poetry.

VINCENT, HENRY (1813–76), Chartist and temperance lecturer. A printer of humble parentage, he was drawn to politics in the 1830s and became a political missionary for the London Working Men's Association and an effective public speaker. The founder editor of the *Western Vindicator*, he was twice imprisoned for his outspoken support of the People's Charter (*see* LOVETT, WILLIAM), but subsequently moderated his opinions and enjoyed a successful career as an advocate of temperance, self-improvement and universal suffrage.

VINE, FREDERICK (1939–), geologist. Vine studied natural sciences at Cambridge University, where he researched geology under the marine geologist Drummond Matthews. In 1967 they jointly announced paleomagnetic evidence in favour of the American geophysicist H. H. Hess's explanation of continental drift by sea-floor spreading. This work informed the most sophisticated development in earth sciences, plate tectonics. Since 1970 Vine has been based at the University of East Anglia.

VINSAUF, GEOFFREY DE (*fl.* 1200), poet. Known as Anglicus, 'the Englishman', and author of *Poetria Nova*, the most influential teaching aid

continued on page 803

VICTORIA (1819–1901)
Queen of the United Kingdom of Great Britain and Ireland (1837–1901) and
Empress of India (1877–1901)

The longest-reigning monarch in British history, Alexandrina Victoria was born at Kensington Palace on 24 May 1819, the only child of GEORGE III's fourth son, the Duke of Kent, and Princess Victoria of Saxe-Coburg-Gotha. Her birth made Victoria an immediate contender in the 'unseemly race to the throne' that was occasioned when the wife of the Prince Regent, Princess Charlotte, died in childbirth in 1817, and none of the remaining 12 offspring of George III had a legitimate heir. Her father died when Victoria was eight months old and, with the succession unsecured, she had a circumscribed and lonely childhood with her protective and ambitious mother and her mother's adviser Sir John Conway, being groomed for a role which it was by no means certain that she would take. Not until 1830, when WILLIAM IV succeeded his brother George IV, was it clear that Victoria would one day be Queen. On William's death in 1837, she ascended the throne at the age of 18, vowing that although she was 'very young, and perhaps in many, though not in all things, inexperienced … I am sure, that very few have more real good will and more real desire to do what is right than I have'.

The young Queen immediately commanded the admiration of her ministers, and the contrast between her youth and the dissolute and world-weary attitude of her predecessors seemed to offer a monarchy that had fallen into contempt with the public a hope of rejuvenation and respect. Nevertheless, the early years of the reign were not easy: Victoria's youthful enthusiasm for the job was soon tempered by the insistent demands of the 'trade of sovereign' (as her uncle and close adviser in those early years, Leopold, later King of the Belgians, instructed her it was), and her inexperience and lack of judgement were manifest in such incidents as the Lady Flora HASTINGS affair. In the circumstances, Victoria's dependence on her Whig Prime Minister, Lord Melbourne (see LAMB, WILLIAM) who took a close fatherly interest in guiding his sovereign through the niceties of her constitutional position, was unsurprising. Nevertheless, Melbourne's political tutelage did not go unremarked and set the pattern throughout Victoria's reign of conflating the personal with the political while imagining that she was transcending politics – a tendency that precipitated a crisis in 1839 when it seemed to her that the conservative Sir Robert PEEL, when trying to form a Tory government, was interfering with the royal prerogative in requesting the replacement of her Whig Ladies of the Bedchamber.

In Nov. 1840, Victoria married her first cousin Prince ALBERT of Saxe-Coburg-Gotha and for the next 20 years they were inseparable. Victoria bore nine children. The portrayal of her happy domestic life did much to differentiate her reign from those of her 'wicked uncles' who had shown such aristocratic indifference to the duties of high office, and Victoria and Albert both regarded their evident sense of duty as the strongest card they had to play in sustaining the monarchy. The middle-class morality which they were seen to represent contrasted with the dynastic achievements of their descendants who were to succeed to the thrones of Germany, Russia, Sweden, Denmark, Spain, Greece, Romania, Yugoslavia and Britain, and with the visible pomp and display of monarchy which increased in inverse proportion to the monarch's declining constitutional influence.

Whereas at first Albert's constitutional role was subservient to that of his wife, as her pregnancies progressed the marriage increasingly became a constitutional as well as a domestic partnership, and in the view of the constitutional expert Walter BAGEHOT it was akin to having 'a family on the throne'. The couple's ideal of a constitutional monarchy that transcended transient political parties but exerted an independent influence on the nation was realized to a considerable extent during the years 1846–59, when no single party could command an overall majority in the Commons. The Queen thus determined the composition of several ministries, dismissing her errant Foreign Secretary, Palmerston (see TEMPLE, HENRY), in 1851, and exercising her personal choice, though her options were limited, in appointing Aberdeen (see GORDON, GEORGE) and Rosebery (see PRIMROSE, ARCHIBALD). Her working out of the role of a constitutional monarch – a question that had been endemic in British politics since 1688 – was gradually reduced as the electoral franchise was extended and the grip of party became more tenacious: she found herself powerless to prevent GLADSTONE becoming Prime Minister in 1880.

Whereas events taught Victoria that the powers of a constitutional monarch were circumscribed at home, she was adamant that 'the right of supervision and control belong[ed] to the Crown in Foreign Policy'. This led to a number of clashes with Palmerston, her independent-minded Foreign Secretary, while her strong support for British interests abroad led her to take an active and informed interest in the Crimean War (1853–6), where Britain was in alliance with Russia and France against the crumbling Ottoman empire and, later in her reign, in protecting and forwarding British imperial interests and annexations in the Sudan and South Africa.

Her inherited family connections gave her a perspective on foreign policy. Her view was coloured by concerns for the European dynasties into which her children had married, especially the German royal families, and this too led to conflict with her ministers on several occasions (for example, over Schleswig-Holstein in 1864).

In matters of social concern, Victoria was sympathetic to individual hardship, particularly if she knew the person concerned, and took an interest in a number of philanthropic enterprises, especially where the welfare of soldiers wounded in wars which she had been keen to prosecute was concerned. But she had no sympathy with organized political protest such as the Chartist movement, which was active in its demands for greater political accountability in the 1840s, nationalist demands in Ireland for land reform and later for Home Rule, or nascent socialism, all of which she regarded as examples of the populace being incited by rabble-rousers with sectional interests that were inimical to the cohesion and unity of her nation.

Albert died from typhoid fever in Dec. 1861 aged 42, and Victoria's overwhelming grief made her largely withdraw from public life for more than a decade, spending long months at Balmoral, her home in the Scottish Highlands, or at Osborne on the Isle of Wight, confining her duties to advising her ministers (largely by post) and unveiling a series of memorials to her departed husband.

This perceived dereliction of public duty – Victoria declined to open Parliament personally on more than seven occasions after Albert's death – coupled with unsubstantiated rumours about her relationship with her Scottish gillie, John Brown, led to a flurry of republicanism, but by the late 1870s the Prime Minister, Benjamin DISRAELI, had coaxed her back into public view. Although she described herself as a Liberal and was an advocate of Free Trade and religious tolerance, Victoria's greatest rapport, both personal and political, was with the Conservative Disraeli, rather than with the Liberal leader Gladstone, whose policies, particularly his advocacy of Home Rule for Ireland and vocal support for nationalist movements in the Balkans, she fervently opposed.

In 1877 Disraeli created his 'faery Queen' (as he frequently referred to Victoria) Empress of India. It was a title that delighted her and one that she used at home, as well as 'east of Suez', where its use was deemed to be appropriate. Although she never visited the subcontinent herself, she took a keen interest in Indian affairs and artefacts and formed a close association with an Indian servant, Abdul Karim, whom she elevated to be her *Munshi* (teacher) as she laboured to learn Hindi.

In the last decades of her life, Victoria resumed her political and constitutional interests with vigour, to the detriment of her somewhat wayward son and heir, EDWARD VII, who was denied access to many vital State papers until 1892. She herself was indefatigable in studying voluminous papers and corresponding with her ministers, insisting on frequent consultation. She was no less assiduous in documenting her own life in a daily journal that she had kept since the age of 13, in copious correspondence which she exchanged with her far-flung family on all matters personal and political, of great moment and of the smallest detail, and in her published *Leaves from the Journal of my Life in the Highlands* (1868), illustrated with her own watercolour sketches. By the time of her national jubilees (Golden in 1887 and Diamond in 1897), which were orchestrated to show Victoria in her roles of triumphantly surviving European monarch and head of a great and loyal Empire, the popularity of the diminutive widow dressed almost always and entirely in black was assured, and the almost wholly ceremonial role of the British monarchy was firmly established.

When Victoria died at Osborne on 22 Jan. 1901, after a reign of 63 years, she was the matriarch of European royalty, she had transformed the standing of the monarchy, and the monarch had become the single most obvious link that held together the world's greatest empire: by the 1890s one person in four on earth was a subject of Queen Victoria. Her name is synonymous with the nineteenth century in style as in achievement. After a widowhood that had lasted nearly 40 years, Victoria was buried alongside her beloved Albert at Frogmore, Windsor. One of the mourners at her funeral was her grandson Kaiser Wilhelm II of Germany, who would declare war on Britain some 13 years later in Aug. 1914.

Monica Charlot, Victoria the Young Queen (1991)
Elizabeth Longford, Victoria RI (1964)

VILLIERS, GEORGE (4th [1st Villiers] Duke of Buckingham) (1592–1628)
Politician

A Leics. gentleman whose career was built on his charm, good looks and JAMES I's love. He was introduced to the King in 1614 by the unlikely combination of ANNE OF DENMARK and Archbishop George ABBOT, backed by William HERBERT, Earl of Pembroke, who aimed to undermine James's passion for Robert CARR and thus attack the power of Carr's relatives the HOWARDS. James gave the new favourite the affectionate nickname 'Steenie', in allusion to St Stephen whom the Bible describes as having 'the face of an angel'. Soon he was made a Cupbearer (an office in the King's Privy Chamber), and in 1615 Gentleman of the Bedchamber. He was made Master of the Horse in 1616; this required his constant attendance on the King outside the palace, so in combination with his office in the royal private apartments he now had an unrivalled degree of access to James, an advantage which he exploited to the full. A barony, viscountcy and earldom followed in quick succession before he was created Marquess in 1618, rounding it off with the dukedom in 1623. He was created Lord Admiral in 1619, an office which he held until his assassination. He was not entirely incompetent in this role, promoting the building of small manoeuvrable frigates to increase the navy's effectiveness. His proclaimed commitment to reform and vigorous government was compromised by massive and blatant corruption to enrich himself and his insatiable extended family; he used his administrative abilities mainly to benefit himself. Successive politicians tried to undermine his position (including an attempt at impeachment in 1621, headed by Edward COKE) but they succeeded only in destroying their own careers. He imported his relatives virtually to monopolize office in the Bedchamber, and used this power-base to act as general broker for royal patronage and favour, building up a huge private fortune in the process; he was prominent in the sale of peerages and took a large share of the proceeds.

Buckingham recognized that too great a dependence on the aging King's favour was dangerous, and, astutely, he allied with James's son the future CHARLES I; from 1622 they were working together in government. Their first preoccupation was to move James from his inactive foreign policy, initially into close alliance with Spain. Buckingham persuaded James in 1623 to sanction an expedition with Charles to Spain; the pair travelled to Madrid in nominal disguise, to win Charles a Spanish princess as bride. While there, Buckingham quarrelled bitterly with the resident English Ambassador, John DIGBY, Earl of Bristol, beginning a long-running feud between the two men. The marriage venture caused deep apprehension in England, which turned to extravagant national celebration when Charles and Buckingham returned empty-handed; they were now determined on war with Spain. They used Parliament to press a very reluctant James into declaring war and to destroy Lionel CRANFIELD, who opposed their schemes. By the time of James's death, such bullying was eroding the King's affection for his favourite, but Buckingham was secure in the esteem of the new King – a remarkable tribute to his ability as a manipulator; once more he was made Master of the Horse, and now for the first time he was able to exclude all his main enemies from any significant role in government. Recognizing Charles's enthusiasm for Arminian clergy in the Church, he turned to promoting their interests, especially through William LAUD (who recorded an erotic dream about him in his diary). By now he had many enemies and, after renewed attacks on him in the 1625 Parliament, there was a further attempt in the 1626 Parliament, led by Thomas HOWARD, Earl of Arundel, but also by agents of his one-time promoter William Herbert, Earl of Pembroke. Efforts to silence opposition by arresting Arundel and the Earl of Bristol produced a storm of protest that this was an assault on parliamentary privilege, and Buckingham was saved only when Charles dissolved Parliament. He signalled his escape by promoting purges of his enemies from local office. War was now declared with France as well as Spain, and Buckingham led an expedition to aid the Huguenot stronghold of La Rochelle (1627). It was disastrously badly organized, and he was forced to withdraw after a siege of the Île de Rhé left half his army dead. Further attacks in the 1628 Parliament were inevitable and once more fruitless. Buckingham's power ended only when he was assassinated by a discontented army officer, John Felton, while preparing at Portsmouth for another expedition to La Rochelle. Charles was appalled at the level of national rejoicing at his death.

Roger Lockyer, Buckingham: The Life and Political Career of George Villiers, First Duke of Buckingham, 1592–1618 (1981) on the art of Latin poetry written in medieval Europe, he was referred to by CHAUCER as 'my dear and sovereign master', probably teasingly since, although Vinsauf advised the budding poet to avoid 'lofty eloquence: speak as the many, think as the few', his surviving work, such as the lament on the death of RICHARD I, suggests that he did not always follow his own precepts.

VIVES, JUAN LUIS (1492–1540), scholar. Born in Valencia, he went to Paris and the Netherlands, where he lectured at Leuven. Introduced to HENRY VIII and CATHERINE OF ARAGON on their visit to Bruges in 1521–2, he was invited to England and became a fellow of Corpus Christi College, Oxford, a new humanist foundation based on the Spanish university of Alcalá. Unhappy at the annulment proceedings of the royal marriage but infuriating both sides by his waverings, he left England for good in 1528, and published his major treatises on philosophy and education abroad.

VORTEPOR (*fl.* early sixth century), King of Dyfed. One of the British kings denounced by GILDAS as tyrant of the Demetae for laxity and corruption at the time of the invasions of Britain by the Angles and Saxons. Little is otherwise known of Vortepor. By Gildas's account, he had succeeded a more renowned father to the kingship and was an old man when Gildas wrote.

VORTIGERN, legendary British ruler. This name was given by BEDE to a British ruler said by GILDAS (who did not name him) to have invited Germanic tribesmen to fight on his behalf against the Picts and Scots, and who was overwhelmed and defeated by these newcomers. By the time of NENNIUS, many legends had developed around Vortigern's career, all concerned with weakness and treachery. The pattern of events in which he was supposedly involved is a plausible one and, if he did exist, it must have been at some time during the fifth century. The *Historia Brittonum* of Nennius mentions that CADELL succeeded him as King in Powys.

VOYSEY, C(HARLES) F(RANCIS) A(NNERSLEY) (1857–1941), architect. Son of a Yorks. clergyman who was tried for heresy (1871) for denying the existence of hell, Voysey was articled to an architect in 1874 and set up his own practice in London in 1882. During the 1880s he mainly designed wallpaper and textiles. In 1888 some of his house plans were featured in *The Architect* and a rush of commissions followed (including one from H. G. WELLS in 1908), for which he designed (often large) cottage-style houses with low-ceilinged rooms and overhanging roofs, using local materials where possible and designing details like fireplaces, hinges and locks himself. He was elected to the Art Workers' Guild in 1884: his designs for wallpaper, clocks and carpets amply fulfilled the Arts and Crafts movement's aim for high standards of craftsmanship, while educating the public to demand such standards in an industrial age of mass production.

W

WACE (*fl.* 1160), poet. A Norman court poet patronized by HENRY II, he wrote his *Roman de Brut*, a version of GEOFFREY OF MONMOUTH's *Historia Regum Britanniae*, in Anglo-Norman verse, completed by 1155, that took the story of King ARTHUR and the Round Table (a detail that first appears in Wace) to the wider world. He left unfinished his verse chronicle of the dukes of Normandy, the *Roman de Rou*, when he lost his role as the Henrician court's vernacular chronicler to Benoit de Sainte-Maure.

WADDING, LUKE (?–1657), historian. From an Old English Waterford family, he became a Franciscan friar and founded the Franciscan college of St Isidore in Rome (1625). He produced a definitive edition of St Francis (1623) and (building on Hugh MACCAGHWELL's work) of DUNS SCOTUS (1639); he wrote extensively on Franciscan history. After the Irish rebellion (1641) he was prominent in organizing the return of experienced soldiers from Europe to help the Catholic Confederates; Confederate representative in Rome, he tried to steer clear of Gaelic–English quarrels, but his background made him a prime target of O'FERRALL in the *Commentarius Rinuccinianus*.

WADE, GEORGE (1673–1748), soldier and road-builder. He embarked on a military career in 1690, ending the War of the Spanish Succession with the rank of Major General. He helped foil the Jacobite rebellion in the West Country in 1715, assisted by Ralph ALLEN, then a post office clerk, who became his protégé and married his daughter. He became MP for Bath in 1722. After successfully suppressing riots against the Malt Tax in 1725, he was appointed Commander-in-Chief in Scotland in 1726 and built a network of military roads, later extended by William ROY. In 1743 he was made Field Marshal and Commander-in-Chief in Flanders but, in failing health, could not reach agreement with his Dutch and Austrian allies, contributing to ineffective action against the French. In 1744 he returned as Commander-in-Chief to England where the next year he failed to anticipate Charles Edward STUART's invading via Carlisle rather than Newcastle and so retired in favour of Cumberland (*see* WILLIAM AUGUSTUS).

WADHAM, LADY DOROTHY (née Petre) (1534–1618), educational patron. Daughter of the long-serving Royal Secretary, Sir William Petre, himself a major benefactor of Exeter College, Oxford, she married Sir Nicholas Wadham in 1555. He was a wealthy Soms. gentleman who having studied at Oxford concentrated on farming and took no part in public affairs. After his death, probably to fulfil an agreement between them, she began preparations for an Oxford college in their names, taking a close personal interest in it, and living to see it completed in 1613. The original buildings remain remarkably unaltered.

WÆRBURH (OR WERBERGA), ST (?–*c.* 700). A daughter of King WULFHERE of Mercia who, with the encouragement of her uncle King ETHELRED, founded a number of monasteries throughout Mercia. One of many women who took an active role in the development of monasticism in the century after the conversion of the English to Christianity, she was buried at Chester.

WÆRFERTH, Bishop of Worcester (872–914 or 915). A native of Mercia recruited by ALFRED THE GREAT to assist in the development of his educational programme, Wærferth was responsible for translating Gregory the Great's *Dialogues* into Old English. A member of the King's group of court scholars, he also co-operated with his daughter ETHELFLÆD in developing fortifications within Mercia.

WAITE, TERENCE (TERRY) (1939–), theologian and hostage. A lay training adviser to the Bishop of Bristol (1964–8) and the Archbishop of Uganda, Rwanda and Burundi (1968–71), he then worked as adviser to the Archbishop of Canterbury, Dr Robert RUNCIE, from 1980 and undertook a number of diplomatic missions. In 1987, while investigating the taking of hostages in Beirut by the Islamic Jihad, he disappeared, and despite worldwide pressure he and his fellow hostages were not released until 1991.

WAKE, WILLIAM (1657–1737), Archbishop of Canterbury (1716–37). His father was an MP and diplomat and Wake established political connections early in his career, as chaplain to CHARLES II's Ambassador to France from 1682 to 1685. Wake became a chaplain to WILLIAM III and MARY II and was also their Deputy Clerk of the Closet; he held further clerical posts until appointed Archbishop of Canterbury. Wake believed in reconciliation with the Nonconformists through the reform of the Prayer Book, but was opposed to the repeal of the Test and Corporation Acts. From 1717 to 1720 he negotiated with several French clergy about the possibility of the Gallican Church declaring its independence from Rome and allying with the Church of England. Wake gained a reputation for ineffectiveness and corruption as he grew older, distributing lucrative sinecures to his family.

WAKEFIELD, GILBERT (1756–1801), theologian and radical. He initially followed in the footsteps of his Notts. clergyman father, attending Jesus College, Cambridge, where he was elected a Fellow and ordained Deacon. He served briefly as a curate in Liverpool, where he became a critic of the slave trade. He was among those influenced by controversy about the Thirty-Nine Articles of the Church of England in the early 1770s (*see also* BLACKBURNE, FRANCIS) to leave the Church. He took a teaching post at the Dissenting college, Warrington Academy, in 1779 and remained there until 1783; he then settled in Nottingham, where he sought private pupils and moved in radical circles. His *Silva Critica*, published 1789–95, sought to interpret biblical writing through classical philosophy. In 1790 he moved to London, where he produced translations of the classics and the New Testament. He also wrote against the war with Revolutionary France and against PITT THE YOUNGER's policies in general. In 1798 he wrote a reply to a loyalist tract by Richard WATSON, Bishop of Llandaff, in which he argued that the poor would lose nothing by a French invasion, also condemning the political and ecclesiastical structures in England. He was prosecuted and sentenced to two years in prison. During this period he and his family were financially supported by his friends and opposition leaders including Charles James FOX.

WALCHER (?–1080), churchman. He and his staff were murdered in 1080, victims of the ethnic tension caused by the Norman Conquest. A churchman from Liège, he was appointed Bishop of Durham by WILLIAM I THE CONQUEROR in 1071 and then given responsibility for ruling Northumbria after the English Earl, WALTHEOF, rebelled in 1075. When his foreign advisers were blamed for the death of a Northumbrian noble, he tried to negotiate but he and his followers were trapped inside the church of St Michael's, Gateshead (Co. Durham), and killed.

WALKER, JOHN (1674–1747), historian *see* CALAMY, EDMUND

WALKER, JOHN (1781–1859), chemist and inventor of the modern match. Walker's breakthrough came by accident in 1826 while he was preparing a mixture of potassium chlorate, an oxidizing agent, and black antimony sulphade, which has a low kindling temperature. By 1827 Walker was selling his matches or 'friction lights' as he called them at 100 for a shilling. His refusal to take out a patent gave the lead in match manufacture to others. But for the discovery of Walker's day book, his small but significant contribution to the industrial revolution might never have been known.

WALKER, PETER (Baron Walker of Worcester) (1932–), politician. Walker chaired the Young Conservatives from 1958 until 1960 the following year was elected MP for Worcester, which he represented until 1992. In 1965 he organized Edward HEATH's campaign for the leadership of the party, and was rewarded with the positions of Secretary of State for the Environment (1970–2) and then for Trade and Industry (1972–4). Despite being an avowed Heathite, Walker proved very useful to Margaret THATCHER as Secretary of State for Energy (1983–7), maintaining an appearance of official aloofness from the miners' strike of 1984–5 while using the media skilfully to counteract the miners and put the government's case. He ended his political career as a highly interventionist Secretary of State for Wales.

WALLACE, ALFRED RUSSEL (1823–1913), naturalist. Born to a humble Welsh family, Wallace moved to London in 1837, where he worked as a surveyor and developed interests in natural history, secularism and socialism. In 1844 he became a schoolteacher in Leicester, where he deepened his knowledge of natural history and evolutionary theories. He travelled in the Amazon (1848–52), where he collected a large number of natural historical specimens, most of which were unfortunately lost at sea. Between 1854 and 1862 he conducted an exploration of the Malay archipelago, where he travelled over 14,000 miles and gathered some 127,000 specimens. In 1855 he published a paper arguing that an evolutionary law explained how species had been introduced and geographically distributed. Three years later he used Thomas MALTHUS's work on population to formulate a theory of the evolution of species by natural selection, a theory showing how only the fittest species win the struggle for existence. He sent his work to Charles DARWIN, who, surprised that Wallace had anticipated his own theory of evolution, hastened the completion of his *On the Origin of Species* (1859). In July 1858 Wallace's and Darwin's papers on natural selection were jointly presented at the Linnaean Society in London. Later, this led to Wallace's reputation as the joint originator of the 'natural selection' theory of evolution. In 1862, when Wallace returned to England, he published interpretations of his Malayan expedition which included numerous articles attempting to strengthen the evolutionary theory, and the best-known of his many travel books, *The Malay Archipelago* (1869). He was a leading proponent of Darwinism, even though his views often diverged radically from Darwin's. In his *Contributions to the Theory of Natural Selection* (1870) he insisted that the human being's higher mental attributes could not have arisen by natural selection alone and ascribed such attributes to a spiritual agency.

Wallace is also renowned as a pioneer of zoogeography. He showed that the Malay archipelago consists of two distinct zoological regions separated by an imaginary line (Wallace's Line), and wrote *The Geographical Distribution of Animals* (1876), which explained zoo-geographic data in terms of evolutionary laws. In the last decades of his life he was actively involved in a number of controversial causes, campaigning against vaccination and supporting land nationalization, psychical research, socialism and women's suffrage.

WALLACE, WILLIAM (?–1305), soldier. A hero of the War of Scottish Independence, he came to prominence in 1296–7 after the defeat of JOHN BALLIOL and at a time when the Scottish aristocracy was prepared to capitulate to EDWARD I. At this critical moment in Scottish history the fierce resistance of two esquires, Wallace and Andrew MORAY, enabled them to raise an army capable of inflicting a humiliating defeat upon an over-confident enemy at the Battle of Stirling Bridge (11 Sept. 1297). By crossing the bridge to the north bank of the Forth the English vanguard allowed itself to be separated from the rest of the army and it paid the price. It was slaughtered and one of its commanders, Cressingham, was killed and skinned. Moray, however, was mortally wounded. For the next 10 months Wallace was the unrivalled leader of the Scots until he unwisely engaged Edward I's army at Falkirk (Stirlings.) (22 July 1298). This time his army, largely composed of spearmen drawn up in defensive formations known as schiltrons, was easily defeated by the overwhelming superiority of the English in both archers and cavalry. He fought on, once again in relative obscurity, until 1305 when he was betrayed to the English and executed at

Smithfield (London). But he had inspired a patriotic resistance which outlasted his defeat and death, even influencing twentieth-century Scottish nationalism.

WALLER, EDMUND (1606–87), politician and poet. From Bucks. and Cambridge-educated, he was a veteran Parliamentarian, sitting for six different constituencies between 1624 and 1685. Royalist on the outbreak of the First Civil War (1642) he was involved in a failed plot to seize London for CHARLES I, was imprisoned and then banished to France. Pardoned thanks to his relative Oliver CROMWELL in 1651, he succcessively wrote verses praising Cromwell, verses celebrating Cromwell's death, and verses celebrating CHARLES II's restoration. He strongly advocated religious toleration.

WALLIS, SIR BARNES (1887–1979), engineer. Wallis served an apprenticeship in marine engineering and in 1913 moved to Vickers. During the First World War he worked on airship design, and subsequently on aeroplanes; the geodetic design of the Wellington, his most successful model of the Second World War, was a logical development of his work in the 1910s. In 1941 Wallis learned that the dams of the Ruhr were the key to German industrial production. In the teeth of official opposition he designed and built spherical 'bouncing bombs' which enabled the RAF's elite 617 squadron to destroy two dams in May 1943, causing considerable panic in Germany though little long term damage to the German war effort. He subsequently designed the Tallboy and the Grand Slam, huge bombs that could penetrate layers of reinforced concrete on the roofs of U-boat pens. Wallis continued to work until 1971, one of his last designs being the swing wing incorporated into the American F1-11 fighter-bomber, an aircraft which was still operational at the end of the twentieth century.

WALLIS, JOHN (1616–1703), mathematician. He went up to Emmanuel, Cambridge, in 1632, was ordained in 1640 and worked for Parliament deciphering Royalist correspondence during the Civil Wars. In 1649 he was appointed Savilian Professor of Geometry at Oxford. Through the 1640s and 1650s he was a member of Robert BOYLE's 'invisible college'. At the Restoration he claimed successfully that he had been selective in what he had chosen to decipher, and thus had served the monarch's cause; in 1662 he was among the founders of the Royal Society. In his first mathematical treatise, *Arithmetica Infinitorum* (1655), Wallis expressed the value of π (*pi*), arrived at by 'interpolation' (a term which he coined) from infinite series. He also made the mathematical work of Descartes better known, invented ∞ as the symbol for infinity, and devised an effective system for teaching the deaf to speak. His collected mathematical works were published between 1693 and 1699 at Oxford. Some of his last years were spent again dealing with secret correspondence, this time for WILLIAM III.

WALLMODEN, AMALIE SOPHIE MARIANNE (née von Wendt) (1704–65) (Countess of Yarmouth), royal mistress. A member of the Hanoverian administrative elite, she attracted GEORGE II on his visit to Hanover in 1735, and the liaison was approved by Queen CAROLINE. After Caroline's death she divorced her husband and moved to London where she was established as George II's mistress and made Countess (1740). She was politically influential and eased the relations between George II and his ministers but does not appear to have taken a partisan role.

WALPOLE, HORACE (HORATIO) (5th [4th Walpole] Earl of Orford) (1717–97), novelist and connoisseur. The dilettante fourth son of Sir Robert Walpole, he was educated at Eton and Cambridge. As an adult, he lived off the proceeds of sinecure offices and a legacy. Strawberry Hill (in Twickenham, outside London), the villa which he rebuilt in picturesque Gothic style, was a noted exemplar of that fashion. He established a private press there in 1757, and published fine editions of the classics and some of his own works, including *Anecdotes of Painting in England* (1762). His *The Castle of Otranto* (1764) was a pioneering Gothic novel. He sat in Parliament (1741–67), latterly in opposition. His posthumously published political *Memoirs* expounded the view that GEORGE III and Bute (*see* STUART, JOHN) had plotted to reassert royal power. He corresponded voluminously, most frequently with Horace Mann, British minister in Florence; other correspondents included Thomas GRAY. His anecdotes are often cited by historians.

WALPOLE, SIR ROBERT *see* essay on pages 808–09

WALSH, PETER (?1618–88), churchman. Old English gentry from Kildare, he joined the Franciscans at Leuven; back in Ireland as lecturer at Kilkenny during the Civil Wars, he was a strong opponent of RINUCCINI and advocate of a compromise peace with James BUTLER, Duke of Ormond, and the Royalist armies. He went into exile from 1652 in London. From 1660 to 1669, backed by Ormond, he wrote and campaigned urging Roman Catholics to promise total secular loyalty to the English Crown in return for toleration; repudiated by Rome, he was excommunicated.

WALSINGHAM, FRANCIS *see* essay on page 810

WALSINGHAM, THOMAS (?–*c.* 1422), chronicler. A Benedictine monk of St Albans (Herts.), he revived the abbey's tradition of history-writing. His main work was a massive history of England conceived as a continuation of Matthew PARIS's *Chronica Majora*. Walsingham's strong views on prominent contemporaries JOHN OF GAUNT, WYCLIF, PERRERS and the leaders of the Peasants' Revolt, for example, were expressed freely in his original version, completed *c.* 1392. When he returned to writing history after the deposition of RICHARD II, his new enthusiasm for the Lancastrian dynasty made him extensively revise his earlier work as well as continuing it to 1420.

WALTER, HUBERT (*c.* 1140–1205), Archbishop of Canterbury (1193–1205). Being a nephew of Ranulf GLANVIL eased his path into HENRY II's service but it was under RICHARD I that his career really flourished. Richard made him Bishop of Salisbury in 1189, employed him as chief of staff on crusade and was so impressed by his performance in these challenging circumstances that in 1193 he promoted him to take charge of both secular and ecclesiastical government in England as Justiciar and Archbishop of Canterbury. While the King was in France, he governed England; he would later rightly be called 'one of the greatest royal ministers of all time'.

In 1195 he was made Papal Legate and, on JOHN's accession, was appointed Chancellor. The great series of Chancery rolls, for centuries the central records of English government, date from his period in office. As Archbishop, although clearly appointed for entirely secular reasons, he proved to be an active and responsible head of the English Church who found time to summon and preside over reforming provincial and legatine councils.

WALTER, JOHN (1739–1812), founder of *The Times*. He began his career in his father's coal business, but sold it in 1781 to help repay the debts incurred as an insurance underwriter during the War of American Independence. He bought the patent for the 'logographic' printing process and started to print first books and then in 1785 a newspaper, *The Daily Universal Register*, which in 1788 he renamed *The Times*. He was imprisoned in 1789 after he printed the claim that GEORGE III's sons were insincere in their pleasure at the King's recovery, the paragraphs in question having been supplied by the Secretary to the Treasury. In 1803 he handed sole control of the newspaper to his son John (1776–1845) who sought to increase the newspaper's authority and independence. The Walter family owned *The Times* until 1908 and sold the last of their shares in 1964.

WALPOLE, SIR ROBERT (2nd [1st Walpole] Earl of Orford) (1676–1745)
Politician and Prime Minister (1721–42)

An early product of, and skilled operator within, the new system of parliamentary government, Walpole commanded the heights of politics longer than any other eighteenth-century politician.

Younger son of a Norfolk county family, he was educated at Eton and King's College, Cambridge, until summoned home on his brother's death in 1698. His father arranged his marriage to the daughter of a wealthy Kentish timber merchant. Walpole entered Parliament in 1701, sitting for the small borough of Castle Rising, later for King's Lynn.

In 1701 party feeling ran high. The Whigs were in trouble because of their unpopular foreign policies, yet it was to them Walpole turned, allying himself with a Norfolk group linked with the leading Junto Whigs, becoming close to Lord Orford (see RUSSELL, EDWARD), whose title he would later take. Through his neighbour Lord Townshend (see TOWNSHEND, CHARLES), who had been his father's ward, he entered aristocratic Whig circles. In 1703 he was elected to the elite Whig Kit-Cat Club (see CAT, CHRISTOPHER). In Parliament, he showed mettle as a critic of Tory policies.

In 1705 ruling ministers Marlborough (see CHURCHILL, JOHN), GODOLPHIN and Robert HARLEY decided to reduce their dependence on the Tories. Walpole gained his first post, at the Admiralty, showing administrative talent. He defended the government against attack from the excluded of both parties (including his former Junto associates) and was rewarded by promotion in 1708 to Secretary at War (a demanding post, with the Spanish Succession War still raging) and in 1710 to the financially valuable post of Treasurer of the Navy. Whig strength both in Parliament and in government peaked between 1708 and early 1710, and he was able to rebuild links with the Junto Whigs. He served as a manager presenting to the Lords the case for impeaching Tory cleric Henry SACHEVERELL. When Sacheverell received only a light sentence and there were popular demonstrations in his favour, it became clear that the Whigs had overreached themselves. Walpole lost both his posts, and faced charges of corruption. Since he was to the fore in attacking Tory moves towards peace, there was political advantage in pressing these: in 1712 he was expelled from the Commons and imprisoned in the Tower.

Returned to Parliament in 1713, he responded to Queen ANNE's evidently declining health by emphasizing Whig loyalty to the Protestant succession and questioning Tory intentions.

GEORGE I on his accession showed himself well disposed to the Whigs. Walpole gained the lucrative post of Paymaster General; his friend Townshend (recently married to Walpole's sister) became a Secretary of State. Walpole led the parliamentary attack on the Tories, serving as chairman of the Committee of Secrecy which investigated the activities of Anne's last ministry. He helped panic Bolingbroke (see ST JOHN, HENRY) into fleeing abroad and brought impeachment charges against him and other Tory leaders. He was made First Lord of the Treasury and Chancellor of the Exchequer.

A rift however developed among leading Whigs. STANHOPE, also a Secretary of State, and Sunderland (see SPENCER, CHARLES), Lord Privy Seal, feared the growing power of Walpole and Townshend and their hostility to a forward policy in the Baltic. The King's preference for Stanhope and Sunderland was strengthened by their suggestion that Walpole and Townshend had links with the oppositionally inclined Prince of Wales (the future GEORGE II). Townshend was dismissed, and Walpole resigned. For some years the two joined with the Tories to harry the ministry, scotching ministerial plans to entrench their position by a Peerage Bill (to prevent new creations such as Anne had used to force peace proposals through the Lords). In the spring of 1720 relations were patched up; Walpole and Townshend returned to office, Walpole again as Paymaster General.

Walpole's route to power was unexpectedly cleared by the bursting of the South Sea Bubble in the summer of 1720 (the financial collapse that followed the bidding up of South Sea Stock, which the government had facilitated by promoting the fortunes of the company in exchange for its assuming part of the national debt). Stanhope and Sunderland lost popularity. Walpole, out of office when the scheme was approved, seemed to have clean hands and helped restore public confidence. He also protected Stanhope and Sunderland from parliamentary vengeance, earning the charge of serving as a 'screen'. They resented his recovery – he regained the positions of First Lord of the Treasury and Chancellor of the Exchequer in 1721, while Townshend was reinstated as Secretary of State – but neither lived long enough to challenge his new eminence.

Walpole was to remain First Lord of the Treasury for 20 years. Crucial to this achievement were his administrative skills and his success in making his regime palatable to most MPs, both of which made him invaluable to the King. In 1727, when the new King George II was disposed to favour Spencer COMPTON over Walpole, Walpole's ability to deliver a generous financial settlement tipped the balance in his favour. He also had good relations with the new Queen CAROLINE.

The years of war, during which Walpole had served his political apprenticeship, had left both Britain and France exhausted. Furthermore, neither dynasty was secure: the French King Louis XV had come to the throne as a minor; the Hanoverians could not count on the loyalty of their British subjects. Peace therefore had attractions for both parties, making it possible to keep taxes down and ensuring that Walpolean Whiggery was more acceptable to many people than Junto Whiggery. Walpole also generally discouraged initiatives that might upset the precarious religious truce: thus when in the 1730s Dissenters campaigned for the repeal of the Test and Corporation Acts (restricting their access to public office) he refused to help, saying that the time was not ripe.

Walpole's methods of governing had limitations, however, and opposition to him gradually gathered force until finally it brought him down. One notable feature of his regime was his continuing insistence that Whigs be given preference in appointments, both national and local. Tories who set aside their old loyalties might hope for favour; as Tories, they could not prosper. There may have been an element of political calculation here. The Whigs had laid the foundations for their triumph by charging Tory leaders with crypto-Jacobitism, depriving them of potential support. In 1722 Walpole manipulated evidence of Tory Jacobite plots (see LAYER and ATTERBURY) to the same end. Probably his outlook had also been permanently marked by the partisan passions of his early experience. His intransigence towards Tories was in some respects disadvantageous. It helped to keep an important section of the nation alienated and frustrated.

A second marked characteristic of Walpole's rule was his unwillingness to share power with more than a few trusted associates. In 1725, when hard pressed by the ambitious William PULTENEY, he had him dismissed from office: Pulteney moved into opposition. In 1730 Walpole fell out with his brother-in-law Townshend, and replaced him with the more biddable Duke of Newcastle (see PELHAM-HOLLES, THOMAS), whom Walpole trusted with many responsibilities, admitting few others to his confidence.

Walpole's personal style also antagonized many, and provided ammunition to critics. He all too plainly revelled in wealth and power. During the 1720s he rebuilt his family home at Houghton (Norfolk) in the style of a palace and amassed an extraordinary picture collection (bought after his death by Catherine the Great, and still in Russia to this day). Though remaining a commoner (his power base was, after all, in the Commons), he had more the manner of a prince; contemporaries called him the Great Man. He was cynical and worldly, and presided over a political and financial milieu repeatedly soiled with corruption scandals. His Lord Chancellor, Macclesfield (see PARKER, THOMAS), was impeached for corruption in 1724.

In the late 1720s Walpole's Whig and Tory opponents began to coalesce in a 'Country' opposition. Bolingbroke, back in England, sponsored an opposition journal, *The Craftsman*, which attacked Walpole as a corrupt, power-hungry politician – effectively enough for the government to harass the journal through the courts. As the 1734 general election approached, Walpole's opponents exploited his attempt to extend the responsibilities of the unpopular excise service to raise fears of a 'general excise', levied by excise officers intruding into the homes of freeborn Englishmen. Walpole lost support in the boroughs. In the late 1730s he lost support in Scotland, most crucially that of the powerful John CAMPBELL, by his heavy-handed treatment of Edinburgh after the PORTEOUS Riots. In 1739 he lost control of foreign policy: chauvinistic extra-parliamentary pressure and the urgings of his colleagues combined to push him into a mismanaged war against Spain. In the 1741 election enough opposition to him had massed for it to become clear, on the meeting of the new Parliament, that he could no longer command the Commons. Despite George II's pleas he resigned early in 1742, accepting a peerage as Earl of Orford.

Pulteney and others of the 'Country' critics, absorbed into a new administration, did not usher in the new political era that they had promised, encouraging subsequent public cynicism about the motives of self-proclaimed 'patriots'. But the political scene did change in certain ways. The PELHAM brothers, who dominated politics for most of the next decade, tried to incorporate more sectors of opinion into government. The term Prime Minister increasingly became a standard term for the leading minister, but none of Walpole's successors flaunted their ambition or success as he had done.

J. H. Plumb, *Sir Robert Walpole* (2 vols, 1956–60)
Brian W. Hill, *Sir Robert Walpole, Sole and Prime Minister* (1989)

WALSINGHAM, SIR FRANCIS (?1532–90)
Politician

Walsingham came from a prosperous London mercantile family who had set up as Kentish gentry; his mother was sister to the prominent evangelical Henrician courtier Sir Anthony DENNY, and when Francis was a boy she married a distant cousin of ELIZABETH I. It is likely that the militant Protestantism which characterized his political career was already developing in the 1540s, and was reinforced by his time at King's, Cambridge; there he probably met William CECIL, the son-in-law of Sir John CHEKE, Provost of King's, beginning a lifelong friendship. From 1550 he travelled abroad, and left again after MARY I's accession, after probable involvement in the enterprises of JANE GREY and Thomas WYATT. He studied law at Padua and visited Switzerland. He returned quickly to England on ELIZABETH I's accession, and was soon involved in government business for Cecil. Cecil secured one of the Earl of Bedford's seats in the Commons for him; thereafter he sat in most Parliaments until his death. By 1568 he was being used by Cecil and Elizabeth in diplomacy and foreign affairs. He was Ambassador to France from 1570–3, years which spanned the crisis in Anglo-French relations caused by the atrocities against French Protestants during the Massacre of St Bartholomew in Aug. 1572; his house became a refuge for Huguenots. He was made Principal Secretary in 1573, specializing in foreign affairs, and he kept this office until his death. His diplomatic missions later included embassies to the Netherlands in 1578, to France in 1581 and to Scotland in 1583.

Walsingham was one of the group of politicians who were enthusiastic for pursuing an aggressive foreign policy in support of international Protestant interests; his daughter married the Puritan hero, Sir Philip SIDNEY. Nevertheless, he often loyally restrained his Puritan instincts, acutely conscious of the dangers of dividing the Protestant cause in the face of the continent-wide Catholic threat. He was much respected by the Queen, even though she did not feel the personal warmth towards him which characterized her relationship with Cecil, was annoyed by his commitment to godly activism and frequently disregarded his advice. Despite frequent bickerings, monarch and minister managed to co-operate for nearly two decades. His particular usefulness to the Queen, which preserved him from dismissal, was his acute instinct for gathering information, honed in his investigations of the RIDOLFI plot in 1570. To keep in touch with events at home and abroad he drew on a variety of sources – members of official missions, trustworthy merchants trading in Europe, and a network of paid agents and informers, some of whom were turncoat Roman Catholics and double agents for rival powers. Walsingham devoted much of his own money to maintaining these contacts. With his files of information, he was able to combat and subvert such conspiracies against Elizabeth as those of Francis THROCKMORTON and Anthony BABINGTON, and it became clear to him that a major participant in such ventures was the imprisoned MARY QUEEN OF SCOTS, whom he regarded with deep abhorrence. His agents provided the vital evidence which connected her to the assassination plans of Babington, although he managed to escape the consequences of Elizabeth's guilty fury at Mary's execution, since he was ill when William DAVISON implemented the death warrant (Jan. 1587).

Difficult times followed, however. Walsingham's intelligence reports revealed the intensity of Spanish preparations for invading England, yet he found it difficult to persuade Cecil to abandon his habitual caution to bring pressure on the Queen to match Spanish aggressive preparations. He was also drawn into personal quarrels with Robert DUDLEY, Earl of Leicester, at a time when these two advocates of a militant anti-Catholic policy ought to have been working together. Partly this was caused by disagreements about responsibility for the burden of debt left by Philip Sidney, but with much justice Walsingham felt that Leicester was badly mishandling his command against the Spaniards in the Netherlands. After Leicester's death he struggled to maintain his huge workload despite increasing bad health, and he died in considerable debt.

Lacking the panache of Leicester or Sidney, Walsingham was nevertheless one of the ablest and most reliable of Elizabeth's ministers. His cultural interests and his influence were attested by the number of books on theology and philosophy dedicated to him. He took a great interest in the overseas voyages of Martin FROBISHER, Francis DRAKE and Humphrey GILBERT. Much of his archive survives, divided between the State Papers, the British Library and Burghley's archive at Hatfield House.

Conyers Read, Mr Secretary Walsingham and the Policy of Queen Elizabeth (3 vols, 1925)

WALTER, LUCY (*c.* 1630–58), royal mistress. She was the daughter of a Pembs. gentleman and niece of the leading Welsh Royalist John Vaughan, Earl of Carbery. In 1648 she became the lover of the future CHARLES II when he was living at the Hague; the relationship ended around 1651, by which time they had had a son, James SCOTT, later Duke of Monmouth. Lucy was later imprisoned in the Tower of London as a spy and died in Paris in 1658. During the Exclusion Crisis (*see* COOPER, ANTHONY ASHLEY) rumours circulated that Charles had married Lucy and that the contract was held in a black box, but the story was denied by Charles and all alleged participants.

WALTER OF COUTANCES (?–1207), prelate and politician. He governed England for two years while RICHARD I was on crusade. His administrative and diplomatic skills brought him promotion as Bishop of Lincoln in 1183 and as Archbishop of Rouen in 1184. He set out on crusade with Richard but news of tension between JOHN and LONGCHAMP caused the King to send him back to resolve the dispute. In 1204 at Rouen he had to come to terms with John's loss of Normandy to King Philip II Augustus of France.

WALTER OF HENLEY (*fl.* 1250), farmer and writer. His *Hosebondrie*, a book which he described as 'teaching the tillage of land and the keeping of cattle, from which great wealth will come to those who follow this teaching', remained the most influential treatise on farm management until the sixteenth century. Translated from the original Anglo-French into English, it was printed by Wynkyn de Worde.

WALTER, THEOBALD (?–1205), courtier. He went to Ireland in 1185 with Prince JOHN, and was granted extensive estates there, including a large part of the kingdom of Limerick. Since, as was often the case, these grants were of land actually in Irish hands, he and his fellow colonists were being authorized to force the Irish to surrender them. He was also granted the office of Butler of Ireland, from which his descendants, earls and dukes of Ormonde, took the surname Butler.

WALTERS, SIR ALAN (1926–), economist. A graduate of London University, he was Cassel Professor of Economics at the London School of Economics and later became Professor of Political Economy at Johns Hopkins University, USA. He was prominent in the Institute of Economic Affairs and one of the earliest British monetarists. This, allied to his Euro-sceptic views, led to his appointment as economic adviser to Margaret THATCHER in 1981. As his ideas on exchange-rate targeting conflicted with those of the Chancellor

of the Exchequer, Nigel LAWSON, Walters became the centre of a major political dispute and the Prime Minister was forced to dispense with his services. His academic interests were originally in the area of road pricing, cost-benefit analysis and econometrics; only later did he become involved in issues of monetary theory.

WALTHEOF (?–1076), Earl of Northumbria. Too young to succeed to the earldom of Northumbria when his father SIWARD died in 1055, he was probably made Earl (of some Midland shires) in 1065. The rest of his short life was overshadowed by the trauma of the Norman Conquest. Initially, as one of the English magnates whom WILLIAM I THE CONQUEROR half trusted, he was confirmed in office, but in 1069 he joined the northern revolt. When he finally submitted, William made further efforts to retain his loyalty, first marrying him to his niece Judith, then giving him the earldom of Northumbria in 1072. In spite of this, Waltheof became involved in the 1075 revolt of the Norman earls, and when this was suppressed he, as an Englishman, was the only one to suffer the death penalty, the last earl executed for rebellion in England until the fourteenth century.

WALTON, IZAAK (1593–1683), writer. From a modest Staffs. background, he became a London merchant and built a reputation for his poetry and personal charm. He favoured the Royalist cause in the Civil Wars and lived in retirement, which led to his best-known work, *The Compleat Angler* (1653). He also published lives of John DONNE, Henry WOTTON, Richard HOOKER, George HERBERT and Robert SANDERSON; subtly moulded to mirror his own moderate sacramental Anglicanism, these have proved very influential. After the Restoration, first Bishop George Morley, then Walton's clergyman son-in-law, were happy to have him as permanent house-guest.

WALTON, SIR WILLIAM (1902–83), composer. Having failed to complete his degree at Oxford, Walton lived for the next 10 years as the 'adopted, or elected brother' of Osbert and Sacheverell Sitwell and achieved notoriety for his collaboration with Edith SITWELL in the entertainment *Façade* (1922). He was declared the leading composer of his generation with the performance, by Paul Hindemith, of his viola concerto (1929), whilst *Belshazzar's Feast* (1931) was considered to be the greatest English choral work since ELGAR's *The Dream of Gerontius*. Walton completed his first symphony in 1935 and his second in 1960. His most important opera, *Troilus and Cressida,* was first performed in 1954 and revived at Covent Garden in 1976. His film music is greatly admired, including the memorable *Spitfire Prelude and*

Fugue from the film score *The First of the Few* (1942) and especially the scores which he wrote for Lawrence OLIVIER's *Henry V* (1944), *Hamlet* (1947) and *Richard III* (1955) and for *The Battle of Britain* (1969).

WALWORTH, WILLIAM (?–1385), politician. Lord Mayor of London during the Peasants' Revolt of 1381, a rich businessman, a member of the Fishmongers' Co., he was an influential figure in both London and national politics in the 1370s and 1380s. At RICHARD II's side when the young King confronted the rebels at Smithfield on 15 June, he won fame and a knighthood by his brutal treatment of Wat TYLER. Amongst his other concerns was a campaign to limit the size of alehouse signs.

WARBECK, PERKIN (?1474–99), conspirator. Possibly a bastard of EDWARD IV, he was apparently from Flanders, where Yorkist conspirators discovered his acting abilities. In 1491 he was taken to Ireland, where his career of impersonation began, first as Edward PLANTAGENET, Earl of Warwick (the nephew of Edward IV), then Richard, the younger Prince in the Tower (*see* EDWARD V). A Europe-wide network of plots against HENRY VII and two failed invasion attempts ended in capture in 1497 after a third landing in Cornwall. Comfortably imprisoned in the Tower, he made escape attempts which were eventually used to justify his execution, along with the real Earl of Warwick.

WARBURG, SIR SIEGMUND (1902–82), banker. Co-founder with Henry Grunfeld (1904–99), a fellow refugee from Nazism, of the City merchant bank S. G. Warburg, Warburg was a member of one of Germany's most prominent families. He and Grunfeld met in The Hague in 1935; their first financial venture, the New Trading Co., was an investment vehicle to allow fellow refugees to get their money out of Germany and invest it safely. Relocated in London, where it was bolstered by connections with New York and by the ROTHSCHILD FAMILY, the company became S. G. Warburg. It took the City by storm, and in the course of the post-war years developed the Eurobond market and perfected the art of the hostile take-over. Warburg, who had taken British citizenship in 1939, resigned the chairmanship of the merchant bank that bore his name in 1964 (Grunfeld becoming Chairman) and resigned as a partner in 1969, although he was prevailed upon to serve as its President (1970–8).

WARBURTON, WILLIAM (1698–1779), religious controversialist. He trained as an attorney, but read much theology, was ordained Deacon in 1723 and, four years later, was given a small living. He became noted as a savage polemicist. His major works were *The Alliance between Church and State* (1736), which defended the prevailing combination of religious toleration and restriction of Dissenters' civil rights as the result of a contract made between Church and State for mutual advantage, and *The Divine Legation of Moses* (1737, 1741), conceived as a refutation of Deism. POPE, who became his friend in the 1740s, left him the rights to all his works. Pope's support also helped him to attain preferment: he became chaplain to FREDERICK, Prince of Wales, in 1737 and to GEORGE II in 1754, Dean of Bristol in 1757 and Bishop of Gloucester in 1779.

WARD, MARY (1585-1645), religious pioneer. Yorks.-born, she went to St Omer (Pas de Calais) in 1606 to become a nun of the Order of Poor Clares. Seeking a more active approach to the female religious life, she gathered in 1609 the nucleus of a new congregation which modelled itself on the Society of Jesus, with the aims of educating women and ministering among them: the Institute of the Blessed Virgin Mary. Soon she had several houses under her control, and in 1629 she journeyed to Rome to seek papal ratification for the institute. Immediately she fell foul of male clerical suspicion of this new departure; in 1630 the institute was suppressed and she was imprisoned in Munich. Obtaining her freedom, she compromised with the Papacy by restructuring her houses on a contemplative, enclosed basis. She spent her last years in England, founding a Yorks. nunnery in 1642 which has been in York as the Bar Convent since 1686, surviving all penal restrictions on Roman Catholics.

WARE, SIR JAMES (1594–1666), historian. Son of a New English royal servant, he studied at Dublin, collected Irish manuscripts in collaboration with traditional Gaelic genealogists, and published much on Irish history; his writings, all in Latin, are notably lacking in religious prejudice. Knighted in 1629 and Auditor General of Ireland 1632–49, he was restored to his post in 1660, having spent some time during the Civil Wars in prison in London and then the years 1651–60 in London exile.

WARENNE, JOHN DE (7th Earl of Surrey and Earl Warenne) (*c.* 1231–1304), soldier and royal servant. He succeeded his father William in 1240 and became one of EDWARD I's principal captains in the wars in Wales and Scotland. Left in command of Scotland in 1297, he overslept on the morning of the Battle of Stirling Bridge, and was humiliatingly defeated by William WALLACE and Andrew MORAY.

WARHAM, WILLIAM (*c.* 1456–1532), Archbishop of Canterbury (1503–32). A civil lawyer trained at Oxford, he was a useful diplomat under HENRY VII and was rewarded with the bishopric of London (1502) and the archbishopric of Canterbury (1503), becoming Lord Chancellor in 1504. He expressed doubts as to the wisdom of HENRY VIII marrying CATHERINE OF ARAGON, the widow of Prince ARTHUR, but presided at their coronation. Thomas WOLSEY replaced him as Lord Chancellor in 1515, and when, in 1518, Wolsey was also made Legate *a latere* (personal papal representative in England), this encroached on Warham's legatine position as Primate of All England; relations remained cool but correct between them. Warham did nothing to assist Catherine against Henry's efforts from 1527 to have their marriage declared null, but he became increasingly unhappy with the radically anti-papal turn of royal policy after 1530. In 1532 he made a formal but secret protest against royal moves to curb the independence of the Church, and was contemplating speaking out openly. He drew back, however, from such defiance of the monarchy which he had served all his life, and he agreed to the Submission of the Clergy by which, in May 1532, the English Church's legislative bodies, the convocations of Canterbury and York, surrendered their power to make laws independently of the King and Parliament. His death soon after enabled Henry to appoint Thomas CRANMER as Archbishop to act as a reliable agent of royal policy. Warham was a good example of the late medieval English Church hierarchy: pious, energetic and a great builder, generous patron of humanist scholars including ERASMUS, and deeply hostile to those who wanted radical change in the Church.

WARTON, JOSEPH (1722–1800), poet and critic. The elder son of Thomas Warton, Headmaster of Winchester, and brother of the poet Thomas WARTON, Joseph Warton followed a career in the Church and then in teaching, also becoming Headmaster of Winchester in 1766. He published two very successful volumes of poems in the 1740s but his criticism, particularly his *Essay on the Genius and Writings of Pope* (two vols, 1757–82), was more influential. An admirer of POPE, he rebuked the Augustans for their emphasis on moralizing, and instead called for more imagination, innovation and emotion rather than adherence to supposed rules of composition.

WARTON, THOMAS (1728–90), poet and critic. The younger brother of Joseph WARTON, he became a Fellow of Trinity College, Oxford, where he established his reputation as a poet with work such as *The Triumph of Isis* (1749), a defence of the university, and the humorous anthology, *The Oxford Sausage* (1764). Warton travelled the country studying then neglected Gothic architecture and attempted the rehabilitation of medieval literature in his *History of English Poetry* (three vols, 1774–81) based upon an abortive scheme of Thomas GRAY. His *Observations on the Faerie Queene* (1754) drew parallels between SPENSER and the work of other poets. Although he and Samuel JOHNSON disagreed on many questions, Warton was from 1782 a member of Johnson's literary club. He was Poet Laureate (1785–90).

WARWICK, EARL OF, 10TH *see* BEAUCHAMP, GUY; **13TH** *see* BEAUCHAMP, RICHARD; **18TH** *see* PLANTAGENET, EDWARD; **19TH** *see* DUDLEY, JOHN; **21ST** *see* DUDLEY, AMBROSE; **23RD** *see* RICH, ROBERT

WASHINGTON, GEORGE (1732–99), first President of the United States of America (1789–97). A Virginia gentleman, his family's origins were in northern England, both landowning and mercantile. After serving in the army fighting the French (1755–9), he became a champion of colonial independence. He was one of the principal leaders in the War of American Independence, and was chosen to command the Continental Army in 1775, moulding it despite considerable privations (especially in winter) and defeats as well as victories, eventually to rout the British forces under CORNWALLIS at Yorktown. After the war his role became political, in the disputes between the new states over federal powers. He presided over the federal convention of 1787 which adopted the Constitution, under which he was elected the first President. He assumed office, in New York, in 1789 and retired in 1797 having served as a great federalist statesman. The new capital city of the USA, on the border between Virginia and Maryland, was named after him.

WASTELL, JOHN (?–after 1516), architect. From Bury St Edmunds (Suff.) he worked for the abbey there. Apart from the central Bell Harry tower of Canterbury Cathedral, his important works are all East Anglian; besides major parish church enlargements and eastern chapels at Peterborough Abbey (now Cathedral), he completed King's College Chapel, Cambridge (1508–13), designing its famous fan vaulting (*see also* VERTUE, William).

WATERHOUSE, ALFRED (1830–1905), architect. Liverpool-born leader of the Gothic revivalists, Waterhouse designed the assize courts (1859) and the town hall (1869–77) in Manchester, the Natural History Museum, South Kensington (1873–81) and the headquarters of the Prudential Assurance Company, High Holborn (started in 1876) in London, a number of Congregational churches, and colleges including Owen's College, Manchester, and Caius College, Cambridge. His preference for red brick and terracotta gave rise to the prefix 'red brick' for the new colleges and universities of the early twentieth century.

WATSON-WATT, SIR ROBERT (1892–1973), radar pioneer. During the First World War Watson-Watt worked at the Meteorological Office and developed a technique for locating distant thunderstorms by using radio waves. After the war he worked on radio beacons and direction-finding at the National Physical Laboratory, and in 1935 started developing his system for locating and ranging aircraft by reflecting radio waves from them (radio detection and ranging, or radar). Following successful initial trials, the government agreed to support his scheme for detecting enemy aircraft. By 1940 he had helped construct radio transmitters and receivers along the British east coast, and he later built radar systems for use in ships and aeroplanes. Radar proved crucial to Britain's defence against German bombers in the Second World War.

WATSON-WENTWORTH, CHARLES (2nd Marquess of Rockingham) *see* essay on page 815

WATT, A(LEXANDER) P(OLLOCK) (?1837–1914), literary agent. Watt is generally credited with being Britain's first full-time literary agent, acting on behalf of authors as they were starting to consider themselves as professionals. He joined the London office of his brother-in-law, the Glasgow publisher Alexander Strachan, in 1871 and in 1878 undertook to market the fiction of one of Strachan's most successful authors, George MacDonald, when Strachan could no longer afford to publish him. He subsequently handled such clients as Arthur Conan DOYLE and Rudyard KIPLING. The 1891 US Copyright Act, which extended protection to British books, made a literary agent, in Watt's own words, 'not only a convenience but an absolute necessity', and he opened an office in New York. Some publishers thought him a parasite, others were grateful that he made the often tricky business of handling authors his business.

WATT, JAMES (1736–1819), inventor. The son of a Greenock instrument-maker and merchant, Watt developed mechanical skills in his father's workshop, learnt the instrument-making trade in Glasgow and London, and in 1757 established his own workshop and instrument-making firm at Glasgow University. The Scottish natural philosophers John Robson and Joseph BLACK sparked Watt's interests in steam power, and in 1764, when he repaired a university model of the NEWCOMEN steam engine, he developed a method of making the engine more efficient, economic and reliable:

in his version of the engine the cylinder was kept hot and the spent steam was driven out of the cylinder and condensed in a separate vessel. In 1768 he became a partner to the inventor John Roebuck in a scheme for working Watt's steam engine which he patented in 1769. The partnership dissolved in 1773 owing to flaws in the engine's construction and Roebuck's bankruptcy. Between 1767 and 1774 Watt earned a living as a canal surveyor and in 1769 met the wealthy manufacturer Matthew BOULTON, who was keen to exploit Watt's engine. In 1775 Boulton secured an extension of Watt's steam engine patent and entered into partnership with the inventor, developing and building steam engines in the Soho foundry near Birmingham. From 1774 Watt added a number of crucial features to his engine, including a mechanism for making it double-acting, an automatic centrifugal governor and sun-and-planet gearing. He also devised the term horse-power to rate the steam engine's efficiency: the unit of power is named after him. By the early 1780s Watt had completed an improved version of the engine and within years was enjoying rising sales of the engine to cotton and woollen mills. Although Watt is not credited with the invention of the steam engine, his improved version of the machine played a crucial part in the industrial revolution.

WATTS, CHARLIE (1941–), musician *see* JAGGER, MICK

WATTS, G(EORGE) F(REDERICK) (1817–1904), artist. Regarded by LEIGHTON as 'England's Michelangelo', Watts was a painter in the grand Victorian style: the Elgin marbles were his idea of perfection. But he also put to practical effect his belief that art and beauty were forces for good by working with the Home Arts and Industries Association, which encouraged sick and unemployed people to spend their time productively doing arts and crafts, and Watts exhibited his paintings in London's East End in an attempt to 'bring art to the people'.

He studied at the Royal Academy Schools and was introduced into London society by Lord Holland, whom he met in Florence where he had gone to study the Renaissance painters. The introduction enabled him (then briefly married to the young Ellen TERRY) to finance by painting portraits what he considered his 'real art', allegorical paintings, like the extraordinary, and extraordinarily popular, *Hope* (1886). He painted TENNYSON, GLADSTONE, MANNING, CARLYLE, William MORRIS, John Stuart MILL, Matthew ARNOLD, Dante Gabriel ROSSETTI and a host of others. He sculpted the equestrian statue *Physical Energy*, one cast of which is part of a monument to Cecil RHODES,

continued on page 816

WATSON-WENTWORTH, CHARLES (2nd Marquess of Rockingham) (1730–82)
Politician and Prime Minister (1765–6, 1782)

In 1750 he succeeded to his father's title and major political interest in Yorks. A lord of the bedchamber from 1751, Rockingham was disturbed by former Tories gaining court positions at the accession of GEORGE III (1760). He resigned in 1762, casting his fortunes with opposition Whiggery.

Rockingham was not naturally assertive, he hardly spoke in Parliament, but veteran Whigs such as Newcastle (*see* PELHAM-HOLLES, THOMAS) and Hardwicke (*see* YORKE, PHILIP) were aged or dying, and many who shared their distrust of the new King were too young and inexperienced to take the lead. Rockingham therefore emerged as leader of a group of disgruntled Old Corps Whigs, termed Rockinghamite Whigs. They believed themselves to be the true heirs of the Whig tradition and, encouraged by their ideologue BURKE, defended party as not faction but 'honourable connection'. The historian Sir Lewis NAMIER credited them with bringing about the 'birth of party'. Many Rockinghamites also admired the fiery William PITT (who became Lord Chatham in 1766), and would have preferred to see him among their number. Pitt's differing political attitudes, and prima-donna-ish temperament, made this difficult. Though they sometimes co-operated, Rockinghamite and Chathamite Whigs mostly acted as independent opposition groupings.

Rockingham came formally to the fore when he was made first Lord of the Treasury in the ministry put together by Cumberland (*see* WILLIAM, AUGUSTUS) in 1765. This courted popularity at home and in the colonies by repealing Bute's (*see* STUART, JOHN) cider excise and George GRENVILLE's Stamp Act. A quarrel with the King over appointments led to Rockingham's fall in 1766; those who left with him became his core followers. He presided over fierce opposition to Grafton (*see* FITZROY, AUGUSTUS). Against the background of agitation over WILKES, Rockinghamites and Chathamites attempted to unite and storm their way into office, but the rise of Lord NORTH ended these fancies. Maintaining effective opposition to the competent and pragmatic North initially proved difficult. Even when war with America broke out, Rockinghamite attempts to convince the public that Americans were victims fell on largely deaf ears. When first the French, then the Spanish, allied with the Americans (1778–9), even the Rockinghams saw no alternative but to support the war.

It remained open to them to criticize its conduct and the ways in which peoples historically associated with Britain were handled. They began to argue the case for recognizing American independence and that the serious effects of the war on the Irish economy highlighted long-standing injustices in British treatment of Ireland; Rockingham, like many of his team, was a major Irish landowner, giving Irish issues special interest and ensuring that the group had kinsmen and friends among Irish critics of government. In 1780 discontent with the conduct of the war led Christopher WYVILL, a Yorkshire gentleman, to launch his politically reformist 'Association'. Like the Wilkite movement of the previous decade, this faced the Rockinghamites with a complex challenge. The latent radicalism of the movement disturbed them, yet they could not afford to ignore a popular groundswell against a regime which they too opposed. Accordingly, they did their best to harness it for their own purposes, arguing, for example, that criticism should focus on the court rather than Parliament, and that the best way forward lay in 'economical reforms' that would limit ministers' capacity to win MPs' votes by offering government jobs and other patronage. North considered adding members of the group to a reconstructed ministry, but their insistence on entering only on their own terms, including recognition of American independence and economical reforms, confirmed the King's prejudice against them.

When the failure of British arms in America made North's position untenable (1782) he resigned. The King despaired to find himself at the mercy of the erstwhile opposition, but had little alternative save to appoint Rockingham to the Treasury, to preside over a mixture of his followers and those of the recently deceased Chatham. Rockingham's second ministry went some way towards making good former promises, moving towards ending the war in America and giving Ireland 'legislative independence' by repealing the Declaratory Act 1720 (which proclaimed the British Parliament's right to legislate for Ireland) and by encouraging the Irish Parliament to repeal Poynings' Law (which made Irish legislation subject to approval from both Irish and British Privy Councils). It also enacted limited measures of economic reform. Rockingham's sudden death in July 1782 precipitated a latent split among his colleagues, a group led by Charles James FOX refusing to serve under the leader of the Chathamites, Shelburne (*see* PETTY, WILLIAM).

Though Rockingham was not an assertive figure, some political skill is suggested by his ability to hold together a group of talented but independent-minded followers.

Ross J. Hoffman, The Marquis: A Study of Lord Rockingham 1730–1782 (1973) another can be seen in Kensington Gardens, but Watts's own energy gave out before it was completed, after a long life of quintessential Victorian confidence and productivity.

WAUGH, EVELYN (1903–66), novelist. Following his Oxford education, he had a short stint as a schoolmaster, which formed the background to his first novel, *Decline and Fall* (1928). Its success allowed him to devote himself to writing a series of black comic novels, including *Vile Bodies* (1930), *Black Mischief* (1932) and *Scoop* (1938). In 1930, he converted to Roman Catholicism, an element which often appeared in his novels (e.g. *Brideshead Revisited,* 1945) and which emphasized his increasingly self-conscious isolation from contemporary changes in British society and politics. The *Ordeal of Gilbert Pinfold* (1958) was a semi-autobiographical account of a near mental breakdown. Waugh is now considered one of Britain's finest twentieth-century prose writers.

WAVELL, ARCHIBALD (Earl Wavell) (1883–1950), Viceroy of India. Wavell, who served in the Boer War and both world wars, was a soldier and administrator who was to be remembered as the 'undistinguished slave of duty'. After his 1941 counter-offensive in North Africa had failed, Wavell exchanged posts with AUCHINLECK to become Commander-in-Chief, India. Both Malaya and Burma were lost to the Japanese; in 1943, being known as 'a man willing to shoulder an unpopular burden,' he was made Viceroy of India. Among his first acts were measures to relieve the terrible Bengal famine, but the cementing of his reputation was the Simla conference of June 1945, convened for politically eminent men to advise the Viceroy and break the political impasse. The conference broke down amid squabbling between the Indian National Congress and the All-India Muslim League under JINNAH. Partition between India and Pakistan soon proved the only viable political solution. After the installation of an interim government, Wavell was relieved of his post in March 1947. Louis MOUNTBATTEN oversaw the final months of the Indian Empire and independence.

WAVRIN, JEAN DE (*c.* 1394–*c.* 1472), historian. Soldier and councillor in the service of the dukes of Burgundy, he was amazed, he said, that no Englishman had commemorated the 'lofty enterprises' of the 'excellent and valiant kings of England', and he decided to remedy the situation. His long *Recueil des Croniques et Anchiennes Istories de la Grant Bretaigne, a present nomme Engleterre* covered the period from the fall of Troy to his own day. He presented a copy to EDWARD IV.

WEBB, BEATRICE *see* essay on pages 818–19

WEBB, BENEDICT (1563–after 1626), entrepreneur and autobiographer. From a line of Gloucs. clothiers, he worked in London and in France and Italy, copying techniques and returning to exploit them in Taunton (Soms.) and Gloucs. He was influential in representing clothiers' interests to government. He introduced the cultivation of rape to provide oil for dressing cloth and introduced the French style of mill for rape-seed oil. A short autobiography trumpeted his achievements.

WEBB, MATTHEW (1848–83), swimmer. The first man to swim the English Channel, he was a merchant seaman, popularly known as Captain Webb. The swim lasted from 1 p.m. on 24 Aug. 1875 when he entered the sea at Dover, until 10.40 the next morning when he struggled ashore at Cap Gris Nez. It was his second attempt: he had been blown off course the first time but this time, encased in porpoise oil and sipping cod liver oil, beef tea and brandy as he cleaved, breast stroke, through the waves, he succeeded. The public were thrilled: classicists thought it a feat that beat crossing the Hellespont, and Webb resolved to become a swimming showman. In 1893 he drowned in a whirlpool during an attempt to swim from the USA to Canada via the Niagara Falls.

WEBB, PHILIP (1831–1915), architect. One of the great architects of the late Victorian English revival, Webb designed the Red House for William MORRIS at Bexleyheath (Kent), including many of the fixtures and fittings, worked with Morris's design firm, and was active with Morris in founding the 'anti-scrape society' (the Society for the Protection of Ancient Buildings). His output was modest – 'Clouds' (Wilts.) was among his finest work – but it has proved highly influential. Many of the gables and turrets, hanging tiles and pitched roofs seen in suburbia today owe a debt to Webb.

WEBB, SIDNEY (1st Baron Passfield) (1859–1947), political theorist and social reformer. The son of a London hairdresser and milliner and a poorly paid accountant, he was, in the words of his future wife, 'isolated from his own class by his superior tastes'. At 16 Webb started work as a City clerk while attending evening classes in order to pass the necessary exams to enter the Civil Service (1878). There he became a first-division clerk in the Colonial Office, studying for a law degree in the evenings. In 1885 he joined the Fabian Society, which rejected Marxist revolutionary socialism in favour of a gradualist policy of 'permeation' by education and persuasion. His contribution to *Fabian Essays in Socialism* (1889) argued that the growth of local government had, *de facto*, brought about a collectivist State. In 1892 he was elected to the newly established London County Council.

He married Beatrice Potter (*see* WEBB, BEATRICE) in 1892 and the couple embarked on a working partnership of social research. Sidney had a particular interest in education, contrasting the English system unfavourably with the German technical education which he had observed as a young man, and he was a force behind the 1902 and 1903 Education Acts. Disillusion with the Liberal Party, particularly after the Poor Law Commission Report of 1909, led the Webbs eventually to the Labour Party, and in 1916 Sidney was elected to the party executive, where he set about drawing up a blueprint for a prudent socialist future: he drafted the famous 1918 constitution, Clause Four of which prescribed 'the common ownership of the means of production', only finally set aside in the 1990s. In 1922 he was elected Labour MP for Seaham (Co. Durham), and in 1924 became a member of the first Labour Cabinet as President of the Board of Trade; he was Secretary of State for the Colonies in the second. But his parliamentary career was not distinguished, and in 1931 he refused to serve in Ramsay MACDONALD's coalition and turned his attention to the Soviet Union as the only place where the workers' State had been successfully established. George Bernard SHAW regarded Webb 'as the ablest man in England', and the information and analyses that the Webbs stacked up during long and prodigiously energetic lifetimes remain a remarkable monument to their industry, though its actual political results are harder to quantify.

WEBSTER, ALEXANDER (1707–84), statistician. He followed his father into the Church of Scotland ministry. Gathering evidence from ministers in every parish, he successfully developed actuarial tables by which pensions for the widows of ministers could be calculated. In 1755 Webster estimated that the population of Scotland was over 1,265,000, and had recovered from the famine years at the end of the seventeenth century.

WEBSTER, JOHN (?1580–?1625), dramatist. A London tailor's son, he collaborated with other writers including Thomas DEKKER and Michael DRAYTON in writing, and produced works for civic pageantry. His own plays, notably *The White Devil* (1608) and *The Duchess of Malfi* (c. 1614), are the ultimate Jacobean tragedies in their gruesome plots and vivid language.

WEDGWOOD, JOSIAH (1730–95), pottery manufacturer. The son of a potter, in what was already the specialized pottery district of Staffs., he left school at nine, when his father died, and began working for his brothers. Having completed an apprenticeship, he set up in business for himself in 1759. He adopted an experimental and innovative approach to manufacture, design,

workplace organization and marketing. In 1769 he opened a new factory at Etruria and, with his partner Thomas Bentley, Chelsea works in 1770, producing for both the luxury and the more popular market. An early exponent of the neoclassical style, Wedgwood employed FLAXMAN among his designers. Wedgwood moved in Dissenting and liberal circles. His medallion depicting a slave, with the inscription 'Am I Not a Man and a Brother?', helped to popularize an emblem of the early anti-slavery movement.

WEELKES, THOMAS (c. 1575–1623), composer. Organist of Winchester College (1600) and later Chichester Cathedral (c. 1603), he wrote madrigals, English choral Church music and instrumental pieces.

WEEVER, JOHN (1576–1632), antiquary and poet. Lancs.-born, he studied at Cambridge and published *Epigrammes* in 1599 which include verses addressed to William SHAKESPEARE, Edmund SPENSER, Ben JONSON etc. He may have acted with Shakespeare. He published the results of his antiquarian tours in *Ancient Funerall Monuments* (1631), which has great value in recording Church antiquities later destroyed.

WEINSTOCK, ARNOLD (Baron Weinstock of Bowden) (1924–), manufacturer. Co-founder of Radio & Allied Industries in 1954, that grew by reverse take-over into the electronics giant General Electric Co. (GEC), Weinstock was the son of a Polish-born tailor from north London. He had a varied, undistinguished education and early employment before starting Radio & Allied with his brother-in-law Michael Sobell. The company thrived in the early television boom of the 1950s; the ailing GEC was acquired in 1963 and the new combine took its name. Weinstock, GEC's Managing Director for the remainder of his working life, began a ruthless cost- and job-cutting policy and embarked on a series of highly contested business take-overs, notably of AEI (Allied Electrical Industries) and English Electric in 1967–8. Weinstock was the businessman's businessman of the 1970s, came to be seen as an arch business conservative in the 1980s and finally in the 1990s as a reinvigorated man when GEC acquired Plessey, Ferranti's defence companies and links with Siemens in Germany.

WEISZ, VICTOR ('VICKY') (1913–66), cartoonist. Son of Hungarian Jews, he was born in Berlin and the political cartoons which he started to draw in his teens meant that he had to flee Nazi Germany, arriving in London in 1935. In 1941 he was appointed staff cartoonist of the Liberal *News*
continued on page 820

WEBB, BEATRICE (née Potter) (1858–1953)
Social reformer

She was born and grew up in Glos., the rather frail, second youngest of the nine daughters of Richard Potter, a railway magnate, who 'genuinely believed that women were superior to men, and acted as if he did'. Both her grandfathers were Liberal MPs, and her parents moved in an intellectual and liberal circle which included T. H. HUXLEY and Herbert SPENCER. The young Potter daughters were encouraged to read widely and participate in adult conversation. In 1877, when she was 18, Beatrice was presented at court, but her anxieties and puritanical inclination led her to seek restlessly for some intellectual purpose to her life, a 'craft' that she could practise for the benefit of society.

After the death of her mother Beatrice decided on a taxing course of political self-education and charitable work to educate the poor. In 1883 she met the radical Liberal politician Joseph CHAMBERLAIN, who profoundly attracted her. Their 'romance' was a tortured affair, with Beatrice mesmerized by the much older Chamberlain's charisma and political stature, while being appalled at his conventional view of a wife's role. When she asked if he would allow dissent to be expressed in his household and he said no, 'that little word ended our intercourse'. The interlude did nothing for Miss Potter's emotional well-being or intellectual confidence, and for the next three years she threw herself with desperate vigour into study to forget the man with whom she had believed herself to be in love. Her interest in finding out for herself about social problems and their possible resolution sent her to Lancs. to investigate the lives of the cotton workers.

Returning to London, she started to work with Canon Barnett of Toynbee Hall and the social investigator Charles BOOTH, who was married to her cousin. It was Booth's work that convinced her that there could be no solution to the problem of poverty until a statistical survey had audited its extent, location and nature. In 1886 she wrote an article in the *Pall Mall Gazette*, 'A Lady's View of the Unemployed in the East End', complaining of the unscientific nature of the solution to the current problem of high unemployment in the East End of London. Further social investigation followed when Beatrice volunteered to survey London's docklands for Booth's project. By now convinced that she had found '*the* work I have always longed to do … the realization of my youthful ambition', she moved on to study the sweating system in the East End where, in the

interests of research, Beatrice disguised herself as a rag-trade worker, albeit not a very adroit one, and published her observations in *Nineteenth Century*, in which she unequivocally recognized the need for the regulation of labour. In May 1888 she was called to give evidence to the House of Lords Select Committee on Sweating, and vividly portrayed the appalling conditions in which women in particular worked for a pittance, victims of a capitalist system which was built on 'the evil spirit of the age, unrestricted competition'. But despite her growing expertise, she was disinclined to devote herself to investigating the conditions of women, whom she seemed reluctant to see as a special category. Indeed, she had signed the manifesto of the novelist Mrs Humphrey Ward against women's suffrage, feeling that she personally had not been prevented from achieving what she had wanted in a career by being a woman; indeed it had been a positive advantage.

In 1889 she left her work with Booth: she wanted to explore political and economic solutions to the social problems that their inquiries had revealed, and the Co-operative movement which had first interested her in Lancs. seemed a possible alternative to conventional capitalist enterprise. She resolved to work on a history of the movement, and a friend suggested she should meet Sidney WEBB, whose essay on the 'historic basis' of Fabianism she had just read and much admired. She 'like[d] the man', considered him a 'loophole into the socialist party' which she was teetering on the edge of joining, but found him physically and socially unappealing with his 'tiny tadpole body … Cockney pronunciation, poverty'. But the self-educated minor civil servant, son of a clerk, found the willowy, ethereally beautiful, upper-class Miss Potter utterly compelling. Throughout that summer Beatrice sternly rebuffed Webb's passionate declarations of love while asking for his help in explaining the diagrams in Alfred MARSHALL's *Principles of Economics* and advising him to work at his pronunciation. At last Beatrice relented and the pair were married on 23 July 1892.

It was an avowedly rational union: Sidney had urged marriage on the basis that together they could accomplish more than they could apart (he had even drawn a diagram to prove it), while Beatrice calculated, 'we are both of us second-rate minds, but we are curiously combined – I am the investigator, and he the executor – and we have a wide and varied experience of men and things between us. I also have an unearned salary.' This forms our unique circumstance.' But as well as shared intellectual capital, working methods and political aims, the marriage also brought emotional contentment, security and companionship to Sidney, as well as to Beatrice, who had perhaps sounded a little hollow in her espousal of 'glorious spinsterhood'. The 'firm of Webb', as Beatrice called it, was protean in social reform projects, in promoting trade unionism (Beatrice had been particularly impressed by the London dock strike of 1890), and in working for the reform of local government, the extension of education and the relief of poverty. Their works were jointly researched (with Beatrice better on the people side and Sidney a genius at absorbing and distilling facts) and authored: *A History of Trade Unionism* (1894) and *Industrial Democracy* (1897), both of which were concerned with the issues of organized labour in a democratic society. The first book of the Webbs' monumental 11-volume history of English local government appeared in 1903, the last in 1929.

As Fabians, the Webbs believed in a policy of persuasion, and they held dinner parties in their home near the House of Commons to which they invited politicians and those with the facts that the Webbs thought the politicians needed. (These intellectually rich but ascetic evenings were parodied in *The New Machiavelli* (1911) by a fellow Fabian, H. G. WELLS, in which Beatrice features as Altiora Bailey.) In 1913 their drawing-room conversations were extended in print with the founding of the weekly journal the *New Statesman*. But their belief in rational intellect rather than material politics made them unreliable political weather-vanes, putting their trust in New Liberalism rather than the burgeoning Labour Party in the years before the First World War. In 1909 Beatrice was invited to be a member of the Royal Commission on the Poor Law and the Relief of Distress, but when the report was published in 1909 the Webbs dissented from its recommendations; they published a minority report recommending that the Poor Law should be abandoned altogether and government ministries developed to provide a range of social services, including what was essentially a National Health Service in embryo. It was an attempt to address the structural causes of problems rather than deal with their consequences, but it appeared too much like coercive State intervention on a grand scale, and the more modest, and more partial, reforms of LLOYD GEORGE won the day.

By 1912 Beatrice, disillusioned with the Liberals (the 'Limps' as she called them) had joined the Independent Labour Party. After the First World War she encouraged Sidney in his bid to enter Parliament in the Labour interest and founded the Half-Circle Club in 1920 to prepare Labour MPs' wives for the day when their husbands would take ministerial office. When that happened in 1924, Beatrice felt somewhat isolated, spending her time with Sidney's constituents in Co. Durham, at Passfield Corner, the house they had bought in Hants, or engaged in her 'creative writing'. Her autobiography, *My Apprenticeship*, was published in 1926 to the considerable surprise of those who had thought of Beatrice as little but a dry gradgrind. Sidney was elevated to the peerage in 1929, but Beatrice resolutely refused to call herself Lady Passfield even when the wife of Stanley BALDWIN insisted, 'we shall call you that whether you like it or not'.

In May 1932 the Webbs, inspired by the eulogies of fellow left-wing intellectuals like George Bernard SHAW and Bertrand RUSSELL, visited the Soviet Union. The Russian Communist Party had revered the authors of the *History of Trade Unionism* (Lenin himself had translated it) and they were royally received. For their part the Webbs embraced the Soviet Union with fervour, marvelling at Stalin's collectivist farms and Pioneers of Communist Youth. Excusing rumours of terrorism as the 'war measures' of an emerging society that was solving the economic problems of production and consumption, they published *Soviet Communism: A New Civilisation?* on their return, to the dismay of many of their friends and admirers. Beatrice's final political pamphlet, 'The Truth about Soviet Russia', which continued to vindicate Stalin, was published in 1942

In mid April 1943 Beatrice wrote the last entry in the diaries she had been keeping since girlhood and which now totalled three million words. On 30 April she died: Sidney kept her ashes in a box on the mantelpiece. He died four years later: *Our Partnership* (Beatrice's account of their marriage published posthumously) was over. Its fruits persist in the continuation of the *New Statesman*, the London School of Economics (which they were instrumental in founding in 1894), a regard for the social sciences as the basis for action and the belief in politics as the enactment of moral responsibility.

Norman and Jeanne Mackenzie (eds), The Diaries of Beatrice Webb (4 vols, 1982–5)
Carole Seymour-Jones, Beatrice Webb: Woman of Conflict (1992)

Chronicle, and in 1953 joined the Labour-supporting *Daily Mirror*, moving to the *Evening Standard* in 1958, where his angry socialist cartoons with their distrust of the Soviet Union, antipathy towards the USA and humanitarian reproach for the poor and wretched of the earth were as powerful as any written comment. A contributor to the *New Statesman*, a leading supporter of the Campaign for Nuclear Disarmament (CND), and the creator of 'Supermac', which did little to help MACMILLAN's image in the final years of his premiership, the angst-ridden Vicky killed himself when he was 52 and still a prolific cartoonist.

WEIZMANN, CHAIM (1874–1952), scientist, Zionist leader and first President of Israel. Born in Russian Poland, he studied in Germany before taking up a post as a biochemist at Manchester University in 1906. A British subject from 1910, he became active in the campaign for a Jewish homeland in Palestine. As Director of the Admiralty laboratories (1916–19), he made important discoveries which assisted the wartime munitions industry. His good connections with the British government led to his participation in the negotiations that produced the BALFOUR Declaration, outlining British support for a Jewish homeland in Palestine. He served as President of the World Zionist Organization (1920–31, 1935–46) and of the Jewish Agency from 1929. He became President of an independent Israel in 1949.

WELLCOME, SIR HENRY (1853–1936), drug manufacturer. Raised in Minnesota, USA, Wellcome worked in a drugstore before studying pharmacy in Philadelphia. In 1880, after several apprenticeships, he joined Silas Burroughs to form Burroughs, Wellcome & Co., a prosperous London-based drug manufacturers which produced compressed drugs under the trade name Tabloid. On Burroughs's death in 1895 Wellcome bought what had become a highly lucrative business and used his fortune to support scientific research, founding the Wellcome Physiological Research Laboratories (1894) and the Wellcome Tropical Research Laboratories, Khartoum (1901). In 1924 he transformed his pharmaceutical firm and medical research organization into the Wellcome Foundation, the largest private organization funding research into medicine and its history.

WELLES, ROBERT (?–1470), rebel leader. Leader of the Lincolnshire rising against EDWARD IV in March 1470. When the King intervened in his father's feud with a neighbour, as self-styled 'great captain of the commons of Lincolnshire', he called upon the people to resist. At Empingham, near Stamford, the rebels were defeated and shed their defensive clothing so fast as to give the skirmish the name 'Lose-cote Field'. Fearful that they had been plotting with Warwick (*see* NEVILLE, RICHARD) to put Clarence (*see* PLANTAGENET, GEORGE) on the throne, Edward had both Robert and his father Richard Welles beheaded.

WELLESLEY, SIR ARTHUR (1st Duke of Wellington) *see* essay on page 821

WELLESLEY, RICHARD (2nd Earl Mornington, 1st Marquess of Wellesley) (1760–1842), Governor General of India. Wellesley significantly extended British power and influence in India between 1797 and 1805. An MP in 1784, a Lord of the Treasury in 1786 and a Commissioner of the East India Co. from 1793, as Governor General he pledged to fight French interest in India, receiving active support from William PITT THE YOUNGER and Henry DUNDAS. His first significant move was against Tipu Sultan, ruler of Mysore, an adherent of France, who in 1799 was decisively defeated at Seringapatam. Victory earned Wellesley an Irish peerage (a double-gilt potato, he derisively called it) and the room to manoeuvre towards a system of subsidiary alliances with client kingdoms. Territory was also ceded to direct British rule, in some cases through force. His brother Arthur WELLESLEY led campaigns to annex territory in south India. Tension between Richard Wellesley and the East India Co. mounted, but he was seemingly vindicated by quelling the rebellious Maratha chiefs in 1802–3. Only when the Marathas rose in 1805 and the British were defeated at Bharatpur, did the company demand his recall. Ambassador to Spain in 1809, and Foreign Secretary until 1812, his final public office was as Lord Lieutenant of Ireland (1821–8 and 1833–4).

WELLINGTON, 1ST DUKE OF *see* WELLESLEY, ARTHUR, essay on page 821

WELLS, H(ERBERT) G(EORGE) (1866–1946), writer and Fabian socialist. From a lower middle-class home in Bromley (Kent), Wells's first job was as an apprentice draper. At the Normal School of Science, Kensington (now Imperial College), he studied under T. H. HUXLEY and started writing on science and the social sciences, showing an interest in eugenics and a distaste for 'the masses', from whence he had so recently sprung. His writings from this period include *Anticipations of the Reaction of Mechanical and Scientific Progress upon Human Life and Thought* (1901) and *A Modern Utopia* (1905).

From 1903 to 1908 Wells was a disputatious member of the Fabian Society (1884), which favoured a gradualist approach of education and

continued on page 822

WELLESLEY, SIR ARTHUR 821

WELLESLEY, SIR ARTHUR ('THE IRON DUKE')
(1st Duke of Wellington) (1769–1852)
Soldier, politician and Prime Minister (1828–30)

Born into the impoverished Irish aristocracy, educated at Eton, Wellesley finished his education at a French military academy at Angers, and his elder brother lent him money to purchase a commission as an ensign in the 73rd Highlanders in 1787. Over the next six years, he purchased his way up to be lieutenant colonel of the 33rd Foot, which regiment he commanded in the disastrous Flanders campaign (1794–5). His fortunes changed decisively when he sailed with his regiment for India in 1797, where he served as Governor of Mysore (1799) and became a Major-General (1802), after which he fought in the Second Maratha War (1803–5). Returning to England he became MP for Rye in 1806. As Chief Secretary for Ireland (1807–9) he was firm but fair-minded, criticizing absentee landlords and prohibiting triumphalist processions on the anniversary of the defeat of the United Irishmen.

It was the Peninsular War that confirmed Wellesley's military reputation. After Sir John MOORE's abortive Corunna campaign, Wellesley led the British army and its Portuguese allies into a five-year campaign against the French. His success was largely due to the British navy which supplied him with provisions or the wherewithal to obtain them from the local population, whereas the much larger French armies were forced to scavenge from the land. He won a series of battles against the French, and was able to sit out a French onslaught ensconced in a coastal stronghold in the Torres Vedras campaign of 1811–12. He conducted successful sieges against French-held fortresses, caught the retreating French forces at the Battle of Salamanca on 23 July 1812 and moved to capture Madrid on 12 Aug. Napoleon's withdrawal of forces for the Russian campaign allowed Wellesley to regroup and pursue the French back onto their own soil, winning the victories at Orthez (27 Feb. 1814) and Toulouse (10 April).

Wellesley was created Duke of Wellington and after Napoleon's abdication, appointed Ambassador to the French court, accompanying Castlereagh (see STEWART, ROBERT) to the Congress of Vienna. On the news of Napoleon's return, Wellington was made Commander-in-Chief of the British forces in March 1815. He marched to meet Napoleon, intervening in the Franco-Prussian Battle of Ligny on 16 June at Quatre Bras, and narrowly avoided capture. But it was not until 18 June that the British encountered the full French army at Waterloo. Wellington's army held firm against five major attacks by the French forces; he finally ordered the counter-attack, and drove the French armies from the field, pushing them back to Paris, from where Napoleon was again sent into exile, this time to St Helena, and Wellington was put in charge of the allied army of occupation. His military success was largely due to his brilliance as a defensive tactician, stringent in the conservation of his forces, always poised to take advantage of the enemy's mistakes or weakness and able to judge exactly when to counter-attack without unnecessary loss of life.

By now a wealthy man, Wellington could have retired to the life of a country gentleman, but in his remaining 37 years he crammed in enough for two or three ordinary careers. He advised the government on the employment of military force to deal with insurrections both in Ireland and England, and organized the defence of London which many thought would be under attack from Chartist demonstrations. He also vigorously opposed any social reform of the British army, refusing to countenance soldier education, the abolition of flogging, short-term enlistment and various other schemes to civilize the 'brutal, licentious lobster' and turn him into a professional soldier. Wellington had fought and won with armies composed of the 'scum of the earth', and saw no reason to experiment with a more enlightened regime.

Wellington became Prime Minister at the beginning of 1828 when the demand for Catholic Emancipation was at its height. Supported by his Home Secretary Sir Robert PEEL, he agreed to the conditions laid down by GEORGE IV that emancipation should not become a government issue. But after the Co. Clare by-election he recognized that further deferment could only result in civil war. The King was won round only after Wellington and Peel threatened to resign. Catholic Emancipation split the Tories and brought the Whigs to power in 1830, after which Wellington became the elder statesman of the Tory party. He served briefly as Foreign Secretary in Peel's minority government of 1834–5 and was Minister without Portfolio during Peel's second ministry of 1841–6. His sense of duty and discipline and concern for order gave his Toryism a pragmatism that was lacking among the ultra-Tories with whom he tended to identify.

Elizabeth Longford, Wellington: The Years of the Sword (1969); Wellington: Pillar of State (1972) the permeation of local government to bring about socialism. For much of his life he experimented with forms of organization to implement his political vision, serving briefly as Minister of Information in the First World War (largely as a result of the publication in 1914 of his book *The War That Will End War*); striving to shape a League of Nations that was compatible with his own view of world citizenship; visiting Russia in 1920 to meet Lenin; travelling to see Stalin and, separately, F. D. Roosevelt in 1934; twice standing unsuccessfully for Labour and pursuing a role as educator with the publication of such books as *The Outline of History* (1920).

Success came with his works of fiction, many of which (*The Time Machine* (1895), *The Island of Dr Moreau* (1896), *The Invisible Man* (1897), *The War of the Worlds* (1898) and *The First Men on the Moon* (1901)) were based on his acquaintance with the sciences, and his concern with prevailing Edwardian social issues. In this category could be included his most enduring novels, some of which also reflect the distaste he felt for his experiences as a child and a young man: *Love and Mr Lewisham* (1900), *Kipps* (1905), *Tono-Bungay* (1909), *Ann Veronica* (1909), which scandalized with its advocacy of women's emancipation, *The History of Mr Polly* (1910) and *The New Machiavelli* (1911), a thinly veiled portrait of Sidney and Beatrice WEBB. Wells, who was married twice, also had an active extramarital life which has been well documented, particularly by the illegitimate son he had with the writer Rebecca WEST.

WELSH, JANE (1801–66), intellectual and wife to Carlyle *see* CARLYLE, THOMAS

WENTWORTH, ANN (*fl.* 1516), visionary. Twelve-year-old daughter of Sir Roger Wentworth, a leading magnate in Essex, in 1515 she began suffering violent fits which were cured by visions of Our Lady of Ipswich, and she became the centre of revivalist excitement at Ipswich's Marian shrine, attracting large crowds which subsequently included CATHERINE OF ARAGON and Thomas WOLSEY. She soon retired into obscurity as a nun in the Minories, London; her demonstrations were a decade too early to take on the political significance accorded Elizabeth BARTON.

WENTWORTH, PETER (1524–97), parliamentarian. Son of a Bucks. knight, he was reared in a radically Protestant atmosphere and after entering Parliament in 1571 became an outspoken Puritan voice in the Commons. In his anxiety to see further Church reform and the execution of MARY QUEEN OF SCOTS, he agitated for parliamentary freedom of speech in 1576, earning brief impris-

onment. From 1587 he caused equal fuss and underwent longer imprisonment for urging a long-suffering ELIZABETH I to settle the royal succession.

WENTWORTH, THOMAS *see* essay on page 823

WENTWORTH-FITZWILLIAM, WILLIAM (2nd Earl Fitzwilliam) (1748–1833), politician. Heir to Rockingham's (*see* WENTWORTH, CHARLES) Yorks. estate, and to his political influence there, Fitzwilliam nevertheless remained a second-rank politician. A devoted friend of both BURKE and Charles James FOX, he trod a complicated political course during the 1790s. Having transferred his support to PITT THE YOUNGER in 1794, he was made Lord Lieutenant of Ireland but, having indicated warmer support for Catholic Emancipation than Pitt was prepared to endorse, resigned in bad humour. He allied with the Whigs, and was consequently usually in opposition during the early nineteenth century. In 1819 he resigned as Lord Lieutenant of the West Riding in protest over the Peterloo Massacre, when 11 people were killed in a savage repression of a meeting to hear 'Orator Hunt' (*see* HUNT, HENRY) speak in Manchester.

WESKER, ARNOLD (1932–), playwright. From a Jewish immigrant, communist family in the East End of London, he drew on his experience of short-term jobs, including his time as a pastry cook and as an airman in the RAF, for his early plays, *The Kitchen* (1959), his trilogy *Chicken Soup with Barley* (1957), *Roots* (1959), *I'm Talking about Jerusalem* (1960) and *Chips with Everything* (1962). His work came to exemplify the term 'kitchen sink drama'– a social realist slice of working-class life rather than a portrayal of the upper-class drawing-room – a culture shift that was apparent in work from playwrights like John OSBORNE and in novels, films and paintings in the late 1950s. At Centre 42 (1961–70), a company committed to bringing socialist-inspired theatre to working-class people, Wesker directed several of his own plays, premiering some overseas, in Cuba and Yugoslavia among other places.

WESLEY, CHARLES (1707–88), Methodist and writer of hymns. The younger brother of John WESLEY, Charles and his friends were the first Methodists. Like his brother he joined the mission to Georgia, and, following a similar conversion experience, Charles also undertook itinerant preaching, but was more sensitive than John Wesley to claims that their activities were causing a separation within the Church. After 1756 he stopped itinerant preaching and tried to persuade Methodist preachers to seek ordination

continued on page 824

WENTWORTH, THOMAS (Baron and Viscount Wentworth, 1st Earl of Strafford) (1593–1641)
Politician

A leading Yorks. gentleman, he was knighted when only 18, and was then sent to travel on the continent before his first service as knight of the shire for Yorkshire in the 1614 Addled Parliament. He was prominent in Parliamentary opposition to arbitrary royal government and financial exactions (including to the Forced Loan of 1626–7), until after the 1628 Parliament, when CHARLES I gave him a barony and the presidency of the Council of the North; the interpretation of his sudden dramatic change of stance remains controversial. His relations with Lord Treasurer Richard WESTON (who had played a major part in securing him his peerage) soon deteriorated, and from 1630 he grew increasingly close to William LAUD, leaving behind his previous adherence to the Calvinist churchmanship of Archbishop ABBOT; throughout the 1630s the friendship and cooperation of Wentworth and Laud remained constant. Wentworth had become increasingly prominent on the Irish committee of the Privy Council, and in 1632 he was made Lord Deputy in Ireland, charged with increasing royal revenue and bringing an end to corruption and waste. To do so, he ruthlessly and tactlessly promoted the royal policy of 'Thorough', first making an unexpected alliance with the overwhelmingly Roman Catholic Old English against the predominantly Protestant New English settlers, but he alienated the Old English by investigating insecure land titles in the Crown's interest. Such was his success in the short term that in 1634 he gained Charles's permission to hold a Parliament (in contrast to its complete abeyance in England); it was dissolved in April 1635. In this he exploited the rivalry of New and Old English. His backing of a new plantation scheme in Connacht (1635) aroused fury among the Old English for its threat to their interests, while the simultaneous Crown seizure of Londonderry appalled the New English and their contacts in England. Wentworth allowed a good deal of latitude to Roman Catholic clergy; he also backed moves to bring the Church of Ireland into line with Laud's English religious policies, in opposition to its generally Calvinist-sympathizing leadership. He was as energetic in reclaiming lands for the Church as for the Crown, an unprecedented move which created much alarm back in England; additionally he made a huge profit for himself in lands and revenues from his lease of the Customs. He was recalled to England in 1639 to help the King in the gathering crisis, and Charles granted him an earldom (1640); his success in the Short Parliament (1640) in rallying the House of Lords to support Charles was in dismal contrast to the King's mishandling of the Commons. Reluctant to see Parliament dissolved, he nevertheless subsequently urged Charles to use emergency powers to take control in England, and seems to have recommended impeaching opposition leaders for their treasonable contacts with the Scots who had been fighting the Crown (and for whom he had a deep contempt). On the collapse of the royal regime, he was a prime target for revenge, particularly from the champion of the New English, Richard BOYLE, Earl of Cork, whose Irish estates had suffered the most from the campaign to strengthen the Church. After a tumultuous and blatantly unfair parliamentary trial, Charles abandoned Wentworth, assenting to his attainder and his execution on Tower Hill in 1641. There was widespread rejoicing and much exultant pamphleteering at his death.

Wentworth was a magnetic personality whose energy and efficiency allowed little belief in compromise and little respect for his opponents' judgement. His career has remained controversial between Whig and Tory historians in similar fashion to that of his master, and his time in Ireland has attracted argument about its significance: were his policies a dress rehearsal for similar royal ruthlessness in England or an attempt to face the problems of Irish government in a distinctive way? A revived interest in Wentworth emerged among French conservatives at the time of the 1789 Revolution, and in 1796 one of his French admirers published the first biography of him; the climax of sympathy for his qualities and his tragedy comes in the masterly modern life by C. V. Wedgwood. Studies of his Irish policy by Hugh Kearney and Terence Ranger damningly stressed the absolutism and selfish factionalism displayed in his Irish policy, whereas J. P. Cooper emphasized his principled loyalty to Charles. His rich archive of papers now in Sheffield City Archives is one of the most revealing sources for high politics in the early Stuart period, yet historians in the past relied on eighteenth-century selections, and the full range of the papers has begun to be exploited only in the last 50 years.

C. V. Wedgwood, Thomas Wentworth First Earl of Strafford 1593–1641: A Revaluation (1961) within the Established Church. In 1784 he denounced his brother's ordination of Methodist ministers, and before his death insisted that he should be buried in consecrated ground rather than the City Road Methodist chapel (London) that he had helped found.

WESLEY, JOHN (1703–91), founder of Methodism. Lincs. born, the son of a clergyman who, though raised as a Dissenter, favoured the High Church, Wesley was educated at Oxford where he became a college tutor and, together with his younger brother Charles WESLEY, was a member of the High Church 'Holy Club' for religious study and devotion as well as pastoral work among prisoners and the poor. He was ordained Deacon in 1725, elected Fellow of Lincoln 1726 and ordained priest in 1728. In 1735, Wesley was appointed to minister to colonists in Georgia, but having aroused antagonism, he returned two years later. Contact with the Moravian brethren and their devotional practices provided the context for a religious experience at a meeting in Aldersgate, London in 1738, which fired his interest in the relationship between conversion and faith.

Following the example of George WHITEFIELD, whom he had first encountered in the Holy Club, Wesley began to travel and preach in the open air, attracting large crowds. He encouraged the formation of Methodist societies for devotional purposes, and devised an organizational structure that effectively bound these bodies together; the first of a series of annual conferences was held in 1744. By 1767 Wesleyan Methodist societies totalled some 25,000 members – the vast majority in England – which made them a relatively small, but not inconsiderable group by the standards of the old Dissenting sects. He claimed that his efforts were intended to strengthen the established Church, but in practice, his network of lay preachers – humble men by the standards of the Anglican clergy – was not easily accommodated within the establishment. After his death, when Methodist membership had grown to over 70,000, a formal separation took place.

In some ways very much a man of his age, with an interest in science and the systematic study of religious experience, Wesley was an inspired popularizer, warily sympathetic to the ways in which poorer people spontaneously expressed their fears, hopes and beliefs. A very effective orate and prolific writer, he tried to make suitable contemporary works of fiction and non-fiction accessible to a wide audience by abridging and rewriting them.

WEST, BENJAMIN (1738–1820), painter. He came from a Quaker family in Pennsylvania and travelled to London in 1763, where he became established as a fashionable portrait-painter and abandoned his Quaker beliefs for Anglicanism. West's ambition to move into history-painting was helped by a commission from Robert Hay Drummond, Archbishop of York, who recommended him to GEORGE III (1766). West caused great controversy when he made it known that his *Death of WOLFE* (completed 1770) would show the subjects in modern rather than the usual classical costume, and Joshua REYNOLDS and Hay Drummond pleaded with him to change his mind. The *Death of Wolfe* was West's most successful painting and he followed it with other modern historical subjects. The favourite painter of George III, from 1772 West undertook a series of historical works at Windsor, including eight illustrations of the life of EDWARD III at St George's Hall. He was President of the Royal Academy from 1792 until his death.

WEST, DAME REBECCA (originally Cicily Fairfield Andrews) (1892–1983), writer. First an actress (her pseudonym comes from the part she played in Ibsen's *Rosmersholm* in 1911), she joined the staff of *The Freewoman*, a feminist periodical which her mother had not allowed her to read, and then started to write her acerbic pieces for the socialist periodical *The Clarion*. In 1913, after critically reviewing his novel *Marriage*, she met and started what was to be a destructive and painful affair with the married writer H G. WELLS; their son Anthony was born in 1914, when it was socially unacceptable to be an unmarried mother. In 1916 she published a well-received biography of Henry James and her first work of fiction, *The Return of the Soldier*. It was followed at lengthy intervals by *The Thinking Reed* (1936), *The Fountain Overflows* (1956) and *The Birds Fall Down* (1966), which give a telling picture of the frustrations of being a woman in the early twentieth century. In 1937 she paid three visits to Yugoslavia: the controversial 500,000-word, two-volume *Black Lamb and Grey Falcon* (1941) was as much about West as about Yugoslavia. In 1945 she was commissioned to cover the trial of 'Lord Haw Haw' (William JOYCE) for the *New Yorker*, and the resultant book, *The Meaning of Treason* (1949), was revised in 1965 to include other traitors (BURGESS, MACLEAN, PHILBY and George BLAKE). A nostalgic view of a world she had lost, *1900* (1983), was her last book published in her lifetime: others, *romans-à-clef*, came posthumously.

WESTMORELAND, EARL OF, 1ST *see* NEVILLE, RALPH; **6TH** *see* NEVILLE, CHARLES

WESTON, SIR AYLMER (1864–1940), soldier. Educated at Woolwich, he was commissioned into the Royal Engineers in 1884. In 1899 in South Africa he commanded the 1st Mounted Engineers, a unit that operated in enemy territory, disrupting Boer communications. A competent soldier in colonial campaigns, Weston proved incapable of command in more complex situations, his handling of the Cape Hellas landings on 25 April 1915 proving little short of disastrous. Protected by the military establishment, he went on to command VIII Corps on the Western Front. Regarded by his men as the very embodiment of the amiable colonial soldier, he was totally out of his depth in modern high-technology warfare, and his post-war letters to the *Daily Telegraph* provided cartoonist David Low with the idea for 'Colonel Blimp'.

WESTON, RICHARD (1st Earl of Portland) (1577–1635), royal servant. From an Essex Roman Catholic knightly family, he studied at Cambridge and was frequently an MP between 1601 and 1626. He undertook several embassies and from 1621 held offices in the Exchequer, culminating in the lord treasurership in 1628. Unpopular because of his suspected Roman Catholicism but also disliked by HENRIETTA MARIA, he was saved from impeachment only by the dissolution of Parliament in 1629. Consistently opposed to military involvements, he engineered peace with Spain in 1630, and a further secret treaty in 1634; he was made Earl in 1633.

WESTWOOD, VIVIENNE (1941–), fashion designer. Westwood first attracted attention in 1971, when she opened a shop in London's King's Road with her then partner Malcolm MCLAREN. It became a focus for the newly emerging punk movement, which seized on her clothes of rubber and leather and her use of the safety pin, which became the iconic fashion device of the punks. From the early 1980s Westwood achieved international recognition as a fashion designer and she was named designer of the year for her increasingly flamboyant theatrical designs.

WEYMOUTH, 3RD VISCOUNT *see* THYNNE, THOMAS

WHARTON, PHILIP (4th Baron Wharton) (1613–96), politician. Longevity allowed this radically minded nobleman to sustain his staunchly independent stance through to the end of the century. A strong opponent of the court, Wharton signed the petition of 12 peers against royal misgovernment in 1640. He was chosen to command Parliament's army in Ireland in 1642. He commanded a Parliamentary regiment at the Royalist defeat at Edgehill (23 Oct. 1642), after which he was said to have hidden in a saw-pit,

from which he derived his nickname, Saw-Pit Wharton. Active in Parliament, he supported the Self-Denying Ordinance of 1644–5 which led to the resignation of most current commanders and the formation of the New Model Army. He disapproved of the execution of CHARLES I in Jan. 1649, was close to Oliver CROMWELL but welcomed the restoration of CHARLES II. Dissatisfied with the Anglican religious settlement, he became a Dissenter. In 1676–7 he was imprisoned with three other peers for claiming that Parliament's prorogation for 15 months amounted to a dissolution. He left for Flanders and Germany at the accession of JAMES II, and was a strong supporter of William of Orange (the future WILLIAM III). Made a Privy Councillor in 1689, he was precluded by age from playing a significant part in the new era.

WHARTON, PHILIP (1st Duke of Wharton) (1698–1731), politician. He was the son of Thomas WHARTON, to whom WILLIAM III felt so indebted that he stood godfather to his son. The son, however, was to prove more rakish than his father, and recklessly squandered his extraordinary advantages. He contracted a runaway 'Fleet marriage' (one carried out clandestinely by a disreputable clergyman). Sent to Geneva to learn good doctrine, he wandered further afield and accepted a title from the Old Pretender (*see* STUART, JAMES EDWARD), but converted to Whiggery before the Hanoverian succession. In recognition of his father's merits, and his own wayward talents, his inherited Irish title was raised to an English dukedom, the highest rank of the peerage and a most unusual honour, in 1718. He nonetheless set up as captain of the notorious Hell Fire Club, the subject of a royal proclamation in 1721. In 1723 he sponsored an opposition journal, the *True Briton*. In 1725 he went to Vienna, where he became an open adherent of the Pretender (*see* STUART, JAMES), who rewarded him with further titles and honours. He was convicted of high treason in his absence, and spent his final years roaming about Europe in a state of drunkenness and beggary.

WHARTON, THOMAS (5th Baron and 1st Marquess of Wharton) (1648–1715), politican. A rakehell who renounced his father's puritan piety, he was first returned to the Commons in 1673, and served regularly until his father's death removed him to the Lords in 1696. A firm supporter of the future WILLIAM III (and author of the catchy ballad 'Lilliburlero', which he claimed helped to drive JAMES II from his throne and which introduces the BBC World Service today), he was rewarded with the post of Comptroller of the Household in 1689. He was to hold a series of other posts during his career, including a brief spell as Lord Lieutenant of Ireland (1708–10) and Lord Privy Seal under GEORGE I. But his real contribution to the Junto was as a parliamentary debater and organizer, as well as enthusiastic electioneer, putting his income of £16,000 a year at the service of the 'honest interest' in over a dozen constituencies from his home county of Bucks. to Cumb. His son Philip, 1st Duke of WHARTON, was a grievous disappointment to the ageing Wharton, and in his will he diverted from him all he could for the benefit of his two daughters.

WHEATSTONE, SIR CHARLES (1802–75), inventor and pioneer of the electric telegraph. Wheatstone learned instrument-making in the family firm and studied natural philosophical subjects. He subsequently conducted important researches in acoustics, optics and the speed of electrical fluid, developed a technique of accurately measuring resistance (later called the Wheatstone bridge) and invented instruments such as the stereoscope (1838) and the concertina (1844). Professor of Experimental Philosophy at King's College, London (1834–75), he is best known for his collaboration, from the late 1830s, with William Fothergill Cooke, on the invention and marketing of the first British electric telegraph apparatus. He broke with Cooke in 1845 but thereafter built a scientific reputation and a fortune from telegraphic invention.

WHEELER, SIR MORTIMER (1890–1976), archaeologist. Wheeler was Keeper of Archaeology at the National Museum of Wales (1920–6). In the 1920s he developed his new technically rigorous methods for the recovery and examination of archaeological remains in excavations at Segontium and Brecon Gaer (Wales), Caerleon (Mon.) and Lydney (Glos.). During the 1930s he further developed these techniques on celebrated excavations at Verulamium (St Albans, Herts.) and Maiden Castle (Dorset). He was Keeper of the London Museum (1926–44), Director General of Archaeology in India (1944–7), Professor of Archaeology of the Roman Provinces at the Institute of Archaeology, London (1948–55), and a successful popularizer of archaeology.

WHELDON, SIR HUW (1916–86), television executive. Editor of the ground-breaking and influential BBC arts programme *Monitor* (1957–64), he joined the BBC in 1952 and rose through the corporation's hierarchy to become managing director (1968–75).

WHEWELL, WILLIAM (1794–1866), mathematician and philosopher. With his friends Charles BABBAGE and John HERSCHEL Whewell introduced continental techniques of mathematics to Cambridge, where he spent his career. During the 1820s he was ordained, developed interests in architecture and was appointed Professor of Mineralogy (1825): he developed mineralogical classification and pioneered mathematical crystallography. He worked hard to make physical sciences theologically safe and was responsible for introducing many words, including 'scientist', 'anode' and 'cathode'. In the 1830s he helped launch the British Association for the Advancement of Science and wrote the influential *History of the Inductive Sciences* (1837) and *The Philosophy of the Inductive Sciences* (1840). Appointed Professor of Moral Philosophy (1838) and Master of Trinity College in 1841, he introduced the natural sciences tripos and brought mechanical subjects into the mathematics tripos. He was involved in some key nineteenth-century intellectual controversies: he fiercely attacked utilitarianism and the doctrine of the plurality of worlds. Whewell's reputation as a polymath rests on the fact that he wrote on a vast range of subjects including mathematics, moral philosophy, religion, natural philosophy, political economy, architecture, poetry and the classics.

WHICHCOTE, BENJAMIN (1609–83), philosopher and Cambridge Platonist. Son of a Salop. gentleman, he was educated at Emmanuel College, Cambridge, of which he became a Fellow in 1633. In 1636 he became a university preacher and Sunday afternoon lecturer at Trinity College chapel, where he gained a reputation for sermons that concentrated on the nature and reason of the universe rather than arguments of doctrine. In 1644, despite his refusal to sign the Covenant, he was appointed Provost of King's College by Parliament, and Vice-Chancellor in 1651. His correspondence with Tuckney, Master of Emmanuel, where Whichcote argued against puritan Christianity and in favour of private judgement and rationality, was not published until 1753 but came to be regarded as the classic expression of Cambridge Platonism. This term has been used to designate the ideas of a group of men active between the 1630s and 1680s, concentrated in Emmanuel and Christ's colleges, who strove to reconcile reason and faith, the new natural philosophy and Christian revelation, and who drew on Plato's ideas for this purpose. Critics of empiricism, the idea that knowledge is built up from experience, they stressed the role of reason; at the same time they were critical of mechanical philosophy, which seemed to leave no room for spirit and God. Whichcote was ejected from Cambridge at the

Restoration; he subsequently had parishes in London and Cambs.

WHINFIELD, JOHN (1901–66), chemist. Whinfield studied chemistry at Cambridge and acquired skills in textile chemistry in Charles CROSS's and E. J. Bevan's laboratory and as a research chemist in the Calico Printers' Association. In 1941, inspired by Wallace Carothers's invention of nylon, he and James Dickson patented a technique for turning polymerized condensate of terephthalic acid and ethylene glycol into a strong fibre suitable for the textile trade. The commercial possibilities of the Whinfield–Dickson patent were not exploited until after the Second World War: in 1947 Imperial Chemical Industries marketed it as Terylene and Dupont as Dacron.

WHISTLER, JAMES MCNEILL (1834–1903), artist. Born in Massachusetts, he lived for part of his childhood in Russia, where his father worked as an engineer on the St Petersburg–Moscow railway. Expelled from the Military Academy at West Point, Whistler went to Paris to study painting when he was 21, arriving in London in 1859, where he was to live for the next 40 years, though he travelled frequently between France and England and formed an important bridge between the avant-garde of the two countries. Influenced by the newly popular Japanese art, Whistler's series of *Nocturnes* brought him fame, but also derision from John RUSKIN, the most influential critic of the age, who accused him in 1877 of 'flinging a pot of paint in the public's face'. Whistler, a monocled dandy, was incensed by the view that art had to be judged by its faithfulness to nature, since if that were the case 'the king of artists would be the photographer'; he sued for libel and though he won was bankrupt as a result and fled to Venice. On his return to London, his views on art and art critics were the subject of his famous 'Ten O'Clock Lectures', published as *The Gentle Art of Making Enemies* (1890). Whistler's aim was to revitalize British portraiture: his painting of his mother (1871) is one of the most famous portraits in Western art, while his portrayals of society women brought him a stream of commissions that has left a galaxy of Edwardian beauties hanging in art galleries in Britain and the USA.

WHISTON, WILLIAM (1667–1752), scientist and controversialist. The son of a clergyman, he studied at Cambridge and was ordained in 1693. In 1696 he published *A New Theory of the Earth*, an attempt to reconcile the biblical account of creation with Newtonian science. He succeeded NEWTON as Lucasian Professor at Cambridge in 1703. Having concluded that the doctrine of the Trinity was erroneous, he was deprived of his professorship in 1710. His *Primitive Christianity Revived* (1711) was prosecuted by Convocation in 1714, but the case was dropped. He gave scientific lectures in London, and regained some prosperity and respect through his friendship with Queen CAROLINE. He actively sought a method for determining longitude (a problem which John HARRISON solved). Increasingly eccentric in old age, he came to believe that the millennium was due. He took an interest in the *cause célèbre* of Mary TOFTS, said to have given birth to rabbits, and claimed that this had been predicted in the apocryphal biblical book of Esdras.

WHITAKER, THOMAS KENNETH (1916–) Irish economist. From an Ulster Catholic background, appointed Secretary of the Irish Republic's Department of Finance in 1955, he was responsible for the creation and publication in 1958 of the First Programme for Economic Development, which recognized that the policy of economic self-sufficiency had failed and set out targets for industrial expansion based on free trade and economic planning. While a shift in economic attitudes was already under way, the programme associated Whitaker and Sean LEMASS with the economic growth and renewed hopes of the 1960s after the depression of the 1950s. Whitaker became Governor of the Central Bank (1969–76) and Senator (1977–82). Prominent in many other bodies set up to encourage industrial development and cross-border reconciliation, he is recognized as one of Ireland's foremost public servants.

WHITBREAD, SAMUEL (I) (1720–96) and **SAMUEL (II)** (1764–1815), brewers and politicians. The elder Samuel was the son of a Beds. farmer who in 1736 apprenticed him to a London brewer. In 1742 he bought a share in a small brewery for £2–3,000; by 1761 he was the sole shareholder in the leading brewery in London, worth £116,000. He became a substantial landowner in Beds. and then an MP from 1768, generally voting with NORTH's ministry, and later with PITT THE YOUNGER. He was a generous benefactor to charitable causes, including those against slavery and in favour of prison reform, the latter led by his cousin John HOWARD. The younger Samuel Whitbread broke with his father over politics, following him as MP for Bedford in 1790 as an avowed follower of Charles James FOX. He led the ultimately unsuccessful campaign to impeach Henry DUNDAS, Lord Melville, for his alleged misconduct as Paymaster General, in 1805. Throughout his political career he supported peace with revolutionary and then Napoleonic France, and his opposition to the war contributed to a breach with his brother-in-law Charles GREY after 1808, which damaged the effectiveness of the opposition. He was a member of a radical faction among the Whigs, termed 'the mountain'. Whitbread remained actively interested in the brewery as well as his estates; he also acquired an interest in the financially precarious Theatre Royal, Drury Lane, and it was after a quarrel with his manager there that he cut his own throat in 1815. The Whitbread firm remained in the hands of family members and other partners until it became a public company in 1889.

WHITCHURCH, EDWARD (?–1561), printer. Based in London, he was enthusiastic for the Reformation and was a partner of Richard GRAFTON in various Protestant printing enterprises, including the 'Matthew Bible' (*see* ROGERS, JOHN), the Great Bible (1539), the official Homilies (1547) and the 1549 and 1552 Prayer Books. He looked after Archbishop CRANMER's family after his burning, and married his widow.

WHITE, GORDON (Baron White of Hull) (1923–95), entrepreneur. He joined his family publishing business and met James HANSON in the 1950s. When their respective businesses were both taken over by the Wiles group, White and Hanson set up business together, later buying out Wiles and renaming it Hanson Trust. From greetings-card manufacturers to multinational traders in companies, Hanson Trust grew to be by the 1980s one of the most successful companies on both sides of the Atlantic. White organized the US operations, arriving in New York in 1973 and buying a fish-processing company, the first of many that he built into a $6-billion conglomerate of low-technology enterprises. One of the colourful businessmen courted and ennobled by Margaret THATCHER, he was never a stranger to the gossip columns.

WHITEFIELD, GEORGE (1714–70), Evangelical preacher. Son of a Glos. innkeeper, he left school at 15, but in 1732 went to Oxford University. There he met Charles and John WESLEY and became a leading member of the Holy Club. Ordained in 1736, he developed an extremely effective popular preaching style. He went to Georgia in 1737–8, where he came into contact with nascent American Evangelism, and, on his return, preached in the open air. He attracted a huge popular following, although he was attacked for his unconventional conduct, unorthodox interpretation of the scriptures and lack of intellectual rigour. He spent the rest of his life travelling between America and England on Evangelical missions. In the early 1740s, he broke with Wesley because of doctrinal differences, Whitefield a strict Calvinist.

WHITEHEAD, A(LFRED) N(ORTH) (1861–1947), mathematician and logician. From a line of clerics and teachers, Whitehead was educated at Cambridge and elected a Fellow of Trinity College, Cambridge, in 1884. He was an uncommonly good teacher, and one his most gifted pupils was Bertrand RUSSELL, with whom he collaborated on establishing the logical foundations of mathematics: the result of this stupendous scholarly ambition was the revolutionary three-volume *Principia Mathematica* (1910–13) (a fourth, by Whitehead alone on geometry, never materialized), which has been considered the most important work on logic since Aristotle.

At Cambridge Whitehead had been a pure mathematician, publishing *A Treatise on Universal Algebra* (1893) and numerous papers, including the famous 'On Mathematical Concepts in the Material World' (1906). In 1910 he resigned his Trinity fellowship and went to London to take up the post of Professor of Applied Mathematics at Imperial College (1914–24). There his scholarly inquiries turned to the philosophy of science, and among his published works were *The Concept of Nature* (1920) and *The Principle of Relativity* (1922).

When he was 62 Whitehead moved to Harvard, where he was Professor of Philosophy and his concern was with what he termed the 'philosophy of organism', considering metaphysical questions, the relation between God and the universe, which resulted in such difficult works as *Process and Reality: An Essay in Cosmology* (1929) and *Nature and Life* (1934).

WHITEHOUSE, MARY (1910–), campaigner. A Ches. schoolteacher, Whitehouse started the 'Clean Up TV Campaign' in 1964, which metamorphosed into the National Viewers and Listeners Association (NVALA) a year later. A moral crusade of the so-called 'silent majority', NVALA based its campaign on the as yet unproven belief that violence and sex on television encourage similar behaviour particularly in the young, and that in the so-called 'permissive society' the Church, government and the media have abdicated their role as guardians of the morals and behaviour of the nation. The campaigns of the NVLA have included support for a Private Member's Bill in 1984 for the official classification of videos.

WHITELAW, WILLIAM (1st Viscount Whitelaw of Penrith) (1918–99), politician. Whitelaw was the great unsung hero of the early THATCHER years. As a Tory grandee he loyally guarded her against attacks from the Left and, with his fund of experience, gave her excellent counsel. Whitelaw was very much a Conservative of the old school, Winchester and Cambridge followed by a spell in the Guards. A farmer and landowner, he was elected for his own part of the country, Selkirk and the Borders, in 1955, and made a career in the Whips' Office which, in those days, was not the springboard for further promotion. As a Guardsman and a farmer, Whitelaw touched the contemporary party at its two main sources of MPs, which made him an ideal Whip, serving in the office (1959–62). He was chief opposition Whip (1964–70), and became Leader of the House under Edward HEATH. His period as Northern Ireland Secretary (1972–3) was marked by the failed attempt to set up a power-sharing assembly, and by his own secret attempts to negotiate with the IRA. As Secretary of State for Employment (1973–4), he found himself at the centre of the dispute with the miners, and was one of those who advised Heath to go to the country.

As Chairman of the Conservative Party for the next year Whitelaw presided over two unsuccessful elections but supported Heath loyally. When Heath was defeated in the leadership ballot by Thatcher in Feb. 1975, Whitelaw himself stood in the second round against her but lost. He took his defeat like the gentleman he was and served Thatcher loyally as deputy leader until the 1979 election victory, when he became Home Secretary. He stayed on after 1983 as Lord President of the Council and Leader of the Lords, having been rewarded by Thatcher with the first hereditary peerage for many years. He retired in 1988.

WHITELOCKE, BULSTRODE (1605–75), administrator. A lawyer, he worked busily for Parliament during the Civil Wars (1642–8) and for the regimes of the 1650s, in diplomacy and home affairs, always favouring moderation. He lived in comfortable retirement after the restoration of CHARLES II. He is important because he knew everybody and wrote extensive journals, fully edited in 1990.

WHITFORD, RICHARD (c. 1470–?1541), devotional writer. A Cambridge don from Clwyd who was a friend of ERASMUS and chaplain to Bishop Richard FOX, he entered Syon Abbey c. 1507. He produced a stream of devotional and polemic books designed to challenge Lutheranism, although he reluctantly took the 1536 Oath of Royal Supremacy. After the dissolution of Syon, he lived in London. An English translation of Thomas à Kempis's *Imitation of Christ* has, probably wrongly, been attributed to him.

WHITGIFT, JOHN (1532–1604), Archbishop of Canterbury (1583–1604). Born in Lincs., Whitgift began his career as a Cambridge don. Despite his Calvinist sympathies, he was very concerned to enforce Church order; his brisk disciplining of non-conforming Puritans attracted ELIZABETH I and led to the bishopric of Worcester in 1577, and in 1583 the archbishopric of Canterbury. He immediately confronted the Puritan clergy. Although government nervousness at the ensuing rows somewhat restrained him, he relied on Christopher HATTON's support against the discreet hostility of William CECIL, and encouraged much gradual reform in the Church. In 1595 he drew up a series of doctrinal articles (the Lambeth Articles) to end a row at Cambridge University caused by attacks on Calvinist doctrines of salvation. Argument continues about their theological character, but they were sufficiently thoroughgoing a statement of Calvinist views for later Puritans to appeal to them. Elizabeth I was annoyed that a clergyman should attempt to decide theology for her Church, and refused to give the Lambeth Articles official status.

WHITTINGHAM, WILLIAM (c. 1524–79), churchman and writer. An evangelical Oxford don who took refuge in Frankfurt and Geneva under MARY I, he was a keen supporter of John KNOX and was one of the main translators of the Geneva Bible (1557–60). Although apparently never ordained, he was Dean of Durham from 1563, doing much to wreck antiquities in the cathedral in his iconoclastic zeal; his wife burned the banner of St CUTHBERT.

WHITTINGTON, RICHARD (?–1423), businessman and philanthropist. A wealthy London entrepreneur and benefactor, he was deeply involved in the city's financial dealings with RICHARD II, HENRY IV and HENRY V. Although he was three times Lord Mayor of London and married Alice FitzWarin, there is otherwise little to connect him with the story of the young Dick Whittington whose cat helped him to prosperity, a common motif in European folklore which first appeared in a seventeenth-century ballad.

WHITTLE, SIR FRANK (1907–96), aeronautical engineer. Whittle developed aeronautical skills in the Royal Air Force and engineering expertise at Cambridge. In 1930, while a flying cadet in the RAF, he patented a gas-turbine propulsion engine, which permitted faster, higher-altitude flight, and in 1936 established a company for developing aircraft powered by his engine. A year later he had built his engine but it was 1939 before he secured Air Ministry funds for building his aeroplane. Whittle's engine powered the first British jet aircraft (launched 1941) and the first British military fighter, the *Meteor* (launched 1944).

WHITWORTH, JOSEPH (1803–87), engineer. Whitworth developed mechanical expertise in a Derb. cotton mill and as a mechanic in Manchester, and learnt precision engineering from Henry MAUDSLAY and Joseph Clement in London. In 1833 he started his own prosperous engineering firm in Manchester and gradually built a reputation as the foremost producer of high-precision machine-tools, from textile machines to cutting engines. He was also celebrated as the engineer of truly plane surfaces and as designer of a system of standard measures and gauges, notably screw threads. In 1857 he designed an accurate rifle, which was rejected by the War Office, and in the 1870s he mass-produced fluid-compressed steel for heavy artillery. He devoted much of his fortune to technical education.

WHYMPER, EDWARD (1840–1911), mountaineer. Cashing in on the Victorian Romantic fascination for mountains in 1860, Whymper accepted a commission to produce engravings of the Swiss Alps. He found himself to be a natural mountaineer and decided to try to beat the Italians to the top of the Matterhorn, as yet unscaled. On his fifth attempt, in 1865, he and his party found an untried route and rapidly reached the summit. But tragedy struck on the descent when the rope broke, sending four to their deaths on the glaciers below. There was outrage at home at such waste of young lives, but Whymper's justificatory *Scrambles among the Alps* (1871) proved a best-seller, and he continued to climb, collect specimens, take photographs and compile data on what the human body could expect at exceptionally high altitudes.

WIGG, GEORGE (1900–83), politician. A professional soldier elected as Labour MP for Dudley in the west Midlands in 1945, he was a formidable opponent of the then Secretary of State for War, John PROFUMO, whom he delightedly pursued in the Commons for his lies over his affair with Christine Keeler (1963). Campaign manager for Harold WILSON on the death of Hugh GAITSKELL, the arch-intriguer Wigg was rewarded with the post of Paymaster General (1964) with responsibility for security matters, with direct access to Wilson. But in 1967 a harried Wilson sent Wigg to the Lords and gave him the chairmanship of the Horserace Betting Levy Board.

WIGLAF, King of Mercia (827–9, 830–c. 838). Although not a member of the Mercian royal kindred, Wiglaf seized power after the death of King BEORNWULF. He was not able to recover the Mercian hegemony which was destroyed by Beornwulf's defeat at the Battle of Ellendun at the hands of King EGBERT of Wessex, and was even temporarily expelled from his kingdom. The weakening of Mercian power anticipates the kingdom's defeat by the Vikings in the time of Kings BURGRED and CEOLWULF II.

WIGMORE, BARON *see* MORTIMER, ROGER

WIHTRED, King of Kent (690–725). A ruler of some importance, he restored Kentish kingship after the confused period which had followed the deaths of HLOTHERE and EADRIC and freed Kent from the domination exercised by King CADWALLA of Wessex. Maintaining a Kentish tradition which went back to ETHELBERT, he issued a law-code which gave especially privileged treatment to the Church. He also had an extensive coinage of the early medieval money known as *sceattas* minted on his behalf. His career illustrates the achievements of the lesser kingdoms of England in the years before Wessex and Mercia achieved a near-permanent domination over smaller kingdoms. His co-operation with Archbishop BERHTWALD of Canterbury was a notable instance of collaboration between secular and religious authorities. He was succeeded by his son ETHELBERT.

WILBERFORCE, SAMUEL (1805–73), Anglican prelate. Son of William WILBERFORCE, he was ordained in 1828, became chaplain to ALBERT the Prince Consort, and from 1845 was Bishop of Oxford. He engaged in the controversies over biblical criticism, provoked by the publication of essays and reviews, and famously debated with T. H. HUXLEY the implications of natural evolution. He played a leading role in the revival of Convocation (1852) and founded Cuddesdon Theological College opposite his palace near Oxford. His nickname 'Soapy Sam' reflected his evident ease in the role of courtly bishop.

WILBERFORCE, WILLIAM *see* essay on pages 832–33

WILD, JONATHAN (?1682–1725), criminal. A London bucklemaker, having developed a network of connections among thieves, he opened a 'lost property' agency, for the sale back to their owners of goods whose theft he had planned. He titled himself 'thief-taker general', and claimed to be a public benefactor, regularly handing over to justice a selection of his criminal associates. Having been exposed, he was executed as a receiver of stolen property. He was the model for Peachum in GAY's *Beggar's Opera* (1728), and the subject of Henry FIELDING's novel, *Jonathan Wild the Great* (1743). Both authors implied that Wild's activities were analogous to those of contemporary politicians, whose clientage networks, they suggested, were based on similarly illicit understandings.

WILDE, JANE FRANCESCA (née Elgee) (1821–96), poet. 'A very odd and original lady', granddaughter of an archdeacon from Co. Wexford, she took the name 'Speranza' (Italian for 'hope') for the nationalist poetry she wrote for *The Nation* (edited by Charles Gavan DUFFY). A striking woman of great presence and a fine linguist, she published 13 books, including poetry, Irish myths and legends, and translations, of which Meinhold's *Sidonia the Sorceress* is the best known. In 1851 she married the oculist William Wilde: their home in Dublin's Merrion Square became a focus of Irish literary, theatrical and political life. Her second son was Oscar WILDE, who was devoted to her: she died while he was in Reading gaol. He was refused permission to go to her bedside: 'her death was so terrible to me that I, once lord of language, have no words with which to express my anger and shame'.

WILDE, OSCAR *see* essay on page 834

WILDMAN, SIR JOHN (*c.* 1621–93), conspirator. He was educated at Cambridge and studied law in London. In 1647 he became the leading spokesman for the regiments of the New Model Army in arguing against negotiations with CHARLES I, and accompanied the agents of five dissentient regiments to the general meeting of the army at Putney in Oct. He became an officer some time in the 1650s, and from 1655 was regularly referred to as Major. Elected MP in 1654, he plotted the overthrow of Oliver CROMWELL, with both Royalists and Levellers, and was imprisoned. In 1659, employed by the Council of Officers to draw up a form of government, he plotted to overthrow them, and helped seize Windsor Castle for Parliament.

Suspected of involvement in republican plots after the restoration of CHARLES II, he was imprisoned for a further six years. He was closely involved with Algernon SIDNEY, and in 1683 was imprisoned for involvement in the Rye House Plot to assassinate the King and the Duke of York (the future JAMES II). After the unsuccessful rising of James SCOTT, Duke of Monmouth, in 1685, in which he did not participate, he fled to the Netherlands, returning with William of Orange (the future WILLIAM III) in 1688, and writing many anonymous pamphlets. Made Postmaster General

in 1689, he was dismissed for using his position to discredit political opponents by means of forged letters.

WILFRID, ST (634–709), Bishop of York (664–78). Of Northumbrian descent, he was one of the most important and controversial figures of the conversion period. A great deal is known about his career from the biography composed by his chaplain EDDIUS STEPHANUS and from BEDE. Having spent important formative years in France and at Rome, he returned to England imbued with Gaulish ideas on episcopal dignity and with a strong devotion to the Papacy. Encouraged by his installation at Ripon in 660 by King ALHFRITH of Deira, he pushed for the adoption of Roman ideas in northern England. As a result, he was the leading protagonist on the Roman side at the Synod of Whitby (664) against the monk of Iona and Bishop of Northumbria, St COLMAN, an event which was a major turning-point in the penetration of northern Britain and Ireland by papal authority. Wilfrid's habit of appealing for papal support was also greatly to reinforce England's strong connections with Rome.

Appointed Bishop of York in 664, for the rest of his life he was involved in disputes with Kings ECGFRITH and Aldfrith of Northumbria, and with Archbishops St THEODORE OF TARSUS and BERHT-WALD of Canterbury, who sought, successfully, to divide Wilfrid's large diocese. During his exiles from Northumbria in 678 and 680, which resulted from his quarrels with Ecgfrith, he undertook missionary work in southern England, becoming the head of a confederation of monasteries in several kingdoms. He was a great builder, although now only the crypts of his churches at Hexham and Ripon survive.

WILKES, JOHN *see* essay on page 835

WILKINS, JOHN (1614–72), churchman and scientist. His first work, published in 1638, appeared to demonstrate that the moon was habitable. His subsequent works attempted to show how travel to the moon was possible, and argued that the earth was a planet. Son of an Oxford goldsmith noted for his love of experiments, he studied at the university, took orders, and became chaplain to the Prince Palatine, Charles Lewis, nephew of CHARLES I and older brother of Prince RUPERT. In the Civil Wars he supported the Parliament. An active member of Robert BOYLE's 'invisible college', the precursor of the Royal Society, he was appointed Warden of Wadham College, Oxford, in 1648, which he turned into the centre of intellectual life in the city. In 1652 he married Oliver CROMWELL's sister. He moved to the presidency of Trinity College, Cambridge, in

continued on page 836

WILBERFORCE, WILLIAM (1759–1833)
Evangelical philanthropist

Son of a prosperous Hull merchant, he came under Methodist influence in childhood, when he spent holidays with an aunt who was half-sister to John THORNTON and admired WHITEFIELD. His parents weaned him from this. After Cambridge, he served as MP for Hull, then for Yorks. In 1785, however, while on a continental tour, he experienced a 'conversion'. Back in England, he sought out Methodist advisers and read widely for himself. He came to espouse a form of 'moderate Calvinism', which set him apart from the Arminian followers of John WESLEY, but linked him with a wider movement of Calvinist revival.

Without this transforming experience he might have had a successful conventional political career. As it was, he remained embedded in mainstream politics, continuing to serve as MP for Yorks., which required him to pay attention to many issues affecting this populous manufacturing county, until 1812, when age and family responsibilities led him to retire to a less demanding borough seat. His Christian conscience, however, impelled him to develop a new form of public life, devoted to promoting moral and social reform at the highest levels of government and society.

The two causes to which he first attended were the 'reformation of manners' and the abolition of slavery. The reformation of manners campaign built on efforts by magistrates and other local government officers. Wilberforce persuaded the King to issue a 'proclamation against vice and immorality' (something conventionally issued at the beginning of a reign, sometimes on other occasions), and then recruited bishops, peers, MPs, philanthropic activists and local magistrates into a Society for the Enforcement of his Majesty's Proclamation. No subsequent campaign of his would draw so much support from the social and political establishment. His anti-slavery efforts associated him with what was to be a more customary mix of Dissenters and radicals as well as many ordinary people moved by this 'cause of humanity'. Quakers had been working to mobilize support for the abolition of the slave trade from the early 1780s; Wilberforce's support came when the movement was taking off as a humanitarian campaign of unprecedented scale and force. His contribution was to spearhead its crucial parliamentary campaign. In 1790 he first moved what would become his annual motion for abolition.

The early 1790s saw the formation of what was subsequently termed the Clapham Sect: a group of Evangelicals living in this fashionable London suburb. Henry THORNTON and his brothers – sons of John Thornton – formed the nucleus of the group, which appointed John VENN as rector and encouraged Wilberforce and fellow Evangelicals Charles Grant and Edward Eliot to settle nearby.

The outbreak of war with revolutionary France in 1793 decreased the chance of persuading Parliament to sacrifice property to human rights by prohibiting trade in slaves. Wilberforce did not abandon hope and found new outlets for his energies. Concern about the state of England's labouring classes was sharpened in the 1790s both by the belief that unalloyed misery provided fuel for revolutionaries and by the escalating poverty associated with a bad harvest and soaring prices in 1795–6. In response, Sir Thomas BERNARD established a Society for Bettering the Condition of the Poor, which took over members from the flagging Proclamation Society. Wilberforce was active in the new body. He also took an interest in dispatching Christian missionaries overseas, encouraged both by the growth of Evangelicalism and by millenarian expectations which the French Revolution helped to foster. He supported the interdenominational but chiefly dissenting London Missionary Society, and in 1799 helped found the Church Missionary Society, along with Charles Grant, who as an East India Company official had a special interest in Indian missions. Both also supported the interdenominational British and Foreign Bible Society.

In 1797 Wilberforce published *A Practical View of the Prevailing Religious System of Professed Christians in the Higher and Middle Classes of the Country contrasted with Real Christianity*. Here he set out the principles which governed his own life, arguing that mere occasional observance was not enough. Serious Christians should regard all 'their bodily and mental faculties … their substance, their authority, their time, their influence … as so many instruments to be consecrated to the honour and employed in the service of God'. A few months later, he married the daughter of a country banker near Birmingham, who shared his pious cast of mind. The first of their six children was born the following year.

In 1802 the Clapham Evangelicals launched a magazine, the *Christian Observer*, to express their views, under the editorship of Zachary Macaulay who complained about the difficulties of maintaining the middle ground between warring camps: 'The Dissenters make a violent clamour against it as being High Church, while the High

Church abuse it as being favourable to Methodists.' This captured the Evanglicals' position in general, yet in many respects the middle ground was a position of strength. It made it possible to operate with any of a number of allies, whichever best served their current purpose.

The early nineteenth century saw the Evangelicals making common cause with radicals in attacking corruption in high places. Their votes against government, against Melville (see DUNDAS, HENRY) in 1805 or in the scandal over the role of the mistress of the Duke of York (see FREDERICK AUGUSTUS) in the sale of army commissions (1809) were more embarrassing because they were *not* habitual oppositionists; their attitude helped erode the legitimacy of 'old corruption'.

Pitt's death in 1806 opened the way for the appointment of a cross-party 'Ministry of all the Talents'. Charles James FOX and other Whigs now brought into government gave the abolition movement powerful support. The abolition of the slave trade was finally carried in 1807.

In line with Wilberforce's constituency obligations, he chaired a parliamentary committee considering the wish of small Yorks. clothiers to preserve the domestic, as opposed to the factory, system, by reinforcing old laws against taking on large numbers of apprentices. The committee recommended against trying to constrain the spread of new technologies. Though the issue was divisive in Yorks. (and Wilberforce's opponents also criticized his anti-slavery stance) he held on to his seat, as again in the hotly contested 1807 election.

The issue of Catholic emancipation (allowing Catholics to sit in Parliament) rose in importance in the early nineteenth century. Many of Wilberforce's friends opposed emancipation but, while sharing their dislike of Catholicism, he was a supporter. Treating Catholics oppressively, he argued, enhanced the influence of priests within Catholic (especially Irish Catholic) culture, whereas the goal should be to integrate them into wider British society.

Wilberforce hoped to seize the occasion of peace negotiations at the end of the Napoleonic Wars to have the slave trade declared illegal by all European powers. A massive British petitioning campaign helped persuade British politicians to make this national policy at the Vienna Peace Conference. In fact, no more was achieved than a declaration condemning the trade and resolving to end it as soon as possible. Wilberforce however proceeded to obtain the support of the Pope, and, with his aid and financial inducements, Spain and Portugal were brought into line.

During the post-war years of popular agitation and disturbance, associated with economic hardship and the demand for an extension of political rights, Wilberforce set his face against popular radicalism, disliking its disorderly and subversive qualities, and particularly its anti-religious, sometimes blasphemous aspect. He supported the suspension of *habeas corpus*, though he criticized the government's use of spies and *agents provocateurs*. He opposed the motion for an inquiry into the Peterloo Massacre, when troops shot and killed members of a crowd gathered for a parliamentary reform demonstration in Manchester in 1819. He continued, however, to favour some reforming measures, notably 'penal reform' (the movement to reduce resort to the death penalty) and factory reform (limiting the working day and requiring the education of child workers).

The abolition of the slave trade opened the way for a movement to emancipate slaves. Deciding himself too old and ill to take the lead, Wilberforce nominated Thomas Fowell BUXTON, already prominent as a penal reformer. Wilberforce helped to found and became an active member of the Anti-Slavery Society (1822); he also prepared an opening manifesto.

In 1825 he retired from Parliament, rejecting a suggestion that he enter the Lords on the grounds that he had done no more than he was obliged to do as a Christian and, moreover, aristocratic society would be bad for his children. His sons were in fact to distance themselves from their father's Evangelicalism.

Wilberforce has always divided opinion. Some thought him a saint, or a humanitarian hero; others, a sanctimonious hypocrite. Some reformers, though prepared to work with him, saw his reforming interests as aberrations from an essentially conservative position. His anti-slavery stance has been particularly controversial. Some charged him with caring about slaves but ignoring the poor at home (an accusation that was scarcely fair). The campaign against the slave trade has itself been 'debunked' on the grounds that it arose only when profits from the trade declined, though few historians now accept that analysis. One does not have to think Wilberforce a saint to absolve him of some of these charges of inconsistency, arising as they do from an attempt to force him into ideological moulds not his own. His idiosyncratic career had much consistency in its own terms.

Robin Furneaux, William Wilberforce (1974)

WILDE, OSCAR FINGAL O'FLAHERTIE WILLS (1854-1900)
Poet, dramatist and critic

The second son of Jane Francesca WILDE, a journalist and poet, and Dr (later Sir) William Wilde, a surgeon and oculist, Oscar read classics first at Trinity College, Dublin then Magdalen College, Oxford where he was known as 'O'Flighty' to the Oxford hearties for his long hair, epigrammatic conversational style and aesthetic sensibilities. Despite his affectation as a dilettante, Wilde was an assiduous and brilliant scholar winning the Newdigate Prize for Poetry. But he had no clear idea how a genius was to earn a living, though he had resolved 'somehow or other I'll be famous, and if not famous, I'll be notorious'. In 1871 Wilde was invited to lecture in America as the personification of the limp, lilly-clutching aesthete in GILBERT and SULLIVAN's musical *Patience*. Dressed in velvet and fur, Byronic shirts and the knee breeches and stockings of his Masonic lodge, he took America by storm.

In May 1884 Wilde married Constance Lloyd and they moved into a house in Tite Street, Chelsea. Cyril was born in 1885 and Vyvan a year later, and Oscar's vermilion study decorated with peacock feathers became a night nursery. Though he remained fond of Constance their marital relations ceased.

In 1887 Wilde was appointed editor of *The Lady's World* but soon the routines of the magazine began to oppress this 'Pegasus in harness', and in 1889, he was sacked. He was contributing essays to magazines and journals: 'The Portrait of Mr WH' (1889) mused on the identity of the young man to whom Shakespeare's sonnets are addressed, while essays that first appeared in *The Nineteenth Century* and *The Fortnightly Review* including 'The Truth of Masks', 'The Decay of Lying', 'The Critic as Artist', were republished as a book. But it was his 'first long story', *The Picture of Dorian Gray* (1890), the tale of a man who retains his youthful looks as his painted images fades, that caused a sensation. Wilde insisted that it was 'a real work of art with a strong ethical message in it', but was received with almost universal condemnation as a 'tale spawned from the leprous literature of the French *décadents* – a poisonous book'.

Despairing of English morality masquerading as criticism, Wilde left for Paris, where he wrote another scandalous play which was never performed in England in his lifetime, *Salomé*, about the woman who danced before King Herod carrying the severed head of John the Baptist. In the spring of 1892, Wilde, in London to supervise the rehearsals of his first play for the London stage, *Lady Windermere's Fan*, started a relationship with Lord Alfred DOUGLAS, known as 'Bosie', that eclipsed all his earlier passions for young men. Yet as he was drawn more deeply into this intense and draining relationship, his literary and financial star was rising: *A Woman of No Importance* opened in April 1893, and though the critics were divided, the story of deception and revelation (a 'woman's play' wrote Wilde) ran for 118 performances. *An Ideal Husband* opened in Jan. 1985: it had, wrote George Bernard SHAW, 'the property of making his critics dull. Mr Wilde is to me our only thorough playwright.' *The Importance of Being Earnest* was a triumph when it opened on 14 Feb. 1895, but Wilde's pleasure was short-lived.

Bosie's father, the unstable Marquis of Queensberry (*see* DOUGLAS, JOHN SHOLTO), left a card at Wilde's club, accusing him of 'posing as somdomite' [*sic*]. Wilde, egged on by Bosie who was at war with his father, issued a writ against Queensberry, alleging libel. The case came to trial on 3 April 1895. The defence, led by Edward CARSON, conflated Wilde's 'immoral works' and his association with a string of young working-class boys. The civil case against Queensberry was lost and Wilde was arrested. His trial on charges of gross indecency opened on 26 April 1895. A dreary succession of 'boys' told of presents, flirtations and 'acts of sodomy' which Wilde denied, though he admitted that he was 'a lover of youth'. Again it was his writing and its power to corrupt that was on trial too, and Wilde mounted a magnificent defence of the 'love that dare not speak its name' at which the gallery 'burst into applause'. Wilde was found guilty and received the maximum sentence of two years' hard labour, the judge describing the case as the worst he had ever tried.

In prison Wilde wrote an indictment of the justice system, *The Ballad of Reading Goal* (1898), and started *De Profundis*, an outpouring of his bitterness against the man who still 'walked free among the flowers' whilst he languished in a prison cell. But on his release in May 1899, Wilde soon weakened and responded to his 'darling boy', meeting with Bosie, as, under the name of Sebastian Melmoth, he wandered Europe from Dieppe to Naples to Paris where he died, fortified by the rites of the Roman Catholic church, in a small left-bank hotel.

Rupert Hart-Davis (ed.), *The Letters of Oscar Wilde (1962)*
Richard Ellman, *Oscar Wilde (1987)*

WILKES, JOHN (1725–97)
Radical

Son of a prosperous London distiller and his Presbyterian wife, he was educated at Leiden University in the Dutch Republic; not unusual for those unsympathetic to the exclusive Anglicanism of Oxford and Cambridge. A fellow student remembered him both for his ugliness (he had a pronounced squint) and for 'the daring profligacy for which he was afterwards notorious'. He was fond of learning, but 'passionately desirous of being thought something extraordinary'.

In 1747 he returned home to marry a woman 10 years older, heiress to the manor of Aylesbury. The marriage gave him the means to live as a gentleman, but was unhappy, and in 1757 they separated. He developed a set of well-connected but rakish friends, including Sir Francis DASH-WOOD and Lord Sandwich (see MONTAGU, JOHN), whom he joined in blasphemous and erotic antics, and with whom he shared his pornographic satire of POPE's poem *Essay on Man*, the *Essay on Woman*.

In 1757 he was elected MP for Aylesbury at a by-election and entered Parliament as a supporter of PITT THE ELDER, becoming especially close to Pitt's cousin, Lord Temple (see GRENVILLE-TEMPLE, RICHARD). When Pitt fell from power in 1761, Wilkes emerged as a vigorous critic of the new regime, associated first informally then formally with GEORGE III's favourite Lord Bute (see STUART, JOHN). He spoke against it in Parliament and wrote against it in a weekly essay paper, the *North Briton*, a riposte to SMOLLETT's pro-government *Briton*. The title of Wilkes's paper hinted at the Scottish flavour of the new regime (both Bute and Smollett were Scots). According to a prejudice which Wilkes encouraged, unlike freedom-loving Englishmen, Scots had a taste for authoritarian government, as previously manifested in their support for the dethroned Stuarts (see STUART, JAMES and CHARLES).

The King and his ministers were much disturbed by the tone, and success, of Wilkes's paper, and when he attacked the King's speech in issue number 45 both he and his printers were charged with seditious libel. The move backfired as Wilkes argued successfully that his arrest breached parliamentary privilege; the general warrants issued for the arrest of his publishers were judged unconstitutional. Wilkes became widely identified with the cause of 'liberty', and became a popular hero, at least in England (his anti-Scottish stance lost him friends north of the border). His supporters employed 'number 45' as a symbol, holding dinners for 45, for example. Determined to rid themselves of this pest, the ministry had him expelled from Parliament, and pursued libel prosecutions in relation both to the *North Briton* and to the *Essay on Woman* (treacherously dragged up against him by his old friend Sandwich). Wilkes fled abroad.

Returning in 1768, determined to re-establish himself, he succeeded in winning election for the populous county of Middx., where high metropolitan land-values helped to ensure that many 'middling sort' of people qualified as electors. He then surrendered to the court of King's Bench and was imprisoned for two years. Unable to let the situation rest, the Grafton ministry (see FITZROY, AUGUSTUS) had him expelled from Parliament once again for a libel in relation to the St George's Field massacre, when troops had shot and killed spectators gathered outside the prison to hail Wilkes. The result was that the Middx. electors three times re-elected him, despite Parliament's repeated refusal to seat him. Wilkes once more emerged as a representative of the 'common man', fighting for his rights against an overbearing government. Wilkes's closest associates formed the Society of Supporters of the Bill of Rights, to promote his cause; the Rockinghamite and Chathamite Whigs (see WATSON-WENTWORTH, CHARLES and PITT THE ELDER), though lacking enthusiasm for some of his supporters' more radical demands, saw advantage to the opposition in associating with (and trying to control) the movement, and helped to organize petitions in his favour.

Released in 1770, Wilkes was elected an alderman of London, becoming Lord Mayor in 1774. In the same year he was again elected MP for Middx. and this time seated. He remained a supporter of reformist causes into the 1780s, opposing the War of American Independence and backing Christopher WYVILL's 'Association', but his days as darling of the mob were over. As an advocate of religious toleration, he opposed the mob in the anti-Catholic Gordon Riots. After 1784, his support for PITT THE YOUNGER increasingly estranged him from radical causes.

Wilkes's devil-may-care style enhanced his popular appeal, though it alienated more respectable radicals. His sincerity has often been questioned but, though he loved to provoke, there was consistency in his stances. His commitments were, above all, to broadly conceived 'rights'. Though parliamentary reform was for him only one among other concerns, the Middx. election may have helped to bring that issue to the fore in the radical agenda.

Peter D. G. Thomas, John Wilkes: A Friend to Liberty (1996)

1659 but was deprived at the Restoration. The first Secretary of the Royal Society (1662) and Bishop of Chester (1668), he interpreted the Act of Uniformity liberally in order to accommodate Dissenting clergy.

WILKINSON, ELLEN *see* essay on page 837

WILKINSON, JOAN (OR JANE) (née North) (?–1557), religious activist. Daughter of a London merchant, she became silkwoman to ANNE BOLEYN and an enthusiastic evangelical; she married William Wilkinson, a wealthy London merchant. Her brother Edward (c. 1496–1565) became a leading royal financial official and in 1554, a religious conservative, gained a peerage; his protection may have been useful in her exile under MARY I. While in Frankfurt, she used her wealth to sustain exiles and victims of persecution, and maintained close links with London; her gender has obscured her crucial part in Marian Protestantism. *See also* WILLOUGHBY, CATHERINE.

WILKINSON, JOHN (1728–1808), ironmaster. The son of a Cumb. ironmaster, John and his brother William expanded the business, acquiring furnaces at Bersham, near Wrexham, Broseley (Salop.) and Bradley (Staffs.). Wilkinson dramatically expanded the range of iron goods which he produced and promoted them with an unprecedented commercial flair, for which he became known as 'iron-mad' Wilkinson. In 1774 he devised a cannon-boring machine, which was adapted to make cylinders for the steam engines of Matthew BOULTON and James WATT. Wilkinson's enthusiasm for iron soon extended to the new steam engine; he installed an engine to blast air into Broseley furnace, and installed a Boulton and Watt engine when he modernized the Paris waterworks in the 1780s. Also an arms manufacturer, Wilkinson illicitly supplied the French and Americans.

WILLIAM I THE CONQUEROR *see* essay on pages 838–39

WILLIAM I THE LION (1142?–1214), King of Scots. Second son of HENRY OF NORTHUMBRIA, he was invested with the earldom after his father's death in 1152, while he was still a child, but his older brother MAEL COLUIM IV was unable to prevent HENRY II from reclaiming the earldom for the English Crown. William succeeded to the Scottish throne after Mael Coluim's death in 1165. The rebellion of 1173–4 against Henry gave William his opportunity but his invasions of Northumbria ended disastrously when he was taken by surprise at Alnwick (Northumb.) and captured. To obtain his freedom he had to accept the Treaty of Falaise (named after one of the

Norman castles in which he was kept prisoner). According to its terms he had to do homage to Henry for Scotland, and the Scottish nobles had to swear allegiance to Henry and hand over sons as hostages. English garrisons were installed in the castles of Edinburgh, Berwick and Roxburgh. Edinburgh was restored in 1185 as Henry's gift to his vassal when he arranged his marriage to Ermengarde of Beaumont, but it was not until the accession of RICHARD I in 1189 and the agreement known as the Quit-claim of Canterbury, that William was fully able to recover Scottish independence in return for a payment of 10,000 marks. Subsequently William contributed to the ransom by which Richard was freed from imprisonment in Germany. Although after 1174 he never again invaded Northumbria he did not let either Richard or JOHN forget that he claimed it. Exasperated by this, in 1209 John took advantage of William's illness to march against Scotland, forcing the Scottish King to hand over two daughters as hostages. For much of his reign his right to the throne was challenged by the MacWilliam dynasty, descendants of William, son of DUNCAN II. Donald MacWilliam rebelled in 1187 and Donald's son Guthred in 1211–12; both lost their heads. Despite these difficulties William's reign witnessed the extension of royal authority northwards across the Moray Firth. Why later writers came to call him 'the Lion' is not clear; perhaps because in one obituary he was referred to as 'the lion of justice'.

WILLIAM II RUFUS (c. 1058–1100), King of England (1087–1100). The name Rufus by which he is and was familiarly known derived from either his red hair or his ruddy complexion. The second son of WILLIAM I THE CONQUEROR, he was able to remain on good terms with his father, an advantage that eventually allowed him to succeed as King of England in 1087, but his elder brother, ROBERT II Curthose, having secured Normandy, disputed his title to England. In consequence, William Rufus faced revolts in 1088 and 1095, as well as a war of succession that lasted until 1096 when Robert joined the First Crusade. To finance this enterprise, he mortgaged his duchy to Rufus.

Over the next few years, Rufus established a formidable military reputation during the near-permanent warfare among the princes of northern France. He also came to be known as a chivalrous and generous leader of knights. But these secular qualities cut no ice with churchmen; moreover, most of these were appalled by what they regarded as William Rufus's rapacious disregard for their property rights. His quarrels with Archbishop ANSELM of Canterbury were fierce enough to drive the Archbishop into exile. In an age when most chroniclers were monks, William Rufus got a very

continued on page 840

WILKINSON, ELLEN (1891–1947)
Politician

'Red Ellen' (so called as much for her titian hair and her fiery temper as for her left-wing politics), forever associated with the 'hungry thirties', was born of a working-class family in Ardwick, Manchester, and in 1909 won a scholarship to read history at Manchester University. Shaped by the Methodism of her father, which remained 'a special glow' all her life, Wilkinson had joined the Independent Labour Party (ILP) at 16 and at university became a member of the Fabian Society and, on graduating, a full-time organizer of the National Union of Women's Suffrage Societies (NUWSS) in Manchester. In 1915 during the First World War her experience of women's work in munitions helped her secure the job of National Women's Organizer to the Amalgamated Union of Co-operative Workers (AUCW), which catered mainly to shop assistants and factory workers.

A dynamic organizer and effective speaker, Wilkinson was a founder member of the British Communist Party and in 1921 went to Moscow with a fellow Communist, Harry POLLITT, where the Red International of Labour Unions (RILU) was established to 'win unions from the policy of class collaboration to that of class struggle', though she was unsuccessful in persuading her own union to affiliate. But disenchantment was swift: it was rumoured that the Comintern was insisting that all constituent Communist parties would be required to accept central direction. Wilkinson was among those who resigned in 1924. In the autumn of 1923 she had been elected on to Manchester City Council, and fought her first parliamentary election at Ashton-under-Lyne, and in 1924 was elected Labour MP for Middlesbrough East. The only woman on the Labour benches and the youngest MP, she attracted condescending publicity, her 'elfin stature' (she was 4 feet 11 inches tall) seemed to excuse (at first) the fact that she 'represented the extreme left wing of the Labour Party'. 'Our Ellen' capitalized on the attention and proved a formidable parliamentarian, promoting the rights of women and the needs of her constituents and all other working people. Tireless in the 1926 General Strike she toured the north to co-ordinate activity and disseminate information. She co-authored *A Worker's History of the Great Strike*, which castigated the TUC for its 'betrayal' of the strikers by refusing to turn industrial into political action, and chaired the Women's Committee for Relief of Miners' Wives and Children to alleviate the suffering caused by the strike.

Labour won the 1929 General Election, the first in which some five million women over 21 voted, enfranchised by an Act the previous year. But it was a minority government again and Wilkinson, appointed Private Parliamentary Secretary to Susan Lawrence, the Parliamentary Secretary to the Minister of Health, made no secret of her irritation at the caution of the Labour leader, Ramsay MACDONALD.

In the 1931 election she lost her seat and turned to journalism, contributing regularly to *Time and Tide* and briefly to *Tribune*. She also wrote political novels, and her greatest success was the one she wrote about the town that elected her as its MP in 1935, Jarrow. *The Town that was Murdered* (1939), 'a picture of capitalism at work', was an indictment of the politics that made Jarrow 'a workhouse without walls', where the decline of the shipbuilding industry meant that nearly 80 per cent of the workforce was unemployed and death rates were among the highest in the country. In order to draw the nation's attention to the plight of the unemployed and galvanize the government into some regeneration of local industry, a march was organized from Jarrow to London in Oct. 1936. It became a symbol of the dignity and the hopelessness of the 1930s, and Wilkinson joined 200 of her (male) constituents on stretches of 'the folk crusade ... of moral indignation'.

In 1940 Wilkinson was appointed a Parliamentary Secretary to Herbert MORRISON, the Home Secretary, whose bid for the leadership of the Party she had supported in opposition to Clement ATTLEE despite their fundamental political differences, though not necessarily because of their (probable) long affair. Her particular responsibility was air-raid shelter provision. In the 1945 Labour government she was Minister of Education, charged with the implementation of R. A. BUTLER's 1944 Education Act. A believer in 'parity of esteem', who raised the school-leaving age to 15, Wilkinson has been criticized for her lack of direction as minister and her defence of the tripartite system of grammar, technical and secondary education against the cause of comprehensive education.

An asthmatic, by 1946 she was seriously unwell, and in Feb. 1947 died aged 55. Hailed as Britain's *La Pasionaria*, Wilkinson proved a creditable example of what a woman of conviction can achieve in politics, and was a committed, effective and inspiring crusader for social justice.

Betty D. Vernon, Ellen Wilkinson, 1891–1947 (1982)

WILLIAM I THE CONQUEROR (1027 or 1028–87)
Duke of Normandy

King of England (1066–87). The architect of the Norman Conquest of England, William was known as the Conqueror from the thirteenth century onwards. He was only eight when he succeeded his father, ROBERT I, as Duke of Normandy in 1035. His mother Herleva, although not of aristocratic birth, was an established partner of Robert. Yet in the eyes of the Church they were not married, so to many contemporaries William was the Bastard.

But he was his father's only son, and his succession had the prior agreement of his lord, the King of France, as well as of the Norman magnates. Not long after William's birth, his mother was given in marriage to one of Robert's followers, and by him she had two more sons, Robert of Mortain and ODO OF BAYEUX; his half-brothers were to be William's most important advisers and supporters.

His early years were turbulent, as various aristocratic factions fought and killed each other in the struggle for control of the boy-duke. But it was only after he was old enough to assume power for himself that he faced rebellions led by kinsmen with rival claims to the ducal throne. These he defeated in 1047 and 1053–4. In the 1050s he also faced and defeated invasions launched by neighbouring French princes. In these years he proved himself a master of the art of war. After the deaths in 1060 of his two principal enemies, King Henry I of France and Count Geoffrey Martel of Anjou, William was able to seize the initiative. In 1063 he made his first conquest, Maine, a county hitherto under the domination of Anjou.

Then, after the death of EDWARD THE CONFESSOR in Jan. 1066, he claimed the English throne in opposition to HAROLD II. According to Norman sources, Edward had first promised (perhaps in 1051) that William should be his successor and then many years later, probably in 1064, had sent Harold to Normandy as his ambassador to confirm the promise. Since Harold had sworn to the promise on oath, the Norman case was that he had no right to accept Edward's deathbed designation of him as successor. No one in England, however, accepted the Norman case; nor, if they had known of it, would they have been impressed by William's parade of a papal banner. Only by conquest could the Bastard become King. In response to William's preparations for war (later depicted in the Bayeux Tapestry), by the early summer of 1066 Harold had mustered an army and a fleet along the south coast. But perhaps by judgement as much as by the luck of wind direction, William's crossing was delayed until late Sept., after Harold had been forced to disband his own fleet and at a time when he had been called away to Yorks. to deal with an invasion launched by the Norwegian king, HARALD HARDRAADA. William landed at Pevensey (Sussex) on 28 Sept. On 14 Oct. a few miles inland he won the Battle of Hastings, partly by luck, partly by his own good reconnaissance and tactical skill. The killing of Harold II and his brothers GYRTH and LEOFWINE in this battle left the English without a credible alternative around whom they could unite, and the damage caused by William's ravaging army brought about the surrender of London. On Christmas Day 1066 William was acclaimed King in Westminster Abbey. The shouts of acclamation, in English as well as French, alarmed the Norman guards posted outside and they set fire to houses adjoining the abbey. The church was virtually emptied as people rushed out to fight the fire or to loot. Only the monks and a few bishops remained to complete the consecration of a King who was trembling violently.

William had good reason to tremble. Initially he tried to rule with the aid of an aristocracy which was English as well as French, but trusted only the latter, and this half-hearted policy was doomed to fail. There were English revolts against Norman rule in every year from 1067 to 1070. In the early years the conquerors had to live like an army of occupation, living, eating and sleeping in castles, strongholds from which a few men could dominate a hostile population, and of a type rarely found in England before the Norman Conquest. There may have been no more than 10,000 Frenchmen in the midst of a population of one or two million. It took six years of campaigning before the English finally admitted defeat. The north in particular posed huge military and political problems; hence the systematically brutal 'harrying of the north' during the winter of 1069–70. The 1072 invasion of Scotland deterred King MAEL COLUIM III CENN MÓR from helping English exiles, but the north remained difficult to govern, as Bishop WALCHER of Durham found to his cost. The years of insecurity had a profound effect on subsequent history. In 1070 William had some English bishops deposed and thereafter appointed no Englishman to either bishopric or abbey; foreigners such as LANFRANC were preferred. Although none of the leaders of these early revolts was put to death (for as a chivalrous Frenchman William prided himself on clemency), the imprisonment and loss of estates which they suffered inevitably caused great resentment A series of confiscations culminated in a policy of wholesale transfer of lordship over land into French hands. By 1086, as the Domesday Book reveals, there were only four major landholders of English birth left. Although the economic and social system hardly changed, the country was now totally dominated by a northern French aristocracy. Since the new elite kept their lands and connections on the continent a new cross-Channel political community was created.

In 1073 William took an army which included English contingents to reconquer Maine. Inevitably the demands made on his resources and energy by the conquest of England had led to a loosening of his grip on politics in northern France. A new generation of rivals, led by Philip I of France and Count Fulk le Rechin of Anjou, naturally alarmed by the success of his conquest of so rich a land as England kept William on the defensive for the rest of his life. His last 10 years were further troubled by quarrels with his eldest son (see ROBERT II) and with the ambitious Odo of Bayeux. This left time for no more than occasional visits to England, usually to deal with crises such as the 1075 revolt in which Earl WALTHEOF was implicated. On one visit, in 1081, he led an army to St David's; no previous king of England had been seen so far west in Wales. It was in the context of measures taken to deal with another emergency, the quartering and provisioning of a large army to meet a threatened invasion from Denmark, that, at Christmas 1085, William decided to initiate the survey which resulted in the Domesday Book. In the words of the *Anglo-Saxon Chronicle*, 'the King had much thought and very deep discussion with his council about this country – how it was held and with what sort of people. Then he sent his men into every shire and had them find out ... he had a record made of what or how much, in land and in livestock, everybody who was holding land in England held, and how much it was all

worth. So very thoroughly did he have the enquiry carried out that – it is shameful to say it, but it did not seem shameful to him to do it – not one ox, nor one cow, nor one pig escaped notice in his survey.' Although this is an exaggeration, the Domesday Book is the most remarkable statistical document in European history; there is nothing else on this scale before the nineteenth century. The fact that in making the survey William's government was able to utilize Anglo-Saxon administrative records indicates the extent to which he relied on mechanisms inherited from the late Old English nation state. The survey's scale, however, marks the heel of the conqueror. It set the seal on the dispossession of the old aristocracy and validated the title of a kleptocracy.

According to WILLIAM OF MALMESBURY, as a young man Duke William was so chaste that people thought him impotent. Since his marriage (c. 1050) to MATILDA OF FLANDERS produced nine children, this seems improbable. In Sept. 1087 he died at Rouen after a fall from his horse while campaigning against Philip of France. He had been tempted to disinherit Robert, but in the end agreed that his ancestral lands (Normandy) should go to the first-born, leaving his conquest to his second son, WILLIAM II RUFUS. He was buried in his own foundation, St Stephen's in Caen. His corpulent body was too big for the sarcophagus that had been prepared, and it burst when they tried to force it in – an unlucky end for a lucky bastard. As the organizing genius of the Norman Conquest William had completed a more far-reaching transformation of English society than any ruler before or since. From now on the histories of England and France, especially Normandy, were to be inextricably interwoven, while old English ties with Scandinavia were weakened. William's conquest had brought England into a French orbit, with profound consequences for the future development of English art and culture, above all for the formation of the English language. The pre-eminence of French schools and fashions in the music, literature and architecture of the twelfth and thirteenth centuries meant that a conquered and forcibly Frenchified England was now in the mainstream of European culture.

David Bates, William the Conqueror (1989

bad press, and his sudden death in the New Forest, probably in a hunting accident, was readily interpreted as God's punishment of an irreligious man. (The interpretation was confirmed when the tower of Winchester Cathedral fell down after he was buried under it.)

William Rufus died unmarried and with no acknowledged illegitimate children, which has sometimes inclined modern historians to interpret contemporary denunciations of the 'effeminate' long hair and fashionable styles of dress of his courtiers as evidence of the King's own homosexuality. This is to read a great deal into the words of monks profoundly out of sympathy with the worldly lifestyle enjoyed at Rufus's court. GAIMAR, by contrast, remembered William as a fine, generous and good-tempered King. One of his buildings still stands: Westminster Hall, in its day the greatest royal hall in Europe.

WILLIAM III *see* essay on page 842–43

WILLIAM IV (1765–1837), King of Great Britain and Ireland (1830–7), the 'sailor king'. The third son of GEORGE III, he joined the Royal Navy in 1779 and served in America and the West Indies. In 1789 he was made Duke of Clarence, and was promoted Admiral of the Fleet in 1811 and Lord High Admiral in 1827. A popular if somewhat eccentric figure, he married Princess Adelaide, daughter of the Duke of Saxe-Meiningen, in 1818, but their two daughters both died in infancy. He had previously lived with the actress Dorothy Jordan from 1790 to 1811 and they had 10 children. The death of the Duke of York in 1827 made him heir presumptive to the throne, to which he succeeded three years later. As King his most important public act related to the crisis that preceded the passage of the 1832 Reform Act; the King's hostility to reform was, indeed, a key element in the crisis. From 1830 to 1832 the House of Lords, with the Crown's encouragement, resisted the Reform Bill, twice rejecting the measure. After a dissolution the Whigs returned to power under Charles GREY with a huge majority and persuaded the King to create sufficient peers to pass the Bill if it were rejected in the Lords again. When opposition was renewed in the Upper House, the King changed his mind and tried to withdraw from his undertaking to create 50 new peerages; the ministry resigned. The King tried to form another ministry under Wellington (*see* WELLESLEY, ARTHUR), but failed and surrendered. In doing so he avoided internal disorder but set in motion the transformation of the constitutional balance between Crown and Parliament. When in 1834 he ignored parliamentary support for PEEL and replaced him with Melbourne (*see* LAMB, WILLIAM), he was the last British monarch to try to choose the Prime Minister in opposition to the wishes of Parliament. William died without a legitimate heir and the crown passed to his niece, VICTORIA.

WILLIAM AUGUSTUS (3rd Duke of Cumberland) (1721–65), second son of GEORGE II. Educated for a military career, he first came to prominence at the Battle of Fontenoy of 30 April to 11 May 1745, when he commanded the British, Hanoverian, Austrian and Dutch forces sent to relieve Tournai in the Austrian Netherlands (now Belgium). Although they were defeated their retreat was seen as a heroic act. Recalled to Britain in the face of Charles STUART's invasion, he successfully pursued the Jacobite army to Culloden near Inverness (on the estate of Duncan FORBES) where it was defeated in April 1746. He acquired the nickname 'the Butcher' for the cruelty which he displayed. After the death of his elder brother FREDERICK, his political importance increased: Frederick's son was still a child, and, if the ailing George II had died, Cumberland might be expected to dominate. Anxious Whig politicians and Frederick's widow AUGUSTA strove to limit his influence. During the Seven Years War much was expected of his military prowess, but his campaigns were unsuccessful and after surrendering the British and allied forces at the Convention of Kloster-Zeven in 1757 he retired from his military career. He continued to wield influence as a political patron, playing a crucial part in the formation of the first Rockingham (*see* WATSON-WENTWORTH, CHARLES) ministry.

WILLIAM OF MALMESBURY (*c*. 1095–?1143), historian. He was a monk of Malmesbury (Wilts.), whose breadth of reading, devotion to classical culture, acute sense of style and textual criticism, all combined with his patriotism to make him (as he said himself) the greatest English historian since BEDE. After extensive research in the libraries of the cathedrals and major abbeys of the land, he composed what remained for some centuries the standard history of the English from 'the time of their arrival in Britain' to his own day. He did this in two complementary works, both completed by 1125 and both written in a lively and anecdotal style: the *Gesta Regum Anglorum* (The Deeds of the Kings), and the *Gesta Pontificum* (The Deeds of the Bishops), the latter a diocese by diocese history and topographical survey, a wholly original concept which showed that he had used his travels to observe buildings as well as to read manuscripts. He also wrote a remarkable research monograph, *The History of Glastonbury*, a book of miracles, *Miracles of the Virgin,* and lives of WULFSTAN and other saints, before carrying the national history up to 1142 in his *Historia Novella* (Recent History). He produced a three-theme history: the first was the making of the English into one people, the second the political unification of England under one king, the third the social and moral progress of the English as, under the influence of Christianity and French court culture (he was acutely aware that the blood of both Normans and English ran in his veins), they advanced, as he saw it, from barbarism to civilization. The third of these themes led to his taking a condescending view of less advanced Celtic peoples in Britain and Ireland. His approach presumably pleased his patrons at the royal court, MATILDA II and ROBERT OF GLOUCESTER. It also in effect laid down guidelines for most subsequent English historical writing.

WILLIAM OF NAYLAND *see* JONES, WILLIAM

WILLIAM OF NEWBURGH (*c.* 1135–?1198), historian. An Augustinian canon from Yorks., in the late 1190s he wrote the *Historia Rerum Anglicarum* (History of English Affairs) covering the period from the Norman Conquest to his own day. His judicious approach, for example his cool treatment of BECKET, has won him many modern admirers. Although he liked a good story, and included several about what would now be called 'zombies', his critical sense was affronted by tales of King ARTHUR and MERLIN; in his preface, he denounces GEOFFREY OF MONMOUTH as a writer of fiction masquerading as history.

WILLIAM OF NORWICH, ST (*c.* 1132–44), child 'martyr'. His mutilated body, buried in Norwich Cathedral, became the focus of a controversial cult. According to Thomas of Monmouth's *Life and Martyrdom of St William of Norwich* (written *c.* 1172), he, like the later Little St HUGH OF LINCOLN, was the Christian victim of a Jewish ritual murder. As the first occasion when this false 'blood-libel' accusation was made, the case of William of Norwich marks a key moment in the history of European anti-Semitism.

WILLIAM OF OCKHAM (OR OCCAM) (*c.* 1289–1349), theologian. Presumably born at Occam (Surrey) and educated at Oxford and Paris, he wrote books on logic, theology and political theory, and defended the Franciscan order and its doctrine of evangelical poverty. He was imprisoned by the Pope in 1328, and was excommunicated when he escaped to the court of Louis of Bavaria. In his responses to papal attacks he accused Popes John XXII and Benedict XII of heresies and errors. For him faith and the revealed truth of the Bible were beyond reasoned argument. In matters of logic he insisted that assumptions should be as few as possible, 'Occam's razor'.

WILLIAM OF ST CALAIS (?–1096), prelate. A Norman from Bayeux, as Abbot of St Vincent at Le Mans, he was WILLIAM I THE CONQUEROR's choice to succeed WALCHER as Bishop of Durham. WILLIAM II suspected him of complicity in the rebellion of 1088, and had him tried and exiled. But he made his peace with the King and in 1091 returned to the city, on which he left an enduring mark: he replaced the cathedral canons with monks and began building the present magnificent cathedral church.

WILLIAM OF SENS (*fl.* 1174–84), architect. A French master mason, he was appointed by the monks of Canterbury to rebuild the eastern part of the cathedral, which had been severely damaged by fire in 1174. The rebuilding was chronicled in detail by GERVASE OF CANTERBURY. William is credited with the introduction to England of the Gothic style of architecture.

WILLIAM OF WYKEHAM (1324–1404), patron of education. Having entered EDWARD III's service as EDINGTON's protégé, in 1356 he was appointed Clerk of Works at Windsor, and he turned it into the greatest castle in England. He rapidly became Edward's most trusted minister, first Chief Keeper and Surveyor of the King's Works, then Royal Secretary in 1361, Keeper of the Privy Seal in 1363 and Chancellor in 1367. According to FROISSART, 'Without him nothing was done.' In 1366 the King prevailed upon Pope Urban V to make him, despite his academic shortcomings, Bishop of Winchester.

During the years of peace (1360–9), administration was allowed to become slack, and when the renewal of the Hundred Years War made this apparent, William was dismissed at Parliament's insistence (1371). He joined in the Good Parliament's criticism of the court; as a result, JOHN OF GAUNT, who saw this as a betrayal, had him convicted of embezzlement in Nov. 1376. His estates were confiscated but, after a protest from the clergy, were restored in 1377. Two years later he founded New College, Oxford, then Winchester school in 1382, both on a lavish scale. Between 1389 and 1391, in his new role as respected elder statesman, he served as RICHARD II's Chancellor, but after 1394 he devoted most of his energy and money to rebuilding the nave of Winchester Cathedral, where he now lies buried in a sumptuous chantry chapel.

WILLIAM OF YORK *see* FITZHERBERT, WILLIAM

WILLIAMS, BETTY (1943–), Irish peace activist *see* MAGUIRE, MAIREAD

WILLIAMS, EDWARD *see* essay on page 844

WILLIAM III (also known as William of Orange) (1650–1702)
King of England, Scotland, and Ireland (1689–1702)

The posthumous and only son of William II, Prince of Orange, Stadtholder of the Netherlands (a military post, whose powers varied as the States decided). During William's boyhood, the de Witt brothers dominated the Dutch Republic, and it was agreed the stadholdership should lapse. William was brought up by his mother Mary, daughter of CHARLES I (she died when he was 14), and various Dutch tutors. Johan de Witt himself gave him lessons in politics. He encountered his Stuart cousin Charles (later CHARLES II), then in exile on the continent. A lasting friend from this era was Hans Willem BENTINCK, initially William's page.

Dutch commercial prowess caused jealousy in both England and France. A First Dutch War was fought from 1650 to 1652, and again from 1665 to 1667. In the Second Dutch War the French allied with the Dutch, and the English were hard pressed. Most difficult for the Netherlands was the Third Dutch War (1672–4), when the English and French allied. The de Witt brothers were blamed and murdered; William was made Captain General and Admiral General in 1672, and in 1673 was appointed to the newly revived office of Stadholder, made hereditary in 1674.

In 1674 England and the Netherlands made a separate peace. (Peace with France was concluded only in 1678.) Danby (see OSBORNE, THOMAS), now the leading English minister, was keen to cement Anglo-Dutch relations, and promoted a marriage, which took place in 1677, between William and MARY, eldest daughter of James, Duke of York (later JAMES II). When from 1679 to 1681 English Parliaments repeatedly called for the exclusion of the Catholic James from the line of succession, one possibility considered was to turn to Mary, as next heir, and her husband. Some thought that William should go to England to promote his case, but he went only after Charles had dismissed his last Parliament, when he met members of the Whig opposition, including Arthur CAPEL, Earl of Essex, and Lord William RUSSELL.

In 1683 the Rye House Plot to assassinate Charles and James was uncovered. The Whig lords were executed; Charles's illegitimate son James SCOTT, Duke of Monmouth, who had knowledge of the plot, was sent abroad. He spent much time in the Netherlands and was well received by William. But when Monmouth tried to lead a rebellion in England after Charles's death in 1685, William sent British regiments in Dutch service to help crush the rebels.

Many English political exiles headed for the Netherlands, including Shaftesbury (see COOPER, ANTHONY ASHLEY) and John LOCKE, though William had no contact with most of them. Meanwhile in 1687 William sent his envoy Dijkvelt to England, to argue with James about his style of rule, and ensure that he had no plans to tamper with the succession. Dijkvelt had many interviews with English politicians, forging links that would help William later.

James's Catholicizing policies were increasingly alienating English opinion. The birth of his son in June 1688 encouraged some to look for a way out. In July, the 'immortal Seven', leading figures all, wrote to William to ask him to come with an army to lend support to a rising. William published a *Declaration* proclaiming it proper to use force against tyrannical monarchs and his own intention of restoring England's laws and liberties, and set sail with some 20,000 men, arriving in England on 5 Nov. The train of events which his arrival touched off would be termed the Glorious Revolution, because it entailed (in England at least) a relatively bloodless but radical change.

William's motives are disputed. He had long taken a close interest in English politics, and was keen to secure consistent British support against the French. European affairs seemed to be at a critical point: the new Elector of Brandenburg was prepared to join the anti-French alliance that William had long laboured to construct, while in Sept. large numbers of French troops were sent into Germany. What is not clear is to what lengths William was prepared to go to achieve this. James helped to clear the way for a change of regime by fleeing. When he was stopped and brought back, William decided the issue by pressing him to leave again.

Power had meanwhile passed into the hands of an assembly of peers in the London Guildhall under Rochester (see HYDE, LAURENCE) and Halifax (see SAVILE, GEORGE). The peers, and an Assembly of Commoners summoned by William (consisting of MPs from Charles II's Parliaments and London aldermen and common councilmen) asked him to take charge of the government. Elections in Jan. 1689 produced a Convention Parliament, which began to work out the terms of the revolution settlement. William was unwilling to serve as regent or to let Mary reign alone (which Mary also did not wish); Parliament offered them the Crown as joint monarchs in Feb. 1689. The Scots Parliament followed suit, and they were crowned for their joint lives in April. The succession was settled in favour of Mary's children if any, then ANNE and her children, then William's children by any later marriage.

The settlement included a statement of certain fundamental liberties, the Bill of Rights. The Crown was denied the power to suspend or dispense with laws, a power which Charles and James were thought to have abused to further their religious policies. It was also provided that the monarch might not be and might not marry a Catholic. Parliamentary consent was henceforth needed for an army to be kept in being in peacetime. Otherwise, royal power was not significantly constrained.

Britain declared war on France in May, soon to be joined by the United Provinces and the Holy Roman Empire. William also had rebels at home to be dealt with. Scots rebels under John GRAHAM, Earl of Dundee, were defeated in Aug.; fighting in Ireland, where James had convoked a Jacobite Parliament, continued until the Battle of the Boyne in July 1690, after which James returned to France. Irish Catholic resistance ended with the surrender of Limerick in Oct. 1691.

European war continued for several years. By 1692 the Allies had overcome the French fleet, though privateering continued to menace commerce. English military effort focused on campaigns in the Netherlands. The Grand Alliance began to crumble in 1696. In May 1697 a peace conference assembled; the Treaty of Ryswick was signed in Sept. In this, France effectively recognized William as King of Great Britain and Ireland (Mary had died in 1694).

As King, William proved vigorous and assertive, but the needs of war determined that he was often out of the country. Seeing the war as fought for the defence of the Protestant faith and the traditional constitution, Parliament was prepared to grant him substantial resources but anxiety lest they lose their regained liberty spurred MPs to search for ways of controlling the King: for example, they granted only a reduced civil list, rather than the customary more generous financial settlement, making him dependent on Parliament for annual supplies. Similarly they forced him to accept a Triennial Act, requiring elections at least every three years. Parliament and the King repeatedly did battle over such issues. William used his veto more frequently than his predecessors but often had to back down in the end.

William had been determined not to fall under the control of any political party, and his first ministries contained a mixture of Whigs and Tories. Tories, however, tended to be critical of government growth and taxes associated with war. These complaints were echoed by certain 'Country' Whigs, notably Paul Foley and Robert HARLEY. William became increasingly dependent on the talents of the so-called Whig Junto. In 1696 they seized the opportunity provided by an attempt to assassinate William to try to drive from public office all those not committed to the view that he was not merely *de facto* but legitimate monarch. This party extremism prompted a Tory backlash in the last years of the decade.

Peace did not resolve the differences between the King and the English Parliament. There was a battle over what should happen to the standing army in peacetime; in the end it was kept in being but in much smaller numbers than William had wished. MPs opposed William's plans for fuller union with Scotland and invalidated his Irish land settlement. They were particularly irate about rewards lavished on Dutch favourites, Bentinck, who was made Earl of Portland, and Arnold Joost van KEPPEL, made Earl of Albemarle.

Accepting the need to come to terms with his critics, William brought Rochester and GODOLPHIN into the ministry, and in 1701 backed Harley to become Speaker of the Commons . These ministers dealt with the issues arising from the death of Anne's last surviving child by shepherding an Act of Settlement through Parliament, under whose terms the Hanoverian GEORGE I would ultimately succeed, but attached a set of provisions designed drastically to curb the power of future ministries. The fury with which they pursued the Junto lords alienated William, and he attempted to construct a ministry more to his taste.

He had little time left. He died in March 1702 from complications resulting from a fall from his horse, which stumbled on a molehill at Hampton Court. Jacobites toasted 'the little gentleman in black velvet'. Many honoured the King's memory, but none more so than the Protestant Irish. His adoption as a symbol of militant Irish Protestantism has ensured that, centuries after his death, his legacy remains controversial.

Bryan Bevan, King William III: Prince of Orange, the First European (1997)

WILLIAMS, EDWARD (pen name Iolo Morganwg) (1747–1826)
Welsh poet, antiquarian, literary forger and reviver of bardic tradition

The son of a stonemason from Llancarfan, Glam., whose mother had been raised as the 'poor relation' of a minor gentry family, he acquired his early knowledge of Welsh literature and culture from her. He was also influenced by Thomas Richards, who published the first modern Welsh thesaurus in 1753, and John Walters, who began publishing his Welsh dictionary in 1770; he helped Walters to invent new Welsh words, and construct fictional etymologies for them, thus first demonstrating his capacity for literary deception.

In 1773 he moved to London, where he became active in the Gwyneddigion Society of Welsh literary enthusiasts. Returning to Glam., he tried and failed at various business ventures, including farming and bookselling. Throughout this period he studied the work of the fifteenth-century poet DAFYDD AP GWILYM, and sent his imitations to London Welsh literary enthusiasts Owen Jones (Owain Myfir) and William Owen, who took them to be genuine. When in 1789 they published the *Barddoniaeth Dafydd ap Gwilym*, collecting all Dafydd's known poems, the 'newly-discovered' poems in the appendix were in fact by Williams.

By this time Williams was signing his acknowledged work with the bardic alias 'Iolo Morganwg'. On his return to London in 1791 he found a receptive audience for his interpretation of Welsh cultural history. He claimed to be a descendant of the ancient Druids and as such inheritor of a genuine Druidic bardic tradition found only in Glam. and superior to the north Welsh literary culture of the Lewis MORRIS circle. Iolo rejected origin legends favoured by previous Welsh writers: in his view, the Welsh, ancient and modern, were not a branch of a larger race, but unique in their traditions and their relationship with the island of Britain. When authentic works documenting his theories were lacking, he composed them, and attributed them to former bards. Iolo took laudanum as a treatment for asthma; biographers have charitably speculated that this affected his ability to tell fact from fantasy. His obsession with his own version of Welsh literary history led him to hold a *gorsedd*, or bardic gathering, on Primrose Hill near London in 1792. This was followed by others, which were accepted by most as authentic.

Poems Lyric and Pastoral (1794) revealed him to be an indifferent English poet, but the volume's subscription list was headed by the Prince of Wales (later GEORGE IV) and President George WASHINGTON; its mix of reverence for Welsh tradition and political radicalism helped it to find an audience. Iolo returned to Wales and continued collecting, commenting on and (unbeknown to his contemporaries) adding to the output of Welsh authors of previous centuries. He also travelled Wales for the Board of Agriculture inspecting farming customs. He never finished any of his reports, but his observations survived in manuscript and proved valuable to later historians of Wales.

Between 1801 and 1807, with William Owen and Owain Myfir, he produced *The Myvyrian Archaiology*, conceived as a working compendium of Welsh literature of the sixth to fourteenth centuries. Iolo was responsible for large numbers of poems, including the entire third volume.

He died in 1826, leaving most of his writing still in manuscript. His son Taliesin believed his father's manuscripts to be truly copies of the work of past bards, and prepared them for the press. *Cyfrinach y Beirdd* (Secrets of the Bards) was published in 1829.

The forgeries of Iolo Morganwg were accepted as genuine until the early twentieth century. Since that time scholars have worked to separate Iolo's inventions from the canon of medieval Welsh literature. He has also been recognized as a great poet in his own right, with genuine insight into early Welsh literature.

Iolo was the first writer to make a serious case for the foundation of institutions such as a national library, museum, manuscript society and universities for Wales, and their eventual establishment owes something to his advocacy: he remains the most influential person in the revival of Welsh intellectual life in the late eighteenth and early nineteenth centuries.

Prys Morgan, Iolo Morganwg (1978)
Ceri Lewis, Iolo Morganwg (Welsh edn, 1995)

WILLIAMS, JOHN (1582–1650), churchman. A Welsh Cambridge don and deviously able politician, he became Bishop of Lincoln and Lord Keeper of the Great Seal in 1621, gaining great favour from George VILLIERS, Duke of Buckingham. He conducted a long feud with William LAUD about the theology and positioning of altars (holy tables) in churches, which resulted in Laud getting him suspended and imprisoned (1637–40). Predictably he was made Archbishop of York on Laud's fall (1641), but retired to north Wales. He was a major benefactor to his old college, St John's, and also Lincoln College, Oxford.

WILLIAMS, MARCIA (Baroness Falkender of West Haddon) (1932–), political secretary. As private secretary to Harold WILSON (1956–83), Marcia Williams came to be regarded in the 1970s as the power behind the throne, because she was alleged to yield so much influence over him. Lampooned by *Private Eye* as Lady Forkbender after her elevation in 1974, her secret lay in her forceful personality and her efficiency. She was, in effect, Wilson's 'kitchen cabinet', and the resignation honours list of 1974 written on her lavender note-paper caused considerable scandal because of the nature of the peerages it created, including that of Lord Kagan, later jailed for fraud.

WILLIAMS, RAYMOND (1921–88), socialist critic and cultural theorist. More than any other single writer Williams shaped what have come to be known as cultural studies, insisting from his earliest writings in the 1950s that culture was 'ordinary'. Williams's background, the distinctive radicalism of the Welsh working class, resonates through his writing. He was concerned not only with forms of cultural production such as literature, but with culture as 'a whole way of life' in which the creation, communication and reception of meaning came to be embodied in the forms and institutions of social life. Thus in *Culture and Society* (1958) and *The Long Revolution* (1961), written while teaching in adult education before moving to Cambridge University in 1961, he extended the study of culture from the analysis of what had generally been seen, following earlier writers like Matthew ARNOLD and T. S. ELIOT, as the 'best' art and literature produced within a society to such forms as the press and television and also to the cultures of whole social classes. Culture can never, in Williams's accounts, be understood outside relations of power, particularly those of class power, an analysis exemplified in his outstanding *The Country and the City* (1973). *Marxism and Literature* (1977) contained a highly original cultural theory suffused with a critical dialogue with the whole European tradition of Marxist thought. *Towards 2000* (1983) was an attempt to rethink socialism in the light of the major changes in society, culture and politics since the 1960s. While he was an independent socialist whose influence is most evident within the academy, he was also deeply immersed, as a public intellectual, in the practical politics of the Left, from the creation of the 'New Left' of 1956–62 to the causes of 'green socialist' and European-wide politics in the 1980s.

WILLIAMS, SHIRLEY (née Caitlin) (Baroness Williams of Crosby) (1930–), politician. The daughter of Vera BRITTAIN, she was educated at Somerville College, Oxford. Elected Labour MP for Hitchin (Herts.) in 1964 Williams held junior office under Harold WILSON and when Labour returned to office in 1974 was appointed to the newly created post of Secretary of State for Prices and Consumer Protection, but it was as Education Secretary from 1976 that she first became well known, initiating a series of nationwide debates on comprehensive education. Always on the right wing of the party, in 1980 she publicly stated, alongside David OWEN and William RODGERS, that she would leave the Labour Party if it committed itself to leaving the EEC, and the following year these three, with the former Labour Chancellor Roy JENKINS, announced the formation of the Social Democratic Party. Williams returned to Parliament eight months later, overturning a Tory majority of almost 20,000 in a sensational by-election win at Crosby (Lancs.), but lost the seat in 1983. She has sat in the House of Lords since 1993.

WILLIAMSON, SIR JOSEPH (1633–1701), royal servant. Son of a Cumb. clergyman, he came to London to act as clerk to his local MP, and was by him sent to Westminster school, from where he went on to Oxford. He joined the staff of the secretaries of state in 1660, where he managed the paper and post offices, receiving reports and issuing orders to English agents abroad. He helped to start the official newspaper, the *London Gazette*, which he edited for several years. In 1674 he succeeded his mentor Arlington as Secretary of State (*see* BENNETT, HENRY). CHARLES II trusted him as he was without a landed interest of his own and thus dependent on continued government employment. He faithfully carried out his duties, but in 1679 was committed to the Tower by the Commons for approving money grants made by Charles to Catholics, and Charles replaced him with the Whiggish Sunderland (*see* SPENCER, CHARLES). After his release he continued to sit in the Commons, where in 1690 he famously remarked 'when Princes have not needed money they have not needed us'. Rehabilitated by WILLIAM III, he took part in negotiating the Treaty of Ryswick in 1697.

WILLIBALD, ST (?700–86), Bishop of Eichstätt. A relative of St BONIFACE, he is famous as the first Englishman known to have travelled in the Middle East. His account of his travels, including his pilgrimage to Jerusalem, was written down in his old age by a nun named HUNEBERC, in the text known as the *Hodoeporicon*. On his return, he was sent by the Pope to join the English missionaries already active in Germany, where he remained a missionary bishop for the last 40 years of his life.

WILLIBRORD, ST (658–739), Archbishop of Utrecht. A pupil of St WILFRID (in England) and St EGBERT OF IONA (in Ireland), in 690 he set out with 11 companions to convert the pagan Frisians, and became one of the most important of the Anglo-Saxon missionaries to the continent. Although less is known about him than about his near-contemporary St BONIFACE, it is clear that his career followed a similar pattern, especially with regard to co-operation with the Carolingians and the Papacy. His strenuous missionary work even led him to attempt the conversion of the Danes.

WILLIS, THOMAS (1621–75), physician. The son of a Wilts. landowner's steward, he was educated at Christ Church, Oxford, where his studies were interrupted by the Civil Wars. A Royalist, he was excluded from academic advancement under the Commonwealth, and practised as a physician while hosting Anglican services. In 1660 he became Professor of Natural Philosophy, his pupils including Richard LOWER and John MAYOW. While at Oxford Willis performed several experiments on the brains of animals and human beings and in 1664 published a ground-breaking survey of the nervous system, establishing a relationship between brain, muscles and circulation. Willis moved to London in 1666 and established a fashionable practice as well as a reputation for the study of nervous ailments, of varieties which would later be distinguished according to their psychological or physiological causes; he also identified sugar diabetes as a distinct disease, without being able to establish its origins.

WILLOCK, JOHN (?–1585), churchman. From Ayr, he was (like John KNOX) an international figure with eyes on both Scottish and English reformations. After studies in Glasgow and Cologne, he ministered in London from the 1530s, as well as preaching in Scotland; exiled in Emden under MARY I, he was prominent in the Protestant Scottish national revolution from 1558. After that he achieved the remarkable geographical feat of being rector of Loughborough (Leics.) and superintendent of Glasgow and western Scotland, apparently functioning in both places.

WILLOUGHBY, CATHERINE (Baroness Willoughby of Eresby, Duchess of Suffolk) (1519–80), Protestant activist. Daughter and heiress of Lord Willoughby by his wife, a Spanish lady-in-waiting of CATHERINE OF ARAGON, she became in 1533 fourth wife of her guardian Charles BRANDON, Duke of Suffolk, and steered him towards her own strong evangelical faith. Their two sons died in 1551 of the sweating sickness. In exile under MARY I she proved a major sustainer of less wealthy exiles (*see* WILKINSON, JOAN); her son Peregrine BERTIE (by her second husband, one of her household officials) was born at Wesel.

WILLOUGHBY, SIR HUGH (?–1554), explorer. From a Notts. knightly family, he served in Scotland in the 1540s under Edward SEYMOUR, the future Duke of Somerset, but Seymour's fall damaged his promotion prospects and he turned to maritime ventures in association with Richard CHANCELLOR and Sebastian CABOT. Their venture of 1553 was an attempt to find a north-east passage to Asia around Scandinavia and Russia. Willoughby died on the Norwegian coast. His journal, found years later with his frozen corpse, was published by Richard HAKLUYT.

WILLOUGHBY OF ERESBY, 13TH BARON
see BERTIE, PEREGRINE

WILLS, W(ILLIAM) H(ENRY) (Baron Winterstoke of Blagdon) (1830–1911) and **SIR G(EORGE) A(LFRED)** (1854–1928), manufacturers. The Willses were one of the leading families of Bristol, of the British tobacco industry and of Congregationalism; the firm of W. D. & H. O. Wills had been founded by Henry Overton Wills I (1761–1826) and William Day Wills (1797–1865). William Henry, son of the latter, entered the firm in 1846; after 1865 he and his cousin Henry Overton III (1828–1911) assumed overall control. Steady expansion was accompanied by increasing national recognition of their company; the four sons of Henry Overton III were encouraged by their uncle in the early 1880s in the patenting of new cigarette-making machinery and the launch of the 'penny Woodbine' cigarette brand that made Wills a household name and the family members super-rich. William Henry's personal income quadrupled between 1894 and 1901, and he and his cousin were significant benefactors to their native city and the new University of Bristol. William Henry was Liberal MP for Coventry (1880–5), and subsequently for East Bristol (1895–1900). In 1901, to counter the American 'invasion' of the British tobacco market, he led 13 manufacturers into an alliance as Imperial Tobacco; when terms of trade were agreed with

American interests, British American Tobacco was subsequently formed. Of William Henry's four nephews, the leader was George Alfred, who succeeded his uncle as Chairman of Imperial (1911–24). His many business ventures included brand promotion and the building of a state-of-the-art factory.

WILMINGTON, 1ST EARL OF see COMPTON, SPENCER

WILMOT, JOHN (2nd Earl of Rochester) (1647–80), poet and courtier. The son of a leading Royalist, he was educated at Oxford, then toured France and Italy. He presented himself at court to CHARLES II in 1664 and became one of his close companions, despite the fact that Charles was occasionally the focus of Rochester's satirical humour, as in his aphorism that Charles 'never said a foolish thing, nor ever did a wise one'. Moving among the set who made Charles's court a byword for immorality, Rochester was a heavy drinker and notorious womanizer; when the wealthy young woman whom he wished to wed resisted his advances, he abducted her, for which he was briefly imprisoned in the Tower (they did nevertheless subsequently marry). Several writers benefited from Rochester's patronage including DRYDEN, OTWAY and SETTLE; ETHEREDGE satirized his friend as Dorimant in *She Wou'd if She Cou'd*. On his deathbed Rochester called for Gilbert BURNET, and repented his misspent life. After his death his works began to appear in print and a collection was published in 1714. Although his poems are conversational, light and whimsical in tone, often sexually frank, some critics see in them a deeper sense of malaise.

WILMUT, IAN (1944–), pioneer of cloning. Wilmut researched the freezing of boar semen at Cambridge University (1971–3) and in 1973 began studying the production of animals from frozen embryos at the privately funded Animal Breeding Research Station (now the Roslin Institute) near Edinburgh. In 1997 Wilmut and his team caused a worldwide sensation when they announced that they had, in 1996, successfully cloned a sheep (later named Dolly). Their experiment involved fusing a mammary cell (containing genetic information) from one ewe with unfertilized egg cells (from which genetic information was removed) from another ewe. A growing embryo resulted which was then implanted in a surrogate mother. This work prompted others to clone animals and raised fears about human cloning. Although Wilmut opposes human cloning he upholds the benefits to humans of cloning animals. In early 2000 Wilmut's cloning technique was granted a patent.

WILSON, CHARLES (1869–1959), physicist. Professor of Natural Philosophy (1925–34) at Cambridge University, Wilson was interested in atmospheric physics and from the mid 1890s sought to reproduce artificial clouds in the laboratory, claiming in 1896–7 that ions could act as sites for the formation of water droplets in dust-free supersaturated air. This, in turn, led to his development in 1911 of the 'cloud chamber', an apparatus for displaying the path of electrons and radioactive emanations as a track of tiny water droplets. His apparatus has since been widely exploited by physicists to produce evidence for new sub-atomic particles. His work on atmospheric physics also led to a technique for protecting barrage balloons from lightning. He shared the 1927 Nobel Prize for Physics with the American physicist Arthur Compton.

WILSON, COLIN (1931–), writer. The paradigmatic alienated provincial 'angry young man' of the 1950s, 24-year-old Leicester-born Wilson rocketed to fame with his version of existential philosophy, *The Outsider* (1956), which appeared in the week that John OSBORNE's play *Look Back in Anger* opened. Hailed as a writer of 'luminous intelligence' whose book was a sell-out success, he was, despite a prolific subsequent output of novels and works of philosophy, the paranormal and the occult, never to repeat his remarkable début.

WILSON, HAROLD see essay on pages 848–49

WILSON, SIR HENRY (1864–1922), soldier. After consistently failing to pass entrance examinations for Woolwich and Sandhurst, Wilson, an Anglo-Irish gentleman, obtained a commission in the Rifle Brigade, after which he served in intelligence before going to the Boer War. Taken up by Commander-in-Chief Lord ROBERTS as a surrogate son (his own son had been killed in Wilson's presence at Colenso), Wilson became Commandant of the Staff College in 1907 and Director of Military Operations in 1910. Largely responsible for plans that committed Britain to France in the event of a European war, in 1914 Wilson ran the British Expeditionary Force's HQ during the retreat from Mons. Increasingly important staff jobs – he was senior liaison officer with the French until declared *persona non grata* by Pétain – led to a major role in LLOYD GEORGE's ultimately successful plot to dismiss Sir William ROBERTSON as Chief of the Imperial General Staff, a position which then fell to Wilson. Fanatically opposed to Irish Home Rule, Wilson came to detest Lloyd George's post-war compromise with Sinn Fein. Retiring in 1922, he was elected Conservative member for an Ulster constituency

continued on page 850

WILSON, HAROLD (Baron Wilson of Rievaulx) (1916–95)
Politician and Prime Minister (1964–70, 1974–6)

Wilson's image as the classic example of the grammar-school boy made good contains an important element of truth: all his life he strove to win what Lord Birkenhead (*see* SMITH, F. E.) had called 'the glittering prizes', and his tragedy was that the gods granted him his wishes.

Although he liked to project himself as a down-to-earth Yorkshireman, having been born in Huddersfield, he was brought up on the Wirral and educated at Wirral grammar school, where despite later claims no one noticed him going bare-foot to school. But his background was a humble one and, as a scholarship boy at Oxford, he was notable for his diligence and intelligence rather than for his attendance at the Union debating society. An expert economist, Wilson spent the war at the Board of Trade and in Whitehall, where he gained a reputation as a master of detail. He became an MP in 1945 and, when he entered the Cabinet in 1947 as President of the Board of Trade, he was the youngest minister since PITT THE YOUNGER; that was the sort of detail which Wilson himself relished.

At this period of his career Wilson was the epitome of the 'man from Whitehall' who 'knew best'. With his Oxford accent, his pin-stripe suit and his encyclopaedic memory, he symbolized the new Labour Party of ATTLEE's day, with its faith in planning and 'big government'. He was particularly assiduous in promoting British trade with the Soviet Union, an activity which in the twilight of his career would encourage lurid rumours about his connections with the Russian secret service. Such was his reputation as one of Attlee's protégés that his resignation from the Cabinet in 1951 came as something of a shock. That Aneurin BEVAN, the siren figure of the Left, should have resigned over the imposition of prescription charges was understandable and even predictable but that Wilson should also go was not; it was the first sign of his abilities as a political tactician, since in the event it gave him a useful store of credit with the left wing of the Labour Party after the 1951 election defeat.

The 1950s were a decade of disappointment for Wilson. His more charismatic contemporary, Hugh GAITSKELL, became Labour leader following Attlee's resignation in 1955 and, given his distrust of Wilson, there seemed little hope that Wilson's ambition for the highest office would ever be realized. His decision to stand against Gaitskell for the party leadership in 1961 marked the low point of his career. But two years later Gaitskell was dead and Wilson was leader of the Labour Party and prospective Prime Minister: it was little wonder that he should once have remarked that 'a week is a long time in politics'.

Fate's timing seemed to have been impeccable. By the time of Gaitskell's death, the Conservatives under MACMILLAN were already showing signs of the internal disarray and battle-weariness which was so marked a feature of their last 18 months in office; that Macmillan's resignation should have brought DOUGLAS-HOME to power was an uncovenanted blessing for Wilson. The 'satire boom' and the advent of the 'swinging sixties' created a climate which was as inimical to Home as it was congenial for Wilson. The latter played up his Merseyside links, flattened his accent, flourished his pipe (when in private he preferred cigars) and set himself up as a man of the people in contrast to the 'fourteenth Earl Home'. Where Home confessed to doing his economics with match-sticks, Wilson made great play with his credentials as an economist and before the 1964 election promised to modernize Britain in the 'white-heat of the technological revolution'.

In the event the election delivered a tiny majority of five. But it was here that Wilson proved himself a master of political tactics. He missed no opportunity to pose on the world stage, and liked to compare himself with US President Lyndon Johnson, whom, truth to tell, he resembled not at all. He identified himself with the youth culture of the 1960s with populist gestures such as awarding the Beatles the MBE and celebrating England's 1966 victory in football's World Cup; his professed liking for HP sauce and the TV soap-opera, *Coronation Street*, cemented his credentials as an ordinary chap. Faced with the wooden and uncharismatic Edward HEATH and a Tory Party in disarray, Wilson romped home in the 1966 election with a majority of 97.

Wilson's professed aim was to make Labour 'the natural party of government' but in the event he proved more adept at dealing with social than with economic issues. In tune with the mood of the 1960s his government passed liberalizing measures in the fields of capital punishment, abortion, homosexuality and divorce but elsewhere the record was less impressive. On the central issue of the economy, Wilson's much-vaunted 'National

Plan' turned out to be neither national nor much of a plan; the powerful trade-union bosses refused to allow incomes to be controlled, while prices proved immune to the government's plans. The late 1960s saw a simultaneous rise in unemployment and inflation, something the economists said could not happen but which happened all the same. Wilson's attempt in 1969 to impose controls on the trade unions with his 'In place of strife' White paper provoked so much strife within his own party that it had to be dropped.

Like many prime ministers, Wilson sought solace from his domestic woes in foreign affairs but here too achievement eluded him. Having been opposed to Macmillan's policy of joining the Common Market, Wilson adopted it for himself once in office; but de Gaulle was no more ready to let Britain join in 1968 than he had been in 1962. For all his boasting about the Anglo-American connection, Wilson's gestures towards helping America in Vietnam failed to gain American gratitude (because they were no more than gestures) but did arouse domestic opposition from those who were implacably opposed to US involvement in Vietnam. Throughout his period in office the thorny issue of Rhodesia, whose unilateral declaration of independence (UDI) in 1965 had led to cries for sanctions, dogged his footsteps. Characteristically dramatic gestures such as meetings on warships with the Rhodesian leader, Ian SMITH, failed to produce any results.

Wilson always deprecated appeals to the 'Dunkirk spirit' and then proceeded to appeal to it himself in 1967 when the government was forced to devalue the pound. His television statement that 'the pound in your pocket has not been devalued' was widely thought to lack conviction and was often quoted against him later. The brief economic revival of 1969–70 was widely expected to bring Labour victory in 1970 despite the government's patchy record but instead the electorate insisted on voting in a way which was inconsistent with the opinion polls and, to everyone's surprise, Edward Heath found himself Prime Minister.

Wilson was not a good leader of the opposition. He gave the impression of a man who had had the stuffing knocked out of him, and he did little to counteract the Labour Party's leftwards drift. The industrial relations and economic difficulties which afflicted the Conservatives gave Labour an opportunity to win support without putting forward anything new by way of policies, and Wilson's own willingness to tolerate the anti-European line favoured on the left of his party was a sign of ruthless opportunism, or weakness, according to taste.

The first election of 1974 allowed Wilson into office with a minority; the second gave him a marginal majority. His second period at 10 Downing Street was a disappointment to those who had hoped for firm leadership. Wilson's unwillingness and inability to impose unity on his own party resulted in his decision to hold a referendum on the Common Market in 1975, and accounted for the fact that he made it an 'open question' as far as the Cabinet was concerned. The spectacle of members of the Labour government campaigning against each other in the referendum campaign did nothing for Cabinet unity, and the eventual victory for the 'yes' campaign could not be unambiguously interpreted as a positive vote for Wilson himself.

By early 1976 Britain's economic situation was so serious that a loan from the International Monetary Fund was widely held to be the only option for the government. Faced with opposition from his own left wing, problems with the trade unions, and an intractable economic situation, it was difficult to see what even Wilson's legendary abilities as an escapologist could produce; to the amazement of everyone he resigned suddenly in March, making way for the older James CALLAGHAN, and leaving behind him a furore over his final honours list, which included a peerage for his private secretary, Marcia WILLIAMS. Rumours abounded: there was some secret scandal which would eventually come out; it was a plot by MI5; Wilson had some ulterior motive; no one could explain why a man so devoted to politics had suddenly cut and run.

It was only much later that it became apparent that Wilson was suffering from a disease which was affecting his legendary memory and his ability to concentrate, and that he wanted to bow out before he shared the fate of Ramsay MACDONALD. There followed a long and distressing descent into ill health. Wilson's enemies said that his opportunism betrayed socialism; but when their turn came in the 1980s they made Labour unelectable; only a return to Wilsonian pragmatism under Tony BLAIR would change this.

Ben Pimlott, Harold Wilson (1992

and was creating a mass anti-republican movement when he was assassinated by the Irish Republican Army.

WILSON, HENRY (1881–1964), soldier. Educated at Eton and Sandhurst, Wilson served in South Africa with the Greenjackets (1900–2) and in France on various divisional staffs (1915–18). Appointed to command the British army in the Middle East in 1939, Wilson oversaw the spectacular British victory over the Italians (Dec. 1940–Feb. 1941), commanded and successfully evacuated British forces from Greece (March–May 1941) and reoccupied Iraq (June–July 1941), eventually taking over the new Persia–Iraq command. Commander-in-Chief Middle East, Supreme Commander in the Mediterranean and finally, from Jan. 1945, head of the joint staff mission in Washington, nicknamed 'Jumbo' because of his size, Wilson was a political rather than an operational soldier, his role in the Mediterranean being virtually that of pro-consul.

WILSON, SIR HORACE (1882–1972), civil servant. Educated at the London School of Economics, he enjoyed rapid promotion in the Civil Service, becoming the leading expert on industrial relations at a time when industrial disputes were an increasingly important feature of British politics in the wake of the First World War. Appointed Permanent Secretary at the Ministry of Labour before he was 40, Wilson was chief industrial adviser to the government in 1930, and when Stanley BALDWIN moved into 10 Downing Street in 1935 Wilson went with him as, in effect, his chief adviser across the whole range of policy issues. He continued to perform this role for Neville CHAMBERLAIN during his premiership (1937–40). As Chamberlain's *éminence grise*, Wilson was inevitably drawn into the politics of appeasement and became one of the policy's most energetic proponents. He played a key role in the negotiations that led up to the Munich conference in Sept. 1938. His critics alleged that he was singularly ill qualified to dispense advice on foreign affairs and that he was more partisan in supporting Chamberlain's policies than he should have been as a civil servant. As soon as CHURCHILL replaced Chamberlain as Prime Minister in May 1940, Wilson was removed from No. 10. He remained as head of the Treasury until the end of the war.

WILSON, JOSEPH (1858–1929), trade-union leader. Born in Sunderland, he became a seaman when he was 13, working in a variety of jobs. After marrying in 1879 he left the ships and opened, first, a cook shop then a temperance hotel and restaurant in Sunderland. But he had already gained experience of trade unionism and in 1883 joined the North of England Sailors' and Seagoing Firemen's Friendly Society, which had been established in 1879. By 1885 he had become President but after an internal union dispute he left to form the Amalgamated Sailors' and Firemen's Union (from 1894 the National Sailors' and Firemen's Union). From then on he became the dominating figure in the complex history of unionism within the shipping industry. Although he was an important figure in establishing unionism within the industry before the First World War, during the war years and later he became increasingly conservative and by the 1920s was leading the seamen's union as, in effect, a company union. He was Liberal MP for Middlesbrough (1892–1900) and coalition Liberal MP for South Shields (1918–22). After 1917 he typified the strand of labour politics which was fiercely anti-communist.

WILSON, RICHARD (1714–82), painter. After spending the 1730s and 1740s in London as a portrait and landscape painter, he travelled to Italy in 1749 and remained there until 1757 teaching art; his pupils included visiting British noblemen. He then returned to England to concentrate exclusively on landscapes. Although at first praised for Italianizing British landscapes, after 1769 his celebrations of large estates and paternalist ideology fell out of fashion. In 1780 a deputation from the Royal Academy (of which Wilson was a founding Fellow) urged him to adopt a more commercial style but he refused despite his poverty. In 1781 the death of his brother enabled him to retire to the family estate near Llanberis, north Wales.

WILTSHIRE, 13TH EARL OF *see* PAULET, WILLIAM

WIMUND (?–c. 1152), prelate. A former monk and Bishop of the Isles, he led a series of raids on DAVID I's Scotland claiming that as a descendant of the kings of Moray he had been unjustly deprived of his rights. He was eventually trapped, blinded, castrated and sent to the monastery of Byland (Yorks.), where he lived out his days, insisting, according to WILLIAM OF NEWBURGH, that if his enemies had left him just the eye of a sparrow he would have made them pay.

WINCHELSEA, ROBERT DE (?–1313), Archbishop of Canterbury (1293–1313). From the time that he, a former Chancellor of Oxford University, was elected Archbishop in 1293, he found himself almost always at odds with the Crown, being a resolute upholder of clerical authority over civil. EDWARD I outlawed him and the rest of the English clergy in 1296 when he obeyed a papal bull ordering the clergy to pay State taxes only with the Pope's permission. He compromised only after Pope Boniface VIII had done so too. Edward persuaded a later pope to suspend him. Although restored when EDWARD II came to the throne, he soon joined the opposition to him.

WINCHESTER, 1ST MARQUESS OF *see* PAULET, WILLIAM

WINCHILSEA, COUNTESS OF *see* FINCH, ANNE

WINDSOR, DUCHESS OF *see* SIMPSON, WALLIS

WINDSOR, DUKE OF *see* EDWARD VIII

WINGATE, ORDE (1903–44), soldier. Educated at Woolwich, he was commissioned into the Royal Artillery in 1923. Wingate subsequently transferred to the Sudan Defence Force, led an expedition into Libya looking for the lost oasis of Zerzura and also explored routes which proved useful during the Second World War. Posted to Palestine in 1936, Wingate, a fanatical Zionist, helped organize the Haganah (Jewish Defence Force), and was wounded in 1938 in a skirmish with Arab guerrillas. With Italy's entry into the war in June 1940, Wingate led a force of Ethiopian irregulars into Italian-occupied Abyssinia, and in the spring of 1941 helped put Haile Selasse back on his throne in Addis Ababa. Having established a reputation as an unconventional soldier, in 1943 Wingate recruited, trained and then led the Chindits deep into Japanese-occupied Burma, an exploit which attracted the attention of CHURCHILL, who took Wingate to the Quebec conference in the autumn of 1943. Having gained the support of the Americans and the Prime Minister, but strongly opposed by 14th Army Commander SLIM, in March 1944 Wingate launched a massive glider-borne Chindit assault onto the Japanese lines of communication in northern Burma but was himself killed on 21 March in an air crash.

WINGFIELD, HUMPHREY (before 1481–1545), parliamentarian. One of 12 sons in a knightly Suffolk family, he made his own career in the law, became a major royal and ducal administrator in East Anglia and was Speaker of the Commons from 1533 in the Reformation Parliament. He ran a remarkable humanist school in his house which sent students to St John's College, Cambridge (*see* ASCHAM, ROGER; CHRISTOPHERSON, JOHN). He seems to have won the trust of all sides in the snake-pit of early Tudor politics.

WINRAM, JOHN (?1492–1582), churchman. After studies at St Andrews he became sub-prior of the cathedral. He stood aloof from George WISHART's burning, and although present at the burning of a St Andrews Protestant in 1558 rapidly joined the Reformation thereafter, helping to draw up the new Kirk's first *Book of Discipline* (blueprint for Church reform) in 1560. He was an energetic superintendent of Fife (1561–72) and of Strathearn (1572–4). Scholarly and of an older generation than most Scottish reformers, he was a force for moderation in Scotland's Reformation.

WINSTANLEY, GERRARD (1609–76), political leader. He led a group known as the True Levellers or Diggers, who from April 1649 set up communal farming settlements on former Crown and common land, most famously at St George's Hill and later Cobham (Surrey). By spring 1650 local opposition combined with army hostility had destroyed them, though the movement had inspired about 10 communities in the home counties and as far away as the Midlands. His pamphlets express radical views on sharing property, although the mystical religion which he propounds still arouses controversy among historians. He became a Quaker, spent his later years obscurely as a merchant and died in London.

WINSTANLEY, HENRY (1644–1703), engineer and architect. Born in Saffron Walden (Essex), Winstanley learned construction techniques working at Audley End, the mansion nearby sold by the 3rd Howard Earl of Suffolk to CHARLES II in 1666. Charles made Winstanley supervisor of architectural work at Audley End and at Newmarket Palace. Winstanley became known for his interest in gadgetry and exhibited an indoor waterfall in Piccadilly. From 1696 he was engaged on the first Eddystone lighthouse near Plymouth. The building was mainly of wood and was damaged several times during construction. In Nov. 1703 Winstanley was killed by tidal waves when at the lighthouse, which was destroyed; it was reconstructed to a modified version of Winstanley's plan and stood until John SMEATON was commissioned to build a more durable lighthouse.

WINTERHALTER, FRANZ (1805–73), court painter. Born in Germany, Winterhalter became the pre-eminent royal portraitist of the mid-nineteenth century, painting at the court of Louis-Philippe of France and receiving the first of several commissions to paint Queen VICTORIA in 1841. She much admired his work and became an avid collector.

WINTHROP, JOHN (1588–1649), colonist. A minor Suffolk gentleman and lawyer whose financial troubles and Puritan enthusiasm drove him to the new colony of Massachusetts in 1630; thereafter he took a leading role in the colony's government, 12 times as elected Governor, and established the town of Boston. His journal and papers are an invaluable record of the formative years of the New England colonies.

WINZET (OR WINGATE), NINIAN (1518–92), churchman. Provost of Linlithgow (Lothian), Winzet was ejected in 1561 for his vocal opposition to the Reformation, and in 1562 went into exile abroad; from 1577 he was Abbot of a Benedictine monastery at Regensburg. He wrote vigorous defences of traditional religion and attacks on John KNOX and others, both in Scots and in Latin.

WISE, ERNIE (originally Earnest Wiseman) (1925–99), comedian *see* MORECAMBE, ERIC

WISE, HENRY (1653–1738), garden designer. In the reign of JAMES II he became the partner of George LONDON, who owned the largest nursery in south-east England, at Brompton (Middx.), and so was able to use a wide variety of plants in his designs. From 1689 he and London were joint Deputy Superintendents of the royal gardens. Among his works outside London were the gardens of Blenheim Palace (Oxon.) and Melbourne (Derb.).

WISEMAN, NICHOLAS (1802–65), Cardinal. Of Irish birth, Wiseman was a scholar in Rome and rector of the English College there before being appointed in 1850 by Pope Pius IX as the first Cardinal Archbishop of Westminster since the Reformation, at a time when the number of Roman Catholics was swelling in England (a result of immigration from Ireland, following the Famine, and of the conversion of clerics such as MANNING and NEWMAN). But in a fundamentally Protestant nation it was not a popular move: *The Times* saw it as 'a gross act of impertinence' and Catholic archbishops were hurriedly deprived of the right to territorial titles.

WISHART, GEORGE (*c.* 1513–46), martyr. He fled Scotland in 1538 as a heretic, and though finding some powerful evangelical patrons in England had similar troubles there, which led to travels in Europe. He may have been the Wishart who proposed assassinating Cardinal BEATON (an old family acquaintance) to the English government in 1544; he had by then returned to Scotland and preached actively for the Reformation, supported by John KNOX. Arrested by Patrick HEPBURN, Earl of Bothwell, he was burned in St Andrews by Beaton.

WITTGENSTEIN, LUDWIG (1889–1951), philosopher. Perhaps the greatest philosopher of the twentieth century, Wittgenstein was born into a wealthy and highly cultivated Viennese family and later naturalized as British. Educated to a curriculum of his father's devising, he obtained only one academic qualification, his Cambridge PhD gained at the age of 40. While studying aero-nautical engineering at Manchester University, he became interested in philosophical questions about the foundations of mathematics: Bertrand RUSSELL's *Principles of Mathematics* had a profound effect upon him. He began studying with Russell at Cambridge in 1912. Within two years he began to write what would become the only work published in his lifetime and considered by many the greatest work in philosophy, the *Tractatus Logico-Philosophicus*. Completed while a prisoner of war in Italy, published first in German (1921) and then in English (1922), the work's bold thesis was that many of the traditional questions preoccupying philosophers were illusory, arising from misunderstandings about language. The task of philosophy was to come to an understanding of how language works and thereby to make the nature of our thoughts clear. The impact of the work was immediate, influencing Russell, the Vienna school and A. J. AYER. After the war Wittgenstein remained in Austria and worked successively as a schoolteacher, gardener and architect before returning to Cambridge and philosophy in 1950, where he remained for the rest of his career. Uncompromising in thought and the perfection of his writings, his *Philosophical Investigations*, published posthumously in 1953, challenged the central thesis of the *Tractatus*.

WODEHOUSE, SIR P(ELHAM) G(RENVILLE) (1881–1975), humorist. His career began in banking in Hong Kong, but by 1903 Wodehouse was a writer, producing humorous stories for boys' magazines, *Punch* and *The Strand* magazine. The first of his 120 books was published in 1903, and *The Man With Two Left Feet* (1917) introduced his characters Bertie Wooster and Jeeves and they, along with a cast of such upper-class eccentrics, bounders, maiden aunts and pretty girls as Lord Emsworth, Psmith, Aunt Dahlia and Gussy Finknottle, have enjoyed a persistent success as the evocation of a sunlit, amiable, confident England that never was. During the Second World War, Wodehouse's broadcasts to America as a German internee cast doubts on his Allied patriotism, and he did not live in Britain again.

WOLFE, JAMES (1727–59), soldier. Son of an army officer, he was commissioned in his father's regiment of marines in 1741, and fought at Dettingen and Culloden. In the Seven Years War, he took part in successful attacks on Rochefort and Louisbourg; GEORGE II reputedly said, when told that Wolfe was mad, that he wished that this commander would bite some of the other generals. Promoted to Major General, Wolfe was put in charge of the expedition against Quebec; he was killed in the final battle, in which the French were defeated. The event was commemorated by Benjamin WEST in a renowned heroic painting, exhibited at the Royal Academy in 1770, which captured the public's imagination.

WOLFENDEN, JOHN (Baron Wolfenden of Westcott) (1908–85), public servant. Although largely known for giving his name to the 1957 report which led to the decriminalization of homosexuality, Wolfenden had a long, diverse and distinguished career as an educationalist and chairman of several public bodies. After five years as a tutor in philosophy at Magdalen College, Oxford, he was appointed Headmaster of Uppingham school (Rutland) in 1934, aged only 26. He remained in this post for 10 years, before becoming Headmaster of Shrewsbury school and, in 1950, Vice-Chancellor of Reading University. Wolfenden chaired numerous government committees on education and social services, notably the Committee on Homosexual Offences and Prostitution, which sat from 1954 until 1957 and laid the foundations for the Labour government's Sexual Offences Act of 1967 allowing private homosexual acts between consenting adult males. In 1963 he became Chairman of the University Grants Committee, a position which he held until 1969, having overseen a period of exceptionally rapid expansion.

WOLFSON, SIR ISAAC (1897–1991), entrepreneur. Glasgow-born, of Polish-Jewish extraction, Wolfson was a travelling salesman before he set up business in London selling clocks and furnishings. After supplying clocks to Great Universal Stores (GUS), a Manchester mail-order company, he was recruited as its chief buyer, and then in the 1932 slump bought a large stake in the company and became its Managing Director. Turning the business round, he achieved significant growth through the 1930s and 1940s, largely through acquisition of ailing and under-performing furnishing and mail-order companies. With retail chain stores added to the group in the 1950s, GUS came to comprise 250 different companies, over which he and his family exercised considerable control. He finally stepped down in 1987 and retired to Israel; by that time GUS itself was seen as under-performing, and management reorganization followed a business credit agreement made in 1986 with retail rivals Harris Queensway. Wolfson's philanthropy to education, medicine and Israel was considerable: apart from him only the deity and certain saints have colleges at both Oxford and Cambridge named after them.

WOLLSTONECRAFT, MARY *see* essay on page 854

WOLSELEY, GARNET (1st Viscount Wolseley) (1833–1913), soldier. One of seven children born to an Anglo-Irish major whose early death left his family in poverty, Wolseley knew his only chance of advancement lay on the battlefield. Displaying near suicidal bravery, he fought in Burma (1852–3), the Crimea (1854–6), the Indian mutiny (1857–8), and China (1860), where he lost an eye; visited and reported on the Confederate army in America (1863); and in 1870 commanded the expedition along the Red River which suppressed Louis Riell's rebellion in the Canadian west. Promoted Major-General, back in Africa in 1873 Wolsely put down the Ashanti. In 1879 he arrived in Natal just too late to put down the Zulus, in 1882 commanded the conquest of Egypt and in 1884–5 led the expedition up the Nile to rescue General GORDON in Khartoum. Wolseley supported the abolition of purchase, and as Adjutant General fought bitter battles with GEORGE, Duke of Cambridge, and Lord Frederick ROBERTS; by promoting the careers of young officers he deemed exceptional, he formed an embryonic general staff which became known as the Wolseley 'ring'. Enormously popular (the modern Major-General in GILBERT and SULLIVAN's *The Pirates of Penzance* was always made up to look like Wolseley), by 1900 his judgement was being questioned as key members of his ring failed the test of modern combat.

WOLSEY, THOMAS *see* essay on pages 856–57

WOLSTENHOLME ELMY, ELIZABETH (?1834–1913), educationalist and women's suffragist. The largely self-educated daughter of a Methodist minister from Eccles (Lancs.), at 19 she founded a school of her own near Manchester; in 1865, as a well-known headmistress, she established the Manchester Schoolmistresses' Association and became a keen advocate of educational opportunities for women in the North of England Council for the Higher Education of Women. She also worked from the beginning with Manchester women's suffrage campaigners. Remarkably, she spanned the earliest and the later years of the campaign, joining in 1905 the Women's Social and Political Union. She had also been involved in the Married Women's Property Committee (1868–82), to secure possession of property and earnings for married women, and the campaign for the repeal of the Contagious Diseases Acts. In 1874 she married Benjamin Elmy, a fellow free-thinker and supporter of women's suffrage.

WOOD, EDWARD (6th [1st Wood] Earl of Halifax) *see* essay on page 858

WOOD, SIR HENRY (1838–1919), soldier. Youngest son of an Anglican clergyman, he was

continued on page 855

WOLLSTONECRAFT, MARY (1759–97)
Writer and feminist

Her father, a handkerchief-weaver in Spitalfields, failed in business. The family lived on a series of farms around London, moving to Yorks. in 1765. Wollstonecraft's parents believed that girls needed only a rudimentary education, but she was encouraged by a friend's father and later, in London, by an elderly clergyman and his wife. In 1777, after further family crises, she became paid companion to an elderly lady, Mrs Dawson, one of the few posts available to a middle-class young woman. This allowed her to see fashionable society close to.

In 1784, having (in her view) rescued her younger sister from an abusive husband, Wollstonecraft, her two sisters and friend Fanny Blood established a school for girls at Newington Green. Her friends in intellectual circles there included Richard PRICE and Thomas DAY, who introduced her to other writers. Although her school failed, she wrote *Thoughts on the Education of Daughters* (1786), which, inspired by the educational ideas of Rousseau and BENTHAM, rejected teaching by rote and argued that women should have greater employment opportunities and be paid enough to keep them in old age.

When the Newington Green household broke up, Wollstonecraft served as governess to the children of Viscount and Viscountess Kingsborough at Mitchelstown Castle in Ireland, but their fashionable radicalism and profligate lifestyle disturbed her. She was dismissed, her experiences contributing to her autobiographical novel *Mary* (1788). She became a writer and translator in London, mainly for Joseph Johnson's *Analytical Review*, which also published Joseph PRIESTLEY, Richard Lovell EDGEWORTH and Erasmus DARWIN. She completed *Original Stories* (1788), a collection of fables for children highlighting the wretchedness of the poor.

Johnson's circle welcomed the French Revolution and when in 1790 BURKE published *Reflections on the Revolution in France*, Wollstonecraft responded with *A Vindication of the Rights of Men*. It described her ideal society, in which hard work and ability would be rewarded for women as well as men, irrespective of social class, and in which practices that penalized the unfortunate, such as game laws, slavery and the press gang, would be abolished. The work established her as a leading revolutionary thinker alongside Thomas PAINE.

Paine is sometimes credited with suggesting to her the subject of her next book, *A Vindication of the Rights of Women* (1792), which argued that by limiting women's participation society was wasting its assets. Girls should be encouraged to develop their mental and physical abilities alongside boys at co-educational schools, to enter diverse careers, to vote and to sit in Parliament. Wollstonecraft saw men as imposing sexual identity upon women; she saw sexuality's only value as lying in parenthood and was the first to call marriage 'legal prostitution'. The *Vindication* was rejected by conservative women writers such as Hannah MORE but gained Wollstonecraft disciples including Mary Hays and Anna SEWARD. It was translated into German, Italian and French.

In late 1792, as anti-radical agitation increased, Wollstonecraft left for France. When war broke out between England and France in 1793 she was trapped. She wrote *A Historical and Moral View of the French Revolution* (1794), and had an affair with an American captain, Gilbert Imlay. Being registered as his wife at the American embassy helped her evade arrest when other English exiles were imprisoned during the Terror. With their young child, she went to Scandinavia in search of compensation for bullion seized from a ship of Imlay's.

Abandoned by Imlay in London, Wollstonecraft returned to what was left of her old circle, renewing an earlier acquaintance with William GODWIN, and they became lovers. Godwin had expressed views compatible with Mary's in *Political Justice*, although he was less willing to allow women full economic independence. Wollstonecraft wrote her novel, *The Wrongs of Women, or Maria* (1796), about the middle-class Maria, who struggles against and escapes from her cruel husband only to find that the law is on his side, and the workhouse warder Jemima, bred in poverty and at various times rape victim, prostitute, housemaid, washerwoman and workhouse inmate. Maria's 'refinement' fails to give her the status of an individual in society; she and Jemima are shown to suffer from the same discrimination. The novel develops the arguments made in the *Vindication*, allowing women to be sexual actors. It was unfinished at her death and was published among her posthumous works (1798).

Early in 1797 Wollstonecraft realized that she was again pregnant; she and Godwin married in church despite Godwin's atheism, and their daughter Mary, later Mary SHELLEY, was born late Aug. Wollstonecraft died from an infection arising from the non-delivery of the placenta. Her reputation suffered in the conservative moral climate of the nineteenth century, but recovered in the second half of the twentieth when she was claimed, with justification, as a prophet of the feminist movement.

Claire Tomalin, The Life and Death of Mary Wollstonecraft (1992) forced by family poverty to leave Marlborough at 14 and join the Royal Navy. Wounded while serving with the Naval Brigade in the Crimea (1855), Wood transferred to a cavalry regiment destined for India, was awarded the Victoria Cross in the suppression of the Indian mutiny and distinguished himself academically at Staff College (1862–4). Wood's advancement was assured when in 1873 WOLSELEY selected him to serve in the Ashanti expedition; thereafter he served with Wolseley against the Zulus (1879) and in Egypt (1882), eventually replacing him as Quartermaster General (1893). As Adjutant General in 1899 Wood oversaw the creation of the largest army Britain had yet deployed. Wood's retirement (1903) marked the end of the influence of the Wolseley ring.

WOOD, SIR HENRY (1869–1944), musician. Wood, whose name is synonymous with the annual Promenade Concerts, made his début as a conductor with the Clapton Music Society in 1888. In 1892 he conducted the English première of Tchaikovsky's *Eugene Onegin*. The following year Robert Newman, manager of the new Queen's Hall (London), suggested the idea of promenade concerts, a festival series offering an adventurous mixture of new pieces with traditional favourites and enabling concert goers to purchase cheap tickets on the day of performance. A new and permanent orchestra was assembled under Wood's direction, and its first Promenade Concert was performed on 10 Aug. 1895. Wood remained in sole charge of the orchestra and the Proms until 1940. After the Queen's Hall was destroyed in an air raid in 1941, the Proms were moved to the Royal Albert Hall, and Wood was joined by Adrian Boult as an associate conductor. A vigorous and extremely hard-working conductor, his style appealed to a wide audience.

WOOD, JOHN THE ELDER (1704–54) and **JOHN THE YOUNGER** (1728–81), architects. The older John Wood, the son of a Bath builder, learned new architectural techniques when working in London as a young man and argued that new streets and squares in the Palladian style would suit Bath's growing reputation as a fashionable resort. He succeeded, despite the opposition of the city authorities, by buying land himself and sub-leasing it on the condition that leaseholders built according to his elevations. Wood also built and designed several country houses in the west of England, including Prior Park, near Bath, for Ralph ALLEN, and worked in other growing towns such as Liverpool. His main work in Bath, the Circus and Forum, progressed slowly and was only after his death completed by his son, John Wood. The younger Wood continued the reconstruction of Bath in the same style as his father, most notably with the New Assembly Rooms and the Hot Bath.

WOOD, SIR KINGSLEY (1881–1943), politician. He served as Postmaster General (1931–5) and Minister of Health (1935–8) in the National government. As Air Minister (1938–40) and member of the War Cabinet under Neville CHAMBERLAIN, he oversaw the rapid expansion of the Royal Air Force and the introduction of radar defences in southern England. He became Winston CHURCHILL's Chancellor of the Exchequer in Nov. 1940, introducing compulsory savings and a system of automatic taxation ('pay as you earn', PAYE) to help meet the costs of the war. Influenced by KEYNES, he used the budget as an instrument of broad economic policy, especially to prevent inflation. He died in office.

WOOD, ROBERT (*c*. 1717–71), antiquarian. A member of the Irish gentry, he spent much of his life on an extended Grand Tour. In the early 1740s and again 10 years later, he explored the eastern Mediterranean. In May 1751 he met Nicholas REVETT and James STUART in Athens, and later published two works on the *Ruins of Palmyra* (1753) and the *Ruins of Balbec* (1757). Elected to the Society of Dilettanti in 1763, he raised money for Revett's 1764–6 expedition to Asia Minor, but by this time he had been claimed by politics and although he left office with his superior Lord Weymouth (*see* THYNNE, THOMAS) in 1770 he died before he could write up all his archaeological studies.

WOOD, WILLIAM (1671–1730), coinage manufacturer. Owner of the largest metalworking business in early eighteenth-century England, in 1722 he was awarded a patent to coin halfpence and farthings for Ireland. Critics, including Jonathan SWIFT in *The Drapier's Letters*, claimed that Wood stood to make excessive profits because of the difference between the intrinsic and the face value of the coins and also that the evident over-production of the new coins would disrupt the economy. The news that the patent had been auctioned off by GEORGE I's mistress the Duchess of Kendal (*see* SCHULENBERG, MELUSINE VON DER) further discredited the currency. Robert WALPOLE was inclined to read Irish opposition as a challenge to Ireland's constitutional subordination, but senior members of the Irish administration also opposed the currency and Wood's patent was withdrawn in 1725.

WOODCOCK, GEORGE (1904–79), trade-union leader. Son of a Lancs. cotton weaver, he benefited from trade-union sponsorship to study at Ruskin and then New College, Oxford. A civil servant (1934–6), Woodcock was appointed head of the Trades Union Congress (TUC) research and economic department (1937–47), becoming general secretary (1960–9) and giving the TUC a
continued on page 859

WOLSEY, THOMAS (?1472–1530)
Statesman

A prosperous Ipswich butcher's son, he had most of his education at Magdalen College, Oxford, and became a fellow before 1497; he is said to have been dismissed as college bursar for some characteristic impetuous extravagance in financing the building of Magdalen Tower. He became chaplain to Henry Deane, Archbishop of Canterbury (1501) and, after Deane's death, to Sir Richard Nanfan, Deputy Governor of Calais (1503).

Wolsey gained a royal chaplaincy *c.* 1507; he began to be employed in diplomatic missions and became Dean of Lincoln in Feb. 1509. His rise was meteoric when HENRY VIII (two of whose childhood tutors had been Magdalen men) realized that he was ideally suited to the tedious work of government. In Nov. 1509 he was appointed Royal Almoner and became a Royal Councillor in 1511; by 1513 he had sidelined the older Councillors in exercising power, which conveniently freed Henry from their restraining influence.

From 1515 the King and Wolsey decided policy between them, and only then referred it to other Councillors; Wolsey exercised a degree of control over diplomacy, provision for war and government in Church and State enjoyed by no other Tudor minister. He devoted much energy to diplomacy in an effort to promote Henry's greatness in Europe, but the difficulty of making England appear more important than it actually was is reflected in the puzzling contradictions of the results: attempts at close alliance with France in 1514, 1518 and 1526–7, together with aggressive moves and international diplomacy aimed against France in 1516–17 and 1521–5, and attempts to act as a peace-broker for all Europe in 1518, 1521 and 1527–9.

Henry rewarded him for this 'busyness' by obtaining his elevation to Cardinal in 1515 and appointing him Lord Chancellor, uniquely (though in the end inaccurately) as a grant for life. Wolsey also accumulated an astonishing array of Church offices: briefly Bishop of Lincoln, and of Tournai (1514); Archbishop of York (1514–30); Bishop of Bath and Wells (1518–23); of Durham (1523–9); of Winchester (1529–30); even Abbot of St Albans. William WARHAM's inconvenient longevity withheld the archbishopric of Canterbury, and Henry failed to win his election as Pope in 1521, 1523 and 1529; nevertheless his appointment as Papal Legate *a latere* (1518) gave him unique power in the English Church, effectively making him Pope in England, outranking Warham. He also secured a variety of profitable Church offices to support his bastard son Thomas Winter in the acquisition of a humanist education (Winter at least acquired beautiful italic handwriting).

Wolsey's fitful and frequently self-promoting use of his legatine powers for Church reform provoked conservative fury, and deprived him of the support of respected senior clergy who were his natural allies.

Unusually among English bishops, he spent little time in his dioceses. He could be regarded by senior churchmen as soft on heresy, although he was fairly energetic against Lutheranism when it appeared, and his efforts to get religious reformers to recant might now be seen as a more subtle and effective strategy than creating martyrs at the stake.

His one major programme of change in the Church was to close a clutch of small monasteries in the south-east, in order to finance colleges at Ipswich and Oxford (grandiose imitations of the twinned foundations of Eton and King's, Cambridge). The dissolutions might be considered a sensible redeployment of resources, but they were too closely associated with his self-indulgence, and they aroused local fury, even riots when some of the monasteries were closed. Wolsey succeeded in alienating virtually the entire monastic world, even attacking the independence of the Observant Friars, one of the few religious orders in England which needed no reform.

Wolsey was more interested in secular government (which had given him his earliest power) than in Church reform. His greatest talent and concern lay in administering justice, despite his lack of formal legal training. He devoted particular energy to restructuring the equity and prerogative courts: he very frequently sat as judge in Chancery and encouraged a boom in its business in property disputes, but he also tried to solve the perennial problem of bringing effective justice to particularly complex disputes which polarized whole areas. Wolsey saw that the only effective way of intervening in such feuds was to bring in the greatest power in the land, so he made a point of using the Royal Council as a regular court.

This also became the place where Wolsey most frequently demonstrated his power, because he could use the Council's authority in any way that he liked. He effectively separated the Council's judicial function, which might otherwise have swamped his other activities, as the work of the

Court of Star Chamber (named from the room in which the Council met for judicial business), and he used summons to Star Chamber as the way in which central government controlled the localities.

He also reorganized the Council in the North and the Council in the Marches of Wales to make them more effective instruments of Westminster government and justice, and made a point of regularly summoning Justices of the Peace to Westminster to account for themselves and receive royal instructions.

The nobility and gentry hated Wolsey as an upstart who stood in the way of their securing the share of political spoils; the execution of Edward STAFFORD, Duke of Buckingham, in 1521 was widely and unjustly blamed on Wolsey's jealousy of ancient lineage. His constant danger was therefore his isolation; he was entirely dependent on the King's favour, which was in turn dependent on Wolsey's continuing to make a success of government – in particular, providing money for the King's military adventures abroad.

His reputation for omnicompetence first took a blow in 1525, with the failure of his Amicable Grant scheme, intended to raise an extra-parliamentary lump sum for war with France. This was the last straw after three years in which Wolsey had fronted a series of demands for money, both loans and parliamentary taxation: faced with a tax strike, he had to back down, abandon the grant and rein in royal aggression. He was forced to surrender Hampton Court for the King's use, and there was an attempt to restore real power to the Council in a reorganization, the Eltham Ordinance (1526), which Wolsey avoided implementing in full.

The irreparable error was Wolsey's failure to solve, from 1527, the problem of securing an annulment of Henry's marriage to CATHERINE OF ARAGON. His enemies were delighted to turn on him, and, with increasing hostility from ANNE BOLEYN, Henry's affection cooled. The worst blow was the failure of a papal tribunal headed by Wolsey and Cardinal Lorenzo Campeggio, sitting at Blackfriars, London, in summer 1529, to make any progress on the annulment; the case was revoked to Rome.

In Oct. Wolsey was indicted on charges of *praemunire*, i.e. exercising a foreign jurisdiction – the papal jurisdiction which Henry had been instrumental in securing for him. He was dismissed as Lord Chancellor, and lost his Westminster palace, York Place, to the King (it was renamed Whitehall). He was sent to his archdiocese of York, travelling in unwisely magnificent state; he watched in increasing despair as his enemies secured new humiliations, particularly the confiscation of his colleges (Henry soon revived Cardinal College, Oxford, eventually as Christ Church). Arrested on treason charges arising from rather pathetic negotiations with French agents, Wolsey died at Leicester on his way south.

Wolsey has never found many defenders, being seen by Catholic historians as an embarrassment and by Protestants as the perfect symbol of a corrupt Church, despite the admiring early life written by his devoted gentleman usher George Cavendish.

He ought, however, to be judged alongside other cardinal-ministers of the period, David BEATON in Scotland, who unlike Wolsey lived as if he were a married layman, or the French Cardinal François de Tournon (d. 1562), who collected two Italian bishoprics and 27 abbeys and priories, besides four archbishoprics in succession.

The problem was that no English figure directly compared to Wolsey, while there was a very damaging direct contrast between Wolsey's origins and his manifest desire to be more magnificent than anyone else. He loved spending money on building, the arts, music, ceremonial and simply enjoying himself: it was the reward for being a workaholic.

In building he outdid all his contemporaries except HENRY VII and Henry VIII and indeed until his fall he outdid Henry VIII. All this magnificence also undermined his genuine efforts to set moral standards, for instance a unique attempt to regulate people's diets and his better-known laws against excessive expenditure on dress, dicing and gambling. It also annoyed the nobility, who were accustomed to setting the pace in showing off and spending money.

Undoubtedly he squandered much of his great ability and his powers in Church and State, but his overwhelming and understandable priority was to do Henry's bidding. His reforms in the secular courts and his close attention to central intervention in local government have been revealed by recent research as of lasting significance: the 'Tudor Revolution in Government' with which Geoffrey ELTON credited Thomas CROMWELL was thus in many ways anticipated in the work of his master.

S. J. Gunn and P. G. Lindley (eds), Cardinal Wolsey: Church, State and Art (1991)

WOOD, EDWARD (3rd Viscount, 6th [1st Wood] Earl of Halifax) (1881–1959)
Politician

Wood's background was impeccably north country Whig. His grandfather was a member of the Palmerston (see TEMPLE, HENRY) and GLADSTONE Cabinets, his father a devout High Anglican; Wood himself was equal parts Whig and High Anglican, even though his political career was to be spent in the ranks of the Conservative Party. Like many Whigs, Wood's family took flight from the Liberal Party after the Home Rule crisis of 1886 but they brought with them into the Unionist coalition many liberal attitudes which would, in time, profoundly affect the Conservative Party of which Halifax himself would be such an ornament.

A scholarly young man who won an All Souls fellowship, Wood decided to join the army in 1914 despite the disability of a withered left arm. He served with distinction, and after the war entered Parliament as a Conservative MP, where, along with the young Lord George Ambrose Lloyd, he wrote an influential book on the future of Conservatism, *The Great Opportunity* (1919), but it was in the field of external rather than internal politics that Wood's liberal conservatism was destined to operate.

Wood was one of those younger Conservatives who benefited from the split in the party consequent on the 1922 revolt against the LLOYD GEORGE coalition and, after serving under Bonar LAW and BALDWIN, the latter appointed him as Viceroy of India in 1925. Lord Irwin, as he became, belonged firmly in the camp of those who believed that the future of the Empire lay in a devolution of central power to the colonial possessions, and his partnership with Baldwin's India Secretary, the diehard Lord Birkenhead (*see* SMITH, F. E.), was an uneasy one. He was happier under a Labour government and was, in Oct. 1929, responsible for the Irwin declaration which pronounced that dominion status was the goal of British rule in India. This created great divisions in the Conservative Party but Irwin won the support of his friend Baldwin and, after his return to England in 1933, campaigned for the National government's India Bill against the opposition of CHURCHILL and the imperialist wing of the Conservative Party.

Neville CHAMBERLAIN appointed him Lord President of the Council in 1937, and the following year, after EDEN's resignation, Halifax (as he had become in 1934) became Foreign Secretary. Halifax saw himself as a realist, taking the view that however little he liked the dictators they were facts of life and had to be dealt with. His first priority was to get on better terms with Mussolini before trying to do the same with Hitler. His efforts were overtaken by the Munich crisis, and he supported Chamberlain's visit to Berchtesgaden in Sept. 1938 but was horrified by the terms which Chamberlain brought back from a second meeting with Hitler at Bad Godesberg. It was Halifax's opposition which persuaded Chamberlain not to accept Hitler's terms and, while he was happy with the Munich settlement, he urged Chamberlain to widen his government's support by bringing back Eden. After *Kristallnacht* (9 Nov. 1938) the persecution of the Jews helped to convince Halifax that Hitler's regime might need dealing with by non-diplomatic means. It was largely through his prompting that Chamberlain gave the guarantee to Poland in March 1939 which led Britain into war in Sept.

Halifax was a more emollient political figure than Chamberlain and, when the latter decided to resign in May 1940, he was almost everyone's first choice for premier; the one dissentient voice was his own, and so the post went to Churchill. Halifax tried to persuade Churchill of the need to negotiate with Hitler in late May 1940, but Churchill's rhetorical mastery and the adoption of a policy of 'no surrender' lessened Halifax's influence, which was further undermined by the publication of *Guilty Men* (1940) by Michael FOOT and Frank Owen, which blamed him and Chamberlain for the failures of the appeasement years. But he remained a major figure in the party, and Churchill was happy to send him to Washington as Ambassador at the end of 1940.

Halifax's aristocratic manner ensured that his initial months as Ambassador in America would be uneasy ones but he quickly set about making friends with the most influential members of the Roosevelt administration and, by 1945, had made such a success of the job that he was kept on by Ernest BEVIN when Labour came to power. After his retirement in 1946 he played no part in national politics.

Halifax presided over British foreign policy at just the point where pretensions to world power had outstripped the capacity to maintain them, but he played a notable role in securing the American alliance which would allow his post-war successors to retain them until the Suez fiasco of 1956.

Andrew Roberts, The Holy Fox: A Biography of Lord Halifax (1991) weight that enabled it to be a forceful partner to government. In the belief that co-operation was essential to safeguard full employment, Woodcock managed to persuade the TUC to take part in the Conservative government's National Development Council in 1962 and to agree that under the Labour government the TUC should in effect agree in advance the wage claims of individual unions, a role which it had never had before. Seen as a sometimes rather distant figure, Woodcock's intellectual grasp and practical experience informed the work of the Donovan Commission on Trades Unions and Employers Associations (1965–8), on which he sat. Harold WILSON appointed him to chair the Commission on Industrial Relations, but he resigned in 1971 when Edward HEATH's government proposed making the commission an enforcing body.

WOODFORDE, JAMES ('PARSON') (1740–1802), clergyman and diarist. His diaries, first published in 1924–31, have been much cited for their account of eighteenth-century clerical and rural life. Spanning the years 1758–1802, from the time of Woodforde's studies at Oxford to his tenure (from 1774 until his death) of the rectory of Weston Longville (Norfolk), they record a largely placid life, and suggest a preoccupation with material comforts. By no means all eighteenth-century clergy were as comfortable or as complacent.

WOODVILLE, ANTHONY (2nd Earl Rivers) (c. 1440–83), royal servant. He inherited the newly created earldom from his father in 1469. As brother of EDWARD IV's Queen, ELIZABETH WOODVILLE, and one of the most cultivated figures at court, well known for his literary and chivalrous tastes, he was an obvious choice for governor of the heir to the throne's household, a post he held from 1473. In April 1483 he was escorting EDWARD V to London for his coronation when he was, to his evident surprise, arrested by Richard of Gloucester, and was summarily executed on 25 June, the day before his captor was proclaimed King as RICHARD III.

WOODWARD, JOHN FORSTER (1932–), sailor. A submariner, as Director of Naval Plans (1978–81) he was widely regarded as the navy's leading expert on under-water operations. Unexpectedly chosen to command a force of surface ships tasked with retaking the Falkland Islands, Woodward was not reassured when told that the Admiralty needed someone important enough to sack if things went wrong. Problems of logistics and the sub-Antarctic weather were compounded by a totally inadequate air defence. After losing several ships to Argentine bombs and missiles Woodward kept his major units so far to the north-east of the islands that British land forces accused the navy of being on the 'South Africa station'. In fact Woodward's destroyers and frigates gave land forces considerable naval gunfire support, suffering further casualties to land-based Argentine missiles. Achieving success in extremely difficult circumstances, Woodward was promoted to Deputy Chief of the Defence Staff in 1983 and Commander-in-Chief Naval Home Command in 1987.

WOOLF, GUSTAV WILHELM (1834–1913), shipbuilder see HARLAND, SIR EDWARD

WOOLF, LEONARD (1880–1969), writer and publisher. Son of a Jewish barrister, a member of the Apostles at Cambridge, where he was greatly influenced by G. E. MOORE, Woolf went to Ceylon (1904–11) as a member of the Colonial Service. On his return to England on leave in 1911 he proposed to Virginia Stephen (see WOOLF, VIRGINIA) and published the first of several novels about his life in the colonies. Leonard and Virginia were married in 1912 and in 1917 started the Hogarth Press, which was to publish several novels by members of the Bloomsbury group, as well as Leonard's own works on politics and international affairs. A Fabian and a supporter of the Co-operative movement, he was joint editor of the *Political Quarterly* (1931–59), and wrote five volumes of autobiography, which remain a sober source for the political realities of the period, but his name is heard more often today in debate over his possible responsibility for his wife's mental instability.

WOOLF, VIRGINIA (née Stephen) (1882–1941), novelist. Born into a literary family, she moved with her sister (see BELL, VANESSA) and brothers to Gordon Square near the British Museum after the death of their father, Leslie STEPHEN, in 1904, so forming the nucleus of the literary and artistic circle that would be known as the Bloomsbury group. This loose association of gifted and productive people included at various times such luminaries as the economist and writer J. M. KEYNES, the writers E. M. FORSTER, Lytton STRACHEY and Desmond MacCarthy, the philosopher G. E. MOORE, the painters Duncan GRANT and Dora CARRINGTON, the art critic Roger FRY and later the writer David GARNETT. They were united in their scorn for what they regarded as Victorian vulgarity and narrowness of vision. Elitist in their social attitudes, unspecifically left-wing in their politics, agnostic and avant-garde in artistic, personal and sexual matters, they appear both collectively and individually to have an abiding fascination for those interested in British culture and society. In 1912 Virginia married the ex-civil servant and writer Leonard WOOLF and in 1917 they set up the Hogarth Press, which published many such distinguished writers as Katherine

MANSFIELD, T. S. ELIOT and Virginia herself, often jacketed with illustrations by Vanessa. Virginia's first novel, *The Voyage Out*, was published in 1915. As a literary critic she urged a move away from 'realism' to a more interior, experimental 'stream of consciousness' style as exemplified by *Mrs Dalloway* (1925), *To the Lighthouse* (1927) and particularly *The Waves* (1931), all of them establishing her as one of the leading exponents of 'modernism'; her polemical *A Room of One's Own* (1929) is now regarded as a feminist classic. Long troubled by mental breakdowns, she committed suicide, after completing *Between the Acts* (1941), by walking into the River Ouse near Rodmell (Sussex) where the Woolfs had a house.

WOOLTON, 1ST EARL OF *see* MARQUIS, FREDERICK JAMES

WORCESTER, EARL OF, 2ND *see* PERCY, THOMAS; **4TH** *see* TIPTOFT, JOHN

WORCESTER, WILLIAM (1415–82), writer. After a lifetime devoted to the complex business interests of Sir John FASTOLF, in 1478 he was finally free to indulge his passion for antiquarian studies. As he rode about Britain, he recorded on sheets of paper he kept in his saddlebag the curiosities and places of interest which he encountered. The result was the *Itinerary*, the notebook of his travels between 1478 and 1480 and the earliest historical guidebook written in England. Earlier, while Fastolf's secretary, he had responded to the loss of Normandy by writing the *Boke of Noblesse* in the forlorn hope of persuading HENRY VI to carry on the fight.

WORDSWORTH, DOROTHY (1771–1855), journal and letter writer. Sister of the more famous William, nothing that Dorothy wrote was published in her lifetime save for a poem entitled 'To a Child', which was included in William WORDSWORTH's *Poems* (1815). Yet her letters and journals, which she started in 1798 'to give William pleasure', and on which he drew for *Guide to the Lakes* (1823), vividly detail the landscape of the Lake District where she lived for most of her life with her beloved brother even after he married and had a family. They are a record of her passionate affinity with nature, the domestic activities of the household to which COLERIDGE was a sometime frequent visitor and the hard lives of her fellow Lakelanders during the Napoleonic Wars and the enclosure of land.

WORDSWORTH, WILLIAM (1770–1850), poet. The most celebrated of the Lakeland Romantic poets, he was born at Cockermouth (Cumb.). By 1783 the Wordsworth children were orphans, and William and his sister Dorothy WORDSWORTH, to whom he was particularly close, were parted. In 1787 he went up to St John's College, Cambridge, but found the precious and competitive intellectual world there uncongenial and in 1791 set off for France, which had been, since 1789, in a state of revolutionary tumult. He found the year he spent there sublime and, inspired with the notions of liberty, equality and fraternity for all citizens, planned to join the Girondist army. He also fathered a daughter with Annette Vallon, a Blois surgeon's daughter. Lack of funds dictated his return to England in Dec. 1792 to an uncertain future and a sense of moral guilt and intellectual confusion. Still fuelled with revolutionary fervour, he was appalled at the coming to power of Robespierre with the advent of the Jacobin 'reign of terror', but he was equally unhappy to see Britain at war with France, and he fell into a deep depression, recounted in *The Borderers* (1796–7, published 1842).

In 1795 a legacy allowed Wordsworth to support himself as a poet, and to be reunited with Dorothy. He composed *Lyrical Ballads*, a landmark in English Romanticism, and sections of what was later to become 'The Prelude'. In 1799 he and Dorothy returned to the Lake District, settling at Dove Cottage, Grasmere. There he wrote most of his greatest poems, which were published in a second edition of *Lyrical Ballads* (2 vols, 1800, with the controversial preface setting out poetic rules), *Poems in Two Volumes* (1807, containing 'Intimations of Immortality'), *The Excursion* (1814), *The White Doe of Rylstone* (1815), *Poems, including Lyrical Ballads* (1815), *Peter Bell: A Tale in Verse* (1819) and *The Waggoners* (1819).

By now a man of some substance, his appointment in 1813 to the sinecure of distributor of stamps for Westmorland enabled him and his family (his wife Mary Hutchinson, whom he had married in 1802, five children and Dorothy) to move to Rydal Mount, Ambleside, where he lived for the rest of his life. But the fiery, revolutionary youth had metamorphosed into a patrician, conservative patriot who (much to the disgust of KEATS) could be found canvassing for the local Tory Lord Lonsdale, was awarded a civil list pension and in 1842 was appointed Poet Laureate in succession to SOUTHEY.

WOTTON, SIR HENRY (1568–1639), scholar. From a Kent knightly family, he studied at Oxford, travelled in Europe and was in the service of Robert DEVEREUX, Earl of Essex, who used him to gather information. He settled in Venice, frequently serving as Ambassador there and elsewhere in Europe between 1604 and 1624 (inventing the famous definition of an ambassador as a man sent abroad to lie for his country).

From 1639 he was Provost of Eton. He wrote on a variety of subjects, including architecture and international relations, and published poetry. Izaak WALTON wrote his life.

WREN, SIR CHRISTOPHER (1632–1723), architect. Son of a clergyman, Wren went to Oxford, where he conducted scientific experiments and was elected a Fellow in 1653. In 1657 he became Professor of Astronomy at Gresham College, London; from 1661 until 1673 he was Savilian Professor of Astronomy at Oxford. His interests ranged over mathematics, optics, anatomy and medicine; the use of the barometer to study weather is attributed to him. He played an important role in the foundation of the Royal Society, becoming its President in 1680. In 1661 CHARLES II invited him to serve as assistant to the Surveyor General of the King's Works, and in 1669 he was made Surveyor General. Architecture ultimately became his pre-eminent interest: he was the principal architect for the rebuilding of London after the Great Fire (1666), designing St Paul's Cathedral and many churches and livery houses in what has been termed a 'half-Baroque' style. Other works included the Sheldonian Theatre, Oxford (one of his first major commissions), and the hospitals at Chelsea, Greenwich and Kilmainham (Dublin). Wren served as an MP in 1685, 1689, 1690 and 1701. His buildings temporarily fell from favour with the rise of Palladianism, championed by Colen CAMPBELL and Lord Burlington (*see* BOYLE, ROBERT) from the 1710s.

WREN, MATTHEW (1585–1667), churchman. A Cambridge don who became chaplain to the future CHARLES I in 1622, he was an aggressive Arminian supporter of William LAUD, and became Bishop of Hereford in 1634. As Bishop of Norwich from 1635 he caused uproar in East Anglia by his campaigns against Puritans, prompting many to leave for the North American settlements. Moved to Ely in 1638, he was arrested in 1642 and imprisoned until 1660, when he regained his diocese. In his building projects thereafter, he was one of the first patrons of his nephew Christopher WREN.

WRIGHT, JOSEPH (also known as Wright of Derby) (1734–97), painter. Son of a Derby attorney, he was educated at the local grammar school. His artistic talents attracted attention, and he was sent to study with the painter Thomas Hudson, after which he returned to Derby and set up as a portrait-painter. He is chiefly known for his paintings of figures illuminated by artificial light, reflecting the philosophical and technological interests of eighteenth-century society. The most famous of these is probably *An Experiment with a Bird in the Air Pump* (1769). His scientific subjects made his reputation in London but he remained close to provincial circles, including that of Erasmus DARWIN. On his visit to Italy in 1773 he was inspired by the eruption of Vesuvius, which led him to paint 18 pictures of the subject up to 1794.

WRIOTHESLEY, THOMAS (5th [4th Wriothesley] Earl of Southampton) (1607–67), politician. Educated at Oxford, and then spending some years on the continent, he strove to take a pacific line in Parliament in 1640–1, but increasingly sided with CHARLES I, and became one of his closest advisers during the First English Civil War, representing him in peace negotiations from 1643 to 1645. He was allowed to compound for (i.e. buy back) his estates, and lived in retirement until the restoration of CHARLES II, when he again played a moderate part, urging mercy to those who had signed Charles I's death warrant. Favoured by Edward HYDE, Earl of Clarendon, he served as Lord Treasurer from 1660 until his death in 1667. Proud of his own avoidance of corruption, he was dismayed by the extravagance of Charles II's court and withdrew from active business, perhaps being left in office because otherwise he would have been a magnet for opponents of the court.

WROTH, MARY (née Sidney) (*c.* 1586–*c.* 1652), poet. Niece of Sir Philip SIDNEY, she married in 1602 Sir Robert Wroth; their house became a centre of hospitality and literary patronage. Her attentions to her cousin William HERBERT (she was a great beauty) infuriated his mother, the poet Mary HERBERT, Countess of Pembroke. Her cheerfully erotic poetry is better than her prose, and is consciously in debt to Sidney.

WROTH, WILLIAM (1576–1641), Congregationalist pioneer. Rector of Llanfaches (Glamorgan), he had a conversion experience and became a celebrated preacher, attracting the hostile attention of William LAUD from 1635. Resigning his living in 1639, he established Wales's first Independent Church at Llanfaches.

WULFHERE, King of Mercia (658–75). The son of PENDA of Mercia, he reasserted Mercian domination over southern Britain after the short period of Northumbrian supremacy that had followed his father's defeat and death at the Battle of the Winwæd. Wulfhere's achievements therefore consolidated the Mercian kingdom and helped to lay the basis for the eighth-century achievements of Kings ETHELBALD and OFFA. His daughter, St WÆRBURH, played a notable role in spreading monasticism in Mercia.

WULFNOTH (*c.* 1030–*c.* 1090), youngest son of GODWINE, Earl of Wessex, and brother of King

HAROLD II and Queen EDITH, wife of EDWARD THE CONFESSOR. Taken as a hostage from Godwine by Edward in 1051 as a guarantee of good behaviour, Wulfnoth was sent to Duke William of Normandy, the future WILLIAM I THE CONQUEROR, as a hostage and remained a prisoner until the dying William released him in 1087.

WULFRED (?–832), Archbishop of Canterbury (805–32). As with his predecessors JÆNBERHT and St ETHELHEARD, Wulfred's rule was frequently disrupted by disputes with the kings of Mercia, and he was at one stage exiled from his see by King CENWULF before ultimately achieving some significant successes (see CWENFRYTH). He was also an important reforming archbishop, bringing his Church's organization into line with current continental models and holding major reforming councils of the English Church.

WULFRIC (?–c. 1004), nobleman. A great Mercian nobleman whose loyalty to the kings of Wessex indicates how firmly their power was established in the north Midlands. He supported the Tenth-Century Reform and founded a monastery at Burton-upon-Trent (Staffs.). After his death without a direct male heir, his relatives were killed or mutilated, probably to the benefit of EADRIC STREONA, the arch-villain of ETHELRED II THE UNREADY's reign.

WULFSTAN I (?–955), Archbishop of York (931–55). Initially appointed Archbishop as a protégé of King ATHELSTAN of Wessex to increase southern English and Christian influence within the Scandinavian kingdom of York, Wulfstan took very seriously his duties to the kings of York, participating actively in the campaigns of OLAF GOTHRITHSSON and later supporting ERIC BLOODAXE. He was arrested in 952 by King EADRED and probably never regained his archbishopric, which he had held since 931. His career illustrates graphically the conflicts of loyalty which the existence of distinct spheres of authority created and how they were enhanced when the kings of Wessex sought to impose their rule in the north.

WULFSTAN II (?–1023), Archbishop of York (1002–23). One of the heirs to the literary and educational endeavours of the Tenth-Century Reform, Wulfstan produced a succession of tracts that culminated in his *Institutes of Polity*, and he was also responsible for drafting many of the law-codes of Kings ETHELRED II THE UNREADY and CNUT. His aim was to instruct kings, bishops and others in their Christian responsibilities, emphasizing the threat to society if Christian precepts were not followed and if the conventional medieval division of people into the three groups of those who prayed, fought and worked was not sustained.

WULFSTAN, ST (c. 1010–95), churchman. Bishop of Worcester from 1062, he was the one Old English bishop to remain permanently in office after the Norman Conquest. A contemporary life describes a saintly and gentle man, although he was not canonized until the seventeenth century.

WYATT, JAMES (1746–1813), architect. From a Staffs. family of builders and architects, after studying in Italy he returned to England in 1768 where he became partner to his brother Samuel, master-carpenter at Kedleston (Derb.), then being remodelled by Robert ADAM. Wyatt combined the neoclassicism of the Adams with influences from Italy in his most famous work, the Pantheon on Oxford Street (London), an assembly room intended to rival the outdoor pleasure gardens. It opened in 1772 and enabled Wyatt to build a large independent practice, in both the neoclassical and Gothic styles. His plans to rebuild several medieval cathedrals in eighteenth-century Gothic were condemned by many as inauthentic, particularly at Durham, and gained him a reputation as a 'destroyer'. His success was, however, crowned with royal approval and commissions at Windsor. In 1796 he succeeded William Chambers as Surveyor General and Comptroller of the Office of Works, but he was a poor administrator and at his death was under investigation for malpractice.

WYATT, SIR THOMAS THE ELDER (?1503–42), poet. Son of a Kentish knight, he studied at Cambridge and entered service at court in 1516, leading embassies abroad and becoming prominent in court tournaments. His old liaison with ANNE BOLEYN brought extreme danger on her fall in 1536, but he survived both this and treasonable involvement with Cardinal Reginald POLE in 1540–1. With his close friend Henry HOWARD, Earl of Surrey, he was a pioneer of sonnet form in English, and also wrote verse satires; his poetry was published posthumously.

WYATT, SIR THOMAS THE YOUNGER (?1521–1554). Son of the elder Sir Thomas WYATT, the younger Wyatt embarked on a military career, serving in France initially under the command of his close friend Henry HOWARD, Earl of Surrey, and returning to his native Kent in 1550. His Kentish rising against MARY I in Jan. 1554 was intended to form one component of an attempted Protestant come-back by members of the ousted regime of John DUDLEY, Duke of Northumberland. Elsewhere risings were stillborn, and in Kent the attempt to win popular support by stirring opposition to Mary's planned marriage with PHILIP II was losing momentum, when the government's expeditionary force deserted to the rebels. Wyatt's forces marched to London, but Mary personally

continued on page 864

WYCLIF, JOHN (c. 1330–84)
Theologian

An Oxford academic he became the founder of the first nonconformist movement in English history and his defiance of the Papacy resulted in early Protestants christening him 'the morning-star of the Reformation'. In the words of John FOXE in his *Acts and Monuments* (1563), 'When all the world was in most desperate and vile estate this man stepped forth like a valiant champion, even as the morning-star in the midst of a cloud.'

He may have been born, as tradition asserts, in the Yorks. village of Wycliffe (although his enemies were to say that the true meaning of his name was as a sign of his wicked life), but nothing certain is known of him until he appears as a clerk at Oxford University in 1356. After finishing his arts degree he stayed on to study theology, becoming Doctor of Divinity in 1372 and developing the ideas which took him into heresy. According to his theory of Dominion and Grace, all power and dominion derived from God and ought to belong only to the elect, those who were in a state of grace. On these grounds there could be no special authority for popes since popes might not be among the elect; indeed to all appearances some were in a state of mortal sin, and at a time when the Papacy, based at Avignon, was widely believed to be under the thumb of the French, it was fairly easy for an Englishman to think so. These ideas appealed to an English government which was aiming to bolster its own authority over the nation's Church at the expense of the Papacy. In 1374 Wyclif was attached to a delegation sent to confer with Pope Gregory XI's envoys over such controversial issues as the Pope's right to tax the English Church or make appointments to English benefices. In 1376 he was invited to London to preach against the 'Caesarean clergy', his term for the clergy who rendered Caesar all too much service, men such as WILLIAM OF WYKEHAM, long-serving minister of the Crown and political opponent of JOHN OF GAUNT, Wyclif's patron. His call for the return of the Church to apostolic poverty appealed to many, notably those who stood to gain if Church property were to be forcibly returned to the descendants of original donors. In 1377 Pope Gregory condemned as erroneous 18 propositions taken from Wyclif's writings on dominion, asserting that they were subversive of all authority, in State as well as in Church. Oxford sprang to Wyclif's defence and,

instead of backing down, Wyclif replied with a treatise *On the Truth of Holy Writ* (1378), arguing that the only certain source of authority was God's word as revealed in the Bible. No one should rely upon the interpretation pronounced by a corrupt Church; each member of the elect should read and interpret the Bible for himself. In this lay the inspiration for the Wycliffite translation of the Bible into English in the 1390s. In 1379 he published *De Eucharistia*, arguing that the substance of bread remained after consecration by a priest. But this denial of transubstantiation, the theory behind the central sacrament of the Catholic Church, appealed to no one's vested interests. After this act of intellectual defiance, not even Gaunt would protect him. Early in 1381 he was forced to leave Oxford. Although he condemned the Peasants' Revolt of June 1381, his opponents accused him of encouraging it. He retired to his rectory at Lutterworth (Leics.), and continued to write. He suffered a stroke and died on 31 Dec. 1384.

Meanwhile his followers, expelled from Oxford by William COURTENAY, had begun to preach to the people. As itinerant preachers hounded by the authorities, they were inevitably poor. In the poverty and chastity of their lifestyle these heretics represented ideals which orthodox churchmen espoused in theory but all too often failed to live up to. So the Lollard movement was born. The Church authorities turned to the State for help. In 1401 the Statute *De heretico comburendo* brought in the death penalty for obstinate heretics, and a number were burned at the stake. At first Lollardy enjoyed some support within the establishment (the Lollard knights) but, after the failure of the 1414 rising led by Sir John OLDCASTLE, it became an underground movement of Bible-reading craftsmen, with its own priests, schoolmasters and an extensive literature in English. It became less academic but never lost sight of its intellectual and spiritual debt to its founding father. Yet, as a prophet, Wyclif won greater honour in another country, Bohemia. The great Czech reformer John Hus went to the stake in 1415 for his adherence to Wycliffite ideas, and it was he who wrote, 'Wyclif, Wyclif, you will unsettle many a man's mind.'

Kenneth B. McFarlane, John Wycliffe and the Beginnings of English Nonconformity (1952) steadied panic in the capital and the rebel army disintegrated. Wyatt was executed.

WYCH, RICHARD, ST (St Richard of Chichester) (?1197–1253), churchman. According to his *Life*, he transferred his fiancée to his brother, assuring him that he had never kissed her, then studied at Oxford, becoming Chancellor of the university in 1235. He joined the staff of Edmund RICH and was elected Bishop of Chichester against royal wishes in 1244. Consecrated by Pope Innocent IV in 1245, he was eventually accepted by HENRY III and became, probably under GROSSETESTE's influence, a keen supervisor of his diocesan clergy. An ascetic scholar regarded by the Papacy as a model bishop, he was canonized in 1262.

WYCHERLEY, WILLIAM (1640–1716), playwright. His father was steward to the Marquess of Winchester. He entered the Inner Temple after Oxford but abandoned the law for writing. His most successful plays were *The Country Wife* (1675) and *The Plain Dealer* (1676), which both satirize the social conventions and petty hypocrisies of Restoration society. Wycherley identified with Manly, the hero of *The Plain Dealer*, whose actions demonstrated contempt for social civilities. In 1681–2 he was imprisoned for debt, and after the Duke of York (the future JAMES II) redeemed his losses became a near-recluse, but after the publication of his *Miscellaneous Poems* in 1704, he was 'rediscovered' by POPE.

WYCLIF, JOHN *see* essay on page 863

WYMAN, BILL (1936–), musician *see* JAGGER, MICK

WYNDHAM, SIR WILLIAM (*c.* 1688–1740), Tory politician. A Som. baronet, and MP for the county from 1710, he was close to Bolingbroke (*see* ST JOHN, HENRY) and after Bolingbroke's flight to France intended to lead the western English branch of the 1715 Jacobite rebellion; he was arrested before his plans bore fruit. Thanks to the influence of his Whig father-in-law, the Duke of Somerset, he was never tried. Guided by Bolingbroke, he established himself as one of the leaders of the Tory party in the Commons, moving away from Jacobitism and towards alliances with Whigs. These manoeuvres included an attempted government coalition with Robert WALPOLE in the 1720s, and then more successfully an alliance with

'patriot' Whigs such as PULTENEY who were opposed to Walpole. In the late 1730s he entered the circle of FREDERICK, Prince of Wales, although the relationship foundered in 1738 over Frederick's support for a standing army, which the Tories wanted to see reduced.

WYSTAN (OR WIGSTAN), ST (?–849), Mercian prince. The grandson of King WIGLAF of Mercia, Wystan was murdered by a relative and buried at Repton (Derb.), where, as recent archaeological excavations have shown, the development of a cult of sanctity around him resulted in the church being remodelled. After the Viking conquest of Mercia, Wystan's relics were moved to Evesham (Worcs.) where he continued to be venerated as a saint. Like St CYNEHELM's, his career shows how an Anglo-Saxon nobleman could acquire a reputation for sanctity which may not have been justified by his actual life.

WYVILL, CHRISTOPHER (1740–1822), political and religious reformer. He came from a Yorks. landed family, although his father was an excise supervisor. He was educated at Cambridge, ordained and presented with an Essex living, but paid a curate to discharge his duties (perhaps in part because of his own unorthodox religious views). In 1774 he inherited substantial estates. He is best known for his prominent part in the Association Movement of the 1780s, formed to protest ills in the governmental system, thought to have been revealed by the burdensome and unsuccessful American War of Independence (1776–83). The movement's members called for a combination of more frequent elections, extension of the franchise and redrawing of constituency boundaries, usually together with some measure of 'economical' reform of government offices. The movement ran out of steam as key supporters fell out over tactics, and the fall of NORTH and the ending of the war removed the focuses of their discontent. Wyvill and other leaders then pinned their hopes on PITT THE YOUNGER, who did float an unsuccessful reform motion in Parliament in 1785.

Wyvill published his *Political Papers*, documents which chronicled the Association Movement, in 1794–5. He also supported liberal religious campaigns to relax the requirement that university students and Anglican ministers subscribe to the Thirty-Nine Articles and to extend the rights of Dissenters.

Y

YARMOUTH, COUNTESS OF *see* WALLMODEN, AMALIE SOPHIE MARIANNE

YARRANTON, ANDREW (1616–*c*. 1684), economic improver. A linen-draper before he joined the Parliamentary army during the Civil Wars, he became an ironmonger in 1652 and turned his attention to issues of economic improvement. After several abortive schemes he succeeded in making the Worcs. River Stour navigable from Stourbridge to Kidderminster. Following imprisonment at the Restoration on suspicion of planning a Presbyterian rising, he travelled to Saxony to study tin-plating but was unable to secure the English patent. He then returned to waterways and surveyed several in England and Ireland, including the Dee and the Wilts. and Warws. Avons, and published his plans in *England's Improvement by Sea and Land to outdo the Dutch without Fighting* (1677–81). The book also contained proposals for a land bank and measures to prevent fires in cities.

YEARSLEY, ANNE (née Cromartie) (1756–1806), poet. The daughter of a Bristol milkwoman whose round she inherited, she wrote poetry at home while struggling to bring up six children. The poems were brought to the attention of Hannah MORE, who sponsored their publication in 1784. More and Elizabeth MONTAGU became trustees of the £600 raised by the book and they intended that Yearsley should set up a school under More's guidance. Yearsley, supported by Anna SEWARD and the Earl of Bristol (*see* HERVEY, FREDERICK), saw this as condescension and replied to More's claims that she had effectively written the poems herself with an *Autobiographical Narrative* (1786) and a further volume of poems. With More's opposition, however, her prospects declined. She continued to write, but failed to find an audience.

YEATS, WILLIAM BUTLER (1865–1939), poet. His father was a portrait-painter, his sisters were successful graphic artists, and his brother Jack is regarded as the greatest Irish painter of the twentieth century. His early writings drew on Irish folk tales and the literature of the Celtic Revival. The youthful Yeats was an ardent Irish nationalist, encouraged by his unrequited love for the political activist Maud GONNE. He combined his nationalism with a career as orchestrator of literary movements, founding Irish literary societies and the prototype of an Irish National Theatre in the course of the 1890s. His insistence on aesthetic standards alienated nationalists who saw art as subordinate to political propaganda; this conflict came to a head in 1902–7 when Yeats defended SYNGE's plays against nationalist hostility. His nationalist fervour was briefly rekindled by the Easter Rising (1916), while the First World War and the Irish troubles of 1919–23 encouraged his sense of a worldwide crisis of civilization. He served as a member of the Irish Free State Senate (1922–8), and received the Nobel Prize for Literature in 1923. Yeats identified himself with Anglo-Irish aristocratic civilization against Catholic middle-class values. These attitudes led him to denounce literary censorship, oppose the prohibition of divorce, advocate eugenics and speak favourably of fascism. (He briefly endorsed Eoin O'DUFFY's Blueshirts in the 1930s.) With James JOYCE, Yeats is one of the most important Irish literary voices of the twentieth century.

YEVELE, HENRY (*c*. 1325–1400), architect. Regarded by some of his admirers as the greatest of all English architects, he was undoubtedly a master of the distinctively English perpendicular style. From the late 1350s he was continuously employed by the rich and fashionable, from the royal family downwards, on redesigning and refurbishing of their palaces, manor houses, castles and churches. His workshop was responsible for the design of the tombs of EDWARD THE BLACK PRINCE, EDWARD III, RICHARD II and ANNE OF BOHEMIA. Among the surviving buildings that still bear his imprint are Canterbury Cathedral and Westminster Abbey and Hall.

YOLANDE OF DREUX (*fl*. 1285), Queen of Scots. Daughter of the Count of Dreux, she married 43-year-old ALEXANDER III in 1285, when the King desperately needed a child to ensure the succession. Five months after the marriage, Alexander was killed in an accident. She may well have been pregnant, but if so she suffered a miscarriage. The Scots asked EDWARD I for his advice on the succession, a move which in time they would bitterly regret.

YONGE, CHARLOTTE (1823–1901), novelist. An apologist for the Oxford Movement and a friend of KEBLE, she remained committed to the Church of England and opposed to Catholicism, feminism and socialism. She wrote over 160 titles, mainly romances of upper-class life, of which *The Heir of Radclyffe Hall* (1853) is the best known.

YORK, DUKE OF, 1ST *see* LANGLEY, EDMUND; **2ND** *see* EDWARD OF YORK; **3RD** *see* RICHARD OF YORK; **DUCHESS OF** *see* HYDE, ANNE

YORKE, PHILIP (1st Baron and 1st Earl of Hardwicke) (1690–1764), politician and lawyer. The son of a Dover attorney, Yorke was called to the Bar in 1715. He became a protégé of Thomas PARKER, Lord Macclesfield, and entered Parliament in 1719, where he established himself as an effective government spokesman and was rewarded for his defence of Robert WALPOLE in the excise debate of March 1733 with a peerage and the office of Lord Chief Justice. Hardwicke established a strong partnership with Thomas PELHAM-HOLLES, Duke of Newcastle, in the management of the Lords. In 1737 he became Lord Chancellor, an office which he retained under Wilmington (*see* COMPTON, SPENCER) and PELHAM. He was responsible for much legislation, including the repressive measures against Highland costume after the 1745 rebellion, but is perhaps best remembered for the 1753 Marriage Act which curbed clandestine marriages, most notoriously those conducted in the Fleet prison, and so protected the inheritance of landed estates. The Act provoked grievances as, with few exceptions, the only legal marriages were those performed in the Church of England and those under 21 had to obtain parental consent. Hardwicke was made an earl when Newcastle became Prime Minister, but left office with him in 1756. In his last years, he helped broker the coalitions of the early part of GEORGE III's reign.

YOUNG, ARTHUR (1741–1820), writer. Son of a clergyman, he was apprenticed to a counting house in King's Lynn (Norfolk), but, hoping to make a living as a writer, went to London. In 1763 he inherited a farm, and thereafter wrote chiefly on agricultural topics, but sometimes more generally on social and economic issues. His *Six Weeks Tour through the Southern Counties of England and Wales* (1768), a survey of farming practice, made his reputation; on subsequent tours, he was entertained by noblemen and gentry.

He pioneered the collection of empirical and statistical data relating to both rural economy and society, and championed agricultural against manufacturing interests. In 1779 he became agent to Lord Kingsborough in Co. Cork, gaining material there for an Irish *Tour*. Between 1784 and 1809, he produced (and largely wrote) the periodical *Annals of Agriculture*. He visited France three times between 1787 and 1789, collecting material for another *Tour*, and witnessed the outbreak of the Revolution, which he recorded in this *Tour*. His zeal for improvement, which reflected the mood of the time, brought reward in 1794 when he was made Secretary to the newly founded Board of Agriculture under Sir John SINCLAIR.

YOUNG, DAVID (Baron Young of Graffham) (1932–), politician. As Prime Minister, Margaret THATCHER had a penchant for the advice of successful businessmen, and Young, who had made a career in business, was appointed by her in 1982 to head the Manpower Services Commission, which was designed to deal with rising unemployment. Young's 'can-do' style appealed to her and she famously said of him that 'where other people bring me problems, David brings me solutions'. Young was given a life peerage in 1983 and made a minister at the Department of Trade and Industry, before going on to be Secretary of State for Employment (1985–7) and Secretary of State for Trade and Industry (1987–9). He played a notable part, along with the party Chairman, Norman TEBBIT, in organizing the election victory of 1987, but he and Tebbit did not always enjoy cordial relations. He was party Chairman (1989–90), resigning with his patron.

YOUNG, EDWARD (1683–1765), poet and playwright. The son of a churchman, he became a Fellow of All Souls, Oxford, in 1708. Part of the literary circle of Joseph ADDISON though a High Churchman, he strove to maintain good relations with both Whigs and Tories. He had two plays performed at Drury Lane in 1719 and 1721 but afterwards chiefly wrote poems, often on political themes. The work for which he is best remembered is *Night Thoughts*, composed in response to the death of his wife, stepdaughter and stepson-in-law between 1736 and 1741. Its success and that of its sequels enabled him to live in comfort as rector of Welwyn (Herts.).

YOUNG, MICHAEL (Baron Young of Dartington) (1915–), educationalist. Baron Young studied sociology and law, and after becoming a barrister published a number of important books, most notably *The Rise of the Meritocracy* (1958). Secretary of the research department of the Labour Party (1945–51), he drafted the 1945 General Election manifesto, 'Let Us Face the Future'. In 1965 he was elected President of the Consumers'

Association, whose journal *Which* became one of the leading expressions of consumer protection throughout the world. A man of varied interests, Young was a pivotal figure in the National Extension College, furthered the cause of 'distance learning' (or learning by correspondence) in Britain and made a significant contribution to its advance in the Third World.

YOUNG, THOMAS (1773–1829), natural philosopher. Young studied languages and natural philosophy in his youth and between 1793 and 1796 studied medicine in London, Edinburgh and Göttingen. In 1797 he inherited an uncle's fortune and subsequently studied medicine at Cambridge (1797–9), ran a private medical practice in London (1799–1814) and became Professor of Natural Philosophy at the Royal Institution (1801–3). In 1811 he was appointed physician at St George's Hospital, London. He published on astigmatism and capillary action but is best known for his formulation, in the early 1800s, of the wave theory of light and for identifying the phenomenon of optical interference.

YULE, SIR HENRY (1820–89), lexicographer. A public servant in India for 20 years, having joined the Bengal Engineers in 1840, Yule was involved in irrigation projects as well as a succession of wars. His extensive travels gave him unrivalled knowledge of the subcontinent, that bore fruit in many publications, often editions of exploration accounts for the HAKLUYT Society. His *Hobson–Jobson: A Glossary of Anglo-Indian Colloquial Words and Phrases* (1886), compiled jointly with Arthur Burnell, cemented the position of many borrowings from Anglo-India in the English language, from *chit* and *pyjamas* to *wallah* and *kedgeree*.

YWAIN, SON OF BILI (*fl.* mid seventh century), King of the Strathclyde Britons. Ywain defeated and killed DOMNALL BRECC, King of Dál Riata, at the Battle of Strathcarron in *c.* 642 and may have acquired some domination over Dál Riata as a result. A further reflection of his power may well lie in the fact that his brother, BRIDEI, SON OF BELI, subsequently became King of Fortriu, in southern Pictland. The date of Ywain's death is unknown, but the record of 'Guret King of Dumbarton' in the *Annals of Ulster* under 658 indicates it must have been before this date.

YWAIN, SON OF DYFNWAL (*fl.* 934–7), King of Strathclyde. Ywain was a nephew of CONSTANTÍN II, King of the Scots. He, together with Constantín, was routed by the English King ATHELSTAN in 934. In 937 he was again on the losing side, supporting Constantín and OLAF GOTHFRITHSSON at the Battle of Brunanburh. The date of Ywain's death is uncertain, but must have been before 943.

YWAIN THE BALD (?–?1018), King of Strathclyde. The last of the line of the kings of Strathclyde, Ywain may have been a son of DYFNWAL, SON OF YWAIN, and thus would have succeeded his brother Mael Coluim in 997. It is likely that he was killed at the Battle of Carham in 1018 fighting alongside MAEL COLUIM II, King of the Scots, following which Strathclyde was essentially incorporated into the kingdom of the Scots under client Scottish kings.

Z

ZANGWILL, ISRAEL (1864–1926) novelist and translator. The son of Russian-Jewish parents, he was born in London and educated at university there. His first successful novel, *Children of the Ghetto* (1892), established him as a powerful voice of the Jewish immigrant experience and a spokesman for Jewish rights, a reputation consolidated with *The King of Schnorrers* (1894) and other novels and works of non-fiction. His play *The Melting Pot* (1909) coined the phrase for a multicultural society.

ZOFFANY, JOHANN (1734 or 1735–1810), painter. Born in Germany, he studied in Italy and settled in England when he was 25. Influenced by HOGARTH among other artists, he received many commissions from GEORGE III and Queen CHARLOTTE; George III sent him to Italy to paint antiquities and he also worked for the theatre and depicted scenes from contemporary history. His paintings were celebrated by contemporaries and later critics mostly for the way in which they captured the nature of eighteenth-century English society. In 1768 he was one of the 40 original members of the Royal Academy.

ZUCKERMAN, SOLLY (Baron Zuckerman) (1904–93), scientist. Beginning his academic career as an anatomist, moving from his native South Africa to London to train, Zuckerman became one of the most influential scientific brains in wartime. From studying the effects of bombing on the human body, he acquired skills in planning bombing operations that won him a place in the counsels of TEDDER and Eisenhower. As chief scientific adviser to a succession of Conservative and Labour defence ministers from the late 1950s, thereafter as chief scientific adviser to the Cabinet Office during the 'white heat of the technological revolution' years of the administrations of Harold WILSON, he wielded considerable authority, streamlining decisions and appraisals. On retiring from public service in 1971, he became an outspoken critic of tactical nuclear weapons.

ZWINGLI, HULDRYCH (1484–1531), theologian. The pioneer of the reformed branch of Protestant Christianity, from 1518 he was leader of the Zürich Reformation, dying in battle during a Swiss civil war. His Reformation differed from Martin LUTHER's, in particular on the nature of the Eucharist: Luther maintaining that Christ's presence in bread and wine was a physical or corporal reality, Zwingli maintaining that it was spiritual or symbolic (John CALVIN sought a middle path, but alienated Lutherans). Contacts between Switzerland and England began in the early 1530s; ultimately the Swiss Reformation was more influential than Lutheranism on English Protestantism.

KINGS & QUEENS OF THE ENGLISH, ENGLAND & BRITAIN

Edward the Elder	899–924	Henry VI	1422–61, 1470–1
Athelstan	924–39	Edward IV	1461–70, 1471–83
Edmund	939–46	Edward V	1483
Eadred	946–55	Richard III	1483–5
Eadwig	955–59	Henry VII	1485–1509
Edgar	959–75	Henry VIII	1509–47
Edward the Martyr	975–78	Edward VI	1547–53
Ethelred II the Unready	978–1016	Lady Jane Grey	1553
Edmund Ironside	1016	Mary I	1553–8
Cnut	1016–35	Elizabeth I	1558–1603
Harold I Harefoot	1037–40	James I	1603–25
Harthacnut	1040–42	Charles I	1625–49
Edward the Confessor	1042–66	Charles II	1660–85
Harold II	1066	James II	1685–8
William I	1066–87	William III & Mary II	1688–94
William II	1087–1100	William III	1694–1702
Henry I	1100–35	Anne	1702–14
Stephen	1135–54	George I	1714–27
Henry II	1154–89	George II	1727–60
Richard I	1189–99	George III	1760–1820
John	1199–1216	George IV	1820–30
Henry III	1216–72	William IV	1830–7
Edward I	1272–1307	Victoria	1837–1901
Edward II	1307–27	Edward VII	1901–10
Edward III	1327–77	George V	1910–36
Richard II	1377–99	Edward VIII	1936
Henry IV	1399–1413	George VI	1936–52
Henry V	1413–22	Elizabeth II	1952–

BRITISH PRIME MINISTERS

Robert Walpole, 2nd Earl of Orford	1721–42
Spencer Compton, 1st Earl of Wilmington	1742–3
Henry Pelham	1743–54
Thomas Pelham-Holles, 4th Duke of Newcastle	1754–6
William Cavendish, 4th Duke of Devonshire	1756–7
William Pitt the Elder	1757–61
Thomas Pelham-Holles, 4th Duke of Newcastle	1757–62
John Stuart, 3rd Earl of Bute	1762–3
George Grenville	1763–5
Charles Wentworth, 2nd Marquess of Rockingham	1765–6
William Pitt the Elder	1766–7
Augustus Fitzroy, 3rd Duke of Grafton	1767–70
Frederick North, 2nd Earl of Guildford	1770–82
Charles Wentworth, 2nd Marquess of Rockingham	1782
William Petty, Earl of Shelburne	1782–3
William Cavendish Bentinck, 3rd Duke of Portland	1783
William Pitt the Younger	1783–1801
Henry Addington	1801–4
William Pitt the Younger	1804–6
William Grenville, 1st Baron Grenville	1806–7
William Cavendish Bentinck, 3rd Duke of Portland	1807–9
Spencer Perceval	1809–12
Robert Jenkinson, 2nd Earl of Liverpool	1812–27

George Canning	1827
Frederick Robinson, Viscount Goderich, 1st Earl of Ripon	1827–8
Arthur Wellesley, 1st Duke of Wellington	1828–30
Charles Grey, 2nd Earl Grey	1830–4
William Lamb, 2nd Viscount Melbourne	1834
Robert Peel	1834–5
William Lamb, 2nd Viscount Melbourne	1835–41
Robert Peel	1841–6
Lord John Russell, 1st Earl Russell	1846–52
Edward Stanley, 23rd Earl of Derby	1852
George Gordon, 4th Earl of Aberdeen	1852–5
John Temple, 3rd Viscount Palmerston	1855–8
Edward Stanley, 23rd Earl of Derby	1858–9
John Temple, 3rd Viscount Palmerston	1859–65
Lord John Russell, 1st Earl Russell	1865–6
Edward Stanley, 23rd Earl of Derby	1866–8
Benjamin Disraeli, 1st Earl of Beaconsfield	1868
W. E. Gladstone	1868–74
Benjamin Disraeli, 1st Earl of Beaconsfield	1874–80
W. E. Gladstone	1880–5
Robert Cecil, 3rd Marquess of Salisbury	1885–6
W. E. Gladstone	1886
Robert Cecil, 3rd Marquess of Salisbury	1886–92
W. E. Gladstone	1892–4
Archibald Primrose, 5th Earl of Rosebery	1894–5
Robert Cecil, 3rd Marquess of Salisbury	1895–1902
A. J. Balfour	1902–5
Henry Campbell-Bannerman	1905–8
H. H. Asquith	1908–16
Andrew Bonar Law	1922–3
Stanley Baldwin	1923–4
Ramsay MacDonald	1924
Stanley Baldwin	1924–9
Ramsey MacDonald	1929–35
Stanley Baldwin	1935–7
Neville Chamberlain	1937–40
Winston Churchill	1940–5
Clement Attlee	1945–51
Winston Churchill	1951–5
Anthony Eden	1955–7
Harold Macmillan	1957–63
Alec Douglas-Home	1963–4
Harold Wilson	1964–70
Edward Heath	1970–4
Harold Wilson	1974–6
James Callaghan	1976–9
Margaret Thatcher	1979–90
John Major	1990–7
Tony Blair	1997–